America's
Top-Rated Cities:
A Statistical Handbook

Volume 1

2014
Twenty-First Edition

America's
Top-Rated Cities:
A Statistical Handbook

Volume 1: Southern Region

PUBLISHER: Leslie Mackenzie
EDITORIAL DIRECTOR: Laura Mars
EDITOR: David Garoogian

RESEARCHERS & WRITERS: Allison Blake; Denise Lenchner; Veronica Towers
PRODUCTION MANAGER: Kristen Thatcher
MARKETING DIRECTOR: Jessica Moody

A Universal Reference Book
Grey House Publishing, Inc.
4919 Route 22
Amenia, NY 12501
518.789.8700
Fax 845.373.6390
www.greyhouse.com
e-mail: books @greyhouse.com

Twenty-first Edition
Printed in Canada

Publisher's Cataloging-in-Publication Data
(Prepared by The Donohue Group, Inc.)

America's top-rated cities. Vol. I, Southern region : a statistical handbook. — 1992-

    v. : ill. ; cm.
    Annual, 1995-
    Irregular, 1992-1993
    ISSN: 1082-7102

1. Cities and towns--Ratings--Southern States--Statistics--Periodicals. 2. Cities and towns--Southern States--Statistics--Periodicals. 3. Social indicators--Southern States--Periodicals. 4. Quality of life--Southern States--Statistics--Periodicals.
5. Southern States--Social conditions--Statistics--Periodicals. I. Title: America's top rated cities. II. Title: Southern region

HT123.5.S6 A44
307.76/0973/05   95644648

4-Volume Set   ISBN: 978-1-61925-264-6
Volume 1   ISBN: 978-1-61925-265-3
Volume 2   ISBN: 978-1-61925-266-0
Volume 3   ISBN: 978-1-61925-267-7
Volume 4   ISBN: 978-1-61925-268-4

Abilene, Texas

Athens, Georgia

Atlanta, Georgia

Austin, Texas

Cape Coral, Florida

Charleston, South Carolina

Clarksville, Tennessee

Dallas, Texas

El Paso, Texas

Fort Worth, Texas

Gainesville, Florida

Houston, Texas

McAllen, Texas

Miami, Florida

Midland, Texas

Montgomery, Alabama

Introduction

This twenty-first edition of *America's Top Rated Cities* is a concise, statistical, 4-volume work identifying America's top-rated cities with populations of at least 100,000. It profiles 100 cities that have received high marks for business and living from prominent sources such as *Forbes, U.S. News & World Report, BusinessWeek, Inc., Fortune, Men's Health, The Wall Street Journal, Cosmopolitan,* and *CNNMoney.*

Each volume covers a different region of the country—Southern, Western, Central and Eastern—and includes a detailed Table of Contents, City Chapters, Appendices, and Maps. Each City Chapter incorporates information from hundreds of resources to create the following major sections:

- **Background**—lively narrative of significant, up-to-date news for both businesses and residents. These combine historical facts with current developments, "known-for" annual events, and climate data.
- **Rankings**—fun-to-read, bulleted survey results from over 300 books, magazines, and online articles, ranging from general (Great Places to Live), to specific (Best Cities for Newlyweds), and everything in between.
- **Statistical Tables**—121 tables and detailed topics—several new and expanded—that offer an unparalleled view of each city's Business and Living Environments. They are carefully organized with data that is easy to read and understand.
- **Appendices**—five in all, follow each volume of City Chapters. These range from listings of Metropolitan Statistical Areas to Comparative Statistics for all 100 cities.

This new edition of *America's Top Rated Cities* includes cities that not only surveyed well, but ranked highest using our unique weighting system. We looked at violent crime, property crime, population growth, median household income, educational attainment, and unemployment. You'll find that a number of American cities remain "top-rated" despite less-than-stellar numbers. Miami, for example, is known for high crime and unemployment, but also for its unique location—as both a valuable business port and popular vacation spot. New York and Los Angeles have relatively low high school graduation rates, but both of these cities make up for it in other ways. A final consideration is location—we strive to include as many states in the country as possible.

Part of this year's city criteria is that it be the "primary" city in a given metropolitan area. For example, if the metro area is Raleigh-Cary, NC, we would consider Raleigh, not Cary. This allows for a more equitable core city to core city comparison. In general, the core city of a metro area is defined as having substantial influence on neighboring cities.

The following 14 cities have never before appeared as a top-rated city:
- SOUTHERN: Abilene, TX; Lafayette, LA; Lubbock, TX; Midland, TX; Montgomery, AL
- WESTERN: Salem, OR
- CENTRAL: Davenport, IA; Peoria, IL; Rochester, MN; Topeka, KS
- EASTERN: Erie, PA; Fayetteville, NC; Wilmington, NC; Worcester, MA

The following 21 cities have regained their top-city status after being removed from the list for one, or many, years:
- SOUTHERN: Gainesville, FL; Tallahassee, FL
- WESTERN: Oxnard, CA; Phoenix, AZ; Reno, NV; Riverside, CA; Salt Lake City, UT; Santa Rosa, CA; Spokane, WA
- CENTRAL: Des Moines, IA; Grand Rapids, MI; Green Bay, WI; Minneapolis, MN; Oklahoma City, OK; Springfield, MO; Tulsa, OK; Wichita, KS
- EASTERN: Baltimore, MD; Cincinnati, OH; Louisville, KY; Richmond, VA

Praise for previous editions:

> "...[ATRC] has...proven its worth to a wide audience...from businesspeople and corporations planning to launch, relocate, or expand their operations to market researchers, real estate professionals, urban planners, job-seekers, students...interested in...reliable, attractively presented statistical information about larger U.S. cities."
> —ARBA

> "...For individuals or businesses looking to relocate, this resource conveniently reports rankings from more than 300 sources for the top 100 US cities. Recommended..."
> —Choice

> "...While patrons are becoming increasingly comfortable locating statistical data online, there is still something to be said for the ease associated with such a compendium of otherwise scattered data. A well-organized and appropriate update...
> —Library Journal

BACKGROUND

Each city begins with an informative Background that combines history with current events. These narratives often reflect changes that have occurred during the past year, and touch on the city's environment, politics, employment, cultural offerings, and climate, often including interesting trivia. For example: The unique craft of cowboy boot making is demonstrated at the Abilene Historical Museum; Peregrine Falcons were rehabilitated and released into the wild from Boise City's World Center for Birds of Prey; Gainesville is home to a 6,800 square-foot living Butterfly Rainforest, and Grand Rapids was the first city to introduce fluoride into its drinking water in 1945.

RANKINGS

This section has rankings from a possible 327 books, articles, and reports. For easy reference, these Rankings are categorized into 17 topics including Business/Finance, Dating/Romance, and Health/Fitness.

The Rankings are presented in an easy-to-read, bulleted format and include results from both annual surveys and one-shot studies. **Fastest-Growing Wages . . . Most Well-Read . . . Most Playful . . . Most Wired. . . Healthiest for Women . . . Best for Minority Entrepreneurs . . . Safest . . . Best to Grow Old . . . Most Polite . . . Best for Moviemakers . . . Most Frugal . . . Noisiest . . . Sex Happy . . . Most Vegetarian-Friendly . . . Least Stressful . . . Hottest Cities of the Future . . . Most Political . . . Most Charitable . . . Most Tax Friendly . . . Best for Telecommuters . . . Best for Singles . . . Greediest . . . Gayest . . . Best for Cats . . . Most Tattooed . . . Best for Wheelchair Users,** and more.

Sources for these Rankings include both well-known magazines and other media, including *Forbes, Fortune, Inc. Magazine, Working Mother, BusinessWeek, Kiplinger's Personal Finance, Men's Journal,* and *Travel + Leisure,* as well as resources not as well known, such as the *Asthma & Allergy Foundation of America, Christopher & Dana Reeve Foundation, The Advocate, Black Enterprise, National Civic League, The National Coalition for the Homeless, MovieMaker Magazine, Center for Digital Government, U.S. Conference of Mayors,* and the *Milken Institute.*

Since rankings cover a variety of geographic areas-metropolitan statistical areas, metropolitan divisions, cities, etc.- rankings can apply to one or all of these areas; see Appendix B for full geographic definitions.

STATISTICAL TABLES

Each city chapter includes a possible 121 tables and detailed topics—67 in BUSINESS and 54 in LIVING. Over 90% of statistical data has been updated. New topics include *Chronic Health Indicators, Air Quality Trends: Ozone,* and *Gross Rent.* Expanded topics include the addition of podiatrists, chiropractors, and optometrists to *Number of Medical Professionals* and the year established to *Professional Sports Teams.*

Business Environment includes hard facts and figures on 12 topics, including City Finances, Demographics, Income, Economy, Employment, and Real Estate. *Living Environment* includes 11 topics, such as Cost of Living, Housing, Health, Education, Safety, Recreation, and Climate.

To compile the Statistical Tables, our editors have again turned to a wide range of sources, some well known, such as the *U.S. Census Bureau, U.S. Environmental Protection Agency, Bureau of Labor Statistics, Centers for Disease Control and Prevention,* and the *Federal Bureau of Investigation,* and some more obscure, like *The Council for Community and Economic Research, Texas Transportation Institute,* and *Federation of Tax Administrators.*

APPENDICES: Data for all cities appear in all volumes.
- **Appendix A**—*Comparative Statistics*
- **Appendix B**—*Metropolitan Area Definitions*
- **Appendix C**—*Government Type and County*
- **Appendix D**—*Chambers of Commerce and Economic Development Organizations*
- **Appendix E**—*State Departments of Labor and Employment*

Material provided by public and private agencies and organizations was supplemented by original research, numerous library sources and Internet sites. *America's Top-Rated Cities, 2014,* is designed for a wide range of readers: private individuals considering relocating a residence or business; professionals considering expanding their businesses or changing careers; corporations considering relocation, opening up additional offices or creating new divisions; government agencies; general and market researchers; real estate consultants; human resource personnel; urban planners; investors; and urban government students.

Customers who purchase the four-volume set receive free online access to *America's Top Rated Cities* to: download city reports; sort and rank by 50-plus data points; and access data for 200 more cities than in the print version.

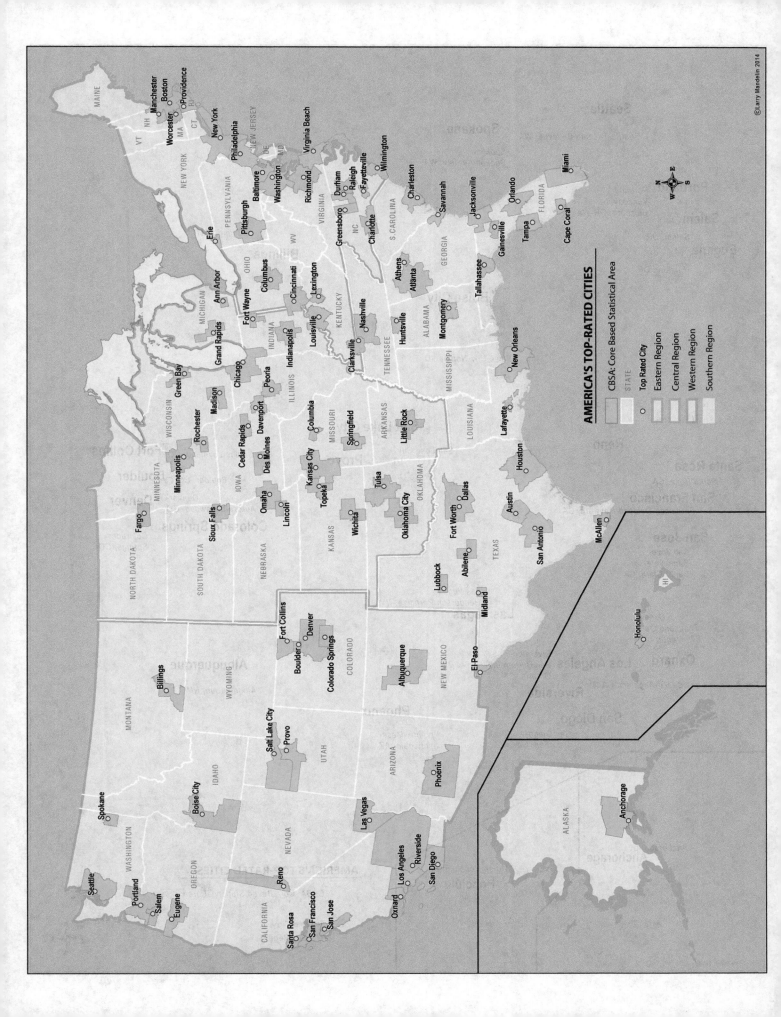

AMERICA'S TOP-RATED CITIES

CBSA: Core Based Statistical Area	
STATE	
	Top Rated City
	Eastern Region
	Central Region
	Western Region
	Southern Region

©Larry Mandelin 2014

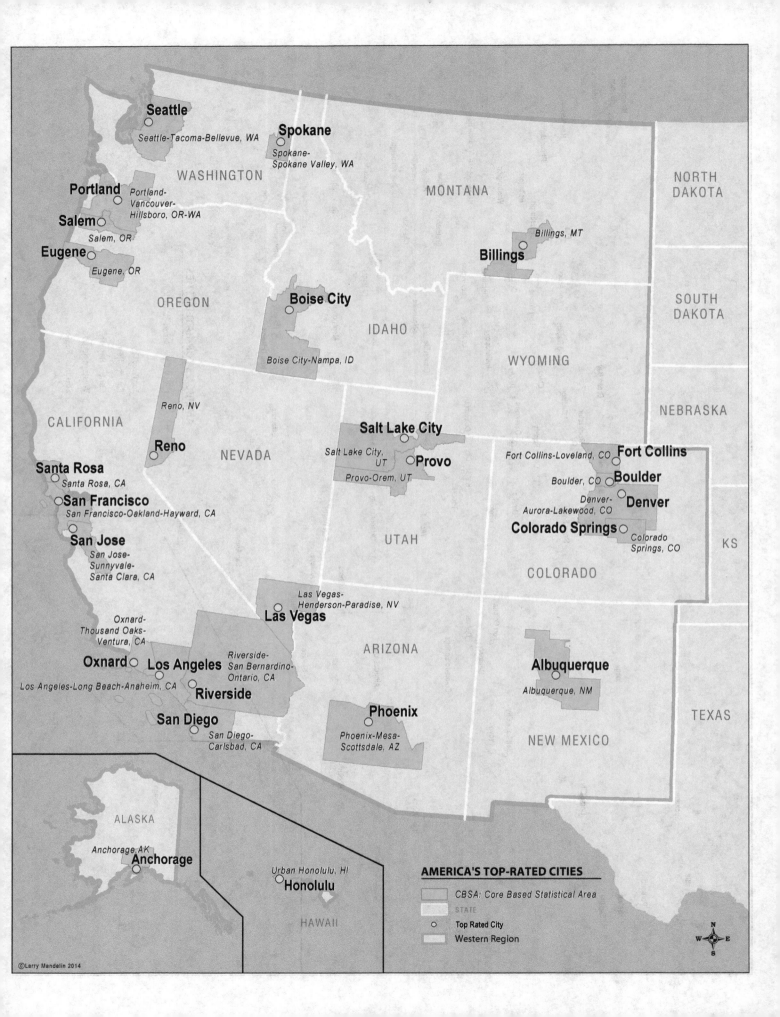

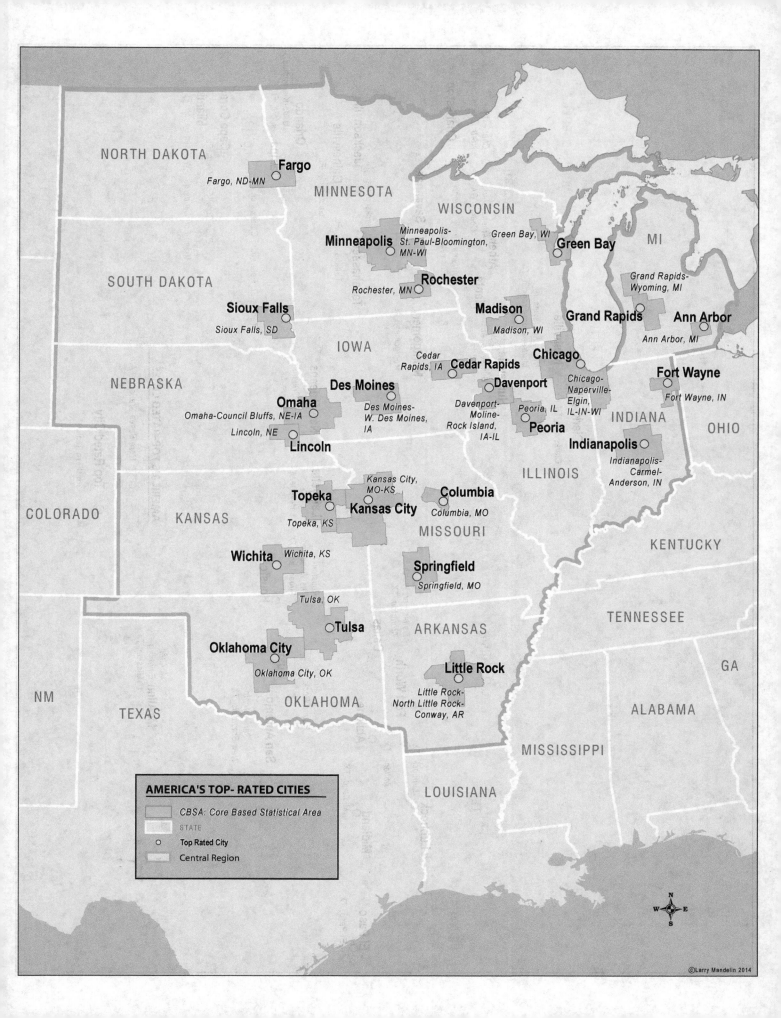

NORTH DAKOTA

Fargo
Fargo, ND-MN

MINNESOTA

WISCONSIN

Green Bay, WI

MI

Minneapolis
*Minneapolis-
St. Paul-Bloomington,
MN-WI*

Green Bay

SOUTH DAKOTA

Rochester
Rochester, MN

Grand Rapids-
Wyoming, MI

Sioux Falls
Sioux Falls, SD

Madison
Madison, WI

Grand Rapids

Ann Arbor
Ann Arbor, MI

IOWA

Cedar
Rapids, IA

Cedar Rapids

Chicago

NEBRASKA

Des Moines

Davenport

Chicago-
Naperville-
Elgin,
IL-IN-WI

Fort Wayne
Fort Wayne, IN

Omaha
Omaha-Council Bluffs, NE-IA

*Des Moines-
W. Des Moines,
IA*

Davenport-
Moline-
Rock Island,
IA-IL

Peoria, IL

INDIANA

OHIO

Lincoln, NE

Lincoln

Peoria

Indianapolis

Kansas City,
MO-KS

Columbia
Columbia, MO

Indianapolis-
Carmel-
Anderson, IN

COLORADO

KANSAS

Topeka

Kansas City

ILLINOIS

KENTUCKY

Topeka, KS

MISSOURI

Wichita
Wichita, KS

Springfield
Springfield, MO

TENNESSEE

Tulsa, OK

NM

Tulsa

ARKANSAS

GA

Oklahoma City

Little Rock

TEXAS

Oklahoma City, OK

OKLAHOMA

*Little Rock-
North Little Rock-
Conway, AR*

ALABAMA

MISSISSIPPI

LOUISIANA

AMERICA'S TOP- RATED CITIES

CBSA: Core Based Statistical Area

STATE

o Top Rated City

Central Region

N
W E
S

©Larry Mandelin 2014

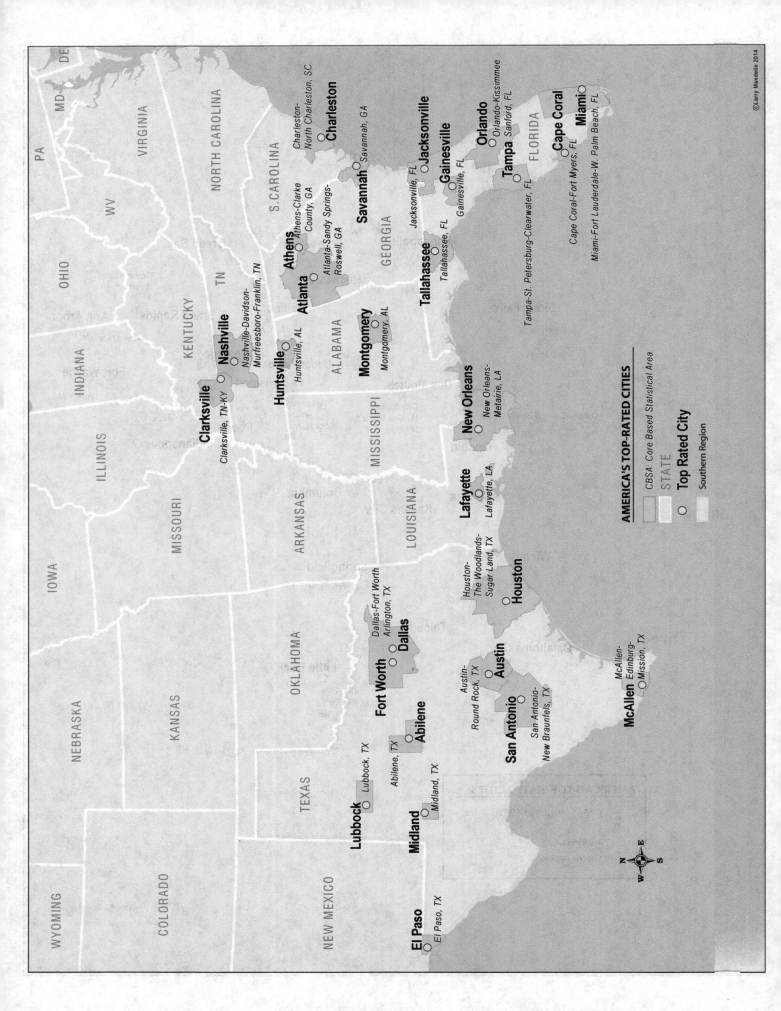

AMERICA'S TOP-RATED CITIES

©Larry Mandelin 2014

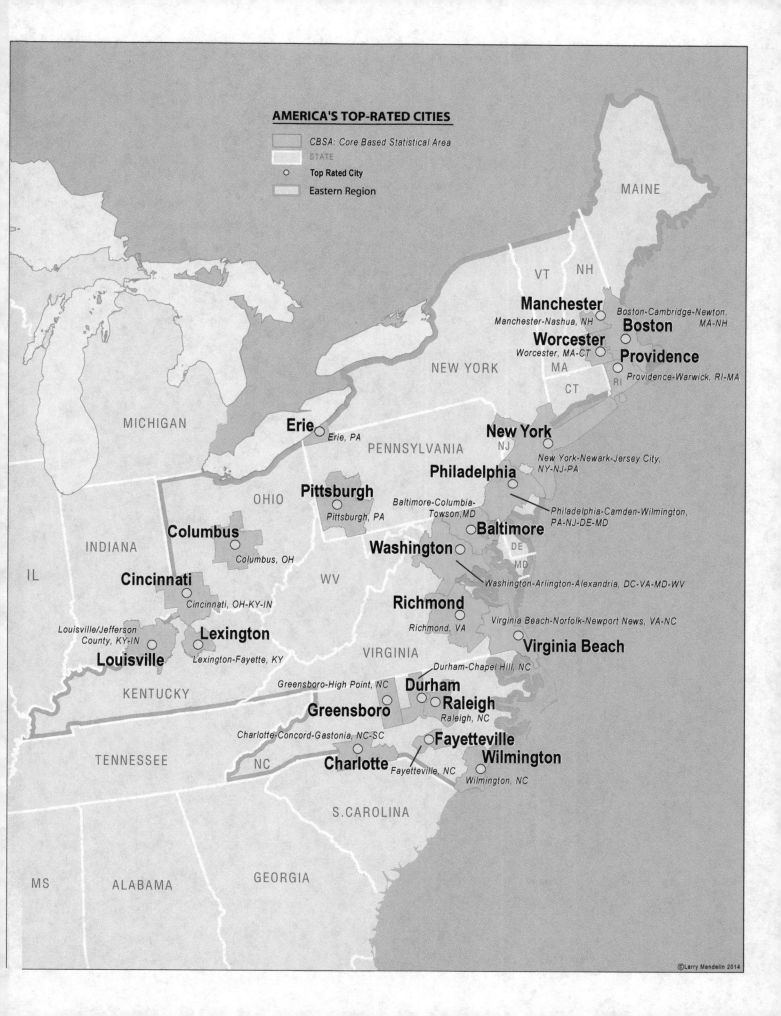

AMERICA'S TOP-RATED CITIES

- CBSA: Core Based Statistical Area
- STATE
- ○ Top Rated City
- Eastern Region

MAINE

VT   NH

Manchester
Manchester-Nashua, NH

Boston
Boston-Cambridge-Newton, MA-NH

Worcester
Worcester, MA-CT

Providence
Providence-Warwick, RI-MA

MA

CT

RI

NEW YORK

MICHIGAN

Erie
Erie, PA

PENNSYLVANIA

New York
New York-Newark-Jersey City, NY-NJ-PA

NJ

Philadelphia
Philadelphia-Camden-Wilmington, PA-NJ-DE-MD

Pittsburgh
Pittsburgh, PA

OHIO

Baltimore-Columbia-Towson, MD

Baltimore

DE

MD

Columbus
Columbus, OH

INDIANA

Washington
Washington-Arlington-Alexandria, DC-VA-MD-WV

IL

WV

Cincinnati
Cincinnati, OH-KY-IN

Richmond
Richmond, VA

Virginia Beach-Norfolk-Newport News, VA-NC

Louisville/Jefferson County, KY-IN

Lexington
Lexington-Fayette, KY

VIRGINIA

Virginia Beach

Louisville

KENTUCKY

Durham-Chapel Hill, NC

Greensboro-High Point, NC

Durham

Raleigh
Raleigh, NC

Greensboro

TENNESSEE

Charlotte-Concord-Gastonia, NC-SC

NC

Fayetteville

Wilmington

Charlotte
Fayetteville, NC

Wilmington, NC

S.CAROLINA

MS   ALABAMA   GEORGIA

©Larry Mandelin 2014

Abilene, Texas

Background

Abilene originated as a planned community of sorts. Dubbed the "Future Great City of West Texas" by J. Stoddard Johnston and other Texas and Pacific Railroad officials who, with local ranchers and land speculators, planned the town site as a station for the Texas and Pacific Railroad. As with its namesake, Abilene Kansas, town originators foresaw a rail and cattle town. Ranching, railroads and later, oil would generate a vibrant economy in the otherwise rugged landscape. With an annual, average rainfall of just 23.59 inches, it was with some foresight that early urban planners excavated several lakes (Lytle, Abilene, Kirby and Fort Phantom Hill) to provide a reliable water supply, making the arid landscape of Abilene more habitable.

Though Abilene was officially chartered in 1883, World War II put the town on the map. In 1940, Camp Barkeley was installed, the Army's largest training facility during World War II. By the end of the war, over 1,500,000 soldiers infused millions of dollars into the local economy. However, not all of those millions were totally welcomed. Since its inception, Abilene had been billed as a wholesome, family environment. Since 1903, the town had been dry and saloons had been banished. When, in March of 1941, Camp Barkeley released roughly 1,300 soldiers with weekend passes, the town was overwhelmed. Before long, prostitution and bootleg whiskey were rampant. In response, the town built several USO clubs and launched a "Bluebonnet Brigade" of more than 1,100 well-screened young women, and dozens of chaperones, to help with the restlessness of young soldiers'—some think this was the inspiration for the line "…women there don't treat you mean…" in Bob Gibson's famous song, "Abilene, Abilene." After the war, the camp was disassembled and civic leaders campaigned hard to fill the void with a new installation. Dyess Air Force Base was established in 1956.

Abilene's early Christian roots have engendered three Christian universities: Hardin-Simmons University, Abilene Christian University, and McMurry University. Texas Technical University has a School of Nursing and a School of Pharmacy in Abilene. In addition, Dyess Air Force Base operates a branch of Embry-Riddle Aeronautical University, a leader in aviation and aerospace sciences.

In 1982, Abilene began a revitalization effort for its downtown district—the first city in Texas to do so. Much of Abilene's historic downtown had been designed and constructed by David Castle (often referred to as the "Architect of Abilene") in the 1920s. One of his best-known buildings, The Grace, had originally been built as a hotel near the rail depot, where weary travellers could find rest. But when rail travel declined, the hotel closed and the building fell into disrepair. It has since been renovated and houses three museums: the Abilene Historical Museum, the Children's Museum, and the Mallouf Boot Shop, a permanent exhibit of the unique craft of cowboy boot making. Another of Castle's constructions, the Paramount Theatre, now shows classic films and hosts numerous plays and concerts. Abilene also presents regularly scheduled cultural events. On the second Saturday of each month street vendors, live entertainment, and sidewalk sales line Cypress Street for "Downtown Dayz," and the Center for Contemporary Arts hosts "Artwalk" and other venues celebrating visual and performing arts. Abilene is also home to the National Center for Children's Illustrated Literature.

The warm and dry climate makes Abilene a popular spot for numerous outdoor sports and activities, from hunting and fishing, to golf. In 1981, the PGA tour added the Fairway Oaks Golf and Racquet Club to its roster. Each year, in September, Abilene hosts the West Texas Fair and Rodeo.

Rankings

Business/Finance Rankings

- The Abilene metro area appeared on the Milken Institute "2013 Best Performing Cities" list. Rank: #47 out of 179 small metro areas. Criteria: job growth; wage and salary growth; high-tech output growth. *Milken Institute, "Best-Performing Cities 2013," December 2013*

- *Forbes* ranked 184 smaller metro areas in the U.S. in terms of the "Best Small Places for Business and Careers." The Abilene metro area was ranked #46. Criteria: costs (business and living); job growth (past and projected); income growth; educational attainment (college and high school); projected economic growth; cultural and recreational opportunities; net migration patterns; number of highly ranked colleges. *Forbes, "The Best Small Places for Business and Careers," August 7, 2013*

Environmental Rankings

- The Abilene metro area came in at #320 for the relative comfort of its climate on Sperling's list of "chill cities," as measured by the Sperling Heat Index. All 361 metro areas are included. Criteria included daytime high temperatures, nighttime low temperatures, dew point, and relative humidity at the high temperatures. *www.bertsperling.com, "Sperling's Chill Cities," July 18, 2013*

- Sperling's BestPlaces assessed 379 metropolitan areas of the United States for the likelihood of dangerously extreme weather events or earthquakes. In general the Southeast and South-Central regions have the highest risk of weather extremes and earthquakes, while the Pacific Northwest enjoys the lowest risk. Of the least risky metropolitan areas, the Abilene metro area was ranked #317. *www.bestplaces.net, "Safest Places from Natural Disasters," April 2011*

- Abilene was selected as one of 22 "Smarter Cities" for energy by the Natural Resources Defense Council. Criteria: investment in green power; energy efficiency measures; conservation. *Natural Resources Defense Council, "2010 Smarter Cities," July 19, 2010*

Real Estate Rankings

- Abilene was ranked #113 out of 224 metro areas in terms of housing affordability in 2013 by the National Association of Home Builders (#1 = most affordable). The NAHB-Wells Fargo Housing Opportunity Index (HOI) for a given area is defined as the share of homes sold in that area that would have been affordable to a family earning the local median income, based on standard mortgage underwriting criteria. *National Association of Home Builders®, NAHB-Wells Fargo Housing Opportunity Index, 4th Quarter 2013*

Safety Rankings

- The National Insurance Crime Bureau ranked 380 metro areas in the U.S. in terms of per capita rates of vehicle theft. The Abilene metro area ranked #252 (#1 = highest rate). Criteria: number of vehicle theft offenses per 100,000 inhabitants in 2012. *National Insurance Crime Bureau, "Hot Spots 2012," June 26, 2013*

Seniors/Retirement Rankings

- From its Best Cities for Successful Aging indexes, the Milken Institute generated rankings for metropolitan areas, weighing data in eight categories—general indicators, health care, wellness, living arrangements, transportation and general accessibility, financial well-being, education and employment, and community participation. The Abilene metro area was ranked #95 overall in the small metro area category. *Milken Institute, "Best Cities for Successful Aging," July 2012*

- Abilene made the 2014 *Forbes* list of "25 Best Places to Retire." Criteria include: housing and living costs; tax climate for retirees; weather and air quality; crime rates; doctor availability; active-lifestyle rankings for walkability, bicycling and volunteering. *Forbes.com, "The Best Places to Retire in 2014," January 16, 2014*

Business Environment

CITY FINANCES

City Government Finances

Component	2011 ($000)	2011 ($ per capita)
Total Revenues	158,704	1,366
Total Expenditures	143,448	1,234
Debt Outstanding	143,749	1,237
Cash and Securities[1]	96,428	830

Note: (1) Cash and security holdings of a government at the close of its fiscal year, including those of its dependent agencies, utilities, and liquor stores.
Source: U.S Census Bureau, State & Local Government Finances 2011

City Government Revenue by Source

Source	2011 ($000)	2011 ($ per capita)
General Revenue		
From Federal Government	13,753	118
From State Government	5,540	48
From Local Governments	2	0
Taxes		
Property	33,336	287
Sales and Gross Receipts	41,922	361
Personal Income	0	0
Corporate Income	0	0
Motor Vehicle License	0	0
Other Taxes	1,223	11
Current Charges	27,654	238
Liquor Store	0	0
Utility	25,356	218
Employee Retirement	0	0

Source: U.S Census Bureau, State & Local Government Finances 2011

City Government Expenditures by Function

Function	2011 ($000)	2011 ($ per capita)	2011 (%)
General Direct Expenditures			
Air Transportation	7,274	63	5.1
Corrections	0	0	0.0
Education	0	0	0.0
Employment Security Administration	0	0	0.0
Financial Administration	5,361	46	3.7
Fire Protection	16,355	141	11.4
General Public Buildings	1,487	13	1.0
Governmental Administration, Other	2,638	23	1.8
Health	4,500	39	3.1
Highways	11,304	97	7.9
Hospitals	0	0	0.0
Housing and Community Development	2,008	17	1.4
Interest on General Debt	4,051	35	2.8
Judicial and Legal	1,504	13	1.0
Libraries	2,897	25	2.0
Parking	0	0	0.0
Parks and Recreation	6,156	53	4.3
Police Protection	21,386	184	14.9
Public Welfare	0	0	0.0
Sewerage	7,982	69	5.6
Solid Waste Management	9,335	80	6.5
Veterans' Services	0	0	0.0
Liquor Store	0	0	0.0
Utility	24,820	214	17.3
Employee Retirement	0	0	0.0

Source: U.S Census Bureau, State & Local Government Finances 2011

DEMOGRAPHICS

Population Growth

Area	1990 Census	2000 Census	2010 Census	Population Growth (%) 1990-2000	Population Growth (%) 2000-2010
City	106,927	115,930	117,063	8.4	1.0
MSA[1]	148,004	160,245	165,252	8.3	3.1
U.S.	248,709,873	281,421,906	308,745,538	13.2	9.7

Note: (1) Figures cover the Abilene, TX Metropolitan Statistical Area—see Appendix B for areas included
Source: U.S. Census Bureau, Census 1990, 2000, 2010

Household Size

Area	Persons in Household (%) One	Two	Three	Four	Five	Six	Seven or More	Average Household Size
City	29.2	35.3	15.0	11.7	5.3	2.4	1.1	2.55
MSA[1]	28.5	36.8	14.7	11.4	5.4	2.2	1.0	2.55
U.S.	27.6	33.5	15.7	13.2	6.1	2.4	1.5	2.63

Note: (1) Figures cover the Abilene, TX Metropolitan Statistical Area—see Appendix B for areas included
Source: U.S. Census Bureau, 2010-2012 American Community Survey 3-Year Estimates

Race

Area	White Alone[2] (%)	Black Alone[2] (%)	Asian Alone[2] (%)	AIAN[3] Alone[2] (%)	NHOPI[4] Alone[2] (%)	Other Race Alone[2] (%)	Two or More Races (%)
City	80.3	10.3	1.8	0.5	0.0	4.2	2.9
MSA[1]	83.7	8.1	1.5	0.4	0.0	3.7	2.6
U.S.	74.0	12.6	4.9	0.8	0.2	4.7	2.8

Note: (1) Figures cover the Abilene, TX Metropolitan Statistical Area—see Appendix B for areas included; (2) Alone is defined as not being in combination with one or more other races; (3) American Indian and Alaska Native; (4) Native Hawaiian and Other Pacific Islander
Source: U.S. Census Bureau, 2010-2012 American Community Survey 3-Year Estimates

Hispanic or Latino Origin

Area	Total (%)	Mexican (%)	Puerto Rican (%)	Cuban (%)	Other (%)
City	25.1	22.4	0.5	0.1	2.1
MSA[1]	21.7	19.3	0.4	0.1	1.9
U.S.	16.6	10.7	1.6	0.6	3.7

Note: Persons of Hispanic or Latino origin can be of any race; (1) Figures cover the Abilene, TX Metropolitan Statistical Area—see Appendix B for areas included
Source: U.S. Census Bureau, 2010-2012 American Community Survey 3-Year Estimates

Segregation

Type	Segregation Indices[1] 1990	2000	2010	2010 Rank[2]	Percent Change 1990-2000	1990-2010	2000-2010
Black/White	n/a	n/a	n/a	n/a	n/a	n/a	n/a
Asian/White	n/a	n/a	n/a	n/a	n/a	n/a	n/a
Hispanic/White	n/a	n/a	n/a	n/a	n/a	n/a	n/a

Note: All figures cover the Metropolitan Statistical Area—see Appendix B for areas included; Figures are based on an analysis of 1990, 2000, and 2010 Census Decennial Census tract data by William H. Frey, Brookings Institution and the University of Michigan Social Science Data Analysis Network. In this analysis all racial groups (whites, blacks, and asians) are non-Hispanic members of those races. Hispanics are shown as a separate category;
(1) Segregation Indices are Dissimilarity Indices that measure the degree to which the minority group is distributed differently than whites across census tracts. They range from 0 (complete integration) to 100 (complete segregation) where the value indicates the percentage of the minority group that needs to move to be distributed exactly like whites; (2) Ranges from 1 (most segregated) to 102 (least segregated); n/a not available.
Source: www.CensusScope.org

Ancestry

Area	German	Irish	English	American	Italian	Polish	French[2]	Scottish	Dutch
City	12.4	9.2	7.3	6.0	1.3	0.6	2.0	1.6	0.8
MSA[1]	12.1	9.7	7.9	7.3	1.4	0.5	1.9	1.7	0.8
U.S.	15.2	11.1	8.2	7.2	5.6	3.1	2.8	1.7	1.4

Note: Figures are the percentage of the total population reporting a particular ancestry. The nine most commonly reported ancestries in the U.S. are shown. Figures include multiple ancestries (e.g. if a person reported being Irish and Italian, they were included in both columns); (1) Figures cover the Abilene, TX Metropolitan Statistical Area—see Appendix B for areas included; (2) Excludes Basque
Source: U.S. Census Bureau, 2010-2012 American Community Survey 3-Year Estimates

Foreign-Born Population

Area	Percent of Population Born in								
	Any Foreign Country	Mexico	Asia	Europe	Carribean	South America	Central America[2]	Africa	Canada
City	n/a	n/a	n/a	n/a	n/a	n/a	n/a	n/a	n/a
MSA[1]	n/a	n/a	n/a	n/a	n/a	n/a	n/a	n/a	n/a
U.S.	13.0	3.7	3.7	1.6	1.2	0.9	1.0	0.5	0.3

Note: (1) Figures cover the Abilene, TX Metropolitan Statistical Area—see Appendix B for areas included; (2) Excludes Mexico.
Source: U.S. Census Bureau, 2010-2012 American Community Survey 3-Year Estimates

Marital Status

Area	Never Married	Now Married[2]	Separated	Widowed	Divorced
City	35.3	43.2	2.4	6.8	12.2
MSA[1]	31.3	46.9	2.3	7.0	12.5
U.S.	32.4	48.4	2.2	6.0	11.0

Note: Figures are percentages and cover the population 15 years of age and older; (1) Figures cover the Abilene, TX Metropolitan Statistical Area—see Appendix B for areas included; (2) Excludes separated
Source: U.S. Census Bureau, 2010-2012 American Community Survey 3-Year Estimates

Age

Area	Percent of Population									Median Age
	Under Age 5	Age 5–19	Age 20–34	Age 35–44	Age 45–54	Age 55–64	Age 65–74	Age 75–84	Age 85+	
City	7.4	19.1	27.4	11.2	12.3	10.2	6.4	4.2	1.9	31.9
MSA[1]	6.9	19.9	23.6	11.5	13.0	11.3	7.4	4.7	1.8	34.7
U.S.	6.4	20.1	20.5	13.1	14.3	12.2	7.3	4.2	1.8	37.3

Note: (1) Figures cover the Abilene, TX Metropolitan Statistical Area—see Appendix B for areas included
Source: U.S. Census Bureau, 2010-2012 American Community Survey 3-Year Estimates

Gender

Area	Males	Females	Males per 100 Females
City	61,444	58,583	104.9
MSA[1]	83,952	82,388	101.9
U.S.	153,276,055	158,333,314	96.8

Note: (1) Figures cover the Abilene, TX Metropolitan Statistical Area—see Appendix B for areas included
Source: U.S. Census Bureau, 2010-2012 American Community Survey 3-Year Estimates

Religious Groups by Family

Area	Catholic	Baptist	Non-Den.	Methodist[2]	Lutheran	LDS[3]	Pentecostal	Presbyterian[4]	Muslim[5]	Judaism
MSA[1]	5.3	40.3	4.7	6.3	1.1	1.0	1.7	1.0	<0.1	<0.1
U.S.	19.1	9.3	4.0	4.0	2.3	2.0	1.9	1.6	0.8	0.7

Note: Figures are the number of adherents as a percentage of the total population; (1) Figures cover the Abilene, TX Metropolitan Statistical Area—see Appendix B for areas included; (2) Methodist/Pietist; (3) Latter Day Saints; (4) Reformed; (5) Figures are estimates
Source: Association of Statisticians of American Religious Bodies, 2010 U.S. Religion Census: Religious Congregations & Membership Study

Religious Groups by Tradition

Area	Catholic	Evangelical Protestant	Mainline Protestant	Other Tradition	Black Protestant	Orthodox
MSA[1]	5.3	47.4	9.0	1.1	0.4	<0.1
U.S.	19.1	16.2	7.3	4.3	1.6	0.3

Note: Figures are the number of adherents as a percentage of the total population; (1) Figures cover the Abilene, TX Metropolitan Statistical Area—see Appendix B for areas included
Source: Association of Statisticians of American Religious Bodies, 2010 U.S. Religion Census: Religious Congregations & Membership Study

ECONOMY

Gross Metropolitan Product

Area	2011	2012	2013	2014	Rank[2]
MSA[1]	5.6	6.0	6.2	6.5	244

Note: Figures are in billions of dollars; (1) Figures cover the Abilene, TX Metropolitan Statistical Area—see Appendix B for areas included; (2) Rank is based on 2014 data and ranges from 1 to 363
Source: The United States Conference of Mayors, U.S. Metro Economies: Outlook—Gross Metropolitan Product, with Metro Employment Projections, November 2013

Economic Growth

Area	2011 (%)	2012 (%)	2013 (%)	2014 (%)	Rank[2]
MSA[1]	1.3	4.9	2.6	2.0	40
U.S.	1.6	2.5	1.7	2.5	–

Note: Figures are real gross metropolitan product (GMP) growth rates and represent annual average percent change; (1) Figures cover the Abilene, TX Metropolitan Statistical Area—see Appendix B for areas included; (2) Rank is based on 2013 data and ranges from 1 to 363
Source: The United States Conference of Mayors, U.S. Metro Economies: Outlook—Gross Metropolitan Product, with Metro Employment Projections, November 2013

Metropolitan Area Exports

Area	2007	2008	2009	2010	2011	2012	Rank[2]
MSA[1]	53.2	54.4	39.2	46.8	41.2	92.9	341

Note: Figures are in millions of dollars; (1) Figures cover the Abilene, TX Metropolitan Statistical Area—see Appendix B for areas included; (2) Rank is based on 2012 data and ranges from 1 to 369
Source: U.S. Department of Commerce, International Trade Administration, Office of Trade & Industry Information, Manufacturing & Services, data extracted April 1, 2014

INCOME

Income

Area	Per Capita ($)	Median Household ($)	Average Household ($)
City	20,195	41,460	54,290
MSA[1]	21,548	42,724	57,470
U.S.	27,385	51,771	71,579

Note: (1) Figures cover the Abilene, TX Metropolitan Statistical Area—see Appendix B for areas included
Source: U.S. Census Bureau, 2010-2012 American Community Survey 3-Year Estimates

Household Income Distribution

Area	Percent of Households Earning							
	Under $15,000	$15,000 -24,999	$25,000 -34,999	$35,000 -49,999	$50,000 -74,999	$75,000 -99,000	$100,000 -149,999	$150,000 and up
City	16.4	13.3	12.7	15.9	19.3	9.8	8.4	4.3
MSA[1]	15.3	13.3	12.5	15.4	19.6	9.8	9.1	4.9
U.S.	13.1	11.0	10.5	13.7	18.1	11.9	12.5	9.1

Note: (1) Figures cover the Abilene, TX Metropolitan Statistical Area—see Appendix B for areas included
Source: U.S. Census Bureau, 2010-2012 American Community Survey 3-Year Estimates

Poverty Rate

Area	All Ages	Under 18 Years Old	18 to 64 Years Old	65 Years and Over
City	20.3	23.5	20.9	11.2
MSA[1]	18.4	22.2	18.5	11.2
U.S.	15.7	22.2	14.6	9.3

*Note: Figures are percentage of people whose income during the past 12 months was below the poverty level;
(1) Figures cover the Abilene, TX Metropolitan Statistical Area—see Appendix B for areas included
Source: U.S. Census Bureau, 2010-2012 American Community Survey 3-Year Estimates*

Personal Bankruptcy Filing Rate

Area	2008	2009	2010	2011	2012	2013
Taylor County	2.48	2.42	2.09	2.10	1.87	1.54
U.S.	3.53	4.61	4.97	4.37	3.76	3.29

*Note: Numbers are per 1,000 population and include Chapter 7 and Chapter 13 filings
Source: Federal Deposit Insurance Corporation, Regional Economic Conditions, March 20, 2014*

EMPLOYMENT

Labor Force and Employment

Area	Civilian Labor Force			Workers Employed		
	Dec. 2012	Dec. 2013	% Chg.	Dec. 2012	Dec. 2013	% Chg.
City	58,388	59,322	1.6	55,629	56,690	1.9
MSA[1]	84,362	85,707	1.6	80,437	81,972	1.9
U.S.	154,904,000	154,408,000	-0.3	143,060,000	144,423,000	1.0

*Note: Data is not seasonally adjusted and covers workers 16 years of age and older; (1) Metropolitan Statistical Area—see Appendix B for areas included
Source: Bureau of Labor Statistics, Local Area Unemployment Statistics*

Unemployment Rate

Area	2013											
	Jan.	Feb.	Mar.	Apr.	May	Jun.	Jul.	Aug.	Sep.	Oct.	Nov.	Dec.
City	5.5	5.1	5.0	4.8	5.4	5.9	5.6	5.1	5.1	4.8	4.6	4.4
MSA[1]	5.4	5.1	4.9	4.8	5.3	5.7	5.5	5.0	5.0	4.7	4.5	4.4
U.S.	8.5	8.1	7.6	7.1	7.3	7.8	7.7	7.3	7.0	7.0	6.6	6.5

*Note: Data is not seasonally adjusted and covers workers 16 years of age and older; All figures are percentages;
(1) Metropolitan Statistical Area—see Appendix B for areas included
Source: Bureau of Labor Statistics, Local Area Unemployment Statistics*

Employment by Occupation

Occupation Classification	City (%)	MSA[1] (%)	U.S. (%)
Management, Business, Science, and Arts	30.4	30.6	36.0
Natural Resources, Construction, and Maintenance	9.3	11.1	9.1
Production, Transportation, and Material Moving	9.8	10.4	12.0
Sales and Office	28.1	27.3	24.7
Service	22.4	20.6	18.2

*Note: Figures cover employed civilians 16 years of age and older; (1) Figures cover the Abilene, TX Metropolitan Statistical Area—see Appendix B for areas included
Source: U.S. Census Bureau, 2010-2012 American Community Survey 3-Year Estimates*

Employment by Industry

| Sector | MSA[1] | | U.S. |
	Number of Employees	Percent of Total	Percent of Total
Construction	n/a	n/a	4.2
Education and Health Services	13,100	19.3	15.5
Financial Activities	3,800	5.6	5.7
Government	12,700	18.7	16.1
Information	1,200	1.8	1.9
Leisure and Hospitality	7,600	11.2	10.2
Manufacturing	2,700	4.0	8.7
Mining and Logging	n/a	n/a	0.6
Other Services	2,800	4.1	3.9
Professional and Business Services	5,200	7.7	13.7
Retail Trade	8,600	12.7	11.4
Transportation and Utilities	1,900	2.8	3.8
Wholesale Trade	2,800	4.1	4.2

Note: Figures cover non-farm employment as of December 2013 and are not seasonally adjusted;
(1) Metropolitan Statistical Area—see Appendix B for areas included; n/a not available
Source: Bureau of Labor Statistics, Current Employment Statistics, Employment, Hours, and Earnings

Occupations with Greatest Projected Employment Growth: 2010 – 2020

Occupation[1]	2010 Employment	2020 Projected Employment	Numeric Employment Change	Percent Employment Change
Combined Food Preparation and Serving Workers, Including Fast Food	243,530	322,520	78,990	32.4
Elementary School Teachers, Except Special Education	166,090	233,860	67,780	40.8
Personal Care Aides	133,820	199,970	66,150	49.4
Retail Salespersons	370,620	433,180	62,560	16.9
Registered Nurses	184,700	245,870	61,160	33.1
Waiters and Waitresses	190,870	244,610	53,730	28.2
Office Clerks, General	262,740	314,810	52,070	19.8
Cashiers	250,510	292,730	42,220	16.9
Home Health Aides	82,420	123,970	41,550	50.4
Customer Service Representatives	200,880	241,030	40,160	20.0

Note: Projections cover Texas; (1) Sorted by numeric employment change
Source: www.projectionscentral.com, State Occupational Projections, 2010–2020 Long-Term Projections

Fastest Growing Occupations: 2010 – 2020

Occupation[1]	2010 Employment	2020 Projected Employment	Numeric Employment Change	Percent Employment Change
Biomedical Engineers	1,440	2,490	1,050	72.9
Diagnostic Medical Sonographers	3,560	5,410	1,850	51.9
Derrick Operators, Oil and Gas	7,190	10,860	3,670	51.1
Home Health Aides	82,420	123,970	41,550	50.4
Personal Care Aides	133,820	199,970	66,150	49.4
Service Unit Operators, Oil, Gas, and Mining	17,870	26,460	8,590	48.0
Special Education Teachers, Middle School	6,170	8,950	2,780	45.1
Special Education Teachers, Preschool, Kindergarten, and Elementary School	12,940	18,750	5,810	44.9
Rotary Drill Operators, Oil and Gas	7,160	10,340	3,180	44.4
Roustabouts, Oil and Gas	17,800	25,580	7,790	43.8

Note: Projections cover Texas; (1) Sorted by percent employment change and excludes occupations with numeric employment change less than 100
Source: www.projectionscentral.com, State Occupational Projections, 2010–2020 Long-Term Projections

Average Wages

Occupation	$/Hr.	Occupation	$/Hr.
Accountants and Auditors	27.43	Maids and Housekeeping Cleaners	8.54
Automotive Mechanics	16.42	Maintenance and Repair Workers	13.87
Bookkeepers	14.82	Marketing Managers	n/a
Carpenters	12.98	Nuclear Medicine Technologists	n/a
Cashiers	9.17	Nurses, Licensed Practical	18.56
Clerks, General Office	13.24	Nurses, Registered	28.14
Clerks, Receptionists/Information	10.53	Nursing Assistants	10.88
Clerks, Shipping/Receiving	13.69	Packers and Packagers, Hand	9.20
Computer Programmers	27.23	Physical Therapists	40.86
Computer Systems Analysts	32.18	Postal Service Mail Carriers	24.24
Computer User Support Specialists	17.64	Real Estate Brokers	n/a
Cooks, Restaurant	9.42	Retail Salespersons	13.62
Dentists	103.87	Sales Reps., Exc. Tech./Scientific	23.66
Electrical Engineers	37.88	Sales Reps., Tech./Scientific	36.44
Electricians	18.68	Secretaries, Exc. Legal/Med./Exec.	12.92
Financial Managers	56.69	Security Guards	10.71
First-Line Supervisors/Managers, Sales	22.73	Surgeons	n/a
Food Preparation Workers	9.26	Teacher Assistants	9.90
General and Operations Managers	43.14	Teachers, Elementary School	21.30
Hairdressers/Cosmetologists	11.06	Teachers, Secondary School	22.00
Internists	n/a	Telemarketers	n/a
Janitors and Cleaners	9.79	Truck Drivers, Heavy/Tractor-Trailer	18.97
Landscaping/Groundskeeping Workers	10.35	Truck Drivers, Light/Delivery Svcs.	11.41
Lawyers	50.25	Waiters and Waitresses	8.74

Note: Wage data covers the Abilene, TX Metropolitan Statistical Area—see Appendix B for areas included. Hourly wages for elementary/secondary school teachers and teacher assistants were calculated by the editors from annual wage data assuming a 40 hour work week; n/a not available.
Source: Bureau of Labor Statistics, Metro Area Occupational Employment and Wage Estimates, May 2013

RESIDENTIAL REAL ESTATE

Building Permits

Area	Single-Family			Multi-Family			Total		
	2012	2013	Pct. Chg.	2012	2013	Pct. Chg.	2012	2013	Pct. Chg.
City	233	280	20.2	206	2	-99.0	439	282	-35.8
MSA[1]	241	292	21.2	214	14	-93.5	455	306	-32.7
U.S.	518,695	620,802	19.7	310,963	370,020	19.0	829,658	990,822	19.4

Note: (1) Metropolitan Statistical Area—see Appendix B for areas included; figures represent new, privately-owned housing units authorized (unadjusted data); All permit data are based on estimates with imputation.
Source: U.S. Census Bureau, Manufacturing, Mining, and Construction Statistics, Building Permits, 2012, 2013

Homeownership Rate

Area	2006 (%)	2007 (%)	2008 (%)	2009 (%)	2010 (%)	2011 (%)	2012 (%)	2013 (%)
MSA[1]	n/a	n/a	n/a	n/a	n/a	n/a	n/a	n/a
U.S.	68.8	68.1	67.8	67.4	66.9	66.1	65.4	65.1

Note: (1) Figures cover the Abilene, TX Metropolitan Statistical Area—see Appendix B for areas included; n/a not available
Source: U.S. Census Bureau, Housing Vacancies and Homeownership Annual Statistics: 2013

Housing Vacancy Rates

Area	Gross Vacancy Rate[2] (%)			Year-Round Vacancy Rate[3] (%)			Rental Vacancy Rate[4] (%)			Homeowner Vacancy Rate[5] (%)		
	2011	2012	2013	2011	2012	2013	2011	2012	2013	2011	2012	2013
MSA[1]	n/a	n/a	n/a	n/a	n/a	n/a	n/a	n/a	n/a	n/a	n/a	n/a
U.S.	14.2	13.8	13.8	11.1	10.8	10.7	9.5	8.7	8.3	2.5	2.0	2.0

Note: (1) Figures cover the Abilene, TX Metropolitan Statistical Area—see Appendix B for areas included; (2) The percentage of the total housing inventory that is vacant; (3) The percentage of the housing inventory (excluding seasonal units) that is year-round vacant; (4) The percentage of rental inventory that is vacant for rent; (5) The percentage of homeowner inventory that is vacant for sale; n/a not available
Source: U.S. Census Bureau, Housing Vacancies and Homeownership Annual Statistics: 2013

TAXES

State Corporate Income Tax Rates

State	Tax Rate (%)	Income Brackets ($)	Num. of Brackets	Financial Institution Tax Rate (%)[a]	Federal Income Tax Ded.
Texas	(x)	–	–	(x)	No

Note: Tax rates as of January 1, 2014; (a) Rates listed are the corporate income tax rate applied to financial institutions or excise taxes based on income. Some states have other taxes based upon the value of deposits or shares; (x) Texas imposes a Franchise Tax, otherwise known as margin tax, imposed on entities with more than $1,030,000 total revenues at rate of 1%, or 0.5% for entities primarily engaged in retail or wholesale trade, on lesser of 70% of total revenues or 100% of gross receipts after deductions for either compensation or cost of goods sold.
Source: Federation of Tax Administrators, "State Corporate Income Tax Rates, 2014"

State Individual Income Tax Rates

State	Tax Rate (%)	Income Brackets ($)	Num. of Brackets	Personal Exempt. ($)[1] Single	Personal Exempt. ($)[1] Dependents	Fed. Inc. Tax Ded.
Texas	None	–	–	–	–	–

Note: Tax rates as of January 1, 2014; Local- and county-level taxes are not included; n/a not applicable;
(1) Married joint filers generally receive double the single exemption
Source: Federation of Tax Administrators, "State Individual Income Tax Rates, 2014"

Various State and Local Tax Rates

State	State and Local Sales and Use (%)	State Sales and Use (%)	Gasoline[1] (¢/gal.)	Cigarette[2] ($/pack)	Spirits[3] ($/gal.)	Wine[4] ($/gal.)	Beer[5] ($/gal.)
Texas	8.25	6.25	20.00	1.410	2.40 (f)	0.20	0.20

Note: All tax rates as of January 1, 2014; (1) The American Petroleum Institute has developed a methodology for determining the average tax rate on a gallon of fuel. Rates may include any of the following: excise taxes, environmental fees, storage tank fees, other fees or taxes, general sales tax, and local taxes. In states where gasoline is subject to the general sales tax, or where the fuel tax is based on the average sale price, the average rate determined by API is sensitive to changes in the price of gasoline. States that fully or partially apply general sales taxes to gasoline: CA, CO, GA, IL, IN, MI, NY; (2) The federal excise tax of $1.0066 per pack and local taxes are not included; (3) Rates are those applicable to off-premise sales of 40% alcohol by volume (a.b.v.) distilled spirits in 750ml containers. Local excise taxes are excluded; (4) Rates are those applicable to off-premise sales of 11% a.b.v. non-carbonated wine in 750ml containers; (5) Rates are those applicable to off-premise sales of 4.7% a.b.v. beer in 12 ounce containers; (f) Different rates also applicable according to alcohol content, place of production, size of container, or place purchased (on- or off-premise or onboard airlines).
Source: Tax Foundation, 2014 Facts & Figures: How Does Your State Compare?

State Business Tax Climate Index Rankings

State	Overall Rank	Corporate Tax Index Rank	Individual Income Tax Index Rank	Sales Tax Index Rank	Unemployment Insurance Tax Index Rank	Property Tax Index Rank
Texas	11	38	7	36	14	35

Note: The index is a measure of how each state's tax laws affect economic performance. The lower the rank, the more favorable a state's tax system is for business. States without a given tax are given a ranking of 1. The scores/rankings for the District of Columbia do not affect other states. The 2014 index represents the tax climate as of July 1, 2013.
Source: Tax Foundation, State Business Tax Climate Index 2014

COMMERCIAL UTILITIES

Typical Monthly Electric Bills

Area	Commercial Service ($/month) 1,500 kWh	Commercial Service ($/month) 40 kW demand 14,000 kWh	Industrial Service ($/month) 1,000 kW demand 200,000 kWh	Industrial Service ($/month) 50,000 kW demand 15,000,000 kWh
City	n/a	n/a	n/a	n/a
Average[1]	197	1,636	25,662	1,485,307

Note: Based on total rates in effect July 1, 2013; (1) average based on 180 utilities surveyed; n/a not available
Source: Edison Electric Institute, Typical Bills and Average Rates Report, Summer 2013

TRANSPORTATION

Means of Transportation to Work

Area	Car/Truck/Van		Public Transportation			Bicycle	Walked	Other Means	Worked at Home
	Drove Alone	Car-pooled	Bus	Subway	Railroad				
City	80.3	10.2	1.1	0.0	0.0	0.2	2.9	2.7	2.5
MSA[1]	80.1	11.1	0.8	0.0	0.0	0.2	2.5	2.7	2.4
U.S.	76.4	9.7	2.6	1.7	0.5	0.6	2.8	1.3	4.3

Note: Figures are percentages and cover workers 16 years of age and older; (1) Figures cover the Abilene, TX Metropolitan Statistical Area—see Appendix B for areas included
Source: U.S. Census Bureau, 2010-2012 American Community Survey 3-Year Estimates

Travel Time to Work

Area	Less Than 10 Minutes	10 to 19 Minutes	20 to 29 Minutes	30 to 44 Minutes	45 to 59 Minutes	60 to 89 Minutes	90 Minutes or More
City	24.2	56.3	11.3	3.9	1.7	1.6	1.1
MSA[1]	24.2	47.2	15.5	7.6	2.3	1.8	1.5
U.S.	13.5	29.8	20.9	20.1	7.5	5.6	2.5

Note: Figures are percentages and include workers 16 years old and over; (1) Figures cover the Abilene, TX Metropolitan Statistical Area—see Appendix B for areas included
Source: U.S. Census Bureau, 2010-2012 American Community Survey 3-Year Estimates

Travel Time Index

Area	1985	1990	1995	2000	2005	2010	2011
Urban Area[1]	n/a	n/a	n/a	n/a	n/a	n/a	n/a
Average[2]	1.09	1.14	1.16	1.19	1.23	1.18	1.18

Note: Travel Time Index—the ratio of travel time in the peak period to the travel time at free-flow conditions. For example, a value of 1.30 indicates a 20-minute free-flow trip takes 26 minutes in the peak. Free-flow speeds (60 mph on freeways and 35 mph on principal arterials) are used as the comparison threshold; (1) Data for the Abilene, TX urban area was not available; (2) average of 498 urban areas
Source: Texas Transportation Institute, Urban Mobility Report 2012, December 2012

Public Transportation

Agency Name / Mode of Transportation	Vehicles Operated in Maximum Service	Annual Unlinked Passenger Trips (in thous.)	Annual Passenger Miles (in thous.)
CityLink Transit			
Bus (directly operated)	12	507.5	n/a
Demand Response (directly operated)	17	102.9	n/a

Source: Federal Transit Administration, National Transit Database, 2012

Air Transportation

Airport Name and Code / Type of Service	Passenger Airlines[1]	Passenger Enplanements	Freight Carriers[2]	Freight (lbs.)
Abilene Regional Airport (ABI)				
Domestic service (U.S. carriers - 2013)	6	82,616	2	600,792
International service (U.S. carriers - 2012)	0	0	0	0

Note: (1) Includes all U.S.-based major, minor and commuter airlines that carried at least one passenger during the year; (2) Includes all U.S.-based airlines and freight carriers that transported at least one lb. of freight during the year.
Source: Bureau of Transportation Statistics, The Intermodal Transportation Database, Air Carriers: T-100 Domestic Market (U.S. Carriers), 2013; Bureau of Transportation Statistics, The Intermodal Transportation Database, Air Carriers: T-100 International Market (U.S. Carriers), 2012

Other Transportation Statistics

Major Highways:	I-20
Amtrak Service:	No
Major Waterways/Ports:	None

Source: Amtrak.com; Google Maps

BUSINESSES

Major Business Headquarters

Company Name	Rankings	
	Fortune[1]	Forbes[2]
No companies listed	-	-

Note: (1) Fortune 500—companies that produce a 10-K are ranked 1 to 500 based on 2012 revenue; (2) all private companies with at least $2 billion in annual revenue through the end of their most current fiscal year are ranked 1 to 224; companies listed are headquartered in the city; dashes indicate no ranking
Source: Fortune, "Fortune 500," May 20, 2013; Forbes, "America's Largest Private Companies," December 18, 2013

Minority- and Women-Owned Businesses

Group	All Firms		Firms with Paid Employees			
	Firms	Sales ($000)	Firms	Sales ($000)	Employees	Payroll ($000)
Asian	(s)	(s)	(s)	(s)	(s)	(s)
Black	(s)	(s)	(s)	(s)	(s)	(s)
Hispanic	(s)	(s)	(s)	(s)	(s)	(s)
Women	2,267	236,656	266	176,748	1,345	32,405
All Firms	10,332	9,178,021	2,673	8,763,509	49,395	1,294,341

Note: Figures cover firms located in the city; minority- and women-owned business are defined as firms in which the corresponding group own 51% or more of the stock or equity of the company; (s) estimates are suppressed when publication standards are not met
Source: U.S. Census Bureau, 2007 Economic Census, Survey of Business Owners (2012 Survey of Business Owners data will be released starting in June 2015)

HOTELS & CONVENTION CENTERS

Hotels/Motels

Area	5 Star		4 Star		3 Star		2 Star		1 Star		Not Rated	
	Num.	Pct.[3]	Num.	Pct.[3]	Num.	Pct.[3]	Num.	Pct.[3]	Num.	Pct.[3]	Num.	Pct.[3]
City[1]	0	0.0	0	0.0	4	10.8	24	64.9	2	5.4	7	18.9
Total[2]	142	0.9	1,005	6.0	5,147	30.9	8,578	51.4	408	2.4	1,397	8.4

Note: (1) Figures cover Abilene and vicinity; (2) Figures cover all 100 cities in this book; (3) Percentage of hotels which have a given star rating; Star ratings are determined by expedia.com and offer an indication of the general quality of a particular hotel.
Source: expedia.com, April 7, 2014

Major Convention Centers

Name	Overall Space (sq. ft.)	Exhibit Space (sq. ft.)	Meeting Space (sq. ft.)	Meeting Rooms
Abilene Civic Center	113,218	20,000	n/a	n/a

Note: Table includes convention centers located in the Abilene, TX metro area; n/a not available
Source: Original research

Living Environment

COST OF LIVING

Cost of Living Index

Composite Index	Groceries	Housing	Utilities	Trans-portation	Health Care	Misc. Goods/ Services
n/a	n/a	n/a	n/a	n/a	n/a	n/a

Note: The Cost of Living Index measures regional differences in the cost of consumer goods and services, excluding taxes and non-consumer expenditures, for professional and managerial households in the top income quintile. It is based on more than 50,000 prices covering almost 60 different items for which prices are collected three times a year by chambers of commerce, economic development organizations or university applied economic centers in each participating urban area. The numbers shown should be read as a percentage above or below the national average of 100. For example, a value of 115.4 in the groceries column indicates that grocery prices are 15.4% higher than the national average. Small differences in the index numbers should not be interpreted as significant; n/a not available.
Source: The Council for Community and Economic Research, ACCRA Cost of Living Index, 2013

Grocery Prices

Area[1]	T-Bone Steak ($/pound)	Frying Chicken ($/pound)	Whole Milk ($/half gal.)	Eggs ($/dozen)	Orange Juice ($/64 oz.)	Coffee ($/11.5 oz.)
City[2]	n/a	n/a	n/a	n/a	n/a	n/a
Avg.	10.19	1.28	2.34	1.81	3.48	4.39
Min.	8.56	0.94	1.44	1.19	2.78	3.40
Max.	14.82	2.28	3.56	3.73	6.23	7.32

Note: (1) Values for the local area are compared with the average, minimum and maximum values for all 327 areas in the Cost of Living Index; (2) Figures cover the Abilene TX urban area; n/a not available; **T-Bone Steak** (price per pound); **Frying Chicken** (price per pound, whole fryer); **Whole Milk** (half gallon carton); **Eggs** (price per dozen, Grade A, large); **Orange Juice** (64 oz. Tropicana or Florida Natural); **Coffee** (11.5 oz. can, vacuum-packed, Maxwell House, Hills Bros, or Folgers).
Source: The Council for Community and Economic Research, ACCRA Cost of Living Index, 2013

Housing and Utility Costs

Area[1]	New Home Price ($)	Apartment Rent ($/month)	All Electric ($/month)	Part Electric ($/month)	Other Energy ($/month)	Telephone ($/month)
City[2]	n/a	n/a	n/a	n/a	n/a	n/a
Avg.	295,864	900	171.38	91.82	70.12	27.73
Min.	185,506	458	117.80	48.81	33.67	17.16
Max.	1,358,917	3,783	441.68	171.40	372.65	39.47

Note: (1) Values for the local area are compared with the average, minimum and maximum values for all 327 areas in the Cost of Living Index; (2) Figures cover the Abilene TX urban area; n/a not available; **New Home Price** (2,400 sf living area, 8,000 sf lot, in urban area with full utilities); **Apartment Rent** (950 sf 2 bedroom/1.5 or 2 bath, unfurnished, excluding all utilities except water); **All Electric** (average monthly cost for an all-electric home); **Part Electric** (average monthly cost for a part-electric home); **Other Energy** (average monthly cost for natural gas, fuel oil, coal, wood, and any other forms of energy except electricity); **Telephone** (price includes basic monthly rate for a private residential line plus additional local usage charges incurred by a family of four).
Source: The Council for Community and Economic Research, ACCRA Cost of Living Index, 2013

Health Care, Transportation, and Other Costs

Area[1]	Doctor ($/visit)	Dentist ($/visit)	Optometrist ($/visit)	Gasoline ($/gallon)	Beauty Salon ($/visit)	Men's Shirt ($)
City[2]	n/a	n/a	n/a	n/a	n/a	n/a
Avg.	101.40	86.48	96.16	3.44	33.87	26.55
Min.	61.67	50.83	50.12	3.08	18.92	12.48
Max.	182.71	152.50	223.78	4.33	68.22	52.03

Note: (1) Values for the local area are compared with the average, minimum and maximum values for all 327 areas in the Cost of Living Index; (2) Figures cover the Abilene TX urban area; n/a not available; **Doctor** (general practitioners routine exam of an established patient); **Dentist** (adult teeth cleaning and periodic oral examination); **Optometrist** (full vision eye exam for established adult patient); **Gasoline** (one gallon regular unleaded, national brand, including all taxes, cash price at self-service pump if available); **Beauty Salon** (woman's shampoo, trim, and blow-dry); **Men's Shirt** (cotton/polyester dress shirt, pinpoint weave, long sleeves).
Source: The Council for Community and Economic Research, ACCRA Cost of Living Index, 2013

HOUSING

House Price Index (HPI)

Area	National Ranking[2]	Quarterly Change (%)	One-Year Change (%)	Five-Year Change (%)
MSA[1]	(a)	n/a	5.43	6.70
U.S.[3]	–	1.20	7.69	4.18

Note: The HPI is a weighted repeat sales index. It measures average price changes in repeat sales or refinancings on the same properties. This information is obtained by reviewing repeat mortgage transactions on single-family properties whose mortgages have been purchased or securitized by Fannie Mae or Freddie Mac in January 1975; (1) Abilene, TX Metropolitan Statistical Area—see Appendix B for areas included; (2) Rankings are based on annual percentage change for all metro areas containing at least 15,000 transactions over the last 10 years and ranges from 1 to 283; (3) figures based on a weighted average of Census Division estimates using a seasonally adjusted, purchase-only index; all figures are for the period ending December 31, 2013; n/a not available; (a) Not ranked because of increased index variability due to smaller sample size
Source: Federal Housing Finance Agency, House Price Index, February 25, 2014

Median Single-Family Home Prices

Area	2011	2012	2013p	Percent Change 2012 to 2013
MSA[1]	119.2	124.6	129.7	4.1
U.S. Average	166.2	177.2	197.4	11.4

Note: Figures are median sales prices of existing single-family homes in thousands of dollars; (p) preliminary; n/a not available; (1) Abilene, TX Metropolitan Statistical Area—see Appendix B for areas included
Source: National Association of Realtors, Median Sales Price of Existing Single-Family Homes for Metropolitan Areas, 4th Quarter 2013

Qualifying Income Based on Median Sales Price of Existing Single-Family Homes

Area	With 5% Down ($)	With 10% Down ($)	With 20% Down ($)
MSA[1]	28,473	26,974	23,977
U.S. Average	45,395	43,006	38,228

Note: Figures are preliminary; Qualifying income is based on a mortgage rate of 4.4%. Monthly principal and interest payment is limited to 25% of income; n/a not available; (1) Abilene, TX Metropolitan Statistical Area—see Appendix B for areas included
Source: National Association of Realtors, Qualifying Income Based on Median Sales Price of Existing Single-Family Homes for Metropolitan Areas, 4th Quarter 2013

Median Apartment Condo-Coop Home Prices

Area	2011	2012	2013p	Percent Change 2012 to 2013
MSA[1]	n/a	n/a	n/a	n/a
U.S. Average	165.1	173.7	194.9	12.2

Note: Figures are median sales prices of existing apartment condo-coop homes in thousands of dollars; (p) preliminary; n/a not available; (1) Abilene, TX Metropolitan Statistical Area—see Appendix B for areas included
Source: National Association of Realtors, Median Sales Price of Existing Apartment Condo-Coop Homes for Metropolitan Areas, 4th Quarter 2013

Gross Monthly Rent

Area	Under $200	$200 -299	$300 -499	$500 -749	$750 -999	$1,000 -1,499	$1,500 and up	Median ($)
City	1.5	0.7	10.6	35.9	27.4	18.2	5.6	761
MSA[1]	1.8	1.5	11.9	35.6	27.4	16.3	5.4	745
U.S.	1.7	3.3	8.1	22.7	24.3	25.7	14.3	889

Note: Figures are percentages except for Median; Gross rent is the contract rent plus the estimated average monthly cost of utilities (electricity, gas, and water and sewer) and fuels (oil, coal, kerosene, wood, etc.) if these are paid by the renter (or paid for the renter by someone else); (1) Figures cover the Abilene, TX Metropolitan Statistical Area—see Appendix B for areas included
Source: U.S. Census Bureau, 2010-2012 American Community Survey 3-Year Estimates

Year Housing Structure Built

Area	2010 or Later	2000 -2009	1990 -1999	1980 -1989	1970 -1979	1960 -1969	1950 -1959	1940 -1949	Before 1940	Median Year
City	0.7	9.8	8.9	17.2	13.7	12.4	20.4	7.1	9.7	1970
MSA[1]	0.9	11.2	9.1	17.6	14.9	11.0	17.1	7.4	10.6	1973
U.S.	0.5	14.9	13.8	13.9	15.9	11.1	10.9	5.5	13.5	1976

Note: Figures are percentages except for Median Year; (1) Figures cover the Abilene, TX Metropolitan Statistical Area—see Appendix B for areas included
Source: U.S. Census Bureau, 2010-2012 American Community Survey 3-Year Estimates

HEALTH

Health Risk Data

Category	MSA[1] (%)	U.S. (%)
Adults aged 18–64 who have any kind of health care coverage	n/a	79.6
Adults who reported being in good or excellent health	n/a	83.1
Adults who are current smokers	n/a	19.6
Adults who are heavy drinkers[2]	n/a	6.1
Adults who are binge drinkers[3]	n/a	16.9
Adults who are overweight (BMI 25.0 - 29.9)	n/a	35.8
Adults who are obese (BMI 30.0 - 99.8)	n/a	27.6
Adults who participated in any physical activities in the past month	n/a	77.1
Adults 50+ who have ever had a sigmoidoscopy or colonoscopy	n/a	67.3
Women aged 40+ who have had a mammogram within the past two years	n/a	74.0
Men aged 40+ who have had a PSA test within the past two years	n/a	45.2
Adults aged 65+ who have had flu shot within the past year	n/a	60.1
Adults who always wear a seatbelt	n/a	93.8

Note: Data as of 2012 unless otherwise noted; n/a not available; (1) Figures cover the Abilene, TX Metropolitan Statistical Area—see Appendix B for areas included; (2) Heavy drinkers are classified as males having more than two drinks per day or females having more than one drink per day; (3) Binge drinkers are classified as males having five or more drinks on one occasion or females having four or more drinks on one occasion
Source: Centers for Disease Control and Prevention, Behaviorial Risk Factor Surveillance System, SMART: Selected Metropolitan/Micropolitan Area Risk Trends, 2012

Chronic Health Indicators

Category	MSA[1] (%)	U.S. (%)
Adults who have ever been told they had a heart attack	n/a	4.5
Adults who have ever been told they had a stroke	n/a	2.9
Adults who have been told they currently have asthma	n/a	8.9
Adults who have ever been told they have arthritis	n/a	25.7
Adults who have ever been told they have diabetes[2]	n/a	9.7
Adults who have ever been told they had skin cancer	n/a	5.7
Adults who have ever been told they had any other types of cancer	n/a	6.5
Adults who have ever been told they have COPD	n/a	6.2
Adults who have ever been told they have kidney disease	n/a	2.5
Adults who have ever been told they have a form of depression	n/a	18.0

Note: Data as of 2012 unless otherwise noted; n/a not available; (1) Figures cover the Abilene, TX Metropolitan Statistical Area—see Appendix B for areas included; (2) Figures do not include pregnancy-related, borderline, or pre-diabetes
Source: Centers for Disease Control and Prevention, Behaviorial Risk Factor Surveillance System, SMART: Selected Metropolitan/Micropolitan Area Risk Trends, 2012

Mortality Rates for the Top 10 Causes of Death in the U.S.

ICD-10[a] Sub-Chapter	ICD-10[a] Code	Age-Adjusted Mortality Rate[1] per 100,000 population	
		County[2]	U.S.
Malignant neoplasms	C00-C97	187.0	174.2
Ischaemic heart diseases	I20-I25	153.6	119.1
Other forms of heart disease	I30-I51	49.3	49.6
Chronic lower respiratory diseases	J40-J47	46.0	43.2
Cerebrovascular diseases	I60-I69	59.9	40.3
Organic, including symptomatic, mental disorders	F01-F09	29.3	30.5
Other degenerative diseases of the nervous system	G30-G31	41.0	26.3
Other external causes of accidental injury	W00-X59	25.1	25.1
Diabetes mellitus	E10-E14	30.3	21.3
Hypertensive diseases	I10-I15	22.1	18.8

Note: (a) ICD-10 = International Classification of Diseases 10th Revision; (1) Mortality rates are a three year average covering 2008-2010; (2) Figures cover Taylor County
Source: Centers for Disease Control and Prevention, National Center for Health Statistics. Compressed Mortality File 1999-2010 on CDC WONDER Online Database, released January 2013. Data are compiled from the Compressed Mortality File 1999-2010, Series 20 No. 2P, 2013.

Mortality Rates for Selected Causes of Death

ICD-10[a] Sub-Chapter	ICD-10[a] Code	Age-Adjusted Mortality Rate[1] per 100,000 population	
		County[2]	U.S.
Assault	X85-Y09	*4.2	5.5
Diseases of the liver	K70-K76	17.9	12.4
Human immunodeficiency virus (HIV) disease	B20-B24	Suppressed	3.0
Influenza and pneumonia	J09-J18	17.7	16.4
Intentional self-harm	X60-X84	13.2	11.8
Malnutrition	E40-E46	Suppressed	0.8
Obesity and other hyperalimentation	E65-E68	Suppressed	1.6
Renal failure	N17-N19	13.2	13.6
Transport accidents	V01-V99	17.8	12.6
Viral hepatitis	B15-B19	*3.7	2.2

Note: (a) ICD-10 = International Classification of Diseases 10th Revision; (1) Mortality rates are a three year average covering 2008-2010; (2) Figures cover Taylor County; (*) Unreliable data as per CDC
Source: Centers for Disease Control and Prevention, National Center for Health Statistics. Compressed Mortality File 1999-2010 on CDC WONDER Online Database, released January 2013. Data are compiled from the Compressed Mortality File 1999-2010, Series 20 No. 2P, 2013.

Health Insurance Coverage

Area	With Health Insurance	With Private Health Insurance	With Public Health Insurance	Without Health Insurance	Population Under Age 18 Without Health Insurance
City	80.8	59.8	33.3	19.2	9.4
MSA[1]	80.5	60.3	32.9	19.5	10.8
U.S.	84.9	65.4	30.4	15.1	7.5

Note: Figures are percentages that cover the civilian noninstitutionalized population; (1) Figures cover the Abilene, TX Metropolitan Statistical Area—see Appendix B for areas included
Source: U.S. Census Bureau, 2010-2012 American Community Survey 3-Year Estimates

Number of Medical Professionals

Area[1]	MDs[2]	DOs[2,3]	Dentists	Podiatrists	Chiropractors	Optometrists
Local (number)	273	29	84	8	23	23
Local (rate[4])	205.7	21.8	62.7	6.0	17.2	17.2
U.S. (rate[4])	267.6	19.6	61.7	5.6	24.7	14.5

Note: Data as of 2012 unless noted; (1) Local data covers Taylor County; (2) Data as of 2011; (3) Doctor of Osteopathic Medicine; (4) rate per 100,000 population
Source: Area Resource File (ARF) 2012-2013. U.S. Department of Health and Human Services, Health Resources and Services Administration, Bureau of Health Professions

EDUCATION

Public School District Statistics

District Name	Schls	Pupils	Pupil/Teacher Ratio	Minority Pupils[1] (%)	Free Lunch Eligible[2] (%)	IEP[3] (%)
Abilene ISD	39	17,177	15.4	58.8	54.5	12.8
Wylie ISD	5	3,399	16.3	21.9	10.6	7.3

Note: Table includes school districts with 2,000 or more students; (1) Percentage of students that are not non-Hispanic white; (2) Percentage of students that are eligible for the free lunch program; (3) Percentage of students that have an Individualized Education Program.
Source: U.S. Department of Education, National Center for Education Statistics, Common Core of Data, Local Education Agency (School District) Universe Survey: School Year 2011-2012; U.S. Department of Education, National Center for Education Statistics, Common Core of Data, Public Elementary/Secondary School Universe Survey: School Year 2011-2012

Highest Level of Education

Area	Less than H.S.	H.S. Diploma	Some College, No Deg.	Associate Degree	Bachelor's Degree	Master's Degree	Prof. School Degree	Doctorate Degree
City	17.7	28.2	25.4	6.6	14.8	5.1	1.3	1.0
MSA[1]	16.8	30.4	25.5	6.3	14.1	4.8	1.2	0.9
U.S.	14.1	28.3	21.3	7.8	18.0	7.5	1.9	1.2

Note: Figures cover persons age 25 and over; (1) Figures cover the Abilene, TX Metropolitan Statistical Area—see Appendix B for areas included
Source: U.S. Census Bureau, 2010-2012 American Community Survey 3-Year Estimates

Educational Attainment by Race

Area	High School Graduate or Higher (%)					Bachelor's Degree or Higher (%)				
	Total	White	Black	Asian	Hisp.[2]	Total	White	Black	Asian	Hisp.[2]
City	82.3	84.7	71.7	82.6	61.7	22.1	24.2	9.1	30.6	6.8
MSA[1]	83.2	85.5	69.5	83.4	61.4	20.9	22.4	8.4	31.8	6.2
U.S.	85.9	88.1	82.5	85.5	63.1	28.6	30.0	18.4	50.2	13.4

Note: Figures shown cover persons 25 years old and over; (1) Figures cover the Abilene, TX Metropolitan Statistical Area—see Appendix B for areas included; (2) People of Hispanic origin can be of any race
Source: U.S. Census Bureau, 2010-2012 American Community Survey 3-Year Estimates

School Enrollment by Grade and Control

Area	Preschool (%)		Kindergarten (%)		Grades 1 - 4 (%)		Grades 5 - 8 (%)		Grades 9 - 12 (%)	
	Public	Private	Public	Private	Public	Private	Public	Private	Public	Private
City	78.7	21.3	99.0	1.0	94.3	5.7	91.9	8.1	94.9	5.1
MSA[1]	78.5	21.5	98.4	1.6	94.3	5.7	93.2	6.8	93.9	6.1
U.S.	56.9	43.1	87.8	12.2	89.9	10.1	90.0	10.0	90.8	9.2

Note: Figures shown cover persons 3 years old and over; (1) Figures cover the Abilene, TX Metropolitan Statistical Area—see Appendix B for areas included
Source: U.S. Census Bureau, 2010-2012 American Community Survey 3-Year Estimates

Average Salaries of Public School Classroom Teachers

Area	2012-13		2013-14		Percent Change 2012-13 to 2013-14	Percent Change 2003-04 to 2013-14
	Dollars	Rank[1]	Dollars	Rank[1]		
Texas	48,819	35	49,270	35	0.92	21.7
U.S. Average	56,103	–	56,689	–	1.04	21.8

Note: (1) State rank ranges from 1 to 51 where 1 indicates highest salary.
Source: National Education Association, Rankings & Estimates: Rankings of the States 2013 and Estimates of School Statistics 2014, March 2014

Higher Education

Four-Year Colleges			Two-Year Colleges			Medical Schools[1]	Law Schools[2]	Voc/ Tech[3]
Public	Private Non-profit	Private For-profit	Public	Private Non-profit	Private For-profit			
0	3	0	0	0	0	0	0	2

Note: Figures cover institutions located within the city limits and include main campuses only; (1) includes schools accredited by the Liaison Committee on Medical Education and the American Osteopathic Association's Commission on Osteopathic College Accreditation; (2) includes ABA-accredited schools, schools with provisional ABA accreditation, and state accredited schools; (3) includes all schools with programs that are less than 2 years.
Source: National Center for Education Statistics, Integrated Postsecondary Education System (IPEDS), 2012-13; Association of American Medical Colleges, Member List, April 24, 2014; American Osteopathic Association, Member List, April 24, 2014; Law School Admission Council, Official Guide to ABA-Approved Law Schools Online, April 24, 2014; Wikipedia, List of Medical Schools in the United States, April 24, 2014; Wikipedia, List of Law Schools in the United States, April 24, 2014

PRESIDENTIAL ELECTION

2012 Presidential Election Results

Area	Obama	Romney	Other
Taylor County	22.5	76.1	1.4
U.S.	51.0	47.2	1.8

Note: Results are percentages and may not add to 100% due to rounding
Source: Dave Leip's Atlas of U.S. Presidential Elections

EMPLOYERS

Major Employers

Company Name	Industry
Abilene Christian University	Education
Abilene Diagnostic Clinic	Medical
Abilene ISD	Education
Abilene Regional Medical Center	Medical
Abilene State Supported Living Center	Government
BlueCross BlueShield of Texas	Telecommunications
Cisco College	Education
City of Abilene	Government
Coca-Cola Refreshments USA	Manufacturing
Dyess Air Force Base	Government
Eagle Aviation Services	Other
Fehr Foods	Manufacturing
First Financial Bank	Finance
Hardin-Simmons University	Education
Hendrick Health System	Medical
Lauren Engineers	Other
McMurry University	Education
Rentech Boiler Systems	Manufacturing
Sears Methodist Retirement	Medical
Smith Pipe	Manufacturing
Taylor County	Government
Teleperformance USA	Telecommunications
TX Dept. of Criminal Justice	Government
US Postal Service	Government
Wylie ISD	Education

Note: Companies shown are located within the Abilene, TX Metropolitan Statistical Area.
Source: Hoovers.com; Wikipedia

PUBLIC SAFETY

Crime Rate

Area	All Crimes	Violent Crimes				Property Crimes		
		Murder	Forcible Rape	Robbery	Aggrav. Assault	Burglary	Larceny -Theft	Motor Vehicle Theft
City	4,058.0	2.5	31.7	105.9	253.6	865.0	2,656.7	142.6
Suburbs[1]	1,570.7	0.0	14.3	18.4	136.7	424.3	909.8	67.3
Metro[2]	3,336.1	1.8	26.6	80.5	219.6	737.1	2,149.7	120.8
U.S.	3,246.1	4.7	26.9	112.9	242.3	670.2	1,959.3	229.7

Note: Figures are crimes per 100,000 population; (1) All areas within the metro area that are located outside the city limits; (2) Figures cover the Abilene, TX Metropolitan Statistical Area—see Appendix B for areas included
Source: FBI Uniform Crime Reports, 2012

Hate Crimes

Area	Number of Quarters Reported	Bias Motivation				
		Race	Religion	Sexual Orientation	Ethnicity	Disability
City	4	0	0	0	0	0
U.S.	4	2,797	1,099	1,135	667	92

Source: Federal Bureau of Investigation, Hate Crime Statistics 2012

Identity Theft Consumer Complaints

Area	Complaints	Complaints per 100,000 Population	Rank[2]
MSA[1]	73	44.2	317
U.S.	290,056	91.8	-

Note: (1) Figures cover the Abilene, TX Metropolitan Statistical Area—see Appendix B for areas included; (2) Rank ranges from 1 to 377 where 1 indicates greatest number of identity theft complaints per 100,000 population
Source: Federal Trade Commission, Consumer Sentinel Network Data Book for January–December 2013

Fraud and Other Consumer Complaints

Area	Complaints	Complaints per 100,000 Population	Rank[2]
MSA[1]	452	273.5	344
U.S.	1,811,724	595.2	-

Note: (1) Figures cover the Abilene, TX Metropolitan Statistical Area—see Appendix B for areas included; (2) Rank ranges from 1 to 377 where 1 indicates greatest number of identity theft complaints per 100,000 population
Source: Federal Trade Commission, Consumer Sentinel Network Data Book for January–December 2013

RECREATION

Culture

Dance[1]	Theatre[1]	Instrumental Music[1]	Vocal Music[1]	Series and Festivals	Museums and Art Galleries[2]	Zoos and Aquariums[3]
0	0	1	0	0	7	1

Note: (1) Number of professional perfoming groups; (2) Based on organizations with primary SIC code 8412; (3) AZA-accredited
Source: The Grey House Performing Arts Directory, 2013; Association of Zoos & Aquariums, AZA Member Zoos & Aquariums, April 2014; www.AccuLeads.com, May 1, 2014

Professional Sports Teams

Team Name	League	Year Established
No teams are located in the metro area		

Source: Wikipedia, Major Professional Sports Teams of the United States and Canada, April 25, 2014

CLIMATE

Average and Extreme Temperatures

Temperature	Jan	Feb	Mar	Apr	May	Jun	Jul	Aug	Sep	Oct	Nov	Dec	Yr.
Extreme High (°F)	88	89	97	99	107	109	110	107	106	103	92	89	110
Average High (°F)	55	60	68	78	84	91	95	94	87	78	66	58	76
Average Temp. (°F)	44	48	56	65	73	80	84	83	76	66	54	46	65
Average Low (°F)	31	36	43	53	61	69	72	72	65	54	42	34	53
Extreme Low (°F)	-1	-7	9	25	36	47	57	55	38	28	14	-7	-7

Note: Figures cover the years 1948-1990
Source: National Climatic Data Center, International Station Meteorological Climate Summary, 9/96

Average Precipitation/Snowfall/Humidity

Precip./Humidity	Jan	Feb	Mar	Apr	May	Jun	Jul	Aug	Sep	Oct	Nov	Dec	Yr.
Avg. Precip. (in.)	0.9	1.1	1.1	2.1	3.4	2.7	2.3	2.4	2.8	2.5	1.3	1.0	23.6
Avg. Snowfall (in.)	2	1	1	0	0	0	0	0	0	Tr	1	1	5
Avg. Rel. Hum. 6am (%)	72	73	69	72	79	78	73	73	77	76	73	71	74
Avg. Rel. Hum. 3pm (%)	44	44	37	38	43	41	38	37	43	43	42	43	41

Note: Figures cover the years 1948-1990; Tr = Trace amounts (<0.05 in. of rain; <0.5 in. of snow)
Source: National Climatic Data Center, International Station Meteorological Climate Summary, 9/96

Weather Conditions

Temperature			Daytime Sky			Precipitation		
10°F & below	32°F & below	90°F & above	Clear	Partly cloudy	Cloudy	0.01 inch or more precip.	0.1 inch or more snow/ice	Thunder-storms
2	52	102	141	125	99	65	4	43

Note: Figures are average number of days per year and cover the years 1948-1990
Source: National Climatic Data Center, International Station Meteorological Climate Summary, 9/96

HAZARDOUS WASTE

Superfund Sites

Abilene has no sites on the EPA's Superfund Final National Priorities List.
U.S. Environmental Protection Agency, Final National Priorities List, April 26, 2014

AIR & WATER QUALITY

Air Quality Index

Area	Percent of Days when Air Quality was...[2]					AQI Statistics[2]	
	Good	Moderate	Unhealthy for Sensitive Groups	Unhealthy	Very Unhealthy	Maximum	Median
MSA[1]	n/a	n/a	n/a	n/a	n/a	n/a	n/a

Note: (1) Data covers the Abilene, TX Metropolitan Statistical Area—see Appendix B for areas included;
(2) Based on days with AQI data in 2013. Air Quality Index (AQI) is an index for reporting daily air quality.
EPA calculates the AQI for five major air pollutants regulated by the Clean Air Act: ground-level ozone,
particle pollution (aka particulate matter), carbon monoxide, sulfur dioxide, and nitrogen dioxide. The AQI runs
from 0 to 500. The higher the AQI value, the greater the level of air pollution and the greater the health
concern. There are six AQI categories: "Good" AQI is between 0 and 50. Air quality is considered satisfactory;
"Moderate" AQI is between 51 and 100. Air quality is acceptable; "Unhealthy for Sensitive Groups" When
AQI values are between 101 and 150, members of sensitive groups may experience health effects; "Unhealthy"
When AQI values are between 151 and 200 everyone may begin to experience health effects; "Very Unhealthy"
AQI values between 201 and 300 trigger a health alert; "Hazardous" AQI values over 300 trigger warnings of
emergency conditions (not shown).
Source: U.S. Environmental Protection Agency, Air Quality Index Report, 2013

Air Quality Index Pollutants

Area	Percent of Days when AQI Pollutant was...[2]					
	Carbon Monoxide	Nitrogen Dioxide	Ozone	Sulfur Dioxide	Particulate Matter 2.5	Particulate Matter 10
MSA[1]	n/a	n/a	n/a	n/a	n/a	n/a

Note: (1) Data covers the Abilene, TX Metropolitan Statistical Area—see Appendix B for areas included; (2) Based on days with AQI data in 2013. The Air Quality Index (AQI) is an index for reporting daily air quality. EPA calculates the AQI for five major air pollutants regulated by the Clean Air Act: ground-level ozone, particle pollution (also known as particulate matter), carbon monoxide, sulfur dioxide, and nitrogen dioxide. The AQI runs from 0 to 500. The higher the AQI value, the greater the level of air pollution and the greater the health concern.
Source: U.S. Environmental Protection Agency, Air Quality Index Report, 2013

Air Quality Trends: Ozone

	2003	2004	2005	2006	2007	2008	2009	2010	2011	2012
MSA[1]	n/a	n/a	n/a	n/a	n/a	n/a	n/a	n/a	n/a	n/a

Note: (1) Data covers the Abilene, TX Metropolitan Statistical Area—see Appendix B for areas included; n/a not available. The values shown are the composite ozone concentration averages among trend sites based on the highest fourth daily maximum 8-hour concentration in parts per million. These trends are based on sites having an adequate record of monitoring data during the trend period. Data from exceptional events are included.
Source: U.S. Environmental Protection Agency, Air Quality Monitoring Information, "Air Quality Trends by City, 2000-2012"

Maximum Air Pollutant Concentrations: Particulate Matter, Ozone, CO and Lead

	Particulate Matter 10 (ug/m³)	Particulate Matter 2.5 Wtd AM (ug/m³)	Particulate Matter 2.5 24-Hr (ug/m³)	Ozone (ppm)	Carbon Monoxide (ppm)	Lead (ug/m³)
MSA[1] Level	n/a	n/a	n/a	n/a	n/a	n/a
NAAQS[2]	150	15	35	0.075	9	0.15
Met NAAQS[2]	Yes	Yes	Yes	Yes	Yes	Yes

Note: (1) Data covers the Abilene, TX Metropolitan Statistical Area—see Appendix B for areas included; Data from exceptional events are included; (2) National Ambient Air Quality Standards; ppm = parts per million; ug/m³ = micrograms per cubic meter; n/a not available.
Concentrations: Particulate Matter 10 (coarse particulate)—highest second maximum 24-hour concentration; Particulate Matter 2.5 Wtd AM (fine particulate)—highest weighted annual mean concentration; Particulate Matter 2.5 24-Hour (fine particulate)—highest 98th percentile 24-hour concentration; Ozone—highest fourth daily maximum 8-hour concentration; Carbon Monoxide—highest second maximum non-overlapping 8-hour concentration; Lead—maximum running 3-month average
Source: U.S. Environmental Protection Agency, Air Quality Monitoring Information, "Air Quality Statistics by City, 2012"

Maximum Air Pollutant Concentrations: Nitrogen Dioxide and Sulfur Dioxide

	Nitrogen Dioxide AM (ppb)	Nitrogen Dioxide 1-Hr (ppb)	Sulfur Dioxide AM (ppb)	Sulfur Dioxide 1-Hr (ppb)	Sulfur Dioxide 24-Hr (ppb)
MSA[1] Level	n/a	n/a	n/a	n/a	n/a
NAAQS[2]	53	100	30	75	140
Met NAAQS[2]	Yes	Yes	Yes	Yes	Yes

Note: (1) Data covers the Abilene, TX Metropolitan Statistical Area—see Appendix B for areas included; Data from exceptional events are included; (2) National Ambient Air Quality Standards; ppm = parts per million; ug/m³ = micrograms per cubic meter; n/a not available.
Concentrations: Nitrogen Dioxide AM—highest arithmetic mean concentration; Nitrogen Dioxide 1-Hr—highest 98th percentile 1-hour daily maximum concentration; Sulfur Dioxide AM—highest annual mean concentration; Sulfur Dioxide 1-Hr—highest 99th percentile 1-hour daily maximum concentration; Sulfur Dioxide 24-Hr—highest second maximum 24-hour concentration
Source: U.S. Environmental Protection Agency, Air Quality Monitoring Information, "Air Quality Statistics by City, 2012"

Drinking Water

Water System Name	Pop. Served	Primary Water Source Type	Violations[1]	
			Health Based	Monitoring/ Reporting
City of Abilene	116,412	Surface	0	0

Note: (1) Based on violation data from January 1, 2013 to December 31, 2013 (includes unresolved violations from earlier years)
Source: U.S. Environmental Protection Agency, Office of Ground Water and Drinking Water, Safe Drinking Water Information System (based on data extracted February 10, 2014)

Athens, Georgia

Background

Athens, home to the University of Georgia, retains its old charms while cultivating the new. Antebellum homes that grace the city still stand because Gen. William Tecumseh Sherman's March to the Sea took a route that left this northeast Georgia town intact (while burning Atlanta, about 60 miles to the southwest). The Athens Music History Walking Tour, available through the local convention and visitors' bureau, stops at Weaver D's soul food restaurant with the slogan, "Automatic for the People," that went national as the name of locally-grown REM's 1992 album. The college music scene that spawned the B-52s and the Indigo Girls in the 1970s and 1980s, continues to support a thriving music industry. In 2002, the *New York Times* called Athens "Live Music Central."

Present-day Athens started as a small settlement where an old Cherokee trail crossed the Oconee River. In 1785 the state's General Assembly chartered the university, which established a campus here in 1801. Three years later, the school held its first graduation ceremony. The city was named for the ancient Greece's center of learning.

Undoubtedly the major influence in the city and surrounding Clarke County, the University of Georgia is also the area's largest employer. The comprehensive land grant and sea-grant institution offers all levels of degree programs in numerous disciplines. Other educational institutions in Athens are the Navy Supply School, Athens Technical College, and branches of Piedmont College and Old Dominion University.

Other major employers are focused on health care, government, and manufacturing. They include Athens Regional Medical Center and St. Mary's Health Care System, which have enlarged their facilities and specialized in areas including oncology, pediatrics and heart disease. In March 2010, St. Mary's was the first area hospital to implement the next generation of minimally invasive surgery using a hi-tech assistive robot. Manufacturing is a major employment sector.

The city's official government merged with its home county in 1991, creating the Unified Government of Athens-Clark County.

With its shops, boutiques and restaurants, Athens offers plenty to do. The Georgia State Museum of Art, Museum of Natural History, and the State Botanical Garden here are affiliated with the university. The restored 1910 Morton Theater once hosted Cab Calloway, Duke Ellington, and Louis Armstrong, and now hosts dramatic and musical performances. Undoubtedly the strong presence of young people in Athens has contributed to the burgeoning artistic scene there. The city center is home to bars, galleries, cafes, and music venues that cater to the city's creative climate. The annual AthFest in June, hosts 120 bands to support local education. The city's charms, attractive to all ages, have not gone unnoticed by the media. Athens has been named one of the best places for small business, the best college town for retirees, and the best place to recapture your youth. The city also has a lively bicycle culture, and hosts several annual bicycle races.

The climate is mild, with average temperatures about 20 degrees warmer than the U.S. average. Snowfall is next to nothing, but precipitation is at its highest from January-March. Spring is lovely, with three to four inches of rain, sunshine up to 70 percent of the time starting in April, and temperatures averaging in the 70s.

Rankings

Business/Finance Rankings

- Athens was identified as one of "America's Hardest-Working Towns." The city ranked #15 out of 25. Criteria: average hours worked per capita; willingness to work during personal time; number of dual income households; local employment rate. *Parade, "What is America's Hardest-Working Town?," April 15, 2012*

- The Athens metro area appeared on the Milken Institute "2013 Best Performing Cities" list. Rank: #94 out of 179 small metro areas. Criteria: job growth; wage and salary growth; high-tech output growth. *Milken Institute, "Best-Performing Cities 2013," December 2013*

- *Forbes* ranked 184 smaller metro areas in the U.S. in terms of the "Best Small Places for Business and Careers." The Athens metro area was ranked #33. Criteria: costs (business and living); job growth (past and projected); income growth; educational attainment (college and high school); projected economic growth; cultural and recreational opportunities; net migration patterns; number of highly ranked colleges. *Forbes, "The Best Small Places for Business and Careers," August 7, 2013*

Culture/Performing Arts Rankings

- Athens was selected as one of America's top cities for the arts. The city ranked #13 in the mid-sized city (population 100,000 to 499,999) category. Criteria: readers' top choices for arts travel destinations based on the richness and variety of visual arts sites, activities and events. *American Style, "2012 Top 25 Arts Destinations," June 2012*

Environmental Rankings

- The Athens metro area came in at #257 for the relative comfort of its climate on Sperling's list of "chill cities," as measured by the Sperling Heat Index. All 361 metro areas are included. Criteria included daytime high temperatures, nighttime low temperatures, dew point, and relative humidity at the high temperatures. *www.bertsperling.com, "Sperling's Chill Cities," July 18, 2013*

- Sperling's BestPlaces assessed 379 metropolitan areas of the United States for the likelihood of dangerously extreme weather events or earthquakes. In general the Southeast and South-Central regions have the highest risk of weather extremes and earthquakes, while the Pacific Northwest enjoys the lowest risk. Of the least risky metropolitan areas, the Athens metro area was ranked #323. *www.bestplaces.net, "Safest Places from Natural Disasters," April 2011*

- Athens was selected as one of 22 "Smarter Cities" for energy by the Natural Resources Defense Council. Criteria: investment in green power; energy efficiency measures; conservation. *Natural Resources Defense Council, "2010 Smarter Cities," July 19, 2010*

- Athens was highlighted as one of the top 25 cleanest metro areas for short-term particle pollution (24-hour PM 2.5) in the U.S. during 2008 through 2010. Monitors in these cities reported no days with unhealthful PM 2.5 levels. *American Lung Association, State of the Air 2012*

Real Estate Rankings

- Athens was ranked #85 out of 283 metro areas in terms of house price appreciation in 2013 (#1 = highest rate). *Federal Housing Finance Agency, House Price Index, 4th Quarter 2013*

- Athens was selected as one of the best college towns for renters by ApartmentRatings.com." The area ranked #34 out of 87. Overall satisfaction ratings were ranked using thousands of user submitted scores for hundreds of apartment complexes located in cities and towns that are home to the 100 largest four-year institutions in the U.S. *ApartmentRatings.com, "2011 College Town Renter Satisfaction Rankings"*

Safety Rankings

- The National Insurance Crime Bureau ranked 380 metro areas in the U.S. in terms of per capita rates of vehicle theft. The Athens metro area ranked #159 (#1 = highest rate). Criteria: number of vehicle theft offenses per 100,000 inhabitants in 2012. *National Insurance Crime Bureau, "Hot Spots 2012," June 26, 2013*

Seniors/Retirement Rankings

- From its Best Cities for Successful Aging indexes, the Milken Institute generated rankings for metropolitan areas, weighing data in eight categories—general indicators, health care, wellness, living arrangements, transportation and general accessibility, financial well-being, education and employment, and community participation. The Athens metro area was ranked #61 overall in the small metro area category. *Milken Institute, "Best Cities for Successful Aging," July 2012*

- Athens was chosen in the "College Town" category of CNNMoney's list of the 25 best places to retire." Criteria include: type of location (big city, small town, resort area, college town); median home prices; top state income tax rate. *CNNMoney, "25 Best Places to Retire," December 17, 2012*

- Athens was identified as one of the most popular places to retire by *Topretirements.com*. The list reflects the 100 cities (out of 900+ total cities reviewed) that visitors to the website are most interested in for retirement. *Topretirements.com, "Most Popular Places to Retire for 2014," February 25, 2014*

Sports/Recreation Rankings

- Athens appeared on the *Sporting News* list of the "Best Sports Cities" for 2011. The area ranked #78 out of 271. Criteria: the magazine takes a 12-month snapshot of each city's sports, putting a heavy premium on regular-season won-lost records (from the most recently completed season). Other criteria include: playoff berths, bowl appearances and tournament bids; championships; applicable power ratings; quality of competition; overall fan fervor (measured in part by attendance); abundance of teams (rewarding quality over quantity); stadium and arena quality; ticket availability and prices; franchise ownership; and marquee appeal of athletes. *Sporting News, "Best Sports Cities 2011," October 4, 2011*

- Athens appeared on the *Sporting News* list of the "Best Sports Cities" for 2011. The area ranked #78 out of 271. Criteria: a 12-month snapshot of regular-season won-lost records (from the most recently completed season). Other criteria include: playoff berths, bowl appearances and tournament bids; championships; applicable power ratings; quality of competition; overall fan fervor (measured in part by attendance); abundance of teams (quality over quantity); stadium and arena quality; ticket availability and prices; franchise ownership; and marquee appeal of athletes. *Sporting News, "Best Sports Cities 2011," October 4, 2011*

- Athens was chosen as a bicycle friendly community by the League of American Bicyclists. A "Bicycle Friendly Community" welcomes cyclists by providing safe accommodation for cycling and encouraging people to bike for transportation and recreation. There are four award levels: Platinum; Gold; Silver; and Bronze. The community achieved an award level of Bronze. *League of American Bicyclists, "Bicycle Friendly Community Master List," Fall 2013*

Business Environment

CITY FINANCES

City Government Finances

Component	2011 ($000)	2011 ($ per capita)
Total Revenues	225,435	1,976
Total Expenditures	261,285	2,291
Debt Outstanding	262,424	2,301
Cash and Securities[1]	207,144	1,816

Note: (1) Cash and security holdings of a government at the close of its fiscal year, including those of its dependent agencies, utilities, and liquor stores.
Source: U.S Census Bureau, State & Local Government Finances 2011

City Government Revenue by Source

Source	2011 ($000)	2011 ($ per capita)
General Revenue		
From Federal Government	3,829	34
From State Government	19,932	175
From Local Governments	41,246	362
Taxes		
Property	50,127	439
Sales and Gross Receipts	18,261	160
Personal Income	0	0
Corporate Income	0	0
Motor Vehicle License	0	0
Other Taxes	3,717	33
Current Charges	43,098	378
Liquor Store	0	0
Utility	23,992	210
Employee Retirement	0	0

Source: U.S Census Bureau, State & Local Government Finances 2011

City Government Expenditures by Function

Function	2011 ($000)	2011 ($ per capita)	2011 (%)
General Direct Expenditures			
Air Transportation	1,145	10	0.4
Corrections	18,240	160	7.0
Education	0	0	0.0
Employment Security Administration	0	0	0.0
Financial Administration	4,319	38	1.7
Fire Protection	12,868	113	4.9
General Public Buildings	6,170	54	2.4
Governmental Administration, Other	14,796	130	5.7
Health	11,490	101	4.4
Highways	8,011	70	3.1
Hospitals	0	0	0.0
Housing and Community Development	6,345	56	2.4
Interest on General Debt	386	3	0.1
Judicial and Legal	9,706	85	3.7
Libraries	6,438	56	2.5
Parking	887	8	0.3
Parks and Recreation	11,467	101	4.4
Police Protection	23,839	209	9.1
Public Welfare	463	4	0.2
Sewerage	29,936	262	11.5
Solid Waste Management	5,700	50	2.2
Veterans' Services	0	0	0.0
Liquor Store	0	0	0.0
Utility	54,268	476	20.8
Employee Retirement	0	0	0.0

Source: U.S Census Bureau, State & Local Government Finances 2011

DEMOGRAPHICS

Population Growth

Area	1990 Census	2000 Census	2010 Census	Population Growth (%)	
				1990-2000	2000-2010
City	86,561	100,266	115,452	15.8	15.1
MSA[1]	136,025	166,079	192,541	22.1	15.9
U.S.	248,709,873	281,421,906	308,745,538	13.2	9.7

Note: (1) Figures cover the Athens-Clarke County, GA Metropolitan Statistical Area—see Appendix B for areas included
Source: U.S. Census Bureau, Census 1990, 2000, 2010

Household Size

Area	Persons in Household (%)							Average Household Size
	One	Two	Three	Four	Five	Six	Seven or More	
City	32.8	34.3	13.8	12.8	4.1	1.7	0.6	2.66
MSA[1]	27.9	35.3	15.0	14.2	4.8	1.9	0.9	2.75
U.S.	27.6	33.5	15.7	13.2	6.1	2.4	1.5	2.63

Note: (1) Figures cover the Athens-Clarke County, GA Metropolitan Statistical Area—see Appendix B for areas included
Source: U.S. Census Bureau, 2010-2012 American Community Survey 3-Year Estimates

Race

Area	White Alone[2] (%)	Black Alone[2] (%)	Asian Alone[2] (%)	AIAN[3] Alone[2] (%)	NHOPI[4] Alone[2] (%)	Other Race Alone[2] (%)	Two or More Races (%)
City	65.8	26.2	4.0	0.2	0.0	1.3	2.4
MSA[1]	73.9	19.3	3.2	0.2	0.0	1.2	2.2
U.S.	74.0	12.6	4.9	0.8	0.2	4.7	2.8

Note: (1) Figures cover the Athens-Clarke County, GA Metropolitan Statistical Area—see Appendix B for areas included; (2) Alone is defined as not being in combination with one or more other races; (3) American Indian and Alaska Native; (4) Native Hawaiian and Other Pacific Islander
Source: U.S. Census Bureau, 2010-2012 American Community Survey 3-Year Estimates

Hispanic or Latino Origin

Area	Total (%)	Mexican (%)	Puerto Rican (%)	Cuban (%)	Other (%)
City	10.6	7.3	0.3	0.4	2.6
MSA[1]	8.1	5.5	0.4	0.3	2.0
U.S.	16.6	10.7	1.6	0.6	3.7

Note: Persons of Hispanic or Latino origin can be of any race; (1) Figures cover the Athens-Clarke County, GA Metropolitan Statistical Area—see Appendix B for areas included
Source: U.S. Census Bureau, 2010-2012 American Community Survey 3-Year Estimates

Segregation

Type	Segregation Indices[1]				Percent Change		
	1990	2000	2010	2010 Rank[2]	1990-2000	1990-2010	2000-2010
Black/White	n/a	n/a	n/a	n/a	n/a	n/a	n/a
Asian/White	n/a	n/a	n/a	n/a	n/a	n/a	n/a
Hispanic/White	n/a	n/a	n/a	n/a	n/a	n/a	n/a

Note: All figures cover the Metropolitan Statistical Area—see Appendix B for areas included; Figures are based on an analysis of 1990, 2000, and 2010 Census Decennial Census tract data by William H. Frey, Brookings Institution and the University of Michigan Social Science Data Analysis Network. In this analysis all racial groups (whites, blacks, and asians) are non-Hispanic members of those races. Hispanics are shown as a separate category;
(1) Segregation Indices are Dissimilarity Indices that measure the degree to which the minority group is distributed differently than whites across census tracts. They range from 0 (complete integration) to 100 (complete segregation) where the value indicates the percentage of the minority group that needs to move to be distributed exactly like whites; (2) Ranges from 1 (most segregated) to 102 (least segregated); n/a not available.
Source: www.CensusScope.org

Ancestry

Area	German	Irish	English	American	Italian	Polish	French[2]	Scottish	Dutch
City	9.6	8.1	8.5	10.2	2.0	2.2	1.6	3.5	0.8
MSA[1]	9.5	9.1	9.7	15.7	2.0	1.6	1.7	3.3	0.7
U.S.	15.2	11.1	8.2	7.2	5.6	3.1	2.8	1.7	1.4

Note: Figures are the percentage of the total population reporting a particular ancestry. The nine most commonly reported ancestries in the U.S. are shown. Figures include multiple ancestries (e.g. if a person reported being Irish and Italian, they were included in both columns); (1) Figures cover the Athens-Clarke County, GA Metropolitan Statistical Area—see Appendix B for areas included; (2) Excludes Basque
Source: U.S. Census Bureau, 2010-2012 American Community Survey 3-Year Estimates

Foreign-Born Population

Area	Percent of Population Born in								
	Any Foreign Country	Mexico	Asia	Europe	Carribean	South America	Central America[2]	Africa	Canada
City	n/a	n/a	n/a	n/a	n/a	n/a	n/a	n/a	n/a
MSA[1]	7.6	2.9	2.3	0.7	0.1	0.5	0.7	0.3	0.2
U.S.	13.0	3.7	3.7	1.6	1.2	0.9	1.0	0.5	0.3

Note: (1) Figures cover the Athens-Clarke County, GA Metropolitan Statistical Area—see Appendix B for areas included; (2) Excludes Mexico.
Source: U.S. Census Bureau, 2010-2012 American Community Survey 3-Year Estimates

Marital Status

Area	Never Married	Now Married[2]	Separated	Widowed	Divorced
City	56.5	30.1	1.7	4.0	7.7
MSA[1]	44.1	40.7	1.7	4.9	8.6
U.S.	32.4	48.4	2.2	6.0	11.0

Note: Figures are percentages and cover the population 15 years of age and older; (1) Figures cover the Athens-Clarke County, GA Metropolitan Statistical Area—see Appendix B for areas included; (2) Excludes separated
Source: U.S. Census Bureau, 2010-2012 American Community Survey 3-Year Estimates

Age

Area	Percent of Population									Median Age
	Under Age 5	Age 5–19	Age 20–34	Age 35–44	Age 45–54	Age 55–64	Age 65–74	Age 75–84	Age 85+	
City	5.9	20.8	37.9	10.2	8.7	7.8	4.9	2.8	1.0	25.9
MSA[1]	6.0	21.1	29.3	11.4	11.6	10.1	6.2	3.0	1.2	30.1
U.S.	6.4	20.1	20.5	13.1	14.3	12.2	7.3	4.2	1.8	37.3

Note: (1) Figures cover the Athens-Clarke County, GA Metropolitan Statistical Area—see Appendix B for areas included
Source: U.S. Census Bureau, 2010-2012 American Community Survey 3-Year Estimates

Gender

Area	Males	Females	Males per 100 Females
City	55,698	61,633	90.4
MSA[1]	93,538	101,323	92.3
U.S.	153,276,055	158,333,314	96.8

Note: (1) Figures cover the Athens-Clarke County, GA Metropolitan Statistical Area—see Appendix B for areas included
Source: U.S. Census Bureau, 2010-2012 American Community Survey 3-Year Estimates

Religious Groups by Family

Area	Catholic	Baptist	Non-Den.	Methodist[2]	Lutheran	LDS[3]	Pentecostal	Presbyterian[4]	Muslim[5]	Judaism
MSA[1]	4.4	16.3	2.3	8.4	0.4	0.8	2.8	2.0	0.4	0.2
U.S.	19.1	9.3	4.0	4.0	2.3	2.0	1.9	1.6	0.8	0.7

Note: Figures are the number of adherents as a percentage of the total population; (1) Figures cover the Athens-Clarke County, GA Metropolitan Statistical Area—see Appendix B for areas included; (2) Methodist/Pietist; (3) Latter Day Saints; (4) Reformed; (5) Figures are estimates
Source: Association of Statisticians of American Religious Bodies, 2010 U.S. Religion Census: Religious Congregations & Membership Study

Religious Groups by Tradition

Area	Catholic	Evangelical Protestant	Mainline Protestant	Other Tradition	Black Protestant	Orthodox
MSA[1]	4.4	21.1	9.8	1.7	2.5	0.1
U.S.	19.1	16.2	7.3	4.3	1.6	0.3

Note: Figures are the number of adherents as a percentage of the total population; (1) Figures cover the Athens-Clarke County, GA Metropolitan Statistical Area—see Appendix B for areas included
Source: Association of Statisticians of American Religious Bodies, 2010 U.S. Religion Census: Religious Congregations & Membership Study

ECONOMY

Gross Metropolitan Product

Area	2011	2012	2013	2014	Rank[2]
MSA[1]	6.6	6.8	7.0	7.3	224

Note: Figures are in billions of dollars; (1) Figures cover the Athens-Clarke County, GA Metropolitan Statistical Area—see Appendix B for areas included; (2) Rank is based on 2014 data and ranges from 1 to 363
Source: The United States Conference of Mayors, U.S. Metro Economies: Outlook—Gross Metropolitan Product, with Metro Employment Projections, November 2013

Economic Growth

Area	2011 (%)	2012 (%)	2013 (%)	2014 (%)	Rank[2]
MSA[1]	-0.7	1.2	0.8	1.7	175
U.S.	1.6	2.5	1.7	2.5	–

Note: Figures are real gross metropolitan product (GMP) growth rates and represent annual average percent change; (1) Figures cover the Athens-Clarke County, GA Metropolitan Statistical Area—see Appendix B for areas included; (2) Rank is based on 2013 data and ranges from 1 to 363
Source: The United States Conference of Mayors, U.S. Metro Economies: Outlook—Gross Metropolitan Product, with Metro Employment Projections, November 2013

Metropolitan Area Exports

Area	2007	2008	2009	2010	2011	2012	Rank[2]
MSA[1]	182.2	171.4	214.6	194.6	221.6	229.7	287

Note: Figures are in millions of dollars; (1) Figures cover the Athens-Clarke County, GA Metropolitan Statistical Area—see Appendix B for areas included; (2) Rank is based on 2012 data and ranges from 1 to 369
Source: U.S. Department of Commerce, International Trade Administration, Office of Trade & Industry Information, Manufacturing & Services, data extracted April 1, 2014

INCOME

Income

Area	Per Capita ($)	Median Household ($)	Average Household ($)
City	18,760	32,809	50,939
MSA[1]	21,698	41,339	59,744
U.S.	27,385	51,771	71,579

Note: (1) Figures cover the Athens-Clarke County, GA Metropolitan Statistical Area—see Appendix B for areas included
Source: U.S. Census Bureau, 2010-2012 American Community Survey 3-Year Estimates

Household Income Distribution

Area	Percent of Households Earning							
	Under $15,000	$15,000 -24,999	$25,000 -34,999	$35,000 -49,999	$50,000 -74,999	$75,000 -99,000	$100,000 -149,999	$150,000 and up
City	28.0	13.3	10.7	12.8	15.1	7.1	6.9	6.1
MSA[1]	20.9	12.3	10.7	13.4	16.4	9.8	9.1	7.4
U.S.	13.1	11.0	10.5	13.7	18.1	11.9	12.5	9.1

Note: (1) Figures cover the Athens-Clarke County, GA Metropolitan Statistical Area—see Appendix B for areas included
Source: U.S. Census Bureau, 2010-2012 American Community Survey 3-Year Estimates

Poverty Rate

Area	All Ages	Under 18 Years Old	18 to 64 Years Old	65 Years and Over
City	35.8	34.7	39.3	11.2
MSA[1]	26.1	24.5	29.3	9.3
U.S.	15.7	22.2	14.6	9.3

Note: Figures are percentage of people whose income during the past 12 months was below the poverty level; (1) Figures cover the Athens-Clarke County, GA Metropolitan Statistical Area—see Appendix B for areas included
Source: U.S. Census Bureau, 2010-2012 American Community Survey 3-Year Estimates

Personal Bankruptcy Filing Rate

Area	2008	2009	2010	2011	2012	2013
Clarke County	2.89	3.46	3.52	3.77	3.43	3.31
U.S.	3.53	4.61	4.97	4.37	3.76	3.29

Note: Numbers are per 1,000 population and include Chapter 7 and Chapter 13 filings
Source: Federal Deposit Insurance Corporation, Regional Economic Conditions, March 20, 2014

EMPLOYMENT

Labor Force and Employment

Area	Civilian Labor Force			Workers Employed		
	Dec. 2012	Dec. 2013	% Chg.	Dec. 2012	Dec. 2013	% Chg.
City	69,635	68,686	-1.4	64,973	64,893	-0.1
MSA[1]	114,803	113,199	-1.4	107,437	107,305	-0.1
U.S.	154,904,000	154,408,000	-0.3	143,060,000	144,423,000	1.0

Note: Data is not seasonally adjusted and covers workers 16 years of age and older; (1) Metropolitan Statistical Area—see Appendix B for areas included
Source: Bureau of Labor Statistics, Local Area Unemployment Statistics

Unemployment Rate

Area	2013											
	Jan.	Feb.	Mar.	Apr.	May	Jun.	Jul.	Aug.	Sep.	Oct.	Nov.	Dec.
City	6.9	6.4	6.2	5.9	6.6	7.7	7.3	6.6	6.1	6.2	5.4	5.5
MSA[1]	6.5	6.1	5.9	5.5	6.2	7.2	6.9	6.1	5.6	5.8	5.0	5.2
U.S.	8.5	8.1	7.6	7.1	7.3	7.8	7.7	7.3	7.0	7.0	6.6	6.5

Note: Data is not seasonally adjusted and covers workers 16 years of age and older; All figures are percentages; (1) Metropolitan Statistical Area—see Appendix B for areas included
Source: Bureau of Labor Statistics, Local Area Unemployment Statistics

Employment by Occupation

Occupation Classification	City (%)	MSA[1] (%)	U.S. (%)
Management, Business, Science, and Arts	39.9	39.6	36.0
Natural Resources, Construction, and Maintenance	5.2	6.5	9.1
Production, Transportation, and Material Moving	11.7	12.5	12.0
Sales and Office	22.5	23.5	24.7
Service	20.7	17.8	18.2

Note: Figures cover employed civilians 16 years of age and older; (1) Figures cover the Athens-Clarke County, GA Metropolitan Statistical Area—see Appendix B for areas included
Source: U.S. Census Bureau, 2010-2012 American Community Survey 3-Year Estimates

Employment by Industry

Sector	MSA[1]		U.S.
	Number of Employees	Percent of Total	Percent of Total
Construction	n/a	n/a	4.2
Education and Health Services	n/a	n/a	15.5
Financial Activities	n/a	n/a	5.7
Government	31,700	34.6	16.1
Information	n/a	n/a	1.9
Leisure and Hospitality	9,200	10.0	10.2
Manufacturing	n/a	n/a	8.7
Mining and Logging	n/a	n/a	0.6
Other Services	n/a	n/a	3.9
Professional and Business Services	7,200	7.9	13.7
Retail Trade	9,900	10.8	11.4
Transportation and Utilities	n/a	n/a	3.8
Wholesale Trade	n/a	n/a	4.2

Note: Figures cover non-farm employment as of December 2013 and are not seasonally adjusted;
(1) Metropolitan Statistical Area—see Appendix B for areas included; n/a not available
Source: Bureau of Labor Statistics, Current Employment Statistics, Employment, Hours, and Earnings

Occupations with Greatest Projected Employment Growth: 2010 – 2020

Occupation[1]	2010 Employment	2020 Projected Employment	Numeric Employment Change	Percent Employment Change
Combined Food Preparation and Serving Workers, Including Fast Food	98,330	120,660	22,330	22.7
Registered Nurses	69,190	90,020	20,830	30.1
Retail Salespersons	143,460	157,600	14,130	9.9
Office Clerks, General	81,710	93,640	11,930	14.6
Postsecondary Teachers	36,620	47,350	10,730	29.3
Waiters and Waitresses	62,600	72,990	10,390	16.6
Customer Service Representatives	91,150	101,390	10,240	11.2
Janitors and Cleaners, Except Maids and Housekeeping Cleaners	73,670	82,570	8,900	12.1
Laborers and Freight, Stock, and Material Movers, Hand	82,360	90,940	8,580	10.4
Elementary School Teachers, Except Special Education	45,250	53,470	8,220	18.2

Note: Projections cover Georgia; (1) Sorted by numeric employment change
Source: www.projectionscentral.com, State Occupational Projections, 2010–2020 Long-Term Projections

Fastest Growing Occupations: 2010 – 2020

Occupation[1]	2010 Employment	2020 Projected Employment	Numeric Employment Change	Percent Employment Change
Biomedical Engineers	170	280	110	64.7
Marriage and Family Therapists	290	460	160	55.3
Home Health Aides	11,790	18,070	6,270	53.2
Diagnostic Medical Sonographers	1,110	1,650	540	48.5
Medical Scientists, Except Epidemiologists	500	730	230	46.6
Personal Care Aides	9,550	13,870	4,320	45.2
Mental Health Counselors	2,030	2,870	840	41.3
Helpers—Carpenters	1,500	2,100	610	40.5
Cardiovascular Technologists and Technicians	1,030	1,400	370	36.0
Medical Secretaries	15,780	21,440	5,660	35.9

Note: Projections cover Georgia; (1) Sorted by percent employment change and excludes occupations with
numeric employment change less than 100
Source: www.projectionscentral.com, State Occupational Projections, 2010–2020 Long-Term Projections

Average Wages

Occupation	$/Hr.	Occupation	$/Hr.
Accountants and Auditors	26.22	Maids and Housekeeping Cleaners	9.62
Automotive Mechanics	19.62	Maintenance and Repair Workers	16.79
Bookkeepers	15.14	Marketing Managers	53.90
Carpenters	13.35	Nuclear Medicine Technologists	n/a
Cashiers	9.24	Nurses, Licensed Practical	18.64
Clerks, General Office	11.17	Nurses, Registered	29.33
Clerks, Receptionists/Information	12.30	Nursing Assistants	9.81
Clerks, Shipping/Receiving	13.86	Packers and Packagers, Hand	9.29
Computer Programmers	26.99	Physical Therapists	36.78
Computer Systems Analysts	30.82	Postal Service Mail Carriers	23.23
Computer User Support Specialists	17.19	Real Estate Brokers	n/a
Cooks, Restaurant	9.71	Retail Salespersons	10.51
Dentists	n/a	Sales Reps., Exc. Tech./Scientific	24.97
Electrical Engineers	33.72	Sales Reps., Tech./Scientific	n/a
Electricians	18.25	Secretaries, Exc. Legal/Med./Exec.	14.32
Financial Managers	48.93	Security Guards	13.49
First-Line Supervisors/Managers, Sales	17.60	Surgeons	n/a
Food Preparation Workers	9.44	Teacher Assistants	8.70
General and Operations Managers	43.42	Teachers, Elementary School	25.30
Hairdressers/Cosmetologists	14.05	Teachers, Secondary School	25.30
Internists	n/a	Telemarketers	8.69
Janitors and Cleaners	10.93	Truck Drivers, Heavy/Tractor-Trailer	20.40
Landscaping/Groundskeeping Workers	10.04	Truck Drivers, Light/Delivery Svcs.	15.44
Lawyers	58.06	Waiters and Waitresses	9.03

Note: Wage data covers the Athens-Clarke County, GA Metropolitan Statistical Area—see Appendix B for areas included. Hourly wages for elementary/secondary school teachers and teacher assistants were calculated by the editors from annual wage data assuming a 40 hour work week; n/a not available.
Source: Bureau of Labor Statistics, Metro Area Occupational Employment and Wage Estimates, May 2013

RESIDENTIAL REAL ESTATE

Building Permits

Area	Single-Family			Multi-Family			Total		
	2012	2013	Pct. Chg.	2012	2013	Pct. Chg.	2012	2013	Pct. Chg.
City	185	143	-22.7	168	351	108.9	353	494	39.9
MSA[1]	447	698	56.2	172	381	121.5	619	1,079	74.3
U.S.	518,695	620,802	19.7	310,963	370,020	19.0	829,658	990,822	19.4

Note: (1) Metropolitan Statistical Area—see Appendix B for areas included; figures represent new, privately-owned housing units authorized (unadjusted data); All permit data are based on estimates with imputation.
Source: U.S. Census Bureau, Manufacturing, Mining, and Construction Statistics, Building Permits, 2012, 2013

Homeownership Rate

Area	2006 (%)	2007 (%)	2008 (%)	2009 (%)	2010 (%)	2011 (%)	2012 (%)	2013 (%)
MSA[1]	n/a	n/a	n/a	n/a	n/a	n/a	n/a	n/a
U.S.	68.8	68.1	67.8	67.4	66.9	66.1	65.4	65.1

Note: (1) Figures cover the Athens-Clarke County, GA Metropolitan Statistical Area—see Appendix B for areas included; n/a not available
Source: U.S. Census Bureau, Housing Vacancies and Homeownership Annual Statistics: 2013

Housing Vacancy Rates

Area	Gross Vacancy Rate[2] (%)			Year-Round Vacancy Rate[3] (%)			Rental Vacancy Rate[4] (%)			Homeowner Vacancy Rate[5] (%)		
	2011	2012	2013	2011	2012	2013	2011	2012	2013	2011	2012	2013
MSA[1]	n/a	n/a	n/a	n/a	n/a	n/a	n/a	n/a	n/a	n/a	n/a	n/a
U.S.	14.2	13.8	13.8	11.1	10.8	10.7	9.5	8.7	8.3	2.5	2.0	2.0

Note: (1) Figures cover the Athens-Clarke County, GA Metropolitan Statistical Area—see Appendix B for areas included; (2) The percentage of the total housing inventory that is vacant; (3) The percentage of the housing inventory (excluding seasonal units) that is year-round vacant; (4) The percentage of rental inventory that is vacant for rent; (5) The percentage of homeowner inventory that is vacant for sale; n/a not available
Source: U.S. Census Bureau, Housing Vacancies and Homeownership Annual Statistics: 2013

TAXES

State Corporate Income Tax Rates

State	Tax Rate (%)	Income Brackets ($)	Num. of Brackets	Financial Institution Tax Rate (%)[a]	Federal Income Tax Ded.
Georgia	6.0	Flat rate	1	6.0	No

Note: Tax rates as of January 1, 2014; (a) Rates listed are the corporate income tax rate applied to financial institutions or excise taxes based on income. Some states have other taxes based upon the value of deposits or shares.
Source: Federation of Tax Administrators, "State Corporate Income Tax Rates, 2014"

State Individual Income Tax Rates

State	Tax Rate (%)	Income Brackets ($)	Num. of Brackets	Personal Exempt. ($)[1] Single	Personal Exempt. ($)[1] Dependents	Fed. Inc. Tax Ded.
Georgia	1.0 - 6.0	750 - 7,001 (h)	6	2,700	3,000	No

Note: Tax rates as of January 1, 2014; Local- and county-level taxes are not included; n/a not applicable; (1) Married joint filers generally receive double the single exemption; (h) The Georgia income brackets reported are for single individuals. For married couples filing jointly, the same tax rates apply to income brackets ranging from $1,000, to $10,000.
Source: Federation of Tax Administrators, "State Individual Income Tax Rates, 2014"

Various State and Local Tax Rates

State	State and Local Sales and Use (%)	State Sales and Use (%)	Gasoline[1] (¢/gal.)	Cigarette[2] ($/pack)	Spirits[3] ($/gal.)	Wine[4] ($/gal.)	Beer[5] ($/gal.)
Georgia	7.0	4.00	28.45	0.370	3.79 (f)	1.51	1.01 (q)

Note: All tax rates as of January 1, 2014; (1) The American Petroleum Institute has developed a methodology for determining the average tax rate on a gallon of fuel. Rates may include any of the following: excise taxes, environmental fees, storage tank fees, other fees or taxes, general sales tax, and local taxes. In states where gasoline is subject to the general sales tax, or where the fuel tax is based on the average sale price, the average rate determined by API is sensitive to changes in the price of gasoline. States that fully or partially apply general sales taxes to gasoline: CA, CO, GA, IL, IN, MI, NY; (2) The federal excise tax of $1.0066 per pack and local taxes are not included; (3) Rates are those applicable to off-premise sales of 40% alcohol by volume (a.b.v.) distilled spirits in 750ml containers. Local excise taxes are excluded; (4) Rates are those applicable to off-premise sales of 11% a.b.v. non-carbonated wine in 750ml containers; (5) Rates are those applicable to off-premise sales of 4.7% a.b.v. beer in 12 ounce containers; (f) Different rates also applicable according to alcohol content, place of production, size of container, or place purchased (on- or off-premise or onboard airlines); (q) Includes statewide local rate in Alabama ($0.52) and Georgia ($0.53).
Source: Tax Foundation, 2014 Facts & Figures: How Does Your State Compare?

State Business Tax Climate Index Rankings

State	Overall Rank	Corporate Tax Index Rank	Individual Income Tax Index Rank	Sales Tax Index Rank	Unemployment Insurance Tax Index Rank	Property Tax Index Rank
Georgia	32	8	41	12	24	31

Note: The index is a measure of how each state's tax laws affect economic performance. The lower the rank, the more favorable a state's tax system is for business. States without a given tax are given a ranking of 1. The scores/rankings for the District of Columbia do not affect other states. The 2014 index represents the tax climate as of July 1, 2013.
Source: Tax Foundation, State Business Tax Climate Index 2014

COMMERCIAL UTILITIES

Typical Monthly Electric Bills

Area	Commercial Service ($/month) 1,500 kWh	Commercial Service ($/month) 40 kW demand 14,000 kWh	Industrial Service ($/month) 1,000 kW demand 200,000 kWh	Industrial Service ($/month) 50,000 kW demand 15,000,000 kWh
City	n/a	n/a	n/a	n/a
Average[1]	197	1,636	25,662	1,485,307

Note: Based on total rates in effect July 1, 2013; (1) average based on 180 utilities surveyed; n/a not available
Source: Edison Electric Institute, Typical Bills and Average Rates Report, Summer 2013

TRANSPORTATION

Means of Transportation to Work

| Area | Car/Truck/Van | | Public Transportation | | | Bicycle | Walked | Other Means | Worked at Home |
	Drove Alone	Car-pooled	Bus	Subway	Railroad				
City	72.5	10.5	3.0	0.0	0.0	2.1	5.7	1.9	4.2
MSA[1]	77.3	9.4	1.8	0.0	0.0	1.3	3.9	1.6	4.7
U.S.	76.4	9.7	2.6	1.7	0.5	0.6	2.8	1.3	4.3

Note: Figures are percentages and cover workers 16 years of age and older; (1) Figures cover the Athens-Clarke County, GA Metropolitan Statistical Area—see Appendix B for areas included
Source: U.S. Census Bureau, 2010-2012 American Community Survey 3-Year Estimates

Travel Time to Work

Area	Less Than 10 Minutes	10 to 19 Minutes	20 to 29 Minutes	30 to 44 Minutes	45 to 59 Minutes	60 to 89 Minutes	90 Minutes or More
City	17.5	49.9	17.2	7.7	2.8	2.9	2.0
MSA[1]	13.7	42.7	21.4	13.1	3.5	3.2	2.4
U.S.	13.5	29.8	20.9	20.1	7.5	5.6	2.5

Note: Figures are percentages and include workers 16 years old and over; (1) Figures cover the Athens-Clarke County, GA Metropolitan Statistical Area—see Appendix B for areas included
Source: U.S. Census Bureau, 2010-2012 American Community Survey 3-Year Estimates

Travel Time Index

Area	1985	1990	1995	2000	2005	2010	2011
Urban Area[1]	n/a	n/a	n/a	n/a	n/a	n/a	n/a
Average[2]	1.09	1.14	1.16	1.19	1.23	1.18	1.18

Note: Travel Time Index—the ratio of travel time in the peak period to the travel time at free-flow conditions. For example, a value of 1.30 indicates a 20-minute free-flow trip takes 26 minutes in the peak. Free-flow speeds (60 mph on freeways and 35 mph on principal arterials) are used as the comparison threshold; (1) Data for the Athens-Clarke County, GA urban area was not available; (2) average of 498 urban areas
Source: Texas Transportation Institute, Urban Mobility Report 2012, December 2012

Public Transportation

Agency Name / Mode of Transportation	Vehicles Operated in Maximum Service	Annual Unlinked Passenger Trips (in thous.)	Annual Passenger Miles (in thous.)
Athens Transit System			
Bus (directly operated)	22	1,789.7	5,188.4
Demand Response (directly operated)	3	9.2	53.0

Source: Federal Transit Administration, National Transit Database, 2012

Air Transportation

Airport Name and Code / Type of Service	Passenger Airlines[1]	Passenger Enplanements	Freight Carriers[2]	Freight (lbs.)
Athens Municipal (AHN)				
Domestic service (U.S. carriers - 2013)	3	1,921	0	0
International service (U.S. carriers - 2012)	0	0	0	0

Note: (1) Includes all U.S.-based major, minor and commuter airlines that carried at least one passenger during the year; (2) Includes all U.S.-based airlines and freight carriers that transported at least one lb. of freight during the year.
Source: Bureau of Transportation Statistics, The Intermodal Transportation Database, Air Carriers: T-100 Domestic Market (U.S. Carriers), 2013; Bureau of Transportation Statistics, The Intermodal Transportation Database, Air Carriers: T-100 International Market (U.S. Carriers), 2012

Other Transportation Statistics

Major Highways:	CR-82 connecting to I-85 (18 miles)
Amtrak Service:	No
Major Waterways/Ports:	None

Source: Amtrak.com; Google Maps

BUSINESSES

Major Business Headquarters

Company Name	Rankings	
	Fortune[1]	Forbes[2]
No companies listed	-	-

Note: (1) Fortune 500—companies that produce a 10-K are ranked 1 to 500 based on 2012 revenue; (2) all private companies with at least $2 billion in annual revenue through the end of their most current fiscal year are ranked 1 to 224; companies listed are headquartered in the city; dashes indicate no ranking
Source: Fortune, "Fortune 500," May 20, 2013; Forbes, "America's Largest Private Companies," December 18, 2013

Minority- and Women-Owned Businesses

Group	All Firms		Firms with Paid Employees			
	Firms	Sales ($000)	Firms	Sales ($000)	Employees	Payroll ($000)
Asian	330	285,670	161	280,037	1,813	40,491
Black	(s)	(s)	(s)	(s)	(s)	(s)
Hispanic	311	22,829	16	11,624	81	2,166
Women	2,687	605,533	366	562,480	4,810	119,645
All Firms	10,181	8,756,927	2,435	8,454,434	48,844	1,391,992

Note: Figures cover firms located in the city; minority- and women-owned business are defined as firms in which the corresponding group own 51% or more of the stock or equity of the company; (s) estimates are suppressed when publication standards are not met
Source: U.S. Census Bureau, 2007 Economic Census, Survey of Business Owners (2012 Survey of Business Owners data will be released starting in June 2015)

HOTELS & CONVENTION CENTERS

Hotels/Motels

Area	5 Star		4 Star		3 Star		2 Star		1 Star		Not Rated	
	Num.	Pct.[3]	Num.	Pct.[3]	Num.	Pct.[3]	Num.	Pct.[3]	Num.	Pct.[3]	Num.	Pct.[3]
City[1]	0	0.0	1	1.2	12	14.0	56	65.1	2	2.3	15	17.4
Total[2]	142	0.9	1,005	6.0	5,147	30.9	8,578	51.4	408	2.4	1,397	8.4

Note: (1) Figures cover Athens and vicinity; (2) Figures cover all 100 cities in this book; (3) Percentage of hotels which have a given star rating; Star ratings are determined by expedia.com and offer an indication of the general quality of a particular hotel.
Source: expedia.com, April 7, 2014

Major Convention Centers

Name	Overall Space (sq. ft.)	Exhibit Space (sq. ft.)	Meeting Space (sq. ft.)	Meeting Rooms
The Classic Center	104,540	56,000	n/a	35

Note: Table includes convention centers located in the Athens-Clarke County, GA metro area; n/a not available
Source: Original research

Living Environment

COST OF LIVING

Cost of Living Index

Composite Index	Groceries	Housing	Utilities	Trans-portation	Health Care	Misc. Goods/ Services
n/a	n/a	n/a	n/a	n/a	n/a	n/a

Note: The Cost of Living Index measures regional differences in the cost of consumer goods and services, excluding taxes and non-consumer expenditures, for professional and managerial households in the top income quintile. It is based on more than 50,000 prices covering almost 60 different items for which prices are collected three times a year by chambers of commerce, economic development organizations or university applied economic centers in each participating urban area. The numbers shown should be read as a percentage above or below the national average of 100. For example, a value of 115.4 in the groceries column indicates that grocery prices are 15.4% higher than the national average. Small differences in the index numbers should not be interpreted as significant; n/a not available.
Source: The Council for Community and Economic Research, ACCRA Cost of Living Index, 2013

Grocery Prices

Area[1]	T-Bone Steak ($/pound)	Frying Chicken ($/pound)	Whole Milk ($/half gal.)	Eggs ($/dozen)	Orange Juice ($/64 oz.)	Coffee ($/11.5 oz.)
City[2]	n/a	n/a	n/a	n/a	n/a	n/a
Avg.	10.19	1.28	2.34	1.81	3.48	4.39
Min.	8.56	0.94	1.44	1.19	2.78	3.40
Max.	14.82	2.28	3.56	3.73	6.23	7.32

Note: (1) Values for the local area are compared with the average, minimum and maximum values for all 327 areas in the Cost of Living Index; (2) Figures cover the Athens GA urban area; n/a not available; **T-Bone Steak** (price per pound); **Frying Chicken** (price per pound, whole fryer); **Whole Milk** (half gallon carton); **Eggs** (price per dozen, Grade A, large); **Orange Juice** (64 oz. Tropicana or Florida Natural); **Coffee** (11.5 oz. can, vacuum-packed, Maxwell House, Hills Bros, or Folgers).
Source: The Council for Community and Economic Research, ACCRA Cost of Living Index, 2013

Housing and Utility Costs

Area[1]	New Home Price ($)	Apartment Rent ($/month)	All Electric ($/month)	Part Electric ($/month)	Other Energy ($/month)	Telephone ($/month)
City[2]	n/a	n/a	n/a	n/a	n/a	n/a
Avg.	295,864	900	171.38	91.82	70.12	27.73
Min.	185,506	458	117.80	48.81	33.67	17.16
Max.	1,358,917	3,783	441.68	171.40	372.65	39.47

Note: (1) Values for the local area are compared with the average, minimum and maximum values for all 327 areas in the Cost of Living Index; (2) Figures cover the Athens GA urban area; n/a not available; **New Home Price** (2,400 sf living area, 8,000 sf lot, in urban area with full utilities); **Apartment Rent** (950 sf 2 bedroom/1.5 or 2 bath, unfurnished, excluding all utilities except water); **All Electric** (average monthly cost for an all-electric home); **Part Electric** (average monthly cost for a part-electric home); **Other Energy** (average monthly cost for natural gas, fuel oil, coal, wood, and any other forms of energy except electricity); **Telephone** (price includes basic monthly rate for a private residential line plus additional local usage charges incurred by a family of four).
Source: The Council for Community and Economic Research, ACCRA Cost of Living Index, 2013

Health Care, Transportation, and Other Costs

Area[1]	Doctor ($/visit)	Dentist ($/visit)	Optometrist ($/visit)	Gasoline ($/gallon)	Beauty Salon ($/visit)	Men's Shirt ($)
City[2]	n/a	n/a	n/a	n/a	n/a	n/a
Avg.	101.40	86.48	96.16	3.44	33.87	26.55
Min.	61.67	50.83	50.12	3.08	18.92	12.48
Max.	182.71	152.50	223.78	4.33	68.22	52.03

Note: (1) Values for the local area are compared with the average, minimum and maximum values for all 327 areas in the Cost of Living Index; (2) Figures cover the Athens GA urban area; n/a not available; **Doctor** (general practitioners routine exam of an established patient); **Dentist** (adult teeth cleaning and periodic oral examination); **Optometrist** (full vision eye exam for established adult patient); **Gasoline** (one gallon regular unleaded, national brand, including all taxes, cash price at self-service pump if available); **Beauty Salon** (woman's shampoo, trim, and blow-dry); **Men's Shirt** (cotton/polyester dress shirt, pinpoint weave, long sleeves).
Source: The Council for Community and Economic Research, ACCRA Cost of Living Index, 2013

HOUSING

House Price Index (HPI)

Area	National Ranking[2]	Quarterly Change (%)	One-Year Change (%)	Five-Year Change (%)
MSA[1]	85	2.17	5.31	-12.78
U.S.[3]	–	1.20	7.69	4.18

Note: The HPI is a weighted repeat sales index. It measures average price changes in repeat sales or refinancings on the same properties. This information is obtained by reviewing repeat mortgage transactions on single-family properties whose mortgages have been purchased or securitized by Fannie Mae or Freddie Mac in January 1975; (1) Athens-Clarke County, GA Metropolitan Statistical Area—see Appendix B for areas included; (2) Rankings are based on annual percentage change for all metro areas containing at least 15,000 transactions over the last 10 years and ranges from 1 to 283; (3) figures based on a weighted average of Census Division estimates using a seasonally adjusted, purchase-only index; all figures are for the period ending December 31, 2013
Source: Federal Housing Finance Agency, House Price Index, February 25, 2014

Median Single-Family Home Prices

Area	2011	2012	2013p	Percent Change 2012 to 2013
MSA[1]	n/a	n/a	n/a	n/a
U.S. Average	166.2	177.2	197.4	11.4

Note: Figures are median sales prices of existing single-family homes in thousands of dollars; (p) preliminary; n/a not available; (1) Athens-Clarke County, GA Metropolitan Statistical Area—see Appendix B for areas included
Source: National Association of Realtors, Median Sales Price of Existing Single-Family Homes for Metropolitan Areas, 4th Quarter 2013

Qualifying Income Based on Median Sales Price of Existing Single-Family Homes

Area	With 5% Down ($)	With 10% Down ($)	With 20% Down ($)
MSA[1]	n/a	n/a	n/a
U.S. Average	45,395	43,006	38,228

Note: Figures are preliminary; Qualifying income is based on a mortgage rate of 4.4%. Monthly principal and interest payment is limited to 25% of income; n/a not available; (1) Athens-Clarke County, GA Metropolitan Statistical Area—see Appendix B for areas included
Source: National Association of Realtors, Qualifying Income Based on Median Sales Price of Existing Single-Family Homes for Metropolitan Areas, 4th Quarter 2013

Median Apartment Condo-Coop Home Prices

Area	2011	2012	2013p	Percent Change 2012 to 2013
MSA[1]	n/a	n/a	n/a	n/a
U.S. Average	165.1	173.7	194.9	12.2

Note: Figures are median sales prices of existing apartment condo-coop homes in thousands of dollars; (p) preliminary; n/a not available; (1) Athens-Clarke County, GA Metropolitan Statistical Area—see Appendix B for areas included
Source: National Association of Realtors, Median Sales Price of Existing Apartment Condo-Coop Homes for Metropolitan Areas, 4th Quarter 2013

Gross Monthly Rent

Area	Under $200	$200 -299	$300 -499	$500 -749	$750 -999	$1,000 -1,499	$1,500 and up	Median ($)
City	2.7	2.8	8.6	35.2	27.1	16.3	7.2	755
MSA[1]	2.4	2.9	8.7	34.1	28.1	16.5	7.3	766
U.S.	1.7	3.3	8.1	22.7	24.3	25.7	14.3	889

Note: Figures are percentages except for Median; Gross rent is the contract rent plus the estimated average monthly cost of utilities (electricity, gas, and water and sewer) and fuels (oil, coal, kerosene, wood, etc.) if these are paid by the renter (or paid for the renter by someone else); (1) Figures cover the Athens-Clarke County, GA Metropolitan Statistical Area—see Appendix B for areas included
Source: U.S. Census Bureau, 2010-2012 American Community Survey 3-Year Estimates

Year Housing Structure Built

Area	2010 or Later	2000 -2009	1990 -1999	1980 -1989	1970 -1979	1960 -1969	1950 -1959	1940 -1949	Before 1940	Median Year
City	0.2	18.0	19.4	20.9	17.8	10.3	5.8	2.9	4.7	1984
MSA[1]	0.2	18.8	20.7	20.2	17.6	9.2	5.1	2.7	5.4	1985
U.S.	0.5	14.9	13.8	13.9	15.9	11.1	10.9	5.5	13.5	1976

Note: Figures are percentages except for Median Year; (1) Figures cover the Athens-Clarke County, GA Metropolitan Statistical Area—see Appendix B for areas included
Source: U.S. Census Bureau, 2010-2012 American Community Survey 3-Year Estimates

HEALTH

Health Risk Data

Category	MSA[1] (%)	U.S. (%)
Adults aged 18–64 who have any kind of health care coverage	n/a	79.6
Adults who reported being in good or excellent health	n/a	83.1
Adults who are current smokers	n/a	19.6
Adults who are heavy drinkers[2]	n/a	6.1
Adults who are binge drinkers[3]	n/a	16.9
Adults who are overweight (BMI 25.0 - 29.9)	n/a	35.8
Adults who are obese (BMI 30.0 - 99.8)	n/a	27.6
Adults who participated in any physical activities in the past month	n/a	77.1
Adults 50+ who have ever had a sigmoidoscopy or colonoscopy	n/a	67.3
Women aged 40+ who have had a mammogram within the past two years	n/a	74.0
Men aged 40+ who have had a PSA test within the past two years	n/a	45.2
Adults aged 65+ who have had flu shot within the past year	n/a	60.1
Adults who always wear a seatbelt	n/a	93.8

Note: Data as of 2012 unless otherwise noted; n/a not available; (1) Figures cover the Athens-Clarke County, GA Metropolitan Statistical Area—see Appendix B for areas included; (2) Heavy drinkers are classified as males having more than two drinks per day or females having more than one drink per day; (3) Binge drinkers are classified as males having five or more drinks on one occasion or females having four or more drinks on one occasion
Source: Centers for Disease Control and Prevention, Behaviorial Risk Factor Surveillance System, SMART: Selected Metropolitan/Micropolitan Area Risk Trends, 2012

Chronic Health Indicators

Category	MSA[1] (%)	U.S. (%)
Adults who have ever been told they had a heart attack	n/a	4.5
Adults who have ever been told they had a stroke	n/a	2.9
Adults who have been told they currently have asthma	n/a	8.9
Adults who have ever been told they have arthritis	n/a	25.7
Adults who have ever been told they have diabetes[2]	n/a	9.7
Adults who have ever been told they had skin cancer	n/a	5.7
Adults who have ever been told they had any other types of cancer	n/a	6.5
Adults who have ever been told they have COPD	n/a	6.2
Adults who have ever been told they have kidney disease	n/a	2.5
Adults who have ever been told they have a form of depression	n/a	18.0

Note: Data as of 2012 unless otherwise noted; n/a not available; (1) Figures cover the Athens-Clarke County, GA Metropolitan Statistical Area—see Appendix B for areas included; (2) Figures do not include pregnancy-related, borderline, or pre-diabetes
Source: Centers for Disease Control and Prevention, Behaviorial Risk Factor Surveillance System, SMART: Selected Metropolitan/Micropolitan Area Risk Trends, 2012

Mortality Rates for the Top 10 Causes of Death in the U.S.

ICD-10[a] Sub-Chapter	ICD-10[a] Code	Age-Adjusted Mortality Rate[1] per 100,000 population	
		County[2]	U.S.
Malignant neoplasms	C00-C97	174.0	174.2
Ischaemic heart diseases	I20-I25	84.6	119.1
Other forms of heart disease	I30-I51	61.9	49.6
Chronic lower respiratory diseases	J40-J47	37.1	43.2
Cerebrovascular diseases	I60-I69	39.6	40.3
Organic, including symptomatic, mental disorders	F01-F09	41.9	30.5
Other degenerative diseases of the nervous system	G30-G31	22.6	26.3
Other external causes of accidental injury	W00-X59	19.3	25.1
Diabetes mellitus	E10-E14	23.7	21.3
Hypertensive diseases	I10-I15	30.1	18.8

Note: (a) ICD-10 = International Classification of Diseases 10th Revision; (1) Mortality rates are a three year average covering 2008-2010; (2) Figures cover Clarke County
Source: Centers for Disease Control and Prevention, National Center for Health Statistics. Compressed Mortality File 1999-2010 on CDC WONDER Online Database, released January 2013. Data are compiled from the Compressed Mortality File 1999-2010, Series 20 No. 2P, 2013.

Mortality Rates for Selected Causes of Death

ICD-10[a] Sub-Chapter	ICD-10[a] Code	Age-Adjusted Mortality Rate[1] per 100,000 population	
		County[2]	U.S.
Assault	X85-Y09	*5.4	5.5
Diseases of the liver	K70-K76	15.2	12.4
Human immunodeficiency virus (HIV) disease	B20-B24	*4.5	3.0
Influenza and pneumonia	J09-J18	13.2	16.4
Intentional self-harm	X60-X84	12.8	11.8
Malnutrition	E40-E46	Suppressed	0.8
Obesity and other hyperalimentation	E65-E68	Suppressed	1.6
Renal failure	N17-N19	12.5	13.6
Transport accidents	V01-V99	14.0	12.6
Viral hepatitis	B15-B19	Suppressed	2.2

Note: (a) ICD-10 = International Classification of Diseases 10th Revision; (1) Mortality rates are a three year average covering 2008-2010; (2) Figures cover Clarke County; (*) Unreliable data as per CDC
Source: Centers for Disease Control and Prevention, National Center for Health Statistics. Compressed Mortality File 1999-2010 on CDC WONDER Online Database, released January 2013. Data are compiled from the Compressed Mortality File 1999-2010, Series 20 No. 2P, 2013.

Health Insurance Coverage

Area	With Health Insurance	With Private Health Insurance	With Public Health Insurance	Without Health Insurance	Population Under Age 18 Without Health Insurance
City	83.5	68.3	22.5	16.5	6.8
MSA[1]	84.7	68.9	24.2	15.3	6.1
U.S.	84.9	65.4	30.4	15.1	7.5

Note: Figures are percentages that cover the civilian noninstitutionalized population; (1) Figures cover the Athens-Clarke County, GA Metropolitan Statistical Area—see Appendix B for areas included
Source: U.S. Census Bureau, 2010-2012 American Community Survey 3-Year Estimates

Number of Medical Professionals

Area[1]	MDs[2]	DOs[2,3]	Dentists	Podiatrists	Chiropractors	Optometrists
Local (number)	328	10	63	6	23	20
Local (rate[4])	276.6	8.4	52.4	5.0	19.1	16.6
U.S. (rate[4])	267.6	19.6	61.7	5.6	24.7	14.5

Note: Data as of 2012 unless noted; (1) Local data covers Clarke County; (2) Data as of 2011; (3) Doctor of Osteopathic Medicine; (4) rate per 100,000 population
Source: Area Resource File (ARF) 2012-2013. U.S. Department of Health and Human Services, Health Resources and Services Administration, Bureau of Health Professions

EDUCATION

Public School District Statistics

District Name	Schls	Pupils	Pupil/ Teacher Ratio	Minority Pupils[1] (%)	Free Lunch Eligible[2] (%)	IEP[3] (%)
Clarke County	21	12,444	12.3	80.9	72.6	11.9

Note: Table includes school districts with 2,000 or more students; (1) Percentage of students that are not non-Hispanic white; (2) Percentage of students that are eligible for the free lunch program; (3) Percentage of students that have an Individualized Education Program.
Source: U.S. Department of Education, National Center for Education Statistics, Common Core of Data, Local Education Agency (School District) Universe Survey: School Year 2011-2012; U.S. Department of Education, National Center for Education Statistics, Common Core of Data, Public Elementary/Secondary School Universe Survey: School Year 2011-2012

Highest Level of Education

Area	Less than H.S.	H.S. Diploma	Some College, No Deg.	Associate Degree	Bachelor's Degree	Master's Degree	Prof. School Degree	Doctorate Degree
City	14.2	22.5	17.9	5.0	19.8	12.1	3.1	5.3
MSA[1]	14.5	26.6	18.9	5.3	17.7	10.5	2.7	3.8
U.S.	14.1	28.3	21.3	7.8	18.0	7.5	1.9	1.2

Note: Figures cover persons age 25 and over; (1) Figures cover the Athens-Clarke County, GA Metropolitan Statistical Area—see Appendix B for areas included
Source: U.S. Census Bureau, 2010-2012 American Community Survey 3-Year Estimates

Educational Attainment by Race

Area	High School Graduate or Higher (%)					Bachelor's Degree or Higher (%)				
	Total	White	Black	Asian	Hisp.[2]	Total	White	Black	Asian	Hisp.[2]
City	85.8	89.8	77.1	92.0	55.6	40.4	52.5	10.9	70.5	10.5
MSA[1]	85.5	88.7	75.2	89.6	57.2	34.8	40.2	11.2	66.6	10.7
U.S.	85.9	88.1	82.5	85.5	63.1	28.6	30.0	18.4	50.2	13.4

Note: Figures shown cover persons 25 years old and over; (1) Figures cover the Athens-Clarke County, GA Metropolitan Statistical Area—see Appendix B for areas included; (2) People of Hispanic origin can be of any race
Source: U.S. Census Bureau, 2010-2012 American Community Survey 3-Year Estimates

School Enrollment by Grade and Control

Area	Preschool (%)		Kindergarten (%)		Grades 1 - 4 (%)		Grades 5 - 8 (%)		Grades 9 - 12 (%)	
	Public	Private	Public	Private	Public	Private	Public	Private	Public	Private
City	60.5	39.5	84.6	15.4	93.9	6.1	86.0	14.0	90.8	9.2
MSA[1]	64.4	35.6	87.3	12.7	93.9	6.1	85.7	14.3	89.9	10.1
U.S.	56.9	43.1	87.8	12.2	89.9	10.1	90.0	10.0	90.8	9.2

Note: Figures shown cover persons 3 years old and over; (1) Figures cover the Athens-Clarke County, GA Metropolitan Statistical Area—see Appendix B for areas included
Source: U.S. Census Bureau, 2010-2012 American Community Survey 3-Year Estimates

Average Salaries of Public School Classroom Teachers

Area	2012-13		2013-14		Percent Change 2012-13 to 2013-14	Percent Change 2003-04 to 2013-14
	Dollars	Rank[1]	Dollars	Rank[1]		
Georgia	52,880	22	52,924	23	0.08	15.1
U.S. Average	56,103	–	56,689	–	1.04	21.8

Note: (1) State rank ranges from 1 to 51 where 1 indicates highest salary.
Source: National Education Association, Rankings & Estimates: Rankings of the States 2013 and Estimates of School Statistics 2014, March 2014

Higher Education

Four-Year Colleges			Two-Year Colleges			Medical Schools[1]	Law Schools[2]	Voc/ Tech[3]
Public	Private Non-profit	Private For-profit	Public	Private Non-profit	Private For-profit			
1	0	0	1	0	0	0	1	1

Note: Figures cover institutions located within the city limits and include main campuses only; (1) includes schools accredited by the Liaison Committee on Medical Education and the American Osteopathic Association's Commission on Osteopathic College Accreditation; (2) includes ABA-accredited schools, schools with provisional ABA accreditation, and state accredited schools; (3) includes all schools with programs that are less than 2 years.
Source: National Center for Education Statistics, Integrated Postsecondary Education System (IPEDS), 2012-13; Association of American Medical Colleges, Member List, April 24, 2014; American Osteopathic Association, Member List, April 24, 2014; Law School Admission Council, Official Guide to ABA-Approved Law Schools Online, April 24, 2014; Wikipedia, List of Medical Schools in the United States, April 24, 2014; Wikipedia, List of Law Schools in the United States, April 24, 2014

According to *U.S. News & World Report,* the Athens-Clarke County, GA metro area is home to one of the best national universities in the U.S.: **University of Georgia** (#60). The indicators used to capture academic quality fall into a number of categories: assessment by administrators at peer institutions; retention of students; faculty resources; student selectivity; financial resources; alumni giving; high school counselor ratings of colleges; and graduation rate. *U.S. News & World Report, "America's Best Colleges 2014"*

According to *U.S. News & World Report,* the Athens-Clarke County, GA metro area is home to one of the top 100 law schools in the U.S.: **University of Georgia** (#33). The rankings are based on a weighted average of 12 measures of quality: peer assessment score; assessment score by lawyers/judges; median LSAT scores; median undergrad GPA; acceptance rate; employment rates for graduates; placement success; bar passage rate; faculty resources; expenditures per student; student/faculty ratio; and library resources. *U.S. News & World Report, "America's Best Graduate Schools, Law, 2014"*

According to *U.S. News & World Report,* the Athens-Clarke County, GA metro area is home to one of the top 100 business schools in the U.S.: **University of Georgia (Terry)** (#52). The rankings are based on a weighted average of the following nine measures: quality assessment; peer assessment; recruiter assessment; placement success; mean starting salary and bonus; student selectivity; mean GMAT and GRE scores; mean undergraduate GPA; and acceptance rate. *U.S. News & World Report, "America's Best Graduate Schools, Business, 2014"*

PRESIDENTIAL ELECTION

2012 Presidential Election Results

Area	Obama	Romney	Other
Clarke County	63.3	34.4	2.4
U.S.	51.0	47.2	1.8

Note: Results are percentages and may not add to 100% due to rounding
Source: Dave Leip's Atlas of U.S. Presidential Elections

EMPLOYERS

Major Employers

Company Name	Industry
Agricultural Research Service	Regulation of agricultural marketing
Athens Regional Medical Center	General medical and surgical hospitals
Athens-Clarke County, Unified Govt of	Executive offices, local government
Athens-Clarke County, Unified Govt of	Air, water, & solid waste management, county govt
Carrier Corporation	Refrigeration equipment, complete
Certainteed Corporation	Insulation: rock wool, slag, and silica minerals
Flowers	Gifts and novelties
Georgia Power Company	Electric services
Island Apparel	Men's and boy's trousers and slacks
McLane/Southeast	Groceries, general line
Power Partners	Power, distribution and specialty transformers
St Mary's Health Care System	General medical and surgical hospitals
The University of Georgia	Colleges and universities
The University of Georgia	Vocational schools
United States Postal Service	U.s. postal service
University of Georgia Athletic Assn	Athletic organizations
Wal-Mart Stores	Department stores, discount

Note: Companies shown are located within the Athens-Clarke County, GA Metropolitan Statistical Area.
Source: Hoovers.com; Wikipedia

PUBLIC SAFETY

Crime Rate

Area	All Crimes	Violent Crimes				Property Crimes		
		Murder	Forcible Rape	Robbery	Aggrav. Assault	Burglary	Larceny -Theft	Motor Vehicle Theft
City	4,304.6	4.3	40.9	134.5	207.7	978.2	2,732.9	206.0
Suburbs[1]	2,849.0	1.3	26.9	26.9	164.3	537.7	1,955.8	136.0
Metro[2]	3,724.0	3.1	35.3	91.6	190.4	802.5	2,423.0	178.1
U.S.	3,246.1	4.7	26.9	112.9	242.3	670.2	1,959.3	229.7

Note: Figures are crimes per 100,000 population; (1) All areas within the metro area that are located outside the city limits; (2) Figures cover the Athens-Clarke County, GA Metropolitan Statistical Area—see Appendix B for areas included
Source: FBI Uniform Crime Reports, 2012

Hate Crimes

Area	Number of Quarters Reported	Bias Motivation				
		Race	Religion	Sexual Orientation	Ethnicity	Disability
Area[2]	2	0	0	0	0	0
U.S.	4	2,797	1,099	1,135	667	92

Note: (2) Figures cover Athens-Clarke County.
Source: Federal Bureau of Investigation, Hate Crime Statistics 2012

Identity Theft Consumer Complaints

Area	Complaints	Complaints per 100,000 Population	Rank[2]
MSA[1]	166	86.2	80
U.S.	290,056	91.8	-

Note: (1) Figures cover the Athens-Clarke County, GA Metropolitan Statistical Area—see Appendix B for areas included; (2) Rank ranges from 1 to 377 where 1 indicates greatest number of identity theft complaints per 100,000 population
Source: Federal Trade Commission, Consumer Sentinel Network Data Book for January–December 2013

RECREATION

Fraud and Other Consumer Complaints

Area	Complaints	Complaints per 100,000 Population	Rank[2]
MSA[1]	563	292.4	317
U.S.	1,811,724	595.2	-

Note: (1) Figures cover the Athens-Clarke County, GA Metropolitan Statistical Area—see Appendix B for areas included; (2) Rank ranges from 1 to 377 where 1 indicates greatest number of identity theft complaints per 100,000 population
Source: Federal Trade Commission, Consumer Sentinel Network Data Book for January–December 2013

Culture

Dance[1]	Theatre[1]	Instrumental Music[1]	Vocal Music[1]	Series and Festivals	Museums and Art Galleries[2]	Zoos and Aquariums[3]
2	2	0	0	1	11	0

Note: (1) Number of professional performing groups; (2) Based on organizations with primary SIC code 8412; (3) AZA-accredited
Source: The Grey House Performing Arts Directory, 2013; Association of Zoos & Aquariums, AZA Member Zoos & Aquariums, April 2014; www.AccuLeads.com, May 1, 2014

Professional Sports Teams

Team Name	League	Year Established
No teams are located in the metro area		

Source: Wikipedia, Major Professional Sports Teams of the United States and Canada, April 25, 2014

CLIMATE

Average and Extreme Temperatures

Temperature	Jan	Feb	Mar	Apr	May	Jun	Jul	Aug	Sep	Oct	Nov	Dec	Yr.
Extreme High (°F)	79	80	85	93	95	101	105	102	98	95	84	77	105
Average High (°F)	52	56	64	73	80	86	88	88	82	73	63	54	72
Average Temp. (°F)	43	46	53	62	70	77	79	79	73	63	53	45	62
Average Low (°F)	33	36	42	51	59	66	70	69	64	52	42	35	52
Extreme Low (°F)	-8	5	10	26	37	46	53	55	36	28	3	0	-8

Note: Figures cover the years 1945-1990
Source: National Climatic Data Center, International Station Meteorological Climate Summary, 9/96

Average Precipitation/Snowfall/Humidity

Precip./Humidity	Jan	Feb	Mar	Apr	May	Jun	Jul	Aug	Sep	Oct	Nov	Dec	Yr.
Avg. Precip. (in.)	4.7	4.6	5.7	4.3	4.0	3.5	5.1	3.6	3.4	2.8	3.8	4.2	49.8
Avg. Snowfall (in.)	1	1	Tr	Tr	0	0	0	0	0	0	Tr	Tr	2
Avg. Rel. Hum. 7am (%)	79	77	78	78	82	83	88	89	88	84	81	79	82
Avg. Rel. Hum. 4pm (%)	56	50	48	45	49	52	57	56	56	51	52	55	52

Note: Figures cover the years 1945-1990; Tr = Trace amounts (<0.05 in. of rain; <0.5 in. of snow)
Source: National Climatic Data Center, International Station Meteorological Climate Summary, 9/96

Weather Conditions

Temperature			Daytime Sky			Precipitation		
10°F & below	32°F & below	90°F & above	Clear	Partly cloudy	Cloudy	0.01 inch or more precip.	0.1 inch or more snow/ice	Thunder-storms
1	49	38	98	147	120	116	3	48

Note: Figures are average number of days per year and cover the years 1945-1990
Source: National Climatic Data Center, International Station Meteorological Climate Summary, 9/96

HAZARDOUS WASTE

Superfund Sites

Athens has no sites on the EPA's Superfund Final National Priorities List.
U.S. Environmental Protection Agency, Final National Priorities List, April 26, 2014

AIR & WATER QUALITY

Air Quality Index

Area	Percent of Days when Air Quality was...[2]					AQI Statistics[2]	
	Good	Moderate	Unhealthy for Sensitive Groups	Unhealthy	Very Unhealthy	Maximum	Median
MSA[1]	74.5	25.5	0.0	0.0	0.0	91	39

*Note: (1) Data covers the Athens-Clarke County, GA Metropolitan Statistical Area—see Appendix B for areas included; (2) Based on 365 days with AQI data in 2013. Air Quality Index (AQI) is an index for reporting daily air quality. EPA calculates the AQI for five major air pollutants regulated by the Clean Air Act: ground-level ozone, particle pollution (aka particulate matter), carbon monoxide, sulfur dioxide, and nitrogen dioxide. The AQI runs from 0 to 500. The higher the AQI value, the greater the level of air pollution and the greater the health concern. There are six AQI categories: "Good" AQI is between 0 and 50. Air quality is considered satisfactory; "Moderate" AQI is between 51 and 100. Air quality is acceptable; "Unhealthy for Sensitive Groups" When AQI values are between 101 and 150, members of sensitive groups may experience health effects; "Unhealthy" When AQI values are between 151 and 200 everyone may begin to experience health effects; "Very Unhealthy" AQI values between 201 and 300 trigger a health alert; "Hazardous" AQI values over 300 trigger warnings of emergency conditions (not shown).
Source: U.S. Environmental Protection Agency, Air Quality Index Report, 2013*

Air Quality Index Pollutants

Area	Percent of Days when AQI Pollutant was...[2]					
	Carbon Monoxide	Nitrogen Dioxide	Ozone	Sulfur Dioxide	Particulate Matter 2.5	Particulate Matter 10
MSA[1]	0.0	0.0	21.6	0.0	78.4	0.0

*Note: (1) Data covers the Athens-Clarke County, GA Metropolitan Statistical Area—see Appendix B for areas included; (2) Based on 365 days with AQI data in 2013. The Air Quality Index (AQI) is an index for reporting daily air quality. EPA calculates the AQI for five major air pollutants regulated by the Clean Air Act: ground-level ozone, particle pollution (also known as particulate matter), carbon monoxide, sulfur dioxide, and nitrogen dioxide. The AQI runs from 0 to 500. The higher the AQI value, the greater the level of air pollution and the greater the health concern.
Source: U.S. Environmental Protection Agency, Air Quality Index Report, 2013*

Air Quality Trends: Ozone

	2003	2004	2005	2006	2007	2008	2009	2010	2011	2012
MSA[1]	0.072	0.078	0.082	0.086	0.083	0.077	0.067	0.073	0.075	0.071

*Note: (1) Data covers the Athens-Clarke County, GA Metropolitan Statistical Area—see Appendix B for areas included. The values shown are the composite ozone concentration averages among trend sites based on the highest fourth daily maximum 8-hour concentration in parts per million. These trends are based on sites having an adequate record of monitoring data during the trend period. Data from exceptional events are included.
Source: U.S. Environmental Protection Agency, Air Quality Monitoring Information, "Air Quality Trends by City, 2000-2012"*

Maximum Air Pollutant Concentrations: Particulate Matter, Ozone, CO and Lead

	Particulate Matter 10 (ug/m³)	Particulate Matter 2.5 Wtd AM (ug/m³)	Particulate Matter 2.5 24-Hr (ug/m³)	Ozone (ppm)	Carbon Monoxide (ppm)	Lead (ug/m³)
MSA[1] Level	n/a	n/a	n/a	0.071	n/a	n/a
NAAQS[2]	150	15	35	0.075	9	0.15
Met NAAQS[2]	n/a	n/a	n/a	Yes	n/a	n/a

*Note: (1) Data covers the Athens-Clarke County, GA Metropolitan Statistical Area—see Appendix B for areas included; Data from exceptional events are included; (2) National Ambient Air Quality Standards; ppm = parts per million; ug/m³ = micrograms per cubic meter; n/a not available.
Concentrations: Particulate Matter 10 (coarse particulate)—highest second maximum 24-hour concentration; Particulate Matter 2.5 Wtd AM (fine particulate)—highest weighted annual mean concentration; Particulate Matter 2.5 24-Hour (fine particulate)—highest 98th percentile 24-hour concentration; Ozone—highest fourth daily maximum 8-hour concentration; Carbon Monoxide—highest second maximum non-overlapping 8-hour concentration; Lead—maximum running 3-month average
Source: U.S. Environmental Protection Agency, Air Quality Monitoring Information, "Air Quality Statistics by City, 2012"*

Maximum Air Pollutant Concentrations: Nitrogen Dioxide and Sulfur Dioxide

	Nitrogen Dioxide AM (ppb)	Nitrogen Dioxide 1-Hr (ppb)	Sulfur Dioxide AM (ppb)	Sulfur Dioxide 1-Hr (ppb)	Sulfur Dioxide 24-Hr (ppb)
MSA[1] Level	n/a	n/a	n/a	n/a	n/a
NAAQS[2]	53	100	30	75	140
Met NAAQS[2]	n/a	n/a	n/a	n/a	n/a

Note: (1) Data covers the Athens-Clarke County, GA Metropolitan Statistical Area—see Appendix B for areas included; Data from exceptional events are included; (2) National Ambient Air Quality Standards; ppm = parts per million; ug/m^3 = micrograms per cubic meter; n/a not available.
Concentrations: Nitrogen Dioxide AM—highest arithmetic mean concentration; Nitrogen Dioxide 1-Hr—highest 98th percentile 1-hour daily maximum concentration; Sulfur Dioxide AM—highest annual mean concentration; Sulfur Dioxide 1-Hr—highest 99th percentile 1-hour daily maximum concentration; Sulfur Dioxide 24-Hr—highest second maximum 24-hour concentration
Source: U.S. Environmental Protection Agency, Air Quality Monitoring Information, "Air Quality Statistics by City, 2012"

Drinking Water

Water System Name	Pop. Served	Primary Water Source Type	Violations[1] Health Based	Violations[1] Monitoring/ Reporting
Athens-Clarke Co. Water System	102,811	Surface	0	0

Note: (1) Based on violation data from January 1, 2013 to December 31, 2013 (includes unresolved violations from earlier years)
Source: U.S. Environmental Protection Agency, Office of Ground Water and Drinking Water, Safe Drinking Water Information System (based on data extracted February 10, 2014)

Atlanta, Georgia

Background

Atlanta was born of a rough-and-tumble past, first as a natural outgrowth of a thriving railroad network in the 1840s, and second as a resilient go-getter that proudly rose again above the rubble of the Civil War.

Blanketed over the rolling hills of the Piedmont Plateau, at the foot of the Blue Ridge Mountains, Georgia's capital stands 1,000 feet above sea level. Atlanta is located in the northwest corner of Georgia where the terrain is rolling to hilly, and slopes downward to the east, west, and south.

Atlanta proper begins at the "terminus," or zero mile mark, of the now defunct Western and Atlantic Railroad Line. However its metropolitan area comprises 28 counties that include Fulton, DeKalb, Clayton and Gwinnet, among others. Population-wise, Atlanta is the largest city in the southeast United States, and has been growing at a steady rate for the last decade. In 2007, the census bureau declared Atlanta the fastest growing metropolitan area in the nation. Understandably, the city contributes to nearly two thirds of the state's economy.

Within the city itself, Atlanta's has a diversified economy that allows for employment in a variety of sectors such as manufacturing, retail, and government. The city hosts many of the nation's Fortune 500 company headquarters, including CNN headquarters, as well as the nation's Centers for Disease Control and Prevention (CDC).

These accomplishments are the result of an involved city government that seeks to work closely with its business community, due in part to a change in the city charter in 1974, when greater administrative powers were vested in the mayoral office, and the city inaugurated its first black mayor.

As middle class residents, both white and black, continue to move to the suburbs separating themselves from Atlanta's old downtown, the city faces the complex issue of where it plans to move as an urban center in light of the conflict between the city and its surroundings.

While schools in the city remain predominantly black and schools in its suburbs predominantly white, Atlanta boasts a racially progressive climate. The Martin Luther King, Jr. Historic Site and Preservation District is located in the Sweet Auburn neighborhood, which includes King's birth home and the Ebenezer Baptist Church, where both he and his father preached. The city's consortium of black colleges that includes Morehouse College and the Interdenominational Theological Center testifies to the city's appreciation for a people who have always been one-third of Atlanta's population. Atlanta has become a major regional center for film and television production in recent years, with Tyler Perry Studios, TurnerStudios and EVE/ScreenGems Studio in the city.

Indeed, King is one of Atlanta's two Nobel Peace Prize winners. The second, former President Jimmy Carter, famously of Plains, Georgia, also brings his name to Atlanta as namesake to the Carter Center. Devoted to human rights, the center is operated with neighboring Emory University, and sits adjacent to the Jimmy Carter Library and Museum on a hill overlooking the city. Habitat for Humanity, also founded by Carter, moved its international administrative headquarters to Atlanta in 2006.

Hartsfield-Jackson Atlanta International Airport, the world's busiest passenger airport, underwent significant expansion in recent years. MARTA, the city's public transport system, is the nation's 9th largest and transports on average 500,000 passengers daily on a 48-mile, 38-station rapid rail system with connections to hundreds of bus routes.

The Appalachian chain of mountains, the Gulf of Mexico, and the Atlantic Ocean influence Atlanta's climate. Temperatures are moderate to hot throughout the year, but extended periods of heat are unusual and 100-degree heat is rarely experienced. Atlanta winters are mild with a few, short-lived cold spells. Summers can be humid. A rare event occurred in March 2008, when a tornado caused considerable damage to the city.

Rankings

General Rankings

- Atlanta was identified as one of America's fastest-growing cities in terms of population and economy by *Forbes*. The area ranked #12 out of 20. The 100 most populous metro areas in the U.S. were evaluated on the following criteria: estimated population growth; job growth; gross metropolitan product growth; unemployment; median salaries for college-educated workers. *Forbes, "America's Fastest-Growing Cities 2014," February 14, 2014*

- Among the 50 largest U.S. cities, Atlanta placed #7 in Vocativ's "semi-exhaustive, mostly scientific" city Livability Index for people aged 35 and under. Average salary, unemployment rates, rents, and other living costs were considered, along with bike lanes, low-cost broadband, cheap takeout, self-service laundries, the price of a pint of Guinness, music venues, and vintage clothing stores. *vocative.com, "The Livability Index: The Best U.S. Cities for People 35 and Under," November 7, 2013*

- Atlanta was selected as one of America's best cities by *Bloomberg Businessweek*. The city ranked #16 out of 50. Criteria: leisure attributes (the number of restaurants, bars, libraries, museums, professional sports teams, and park acres by population); educational attributes (public school performance, the number of colleges, and graduate degree holders); economic factors (2011 income and June and July 2012 unemployment); crime; and air quality. *Bloomberg BusinessWeek, "America's Best Cities," September 26, 2012*

- Atlanta was selected as one of "America's Favorite Cities." The city ranked #26 in the "Quality of Life and Visitor Experience: Cleanliness" category. Respondents to an online survey were asked to rate 35 top urban destinations in the U.S. from a visitor's perspective. Criteria: cleanliness. *Travel + Leisure, "America's Favorite Cities 2013"*

- Atlanta was selected as one of "America's Favorite Cities." The city ranked #21 in the "Type of Trip: Gay-friendly" category. Respondents to an online survey were asked to rate 35 top urban destinations in the U.S. from a visitor's perspective. Criteria: gay-friendly. *Travel + Leisure, "America's Favorite Cities 2013"*

Business/Finance Rankings

- Measuring indicators of "tolerance"—the nonjudgmental environment that "attracts open-minded and new-thinking kinds of people"— as well as concentrations of technological and economic innovators, analysts identified the most creative American metro areas. On the resulting 2012 Creativity Index, the Atlanta metro area placed #19. *www.thedailybeast.com, "Boulder, Ann Arbor, Tucson & More: 20 Most Creative U.S. Cities," June 26, 2012*

- Atlanta was the #1-ranked city for savers, according to the finance site GoBankingRates, which considered the prospects for savers in a tough savings economy by looking for higher interest yields, lower taxes, more jobs with higher incomes, and less expensive housing costs. *www.gobankingrates.com, "Best Cities for Saving Money," February 24, 2014*

- The editors of *Kiplinger's Personal Finance Magazine* named Atlanta to their list of ten of the best metro areas for start-ups. Criteria included a well-educated workforce and low living costs for self-employed people, as measured by the Council for Community and Economic Research, as well as areas with lots of start-up investment dollars and low business costs. *www.kiplinger.com, "10 Great Cities for Starting a Business," January 2013*

- Based on a minimum of 500 social media reviews per metro area, the employment opinion group Glassdoor surveyed 50 of the largest U.S. metro areas on measures including compensation and benefits, satisfaction with management, business outlook, and number of employers hiring. The Atlanta metro area was ranked #27 in overall employee satisfaction. *www.glassdoor.com, "Employment Satisfaction Report Card by City," June 21, 2013*

- In its Competitive Alternatives report, consulting firm KPMG analyzed the 27 largest metropolitan statistical areas according to 26 cost components (such as taxes, labor costs, and utilities) and 30 non-cost-related variables (such as crime rates and number of universities). The business website 24/7 Wall Street examined the KPMG findings, adding to the mix current unemployment rates, GDP, median income, and employment decline during the last recession and "projected" recovery. It identified the Atlanta metro area as #2 among the ten best American cities for business. *247wallst.com, "Best American Cities for Business," April 4, 2012*

- The financial literacy site NerdWallet.com set out to identify the 20 most promising cities for job seekers, analyzing data for the nation's 50 largest cities. Atlanta was ranked #11. Criteria: unemployment rate; population growth; median income; selected monthly owner costs. *NerdWallet.com, "Best Cities for Job Seekers," January 7, 2014*

- The Brookings Institution ranked the 50 largest cities in the U.S. based on income inequality. Atlanta was ranked #1. (#1 = greatest inequality). Criteria: the cities were ranked based on the "95/20 ratio." This figure represents the income at which a household earns more than 95 percent of all other households, divided by the income at which a household earns more than only 20 percent of all other households. *Brookings Institution, "Income Inequality in America's 50 Largest Cities, 2007-2012," February 20, 2014*

- Atlanta was ranked #39 out of 100 metro areas in terms of economic performance (#1 = best) during the recession and recovery from trough quarter through the second quarter of 2013. Criteria: percent change in employment; percentage point change in unemployment rate; percent change in gross metropolitan product; percent change in House Price Index. *Brookings Institution, MetroMonitor: Tracking Economic Recession and Recovery in America's 100 Largest Metropolitan Areas, September 2013*

- Payscale.com ranked the 20 largest metro areas in terms of wage growth. The Atlanta metro area ranked #16. Criteria: private-sector wage growth between the 4th quarter of 2012 and the 4th quarter of 2013. *PayScale, "Wage Trends by Metro Area," 4th Quarter, 2013*

- Atlanta was identified as one of America's most frugal metro areas by *Coupons.com*. The city ranked #1 out of 25. Criteria: online coupon usage. *Coupons.com, "Top 25 Most Frugal Cities of 2012," February 19, 2013*

- Atlanta was identified as one of America's most frugal metro areas by *Coupons.com*. The city ranked #3 out of 25. Criteria: Grocery IQ and coupons.com mobile app usage. *Coupons.com, "Top 25 Most On-the-Go Frugal Cities of 2012," February 19, 2013*

- Atlanta was identified as one of the top 25 U.S. cities with the most credit card debt by credit reporting bureau Experian. The city was ranked #3. *Experian, March 4, 2011*

- Atlanta was cited as one of America's top metros for new and expanded facility projects in 2013. The area ranked #4 in the large metro area category (population over 1 million). *Site Selection, "Top Metros of 2013," March 2014*

- Atlanta was identified as one of the best cities for college graduates to find work—and live. The city ranked #6 out of 15. Criteria: job availability; average salary; average rent. *CareerBuilder.com, "15 Best Cities for College Grads to Find Work—and Live," June 5, 2012*

- The Atlanta metro area appeared on the Milken Institute "2013 Best Performing Cities" list. Rank: #41 out of 200 large metro areas. Criteria: job growth; wage and salary growth; high-tech output growth. *Milken Institute, "Best-Performing Cities 2013," December 2013*

- *Forbes* ranked the 200 most populous metro areas in the U.S. in terms of the "Best Places for Business and Careers." The Atlanta metro area was ranked #22. Criteria: costs (business and living); job growth (past and projected); income growth; educational attainment (college and high school); projected economic growth; cultural and recreational opportunities; net migration patterns; number of highly ranked colleges. *Forbes, "The Best Places for Business and Careers," August 7, 2013*

Children/Family Rankings

- Atlanta was selected as one of the best cities for families to live by *Parenting* magazine. The city ranked #55 out of 100. Criteria: education; health; community; *Parenting's* Culture & Charm Index. *Parenting.com, "The 2012 Best Cities for Families List"*

Culture/Performing Arts Rankings

- Atlanta was selected as one of 10 best U.S. cities to be a moviemaker. The city was ranked #10. Criteria: film community; access to new films; access to equipment; cost of living; tax incentives. *MovieMaker Magazine, "Top 10 Cities to be a Moviemaker: 2013," March 5, 2013*

- Atlanta was selected as one of "America's Favorite Cities." The city ranked #27 in the "Culture: Museum/Galleries" category. Respondents to an online survey were asked to rate 35 top urban destinations in the U.S. from a visitor's perspective. Criteria: number and quality of museums and galleries. *Travelandleisure.com, "America's Favorite Cities 2013"*

- Atlanta was selected as one of America's top cities for the arts. The city ranked #8 in the mid-sized city (population 100,000 to 499,999) category. Criteria: readers' top choices for arts travel destinations based on the richness and variety of visual arts sites, activities and events. *American Style, "2012 Top 25 Arts Destinations," June 2012*

Dating/Romance Rankings

- CreditDonkey, a financial education website, sought out the ten best U.S. cities for newlyweds, considering the number of married couples, divorce rate, average credit score, and average number of hours worked per week in metro areas with a million or more residents. The Atlanta metro area placed #1. *www.creditdonkey.com, "Study: Best Cities for Newlyweds," November 30, 2013*

- Of the 100 U.S. cities surveyed by *Men's Health* in its quest to identify the nation's best cities for dating and forming relationships, Atlanta was ranked #1 for online dating (#1 = best). *Men's Health, "The Best and Worst Cities for Online Dating," January 30, 2013*

Education Rankings

- *Men's Health* ranked 100 U.S. cities in terms of their education levels. Atlanta was ranked #25 (#1 = most educated city). Criteria: high school graduation rates; school enrollment; educational attainment; number of households who have outstanding student loans; number of households whose members have taken adult-education courses. *Men's Health, "Where School Is In: The Most and Least Educated Cities," September 12, 2011*

- Atlanta was selected as one of the most well-read cities in America by Amazon.com. The city ranked #16 of 20. Cities with populations greater than 100,000 were evaluated based on per capita sales of books, magazines and newspapers. *Amazon.com, "The 20 Most Well-Read Cities in America," April 28, 2013*

- Atlanta was selected as one of America's most literate cities. The city ranked #4 out of the 77 largest U.S. cities. Criteria: number of booksellers; library resources; Internet resources; educational attainment; periodical publishing resources; newspaper circulation. *Central Connecticut State University, "America's Most Literate Cities, 2013"*

Environmental Rankings

- The Atlanta metro area came in at #246 for the relative comfort of its climate on Sperling's list of "chill cities," as measured by the Sperling Heat Index. All 361 metro areas are included. Criteria included daytime high temperatures, nighttime low temperatures, dew point, and relative humidity at the high temperatures. *www.bertsperling.com, "Sperling's Chill Cities," July 18, 2013*

- Sperling's BestPlaces assessed 379 metropolitan areas of the United States for the likelihood of dangerously extreme weather events or earthquakes. In general the Southeast and South-Central regions have the highest risk of weather extremes and earthquakes, while the Pacific Northwest enjoys the lowest risk. Of the least risky metropolitan areas, the Atlanta metro area was ranked #358. *www.bestplaces.net, "Safest Places from Natural Disasters," April 2011*

- Atlanta was identified as one of North America's greenest metropolitan areas. The area ranked #21. The Green City Index is comprised of 31 indicators, and scores cities across nine categories: carbon dioxide; energy; land use; buildings; transport; water; waste; air quality; environmental governance. The 27 largest metropolitan areas in the U.S. and Canada were considered. *Economist Intelligence Unit, sponsored by Siemens, "U.S. and Canada Green City Index, 2011"*

- The U.S. Environmental Protection Agency (EPA) released a list of U.S. metropolitan areas with the most ENERGY STAR certified buildings in 2012. The Atlanta metro area was ranked #5 out of 25. *U.S. Environmental Protection Agency, "Top Cities With the Most ENERGY STAR Certified Buildings in 2012," March 12, 2013*

- Atlanta was selected as one of 22 "Smarter Cities" for energy by the Natural Resources Defense Council. Criteria: investment in green power; energy efficiency measures; conservation. *Natural Resources Defense Council, "2010 Smarter Cities," July 19, 2010*

- Atlanta was highlighted as one of the 25 metro areas most polluted by year-round particle pollution (Annual PM 2.5) in the U.S. during 2008 through 2010. The area ranked #18. *American Lung Association, State of the Air 2012*

Food/Drink Rankings

- *Men's Health* ranked 100 major U.S. cities in terms of alcohol intoxication. Atlanta ranked #13 (#1 = most sober).Criteria: binge drinking; alcohol-related traffic accidents, arrests, and fatalities. *Men's Health, "The Drunkest Cities in America," November 19, 2013*

Health/Fitness Rankings

- For each of the 50 most populous metro areas in the United States, the American College of Sports Medicine's American Fitness Index evaluated infrastructure, community assets, and policies that encourage healthy and fit lifestyles, including preventive health behaviors, levels of chronic disease conditions, health care access, and community resources and policies that support physical activity. The Atlanta metro area ranked #21 for "community fitness." Personal health indicators were considered as well as community and environmental indicators. *www.americanfitnessindex.org, "ACSM American Fitness Index Health and Community Fitness Status of the 50 Largest Metropolitan Areas," May 2013*

- The Atlanta metro area was identified as one of the worst cities for bed bugs in America by pest control company Orkin. The area ranked #15 out of 50 based on the number of bed bug treatments Orkin performed from January to December 2013. *Orkin, "Chicago Tops Bed Bug Cities List for Second Year in a Row," January 16, 2014*

- Atlanta was selected as one of the 25 fattest cities in America by *Men's Fitness Online*. It ranked #20 out of America's 50 largest cities. Criteria: fitness centers and sport stores; nutrition; sports participation; TV viewing; overweight/sedentary; junk food; air quality; geography; commute; parks and open space; city recreational facilities; access to healthcare; motivation; mayor and city initiatives; state obesity initiatives. *Men's Fitness, "The Fittest and Fattest Cities in America," March 5, 2012*

- Atlanta was identified as a "2013 Spring Allergy Capital." The area ranked #72 out of 100. Three groups of factors were used to identify the most severe cities for people with allergies during the spring season: annual pollen levels; medicine utilization; access to board-certified allergists. *Asthma and Allergy Foundation of America, "Spring Allergy Capitals 2013"*

- Atlanta was identified as a "2013 Fall Allergy Capital." The area ranked #74 out of 100. Three groups of factors were used to identify the most severe cities for people with allergies during the fall season: annual pollen levels; medicine utilization; access to board-certified allergists. *Asthma and Allergy Foundation of America, "Fall Allergy Capitals 2013"*

- Atlanta was identified as a "2013 Asthma Capital." The area ranked #9 out of the nation's 100 largest metropolitan areas. Twelve factors were used to identify the most challenging places to live for people with asthma: estimated prevalence; self-reported prevalence; crude death rate for asthma; annual pollen score; annual air quality; public smoking laws; number of board-certified asthma specialists; school inhaler access laws; rescue medication use; controller medication use; uninsured rate; poverty rate. *Asthma and Allergy Foundation of America, "Asthma Capitals 2013"*

- *Men's Health* ranked 100 major U.S. cities in terms of the best and worst cities for men. Atlanta ranked #28. Criteria: thirty-three data points were examined covering health, fitness, and quality of life. *Men's Health, "The Best & Worst Cities for Men 2014," December 6, 2013*

- Atlanta was selected as one of the best metropolitan areas for hospital care in America by *HealthGrades.com*. The rankings are based on a comprehensive study of patient death and complication rates in the nation's nearly 5,000 hospitals. Hospitals performing in the top 5% nationwide across 26 different medical procedures and diagnoses were identified. *HealthGrades.com* then ranked cities by the highest percentage of these Distinguished Hospitals for Clinical Excellence™. The Atlanta metro area ranked #50. *HealthGrades.com, "America's Top 50 Cities for Hospital Care," January 21, 2012*

- The American Academy of Dermatology ranked 26 U.S. metropolitan regions in terms of their residents knowledge, attitude and behaviors towards tanning, sun protection and skin cancer detection. The Atlanta metro area ranked #7. The results of the study are based on an online survey of over 7,000 adults nationwide. *American Academy of Dermatology, "Suntelligence: How Sun Smart is Your City?," May 3, 2010*

- The Atlanta metro area appeared in the 2013 Gallup-Healthways Well-Being Index. The area ranked #42 out of 189. The Gallup-Healthways Well-Being Index score is an average of six sub-indexes, which individually examine life evaluation, emotional health, work environment, physical health, healthy behaviors, and access to basic necessities. Results are based on telephone interviews conducted as part of the Gallup-Healthways Well-Being Index survey January 2–December 29, 2012, and January 2–December 30, 2013, with a random sample of 531,630 adults, aged 18 and older, living in metropolitan areas in the 50 U.S. states and the District of Columbia. *Gallup-Healthways, "State of American Well-Being," March 25, 2014*

- The Atlanta metro area was identified as one of "America's Most Stressful Cities" by *Sperling's BestPlaces*. The metro area ranked #15 out of 50. Criteria: unemployment rate; suicide rate; commute time; mental health; poor rest; alcohol use; violent crime rate; property crime rate; cloudy days annually. *Sperling's BestPlaces, www.BestPlaces.net, "Stressful Cities 2012*

- *Men's Health* ranked 100 U.S. cities in terms of their activity levels. Atlanta was ranked #8 (#1 = most active city). Criteria: where and how often residents exercise; percentage of households that watch more than 15 hours of cable television a week and buy more than 11 video games a year; death rate from deep-vein thrombosis, a condition linked to sitting for extended periods of time. *Men's Health, "Where Sit Happens: The Most and Least Active Cities in America," June 20, 2011*

- Atlanta was selected as one of the "20 Most Livable U.S. Cities for Wheelchair Users" by the Christopher & Dana Reeve Foundation. The city ranked #20. Criteria: Medicaid eligibility and spending; access to physicians and rehabilitation facilities; access to fitness facilities and recreation; access to paratransit; percentage of people living with disabilities who are employed; clean air; climate. *Christopher & Dana Reeve Foundation, "20 Most Livable U.S. Cities for Wheelchair Users," July 26, 2010*

Real Estate Rankings

- On the list compiled by Penske Truck Rental, the Atlanta metro area was named the #1 moving destination in 2013, based on one-way consumer truck rental reservations made through Penske's website and reservations call center. *blog.gopenske.com, "Penske Truck Rental's 2013 Top Moving Destinations List," January 22, 2014*

- The Atlanta metro area was identified as one of the top 20 housing markets to invest in for 2014 by *Forbes*. The area ranked #6. Criteria: high population and job growth; relatively low home prices which are below equilibrium home price (EHP). The EHP is what the average price for a market should be, if speculation, weird distortions in local income, and other factors (like the housing collapse) weren't present in the market. *Forbes.com, "Best Buy Cities: Where to Invest in Housing in 2014," December 25, 2013*

- *Kiplinger* looked at metro areas with populations above 250,000 to identify the cities in which home prices have risen most, drawing on sales, supply, foreclosure, and market data from Realtors' associations and industry analysts. U.S. Bureau of Labor Statistics unemployment figures were also considered. Atlanta ranked #10. *Kiplinger, "12 Cities Where Home Prices Have Risen Most," May 2013*

- Atlanta was ranked #66 out of 283 metro areas in terms of house price appreciation in 2013 (#1 = highest rate). *Federal Housing Finance Agency, House Price Index, 4th Quarter 2013*

- Atlanta was selected as one of the 10 U.S. metro areas that "Offer the Best Bang for Your Buck." The area ranked #6. Criteria: average home price per square foot. *CNBC, "Cities That Offer the Best Bang for Your Buck," December 15, 2011*

- The Atlanta metro area was identified as one of the 20 best housing markets in the U.S. in 2013. The area ranked #1 out of 173 markets with a home price appreciation of 33.2%. Criteria: year-over-year change of median sales price of existing single-family homes between the 4th quarter of 2012 and the 4th quarter of 2013. *National Association of Realtors®, Median Sales Price of Existing Single-Family Homes for Metropolitan Areas, 4th Quarter 2013*

- The Atlanta metro area was identified as one of the 10 best condo markets in the U.S. in 2013. The area ranked #2 out of 64 markets with a price appreciation of 46.4%. Criteria: year-over-year change of median sales price of existing apartment condo-coop homes between the 4th quarter of 2012 and the 4th quarter of 2013. *National Association of Realtors®, Median Sales Price of Existing Apartment Condo-Coop Homes for Metropolitan Areas, 4th Quarter 2013*

- Atlanta was ranked #94 out of 224 metro areas in terms of housing affordability in 2013 by the National Association of Home Builders (#1 = most affordable). The NAHB-Wells Fargo Housing Opportunity Index (HOI) for a given area is defined as the share of homes sold in that area that would have been affordable to a family earning the local median income, based on standard mortgage underwriting criteria. *National Association of Home Builders®, NAHB-Wells Fargo Housing Opportunity Index, 4th Quarter 2013*

- Atlanta was selected as one of the best college towns for renters by ApartmentRatings.com." The area ranked #35 out of 87. Overall satisfaction ratings were ranked using thousands of user submitted scores for hundreds of apartment complexes located in cities and towns that are home to the 100 largest four-year institutions in the U.S. *ApartmentRatings.com, "2011 College Town Renter Satisfaction Rankings"*

- The Atlanta metro area was identified as one of the 10 best U.S. markets to invest in single-family homes as rental properties by HomeVestors and Local Market Monitor. The area ranked #5. Criteria: risk-return premium relative to national average. *HomeVestors and Local Market Monitor, "Year-End Top 10 Real Estate Markets," December 20, 2013*

Safety Rankings

- Business Insider looked at the FBI's Uniform Crime Report to identify the U.S. cities with the most violent crime per capita, excluding localities with fewer than 100,000 residents. To judge by its relatively high murder, rape, and robbery data, Atlanta was ranked #23 (#1 = worst) among the 25 most dangerous cities. *www.businessinsider.com, "The 25 Most Dangerous Cities in America," June 13, 2013*

- Symantec, in partnership with Sperling's BestPlaces, ranked the 50 largest cities in the U.S. in terms of their vulnerability to cybercrime. The city ranked #4. Criteria: number of cyberattacks and potential infections; level of Internet access; expenditures on smartphones and computer hardware/software; wireless hotspots; broadband connectivity; Internet usage; online purchases. *Symantec, "Riskiest Online Cities of 2012" February 15, 2012*

- Allstate ranked the 200 largest cities in America in terms of driver safety. Atlanta ranked #164. Allstate researchers analyzed internal property damage claims over a two-year period from January 2010 to December 2011. A weighted average of the two-year numbers determined the annual percentages. *Allstate, "Allstate America's Best Drivers Report®, August 27, 2013"*

- The Atlanta metro area was identified as one of "America's Most Dangerous Cities" by *Forbes*. The area ranked #9 out of 10. Criteria: violent crime (murder and non-negligent manslaughter, forcible rape, robbery, and aggravated assault) rates per capita. The editors only considered metropolitan areas with populations above 200,000. *Forbes, "America's Most Dangerous Cities 2013," October 22, 2013*

- Atlanta was identified as one of the most dangerous cities in America by *The Business Insider*. Criteria: cities with 100,000 residents or more were ranked by violent crime rate in 2011. Violent crimes include for murder, rape, robbery, and aggravated assault. The city ranked #8 out of 25. *The Business Insider, "The 25 Most Dangerous Cities in America," November 4, 2012*

- The National Insurance Crime Bureau ranked 380 metro areas in the U.S. in terms of per capita rates of vehicle theft. The Atlanta metro area ranked #36 (#1 = highest rate). Criteria: number of vehicle theft offenses per 100,000 inhabitants in 2012. *National Insurance Crime Bureau, "Hot Spots 2012," June 26, 2013*

- The Atlanta metro area was identified as one of the most dangerous metro areas for pedestrians by Transportation for America. The metro area ranked #11 out of 52 metro areas with over 1 million residents. Criteria: area's population divided by the number of pedestrian fatalities in that area. *Transportation for America, "Dangerous by Design 2011"*

Seniors/Retirement Rankings

- From its Best Cities for Successful Aging indexes, the Milken Institute generated rankings for metropolitan areas, weighing data in eight categories—general indicators, health care, wellness, living arrangements, transportation and general accessibility, financial well-being, education and employment, and community participation. The Atlanta metro area was ranked #70 overall in the large metro area category. *Milken Institute, "Best Cities for Successful Aging," July 2012*

- Bankers Life and Casualty Company, in partnership with Sperling's BestPlaces, ranked the nation's 50 largest metro areas in terms of the "Best U.S. Cities for Seniors." The Atlanta metro area ranked #39. Criteria: healthcare; transportation; housing; environment; economy; health and longevity; social and spiritual life; crime. *Bankers Life and Casualty Company, Center for a Secure Retirement, "Best U.S. Cities for Seniors 2011," September 2011*

Sports/Recreation Rankings

- Atlanta was selected as one of "America's Most Miserable Sports Cities" by *Forbes*. The city was ranked #2. Criteria: postseason losses; years since last title; ratio of cumulative seasons to championships won. Contenders were limited to cities with at least 75 total seasons of NFL, NBA, NHL and MLB play. *Forbes, "America's Most Miserable Sports Cities," July 31, 2013*

- Atlanta appeared on the *Sporting News* list of the "Best Sports Cities" for 2011. The area ranked #7 out of 271. Criteria: the magazine takes a 12-month snapshot of each city's sports, putting a heavy premium on regular-season won-lost records (from the most recently completed season). Other criteria include: playoff berths, bowl appearances and tournament bids; championships; applicable power ratings; quality of competition; overall fan fervor (measured in part by attendance); abundance of teams (rewarding quality over quantity); stadium and arena quality; ticket availability and prices; franchise ownership; and marquee appeal of athletes. *Sporting News, "Best Sports Cities 2011," October 4, 2011*

- Atlanta appeared on the *Sporting News* list of the "Best Sports Cities" for 2011. The area ranked #7 out of 271. Criteria: a 12-month snapshot of regular-season won-lost records (from the most recently completed season). Other criteria include: playoff berths, bowl appearances and tournament bids; championships; applicable power ratings; quality of competition; overall fan fervor (measured in part by attendance); abundance of teams (quality over quantity); stadium and arena quality; ticket availability and prices; franchise ownership; and marquee appeal of athletes. *Sporting News, "Best Sports Cities 2011," October 4, 2011*

- Atlanta was selected as one of the most playful cities in the U.S. by KaBOOM! The organization's Playful City USA initiative honors cities and towns across the nation for a vision, plan and commitment to creating an agenda for play. Criteria: creating a local play commission or task force; designing an annual action plan for play; conducting a play space audit; outlining a financial investment in play for the current fiscal year; and proclaiming and celebrating an annual "play day." *KaBOOM! National Campaign for Play, "2013 Playful City USA Communities"*

Transportation Rankings

- NerdWallet surveyed average annual car insurance premiums in 125 U.S. cities to identify the least expensive U.S. cities in which to insure a car. Locations with no-fault insurance laws was a strong determinant. Atlanta came in at #26 for the most expensive rates. *www.nerdwallet.com, "Best Cities for Cheap Car Insurance," February 3, 2014*

- Atlanta was identified as one of the most congested metro areas in the U.S. The area ranked #7 out of 10. Criteria: yearly delay per auto commuter in hours. *Texas A&M Transportation Institute, "2012 Urban Mobility Report," December 2012*

- The Atlanta metro area appeared on *Forbes* list of places with the most extreme commutes. The metro area ranked #7 out of 10. Criteria: average travel time; percentage of mega commuters. Mega-commuters travel more than 90 minutes and 50 miles each way to work. *Forbes.com, "The Cities with the Most Extreme Commutes," March 5, 2013*

Women/Minorities Rankings

- The Daily Beast surveyed the nation's cities for highest percentage of singles and lowest divorce rate, plus other measures, to determine "emotional intelligence"—happiness, confidence, kindness—which, researchers say, has a strong correlation with people's satisfaction with their romantic relationships. Atlanta placed #4. *www.thedailybeast.com, "Best Cities to Find Love and Stay in Love," February 14, 2014*

- *Women's Health* examined U.S. cities and identified the 100 best cities for women. Atlanta was ranked #39. Criteria: 30 categories were examined from obesity and breast cancer rates to commuting times and hours spent working out. *Women's Health, "Best Cities for Women 2012"*

- Atlanta was selected as one of the gayest cities in America by *The Advocate*. The city ranked #5 out of 15. This year's criteria include points for a city's LGBT elected officials (and fractional points for the state's elected officials), points for the percentage of the population comprised by lesbian-coupled households, a point for a gay rodeo association, points for bars listed in *Out* magazine's 200 Best Bars list, a point per women's college, and points for concert performances by Mariah Carey, Pink, Lady Gaga, or the Jonas Brothers. The raw score is divided by the population to provide a ranking based on a per capita LGBT quotient. *The Advocate, "2014's Gayest Cities in America" January 6, 2014*

- The Atlanta metro area appeared on *Forbes'* list of the "Best Cities for Minority Entrepreneurs." The area ranked #5 out of 10. Criteria: 52 metropolitan statistical areas were examined. For each ethnicity (African Americans, Asians and Hispanics), the editors measured housing affordability, population growth, income growth, and entrepreneurship (per capita self-employment). *Forbes, "Best Cities for Minority Entrepreneurs," March 23, 2011*

Miscellaneous Rankings

- The watchdog site Charity Navigator conducts an annual study of charities in the nation's major markets both to analyze statistical differences in their financial, accountability, and transparency practices and to track year-to-year variations in individual communities. The Atlanta metro area was ranked #27 among the 30 metro markets. *www.charitynavigator.org, "Metro Market Study 2013," June 1, 2013*

- The Harris Poll's Happiness Index survey revealed that of the top ten U.S. markets, the Atlanta metro area residents ranked #4 in happiness. Criteria included strong assent to positive statements and strong disagreement with negative ones, and degree of agreement with a series of statements about respondents' personal relationships and general outlook. The online survey was conducted between July 14 and July 30, 2013. *www.harrisinteractive.com, "Dallas/Fort Worth Is "Happiest" City among America's Top Ten Markets," September 4, 2013*

- Market analyst Scarborough Research surveyed adults who had done volunteer work over the previous 12 months to find out where volunteers are concentrated. The Atlanta metro area made the list for highest volunteer participation. *Scarborough Research, "Salt Lake City, UT; Minneapolis, MN; and Des Moines, IA Lend a Helping Hand," November 27, 2012*

- Atlanta was selected as one of America's funniest cities by the Humor Research Lab at the University of Colorado. The city ranked #3 out of 10. Criteria: frequency of visits to comedy websites; number of comedy clubs per square mile; traveling comedians' ratings of each city's comedy-club audiences; number of famous comedians born in each city per capita; number of famous funny tweeters living in each city per capita; number of comedy radio stations available in each city; frequency of humor-related web searches originating in each city. *The New York Times, "So These Professors Walk Into a Comedy Club...," April 20, 2014*

- *Men's Health* ranked 100 U.S. cities by their level of sadness. Atlanta was ranked #87 (#1 = saddest city). Criteria: suicide rates; unemployment rates; percentage of households that use antidepressants; percent of population who report feeling blue all or most of the time. *Men's Health, "Frown Towns," November 28, 2011*

- Energizer Personal Care, the makers of Edge® shave gel, in partnership with Sperling's BestPlaces, ranked 50 major metro areas in terms of everyday irritations. The Atlanta metro area ranked #5. Criteria: high male-to-female ratio; poor sports team performance and high ticket prices; slow traffic; lack of job availability; unaffordable housing; extreme weather; lack of nightlife and fitness options. *Energizer Personal Care, "Most Irritatng Cities for Guys," August 26, 2013*

- Mars Chocolate North America, the makers of COMBOS®, in partnership with Sperling's BestPlaces, ranked 50 major metro areas in terms of their "manliness." The Atlanta metro area ranked #17. Criteria: number of professional sports teams; number of nearby NASCAR tracks and racing events; manly lifestyle; concentration of manly retail stores; manly occupations per capita; salty snack sales; "Board of Manliness" rankings. *Mars Chocolate North America, "America's Manliest Cities 2012"*

- The Atlanta metro area was selected as one of "America's Most Miserable Cities" by *Forbes.com.* The metro area ranked #16 out of 20. Criteria: violent crime; unemployment; foreclosures; income and property taxes; home prices; commute times; climate. *Forbes.com, "America's Most Miserable Cities" February 22, 2013*

- The National Alliance to End Homelessness ranked the 100 most populous metro areas in terms the rate of homelessness. The Atlanta metro area ranked #61. Criteria: number of homeless people per 10,000 population in 2011. *National Alliance to End Homelessness, The State of Homelessness in America 2012*

Business Environment

CITY FINANCES

City Government Finances

Component	2011 ($000)	2011 ($ per capita)
Total Revenues	2,575,203	4,960
Total Expenditures	2,327,660	4,484
Debt Outstanding	7,451,996	14,354
Cash and Securities[1]	4,825,323	9,295

Note: (1) Cash and security holdings of a government at the close of its fiscal year, including those of its dependent agencies, utilities, and liquor stores.
Source: U.S Census Bureau, State & Local Government Finances 2011

City Government Revenue by Source

Source	2011 ($000)	2011 ($ per capita)
General Revenue		
From Federal Government	41,172	79
From State Government	17,109	33
From Local Governments	204,373	394
Taxes		
Property	338,093	651
Sales and Gross Receipts	153,203	295
Personal Income	0	0
Corporate Income	0	0
Motor Vehicle License	0	0
Other Taxes	66,098	127
Current Charges	930,692	1,793
Liquor Store	0	0
Utility	266,017	512
Employee Retirement	406,607	783

Source: U.S Census Bureau, State & Local Government Finances 2011

City Government Expenditures by Function

Function	2011 ($000)	2011 ($ per capita)	2011 (%)
General Direct Expenditures			
Air Transportation	764,179	1,472	32.8
Corrections	20,747	40	0.9
Education	0	0	0.0
Employment Security Administration	0	0	0.0
Financial Administration	39,776	77	1.7
Fire Protection	82,489	159	3.5
General Public Buildings	16,288	31	0.7
Governmental Administration, Other	42,512	82	1.8
Health	822	2	0.0
Highways	40,830	79	1.8
Hospitals	0	0	0.0
Housing and Community Development	22,824	44	1.0
Interest on General Debt	121,535	234	5.2
Judicial and Legal	11,802	23	0.5
Libraries	0	0	0.0
Parking	0	0	0.0
Parks and Recreation	82,257	158	3.5
Police Protection	166,715	321	7.2
Public Welfare	23,346	45	1.0
Sewerage	184,652	356	7.9
Solid Waste Management	34,433	66	1.5
Veterans' Services	0	0	0.0
Liquor Store	0	0	0.0
Utility	407,856	786	17.5
Employee Retirement	187,495	361	8.1

Source: U.S Census Bureau, State & Local Government Finances 2011

DEMOGRAPHICS

Population Growth

Area	1990 Census	2000 Census	2010 Census	Population Growth (%)	
				1990-2000	2000-2010
City	394,092	416,474	420,003	5.7	0.8
MSA[1]	3,069,411	4,247,981	5,268,860	38.4	24.0
U.S.	248,709,873	281,421,906	308,745,538	13.2	9.7

Note: (1) Figures cover the Atlanta-Sandy Springs-Roswell, GA Metropolitan Statistical Area—see Appendix B for areas included
Source: U.S. Census Bureau, Census 1990, 2000, 2010

Household Size

Area	Persons in Household (%)							Average Household Size
	One	Two	Three	Four	Five	Six	Seven or More	
City	45.6	29.2	11.8	7.8	3.2	1.6	0.7	2.27
MSA[1]	26.6	31.2	16.8	14.8	6.6	2.5	1.6	2.78
U.S.	27.6	33.5	15.7	13.2	6.1	2.4	1.5	2.63

Note: (1) Figures cover the Atlanta-Sandy Springs-Roswell, GA Metropolitan Statistical Area—see Appendix B for areas included
Source: U.S. Census Bureau, 2010-2012 American Community Survey 3-Year Estimates

Race

Area	White Alone[2] (%)	Black Alone[2] (%)	Asian Alone[2] (%)	AIAN[3] Alone[2] (%)	NHOPI[4] Alone[2] (%)	Other Race Alone[2] (%)	Two or More Races (%)
City	39.3	53.4	3.6	0.2	0.0	1.5	1.9
MSA[1]	56.2	32.7	5.0	0.3	0.0	3.8	2.1
U.S.	74.0	12.6	4.9	0.8	0.2	4.7	2.8

Note: (1) Figures cover the Atlanta-Sandy Springs-Roswell, GA Metropolitan Statistical Area—see Appendix B for areas included; (2) Alone is defined as not being in combination with one or more other races; (3) American Indian and Alaska Native; (4) Native Hawaiian and Other Pacific Islander
Source: U.S. Census Bureau, 2010-2012 American Community Survey 3-Year Estimates

Hispanic or Latino Origin

Area	Total (%)	Mexican (%)	Puerto Rican (%)	Cuban (%)	Other (%)
City	5.7	3.3	0.6	0.2	1.5
MSA[1]	10.5	6.0	0.9	0.4	3.2
U.S.	16.6	10.7	1.6	0.6	3.7

Note: Persons of Hispanic or Latino origin can be of any race; (1) Figures cover the Atlanta-Sandy Springs-Roswell, GA Metropolitan Statistical Area—see Appendix B for areas included
Source: U.S. Census Bureau, 2010-2012 American Community Survey 3-Year Estimates

Segregation

Type	Segregation Indices[1]				Percent Change		
	1990	2000	2010	2010 Rank[2]	1990-2000	1990-2010	2000-2010
Black/White	66.3	64.3	59.0	41	-2.0	-7.2	-5.3
Asian/White	42.5	46.9	48.5	10	4.4	6.0	1.5
Hispanic/White	35.3	51.6	49.5	27	16.3	14.1	-2.1

Note: All figures cover the Metropolitan Statistical Area—see Appendix B for areas included; Figures are based on an analysis of 1990, 2000, and 2010 Census Decennial Census tract data by William H. Frey, Brookings Institution and the University of Michigan Social Science Data Analysis Network. In this analysis all racial groups (whites, blacks, and asians) are non-Hispanic members of those races. Hispanics are shown as a separate category;
(1) Segregation Indices are Dissimilarity Indices that measure the degree to which the minority group is distributed differently than whites across census tracts. They range from 0 (complete integration) to 100 (complete segregation) where the value indicates the percentage of the minority group that needs to move to be distributed exactly like whites; (2) Ranges from 1 (most segregated) to 102 (least segregated); n/a not available.
Source: www.CensusScope.org

Ancestry

Area	German	Irish	English	American	Italian	Polish	French[2]	Scottish	Dutch
City	6.2	5.0	6.5	7.1	1.9	1.3	1.3	2.1	0.6
MSA[1]	7.7	7.6	7.6	9.8	2.6	1.3	1.5	1.8	0.8
U.S.	15.2	11.1	8.2	7.2	5.6	3.1	2.8	1.7	1.4

Note: Figures are the percentage of the total population reporting a particular ancestry. The nine most commonly reported ancestries in the U.S. are shown. Figures include multiple ancestries (e.g. if a person reported being Irish and Italian, they were included in both columns); (1) Figures cover the Atlanta-Sandy Springs-Roswell, GA Metropolitan Statistical Area—see Appendix B for areas included; (2) Excludes Basque
Source: U.S. Census Bureau, 2010-2012 American Community Survey 3-Year Estimates

Foreign-Born Population

Area	Any Foreign Country	Mexico	Asia	Europe	Carribean	South America	Central America[2]	Africa	Canada
City	8.2	1.8	2.7	1.3	0.6	0.5	0.3	0.7	0.1
MSA[1]	13.3	3.2	3.9	1.2	1.5	0.9	1.1	1.3	0.2
U.S.	13.0	3.7	3.7	1.6	1.2	0.9	1.0	0.5	0.3

Note: (1) Figures cover the Atlanta-Sandy Springs-Roswell, GA Metropolitan Statistical Area—see Appendix B for areas included; (2) Excludes Mexico.
Source: U.S. Census Bureau, 2010-2012 American Community Survey 3-Year Estimates

Marital Status

Area	Never Married	Now Married[2]	Separated	Widowed	Divorced
City	54.2	26.8	2.6	5.4	11.1
MSA[1]	33.9	47.9	2.4	4.7	11.0
U.S.	32.4	48.4	2.2	6.0	11.0

Note: Figures are percentages and cover the population 15 years of age and older; (1) Figures cover the Atlanta-Sandy Springs-Roswell, GA Metropolitan Statistical Area—see Appendix B for areas included; (2) Excludes separated
Source: U.S. Census Bureau, 2010-2012 American Community Survey 3-Year Estimates

Age

Area	Under Age 5	Age 5–19	Age 20–34	Age 35–44	Age 45–54	Age 55–64	Age 65–74	Age 75–84	Age 85+	Median Age
City	6.4	16.4	30.4	15.0	12.2	9.8	5.5	2.8	1.5	33.2
MSA[1]	7.0	21.9	20.9	15.5	14.6	10.8	5.7	2.7	1.0	35.2
U.S.	6.4	20.1	20.5	13.1	14.3	12.2	7.3	4.2	1.8	37.3

Note: (1) Figures cover the Atlanta-Sandy Springs-Roswell, GA Metropolitan Statistical Area—see Appendix B for areas included
Source: U.S. Census Bureau, 2010-2012 American Community Survey 3-Year Estimates

Gender

Area	Males	Females	Males per 100 Females
City	214,757	217,995	98.5
MSA[1]	2,609,093	2,752,059	94.8
U.S.	153,276,055	158,333,314	96.8

Note: (1) Figures cover the Atlanta-Sandy Springs-Roswell, GA Metropolitan Statistical Area—see Appendix B for areas included
Source: U.S. Census Bureau, 2010-2012 American Community Survey 3-Year Estimates

Religious Groups by Family

Area	Catholic	Baptist	Non-Den.	Methodist[2]	Lutheran	LDS[3]	Pente-costal	Presby-terian[4]	Muslim[5]	Judaism
MSA[1]	7.5	17.5	6.9	7.9	0.5	0.8	2.6	1.8	0.8	0.6
U.S.	19.1	9.3	4.0	4.0	2.3	2.0	1.9	1.6	0.8	0.7

Note: Figures are the number of adherents as a percentage of the total population; (1) Figures cover the Atlanta-Sandy Springs-Roswell, GA Metropolitan Statistical Area—see Appendix B for areas included; (2) Methodist/Pietist; (3) Latter Day Saints; (4) Reformed; (5) Figures are estimates
Source: Association of Statisticians of American Religious Bodies, 2010 U.S. Religion Census: Religious Congregations & Membership Study

Religious Groups by Tradition

Area	Catholic	Evangelical Protestant	Mainline Protestant	Other Tradition	Black Protestant	Orthodox
MSA[1]	7.5	26.1	9.8	2.9	3.2	0.3
U.S.	19.1	16.2	7.3	4.3	1.6	0.3

Note: Figures are the number of adherents as a percentage of the total population; (1) Figures cover the Atlanta-Sandy Springs-Roswell, GA Metropolitan Statistical Area—see Appendix B for areas included
Source: Association of Statisticians of American Religious Bodies, 2010 U.S. Religion Census: Religious Congregations & Membership Study

ECONOMY

Gross Metropolitan Product

Area	2011	2012	2013	2014	Rank[2]
MSA[1]	282.0	294.0	304.9	320.9	10

Note: Figures are in billions of dollars; (1) Figures cover the Atlanta-Sandy Springs-Roswell, GA Metropolitan Statistical Area—see Appendix B for areas included; (2) Rank is based on 2014 data and ranges from 1 to 363
Source: The United States Conference of Mayors, U.S. Metro Economies: Outlook—Gross Metropolitan Product, with Metro Employment Projections, November 2013

Economic Growth

Area	2011 (%)	2012 (%)	2013 (%)	2014 (%)	Rank[2]
MSA[1]	2.6	2.6	2.4	3.4	52
U.S.	1.6	2.5	1.7	2.5	–

Note: Figures are real gross metropolitan product (GMP) growth rates and represent annual average percent change; (1) Figures cover the Atlanta-Sandy Springs-Roswell, GA Metropolitan Statistical Area—see Appendix B for areas included; (2) Rank is based on 2013 data and ranges from 1 to 363
Source: The United States Conference of Mayors, U.S. Metro Economies: Outlook—Gross Metropolitan Product, with Metro Employment Projections, November 2013

Metropolitan Area Exports

Area	2007	2008	2009	2010	2011	2012	Rank[2]
MSA[1]	12,551.0	14,432.9	13,405.9	15,009.7	17,229.1	18,169.1	17

Note: Figures are in millions of dollars; (1) Figures cover the Atlanta-Sandy Springs-Roswell, GA Metropolitan Statistical Area—see Appendix B for areas included; (2) Rank is based on 2012 data and ranges from 1 to 369
Source: U.S. Department of Commerce, International Trade Administration, Office of Trade & Industry Information, Manufacturing & Services, data extracted April 1, 2014

INCOME

Income

Area	Per Capita ($)	Median Household ($)	Average Household ($)
City	34,041	44,784	78,505
MSA[1]	27,642	54,807	75,230
U.S.	27,385	51,771	71,579

Note: (1) Figures cover the Atlanta-Sandy Springs-Roswell, GA Metropolitan Statistical Area—see Appendix B for areas included
Source: U.S. Census Bureau, 2010-2012 American Community Survey 3-Year Estimates

Household Income Distribution

Area	Percent of Households Earning							
	Under $15,000	$15,000 -24,999	$25,000 -34,999	$35,000 -49,999	$50,000 -74,999	$75,000 -99,000	$100,000 -149,999	$150,000 and up
City	21.5	10.9	9.9	10.9	15.4	8.7	10.2	12.5
MSA[1]	12.0	9.9	10.1	13.7	18.6	12.0	13.3	10.4
U.S.	13.1	11.0	10.5	13.7	18.1	11.9	12.5	9.1

Note: (1) Figures cover the Atlanta-Sandy Springs-Roswell, GA Metropolitan Statistical Area—see Appendix B for areas included
Source: U.S. Census Bureau, 2010-2012 American Community Survey 3-Year Estimates

Poverty Rate

Area	All Ages	Under 18 Years Old	18 to 64 Years Old	65 Years and Over
City	26.0	39.2	23.1	20.1
MSA[1]	16.0	22.5	14.2	9.8
U.S.	15.7	22.2	14.6	9.3

Note: Figures are percentage of people whose income during the past 12 months was below the poverty level; (1) Figures cover the Atlanta-Sandy Springs-Roswell, GA Metropolitan Statistical Area—see Appendix B for areas included
Source: U.S. Census Bureau, 2010-2012 American Community Survey 3-Year Estimates

Personal Bankruptcy Filing Rate

Area	2008	2009	2010	2011	2012	2013
Fulton County	5.68	7.45	8.21	7.57	6.23	5.48
U.S.	3.53	4.61	4.97	4.37	3.76	3.29

Note: Numbers are per 1,000 population and include Chapter 7 and Chapter 13 filings
Source: Federal Deposit Insurance Corporation, Regional Economic Conditions, March 20, 2014

EMPLOYMENT

Labor Force and Employment

Area	Civilian Labor Force			Workers Employed		
	Dec. 2012	Dec. 2013	% Chg.	Dec. 2012	Dec. 2013	% Chg.
City	197,605	193,652	-2.0	176,010	176,555	0.3
MSA[1]	2,773,421	2,734,954	-1.4	2,540,260	2,548,119	0.3
U.S.	154,904,000	154,408,000	-0.3	143,060,000	144,423,000	1.0

Note: Data is not seasonally adjusted and covers workers 16 years of age and older; (1) Metropolitan Statistical Area—see Appendix B for areas included
Source: Bureau of Labor Statistics, Local Area Unemployment Statistics

Unemployment Rate

Area	2013											
	Jan.	Feb.	Mar.	Apr.	May	Jun.	Jul.	Aug.	Sep.	Oct.	Nov.	Dec.
City	11.1	10.3	9.9	9.6	10.4	11.4	10.9	10.4	9.6	9.8	9.1	8.8
MSA[1]	8.7	8.3	7.9	7.6	8.2	8.8	8.6	7.9	7.4	7.7	7.0	6.8
U.S.	8.5	8.1	7.6	7.1	7.3	7.8	7.7	7.3	7.0	7.0	6.6	6.5

Note: Data is not seasonally adjusted and covers workers 16 years of age and older; All figures are percentages; (1) Metropolitan Statistical Area—see Appendix B for areas included
Source: Bureau of Labor Statistics, Local Area Unemployment Statistics

Employment by Occupation

Occupation Classification	City (%)	MSA[1] (%)	U.S. (%)
Management, Business, Science, and Arts	49.7	39.1	36.0
Natural Resources, Construction, and Maintenance	4.2	8.2	9.1
Production, Transportation, and Material Moving	7.8	10.8	12.0
Sales and Office	22.2	25.9	24.7
Service	16.1	16.0	18.2

Note: Figures cover employed civilians 16 years of age and older; (1) Figures cover the Atlanta-Sandy Springs-Roswell, GA Metropolitan Statistical Area—see Appendix B for areas included
Source: U.S. Census Bureau, 2010-2012 American Community Survey 3-Year Estimates

Employment by Industry

Sector	MSA[1]		U.S.
	Number of Employees	Percent of Total	Percent of Total
Construction	95,300	3.9	4.2
Education and Health Services	299,300	12.2	15.5
Financial Activities	159,000	6.5	5.7
Government	319,100	13.0	16.1
Information	85,000	3.5	1.9
Leisure and Hospitality	249,500	10.2	10.2
Manufacturing	151,000	6.2	8.7
Mining and Logging	1,200	<0.1	0.6
Other Services	92,600	3.8	3.9
Professional and Business Services	441,900	18.0	13.7
Retail Trade	272,100	11.1	11.4
Transportation and Utilities	132,500	5.4	3.8
Wholesale Trade	150,800	6.2	4.2

Note: Figures cover non-farm employment as of December 2013 and are not seasonally adjusted;
(1) Metropolitan Statistical Area—see Appendix B for areas included
Source: Bureau of Labor Statistics, Current Employment Statistics, Employment, Hours, and Earnings

Occupations with Greatest Projected Employment Growth: 2010 – 2020

Occupation[1]	2010 Employment	2020 Projected Employment	Numeric Employment Change	Percent Employment Change
Combined Food Preparation and Serving Workers, Including Fast Food	98,330	120,660	22,330	22.7
Registered Nurses	69,190	90,020	20,830	30.1
Retail Salespersons	143,460	157,600	14,130	9.9
Office Clerks, General	81,710	93,640	11,930	14.6
Postsecondary Teachers	36,620	47,350	10,730	29.3
Waiters and Waitresses	62,600	72,990	10,390	16.6
Customer Service Representatives	91,150	101,390	10,240	11.2
Janitors and Cleaners, Except Maids and Housekeeping Cleaners	73,670	82,570	8,900	12.1
Laborers and Freight, Stock, and Material Movers, Hand	82,360	90,940	8,580	10.4
Elementary School Teachers, Except Special Education	45,250	53,470	8,220	18.2

Note: Projections cover Georgia; (1) Sorted by numeric employment change
Source: www.projectionscentral.com, State Occupational Projections, 2010–2020 Long-Term Projections

Fastest Growing Occupations: 2010 – 2020

Occupation[1]	2010 Employment	2020 Projected Employment	Numeric Employment Change	Percent Employment Change
Biomedical Engineers	170	280	110	64.7
Marriage and Family Therapists	290	460	160	55.3
Home Health Aides	11,790	18,070	6,270	53.2
Diagnostic Medical Sonographers	1,110	1,650	540	48.5
Medical Scientists, Except Epidemiologists	500	730	230	46.6
Personal Care Aides	9,550	13,870	4,320	45.2
Mental Health Counselors	2,030	2,870	840	41.3
Helpers—Carpenters	1,500	2,100	610	40.5
Cardiovascular Technologists and Technicians	1,030	1,400	370	36.0
Medical Secretaries	15,780	21,440	5,660	35.9

Note: Projections cover Georgia; (1) Sorted by percent employment change and excludes occupations with numeric employment change less than 100
Source: www.projectionscentral.com, State Occupational Projections, 2010–2020 Long-Term Projections

Average Wages

Occupation	$/Hr.	Occupation	$/Hr.
Accountants and Auditors	36.56	Maids and Housekeeping Cleaners	9.14
Automotive Mechanics	19.69	Maintenance and Repair Workers	18.34
Bookkeepers	18.07	Marketing Managers	64.06
Carpenters	21.86	Nuclear Medicine Technologists	34.66
Cashiers	9.32	Nurses, Licensed Practical	19.02
Clerks, General Office	13.52	Nurses, Registered	30.95
Clerks, Receptionists/Information	13.47	Nursing Assistants	11.11
Clerks, Shipping/Receiving	14.19	Packers and Packagers, Hand	10.47
Computer Programmers	45.14	Physical Therapists	37.96
Computer Systems Analysts	36.84	Postal Service Mail Carriers	24.72
Computer User Support Specialists	24.72	Real Estate Brokers	43.11
Cooks, Restaurant	10.64	Retail Salespersons	11.95
Dentists	91.04	Sales Reps., Exc. Tech./Scientific	30.79
Electrical Engineers	41.62	Sales Reps., Tech./Scientific	38.95
Electricians	22.84	Secretaries, Exc. Legal/Med./Exec.	16.85
Financial Managers	61.89	Security Guards	11.48
First-Line Supervisors/Managers, Sales	20.29	Surgeons	120.81
Food Preparation Workers	10.03	Teacher Assistants	10.30
General and Operations Managers	57.36	Teachers, Elementary School	26.20
Hairdressers/Cosmetologists	12.42	Teachers, Secondary School	27.10
Internists	112.68	Telemarketers	13.99
Janitors and Cleaners	11.69	Truck Drivers, Heavy/Tractor-Trailer	20.41
Landscaping/Groundskeeping Workers	12.60	Truck Drivers, Light/Delivery Svcs.	16.93
Lawyers	69.70	Waiters and Waitresses	9.19

Note: Wage data covers the Atlanta-Sandy Springs-Marietta, GA Metropolitan Statistical Area—see Appendix B for areas included. Hourly wages for elementary/secondary school teachers and teacher assistants were calculated by the editors from annual wage data assuming a 40 hour work week; n/a not available.
Source: Bureau of Labor Statistics, Metro Area Occupational Employment and Wage Estimates, May 2013

RESIDENTIAL REAL ESTATE

Building Permits

Area	Single-Family			Multi-Family			Total		
	2012	2013	Pct. Chg.	2012	2013	Pct. Chg.	2012	2013	Pct. Chg.
City	359	473	31.8	1,764	5,070	187.4	2,123	5,543	161.1
MSA[1]	9,167	14,824	61.7	5,213	9,473	81.7	14,380	24,297	69.0
U.S.	518,695	620,802	19.7	310,963	370,020	19.0	829,658	990,822	19.4

Note: (1) Metropolitan Statistical Area—see Appendix B for areas included; figures represent new, privately-owned housing units authorized (unadjusted data); All permit data are based on estimates with imputation.
Source: U.S. Census Bureau, Manufacturing, Mining, and Construction Statistics, Building Permits, 2012, 2013

Homeownership Rate

Area	2006 (%)	2007 (%)	2008 (%)	2009 (%)	2010 (%)	2011 (%)	2012 (%)	2013 (%)
MSA[1]	67.9	66.4	67.5	67.7	67.2	65.8	62.1	61.6
U.S.	68.8	68.1	67.8	67.4	66.9	66.1	65.4	65.1

Note: (1) Figures cover the Atlanta-Sandy Springs-Roswell, GA Metropolitan Statistical Area—see Appendix B for areas included
Source: U.S. Census Bureau, Housing Vacancies and Homeownership Annual Statistics: 2013

Housing Vacancy Rates

Area	Gross Vacancy Rate[2] (%)			Year-Round Vacancy Rate[3] (%)			Rental Vacancy Rate[4] (%)			Homeowner Vacancy Rate[5] (%)		
	2011	2012	2013	2011	2012	2013	2011	2012	2013	2011	2012	2013
MSA[1]	12.8	12.5	12.4	12.4	12.2	11.8	11.6	10.6	10.2	4.3	2.6	2.1
U.S.	14.2	13.8	13.8	11.1	10.8	10.7	9.5	8.7	8.3	2.5	2.0	2.0

Note: (1) Figures cover the Atlanta-Sandy Springs-Roswell, GA Metropolitan Statistical Area—see Appendix B for areas included; (2) The percentage of the total housing inventory that is vacant; (3) The percentage of the housing inventory (excluding seasonal units) that is year-round vacant; (4) The percentage of rental inventory that is vacant for rent; (5) The percentage of homeowner inventory that is vacant for sale
Source: U.S. Census Bureau, Housing Vacancies and Homeownership Annual Statistics: 2013

TAXES

State Corporate Income Tax Rates

State	Tax Rate (%)	Income Brackets ($)	Num. of Brackets	Financial Institution Tax Rate (%)[a]	Federal Income Tax Ded.
Georgia	6.0	Flat rate	1	6.0	No

Note: Tax rates as of January 1, 2014; (a) Rates listed are the corporate income tax rate applied to financial institutions or excise taxes based on income. Some states have other taxes based upon the value of deposits or shares.
Source: Federation of Tax Administrators, "State Corporate Income Tax Rates, 2014"

State Individual Income Tax Rates

State	Tax Rate (%)	Income Brackets ($)	Num. of Brackets	Personal Exempt. ($)[1] Single	Personal Exempt. ($)[1] Dependents	Fed. Inc. Tax Ded.
Georgia	1.0 - 6.0	750 - 7,001 (h)	6	2,700	3,000	No

Note: Tax rates as of January 1, 2014; Local- and county-level taxes are not included; n/a not applicable; (1) Married joint filers generally receive double the single exemption; (h) The Georgia income brackets reported are for single individuals. For married couples filing jointly, the same tax rates apply to income brackets ranging from $1,000, to $10,000.
Source: Federation of Tax Administrators, "State Individual Income Tax Rates, 2014"

Various State and Local Tax Rates

State	State and Local Sales and Use (%)	State Sales and Use (%)	Gasoline[1] (¢/gal.)	Cigarette[2] ($/pack)	Spirits[3] ($/gal.)	Wine[4] ($/gal.)	Beer[5] ($/gal.)
Georgia	8.0	4.00	28.45	0.370	3.79 (f)	1.51	1.01 (q)

Note: All tax rates as of January 1, 2014; (1) The American Petroleum Institute has developed a methodology for determining the average tax rate on a gallon of fuel. Rates may include any of the following: excise taxes, environmental fees, storage tank fees, other fees or taxes, general sales tax, and local taxes. In states where gasoline is subject to the general sales tax, or where the fuel tax is based on the average sale price, the average rate determined by API is sensitive to changes in the price of gasoline. States that fully or partially apply general sales taxes to gasoline: CA, CO, GA, IL, IN, MI, NY; (2) The federal excise tax of $1.0066 per pack and local taxes are not included; (3) Rates are those applicable to off-premise sales of 40% alcohol by volume (a.b.v.) distilled spirits in 750ml containers. Local excise taxes are excluded; (4) Rates are those applicable to off-premise sales of 11% a.b.v. non-carbonated wine in 750ml containers; (5) Rates are those applicable to off-premise sales of 4.7% a.b.v. beer in 12 ounce containers; (f) Different rates also applicable according to alcohol content, place of production, size of container, or place purchased (on- or off-premise or onboard airlines); (q) Includes statewide local rate in Alabama ($0.52) and Georgia ($0.53).
Source: Tax Foundation, 2014 Facts & Figures: How Does Your State Compare?

State Business Tax Climate Index Rankings

State	Overall Rank	Corporate Tax Index Rank	Individual Income Tax Index Rank	Sales Tax Index Rank	Unemployment Insurance Tax Index Rank	Property Tax Index Rank
Georgia	32	8	41	12	24	31

Note: The index is a measure of how each state's tax laws affect economic performance. The lower the rank, the more favorable a state's tax system is for business. States without a given tax are given a ranking of 1. The scores/rankings for the District of Columbia do not affect other states. The 2014 index represents the tax climate as of July 1, 2013.
Source: Tax Foundation, State Business Tax Climate Index 2014

COMMERCIAL REAL ESTATE

Office Market

Market Area	Inventory (sq. ft.)	Vacancy Rate (%)	Under Construction (sq. ft.)	YTD Net Absorption (sq. ft.)	Total Average Asking Rent ($/sq. ft./year)
Atlanta	144,119,031	20.6	550,000	2,300,806	20.26
National	4,726,900,879	15.0	55,419,286	42,829,434	26.27

Source: Newmark Grubb Knight Frank, National Office Market Report, 4th Quarter 2013

Industrial/Warehouse/R&D Market

Market Area	Inventory (sq. ft.)	Vacancy Rate (%)	Under Construction (sq. ft.)	YTD Net Absorption (sq. ft.)	Total Average Asking Rent ($/sq. ft./year)
Atlanta	596,340,412	11.7	555,126	11,006,287	3.77
National	14,022,031,238	7.9	83,249,164	156,549,903	5.40

Source: Newmark Grubb Knight Frank, National Industrial Market Report, 4th Quarter 2013

COMMERCIAL UTILITIES

Typical Monthly Electric Bills

Area	Commercial Service ($/month)		Industrial Service ($/month)	
	1,500 kWh	40 kW demand 14,000 kWh	1,000 kW demand 200,000 kWh	50,000 kW demand 15,000,000 kWh
City	250	1,592	30,725	1,512,982
Average[1]	197	1,636	25,662	1,485,307

Note: Based on total rates in effect July 1, 2013; (1) average based on 180 utilities surveyed
Source: Edison Electric Institute, Typical Bills and Average Rates Report, Summer 2013

TRANSPORTATION

Means of Transportation to Work

Area	Car/Truck/Van		Public Transportation			Bicycle	Walked	Other Means	Worked at Home
	Drove Alone	Car-pooled	Bus	Subway	Railroad				
City	67.4	7.8	7.0	2.9	0.3	1.0	4.8	1.6	7.3
MSA[1]	77.8	10.4	2.3	0.7	0.1	0.2	1.4	1.4	5.7
U.S.	76.4	9.7	2.6	1.7	0.5	0.6	2.8	1.3	4.3

Note: Figures are percentages and cover workers 16 years of age and older; (1) Figures cover the Atlanta-Sandy Springs-Roswell, GA Metropolitan Statistical Area—see Appendix B for areas included
Source: U.S. Census Bureau, 2010-2012 American Community Survey 3-Year Estimates

Travel Time to Work

Area	Less Than 10 Minutes	10 to 19 Minutes	20 to 29 Minutes	30 to 44 Minutes	45 to 59 Minutes	60 to 89 Minutes	90 Minutes or More
City	8.9	31.5	26.6	20.5	5.6	4.2	2.7
MSA[1]	8.0	23.3	20.2	25.3	11.7	8.6	2.9
U.S.	13.5	29.8	20.9	20.1	7.5	5.6	2.5

Note: Figures are percentages and include workers 16 years old and over; (1) Figures cover the Atlanta-Sandy Springs-Roswell, GA Metropolitan Statistical Area—see Appendix B for areas included
Source: U.S. Census Bureau, 2010-2012 American Community Survey 3-Year Estimates

Travel Time Index

Area	1985	1990	1995	2000	2005	2010	2011
Urban Area[1]	1.10	1.13	1.21	1.26	1.29	1.24	1.24
Average[2]	1.09	1.14	1.16	1.19	1.23	1.18	1.18

Note: Travel Time Index—the ratio of travel time in the peak period to the travel time at free-flow conditions. For example, a value of 1.30 indicates a 20-minute free-flow trip takes 26 minutes in the peak. Free-flow speeds (60 mph on freeways and 35 mph on principal arterials) are used as the comparison threshold; (1) Covers the Atlanta GA urban area; (2) average of 498 urban areas
Source: Texas Transportation Institute, Urban Mobility Report 2012, December 2012

Public Transportation

Agency Name / Mode of Transportation	Vehicles Operated in Maximum Service	Annual Unlinked Passenger Trips (in thous.)	Annual Passenger Miles (in thous.)
Metropolitan Atlanta Rapid Transit Authority (MARTA)			
Bus (directly operated)	443	61,596.7	228,212.5
Demand Response (directly operated)	154	581.5	7,875.8
Heavy Rail (directly operated)	182	72,711.5	463,168.6

Source: Federal Transit Administration, National Transit Database, 2012

Air Transportation

Airport Name and Code / Type of Service	Passenger Airlines[1]	Passenger Enplanements	Freight Carriers[2]	Freight (lbs.)
Hartsfield-Jackson Atlanta International Airport (ATL)				
Domestic service (U.S. carriers - 2013)	35	40,354,275	22	268,746,257
International service (U.S. carriers - 2012)	15	4,173,154	11	116,259,080

Note: (1) Includes all U.S.-based major, minor and commuter airlines that carried at least one passenger during the year; (2) Includes all U.S.-based airlines and freight carriers that transported at least one lb. of freight during the year.
Source: Bureau of Transportation Statistics, The Intermodal Transportation Database, Air Carriers: T-100 Domestic Market (U.S. Carriers), 2013; Bureau of Transportation Statistics, The Intermodal Transportation Database, Air Carriers: T-100 International Market (U.S. Carriers), 2012

Other Transportation Statistics

Major Highways:	I-20; I-75; I-85
Amtrak Service:	Yes
Major Waterways/Ports:	None

Source: Amtrak.com; Google Maps

BUSINESSES

Major Business Headquarters

Company Name	Rankings	
	Fortune[1]	Forbes[2]
Coca-Cola	57	-
Coca-Cola Enterprises	339	-
Cox Enterprises	-	17
Delta Air Lines	83	-
First Data	254	31
Genuine Parts	214	-
HD Supply	330	44
Home Depot	34	-
Newell Rubbermaid	433	-
RaceTrac Petroleum	-	39
Southern	171	-
SunTrust Banks	239	-
Travelport	-	221
United Parcel Service	53	-

Note: (1) Fortune 500—companies that produce a 10-K are ranked 1 to 500 based on 2012 revenue; (2) all private companies with at least $2 billion in annual revenue through the end of their most current fiscal year are ranked 1 to 224; companies listed are headquartered in the city; dashes indicate no ranking Source: Fortune, "Fortune 500," May 20, 2013; Forbes, "America's Largest Private Companies," December 18, 2013

Fast-Growing Businesses

According to *Inc.*, Atlanta is home to 10 of America's 500 fastest-growing private companies: **Innovolt** (#31); **GSC Packaging** (#64); **Cloud Sherpas** (#142); **TracePoint Consulting** (#170); **Xtreme Solutions** (#237); **Caduceus Healthcare** (#301); **MiLend** (#324); **PalmerHouse Properties** (#404); **RePay** (#440); **StandBy Talent Staffing Services** (#447). Criteria: must be an independent, privately-held, for-profit, U.S. corporation, proprietorship or partnership; revenues must be at least $100,000 in 2009 and $2 million in 2012; must have four-year operating/sales history. Holding companies, regulated banks, and utilities were excluded. *Inc., "America's 500 Fastest-Growing Private Companies," September 2013*

According to *Fortune*, Atlanta is home to two of the 100 fastest-growing companies in the world: **Ocwen Financial** (#12); **RPC** (#16). Companies were ranked by their revenue growth rate; their EPS growth rate; and their three-year annualized total return to investors for the period ending June 30, 2013. Criteria for inclusion: a company, foreign or domestic, must trade on a major U.S. stock exchange; must file quarterly reports with the SEC; must have a minimum market capitalization of $250 million; must have a stock price of at least $5 on June 29, 2013; must have been trading continuously since June 30, 2009; must have revenue and net income for the four quarters ended on or before April 30, 2013, of at least $50 million and $10 million, respectively; and must have posted a compound annual growth in revenue and earnings per share of at least

20% annually over the three years ending on or before April 30, 2013. REITs, limited-liability companies, limited parterships, companies about to be acquired, and companies that lost money in the quarter ending April 30, 2013 were excluded. *Fortune, "100 Fastest-Growing Companies," August 29, 2013*

According to Deloitte, Atlanta is home to four of North America's 500 fastest-growing high-technology companies: **Innovolt** (#29); **AirWatch** (#119); **Vocalocity** (#188); **PrimeRevenue** (#291). Companies are ranked by percentage growth in revenue over a five-year period. Criteria for inclusion: company must be headquartered within North America; must own proprietary intellectual property or proprietary technology that contributes to a significant portion of the company's operating revenue, or devote a significant proportion of revenues to research and development of technology; must have been in business for a minumum of five years with 2008 operating revenues of at least $50,000 USD/CD and 2012 operating revenues of at least $5 million USD/CD. *Deloitte Touche Tohmatsu, 2013 Technology Fast 500*^{TM}

Minority Business Opportunity

Atlanta is home to four companies which are on the *Black Enterprise* Industrial/Service 100 list (100 largest companies based on gross sales): **H. J. Russell & Co.** (#15); **The Gourmet Cos.** (#19); **Jackmont Hospitality** (#39); **B & S Electric Supply Co.** (#63). Criteria: operational in previous calendar year; at least 51% black-owned and manufactures/owns the product it sells or provides industrial or consumer services. Brokerages, real estate firms and firms that provide professional services are not eligible. *Black Enterprise, B.E. 100s, 2013*

Atlanta is home to two companies which are on the *Black Enterprise* Auto Dealer 60 list (60 largest dealers based on gross sales): **Mercedes-Benz of Buckhead** (#12); **Malcolm Cunningham Ford Lincoln** (#33). Criteria: company must be operational in previous calendar year and be at least 51% black-owned. *Black Enterprise, B.E. 100s, 2013*

Atlanta is home to two companies which are on the *Black Enterprise* Bank 20 list (20 largest banks based on total assets, capital, deposits and loans, including mortgage-backed securities for the calendar year): **Citizens Bancshares Corporation (Citizens Trust Bank)** (#5); **Capitol City Bank & Trust Co. (Capitol City Bank)** (#9). Only commercial banks or savings and loans that are classified by the Federal Reserve as black institutions and have been fully operational for the previous calendar year were considered. *Black Enterprise, B.E. 100s, 2013*

Atlanta is home to two companies which are on the *Black Enterprise* Asset Manager 15 list (15 largest asset management firms based on assets under management): **EARNEST Partners** (#2); **Herndon Capital Management** (#3). Criteria: company must have been operational in previous calendar year and be at least 51% black-owned. *Black Enterprise, B.E. 100s, 2013*

Atlanta is home to three companies which are on the *Hispanic Business* 500 list (500 largest U.S. Hispanic-owned companies based on 2012 revenue): **Precision 2000** (#293); **Caduceus Healthcare** (#406); **GSB Architects** (#468). Companies included must show at least 51 percent ownership by Hispanic U.S. citizens, and must maintain headquarters in one of the 50 states or Washington, D.C. *Hispanic Business, "Hispanic Business 500," June 20, 2013*

Atlanta is home to two companies which are on the *Hispanic Business* Fastest-Growing 100 list (greatest sales growth from 2008 to 2012): **Precision 2000** (#75); **GSB Architects** (#85). Companies included must show at least 51 percent ownership by Hispanic U.S. citizens, and must maintain headquarters in one of the 50 states or Washington, D.C. In addition, companies must have minimum revenues of $200,000 for calendar year 2008. *Hispanic Business, June20, 2013*

Minority- and Women-Owned Businesses

Group	All Firms		Firms with Paid Employees			
	Firms	Sales ($000)	Firms	Sales ($000)	Employees	Payroll ($000)
Asian	2,257	1,178,708	1,025	1,131,161	5,837	164,452
Black	15,738	1,256,723	981	895,035	7,367	230,657
Hispanic	1,240	415,116	200	356,231	2,051	78,188
Women	17,047	5,316,681	2,348	4,800,357	24,541	851,096
All Firms	50,966	105,935,888	12,824	103,541,309	347,658	19,829,323

Note: Figures cover firms located in the city; minority- and women-owned business are defined as firms in which the corresponding group own 51% or more of the stock or equity of the company
Source: U.S. Census Bureau, 2007 Economic Census, Survey of Business Owners (2012 Survey of Business Owners data will be released starting in June 2015)

**HOTELS &
CONVENTION
CENTERS**

Hotels/Motels

Area	5 Star Num.	5 Star Pct.[3]	4 Star Num.	4 Star Pct.[3]	3 Star Num.	3 Star Pct.[3]	2 Star Num.	2 Star Pct.[3]	1 Star Num.	1 Star Pct.[3]	Not Rated Num.	Not Rated Pct.[3]
City[1]	6	1.1	23	4.3	146	27.2	302	56.2	24	4.5	36	6.7
Total[2]	142	0.9	1,005	6.0	5,147	30.9	8,578	51.4	408	2.4	1,397	8.4

Note: (1) Figures cover Atlanta and vicinity; (2) Figures cover all 100 cities in this book; (3) Percentage of hotels which have a given star rating; Star ratings are determined by expedia.com and offer an indication of the general quality of a particular hotel.
Source: expedia.com, April 7, 2014

The Atlanta-Sandy Springs-Roswell, GA metro area is home to three of the best hotels in the U.S. according to *Travel & Leisure*: **The St. Regis Atlanta**; **Four Seasons Hotel**; **Ritz-Carlton, Buckhead**. Criteria: service; location; rooms; food; and value. The list includes the top 200 hotels in the U.S. *Travel & Leisure, "T+L 500, The World's Best Hotels 2014"*

The Atlanta-Sandy Springs-Roswell, GA metro area is home to one of the best hotels in the world according to *Condé Nast Traveler*: **The St. Regis Atlanta**. The selections are based on over 79,000 responses to the magazine's annual Readers' Choice Survey. The list includes the top 200 hotels in the U.S. *Condé Nast Traveler, "Gold List 2014, The World's Best Places to Stay"*

Major Convention Centers

Name	Overall Space (sq. ft.)	Exhibit Space (sq. ft.)	Meeting Space (sq. ft.)	Meeting Rooms
AmericasMart Atlanta	n/a	441,000	n/a	38
Cobb Galleria Centre	320,000	144,000	20,000	20
Georgia International Convention Center	n/a	150,000	16,000	n/a
Georgia World Congress Center	3,900,000	1,400,000	n/a	106

Note: Table includes convention centers located in the Atlanta-Sandy Springs-Roswell, GA metro area; n/a not available
Source: Original research

Living Environment

COST OF LIVING

Cost of Living Index

Composite Index	Groceries	Housing	Utilities	Trans- portation	Health Care	Misc. Goods/ Services
94.9	91.2	87.1	92.0	102.0	102.5	99.6

Note: The Cost of Living Index measures regional differences in the cost of consumer goods and services, excluding taxes and non-consumer expenditures, for professional and managerial households in the top income quintile. It is based on more than 50,000 prices covering almost 60 different items for which prices are collected three times a year by chambers of commerce, economic development organizations or university applied economic centers in each participating urban area. The numbers shown should be read as a percentage above or below the national average of 100. For example, a value of 115.4 in the groceries column indicates that grocery prices are 15.4% higher than the national average. Small differences in the index numbers should not be interpreted as significant; Figures cover the Atlanta GA urban area.
Source: The Council for Community and Economic Research, ACCRA Cost of Living Index, 2013

Grocery Prices

Area[1]	T-Bone Steak ($/pound)	Frying Chicken ($/pound)	Whole Milk ($/half gal.)	Eggs ($/dozen)	Orange Juice ($/64 oz.)	Coffee ($/11.5 oz.)
City[2]	11.52	1.09	2.22	1.66	3.41	4.93
Avg.	10.19	1.28	2.34	1.81	3.48	4.39
Min.	8.56	0.94	1.44	1.19	2.78	3.40
Max.	14.82	2.28	3.56	3.73	6.23	7.32

Note: (1) Values for the local area are compared with the average, minimum and maximum values for all 327 areas in the Cost of Living Index; (2) Figures cover the Atlanta GA urban area; **T-Bone Steak** *(price per pound);* **Frying Chicken** *(price per pound, whole fryer);* **Whole Milk** *(half gallon carton);* **Eggs** *(price per dozen, Grade A, large);* **Orange Juice** *(64 oz. Tropicana or Florida Natural);* **Coffee** *(11.5 oz. can, vacuum-packed, Maxwell House, Hills Bros, or Folgers).*
Source: The Council for Community and Economic Research, ACCRA Cost of Living Index, 2013

Housing and Utility Costs

Area[1]	New Home Price ($)	Apartment Rent ($/month)	All Electric ($/month)	Part Electric ($/month)	Other Energy ($/month)	Telephone ($/month)
City[2]	239,252	964	-	94.08	58.37	25.06
Avg.	295,864	900	171.38	91.82	70.12	27.73
Min.	185,506	458	117.80	48.81	33.67	17.16
Max.	1,358,917	3,783	441.68	171.40	372.65	39.47

Note: (1) Values for the local area are compared with the average, minimum and maximum values for all 327 areas in the Cost of Living Index; (2) Figures cover the Atlanta GA urban area; **New Home Price** *(2,400 sf living area, 8,000 sf lot, in urban area with full utilities);* **Apartment Rent** *(950 sf 2 bedroom/1.5 or 2 bath, unfurnished, excluding all utilities except water);* **All Electric** *(average monthly cost for an all-electric home);* **Part Electric** *(average monthly cost for a part-electric home);* **Other Energy** *(average monthly cost for natural gas, fuel oil, coal, wood, and any other forms of energy except electricity);* **Telephone** *(price includes basic monthly rate for a private residential line plus additional local usage charges incurred by a family of four).*
Source: The Council for Community and Economic Research, ACCRA Cost of Living Index, 2013

Health Care, Transportation, and Other Costs

Area[1]	Doctor ($/visit)	Dentist ($/visit)	Optometrist ($/visit)	Gasoline ($/gallon)	Beauty Salon ($/visit)	Men's Shirt ($)
City[2]	97.60	99.69	76.89	3.42	42.10	24.19
Avg.	101.40	86.48	96.16	3.44	33.87	26.55
Min.	61.67	50.83	50.12	3.08	18.92	12.48
Max.	182.71	152.50	223.78	4.33	68.22	52.03

Note: (1) Values for the local area are compared with the average, minimum and maximum values for all 327 areas in the Cost of Living Index; (2) Figures cover the Atlanta GA urban area; **Doctor** *(general practitioners routine exam of an established patient);* **Dentist** *(adult teeth cleaning and periodic oral examination);* **Optometrist** *(full vision eye exam for established adult patient);* **Gasoline** *(one gallon regular unleaded, national brand, including all taxes, cash price at self-service pump if available);* **Beauty Salon** *(woman's shampoo, trim, and blow-dry);* **Men's Shirt** *(cotton/polyester dress shirt, pinpoint weave, long sleeves).*
Source: The Council for Community and Economic Research, ACCRA Cost of Living Index, 2013

HOUSING

House Price Index (HPI)

Area	National Ranking[2]	Quarterly Change (%)	One-Year Change (%)	Five-Year Change (%)
MSA[1]	66	1.07	7.12	-13.81
U.S.[3]	–	1.20	7.69	4.18

Note: The HPI is a weighted repeat sales index. It measures average price changes in repeat sales or refinancings on the same properties. This information is obtained by reviewing repeat mortgage transactions on single-family properties whose mortgages have been purchased or securitized by Fannie Mae or Freddie Mac in January 1975; (1) Atlanta-Sandy Springs-Roswell, GA Metropolitan Statistical Area—see Appendix B for areas included; (2) Rankings are based on annual percentage change for all metro areas containing at least 15,000 transactions over the last 10 years and ranges from 1 to 283; (3) figures based on a weighted average of Census Division estimates using a seasonally adjusted, purchase-only index; all figures are for the period ending December 31, 2013
Source: Federal Housing Finance Agency, House Price Index, February 25, 2014

Median Single-Family Home Prices

Area	2011	2012	2013p	Percent Change 2012 to 2013
MSA[1]	98.6	101.4	139.5	37.6
U.S. Average	166.2	177.2	197.4	11.4

Note: Figures are median sales prices of existing single-family homes in thousands of dollars; (p) preliminary; n/a not available; (1) Atlanta-Sandy Springs-Roswell, GA Metropolitan Statistical Area—see Appendix B for areas included
Source: National Association of Realtors, Median Sales Price of Existing Single-Family Homes for Metropolitan Areas, 4th Quarter 2013

Qualifying Income Based on Median Sales Price of Existing Single-Family Homes

Area	With 5% Down ($)	With 10% Down ($)	With 20% Down ($)
MSA[1]	32,830	31,103	27,647
U.S. Average	45,395	43,006	38,228

Note: Figures are preliminary; Qualifying income is based on a mortgage rate of 4.4%. Monthly principal and interest payment is limited to 25% of income; n/a not available; (1) Atlanta-Sandy Springs-Roswell, GA Metropolitan Statistical Area—see Appendix B for areas included
Source: National Association of Realtors, Qualifying Income Based on Median Sales Price of Existing Single-Family Homes for Metropolitan Areas, 4th Quarter 2013

Median Apartment Condo-Coop Home Prices

Area	2011	2012	2013p	Percent Change 2012 to 2013
MSA[1]	38.8	76.9	117.3	52.5
U.S. Average	165.1	173.7	194.9	12.2

Note: Figures are median sales prices of existing apartment condo-coop homes in thousands of dollars; (p) preliminary; n/a not available; (1) Atlanta-Sandy Springs-Roswell, GA Metropolitan Statistical Area—see Appendix B for areas included
Source: National Association of Realtors, Median Sales Price of Existing Apartment Condo-Coop Homes for Metropolitan Areas, 4th Quarter 2013

Gross Monthly Rent

Area	Under $200	$200 -299	$300 -499	$500 -749	$750 -999	$1,000 -1,499	$1,500 and up	Median ($)
City	3.4	4.5	5.7	15.3	28.8	30.8	11.6	935
MSA[1]	1.1	1.7	3.2	18.7	33.2	33.3	8.8	940
U.S.	1.7	3.3	8.1	22.7	24.3	25.7	14.3	889

Note: Figures are percentages except for Median; Gross rent is the contract rent plus the estimated average monthly cost of utilities (electricity, gas, and water and sewer) and fuels (oil, coal, kerosene, wood, etc.) if these are paid by the renter (or paid for the renter by someone else); (1) Figures cover the Atlanta-Sandy Springs-Roswell, GA Metropolitan Statistical Area—see Appendix B for areas included
Source: U.S. Census Bureau, 2010-2012 American Community Survey 3-Year Estimates

Year Housing Structure Built

Area	2010 or Later	2000 -2009	1990 -1999	1980 -1989	1970 -1979	1960 -1969	1950 -1959	1940 -1949	Before 1940	Median Year
City	0.7	25.2	10.6	8.3	9.5	13.3	12.6	6.9	12.9	1975
MSA[1]	0.5	27.0	22.3	18.5	13.5	7.9	5.1	2.1	3.1	1990
U.S.	0.5	14.9	13.8	13.9	15.9	11.1	10.9	5.5	13.5	1976

Note: Figures are percentages except for Median Year; (1) Figures cover the Atlanta-Sandy Springs-Roswell, GA Metropolitan Statistical Area—see Appendix B for areas included
Source: U.S. Census Bureau, 2010-2012 American Community Survey 3-Year Estimates

HEALTH

Health Risk Data

Category	MSA[1] (%)	U.S. (%)
Adults aged 18–64 who have any kind of health care coverage	74.3	79.6
Adults who reported being in good or excellent health	86.5	83.1
Adults who are current smokers	17.3	19.6
Adults who are heavy drinkers[2]	4.6	6.1
Adults who are binge drinkers[3]	14.6	16.9
Adults who are overweight (BMI 25.0 - 29.9)	34.4	35.8
Adults who are obese (BMI 30.0 - 99.8)	26.5	27.6
Adults who participated in any physical activities in the past month	81.0	77.1
Adults 50+ who have ever had a sigmoidoscopy or colonoscopy	70.3	67.3
Women aged 40+ who have had a mammogram within the past two years	75.7	74.0
Men aged 40+ who have had a PSA test within the past two years	54.7	45.2
Adults aged 65+ who have had flu shot within the past year	57.2	60.1
Adults who always wear a seatbelt	96.3	93.8

Note: Data as of 2012 unless otherwise noted; (1) Figures cover the Atlanta-Sandy Springs-Marietta, GA Metropolitan Statistical Area—see Appendix B for areas included; (2) Heavy drinkers are classified as males having more than two drinks per day or females having more than one drink per day; (3) Binge drinkers are classified as males having five or more drinks on one occasion or females having four or more drinks on one occasion
Source: Centers for Disease Control and Prevention, Behaviorial Risk Factor Surveillance System, SMART: Selected Metropolitan/Micropolitan Area Risk Trends, 2012

Chronic Health Indicators

Category	MSA[1] (%)	U.S. (%)
Adults who have ever been told they had a heart attack	3.7	4.5
Adults who have ever been told they had a stroke	2.9	2.9
Adults who have been told they currently have asthma	8.0	8.9
Adults who have ever been told they have arthritis	20.7	25.7
Adults who have ever been told they have diabetes[2]	8.9	9.7
Adults who have ever been told they had skin cancer	5.2	5.7
Adults who have ever been told they had any other types of cancer	5.2	6.5
Adults who have ever been told they have COPD	5.2	6.2
Adults who have ever been told they have kidney disease	3.0	2.5
Adults who have ever been told they have a form of depression	14.5	18.0

Note: Data as of 2012 unless otherwise noted; (1) Figures cover the Atlanta-Sandy Springs-Marietta, GA Metropolitan Statistical Area—see Appendix B for areas included; (2) Figures do not include pregnancy-related, borderline, or pre-diabetes
Source: Centers for Disease Control and Prevention, Behaviorial Risk Factor Surveillance System, SMART: Selected Metropolitan/Micropolitan Area Risk Trends, 2012

Mortality Rates for the Top 10 Causes of Death in the U.S.

ICD-10[a] Sub-Chapter	ICD-10[a] Code	Age-Adjusted Mortality Rate[1] per 100,000 population	
		County[2]	U.S.
Malignant neoplasms	C00-C97	173.6	174.2
Ischaemic heart diseases	I20-I25	80.0	119.1
Other forms of heart disease	I30-I51	74.3	49.6
Chronic lower respiratory diseases	J40-J47	30.6	43.2
Cerebrovascular diseases	I60-I69	47.7	40.3
Organic, including symptomatic, mental disorders	F01-F09	53.6	30.5
Other degenerative diseases of the nervous system	G30-G31	18.0	26.3
Other external causes of accidental injury	W00-X59	26.0	25.1
Diabetes mellitus	E10-E14	18.3	21.3
Hypertensive diseases	I10-I15	44.6	18.8

Note: (a) ICD-10 = International Classification of Diseases 10th Revision; (1) Mortality rates are a three year average covering 2008-2010; (2) Figures cover Fulton County
Source: Centers for Disease Control and Prevention, National Center for Health Statistics. Compressed Mortality File 1999-2010 on CDC WONDER Online Database, released January 2013. Data are compiled from the Compressed Mortality File 1999-2010, Series 20 No. 2P, 2013.

Mortality Rates for Selected Causes of Death

ICD-10[a] Sub-Chapter	ICD-10[a] Code	Age-Adjusted Mortality Rate[1] per 100,000 population	
		County[2]	U.S.
Assault	X85-Y09	11.4	5.5
Diseases of the liver	K70-K76	10.8	12.4
Human immunodeficiency virus (HIV) disease	B20-B24	15.3	3.0
Influenza and pneumonia	J09-J18	16.9	16.4
Intentional self-harm	X60-X84	9.5	11.8
Malnutrition	E40-E46	1.1	0.8
Obesity and other hyperalimentation	E65-E68	1.0	1.6
Renal failure	N17-N19	23.5	13.6
Transport accidents	V01-V99	10.9	12.6
Viral hepatitis	B15-B19	1.3	2.2

Note: (a) ICD-10 = International Classification of Diseases 10th Revision; (1) Mortality rates are a three year average covering 2008-2010; (2) Figures cover Fulton County
Source: Centers for Disease Control and Prevention, National Center for Health Statistics. Compressed Mortality File 1999-2010 on CDC WONDER Online Database, released January 2013. Data are compiled from the Compressed Mortality File 1999-2010, Series 20 No. 2P, 2013.

Health Insurance Coverage

Area	With Health Insurance	With Private Health Insurance	With Public Health Insurance	Without Health Insurance	Population Under Age 18 Without Health Insurance
City	80.7	59.8	27.6	19.3	7.2
MSA[1]	80.8	65.0	23.5	19.2	9.7
U.S.	84.9	65.4	30.4	15.1	7.5

Note: Figures are percentages that cover the civilian noninstitutionalized population; (1) Figures cover the Atlanta-Sandy Springs-Roswell, GA Metropolitan Statistical Area—see Appendix B for areas included
Source: U.S. Census Bureau, 2010-2012 American Community Survey 3-Year Estimates

Number of Medical Professionals

Area[1]	MDs[2]	DOs[2,3]	Dentists	Podiatrists	Chiropractors	Optometrists
Local (number)	4,585	81	625	38	445	135
Local (rate[4])	482.7	8.5	64.0	3.9	45.5	13.8
U.S. (rate[4])	267.6	19.6	61.7	5.6	24.7	14.5

Note: Data as of 2012 unless noted; (1) Local data covers Fulton County; (2) Data as of 2011; (3) Doctor of Osteopathic Medicine; (4) rate per 100,000 population
Source: Area Resource File (ARF) 2012-2013. U.S. Department of Health and Human Services, Health Resources and Services Administration, Bureau of Health Professions

Best Hospitals

According to *U.S. News,* the Atlanta-Sandy Springs-Roswell, GA metro area is home to two of the best hospitals in the U.S.: **Emory University Hospital** (5 specialties); **Shepherd Center** (1 specialty). The hospitals listed were nationally ranked in at least one adult specialty. Only 147 hospitals nationwide were nationally ranked in one or more specialties. Eighteen hospitals in the U.S. made the Honor Roll by ranking near the top in at least six specialties.*U.S. News Online, "America's Best Hospitals 2013-14"*

According to *U.S. News,* the Atlanta-Sandy Springs-Roswell, GA metro area is home to one of the best children's hospitals in the U.S.: **Children's Healthcare of Atlanta**. The hospital listed was highly ranked in at least one pediatric specialty. Eighty-seven hospitals in the U.S. ranked in at least one specialty. Ten children's hospitals in the U.S. made the Honor Roll by ranking near the top in three or more specialties.*U.S. News Online, "America's Best Children's Hospitals 2013-14"*

EDUCATION

Public School District Statistics

District Name	Schls	Pupils	Pupil/ Teacher Ratio	Minority Pupils[1] (%)	Free Lunch Eligible[2] (%)	IEP[3] (%)
Atlanta Public Schools	108	50,009	13.8	86.9	71.5	9.0
Fulton County	104	92,604	14.9	67.0	40.1	10.3

Note: Table includes school districts with 2,000 or more students; (1) Percentage of students that are not non-Hispanic white; (2) Percentage of students that are eligible for the free lunch program; (3) Percentage of students that have an Individualized Education Program.
Source: U.S. Department of Education, National Center for Education Statistics, Common Core of Data, Local Education Agency (School District) Universe Survey: School Year 2011-2012; U.S. Department of Education, National Center for Education Statistics, Common Core of Data, Public Elementary/Secondary School Universe Survey: School Year 2011-2012

Best High Schools

High School Name	Rank[1]	Grad. Rate[2] (%)	Coll.[3] (%)	AP/IB/ AICE Tests[4]	AP/IB/ AICE Score[5]	SAT Score[6]	ACT Score[6]
Lakeside H.S., DeKalb	1759	63	96	0.6	2.9	1529	23.5

Note: (1) Public schools are ranked from 1 to 2,000 based on the following self-reported statistics (with the corresponding weight used in calculating their overall score). Schools that were newly founded and did not have a graduating senior class in 2012 were excluded; (2) Four-year, on-time graduation rate (25%); (3) Percent of 2011 graduates who were accepted to college (25%); (4) AP/IB/AICE tests taken per student (25%); (5) Average AP/IB/AICE exam score (10%); (6) Average SAT and/or ACT score (10%); Percent of students enrolled in at least one AP/IB/AICE course (5%)—data not shown
Source: Newsweek and The Daily Beast, "America's Best High Schools 2013"

Highest Level of Education

Area	Less than H.S.	H.S. Diploma	Some College, No Deg.	Associate Degree	Bachelor's Degree	Master's Degree	Prof. School Degree	Doctorate Degree
City	12.1	20.4	16.7	4.3	27.7	12.3	4.5	2.0
MSA[1]	12.5	24.9	20.9	7.0	22.6	8.7	2.2	1.3
U.S.	14.1	28.3	21.3	7.8	18.0	7.5	1.9	1.2

Note: Figures cover persons age 25 and over; (1) Figures cover the Atlanta-Sandy Springs-Roswell, GA Metropolitan Statistical Area—see Appendix B for areas included
Source: U.S. Census Bureau, 2010-2012 American Community Survey 3-Year Estimates

Educational Attainment by Race

Area	High School Graduate or Higher (%)					Bachelor's Degree or Higher (%)				
	Total	White	Black	Asian	Hisp.[2]	Total	White	Black	Asian	Hisp.[2]
City	87.9	95.8	81.2	95.6	74.1	46.5	73.0	22.5	82.2	36.2
MSA[1]	87.5	89.0	88.2	86.9	59.7	34.7	38.5	26.9	52.5	15.6
U.S.	85.9	88.1	82.5	85.5	63.1	28.6	30.0	18.4	50.2	13.4

Note: Figures shown cover persons 25 years old and over; (1) Figures cover the Atlanta-Sandy Springs-Roswell, GA Metropolitan Statistical Area—see Appendix B for areas included; (2) People of Hispanic origin can be of any race
Source: U.S. Census Bureau, 2010-2012 American Community Survey 3-Year Estimates

School Enrollment by Grade and Control

Area	Preschool (%)		Kindergarten (%)		Grades 1 - 4 (%)		Grades 5 - 8 (%)		Grades 9 - 12 (%)	
	Public	Private	Public	Private	Public	Private	Public	Private	Public	Private
City	54.6	45.4	82.9	17.1	85.2	14.8	83.6	16.4	81.6	18.4
MSA[1]	53.5	46.5	88.5	11.5	90.4	9.6	89.6	10.4	90.9	9.1
U.S.	56.9	43.1	87.8	12.2	89.9	10.1	90.0	10.0	90.8	9.2

Note: Figures shown cover persons 3 years old and over; (1) Figures cover the Atlanta-Sandy Springs-Roswell, GA Metropolitan Statistical Area—see Appendix B for areas included
Source: U.S. Census Bureau, 2010-2012 American Community Survey 3-Year Estimates

Average Salaries of Public School Classroom Teachers

Area	2012-13		2013-14		Percent Change 2012-13 to 2013-14	Percent Change 2003-04 to 2013-14
	Dollars	Rank[1]	Dollars	Rank[1]		
Georgia	52,880	22	52,924	23	0.08	15.1
U.S. Average	56,103	–	56,689	–	1.04	21.8

Note: (1) State rank ranges from 1 to 51 where 1 indicates highest salary.
Source: National Education Association, Rankings & Estimates: Rankings of the States 2013 and Estimates of School Statistics 2014, March 2014

Higher Education

Four-Year Colleges			Two-Year Colleges			Medical Schools[1]	Law Schools[2]	Voc/Tech[3]
Public	Private Non-profit	Private For-profit	Public	Private Non-profit	Private For-profit			
3	11	12	2	0	8	2	3	5

Note: Figures cover institutions located within the city limits and include main campuses only; (1) includes schools accredited by the Liaison Committee on Medical Education and the American Osteopathic Association's Commission on Osteopathic College Accreditation; (2) includes ABA-accredited schools, schools with provisional ABA accreditation, and state accredited schools; (3) includes all schools with programs that are less than 2 years.
Source: National Center for Education Statistics, Integrated Postsecondary Education System (IPEDS), 2012-13; Association of American Medical Colleges, Member List, April 24, 2014; American Osteopathic Association, Member List, April 24, 2014; Law School Admission Council, Official Guide to ABA-Approved Law Schools Online, April 24, 2014; Wikipedia, List of Medical Schools in the United States, April 24, 2014; Wikipedia, List of Law Schools in the United States, April 24, 2014

According to U.S. News & World Report, the Atlanta-Sandy Springs-Roswell, GA metro area is home to two of the best national universities in the U.S.: **Emory University** (#20); **Georgia Institute of Technology** (#36). The indicators used to capture academic quality fall into a number of categories: assessment by administrators at peer institutions; retention of students; faculty resources; student selectivity; financial resources; alumni giving; high school counselor ratings of colleges; and graduation rate. U.S. News & World Report, "America's Best Colleges 2014"

According to U.S. News & World Report, the Atlanta-Sandy Springs-Roswell, GA metro area is home to four of the best liberal arts colleges in the U.S.: **Spelman College** (#65); **Agnes Scott College** (#89); **Morehouse College** (#126); **Oglethorpe University** (#165). The indicators used to capture academic quality fall into a number of categories: assessment by administrators at peer institutions; retention of students; faculty resources; student selectivity; financial resources; alumni giving; high school counselor ratings of colleges; and graduation rate. U.S. News & World Report, "America's Best Colleges 2014"

According to U.S. News & World Report, the Atlanta-Sandy Springs-Roswell, GA metro area is home to two of the top 100 law schools in the U.S.: **Emory University** (#23); **Georgia State University** (#54). The rankings are based on a weighted average of 12 measures of quality: peer assessment score; assessment score by lawyers/judges; median LSAT scores; median undergrad GPA; acceptance rate; employment rates for graduates; placement success; bar passage rate; faculty resources; expenditures per student; student/faculty ratio; and library resources. U.S. News & World Report, "America's Best Graduate Schools, Law, 2014"

According to U.S. News & World Report, the Atlanta-Sandy Springs-Roswell, GA metro area is home to two of the top 100 business schools in the U.S.: **Emory University (Goizueta)** (#18); **Georgia Institute of Technology (Scheller)** (#27). The rankings are based on a weighted average of the following nine measures: quality assessment; peer assessment; recruiter assessment; placement success; mean starting salary and bonus; student selectivity; mean GMAT and GRE scores; mean undergraduate GPA; and acceptance rate. U.S. News & World Report, "America's Best Graduate Schools, Business, 2014"

PRESIDENTIAL ELECTION

2012 Presidential Election Results

Area	Obama	Romney	Other
Fulton County	64.3	34.5	1.2
U.S.	51.0	47.2	1.8

Note: Results are percentages and may not add to 100% due to rounding
Source: Dave Leip's Atlas of U.S. Presidential Elections

EMPLOYERS

Major Employers

Company Name	Industry
Apartments.Com	Apartment locating service
Aquilex Holdings	Facilities support services
AT&T Corp.	Engineering services
Behavioral Health, Georgia Department of	Administration of public health programs
Clayton County Board of Education	Public elementary and secondary schools
County of Gwinnett	County commissioner
Delta Air Lines	Air transportation, scheduled
Georgia Department of Human Resoures	Administration of public health programs
Georgia Department of Transportation	Regulation, administration of transportation
Internal Revenue Service	Taxation department, government
Lockheed Martin Aeronautical Company	Aircraft
NCR Corporation	Calculating and accounting equipment
Progressive Logistics Services	Labor organizations
Robert Half International	Employment agencies
The Army, United States Department of	Army
The Coca-Cola Company	Bottled and canned soft drinks
The Fulton-Dekalb Hospital Authority	General medical and surgical hospitals
The Home Depot	Hardware stores
WellStar Kennestone Hospital	General medical and surgical hospitals
World Travel Partners Group	Travel agencies

Note: Companies shown are located within the Atlanta-Sandy Springs-Roswell, GA Metropolitan Statistical Area.
Source: Hoovers.com; Wikipedia

Best Companies to Work For

Alston & Bird; Children's Healthcare of Atlanta, headquartered in Atlanta, are among "The 100 Best Companies to Work For." To pick the 100 Best Companies to Work For, *Fortune* partnered with the Great Place to Work Institute. Two hundred fifty seven firms participated in this year's survey. Two-thirds of a company's score is based on the results of the Institute's Trust Index survey, which is sent to a random sample of employees from each company. The questions related to attitudes about management's credibility, job satisfaction, and camaraderie. The other third of the scoring is based on the company's responses to the Institute's Culture Audit, which includes detailed questions about pay and benefit programs, and a series of open-ended questions about hiring practices, internal communication, training, recognition programs, and diversity efforts. Any company that is at least five years old with more than 1,000 U.S. employees is eligible. *Fortune, "The 100 Best Companies to Work For," 2014*

Children's Healthcare of Atlanta; Turner Broadcasting System, headquartered in Atlanta, are among the "100 Best Companies for Working Mothers." Criteria: workforce representation; child care; flexibility programs; and leave policies. This year *Working Mother* gave particular weight to flexible work arrangements, women's advancement programs, and paid maternity leave. *Working Mother, "100 Best Companies 2013"*

Southern Company, headquartered in Atlanta, is among the "50 Best Employers for Workers Over 50." Criteria: recruiting practices; opportunities for training, education, and career development; workplace accommodations; alternative work options, such as flexible scheduling, job sharing, and phased retirement; employee health and pension benefits; and retiree benefits. Employers with at least 50 employees based in the U.S. are eligible, including for-profit companies, not-for-profit organizations, and government employers. *AARP, "2013 AARP Best Employers for Workers Over 50"*

Coca-Cola Enterprises; NIIT Technologies; Southern Co, headquartered in Atlanta, are among the "100 Best Places to Work in IT." To qualify, companies, both public and private, had to have a minimum of 50 IT employees and were selected based on average salary and bonus increases, the percentage of IT staffers promoted, IT staff turnover rates, training and development programs, and the percentage of women and minorities in IT staff and management positions. In addition, *Computerworld* looked at retention efforts, programs for recognizing and rewarding outstanding performances, and benefits such as flextime, elder care and child care, and reimbursement for college tuition and the cost of pursuing technology certifications. *Computerworld, "100 Best Places to Work in IT 2013"*

PUBLIC SAFETY

Crime Rate

Area	All Crimes	Violent Crimes				Property Crimes		
		Murder	Forcible Rape	Robbery	Aggrav. Assault	Burglary	Larceny -Theft	Motor Vehicle Theft
City	7,912.5	19.0	25.9	520.8	813.4	1,416.8	3,938.3	1,178.4
Suburbs[1]	3,431.7	5.0	19.6	122.2	177.0	824.3	1,978.8	304.9
Metro[2]	3,792.0	6.1	20.1	154.2	228.2	871.9	2,136.4	375.1
U.S.	3,246.1	4.7	26.9	112.9	242.3	670.2	1,959.3	229.7

Note: Figures are crimes per 100,000 population; (1) All areas within the metro area that are located outside the city limits; (2) Figures cover the Atlanta-Sandy Springs-Roswell, GA Metropolitan Statistical Area—see Appendix B for areas included
Source: FBI Uniform Crime Reports, 2012

Hate Crimes

Area	Number of Quarters Reported	Bias Motivation				
		Race	Religion	Sexual Orientation	Ethnicity	Disability
City	3	0	0	0	0	0
U.S.	4	2,797	1,099	1,135	667	92

Source: Federal Bureau of Investigation, Hate Crime Statistics 2012

Identity Theft Consumer Complaints

Area	Complaints	Complaints per 100,000 Population	Rank[2]
MSA[1]	9,022	170.7	7
U.S.	290,056	91.8	-

Note: (1) Figures cover the Atlanta-Sandy Springs-Roswell, GA Metropolitan Statistical Area—see Appendix B for areas included; (2) Rank ranges from 1 to 377 where 1 indicates greatest number of identity theft complaints per 100,000 population
Source: Federal Trade Commission, Consumer Sentinel Network Data Book for January–December 2013

Fraud and Other Consumer Complaints

Area	Complaints	Complaints per 100,000 Population	Rank[2]
MSA[1]	25,389	480.2	29
U.S.	1,811,724	595.2	-

Note: (1) Figures cover the Atlanta-Sandy Springs-Roswell, GA Metropolitan Statistical Area—see Appendix B for areas included; (2) Rank ranges from 1 to 377 where 1 indicates greatest number of identity theft complaints per 100,000 population
Source: Federal Trade Commission, Consumer Sentinel Network Data Book for January–December 2013

RECREATION

Culture

Dance[1]	Theatre[1]	Instrumental Music[1]	Vocal Music[1]	Series and Festivals	Museums and Art Galleries[2]	Zoos and Aquariums[3]
5	20	5	8	9	46	2

Note: (1) Number of professional perfoming groups; (2) Based on organizations with primary SIC code 8412; (3) AZA-accredited
Source: The Grey House Performing Arts Directory, 2013; Association of Zoos & Aquariums, AZA Member Zoos & Aquariums, April 2014; www.AccuLeads.com, May 1, 2014

Professional Sports Teams

Team Name	League	Year Established
Atlanta Braves	Major League Baseball (MLB)	1966
Atlanta Falcons	National Football League (NFL)	1966
Atlanta Hawks	National Basketball Association (NBA)	1968

Note: Includes teams located in the Atlanta-Sandy Springs-Roswell, GA Metropolitan Statistical Area.
Source: Wikipedia, Major Professional Sports Teams of the United States and Canada

CLIMATE

Average and Extreme Temperatures

Temperature	Jan	Feb	Mar	Apr	May	Jun	Jul	Aug	Sep	Oct	Nov	Dec	Yr.
Extreme High (°F)	79	80	85	93	95	101	105	102	98	95	84	77	105
Average High (°F)	52	56	64	73	80	86	88	88	82	73	63	54	72
Average Temp. (°F)	43	46	53	62	70	77	79	79	73	63	53	45	62
Average Low (°F)	33	36	42	51	59	66	70	69	64	52	42	35	52
Extreme Low (°F)	-8	5	10	26	37	46	53	55	36	28	3	0	-8

Note: Figures cover the years 1945-1990
Source: National Climatic Data Center, International Station Meteorological Climate Summary, 9/96

Average Precipitation/Snowfall/Humidity

Precip./Humidity	Jan	Feb	Mar	Apr	May	Jun	Jul	Aug	Sep	Oct	Nov	Dec	Yr.
Avg. Precip. (in.)	4.7	4.6	5.7	4.3	4.0	3.5	5.1	3.6	3.4	2.8	3.8	4.2	49.8
Avg. Snowfall (in.)	1	1	Tr	Tr	0	0	0	0	0	0	Tr	Tr	2
Avg. Rel. Hum. 7am (%)	79	77	78	78	82	83	88	89	88	84	81	79	82
Avg. Rel. Hum. 4pm (%)	56	50	48	45	49	52	57	56	56	51	52	55	52

Note: Figures cover the years 1945-1990; Tr = Trace amounts (<0.05 in. of rain; <0.5 in. of snow)
Source: National Climatic Data Center, International Station Meteorological Climate Summary, 9/96

Weather Conditions

Temperature			Daytime Sky			Precipitation		
10°F & below	32°F & below	90°F & above	Clear	Partly cloudy	Cloudy	0.01 inch or more precip.	0.1 inch or more snow/ice	Thunder-storms
1	49	38	98	147	120	116	3	48

Note: Figures are average number of days per year and cover the years 1945-1990
Source: National Climatic Data Center, International Station Meteorological Climate Summary, 9/96

HAZARDOUS WASTE

Superfund Sites

Atlanta has no sites on the EPA's Superfund Final National Priorities List.
U.S. Environmental Protection Agency, Final National Priorities List, April 26, 2014

AIR & WATER QUALITY

Air Quality Index

Area	Percent of Days when Air Quality was...[2]					AQI Statistics[2]	
	Good	Moderate	Unhealthy for Sensitive Groups	Unhealthy	Very Unhealthy	Maximum	Median
MSA[1]	47.9	51.2	0.5	0.3	0.0	151	52

Note: (1) Data covers the Atlanta-Sandy Springs-Roswell, GA Metropolitan Statistical Area—see Appendix B for areas included; (2) Based on 365 days with AQI data in 2013. Air Quality Index (AQI) is an index for reporting daily air quality. EPA calculates the AQI for five major air pollutants regulated by the Clean Air Act: ground-level ozone, particle pollution (aka particulate matter), carbon monoxide, sulfur dioxide, and nitrogen dioxide. The AQI runs from 0 to 500. The higher the AQI value, the greater the level of air pollution and the greater the health concern. There are six AQI categories: "Good" AQI is between 0 and 50. Air quality is considered satisfactory; "Moderate" AQI is between 51 and 100. Air quality is acceptable; "Unhealthy for Sensitive Groups" When AQI values are between 101 and 150, members of sensitive groups may experience health effects; "Unhealthy" When AQI values are between 151 and 200 everyone may begin to experience health effects; "Very Unhealthy" AQI values between 201 and 300 trigger a health alert; "Hazardous" AQI values over 300 trigger warnings of emergency conditions (not shown).
Source: U.S. Environmental Protection Agency, Air Quality Index Report, 2013

Air Quality Index Pollutants

| Area | Percent of Days when AQI Pollutant was...[2] | | | | | |
	Carbon Monoxide	Nitrogen Dioxide	Ozone	Sulfur Dioxide	Particulate Matter 2.5	Particulate Matter 10
MSA[1]	0.0	1.9	20.8	0.0	77.3	0.0

Note: (1) Data covers the Atlanta-Sandy Springs-Roswell, GA Metropolitan Statistical Area—see Appendix B for areas included; (2) Based on 365 days with AQI data in 2013. The Air Quality Index (AQI) is an index for reporting daily air quality. EPA calculates the AQI for five major air pollutants regulated by the Clean Air Act: ground-level ozone, particle pollution (also known as particulate matter), carbon monoxide, sulfur dioxide, and nitrogen dioxide. The AQI runs from 0 to 500. The higher the AQI value, the greater the level of air pollution and the greater the health concern.
Source: U.S. Environmental Protection Agency, Air Quality Index Report, 2013

Air Quality Trends: Ozone

	2003	2004	2005	2006	2007	2008	2009	2010	2011	2012
MSA[1]	0.083	0.081	0.085	0.092	0.091	0.080	0.072	0.074	0.078	0.077

Note: (1) Data covers the Atlanta-Sandy Springs-Roswell, GA Metropolitan Statistical Area—see Appendix B for areas included. The values shown are the composite ozone concentration averages among trend sites based on the highest fourth daily maximum 8-hour concentration in parts per million. These trends are based on sites having an adequate record of monitoring data during the trend period. Data from exceptional events are included.
Source: U.S. Environmental Protection Agency, Air Quality Monitoring Information, "Air Quality Trends by City, 2000-2012"

Maximum Air Pollutant Concentrations: Particulate Matter, Ozone, CO and Lead

	Particulate Matter 10 (ug/m^3)	Particulate Matter 2.5 Wtd AM (ug/m^3)	Particulate Matter 2.5 24-Hr (ug/m^3)	Ozone (ppm)	Carbon Monoxide (ppm)	Lead (ug/m^3)
MSA[1] Level	38	11	21	0.088	1	0.03
NAAQS[2]	150	15	35	0.075	9	0.15
Met NAAQS[2]	Yes	Yes	Yes	No	Yes	Yes

Note: (1) Data covers the Atlanta-Sandy Springs-Roswell, GA Metropolitan Statistical Area—see Appendix B for areas included; Data from exceptional events are included; (2) National Ambient Air Quality Standards; ppm = parts per million; ug/m^3 = micrograms per cubic meter; n/a not available.
Concentrations: Particulate Matter 10 (coarse particulate)—highest second maximum 24-hour concentration; Particulate Matter 2.5 Wtd AM (fine particulate)—highest weighted annual mean concentration; Particulate Matter 2.5 24-Hour (fine particulate)—highest 98th percentile 24-hour concentration; Ozone—highest fourth daily maximum 8-hour concentration; Carbon Monoxide—highest second maximum non-overlapping 8-hour concentration; Lead—maximum running 3-month average
Source: U.S. Environmental Protection Agency, Air Quality Monitoring Information, "Air Quality Statistics by City, 2012"

Maximum Air Pollutant Concentrations: Nitrogen Dioxide and Sulfur Dioxide

	Nitrogen Dioxide AM (ppb)	Nitrogen Dioxide 1-Hr (ppb)	Sulfur Dioxide AM (ppb)	Sulfur Dioxide 1-Hr (ppb)	Sulfur Dioxide 24-Hr (ppb)
MSA[1] Level	12	53	n/a	11	n/a
NAAQS[2]	53	100	30	75	140
Met NAAQS[2]	Yes	Yes	n/a	Yes	n/a

Note: (1) Data covers the Atlanta-Sandy Springs-Roswell, GA Metropolitan Statistical Area—see Appendix B for areas included; Data from exceptional events are included; (2) National Ambient Air Quality Standards; ppm = parts per million; ug/m^3 = micrograms per cubic meter; n/a not available.
Concentrations: Nitrogen Dioxide AM—highest arithmetic mean concentration; Nitrogen Dioxide 1-Hr—highest 98th percentile 1-hour daily maximum concentration; Sulfur Dioxide AM—highest annual mean concentration; Sulfur Dioxide 1-Hr—highest 99th percentile 1-hour daily maximum concentration; Sulfur Dioxide 24-Hr—highest second maximum 24-hour concentration
Source: U.S. Environmental Protection Agency, Air Quality Monitoring Information, "Air Quality Statistics by City, 2012"

Drinking Water

Water System Name	Pop. Served	Primary Water Source Type	Violations[1]	
			Health Based	Monitoring/ Reporting
Atlanta	650,000	Surface	1	0

Note: (1) Based on violation data from January 1, 2013 to December 31, 2013 (includes unresolved violations from earlier years)
Source: U.S. Environmental Protection Agency, Office of Ground Water and Drinking Water, Safe Drinking Water Information System (based on data extracted February 10, 2014)

Austin, Texas

Background

Starting out in 1730 as a peaceful Spanish mission on the north bank of the Colorado River in south-central Texas, Austin soon engaged in an imbroglio of territorial wars, beginning when the "Father of Texas," Stephen F. Austin, annexed the territory from Mexico in 1833 as his own. Later, the Republic of Texas named the territory Austin in honor of the colonizer, and conferred upon it state capital status. Challenges to this decision ensued, ranging from an invasion by the Mexican government to reclaim its land, to Sam Houston's call that the capital ought to move from Austin to Houston.

During peaceful times, however, Austin has been called the "City of the Violet Crown." Coined by the short story writer, William Sydney Porter, or O. Henry, the name refers to the purple mist that circles the surrounding hills of the Colorado River Valley.

This city of technological innovation is home to a strong computer and electronics industry. Austin offers more free wireless spots—including its city parks—per capita than any other city in the nation, and its technology focus has traditionally drawn numerous high-tech companies. Samsung Electronics' major computer chip plant was built in Austin in the late 1990s with expansions and a new facility, nine football fields big, since. Along with this technology growth has come the problem of increased traffic, especially on Interstate 35, the main highway linking the U.S. and Mexico. A recently developed 89-mile bypass has helped to relieve some of the traffic difficulties long associated with I-35. In May 2010, Facebook opened a sales and operations facility in the city.

In addition to its traditional business community, Austin is home to the main campus of the University of Texas. The university provides Austin with even further diverse lifestyles; today there is a solid mix of white-collar workers, students, professors, blue-collar workers, musicians and artists, and members of the booming tech industry who all call themselves Austinites.

The influx of young people centered on university life has contributed to the city's growth as a thriving live music scene. It is so important to the city that its local government maintains the Austin Music Commission to promote the local music industry.

A notable industry conference takes place here each spring. The South by Southwest Conference (SXSW) showcases more than 2,000 performers at 90+ venues throughout the city. The growing film and interactive industries have been added to the conference in recent years.

The civic-minded city, whose mayor is working toward making Austin the nation's fittest city, is operating from a new city hall, which was completed in late 2004. The building, at about 115,000 square feet, is also home to a public plaza facing Town Lake. One of the town's cultural hubs, the Long Center for the Performing Arts, underwent renovation in 2006, and reopened in 2008.

It is most likely Austinites' pride in their creative and independent culture that has spawned a movement to keep the city from too much corporate development. The slogan "Keep Austin Weird" was adopted by the Austin Independent Business Alliance in 2003 as a way to promote local and alternative business.

The city sits at a desirable location along the Colorado River, and many recreational activities center on the water. For instance, Austin boasts three spring-fed swimming pools enjoyed by its residents, as well as the Lance Armstrong Crosstown Bikeway. The city has more than 100 miles of bike paths.

The climate of Austin is subtropical with hot summers. Winters are mild, with below-freezing temperatures occurring on an average of 25 days a year. Cold spells are short, seldom lasting more than two days. Daytime temperatures in summer are hot, while summer nights are usually pleasant.

Rankings

General Rankings

- *Business Insider* projected current trends well into the future to compile its list of the "15 Hottest American Cities of the Future." To such metrics as job and population growth, demographics, affordability, livability, and residents' health and welfare, analysts added innovation in technology and sustainability as well as a culture favoring youth and creativity. Judging by these combined factors, Austin ranked #3. *Business Insider, "The Fifteen Hottest American Cities of the Future," June 18, 2012*

- Austin was identified as one of America's fastest-growing cities in terms of population and economy by *Forbes*. The area ranked #1 out of 20. The 100 most populous metro areas in the U.S. were evaluated on the following criteria: estimated population growth; job growth; gross metropolitan product growth; unemployment; median salaries for college-educated workers. *Forbes, "America's Fastest-Growing Cities 2014," February 14, 2014*

- Austin was identified as one of America's fastest-growing major metropolitan areas in terms of population by CNNMoney.com. The area ranked #1 out of 10. Criteria: population growth between July 2012 and July 2013. *CNNMoney, "10 Fastest-Growing Cities," March 28, 2014*

- Among the 50 largest U.S. cities, Austin placed #2 in Vocativ's "semi-exhaustive, mostly scientific" city Livability Index for people aged 35 and under. Average salary, unemployment rates, rents, and other living costs were considered, along with bike lanes, low-cost broadband, cheap takeout, self-service laundries, the price of a pint of Guinness, music venues, and vintage clothing stores. *vocative.com, "The Livability Index: The Best U.S. Cities for People 35 and Under," November 7, 2013*

- Austin was selected as one of America's best cities by *Bloomberg Businessweek*. The city ranked #8 out of 50. Criteria: leisure attributes (the number of restaurants, bars, libraries, museums, professional sports teams, and park acres by population); educational attributes (public school performance, the number of colleges, and graduate degree holders); economic factors (2011 income and June and July 2012 unemployment); crime; and air quality. *Bloomberg BusinessWeek, "America's Best Cities," September 26, 2012*

- Austin appeared on RelocateAmerica's list of best places to live in America. The annual "Top 100 Places to Live" list recognizes the top communities as nominated by their residents & local businesses. RelocateAmerica's Research Group determined the list based on review of various data gathered for economic, employment, housing, education, industry, opportunity, environment and recreation along with feedback from area leaders and residents. *RelocateAmerica.com, "Top 100 Places to Live for 2011"*

- Austin was selected as one of "America's Top 10 Places to Live" by *RelocateAmerica.com*. The city ranked #1. Criteria: real estate and housing; economic health; recreation; safety; input from local residents, business and community leaders. *RelocateAmerica.com, "Top 10 Places to Live for 2011"*

- Austin was selected as one of "America's Favorite Cities." The city ranked #17 in the "Quality of Life and Visitor Experience: Cleanliness" category. Respondents to an online survey were asked to rate 35 top urban destinations in the U.S. from a visitor's perspective. Criteria: cleanliness. *Travel + Leisure, "America's Favorite Cities 2013"*

- Austin was selected as one of "America's Favorite Cities." The city ranked #17 in the "Type of Trip: Gay-friendly" category. Respondents to an online survey were asked to rate 35 top urban destinations in the U.S. from a visitor's perspective. Criteria: gay-friendly. *Travel + Leisure, "America's Favorite Cities 2013"*

Business/Finance Rankings

- Measuring indicators of "tolerance"—the nonjudgmental environment that "attracts open-minded and new-thinking kinds of people"— as well as concentrations of technological and economic innovators, analysts identified the most creative American metro areas. On the resulting 2012 Creativity Index, the Austin metro area placed #16. *www.thedailybeast.com, "Boulder, Ann Arbor, Tucson & More: 20 Most Creative U.S. Cities," June 26, 2012*

- The personal finance site NerdWallet scored the nation's 20 largest American cities according to how friendly a business climate they offer to would-be entrepreneurs. Criteria inlcuded local taxes (state, city, payroll, property), growth rate, and the regulatory environment as judged by small business owners. On the resulting list of most welcoming cities, Austin ranked #1. *www.nerdwallet.com, "Top 10 Best Cities for Small Business," August 26, 2013*

- Recognizing the sizeable percentage of American workers who are self-employed, NerdWallet editors assessed the country's cities according to percentage of freelancers, median rental costs, and affordability of median healthcare costs. By these criteria, Austin placed #4 among the best cities for independent workers. *www.nerdwallet.com, "Best Cities for Freelancers," February 25, 2014*

- In order to help veterans transition from the military to civilian life, USAA and Hiring Our Heroes worked with Sperlings's BestPlaces to develop a list of the major metropolitan areas where military-skills-related employment is strongest. Criteria included job prospects, unemployment, number of government jobs, recent job growth, accessible health resources, and colleges and universities. Metro areas with a violent crime rate or high cost of living were excluded. At #5, the Austin metro area made the top ten. *www.usaa.com, "2013 Best Places for Veterans: Jobs," November 2013*

- The finance website Wall St. Cheat Sheet reported on the prospects for high-wage job creation in the nation's largest metro areas over the next five years and ranked them accordingly, drawing on in-depth analysis by CareerBuilder and Economic Modeling Specialists International (EMSI). The Austin metro area placed #2 on the Wall St. Cheat Sheet list. *wallstcheatsheet.com, "Top 10 Cities for High-Wage Job Growth," December 8, 2013*

- Austin was the #7-ranked city in a Seedtable analysis of the world's most active cities for start-up companies, as reported by Statista. *www.statista.com, "San Francisco Has the Most Active Start-Up Scene," August 21, 2013*

- Based on a minimum of 500 social media reviews per metro area, the employment opinion group Glassdoor surveyed 50 of the largest U.S. metro areas on measures including compensation and benefits, satisfaction with management, business outlook, and number of employers hiring. The Austin metro area was ranked #10 in overall employee satisfaction. *www.glassdoor.com, "Employment Satisfaction Report Card by City," June 21, 2013*

- The financial literacy site NerdWallet.com set out to identify the 20 most promising cities for job seekers, analyzing data for the nation's 50 largest cities. Austin was ranked #1. Criteria: unemployment rate; population growth; median income; selected monthly owner costs. *NerdWallet.com, "Best Cities for Job Seekers," January 7, 2014*

- The Brookings Institution ranked the 50 largest cities in the U.S. based on income inequality. Austin was ranked #24. (#1 = greatest ineqality). Criteria: the cities were ranked based on the "95/20 ratio." This figure represents the income at which a household earns more than 95 percent of all other households, divided by the income at which a household earns more than only 20 percent of all other households. *Brookings Institution, "Income Inequality in America's 50 Largest Cities, 2007-2012," February 20, 2014*

- *Forbes* ranked the largest metro areas in the U.S. in terms of the "Best Cities for Young Professionals." The Austin metro area ranked #11 out of 15. Criteria: job growth; unemployment rate; median salary of college graduates age 24 to 34; cost of living; number of small businesses per capita; number of large companies; percentage of population 25 years of age and older with college degrees. *Forbes.com, "America's Best Cities for Young Professionals," July 12, 2011*

- Austin was ranked #2 out of 100 metro areas in terms of economic performance (#1 = best) during the recession and recovery from trough quarter through the second quarter of 2013. Criteria: percent change in employment; percentage point change in unemployment rate; percent change in gross metropolitan product; percent change in House Price Index. *Brookings Institution, MetroMonitor: Tracking Economic Recession and Recovery in America's 100 Largest Metropolitan Areas, September 2013*

- Austin was identified as one of the best places for finding a job by *U.S. News & World Report*. The city ranked #5 out of 10. Criteria: strong job market. *U.S. News & World Report, "The 10 Best Cities to Find Jobs," June 17, 2013*

- Austin was identified as one of America's most frugal metro areas by *Coupons.com*. The city ranked #18 out of 25. Criteria: Grocery IQ and coupons.com mobile app usage. *Coupons.com, "Top 25 Most On-the-Go Frugal Cities of 2012," February 19, 2013*

- Austin was identified as one of America's "10 Best Cities to Get a Job" by *U.S. News & World Report*. The city ranked #6. Criteria: number of available jobs; unemployment rate. *U.S. News & World Report, "10 Best Cities to Get a Job," February 1, 2011*

- Austin was identified as one of the top 25 U.S. cities with the most credit card debt by credit reporting bureau Experian. The city was ranked #8. *Experian, March 4, 2011*

- The Austin metro area appeared on the Milken Institute "2013 Best Performing Cities" list. Rank: #1 out of 200 large metro areas. Criteria: job growth; wage and salary growth; high-tech output growth. *Milken Institute, "Best-Performing Cities 2013," December 2013*

- *Forbes* ranked the 200 most populous metro areas in the U.S. in terms of the "Best Places for Business and Careers." The Austin metro area was ranked #14. Criteria: costs (business and living); job growth (past and projected); income growth; educational attainment (college and high school); projected economic growth; cultural and recreational opportunities; net migration patterns; number of highly ranked colleges. *Forbes, "The Best Places for Business and Careers," August 7, 2013*

Children/Family Rankings

- Austin was selected as one of the best cities for families to live by *Parenting* magazine. The city ranked #4 out of 100. Criteria: education; health; community; *Parenting's* Culture & Charm Index. *Parenting.com, "The 2012 Best Cities for Families List"*

Culture/Performing Arts Rankings

- Austin was selected as one of 10 best U.S. cities to be a moviemaker. The city was ranked #1. Criteria: film community; access to new films; access to equipment; cost of living; tax incentives. *MovieMaker Magazine, "Top 10 Cities to be a Moviemaker: 2013," March 5, 2013*

- Austin was selected as one of "America's Favorite Cities." The city ranked #29 in the "Culture: Museum/Galleries" category. Respondents to an online survey were asked to rate 35 top urban destinations in the U.S. from a visitor's perspective. Criteria: number and quality of museums and galleries. *Travelandleisure.com, "America's Favorite Cities 2013"*

- Austin was selected as one of America's top cities for the arts. The city ranked #9 in the big city (population 500,000 and over) category. Criteria: readers' top choices for arts travel destinations based on the richness and variety of visual arts sites, activities and events. *American Style, "2012 Top 25 Arts Destinations," June 2012*

Dating/Romance Rankings

- A *Cosmopolitan* magazine article surveyed the gender balance and other factors to arrive at a list of the best and worst cities for women to meet single guys. Austin was #8 among the best for single women looking for dates. *www.cosmopolitan.com, "Working the Ratio," October 1, 2013*

- Of the 100 U.S. cities surveyed by *Men's Health* in its quest to identify the nation's best cities for dating and forming relationships, Austin was ranked #11 for online dating (#1 = best). *Men's Health, "The Best and Worst Cities for Online Dating," January 30, 2013*

- Austin was selected as one of America's best cities for singles by the readers of *Travel + Leisure* in their annual "America's Favorite Cities" survey. The city was ranked #7 out of 20. *Travel + Leisure, "America's Best Cities for Singles," July 2012*

- Austin was selected as one of the best cities for newlyweds by *Rent.com*. The city ranked #1 of 10. Criteria: cost of living; mean annual income; unemployment rate. *Rent.com, "10 Best Cities for Newlyweds," March 20, 2012*

- Austin was selected as one of "America's Best Cities for Dating" by *Yahoo! Travel*. Criteria: high proportion of singles; excellent dating venues and/or stunning natural settings. *Yahoo! Travel, "America's Best Cities for Dating," February 7, 2012*

- Austin was selected as one of the best cities for single women in America by *SingleMindedWomen.com*. The city ranked #10. Criteria: ratio of women to men; singles population; healthy lifestyle; employment opportunities; cost of living; access to travel; entertainment options; social opportunities. *SingleMindedWomen.com, "Top 10 Cities for Single Women," 2011*

Education Rankings

- Based on a Brookings Institution study, *24/7 Wall St.* identified the ten U.S. metropolitan areas with the most average patent filings per million residents between 2007 and 2011. Austin ranked #9. *24/7 Wall St., "America's Most Innovative Cities," February 1, 2013*

- The Austin metro area was selected as one of America's most innovative cities" by *The Business Insider*. The metro area was ranked #9 out of 20. Criteria: patents per capita. *The Business Insider, "The 20 Most Innovative Cities in the U.S.," February 1, 2013*

- *Men's Health* ranked 100 U.S. cities in terms of their education levels. Austin was ranked #31 (#1 = most educated city). Criteria: high school graduation rates; school enrollment; educational attainment; number of households who have outstanding student loans; number of households whose members have taken adult-education courses. *Men's Health, "Where School Is In: The Most and Least Educated Cities," September 12, 2011*

- Austin was selected as one of "America's Geekiest Cities" by *Forbes.com*. The city ranked #12 of 20. Criteria: percentage of workers with jobs in science, technology, engineering and mathematics. *Forbes.com, "America's Geekiest Cities," August 5, 2011*

- Austin was selected as one of America's most literate cities. The city ranked #21 out of the 77 largest U.S. cities. Criteria: number of booksellers; library resources; Internet resources; educational attainment; periodical publishing resources; newspaper circulation. *Central Connecticut State University, "America's Most Literate Cities, 2013"*

- Austin was identified as one of "America's Smartest Cities" by *The Daily Beast* using data from Lumos Labs. The metro area ranked #9 out of 25. Criteria: with data collected from more than 1 million users as part of its human cognition project, Lumos Labs was able to analyze performance for nearly 200 metro areas in five cognitive areas: memory, processing speed, flexibility, attention, and problem solving. The median Lumos Lab score was worth 50 percent of the final, weighted ranking. The other half of the ranking was based on the percentage of adults over age 25 with a bachelor's and/or master's degree. *The Daily Beast, "America's Smartest Cities 2012" August 16, 2012*

- Austin was identified as one of America's most inventive cities by *The Daily Beast*. The city ranked #14 out of 25. The 200 largest cities in the U.S. were ranked by the number of patents (applied and approved) per capita. *The Daily Beast, "The 25 Most Inventive Cities," October 2, 2011*

Environmental Rankings

- The Austin metro area came in at #346 for the relative comfort of its climate on Sperling's list of "chill cities," as measured by the Sperling Heat Index. All 361 metro areas are included. Criteria included daytime high temperatures, nighttime low temperatures, dew point, and relative humidity at the high temperatures. *www.bertsperling.com, "Sperling's Chill Cities," July 18, 2013*

- Sperling's BestPlaces assessed 379 metropolitan areas of the United States for the likelihood of dangerously extreme weather events or earthquakes. In general the Southeast and South-Central regions have the highest risk of weather extremes and earthquakes, while the Pacific Northwest enjoys the lowest risk. Of the least risky metropolitan areas, the Austin metro area was ranked #373. *www.bestplaces.net, "Safest Places from Natural Disasters," April 2011*

- Austin was selected as one of 22 "Smarter Cities" for energy by the Natural Resources Defense Council. The city appeared as one of 12 cities in the large city (population 250,000 and over) category. Criteria: investment in green power; energy efficiency measures; conservation. *Natural Resources Defense Council, "2010 Smarter Cities," July 19, 2010*

- Austin was highlighted as one of the top 25 cleanest metro areas for short-term particle pollution (24-hour PM 2.5) in the U.S. during 2008 through 2010. Monitors in these cities reported no days with unhealthful PM 2.5 levels. *American Lung Association, State of the Air 2012*

Food/Drink Rankings

- According to Fodor's Travel, Austin placed #373 among the best U.S. cities for food-truck cuisine. *www.fodors.com, "America's Best Food Truck Cities," December 20, 2013*

- *Men's Health* ranked 100 major U.S. cities in terms of alcohol intoxication. Austin ranked #93 (#1 = most sober).Criteria: binge drinking; alcohol-related traffic accidents, arrests, and fatalities. *Men's Health, "The Drunkest Cities in America," November 19, 2013*

- Austin was identified as one of "America's Drunkest Cities of 2011" by *The Daily Beast.* The city ranked #7 out of 25. Criteria: binge drinking; drinks consumed per month. *The Daily Beast, "Tipsy Towns: Where are America's Drunkest Cities?," December 31, 2011*

- Austin was identified as one of the most vegetarian-friendly cities in America by GrubHub.com, the nation's largest food ordering service. The city ranked #6 out of 10. Criteria: percentage of vegetarian restaurants. *GrubHub.com, "Top Vegetarian-Friendly Cities," July 18, 2012*

- Austin was selected as one of the seven best cities for barbeque by *U.S. News & World Report.* The city was ranked #5. *U.S. New & World Report, "America's Best BBQ Cities," February 29, 2012*

- Austin was selected as one of America's 10 most vegan-friendly cities. The city was ranked #1. *People for the Ethical Treatment of Animals, "Top Vegan-Friendly Cities of 2013," June 11, 2013*

Health/Fitness Rankings

- For each of the 50 most populous metro areas in the United States, the American College of Sports Medicine's American Fitness Index evaluated infrastructure, community assets, and policies that encourage healthy and fit lifestyles, including preventive health behaviors, levels of chronic disease conditions, health care access, and community resources and policies that support physical activity. The Austin metro area ranked #11 for "community fitness." Personal health indicators were considered as well as community and environmental indicators. *www.americanfitnessindex.org, "ACSM American Fitness Index Health and Community Fitness Status of the 50 Largest Metropolitan Areas," May 2013*

- Austin was selected as one of the 25 fittest cities in America by *Men's Fitness Online.* It ranked #12 out of America's 50 largest cities. Criteria: fitness centers and sport stores; nutrition; sports participation; TV viewing; overweight/sedentary; junk food; air quality; geography; commute; parks and open space; city recreational facilities; access to healthcare; motivation; mayor and city initiatives; state obesity initiatives. *Men's Fitness, "The Fittest and Fattest Cities in America," March 5, 2012*

- Austin was identified as a "2013 Spring Allergy Capital." The area ranked #64 out of 100. Three groups of factors were used to identify the most severe cities for people with allergies during the spring season: annual pollen levels; medicine utilization; access to board-certified allergists. *Asthma and Allergy Foundation of America, "Spring Allergy Capitals 2013"*

- Austin was identified as a "2013 Fall Allergy Capital." The area ranked #45 out of 100. Three groups of factors were used to identify the most severe cities for people with allergies during the fall season: annual pollen levels; medicine utilization; access to board-certified allergists. *Asthma and Allergy Foundation of America, "Fall Allergy Capitals 2013"*

- Austin was identified as a "2013 Asthma Capital." The area ranked #93 out of the nation's 100 largest metropolitan areas. Twelve factors were used to identify the most challenging places to live for people with asthma: estimated prevalence; self-reported prevalence; crude death rate for asthma; annual pollen score; annual air quality; public smoking laws; number of board-certified asthma specialists; school inhaler access laws; rescue medication use; controller medication use; uninsured rate; poverty rate. *Asthma and Allergy Foundation of America, "Asthma Capitals 2013"*

- *Men's Health* ranked 100 major U.S. cities in terms of the best and worst cities for men. Austin ranked #7. Criteria: thirty-three data points were examined covering health, fitness, and quality of life. *Men's Health, "The Best & Worst Cities for Men 2014," December 6, 2013*

- *Men's Health* ranked 100 U.S. cities in terms of the best and worst cities for women. Austin was ranked among the ten best at #5. Criteria: dozens of statistical parameters of long life in the categories of health, quality of life, and fitness. *Men's Health, "The 10 Best and Worst Cities for Women 2011," January/February 2011*

- Breathe Right Nasal Strips, in partnership with Sperling's BestPlaces, analyzed 50 metro areas and identified those U.S. cities most challenged by chronic nasal congestion. The Austin metro area ranked #14. Criteria: tree, grass and weed pollens; molds and spores; air pollution; climate; smoking; purchase habits of congestion products; prescriptions of drugs for congestion relief; incidence of influenza. *Breathe Right Nasal Strips, "Most Congested Cities," October 3, 2011*

- Austin was selected as one of the best metropolitan areas for hospital care in America by *HealthGrades.com*. The rankings are based on a comprehensive study of patient death and complication rates in the nation's nearly 5,000 hospitals. Hospitals performing in the top 5% nationwide across 26 different medical procedures and diagnoses were identified. *HealthGrades.com* then ranked cities by the highest percentage of these Distinguished Hospitals for Clinical Excellence™. The Austin metro area ranked #45. *HealthGrades.com, "America's Top 50 Cities for Hospital Care," January 21, 2012*

- The Austin metro area appeared in the 2013 Gallup-Healthways Well-Being Index. The area ranked #30 out of 189. The Gallup-Healthways Well-Being Index score is an average of six sub-indexes, which individually examine life evaluation, emotional health, work environment, physical health, healthy behaviors, and access to basic necessities. Results are based on telephone interviews conducted as part of the Gallup-Healthways Well-Being Index survey January 2–December 29, 2012, and January 2–December 30, 2013, with a random sample of 531,630 adults, aged 18 and older, living in metropolitan areas in the 50 U.S. states and the District of Columbia. *Gallup-Healthways, "State of American Well-Being," March 25, 2014*

- The Austin metro area was identified as one of "America's Most Stressful Cities" by *Sperling's BestPlaces*. The metro area ranked #38 out of 50. Criteria: unemployment rate; suicide rate; commute time; mental health; poor rest; alcohol use; violent crime rate; property crime rate; cloudy days annually. *Sperling's BestPlaces, www.BestPlaces.net, "Stressful Cities 2012*

- *Men's Health* ranked 100 U.S. cities in terms of their activity levels. Austin was ranked #14 (#1 = most active city). Criteria: where and how often residents exercise; percentage of households that watch more than 15 hours of cable television a week and buy more than 11 video games a year; death rate from deep-vein thrombosis, a condition linked to sitting for extended periods of time. *Men's Health, "Where Sit Happens: The Most and Least Active Cities in America," June 20, 2011*

Pet Rankings

- Austin was selected as one of the best cities for dogs by real estate website Estately.com. The city was ranked #4. Criteria: weather; walkability; yard sizes; dog activities; meetup groups; availability of dogsitters. *Estately.com, "17 Best U.S. Cities for Dogs," May 14, 2013*

Real Estate Rankings

- NerdWallet identified the 10 U.S. cities among the 25 largest, most hospitable for recent college graduates, based on demographics; social life; accessibility; cost of living; and economic opportunity. Austin placed #8 as a destination for new young graduates. *http://www.nerdwallet.com, "Best Cities for Fresh College Graduates," May 30, 2013*

- The PricewaterhouseCoopers and Urban Land Institute report *Emerging Trends in Real Estate* forecasts that improvements in leasing, rents, and pricing will fuel recovery in all property sectors in 2013. Austin was ranked #4 among the top ten markets to watch in 2013. *PricewaterhouseCoopers/Urban Land Institute, "U.S. Commercial Real Estate Recovery to Advance in 2013," October 17, 2012*

- Austin was ranked #46 out of 283 metro areas in terms of house price appreciation in 2013 (#1 = highest rate). *Federal Housing Finance Agency, House Price Index, 4th Quarter 2013*

- The Austin metro area was identified as one of the 15 worst housing markets for the next five years." Criteria: projected annualized change in home prices between the fourth quarter 2012 and the fourth quarter 2017. *The Business Insider, "The 15 Worst Housing Markets for the Next Five Years," May 22, 2013*

- The Austin metro area was identified as one of the 10 worst condo markets in the U.S. in 2013. The area ranked #10 out of 64 markets with a price appreciation of -0.6%. Criteria: year-over-year change of median sales price of existing apartment condo-coop homes between the 4th quarter of 2012 and the 4th quarter of 2013. *National Association of Realtors®, Median Sales Price of Existing Apartment Condo-Coop Homes for Metropolitan Areas, 4th Quarter 2013*

- Austin was ranked #176 out of 224 metro areas in terms of housing affordability in 2013 by the National Association of Home Builders (#1 = most affordable). The NAHB-Wells Fargo Housing Opportunity Index (HOI) for a given area is defined as the share of homes sold in that area that would have been affordable to a family earning the local median income, based on standard mortgage underwriting criteria. *National Association of Home Builders®, NAHB-Wells Fargo Housing Opportunity Index, 4th Quarter 2013*

- Austin was selected as one of the best college towns for renters by ApartmentRatings.com." The area ranked #44 out of 87. Overall satisfaction ratings were ranked using thousands of user submitted scores for hundreds of apartment complexes located in cities and towns that are home to the 100 largest four-year institutions in the U.S. *ApartmentRatings.com, "2011 College Town Renter Satisfaction Rankings"*

- The nation's largest metro areas were analyzed in terms of the worst places to buy foreclosures in 2013. The Austin metro area ranked #17 out of 20. Criteria: RealtyTrac scored all metro areas with a population of 500,000 or more by summing up four numbers: months' supply of foreclosure inventory; percentage of foreclosure sales; foreclosure discount; percentage increase in foreclosure activity in 2012. *RealtyTrac, "2012 Year-End Metropolitan Foreclosure Market Report," January 28, 2013*

Safety Rankings

- Symantec, in partnership with Sperling's BestPlaces, ranked the 50 largest cities in the U.S. in terms of their vulnerability to cybercrime. The city ranked #10. Criteria: number of cyberattacks and potential infections; level of Internet access; expenditures on smartphones and computer hardware/software; wireless hotspots; broadband connectivity; Internet usage; online purchases. *Symantec, "Riskiest Online Cities of 2012" February 15, 2012*

- Farmers Insurance, in partnership with Sperling's BestPlaces, ranked metro areas in the U.S. and identified the "Most Secure Places to Live." The Austin metro area ranked #4 out of the top 20 in the large metro area category (500,000 or more residents). Criteria: economic stability; crime statistics; extreme weather; risk of natural disasters; housing depreciation; foreclosures; air quality; environmental hazards; life expectancy; motor vehicle fatalities; and employment numbers. *Farmers Insurance Group of Companies, "Most Secure U.S. Places to Live in the U.S.," June 25, 2013*

- Allstate ranked the 200 largest cities in America in terms of driver safety. Austin ranked #155. Allstate researchers analyzed internal property damage claims over a two-year period from January 2010 to December 2011. A weighted average of the two-year numbers determined the annual percentages. *Allstate, "Allstate America's Best Drivers Report®, August 27, 2013"*

- Austin was identified as one of the safest large cities in America by CQ Press. All 32 cities with populations of 500,000 or more that reported crime rates in 2012 for murder, rape, robbery, aggravated assault, burglary, and motor vehicle thefts were ranked. The city ranked #3 out of the top 10. *CQ Press, City Crime Rankings 2014*

- The National Insurance Crime Bureau ranked 380 metro areas in the U.S. in terms of per capita rates of vehicle theft. The Austin metro area ranked #134 (#1 = highest rate). Criteria: number of vehicle theft offenses per 100,000 inhabitants in 2012. *National Insurance Crime Bureau, "Hot Spots 2012," June 26, 2013*

- The Austin metro area was identified as one of the most dangerous metro areas for pedestrians by Transportation for America. The metro area ranked #18 out of 52 metro areas with over 1 million residents. Criteria: area's population divided by the number of pedestrian fatalities in that area. *Transportation for America, "Dangerous by Design 2011"*

Seniors/Retirement Rankings

- From its Best Cities for Successful Aging indexes, the Milken Institute generated rankings for metropolitan areas, weighing data in eight categories—general indicators, health care, wellness, living arrangements, transportation and general accessibility, financial well-being, education and employment, and community participation. The Austin metro area was ranked #41 overall in the large metro area category. *Milken Institute, "Best Cities for Successful Aging," July 2012*

- Austin made the 2014 *Forbes* list of "25 Best Places to Retire." Criteria include: housing and living costs; tax climate for retirees; weather and air quality; crime rates; doctor availability; active-lifestyle rankings for walkability, bicycling and volunteering. *Forbes.com, "The Best Places to Retire in 2014," January 16, 2014*

- Austin was chosen in the "Big City" category of CNNMoney's list of the 25 best places to retire." Criteria include: type of location (big city, small town, resort area, college town); median home prices; top state income tax rate. *CNNMoney, "25 Best Places to Retire," December 17, 2012*

- Bankers Life and Casualty Company, in partnership with Sperling's BestPlaces, ranked the nation's 50 largest metro areas in terms of the "Best U.S. Cities for Seniors." The Austin metro area ranked #24. Criteria: healthcare; transportation; housing; environment; economy; health and longevity; social and spiritual life; crime. *Bankers Life and Casualty Company, Center for a Secure Retirement, "Best U.S. Cities for Seniors 2011," September 2011*

- Austin was identified as one of the most popular places to retire by *Topretirements.com*. The list reflects the 100 cities (out of 900+ total cities reviewed) that visitors to the website are most interested in for retirement. *Topretirements.com, "Most Popular Places to Retire for 2014," February 25, 2014*

- Austin was selected as one of the best places to retire by *CNNMoney.com*. Criteria: low cost of living; low violent-crime rate; good medical care; large population over age 50; abundant amenities for retirees. *CNNMoney.com, "Best Places to Retire 2011"*

Sports/Recreation Rankings

- Austin appeared on the *Sporting News* list of the "Best Sports Cities" for 2011. The area ranked #76 out of 271. Criteria: the magazine takes a 12-month snapshot of each city's sports, putting a heavy premium on regular-season won-lost records (from the most recently completed season). Other criteria include: playoff berths, bowl appearances and tournament bids; championships; applicable power ratings; quality of competition; overall fan fervor (measured in part by attendance); abundance of teams (rewarding quality over quantity); stadium and arena quality; ticket availability and prices; franchise ownership; and marquee appeal of athletes. *Sporting News, "Best Sports Cities 2011," October 4, 2011*

- Austin appeared on the *Sporting News* list of the "Best Sports Cities" for 2011. The area ranked #76 out of 271. Criteria: a 12-month snapshot of regular-season won-lost records (from the most recently completed season). Other criteria include: playoff berths, bowl appearances and tournament bids; championships; applicable power ratings; quality of competition; overall fan fervor (measured in part by attendance); abundance of teams (quality over quantity); stadium and arena quality; ticket availability and prices; franchise ownership; and marquee appeal of athletes. *Sporting News, "Best Sports Cities 2011," October 4, 2011*

- Austin was chosen as a bicycle friendly community by the League of American Bicyclists. A "Bicycle Friendly Community" welcomes cyclists by providing safe accommodation for cycling and encouraging people to bike for transportation and recreation. There are four award levels: Platinum; Gold; Silver; and Bronze. The community achieved an award level of Silver. *League of American Bicyclists, "Bicycle Friendly Community Master List," Fall 2013*

- Austin was selected as one of the most playful cities in the U.S. by KaBOOM! The organization's Playful City USA initiative honors cities and towns across the nation for a vision, plan and commitment to creating an agenda for play. Criteria: creating a local play commission or task force; designing an annual action plan for play; conducting a play space audit; outlining a financial investment in play for the current fiscal year; and proclaiming and celebrating an annual "play day." *KaBOOM! National Campaign for Play, "2013 Playful City USA Communities"*

- Austin was chosen as one of America's best cities for bicycling. The city ranked #13 out of 50. Criteria: robust cycling infrastructure; vibrant bike culture. The editors only considered cities with populations of 95,000 or more. *Bicycling, "America's Top 50 Bike-Friendly Cities," May 23, 2012*

Transportation Rankings

- Austin appeared on *Trapster.com's* list of the 10 most-active U.S. cities for speed traps. The city ranked #10 of 10. *Trapster.com* is a community platform accessed online and via smartphone app that alerts drivers to traps, hazards and other traffic issues nearby. *Trapster.com, "Speeders Beware: Cities With the Most Speed Traps," February 10, 2012*

- Austin was identified as one of America's "10 Best Cities for Public Transportation" by *U.S. News & World Report*. The city ranked #9. The ten cities selected had the best combination of public transportation investment, ridership, and safety. *U.S. News & World Report, "10 Best Cities for Public Transportation," February 8, 2011*

- Austin was identified as one of America's worst cities for speed traps by the National Motorists Association. The city ranked #9 out of 25. Criteria: speed trap locations per 100,000 residents. *National Motorists Association, September 2011*

Women/Minorities Rankings

- To determine the best metro areas for working women, the personal finance website NerdWallet considered city size as well as relevant economic metrics—high salaries, narrow pay differential by gender, prevalence of women in the highest-paying industries, and population growth over 2010–2012. Of the large U.S. cities examined, the Austin metro area held the #4 position. *www.nerdwallet.com, "Best Places for Women in the Workforce," May 19, 2013*

- *Women's Health* examined U.S. cities and identified the 100 best cities for women. Austin was ranked #9. Criteria: 30 categories were examined from obesity and breast cancer rates to commuting times and hours spent working out. *Women's Health, "Best Cities for Women 2012"*

- Austin was selected as one of the 25 healthiest cities for Latinas by *Latina Magazine*. The city ranked #2. Criteria: U.S. cities with populations over 500,000 residents were evaluated on the following criteria: percentage of 18-34 year-olds per city; Latino college graduation rates; number of colleges and universities; affordability; housing costs; income growth over time; average salary; percentage of singles; climate; safety; how the city's diversity compares to the national average; opportunities for minority entrepreneurs. *Latina Magazine, "Top 15 U.S. Cities for Young Latinos to Live In," August 19, 2011*

- Austin was selected as one of the best cities for young Latinos in 2013 by mun2, a national cable television broadcast network. The city ranked #2. Criteria: U.S. cities with populations over 500,000 residents were evaluated on the following criteria: number of young latinos; jobs; friendliness; cost of living; fun. *mun2.tv, "Best Cities for Young Latinos 2013*

- The Austin metro area appeared on *Forbes'* list of the "Best Cities for Minority Entrepreneurs." The area ranked #2 out of 10. Criteria: 52 metropolitan statistical areas were examined. For each ethnicity (African Americans, Asians and Hispanics), the editors measured housing affordability, population growth, income growth, and entrepreneurship (per capita self-employment). *Forbes, "Best Cities for Minority Entrepreneurs," March 23, 2011*

Miscellaneous Rankings

- Austin was selected as a 2013 Digital Cities Survey winner. The city ranked #6 in the large city (250,000 or more population) category. The survey examined and assessed how city governments are utilizing information technology to operate and deliver quality service to their customers and citizens. Survey questions focused on implementation and adoption of online service delivery; planning and governance; and the infrastructure and architecture that make the transformation to digital government possible. *Center for Digital Government, "2013 Digital Cities Survey," November 7, 2013*

- *Travel + Leisure* invited readers to rate cities on indicators such as aloofness, "smarty-pants residents," highbrow cultural offerings, high-end shopping, artisanal coffeehouses, conspicuous eco-consciousness, and more in order to identify the nation's snobbiest cities. Cities large and small made the list; among them was Austin, at #19. *www.travelandleisure.com, "America's Snobbiest Cities, June 2013*

- In *Condé Nast Traveler* magazine's 2013 Readers' Choice Survey, Austin made the top ten list of friendliest American cities, at #5. *www.cntraveler.com, "The Friendliest and Unfriendliest Cities in the U.S.," July 30, 2013*

- Ink Army reported on a survey by the website TotalBeauty calculating the number of tattoo shops per 100,000 residents in order to determine the U.S. cities with the most tattoo acceptance. Austin took the #6 slot. *inkarmy.com, "Most Tattoo Friendly Cities in the United States," November 1, 2013*

- Market analyst Scarborough Research surveyed adults who had done volunteer work over the previous 12 months to find out where volunteers are concentrated. The Austin metro area made the list for highest volunteer participation. *Scarborough Research, "Salt Lake City, UT; Minneapolis, MN; and Des Moines, IA Lend a Helping Hand," November 27, 2012*

- Austin was selected as one of the 10 best run cities in America by *24/7 Wall St.* The city ranked #8. Criteria: the 100 largest cities in the U.S. were ranked in terms of economy, job market, crime, and the welfare of its residents. *24/7 Wall St., "The Best and Worst Run Cities in America," January 15, 2013*

- *Men's Health* ranked 100 U.S. cities by their level of sadness. Austin was ranked #19 (#1 = saddest city). Criteria: suicide rates; unemployment rates; percentage of households that use antidepressants; percent of population who report feeling blue all or most of the time. *Men's Health, "Frown Towns," November 28, 2011*

- The Austin metro area was selected as one of "The Best U.S. Cities for Bargain Shopping" by *Forbes.* The area ranked #2 out of 10. Criteria: number of outlet stores; gross leasable retail space in major malls; low consumer price index; low sales tax rate. Indicators were examined in the nation's 50 largest metropolitan areas. *Forbes, "The Best U.S. Cities for Bargain Shopping," January 20, 2012*

- Austin was selected as one of the most tattooed cities in America by *Lovelyish.com.* The city was ranked #6. Criteria: number of tattoo shops per capita. *Lovelyish.com, "Top Ten: Most Tattooed Cities in America," October 17, 2012*

- The National Alliance to End Homelessness ranked the 100 most populous metro areas in terms the rate of homelessness. The Austin metro area ranked #57. Criteria: number of homeless people per 10,000 population in 2011. *National Alliance to End Homelessness, The State of Homelessness in America 2012*

Business Environment

CITY FINANCES

City Government Finances

Component	2011 ($000)	2011 ($ per capita)
Total Revenues	3,104,313	4,178
Total Expenditures	3,102,200	4,175
Debt Outstanding	5,446,752	7,330
Cash and Securities[1]	4,657,143	6,267

Note: (1) Cash and security holdings of a government at the close of its fiscal year, including those of its dependent agencies, utilities, and liquor stores.
Source: U.S Census Bureau, State & Local Government Finances 2011

City Government Revenue by Source

Source	2011 ($000)	2011 ($ per capita)
General Revenue		
From Federal Government	61,319	83
From State Government	27,199	37
From Local Governments	12,673	17
Taxes		
Property	340,804	459
Sales and Gross Receipts	226,982	305
Personal Income	0	0
Corporate Income	0	0
Motor Vehicle License	0	0
Other Taxes	15,716	21
Current Charges	552,564	744
Liquor Store	0	0
Utility	1,326,919	1,786
Employee Retirement	426,705	574

Source: U.S Census Bureau, State & Local Government Finances 2011

City Government Expenditures by Function

Function	2011 ($000)	2011 ($ per capita)	2011 (%)
General Direct Expenditures			
Air Transportation	74,728	101	2.4
Corrections	0	0	0.0
Education	0	0	0.0
Employment Security Administration	0	0	0.0
Financial Administration	27,961	38	0.9
Fire Protection	122,795	165	4.0
General Public Buildings	0	0	0.0
Governmental Administration, Other	27,676	37	0.9
Health	98,653	133	3.2
Highways	109,858	148	3.5
Hospitals	0	0	0.0
Housing and Community Development	56,169	76	1.8
Interest on General Debt	90,551	122	2.9
Judicial and Legal	26,837	36	0.9
Libraries	25,913	35	0.8
Parking	67	< 1	< 0.1
Parks and Recreation	116,101	156	3.7
Police Protection	259,782	350	8.4
Public Welfare	0	0	0.0
Sewerage	170,183	229	5.5
Solid Waste Management	66,688	90	2.1
Veterans' Services	0	0	0.0
Liquor Store	0	0	0.0
Utility	1,467,371	1,975	47.3
Employee Retirement	181,261	244	5.8

Source: U.S Census Bureau, State & Local Government Finances 2011

DEMOGRAPHICS

Population Growth

Area	1990 Census	2000 Census	2010 Census	Population Growth (%) 1990-2000	2000-2010
City	499,053	656,562	790,390	31.6	20.4
MSA[1]	846,217	1,249,763	1,716,289	47.7	37.3
U.S.	248,709,873	281,421,906	308,745,538	13.2	9.7

Note: (1) Figures cover the Austin-Round Rock, TX Metropolitan Statistical Area—see Appendix B for areas included
Source: U.S. Census Bureau, Census 1990, 2000, 2010

Household Size

Area	Persons in Household (%) One	Two	Three	Four	Five	Six	Seven or More	Average Household Size
City	34.0	32.4	14.9	11.0	4.8	1.6	1.3	2.44
MSA[1]	27.7	32.8	15.7	13.8	6.2	2.3	1.5	2.65
U.S.	27.6	33.5	15.7	13.2	6.1	2.4	1.5	2.63

Note: (1) Figures cover the Austin-Round Rock, TX Metropolitan Statistical Area—see Appendix B for areas included
Source: U.S. Census Bureau, 2010-2012 American Community Survey 3-Year Estimates

Race

Area	White Alone[2] (%)	Black Alone[2] (%)	Asian Alone[2] (%)	AIAN[3] Alone[2] (%)	NHOPI[4] Alone[2] (%)	Other Race Alone[2] (%)	Two or More Races (%)
City	72.7	7.9	6.4	0.6	0.1	9.3	2.9
MSA[1]	77.3	7.4	4.9	0.5	0.1	7.2	2.7
U.S.	74.0	12.6	4.9	0.8	0.2	4.7	2.8

Note: (1) Figures cover the Austin-Round Rock, TX Metropolitan Statistical Area—see Appendix B for areas included; (2) Alone is defined as not being in combination with one or more other races; (3) American Indian and Alaska Native; (4) Native Hawaiian and Other Pacific Islander
Source: U.S. Census Bureau, 2010-2012 American Community Survey 3-Year Estimates

Hispanic or Latino Origin

Area	Total (%)	Mexican (%)	Puerto Rican (%)	Cuban (%)	Other (%)
City	35.0	29.9	0.5	0.5	4.1
MSA[1]	31.7	26.5	0.5	0.4	4.3
U.S.	16.6	10.7	1.6	0.6	3.7

Note: Persons of Hispanic or Latino origin can be of any race; (1) Figures cover the Austin-Round Rock, TX Metropolitan Statistical Area—see Appendix B for areas included
Source: U.S. Census Bureau, 2010-2012 American Community Survey 3-Year Estimates

Segregation

Type	Segregation Indices[1] 1990	2000	2010	2010 Rank[2]	Percent Change 1990-2000	1990-2010	2000-2010
Black/White	54.1	52.1	50.1	70	-1.9	-4.0	-2.1
Asian/White	39.4	42.3	41.2	49	2.9	1.8	-1.2
Hispanic/White	41.7	45.6	43.2	51	3.9	1.5	-2.4

Note: All figures cover the Metropolitan Statistical Area—see Appendix B for areas included; Figures are based on an analysis of 1990, 2000, and 2010 Census Decennial Census tract data by William H. Frey, Brookings Institution and the University of Michigan Social Science Data Analysis Network. In this analysis all racial groups (whites, blacks, and asians) are non-Hispanic members of those races. Hispanics are shown as a separate category;
(1) Segregation Indices are Dissimilarity Indices that measure the degree to which the minority group is distributed differently than whites across census tracts. They range from 0 (complete integration) to 100 (complete segregation) where the value indicates the percentage of the minority group that needs to move to be distributed exactly like whites; (2) Ranges from 1 (most segregated) to 102 (least segregated); n/a not available.
Source: www.CensusScope.org

Ancestry

Area	German	Irish	English	American	Italian	Polish	French[2]	Scottish	Dutch
City	12.6	8.6	8.4	4.0	2.9	1.5	3.1	2.3	0.9
MSA[1]	15.0	9.1	9.0	4.7	2.9	1.6	2.8	2.2	1.0
U.S.	15.2	11.1	8.2	7.2	5.6	3.1	2.8	1.7	1.4

Note: Figures are the percentage of the total population reporting a particular ancestry. The nine most commonly reported ancestries in the U.S. are shown. Figures include multiple ancestries (e.g. if a person reported being Irish and Italian, they were included in both columns); (1) Figures cover the Austin-Round Rock, TX Metropolitan Statistical Area—see Appendix B for areas included; (2) Excludes Basque
Source: U.S. Census Bureau, 2010-2012 American Community Survey 3-Year Estimates

Foreign-Born Population

Area	Percent of Population Born in								
	Any Foreign Country	Mexico	Asia	Europe	Carribean	South America	Central America[2]	Africa	Canada
City	18.5	9.6	4.7	1.2	0.4	0.4	1.5	0.4	0.2
MSA[1]	14.6	7.5	3.6	1.1	0.3	0.4	1.0	0.4	0.3
U.S.	13.0	3.7	3.7	1.6	1.2	0.9	1.0	0.5	0.3

Note: (1) Figures cover the Austin-Round Rock, TX Metropolitan Statistical Area—see Appendix B for areas included; (2) Excludes Mexico.
Source: U.S. Census Bureau, 2010-2012 American Community Survey 3-Year Estimates

Marital Status

Area	Never Married	Now Married[2]	Separated	Widowed	Divorced
City	43.8	39.1	2.3	3.4	11.5
MSA[1]	35.8	47.7	2.0	3.6	11.0
U.S.	32.4	48.4	2.2	6.0	11.0

Note: Figures are percentages and cover the population 15 years of age and older; (1) Figures cover the Austin-Round Rock, TX Metropolitan Statistical Area—see Appendix B for areas included; (2) Excludes separated
Source: U.S. Census Bureau, 2010-2012 American Community Survey 3-Year Estimates

Age

Area	Percent of Population									Median Age
	Under Age 5	Age 5–19	Age 20–34	Age 35–44	Age 45–54	Age 55–64	Age 65–74	Age 75–84	Age 85+	
City	7.1	18.3	31.4	15.1	11.9	9.0	4.0	2.2	1.0	31.4
MSA[1]	7.3	20.8	25.3	15.2	13.1	10.0	5.0	2.5	1.0	32.9
U.S.	6.4	20.1	20.5	13.1	14.3	12.2	7.3	4.2	1.8	37.3

Note: (1) Figures cover the Austin-Round Rock, TX Metropolitan Statistical Area—see Appendix B for areas included
Source: U.S. Census Bureau, 2010-2012 American Community Survey 3-Year Estimates

Gender

Area	Males	Females	Males per 100 Females
City	413,718	404,518	102.3
MSA[1]	892,059	888,831	100.4
U.S.	153,276,055	158,333,314	96.8

Note: (1) Figures cover the Austin-Round Rock, TX Metropolitan Statistical Area—see Appendix B for areas included
Source: U.S. Census Bureau, 2010-2012 American Community Survey 3-Year Estimates

Religious Groups by Family

Area	Catholic	Baptist	Non-Den.	Methodist[2]	Lutheran	LDS[3]	Pentecostal	Presbyterian[4]	Muslim[5]	Judaism
MSA[1]	16.0	10.3	4.5	3.6	2.0	1.2	0.8	1.1	1.2	0.3
U.S.	19.1	9.3	4.0	4.0	2.3	2.0	1.9	1.6	0.8	0.7

Note: Figures are the number of adherents as a percentage of the total population; (1) Figures cover the Austin-Round Rock, TX Metropolitan Statistical Area—see Appendix B for areas included; (2) Methodist/Pietist; (3) Latter Day Saints; (4) Reformed; (5) Figures are estimates
Source: Association of Statisticians of American Religious Bodies, 2010 U.S. Religion Census: Religious Congregations & Membership Study

Religious Groups by Tradition

Area	Catholic	Evangelical Protestant	Mainline Protestant	Other Tradition	Black Protestant	Orthodox
MSA[1]	16.0	16.1	6.3	3.9	1.4	0.1
U.S.	19.1	16.2	7.3	4.3	1.6	0.3

Note: Figures are the number of adherents as a percentage of the total population; (1) Figures cover the Austin-Round Rock, TX Metropolitan Statistical Area—see Appendix B for areas included
Source: Association of Statisticians of American Religious Bodies, 2010 U.S. Religion Census: Religious Congregations & Membership Study

ECONOMY

Gross Metropolitan Product

Area	2011	2012	2013	2014	Rank[2]
MSA[1]	91.5	98.7	103.2	109.3	31

Note: Figures are in billions of dollars; (1) Figures cover the Austin-Round Rock, TX Metropolitan Statistical Area—see Appendix B for areas included; (2) Rank is based on 2014 data and ranges from 1 to 363
Source: The United States Conference of Mayors, U.S. Metro Economies: Outlook—Gross Metropolitan Product, with Metro Employment Projections, November 2013

Economic Growth

Area	2011 (%)	2012 (%)	2013 (%)	2014 (%)	Rank[2]
MSA[1]	3.6	6.5	3.4	4.0	12
U.S.	1.6	2.5	1.7	2.5	–

Note: Figures are real gross metropolitan product (GMP) growth rates and represent annual average percent change; (1) Figures cover the Austin-Round Rock, TX Metropolitan Statistical Area—see Appendix B for areas included; (2) Rank is based on 2013 data and ranges from 1 to 363
Source: The United States Conference of Mayors, U.S. Metro Economies: Outlook—Gross Metropolitan Product, with Metro Employment Projections, November 2013

Metropolitan Area Exports

Area	2007	2008	2009	2010	2011	2012	Rank[2]
MSA[1]	8,428.6	7,405.5	5,963.7	8,867.8	8,626.3	8,976.6	35

Note: Figures are in millions of dollars; (1) Figures cover the Austin-Round Rock, TX Metropolitan Statistical Area—see Appendix B for areas included; (2) Rank is based on 2012 data and ranges from 1 to 369
Source: U.S. Department of Commerce, International Trade Administration, Office of Trade & Industry Information, Manufacturing & Services, data extracted April 1, 2014

INCOME

Income

Area	Per Capita ($)	Median Household ($)	Average Household ($)
City	30,880	51,668	74,860
MSA[1]	30,365	58,821	79,799
U.S.	27,385	51,771	71,579

Note: (1) Figures cover the Austin-Round Rock, TX Metropolitan Statistical Area—see Appendix B for areas included
Source: U.S. Census Bureau, 2010-2012 American Community Survey 3-Year Estimates

Household Income Distribution

| Area | Percent of Households Earning | | | | | | | |
	Under $15,000	$15,000 -24,999	$25,000 -34,999	$35,000 -49,999	$50,000 -74,999	$75,000 -99,000	$100,000 -149,999	$150,000 and up
City	13.4	10.0	10.5	14.8	17.2	11.3	12.3	10.5
MSA[1]	10.9	8.9	9.4	13.8	18.2	12.8	14.6	11.4
U.S.	13.1	11.0	10.5	13.7	18.1	11.9	12.5	9.1

Note: (1) Figures cover the Austin-Round Rock, TX Metropolitan Statistical Area—see Appendix B for areas included
Source: U.S. Census Bureau, 2010-2012 American Community Survey 3-Year Estimates

Poverty Rate

Area	All Ages	Under 18 Years Old	18 to 64 Years Old	65 Years and Over
City	20.1	28.4	18.6	9.3
MSA[1]	15.4	20.1	14.7	6.8
U.S.	15.7	22.2	14.6	9.3

Note: Figures are percentage of people whose income during the past 12 months was below the poverty level;
(1) Figures cover the Austin-Round Rock, TX Metropolitan Statistical Area—see Appendix B for areas included
Source: U.S. Census Bureau, 2010-2012 American Community Survey 3-Year Estimates

Personal Bankruptcy Filing Rate

Area	2008	2009	2010	2011	2012	2013
Travis County	1.35	1.81	1.86	1.52	1.37	1.08
U.S.	3.53	4.61	4.97	4.37	3.76	3.29

Note: Numbers are per 1,000 population and include Chapter 7 and Chapter 13 filings
Source: Federal Deposit Insurance Corporation, Regional Economic Conditions, March 20, 2014

EMPLOYMENT

Labor Force and Employment

| Area | Civilian Labor Force | | | Workers Employed | | |
	Dec. 2012	Dec. 2013	% Chg.	Dec. 2012	Dec. 2013	% Chg.
City	464,387	475,873	2.5	442,621	455,863	3.0
MSA[1]	972,339	996,173	2.5	923,238	950,857	3.0
U.S.	154,904,000	154,408,000	-0.3	143,060,000	144,423,000	1.0

Note: Data is not seasonally adjusted and covers workers 16 years of age and older; (1) Metropolitan Statistical Area—see Appendix B for areas included
Source: Bureau of Labor Statistics, Local Area Unemployment Statistics

Unemployment Rate

| Area | 2013 | | | | | | | | | | | |
	Jan.	Feb.	Mar.	Apr.	May	Jun.	Jul.	Aug.	Sep.	Oct.	Nov.	Dec.
City	5.5	5.0	4.9	4.7	5.0	5.4	5.2	4.8	5.0	4.8	4.4	4.2
MSA[1]	5.8	5.4	5.3	5.1	5.4	5.8	5.6	5.2	5.3	5.1	4.7	4.5
U.S.	8.5	8.1	7.6	7.1	7.3	7.8	7.7	7.3	7.0	7.0	6.6	6.5

Note: Data is not seasonally adjusted and covers workers 16 years of age and older; All figures are percentages;
(1) Metropolitan Statistical Area—see Appendix B for areas included
Source: Bureau of Labor Statistics, Local Area Unemployment Statistics

Employment by Occupation

Occupation Classification	City (%)	MSA[1] (%)	U.S. (%)
Management, Business, Science, and Arts	45.0	43.4	36.0
Natural Resources, Construction, and Maintenance	8.1	8.7	9.1
Production, Transportation, and Material Moving	5.8	7.1	12.0
Sales and Office	22.8	24.3	24.7
Service	18.2	16.5	18.2

Note: Figures cover employed civilians 16 years of age and older; (1) Figures cover the Austin-Round Rock, TX Metropolitan Statistical Area—see Appendix B for areas included
Source: U.S. Census Bureau, 2010-2012 American Community Survey 3-Year Estimates

Employment by Industry

| Sector | MSA[1] | | U.S. |
	Number of Employees	Percent of Total	Percent of Total
Construction	n/a	n/a	4.2
Education and Health Services	100,700	11.4	15.5
Financial Activities	49,700	5.6	5.7
Government	169,900	19.2	16.1
Information	23,800	2.7	1.9
Leisure and Hospitality	104,800	11.8	10.2
Manufacturing	53,000	6.0	8.7
Mining and Logging	n/a	n/a	0.6
Other Services	38,000	4.3	3.9
Professional and Business Services	139,300	15.7	13.7
Retail Trade	99,500	11.2	11.4
Transportation and Utilities	15,000	1.7	3.8
Wholesale Trade	45,600	5.2	4.2

Note: Figures cover non-farm employment as of December 2013 and are not seasonally adjusted;
(1) Metropolitan Statistical Area—see Appendix B for areas included; n/a not available
Source: Bureau of Labor Statistics, Current Employment Statistics, Employment, Hours, and Earnings

Occupations with Greatest Projected Employment Growth: 2010 – 2020

Occupation[1]	2010 Employment	2020 Projected Employment	Numeric Employment Change	Percent Employment Change
Combined Food Preparation and Serving Workers, Including Fast Food	243,530	322,520	78,990	32.4
Elementary School Teachers, Except Special Education	166,090	233,860	67,780	40.8
Personal Care Aides	133,820	199,970	66,150	49.4
Retail Salespersons	370,620	433,180	62,560	16.9
Registered Nurses	184,700	245,870	61,160	33.1
Waiters and Waitresses	190,870	244,610	53,730	28.2
Office Clerks, General	262,740	314,810	52,070	19.8
Cashiers	250,510	292,730	42,220	16.9
Home Health Aides	82,420	123,970	41,550	50.4
Customer Service Representatives	200,880	241,030	40,160	20.0

Note: Projections cover Texas; (1) Sorted by numeric employment change
Source: www.projectionscentral.com, State Occupational Projections, 2010–2020 Long-Term Projections

Fastest Growing Occupations: 2010 – 2020

Occupation[1]	2010 Employment	2020 Projected Employment	Numeric Employment Change	Percent Employment Change
Biomedical Engineers	1,440	2,490	1,050	72.9
Diagnostic Medical Sonographers	3,560	5,410	1,850	51.9
Derrick Operators, Oil and Gas	7,190	10,860	3,670	51.1
Home Health Aides	82,420	123,970	41,550	50.4
Personal Care Aides	133,820	199,970	66,150	49.4
Service Unit Operators, Oil, Gas, and Mining	17,870	26,460	8,590	48.0
Special Education Teachers, Middle School	6,170	8,950	2,780	45.1
Special Education Teachers, Preschool, Kindergarten, and Elementary School	12,940	18,750	5,810	44.9
Rotary Drill Operators, Oil and Gas	7,160	10,340	3,180	44.4
Roustabouts, Oil and Gas	17,800	25,580	7,790	43.8

Note: Projections cover Texas; (1) Sorted by percent employment change and excludes occupations with numeric employment change less than 100
Source: www.projectionscentral.com, State Occupational Projections, 2010–2020 Long-Term Projections

Average Wages

Occupation	$/Hr.	Occupation	$/Hr.
Accountants and Auditors	32.18	Maids and Housekeeping Cleaners	9.40
Automotive Mechanics	19.17	Maintenance and Repair Workers	17.03
Bookkeepers	18.54	Marketing Managers	67.44
Carpenters	17.33	Nuclear Medicine Technologists	32.88
Cashiers	10.12	Nurses, Licensed Practical	22.05
Clerks, General Office	15.40	Nurses, Registered	30.98
Clerks, Receptionists/Information	12.42	Nursing Assistants	11.67
Clerks, Shipping/Receiving	13.46	Packers and Packagers, Hand	11.34
Computer Programmers	41.66	Physical Therapists	41.88
Computer Systems Analysts	39.12	Postal Service Mail Carriers	25.00
Computer User Support Specialists	23.74	Real Estate Brokers	30.32
Cooks, Restaurant	11.05	Retail Salespersons	12.53
Dentists	99.44	Sales Reps., Exc. Tech./Scientific	29.84
Electrical Engineers	47.89	Sales Reps., Tech./Scientific	37.48
Electricians	22.17	Secretaries, Exc. Legal/Med./Exec.	15.77
Financial Managers	65.02	Security Guards	12.42
First-Line Supervisors/Managers, Sales	20.04	Surgeons	n/a
Food Preparation Workers	10.21	Teacher Assistants	10.60
General and Operations Managers	57.84	Teachers, Elementary School	22.70
Hairdressers/Cosmetologists	12.37	Teachers, Secondary School	23.50
Internists	119.07	Telemarketers	13.90
Janitors and Cleaners	10.43	Truck Drivers, Heavy/Tractor-Trailer	18.67
Landscaping/Groundskeeping Workers	12.05	Truck Drivers, Light/Delivery Svcs.	16.53
Lawyers	59.97	Waiters and Waitresses	9.34

Note: Wage data covers the Austin-Round Rock-San Marcos, TX Metropolitan Statistical Area—see Appendix B for areas included. Hourly wages for elementary/secondary school teachers and teacher assistants were calculated by the editors from annual wage data assuming a 40 hour work week; n/a not available.
Source: Bureau of Labor Statistics, Metro Area Occupational Employment and Wage Estimates, May 2013

RESIDENTIAL REAL ESTATE

Building Permits

Area	Single-Family			Multi-Family			Total		
	2012	2013	Pct. Chg.	2012	2013	Pct. Chg.	2012	2013	Pct. Chg.
City	2,539	2,573	1.3	7,671	9,261	20.7	10,210	11,834	15.9
MSA[1]	8,229	8,941	8.7	11,334	11,911	5.1	19,563	20,852	6.6
U.S.	518,695	620,802	19.7	310,963	370,020	19.0	829,658	990,822	19.4

Note: (1) Metropolitan Statistical Area—see Appendix B for areas included; figures represent new, privately-owned housing units authorized (unadjusted data); All permit data are based on estimates with imputation.
Source: U.S. Census Bureau, Manufacturing, Mining, and Construction Statistics, Building Permits, 2012, 2013

Homeownership Rate

Area	2006 (%)	2007 (%)	2008 (%)	2009 (%)	2010 (%)	2011 (%)	2012 (%)	2013 (%)
MSA[1]	66.7	66.4	65.5	64.0	65.8	58.4	60.1	59.6
U.S.	68.8	68.1	67.8	67.4	66.9	66.1	65.4	65.1

Note: (1) Figures cover the Austin-Round Rock, TX Metropolitan Statistical Area—see Appendix B for areas included
Source: U.S. Census Bureau, Housing Vacancies and Homeownership Annual Statistics: 2013

Housing Vacancy Rates

Area	Gross Vacancy Rate[2] (%)			Year-Round Vacancy Rate[3] (%)			Rental Vacancy Rate[4] (%)			Homeowner Vacancy Rate[5] (%)		
	2011	2012	2013	2011	2012	2013	2011	2012	2013	2011	2012	2013
MSA[1]	12.6	12.7	12.5	11.7	11.9	11.9	6.4	9.6	12.1	0.6	1.3	1.1
U.S.	14.2	13.8	13.8	11.1	10.8	10.7	9.5	8.7	8.3	2.5	2.0	2.0

Note: (1) Figures cover the Austin-Round Rock, TX Metropolitan Statistical Area—see Appendix B for areas included; (2) The percentage of the total housing inventory that is vacant; (3) The percentage of the housing inventory (excluding seasonal units) that is year-round vacant; (4) The percentage of rental inventory that is vacant for rent; (5) The percentage of homeowner inventory that is vacant for sale
Source: U.S. Census Bureau, Housing Vacancies and Homeownership Annual Statistics: 2013

TAXES

State Corporate Income Tax Rates

State	Tax Rate (%)	Income Brackets ($)	Num. of Brackets	Financial Institution Tax Rate (%)[a]	Federal Income Tax Ded.
Texas	(x)	–	–	(x)	No

Note: Tax rates as of January 1, 2014; (a) Rates listed are the corporate income tax rate applied to financial institutions or excise taxes based on income. Some states have other taxes based upon the value of deposits or shares; (x) Texas imposes a Franchise Tax, otherwise known as margin tax, imposed on entities with more than $1,030,000 total revenues at rate of 1%, or 0.5% for entities primarily engaged in retail or wholesale trade, on lesser of 70% of total revenues or 100%of gross receipts after deductions for either compensation or cost of goods sold.
Source: Federation of Tax Administrators, "State Corporate Income Tax Rates, 2014"

State Individual Income Tax Rates

State	Tax Rate (%)	Income Brackets ($)	Num. of Brackets	Personal Exempt. ($)[1] Single	Dependents	Fed. Inc. Tax Ded.
Texas	None	–	–	–	–	–

Note: Tax rates as of January 1, 2014; Local- and county-level taxes are not included; n/a not applicable; (1) Married joint filers generally receive double the single exemption
Source: Federation of Tax Administrators, "State Individual Income Tax Rates, 2014"

Various State and Local Tax Rates

State	State and Local Sales and Use (%)	State Sales and Use (%)	Gasoline[1] (¢/gal.)	Cigarette[2] ($/pack)	Spirits[3] ($/gal.)	Wine[4] ($/gal.)	Beer[5] ($/gal.)
Texas	8.25	6.25	20.00	1.410	2.40 (f)	0.20	0.20

Note: All tax rates as of January 1, 2014; (1) The American Petroleum Institute has developed a methodology for determining the average tax rate on a gallon of fuel. Rates may include any of the following: excise taxes, environmental fees, storage tank fees, other fees or taxes, general sales tax, and local taxes. In states where gasoline is subject to the general sales tax, or where the fuel tax is based on the average sale price, the average rate determined by API is sensitive to changes in the price of gasoline. States that fully or partially apply general sales taxes to gasoline: CA, CO, GA, IL, IN, MI, NY; (2) The federal excise tax of $1.0066 per pack and local taxes are not included; (3) Rates are those applicable to off-premise sales of 40% alcohol by volume (a.b.v.) distilled spirits in 750ml containers. Local excise taxes are excluded; (4) Rates are those applicable to off-premise sales of 11% a.b.v. non-carbonated wine in 750ml containers; (5) Rates are those applicable to off-premise sales of 4.7% a.b.v. beer in 12 ounce containers; (f) Different rates also applicable according to alcohol content, place of production, size of container, or place purchased (on- or off-premise or onboard airlines).
Source: Tax Foundation, 2014 Facts & Figures: How Does Your State Compare?

State Business Tax Climate Index Rankings

State	Overall Rank	Corporate Tax Index Rank	Individual Income Tax Index Rank	Sales Tax Index Rank	Unemployment Insurance Tax Index Rank	Property Tax Index Rank
Texas	11	38	7	36	14	35

Note: The index is a measure of how each state's tax laws affect economic performance. The lower the rank, the more favorable a state's tax system is for business. States without a given tax are given a ranking of 1. The scores/rankings for the District of Columbia do not affect other states. The 2014 index represents the tax climate as of July 1, 2013.
Source: Tax Foundation, State Business Tax Climate Index 2014

COMMERCIAL REAL ESTATE

Office Market

Market Area	Inventory (sq. ft.)	Vacancy Rate (%)	Under Construction (sq. ft.)	YTD Net Absorption (sq. ft.)	Total Average Asking Rent ($/sq. ft./year)
Austin	58,248,104	12.3	1,624,732	806,416	28.87
National	4,726,900,879	15.0	55,419,286	42,829,434	26.27

Source: Newmark Grubb Knight Frank, National Office Market Report, 4th Quarter 2013

Industrial/Warehouse/R&D Market

Market Area	Inventory (sq. ft.)	Vacancy Rate (%)	Under Construction (sq. ft.)	YTD Net Absorption (sq. ft.)	Total Average Asking Rent ($/sq. ft./year)
Austin	82,622,137	8.1	416,964	1,027,217	7.20
National	14,022,031,238	7.9	83,249,164	156,549,903	5.40

Source: Newmark Grubb Knight Frank, National Industrial Market Report, 4th Quarter 2013

COMMERCIAL UTILITIES

Typical Monthly Electric Bills

Area	Commercial Service ($/month)		Industrial Service ($/month)	
	40 kW demand 5,000 kWh	500 kW demand 100,000 kWh	5,000 kW demand 1,500,000 kWh	70,000 kW demand 50,000,000 kWh
City	798	12,500	150,585	3,136,200

Note: Based on rates in effect January 2, 2013
Source: Memphis Light, Gas and Water, 2013 Utility Bill Comparisons for Selected U.S. Cities

TRANSPORTATION

Means of Transportation to Work

Area	Car/Truck/Van		Public Transportation			Bicycle	Walked	Other Means	Worked at Home
	Drove Alone	Car-pooled	Bus	Subway	Railroad				
City	72.4	10.6	4.1	0.0	0.1	1.5	2.8	1.9	6.6
MSA[1]	75.4	10.9	2.2	0.0	0.1	0.8	2.0	1.6	7.0
U.S.	76.4	9.7	2.6	1.7	0.5	0.6	2.8	1.3	4.3

Note: Figures are percentages and cover workers 16 years of age and older; (1) Figures cover the Austin-Round Rock, TX Metropolitan Statistical Area—see Appendix B for areas included
Source: U.S. Census Bureau, 2010-2012 American Community Survey 3-Year Estimates

Travel Time to Work

Area	Less Than 10 Minutes	10 to 19 Minutes	20 to 29 Minutes	30 to 44 Minutes	45 to 59 Minutes	60 to 89 Minutes	90 Minutes or More
City	11.5	34.6	24.1	20.6	4.5	3.2	1.6
MSA[1]	11.3	29.2	22.3	22.9	7.8	4.7	1.8
U.S.	13.5	29.8	20.9	20.1	7.5	5.6	2.5

Note: Figures are percentages and include workers 16 years old and over; (1) Figures cover the Austin-Round Rock, TX Metropolitan Statistical Area—see Appendix B for areas included
Source: U.S. Census Bureau, 2010-2012 American Community Survey 3-Year Estimates

Travel Time Index

Area	1985	1990	1995	2000	2005	2010	2011
Urban Area[1]	1.12	1.16	1.22	1.26	1.35	1.31	1.32
Average[2]	1.09	1.14	1.16	1.19	1.23	1.18	1.18

Note: Travel Time Index—the ratio of travel time in the peak period to the travel time at free-flow conditions. For example, a value of 1.30 indicates a 20-minute free-flow trip takes 26 minutes in the peak. Free-flow speeds (60 mph on freeways and 35 mph on principal arterials) are used as the comparison threshold; (1) Covers the Austin TX urban area; (2) average of 498 urban areas
Source: Texas Transportation Institute, Urban Mobility Report 2012, December 2012

Public Transportation

Agency Name / Mode of Transportation	Vehicles Operated in Maximum Service	Annual Unlinked Passenger Trips (in thous.)	Annual Passenger Miles (in thous.)
Capital Metropolitan Transportation Authority (CMTA)			
Bus (directly operated)	173	19,010.8	84,687.0
Bus (purchased transportation)	308	14,537.6	46,989.2
Commuter Bus (directly operated)	33	520.8	8,204.2
Commuter Bus (purchased transportation)	33	78.8	1,091.1
Demand Response (directly operated)	91	382.8	2,978.9
Demand Response (purchased transportation)	123	195.5	1,591.8
Demand Response Taxi (purchased transportation)	115	33.4	261.4
Hybrid Rail (purchased transportation)	4	527.4	8,534.2
Vanpool (directly operated)	100	225.2	5,631.7

Source: Federal Transit Administration, National Transit Database, 2012

Air Transportation

Airport Name and Code / Type of Service	Passenger Airlines[1]	Passenger Enplanements	Freight Carriers[2]	Freight (lbs.)
Austin-Bergstrom International (AUS)				
Domestic service (U.S. carriers - 2013)	28	4,872,563	17	73,538,338
International service (U.S. carriers - 2012)	7	15,677	3	10,171,281

Note: (1) Includes all U.S.-based major, minor and commuter airlines that carried at least one passenger during the year; (2) Includes all U.S.-based airlines and freight carriers that transported at least one lb. of freight during the year.
Source: Bureau of Transportation Statistics, The Intermodal Transportation Database, Air Carriers: T-100 Domestic Market (U.S. Carriers), 2013; Bureau of Transportation Statistics, The Intermodal Transportation Database, Air Carriers: T-100 International Market (U.S. Carriers), 2012

Other Transportation Statistics

Major Highways:	I-35
Amtrak Service:	Yes
Major Waterways/Ports:	None

Source: Amtrak.com; Google Maps

BUSINESSES

Major Business Headquarters

Company Name	Rankings	
	Fortune[1]	Forbes[2]
Whole Foods Market	232	-

Note: (1) Fortune 500—companies that produce a 10-K are ranked 1 to 500 based on 2012 revenue; (2) all private companies with at least $2 billion in annual revenue through the end of their most current fiscal year are ranked 1 to 224; companies listed are headquartered in the city; dashes indicate no ranking
Source: Fortune, "Fortune 500," May 20, 2013; Forbes, "America's Largest Private Companies," December 18, 2013

Fast-Growing Businesses

According to *Inc.*, Austin is home to 12 of America's 500 fastest-growing private companies: **MileStone Community Builders** (#6); **Patient Conversation Media** (#22); **Phunware** (#40); **MHD Enterprises** (#61); **Vital Farms** (#85); **Econohomes** (#116); **Camp Gladiator** (#234); **FreightPros** (#282); **Vintage IT Services** (#283); **Adscend Media** (#396); **Luna Data Solutions** (#402); **Kenry Home Improvement** (#424). Criteria: must be an independent, privately-held, for-profit, U.S. corporation, proprietorship or partnership; revenues must be at least $100,000 in 2009 and $2 million in 2012; must have four-year operating/sales history. Holding companies, regulated banks, and utilities were excluded. *Inc., "America's 500 Fastest-Growing Private Companies," September 2013*

According to *Fortune*, Austin is home to two of the 100 fastest-growing companies in the world: **Cirrus Logic** (#69); **SolarWinds** (#82). Companies were ranked by their revenue growth rate; their EPS growth rate; and their three-year annualized total return to investors for the period ending June 30, 2013. Criteria for inclusion: a company, foreign or domestic, must trade on a major U.S. stock exchange; must file quarterly reports with the SEC; must have a minimum market capitalization of $250 million; must have a stock price of at least $5 on June 29, 2013; must have been trading continuously since June 30, 2009; must have revenue and net income for the four quarters ended on or before April 30, 2013, of at least $50 million and $10 million, respectively; and must have posted a compound annual growth in revenue and earnings per share of at least 20% annually over the three years ending on or before April 30, 2013. REITs, limited-liability companies, limited parterships, companies about to be acquired, and companies that lost money in the quarter ending April 30, 2013 were excluded. *Fortune, "100 Fastest-Growing Companies," August 29, 2013*

According to *Initiative for a Competitive Inner City (ICIC)*, Austin is home to three of America's 100 fastest-growing "inner city" companies: **OriGen Biomedical** (#19); **Petrelocation.com** (#39); **Aztec Promotional Group** (#78). Companies were ranked by their five-year compound annual growth rate. Criteria for inclusion: company must be headquartered in or have 51 percent or more of its physical operations in an economically distressed urban area; must be an independent, for-profit corporation, partnership or proprietorship; must have 10 or more employees and have a five-year sales history that includes sales of at least $200,000 in the base year and at least $1 million in the current year with no decrease in sales over the two most recent years. *Initiative for a Competitive Inner City (ICIC), "Inner City 100 Companies, 2013"*

According to Deloitte, Austin is home to seven of North America's 500 fastest-growing high-technology companies: **SailPoint** (#62); **Kinnser Software** (#135); **Bazaarvoice** (#139); **Adometry** (#177); **BuildASign.com** (#277); **HomeAway** (#329); **SolarWinds** (#400). Companies are ranked by percentage growth in revenue over a five-year period. Criteria for inclusion: company must be headquartered within North America; must own proprietary intellectual property or proprietary technology that contributes to a significant portion of the company's operating revenue, or devote a significant proportion of revenues to research and development of technology; must have been in business for a minumum of five years with 2008 operating revenues of at least $50,000 USD/CD and 2012 operating revenues of at least $5 million USD/CD. *Deloitte Touche Tohmatsu, 2013 Technology Fast 500*[TM]

Minority Business Opportunity

Austin is home to two companies which are on the *Black Enterprise* Auto Dealer 60 list (60 largest dealers based on gross sales): **JMC Auto Group** (#32); **Davis Automotive** (#39). Criteria: company must be operational in previous calendar year and be at least 51% black-owned. *Black Enterprise, B.E. 100s, 2013*

Austin is home to two companies which are on the *Hispanic Business* 500 list (500 largest U.S. Hispanic-owned companies based on 2012 revenue): **Venta Financial Group** (#187); **Tramex Travel** (#233). Companies included must show at least 51 percent ownership by Hispanic U.S. citizens, and must maintain headquarters in one of the 50 states or Washington, D.C. *Hispanic Business, "Hispanic Business 500," June 20, 2013*

Minority- and Women-Owned Businesses

Group	All Firms		Firms with Paid Employees			
	Firms	Sales ($000)	Firms	Sales ($000)	Employees	Payroll ($000)
Asian	3,970	4,402,119	1,293	4,268,417	10,160	271,171
Black	3,118	505,907	240	450,953	2,879	71,712
Hispanic	10,546	1,468,542	1,233	1,059,525	10,337	295,270
Women	22,714	4,016,054	3,107	3,369,162	26,252	885,256
All Firms	80,570	127,872,644	18,383	124,575,830	424,724	19,184,572

Note: Figures cover firms located in the city; minority- and women-owned business are defined as firms in which the corresponding group own 51% or more of the stock or equity of the company
Source: U.S. Census Bureau, 2007 Economic Census, Survey of Business Owners (2012 Survey of Business Owners data will be released starting in June 2015)

HOTELS & CONVENTION CENTERS

Hotels/Motels

Area	5 Star		4 Star		3 Star		2 Star		1 Star		Not Rated	
	Num.	Pct.[3]	Num.	Pct.[3]	Num.	Pct.[3]	Num.	Pct.[3]	Num.	Pct.[3]	Num.	Pct.[3]
City[1]	0	0.0	18	7.4	62	25.6	137	56.6	4	1.7	21	8.7
Total[2]	142	0.9	1,005	6.0	5,147	30.9	8,578	51.4	408	2.4	1,397	8.4

Note: (1) Figures cover Austin and vicinity; (2) Figures cover all 100 cities in this book; (3) Percentage of hotels which have a given star rating; Star ratings are determined by expedia.com and offer an indication of the general quality of a particular hotel.
Source: expedia.com, April 7, 2014

The Austin-Round Rock, TX metro area is home to two of the best hotels in the U.S. according to *Travel & Leisure*: **Four Seasons Hotel, Austin**; **The Driskill**. Criteria: service; location; rooms; food; and value. The list includes the top 200 hotels in the U.S. *Travel & Leisure*, "*T+L 500, The World's Best Hotels 2014*"

Major Convention Centers

Name	Overall Space (sq. ft.)	Exhibit Space (sq. ft.)	Meeting Space (sq. ft.)	Meeting Rooms
Austin Convention Center	881,400	246,097	37,170	54

Note: Table includes convention centers located in the Austin-Round Rock, TX metro area; n/a not available
Source: Original research

Living Environment

COST OF LIVING

Cost of Living Index

Composite Index	Groceries	Housing	Utilities	Trans- portation	Health Care	Misc. Goods/ Services
92.9	84.0	86.0	91.1	97.2	99.4	99.8

Note: The Cost of Living Index measures regional differences in the cost of consumer goods and services, excluding taxes and non-consumer expenditures, for professional and managerial households in the top income quintile. It is based on more than 50,000 prices covering almost 60 different items for which prices are collected three times a year by chambers of commerce, economic development organizations or university applied economic centers in each participating urban area. The numbers shown should be read as a percentage above or below the national average of 100. For example, a value of 115.4 in the groceries column indicates that grocery prices are 15.4% higher than the national average. Small differences in the index numbers should not be interpreted as significant; Figures cover the Austin TX urban area.
Source: The Council for Community and Economic Research, ACCRA Cost of Living Index, 2013

Grocery Prices

Area[1]	T-Bone Steak ($/pound)	Frying Chicken ($/pound)	Whole Milk ($/half gal.)	Eggs ($/dozen)	Orange Juice ($/64 oz.)	Coffee ($/11.5 oz.)
City[2]	8.95	1.25	2.13	1.70	3.17	3.57
Avg.	10.19	1.28	2.34	1.81	3.48	4.39
Min.	8.56	0.94	1.44	1.19	2.78	3.40
Max.	14.82	2.28	3.56	3.73	6.23	7.32

*Note: (1) Values for the local area are compared with the average, minimum and maximum values for all 327 areas in the Cost of Living Index; (2) Figures cover the Austin TX urban area; **T-Bone Steak** (price per pound); **Frying Chicken** (price per pound, whole fryer); **Whole Milk** (half gallon carton); **Eggs** (price per dozen, Grade A, large); **Orange Juice** (64 oz. Tropicana or Florida Natural); **Coffee** (11.5 oz. can, vacuum-packed, Maxwell House, Hills Bros, or Folgers).*
Source: The Council for Community and Economic Research, ACCRA Cost of Living Index, 2013

Housing and Utility Costs

Area[1]	New Home Price ($)	Apartment Rent ($/month)	All Electric ($/month)	Part Electric ($/month)	Other Energy ($/month)	Telephone ($/month)
City[2]	234,211	970	-	89.15	36.67	30.94
Avg.	295,864	900	171.38	91.82	70.12	27.73
Min.	185,506	458	117.80	48.81	33.67	17.16
Max.	1,358,917	3,783	441.68	171.40	372.65	39.47

*Note: (1) Values for the local area are compared with the average, minimum and maximum values for all 327 areas in the Cost of Living Index; (2) Figures cover the Austin TX urban area; **New Home Price** (2,400 sf living area, 8,000 sf lot, in urban area with full utilities); **Apartment Rent** (950 sf 2 bedroom/1.5 or 2 bath, unfurnished, excluding all utilities except water); **All Electric** (average monthly cost for an all-electric home); **Part Electric** (average monthly cost for a part-electric home); **Other Energy** (average monthly cost for natural gas, fuel oil, coal, wood, and any other forms of energy except electricity); **Telephone** (price includes basic monthly rate for a private residential line plus additional local usage charges incurred by a family of four).*
Source: The Council for Community and Economic Research, ACCRA Cost of Living Index, 2013

Health Care, Transportation, and Other Costs

Area[1]	Doctor ($/visit)	Dentist ($/visit)	Optometrist ($/visit)	Gasoline ($/gallon)	Beauty Salon ($/visit)	Men's Shirt ($)
City[2]	100.74	94.53	112.08	3.30	42.60	30.48
Avg.	101.40	86.48	96.16	3.44	33.87	26.55
Min.	61.67	50.83	50.12	3.08	18.92	12.48
Max.	182.71	152.50	223.78	4.33	68.22	52.03

*Note: (1) Values for the local area are compared with the average, minimum and maximum values for all 327 areas in the Cost of Living Index; (2) Figures cover the Austin TX urban area; **Doctor** (general practitioners routine exam of an established patient); **Dentist** (adult teeth cleaning and periodic oral examination); **Optometrist** (full vision eye exam for established adult patient); **Gasoline** (one gallon regular unleaded, national brand, including all taxes, cash price at self-service pump if available); **Beauty Salon** (woman's shampoo, trim, and blow-dry); **Men's Shirt** (cotton/polyester dress shirt, pinpoint weave, long sleeves).*
Source: The Council for Community and Economic Research, ACCRA Cost of Living Index, 2013

HOUSING

House Price Index (HPI)

Area	National Ranking[2]	Quarterly Change (%)	One-Year Change (%)	Five-Year Change (%)
MSA[1]	46	2.40	10.34	12.60
U.S.[3]	–	1.20	7.69	4.18

Note: The HPI is a weighted repeat sales index. It measures average price changes in repeat sales or refinancings on the same properties. This information is obtained by reviewing repeat mortgage transactions on single-family properties whose mortgages have been purchased or securitized by Fannie Mae or Freddie Mac in January 1975; (1) Austin-Round Rock, TX Metropolitan Statistical Area—see Appendix B for areas included; (2) Rankings are based on annual percentage change for all metro areas containing at least 15,000 transactions over the last 10 years and ranges from 1 to 283; (3) figures based on a weighted average of Census Division estimates using a seasonally adjusted, purchase-only index; all figures are for the period ending December 31, 2013
Source: Federal Housing Finance Agency, House Price Index, February 25, 2014

Median Single-Family Home Prices

Area	2011	2012	2013p	Percent Change 2012 to 2013
MSA[1]	193.1	206.0	222.9	8.2
U.S. Average	166.2	177.2	197.4	11.4

Note: Figures are median sales prices of existing single-family homes in thousands of dollars; (p) preliminary; n/a not available; (1) Austin-Round Rock, TX Metropolitan Statistical Area—see Appendix B for areas included
Source: National Association of Realtors, Median Sales Price of Existing Single-Family Homes for Metropolitan Areas, 4th Quarter 2013

Qualifying Income Based on Median Sales Price of Existing Single-Family Homes

Area	With 5% Down ($)	With 10% Down ($)	With 20% Down ($)
MSA[1]	50,859	48,183	42,829
U.S. Average	45,395	43,006	38,228

Note: Figures are preliminary; Qualifying income is based on a mortgage rate of 4.4%. Monthly principal and interest payment is limited to 25% of income; n/a not available; (1) Austin-Round Rock, TX Metropolitan Statistical Area—see Appendix B for areas included
Source: National Association of Realtors, Qualifying Income Based on Median Sales Price of Existing Single-Family Homes for Metropolitan Areas, 4th Quarter 2013

Median Apartment Condo-Coop Home Prices

Area	2011	2012	2013p	Percent Change 2012 to 2013
MSA[1]	168.8	168.8	168.8	0.0
U.S. Average	165.1	173.7	194.9	12.2

Note: Figures are median sales prices of existing apartment condo-coop homes in thousands of dollars; (p) preliminary; n/a not available; (1) Austin-Round Rock, TX Metropolitan Statistical Area—see Appendix B for areas included
Source: National Association of Realtors, Median Sales Price of Existing Apartment Condo-Coop Homes for Metropolitan Areas, 4th Quarter 2013

Gross Monthly Rent

Area	Under $200	$200 -299	$300 -499	$500 -749	$750 -999	$1,000 -1,499	$1,500 and up	Median ($)
City	0.8	1.2	2.3	19.9	31.3	32.2	12.4	954
MSA[1]	0.8	1.1	2.4	18.6	31.0	33.1	13.1	967
U.S.	1.7	3.3	8.1	22.7	24.3	25.7	14.3	889

Note: Figures are percentages except for Median; Gross rent is the contract rent plus the estimated average monthly cost of utilities (electricity, gas, and water and sewer) and fuels (oil, coal, kerosene, wood, etc.) if these are paid by the renter (or paid for the renter by someone else); (1) Figures cover the Austin-Round Rock, TX Metropolitan Statistical Area—see Appendix B for areas included
Source: U.S. Census Bureau, 2010-2012 American Community Survey 3-Year Estimates

Year Housing Structure Built

Area	2010 or Later	2000 -2009	1990 -1999	1980 -1989	1970 -1979	1960 -1969	1950 -1959	1940 -1949	Before 1940	Median Year
City	0.8	22.5	15.6	20.9	19.7	8.2	6.3	3.1	3.0	1985
MSA[1]	1.3	31.2	18.9	19.3	14.7	5.5	4.3	2.2	2.6	1991
U.S.	0.5	14.9	13.8	13.9	15.9	11.1	10.9	5.5	13.5	1976

Note: Figures are percentages except for Median Year; (1) Figures cover the Austin-Round Rock, TX Metropolitan Statistical Area—see Appendix B for areas included
Source: U.S. Census Bureau, 2010-2012 American Community Survey 3-Year Estimates

HEALTH

Health Risk Data

Category	MSA[1] (%)	U.S. (%)
Adults aged 18–64 who have any kind of health care coverage	71.9	79.6
Adults who reported being in good or excellent health	84.2	83.1
Adults who are current smokers	15.2	19.6
Adults who are heavy drinkers[2]	7.5	6.1
Adults who are binge drinkers[3]	17.6	16.9
Adults who are overweight (BMI 25.0 - 29.9)	35.8	35.8
Adults who are obese (BMI 30.0 - 99.8)	25.5	27.6
Adults who participated in any physical activities in the past month	80.2	77.1
Adults 50+ who have ever had a sigmoidoscopy or colonoscopy	68.3	67.3
Women aged 40+ who have had a mammogram within the past two years	71.1	74.0
Men aged 40+ who have had a PSA test within the past two years	40.1	45.2
Adults aged 65+ who have had flu shot within the past year	64.0	60.1
Adults who always wear a seatbelt	97.3	93.8

Note: Data as of 2012 unless otherwise noted; (1) Figures cover the Austin-Round Rock, TX Metropolitan Statistical Area—see Appendix B for areas included; (2) Heavy drinkers are classified as males having more than two drinks per day or females having more than one drink per day; (3) Binge drinkers are classified as males having five or more drinks on one occasion or females having four or more drinks on one occasion
Source: Centers for Disease Control and Prevention, Behaviorial Risk Factor Surveillance System, SMART: Selected Metropolitan/Micropolitan Area Risk Trends, 2012

Chronic Health Indicators

Category	MSA[1] (%)	U.S. (%)
Adults who have ever been told they had a heart attack	2.1	4.5
Adults who have ever been told they had a stroke	1.6	2.9
Adults who have been told they currently have asthma	8.4	8.9
Adults who have ever been told they have arthritis	17.6	25.7
Adults who have ever been told they have diabetes[2]	7.4	9.7
Adults who have ever been told they had skin cancer	5.8	5.7
Adults who have ever been told they had any other types of cancer	4.0	6.5
Adults who have ever been told they have COPD	4.0	6.2
Adults who have ever been told they have kidney disease	2.1	2.5
Adults who have ever been told they have a form of depression	15.6	18.0

Note: Data as of 2012 unless otherwise noted; (1) Figures cover the Austin-Round Rock, TX Metropolitan Statistical Area—see Appendix B for areas included; (2) Figures do not include pregnancy-related, borderline, or pre-diabetes
Source: Centers for Disease Control and Prevention, Behaviorial Risk Factor Surveillance System, SMART: Selected Metropolitan/Micropolitan Area Risk Trends, 2012

Mortality Rates for the Top 10 Causes of Death in the U.S.

ICD-10[a] Sub-Chapter	ICD-10[a] Code	Age-Adjusted Mortality Rate[1] per 100,000 population	
		County[2]	U.S.
Malignant neoplasms	C00-C97	148.1	174.2
Ischaemic heart diseases	I20-I25	82.0	119.1
Other forms of heart disease	I30-I51	39.6	49.6
Chronic lower respiratory diseases	J40-J47	29.6	43.2
Cerebrovascular diseases	I60-I69	37.9	40.3
Organic, including symptomatic, mental disorders	F01-F09	48.1	30.5
Other degenerative diseases of the nervous system	G30-G31	22.7	26.3
Other external causes of accidental injury	W00-X59	31.1	25.1
Diabetes mellitus	E10-E14	17.6	21.3
Hypertensive diseases	I10-I15	21.5	18.8

Note: (a) ICD-10 = International Classification of Diseases 10th Revision; (1) Mortality rates are a three year average covering 2008-2010; (2) Figures cover Travis County
Source: Centers for Disease Control and Prevention, National Center for Health Statistics. Compressed Mortality File 1999-2010 on CDC WONDER Online Database, released January 2013. Data are compiled from the Compressed Mortality File 1999-2010, Series 20 No. 2P, 2013.

Mortality Rates for Selected Causes of Death

ICD-10[a] Sub-Chapter	ICD-10[a] Code	Age-Adjusted Mortality Rate[1] per 100,000 population	
		County[2]	U.S.
Assault	X85-Y09	3.2	5.5
Diseases of the liver	K70-K76	14.0	12.4
Human immunodeficiency virus (HIV) disease	B20-B24	2.9	3.0
Influenza and pneumonia	J09-J18	10.4	16.4
Intentional self-harm	X60-X84	11.5	11.8
Malnutrition	E40-E46	*0.8	0.8
Obesity and other hyperalimentation	E65-E68	1.4	1.6
Renal failure	N17-N19	11.4	13.6
Transport accidents	V01-V99	10.5	12.6
Viral hepatitis	B15-B19	2.8	2.2

Note: (a) ICD-10 = International Classification of Diseases 10th Revision; (1) Mortality rates are a three year average covering 2008-2010; (2) Figures cover Travis County; (*) Unreliable data as per CDC
Source: Centers for Disease Control and Prevention, National Center for Health Statistics. Compressed Mortality File 1999-2010 on CDC WONDER Online Database, released January 2013. Data are compiled from the Compressed Mortality File 1999-2010, Series 20 No. 2P, 2013.

Health Insurance Coverage

Area	With Health Insurance	With Private Health Insurance	With Public Health Insurance	Without Health Insurance	Population Under Age 18 Without Health Insurance
City	78.9	63.0	22.3	21.1	11.2
MSA[1]	81.2	67.1	21.9	18.8	10.4
U.S.	84.9	65.4	30.4	15.1	7.5

Note: Figures are percentages that cover the civilian noninstitutionalized population; (1) Figures cover the Austin-Round Rock, TX Metropolitan Statistical Area—see Appendix B for areas included
Source: U.S. Census Bureau, 2010-2012 American Community Survey 3-Year Estimates

Number of Medical Professionals

Area[1]	MDs[2]	DOs[2,3]	Dentists	Podiatrists	Chiropractors	Optometrists
Local (number)	3,107	160	680	49	325	165
Local (rate[4])	292.5	15.1	62.0	4.5	29.6	15.1
U.S. (rate[4])	267.6	19.6	61.7	5.6	24.7	14.5

Note: Data as of 2012 unless noted; (1) Local data covers Travis County; (2) Data as of 2011; (3) Doctor of Osteopathic Medicine; (4) rate per 100,000 population
Source: Area Resource File (ARF) 2012-2013. U.S. Department of Health and Human Services, Health Resources and Services Administration, Bureau of Health Professions

Best Hospitals

According to *U.S. News*, the Austin-Round Rock, TX metro area is home to one of the best children's hospitals in the U.S.: **Dell Children's Medical Center of Central Texas**. The hospital listed was highly ranked in at least one pediatric specialty. Eighty-seven hospitals in the U.S. ranked in at least one specialty. Ten children's hospitals in the U.S. made the Honor Roll by ranking near the top in three or more specialties.*U.S. News Online, "America's Best Children's Hospitals 2013-14"*

EDUCATION

Public School District Statistics

District Name	Schls	Pupils	Pupil/ Teacher Ratio	Minority Pupils[1] (%)	Free Lunch Eligible[2] (%)	IEP[3] (%)
Austin ISD	122	86,528	15.0	75.6	58.3	10.0
Eanes ISD	9	7,803	14.3	28.0	2.4	7.6
Harmony Science Academy (Austin)	5	2,584	14.3	81.1	41.0	3.6
Lake Travis ISD	8	7,412	15.6	28.1	12.2	7.4

Note: Table includes school districts with 2,000 or more students; (1) Percentage of students that are not non-Hispanic white; (2) Percentage of students that are eligible for the free lunch program; (3) Percentage of students that have an Individualized Education Program.
Source: U.S. Department of Education, National Center for Education Statistics, Common Core of Data, Local Education Agency (School District) Universe Survey: School Year 2011-2012; U.S. Department of Education, National Center for Education Statistics, Common Core of Data, Public Elementary/Secondary School Universe Survey: School Year 2011-2012

Best High Schools

High School Name	Rank[1]	Grad. Rate[2] (%)	Coll.[3] (%)	AP/IB/ AICE Tests[4]	AP/IB/ AICE Score[5]	SAT Score[6]	ACT Score[6]
A N McCallum	1649	90	72	0.4	3.2	1599	20.3
Chaparral Star Academy	410	100	100	0.5	2.8	1661	n/a
James Bowie H.S.	476	97	100	0.3	3.1	1632	24.1
L. C. Anderson H.S.	611	95	91	0.6	3.3	1693	24.7
Lake Travis H.S.	420	98	99	0.4	3.4	1654	24.3
Liberal Arts and Science Academy H.S.	33	100	100	1.3	3.9	1983	28.0
NYOS Charter School	508	100	96	0.4	3.2	1597	n/a
Stephen F. Austin H.S.	1280	91	89	0.4	2.8	1568	22.5
Westlake H.S.	93	97	99	1.2	3.4	1764	26.6
Westwood H.S.	57	100	97	1.1	4.6	1777	26.8

Note: (1) Public schools are ranked from 1 to 2,000 based on the following self-reported statistics (with the corresponding weight used in calculating their overall score). Schools that were newly founded and did not have a graduating senior class in 2012 were excluded; (2) Four-year, on-time graduation rate (25%); (3) Percent of 2011 graduates who were accepted to college (25%); (4) AP/IB/AICE tests taken per student (25%); (5) Average AP/IB/AICE exam score (10%); (6) Average SAT and/or ACT score (10%); Percent of students enrolled in at least one AP/IB/AICE course (5%)—data not shown; n/a not available
Source: Newsweek and The Daily Beast, "America's Best High Schools 2013"

Highest Level of Education

Area	Less than H.S.	H.S. Diploma	Some College, No Deg.	Associate Degree	Bachelor's Degree	Master's Degree	Prof. School Degree	Doctorate Degree
City	13.6	16.8	19.3	5.4	28.5	11.3	2.8	2.3
MSA[1]	12.1	19.4	21.7	6.5	26.6	9.7	2.3	1.7
U.S.	14.1	28.3	21.3	7.8	18.0	7.5	1.9	1.2

Note: Figures cover persons age 25 and over; (1) Figures cover the Austin-Round Rock, TX Metropolitan Statistical Area—see Appendix B for areas included
Source: U.S. Census Bureau, 2010-2012 American Community Survey 3-Year Estimates

Educational Attainment by Race

Area	High School Graduate or Higher (%)					Bachelor's Degree or Higher (%)				
	Total	White	Black	Asian	Hisp.[2]	Total	White	Black	Asian	Hisp.[2]
City	86.4	89.2	88.1	92.9	62.5	44.9	49.2	20.9	69.1	17.8
MSA[1]	87.9	90.0	89.1	92.1	65.8	40.2	42.6	23.1	66.0	17.3
U.S.	85.9	88.1	82.5	85.5	63.1	28.6	30.0	18.4	50.2	13.4

Note: Figures shown cover persons 25 years old and over; (1) Figures cover the Austin-Round Rock, TX Metropolitan Statistical Area—see Appendix B for areas included; (2) People of Hispanic origin can be of any race
Source: U.S. Census Bureau, 2010-2012 American Community Survey 3-Year Estimates

School Enrollment by Grade and Control

Area	Preschool (%)		Kindergarten (%)		Grades 1 - 4 (%)		Grades 5 - 8 (%)		Grades 9 - 12 (%)	
	Public	Private	Public	Private	Public	Private	Public	Private	Public	Private
City	48.3	51.7	88.7	11.3	90.4	9.6	90.9	9.1	93.0	7.0
MSA[1]	50.8	49.2	88.7	11.3	92.4	7.6	92.4	7.6	93.5	6.5
U.S.	56.9	43.1	87.8	12.2	89.9	10.1	90.0	10.0	90.8	9.2

Note: Figures shown cover persons 3 years old and over; (1) Figures cover the Austin-Round Rock, TX Metropolitan Statistical Area—see Appendix B for areas included
Source: U.S. Census Bureau, 2010-2012 American Community Survey 3-Year Estimates

Average Salaries of Public School Classroom Teachers

Area	2012-13		2013-14		Percent Change 2012-13 to 2013-14	Percent Change 2003-04 to 2013-14
	Dollars	Rank[1]	Dollars	Rank[1]		
Texas	48,819	35	49,270	35	0.92	21.7
U.S. Average	56,103	–	56,689	–	1.04	21.8

Note: (1) State rank ranges from 1 to 51 where 1 indicates highest salary.
Source: National Education Association, Rankings & Estimates: Rankings of the States 2013 and Estimates of School Statistics 2014, March 2014

Higher Education

Four-Year Colleges			Two-Year Colleges			Medical Schools[1]	Law Schools[2]	Voc/ Tech[3]
Public	Private Non-profit	Private For-profit	Public	Private Non-profit	Private For-profit			
1	6	8	1	0	8	0	1	9

Note: Figures cover institutions located within the city limits and include main campuses only; (1) includes schools accredited by the Liaison Committee on Medical Education and the American Osteopathic Association's Commission on Osteopathic College Accreditation; (2) includes ABA-accredited schools, schools with provisional ABA accreditation, and state accredited schools; (3) includes all schools with programs that are less than 2 years.
Source: National Center for Education Statistics, Integrated Postsecondary Education System (IPEDS), 2012-13; Association of American Medical Colleges, Member List, April 24, 2014; American Osteopathic Association, Member List, April 24, 2014; Law School Admission Council, Official Guide to ABA-Approved Law Schools Online, April 24, 2014; Wikipedia, List of Medical Schools in the United States, April 24, 2014; Wikipedia, List of Law Schools in the United States, April 24, 2014

According to *U.S. News & World Report,* the Austin-Round Rock, TX metro area is home to one of the best national universities in the U.S.: **University of Texas–Austin** (#52). The indicators used to capture academic quality fall into a number of categories: assessment by administrators at peer institutions; retention of students; faculty resources; student selectivity; financial resources; alumni giving; high school counselor ratings of colleges; and graduation rate. *U.S. News & World Report, "America's Best Colleges 2014"*

According to *U.S. News & World Report,* the Austin-Round Rock, TX metro area is home to one of the best liberal arts colleges in the U.S.: **Southwestern University** (#65). The indicators used to capture academic quality fall into a number of categories: assessment by administrators at peer institutions; retention of students; faculty resources; student selectivity; financial resources; alumni giving; high school counselor ratings of colleges; and graduation rate. *U.S. News & World Report, "America's Best Colleges 2014"*

According to *U.S. News & World Report*, the Austin-Round Rock, TX metro area is home to one of the top 100 law schools in the U.S.: **University of Texas–Austin** (#15). The rankings are based on a weighted average of 12 measures of quality: peer assessment score; assessment score by lawyers/judges; median LSAT scores; median undergrad GPA; acceptance rate; employment rates for graduates; placement success; bar passage rate; faculty resources; expenditures per student; student/faculty ratio; and library resources. *U.S. News & World Report, "America's Best Graduate Schools, Law, 2014"*

According to *U.S. News & World Report*, the Austin-Round Rock, TX metro area is home to one of the top 100 business schools in the U.S.: **University of Texas–Austin (McCombs)** (#17). The rankings are based on a weighted average of the following nine measures: quality assessment; peer assessment; recruiter assessment; placement success; mean starting salary and bonus; student selectivity; mean GMAT and GRE scores; mean undergraduate GPA; and acceptance rate. *U.S. News & World Report, "America's Best Graduate Schools, Business, 2014"*

PRESIDENTIAL ELECTION

2012 Presidential Election Results

Area	Obama	Romney	Other
Travis County	60.1	36.2	3.6
U.S.	51.0	47.2	1.8

Note: Results are percentages and may not add to 100% due to rounding
Source: Dave Leip's Atlas of U.S. Presidential Elections

EMPLOYERS

Major Employers

Company Name	Industry
3M Company	Tape, pressure sensitive: made from purchased materials
Attorney General, Texas	Attorney general's office
Dell	Electronic computers
Dell USA Corporation	Business management
Environmental Quality, Texas Comm On	Air, water, & solid waste management
Freescale Semiconductor	Semiconductors and related devices
Hospital Housekeeping Systems GP	Cleaning service, industrial or commercial
Internal Revenue Service	Taxation department, government
Legislative Office, Texas	Legislative bodies
Nextel of Texas	Radiotelephone communication
Pleasant Hill Preservation LP	Apartment building operators
State Farm	Automobile insurance
Texas Department of Public Safety	Public order and safety statistics centers
Texas Department of State Health Services	Administration of public health programs
Texas State University-San Marcos	Colleges and universities
Texas Workforce Commission	Administration of social and manpower programs
Univ of Texas System	Generation, electric power
University of Texas at Austin	University

Note: Companies shown are located within the Austin-Round Rock, TX Metropolitan Statistical Area.
Source: Hoovers.com; Wikipedia

Best Companies to Work For

National Instruments; Whole Foods Market, headquartered in Austin, are among "The 100 Best Companies to Work For." To pick the 100 Best Companies to Work For, *Fortune* partnered with the Great Place to Work Institute. Two hundred fifty seven firms participated in this year's survey. Two-thirds of a company's score is based on the results of the Institute's Trust Index survey, which is sent to a random sample of employees from each company. The questions related to attitudes about management's credibility, job satisfaction, and camaraderie. The other third of the scoring is based on the company's responses to the Institute's Culture Audit, which includes detailed questions about pay and benefit programs, and a series of open-ended questions about hiring practices, internal communication, training, recognition programs, and diversity efforts. Any company that is at least five years old with more than 1,000 U.S. employees is eligible. *Fortune, "The 100 Best Companies to Work For," 2014*

PUBLIC SAFETY

Crime Rate

Area	All Crimes	Violent Crimes				Property Crimes		
		Murder	Forcible Rape	Robbery	Aggrav. Assault	Burglary	Larceny -Theft	Motor Vehicle Theft
City	5,628.2	3.7	25.1	117.4	262.6	869.7	4,071.7	277.9
Suburbs[1]	2,101.1	0.8	25.0	22.2	145.8	402.0	1,434.1	71.2
Metro[2]	3,723.9	2.2	25.0	66.0	199.5	617.2	2,647.7	166.3
U.S.	3,246.1	4.7	26.9	112.9	242.3	670.2	1,959.3	229.7

Note: Figures are crimes per 100,000 population; (1) All areas within the metro area that are located outside the city limits; (2) Figures cover the Austin-Round Rock, TX Metropolitan Statistical Area—see Appendix B for areas included
Source: FBI Uniform Crime Reports, 2012

Hate Crimes

Area	Number of Quarters Reported	Bias Motivation				
		Race	Religion	Sexual Orientation	Ethnicity	Disability
City	4	3	2	1	0	0
U.S.	4	2,797	1,099	1,135	667	92

Source: Federal Bureau of Investigation, Hate Crime Statistics 2012

Identity Theft Consumer Complaints

Area	Complaints	Complaints per 100,000 Population	Rank[2]
MSA[1]	1,462	85.2	85
U.S.	290,056	91.8	-

Note: (1) Figures cover the Austin-Round Rock, TX Metropolitan Statistical Area—see Appendix B for areas included; (2) Rank ranges from 1 to 377 where 1 indicates greatest number of identity theft complaints per 100,000 population
Source: Federal Trade Commission, Consumer Sentinel Network Data Book for January–December 2013

Fraud and Other Consumer Complaints

Area	Complaints	Complaints per 100,000 Population	Rank[2]
MSA[1]	7,682	447.6	52
U.S.	1,811,724	595.2	-

Note: (1) Figures cover the Austin-Round Rock, TX Metropolitan Statistical Area—see Appendix B for areas included; (2) Rank ranges from 1 to 377 where 1 indicates greatest number of identity theft complaints per 100,000 population
Source: Federal Trade Commission, Consumer Sentinel Network Data Book for January–December 2013

RECREATION

Culture

Dance[1]	Theatre[1]	Instrumental Music[1]	Vocal Music[1]	Series and Festivals	Museums and Art Galleries[2]	Zoos and Aquariums[3]
3	7	3	4	4	50	0

Note: (1) Number of professional perfoming groups; (2) Based on organizations with primary SIC code 8412; (3) AZA-accredited
Source: The Grey House Performing Arts Directory, 2013; Association of Zoos & Aquariums, AZA Member Zoos & Aquariums, April 2014; www.AccuLeads.com, May 1, 2014

Professional Sports Teams

Team Name	League	Year Established
No teams are located in the metro area		

Source: Wikipedia, Major Professional Sports Teams of the United States and Canada, April 25, 2014

CLIMATE

Average and Extreme Temperatures

Temperature	Jan	Feb	Mar	Apr	May	Jun	Jul	Aug	Sep	Oct	Nov	Dec	Yr.
Extreme High (°F)	90	97	98	98	100	105	109	106	104	98	91	90	109
Average High (°F)	60	64	72	79	85	91	95	96	90	81	70	63	79
Average Temp. (°F)	50	53	61	69	75	82	85	85	80	70	60	52	69
Average Low (°F)	39	43	50	58	65	72	74	74	69	59	49	41	58
Extreme Low (°F)	-2	7	18	35	43	53	64	61	47	32	20	4	-2

Note: Figures cover the years 1948-1990
Source: National Climatic Data Center, International Station Meteorological Climate Summary, 9/96

Average Precipitation/Snowfall/Humidity

Precip./Humidity	Jan	Feb	Mar	Apr	May	Jun	Jul	Aug	Sep	Oct	Nov	Dec	Yr.
Avg. Precip. (in.)	1.6	2.3	1.8	2.9	4.3	3.5	1.9	1.9	3.3	3.5	2.1	1.9	31.1
Avg. Snowfall (in.)	1	Tr	Tr	0	0	0	0	0	0	0	Tr	Tr	1
Avg. Rel. Hum. 6am (%)	79	80	79	83	88	89	88	87	86	84	81	79	84
Avg. Rel. Hum. 3pm (%)	53	51	47	50	53	49	43	42	47	47	49	51	48

Note: Figures cover the years 1948-1990; Tr = Trace amounts (<0.05 in. of rain; <0.5 in. of snow)
Source: National Climatic Data Center, International Station Meteorological Climate Summary, 9/96

Weather Conditions

Temperature			Daytime Sky			Precipitation		
10°F & below	32°F & below	90°F & above	Clear	Partly cloudy	Cloudy	0.01 inch or more precip.	0.1 inch or more snow/ice	Thunder-storms
< 1	20	111	105	148	112	83	1	41

Note: Figures are average number of days per year and cover the years 1948-1990
Source: National Climatic Data Center, International Station Meteorological Climate Summary, 9/96

HAZARDOUS WASTE

Superfund Sites

Austin has no sites on the EPA's Superfund Final National Priorities List.
U.S. Environmental Protection Agency, Final National Priorities List, April 26, 2014

AIR & WATER QUALITY

Air Quality Index

Area	Percent of Days when Air Quality was...[2]					AQI Statistics[2]	
	Good	Moderate	Unhealthy for Sensitive Groups	Unhealthy	Very Unhealthy	Maximum	Median
MSA[1]	73.7	26.0	0.3	0.0	0.0	109	41

Note: (1) Data covers the Austin-Round Rock, TX Metropolitan Statistical Area—see Appendix B for areas included; (2) Based on 365 days with AQI data in 2013. Air Quality Index (AQI) is an index for reporting daily air quality. EPA calculates the AQI for five major air pollutants regulated by the Clean Air Act: ground-level ozone, particle pollution (aka particulate matter), carbon monoxide, sulfur dioxide, and nitrogen dioxide. The AQI runs from 0 to 500. The higher the AQI value, the greater the level of air pollution and the greater the health concern. There are six AQI categories: "Good" AQI is between 0 and 50. Air quality is considered satisfactory; "Moderate" AQI is between 51 and 100. Air quality is acceptable; "Unhealthy for Sensitive Groups" When AQI values are between 101 and 150, members of sensitive groups may experience health effects; "Unhealthy" When AQI values are between 151 and 200 everyone may begin to experience health effects; "Very Unhealthy" AQI values between 201 and 300 trigger a health alert; "Hazardous" AQI values over 300 trigger warnings of emergency conditions (not shown).
Source: U.S. Environmental Protection Agency, Air Quality Index Report, 2013

Air Quality Index Pollutants

Area	Percent of Days when AQI Pollutant was...[2]					
	Carbon Monoxide	Nitrogen Dioxide	Ozone	Sulfur Dioxide	Particulate Matter 2.5	Particulate Matter 10
MSA[1]	0.0	0.3	51.5	0.0	48.2	0.0

Note: (1) Data covers the Austin-Round Rock, TX Metropolitan Statistical Area—see Appendix B for areas included; (2) Based on 365 days with AQI data in 2013. The Air Quality Index (AQI) is an index for reporting daily air quality. EPA calculates the AQI for five major air pollutants regulated by the Clean Air Act: ground-level ozone, particle pollution (also known as particulate matter), carbon monoxide, sulfur dioxide, and nitrogen dioxide. The AQI runs from 0 to 500. The higher the AQI value, the greater the level of air pollution and the greater the health concern.
Source: U.S. Environmental Protection Agency, Air Quality Index Report, 2013

Air Quality Trends: Ozone

	2003	2004	2005	2006	2007	2008	2009	2010	2011	2012
MSA[1]	0.083	0.081	0.081	0.083	0.073	0.072	0.073	0.072	0.074	0.075

Note: (1) Data covers the Austin-Round Rock, TX Metropolitan Statistical Area—see Appendix B for areas included. The values shown are the composite ozone concentration averages among trend sites based on the highest fourth daily maximum 8-hour concentration in parts per million. These trends are based on sites having an adequate record of monitoring data during the trend period. Data from exceptional events are included.
Source: U.S. Environmental Protection Agency, Air Quality Monitoring Information, "Air Quality Trends by City, 2000-2012"

Maximum Air Pollutant Concentrations: Particulate Matter, Ozone, CO and Lead

	Particulate Matter 10 (ug/m^3)	Particulate Matter 2.5 Wtd AM (ug/m^3)	Particulate Matter 2.5 24-Hr (ug/m^3)	Ozone (ppm)	Carbon Monoxide (ppm)	Lead (ug/m^3)
MSA[1] Level	32	7.8	17	0.076	0	n/a
NAAQS[2]	150	15	35	0.075	9	0.15
Met NAAQS[2]	Yes	Yes	Yes	No	Yes	n/a

Note: (1) Data covers the Austin-Round Rock, TX Metropolitan Statistical Area—see Appendix B for areas included; Data from exceptional events are included; (2) National Ambient Air Quality Standards; ppm = parts per million; ug/m^3 = micrograms per cubic meter; n/a not available.
Concentrations: Particulate Matter 10 (coarse particulate)—highest second maximum 24-hour concentration; Particulate Matter 2.5 Wtd AM (fine particulate)—highest weighted annual mean concentration; Particulate Matter 2.5 24-Hour (fine particulate)—highest 98th percentile 24-hour concentration; Ozone—highest fourth daily maximum 8-hour concentration; Carbon Monoxide—highest second maximum non-overlapping 8-hour concentration; Lead—maximum running 3-month average
Source: U.S. Environmental Protection Agency, Air Quality Monitoring Information, "Air Quality Statistics by City, 2012"

Maximum Air Pollutant Concentrations: Nitrogen Dioxide and Sulfur Dioxide

	Nitrogen Dioxide AM (ppb)	Nitrogen Dioxide 1-Hr (ppb)	Sulfur Dioxide AM (ppb)	Sulfur Dioxide 1-Hr (ppb)	Sulfur Dioxide 24-Hr (ppb)
MSA[1] Level	n/a	n/a	n/a	n/a	n/a
NAAQS[2]	53	100	30	75	140
Met NAAQS[2]	n/a	n/a	n/a	n/a	n/a

Note: (1) Data covers the Austin-Round Rock, TX Metropolitan Statistical Area—see Appendix B for areas included; Data from exceptional events are included; (2) National Ambient Air Quality Standards; ppm = parts per million; ug/m^3 = micrograms per cubic meter; n/a not available.
Concentrations: Nitrogen Dioxide AM—highest arithmetic mean concentration; Nitrogen Dioxide 1-Hr—highest 98th percentile 1-hour daily maximum concentration; Sulfur Dioxide AM—highest annual mean concentration; Sulfur Dioxide 1-Hr—highest 99th percentile 1-hour daily maximum concentration; Sulfur Dioxide 24-Hr—highest second maximum 24-hour concentration
Source: U.S. Environmental Protection Agency, Air Quality Monitoring Information, "Air Quality Statistics by City, 2012"

Drinking Water

Water System Name	Pop. Served	Primary Water Source Type	Violations[1] Health Based	Violations[1] Monitoring/ Reporting
Austin Water & Wastewater	903,570	Surface	0	0

Note: (1) Based on violation data from January 1, 2013 to December 31, 2013 (includes unresolved violations from earlier years)
Source: U.S. Environmental Protection Agency, Office of Ground Water and Drinking Water, Safe Drinking Water Information System (based on data extracted February 10, 2014)

Cape Coral, Florida

Background

Tucked along Florida's Gulf Coast 71 miles south of Sarasota, Cape Coral is a mid-twentieth century community grown from a development launched in 1957. Today, at 115 square miles, it is Florida's third-largest city by land mass and the most populous city between Tampa and Miami. To the east across the Caloosahatchie River lies Fort Myers, and to the west across Pine Island and Pine Island sound lie the fabled barrier islands of Captiva and Sanibel by Pine Island and Pine Island Sound.

Baltimore brothers Leonard and Jack Rosen purchased the former Redfish Point for $678,000 and renamed the property Cape Coral. By June of the following year "the Cape," as it is known, was receiving its first residents. The city incorporated in 1970 when its population reached 11,470.

Despite the city's relative youth, this self-named "Waterfront Wonderland" has developed an interest in its roots. It fosters a Cape Coral Historical Museum that is housed in the original snack bar from the local country club, and one of its oldest historical documents is the Cape's 1961 phone book.

Four hundred precious miles of salt water and fresh water canals slice through the city, providing water access to abundant recreational boaters and numerous opportunities for waterfront living.

Following the economic downturn, Cape Coral is rebounding nicely. It was named a "most improved" housing market in a National Association of Builders report, and Realty Trac showed improvement in the area's foreclosures at the same time. The Army Reserve purchased a 15-acre Cape Coral site for use as an Army Reserve Training Center for local reservists.

Industry-wise, Cape Coral has Foreign Trade Zones in two of its three industrial parks, the 92.5 acre North Cape Industrial Park—home to light manufacturers, service industry and warehouses—and the Mid Cape Commerce Park which, at 143.37 acres, is comprised of service industries and warehouses. In addition, a VA Clinic was recently built by the U.S. Dept. of Veteran's Affairs at the Hancock Creek Commerce Park and Indian Oaks Trade Centre.

The VA Clinic provides a full range of services ranging from mental health and diagnostic radiology to urology and a full complement of imaging services such as CT scans and nuclear medicine. It is the centerpiece of a Veterans Investment Zone initiative that is proposed to draw office, medical parks, assisted living facilities and the like.

Today the U.S. Bureau of Labor Statistics tracks Cape Coral's success in conjunction with that of nearby Fort Myers, and the region boasts trade, transportation and utilities as its largest economic sector. Essentially, this is a retirement and tourism destination.

Significant recreational opportunities are available in the area, and include the Four Mile Cove Ecological Preserve with its nature trail, picnic area, and warm weather kayak rentals. The Cape Coral Yacht Club, located where the city first began, includes a fishing pier, beach, and community pool. The 18-hole public Coral Oaks Golf Course (replete with pro shop and pub), the Northwest Softball Complex, the William Bill Austen Youth Center Eagle Skate Park, the Strausser BMX Sports Complex, and even the Pelican Sport Soccer Complex show the city's diverse recreational opportunities.

To the east of Cape Coral—on the other side of Fort Myers—is both the Florida Gulf Coast University and Southwest Florida International Airport.

Cape Coral's climate borders on perfect, with an average 335 days per year of sunshine (albeit hot and humid ones in summer time). Annual rainfall is 53.37 inches, with the most rain coming in summer. The city dries out from October into May.

Rankings

General Rankings

- Cape Coral was identified as one of America's fastest-growing cities in terms of population and economy by *Forbes*. The area ranked #14 out of 20. The 100 most populous metro areas in the U.S. were evaluated on the following criteria: estimated population growth; job growth; gross metropolitan product growth; unemployment; median salaries for college-educated workers. *Forbes, "America's Fastest-Growing Cities 2014," February 14, 2014*

Business/Finance Rankings

- Building on the U.S. Department of Labor's Occupational Information Network Data Collection Program, the Brookings Institution defined STEM occupations and job opportunities for STEM workers at various levels of educational attainment. The Cape Coral metro area was one of the ten metro areas where workers in low-education-level STEM jobs earn the highest relative wages. *www.brookings.edu, "The Hidden Stem Economy," June 10, 2013*

- Building on the U.S. Department of Labor's Occupational Information Network Data Collection Program, the Brookings Institution defined STEM occupations and job opportunities for STEM workers at various levels of educational attainment. The Cape Coral metro area was placed among the ten large metro areas with the lowest demand for high-level STEM knowledge. *www.brookings.edu, "The Hidden Stem Economy," June 10, 2013*

- Cape Coral was ranked #10 out of 100 metro areas in terms of economic performance (#1 = best) during the recession and recovery from trough quarter through the second quarter of 2013. Criteria: percent change in employment; percentage point change in unemployment rate; percent change in gross metropolitan product; percent change in House Price Index. *Brookings Institution, MetroMonitor: Tracking Economic Recession and Recovery in America's 100 Largest Metropolitan Areas, September 2013*

- The Cape Coral metro area appeared on the Milken Institute "2013 Best Performing Cities" list. Rank: #164 out of 200 large metro areas. Criteria: job growth; wage and salary growth; high-tech output growth. *Milken Institute, "Best-Performing Cities 2013," December 2013*

- *Forbes* ranked the 200 most populous metro areas in the U.S. in terms of the "Best Places for Business and Careers." The Cape Coral metro area was ranked #117. Criteria: costs (business and living); job growth (past and projected); income growth; educational attainment (college and high school); projected economic growth; cultural and recreational opportunities; net migration patterns; number of highly ranked colleges. *Forbes, "The Best Places for Business and Careers," August 7, 2013*

Environmental Rankings

- The Cape Coral metro area came in at #347 for the relative comfort of its climate on Sperling's list of "chill cities," as measured by the Sperling Heat Index. All 361 metro areas are included. Criteria included daytime high temperatures, nighttime low temperatures, dew point, and relative humidity at the high temperatures. *www.bertsperling.com, "Sperling's Chill Cities," July 18, 2013*

- Sperling's BestPlaces assessed 379 metropolitan areas of the United States for the likelihood of dangerously extreme weather events or earthquakes. In general the Southeast and South-Central regions have the highest risk of weather extremes and earthquakes, while the Pacific Northwest enjoys the lowest risk. Of the least risky metropolitan areas, the Cape Coral metro area was ranked #335. *www.bestplaces.net, "Safest Places from Natural Disasters," April 2011*

- Cape Coral was selected as one of 22 "Smarter Cities" for energy by the Natural Resources Defense Council. Criteria: investment in green power; energy efficiency measures; conservation. *Natural Resources Defense Council, "2010 Smarter Cities," July 19, 2010*

- Cape Coral was highlighted as one of the cleanest metro areas for ozone air pollution in the U.S. during 2008 through 2010. The list represents cities with no monitored ozone air pollution in unhealthful ranges. *American Lung Association, State of the Air 2012*

- Cape Coral was highlighted as one of the top 25 cleanest metro areas for year-round particle pollution (Annual PM 2.5) in the U.S. during 2008 through 2010. The area ranked #20. *American Lung Association, State of the Air 2012*

- Cape Coral was highlighted as one of the top 25 cleanest metro areas for short-term particle pollution (24-hour PM 2.5) in the U.S. during 2008 through 2010. Monitors in these cities reported no days with unhealthful PM 2.5 levels. *American Lung Association, State of the Air 2012*

Health/Fitness Rankings

- Cape Coral was identified as a "2013 Spring Allergy Capital." The area ranked #73 out of 100. Three groups of factors were used to identify the most severe cities for people with allergies during the spring season: annual pollen levels; medicine utilization; access to board-certified allergists. *Asthma and Allergy Foundation of America, "Spring Allergy Capitals 2013"*

- Cape Coral was identified as a "2013 Fall Allergy Capital." The area ranked #65 out of 100. Three groups of factors were used to identify the most severe cities for people with allergies during the fall season: annual pollen levels; medicine utilization; access to board-certified allergists. *Asthma and Allergy Foundation of America, "Fall Allergy Capitals 2013"*

- Cape Coral was identified as a "2013 Asthma Capital." The area ranked #95 out of the nation's 100 largest metropolitan areas. Twelve factors were used to identify the most challenging places to live for people with asthma: estimated prevalence; self-reported prevalence; crude death rate for asthma; annual pollen score; annual air quality; public smoking laws; number of board-certified asthma specialists; school inhaler access laws; rescue medication use; controller medication use; uninsured rate; poverty rate. *Asthma and Allergy Foundation of America, "Asthma Capitals 2013"*

- Cape Coral was selected as one of the best metropolitan areas for hospital care in America by *HealthGrades.com*. The rankings are based on a comprehensive study of patient death and complication rates in the nation's nearly 5,000 hospitals. Hospitals performing in the top 5% nationwide across 26 different medical procedures and diagnoses were identified. *HealthGrades.com* then ranked cities by the highest percentage of these Distinguished Hospitals for Clinical Excellence™. The Cape Coral metro area ranked #11. *HealthGrades.com, "America's Top 50 Cities for Hospital Care," January 21, 2012*

- The Cape Coral metro area appeared in the 2013 Gallup-Healthways Well-Being Index. The area ranked #149 out of 189. The Gallup-Healthways Well-Being Index score is an average of six sub-indexes, which individually examine life evaluation, emotional health, work environment, physical health, healthy behaviors, and access to basic necessities. Results are based on telephone interviews conducted as part of the Gallup-Healthways Well-Being Index survey January 2–December 29, 2012, and January 2–December 30, 2013, with a random sample of 531,630 adults, aged 18 and older, living in metropolitan areas in the 50 U.S. states and the District of Columbia. *Gallup-Healthways, "State of American Well-Being," March 25, 2014*

Real Estate Rankings

- Cape Coral was identified as one of the "Top Turnaround Housing Markets for 2012." The area ranked #4 out of 10. Criteria: year-over-year median home price appreciation; year-over-year median inventory age; year-over-year inventory reduction. *AOL Real Estate, "Top Turnaround Housing Markets for 2012," February 4, 2012*

- Cape Coral was ranked #39 out of 283 metro areas in terms of house price appreciation in 2013 (#1 = highest rate). *Federal Housing Finance Agency, House Price Index, 4th Quarter 2013*

- The Cape Coral metro area was identified as one of the 20 best housing markets in the U.S. in 2013. The area ranked #8 out of 173 markets with a home price appreciation of 21.6%. Criteria: year-over-year change of median sales price of existing single-family homes between the 4th quarter of 2012 and the 4th quarter of 2013. *National Association of Realtors®, Median Sales Price of Existing Single-Family Homes for Metropolitan Areas, 4th Quarter 2013*

- Cape Coral was ranked #147 out of 224 metro areas in terms of housing affordability in 2013 by the National Association of Home Builders (#1 = most affordable). The NAHB-Wells Fargo Housing Opportunity Index (HOI) for a given area is defined as the share of homes sold in that area that would have been affordable to a family earning the local median income, based on standard mortgage underwriting criteria. *National Association of Home Builders®, NAHB-Wells Fargo Housing Opportunity Index, 4th Quarter 2013*

Safety Rankings

- Allstate ranked the 200 largest cities in America in terms of driver safety. Cape Coral ranked #40. Allstate researchers analyzed internal property damage claims over a two-year period from January 2010 to December 2011. A weighted average of the two-year numbers determined the annual percentages. *Allstate, "Allstate America's Best Drivers Report®, August 27, 2013"*

- The National Insurance Crime Bureau ranked 380 metro areas in the U.S. in terms of per capita rates of vehicle theft. The Cape Coral metro area ranked #195 (#1 = highest rate). Criteria: number of vehicle theft offenses per 100,000 inhabitants in 2012. *National Insurance Crime Bureau, "Hot Spots 2012," June 26, 2013*

Seniors/Retirement Rankings

- From its Best Cities for Successful Aging indexes, the Milken Institute generated rankings for metropolitan areas, weighing data in eight categories—general indicators, health care, wellness, living arrangements, transportation and general accessibility, financial well-being, education and employment, and community participation. The Cape Coral metro area was ranked #46 overall in the large metro area category. *Milken Institute, "Best Cities for Successful Aging," July 2012*

- Cape Coral made the 2014 *Forbes* list of "25 Best Places to Retire." Criteria include: housing and living costs; tax climate for retirees; weather and air quality; crime rates; doctor availability; active-lifestyle rankings for walkability, bicycling and volunteering. *Forbes.com, "The Best Places to Retire in 2014," January 16, 2014*

- Cape Coral was selected as one of the best places to retire by *CNNMoney.com*. Criteria: low cost of living; low violent-crime rate; good medical care; large population over age 50; abundant amenities for retirees. *CNNMoney.com, "Best Places to Retire 2011"*

Miscellaneous Rankings

- The National Alliance to End Homelessness ranked the 100 most populous metro areas in terms the rate of homelessness. The Cape Coral metro area ranked #43. Criteria: number of homeless people per 10,000 population in 2011. *National Alliance to End Homelessness, The State of Homelessness in America 2012*

Business Environment

CITY FINANCES

City Government Finances

Component	2011 ($000)	2011 ($ per capita)
Total Revenues	277,088	1,765
Total Expenditures	287,254	1,830
Debt Outstanding	919,504	5,857
Cash and Securities[1]	433,044	2,759

Note: (1) Cash and security holdings of a government at the close of its fiscal year, including those of its dependent agencies, utilities, and liquor stores.
Source: U.S Census Bureau, State & Local Government Finances 2011

City Government Revenue by Source

Source	2011 ($000)	2011 ($ per capita)
General Revenue		
From Federal Government	7,598	48
From State Government	15,501	99
From Local Governments	3,647	23
Taxes		
Property	82,845	528
Sales and Gross Receipts	19,445	124
Personal Income	0	0
Corporate Income	0	0
Motor Vehicle License	0	0
Other Taxes	3,470	22
Current Charges	54,193	345
Liquor Store	0	0
Utility	28,583	182
Employee Retirement	4,412	28

Source: U.S Census Bureau, State & Local Government Finances 2011

City Government Expenditures by Function

Function	2011 ($000)	2011 ($ per capita)	2011 (%)
General Direct Expenditures			
Air Transportation	0	0	0.0
Corrections	0	0	0.0
Education	15,686	100	5.5
Employment Security Administration	0	0	0.0
Financial Administration	16,759	107	5.8
Fire Protection	24,713	157	8.6
General Public Buildings	0	0	0.0
Governmental Administration, Other	3,552	23	1.2
Health	0	0	0.0
Highways	44,483	283	15.5
Hospitals	0	0	0.0
Housing and Community Development	8,509	54	3.0
Interest on General Debt	8,676	55	3.0
Judicial and Legal	932	6	0.3
Libraries	0	0	0.0
Parking	26	< 1	< 0.1
Parks and Recreation	17,005	108	5.9
Police Protection	37,387	238	13.0
Public Welfare	0	0	0.0
Sewerage	20,058	128	7.0
Solid Waste Management	0	0	0.0
Veterans' Services	0	0	0.0
Liquor Store	0	0	0.0
Utility	41,968	267	14.6
Employee Retirement	10,652	68	3.7

Source: U.S Census Bureau, State & Local Government Finances 2011

DEMOGRAPHICS

Population Growth

Area	1990 Census	2000 Census	2010 Census	Population Growth (%)	
				1990-2000	2000-2010
City	75,507	102,286	154,305	35.5	50.9
MSA[1]	335,113	440,888	618,754	31.6	40.3
U.S.	248,709,873	281,421,906	308,745,538	13.2	9.7

Note: (1) Figures cover the Cape Coral-Fort Myers, FL Metropolitan Statistical Area—see Appendix B for areas included
Source: U.S. Census Bureau, Census 1990, 2000, 2010

Household Size

Area	Persons in Household (%)							Average Household Size
	One	Two	Three	Four	Five	Six	Seven or More	
City	22.5	41.3	15.7	11.6	6.1	1.7	1.0	2.84
MSA[1]	28.4	43.5	12.0	9.4	4.1	1.7	0.8	2.62
U.S.	27.6	33.5	15.7	13.2	6.1	2.4	1.5	2.63

Note: (1) Figures cover the Cape Coral-Fort Myers, FL Metropolitan Statistical Area—see Appendix B for areas included
Source: U.S. Census Bureau, 2010-2012 American Community Survey 3-Year Estimates

Race

Area	White Alone[2] (%)	Black Alone[2] (%)	Asian Alone[2] (%)	AIAN[3] Alone[2] (%)	NHOPI[4] Alone[2] (%)	Other Race Alone[2] (%)	Two or More Races (%)
City	91.2	3.5	1.6	0.5	0.0	1.7	1.4
MSA[1]	84.1	8.2	1.6	0.4	0.0	4.1	1.6
U.S.	74.0	12.6	4.9	0.8	0.2	4.7	2.8

Note: (1) Figures cover the Cape Coral-Fort Myers, FL Metropolitan Statistical Area—see Appendix B for areas included; (2) Alone is defined as not being in combination with one or more other races; (3) American Indian and Alaska Native; (4) Native Hawaiian and Other Pacific Islander
Source: U.S. Census Bureau, 2010-2012 American Community Survey 3-Year Estimates

Hispanic or Latino Origin

Area	Total (%)	Mexican (%)	Puerto Rican (%)	Cuban (%)	Other (%)
City	18.2	1.8	5.3	5.9	5.3
MSA[1]	18.6	5.8	4.3	3.8	4.8
U.S.	16.6	10.7	1.6	0.6	3.7

Note: Persons of Hispanic or Latino origin can be of any race; (1) Figures cover the Cape Coral-Fort Myers, FL Metropolitan Statistical Area—see Appendix B for areas included
Source: U.S. Census Bureau, 2010-2012 American Community Survey 3-Year Estimates

Segregation

Type	Segregation Indices[1]				Percent Change		
	1990	2000	2010	2010 Rank[2]	1990-2000	1990-2010	2000-2010
Black/White	76.8	69.4	61.6	35	-7.5	-15.3	-7.8
Asian/White	23.3	28.5	25.3	96	5.3	2.0	-3.3
Hispanic/White	36.1	40.8	40.2	63	4.7	4.1	-0.6

Note: All figures cover the Metropolitan Statistical Area—see Appendix B for areas included; Figures are based on an analysis of 1990, 2000, and 2010 Census Decennial Census tract data by William H. Frey, Brookings Institution and the University of Michigan Social Science Data Analysis Network. In this analysis all racial groups (whites, blacks, and asians) are non-Hispanic members of those races. Hispanics are shown as a separate category;
(1) Segregation Indices are Dissimilarity Indices that measure the degree to which the minority group is distributed differently than whites across census tracts. They range from 0 (complete integration) to 100 (complete segregation) where the value indicates the percentage of the minority group that needs to move to be distributed exactly like whites; (2) Ranges from 1 (most segregated) to 102 (least segregated); n/a not available.
Source: www.CensusScope.org

Ancestry

Area	German	Irish	English	American	Italian	Polish	French[2]	Scottish	Dutch
City	19.2	16.0	8.9	10.6	12.3	4.5	3.1	1.4	1.4
MSA[1]	15.8	12.6	9.5	13.6	8.1	3.8	2.9	1.6	1.3
U.S.	15.2	11.1	8.2	7.2	5.6	3.1	2.8	1.7	1.4

Note: Figures are the percentage of the total population reporting a particular ancestry. The nine most commonly reported ancestries in the U.S. are shown. Figures include multiple ancestries (e.g. if a person reported being Irish and Italian, they were included in both columns); (1) Figures cover the Cape Coral-Fort Myers, FL Metropolitan Statistical Area—see Appendix B for areas included; (2) Excludes Basque
Source: U.S. Census Bureau, 2010-2012 American Community Survey 3-Year Estimates

Foreign-Born Population

Area	Percent of Population Born in								
	Any Foreign Country	Mexico	Asia	Europe	Carribean	South America	Central America[2]	Africa	Canada
City	13.6	0.5	1.3	3.1	5.1	2.4	0.9	0.1	0.3
MSA[1]	14.9	2.8	1.2	2.3	4.4	1.7	1.4	0.1	0.9
U.S.	13.0	3.7	3.7	1.6	1.2	0.9	1.0	0.5	0.3

Note: (1) Figures cover the Cape Coral-Fort Myers, FL Metropolitan Statistical Area—see Appendix B for areas included; (2) Excludes Mexico.
Source: U.S. Census Bureau, 2010-2012 American Community Survey 3-Year Estimates

Marital Status

Area	Never Married	Now Married[2]	Separated	Widowed	Divorced
City	25.1	52.3	1.9	7.1	13.7
MSA[1]	25.9	50.4	2.1	8.2	13.4
U.S.	32.4	48.4	2.2	6.0	11.0

Note: Figures are percentages and cover the population 15 years of age and older; (1) Figures cover the Cape Coral-Fort Myers, FL Metropolitan Statistical Area—see Appendix B for areas included; (2) Excludes separated
Source: U.S. Census Bureau, 2010-2012 American Community Survey 3-Year Estimates

Age

Area	Percent of Population									Median Age
	Under Age 5	Age 5–19	Age 20–34	Age 35–44	Age 45–54	Age 55–64	Age 65–74	Age 75–84	Age 85+	
City	5.9	19.9	14.6	13.1	14.5	14.0	10.4	5.2	2.4	42.2
MSA[1]	5.2	16.3	16.0	11.2	13.0	14.1	13.6	7.5	3.1	46.0
U.S.	6.4	20.1	20.5	13.1	14.3	12.2	7.3	4.2	1.8	37.3

Note: (1) Figures cover the Cape Coral-Fort Myers, FL Metropolitan Statistical Area—see Appendix B for areas included
Source: U.S. Census Bureau, 2010-2012 American Community Survey 3-Year Estimates

Gender

Area	Males	Females	Males per 100 Females
City	78,211	79,722	98.1
MSA[1]	310,415	322,084	96.4
U.S.	153,276,055	158,333,314	96.8

Note: (1) Figures cover the Cape Coral-Fort Myers, FL Metropolitan Statistical Area—see Appendix B for areas included
Source: U.S. Census Bureau, 2010-2012 American Community Survey 3-Year Estimates

Religious Groups by Family

Area	Catholic	Baptist	Non-Den.	Methodist[2]	Lutheran	LDS[3]	Pentecostal	Presbyterian[4]	Muslim[5]	Judaism
MSA[1]	16.2	5.0	3.0	2.5	1.2	0.5	4.4	1.4	0.9	0.2
U.S.	19.1	9.3	4.0	4.0	2.3	2.0	1.9	1.6	0.8	0.7

Note: Figures are the number of adherents as a percentage of the total population; (1) Figures cover the Cape Coral-Fort Myers, FL Metropolitan Statistical Area—see Appendix B for areas included; (2) Methodist/Pietist; (3) Latter Day Saints; (4) Reformed; (5) Figures are estimates
Source: Association of Statisticians of American Religious Bodies, 2010 U.S. Religion Census: Religious Congregations & Membership Study

Religious Groups by Tradition

Area	Catholic	Evangelical Protestant	Mainline Protestant	Other Tradition	Black Protestant	Orthodox
MSA[1]	16.2	14.3	4.6	2.0	0.3	0.2
U.S.	19.1	16.2	7.3	4.3	1.6	0.3

Note: Figures are the number of adherents as a percentage of the total population; (1) Figures cover the Cape Coral-Fort Myers, FL Metropolitan Statistical Area—see Appendix B for areas included
Source: Association of Statisticians of American Religious Bodies, 2010 U.S. Religion Census: Religious Congregations & Membership Study

ECONOMY

Gross Metropolitan Product

Area	2011	2012	2013	2014	Rank[2]
MSA[1]	20.1	20.9	21.4	22.4	100

Note: Figures are in billions of dollars; (1) Figures cover the Cape Coral-Fort Myers, FL Metropolitan Statistical Area—see Appendix B for areas included; (2) Rank is based on 2014 data and ranges from 1 to 363
Source: The United States Conference of Mayors, U.S. Metro Economies: Outlook—Gross Metropolitan Product, with Metro Employment Projections, November 2013

Economic Growth

Area	2011 (%)	2012 (%)	2013 (%)	2014 (%)	Rank[2]
MSA[1]	0.5	2.2	1.1	2.6	145
U.S.	1.6	2.5	1.7	2.5	–

Note: Figures are real gross metropolitan product (GMP) growth rates and represent annual average percent change; (1) Figures cover the Cape Coral-Fort Myers, FL Metropolitan Statistical Area—see Appendix B for areas included; (2) Rank is based on 2013 data and ranges from 1 to 363
Source: The United States Conference of Mayors, U.S. Metro Economies: Outlook—Gross Metropolitan Product, with Metro Employment Projections, November 2013

Metropolitan Area Exports

Area	2007	2008	2009	2010	2011	2012	Rank[2]
MSA[1]	198.3	282.8	237.5	298.0	305.1	509.8	205

Note: Figures are in millions of dollars; (1) Figures cover the Cape Coral-Fort Myers, FL Metropolitan Statistical Area—see Appendix B for areas included; (2) Rank is based on 2012 data and ranges from 1 to 369
Source: U.S. Department of Commerce, International Trade Administration, Office of Trade & Industry Information, Manufacturing & Services, data extracted April 1, 2014

INCOME

Income

Area	Per Capita ($)	Median Household ($)	Average Household ($)
City	22,522	47,586	59,540
MSA[1]	26,278	46,022	65,020
U.S.	27,385	51,771	71,579

Note: (1) Figures cover the Cape Coral-Fort Myers, FL Metropolitan Statistical Area—see Appendix B for areas included
Source: U.S. Census Bureau, 2010-2012 American Community Survey 3-Year Estimates

Household Income Distribution

Area	Percent of Households Earning							
	Under $15,000	$15,000 -24,999	$25,000 -34,999	$35,000 -49,999	$50,000 -74,999	$75,000 -99,000	$100,000 -149,999	$150,000 and up
City	11.3	11.7	12.9	16.2	20.6	11.9	10.6	4.9
MSA[1]	11.9	12.5	13.2	16.2	18.9	10.4	10.1	6.8
U.S.	13.1	11.0	10.5	13.7	18.1	11.9	12.5	9.1

Note: (1) Figures cover the Cape Coral-Fort Myers, FL Metropolitan Statistical Area—see Appendix B for areas included
Source: U.S. Census Bureau, 2010-2012 American Community Survey 3-Year Estimates

Poverty Rate

Area	All Ages	Under 18 Years Old	18 to 64 Years Old	65 Years and Over
City	15.1	21.6	14.5	8.7
MSA[1]	16.1	27.3	16.3	6.9
U.S.	15.7	22.2	14.6	9.3

Note: Figures are percentage of people whose income during the past 12 months was below the poverty level;
(1) Figures cover the Cape Coral-Fort Myers, FL Metropolitan Statistical Area—see Appendix B for areas included
Source: U.S. Census Bureau, 2010-2012 American Community Survey 3-Year Estimates

Personal Bankruptcy Filing Rate

Area	2008	2009	2010	2011	2012	2013
Lee County	4.92	7.38	7.32	5.30	3.73	2.92
U.S.	3.53	4.61	4.97	4.37	3.76	3.29

Note: Numbers are per 1,000 population and include Chapter 7 and Chapter 13 filings
Source: Federal Deposit Insurance Corporation, Regional Economic Conditions, March 20, 2014

EMPLOYMENT

Labor Force and Employment

Area	Civilian Labor Force			Workers Employed		
	Dec. 2012	Dec. 2013	% Chg.	Dec. 2012	Dec. 2013	% Chg.
City	79,099	79,040	-0.1	72,936	74,536	2.2
MSA[1]	288,827	288,702	0.0	266,079	271,916	2.2
U.S.	154,904,000	154,408,000	-0.3	143,060,000	144,423,000	1.0

Note: Data is not seasonally adjusted and covers workers 16 years of age and older; (1) Metropolitan Statistical Area—see Appendix B for areas included
Source: Bureau of Labor Statistics, Local Area Unemployment Statistics

Unemployment Rate

Area	2013											
	Jan.	Feb.	Mar.	Apr.	May	Jun.	Jul.	Aug.	Sep.	Oct.	Nov.	Dec.
City	8.0	7.4	6.9	6.6	6.7	7.1	7.2	6.9	6.5	6.2	6.2	5.7
MSA[1]	7.9	7.4	6.8	6.7	7.0	7.5	7.6	7.3	7.0	6.5	6.3	5.8
U.S.	8.5	8.1	7.6	7.1	7.3	7.8	7.7	7.3	7.0	7.0	6.6	6.5

Note: Data is not seasonally adjusted and covers workers 16 years of age and older; All figures are percentages;
(1) Metropolitan Statistical Area—see Appendix B for areas included
Source: Bureau of Labor Statistics, Local Area Unemployment Statistics

Employment by Occupation

Occupation Classification	City (%)	MSA[1] (%)	U.S. (%)
Management, Business, Science, and Arts	29.4	29.1	36.0
Natural Resources, Construction, and Maintenance	11.2	10.5	9.1
Production, Transportation, and Material Moving	7.4	7.6	12.0
Sales and Office	29.7	28.8	24.7
Service	22.3	23.9	18.2

Note: Figures cover employed civilians 16 years of age and older; (1) Figures cover the Cape Coral-Fort Myers, FL Metropolitan Statistical Area—see Appendix B for areas included
Source: U.S. Census Bureau, 2010-2012 American Community Survey 3-Year Estimates

Employment by Industry

| Sector | MSA[1] | | U.S. |
	Number of Employees	Percent of Total	Percent of Total
Construction	n/a	n/a	4.2
Education and Health Services	25,300	11.3	15.5
Financial Activities	11,600	5.2	5.7
Government	39,200	17.5	16.1
Information	3,200	1.4	1.9
Leisure and Hospitality	35,100	15.6	10.2
Manufacturing	4,900	2.2	8.7
Mining and Logging	n/a	n/a	0.6
Other Services	9,200	4.1	3.9
Professional and Business Services	29,100	13.0	13.7
Retail Trade	38,200	17.0	11.4
Transportation and Utilities	4,200	1.9	3.8
Wholesale Trade	6,800	3.0	4.2

Note: Figures cover non-farm employment as of December 2013 and are not seasonally adjusted; (1) Metropolitan Statistical Area—see Appendix B for areas included; n/a not available
Source: Bureau of Labor Statistics, Current Employment Statistics, Employment, Hours, and Earnings

Occupations with Greatest Projected Employment Growth: 2010 – 2020

Occupation[1]	2010 Employment	2020 Projected Employment	Numeric Employment Change	Percent Employment Change
Retail Salespersons	290,200	345,860	55,660	19.2
Combined Food Preparation and Serving Workers, Including Fast Food	154,650	193,760	39,110	25.3
Registered Nurses	165,400	202,190	36,790	22.3
Waiters and Waitresses	174,630	210,650	36,010	20.6
Customer Service Representatives	165,950	194,220	28,260	17.0
Cashiers	200,040	225,430	25,400	12.7
Office Clerks, General	142,480	164,800	22,330	15.7
Landscaping and Groundskeeping Workers	93,350	115,400	22,050	23.6
Postsecondary Teachers	75,610	94,190	18,580	24.6
Cooks, Restaurant	76,000	94,180	18,190	23.9

Note: Projections cover Florida; (1) Sorted by numeric employment change
Source: www.projectionscentral.com, State Occupational Projections, 2010–2020 Long-Term Projections

Fastest Growing Occupations: 2010 – 2020

Occupation[1]	2010 Employment	2020 Projected Employment	Numeric Employment Change	Percent Employment Change
Layout Workers, Metal and Plastic	230	380	150	65.2
Biomedical Engineers	620	990	370	60.2
Helpers—Carpenters	1,120	1,770	650	58.0
Biochemists and Biophysicists	650	1,000	350	53.6
Medical Scientists, Except Epidemiologists	2,850	4,370	1,520	53.5
Helpers—Brickmasons, Blockmasons, Stonemasons, and Tile and Marble Setters	810	1,240	430	52.6
Reinforcing Iron and Rebar Workers	940	1,370	430	46.1
Home Health Aides	28,580	41,010	12,430	43.5
Stonemasons	550	790	240	42.9
Personal Care Aides	16,880	23,920	7,040	41.7

Note: Projections cover Florida; (1) Sorted by percent employment change and excludes occupations with numeric employment change less than 100
Source: www.projectionscentral.com, State Occupational Projections, 2010–2020 Long-Term Projections

Average Wages

Occupation	$/Hr.	Occupation	$/Hr.
Accountants and Auditors	32.91	Maids and Housekeeping Cleaners	10.00
Automotive Mechanics	18.63	Maintenance and Repair Workers	15.96
Bookkeepers	16.17	Marketing Managers	51.96
Carpenters	19.17	Nuclear Medicine Technologists	36.35
Cashiers	9.72	Nurses, Licensed Practical	19.78
Clerks, General Office	13.10	Nurses, Registered	28.94
Clerks, Receptionists/Information	12.80	Nursing Assistants	12.72
Clerks, Shipping/Receiving	12.50	Packers and Packagers, Hand	9.05
Computer Programmers	44.91	Physical Therapists	40.30
Computer Systems Analysts	45.79	Postal Service Mail Carriers	24.25
Computer User Support Specialists	19.67	Real Estate Brokers	n/a
Cooks, Restaurant	11.37	Retail Salespersons	11.83
Dentists	47.08	Sales Reps., Exc. Tech./Scientific	24.18
Electrical Engineers	32.63	Sales Reps., Tech./Scientific	29.78
Electricians	16.91	Secretaries, Exc. Legal/Med./Exec.	14.54
Financial Managers	49.70	Security Guards	11.15
First-Line Supervisors/Managers, Sales	20.90	Surgeons	n/a
Food Preparation Workers	10.08	Teacher Assistants	13.20
General and Operations Managers	52.27	Teachers, Elementary School	23.40
Hairdressers/Cosmetologists	15.40	Teachers, Secondary School	24.10
Internists	102.76	Telemarketers	9.65
Janitors and Cleaners	11.52	Truck Drivers, Heavy/Tractor-Trailer	16.06
Landscaping/Groundskeeping Workers	11.41	Truck Drivers, Light/Delivery Svcs.	14.10
Lawyers	40.19	Waiters and Waitresses	9.67

Note: Wage data covers the Cape Coral-Fort Myers, FL Metropolitan Statistical Area—see Appendix B for areas included. Hourly wages for elementary/secondary school teachers and teacher assistants were calculated by the editors from annual wage data assuming a 40 hour work week; n/a not available.
Source: Bureau of Labor Statistics, Metro Area Occupational Employment and Wage Estimates, May 2013

RESIDENTIAL REAL ESTATE

Building Permits

Area	Single-Family			Multi-Family			Total		
	2012	2013	Pct. Chg.	2012	2013	Pct. Chg.	2012	2013	Pct. Chg.
City	330	492	49.1	16	6	-62.5	346	498	43.9
MSA[1]	1,806	2,531	40.1	237	645	172.2	2,043	3,176	55.5
U.S.	518,695	620,802	19.7	310,963	370,020	19.0	829,658	990,822	19.4

Note: (1) Metropolitan Statistical Area—see Appendix B for areas included; figures represent new, privately-owned housing units authorized (unadjusted data); All permit data are based on estimates with imputation.
Source: U.S. Census Bureau, Manufacturing, Mining, and Construction Statistics, Building Permits, 2012, 2013

Homeownership Rate

Area	2006 (%)	2007 (%)	2008 (%)	2009 (%)	2010 (%)	2011 (%)	2012 (%)	2013 (%)
MSA[1]	n/a	n/a	n/a	n/a	n/a	n/a	n/a	n/a
U.S.	68.8	68.1	67.8	67.4	66.9	66.1	65.4	65.1

Note: (1) Figures cover the Cape Coral-Fort Myers, FL Metropolitan Statistical Area—see Appendix B for areas included; n/a not available
Source: U.S. Census Bureau, Housing Vacancies and Homeownership Annual Statistics: 2013

Housing Vacancy Rates

Area	Gross Vacancy Rate[2] (%)			Year-Round Vacancy Rate[3] (%)			Rental Vacancy Rate[4] (%)			Homeowner Vacancy Rate[5] (%)		
	2011	2012	2013	2011	2012	2013	2011	2012	2013	2011	2012	2013
MSA[1]	n/a	n/a	n/a	n/a	n/a	n/a	n/a	n/a	n/a	n/a	n/a	n/a
U.S.	14.2	13.8	13.8	11.1	10.8	10.7	9.5	8.7	8.3	2.5	2.0	2.0

Note: (1) Figures cover the Cape Coral-Fort Myers, FL Metropolitan Statistical Area—see Appendix B for areas included; (2) The percentage of the total housing inventory that is vacant; (3) The percentage of the housing inventory (excluding seasonal units) that is year-round vacant; (4) The percentage of rental inventory that is vacant for rent; (5) The percentage of homeowner inventory that is vacant for sale; n/a not available
Source: U.S. Census Bureau, Housing Vacancies and Homeownership Annual Statistics: 2013

TAXES

State Corporate Income Tax Rates

State	Tax Rate (%)	Income Brackets ($)	Num. of Brackets	Financial Institution Tax Rate (%)[a]	Federal Income Tax Ded.
Florida	5.5 (f)	Flat rate	1	5.5 (f)	No

Note: Tax rates as of January 1, 2014; (a) Rates listed are the corporate income tax rate applied to financial institutions or excise taxes based on income. Some states have other taxes based upon the value of deposits or shares; (f) An exemption of $50,000 is allowed. Florida's Alternative Minimum Tax rate is 3.3%.
Source: Federation of Tax Administrators, "State Corporate Income Tax Rates, 2014"

State Individual Income Tax Rates

State	Tax Rate (%)	Income Brackets ($)	Num. of Brackets	Personal Exempt. ($)[1] Single	Personal Exempt. ($)[1] Dependents	Fed. Inc. Tax Ded.
Florida	None	–	–	–	–	–

Note: Tax rates as of January 1, 2014; Local- and county-level taxes are not included; n/a not applicable; (1) Married joint filers generally receive double the single exemption
Source: Federation of Tax Administrators, "State Individual Income Tax Rates, 2014"

Various State and Local Tax Rates

State	State and Local Sales and Use (%)	State Sales and Use (%)	Gasoline[1] (¢/gal.)	Cigarette[2] ($/pack)	Spirits[3] ($/gal.)	Wine[4] ($/gal.)	Beer[5] ($/gal.)
Florida	6.0	6.00	36.03	1.339	6.50 (f)	2.25	0.48

Note: All tax rates as of January 1, 2014; (1) The American Petroleum Institute has developed a methodology for determining the average tax rate on a gallon of fuel. Rates may include any of the following: excise taxes, environmental fees, storage tank fees, other fees or taxes, general sales tax, and local taxes. In states where gasoline is subject to the general sales tax, or where the fuel tax is based on the average sale price, the average rate determined by API is sensitive to changes in the price of gasoline. States that fully or partially apply general sales taxes to gasoline: CA, CO, GA, IL, IN, MI, NY; (2) The federal excise tax of $1.0066 per pack and local taxes are not included; (3) Rates are those applicable to off-premise sales of 40% alcohol by volume (a.b.v.) distilled spirits in 750ml containers. Local excise taxes are excluded; (4) Rates are those applicable to off-premise sales of 11% a.b.v. non-carbonated wine in 750ml containers; (5) Rates are those applicable to off-premise sales of 4.7% a.b.v. beer in 12 ounce containers; (f) Different rates also applicable according to alcohol content, place of production, size of container, or place purchased (on- or off-premise or onboard airlines).
Source: Tax Foundation, 2014 Facts & Figures: How Does Your State Compare?

State Business Tax Climate Index Rankings

State	Overall Rank	Corporate Tax Index Rank	Individual Income Tax Index Rank	Sales Tax Index Rank	Unemployment Insurance Tax Index Rank	Property Tax Index Rank
Florida	5	13	1	18	6	16

Note: The index is a measure of how each state's tax laws affect economic performance. The lower the rank, the more favorable a state's tax system is for business. States without a given tax are given a ranking of 1. The scores/rankings for the District of Columbia do not affect other states. The 2014 index represents the tax climate as of July 1, 2013.
Source: Tax Foundation, State Business Tax Climate Index 2014

COMMERCIAL UTILITIES

Typical Monthly Electric Bills

Area	Commercial Service ($/month) 1,500 kWh	Commercial Service ($/month) 40 kW demand 14,000 kWh	Industrial Service ($/month) 1,000 kW demand 200,000 kWh	Industrial Service ($/month) 50,000 kW demand 15,000,000 kWh
City	n/a	n/a	n/a	n/a
Average[1]	197	1,636	25,662	1,485,307

Note: Based on total rates in effect July 1, 2013; (1) average based on 180 utilities surveyed; n/a not available
Source: Edison Electric Institute, Typical Bills and Average Rates Report, Summer 2013

TRANSPORTATION

Means of Transportation to Work

Area	Car/Truck/Van		Public Transportation			Bicycle	Walked	Other Means	Worked at Home
	Drove Alone	Car-pooled	Bus	Subway	Railroad				
City	83.7	9.0	0.6	0.0	0.0	0.5	0.8	1.5	4.0
MSA[1]	76.6	12.1	1.3	0.0	0.0	1.0	1.0	2.2	5.8
U.S.	76.4	9.7	2.6	1.7	0.5	0.6	2.8	1.3	4.3

Note: Figures are percentages and cover workers 16 years of age and older; (1) Figures cover the Cape Coral-Fort Myers, FL Metropolitan Statistical Area—see Appendix B for areas included
Source: U.S. Census Bureau, 2010-2012 American Community Survey 3-Year Estimates

Travel Time to Work

Area	Less Than 10 Minutes	10 to 19 Minutes	20 to 29 Minutes	30 to 44 Minutes	45 to 59 Minutes	60 to 89 Minutes	90 Minutes or More
City	8.3	25.9	23.0	26.4	10.1	4.0	2.3
MSA[1]	9.1	28.2	21.6	25.5	8.7	4.4	2.6
U.S.	13.5	29.8	20.9	20.1	7.5	5.6	2.5

Note: Figures are percentages and include workers 16 years old and over; (1) Figures cover the Cape Coral-Fort Myers, FL Metropolitan Statistical Area—see Appendix B for areas included
Source: U.S. Census Bureau, 2010-2012 American Community Survey 3-Year Estimates

Travel Time Index

Area	1985	1990	1995	2000	2005	2010	2011
Urban Area[1]	1.10	1.13	1.21	1.15	1.18	1.15	1.15
Average[2]	1.09	1.14	1.16	1.19	1.23	1.18	1.18

Note: Travel Time Index—the ratio of travel time in the peak period to the travel time at free-flow conditions. For example, a value of 1.30 indicates a 20-minute free-flow trip takes 26 minutes in the peak. Free-flow speeds (60 mph on freeways and 35 mph on principal arterials) are used as the comparison threshold; (1) Covers the Cape Coral FL urban area; (2) average of 498 urban areas
Source: Texas Transportation Institute, Urban Mobility Report 2012, December 2012

Public Transportation

Agency Name / Mode of Transportation	Vehicles Operated in Maximum Service	Annual Unlinked Passenger Trips (in thous.)	Annual Passenger Miles (in thous.)
Lee County Transit (LeeTran)			
Bus (directly operated)	46	3,754.1	20,790.1
Demand Response (directly operated)	36	102.3	1,085.2
Vanpool (purchased transportation)	11	39.5	1,644.4

Source: Federal Transit Administration, National Transit Database, 2012

Air Transportation

Airport Name and Code / Type of Service	Passenger Airlines[1]	Passenger Enplanements	Freight Carriers[2]	Freight (lbs.)
Southwest Florida International Airport (RSW)				
Domestic service (U.S. carriers - 2013)	23	3,637,566	10	9,274,991
International service (U.S. carriers - 2012)	4	824	1	1,821

Note: (1) Includes all U.S.-based major, minor and commuter airlines that carried at least one passenger during the year; (2) Includes all U.S.-based airlines and freight carriers that transported at least one lb. of freight during the year.
Source: Bureau of Transportation Statistics, The Intermodal Transportation Database, Air Carriers: T-100 Domestic Market (U.S. Carriers), 2013; Bureau of Transportation Statistics, The Intermodal Transportation Database, Air Carriers: T-100 International Market (U.S. Carriers), 2012

Other Transportation Statistics

Major Highways:	I-75
Amtrak Service:	Bus service only (station is in Ft. Myers)
Major Waterways/Ports:	Gulf of Mexico; Caloosahatchee River

Source: Amtrak.com; Google Maps

BUSINESSES

Major Business Headquarters

Company Name	Rankings	
	Fortune[1]	Forbes[2]
No companies listed		

Note: (1) Fortune 500—companies that produce a 10-K are ranked 1 to 500 based on 2012 revenue; (2) all private companies with at least $2 billion in annual revenue through the end of their most current fiscal year are ranked 1 to 224; companies listed are headquartered in the city; dashes indicate no ranking
Source: Fortune, "Fortune 500," May 20, 2013; Forbes, "America's Largest Private Companies," December 18, 2013

Minority- and Women-Owned Businesses

Group	All Firms		Firms with Paid Employees			
	Firms	Sales ($000)	Firms	Sales ($000)	Employees	Payroll ($000)
Asian	374	46,704	(s)	(s)	(s)	(s)
Black	741	36,991	65	16,996	322	4,468
Hispanic	3,487	149,403	(s)	(s)	(s)	(s)
Women	5,213	365,051	505	252,724	2,110	58,541
All Firms	18,476	4,711,956	3,366	4,140,517	26,555	820,005

Note: Figures cover firms located in the city; minority- and women-owned business are defined as firms in which the corresponding group own 51% or more of the stock or equity of the company; (s) estimates are suppressed when publication standards are not met
Source: U.S. Census Bureau, 2007 Economic Census, Survey of Business Owners (2012 Survey of Business Owners data will be released starting in June 2015)

HOTELS & CONVENTION CENTERS

Hotels/Motels

Area	5 Star		4 Star		3 Star		2 Star		1 Star		Not Rated	
	Num.	Pct.[3]	Num.	Pct.[3]	Num.	Pct.[3]	Num.	Pct.[3]	Num.	Pct.[3]	Num.	Pct.[3]
City[1]	0	0.0	2	2.4	29	34.5	45	53.6	1	1.2	7	8.3
Total[2]	142	0.9	1,005	6.0	5,147	30.9	8,578	51.4	408	2.4	1,397	8.4

Note: (1) Figures cover Cape Coral and vicinity; (2) Figures cover all 100 cities in this book; (3) Percentage of hotels which have a given star rating; Star ratings are determined by expedia.com and offer an indication of the general quality of a particular hotel.
Source: expedia.com, April 7, 2014

Major Convention Centers

Name	Overall Space (sq. ft.)	Exhibit Space (sq. ft.)	Meeting Space (sq. ft.)	Meeting Rooms

There are no major convention centers located in the metro area
Source: Original research

Living Environment

COST OF LIVING

Cost of Living Index

Composite Index	Groceries	Housing	Utilities	Trans-portation	Health Care	Misc. Goods/Services
97.4	91.9	93.2	98.1	109.1	98.1	98.3

Note: The Cost of Living Index measures regional differences in the cost of consumer goods and services, excluding taxes and non-consumer expenditures, for professional and managerial households in the top income quintile. It is based on more than 50,000 prices covering almost 60 different items for which prices are collected three times a year by chambers of commerce, economic development organizations or university applied economic centers in each participating urban area. The numbers shown should be read as a percentage above or below the national average of 100. For example, a value of 115.4 in the groceries column indicates that grocery prices are 15.4% higher than the national average. Small differences in the index numbers should not be interpreted as significant; Figures cover the Cape Coral-Fort Myers FL urban area.
Source: The Council for Community and Economic Research, ACCRA Cost of Living Index, 2013

Grocery Prices

Area[1]	T-Bone Steak ($/pound)	Frying Chicken ($/pound)	Whole Milk ($/half gal.)	Eggs ($/dozen)	Orange Juice ($/64 oz.)	Coffee ($/11.5 oz.)
City[2]	10.66	1.13	2.60	1.79	3.42	4.11
Avg.	10.19	1.28	2.34	1.81	3.48	4.39
Min.	8.56	0.94	1.44	1.19	2.78	3.40
Max.	14.82	2.28	3.56	3.73	6.23	7.32

Note: (1) Values for the local area are compared with the average, minimum and maximum values for all 327 areas in the Cost of Living Index; (2) Figures cover the Cape Coral-Fort Myers FL urban area; T-Bone Steak (price per pound); Frying Chicken (price per pound, whole fryer); Whole Milk (half gallon carton); Eggs (price per dozen, Grade A, large); Orange Juice (64 oz. Tropicana or Florida Natural); Coffee (11.5 oz. can, vacuum-packed, Maxwell House, Hills Bros, or Folgers).
Source: The Council for Community and Economic Research, ACCRA Cost of Living Index, 2013

Housing and Utility Costs

Area[1]	New Home Price ($)	Apartment Rent ($/month)	All Electric ($/month)	Part Electric ($/month)	Other Energy ($/month)	Telephone ($/month)
City[2]	271,536	847	189.95	-	-	20.00
Avg.	295,864	900	171.38	91.82	70.12	27.73
Min.	185,506	458	117.80	48.81	33.67	17.16
Max.	1,358,917	3,783	441.68	171.40	372.65	39.47

Note: (1) Values for the local area are compared with the average, minimum and maximum values for all 327 areas in the Cost of Living Index; (2) Figures cover the Cape Coral-Fort Myers FL urban area; New Home Price (2,400 sf living area, 8,000 sf lot, in urban area with full utilities); Apartment Rent (950 sf 2 bedroom/1.5 or 2 bath, unfurnished, excluding all utilities except water); All Electric (average monthly cost for an all-electric home); Part Electric (average monthly cost for a part-electric home); Other Energy (average monthly cost for natural gas, fuel oil, coal, wood, and any other forms of energy except electricity); Telephone (price includes basic monthly rate for a private residential line plus additional local usage charges incurred by a family of four).
Source: The Council for Community and Economic Research, ACCRA Cost of Living Index, 2013

Health Care, Transportation, and Other Costs

Area[1]	Doctor ($/visit)	Dentist ($/visit)	Optometrist ($/visit)	Gasoline ($/gallon)	Beauty Salon ($/visit)	Men's Shirt ($)
City[2]	85.97	85.69	86.36	3.54	35.31	20.52
Avg.	101.40	86.48	96.16	3.44	33.87	26.55
Min.	61.67	50.83	50.12	3.08	18.92	12.48
Max.	182.71	152.50	223.78	4.33	68.22	52.03

Note: (1) Values for the local area are compared with the average, minimum and maximum values for all 327 areas in the Cost of Living Index; (2) Figures cover the Cape Coral-Fort Myers FL urban area; Doctor (general practitioners routine exam of an established patient); Dentist (adult teeth cleaning and periodic oral examination); Optometrist (full vision eye exam for established adult patient); Gasoline (one gallon regular unleaded, national brand, including all taxes, cash price at self-service pump if available); Beauty Salon (woman's shampoo, trim, and blow-dry); Men's Shirt (cotton/polyester dress shirt, pinpoint weave, long sleeves).
Source: The Council for Community and Economic Research, ACCRA Cost of Living Index, 2013

HOUSING

House Price Index (HPI)

Area	National Ranking[2]	Quarterly Change (%)	One-Year Change (%)	Five-Year Change (%)
MSA[1]	39	2.14	11.67	4.86
U.S.[3]	–	1.20	7.69	4.18

Note: The HPI is a weighted repeat sales index. It measures average price changes in repeat sales or refinancings on the same properties. This information is obtained by reviewing repeat mortgage transactions on single-family properties whose mortgages have been purchased or securitized by Fannie Mae or Freddie Mac in January 1975; (1) Cape Coral-Fort Myers, FL Metropolitan Statistical Area—see Appendix B for areas included; (2) Rankings are based on annual percentage change for all metro areas containing at least 15,000 transactions over the last 10 years and ranges from 1 to 283; (3) figures based on a weighted average of Census Division estimates using a seasonally adjusted, purchase-only index; all figures are for the period ending December 31, 2013
Source: Federal Housing Finance Agency, House Price Index, February 25, 2014

Median Single-Family Home Prices

Area	2011	2012	2013p	Percent Change 2012 to 2013
MSA[1]	102.9	128.1	166.1	29.7
U.S. Average	166.2	177.2	197.4	11.4

Note: Figures are median sales prices of existing single-family homes in thousands of dollars; (p) preliminary; n/a not available; (1) Cape Coral-Fort Myers, FL Metropolitan Statistical Area—see Appendix B for areas included
Source: National Association of Realtors, Median Sales Price of Existing Single-Family Homes for Metropolitan Areas, 4th Quarter 2013

Qualifying Income Based on Median Sales Price of Existing Single-Family Homes

Area	With 5% Down ($)	With 10% Down ($)	With 20% Down ($)
MSA[1]	38,087	36,082	32,073
U.S. Average	45,395	43,006	38,228

Note: Figures are preliminary; Qualifying income is based on a mortgage rate of 4.4%. Monthly principal and interest payment is limited to 25% of income; n/a not available; (1) Cape Coral-Fort Myers, FL Metropolitan Statistical Area—see Appendix B for areas included
Source: National Association of Realtors, Qualifying Income Based on Median Sales Price of Existing Single-Family Homes for Metropolitan Areas, 4th Quarter 2013

Median Apartment Condo-Coop Home Prices

Area	2011	2012	2013p	Percent Change 2012 to 2013
MSA[1]	n/a	n/a	146.9	n/a
U.S. Average	165.1	173.7	194.9	12.2

Note: Figures are median sales prices of existing apartment condo-coop homes in thousands of dollars; (p) preliminary; n/a not available; (1) Cape Coral-Fort Myers, FL Metropolitan Statistical Area—see Appendix B for areas included
Source: National Association of Realtors, Median Sales Price of Existing Apartment Condo-Coop Homes for Metropolitan Areas, 4th Quarter 2013

Gross Monthly Rent

Area	Under $200	$200 -299	$300 -499	$500 -749	$750 -999	$1,000 -1,499	$1,500 and up	Median ($)
City	0.0	0.0	1.0	12.2	35.1	40.2	11.4	1,014
MSA[1]	0.6	1.3	3.7	22.8	34.0	28.0	9.7	909
U.S.	1.7	3.3	8.1	22.7	24.3	25.7	14.3	889

Note: Figures are percentages except for Median; Gross rent is the contract rent plus the estimated average monthly cost of utilities (electricity, gas, and water and sewer) and fuels (oil, coal, kerosene, wood, etc.) if these are paid by the renter (or paid for the renter by someone else); (1) Figures cover the Cape Coral-Fort Myers, FL Metropolitan Statistical Area—see Appendix B for areas included
Source: U.S. Census Bureau, 2010-2012 American Community Survey 3-Year Estimates

Year Housing Structure Built

Area	2010 or Later	2000 -2009	1990 -1999	1980 -1989	1970 -1979	1960 -1969	1950 -1959	1940 -1949	Before 1940	Median Year
City	0.2	45.2	14.5	20.6	12.5	6.1	0.6	0.3	0.1	1997
MSA[1]	0.2	34.4	18.1	21.6	15.8	5.7	2.8	0.6	0.7	1992
U.S.	0.5	14.9	13.8	13.9	15.9	11.1	10.9	5.5	13.5	1976

Note: Figures are percentages except for Median Year; (1) Figures cover the Cape Coral-Fort Myers, FL Metropolitan Statistical Area—see Appendix B for areas included
Source: U.S. Census Bureau, 2010-2012 American Community Survey 3-Year Estimates

HEALTH

Health Risk Data

Category	MSA[1] (%)	U.S. (%)
Adults aged 18–64 who have any kind of health care coverage	n/a	79.6
Adults who reported being in good or excellent health	n/a	83.1
Adults who are current smokers	n/a	19.6
Adults who are heavy drinkers[2]	n/a	6.1
Adults who are binge drinkers[3]	n/a	16.9
Adults who are overweight (BMI 25.0 - 29.9)	n/a	35.8
Adults who are obese (BMI 30.0 - 99.8)	n/a	27.6
Adults who participated in any physical activities in the past month	n/a	77.1
Adults 50+ who have ever had a sigmoidoscopy or colonoscopy	n/a	67.3
Women aged 40+ who have had a mammogram within the past two years	n/a	74.0
Men aged 40+ who have had a PSA test within the past two years	n/a	45.2
Adults aged 65+ who have had flu shot within the past year	n/a	60.1
Adults who always wear a seatbelt	n/a	93.8

Note: Data as of 2012 unless otherwise noted; n/a not available; (1) Figures cover the Cape Coral-Fort Myers, FL Metropolitan Statistical Area—see Appendix B for areas included; (2) Heavy drinkers are classified as males having more than two drinks per day or females having more than one drink per day; (3) Binge drinkers are classified as males having five or more drinks on one occasion or females having four or more drinks on one occasion
Source: Centers for Disease Control and Prevention, Behaviorial Risk Factor Surveillance System, SMART: Selected Metropolitan/Micropolitan Area Risk Trends, 2012

Chronic Health Indicators

Category	MSA[1] (%)	U.S. (%)
Adults who have ever been told they had a heart attack	n/a	4.5
Adults who have ever been told they had a stroke	n/a	2.9
Adults who have been told they currently have asthma	n/a	8.9
Adults who have ever been told they have arthritis	n/a	25.7
Adults who have ever been told they have diabetes[2]	n/a	9.7
Adults who have ever been told they had skin cancer	n/a	5.7
Adults who have ever been told they had any other types of cancer	n/a	6.5
Adults who have ever been told they have COPD	n/a	6.2
Adults who have ever been told they have kidney disease	n/a	2.5
Adults who have ever been told they have a form of depression	n/a	18.0

Note: Data as of 2012 unless otherwise noted; n/a not available; (1) Figures cover the Cape Coral-Fort Myers, FL Metropolitan Statistical Area—see Appendix B for areas included; (2) Figures do not include pregnancy-related, borderline, or pre-diabetes
Source: Centers for Disease Control and Prevention, Behaviorial Risk Factor Surveillance System, SMART: Selected Metropolitan/Micropolitan Area Risk Trends, 2012

Mortality Rates for the Top 10 Causes of Death in the U.S.

ICD-10[a] Sub-Chapter	ICD-10[a] Code	Age-Adjusted Mortality Rate[1] per 100,000 population	
		County[2]	U.S.
Malignant neoplasms	C00-C97	146.6	174.2
Ischaemic heart diseases	I20-I25	106.0	119.1
Other forms of heart disease	I30-I51	24.8	49.6
Chronic lower respiratory diseases	J40-J47	35.3	43.2
Cerebrovascular diseases	I60-I69	26.3	40.3
Organic, including symptomatic, mental disorders	F01-F09	33.3	30.5
Other degenerative diseases of the nervous system	G30-G31	16.9	26.3
Other external causes of accidental injury	W00-X59	32.9	25.1
Diabetes mellitus	E10-E14	15.8	21.3
Hypertensive diseases	I10-I15	17.4	18.8

Note: (a) ICD-10 = International Classification of Diseases 10th Revision; (1) Mortality rates are a three year average covering 2008-2010; (2) Figures cover Lee County
Source: Centers for Disease Control and Prevention, National Center for Health Statistics. Compressed Mortality File 1999-2010 on CDC WONDER Online Database, released January 2013. Data are compiled from the Compressed Mortality File 1999-2010, Series 20 No. 2P, 2013.

Mortality Rates for Selected Causes of Death

ICD-10[a] Sub-Chapter	ICD-10[a] Code	Age-Adjusted Mortality Rate[1] per 100,000 population	
		County[2]	U.S.
Assault	X85-Y09	7.8	5.5
Diseases of the liver	K70-K76	13.3	12.4
Human immunodeficiency virus (HIV) disease	B20-B24	2.5	3.0
Influenza and pneumonia	J09-J18	7.2	16.4
Intentional self-harm	X60-X84	16.1	11.8
Malnutrition	E40-E46	*0.4	0.8
Obesity and other hyperalimentation	E65-E68	0.9	1.6
Renal failure	N17-N19	6.8	13.6
Transport accidents	V01-V99	15.0	12.6
Viral hepatitis	B15-B19	1.5	2.2

Note: (a) ICD-10 = International Classification of Diseases 10th Revision; (1) Mortality rates are a three year average covering 2008-2010; (2) Figures cover Lee County; (*) Unreliable data as per CDC
Source: Centers for Disease Control and Prevention, National Center for Health Statistics. Compressed Mortality File 1999-2010 on CDC WONDER Online Database, released January 2013. Data are compiled from the Compressed Mortality File 1999-2010, Series 20 No. 2P, 2013.

Health Insurance Coverage

Area	With Health Insurance	With Private Health Insurance	With Public Health Insurance	Without Health Insurance	Population Under Age 18 Without Health Insurance
City	78.8	57.5	34.3	21.2	11.9
MSA[1]	78.7	56.6	39.4	21.3	14.2
U.S.	84.9	65.4	30.4	15.1	7.5

Note: Figures are percentages that cover the civilian noninstitutionalized population; (1) Figures cover the Cape Coral-Fort Myers, FL Metropolitan Statistical Area—see Appendix B for areas included
Source: U.S. Census Bureau, 2010-2012 American Community Survey 3-Year Estimates

Number of Medical Professionals

Area[1]	MDs[2]	DOs[2,3]	Dentists	Podiatrists	Chiropractors	Optometrists
Local (number)	1,114	172	279	50	167	87
Local (rate[4])	176.5	27.3	43.3	7.8	25.9	13.5
U.S. (rate[4])	267.6	19.6	61.7	5.6	24.7	14.5

Note: Data as of 2012 unless noted; (1) Local data covers Lee County; (2) Data as of 2011; (3) Doctor of Osteopathic Medicine; (4) rate per 100,000 population
Source: Area Resource File (ARF) 2012-2013. U.S. Department of Health and Human Services, Health Resources and Services Administration, Bureau of Health Professions

EDUCATION

Public School District Statistics

District Name	Schls	Pupils	Pupil/ Teacher Ratio	Minority Pupils[1] (%)	Free Lunch Eligible[2] (%)	IEP[3] (%)
Lee County Public Schools	129	83,895	16.1	52.4	55.6	13.8

Note: Table includes school districts with 2,000 or more students; (1) Percentage of students that are not non-Hispanic white; (2) Percentage of students that are eligible for the free lunch program; (3) Percentage of students that have an Individualized Education Program.
Source: U.S. Department of Education, National Center for Education Statistics, Common Core of Data, Local Education Agency (School District) Universe Survey: School Year 2011-2012; U.S. Department of Education, National Center for Education Statistics, Common Core of Data, Public Elementary/Secondary School Universe Survey: School Year 2011-2012

Highest Level of Education

Area	Less than H.S.	H.S. Diploma	Some College, No Deg.	Associate Degree	Bachelor's Degree	Master's Degree	Prof. School Degree	Doctorate Degree
City	10.2	38.6	23.6	8.0	12.8	4.9	1.1	0.7
MSA[1]	13.2	33.0	22.0	7.8	15.0	6.0	1.9	1.1
U.S.	14.1	28.3	21.3	7.8	18.0	7.5	1.9	1.2

Note: Figures cover persons age 25 and over; (1) Figures cover the Cape Coral-Fort Myers, FL Metropolitan Statistical Area—see Appendix B for areas included
Source: U.S. Census Bureau, 2010-2012 American Community Survey 3-Year Estimates

Educational Attainment by Race

Area	High School Graduate or Higher (%)					Bachelor's Degree or Higher (%)				
	Total	White	Black	Asian	Hisp.[2]	Total	White	Black	Asian	Hisp.[2]
City	89.8	90.2	88.9	75.9	75.1	19.5	19.9	10.4	29.0	15.3
MSA[1]	86.8	89.3	71.0	80.9	64.7	24.1	25.6	10.2	37.4	11.3
U.S.	85.9	88.1	82.5	85.5	63.1	28.6	30.0	18.4	50.2	13.4

Note: Figures shown cover persons 25 years old and over; (1) Figures cover the Cape Coral-Fort Myers, FL Metropolitan Statistical Area—see Appendix B for areas included; (2) People of Hispanic origin can be of any race
Source: U.S. Census Bureau, 2010-2012 American Community Survey 3-Year Estimates

School Enrollment by Grade and Control

Area	Preschool (%)		Kindergarten (%)		Grades 1 - 4 (%)		Grades 5 - 8 (%)		Grades 9 - 12 (%)	
	Public	Private	Public	Private	Public	Private	Public	Private	Public	Private
City	65.6	34.4	92.8	7.2	92.3	7.7	95.2	4.8	93.6	6.4
MSA[1]	61.1	38.9	93.7	6.3	93.3	6.7	90.3	9.7	92.5	7.5
U.S.	56.9	43.1	87.8	12.2	89.9	10.1	90.0	10.0	90.8	9.2

Note: Figures shown cover persons 3 years old and over; (1) Figures cover the Cape Coral-Fort Myers, FL Metropolitan Statistical Area—see Appendix B for areas included
Source: U.S. Census Bureau, 2010-2012 American Community Survey 3-Year Estimates

Average Salaries of Public School Classroom Teachers

Area	2012-13		2013-14		Percent Change 2012-13 to 2013-14	Percent Change 2003-04 to 2013-14
	Dollars	Rank[1]	Dollars	Rank[1]		
Florida	46,598	45	46,691	45	0.20	15.0
U.S. Average	56,103	–	56,689	–	1.04	21.8

Note: (1) State rank ranges from 1 to 51 where 1 indicates highest salary.
Source: National Education Association, Rankings & Estimates: Rankings of the States 2013 and Estimates of School Statistics 2014, March 2014

Higher Education

	Four-Year Colleges			Two-Year Colleges		Medical Schools[1]	Law Schools[2]	Voc/ Tech[3]
Public	Private Non-profit	Private For-profit	Public	Private Non-profit	Private For-profit			
0	0	0	0	0	0	0	0	1

Note: Figures cover institutions located within the city limits and include main campuses only; (1) includes schools accredited by the Liaison Committee on Medical Education and the American Osteopathic Association's Commission on Osteopathic College Accreditation; (2) includes ABA-accredited schools, schools with provisional ABA accreditation, and state accredited schools; (3) includes all schools with programs that are less than 2 years.
Source: National Center for Education Statistics, Integrated Postsecondary Education System (IPEDS), 2012-13; Association of American Medical Colleges, Member List, April 24, 2014; American Osteopathic Association, Member List, April 24, 2014; Law School Admission Council, Official Guide to ABA-Approved Law Schools Online, April 24, 2014; Wikipedia, List of Medical Schools in the United States, April 24, 2014; Wikipedia, List of Law Schools in the United States, April 24, 2014

PRESIDENTIAL ELECTION

2012 Presidential Election Results

Area	Obama	Romney	Other
Lee County	41.4	57.9	0.7
U.S.	51.0	47.2	1.8

Note: Results are percentages and may not add to 100% due to rounding
Source: Dave Leip's Atlas of U.S. Presidential Elections

EMPLOYERS

Major Employers

Company Name	Industry
Aris Horticulture	Flowers: grown under cover
Chico's FAS	Women's clothing stores
Christian & Missionary Alliance Fndn	Retirement hotel operation
City of Cape Coral	City and town managers' office
County of Lee	Sheriffs' office
Crowther Roofing & Sheet Metal of FL	Roofing contractor
Doctors Osteopathic Medical Center	General medical and surgical hospitals
Edison State College	Community college
Florida Department of Military	National guard
General Electric Company	Aircraft engines and engine parts
K Corp Lee	Restaurant management
Lee Memorial Health System	General medical and surgical hospitals
Lee Memorial Health System Foundation	Health systems agency
MCI Communications Services	Telephone communication, except radio
Raymond Building Supply Corporation	Lumber plywood, and millwork
Robby & Stucky Limited	Furniture stores
Schear Corp.	Multi-family dwellings, new construction
Sunshine Masonry	Concrete block masonry laying
United States Postal Service	U.s. postal service
Wal-Mart Stores	Department stores, discount

Note: Companies shown are located within the Cape Coral-Fort Myers, FL Metropolitan Statistical Area.
Source: Hoovers.com; Wikipedia

PUBLIC SAFETY

Crime Rate

Area	All Crimes	Violent Crimes				Property Crimes		
		Murder	Forcible Rape	Robbery	Aggrav. Assault	Burglary	Larceny -Theft	Motor Vehicle Theft
City	2,349.3	2.5	10.0	25.7	105.2	538.8	1,595.6	71.4
Suburbs[1]	2,811.7	8.5	19.4	106.6	282.9	689.3	1,536.5	168.4
Metro[2]	2,696.3	7.0	17.0	86.4	238.6	651.8	1,551.2	144.2
U.S.	3,246.1	4.7	26.9	112.9	242.3	670.2	1,959.3	229.7

Note: Figures are crimes per 100,000 population; (1) All areas within the metro area that are located outside the city limits; (2) Figures cover the Cape Coral-Fort Myers, FL Metropolitan Statistical Area—see Appendix B for areas included
Source: FBI Uniform Crime Reports, 2012

Hate Crimes

Area	Number of Quarters Reported	Bias Motivation				
		Race	Religion	Sexual Orientation	Ethnicity	Disability
City	4	1	0	0	0	0
U.S.	4	2,797	1,099	1,135	667	92

Source: Federal Bureau of Investigation, Hate Crime Statistics 2012

Identity Theft Consumer Complaints

Area	Complaints	Complaints per 100,000 Population	Rank[2]
MSA[1]	1,082	174.9	6
U.S.	290,056	91.8	-

Note: (1) Figures cover the Cape Coral-Fort Myers, FL Metropolitan Statistical Area—see Appendix B for areas included; (2) Rank ranges from 1 to 377 where 1 indicates greatest number of identity theft complaints per 100,000 population
Source: Federal Trade Commission, Consumer Sentinel Network Data Book for January–December 2013

Fraud and Other Consumer Complaints

Area	Complaints	Complaints per 100,000 Population	Rank[2]
MSA[1]	2,780	449.3	49
U.S.	1,811,724	595.2	-

Note: (1) Figures cover the Cape Coral-Fort Myers, FL Metropolitan Statistical Area—see Appendix B for areas included; (2) Rank ranges from 1 to 377 where 1 indicates greatest number of identity theft complaints per 100,000 population
Source: Federal Trade Commission, Consumer Sentinel Network Data Book for January–December 2013

RECREATION

Culture

Dance[1]	Theatre[1]	Instrumental Music[1]	Vocal Music[1]	Series and Festivals	Museums and Art Galleries[2]	Zoos and Aquariums[3]
0	0	0	0	0	1	0

Note: (1) Number of professional perfoming groups; (2) Based on organizations with primary SIC code 8412; (3) AZA-accredited
Source: The Grey House Performing Arts Directory, 2013; Association of Zoos & Aquariums, AZA Member Zoos & Aquariums, April 2014; www.AccuLeads.com, May 1, 2014

Professional Sports Teams

Team Name	League	Year Established
No teams are located in the metro area		

Source: Wikipedia, Major Professional Sports Teams of the United States and Canada, April 25, 2014

CLIMATE

Average and Extreme Temperatures

Temperature	Jan	Feb	Mar	Apr	May	Jun	Jul	Aug	Sep	Oct	Nov	Dec	Yr.
Extreme High (°F)	88	91	93	96	99	103	98	98	96	95	95	90	103
Average High (°F)	75	76	80	85	89	91	91	92	90	86	80	76	84
Average Temp. (°F)	65	65	70	74	79	82	83	83	82	77	71	66	75
Average Low (°F)	54	54	59	62	68	73	74	75	74	68	61	55	65
Extreme Low (°F)	28	32	33	39	52	60	66	67	64	48	34	26	26

Note: Figures cover the years 1948-1995
Source: National Climatic Data Center, International Station Meteorological Climate Summary, 9/96

Average Precipitation/Snowfall/Humidity

Precip./Humidity	Jan	Feb	Mar	Apr	May	Jun	Jul	Aug	Sep	Oct	Nov	Dec	Yr.
Avg. Precip. (in.)	2.0	2.2	2.6	1.7	3.6	9.3	8.9	8.9	8.2	3.5	1.4	1.5	53.9
Avg. Snowfall (in.)	0	0	0	0	0	0	0	0	0	0	0	0	0
Avg. Rel. Hum. 7am (%)	90	89	89	88	87	89	90	91	92	90	90	90	90
Avg. Rel. Hum. 4pm (%)	56	54	52	50	53	64	68	67	66	59	58	57	59

Note: Figures cover the years 1948-1995; Tr = Trace amounts (<0.05 in. of rain; <0.5 in. of snow)
Source: National Climatic Data Center, International Station Meteorological Climate Summary, 9/96

Weather Conditions

Temperature			Daytime Sky			Precipitation		
32°F & below	45°F & below	90°F & above	Clear	Partly cloudy	Cloudy	0.01 inch or more precip.	0.1 inch or more snow/ice	Thunder-storms
1	18	115	93	220	52	110	0	92

Note: Figures are average number of days per year and cover the years 1948-1995
Source: National Climatic Data Center, International Station Meteorological Climate Summary, 9/96

HAZARDOUS WASTE

Superfund Sites

Cape Coral has no sites on the EPA's Superfund Final National Priorities List.
U.S. Environmental Protection Agency, Final National Priorities List, April 26, 2014

AIR & WATER QUALITY

Air Quality Index

Area	Percent of Days when Air Quality was...[2]					AQI Statistics[2]	
	Good	Moderate	Unhealthy for Sensitive Groups	Unhealthy	Very Unhealthy	Maximum	Median
MSA[1]	90.1	9.9	0.0	0.0	0.0	77	33

Note: (1) Data covers the Cape Coral-Fort Myers, FL Metropolitan Statistical Area—see Appendix B for areas included; (2) Based on 365 days with AQI data in 2013. Air Quality Index (AQI) is an index for reporting daily air quality. EPA calculates the AQI for five major air pollutants regulated by the Clean Air Act: ground-level ozone, particle pollution (aka particulate matter), carbon monoxide, sulfur dioxide, and nitrogen dioxide. The AQI runs from 0 to 500. The higher the AQI value, the greater the level of air pollution and the greater the health concern. There are six AQI categories: "Good" AQI is between 0 and 50. Air quality is considered satisfactory; "Moderate" AQI is between 51 and 100. Air quality is acceptable; "Unhealthy for Sensitive Groups" When AQI values are between 101 and 150, members of sensitive groups may experience health effects; "Unhealthy" When AQI values are between 151 and 200 everyone may begin to experience health effects; "Very Unhealthy" AQI values between 201 and 300 trigger a health alert; "Hazardous" AQI values over 300 trigger warnings of emergency conditions (not shown).
Source: U.S. Environmental Protection Agency, Air Quality Index Report, 2013

Air Quality Index Pollutants

Area	Percent of Days when AQI Pollutant was...[2]					
	Carbon Monoxide	Nitrogen Dioxide	Ozone	Sulfur Dioxide	Particulate Matter 2.5	Particulate Matter 10
MSA[1]	0.0	0.0	57.3	0.0	42.7	0.0

Note: (1) Data covers the Cape Coral-Fort Myers, FL Metropolitan Statistical Area—see Appendix B for areas included; (2) Based on 365 days with AQI data in 2013. The Air Quality Index (AQI) is an index for reporting daily air quality. EPA calculates the AQI for five major air pollutants regulated by the Clean Air Act: ground-level ozone, particle pollution (also known as particulate matter), carbon monoxide, sulfur dioxide, and nitrogen dioxide. The AQI runs from 0 to 500. The higher the AQI value, the greater the level of air pollution and the greater the health concern.
Source: U.S. Environmental Protection Agency, Air Quality Index Report, 2013

Air Quality Trends: Ozone

	2003	2004	2005	2006	2007	2008	2009	2010	2011	2012
MSA[1]	0.074	0.072	0.070	0.070	0.069	0.068	0.062	0.064	0.062	0.063

Note: (1) Data covers the Cape Coral-Fort Myers, FL Metropolitan Statistical Area—see Appendix B for areas included. The values shown are the composite ozone concentration averages among trend sites based on the highest fourth daily maximum 8-hour concentration in parts per million. These trends are based on sites having an adequate record of monitoring data during the trend period. Data from exceptional events are included.
Source: U.S. Environmental Protection Agency, Air Quality Monitoring Information, "Air Quality Trends by City, 2000-2012"

Maximum Air Pollutant Concentrations: Particulate Matter, Ozone, CO and Lead

	Particulate Matter 10 (ug/m³)	Particulate Matter 2.5 Wtd AM (ug/m³)	Particulate Matter 2.5 24-Hr (ug/m³)	Ozone (ppm)	Carbon Monoxide (ppm)	Lead (ug/m³)
MSA[1] Level	57	6.7	14	0.065	n/a	n/a
NAAQS[2]	150	15	35	0.075	9	0.15
Met NAAQS[2]	Yes	Yes	Yes	Yes	n/a	n/a

Note: (1) Data covers the Cape Coral-Fort Myers, FL Metropolitan Statistical Area—see Appendix B for areas included; Data from exceptional events are included; (2) National Ambient Air Quality Standards; ppm = parts per million; ug/m³ = micrograms per cubic meter; n/a not available.
Concentrations: Particulate Matter 10 (coarse particulate)—highest second maximum 24-hour concentration; Particulate Matter 2.5 Wtd AM (fine particulate)—highest weighted annual mean concentration; Particulate Matter 2.5 24-Hour (fine particulate)—highest 98th percentile 24-hour concentration; Ozone—highest fourth daily maximum 8-hour concentration; Carbon Monoxide—highest second maximum non-overlapping 8-hour concentration; Lead—maximum running 3-month average
Source: U.S. Environmental Protection Agency, Air Quality Monitoring Information, "Air Quality Statistics by City, 2012"

Maximum Air Pollutant Concentrations: Nitrogen Dioxide and Sulfur Dioxide

	Nitrogen Dioxide AM (ppb)	Nitrogen Dioxide 1-Hr (ppb)	Sulfur Dioxide AM (ppb)	Sulfur Dioxide 1-Hr (ppb)	Sulfur Dioxide 24-Hr (ppb)
MSA[1] Level	n/a	n/a	n/a	n/a	n/a
NAAQS[2]	53	100	30	75	140
Met NAAQS[2]	n/a	n/a	n/a	n/a	n/a

Note: (1) Data covers the Cape Coral-Fort Myers, FL Metropolitan Statistical Area—see Appendix B for areas included; Data from exceptional events are included; (2) National Ambient Air Quality Standards; ppm = parts per million; ug/m³ = micrograms per cubic meter; n/a not available.
Concentrations: Nitrogen Dioxide AM—highest arithmetic mean concentration; Nitrogen Dioxide 1-Hr—highest 98th percentile 1-hour daily maximum concentration; Sulfur Dioxide AM—highest annual mean concentration; Sulfur Dioxide 1-Hr—highest 99th percentile 1-hour daily maximum concentration; Sulfur Dioxide 24-Hr—highest second maximum 24-hour concentration
Source: U.S. Environmental Protection Agency, Air Quality Monitoring Information, "Air Quality Statistics by City, 2012"

Drinking Water

Water System Name	Pop. Served	Primary Water Source Type	Violations[1] Health Based	Violations[1] Monitoring/ Reporting
City of Cape Coral	123,059	Ground	0	0

Note: (1) Based on violation data from January 1, 2013 to December 31, 2013 (includes unresolved violations from earlier years)
Source: U.S. Environmental Protection Agency, Office of Ground Water and Drinking Water, Safe Drinking Water Information System (based on data extracted February 10, 2014)

Charleston, South Carolina

Background

Charleston is located on the state's Atlantic coastline, 110 miles southeast of Columbia and 100 miles north of Savannah, Georgia. The city, named for King Charles II of England, is the county seat of Charleston County. Charleston is located on a bay at the end of a peninsula between the Ashley and Cooper rivers. The terrain is low-lying and coastal with nearby islands and inlets.

In 1670, English colonists established a nearby settlement, and subsequently moved to Charleston's present site. Charleston became an early trading center for rice, indigo, cotton and other goods. As the plantation economy grew, Charleston became a slave-trading center. In 1861, the Confederacy fired the cannon shot that launched the Civil War from the city's Battery, aimed at the Union's Fort Sumter in Charleston Harbor. Charleston was under siege during the Civil War, and experienced many difficulties during Reconstruction. Manufacturing industries including textiles and ironwork became important in the nineteenth century.

Charleston is part of a larger metropolitan area that includes North Charleston and Mount Pleasant and covers Charleston, Berkley and Dorchester counties. This area is a regional commercial and cultural center and a southern transportation hub whose port is among the nation's busiest shipping facilities. Charleston's other contemporary economic sectors include manufacturing, health care, business and professional services, defense activity, retail and wholesale trade, tourism, education and construction.

Charleston is a popular tourist area, based on its scenery, history and recreation. The city's center is well known for its historic neighborhoods with distinctive early southern architecture and ambiance. As one of the first American cities in the early twentieth century to actively encourage historic restoration and preservation, Charleston has more recently undertaken numerous revitalization initiatives, including the Charleston Place Hotel and retail complex, and Waterfront Park. North Charleston and other communities are also growing with industry and suburban development.

The founding of the Charleston Naval Shipyard stimulated a military-based economy after 1901. Numerous other defense facilities were later established, including the Charleston Air Force Base, located in North Charleston. Several military facilities were closed in the 1990s, including the shipyard, although other defense-related operations have remained.

In 2000, the Confederate submarine the *HL Hunley,* which sank in 1864, was raised, and brought to a conservation laboratory at the old Charleston Naval Base. Author Patricia Cornwell has taken a great interest in the project, and is involved in the creation of a museum to house the submarine. Also, an International Museum of African American History, will sit across from Liberty Square.

Charleston is a center for health care and medical research. SPAWAR (US Navy Space and Naval Warfare Systems Command) is the area's largest single employer followed by the Medical University of South Carolina, founded in 1824, with approximately 8,000 employees. Other area educational institutions include The College of Charleston, The Citadel Military College, Trident Technical College, Charleston Southern University, and a campus of Johnson and Wales University offering culinary and hospitality education.

The Charleston area has numerous parks, including one with a skateboard center, and public waterfront areas. Coastal recreation activities such as boating, swimming, fishing and beaches are popular, as are golf and other land sports.

The Charleston Museum is the nation's oldest, founded in 1773. There are also several former plantations in the area, including Boone Hall Plantation, Drayton Hall, Magnolia Plantation, and Middleton Place. Other attractions include the South Carolina Aquarium with its IMAX Theater, the American Military Museum, the Drayton Hall Plantation Museum, the Gibbes Museum of Art and the Karpeles Manuscript Museum. A North Charleston Convention Center and Performing Arts Center complex opened in 1999. Cultural organizations include the Spoleto Festival USA annual summer arts festival. The fifth annual Charleston International Film Festival, CIFF, was held in 2011.

The Arthur Ravenel Jr. Bridge is the longest cable-stayed bridge in all of the Americas, running across Charleston's Cooper River.

The nearby Atlantic Ocean moderates the climate, especially in winter, and keeps summer a bit cooler than expected. Expect Indian summers in fall, and a possible hurricane, while spring sharply turns from the cold winds of March to lovely May. Severe storms are possible.

Rankings

General Rankings

- Charleston was selected as one of "America's Favorite Cities." The city ranked #3 in the "Quality of Life and Visitor Experience: Cleanliness" category. Respondents to an online survey were asked to rate 35 top urban destinations in the U.S. from a visitor's perspective. Criteria: cleanliness. *Travel + Leisure, "America's Favorite Cities 2013"*

- Charleston was selected as one of "America's Favorite Cities." The city ranked #25 in the "Type of Trip: Gay-friendly" category. Respondents to an online survey were asked to rate 35 top urban destinations in the U.S. from a visitor's perspective. Criteria: gay-friendly. *Travel + Leisure, "America's Favorite Cities 2013"*

- Charleston appeared on *Travel + Leisure's* list of the ten best cities in the U.S. and Canada. The city was ranked #1. Criteria: activities/attractions; culture/arts; restaurants/food; people; and value. *Travel + Leisure, "The World's Best Awards 2013"*

- *Condé Nast Traveler* polled 79,268 readers for travel satisfaction. American cities were ranked based on the following criteria: friendliness; atmosphere/ambiance; culture/sites; restaurants; lodging; and shopping. Charleston appeared in the top 10, ranking #1. *Condé Nast Traveler, Readers' Choice Awards 2013, "Top 10 Cities in the United States"*

Business/Finance Rankings

- Charleston was ranked #17 out of 100 metro areas in terms of economic performance (#1 = best) during the recession and recovery from trough quarter through the second quarter of 2013. Criteria: percent change in employment; percentage point change in unemployment rate; percent change in gross metropolitan product; percent change in House Price Index. *Brookings Institution, MetroMonitor: Tracking Economic Recession and Recovery in America's 100 Largest Metropolitan Areas, September 2013*

- The Charleston metro area appeared on the Milken Institute "2013 Best Performing Cities" list. Rank: #11 out of 200 large metro areas. Criteria: job growth; wage and salary growth; high-tech output growth. *Milken Institute, "Best-Performing Cities 2013," December 2013*

- *Forbes* ranked the 200 most populous metro areas in the U.S. in terms of the "Best Places for Business and Careers." The Charleston metro area was ranked #61. Criteria: costs (business and living); job growth (past and projected); income growth; educational attainment (college and high school); projected economic growth; cultural and recreational opportunities; net migration patterns; number of highly ranked colleges. *Forbes, "The Best Places for Business and Careers," August 7, 2013*

Children/Family Rankings

- Charleston was selected as one of the best cities for families to live by *Parenting* magazine. The city ranked #24 out of 100. Criteria: education; health; community; *Parenting's* Culture & Charm Index. *Parenting.com, "The 2012 Best Cities for Families List"*

- Charleston was chosen as one of America's 100 best communities for young people. The winners were selected based upon detailed information provided about each community's efforts to fulfill five essential promises critical to the well-being of young people: caring adults who are actively involved in their lives; safe places in which to learn and grow; a healthy start toward adulthood; an effective education that builds marketable skills; and opportunities to help others. *America's Promise Alliance, "100 Best Communities for Young People, 2012"*

Culture/Performing Arts Rankings

- Charleston was selected as one of "America's Favorite Cities." The city ranked #14 in the "Culture: Museum/Galleries" category. Respondents to an online survey were asked to rate 35 top urban destinations in the U.S. from a visitor's perspective. Criteria: number and quality of museums and galleries. *Travelandleisure.com, "America's Favorite Cities 2013"*

- Charleston was selected as one of America's top cities for the arts. The city ranked #10 in the mid-sized city (population 100,000 to 499,999) category. Criteria: readers' top choices for arts travel destinations based on the richness and variety of visual arts sites, activities and events. *American Style, "2012 Top 25 Arts Destinations," June 2012*

Environmental Rankings

- The Charleston metro area came in at #307 for the relative comfort of its climate on Sperling's list of "chill cities," as measured by the Sperling Heat Index. All 361 metro areas are included. Criteria included daytime high temperatures, nighttime low temperatures, dew point, and relative humidity at the high temperatures. *www.bertsperling.com, "Sperling's Chill Cities," July 18, 2013*

- Sperling's BestPlaces assessed 379 metropolitan areas of the United States for the likelihood of dangerously extreme weather events or earthquakes. In general the Southeast and South-Central regions have the highest risk of weather extremes and earthquakes, while the Pacific Northwest enjoys the lowest risk. Of the least risky metropolitan areas, the Charleston metro area was ranked #250. *www.bestplaces.net, "Safest Places from Natural Disasters," April 2011*

- Charleston was selected as one of 22 "Smarter Cities" for energy by the Natural Resources Defense Council. Criteria: investment in green power; energy efficiency measures; conservation. *Natural Resources Defense Council, "2010 Smarter Cities," July 19, 2010*

- Charleston was highlighted as one of the cleanest metro areas for ozone air pollution in the U.S. during 2008 through 2010. The list represents cities with no monitored ozone air pollution in unhealthful ranges. *American Lung Association, State of the Air 2012*

Food/Drink Rankings

- Charleston was identified as one of "America's Drunkest Cities of 2011" by *The Daily Beast*. The city ranked #12 out of 25. Criteria: binge drinking; drinks consumed per month. *The Daily Beast, "Tipsy Towns: Where are America's Drunkest Cities?," December 31, 2011*

Health/Fitness Rankings

- Charleston was identified as a "2013 Spring Allergy Capital." The area ranked #32 out of 100. Three groups of factors were used to identify the most severe cities for people with allergies during the spring season: annual pollen levels; medicine utilization; access to board-certified allergists. *Asthma and Allergy Foundation of America, "Spring Allergy Capitals 2013"*

- Charleston was identified as a "2013 Fall Allergy Capital." The area ranked #26 out of 100. Three groups of factors were used to identify the most severe cities for people with allergies during the fall season: annual pollen levels; medicine utilization; access to board-certified allergists. *Asthma and Allergy Foundation of America, "Fall Allergy Capitals 2013"*

- Charleston was identified as a "2013 Asthma Capital." The area ranked #71 out of the nation's 100 largest metropolitan areas. Twelve factors were used to identify the most challenging places to live for people with asthma: estimated prevalence; self-reported prevalence; crude death rate for asthma; annual pollen score; annual air quality; public smoking laws; number of board-certified asthma specialists; school inhaler access laws; rescue medication use; controller medication use; uninsured rate; poverty rate. *Asthma and Allergy Foundation of America, "Asthma Capitals 2013"*

- The Charleston metro area appeared in the 2013 Gallup-Healthways Well-Being Index. The area ranked #111 out of 189. The Gallup-Healthways Well-Being Index score is an average of six sub-indexes, which individually examine life evaluation, emotional health, work environment, physical health, healthy behaviors, and access to basic necessities. Results are based on telephone interviews conducted as part of the Gallup-Healthways Well-Being Index survey January 2–December 29, 2012, and January 2–December 30, 2013, with a random sample of 531,630 adults, aged 18 and older, living in metropolitan areas in the 50 U.S. states and the District of Columbia. *Gallup-Healthways, "State of American Well-Being," March 25, 2014*

Real Estate Rankings

- Using data from the housing-market research firm RealtyTrac, Yahoo! Finance researchers listed the housing markets in which housing affordability is deteriorating most, factoring in interest rates as well as median home prices. The Charleston metro area was among the least affordable housing markets according to the percentage difference in the income required to buy a home in December 2013 as opposed to in December 2012. *news.yahoo.com, "10 Cities Where Ordinary People Can No Longer Afford Homes," March 5, 2014*

- Charleston was ranked #95 out of 283 metro areas in terms of house price appreciation in 2013 (#1 = highest rate). *Federal Housing Finance Agency, House Price Index, 4th Quarter 2013*

- The Charleston metro area was identified as one of the 20 least affordable housing markets in the U.S. in 2013. The area ranked #20 out of 173 markets. Criteria: whether or not a typical family could qualify for a mortgage loan on a typical home. *National Association of Realtors®, Affordability Index of Existing Single-Family Homes for Metropolitan Areas, 2013*

- Charleston was ranked #178 out of 224 metro areas in terms of housing affordability in 2013 by the National Association of Home Builders (#1 = most affordable). The NAHB-Wells Fargo Housing Opportunity Index (HOI) for a given area is defined as the share of homes sold in that area that would have been affordable to a family earning the local median income, based on standard mortgage underwriting criteria. *National Association of Home Builders®, NAHB-Wells Fargo Housing Opportunity Index, 4th Quarter 2013*

Safety Rankings

- The National Insurance Crime Bureau ranked 380 metro areas in the U.S. in terms of per capita rates of vehicle theft. The Charleston metro area ranked #45 (#1 = highest rate). Criteria: number of vehicle theft offenses per 100,000 inhabitants in 2012. *National Insurance Crime Bureau, "Hot Spots 2012," June 26, 2013*

Seniors/Retirement Rankings

- From its Best Cities for Successful Aging indexes, the Milken Institute generated rankings for metropolitan areas, weighing data in eight categories—general indicators, health care, wellness, living arrangements, transportation and general accessibility, financial well-being, education and employment, and community participation. The Charleston metro area was ranked #27 overall in the large metro area category. *Milken Institute, "Best Cities for Successful Aging," July 2012*

- Charleston made the 2014 *Forbes* list of "25 Best Places to Retire." Criteria include: housing and living costs; tax climate for retirees; weather and air quality; crime rates; doctor availability; active-lifestyle rankings for walkability, bicycling and volunteering. *Forbes.com, "The Best Places to Retire in 2014," January 16, 2014*

- Charleston was identified as one of the most popular places to retire by *Topretirements.com*. The list reflects the 100 cities (out of 900+ total cities reviewed) that visitors to the website are most interested in for retirement. *Topretirements.com, "Most Popular Places to Retire for 2014," February 25, 2014*

- Charleston was selected as one of "The Best Retirement Places" by *Forbes*. The magazine considered a wide range of factors such as climate, availability of doctors, driving environment, and crime rates, but focused especially on tax burden and cost of living. *Forbes, "The Best Retirement Places," March 27, 2011*

Sports/Recreation Rankings

- Charleston appeared on the *Sporting News* list of the "Best Sports Cities" for 2011. The area ranked #173 out of 271. Criteria: the magazine takes a 12-month snapshot of each city's sports, putting a heavy premium on regular-season won-lost records (from the most recently completed season). Other criteria include: playoff berths, bowl appearances and tournament bids; championships; applicable power ratings; quality of competition; overall fan fervor (measured in part by attendance); abundance of teams (rewarding quality over quantity); stadium and arena quality; ticket availability and prices; franchise ownership; and marquee appeal of athletes. *Sporting News, "Best Sports Cities 2011," October 4, 2011*

- Charleston appeared on the *Sporting News* list of the "Best Sports Cities" for 2011. The area ranked #173 out of 271. Criteria: a 12-month snapshot of regular-season won-lost records (from the most recently completed season). Other criteria include: playoff berths, bowl appearances and tournament bids; championships; applicable power ratings; quality of competition; overall fan fervor (measured in part by attendance); abundance of teams (quality over quantity); stadium and arena quality; ticket availability and prices; franchise ownership; and marquee appeal of athletes. *Sporting News, "Best Sports Cities 2011," October 4, 2011*

- Charleston was chosen as a bicycle friendly community by the League of American Bicyclists. A "Bicycle Friendly Community" welcomes cyclists by providing safe accommodation for cycling and encouraging people to bike for transportation and recreation. There are four award levels: Platinum; Gold; Silver; and Bronze. The community achieved an award level of Bronze. *League of American Bicyclists, "Bicycle Friendly Community Master List," Fall 2013*

- Charleston was chosen as one of America's best cities for bicycling. The city ranked #48 out of 50. Criteria: robust cycling infrastructure; vibrant bike culture. The editors only considered cities with populations of 95,000 or more. *Bicycling, "America's Top 50 Bike-Friendly Cities," May 23, 2012*

Miscellaneous Rankings

- *Travel + Leisure* invited readers to rate cities on indicators such as aloofness, "smarty-pants residents," highbrow cultural offerings, high-end shopping, artisanal coffeehouses, conspicuous eco-consciousness, and more in order to identify the nation's snobbiest cities. Cities large and small made the list; among them was Charleston, at #10. *www.travelandleisure.com, "America's Snobbiest Cities, June 2013*

- In *Condé Nast Traveler* magazine's 2013 Readers' Choice Survey, Charleston made the top ten list of friendliest American cities, at #1. *www.cntraveler.com, "The Friendliest and Unfriendliest Cities in the U.S.," July 30, 2013*

- Charleston appeared on *Travel + Leisure's* list of America's most attractive people. Criteria: cities were selected by readers in their annual America's Favorite Cities survey. The city ranked #10 out of 10. *Travel + Leisure, "America's Most and Least Attractive People," November 2013*

- Charleston was selected as one of "America's Best Cities for Hipsters" by *Travel + Leisure*. The city was ranked #7 out of 20. Criteria: live music; coffee bars; independent boutiques; best microbrews; offbeat and tech-savvy locals. *Travel + Leisure, "America's Best Cities for Hipsters," November 2013*

- The National Alliance to End Homelessness ranked the 100 most populous metro areas in terms the rate of homelessness. The Charleston metro area ranked #91. Criteria: number of homeless people per 10,000 population in 2011. *National Alliance to End Homelessness, The State of Homelessness in America 2012*

- Charleston was selected as one of America's best-mannered cities. The area ranked #1. The general public determined the winners by casting votes online. *The Charleston School of Protocol and Etiquette, "2012 Most Mannerly City in America Contest," January 31, 2013*

Business Environment

CITY FINANCES

City Government Finances

Component	2011 ($000)	2011 ($ per capita)
Total Revenues	185,134	1,683
Total Expenditures	147,497	1,341
Debt Outstanding	687,771	6,252
Cash and Securities[1]	88,538	805

Note: (1) Cash and security holdings of a government at the close of its fiscal year, including those of its dependent agencies, utilities, and liquor stores.
Source: U.S Census Bureau, State & Local Government Finances 2011

City Government Revenue by Source

Source	2011 ($000)	2011 ($ per capita)
General Revenue		
From Federal Government	0	0
From State Government	15,237	138
From Local Governments	0	0
Taxes		
Property	57,347	521
Sales and Gross Receipts	31,531	287
Personal Income	0	0
Corporate Income	0	0
Motor Vehicle License	0	0
Other Taxes	39,558	360
Current Charges	29,246	266
Liquor Store	0	0
Utility	0	0
Employee Retirement	0	0

Source: U.S Census Bureau, State & Local Government Finances 2011

City Government Expenditures by Function

Function	2011 ($000)	2011 ($ per capita)	2011 (%)
General Direct Expenditures			
Air Transportation	0	0	0.0
Corrections	0	0	0.0
Education	0	0	0.0
Employment Security Administration	0	0	0.0
Financial Administration	7,242	66	4.9
Fire Protection	21,091	192	14.3
General Public Buildings	5,186	47	3.5
Governmental Administration, Other	3,364	31	2.3
Health	0	0	0.0
Highways	3,936	36	2.7
Hospitals	0	0	0.0
Housing and Community Development	3,424	31	2.3
Interest on General Debt	23,912	217	16.2
Judicial and Legal	2,683	24	1.8
Libraries	0	0	0.0
Parking	8,282	75	5.6
Parks and Recreation	17,317	157	11.7
Police Protection	36,812	335	25.0
Public Welfare	646	6	0.4
Sewerage	0	0	0.0
Solid Waste Management	0	0	0.0
Veterans' Services	0	0	0.0
Liquor Store	0	0	0.0
Utility	0	0	0.0
Employee Retirement	0	0	0.0

Source: U.S Census Bureau, State & Local Government Finances 2011

DEMOGRAPHICS

Population Growth

Area	1990 Census	2000 Census	2010 Census	Population Growth (%) 1990-2000	Population Growth (%) 2000-2010
City	96,102	96,650	120,083	0.6	24.2
MSA[1]	506,875	549,033	664,607	8.3	21.1
U.S.	248,709,873	281,421,906	308,745,538	13.2	9.7

Note: (1) Figures cover the Charleston-North Charleston, SC Metropolitan Statistical Area—see Appendix B for areas included
Source: U.S. Census Bureau, Census 1990, 2000, 2010

Household Size

Area	Persons in Household (%) One	Two	Three	Four	Five	Six	Seven or More	Average Household Size
City	35.8	36.2	14.4	9.8	2.9	0.6	0.4	2.25
MSA[1]	28.4	34.4	16.9	12.7	4.9	1.8	0.9	2.57
U.S.	27.6	33.5	15.7	13.2	6.1	2.4	1.5	2.63

Note: (1) Figures cover the Charleston-North Charleston, SC Metropolitan Statistical Area—see Appendix B for areas included
Source: U.S. Census Bureau, 2010-2012 American Community Survey 3-Year Estimates

Race

Area	White Alone[2] (%)	Black Alone[2] (%)	Asian Alone[2] (%)	AIAN[3] Alone[2] (%)	NHOPI[4] Alone[2] (%)	Other Race Alone[2] (%)	Two or More Races (%)
City	71.0	25.5	1.3	0.1	0.1	0.4	1.5
MSA[1]	67.0	27.4	1.6	0.4	0.1	1.2	2.3
U.S.	74.0	12.6	4.9	0.8	0.2	4.7	2.8

Note: (1) Figures cover the Charleston-North Charleston, SC Metropolitan Statistical Area—see Appendix B for areas included; (2) Alone is defined as not being in combination with one or more other races; (3) American Indian and Alaska Native; (4) Native Hawaiian and Other Pacific Islander
Source: U.S. Census Bureau, 2010-2012 American Community Survey 3-Year Estimates

Hispanic or Latino Origin

Area	Total (%)	Mexican (%)	Puerto Rican (%)	Cuban (%)	Other (%)
City	3.0	1.0	1.0	0.4	0.6
MSA[1]	5.4	3.1	0.8	0.2	1.3
U.S.	16.6	10.7	1.6	0.6	3.7

Note: Persons of Hispanic or Latino origin can be of any race; (1) Figures cover the Charleston-North Charleston, SC Metropolitan Statistical Area—see Appendix B for areas included
Source: U.S. Census Bureau, 2010-2012 American Community Survey 3-Year Estimates

Segregation

Type	Segregation Indices[1] 1990	2000	2010	2010 Rank[2]	Percent Change 1990-2000	1990-2010	2000-2010
Black/White	47.4	44.2	41.5	88	-3.2	-5.9	-2.7
Asian/White	34.4	34.2	33.4	84	-0.3	-1.1	-0.8
Hispanic/White	26.6	32.2	39.8	66	5.6	13.2	7.6

Note: All figures cover the Metropolitan Statistical Area—see Appendix B for areas included; Figures are based on an analysis of 1990, 2000, and 2010 Census Decennial Census tract data by William H. Frey, Brookings Institution and the University of Michigan Social Science Data Analysis Network. In this analysis all racial groups (whites, blacks, and asians) are non-Hispanic members of those races. Hispanics are shown as a separate category;
(1) Segregation Indices are Dissimilarity Indices that measure the degree to which the minority group is distributed differently than whites across census tracts. They range from 0 (complete integration) to 100 (complete segregation) where the value indicates the percentage of the minority group that needs to move to be distributed exactly like whites; (2) Ranges from 1 (most segregated) to 102 (least segregated); n/a not available.
Source: www.CensusScope.org

Ancestry

Area	German	Irish	English	American	Italian	Polish	French[2]	Scottish	Dutch
City	12.2	11.3	11.9	11.4	4.3	1.9	3.0	3.4	1.2
MSA[1]	11.7	10.3	9.0	13.2	3.6	1.9	2.7	2.6	1.1
U.S.	15.2	11.1	8.2	7.2	5.6	3.1	2.8	1.7	1.4

Note: Figures are the percentage of the total population reporting a particular ancestry. The nine most commonly reported ancestries in the U.S. are shown. Figures include multiple ancestries (e.g. if a person reported being Irish and Italian, they were included in both columns); (1) Figures cover the Charleston-North Charleston, SC Metropolitan Statistical Area—see Appendix B for areas included; (2) Excludes Basque
Source: U.S. Census Bureau, 2010-2012 American Community Survey 3-Year Estimates

Foreign-Born Population

Area	Percent of Population Born in								
	Any Foreign Country	Mexico	Asia	Europe	Carribean	South America	Central America[2]	Africa	Canada
City	n/a	n/a	n/a	n/a	n/a	n/a	n/a	n/a	n/a
MSA[1]	5.2	1.5	1.2	1.0	0.3	0.3	0.5	0.1	0.2
U.S.	13.0	3.7	3.7	1.6	1.2	0.9	1.0	0.5	0.3

Note: (1) Figures cover the Charleston-North Charleston, SC Metropolitan Statistical Area—see Appendix B for areas included; (2) Excludes Mexico.
Source: U.S. Census Bureau, 2010-2012 American Community Survey 3-Year Estimates

Marital Status

Area	Never Married	Now Married[2]	Separated	Widowed	Divorced
City	44.2	38.1	2.6	5.5	9.5
MSA[1]	33.7	46.5	3.2	5.7	10.9
U.S.	32.4	48.4	2.2	6.0	11.0

Note: Figures are percentages and cover the population 15 years of age and older; (1) Figures cover the Charleston-North Charleston, SC Metropolitan Statistical Area—see Appendix B for areas included; (2) Excludes separated
Source: U.S. Census Bureau, 2010-2012 American Community Survey 3-Year Estimates

Age

Area	Percent of Population									Median Age
	Under Age 5	Age 5–19	Age 20–34	Age 35–44	Age 45–54	Age 55–64	Age 65–74	Age 75–84	Age 85+	
City	5.7	16.1	30.7	12.3	11.8	11.2	6.9	3.8	1.6	33.2
MSA[1]	6.8	19.1	23.2	13.0	13.8	12.0	7.2	3.4	1.3	35.5
U.S.	6.4	20.1	20.5	13.1	14.3	12.2	7.3	4.2	1.8	37.3

Note: (1) Figures cover the Charleston-North Charleston, SC Metropolitan Statistical Area—see Appendix B for areas included
Source: U.S. Census Bureau, 2010-2012 American Community Survey 3-Year Estimates

Gender

Area	Males	Females	Males per 100 Females
City	58,093	65,133	89.2
MSA[1]	333,074	349,170	95.4
U.S.	153,276,055	158,333,314	96.8

Note: (1) Figures cover the Charleston-North Charleston, SC Metropolitan Statistical Area—see Appendix B for areas included
Source: U.S. Census Bureau, 2010-2012 American Community Survey 3-Year Estimates

Religious Groups by Family

Area	Catholic	Baptist	Non-Den.	Methodist[2]	Lutheran	LDS[3]	Pentecostal	Presbyterian[4]	Muslim[5]	Judaism
MSA[1]	6.2	12.4	7.1	10.0	1.1	1.0	2.0	2.4	0.2	0.3
U.S.	19.1	9.3	4.0	4.0	2.3	2.0	1.9	1.6	0.8	0.7

Note: Figures are the number of adherents as a percentage of the total population; (1) Figures cover the Charleston-North Charleston, SC Metropolitan Statistical Area—see Appendix B for areas included; (2) Methodist/Pietist; (3) Latter Day Saints; (4) Reformed; (5) Figures are estimates
Source: Association of Statisticians of American Religious Bodies, 2010 U.S. Religion Census: Religious Congregations & Membership Study

Religious Groups by Tradition

Area	Catholic	Evangelical Protestant	Mainline Protestant	Other Tradition	Black Protestant	Orthodox
MSA[1]	6.2	19.7	11.2	1.9	7.3	0.1
U.S.	19.1	16.2	7.3	4.3	1.6	0.3

Note: Figures are the number of adherents as a percentage of the total population; (1) Figures cover the Charleston-North Charleston, SC Metropolitan Statistical Area—see Appendix B for areas included
Source: Association of Statisticians of American Religious Bodies, 2010 U.S. Religion Census: Religious Congregations & Membership Study

ECONOMY

Gross Metropolitan Product

Area	2011	2012	2013	2014	Rank[2]
MSA[1]	29.7	31.0	31.8	33.4	74

Note: Figures are in billions of dollars; (1) Figures cover the Charleston-North Charleston, SC Metropolitan Statistical Area—see Appendix B for areas included; (2) Rank is based on 2014 data and ranges from 1 to 363
Source: The United States Conference of Mayors, U.S. Metro Economies: Outlook—Gross Metropolitan Product, with Metro Employment Projections, November 2013

Economic Growth

Area	2011 (%)	2012 (%)	2013 (%)	2014 (%)	Rank[2]
MSA[1]	4.2	2.9	1.2	3.2	134
U.S.	1.6	2.5	1.7	2.5	–

Note: Figures are real gross metropolitan product (GMP) growth rates and represent annual average percent change; (1) Figures cover the Charleston-North Charleston, SC Metropolitan Statistical Area—see Appendix B for areas included; (2) Rank is based on 2013 data and ranges from 1 to 363
Source: The United States Conference of Mayors, U.S. Metro Economies: Outlook—Gross Metropolitan Product, with Metro Employment Projections, November 2013

Metropolitan Area Exports

Area	2007	2008	2009	2010	2011	2012	Rank[2]
MSA[1]	1,842.9	2,005.5	1,455.7	2,120.0	2,299.4	2,429.8	87

Note: Figures are in millions of dollars; (1) Figures cover the Charleston-North Charleston, SC Metropolitan Statistical Area—see Appendix B for areas included; (2) Rank is based on 2012 data and ranges from 1 to 369
Source: U.S. Department of Commerce, International Trade Administration, Office of Trade & Industry Information, Manufacturing & Services, data extracted April 1, 2014

INCOME

Income

Area	Per Capita ($)	Median Household ($)	Average Household ($)
City	31,728	50,602	72,430
MSA[1]	26,490	50,660	67,011
U.S.	27,385	51,771	71,579

Note: (1) Figures cover the Charleston-North Charleston, SC Metropolitan Statistical Area—see Appendix B for areas included
Source: U.S. Census Bureau, 2010-2012 American Community Survey 3-Year Estimates

Household Income Distribution

Area	Percent of Households Earning							
	Under $15,000	$15,000 -24,999	$25,000 -34,999	$35,000 -49,999	$50,000 -74,999	$75,000 -99,000	$100,000 -149,999	$150,000 and up
City	17.6	9.8	9.6	12.4	16.5	11.8	11.5	10.6
MSA[1]	13.7	10.9	10.4	14.3	19.4	11.9	11.6	7.9
U.S.	13.1	11.0	10.5	13.7	18.1	11.9	12.5	9.1

Note: (1) Figures cover the Charleston-North Charleston, SC Metropolitan Statistical Area—see Appendix B for areas included
Source: U.S. Census Bureau, 2010-2012 American Community Survey 3-Year Estimates

Poverty Rate

Area	All Ages	Under 18 Years Old	18 to 64 Years Old	65 Years and Over
City	21.2	28.8	21.3	10.0
MSA[1]	16.1	22.6	15.0	9.2
U.S.	15.7	22.2	14.6	9.3

Note: Figures are percentage of people whose income during the past 12 months was below the poverty level;
(1) Figures cover the Charleston-North Charleston, SC Metropolitan Statistical Area—see Appendix B for areas included
Source: U.S. Census Bureau, 2010-2012 American Community Survey 3-Year Estimates

Personal Bankruptcy Filing Rate

Area	2008	2009	2010	2011	2012	2013
Charleston County	1.45	1.71	1.88	1.51	1.36	1.36
U.S.	3.53	4.61	4.97	4.37	3.76	3.29

Note: Numbers are per 1,000 population and include Chapter 7 and Chapter 13 filings
Source: Federal Deposit Insurance Corporation, Regional Economic Conditions, March 20, 2014

EMPLOYMENT

Labor Force and Employment

Area	Civilian Labor Force			Workers Employed		
	Dec. 2012	Dec. 2013	% Chg.	Dec. 2012	Dec. 2013	% Chg.
City	61,564	61,147	-0.7	57,591	58,429	1.5
MSA[1]	330,542	328,726	-0.5	307,190	311,663	1.5
U.S.	154,904,000	154,408,000	-0.3	143,060,000	144,423,000	1.0

Note: Data is not seasonally adjusted and covers workers 16 years of age and older; (1) Metropolitan Statistical Area—see Appendix B for areas included
Source: Bureau of Labor Statistics, Local Area Unemployment Statistics

Unemployment Rate

Area	2013											
	Jan.	Feb.	Mar.	Apr.	May	Jun.	Jul.	Aug.	Sep.	Oct.	Nov.	Dec.
City	6.6	6.0	5.6	5.2	5.8	6.8	6.1	6.3	5.6	5.2	4.8	4.4
MSA[1]	7.3	6.8	6.4	5.9	6.4	7.3	6.7	6.9	6.3	6.0	5.5	5.2
U.S.	8.5	8.1	7.6	7.1	7.3	7.8	7.7	7.3	7.0	7.0	6.6	6.5

Note: Data is not seasonally adjusted and covers workers 16 years of age and older; All figures are percentages;
(1) Metropolitan Statistical Area—see Appendix B for areas included
Source: Bureau of Labor Statistics, Local Area Unemployment Statistics

Employment by Occupation

Occupation Classification	City (%)	MSA[1] (%)	U.S. (%)
Management, Business, Science, and Arts	44.4	35.0	36.0
Natural Resources, Construction, and Maintenance	5.1	10.0	9.1
Production, Transportation, and Material Moving	6.5	11.0	12.0
Sales and Office	23.1	25.3	24.7
Service	20.9	18.8	18.2

Note: Figures cover employed civilians 16 years of age and older; (1) Figures cover the Charleston-North Charleston, SC Metropolitan Statistical Area—see Appendix B for areas included
Source: U.S. Census Bureau, 2010-2012 American Community Survey 3-Year Estimates

Employment by Industry

| Sector | MSA[1] | | U.S. |
	Number of Employees	Percent of Total	Percent of Total
Construction	n/a	n/a	4.2
Education and Health Services	36,000	11.6	15.5
Financial Activities	12,900	4.1	5.7
Government	62,400	20.1	16.1
Information	5,200	1.7	1.9
Leisure and Hospitality	37,600	12.1	10.2
Manufacturing	24,100	7.8	8.7
Mining and Logging	n/a	n/a	0.6
Other Services	13,000	4.2	3.9
Professional and Business Services	44,500	14.3	13.7
Retail Trade	38,300	12.3	11.4
Transportation and Utilities	14,000	4.5	3.8
Wholesale Trade	8,000	2.6	4.2

Note: Figures cover non-farm employment as of December 2013 and are not seasonally adjusted;
(1) Metropolitan Statistical Area—see Appendix B for areas included; n/a not available
Source: Bureau of Labor Statistics, Current Employment Statistics, Employment, Hours, and Earnings

Occupations with Greatest Projected Employment Growth: 2010 – 2020

Occupation[1]	2010 Employment	2020 Projected Employment	Numeric Employment Change	Percent Employment Change
Retail Salespersons	65,490	76,560	11,070	16.9
Registered Nurses	42,330	53,180	10,850	25.6
Office Clerks, General	37,790	44,370	6,580	17.4
Combined Food Preparation and Serving Workers, Including Fast Food	35,990	42,390	6,390	17.8
Cashiers	57,730	63,750	6,020	10.4
Customer Service Representatives	35,330	40,470	5,130	14.5
Nursing Aides, Orderlies, and Attendants	20,320	25,400	5,080	25.0
Personal Care Aides	8,300	13,300	5,000	60.2
Laborers and Freight, Stock, and Material Movers, Hand	32,510	37,460	4,950	15.2
Landscaping and Groundskeeping Workers	22,320	27,090	4,770	21.4

Note: Projections cover South Carolina; (1) Sorted by numeric employment change
Source: www.projectionscentral.com, State Occupational Projections, 2010–2020 Long-Term Projections

Fastest Growing Occupations: 2010 – 2020

Occupation[1]	2010 Employment	2020 Projected Employment	Numeric Employment Change	Percent Employment Change
Personal Care Aides	8,300	13,300	5,000	60.2
Veterinary Technologists and Technicians	1,220	1,880	660	53.7
Helpers—Brickmasons, Blockmasons, Stonemasons, and Tile and Marble Setters	450	690	240	52.8
Helpers—Carpenters	1,090	1,590	490	45.2
Market Research Analysts and Marketing Specialists	1,940	2,730	790	40.8
Medical Secretaries	6,330	8,910	2,580	40.8
Diagnostic Medical Sonographers	720	1,020	290	40.6
Physical Therapist Assistants	1,030	1,440	410	39.7
Helpers—Pipelayers, Plumbers, Pipefitters, and Steamfitters	1,210	1,690	480	39.4
Dental Hygienists	2,430	3,380	950	39.2

Note: Projections cover South Carolina; (1) Sorted by percent employment change and excludes occupations
with numeric employment change less than 100
Source: www.projectionscentral.com, State Occupational Projections, 2010–2020 Long-Term Projections

Average Wages

Occupation	$/Hr.	Occupation	$/Hr.
Accountants and Auditors	28.92	Maids and Housekeeping Cleaners	9.35
Automotive Mechanics	20.06	Maintenance and Repair Workers	17.87
Bookkeepers	16.48	Marketing Managers	53.11
Carpenters	17.86	Nuclear Medicine Technologists	32.35
Cashiers	9.45	Nurses, Licensed Practical	20.18
Clerks, General Office	12.58	Nurses, Registered	32.16
Clerks, Receptionists/Information	13.41	Nursing Assistants	11.10
Clerks, Shipping/Receiving	15.68	Packers and Packagers, Hand	9.94
Computer Programmers	32.89	Physical Therapists	36.90
Computer Systems Analysts	31.81	Postal Service Mail Carriers	23.89
Computer User Support Specialists	22.77	Real Estate Brokers	26.30
Cooks, Restaurant	10.15	Retail Salespersons	11.52
Dentists	88.16	Sales Reps., Exc. Tech./Scientific	27.76
Electrical Engineers	38.32	Sales Reps., Tech./Scientific	40.46
Electricians	18.98	Secretaries, Exc. Legal/Med./Exec.	15.32
Financial Managers	50.16	Security Guards	13.52
First-Line Supervisors/Managers, Sales	19.38	Surgeons	n/a
Food Preparation Workers	10.20	Teacher Assistants	11.50
General and Operations Managers	50.21	Teachers, Elementary School	24.70
Hairdressers/Cosmetologists	11.03	Teachers, Secondary School	25.40
Internists	73.51	Telemarketers	9.57
Janitors and Cleaners	10.54	Truck Drivers, Heavy/Tractor-Trailer	19.36
Landscaping/Groundskeeping Workers	10.92	Truck Drivers, Light/Delivery Svcs.	15.63
Lawyers	48.58	Waiters and Waitresses	9.42

Note: Wage data covers the Charleston-North Charleston-Summerville, SC Metropolitan Statistical Area—see Appendix B for areas included. Hourly wages for elementary/secondary school teachers and teacher assistants were calculated by the editors from annual wage data assuming a 40 hour work week; n/a not available.
Source: Bureau of Labor Statistics, Metro Area Occupational Employment and Wage Estimates, May 2013

RESIDENTIAL REAL ESTATE

Building Permits

Area	Single-Family			Multi-Family			Total		
	2012	2013	Pct. Chg.	2012	2013	Pct. Chg.	2012	2013	Pct. Chg.
City	477	576	20.8	338	351	3.8	815	927	13.7
MSA[1]	3,132	3,779	20.7	1,461	1,638	12.1	4,593	5,417	17.9
U.S.	518,695	620,802	19.7	310,963	370,020	19.0	829,658	990,822	19.4

Note: (1) Metropolitan Statistical Area—see Appendix B for areas included; figures represent new, privately-owned housing units authorized (unadjusted data); All permit data are based on estimates with imputation.
Source: U.S. Census Bureau, Manufacturing, Mining, and Construction Statistics, Building Permits, 2012, 2013

Homeownership Rate

Area	2006 (%)	2007 (%)	2008 (%)	2009 (%)	2010 (%)	2011 (%)	2012 (%)	2013 (%)
MSA[1]	n/a	n/a	n/a	n/a	n/a	n/a	n/a	n/a
U.S.	68.8	68.1	67.8	67.4	66.9	66.1	65.4	65.1

Note: (1) Figures cover the Charleston-North Charleston, SC Metropolitan Statistical Area—see Appendix B for areas included; n/a not available
Source: U.S. Census Bureau, Housing Vacancies and Homeownership Annual Statistics: 2013

Housing Vacancy Rates

Area	Gross Vacancy Rate[2] (%)			Year-Round Vacancy Rate[3] (%)			Rental Vacancy Rate[4] (%)			Homeowner Vacancy Rate[5] (%)		
	2011	2012	2013	2011	2012	2013	2011	2012	2013	2011	2012	2013
MSA[1]	n/a	n/a	n/a	n/a	n/a	n/a	n/a	n/a	n/a	n/a	n/a	n/a
U.S.	14.2	13.8	13.8	11.1	10.8	10.7	9.5	8.7	8.3	2.5	2.0	2.0

Note: (1) Figures cover the Charleston-North Charleston, SC Metropolitan Statistical Area—see Appendix B for areas included; (2) The percentage of the total housing inventory that is vacant; (3) The percentage of the housing inventory (excluding seasonal units) that is year-round vacant; (4) The percentage of rental inventory that is vacant for rent; (5) The percentage of homeowner inventory that is vacant for sale; n/a not available
Source: U.S. Census Bureau, Housing Vacancies and Homeownership Annual Statistics: 2013

TAXES

State Corporate Income Tax Rates

State	Tax Rate (%)	Income Brackets ($)	Num. of Brackets	Financial Institution Tax Rate (%)[a]	Federal Income Tax Ded.
South Carolina	5.0	Flat rate	1	4.5 (w)	No

Note: Tax rates as of January 1, 2014; (a) Rates listed are the corporate income tax rate applied to financial institutions or excise taxes based on income. Some states have other taxes based upon the value of deposits or shares; (w) South Carolina taxes savings and loans at a 6% rate.
Source: Federation of Tax Administrators, "State Corporate Income Tax Rates, 2014"

State Individual Income Tax Rates

State	Tax Rate (%)	Income Brackets ($)	Num. of Brackets	Personal Exempt. ($)[1] Single	Personal Exempt. ($)[1] Dependents	Fed. Inc. Tax Ded.
South Carolina (a)	0.0 - 7.0	2,880 - 14,400	6	3,950 (d)	3,950 (d)	No

Note: Tax rates as of January 1, 2014; Local- and county-level taxes are not included; n/a not applicable; (1) Married joint filers generally receive double the single exemption; (a) 17 states have statutory provision for automatically adjusting to the rate of inflation the dollar values of the income tax brackets, standard deductions, and/or personal exemptions. Massachusetts, Michigan, and Nebraska index the personal exemptiononly. Oregon does not index the income brackets for $125,000 and over. Maine has suspended indexing for 2014 and 2015; (d) These states use the personal exemption amounts provided in the federal Internal Revenue Code.
Source: Federation of Tax Administrators, "State Individual Income Tax Rates, 2014"

Various State and Local Tax Rates

State	State and Local Sales and Use (%)	State Sales and Use (%)	Gasoline[1] (¢/gal.)	Cigarette[2] ($/pack)	Spirits[3] ($/gal.)	Wine[4] ($/gal.)	Beer[5] ($/gal.)
South Carolina	8.5	6.00	16.75	0.570	5.42 (i)	1.08	0.77

Note: All tax rates as of January 1, 2014; (1) The American Petroleum Institute has developed a methodology for determining the average tax rate on a gallon of fuel. Rates may include any of the following: excise taxes, environmental fees, storage tank fees, other fees or taxes, general sales tax, and local taxes. In states where gasoline is subject to the general sales tax, or where the fuel tax is based on the average sale price, the average rate determined by API is sensitive to changes in the price of gasoline. States that fully or partially apply general sales taxes to gasoline: CA, CO, GA, IL, IN, MI, NY; (2) The federal excise tax of $1.0066 per pack and local taxes are not included; (3) Rates are those applicable to off-premise sales of 40% alcohol by volume (a.b.v.) distilled spirits in 750ml containers. Local excise taxes are excluded; (4) Rates are those applicable to off-premise sales of 11% a.b.v. non-carbonated wine in 750ml containers; (5) Rates are those applicable to off-premise sales of 4.7% a.b.v. beer in 12 ounce containers; (i) Includes case fees and/or bottle fees which may vary with size of container.
Source: Tax Foundation, 2014 Facts & Figures: How Does Your State Compare?

State Business Tax Climate Index Rankings

State	Overall Rank	Corporate Tax Index Rank	Individual Income Tax Index Rank	Sales Tax Index Rank	Unemployment Insurance Tax Index Rank	Property Tax Index Rank
South Carolina	37	10	40	22	30	21

Note: The index is a measure of how each state's tax laws affect economic performance. The lower the rank, the more favorable a state's tax system is for business. States without a given tax are given a ranking of 1. The scores/rankings for the District of Columbia do not affect other states. The 2014 index represents the tax climate as of July 1, 2013.
Source: Tax Foundation, State Business Tax Climate Index 2014

COMMERCIAL UTILITIES

Typical Monthly Electric Bills

Area	Commercial Service ($/month) 1,500 kWh	Commercial Service ($/month) 40 kW demand 14,000 kWh	Industrial Service ($/month) 1,000 kW demand 200,000 kWh	Industrial Service ($/month) 50,000 kW demand 15,000,000 kWh
City	206	1,846	26,759	1,495,475
Average[1]	197	1,636	25,662	1,485,307

Note: Based on total rates in effect July 1, 2013; (1) average based on 180 utilities surveyed
Source: Edison Electric Institute, Typical Bills and Average Rates Report, Summer 2013

TRANSPORTATION

Means of Transportation to Work

| Area | Car/Truck/Van | | Public Transportation | | | Bicycle | Walked | Other Means | Worked at Home |
	Drove Alone	Car-pooled	Bus	Subway	Railroad				
City	76.4	7.2	2.9	0.0	0.0	2.5	5.6	1.1	4.3
MSA[1]	80.4	9.0	1.3	0.0	0.0	0.9	3.0	0.9	4.4
U.S.	76.4	9.7	2.6	1.7	0.5	0.6	2.8	1.3	4.3

Note: Figures are percentages and cover workers 16 years of age and older; (1) Figures cover the Charleston-North Charleston, SC Metropolitan Statistical Area—see Appendix B for areas included
Source: U.S. Census Bureau, 2010-2012 American Community Survey 3-Year Estimates

Travel Time to Work

Area	Less Than 10 Minutes	10 to 19 Minutes	20 to 29 Minutes	30 to 44 Minutes	45 to 59 Minutes	60 to 89 Minutes	90 Minutes or More
City	13.0	35.0	28.2	16.0	3.5	2.7	1.6
MSA[1]	10.2	29.8	25.7	21.9	7.5	3.3	1.6
U.S.	13.5	29.8	20.9	20.1	7.5	5.6	2.5

Note: Figures are percentages and include workers 16 years old and over; (1) Figures cover the Charleston-North Charleston, SC Metropolitan Statistical Area—see Appendix B for areas included
Source: U.S. Census Bureau, 2010-2012 American Community Survey 3-Year Estimates

Travel Time Index

Area	1985	1990	1995	2000	2005	2010	2011
Urban Area[1]	1.10	1.12	1.14	1.15	1.16	1.15	1.15
Average[2]	1.09	1.14	1.16	1.19	1.23	1.18	1.18

Note: Travel Time Index—the ratio of travel time in the peak period to the travel time at free-flow conditions. For example, a value of 1.30 indicates a 20-minute free-flow trip takes 26 minutes in the peak. Free-flow speeds (60 mph on freeways and 35 mph on principal arterials) are used as the comparison threshold; (1) Covers the Charleston-North Charleston SC urban area; (2) average of 498 urban areas
Source: Texas Transportation Institute, Urban Mobility Report 2012, December 2012

Public Transportation

Agency Name / Mode of Transportation	Vehicles Operated in Maximum Service	Annual Unlinked Passenger Trips (in thous.)	Annual Passenger Miles (in thous.)
Charleston Area Regional Transportation (CARTA)			
Bus (purchased transportation)	81	4,832.1	17,938.2
Demand Response (purchased transportation)	23	72.3	783.4

Source: Federal Transit Administration, National Transit Database, 2012

Air Transportation

Airport Name and Code / Type of Service	Passenger Airlines[1]	Passenger Enplanements	Freight Carriers[2]	Freight (lbs.)
Charleston International Airport (CHS)				
Domestic service (U.S. carriers - 2013)	23	1,438,734	10	9,983,240
International service (U.S. carriers - 2012)	2	86	6	4,621,693

Note: (1) Includes all U.S.-based major, minor and commuter airlines that carried at least one passenger during the year; (2) Includes all U.S.-based airlines and freight carriers that transported at least one lb. of freight during the year.
Source: Bureau of Transportation Statistics, The Intermodal Transportation Database, Air Carriers: T-100 Domestic Market (U.S. Carriers), 2013; Bureau of Transportation Statistics, The Intermodal Transportation Database, Air Carriers: T-100 International Market (U.S. Carriers), 2012

Other Transportation Statistics

Major Highways: I-26; I-95
Amtrak Service: Yes (station is located in North Charleston)
Major Waterways/Ports: Atlantic Ocean

Source: Amtrak.com; Google Maps

BUSINESSES

Major Business Headquarters

Company Name	Rankings	
	Fortune[1]	Forbes[2]
No companies listed	–	–

Note: (1) Fortune 500—companies that produce a 10-K are ranked 1 to 500 based on 2012 revenue; (2) all private companies with at least $2 billion in annual revenue through the end of their most current fiscal year are ranked 1 to 224; companies listed are headquartered in the city; dashes indicate no ranking
Source: Fortune, "Fortune 500," May 20, 2013; Forbes, "America's Largest Private Companies," December 18, 2013

Fast-Growing Businesses

According to *Inc.*, Charleston is home to three of America's 500 fastest-growing private companies: **Sparc** (#14); **BoomTown** (#431); **Blue Acorn** (#474). Criteria: must be an independent, privately-held, for-profit, U.S. corporation, proprietorship or partnership; revenues must be at least $100,000 in 2009 and $2 million in 2012; must have four-year operating/sales history. Holding companies, regulated banks, and utilities were excluded. *Inc., "America's 500 Fastest-Growing Private Companies," September 2013*

According to Deloitte, Charleston is home to one of North America's 500 fastest-growing high-technology companies: **BoomTown** (#52). Companies are ranked by percentage growth in revenue over a five-year period. Criteria for inclusion: company must be headquartered within North America; must own proprietary intellectual property or proprietary technology that contributes to a significant portion of the company's operating revenue, or devote a significant proportion of revenues to research and development of technology; must have been in business for a minumum of five years with 2008 operating revenues of at least $50,000 USD/CD and 2012 operating revenues of at least $5 million USD/CD. *Deloitte Touche Tohmatsu, 2013 Technology Fast 500[TM]*

Minority- and Women-Owned Businesses

Group	All Firms		Firms with Paid Employees			
	Firms	Sales ($000)	Firms	Sales ($000)	Employees	Payroll ($000)
Asian	230	97,937	57	89,149	866	16,742
Black	1,081	64,190	114	37,962	479	11,292
Hispanic	(s)	(s)	(s)	(s)	(s)	(s)
Women	3,766	640,119	657	544,193	4,477	108,612
All Firms	13,392	11,088,365	3,844	10,554,855	62,244	2,129,311

Note: Figures cover firms located in the city; minority- and women-owned business are defined as firms in which the corresponding group own 51% or more of the stock or equity of the company; (s) estimates are suppressed when publication standards are not met
Source: U.S. Census Bureau, 2007 Economic Census, Survey of Business Owners (2012 Survey of Business Owners data will be released starting in June 2015)

HOTELS & CONVENTION CENTERS

Hotels/Motels

Area	5 Star		4 Star		3 Star		2 Star		1 Star		Not Rated	
	Num.	Pct.[3]	Num.	Pct.[3]	Num.	Pct.[3]	Num.	Pct.[3]	Num.	Pct.[3]	Num.	Pct.[3]
City[1]	1	0.7	11	7.7	54	38.0	68	47.9	1	0.7	7	4.9
Total[2]	142	0.9	1,005	6.0	5,147	30.9	8,578	51.4	408	2.4	1,397	8.4

Note: (1) Figures cover Charleston and vicinity; (2) Figures cover all 100 cities in this book; (3) Percentage of hotels which have a given star rating; Star ratings are determined by expedia.com and offer an indication of the general quality of a particular hotel.
Source: expedia.com, April 7, 2014

The Charleston-North Charleston, SC metro area is home to six of the best hotels in the U.S. according to *Travel & Leisure*: **Market Pavilion Hotel**; **Wentworth Mansion**; **French Quarter Inn**; **Sanctuary at Kiawah Island Golf Resort**; **Planters Inn**; **Belmond Charleston Place**. Criteria: service; location; rooms; food; and value. The list includes the top 200 hotels in the U.S. *Travel & Leisure, "T+L 500, The World's Best Hotels 2014"*

The Charleston-North Charleston, SC metro area is home to nine of the best hotels in the world according to *Condé Nast Traveler*: **Charleston Place**; **French Quarter Inn**; **HarbourView Inn**; **John Rutledge House Inn**; **Market Pavilion Hotel**; **Planters Inn**; **Restoration on King**; **Sanctuary at Kiawah Island Golf Resort**; **Wentworth Mansion**. The selections are based on over 79,000 responses to the magazine's annual Readers' Choice Survey. The list includes the top 200 hotels in the U.S. *Condé Nast Traveler, "Gold List 2014, The World's Best Places to Stay"*

Major Convention Centers

Name	Overall Space (sq. ft.)	Exhibit Space (sq. ft.)	Meeting Space (sq. ft.)	Meeting Rooms
Charleston Area Convention Center Complex	n/a	76,960	n/a	n/a

Note: Table includes convention centers located in the Charleston-North Charleston, SC metro area; n/a not available
Source: Original research

Living Environment

COST OF LIVING

Cost of Living Index

Composite Index	Groceries	Housing	Utilities	Trans-portation	Health Care	Misc. Goods/Services
99.8	104.9	88.8	113.5	95.7	103.0	103.4

Note: The Cost of Living Index measures regional differences in the cost of consumer goods and services, excluding taxes and non-consumer expenditures, for professional and managerial households in the top income quintile. It is based on more than 50,000 prices covering almost 60 different items for which prices are collected three times a year by chambers of commerce, economic development organizations or university applied economic centers in each participating urban area. The numbers shown should be read as a percentage above or below the national average of 100. For example, a value of 115.4 in the groceries column indicates that grocery prices are 15.4% higher than the national average. Small differences in the index numbers should not be interpreted as significant; Figures cover the Charleston-N Charleston SC urban area.
Source: The Council for Community and Economic Research, ACCRA Cost of Living Index, 2013

Grocery Prices

Area[1]	T-Bone Steak ($/pound)	Frying Chicken ($/pound)	Whole Milk ($/half gal.)	Eggs ($/dozen)	Orange Juice ($/64 oz.)	Coffee ($/11.5 oz.)
City[2]	10.12	1.46	2.73	1.76	3.54	4.31
Avg.	10.19	1.28	2.34	1.81	3.48	4.39
Min.	8.56	0.94	1.44	1.19	2.78	3.40
Max.	14.82	2.28	3.56	3.73	6.23	7.32

*Note: (1) Values for the local area are compared with the average, minimum and maximum values for all 327 areas in the Cost of Living Index; (2) Figures cover the Charleston-N Charleston SC urban area; **T-Bone Steak** (price per pound); **Frying Chicken** (price per pound, whole fryer); **Whole Milk** (half gallon carton); **Eggs** (price per dozen, Grade A, large); **Orange Juice** (64 oz. Tropicana or Florida Natural); **Coffee** (11.5 oz. can, vacuum-packed, Maxwell House, Hills Bros, or Folgers).*
Source: The Council for Community and Economic Research, ACCRA Cost of Living Index, 2013

Housing and Utility Costs

Area[1]	New Home Price ($)	Apartment Rent ($/month)	All Electric ($/month)	Part Electric ($/month)	Other Energy ($/month)	Telephone ($/month)
City[2]	238,131	1,058	196.23	-	-	28.92
Avg.	295,864	900	171.38	91.82	70.12	27.73
Min.	185,506	458	117.80	48.81	33.67	17.16
Max.	1,358,917	3,783	441.68	171.40	372.65	39.47

*Note: (1) Values for the local area are compared with the average, minimum and maximum values for all 327 areas in the Cost of Living Index; (2) Figures cover the Charleston-N Charleston SC urban area; **New Home Price** (2,400 sf living area, 8,000 sf lot, in urban area with full utilities); **Apartment Rent** (950 sf 2 bedroom/1.5 or 2 bath, unfurnished, excluding all utilities except water); **All Electric** (average monthly cost for an all-electric home); **Part Electric** (average monthly cost for a part-electric home); **Other Energy** (average monthly cost for natural gas, fuel oil, coal, wood, and any other forms of energy except electricity); **Telephone** (price includes basic monthly rate for a private residential line plus additional local usage charges incurred by a family of four).*
Source: The Council for Community and Economic Research, ACCRA Cost of Living Index, 2013

Health Care, Transportation, and Other Costs

Area[1]	Doctor ($/visit)	Dentist ($/visit)	Optometrist ($/visit)	Gasoline ($/gallon)	Beauty Salon ($/visit)	Men's Shirt ($)
City[2]	95.15	92.47	105.89	3.28	42.50	31.50
Avg.	101.40	86.48	96.16	3.44	33.87	26.55
Min.	61.67	50.83	50.12	3.08	18.92	12.48
Max.	182.71	152.50	223.78	4.33	68.22	52.03

*Note: (1) Values for the local area are compared with the average, minimum and maximum values for all 327 areas in the Cost of Living Index; (2) Figures cover the Charleston-N Charleston SC urban area; **Doctor** (general practitioners routine exam of an established patient); **Dentist** (adult teeth cleaning and periodic oral examination); **Optometrist** (full vision eye exam for established adult patient); **Gasoline** (one gallon regular unleaded, national brand, including all taxes, cash price at self-service pump if available); **Beauty Salon** (woman's shampoo, trim, and blow-dry); **Men's Shirt** (cotton/polyester dress shirt, pinpoint weave, long sleeves).*
Source: The Council for Community and Economic Research, ACCRA Cost of Living Index, 2013

HOUSING

House Price Index (HPI)

Area	National Ranking[2]	Quarterly Change (%)	One-Year Change (%)	Five-Year Change (%)
MSA[1]	95	-0.30	4.62	-10.06
U.S.[3]	–	1.20	7.69	4.18

Note: The HPI is a weighted repeat sales index. It measures average price changes in repeat sales or refinancings on the same properties. This information is obtained by reviewing repeat mortgage transactions on single-family properties whose mortgages have been purchased or securitized by Fannie Mae or Freddie Mac in January 1975; (1) Charleston-North Charleston, SC Metropolitan Statistical Area—see Appendix B for areas included; (2) Rankings are based on annual percentage change for all metro areas containing at least 15,000 transactions over the last 10 years and ranges from 1 to 283; (3) figures based on a weighted average of Census Division estimates using a seasonally adjusted, purchase-only index; all figures are for the period ending December 31, 2013
Source: Federal Housing Finance Agency, House Price Index, February 25, 2014

Median Single-Family Home Prices

Area	2011	2012	2013p	Percent Change 2012 to 2013
MSA[1]	197.0	207.5	221.7	6.8
U.S. Average	166.2	177.2	197.4	11.4

Note: Figures are median sales prices of existing single-family homes in thousands of dollars; (p) preliminary; n/a not available; (1) Charleston-North Charleston, SC Metropolitan Statistical Area—see Appendix B for areas included
Source: National Association of Realtors, Median Sales Price of Existing Single-Family Homes for Metropolitan Areas, 4th Quarter 2013

Qualifying Income Based on Median Sales Price of Existing Single-Family Homes

Area	With 5% Down ($)	With 10% Down ($)	With 20% Down ($)
MSA[1]	51,759	49,034	43,586
U.S. Average	45,395	43,006	38,228

Note: Figures are preliminary; Qualifying income is based on a mortgage rate of 4.4%. Monthly principal and interest payment is limited to 25% of income; n/a not available; (1) Charleston-North Charleston, SC Metropolitan Statistical Area—see Appendix B for areas included
Source: National Association of Realtors, Qualifying Income Based on Median Sales Price of Existing Single-Family Homes for Metropolitan Areas, 4th Quarter 2013

Median Apartment Condo-Coop Home Prices

Area	2011	2012	2013p	Percent Change 2012 to 2013
MSA[1]	n/a	n/a	n/a	n/a
U.S. Average	165.1	173.7	194.9	12.2

Note: Figures are median sales prices of existing apartment condo-coop homes in thousands of dollars; (p) preliminary; n/a not available; (1) Charleston-North Charleston, SC Metropolitan Statistical Area—see Appendix B for areas included
Source: National Association of Realtors, Median Sales Price of Existing Apartment Condo-Coop Homes for Metropolitan Areas, 4th Quarter 2013

Gross Monthly Rent

Area	Under $200	$200 -299	$300 -499	$500 -749	$750 -999	$1,000 -1,499	$1,500 and up	Median ($)
City	1.7	3.6	6.4	16.4	27.6	29.8	14.6	958
MSA[1]	0.8	2.0	5.4	18.4	30.4	31.4	11.6	945
U.S.	1.7	3.3	8.1	22.7	24.3	25.7	14.3	889

Note: Figures are percentages except for Median; Gross rent is the contract rent plus the estimated average monthly cost of utilities (electricity, gas, and water and sewer) and fuels (oil, coal, kerosene, wood, etc.) if these are paid by the renter (or paid for the renter by someone else); (1) Figures cover the Charleston-North Charleston, SC Metropolitan Statistical Area—see Appendix B for areas included
Source: U.S. Census Bureau, 2010-2012 American Community Survey 3-Year Estimates

Year Housing Structure Built

Area	2010 or Later	2000 -2009	1990 -1999	1980 -1989	1970 -1979	1960 -1969	1950 -1959	1940 -1949	Before 1940	Median Year
City	0.7	25.4	12.5	13.9	9.6	11.0	7.3	4.3	15.4	1982
MSA[1]	0.8	26.3	16.3	17.4	15.9	9.5	6.3	2.7	4.8	1986
U.S.	0.5	14.9	13.8	13.9	15.9	11.1	10.9	5.5	13.5	1976

Note: Figures are percentages except for Median Year; (1) Figures cover the Charleston-North Charleston, SC Metropolitan Statistical Area—see Appendix B for areas included
Source: U.S. Census Bureau, 2010-2012 American Community Survey 3-Year Estimates

HEALTH

Health Risk Data

Category	MSA[1] (%)	U.S. (%)
Adults aged 18–64 who have any kind of health care coverage	77.7	79.6
Adults who reported being in good or excellent health	84.5	83.1
Adults who are current smokers	20.2	19.6
Adults who are heavy drinkers[2]	8.2	6.1
Adults who are binge drinkers[3]	21.1	16.9
Adults who are overweight (BMI 25.0 - 29.9)	33.9	35.8
Adults who are obese (BMI 30.0 - 99.8)	28.5	27.6
Adults who participated in any physical activities in the past month	79.0	77.1
Adults 50+ who have ever had a sigmoidoscopy or colonoscopy	70.1	67.3
Women aged 40+ who have had a mammogram within the past two years	75.7	74.0
Men aged 40+ who have had a PSA test within the past two years	49.9	45.2
Adults aged 65+ who have had flu shot within the past year	68.1	60.1
Adults who always wear a seatbelt	93.5	93.8

Note: Data as of 2012 unless otherwise noted; (1) Figures cover the Charleston-North Charleston, SC Metropolitan Statistical Area—see Appendix B for areas included; (2) Heavy drinkers are classified as males having more than two drinks per day or females having more than one drink per day; (3) Binge drinkers are classified as males having five or more drinks on one occasion or females having four or more drinks on one occasion
Source: Centers for Disease Control and Prevention, Behaviorial Risk Factor Surveillance System, SMART: Selected Metropolitan/Micropolitan Area Risk Trends, 2012

Chronic Health Indicators

Category	MSA[1] (%)	U.S. (%)
Adults who have ever been told they had a heart attack	4.0	4.5
Adults who have ever been told they had a stroke	3.5	2.9
Adults who have been told they currently have asthma	8.0	8.9
Adults who have ever been told they have arthritis	24.8	25.7
Adults who have ever been told they have diabetes[2]	11.7	9.7
Adults who have ever been told they had skin cancer	6.6	5.7
Adults who have ever been told they had any other types of cancer	6.6	6.5
Adults who have ever been told they have COPD	6.1	6.2
Adults who have ever been told they have kidney disease	2.1	2.5
Adults who have ever been told they have a form of depression	17.3	18.0

Note: Data as of 2012 unless otherwise noted; (1) Figures cover the Charleston-North Charleston, SC Metropolitan Statistical Area—see Appendix B for areas included; (2) Figures do not include pregnancy-related, borderline, or pre-diabetes
Source: Centers for Disease Control and Prevention, Behaviorial Risk Factor Surveillance System, SMART: Selected Metropolitan/Micropolitan Area Risk Trends, 2012

Mortality Rates for the Top 10 Causes of Death in the U.S.

ICD-10[a] Sub-Chapter	ICD-10[a] Code	Age-Adjusted Mortality Rate[1] per 100,000 population	
		County[2]	U.S.
Malignant neoplasms	C00-C97	188.8	174.2
Ischaemic heart diseases	I20-I25	90.8	119.1
Other forms of heart disease	I30-I51	52.7	49.6
Chronic lower respiratory diseases	J40-J47	39.9	43.2
Cerebrovascular diseases	I60-I69	49.8	40.3
Organic, including symptomatic, mental disorders	F01-F09	40.6	30.5
Other degenerative diseases of the nervous system	G30-G31	35.7	26.3
Other external causes of accidental injury	W00-X59	29.4	25.1
Diabetes mellitus	E10-E14	22.1	21.3
Hypertensive diseases	I10-I15	15.5	18.8

Note: (a) ICD-10 = International Classification of Diseases 10th Revision; (1) Mortality rates are a three year average covering 2008-2010; (2) Figures cover Charleston County
Source: Centers for Disease Control and Prevention, National Center for Health Statistics. Compressed Mortality File 1999-2010 on CDC WONDER Online Database, released January 2013. Data are compiled from the Compressed Mortality File 1999-2010, Series 20 No. 2P, 2013.

Mortality Rates for Selected Causes of Death

ICD-10[a] Sub-Chapter	ICD-10[a] Code	Age-Adjusted Mortality Rate[1] per 100,000 population	
		County[2]	U.S.
Assault	X85-Y09	8.9	5.5
Diseases of the liver	K70-K76	12.0	12.4
Human immunodeficiency virus (HIV) disease	B20-B24	5.1	3.0
Influenza and pneumonia	J09-J18	10.9	16.4
Intentional self-harm	X60-X84	13.3	11.8
Malnutrition	E40-E46	*1.5	0.8
Obesity and other hyperalimentation	E65-E68	*1.3	1.6
Renal failure	N17-N19	15.2	13.6
Transport accidents	V01-V99	14.2	12.6
Viral hepatitis	B15-B19	2.5	2.2

Note: (a) ICD-10 = International Classification of Diseases 10th Revision; (1) Mortality rates are a three year average covering 2008-2010; (2) Figures cover Charleston County; (*) Unreliable data as per CDC
Source: Centers for Disease Control and Prevention, National Center for Health Statistics. Compressed Mortality File 1999-2010 on CDC WONDER Online Database, released January 2013. Data are compiled from the Compressed Mortality File 1999-2010, Series 20 No. 2P, 2013.

Health Insurance Coverage

Area	With Health Insurance	With Private Health Insurance	With Public Health Insurance	Without Health Insurance	Population Under Age 18 Without Health Insurance
City	87.2	73.3	24.9	12.8	7.2
MSA[1]	82.9	66.7	27.5	17.1	9.8
U.S.	84.9	65.4	30.4	15.1	7.5

Note: Figures are percentages that cover the civilian noninstitutionalized population; (1) Figures cover the Charleston-North Charleston, SC Metropolitan Statistical Area—see Appendix B for areas included
Source: U.S. Census Bureau, 2010-2012 American Community Survey 3-Year Estimates

Number of Medical Professionals

Area[1]	MDs[2]	DOs[2,3]	Dentists	Podiatrists	Chiropractors	Optometrists
Local (number)	2,713	89	366	18	151	70
Local (rate[4])	758.6	24.9	100.2	4.9	41.4	19.2
U.S. (rate[4])	267.6	19.6	61.7	5.6	24.7	14.5

Note: Data as of 2012 unless noted; (1) Local data covers Charleston County; (2) Data as of 2011; (3) Doctor of Osteopathic Medicine; (4) rate per 100,000 population
Source: Area Resource File (ARF) 2012-2013. U.S. Department of Health and Human Services, Health Resources and Services Administration, Bureau of Health Professions

Best Hospitals

According to *U.S. News,* the Charleston-North Charleston, SC metro area is home to one of the best hospitals in the U.S.: **Medical University of South Carolina** (3 specialties). The hospital listed was nationally ranked in at least one adult specialty. Only 147 hospitals nationwide were nationally ranked in one or more specialties. Eighteen hospitals in the U.S. made the Honor Roll by ranking near the top in at least six specialties.*U.S. News Online, "America's Best Hospitals 2013-14"*

According to *U.S. News,* the Charleston-North Charleston, SC metro area is home to one of the best children's hospitals in the U.S.: **Medical University of South Carolina Children's Hospital.** The hospital listed was highly ranked in at least one pediatric specialty. Eighty-seven hospitals in the U.S. ranked in at least one specialty. Ten children's hospitals in the U.S. made the Honor Roll by ranking near the top in three or more specialties.*U.S. News Online, "America's Best Children's Hospitals 2013-14"*

EDUCATION

Public School District Statistics

District Name	Schls	Pupils	Pupil/ Teacher Ratio	Minority Pupils[1] (%)	Free Lunch Eligible[2] (%)	IEP[3] (%)
Charleston 01	78	44,058	13.7	55.0	46.1	10.2

Note: Table includes school districts with 2,000 or more students; (1) Percentage of students that are not non-Hispanic white; (2) Percentage of students that are eligible for the free lunch program; (3) Percentage of students that have an Individualized Education Program.
Source: U.S. Department of Education, National Center for Education Statistics, Common Core of Data, Local Education Agency (School District) Universe Survey: School Year 2011-2012; U.S. Department of Education, National Center for Education Statistics, Common Core of Data, Public Elementary/Secondary School Universe Survey: School Year 2011-2012

Highest Level of Education

Area	Less than H.S.	H.S. Diploma	Some College, No Deg.	Associate Degree	Bachelor's Degree	Master's Degree	Prof. School Degree	Doctorate Degree
City	7.7	18.4	18.9	6.9	30.3	11.0	4.4	2.5
MSA[1]	12.2	26.1	22.3	8.4	20.2	7.8	1.9	1.2
U.S.	14.1	28.3	21.3	7.8	18.0	7.5	1.9	1.2

Note: Figures cover persons age 25 and over; (1) Figures cover the Charleston-North Charleston, SC Metropolitan Statistical Area—see Appendix B for areas included
Source: U.S. Census Bureau, 2010-2012 American Community Survey 3-Year Estimates

Educational Attainment by Race

Area	High School Graduate or Higher (%)					Bachelor's Degree or Higher (%)				
	Total	White	Black	Asian	Hisp.[2]	Total	White	Black	Asian	Hisp.[2]
City	92.3	96.2	80.1	n/a	89.1	48.2	57.8	15.8	n/a	30.3
MSA[1]	87.8	91.7	79.0	81.8	70.1	31.1	37.6	14.2	38.4	19.8
U.S.	85.9	88.1	82.5	85.5	63.1	28.6	30.0	18.4	50.2	13.4

Note: Figures shown cover persons 25 years old and over; (1) Figures cover the Charleston-North Charleston, SC Metropolitan Statistical Area—see Appendix B for areas included; (2) People of Hispanic origin can be of any race
Source: U.S. Census Bureau, 2010-2012 American Community Survey 3-Year Estimates

School Enrollment by Grade and Control

Area	Preschool (%)		Kindergarten (%)		Grades 1 - 4 (%)		Grades 5 - 8 (%)		Grades 9 - 12 (%)	
	Public	Private	Public	Private	Public	Private	Public	Private	Public	Private
City	35.2	64.8	80.4	19.6	81.3	18.7	81.4	18.6	84.2	15.8
MSA[1]	46.5	53.5	84.2	15.8	88.2	11.8	89.8	10.2	90.2	9.8
U.S.	56.9	43.1	87.8	12.2	89.9	10.1	90.0	10.0	90.8	9.2

Note: Figures shown cover persons 3 years old and over; (1) Figures cover the Charleston-North Charleston, SC Metropolitan Statistical Area—see Appendix B for areas included
Source: U.S. Census Bureau, 2010-2012 American Community Survey 3-Year Estimates

Average Salaries of Public School Classroom Teachers

Area	2012-13		2013-14		Percent Change 2012-13 to 2013-14	Percent Change 2003-04 to 2013-14
	Dollars	Rank[1]	Dollars	Rank[1]		
South Carolina	48,375	38	48,425	39	0.10	17.6
U.S. Average	56,103	–	56,689	–	1.04	21.8

Note: (1) State rank ranges from 1 to 51 where 1 indicates highest salary.
Source: National Education Association, Rankings & Estimates: Rankings of the States 2013 and Estimates of School Statistics 2014, March 2014

Higher Education

Four-Year Colleges			Two-Year Colleges			Medical Schools[1]	Law Schools[2]	Voc/ Tech[3]
Public	Private Non-profit	Private For-profit	Public	Private Non-profit	Private For-profit			
3	1	2	1	0	1	1	1	3

Note: Figures cover institutions located within the city limits and include main campuses only; (1) includes schools accredited by the Liaison Committee on Medical Education and the American Osteopathic Association's Commission on Osteopathic College Accreditation; (2) includes ABA-accredited schools, schools with provisional ABA accreditation, and state accredited schools; (3) includes all schools with programs that are less than 2 years.
Source: National Center for Education Statistics, Integrated Postsecondary Education System (IPEDS), 2012-13; Association of American Medical Colleges, Member List, April 24, 2014; American Osteopathic Association, Member List, April 24, 2014; Law School Admission Council, Official Guide to ABA-Approved Law Schools Online, April 24, 2014; Wikipedia, List of Medical Schools in the United States, April 24, 2014; Wikipedia, List of Law Schools in the United States, April 24, 2014

PRESIDENTIAL ELECTION

2012 Presidential Election Results

Area	Obama	Romney	Other
Charleston County	50.4	48.0	1.6
U.S.	51.0	47.2	1.8

Note: Results are percentages and may not add to 100% due to rounding
Source: Dave Leip's Atlas of U.S. Presidential Elections

EMPLOYERS

Major Employers

Company Name	Industry
Allergy Centers of America	Ears, nose, and throat specialist, physician/surgeon
Alternative Staffing	Help supply services
Behr Heat Transfer Systems	Radiators & radiator shells & cores, motor vehicle
Campground At James Island	Trailer parks and campsites
CELLCO Partnership	Cellular telephone services
College of Charleston	Colleges and universities
County of Charleston	Marshals' office, police
CUMMINS	Internal combustion engines
Kiawah Island Inn Company	Resort hotel
Medical University Hospital Authority	General medical and surgical hospitals
Medical University of South Carolina	General medical and surgical hospitals
Six Continents Hotels	Hotels and motels
The Boeing Company	Airplanes, fixed or rotary wing
Trident Medical Center	General medical and surgical hospitals
United States Department of the Navy	Navy
Veterans Health Administration	General medical and surgical hospitals

Note: Companies shown are located within the Charleston-North Charleston, SC Metropolitan Statistical Area.
Source: Hoovers.com; Wikipedia

PUBLIC SAFETY

Crime Rate

Area	All Crimes	Violent Crimes				Property Crimes		
		Murder	Forcible Rape	Robbery	Aggrav. Assault	Burglary	Larceny -Theft	Motor Vehicle Theft
City	2,962.3	9.7	15.3	84.0	130.0	302.0	2,231.6	189.7
Suburbs[1]	3,850.5	6.4	31.7	91.0	333.2	708.1	2,393.3	286.9
Metro[2]	3,690.8	7.0	28.8	89.7	296.7	635.1	2,364.2	269.4
U.S.	3,246.1	4.7	26.9	112.9	242.3	670.2	1,959.3	229.7

Note: Figures are crimes per 100,000 population; (1) All areas within the metro area that are located outside the city limits; (2) Figures cover the Charleston-North Charleston, SC Metropolitan Statistical Area—see Appendix B for areas included
Source: FBI Uniform Crime Reports, 2012

Hate Crimes

Area	Number of Quarters Reported	Bias Motivation				
		Race	Religion	Sexual Orientation	Ethnicity	Disability
City	4	1	0	0	0	0
U.S.	4	2,797	1,099	1,135	667	92

Source: Federal Bureau of Investigation, Hate Crime Statistics 2012

Identity Theft Consumer Complaints

Area	Complaints	Complaints per 100,000 Population	Rank[2]
MSA[1]	490	73.7	136
U.S.	290,056	91.8	-

Note: (1) Figures cover the Charleston-North Charleston, SC Metropolitan Statistical Area—see Appendix B for areas included; (2) Rank ranges from 1 to 377 where 1 indicates greatest number of identity theft complaints per 100,000 population
Source: Federal Trade Commission, Consumer Sentinel Network Data Book for January–December 2013

Fraud and Other Consumer Complaints

Area	Complaints	Complaints per 100,000 Population	Rank[2]
MSA[1]	3,097	466.0	40
U.S.	1,811,724	595.2	-

Note: (1) Figures cover the Charleston-North Charleston, SC Metropolitan Statistical Area—see Appendix B for areas included; (2) Rank ranges from 1 to 377 where 1 indicates greatest number of identity theft complaints per 100,000 population
Source: Federal Trade Commission, Consumer Sentinel Network Data Book for January–December 2013

RECREATION

Culture

Dance[1]	Theatre[1]	Instrumental Music[1]	Vocal Music[1]	Series and Festivals	Museums and Art Galleries[2]	Zoos and Aquariums[3]
2	1	2	0	4	25	1

Note: (1) Number of professional perfoming groups; (2) Based on organizations with primary SIC code 8412; (3) AZA-accredited
Source: The Grey House Performing Arts Directory, 2013; Association of Zoos & Aquariums, AZA Member Zoos & Aquariums, April 2014; www.AccuLeads.com, May 1, 2014

Professional Sports Teams

Team Name	League	Year Established

No teams are located in the metro area

Source: Wikipedia, Major Professional Sports Teams of the United States and Canada, April 25, 2014

CLIMATE

Average and Extreme Temperatures

Temperature	Jan	Feb	Mar	Apr	May	Jun	Jul	Aug	Sep	Oct	Nov	Dec	Yr.
Extreme High (°F)	83	87	90	94	98	101	104	102	97	94	88	83	104
Average High (°F)	59	62	68	76	83	88	90	89	85	77	69	61	76
Average Temp. (°F)	49	51	57	65	73	78	81	81	76	67	58	51	66
Average Low (°F)	38	40	46	53	62	69	72	72	67	56	46	39	55
Extreme Low (°F)	6	12	15	30	36	50	58	56	42	27	15	8	6

Note: Figures cover the years 1945-1995
Source: National Climatic Data Center, International Station Meteorological Climate Summary, 9/96

Average Precipitation/Snowfall/Humidity

Precip./Humidity	Jan	Feb	Mar	Apr	May	Jun	Jul	Aug	Sep	Oct	Nov	Dec	Yr.
Avg. Precip. (in.)	3.5	3.1	4.4	2.8	4.1	6.0	7.2	6.9	5.6	3.1	2.5	3.1	52.1
Avg. Snowfall (in.)	Tr	Tr	Tr	0	0	0	0	0	0	0	Tr	Tr	1
Avg. Rel. Hum. 7am (%)	83	81	83	84	85	86	88	90	91	89	86	83	86
Avg. Rel. Hum. 4pm (%)	55	52	51	51	56	62	66	66	65	58	56	55	58

Note: Figures cover the years 1945-1995; Tr = Trace amounts (<0.05 in. of rain; <0.5 in. of snow)
Source: National Climatic Data Center, International Station Meteorological Climate Summary, 9/96

Weather Conditions

Temperature			Daytime Sky			Precipitation		
10°F & below	32°F & below	90°F & above	Clear	Partly cloudy	Cloudy	0.01 inch or more precip.	0.1 inch or more snow/ice	Thunder-storms
< 1	33	53	89	162	114	114	1	59

Note: Figures are average number of days per year and cover the years 1945-1995
Source: National Climatic Data Center, International Station Meteorological Climate Summary, 9/96

HAZARDOUS WASTE

Superfund Sites

Charleston has one hazardous waste site on the EPA's Superfund Final National Priorities List: **Koppers Co., Inc. (Charleston Plant).** *U.S. Environmental Protection Agency, Final National Priorities List, April 26, 2014*

AIR & WATER QUALITY

Air Quality Index

Area	Percent of Days when Air Quality was...[2]					AQI Statistics[2]	
	Good	Moderate	Unhealthy for Sensitive Groups	Unhealthy	Very Unhealthy	Maximum	Median
MSA[1]	83.3	16.7	0.0	0.0	0.0	73	36

Note: (1) Data covers the Charleston-North Charleston, SC Metropolitan Statistical Area—see Appendix B for areas included; (2) Based on 365 days with AQI data in 2013. Air Quality Index (AQI) is an index for reporting daily air quality. EPA calculates the AQI for five major air pollutants regulated by the Clean Air Act: ground-level ozone, particle pollution (aka particulate matter), carbon monoxide, sulfur dioxide, and nitrogen dioxide. The AQI runs from 0 to 500. The higher the AQI value, the greater the level of air pollution and the greater the health concern. There are six AQI categories: "Good" AQI is between 0 and 50. Air quality is considered satisfactory; "Moderate" AQI is between 51 and 100. Air quality is acceptable; "Unhealthy for Sensitive Groups" When AQI values are between 101 and 150, members of sensitive groups may experience health effects; "Unhealthy" When AQI values are between 151 and 200 everyone may begin to experience health effects; "Very Unhealthy" AQI values between 201 and 300 trigger a health alert; "Hazardous" AQI values over 300 trigger warnings of emergency conditions (not shown).
Source: U.S. Environmental Protection Agency, Air Quality Index Report, 2013

Air Quality Index Pollutants

Area	Percent of Days when AQI Pollutant was...[2]					
	Carbon Monoxide	Nitrogen Dioxide	Ozone	Sulfur Dioxide	Particulate Matter 2.5	Particulate Matter 10
MSA[1]	0.0	2.5	20.8	0.5	76.2	0.0

Note: (1) Data covers the Charleston-North Charleston, SC Metropolitan Statistical Area—see Appendix B for areas included; (2) Based on 365 days with AQI data in 2013. The Air Quality Index (AQI) is an index for reporting daily air quality. EPA calculates the AQI for five major air pollutants regulated by the Clean Air Act: ground-level ozone, particle pollution (also known as particulate matter), carbon monoxide, sulfur dioxide, and nitrogen dioxide. The AQI runs from 0 to 500. The higher the AQI value, the greater the level of air pollution and the greater the health concern.
Source: U.S. Environmental Protection Agency, Air Quality Index Report, 2013

Air Quality Trends: Ozone

	2003	2004	2005	2006	2007	2008	2009	2010	2011	2012
MSA[1]	0.072	0.072	0.073	0.071	0.065	0.069	0.059	0.067	0.066	0.063

Note: (1) Data covers the Charleston-North Charleston, SC Metropolitan Statistical Area—see Appendix B for areas included. The values shown are the composite ozone concentration averages among trend sites based on the highest fourth daily maximum 8-hour concentration in parts per million. These trends are based on sites having an adequate record of monitoring data during the trend period. Data from exceptional events are included.
Source: U.S. Environmental Protection Agency, Air Quality Monitoring Information, "Air Quality Trends by City, 2000-2012"

Maximum Air Pollutant Concentrations: Particulate Matter, Ozone, CO and Lead

	Particulate Matter 10 (ug/m^3)	Particulate Matter 2.5 Wtd AM (ug/m^3)	Particulate Matter 2.5 24-Hr (ug/m^3)	Ozone (ppm)	Carbon Monoxide (ppm)	Lead (ug/m^3)
MSA[1] Level	41	8.5	21	0.064	n/a	n/a
NAAQS[2]	150	15	35	0.075	9	0.15
Met NAAQS[2]	Yes	Yes	Yes	Yes	n/a	n/a

Note: (1) Data covers the Charleston-North Charleston, SC Metropolitan Statistical Area—see Appendix B for areas included; Data from exceptional events are included; (2) National Ambient Air Quality Standards; ppm = parts per million; ug/m^3 = micrograms per cubic meter; n/a not available.
Concentrations: Particulate Matter 10 (coarse particulate)—highest second maximum 24-hour concentration; Particulate Matter 2.5 Wtd AM (fine particulate)—highest weighted annual mean concentration; Particulate Matter 2.5 24-Hour (fine particulate)—highest 98th percentile 24-hour concentration; Ozone—highest fourth daily maximum 8-hour concentration; Carbon Monoxide—highest second maximum non-overlapping 8-hour concentration; Lead—maximum running 3-month average
Source: U.S. Environmental Protection Agency, Air Quality Monitoring Information, "Air Quality Statistics by City, 2012"

Maximum Air Pollutant Concentrations: Nitrogen Dioxide and Sulfur Dioxide

	Nitrogen Dioxide AM (ppb)	Nitrogen Dioxide 1-Hr (ppb)	Sulfur Dioxide AM (ppb)	Sulfur Dioxide 1-Hr (ppb)	Sulfur Dioxide 24-Hr (ppb)
MSA[1] Level	7	n/a	n/a	17	n/a
NAAQS[2]	53	100	30	75	140
Met NAAQS[2]	Yes	n/a	n/a	Yes	n/a

Note: (1) Data covers the Charleston-North Charleston, SC Metropolitan Statistical Area—see Appendix B for areas included; Data from exceptional events are included; (2) National Ambient Air Quality Standards; ppm = parts per million; ug/m^3 = micrograms per cubic meter; n/a not available.
Concentrations: Nitrogen Dioxide AM—highest arithmetic mean concentration; Nitrogen Dioxide 1-Hr—highest 98th percentile 1-hour daily maximum concentration; Sulfur Dioxide AM—highest annual mean concentration; Sulfur Dioxide 1-Hr—highest 99th percentile 1-hour daily maximum concentration; Sulfur Dioxide 24-Hr—highest second maximum 24-hour concentration
Source: U.S. Environmental Protection Agency, Air Quality Monitoring Information, "Air Quality Statistics by City, 2012"

Drinking Water

Water System Name	Pop. Served	Primary Water Source Type	Violations[1]	
			Health Based	Monitoring/ Reporting
Charleston Water System	214,367	Surface	0	0

Note: (1) Based on violation data from January 1, 2013 to December 31, 2013 (includes unresolved violations from earlier years)
Source: U.S. Environmental Protection Agency, Office of Ground Water and Drinking Water, Safe Drinking Water Information System (based on data extracted February 10, 2014)

Clarksville, Tennessee

Background

Located just south of the Kentucky border and 47 miles north of Nashville, Clarksville is Tennessee's fifth-largest town and has seen significant growth in recent years. Named for Gen. George Rogers Clark, a decorated veteran of the Indian and Revolutionary Wars, the city was found in 1784, and became incorporated by the state of Tennessee when it joined the union in 1796.

Located near the confluence of Red and Cumberland rivers, Clarksville was the site of three Confederate forts that the Union defeated in 1862. Fort Defiance transferred hands and became known as a place where fleeing or freed slaves could find refuge—and jobs. In the 1980s the well-preserved fort passed from the private hands of a local judge to the city itself, and in 2011 an interpretive center and walking trails were unveiled at what is now called Fort Defiance Civil War Park and Interpretive Center. The site features walking trails as well as the 1,500+ square foot center.

Clarksville is home to the 105,000-acre Fort Campbell, established as Camp Campbell in 1942, with nearly two-thirds of its land mass in Tennessee and the rest—including the post office—located in Kentucky. It is home to the world's only air assault division, known as the Screaming Eagles. Two special ops command units, a combat support hospital, and far more make this home to the U.S. Army's most-deployed contingency forces and the its fifth-largest military population. With more than 4,000 civilian jobs, it's the area's largest employer with services on the post ranging from bowling to the commissary to the Fort Campbell Credit Union, as well as medical services and child care.

Austin Peay State University's main campus is in Clarksville, another of the city's major employers, and named for a local son who became governor. The four-year public master's-level university saw its enrollment climb throughout the 2000's, crossing the 10,000 mark in 2009. Austin Peay also operates a center at Fort Campbell with fifteen associate, bachelor and master's level programs.

In 2012, Hemlock Semiconductor Corp, a subsidiary of Dow Corning, opened a $1.2 billion plant to generate polycrystalline silicon used in semiconductor chips and solar products. The state committed $6.4 million to create a new educational center at APSU to train workers, and also is spending $5 million to support Hemlock's worker training.

A 146-acre Liberty Park and Marina redevelopment project was completed in 2012, replete with pavilions, sports fields, picnic shelters, a dog park, and a ten-acre pond with a boardwalk and fishing piers. The Wilma Rudolph Pavilion and Great lawn is named for the great Olympic runner, Clarksville's native daughter. Another recent development came when the city created an Indoor Aquatic Center with an inflatable dome that allows for water sports in winter.

On the cultural side of Clarksville's quality of life, the popular Clarksville Downtown Market—with produce and arts and crafts—is enjoying significant popularity after opening in the summer of 2009.

Clarksville is also home to the state's second largest general museum, called the Customs House Museum and Cultural Center, which has seen a recent facelift. Model trains, a gallery devoted to sports champions, and even a bubble cave are all part of the experience.

The climate in Clarksville means hot summers but relatively moderate winters with average lows reaching 25 degrees in January. Precipitation stays fairly steady year round, getting no higher than 5.39 in March and bottoming out at 3.27 inches in October.

Rankings

Business/Finance Rankings

- The Clarksville metro area appeared on the Milken Institute "2013 Best Performing Cities" list. Rank: #40 out of 200 large metro areas. Criteria: job growth; wage and salary growth; high-tech output growth. *Milken Institute, "Best-Performing Cities 2013," December 2013*

- *Forbes* ranked the 200 most populous metro areas in the U.S. in terms of the "Best Places for Business and Careers." The Clarksville metro area was ranked #144. Criteria: costs (business and living); job growth (past and projected); income growth; educational attainment (college and high school); projected economic growth; cultural and recreational opportunities; net migration patterns; number of highly ranked colleges. *Forbes, "The Best Places for Business and Careers," August 7, 2013*

Environmental Rankings

- The Clarksville metro area came in at #247 for the relative comfort of its climate on Sperling's list of "chill cities," as measured by the Sperling Heat Index. All 361 metro areas are included. Criteria included daytime high temperatures, nighttime low temperatures, dew point, and relative humidity at the high temperatures. *www.bertsperling.com, "Sperling's Chill Cities," July 18, 2013*

- Sperling's BestPlaces assessed 379 metropolitan areas of the United States for the likelihood of dangerously extreme weather events or earthquakes. In general the Southeast and South-Central regions have the highest risk of weather extremes and earthquakes, while the Pacific Northwest enjoys the lowest risk. Of the least risky metropolitan areas, the Clarksville metro area was ranked #197. *www.bestplaces.net, "Safest Places from Natural Disasters," April 2011*

- Clarksville was selected as one of 22 "Smarter Cities" for energy by the Natural Resources Defense Council. Criteria: investment in green power; energy efficiency measures; conservation. *Natural Resources Defense Council, "2010 Smarter Cities," July 19, 2010*

- Clarksville was highlighted as one of the top 25 cleanest metro areas for short-term particle pollution (24-hour PM 2.5) in the U.S. during 2008 through 2010. Monitors in these cities reported no days with unhealthful PM 2.5 levels. *American Lung Association, State of the Air 2012*

Health/Fitness Rankings

- Analysts who tracked obesity rates in 189 of the nation's metro areas found that the Clarksville metro area was one of the ten communities where residents were most likely to be obese, defined as a BMI score of 30 or above. *www.gallup.com, "Boulder, Colo., Residents Still Least Likely to Be Obese," April 4, 2014*

- The Clarksville metro area appeared in the 2013 Gallup-Healthways Well-Being Index. The area ranked #146 out of 189. The Gallup-Healthways Well-Being Index score is an average of six sub-indexes, which individually examine life evaluation, emotional health, work environment, physical health, healthy behaviors, and access to basic necessities. Results are based on telephone interviews conducted as part of the Gallup-Healthways Well-Being Index survey January 2–December 29, 2012, and January 2–December 30, 2013, with a random sample of 531,630 adults, aged 18 and older, living in metropolitan areas in the 50 U.S. states and the District of Columbia. *Gallup-Healthways, "State of American Well-Being," March 25, 2014*

Safety Rankings

- Allstate ranked the 200 largest cities in America in terms of driver safety. Clarksville ranked #69. Allstate researchers analyzed internal property damage claims over a two-year period from January 2010 to December 2011. A weighted average of the two-year numbers determined the annual percentages. *Allstate, "Allstate America's Best Drivers Report®, August 27, 2013"*

- The National Insurance Crime Bureau ranked 380 metro areas in the U.S. in terms of per capita rates of vehicle theft. The Clarksville metro area ranked #255 (#1 = highest rate). Criteria: number of vehicle theft offenses per 100,000 inhabitants in 2012. *National Insurance Crime Bureau, "Hot Spots 2012," June 26, 2013*

Seniors/Retirement Rankings

- From its Best Cities for Successful Aging indexes, the Milken Institute generated rankings for metropolitan areas, weighing data in eight categories—general indicators, health care, wellness, living arrangements, transportation and general accessibility, financial well-being, education and employment, and community participation. The Clarksville metro area was ranked #241 overall in the small metro area category. *Milken Institute, "Best Cities for Successful Aging," July 2012*

- Clarksville was selected as one of the best places to retire by *CNNMoney.com*. Criteria: low cost of living; low violent-crime rate; good medical care; large population over age 50; abundant amenities for retirees. *CNNMoney.com, "Best Places to Retire 2011"*

Sports/Recreation Rankings

- Clarksville appeared on the *Sporting News* list of the "Best Sports Cities" for 2011. The area ranked #156 out of 271. Criteria: the magazine takes a 12-month snapshot of each city's sports, putting a heavy premium on regular-season won-lost records (from the most recently completed season). Other criteria include: playoff berths, bowl appearances and tournament bids; championships; applicable power ratings; quality of competition; overall fan fervor (measured in part by attendance); abundance of teams (rewarding quality over quantity); stadium and arena quality; ticket availability and prices; franchise ownership; and marquee appeal of athletes. *Sporting News, "Best Sports Cities 2011," October 4, 2011*

- Clarksville appeared on the *Sporting News* list of the "Best Sports Cities" for 2011. The area ranked #156 out of 271. Criteria: a 12-month snapshot of regular-season won-lost records (from the most recently completed season). Other criteria include: playoff berths, bowl appearances and tournament bids; championships; applicable power ratings; quality of competition; overall fan fervor (measured in part by attendance); abundance of teams (quality over quantity); stadium and arena quality; ticket availability and prices; franchise ownership; and marquee appeal of athletes. *Sporting News, "Best Sports Cities 2011," October 4, 2011*

Business Environment

CITY FINANCES

City Government Finances

Component	2011 ($000)	2011 ($ per capita)
Total Revenues	382,601	3,207
Total Expenditures	446,236	3,741
Debt Outstanding	873,864	7,326
Cash and Securities[1]	350,094	2,935

Note: (1) Cash and security holdings of a government at the close of its fiscal year, including those of its dependent agencies, utilities, and liquor stores.
Source: U.S Census Bureau, State & Local Government Finances 2011

City Government Revenue by Source

Source	2011 ($000)	2011 ($ per capita)
General Revenue		
From Federal Government	1,473	12
From State Government	19,976	167
From Local Governments	12,139	102
Taxes		
Property	27,846	233
Sales and Gross Receipts	4,537	38
Personal Income	0	0
Corporate Income	0	0
Motor Vehicle License	0	0
Other Taxes	3,666	31
Current Charges	25,055	210
Liquor Store	0	0
Utility	254,679	2,135
Employee Retirement	0	0

Source: U.S Census Bureau, State & Local Government Finances 2011

City Government Expenditures by Function

Function	2011 ($000)	2011 ($ per capita)	2011 (%)
General Direct Expenditures			
Air Transportation	0	0	0.0
Corrections	0	0	0.0
Education	0	0	0.0
Employment Security Administration	0	0	0.0
Financial Administration	3,278	27	0.7
Fire Protection	13,716	115	3.1
General Public Buildings	645	5	0.1
Governmental Administration, Other	1,696	14	0.4
Health	0	0	0.0
Highways	10,273	86	2.3
Hospitals	0	0	0.0
Housing and Community Development	1,659	14	0.4
Interest on General Debt	5,653	47	1.3
Judicial and Legal	347	3	0.1
Libraries	0	0	0.0
Parking	314	3	0.1
Parks and Recreation	6,200	52	1.4
Police Protection	22,919	192	5.1
Public Welfare	0	0	0.0
Sewerage	35,742	300	8.0
Solid Waste Management	0	0	0.0
Veterans' Services	0	0	0.0
Liquor Store	0	0	0.0
Utility	271,484	2,276	60.8
Employee Retirement	0	0	0.0

Source: U.S Census Bureau, State & Local Government Finances 2011

DEMOGRAPHICS

Population Growth

Area	1990 Census	2000 Census	2010 Census	Population Growth (%)	
				1990-2000	2000-2010
City	78,569	103,455	132,929	31.7	28.5
MSA[1]	189,277	232,000	273,949	22.6	18.1
U.S.	248,709,873	281,421,906	308,745,538	13.2	9.7

Note: (1) Figures cover the Clarksville, TN-KY Metropolitan Statistical Area—see Appendix B for areas included
Source: U.S. Census Bureau, Census 1990, 2000, 2010

Household Size

Area	Persons in Household (%)							Average Household Size
	One	Two	Three	Four	Five	Six	Seven or More	
City	22.4	31.1	20.8	15.0	6.6	2.4	1.7	2.71
MSA[1]	22.8	32.4	18.9	14.3	7.2	2.6	1.7	2.68
U.S.	27.6	33.5	15.7	13.2	6.1	2.4	1.5	2.63

Note: (1) Figures cover the Clarksville, TN-KY Metropolitan Statistical Area—see Appendix B for areas included
Source: U.S. Census Bureau, 2010-2012 American Community Survey 3-Year Estimates

Race

Area	White Alone[2] (%)	Black Alone[2] (%)	Asian Alone[2] (%)	AIAN[3] Alone[2] (%)	NHOPI[4] Alone[2] (%)	Other Race Alone[2] (%)	Two or More Races (%)
City	66.6	23.0	2.4	1.1	0.4	1.8	4.7
MSA[1]	74.2	18.0	1.7	0.8	0.4	1.3	3.6
U.S.	74.0	12.6	4.9	0.8	0.2	4.7	2.8

Note: (1) Figures cover the Clarksville, TN-KY Metropolitan Statistical Area—see Appendix B for areas included; (2) Alone is defined as not being in combination with one or more other races; (3) American Indian and Alaska Native; (4) Native Hawaiian and Other Pacific Islander
Source: U.S. Census Bureau, 2010-2012 American Community Survey 3-Year Estimates

Hispanic or Latino Origin

Area	Total (%)	Mexican (%)	Puerto Rican (%)	Cuban (%)	Other (%)
City	9.7	5.0	2.5	0.1	2.1
MSA[1]	7.2	3.9	1.7	0.0	1.5
U.S.	16.6	10.7	1.6	0.6	3.7

Note: Persons of Hispanic or Latino origin can be of any race; (1) Figures cover the Clarksville, TN-KY Metropolitan Statistical Area—see Appendix B for areas included
Source: U.S. Census Bureau, 2010-2012 American Community Survey 3-Year Estimates

Segregation

Type	Segregation Indices[1]				Percent Change		
	1990	2000	2010	2010 Rank[2]	1990-2000	1990-2010	2000-2010
Black/White	n/a	n/a	n/a	n/a	n/a	n/a	n/a
Asian/White	n/a	n/a	n/a	n/a	n/a	n/a	n/a
Hispanic/White	n/a	n/a	n/a	n/a	n/a	n/a	n/a

Note: All figures cover the Metropolitan Statistical Area—see Appendix B for areas included; Figures are based on an analysis of 1990, 2000, and 2010 Census Decennial Census tract data by William H. Frey, Brookings Institution and the University of Michigan Social Science Data Analysis Network. In this analysis all racial groups (whites, blacks, and asians) are non-Hispanic members of those races. Hispanics are shown as a separate category;
(1) Segregation Indices are Dissimilarity Indices that measure the degree to which the minority group is distributed differently than whites across census tracts. They range from 0 (complete integration) to 100 (complete segregation) where the value indicates the percentage of the minority group that needs to move to be distributed exactly like whites; (2) Ranges from 1 (most segregated) to 102 (least segregated); n/a not available.
Source: www.CensusScope.org

Ancestry

Area	German	Irish	English	American	Italian	Polish	French[2]	Scottish	Dutch
City	13.7	10.9	6.5	11.9	2.9	1.8	1.8	1.4	1.1
MSA[1]	13.0	10.5	7.8	16.9	2.8	1.6	1.8	1.9	1.2
U.S.	15.2	11.1	8.2	7.2	5.6	3.1	2.8	1.7	1.4

Note: Figures are the percentage of the total population reporting a particular ancestry. The nine most commonly reported ancestries in the U.S. are shown. Figures include multiple ancestries (e.g. if a person reported being Irish and Italian, they were included in both columns); (1) Figures cover the Clarksville, TN-KY Metropolitan Statistical Area—see Appendix B for areas included; (2) Excludes Basque
Source: U.S. Census Bureau, 2010-2012 American Community Survey 3-Year Estimates

Foreign-Born Population

Area	Percent of Population Born in								
	Any Foreign Country	Mexico	Asia	Europe	Carribean	South America	Central America[2]	Africa	Canada
City	n/a	n/a	n/a	n/a	n/a	n/a	n/a	n/a	n/a
MSA[1]	n/a	n/a	n/a	n/a	n/a	n/a	n/a	n/a	n/a
U.S.	13.0	3.7	3.7	1.6	1.2	0.9	1.0	0.5	0.3

Note: (1) Figures cover the Clarksville, TN-KY Metropolitan Statistical Area—see Appendix B for areas included; (2) Excludes Mexico.
Source: U.S. Census Bureau, 2010-2012 American Community Survey 3-Year Estimates

Marital Status

Area	Never Married	Now Married[2]	Separated	Widowed	Divorced
City	29.2	52.5	2.8	3.7	11.7
MSA[1]	26.5	54.7	2.5	5.1	11.2
U.S.	32.4	48.4	2.2	6.0	11.0

Note: Figures are percentages and cover the population 15 years of age and older; (1) Figures cover the Clarksville, TN-KY Metropolitan Statistical Area—see Appendix B for areas included; (2) Excludes separated
Source: U.S. Census Bureau, 2010-2012 American Community Survey 3-Year Estimates

Age

Area	Percent of Population									Median Age
	Under Age 5	Age 5–19	Age 20–34	Age 35–44	Age 45–54	Age 55–64	Age 65–74	Age 75–84	Age 85+	
City	9.2	21.8	29.9	13.1	11.0	7.7	4.3	2.2	0.8	28.3
MSA[1]	8.6	21.3	26.3	12.8	12.0	9.4	5.6	3.0	1.0	30.6
U.S.	6.4	20.1	20.5	13.1	14.3	12.2	7.3	4.2	1.8	37.3

Note: (1) Figures cover the Clarksville, TN-KY Metropolitan Statistical Area—see Appendix B for areas included
Source: U.S. Census Bureau, 2010-2012 American Community Survey 3-Year Estimates

Gender

Area	Males	Females	Males per 100 Females
City	67,056	70,532	95.1
MSA[1]	139,821	140,411	99.6
U.S.	153,276,055	158,333,314	96.8

Note: (1) Figures cover the Clarksville, TN-KY Metropolitan Statistical Area—see Appendix B for areas included
Source: U.S. Census Bureau, 2010-2012 American Community Survey 3-Year Estimates

Religious Groups by Family

Area	Catholic	Baptist	Non-Den.	Methodist[2]	Lutheran	LDS[3]	Pentecostal	Presbyterian[4]	Muslim[5]	Judaism
MSA[1]	4.1	30.9	2.3	6.2	0.6	1.5	1.8	1.1	0.1	<0.1
U.S.	19.1	9.3	4.0	4.0	2.3	2.0	1.9	1.6	0.8	0.7

Note: Figures are the number of adherents as a percentage of the total population; (1) Figures cover the Clarksville, TN-KY Metropolitan Statistical Area—see Appendix B for areas included; (2) Methodist/Pietist; (3) Latter Day Saints; (4) Reformed; (5) Figures are estimates
Source: Association of Statisticians of American Religious Bodies, 2010 U.S. Religion Census: Religious Congregations & Membership Study

Religious Groups by Tradition

Area	Catholic	Evangelical Protestant	Mainline Protestant	Other Tradition	Black Protestant	Orthodox
MSA[1]	4.1	35.4	7.3	1.7	2.4	<0.1
U.S.	19.1	16.2	7.3	4.3	1.6	0.3

Note: Figures are the number of adherents as a percentage of the total population; (1) Figures cover the
Clarksville, TN-KY Metropolitan Statistical Area—see Appendix B for areas included
Source: Association of Statisticians of American Religious Bodies, 2010 U.S. Religion Census: Religious
Congregations & Membership Study

ECONOMY

Gross Metropolitan Product

Area	2011	2012	2013	2014	Rank[2]
MSA[1]	11.5	11.8	11.9	12.5	163

Note: Figures are in billions of dollars; (1) Figures cover the Clarksville, TN-KY Metropolitan Statistical
Area—see Appendix B for areas included; (2) Rank is based on 2014 data and ranges from 1 to 363
Source: The United States Conference of Mayors, U.S. Metro Economies: Outlook—Gross Metropolitan
Product, with Metro Employment Projections, November 2013

Economic Growth

Area	2011 (%)	2012 (%)	2013 (%)	2014 (%)	Rank[2]
MSA[1]	6.8	0.4	-0.5	2.8	290
U.S.	1.6	2.5	1.7	2.5	–

Note: Figures are real gross metropolitan product (GMP) growth rates and represent annual average percent
change; (1) Figures cover the Clarksville, TN-KY Metropolitan Statistical Area—see Appendix B for areas
included; (2) Rank is based on 2013 data and ranges from 1 to 363
Source: The United States Conference of Mayors, U.S. Metro Economies: Outlook—Gross Metropolitan
Product, with Metro Employment Projections, November 2013

Metropolitan Area Exports

Area	2007	2008	2009	2010	2011	2012	Rank[2]
MSA[1]	309.7	311.4	158.4	238.3	328.8	326.3	246

Note: Figures are in millions of dollars; (1) Figures cover the Clarksville, TN-KY Metropolitan Statistical
Area—see Appendix B for areas included; (2) Rank is based on 2012 data and ranges from 1 to 369
Source: U.S. Department of Commerce, International Trade Administration, Office of Trade & Industry
Information, Manufacturing & Services, data extracted April 1, 2014

INCOME

Income

Area	Per Capita ($)	Median Household ($)	Average Household ($)
City	20,493	44,760	54,454
MSA[1]	21,098	44,361	55,912
U.S.	27,385	51,771	71,579

Note: (1) Figures cover the Clarksville, TN-KY Metropolitan Statistical Area—see Appendix B for areas included
Source: U.S. Census Bureau, 2010-2012 American Community Survey 3-Year Estimates

Household Income Distribution

Area	Under $15,000	$15,000 -24,999	$25,000 -34,999	$35,000 -49,999	$50,000 -74,999	$75,000 -99,000	$100,000 -149,999	$150,000 and up
City	13.9	10.6	12.7	17.8	22.3	11.2	8.4	3.2
MSA[1]	13.8	12.3	12.6	16.8	21.0	11.4	8.4	3.7
U.S.	13.1	11.0	10.5	13.7	18.1	11.9	12.5	9.1

Note: (1) Figures cover the Clarksville, TN-KY Metropolitan Statistical Area—see Appendix B for areas included
Source: U.S. Census Bureau, 2010-2012 American Community Survey 3-Year Estimates

Poverty Rate

Area	All Ages	Under 18 Years Old	18 to 64 Years Old	65 Years and Over
City	18.9	27.8	16.0	10.2
MSA[1]	18.2	26.5	15.9	9.1
U.S.	15.7	22.2	14.6	9.3

Note: Figures are percentage of people whose income during the past 12 months was below the poverty level;
(1) Figures cover the Clarksville, TN-KY Metropolitan Statistical Area—see Appendix B for areas included
Source: U.S. Census Bureau, 2010-2012 American Community Survey 3-Year Estimates

Personal Bankruptcy Filing Rate

Area	2008	2009	2010	2011	2012	2013
Montgomery County	4.14	4.65	5.02	4.47	4.25	4.24
U.S.	3.53	4.61	4.97	4.37	3.76	3.29

Note: Numbers are per 1,000 population and include Chapter 7 and Chapter 13 filings
Source: Federal Deposit Insurance Corporation, Regional Economic Conditions, March 20, 2014

EMPLOYMENT

Labor Force and Employment

Area	Civilian Labor Force			Workers Employed		
	Dec. 2012	Dec. 2013	% Chg.	Dec. 2012	Dec. 2013	% Chg.
City	58,343	56,734	-2.8	53,866	52,473	-2.6
MSA[1]	117,691	114,501	-2.7	108,121	105,574	-2.4
U.S.	154,904,000	154,408,000	-0.3	143,060,000	144,423,000	1.0

Note: Data is not seasonally adjusted and covers workers 16 years of age and older; (1) Metropolitan Statistical Area—see Appendix B for areas included
Source: Bureau of Labor Statistics, Local Area Unemployment Statistics

Unemployment Rate

Area	2013											
	Jan.	Feb.	Mar.	Apr.	May	Jun.	Jul.	Aug.	Sep.	Oct.	Nov.	Dec.
City	8.2	7.7	7.9	7.5	7.8	9.0	8.3	8.1	8.2	8.9	8.0	7.5
MSA[1]	9.0	8.6	8.4	8.4	8.8	9.5	9.4	8.9	8.7	8.9	8.1	7.8
U.S.	8.5	8.1	7.6	7.1	7.3	7.8	7.7	7.3	7.0	7.0	6.6	6.5

Note: Data is not seasonally adjusted and covers workers 16 years of age and older; All figures are percentages;
(1) Metropolitan Statistical Area—see Appendix B for areas included
Source: Bureau of Labor Statistics, Local Area Unemployment Statistics

Employment by Occupation

Occupation Classification	City (%)	MSA[1] (%)	U.S. (%)
Management, Business, Science, and Arts	29.0	29.7	36.0
Natural Resources, Construction, and Maintenance	8.0	10.0	9.1
Production, Transportation, and Material Moving	13.8	16.0	12.0
Sales and Office	28.4	25.6	24.7
Service	20.9	18.6	18.2

Note: Figures cover employed civilians 16 years of age and older; (1) Figures cover the Clarksville, TN-KY Metropolitan Statistical Area—see Appendix B for areas included
Source: U.S. Census Bureau, 2010-2012 American Community Survey 3-Year Estimates

Employment by Industry

| Sector | MSA[1] | | U.S. |
	Number of Employees	Percent of Total	Percent of Total
Construction	n/a	n/a	4.2
Education and Health Services	11,400	12.8	15.5
Financial Activities	3,000	3.4	5.7
Government	21,100	23.6	16.1
Information	1,100	1.2	1.9
Leisure and Hospitality	10,800	12.1	10.2
Manufacturing	9,900	11.1	8.7
Mining and Logging	n/a	n/a	0.6
Other Services	3,000	3.4	3.9
Professional and Business Services	8,700	9.7	13.7
Retail Trade	12,200	13.6	11.4
Transportation and Utilities	2,300	2.6	3.8
Wholesale Trade	n/a	n/a	4.2

Note: Figures cover non-farm employment as of December 2013 and are not seasonally adjusted;
(1) Metropolitan Statistical Area—see Appendix B for areas included; n/a not available
Source: Bureau of Labor Statistics, Current Employment Statistics, Employment, Hours, and Earnings

Occupations with Greatest Projected Employment Growth: 2010 – 2020

Occupation[1]	2010 Employment	2020 Projected Employment	Numeric Employment Change	Percent Employment Change
Registered Nurses	56,290	69,010	12,720	22.6
Office Clerks, General	64,300	75,450	11,150	17.3
Heavy and Tractor-Trailer Truck Drivers	58,680	69,250	10,570	18.0
Personal Care Aides	15,310	24,380	9,070	59.2
Combined Food Preparation and Serving Workers, Including Fast Food	56,520	64,280	7,750	13.7
Janitors and Cleaners, Except Maids and Housekeeping Cleaners	41,370	48,290	6,920	16.7
Security Guards	21,960	28,260	6,300	28.7
Nursing Aides, Orderlies, and Attendants	29,910	35,570	5,650	18.9
First-Line Supervisors of Office and Administrative Support Workers	31,880	37,210	5,330	16.7
Landscaping and Groundskeeping Workers	16,920	22,210	5,290	31.2

Note: Projections cover Tennessee; (1) Sorted by numeric employment change
Source: www.projectionscentral.com, State Occupational Projections, 2010–2020 Long-Term Projections

Fastest Growing Occupations: 2010 – 2020

Occupation[1]	2010 Employment	2020 Projected Employment	Numeric Employment Change	Percent Employment Change
Personal Care Aides	15,310	24,380	9,070	59.2
Meeting, Convention, and Event Planners	950	1,470	520	55.4
Audiologists	280	410	140	50.2
Glaziers	950	1,400	460	48.2
Software Developers, Systems Software	2,590	3,840	1,250	48.2
Helpers—Pipelayers, Plumbers, Pipefitters, and Steamfitters	1,220	1,770	550	45.1
Physician Assistants	1,550	2,240	690	44.3
Diagnostic Medical Sonographers	1,100	1,560	460	41.8
Security and Fire Alarm Systems Installers	1,340	1,890	550	40.9
Tree Trimmers and Pruners	2,260	3,170	920	40.7

Note: Projections cover Tennessee; (1) Sorted by percent employment change and excludes occupations with numeric employment change less than 100
Source: www.projectionscentral.com, State Occupational Projections, 2010–2020 Long-Term Projections

Average Wages

Occupation	$/Hr.	Occupation	$/Hr.
Accountants and Auditors	28.37	Maids and Housekeeping Cleaners	8.59
Automotive Mechanics	17.07	Maintenance and Repair Workers	16.48
Bookkeepers	15.56	Marketing Managers	42.15
Carpenters	18.13	Nuclear Medicine Technologists	n/a
Cashiers	9.05	Nurses, Licensed Practical	18.75
Clerks, General Office	13.06	Nurses, Registered	27.23
Clerks, Receptionists/Information	11.27	Nursing Assistants	11.76
Clerks, Shipping/Receiving	15.98	Packers and Packagers, Hand	12.86
Computer Programmers	27.53	Physical Therapists	36.69
Computer Systems Analysts	32.31	Postal Service Mail Carriers	24.34
Computer User Support Specialists	18.56	Real Estate Brokers	n/a
Cooks, Restaurant	9.56	Retail Salespersons	11.36
Dentists	n/a	Sales Reps., Exc. Tech./Scientific	23.44
Electrical Engineers	35.58	Sales Reps., Tech./Scientific	52.26
Electricians	20.80	Secretaries, Exc. Legal/Med./Exec.	13.22
Financial Managers	29.29	Security Guards	13.43
First-Line Supervisors/Managers, Sales	17.04	Surgeons	n/a
Food Preparation Workers	9.33	Teacher Assistants	11.10
General and Operations Managers	36.00	Teachers, Elementary School	26.60
Hairdressers/Cosmetologists	11.81	Teachers, Secondary School	26.40
Internists	n/a	Telemarketers	n/a
Janitors and Cleaners	11.03	Truck Drivers, Heavy/Tractor-Trailer	15.41
Landscaping/Groundskeeping Workers	11.47	Truck Drivers, Light/Delivery Svcs.	13.76
Lawyers	40.52	Waiters and Waitresses	9.12

Note: Wage data covers the Clarksville, TN-KY Metropolitan Statistical Area—see Appendix B for areas included. Hourly wages for elementary/secondary school teachers and teacher assistants were calculated by the editors from annual wage data assuming a 40 hour work week; n/a not available.
Source: Bureau of Labor Statistics, Metro Area Occupational Employment and Wage Estimates, May 2013

RESIDENTIAL REAL ESTATE

Building Permits

Area	Single-Family			Multi-Family			Total		
	2012	2013	Pct. Chg.	2012	2013	Pct. Chg.	2012	2013	Pct. Chg.
City	937	779	-16.9	421	580	37.8	1,358	1,359	0.1
MSA[1]	1,387	1,256	-9.4	509	586	15.1	1,896	1,842	-2.8
U.S.	518,695	620,802	19.7	310,963	370,020	19.0	829,658	990,822	19.4

Note: (1) Metropolitan Statistical Area—see Appendix B for areas included; figures represent new, privately-owned housing units authorized (unadjusted data); All permit data are based on estimates with imputation.
Source: U.S. Census Bureau, Manufacturing, Mining, and Construction Statistics, Building Permits, 2012, 2013

Homeownership Rate

Area	2006 (%)	2007 (%)	2008 (%)	2009 (%)	2010 (%)	2011 (%)	2012 (%)	2013 (%)
MSA[1]	n/a	n/a	n/a	n/a	n/a	n/a	n/a	n/a
U.S.	68.8	68.1	67.8	67.4	66.9	66.1	65.4	65.1

Note: (1) Figures cover the Clarksville, TN-KY Metropolitan Statistical Area—see Appendix B for areas included; n/a not available
Source: U.S. Census Bureau, Housing Vacancies and Homeownership Annual Statistics: 2013

Housing Vacancy Rates

Area	Gross Vacancy Rate[2] (%)			Year-Round Vacancy Rate[3] (%)			Rental Vacancy Rate[4] (%)			Homeowner Vacancy Rate[5] (%)		
	2011	2012	2013	2011	2012	2013	2011	2012	2013	2011	2012	2013
MSA[1]	n/a	n/a	n/a	n/a	n/a	n/a	n/a	n/a	n/a	n/a	n/a	n/a
U.S.	14.2	13.8	13.8	11.1	10.8	10.7	9.5	8.7	8.3	2.5	2.0	2.0

Note: (1) Figures cover the Clarksville, TN-KY Metropolitan Statistical Area—see Appendix B for areas included; (2) The percentage of the total housing inventory that is vacant; (3) The percentage of the housing inventory (excluding seasonal units) that is year-round vacant; (4) The percentage of rental inventory that is vacant for rent; (5) The percentage of homeowner inventory that is vacant for sale; n/a not available
Source: U.S. Census Bureau, Housing Vacancies and Homeownership Annual Statistics: 2013

TAXES

State Corporate Income Tax Rates

State	Tax Rate (%)	Income Brackets ($)	Num. of Brackets	Financial Institution Tax Rate (%)[a]	Federal Income Tax Ded.
Tennessee	6.5	Flat rate	1	6.5	No

Note: Tax rates as of January 1, 2014; (a) Rates listed are the corporate income tax rate applied to financial institutions or excise taxes based on income. Some states have other taxes based upon the value of deposits or shares.
Source: Federation of Tax Administrators, "State Corporate Income Tax Rates, 2014"

State Individual Income Tax Rates

State	Tax Rate (%)	Income Brackets ($)	Num. of Brackets	Personal Exempt. ($)[1] Single	Dependents	Fed. Inc. Tax Ded.
Tennessee		State income tax of 6% on dividends and interest income only				

Note: Tax rates as of January 1, 2014; Local- and county-level taxes are not included; n/a not applicable; (1) Married joint filers generally receive double the single exemption
Source: Federation of Tax Administrators, "State Individual Income Tax Rates, 2014"

Various State and Local Tax Rates

State	State and Local Sales and Use (%)	State Sales and Use (%)	Gasoline[1] (¢/gal.)	Cigarette[2] ($/pack)	Spirits[3] ($/gal.)	Wine[4] ($/gal.)	Beer[5] ($/gal.)
Tennessee	9.5	7.00	21.40	0.620	4.46 (i)	1.27 (m)	1.17 (t)

Note: All tax rates as of January 1, 2014; (1) The American Petroleum Institute has developed a methodology for determining the average tax rate on a gallon of fuel. Rates may include any of the following: excise taxes, environmental fees, storage tank fees, other fees or taxes, general sales tax, and local taxes. In states where gasoline is subject to the general sales tax, or where the fuel tax is based on the average sale price, the average rate determined by API is sensitive to changes in the price of gasoline. States that fully or partially apply general sales taxes to gasoline: CA, CO, GA, IL, IN, MI, NY; (2) The federal excise tax of $1.0066 per pack and local taxes are not included; (3) Rates are those applicable to off-premise sales of 40% alcohol by volume (a.b.v.) distilled spirits in 750ml containers. Local excise taxes are excluded; (4) Rates are those applicable to off-premise sales of 11% a.b.v. non-carbonated wine in 750ml containers; (5) Rates are those applicable to off-premise sales of 4.7% a.b.v. beer in 12 ounce containers; (i) Includes case fees and/or bottle fees which may vary with size of container; (m) Includes case fees and/or bottle fees which may vary with size of container; (t) Includes the wholesale tax rate of 17%, converted into a gallonage excise tax rate.
Source: Tax Foundation, 2014 Facts & Figures: How Does Your State Compare?

State Business Tax Climate Index Rankings

State	Overall Rank	Corporate Tax Index Rank	Individual Income Tax Index Rank	Sales Tax Index Rank	Unemployment Insurance Tax Index Rank	Property Tax Index Rank
Tennessee	15	14	8	43	27	37

Note: The index is a measure of how each state's tax laws affect economic performance. The lower the rank, the more favorable a state's tax system is for business. States without a given tax are given a ranking of 1. The scores/rankings for the District of Columbia do not affect other states. The 2014 index represents the tax climate as of July 1, 2013.
Source: Tax Foundation, State Business Tax Climate Index 2014

COMMERCIAL UTILITIES

Typical Monthly Electric Bills

Area	Commercial Service ($/month) 1,500 kWh	40 kW demand 14,000 kWh	Industrial Service ($/month) 1,000 kW demand 200,000 kWh	50,000 kW demand 15,000,000 kWh
City	n/a	n/a	n/a	n/a
Average[1]	197	1,636	25,662	1,485,307

Note: Based on total rates in effect July 1, 2013; (1) average based on 180 utilities surveyed; n/a not available
Source: Edison Electric Institute, Typical Bills and Average Rates Report, Summer 2013

TRANSPORTATION

Means of Transportation to Work

Area	Car/Truck/Van		Public Transportation			Bicycle	Walked	Other Means	Worked at Home
	Drove Alone	Car-pooled	Bus	Subway	Railroad				
City	84.8	9.8	0.5	0.0	0.0	0.1	2.1	1.1	1.5
MSA[1]	82.3	10.4	0.5	0.0	0.0	0.1	2.8	1.2	2.7
U.S.	76.4	9.7	2.6	1.7	0.5	0.6	2.8	1.3	4.3

Note: Figures are percentages and cover workers 16 years of age and older; (1) Figures cover the Clarksville, TN-KY Metropolitan Statistical Area—see Appendix B for areas included
Source: U.S. Census Bureau, 2010-2012 American Community Survey 3-Year Estimates

Travel Time to Work

Area	Less Than 10 Minutes	10 to 19 Minutes	20 to 29 Minutes	30 to 44 Minutes	45 to 59 Minutes	60 to 89 Minutes	90 Minutes or More
City	12.9	35.8	25.5	15.8	5.2	4.0	0.9
MSA[1]	14.8	32.9	23.1	17.7	6.2	3.8	1.5
U.S.	13.5	29.8	20.9	20.1	7.5	5.6	2.5

Note: Figures are percentages and include workers 16 years old and over; (1) Figures cover the Clarksville, TN-KY Metropolitan Statistical Area—see Appendix B for areas included
Source: U.S. Census Bureau, 2010-2012 American Community Survey 3-Year Estimates

Travel Time Index

Area	1985	1990	1995	2000	2005	2010	2011
Urban Area[1]	n/a	n/a	n/a	n/a	n/a	n/a	n/a
Average[2]	1.09	1.14	1.16	1.19	1.23	1.18	1.18

Note: Travel Time Index—the ratio of travel time in the peak period to the travel time at free-flow conditions. For example, a value of 1.30 indicates a 20-minute free-flow trip takes 26 minutes in the peak. Free-flow speeds (60 mph on freeways and 35 mph on principal arterials) are used as the comparison threshold; (1) Data for the Clarksville, TN-KY urban area was not available; (2) average of 498 urban areas
Source: Texas Transportation Institute, Urban Mobility Report 2012, December 2012

Public Transportation

Agency Name / Mode of Transportation	Vehicles Operated in Maximum Service	Annual Unlinked Passenger Trips (in thous.)	Annual Passenger Miles (in thous.)
Clarksville Transit System (CTS)			
Bus (directly operated)	16	866.6	4,889.6
Demand Response (directly operated)	8	27.7	183.9

Source: Federal Transit Administration, National Transit Database, 2012

Air Transportation

Airport Name and Code / Type of Service	Passenger Airlines[1]	Passenger Enplanements	Freight Carriers[2]	Freight (lbs.)
Outlaw Field (CKV)				
Domestic service (U.S. carriers - 2013)	1	4	0	0
International service (U.S. carriers - 2012)	0	0	1	13,980

Note: (1) Includes all U.S.-based major, minor and commuter airlines that carried at least one passenger during the year; (2) Includes all U.S.-based airlines and freight carriers that transported at least one lb. of freight during the year.
Source: Bureau of Transportation Statistics, The Intermodal Transportation Database, Air Carriers: T-100 Domestic Market (U.S. Carriers), 2013; Bureau of Transportation Statistics, The Intermodal Transportation Database, Air Carriers: T-100 International Market (U.S. Carriers), 2012

Other Transportation Statistics

Major Highways: I-24; SR-79; SR-41A
Amtrak Service: No
Major Waterways/Ports: Cumberland River
Source: Amtrak.com; Google Maps

BUSINESSES

Major Business Headquarters

Company Name	Rankings	
	Fortune[1]	Forbes[2]
No companies listed	-	-

Note: (1) Fortune 500—companies that produce a 10-K are ranked 1 to 500 based on 2012 revenue; (2) all private companies with at least $2 billion in annual revenue through the end of their most current fiscal year are ranked 1 to 224; companies listed are headquartered in the city; dashes indicate no ranking
Source: Fortune, "Fortune 500," May 20, 2013; Forbes, "America's Largest Private Companies," December 18, 2013

Minority- and Women-Owned Businesses

Group	All Firms		Firms with Paid Employees			
	Firms	Sales ($000)	Firms	Sales ($000)	Employees	Payroll ($000)
Asian	260	74,105	117	68,699	1,187	9,011
Black	760	26,591	44	15,759	233	3,835
Hispanic	(s)	(s)	(s)	(s)	(s)	(s)
Women	2,355	301,725	271	268,592	2,465	51,824
All Firms	7,044	5,624,589	1,770	5,453,404	30,502	781,365

Note: Figures cover firms located in the city; minority- and women-owned business are defined as firms in which the corresponding group own 51% or more of the stock or equity of the company; (s) estimates are suppressed when publication standards are not met
Source: U.S. Census Bureau, 2007 Economic Census, Survey of Business Owners (2012 Survey of Business Owners data will be released starting in June 2015)

HOTELS & CONVENTION CENTERS

Hotels/Motels

Area	5 Star		4 Star		3 Star		2 Star		1 Star		Not Rated	
	Num.	Pct.[3]	Num.	Pct.[3]	Num.	Pct.[3]	Num.	Pct.[3]	Num.	Pct.[3]	Num.	Pct.[3]
City[1]	0	0.0	0	0.0	4	9.3	34	79.1	0	0.0	5	11.6
Total[2]	142	0.9	1,005	6.0	5,147	30.9	8,578	51.4	408	2.4	1,397	8.4

Note: (1) Figures cover Clarksville and vicinity; (2) Figures cover all 100 cities in this book; (3) Percentage of hotels which have a given star rating; Star ratings are determined by expedia.com and offer an indication of the general quality of a particular hotel.
Source: expedia.com, April 7, 2014

Major Convention Centers

Name	Overall Space (sq. ft.)	Exhibit Space (sq. ft.)	Meeting Space (sq. ft.)	Meeting Rooms
There are no major convention centers located in the metro area				

Source: Original research

Living Environment

COST OF LIVING

Cost of Living Index

Composite Index	Groceries	Housing	Utilities	Trans-portation	Health Care	Misc. Goods/Services
n/a	n/a	n/a	n/a	n/a	n/a	n/a

Note: The Cost of Living Index measures regional differences in the cost of consumer goods and services, excluding taxes and non-consumer expenditures, for professional and managerial households in the top income quintile. It is based on more than 50,000 prices covering almost 60 different items for which prices are collected three times a year by chambers of commerce, economic development organizations or university applied economic centers in each participating urban area. The numbers shown should be read as a percentage above or below the national average of 100. For example, a value of 115.4 in the groceries column indicates that grocery prices are 15.4% higher than the national average. Small differences in the index numbers should not be interpreted as significant; n/a not available.
Source: The Council for Community and Economic Research, ACCRA Cost of Living Index, 2013

Grocery Prices

Area[1]	T-Bone Steak ($/pound)	Frying Chicken ($/pound)	Whole Milk ($/half gal.)	Eggs ($/dozen)	Orange Juice ($/64 oz.)	Coffee ($/11.5 oz.)
City[2]	n/a	n/a	n/a	n/a	n/a	n/a
Avg.	10.19	1.28	2.34	1.81	3.48	4.39
Min.	8.56	0.94	1.44	1.19	2.78	3.40
Max.	14.82	2.28	3.56	3.73	6.23	7.32

*Note: (1) Values for the local area are compared with the average, minimum and maximum values for all 327 areas in the Cost of Living Index; (2) Figures cover the Clarksville TN urban area; n/a not available; **T-Bone Steak** (price per pound); **Frying Chicken** (price per pound, whole fryer); **Whole Milk** (half gallon carton); **Eggs** (price per dozen, Grade A, large); **Orange Juice** (64 oz. Tropicana or Florida Natural); **Coffee** (11.5 oz. can, vacuum-packed, Maxwell House, Hills Bros, or Folgers).*
Source: The Council for Community and Economic Research, ACCRA Cost of Living Index, 2013

Housing and Utility Costs

Area[1]	New Home Price ($)	Apartment Rent ($/month)	All Electric ($/month)	Part Electric ($/month)	Other Energy ($/month)	Telephone ($/month)
City[2]	n/a	n/a	n/a	n/a	n/a	n/a
Avg.	295,864	900	171.38	91.82	70.12	27.73
Min.	185,506	458	117.80	48.81	33.67	17.16
Max.	1,358,917	3,783	441.68	171.40	372.65	39.47

*Note: (1) Values for the local area are compared with the average, minimum and maximum values for all 327 areas in the Cost of Living Index; (2) Figures cover the Clarksville TN urban area; n/a not available; **New Home Price** (2,400 sf living area, 8,000 sf lot, in urban area with full utilities); **Apartment Rent** (950 sf 2 bedroom/1.5 or 2 bath, unfurnished, excluding all utilities except water); **All Electric** (average monthly cost for an all-electric home); **Part Electric** (average monthly cost for a part-electric home); **Other Energy** (average monthly cost for natural gas, fuel oil, coal, wood, and any other forms of energy except electricity); **Telephone** (price includes basic monthly rate for a private residential line plus additional local usage charges incurred by a family of four).*
Source: The Council for Community and Economic Research, ACCRA Cost of Living Index, 2013

Health Care, Transportation, and Other Costs

Area[1]	Doctor ($/visit)	Dentist ($/visit)	Optometrist ($/visit)	Gasoline ($/gallon)	Beauty Salon ($/visit)	Men's Shirt ($)
City[2]	n/a	n/a	n/a	n/a	n/a	n/a
Avg.	101.40	86.48	96.16	3.44	33.87	26.55
Min.	61.67	50.83	50.12	3.08	18.92	12.48
Max.	182.71	152.50	223.78	4.33	68.22	52.03

*Note: (1) Values for the local area are compared with the average, minimum and maximum values for all 327 areas in the Cost of Living Index; (2) Figures cover the Clarksville TN urban area; n/a not available; **Doctor** (general practitioners routine exam of an established patient); **Dentist** (adult teeth cleaning and periodic oral examination); **Optometrist** (full vision eye exam for established adult patient); **Gasoline** (one gallon regular unleaded, national brand, including all taxes, cash price at self-service pump if available); **Beauty Salon** (woman's shampoo, trim, and blow-dry); **Men's Shirt** (cotton/polyester dress shirt, pinpoint weave, long sleeves).*
Source: The Council for Community and Economic Research, ACCRA Cost of Living Index, 2013

HOUSING

House Price Index (HPI)

Area	National Ranking[2]	Quarterly Change (%)	One-Year Change (%)	Five-Year Change (%)
MSA[1]	(a)	n/a	-0.03	2.36
U.S.[3]	–	1.20	7.69	4.18

Note: The HPI is a weighted repeat sales index. It measures average price changes in repeat sales or refinancings on the same properties. This information is obtained by reviewing repeat mortgage transactions on single-family properties whose mortgages have been purchased or securitized by Fannie Mae or Freddie Mac in January 1975; (1) Clarksville, TN-KY Metropolitan Statistical Area—see Appendix B for areas included; (2) Rankings are based on annual percentage change for all metro areas containing at least 15,000 transactions over the last 10 years and ranges from 1 to 283; (3) figures based on a weighted average of Census Division estimates using a seasonally adjusted, purchase-only index; all figures are for the period ending December 31, 2013; n/a not available; (a) Not ranked because of increased index variability due to smaller sample size
Source: Federal Housing Finance Agency, House Price Index, February 25, 2014

Median Single-Family Home Prices

Area	2011	2012	2013p	Percent Change 2012 to 2013
MSA[1]	n/a	n/a	n/a	n/a
U.S. Average	166.2	177.2	197.4	11.4

Note: Figures are median sales prices of existing single-family homes in thousands of dollars; (p) preliminary; n/a not available; (1) Clarksville, TN-KY Metropolitan Statistical Area—see Appendix B for areas included
Source: National Association of Realtors, Median Sales Price of Existing Single-Family Homes for Metropolitan Areas, 4th Quarter 2013

Qualifying Income Based on Median Sales Price of Existing Single-Family Homes

Area	With 5% Down ($)	With 10% Down ($)	With 20% Down ($)
MSA[1]	n/a	n/a	n/a
U.S. Average	45,395	43,006	38,228

Note: Figures are preliminary; Qualifying income is based on a mortgage rate of 4.4%. Monthly principal and interest payment is limited to 25% of income; n/a not available; (1) Clarksville, TN-KY Metropolitan Statistical Area—see Appendix B for areas included
Source: National Association of Realtors, Qualifying Income Based on Median Sales Price of Existing Single-Family Homes for Metropolitan Areas, 4th Quarter 2013

Median Apartment Condo-Coop Home Prices

Area	2011	2012	2013p	Percent Change 2012 to 2013
MSA[1]	n/a	n/a	n/a	n/a
U.S. Average	165.1	173.7	194.9	12.2

Note: Figures are median sales prices of existing apartment condo-coop homes in thousands of dollars; (p) preliminary; n/a not available; (1) Clarksville, TN-KY Metropolitan Statistical Area—see Appendix B for areas included
Source: National Association of Realtors, Median Sales Price of Existing Apartment Condo-Coop Homes for Metropolitan Areas, 4th Quarter 2013

Gross Monthly Rent

Area	Under $200	$200 -299	$300 -499	$500 -749	$750 -999	$1,000 -1,499	$1,500 and up	Median ($)
City	1.3	1.4	4.9	31.9	33.2	22.4	5.0	824
MSA[1]	1.3	2.2	9.4	31.8	33.7	17.8	3.8	792
U.S.	1.7	3.3	8.1	22.7	24.3	25.7	14.3	889

Note: Figures are percentages except for Median; Gross rent is the contract rent plus the estimated average monthly cost of utilities (electricity, gas, and water and sewer) and fuels (oil, coal, kerosene, wood, etc.) if these are paid by the renter (or paid for the renter by someone else); (1) Figures cover the Clarksville, TN-KY Metropolitan Statistical Area—see Appendix B for areas included
Source: U.S. Census Bureau, 2010-2012 American Community Survey 3-Year Estimates

Year Housing Structure Built

Area	2010 or Later	2000 -2009	1990 -1999	1980 -1989	1970 -1979	1960 -1969	1950 -1959	1940 -1949	Before 1940	Median Year
City	1.7	27.8	22.1	14.5	13.7	9.2	5.8	2.6	2.6	1991
MSA[1]	1.3	23.3	21.8	13.6	14.7	10.2	6.8	3.1	5.2	1987
U.S.	0.5	14.9	13.8	13.9	15.9	11.1	10.9	5.5	13.5	1976

Note: Figures are percentages except for Median Year; (1) Figures cover the Clarksville, TN-KY Metropolitan Statistical Area—see Appendix B for areas included
Source: U.S. Census Bureau, 2010-2012 American Community Survey 3-Year Estimates

HEALTH

Health Risk Data

Category	MSA[1] (%)	U.S. (%)
Adults aged 18–64 who have any kind of health care coverage	n/a	79.6
Adults who reported being in good or excellent health	n/a	83.1
Adults who are current smokers	n/a	19.6
Adults who are heavy drinkers[2]	n/a	6.1
Adults who are binge drinkers[3]	n/a	16.9
Adults who are overweight (BMI 25.0 - 29.9)	n/a	35.8
Adults who are obese (BMI 30.0 - 99.8)	n/a	27.6
Adults who participated in any physical activities in the past month	n/a	77.1
Adults 50+ who have ever had a sigmoidoscopy or colonoscopy	n/a	67.3
Women aged 40+ who have had a mammogram within the past two years	n/a	74.0
Men aged 40+ who have had a PSA test within the past two years	n/a	45.2
Adults aged 65+ who have had flu shot within the past year	n/a	60.1
Adults who always wear a seatbelt	n/a	93.8

Note: Data as of 2012 unless otherwise noted; n/a not available; (1) Figures cover the Clarksville, TN-KY Metropolitan Statistical Area—see Appendix B for areas included; (2) Heavy drinkers are classified as males having more than two drinks per day or females having more than one drink per day; (3) Binge drinkers are classified as males having five or more drinks on one occasion or females having four or more drinks on one occasion
Source: Centers for Disease Control and Prevention, Behaviorial Risk Factor Surveillance System, SMART: Selected Metropolitan/Micropolitan Area Risk Trends, 2012

Chronic Health Indicators

Category	MSA[1] (%)	U.S. (%)
Adults who have ever been told they had a heart attack	n/a	4.5
Adults who have ever been told they had a stroke	n/a	2.9
Adults who have been told they currently have asthma	n/a	8.9
Adults who have ever been told they have arthritis	n/a	25.7
Adults who have ever been told they have diabetes[2]	n/a	9.7
Adults who have ever been told they had skin cancer	n/a	5.7
Adults who have ever been told they had any other types of cancer	n/a	6.5
Adults who have ever been told they have COPD	n/a	6.2
Adults who have ever been told they have kidney disease	n/a	2.5
Adults who have ever been told they have a form of depression	n/a	18.0

Note: Data as of 2012 unless otherwise noted; n/a not available; (1) Figures cover the Clarksville, TN-KY Metropolitan Statistical Area—see Appendix B for areas included; (2) Figures do not include pregnancy-related, borderline, or pre-diabetes
Source: Centers for Disease Control and Prevention, Behaviorial Risk Factor Surveillance System, SMART: Selected Metropolitan/Micropolitan Area Risk Trends, 2012

Mortality Rates for the Top 10 Causes of Death in the U.S.

ICD-10[a] Sub-Chapter	ICD-10[a] Code	Age-Adjusted Mortality Rate[1] per 100,000 population	
		County[2]	U.S.
Malignant neoplasms	C00-C97	197.6	174.2
Ischaemic heart diseases	I20-I25	150.6	119.1
Other forms of heart disease	I30-I51	44.2	49.6
Chronic lower respiratory diseases	J40-J47	68.2	43.2
Cerebrovascular diseases	I60-I69	75.5	40.3
Organic, including symptomatic, mental disorders	F01-F09	40.4	30.5
Other degenerative diseases of the nervous system	G30-G31	31.9	26.3
Other external causes of accidental injury	W00-X59	29.8	25.1
Diabetes mellitus	E10-E14	27.8	21.3
Hypertensive diseases	I10-I15	17.3	18.8

Note: (a) ICD-10 = International Classification of Diseases 10th Revision; (1) Mortality rates are a three year average covering 2008-2010; (2) Figures cover Montgomery County
Source: Centers for Disease Control and Prevention, National Center for Health Statistics. Compressed Mortality File 1999-2010 on CDC WONDER Online Database, released January 2013. Data are compiled from the Compressed Mortality File 1999-2010, Series 20 No. 2P, 2013.

Mortality Rates for Selected Causes of Death

ICD-10[a] Sub-Chapter	ICD-10[a] Code	Age-Adjusted Mortality Rate[1] per 100,000 population	
		County[2]	U.S.
Assault	X85-Y09	6.4	5.5
Diseases of the liver	K70-K76	13.0	12.4
Human immunodeficiency virus (HIV) disease	B20-B24	*2.5	3.0
Influenza and pneumonia	J09-J18	18.6	16.4
Intentional self-harm	X60-X84	12.7	11.8
Malnutrition	E40-E46	Suppressed	0.8
Obesity and other hyperalimentation	E65-E68	*3.9	1.6
Renal failure	N17-N19	11.8	13.6
Transport accidents	V01-V99	17.0	12.6
Viral hepatitis	B15-B19	*3.3	2.2

Note: (a) ICD-10 = International Classification of Diseases 10th Revision; (1) Mortality rates are a three year average covering 2008-2010; (2) Figures cover Montgomery County; (*) Unreliable data as per CDC
Source: Centers for Disease Control and Prevention, National Center for Health Statistics. Compressed Mortality File 1999-2010 on CDC WONDER Online Database, released January 2013. Data are compiled from the Compressed Mortality File 1999-2010, Series 20 No. 2P, 2013.

Health Insurance Coverage

Area	With Health Insurance	With Private Health Insurance	With Public Health Insurance	Without Health Insurance	Population Under Age 18 Without Health Insurance
City	87.1	70.7	28.5	12.9	4.0
MSA[1]	85.9	69.3	28.8	14.1	6.4
U.S.	84.9	65.4	30.4	15.1	7.5

Note: Figures are percentages that cover the civilian noninstitutionalized population; (1) Figures cover the Clarksville, TN-KY Metropolitan Statistical Area—see Appendix B for areas included
Source: U.S. Census Bureau, 2010-2012 American Community Survey 3-Year Estimates

Number of Medical Professionals

Area[1]	MDs[2]	DOs[2,3]	Dentists	Podiatrists	Chiropractors	Optometrists
Local (number)	184	32	69	4	27	28
Local (rate[4])	104.1	18.1	37.3	2.2	14.6	15.1
U.S. (rate[4])	267.6	19.6	61.7	5.6	24.7	14.5

Note: Data as of 2012 unless noted; (1) Local data covers Montgomery County; (2) Data as of 2011; (3) Doctor of Osteopathic Medicine; (4) rate per 100,000 population
Source: Area Resource File (ARF) 2012-2013. U.S. Department of Health and Human Services, Health Resources and Services Administration, Bureau of Health Professions

EDUCATION

Public School District Statistics

District Name	Schls	Pupils	Pupil/ Teacher Ratio	Minority Pupils[1] (%)	Free Lunch Eligible[2] (%)	IEP[3] (%)
Montgomery County	36	30,614	15.6	42.2	35.7	12.4

Note: Table includes school districts with 2,000 or more students; (1) Percentage of students that are not non-Hispanic white; (2) Percentage of students that are eligible for the free lunch program; (3) Percentage of students that have an Individualized Education Program.
Source: U.S. Department of Education, National Center for Education Statistics, Common Core of Data, Local Education Agency (School District) Universe Survey: School Year 2011-2012; U.S. Department of Education, National Center for Education Statistics, Common Core of Data, Public Elementary/Secondary School Universe Survey: School Year 2011-2012

Highest Level of Education

Area	Less than H.S.	H.S. Diploma	Some College, No Deg.	Associate Degree	Bachelor's Degree	Master's Degree	Prof. School Degree	Doctorate Degree
City	8.8	30.6	28.1	8.6	16.0	6.0	1.0	0.8
MSA[1]	11.6	33.0	27.1	8.2	13.3	5.2	1.1	0.7
U.S.	14.1	28.3	21.3	7.8	18.0	7.5	1.9	1.2

Note: Figures cover persons age 25 and over; (1) Figures cover the Clarksville, TN-KY Metropolitan Statistical Area—see Appendix B for areas included
Source: U.S. Census Bureau, 2010-2012 American Community Survey 3-Year Estimates

Educational Attainment by Race

Area	High School Graduate or Higher (%)					Bachelor's Degree or Higher (%)				
	Total	White	Black	Asian	Hisp.[2]	Total	White	Black	Asian	Hisp.[2]
City	91.2	92.4	89.2	86.1	82.3	23.9	25.2	19.4	32.2	17.8
MSA[1]	88.4	88.9	87.1	85.0	82.0	20.2	20.8	16.0	35.4	14.4
U.S.	85.9	88.1	82.5	85.5	63.1	28.6	30.0	18.4	50.2	13.4

Note: Figures shown cover persons 25 years old and over; (1) Figures cover the Clarksville, TN-KY Metropolitan Statistical Area—see Appendix B for areas included; (2) People of Hispanic origin can be of any race
Source: U.S. Census Bureau, 2010-2012 American Community Survey 3-Year Estimates

School Enrollment by Grade and Control

Area	Preschool (%)		Kindergarten (%)		Grades 1 - 4 (%)		Grades 5 - 8 (%)		Grades 9 - 12 (%)	
	Public	Private	Public	Private	Public	Private	Public	Private	Public	Private
City	60.5	39.5	93.0	7.0	92.8	7.2	94.3	5.7	90.1	9.9
MSA[1]	66.8	33.2	88.4	11.6	89.5	10.5	91.4	8.6	89.4	10.6
U.S.	56.9	43.1	87.8	12.2	89.9	10.1	90.0	10.0	90.8	9.2

Note: Figures shown cover persons 3 years old and over; (1) Figures cover the Clarksville, TN-KY Metropolitan Statistical Area—see Appendix B for areas included
Source: U.S. Census Bureau, 2010-2012 American Community Survey 3-Year Estimates

Average Salaries of Public School Classroom Teachers

Area	2012-13		2013-14		Percent Change 2012-13 to 2013-14	Percent Change 2003-04 to 2013-14
	Dollars	Rank[1]	Dollars	Rank[1]		
Tennessee	47,563	40	48,049	43	1.02	19.2
U.S. Average	56,103	–	56,689	–	1.04	21.8

Note: (1) State rank ranges from 1 to 51 where 1 indicates highest salary.
Source: National Education Association, Rankings & Estimates: Rankings of the States 2013 and Estimates of School Statistics 2014, March 2014

Higher Education

Four-Year Colleges			Two-Year Colleges			Medical Schools[1]	Law Schools[2]	Voc/ Tech[3]
Public	Private Non-profit	Private For-profit	Public	Private Non-profit	Private For-profit			
1	0	1	0	0	2	0	0	1

Note: Figures cover institutions located within the city limits and include main campuses only; (1) includes schools accredited by the Liaison Committee on Medical Education and the American Osteopathic Association's Commission on Osteopathic College Accreditation; (2) includes ABA-accredited schools, schools with provisional ABA accreditation, and state accredited schools; (3) includes all schools with programs that are less than 2 years.
Source: National Center for Education Statistics, Integrated Postsecondary Education System (IPEDS), 2012-13; Association of American Medical Colleges, Member List, April 24, 2014; American Osteopathic Association, Member List, April 24, 2014; Law School Admission Council, Official Guide to ABA-Approved Law Schools Online, April 24, 2014; Wikipedia, List of Medical Schools in the United States, April 24, 2014; Wikipedia, List of Law Schools in the United States, April 24, 2014

PRESIDENTIAL ELECTION

2012 Presidential Election Results

Area	Obama	Romney	Other
Montgomery County	44.0	54.5	1.5
U.S.	51.0	47.2	1.8

Note: Results are percentages and may not add to 100% due to rounding
Source: Dave Leip's Atlas of U.S. Presidential Elections

EMPLOYERS

Major Employers

Company Name	Industry
ABMA	Motor vehicle brake systems and parts
Army & Air Force Exchange Service	Army-navy goods stores
AT&T Corp.	Engineering services
Austin Peay State University	University
Bridgestone Metalpha U.S.A.	Steel tire cords and tire cord fabrics
Flynn Enterprises	Dungarees: men's, youths', and boys'
Gateway Health System	General medical and surgical hospitals
Jennie Stuart Medical Center	General medical and surgical hospitals
Jostens	Rings, finger: precious metal
Martinrea Industries	Body parts, automobile: stamped metal
Metalsa, S.A. De C.V.	Motor vehicle parts and accessories
TG Automotive Sealing Kentucky	Automotive stampings
The Army, United States Department of	General medical and surgical hospitals
The Army, United States Department of	Army
Trigg County Board of Education	Elementary and secondary schools
Wal-Mart Stores	Department stores, discount

Note: Companies shown are located within the Clarksville, TN-KY Metropolitan Statistical Area.
Source: Hoovers.com; Wikipedia

PUBLIC SAFETY

Crime Rate

Area	All Crimes	Violent Crimes				Property Crimes		
		Murder	Forcible Rape	Robbery	Aggrav. Assault	Burglary	Larceny -Theft	Motor Vehicle Theft
City	3,360.6	7.3	33.5	72.1	524.2	710.6	1,891.4	121.6
Suburbs[1]	2,736.0	5.4	30.3	58.2	138.9	676.8	1,699.0	127.3
Metro[2]	3,058.3	6.4	31.9	65.4	337.7	694.2	1,798.3	124.3
U.S.	3,246.1	4.7	26.9	112.9	242.3	670.2	1,959.3	229.7

Note: Figures are crimes per 100,000 population; (1) All areas within the metro area that are located outside the city limits; (2) Figures cover the Clarksville, TN-KY Metropolitan Statistical Area—see Appendix B for areas included
Source: FBI Uniform Crime Reports, 2012

Hate Crimes

Area	Number of Quarters Reported	Bias Motivation				
		Race	Religion	Sexual Orientation	Ethnicity	Disability
City	4	3	1	1	0	1
U.S.	4	2,797	1,099	1,135	667	92

Source: Federal Bureau of Investigation, Hate Crime Statistics 2012

Identity Theft Consumer Complaints

Area	Complaints	Complaints per 100,000 Population	Rank[2]
MSA[1]	143	54.9	251
U.S.	290,056	91.8	-

Note: (1) Figures cover the Clarksville, TN-KY Metropolitan Statistical Area—see Appendix B for areas included; (2) Rank ranges from 1 to 377 where 1 indicates greatest number of identity theft complaints per 100,000 population
Source: Federal Trade Commission, Consumer Sentinel Network Data Book for January–December 2013

Fraud and Other Consumer Complaints

Area	Complaints	Complaints per 100,000 Population	Rank[2]
MSA[1]	1,124	431.3	73
U.S.	1,811,724	595.2	-

Note: (1) Figures cover the Clarksville, TN-KY Metropolitan Statistical Area—see Appendix B for areas included; (2) Rank ranges from 1 to 377 where 1 indicates greatest number of identity theft complaints per 100,000 population
Source: Federal Trade Commission, Consumer Sentinel Network Data Book for January–December 2013

RECREATION

Culture

Dance[1]	Theatre[1]	Instrumental Music[1]	Vocal Music[1]	Series and Festivals	Museums and Art Galleries[2]	Zoos and Aquariums[3]
0	1	0	0	1	2	0

Note: (1) Number of professional performing groups; (2) Based on organizations with primary SIC code 8412; (3) AZA-accredited
Source: The Grey House Performing Arts Directory, 2013; Association of Zoos & Aquariums, AZA Member Zoos & Aquariums, April 2014; www.AccuLeads.com, May 1, 2014

Professional Sports Teams

Team Name	League	Year Established
No teams are located in the metro area		

Source: Wikipedia, Major Professional Sports Teams of the United States and Canada, April 25, 2014

CLIMATE

Average and Extreme Temperatures

Temperature	Jan	Feb	Mar	Apr	May	Jun	Jul	Aug	Sep	Oct	Nov	Dec	Yr.
Extreme High (°F)	78	84	86	91	95	106	107	104	105	94	84	79	107
Average High (°F)	47	51	60	71	79	87	90	89	83	72	60	50	70
Average Temp. (°F)	38	41	50	60	68	76	80	79	72	61	49	41	60
Average Low (°F)	28	31	39	48	57	65	69	68	61	48	39	31	49
Extreme Low (°F)	-17	-13	2	23	34	42	54	49	36	26	-1	-10	-17

Note: Figures cover the years 1948-1990
Source: National Climatic Data Center, International Station Meteorological Climate Summary, 9/96

Average Precipitation/Snowfall/Humidity

Precip./Humidity	Jan	Feb	Mar	Apr	May	Jun	Jul	Aug	Sep	Oct	Nov	Dec	Yr.
Avg. Precip. (in.)	4.4	4.2	5.0	4.1	4.6	3.7	3.8	3.3	3.2	2.6	3.9	4.6	47.4
Avg. Snowfall (in.)	4	3	1	Tr	0	0	0	0	0	Tr	1	1	11
Avg. Rel. Hum. 6am (%)	81	81	80	81	86	86	88	90	90	87	83	82	85
Avg. Rel. Hum. 3pm (%)	61	57	51	48	52	52	54	53	52	49	55	59	54

Note: Figures cover the years 1948-1990; Tr = Trace amounts (<0.05 in. of rain; <0.5 in. of snow)
Source: National Climatic Data Center, International Station Meteorological Climate Summary, 9/96

Weather Conditions

Temperature			Daytime Sky			Precipitation		
10°F & below	32°F & below	90°F & above	Clear	Partly cloudy	Cloudy	0.01 inch or more precip.	0.1 inch or more snow/ice	Thunder-storms
5	76	51	98	135	132	119	8	54

Note: Figures are average number of days per year and cover the years 1948-1990
Source: National Climatic Data Center, International Station Meteorological Climate Summary, 9/96

HAZARDOUS WASTE

Superfund Sites

Clarksville has no sites on the EPA's Superfund Final National Priorities List.
U.S. Environmental Protection Agency, Final National Priorities List, April 26, 2014

AIR & WATER QUALITY

Air Quality Index

Area	Percent of Days when Air Quality was...[2]					AQI Statistics[2]	
	Good	Moderate	Unhealthy for Sensitive Groups	Unhealthy	Very Unhealthy	Maximum	Median
MSA[1]	76.2	23.8	0.0	0.0	0.0	100	41

Note: (1) Data covers the Clarksville, TN-KY Metropolitan Statistical Area—see Appendix B for areas included; (2) Based on 365 days with AQI data in 2013. Air Quality Index (AQI) is an index for reporting daily air quality. EPA calculates the AQI for five major air pollutants regulated by the Clean Air Act: ground-level ozone, particle pollution (aka particulate matter), carbon monoxide, sulfur dioxide, and nitrogen dioxide. The AQI runs from 0 to 500. The higher the AQI value, the greater the level of air pollution and the greater the health concern. There are six AQI categories: "Good" AQI is between 0 and 50. Air quality is considered satisfactory; "Moderate" AQI is between 51 and 100. Air quality is acceptable; "Unhealthy for Sensitive Groups" When AQI values are between 101 and 150, members of sensitive groups may experience health effects; "Unhealthy" When AQI values are between 151 and 200 everyone may begin to experience health effects; "Very Unhealthy" AQI values between 201 and 300 trigger a health alert; "Hazardous" AQI values over 300 trigger warnings of emergency conditions (not shown).
Source: U.S. Environmental Protection Agency, Air Quality Index Report, 2013

Air Quality Index Pollutants

Area	Percent of Days when AQI Pollutant was...[2]					
	Carbon Monoxide	Nitrogen Dioxide	Ozone	Sulfur Dioxide	Particulate Matter 2.5	Particulate Matter 10
MSA[1]	0.0	0.0	43.3	1.9	54.8	0.0

Note: (1) Data covers the Clarksville, TN-KY Metropolitan Statistical Area—see Appendix B for areas included; (2) Based on 365 days with AQI data in 2013. The Air Quality Index (AQI) is an index for reporting daily air quality. EPA calculates the AQI for five major air pollutants regulated by the Clean Air Act: ground-level ozone, particle pollution (also known as particulate matter), carbon monoxide, sulfur dioxide, and nitrogen dioxide. The AQI runs from 0 to 500. The higher the AQI value, the greater the level of air pollution and the greater the health concern.
Source: U.S. Environmental Protection Agency, Air Quality Index Report, 2013

Air Quality Trends: Ozone

	2003	2004	2005	2006	2007	2008	2009	2010	2011	2012
MSA[1]	n/a	n/a	n/a	n/a	n/a	n/a	n/a	n/a	n/a	n/a

Note: (1) Data covers the Clarksville, TN-KY Metropolitan Statistical Area—see Appendix B for areas included; n/a not available. The values shown are the composite ozone concentration averages among trend sites based on the highest fourth daily maximum 8-hour concentration in parts per million. These trends are based on sites having an adequate record of monitoring data during the trend period. Data from exceptional events are included.
Source: U.S. Environmental Protection Agency, Air Quality Monitoring Information, "Air Quality Trends by City, 2000-2012"

Maximum Air Pollutant Concentrations: Particulate Matter, Ozone, CO and Lead

	Particulate Matter 10 (ug/m^3)	Particulate Matter 2.5 Wtd AM (ug/m^3)	Particulate Matter 2.5 24-Hr (ug/m^3)	Ozone (ppm)	Carbon Monoxide (ppm)	Lead (ug/m^3)
MSA[1] Level	29	9.9	20	0.078	n/a	n/a
NAAQS[2]	150	15	35	0.075	9	0.15
Met NAAQS[2]	Yes	Yes	Yes	No	n/a	n/a

Note: (1) Data covers the Clarksville, TN-KY Metropolitan Statistical Area—see Appendix B for areas included; Data from exceptional events are included; (2) National Ambient Air Quality Standards; ppm = parts per million; ug/m^3 = micrograms per cubic meter; n/a not available.
Concentrations: Particulate Matter 10 (coarse particulate)—highest second maximum 24-hour concentration; Particulate Matter 2.5 Wtd AM (fine particulate)—highest weighted annual mean concentration; Particulate Matter 2.5 24-Hour (fine particulate)—highest 98th percentile 24-hour concentration; Ozone—highest fourth daily maximum 8-hour concentration; Carbon Monoxide—highest second maximum non-overlapping 8-hour concentration; Lead—maximum running 3-month average
Source: U.S. Environmental Protection Agency, Air Quality Monitoring Information, "Air Quality Statistics by City, 2012"

Maximum Air Pollutant Concentrations: Nitrogen Dioxide and Sulfur Dioxide

	Nitrogen Dioxide AM (ppb)	Nitrogen Dioxide 1-Hr (ppb)	Sulfur Dioxide AM (ppb)	Sulfur Dioxide 1-Hr (ppb)	Sulfur Dioxide 24-Hr (ppb)
MSA[1] Level	n/a	n/a	n/a	55	n/a
NAAQS[2]	53	100	30	75	140
Met NAAQS[2]	n/a	n/a	n/a	Yes	n/a

Note: (1) Data covers the Clarksville, TN-KY Metropolitan Statistical Area—see Appendix B for areas included; Data from exceptional events are included; (2) National Ambient Air Quality Standards; ppm = parts per million; ug/m^3 = micrograms per cubic meter; n/a not available.
Concentrations: Nitrogen Dioxide AM—highest arithmetic mean concentration; Nitrogen Dioxide 1-Hr—highest 98th percentile 1-hour daily maximum concentration; Sulfur Dioxide AM—highest annual mean concentration; Sulfur Dioxide 1-Hr—highest 99th percentile 1-hour daily maximum concentration; Sulfur Dioxide 24-Hr—highest second maximum 24-hour concentration
Source: U.S. Environmental Protection Agency, Air Quality Monitoring Information, "Air Quality Statistics by City, 2012"

Drinking Water

Water System Name	Pop. Served	Primary Water Source Type	Violations[1] Health Based	Violations[1] Monitoring/ Reporting
Clarksville Water Department	174,740	Surface	0	0

Note: (1) Based on violation data from January 1, 2013 to December 31, 2013 (includes unresolved violations from earlier years)
Source: U.S. Environmental Protection Agency, Office of Ground Water and Drinking Water, Safe Drinking Water Information System (based on data extracted February 10, 2014)

Dallas, Texas

Background

Dallas is one of those cities that offer everything. Founded in 1841 by Tennessee lawyer and trader, John Neely Bryan, Dallas has come to symbolize in modern times all that is big, exciting, and affluent. The city itself is home to 15 billionaires, placing it ninth worldwide among cities with the most billionaires. When combined with the eight billionaires who live in Dallas's neighboring city of Fort Worth, the area has one of the greatest concentrations of billionaires in the world.

Originally one of the largest markets for cotton in the U.S., Dallas moved on to become one of the largest markets for oil in the country. In the 1930s, oil was struck on the eastern fields of Texas. As a result, oil companies were founded and millionaires were made. The face we now associate with Dallas and the state of Texas had emerged.

Today, oil still plays a dominant role in the Dallas economy. Outside of Alaska, Texas holds most of the U.S. oil reserves. For that reason, many oil companies choose to headquarter in the silver skyscrapers of Dallas.

In addition to employment opportunities in the oil industry, the Dallas branch of the Federal Reserve Bank, and a host of other banks and investment firms clustering around the Federal Reserve hub employ thousands. Other opportunities are offered in the aircraft, advertising, motion picture, and publishing industries.

Major employers in the Dallas area include American Airlines (Dallas-Fort Worth Airport); Lockheed Martin (in nearby Fort Worth); University of North Texas in Denton; Parkland Memorial Hospital; and Baylor University Medical center. Vought Aircraft Industries, a major supplier of aircraft components to Boeing, Sikorsky and other aircraft manufacturers, continues to expand its local operations. The city is sometimes referred to as Texas's "Silicon Prairie" because of a high concentration of telecommunications companies.

The Dallas Convention Center, with more than two million square feet of space, is the largest convention center in Texas with more than 1 million square feet of exhibit area, including nearly 800,000 square feet of same level, contiguous prime exhibit space with more than 3.8 million people attending more than 3,600 conventions and spending more than $4.2 billion annually.

Dallas also is busy culturally. A host of independent theater groups is sponsored by Southern Methodist University. The Museum of Art houses an excellent collection of modern art, especially American paintings. The Winspear Opera House, along with 3 other venues that make up the AT&T Performing Arts Center was dedicated in 2009. The Dallas Opera has showcased Maria Callas, Joan Sutherland, and Monserrat Caballe. The city also contains many historical districts such as the Swiss Avenue District, and elegant buildings such as the City Hall Building designed by I.M. Pei. The most notable event held in Dallas is the State Fair of Texas, which has been held annually at Fair Park since 1886. The fair is a massive event for the state of Texas and brings an estimated $350 million to the city's economy annually.

The area's high concentration of wealth undoubtedly contributes to Dallas's wide array of shopping centers and high-end boutiques. Downtown Dallas is home to many cafes, restaurants and clubs. The city's centrally located "Arts District" is appropriately named for the independent theaters and art galleries located in the neighborhood. While northern districts of the city and the central downtown have seen much urban revival in the last 30 years, neighborhoods south of downtown have not experienced the same growth.

Colleges and universities in the Dallas area include Southern Methodist University, University of Dallas, and University of Texas at Dallas. In 2006, University of North Texas opened a branch in the southern part of the city, in part, to help accelerate development south of downtown Dallas.

The city maintains around 21,000 acres of park land, with over 400 parks.

The climate of Dallas is generally temperate. Occasional periods of extreme cold are short-lived, and extremely high temperatures that sometimes occur in summer usually do not last for extended periods.

Rankings

General Rankings

- The Dallas-Fort Worth metro area was identified as one of America's fastest-growing areas in terms of population and economy by *Forbes*. The area ranked #4 out of 20. The 100 most populous metro areas in the U.S. were evaluated on the following criteria: estimated population growth; job growth; gross metropolitan product growth; unemployment; median salaries for college-educated workers. *Forbes, "America's Fastest-Growing Cities 2014," February 14, 2014*

- Among the 50 largest U.S. cities, Dallas placed #32 in Vocativ's "semi-exhaustive, mostly scientific" city Livability Index for people aged 35 and under. Average salary, unemployment rates, rents, and other living costs were considered, along with bike lanes, low-cost broadband, cheap takeout, self-service laundries, the price of a pint of Guinness, music venues, and vintage clothing stores. *vocative.com, "The Livability Index: The Best U.S. Cities for People 35 and Under," November 7, 2013*

- Dallas was selected as one of America's best cities by *Bloomberg Businessweek*. The city ranked #41 out of 50. Criteria: leisure attributes (the number of restaurants, bars, libraries, museums, professional sports teams, and park acres by population); educational attributes (public school performance, the number of colleges, and graduate degree holders); economic factors (2011 income and June and July 2012 unemployment); crime; and air quality. *Bloomberg BusinessWeek, "America's Best Cities," September 26, 2012*

- Dallas appeared on RelocateAmerica's list of best places to live in America. The annual "Top 100 Places to Live" list recognizes the top communities as nominated by their residents & local businesses. RelocateAmerica's Research Group determined the list based on review of various data gathered for economic, employment, housing, education, industry, opportunity, environment and recreation along with feedback from area leaders and residents. *RelocateAmerica.com, "Top 100 Places to Live for 2011"*

- Dallas was selected as one of "America's Top 10 Places to Live" by *RelocateAmerica.com*. The city ranked #5. Criteria: real estate and housing; economic health; recreation; safety; input from local residents, business and community leaders. *RelocateAmerica.com, "Top 10 Places to Live for 2011"*

- Dallas was selected as one of "America's Favorite Cities." The city ranked #25 in the "Quality of Life and Visitor Experience: Cleanliness" category. Respondents to an online survey were asked to rate 35 top urban destinations in the U.S. from a visitor's perspective. Criteria: cleanliness. *Travel + Leisure, "America's Favorite Cities 2013"*

- Dallas was selected as one of "America's Favorite Cities." The city ranked #33 in the "Type of Trip: Gay-friendly" category. Respondents to an online survey were asked to rate 35 top urban destinations in the U.S. from a visitor's perspective. Criteria: gay-friendly. *Travel + Leisure, "America's Favorite Cities 2013"*

Business/Finance Rankings

- The personal finance site NerdWallet scored the nation's 20 largest American cities according to how friendly a business climate they offer to would-be entrepreneurs. Criteria inlcuded local taxes (state, city, payroll, property), growth rate, and the regulatory environment as judged by small business owners. On the resulting list of most welcoming cities, Dallas ranked #3. *www.nerdwallet.com, "Top 10 Best Cities for Small Business," August 26, 2013*

- The editors of *Kiplinger's Personal Finance Magazine* named Dallas-Fort Worth to their list of ten of the best metro areas for start-ups. Criteria included a well-educated workforce and low living costs for self-employed people, as measured by the Council for Community and Economic Research, as well as areas with lots of start-up investment dollars and low business costs. *www.kiplinger.com, "10 Great Cities for Starting a Business," January 2013*

- In order to help veterans transition from the military to civilian life, USAA and Hiring Our Heroes worked with Sperlings's BestPlaces to develop a list of the major metropolitan areas where military-skills-related employment is strongest. Criteria included job prospects, unemployment, number of government jobs, recent job growth, accessible health resources, and colleges and universities. Metro areas with a violent crime rate or high cost of living were excluded. At #2, the Dallas-Fort Worth metro area made the top ten. *www.usaa.com, "2013 Best Places for Veterans: Jobs," November 2013*

- The finance website Wall St. Cheat Sheet reported on the prospects for high-wage job creation in the nation's largest metro areas over the next five years and ranked them accordingly, drawing on in-depth analysis by CareerBuilder and Economic Modeling Specialists International (EMSI). The Dallas-Fort Worth metro area placed #9 on the Wall St. Cheat Sheet list. *wallstcheatsheet.com, "Top 10 Cities for High-Wage Job Growth," December 8, 2013*

- Based on a minimum of 500 social media reviews per metro area, the employment opinion group Glassdoor surveyed 50 of the largest U.S. metro areas on measures including compensation and benefits, satisfaction with management, business outlook, and number of employers hiring. The Dallas-Fort Worth metro area was ranked #28 in overall employee satisfaction. *www.glassdoor.com, "Employment Satisfaction Report Card by City," June 21, 2013*

- In its Competitive Alternatives report, consulting firm KPMG analyzed the 27 largest metropolitan statistical areas according to 26 cost components (such as taxes, labor costs, and utilities) and 30 non-cost-related variables (such as crime rates and number of universities). The business website 24/7 Wall Street examined the KPMG findings, adding to the mix current unemployment rates, GDP, median income, and employment decline during the last recession and "projected" recovery. It identified the Dallas-Fort Worth metro area as #5 among the ten best American cities for business. *247wallst.com, "Best American Cities for Business," April 4, 2012*

- A *Fiscal Times* analysis balancing cost of living with average income to find the cities where residents' dollars go furthest was published by the *Huffington Post*. Based on the Census Bureau's 2010 Cost of Living Index and the National Compensation Survey, Dallas-Fort Worth was ranked the #3 metro area where you can "actually spend less and make more." *Fiscal Times/Huffington Post, "The Best Bang for Your Buck Cities in the United States," June 26, 2012*

- The financial literacy site NerdWallet.com set out to identify the 20 most promising cities for job seekers, analyzing data for the nation's 50 largest cities. Dallas was ranked #13. Criteria: unemployment rate; population growth; median income; selected monthly owner costs. *NerdWallet.com, "Best Cities for Job Seekers," January 7, 2014*

- The Brookings Institution ranked the 50 largest cities in the U.S. based on income inequality. Dallas was ranked #13. (#1 = greatest inequality). Criteria: the cities were ranked based on the "95/20 ratio." This figure represents the income at which a household earns more than 95 percent of all other households, divided by the income at which a household earns more than only 20 percent of all other households. *Brookings Institution, "Income Inequality in America's 50 Largest Cities, 2007-2012," February 20, 2014*

- Dallas-Fort Worth was ranked #20 out of 100 metro areas in terms of economic performance (#1 = best) during the recession and recovery from trough quarter through the second quarter of 2013. Criteria: percent change in employment; percentage point change in unemployment rate; percent change in gross metropolitan product; percent change in House Price Index. *Brookings Institution, MetroMonitor: Tracking Economic Recession and Recovery in America's 100 Largest Metropolitan Areas, September 2013*

- Payscale.com ranked the 20 largest metro areas in terms of wage growth. The Dallas-Fort Worth metro area ranked #12. Criteria: private-sector wage growth between the 4th quarter of 2012 and the 4th quarter of 2013. *PayScale, "Wage Trends by Metro Area," 4th Quarter, 2013*

- Dallas-Fort Worth was identified as one of America's most frugal metro areas by *Coupons.com.* The city ranked #14 out of 25. Criteria: online coupon usage. *Coupons.com, "Top 25 Most Frugal Cities of 2012," February 19, 2013*

- Dallas-Fort Worth was identified as one of America's most frugal metro areas by *Coupons.com.* The city ranked #5 out of 25. Criteria: Grocery IQ and coupons.com mobile app usage. *Coupons.com, "Top 25 Most On-the-Go Frugal Cities of 2012," February 19, 2013*

- Dallas was identified as one of "America's Hardest-Working Towns." The city ranked #25 out of 25. Criteria: average hours worked per capita; willingness to work during personal time; number of dual income households; local employment rate. *Parade, "What is America's Hardest-Working Town?," April 15, 2012*

- Dallas was identified as one of the top 25 U.S. cities with the most credit card debt by credit reporting bureau Experian. The city was ranked #5. *Experian, March 4, 2011*

- Dallas-Fort Worth was cited as one of America's top metros for new and expanded facility projects in 2013. The area ranked #3 in the large metro area category (population over 1 million). *Site Selection, "Top Metros of 2013," March 2014*

- Dallas was identified as one of the best cities for college graduates to find work—and live. The city ranked #5 out of 15. Criteria: job availability; average salary; average rent. *CareerBuilder.com, "15 Best Cities for College Grads to Find Work—and Live," June 5, 2012*

- The Dallas-Fort Worth metro area appeared on the Milken Institute "2013 Best Performing Cities" list. Rank: #7 out of 200 large metro areas. Criteria: job growth; wage and salary growth; high-tech output growth. *Milken Institute, "Best-Performing Cities 2013," December 2013*

- *Forbes* ranked the 200 most populous metro areas in the U.S. in terms of the "Best Places for Business and Careers." The Dallas-Fort Worth metro area was ranked #13. Criteria: costs (business and living); job growth (past and projected); income growth; educational attainment (college and high school); projected economic growth; cultural and recreational opportunities; net migration patterns; number of highly ranked colleges. *Forbes, "The Best Places for Business and Careers," August 7, 2013*

Children/Family Rankings

- Dallas was selected as one of the best cities for families to live by *Parenting* magazine. The city ranked #79 out of 100. Criteria: education; health; community; *Parenting's* Culture & Charm Index. *Parenting.com, "The 2012 Best Cities for Families List"*

Culture/Performing Arts Rankings

- Dallas was selected as one of "America's Favorite Cities." The city ranked #26 in the "Culture: Museum/Galleries" category. Respondents to an online survey were asked to rate 35 top urban destinations in the U.S. from a visitor's perspective. Criteria: number and quality of museums and galleries. *Travelandleisure.com, "America's Favorite Cities 2013"*

- Dallas was selected as one of America's top cities for the arts. The city ranked #19 in the big city (population 500,000 and over) category. Criteria: readers' top choices for arts travel destinations based on the richness and variety of visual arts sites, activities and events. *American Style, "2012 Top 25 Arts Destinations," June 2012*

Dating/Romance Rankings

- A *Cosmopolitan* magazine article surveyed the gender balance and other factors to arrive at a list of the best and worst cities for women to meet single guys. Dallas was #6 among the best for single women looking for dates. *www.cosmopolitan.com, "Working the Ratio," October 1, 2013*

- *Forbes* reports that the Dallas-Fort Worth metro area made Rent.com's Best Cities for Newlyweds survey for 2013, based on Bureau of Labor Statistics and Census Bureau data on number of married couples, percentage of families with children under age six, average annual income, cost of living, and availability of rentals. *www.forbes.com, "The 10 Best Cities for Newlyweds to Live and Work In," May 30, 2013*

- Of the 100 U.S. cities surveyed by *Men's Health* in its quest to identify the nation's best cities for dating and forming relationships, Dallas was ranked #18 for online dating (#1 = best). *Men's Health, "The Best and Worst Cities for Online Dating," January 30, 2013*

- Dallas was selected as one of the best cities for newlyweds by *Rent.com*. The city ranked #3 of 10. Criteria: cost of living; mean annual income; unemployment rate. *Rent.com, "10 Best Cities for Newlyweds," March 20, 2012*

- Dallas was selected as one of the best cities for single women in America by *SingleMindedWomen.com*. The city ranked #9. Criteria: ratio of women to men; singles population; healthy lifestyle; employment opportunities; cost of living; access to travel; entertainment options; social opportunities. *SingleMindedWomen.com, "Top 10 Cities for Single Women," 2011*

Education Rankings

- *Men's Health* ranked 100 U.S. cities in terms of their education levels. Dallas was ranked #86 (#1 = most educated city). Criteria: high school graduation rates; school enrollment; educational attainment; number of households who have outstanding student loans; number of households whose members have taken adult-education courses. *Men's Health, "Where School Is In: The Most and Least Educated Cities," September 12, 2011*

- Dallas was selected as one of America's most literate cities. The city ranked #37 out of the 77 largest U.S. cities. Criteria: number of booksellers; library resources; Internet resources; educational attainment; periodical publishing resources; newspaper circulation. *Central Connecticut State University, "America's Most Literate Cities, 2013"*

Environmental Rankings

- The Dallas-Fort Worth metro area came in at #350 for the relative comfort of its climate on Sperling's list of "chill cities," as measured by the Sperling Heat Index. All 361 metro areas are included. Criteria included daytime high temperatures, nighttime low temperatures, dew point, and relative humidity at the high temperatures. *www.bertsperling.com, "Sperling's Chill Cities," July 18, 2013*

- Sperling's BestPlaces assessed 379 metropolitan areas of the United States for the likelihood of dangerously extreme weather events or earthquakes. In general the Southeast and South-Central regions have the highest risk of weather extremes and earthquakes, while the Pacific Northwest enjoys the lowest risk. Of the least risky metropolitan areas, the Dallas-Fort Worth metro area was ranked #379. *www.bestplaces.net, "Safest Places from Natural Disasters," April 2011*

- Dallas-Fort Worth was identified as one of North America's greenest metropolitan areas. The area ranked #17. The Green City Index is comprised of 31 indicators, and scores cities across nine categories: carbon dioxide; energy; land use; buildings; transport; water; waste; air quality; environmental governance. The 27 largest metropolitan areas in the U.S. and Canada were considered. *Economist Intelligence Unit, sponsored by Siemens, "U.S. and Canada Green City Index, 2011"*

- The U.S. Environmental Protection Agency (EPA) released a list of U.S. metropolitan areas with the most ENERGY STAR certified buildings in 2012. The Dallas-Fort Worth metro area was ranked #8 out of 25. *U.S. Environmental Protection Agency, "Top Cities With the Most ENERGY STAR Certified Buildings in 2012," March 12, 2013*

- Dallas was selected as one of 22 "Smarter Cities" for energy by the Natural Resources Defense Council. The city appeared as one of 12 cities in the large city (population 250,000 and over) category. Criteria: investment in green power; energy efficiency measures; conservation. *Natural Resources Defense Council, "2010 Smarter Cities," July 19, 2010*

- Dallas was selected as one of the five worst summer weather cities in the U.S. by the *Farmers' Almanac*. The city ranked #3. Criteria: average summer and winter temperatures; humidity; precipitation; number of overcast days. The editors only considered cities with populations of 50,000 or more. *Farmers' Almanac, "America's Ten Worst Weather Cities," September 7, 2010*

- Dallas-Fort Worth was highlighted as one of the 25 most ozone-polluted metro areas in the U.S. during 2008 through 2010. The area ranked #8. *American Lung Association, State of the Air 2012*

Food/Drink Rankings

- *Men's Health* ranked 100 major U.S. cities in terms of alcohol intoxication. Dallas ranked #16 (#1 = most sober).Criteria: binge drinking; alcohol-related traffic accidents, arrests, and fatalities. *Men's Health, "The Drunkest Cities in America," November 19, 2013*

- Dallas was identified as one of the most vegetarian-friendly cities in America by GrubHub.com, the nation's largest food ordering service. The city ranked #5 out of 10. Criteria: percentage of vegetarian restaurants. *GrubHub.com, "Top Vegetarian-Friendly Cities," July 18, 2012*

Health/Fitness Rankings

- For each of the 50 most populous metro areas in the United States, the American College of Sports Medicine's American Fitness Index evaluated infrastructure, community assets, and policies that encourage healthy and fit lifestyles, including preventive health behaviors, levels of chronic disease conditions, health care access, and community resources and policies that support physical activity. The Dallas-Fort Worth metro area ranked #44 for "community fitness." Personal health indicators were considered as well as community and environmental indicators. *www.americanfitnessindex.org, "ACSM American Fitness Index Health and Community Fitness Status of the 50 Largest Metropolitan Areas," May 2013*

- The Dallas-Fort Worth metro area was identified as one of the worst cities for bed bugs in America by pest control company Orkin. The area ranked #13 out of 50 based on the number of bed bug treatments Orkin performed from January to December 2013. *Orkin, "Chicago Tops Bed Bug Cities List for Second Year in a Row," January 16, 2014*

- Dallas was identified as one of 15 cities with the highest increase in bed bug activity in the U.S. by pest control provider Terminix. The city ranked #13. Criteria: cities with the largest percentage gains in bed bug customer calls from January–May 2013 compared to the same time period in 2012. *Terminix, "Cities with Highest Increases in Bed Bug Activity," July 9, 2013*

- Dallas was selected as one of the 25 fattest cities in America by *Men's Fitness Online*. It ranked #25 out of America's 50 largest cities. Criteria: fitness centers and sport stores; nutrition; sports participation; TV viewing; overweight/sedentary; junk food; air quality; geography; commute; parks and open space; city recreational facilities; access to healthcare; motivation; mayor and city initiatives; state obesity initiatives. *Men's Fitness, "The Fittest and Fattest Cities in America," March 5, 2012*

- Dallas-Fort Worth was identified as one of "The 8 Most Artery-Clogging Cities in America." The metro area ranked #5. Criteria: obesity rates; heart disease rates. *Prevention, "The 8 Most Artery-Clogging Cities in America," December 2011*

- Dallas-Fort Worth was identified as a "2013 Spring Allergy Capital." The area ranked #23 out of 100. Three groups of factors were used to identify the most severe cities for people with allergies during the spring season: annual pollen levels; medicine utilization; access to board-certified allergists. *Asthma and Allergy Foundation of America, "Spring Allergy Capitals 2013"*

- Dallas-Fort Worth was identified as a "2013 Fall Allergy Capital." The area ranked #18 out of 100. Three groups of factors were used to identify the most severe cities for people with allergies during the fall season: annual pollen levels; medicine utilization; access to board-certified allergists. *Asthma and Allergy Foundation of America, "Fall Allergy Capitals 2013"*

- Dallas-Fort Worth was identified as a "2013 Asthma Capital." The area ranked #49 out of the nation's 100 largest metropolitan areas. Twelve factors were used to identify the most challenging places to live for people with asthma: estimated prevalence; self-reported prevalence; crude death rate for asthma; annual pollen score; annual air quality; public smoking laws; number of board-certified asthma specialists; school inhaler access laws; rescue medication use; controller medication use; uninsured rate; poverty rate. *Asthma and Allergy Foundation of America, "Asthma Capitals 2013"*

- *Men's Health* ranked 100 major U.S. cities in terms of the best and worst cities for men. Dallas ranked #50. Criteria: thirty-three data points were examined covering health, fitness, and quality of life. *Men's Health, "The Best & Worst Cities for Men 2014," December 6, 2013*

- Breathe Right Nasal Strips, in partnership with Sperling's BestPlaces, analyzed 50 metro areas and identified those U.S. cities most challenged by chronic nasal congestion. The Dallas-Fort Worth metro area ranked #7. Criteria: tree, grass and weed pollens; molds and spores; air pollution; climate; smoking; purchase habits of congestion products; prescriptions of drugs for congestion relief; incidence of influenza. *Breathe Right Nasal Strips, "Most Congested Cities," October 3, 2011*

- The American Academy of Dermatology ranked 26 U.S. metropolitan regions in terms of their residents knowledge, attitude and behaviors towards tanning, sun protection and skin cancer detection. The Dallas-Fort Worth metro area ranked #11. The results of the study are based on an online survey of over 7,000 adults nationwide. *American Academy of Dermatology, "Suntelligence: How Sun Smart is Your City?," May 3, 2010*

- The Dallas-Fort Worth metro area appeared in the 2013 Gallup-Healthways Well-Being Index. The area ranked #54 out of 189. The Gallup-Healthways Well-Being Index score is an average of six sub-indexes, which individually examine life evaluation, emotional health, work environment, physical health, healthy behaviors, and access to basic necessities. Results are based on telephone interviews conducted as part of the Gallup-Healthways Well-Being Index survey January 2–December 29, 2012, and January 2–December 30, 2013, with a random sample of 531,630 adults, aged 18 and older, living in metropolitan areas in the 50 U.S. states and the District of Columbia. *Gallup-Healthways, "State of American Well-Being," March 25, 2014*

- The Dallas-Fort Worth metro area was identified as one of "America's Most Stressful Cities" by *Sperling's BestPlaces*. The metro area ranked #43 out of 50. Criteria: unemployment rate; suicide rate; commute time; mental health; poor rest; alcohol use; violent crime rate; property crime rate; cloudy days annually. *Sperling's BestPlaces, www.BestPlaces.net, "Stressful Cities 2012*

- The Dallas-Fort Worth metro area was identified as one of "America's Most Stressful Cities" by *Forbes*. The metro area ranked #9 out of 40. Criteria: housing affordability; unemployment rate; cost of living; air quality; traffic congestion; sunny days; population density. *Forbes.com, "America's Most Stressful Cities," September 23, 2011*

- *Men's Health* ranked 100 U.S. cities in terms of their activity levels. Dallas was ranked #56 (#1 = most active city). Criteria: where and how often residents exercise; percentage of households that watch more than 15 hours of cable television a week and buy more than 11 video games a year; death rate from deep-vein thrombosis, a condition linked to sitting for extended periods of time. *Men's Health, "Where Sit Happens: The Most and Least Active Cities in America," June 20, 2011*

Real Estate Rankings

- On the list compiled by Penske Truck Rental, the Dallas-Fort Worth metro area was named the #3 moving destination in 2013, based on one-way consumer truck rental reservations made through Penske's website and reservations call center. *blog.gopenske.com, "Penske Truck Rental's 2013 Top Moving Destinations List," January 22, 2014*

- The PricewaterhouseCoopers and Urban Land Institute report *Emerging Trends in Real Estate* forecasts that improvements in leasing, rents, and pricing will fuel recovery in all property sectors in 2013. Dallas-Fort Worth was ranked #9 among the top ten markets to watch in 2013. *PricewaterhouseCoopers/Urban Land Institute, "U.S. Commercial Real Estate Recovery to Advance in 2013," October 17, 2012*

- The Dallas-Fort Worth metro area was identified as one of the top 20 housing markets to invest in for 2014 by *Forbes*. The area ranked #2. Criteria: high population and job growth; relatively low home prices which are below equilibrium home price (EHP). The EHP is what the average price for a market should be, if speculation, weird distortions in local income, and other factors (like the housing collapse) weren't present in the market. *Forbes.com, "Best Buy Cities: Where to Invest in Housing in 2014," December 25, 2013*

- Dallas-Fort Worth was ranked #70 out of 283 metro areas in terms of house price appreciation in 2013 (#1 = highest rate). *Federal Housing Finance Agency, House Price Index, 4th Quarter 2013*

- Dallas-Fort Worth was ranked #182 out of 224 metro areas in terms of housing affordability in 2013 by the National Association of Home Builders (#1 = most affordable). The NAHB-Wells Fargo Housing Opportunity Index (HOI) for a given area is defined as the share of homes sold in that area that would have been affordable to a family earning the local median income, based on standard mortgage underwriting criteria. *National Association of Home Builders®, NAHB-Wells Fargo Housing Opportunity Index, 4th Quarter 2013*

- The Dallas-Fort Worth metro area was identified as one of the 10 best U.S. markets to invest in single-family homes as rental properties by HomeVestors and Local Market Monitor. The area ranked #2. Criteria: risk-return premium relative to national average. *HomeVestors and Local Market Monitor, "Year-End Top 10 Real Estate Markets," December 20, 2013*

Safety Rankings

- Symantec, in partnership with Sperling's BestPlaces, ranked the 50 largest cities in the U.S. in terms of their vulnerability to cybercrime. The city ranked #15. Criteria: number of cyberattacks and potential infections; level of Internet access; expenditures on smartphones and computer hardware/software; wireless hotspots; broadband connectivity; Internet usage; online purchases. *Symantec, "Riskiest Online Cities of 2012" February 15, 2012*

- Farmers Insurance, in partnership with Sperling's BestPlaces, ranked metro areas in the U.S. and identified the "Most Secure Places to Live." The Dallas-Fort Worth metro area ranked #10 out of the top 20 in the large metro area category (500,000 or more residents). Criteria: economic stability; crime statistics; extreme weather; risk of natural disasters; housing depreciation; foreclosures; air quality; environmental hazards; life expectancy; motor vehicle fatalities; and employment numbers. *Farmers Insurance Group of Companies, "Most Secure U.S. Places to Live in the U.S.," June 25, 2013*

- Allstate ranked the 200 largest cities in America in terms of driver safety. Dallas ranked #170. Allstate researchers analyzed internal property damage claims over a two-year period from January 2010 to December 2011. A weighted average of the two-year numbers determined the annual percentages. *Allstate, "Allstate America's Best Drivers Report®, August 27, 2013"*

- Dallas was identified as one of the most dangerous large cities in America by CQ Press. All 32 cities with populations of 500,000 or more that reported crime rates in 2012 for murder, rape, robbery, aggravated assault, burglary, and motor vehicle thefts were ranked. The city ranked #10 out of the top 10. *CQ Press, City Crime Rankings 2014*

- The National Insurance Crime Bureau ranked 380 metro areas in the U.S. in terms of per capita rates of vehicle theft. The Dallas-Fort Worth metro area ranked #68 (#1 = highest rate). Criteria: number of vehicle theft offenses per 100,000 inhabitants in 2012. *National Insurance Crime Bureau, "Hot Spots 2012," June 26, 2013*

- The Dallas-Fort Worth metro area was identified as one of the most dangerous metro areas for pedestrians by Transportation for America. The metro area ranked #10 out of 52 metro areas with over 1 million residents. Criteria: area's population divided by the number of pedestrian fatalities in that area. *Transportation for America, "Dangerous by Design 2011"*

Seniors/Retirement Rankings

- From its Best Cities for Successful Aging indexes, the Milken Institute generated rankings for metropolitan areas, weighing data in eight categories—general indicators, health care, wellness, living arrangements, transportation and general accessibility, financial well-being, education and employment, and community participation. The Dallas-Fort Worth metro area was ranked #73 overall in the large metro area category. *Milken Institute, "Best Cities for Successful Aging," July 2012*

- Bankers Life and Casualty Company, in partnership with Sperling's BestPlaces, ranked the nation's 50 largest metro areas in terms of the "Best U.S. Cities for Seniors." The Dallas-Fort Worth metro area ranked #29. Criteria: healthcare; transportation; housing; environment; economy; health and longevity; social and spiritual life; crime. *Bankers Life and Casualty Company, Center for a Secure Retirement, "Best U.S. Cities for Seniors 2011," September 2011*

Sports/Recreation Rankings

- According to the personal finance website NerdWallet, the Dallas-Fort Worth metro area, at #1, is one of the nation's top dozen metro areas for sports fans. Criteria included the presence of all four major sports—MLB, NFL, NHL, and NBA, fan enthusiasm (as measured by game attendance), ticket affordability, and "sports culture," that is, number of sports bars. *www.nerdwallet.com, "Best Cities for Sports Fans," May 5, 2013*

- The sports site Bleacher Report named Dallas as one of the nation's top ten golf cities. Criteria included the concentration of public and private golf courses in a given city and the favored locations of PGA tour events. *BleacherReport.com, "Top 10 U.S. Cities for Golf," September 16, 2013*

- Dallas appeared on the *Sporting News* list of the "Best Sports Cities" for 2011. The area ranked #1 out of 271. Criteria: the magazine takes a 12-month snapshot of each city's sports, putting a heavy premium on regular-season won-lost records (from the most recently completed season). Other criteria include: playoff berths, bowl appearances and tournament bids; championships; applicable power ratings; quality of competition; overall fan fervor (measured in part by attendance); abundance of teams (rewarding quality over quantity); stadium and arena quality; ticket availability and prices; franchise ownership; and marquee appeal of athletes. *Sporting News, "Best Sports Cities 2011," October 4, 2011*

- Dallas appeared on the *Sporting News* list of the "Best Sports Cities" for 2011. The area ranked #1 out of 271. Criteria: a 12-month snapshot of regular-season won-lost records (from the most recently completed season). Other criteria include: playoff berths, bowl appearances and tournament bids; championships; applicable power ratings; quality of competition; overall fan fervor (measured in part by attendance); abundance of teams (quality over quantity); stadium and arena quality; ticket availability and prices; franchise ownership; and marquee appeal of athletes. *Sporting News, "Best Sports Cities 2011," October 4, 2011*

- The Dallas-Fort Worth was selected as one of the best metro areas for golf in America by *Golf Digest*. The Dallas-Fort Worth area was ranked #1 out of 20. Criteria: climate; cost of public golf; quality of public golf; accessibility. *Golf Digest, "The Top 20 Cities for Golf," October 2011*

Women/Minorities Rankings

- To determine the best metro areas for working women, the personal finance website NerdWallet considered city size as well as relevant economic metrics—high salaries, narrow pay differential by gender, prevalence of women in the highest-paying industries, and population growth over 2010–2012. Of the large U.S. cities examined, the Dallas-Fort Worth metro area held the #5 position. *www.nerdwallet.com, "Best Places for Women in the Workforce," May 19, 2013*

- *Women's Health* examined U.S. cities and identified the 100 best cities for women. Dallas was ranked #53. Criteria: 30 categories were examined from obesity and breast cancer rates to commuting times and hours spent working out. *Women's Health, "Best Cities for Women 2012"*

- Dallas was selected as one of the 25 healthiest cities for Latinas by *Latina Magazine*. The city ranked #7. Criteria: U.S. cities with populations over 500,000 residents were evaluated on the following criteria: percentage of 18-34 year-olds per city; Latino college graduation rates; number of colleges and universities; affordability; housing costs; income growth over time; average salary; percentage of singles; climate; safety; how the city's diversity compares to the national average; opportunities for minority entrepreneurs. *Latina Magazine, "Top 15 U.S. Cities for Young Latinos to Live In," August 19, 2011*

- Dallas was selected as one of the best cities for young Latinos in 2013 by mun2, a national cable television broadcast network. The city ranked #8. Criteria: U.S. cities with populations over 500,000 residents were evaluated on the following criteria: number of young latinos; jobs; friendliness; cost of living; fun. *mun2.tv, "Best Cities for Young Latinos 2013*

- The Dallas-Fort Worth metro area appeared on *Forbes'* list of the "Best Cities for Minority Entrepreneurs." The area ranked #8 out of 10. Criteria: 52 metropolitan statistical areas were examined. For each ethnicity (African Americans, Asians and Hispanics), the editors measured housing affordability, population growth, income growth, and entrepreneurship (per capita self-employment). *Forbes, "Best Cities for Minority Entrepreneurs," March 23, 2011*

Miscellaneous Rankings

- The watchdog site Charity Navigator conducts an annual study of charities in the nation's major markets both to analyze statistical differences in their financial, accountability, and transparency practices and to track year-to-year variations in individual communities. The Dallas-Fort Worth metro area was ranked #14 among the 30 metro markets. *www.charitynavigator.org, "Metro Market Study 2013," June 1, 2013*

- The Harris Poll's Happiness Index survey revealed that of the top ten U.S. markets, the Dallas-Fort Worth metro area residents ranked #1 in happiness. Criteria included strong assent to positive statements and strong disagreement with negative ones, and degree of agreement with a series of statements about respondents' personal relationships and general outlook. The online survey was conducted between July 14 and July 30, 2013. *www.harrisinteractive.com, "Dallas/Fort Worth Is "Happiest" City among America's Top Ten Markets," September 4, 2013*

- *Men's Health* ranked 100 U.S. cities by their level of sadness. Dallas was ranked #48 (#1 = saddest city). Criteria: suicide rates; unemployment rates; percentage of households that use antidepressants; percent of population who report feeling blue all or most of the time. *Men's Health, "Frown Towns," November 28, 2011*

- Mars Chocolate North America, the makers of COMBOS®, in partnership with Sperling's BestPlaces, ranked 50 major metro areas in terms of their "manliness." The Dallas-Fort Worth metro area ranked #15. Criteria: number of professional sports teams; number of nearby NASCAR tracks and racing events; manly lifestyle; concentration of manly retail stores; manly occupations per capita; salty snack sales; "Board of Manliness" rankings. *Mars Chocolate North America, "America's Manliest Cities 2012"*

- The National Alliance to End Homelessness ranked the 100 most populous metro areas in terms the rate of homelessness. The Dallas-Fort Worth metro area ranked #87. Criteria: number of homeless people per 10,000 population in 2011. *National Alliance to End Homelessness, The State of Homelessness in America 2012*

Business Environment

CITY FINANCES

City Government Finances

Component	2011 ($000)	2011 ($ per capita)
Total Revenues	3,180,623	2,564
Total Expenditures	3,099,794	2,499
Debt Outstanding	8,939,194	7,206
Cash and Securities[1]	11,371,802	9,167

Note: (1) Cash and security holdings of a government at the close of its fiscal year, including those of its dependent agencies, utilities, and liquor stores.
Source: U.S Census Bureau, State & Local Government Finances 2011

City Government Revenue by Source

Source	2011 ($000)	2011 ($ per capita)
General Revenue		
From Federal Government	61,842	50
From State Government	86,342	70
From Local Governments	10,515	8
Taxes		
Property	660,958	533
Sales and Gross Receipts	354,834	286
Personal Income	0	0
Corporate Income	0	0
Motor Vehicle License	0	0
Other Taxes	31,370	25
Current Charges	1,077,389	869
Liquor Store	0	0
Utility	278,419	224
Employee Retirement	465,188	375

Source: U.S Census Bureau, State & Local Government Finances 2011

City Government Expenditures by Function

Function	2011 ($000)	2011 ($ per capita)	2011 (%)
General Direct Expenditures			
Air Transportation	475,975	384	15.4
Corrections	2,008	2	0.1
Education	0	0	0.0
Employment Security Administration	0	0	0.0
Financial Administration	30,584	25	1.0
Fire Protection	189,706	153	6.1
General Public Buildings	25,016	20	0.8
Governmental Administration, Other	13,715	11	0.4
Health	26,688	22	0.9
Highways	143,389	116	4.6
Hospitals	0	0	0.0
Housing and Community Development	44,266	36	1.4
Interest on General Debt	376,522	304	12.1
Judicial and Legal	23,776	19	0.8
Libraries	36,421	29	1.2
Parking	160	< 1	< 0.1
Parks and Recreation	193,032	156	6.2
Police Protection	377,523	304	12.2
Public Welfare	15,874	13	0.5
Sewerage	220,904	178	7.1
Solid Waste Management	67,993	55	2.2
Veterans' Services	0	0	0.0
Liquor Store	0	0	0.0
Utility	320,429	258	10.3
Employee Retirement	375,004	302	12.1

Source: U.S Census Bureau, State & Local Government Finances 2011

DEMOGRAPHICS

Population Growth

Area	1990 Census	2000 Census	2010 Census	Population Growth (%)	
				1990-2000	2000-2010
City	1,006,971	1,188,580	1,197,816	18.0	0.8
MSA[1]	3,989,294	5,161,544	6,371,773	29.4	23.4
U.S.	248,709,873	281,421,906	308,745,538	13.2	9.7

Note: (1) Figures cover the Dallas-Fort Worth-Arlington, TX Metropolitan Statistical Area—see Appendix B for areas included
Source: U.S. Census Bureau, Census 1990, 2000, 2010

Household Size

Area	Persons in Household (%)							Average Household Size
	One	Two	Three	Four	Five	Six	Seven or More	
City	34.7	28.1	13.8	11.5	6.6	3.0	2.3	2.63
MSA[1]	25.3	30.4	16.7	15.1	7.6	3.0	1.9	2.80
U.S.	27.6	33.5	15.7	13.2	6.1	2.4	1.5	2.63

Note: (1) Figures cover the Dallas-Fort Worth-Arlington, TX Metropolitan Statistical Area—see Appendix B for areas included
Source: U.S. Census Bureau, 2010-2012 American Community Survey 3-Year Estimates

Race

Area	White Alone[2] (%)	Black Alone[2] (%)	Asian Alone[2] (%)	AIAN[3] Alone[2] (%)	NHOPI[4] Alone[2] (%)	Other Race Alone[2] (%)	Two or More Races (%)
City	56.5	24.4	2.9	0.3	0.0	13.8	2.0
MSA[1]	69.2	15.0	5.5	0.5	0.1	7.1	2.6
U.S.	74.0	12.6	4.9	0.8	0.2	4.7	2.8

Note: (1) Figures cover the Dallas-Fort Worth-Arlington, TX Metropolitan Statistical Area—see Appendix B for areas included; (2) Alone is defined as not being in combination with one or more other races; (3) American Indian and Alaska Native; (4) Native Hawaiian and Other Pacific Islander
Source: U.S. Census Bureau, 2010-2012 American Community Survey 3-Year Estimates

Hispanic or Latino Origin

Area	Total (%)	Mexican (%)	Puerto Rican (%)	Cuban (%)	Other (%)
City	42.2	37.5	0.3	0.2	4.3
MSA[1]	27.8	23.8	0.5	0.2	3.3
U.S.	16.6	10.7	1.6	0.6	3.7

Note: Persons of Hispanic or Latino origin can be of any race; (1) Figures cover the Dallas-Fort Worth-Arlington, TX Metropolitan Statistical Area—see Appendix B for areas included
Source: U.S. Census Bureau, 2010-2012 American Community Survey 3-Year Estimates

Segregation

Type	Segregation Indices[1]				Percent Change		
	1990	2000	2010	2010 Rank[2]	1990-2000	1990-2010	2000-2010
Black/White	62.8	59.8	56.6	48	-3.1	-6.2	-3.2
Asian/White	41.8	45.6	46.6	19	3.8	4.8	1.0
Hispanic/White	48.8	52.3	50.3	24	3.5	1.5	-2.0

Note: All figures cover the Metropolitan Statistical Area—see Appendix B for areas included; Figures are based on an analysis of 1990, 2000, and 2010 Census Decennial Census tract data by William H. Frey, Brookings Institution and the University of Michigan Social Science Data Analysis Network. In this analysis all racial groups (whites, blacks, and asians) are non-Hispanic members of those races. Hispanics are shown as a separate category;
(1) Segregation Indices are Dissimilarity Indices that measure the degree to which the minority group is distributed differently than whites across census tracts. They range from 0 (complete integration) to 100 (complete segregation) where the value indicates the percentage of the minority group that needs to move to be distributed exactly like whites; (2) Ranges from 1 (most segregated) to 102 (least segregated); n/a not available.
Source: www.CensusScope.org

Ancestry

Area	German	Irish	English	American	Italian	Polish	French[2]	Scottish	Dutch
City	5.9	4.4	5.0	3.2	1.4	0.8	1.4	1.1	0.5
MSA[1]	10.5	8.2	7.6	6.8	2.2	1.1	2.0	1.7	1.0
U.S.	15.2	11.1	8.2	7.2	5.6	3.1	2.8	1.7	1.4

Note: Figures are the percentage of the total population reporting a particular ancestry. The nine most commonly reported ancestries in the U.S. are shown. Figures include multiple ancestries (e.g. if a person reported being Irish and Italian, they were included in both columns); (1) Figures cover the Dallas-Fort Worth-Arlington, TX Metropolitan Statistical Area—see Appendix B for areas included; (2) Excludes Basque
Source: U.S. Census Bureau, 2010-2012 American Community Survey 3-Year Estimates

Foreign-Born Population

Area	Percent of Population Born in								
	Any Foreign Country	Mexico	Asia	Europe	Carribean	South America	Central America[2]	Africa	Canada
City	24.8	17.1	2.6	0.8	0.2	0.5	2.2	1.3	0.2
MSA[1]	17.6	9.2	4.3	0.8	0.2	0.5	1.3	1.0	0.2
U.S.	13.0	3.7	3.7	1.6	1.2	0.9	1.0	0.5	0.3

Note: (1) Figures cover the Dallas-Fort Worth-Arlington, TX Metropolitan Statistical Area—see Appendix B for areas included; (2) Excludes Mexico.
Source: U.S. Census Bureau, 2010-2012 American Community Survey 3-Year Estimates

Marital Status

Area	Never Married	Now Married[2]	Separated	Widowed	Divorced
City	40.5	39.7	3.6	4.9	11.3
MSA[1]	31.2	50.7	2.6	4.5	11.1
U.S.	32.4	48.4	2.2	6.0	11.0

Note: Figures are percentages and cover the population 15 years of age and older; (1) Figures cover the Dallas-Fort Worth-Arlington, TX Metropolitan Statistical Area—see Appendix B for areas included; (2) Excludes separated
Source: U.S. Census Bureau, 2010-2012 American Community Survey 3-Year Estimates

Age

Area	Percent of Population									Median Age
	Under Age 5	Age 5–19	Age 20–34	Age 35–44	Age 45–54	Age 55–64	Age 65–74	Age 75–84	Age 85+	
City	8.3	20.4	26.4	13.9	12.5	9.4	5.1	2.8	1.3	31.9
MSA[1]	7.6	22.6	21.6	14.8	14.1	10.2	5.4	2.7	1.0	33.7
U.S.	6.4	20.1	20.5	13.1	14.3	12.2	7.3	4.2	1.8	37.3

Note: (1) Figures cover the Dallas-Fort Worth-Arlington, TX Metropolitan Statistical Area—see Appendix B for areas included
Source: U.S. Census Bureau, 2010-2012 American Community Survey 3-Year Estimates

Gender

Area	Males	Females	Males per 100 Females
City	612,684	607,195	100.9
MSA[1]	3,216,334	3,303,515	97.4
U.S.	153,276,055	158,333,314	96.8

Note: (1) Figures cover the Dallas-Fort Worth-Arlington, TX Metropolitan Statistical Area—see Appendix B for areas included
Source: U.S. Census Bureau, 2010-2012 American Community Survey 3-Year Estimates

Religious Groups by Family

Area	Catholic	Baptist	Non-Den.	Methodist[2]	Lutheran	LDS[3]	Pentecostal	Presbyterian[4]	Muslim[5]	Judaism
MSA[1]	13.3	18.7	7.8	5.3	0.8	1.2	2.2	1.0	2.4	0.4
U.S.	19.1	9.3	4.0	4.0	2.3	2.0	1.9	1.6	0.8	0.7

Note: Figures are the number of adherents as a percentage of the total population; (1) Figures cover the Dallas-Fort Worth-Arlington, TX Metropolitan Statistical Area—see Appendix B for areas included; (2) Methodist/Pietist; (3) Latter Day Saints; (4) Reformed; (5) Figures are estimates
Source: Association of Statisticians of American Religious Bodies, 2010 U.S. Religion Census: Religious Congregations & Membership Study

Religious Groups by Tradition

Area	Catholic	Evangelical Protestant	Mainline Protestant	Other Tradition	Black Protestant	Orthodox
MSA[1]	13.3	28.3	7.0	4.8	1.8	0.2
U.S.	19.1	16.2	7.3	4.3	1.6	0.3

Note: Figures are the number of adherents as a percentage of the total population; (1) Figures cover the Dallas-Fort Worth-Arlington, TX Metropolitan Statistical Area—see Appendix B for areas included
Source: Association of Statisticians of American Religious Bodies, 2010 U.S. Religion Census: Religious Congregations & Membership Study

ECONOMY

Gross Metropolitan Product

Area	2011	2012	2013	2014	Rank[2]
MSA[1]	397.0	418.6	436.4	460.9	6

Note: Figures are in billions of dollars; (1) Figures cover the Dallas-Fort Worth-Arlington, TX Metropolitan Statistical Area—see Appendix B for areas included; (2) Rank is based on 2014 data and ranges from 1 to 363
Source: The United States Conference of Mayors, U.S. Metro Economies: Outlook—Gross Metropolitan Product, with Metro Employment Projections, November 2013

Economic Growth

Area	2011 (%)	2012 (%)	2013 (%)	2014 (%)	Rank[2]
MSA[1]	3.2	4.3	3.0	3.7	25
U.S.	1.6	2.5	1.7	2.5	–

Note: Figures are real gross metropolitan product (GMP) growth rates and represent annual average percent change; (1) Figures cover the Dallas-Fort Worth-Arlington, TX Metropolitan Statistical Area—see Appendix B for areas included; (2) Rank is based on 2013 data and ranges from 1 to 363
Source: The United States Conference of Mayors, U.S. Metro Economies: Outlook—Gross Metropolitan Product, with Metro Employment Projections, November 2013

Metropolitan Area Exports

Area	2007	2008	2009	2010	2011	2012	Rank[2]
MSA[1]	22,079.1	22,503.7	19,881.8	22,500.4	26,648.7	27,820.9	8

Note: Figures are in millions of dollars; (1) Figures cover the Dallas-Fort Worth-Arlington, TX Metropolitan Statistical Area—see Appendix B for areas included; (2) Rank is based on 2012 data and ranges from 1 to 369
Source: U.S. Department of Commerce, International Trade Administration, Office of Trade & Industry Information, Manufacturing & Services, data extracted April 1, 2014

INCOME

Income

Area	Per Capita ($)	Median Household ($)	Average Household ($)
City	26,294	41,745	67,684
MSA[1]	28,421	57,109	78,238
U.S.	27,385	51,771	71,579

Note: (1) Figures cover the Dallas-Fort Worth-Arlington, TX Metropolitan Statistical Area—see Appendix B for areas included
Source: U.S. Census Bureau, 2010-2012 American Community Survey 3-Year Estimates

Household Income Distribution

Area	Percent of Households Earning							
	Under $15,000	$15,000 -24,999	$25,000 -34,999	$35,000 -49,999	$50,000 -74,999	$75,000 -99,000	$100,000 -149,999	$150,000 and up
City	16.4	12.9	13.1	14.6	17.1	8.3	8.7	8.9
MSA[1]	10.4	9.7	10.2	13.6	18.5	12.1	14.4	11.0
U.S.	13.1	11.0	10.5	13.7	18.1	11.9	12.5	9.1

Note: (1) Figures cover the Dallas-Fort Worth-Arlington, TX Metropolitan Statistical Area—see Appendix B for areas included
Source: U.S. Census Bureau, 2010-2012 American Community Survey 3-Year Estimates

Poverty Rate

Area	All Ages	Under 18 Years Old	18 to 64 Years Old	65 Years and Over
City	24.2	37.9	19.9	15.4
MSA[1]	15.1	21.8	13.0	9.0
U.S.	15.7	22.2	14.6	9.3

Note: Figures are percentage of people whose income during the past 12 months was below the poverty level; (1) Figures cover the Dallas-Fort Worth-Arlington, TX Metropolitan Statistical Area—see Appendix B for areas included
Source: U.S. Census Bureau, 2010-2012 American Community Survey 3-Year Estimates

Personal Bankruptcy Filing Rate

Area	2008	2009	2010	2011	2012	2013
Dallas County	2.39	2.90	2.86	2.64	2.74	2.20
U.S.	3.53	4.61	4.97	4.37	3.76	3.29

Note: Numbers are per 1,000 population and include Chapter 7 and Chapter 13 filings
Source: Federal Deposit Insurance Corporation, Regional Economic Conditions, March 20, 2014

EMPLOYMENT

Labor Force and Employment

Area	Civilian Labor Force			Workers Employed		
	Dec. 2012	Dec. 2013	% Chg.	Dec. 2012	Dec. 2013	% Chg.
City	586,561	596,415	1.7	549,042	561,247	2.2
MD[1]	2,245,884	2,285,469	1.8	2,113,329	2,160,308	2.2
U.S.	154,904,000	154,408,000	-0.3	143,060,000	144,423,000	1.0

Note: Data is not seasonally adjusted and covers workers 16 years of age and older; (1) Metropolitan Division—see Appendix B for areas included
Source: Bureau of Labor Statistics, Local Area Unemployment Statistics

Unemployment Rate

Area	2013											
	Jan.	Feb.	Mar.	Apr.	May	Jun.	Jul.	Aug.	Sep.	Oct.	Nov.	Dec.
City	7.3	6.9	6.7	6.5	6.9	7.2	6.9	6.5	6.7	6.4	6.1	5.9
MD[1]	6.7	6.4	6.2	6.0	6.3	6.7	6.4	6.0	6.1	5.9	5.7	5.5
U.S.	8.5	8.1	7.6	7.1	7.3	7.8	7.7	7.3	7.0	7.0	6.6	6.5

Note: Data is not seasonally adjusted and covers workers 16 years of age and older; All figures are percentages; (1) Metropolitan Division—see Appendix B for areas included
Source: Bureau of Labor Statistics, Local Area Unemployment Statistics

Employment by Occupation

Occupation Classification	City (%)	MSA[1] (%)	U.S. (%)
Management, Business, Science, and Arts	32.4	37.3	36.0
Natural Resources, Construction, and Maintenance	12.3	9.5	9.1
Production, Transportation, and Material Moving	12.4	11.5	12.0
Sales and Office	23.2	25.7	24.7
Service	19.7	15.9	18.2

Note: Figures cover employed civilians 16 years of age and older; (1) Figures cover the Dallas-Fort Worth-Arlington, TX Metropolitan Statistical Area—see Appendix B for areas included
Source: U.S. Census Bureau, 2010-2012 American Community Survey 3-Year Estimates

Employment by Industry

Sector	MD[1]		U.S.
	Number of Employees	Percent of Total	Percent of Total
Construction	n/a	n/a	4.2
Education and Health Services	269,600	12.2	15.5
Financial Activities	197,400	9.0	5.7
Government	272,700	12.4	16.1
Information	67,000	3.0	1.9
Leisure and Hospitality	213,600	9.7	10.2
Manufacturing	163,500	7.4	8.7
Mining and Logging	n/a	n/a	0.6
Other Services	76,600	3.5	3.9
Professional and Business Services	384,700	17.4	13.7
Retail Trade	230,900	10.5	11.4
Transportation and Utilities	86,000	3.9	3.8
Wholesale Trade	129,100	5.9	4.2

Note: Figures cover non-farm employment as of December 2013 and are not seasonally adjusted;
(1) Metropolitan Division—see Appendix B for areas included; n/a not available
Source: Bureau of Labor Statistics, Current Employment Statistics, Employment, Hours, and Earnings

Occupations with Greatest Projected Employment Growth: 2010 – 2020

Occupation[1]	2010 Employment	2020 Projected Employment	Numeric Employment Change	Percent Employment Change
Combined Food Preparation and Serving Workers, Including Fast Food	243,530	322,520	78,990	32.4
Elementary School Teachers, Except Special Education	166,090	233,860	67,780	40.8
Personal Care Aides	133,820	199,970	66,150	49.4
Retail Salespersons	370,620	433,180	62,560	16.9
Registered Nurses	184,700	245,870	61,160	33.1
Waiters and Waitresses	190,870	244,610	53,730	28.2
Office Clerks, General	262,740	314,810	52,070	19.8
Cashiers	250,510	292,730	42,220	16.9
Home Health Aides	82,420	123,970	41,550	50.4
Customer Service Representatives	200,880	241,030	40,160	20.0

Note: Projections cover Texas; (1) Sorted by numeric employment change
Source: www.projectionscentral.com, State Occupational Projections, 2010–2020 Long-Term Projections

Fastest Growing Occupations: 2010 – 2020

Occupation[1]	2010 Employment	2020 Projected Employment	Numeric Employment Change	Percent Employment Change
Biomedical Engineers	1,440	2,490	1,050	72.9
Diagnostic Medical Sonographers	3,560	5,410	1,850	51.9
Derrick Operators, Oil and Gas	7,190	10,860	3,670	51.1
Home Health Aides	82,420	123,970	41,550	50.4
Personal Care Aides	133,820	199,970	66,150	49.4
Service Unit Operators, Oil, Gas, and Mining	17,870	26,460	8,590	48.0
Special Education Teachers, Middle School	6,170	8,950	2,780	45.1
Special Education Teachers, Preschool, Kindergarten, and Elementary School	12,940	18,750	5,810	44.9
Rotary Drill Operators, Oil and Gas	7,160	10,340	3,180	44.4
Roustabouts, Oil and Gas	17,800	25,580	7,790	43.8

Note: Projections cover Texas; (1) Sorted by percent employment change and excludes occupations with
numeric employment change less than 100
Source: www.projectionscentral.com, State Occupational Projections, 2010–2020 Long-Term Projections

Average Wages

Occupation	$/Hr.	Occupation	$/Hr.
Accountants and Auditors	37.07	Maids and Housekeeping Cleaners	9.06
Automotive Mechanics	19.69	Maintenance and Repair Workers	17.50
Bookkeepers	18.75	Marketing Managers	66.23
Carpenters	14.51	Nuclear Medicine Technologists	33.14
Cashiers	9.45	Nurses, Licensed Practical	22.36
Clerks, General Office	15.35	Nurses, Registered	33.65
Clerks, Receptionists/Information	12.97	Nursing Assistants	12.32
Clerks, Shipping/Receiving	14.76	Packers and Packagers, Hand	10.29
Computer Programmers	38.38	Physical Therapists	45.06
Computer Systems Analysts	41.14	Postal Service Mail Carriers	24.91
Computer User Support Specialists	23.30	Real Estate Brokers	n/a
Cooks, Restaurant	11.30	Retail Salespersons	12.58
Dentists	103.85	Sales Reps., Exc. Tech./Scientific	33.78
Electrical Engineers	46.81	Sales Reps., Tech./Scientific	36.24
Electricians	20.44	Secretaries, Exc. Legal/Med./Exec.	16.42
Financial Managers	65.14	Security Guards	13.08
First-Line Supervisors/Managers, Sales	21.17	Surgeons	95.05
Food Preparation Workers	9.81	Teacher Assistants	10.70
General and Operations Managers	63.07	Teachers, Elementary School	25.00
Hairdressers/Cosmetologists	13.42	Teachers, Secondary School	25.80
Internists	94.24	Telemarketers	n/a
Janitors and Cleaners	10.00	Truck Drivers, Heavy/Tractor-Trailer	19.20
Landscaping/Groundskeeping Workers	11.31	Truck Drivers, Light/Delivery Svcs.	15.72
Lawyers	65.75	Waiters and Waitresses	10.24

Note: Wage data covers the Dallas-Plano-Irving, TX Metropolitan Division—see Appendix B for areas included.
Hourly wages for elementary/secondary school teachers and teacher assistants were calculated by the editors
from annual wage data assuming a 40 hour work week; n/a not available.
Source: Bureau of Labor Statistics, Metro Area Occupational Employment and Wage Estimates, May 2013

RESIDENTIAL REAL ESTATE

Building Permits

Area	Single-Family			Multi-Family			Total		
	2012	2013	Pct. Chg.	2012	2013	Pct. Chg.	2012	2013	Pct. Chg.
City	936	1,075	14.9	6,149	7,559	22.9	7,085	8,634	21.9
MSA[1]	18,090	21,224	17.3	16,952	16,686	-1.6	35,042	37,910	8.2
U.S.	518,695	620,802	19.7	310,963	370,020	19.0	829,658	990,822	19.4

Note: (1) Metropolitan Statistical Area—see Appendix B for areas included; figures represent new, privately-
owned housing units authorized (unadjusted data); All permit data are based on estimates with imputation.
Source: U.S. Census Bureau, Manufacturing, Mining, and Construction Statistics, Building Permits, 2012, 2013

Homeownership Rate

Area	2006 (%)	2007 (%)	2008 (%)	2009 (%)	2010 (%)	2011 (%)	2012 (%)	2013 (%)
MSA[1]	60.7	60.9	60.9	61.6	63.8	62.6	61.8	59.9
U.S.	68.8	68.1	67.8	67.4	66.9	66.1	65.4	65.1

Note: (1) Figures cover the Dallas-Fort Worth-Arlington, TX Metropolitan Statistical Area—see Appendix B for
areas included
Source: U.S. Census Bureau, Housing Vacancies and Homeownership Annual Statistics: 2013

Housing Vacancy Rates

Area	Gross Vacancy Rate[2] (%)			Year-Round Vacancy Rate[3] (%)			Rental Vacancy Rate[4] (%)			Homeowner Vacancy Rate[5] (%)		
	2011	2012	2013	2011	2012	2013	2011	2012	2013	2011	2012	2013
MSA[1]	9.8	8.7	9.0	9.6	8.4	8.8	11.8	9.2	8.2	2.0	2.1	1.9
U.S.	14.2	13.8	13.8	11.1	10.8	10.7	9.5	8.7	8.3	2.5	2.0	2.0

Note: (1) Figures cover the Dallas-Fort Worth-Arlington, TX Metropolitan Statistical Area—see Appendix B for
areas included; (2) The percentage of the total housing inventory that is vacant; (3) The percentage of the
housing inventory (excluding seasonal units) that is year-round vacant; (4) The percentage of rental inventory
that is vacant for rent; (5) The percentage of homeowner inventory that is vacant for sale
Source: U.S. Census Bureau, Housing Vacancies and Homeownership Annual Statistics: 2013

TAXES

State Corporate Income Tax Rates

State	Tax Rate (%)	Income Brackets ($)	Num. of Brackets	Financial Institution Tax Rate (%)[a]	Federal Income Tax Ded.
Texas	(x)	–	–	(x)	No

Note: Tax rates as of January 1, 2014; (a) Rates listed are the corporate income tax rate applied to financial institutions or excise taxes based on income. Some states have other taxes based upon the value of deposits or shares; (x) Texas imposes a Franchise Tax, otherwise known as margin tax, imposed on entities with more than $1,030,000 total revenues at rate of 1%, or 0.5% for entities primarily engaged in retail or wholesale trade, on lesser of 70% of total revenues or 100% of gross receipts after deductions for either compensation or cost of goods sold.
Source: Federation of Tax Administrators, "State Corporate Income Tax Rates, 2014"

State Individual Income Tax Rates

State	Tax Rate (%)	Income Brackets ($)	Num. of Brackets	Personal Exempt. ($)[1] Single	Personal Exempt. ($)[1] Dependents	Fed. Inc. Tax Ded.
Texas	None	–	–	–	–	–

Note: Tax rates as of January 1, 2014; Local- and county-level taxes are not included; n/a not applicable;
(1) Married joint filers generally receive double the single exemption
Source: Federation of Tax Administrators, "State Individual Income Tax Rates, 2014"

Various State and Local Tax Rates

State	State and Local Sales and Use (%)	State Sales and Use (%)	Gasoline[1] (¢/gal.)	Cigarette[2] ($/pack)	Spirits[3] ($/gal.)	Wine[4] ($/gal.)	Beer[5] ($/gal.)
Texas	8.25	6.25	20.00	1.410	2.40 (f)	0.20	0.20

Note: All tax rates as of January 1, 2014; (1) The American Petroleum Institute has developed a methodology for determining the average tax rate on a gallon of fuel. Rates may include any of the following: excise taxes, environmental fees, storage tank fees, other fees or taxes, general sales tax, and local taxes. In states where gasoline is subject to the general sales tax, or where the fuel tax is based on the average sale price, the average rate determined by API is sensitive to changes in the price of gasoline. States that fully or partially apply general sales taxes to gasoline: CA, CO, GA, IL, IN, MI, NY; (2) The federal excise tax of $1.0066 per pack and local taxes are not included; (3) Rates are those applicable to off-premise sales of 40% alcohol by volume (a.b.v.) distilled spirits in 750ml containers. Local excise taxes are excluded; (4) Rates are those applicable to off-premise sales of 11% a.b.v. non-carbonated wine in 750ml containers; (5) Rates are those applicable to off-premise sales of 4.7% a.b.v. beer in 12 ounce containers; (f) Different rates also applicable according to alcohol content, place of production, size of container, or place purchased (on- or off-premise or onboard airlines).
Source: Tax Foundation, 2014 Facts & Figures: How Does Your State Compare?

State Business Tax Climate Index Rankings

State	Overall Rank	Corporate Tax Index Rank	Individual Income Tax Index Rank	Sales Tax Index Rank	Unemployment Insurance Tax Index Rank	Property Tax Index Rank
Texas	11	38	7	36	14	35

Note: The index is a measure of how each state's tax laws affect economic performance. The lower the rank, the more favorable a state's tax system is for business. States without a given tax are given a ranking of 1. The scores/rankings for the District of Columbia do not affect other states. The 2014 index represents the tax climate as of July 1, 2013.
Source: Tax Foundation, State Business Tax Climate Index 2014

COMMERCIAL REAL ESTATE

Office Market

Market Area	Inventory (sq. ft.)	Vacancy Rate (%)	Under Construction (sq. ft.)	YTD Net Absorption (sq. ft.)	Total Average Asking Rent ($/sq. ft./year)
Dallas-Fort Worth	230,553,509	19.0	4,635,881	3,337,229	20.73
National	4,726,900,879	15.0	55,419,286	42,829,434	26.27

Source: Newmark Grubb Knight Frank, National Office Market Report, 4th Quarter 2013

Industrial/Warehouse/R&D Market

Market Area	Inventory (sq. ft.)	Vacancy Rate (%)	Under Construction (sq. ft.)	YTD Net Absorption (sq. ft.)	Total Average Asking Rent ($/sq. ft./year)
Dallas-Fort Worth	744,670,654	7.1	10,438,464	16,953,296	5.10
National	14,022,031,238	7.9	83,249,164	156,549,903	5.40

Source: Newmark Grubb Knight Frank, National Industrial Market Report, 4th Quarter 2013

COMMERCIAL UTILITIES

Typical Monthly Electric Bills

Area	Commercial Service ($/month)		Industrial Service ($/month)	
	1,500 kWh	40 kW demand 14,000 kWh	1,000 kW demand 200,000 kWh	50,000 kW demand 15,000,000 kWh
City	n/a	n/a	n/a	n/a
Average[1]	197	1,636	25,662	1,485,307

Note: Based on total rates in effect July 1, 2013; (1) average based on 180 utilities surveyed; n/a not available
Source: Edison Electric Institute, Typical Bills and Average Rates Report, Summer 2013

TRANSPORTATION

Means of Transportation to Work

Area	Car/Truck/Van		Public Transportation			Bicycle	Walked	Other Means	Worked at Home
	Drove Alone	Car-pooled	Bus	Subway	Railroad				
City	77.7	10.7	3.3	0.3	0.3	0.2	1.8	1.6	4.1
MSA[1]	81.1	10.2	1.0	0.1	0.3	0.2	1.2	1.3	4.6
U.S.	76.4	9.7	2.6	1.7	0.5	0.6	2.8	1.3	4.3

Note: Figures are percentages and cover workers 16 years of age and older; (1) Figures cover the Dallas-Fort Worth-Arlington, TX Metropolitan Statistical Area—see Appendix B for areas included
Source: U.S. Census Bureau, 2010-2012 American Community Survey 3-Year Estimates

Travel Time to Work

Area	Less Than 10 Minutes	10 to 19 Minutes	20 to 29 Minutes	30 to 44 Minutes	45 to 59 Minutes	60 to 89 Minutes	90 Minutes or More
City	9.0	29.6	23.1	25.3	7.0	4.4	1.7
MSA[1]	10.0	26.7	21.3	25.1	9.5	5.6	1.8
U.S.	13.5	29.8	20.9	20.1	7.5	5.6	2.5

Note: Figures are percentages and include workers 16 years old and over; (1) Figures cover the Dallas-Fort Worth-Arlington, TX Metropolitan Statistical Area—see Appendix B for areas included
Source: U.S. Census Bureau, 2010-2012 American Community Survey 3-Year Estimates

Travel Time Index

Area	1985	1990	1995	2000	2005	2010	2011
Urban Area[1]	1.08	1.12	1.16	1.22	1.30	1.25	1.26
Average[2]	1.09	1.14	1.16	1.19	1.23	1.18	1.18

Note: Travel Time Index—the ratio of travel time in the peak period to the travel time at free-flow conditions. For example, a value of 1.30 indicates a 20-minute free-flow trip takes 26 minutes in the peak. Free-flow speeds (60 mph on freeways and 35 mph on principal arterials) are used as the comparison threshold; (1) Covers the Dallas-Fort Worth-Arlington TX urban area; (2) average of 498 urban areas
Source: Texas Transportation Institute, Urban Mobility Report 2012, December 2012

Public Transportation

Agency Name / Mode of Transportation	Vehicles Operated in Maximum Service	Annual Unlinked Passenger Trips (in thous.)	Annual Passenger Miles (in thous.)
Dallas Area Rapid Transit Authority (DART)			
Bus (directly operated)	509	38,378.9	161,289.3
Commuter Rail (purchased transportation)	23	2,252.1	43,186.4
Demand Response (purchased transportation)	200	1,141.0	12,798.9
Light Rail (directly operated)	100	27,653.9	214,583.6
Vanpool (directly operated)	198	1,033.0	40,576.3

Source: Federal Transit Administration, National Transit Database, 2012

Air Transportation

Airport Name and Code / Type of Service	Passenger Airlines[1]	Passenger Enplanements	Freight Carriers[2]	Freight (lbs.)
Dallas-Fort Worth International (DFW)				
Domestic service (U.S. carriers - 2013)	26	25,820,977	20	328,889,605
International service (U.S. carriers - 2012)	11	2,426,715	4	66,271,050
Dallas Love Field (DAL)				
Domestic service (U.S. carriers - 2013)	18	4,016,160	8	9,764,315
International service (U.S. carriers - 2012)	7	1,563	2	69,530

Note: (1) Includes all U.S.-based major, minor and commuter airlines that carried at least one passenger during the year; (2) Includes all U.S.-based airlines and freight carriers that transported at least one lb. of freight during the year.
Source: Bureau of Transportation Statistics, The Intermodal Transportation Database, Air Carriers: T-100 Domestic Market (U.S. Carriers), 2013; Bureau of Transportation Statistics, The Intermodal Transportation Database, Air Carriers: T-100 International Market (U.S. Carriers), 2012

Other Transportation Statistics

Major Highways:	I-20; I-30; I-35E; I-45
Amtrak Service:	Yes
Major Waterways/Ports:	None

Source: Amtrak.com; Google Maps

BUSINESSES

Major Business Headquarters

Company Name	Rankings	
	Fortune[1]	Forbes[2]
AT&T	11	-
Celanese	396	-
Dean Foods	217	-
Energy Future Holdings	447	63
Energy Transfer Equity	161	-
Glazer's	-	114
HollyFrontier	143	-
Hunt Consolidated/Hunt Oil	-	106
Neiman Marcus Group	-	82
Sammons Enterprises	-	123
Southwest Airlines	164	-
Tenet Healthcare	269	-
Texas Instruments	218	-

Note: (1) Fortune 500—companies that produce a 10-K are ranked 1 to 500 based on 2012 revenue; (2) all private companies with at least $2 billion in annual revenue through the end of their most current fiscal year are ranked 1 to 224; companies listed are headquartered in the city; dashes indicate no ranking Source: Fortune, "Fortune 500," May 20, 2013; Forbes, "America's Largest Private Companies," December 18, 2013

Fast-Growing Businesses

According to *Inc.*, Dallas is home to five of America's 500 fastest-growing private companies: **Apex Resources** (#143); **Dhaliwal Laboratories** (#146); **Bottle Rocket Apps** (#284); **Frontline Source Group** (#452); **Mpact Financial Group** (#500). Criteria: must be an independent, privately-held, for-profit, U.S. corporation, proprietorship or partnership; revenues must be at least $100,000 in 2009 and $2 million in 2012; must have four-year operating/sales history. Holding companies, regulated banks, and utilities were excluded. *Inc., "America's 500 Fastest-Growing Private Companies," September 2013*

According to *Fortune*, Dallas is home to three of the 100 fastest-growing companies in the world: **HollyFrontier** (#2); **Primoris Services** (#44); **Trinity Industries** (#52). Companies were ranked by their revenue growth rate; their EPS growth rate; and their three-year annualized total return to investors for the period ending June 30, 2013. Criteria for inclusion: a company, foreign or domestic, must trade on a major U.S. stock exchange; must file quarterly reports with the SEC; must have a minimum market capitalization of $250 million; must have a stock price of at least $5 on June 29, 2013; must have been trading continuously since June 30, 2009; must have revenue and net income for the four quarters ended on or before April 30, 2013, of at least $50 million and $10 million, respectively; and must have posted a compound annual growth in revenue and earnings per share of at least 20% annually over the three years ending on or before April 30, 2013. REITs, limited-liability companies, limited parterships, companies about to be acquired, and companies that lost money in the quarter ending April 30, 2013 were excluded. *Fortune, "100 Fastest-Growing Companies," August 29, 2013*

According to *Initiative for a Competitive Inner City (ICIC)*, Dallas is home to two of America's 100 fastest-growing "inner city" companies: **Aspenmark Roofing & Solar** (#9); **Xtra 21 Express Trucking** (#17). Companies were ranked by their five-year compound annual growth rate. Criteria for inclusion: company must be headquartered in or have 51 percent or more of its physical operations in an economically distressed urban area; must be an independent, for-profit corporation, partnership or proprietorship; must have 10 or more employees and have a five-year sales history that includes sales of at least $200,000 in the base year and at least $1 million in the current year with no decrease in sales over the two most recent years. *Initiative for a Competitive Inner City (ICIC), "Inner City 100 Companies, 2013"*

According to Deloitte, Dallas is home to one of North America's 500 fastest-growing high-technology companies: **One Technologies** (#306). Companies are ranked by percentage growth in revenue over a five-year period. Criteria for inclusion: company must be headquartered within North America; must own proprietary intellectual property or proprietary technology that contributes to a significant portion of the company's operating revenue, or devote a significant proportion of revenues to research and development of technology; must have been in business for a minumum of five years with 2008 operating revenues of at least $50,000 USD/CD and 2012 operating revenues of at least $5 million USD/CD. *Deloitte Touche Tohmatsu, 2013 Technology Fast 500*^{TM}

Minority Business Opportunity

Dallas is home to three companies which are on the *Black Enterprise* Industrial/Service 100 list (100 largest companies based on gross sales): **Facility Interiors** (#33); **Parrish Restaurants Ltd.** (#49); **On-Target Supplies & Logistics** (#84). Criteria: operational in previous calendar year; at least 51% black-owned and manufactures/owns the product it sells or provides industrial or consumer services. Brokerages, real estate firms and firms that provide professional services are not eligible. *Black Enterprise, B.E. 100s, 2013*

Dallas is home to two companies which are on the *Black Enterprise* Private Equity 15 list (15 largest private equity firms based on capital under management): **Pharos Capital Group** (#6); **21st Century Group** (#13). Criteria: company must be operational in previous calendar year and be at least 51% black-owned. *Black Enterprise, B.E. 100s, 2013*

Dallas is home to eight companies which are on the *Hispanic Business* 500 list (500 largest U.S. Hispanic-owned companies based on 2012 revenue): **Sun Holdings** (#21); **Pinnacle Technical Resources** (#33); **Gilbert May** (#113); **Aguirre Roden** (#175); **ROC Construction** (#271); **Alman Electric** (#285); **Pursuit of Excellence HR** (#330); **Carrco Painting Contractor** (#341). Companies included must show at least 51 percent ownership by Hispanic U.S. citizens, and must maintain headquarters in one of the 50 states or Washington, D.C. *Hispanic Business, "Hispanic Business 500," June 20, 2013*

Dallas is home to one company which is on the *Hispanic Business* Fastest-Growing 100 list (greatest sales growth from 2008 to 2012): **Sun Holdings** (#40). Companies included must show at least 51 percent ownership by Hispanic U.S. citizens, and must maintain headquarters in one of the 50 states or Washington, D.C. In addition, companies must have minimum revenues of $200,000 for calendar year 2008. *Hispanic Business, June20, 2013*

Minority- and Women-Owned Businesses

Group	All Firms		Firms with Paid Employees			
	Firms	Sales ($000)	Firms	Sales ($000)	Employees	Payroll ($000)
Asian	5,977	3,165,560	2,181	3,012,132	15,033	478,254
Black	16,319	1,212,849	770	906,803	7,562	204,412
Hispanic	18,162	3,358,739	1,989	2,603,364	27,163	712,610
Women	33,387	9,048,065	4,057	8,115,528	47,614	1,543,965
All Firms	121,276	185,276,034	26,420	179,315,299	723,706	36,948,202

Note: Figures cover firms located in the city; minority- and women-owned business are defined as firms in which the corresponding group own 51% or more of the stock or equity of the company
Source: U.S. Census Bureau, 2007 Economic Census, Survey of Business Owners (2012 Survey of Business Owners data will be released starting in June 2015)

**HOTELS &
CONVENTION
CENTERS**

Hotels/Motels

Area	5 Star Num.	5 Star Pct.[3]	4 Star Num.	4 Star Pct.[3]	3 Star Num.	3 Star Pct.[3]	2 Star Num.	2 Star Pct.[3]	1 Star Num.	1 Star Pct.[3]	Not Rated Num.	Not Rated Pct.[3]
City[1]	3	0.6	32	6.1	169	32.0	288	54.5	8	1.5	28	5.3
Total[2]	142	0.9	1,005	6.0	5,147	30.9	8,578	51.4	408	2.4	1,397	8.4

Note: (1) Figures cover Dallas and vicinity; (2) Figures cover all 100 cities in this book; (3) Percentage of hotels which have a given star rating; Star ratings are determined by expedia.com and offer an indication of the general quality of a particular hotel.
Source: expedia.com, April 7, 2014

The Dallas-Plano-Irving, TX metro area is home to two of the best hotels in the U.S. according to *Travel & Leisure*: **Ritz-Carlton, Dallas; Rosewood Mansion on Turtle Creek**. Criteria: service; location; rooms; food; and value. The list includes the top 200 hotels in the U.S. *Travel & Leisure, "T+L 500, The World's Best Hotels 2014"*

The Dallas-Plano-Irving, TX metro area is home to three of the best hotels in the world according to *Condé Nast Traveler*: **Ritz-Carlton; Rosewood Crescent Hotel; Rosewood Mansion on Turtle Creek**. The selections are based on over 79,000 responses to the magazine's annual Readers' Choice Survey. The list includes the top 200 hotels in the U.S. *Condé Nast Traveler, "Gold List 2014, The World's Best Places to Stay"*

Major Convention Centers

Name	Overall Space (sq. ft.)	Exhibit Space (sq. ft.)	Meeting Space (sq. ft.)	Meeting Rooms
Dallas Convention Center	2,000,000	929,726	n/a	96
Fort Worth Convention Center	n/a	253,226	58,849	41
Frisco Conference Center	90,000	n/a	n/a	14

Note: Table includes convention centers located in the Dallas-Fort Worth-Arlington, TX metro area; n/a not available
Source: Original research

Living Environment

COST OF LIVING

Cost of Living Index

Composite Index	Groceries	Housing	Utilities	Trans-portation	Health Care	Misc. Goods/Services
95.6	92.3	75.5	106.9	102.2	99.1	106.2

Note: The Cost of Living Index measures regional differences in the cost of consumer goods and services, excluding taxes and non-consumer expenditures, for professional and managerial households in the top income quintile. It is based on more than 50,000 prices covering almost 60 different items for which prices are collected three times a year by chambers of commerce, economic development organizations or university applied economic centers in each participating urban area. The numbers shown should be read as a percentage above or below the national average of 100. For example, a value of 115.4 in the groceries column indicates that grocery prices are 15.4% higher than the national average. Small differences in the index numbers should not be interpreted as significant; Figures cover the Dallas TX urban area.
Source: The Council for Community and Economic Research, ACCRA Cost of Living Index, 2013

Grocery Prices

Area[1]	T-Bone Steak ($/pound)	Frying Chicken ($/pound)	Whole Milk ($/half gal.)	Eggs ($/dozen)	Orange Juice ($/64 oz.)	Coffee ($/11.5 oz.)
City[2]	10.54	1.19	2.18	1.71	3.61	4.46
Avg.	10.19	1.28	2.34	1.81	3.48	4.39
Min.	8.56	0.94	1.44	1.19	2.78	3.40
Max.	14.82	2.28	3.56	3.73	6.23	7.32

Note: (1) Values for the local area are compared with the average, minimum and maximum values for all 327 areas in the Cost of Living Index; (2) Figures cover the Dallas TX urban area; **T-Bone Steak** (price per pound); **Frying Chicken** (price per pound, whole fryer); **Whole Milk** (half gallon carton); **Eggs** (price per dozen, Grade A, large); **Orange Juice** (64 oz. Tropicana or Florida Natural); **Coffee** (11.5 oz. can, vacuum-packed, Maxwell House, Hills Bros, or Folgers).
Source: The Council for Community and Economic Research, ACCRA Cost of Living Index, 2013

Housing and Utility Costs

Area[1]	New Home Price ($)	Apartment Rent ($/month)	All Electric ($/month)	Part Electric ($/month)	Other Energy ($/month)	Telephone ($/month)
City[2]	214,062	818	-	134.32	46.62	28.15
Avg.	295,864	900	171.38	91.82	70.12	27.73
Min.	185,506	458	117.80	48.81	33.67	17.16
Max.	1,358,917	3,783	441.68	171.40	372.65	39.47

Note: (1) Values for the local area are compared with the average, minimum and maximum values for all 327 areas in the Cost of Living Index; (2) Figures cover the Dallas TX urban area; **New Home Price** (2,400 sf living area, 8,000 sf lot, in urban area with full utilities); **Apartment Rent** (950 sf 2 bedroom/1.5 or 2 bath, unfurnished, excluding all utilities except water); **All Electric** (average monthly cost for an all-electric home); **Part Electric** (average monthly cost for a part-electric home); **Other Energy** (average monthly cost for natural gas, fuel oil, coal, wood, and any other forms of energy except electricity); **Telephone** (price includes basic monthly rate for a private residential line plus additional local usage charges incurred by a family of four).
Source: The Council for Community and Economic Research, ACCRA Cost of Living Index, 2013

Health Care, Transportation, and Other Costs

Area[1]	Doctor ($/visit)	Dentist ($/visit)	Optometrist ($/visit)	Gasoline ($/gallon)	Beauty Salon ($/visit)	Men's Shirt ($)
City[2]	106.67	86.19	93.70	3.40	39.02	35.25
Avg.	101.40	86.48	96.16	3.44	33.87	26.55
Min.	61.67	50.83	50.12	3.08	18.92	12.48
Max.	182.71	152.50	223.78	4.33	68.22	52.03

Note: (1) Values for the local area are compared with the average, minimum and maximum values for all 327 areas in the Cost of Living Index; (2) Figures cover the Dallas TX urban area; **Doctor** (general practitioners routine exam of an established patient); **Dentist** (adult teeth cleaning and periodic oral examination); **Optometrist** (full vision eye exam for established adult patient); **Gasoline** (one gallon regular unleaded, national brand, including all taxes, cash price at self-service pump if available); **Beauty Salon** (woman's shampoo, trim, and blow-dry); **Men's Shirt** (cotton/polyester dress shirt, pinpoint weave, long sleeves).
Source: The Council for Community and Economic Research, ACCRA Cost of Living Index, 2013

HOUSING

House Price Index (HPI)

Area	National Ranking[2]	Quarterly Change (%)	One-Year Change (%)	Five-Year Change (%)
MD[1]	70	1.18	6.77	6.22
U.S.[3]	–	1.20	7.69	4.18

Note: The HPI is a weighted repeat sales index. It measures average price changes in repeat sales or refinancings on the same properties. This information is obtained by reviewing repeat mortgage transactions on single-family properties whose mortgages have been purchased or securitized by Fannie Mae or Freddie Mac in January 1975; (1) Dallas-Plano-Irving, TX Metropolitan Division—see Appendix B for areas included; (2) Rankings are based on annual percentage change for all metro areas containing at least 15,000 transactions over the last 10 years and ranges from 1 to 283; (3) figures based on a weighted average of Census Division estimates using a seasonally adjusted, purchase-only index; all figures are for the period ending December 31, 2013
Source: Federal Housing Finance Agency, House Price Index, February 25, 2014

Median Single-Family Home Prices

Area	2011	2012	2013[p]	Percent Change 2012 to 2013
MSA[1]	148.9	159.3	175.6	10.2
U.S. Average	166.2	177.2	197.4	11.4

Note: Figures are median sales prices of existing single-family homes in thousands of dollars; (p) preliminary; n/a not available; (1) Dallas-Fort Worth-Arlington, TX Metropolitan Statistical Area—see Appendix B for areas included
Source: National Association of Realtors, Median Sales Price of Existing Single-Family Homes for Metropolitan Areas, 4th Quarter 2013

Qualifying Income Based on Median Sales Price of Existing Single-Family Homes

Area	With 5% Down ($)	With 10% Down ($)	With 20% Down ($)
MSA[1]	40,093	37,983	33,762
U.S. Average	45,395	43,006	38,228

Note: Figures are preliminary; Qualifying income is based on a mortgage rate of 4.4%. Monthly principal and interest payment is limited to 25% of income; n/a not available; (1) Dallas-Fort Worth-Arlington, TX Metropolitan Statistical Area—see Appendix B for areas included
Source: National Association of Realtors, Qualifying Income Based on Median Sales Price of Existing Single-Family Homes for Metropolitan Areas, 4th Quarter 2013

Median Apartment Condo-Coop Home Prices

Area	2011	2012	2013[p]	Percent Change 2012 to 2013
MSA[1]	126.0	142.1	155.7	9.6
U.S. Average	165.1	173.7	194.9	12.2

Note: Figures are median sales prices of existing apartment condo-coop homes in thousands of dollars; (p) preliminary; n/a not available; (1) Dallas-Fort Worth-Arlington, TX Metropolitan Statistical Area—see Appendix B for areas included
Source: National Association of Realtors, Median Sales Price of Existing Apartment Condo-Coop Homes for Metropolitan Areas, 4th Quarter 2013

Gross Monthly Rent

Area	Under $200	$200 -299	$300 -499	$500 -749	$750 -999	$1,000 -1,499	$1,500 and up	Median ($)
City	1.2	1.6	4.9	32.9	30.0	21.6	7.8	816
MSA[1]	0.9	1.2	4.0	26.2	30.5	27.2	9.9	884
U.S.	1.7	3.3	8.1	22.7	24.3	25.7	14.3	889

Note: Figures are percentages except for Median; Gross rent is the contract rent plus the estimated average monthly cost of utilities (electricity, gas, and water and sewer) and fuels (oil, coal, kerosene, wood, etc.) if these are paid by the renter (or paid for the renter by someone else); (1) Figures cover the Dallas-Fort Worth-Arlington, TX Metropolitan Statistical Area—see Appendix B for areas included
Source: U.S. Census Bureau, 2010-2012 American Community Survey 3-Year Estimates

Year Housing Structure Built

Area	2010 or Later	2000 -2009	1990 -1999	1980 -1989	1970 -1979	1960 -1969	1950 -1959	1940 -1949	Before 1940	Median Year
City	0.6	12.8	9.2	17.3	19.7	14.8	13.8	6.2	5.6	1975
MSA[1]	0.9	23.6	16.2	19.7	15.6	9.7	7.9	3.2	3.1	1985
U.S.	0.5	14.9	13.8	13.9	15.9	11.1	10.9	5.5	13.5	1976

Note: Figures are percentages except for Median Year; (1) Figures cover the Dallas-Fort Worth-Arlington, TX Metropolitan Statistical Area—see Appendix B for areas included
Source: U.S. Census Bureau, 2010-2012 American Community Survey 3-Year Estimates

HEALTH

Health Risk Data

Category	MD[1] (%)	U.S. (%)
Adults aged 18–64 who have any kind of health care coverage	63.9	79.6
Adults who reported being in good or excellent health	83.3	83.1
Adults who are current smokers	15.8	19.6
Adults who are heavy drinkers[2]	5.0	6.1
Adults who are binge drinkers[3]	16.0	16.9
Adults who are overweight (BMI 25.0 - 29.9)	36.5	35.8
Adults who are obese (BMI 30.0 - 99.8)	26.1	27.6
Adults who participated in any physical activities in the past month	75.1	77.1
Adults 50+ who have ever had a sigmoidoscopy or colonoscopy	63.6	67.3
Women aged 40+ who have had a mammogram within the past two years	70.3	74.0
Men aged 40+ who have had a PSA test within the past two years	44.4	45.2
Adults aged 65+ who have had flu shot within the past year	56.2	60.1
Adults who always wear a seatbelt	n/a	93.8

Note: Data as of 2012 unless otherwise noted; n/a not available; (1) Figures cover the Dallas-Plano-Irving, TX Metropolitan Division—see Appendix B for areas included; (2) Heavy drinkers are classified as males having more than two drinks per day or females having more than one drink per day; (3) Binge drinkers are classified as males having five or more drinks on one occasion or females having four or more drinks on one occasion
Source: Centers for Disease Control and Prevention, Behaviorial Risk Factor Surveillance System, SMART: Selected Metropolitan/Micropolitan Area Risk Trends, 2012

Chronic Health Indicators

Category	MD[1] (%)	U.S. (%)
Adults who have ever been told they had a heart attack	3.8	4.5
Adults who have ever been told they had a stroke	2.2	2.9
Adults who have been told they currently have asthma	8.0	8.9
Adults who have ever been told they have arthritis	19.3	25.7
Adults who have ever been told they have diabetes[2]	9.9	9.7
Adults who have ever been told they had skin cancer	4.6	5.7
Adults who have ever been told they had any other types of cancer	5.9	6.5
Adults who have ever been told they have COPD	4.2	6.2
Adults who have ever been told they have kidney disease	4.3	2.5
Adults who have ever been told they have a form of depression	13.3	18.0

Note: Data as of 2012 unless otherwise noted; (1) Figures cover the Dallas-Plano-Irving, TX Metropolitan Division—see Appendix B for areas included; (2) Figures do not include pregnancy-related, borderline, or pre-diabetes
Source: Centers for Disease Control and Prevention, Behaviorial Risk Factor Surveillance System, SMART: Selected Metropolitan/Micropolitan Area Risk Trends, 2012

Mortality Rates for the Top 10 Causes of Death in the U.S.

ICD-10[a] Sub-Chapter	ICD-10[a] Code	Age-Adjusted Mortality Rate[1] per 100,000 population	
		County[2]	U.S.
Malignant neoplasms	C00-C97	170.7	174.2
Ischaemic heart diseases	I20-I25	108.8	119.1
Other forms of heart disease	I30-I51	50.7	49.6
Chronic lower respiratory diseases	J40-J47	40.5	43.2
Cerebrovascular diseases	I60-I69	48.8	40.3
Organic, including symptomatic, mental disorders	F01-F09	37.0	30.5
Other degenerative diseases of the nervous system	G30-G31	32.0	26.3
Other external causes of accidental injury	W00-X59	23.2	25.1
Diabetes mellitus	E10-E14	21.1	21.3
Hypertensive diseases	I10-I15	27.3	18.8

Note: (a) ICD-10 = International Classification of Diseases 10th Revision; (1) Mortality rates are a three year average covering 2008-2010; (2) Figures cover Dallas County
Source: Centers for Disease Control and Prevention, National Center for Health Statistics. Compressed Mortality File 1999-2010 on CDC WONDER Online Database, released January 2013. Data are compiled from the Compressed Mortality File 1999-2010, Series 20 No. 2P, 2013.

Mortality Rates for Selected Causes of Death

ICD-10[a] Sub-Chapter	ICD-10[a] Code	Age-Adjusted Mortality Rate[1] per 100,000 population	
		County[2]	U.S.
Assault	X85-Y09	8.4	5.5
Diseases of the liver	K70-K76	12.2	12.4
Human immunodeficiency virus (HIV) disease	B20-B24	6.3	3.0
Influenza and pneumonia	J09-J18	15.4	16.4
Intentional self-harm	X60-X84	10.3	11.8
Malnutrition	E40-E46	1.0	0.8
Obesity and other hyperalimentation	E65-E68	2.2	1.6
Renal failure	N17-N19	17.2	13.6
Transport accidents	V01-V99	10.8	12.6
Viral hepatitis	B15-B19	2.2	2.2

Note: (a) ICD-10 = International Classification of Diseases 10th Revision; (1) Mortality rates are a three year average covering 2008-2010; (2) Figures cover Dallas County
Source: Centers for Disease Control and Prevention, National Center for Health Statistics. Compressed Mortality File 1999-2010 on CDC WONDER Online Database, released January 2013. Data are compiled from the Compressed Mortality File 1999-2010, Series 20 No. 2P, 2013.

Health Insurance Coverage

Area	With Health Insurance	With Private Health Insurance	With Public Health Insurance	Without Health Insurance	Population Under Age 18 Without Health Insurance
City	69.0	45.0	29.9	31.0	16.7
MSA[1]	77.7	61.1	23.3	22.3	13.3
U.S.	84.9	65.4	30.4	15.1	7.5

Note: Figures are percentages that cover the civilian noninstitutionalized population; (1) Figures cover the Dallas-Fort Worth-Arlington, TX Metropolitan Statistical Area—see Appendix B for areas included
Source: U.S. Census Bureau, 2010-2012 American Community Survey 3-Year Estimates

Number of Medical Professionals

Area[1]	MDs[2]	DOs[2,3]	Dentists	Podiatrists	Chiropractors	Optometrists
Local (number)	7,444	470	1,761	91	763	292
Local (rate[4])	309.1	19.5	71.8	3.7	31.1	11.9
U.S. (rate[4])	267.6	19.6	61.7	5.6	24.7	14.5

Note: Data as of 2012 unless noted; (1) Local data covers Dallas County; (2) Data as of 2011; (3) Doctor of Osteopathic Medicine; (4) rate per 100,000 population
Source: Area Resource File (ARF) 2012-2013. U.S. Department of Health and Human Services, Health Resources and Services Administration, Bureau of Health Professions

Best Hospitals

According to *U.S. News,* the Dallas-Plano-Irving, TX metro area is home to two of the best hospitals in the U.S.: **Baylor University Medical Center** (7 specialties); **University of Texas Southwestern Medical Center** (4 specialties). The hospitals listed were nationally ranked in at least one adult specialty. Only 147 hospitals nationwide were nationally ranked in one or more specialties. Eighteen hospitals in the U.S. made the Honor Roll by ranking near the top in at least six specialties.*U.S. News Online, "America's Best Hospitals 2013-14"*

According to *U.S. News,* the Dallas-Plano-Irving, TX metro area is home to one of the best children's hospitals in the U.S.: **Children's Medical Center of Dallas**. The hospital listed was highly ranked in at least one pediatric specialty. Eighty-seven hospitals in the U.S. ranked in at least one specialty. Ten children's hospitals in the U.S. made the Honor Roll by ranking near the top in three or more specialties.*U.S. News Online, "America's Best Children's Hospitals 2013-14"*

EDUCATION

Public School District Statistics

District Name	Schls	Pupils	Pupil/ Teacher Ratio	Minority Pupils[1] (%)	Free Lunch Eligible[2] (%)	IEP[3] (%)
Dallas Can Academy Charter	4	2,146	18.8	97.3	89.2	13.4
Dallas ISD	239	157,575	15.3	95.3	81.6	7.6
Highland Park ISD	7	6,804	15.9	10.4	n/a	8.0

Note: Table includes school districts with 2,000 or more students; (1) Percentage of students that are not non-Hispanic white; (2) Percentage of students that are eligible for the free lunch program; (3) Percentage of students that have an Individualized Education Program.
Source: U.S. Department of Education, National Center for Education Statistics, Common Core of Data, Local Education Agency (School District) Universe Survey: School Year 2011-2012; U.S. Department of Education, National Center for Education Statistics, Common Core of Data, Public Elementary/Secondary School Universe Survey: School Year 2011-2012

Best High Schools

High School Name	Rank[1]	Grad. Rate[2] (%)	Coll.[3] (%)	AP/IB/ AICE Tests[4]	AP/IB/ AICE Score[5]	SAT Score[6]	ACT Score[6]
Booker T. Washington H.S. for the Performing and Visual Arts	221	100	97	1.0	2.7	1577	22.6
Harmony Science Academy Dallas	685	100	100	0.4	2.8	1460	n/a
Highland Park H.S.	86	100	95	1.3	3.2	1792	26.6
Hillcrest H.S.	1859	88	72	0.5	2.8	932	20.0
Judge Barefoot Sanders Law Magnet	225	100	98	1.2	2.0	1516	21.4
Lake Highlands H.S.	1762	94	64	0.5	2.7	1504	21.9
Rosie C. Sorrells School of Education and Social Services at Yvonne	501	100	95	0.9	2.0	1400	21.0
School of Business and Management	328	99	95	1.0	2.7	1472	21.0
School of Health Professions	661	100	94	1.0	2.0	1500	21.3
School of Science/Engineering Magnet	4	100	100	3.9	2.6	1786	26.8
Skyline H.S. and Career and Development Center	1767	86	94	0.2	2.1	1284	17.9
The School for the Talented and Gifted Magnet H.S.	5	90	100	3.9	3.4	1914	27.7
Trindidad Garza Early College H.S.	890	100	100	0.4	2.4	1371	17.1
Uplift Hampton Preparatory School	859	85	100	1.4	1.4	1284	n/a
Uplift Peak Preparatory School	732	100	100	1.1	1.6	1334	17.3
Uplift Williams Preparatory School	493	100	100	1.0	1.9	1387	17.5
Warren Travis White	1880	81	90	0.7	1.4	1283	18.0

Note: (1) Public schools are ranked from 1 to 2,000 based on the following self-reported statistics (with the corresponding weight used in calculating their overall score). Schools that were newly founded and did not have a graduating senior class in 2012 were excluded; (2) Four-year, on-time graduation rate (25%); (3) Percent of 2011 graduates who were accepted to college (25%); (4) AP/IB/AICE tests taken per student (25%); (5) Average AP/IB/AICE exam score (10%); (6) Average SAT and/or ACT score (10%); Percent of students enrolled in at least one AP/IB/AICE course (5%)—data not shown; n/a not available
Source: Newsweek and The Daily Beast, "America's Best High Schools 2013"

Highest Level of Education

Area	Less than H.S.	H.S. Diploma	Some College, No Deg.	Associate Degree	Bachelor's Degree	Master's Degree	Prof. School Degree	Doctorate Degree
City	26.2	22.4	17.8	4.4	18.4	7.0	2.7	1.1
MSA[1]	16.3	23.0	22.8	6.5	21.2	7.7	1.6	1.0
U.S.	14.1	28.3	21.3	7.8	18.0	7.5	1.9	1.2

Note: Figures cover persons age 25 and over; (1) Figures cover the Dallas-Fort Worth-Arlington, TX Metropolitan Statistical Area—see Appendix B for areas included
Source: U.S. Census Bureau, 2010-2012 American Community Survey 3-Year Estimates

Educational Attainment by Race

Area	High School Graduate or Higher (%)					Bachelor's Degree or Higher (%)				
	Total	White	Black	Asian	Hisp.[2]	Total	White	Black	Asian	Hisp.[2]
City	73.8	75.3	82.9	83.1	44.3	29.2	38.0	15.0	56.5	8.2
MSA[1]	83.7	85.4	88.4	86.9	54.7	31.4	33.4	23.0	54.3	10.9
U.S.	85.9	88.1	82.5	85.5	63.1	28.6	30.0	18.4	50.2	13.4

Note: Figures shown cover persons 25 years old and over; (1) Figures cover the Dallas-Fort Worth-Arlington, TX Metropolitan Statistical Area—see Appendix B for areas included; (2) People of Hispanic origin can be of any race
Source: U.S. Census Bureau, 2010-2012 American Community Survey 3-Year Estimates

School Enrollment by Grade and Control

Area	Preschool (%)		Kindergarten (%)		Grades 1 - 4 (%)		Grades 5 - 8 (%)		Grades 9 - 12 (%)	
	Public	Private	Public	Private	Public	Private	Public	Private	Public	Private
City	70.8	29.2	89.1	10.9	91.7	8.3	90.3	9.7	90.8	9.2
MSA[1]	55.6	44.4	90.2	9.8	92.2	7.8	92.4	7.6	92.7	7.3
U.S.	56.9	43.1	87.8	12.2	89.9	10.1	90.0	10.0	90.8	9.2

Note: Figures shown cover persons 3 years old and over; (1) Figures cover the Dallas-Fort Worth-Arlington, TX Metropolitan Statistical Area—see Appendix B for areas included
Source: U.S. Census Bureau, 2010-2012 American Community Survey 3-Year Estimates

Average Salaries of Public School Classroom Teachers

Area	2012-13		2013-14		Percent Change 2012-13 to 2013-14	Percent Change 2003-04 to 2013-14
	Dollars	Rank[1]	Dollars	Rank[1]		
Texas	48,819	35	49,270	35	0.92	21.7
U.S. Average	56,103	–	56,689	–	1.04	21.8

Note: (1) State rank ranges from 1 to 51 where 1 indicates highest salary.
Source: National Education Association, Rankings & Estimates: Rankings of the States 2013 and Estimates of School Statistics 2014, March 2014

Higher Education

Four-Year Colleges			Two-Year Colleges			Medical Schools[1]	Law Schools[2]	Voc/ Tech[3]
Public	Private Non-profit	Private For-profit	Public	Private Non-profit	Private For-profit			
1	7	5	3	1	10	1	1	15

Note: Figures cover institutions located within the city limits and include main campuses only; (1) includes schools accredited by the Liaison Committee on Medical Education and the American Osteopathic Association's Commission on Osteopathic College Accreditation; (2) includes ABA-accredited schools, schools with provisional ABA accreditation, and state accredited schools; (3) includes all schools with programs that are less than 2 years.
Source: National Center for Education Statistics, Integrated Postsecondary Education System (IPEDS), 2012-13; Association of American Medical Colleges, Member List, April 24, 2014; American Osteopathic Association, Member List, April 24, 2014; Law School Admission Council, Official Guide to ABA-Approved Law Schools Online, April 24, 2014; Wikipedia, List of Medical Schools in the United States, April 24, 2014; Wikipedia, List of Law Schools in the United States, April 24, 2014

According to *U.S. News & World Report*, the Dallas-Plano-Irving, TX metro division is home to two of the best national universities in the U.S.: **Southern Methodist University** (#60); **University of Texas–Dallas** (#142). The indicators used to capture academic quality fall into a number of categories: assessment by administrators at peer institutions; retention of students; faculty resources; student selectivity; financial resources; alumni giving; high school counselor ratings of colleges; and graduation rate. *U.S. News & World Report, "America's Best Colleges 2014"*

According to *U.S. News & World Report*, the Dallas-Plano-Irving, TX metro division is home to one of the top 100 law schools in the U.S.: **Southern Methodist University (Dedman)** (#48). The rankings are based on a weighted average of 12 measures of quality: peer assessment score; assessment score by lawyers/judges; median LSAT scores; median undergrad GPA; acceptance rate; employment rates for graduates; placement success; bar passage rate; faculty resources; expenditures per student; student/faculty ratio; and library resources. *U.S. News & World Report, "America's Best Graduate Schools, Law, 2014"*

According to *U.S. News & World Report*, the Dallas-Plano-Irving, TX metro division is home to two of the top 100 business schools in the U.S.: **University of Texas–Dallas** (#37); **Southern Methodist University (Cox)** (#52). The rankings are based on a weighted average of the following nine measures: quality assessment; peer assessment; recruiter assessment; placement success; mean starting salary and bonus; student selectivity; mean GMAT and GRE scores; mean undergraduate GPA; and acceptance rate. *U.S. News & World Report, "America's Best Graduate Schools, Business, 2014"*

PRESIDENTIAL ELECTION

2012 Presidential Election Results

Area	Obama	Romney	Other
Dallas County	57.1	41.7	1.2
U.S.	51.0	47.2	1.8

Note: Results are percentages and may not add to 100% due to rounding
Source: Dave Leip's Atlas of U.S. Presidential Elections

EMPLOYERS

Major Employers

Company Name	Industry
AMR Corporation	Air transportation, scheduled
Associates First Capital Corporation	Mortgage bankers
Baylor University Medical Center	General medical and surgical hospitals
Children's Medical Center Dallas	Specialty hospitals, except psychiatric
Combat Support Associates	Engineering services
County of Dallas	County supervisors' and executives' office
Dallas County Hospital District	General medical and surgical hospitals
Fort Worth Independent School District	Public elementary and secondary schools
Housewares Holding Company	Toasters, electric: household
HP Enterprise Services	Computer integrated systems design
J.C. Penney Company	Department stores
JCP Publications Corp.	Department stores
L-3 Communications Corporation	Business economic service
Odyssey HealthCare	Home health care services
Romano's Macaroni Grill	Italian restaurant
SFG Management Limited Liability	Milk processing (pasteurizing, homogenizing, bottling)
Texas Instruments Incorporated	Semiconductors and related devices
University of North Texas	Colleges and universities
University of Texas SW Medical Center	Accident and health insurance
Verizon Business Global	Telephone communication, except radio

Note: Companies shown are located within the Dallas-Fort Worth-Arlington, TX Metropolitan Statistical Area.
Source: Hoovers.com; Wikipedia

Best Companies to Work For

TDIndustries, headquartered in Dallas, is among "The 100 Best Companies to Work For." To pick the 100 Best Companies to Work For, *Fortune* partnered with the Great Place to Work Institute. Two hundred fifty seven firms participated in this year's survey. Two-thirds of a company's score is based on the results of the Institute's Trust Index survey, which is sent to a random sample of employees from each company. The questions related to attitudes about management's credibility, job satisfaction, and camaraderie. The other third of the scoring is based on the company's responses to the Institute's Culture Audit, which includes detailed questions about pay and benefit programs, and a series of open-ended questions about hiring practices, internal communication, training, recognition programs, and diversity efforts. Any company that is at least five years old with more than 1,000 U.S. employees is eligible. *Fortune, "The 100 Best Companies to Work For," 2014*

Ryan; Texas Instruments, headquartered in Dallas, are among the "100 Best Companies for Working Mothers." Criteria: workforce representation; child care; flexibility programs; and leave policies. This year *Working Mother* gave particular weight to flexible work arrangements, women's advancement programs, and paid maternity leave. *Working Mother, "100 Best Companies 2013"*

AT&T, headquartered in Dallas, is among the "100 Best Places to Work in IT." To qualify, companies, both public and private, had to have a minimum of 50 IT employees and were selected based on average salary and bonus increases, the percentage of IT staffers promoted, IT staff turnover rates, training and development programs, and the percentage of women and minorities in IT staff and management positions. In addition, *Computerworld* looked at retention efforts, programs for recognizing and rewarding outstanding performances, and benefits such as flextime, elder care and child care, and reimbursement for college tuition and the cost of pursuing technology certifications. *Computerworld, "100 Best Places to Work in IT 2013"*

AT&T; Texas Instruments, headquartered in Dallas, are among the "Top Companies for Executive Women." To be named to the list, companies with a minimum of two women on the board complete a comprehensive application that focuses on the number of women in senior ranks. In addition to assessing corporate programs and policies dedicated to advancing women, NAFE examined the number of women in each company overall, in senior management, and on its board of directors, paying particular attention to the number of women with profit-and-loss responsibility. *National Association for Female Executives, "2013 NAFE Top 50 Companies for Executive Women"*

PUBLIC SAFETY

Crime Rate

Area	All Crimes	Violent Crimes				Property Crimes		
		Murder	Forcible Rape	Robbery	Aggrav. Assault	Burglary	Larceny -Theft	Motor Vehicle Theft
City	5,048.5	12.4	39.1	329.7	293.7	1,296.0	2,508.8	568.8
Suburbs[1]	2,786.9	1.3	20.0	52.8	115.4	573.7	1,846.4	177.1
Metro[2]	3,424.2	4.4	25.4	130.9	165.7	777.2	2,033.1	287.5
U.S.	3,246.1	4.7	26.9	112.9	242.3	670.2	1,959.3	229.7

Note: Figures are crimes per 100,000 population; (1) All areas within the metro area that are located outside the city limits; (2) Figures cover the Dallas-Plano-Irving, TX Metropolitan Division—see Appendix B for areas included
Source: FBI Uniform Crime Reports, 2012

Hate Crimes

Area	Number of Quarters Reported	Bias Motivation				
		Race	Religion	Sexual Orientation	Ethnicity	Disability
City	4	7	5	10	8	0
U.S.	4	2,797	1,099	1,135	667	92

Source: Federal Bureau of Investigation, Hate Crime Statistics 2012

Identity Theft Consumer Complaints

Area	Complaints	Complaints per 100,000 Population	Rank[2]
MSA[1]	7,378	114.8	34
U.S.	290,056	91.8	-

Note: (1) Figures cover the Dallas-Fort Worth-Arlington, TX Metropolitan Statistical Area—see Appendix B for areas included; (2) Rank ranges from 1 to 377 where 1 indicates greatest number of identity theft complaints per 100,000 population
Source: Federal Trade Commission, Consumer Sentinel Network Data Book for January–December 2013

Fraud and Other Consumer Complaints

Area	Complaints	Complaints per 100,000 Population	Rank[2]
MSA[1]	29,924	465.7	41
U.S.	1,811,724	595.2	-

Note: (1) Figures cover the Dallas-Fort Worth-Arlington, TX Metropolitan Statistical Area—see Appendix B for areas included; (2) Rank ranges from 1 to 377 where 1 indicates greatest number of identity theft complaints per 100,000 population
Source: Federal Trade Commission, Consumer Sentinel Network Data Book for January–December 2013

RECREATION

Culture

Dance[1]	Theatre[1]	Instrumental Music[1]	Vocal Music[1]	Series and Festivals	Museums and Art Galleries[2]	Zoos and Aquariums[3]
2	16	8	3	6	43	2

Note: (1) Number of professional perfoming groups; (2) Based on organizations with primary SIC code 8412; (3) AZA-accredited
Source: The Grey House Performing Arts Directory, 2013; Association of Zoos & Aquariums, AZA Member Zoos & Aquariums, April 2014; www.AccuLeads.com, May 1, 2014

Professional Sports Teams

Team Name	League	Year Established
Dallas Cowboys	National Football League (NFL)	1960
Dallas Mavericks	National Basketball Association (NBA)	1980
Dallas Stars	National Hockey League (NHL)	1993
FC Dallas	Major League Soccer (MLS)	1996
Texas Rangers	Major League Baseball (MLB)	1972

Note: Includes teams located in the Dallas-Fort Worth-Arlington, TX Metropolitan Statistical Area.
Source: Wikipedia, Major Professional Sports Teams of the United States and Canada

CLIMATE

Average and Extreme Temperatures

Temperature	Jan	Feb	Mar	Apr	May	Jun	Jul	Aug	Sep	Oct	Nov	Dec	Yr.
Extreme High (°F)	85	90	100	100	101	112	111	109	107	101	91	87	112
Average High (°F)	55	60	68	76	84	92	96	96	89	79	67	58	77
Average Temp. (°F)	45	50	57	66	74	82	86	86	79	68	56	48	67
Average Low (°F)	35	39	47	56	64	72	76	75	68	57	46	38	56
Extreme Low (°F)	-2	9	12	30	39	53	58	58	42	24	16	0	-2

Note: Figures cover the years 1945-1993
Source: National Climatic Data Center, International Station Meteorological Climate Summary, 9/96

Average Precipitation/Snowfall/Humidity

Precip./Humidity	Jan	Feb	Mar	Apr	May	Jun	Jul	Aug	Sep	Oct	Nov	Dec	Yr.
Avg. Precip. (in.)	1.9	2.3	2.6	3.8	4.9	3.4	2.1	2.3	2.9	3.3	2.3	2.1	33.9
Avg. Snowfall (in.)	1	1	Tr	Tr	0	0	0	0	0	Tr	Tr	Tr	3
Avg. Rel. Hum. 6am (%)	78	77	75	77	82	81	77	76	80	79	78	77	78
Avg. Rel. Hum. 3pm (%)	53	51	47	49	51	48	43	41	46	46	48	51	48

Note: Figures cover the years 1945-1993; Tr = Trace amounts (<0.05 in. of rain; <0.5 in. of snow)
Source: National Climatic Data Center, International Station Meteorological Climate Summary, 9/96

Weather Conditions

Temperature			Daytime Sky			Precipitation		
10°F & below	32°F & below	90°F & above	Clear	Partly cloudy	Cloudy	0.01 inch or more precip.	0.1 inch or more snow/ice	Thunder-storms
1	34	102	108	160	97	78	2	49

Note: Figures are average number of days per year and cover the years 1945-1993
Source: National Climatic Data Center, International Station Meteorological Climate Summary, 9/96

HAZARDOUS WASTE

Superfund Sites

Dallas has one hazardous waste site on the EPA's Superfund Final National Priorities List: **RSR Corp.** *U.S. Environmental Protection Agency, Final National Priorities List, April 26, 2014*

AIR & WATER QUALITY

Air Quality Index

Area	Percent of Days when Air Quality was...[2]					AQI Statistics[2]	
	Good	Moderate	Unhealthy for Sensitive Groups	Unhealthy	Very Unhealthy	Maximum	Median
MSA[1]	42.7	48.2	8.8	0.3	0.0	161	54

Note: (1) Data covers the Dallas-Fort Worth-Arlington, TX Metropolitan Statistical Area—see Appendix B for areas included; (2) Based on 365 days with AQI data in 2013. Air Quality Index (AQI) is an index for reporting daily air quality. EPA calculates the AQI for five major air pollutants regulated by the Clean Air Act: ground-level ozone, particle pollution (aka particulate matter), carbon monoxide, sulfur dioxide, and nitrogen dioxide. The AQI runs from 0 to 500. The higher the AQI value, the greater the level of air pollution and the greater the health concern. There are six AQI categories: "Good" AQI is between 0 and 50. Air quality is considered satisfactory; "Moderate" AQI is between 51 and 100. Air quality is acceptable; "Unhealthy for Sensitive Groups" When AQI values are between 101 and 150, members of sensitive groups may experience health effects; "Unhealthy" When AQI values are between 151 and 200 everyone may begin to experience health effects; "Very Unhealthy" AQI values between 201 and 300 trigger a health alert; "Hazardous" AQI values over 300 trigger warnings of emergency conditions (not shown).
Source: U.S. Environmental Protection Agency, Air Quality Index Report, 2013

Air Quality Index Pollutants

Area	Percent of Days when AQI Pollutant was...[2]					
	Carbon Monoxide	Nitrogen Dioxide	Ozone	Sulfur Dioxide	Particulate Matter 2.5	Particulate Matter 10
MSA[1]	0.0	4.7	38.4	0.0	55.6	1.4

Note: (1) Data covers the Dallas-Fort Worth-Arlington, TX Metropolitan Statistical Area—see Appendix B for areas included; (2) Based on 365 days with AQI data in 2013. The Air Quality Index (AQI) is an index for reporting daily air quality. EPA calculates the AQI for five major air pollutants regulated by the Clean Air Act: ground-level ozone, particle pollution (also known as particulate matter), carbon monoxide, sulfur dioxide, and nitrogen dioxide. The AQI runs from 0 to 500. The higher the AQI value, the greater the level of air pollution and the greater the health concern.
Source: U.S. Environmental Protection Agency, Air Quality Index Report, 2013

Air Quality Trends: Ozone

	2003	2004	2005	2006	2007	2008	2009	2010	2011	2012
MSA[1]	0.089	0.087	0.093	0.089	0.081	0.077	0.080	0.076	0.085	0.083

Note: (1) Data covers the Dallas-Fort Worth-Arlington, TX Metropolitan Statistical Area—see Appendix B for areas included. The values shown are the composite ozone concentration averages among trend sites based on the highest fourth daily maximum 8-hour concentration in parts per million. These trends are based on sites having an adequate record of monitoring data during the trend period. Data from exceptional events are included.
Source: U.S. Environmental Protection Agency, Air Quality Monitoring Information, "Air Quality Trends by City, 2000-2012"

Maximum Air Pollutant Concentrations: Particulate Matter, Ozone, CO and Lead

	Particulate Matter 10 (ug/m³)	Particulate Matter 2.5 Wtd AM (ug/m³)	Particulate Matter 2.5 24-Hr (ug/m³)	Ozone (ppm)	Carbon Monoxide (ppm)	Lead (ug/m³)
MSA[1] Level	66	10.7	22	0.092	1	0.42
NAAQS[2]	150	15	35	0.075	9	0.15
Met NAAQS[2]	Yes	Yes	Yes	No	Yes	No

Note: (1) Data covers the Dallas-Fort Worth-Arlington, TX Metropolitan Statistical Area—see Appendix B for areas included; Data from exceptional events are included; (2) National Ambient Air Quality Standards; ppm = parts per million; ug/m³ = micrograms per cubic meter; n/a not available.
Concentrations: Particulate Matter 10 (coarse particulate)—highest second maximum 24-hour concentration; Particulate Matter 2.5 Wtd AM (fine particulate)—highest weighted annual mean concentration; Particulate Matter 2.5 24-Hour (fine particulate)—highest 98th percentile 24-hour concentration; Ozone—highest fourth daily maximum 8-hour concentration; Carbon Monoxide—highest second maximum non-overlapping 8-hour concentration; Lead—maximum running 3-month average
Source: U.S. Environmental Protection Agency, Air Quality Monitoring Information, "Air Quality Statistics by City, 2012"

Maximum Air Pollutant Concentrations: Nitrogen Dioxide and Sulfur Dioxide

	Nitrogen Dioxide AM (ppb)	Nitrogen Dioxide 1-Hr (ppb)	Sulfur Dioxide AM (ppb)	Sulfur Dioxide 1-Hr (ppb)	Sulfur Dioxide 24-Hr (ppb)
MSA[1] Level	12	53	n/a	15	n/a
NAAQS[2]	53	100	30	75	140
Met NAAQS[2]	Yes	Yes	n/a	Yes	n/a

Note: (1) Data covers the Dallas-Fort Worth-Arlington, TX Metropolitan Statistical Area—see Appendix B for areas included; Data from exceptional events are included; (2) National Ambient Air Quality Standards; ppm = parts per million; ug/m³ = micrograms per cubic meter; n/a not available.
Concentrations: Nitrogen Dioxide AM—highest arithmetic mean concentration; Nitrogen Dioxide 1-Hr—highest 98th percentile 1-hour daily maximum concentration; Sulfur Dioxide AM—highest annual mean concentration; Sulfur Dioxide 1-Hr—highest 99th percentile 1-hour daily maximum concentration; Sulfur Dioxide 24-Hr—highest second maximum 24-hour concentration
Source: U.S. Environmental Protection Agency, Air Quality Monitoring Information, "Air Quality Statistics by City, 2012"

Drinking Water

			Violations[1]	
Water System Name	Pop. Served	Primary Water Source Type	Health Based	Monitoring/ Reporting
Dallas Water Utility	1,253,000	Surface	0	0

Note: (1) Based on violation data from January 1, 2013 to December 31, 2013 (includes unresolved violations from earlier years)
Source: U.S. Environmental Protection Agency, Office of Ground Water and Drinking Water, Safe Drinking Water Information System (based on data extracted February 10, 2014)

El Paso, Texas

Background

El Paso is so named because it sits in a spectacular pass through the Franklin Mountains, at an average elevation of 3,700 feet and in direct view of peaks that rise to 7,200 feet. El Paso is the fourth-largest city in Texas. It lies just south of New Mexico on the Rio Grande and just north of Juarez, Mexico.

The early Spanish explorer Alvar Nunez Cabeza de Vaca (circa 1530) probably passed through this area, but the city was named in 1598 by Juan de Onante, who dubbed it El Paso del Rio del Norte, or The Pass at the River of the North. It was also Onante who declared the area Spanish, on the authority of King Philip II, but a mission was not established until 1649. For some time, El Paso del Norte was the seat of government for northern Mexico, but settlement in and around the present-day city was sparse for many years.

This changed considerably by 1807, when Zebulon A. Pike, a United States Army officer, was interned in El Paso after being convicted of trespassing on Spanish territory. He found the area pleasant and well tended, with many irrigated fields and vineyards and a thriving trade in brandy and wine. In spite of Pike's stay there, though, El Paso remained for many years a largely Mexican region, escaping most of the military action connected to the Texas Revolution.

In the wake of the Mexican War (1846-1848) and in response to the California gold rush in 1849, El Paso emerged as a significant way station on the road West. A federal garrison, Fort Bliss, was established there in 1849, and was briefly occupied by Confederate sympathizers in 1862. Federal forces quickly reoccupied the fort, however, and the area was firmly controlled by Union armies. El Paso was incorporated in 1873, and after 1881, growth accelerated considerably with the building of rail links through the city, giving rise to ironworks, mills, and breweries.

During the Mexican Revolution (1911), El Paso was an important and disputed city, with Pancho Villa himself a frequent visitor, and many of his followers residents of the town. Mexico's national history, in fact, continued to affect El Paso until 1967 when, by way of settling a historic border dispute, 437 acres of the city was ceded to Mexico. Much of the disputed area on both sides of the border was made into parkland. The U.S. National Parks Service maintains the Chamizal Park on the U.S. side and it plays host to a variety of community events during the year including the Chamizal Film Festival and the summer concert series, Music Under the Stars.

One of the major points of entry to the U.S. from Mexico, El Paso is a vitally important international city and a burgeoning center of rail, road, and air transportation. During the 1990s, the city's economy shifted more toward a service-oriented economy and away from a manufacturing base.

Transportation services and motor freight transportation and warehousing has been increasing, and tourism is becoming a growing segment of the economy. Government and military are also sources of employment, with Ft. Bliss being the largest Air Defense Artillery Training Center in the world. The city hosts the University of Texas at El Paso, and a community college. Cultural amenities include the Tigua Indian Cultural Center, a Wilderness Park Museum, the El Paso Zoo, museums, a symphony orchestra, a ballet company, and many theaters. The city's "Wild West" qualities have long made it a popular destination for musicians-many of whom have recorded albums at El Paso's Sonic Ranch recording studio.

El Paso 2015 downtown renovation project began in 2006, with the goal of increasing El Paso's aesthetic appeal. Completed are an open-air mall and "lifestyle center" in the city's central area, Doubletree by Hilton Hotel, and renovations of several historic downtown buildings.

In August 2007, El Paso became the site of the world's largest inland desalination plant, designed to produce 27.5 million gallons of fresh water daily making it a critical component of the region's water portfolio.

The weather in El Paso is of the mountain-desert type, with very little precipitation. Summers are hot, humidity is low and winters are mild. However, temperatures in the flat Rio Grande Valley nearby are notably cooler at night year-round. There is plenty of sunshine and clear skies 202 days of the year.

Rankings

General Rankings

- El Paso appeared on RelocateAmerica's list of best places to live in America. The annual "Top 100 Places to Live" list recognizes the top communities as nominated by their residents & local businesses. RelocateAmerica's Research Group determined the list based on review of various data gathered for economic, employment, housing, education, industry, opportunity, environment and recreation along with feedback from area leaders and residents. *RelocateAmerica.com, "Top 100 Places to Live for 2011"*

Business/Finance Rankings

- TransUnion ranked the nation's metro areas by average credit score, calculated on the VantageScore system, developed by the three major credit-reporting bureaus—TransUnion, Experian, and Equifax. The El Paso metro area was among the ten cities with the lowest collective credit score, meaning that its residents posed the highest average consumer credit risk. *www.usatoday.com, "Metro Areas' Average Credit Rating Revealed," February 7, 2013*

- Building on the U.S. Department of Labor's Occupational Information Network Data Collection Program, the Brookings Institution defined STEM occupations and job opportunities for STEM workers at various levels of educational attainment. The El Paso metro area was one of the ten metro areas where workers in low-education-level STEM jobs earn the lowest relative wages. *www.brookings.edu, "The Hidden Stem Economy," June 10, 2013*

- The Brookings Institution ranked the 50 largest cities in the U.S. based on income inequality. El Paso was ranked #29. (#1 = greatest ineqality). Criteria: the cities were ranked based on the "95/20 ratio." This figure represents the income at which a household earns more than 95 percent of all other households, divided by the income at which a household earns more than only 20 percent of all other households. *Brookings Institution, "Income Inequality in America's 50 Largest Cities, 2007-2012," February 20, 2014*

- CareerBliss, an employment and careers website, analyzed U.S. Bureau of Labor Statistics data, more than 14,000 company reviews from employees and former employees, and job openings over a six-month period to arrive at its list of the 20 worst places in the United States to look for a job. El Paso was ranked #6. *CareerBliss.com, "20 Worst Cities to Find a Job for 2012," October 11, 2012*

- El Paso was ranked #38 out of 100 metro areas in terms of economic performance (#1 = best) during the recession and recovery from trough quarter through the second quarter of 2013. Criteria: percent change in employment; percentage point change in unemployment rate; percent change in gross metropolitan product; percent change in House Price Index. *Brookings Institution, MetroMonitor: Tracking Economic Recession and Recovery in America's 100 Largest Metropolitan Areas, September 2013*

- The El Paso metro area was identified as one of 10 best-paying cities for women. The metro area ranked #7. Criteria: *24/7 Wall St.* identified the metropolitan areas that have the smallest pay disparity between men and women by comparing the median earnings for the past 12 months of both men and women working full-time in the country's 100 largest metropolitan statistical areas. *24/7 Wall St., "10 Best-Paying Cities for Women," April 14, 2013*

- The El Paso metro area was identified as one of the most debt-ridden places in America by credit reporting agency Equifax. The metro area was ranked #2. Criteria: proportion of average yearly income owed to credit card companies. *Equifax, "The Most Debt-Ridden Cities in America," February 23, 2012*

- The El Paso metro area appeared on the Milken Institute "2013 Best Performing Cities" list. Rank: #35 out of 200 large metro areas. Criteria: job growth; wage and salary growth; high-tech output growth. *Milken Institute, "Best-Performing Cities 2013," December 2013*

- *Forbes* ranked the 200 most populous metro areas in the U.S. in terms of the "Best Places for Business and Careers." The El Paso metro area was ranked #53. Criteria: costs (business and living); job growth (past and projected); income growth; educational attainment (college and high school); projected economic growth; cultural and recreational opportunities; net migration patterns; number of highly ranked colleges. *Forbes, "The Best Places for Business and Careers," August 7, 2013*

Children/Family Rankings

• El Paso was selected as one of the best cities for families to live by *Parenting* magazine. The city ranked #52 out of 100. Criteria: education; health; community; *Parenting's* Culture & Charm Index. *Parenting.com, "The 2012 Best Cities for Families List"*

Dating/Romance Rankings

• Of the 100 U.S. cities surveyed by *Men's Health* in its quest to identify the nation's best cities for dating and forming relationships, El Paso was ranked #83 for online dating (#1 = best). *Men's Health, "The Best and Worst Cities for Online Dating," January 30, 2013*

Education Rankings

• *Men's Health* ranked 100 U.S. cities in terms of their education levels. El Paso was ranked #77 (#1 = most educated city). Criteria: high school graduation rates; school enrollment; educational attainment; number of households who have outstanding student loans; number of households whose members have taken adult-education courses. *Men's Health, "Where School Is In: The Most and Least Educated Cities," September 12, 2011*

• El Paso was selected as one of America's most literate cities. The city ranked #74 out of the 77 largest U.S. cities. Criteria: number of booksellers; library resources; Internet resources; educational attainment; periodical publishing resources; newspaper circulation. *Central Connecticut State University, "America's Most Literate Cities, 2013"*

Environmental Rankings

• The El Paso metro area came in at #273 for the relative comfort of its climate on Sperling's list of "chill cities," as measured by the Sperling Heat Index. All 361 metro areas are included. Criteria included daytime high temperatures, nighttime low temperatures, dew point, and relative humidity at the high temperatures. *www.bertsperling.com, "Sperling's Chill Cities," July 18, 2013*

• Sperling's BestPlaces assessed 379 metropolitan areas of the United States for the likelihood of dangerously extreme weather events or earthquakes. In general the Southeast and South-Central regions have the highest risk of weather extremes and earthquakes, while the Pacific Northwest enjoys the lowest risk. Of the least risky metropolitan areas, the El Paso metro area was ranked #86. *www.bestplaces.net, "Safest Places from Natural Disasters," April 2011*

• El Paso was selected as one of 22 "Smarter Cities" for energy by the Natural Resources Defense Council. The city appeared as one of 12 cities in the large city (population 250,000 and over) category. Criteria: investment in green power; energy efficiency measures; conservation. *Natural Resources Defense Council, "2010 Smarter Cities," July 19, 2010*

Food/Drink Rankings

• *Men's Health* ranked 100 major U.S. cities in terms of alcohol intoxication. El Paso ranked #84 (#1 = most sober).Criteria: binge drinking; alcohol-related traffic accidents, arrests, and fatalities. *Men's Health, "The Drunkest Cities in America," November 19, 2013*

Health/Fitness Rankings

• El Paso was selected as one of the 25 fattest cities in America by *Men's Fitness Online*. It ranked #7 out of America's 50 largest cities. Criteria: fitness centers and sport stores; nutrition; sports participation; TV viewing; overweight/sedentary; junk food; air quality; geography; commute; parks and open space; city recreational facilities; access to healthcare; motivation; mayor and city initiatives; state obesity initiatives. *Men's Fitness, "The Fittest and Fattest Cities in America," March 5, 2012*

• El Paso was identified as a "2013 Spring Allergy Capital." The area ranked #80 out of 100. Three groups of factors were used to identify the most severe cities for people with allergies during the spring season: annual pollen levels; medicine utilization; access to board-certified allergists. *Asthma and Allergy Foundation of America, "Spring Allergy Capitals 2013"*

- El Paso was identified as a "2013 Fall Allergy Capital." The area ranked #52 out of 100. Three groups of factors were used to identify the most severe cities for people with allergies during the fall season: annual pollen levels; medicine utilization; access to board-certified allergists. *Asthma and Allergy Foundation of America, "Fall Allergy Capitals 2013"*

- El Paso was identified as a "2013 Asthma Capital." The area ranked #45 out of the nation's 100 largest metropolitan areas. Twelve factors were used to identify the most challenging places to live for people with asthma: estimated prevalence; self-reported prevalence; crude death rate for asthma; annual pollen score; annual air quality; public smoking laws; number of board-certified asthma specialists; school inhaler access laws; rescue medication use; controller medication use; uninsured rate; poverty rate. *Asthma and Allergy Foundation of America, "Asthma Capitals 2013"*

- *Men's Health* ranked 100 major U.S. cities in terms of the best and worst cities for men. El Paso ranked #60. Criteria: thirty-three data points were examined covering health, fitness, and quality of life. *Men's Health, "The Best & Worst Cities for Men 2014," December 6, 2013*

- The El Paso metro area appeared in the 2013 Gallup-Healthways Well-Being Index. The area ranked #68 out of 189. The Gallup-Healthways Well-Being Index score is an average of six sub-indexes, which individually examine life evaluation, emotional health, work environment, physical health, healthy behaviors, and access to basic necessities. Results are based on telephone interviews conducted as part of the Gallup-Healthways Well-Being Index survey January 2–December 29, 2012, and January 2–December 30, 2013, with a random sample of 531,630 adults, aged 18 and older, living in metropolitan areas in the 50 U.S. states and the District of Columbia. *Gallup-Healthways, "State of American Well-Being," March 25, 2014*

- *Men's Health* ranked 100 U.S. cities in terms of their activity levels. El Paso was ranked #73 (#1 = most active city). Criteria: where and how often residents exercise; percentage of households that watch more than 15 hours of cable television a week and buy more than 11 video games a year; death rate from deep-vein thrombosis, a condition linked to sitting for extended periods of time. *Men's Health, "Where Sit Happens: The Most and Least Active Cities in America," June 20, 2011*

Real Estate Rankings

- *Forbes* reported that El Paso ranked #3 on its list of cities where renters could get the best value for their money, based on current rental prices, price per square foot, year-over-year changes in rent cost, and cost of renting compared with the cost of purchasing a home. *www.forbes.com, "Renting? Cities to Get the Most Bang for Your Buck," July 19, 2013*

- El Paso was ranked #203 out of 283 metro areas in terms of house price appreciation in 2013 (#1 = highest rate). *Federal Housing Finance Agency, House Price Index, 4th Quarter 2013*

- El Paso was ranked #188 out of 224 metro areas in terms of housing affordability in 2013 by the National Association of Home Builders (#1 = most affordable). The NAHB-Wells Fargo Housing Opportunity Index (HOI) for a given area is defined as the share of homes sold in that area that would have been affordable to a family earning the local median income, based on standard mortgage underwriting criteria. *National Association of Home Builders®, NAHB-Wells Fargo Housing Opportunity Index, 4th Quarter 2013*

- The nation's largest metro areas were analyzed in terms of the best places to buy foreclosures in 2013. The El Paso metro area ranked #11 out of 20. Criteria: RealtyTrac scored all metro areas with a population of 500,000 or more by summing up four numbers: months' supply of foreclosure inventory; percentage of foreclosure sales; foreclosure discount; percentage increase in foreclosure activity in 2012. *RealtyTrac, "2012 Year-End Metropolitan Foreclosure Market Report," January 28, 2013*

Safety Rankings

- In search of the nation's safest cities, Business Insider looked at the FBI's preliminary Uniform Crime Report, excluding localities with fewer than 200,000 residents. To judge by its low murder, rape, and robbery data, El Paso made the 20 safest cities list, at #14. *www.businessinsider.com, "The 20 Safest Cities in America," July 25, 2013*

- Symantec, in partnership with Sperling's BestPlaces, ranked the 50 largest cities in the U.S. in terms of their vulnerability to cybercrime. The city ranked #49. Criteria: number of cyberattacks and potential infections; level of Internet access; expenditures on smartphones and computer hardware/software; wireless hotspots; broadband connectivity; Internet usage; online purchases. *Symantec, "Riskiest Online Cities of 2012" February 15, 2012*

- Farmers Insurance, in partnership with Sperling's BestPlaces, ranked metro areas in the U.S. and identified the "Most Secure Places to Live." The El Paso metro area ranked #17 out of the top 20 in the large metro area category (500,000 or more residents). Criteria: economic stability; crime statistics; extreme weather; risk of natural disasters; housing depreciation; foreclosures; air quality; environmental hazards; life expectancy; motor vehicle fatalities; and employment numbers. *Farmers Insurance Group of Companies, "Most Secure U.S. Places to Live in the U.S.," June 25, 2013*

- Allstate ranked the 200 largest cities in America in terms of driver safety. El Paso ranked #76. Allstate researchers analyzed internal property damage claims over a two-year period from January 2010 to December 2011. A weighted average of the two-year numbers determined the annual percentages. *Allstate, "Allstate America's Best Drivers Report®, August 27, 2013"*

- El Paso was identified as one of the safest large cities in America by CQ Press. All 32 cities with populations of 500,000 or more that reported crime rates in 2012 for murder, rape, robbery, aggravated assault, burglary, and motor vehicle thefts were ranked. The city ranked #1 out of the top 10. *CQ Press, City Crime Rankings 2014*

- The National Insurance Crime Bureau ranked 380 metro areas in the U.S. in terms of per capita rates of vehicle theft. The El Paso metro area ranked #80 (#1 = highest rate). Criteria: number of vehicle theft offenses per 100,000 inhabitants in 2012. *National Insurance Crime Bureau, "Hot Spots 2012," June 26, 2013*

Seniors/Retirement Rankings

- From its Best Cities for Successful Aging indexes, the Milken Institute generated rankings for metropolitan areas, weighing data in eight categories—general indicators, health care, wellness, living arrangements, transportation and general accessibility, financial well-being, education and employment, and community participation. The El Paso metro area was ranked #91 overall in the large metro area category. *Milken Institute, "Best Cities for Successful Aging," July 2012*

Sports/Recreation Rankings

- El Paso appeared on the *Sporting News* list of the "Best Sports Cities" for 2011. The area ranked #105 out of 271. Criteria: the magazine takes a 12-month snapshot of each city's sports, putting a heavy premium on regular-season won-lost records (from the most recently completed season). Other criteria include: playoff berths, bowl appearances and tournament bids; championships; applicable power ratings; quality of competition; overall fan fervor (measured in part by attendance); abundance of teams (rewarding quality over quantity); stadium and arena quality; ticket availability and prices; franchise ownership; and marquee appeal of athletes. *Sporting News, "Best Sports Cities 2011," October 4, 2011*

- El Paso appeared on the *Sporting News* list of the "Best Sports Cities" for 2011. The area ranked #105 out of 271. Criteria: a 12-month snapshot of regular-season won-lost records (from the most recently completed season). Other criteria include: playoff berths, bowl appearances and tournament bids; championships; applicable power ratings; quality of competition; overall fan fervor (measured in part by attendance); abundance of teams (quality over quantity); stadium and arena quality; ticket availability and prices; franchise ownership; and marquee appeal of athletes. *Sporting News, "Best Sports Cities 2011," October 4, 2011*

Women/Minorities Rankings

- To determine the best metro areas for working women, the personal finance website NerdWallet considered city size as well as relevant economic metrics—high salaries, narrow pay differential by gender, prevalence of women in the highest-paying industries, and population growth over 2010–2012. Of the medium-sized U.S. cities examined, the El Paso metro area held the #7 position. *www.nerdwallet.com, "Best Places for Women in the Workforce," May 19, 2013*

- *Women's Health* examined U.S. cities and identified the 100 best cities for women. El Paso was ranked #42. Criteria: 30 categories were examined from obesity and breast cancer rates to commuting times and hours spent working out. *Women's Health, "Best Cities for Women 2012"*

- El Paso was selected as one of the 25 healthiest cities for Latinas by *Latina Magazine*. The city ranked #14. Criteria: U.S. cities with populations over 500,000 residents were evaluated on the following criteria: percentage of 18-34 year-olds per city; Latino college graduation rates; number of colleges and universities; affordability; housing costs; income growth over time; average salary; percentage of singles; climate; safety; how the city's diversity compares to the national average; opportunities for minority entrepreneurs. *Latina Magazine, "Top 15 U.S. Cities for Young Latinos to Live In," August 19, 2011*

Miscellaneous Rankings

- *Men's Health* ranked 100 U.S. cities by their level of sadness. El Paso was ranked #58 (#1 = saddest city). Criteria: suicide rates; unemployment rates; percentage of households that use antidepressants; percent of population who report feeling blue all or most of the time. *Men's Health, "Frown Towns," November 28, 2011*

- The National Alliance to End Homelessness ranked the 100 most populous metro areas in terms the rate of homelessness. The El Paso metro area ranked #37. Criteria: number of homeless people per 10,000 population in 2011. *National Alliance to End Homelessness, The State of Homelessness in America 2012*

Business Environment

CITY FINANCES

City Government Finances

Component	2011 ($000)	2011 ($ per capita)
Total Revenues	934,429	1,540
Total Expenditures	828,363	1,365
Debt Outstanding	1,492,055	2,458
Cash and Securities[1]	1,608,530	2,650

Note: (1) Cash and security holdings of a government at the close of its fiscal year, including those of its dependent agencies, utilities, and liquor stores.
Source: U.S Census Bureau, State & Local Government Finances 2011

City Government Revenue by Source

Source	2011 ($000)	2011 ($ per capita)
General Revenue		
From Federal Government	62,566	103
From State Government	27,098	45
From Local Governments	6,944	11
Taxes		
Property	189,453	312
Sales and Gross Receipts	153,720	253
Personal Income	0	0
Corporate Income	0	0
Motor Vehicle License	0	0
Other Taxes	14,438	24
Current Charges	182,095	300
Liquor Store	0	0
Utility	94,736	156
Employee Retirement	153,302	253

Source: U.S Census Bureau, State & Local Government Finances 2011

City Government Expenditures by Function

Function	2011 ($000)	2011 ($ per capita)	2011 (%)
General Direct Expenditures			
Air Transportation	32,295	53	3.9
Corrections	0	0	0.0
Education	0	0	0.0
Employment Security Administration	0	0	0.0
Financial Administration	8,305	14	1.0
Fire Protection	73,798	122	8.9
General Public Buildings	11,314	19	1.4
Governmental Administration, Other	10,104	17	1.2
Health	19,603	32	2.4
Highways	49,963	82	6.0
Hospitals	0	0	0.0
Housing and Community Development	18,470	30	2.2
Interest on General Debt	50,736	84	6.1
Judicial and Legal	9,012	15	1.1
Libraries	8,210	14	1.0
Parking	0	0	0.0
Parks and Recreation	46,686	77	5.6
Police Protection	105,366	174	12.7
Public Welfare	2,694	4	0.3
Sewerage	58,320	96	7.0
Solid Waste Management	20,607	34	2.5
Veterans' Services	0	0	0.0
Liquor Store	0	0	0.0
Utility	163,010	269	19.7
Employee Retirement	81,683	135	9.9

Source: U.S Census Bureau, State & Local Government Finances 2011

DEMOGRAPHICS

Population Growth

Area	1990 Census	2000 Census	2010 Census	Population Growth (%) 1990-2000	Population Growth (%) 2000-2010
City	515,541	563,662	649,121	9.3	15.2
MSA[1]	591,610	679,622	800,647	14.9	17.8
U.S.	248,709,873	281,421,906	308,745,538	13.2	9.7

Note: (1) Figures cover the El Paso, TX Metropolitan Statistical Area—see Appendix B for areas included
Source: U.S. Census Bureau, Census 1990, 2000, 2010

Household Size

Area	Persons in Household (%) One	Two	Three	Four	Five	Six	Seven or More	Average Household Size
City	22.4	26.6	19.0	16.8	9.2	3.7	2.3	3.02
MSA[1]	20.5	25.8	19.3	17.4	10.1	4.1	2.8	3.13
U.S.	27.6	33.5	15.7	13.2	6.1	2.4	1.5	2.63

Note: (1) Figures cover the El Paso, TX Metropolitan Statistical Area—see Appendix B for areas included
Source: U.S. Census Bureau, 2010-2012 American Community Survey 3-Year Estimates

Race

Area	White Alone[2] (%)	Black Alone[2] (%)	Asian Alone[2] (%)	AIAN[3] Alone[2] (%)	NHOPI[4] Alone[2] (%)	Other Race Alone[2] (%)	Two or More Races (%)
City	81.8	3.4	1.3	0.5	0.1	10.8	2.1
MSA[1]	80.4	3.3	1.1	0.5	0.1	12.4	2.2
U.S.	74.0	12.6	4.9	0.8	0.2	4.7	2.8

Note: (1) Figures cover the El Paso, TX Metropolitan Statistical Area—see Appendix B for areas included; (2) Alone is defined as not being in combination with one or more other races; (3) American Indian and Alaska Native; (4) Native Hawaiian and Other Pacific Islander
Source: U.S. Census Bureau, 2010-2012 American Community Survey 3-Year Estimates

Hispanic or Latino Origin

Area	Total (%)	Mexican (%)	Puerto Rican (%)	Cuban (%)	Other (%)
City	80.0	76.2	1.0	0.3	2.5
MSA[1]	81.7	78.1	0.9	0.2	2.4
U.S.	16.6	10.7	1.6	0.6	3.7

Note: Persons of Hispanic or Latino origin can be of any race; (1) Figures cover the El Paso, TX Metropolitan Statistical Area—see Appendix B for areas included
Source: U.S. Census Bureau, 2010-2012 American Community Survey 3-Year Estimates

Segregation

Type	Segregation Indices[1] 1990	2000	2010	2010 Rank[2]	Percent Change 1990-2000	Percent Change 1990-2010	Percent Change 2000-2010
Black/White	37.5	36.2	30.7	100	-1.3	-6.8	-5.5
Asian/White	23.8	21.9	22.2	100	-1.9	-1.7	0.2
Hispanic/White	49.7	45.2	43.3	50	-4.5	-6.5	-1.9

Note: All figures cover the Metropolitan Statistical Area—see Appendix B for areas included; Figures are based on an analysis of 1990, 2000, and 2010 Census Decennial Census tract data by William H. Frey, Brookings Institution and the University of Michigan Social Science Data Analysis Network. In this analysis all racial groups (whites, blacks, and asians) are non-Hispanic members of those races. Hispanics are shown as a separate category;
(1) Segregation Indices are Dissimilarity Indices that measure the degree to which the minority group is distributed differently than whites across census tracts. They range from 0 (complete integration) to 100 (complete segregation) where the value indicates the percentage of the minority group that needs to move to be distributed exactly like whites; (2) Ranges from 1 (most segregated) to 102 (least segregated); n/a not available.
Source: www.CensusScope.org

Ancestry

Area	German	Irish	English	American	Italian	Polish	French[2]	Scottish	Dutch
City	3.7	2.8	1.8	4.3	1.1	0.4	0.7	0.5	0.2
MSA[1]	3.3	2.6	1.6	3.9	1.0	0.4	0.6	0.4	0.2
U.S.	15.2	11.1	8.2	7.2	5.6	3.1	2.8	1.7	1.4

Note: Figures are the percentage of the total population reporting a particular ancestry. The nine most commonly reported ancestries in the U.S. are shown. Figures include multiple ancestries (e.g. if a person reported being Irish and Italian, they were included in both columns); (1) Figures cover the El Paso, TX Metropolitan Statistical Area—see Appendix B for areas included; (2) Excludes Basque
Source: U.S. Census Bureau, 2010-2012 American Community Survey 3-Year Estimates

Foreign-Born Population

Area	Any Foreign Country	Mexico	Asia	Europe	Carribean	South America	Central America[2]	Africa	Canada
City	24.6	22.2	1.0	0.5	0.3	0.2	0.3	0.1	0.1
MSA[1]	25.7	23.5	0.9	0.4	0.2	0.2	0.3	0.0	0.1
U.S.	13.0	3.7	3.7	1.6	1.2	0.9	1.0	0.5	0.3

Note: (1) Figures cover the El Paso, TX Metropolitan Statistical Area—see Appendix B for areas included; (2) Excludes Mexico.
Source: U.S. Census Bureau, 2010-2012 American Community Survey 3-Year Estimates

Marital Status

Area	Never Married	Now Married[2]	Separated	Widowed	Divorced
City	31.6	47.8	3.5	5.7	11.4
MSA[1]	32.1	47.8	3.8	5.5	10.8
U.S.	32.4	48.4	2.2	6.0	11.0

Note: Figures are percentages and cover the population 15 years of age and older; (1) Figures cover the El Paso, TX Metropolitan Statistical Area—see Appendix B for areas included; (2) Excludes separated
Source: U.S. Census Bureau, 2010-2012 American Community Survey 3-Year Estimates

Age

Area	Under Age 5	Age 5–19	Age 20–34	Age 35–44	Age 45–54	Age 55–64	Age 65–74	Age 75–84	Age 85+	Median Age
City	7.8	23.9	21.6	12.7	12.8	10.0	6.0	3.9	1.4	32.4
MSA[1]	8.1	25.0	21.7	13.0	12.4	9.5	5.6	3.5	1.3	31.2
U.S.	6.4	20.1	20.5	13.1	14.3	12.2	7.3	4.2	1.8	37.3

Note: (1) Figures cover the El Paso, TX Metropolitan Statistical Area—see Appendix B for areas included
Source: U.S. Census Bureau, 2010-2012 American Community Survey 3-Year Estimates

Gender

Area	Males	Females	Males per 100 Females
City	317,940	344,767	92.2
MSA[1]	397,109	419,186	94.7
U.S.	153,276,055	158,333,314	96.8

Note: (1) Figures cover the El Paso, TX Metropolitan Statistical Area—see Appendix B for areas included
Source: U.S. Census Bureau, 2010-2012 American Community Survey 3-Year Estimates

Religious Groups by Family

Area	Catholic	Baptist	Non-Den.	Methodist[2]	Lutheran	LDS[3]	Pentecostal	Presbyterian[4]	Muslim[5]	Judaism
MSA[1]	43.2	3.8	5.0	0.9	0.3	1.6	1.4	0.2	0.1	0.2
U.S.	19.1	9.3	4.0	4.0	2.3	2.0	1.9	1.6	0.8	0.7

Note: Figures are the number of adherents as a percentage of the total population; (1) Figures cover the El Paso, TX Metropolitan Statistical Area—see Appendix B for areas included; (2) Methodist/Pietist; (3) Latter Day Saints; (4) Reformed; (5) Figures are estimates
Source: Association of Statisticians of American Religious Bodies, 2010 U.S. Religion Census: Religious Congregations & Membership Study

Religious Groups by Tradition

Area	Catholic	Evangelical Protestant	Mainline Protestant	Other Tradition	Black Protestant	Orthodox
MSA[1]	43.2	10.9	1.3	2.1	0.2	0.1
U.S.	19.1	16.2	7.3	4.3	1.6	0.3

Note: Figures are the number of adherents as a percentage of the total population; (1) Figures cover the El Paso, TX Metropolitan Statistical Area—see Appendix B for areas included
Source: Association of Statisticians of American Religious Bodies, 2010 U.S. Religion Census: Religious Congregations & Membership Study

ECONOMY

Gross Metropolitan Product

Area	2011	2012	2013	2014	Rank[2]
MSA[1]	29.0	29.6	29.8	31.2	78

Note: Figures are in billions of dollars; (1) Figures cover the El Paso, TX Metropolitan Statistical Area—see Appendix B for areas included; (2) Rank is based on 2014 data and ranges from 1 to 363
Source: The United States Conference of Mayors, U.S. Metro Economies: Outlook—Gross Metropolitan Product, with Metro Employment Projections, November 2013

Economic Growth

Area	2011 (%)	2012 (%)	2013 (%)	2014 (%)	Rank[2]
MSA[1]	4.3	0.5	-0.6	2.6	296
U.S.	1.6	2.5	1.7	2.5	–

Note: Figures are real gross metropolitan product (GMP) growth rates and represent annual average percent change; (1) Figures cover the El Paso, TX Metropolitan Statistical Area—see Appendix B for areas included; (2) Rank is based on 2013 data and ranges from 1 to 363
Source: The United States Conference of Mayors, U.S. Metro Economies: Outlook—Gross Metropolitan Product, with Metro Employment Projections, November 2013

Metropolitan Area Exports

Area	2007	2008	2009	2010	2011	2012	Rank[2]
MSA[1]	9,608.0	9,390.5	7,748.0	10,315.9	11,615.9	12,796.9	26

Note: Figures are in millions of dollars; (1) Figures cover the El Paso, TX Metropolitan Statistical Area—see Appendix B for areas included; (2) Rank is based on 2012 data and ranges from 1 to 369
Source: U.S. Department of Commerce, International Trade Administration, Office of Trade & Industry Information, Manufacturing & Services, data extracted April 1, 2014

INCOME

Income

Area	Per Capita ($)	Median Household ($)	Average Household ($)
City	19,472	40,920	57,117
MSA[1]	18,183	39,821	55,130
U.S.	27,385	51,771	71,579

Note: (1) Figures cover the El Paso, TX Metropolitan Statistical Area—see Appendix B for areas included
Source: U.S. Census Bureau, 2010-2012 American Community Survey 3-Year Estimates

Household Income Distribution

Area	Percent of Households Earning							
	Under $15,000	$15,000 -24,999	$25,000 -34,999	$35,000 -49,999	$50,000 -74,999	$75,000 -99,000	$100,000 -149,999	$150,000 and up
City	17.4	13.9	12.1	15.5	16.9	9.6	9.2	5.4
MSA[1]	17.8	14.3	12.7	15.2	17.1	9.3	8.5	5.0
U.S.	13.1	11.0	10.5	13.7	18.1	11.9	12.5	9.1

Note: (1) Figures cover the El Paso, TX Metropolitan Statistical Area—see Appendix B for areas included
Source: U.S. Census Bureau, 2010-2012 American Community Survey 3-Year Estimates

Poverty Rate

Area	All Ages	Under 18 Years Old	18 to 64 Years Old	65 Years and Over
City	21.9	30.5	18.5	18.4
MSA[1]	24.0	33.4	20.2	19.3
U.S.	15.7	22.2	14.6	9.3

*Note: Figures are percentage of people whose income during the past 12 months was below the poverty level;
(1) Figures cover the El Paso, TX Metropolitan Statistical Area—see Appendix B for areas included
Source: U.S. Census Bureau, 2010-2012 American Community Survey 3-Year Estimates*

Personal Bankruptcy Filing Rate

Area	2008	2009	2010	2011	2012	2013
El Paso County	2.87	3.71	3.41	3.13	2.99	2.61
U.S.	3.53	4.61	4.97	4.37	3.76	3.29

*Note: Numbers are per 1,000 population and include Chapter 7 and Chapter 13 filings
Source: Federal Deposit Insurance Corporation, Regional Economic Conditions, March 20, 2014*

EMPLOYMENT

Labor Force and Employment

Area	Civilian Labor Force			Workers Employed		
	Dec. 2012	Dec. 2013	% Chg.	Dec. 2012	Dec. 2013	% Chg.
City	271,850	270,705	-0.4	250,664	251,186	0.2
MSA[1]	323,811	322,443	-0.4	296,188	296,805	0.2
U.S.	154,904,000	154,408,000	-0.3	143,060,000	144,423,000	1.0

*Note: Data is not seasonally adjusted and covers workers 16 years of age and older; (1) Metropolitan Statistical Area—see Appendix B for areas included
Source: Bureau of Labor Statistics, Local Area Unemployment Statistics*

Unemployment Rate

Area	2013											
	Jan.	Feb.	Mar.	Apr.	May	Jun.	Jul.	Aug.	Sep.	Oct.	Nov.	Dec.
City	8.7	8.3	8.1	8.0	8.5	9.0	8.6	8.0	8.1	7.8	7.5	7.2
MSA[1]	9.5	9.1	8.9	8.7	9.2	9.8	9.3	8.7	8.8	8.5	8.2	8.0
U.S.	8.5	8.1	7.6	7.1	7.3	7.8	7.7	7.3	7.0	7.0	6.6	6.5

*Note: Data is not seasonally adjusted and covers workers 16 years of age and older; All figures are percentages;
(1) Metropolitan Statistical Area—see Appendix B for areas included
Source: Bureau of Labor Statistics, Local Area Unemployment Statistics*

Employment by Occupation

Occupation Classification	City (%)	MSA[1] (%)	U.S. (%)
Management, Business, Science, and Arts	31.6	29.5	36.0
Natural Resources, Construction, and Maintenance	8.5	9.9	9.1
Production, Transportation, and Material Moving	11.5	12.6	12.0
Sales and Office	27.5	26.6	24.7
Service	20.9	21.3	18.2

*Note: Figures cover employed civilians 16 years of age and older; (1) Figures cover the El Paso, TX Metropolitan Statistical Area—see Appendix B for areas included
Source: U.S. Census Bureau, 2010-2012 American Community Survey 3-Year Estimates*

Employment by Industry

| Sector | MSA[1] | | U.S. |
	Number of Employees	Percent of Total	Percent of Total
Construction	n/a	n/a	4.2
Education and Health Services	39,500	13.6	15.5
Financial Activities	12,100	4.2	5.7
Government	69,700	24.0	16.1
Information	5,800	2.0	1.9
Leisure and Hospitality	30,500	10.5	10.2
Manufacturing	17,500	6.0	8.7
Mining and Logging	n/a	n/a	0.6
Other Services	9,600	3.3	3.9
Professional and Business Services	29,800	10.3	13.7
Retail Trade	39,500	13.6	11.4
Transportation and Utilities	14,000	4.8	3.8
Wholesale Trade	10,000	3.4	4.2

Note: Figures cover non-farm employment as of December 2013 and are not seasonally adjusted;
(1) Metropolitan Statistical Area—see Appendix B for areas included; n/a not available
Source: Bureau of Labor Statistics, Current Employment Statistics, Employment, Hours, and Earnings

Occupations with Greatest Projected Employment Growth: 2010 – 2020

Occupation[1]	2010 Employment	2020 Projected Employment	Numeric Employment Change	Percent Employment Change
Combined Food Preparation and Serving Workers, Including Fast Food	243,530	322,520	78,990	32.4
Elementary School Teachers, Except Special Education	166,090	233,860	67,780	40.8
Personal Care Aides	133,820	199,970	66,150	49.4
Retail Salespersons	370,620	433,180	62,560	16.9
Registered Nurses	184,700	245,870	61,160	33.1
Waiters and Waitresses	190,870	244,610	53,730	28.2
Office Clerks, General	262,740	314,810	52,070	19.8
Cashiers	250,510	292,730	42,220	16.9
Home Health Aides	82,420	123,970	41,550	50.4
Customer Service Representatives	200,880	241,030	40,160	20.0

Note: Projections cover Texas; (1) Sorted by numeric employment change
Source: www.projectionscentral.com, State Occupational Projections, 2010–2020 Long-Term Projections

Fastest Growing Occupations: 2010 – 2020

Occupation[1]	2010 Employment	2020 Projected Employment	Numeric Employment Change	Percent Employment Change
Biomedical Engineers	1,440	2,490	1,050	72.9
Diagnostic Medical Sonographers	3,560	5,410	1,850	51.9
Derrick Operators, Oil and Gas	7,190	10,860	3,670	51.1
Home Health Aides	82,420	123,970	41,550	50.4
Personal Care Aides	133,820	199,970	66,150	49.4
Service Unit Operators, Oil, Gas, and Mining	17,870	26,460	8,590	48.0
Special Education Teachers, Middle School	6,170	8,950	2,780	45.1
Special Education Teachers, Preschool, Kindergarten, and Elementary School	12,940	18,750	5,810	44.9
Rotary Drill Operators, Oil and Gas	7,160	10,340	3,180	44.4
Roustabouts, Oil and Gas	17,800	25,580	7,790	43.8

Note: Projections cover Texas; (1) Sorted by percent employment change and excludes occupations with numeric employment change less than 100
Source: www.projectionscentral.com, State Occupational Projections, 2010–2020 Long-Term Projections

Average Wages

Occupation	$/Hr.	Occupation	$/Hr.
Accountants and Auditors	28.26	Maids and Housekeeping Cleaners	8.80
Automotive Mechanics	15.93	Maintenance and Repair Workers	12.72
Bookkeepers	15.14	Marketing Managers	55.22
Carpenters	13.85	Nuclear Medicine Technologists	n/a
Cashiers	8.90	Nurses, Licensed Practical	20.50
Clerks, General Office	11.88	Nurses, Registered	31.00
Clerks, Receptionists/Information	10.48	Nursing Assistants	10.82
Clerks, Shipping/Receiving	12.21	Packers and Packagers, Hand	9.06
Computer Programmers	33.64	Physical Therapists	48.95
Computer Systems Analysts	34.01	Postal Service Mail Carriers	23.89
Computer User Support Specialists	21.32	Real Estate Brokers	n/a
Cooks, Restaurant	9.33	Retail Salespersons	10.96
Dentists	104.40	Sales Reps., Exc. Tech./Scientific	21.60
Electrical Engineers	45.11	Sales Reps., Tech./Scientific	38.11
Electricians	18.79	Secretaries, Exc. Legal/Med./Exec.	12.87
Financial Managers	48.22	Security Guards	10.13
First-Line Supervisors/Managers, Sales	20.29	Surgeons	n/a
Food Preparation Workers	8.84	Teacher Assistants	10.60
General and Operations Managers	47.02	Teachers, Elementary School	24.60
Hairdressers/Cosmetologists	9.84	Teachers, Secondary School	24.80
Internists	n/a	Telemarketers	9.49
Janitors and Cleaners	9.82	Truck Drivers, Heavy/Tractor-Trailer	17.61
Landscaping/Groundskeeping Workers	9.83	Truck Drivers, Light/Delivery Svcs.	14.03
Lawyers	64.13	Waiters and Waitresses	8.51

*Note: Wage data covers the El Paso, TX Metropolitan Statistical Area—see Appendix B for areas included.
Hourly wages for elementary/secondary school teachers and teacher assistants were calculated by the editors
from annual wage data assuming a 40 hour work week; n/a not available.
Source: Bureau of Labor Statistics, Metro Area Occupational Employment and Wage Estimates, May 2013*

RESIDENTIAL REAL ESTATE

Building Permits

Area	Single-Family			Multi-Family			Total		
	2012	2013	Pct. Chg.	2012	2013	Pct. Chg.	2012	2013	Pct. Chg.
City	2,815	2,271	-19.3	1,177	1,408	19.6	3,992	3,679	-7.8
MSA[1]	3,176	2,613	-17.7	1,179	1,484	25.9	4,355	4,097	-5.9
U.S.	518,695	620,802	19.7	310,963	370,020	19.0	829,658	990,822	19.4

*Note: (1) Metropolitan Statistical Area—see Appendix B for areas included; figures represent new, privately-
owned housing units authorized (unadjusted data); All permit data are based on estimates with imputation.
Source: U.S. Census Bureau, Manufacturing, Mining, and Construction Statistics, Building Permits, 2012, 2013*

Homeownership Rate

Area	2006 (%)	2007 (%)	2008 (%)	2009 (%)	2010 (%)	2011 (%)	2012 (%)	2013 (%)
MSA[1]	65.0	68.2	64.8	63.8	70.1	72.0	67.4	69.3
U.S.	68.8	68.1	67.8	67.4	66.9	66.1	65.4	65.1

*Note: (1) Figures cover the El Paso, TX Metropolitan Statistical Area—see Appendix B for areas included
Source: U.S. Census Bureau, Housing Vacancies and Homeownership Annual Statistics: 2013*

Housing Vacancy Rates

Area	Gross Vacancy Rate[2] (%)			Year-Round Vacancy Rate[3] (%)			Rental Vacancy Rate[4] (%)			Homeowner Vacancy Rate[5] (%)		
	2011	2012	2013	2011	2012	2013	2011	2012	2013	2011	2012	2013
MSA[1]	6.5	4.3	8.8	5.9	4.3	8.6	9.2	8.2	7.9	1.3	0.1	2.9
U.S.	14.2	13.8	13.8	11.1	10.8	10.7	9.5	8.7	8.3	2.5	2.0	2.0

*Note: (1) Figures cover the El Paso, TX Metropolitan Statistical Area—see Appendix B for areas included; (2)
The percentage of the total housing inventory that is vacant; (3) The percentage of the housing inventory
(excluding seasonal units) that is year-round vacant; (4) The percentage of rental inventory that is vacant for
rent; (5) The percentage of homeowner inventory that is vacant for sale
Source: U.S. Census Bureau, Housing Vacancies and Homeownership Annual Statistics: 2013*

TAXES

State Corporate Income Tax Rates

State	Tax Rate (%)	Income Brackets ($)	Num. of Brackets	Financial Institution Tax Rate (%)[a]	Federal Income Tax Ded.
Texas	(x)	–	–	(x)	No

Note: Tax rates as of January 1, 2014; (a) Rates listed are the corporate income tax rate applied to financial institutions or excise taxes based on income. Some states have other taxes based upon the value of deposits or shares; (x) Texas imposes a Franchise Tax, otherwise known as margin tax, imposed on entities with more than $1,030,000 total revenues at rate of 1%, or 0.5% for entities primarily engaged in retail or wholesale trade, on lesser of 70% of total revenues or 100% of gross receipts after deductions for either compensation or cost of goods sold.
Source: Federation of Tax Administrators, "State Corporate Income Tax Rates, 2014"

State Individual Income Tax Rates

State	Tax Rate (%)	Income Brackets ($)	Num. of Brackets	Personal Exempt. ($)[1] Single	Personal Exempt. ($)[1] Dependents	Fed. Inc. Tax Ded.
Texas	None	–	–	–	–	–

Note: Tax rates as of January 1, 2014; Local- and county-level taxes are not included; n/a not applicable;
(1) Married joint filers generally receive double the single exemption
Source: Federation of Tax Administrators, "State Individual Income Tax Rates, 2014"

Various State and Local Tax Rates

State	State and Local Sales and Use (%)	State Sales and Use (%)	Gasoline[1] (¢/gal.)	Cigarette[2] ($/pack)	Spirits[3] ($/gal.)	Wine[4] ($/gal.)	Beer[5] ($/gal.)
Texas	8.25	6.25	20.00	1.410	2.40 (f)	0.20	0.20

Note: All tax rates as of January 1, 2014; (1) The American Petroleum Institute has developed a methodology for determining the average tax rate on a gallon of fuel. Rates may include any of the following: excise taxes, environmental fees, storage tank fees, other fees or taxes, general sales tax, and local taxes. In states where gasoline is subject to the general sales tax, or where the fuel tax is based on the average sale price, the average rate determined by API is sensitive to changes in the price of gasoline. States that fully or partially apply general sales taxes to gasoline: CA, CO, GA, IL, IN, MI, NY; (2) The federal excise tax of $1.0066 per pack and local taxes are not included; (3) Rates are those applicable to off-premise sales of 40% alcohol by volume (a.b.v.) distilled spirits in 750ml containers. Local excise taxes are excluded; (4) Rates are those applicable to off-premise sales of 11% a.b.v. non-carbonated wine in 750ml containers; (5) Rates are those applicable to off-premise sales of 4.7% a.b.v. beer in 12 ounce containers; (f) Different rates also applicable according to alcohol content, place of production, size of container, or place purchased (on- or off-premise or onboard airlines).
Source: Tax Foundation, 2014 Facts & Figures: How Does Your State Compare?

State Business Tax Climate Index Rankings

State	Overall Rank	Corporate Tax Index Rank	Individual Income Tax Index Rank	Sales Tax Index Rank	Unemployment Insurance Tax Index Rank	Property Tax Index Rank
Texas	11	38	7	36	14	35

Note: The index is a measure of how each state's tax laws affect economic performance. The lower the rank, the more favorable a state's tax system is for business. States without a given tax are given a ranking of 1. The scores/rankings for the District of Columbia do not affect other states. The 2014 index represents the tax climate as of July 1, 2013.
Source: Tax Foundation, State Business Tax Climate Index 2014

COMMERCIAL UTILITIES

Typical Monthly Electric Bills

Area	Commercial Service ($/month) 1,500 kWh	Commercial Service ($/month) 40 kW demand 14,000 kWh	Industrial Service ($/month) 1,000 kW demand 200,000 kWh	Industrial Service ($/month) 50,000 kW demand 15,000,000 kWh
City	215	1,645	30,745	1,672,965
Average[1]	197	1,636	25,662	1,485,307

Note: Based on total rates in effect July 1, 2013; (1) average based on 180 utilities surveyed
Source: Edison Electric Institute, Typical Bills and Average Rates Report, Summer 2013

TRANSPORTATION

Means of Transportation to Work

Area	Car/Truck/Van		Public Transportation			Bicycle	Walked	Other Means	Worked at Home
	Drove Alone	Car-pooled	Bus	Subway	Railroad				
City	79.5	11.2	2.0	0.0	0.0	0.1	1.9	2.6	2.7
MSA[1]	79.1	11.2	1.8	0.0	0.0	0.1	2.1	2.8	2.9
U.S.	76.4	9.7	2.6	1.7	0.5	0.6	2.8	1.3	4.3

Note: Figures are percentages and cover workers 16 years of age and older; (1) Figures cover the El Paso, TX Metropolitan Statistical Area—see Appendix B for areas included
Source: U.S. Census Bureau, 2010-2012 American Community Survey 3-Year Estimates

Travel Time to Work

Area	Less Than 10 Minutes	10 to 19 Minutes	20 to 29 Minutes	30 to 44 Minutes	45 to 59 Minutes	60 to 89 Minutes	90 Minutes or More
City	9.5	32.5	29.2	21.5	3.9	2.1	1.3
MSA[1]	9.8	31.2	28.3	22.5	4.3	2.6	1.4
U.S.	13.5	29.8	20.9	20.1	7.5	5.6	2.5

Note: Figures are percentages and include workers 16 years old and over; (1) Figures cover the El Paso, TX Metropolitan Statistical Area—see Appendix B for areas included
Source: U.S. Census Bureau, 2010-2012 American Community Survey 3-Year Estimates

Travel Time Index

Area	1985	1990	1995	2000	2005	2010	2011
Urban Area[1]	1.05	1.08	1.12	1.21	1.23	1.21	1.21
Average[2]	1.09	1.14	1.16	1.19	1.23	1.18	1.18

Note: Travel Time Index—the ratio of travel time in the peak period to the travel time at free-flow conditions. For example, a value of 1.30 indicates a 20-minute free-flow trip takes 26 minutes in the peak. Free-flow speeds (60 mph on freeways and 35 mph on principal arterials) are used as the comparison threshold; (1) Covers the El Paso TX-NM urban area; (2) average of 498 urban areas
Source: Texas Transportation Institute, Urban Mobility Report 2012, December 2012

Public Transportation

Agency Name / Mode of Transportation	Vehicles Operated in Maximum Service	Annual Unlinked Passenger Trips (in thous.)	Annual Passenger Miles (in thous.)
Mass Transit Department-City of El Paso (Sun Metro)			
Bus (directly operated)	122	16,390.6	84,063.0
Demand Response (directly operated)	49	238.1	2,379.0
Demand Response Taxi (purchased transportation)	60	27.2	273.5

Source: Federal Transit Administration, National Transit Database, 2012

Air Transportation

Airport Name and Code / Type of Service	Passenger Airlines[1]	Passenger Enplanements	Freight Carriers[2]	Freight (lbs.)
El Paso International (ELP)				
Domestic service (U.S. carriers - 2013)	20	1,351,599	16	90,092,236
International service (U.S. carriers - 2012)	4	6,491	5	1,299,792

Note: (1) Includes all U.S.-based major, minor and commuter airlines that carried at least one passenger during the year; (2) Includes all U.S.-based airlines and freight carriers that transported at least one lb. of freight during the year.
Source: Bureau of Transportation Statistics, The Intermodal Transportation Database, Air Carriers: T-100 Domestic Market (U.S. Carriers), 2013; Bureau of Transportation Statistics, The Intermodal Transportation Database, Air Carriers: T-100 International Market (U.S. Carriers), 2012

Other Transportation Statistics

Major Highways:	I-10
Amtrak Service:	Yes
Major Waterways/Ports:	Rio Grande

Source: Amtrak.com; Google Maps

BUSINESSES

Major Business Headquarters

Company Name	Rankings	
	Fortune[1]	Forbes[2]
Western Refining	283	-

Note: (1) Fortune 500—companies that produce a 10-K are ranked 1 to 500 based on 2012 revenue; (2) all private companies with at least $2 billion in annual revenue through the end of their most current fiscal year are ranked 1 to 224; companies listed are headquartered in the city; dashes indicate no ranking
Source: Fortune, "Fortune 500," May 20, 2013; Forbes, "America's Largest Private Companies," December 18, 2013

Minority Business Opportunity

El Paso is home to 28 companies which are on the *Hispanic Business* 500 list (500 largest U.S. Hispanic-owned companies based on 2012 revenue): **Fred Loya Insurance** (#19); **Bravo Southwest LP** (#71); **R. M. Personnel** (#155); **Integrated Human Capital/Santana Group** (#157); **dmDickason Personnel Services** (#195); **JACO General Contractors** (#254); **Miratek Corp.** (#275); **Thrifty Car Sales** (#312); **LGA Trucking** (#339); **Mike Garcia Merchant Security** (#354); **Aztec Contractors** (#402); **MFH Environmental Corp.** (#416); **Milvian Solutions** (#426); **Five Star Automatic Fire Protection** (#431); **American Packaging and Supply Co.** (#436); **Cesar-Scott** (#437); **El Paso Sanitation Systems** (#449); **Dynatec Scientific Laboratories** (#451); **H.G. Arias & Associates LP** (#462); **Servpro of West El Paso** (#464); **DataXport.Net** (#472); **Arrow Discount Automotive** (#474); **Accurate Collision Center** (#479); **ASEO** (#480); **Paul Meza CPA Firm** (#483); **The Saucedo Co.** (#487); **ENCON International** (#494); **Kuzzy Industrial Supplier** (#498). Companies included must show at least 51 percent ownership by Hispanic U.S. citizens, and must maintain headquarters in one of the 50 states or Washington, D.C. *Hispanic Business, "Hispanic Business 500," June 20, 2013*

El Paso is home to six companies which are on the *Hispanic Business* Fastest-Growing 100 list (greatest sales growth from 2008 to 2012): **LGA Trucking** (#28); **Integrated Human Capital/Santana Group** (#30); **Bravo Southwest** (#70); **Milvian Solutions** (#80); **Fred Loya Insurance** (#81); **dmDickason Personnel Services** (#96). Companies included must show at least 51 percent ownership by Hispanic U.S. citizens, and must maintain headquarters in one of the 50 states or Washington, D.C. In addition, companies must have minimum revenues of $200,000 for calendar year 2008. *Hispanic Business, June 20, 2013*

Minority- and Women-Owned Businesses

Group	All Firms		Firms with Paid Employees			
	Firms	Sales ($000)	Firms	Sales ($000)	Employees	Payroll ($000)
Asian	1,115	189,485	432	173,094	2,805	43,016
Black	1,197	57,643	(s)	(s)	(s)	(s)
Hispanic	31,640	5,521,058	3,924	4,565,644	29,777	798,704
Women	14,792	1,952,682	1,609	1,638,631	17,694	375,970
All Firms	52,897	45,727,653	9,346	44,068,193	181,930	5,012,823

Note: Figures cover firms located in the city; minority- and women-owned business are defined as firms in which the corresponding group own 51% or more of the stock or equity of the company; (s) estimates are suppressed when publication standards are not met
Source: U.S. Census Bureau, 2007 Economic Census, Survey of Business Owners (2012 Survey of Business Owners data will be released starting in June 2015)

HOTELS & CONVENTION CENTERS

Hotels/Motels

Area	5 Star		4 Star		3 Star		2 Star		1 Star		Not Rated	
	Num.	Pct.[3]	Num.	Pct.[3]	Num.	Pct.[3]	Num.	Pct.[3]	Num.	Pct.[3]	Num.	Pct.[3]
City[1]	0	0.0	1	1.1	31	34.4	50	55.6	0	0.0	8	8.9
Total[2]	142	0.9	1,005	6.0	5,147	30.9	8,578	51.4	408	2.4	1,397	8.4

Note: (1) Figures cover El Paso and vicinity; (2) Figures cover all 100 cities in this book; (3) Percentage of hotels which have a given star rating; Star ratings are determined by expedia.com and offer an indication of the general quality of a particular hotel.
Source: expedia.com, April 7, 2014

Major Convention Centers

Name	Overall Space (sq. ft.)	Exhibit Space (sq. ft.)	Meeting Space (sq. ft.)	Meeting Rooms
Judson F. Williams Convention Center	n/a	80,000	14,900	17

Note: Table includes convention centers located in the El Paso, TX metro area; n/a not available
Source: Original research

Living Environment

COST OF LIVING

Cost of Living Index

Composite Index	Groceries	Housing	Utilities	Trans-portation	Health Care	Misc. Goods/ Services
91.2	90.8	84.0	87.2	97.5	89.9	96.1

Note: The Cost of Living Index measures regional differences in the cost of consumer goods and services, excluding taxes and non-consumer expenditures, for professional and managerial households in the top income quintile. It is based on more than 50,000 prices covering almost 60 different items for which prices are collected three times a year by chambers of commerce, economic development organizations or university applied economic centers in each participating urban area. The numbers shown should be read as a percentage above or below the national average of 100. For example, a value of 115.4 in the groceries column indicates that grocery prices are 15.4% higher than the national average. Small differences in the index numbers should not be interpreted as significant; Figures cover the El Paso TX urban area.
Source: The Council for Community and Economic Research, ACCRA Cost of Living Index, 2013

Grocery Prices

Area[1]	T-Bone Steak ($/pound)	Frying Chicken ($/pound)	Whole Milk ($/half gal.)	Eggs ($/dozen)	Orange Juice ($/64 oz.)	Coffee ($/11.5 oz.)
City[2]	10.28	1.15	2.13	1.66	3.25	4.96
Avg.	10.19	1.28	2.34	1.81	3.48	4.39
Min.	8.56	0.94	1.44	1.19	2.78	3.40
Max.	14.82	2.28	3.56	3.73	6.23	7.32

Note: (1) Values for the local area are compared with the average, minimum and maximum values for all 327 areas in the Cost of Living Index; (2) Figures cover the El Paso TX urban area; **T-Bone Steak** *(price per pound);* **Frying Chicken** *(price per pound, whole fryer);* **Whole Milk** *(half gallon carton);* **Eggs** *(price per dozen, Grade A, large);* **Orange Juice** *(64 oz. Tropicana or Florida Natural);* **Coffee** *(11.5 oz. can, vacuum-packed, Maxwell House, Hills Bros, or Folgers).*
Source: The Council for Community and Economic Research, ACCRA Cost of Living Index, 2013

Housing and Utility Costs

Area[1]	New Home Price ($)	Apartment Rent ($/month)	All Electric ($/month)	Part Electric ($/month)	Other Energy ($/month)	Telephone ($/month)
City[2]	232,054	922	-	97.59	33.67	26.95
Avg.	295,864	900	171.38	91.82	70.12	27.73
Min.	185,506	458	117.80	48.81	33.67	17.16
Max.	1,358,917	3,783	441.68	171.40	372.65	39.47

Note: (1) Values for the local area are compared with the average, minimum and maximum values for all 327 areas in the Cost of Living Index; (2) Figures cover the El Paso TX urban area; **New Home Price** *(2,400 sf living area, 8,000 sf lot, in urban area with full utilities);* **Apartment Rent** *(950 sf 2 bedroom/1.5 or 2 bath, unfurnished, excluding all utilities except water);* **All Electric** *(average monthly cost for an all-electric home);* **Part Electric** *(average monthly cost for a part-electric home);* **Other Energy** *(average monthly cost for natural gas, fuel oil, coal, wood, and any other forms of energy except electricity);* **Telephone** *(price includes basic monthly rate for a private residential line plus additional local usage charges incurred by a family of four).*
Source: The Council for Community and Economic Research, ACCRA Cost of Living Index, 2013

Health Care, Transportation, and Other Costs

Area[1]	Doctor ($/visit)	Dentist ($/visit)	Optometrist ($/visit)	Gasoline ($/gallon)	Beauty Salon ($/visit)	Men's Shirt ($)
City[2]	83.33	77.83	83.33	3.27	32.17	24.94
Avg.	101.40	86.48	96.16	3.44	33.87	26.55
Min.	61.67	50.83	50.12	3.08	18.92	12.48
Max.	182.71	152.50	223.78	4.33	68.22	52.03

Note: (1) Values for the local area are compared with the average, minimum and maximum values for all 327 areas in the Cost of Living Index; (2) Figures cover the El Paso TX urban area; **Doctor** *(general practitioners routine exam of an established patient);* **Dentist** *(adult teeth cleaning and periodic oral examination);* **Optometrist** *(full vision eye exam for established adult patient);* **Gasoline** *(one gallon regular unleaded, national brand, including all taxes, cash price at self-service pump if available);* **Beauty Salon** *(woman's shampoo, trim, and blow-dry);* **Men's Shirt** *(cotton/polyester dress shirt, pinpoint weave, long sleeves).*
Source: The Council for Community and Economic Research, ACCRA Cost of Living Index, 2013

HOUSING

House Price Index (HPI)

Area	National Ranking[2]	Quarterly Change (%)	One-Year Change (%)	Five-Year Change (%)
MSA[1]	203	-1.67	0.47	-5.06
U.S.[3]	–	1.20	7.69	4.18

Note: The HPI is a weighted repeat sales index. It measures average price changes in repeat sales or refinancings on the same properties. This information is obtained by reviewing repeat mortgage transactions on single-family properties whose mortgages have been purchased or securitized by Fannie Mae or Freddie Mac in January 1975; (1) El Paso, TX Metropolitan Statistical Area—see Appendix B for areas included; (2) Rankings are based on annual percentage change for all metro areas containing at least 15,000 transactions over the last 10 years and ranges from 1 to 283; (3) figures based on a weighted average of Census Division estimates using a seasonally adjusted, purchase-only index; all figures are for the period ending December 31, 2013
Source: Federal Housing Finance Agency, House Price Index, February 25, 2014

Median Single-Family Home Prices

Area	2011	2012	2013p	Percent Change 2012 to 2013
MSA[1]	134.3	138.6	141.2	1.9
U.S. Average	166.2	177.2	197.4	11.4

Note: Figures are median sales prices of existing single-family homes in thousands of dollars; (p) preliminary; n/a not available; (1) El Paso, TX Metropolitan Statistical Area—see Appendix B for areas included
Source: National Association of Realtors, Median Sales Price of Existing Single-Family Homes for Metropolitan Areas, 4th Quarter 2013

Qualifying Income Based on Median Sales Price of Existing Single-Family Homes

Area	With 5% Down ($)	With 10% Down ($)	With 20% Down ($)
MSA[1]	33,130	31,386	27,899
U.S. Average	45,395	43,006	38,228

Note: Figures are preliminary; Qualifying income is based on a mortgage rate of 4.4%. Monthly principal and interest payment is limited to 25% of income; n/a not available; (1) El Paso, TX Metropolitan Statistical Area—see Appendix B for areas included
Source: National Association of Realtors, Qualifying Income Based on Median Sales Price of Existing Single-Family Homes for Metropolitan Areas, 4th Quarter 2013

Median Apartment Condo-Coop Home Prices

Area	2011	2012	2013p	Percent Change 2012 to 2013
MSA[1]	n/a	n/a	n/a	n/a
U.S. Average	165.1	173.7	194.9	12.2

Note: Figures are median sales prices of existing apartment condo-coop homes in thousands of dollars; (p) preliminary; n/a not available; (1) El Paso, TX Metropolitan Statistical Area—see Appendix B for areas included
Source: National Association of Realtors, Median Sales Price of Existing Apartment Condo-Coop Homes for Metropolitan Areas, 4th Quarter 2013

Gross Monthly Rent

Area	Under $200	$200 -299	$300 -499	$500 -749	$750 -999	$1,000 -1,499	$1,500 and up	Median ($)
City	3.9	4.5	14.4	31.2	23.5	18.3	4.2	723
MSA[1]	3.8	4.3	15.5	31.0	23.3	18.0	4.2	718
U.S.	1.7	3.3	8.1	22.7	24.3	25.7	14.3	889

Note: Figures are percentages except for Median; Gross rent is the contract rent plus the estimated average monthly cost of utilities (electricity, gas, and water and sewer) and fuels (oil, coal, kerosene, wood, etc.) if these are paid by the renter (or paid for the renter by someone else); (1) Figures cover the El Paso, TX Metropolitan Statistical Area—see Appendix B for areas included
Source: U.S. Census Bureau, 2010-2012 American Community Survey 3-Year Estimates

Year Housing Structure Built

Area	2010 or Later	2000 -2009	1990 -1999	1980 -1989	1970 -1979	1960 -1969	1950 -1959	1940 -1949	Before 1940	Median Year
City	1.5	16.7	13.3	15.2	18.4	12.8	12.9	4.0	5.1	1978
MSA[1]	1.8	19.1	14.6	16.0	17.4	11.5	11.5	3.7	4.7	1981
U.S.	0.5	14.9	13.8	13.9	15.9	11.1	10.9	5.5	13.5	1976

Note: Figures are percentages except for Median Year; (1) Figures cover the El Paso, TX Metropolitan Statistical Area—see Appendix B for areas included
Source: U.S. Census Bureau, 2010-2012 American Community Survey 3-Year Estimates

HEALTH

Health Risk Data

Category	MSA[1] (%)	U.S. (%)
Adults aged 18–64 who have any kind of health care coverage	52.1	79.6
Adults who reported being in good or excellent health	76.6	83.1
Adults who are current smokers	15.1	19.6
Adults who are heavy drinkers[2]	5.2	6.1
Adults who are binge drinkers[3]	21.0	16.9
Adults who are overweight (BMI 25.0 - 29.9)	36.6	35.8
Adults who are obese (BMI 30.0 - 99.8)	29.4	27.6
Adults who participated in any physical activities in the past month	68.0	77.1
Adults 50+ who have ever had a sigmoidoscopy or colonoscopy	50.0	67.3
Women aged 40+ who have had a mammogram within the past two years	65.8	74.0
Men aged 40+ who have had a PSA test within the past two years	36.5	45.2
Adults aged 65+ who have had flu shot within the past year	50.9	60.1
Adults who always wear a seatbelt	n/a	93.8

Note: Data as of 2012 unless otherwise noted; n/a not available; (1) Figures cover the El Paso, TX Metropolitan Statistical Area—see Appendix B for areas included; (2) Heavy drinkers are classified as males having more than two drinks per day or females having more than one drink per day; (3) Binge drinkers are classified as males having five or more drinks on one occasion or females having four or more drinks on one occasion
Source: Centers for Disease Control and Prevention, Behaviorial Risk Factor Surveillance System, SMART: Selected Metropolitan/Micropolitan Area Risk Trends, 2012

Chronic Health Indicators

Category	MSA[1] (%)	U.S. (%)
Adults who have ever been told they had a heart attack	n/a	4.5
Adults who have ever been told they had a stroke	n/a	2.9
Adults who have been told they currently have asthma	7.5	8.9
Adults who have ever been told they have arthritis	19.6	25.7
Adults who have ever been told they have diabetes[2]	14.1	9.7
Adults who have ever been told they had skin cancer	n/a	5.7
Adults who have ever been told they had any other types of cancer	5.8	6.5
Adults who have ever been told they have COPD	4.1	6.2
Adults who have ever been told they have kidney disease	n/a	2.5
Adults who have ever been told they have a form of depression	17.2	18.0

Note: Data as of 2012 unless otherwise noted; n/a not available; (1) Figures cover the El Paso, TX Metropolitan Statistical Area—see Appendix B for areas included; (2) Figures do not include pregnancy-related, borderline, or pre-diabetes
Source: Centers for Disease Control and Prevention, Behaviorial Risk Factor Surveillance System, SMART: Selected Metropolitan/Micropolitan Area Risk Trends, 2012

Mortality Rates for the Top 10 Causes of Death in the U.S.

ICD-10[a] Sub-Chapter	ICD-10[a] Code	Age-Adjusted Mortality Rate[1] per 100,000 population	
		County[2]	U.S.
Malignant neoplasms	C00-C97	148.6	174.2
Ischaemic heart diseases	I20-I25	81.6	119.1
Other forms of heart disease	I30-I51	36.6	49.6
Chronic lower respiratory diseases	J40-J47	36.1	43.2
Cerebrovascular diseases	I60-I69	43.7	40.3
Organic, including symptomatic, mental disorders	F01-F09	21.3	30.5
Other degenerative diseases of the nervous system	G30-G31	27.9	26.3
Other external causes of accidental injury	W00-X59	19.3	25.1
Diabetes mellitus	E10-E14	29.4	21.3
Hypertensive diseases	I10-I15	35.8	18.8

Note: (a) ICD-10 = International Classification of Diseases 10th Revision; (1) Mortality rates are a three year average covering 2008-2010; (2) Figures cover El Paso County
Source: Centers for Disease Control and Prevention, National Center for Health Statistics. Compressed Mortality File 1999-2010 on CDC WONDER Online Database, released January 2013. Data are compiled from the Compressed Mortality File 1999-2010, Series 20 No. 2P, 2013.

Mortality Rates for Selected Causes of Death

ICD-10[a] Sub-Chapter	ICD-10[a] Code	Age-Adjusted Mortality Rate[1] per 100,000 population	
		County[2]	U.S.
Assault	X85-Y09	2.5	5.5
Diseases of the liver	K70-K76	26.3	12.4
Human immunodeficiency virus (HIV) disease	B20-B24	2.5	3.0
Influenza and pneumonia	J09-J18	9.8	16.4
Intentional self-harm	X60-X84	7.9	11.8
Malnutrition	E40-E46	1.8	0.8
Obesity and other hyperalimentation	E65-E68	1.7	1.6
Renal failure	N17-N19	14.7	13.6
Transport accidents	V01-V99	12.5	12.6
Viral hepatitis	B15-B19	3.7	2.2

Note: (a) ICD-10 = International Classification of Diseases 10th Revision; (1) Mortality rates are a three year average covering 2008-2010; (2) Figures cover El Paso County
Source: Centers for Disease Control and Prevention, National Center for Health Statistics. Compressed Mortality File 1999-2010 on CDC WONDER Online Database, released January 2013. Data are compiled from the Compressed Mortality File 1999-2010, Series 20 No. 2P, 2013.

Health Insurance Coverage

Area	With Health Insurance	With Private Health Insurance	With Public Health Insurance	Without Health Insurance	Population Under Age 18 Without Health Insurance
City	73.4	48.1	32.7	26.6	12.8
MSA[1]	71.8	45.4	33.0	28.2	13.7
U.S.	84.9	65.4	30.4	15.1	7.5

Note: Figures are percentages that cover the civilian noninstitutionalized population; (1) Figures cover the El Paso, TX Metropolitan Statistical Area—see Appendix B for areas included
Source: U.S. Census Bureau, 2010-2012 American Community Survey 3-Year Estimates

Number of Medical Professionals

Area[1]	MDs[2]	DOs[2,3]	Dentists	Podiatrists	Chiropractors	Optometrists
Local (number)	1,436	107	293	30	69	64
Local (rate[4])	175.5	13.1	35.4	3.6	8.3	7.7
U.S. (rate[4])	267.6	19.6	61.7	5.6	24.7	14.5

Note: Data as of 2012 unless noted; (1) Local data covers El Paso County; (2) Data as of 2011; (3) Doctor of Osteopathic Medicine; (4) rate per 100,000 population
Source: Area Resource File (ARF) 2012-2013. U.S. Department of Health and Human Services, Health Resources and Services Administration, Bureau of Health Professions

EDUCATION

Public School District Statistics

District Name	Schls	Pupils	Pupil/ Teacher Ratio	Minority Pupils[1] (%)	Free Lunch Eligible[2] (%)	IEP[3] (%)
Canutillo ISD	10	6,031	16.5	95.5	63.3	8.5
Clint ISD	14	11,886	18.6	96.2	42.8	7.1
El Paso ISD	97	64,214	15.2	89.1	62.2	8.8
Socorro ISD	44	43,672	18.1	94.4	59.5	7.9
Ysleta ISD	63	44,376	14.4	97.8	63.9	10.0

Note: Table includes school districts with 2,000 or more students; (1) Percentage of students that are not non-Hispanic white; (2) Percentage of students that are eligible for the free lunch program; (3) Percentage of students that have an Individualized Education Program.
Source: U.S. Department of Education, National Center for Education Statistics, Common Core of Data, Local Education Agency (School District) Universe Survey: School Year 2011-2012; U.S. Department of Education, National Center for Education Statistics, Common Core of Data, Public Elementary/Secondary School Universe Survey: School Year 2011-2012

Best High Schools

High School Name	Rank[1]	Grad. Rate[2] (%)	Coll.[3] (%)	AP/IB/ AICE Tests[4]	AP/IB/ AICE Score[5]	SAT Score[6]	ACT Score[6]
Bel Air H.S.	1839	88	91	0.3	2.1	805	18.9
Coronado H.S.	1208	99	82	0.4	3.0	1462	22.5
Franklin H.S.	1578	90	84	0.2	2.8	1445	22.9
Harmony Science Academy El Paso	1041	79	100	0.8	2.4	1423	27.0

Note: (1) Public schools are ranked from 1 to 2,000 based on the following self-reported statistics (with the corresponding weight used in calculating their overall score). Schools that were newly founded and did not have a graduating senior class in 2012 were excluded; (2) Four-year, on-time graduation rate (25%); (3) Percent of 2011 graduates who were accepted to college (25%); (4) AP/IB/AICE tests taken per student (25%); (5) Average AP/IB/AICE exam score (10%); (6) Average SAT and/or ACT score (10%); Percent of students enrolled in at least one AP/IB/AICE course (5%)—data not shown
Source: Newsweek and The Daily Beast, "America's Best High Schools 2013"

Highest Level of Education

Area	Less than H.S.	H.S. Diploma	Some College, No Deg.	Associate Degree	Bachelor's Degree	Master's Degree	Prof. School Degree	Doctorate Degree
City	23.4	23.9	23.0	7.2	15.1	5.4	1.3	0.7
MSA[1]	25.8	24.0	22.6	7.0	13.9	4.9	1.1	0.6
U.S.	14.1	28.3	21.3	7.8	18.0	7.5	1.9	1.2

Note: Figures cover persons age 25 and over; (1) Figures cover the El Paso, TX Metropolitan Statistical Area—see Appendix B for areas included
Source: U.S. Census Bureau, 2010-2012 American Community Survey 3-Year Estimates

Educational Attainment by Race

Area	High School Graduate or Higher (%)					Bachelor's Degree or Higher (%)				
	Total	White	Black	Asian	Hisp.[2]	Total	White	Black	Asian	Hisp.[2]
City	76.6	77.4	92.2	87.7	71.6	22.6	22.8	28.6	49.1	17.9
MSA[1]	74.2	75.4	92.6	88.1	69.1	20.6	21.0	28.2	49.1	16.1
U.S.	85.9	88.1	82.5	85.5	63.1	28.6	30.0	18.4	50.2	13.4

Note: Figures shown cover persons 25 years old and over; (1) Figures cover the El Paso, TX Metropolitan Statistical Area—see Appendix B for areas included; (2) People of Hispanic origin can be of any race
Source: U.S. Census Bureau, 2010-2012 American Community Survey 3-Year Estimates

School Enrollment by Grade and Control

Area	Preschool (%)		Kindergarten (%)		Grades 1 - 4 (%)		Grades 5 - 8 (%)		Grades 9 - 12 (%)	
	Public	Private	Public	Private	Public	Private	Public	Private	Public	Private
City	80.9	19.1	94.7	5.3	93.9	6.1	94.5	5.5	95.4	4.6
MSA[1]	83.8	16.2	95.5	4.5	95.1	4.9	95.4	4.6	96.3	3.7
U.S.	56.9	43.1	87.8	12.2	89.9	10.1	90.0	10.0	90.8	9.2

Note: Figures shown cover persons 3 years old and over; (1) Figures cover the El Paso, TX Metropolitan Statistical Area—see Appendix B for areas included
Source: U.S. Census Bureau, 2010-2012 American Community Survey 3-Year Estimates

Average Salaries of Public School Classroom Teachers

Area	2012-13		2013-14		Percent Change 2012-13 to 2013-14	Percent Change 2003-04 to 2013-14
	Dollars	Rank[1]	Dollars	Rank[1]		
Texas	48,819	35	49,270	35	0.92	21.7
U.S. Average	56,103	–	56,689	–	1.04	21.8

Note: (1) State rank ranges from 1 to 51 where 1 indicates highest salary.
Source: National Education Association, Rankings & Estimates: Rankings of the States 2013 and Estimates of School Statistics 2014, March 2014

Higher Education

Four-Year Colleges			Two-Year Colleges			Medical Schools[1]	Law Schools[2]	Voc/ Tech[3]
Public	Private Non-profit	Private For-profit	Public	Private Non-profit	Private For-profit			
1	0	1	1	0	8	1	0	6

Note: Figures cover institutions located within the city limits and include main campuses only; (1) includes schools accredited by the Liaison Committee on Medical Education and the American Osteopathic Association's Commission on Osteopathic College Accreditation; (2) includes ABA-accredited schools, schools with provisional ABA accreditation, and state accredited schools; (3) includes all schools with programs that are less than 2 years.
Source: National Center for Education Statistics, Integrated Postsecondary Education System (IPEDS), 2012-13; Association of American Medical Colleges, Member List, April 24, 2014; American Osteopathic Association, Member List, April 24, 2014; Law School Admission Council, Official Guide to ABA-Approved Law Schools Online, April 24, 2014; Wikipedia, List of Medical Schools in the United States, April 24, 2014; Wikipedia, List of Law Schools in the United States, April 24, 2014

PRESIDENTIAL ELECTION

2012 Presidential Election Results

Area	Obama	Romney	Other
El Paso County	65.6	33.0	1.3
U.S.	51.0	47.2	1.8

Note: Results are percentages and may not add to 100% due to rounding
Source: Dave Leip's Atlas of U.S. Presidential Elections

EMPLOYERS

Major Employers

Company Name	Industry
AHAC	Employmant agencies
Automatic Data Processing	Data processing service
Bureau of Customs and Border Protection	Customs
City of El Paso	Executive/legislative combined
Delphi Automotive Systems	Motor vehicle parts/accessories
Delphi Automotive Systems Corporation	Automotive, electrical equipment
El paso County Hospital Direct	General medical/surgical hospitals
El Paso Electric Company	Electric services
Elcom	Electrical circuits
Furukawa Wiring Systems America	Public building /related furniture
Genpact	Data processing/preparation
Justin Brands	Boots/dress or casual mens
Philips Consumer Electronic Company	Cameras/televisions
Redcats USA, LP	Catalog/mail order house
Tenet Hospitals Limited	General medical/surgical hospitals
Texas Tech University	University
Time Warner, Advance Newhouse Prtnrshp	Cable television services
United States Postal Service	Postal service
University of Texas at El Paso	Colleges/universities

Note: Companies shown are located within the El Paso, TX Metropolitan Statistical Area.
Source: Hoovers.com; Wikipedia

PUBLIC SAFETY

Crime Rate

Area	All Crimes	Violent Crimes				Property Crimes		
		Murder	Forcible Rape	Robbery	Aggrav. Assault	Burglary	Larceny -Theft	Motor Vehicle Theft
City	2,852.5	3.4	27.2	69.7	322.9	270.3	1,987.3	171.7
Suburbs[1]	2,117.7	3.1	22.4	23.0	237.2	344.1	1,365.0	123.0
Metro[2]	2,711.1	3.3	26.3	60.7	306.4	284.5	1,867.5	162.3
U.S.	3,246.1	4.7	26.9	112.9	242.3	670.2	1,959.3	229.7

Note: Figures are crimes per 100,000 population; (1) All areas within the metro area that are located outside the city limits; (2) Figures cover the El Paso, TX Metropolitan Statistical Area—see Appendix B for areas included
Source: FBI Uniform Crime Reports, 2012

Hate Crimes

Area	Number of Quarters Reported	Bias Motivation				
		Race	Religion	Sexual Orientation	Ethnicity	Disability
City	4	0	0	3	1	0
U.S.	4	2,797	1,099	1,135	667	92

Source: Federal Bureau of Investigation, Hate Crime Statistics 2012

Identity Theft Consumer Complaints

Area	Complaints	Complaints per 100,000 Population	Rank[2]
MSA[1]	622	77.4	118
U.S.	290,056	91.8	-

Note: (1) Figures cover the El Paso, TX Metropolitan Statistical Area—see Appendix B for areas included; (2) Rank ranges from 1 to 377 where 1 indicates greatest number of identity theft complaints per 100,000 population
Source: Federal Trade Commission, Consumer Sentinel Network Data Book for January–December 2013

Fraud and Other Consumer Complaints

Area	Complaints	Complaints per 100,000 Population	Rank[2]
MSA[1]	2,407	299.3	306
U.S.	1,811,724	595.2	-

Note: (1) Figures cover the El Paso, TX Metropolitan Statistical Area—see Appendix B for areas included; (2) Rank ranges from 1 to 377 where 1 indicates greatest number of identity theft complaints per 100,000 population
Source: Federal Trade Commission, Consumer Sentinel Network Data Book for January–December 2013

RECREATION

Culture

Dance[1]	Theatre[1]	Instrumental Music[1]	Vocal Music[1]	Series and Festivals	Museums and Art Galleries[2]	Zoos and Aquariums[3]
0	2	2	1	4	17	1

Note: (1) Number of professional perfoming groups; (2) Based on organizations with primary SIC code 8412; (3) AZA-accredited
Source: The Grey House Performing Arts Directory, 2013; Association of Zoos & Aquariums, AZA Member Zoos & Aquariums, April 2014; www.AccuLeads.com, May 1, 2014

Professional Sports Teams

Team Name	League	Year Established
No teams are located in the metro area		

Source: Wikipedia, Major Professional Sports Teams of the United States and Canada, April 25, 2014

CLIMATE

Average and Extreme Temperatures

Temperature	Jan	Feb	Mar	Apr	May	Jun	Jul	Aug	Sep	Oct	Nov	Dec	Yr.
Extreme High (°F)	80	83	89	98	104	114	112	108	104	96	87	80	114
Average High (°F)	57	63	70	79	87	96	95	93	88	79	66	58	78
Average Temp. (°F)	44	49	56	64	73	81	83	81	75	65	52	45	64
Average Low (°F)	31	35	41	49	58	66	70	68	62	50	38	32	50
Extreme Low (°F)	-8	8	14	23	31	46	57	56	42	25	1	5	-8

Note: Figures cover the years 1948-1995
Source: National Climatic Data Center, International Station Meteorological Climate Summary, 9/96

Average Precipitation/Snowfall/Humidity

Precip./Humidity	Jan	Feb	Mar	Apr	May	Jun	Jul	Aug	Sep	Oct	Nov	Dec	Yr.
Avg. Precip. (in.)	0.4	0.4	0.3	0.2	0.3	0.7	1.6	1.5	1.4	0.7	0.3	0.6	8.6
Avg. Snowfall (in.)	1	1	Tr	Tr	0	0	0	0	0	Tr	1	2	6
Avg. Rel. Hum. 6am (%)	68	60	50	43	44	46	63	69	72	66	63	68	59
Avg. Rel. Hum. 3pm (%)	34	27	21	17	17	17	28	30	32	29	30	36	26

Note: Figures cover the years 1948-1995; Tr = Trace amounts (<0.05 in. of rain; <0.5 in. of snow)
Source: National Climatic Data Center, International Station Meteorological Climate Summary, 9/96

Weather Conditions

Temperature			Daytime Sky			Precipitation		
10°F & below	32°F & below	90°F & above	Clear	Partly cloudy	Cloudy	0.01 inch or more precip.	0.1 inch or more snow/ice	Thunder-storms
1	59	106	147	164	54	49	3	35

Note: Figures are average number of days per year and cover the years 1948-1995
Source: National Climatic Data Center, International Station Meteorological Climate Summary, 9/96

HAZARDOUS WASTE

Superfund Sites

El Paso has no sites on the EPA's Superfund Final National Priorities List.
U.S. Environmental Protection Agency, Final National Priorities List, April 26, 2014

AIR & WATER QUALITY

Air Quality Index

Area	Percent of Days when Air Quality was...[2]					AQI Statistics[2]	
	Good	Moderate	Unhealthy for Sensitive Groups	Unhealthy	Very Unhealthy	Maximum	Median
MSA[1]	49.0	48.2	1.9	0.8	0.0	168	51

Note: (1) Data covers the El Paso, TX Metropolitan Statistical Area—see Appendix B for areas included; (2) Based on 365 days with AQI data in 2013. Air Quality Index (AQI) is an index for reporting daily air quality. EPA calculates the AQI for five major air pollutants regulated by the Clean Air Act: ground-level ozone, particle pollution (aka particulate matter), carbon monoxide, sulfur dioxide, and nitrogen dioxide. The AQI runs from 0 to 500. The higher the AQI value, the greater the level of air pollution and the greater the health concern. There are six AQI categories: "Good" AQI is between 0 and 50. Air quality is considered satisfactory; "Moderate" AQI is between 51 and 100. Air quality is acceptable; "Unhealthy for Sensitive Groups" When AQI values are between 101 and 150, members of sensitive groups may experience health effects; "Unhealthy" When AQI values are between 151 and 200 everyone may begin to experience health effects; "Very Unhealthy" AQI values between 201 and 300 trigger a health alert; "Hazardous" AQI values over 300 trigger warnings of emergency conditions (not shown).
Source: U.S. Environmental Protection Agency, Air Quality Index Report, 2013

Air Quality Index Pollutants

Area	Percent of Days when AQI Pollutant was...[2]					
	Carbon Monoxide	Nitrogen Dioxide	Ozone	Sulfur Dioxide	Particulate Matter 2.5	Particulate Matter 10
MSA[1]	0.0	13.4	28.2	0.0	53.7	4.7

Note: (1) Data covers the El Paso, TX Metropolitan Statistical Area—see Appendix B for areas included; (2) Based on 365 days with AQI data in 2013. The Air Quality Index (AQI) is an index for reporting daily air quality. EPA calculates the AQI for five major air pollutants regulated by the Clean Air Act: ground-level ozone, particle pollution (also known as particulate matter), carbon monoxide, sulfur dioxide, and nitrogen dioxide. The AQI runs from 0 to 500. The higher the AQI value, the greater the level of air pollution and the greater the health concern.
Source: U.S. Environmental Protection Agency, Air Quality Index Report, 2013

Air Quality Trends: Ozone

	2003	2004	2005	2006	2007	2008	2009	2010	2011	2012
MSA[1]	0.071	0.074	0.077	0.077	0.074	0.074	0.068	0.068	0.069	0.067

Note: (1) Data covers the El Paso, TX Metropolitan Statistical Area—see Appendix B for areas included. The values shown are the composite ozone concentration averages among trend sites based on the highest fourth daily maximum 8-hour concentration in parts per million. These trends are based on sites having an adequate record of monitoring data during the trend period. Data from exceptional events are included.
Source: U.S. Environmental Protection Agency, Air Quality Monitoring Information, "Air Quality Trends by City, 2000-2012"

Maximum Air Pollutant Concentrations: Particulate Matter, Ozone, CO and Lead

	Particulate Matter 10 (ug/m^3)	Particulate Matter 2.5 Wtd AM (ug/m^3)	Particulate Matter 2.5 24-Hr (ug/m^3)	Ozone (ppm)	Carbon Monoxide (ppm)	Lead (ug/m^3)
MSA[1] Level	643	9.9	21	0.074	4	0.03
NAAQS[2]	150	15	35	0.075	9	0.15
Met NAAQS[2]	No	Yes	Yes	Yes	Yes	Yes

Note: (1) Data covers the El Paso, TX Metropolitan Statistical Area—see Appendix B for areas included; Data from exceptional events are included; (2) National Ambient Air Quality Standards; ppm = parts per million; ug/m^3 = micrograms per cubic meter; n/a not available.
Concentrations: Particulate Matter 10 (coarse particulate)—highest second maximum 24-hour concentration; Particulate Matter 2.5 Wtd AM (fine particulate)—highest weighted annual mean concentration; Particulate Matter 2.5 24-Hour (fine particulate)—highest 98th percentile 24-hour concentration; Ozone—highest fourth daily maximum 8-hour concentration; Carbon Monoxide—highest second maximum non-overlapping 8-hour concentration; Lead—maximum running 3-month average
Source: U.S. Environmental Protection Agency, Air Quality Monitoring Information, "Air Quality Statistics by City, 2012"

Maximum Air Pollutant Concentrations: Nitrogen Dioxide and Sulfur Dioxide

	Nitrogen Dioxide AM (ppb)	Nitrogen Dioxide 1-Hr (ppb)	Sulfur Dioxide AM (ppb)	Sulfur Dioxide 1-Hr (ppb)	Sulfur Dioxide 24-Hr (ppb)
MSA[1] Level	16	59	n/a	5	n/a
NAAQS[2]	53	100	30	75	140
Met NAAQS[2]	Yes	Yes	n/a	Yes	n/a

Note: (1) Data covers the El Paso, TX Metropolitan Statistical Area—see Appendix B for areas included; Data from exceptional events are included; (2) National Ambient Air Quality Standards; ppm = parts per million; ug/m^3 = micrograms per cubic meter; n/a not available.
Concentrations: Nitrogen Dioxide AM—highest arithmetic mean concentration; Nitrogen Dioxide 1-Hr—highest 98th percentile 1-hour daily maximum concentration; Sulfur Dioxide AM—highest annual mean concentration; Sulfur Dioxide 1-Hr—highest 99th percentile 1-hour daily maximum concentration; Sulfur Dioxide 24-Hr—highest second maximum 24-hour concentration
Source: U.S. Environmental Protection Agency, Air Quality Monitoring Information, "Air Quality Statistics by City, 2012"

Drinking Water

Water System Name	Pop. Served	Primary Water Source Type	Violations[1]	
			Health Based	Monitoring/ Reporting
El Paso Water Utilities	631,253	Surface	0	0

Note: (1) Based on violation data from January 1, 2013 to December 31, 2013 (includes unresolved violations from earlier years)
Source: U.S. Environmental Protection Agency, Office of Ground Water and Drinking Water, Safe Drinking Water Information System (based on data extracted February 10, 2014)

Drinking Water

Water System Name	Pop. Served	Primary Water Source type	Violations	
			Health based	Monitoring Reporting
El Paso Water Utilities	6/1/2025	Surface	0	0

Note: (*) Reflects violation data from January 1, 2015 to December 31, 2015 (includes unresolved violations from earlier years)

Source: U.S. Environmental Protection Agency, Office of Ground Water and Drinking Water, Safe Drinking Water Information System (based on data accessed February 22, 2016).

Fort Worth, Texas

Background

Fort Worth lies in north central Texas near the headwaters of the Trinity River. Despite its modern skyscrapers, multiple freeways, shopping malls, and extensive industry, the city is known for its easygoing, Western atmosphere.

The area has seen many travelers. Nomadic Native Americans of the plains rode through on horses bred from those brought by Spanish explorers. The 1840s saw American-Anglos settle in the region. On June 6, 1849, Major Ripley A. Arnold and his U.S. Cavalry troop established an outpost on the Trinity River to protect settlers moving westward. The fort was named for General William J. Worth, Commander of the U.S. Army's Texas department. When the fort was abandoned in 1853, settlers moved in and converted the vacant barracks into trading establishments and homes, stealing the county seat from Birdville (an act made legal in the 1860 election).

In the 1860s, Fort Worth, which was close to the Chisholm Trail, became an oasis for cowboys traveling to and from Kansas. Although the town's growth virtually stopped during the Civil War, Fort Worth was incorporated as a city in 1873. In a race against time, the final 26 miles of the Texas & Pacific Line were completed and Fort Worth survived to be a part of the West Texas oil boom in 1917.

Real prosperity followed at the end of World War II, when the city became a center for a number of military installations. Aviation has been the city's principal source of economic growth. The city's leading industries include the manufacture of aircraft, automobiles, machinery, and containers, as well as food processing and brewing. Emerging economic sectors in the new century include semiconductor manufacturing, communications equipment manufacturing, corporate offices, and distribution.

Since it first began testing DNA samples in 2003, the DNA Identity Laboratory at the University of North Texas Health Science Center has made nearly 100 matches, helping to solve missing-persons cases and closing criminal cases. The university is also home to the national Osteopathic Research Center, the only academic DNA Lab qualified to work with the FBI, the Texas Center for Health Disparities and the Health Institutes of Texas. Other colleges in Fort Worth include Texas Christian University, Southwestern Baptist Seminary, and Texas Wesleyan University.

Fort Worth's most comprehensive mixed-use project at Walsh Ranch, is nearing completion. With designs for residential, commercial, office and retail development, the 7,275-acre planned community is named after the original owners of the property, F. Howard and Mary D. Walsh, who were well-known ranchers, philanthropists and civic leaders.

The Omni Fort Worth Hotel opened in January of 2009, and is the first new hotel in the city in over 20 years. It was host to the 2011 AFC champion Pittsburgh Steelers during Super Bowl XLV.

The city also boasts the 3,600-acre Greer Island Nature Center and Refuge, which celebrates its 50th anniversary in 2014.

Winter temperatures and rainfall are both modified by the northeast-northwest mountain barrier, which prevents shallow cold air masses from crossing over from the west. Summer temperatures vary with cloud and shower activity, but are generally mild. Summer precipitation is largely from local thunderstorms and varies from year to year. Damaging rains are infrequent. Hurricanes have produced heavy rainfall, but are usually not accompanied by destructive winds.

Rankings

General Rankings

- The Dallas-Fort Worth metro area was identified as one of America's fastest-growing areas in terms of population and economy by *Forbes*. The area ranked #4 out of 20. The 100 most populous metro areas in the U.S. were evaluated on the following criteria: estimated population growth; job growth; gross metropolitan product growth; unemployment; median salaries for college-educated workers. *Forbes, "America's Fastest-Growing Cities 2014," February 14, 2014*

- Fort Worth was selected as one of "America's Favorite Cities." The city ranked #25 in the "Quality of Life and Visitor Experience: Cleanliness" category. Respondents to an online survey were asked to rate 35 top urban destinations in the U.S. from a visitor's perspective. Criteria: cleanliness. *Travel + Leisure, "America's Favorite Cities 2013"*

- Fort Worth was selected as one of "America's Favorite Cities." The city ranked #33 in the "Type of Trip: Gay-friendly" category. Respondents to an online survey were asked to rate 35 top urban destinations in the U.S. from a visitor's perspective. Criteria: gay-friendly. *Travel + Leisure, "America's Favorite Cities 2013"*

Business/Finance Rankings

- The personal finance site NerdWallet scored the nation's 20 largest American cities according to how friendly a business climate they offer to would-be entrepreneurs. Criteria inlcuded local taxes (state, city, payroll, property), growth rate, and the regulatory environment as judged by small business owners. On the resulting list of most welcoming cities, Fort Worth ranked #3. *www.nerdwallet.com, "Top 10 Best Cities for Small Business," August 26, 2013*

- Fort Worth was the #9-ranked city for savers, according to the finance site GoBankingRates, which considered the prospects for savers in a tough savings economy by looking for higher interest yields, lower taxes, more jobs with higher incomes, and less expensive housing costs. *www.gobankingrates.com, "Best Cities for Saving Money," February 24, 2014*

- The editors of *Kiplinger's Personal Finance Magazine* named Dallas-Fort Worth to their list of ten of the best metro areas for start-ups. Criteria included a well-educated workforce and low living costs for self-employed people, as measured by the Council for Community and Economic Research, as well as areas with lots of start-up investment dollars and low business costs. *www.kiplinger.com, "10 Great Cities for Starting a Business," January 2013*

- In order to help veterans transition from the military to civilian life, USAA and Hiring Our Heroes worked with Sperlings's BestPlaces to develop a list of the major metropolitan areas where military-skills-related employment is strongest. Criteria included job prospects, unemployment, number of government jobs, recent job growth, accessible health resources, and colleges and universities. Metro areas with a violent crime rate or high cost of living were excluded. At #2, the Dallas-Fort Worth metro area made the top ten. *www.usaa.com, "2013 Best Places for Veterans: Jobs," November 2013*

- The finance website Wall St. Cheat Sheet reported on the prospects for high-wage job creation in the nation's largest metro areas over the next five years and ranked them accordingly, drawing on in-depth analysis by CareerBuilder and Economic Modeling Specialists International (EMSI). The Dallas-Fort Worth metro area placed #9 on the Wall St. Cheat Sheet list. *wallstcheatsheet.com, "Top 10 Cities for High-Wage Job Growth," December 8, 2013*

- Based on a minimum of 500 social media reviews per metro area, the employment opinion group Glassdoor surveyed 50 of the largest U.S. metro areas on measures including compensation and benefits, satisfaction with management, business outlook, and number of employers hiring. The Dallas-Fort Worth metro area was ranked #28 in overall employee satisfaction. *www.glassdoor.com, "Employment Satisfaction Report Card by City," June 21, 2013*

- In its Competitive Alternatives report, consulting firm KPMG analyzed the 27 largest metropolitan statistical areas according to 26 cost components (such as taxes, labor costs, and utilities) and 30 non-cost-related variables (such as crime rates and number of universities). The business website 24/7 Wall Street examined the KPMG findings, adding to the mix current unemployment rates, GDP, median income, and employment decline during the last recession and "projected" recovery. It identified the Dallas-Fort Worth metro area as #5 among the ten best American cities for business. *247wallst.com, "Best American Cities for Business," April 4, 2012*

- A *Fiscal Times* analysis balancing cost of living with average income to find the cities where residents' dollars go furthest was published by the *Huffington Post.* Based on the Census Bureau's 2010 Cost of Living Index and the National Compensation Survey, Dallas-Fort Worth was ranked the #3 metro area where you can "actually spend less and make more." *Fiscal Times/Huffington Post, "The Best Bang for Your Buck Cities in the United States," June 26, 2012*

- The financial literacy site NerdWallet.com set out to identify the 20 most promising cities for job seekers, analyzing data for the nation's 50 largest cities. Fort Worth was ranked #3. Criteria: unemployment rate; population growth; median income; selected monthly owner costs. *NerdWallet.com, "Best Cities for Job Seekers," January 7, 2014*

- The Brookings Institution ranked the 50 largest cities in the U.S. based on income inequality. Fort Worth was ranked #44. (#1 = greatest inequality). Criteria: the cities were ranked based on the "95/20 ratio." This figure represents the income at which a household earns more than 95 percent of all other households, divided by the income at which a household earns more than only 20 percent of all other households. *Brookings Institution, "Income Inequality in America's 50 Largest Cities, 2007-2012," February 20, 2014*

- Dallas-Fort Worth was ranked #20 out of 100 metro areas in terms of economic performance (#1 = best) during the recession and recovery from trough quarter through the second quarter of 2013. Criteria: percent change in employment; percentage point change in unemployment rate; percent change in gross metropolitan product; percent change in House Price Index. *Brookings Institution, MetroMonitor: Tracking Economic Recession and Recovery in America's 100 Largest Metropolitan Areas, September 2013*

- Payscale.com ranked the 20 largest metro areas in terms of wage growth. The Dallas-Fort Worth metro area ranked #12. Criteria: private-sector wage growth between the 4th quarter of 2012 and the 4th quarter of 2013. *PayScale, "Wage Trends by Metro Area," 4th Quarter, 2013*

- Dallas-Fort Worth was identified as one of America's most frugal metro areas by *Coupons.com.* The city ranked #14 out of 25. Criteria: online coupon usage. *Coupons.com, "Top 25 Most Frugal Cities of 2012," February 19, 2013*

- Dallas-Fort Worth was identified as one of America's most frugal metro areas by *Coupons.com.* The city ranked #5 out of 25. Criteria: Grocery IQ and coupons.com mobile app usage. *Coupons.com, "Top 25 Most On-the-Go Frugal Cities of 2012," February 19, 2013*

- Dallas-Fort Worth was cited as one of America's top metros for new and expanded facility projects in 2013. The area ranked #3 in the large metro area category (population over 1 million). *Site Selection, "Top Metros of 2013," March 2014*

- The Dallas-Fort Worth metro area appeared on the Milken Institute "2013 Best Performing Cities" list. Rank: #16 out of 200 large metro areas. Criteria: job growth; wage and salary growth; high-tech output growth. *Milken Institute, "Best-Performing Cities 2013," December 2013*

- *Forbes* ranked the 200 most populous metro areas in the U.S. in terms of the "Best Places for Business and Careers." The Dallas-Fort Worth metro area was ranked #15. Criteria: costs (business and living); job growth (past and projected); income growth; educational attainment (college and high school); projected economic growth; cultural and recreational opportunities; net migration patterns; number of highly ranked colleges. *Forbes, "The Best Places for Business and Careers," August 7, 2013*

Children/Family Rankings

- Fort Worth was selected as one of the best cities for families to live by *Parenting* magazine. The city ranked #90 out of 100. Criteria: education; health; community; *Parenting's* Culture & Charm Index. *Parenting.com, "The 2012 Best Cities for Families List"*

Culture/Performing Arts Rankings

- Fort Worth was selected as one of "America's Favorite Cities." The city ranked #26 in the "Culture: Museum/Galleries" category. Respondents to an online survey were asked to rate 35 top urban destinations in the U.S. from a visitor's perspective. Criteria: number and quality of museums and galleries. *Travelandleisure.com, "America's Favorite Cities 2013"*

Dating/Romance Rankings

- *Forbes* reports that the Dallas-Fort Worth metro area made Rent.com's Best Cities for Newlyweds survey for 2013, based on Bureau of Labor Statistics and Census Bureau data on number of married couples, percentage of families with children under age six, average annual income, cost of living, and availability of rentals. *www.forbes.com, "The 10 Best Cities for Newlyweds to Live and Work In," May 30, 2013*

- Of the 100 U.S. cities surveyed by *Men's Health* in its quest to identify the nation's best cities for dating and forming relationships, Fort Worth was ranked #54 for online dating (#1 = best). *Men's Health, "The Best and Worst Cities for Online Dating," January 30, 2013*

Education Rankings

- *Men's Health* ranked 100 U.S. cities in terms of their education levels. Fort Worth was ranked #87 (#1 = most educated city). Criteria: high school graduation rates; school enrollment; educational attainment; number of households who have outstanding student loans; number of households whose members have taken adult-education courses. *Men's Health, "Where School Is In: The Most and Least Educated Cities," September 12, 2011*

- Fort Worth was selected as one of America's most literate cities. The city ranked #49 out of the 77 largest U.S. cities. Criteria: number of booksellers; library resources; Internet resources; educational attainment; periodical publishing resources; newspaper circulation. *Central Connecticut State University, "America's Most Literate Cities, 2013"*

Environmental Rankings

- The Dallas-Fort Worth metro area came in at #350 for the relative comfort of its climate on Sperling's list of "chill cities," as measured by the Sperling Heat Index. All 361 metro areas are included. Criteria included daytime high temperatures, nighttime low temperatures, dew point, and relative humidity at the high temperatures. *www.bertsperling.com, "Sperling's Chill Cities," July 18, 2013*

- Sperling's BestPlaces assessed 379 metropolitan areas of the United States for the likelihood of dangerously extreme weather events or earthquakes. In general the Southeast and South-Central regions have the highest risk of weather extremes and earthquakes, while the Pacific Northwest enjoys the lowest risk. Of the least risky metropolitan areas, the Dallas-Fort Worth metro area was ranked #371. *www.bestplaces.net, "Safest Places from Natural Disasters," April 2011*

- Dallas-Fort Worth was identified as one of North America's greenest metropolitan areas. The area ranked #17. The Green City Index is comprised of 31 indicators, and scores cities across nine categories: carbon dioxide; energy; land use; buildings; transport; water; waste; air quality; environmental governance. The 27 largest metropolitan areas in the U.S. and Canada were considered. *Economist Intelligence Unit, sponsored by Siemens, "U.S. and Canada Green City Index, 2011"*

- The U.S. Environmental Protection Agency (EPA) released a list of U.S. metropolitan areas with the most ENERGY STAR certified buildings in 2012. The Dallas-Fort Worth metro area was ranked #8 out of 25. *U.S. Environmental Protection Agency, "Top Cities With the Most ENERGY STAR Certified Buildings in 2012," March 12, 2013*

- Fort Worth was selected as one of 22 "Smarter Cities" for energy by the Natural Resources Defense Council. Criteria: investment in green power; energy efficiency measures; conservation. *Natural Resources Defense Council, "2010 Smarter Cities," July 19, 2010*

- Dallas-Fort Worth was highlighted as one of the 25 most ozone-polluted metro areas in the U.S. during 2008 through 2010. The area ranked #8. *American Lung Association, State of the Air 2012*

Food/Drink Rankings

- *Men's Health* ranked 100 major U.S. cities in terms of alcohol intoxication. Fort Worth ranked #74 (#1 = most sober).Criteria: binge drinking; alcohol-related traffic accidents, arrests, and fatalities. *Men's Health, "The Drunkest Cities in America," November 19, 2013*

Health/Fitness Rankings

- For each of the 50 most populous metro areas in the United States, the American College of Sports Medicine's American Fitness Index evaluated infrastructure, community assets, and policies that encourage healthy and fit lifestyles, including preventive health behaviors, levels of chronic disease conditions, health care access, and community resources and policies that support physical activity. The Dallas-Fort Worth metro area ranked #44 for "community fitness." Personal health indicators were considered as well as community and environmental indicators. *www.americanfitnessindex.org, "ACSM American Fitness Index Health and Community Fitness Status of the 50 Largest Metropolitan Areas," May 2013*

- The Dallas-Fort Worth metro area was identified as one of the worst cities for bed bugs in America by pest control company Orkin. The area ranked #13 out of 50 based on the number of bed bug treatments Orkin performed from January to December 2013. *Orkin, "Chicago Tops Bed Bug Cities List for Second Year in a Row," January 16, 2014*

- Fort Worth was identified as one of 15 cities with the highest increase in bed bug activity in the U.S. by pest control provider Terminix. The city ranked #13.Criteria: cities with the largest percentage gains in bed bug customer calls from January–May 2013 compared to the same time period in 2012. *Terminix, "Cities with Highest Increases in Bed Bug Activity," July 9, 2013*

- Dallas-Fort Worth was identified as one of "The 8 Most Artery-Clogging Cities in America." The metro area ranked #5. Criteria: obesity rates; heart disease rates. *Prevention, "The 8 Most Artery-Clogging Cities in America," December 2011*

- Dallas-Fort Worth was identified as a "2013 Spring Allergy Capital." The area ranked #23 out of 100. Three groups of factors were used to identify the most severe cities for people with allergies during the spring season: annual pollen levels; medicine utilization; access to board-certified allergists. *Asthma and Allergy Foundation of America, "Spring Allergy Capitals 2013"*

- Dallas-Fort Worth was identified as a "2013 Fall Allergy Capital." The area ranked #18 out of 100. Three groups of factors were used to identify the most severe cities for people with allergies during the fall season: annual pollen levels; medicine utilization; access to board-certified allergists. *Asthma and Allergy Foundation of America, "Fall Allergy Capitals 2013"*

- Dallas-Fort Worth was identified as a "2013 Asthma Capital." The area ranked #49 out of the nation's 100 largest metropolitan areas. Twelve factors were used to identify the most challenging places to live for people with asthma: estimated prevalence; self-reported prevalence; crude death rate for asthma; annual pollen score; annual air quality; public smoking laws; number of board-certified asthma specialists; school inhaler access laws; rescue medication use; controller medication use; uninsured rate; poverty rate. *Asthma and Allergy Foundation of America, "Asthma Capitals 2013"*

- *Men's Health* ranked 100 major U.S. cities in terms of the best and worst cities for men. Fort Worth ranked #35. Criteria: thirty-three data points were examined covering health, fitness, and quality of life. *Men's Health, "The Best & Worst Cities for Men 2014," December 6, 2013*

- Breathe Right Nasal Strips, in partnership with Sperling's BestPlaces, analyzed 50 metro areas and identified those U.S. cities most challenged by chronic nasal congestion. The Dallas-Fort Worth metro area ranked #7. Criteria: tree, grass and weed pollens; molds and spores; air pollution; climate; smoking; purchase habits of congestion products; prescriptions of drugs for congestion relief; incidence of influenza. *Breathe Right Nasal Strips, "Most Congested Cities," October 3, 2011*

- The American Academy of Dermatology ranked 26 U.S. metropolitan regions in terms of their residents knowledge, attitude and behaviors towards tanning, sun protection and skin cancer detection. The Dallas-Fort Worth metro area ranked #11. The results of the study are based on an online survey of over 7,000 adults nationwide. *American Academy of Dermatology, "Suntelligence: How Sun Smart is Your City?," May 3, 2010*

- The Dallas-Fort Worth metro area appeared in the 2013 Gallup-Healthways Well-Being Index. The area ranked #54 out of 189. The Gallup-Healthways Well-Being Index score is an average of six sub-indexes, which individually examine life evaluation, emotional health, work environment, physical health, healthy behaviors, and access to basic necessities. Results are based on telephone interviews conducted as part of the Gallup-Healthways Well-Being Index survey January 2–December 29, 2012, and January 2–December 30, 2013, with a random sample of 531,630 adults, aged 18 and older, living in metropolitan areas in the 50 U.S. states and the District of Columbia. *Gallup-Healthways, "State of American Well-Being," March 25, 2014*

- The Dallas-Fort Worth metro area was identified as one of "America's Most Stressful Cities" by *Sperling's BestPlaces*. The metro area ranked #33 out of 50. Criteria: unemployment rate; suicide rate; commute time; mental health; poor rest; alcohol use; violent crime rate; property crime rate; cloudy days annually. *Sperling's BestPlaces, www.BestPlaces.net, "Stressful Cities 2012*

- The Dallas-Fort Worth metro area was identified as one of "America's Most Stressful Cities" by *Forbes*. The metro area ranked #9 out of 40. Criteria: housing affordability; unemployment rate; cost of living; air quality; traffic congestion; sunny days; population density. *Forbes.com, "America's Most Stressful Cities," September 23, 2011*

- *Men's Health* ranked 100 U.S. cities in terms of their activity levels. Fort Worth was ranked #50 (#1 = most active city). Criteria: where and how often residents exercise; percentage of households that watch more than 15 hours of cable television a week and buy more than 11 video games a year; death rate from deep-vein thrombosis, a condition linked to sitting for extended periods of time. *Men's Health, "Where Sit Happens: The Most and Least Active Cities in America," June 20, 2011*

- Fort Worth was selected as one of the "20 Most Livable U.S. Cities for Wheelchair Users" by the Christopher & Dana Reeve Foundation. The city ranked #14. Criteria: Medicaid eligibility and spending; access to physicians and rehabilitation facilities; access to fitness facilities and recreation; access to paratransit; percentage of people living with disabilities who are employed; clean air; climate. *Christopher & Dana Reeve Foundation, "20 Most Livable U.S. Cities for Wheelchair Users," July 26, 2010*

Real Estate Rankings

- Based on the home-price forecasts compiled by the real-estate valuation firm CoreLogic Case-Shiller, the finance website CNNMoney reported that in 2014, the Dallas-Fort Worth metro area is expected to place #2 among American metro areas in terms of increases in residential real estate prices. *money.cnn.com, "10 Hottest Housing Markets for 2014," January 23, 2014*

- On the list compiled by Penske Truck Rental, the Dallas-Fort Worth metro area was named the #3 moving destination in 2013, based on one-way consumer truck rental reservations made through Penske's website and reservations call center. *blog.gopenske.com, "Penske Truck Rental's 2013 Top Moving Destinations List," January 22, 2014*

- The PricewaterhouseCoopers and Urban Land Institute report *Emerging Trends in Real Estate* forecasts that improvements in leasing, rents, and pricing will fuel recovery in all property sectors in 2013. Dallas-Fort Worth was ranked #9 among the top ten markets to watch in 2013. *PricewaterhouseCoopers/Urban Land Institute, "U.S. Commercial Real Estate Recovery to Advance in 2013," October 17, 2012*

- The Dallas-Fort Worth metro area was identified as one of the top 20 housing markets to invest in for 2014 by *Forbes*. The area ranked #1. Criteria: high population and job growth; relatively low home prices which are below equilibrium home price (EHP). The EHP is what the average price for a market should be, if speculation, weird distortions in local income, and other factors (like the housing collapse) weren't present in the market. *Forbes.com, "Best Buy Cities: Where to Invest in Housing in 2014," December 25, 2013*

- Dallas-Fort Worth was ranked #82 out of 283 metro areas in terms of house price appreciation in 2013 (#1 = highest rate). *Federal Housing Finance Agency, House Price Index, 4th Quarter 2013*

- Dallas-Fort Worth was ranked #148 out of 224 metro areas in terms of housing affordability in 2013 by the National Association of Home Builders (#1 = most affordable). The NAHB-Wells Fargo Housing Opportunity Index (HOI) for a given area is defined as the share of homes sold in that area that would have been affordable to a family earning the local median income, based on standard mortgage underwriting criteria. *National Association of Home Builders®, NAHB-Wells Fargo Housing Opportunity Index, 4th Quarter 2013*

- The Dallas-Fort Worth metro area was identified as one of the 10 best U.S. markets to invest in single-family homes as rental properties by HomeVestors and Local Market Monitor. The area ranked #1. Criteria: risk-return premium relative to national average. *HomeVestors and Local Market Monitor, "Year-End Top 10 Real Estate Markets," December 20, 2013*

Safety Rankings

- Symantec, in partnership with Sperling's BestPlaces, ranked the 50 largest cities in the U.S. in terms of their vulnerability to cybercrime. The city ranked #32. Criteria: number of cyberattacks and potential infections; level of Internet access; expenditures on smartphones and computer hardware/software; wireless hotspots; broadband connectivity; Internet usage; online purchases. *Symantec, "Riskiest Online Cities of 2012" February 15, 2012*

- Farmers Insurance, in partnership with Sperling's BestPlaces, ranked metro areas in the U.S. and identified the "Most Secure Places to Live." The Dallas-Fort Worth metro area ranked #10 out of the top 20 in the large metro area category (500,000 or more residents). Criteria: economic stability; crime statistics; extreme weather; risk of natural disasters; housing depreciation; foreclosures; air quality; environmental hazards; life expectancy; motor vehicle fatalities; and employment numbers. *Farmers Insurance Group of Companies, "Most Secure U.S. Places to Live in the U.S.," June 25, 2013*

- Allstate ranked the 200 largest cities in America in terms of driver safety. Fort Worth ranked #138. Allstate researchers analyzed internal property damage claims over a two-year period from January 2010 to December 2011. A weighted average of the two-year numbers determined the annual percentages. *Allstate, "Allstate America's Best Drivers Report®, August 27, 2013"*

- The National Insurance Crime Bureau ranked 380 metro areas in the U.S. in terms of per capita rates of vehicle theft. The Dallas-Fort Worth metro area ranked #68 (#1 = highest rate). Criteria: number of vehicle theft offenses per 100,000 inhabitants in 2012. *National Insurance Crime Bureau, "Hot Spots 2012," June 26, 2013*

- The Dallas-Fort Worth metro area was identified as one of the most dangerous metro areas for pedestrians by Transportation for America. The metro area ranked #10 out of 52 metro areas with over 1 million residents. Criteria: area's population divided by the number of pedestrian fatalities in that area. *Transportation for America, "Dangerous by Design 2011"*

Seniors/Retirement Rankings

- From its Best Cities for Successful Aging indexes, the Milken Institute generated rankings for metropolitan areas, weighing data in eight categories—general indicators, health care, wellness, living arrangements, transportation and general accessibility, financial well-being, education and employment, and community participation. The Dallas-Fort Worth metro area was ranked #73 overall in the large metro area category. *Milken Institute, "Best Cities for Successful Aging," July 2012*

- *Forbes* selected the Dallas-Fort Worth metro area as one of 25 "Best Places for a Working Retirement." Criteria: affordability; improving, above-average economies and job prospects; and a favorable tax climate for retirees. *Forbes.com, "Best Places for a Working Retirement in 2013," February 4, 2013*

- Fort Worth earned a spot on the AARP's list of "10 Great Sunny Places to Retire." Criteria: minimum of 250 sunny days per year; distinct cultural identity; recreational amenities for retirees; striking outdoor setting; low crime rate; robust economy; and healthy lifestyle. *AARP.org, "Best Places to Retire 2012," November 2011*

- Bankers Life and Casualty Company, in partnership with Sperling's BestPlaces, ranked the nation's 50 largest metro areas in terms of the "Best U.S. Cities for Seniors." The Dallas-Fort Worth metro area ranked #33. Criteria: healthcare; transportation; housing; environment; economy; health and longevity; social and spiritual life; crime. *Bankers Life and Casualty Company, Center for a Secure Retirement, "Best U.S. Cities for Seniors 2011," September 2011*

Sports/Recreation Rankings

- According to the personal finance website NerdWallet, the Dallas-Fort Worth metro area, at #1, is one of the nation's top dozen metro areas for sports fans. Criteria included the presence of all four major sports—MLB, NFL, NHL, and NBA, fan enthusiasm (as measured by game attendance), ticket affordability, and "sports culture," that is, number of sports bars. *www.nerdwallet.com, "Best Cities for Sports Fans," May 5, 2013*

- Fort Worth appeared on the *Sporting News* list of the "Best Sports Cities" for 2011. The area ranked #1 out of 271. Criteria: the magazine takes a 12-month snapshot of each city's sports, putting a heavy premium on regular-season won-lost records (from the most recently completed season). Other criteria include: playoff berths, bowl appearances and tournament bids; championships; applicable power ratings; quality of competition; overall fan fervor (measured in part by attendance); abundance of teams (rewarding quality over quantity); stadium and arena quality; ticket availability and prices; franchise ownership; and marquee appeal of athletes. *Sporting News, "Best Sports Cities 2011," October 4, 2011*

- Fort Worth appeared on the *Sporting News* list of the "Best Sports Cities" for 2011. The area ranked #1 out of 271. Criteria: a 12-month snapshot of regular-season won-lost records (from the most recently completed season). Other criteria include: playoff berths, bowl appearances and tournament bids; championships; applicable power ratings; quality of competition; overall fan fervor (measured in part by attendance); abundance of teams (quality over quantity); stadium and arena quality; ticket availability and prices; franchise ownership; and marquee appeal of athletes. *Sporting News, "Best Sports Cities 2011," October 4, 2011*

- The Dallas-Fort Worth was selected as one of the best metro areas for golf in America by *Golf Digest*. The Dallas-Fort Worth area was ranked #1 out of 20. Criteria: climate; cost of public golf; quality of public golf; accessibility. *Golf Digest, "The Top 20 Cities for Golf," October 2011*

Women/Minorities Rankings

- To determine the best metro areas for working women, the personal finance website NerdWallet considered city size as well as relevant economic metrics—high salaries, narrow pay differential by gender, prevalence of women in the highest-paying industries, and population growth over 2010–2012. Of the large U.S. cities examined, the Dallas-Fort Worth metro area held the #5 position. *www.nerdwallet.com, "Best Places for Women in the Workforce," May 19, 2013*

- *Women's Health* examined U.S. cities and identified the 100 best cities for women. Fort Worth was ranked #43. Criteria: 30 categories were examined from obesity and breast cancer rates to commuting times and hours spent working out. *Women's Health, "Best Cities for Women 2012"*

- The Dallas-Fort Worth metro area appeared on *Forbes'* list of the "Best Cities for Minority Entrepreneurs." The area ranked #43 out of 10. Criteria: 52 metropolitan statistical areas were examined. For each ethnicity (African Americans, Asians and Hispanics), the editors measured housing affordability, population growth, income growth, and entrepreneurship (per capita self-employment). *Forbes, "Best Cities for Minority Entrepreneurs," March 23, 2011*

Miscellaneous Rankings

- The watchdog site Charity Navigator conducts an annual study of charities in the nation's major markets both to analyze statistical differences in their financial, accountability, and transparency practices and to track year-to-year variations in individual communities. The Dallas-Fort Worth metro area was ranked #14 among the 30 metro markets. *www.charitynavigator.org, "Metro Market Study 2013," June 1, 2013*

- The Harris Poll's Happiness Index survey revealed that of the top ten U.S. markets, the Dallas-Fort Worth metro area residents ranked #1 in happiness. Criteria included strong assent to positive statements and strong disagreement with negative ones, and degree of agreement with a series of statements about respondents' personal relationships and general outlook. The online survey was conducted between July 14 and July 30, 2013. *www.harrisinteractive.com, "Dallas/Fort Worth Is "Happiest" City among America's Top Ten Markets," September 4, 2013*

- *Men's Health* ranked 100 U.S. cities by their level of sadness. Fort Worth was ranked #43 (#1 = saddest city). Criteria: suicide rates; unemployment rates; percentage of households that use antidepressants; percent of population who report feeling blue all or most of the time. *Men's Health, "Frown Towns," November 28, 2011*

- Mars Chocolate North America, the makers of COMBOS®, in partnership with Sperling's BestPlaces, ranked 50 major metro areas in terms of their "manliness." The Dallas-Fort Worth metro area ranked #15. Criteria: number of professional sports teams; number of nearby NASCAR tracks and racing events; manly lifestyle; concentration of manly retail stores; manly occupations per capita; salty snack sales; "Board of Manliness" rankings. *Mars Chocolate North America, "America's Manliest Cities 2012"*

- The National Alliance to End Homelessness ranked the 100 most populous metro areas in terms the rate of homelessness. The Dallas-Fort Worth metro area ranked #87. Criteria: number of homeless people per 10,000 population in 2011. *National Alliance to End Homelessness, The State of Homelessness in America 2012*

Business Environment

CITY FINANCES

City Government Finances

Component	2011 ($000)	2011 ($ per capita)
Total Revenues	1,433,570	2,103
Total Expenditures	1,309,477	1,921
Debt Outstanding	2,254,899	3,307
Cash and Securities[1]	3,576,963	5,246

Note: (1) Cash and security holdings of a government at the close of its fiscal year, including those of its dependent agencies, utilities, and liquor stores.
Source: U.S Census Bureau, State & Local Government Finances 2011

City Government Revenue by Source

Source	2011 ($000)	2011 ($ per capita)
General Revenue		
From Federal Government	30,975	45
From State Government	40,473	59
From Local Governments	94	0
Taxes		
Property	375,146	550
Sales and Gross Receipts	206,510	303
Personal Income	0	0
Corporate Income	0	0
Motor Vehicle License	0	0
Other Taxes	24,112	35
Current Charges	241,890	355
Liquor Store	0	0
Utility	178,496	262
Employee Retirement	188,428	276

Source: U.S Census Bureau, State & Local Government Finances 2011

City Government Expenditures by Function

Function	2011 ($000)	2011 ($ per capita)	2011 (%)
General Direct Expenditures			
Air Transportation	11,436	17	0.9
Corrections	0	0	0.0
Education	0	0	0.0
Employment Security Administration	0	0	0.0
Financial Administration	8,187	12	0.6
Fire Protection	106,260	156	8.1
General Public Buildings	6,547	10	0.5
Governmental Administration, Other	13,453	20	1.0
Health	18,615	27	1.4
Highways	97,696	143	7.5
Hospitals	0	0	0.0
Housing and Community Development	17,233	25	1.3
Interest on General Debt	61,262	90	4.7
Judicial and Legal	20,150	30	1.5
Libraries	20,017	29	1.5
Parking	14,009	21	1.1
Parks and Recreation	46,521	68	3.6
Police Protection	220,614	324	16.8
Public Welfare	0	0	0.0
Sewerage	157,583	231	12.0
Solid Waste Management	38,698	57	3.0
Veterans' Services	0	0	0.0
Liquor Store	0	0	0.0
Utility	197,570	290	15.1
Employee Retirement	110,700	162	8.5

Source: U.S Census Bureau, State & Local Government Finances 2011

DEMOGRAPHICS

Population Growth

Area	1990 Census	2000 Census	2010 Census	Population Growth (%)	
				1990-2000	2000-2010
City	448,311	534,694	741,206	19.3	38.6
MSA[1]	3,989,294	5,161,544	6,371,773	29.4	23.4
U.S.	248,709,873	281,421,906	308,745,538	13.2	9.7

Note: (1) Figures cover the Dallas-Fort Worth-Arlington, TX Metropolitan Statistical Area—see Appendix B for areas included
Source: U.S. Census Bureau, Census 1990, 2000, 2010

Household Size

Area	Persons in Household (%)							Average Household Size
	One	Two	Three	Four	Five	Six	Seven or More	
City	27.8	27.7	15.7	15.0	8.0	3.5	2.3	2.83
MSA[1]	25.3	30.4	16.7	15.1	7.6	3.0	1.9	2.80
U.S.	27.6	33.5	15.7	13.2	6.1	2.4	1.5	2.63

Note: (1) Figures cover the Dallas-Fort Worth-Arlington, TX Metropolitan Statistical Area—see Appendix B for areas included
Source: U.S. Census Bureau, 2010-2012 American Community Survey 3-Year Estimates

Race

Area	White Alone[2] (%)	Black Alone[2] (%)	Asian Alone[2] (%)	AIAN[3] Alone[2] (%)	NHOPI[4] Alone[2] (%)	Other Race Alone[2] (%)	Two or More Races (%)
City	66.6	18.9	3.8	0.7	0.2	7.5	2.4
MSA[1]	69.2	15.0	5.5	0.5	0.1	7.1	2.6
U.S.	74.0	12.6	4.9	0.8	0.2	4.7	2.8

Note: (1) Figures cover the Dallas-Fort Worth-Arlington, TX Metropolitan Statistical Area—see Appendix B for areas included; (2) Alone is defined as not being in combination with one or more other races; (3) American Indian and Alaska Native; (4) Native Hawaiian and Other Pacific Islander
Source: U.S. Census Bureau, 2010-2012 American Community Survey 3-Year Estimates

Hispanic or Latino Origin

Area	Total (%)	Mexican (%)	Puerto Rican (%)	Cuban (%)	Other (%)
City	33.9	30.6	0.7	0.2	2.5
MSA[1]	27.8	23.8	0.5	0.2	3.3
U.S.	16.6	10.7	1.6	0.6	3.7

Note: Persons of Hispanic or Latino origin can be of any race; (1) Figures cover the Dallas-Fort Worth-Arlington, TX Metropolitan Statistical Area—see Appendix B for areas included
Source: U.S. Census Bureau, 2010-2012 American Community Survey 3-Year Estimates

Segregation

Type	Segregation Indices[1]				Percent Change		
	1990	2000	2010	2010 Rank[2]	1990-2000	1990-2010	2000-2010
Black/White	62.8	59.8	56.6	48	-3.1	-6.2	-3.2
Asian/White	41.8	45.6	46.6	19	3.8	4.8	1.0
Hispanic/White	48.8	52.3	50.3	24	3.5	1.5	-2.0

Note: All figures cover the Metropolitan Statistical Area—see Appendix B for areas included; Figures are based on an analysis of 1990, 2000, and 2010 Census Decennial Census tract data by William H. Frey, Brookings Institution and the University of Michigan Social Science Data Analysis Network. In this analysis all racial groups (whites, blacks, and asians) are non-Hispanic members of those races. Hispanics are shown as a separate category;
(1) Segregation Indices are Dissimilarity Indices that measure the degree to which the minority group is distributed differently than whites across census tracts. They range from 0 (complete integration) to 100 (complete segregation) where the value indicates the percentage of the minority group that needs to move to be distributed exactly like whites; (2) Ranges from 1 (most segregated) to 102 (least segregated); n/a not available.
Source: www.CensusScope.org

Ancestry

Area	German	Irish	English	American	Italian	Polish	French[2]	Scottish	Dutch
City	9.0	7.3	5.7	7.4	1.8	1.0	1.5	1.6	0.8
MSA[1]	10.5	8.2	7.6	6.8	2.2	1.1	2.0	1.7	1.0
U.S.	15.2	11.1	8.2	7.2	5.6	3.1	2.8	1.7	1.4

Note: Figures are the percentage of the total population reporting a particular ancestry. The nine most commonly reported ancestries in the U.S. are shown. Figures include multiple ancestries (e.g. if a person reported being Irish and Italian, they were included in both columns); (1) Figures cover the Dallas-Fort Worth-Arlington, TX Metropolitan Statistical Area—see Appendix B for areas included; (2) Excludes Basque
Source: U.S. Census Bureau, 2010-2012 American Community Survey 3-Year Estimates

Foreign-Born Population

Area	Percent of Population Born in								
	Any Foreign Country	Mexico	Asia	Europe	Carribean	South America	Central America[2]	Africa	Canada
City	17.6	11.5	3.2	0.8	0.2	0.4	0.7	0.6	0.1
MSA[1]	17.6	9.2	4.3	0.8	0.2	0.5	1.3	1.0	0.2
U.S.	13.0	3.7	3.7	1.6	1.2	0.9	1.0	0.5	0.3

Note: (1) Figures cover the Dallas-Fort Worth-Arlington, TX Metropolitan Statistical Area—see Appendix B for areas included; (2) Excludes Mexico.
Source: U.S. Census Bureau, 2010-2012 American Community Survey 3-Year Estimates

Marital Status

Area	Never Married	Now Married[2]	Separated	Widowed	Divorced
City	33.4	46.6	3.1	4.7	12.3
MSA[1]	31.2	50.7	2.6	4.5	11.1
U.S.	32.4	48.4	2.2	6.0	11.0

Note: Figures are percentages and cover the population 15 years of age and older; (1) Figures cover the Dallas-Fort Worth-Arlington, TX Metropolitan Statistical Area—see Appendix B for areas included; (2) Excludes separated
Source: U.S. Census Bureau, 2010-2012 American Community Survey 3-Year Estimates

Age

Area	Percent of Population									Median Age
	Under Age 5	Age 5–19	Age 20–34	Age 35–44	Age 45–54	Age 55–64	Age 65–74	Age 75–84	Age 85+	
City	8.9	23.1	23.3	14.6	12.7	9.1	4.6	2.6	1.1	31.6
MSA[1]	7.6	22.6	21.6	14.8	14.1	10.2	5.4	2.7	1.0	33.7
U.S.	6.4	20.1	20.5	13.1	14.3	12.2	7.3	4.2	1.8	37.3

Note: (1) Figures cover the Dallas-Fort Worth-Arlington, TX Metropolitan Statistical Area—see Appendix B for areas included
Source: U.S. Census Bureau, 2010-2012 American Community Survey 3-Year Estimates

Gender

Area	Males	Females	Males per 100 Females
City	369,818	392,044	94.3
MSA[1]	3,216,334	3,303,515	97.4
U.S.	153,276,055	158,333,314	96.8

Note: (1) Figures cover the Dallas-Fort Worth-Arlington, TX Metropolitan Statistical Area—see Appendix B for areas included
Source: U.S. Census Bureau, 2010-2012 American Community Survey 3-Year Estimates

Religious Groups by Family

Area	Catholic	Baptist	Non-Den.	Methodist[2]	Lutheran	LDS[3]	Pente-costal	Presby-terian[4]	Muslim[5]	Judaism
MSA[1]	13.3	18.7	7.8	5.3	0.8	1.2	2.2	1.0	2.4	0.4
U.S.	19.1	9.3	4.0	4.0	2.3	2.0	1.9	1.6	0.8	0.7

Note: Figures are the number of adherents as a percentage of the total population; (1) Figures cover the Dallas-Fort Worth-Arlington, TX Metropolitan Statistical Area—see Appendix B for areas included; (2) Methodist/Pietist; (3) Latter Day Saints; (4) Reformed; (5) Figures are estimates
Source: Association of Statisticians of American Religious Bodies, 2010 U.S. Religion Census: Religious Congregations & Membership Study

Religious Groups by Tradition

Area	Catholic	Evangelical Protestant	Mainline Protestant	Other Tradition	Black Protestant	Orthodox
MSA[1]	13.3	28.3	7.0	4.8	1.8	0.2
U.S.	19.1	16.2	7.3	4.3	1.6	0.3

Note: Figures are the number of adherents as a percentage of the total population; (1) Figures cover the Dallas-Fort Worth-Arlington, TX Metropolitan Statistical Area—see Appendix B for areas included
Source: Association of Statisticians of American Religious Bodies, 2010 U.S. Religion Census: Religious Congregations & Membership Study

ECONOMY

Gross Metropolitan Product

Area	2011	2012	2013	2014	Rank[2]
MSA[1]	397.0	418.6	436.4	460.9	6

Note: Figures are in billions of dollars; (1) Figures cover the Dallas-Fort Worth-Arlington, TX Metropolitan Statistical Area—see Appendix B for areas included; (2) Rank is based on 2014 data and ranges from 1 to 363
Source: The United States Conference of Mayors, U.S. Metro Economies: Outlook—Gross Metropolitan Product, with Metro Employment Projections, November 2013

Economic Growth

Area	2011 (%)	2012 (%)	2013 (%)	2014 (%)	Rank[2]
MSA[1]	3.2	4.3	3.0	3.7	25
U.S.	1.6	2.5	1.7	2.5	–

Note: Figures are real gross metropolitan product (GMP) growth rates and represent annual average percent change; (1) Figures cover the Dallas-Fort Worth-Arlington, TX Metropolitan Statistical Area—see Appendix B for areas included; (2) Rank is based on 2013 data and ranges from 1 to 363
Source: The United States Conference of Mayors, U.S. Metro Economies: Outlook—Gross Metropolitan Product, with Metro Employment Projections, November 2013

Metropolitan Area Exports

Area	2007	2008	2009	2010	2011	2012	Rank[2]
MSA[1]	22,079.1	22,503.7	19,881.8	22,500.4	26,648.7	27,820.9	8

Note: Figures are in millions of dollars; (1) Figures cover the Dallas-Fort Worth-Arlington, TX Metropolitan Statistical Area—see Appendix B for areas included; (2) Rank is based on 2012 data and ranges from 1 to 369
Source: U.S. Department of Commerce, International Trade Administration, Office of Trade & Industry Information, Manufacturing & Services, data extracted April 1, 2014

INCOME

Income

Area	Per Capita ($)	Median Household ($)	Average Household ($)
City	23,597	50,129	65,747
MSA[1]	28,421	57,109	78,238
U.S.	27,385	51,771	71,579

Note: (1) Figures cover the Dallas-Fort Worth-Arlington, TX Metropolitan Statistical Area—see Appendix B for areas included
Source: U.S. Census Bureau, 2010-2012 American Community Survey 3-Year Estimates

Household Income Distribution

Area	Percent of Households Earning							
	Under $15,000	$15,000 -24,999	$25,000 -34,999	$35,000 -49,999	$50,000 -74,999	$75,000 -99,000	$100,000 -149,999	$150,000 and up
City	13.6	11.6	10.9	13.7	19.1	12.6	11.7	6.8
MSA[1]	10.4	9.7	10.2	13.6	18.5	12.1	14.4	11.0
U.S.	13.1	11.0	10.5	13.7	18.1	11.9	12.5	9.1

Note: (1) Figures cover the Dallas-Fort Worth-Arlington, TX Metropolitan Statistical Area—see Appendix B for areas included
Source: U.S. Census Bureau, 2010-2012 American Community Survey 3-Year Estimates

Poverty Rate

Area	All Ages	Under 18 Years Old	18 to 64 Years Old	65 Years and Over
City	19.5	27.0	16.8	12.3
MSA[1]	15.1	21.8	13.0	9.0
U.S.	15.7	22.2	14.6	9.3

Note: Figures are percentage of people whose income during the past 12 months was below the poverty level; (1) Figures cover the Dallas-Fort Worth-Arlington, TX Metropolitan Statistical Area—see Appendix B for areas included
Source: U.S. Census Bureau, 2010-2012 American Community Survey 3-Year Estimates

Personal Bankruptcy Filing Rate

Area	2008	2009	2010	2011	2012	2013
Tarrant County	3.02	3.74	3.76	3.20	3.11	2.57
U.S.	3.53	4.61	4.97	4.37	3.76	3.29

Note: Numbers are per 1,000 population and include Chapter 7 and Chapter 13 filings
Source: Federal Deposit Insurance Corporation, Regional Economic Conditions, March 20, 2014

EMPLOYMENT

Labor Force and Employment

Area	Civilian Labor Force			Workers Employed		
	Dec. 2012	Dec. 2013	% Chg.	Dec. 2012	Dec. 2013	% Chg.
City	360,346	368,237	2.2	339,337	348,449	2.7
MD[1]	1,123,153	1,148,399	2.2	1,059,051	1,087,543	2.7
U.S.	154,904,000	154,408,000	-0.3	143,060,000	144,423,000	1.0

Note: Data is not seasonally adjusted and covers workers 16 years of age and older; (1) Metropolitan Division—see Appendix B for areas included
Source: Bureau of Labor Statistics, Local Area Unemployment Statistics

Unemployment Rate

Area	2013											
	Jan.	Feb.	Mar.	Apr.	May	Jun.	Jul.	Aug.	Sep.	Oct.	Nov.	Dec.
City	6.7	6.3	6.3	6.0	6.5	6.9	6.6	6.2	6.1	5.9	5.6	5.4
MD[1]	6.8	6.2	6.1	5.8	6.2	6.6	6.3	5.9	5.9	5.7	5.5	5.3
U.S.	8.5	8.1	7.6	7.1	7.3	7.8	7.7	7.3	7.0	7.0	6.6	6.5

Note: Data is not seasonally adjusted and covers workers 16 years of age and older; All figures are percentages; (1) Metropolitan Division—see Appendix B for areas included
Source: Bureau of Labor Statistics, Local Area Unemployment Statistics

Employment by Occupation

Occupation Classification	City (%)	MSA[1] (%)	U.S. (%)
Management, Business, Science, and Arts	33.6	37.3	36.0
Natural Resources, Construction, and Maintenance	10.2	9.5	9.1
Production, Transportation, and Material Moving	14.7	11.5	12.0
Sales and Office	24.2	25.7	24.7
Service	17.3	15.9	18.2

Note: Figures cover employed civilians 16 years of age and older; (1) Figures cover the Dallas-Fort Worth-Arlington, TX Metropolitan Statistical Area—see Appendix B for areas included
Source: U.S. Census Bureau, 2010-2012 American Community Survey 3-Year Estimates

Employment by Industry

| Sector | MD[1] | | U.S. |
	Number of Employees	Percent of Total	Percent of Total
Construction	n/a	n/a	4.2
Education and Health Services	117,900	12.6	15.5
Financial Activities	54,100	5.8	5.7
Government	128,800	13.7	16.1
Information	13,300	1.4	1.9
Leisure and Hospitality	103,200	11.0	10.2
Manufacturing	93,900	10.0	8.7
Mining and Logging	n/a	n/a	0.6
Other Services	36,300	3.9	3.9
Professional and Business Services	108,300	11.6	13.7
Retail Trade	106,900	11.4	11.4
Transportation and Utilities	68,800	7.3	3.8
Wholesale Trade	43,600	4.7	4.2

Note: Figures cover non-farm employment as of December 2013 and are not seasonally adjusted;
(1) Metropolitan Division—see Appendix B for areas included; n/a not available
Source: Bureau of Labor Statistics, Current Employment Statistics, Employment, Hours, and Earnings

Occupations with Greatest Projected Employment Growth: 2010 – 2020

Occupation[1]	2010 Employment	2020 Projected Employment	Numeric Employment Change	Percent Employment Change
Combined Food Preparation and Serving Workers, Including Fast Food	243,530	322,520	78,990	32.4
Elementary School Teachers, Except Special Education	166,090	233,860	67,780	40.8
Personal Care Aides	133,820	199,970	66,150	49.4
Retail Salespersons	370,620	433,180	62,560	16.9
Registered Nurses	184,700	245,870	61,160	33.1
Waiters and Waitresses	190,870	244,610	53,730	28.2
Office Clerks, General	262,740	314,810	52,070	19.8
Cashiers	250,510	292,730	42,220	16.9
Home Health Aides	82,420	123,970	41,550	50.4
Customer Service Representatives	200,880	241,030	40,160	20.0

Note: Projections cover Texas; (1) Sorted by numeric employment change
Source: www.projectionscentral.com, State Occupational Projections, 2010–2020 Long-Term Projections

Fastest Growing Occupations: 2010 – 2020

Occupation[1]	2010 Employment	2020 Projected Employment	Numeric Employment Change	Percent Employment Change
Biomedical Engineers	1,440	2,490	1,050	72.9
Diagnostic Medical Sonographers	3,560	5,410	1,850	51.9
Derrick Operators, Oil and Gas	7,190	10,860	3,670	51.1
Home Health Aides	82,420	123,970	41,550	50.4
Personal Care Aides	133,820	199,970	66,150	49.4
Service Unit Operators, Oil, Gas, and Mining	17,870	26,460	8,590	48.0
Special Education Teachers, Middle School	6,170	8,950	2,780	45.1
Special Education Teachers, Preschool, Kindergarten, and Elementary School	12,940	18,750	5,810	44.9
Rotary Drill Operators, Oil and Gas	7,160	10,340	3,180	44.4
Roustabouts, Oil and Gas	17,800	25,580	7,790	43.8

Note: Projections cover Texas; (1) Sorted by percent employment change and excludes occupations with numeric employment change less than 100
Source: www.projectionscentral.com, State Occupational Projections, 2010–2020 Long-Term Projections

Average Wages

Occupation	$/Hr.	Occupation	$/Hr.
Accountants and Auditors	34.18	Maids and Housekeeping Cleaners	9.18
Automotive Mechanics	19.54	Maintenance and Repair Workers	16.15
Bookkeepers	17.62	Marketing Managers	53.94
Carpenters	14.67	Nuclear Medicine Technologists	35.60
Cashiers	10.01	Nurses, Licensed Practical	22.36
Clerks, General Office	14.85	Nurses, Registered	33.60
Clerks, Receptionists/Information	12.80	Nursing Assistants	11.89
Clerks, Shipping/Receiving	14.27	Packers and Packagers, Hand	11.04
Computer Programmers	39.47	Physical Therapists	41.45
Computer Systems Analysts	38.95	Postal Service Mail Carriers	24.79
Computer User Support Specialists	24.54	Real Estate Brokers	n/a
Cooks, Restaurant	10.68	Retail Salespersons	11.78
Dentists	77.20	Sales Reps., Exc. Tech./Scientific	32.63
Electrical Engineers	44.46	Sales Reps., Tech./Scientific	36.55
Electricians	19.21	Secretaries, Exc. Legal/Med./Exec.	15.36
Financial Managers	57.15	Security Guards	14.30
First-Line Supervisors/Managers, Sales	21.00	Surgeons	n/a
Food Preparation Workers	9.59	Teacher Assistants	8.90
General and Operations Managers	55.07	Teachers, Elementary School	25.40
Hairdressers/Cosmetologists	12.29	Teachers, Secondary School	26.30
Internists	104.23	Telemarketers	11.19
Janitors and Cleaners	10.62	Truck Drivers, Heavy/Tractor-Trailer	19.47
Landscaping/Groundskeeping Workers	11.14	Truck Drivers, Light/Delivery Svcs.	15.61
Lawyers	54.57	Waiters and Waitresses	9.29

Note: Wage data covers the Fort Worth-Arlington, TX Metropolitan Division—see Appendix B for areas included. Hourly wages for elementary/secondary school teachers and teacher assistants were calculated by the editors from annual wage data assuming a 40 hour work week; n/a not available.
Source: Bureau of Labor Statistics, Metro Area Occupational Employment and Wage Estimates, May 2013

RESIDENTIAL REAL ESTATE

Building Permits

Area	Single-Family			Multi-Family			Total		
	2012	2013	Pct. Chg.	2012	2013	Pct. Chg.	2012	2013	Pct. Chg.
City	2,716	3,321	22.3	1,485	2,334	57.2	4,201	5,655	34.6
MSA[1]	18,090	21,224	17.3	16,952	16,686	-1.6	35,042	37,910	8.2
U.S.	518,695	620,802	19.7	310,963	370,020	19.0	829,658	990,822	19.4

Note: (1) Metropolitan Statistical Area—see Appendix B for areas included; figures represent new, privately-owned housing units authorized (unadjusted data); All permit data are based on estimates with imputation.
Source: U.S. Census Bureau, Manufacturing, Mining, and Construction Statistics, Building Permits, 2012, 2013

Homeownership Rate

Area	2006 (%)	2007 (%)	2008 (%)	2009 (%)	2010 (%)	2011 (%)	2012 (%)	2013 (%)
MSA[1]	60.7	60.9	60.9	61.6	63.8	62.6	61.8	59.9
U.S.	68.8	68.1	67.8	67.4	66.9	66.1	65.4	65.1

Note: (1) Figures cover the Dallas-Fort Worth-Arlington, TX Metropolitan Statistical Area—see Appendix B for areas included
Source: U.S. Census Bureau, Housing Vacancies and Homeownership Annual Statistics: 2013

Housing Vacancy Rates

Area	Gross Vacancy Rate[2] (%)			Year-Round Vacancy Rate[3] (%)			Rental Vacancy Rate[4] (%)			Homeowner Vacancy Rate[5] (%)		
	2011	2012	2013	2011	2012	2013	2011	2012	2013	2011	2012	2013
MSA[1]	9.8	8.7	9.0	9.6	8.4	8.8	11.8	9.2	8.2	2.0	2.1	1.9
U.S.	14.2	13.8	13.8	11.1	10.8	10.7	9.5	8.7	8.3	2.5	2.0	2.0

Note: (1) Figures cover the Dallas-Fort Worth-Arlington, TX Metropolitan Statistical Area—see Appendix B for areas included; (2) The percentage of the total housing inventory that is vacant; (3) The percentage of the housing inventory (excluding seasonal units) that is year-round vacant; (4) The percentage of rental inventory that is vacant for rent; (5) The percentage of homeowner inventory that is vacant for sale
Source: U.S. Census Bureau, Housing Vacancies and Homeownership Annual Statistics: 2013

TAXES

State Corporate Income Tax Rates

State	Tax Rate (%)	Income Brackets ($)	Num. of Brackets	Financial Institution Tax Rate (%)[a]	Federal Income Tax Ded.
Texas	(x)	–	–	(x)	No

Note: Tax rates as of January 1, 2014; (a) Rates listed are the corporate income tax rate applied to financial institutions or excise taxes based on income. Some states have other taxes based upon the value of deposits or shares; (x) Texas imposes a Franchise Tax, otherwise known as margin tax, imposed on entities with more than $1,030,000 total revenues at rate of 1%, or 0.5% for entities primarily engaged in retail or wholesale trade, on lesser of 70% of total revenues or 100% of gross receipts after deductions for either compensation or cost of goods sold.
Source: Federation of Tax Administrators, "State Corporate Income Tax Rates, 2014"

State Individual Income Tax Rates

State	Tax Rate (%)	Income Brackets ($)	Num. of Brackets	Personal Exempt. ($)[1] Single	Personal Exempt. ($)[1] Dependents	Fed. Inc. Tax Ded.
Texas	None	–	–	–	–	–

Note: Tax rates as of January 1, 2014; Local- and county-level taxes are not included; n/a not applicable; (1) Married joint filers generally receive double the single exemption
Source: Federation of Tax Administrators, "State Individual Income Tax Rates, 2014"

Various State and Local Tax Rates

State	State and Local Sales and Use (%)	State Sales and Use (%)	Gasoline[1] (¢/gal.)	Cigarette[2] ($/pack)	Spirits[3] ($/gal.)	Wine[4] ($/gal.)	Beer[5] ($/gal.)
Texas	8.25	6.25	20.00	1.410	2.40 (f)	0.20	0.20

Note: All tax rates as of January 1, 2014; (1) The American Petroleum Institute has developed a methodology for determining the average tax rate on a gallon of fuel. Rates may include any of the following: excise taxes, environmental fees, storage tank fees, other fees or taxes, general sales tax, and local taxes. In states where gasoline is subject to the general sales tax, or where the fuel tax is based on the average sale price, the average rate determined by API is sensitive to changes in the price of gasoline. States that fully or partially apply general sales taxes to gasoline: CA, CO, GA, IL, IN, MI, NY; (2) The federal excise tax of $1.0066 per pack and local taxes are not included; (3) Rates are those applicable to off-premise sales of 40% alcohol by volume (a.b.v.) distilled spirits in 750ml containers. Local excise taxes are excluded; (4) Rates are those applicable to off-premise sales of 11% a.b.v. non-carbonated wine in 750ml containers; (5) Rates are those applicable to off-premise sales of 4.7% a.b.v. beer in 12 ounce containers; (f) Different rates also applicable according to alcohol content, place of production, size of container, or place purchased (on- or off-premise or onboard airlines).
Source: Tax Foundation, 2014 Facts & Figures: How Does Your State Compare?

State Business Tax Climate Index Rankings

State	Overall Rank	Corporate Tax Index Rank	Individual Income Tax Index Rank	Sales Tax Index Rank	Unemployment Insurance Tax Index Rank	Property Tax Index Rank
Texas	11	38	7	36	14	35

Note: The index is a measure of how each state's tax laws affect economic performance. The lower the rank, the more favorable a state's tax system is for business. States without a given tax are given a ranking of 1. The scores/rankings for the District of Columbia do not affect other states. The 2014 index represents the tax climate as of July 1, 2013.
Source: Tax Foundation, State Business Tax Climate Index 2014

COMMERCIAL REAL ESTATE

Office Market

Market Area	Inventory (sq. ft.)	Vacancy Rate (%)	Under Construction (sq. ft.)	YTD Net Absorption (sq. ft.)	Total Average Asking Rent ($/sq. ft./year)
Dallas-Fort Worth	230,553,509	19.0	4,635,881	3,337,229	20.73
National	4,726,900,879	15.0	55,419,286	42,829,434	26.27

Source: Newmark Grubb Knight Frank, National Office Market Report, 4th Quarter 2013

Industrial/Warehouse/R&D Market

Market Area	Inventory (sq. ft.)	Vacancy Rate (%)	Under Construction (sq. ft.)	YTD Net Absorption (sq. ft.)	Total Average Asking Rent ($/sq. ft./year)
Dallas-Fort Worth	744,670,654	7.1	10,438,464	16,953,296	5.10
National	14,022,031,238	7.9	83,249,164	156,549,903	5.40

Source: Newmark Grubb Knight Frank, National Industrial Market Report, 4th Quarter 2013

COMMERCIAL UTILITIES

Typical Monthly Electric Bills

Area	Commercial Service ($/month)		Industrial Service ($/month)	
	1,500 kWh	40 kW demand 14,000 kWh	1,000 kW demand 200,000 kWh	50,000 kW demand 15,000,000 kWh
City	n/a	n/a	n/a	n/a
Average[1]	197	1,636	25,662	1,485,307

Note: Based on total rates in effect July 1, 2013; (1) average based on 180 utilities surveyed; n/a not available
Source: Edison Electric Institute, Typical Bills and Average Rates Report, Summer 2013

TRANSPORTATION

Means of Transportation to Work

Area	Car/Truck/Van		Public Transportation			Bicycle	Walked	Other Means	Worked at Home
	Drove Alone	Car-pooled	Bus	Subway	Railroad				
City	82.0	10.9	0.7	0.0	0.3	0.2	1.2	1.5	3.2
MSA[1]	81.1	10.2	1.0	0.1	0.3	0.2	1.2	1.3	4.6
U.S.	76.4	9.7	2.6	1.7	0.5	0.6	2.8	1.3	4.3

Note: Figures are percentages and cover workers 16 years of age and older; (1) Figures cover the Dallas-Fort Worth-Arlington, TX Metropolitan Statistical Area—see Appendix B for areas included
Source: U.S. Census Bureau, 2010-2012 American Community Survey 3-Year Estimates

Travel Time to Work

Area	Less Than 10 Minutes	10 to 19 Minutes	20 to 29 Minutes	30 to 44 Minutes	45 to 59 Minutes	60 to 89 Minutes	90 Minutes or More
City	9.2	29.2	23.2	23.3	8.0	5.7	1.5
MSA[1]	10.0	26.7	21.3	25.1	9.5	5.6	1.8
U.S.	13.5	29.8	20.9	20.1	7.5	5.6	2.5

Note: Figures are percentages and include workers 16 years old and over; (1) Figures cover the Dallas-Fort Worth-Arlington, TX Metropolitan Statistical Area—see Appendix B for areas included
Source: U.S. Census Bureau, 2010-2012 American Community Survey 3-Year Estimates

Travel Time Index

Area	1985	1990	1995	2000	2005	2010	2011
Urban Area[1]	1.08	1.12	1.16	1.22	1.30	1.25	1.26
Average[2]	1.09	1.14	1.16	1.19	1.23	1.18	1.18

Note: Travel Time Index—the ratio of travel time in the peak period to the travel time at free-flow conditions.
For example, a value of 1.30 indicates a 20-minute free-flow trip takes 26 minutes in the peak. Free-flow speeds
(60 mph on freeways and 35 mph on principal arterials) are used as the comparison threshold; (1) Covers the
Dallas-Fort Worth-Arlington TX urban area; (2) average of 498 urban areas
Source: Texas Transportation Institute, Urban Mobility Report 2012, December 2012

Public Transportation

Agency Name / Mode of Transportation	Vehicles Operated in Maximum Service	Annual Unlinked Passenger Trips (in thous.)	Annual Passenger Miles (in thous.)
Fort Worth Transportation Authority (The T)			
Bus (directly operated)	126	7,358.3	38,429.3
Bus (purchased transportation)	4	81.0	339.3
Demand Response (directly operated)	29	159.0	1,704.2
Demand Response (purchased transportation)	43	242.0	2,547.0

Source: Federal Transit Administration, National Transit Database, 2012

Air Transportation

Airport Name and Code / Type of Service	Passenger Airlines[1]	Passenger Enplanements	Freight Carriers[2]	Freight (lbs.)
Dallas-Fort Worth International (DFW)				
Domestic service (U.S. carriers - 2013)	26	25,820,977	20	328,889,605
International service (U.S. carriers - 2012)	11	2,426,715	4	66,271,050
Dallas Love Field (DAL)				
Domestic service (U.S. carriers - 2013)	18	4,016,160	8	9,764,315
International service (U.S. carriers - 2012)	7	1,563	2	69,530

Note: (1) Includes all U.S.-based major, minor and commuter airlines that carried at least one passenger during the year; (2) Includes all U.S.-based airlines and freight carriers that transported at least one lb. of freight during the year.
Source: Bureau of Transportation Statistics, The Intermodal Transportation Database, Air Carriers: T-100 Domestic Market (U.S. Carriers), 2013; Bureau of Transportation Statistics, The Intermodal Transportation Database, Air Carriers: T-100 International Market (U.S. Carriers), 2012

Other Transportation Statistics

Major Highways:	I-20; I-35W; I-30
Amtrak Service:	Yes
Major Waterways/Ports:	None

Source: Amtrak.com; Google Maps

BUSINESSES

Major Business Headquarters

Company Name	Rankings	
	Fortune[1]	Forbes[2]
AMR	121	
Ben E Keith	-	139

Note: (1) Fortune 500—companies that produce a 10-K are ranked 1 to 500 based on 2012 revenue; (2) all private companies with at least $2 billion in annual revenue through the end of their most current fiscal year are ranked 1 to 224; companies listed are headquartered in the city; dashes indicate no ranking Source: Fortune, "Fortune 500," May 20, 2013; Forbes, "America's Largest Private Companies," December 18, 2013

Fast-Growing Businesses

According to *Initiative for a Competitive Inner City (ICIC)*, Fort Worth is home to one of America's 100 fastest-growing "inner city" companies: **Kemp and Sons General Services** (#10). Companies were ranked by their five-year compound annual growth rate. Criteria for inclusion: company must be headquartered in or have 51 percent or more of its physical operations in an economically distressed urban area; must be an independent, for-profit corporation, partnership or proprietorship; must have 10 or more employees and have a five-year sales history that includes sales of at least $200,000 in the base year and at least $1 million in the current year with no decrease in sales over the two most recent years. *Initiative for a Competitive Inner City (ICIC), "Inner City 100 Companies, 2013"*

Minority Business Opportunity

Fort Worth is home to one company which is on the *Black Enterprise* Asset Manager 15 list (15 largest asset management firms based on assets under management): **American Beacon Advisors** (#1). Criteria: company must have been operational in previous calendar year and be at least 51% black-owned. *Black Enterprise, B.E. 100s, 2013*

Fort Worth is home to four companies which are on the *Hispanic Business* 500 list (500 largest U.S. Hispanic-owned companies based on 2012 revenue): **Thos. S. Byrne Ltd.** (#32); **Elite Staffing Services** (#320); **Ponce Contractors** (#405); **Open Integration Consulting** (#481). Companies included must show at least 51 percent ownership by Hispanic U.S. citizens, and must maintain headquarters in one of the 50 states or Washington, D.C. *Hispanic Business, "Hispanic Business 500," June 20, 2013*

Fort Worth is home to two companies which are on the *Hispanic Business* Fastest-Growing 100 list (greatest sales growth from 2008 to 2012): **Open Integration Consulting** (#53); **Thos. S. Byrne Ltd** (#66). Companies included must show at least 51 percent ownership by Hispanic U.S. citizens, and must maintain headquarters in one of the 50 states or Washington, D.C. In addition, companies must have minimum revenues of $200,000 for calendar year 2008. *Hispanic Business, June20, 2013*

Minority- and Women-Owned Businesses

Group	All Firms		Firms with Paid Employees			
	Firms	Sales ($000)	Firms	Sales ($000)	Employees	Payroll ($000)
Asian	2,530	1,131,325	588	1,054,655	2,854	114,999
Black	7,643	209,790	172	92,162	1,219	31,476
Hispanic	8,168	828,355	625	556,625	7,700	171,154
Women	16,515	3,158,441	1,533	2,784,740	13,109	395,861
All Firms	54,911	85,076,401	10,416	83,106,496	311,610	13,842,330

Note: Figures cover firms located in the city; minority- and women-owned business are defined as firms in which the corresponding group own 51% or more of the stock or equity of the company
Source: U.S. Census Bureau, 2007 Economic Census, Survey of Business Owners (2012 Survey of Business Owners data will be released starting in June 2015)

HOTELS & CONVENTION CENTERS

Hotels/Motels

Area	5 Star		4 Star		3 Star		2 Star		1 Star		Not Rated	
	Num.	Pct.[3]	Num.	Pct.[3]	Num.	Pct.[3]	Num.	Pct.[3]	Num.	Pct.[3]	Num.	Pct.[3]
City[1]	0	0.0	4	1.9	58	26.9	134	62.0	3	1.4	17	7.9
Total[2]	142	0.9	1,005	6.0	5,147	30.9	8,578	51.4	408	2.4	1,397	8.4

Note: (1) Figures cover Fort Worth and vicinity; (2) Figures cover all 100 cities in this book; (3) Percentage of hotels which have a given star rating; Star ratings are determined by expedia.com and offer an indication of the general quality of a particular hotel.
Source: expedia.com, April 7, 2014

Major Convention Centers

Name	Overall Space (sq. ft.)	Exhibit Space (sq. ft.)	Meeting Space (sq. ft.)	Meeting Rooms
Dallas Convention Center	2,000,000	929,726	n/a	96
Fort Worth Convention Center	n/a	253,226	58,849	41
Frisco Conference Center	90,000	n/a	n/a	14

Note: Table includes convention centers located in the Dallas-Fort Worth-Arlington, TX metro area; n/a not available
Source: Original research

Living Environment

COST OF LIVING

Cost of Living Index

Composite Index	Groceries	Housing	Utilities	Trans-portation	Health Care	Misc. Goods/Services
97.1	93.6	85.6	99.6	101.8	104.1	103.9

Note: The Cost of Living Index measures regional differences in the cost of consumer goods and services, excluding taxes and non-consumer expenditures, for professional and managerial households in the top income quintile. It is based on more than 50,000 prices covering almost 60 different items for which prices are collected three times a year by chambers of commerce, economic development organizations or university applied economic centers in each participating urban area. The numbers shown should be read as a percentage above or below the national average of 100. For example, a value of 115.4 in the groceries column indicates that grocery prices are 15.4% higher than the national average. Small differences in the index numbers should not be interpreted as significant; Figures cover the Fort Worth TX urban area.
Source: The Council for Community and Economic Research, ACCRA Cost of Living Index, 2013

Grocery Prices

Area[1]	T-Bone Steak ($/pound)	Frying Chicken ($/pound)	Whole Milk ($/half gal.)	Eggs ($/dozen)	Orange Juice ($/64 oz.)	Coffee ($/11.5 oz.)
City[2]	9.66	1.29	2.33	1.74	3.35	4.06
Avg.	10.19	1.28	2.34	1.81	3.48	4.39
Min.	8.56	0.94	1.44	1.19	2.78	3.40
Max.	14.82	2.28	3.56	3.73	6.23	7.32

*Note: (1) Values for the local area are compared with the average, minimum and maximum values for all 327 areas in the Cost of Living Index; (2) Figures cover the Fort Worth TX urban area; **T-Bone Steak** (price per pound); **Frying Chicken** (price per pound, whole fryer); **Whole Milk** (half gallon carton); **Eggs** (price per dozen, Grade A, large); **Orange Juice** (64 oz. Tropicana or Florida Natural); **Coffee** (11.5 oz. can, vacuum-packed, Maxwell House, Hills Bros, or Folgers).*
Source: The Council for Community and Economic Research, ACCRA Cost of Living Index, 2013

Housing and Utility Costs

Area[1]	New Home Price ($)	Apartment Rent ($/month)	All Electric ($/month)	Part Electric ($/month)	Other Energy ($/month)	Telephone ($/month)
City[2]	214,551	1,179	-	133.76	46.62	23.34
Avg.	295,864	900	171.38	91.82	70.12	27.73
Min.	185,506	458	117.80	48.81	33.67	17.16
Max.	1,358,917	3,783	441.68	171.40	372.65	39.47

*Note: (1) Values for the local area are compared with the average, minimum and maximum values for all 327 areas in the Cost of Living Index; (2) Figures cover the Fort Worth TX urban area; **New Home Price** (2,400 sf living area, 8,000 sf lot, in urban area with full utilities); **Apartment Rent** (950 sf 2 bedroom/1.5 or 2 bath, unfurnished, excluding all utilities except water); **All Electric** (average monthly cost for an all-electric home); **Part Electric** (average monthly cost for a part-electric home); **Other Energy** (average monthly cost for natural gas, fuel oil, coal, wood, and any other forms of energy except electricity); **Telephone** (price includes basic monthly rate for a private residential line plus additional local usage charges incurred by a family of four).*
Source: The Council for Community and Economic Research, ACCRA Cost of Living Index, 2013

Health Care, Transportation, and Other Costs

Area[1]	Doctor ($/visit)	Dentist ($/visit)	Optometrist ($/visit)	Gasoline ($/gallon)	Beauty Salon ($/visit)	Men's Shirt ($)
City[2]	96.72	100.50	82.11	3.35	38.39	36.00
Avg.	101.40	86.48	96.16	3.44	33.87	26.55
Min.	61.67	50.83	50.12	3.08	18.92	12.48
Max.	182.71	152.50	223.78	4.33	68.22	52.03

*Note: (1) Values for the local area are compared with the average, minimum and maximum values for all 327 areas in the Cost of Living Index; (2) Figures cover the Fort Worth TX urban area; **Doctor** (general practitioners routine exam of an established patient); **Dentist** (adult teeth cleaning and periodic oral examination); **Optometrist** (full vision eye exam for established adult patient); **Gasoline** (one gallon regular unleaded, national brand, including all taxes, cash price at self-service pump if available); **Beauty Salon** (woman's shampoo, trim, and blow-dry); **Men's Shirt** (cotton/polyester dress shirt, pinpoint weave, long sleeves).*
Source: The Council for Community and Economic Research, ACCRA Cost of Living Index, 2013

HOUSING

House Price Index (HPI)

Area	National Ranking[2]	Quarterly Change (%)	One-Year Change (%)	Five-Year Change (%)
MD[1]	82	0.99	5.42	4.04
U.S.[3]	–	1.20	7.69	4.18

Note: The HPI is a weighted repeat sales index. It measures average price changes in repeat sales or refinancings on the same properties. This information is obtained by reviewing repeat mortgage transactions on single-family properties whose mortgages have been purchased or securitized by Fannie Mae or Freddie Mac in January 1975; (1) Fort Worth-Arlington, TX Metropolitan Division—see Appendix B for areas included; (2) Rankings are based on annual percentage change for all metro areas containing at least 15,000 transactions over the last 10 years and ranges from 1 to 283; (3) figures based on a weighted average of Census Division estimates using a seasonally adjusted, purchase-only index; all figures are for the period ending December 31, 2013
Source: Federal Housing Finance Agency, House Price Index, February 25, 2014

Median Single-Family Home Prices

Area	2011	2012	2013p	Percent Change 2012 to 2013
MSA[1]	148.9	159.3	175.6	10.2
U.S. Average	166.2	177.2	197.4	11.4

Note: Figures are median sales prices of existing single-family homes in thousands of dollars; (p) preliminary; n/a not available; (1) Dallas-Fort Worth-Arlington, TX Metropolitan Statistical Area—see Appendix B for areas included
Source: National Association of Realtors, Median Sales Price of Existing Single-Family Homes for Metropolitan Areas, 4th Quarter 2013

Qualifying Income Based on Median Sales Price of Existing Single-Family Homes

Area	With 5% Down ($)	With 10% Down ($)	With 20% Down ($)
MSA[1]	40,093	37,983	33,762
U.S. Average	45,395	43,006	38,228

Note: Figures are preliminary; Qualifying income is based on a mortgage rate of 4.4%. Monthly principal and interest payment is limited to 25% of income; n/a not available; (1) Dallas-Fort Worth-Arlington, TX Metropolitan Statistical Area—see Appendix B for areas included
Source: National Association of Realtors, Qualifying Income Based on Median Sales Price of Existing Single-Family Homes for Metropolitan Areas, 4th Quarter 2013

Median Apartment Condo-Coop Home Prices

Area	2011	2012	2013p	Percent Change 2012 to 2013
MSA[1]	126.0	142.1	155.7	9.6
U.S. Average	165.1	173.7	194.9	12.2

Note: Figures are median sales prices of existing apartment condo-coop homes in thousands of dollars; (p) preliminary; n/a not available; (1) Dallas-Fort Worth-Arlington, TX Metropolitan Statistical Area—see Appendix B for areas included
Source: National Association of Realtors, Median Sales Price of Existing Apartment Condo-Coop Homes for Metropolitan Areas, 4th Quarter 2013

Gross Monthly Rent

Area	Under $200	$200 -299	$300 -499	$500 -749	$750 -999	$1,000 -1,499	$1,500 and up	Median ($)
City	1.6	1.8	6.6	28.8	27.6	25.0	8.5	839
MSA[1]	0.9	1.2	4.0	26.2	30.5	27.2	9.9	884
U.S.	1.7	3.3	8.1	22.7	24.3	25.7	14.3	889

Note: Figures are percentages except for Median; Gross rent is the contract rent plus the estimated average monthly cost of utilities (electricity, gas, and water and sewer) and fuels (oil, coal, kerosene, wood, etc.) if these are paid by the renter (or paid for the renter by someone else); (1) Figures cover the Dallas-Fort Worth-Arlington, TX Metropolitan Statistical Area—see Appendix B for areas included
Source: U.S. Census Bureau, 2010-2012 American Community Survey 3-Year Estimates

Year Housing Structure Built

Area	2010 or Later	2000 -2009	1990 -1999	1980 -1989	1970 -1979	1960 -1969	1950 -1959	1940 -1949	Before 1940	Median Year
City	1.1	27.9	11.0	14.8	10.7	9.3	11.9	6.0	7.2	1983
MSA[1]	0.9	23.6	16.2	19.7	15.6	9.7	7.9	3.2	3.1	1985
U.S.	0.5	14.9	13.8	13.9	15.9	11.1	10.9	5.5	13.5	1976

Note: Figures are percentages except for Median Year; (1) Figures cover the Dallas-Fort Worth-Arlington, TX Metropolitan Statistical Area—see Appendix B for areas included
Source: U.S. Census Bureau, 2010-2012 American Community Survey 3-Year Estimates

HEALTH

Health Risk Data

Category	MD[1] (%)	U.S. (%)
Adults aged 18–64 who have any kind of health care coverage	70.7	79.6
Adults who reported being in good or excellent health	84.3	83.1
Adults who are current smokers	20.5	19.6
Adults who are heavy drinkers[2]	7.1	6.1
Adults who are binge drinkers[3]	17.5	16.9
Adults who are overweight (BMI 25.0 - 29.9)	37.2	35.8
Adults who are obese (BMI 30.0 - 99.8)	30.0	27.6
Adults who participated in any physical activities in the past month	71.2	77.1
Adults 50+ who have ever had a sigmoidoscopy or colonoscopy	67.3	67.3
Women aged 40+ who have had a mammogram within the past two years	73.2	74.0
Men aged 40+ who have had a PSA test within the past two years	43.7	45.2
Adults aged 65+ who have had flu shot within the past year	60.0	60.1
Adults who always wear a seatbelt	97.2	93.8

Note: Data as of 2012 unless otherwise noted; (1) Figures cover the Fort Worth-Arlington, TX Metropolitan Division—see Appendix B for areas included; (2) Heavy drinkers are classified as males having more than two drinks per day or females having more than one drink per day; (3) Binge drinkers are classified as males having five or more drinks on one occasion or females having four or more drinks on one occasion
Source: Centers for Disease Control and Prevention, Behaviorial Risk Factor Surveillance System, SMART: Selected Metropolitan/Micropolitan Area Risk Trends, 2012

Chronic Health Indicators

Category	MD[1] (%)	U.S. (%)
Adults who have ever been told they had a heart attack	4.0	4.5
Adults who have ever been told they had a stroke	2.7	2.9
Adults who have been told they currently have asthma	7.2	8.9
Adults who have ever been told they have arthritis	21.3	25.7
Adults who have ever been told they have diabetes[2]	9.7	9.7
Adults who have ever been told they had skin cancer	5.9	5.7
Adults who have ever been told they had any other types of cancer	4.6	6.5
Adults who have ever been told they have COPD	5.4	6.2
Adults who have ever been told they have kidney disease	2.1	2.5
Adults who have ever been told they have a form of depression	13.8	18.0

Note: Data as of 2012 unless otherwise noted; (1) Figures cover the Fort Worth-Arlington, TX Metropolitan Division—see Appendix B for areas included; (2) Figures do not include pregnancy-related, borderline, or pre-diabetes
Source: Centers for Disease Control and Prevention, Behaviorial Risk Factor Surveillance System, SMART: Selected Metropolitan/Micropolitan Area Risk Trends, 2012

Mortality Rates for the Top 10 Causes of Death in the U.S.

ICD-10[a] Sub-Chapter	ICD-10[a] Code	Age-Adjusted Mortality Rate[1] per 100,000 population	
		County[2]	U.S.
Malignant neoplasms	C00-C97	172.1	174.2
Ischaemic heart diseases	I20-I25	119.0	119.1
Other forms of heart disease	I30-I51	48.8	49.6
Chronic lower respiratory diseases	J40-J47	49.5	43.2
Cerebrovascular diseases	I60-I69	50.9	40.3
Organic, including symptomatic, mental disorders	F01-F09	47.7	30.5
Other degenerative diseases of the nervous system	G30-G31	25.4	26.3
Other external causes of accidental injury	W00-X59	19.6	25.1
Diabetes mellitus	E10-E14	20.3	21.3
Hypertensive diseases	I10-I15	22.3	18.8

Note: (a) ICD-10 = International Classification of Diseases 10th Revision; (1) Mortality rates are a three year average covering 2008-2010; (2) Figures cover Tarrant County
Source: Centers for Disease Control and Prevention, National Center for Health Statistics. Compressed Mortality File 1999-2010 on CDC WONDER Online Database, released January 2013. Data are compiled from the Compressed Mortality File 1999-2010, Series 20 No. 2P, 2013.

Mortality Rates for Selected Causes of Death

ICD-10[a] Sub-Chapter	ICD-10[a] Code	Age-Adjusted Mortality Rate[1] per 100,000 population	
		County[2]	U.S.
Assault	X85-Y09	5.1	5.5
Diseases of the liver	K70-K76	15.1	12.4
Human immunodeficiency virus (HIV) disease	B20-B24	2.8	3.0
Influenza and pneumonia	J09-J18	13.9	16.4
Intentional self-harm	X60-X84	10.4	11.8
Malnutrition	E40-E46	1.4	0.8
Obesity and other hyperalimentation	E65-E68	1.4	1.6
Renal failure	N17-N19	15.6	13.6
Transport accidents	V01-V99	11.4	12.6
Viral hepatitis	B15-B19	2.5	2.2

Note: (a) ICD-10 = International Classification of Diseases 10th Revision; (1) Mortality rates are a three year average covering 2008-2010; (2) Figures cover Tarrant County
Source: Centers for Disease Control and Prevention, National Center for Health Statistics. Compressed Mortality File 1999-2010 on CDC WONDER Online Database, released January 2013. Data are compiled from the Compressed Mortality File 1999-2010, Series 20 No. 2P, 2013.

Health Insurance Coverage

Area	With Health Insurance	With Private Health Insurance	With Public Health Insurance	Without Health Insurance	Population Under Age 18 Without Health Insurance
City	75.8	54.8	26.9	24.2	13.0
MSA[1]	77.7	61.1	23.3	22.3	13.3
U.S.	84.9	65.4	30.4	15.1	7.5

Note: Figures are percentages that cover the civilian noninstitutionalized population; (1) Figures cover the Dallas-Fort Worth-Arlington, TX Metropolitan Statistical Area—see Appendix B for areas included
Source: U.S. Census Bureau, 2010-2012 American Community Survey 3-Year Estimates

Number of Medical Professionals

Area[1]	MDs[2]	DOs[2,3]	Dentists	Podiatrists	Chiropractors	Optometrists
Local (number)	3,190	676	973	77	424	238
Local (rate[4])	172.6	36.6	51.7	4.1	22.5	12.6
U.S. (rate[4])	267.6	19.6	61.7	5.6	24.7	14.5

Note: Data as of 2012 unless noted; (1) Local data covers Tarrant County; (2) Data as of 2011; (3) Doctor of Osteopathic Medicine; (4) rate per 100,000 population
Source: Area Resource File (ARF) 2012-2013. U.S. Department of Health and Human Services, Health Resources and Services Administration, Bureau of Health Professions

Best Hospitals

According to *U.S. News*, the Fort Worth-Arlington, TX metro area is home to one of the best children's hospitals in the U.S.: **Cook Children's Medical Center**. The hospital listed was highly ranked in at least one pediatric specialty. Eighty-seven hospitals in the U.S. ranked in at least one specialty. Ten children's hospitals in the U.S. made the Honor Roll by ranking near the top in three or more specialties.*U.S. News Online, "America's Best Children's Hospitals 2013-14"*

EDUCATION

Public School District Statistics

District Name	Schls	Pupils	Pupil/ Teacher Ratio	Minority Pupils[1] (%)	Free Lunch Eligible[2] (%)	IEP[3] (%)
Castleberry ISD	7	3,672	17.2	77.8	74.6	7.9
Eagle Mt-Saginaw ISD	26	17,155	16.7	51.5	31.4	8.1
Fort Worth ISD	145	83,109	16.2	86.3	71.4	5.5
Harmony Science Acad (Fort Worth)	4	2,396	14.1	74.4	35.4	3.0

Note: Table includes school districts with 2,000 or more students; (1) Percentage of students that are not non-Hispanic white; (2) Percentage of students that are eligible for the free lunch program; (3) Percentage of students that have an Individualized Education Program.
Source: U.S. Department of Education, National Center for Education Statistics, Common Core of Data, Local Education Agency (School District) Universe Survey: School Year 2011-2012; U.S. Department of Education, National Center for Education Statistics, Common Core of Data, Public Elementary/Secondary School Universe Survey: School Year 2011-2012

Best High Schools

High School Name	Rank[1]	Grad. Rate[2] (%)	Coll.[3] (%)	AP/IB/ AICE Tests[4]	AP/IB/ AICE Score[5]	SAT Score[6]	ACT Score[6]
Fort Worth Academy of Fine Arts	516	100	96	0.6	2.1	1582	22.3
Green B. Trimble Technical H.S.	1873	95	76	0.3	2.1	1296	18.2
Harmony School of Innovation Fort Worth	246	100	100	0.5	3.2	1623	27.0
R. L. Paschal H.S.	1676	90	70	0.5	3.0	1593	23.5

Note: (1) Public schools are ranked from 1 to 2,000 based on the following self-reported statistics (with the corresponding weight used in calculating their overall score). Schools that were newly founded and did not have a graduating senior class in 2012 were excluded; (2) Four-year, on-time graduation rate (25%); (3) Percent of 2011 graduates who were accepted to college (25%); (4) AP/IB/AICE tests taken per student (25%); (5) Average AP/IB/AICE exam score (10%); (6) Average SAT and/or ACT score (10%); Percent of students enrolled in at least one AP/IB/AICE course (5%)—data not shown
Source: Newsweek and The Daily Beast, "America's Best High Schools 2013"

Highest Level of Education

Area	Less than H.S.	H.S. Diploma	Some College, No Deg.	Associate Degree	Bachelor's Degree	Master's Degree	Prof. School Degree	Doctorate Degree
City	20.6	24.3	23.5	5.8	17.7	6.0	1.4	0.8
MSA[1]	16.3	23.0	22.8	6.5	21.2	7.7	1.6	1.0
U.S.	14.1	28.3	21.3	7.8	18.0	7.5	1.9	1.2

Note: Figures cover persons age 25 and over; (1) Figures cover the Dallas-Fort Worth-Arlington, TX Metropolitan Statistical Area—see Appendix B for areas included
Source: U.S. Census Bureau, 2010-2012 American Community Survey 3-Year Estimates

Educational Attainment by Race

Area	High School Graduate or Higher (%)					Bachelor's Degree or Higher (%)				
	Total	White	Black	Asian	Hisp.[2]	Total	White	Black	Asian	Hisp.[2]
City	79.4	81.1	85.2	79.7	51.3	25.9	29.8	16.2	37.5	8.6
MSA[1]	83.7	85.4	88.4	86.9	54.7	31.4	33.4	23.0	54.3	10.9
U.S.	85.9	88.1	82.5	85.5	63.1	28.6	30.0	18.4	50.2	13.4

Note: Figures shown cover persons 25 years old and over; (1) Figures cover the Dallas-Fort Worth-Arlington, TX Metropolitan Statistical Area—see Appendix B for areas included; (2) People of Hispanic origin can be of any race
Source: U.S. Census Bureau, 2010-2012 American Community Survey 3-Year Estimates

School Enrollment by Grade and Control

Area	Preschool (%)		Kindergarten (%)		Grades 1 - 4 (%)		Grades 5 - 8 (%)		Grades 9 - 12 (%)	
	Public	Private	Public	Private	Public	Private	Public	Private	Public	Private
City	62.5	37.5	92.7	7.3	91.9	8.1	92.1	7.9	93.2	6.8
MSA[1]	55.6	44.4	90.2	9.8	92.2	7.8	92.4	7.6	92.7	7.3
U.S.	56.9	43.1	87.8	12.2	89.9	10.1	90.0	10.0	90.8	9.2

Note: Figures shown cover persons 3 years old and over; (1) Figures cover the Dallas-Fort Worth-Arlington, TX Metropolitan Statistical Area—see Appendix B for areas included
Source: U.S. Census Bureau, 2010-2012 American Community Survey 3-Year Estimates

Average Salaries of Public School Classroom Teachers

Area	2012-13		2013-14		Percent Change 2012-13 to 2013-14	Percent Change 2003-04 to 2013-14
	Dollars	Rank[1]	Dollars	Rank[1]		
Texas	48,819	35	49,270	35	0.92	21.7
U.S. Average	56,103	–	56,689	–	1.04	21.8

Note: (1) State rank ranges from 1 to 51 where 1 indicates highest salary.
Source: National Education Association, Rankings & Estimates: Rankings of the States 2013 and Estimates of School Statistics 2014, March 2014

Higher Education

Four-Year Colleges			Two-Year Colleges			Medical Schools[1]	Law Schools[2]	Voc/ Tech[3]
Public	Private Non-profit	Private For-profit	Public	Private Non-profit	Private For-profit			
1	3	2	1	1	2	1	1	3

Note: Figures cover institutions located within the city limits and include main campuses only; (1) includes schools accredited by the Liaison Committee on Medical Education and the American Osteopathic Association's Commission on Osteopathic College Accreditation; (2) includes ABA-accredited schools, schools with provisional ABA accreditation, and state accredited schools; (3) includes all schools with programs that are less than 2 years.
Source: National Center for Education Statistics, Integrated Postsecondary Education System (IPEDS), 2012-13; Association of American Medical Colleges, Member List, April 24, 2014; American Osteopathic Association, Member List, April 24, 2014; Law School Admission Council, Official Guide to ABA-Approved Law Schools Online, April 24, 2014; Wikipedia, List of Medical Schools in the United States, April 24, 2014; Wikipedia, List of Law Schools in the United States, April 24, 2014

According to U.S. News & World Report, the Fort Worth-Arlington, TX metro division is home to one of the best national universities in the U.S.: **Texas Christian University** (#82). The indicators used to capture academic quality fall into a number of categories: assessment by administrators at peer institutions; retention of students; faculty resources; student selectivity; financial resources; alumni giving; high school counselor ratings of colleges; and graduation rate. U.S. News & World Report, "America's Best Colleges 2014"

According to U.S. News & World Report, the Fort Worth-Arlington, TX metro division is home to one of the top 100 business schools in the U.S.: **Texas Christian University** (Neeley) (#79). The rankings are based on a weighted average of the following nine measures: quality assessment; peer assessment; recruiter assessment; placement success; mean starting salary and bonus; student selectivity; mean GMAT and GRE scores; mean undergraduate GPA; and acceptance rate. U.S. News & World Report, "America's Best Graduate Schools, Business, 2014"

PRESIDENTIAL ELECTION

2012 Presidential Election Results

Area	Obama	Romney	Other
Tarrant County	41.4	57.1	1.4
U.S.	51.0	47.2	1.8

Note: Results are percentages and may not add to 100% due to rounding
Source: Dave Leip's Atlas of U.S. Presidential Elections

EMPLOYERS

Major Employers

Company Name	Industry
AMR Corporation	Air transportation, scheduled
Associates First Capital Corporation	Mortgage bankers
Baylor University Medical Center	General medical and surgical hospitals
Children's Medical Center Dallas	Specialty hospitals, except psychiatric
Combat Support Associates	Engineering services
County of Dallas	County supervisors' and executives' office
Dallas County Hospital District	General medical and surgical hospitals
Fort Worth Independent School District	Public elementary and secondary schools
Housewares Holding Company	Toasters, electric: household
HP Enterprise Services	Computer integrated systems design
J.C. Penney Company	Department stores
JCP Publications Corp.	Department stores
L-3 Communications Corporation	Business economic service
Odyssey HealthCare	Home health care services
Romano's Macaroni Grill	Italian restaurant
SFG Management Limited Liability	Milk processing (pasteurizing, homogenizing, bottling)
Texas Instruments Incorporated	Semiconductors and related devices
University of North Texas	Colleges and universities
University of Texas SW Medical Center	Accident and health insurance
Verizon Business Global	Telephone communication, except radio

Note: Companies shown are located within the Dallas-Fort Worth-Arlington, TX Metropolitan Statistical Area.
Source: Hoovers.com; Wikipedia

Best Companies to Work For

BNSF Railway, headquartered in Fort Worth, is among the "100 Best Places to Work in IT." To qualify, companies, both public and private, had to have a minimum of 50 IT employees and were selected based on average salary and bonus increases, the percentage of IT staffers promoted, IT staff turnover rates, training and development programs, and the percentage of women and minorities in IT staff and management positions. In addition, *Computerworld* looked at retention efforts, programs for recognizing and rewarding outstanding performances, and benefits such as flextime, elder care and child care, and reimbursement for college tuition and the cost of pursuing technology certifications. *Computerworld, "100 Best Places to Work in IT 2013"*

PUBLIC SAFETY

Crime Rate

Area	All Crimes	Violent Crimes				Property Crimes		
		Murder	Forcible Rape	Robbery	Aggrav. Assault	Burglary	Larceny -Theft	Motor Vehicle Theft
City	4,809.5	5.7	50.8	166.2	364.8	1,096.2	2,811.1	314.8
Suburbs[1]	3,143.3	2.6	25.4	63.9	182.3	641.5	2,058.6	168.9
Metro[2]	3,707.5	3.6	34.0	98.6	244.1	795.5	2,313.4	218.3
U.S.	3,246.1	4.7	26.9	112.9	242.3	670.2	1,959.3	229.7

Note: Figures are crimes per 100,000 population; (1) All areas within the metro area that are located outside the city limits; (2) Figures cover the Fort Worth-Arlington, TX Metropolitan Division—see Appendix B for areas included
Source: FBI Uniform Crime Reports, 2012

Hate Crimes

Area	Number of Quarters Reported	Bias Motivation				
		Race	Religion	Sexual Orientation	Ethnicity	Disability
City	4	10	1	3	0	0
U.S.	4	2,797	1,099	1,135	667	92

Source: Federal Bureau of Investigation, Hate Crime Statistics 2012

Identity Theft Consumer Complaints

Area	Complaints	Complaints per 100,000 Population	Rank[2]
MSA[1]	7,378	114.8	34
U.S.	290,056	91.8	-

Note: (1) Figures cover the Dallas-Fort Worth-Arlington, TX Metropolitan Statistical Area—see Appendix B for areas included; (2) Rank ranges from 1 to 377 where 1 indicates greatest number of identity theft complaints per 100,000 population
Source: Federal Trade Commission, Consumer Sentinel Network Data Book for January–December 2013

Fraud and Other Consumer Complaints

Area	Complaints	Complaints per 100,000 Population	Rank[2]
MSA[1]	29,924	465.7	41
U.S.	1,811,724	595.2	-

Note: (1) Figures cover the Dallas-Fort Worth-Arlington, TX Metropolitan Statistical Area—see Appendix B for areas included; (2) Rank ranges from 1 to 377 where 1 indicates greatest number of identity theft complaints per 100,000 population
Source: Federal Trade Commission, Consumer Sentinel Network Data Book for January–December 2013

RECREATION

Culture

Dance[1]	Theatre[1]	Instrumental Music[1]	Vocal Music[1]	Series and Festivals	Museums and Art Galleries[2]	Zoos and Aquariums[3]
3	8	3	4	3	43	1

Note: (1) Number of professional performing groups; (2) Based on organizations with primary SIC code 8412; (3) AZA-accredited
Source: The Grey House Performing Arts Directory, 2013; Association of Zoos & Aquariums, AZA Member Zoos & Aquariums, April 2014; www.AccuLeads.com, May 1, 2014

Professional Sports Teams

Team Name	League	Year Established
Dallas Cowboys	National Football League (NFL)	1960
Dallas Mavericks	National Basketball Association (NBA)	1980
Dallas Stars	National Hockey League (NHL)	1993
FC Dallas	Major League Soccer (MLS)	1996
Texas Rangers	Major League Baseball (MLB)	1972

Note: Includes teams located in the Dallas-Fort Worth-Arlington, TX Metropolitan Statistical Area.
Source: Wikipedia, Major Professional Sports Teams of the United States and Canada

CLIMATE

Average and Extreme Temperatures

Temperature	Jan	Feb	Mar	Apr	May	Jun	Jul	Aug	Sep	Oct	Nov	Dec	Yr.
Extreme High (°F)	88	88	96	98	103	113	110	108	107	106	89	90	113
Average High (°F)	54	59	67	76	83	92	96	96	88	79	67	58	76
Average Temp. (°F)	44	49	57	66	73	81	85	85	78	68	56	47	66
Average Low (°F)	33	38	45	54	63	71	75	74	67	56	45	37	55
Extreme Low (°F)	4	6	11	29	41	51	59	56	43	29	19	-1	-1

Note: Figures cover the years 1953-1990
Source: National Climatic Data Center, International Station Meteorological Climate Summary, 9/96

Average Precipitation/Snowfall/Humidity

Precip./Humidity	Jan	Feb	Mar	Apr	May	Jun	Jul	Aug	Sep	Oct	Nov	Dec	Yr.
Avg. Precip. (in.)	1.8	2.2	2.6	3.7	4.9	2.8	2.1	1.9	3.0	3.3	2.1	1.7	32.3
Avg. Snowfall (in.)	1	1	Tr	0	0	0	0	0	0	0	Tr	Tr	3
Avg. Rel. Hum. 6am (%)	79	79	79	81	86	85	80	79	83	82	80	79	81
Avg. Rel. Hum. 3pm (%)	52	51	48	50	53	47	42	41	46	47	49	51	48

Note: Figures cover the years 1953-1990; Tr = Trace amounts (<0.05 in. of rain; <0.5 in. of snow)
Source: National Climatic Data Center, International Station Meteorological Climate Summary, 9/96

Weather Conditions

	Temperature			Daytime Sky			Precipitation		
10°F & below	32°F & below	90°F & above	Clear	Partly cloudy	Cloudy	0.01 inch or more precip.	0.1 inch or more snow/ice	Thunder-storms
1	40	100	123	136	106	79	3	47

Note: Figures are average number of days per year and cover the years 1953-1990
Source: National Climatic Data Center, International Station Meteorological Climate Summary, 9/96

HAZARDOUS WASTE

Superfund Sites

Fort Worth has one hazardous waste site on the EPA's Superfund Final National Priorities List: **Air Force Plant #4 (General Dynamics)**. *U.S. Environmental Protection Agency, Final National Priorities List, April 26, 2014*

AIR & WATER QUALITY

Air Quality Index

Area	Percent of Days when Air Quality was...[2]					AQI Statistics[2]	
	Good	Moderate	Unhealthy for Sensitive Groups	Unhealthy	Very Unhealthy	Maximum	Median
MSA[1]	42.7	48.2	8.8	0.3	0.0	161	54

Note: (1) Data covers the Dallas-Fort Worth-Arlington, TX Metropolitan Statistical Area—see Appendix B for areas included; (2) Based on 365 days with AQI data in 2013. Air Quality Index (AQI) is an index for reporting daily air quality. EPA calculates the AQI for five major air pollutants regulated by the Clean Air Act: ground-level ozone, particle pollution (aka particulate matter), carbon monoxide, sulfur dioxide, and nitrogen dioxide. The AQI runs from 0 to 500. The higher the AQI value, the greater the level of air pollution and the greater the health concern. There are six AQI categories: "Good" AQI is between 0 and 50. Air quality is considered satisfactory; "Moderate" AQI is between 51 and 100. Air quality is acceptable; "Unhealthy for Sensitive Groups" When AQI values are between 101 and 150, members of sensitive groups may experience health effects; "Unhealthy" When AQI values are between 151 and 200 everyone may begin to experience health effects; "Very Unhealthy" AQI values between 201 and 300 trigger a health alert; "Hazardous" AQI values over 300 trigger warnings of emergency conditions (not shown).
Source: U.S. Environmental Protection Agency, Air Quality Index Report, 2013

Air Quality Index Pollutants

Area	Percent of Days when AQI Pollutant was...[2]					
	Carbon Monoxide	Nitrogen Dioxide	Ozone	Sulfur Dioxide	Particulate Matter 2.5	Particulate Matter 10
MSA[1]	0.0	4.7	38.4	0.0	55.6	1.4

Note: (1) Data covers the Dallas-Fort Worth-Arlington, TX Metropolitan Statistical Area—see Appendix B for areas included; (2) Based on 365 days with AQI data in 2013. The Air Quality Index (AQI) is an index for reporting daily air quality. EPA calculates the AQI for five major air pollutants regulated by the Clean Air Act: ground-level ozone, particle pollution (also known as particulate matter), carbon monoxide, sulfur dioxide, and nitrogen dioxide. The AQI runs from 0 to 500. The higher the AQI value, the greater the level of air pollution and the greater the health concern.
Source: U.S. Environmental Protection Agency, Air Quality Index Report, 2013

Air Quality Trends: Ozone

	2003	2004	2005	2006	2007	2008	2009	2010	2011	2012
MSA[1]	0.089	0.087	0.093	0.089	0.081	0.077	0.080	0.076	0.085	0.083

Note: (1) Data covers the Dallas-Fort Worth-Arlington, TX Metropolitan Statistical Area—see Appendix B for areas included. The values shown are the composite ozone concentration averages among trend sites based on the highest fourth daily maximum 8-hour concentration in parts per million. These trends are based on sites having an adequate record of monitoring data during the trend period. Data from exceptional events are included.
Source: U.S. Environmental Protection Agency, Air Quality Monitoring Information, "Air Quality Trends by City, 2000-2012"

Maximum Air Pollutant Concentrations: Particulate Matter, Ozone, CO and Lead

	Particulate Matter 10 (ug/m³)	Particulate Matter 2.5 Wtd AM (ug/m³)	Particulate Matter 2.5 24-Hr (ug/m³)	Ozone (ppm)	Carbon Monoxide (ppm)	Lead (ug/m³)
MSA[1] Level	66	10.7	22	0.092	1	0.42
NAAQS[2]	150	15	35	0.075	9	0.15
Met NAAQS[2]	Yes	Yes	Yes	No	Yes	No

Note: (1) Data covers the Dallas-Fort Worth-Arlington, TX Metropolitan Statistical Area—see Appendix B for areas included; Data from exceptional events are included; (2) National Ambient Air Quality Standards; ppm = parts per million; ug/m³ = micrograms per cubic meter; n/a not available.
Concentrations: Particulate Matter 10 (coarse particulate)—highest second maximum 24-hour concentration; Particulate Matter 2.5 Wtd AM (fine particulate)—highest weighted annual mean concentration; Particulate Matter 2.5 24-Hour (fine particulate)—highest 98th percentile 24-hour concentration; Ozone—highest fourth daily maximum 8-hour concentration; Carbon Monoxide—highest second maximum non-overlapping 8-hour concentration; Lead—maximum running 3-month average
Source: U.S. Environmental Protection Agency, Air Quality Monitoring Information, "Air Quality Statistics by City, 2012"

Maximum Air Pollutant Concentrations: Nitrogen Dioxide and Sulfur Dioxide

	Nitrogen Dioxide AM (ppb)	Nitrogen Dioxide 1-Hr (ppb)	Sulfur Dioxide AM (ppb)	Sulfur Dioxide 1-Hr (ppb)	Sulfur Dioxide 24-Hr (ppb)
MSA[1] Level	12	53	n/a	15	n/a
NAAQS[2]	53	100	30	75	140
Met NAAQS[2]	Yes	Yes	n/a	Yes	n/a

Note: (1) Data covers the Dallas-Fort Worth-Arlington, TX Metropolitan Statistical Area—see Appendix B for areas included; Data from exceptional events are included; (2) National Ambient Air Quality Standards; ppm = parts per million; ug/m³ = micrograms per cubic meter; n/a not available.
Concentrations: Nitrogen Dioxide AM—highest arithmetic mean concentration; Nitrogen Dioxide 1-Hr—highest 98th percentile 1-hour daily maximum concentration; Sulfur Dioxide AM—highest annual mean concentration; Sulfur Dioxide 1-Hr—highest 99th percentile 1-hour daily maximum concentration; Sulfur Dioxide 24-Hr—highest second maximum 24-hour concentration
Source: U.S. Environmental Protection Agency, Air Quality Monitoring Information, "Air Quality Statistics by City, 2012"

Drinking Water

Water System Name	Pop. Served	Primary Water Source Type	Violations[1] Health Based	Monitoring/ Reporting
City of Fort Worth	748,450	Surface	0	0

Note: (1) Based on violation data from January 1, 2013 to December 31, 2013 (includes unresolved violations from earlier years)
Source: U.S. Environmental Protection Agency, Office of Ground Water and Drinking Water, Safe Drinking Water Information System (based on data extracted February 10, 2014)

Gainesville, Florida

Background

Gainesville is the cultural and educational hub of North Florida, located partway between the Atlantic Ocean and Gulf of Mexico. Alachua County's largest city has grown with a population drawn to its subtropical locale and its heartbeat and largest employer, the colossal University of Florida (UF). Innovation is the name of the game when it comes to the region's push for businesses emerging from the university's numerous research centers. In addition, Gainesville is only a short drive to rural Florida habitat. Ten miles south are the bison, alligators, and 270 bird species found at Paynes Prairie Preserve. Plus, North Florida has the world's largest concentration of freshwater springs.

Originally a Timucuan Indian village, present-day Gainesville was part of a Spanish land grant by 1817. The United States annexed Florida in 1825, and just over a quarter-century later came plans for the Florida Railroad. In 1853, the local citizenry opted to create a new county seat along the railroad line, and Gainesville was founded and named for Seminole Indian War General Edmund P. Gaines. After the Civil War, a Union veteran established a successful cotton shipping station here, and in 1906 UF was founded. Through the years, fire and development has destroyed many of Gainesville's early buildings; a few remain including the Hippodrome State Theatre which was once the local Federal Building.

Emerging from the University of Florida (the nation's fifth largest university), are projects from dozens of research centers and institutes. An early success was Gatorade, invented in 1965 to hydrate the Gator football team. Alternative energy research draws accolades, and the city proper became the nation's first to implement a solar feed-in tariff, which means consumers who invest in the appropriate technology can sell their electricity back to the utility. The university's Sid Martin Biotechnology Incubator was ranked "World's Best University Biotechnology Incubator" by an international study conducted by the Sweden-based research group UBI in 2013. The university's annual economic impact is more than $8.76 billion, and state-wide its activities are estimated to generate more than 106,000 jobs.

In addition to the biotechnology incubator, the city is also home to the Florida Innovation Hub, the first building of the 40-acre Innovation Square package situated as a bridge between the campus and Gainesville's downtown. Eventually, over five million square feet of space will be filled with residences, retail, hotels and open space. The Hub is a 48,000 square-foot facility that incubates start-up companies that emerge from university research. Its Office of Technology Licensing aids the push to grow new business. Also at the square: the UF Innovation Academy, an undergraduate program focusing on entrepreneurial-minded students.

A long list of rankings lauds Gainesville's quality of life for young people and retirees. As with many college towns, there's long been a happening music scene. Tom Petty and the Heartbreakers emerged from Gainesville. Cultural resources include the Florida Museum of Natural History, founded in 1891, fueled by donations from interested professors. In addition to its central museum and collections, it operates the Randell Research Center (a significant Calusa Indian archaeological site-and an ancient ecological site-in Lee County northwest of Fort Myers) and the McGuire Center for Lepidoptera and Biodiversity that boasts one of the world's largest butterfly and moth collections. Public exhibitions include the 6800 square-foot living Butterfly Rainforest.

In addition, UF's Harn Museum of Art exhibits traveling shows and collections of photography and Ancient American, Asian, African, modern and contemporary art. Also in the city are the Hippodrome State Theatre, showcasing cinema and traveling theater, and the Curtis M. Phillips Center for Performing Arts.

Famously humid, Gainesville's subtropical climate means freezes are not unheard of in winter, with December through February average highs in the 50s. June through August is notably wet, averaging more than six inches of rain the first two months of summer and eight inches in August. Equally notable, Gainesville's inland location tends to mitigate the threat of hurricanes that face Florida's coasts. Temperatures often climb into the 90s from April to October.

Rankings

Business/Finance Rankings

- Gainesville was identified as one of "America's Hardest-Working Towns." The city ranked #6 out of 25. Criteria: average hours worked per capita; willingness to work during personal time; number of dual income households; local employment rate. *Parade, "What is America's Hardest-Working Town?," April 15, 2012*

- The Gainesville metro area appeared on the Milken Institute "2013 Best Performing Cities" list. Rank: #124 out of 200 large metro areas. Criteria: job growth; wage and salary growth; high-tech output growth. *Milken Institute, "Best-Performing Cities 2013," December 2013*

- *Forbes* ranked the 200 most populous metro areas in the U.S. in terms of the "Best Places for Business and Careers." The Gainesville metro area was ranked #49. Criteria: costs (business and living); job growth (past and projected); income growth; educational attainment (college and high school); projected economic growth; cultural and recreational opportunities; net migration patterns; number of highly ranked colleges. *Forbes, "The Best Places for Business and Careers," August 7, 2013*

Education Rankings

- Gainesville was selected as one of the most well-read cities in America by Amazon.com. The city ranked #15 of 20. Cities with populations greater than 100,000 were evaluated based on per capita sales of books, magazines and newspapers. *Amazon.com, "The 20 Most Well-Read Cities in America," April 28, 2013*

- Gainesville was identified as one of "America's Smartest Cities" by *The Daily Beast* using data from Lumos Labs. The metro area ranked #13 out of 25. Criteria: with data collected from more than 1 million users as part of its human cognition project, Lumos Labs was able to analyze performance for nearly 200 metro areas in five cognitive areas: memory, processing speed, flexibility, attention, and problem solving. The median Lumos Lab score was worth 50 percent of the final, weighted ranking. The other half of the ranking was based on the percentage of adults over age 25 with a bachelor's and/or master's degree. *The Daily Beast, "America's Smartest Cities 2012" August 16, 2012*

Environmental Rankings

- The Gainesville metro area came in at #295 for the relative comfort of its climate on Sperling's list of "chill cities," as measured by the Sperling Heat Index. All 361 metro areas are included. Criteria included daytime high temperatures, nighttime low temperatures, dew point, and relative humidity at the high temperatures. *www.bertsperling.com, "Sperling's Chill Cities," July 18, 2013*

- Sperling's BestPlaces assessed 379 metropolitan areas of the United States for the likelihood of dangerously extreme weather events or earthquakes. In general the Southeast and South-Central regions have the highest risk of weather extremes and earthquakes, while the Pacific Northwest enjoys the lowest risk. Of the least risky metropolitan areas, the Gainesville metro area was ranked #291. *www.bestplaces.net, "Safest Places from Natural Disasters," April 2011*

- Gainesville was selected as one of 22 "Smarter Cities" for energy by the Natural Resources Defense Council. Criteria: investment in green power; energy efficiency measures; conservation. *Natural Resources Defense Council, "2010 Smarter Cities," July 19, 2010*

- Gainesville was highlighted as one of the cleanest metro areas for ozone air pollution in the U.S. during 2008 through 2010. The list represents cities with no monitored ozone air pollution in unhealthful ranges. *American Lung Association, State of the Air 2012*

- Gainesville was highlighted as one of the top 25 cleanest metro areas for short-term particle pollution (24-hour PM 2.5) in the U.S. during 2008 through 2010. Monitors in these cities reported no days with unhealthful PM 2.5 levels. *American Lung Association, State of the Air 2012*

Health/Fitness Rankings

- The Gainesville metro area appeared in the 2013 Gallup-Healthways Well-Being Index. The area ranked #112 out of 189. The Gallup-Healthways Well-Being Index score is an average of six sub-indexes, which individually examine life evaluation, emotional health, work environment, physical health, healthy behaviors, and access to basic necessities. Results are based on telephone interviews conducted as part of the Gallup-Healthways Well-Being Index survey January 2–December 29, 2012, and January 2–December 30, 2013, with a random sample of 531,630 adults, aged 18 and older, living in metropolitan areas in the 50 U.S. states and the District of Columbia. *Gallup-Healthways, "State of American Well-Being," March 25, 2014*

Real Estate Rankings

- Gainesville was ranked #51 out of 224 metro areas in terms of housing affordability in 2013 by the National Association of Home Builders (#1 = most affordable). The NAHB-Wells Fargo Housing Opportunity Index (HOI) for a given area is defined as the share of homes sold in that area that would have been affordable to a family earning the local median income, based on standard mortgage underwriting criteria. *National Association of Home Builders®, NAHB-Wells Fargo Housing Opportunity Index, 4th Quarter 2013*

- Gainesville was selected as one of the best college towns for renters by ApartmentRatings.com." The area ranked #26 out of 87. Overall satisfaction ratings were ranked using thousands of user submitted scores for hundreds of apartment complexes located in cities and towns that are home to the 100 largest four-year institutions in the U.S. *ApartmentRatings.com, "2011 College Town Renter Satisfaction Rankings"*

Safety Rankings

- The National Insurance Crime Bureau ranked 380 metro areas in the U.S. in terms of per capita rates of vehicle theft. The Gainesville metro area ranked #211 (#1 = highest rate). Criteria: number of vehicle theft offenses per 100,000 inhabitants in 2012. *National Insurance Crime Bureau, "Hot Spots 2012," June 26, 2013*

Seniors/Retirement Rankings

- From its Best Cities for Successful Aging indexes, the Milken Institute generated rankings for metropolitan areas, weighing data in eight categories—general indicators, health care, wellness, living arrangements, transportation and general accessibility, financial well-being, education and employment, and community participation. The Gainesville metro area was ranked #6 overall in the small metro area category. *Milken Institute, "Best Cities for Successful Aging," July 2012*

- The AARP named Gainesville one of the "10 Best Places to Live on $100 a Day." Analysts looked at 200 cities to arrive at their 10-best list. Criteria includes: cost of living; quality-of-life; arts and culture; educational institutions; restaurants; community life; health care; natural setting; sunny days per year; and overall vibe. *AARP The Magazine, "10 Best Places to Live on $100 a Day," July 2012*

- Gainesville was identified as one of the most popular places to retire by *Topretirements.com*. The list reflects the 100 cities (out of 900+ total cities reviewed) that visitors to the website are most interested in for retirement. *Topretirements.com, "Most Popular Places to Retire for 2014," February 25, 2014*

Sports/Recreation Rankings

- Gainesville appeared on the *Sporting News* list of the "Best Sports Cities" for 2011. The area ranked #55 out of 271. Criteria: the magazine takes a 12-month snapshot of each city's sports, putting a heavy premium on regular-season won-lost records (from the most recently completed season). Other criteria include: playoff berths, bowl appearances and tournament bids; championships; applicable power ratings; quality of competition; overall fan fervor (measured in part by attendance); abundance of teams (rewarding quality over quantity); stadium and arena quality; ticket availability and prices; franchise ownership; and marquee appeal of athletes. *Sporting News, "Best Sports Cities 2011," October 4, 2011*

- Gainesville appeared on the *Sporting News* list of the "Best Sports Cities" for 2011. The area ranked #55 out of 271. Criteria: a 12-month snapshot of regular-season won-lost records (from the most recently completed season). Other criteria include: playoff berths, bowl appearances and tournament bids; championships; applicable power ratings; quality of competition; overall fan fervor (measured in part by attendance); abundance of teams (quality over quantity); stadium and arena quality; ticket availability and prices; franchise ownership; and marquee appeal of athletes. *Sporting News, "Best Sports Cities 2011," October 4, 2011*

- Gainesville was chosen as a bicycle friendly community by the League of American Bicyclists. A "Bicycle Friendly Community" welcomes cyclists by providing safe accommodation for cycling and encouraging people to bike for transportation and recreation. There are four award levels: Platinum; Gold; Silver; and Bronze. The community achieved an award level of Silver. *League of American Bicyclists, "Bicycle Friendly Community Master List," Fall 2013*

- Gainesville was chosen as one of America's best cities for bicycling. The city ranked #37 out of 50. Criteria: robust cycling infrastructure; vibrant bike culture. The editors only considered cities with populations of 95,000 or more. *Bicycling, "America's Top 50 Bike-Friendly Cities," May 23, 2012*

Miscellaneous Rankings

- Using Musicmetric's Digital Music Index (DMI), CNBC ranked results for music piracy by way of the file-sharing protocol BitTorrent. Gainesville was ranked #1 among American cities. *CNBC.com, "Florida City Named 'Pirate Capital' of Music World," October 8, 2012*

Business Environment

CITY FINANCES

City Government Finances

Component	2011 ($000)	2011 ($ per capita)
Total Revenues	606,290	5,301
Total Expenditures	568,495	4,970
Debt Outstanding	1,074,920	9,398
Cash and Securities[1]	927,194	8,107

Note: (1) Cash and security holdings of a government at the close of its fiscal year, including those of its dependent agencies, utilities, and liquor stores.
Source: U.S Census Bureau, State & Local Government Finances 2011

City Government Revenue by Source

Source	2011 ($000)	2011 ($ per capita)
General Revenue		
From Federal Government	14,818	130
From State Government	11,100	97
From Local Governments	1,192	10
Taxes		
Property	28,915	253
Sales and Gross Receipts	33,002	289
Personal Income	0	0
Corporate Income	0	0
Motor Vehicle License	0	0
Other Taxes	4,142	36
Current Charges	66,216	579
Liquor Store	0	0
Utility	336,792	2,945
Employee Retirement	61,162	535

Source: U.S Census Bureau, State & Local Government Finances 2011

City Government Expenditures by Function

Function	2011 ($000)	2011 ($ per capita)	2011 (%)
General Direct Expenditures			
Air Transportation	0	0	0.0
Corrections	0	0	0.0
Education	0	0	0.0
Employment Security Administration	0	0	0.0
Financial Administration	7,499	66	1.3
Fire Protection	15,007	131	2.6
General Public Buildings	2,936	26	0.5
Governmental Administration, Other	5,581	49	1.0
Health	297	3	0.1
Highways	20,625	180	3.6
Hospitals	0	0	0.0
Housing and Community Development	7,136	62	1.3
Interest on General Debt	14,715	129	2.6
Judicial and Legal	1,431	13	0.3
Libraries	0	0	0.0
Parking	466	4	0.1
Parks and Recreation	14,914	130	2.6
Police Protection	38,851	340	6.8
Public Welfare	821	7	0.1
Sewerage	24,731	216	4.4
Solid Waste Management	7,859	69	1.4
Veterans' Services	0	0	0.0
Liquor Store	0	0	0.0
Utility	335,146	2,930	59.0
Employee Retirement	29,827	261	5.2

Source: U.S Census Bureau, State & Local Government Finances 2011

DEMOGRAPHICS

Population Growth

Area	1990 Census	2000 Census	2010 Census	Population Growth (%) 1990-2000	Population Growth (%) 2000-2010
City	90,519	95,447	124,354	5.4	30.3
MSA[1]	191,263	232,392	264,275	21.5	13.7
U.S.	248,709,873	281,421,906	308,745,538	13.2	9.7

Note: (1) Figures cover the Gainesville, FL Metropolitan Statistical Area—see Appendix B for areas included
Source: U.S. Census Bureau, Census 1990, 2000, 2010

Household Size

Area	Persons in Household (%) One	Two	Three	Four	Five	Six	Seven or More	Average Household Size
City	37.0	35.6	14.9	9.1	2.2	0.8	0.3	2.39
MSA[1]	31.6	37.1	15.7	10.1	3.7	1.1	0.7	2.48
U.S.	27.6	33.5	15.7	13.2	6.1	2.4	1.5	2.63

Note: (1) Figures cover the Gainesville, FL Metropolitan Statistical Area—see Appendix B for areas included
Source: U.S. Census Bureau, 2010-2012 American Community Survey 3-Year Estimates

Race

Area	White Alone[2] (%)	Black Alone[2] (%)	Asian Alone[2] (%)	AIAN[3] Alone[2] (%)	NHOPI[4] Alone[2] (%)	Other Race Alone[2] (%)	Two or More Races (%)
City	65.8	22.8	6.9	0.3	0.1	1.1	3.0
MSA[1]	71.3	19.4	5.1	0.3	0.1	1.0	2.8
U.S.	74.0	12.6	4.9	0.8	0.2	4.7	2.8

Note: (1) Figures cover the Gainesville, FL Metropolitan Statistical Area—see Appendix B for areas included; (2) Alone is defined as not being in combination with one or more other races; (3) American Indian and Alaska Native; (4) Native Hawaiian and Other Pacific Islander
Source: U.S. Census Bureau, 2010-2012 American Community Survey 3-Year Estimates

Hispanic or Latino Origin

Area	Total (%)	Mexican (%)	Puerto Rican (%)	Cuban (%)	Other (%)
City	10.2	1.2	2.1	2.7	4.1
MSA[1]	8.4	1.3	2.0	2.0	3.2
U.S.	16.6	10.7	1.6	0.6	3.7

Note: Persons of Hispanic or Latino origin can be of any race; (1) Figures cover the Gainesville, FL Metropolitan Statistical Area—see Appendix B for areas included
Source: U.S. Census Bureau, 2010-2012 American Community Survey 3-Year Estimates

Segregation

Type	Segregation Indices[1] 1990	2000	2010	2010 Rank[2]	Percent Change 1990-2000	Percent Change 1990-2010	Percent Change 2000-2010
Black/White	n/a	n/a	n/a	n/a	n/a	n/a	n/a
Asian/White	n/a	n/a	n/a	n/a	n/a	n/a	n/a
Hispanic/White	n/a	n/a	n/a	n/a	n/a	n/a	n/a

Note: All figures cover the Metropolitan Statistical Area—see Appendix B for areas included; Figures are based on an analysis of 1990, 2000, and 2010 Census Decennial Census tract data by William H. Frey, Brookings Institution and the University of Michigan Social Science Data Analysis Network. In this analysis all racial groups (whites, blacks, and asians) are non-Hispanic members of those races. Hispanics are shown as a separate category;
(1) Segregation Indices are Dissimilarity Indices that measure the degree to which the minority group is distributed differently than whites across census tracts. They range from 0 (complete integration) to 100 (complete segregation) where the value indicates the percentage of the minority group that needs to move to be distributed exactly like whites; (2) Ranges from 1 (most segregated) to 102 (least segregated); n/a not available.
Source: www.CensusScope.org

Ancestry

Area	German	Irish	English	American	Italian	Polish	French[2]	Scottish	Dutch
City	11.6	10.8	8.5	4.1	5.8	3.2	2.7	2.1	0.7
MSA[1]	13.3	11.2	10.2	6.1	5.0	2.8	2.7	2.0	1.3
U.S.	15.2	11.1	8.2	7.2	5.6	3.1	2.8	1.7	1.4

Note: Figures are the percentage of the total population reporting a particular ancestry. The nine most commonly reported ancestries in the U.S. are shown. Figures include multiple ancestries (e.g. if a person reported being Irish and Italian, they were included in both columns); (1) Figures cover the Gainesville, FL Metropolitan Statistical Area—see Appendix B for areas included; (2) Excludes Basque
Source: U.S. Census Bureau, 2010-2012 American Community Survey 3-Year Estimates

Foreign-Born Population

Area	Any Foreign Country	Mexico	Asia	Europe	Carribean	South America	Central America[2]	Africa	Canada
City	12.7	0.4	5.4	1.7	2.0	2.0	0.4	0.4	0.3
MSA[1]	10.3	0.4	3.9	1.6	1.6	1.6	0.4	0.4	0.3
U.S.	13.0	3.7	3.7	1.6	1.2	0.9	1.0	0.5	0.3

Note: (1) Figures cover the Gainesville, FL Metropolitan Statistical Area—see Appendix B for areas included; (2) Excludes Mexico.
Source: U.S. Census Bureau, 2010-2012 American Community Survey 3-Year Estimates

Marital Status

Area	Never Married	Now Married[2]	Separated	Widowed	Divorced
City	62.5	24.1	1.6	4.0	7.7
MSA[1]	45.6	37.9	1.7	4.8	9.9
U.S.	32.4	48.4	2.2	6.0	11.0

Note: Figures are percentages and cover the population 15 years of age and older; (1) Figures cover the Gainesville, FL Metropolitan Statistical Area—see Appendix B for areas included; (2) Excludes separated
Source: U.S. Census Bureau, 2010-2012 American Community Survey 3-Year Estimates

Age

Area	Under Age 5	Age 5–19	Age 20–34	Age 35–44	Age 45–54	Age 55–64	Age 65–74	Age 75–84	Age 85+	Median Age
City	4.3	18.1	44.0	8.1	7.9	9.2	3.9	3.1	1.3	24.9
MSA[1]	5.3	18.4	31.2	10.3	11.7	11.5	6.3	3.6	1.5	30.8
U.S.	6.4	20.1	20.5	13.1	14.3	12.2	7.3	4.2	1.8	37.3

Note: (1) Figures cover the Gainesville, FL Metropolitan Statistical Area—see Appendix B for areas included
Source: U.S. Census Bureau, 2010-2012 American Community Survey 3-Year Estimates

Gender

Area	Males	Females	Males per 100 Females
City	60,145	65,128	92.3
MSA[1]	129,927	136,437	95.2
U.S.	153,276,055	158,333,314	96.8

Note: (1) Figures cover the Gainesville, FL Metropolitan Statistical Area—see Appendix B for areas included
Source: U.S. Census Bureau, 2010-2012 American Community Survey 3-Year Estimates

Religious Groups by Family

Area	Catholic	Baptist	Non-Den.	Methodist[2]	Lutheran	LDS[3]	Pentecostal	Presbyterian[4]	Muslim[5]	Judaism
MSA[1]	7.6	12.3	4.3	6.4	0.5	1.0	3.5	1.1	1.1	0.4
U.S.	19.1	9.3	4.0	4.0	2.3	2.0	1.9	1.6	0.8	0.7

Note: Figures are the number of adherents as a percentage of the total population; (1) Figures cover the Gainesville, FL Metropolitan Statistical Area—see Appendix B for areas included; (2) Methodist/Pietist; (3) Latter Day Saints; (4) Reformed; (5) Figures are estimates
Source: Association of Statisticians of American Religious Bodies, 2010 U.S. Religion Census: Religious Congregations & Membership Study

Religious Groups by Tradition

Area	Catholic	Evangelical Protestant	Mainline Protestant	Other Tradition	Black Protestant	Orthodox
MSA[1]	7.6	20.4	7.0	4.2	2.2	0.1
U.S.	19.1	16.2	7.3	4.3	1.6	0.3

Note: Figures are the number of adherents as a percentage of the total population; (1) Figures cover the Gainesville, FL Metropolitan Statistical Area—see Appendix B for areas included
Source: Association of Statisticians of American Religious Bodies, 2010 U.S. Religion Census: Religious Congregations & Membership Study

ECONOMY

Gross Metropolitan Product

Area	2011	2012	2013	2014	Rank[2]
MSA[1]	10.3	10.5	10.7	11.1	176

Note: Figures are in billions of dollars; (1) Figures cover the Gainesville, FL Metropolitan Statistical Area—see Appendix B for areas included; (2) Rank is based on 2014 data and ranges from 1 to 363
Source: The United States Conference of Mayors, U.S. Metro Economies: Outlook—Gross Metropolitan Product, with Metro Employment Projections, November 2013

Economic Growth

Area	2011 (%)	2012 (%)	2013 (%)	2014 (%)	Rank[2]
MSA[1]	0.0	-0.6	0.6	1.7	200
U.S.	1.6	2.5	1.7	2.5	–

Note: Figures are real gross metropolitan product (GMP) growth rates and represent annual average percent change; (1) Figures cover the Gainesville, FL Metropolitan Statistical Area—see Appendix B for areas included; (2) Rank is based on 2013 data and ranges from 1 to 363
Source: The United States Conference of Mayors, U.S. Metro Economies: Outlook—Gross Metropolitan Product, with Metro Employment Projections, November 2013

Metropolitan Area Exports

Area	2007	2008	2009	2010	2011	2012	Rank[2]
MSA[1]	227.5	285.5	233.2	277.7	305.1	348.6	238

Note: Figures are in millions of dollars; (1) Figures cover the Gainesville, FL Metropolitan Statistical Area—see Appendix B for areas included; (2) Rank is based on 2012 data and ranges from 1 to 369
Source: U.S. Department of Commerce, International Trade Administration, Office of Trade & Industry Information, Manufacturing & Services, data extracted April 1, 2014

INCOME

Income

Area	Per Capita ($)	Median Household ($)	Average Household ($)
City	19,445	31,294	48,531
MSA[1]	24,223	41,405	60,928
U.S.	27,385	51,771	71,579

Note: (1) Figures cover the Gainesville, FL Metropolitan Statistical Area—see Appendix B for areas included
Source: U.S. Census Bureau, 2010-2012 American Community Survey 3-Year Estimates

Household Income Distribution

Area	Under $15,000	$15,000 -24,999	$25,000 -34,999	$35,000 -49,999	$50,000 -74,999	$75,000 -99,000	$100,000 -149,999	$150,000 and up
			Percent of Households Earning					
City	27.6	14.0	12.5	12.3	14.5	6.8	7.7	4.5
MSA[1]	20.6	12.3	10.8	12.8	16.1	10.1	10.5	6.7
U.S.	13.1	11.0	10.5	13.7	18.1	11.9	12.5	9.1

Note: (1) Figures cover the Gainesville, FL Metropolitan Statistical Area—see Appendix B for areas included
Source: U.S. Census Bureau, 2010-2012 American Community Survey 3-Year Estimates

Poverty Rate

Area	All Ages	Under 18 Years Old	18 to 64 Years Old	65 Years and Over
City	36.1	29.7	40.4	8.9
MSA[1]	25.5	25.0	28.5	8.8
U.S.	15.7	22.2	14.6	9.3

*Note: Figures are percentage of people whose income during the past 12 months was below the poverty level;
(1) Figures cover the Gainesville, FL Metropolitan Statistical Area—see Appendix B for areas included
Source: U.S. Census Bureau, 2010-2012 American Community Survey 3-Year Estimates*

Personal Bankruptcy Filing Rate

Area	2008	2009	2010	2011	2012	2013
Alachua County	1.46	1.90	1.99	1.81	1.62	1.29
U.S.	3.53	4.61	4.97	4.37	3.76	3.29

*Note: Numbers are per 1,000 population and include Chapter 7 and Chapter 13 filings
Source: Federal Deposit Insurance Corporation, Regional Economic Conditions, March 20, 2014*

EMPLOYMENT

Labor Force and Employment

Area	Civilian Labor Force			Workers Employed		
	Dec. 2012	Dec. 2013	% Chg.	Dec. 2012	Dec. 2013	% Chg.
City	65,566	65,672	0.2	61,555	62,366	1.3
MSA[1]	142,757	142,789	0.0	134,185	135,953	1.3
U.S.	154,904,000	154,408,000	-0.3	143,060,000	144,423,000	1.0

*Note: Data is not seasonally adjusted and covers workers 16 years of age and older; (1) Metropolitan Statistical
Area—see Appendix B for areas included
Source: Bureau of Labor Statistics, Local Area Unemployment Statistics*

Unemployment Rate

Area	2013											
	Jan.	Feb.	Mar.	Apr.	May	Jun.	Jul.	Aug.	Sep.	Oct.	Nov.	Dec.
City	6.2	5.7	5.4	4.8	5.5	6.3	6.5	5.7	5.5	4.8	5.1	5.0
MSA[1]	6.1	5.6	5.2	4.8	5.3	6.0	6.0	5.5	5.3	4.8	4.9	4.8
U.S.	8.5	8.1	7.6	7.1	7.3	7.8	7.7	7.3	7.0	7.0	6.6	6.5

*Note: Data is not seasonally adjusted and covers workers 16 years of age and older; All figures are percentages;
(1) Metropolitan Statistical Area—see Appendix B for areas included
Source: Bureau of Labor Statistics, Local Area Unemployment Statistics*

Employment by Occupation

Occupation Classification	City (%)	MSA[1] (%)	U.S. (%)
Management, Business, Science, and Arts	42.8	44.2	36.0
Natural Resources, Construction, and Maintenance	4.5	5.6	9.1
Production, Transportation, and Material Moving	5.7	6.3	12.0
Sales and Office	24.2	23.8	24.7
Service	22.8	20.1	18.2

*Note: Figures cover employed civilians 16 years of age and older; (1) Figures cover the Gainesville, FL
Metropolitan Statistical Area—see Appendix B for areas included
Source: U.S. Census Bureau, 2010-2012 American Community Survey 3-Year Estimates*

Employment by Industry

| Sector | MSA[1] | | U.S. |
	Number of Employees	Percent of Total	Percent of Total
Construction	n/a	n/a	4.2
Education and Health Services	24,000	18.2	15.5
Financial Activities	6,200	4.7	5.7
Government	42,600	32.4	16.1
Information	1,500	1.1	1.9
Leisure and Hospitality	13,900	10.6	10.2
Manufacturing	4,600	3.5	8.7
Mining and Logging	n/a	n/a	0.6
Other Services	4,000	3.0	3.9
Professional and Business Services	11,500	8.7	13.7
Retail Trade	13,900	10.6	11.4
Transportation and Utilities	2,700	2.1	3.8
Wholesale Trade	2,700	2.1	4.2

Note: Figures cover non-farm employment as of December 2013 and are not seasonally adjusted;
(1) Metropolitan Statistical Area—see Appendix B for areas included; n/a not available
Source: Bureau of Labor Statistics, Current Employment Statistics, Employment, Hours, and Earnings

Occupations with Greatest Projected Employment Growth: 2010 – 2020

Occupation[1]	2010 Employment	2020 Projected Employment	Numeric Employment Change	Percent Employment Change
Retail Salespersons	290,200	345,860	55,660	19.2
Combined Food Preparation and Serving Workers, Including Fast Food	154,650	193,760	39,110	25.3
Registered Nurses	165,400	202,190	36,790	22.3
Waiters and Waitresses	174,630	210,650	36,010	20.6
Customer Service Representatives	165,950	194,220	28,260	17.0
Cashiers	200,040	225,430	25,400	12.7
Office Clerks, General	142,480	164,800	22,330	15.7
Landscaping and Groundskeeping Workers	93,350	115,400	22,050	23.6
Postsecondary Teachers	75,610	94,190	18,580	24.6
Cooks, Restaurant	76,000	94,180	18,190	23.9

Note: Projections cover Florida; (1) Sorted by numeric employment change
Source: www.projectionscentral.com, State Occupational Projections, 2010–2020 Long-Term Projections

Fastest Growing Occupations: 2010 – 2020

Occupation[1]	2010 Employment	2020 Projected Employment	Numeric Employment Change	Percent Employment Change
Layout Workers, Metal and Plastic	230	380	150	65.2
Biomedical Engineers	620	990	370	60.2
Helpers—Carpenters	1,120	1,770	650	58.0
Biochemists and Biophysicists	650	1,000	350	53.6
Medical Scientists, Except Epidemiologists	2,850	4,370	1,520	53.5
Helpers—Brickmasons, Blockmasons, Stonemasons, and Tile and Marble Setters	810	1,240	430	52.6
Reinforcing Iron and Rebar Workers	940	1,370	430	46.1
Home Health Aides	28,580	41,010	12,430	43.5
Stonemasons	550	790	240	42.9
Personal Care Aides	16,880	23,920	7,040	41.7

Note: Projections cover Florida; (1) Sorted by percent employment change and excludes occupations with numeric employment change less than 100
Source: www.projectionscentral.com, State Occupational Projections, 2010–2020 Long-Term Projections

Average Wages

Occupation	$/Hr.	Occupation	$/Hr.
Accountants and Auditors	27.91	Maids and Housekeeping Cleaners	9.44
Automotive Mechanics	18.50	Maintenance and Repair Workers	16.67
Bookkeepers	16.42	Marketing Managers	53.76
Carpenters	17.40	Nuclear Medicine Technologists	n/a
Cashiers	8.96	Nurses, Licensed Practical	19.90
Clerks, General Office	12.60	Nurses, Registered	28.53
Clerks, Receptionists/Information	11.14	Nursing Assistants	10.88
Clerks, Shipping/Receiving	14.29	Packers and Packagers, Hand	10.59
Computer Programmers	27.73	Physical Therapists	36.44
Computer Systems Analysts	37.77	Postal Service Mail Carriers	23.80
Computer User Support Specialists	19.94	Real Estate Brokers	n/a
Cooks, Restaurant	10.26	Retail Salespersons	11.11
Dentists	75.62	Sales Reps., Exc. Tech./Scientific	22.34
Electrical Engineers	36.41	Sales Reps., Tech./Scientific	33.50
Electricians	19.03	Secretaries, Exc. Legal/Med./Exec.	13.86
Financial Managers	61.28	Security Guards	12.24
First-Line Supervisors/Managers, Sales	18.58	Surgeons	n/a
Food Preparation Workers	10.19	Teacher Assistants	9.40
General and Operations Managers	50.33	Teachers, Elementary School	22.10
Hairdressers/Cosmetologists	12.75	Teachers, Secondary School	24.90
Internists	101.18	Telemarketers	9.47
Janitors and Cleaners	10.22	Truck Drivers, Heavy/Tractor-Trailer	15.04
Landscaping/Groundskeeping Workers	11.02	Truck Drivers, Light/Delivery Svcs.	15.26
Lawyers	51.94	Waiters and Waitresses	9.90

Note: Wage data covers the Gainesville, FL Metropolitan Statistical Area—see Appendix B for areas included. Hourly wages for elementary/secondary school teachers and teacher assistants were calculated by the editors from annual wage data assuming a 40 hour work week; n/a not available.
Source: Bureau of Labor Statistics, Metro Area Occupational Employment and Wage Estimates, May 2013

RESIDENTIAL REAL ESTATE

Building Permits

Area	Single-Family			Multi-Family			Total		
	2012	2013	Pct. Chg.	2012	2013	Pct. Chg.	2012	2013	Pct. Chg.
City	51	63	23.5	225	240	6.7	276	303	9.8
MSA[1]	397	558	40.6	227	242	6.6	624	800	28.2
U.S.	518,695	620,802	19.7	310,963	370,020	19.0	829,658	990,822	19.4

Note: (1) Metropolitan Statistical Area—see Appendix B for areas included; figures represent new, privately-owned housing units authorized (unadjusted data); All permit data are based on estimates with imputation.
Source: U.S. Census Bureau, Manufacturing, Mining, and Construction Statistics, Building Permits, 2012, 2013

Homeownership Rate

Area	2006 (%)	2007 (%)	2008 (%)	2009 (%)	2010 (%)	2011 (%)	2012 (%)	2013 (%)
MSA[1]	n/a	n/a	n/a	n/a	n/a	n/a	n/a	n/a
U.S.	68.8	68.1	67.8	67.4	66.9	66.1	65.4	65.1

Note: (1) Figures cover the Gainesville, FL Metropolitan Statistical Area—see Appendix B for areas included; n/a not available
Source: U.S. Census Bureau, Housing Vacancies and Homeownership Annual Statistics: 2013

Housing Vacancy Rates

Area	Gross Vacancy Rate[2] (%)			Year-Round Vacancy Rate[3] (%)			Rental Vacancy Rate[4] (%)			Homeowner Vacancy Rate[5] (%)		
	2011	2012	2013	2011	2012	2013	2011	2012	2013	2011	2012	2013
MSA[1]	n/a	n/a	n/a	n/a	n/a	n/a	n/a	n/a	n/a	n/a	n/a	n/a
U.S.	14.2	13.8	13.8	11.1	10.8	10.7	9.5	8.7	8.3	2.5	2.0	2.0

Note: (1) Figures cover the Gainesville, FL Metropolitan Statistical Area—see Appendix B for areas included; (2) The percentage of the total housing inventory that is vacant; (3) The percentage of the housing inventory (excluding seasonal units) that is year-round vacant; (4) The percentage of rental inventory that is vacant for rent; (5) The percentage of homeowner inventory that is vacant for sale; n/a not available
Source: U.S. Census Bureau, Housing Vacancies and Homeownership Annual Statistics: 2013

TAXES

State Corporate Income Tax Rates

State	Tax Rate (%)	Income Brackets ($)	Num. of Brackets	Financial Institution Tax Rate (%)[a]	Federal Income Tax Ded.
Florida	5.5 (f)	Flat rate	1	5.5 (f)	No

Note: Tax rates as of January 1, 2014; (a) Rates listed are the corporate income tax rate applied to financial institutions or excise taxes based on income. Some states have other taxes based upon the value of deposits or shares; (f) An exemption of $50,000 is allowed. Florida's Alternative Minimum Tax rate is 3.3%.
Source: Federation of Tax Administrators, "State Corporate Income Tax Rates, 2014"

State Individual Income Tax Rates

State	Tax Rate (%)	Income Brackets ($)	Num. of Brackets	Personal Exempt. ($)[1] Single	Personal Exempt. ($)[1] Dependents	Fed. Inc. Tax Ded.
Florida	None	–	–	–	–	–

Note: Tax rates as of January 1, 2014; Local- and county-level taxes are not included; n/a not applicable; (1) Married joint filers generally receive double the single exemption
Source: Federation of Tax Administrators, "State Individual Income Tax Rates, 2014"

Various State and Local Tax Rates

State	State and Local Sales and Use (%)	State Sales and Use (%)	Gasoline[1] (¢/gal.)	Cigarette[2] ($/pack)	Spirits[3] ($/gal.)	Wine[4] ($/gal.)	Beer[5] ($/gal.)
Florida	6.0	6.00	36.03	1.339	6.50 (f)	2.25	0.48

Note: All tax rates as of January 1, 2014; (1) The American Petroleum Institute has developed a methodology for determining the average tax rate on a gallon of fuel. Rates may include any of the following: excise taxes, environmental fees, storage tank fees, other fees or taxes, general sales tax, and local taxes. In states where gasoline is subject to the general sales tax, or where the fuel tax is based on the average sale price, the average rate determined by API is sensitive to changes in the price of gasoline. States that fully or partially apply general sales taxes to gasoline: CA, CO, GA, IL, IN, MI, NY; (2) The federal excise tax of $1.0066 per pack and local taxes are not included; (3) Rates are those applicable to off-premise sales of 40% alcohol by volume (a.b.v.) distilled spirits in 750ml containers. Local excise taxes are excluded; (4) Rates are those applicable to off-premise sales of 11% a.b.v. non-carbonated wine in 750ml containers; (5) Rates are those applicable to off-premise sales of 4.7% a.b.v. beer in 12 ounce containers; (f) Different rates also applicable according to alcohol content, place of production, size of container, or place purchased (on- or off-premise or onboard airlines).
Source: Tax Foundation, 2014 Facts & Figures: How Does Your State Compare?

State Business Tax Climate Index Rankings

State	Overall Rank	Corporate Tax Index Rank	Individual Income Tax Index Rank	Sales Tax Index Rank	Unemployment Insurance Tax Index Rank	Property Tax Index Rank
Florida	5	13	1	18	6	16

Note: The index is a measure of how each state's tax laws affect economic performance. The lower the rank, the more favorable a state's tax system is for business. States without a given tax are given a ranking of 1. The scores/rankings for the District of Columbia do not affect other states. The 2014 index represents the tax climate as of July 1, 2013.
Source: Tax Foundation, State Business Tax Climate Index 2014

COMMERCIAL UTILITIES

Typical Monthly Electric Bills

Area	Commercial Service ($/month) 1,500 kWh	Commercial Service ($/month) 40 kW demand 14,000 kWh	Industrial Service ($/month) 1,000 kW demand 200,000 kWh	Industrial Service ($/month) 50,000 kW demand 15,000,000 kWh
City	n/a	n/a	n/a	n/a
Average[1]	197	1,636	25,662	1,485,307

Note: Based on total rates in effect July 1, 2013; (1) average based on 180 utilities surveyed; n/a not available
Source: Edison Electric Institute, Typical Bills and Average Rates Report, Summer 2013

TRANSPORTATION

Means of Transportation to Work

Area	Car/Truck/Van		Public Transportation			Bicycle	Walked	Other Means	Worked at Home
	Drove Alone	Car-pooled	Bus	Subway	Railroad				
City	63.4	11.8	7.4	0.0	0.0	6.3	5.2	1.7	4.1
MSA[1]	72.9	11.1	4.2	0.0	0.0	3.2	3.1	1.3	4.3
U.S.	76.4	9.7	2.6	1.7	0.5	0.6	2.8	1.3	4.3

Note: Figures are percentages and cover workers 16 years of age and older; (1) Figures cover the Gainesville, FL Metropolitan Statistical Area—see Appendix B for areas included
Source: U.S. Census Bureau, 2010-2012 American Community Survey 3-Year Estimates

Travel Time to Work

Area	Less Than 10 Minutes	10 to 19 Minutes	20 to 29 Minutes	30 to 44 Minutes	45 to 59 Minutes	60 to 89 Minutes	90 Minutes or More
City	18.1	50.9	19.3	8.1	1.8	1.2	0.6
MSA[1]	14.0	39.7	23.1	15.8	4.0	2.2	1.2
U.S.	13.5	29.8	20.9	20.1	7.5	5.6	2.5

Note: Figures are percentages and include workers 16 years old and over; (1) Figures cover the Gainesville, FL Metropolitan Statistical Area—see Appendix B for areas included
Source: U.S. Census Bureau, 2010-2012 American Community Survey 3-Year Estimates

Travel Time Index

Area	1985	1990	1995	2000	2005	2010	2011
Urban Area[1]	n/a	n/a	n/a	n/a	n/a	n/a	n/a
Average[2]	1.09	1.14	1.16	1.19	1.23	1.18	1.18

Note: Travel Time Index—the ratio of travel time in the peak period to the travel time at free-flow conditions. For example, a value of 1.30 indicates a 20-minute free-flow trip takes 26 minutes in the peak. Free-flow speeds (60 mph on freeways and 35 mph on principal arterials) are used as the comparison threshold; (1) Data for the Gainesville, FL urban area was not available; (2) average of 498 urban areas
Source: Texas Transportation Institute, Urban Mobility Report 2012, December 2012

Public Transportation

Agency Name / Mode of Transportation	Vehicles Operated in Maximum Service	Annual Unlinked Passenger Trips (in thous.)	Annual Passenger Miles (in thous.)
Gainesville Regional Transit System (RTS)			
Bus (directly operated)	97	10,652.2	26,097.8
Demand Response (purchased transportation)	35	49.5	455.5

Source: Federal Transit Administration, National Transit Database, 2012

Air Transportation

Airport Name and Code / Type of Service	Passenger Airlines[1]	Passenger Enplanements	Freight Carriers[2]	Freight (lbs.)
Gainesville Regional Airport (GNV)				
Domestic service (U.S. carriers - 2013)	11	197,978	2	2,234
International service (U.S. carriers - 2012)	0	0	0	0

Note: (1) Includes all U.S.-based major, minor and commuter airlines that carried at least one passenger during the year; (2) Includes all U.S.-based airlines and freight carriers that transported at least one lb. of freight during the year.
Source: Bureau of Transportation Statistics, The Intermodal Transportation Database, Air Carriers: T-100 Domestic Market (U.S. Carriers), 2013; Bureau of Transportation Statistics, The Intermodal Transportation Database, Air Carriers: T-100 International Market (U.S. Carriers), 2012

Other Transportation Statistics

Major Highways:	I-75
Amtrak Service:	Yes (train station is located in Waldo
Major Waterways/Ports:	None

Source: Amtrak.com; Google Maps

BUSINESSES

Major Business Headquarters

Company Name	Rankings	
	Fortune[1]	Forbes[2]
No companies listed	-	-

Note: (1) Fortune 500—companies that produce a 10-K are ranked 1 to 500 based on 2012 revenue; (2) all private companies with at least $2 billion in annual revenue through the end of their most current fiscal year are ranked 1 to 224; companies listed are headquartered in the city; dashes indicate no ranking
Source: Fortune, "Fortune 500," May 20, 2013; Forbes, "America's Largest Private Companies," December 18, 2013

Fast-Growing Businesses

According to *Inc.*, Gainesville is home to one of America's 500 fastest-growing private companies: **Reserveage Organics** (#363). Criteria: must be an independent, privately-held, for-profit, U.S. corporation, proprietorship or partnership; revenues must be at least $100,000 in 2009 and $2 million in 2012; must have four-year operating/sales history. Holding companies, regulated banks, and utilities were excluded. *Inc., "America's 500 Fastest-Growing Private Companies," September 2013*

Minority- and Women-Owned Businesses

Group	All Firms		Firms with Paid Employees			
	Firms	Sales ($000)	Firms	Sales ($000)	Employees	Payroll ($000)
Asian	407	97,010	152	93,107	583	12,034
Black	919	146,222	122	135,251	587	17,559
Hispanic	753	207,434	193	168,321	856	28,036
Women	3,387	629,433	498	532,285	4,359	114,296
All Firms	10,976	10,487,232	3,219	10,132,351	60,343	2,193,878

Note: Figures cover firms located in the city; minority- and women-owned business are defined as firms in which the corresponding group own 51% or more of the stock or equity of the company
Source: U.S. Census Bureau, 2007 Economic Census, Survey of Business Owners (2012 Survey of Business Owners data will be released starting in June 2015)

**HOTELS &
CONVENTION
CENTERS**

Hotels/Motels

Area	5 Star		4 Star		3 Star		2 Star		1 Star		Not Rated	
	Num.	Pct.[3]	Num.	Pct.[3]	Num.	Pct.[3]	Num.	Pct.[3]	Num.	Pct.[3]	Num.	Pct.[3]
City[1]	0	0.0	0	0.0	12	14.0	51	59.3	6	7.0	17	19.8
Total[2]	142	0.9	1,005	6.0	5,147	30.9	8,578	51.4	408	2.4	1,397	8.4

Note: (1) Figures cover Gainesville and vicinity; (2) Figures cover all 100 cities in this book; (3) Percentage of hotels which have a given star rating; Star ratings are determined by expedia.com and offer an indication of the general quality of a particular hotel.
Source: expedia.com, April 7, 2014

Major Convention Centers

Name	Overall Space (sq. ft.)	Exhibit Space (sq. ft.)	Meeting Space (sq. ft.)	Meeting Rooms

There are no major convention centers located in the metro area
Source: Original research

Living Environment

COST OF LIVING

Cost of Living Index

Composite Index	Groceries	Housing	Utilities	Trans-portation	Health Care	Misc. Goods/ Services
98.7	97.3	94.1	106.1	104.1	101.2	98.1

Note: The Cost of Living Index measures regional differences in the cost of consumer goods and services, excluding taxes and non-consumer expenditures, for professional and managerial households in the top income quintile. It is based on more than 50,000 prices covering almost 60 different items for which prices are collected three times a year by chambers of commerce, economic development organizations or university applied economic centers in each participating urban area. The numbers shown should be read as a percentage above or below the national average of 100. For example, a value of 115.4 in the groceries column indicates that grocery prices are 15.4% higher than the national average. Small differences in the index numbers should not be interpreted as significant; Figures cover the Gainesville FL urban area.
Source: The Council for Community and Economic Research, ACCRA Cost of Living Index, 2013

Grocery Prices

Area[1]	T-Bone Steak ($/pound)	Frying Chicken ($/pound)	Whole Milk ($/half gal.)	Eggs ($/dozen)	Orange Juice ($/64 oz.)	Coffee ($/11.5 oz.)
City[2]	10.33	1.31	2.70	1.93	3.67	4.19
Avg.	10.19	1.28	2.34	1.81	3.48	4.39
Min.	8.56	0.94	1.44	1.19	2.78	3.40
Max.	14.82	2.28	3.56	3.73	6.23	7.32

*Note: (1) Values for the local area are compared with the average, minimum and maximum values for all 327 areas in the Cost of Living Index; (2) Figures cover the Gainesville FL urban area; **T-Bone Steak** (price per pound); **Frying Chicken** (price per pound, whole fryer); **Whole Milk** (half gallon carton); **Eggs** (price per dozen, Grade A, large); **Orange Juice** (64 oz. Tropicana or Florida Natural); **Coffee** (11.5 oz. can, vacuum-packed, Maxwell House, Hills Bros, or Folgers).*
Source: The Council for Community and Economic Research, ACCRA Cost of Living Index, 2013

Housing and Utility Costs

Area[1]	New Home Price ($)	Apartment Rent ($/month)	All Electric ($/month)	Part Electric ($/month)	Other Energy ($/month)	Telephone ($/month)
City[2]	271,646	900	-	121.68	45.26	31.06
Avg.	295,864	900	171.38	91.82	70.12	27.73
Min.	185,506	458	117.80	48.81	33.67	17.16
Max.	1,358,917	3,783	441.68	171.40	372.65	39.47

*Note: (1) Values for the local area are compared with the average, minimum and maximum values for all 327 areas in the Cost of Living Index; (2) Figures cover the Gainesville FL urban area; **New Home Price** (2,400 sf living area, 8,000 sf lot, in urban area with full utilities); **Apartment Rent** (950 sf 2 bedroom/1.5 or 2 bath, unfurnished, excluding all utilities except water); **All Electric** (average monthly cost for an all-electric home); **Part Electric** (average monthly cost for a part-electric home); **Other Energy** (average monthly cost for natural gas, fuel oil, coal, wood, and any other forms of energy except electricity); **Telephone** (price includes basic monthly rate for a private residential line plus additional local usage charges incurred by a family of four).*
Source: The Council for Community and Economic Research, ACCRA Cost of Living Index, 2013

Health Care, Transportation, and Other Costs

Area[1]	Doctor ($/visit)	Dentist ($/visit)	Optometrist ($/visit)	Gasoline ($/gallon)	Beauty Salon ($/visit)	Men's Shirt ($)
City[2]	93.97	94.69	78.59	3.59	37.00	31.95
Avg.	101.40	86.48	96.16	3.44	33.87	26.55
Min.	61.67	50.83	50.12	3.08	18.92	12.48
Max.	182.71	152.50	223.78	4.33	68.22	52.03

*Note: (1) Values for the local area are compared with the average, minimum and maximum values for all 327 areas in the Cost of Living Index; (2) Figures cover the Gainesville FL urban area; **Doctor** (general practitioners routine exam of an established patient); **Dentist** (adult teeth cleaning and periodic oral examination); **Optometrist** (full vision eye exam for established adult patient); **Gasoline** (one gallon regular unleaded, national brand, including all taxes, cash price at self-service pump if available); **Beauty Salon** (woman's shampoo, trim, and blow-dry); **Men's Shirt** (cotton/polyester dress shirt, pinpoint weave, long sleeves).*
Source: The Council for Community and Economic Research, ACCRA Cost of Living Index, 2013

HOUSING

House Price Index (HPI)

Area	National Ranking[2]	Quarterly Change (%)	One-Year Change (%)	Five-Year Change (%)
MSA[1]	(a)	n/a	1.04	-23.19
U.S.[3]	–	1.20	7.69	4.18

Note: The HPI is a weighted repeat sales index. It measures average price changes in repeat sales or refinancings on the same properties. This information is obtained by reviewing repeat mortgage transactions on single-family properties whose mortgages have been purchased or securitized by Fannie Mae or Freddie Mac in January 1975; (1) Gainesville, FL Metropolitan Statistical Area—see Appendix B for areas included; (2) Rankings are based on annual percentage change for all metro areas containing at least 15,000 transactions over the last 10 years and ranges from 1 to 283; (3) figures based on a weighted average of Census Division estimates using a seasonally adjusted, purchase-only index; all figures are for the period ending December 31, 2013; n/a not available; (a) Not ranked because of increased index variability due to smaller sample size
Source: Federal Housing Finance Agency, House Price Index, February 25, 2014

Median Single-Family Home Prices

Area	2011	2012	2013p	Percent Change 2012 to 2013
MSA[1]	148.6	145.6	167.3	14.9
U.S. Average	166.2	177.2	197.4	11.4

Note: Figures are median sales prices of existing single-family homes in thousands of dollars; (p) preliminary; n/a not available; (1) Gainesville, FL Metropolitan Statistical Area—see Appendix B for areas included
Source: National Association of Realtors, Median Sales Price of Existing Single-Family Homes for Metropolitan Areas, 4th Quarter 2013

Qualifying Income Based on Median Sales Price of Existing Single-Family Homes

Area	With 5% Down ($)	With 10% Down ($)	With 20% Down ($)
MSA[1]	38,387	36,366	32,326
U.S. Average	45,395	43,006	38,228

Note: Figures are preliminary; Qualifying income is based on a mortgage rate of 4.4%. Monthly principal and interest payment is limited to 25% of income; n/a not available; (1) Gainesville, FL Metropolitan Statistical Area—see Appendix B for areas included
Source: National Association of Realtors, Qualifying Income Based on Median Sales Price of Existing Single-Family Homes for Metropolitan Areas, 4th Quarter 2013

Median Apartment Condo-Coop Home Prices

Area	2011	2012	2013p	Percent Change 2012 to 2013
MSA[1]	n/a	n/a	n/a	n/a
U.S. Average	165.1	173.7	194.9	12.2

Note: Figures are median sales prices of existing apartment condo-coop homes in thousands of dollars; (p) preliminary; n/a not available; (1) Gainesville, FL Metropolitan Statistical Area—see Appendix B for areas included
Source: National Association of Realtors, Median Sales Price of Existing Apartment Condo-Coop Homes for Metropolitan Areas, 4th Quarter 2013

Gross Monthly Rent

Area	Under $200	$200 -299	$300 -499	$500 -749	$750 -999	$1,000 -1,499	$1,500 and up	Median ($)
City	1.0	2.7	6.1	27.3	28.3	24.6	9.8	845
MSA[1]	0.8	2.3	6.2	24.6	29.4	25.8	11.0	875
U.S.	1.7	3.3	8.1	22.7	24.3	25.7	14.3	889

Note: Figures are percentages except for Median; Gross rent is the contract rent plus the estimated average monthly cost of utilities (electricity, gas, and water and sewer) and fuels (oil, coal, kerosene, wood, etc.) if these are paid by the renter (or paid for the renter by someone else); (1) Figures cover the Gainesville, FL Metropolitan Statistical Area—see Appendix B for areas included
Source: U.S. Census Bureau, 2010-2012 American Community Survey 3-Year Estimates

Year Housing Structure Built

Area	2010 or Later	2000 -2009	1990 -1999	1980 -1989	1970 -1979	1960 -1969	1950 -1959	1940 -1949	Before 1940	Median Year
City	0.3	15.4	14.3	19.6	22.8	13.1	7.1	2.8	4.5	1980
MSA[1]	0.5	21.3	20.2	19.8	18.1	9.4	5.5	1.9	3.2	1986
U.S.	0.5	14.9	13.8	13.9	15.9	11.1	10.9	5.5	13.5	1976

Note: Figures are percentages except for Median Year; (1) Figures cover the Gainesville, FL Metropolitan Statistical Area—see Appendix B for areas included
Source: U.S. Census Bureau, 2010-2012 American Community Survey 3-Year Estimates

HEALTH

Health Risk Data

Category	MSA[1] (%)	U.S. (%)
Adults aged 18–64 who have any kind of health care coverage	n/a	79.6
Adults who reported being in good or excellent health	n/a	83.1
Adults who are current smokers	n/a	19.6
Adults who are heavy drinkers[2]	n/a	6.1
Adults who are binge drinkers[3]	n/a	16.9
Adults who are overweight (BMI 25.0 - 29.9)	n/a	35.8
Adults who are obese (BMI 30.0 - 99.8)	n/a	27.6
Adults who participated in any physical activities in the past month	n/a	77.1
Adults 50+ who have ever had a sigmoidoscopy or colonoscopy	n/a	67.3
Women aged 40+ who have had a mammogram within the past two years	n/a	74.0
Men aged 40+ who have had a PSA test within the past two years	n/a	45.2
Adults aged 65+ who have had flu shot within the past year	n/a	60.1
Adults who always wear a seatbelt	n/a	93.8

Note: Data as of 2012 unless otherwise noted; n/a not available; (1) Figures cover the Gainesville, FL Metropolitan Statistical Area—see Appendix B for areas included; (2) Heavy drinkers are classified as males having more than two drinks per day or females having more than one drink per day; (3) Binge drinkers are classified as males having five or more drinks on one occasion or females having four or more drinks on one occasion
Source: Centers for Disease Control and Prevention, Behaviorial Risk Factor Surveillance System, SMART: Selected Metropolitan/Micropolitan Area Risk Trends, 2012

Chronic Health Indicators

Category	MSA[1] (%)	U.S. (%)
Adults who have ever been told they had a heart attack	n/a	4.5
Adults who have ever been told they had a stroke	n/a	2.9
Adults who have been told they currently have asthma	n/a	8.9
Adults who have ever been told they have arthritis	n/a	25.7
Adults who have ever been told they have diabetes[2]	n/a	9.7
Adults who have ever been told they had skin cancer	n/a	5.7
Adults who have ever been told they had any other types of cancer	n/a	6.5
Adults who have ever been told they have COPD	n/a	6.2
Adults who have ever been told they have kidney disease	n/a	2.5
Adults who have ever been told they have a form of depression	n/a	18.0

Note: Data as of 2012 unless otherwise noted; n/a not available; (1) Figures cover the Gainesville, FL Metropolitan Statistical Area—see Appendix B for areas included; (2) Figures do not include pregnancy-related, borderline, or pre-diabetes
Source: Centers for Disease Control and Prevention, Behaviorial Risk Factor Surveillance System, SMART: Selected Metropolitan/Micropolitan Area Risk Trends, 2012

Mortality Rates for the Top 10 Causes of Death in the U.S.

ICD-10[a] Sub-Chapter	ICD-10[a] Code	Age-Adjusted Mortality Rate[1] per 100,000 population	
		County[2]	U.S.
Malignant neoplasms	C00-C97	184.2	174.2
Ischaemic heart diseases	I20-I25	97.5	119.1
Other forms of heart disease	I30-I51	40.4	49.6
Chronic lower respiratory diseases	J40-J47	36.4	43.2
Cerebrovascular diseases	I60-I69	40.9	40.3
Organic, including symptomatic, mental disorders	F01-F09	45.7	30.5
Other degenerative diseases of the nervous system	G30-G31	28.0	26.3
Other external causes of accidental injury	W00-X59	29.6	25.1
Diabetes mellitus	E10-E14	25.1	21.3
Hypertensive diseases	I10-I15	20.8	18.8

Note: (a) ICD-10 = International Classification of Diseases 10th Revision; (1) Mortality rates are a three year average covering 2008-2010; (2) Figures cover Alachua County
Source: Centers for Disease Control and Prevention, National Center for Health Statistics. Compressed Mortality File 1999-2010 on CDC WONDER Online Database, released January 2013. Data are compiled from the Compressed Mortality File 1999-2010, Series 20 No. 2P, 2013.

Mortality Rates for Selected Causes of Death

ICD-10[a] Sub-Chapter	ICD-10[a] Code	Age-Adjusted Mortality Rate[1] per 100,000 population	
		County[2]	U.S.
Assault	X85-Y09	3.8	5.5
Diseases of the liver	K70-K76	14.2	12.4
Human immunodeficiency virus (HIV) disease	B20-B24	5.7	3.0
Influenza and pneumonia	J09-J18	9.3	16.4
Intentional self-harm	X60-X84	12.2	11.8
Malnutrition	E40-E46	Suppressed	0.8
Obesity and other hyperalimentation	E65-E68	*2.4	1.6
Renal failure	N17-N19	10.6	13.6
Transport accidents	V01-V99	12.6	12.6
Viral hepatitis	B15-B19	*1.9	2.2

Note: (a) ICD-10 = International Classification of Diseases 10th Revision; (1) Mortality rates are a three year average covering 2008-2010; (2) Figures cover Alachua County; (*) Unreliable data as per CDC
Source: Centers for Disease Control and Prevention, National Center for Health Statistics. Compressed Mortality File 1999-2010 on CDC WONDER Online Database, released January 2013. Data are compiled from the Compressed Mortality File 1999-2010, Series 20 No. 2P, 2013.

Health Insurance Coverage

Area	With Health Insurance	With Private Health Insurance	With Public Health Insurance	Without Health Insurance	Population Under Age 18 Without Health Insurance
City	82.1	69.2	20.1	17.9	7.5
MSA[1]	83.8	68.3	25.3	16.2	8.5
U.S.	84.9	65.4	30.4	15.1	7.5

Note: Figures are percentages that cover the civilian noninstitutionalized population; (1) Figures cover the Gainesville, FL Metropolitan Statistical Area—see Appendix B for areas included
Source: U.S. Census Bureau, 2010-2012 American Community Survey 3-Year Estimates

Number of Medical Professionals

Area[1]	MDs[2]	DOs[2,3]	Dentists	Podiatrists	Chiropractors	Optometrists
Local (number)	2,126	68	386	11	63	33
Local (rate[4])	851.6	27.2	153.3	4.4	25.0	13.1
U.S. (rate[4])	267.6	19.6	61.7	5.6	24.7	14.5

Note: Data as of 2012 unless noted; (1) Local data covers Alachua County; (2) Data as of 2011; (3) Doctor of Osteopathic Medicine; (4) rate per 100,000 population
Source: Area Resource File (ARF) 2012-2013. U.S. Department of Health and Human Services, Health Resources and Services Administration, Bureau of Health Professions

Best Hospitals

According to *U.S. News,* the Gainesville, FL metro area is home to one of the best hospitals in the U.S.: **Shands at the University of Florida** (5 specialties). The hospital listed was nationally ranked in at least one adult specialty. Only 147 hospitals nationwide were nationally ranked in one or more specialties. Eighteen hospitals in the U.S. made the Honor Roll by ranking near the top in at least six specialties.*U.S. News Online, "America's Best Hospitals 2013-14"*

According to *U.S. News,* the Gainesville, FL metro area is home to one of the best children's hospitals in the U.S.: **Shands Children's Hospital at the University of Florida**. The hospital listed was highly ranked in at least one pediatric specialty. Eighty-seven hospitals in the U.S. ranked in at least one specialty. Ten children's hospitals in the U.S. made the Honor Roll by ranking near the top in three or more specialties.*U.S. News Online, "America's Best Children's Hospitals 2013-14"*

EDUCATION

Public School District Statistics

District Name	Schls	Pupils	Pupil/ Teacher Ratio	Minority Pupils[1] (%)	Free Lunch Eligible[2] (%)	IEP[3] (%)
Alachua County Public Schools	69	27,480	15.7	53.2	42.2	15.1

Note: Table includes school districts with 2,000 or more students; (1) Percentage of students that are not non-Hispanic white; (2) Percentage of students that are eligible for the free lunch program; (3) Percentage of students that have an Individualized Education Program.
Source: U.S. Department of Education, National Center for Education Statistics, Common Core of Data, Local Education Agency (School District) Universe Survey: School Year 2011-2012; U.S. Department of Education, National Center for Education Statistics, Common Core of Data, Public Elementary/Secondary School Universe Survey: School Year 2011-2012

Best High Schools

High School Name	Rank[1]	Grad. Rate[2] (%)	Coll.[3] (%)	AP/IB/ AICE Tests[4]	AP/IB/ AICE Score[5]	SAT Score[6]	ACT Score[6]
Eastside H.S.	326	85	85	1.9	2.9	1875	20.0
Gainesville H.S.	1366	90	80	0.6	2.9	1620	21.0

Note: (1) Public schools are ranked from 1 to 2,000 based on the following self-reported statistics (with the corresponding weight used in calculating their overall score). Schools that were newly founded and did not have a graduating senior class in 2012 were excluded; (2) Four-year, on-time graduation rate (25%); (3) Percent of 2011 graduates who were accepted to college (25%); (4) AP/IB/AICE tests taken per student (25%); (5) Average AP/IB/AICE exam score (10%); (6) Average SAT and/or ACT score (10%); Percent of students enrolled in at least one AP/IB/AICE course (5%)—data not shown
Source: Newsweek and The Daily Beast, "America's Best High Schools 2013"

Highest Level of Education

Area	Less than H.S.	H.S. Diploma	Some College, No Deg.	Associate Degree	Bachelor's Degree	Master's Degree	Prof. School Degree	Doctorate Degree
City	8.7	20.3	17.8	10.5	20.6	12.0	3.9	6.2
MSA[1]	9.5	23.0	18.5	10.7	20.0	10.0	3.8	4.6
U.S.	14.1	28.3	21.3	7.8	18.0	7.5	1.9	1.2

Note: Figures cover persons age 25 and over; (1) Figures cover the Gainesville, FL Metropolitan Statistical Area—see Appendix B for areas included
Source: U.S. Census Bureau, 2010-2012 American Community Survey 3-Year Estimates

Educational Attainment by Race

Area	High School Graduate or Higher (%)					Bachelor's Degree or Higher (%)				
	Total	White	Black	Asian	Hisp.[2]	Total	White	Black	Asian	Hisp.[2]
City	91.3	94.3	82.4	95.6	89.3	42.8	50.0	13.6	77.3	43.4
MSA[1]	90.5	92.9	80.5	93.2	89.3	38.3	42.3	13.0	71.7	44.9
U.S.	85.9	88.1	82.5	85.5	63.1	28.6	30.0	18.4	50.2	13.4

Note: Figures shown cover persons 25 years old and over; (1) Figures cover the Gainesville, FL Metropolitan Statistical Area—see Appendix B for areas included; (2) People of Hispanic origin can be of any race
Source: U.S. Census Bureau, 2010-2012 American Community Survey 3-Year Estimates

School Enrollment by Grade and Control

Area	Preschool (%)		Kindergarten (%)		Grades 1 - 4 (%)		Grades 5 - 8 (%)		Grades 9 - 12 (%)	
	Public	Private	Public	Private	Public	Private	Public	Private	Public	Private
City	51.6	48.4	74.4	25.6	89.6	10.4	90.7	9.3	93.9	6.1
MSA[1]	46.5	53.5	82.1	17.9	86.2	13.8	87.8	12.2	86.0	14.0
U.S.	56.9	43.1	87.8	12.2	89.9	10.1	90.0	10.0	90.8	9.2

Note: Figures shown cover persons 3 years old and over; (1) Figures cover the Gainesville, FL Metropolitan Statistical Area—see Appendix B for areas included
Source: U.S. Census Bureau, 2010-2012 American Community Survey 3-Year Estimates

Average Salaries of Public School Classroom Teachers

Area	2012-13		2013-14		Percent Change 2012-13 to 2013-14	Percent Change 2003-04 to 2013-14
	Dollars	Rank[1]	Dollars	Rank[1]		
Florida	46,598	45	46,691	45	0.20	15.0
U.S. Average	56,103	–	56,689	–	1.04	21.8

Note: (1) State rank ranges from 1 to 51 where 1 indicates highest salary.
Source: National Education Association, Rankings & Estimates: Rankings of the States 2013 and Estimates of School Statistics 2014, March 2014

Higher Education

Four-Year Colleges			Two-Year Colleges			Medical Schools[1]	Law Schools[2]	Voc/ Tech[3]
Public	Private Non-profit	Private For-profit	Public	Private Non-profit	Private For-profit			
2	2	1	0	1	0	1	1	2

Note: Figures cover institutions located within the city limits and include main campuses only; (1) includes schools accredited by the Liaison Committee on Medical Education and the American Osteopathic Association's Commission on Osteopathic College Accreditation; (2) includes ABA-accredited schools, schools with provisional ABA accreditation, and state accredited schools; (3) includes all schools with programs that are less than 2 years.
Source: National Center for Education Statistics, Integrated Postsecondary Education System (IPEDS), 2012-13; Association of American Medical Colleges, Member List, April 24, 2014; American Osteopathic Association, Member List, April 24, 2014; Law School Admission Council, Official Guide to ABA-Approved Law Schools Online, April 24, 2014; Wikipedia, List of Medical Schools in the United States, April 24, 2014; Wikipedia, List of Law Schools in the United States, April 24, 2014

According to U.S. News & World Report, the Gainesville, FL metro area is home to one of the best national universities in the U.S.: **University of Florida** (#49). The indicators used to capture academic quality fall into a number of categories: assessment by administrators at peer institutions; retention of students; faculty resources; student selectivity; financial resources; alumni giving; high school counselor ratings of colleges; and graduation rate. U.S. News & World Report, "America's Best Colleges 2014"

According to U.S. News & World Report, the Gainesville, FL metro area is home to one of the top 100 law schools in the U.S.: **University of Florida (Levin)** (#46). The rankings are based on a weighted average of 12 measures of quality: peer assessment score; assessment score by lawyers/judges; median LSAT scores; median undergrad GPA; acceptance rate; employment rates for graduates; placement success; bar passage rate; faculty resources; expenditures per student; student/faculty ratio; and library resources. U.S. News & World Report, "America's Best Graduate Schools, Law, 2014"

According to U.S. News & World Report, the Gainesville, FL metro area is home to one of the top 100 business schools in the U.S.: **University of Florida (Hough)** (#36). The rankings are based on a weighted average of the following nine measures: quality assessment; peer assessment; recruiter assessment; placement success; mean starting salary and bonus; student selectivity; mean GMAT and GRE scores; mean undergraduate GPA; and acceptance rate. U.S. News & World Report, "America's Best Graduate Schools, Business, 2014"

PRESIDENTIAL ELECTION

2012 Presidential Election Results

Area	Obama	Romney	Other
Alachua County	57.9	40.5	1.6
U.S.	51.0	47.2	1.8

Note: Results are percentages and may not add to 100% due to rounding
Source: Dave Leip's Atlas of U.S. Presidential Elections

EMPLOYERS

Major Employers

Company Name	Industry
Alachua County	Government
Alachua County School Board	Public education
AvMed Health Plan	Health plans
City of Gainesville	City government
Cox Communications	Communication
Dollar General Distribution Center	Retail
Driltech Mission	Manufacturing
ESE (Now Mactech)	Management services
Florida Farm Bureau	Agricultural association
Gator Dining Services	Food service
Hunter Marine Corporation	Sailboats
Meridian Behavioral Health Care	Mental healthcare
Nationwide Insurance Company	Insurance
North Florida Regional Medical Center	Healthcare
Publix Supermarkets	Grocery
Regeneration Technologies	Orthopedic/cardio implants
Santa Fe Community College	Education
Shands Hospital	Healthcare
Tower Hill Insurance Group	Insurance
U.S. Postal Services	Government
UF Athletic Association	Athletics
University of Florida	Education
Veterans Affairs Medical Center	Healthcare
Wal-Mart Distribution Center	Grocery
Wal-Mart Stores	Grocery

Note: Companies shown are located within the Gainesville, FL Metropolitan Statistical Area.
Source: Hoovers.com; Wikipedia

PUBLIC SAFETY

Crime Rate

Area	All Crimes	Violent Crimes				Property Crimes		
		Murder	Forcible Rape	Robbery	Aggrav. Assault	Burglary	Larceny -Theft	Motor Vehicle Theft
City	4,764.0	4.7	58.3	134.6	472.3	794.3	3,111.7	188.1
Suburbs[1]	3,054.6	2.8	44.8	58.1	395.2	700.9	1,759.1	93.7
Metro[2]	3,858.8	3.7	51.1	94.1	431.5	744.8	2,395.5	138.1
U.S.	3,246.1	4.7	26.9	112.9	242.3	670.2	1,959.3	229.7

Note: Figures are crimes per 100,000 population; (1) All areas within the metro area that are located outside the city limits; (2) Figures cover the Gainesville, FL Metropolitan Statistical Area—see Appendix B for areas included
Source: FBI Uniform Crime Reports, 2012

Hate Crimes

Area	Number of Quarters Reported	Bias Motivation				
		Race	Religion	Sexual Orientation	Ethnicity	Disability
City	4	4	0	1	0	0
U.S.	4	2,797	1,099	1,135	667	92

Source: Federal Bureau of Investigation, Hate Crime Statistics 2012

Identity Theft Consumer Complaints

Area	Complaints	Complaints per 100,000 Population	Rank[2]
MSA[1]	324	122.6	21
U.S.	290,056	91.8	-

Note: (1) Figures cover the Gainesville, FL Metropolitan Statistical Area—see Appendix B for areas included; (2) Rank ranges from 1 to 377 where 1 indicates greatest number of identity theft complaints per 100,000 population
Source: Federal Trade Commission, Consumer Sentinel Network Data Book for January–December 2013

Fraud and Other Consumer Complaints

Area	Complaints	Complaints per 100,000 Population	Rank[2]
MSA[1]	1,147	434.0	69
U.S.	1,811,724	595.2	-

Note: (1) Figures cover the Gainesville, FL Metropolitan Statistical Area—see Appendix B for areas included; (2) Rank ranges from 1 to 377 where 1 indicates greatest number of identity theft complaints per 100,000 population
Source: Federal Trade Commission, Consumer Sentinel Network Data Book for January–December 2013

RECREATION

Culture

Dance[1]	Theatre[1]	Instrumental Music[1]	Vocal Music[1]	Series and Festivals	Museums and Art Galleries[2]	Zoos and Aquariums[3]
1	1	1	0	0	11	1

Note: (1) Number of professional performing groups; (2) Based on organizations with primary SIC code 8412; (3) AZA-accredited
Source: The Grey House Performing Arts Directory, 2013; Association of Zoos & Aquariums, AZA Member Zoos & Aquariums, April 2014; www.AccuLeads.com, May 1, 2014

Professional Sports Teams

Team Name	League	Year Established
No teams are located in the metro area		

Source: Wikipedia, Major Professional Sports Teams of the United States and Canada, April 25, 2014

CLIMATE

Average and Extreme Temperatures

Temperature	Jan	Feb	Mar	Apr	May	Jun	Jul	Aug	Sep	Oct	Nov	Dec	Yr.
Extreme High (°F)	83	85	90	95	98	102	99	99	95	92	88	85	102
Average High (°F)	66	68	74	81	86	89	90	90	87	81	74	68	79
Average Temp. (°F)	55	57	63	69	75	79	81	81	78	71	63	56	69
Average Low (°F)	43	45	50	56	63	69	71	71	69	60	51	44	58
Extreme Low (°F)	10	19	28	35	42	50	62	62	48	33	28	13	10

Note: Figures cover the years 1962-1995
Source: National Climatic Data Center, International Station Meteorological Climate Summary, 9/96

Average Precipitation/Snowfall/Humidity

Precip./Humidity	Jan	Feb	Mar	Apr	May	Jun	Jul	Aug	Sep	Oct	Nov	Dec	Yr.
Avg. Precip. (in.)	3.7	4.0	3.9	2.3	3.3	6.9	6.5	7.7	5.1	2.8	2.2	2.6	50.9
Avg. Snowfall (in.)	0	Tr	0	0	0	0	0	0	0	0	0	Tr	Tr
Avg. Rel. Hum. 7am (%)	90	90	92	92	91	93	94	96	96	94	94	92	93
Avg. Rel. Hum. 4pm (%)	60	55	52	50	51	61	67	67	67	63	63	61	60

Note: Figures cover the years 1962-1995; Tr = Trace amounts (<0.05 in. of rain; <0.5 in. of snow)
Source: National Climatic Data Center, International Station Meteorological Climate Summary, 9/96

Weather Conditions

Temperature			Daytime Sky			Precipitation		
32°F & below	45°F & below	90°F & above	Clear	Partly cloudy	Cloudy	0.01 inch or more precip.	0.1 inch or more snow/ice	Thunder-storms
16	73	77	88	196	81	119	0	78

Note: Figures are average number of days per year and cover the years 1962-1995
Source: National Climatic Data Center, International Station Meteorological Climate Summary, 9/96

HAZARDOUS WASTE

Superfund Sites

Gainesville has one hazardous waste site on the EPA's Superfund Final National Priorities List: **Cabot/Koppers.** *U.S. Environmental Protection Agency, Final National Priorities List, April 26, 2014*

**AIR & WATER
QUALITY**

Air Quality Index

Area	Percent of Days when Air Quality was...[2]					AQI Statistics[2]	
	Good	Moderate	Unhealthy for Sensitive Groups	Unhealthy	Very Unhealthy	Maximum	Median
MSA[1]	91.8	8.2	0.0	0.0	0.0	84	33

Note: (1) Data covers the Gainesville, FL Metropolitan Statistical Area—see Appendix B for areas included; (2) Based on 365 days with AQI data in 2013. Air Quality Index (AQI) is an index for reporting daily air quality. EPA calculates the AQI for five major air pollutants regulated by the Clean Air Act: ground-level ozone, particle pollution (aka particulate matter), carbon monoxide, sulfur dioxide, and nitrogen dioxide. The AQI runs from 0 to 500. The higher the AQI value, the greater the level of air pollution and the greater the health concern. There are six AQI categories: "Good" AQI is between 0 and 50. Air quality is considered satisfactory; "Moderate" AQI is between 51 and 100. Air quality is acceptable; "Unhealthy for Sensitive Groups" When AQI values are between 101 and 150, members of sensitive groups may experience health effects; "Unhealthy" When AQI values are between 151 and 200 everyone may begin to experience health effects; "Very Unhealthy" AQI values between 201 and 300 trigger a health alert; "Hazardous" AQI values over 300 trigger warnings of emergency conditions (not shown).
Source: U.S. Environmental Protection Agency, Air Quality Index Report, 2013

Air Quality Index Pollutants

Area	Percent of Days when AQI Pollutant was...[2]					
	Carbon Monoxide	Nitrogen Dioxide	Ozone	Sulfur Dioxide	Particulate Matter 2.5	Particulate Matter 10
MSA[1]	0.0	0.0	53.2	0.0	46.8	0.0

Note: (1) Data covers the Gainesville, FL Metropolitan Statistical Area—see Appendix B for areas included; (2) Based on 365 days with AQI data in 2013. The Air Quality Index (AQI) is an index for reporting daily air quality. EPA calculates the AQI for five major air pollutants regulated by the Clean Air Act: ground-level ozone, particle pollution (also known as particulate matter), carbon monoxide, sulfur dioxide, and nitrogen dioxide. The AQI runs from 0 to 500. The higher the AQI value, the greater the level of air pollution and the greater the health concern.
Source: U.S. Environmental Protection Agency, Air Quality Index Report, 2013

Air Quality Trends: Ozone

	2003	2004	2005	2006	2007	2008	2009	2010	2011	2012
MSA[1]	0.071	0.075	0.073	0.075	0.078	0.069	0.056	0.069	0.064	0.064

Note: (1) Data covers the Gainesville, FL Metropolitan Statistical Area—see Appendix B for areas included. The values shown are the composite ozone concentration averages among trend sites based on the highest fourth daily maximum 8-hour concentration in parts per million. These trends are based on sites having an adequate record of monitoring data during the trend period. Data from exceptional events are included.
Source: U.S. Environmental Protection Agency, Air Quality Monitoring Information, "Air Quality Trends by City, 2000-2012"

Maximum Air Pollutant Concentrations: Particulate Matter, Ozone, CO and Lead

	Particulate Matter 10 (ug/m^3)	Particulate Matter 2.5 Wtd AM (ug/m^3)	Particulate Matter 2.5 24-Hr (ug/m^3)	Ozone (ppm)	Carbon Monoxide (ppm)	Lead (ug/m^3)
MSA[1] Level	n/a	7	17	0.064	n/a	n/a
NAAQS[2]	150	15	35	0.075	9	0.15
Met NAAQS[2]	n/a	Yes	Yes	Yes	n/a	n/a

Note: (1) Data covers the Gainesville, FL Metropolitan Statistical Area—see Appendix B for areas included; Data from exceptional events are included; (2) National Ambient Air Quality Standards; ppm = parts per million; ug/m^3 = micrograms per cubic meter; n/a not available.
Concentrations: Particulate Matter 10 (coarse particulate)—highest second maximum 24-hour concentration; Particulate Matter 2.5 Wtd AM (fine particulate)—highest weighted annual mean concentration; Particulate Matter 2.5 24-Hour (fine particulate)—highest 98th percentile 24-hour concentration; Ozone—highest fourth daily maximum 8-hour concentration; Carbon Monoxide—highest second maximum non-overlapping 8-hour concentration; Lead—maximum running 3-month average
Source: U.S. Environmental Protection Agency, Air Quality Monitoring Information, "Air Quality Statistics by City, 2012"

Maximum Air Pollutant Concentrations: Nitrogen Dioxide and Sulfur Dioxide

	Nitrogen Dioxide AM (ppb)	Nitrogen Dioxide 1-Hr (ppb)	Sulfur Dioxide AM (ppb)	Sulfur Dioxide 1-Hr (ppb)	Sulfur Dioxide 24-Hr (ppb)
MSA[1] Level	n/a	n/a	n/a	n/a	n/a
NAAQS[2]	53	100	30	75	140
Met NAAQS[2]	n/a	n/a	n/a	n/a	n/a

Note: (1) Data covers the Gainesville, FL Metropolitan Statistical Area—see Appendix B for areas included; Data from exceptional events are included; (2) National Ambient Air Quality Standards; ppm = parts per million; ug/m³ = micrograms per cubic meter; n/a not available.
Concentrations: Nitrogen Dioxide AM—highest arithmetic mean concentration; Nitrogen Dioxide 1-Hr—highest 98th percentile 1-hour daily maximum concentration; Sulfur Dioxide AM—highest annual mean concentration; Sulfur Dioxide 1-Hr—highest 99th percentile 1-hour daily maximum concentration; Sulfur Dioxide 24-Hr—highest second maximum 24-hour concentration
Source: U.S. Environmental Protection Agency, Air Quality Monitoring Information, "Air Quality Statistics by City, 2012"

Drinking Water

Water System Name	Pop. Served	Primary Water Source Type	Violations[1] Health Based	Violations[1] Monitoring/ Reporting
GRU - Murphree WTP	181,468	Ground	0	0

Note: (1) Based on violation data from January 1, 2013 to December 31, 2013 (includes unresolved violations from earlier years)
Source: U.S. Environmental Protection Agency, Office of Ground Water and Drinking Water, Safe Drinking Water Information System (based on data extracted February 10, 2014)

Houston, Texas

Background

Back in 1836, brothers John K. and Augustus C. Allen bought a 6,642-acre tract of marshy, mosquito-infested land 56 miles north of the Gulf of Mexico and named it Houston, after the hero of San Jacinto. From that moment on, Houston has experienced continued growth.

By the end of its first year in the Republic of Texas, Houston claimed 1,500 residents, one theater, and interestingly, no churches. The first churches came three years later. By the end of its second year, Houston saw its first steamship, establishing its position as one of the top-ranking ports in the country.

Certainly, Houston owes much to the Houston ship channel, the "golden strip" on which oil refineries, chemical plants, cement factories, and grain elevators conduct their bustling economic activity. The diversity of these industries is a testament to Houston's economy in general.

Tonnage through the Port of Houston has grown to the point of its claim of being number one in the nation for foreign tonnage. The port is important to the cruise industry as well, and the Norwegian Cruise Line has sailed from Houston since 2003.

As Texas' biggest city, Houston has also enjoyed manufacturing expansion in its diversified economy. The city is home to the second largest number of Fortune 500 companies, second only to New York City.

Houston is also one of the major scientific research areas in the world. The presence of the Johnson Space Center has spawned a number of related industries in medical and technological research. The Texas Medical Center oversees a network of 45 medical institutions, including St. Luke's Episcopal Hospital, the Texas Children's Hospital, and the Methodist Hospital. As a city whose reputation rests upon advanced research, Houston is also devoted to education and the arts. Rice University, for example, whose admission standards rank as one of the highest in the nation, is located in Houston, as are Dominican College and the University of St. Thomas.

Today, this relatively young city is home to a diverse range of ethnicities, including Mexican-American, Nigerian, American-Indian and Pakistani.

Houston also is patron to the Museum of Fine Arts, the Contemporary Arts Museum, and the Houston Ballet and Grand Opera. A host of smaller cultural institutions, such as the Gilbert and Sullivan Society, the Virtuoso Quartet, and the Houston Harpsichord Society enliven the scene. Two privately funded museums, the Holocaust Museum Houston and the Houston Museum of Natural Science, are historical and educational attractions, and a new baseball stadium, Minute Maid Park, was completed in 2000 in the city's downtown.

Houstonians are eagerly embracing continued revitalization. This urban comeback has resulted in a virtual explosion of dining and entertainment options in the heart of the city. The opening of the Bayou Place, Houston's largest entertainment complex, has especially generated excitement, providing a variety of restaurants and entertainment options in one facility. A new highly active urban park opened in 2007 on 12 acres in front of the George R. Brown Convention Center. Reliant Stadium, located in downtown Houston, is home to the NFL's Houston Texans. The stadium hosted Superbowl XXXVIII in 2004 and WrestleMania XXV in the spring of 2009. In fact, the city has sports teams for every major professional league except the National Hockey League.

Located in the flat coastal plains, Houston's climate is predominantly marine. The terrain includes many small streams and bayous, which, together with the nearness to Galveston Bay, favor the development of fog. Temperatures are moderated by the influence of winds from the Gulf of Mexico, which is 50 miles away. Mild winters are the norm, as is abundant rainfall. Polar air penetrates the area frequently enough to provide variability in the weather.

Rankings

General Rankings

- Houston was identified as one of America's fastest-growing cities in terms of population and economy by *Forbes*. The area ranked #10 out of 20. The 100 most populous metro areas in the U.S. were evaluated on the following criteria: estimated population growth; job growth; gross metropolitan product growth; unemployment; median salaries for college-educated workers. *Forbes, "America's Fastest-Growing Cities 2014," February 14, 2014*

- Houston was identified as one of America's fastest-growing major metropolitan areas in terms of population by CNNMoney.com. The area ranked #2 out of 10. Criteria: population growth between July 2012 and July 2013. *CNNMoney, "10 Fastest-Growing Cities," March 28, 2014*

- Among the 50 largest U.S. cities, Houston placed #30 in Vocativ's "semi-exhaustive, mostly scientific" city Livability Index for people aged 35 and under. Average salary, unemployment rates, rents, and other living costs were considered, along with bike lanes, low-cost broadband, cheap takeout, self-service laundries, the price of a pint of Guinness, music venues, and vintage clothing stores. *vocative.com, "The Livability Index: The Best U.S. Cities for People 35 and Under," November 7, 2013*

- Houston was selected as one of America's best cities by *Bloomberg Businessweek*. The city ranked #22 out of 50. Criteria: leisure attributes (the number of restaurants, bars, libraries, museums, professional sports teams, and park acres by population); educational attributes (public school performance, the number of colleges, and graduate degree holders); economic factors (2011 income and June and July 2012 unemployment); crime; and air quality. *Bloomberg BusinessWeek, "America's Best Cities," September 26, 2012*

- Houston was selected as one of "America's Favorite Cities." The city ranked #24 in the "Quality of Life and Visitor Experience: Cleanliness" category. Respondents to an online survey were asked to rate 35 top urban destinations in the U.S. from a visitor's perspective. Criteria: cleanliness. *Travel + Leisure, "America's Favorite Cities 2013"*

- Houston was selected as one of "America's Favorite Cities." The city ranked #26 in the "Type of Trip: Gay-friendly" category. Respondents to an online survey were asked to rate 35 top urban destinations in the U.S. from a visitor's perspective. Criteria: gay-friendly. *Travel + Leisure, "America's Favorite Cities 2013"*

Business/Finance Rankings

- The personal finance site NerdWallet scored the nation's 20 largest American cities according to how friendly a business climate they offer to would-be entrepreneurs. Criteria inlcuded local taxes (state, city, payroll, property), growth rate, and the regulatory environment as judged by small business owners. On the resulting list of most welcoming cities, Houston ranked #5. *www.nerdwallet.com, "Top 10 Best Cities for Small Business," August 26, 2013*

- Houston was the #4-ranked city for savers, according to the finance site GoBankingRates, which considered the prospects for savers in a tough savings economy by looking for higher interest yields, lower taxes, more jobs with higher incomes, and less expensive housing costs. *www.gobankingrates.com, "Best Cities for Saving Money," February 24, 2014*

- In order to help veterans transition from the military to civilian life, USAA and Hiring Our Heroes worked with Sperlings's BestPlaces to develop a list of the major metropolitan areas where military-skills-related employment is strongest. Criteria included job prospects, unemployment, number of government jobs, recent job growth, accessible health resources, and colleges and universities. Metro areas with a violent crime rate or high cost of living were excluded. At #1, the Houston metro area made the top ten. *www.usaa.com, "2013 Best Places for Veterans: Jobs," November 2013*

- The finance website Wall St. Cheat Sheet reported on the prospects for high-wage job creation in the nation's largest metro areas over the next five years and ranked them accordingly, drawing on in-depth analysis by CareerBuilder and Economic Modeling Specialists International (EMSI). The Houston metro area placed #4 on the Wall St. Cheat Sheet list. *wallstcheatsheet.com, "Top 10 Cities for High-Wage Job Growth," December 8, 2013*

- Building on the U.S. Department of Labor's Occupational Information Network Data Collection Program, the Brookings Institution defined STEM occupations and job opportunities for STEM workers at various levels of educational attainment. The Houston metro area was placed among the ten large metro areas with the highest demand for high-level STEM knowledge. *www.brookings.edu, "The Hidden Stem Economy," June 10, 2013*

- Analysts for the business website 24/7 Wall Street looked at the local government report "Tax Rates and Tax Burdens in the District of Columbia—A Nationwide Comparison" to determine where a family of three at two different income levels would pay the least and the most in state and local taxes. Among the ten cities with the lowest state and local tax burdens was Houston, at #3. *247wallst.com, American Cities with the Highest (and Lowest) Taxes, February 25, 2013*

- Based on a minimum of 500 social media reviews per metro area, the employment opinion group Glassdoor surveyed 50 of the largest U.S. metro areas on measures including compensation and benefits, satisfaction with management, business outlook, and number of employers hiring. The Houston metro area was ranked #19 in overall employee satisfaction. *www.glassdoor.com, "Employment Satisfaction Report Card by City," June 21, 2013*

- A *Fiscal Times* analysis balancing cost of living with average income to find the cities where residents' dollars go furthest was published by the *Huffington Post*. Based on the Census Bureau's 2010 Cost of Living Index and the National Compensation Survey, Houston was ranked the #5 metro area where you can "actually spend less and make more." *Fiscal Times/Huffington Post, "The Best Bang for Your Buck Cities in the United States," June 26, 2012*

- The financial literacy site NerdWallet.com set out to identify the 20 most promising cities for job seekers, analyzing data for the nation's 50 largest cities. Houston was ranked #18. Criteria: unemployment rate; population growth; median income; selected monthly owner costs. *NerdWallet.com, "Best Cities for Job Seekers," January 7, 2014*

- The Brookings Institution ranked the 50 largest cities in the U.S. based on income inequality. Houston was ranked #11. (#1 = greatest inequality). Criteria: the cities were ranked based on the "95/20 ratio." This figure represents the income at which a household earns more than 95 percent of all other households, divided by the income at which a household earns more than only 20 percent of all other households. *Brookings Institution, "Income Inequality in America's 50 Largest Cities, 2007-2012," February 20, 2014*

- Houston was ranked #12 out of 100 metro areas in terms of economic performance (#1 = best) during the recession and recovery from trough quarter through the second quarter of 2013. Criteria: percent change in employment; percentage point change in unemployment rate; percent change in gross metropolitan product; percent change in House Price Index. *Brookings Institution, MetroMonitor: Tracking Economic Recession and Recovery in America's 100 Largest Metropolitan Areas, September 2013*

- Houston was identified as one of the best places for finding a job by *U.S. News & World Report*. The city ranked #9 out of 10. Criteria: strong job market. *U.S. News & World Report, "The 10 Best Cities to Find Jobs," June 17, 2013*

- Payscale.com ranked the 20 largest metro areas in terms of wage growth. The Houston metro area ranked #15. Criteria: private-sector wage growth between the 4th quarter of 2012 and the 4th quarter of 2013. *PayScale, "Wage Trends by Metro Area," 4th Quarter, 2013*

- Houston was identified as one of America's most frugal metro areas by *Coupons.com*. The city ranked #23 out of 25. Criteria: Grocery IQ and coupons.com mobile app usage. *Coupons.com, "Top 25 Most On-the-Go Frugal Cities of 2012," February 19, 2013*

- Houston was cited as one of America's top metros for new and expanded facility projects in 2013. The area ranked #2 in the large metro area category (population over 1 million). *Site Selection, "Top Metros of 2013," March 2014*

- Houston was identified as one of the best cities for college graduates to find work—and live. The city ranked #8 out of 15. Criteria: job availability; average salary; average rent. *CareerBuilder.com, "15 Best Cities for College Grads to Find Work—and Live," June 5, 2012*

- Houston was identified as one of the happiest cities to work in by CareerBliss.com, an online community for career advancement. The city ranked #6 out of 10. Criteria: independent company reviews from employees all over the country on: relationship with their boss and co-workers; work environment; job resources; compensation; growth opportunities; company culture; company reputation; daily tasks; job control over work performed on a daily basis. *CareerBliss.com, "Top 10 Happiest and Unhappiest Cities to Work in 2014," February 10, 2014*

- Houston was identified as one of the happiest cities for young professionals by *CareerBliss.com*, an online community for career advancement. The city ranked #8. Criteria: more than 45,000 young professionals were asked to rate key factors that affect workplace happiness including: work-life balance; compensation; company culture; overall work environment; company reputation; relationships with managers and co-workers; opportunities for growth; job resources; daily tasks; job autonomy. Young professionals are defined as having less than 10 years of work experience. *CareerBliss.com, "Happiest Cities for Young Professionals," April 26, 2013*

- The Houston metro area appeared on the Milken Institute "2013 Best Performing Cities" list. Rank: #8 out of 200 large metro areas. Criteria: job growth; wage and salary growth; high-tech output growth. *Milken Institute, "Best-Performing Cities 2013," December 2013*

- *Forbes* ranked the 200 most populous metro areas in the U.S. in terms of the "Best Places for Business and Careers." The Houston metro area was ranked #25. Criteria: costs (business and living); job growth (past and projected); income growth; educational attainment (college and high school); projected economic growth; cultural and recreational opportunities; net migration patterns; number of highly ranked colleges. *Forbes, "The Best Places for Business and Careers," August 7, 2013*

Children/Family Rankings

- Houston was selected as one of the best cities for families to live by *Parenting* magazine. The city ranked #88 out of 100. Criteria: education; health; community; *Parenting's* Culture & Charm Index. *Parenting.com, "The 2012 Best Cities for Families List"*

Culture/Performing Arts Rankings

- Houston was selected as one of "America's Favorite Cities." The city ranked #12 in the "Culture: Museum/Galleries" category. Respondents to an online survey were asked to rate 35 top urban destinations in the U.S. from a visitor's perspective. Criteria: number and quality of museums and galleries. *Travelandleisure.com, "America's Favorite Cities 2013"*

- Houston was selected as one of America's top cities for the arts. The city ranked #22 in the big city (population 500,000 and over) category. Criteria: readers' top choices for arts travel destinations based on the richness and variety of visual arts sites, activities and events. *American Style, "2012 Top 25 Arts Destinations," June 2012*

Dating/Romance Rankings

- A *Cosmopolitan* magazine article surveyed the gender balance and other factors to arrive at a list of the best and worst cities for women to meet single guys. Houston was #3 among the best for single women looking for dates. *www.cosmopolitan.com, "Working the Ratio," October 1, 2013*

- *Forbes* reports that the Houston metro area made Rent.com's Best Cities for Newlyweds survey for 2013, based on Bureau of Labor Statistics and Census Bureau data on number of married couples, percentage of families with children under age six, average annual income, cost of living, and availability of rentals. *www.forbes.com, "The 10 Best Cities for Newlyweds to Live and Work In," May 30, 2013*

- Of the 100 U.S. cities surveyed by *Men's Health* in its quest to identify the nation's best cities for dating and forming relationships, Houston was ranked #16 for online dating (#1 = best). *Men's Health, "The Best and Worst Cities for Online Dating," January 30, 2013*

- Houston was selected as one of America's best cities for singles by the readers of *Travel + Leisure* in their annual "America's Favorite Cities" survey. The city was ranked #20 out of 20. *Travel + Leisure, "America's Best Cities for Singles," July 2012*

- Houston was selected as one of the least romantic cities in the U.S. by video-rental kiosk company Redbox. The city ranked #7 out of 10. Criteria: number of romance-related rentals in 2012. *Redbox, "10 Most/Least Romantic Cities," February 12, 2013*

- Houston was selected as one of the best cities for newlyweds by *Rent.com*. The city ranked #5 of 10. Criteria: cost of living; mean annual income; unemployment rate. *Rent.com, "10 Best Cities for Newlyweds," March 20, 2012*

Education Rankings

- *Men's Health* ranked 100 U.S. cities in terms of their education levels. Houston was ranked #82 (#1 = most educated city). Criteria: high school graduation rates; school enrollment; educational attainment; number of households who have outstanding student loans; number of households whose members have taken adult-education courses. *Men's Health, "Where School Is In: The Most and Least Educated Cities," September 12, 2011*

- Houston was selected as one of America's most literate cities. The city ranked #56 out of the 77 largest U.S. cities. Criteria: number of booksellers; library resources; Internet resources; educational attainment; periodical publishing resources; newspaper circulation. *Central Connecticut State University, "America's Most Literate Cities, 2013"*

Environmental Rankings

- The Houston metro area came in at #348 for the relative comfort of its climate on Sperling's list of "chill cities," as measured by the Sperling Heat Index. All 361 metro areas are included. Criteria included daytime high temperatures, nighttime low temperatures, dew point, and relative humidity at the high temperatures. *www.bertsperling.com, "Sperling's Chill Cities," July 18, 2013*

- Sperling's BestPlaces assessed 379 metropolitan areas of the United States for the likelihood of dangerously extreme weather events or earthquakes. In general the Southeast and South-Central regions have the highest risk of weather extremes and earthquakes, while the Pacific Northwest enjoys the lowest risk. Of the least risky metropolitan areas, the Houston metro area was ranked #376. *www.bestplaces.net, "Safest Places from Natural Disasters," April 2011*

- Houston was identified as one of America's dirtiest metro areas by *Forbes*. The area ranked #13 out of 20. Criteria: air quality; water quality; toxic releases; superfund sites. *Forbes, "America's 20 Dirtiest Cities," December 10, 2012*

- Houston was identified as one of North America's greenest metropolitan areas. The area ranked #16. The Green City Index is comprised of 31 indicators, and scores cities across nine categories: carbon dioxide; energy; land use; buildings; transport; water; waste; air quality; environmental governance. The 27 largest metropolitan areas in the U.S. and Canada were considered. *Economist Intelligence Unit, sponsored by Siemens, "U.S. and Canada Green City Index, 2011"*

- The U.S. Environmental Protection Agency (EPA) released a list of U.S. metropolitan areas with the most ENERGY STAR certified buildings in 2012. The Houston metro area was ranked #7 out of 25. *U.S. Environmental Protection Agency, "Top Cities With the Most ENERGY STAR Certified Buildings in 2012," March 12, 2013*

- Houston was selected as one of 22 "Smarter Cities" for energy by the Natural Resources Defense Council. Criteria: investment in green power; energy efficiency measures; conservation. *Natural Resources Defense Council, "2010 Smarter Cities," July 19, 2010*

- The Houston metro area was selected as one of "America's Most Toxic Cities" by *Forbes*. The metro area ranked #7 out of 10. The 80 largest metropolitan areas were ranked on the following criteria: air quality; water quality; Superfund sites; toxic releases. *Forbes, "America's Most Toxic Cities, 2011," February 28, 2011*

- Houston was highlighted as one of the 25 most ozone-polluted metro areas in the U.S. during 2008 through 2010. The area ranked #7. *American Lung Association, State of the Air 2012*

Food/Drink Rankings

- *Men's Health* ranked 100 major U.S. cities in terms of alcohol intoxication. Houston ranked #50 (#1 = most sober).Criteria: binge drinking; alcohol-related traffic accidents, arrests, and fatalities. *Men's Health, "The Drunkest Cities in America," November 19, 2013*

- Houston was identified as one of "America's Drunkest Cities of 2011" by *The Daily Beast*. The city ranked #25 out of 25. Criteria: binge drinking; drinks consumed per month. *The Daily Beast, "Tipsy Towns: Where are America's Drunkest Cities?," December 31, 2011*

- Houston was identified as one of the most vegetarian-friendly cities in America by GrubHub.com, the nation's largest food ordering service. The city ranked #4 out of 10. Criteria: percentage of vegetarian restaurants. *GrubHub.com, "Top Vegetarian-Friendly Cities," July 18, 2012*

- Houston was selected as one of America's best cities for hamburgers by the readers of *Travel + Leisure* in their annual America's Favorite Cities survey. The city was ranked #4 out of 10. *Travel + Leisure, "America's Best Burger Cities," August 25, 2013*

Health/Fitness Rankings

- For each of the 50 most populous metro areas in the United States, the American College of Sports Medicine's American Fitness Index evaluated infrastructure, community assets, and policies that encourage healthy and fit lifestyles, including preventive health behaviors, levels of chronic disease conditions, health care access, and community resources and policies that support physical activity. The Houston metro area ranked #43 for "community fitness." Personal health indicators were considered as well as community and environmental indicators. *www.americanfitnessindex.org, "ACSM American Fitness Index Health and Community Fitness Status of the 50 Largest Metropolitan Areas," May 2013*

- The Houston metro area was identified as one of the worst cities for bed bugs in America by pest control company Orkin. The area ranked #16 out of 50 based on the number of bed bug treatments Orkin performed from January to December 2013. *Orkin, "Chicago Tops Bed Bug Cities List for Second Year in a Row," January 16, 2014*

- Houston was identified as one of 15 cities with the highest increase in bed bug activity in the U.S. by pest control provider Terminix. The city ranked #15.Criteria: cities with the largest percentage gains in bed bug customer calls from January–May 2013 compared to the same time period in 2012. *Terminix, "Cities with Highest Increases in Bed Bug Activity," July 9, 2013*

- Houston was selected as one of the 25 fattest cities in America by *Men's Fitness Online*. It ranked #1 out of America's 50 largest cities. Criteria: fitness centers and sport stores; nutrition; sports participation; TV viewing; overweight/sedentary; junk food; air quality; geography; commute; parks and open space; city recreational facilities; access to healthcare; motivation; mayor and city initiatives; state obesity initiatives. *Men's Fitness, "The Fittest and Fattest Cities in America," March 5, 2012*

- Houston was identified as a "2013 Spring Allergy Capital." The area ranked #58 out of 100. Three groups of factors were used to identify the most severe cities for people with allergies during the spring season: annual pollen levels; medicine utilization; access to board-certified allergists. *Asthma and Allergy Foundation of America, "Spring Allergy Capitals 2013"*

- Houston was identified as a "2013 Fall Allergy Capital." The area ranked #32 out of 100. Three groups of factors were used to identify the most severe cities for people with allergies during the fall season: annual pollen levels; medicine utilization; access to board-certified allergists. *Asthma and Allergy Foundation of America, "Fall Allergy Capitals 2013"*

- Houston was identified as a "2013 Asthma Capital." The area ranked #74 out of the nation's 100 largest metropolitan areas. Twelve factors were used to identify the most challenging places to live for people with asthma: estimated prevalence; self-reported prevalence; crude death rate for asthma; annual pollen score; annual air quality; public smoking laws; number of board-certified asthma specialists; school inhaler access laws; rescue medication use; controller medication use; uninsured rate; poverty rate. *Asthma and Allergy Foundation of America, "Asthma Capitals 2013"*

- *Men's Health* ranked 100 major U.S. cities in terms of the best and worst cities for men. Houston ranked #55. Criteria: thirty-three data points were examined covering health, fitness, and quality of life. *Men's Health, "The Best & Worst Cities for Men 2014," December 6, 2013*

- Breathe Right Nasal Strips, in partnership with Sperling's BestPlaces, analyzed 50 metro areas and identified those U.S. cities most challenged by chronic nasal congestion. The Houston metro area ranked #9. Criteria: tree, grass and weed pollens; molds and spores; air pollution; climate; smoking; purchase habits of congestion products; prescriptions of drugs for congestion relief; incidence of influenza. *Breathe Right Nasal Strips, "Most Congested Cities," October 3, 2011*

- Houston was selected as one of the best metropolitan areas for hospital care in America by *HealthGrades.com*. The rankings are based on a comprehensive study of patient death and complication rates in the nation's nearly 5,000 hospitals. Hospitals performing in the top 5% nationwide across 26 different medical procedures and diagnoses were identified. *HealthGrades.com* then ranked cities by the highest percentage of these Distinguished Hospitals for Clinical Excellence™. The Houston metro area ranked #37. *HealthGrades.com, "America's Top 50 Cities for Hospital Care," January 21, 2012*

- The American Academy of Dermatology ranked 26 U.S. metropolitan regions in terms of their residents knowledge, attitude and behaviors towards tanning, sun protection and skin cancer detection. The Houston metro area ranked #12. The results of the study are based on an online survey of over 7,000 adults nationwide. *American Academy of Dermatology, "Suntelligence: How Sun Smart is Your City?," May 3, 2010*

- The Houston metro area appeared in the 2013 Gallup-Healthways Well-Being Index. The area ranked #60 out of 189. The Gallup-Healthways Well-Being Index score is an average of six sub-indexes, which individually examine life evaluation, emotional health, work environment, physical health, healthy behaviors, and access to basic necessities. Results are based on telephone interviews conducted as part of the Gallup-Healthways Well-Being Index survey January 2–December 29, 2012, and January 2–December 30, 2013, with a random sample of 531,630 adults, aged 18 and older, living in metropolitan areas in the 50 U.S. states and the District of Columbia. *Gallup-Healthways, "State of American Well-Being," March 25, 2014*

- The Houston metro area was identified as one of "America's Most Stressful Cities" by *Sperling's BestPlaces*. The metro area ranked #26 out of 50. Criteria: unemployment rate; suicide rate; commute time; mental health; poor rest; alcohol use; violent crime rate; property crime rate; cloudy days annually. *Sperling's BestPlaces, www.BestPlaces.net, "Stressful Cities 2012*

- The Houston metro area was identified as one of "America's Most Stressful Cities" by *Forbes*. The metro area ranked #11 out of 40. Criteria: housing affordability; unemployment rate; cost of living; air quality; traffic congestion; sunny days; population density. *Forbes.com, "America's Most Stressful Cities," September 23, 2011*

- *Men's Health* ranked 100 U.S. cities in terms of their activity levels. Houston was ranked #70 (#1 = most active city). Criteria: where and how often residents exercise; percentage of households that watch more than 15 hours of cable television a week and buy more than 11 video games a year; death rate from deep-vein thrombosis, a condition linked to sitting for extended periods of time. *Men's Health, "Where Sit Happens: The Most and Least Active Cities in America," June 20, 2011*

Real Estate Rankings

- On the list compiled by Penske Truck Rental, the Houston metro area was named the #6 moving destination in 2013, based on one-way consumer truck rental reservations made through Penske's website and reservations call center. *blog.gopenske.com, "Penske Truck Rental's 2013 Top Moving Destinations List," January 22, 2014*

- The PricewaterhouseCoopers and Urban Land Institute report *Emerging Trends in Real Estate* forecasts that improvements in leasing, rents, and pricing will fuel recovery in all property sectors in 2013. Houston was ranked #5 among the top ten markets to watch in 2013. *PricewaterhouseCoopers/Urban Land Institute, "U.S. Commercial Real Estate Recovery to Advance in 2013," October 17, 2012*

- The Houston metro area was identified as one of the top 20 housing markets to invest in for 2014 by *Forbes*. The area ranked #5. Criteria: high population and job growth; relatively low home prices which are below equilibrium home price (EHP). The EHP is what the average price for a market should be, if speculation, weird distortions in local income, and other factors (like the housing collapse) weren't present in the market. *Forbes.com, "Best Buy Cities: Where to Invest in Housing in 2014," December 25, 2013*

- Houston ranked #6 in a *Forbes* study of the rental housing market in the nation's 44 largest metropolitan areas to determine the cities that are best for renters. Criteria: average rent in 2012's first quarter, year-over-year change in that figure, vacancy rate, and average monthly rent payment compared with average monthly mortgage payment. *Forbes.com, "The Best and Worst Cities for Renters," June 14, 2012*

- Houston was ranked #69 out of 283 metro areas in terms of house price appreciation in 2013 (#1 = highest rate). *Federal Housing Finance Agency, House Price Index, 4th Quarter 2013*

- Houston was selected as one of the eight best cities in the U.S. for real estate investment. The city ranked #3. *Association of Foreign Investors in Real Estate, "Ranking of USA Cities for Real Estate Investment, 2013"*

- Houston was ranked #183 out of 224 metro areas in terms of housing affordability in 2013 by the National Association of Home Builders (#1 = most affordable). The NAHB-Wells Fargo Housing Opportunity Index (HOI) for a given area is defined as the share of homes sold in that area that would have been affordable to a family earning the local median income, based on standard mortgage underwriting criteria. *National Association of Home Builders®, NAHB-Wells Fargo Housing Opportunity Index, 4th Quarter 2013*

- Houston was selected as one of the best college towns for renters by ApartmentRatings.com." The area ranked #58 out of 87. Overall satisfaction ratings were ranked using thousands of user submitted scores for hundreds of apartment complexes located in cities and towns that are home to the 100 largest four-year institutions in the U.S. *ApartmentRatings.com, "2011 College Town Renter Satisfaction Rankings"*

- The Houston metro area was identified as one of the 10 best U.S. markets to invest in single-family homes as rental properties by HomeVestors and Local Market Monitor. The area ranked #5. Criteria: risk-return premium relative to national average. *HomeVestors and Local Market Monitor, "Year-End Top 10 Real Estate Markets," December 20, 2013*

Safety Rankings

- Symantec, in partnership with Sperling's BestPlaces, ranked the 50 largest cities in the U.S. in terms of their vulnerability to cybercrime. The city ranked #24. Criteria: number of cyberattacks and potential infections; level of Internet access; expenditures on smartphones and computer hardware/software; wireless hotspots; broadband connectivity; Internet usage; online purchases. *Symantec, "Riskiest Online Cities of 2012" February 15, 2012*

- Allstate ranked the 200 largest cities in America in terms of driver safety. Houston ranked #151. Allstate researchers analyzed internal property damage claims over a two-year period from January 2010 to December 2011. A weighted average of the two-year numbers determined the annual percentages. *Allstate, "Allstate America's Best Drivers Report®, August 27, 2013"*

- Houston was identified as one of the most dangerous large cities in America by CQ Press. All 32 cities with populations of 500,000 or more that reported crime rates in 2012 for murder, rape, robbery, aggravated assault, burglary, and motor vehicle thefts were ranked. The city ranked #9 out of the top 10. *CQ Press, City Crime Rankings 2014*

- The National Insurance Crime Bureau ranked 380 metro areas in the U.S. in terms of per capita rates of vehicle theft. The Houston metro area ranked #28 (#1 = highest rate). Criteria: number of vehicle theft offenses per 100,000 inhabitants in 2012. *National Insurance Crime Bureau, "Hot Spots 2012," June 26, 2013*

- The Houston metro area was identified as one of the most dangerous metro areas for pedestrians by Transportation for America. The metro area ranked #9 out of 52 metro areas with over 1 million residents. Criteria: area's population divided by the number of pedestrian fatalities in that area. *Transportation for America, "Dangerous by Design 2011"*

Seniors/Retirement Rankings

- From its Best Cities for Successful Aging indexes, the Milken Institute generated rankings for metropolitan areas, weighing data in eight categories—general indicators, health care, wellness, living arrangements, transportation and general accessibility, financial well-being, education and employment, and community participation. The Houston metro area was ranked #83 overall in the large metro area category. *Milken Institute, "Best Cities for Successful Aging," July 2012*

- Bankers Life and Casualty Company, in partnership with Sperling's BestPlaces, ranked the nation's 50 largest metro areas in terms of the "Best U.S. Cities for Seniors." The Houston metro area ranked #45. Criteria: healthcare; transportation; housing; environment; economy; health and longevity; social and spiritual life; crime. *Bankers Life and Casualty Company, Center for a Secure Retirement, "Best U.S. Cities for Seniors 2011," September 2011*

Sports/Recreation Rankings

- Houston was selected as one of "America's Most Miserable Sports Cities" by *Forbes*. The city was ranked #8. Criteria: postseason losses; years since last title; ratio of cumulative seasons to championships won. Contenders were limited to cities with at least 75 total seasons of NFL, NBA, NHL and MLB play. *Forbes, "America's Most Miserable Sports Cities," July 31, 2013*

- Houston appeared on the *Sporting News* list of the "Best Sports Cities" for 2011. The area ranked #24 out of 271. Criteria: the magazine takes a 12-month snapshot of each city's sports, putting a heavy premium on regular-season won-lost records (from the most recently completed season). Other criteria include: playoff berths, bowl appearances and tournament bids; championships; applicable power ratings; quality of competition; overall fan fervor (measured in part by attendance); abundance of teams (rewarding quality over quantity); stadium and arena quality; ticket availability and prices; franchise ownership; and marquee appeal of athletes. *Sporting News, "Best Sports Cities 2011," October 4, 2011*

- Houston appeared on the *Sporting News* list of the "Best Sports Cities" for 2011. The area ranked #24 out of 271. Criteria: a 12-month snapshot of regular-season won-lost records (from the most recently completed season). Other criteria include: playoff berths, bowl appearances and tournament bids; championships; applicable power ratings; quality of competition; overall fan fervor (measured in part by attendance); abundance of teams (quality over quantity); stadium and arena quality; ticket availability and prices; franchise ownership; and marquee appeal of athletes. *Sporting News, "Best Sports Cities 2011," October 4, 2011*

- Houston was chosen as a bicycle friendly community by the League of American Bicyclists. A "Bicycle Friendly Community" welcomes cyclists by providing safe accommodation for cycling and encouraging people to bike for transportation and recreation. There are four award levels: Platinum; Gold; Silver; and Bronze. The community achieved an award level of Bronze. *League of American Bicyclists, "Bicycle Friendly Community Master List," Fall 2013*

- The Houston was selected as one of the best metro areas for golf in America by *Golf Digest*. The Houston area was ranked #8 out of 20. Criteria: climate; cost of public golf; quality of public golf; accessibility. *Golf Digest, "The Top 20 Cities for Golf," October 2011*

Transportation Rankings

- NerdWallet surveyed average annual car insurance premiums in 125 U.S. cities to identify the least expensive U.S. cities in which to insure a car. Locations with no-fault insurance laws was a strong determinant. Houston came in at #28 for the most expensive rates. *www.nerdwallet.com, "Best Cities for Cheap Car Insurance," February 3, 2014*

- Houston appeared on *Trapster.com's* list of the 10 most-active U.S. cities for speed traps. The city ranked #3 of 10. *Trapster.com* is a community platform accessed online and via smartphone app that alerts drivers to traps, hazards and other traffic issues nearby. *Trapster.com, "Speeders Beware: Cities With the Most Speed Traps," February 10, 2012*

- Houston was identified as one of America's worst cities for speed traps by the National Motorists Association. The city ranked #18 out of 25. Criteria: speed trap locations per 100,000 residents. *National Motorists Association, September 2011*

- Houston was identified as one of the most congested metro areas in the U.S. The area ranked #6 out of 10. Criteria: yearly delay per auto commuter in hours. *Texas A&M Transportation Institute, "2012 Urban Mobility Report," December 2012*

Women/Minorities Rankings

- *Women's Health* examined U.S. cities and identified the 100 best cities for women. Houston was ranked #46. Criteria: 30 categories were examined from obesity and breast cancer rates to commuting times and hours spent working out. *Women's Health, "Best Cities for Women 2012"*

- Houston was selected as one of the 25 healthiest cities for Latinas by *Latina Magazine*. The city ranked #11. Criteria: U.S. cities with populations over 500,000 residents were evaluated on the following criteria: percentage of 18-34 year-olds per city; Latino college graduation rates; number of colleges and universities; affordability; housing costs; income growth over time; average salary; percentage of singles; climate; safety; how the city's diversity compares to the national average; opportunities for minority entrepreneurs. *Latina Magazine, "Top 15 U.S. Cities for Young Latinos to Live In," August 19, 2011*

- The Houston metro area appeared on *Forbes'* list of the "Best Cities for Minority Entrepreneurs." The area ranked #11 out of 10. Criteria: 52 metropolitan statistical areas were examined. For each ethnicity (African Americans, Asians and Hispanics), the editors measured housing affordability, population growth, income growth, and entrepreneurship (per capita self-employment). *Forbes, "Best Cities for Minority Entrepreneurs," March 23, 2011*

Miscellaneous Rankings

- *Travel + Leisure* invited readers to rate cities on indicators such as aloofness, "smarty-pants residents," highbrow cultural offerings, high-end shopping, artisanal coffeehouses, conspicuous eco-consciousness, and more in order to identify the nation's snobbiest cities. Cities large and small made the list; among them was Houston, at #17. *www.travelandleisure.com, "America's Snobbiest Cities, June 2013*

- The watchdog site Charity Navigator conducts an annual study of charities in the nation's major markets both to analyze statistical differences in their financial, accountability, and transparency practices and to track year-to-year variations in individual communities. The Houston metro area was ranked #2 among the 30 metro markets. *www.charitynavigator.org, "Metro Market Study 2013," June 1, 2013*

- The Harris Poll's Happiness Index survey revealed that of the top ten U.S. markets, the Houston metro area residents ranked #2 in happiness. Criteria included strong assent to positive statements and strong disagreement with negative ones, and degree of agreement with a series of statements about respondents' personal relationships and general outlook. The online survey was conducted between July 14 and July 30, 2013. *www.harrisinteractive.com, "Dallas/Fort Worth Is "Happiest" City among America's Top Ten Markets," September 4, 2013*

- *Men's Health* ranked 100 U.S. cities by their level of sadness. Houston was ranked #49 (#1 = saddest city). Criteria: suicide rates; unemployment rates; percentage of households that use antidepressants; percent of population who report feeling blue all or most of the time. *Men's Health, "Frown Towns," November 28, 2011*

- Energizer Personal Care, the makers of Edge® shave gel, in partnership with Sperling's BestPlaces, ranked 50 major metro areas in terms of everyday irritations. The Houston metro area ranked #8. Criteria: high male-to-female ratio; poor sports team performance and high ticket prices; slow traffic; lack of job availability; unaffordable housing; extreme weather; lack of nightlife and fitness options. *Energizer Personal Care, "Most Irritatng Cities for Guys," August 26, 2013*

- Mars Chocolate North America, the makers of COMBOS®, in partnership with Sperling's BestPlaces, ranked 50 major metro areas in terms of their "manliness." The Houston metro area ranked #6. Criteria: number of professional sports teams; number of nearby NASCAR tracks and racing events; manly lifestyle; concentration of manly retail stores; manly occupations per capita; salty snack sales; "Board of Manliness" rankings. *Mars Chocolate North America, "America's Manliest Cities 2012"*

- The National Alliance to End Homelessness ranked the 100 most populous metro areas in terms the rate of homelessness. The Houston metro area ranked #50. Criteria: number of homeless people per 10,000 population in 2011. *National Alliance to End Homelessness, The State of Homelessness in America 2012*

- The financial education website CreditDonkey compiled a list of the ten "best" cities of the future, based on percentage of housing built in 1990 or later, population change since 2010, and construction jobs as a percentage of population. Also considered were two more futuristic criteria: number of DeLorean cars available for purchase and number of spaceport companies and proposed spaceports. Houston was scored #9. *www.creditDonkey.com, "In the Future, Almost All of America's 'Best' Cities Will Be on the West Coast, Report Says," February 14, 2014*

Business Environment

CITY FINANCES

City Government Finances

Component	2011 ($000)	2011 ($ per capita)
Total Revenues	5,692,824	2,578
Total Expenditures	4,355,069	1,972
Debt Outstanding	13,950,200	6,318
Cash and Securities[1]	12,514,433	5,667

Note: (1) Cash and security holdings of a government at the close of its fiscal year, including those of its dependent agencies, utilities, and liquor stores.
Source: U.S Census Bureau, State & Local Government Finances 2011

City Government Revenue by Source

Source	2011 ($000)	2011 ($ per capita)
General Revenue		
From Federal Government	171,086	77
From State Government	138,279	63
From Local Governments	50,612	23
Taxes		
Property	1,021,295	463
Sales and Gross Receipts	745,600	338
Personal Income	0	0
Corporate Income	0	0
Motor Vehicle License	0	0
Other Taxes	66,124	30
Current Charges	1,018,977	461
Liquor Store	0	0
Utility	448,966	203
Employee Retirement	1,676,402	759

Source: U.S Census Bureau, State & Local Government Finances 2011

City Government Expenditures by Function

Function	2011 ($000)	2011 ($ per capita)	2011 (%)
General Direct Expenditures			
Air Transportation	446,010	202	10.2
Corrections	23,156	10	0.5
Education	0	0	0.0
Employment Security Administration	0	0	0.0
Financial Administration	48,966	22	1.1
Fire Protection	261,995	119	6.0
General Public Buildings	54,667	25	1.3
Governmental Administration, Other	46,942	21	1.1
Health	107,844	49	2.5
Highways	184,947	84	4.2
Hospitals	0	0	0.0
Housing and Community Development	107,300	49	2.5
Interest on General Debt	585,034	265	13.4
Judicial and Legal	43,933	20	1.0
Libraries	50,876	23	1.2
Parking	6,933	3	0.2
Parks and Recreation	147,477	67	3.4
Police Protection	617,839	280	14.2
Public Welfare	0	0	0.0
Sewerage	212,280	96	4.9
Solid Waste Management	70,442	32	1.6
Veterans' Services	0	0	0.0
Liquor Store	0	0	0.0
Utility	291,782	132	6.7
Employee Retirement	505,484	229	11.6

Source: U.S Census Bureau, State & Local Government Finances 2011

DEMOGRAPHICS

Population Growth

Area	1990 Census	2000 Census	2010 Census	Population Growth (%)	
				1990-2000	2000-2010
City	1,697,610	1,953,631	2,099,451	15.1	7.5
MSA[1]	3,767,335	4,715,407	5,946,800	25.2	26.1
U.S.	248,709,873	281,421,906	308,745,538	13.2	9.7

Note: (1) Figures cover the Houston-The Woodlands-Sugar Land, TX Metropolitan Statistical Area—see Appendix B for areas included
Source: U.S. Census Bureau, Census 1990, 2000, 2010

Household Size

Area	Persons in Household (%)							Average Household Size
	One	Two	Three	Four	Five	Six	Seven or More	
City	32.2	28.5	15.3	12.1	7.0	2.8	2.2	2.73
MSA[1]	24.4	29.8	16.9	15.3	8.1	3.2	2.2	2.92
U.S.	27.6	33.5	15.7	13.2	6.1	2.4	1.5	2.63

Note: (1) Figures cover the Houston-The Woodlands-Sugar Land, TX Metropolitan Statistical Area—see Appendix B for areas included
Source: U.S. Census Bureau, 2010-2012 American Community Survey 3-Year Estimates

Race

Area	White Alone[2] (%)	Black Alone[2] (%)	Asian Alone[2] (%)	AIAN[3] Alone[2] (%)	NHOPI[4] Alone[2] (%)	Other Race Alone[2] (%)	Two or More Races (%)
City	57.5	23.3	6.1	0.4	0.0	10.9	1.7
MSA[1]	65.7	17.2	6.7	0.4	0.1	7.9	2.0
U.S.	74.0	12.6	4.9	0.8	0.2	4.7	2.8

Note: (1) Figures cover the Houston-The Woodlands-Sugar Land, TX Metropolitan Statistical Area—see Appendix B for areas included; (2) Alone is defined as not being in combination with one or more other races; (3) American Indian and Alaska Native; (4) Native Hawaiian and Other Pacific Islander
Source: U.S. Census Bureau, 2010-2012 American Community Survey 3-Year Estimates

Hispanic or Latino Origin

Area	Total (%)	Mexican (%)	Puerto Rican (%)	Cuban (%)	Other (%)
City	43.9	33.3	0.5	0.3	9.8
MSA[1]	35.7	27.7	0.5	0.3	7.1
U.S.	16.6	10.7	1.6	0.6	3.7

Note: Persons of Hispanic or Latino origin can be of any race; (1) Figures cover the Houston-The Woodlands-Sugar Land, TX Metropolitan Statistical Area—see Appendix B for areas included
Source: U.S. Census Bureau, 2010-2012 American Community Survey 3-Year Estimates

Segregation

Type	Segregation Indices[1]				Percent Change		
	1990	2000	2010	2010 Rank[2]	1990-2000	1990-2010	2000-2010
Black/White	65.5	65.7	61.4	36	0.1	-4.1	-4.2
Asian/White	48.0	51.4	50.4	7	3.4	2.4	-1.0
Hispanic/White	47.8	53.4	52.5	18	5.6	4.7	-0.9

Note: All figures cover the Metropolitan Statistical Area—see Appendix B for areas included; Figures are based on an analysis of 1990, 2000, and 2010 Census Decennial Census tract data by William H. Frey, Brookings Institution and the University of Michigan Social Science Data Analysis Network. In this analysis all racial groups (whites, blacks, and asians) are non-Hispanic members of those races. Hispanics are shown as a separate category;
(1) Segregation Indices are Dissimilarity Indices that measure the degree to which the minority group is distributed differently than whites across census tracts. They range from 0 (complete integration) to 100 (complete segregation) where the value indicates the percentage of the minority group that needs to move to be distributed exactly like whites; (2) Ranges from 1 (most segregated) to 102 (least segregated); n/a not available.
Source: www.CensusScope.org

Ancestry

Area	German	Irish	English	American	Italian	Polish	French[2]	Scottish	Dutch
City	5.4	3.7	3.9	3.3	1.5	0.9	1.7	0.9	0.5
MSA[1]	8.9	6.1	5.5	5.0	2.0	1.3	2.3	1.2	0.7
U.S.	15.2	11.1	8.2	7.2	5.6	3.1	2.8	1.7	1.4

Note: Figures are the percentage of the total population reporting a particular ancestry. The nine most commonly reported ancestries in the U.S. are shown. Figures include multiple ancestries (e.g. if a person reported being Irish and Italian, they were included in both columns); (1) Figures cover the Houston-The Woodlands-Sugar Land, TX Metropolitan Statistical Area—see Appendix B for areas included; (2) Excludes Basque
Source: U.S. Census Bureau, 2010-2012 American Community Survey 3-Year Estimates

Foreign-Born Population

Area	Percent of Population Born in								
	Any Foreign Country	Mexico	Asia	Europe	Carribean	South America	Central America[2]	Africa	Canada
City	28.1	13.4	5.4	1.1	0.5	1.0	5.4	1.1	0.2
MSA[1]	22.1	9.9	5.3	1.0	0.5	0.9	3.4	0.9	0.2
U.S.	13.0	3.7	3.7	1.6	1.2	0.9	1.0	0.5	0.3

Note: (1) Figures cover the Houston-The Woodlands-Sugar Land, TX Metropolitan Statistical Area—see Appendix B for areas included; (2) Excludes Mexico.
Source: U.S. Census Bureau, 2010-2012 American Community Survey 3-Year Estimates

Marital Status

Area	Never Married	Now Married[2]	Separated	Widowed	Divorced
City	39.3	41.5	3.6	4.9	10.7
MSA[1]	32.4	49.7	2.9	4.6	10.3
U.S.	32.4	48.4	2.2	6.0	11.0

Note: Figures are percentages and cover the population 15 years of age and older; (1) Figures cover the Houston-The Woodlands-Sugar Land, TX Metropolitan Statistical Area—see Appendix B for areas included; (2) Excludes separated
Source: U.S. Census Bureau, 2010-2012 American Community Survey 3-Year Estimates

Age

Area	Percent of Population									Median Age
	Under Age 5	Age 5–19	Age 20–34	Age 35–44	Age 45–54	Age 55–64	Age 65–74	Age 75–84	Age 85+	Median Age
City	7.9	20.5	25.7	14.0	12.8	9.8	5.2	2.8	1.2	32.4
MSA[1]	7.8	22.6	21.9	14.4	13.8	10.6	5.3	2.6	1.0	33.4
U.S.	6.4	20.1	20.5	13.1	14.3	12.2	7.3	4.2	1.8	37.3

Note: (1) Figures cover the Houston-The Woodlands-Sugar Land, TX Metropolitan Statistical Area—see Appendix B for areas included
Source: U.S. Census Bureau, 2010-2012 American Community Survey 3-Year Estimates

Gender

Area	Males	Females	Males per 100 Females
City	1,069,485	1,060,631	100.8
MSA[1]	3,027,722	3,058,151	99.0
U.S.	153,276,055	158,333,314	96.8

Note: (1) Figures cover the Houston-The Woodlands-Sugar Land, TX Metropolitan Statistical Area—see Appendix B for areas included
Source: U.S. Census Bureau, 2010-2012 American Community Survey 3-Year Estimates

Religious Groups by Family

Area	Catholic	Baptist	Non-Den.	Methodist[2]	Lutheran	LDS[3]	Pente-costal	Presby-terian[4]	Muslim[5]	Judaism
MSA[1]	17.1	16.0	7.3	4.9	1.1	1.1	1.5	0.9	2.7	0.4
U.S.	19.1	9.3	4.0	4.0	2.3	2.0	1.9	1.6	0.8	0.7

Note: Figures are the number of adherents as a percentage of the total population; (1) Figures cover the Houston-The Woodlands-Sugar Land, TX Metropolitan Statistical Area—see Appendix B for areas included; (2) Methodist/Pietist; (3) Latter Day Saints; (4) Reformed; (5) Figures are estimates
Source: Association of Statisticians of American Religious Bodies, 2010 U.S. Religion Census: Religious Congregations & Membership Study

Religious Groups by Tradition

Area	Catholic	Evangelical Protestant	Mainline Protestant	Other Tradition	Black Protestant	Orthodox
MSA[1]	17.1	24.9	6.7	4.9	1.3	0.2
U.S.	19.1	16.2	7.3	4.3	1.6	0.3

Note: Figures are the number of adherents as a percentage of the total population; (1) Figures cover the Houston-The Woodlands-Sugar Land, TX Metropolitan Statistical Area—see Appendix B for areas included
Source: Association of Statisticians of American Religious Bodies, 2010 U.S. Religion Census: Religious Congregations & Membership Study

ECONOMY

Gross Metropolitan Product

Area	2011	2012	2013	2014	Rank[2]
MSA[1]	425.5	449.7	463.7	488.7	4

Note: Figures are in billions of dollars; (1) Figures cover the Houston-The Woodlands-Sugar Land, TX Metropolitan Statistical Area—see Appendix B for areas included; (2) Rank is based on 2014 data and ranges from 1 to 363
Source: The United States Conference of Mayors, U.S. Metro Economies: Outlook—Gross Metropolitan Product, with Metro Employment Projections, November 2013

Economic Growth

Area	2011 (%)	2012 (%)	2013 (%)	2014 (%)	Rank[2]
MSA[1]	4.2	5.3	2.0	3.5	75
U.S.	1.6	2.5	1.7	2.5	–

Note: Figures are real gross metropolitan product (GMP) growth rates and represent annual average percent change; (1) Figures cover the Houston-The Woodlands-Sugar Land, TX Metropolitan Statistical Area—see Appendix B for areas included; (2) Rank is based on 2013 data and ranges from 1 to 363
Source: The United States Conference of Mayors, U.S. Metro Economies: Outlook—Gross Metropolitan Product, with Metro Employment Projections, November 2013

Metropolitan Area Exports

Area	2007	2008	2009	2010	2011	2012	Rank[2]
MSA[1]	62,814.7	80,015.1	65,820.9	80,569.7	104,457.3	110,297.8	1

Note: Figures are in millions of dollars; (1) Figures cover the Houston-The Woodlands-Sugar Land, TX Metropolitan Statistical Area—see Appendix B for areas included; (2) Rank is based on 2012 data and ranges from 1 to 369
Source: U.S. Department of Commerce, International Trade Administration, Office of Trade & Industry Information, Manufacturing & Services, data extracted April 1, 2014

INCOME

Income

Area	Per Capita ($)	Median Household ($)	Average Household ($)
City	26,335	43,792	69,421
MSA[1]	28,059	56,080	79,881
U.S.	27,385	51,771	71,579

Note: (1) Figures cover the Houston-The Woodlands-Sugar Land, TX Metropolitan Statistical Area—see Appendix B for areas included
Source: U.S. Census Bureau, 2010-2012 American Community Survey 3-Year Estimates

Household Income Distribution

Area	Percent of Households Earning							
	Under $15,000	$15,000 -24,999	$25,000 -34,999	$35,000 -49,999	$50,000 -74,999	$75,000 -99,000	$100,000 -149,999	$150,000 and up
City	16.1	12.9	12.1	14.0	15.8	9.9	9.7	9.4
MSA[1]	11.5	10.1	10.2	13.0	17.3	12.0	13.8	12.1
U.S.	13.1	11.0	10.5	13.7	18.1	11.9	12.5	9.1

Note: (1) Figures cover the Houston-The Woodlands-Sugar Land, TX Metropolitan Statistical Area—see Appendix B for areas included
Source: U.S. Census Bureau, 2010-2012 American Community Survey 3-Year Estimates

Poverty Rate

Area	All Ages	Under 18 Years Old	18 to 64 Years Old	65 Years and Over
City	23.5	36.3	19.7	14.4
MSA[1]	16.8	24.6	14.2	10.5
U.S.	15.7	22.2	14.6	9.3

Note: Figures are percentage of people whose income during the past 12 months was below the poverty level; (1) Figures cover the Houston-The Woodlands-Sugar Land, TX Metropolitan Statistical Area—see Appendix B for areas included
Source: U.S. Census Bureau, 2010-2012 American Community Survey 3-Year Estimates

Personal Bankruptcy Filing Rate

Area	2008	2009	2010	2011	2012	2013
Harris County	1.52	1.78	2.08	1.95	1.64	1.36
U.S.	3.53	4.61	4.97	4.37	3.76	3.29

Note: Numbers are per 1,000 population and include Chapter 7 and Chapter 13 filings
Source: Federal Deposit Insurance Corporation, Regional Economic Conditions, March 20, 2014

EMPLOYMENT

Labor Force and Employment

Area	Civilian Labor Force			Workers Employed		
	Dec. 2012	Dec. 2013	% Chg.	Dec. 2012	Dec. 2013	% Chg.
City	1,038,662	1,062,784	2.3	974,997	1,004,714	3.0
MSA[1]	3,055,533	3,131,593	2.5	2,872,966	2,960,533	3.0
U.S.	154,904,000	154,408,000	-0.3	143,060,000	144,423,000	1.0

Note: Data is not seasonally adjusted and covers workers 16 years of age and older; (1) Metropolitan Statistical Area—see Appendix B for areas included
Source: Bureau of Labor Statistics, Local Area Unemployment Statistics

Unemployment Rate

Area	2013											
	Jan.	Feb.	Mar.	Apr.	May	Jun.	Jul.	Aug.	Sep.	Oct.	Nov.	Dec.
City	6.9	6.4	6.2	6.1	6.5	6.9	6.6	6.2	6.3	6.0	5.7	5.5
MSA[1]	6.7	6.3	6.1	6.0	6.3	6.7	6.5	6.1	6.2	5.9	5.6	5.5
U.S.	8.5	8.1	7.6	7.1	7.3	7.8	7.7	7.3	7.0	7.0	6.6	6.5

Note: Data is not seasonally adjusted and covers workers 16 years of age and older; All figures are percentages; (1) Metropolitan Statistical Area—see Appendix B for areas included
Source: Bureau of Labor Statistics, Local Area Unemployment Statistics

Employment by Occupation

Occupation Classification	City (%)	MSA[1] (%)	U.S. (%)
Management, Business, Science, and Arts	33.0	35.8	36.0
Natural Resources, Construction, and Maintenance	12.2	11.1	9.1
Production, Transportation, and Material Moving	12.7	12.4	12.0
Sales and Office	22.5	24.0	24.7
Service	19.7	16.7	18.2

Note: Figures cover employed civilians 16 years of age and older; (1) Figures cover the Houston-The Woodlands-Sugar Land, TX Metropolitan Statistical Area—see Appendix B for areas included
Source: U.S. Census Bureau, 2010-2012 American Community Survey 3-Year Estimates

Employment by Industry

| Sector | MSA[1] | | U.S. |
	Number of Employees	Percent of Total	Percent of Total
Construction	188,900	6.7	4.2
Education and Health Services	340,100	12.0	15.5
Financial Activities	141,200	5.0	5.7
Government	378,400	13.3	16.1
Information	32,900	1.2	1.9
Leisure and Hospitality	277,900	9.8	10.2
Manufacturing	255,600	9.0	8.7
Mining and Logging	107,400	3.8	0.6
Other Services	99,500	3.5	3.9
Professional and Business Services	431,000	15.2	13.7
Retail Trade	298,400	10.5	11.4
Transportation and Utilities	135,000	4.8	3.8
Wholesale Trade	153,800	5.4	4.2

Note: Figures cover non-farm employment as of December 2013 and are not seasonally adjusted;
(1) Metropolitan Statistical Area—see Appendix B for areas included
Source: Bureau of Labor Statistics, Current Employment Statistics, Employment, Hours, and Earnings

Occupations with Greatest Projected Employment Growth: 2010 – 2020

Occupation[1]	2010 Employment	2020 Projected Employment	Numeric Employment Change	Percent Employment Change
Combined Food Preparation and Serving Workers, Including Fast Food	243,530	322,520	78,990	32.4
Elementary School Teachers, Except Special Education	166,090	233,860	67,780	40.8
Personal Care Aides	133,820	199,970	66,150	49.4
Retail Salespersons	370,620	433,180	62,560	16.9
Registered Nurses	184,700	245,870	61,160	33.1
Waiters and Waitresses	190,870	244,610	53,730	28.2
Office Clerks, General	262,740	314,810	52,070	19.8
Cashiers	250,510	292,730	42,220	16.9
Home Health Aides	82,420	123,970	41,550	50.4
Customer Service Representatives	200,880	241,030	40,160	20.0

Note: Projections cover Texas; (1) Sorted by numeric employment change
Source: www.projectionscentral.com, State Occupational Projections, 2010–2020 Long-Term Projections

Fastest Growing Occupations: 2010 – 2020

Occupation[1]	2010 Employment	2020 Projected Employment	Numeric Employment Change	Percent Employment Change
Biomedical Engineers	1,440	2,490	1,050	72.9
Diagnostic Medical Sonographers	3,560	5,410	1,850	51.9
Derrick Operators, Oil and Gas	7,190	10,860	3,670	51.1
Home Health Aides	82,420	123,970	41,550	50.4
Personal Care Aides	133,820	199,970	66,150	49.4
Service Unit Operators, Oil, Gas, and Mining	17,870	26,460	8,590	48.0
Special Education Teachers, Middle School	6,170	8,950	2,780	45.1
Special Education Teachers, Preschool, Kindergarten, and Elementary School	12,940	18,750	5,810	44.9
Rotary Drill Operators, Oil and Gas	7,160	10,340	3,180	44.4
Roustabouts, Oil and Gas	17,800	25,580	7,790	43.8

Note: Projections cover Texas; (1) Sorted by percent employment change and excludes occupations with numeric employment change less than 100
Source: www.projectionscentral.com, State Occupational Projections, 2010–2020 Long-Term Projections

Average Wages

Occupation	$/Hr.	Occupation	$/Hr.
Accountants and Auditors	38.74	Maids and Housekeeping Cleaners	8.98
Automotive Mechanics	19.17	Maintenance and Repair Workers	17.78
Bookkeepers	18.62	Marketing Managers	70.33
Carpenters	16.62	Nuclear Medicine Technologists	33.26
Cashiers	9.40	Nurses, Licensed Practical	22.88
Clerks, General Office	15.80	Nurses, Registered	36.56
Clerks, Receptionists/Information	12.86	Nursing Assistants	12.06
Clerks, Shipping/Receiving	14.39	Packers and Packagers, Hand	11.38
Computer Programmers	39.02	Physical Therapists	42.08
Computer Systems Analysts	49.83	Postal Service Mail Carriers	24.51
Computer User Support Specialists	27.90	Real Estate Brokers	48.51
Cooks, Restaurant	10.16	Retail Salespersons	12.40
Dentists	80.85	Sales Reps., Exc. Tech./Scientific	35.33
Electrical Engineers	49.20	Sales Reps., Tech./Scientific	46.06
Electricians	22.65	Secretaries, Exc. Legal/Med./Exec.	16.39
Financial Managers	68.99	Security Guards	11.75
First-Line Supervisors/Managers, Sales	21.30	Surgeons	84.40
Food Preparation Workers	9.38	Teacher Assistants	9.90
General and Operations Managers	63.07	Teachers, Elementary School	24.90
Hairdressers/Cosmetologists	14.85	Teachers, Secondary School	25.50
Internists	84.76	Telemarketers	12.17
Janitors and Cleaners	9.66	Truck Drivers, Heavy/Tractor-Trailer	22.66
Landscaping/Groundskeeping Workers	11.34	Truck Drivers, Light/Delivery Svcs.	16.51
Lawyers	76.17	Waiters and Waitresses	9.73

Note: Wage data covers the Houston-Sugar Land-Baytown, TX Metropolitan Statistical Area—see Appendix B for areas included. Hourly wages for elementary/secondary school teachers and teacher assistants were calculated by the editors from annual wage data assuming a 40 hour work week; n/a not available.
Source: Bureau of Labor Statistics, Metro Area Occupational Employment and Wage Estimates, May 2013

RESIDENTIAL REAL ESTATE

Building Permits

Area	Single-Family			Multi-Family			Total		
	2012	2013	Pct. Chg.	2012	2013	Pct. Chg.	2012	2013	Pct. Chg.
City	3,513	5,198	48.0	9,020	8,845	-1.9	12,533	14,043	12.0
MSA[1]	28,628	34,542	20.7	14,662	16,791	14.5	43,290	51,333	18.6
U.S.	518,695	620,802	19.7	310,963	370,020	19.0	829,658	990,822	19.4

Note: (1) Metropolitan Statistical Area—see Appendix B for areas included; figures represent new, privately-owned housing units authorized (unadjusted data); All permit data are based on estimates with imputation.
Source: U.S. Census Bureau, Manufacturing, Mining, and Construction Statistics, Building Permits, 2012, 2013

Homeownership Rate

Area	2006 (%)	2007 (%)	2008 (%)	2009 (%)	2010 (%)	2011 (%)	2012 (%)	2013 (%)
MSA[1]	63.5	64.5	64.8	63.6	61.4	61.3	62.1	60.5
U.S.	68.8	68.1	67.8	67.4	66.9	66.1	65.4	65.1

Note: (1) Figures cover the Houston-The Woodlands-Sugar Land, TX Metropolitan Statistical Area—see Appendix B for areas included
Source: U.S. Census Bureau, Housing Vacancies and Homeownership Annual Statistics: 2013

Housing Vacancy Rates

Area	Gross Vacancy Rate[2] (%)			Year-Round Vacancy Rate[3] (%)			Rental Vacancy Rate[4] (%)			Homeowner Vacancy Rate[5] (%)		
	2011	2012	2013	2011	2012	2013	2011	2012	2013	2011	2012	2013
MSA[1]	11.8	9.8	9.6	11.4	9.4	9.0	16.5	11.4	10.0	2.0	1.9	2.3
U.S.	14.2	13.8	13.8	11.1	10.8	10.7	9.5	8.7	8.3	2.5	2.0	2.0

Note: (1) Figures cover the Houston-The Woodlands-Sugar Land, TX Metropolitan Statistical Area—see Appendix B for areas included; (2) The percentage of the total housing inventory that is vacant; (3) The percentage of the housing inventory (excluding seasonal units) that is year-round vacant; (4) The percentage of rental inventory that is vacant for rent; (5) The percentage of homeowner inventory that is vacant for sale
Source: U.S. Census Bureau, Housing Vacancies and Homeownership Annual Statistics: 2013

TAXES

State Corporate Income Tax Rates

State	Tax Rate (%)	Income Brackets ($)	Num. of Brackets	Financial Institution Tax Rate (%)[a]	Federal Income Tax Ded.
Texas	(x)	–	–	(x)	No

Note: Tax rates as of January 1, 2014; (a) Rates listed are the corporate income tax rate applied to financial institutions or excise taxes based on income. Some states have other taxes based upon the value of deposits or shares; (x) Texas imposes a Franchise Tax, otherwise known as margin tax, imposed on entities with more than $1,030,000 total revenues at rate of 1%, or 0.5% for entities primarily engaged in retail or wholesale trade, on lesser of 70% of total revenues or 100% of gross receipts after deductions for either compensation or cost of goods sold.
Source: Federation of Tax Administrators, "State Corporate Income Tax Rates, 2014"

State Individual Income Tax Rates

State	Tax Rate (%)	Income Brackets ($)	Num. of Brackets	Personal Exempt. ($)[1] Single	Personal Exempt. ($)[1] Dependents	Fed. Inc. Tax Ded.
Texas	None	–	–	–	–	–

Note: Tax rates as of January 1, 2014; Local- and county-level taxes are not included; n/a not applicable;
(1) Married joint filers generally receive double the single exemption
Source: Federation of Tax Administrators, "State Individual Income Tax Rates, 2014"

Various State and Local Tax Rates

State	State and Local Sales and Use (%)	State Sales and Use (%)	Gasoline[1] (¢/gal.)	Cigarette[2] ($/pack)	Spirits[3] ($/gal.)	Wine[4] ($/gal.)	Beer[5] ($/gal.)
Texas	8.25	6.25	20.00	1.410	2.40 (f)	0.20	0.20

Note: All tax rates as of January 1, 2014; (1) The American Petroleum Institute has developed a methodology for determining the average tax rate on a gallon of fuel. Rates may include any of the following: excise taxes, environmental fees, storage tank fees, other fees or taxes, general sales tax, and local taxes. In states where gasoline is subject to the general sales tax, or where the fuel tax is based on the average sale price, the average rate determined by API is sensitive to changes in the price of gasoline. States that fully or partially apply general sales taxes to gasoline: CA, CO, GA, IL, IN, MI, NY; (2) The federal excise tax of $1.0066 per pack and local taxes are not included; (3) Rates are those applicable to off-premise sales of 40% alcohol by volume (a.b.v.) distilled spirits in 750ml containers. Local excise taxes are excluded; (4) Rates are those applicable to off-premise sales of 11% a.b.v. non-carbonated wine in 750ml containers; (5) Rates are those applicable to off-premise sales of 4.7% a.b.v. beer in 12 ounce containers; (f) Different rates also applicable according to alcohol content, place of production, size of container, or place purchased (on- or off-premise or onboard airlines).
Source: Tax Foundation, 2014 Facts & Figures: How Does Your State Compare?

State Business Tax Climate Index Rankings

State	Overall Rank	Corporate Tax Index Rank	Individual Income Tax Index Rank	Sales Tax Index Rank	Unemployment Insurance Tax Index Rank	Property Tax Index Rank
Texas	11	38	7	36	14	35

Note: The index is a measure of how each state's tax laws affect economic performance. The lower the rank, the more favorable a state's tax system is for business. States without a given tax are given a ranking of 1. The scores/rankings for the District of Columbia do not affect other states. The 2014 index represents the tax climate as of July 1, 2013.
Source: Tax Foundation, State Business Tax Climate Index 2014

COMMERCIAL REAL ESTATE

Office Market

Market Area	Inventory (sq. ft.)	Vacancy Rate (%)	Under Construction (sq. ft.)	YTD Net Absorption (sq. ft.)	Total Average Asking Rent ($/sq. ft./year)
Houston	212,069,437	14.3	7,189,068	3,155,435	25.71
National	4,726,900,879	15.0	55,419,286	42,829,434	26.27

Source: Newmark Grubb Knight Frank, National Office Market Report, 4th Quarter 2013

Industrial/Warehouse/R&D Market

Market Area	Inventory (sq. ft.)	Vacancy Rate (%)	Under Construction (sq. ft.)	YTD Net Absorption (sq. ft.)	Total Average Asking Rent ($/sq. ft./year)
Houston	425,794,316	4.8	5,891,998	5,611,128	5.47
National	14,022,031,238	7.9	83,249,164	156,549,903	5.40

Source: Newmark Grubb Knight Frank, National Industrial Market Report, 4th Quarter 2013

COMMERCIAL UTILITIES

Typical Monthly Electric Bills

Area	Commercial Service ($/month)		Industrial Service ($/month)	
	1,500 kWh	40 kW demand 14,000 kWh	1,000 kW demand 200,000 kWh	50,000 kW demand 15,000,000 kWh
City	n/a	n/a	n/a	n/a
Average[1]	197	1,636	25,662	1,485,307

Note: Based on total rates in effect July 1, 2013; (1) average based on 180 utilities surveyed; n/a not available
Source: Edison Electric Institute, Typical Bills and Average Rates Report, Summer 2013

TRANSPORTATION

Means of Transportation to Work

Area	Car/Truck/Van		Public Transportation			Bicycle	Walked	Other Means	Worked at Home
	Drove Alone	Car-pooled	Bus	Subway	Railroad				
City	75.8	12.2	4.3	0.0	0.0	0.4	2.1	2.0	3.1
MSA[1]	79.9	11.1	2.4	0.0	0.0	0.3	1.4	1.6	3.4
U.S.	76.4	9.7	2.6	1.7	0.5	0.6	2.8	1.3	4.3

Note: Figures are percentages and cover workers 16 years of age and older; (1) Figures cover the Houston-The Woodlands-Sugar Land, TX Metropolitan Statistical Area—see Appendix B for areas included
Source: U.S. Census Bureau, 2010-2012 American Community Survey 3-Year Estimates

Travel Time to Work

Area	Less Than 10 Minutes	10 to 19 Minutes	20 to 29 Minutes	30 to 44 Minutes	45 to 59 Minutes	60 to 89 Minutes	90 Minutes or More
City	8.6	28.0	24.4	25.2	7.2	5.0	1.7
MSA[1]	8.7	25.2	21.1	25.5	10.3	7.1	2.0
U.S.	13.5	29.8	20.9	20.1	7.5	5.6	2.5

Note: Figures are percentages and include workers 16 years old and over; (1) Figures cover the Houston-The Woodlands-Sugar Land, TX Metropolitan Statistical Area—see Appendix B for areas included
Source: U.S. Census Bureau, 2010-2012 American Community Survey 3-Year Estimates

Travel Time Index

Area	1985	1990	1995	2000	2005	2010	2011
Urban Area[1]	1.23	1.22	1.19	1.25	1.31	1.26	1.26
Average[2]	1.09	1.14	1.16	1.19	1.23	1.18	1.18

Note: Travel Time Index—the ratio of travel time in the peak period to the travel time at free-flow conditions. For example, a value of 1.30 indicates a 20-minute free-flow trip takes 26 minutes in the peak. Free-flow speeds (60 mph on freeways and 35 mph on principal arterials) are used as the comparison threshold; (1) Covers the Houston TX urban area; (2) average of 498 urban areas
Source: Texas Transportation Institute, Urban Mobility Report 2012, December 2012

Public Transportation

Agency Name / Mode of Transportation	Vehicles Operated in Maximum Service	Annual Unlinked Passenger Trips (in thous.)	Annual Passenger Miles (in thous.)
Metropolitan Transit Authority of Harris County (METRO)			
Bus (directly operated)	639	47,000.4	234,355.4
Bus (purchased transportation)	130	11,099.7	54,030.8
Commuter Bus (directly operated)	216	5,627.5	98,446.3
Commuter Bus (purchased transportation)	62	1,739.8	33,210.7
Demand Response (purchased transportation)	275	1,486.9	17,543.9
Demand Response Taxi (purchased transportation)	129	181.7	1,305.5
Light Rail (directly operated)	18	11,276.8	26,154.2
Vanpool (purchased transportation)	720	2,478.6	69,505.3

Source: Federal Transit Administration, National Transit Database, 2012

Air Transportation

Airport Name and Code / Type of Service	Passenger Airlines[1]	Passenger Enplanements	Freight Carriers[2]	Freight (lbs.)
George Bush Intercontinental (IAH)				
Domestic service (U.S. carriers - 2013)	29	14,568,518	22	186,438,207
International service (U.S. carriers - 2012)	16	3,374,872	15	82,395,056
William P. Hobby (HOU)				
Domestic service (U.S. carriers - 2013)	19	5,371,688	8	14,730,244
International service (U.S. carriers - 2012)	2	406	1	3,218

Note: (1) Includes all U.S.-based major, minor and commuter airlines that carried at least one passenger during the year; (2) Includes all U.S.-based airlines and freight carriers that transported at least one lb. of freight during the year.
Source: Bureau of Transportation Statistics, The Intermodal Transportation Database, Air Carriers: T-100 Domestic Market (U.S. Carriers), 2013; Bureau of Transportation Statistics, The Intermodal Transportation Database, Air Carriers: T-100 International Market (U.S. Carriers), 2012

Other Transportation Statistics

Major Highways:	I-10; I-45
Amtrak Service:	Yes
Major Waterways/Ports:	Gulf of Mexico; Port of Houston

Source: Amtrak.com; Google Maps

BUSINESSES

Major Business Headquarters

Company Name	Rankings	
	Fortune[1]	Forbes[2]
Apache	167	-
Baker Hughes	135	-
Calpine	459	-
Cameron International	310	-
CenterPoint Energy	344	-
ConocoPhillips	45	-
EOG Resources	233	-
Enbridge Energy Partners	381	-
Enterprise Products Partners	64	-
FMC Technologies	417	-
Grocers Supply	-	134
Group 1 Automotive	343	-
Gulf States Toyota	-	51
Halliburton	106	-
KBR	334	-
Kinder Morgan	265	-
Landry's	-	190
MRC Global	451	-
Marathon Oil	174	-
National Oilwell Varco	144	-
Phillips 66	4	-

Plains All American Pipeline	77	-
Quanta Services	397	-
Republic National Distributing Company	-	79
Spectra Energy	475	-
Sysco	65	-
Targa Resources	435	-
Tauber Oil	-	70
Waste Management	200	-

Note: (1) Fortune 500—companies that produce a 10-K are ranked 1 to 500 based on 2012 revenue; (2) all private companies with at least $2 billion in annual revenue through the end of their most current fiscal year are ranked 1 to 224; companies listed are headquartered in the city; dashes indicate no ranking Source: Fortune, "Fortune 500," May 20, 2013; Forbes, "America's Largest Private Companies," December 18, 2013

Fast-Growing Businesses

According to *Inc.*, Houston is home to five of America's 500 fastest-growing private companies: **ethosIQ** (#65); **EDJ Precision** (#165); **Team Trident** (#233); **HPI** (#383); **Worldwide Power Products** (#458). Criteria: must be an independent, privately-held, for-profit, U.S. corporation, proprietorship or partnership; revenues must be at least $100,000 in 2009 and $2 million in 2012; must have four-year operating/sales history. Holding companies, regulated banks, and utilities were excluded. *Inc., "America's 500 Fastest-Growing Private Companies," September 2013*

According to *Fortune*, Houston is home to eight of the 100 fastest-growing companies in the world: **EPL Oil & Gas** (#11); **Geospace Technologies** (#18); **Rosetta Resources** (#25); **Adams Resources & Energy** (#30); **Patterson-UTI Energy** (#31); **Oil States International** (#32); **DXP Enterprises** (#47); **Superior Energy Services** (#56). Companies were ranked by their revenue growth rate; their EPS growth rate; and their three-year annualized total return to investors for the period ending June 30, 2013. Criteria for inclusion: a company, foreign or domestic, must trade on a major U.S. stock exchange; must file quarterly reports with the SEC; must have a minimum market capitalization of $250 million; must have a stock price of at least $5 on June 29, 2013; must have been trading continuously since June 30, 2009; must have revenue and net income for the four quarters ended on or before April 30, 2013, of at least $50 million and $10 million, respectively; and must have posted a compound annual growth in revenue and earnings per share of at least 20% annually over the three years ending on or before April 30, 2013. REITs, limited-liability companies, limited parterships, companies about to be acquired, and companies that lost money in the quarter ending April 30, 2013 were excluded. *Fortune, "100 Fastest-Growing Companies," August 29, 2013*

According to *Initiative for a Competitive Inner City (ICIC)*, Houston is home to three of America's 100 fastest-growing "inner city" companies: **PMG Project Management Group** (#21); **Clinical Trial Network** (#67); **Pipe Wrap** (#82). Companies were ranked by their five-year compound annual growth rate. Criteria for inclusion: company must be headquartered in or have 51 percent or more of its physical operations in an economically distressed urban area; must be an independent, for-profit corporation, partnership or proprietorship; must have 10 or more employees and have a five-year sales history that includes sales of at least $200,000 in the base year and at least $1 million in the current year with no decrease in sales over the two most recent years. *Initiative for a Competitive Inner City (ICIC), "Inner City 100 Companies, 2013"*

Minority Business Opportunity

Houston is home to two companies which are on the *Black Enterprise* Industrial/Service 100 list (100 largest companies based on gross sales): **The Lewis Group** (#25); **Chase Source** (#93). Criteria: operational in previous calendar year; at least 51% black-owned and manufactures/owns the product it sells or provides industrial or consumer services. Brokerages, real estate firms and firms that provide professional services are not eligible. *Black Enterprise, B.E. 100s, 2013*

Houston is home to two companies which are on the *Black Enterprise* Auto Dealer 60 list (60 largest dealers based on gross sales): **Barnett Auto Group** (#26); **J Davis Automotive Group** (#28). Criteria: company must be operational in previous calendar year and be at least 51% black-owned. *Black Enterprise, B.E. 100s, 2013*

Houston is home to one company which is on the *Black Enterprise* Asset Manager 15 list (15 largest asset management firms based on assets under management): **Smith Graham & Co. Investment Advisors** (#6). Criteria: company must have been operational in previous calendar year and be at least 51% black-owned. *Black Enterprise, B.E. 100s, 2013*

Houston is home to 17 companies which are on the *Hispanic Business* 500 list (500 largest U.S. Hispanic-owned companies based on 2012 revenue): **G&A Partners** (#16); **Petro Amigos Supply** (#20); **The Plaza Group** (#29); **MEI Technologies (MEIT)** (#53); **Tejas Office Products** (#134); **Lopez Negrete Communications** (#167); **Reytec Construction Resources** (#173); **MCA Communications** (#177); **Today's Business Solutions** (#194); **Tube America** (#273); **Traf-Tex** (#310); **Nino Properties** (#401); **Navarro Insurance Group** (#458); **Translation Source** (#460); **Transfinance Corp.** (#465); **Perches Land Services** (#475); **CapWest Companies** (#490). Companies included must show at least 51 percent ownership by Hispanic U.S. citizens, and must maintain headquarters in one of the 50 states or Washington, D.C. *Hispanic Business, "Hispanic Business 500," June 20, 2013*

Houston is home to five companies which are on the *Hispanic Business* Fastest-Growing 100 list (greatest sales growth from 2008 to 2012): **Tejas Office Products** (#18); **Today's Business Solutions** (#27); **Petro Amigos Supply** (#64); **G&A Partners** (#65); **Translation Source** (#83). Companies included must show at least 51 percent ownership by Hispanic U.S. citizens, and must maintain headquarters in one of the 50 states or Washington, D.C. In addition, companies must have minimum revenues of $200,000 for calendar year 2008. *Hispanic Business, June 20, 2013*

Minority- and Women-Owned Businesses

Group	All Firms		Firms with Paid Employees			
	Firms	Sales ($000)	Firms	Sales ($000)	Employees	Payroll ($000)
Asian	22,826	10,793,503	6,878	10,053,255	47,323	1,317,131
Black	33,061	2,077,993	1,757	1,492,851	27,498	530,585
Hispanic	51,205	10,505,159	4,071	8,548,735	42,665	1,526,879
Women	63,416	17,883,106	7,340	16,317,650	88,123	3,246,910
All Firms	219,284	514,239,417	48,175	505,797,015	1,442,271	76,231,379

Note: Figures cover firms located in the city; minority- and women-owned business are defined as firms in which the corresponding group own 51% or more of the stock or equity of the company
Source: U.S. Census Bureau, 2007 Economic Census, Survey of Business Owners (2012 Survey of Business Owners data will be released starting in June 2015)

HOTELS & CONVENTION CENTERS

Hotels/Motels

Area	5 Star		4 Star		3 Star		2 Star		1 Star		Not Rated	
	Num.	Pct.[3]	Num.	Pct.[3]	Num.	Pct.[3]	Num.	Pct.[3]	Num.	Pct.[3]	Num.	Pct.[3]
City[1]	3	0.6	23	4.3	135	25.0	317	58.8	3	0.6	58	10.8
Total[2]	142	0.9	1,005	6.0	5,147	30.9	8,578	51.4	408	2.4	1,397	8.4

Note: (1) Figures cover Houston and vicinity; (2) Figures cover all 100 cities in this book; (3) Percentage of hotels which have a given star rating; Star ratings are determined by expedia.com and offer an indication of the general quality of a particular hotel.
Source: expedia.com, April 7, 2014

The Houston-The Woodlands-Sugar Land, TX metro area is home to two of the best hotels in the world according to *Condé Nast Traveler*: **Hotel Granduca**; **Hotel Sorella**. The selections are based on over 79,000 responses to the magazine's annual Readers' Choice Survey. The list includes the top 200 hotels in the U.S. *Condé Nast Traveler, "Gold List 2014, The World's Best Places to Stay"*

Major Convention Centers

Name	Overall Space (sq. ft.)	Exhibit Space (sq. ft.)	Meeting Space (sq. ft.)	Meeting Rooms
George R. Brown Convention Center	1,200,000	862,000	185,000	100
Reliant Center	1,400,000	706,000	n/a	n/a

Note: Table includes convention centers located in the Houston-The Woodlands-Sugar Land, TX metro area; n/a not available
Source: Original research

Living Environment

COST OF LIVING

Cost of Living Index

Composite Index	Groceries	Housing	Utilities	Trans-portation	Health Care	Misc. Goods/Services
98.8	79.5	107.3	103.2	95.4	96.4	100.2

Note: The Cost of Living Index measures regional differences in the cost of consumer goods and services, excluding taxes and non-consumer expenditures, for professional and managerial households in the top income quintile. It is based on more than 50,000 prices covering almost 60 different items for which prices are collected three times a year by chambers of commerce, economic development organizations or university applied economic centers in each participating urban area. The numbers shown should be read as a percentage above or below the national average of 100. For example, a value of 115.4 in the groceries column indicates that grocery prices are 15.4% higher than the national average. Small differences in the index numbers should not be interpreted as significant; Figures cover the Houston TX urban area.
Source: The Council for Community and Economic Research, ACCRA Cost of Living Index, 2013

Grocery Prices

Area[1]	T-Bone Steak ($/pound)	Frying Chicken ($/pound)	Whole Milk ($/half gal.)	Eggs ($/dozen)	Orange Juice ($/64 oz.)	Coffee ($/11.5 oz.)
City[2]	9.80	1.00	2.11	1.52	3.16	4.01
Avg.	10.19	1.28	2.34	1.81	3.48	4.39
Min.	8.56	0.94	1.44	1.19	2.78	3.40
Max.	14.82	2.28	3.56	3.73	6.23	7.32

*Note: (1) Values for the local area are compared with the average, minimum and maximum values for all 327 areas in the Cost of Living Index; (2) Figures cover the Houston TX urban area; **T-Bone Steak** (price per pound); **Frying Chicken** (price per pound, whole fryer); **Whole Milk** (half gallon carton); **Eggs** (price per dozen, Grade A, large); **Orange Juice** (64 oz. Tropicana or Florida Natural); **Coffee** (11.5 oz. can, vacuum-packed, Maxwell House, Hills Bros, or Folgers).*
Source: The Council for Community and Economic Research, ACCRA Cost of Living Index, 2013

Housing and Utility Costs

Area[1]	New Home Price ($)	Apartment Rent ($/month)	All Electric ($/month)	Part Electric ($/month)	Other Energy ($/month)	Telephone ($/month)
City[2]	248,558	1,435	-	119.33	45.38	29.59
Avg.	295,864	900	171.38	91.82	70.12	27.73
Min.	185,506	458	117.80	48.81	33.67	17.16
Max.	1,358,917	3,783	441.68	171.40	372.65	39.47

*Note: (1) Values for the local area are compared with the average, minimum and maximum values for all 327 areas in the Cost of Living Index; (2) Figures cover the Houston TX urban area; **New Home Price** (2,400 sf living area, 8,000 sf lot, in urban area with full utilities); **Apartment Rent** (950 sf 2 bedroom/1.5 or 2 bath, unfurnished, excluding all utilities except water); **All Electric** (average monthly cost for an all-electric home); **Part Electric** (average monthly cost for a part-electric home); **Other Energy** (average monthly cost for natural gas, fuel oil, coal, wood, and any other forms of energy except electricity); **Telephone** (price includes basic monthly rate for a private residential line plus additional local usage charges incurred by a family of four).*
Source: The Council for Community and Economic Research, ACCRA Cost of Living Index, 2013

Health Care, Transportation, and Other Costs

Area[1]	Doctor ($/visit)	Dentist ($/visit)	Optometrist ($/visit)	Gasoline ($/gallon)	Beauty Salon ($/visit)	Men's Shirt ($)
City[2]	90.61	86.57	89.60	3.38	46.10	24.22
Avg.	101.40	86.48	96.16	3.44	33.87	26.55
Min.	61.67	50.83	50.12	3.08	18.92	12.48
Max.	182.71	152.50	223.78	4.33	68.22	52.03

*Note: (1) Values for the local area are compared with the average, minimum and maximum values for all 327 areas in the Cost of Living Index; (2) Figures cover the Houston TX urban area; **Doctor** (general practitioners routine exam of an established patient); **Dentist** (adult teeth cleaning and periodic oral examination); **Optometrist** (full vision eye exam for established adult patient); **Gasoline** (one gallon regular unleaded, national brand, including all taxes, cash price at self-service pump if available); **Beauty Salon** (woman's shampoo, trim, and blow-dry); **Men's Shirt** (cotton/polyester dress shirt, pinpoint weave, long sleeves).*
Source: The Council for Community and Economic Research, ACCRA Cost of Living Index, 2013

HOUSING

House Price Index (HPI)

Area	National Ranking[2]	Quarterly Change (%)	One-Year Change (%)	Five-Year Change (%)
MSA[1]	69	1.85	6.81	9.89
U.S.[3]	–	1.20	7.69	4.18

Note: The HPI is a weighted repeat sales index. It measures average price changes in repeat sales or refinancings on the same properties. This information is obtained by reviewing repeat mortgage transactions on single-family properties whose mortgages have been purchased or securitized by Fannie Mae or Freddie Mac in January 1975; (1) Houston-The Woodlands-Sugar Land, TX Metropolitan Statistical Area—see Appendix B for areas included; (2) Rankings are based on annual percentage change for all metro areas containing at least 15,000 transactions over the last 10 years and ranges from 1 to 283; (3) figures based on a weighted average of Census Division estimates using a seasonally adjusted, purchase-only index; all figures are for the period ending December 31, 2013
Source: Federal Housing Finance Agency, House Price Index, February 25, 2014

Median Single-Family Home Prices

Area	2011	2012	2013p	Percent Change 2012 to 2013
MSA[1]	155.7	164.8	181.3	10.0
U.S. Average	166.2	177.2	197.4	11.4

Note: Figures are median sales prices of existing single-family homes in thousands of dollars; (p) preliminary; n/a not available; (1) Houston-The Woodlands-Sugar Land, TX Metropolitan Statistical Area—see Appendix B for areas included
Source: National Association of Realtors, Median Sales Price of Existing Single-Family Homes for Metropolitan Areas, 4th Quarter 2013

Qualifying Income Based on Median Sales Price of Existing Single-Family Homes

Area	With 5% Down ($)	With 10% Down ($)	With 20% Down ($)
MSA[1]	42,029	39,817	35,393
U.S. Average	45,395	43,006	38,228

Note: Figures are preliminary; Qualifying income is based on a mortgage rate of 4.4%. Monthly principal and interest payment is limited to 25% of income; n/a not available; (1) Houston-The Woodlands-Sugar Land, TX Metropolitan Statistical Area—see Appendix B for areas included
Source: National Association of Realtors, Qualifying Income Based on Median Sales Price of Existing Single-Family Homes for Metropolitan Areas, 4th Quarter 2013

Median Apartment Condo-Coop Home Prices

Area	2011	2012	2013p	Percent Change 2012 to 2013
MSA[1]	123.5	134.6	142.0	5.5
U.S. Average	165.1	173.7	194.9	12.2

Note: Figures are median sales prices of existing apartment condo-coop homes in thousands of dollars; (p) preliminary; n/a not available; (1) Houston-The Woodlands-Sugar Land, TX Metropolitan Statistical Area—see Appendix B for areas included
Source: National Association of Realtors, Median Sales Price of Existing Apartment Condo-Coop Homes for Metropolitan Areas, 4th Quarter 2013

Gross Monthly Rent

Area	Under $200	$200 -299	$300 -499	$500 -749	$750 -999	$1,000 -1,499	$1,500 and up	Median ($)
City	1.0	1.3	5.3	31.5	29.5	22.8	8.7	830
MSA[1]	0.8	1.3	4.8	26.9	29.7	26.2	10.1	876
U.S.	1.7	3.3	8.1	22.7	24.3	25.7	14.3	889

Note: Figures are percentages except for Median; Gross rent is the contract rent plus the estimated average monthly cost of utilities (electricity, gas, and water and sewer) and fuels (oil, coal, kerosene, wood, etc.) if these are paid by the renter (or paid for the renter by someone else); (1) Figures cover the Houston-The Woodlands-Sugar Land, TX Metropolitan Statistical Area—see Appendix B for areas included
Source: U.S. Census Bureau, 2010-2012 American Community Survey 3-Year Estimates

Year Housing Structure Built

Area	2010 or Later	2000 -2009	1990 -1999	1980 -1989	1970 -1979	1960 -1969	1950 -1959	1940 -1949	Before 1940	Median Year
City	0.7	15.7	8.9	13.9	25.2	14.9	11.2	5.0	4.5	1976
MSA[1]	1.2	25.3	14.4	16.5	20.2	9.6	6.9	3.0	2.8	1985
U.S.	0.5	14.9	13.8	13.9	15.9	11.1	10.9	5.5	13.5	1976

Note: Figures are percentages except for Median Year; (1) Figures cover the Houston-The Woodlands-Sugar Land, TX Metropolitan Statistical Area—see Appendix B for areas included
Source: U.S. Census Bureau, 2010-2012 American Community Survey 3-Year Estimates

HEALTH

Health Risk Data

Category	MSA[1] (%)	U.S. (%)
Adults aged 18–64 who have any kind of health care coverage	64.1	79.6
Adults who reported being in good or excellent health	80.9	83.1
Adults who are current smokers	16.6	19.6
Adults who are heavy drinkers[2]	5.6	6.1
Adults who are binge drinkers[3]	15.1	16.9
Adults who are overweight (BMI 25.0 - 29.9)	35.9	35.8
Adults who are obese (BMI 30.0 - 99.8)	26.6	27.6
Adults who participated in any physical activities in the past month	73.0	77.1
Adults 50+ who have ever had a sigmoidoscopy or colonoscopy	65.1	67.3
Women aged 40+ who have had a mammogram within the past two years	69.1	74.0
Men aged 40+ who have had a PSA test within the past two years	41.9	45.2
Adults aged 65+ who have had flu shot within the past year	61.7	60.1
Adults who always wear a seatbelt	97.0	93.8

Note: Data as of 2012 unless otherwise noted; (1) Figures cover the Houston-Sugar Land-Baytown, TX Metropolitan Statistical Area—see Appendix B for areas included; (2) Heavy drinkers are classified as males having more than two drinks per day or females having more than one drink per day; (3) Binge drinkers are classified as males having five or more drinks on one occasion or females having four or more drinks on one occasion
Source: Centers for Disease Control and Prevention, Behaviorial Risk Factor Surveillance System, SMART: Selected Metropolitan/Micropolitan Area Risk Trends, 2012

Chronic Health Indicators

Category	MSA[1] (%)	U.S. (%)
Adults who have ever been told they had a heart attack	3.0	4.5
Adults who have ever been told they had a stroke	2.7	2.9
Adults who have been told they currently have asthma	5.1	8.9
Adults who have ever been told they have arthritis	19.5	25.7
Adults who have ever been told they have diabetes[2]	10.5	9.7
Adults who have ever been told they had skin cancer	4.5	5.7
Adults who have ever been told they had any other types of cancer	4.9	6.5
Adults who have ever been told they have COPD	5.0	6.2
Adults who have ever been told they have kidney disease	2.2	2.5
Adults who have ever been told they have a form of depression	15.6	18.0

Note: Data as of 2012 unless otherwise noted; (1) Figures cover the Houston-Sugar Land-Baytown, TX Metropolitan Statistical Area—see Appendix B for areas included; (2) Figures do not include pregnancy-related, borderline, or pre-diabetes
Source: Centers for Disease Control and Prevention, Behaviorial Risk Factor Surveillance System, SMART: Selected Metropolitan/Micropolitan Area Risk Trends, 2012

Mortality Rates for the Top 10 Causes of Death in the U.S.

ICD-10[a] Sub-Chapter	ICD-10[a] Code	Age-Adjusted Mortality Rate[1] per 100,000 population	
		County[2]	U.S.
Malignant neoplasms	C00-C97	165.1	174.2
Ischaemic heart diseases	I20-I25	112.3	119.1
Other forms of heart disease	I30-I51	51.9	49.6
Chronic lower respiratory diseases	J40-J47	34.0	43.2
Cerebrovascular diseases	I60-I69	46.0	40.3
Organic, including symptomatic, mental disorders	F01-F09	37.9	30.5
Other degenerative diseases of the nervous system	G30-G31	20.6	26.3
Other external causes of accidental injury	W00-X59	24.7	25.1
Diabetes mellitus	E10-E14	21.9	21.3
Hypertensive diseases	I10-I15	20.8	18.8

Note: (a) ICD-10 = International Classification of Diseases 10th Revision; (1) Mortality rates are a three year average covering 2008-2010; (2) Figures cover Harris County
Source: Centers for Disease Control and Prevention, National Center for Health Statistics. Compressed Mortality File 1999-2010 on CDC WONDER Online Database, released January 2013. Data are compiled from the Compressed Mortality File 1999-2010, Series 20 No. 2P, 2013.

Mortality Rates for Selected Causes of Death

ICD-10[a] Sub-Chapter	ICD-10[a] Code	Age-Adjusted Mortality Rate[1] per 100,000 population	
		County[2]	U.S.
Assault	X85-Y09	9.6	5.5
Diseases of the liver	K70-K76	13.9	12.4
Human immunodeficiency virus (HIV) disease	B20-B24	6.5	3.0
Influenza and pneumonia	J09-J18	15.3	16.4
Intentional self-harm	X60-X84	11.0	11.8
Malnutrition	E40-E46	1.8	0.8
Obesity and other hyperalimentation	E65-E68	1.4	1.6
Renal failure	N17-N19	18.3	13.6
Transport accidents	V01-V99	12.1	12.6
Viral hepatitis	B15-B19	2.2	2.2

Note: (a) ICD-10 = International Classification of Diseases 10th Revision; (1) Mortality rates are a three year average covering 2008-2010; (2) Figures cover Harris County
Source: Centers for Disease Control and Prevention, National Center for Health Statistics. Compressed Mortality File 1999-2010 on CDC WONDER Online Database, released January 2013. Data are compiled from the Compressed Mortality File 1999-2010, Series 20 No. 2P, 2013.

Health Insurance Coverage

Area	With Health Insurance	With Private Health Insurance	With Public Health Insurance	Without Health Insurance	Population Under Age 18 Without Health Insurance
City	70.5	46.4	30.0	29.5	16.7
MSA[1]	75.7	57.0	25.0	24.3	14.4
U.S.	84.9	65.4	30.4	15.1	7.5

Note: Figures are percentages that cover the civilian noninstitutionalized population; (1) Figures cover the Houston-The Woodlands-Sugar Land, TX Metropolitan Statistical Area—see Appendix B for areas included
Source: U.S. Census Bureau, 2010-2012 American Community Survey 3-Year Estimates

Number of Medical Professionals

Area[1]	MDs[2]	DOs[2,3]	Dentists	Podiatrists	Chiropractors	Optometrists
Local (number)	12,354	379	2,548	190	869	719
Local (rate[4])	295.8	9.1	59.9	4.5	20.4	16.9
U.S. (rate[4])	267.6	19.6	61.7	5.6	24.7	14.5

Note: Data as of 2012 unless noted; (1) Local data covers Harris County; (2) Data as of 2011; (3) Doctor of Osteopathic Medicine; (4) rate per 100,000 population
Source: Area Resource File (ARF) 2012-2013. U.S. Department of Health and Human Services, Health Resources and Services Administration, Bureau of Health Professions

Best Hospitals

According to *U.S. News,* the Houston-The Woodlands-Sugar Land, TX metro area is home to five of the best hospitals in the U.S.: **Memorial Hermann-Texas Medical Center** (1 specialty); **Menninger Clinic** (1 specialty); **Houston Methodist Hospital** (12 specialties); **St. Luke's Episcopal Hospital** (4 specialties); **University of Texas M.D. Anderson Cancer Center** (4 specialty). The hospitals listed were nationally ranked in at least one adult specialty. Only 147 hospitals nationwide were nationally ranked in one or more specialties. Eighteen hospitals in the U.S. made the Honor Roll by ranking near the top in at least six specialties.*U.S. News Online, "America's Best Hospitals 2013-14"*

According to *U.S. News,* the Houston-The Woodlands-Sugar Land, TX metro area is home to three of the best children's hospitals in the U.S.: **Children's Cancer Hospital-Univ. of Texas M.D. Anderson Cancer Center; Children's Memorial Hermann Hospital; Texas Children's Hospital** (Honor Roll). The hospitals listed were highly ranked in at least one pediatric specialty. Eighty-seven hospitals in the U.S. ranked in at least one specialty. Ten children's hospitals in the U.S. made the Honor Roll by ranking near the top in three or more specialties.*U.S. News Online, "America's Best Children's Hospitals 2013-14"*

EDUCATION

Public School District Statistics

District Name	Schls	Pupils	Pupil/ Teacher Ratio	Minority Pupils[1] (%)	Free Lunch Eligible[2] (%)	IEP[3] (%)
Aldine ISD	75	64,300	17.0	97.9	77.6	7.0
Alief ISD	46	45,410	15.3	96.4	73.3	7.3
Cypress-Fairbanks ISD	83	107,960	17.3	70.0	40.0	7.3
Galena Park ISD	24	21,861	14.6	94.3	70.4	8.7
Harmony School of Excellence	6	3,325	16.6	81.4	34.7	2.9
Harmony Science Academy	6	3,116	14.3	83.8	49.2	2.9
Houston ISD	281	203,066	18.6	91.9	37.8	7.8
Kipp Inc Charter	15	5,827	18.1	98.9	82.5	3.4
North Forest ISD	13	6,938	16.5	n/a	99.5	8.6
Sheldon ISD	12	7,159	15.7	87.2	68.6	6.2
Spring Branch ISD	49	33,687	15.5	71.8	53.5	7.9
Spring ISD	41	36,513	17.5	87.1	63.5	8.3
Yes Prep Public Schools Inc	9	5,028	16.7	n/a	47.1	5.2

Note: Table includes school districts with 2,000 or more students; (1) Percentage of students that are not non-Hispanic white; (2) Percentage of students that are eligible for the free lunch program; (3) Percentage of students that have an Individualized Education Program.
Source: U.S. Department of Education, National Center for Education Statistics, Common Core of Data, Local Education Agency (School District) Universe Survey: School Year 2011-2012; U.S. Department of Education, National Center for Education Statistics, Common Core of Data, Public Elementary/Secondary School Universe Survey: School Year 2011-2012

Best High Schools

High School Name	Rank[1]	Grad. Rate[2] (%)	Coll.[3] (%)	AP/IB/ AICE Tests[4]	AP/IB/ AICE Score[5]	SAT Score[6]	ACT Score[6]
Alief Kerr H.S.	1221	100	81	0.5	2.7	1583	23.1
Carnegie Vanguard H.S.	28	100	93	1.9	3.1	1883	28.2
Challenge H.S.	1646	82	81	0.8	2.2	1486	20.8
Clear Horizons Early College H.S.	201	100	100	0.5	2.7	1756	25.3
Clear Lake H.S.	392	97	94	0.6	3.6	1678	25.4
Cypress Creek H.S.	1197	91	94	0.3	2.8	1505	21.9
Cypress Falls H.S.	1715	92	80	0.2	3.0	1471	21.0
DeBakey H.S.	85	100	93	1.1	3.9	1844	26.3
East Early College H.S.	1169	100	86	0.7	1.9	1423	19.6
Eastwood Academy	1022	100	71	1.4	2.4	1375	19.0
Energized for STEM Academy	434	89	76	3.1	1.0	1339	21.4
H.S. for Law Enforcement and Criminal Justice	1359	98	77	1.2	1.5	1308	19.4
Harmony School of Advancement*	1040	100	100	0.6	3.2	1571	n/a
Harmony Science Academy	414	100	100	0.6	2.9	1469	n/a
KIPP Houston H.S.	601	96	99	0.9	2.0	1603	19.4
Lamar H.S.	1510	93	74	0.6	1.6	1474	23.3
Memorial H.S.	254	94	96	0.7	4.0	1718	26.0
Stratford H.S.	774	94	92	0.7	2.8	1620	24.5
The H.S. for the Performing and Visual Arts	597	100	84	1.0	2.4	1664	24.7
Westchester Academy for International Studies	924	100	70	0.9	2.3	1559	23.4
Westside H.S.	1958	89	64	0.6	2.5	1400	22.0
YES Prep Public Schools - North Central	370	92	100	0.8	3.2	1570	n/a
YES Prep Public Schools - Southeast	849	93	100	0.4	2.7	1563	n/a

Note: (1) Public schools are ranked from 1 to 2,000 based on the following self-reported statistics (with the corresponding weight used in calculating their overall score). Schools that were newly founded and did not have a graduating senior class in 2012 were excluded; (2) Four-year, on-time graduation rate (25%); (3) Percent of 2011 graduates who were accepted to college (25%); (4) AP/IB/AICE tests taken per student (25%); (5) Average AP/IB/AICE exam score (10%); (6) Average SAT and/or ACT score (10%); Percent of students enrolled in at least one AP/IB/AICE course (5%)—data not shown; n/a not available; (*) A correction to this school's data was submitted after the list was tabulated and is therefore not reflected in the ranking order
Source: Newsweek and The Daily Beast, "America's Best High Schools 2013"

Highest Level of Education

Area	Less than H.S.	H.S. Diploma	Some College, No Deg.	Associate Degree	Bachelor's Degree	Master's Degree	Prof. School Degree	Doctorate Degree
City	24.8	22.4	19.3	4.6	18.0	7.0	2.3	1.5
MSA[1]	19.0	23.8	22.0	6.2	19.0	6.8	1.9	1.3
U.S.	14.1	28.3	21.3	7.8	18.0	7.5	1.9	1.2

Note: Figures cover persons age 25 and over; (1) Figures cover the Houston-The Woodlands-Sugar Land, TX Metropolitan Statistical Area—see Appendix B for areas included
Source: U.S. Census Bureau, 2010-2012 American Community Survey 3-Year Estimates

Educational Attainment by Race

Area	High School Graduate or Higher (%)					Bachelor's Degree or Higher (%)				
	Total	White	Black	Asian	Hisp.[2]	Total	White	Black	Asian	Hisp.[2]
City	75.2	75.2	84.4	84.0	51.2	28.9	33.6	19.0	53.4	10.1
MSA[1]	81.0	81.9	87.6	85.1	57.2	29.0	30.3	23.3	50.6	11.6
U.S.	85.9	88.1	82.5	85.5	63.1	28.6	30.0	18.4	50.2	13.4

Note: Figures shown cover persons 25 years old and over; (1) Figures cover the Houston-The Woodlands-Sugar Land, TX Metropolitan Statistical Area—see Appendix B for areas included; (2) People of Hispanic origin can be of any race
Source: U.S. Census Bureau, 2010-2012 American Community Survey 3-Year Estimates

School Enrollment by Grade and Control

Area	Preschool (%)		Kindergarten (%)		Grades 1 - 4 (%)		Grades 5 - 8 (%)		Grades 9 - 12 (%)	
	Public	Private	Public	Private	Public	Private	Public	Private	Public	Private
City	67.0	33.0	92.2	7.8	93.5	6.5	93.7	6.3	93.1	6.9
MSA[1]	57.0	43.0	90.6	9.4	93.8	6.2	94.4	5.6	93.9	6.1
U.S.	56.9	43.1	87.8	12.2	89.9	10.1	90.0	10.0	90.8	9.2

Note: Figures shown cover persons 3 years old and over; (1) Figures cover the Houston-The Woodlands-Sugar Land, TX Metropolitan Statistical Area—see Appendix B for areas included
Source: U.S. Census Bureau, 2010-2012 American Community Survey 3-Year Estimates

Average Salaries of Public School Classroom Teachers

Area	2012-13		2013-14		Percent Change 2012-13 to 2013-14	Percent Change 2003-04 to 2013-14
	Dollars	Rank[1]	Dollars	Rank[1]		
Texas	48,819	35	49,270	35	0.92	21.7
U.S. Average	56,103	–	56,689	–	1.04	21.8

Note: (1) State rank ranges from 1 to 51 where 1 indicates highest salary.
Source: National Education Association, Rankings & Estimates: Rankings of the States 2013 and Estimates of School Statistics 2014, March 2014

Higher Education

Four-Year Colleges			Two-Year Colleges			Medical Schools[1]	Law Schools[2]	Voc/ Tech[3]
Public	Private Non-profit	Private For-profit	Public	Private Non-profit	Private For-profit			
6	8	9	1	3	12	2	3	33

Note: Figures cover institutions located within the city limits and include main campuses only; (1) includes schools accredited by the Liaison Committee on Medical Education and the American Osteopathic Association's Commission on Osteopathic College Accreditation; (2) includes ABA-accredited schools, schools with provisional ABA accreditation, and state accredited schools; (3) includes all schools with programs that are less than 2 years.
Source: National Center for Education Statistics, Integrated Postsecondary Education System (IPEDS), 2012-13; Association of American Medical Colleges, Member List, April 24, 2014; American Osteopathic Association, Member List, April 24, 2014; Law School Admission Council, Official Guide to ABA-Approved Law Schools Online, April 24, 2014; Wikipedia, List of Medical Schools in the United States, April 24, 2014; Wikipedia, List of Law Schools in the United States, April 24, 2014

According to *U.S. News & World Report*, the Houston-The Woodlands-Sugar Land, TX metro area is home to two of the best national universities in the U.S.: **Rice University** (#18); **University of Houston** (#190). The indicators used to capture academic quality fall into a number of categories: assessment by administrators at peer institutions; retention of students; faculty resources; student selectivity; financial resources; alumni giving; high school counselor ratings of colleges; and graduation rate. *U.S. News & World Report*, "America's Best Colleges 2014"

According to *U.S. News & World Report*, the Houston-The Woodlands-Sugar Land, TX metro area is home to one of the top 100 law schools in the U.S.: **University of Houston** (#48). The rankings are based on a weighted average of 12 measures of quality: peer assessment score; assessment score by lawyers/judges; median LSAT scores; median undergrad GPA; acceptance rate; employment rates for graduates; placement success; bar passage rate; faculty resources; expenditures per student; student/faculty ratio; and library resources. *U.S. News & World Report*, "America's Best Graduate Schools, Law, 2014"

According to *U.S. News & World Report*, the Houston-The Woodlands-Sugar Land, TX metro area is home to two of the top 100 business schools in the U.S.: **Rice University (Jones)** (#30); **University of Houston (Bauer)** (#96). The rankings are based on a weighted average of the following nine measures: quality assessment; peer assessment; recruiter assessment; placement success; mean starting salary and bonus; student selectivity; mean GMAT and GRE scores; mean undergraduate GPA; and acceptance rate. *U.S. News & World Report*, "America's Best Graduate Schools, Business, 2014"

PRESIDENTIAL ELECTION

2012 Presidential Election Results

Area	Obama	Romney	Other
Harris County	49.4	49.3	1.3
U.S.	51.0	47.2	1.8

Note: Results are percentages and may not add to 100% due to rounding
Source: Dave Leip's Atlas of U.S. Presidential Elections

EMPLOYERS

Major Employers

Company Name	Industry
Christus Health Gulf Coast	Management consulting services
Conoco Phillips	Petroleum refining
Continental Airlines	Air trans scheduled
Dibellos Dynamic Orthotics & Prosthetics	Surgical appliances and supplies
El Paso E&P Company	Petroleum refining
F Charles Brunicardi MD	Accounting assoc
Grey Wolf	Drilling oil and gas wells
Kellogg Brown &Root	Industrial plant construction
Mustang Engineers and Constructors	Construction management consultant
Philip Industrial Services	Environmental consultant
Philips Petroleum Company	Oil and gas exploration services
Quaker State Corp	Lubricating oils and greases
St Lukes Episcopal Health System	General medical/surgical hospitals
Texas Childrens Hospital	Specialty hosp
The Methodist Hospital	General medical/surgical hospitals
Tracer Industries	Plumbing
Univ of Texas Medical Branch at Galveston	Accident and health ins
University of Houston System	University
University of Texas System	General medical/surgical hospitals
US Dept of Veteran Affairs	Administration of veterans affairs
Veterans Health Administration	Administration of veterans affairs

Note: Companies shown are located within the Houston-The Woodlands-Sugar Land, TX Metropolitan Statistical Area.
Source: Hoovers.com; Wikipedia

Best Companies to Work For

Camden Property Trust; David Weekley Homes; EOG Resources; Hilcorp; Houston Methodist, headquartered in Houston, are among "The 100 Best Companies to Work For." To pick the 100 Best Companies to Work For, *Fortune* partnered with the Great Place to Work Institute. Two hundred fifty seven firms participated in this year's survey. Two-thirds of a company's score is based on the results of the Institute's Trust Index survey, which is sent to a random sample of employees from each company. The questions related to attitudes about management's credibility, job satisfaction, and camaraderie. The other third of the scoring is based on the company's responses to the Institute's Culture Audit, which includes detailed questions about pay and benefit programs, and a series of open-ended questions about hiring practices, internal communication, training, recognition programs, and diversity efforts. Any company that is at least five years old with more than 1,000 U.S. employees is eligible. *Fortune, "The 100 Best Companies to Work For," 2014*

MEI Technologies; The University of Texas MD Anderson Cancer Center, headquartered in Houston, are among the "50 Best Employers for Workers Over 50." Criteria: recruiting practices; opportunities for training, education, and career development; workplace accommodations; alternative work options, such as flexible scheduling, job sharing, and phased retirement; employee health and pension benefits; and retiree benefits. Employers with at least 50 employees based in the U.S. are eligible, including for-profit companies, not-for-profit organizations, and government employers. *AARP, "2013 AARP Best Employers for Workers Over 50"*

LINN Energy; Noah Consulting; Transocean, headquartered in Houston, are among the "100 Best Places to Work in IT." To qualify, companies, both public and private, had to have a minimum of 50 IT employees and were selected based on average salary and bonus increases, the percentage of IT staffers promoted, IT staff turnover rates, training and development programs, and the percentage of women and minorities in IT staff and management positions. In addition,

Computerworld looked at retention efforts, programs for recognizing and rewarding outstanding performances, and benefits such as flextime, elder care and child care, and reimbursement for college tuition and the cost of pursuing technology certifications. *Computerworld, "100 Best Places to Work in IT 2013"*

PUBLIC SAFETY

Crime Rate

Area	All Crimes	Violent Crimes				Property Crimes		
		Murder	Forcible Rape	Robbery	Aggrav. Assault	Burglary	Larceny-Theft	Motor Vehicle Theft
City	5,938.1	10.0	30.5	431.0	521.0	1,223.1	3,122.2	600.3
Suburbs[1]	n/a	3.3	21.0	104.2	196.8	n/a	1,848.3	256.8
Metro[2]	n/a	5.7	24.4	219.9	311.6	n/a	2,299.3	378.4
U.S.	3,246.1	4.7	26.9	112.9	242.3	670.2	1,959.3	229.7

Note: Figures are crimes per 100,000 population; (1) All areas within the metro area that are located outside the city limits; (2) Figures cover the Houston-The Woodlands-Sugar Land, TX Metropolitan Statistical Area—see Appendix B for areas included
Source: FBI Uniform Crime Reports, 2012

Hate Crimes

Area	Number of Quarters Reported	Bias Motivation				
		Race	Religion	Sexual Orientation	Ethnicity	Disability
City	4	4	1	4	4	0
U.S.	4	2,797	1,099	1,135	667	92

Source: Federal Bureau of Investigation, Hate Crime Statistics 2012

Identity Theft Consumer Complaints

Area	Complaints	Complaints per 100,000 Population	Rank[2]
MSA[1]	6,198	104.7	43
U.S.	290,056	91.8	-

Note: (1) Figures cover the Houston-The Woodlands-Sugar Land, TX Metropolitan Statistical Area—see Appendix B for areas included; (2) Rank ranges from 1 to 377 where 1 indicates greatest number of identity theft complaints per 100,000 population
Source: Federal Trade Commission, Consumer Sentinel Network Data Book for January–December 2013

Fraud and Other Consumer Complaints

Area	Complaints	Complaints per 100,000 Population	Rank[2]
MSA[1]	23,984	405.1	109
U.S.	1,811,724	595.2	-

Note: (1) Figures cover the Houston-The Woodlands-Sugar Land, TX Metropolitan Statistical Area—see Appendix B for areas included; (2) Rank ranges from 1 to 377 where 1 indicates greatest number of identity theft complaints per 100,000 population
Source: Federal Trade Commission, Consumer Sentinel Network Data Book for January–December 2013

RECREATION

Culture

Dance[1]	Theatre[1]	Instrumental Music[1]	Vocal Music[1]	Series and Festivals	Museums and Art Galleries[2]	Zoos and Aquariums[3]
7	11	7	4	11	91	2

Note: (1) Number of professional performing groups; (2) Based on organizations with primary SIC code 8412; (3) AZA-accredited
Source: The Grey House Performing Arts Directory, 2013; Association of Zoos & Aquariums, AZA Member Zoos & Aquariums, April 2014; www.AccuLeads.com, May 1, 2014

Professional Sports Teams

Team Name	League	Year Established
Houston Astros	Major League Baseball (MLB)	1962
Houston Dynamo	Major League Soccer (MLS)	2006
Houston Rockets	National Basketball Association (NBA)	1971
Houston Texans	National Football League (NFL)	2002

Note: Includes teams located in the Houston-The Woodlands-Sugar Land, TX Metropolitan Statistical Area.
Source: Wikipedia, Major Professional Sports Teams of the United States and Canada

CLIMATE

Average and Extreme Temperatures

Temperature	Jan	Feb	Mar	Apr	May	Jun	Jul	Aug	Sep	Oct	Nov	Dec	Yr.
Extreme High (°F)	84	91	91	95	97	103	104	107	102	94	89	83	107
Average High (°F)	61	65	73	79	85	91	93	93	89	81	72	65	79
Average Temp. (°F)	51	54	62	69	75	81	83	83	79	70	61	54	69
Average Low (°F)	41	43	51	58	65	71	73	73	68	58	50	43	58
Extreme Low (°F)	12	20	22	31	44	52	62	62	48	32	19	7	7

Note: Figures cover the years 1969-1990
Source: National Climatic Data Center, International Station Meteorological Climate Summary, 9/96

Average Precipitation/Snowfall/Humidity

Precip./Humidity	Jan	Feb	Mar	Apr	May	Jun	Jul	Aug	Sep	Oct	Nov	Dec	Yr.
Avg. Precip. (in.)	3.3	2.7	3.3	3.3	5.6	4.9	3.7	3.7	4.8	4.7	3.7	3.3	46.9
Avg. Snowfall (in.)	Tr	Tr	0	0	0	0	0	0	0	0	Tr	Tr	Tr
Avg. Rel. Hum. 6am (%)	85	86	87	89	91	92	93	93	93	91	89	86	90
Avg. Rel. Hum. 3pm (%)	58	55	54	54	57	56	55	55	57	53	55	57	55

Note: Figures cover the years 1969-1990; Tr = Trace amounts (<0.05 in. of rain; <0.5 in. of snow)
Source: National Climatic Data Center, International Station Meteorological Climate Summary, 9/96

Weather Conditions

Temperature			Daytime Sky			Precipitation		
32°F & below	45°F & below	90°F & above	Clear	Partly cloudy	Cloudy	0.01 inch or more precip.	0.1 inch or more snow/ice	Thunder-storms
21	87	96	83	168	114	101	1	62

Note: Figures are average number of days per year and cover the years 1969-1990
Source: National Climatic Data Center, International Station Meteorological Climate Summary, 9/96

HAZARDOUS WASTE

Superfund Sites

Houston has seven hazardous waste sites on the EPA's Superfund Final National Priorities List: **Crystal Chemical Co.; Geneva Industries/Fuhrmann Energy; Jones Road Ground Water Plume; Many Diversified Interests, Inc.; North Cavalcade Street; Sol Lynn/Industrial Transformers; South Cavalcade Street**. *U.S. Environmental Protection Agency, Final National Priorities List, April 26, 2014*

AIR & WATER QUALITY

Air Quality Index

Area	Percent of Days when Air Quality was...[2]					AQI Statistics[2]	
	Good	Moderate	Unhealthy for Sensitive Groups	Unhealthy	Very Unhealthy	Maximum	Median
MSA[1]	46.8	47.9	4.9	0.3	0.0	172	52

Note: (1) Data covers the Houston-The Woodlands-Sugar Land, TX Metropolitan Statistical Area—see Appendix B for areas included; (2) Based on 365 days with AQI data in 2013. Air Quality Index (AQI) is an index for reporting daily air quality. EPA calculates the AQI for five major air pollutants regulated by the Clean Air Act: ground-level ozone, particle pollution (aka particulate matter), carbon monoxide, sulfur dioxide, and nitrogen dioxide. The AQI runs from 0 to 500. The higher the AQI value, the greater the level of air pollution and the greater the health concern. There are six AQI categories: "Good" AQI is between 0 and 50. Air quality is considered satisfactory; "Moderate" AQI is between 51 and 100. Air quality is acceptable; "Unhealthy for Sensitive Groups" When AQI values are between 101 and 150, members of sensitive groups may experience health effects; "Unhealthy" When AQI values are between 151 and 200 everyone may begin to experience health effects; "Very Unhealthy" AQI values between 201 and 300 trigger a health alert; "Hazardous" AQI values over 300 trigger warnings of emergency conditions (not shown).
Source: U.S. Environmental Protection Agency, Air Quality Index Report, 2013

Air Quality Index Pollutants

Area	Percent of Days when AQI Pollutant was...[2]					
	Carbon Monoxide	Nitrogen Dioxide	Ozone	Sulfur Dioxide	Particulate Matter 2.5	Particulate Matter 10
MSA[1]	0.0	6.8	26.6	1.6	63.8	1.1

Note: (1) Data covers the Houston-The Woodlands-Sugar Land, TX Metropolitan Statistical Area—see Appendix B for areas included; (2) Based on 365 days with AQI data in 2013. The Air Quality Index (AQI) is an index for reporting daily air quality. EPA calculates the AQI for five major air pollutants regulated by the Clean Air Act: ground-level ozone, particle pollution (also known as particulate matter), carbon monoxide, sulfur dioxide, and nitrogen dioxide. The AQI runs from 0 to 500. The higher the AQI value, the greater the level of air pollution and the greater the health concern.
Source: U.S. Environmental Protection Agency, Air Quality Index Report, 2013

Air Quality Trends: Ozone

	2003	2004	2005	2006	2007	2008	2009	2010	2011	2012
MSA[1]	0.097	0.092	0.087	0.090	0.079	0.074	0.079	0.078	0.082	0.081

Note: (1) Data covers the Houston-The Woodlands-Sugar Land, TX Metropolitan Statistical Area—see Appendix B for areas included. The values shown are the composite ozone concentration averages among trend sites based on the highest fourth daily maximum 8-hour concentration in parts per million. These trends are based on sites having an adequate record of monitoring data during the trend period. Data from exceptional events are included.
Source: U.S. Environmental Protection Agency, Air Quality Monitoring Information, "Air Quality Trends by City, 2000-2012"

Maximum Air Pollutant Concentrations: Particulate Matter, Ozone, CO and Lead

	Particulate Matter 10 (ug/m^3)	Particulate Matter 2.5 Wtd AM (ug/m^3)	Particulate Matter 2.5 24-Hr (ug/m^3)	Ozone (ppm)	Carbon Monoxide (ppm)	Lead (ug/m^3)
MSA[1] Level	128	11.8	26	0.087	2	0.01
NAAQS[2]	150	15	35	0.075	9	0.15
Met NAAQS[2]	Yes	Yes	Yes	No	Yes	Yes

Note: (1) Data covers the Houston-The Woodlands-Sugar Land, TX Metropolitan Statistical Area—see Appendix B for areas included; Data from exceptional events are included; (2) National Ambient Air Quality Standards; ppm = parts per million; ug/m^3 = micrograms per cubic meter; n/a not available.
Concentrations: Particulate Matter 10 (coarse particulate)—highest second maximum 24-hour concentration; Particulate Matter 2.5 Wtd AM (fine particulate)—highest weighted annual mean concentration; Particulate Matter 2.5 24-Hour (fine particulate)—highest 98th percentile 24-hour concentration; Ozone—highest fourth daily maximum 8-hour concentration; Carbon Monoxide—highest second maximum non-overlapping 8-hour concentration; Lead—maximum running 3-month average
Source: U.S. Environmental Protection Agency, Air Quality Monitoring Information, "Air Quality Statistics by City, 2012"

Maximum Air Pollutant Concentrations: Nitrogen Dioxide and Sulfur Dioxide

	Nitrogen Dioxide AM (ppb)	Nitrogen Dioxide 1-Hr (ppb)	Sulfur Dioxide AM (ppb)	Sulfur Dioxide 1-Hr (ppb)	Sulfur Dioxide 24-Hr (ppb)
MSA[1] Level	15	60	n/a	29	n/a
NAAQS[2]	53	100	30	75	140
Met NAAQS[2]	Yes	Yes	n/a	Yes	n/a

Note: (1) Data covers the Houston-The Woodlands-Sugar Land, TX Metropolitan Statistical Area—see Appendix B for areas included; Data from exceptional events are included; (2) National Ambient Air Quality Standards; ppm = parts per million; ug/m³ = micrograms per cubic meter; n/a not available.
Concentrations: Nitrogen Dioxide AM—highest arithmetic mean concentration; Nitrogen Dioxide 1-Hr—highest 98th percentile 1-hour daily maximum concentration; Sulfur Dioxide AM—highest annual mean concentration; Sulfur Dioxide 1-Hr—highest 99th percentile 1-hour daily maximum concentration; Sulfur Dioxide 24-Hr—highest second maximum 24-hour concentration
Source: U.S. Environmental Protection Agency, Air Quality Monitoring Information, "Air Quality Statistics by City, 2012"

Drinking Water

Water System Name	Pop. Served	Primary Water Source Type	Violations[1] Health Based	Violations[1] Monitoring/ Reporting
City of Houston	2,099,000	Surface	0	5

Note: (1) Based on violation data from January 1, 2013 to December 31, 2013 (includes unresolved violations from earlier years)
Source: U.S. Environmental Protection Agency, Office of Ground Water and Drinking Water, Safe Drinking Water Information System (based on data extracted February 10, 2014)

Huntsville, Alabama

Background

The seat of Madison County, Huntsville is richly evocative of the antebellum Deep South. It is also a uniquely cosmopolitan town that remains one of the South's fastest growing, with the highest per capita income in the Southeast.

Huntsville became the seat of Madison County, named for President James Madison, when that jurisdiction was created in 1808. Originally home to Cherokee and Chickasaw Indians, the Huntsville area was rich in forests and game animals. The town itself is named for John Hunt, a Virginia Revolutionary War veteran who built a cabin in 1805 on what is now the corner of Bank Street and Oak Avenue.

The fertility of the valley began to attract both smaller farmers and wealthy plantation investors. Leroy Pope, having donated land to the embryonic municipality, wished to rename it Twickenham, after a London suburb that was home to his relative, the poet Alexander Pope. However, resentment against all things British, which surged following the War of 1812, was sufficient to reestablish Huntsville under its original moniker.

Huntsville was the largest town in the Alabama Territory by 1819, the same year Alabama received statehood. The town was the site of the state's first constitutional convention and briefly served as the state capital. It quickly became a major hub for the sale and processing of corn, tobacco, and cotton, with the last crop becoming the economic mainstay. The establishment of textile mills allowed the town to benefit from both primary production and finished products. In 1852, the last leg of the Memphis and Charleston Railway was completed, establishing Huntsville as a major center in a larger regional marketplace. By the middle of the nineteenth century, the region's planters, merchants, and shippers had transformed Huntsville into one of the main commercial cities in the South.

Because many wealthy residents had remained loyal to the Union at the outset of the Civil War, the town was largely undamaged by occupying forces and, as a result, Huntsville boasts one of the largest collections of undamaged antebellum houses in the South. Walking tours of the Twickenham historic district offer the charms of the 1819 Weeden House Museum and the 1860 Huntsville Depot Museum. Restored nineteenth-century cabins and farm buildings are displayed at the mountaintop Burritt Museum and Park.

Huntsville's U.S. Space and Rocket Center, the state's largest tourist attraction, showcases space technology. It is also the home of Space Camp, providing residential and day camp educational opportunities for children and adults designed to promote science, engineering, aviation and exploration. The Huntsville Botanical Garden, features year-long floral and aquatic gardens, and the Huntsville Museum of Art features both contemporary and classical exhibits.

The city's modern Von Braun Center hosts national and international trade shows and conventions and local sports teams; it also has a concert hall and playhouse. The city also has an outstanding symphony orchestra.

Institutions of higher learning include the University of Alabama in Huntsville (established 1950), and Oakwood College (1896), while Alabama A&M University (1875) is in nearby Normal, Alabama.

Redstone Arsenal, home to the U.S. Army Aviation and Missile Command, is the main engine that propelled Huntsville into the high-tech hub it is today, and is the United States' most crucial strategic and research site for the development and implementation of rocketry, aviation, and related programs. In 1950, German rocket scientists, most notably the famous Wernher von Braun, came to the Redstone Arsenal to develop rockets for the U.S. Army. Within the decade, the Redstone complex had developed the rocket that launched America's first satellite into space, and later, the rockets that put astronauts into space and eventually landed them on the moon.

Despite the economic downturn of the early 1990s, Huntsville has seen progress on the manufacturing front. More than forty Fortune 500 companies have operations in Huntsville.

Huntsville enjoys a mild, temperate climate. Only four to five weeks during the middle of winter see temperatures below freezing. While substantial winter weather and blizzards were frequent in the 1990s, Huntsville has now gone over 13 years without significant snowfall. Rainfall is fairly abundant.

Rankings

General Rankings

- Huntsville appeared on RelocateAmerica's list of best places to live in America. The annual "Top 100 Places to Live" list recognizes the top communities as nominated by their residents & local businesses. RelocateAmerica's Research Group determined the list based on review of various data gathered for economic, employment, housing, education, industry, opportunity, environment and recreation along with feedback from area leaders and residents. *RelocateAmerica.com, "Top 100 Places to Live for 2011"*

- Huntsville was selected as one of the "Best Places to Live" by *Men's Journal*. Criteria: "18 towns were selected that are perfecting the art of living well—places where conservation is more important than development, bike makers and breweries and farmers thrive, and Whole Foods is considered a big-box store." *Men's Journal, "Best Place to Live 2011: Think Small, Live Big," April 2011*

Business/Finance Rankings

- The Huntsville metro area appeared on the Milken Institute "2013 Best Performing Cities" list. Rank: #101 out of 200 large metro areas. Criteria: job growth; wage and salary growth; high-tech output growth. *Milken Institute, "Best-Performing Cities 2013," December 2013*

- *Forbes* ranked the 200 most populous metro areas in the U.S. in terms of the "Best Places for Business and Careers." The Huntsville metro area was ranked #62. Criteria: costs (business and living); job growth (past and projected); income growth; educational attainment (college and high school); projected economic growth; cultural and recreational opportunities; net migration patterns; number of highly ranked colleges. *Forbes, "The Best Places for Business and Careers," August 7, 2013*

Education Rankings

- Huntsville was selected as one of "America's Geekiest Cities" by *Forbes.com*. The city ranked #4 of 20. Criteria: percentage of workers with jobs in science, technology, engineering and mathematics. *Forbes.com, "America's Geekiest Cities," August 5, 2011*

Environmental Rankings

- The Huntsville metro area came in at #258 for the relative comfort of its climate on Sperling's list of "chill cities," as measured by the Sperling Heat Index. All 361 metro areas are included. Criteria included daytime high temperatures, nighttime low temperatures, dew point, and relative humidity at the high temperatures. *www.bertsperling.com, "Sperling's Chill Cities," July 18, 2013*

- Sperling's BestPlaces assessed 379 metropolitan areas of the United States for the likelihood of dangerously extreme weather events or earthquakes. In general the Southeast and South-Central regions have the highest risk of weather extremes and earthquakes, while the Pacific Northwest enjoys the lowest risk. Of the least risky metropolitan areas, the Huntsville metro area was ranked #351. *www.bestplaces.net, "Safest Places from Natural Disasters," April 2011*

- Huntsville was selected as one of 22 "Smarter Cities" for energy by the Natural Resources Defense Council. Criteria: investment in green power; energy efficiency measures; conservation. *Natural Resources Defense Council, "2010 Smarter Cities," July 19, 2010*

- Huntsville was highlighted as one of the top 25 cleanest metro areas for short-term particle pollution (24-hour PM 2.5) in the U.S. during 2008 through 2010. Monitors in these cities reported no days with unhealthful PM 2.5 levels. *American Lung Association, State of the Air 2012*

Health/Fitness Rankings

- The Huntsville metro area appeared in the 2013 Gallup-Healthways Well-Being Index. The area ranked #81 out of 189. The Gallup-Healthways Well-Being Index score is an average of six sub-indexes, which individually examine life evaluation, emotional health, work environment, physical health, healthy behaviors, and access to basic necessities. Results are based on telephone interviews conducted as part of the Gallup-Healthways Well-Being Index survey January 2–December 29, 2012, and January 2–December 30, 2013, with a random sample of 531,630 adults, aged 18 and older, living in metropolitan areas in the 50 U.S. states and the District of Columbia. *Gallup-Healthways, "State of American Well-Being," March 25, 2014*

Real Estate Rankings

- Huntsville was ranked #275 out of 283 metro areas in terms of house price appreciation in 2013 (#1 = highest rate). *Federal Housing Finance Agency, House Price Index, 4th Quarter 2013*

- The Huntsville metro area was identified as one of the 20 worst housing markets in the U.S. in 2013. The area ranked #20 out of 173 markets with a home price appreciation of -4.1%. Criteria: year-over-year change of median sales price of existing single-family homes between the 4th quarter of 2012 and the 4th quarter of 2013. *National Association of Realtors®, Median Sales Price of Existing Single-Family Homes for Metropolitan Areas, 4th Quarter 2013*

Safety Rankings

- Allstate ranked the 200 largest cities in America in terms of driver safety. Huntsville ranked #7. Allstate researchers analyzed internal property damage claims over a two-year period from January 2010 to December 2011. A weighted average of the two-year numbers determined the annual percentages. *Allstate, "Allstate America's Best Drivers Report®, August 27, 2013"*

- The National Insurance Crime Bureau ranked 380 metro areas in the U.S. in terms of per capita rates of vehicle theft. The Huntsville metro area ranked #185 (#1 = highest rate). Criteria: number of vehicle theft offenses per 100,000 inhabitants in 2012. *National Insurance Crime Bureau, "Hot Spots 2012," June 26, 2013*

Seniors/Retirement Rankings

- From its Best Cities for Successful Aging indexes, the Milken Institute generated rankings for metropolitan areas, weighing data in eight categories—general indicators, health care, wellness, living arrangements, transportation and general accessibility, financial well-being, education and employment, and community participation. The Huntsville metro area was ranked #152 overall in the small metro area category. *Milken Institute, "Best Cities for Successful Aging," July 2012*

- Huntsville was chosen in the "College Town" category of CNNMoney's list of the 25 best places to retire." Criteria include: type of location (big city, small town, resort area, college town); median home prices; top state income tax rate. *CNNMoney, "25 Best Places to Retire," December 17, 2012*

- Huntsville was selected as one of the best places to retire by *CNNMoney.com*. Criteria: low cost of living; low violent-crime rate; good medical care; large population over age 50; abundant amenities for retirees. *CNNMoney.com, "Best Places to Retire 2011"*

Sports/Recreation Rankings

- Huntsville appeared on the *Sporting News* list of the "Best Sports Cities" for 2011. The area ranked #255 out of 271. Criteria: the magazine takes a 12-month snapshot of each city's sports, putting a heavy premium on regular-season won-lost records (from the most recently completed season). Other criteria include: playoff berths, bowl appearances and tournament bids; championships; applicable power ratings; quality of competition; overall fan fervor (measured in part by attendance); abundance of teams (rewarding quality over quantity); stadium and arena quality; ticket availability and prices; franchise ownership; and marquee appeal of athletes. *Sporting News, "Best Sports Cities 2011," October 4, 2011*

- Huntsville appeared on the *Sporting News* list of the "Best Sports Cities" for 2011. The area ranked #255 out of 271. Criteria: a 12-month snapshot of regular-season won-lost records (from the most recently completed season). Other criteria include: playoff berths, bowl appearances and tournament bids; championships; applicable power ratings; quality of competition; overall fan fervor (measured in part by attendance); abundance of teams (quality over quantity); stadium and arena quality; ticket availability and prices; franchise ownership; and marquee appeal of athletes. *Sporting News, "Best Sports Cities 2011," October 4, 2011*

- Huntsville was selected as one of the most playful cities in the U.S. by KaBOOM! The organization's Playful City USA initiative honors cities and towns across the nation for a vision, plan and commitment to creating an agenda for play. Criteria: creating a local play commission or task force; designing an annual action plan for play; conducting a play space audit; outlining a financial investment in play for the current fiscal year; and proclaiming and celebrating an annual "play day." *KaBOOM! National Campaign for Play, "2013 Playful City USA Communities"*

Business Environment

CITY FINANCES

City Government Finances

Component	2011 ($000)	2011 ($ per capita)
Total Revenues	869,139	5,073
Total Expenditures	865,208	5,050
Debt Outstanding	748,132	4,367
Cash and Securities[1]	444,590	2,595

Note: (1) Cash and security holdings of a government at the close of its fiscal year, including those of its dependent agencies, utilities, and liquor stores.
Source: U.S Census Bureau, State & Local Government Finances 2011

City Government Revenue by Source

Source	2011 ($000)	2011 ($ per capita)
General Revenue		
From Federal Government	1,366	8
From State Government	20,700	121
From Local Governments	0	0
Taxes		
Property	57,285	334
Sales and Gross Receipts	153,372	895
Personal Income	0	0
Corporate Income	0	0
Motor Vehicle License	0	0
Other Taxes	3,643	21
Current Charges	55,388	323
Liquor Store	0	0
Utility	545,058	3,181
Employee Retirement	0	0

Source: U.S Census Bureau, State & Local Government Finances 2011

City Government Expenditures by Function

Function	2011 ($000)	2011 ($ per capita)	2011 (%)
General Direct Expenditures			
Air Transportation	0	0	0.0
Corrections	0	0	0.0
Education	15,062	88	1.7
Employment Security Administration	0	0	0.0
Financial Administration	9,051	53	1.0
Fire Protection	28,602	167	3.3
General Public Buildings	0	0	0.0
Governmental Administration, Other	9,177	54	1.1
Health	2,476	14	0.3
Highways	20,491	120	2.4
Hospitals	0	0	0.0
Housing and Community Development	7,948	46	0.9
Interest on General Debt	20,727	121	2.4
Judicial and Legal	1,626	9	0.2
Libraries	5,786	34	0.7
Parking	1,605	9	0.2
Parks and Recreation	21,347	125	2.5
Police Protection	43,915	256	5.1
Public Welfare	530	3	0.1
Sewerage	36,761	215	4.2
Solid Waste Management	0	0	0.0
Veterans' Services	0	0	0.0
Liquor Store	0	0	0.0
Utility	545,235	3,182	63.0
Employee Retirement	0	0	0.0

Source: U.S Census Bureau, State & Local Government Finances 2011

DEMOGRAPHICS

Population Growth

Area	1990 Census	2000 Census	2010 Census	Population Growth (%)	
				1990-2000	2000-2010
City	161,842	158,216	180,105	-2.2	13.8
MSA[1]	293,047	342,376	417,593	16.8	22.0
U.S.	248,709,873	281,421,906	308,745,538	13.2	9.7

Note: (1) Figures cover the Huntsville, AL Metropolitan Statistical Area—see Appendix B for areas included
Source: U.S. Census Bureau, Census 1990, 2000, 2010

Household Size

Area	Persons in Household (%)							Average Household Size
	One	Two	Three	Four	Five	Six	Seven or More	
City	36.7	33.8	13.7	10.2	3.7	1.1	0.6	2.33
MSA[1]	29.4	34.7	15.9	12.7	5.0	1.5	0.8	2.51
U.S.	27.6	33.5	15.7	13.2	6.1	2.4	1.5	2.63

Note: (1) Figures cover the Huntsville, AL Metropolitan Statistical Area—see Appendix B for areas included
Source: U.S. Census Bureau, 2010-2012 American Community Survey 3-Year Estimates

Race

Area	White Alone[2] (%)	Black Alone[2] (%)	Asian Alone[2] (%)	AIAN[3] Alone[2] (%)	NHOPI[4] Alone[2] (%)	Other Race Alone[2] (%)	Two or More Races (%)
City	62.2	31.0	2.3	0.4	0.1	1.0	3.0
MSA[1]	71.6	22.0	2.1	0.7	0.1	1.2	2.5
U.S.	74.0	12.6	4.9	0.8	0.2	4.7	2.8

Note: (1) Figures cover the Huntsville, AL Metropolitan Statistical Area—see Appendix B for areas included; (2) Alone is defined as not being in combination with one or more other races; (3) American Indian and Alaska Native; (4) Native Hawaiian and Other Pacific Islander
Source: U.S. Census Bureau, 2010-2012 American Community Survey 3-Year Estimates

Hispanic or Latino Origin

Area	Total (%)	Mexican (%)	Puerto Rican (%)	Cuban (%)	Other (%)
City	6.0	4.0	0.7	0.1	1.2
MSA[1]	4.9	3.4	0.6	0.1	0.8
U.S.	16.6	10.7	1.6	0.6	3.7

Note: Persons of Hispanic or Latino origin can be of any race; (1) Figures cover the Huntsville, AL Metropolitan Statistical Area—see Appendix B for areas included
Source: U.S. Census Bureau, 2010-2012 American Community Survey 3-Year Estimates

Segregation

Type	Segregation Indices[1]				Percent Change		
	1990	2000	2010	2010 Rank[2]	1990-2000	1990-2010	2000-2010
Black/White	n/a	n/a	n/a	n/a	n/a	n/a	n/a
Asian/White	n/a	n/a	n/a	n/a	n/a	n/a	n/a
Hispanic/White	n/a	n/a	n/a	n/a	n/a	n/a	n/a

Note: All figures cover the Metropolitan Statistical Area—see Appendix B for areas included; Figures are based on an analysis of 1990, 2000, and 2010 Census Decennial Census tract data by William H. Frey, Brookings Institution and the University of Michigan Social Science Data Analysis Network. In this analysis all racial groups (whites, blacks, and asians) are non-Hispanic members of those races. Hispanics are shown as a separate category;
(1) Segregation Indices are Dissimilarity Indices that measure the degree to which the minority group is distributed differently than whites across census tracts. They range from 0 (complete integration) to 100 (complete segregation) where the value indicates the percentage of the minority group that needs to move to be distributed exactly like whites; (2) Ranges from 1 (most segregated) to 102 (least segregated); n/a not available.
Source: www.CensusScope.org

Ancestry

Area	German	Irish	English	American	Italian	Polish	French[2]	Scottish	Dutch
City	9.8	8.4	9.5	10.8	2.5	1.1	2.0	2.6	1.1
MSA[1]	9.5	8.9	9.5	15.8	2.1	1.1	2.1	2.1	1.0
U.S.	15.2	11.1	8.2	7.2	5.6	3.1	2.8	1.7	1.4

Note: Figures are the percentage of the total population reporting a particular ancestry. The nine most commonly reported ancestries in the U.S. are shown. Figures include multiple ancestries (e.g. if a person reported being Irish and Italian, they were included in both columns); (1) Figures cover the Huntsville, AL Metropolitan Statistical Area—see Appendix B for areas included; (2) Excludes Basque
Source: U.S. Census Bureau, 2010-2012 American Community Survey 3-Year Estimates

Foreign-Born Population

Area	Percent of Population Born in								
	Any Foreign Country	Mexico	Asia	Europe	Carribean	South America	Central America[2]	Africa	Canada
City	6.5	1.6	2.0	0.8	0.5	0.2	0.4	0.9	0.1
MSA[1]	5.1	1.4	1.7	0.7	0.3	0.2	0.2	0.4	0.1
U.S.	13.0	3.7	3.7	1.6	1.2	0.9	1.0	0.5	0.3

Note: (1) Figures cover the Huntsville, AL Metropolitan Statistical Area—see Appendix B for areas included; (2) Excludes Mexico.
Source: U.S. Census Bureau, 2010-2012 American Community Survey 3-Year Estimates

Marital Status

Area	Never Married	Now Married[2]	Separated	Widowed	Divorced
City	35.3	42.8	2.4	6.2	13.4
MSA[1]	29.2	51.1	1.9	5.9	11.9
U.S.	32.4	48.4	2.2	6.0	11.0

Note: Figures are percentages and cover the population 15 years of age and older; (1) Figures cover the Huntsville, AL Metropolitan Statistical Area—see Appendix B for areas included; (2) Excludes separated
Source: U.S. Census Bureau, 2010-2012 American Community Survey 3-Year Estimates

Age

Area	Percent of Population									Median Age
	Under Age 5	Age 5–19	Age 20–34	Age 35–44	Age 45–54	Age 55–64	Age 65–74	Age 75–84	Age 85+	
City	6.1	18.8	23.0	12.1	14.9	11.1	7.6	4.4	2.0	36.6
MSA[1]	6.2	19.9	20.3	13.3	15.9	11.9	7.2	3.8	1.5	37.7
U.S.	6.4	20.1	20.5	13.1	14.3	12.2	7.3	4.2	1.8	37.3

Note: (1) Figures cover the Huntsville, AL Metropolitan Statistical Area—see Appendix B for areas included
Source: U.S. Census Bureau, 2010-2012 American Community Survey 3-Year Estimates

Gender

Area	Males	Females	Males per 100 Females
City	88,848	92,886	95.7
MSA[1]	210,052	215,057	97.7
U.S.	153,276,055	158,333,314	96.8

Note: (1) Figures cover the Huntsville, AL Metropolitan Statistical Area—see Appendix B for areas included
Source: U.S. Census Bureau, 2010-2012 American Community Survey 3-Year Estimates

Religious Groups by Family

Area	Catholic	Baptist	Non-Den.	Methodist[2]	Lutheran	LDS[3]	Pentecostal	Presbyterian[4]	Muslim[5]	Judaism
MSA[1]	4.0	27.6	3.2	7.5	0.7	1.2	1.2	1.7	0.2	0.2
U.S.	19.1	9.3	4.0	4.0	2.3	2.0	1.9	1.6	0.8	0.7

Note: Figures are the number of adherents as a percentage of the total population; (1) Figures cover the Huntsville, AL Metropolitan Statistical Area—see Appendix B for areas included; (2) Methodist/Pietist; (3) Latter Day Saints; (4) Reformed; (5) Figures are estimates
Source: Association of Statisticians of American Religious Bodies, 2010 U.S. Religion Census: Religious Congregations & Membership Study

Religious Groups by Tradition

Area	Catholic	Evangelical Protestant	Mainline Protestant	Other Tradition	Black Protestant	Orthodox
MSA[1]	4.0	33.3	9.7	1.9	1.8	0.1
U.S.	19.1	16.2	7.3	4.3	1.6	0.3

Note: Figures are the number of adherents as a percentage of the total population; (1) Figures cover the Huntsville, AL Metropolitan Statistical Area—see Appendix B for areas included
Source: Association of Statisticians of American Religious Bodies, 2010 U.S. Religion Census: Religious Congregations & Membership Study

ECONOMY

Gross Metropolitan Product

Area	2011	2012	2013	2014	Rank[2]
MSA[1]	21.4	21.7	21.9	22.8	98

Note: Figures are in billions of dollars; (1) Figures cover the Huntsville, AL Metropolitan Statistical Area—see Appendix B for areas included; (2) Rank is based on 2014 data and ranges from 1 to 363
Source: The United States Conference of Mayors, U.S. Metro Economies: Outlook—Gross Metropolitan Product, with Metro Employment Projections, November 2013

Economic Growth

Area	2011 (%)	2012 (%)	2013 (%)	2014 (%)	Rank[2]
MSA[1]	0.8	-0.1	-0.2	2.1	270
U.S.	1.6	2.5	1.7	2.5	–

Note: Figures are real gross metropolitan product (GMP) growth rates and represent annual average percent change; (1) Figures cover the Huntsville, AL Metropolitan Statistical Area—see Appendix B for areas included; (2) Rank is based on 2013 data and ranges from 1 to 363
Source: The United States Conference of Mayors, U.S. Metro Economies: Outlook—Gross Metropolitan Product, with Metro Employment Projections, November 2013

Metropolitan Area Exports

Area	2007	2008	2009	2010	2011	2012	Rank[2]
MSA[1]	1,052.8	1,079.3	1,136.5	986.8	1,293.3	1,491.5	124

Note: Figures are in millions of dollars; (1) Figures cover the Huntsville, AL Metropolitan Statistical Area—see Appendix B for areas included; (2) Rank is based on 2012 data and ranges from 1 to 369
Source: U.S. Department of Commerce, International Trade Administration, Office of Trade & Industry Information, Manufacturing & Services, data extracted April 1, 2014

INCOME

Income

Area	Per Capita ($)	Median Household ($)	Average Household ($)
City	29,484	46,821	68,794
MSA[1]	29,599	54,407	74,576
U.S.	27,385	51,771	71,579

Note: (1) Figures cover the Huntsville, AL Metropolitan Statistical Area—see Appendix B for areas included
Source: U.S. Census Bureau, 2010-2012 American Community Survey 3-Year Estimates

Household Income Distribution

Area	Percent of Households Earning							
	Under $15,000	$15,000 -24,999	$25,000 -34,999	$35,000 -49,999	$50,000 -74,999	$75,000 -99,000	$100,000 -149,999	$150,000 and up
City	16.2	11.7	11.1	13.2	15.8	10.6	12.4	9.1
MSA[1]	12.5	10.3	9.8	13.6	16.5	12.1	14.7	10.4
U.S.	13.1	11.0	10.5	13.7	18.1	11.9	12.5	9.1

Note: (1) Figures cover the Huntsville, AL Metropolitan Statistical Area—see Appendix B for areas included
Source: U.S. Census Bureau, 2010-2012 American Community Survey 3-Year Estimates

Poverty Rate

Area	All Ages	Under 18 Years Old	18 to 64 Years Old	65 Years and Over
City	16.6	24.9	15.8	7.3
MSA[1]	13.0	18.0	12.2	7.3
U.S.	15.7	22.2	14.6	9.3

Note: Figures are percentage of people whose income during the past 12 months was below the poverty level;
(1) Figures cover the Huntsville, AL Metropolitan Statistical Area—see Appendix B for areas included
Source: U.S. Census Bureau, 2010-2012 American Community Survey 3-Year Estimates

Personal Bankruptcy Filing Rate

Area	2008	2009	2010	2011	2012	2013
Madison County	4.45	4.94	5.11	4.78	4.60	4.26
U.S.	3.53	4.61	4.97	4.37	3.76	3.29

Note: Numbers are per 1,000 population and include Chapter 7 and Chapter 13 filings
Source: Federal Deposit Insurance Corporation, Regional Economic Conditions, March 20, 2014

EMPLOYMENT

Labor Force and Employment

Area	Civilian Labor Force			Workers Employed		
	Dec. 2012	Dec. 2013	% Chg.	Dec. 2012	Dec. 2013	% Chg.
City	90,433	88,011	-2.7	85,419	83,636	-2.1
MSA[1]	211,330	205,600	-2.7	199,598	195,434	-2.1
U.S.	154,904,000	154,408,000	-0.3	143,060,000	144,423,000	1.0

Note: Data is not seasonally adjusted and covers workers 16 years of age and older; (1) Metropolitan Statistical Area—see Appendix B for areas included
Source: Bureau of Labor Statistics, Local Area Unemployment Statistics

Unemployment Rate

Area	2013											
	Jan.	Feb.	Mar.	Apr.	May	Jun.	Jul.	Aug.	Sep.	Oct.	Nov.	Dec.
City	6.7	6.9	6.0	5.2	5.6	6.2	5.9	5.9	5.6	5.6	4.9	5.0
MSA[1]	6.6	6.8	5.9	5.2	5.5	5.9	5.6	5.8	5.6	5.6	4.8	4.9
U.S.	8.5	8.1	7.6	7.1	7.3	7.8	7.7	7.3	7.0	7.0	6.6	6.5

Note: Data is not seasonally adjusted and covers workers 16 years of age and older; All figures are percentages;
(1) Metropolitan Statistical Area—see Appendix B for areas included
Source: Bureau of Labor Statistics, Local Area Unemployment Statistics

Employment by Occupation

Occupation Classification	City (%)	MSA[1] (%)	U.S. (%)
Management, Business, Science, and Arts	40.6	41.9	36.0
Natural Resources, Construction, and Maintenance	6.3	7.7	9.1
Production, Transportation, and Material Moving	10.2	11.6	12.0
Sales and Office	24.9	23.6	24.7
Service	18.0	15.2	18.2

Note: Figures cover employed civilians 16 years of age and older; (1) Figures cover the Huntsville, AL Metropolitan Statistical Area—see Appendix B for areas included
Source: U.S. Census Bureau, 2010-2012 American Community Survey 3-Year Estimates

Employment by Industry

| Sector | MSA[1] | | U.S. |
	Number of Employees	Percent of Total	Percent of Total
Construction	n/a	n/a	4.2
Education and Health Services	19,300	9.0	15.5
Financial Activities	6,300	2.9	5.7
Government	48,900	22.9	16.1
Information	2,700	1.3	1.9
Leisure and Hospitality	18,200	8.5	10.2
Manufacturing	22,800	10.7	8.7
Mining and Logging	n/a	n/a	0.6
Other Services	7,000	3.3	3.9
Professional and Business Services	48,500	22.7	13.7
Retail Trade	23,900	11.2	11.4
Transportation and Utilities	2,800	1.3	3.8
Wholesale Trade	5,800	2.7	4.2

Note: Figures cover non-farm employment as of December 2013 and are not seasonally adjusted;
(1) Metropolitan Statistical Area—see Appendix B for areas included; n/a not available
Source: Bureau of Labor Statistics, Current Employment Statistics, Employment, Hours, and Earnings

Occupations with Greatest Projected Employment Growth: 2010 – 2020

Occupation[1]	2010 Employment	2020 Projected Employment	Numeric Employment Change	Percent Employment Change
Registered Nurses	42,890	55,050	12,160	28.3
Retail Salespersons	56,240	65,530	9,300	16.5
Home Health Aides	11,370	19,230	7,860	69.2
Heavy and Tractor-Trailer Truck Drivers	33,910	40,570	6,660	19.6
Office Clerks, General	36,900	43,290	6,400	17.3
Team Assemblers	27,620	33,900	6,280	22.8
Combined Food Preparation and Serving Workers, Including Fast Food	37,800	43,910	6,110	16.2
Laborers and Freight, Stock, and Material Movers, Hand	34,160	39,010	4,850	14.2
Bookkeeping, Accounting, and Auditing Clerks	29,960	34,360	4,390	14.7
Nursing Aides, Orderlies, and Attendants	22,760	27,110	4,350	19.1

Note: Projections cover Alabama; (1) Sorted by numeric employment change
Source: www.projectionscentral.com, State Occupational Projections, 2010–2020 Long-Term Projections

Fastest Growing Occupations: 2010 – 2020

Occupation[1]	2010 Employment	2020 Projected Employment	Numeric Employment Change	Percent Employment Change
Personal Care Aides	4,200	7,190	2,990	71.3
Home Health Aides	11,370	19,230	7,860	69.2
Occupational Therapy Assistants	400	660	260	64.6
Physical Therapist Assistants	1,330	2,050	720	54.1
Metal-Refining Furnace Operators and Tenders	740	1,120	380	50.4
Physical Therapist Aides	690	1,040	350	50.2
Health Educators	450	670	220	49.1
Helpers—Carpenters	1,190	1,780	590	49.1
Marriage and Family Therapists	350	510	170	48.0
Diagnostic Medical Sonographers	980	1,450	470	47.8

Note: Projections cover Alabama; (1) Sorted by percent employment change and excludes occupations with numeric employment change less than 100
Source: www.projectionscentral.com, State Occupational Projections, 2010–2020 Long-Term Projections

Average Wages

Occupation	$/Hr.	Occupation	$/Hr.
Accountants and Auditors	32.82	Maids and Housekeeping Cleaners	9.14
Automotive Mechanics	18.14	Maintenance and Repair Workers	19.52
Bookkeepers	17.17	Marketing Managers	56.43
Carpenters	16.52	Nuclear Medicine Technologists	25.22
Cashiers	8.84	Nurses, Licensed Practical	18.73
Clerks, General Office	11.15	Nurses, Registered	26.74
Clerks, Receptionists/Information	11.72	Nursing Assistants	10.86
Clerks, Shipping/Receiving	15.17	Packers and Packagers, Hand	10.78
Computer Programmers	43.90	Physical Therapists	38.44
Computer Systems Analysts	43.34	Postal Service Mail Carriers	23.71
Computer User Support Specialists	21.85	Real Estate Brokers	n/a
Cooks, Restaurant	9.95	Retail Salespersons	11.46
Dentists	88.17	Sales Reps., Exc. Tech./Scientific	31.78
Electrical Engineers	48.64	Sales Reps., Tech./Scientific	37.45
Electricians	22.76	Secretaries, Exc. Legal/Med./Exec.	16.94
Financial Managers	57.94	Security Guards	12.32
First-Line Supervisors/Managers, Sales	19.98	Surgeons	n/a
Food Preparation Workers	8.46	Teacher Assistants	8.70
General and Operations Managers	65.79	Teachers, Elementary School	24.60
Hairdressers/Cosmetologists	13.19	Teachers, Secondary School	24.00
Internists	n/a	Telemarketers	9.29
Janitors and Cleaners	9.75	Truck Drivers, Heavy/Tractor-Trailer	16.39
Landscaping/Groundskeeping Workers	10.62	Truck Drivers, Light/Delivery Svcs.	14.79
Lawyers	59.69	Waiters and Waitresses	9.19

Note: Wage data covers the Huntsville, AL Metropolitan Statistical Area—see Appendix B for areas included. Hourly wages for elementary/secondary school teachers and teacher assistants were calculated by the editors from annual wage data assuming a 40 hour work week; n/a not available.
Source: Bureau of Labor Statistics, Metro Area Occupational Employment and Wage Estimates, May 2013

RESIDENTIAL REAL ESTATE

Building Permits

Area	Single-Family			Multi-Family			Total		
	2012	2013	Pct. Chg.	2012	2013	Pct. Chg.	2012	2013	Pct. Chg.
City	960	1,000	4.2	420	306	-27.1	1,380	1,306	-5.4
MSA[1]	1,927	1,944	0.9	420	306	-27.1	2,347	2,250	-4.1
U.S.	518,695	620,802	19.7	310,963	370,020	19.0	829,658	990,822	19.4

Note: (1) Metropolitan Statistical Area—see Appendix B for areas included; figures represent new, privately-owned housing units authorized (unadjusted data); All permit data are based on estimates with imputation.
Source: U.S. Census Bureau, Manufacturing, Mining, and Construction Statistics, Building Permits, 2012, 2013

Homeownership Rate

Area	2006 (%)	2007 (%)	2008 (%)	2009 (%)	2010 (%)	2011 (%)	2012 (%)	2013 (%)
MSA[1]	n/a	n/a	n/a	n/a	n/a	n/a	n/a	n/a
U.S.	68.8	68.1	67.8	67.4	66.9	66.1	65.4	65.1

Note: (1) Figures cover the Huntsville, AL Metropolitan Statistical Area—see Appendix B for areas included; n/a not available
Source: U.S. Census Bureau, Housing Vacancies and Homeownership Annual Statistics: 2013

Housing Vacancy Rates

Area	Gross Vacancy Rate[2] (%)			Year-Round Vacancy Rate[3] (%)			Rental Vacancy Rate[4] (%)			Homeowner Vacancy Rate[5] (%)		
	2011	2012	2013	2011	2012	2013	2011	2012	2013	2011	2012	2013
MSA[1]	n/a	n/a	n/a	n/a	n/a	n/a	n/a	n/a	n/a	n/a	n/a	n/a
U.S.	14.2	13.8	13.8	11.1	10.8	10.7	9.5	8.7	8.3	2.5	2.0	2.0

Note: (1) Figures cover the Huntsville, AL Metropolitan Statistical Area—see Appendix B for areas included; (2) The percentage of the total housing inventory that is vacant; (3) The percentage of the housing inventory (excluding seasonal units) that is year-round vacant; (4) The percentage of rental inventory that is vacant for rent; (5) The percentage of homeowner inventory that is vacant for sale; n/a not available
Source: U.S. Census Bureau, Housing Vacancies and Homeownership Annual Statistics: 2013

TAXES

State Corporate Income Tax Rates

State	Tax Rate (%)	Income Brackets ($)	Num. of Brackets	Financial Institution Tax Rate (%)[a]	Federal Income Tax Ded.
Alabama	6.5	Flat rate	1	6.5	Yes

Note: Tax rates as of January 1, 2014; (a) Rates listed are the corporate income tax rate applied to financial institutions or excise taxes based on income. Some states have other taxes based upon the value of deposits or shares.
Source: Federation of Tax Administrators, "State Corporate Income Tax Rates, 2014"

State Individual Income Tax Rates

State	Tax Rate (%)	Income Brackets ($)	Num. of Brackets	Personal Exempt. ($)[1] Single	Personal Exempt. ($)[1] Dependents	Fed. Inc. Tax Ded.
Alabama	2.0 - 5.0	500 (b) - 3,001 (b)	3	1,500	500 (e)	Yes

Note: Tax rates as of January 1, 2014; Local- and county-level taxes are not included; n/a not applicable; (1) Married joint filers generally receive double the single exemption; (b) For joint returns, taxes are twice the tax on half the couple's income; (e) In Alabama, the per-dependent exemption is $1,000 for taxpayers with state AGI of $20,000 or less, $500 with AGI from $20,001 to $100,000, and $300 with AGI over $100,000.
Source: Federation of Tax Administrators, "State Individual Income Tax Rates, 2014"

Various State and Local Tax Rates

State	State and Local Sales and Use (%)	State Sales and Use (%)	Gasoline[1] (¢/gal.)	Cigarette[2] ($/pack)	Spirits[3] ($/gal.)	Wine[4] ($/gal.)	Beer[5] ($/gal.)
Alabama	8.0	4.00	20.95	0.425	18.23 (g)	1.70	1.05 (q)

Note: All tax rates as of January 1, 2014; (1) The American Petroleum Institute has developed a methodology for determining the average tax rate on a gallon of fuel. Rates may include any of the following: excise taxes, environmental fees, storage tank fees, other fees or taxes, general sales tax, and local taxes. In states where gasoline is subject to the general sales tax, or where the fuel tax is based on the average sale price, the average rate determined by API is sensitive to changes in the price of gasoline. States that fully or partially apply general sales taxes to gasoline: CA, CO, GA, IL, IN, MI, NY; (2) The federal excise tax of $1.0066 per pack and local taxes are not included; (3) Rates are those applicable to off-premise sales of 40% alcohol by volume (a.b.v.) distilled spirits in 750ml containers. Local excise taxes are excluded; (4) Rates are those applicable to off-premise sales of 11% a.b.v. non-carbonated wine in 750ml containers; (5) Rates are those applicable to off-premise sales of 4.7% a.b.v. beer in 12 ounce containers; (g) States where the government controls sales. In these "control states," products are subject to ad valorem mark-up and excise taxes. The excise tax rate is calculated using a methodology developed by the Distilled Spirits Council of the United States; (q) Includes statewide local rate in Alabama ($0.52) and Georgia ($0.53).
Source: Tax Foundation, 2014 Facts & Figures: How Does Your State Compare?

State Business Tax Climate Index Rankings

State	Overall Rank	Corporate Tax Index Rank	Individual Income Tax Index Rank	Sales Tax Index Rank	Unemployment Insurance Tax Index Rank	Property Tax Index Rank
Alabama	21	19	22	37	15	10

Note: The index is a measure of how each state's tax laws affect economic performance. The lower the rank, the more favorable a state's tax system is for business. States without a given tax are given a ranking of 1. The scores/rankings for the District of Columbia do not affect other states. The 2014 index represents the tax climate as of July 1, 2013.
Source: Tax Foundation, State Business Tax Climate Index 2014

COMMERCIAL UTILITIES

Typical Monthly Electric Bills

Area	Commercial Service ($/month) 40 kW demand 5,000 kWh	Commercial Service ($/month) 500 kW demand 100,000 kWh	Industrial Service ($/month) 5,000 kW demand 1,500,000 kWh	Industrial Service ($/month) 70,000 kW demand 50,000,000 kWh
City	506	11,265	144,729	2,647,650

Note: Based on rates in effect January 2, 2013
Source: Memphis Light, Gas and Water, 2013 Utility Bill Comparisons for Selected U.S. Cities

TRANSPORTATION

Means of Transportation to Work

Area	Car/Truck/Van		Public Transportation			Bicycle	Walked	Other Means	Worked at Home
	Drove Alone	Car-pooled	Bus	Subway	Railroad				
City	84.7	8.0	0.6	0.0	0.0	0.1	1.3	2.0	3.2
MSA[1]	86.3	7.9	0.3	0.1	0.0	0.1	1.1	1.3	2.8
U.S.	76.4	9.7	2.6	1.7	0.5	0.6	2.8	1.3	4.3

Note: Figures are percentages and cover workers 16 years of age and older; (1) Figures cover the Huntsville, AL Metropolitan Statistical Area—see Appendix B for areas included
Source: U.S. Census Bureau, 2010-2012 American Community Survey 3-Year Estimates

Travel Time to Work

Area	Less Than 10 Minutes	10 to 19 Minutes	20 to 29 Minutes	30 to 44 Minutes	45 to 59 Minutes	60 to 89 Minutes	90 Minutes or More
City	14.5	45.2	24.9	11.4	1.9	1.0	1.0
MSA[1]	11.6	34.5	27.4	19.1	4.4	1.9	1.1
U.S.	13.5	29.8	20.9	20.1	7.5	5.6	2.5

Note: Figures are percentages and include workers 16 years old and over; (1) Figures cover the Huntsville, AL Metropolitan Statistical Area—see Appendix B for areas included
Source: U.S. Census Bureau, 2010-2012 American Community Survey 3-Year Estimates

Travel Time Index

Area	1985	1990	1995	2000	2005	2010	2011
Urban Area[1]	n/a	n/a	n/a	n/a	n/a	n/a	n/a
Average[2]	1.09	1.14	1.16	1.19	1.23	1.18	1.18

Note: Travel Time Index—the ratio of travel time in the peak period to the travel time at free-flow conditions. For example, a value of 1.30 indicates a 20-minute free-flow trip takes 26 minutes in the peak. Free-flow speeds (60 mph on freeways and 35 mph on principal arterials) are used as the comparison threshold; (1) Data for the Huntsville, AL urban area was not available; (2) average of 498 urban areas
Source: Texas Transportation Institute, Urban Mobility Report 2012, December 2012

Public Transportation

Agency Name / Mode of Transportation	Vehicles Operated in Maximum Service	Annual Unlinked Passenger Trips (in thous.)	Annual Passenger Miles (in thous.)
City of Huntsville - Public Transportation Division			
Bus (directly operated)	13	399.8	2,178.0
Demand Response (directly operated)	16	91.8	712.4

Source: Federal Transit Administration, National Transit Database, 2012

Air Transportation

Airport Name and Code / Type of Service	Passenger Airlines[1]	Passenger Enplanements	Freight Carriers[2]	Freight (lbs.)
Huntsville International (HSV)				
Domestic service (U.S. carriers - 2013)	11	504,803	13	15,783,243
International service (U.S. carriers - 2012)	0	0	2	76,216,421

Note: (1) Includes all U.S.-based major, minor and commuter airlines that carried at least one passenger during the year; (2) Includes all U.S.-based airlines and freight carriers that transported at least one lb. of freight during the year.
Source: Bureau of Transportation Statistics, The Intermodal Transportation Database, Air Carriers: T-100 Domestic Market (U.S. Carriers), 2013; Bureau of Transportation Statistics, The Intermodal Transportation Database, Air Carriers: T-100 International Market (U.S. Carriers), 2012

Other Transportation Statistics

Major Highways:	I-65
Amtrak Service:	No
Major Waterways/Ports:	Near the Tennessee River (12 miles)

Source: Amtrak.com; Google Maps

BUSINESSES

Major Business Headquarters

Company Name	Rankings	
	Fortune[1]	Forbes[2]
No companies listed	-	-

Note: (1) Fortune 500—companies that produce a 10-K are ranked 1 to 500 based on 2012 revenue; (2) all private companies with at least $2 billion in annual revenue through the end of their most current fiscal year are ranked 1 to 224; companies listed are headquartered in the city; dashes indicate no ranking
Source: Fortune, "Fortune 500," May 20, 2013; Forbes, "America's Largest Private Companies," December 18, 2013

Fast-Growing Businesses

According to *Inc.*, Huntsville is home to two of America's 500 fastest-growing private companies: **Summit 7 Systems** (#395); **Yorktown Systems Group** (#432). Criteria: must be an independent, privately-held, for-profit, U.S. corporation, proprietorship or partnership; revenues must be at least $100,000 in 2009 and $2 million in 2012; must have four-year operating/sales history. Holding companies, regulated banks, and utilities were excluded. *Inc., "America's 500 Fastest-Growing Private Companies," September 2013*

Minority Business Opportunity

Huntsville is home to one company which is on the *Black Enterprise* Auto Dealer 60 list (60 largest dealers based on gross sales): **Lexus of Huntsville** (#54). Criteria: company must be operational in previous calendar year and be at least 51% black-owned. *Black Enterprise, B.E. 100s, 2013*

Huntsville is home to two companies which are on the *Hispanic Business* 500 list (500 largest U.S. Hispanic-owned companies based on 2012 revenue): **COLSA Corp.** (#37); **SEI Group** (#236). Companies included must show at least 51 percent ownership by Hispanic U.S. citizens, and must maintain headquarters in one of the 50 states or Washington, D.C. *Hispanic Business, "Hispanic Business 500," June 20, 2013*

Minority- and Women-Owned Businesses

Group	All Firms		Firms with Paid Employees			
	Firms	Sales ($000)	Firms	Sales ($000)	Employees	Payroll ($000)
Asian	576	413,879	256	390,751	3,129	137,158
Black	2,007	268,991	157	243,092	1,821	77,246
Hispanic	207	260,684	45	254,977	1,705	111,457
Women	4,347	1,211,336	649	1,117,014	7,744	276,445
All Firms	14,555	28,244,278	4,604	27,652,214	122,186	5,233,410

Note: Figures cover firms located in the city; minority- and women-owned business are defined as firms in which the corresponding group own 51% or more of the stock or equity of the company
Source: U.S. Census Bureau, 2007 Economic Census, Survey of Business Owners (2012 Survey of Business Owners data will be released starting in June 2015)

HOTELS & CONVENTION CENTERS

Hotels/Motels

Area	5 Star		4 Star		3 Star		2 Star		1 Star		Not Rated	
	Num.	Pct.[3]	Num.	Pct.[3]	Num.	Pct.[3]	Num.	Pct.[3]	Num.	Pct.[3]	Num.	Pct.[3]
City[1]	0	0.0	1	1.1	16	18.2	62	70.5	3	3.4	6	6.8
Total[2]	142	0.9	1,005	6.0	5,147	30.9	8,578	51.4	408	2.4	1,397	8.4

Note: (1) Figures cover Huntsville and vicinity; (2) Figures cover all 100 cities in this book; (3) Percentage of hotels which have a given star rating; Star ratings are determined by expedia.com and offer an indication of the general quality of a particular hotel.
Source: expedia.com, April 7, 2014

Major Convention Centers

Name	Overall Space (sq. ft.)	Exhibit Space (sq. ft.)	Meeting Space (sq. ft.)	Meeting Rooms
Von Braun Center	n/a	n/a	170,000	n/a

Note: Table includes convention centers located in the Huntsville, AL metro area; n/a not available
Source: Original research

Living Environment

COST OF LIVING

Cost of Living Index

Composite Index	Groceries	Housing	Utilities	Trans-portation	Health Care	Misc. Goods/ Services
94.2	89.4	79.1	103.7	98.7	96.2	103.2

Note: The Cost of Living Index measures regional differences in the cost of consumer goods and services, excluding taxes and non-consumer expenditures, for professional and managerial households in the top income quintile. It is based on more than 50,000 prices covering almost 60 different items for which prices are collected three times a year by chambers of commerce, economic development organizations or university applied economic centers in each participating urban area. The numbers shown should be read as a percentage above or below the national average of 100. For example, a value of 115.4 in the groceries column indicates that grocery prices are 15.4% higher than the national average. Small differences in the index numbers should not be interpreted as significant; Figures cover the Huntsville AL urban area.
Source: The Council for Community and Economic Research, ACCRA Cost of Living Index, 2013

Grocery Prices

Area[1]	T-Bone Steak ($/pound)	Frying Chicken ($/pound)	Whole Milk ($/half gal.)	Eggs ($/dozen)	Orange Juice ($/64 oz.)	Coffee ($/11.5 oz.)
City[2]	10.28	1.19	2.21	1.55	3.35	4.14
Avg.	10.19	1.28	2.34	1.81	3.48	4.39
Min.	8.56	0.94	1.44	1.19	2.78	3.40
Max.	14.82	2.28	3.56	3.73	6.23	7.32

*Note: (1) Values for the local area are compared with the average, minimum and maximum values for all 327 areas in the Cost of Living Index; (2) Figures cover the Huntsville AL urban area; **T-Bone Steak** (price per pound); **Frying Chicken** (price per pound, whole fryer); **Whole Milk** (half gallon carton); **Eggs** (price per dozen, Grade A, large); **Orange Juice** (64 oz. Tropicana or Florida Natural); **Coffee** (11.5 oz. can, vacuum-packed, Maxwell House, Hills Bros, or Folgers).*
Source: The Council for Community and Economic Research, ACCRA Cost of Living Index, 2013

Housing and Utility Costs

Area[1]	New Home Price ($)	Apartment Rent ($/month)	All Electric ($/month)	Part Electric ($/month)	Other Energy ($/month)	Telephone ($/month)
City[2]	225,591	815	146.54	-	-	34.39
Avg.	295,864	900	171.38	91.82	70.12	27.73
Min.	185,506	458	117.80	48.81	33.67	17.16
Max.	1,358,917	3,783	441.68	171.40	372.65	39.47

*Note: (1) Values for the local area are compared with the average, minimum and maximum values for all 327 areas in the Cost of Living Index; (2) Figures cover the Huntsville AL urban area; **New Home Price** (2,400 sf living area, 8,000 sf lot, in urban area with full utilities); **Apartment Rent** (950 sf 2 bedroom/1.5 or 2 bath, unfurnished, excluding all utilities except water); **All Electric** (average monthly cost for an all-electric home); **Part Electric** (average monthly cost for a part-electric home); **Other Energy** (average monthly cost for natural gas, fuel oil, coal, wood, and any other forms of energy except electricity); **Telephone** (price includes basic monthly rate for a private residential line plus additional local usage charges incurred by a family of four).*
Source: The Council for Community and Economic Research, ACCRA Cost of Living Index, 2013

Health Care, Transportation, and Other Costs

Area[1]	Doctor ($/visit)	Dentist ($/visit)	Optometrist ($/visit)	Gasoline ($/gallon)	Beauty Salon ($/visit)	Men's Shirt ($)
City[2]	79.53	82.56	133.61	3.30	33.00	35.98
Avg.	101.40	86.48	96.16	3.44	33.87	26.55
Min.	61.67	50.83	50.12	3.08	18.92	12.48
Max.	182.71	152.50	223.78	4.33	68.22	52.03

*Note: (1) Values for the local area are compared with the average, minimum and maximum values for all 327 areas in the Cost of Living Index; (2) Figures cover the Huntsville AL urban area; **Doctor** (general practitioners routine exam of an established patient); **Dentist** (adult teeth cleaning and periodic oral examination); **Optometrist** (full vision eye exam for established adult patient); **Gasoline** (one gallon regular unleaded, national brand, including all taxes, cash price at self-service pump if available); **Beauty Salon** (woman's shampoo, trim, and blow-dry); **Men's Shirt** (cotton/polyester dress shirt, pinpoint weave, long sleeves).*
Source: The Council for Community and Economic Research, ACCRA Cost of Living Index, 2013

HOUSING

House Price Index (HPI)

Area	National Ranking[2]	Quarterly Change (%)	One-Year Change (%)	Five-Year Change (%)
MSA[1]	275	-2.36	-2.87	-6.81
U.S.[3]	–	1.20	7.69	4.18

Note: The HPI is a weighted repeat sales index. It measures average price changes in repeat sales or refinancings on the same properties. This information is obtained by reviewing repeat mortgage transactions on single-family properties whose mortgages have been purchased or securitized by Fannie Mae or Freddie Mac in January 1975; (1) Huntsville, AL Metropolitan Statistical Area—see Appendix B for areas included; (2) Rankings are based on annual percentage change for all metro areas containing at least 15,000 transactions over the last 10 years and ranges from 1 to 283; (3) figures based on a weighted average of Census Division estimates using a seasonally adjusted, purchase-only index; all figures are for the period ending December 31, 2013
Source: Federal Housing Finance Agency, House Price Index, February 25, 2014

Median Single-Family Home Prices

Area	2011	2012	2013p	Percent Change 2012 to 2013
MSA[1]	172.8	173.6	171.7	-1.1
U.S. Average	166.2	177.2	197.4	11.4

Note: Figures are median sales prices of existing single-family homes in thousands of dollars; (p) preliminary; n/a not available; (1) Huntsville, AL Metropolitan Statistical Area—see Appendix B for areas included
Source: National Association of Realtors, Median Sales Price of Existing Single-Family Homes for Metropolitan Areas, 4th Quarter 2013

Qualifying Income Based on Median Sales Price of Existing Single-Family Homes

Area	With 5% Down ($)	With 10% Down ($)	With 20% Down ($)
MSA[1]	39,609	37,524	33,355
U.S. Average	45,395	43,006	38,228

Note: Figures are preliminary; Qualifying income is based on a mortgage rate of 4.4%. Monthly principal and interest payment is limited to 25% of income; n/a not available; (1) Huntsville, AL Metropolitan Statistical Area—see Appendix B for areas included
Source: National Association of Realtors, Qualifying Income Based on Median Sales Price of Existing Single-Family Homes for Metropolitan Areas, 4th Quarter 2013

Median Apartment Condo-Coop Home Prices

Area	2011	2012	2013p	Percent Change 2012 to 2013
MSA[1]	n/a	n/a	n/a	n/a
U.S. Average	165.1	173.7	194.9	12.2

Note: Figures are median sales prices of existing apartment condo-coop homes in thousands of dollars; (p) preliminary; n/a not available; (1) Huntsville, AL Metropolitan Statistical Area—see Appendix B for areas included
Source: National Association of Realtors, Median Sales Price of Existing Apartment Condo-Coop Homes for Metropolitan Areas, 4th Quarter 2013

Gross Monthly Rent

Area	Under $200	$200 -299	$300 -499	$500 -749	$750 -999	$1,000 -1,499	$1,500 and up	Median ($)
City	1.7	4.2	12.7	38.8	26.1	12.9	3.6	705
MSA[1]	1.5	4.5	11.4	37.8	25.4	14.9	4.4	715
U.S.	1.7	3.3	8.1	22.7	24.3	25.7	14.3	889

Note: Figures are percentages except for Median; Gross rent is the contract rent plus the estimated average monthly cost of utilities (electricity, gas, and water and sewer) and fuels (oil, coal, kerosene, wood, etc.) if these are paid by the renter (or paid for the renter by someone else); (1) Figures cover the Huntsville, AL Metropolitan Statistical Area—see Appendix B for areas included
Source: U.S. Census Bureau, 2010-2012 American Community Survey 3-Year Estimates

Year Housing Structure Built

Area	2010 or Later	2000 -2009	1990 -1999	1980 -1989	1970 -1979	1960 -1969	1950 -1959	1940 -1949	Before 1940	Median Year
City	0.7	15.3	10.9	16.1	15.4	24.0	10.3	3.5	3.8	1975
MSA[1]	1.2	21.9	18.8	17.5	12.3	15.2	7.3	2.4	3.3	1985
U.S.	0.5	14.9	13.8	13.9	15.9	11.1	10.9	5.5	13.5	1976

Note: Figures are percentages except for Median Year; (1) Figures cover the Huntsville, AL Metropolitan Statistical Area—see Appendix B for areas included
Source: U.S. Census Bureau, 2010-2012 American Community Survey 3-Year Estimates

HEALTH

Health Risk Data

Category	MSA[1] (%)	U.S. (%)
Adults aged 18–64 who have any kind of health care coverage	81.3	79.6
Adults who reported being in good or excellent health	78.8	83.1
Adults who are current smokers	22.0	19.6
Adults who are heavy drinkers[2]	4.1	6.1
Adults who are binge drinkers[3]	11.4	16.9
Adults who are overweight (BMI 25.0 - 29.9)	36.8	35.8
Adults who are obese (BMI 30.0 - 99.8)	29.4	27.6
Adults who participated in any physical activities in the past month	73.8	77.1
Adults 50+ who have ever had a sigmoidoscopy or colonoscopy	68.0	67.3
Women aged 40+ who have had a mammogram within the past two years	81.8	74.0
Men aged 40+ who have had a PSA test within the past two years	44.7	45.2
Adults aged 65+ who have had flu shot within the past year	54.8	60.1
Adults who always wear a seatbelt	94.8	93.8

Note: Data as of 2012 unless otherwise noted; (1) Figures cover the Huntsville, AL Metropolitan Statistical Area—see Appendix B for areas included; (2) Heavy drinkers are classified as males having more than two drinks per day or females having more than one drink per day; (3) Binge drinkers are classified as males having five or more drinks on one occasion or females having four or more drinks on one occasion
Source: Centers for Disease Control and Prevention, Behavioral Risk Factor Surveillance System, SMART: Selected Metropolitan/Micropolitan Area Risk Trends, 2012

Chronic Health Indicators

Category	MSA[1] (%)	U.S. (%)
Adults who have ever been told they had a heart attack	3.9	4.5
Adults who have ever been told they had a stroke	n/a	2.9
Adults who have been told they currently have asthma	8.6	8.9
Adults who have ever been told they have arthritis	29.9	25.7
Adults who have ever been told they have diabetes[2]	8.8	9.7
Adults who have ever been told they had skin cancer	8.1	5.7
Adults who have ever been told they had any other types of cancer	6.4	6.5
Adults who have ever been told they have COPD	6.8	6.2
Adults who have ever been told they have kidney disease	1.8	2.5
Adults who have ever been told they have a form of depression	20.8	18.0

Note: Data as of 2012 unless otherwise noted; n/a not available; (1) Figures cover the Huntsville, AL Metropolitan Statistical Area—see Appendix B for areas included; (2) Figures do not include pregnancy-related, borderline, or pre-diabetes
Source: Centers for Disease Control and Prevention, Behavioral Risk Factor Surveillance System, SMART: Selected Metropolitan/Micropolitan Area Risk Trends, 2012

Mortality Rates for the Top 10 Causes of Death in the U.S.

ICD-10[a] Sub-Chapter	ICD-10[a] Code	Age-Adjusted Mortality Rate[1] per 100,000 population	
		County[2]	U.S.
Malignant neoplasms	C00-C97	176.3	174.2
Ischaemic heart diseases	I20-I25	55.7	119.1
Other forms of heart disease	I30-I51	116.6	49.6
Chronic lower respiratory diseases	J40-J47	44.1	43.2
Cerebrovascular diseases	I60-I69	42.4	40.3
Organic, including symptomatic, mental disorders	F01-F09	34.8	30.5
Other degenerative diseases of the nervous system	G30-G31	31.7	26.3
Other external causes of accidental injury	W00-X59	22.2	25.1
Diabetes mellitus	E10-E14	26.5	21.3
Hypertensive diseases	I10-I15	19.2	18.8

Note: (a) ICD-10 = International Classification of Diseases 10th Revision; (1) Mortality rates are a three year average covering 2008-2010; (2) Figures cover Madison County
Source: Centers for Disease Control and Prevention, National Center for Health Statistics. Compressed Mortality File 1999-2010 on CDC WONDER Online Database, released January 2013. Data are compiled from the Compressed Mortality File 1999-2010, Series 20 No. 2P, 2013.

Mortality Rates for Selected Causes of Death

ICD-10[a] Sub-Chapter	ICD-10[a] Code	Age-Adjusted Mortality Rate[1] per 100,000 population	
		County[2]	U.S.
Assault	X85-Y09	5.5	5.5
Diseases of the liver	K70-K76	12.7	12.4
Human immunodeficiency virus (HIV) disease	B20-B24	2.8	3.0
Influenza and pneumonia	J09-J18	17.0	16.4
Intentional self-harm	X60-X84	12.8	11.8
Malnutrition	E40-E46	*1.5	0.8
Obesity and other hyperalimentation	E65-E68	Suppressed	1.6
Renal failure	N17-N19	20.9	13.6
Transport accidents	V01-V99	13.9	12.6
Viral hepatitis	B15-B19	*1.3	2.2

Note: (a) ICD-10 = International Classification of Diseases 10th Revision; (1) Mortality rates are a three year average covering 2008-2010; (2) Figures cover Madison County; (*) Unreliable data as per CDC
Source: Centers for Disease Control and Prevention, National Center for Health Statistics. Compressed Mortality File 1999-2010 on CDC WONDER Online Database, released January 2013. Data are compiled from the Compressed Mortality File 1999-2010, Series 20 No. 2P, 2013.

Health Insurance Coverage

Area	With Health Insurance	With Private Health Insurance	With Public Health Insurance	Without Health Insurance	Population Under Age 18 Without Health Insurance
City	84.1	69.4	28.6	15.9	4.9
MSA[1]	87.4	73.8	26.2	12.6	3.6
U.S.	84.9	65.4	30.4	15.1	7.5

Note: Figures are percentages that cover the civilian noninstitutionalized population; (1) Figures cover the Huntsville, AL Metropolitan Statistical Area—see Appendix B for areas included
Source: U.S. Census Bureau, 2010-2012 American Community Survey 3-Year Estimates

Number of Medical Professionals

Area[1]	MDs[2]	DOs[2,3]	Dentists	Podiatrists	Chiropractors	Optometrists
Local (number)	862	36	187	14	70	55
Local (rate[4])	253.8	10.6	54.6	4.1	20.4	16.0
U.S. (rate[4])	267.6	19.6	61.7	5.6	24.7	14.5

Note: Data as of 2012 unless noted; (1) Local data covers Madison County; (2) Data as of 2011; (3) Doctor of Osteopathic Medicine; (4) rate per 100,000 population
Source: Area Resource File (ARF) 2012-2013. U.S. Department of Health and Human Services, Health Resources and Services Administration, Bureau of Health Professions

EDUCATION

Public School District Statistics

District Name	Schls	Pupils	Pupil/ Teacher Ratio	Minority Pupils[1] (%)	Free Lunch Eligible[2] (%)	IEP[3] (%)
Huntsville City	50	22,974	15.1	53.0	43.5	10.3
Madison County	29	20,012	16.0	30.4	27.8	10.2

Note: Table includes school districts with 2,000 or more students; (1) Percentage of students that are not non-Hispanic white; (2) Percentage of students that are eligible for the free lunch program; (3) Percentage of students that have an Individualized Education Program.
Source: U.S. Department of Education, National Center for Education Statistics, Common Core of Data, Local Education Agency (School District) Universe Survey: School Year 2011-2012; U.S. Department of Education, National Center for Education Statistics, Common Core of Data, Public Elementary/Secondary School Universe Survey: School Year 2011-2012

Best High Schools

High School Name	Rank[1]	Grad. Rate[2] (%)	Coll.[3] (%)	AP/IB/ AICE Tests[4]	AP/IB/ AICE Score[5]	SAT Score[6]	ACT Score[6]
Huntsville H.S.	750	92	95	0.6	3.2	1653	23.0
New Century Technology H.S.	834	96	97	0.5	2.7	n/a	23.0
Virgil I. Grissom H.S.	1030	88	92	0.6	3.2	1663	23.8

Note: (1) Public schools are ranked from 1 to 2,000 based on the following self-reported statistics (with the corresponding weight used in calculating their overall score). Schools that were newly founded and did not have a graduating senior class in 2012 were excluded; (2) Four-year, on-time graduation rate (25%); (3) Percent of 2011 graduates who were accepted to college (25%); (4) AP/IB/AICE tests taken per student (25%); (5) Average AP/IB/AICE exam score (10%); (6) Average SAT and/or ACT score (10%); Percent of students enrolled in at least one AP/IB/AICE course (5%)—data not shown; n/a not available
Source: Newsweek and The Daily Beast, "America's Best High Schools 2013"

Highest Level of Education

Area	Less than H.S.	H.S. Diploma	Some College, No Deg.	Associate Degree	Bachelor's Degree	Master's Degree	Prof. School Degree	Doctorate Degree
City	10.3	20.5	23.4	7.3	23.4	11.0	2.4	1.8
MSA[1]	11.7	23.7	22.5	7.3	21.7	10.2	1.6	1.4
U.S.	14.1	28.3	21.3	7.8	18.0	7.5	1.9	1.2

Note: Figures cover persons age 25 and over; (1) Figures cover the Huntsville, AL Metropolitan Statistical Area—see Appendix B for areas included
Source: U.S. Census Bureau, 2010-2012 American Community Survey 3-Year Estimates

Educational Attainment by Race

Area	High School Graduate or Higher (%)					Bachelor's Degree or Higher (%)				
	Total	White	Black	Asian	Hisp.[2]	Total	White	Black	Asian	Hisp.[2]
City	89.7	91.7	85.6	89.7	61.3	38.6	44.1	23.7	54.6	19.9
MSA[1]	88.3	89.0	87.0	85.1	62.5	34.8	36.5	27.2	54.4	19.8
U.S.	85.9	88.1	82.5	85.5	63.1	28.6	30.0	18.4	50.2	13.4

Note: Figures shown cover persons 25 years old and over; (1) Figures cover the Huntsville, AL Metropolitan Statistical Area—see Appendix B for areas included; (2) People of Hispanic origin can be of any race
Source: U.S. Census Bureau, 2010-2012 American Community Survey 3-Year Estimates

School Enrollment by Grade and Control

Area	Preschool (%)		Kindergarten (%)		Grades 1 - 4 (%)		Grades 5 - 8 (%)		Grades 9 - 12 (%)	
	Public	Private	Public	Private	Public	Private	Public	Private	Public	Private
City	37.5	62.5	86.6	13.4	84.7	15.3	81.9	18.1	85.8	14.2
MSA[1]	43.8	56.2	84.2	15.8	86.0	14.0	87.4	12.6	87.0	13.0
U.S.	56.9	43.1	87.8	12.2	89.9	10.1	90.0	10.0	90.8	9.2

Note: Figures shown cover persons 3 years old and over; (1) Figures cover the Huntsville, AL Metropolitan Statistical Area—see Appendix B for areas included
Source: U.S. Census Bureau, 2010-2012 American Community Survey 3-Year Estimates

Average Salaries of Public School Classroom Teachers

Area	2012-13		2013-14		Percent Change 2012-13 to 2013-14	Percent Change 2003-04 to 2013-14
	Dollars	Rank[1]	Dollars	Rank[1]		
Alabama	47,949	39	48,413	40	0.97	26.5
U.S. Average	56,103	–	56,689	–	1.04	21.8

Note: (1) State rank ranges from 1 to 51 where 1 indicates highest salary.
Source: National Education Association, Rankings & Estimates: Rankings of the States 2013 and Estimates of School Statistics 2014, March 2014

Higher Education

Four-Year Colleges			Two-Year Colleges			Medical Schools[1]	Law Schools[2]	Voc/ Tech[3]
Public	Private Non-profit	Private For-profit	Public	Private Non-profit	Private For-profit			
1	2	1	1	0	0	0	0	0

Note: Figures cover institutions located within the city limits and include main campuses only; (1) includes schools accredited by the Liaison Committee on Medical Education and the American Osteopathic Association's Commission on Osteopathic College Accreditation; (2) includes ABA-accredited schools, schools with provisional ABA accreditation, and state accredited schools; (3) includes all schools with programs that are less than 2 years.
Source: National Center for Education Statistics, Integrated Postsecondary Education System (IPEDS), 2012-13; Association of American Medical Colleges, Member List, April 24, 2014; American Osteopathic Association, Member List, April 24, 2014; Law School Admission Council, Official Guide to ABA-Approved Law Schools Online, April 24, 2014; Wikipedia, List of Medical Schools in the United States, April 24, 2014; Wikipedia, List of Law Schools in the United States, April 24, 2014

According to *U.S. News & World Report,* the Huntsville, AL metro area is home to one of the best national universities in the U.S.: **University of Alabama–Huntsville** (#181). The indicators used to capture academic quality fall into a number of categories: assessment by administrators at peer institutions; retention of students; faculty resources; student selectivity; financial resources; alumni giving; high school counselor ratings of colleges; and graduation rate. *U.S. News & World Report, "America's Best Colleges 2014"*

PRESIDENTIAL ELECTION

2012 Presidential Election Results

Area	Obama	Romney	Other
Madison County	40.0	58.6	1.4
U.S.	51.0	47.2	1.8

Note: Results are percentages and may not add to 100% due to rounding
Source: Dave Leip's Atlas of U.S. Presidential Elections

EMPLOYERS

Major Employers

Company Name	Industry
Avocent Corporation	Computer peripheral equip
City of Huntsville	Town council
City of Huntsville	Mayor's office
COLSA Corporation	Commercial research laboratory
County of Madison	Executive offices
Dynetics	Engineering laboratory/except testing
General Dynamics C4 Systems	Defense systems equipment
Healthcare Auth - City of Huntsville	General governement
Intergraph Process & Bldg Solutions	Systems software development
Qualitest Products	Drugs and drug proprietaries
Science Applications Int'l Corporation	Computer processing services
Science Applications Int'l Corporation	Commercial research laboratory
Teledyne brown Engineering	Energy research
The Army, United States Department of	Army
The Boeing Company	Aircraft
The Boeing Company	Guided missiles/space vehicles
United States Department of the Army	Army

Note: Companies shown are located within the Huntsville, AL Metropolitan Statistical Area.
Source: Hoovers.com; Wikipedia

PUBLIC SAFETY

Crime Rate

Area	All Crimes	Violent Crimes				Property Crimes		
		Murder	Forcible Rape	Robbery	Aggrav. Assault	Burglary	Larceny -Theft	Motor Vehicle Theft
City	5,964.9	7.6	39.2	248.2	628.2	1,178.6	3,476.5	386.5
Suburbs[1]	2,284.6	3.3	15.2	37.8	162.2	595.5	1,361.8	108.8
Metro[2]	3,867.1	5.1	25.5	128.3	362.6	846.2	2,271.1	228.2
U.S.	3,246.1	4.7	26.9	112.9	242.3	670.2	1,959.3	229.7

Note: Figures are crimes per 100,000 population; (1) All areas within the metro area that are located outside the city limits; (2) Figures cover the Huntsville, AL Metropolitan Statistical Area—see Appendix B for areas included
Source: FBI Uniform Crime Reports, 2012

Hate Crimes

Area	Number of Quarters Reported	Bias Motivation				
		Race	Religion	Sexual Orientation	Ethnicity	Disability
City	n/a	n/a	n/a	n/a	n/a	n/a
U.S.	4	2,797	1,099	1,135	667	92

Note: n/a not available.
Source: Federal Bureau of Investigation, Hate Crime Statistics 2012

Identity Theft Consumer Complaints

Area	Complaints	Complaints per 100,000 Population	Rank[2]
MSA[1]	286	68.5	152
U.S.	290,056	91.8	-

Note: (1) Figures cover the Huntsville, AL Metropolitan Statistical Area—see Appendix B for areas included; (2) Rank ranges from 1 to 377 where 1 indicates greatest number of identity theft complaints per 100,000 population
Source: Federal Trade Commission, Consumer Sentinel Network Data Book for January–December 2013

Fraud and Other Consumer Complaints

Area	Complaints	Complaints per 100,000 Population	Rank[2]
MSA[1]	1,714	410.4	101
U.S.	1,811,724	595.2	-

Note: (1) Figures cover the Huntsville, AL Metropolitan Statistical Area—see Appendix B for areas included; (2) Rank ranges from 1 to 377 where 1 indicates greatest number of identity theft complaints per 100,000 population
Source: Federal Trade Commission, Consumer Sentinel Network Data Book for January–December 2013

RECREATION

Culture

Dance[1]	Theatre[1]	Instrumental Music[1]	Vocal Music[1]	Series and Festivals	Museums and Art Galleries[2]	Zoos and Aquariums[3]
1	1	3	1	2	16	0

Note: (1) Number of professional performing groups; (2) Based on organizations with primary SIC code 8412; (3) AZA-accredited
Source: The Grey House Performing Arts Directory, 2013; Association of Zoos & Aquariums, AZA Member Zoos & Aquariums, April 2014; www.AccuLeads.com, May 1, 2014

Professional Sports Teams

Team Name	League	Year Established

No teams are located in the metro area
Source: Wikipedia, Major Professional Sports Teams of the United States and Canada, April 25, 2014

CLIMATE

Average and Extreme Temperatures

Temperature	Jan	Feb	Mar	Apr	May	Jun	Jul	Aug	Sep	Oct	Nov	Dec	Yr.
Extreme High (°F)	76	82	88	92	96	101	104	103	101	91	84	77	104
Average High (°F)	49	54	63	73	80	87	90	89	83	73	62	52	71
Average Temp. (°F)	39	44	52	61	69	76	80	79	73	62	51	43	61
Average Low (°F)	30	33	41	49	58	65	69	68	62	50	40	33	50
Extreme Low (°F)	-11	5	6	26	36	45	53	52	37	28	15	-3	-11

Note: Figures cover the years 1958-1995
Source: National Climatic Data Center, International Station Meteorological Climate Summary, 9/96

Average Precipitation/Snowfall/Humidity

Precip./Humidity	Jan	Feb	Mar	Apr	May	Jun	Jul	Aug	Sep	Oct	Nov	Dec	Yr.
Avg. Precip. (in.)	5.0	5.0	6.6	4.8	5.1	4.3	4.6	3.5	4.1	3.3	4.7	5.7	56.8
Avg. Snowfall (in.)	2	1	1	Tr	0	0	0	0	0	Tr	Tr	1	4
Avg. Rel. Hum. 7am (%)	82	81	79	78	79	81	84	86	85	86	84	81	82
Avg. Rel. Hum. 4pm (%)	60	56	51	46	51	53	56	55	54	51	55	60	54

Note: Figures cover the years 1958-1995; Tr = Trace amounts (<0.05 in. of rain; <0.5 in. of snow)
Source: National Climatic Data Center, International Station Meteorological Climate Summary, 9/96

Weather Conditions

Temperature			Daytime Sky			Precipitation		
10°F & below	32°F & below	90°F & above	Clear	Partly cloudy	Cloudy	0.01 inch or more precip.	0.1 inch or more snow/ice	Thunder-storms
2	66	49	70	118	177	116	2	54

Note: Figures are average number of days per year and cover the years 1958-1995
Source: National Climatic Data Center, International Station Meteorological Climate Summary, 9/96

HAZARDOUS WASTE

Superfund Sites

Huntsville has one hazardous waste site on the EPA's Superfund Final National Priorities List:
Redstone Arsenal (USARMY/NASA). *U.S. Environmental Protection Agency, Final National Priorities List, April 26, 2014*

AIR & WATER QUALITY

Air Quality Index

Area	Percent of Days when Air Quality was...[2]					AQI Statistics[2]	
	Good	Moderate	Unhealthy for Sensitive Groups	Unhealthy	Very Unhealthy	Maximum	Median
MSA[1]	90.8	9.2	0.0	0.0	0.0	74	37

Note: (1) Data covers the Huntsville, AL Metropolitan Statistical Area—see Appendix B for areas included; (2) Based on 336 days with AQI data in 2013. Air Quality Index (AQI) is an index for reporting daily air quality. EPA calculates the AQI for five major air pollutants regulated by the Clean Air Act: ground-level ozone, particle pollution (aka particulate matter), carbon monoxide, sulfur dioxide, and nitrogen dioxide. The AQI runs from 0 to 500. The higher the AQI value, the greater the level of air pollution and the greater the health concern. There are six AQI categories: "Good" AQI is between 0 and 50. Air quality is considered satisfactory; "Moderate" AQI is between 51 and 100. Air quality is acceptable; "Unhealthy for Sensitive Groups" When AQI values are between 101 and 150, members of sensitive groups may experience health effects; "Unhealthy" When AQI values are between 151 and 200 everyone may begin to experience health effects; "Very Unhealthy" AQI values between 201 and 300 trigger a health alert; "Hazardous" AQI values over 300 trigger warnings of emergency conditions (not shown).
Source: U.S. Environmental Protection Agency, Air Quality Index Report, 2013

Air Quality Index Pollutants

Area	Percent of Days when AQI Pollutant was...[2]					
	Carbon Monoxide	Nitrogen Dioxide	Ozone	Sulfur Dioxide	Particulate Matter 2.5	Particulate Matter 10
MSA[1]	0.0	0.0	61.3	0.0	22.9	15.8

Note: (1) Data covers the Huntsville, AL Metropolitan Statistical Area—see Appendix B for areas included; (2) Based on 336 days with AQI data in 2013. The Air Quality Index (AQI) is an index for reporting daily air quality. EPA calculates the AQI for five major air pollutants regulated by the Clean Air Act: ground-level ozone, particle pollution (also known as particulate matter), carbon monoxide, sulfur dioxide, and nitrogen dioxide. The AQI runs from 0 to 500. The higher the AQI value, the greater the level of air pollution and the greater the health concern.
Source: U.S. Environmental Protection Agency, Air Quality Index Report, 2013

Air Quality Trends: Ozone

	2003	2004	2005	2006	2007	2008	2009	2010	2011	2012
MSA[1]	0.079	0.077	0.075	0.079	0.082	0.073	0.066	0.071	0.072	0.076

Note: (1) Data covers the Huntsville, AL Metropolitan Statistical Area—see Appendix B for areas included. The values shown are the composite ozone concentration averages among trend sites based on the highest fourth daily maximum 8-hour concentration in parts per million. These trends are based on sites having an adequate record of monitoring data during the trend period. Data from exceptional events are included.
Source: U.S. Environmental Protection Agency, Air Quality Monitoring Information, "Air Quality Trends by City, 2000-2012"

Maximum Air Pollutant Concentrations: Particulate Matter, Ozone, CO and Lead

	Particulate Matter 10 (ug/m^3)	Particulate Matter 2.5 Wtd AM (ug/m^3)	Particulate Matter 2.5 24-Hr (ug/m^3)	Ozone (ppm)	Carbon Monoxide (ppm)	Lead (ug/m^3)
MSA[1] Level	38	9.3	19	0.076	n/a	0.01
NAAQS[2]	150	15	35	0.075	9	0.15
Met NAAQS[2]	Yes	Yes	Yes	No	n/a	Yes

Note: (1) Data covers the Huntsville, AL Metropolitan Statistical Area—see Appendix B for areas included; Data from exceptional events are included; (2) National Ambient Air Quality Standards; ppm = parts per million; ug/m^3 = micrograms per cubic meter; n/a not available.
Concentrations: Particulate Matter 10 (coarse particulate)—highest second maximum 24-hour concentration; Particulate Matter 2.5 Wtd AM (fine particulate)—highest weighted annual mean concentration; Particulate Matter 2.5 24-Hour (fine particulate)—highest 98th percentile 24-hour concentration; Ozone—highest fourth daily maximum 8-hour concentration; Carbon Monoxide—highest second maximum non-overlapping 8-hour concentration; Lead—maximum running 3-month average
Source: U.S. Environmental Protection Agency, Air Quality Monitoring Information, "Air Quality Statistics by City, 2012"

Maximum Air Pollutant Concentrations: Nitrogen Dioxide and Sulfur Dioxide

	Nitrogen Dioxide AM (ppb)	Nitrogen Dioxide 1-Hr (ppb)	Sulfur Dioxide AM (ppb)	Sulfur Dioxide 1-Hr (ppb)	Sulfur Dioxide 24-Hr (ppb)
MSA[1] Level	n/a	n/a	n/a	n/a	n/a
NAAQS[2]	53	100	30	75	140
Met NAAQS[2]	n/a	n/a	n/a	n/a	n/a

Note: (1) Data covers the Huntsville, AL Metropolitan Statistical Area—see Appendix B for areas included; Data from exceptional events are included; (2) National Ambient Air Quality Standards; ppm = parts per million; ug/m^3 = micrograms per cubic meter; n/a not available.
Concentrations: Nitrogen Dioxide AM—highest arithmetic mean concentration; Nitrogen Dioxide 1-Hr—highest 98th percentile 1-hour daily maximum concentration; Sulfur Dioxide AM—highest annual mean concentration; Sulfur Dioxide 1-Hr—highest 99th percentile 1-hour daily maximum concentration; Sulfur Dioxide 24-Hr—highest second maximum 24-hour concentration
Source: U.S. Environmental Protection Agency, Air Quality Monitoring Information, "Air Quality Statistics by City, 2012"

Drinking Water

Water System Name	Pop. Served	Primary Water Source Type	Violations[1]	
			Health Based	Monitoring/ Reporting
Huntsville Utilities	219,168	Surface	0	0

Note: (1) Based on violation data from January 1, 2013 to December 31, 2013 (includes unresolved violations from earlier years)
Source: U.S. Environmental Protection Agency, Office of Ground Water and Drinking Water, Safe Drinking Water Information System (based on data extracted February 10, 2014)

Jacksonville, Florida

Background

Modern day Jacksonville is largely a product of the reconstruction that occurred during the 1940s after a fire had razed 147 city blocks a few decades earlier. Lying under the modern structures, however, is a history that dates back earlier than the settlement of Plymouth by the Pilgrims.

Located in the northeast part of Florida on the St. John's River, Jacksonville, the largest city in land area in the contiguous United States, was settled by English, Spanish, and French explorers from the sixteenth through the eighteenth centuries. Sites commemorating their presence include: Fort Caroline National Monument, marking the French settlement led by René de Goulaine Laudonniére in 1564; Spanish Pond one-quarter of a mile east of Fort Caroline, where Spanish forces led by Pedro Menendez captured the Fort; and Fort George Island, from which General James Oglethorpe led English attacks against the Spanish during the eighteenth century.

Jacksonville was attractive to these early settlers because of its easy access to the Atlantic Ocean, which meant a favorable port.

Today, Jacksonville remains an advantageous port and is home to Naval Air Station Jacksonville, a major employer in the area. Jacksonville is the financial hub of Florida, and many companies have headquarters here.

On the cultural front, Jacksonville boasts a range of options, including the Children's Museum, the Jacksonville Symphony Orchestra, the Gator Bowl, and beach facilities. In 2005, the city hosted Super Bowl XXXIX at the former Alltel Stadium (now Jacksonville Municipal Stadium), home of the NFL's Jacksonville Jaguars. The city also boasts the largest urban park system in the United States, providing services at more than 337 locations on more than 80,000 acres located throughout the city. The Jacksonville Jazz Festival, held every April, is the second-largest jazz festival in the nation. The city is home to several theaters, including Little Theatre, which, operating since 1919, is one of the oldest operating community theaters in the nation.

Jacksonville has more than 80,000 acres of parkland throughout the city, and is renowned for its outdoor recreational facilities. The city's most recent park, The Jacksonville Arboretum and Gardens, was opened in the fall of 2008.

Summers are long, warm, and relatively humid. Winters are generally mild, although periodic invasions of cold northern air bring the temperature down. Temperatures along the beaches rarely rise above 90 degrees. Summer coastal thunderstorms usually occur before noon, and move inland in the afternoons. The greatest rainfall, as localized thundershowers, occurs during the summer months. Although the area is in the hurricane belt, this section of the coast has been very fortunate in escaping hurricane-force winds.

Rankings

Business/Finance Rankings

- The personal finance site NerdWallet scored the nation's 20 largest American cities according to how friendly a business climate they offer to would-be entrepreneurs. Criteria inlcuded local taxes (state, city, payroll, property), growth rate, and the regulatory environment as judged by small business owners. On the resulting list of most welcoming cities, Jacksonville ranked #9. *www.nerdwallet.com, "Top 10 Best Cities for Small Business," August 26, 2013*

- Jacksonville was the #2-ranked city for savers, according to the finance site GoBankingRates, which considered the prospects for savers in a tough savings economy by looking for higher interest yields, lower taxes, more jobs with higher incomes, and less expensive housing costs. *www.gobankingrates.com, "Best Cities for Saving Money," February 24, 2014*

- Analysts for the business website 24/7 Wall Street looked at the local government report "Tax Rates and Tax Burdens in the District of Columbia—A Nationwide Comparison" to determine where a family of three at two different income levels would pay the least and the most in state and local taxes. Among the ten cities with the lowest state and local tax burdens was Jacksonville, at #5. *247wallst.com, American Cities with the Highest (and Lowest) Taxes, February 25, 2013*

- Based on a minimum of 500 social media reviews per metro area, the employment opinion group Glassdoor surveyed 50 of the largest U.S. metro areas on measures including compensation and benefits, satisfaction with management, business outlook, and number of employers hiring. The Jacksonville metro area was ranked #35 in overall employee satisfaction. *www.glassdoor.com, "Employment Satisfaction Report Card by City," June 21, 2013*

- In a survey of economic confidence in the nation's 50 largest metropolitan areas conducted January–December 2012, the Jacksonville metro area placed among the bottom five, according to Gallup's 2013 Economic Confidence Index. *Gallup Economy, "D.C. Metro Area Again Leads U.S. in Economic Confidence," March 28, 2013*

- The Brookings Institution ranked the 50 largest cities in the U.S. based on income inequality. Jacksonville was ranked #37. (#1 = greatest ineqality). Criteria: the cities were ranked based on the "95/20 ratio." This figure represents the income at which a household earns more than 95 percent of all other households, divided by the income at which a household earns more than only 20 percent of all other households. *Brookings Institution, "Income Inequality in America's 50 Largest Cities, 2007-2012," February 20, 2014*

- Jacksonville was ranked #37 out of 100 metro areas in terms of economic performance (#1 = best) during the recession and recovery from trough quarter through the second quarter of 2013. Criteria: percent change in employment; percentage point change in unemployment rate; percent change in gross metropolitan product; percent change in House Price Index. *Brookings Institution, MetroMonitor: Tracking Economic Recession and Recovery in America's 100 Largest Metropolitan Areas, September 2013*

- The Jacksonville metro area was identified as one of the most affordable metropolitan areas in America by *Forbes*. The area ranked #15 out of 20. Criteria: the 100 largest metro areas in the U.S. were analyzed based on housing affordability and cost-of-living. *Forbes.com, "America's Most Affordable Cities," March 11, 2014*

- Jacksonville was identified as one of the top 25 U.S. cities with the most credit card debt by credit reporting bureau Experian. The city was ranked #2. *Experian, March 4, 2011*

- The Jacksonville metro area appeared on the Milken Institute "2013 Best Performing Cities" list. Rank: #133 out of 200 large metro areas. Criteria: job growth; wage and salary growth; high-tech output growth. *Milken Institute, "Best-Performing Cities 2013," December 2013*

- *Forbes* ranked the 200 most populous metro areas in the U.S. in terms of the "Best Places for Business and Careers." The Jacksonville metro area was ranked #58. Criteria: costs (business and living); job growth (past and projected); income growth; educational attainment (college and high school); projected economic growth; cultural and recreational opportunities; net migration patterns; number of highly ranked colleges. *Forbes, "The Best Places for Business and Careers," August 7, 2013*

Children/Family Rankings

- Jacksonville was selected as one of the best cities for families to live by *Parenting* magazine. The city ranked #74 out of 100. Criteria: education; health; community; *Parenting's* Culture & Charm Index. *Parenting.com, "The 2012 Best Cities for Families List"*

Culture/Performing Arts Rankings

- Jacksonville was selected as one of America's top cities for the arts. The city ranked #15 in the big city (population 500,000 and over) category. Criteria: readers' top choices for arts travel destinations based on the richness and variety of visual arts sites, activities and events. *American Style, "2012 Top 25 Arts Destinations," June 2012*

Dating/Romance Rankings

- Of the 100 U.S. cities surveyed by *Men's Health* in its quest to identify the nation's best cities for dating and forming relationships, Jacksonville was ranked #21 for online dating (#1 = best). *Men's Health, "The Best and Worst Cities for Online Dating," January 30, 2013*

Education Rankings

- *Men's Health* ranked 100 U.S. cities in terms of their education levels. Jacksonville was ranked #69 (#1 = most educated city). Criteria: high school graduation rates; school enrollment; educational attainment; number of households who have outstanding student loans; number of households whose members have taken adult-education courses. *Men's Health, "Where School Is In: The Most and Least Educated Cities," September 12, 2011*

- Jacksonville was selected as one of America's most literate cities. The city ranked #58 out of the 77 largest U.S. cities. Criteria: number of booksellers; library resources; Internet resources; educational attainment; periodical publishing resources; newspaper circulation. *Central Connecticut State University, "America's Most Literate Cities, 2013"*

Environmental Rankings

- The Jacksonville metro area came in at #314 for the relative comfort of its climate on Sperling's list of "chill cities," as measured by the Sperling Heat Index. All 361 metro areas are included. Criteria included daytime high temperatures, nighttime low temperatures, dew point, and relative humidity at the high temperatures. *www.bertsperling.com, "Sperling's Chill Cities," July 18, 2013*

- Sperling's BestPlaces assessed 379 metropolitan areas of the United States for the likelihood of dangerously extreme weather events or earthquakes. In general the Southeast and South-Central regions have the highest risk of weather extremes and earthquakes, while the Pacific Northwest enjoys the lowest risk. Of the least risky metropolitan areas, the Jacksonville metro area was ranked #330. *www.bestplaces.net, "Safest Places from Natural Disasters," April 2011*

- Jacksonville was selected as one of 22 "Smarter Cities" for energy by the Natural Resources Defense Council. Criteria: investment in green power; energy efficiency measures; conservation. *Natural Resources Defense Council, "2010 Smarter Cities," July 19, 2010*

Food/Drink Rankings

- *Men's Health* ranked 100 major U.S. cities in terms of alcohol intoxication. Jacksonville ranked #65 (#1 = most sober).Criteria: binge drinking; alcohol-related traffic accidents, arrests, and fatalities. *Men's Health, "The Drunkest Cities in America," November 19, 2013*

Health/Fitness Rankings

- For each of the 50 most populous metro areas in the United States, the American College of Sports Medicine's American Fitness Index evaluated infrastructure, community assets, and policies that encourage healthy and fit lifestyles, including preventive health behaviors, levels of chronic disease conditions, health care access, and community resources and policies that support physical activity. The Jacksonville metro area ranked #37 for "community fitness." Personal health indicators were considered as well as community and environmental indicators. *www.americanfitnessindex.org, "ACSM American Fitness Index Health and Community Fitness Status of the 50 Largest Metropolitan Areas," May 2013*

- Jacksonville was given "Well City USA" status by The Wellness Councils of America, whose objective is to engage entire business communities in building healthy workforces. Well City status is met when a minimum of 20 employers who collectively employ at least 20% of the city's workforce become designated Well Workplaces within a three-year period. To date, eleven communities have achieved Well City USA status. *The Wellness Councils of America, "Well City USA, 2014"*

- Jacksonville was selected as one of the 25 fittest cities in America by *Men's Fitness Online*. It ranked #20 out of America's 50 largest cities. Criteria: fitness centers and sport stores; nutrition; sports participation; TV viewing; overweight/sedentary; junk food; air quality; geography; commute; parks and open space; city recreational facilities; access to healthcare; motivation; mayor and city initiatives; state obesity initiatives. *Men's Fitness, "The Fittest and Fattest Cities in America," March 5, 2012*

- Jacksonville was identified as a "2013 Spring Allergy Capital." The area ranked #52 out of 100. Three groups of factors were used to identify the most severe cities for people with allergies during the spring season: annual pollen levels; medicine utilization; access to board-certified allergists. *Asthma and Allergy Foundation of America, "Spring Allergy Capitals 2013"*

- Jacksonville was identified as a "2013 Fall Allergy Capital." The area ranked #59 out of 100. Three groups of factors were used to identify the most severe cities for people with allergies during the fall season: annual pollen levels; medicine utilization; access to board-certified allergists. *Asthma and Allergy Foundation of America, "Fall Allergy Capitals 2013"*

- Jacksonville was identified as a "2013 Asthma Capital." The area ranked #48 out of the nation's 100 largest metropolitan areas. Twelve factors were used to identify the most challenging places to live for people with asthma: estimated prevalence; self-reported prevalence; crude death rate for asthma; annual pollen score; annual air quality; public smoking laws; number of board-certified asthma specialists; school inhaler access laws; rescue medication use; controller medication use; uninsured rate; poverty rate. *Asthma and Allergy Foundation of America, "Asthma Capitals 2013"*

- *Men's Health* ranked 100 major U.S. cities in terms of the best and worst cities for men. Jacksonville ranked #79. Criteria: thirty-three data points were examined covering health, fitness, and quality of life. *Men's Health, "The Best & Worst Cities for Men 2014," December 6, 2013*

- Jacksonville was selected as one of the best metropolitan areas for hospital care in America by *HealthGrades.com*. The rankings are based on a comprehensive study of patient death and complication rates in the nation's nearly 5,000 hospitals. Hospitals performing in the top 5% nationwide across 26 different medical procedures and diagnoses were identified. *HealthGrades.com* then ranked cities by the highest percentage of these Distinguished Hospitals for Clinical Excellence™. The Jacksonville metro area ranked #40. *HealthGrades.com, "America's Top 50 Cities for Hospital Care," January 21, 2012*

- The Jacksonville metro area appeared in the 2013 Gallup-Healthways Well-Being Index. The area ranked #159 out of 189. The Gallup-Healthways Well-Being Index score is an average of six sub-indexes, which individually examine life evaluation, emotional health, work environment, physical health, healthy behaviors, and access to basic necessities. Results are based on telephone interviews conducted as part of the Gallup-Healthways Well-Being Index survey January 2–December 29, 2012, and January 2–December 30, 2013, with a random sample of 531,630 adults, aged 18 and older, living in metropolitan areas in the 50 U.S. states and the District of Columbia. *Gallup-Healthways, "State of American Well-Being," March 25, 2014*

- The Jacksonville metro area was identified as one of "America's Most Stressful Cities" by *Sperling's BestPlaces*. The metro area ranked #4 out of 50. Criteria: unemployment rate; suicide rate; commute time; mental health; poor rest; alcohol use; violent crime rate; property crime rate; cloudy days annually. *Sperling's BestPlaces, www.BestPlaces.net, "Stressful Cities 2012*

- *Men's Health* ranked 100 U.S. cities in terms of their activity levels. Jacksonville was ranked #75 (#1 = most active city). Criteria: where and how often residents exercise; percentage of households that watch more than 15 hours of cable television a week and buy more than 11 video games a year; death rate from deep-vein thrombosis, a condition linked to sitting for extended periods of time. *Men's Health, "Where Sit Happens: The Most and Least Active Cities in America," June 20, 2011*

- *The Daily Beast* identified the 30 U.S. metro areas with the worst smoking habits. The Jacksonville metro area ranked #20. Sixty urban centers with populations of more than one million were ranked based on the following criteria: number of smokers; number of cigarettes smoked per day; fewest attempts to quit. *The Daily Beast, "30 Cities With Smoking Problems," January 3, 2011*

Real Estate Rankings

- Jacksonville ranked #2 in a *Forbes* study of the rental housing market in the nation's 44 largest metropolitan areas to determine the cities that are best for renters. Criteria: average rent in 2012's first quarter, year-over-year change in that figure, vacancy rate, and average monthly rent payment compared with average monthly mortgage payment. *Forbes.com, "The Best and Worst Cities for Renters," June 14, 2012*

- Jacksonville was ranked #65 out of 283 metro areas in terms of house price appreciation in 2013 (#1 = highest rate). *Federal Housing Finance Agency, House Price Index, 4th Quarter 2013*

- The Jacksonville metro area was identified as one of the 20 best housing markets in the U.S. in 2013. The area ranked #7 out of 173 markets with a home price appreciation of 21.8%. Criteria: year-over-year change of median sales price of existing single-family homes between the 4th quarter of 2012 and the 4th quarter of 2013. *National Association of Realtors®, Median Sales Price of Existing Single-Family Homes for Metropolitan Areas, 4th Quarter 2013*

- The Jacksonville metro area was identified as one of the 10 best condo markets in the U.S. in 2013. The area ranked #3 out of 64 markets with a price appreciation of 41.5%. Criteria: year-over-year change of median sales price of existing apartment condo-coop homes between the 4th quarter of 2012 and the 4th quarter of 2013. *National Association of Realtors®, Median Sales Price of Existing Apartment Condo-Coop Homes for Metropolitan Areas, 4th Quarter 2013*

- Jacksonville was ranked #79 out of 224 metro areas in terms of housing affordability in 2013 by the National Association of Home Builders (#1 = most affordable). The NAHB-Wells Fargo Housing Opportunity Index (HOI) for a given area is defined as the share of homes sold in that area that would have been affordable to a family earning the local median income, based on standard mortgage underwriting criteria. *National Association of Home Builders®, NAHB-Wells Fargo Housing Opportunity Index, 4th Quarter 2013*

- The nation's largest metro areas were analyzed in terms of the percentage of households entering some stage of foreclosure in 2013. The Jacksonville metro area ranked #2 out of 10 (#1 = highest foreclosure rate). *RealtyTrac, "2013 Year-End U.S. Foreclosure Market Report™," January 16, 2014*

- The nation's largest metro areas were analyzed in terms of the best places to buy foreclosures in 2013. The Jacksonville metro area ranked #7 out of 20. Criteria: RealtyTrac scored all metro areas with a population of 500,000 or more by summing up four numbers: months' supply of foreclosure inventory; percentage of foreclosure sales; foreclosure discount; percentage increase in foreclosure activity in 2012. *RealtyTrac, "2012 Year-End Metropolitan Foreclosure Market Report," January 28, 2013*

Safety Rankings

- Symantec, in partnership with Sperling's BestPlaces, ranked the 50 largest cities in the U.S. in terms of their vulnerability to cybercrime. The city ranked #40. Criteria: number of cyberattacks and potential infections; level of Internet access; expenditures on smartphones and computer hardware/software; wireless hotspots; broadband connectivity; Internet usage; online purchases. *Symantec, "Riskiest Online Cities of 2012" February 15, 2012*

- Allstate ranked the 200 largest cities in America in terms of driver safety. Jacksonville ranked #73. Allstate researchers analyzed internal property damage claims over a two-year period from January 2010 to December 2011. A weighted average of the two-year numbers determined the annual percentages. *Allstate, "Allstate America's Best Drivers Report®, August 27, 2013"*

- The National Insurance Crime Bureau ranked 380 metro areas in the U.S. in terms of per capita rates of vehicle theft. The Jacksonville metro area ranked #170 (#1 = highest rate). Criteria: number of vehicle theft offenses per 100,000 inhabitants in 2012. *National Insurance Crime Bureau, "Hot Spots 2012," June 26, 2013*

- The Jacksonville metro area was identified as one of the most dangerous metro areas for pedestrians by Transportation for America. The metro area ranked #3 out of 52 metro areas with over 1 million residents. Criteria: area's population divided by the number of pedestrian fatalities in that area. *Transportation for America, "Dangerous by Design 2011"*

Seniors/Retirement Rankings

- From its Best Cities for Successful Aging indexes, the Milken Institute generated rankings for metropolitan areas, weighing data in eight categories—general indicators, health care, wellness, living arrangements, transportation and general accessibility, financial well-being, education and employment, and community participation. The Jacksonville metro area was ranked #40 overall in the large metro area category. *Milken Institute, "Best Cities for Successful Aging," July 2012*

- Jacksonville was identified as one of the most popular places to retire by *Topretirements.com*. The list reflects the 100 cities (out of 900+ total cities reviewed) that visitors to the website are most interested in for retirement. *Topretirements.com, "Most Popular Places to Retire for 2014," February 25, 2014*

- Jacksonville was selected as one of "The Best Retirement Places" by *Forbes*. The magazine considered a wide range of factors such as climate, availability of doctors, driving environment, and crime rates, but focused especially on tax burden and cost of living. *Forbes, "The Best Retirement Places," March 27, 2011*

Sports/Recreation Rankings

- Jacksonville appeared on the *Sporting News* list of the "Best Sports Cities" for 2011. The area ranked #44 out of 271. Criteria: the magazine takes a 12-month snapshot of each city's sports, putting a heavy premium on regular-season won-lost records (from the most recently completed season). Other criteria include: playoff berths, bowl appearances and tournament bids; championships; applicable power ratings; quality of competition; overall fan fervor (measured in part by attendance); abundance of teams (rewarding quality over quantity); stadium and arena quality; ticket availability and prices; franchise ownership; and marquee appeal of athletes. *Sporting News, "Best Sports Cities 2011," October 4, 2011*

- Jacksonville appeared on the *Sporting News* list of the "Best Sports Cities" for 2011. The area ranked #44 out of 271. Criteria: a 12-month snapshot of regular-season won-lost records (from the most recently completed season). Other criteria include: playoff berths, bowl appearances and tournament bids; championships; applicable power ratings; quality of competition; overall fan fervor (measured in part by attendance); abundance of teams (quality over quantity); stadium and arena quality; ticket availability and prices; franchise ownership; and marquee appeal of athletes. *Sporting News, "Best Sports Cities 2011," October 4, 2011*

Transportation Rankings

- Jacksonville was identified as one of America's worst cities for speed traps by the National Motorists Association. The city ranked #12 out of 25. Criteria: speed trap locations per 100,000 residents. *National Motorists Association, September 2011*

Women/Minorities Rankings

- *Women's Health* examined U.S. cities and identified the 100 best cities for women. Jacksonville was ranked #77. Criteria: 30 categories were examined from obesity and breast cancer rates to commuting times and hours spent working out. *Women's Health, "Best Cities for Women 2012"*

- The Jacksonville metro area appeared on *Forbes'* list of the "Best Cities for Minority Entrepreneurs." The area ranked #77 out of 10. Criteria: 52 metropolitan statistical areas were examined. For each ethnicity (African Americans, Asians and Hispanics), the editors measured housing affordability, population growth, income growth, and entrepreneurship (per capita self-employment). *Forbes, "Best Cities for Minority Entrepreneurs," March 23, 2011*

Miscellaneous Rankings

- Jacksonville was selected as a 2013 Digital Cities Survey winner. The city ranked #3 in the large city (250,000 or more population) category. The survey examined and assessed how city governments are utilizing information technology to operate and deliver quality service to their customers and citizens. Survey questions focused on implementation and adoption of online service delivery; planning and governance; and the infrastructure and architecture that make the transformation to digital government possible. *Center for Digital Government, "2013 Digital Cities Survey," November 7, 2013*

- *Men's Health* ranked 100 U.S. cities by their level of sadness. Jacksonville was ranked #88 (#1 = saddest city). Criteria: suicide rates; unemployment rates; percentage of households that use antidepressants; percent of population who report feeling blue all or most of the time. *Men's Health, "Frown Towns," November 28, 2011*

- Mars Chocolate North America, the makers of COMBOS®, in partnership with Sperling's BestPlaces, ranked 50 major metro areas in terms of their "manliness." The Jacksonville metro area ranked #21. Criteria: number of professional sports teams; number of nearby NASCAR tracks and racing events; manly lifestyle; concentration of manly retail stores; manly occupations per capita; salty snack sales; "Board of Manliness" rankings. *Mars Chocolate North America, "America's Manliest Cities 2012"*

- The National Alliance to End Homelessness ranked the 100 most populous metro areas in terms the rate of homelessness. The Jacksonville metro area ranked #14. Criteria: number of homeless people per 10,000 population in 2011. *National Alliance to End Homelessness, The State of Homelessness in America 2012*

Business Environment

CITY FINANCES

City Government Finances

Component	2011 ($000)	2011 ($ per capita)
Total Revenues	3,997,373	4,962
Total Expenditures	4,689,030	5,821
Debt Outstanding	10,456,655	12,980
Cash and Securities[1]	5,532,734	6,868

Note: (1) Cash and security holdings of a government at the close of its fiscal year, including those of its dependent agencies, utilities, and liquor stores.
Source: U.S Census Bureau, State & Local Government Finances 2011

City Government Revenue by Source

Source	2011 ($000)	2011 ($ per capita)
General Revenue		
From Federal Government	90,863	113
From State Government	149,190	185
From Local Governments	3,748	5
Taxes		
Property	493,171	612
Sales and Gross Receipts	360,846	448
Personal Income	0	0
Corporate Income	0	0
Motor Vehicle License	0	0
Other Taxes	55,192	69
Current Charges	485,790	603
Liquor Store	0	0
Utility	1,813,659	2,251
Employee Retirement	154,813	192

Source: U.S Census Bureau, State & Local Government Finances 2011

City Government Expenditures by Function

Function	2011 ($000)	2011 ($ per capita)	2011 (%)
General Direct Expenditures			
Air Transportation	58,688	73	1.3
Corrections	59,179	73	1.3
Education	0	0	0.0
Employment Security Administration	0	0	0.0
Financial Administration	79,589	99	1.7
Fire Protection	126,115	157	2.7
General Public Buildings	12,718	16	0.3
Governmental Administration, Other	21,165	26	0.5
Health	34,714	43	0.7
Highways	123,584	153	2.6
Hospitals	0	0	0.0
Housing and Community Development	6,918	9	0.1
Interest on General Debt	244,402	303	5.2
Judicial and Legal	29,451	37	0.6
Libraries	43,593	54	0.9
Parking	3,584	4	0.1
Parks and Recreation	83,498	104	1.8
Police Protection	297,364	369	6.3
Public Welfare	45,610	57	1.0
Sewerage	138,674	172	3.0
Solid Waste Management	72,235	90	1.5
Veterans' Services	0	0	0.0
Liquor Store	0	0	0.0
Utility	2,300,103	2,855	49.1
Employee Retirement	254,227	316	5.4

Source: U.S Census Bureau, State & Local Government Finances 2011

Jacksonville, Florida   373

DEMOGRAPHICS

Population Growth

Area	1990 Census	2000 Census	2010 Census	Population Growth (%) 1990-2000	Population Growth (%) 2000-2010
City	635,221	735,617	821,784	15.8	11.7
MSA[1]	925,213	1,122,750	1,345,596	21.4	19.8
U.S.	248,709,873	281,421,906	308,745,538	13.2	9.7

Note: (1) Figures cover the Jacksonville, FL Metropolitan Statistical Area—see Appendix B for areas included
Source: U.S. Census Bureau, Census 1990, 2000, 2010

Household Size

Area	Persons in Household (%) One	Two	Three	Four	Five	Six	Seven or More	Average Household Size
City	30.6	33.1	16.6	11.7	4.9	2.0	1.2	2.61
MSA[1]	27.6	35.2	16.3	12.7	5.3	1.9	1.0	2.63
U.S.	27.6	33.5	15.7	13.2	6.1	2.4	1.5	2.63

Note: (1) Figures cover the Jacksonville, FL Metropolitan Statistical Area—see Appendix B for areas included
Source: U.S. Census Bureau, 2010-2012 American Community Survey 3-Year Estimates

Race

Area	White Alone[2] (%)	Black Alone[2] (%)	Asian Alone[2] (%)	AIAN[3] Alone[2] (%)	NHOPI[4] Alone[2] (%)	Other Race Alone[2] (%)	Two or More Races (%)
City	60.5	30.5	4.3	0.3	0.1	1.2	3.2
MSA[1]	70.8	21.6	3.5	0.3	0.1	1.0	2.8
U.S.	74.0	12.6	4.9	0.8	0.2	4.7	2.8

Note: (1) Figures cover the Jacksonville, FL Metropolitan Statistical Area—see Appendix B for areas included;
(2) Alone is defined as not being in combination with one or more other races; (3) American Indian and Alaska
Native; (4) Native Hawaiian and Other Pacific Islander
Source: U.S. Census Bureau, 2010-2012 American Community Survey 3-Year Estimates

Hispanic or Latino Origin

Area	Total (%)	Mexican (%)	Puerto Rican (%)	Cuban (%)	Other (%)
City	8.1	1.8	2.6	1.1	2.6
MSA[1]	7.2	1.6	2.3	0.9	2.3
U.S.	16.6	10.7	1.6	0.6	3.7

Note: Persons of Hispanic or Latino origin can be of any race; (1) Figures cover the Jacksonville, FL
Metropolitan Statistical Area—see Appendix B for areas included
Source: U.S. Census Bureau, 2010-2012 American Community Survey 3-Year Estimates

Segregation

Type	Segregation Indices[1] 1990	2000	2010	2010 Rank[2]	Percent Change 1990-2000	1990-2010	2000-2010
Black/White	57.5	53.9	53.1	59	-3.6	-4.4	-0.8
Asian/White	34.2	37.0	37.5	71	2.8	3.2	0.4
Hispanic/White	22.1	26.6	27.6	98	4.6	5.5	1.0

Note: All figures cover the Metropolitan Statistical Area—see Appendix B for areas included; Figures are based
on an analysis of 1990, 2000, and 2010 Census Decennial Census tract data by William H. Frey, Brookings
Institution and the University of Michigan Social Science Data Analysis Network. In this analysis all racial
groups (whites, blacks, and asians) are non-Hispanic members of those races. Hispanics are shown as a
separate category;
(1) Segregation Indices are Dissimilarity Indices that measure the degree to which the minority group is
distributed differently than whites across census tracts. They range from 0 (complete integration) to 100
(complete segregation) where the value indicates the percentage of the minority group that needs to move to be
distributed exactly like whites; (2) Ranges from 1 (most segregated) to 102 (least segregated); n/a not available.
Source: www.CensusScope.org

Ancestry

Area	German	Irish	English	American	Italian	Polish	French[2]	Scottish	Dutch
City	9.4	9.9	8.4	6.0	4.0	1.4	2.2	1.7	0.9
MSA[1]	11.2	11.8	9.8	8.3	5.1	1.9	2.6	2.1	1.0
U.S.	15.2	11.1	8.2	7.2	5.6	3.1	2.8	1.7	1.4

Note: Figures are the percentage of the total population reporting a particular ancestry. The nine most commonly reported ancestries in the U.S. are shown. Figures include multiple ancestries (e.g. if a person reported being Irish and Italian, they were included in both columns); (1) Figures cover the Jacksonville, FL Metropolitan Statistical Area—see Appendix B for areas included; (2) Excludes Basque
Source: U.S. Census Bureau, 2010-2012 American Community Survey 3-Year Estimates

Foreign-Born Population

Area	Any Foreign Country	Mexico	Asia	Europe	Carribean	South America	Central America[2]	Africa	Canada
City	9.6	0.5	3.7	1.7	1.6	0.9	0.6	0.6	0.2
MSA[1]	7.9	0.4	2.9	1.6	1.2	0.8	0.4	0.4	0.2
U.S.	13.0	3.7	3.7	1.6	1.2	0.9	1.0	0.5	0.3

Note: (1) Figures cover the Jacksonville, FL Metropolitan Statistical Area—see Appendix B for areas included; (2) Excludes Mexico.
Source: U.S. Census Bureau, 2010-2012 American Community Survey 3-Year Estimates

Marital Status

Area	Never Married	Now Married[2]	Separated	Widowed	Divorced
City	33.5	43.6	2.8	6.0	14.1
MSA[1]	30.4	47.6	2.4	5.9	13.7
U.S.	32.4	48.4	2.2	6.0	11.0

Note: Figures are percentages and cover the population 15 years of age and older; (1) Figures cover the Jacksonville, FL Metropolitan Statistical Area—see Appendix B for areas included; (2) Excludes separated
Source: U.S. Census Bureau, 2010-2012 American Community Survey 3-Year Estimates

Age

Area	Under Age 5	Age 5–19	Age 20–34	Age 35–44	Age 45–54	Age 55–64	Age 65–74	Age 75–84	Age 85+	Median Age
City	7.0	19.3	23.0	13.3	14.4	11.7	6.4	3.4	1.5	35.5
MSA[1]	6.4	19.8	20.5	13.3	14.9	12.6	7.3	3.8	1.6	37.6
U.S.	6.4	20.1	20.5	13.1	14.3	12.2	7.3	4.2	1.8	37.3

Note: (1) Figures cover the Jacksonville, FL Metropolitan Statistical Area—see Appendix B for areas included
Source: U.S. Census Bureau, 2010-2012 American Community Survey 3-Year Estimates

Gender

Area	Males	Females	Males per 100 Females
City	401,863	427,672	94.0
MSA[1]	663,092	699,558	94.8
U.S.	153,276,055	158,333,314	96.8

Note: (1) Figures cover the Jacksonville, FL Metropolitan Statistical Area—see Appendix B for areas included
Source: U.S. Census Bureau, 2010-2012 American Community Survey 3-Year Estimates

Religious Groups by Family

Area	Catholic	Baptist	Non-Den.	Methodist[2]	Lutheran	LDS[3]	Pente-costal	Presby-terian[4]	Muslim[5]	Judaism
MSA[1]	9.9	18.5	7.8	4.5	0.7	1.1	1.9	1.6	0.6	0.4
U.S.	19.1	9.3	4.0	4.0	2.3	2.0	1.9	1.6	0.8	0.7

Note: Figures are the number of adherents as a percentage of the total population; (1) Figures cover the Jacksonville, FL Metropolitan Statistical Area—see Appendix B for areas included; (2) Methodist/Pietist; (3) Latter Day Saints; (4) Reformed; (5) Figures are estimates
Source: Association of Statisticians of American Religious Bodies, 2010 U.S. Religion Census: Religious Congregations & Membership Study

Religious Groups by Tradition

Area	Catholic	Evangelical Protestant	Mainline Protestant	Other Tradition	Black Protestant	Orthodox
MSA[1]	9.9	27.1	5.7	2.9	4.2	0.3
U.S.	19.1	16.2	7.3	4.3	1.6	0.3

Note: Figures are the number of adherents as a percentage of the total population; (1) Figures cover the Jacksonville, FL Metropolitan Statistical Area—see Appendix B for areas included
Source: Association of Statisticians of American Religious Bodies, 2010 U.S. Religion Census: Religious Congregations & Membership Study

ECONOMY

Gross Metropolitan Product

Area	2011	2012	2013	2014	Rank[2]
MSA[1]	59.8	62.3	65.1	68.2	47

Note: Figures are in billions of dollars; (1) Figures cover the Jacksonville, FL Metropolitan Statistical Area—see Appendix B for areas included; (2) Rank is based on 2014 data and ranges from 1 to 363
Source: The United States Conference of Mayors, U.S. Metro Economies: Outlook—Gross Metropolitan Product, with Metro Employment Projections, November 2013

Economic Growth

Area	2011 (%)	2012 (%)	2013 (%)	2014 (%)	Rank[2]
MSA[1]	0.6	2.2	3.1	2.8	19
U.S.	1.6	2.5	1.7	2.5	–

Note: Figures are real gross metropolitan product (GMP) growth rates and represent annual average percent change; (1) Figures cover the Jacksonville, FL Metropolitan Statistical Area—see Appendix B for areas included; (2) Rank is based on 2013 data and ranges from 1 to 363
Source: The United States Conference of Mayors, U.S. Metro Economies: Outlook—Gross Metropolitan Product, with Metro Employment Projections, November 2013

Metropolitan Area Exports

Area	2007	2008	2009	2010	2011	2012	Rank[2]
MSA[1]	1,709.3	1,973.5	1,634.4	1,940.5	2,385.2	2,595.0	84

Note: Figures are in millions of dollars; (1) Figures cover the Jacksonville, FL Metropolitan Statistical Area—see Appendix B for areas included; (2) Rank is based on 2012 data and ranges from 1 to 369
Source: U.S. Department of Commerce, International Trade Administration, Office of Trade & Industry Information, Manufacturing & Services, data extracted April 1, 2014

INCOME

Income

Area	Per Capita ($)	Median Household ($)	Average Household ($)
City	24,483	45,577	62,009
MSA[1]	26,938	50,952	69,112
U.S.	27,385	51,771	71,579

Note: (1) Figures cover the Jacksonville, FL Metropolitan Statistical Area—see Appendix B for areas included
Source: U.S. Census Bureau, 2010-2012 American Community Survey 3-Year Estimates

Household Income Distribution

Area				Percent of Households Earning				
	Under $15,000	$15,000 -24,999	$25,000 -34,999	$35,000 -49,999	$50,000 -74,999	$75,000 -99,000	$100,000 -149,999	$150,000 and up
City	15.2	12.1	11.6	14.8	18.6	11.4	10.9	5.5
MSA[1]	13.2	10.8	10.7	14.5	19.1	12.2	12.1	7.4
U.S.	13.1	11.0	10.5	13.7	18.1	11.9	12.5	9.1

Note: (1) Figures cover the Jacksonville, FL Metropolitan Statistical Area—see Appendix B for areas included
Source: U.S. Census Bureau, 2010-2012 American Community Survey 3-Year Estimates

Poverty Rate

Area	All Ages	Under 18 Years Old	18 to 64 Years Old	65 Years and Over
City	17.7	25.5	16.2	9.6
MSA[1]	15.2	21.1	14.4	8.4
U.S.	15.7	22.2	14.6	9.3

Note: Figures are percentage of people whose income during the past 12 months was below the poverty level;
(1) Figures cover the Jacksonville, FL Metropolitan Statistical Area—see Appendix B for areas included
Source: U.S. Census Bureau, 2010-2012 American Community Survey 3-Year Estimates

Personal Bankruptcy Filing Rate

Area	2008	2009	2010	2011	2012	2013
Duval County	4.44	5.80	5.97	5.13	4.36	4.39
U.S.	3.53	4.61	4.97	4.37	3.76	3.29

Note: Numbers are per 1,000 population and include Chapter 7 and Chapter 13 filings
Source: Federal Deposit Insurance Corporation, Regional Economic Conditions, March 20, 2014

EMPLOYMENT

Labor Force and Employment

Area	Civilian Labor Force			Workers Employed		
	Dec. 2012	Dec. 2013	% Chg.	Dec. 2012	Dec. 2013	% Chg.
City	423,087	419,389	-0.9	390,776	395,150	1.1
MSA[1]	699,589	694,256	-0.8	648,259	655,515	1.1
U.S.	154,904,000	154,408,000	-0.3	143,060,000	144,423,000	1.0

Note: Data is not seasonally adjusted and covers workers 16 years of age and older; (1) Metropolitan Statistical Area—see Appendix B for areas included
Source: Bureau of Labor Statistics, Local Area Unemployment Statistics

Unemployment Rate

Area	2013											
	Jan.	Feb.	Mar.	Apr.	May	Jun.	Jul.	Aug.	Sep.	Oct.	Nov.	Dec.
City	7.9	7.4	6.8	6.7	6.9	7.5	6.9	7.3	6.6	6.3	6.1	5.8
MSA[1]	7.5	7.1	6.5	6.4	6.6	7.0	7.0	6.8	6.4	6.1	5.9	5.6
U.S.	8.5	8.1	7.6	7.1	7.3	7.8	7.7	7.3	7.0	7.0	6.6	6.5

Note: Data is not seasonally adjusted and covers workers 16 years of age and older; All figures are percentages;
(1) Metropolitan Statistical Area—see Appendix B for areas included
Source: Bureau of Labor Statistics, Local Area Unemployment Statistics

Employment by Occupation

Occupation Classification	City (%)	MSA[1] (%)	U.S. (%)
Management, Business, Science, and Arts	33.2	35.4	36.0
Natural Resources, Construction, and Maintenance	8.2	8.3	9.1
Production, Transportation, and Material Moving	10.6	10.0	12.0
Sales and Office	29.1	27.9	24.7
Service	18.8	18.4	18.2

Note: Figures cover employed civilians 16 years of age and older; (1) Figures cover the Jacksonville, FL Metropolitan Statistical Area—see Appendix B for areas included
Source: U.S. Census Bureau, 2010-2012 American Community Survey 3-Year Estimates

Employment by Industry

| Sector | MSA[1] | | U.S. |
	Number of Employees	Percent of Total	Percent of Total
Construction	31,100	5.0	4.2
Education and Health Services	91,300	14.6	15.5
Financial Activities	60,900	9.8	5.7
Government	75,600	12.1	16.1
Information	9,100	1.5	1.9
Leisure and Hospitality	74,500	12.0	10.2
Manufacturing	28,300	4.5	8.7
Mining and Logging	400	0.1	0.6
Other Services	20,400	3.3	3.9
Professional and Business Services	99,300	15.9	13.7
Retail Trade	75,000	12.0	11.4
Transportation and Utilities	32,300	5.2	3.8
Wholesale Trade	25,200	4.0	4.2

Note: Figures cover non-farm employment as of December 2013 and are not seasonally adjusted;
(1) Metropolitan Statistical Area—see Appendix B for areas included
Source: Bureau of Labor Statistics, Current Employment Statistics, Employment, Hours, and Earnings

Occupations with Greatest Projected Employment Growth: 2010 – 2020

Occupation[1]	2010 Employment	2020 Projected Employment	Numeric Employment Change	Percent Employment Change
Retail Salespersons	290,200	345,860	55,660	19.2
Combined Food Preparation and Serving Workers, Including Fast Food	154,650	193,760	39,110	25.3
Registered Nurses	165,400	202,190	36,790	22.3
Waiters and Waitresses	174,630	210,650	36,010	20.6
Customer Service Representatives	165,950	194,220	28,260	17.0
Cashiers	200,040	225,430	25,400	12.7
Office Clerks, General	142,480	164,800	22,330	15.7
Landscaping and Groundskeeping Workers	93,350	115,400	22,050	23.6
Postsecondary Teachers	75,610	94,190	18,580	24.6
Cooks, Restaurant	76,000	94,180	18,190	23.9

Note: Projections cover Florida; (1) Sorted by numeric employment change
Source: www.projectionscentral.com, State Occupational Projections, 2010–2020 Long-Term Projections

Fastest Growing Occupations: 2010 – 2020

Occupation[1]	2010 Employment	2020 Projected Employment	Numeric Employment Change	Percent Employment Change
Layout Workers, Metal and Plastic	230	380	150	65.2
Biomedical Engineers	620	990	370	60.2
Helpers—Carpenters	1,120	1,770	650	58.0
Biochemists and Biophysicists	650	1,000	350	53.6
Medical Scientists, Except Epidemiologists	2,850	4,370	1,520	53.5
Helpers—Brickmasons, Blockmasons, Stonemasons, and Tile and Marble Setters	810	1,240	430	52.6
Reinforcing Iron and Rebar Workers	940	1,370	430	46.1
Home Health Aides	28,580	41,010	12,430	43.5
Stonemasons	550	790	240	42.9
Personal Care Aides	16,880	23,920	7,040	41.7

Note: Projections cover Florida; (1) Sorted by percent employment change and excludes occupations with numeric employment change less than 100
Source: www.projectionscentral.com, State Occupational Projections, 2010–2020 Long-Term Projections

Average Wages

Occupation	$/Hr.	Occupation	$/Hr.
Accountants and Auditors	34.05	Maids and Housekeeping Cleaners	9.35
Automotive Mechanics	18.24	Maintenance and Repair Workers	17.27
Bookkeepers	16.66	Marketing Managers	59.89
Carpenters	14.81	Nuclear Medicine Technologists	34.31
Cashiers	9.16	Nurses, Licensed Practical	20.51
Clerks, General Office	13.20	Nurses, Registered	30.37
Clerks, Receptionists/Information	13.25	Nursing Assistants	11.57
Clerks, Shipping/Receiving	14.27	Packers and Packagers, Hand	9.32
Computer Programmers	33.68	Physical Therapists	46.60
Computer Systems Analysts	37.38	Postal Service Mail Carriers	24.69
Computer User Support Specialists	20.85	Real Estate Brokers	n/a
Cooks, Restaurant	11.17	Retail Salespersons	11.47
Dentists	75.89	Sales Reps., Exc. Tech./Scientific	28.88
Electrical Engineers	41.44	Sales Reps., Tech./Scientific	35.44
Electricians	19.69	Secretaries, Exc. Legal/Med./Exec.	14.98
Financial Managers	60.52	Security Guards	10.35
First-Line Supervisors/Managers, Sales	19.05	Surgeons	118.25
Food Preparation Workers	9.83	Teacher Assistants	12.40
General and Operations Managers	55.77	Teachers, Elementary School	24.10
Hairdressers/Cosmetologists	13.48	Teachers, Secondary School	24.50
Internists	100.97	Telemarketers	10.58
Janitors and Cleaners	11.28	Truck Drivers, Heavy/Tractor-Trailer	18.75
Landscaping/Groundskeeping Workers	11.69	Truck Drivers, Light/Delivery Svcs.	15.81
Lawyers	55.10	Waiters and Waitresses	9.66

Note: Wage data covers the Jacksonville, FL Metropolitan Statistical Area—see Appendix B for areas included. Hourly wages for elementary/secondary school teachers and teacher assistants were calculated by the editors from annual wage data assuming a 40 hour work week; n/a not available.
Source: Bureau of Labor Statistics, Metro Area Occupational Employment and Wage Estimates, May 2013

RESIDENTIAL REAL ESTATE

Building Permits

Area	Single-Family			Multi-Family			Total		
	2012	2013	Pct. Chg.	2012	2013	Pct. Chg.	2012	2013	Pct. Chg.
City	1,310	1,844	40.8	2,499	709	-71.6	3,809	2,553	-33.0
MSA[1]	4,579	6,281	37.2	2,587	1,077	-58.4	7,166	7,358	2.7
U.S.	518,695	620,802	19.7	310,963	370,020	19.0	829,658	990,822	19.4

Note: (1) Metropolitan Statistical Area—see Appendix B for areas included; figures represent new, privately-owned housing units authorized (unadjusted data); All permit data are based on estimates with imputation.
Source: U.S. Census Bureau, Manufacturing, Mining, and Construction Statistics, Building Permits, 2012, 2013

Homeownership Rate

Area	2006 (%)	2007 (%)	2008 (%)	2009 (%)	2010 (%)	2011 (%)	2012 (%)	2013 (%)
MSA[1]	70.0	70.9	72.1	72.6	70.0	68.0	66.6	69.9
U.S.	68.8	68.1	67.8	67.4	66.9	66.1	65.4	65.1

Note: (1) Figures cover the Jacksonville, FL Metropolitan Statistical Area—see Appendix B for areas included
Source: U.S. Census Bureau, Housing Vacancies and Homeownership Annual Statistics: 2013

Housing Vacancy Rates

Area	Gross Vacancy Rate[2] (%)			Year-Round Vacancy Rate[3] (%)			Rental Vacancy Rate[4] (%)			Homeowner Vacancy Rate[5] (%)		
	2011	2012	2013	2011	2012	2013	2011	2012	2013	2011	2012	2013
MSA[1]	14.7	15.4	14.2	14.1	14.4	12.7	13.3	11.7	8.4	2.8	1.9	1.5
U.S.	14.2	13.8	13.8	11.1	10.8	10.7	9.5	8.7	8.3	2.5	2.0	2.0

Note: (1) Figures cover the Jacksonville, FL Metropolitan Statistical Area—see Appendix B for areas included; (2) The percentage of the total housing inventory that is vacant; (3) The percentage of the housing inventory (excluding seasonal units) that is year-round vacant; (4) The percentage of rental inventory that is vacant for rent; (5) The percentage of homeowner inventory that is vacant for sale
Source: U.S. Census Bureau, Housing Vacancies and Homeownership Annual Statistics: 2013

TAXES

State Corporate Income Tax Rates

State	Tax Rate (%)	Income Brackets ($)	Num. of Brackets	Financial Institution Tax Rate (%)[a]	Federal Income Tax Ded.
Florida	5.5 (f)	Flat rate	1	5.5 (f)	No

Note: Tax rates as of January 1, 2014; (a) Rates listed are the corporate income tax rate applied to financial institutions or excise taxes based on income. Some states have other taxes based upon the value of deposits or shares; (f) An exemption of $50,000 is allowed. Florida's Alternative Minimum Tax rate is 3.3%.
Source: Federation of Tax Administrators, "State Corporate Income Tax Rates, 2014"

State Individual Income Tax Rates

State	Tax Rate (%)	Income Brackets ($)	Num. of Brackets	Personal Exempt. ($)[1] Single	Personal Exempt. ($)[1] Dependents	Fed. Inc. Tax Ded.
Florida	None	–	–	–	–	–

Note: Tax rates as of January 1, 2014; Local- and county-level taxes are not included; n/a not applicable; (1) Married joint filers generally receive double the single exemption
Source: Federation of Tax Administrators, "State Individual Income Tax Rates, 2014"

Various State and Local Tax Rates

State	State and Local Sales and Use (%)	State Sales and Use (%)	Gasoline[1] (¢/gal.)	Cigarette[2] ($/pack)	Spirits[3] ($/gal.)	Wine[4] ($/gal.)	Beer[5] ($/gal.)
Florida	7.0	6.00	36.03	1.339	6.50 (f)	2.25	0.48

Note: All tax rates as of January 1, 2014; (1) The American Petroleum Institute has developed a methodology for determining the average tax rate on a gallon of fuel. Rates may include any of the following: excise taxes, environmental fees, storage tank fees, other fees or taxes, general sales tax, and local taxes. In states where gasoline is subject to the general sales tax, or where the fuel tax is based on the average sale price, the average rate determined by API is sensitive to changes in the price of gasoline. States that fully or partially apply general sales taxes to gasoline: CA, CO, GA, IL, IN, MI, NY; (2) The federal excise tax of $1.0066 per pack and local taxes are not included; (3) Rates are those applicable to off-premise sales of 40% alcohol by volume (a.b.v.) distilled spirits in 750ml containers. Local excise taxes are excluded; (4) Rates are those applicable to off-premise sales of 11% a.b.v. non-carbonated wine in 750ml containers; (5) Rates are those applicable to off-premise sales of 4.7% a.b.v. beer in 12 ounce containers; (f) Different rates also applicable according to alcohol content, place of production, size of container, or place purchased (on- or off-premise or onboard airlines).
Source: Tax Foundation, 2014 Facts & Figures: How Does Your State Compare?

State Business Tax Climate Index Rankings

State	Overall Rank	Corporate Tax Index Rank	Individual Income Tax Index Rank	Sales Tax Index Rank	Unemployment Insurance Tax Index Rank	Property Tax Index Rank
Florida	5	13	1	18	6	16

Note: The index is a measure of how each state's tax laws affect economic performance. The lower the rank, the more favorable a state's tax system is for business. States without a given tax are given a ranking of 1. The scores/rankings for the District of Columbia do not affect other states. The 2014 index represents the tax climate as of July 1, 2013.
Source: Tax Foundation, State Business Tax Climate Index 2014

COMMERCIAL REAL ESTATE

Office Market

Market Area	Inventory (sq. ft.)	Vacancy Rate (%)	Under Construction (sq. ft.)	YTD Net Absorption (sq. ft.)	Total Average Asking Rent ($/sq. ft./year)
Jacksonville	32,715,487	18.2	210,000	416,133	17.38
National	4,726,900,879	15.0	55,419,286	42,829,434	26.27

Source: Newmark Grubb Knight Frank, National Office Market Report, 4th Quarter 2013

Industrial/Warehouse/R&D Market

Market Area	Inventory (sq. ft.)	Vacancy Rate (%)	Under Construction (sq. ft.)	YTD Net Absorption (sq. ft.)	Total Average Asking Rent ($/sq. ft./year)
Jacksonville	117,643,788	10.4	0	1,360,512	3.86
National	14,022,031,238	7.9	83,249,164	156,549,903	5.40

Source: Newmark Grubb Knight Frank, National Industrial Market Report, 4th Quarter 2013

COMMERCIAL UTILITIES

Typical Monthly Electric Bills

Area	Commercial Service ($/month)		Industrial Service ($/month)	
	40 kW demand 5,000 kWh	500 kW demand 100,000 kWh	5,000 kW demand 1,500,000 kWh	70,000 kW demand 50,000,000 kWh
City	566	12,742	170,357	3,675,318

Note: Based on rates in effect January 2, 2013
Source: Memphis Light, Gas and Water, 2013 Utility Bill Comparisons for Selected U.S. Cities

TRANSPORTATION

Means of Transportation to Work

Area	Car/Truck/Van		Public Transportation			Bicycle	Walked	Other Means	Worked at Home
	Drove Alone	Car-pooled	Bus	Subway	Railroad				
City	80.6	10.3	1.8	0.0	0.0	0.4	1.3	1.1	4.4
MSA[1]	81.3	9.8	1.2	0.0	0.0	0.6	1.3	1.2	4.7
U.S.	76.4	9.7	2.6	1.7	0.5	0.6	2.8	1.3	4.3

Note: Figures are percentages and cover workers 16 years of age and older; (1) Figures cover the Jacksonville, FL Metropolitan Statistical Area—see Appendix B for areas included
Source: U.S. Census Bureau, 2010-2012 American Community Survey 3-Year Estimates

Travel Time to Work

Area	Less Than 10 Minutes	10 to 19 Minutes	20 to 29 Minutes	30 to 44 Minutes	45 to 59 Minutes	60 to 89 Minutes	90 Minutes or More
City	8.2	31.3	30.1	22.1	4.7	2.5	1.1
MSA[1]	9.5	28.1	25.9	23.8	7.8	3.7	1.2
U.S.	13.5	29.8	20.9	20.1	7.5	5.6	2.5

Note: Figures are percentages and include workers 16 years old and over; (1) Figures cover the Jacksonville, FL Metropolitan Statistical Area—see Appendix B for areas included
Source: U.S. Census Bureau, 2010-2012 American Community Survey 3-Year Estimates

Travel Time Index

Area	1985	1990	1995	2000	2005	2010	2011
Urban Area[1]	1.11	1.17	1.25	1.20	1.26	1.14	1.14
Average[2]	1.09	1.14	1.16	1.19	1.23	1.18	1.18

Note: Travel Time Index—the ratio of travel time in the peak period to the travel time at free-flow conditions. For example, a value of 1.30 indicates a 20-minute free-flow trip takes 26 minutes in the peak. Free-flow speeds (60 mph on freeways and 35 mph on principal arterials) are used as the comparison threshold; (1) Covers the Jacksonville FL urban area; (2) average of 498 urban areas
Source: Texas Transportation Institute, Urban Mobility Report 2012, December 2012

Public Transportation

Agency Name / Mode of Transportation	Vehicles Operated in Maximum Service	Annual Unlinked Passenger Trips (in thous.)	Annual Passenger Miles (in thous.)
Jacksonville Transportation Authority (JTA)			
Bus (directly operated)	118	10,906.2	67,442.4
Bus (purchased transportation)	20	594.7	3,009.6
Demand Response (purchased transportation)	76	388.3	4,931.0
Monorail and Automated Guideway (directly operated)	7	817.2	374.9

Source: Federal Transit Administration, National Transit Database, 2012

Air Transportation

Airport Name and Code / Type of Service	Passenger Airlines[1]	Passenger Enplanements	Freight Carriers[2]	Freight (lbs.)
Jacksonville International (JAX)				
Domestic service (U.S. carriers - 2013)	23	2,547,732	13	73,251,601
International service (U.S. carriers - 2012)	5	844	0	0

Note: (1) Includes all U.S.-based major, minor and commuter airlines that carried at least one passenger during the year; (2) Includes all U.S.-based airlines and freight carriers that transported at least one lb. of freight during the year.
Source: Bureau of Transportation Statistics, The Intermodal Transportation Database, Air Carriers: T-100 Domestic Market (U.S. Carriers), 2013; Bureau of Transportation Statistics, The Intermodal Transportation Database, Air Carriers: T-100 International Market (U.S. Carriers), 2012

Other Transportation Statistics

Major Highways:	I-10; I-95
Amtrak Service:	Yes
Major Waterways/Ports:	St. Johns River

Source: Amtrak.com; Google Maps

BUSINESSES

Major Business Headquarters

Company Name	Rankings	
	Fortune[1]	Forbes[2]
CSX	231	-
Fidelity National Financial	353	-
Fidelity National Information Services	434	-

Note: (1) Fortune 500—companies that produce a 10-K are ranked 1 to 500 based on 2012 revenue; (2) all private companies with at least $2 billion in annual revenue through the end of their most current fiscal year are ranked 1 to 224; companies listed are headquartered in the city; dashes indicate no ranking Source: Fortune, "Fortune 500," May 20, 2013; Forbes, "America's Largest Private Companies," December 18, 2013

Fast-Growing Businesses

According to *Inc.*, Jacksonville is home to five of America's 500 fastest-growing private companies: **The HCI Group** (#3); **North Florida Field Services** (#238); **ShayCore Enterprises** (#262); **Colo5** (#392); **GO Auto Recycling** (#401). Criteria: must be an independent, privately-held, for-profit, U.S. corporation, proprietorship or partnership; revenues must be at least $100,000 in 2009 and $2 million in 2012; must have four-year operating/sales history. Holding companies, regulated banks, and utilities were excluded. *Inc., "America's 500 Fastest-Growing Private Companies," September 2013*

According to Deloitte, Jacksonville is home to one of North America's 500 fastest-growing high-technology companies: **Web.com Group** (#330). Companies are ranked by percentage growth in revenue over a five-year period. Criteria for inclusion: company must be headquartered within North America; must own proprietary intellectual property or proprietary technology that contributes to a significant portion of the company's operating revenue, or devote a significant proportion of revenues to research and development of technology; must have been in business for a minumum of five years with 2008 operating revenues of at least $50,000 USD/CD and 2012 operating revenues of at least $5 million USD/CD. *Deloitte Touche Tohmatsu, 2013 Technology Fast 500™*

Minority Business Opportunity

Jacksonville is home to one company which is on the *Black Enterprise* Industrial/Service 100 list (100 largest companies based on gross sales): **Raven Transport Co.** (#35). Criteria: operational in previous calendar year; at least 51% black-owned and manufactures/owns the product it sells or provides industrial or consumer services. Brokerages, real estate firms and firms that provide professional services are not eligible. *Black Enterprise, B.E. 100s, 2013*

Jacksonville is home to one company which is on the *Black Enterprise* Auto Dealer 60 list (60 largest dealers based on gross sales): **Cadillac of Orange Park** (#51). Criteria: company must be operational in previous calendar year and be at least 51% black-owned. *Black Enterprise, B.E. 100s, 2013*

Jacksonville is home to one company which is on the *Hispanic Business* 500 list (500 largest U.S. Hispanic-owned companies based on 2012 revenue): **Information and Computing Services** (#209). Companies included must show at least 51 percent ownership by Hispanic U.S. citizens, and must maintain headquarters in one of the 50 states or Washington, D.C. *Hispanic Business, "Hispanic Business 500," June 20, 2013*

Jacksonville is home to one company which is on the *Hispanic Business* Fastest-Growing 100 list (greatest sales growth from 2008 to 2012): **Information & Computing Services** (#99). Companies included must show at least 51 percent ownership by Hispanic U.S. citizens, and must maintain headquarters in one of the 50 states or Washington, D.C. In addition, companies must have minimum revenues of $200,000 for calendar year 2008. *Hispanic Business, June 20, 2013*

Minority- and Women-Owned Businesses

Group	All Firms		Firms with Paid Employees			
	Firms	Sales ($000)	Firms	Sales ($000)	Employees	Payroll ($000)
Asian	3,275	683,318	873	590,497	5,392	124,476
Black	9,718	373,933	650	208,344	3,220	66,134
Hispanic	4,175	800,765	611	627,534	4,024	117,669
Women	19,155	3,802,252	3,059	3,403,581	22,636	698,117
All Firms	64,101	109,406,895	17,474	107,422,420	431,635	17,490,879

Note: Figures cover firms located in the city; minority- and women-owned business are defined as firms in which the corresponding group own 51% or more of the stock or equity of the company
Source: U.S. Census Bureau, 2007 Economic Census, Survey of Business Owners (2012 Survey of Business Owners data will be released starting in June 2015)

HOTELS & CONVENTION CENTERS

Hotels/Motels

Area	5 Star		4 Star		3 Star		2 Star		1 Star		Not Rated	
	Num.	Pct.[3]	Num.	Pct.[3]	Num.	Pct.[3]	Num.	Pct.[3]	Num.	Pct.[3]	Num.	Pct.[3]
City[1]	1	0.6	10	5.7	57	32.4	95	54.0	3	1.7	10	5.7
Total[2]	142	0.9	1,005	6.0	5,147	30.9	8,578	51.4	408	2.4	1,397	8.4

Note: (1) Figures cover Jacksonville and vicinity; (2) Figures cover all 100 cities in this book; (3) Percentage of hotels which have a given star rating; Star ratings are determined by expedia.com and offer an indication of the general quality of a particular hotel.
Source: expedia.com, April 7, 2014

The Jacksonville, FL metro area is home to four of the best hotels in the U.S. according to *Travel & Leisure*: **Elizabeth Pointe Lodge; Ponte Vedra Inn & Club; Lodge & Club at Ponte Vedra Beach; Ritz-Carlton, Amelia Island**. Criteria: service; location; rooms; food; and value. The list includes the top 200 hotels in the U.S. *Travel & Leisure, "T+L 500, The World's Best Hotels 2014"*

The Jacksonville, FL metro area is home to one of the best hotels in the world according to *Condé Nast Traveler*: **Ritz-Carlton**. The selections are based on over 79,000 responses to the magazine's annual Readers' Choice Survey. The list includes the top 200 hotels in the U.S. *Condé Nast Traveler, "Gold List 2014, The World's Best Places to Stay"*

Major Convention Centers

Name	Overall Space (sq. ft.)	Exhibit Space (sq. ft.)	Meeting Space (sq. ft.)	Meeting Rooms
Prime F. Osborn III Convention Center	296,000	100,000	48,000	22

Note: Table includes convention centers located in the Jacksonville, FL metro area; n/a not available
Source: Original research

Living Environment

COST OF LIVING

Cost of Living Index

Composite Index	Groceries	Housing	Utilities	Trans- portation	Health Care	Misc. Goods/ Services
94.9	95.2	83.3	105.7	104.7	85.1	98.4

Note: The Cost of Living Index measures regional differences in the cost of consumer goods and services, excluding taxes and non-consumer expenditures, for professional and managerial households in the top income quintile. It is based on more than 50,000 prices covering almost 60 different items for which prices are collected three times a year by chambers of commerce, economic development organizations or university applied economic centers in each participating urban area. The numbers shown should be read as a percentage above or below the national average of 100. For example, a value of 115.4 in the groceries column indicates that grocery prices are 15.4% higher than the national average. Small differences in the index numbers should not be interpreted as significant; Figures cover the Jacksonville FL urban area.
Source: The Council for Community and Economic Research, ACCRA Cost of Living Index, 2013

Grocery Prices

Area[1]	T-Bone Steak ($/pound)	Frying Chicken ($/pound)	Whole Milk ($/half gal.)	Eggs ($/dozen)	Orange Juice ($/64 oz.)	Coffee ($/11.5 oz.)
City[2]	10.37	1.50	2.66	1.94	3.49	4.07
Avg.	10.19	1.28	2.34	1.81	3.48	4.39
Min.	8.56	0.94	1.44	1.19	2.78	3.40
Max.	14.82	2.28	3.56	3.73	6.23	7.32

Note: (1) Values for the local area are compared with the average, minimum and maximum values for all 327 areas in the Cost of Living Index; (2) Figures cover the Jacksonville FL urban area; T-Bone Steak (price per pound); Frying Chicken (price per pound, whole fryer); Whole Milk (half gallon carton); Eggs (price per dozen, Grade A, large); Orange Juice (64 oz. Tropicana or Florida Natural); Coffee (11.5 oz. can, vacuum-packed, Maxwell House, Hills Bros, or Folgers).
Source: The Council for Community and Economic Research, ACCRA Cost of Living Index, 2013

Housing and Utility Costs

Area[1]	New Home Price ($)	Apartment Rent ($/month)	All Electric ($/month)	Part Electric ($/month)	Other Energy ($/month)	Telephone ($/month)
City[2]	216,016	1,037	171.80	-	-	29.58
Avg.	295,864	900	171.38	91.82	70.12	27.73
Min.	185,506	458	117.80	48.81	33.67	17.16
Max.	1,358,917	3,783	441.68	171.40	372.65	39.47

Note: (1) Values for the local area are compared with the average, minimum and maximum values for all 327 areas in the Cost of Living Index; (2) Figures cover the Jacksonville FL urban area; New Home Price (2,400 sf living area, 8,000 sf lot, in urban area with full utilities); Apartment Rent (950 sf 2 bedroom/1.5 or 2 bath, unfurnished, excluding all utilities except water); All Electric (average monthly cost for an all-electric home); Part Electric (average monthly cost for a part-electric home); Other Energy (average monthly cost for natural gas, fuel oil, coal, wood, and any other forms of energy except electricity); Telephone (price includes basic monthly rate for a private residential line plus additional local usage charges incurred by a family of four).
Source: The Council for Community and Economic Research, ACCRA Cost of Living Index, 2013

Health Care, Transportation, and Other Costs

Area[1]	Doctor ($/visit)	Dentist ($/visit)	Optometrist ($/visit)	Gasoline ($/gallon)	Beauty Salon ($/visit)	Men's Shirt ($)
City[2]	67.03	88.43	61.02	3.52	43.07	23.47
Avg.	101.40	86.48	96.16	3.44	33.87	26.55
Min.	61.67	50.83	50.12	3.08	18.92	12.48
Max.	182.71	152.50	223.78	4.33	68.22	52.03

Note: (1) Values for the local area are compared with the average, minimum and maximum values for all 327 areas in the Cost of Living Index; (2) Figures cover the Jacksonville FL urban area; Doctor (general practitioners routine exam of an established patient); Dentist (adult teeth cleaning and periodic oral examination); Optometrist (full vision eye exam for established adult patient); Gasoline (one gallon regular unleaded, national brand, including all taxes, cash price at self-service pump if available); Beauty Salon (woman's shampoo, trim, and blow-dry); Men's Shirt (cotton/polyester dress shirt, pinpoint weave, long sleeves).
Source: The Council for Community and Economic Research, ACCRA Cost of Living Index, 2013

HOUSING

House Price Index (HPI)

Area	National Ranking[2]	Quarterly Change (%)	One-Year Change (%)	Five-Year Change (%)
MSA[1]	65	1.46	7.30	-18.23
U.S.[3]	–	1.20	7.69	4.18

Note: The HPI is a weighted repeat sales index. It measures average price changes in repeat sales or refinancings on the same properties. This information is obtained by reviewing repeat mortgage transactions on single-family properties whose mortgages have been purchased or securitized by Fannie Mae or Freddie Mac in January 1975; (1) Jacksonville, FL Metropolitan Statistical Area—see Appendix B for areas included; (2) Rankings are based on annual percentage change for all metro areas containing at least 15,000 transactions over the last 10 years and ranges from 1 to 283; (3) figures based on a weighted average of Census Division estimates using a seasonally adjusted, purchase-only index; all figures are for the period ending December 31, 2013
Source: Federal Housing Finance Agency, House Price Index, February 25, 2014

Median Single-Family Home Prices

Area	2011	2012	2013p	Percent Change 2012 to 2013
MSA[1]	123.6	128.2	160.8	25.4
U.S. Average	166.2	177.2	197.4	11.4

Note: Figures are median sales prices of existing single-family homes in thousands of dollars; (p) preliminary; n/a not available; (1) Jacksonville, FL Metropolitan Statistical Area—see Appendix B for areas included
Source: National Association of Realtors, Median Sales Price of Existing Single-Family Homes for Metropolitan Areas, 4th Quarter 2013

Qualifying Income Based on Median Sales Price of Existing Single-Family Homes

Area	With 5% Down ($)	With 10% Down ($)	With 20% Down ($)
MSA[1]	36,658	34,728	30,870
U.S. Average	45,395	43,006	38,228

Note: Figures are preliminary; Qualifying income is based on a mortgage rate of 4.4%. Monthly principal and interest payment is limited to 25% of income; n/a not available; (1) Jacksonville, FL Metropolitan Statistical Area—see Appendix B for areas included
Source: National Association of Realtors, Qualifying Income Based on Median Sales Price of Existing Single-Family Homes for Metropolitan Areas, 4th Quarter 2013

Median Apartment Condo-Coop Home Prices

Area	2011	2012	2013p	Percent Change 2012 to 2013
MSA[1]	65.5	75.8	102.9	35.8
U.S. Average	165.1	173.7	194.9	12.2

Note: Figures are median sales prices of existing apartment condo-coop homes in thousands of dollars; (p) preliminary; n/a not available; (1) Jacksonville, FL Metropolitan Statistical Area—see Appendix B for areas included
Source: National Association of Realtors, Median Sales Price of Existing Apartment Condo-Coop Homes for Metropolitan Areas, 4th Quarter 2013

Gross Monthly Rent

Area	Under $200	$200 -299	$300 -499	$500 -749	$750 -999	$1,000 -1,499	$1,500 and up	Median ($)
City	1.7	2.3	5.0	20.6	31.0	32.2	7.3	909
MSA[1]	1.4	2.1	4.6	18.8	29.7	33.4	10.0	942
U.S.	1.7	3.3	8.1	22.7	24.3	25.7	14.3	889

Note: Figures are percentages except for Median; Gross rent is the contract rent plus the estimated average monthly cost of utilities (electricity, gas, and water and sewer) and fuels (oil, coal, kerosene, wood, etc.) if these are paid by the renter (or paid for the renter by someone else); (1) Figures cover the Jacksonville, FL Metropolitan Statistical Area—see Appendix B for areas included
Source: U.S. Census Bureau, 2010-2012 American Community Survey 3-Year Estimates

Year Housing Structure Built

Area	2010 or Later	2000 -2009	1990 -1999	1980 -1989	1970 -1979	1960 -1969	1950 -1959	1940 -1949	Before 1940	Median Year
City	0.4	20.9	15.0	16.0	13.8	11.1	12.0	5.5	5.2	1981
MSA[1]	0.5	24.6	17.3	17.8	13.7	8.8	8.9	4.2	4.2	1986
U.S.	0.5	14.9	13.8	13.9	15.9	11.1	10.9	5.5	13.5	1976

Note: Figures are percentages except for Median Year; (1) Figures cover the Jacksonville, FL Metropolitan Statistical Area—see Appendix B for areas included
Source: U.S. Census Bureau, 2010-2012 American Community Survey 3-Year Estimates

HEALTH

Health Risk Data

Category	MSA[1] (%)	U.S. (%)
Adults aged 18–64 who have any kind of health care coverage	80.8	79.6
Adults who reported being in good or excellent health	81.4	83.1
Adults who are current smokers	20.9	19.6
Adults who are heavy drinkers[2]	9.7	6.1
Adults who are binge drinkers[3]	19.3	16.9
Adults who are overweight (BMI 25.0 - 29.9)	36.7	35.8
Adults who are obese (BMI 30.0 - 99.8)	29.2	27.6
Adults who participated in any physical activities in the past month	81.5	77.1
Adults 50+ who have ever had a sigmoidoscopy or colonoscopy	70.4	67.3
Women aged 40+ who have had a mammogram within the past two years	67.8	74.0
Men aged 40+ who have had a PSA test within the past two years	38.7	45.2
Adults aged 65+ who have had flu shot within the past year	55.5	60.1
Adults who always wear a seatbelt	n/a	93.8

Note: Data as of 2012 unless otherwise noted; n/a not available; (1) Figures cover the Jacksonville, FL Metropolitan Statistical Area—see Appendix B for areas included; (2) Heavy drinkers are classified as males having more than two drinks per day or females having more than one drink per day; (3) Binge drinkers are classified as males having five or more drinks on one occasion or females having four or more drinks on one occasion
Source: Centers for Disease Control and Prevention, Behaviorial Risk Factor Surveillance System, SMART: Selected Metropolitan/Micropolitan Area Risk Trends, 2012

Chronic Health Indicators

Category	MSA[1] (%)	U.S. (%)
Adults who have ever been told they had a heart attack	4.5	4.5
Adults who have ever been told they had a stroke	3.1	2.9
Adults who have been told they currently have asthma	10.3	8.9
Adults who have ever been told they have arthritis	26.6	25.7
Adults who have ever been told they have diabetes[2]	11.6	9.7
Adults who have ever been told they had skin cancer	8.5	5.7
Adults who have ever been told they had any other types of cancer	6.2	6.5
Adults who have ever been told they have COPD	7.7	6.2
Adults who have ever been told they have kidney disease	n/a	2.5
Adults who have ever been told they have a form of depression	18.7	18.0

Note: Data as of 2012 unless otherwise noted; n/a not available; (1) Figures cover the Jacksonville, FL Metropolitan Statistical Area—see Appendix B for areas included; (2) Figures do not include pregnancy-related, borderline, or pre-diabetes
Source: Centers for Disease Control and Prevention, Behaviorial Risk Factor Surveillance System, SMART: Selected Metropolitan/Micropolitan Area Risk Trends, 2012

Mortality Rates for the Top 10 Causes of Death in the U.S.

ICD-10[a] Sub-Chapter	ICD-10[a] Code	Age-Adjusted Mortality Rate[1] per 100,000 population	
		County[2]	U.S.
Malignant neoplasms	C00-C97	202.0	174.2
Ischaemic heart diseases	I20-I25	127.6	119.1
Other forms of heart disease	I30-I51	48.5	49.6
Chronic lower respiratory diseases	J40-J47	55.2	43.2
Cerebrovascular diseases	I60-I69	40.6	40.3
Organic, including symptomatic, mental disorders	F01-F09	47.1	30.5
Other degenerative diseases of the nervous system	G30-G31	18.1	26.3
Other external causes of accidental injury	W00-X59	27.7	25.1
Diabetes mellitus	E10-E14	30.7	21.3
Hypertensive diseases	I10-I15	29.8	18.8

Note: (a) ICD-10 = International Classification of Diseases 10th Revision; (1) Mortality rates are a three year average covering 2008-2010; (2) Figures cover Duval County
Source: Centers for Disease Control and Prevention, National Center for Health Statistics. Compressed Mortality File 1999-2010 on CDC WONDER Online Database, released January 2013. Data are compiled from the Compressed Mortality File 1999-2010, Series 20 No. 2P, 2013.

Mortality Rates for Selected Causes of Death

ICD-10[a] Sub-Chapter	ICD-10[a] Code	Age-Adjusted Mortality Rate[1] per 100,000 population	
		County[2]	U.S.
Assault	X85-Y09	12.8	5.5
Diseases of the liver	K70-K76	14.1	12.4
Human immunodeficiency virus (HIV) disease	B20-B24	10.0	3.0
Influenza and pneumonia	J09-J18	19.3	16.4
Intentional self-harm	X60-X84	15.4	11.8
Malnutrition	E40-E46	0.9	0.8
Obesity and other hyperalimentation	E65-E68	2.1	1.6
Renal failure	N17-N19	16.1	13.6
Transport accidents	V01-V99	15.5	12.6
Viral hepatitis	B15-B19	4.0	2.2

Note: (a) ICD-10 = International Classification of Diseases 10th Revision; (1) Mortality rates are a three year average covering 2008-2010; (2) Figures cover Duval County
Source: Centers for Disease Control and Prevention, National Center for Health Statistics. Compressed Mortality File 1999-2010 on CDC WONDER Online Database, released January 2013. Data are compiled from the Compressed Mortality File 1999-2010, Series 20 No. 2P, 2013.

Health Insurance Coverage

Area	With Health Insurance	With Private Health Insurance	With Public Health Insurance	Without Health Insurance	Population Under Age 18 Without Health Insurance
City	82.4	62.0	30.1	17.6	8.9
MSA[1]	84.1	65.9	29.2	15.9	8.3
U.S.	84.9	65.4	30.4	15.1	7.5

Note: Figures are percentages that cover the civilian noninstitutionalized population; (1) Figures cover the Jacksonville, FL Metropolitan Statistical Area—see Appendix B for areas included
Source: U.S. Census Bureau, 2010-2012 American Community Survey 3-Year Estimates

Number of Medical Professionals

Area[1]	MDs[2]	DOs[2,3]	Dentists	Podiatrists	Chiropractors	Optometrists
Local (number)	2,943	212	578	67	182	127
Local (rate[4])	337.6	24.3	65.7	7.6	20.7	14.4
U.S. (rate[4])	267.6	19.6	61.7	5.6	24.7	14.5

Note: Data as of 2012 unless noted; (1) Local data covers Duval County; (2) Data as of 2011; (3) Doctor of Osteopathic Medicine; (4) rate per 100,000 population
Source: Area Resource File (ARF) 2012-2013. U.S. Department of Health and Human Services, Health Resources and Services Administration, Bureau of Health Professions

Best Hospitals

According to *U.S. News,* the Jacksonville, FL metro area is home to two of the best hospitals in the U.S.: **Mayo Clinic** (1 specialty); **Baptist Medical Center** (1 specialty). The hospitals listed were nationally ranked in at least one adult specialty. Only 147 hospitals nationwide were nationally ranked in one or more specialties. Eighteen hospitals in the U.S. made the Honor Roll by ranking near the top in at least six specialties.*U.S. News Online, "America's Best Hospitals 2013-14"*

According to *U.S. News,* the Jacksonville, FL metro area is home to one of the best children's hospitals in the U.S.: **Wolfson Children's Hospital**. The hospital listed was highly ranked in at least one pediatric specialty. Eighty-seven hospitals in the U.S. ranked in at least one specialty. Ten children's hospitals in the U.S. made the Honor Roll by ranking near the top in three or more specialties.*U.S. News Online, "America's Best Children's Hospitals 2013-14"*

EDUCATION

Public School District Statistics

District Name	Schls	Pupils	Pupil/ Teacher Ratio	Minority Pupils[1] (%)	Free Lunch Eligible[2] (%)	IEP[3] (%)
Duval County Public Schools	199	125,429	16.5	60.8	47.3	13.7

Note: Table includes school districts with 2,000 or more students; (1) Percentage of students that are not non-Hispanic white; (2) Percentage of students that are eligible for the free lunch program; (3) Percentage of students that have an Individualized Education Program.
Source: U.S. Department of Education, National Center for Education Statistics, Common Core of Data, Local Education Agency (School District) Universe Survey: School Year 2011-2012; U.S. Department of Education, National Center for Education Statistics, Common Core of Data, Public Elementary/Secondary School Universe Survey: School Year 2011-2012

Best High Schools

High School Name	Rank[1]	Grad. Rate[2] (%)	Coll.[3] (%)	AP/IB/ AICE Tests[4]	AP/IB/ AICE Score[5]	SAT Score[6]	ACT Score[6]
Douglas Anderson School of the Arts	456	95	98	1.1	2.2	1533	21.8
Mandarin H.S.	1129	81	86	1.2	2.4	1496	21.2
Stanton College Preparatory School	10	99	99	2.7	2.7	1824	26.0
The PAXON School for Advanced Studies	35	100	99	2.1	2.0	1604	23.6

Note: (1) Public schools are ranked from 1 to 2,000 based on the following self-reported statistics (with the corresponding weight used in calculating their overall score). Schools that were newly founded and did not have a graduating senior class in 2012 were excluded; (2) Four-year, on-time graduation rate (25%); (3) Percent of 2011 graduates who were accepted to college (25%); (4) AP/IB/AICE tests taken per student (25%); (5) Average AP/IB/AICE exam score (10%); (6) Average SAT and/or ACT score (10%); Percent of students enrolled in at least one AP/IB/AICE course (5%)—data not shown
Source: Newsweek and The Daily Beast, "America's Best High Schools 2013"

Highest Level of Education

Area	Less than H.S.	H.S. Diploma	Some College, No Deg.	Associate Degree	Bachelor's Degree	Master's Degree	Prof. School Degree	Doctorate Degree
City	12.5	29.8	23.8	9.2	17.3	5.1	1.5	0.8
MSA[1]	11.3	28.9	23.4	9.2	18.8	6.0	1.6	1.0
U.S.	14.1	28.3	21.3	7.8	18.0	7.5	1.9	1.2

Note: Figures cover persons age 25 and over; (1) Figures cover the Jacksonville, FL Metropolitan Statistical Area—see Appendix B for areas included
Source: U.S. Census Bureau, 2010-2012 American Community Survey 3-Year Estimates

Educational Attainment by Race

Area	High School Graduate or Higher (%)					Bachelor's Degree or Higher (%)				
	Total	White	Black	Asian	Hisp.[2]	Total	White	Black	Asian	Hisp.[2]
City	87.5	89.1	84.5	86.0	80.7	24.7	27.2	16.0	44.7	21.0
MSA[1]	88.7	90.0	84.6	87.5	82.7	27.3	29.4	16.4	45.2	23.7
U.S.	85.9	88.1	82.5	85.5	63.1	28.6	30.0	18.4	50.2	13.4

Note: Figures shown cover persons 25 years old and over; (1) Figures cover the Jacksonville, FL Metropolitan Statistical Area—see Appendix B for areas included; (2) People of Hispanic origin can be of any race
Source: U.S. Census Bureau, 2010-2012 American Community Survey 3-Year Estimates

School Enrollment by Grade and Control

Area	Preschool (%) Public	Preschool (%) Private	Kindergarten (%) Public	Kindergarten (%) Private	Grades 1 - 4 (%) Public	Grades 1 - 4 (%) Private	Grades 5 - 8 (%) Public	Grades 5 - 8 (%) Private	Grades 9 - 12 (%) Public	Grades 9 - 12 (%) Private
City	54.8	45.2	84.1	15.9	85.9	14.1	85.3	14.7	84.2	15.8
MSA[1]	51.8	48.2	84.9	15.1	86.4	13.6	87.1	12.9	87.3	12.7
U.S.	56.9	43.1	87.8	12.2	89.9	10.1	90.0	10.0	90.8	9.2

Note: Figures shown cover persons 3 years old and over; (1) Figures cover the Jacksonville, FL Metropolitan Statistical Area—see Appendix B for areas included
Source: U.S. Census Bureau, 2010-2012 American Community Survey 3-Year Estimates

Average Salaries of Public School Classroom Teachers

Area	2012-13 Dollars	2012-13 Rank[1]	2013-14 Dollars	2013-14 Rank[1]	Percent Change 2012-13 to 2013-14	Percent Change 2003-04 to 2013-14
Florida	46,598	45	46,691	45	0.20	15.0
U.S. Average	56,103	–	56,689	–	1.04	21.8

Note: (1) State rank ranges from 1 to 51 where 1 indicates highest salary.
Source: National Education Association, Rankings & Estimates: Rankings of the States 2013 and Estimates of School Statistics 2014, March 2014

Higher Education

Four-Year Colleges Public	Four-Year Colleges Private Non-profit	Four-Year Colleges Private For-profit	Two-Year Colleges Public	Two-Year Colleges Private Non-profit	Two-Year Colleges Private For-profit	Medical Schools[1]	Law Schools[2]	Voc/ Tech[3]
2	4	5	0	0	9	0	1	10

Note: Figures cover institutions located within the city limits and include main campuses only; (1) includes schools accredited by the Liaison Committee on Medical Education and the American Osteopathic Association's Commission on Osteopathic College Accreditation; (2) includes ABA-accredited schools, schools with provisional ABA accreditation, and state accredited schools; (3) includes all schools with programs that are less than 2 years.
Source: National Center for Education Statistics, Integrated Postsecondary Education System (IPEDS), 2012-13; Association of American Medical Colleges, Member List, April 24, 2014; American Osteopathic Association, Member List, April 24, 2014; Law School Admission Council, Official Guide to ABA-Approved Law Schools Online, April 24, 2014; Wikipedia, List of Medical Schools in the United States, April 24, 2014; Wikipedia, List of Law Schools in the United States, April 24, 2014

PRESIDENTIAL ELECTION

2012 Presidential Election Results

Area	Obama	Romney	Other
Duval County	47.8	51.4	0.8
U.S.	51.0	47.2	1.8

Note: Results are percentages and may not add to 100% due to rounding
Source: Dave Leip's Atlas of U.S. Presidential Elections

EMPLOYERS

Major Employers

Company Name	Industry
Baptist Health System	Hospital management
Baptist Health System	General medical/surgical hospitals
Baptist Health System Foundation	Individual and family services
Blue Cross Blue Shield of Florida	Hospital and medical service plans
Fidelity National Information Services	Prepackaged software
Jacksonville Electric Authority	Electric services
Kelley Clark	Food brokers
Mayo Clinic Jacksonville	General medical/surgical hospitals
Shands Jacksonville Medical Center	General medical/surgical hospitals
Southern Baptist Hospital of Florida	Hospital medical school affiliated with residency

Note: Companies shown are located within the Jacksonville, FL Metropolitan Statistical Area.
Source: Hoovers.com; Wikipedia

Best Companies to Work For

CSX, headquartered in Jacksonville, is among the "100 Best Places to Work in IT." To qualify, companies, both public and private, had to have a minimum of 50 IT employees and were selected based on average salary and bonus increases, the percentage of IT staffers promoted, IT staff turnover rates, training and development programs, and the percentage of women and minorities in IT staff and management positions. In addition, *Computerworld* looked at retention efforts, programs for recognizing and rewarding outstanding performances, and benefits such as flextime, elder care and child care, and reimbursement for college tuition and the cost of pursuing technology certifications. *Computerworld, "100 Best Places to Work in IT 2013"*

PUBLIC SAFETY

Crime Rate

Area	All Crimes	Violent Crimes				Property Crimes		
		Murder	Forcible Rape	Robbery	Aggrav. Assault	Burglary	Larceny -Theft	Motor Vehicle Theft
City	4,741.9	11.1	40.6	163.1	402.5	907.9	3,021.8	195.0
Suburbs[1]	2,769.3	3.2	15.8	44.4	287.8	488.2	1,845.6	84.4
Metro[2]	3,972.0	8.0	30.9	116.8	357.8	744.0	2,562.7	151.8
U.S.	3,246.1	4.7	26.9	112.9	242.3	670.2	1,959.3	229.7

Note: Figures are crimes per 100,000 population; (1) All areas within the metro area that are located outside the city limits; (2) Figures cover the Jacksonville, FL Metropolitan Statistical Area—see Appendix B for areas included
Source: FBI Uniform Crime Reports, 2012

Hate Crimes

Area	Number of Quarters Reported	Bias Motivation				
		Race	Religion	Sexual Orientation	Ethnicity	Disability
City	4	2	1	1	0	0
U.S.	4	2,797	1,099	1,135	667	92

Source: Federal Bureau of Investigation, Hate Crime Statistics 2012

Identity Theft Consumer Complaints

Area	Complaints	Complaints per 100,000 Population	Rank[2]
MSA[1]	1,692	125.7	17
U.S.	290,056	91.8	

Note: (1) Figures cover the Jacksonville, FL Metropolitan Statistical Area—see Appendix B for areas included; (2) Rank ranges from 1 to 377 where 1 indicates greatest number of identity theft complaints per 100,000 population
Source: Federal Trade Commission, Consumer Sentinel Network Data Book for January–December 2013

Fraud and Other Consumer Complaints

Area	Complaints	Complaints per 100,000 Population	Rank[2]
MSA[1]	7,467	554.9	7
U.S.	1,811,724	595.2	-

Note: (1) Figures cover the Jacksonville, FL Metropolitan Statistical Area—see Appendix B for areas included; (2) Rank ranges from 1 to 377 where 1 indicates greatest number of identity theft complaints per 100,000 population
Source: Federal Trade Commission, Consumer Sentinel Network Data Book for January–December 2013

RECREATION

Culture

Dance[1]	Theatre[1]	Instrumental Music[1]	Vocal Music[1]	Series and Festivals	Museums and Art Galleries[2]	Zoos and Aquariums[3]
2	2	1	0	5	24	1

Note: (1) Number of professional perfoming groups; (2) Based on organizations with primary SIC code 8412; (3) AZA-accredited
Source: The Grey House Performing Arts Directory, 2013; Association of Zoos & Aquariums, AZA Member Zoos & Aquariums, April 2014; www.AccuLeads.com, May 1, 2014

Professional Sports Teams

Team Name	League	Year Established
Jacksonville Jaguars	National Football League (NFL)	1995

Note: Includes teams located in the Jacksonville, FL Metropolitan Statistical Area.
Source: Wikipedia, Major Professional Sports Teams of the United States and Canada

CLIMATE

Average and Extreme Temperatures

Temperature	Jan	Feb	Mar	Apr	May	Jun	Jul	Aug	Sep	Oct	Nov	Dec	Yr.
Extreme High (°F)	84	88	91	95	100	103	103	102	98	96	88	84	103
Average High (°F)	65	68	74	80	86	90	92	91	87	80	73	67	79
Average Temp. (°F)	54	57	62	69	75	80	83	82	79	71	62	56	69
Average Low (°F)	43	45	51	57	64	70	73	73	70	61	51	44	58
Extreme Low (°F)	7	22	23	34	45	47	61	63	48	36	21	11	7

Note: Figures cover the years 1948-1990
Source: National Climatic Data Center, International Station Meteorological Climate Summary, 9/96

Average Precipitation/Snowfall/Humidity

Precip./Humidity	Jan	Feb	Mar	Apr	May	Jun	Jul	Aug	Sep	Oct	Nov	Dec	Yr.
Avg. Precip. (in.)	3.0	3.7	3.8	3.0	3.6	5.3	6.2	7.4	7.8	3.7	2.0	2.6	52.0
Avg. Snowfall (in.)	Tr	Tr	Tr	0	0	0	0	0	0	0	0	Tr	0
Avg. Rel. Hum. 7am (%)	86	86	87	86	86	88	89	91	92	91	89	88	88
Avg. Rel. Hum. 4pm (%)	56	53	50	49	54	61	64	65	66	62	58	58	58

Note: Figures cover the years 1948-1990; Tr = Trace amounts (<0.05 in. of rain; <0.5 in. of snow)
Source: National Climatic Data Center, International Station Meteorological Climate Summary, 9/96

Weather Conditions

Temperature			Daytime Sky			Precipitation		
10°F & below	32°F & below	90°F & above	Clear	Partly cloudy	Cloudy	0.01 inch or more precip.	0.1 inch or more snow/ice	Thunder-storms
< 1	16	83	86	181	98	114	1	65

Note: Figures are average number of days per year and cover the years 1948-1990
Source: National Climatic Data Center, International Station Meteorological Climate Summary, 9/96

HAZARDOUS WASTE

Superfund Sites

Jacksonville has five hazardous waste sites on the EPA's Superfund Final National Priorities List: **Cecil Field Naval Air Station; Fairfax St. Wood Treaters; Jacksonville Naval Air Station; Kerr-McGee Chemical Corp - Jacksonville; Pickettville Road Landfill.** *U.S. Environmental Protection Agency, Final National Priorities List, April 26, 2014*

AIR & WATER QUALITY

Air Quality Index

Area	Percent of Days when Air Quality was...[2]					AQI Statistics[2]	
	Good	Moderate	Unhealthy for Sensitive Groups	Unhealthy	Very Unhealthy	Maximum	Median
MSA[1]	82.2	17.3	0.5	0.0	0.0	111	38

Note: (1) Data covers the Jacksonville, FL Metropolitan Statistical Area—see Appendix B for areas included; (2) Based on 365 days with AQI data in 2013. Air Quality Index (AQI) is an index for reporting daily air quality. EPA calculates the AQI for five major air pollutants regulated by the Clean Air Act: ground-level ozone, particle pollution (aka particulate matter), carbon monoxide, sulfur dioxide, and nitrogen dioxide. The AQI runs from 0 to 500. The higher the AQI value, the greater the level of air pollution and the greater the health concern. There are six AQI categories: "Good" AQI is between 0 and 50. Air quality is considered satisfactory; "Moderate" AQI is between 51 and 100. Air quality is acceptable; "Unhealthy for Sensitive Groups" When AQI values are between 101 and 150, members of sensitive groups may experience health effects; "Unhealthy" When AQI values are between 151 and 200 everyone may begin to experience health effects; "Very Unhealthy" AQI values between 201 and 300 trigger a health alert; "Hazardous" AQI values over 300 trigger warnings of emergency conditions (not shown).
Source: U.S. Environmental Protection Agency, Air Quality Index Report, 2013

Air Quality Index Pollutants

Area	Percent of Days when AQI Pollutant was...[2]					
	Carbon Monoxide	Nitrogen Dioxide	Ozone	Sulfur Dioxide	Particulate Matter 2.5	Particulate Matter 10
MSA[1]	0.0	0.3	38.1	6.6	55.1	0.0

Note: (1) Data covers the Jacksonville, FL Metropolitan Statistical Area—see Appendix B for areas included; (2) Based on 365 days with AQI data in 2013. The Air Quality Index (AQI) is an index for reporting daily air quality. EPA calculates the AQI for five major air pollutants regulated by the Clean Air Act: ground-level ozone, particle pollution (also known as particulate matter), carbon monoxide, sulfur dioxide, and nitrogen dioxide. The AQI runs from 0 to 500. The higher the AQI value, the greater the level of air pollution and the greater the health concern.
Source: U.S. Environmental Protection Agency, Air Quality Index Report, 2013

Air Quality Trends: Ozone

	2003	2004	2005	2006	2007	2008	2009	2010	2011	2012
MSA[1]	0.071	0.074	0.072	0.074	0.073	0.069	0.061	0.067	0.066	0.060

Note: (1) Data covers the Jacksonville, FL Metropolitan Statistical Area—see Appendix B for areas included. The values shown are the composite ozone concentration averages among trend sites based on the highest fourth daily maximum 8-hour concentration in parts per million. These trends are based on sites having an adequate record of monitoring data during the trend period. Data from exceptional events are included.
Source: U.S. Environmental Protection Agency, Air Quality Monitoring Information, "Air Quality Trends by City, 2000-2012"

Maximum Air Pollutant Concentrations: Particulate Matter, Ozone, CO and Lead

	Particulate Matter 10 (ug/m^3)	Particulate Matter 2.5 Wtd AM (ug/m^3)	Particulate Matter 2.5 24-Hr (ug/m^3)	Ozone (ppm)	Carbon Monoxide (ppm)	Lead (ug/m^3)
MSA[1] Level	55	8	22	0.061	1	n/a
NAAQS[2]	150	15	35	0.075	9	0.15
Met NAAQS[2]	Yes	Yes	Yes	Yes	Yes	n/a

Note: (1) Data covers the Jacksonville, FL Metropolitan Statistical Area—see Appendix B for areas included; Data from exceptional events are included; (2) National Ambient Air Quality Standards; ppm = parts per million; ug/m^3 = micrograms per cubic meter; n/a not available.
Concentrations: Particulate Matter 10 (coarse particulate)—highest second maximum 24-hour concentration; Particulate Matter 2.5 Wtd AM (fine particulate)—highest weighted annual mean concentration; Particulate Matter 2.5 24-Hour (fine particulate)—highest 98th percentile 24-hour concentration; Ozone—highest fourth daily maximum 8-hour concentration; Carbon Monoxide—highest second maximum non-overlapping 8-hour concentration; Lead—maximum running 3-month average
Source: U.S. Environmental Protection Agency, Air Quality Monitoring Information, "Air Quality Statistics by City, 2012"

Maximum Air Pollutant Concentrations: Nitrogen Dioxide and Sulfur Dioxide

	Nitrogen Dioxide AM (ppb)	Nitrogen Dioxide 1-Hr (ppb)	Sulfur Dioxide AM (ppb)	Sulfur Dioxide 1-Hr (ppb)	Sulfur Dioxide 24-Hr (ppb)
MSA[1] Level	8	37	n/a	54	n/a
NAAQS[2]	53	100	30	75	140
Met NAAQS[2]	Yes	Yes	n/a	Yes	n/a

Note: (1) Data covers the Jacksonville, FL Metropolitan Statistical Area—see Appendix B for areas included; Data from exceptional events are included; (2) National Ambient Air Quality Standards; ppm = parts per million; ug/m^3 = micrograms per cubic meter; n/a not available.
Concentrations: Nitrogen Dioxide AM—highest arithmetic mean concentration; Nitrogen Dioxide 1-Hr—highest 98th percentile 1-hour daily maximum concentration; Sulfur Dioxide AM—highest annual mean concentration; Sulfur Dioxide 1-Hr—highest 99th percentile 1-hour daily maximum concentration; Sulfur Dioxide 24-Hr—highest second maximum 24-hour concentration
Source: U.S. Environmental Protection Agency, Air Quality Monitoring Information, "Air Quality Statistics by City, 2012"

Drinking Water

Water System Name	Pop. Served	Primary Water Source Type	Violations[1]	
			Health Based	Monitoring/ Reporting
JEA Major Grid	703,750	Ground	0	0

Note: (1) Based on violation data from January 1, 2013 to December 31, 2013 (includes unresolved violations from earlier years)
Source: U.S. Environmental Protection Agency, Office of Ground Water and Drinking Water, Safe Drinking Water Information System (based on data extracted February 10, 2014)

Lafayette, Louisiana

Background

Lafayette's cultural origins originated far north of the city, to Nova Scotia, Canada. In 1755, the British governor, Charles Lawrence, expelled the entire population of Canadians known as the Acadians, whose roots were French and Catholic, when they refused to pledge loyalty to the British crown. Many lost their lives in their quest for a new home, as they settled all along the eastern seaboard of the United States. A large majority of Acadians settled in southern Louisiana, in the area surrounding New Orleans.

Prior to the Acadian expulsion, southern Louisiana had remained fairly unsettled. The first known inhabitants were the Attakapas, a much-feared and brutal tribe of Native Americans. A sparse population of French trappers, traders, and ranchers occupied the region until the Spanish occupation of 1766. The 1789 French Revolution brought teams of French immigrants fleeing the brutal conditions at home. In 1803, the French sold the Louisiana territory to the United States—a transaction known as the Louisiana Purchase.

The most important early event for Lafayette was the donation of land by an Acadian named Jean Mouton, to the Catholic Church. The population began to grow in the parish then known as St. John the Evangelist of Vermillion. Lafayette's original name was Vermillionville, but it was renamed in 1884 in honor of the French Marquis de Lafayette, a Frenchman who fought under General George Washington in the American Revolution. Lafayette has been credited with bringing some of the ideals of the American Revolution to the French, partly precipitating the French Revolution. By his death, Lafayette had visited all 24 of the United States, and was an American citizen.

The word "cajun," is derived from the early Acadian settlers. In French, "Les Acadians" became "le Cadiens," which later became just '"Cadien." The French pronunciation was difficult for non-French Americans to say, so Cadien became Cajun. A primary characteristic of the Acadian/Cajun culture is what's known as "joie de vivre"—joy of living. The Cajun reputation is one of hard work and hard play, full of passion that can turn on a dime. Their greatest contribution to the fabric of America has been their food and their music—both are decidedly spicy.

Geographically, Lafayette is about 40 miles north of the Gulf of Mexico, and 100 miles west of New Orleans. The city is often referred to as the center of Cajun culture not because of its geography, but because of the strong Cajun influence in everyday life. Celebration is a major part of the Cajun culture, and this is reflected in Lafayette's many festivals and cultural traditions. The most famous of dozens of annual festivals is Mari Gras. The Festival International de Louisiana celebrates the French-speaking heritage of much of the population. Festival Acadians celebrates everything that is uniquely Cajun.

While Lafayette is known for its oil and natural gas industries, with over 600 oil-related businesses in Lafayette Parish alone, jobs in healthcare are not far behind. Education is also a big industry in Lafayette, home of the University of Louisiana's Ragin' Cajuns. UL started out as a small agricultural college with about 100 students, and today, over 17,000 students roam the 1,300-acre campus. It is the second largest public university in the state. The university's main focus is hands-on research—dubbed "research for a reason"—meaning that all students are given the opportunity to have a meaningful impact in their area of study. The University of Louisiana is considered among the top universities in computer science, engineering and nursing.

Lafayette's climate is humid and subtropical. It is typical of areas along the Gulf of Mexico with hot, humid summers and mild winters.

Rankings

General Rankings

- Lafayette appeared on RelocateAmerica's list of best places to live in America. The annual "Top 100 Places to Live" list recognizes the top communities as nominated by their residents & local businesses. RelocateAmerica's Research Group determined the list based on review of various data gathered for economic, employment, housing, education, industry, opportunity, environment and recreation along with feedback from area leaders and residents. *RelocateAmerica.com, "Top 100 Places to Live for 2011"*

Business/Finance Rankings

- According to data published by the U.S. Conference of Mayors and produced by IHS Global Insight, the Lafayette metro area was on the list of metro areas with the fastest-shrinking GMP (gross metro product) and negative employment trends, at #4. *247wallst.com, "America's Fastest Growing (and Shrinking) Economies," January 31, 2014*

- To identify the metro areas with the largest gap in income between rich and poor residents, the 24/7 Wall Street research team used the U.S. Census Bureau's 2012 American Community Survey, an index of income disparity, additional income, poverty, and home-value data. The Lafayette metro area placed #7 among metro areas with the widest wealth gap between rich and poor. *247wallst.com, "Cities with the Widest Gap between Rich and Poor," November 4, 2013*

- The Lafayette metro area was identified as one of 10 places with the highest projected job growth through 2015. The metro area was ranked #4. Criteria: 384 metropolitan areas were ranked by projected job growth for first quarter 2012 through fourth quarter 2015. *USAToday.com, "Jobs Rebound Will be Slow," March 7, 2012*

- The Lafayette metro area appeared on the Milken Institute "2013 Best Performing Cities" list. Rank: #24 out of 200 large metro areas. Criteria: job growth; wage and salary growth; high-tech output growth. *Milken Institute, "Best-Performing Cities 2013," December 2013*

- *Forbes* ranked the 200 most populous metro areas in the U.S. in terms of the "Best Places for Business and Careers." The Lafayette metro area was ranked #149. Criteria: costs (business and living); job growth (past and projected); income growth; educational attainment (college and high school); projected economic growth; cultural and recreational opportunities; net migration patterns; number of highly ranked colleges. *Forbes, "The Best Places for Business and Careers," August 7, 2013*

Environmental Rankings

- The Lafayette metro area came in at #322 for the relative comfort of its climate on Sperling's list of "chill cities," as measured by the Sperling Heat Index. All 361 metro areas are included. Criteria included daytime high temperatures, nighttime low temperatures, dew point, and relative humidity at the high temperatures. *www.bertsperling.com, "Sperling's Chill Cities," July 18, 2013*

- Sperling's BestPlaces assessed 379 metropolitan areas of the United States for the likelihood of dangerously extreme weather events or earthquakes. In general the Southeast and South-Central regions have the highest risk of weather extremes and earthquakes, while the Pacific Northwest enjoys the lowest risk. Of the least risky metropolitan areas, the Lafayette metro area was ranked #363. *www.bestplaces.net, "Safest Places from Natural Disasters," April 2011*

- Lafayette was selected as one of 22 "Smarter Cities" for energy by the Natural Resources Defense Council. Criteria: investment in green power; energy efficiency measures; conservation. *Natural Resources Defense Council, "2010 Smarter Cities," July 19, 2010*

Food/Drink Rankings

- In compiling its list of "Top 10 Foodie Cities 2013," the lifestyle website Livability excluded "well-known food-lovers' cities like New York, Chicago, San Francisco and New Orleans" and focused on cities of fewer than 250,000 with "unexpected epicurean delights." Looking at food festivals, farmers' markets, cooking schools, ratio of top-rated restaurants to residents, and more, Livability chose Lafayette as the #6 American foodie town. *livability.com, "Top 10 Foodie Cities 2013: A Second Helping," August 2, 2013*

Health/Fitness Rankings

- The Gallup-Healthways Well-Being Index tracks Americans' optimism about their communities in addition to their satisfaction with the metro areas in which they live. Gallup researchers asked at least 300 adult residents in each of 189 U.S. metropolitan areas whether their metro was improving. The Lafayette metro area placed among the top ten in the percentage of residents who were optimistic about their metro area. *www.gallup.com, "City Satisfaction Highest in Fort Collins-Loveland, Colo.," April 11, 2014*

- The Lafayette metro area appeared in the 2013 Gallup-Healthways Well-Being Index. The area ranked #86 out of 189. The Gallup-Healthways Well-Being Index score is an average of six sub-indexes, which individually examine life evaluation, emotional health, work environment, physical health, healthy behaviors, and access to basic necessities. Results are based on telephone interviews conducted as part of the Gallup-Healthways Well-Being Index survey January 2–December 29, 2012, and January 2–December 30, 2013, with a random sample of 531,630 adults, aged 18 and older, living in metropolitan areas in the 50 U.S. states and the District of Columbia. *Gallup-Healthways, "State of American Well-Being," March 25, 2014*

Real Estate Rankings

- Lafayette was ranked #142 out of 283 metro areas in terms of house price appreciation in 2013 (#1 = highest rate). *Federal Housing Finance Agency, House Price Index, 4th Quarter 2013*

Safety Rankings

- The National Insurance Crime Bureau ranked 380 metro areas in the U.S. in terms of per capita rates of vehicle theft. The Lafayette metro area ranked #263 (#1 = highest rate). Criteria: number of vehicle theft offenses per 100,000 inhabitants in 2012. *National Insurance Crime Bureau, "Hot Spots 2012," June 26, 2013*

Seniors/Retirement Rankings

- From its Best Cities for Successful Aging indexes, the Milken Institute generated rankings for metropolitan areas, weighing data in eight categories—general indicators, health care, wellness, living arrangements, transportation and general accessibility, financial well-being, education and employment, and community participation. The Lafayette metro area was ranked #37 overall in the small metro area category. *Milken Institute, "Best Cities for Successful Aging," July 2012*

- *Forbes* selected the Lafayette metro area as one of 25 "Best Places for a Working Retirement." Criteria: affordability; improving, above-average economies and job prospects; and a favorable tax climate for retirees. *Forbes.com, "Best Places for a Working Retirement in 2013," February 4, 2013*

Sports/Recreation Rankings

- Lafayette appeared on the *Sporting News* list of the "Best Sports Cities" for 2011. The area ranked #184 out of 271. Criteria: the magazine takes a 12-month snapshot of each city's sports, putting a heavy premium on regular-season won-lost records (from the most recently completed season). Other criteria include: playoff berths, bowl appearances and tournament bids; championships; applicable power ratings; quality of competition; overall fan fervor (measured in part by attendance); abundance of teams (rewarding quality over quantity); stadium and arena quality; ticket availability and prices; franchise ownership; and marquee appeal of athletes. *Sporting News, "Best Sports Cities 2011," October 4, 2011*

- Lafayette appeared on the *Sporting News* list of the "Best Sports Cities" for 2011. The area ranked #184 out of 271. Criteria: a 12-month snapshot of regular-season won-lost records (from the most recently completed season). Other criteria include: playoff berths, bowl appearances and tournament bids; championships; applicable power ratings; quality of competition; overall fan fervor (measured in part by attendance); abundance of teams (quality over quantity); stadium and arena quality; ticket availability and prices; franchise ownership; and marquee appeal of athletes. *Sporting News, "Best Sports Cities 2011," October 4, 2011*

Business Environment

CITY FINANCES

City Government Finances

Component	2011 ($000)	2011 ($ per capita)
Total Revenues	627,767	5,529
Total Expenditures	643,406	5,667
Debt Outstanding	1,037,627	9,139
Cash and Securities[1]	804,253	7,083

Note: (1) Cash and security holdings of a government at the close of its fiscal year, including those of its dependent agencies, utilities, and liquor stores.
Source: U.S Census Bureau, State & Local Government Finances 2011

City Government Revenue by Source

Source	2011 ($000)	2011 ($ per capita)
General Revenue		
From Federal Government	31,883	281
From State Government	32,476	286
From Local Governments	5,133	45
Taxes		
Property	100,896	889
Sales and Gross Receipts	89,054	784
Personal Income	0	0
Corporate Income	0	0
Motor Vehicle License	0	0
Other Taxes	5,073	45
Current Charges	77,912	686
Liquor Store	0	0
Utility	257,419	2,267
Employee Retirement	0	0

Source: U.S Census Bureau, State & Local Government Finances 2011

City Government Expenditures by Function

Function	2011 ($000)	2011 ($ per capita)	2011 (%)
General Direct Expenditures			
Air Transportation	12,622	111	2.0
Corrections	22,949	202	3.6
Education	0	0	0.0
Employment Security Administration	0	0	0.0
Financial Administration	13,526	119	2.1
Fire Protection	16,088	142	2.5
General Public Buildings	5,022	44	0.8
Governmental Administration, Other	8,742	77	1.4
Health	4,210	37	0.7
Highways	27,694	244	4.3
Hospitals	0	0	0.0
Housing and Community Development	20,731	183	3.2
Interest on General Debt	28,816	254	4.5
Judicial and Legal	22,118	195	3.4
Libraries	6,996	62	1.1
Parking	701	6	0.1
Parks and Recreation	27,047	238	4.2
Police Protection	52,114	459	8.1
Public Welfare	539	5	0.1
Sewerage	18,821	166	2.9
Solid Waste Management	11,404	100	1.8
Veterans' Services	0	0	0.0
Liquor Store	0	0	0.0
Utility	245,976	2,166	38.2
Employee Retirement	0	0	0.0

Source: U.S Census Bureau, State & Local Government Finances 2011

DEMOGRAPHICS

Population Growth

Area	1990 Census	2000 Census	2010 Census	Population Growth (%)	
				1990-2000	2000-2010
City	104,735	110,257	120,623	5.3	9.4
MSA[1]	208,740	239,086	273,738	14.5	14.5
U.S.	248,709,873	281,421,906	308,745,538	13.2	9.7

Note: (1) Figures cover the Lafayette, LA Metropolitan Statistical Area—see Appendix B for areas included
Source: U.S. Census Bureau, Census 1990, 2000, 2010

Household Size

Area	Persons in Household (%)							Average Household Size
	One	Two	Three	Four	Five	Six	Seven or More	
City	35.4	32.7	15.4	10.8	3.8	0.7	1.1	2.38
MSA[1]	30.3	32.5	16.7	12.8	5.2	1.4	1.1	2.58
U.S.	27.6	33.5	15.7	13.2	6.1	2.4	1.5	2.63

Note: (1) Figures cover the Lafayette, LA Metropolitan Statistical Area—see Appendix B for areas included
Source: U.S. Census Bureau, 2010-2012 American Community Survey 3-Year Estimates

Race

Area	White Alone[2] (%)	Black Alone[2] (%)	Asian Alone[2] (%)	AIAN[3] Alone[2] (%)	NHOPI[4] Alone[2] (%)	Other Race Alone[2] (%)	Two or More Races (%)
City	64.7	30.7	2.1	0.2	0.0	0.5	1.7
MSA[1]	69.4	26.3	1.4	0.3	0.0	0.5	2.0
U.S.	74.0	12.6	4.9	0.8	0.2	4.7	2.8

Note: (1) Figures cover the Lafayette, LA Metropolitan Statistical Area—see Appendix B for areas included; (2) Alone is defined as not being in combination with one or more other races; (3) American Indian and Alaska Native; (4) Native Hawaiian and Other Pacific Islander
Source: U.S. Census Bureau, 2010-2012 American Community Survey 3-Year Estimates

Hispanic or Latino Origin

Area	Total (%)	Mexican (%)	Puerto Rican (%)	Cuban (%)	Other (%)
City	4.4	1.5	0.2	0.2	2.4
MSA[1]	3.7	1.7	0.1	0.1	1.7
U.S.	16.6	10.7	1.6	0.6	3.7

Note: Persons of Hispanic or Latino origin can be of any race; (1) Figures cover the Lafayette, LA Metropolitan Statistical Area—see Appendix B for areas included
Source: U.S. Census Bureau, 2010-2012 American Community Survey 3-Year Estimates

Segregation

Type	Segregation Indices[1]				Percent Change		
	1990	2000	2010	2010 Rank[2]	1990-2000	1990-2010	2000-2010
Black/White	n/a	n/a	n/a	n/a	n/a	n/a	n/a
Asian/White	n/a	n/a	n/a	n/a	n/a	n/a	n/a
Hispanic/White	n/a	n/a	n/a	n/a	n/a	n/a	n/a

Note: All figures cover the Metropolitan Statistical Area—see Appendix B for areas included; Figures are based on an analysis of 1990, 2000, and 2010 Census Decennial Census tract data by William H. Frey, Brookings Institution and the University of Michigan Social Science Data Analysis Network. In this analysis all racial groups (whites, blacks, and asians) are non-Hispanic members of those races. Hispanics are shown as a separate category;
(1) Segregation Indices are Dissimilarity Indices that measure the degree to which the minority group is distributed differently than whites across census tracts. They range from 0 (complete integration) to 100 (complete segregation) where the value indicates the percentage of the minority group that needs to move to be distributed exactly like whites; (2) Ranges from 1 (most segregated) to 102 (least segregated); n/a not available.
Source: www.CensusScope.org

Ancestry

Area	German	Irish	English	American	Italian	Polish	French[2]	Scottish	Dutch
City	9.8	5.7	6.3	7.0	3.6	0.5	19.8	1.4	0.5
MSA[1]	8.9	4.9	4.6	8.9	3.1	0.4	22.0	1.1	0.3
U.S.	15.2	11.1	8.2	7.2	5.6	3.1	2.8	1.7	1.4

Note: Figures are the percentage of the total population reporting a particular ancestry. The nine most commonly reported ancestries in the U.S. are shown. Figures include multiple ancestries (e.g. if a person reported being Irish and Italian, they were included in both columns); (1) Figures cover the Lafayette, LA Metropolitan Statistical Area—see Appendix B for areas included; (2) Excludes Basque
Source: U.S. Census Bureau, 2010-2012 American Community Survey 3-Year Estimates

Foreign-Born Population

Area	Percent of Population Born in								
	Any Foreign Country	Mexico	Asia	Europe	Carribean	South America	Central America[2]	Africa	Canada
City	n/a	n/a	n/a	n/a	n/a	n/a	n/a	n/a	n/a
MSA[1]	n/a	n/a	n/a	n/a	n/a	n/a	n/a	n/a	n/a
U.S.	13.0	3.7	3.7	1.6	1.2	0.9	1.0	0.5	0.3

Note: (1) Figures cover the Lafayette, LA Metropolitan Statistical Area—see Appendix B for areas included; (2) Excludes Mexico.
Source: U.S. Census Bureau, 2010-2012 American Community Survey 3-Year Estimates

Marital Status

Area	Never Married	Now Married[2]	Separated	Widowed	Divorced
City	40.2	38.6	2.2	6.0	13.0
MSA[1]	34.6	45.1	2.2	5.8	12.3
U.S.	32.4	48.4	2.2	6.0	11.0

Note: Figures are percentages and cover the population 15 years of age and older; (1) Figures cover the Lafayette, LA Metropolitan Statistical Area—see Appendix B for areas included; (2) Excludes separated
Source: U.S. Census Bureau, 2010-2012 American Community Survey 3-Year Estimates

Age

Area	Percent of Population									Median Age
	Under Age 5	Age 5–19	Age 20–34	Age 35–44	Age 45–54	Age 55–64	Age 65–74	Age 75–84	Age 85+	
City	5.3	19.9	25.6	12.3	13.9	10.5	6.8	4.0	1.5	34.5
MSA[1]	7.2	20.3	23.7	12.6	14.1	11.3	6.1	3.4	1.3	34.2
U.S.	6.4	20.1	20.5	13.1	14.3	12.2	7.3	4.2	1.8	37.3

Note: (1) Figures cover the Lafayette, LA Metropolitan Statistical Area—see Appendix B for areas included
Source: U.S. Census Bureau, 2010-2012 American Community Survey 3-Year Estimates

Gender

Area	Males	Females	Males per 100 Females
City	59,849	61,895	96.7
MSA[1]	135,466	141,595	95.7
U.S.	153,276,055	158,333,314	96.8

Note: (1) Figures cover the Lafayette, LA Metropolitan Statistical Area—see Appendix B for areas included
Source: U.S. Census Bureau, 2010-2012 American Community Survey 3-Year Estimates

Religious Groups by Family

Area	Catholic	Baptist	Non-Den.	Methodist[2]	Lutheran	LDS[3]	Pente-costal	Presby-terian[4]	Muslim[5]	Judaism
MSA[1]	47.0	14.8	4.0	2.6	0.2	0.4	2.9	0.2	0.1	0.1
U.S.	19.1	9.3	4.0	4.0	2.3	2.0	1.9	1.6	0.8	0.7

Note: Figures are the number of adherents as a percentage of the total population; (1) Figures cover the Lafayette, LA Metropolitan Statistical Area—see Appendix B for areas included; (2) Methodist/Pietist; (3) Latter Day Saints; (4) Reformed; (5) Figures are estimates
Source: Association of Statisticians of American Religious Bodies, 2010 U.S. Religion Census: Religious Congregations & Membership Study

Religious Groups by Tradition

Area	Catholic	Evangelical Protestant	Mainline Protestant	Other Tradition	Black Protestant	Orthodox
MSA[1]	47.0	12.8	3.2	0.8	9.3	0.1
U.S.	19.1	16.2	7.3	4.3	1.6	0.3

Note: Figures are the number of adherents as a percentage of the total population; (1) Figures cover the Lafayette, LA Metropolitan Statistical Area—see Appendix B for areas included
Source: Association of Statisticians of American Religious Bodies, 2010 U.S. Religion Census: Religious Congregations & Membership Study

ECONOMY

Gross Metropolitan Product

Area	2011	2012	2013	2014	Rank[2]
MSA[1]	19.2	17.7	17.2	17.8	126

Note: Figures are in billions of dollars; (1) Figures cover the Lafayette, LA Metropolitan Statistical Area—see Appendix B for areas included; (2) Rank is based on 2014 data and ranges from 1 to 363
Source: The United States Conference of Mayors, U.S. Metro Economies: Outlook—Gross Metropolitan Product, with Metro Employment Projections, November 2013

Economic Growth

Area	2011 (%)	2012 (%)	2013 (%)	2014 (%)	Rank[2]
MSA[1]	1.0	-8.1	-4.2	1.6	361
U.S.	1.6	2.5	1.7	2.5	–

Note: Figures are real gross metropolitan product (GMP) growth rates and represent annual average percent change; (1) Figures cover the Lafayette, LA Metropolitan Statistical Area—see Appendix B for areas included; (2) Rank is based on 2013 data and ranges from 1 to 363
Source: The United States Conference of Mayors, U.S. Metro Economies: Outlook—Gross Metropolitan Product, with Metro Employment Projections, November 2013

Metropolitan Area Exports

Area	2007	2008	2009	2010	2011	2012	Rank[2]
MSA[1]	587.3	762.7	657.0	488.1	655.9	726.0	182

Note: Figures are in millions of dollars; (1) Figures cover the Lafayette, LA Metropolitan Statistical Area—see Appendix B for areas included; (2) Rank is based on 2012 data and ranges from 1 to 369
Source: U.S. Department of Commerce, International Trade Administration, Office of Trade & Industry Information, Manufacturing & Services, data extracted April 1, 2014

INCOME

Income

Area	Per Capita ($)	Median Household ($)	Average Household ($)
City	27,580	43,928	64,837
MSA[1]	26,809	47,146	67,314
U.S.	27,385	51,771	71,579

Note: (1) Figures cover the Lafayette, LA Metropolitan Statistical Area—see Appendix B for areas included
Source: U.S. Census Bureau, 2010-2012 American Community Survey 3-Year Estimates

Household Income Distribution

Area	Percent of Households Earning							
	Under $15,000	$15,000 -24,999	$25,000 -34,999	$35,000 -49,999	$50,000 -74,999	$75,000 -99,000	$100,000 -149,999	$150,000 and up
City	18.5	13.3	9.0	14.0	16.2	9.6	11.0	8.3
MSA[1]	16.9	12.3	9.7	12.9	17.1	11.0	11.5	8.6
U.S.	13.1	11.0	10.5	13.7	18.1	11.9	12.5	9.1

Note: (1) Figures cover the Lafayette, LA Metropolitan Statistical Area—see Appendix B for areas included
Source: U.S. Census Bureau, 2010-2012 American Community Survey 3-Year Estimates

Poverty Rate

Area	All Ages	Under 18 Years Old	18 to 64 Years Old	65 Years and Over
City	20.6	26.7	20.7	9.4
MSA[1]	18.5	25.3	16.9	11.6
U.S.	15.7	22.2	14.6	9.3

Note: Figures are percentage of people whose income during the past 12 months was below the poverty level;
(1) Figures cover the Lafayette, LA Metropolitan Statistical Area—see Appendix B for areas included
Source: U.S. Census Bureau, 2010-2012 American Community Survey 3-Year Estimates

Personal Bankruptcy Filing Rate

Area	2008	2009	2010	2011	2012	2013
Lafayette Parish	2.50	2.97	3.00	2.75	2.52	2.25
U.S.	3.53	4.61	4.97	4.37	3.76	3.29

Note: Numbers are per 1,000 population and include Chapter 7 and Chapter 13 filings
Source: Federal Deposit Insurance Corporation, Regional Economic Conditions, March 20, 2014

EMPLOYMENT

Labor Force and Employment

Area	Civilian Labor Force			Workers Employed		
	Dec. 2012	Dec. 2013	% Chg.	Dec. 2012	Dec. 2013	% Chg.
City	63,962	65,811	2.9	61,411	63,563	3.5
MSA[1]	141,028	145,012	2.8	135,418	140,163	3.5
U.S.	154,904,000	154,408,000	-0.3	143,060,000	144,423,000	1.0

Note: Data is not seasonally adjusted and covers workers 16 years of age and older; (1) Metropolitan Statistical Area—see Appendix B for areas included
Source: Bureau of Labor Statistics, Local Area Unemployment Statistics

Unemployment Rate

Area	2013											
	Jan.	Feb.	Mar.	Apr.	May	Jun.	Jul.	Aug.	Sep.	Oct.	Nov.	Dec.
City	5.5	4.2	4.3	4.6	5.5	6.1	5.4	5.4	4.9	4.7	4.3	3.4
MSA[1]	5.4	4.2	4.3	4.6	5.3	6.0	5.4	5.3	4.8	4.6	4.2	3.3
U.S.	8.5	8.1	7.6	7.1	7.3	7.8	7.7	7.3	7.0	7.0	6.6	6.5

Note: Data is not seasonally adjusted and covers workers 16 years of age and older; All figures are percentages;
(1) Metropolitan Statistical Area—see Appendix B for areas included
Source: Bureau of Labor Statistics, Local Area Unemployment Statistics

Employment by Occupation

Occupation Classification	City (%)	MSA[1] (%)	U.S. (%)
Management, Business, Science, and Arts	36.2	31.7	36.0
Natural Resources, Construction, and Maintenance	9.1	11.6	9.1
Production, Transportation, and Material Moving	8.3	11.5	12.0
Sales and Office	25.1	26.0	24.7
Service	21.3	19.2	18.2

Note: Figures cover employed civilians 16 years of age and older; (1) Figures cover the Lafayette, LA Metropolitan Statistical Area—see Appendix B for areas included
Source: U.S. Census Bureau, 2010-2012 American Community Survey 3-Year Estimates

Employment by Industry

| Sector | MSA[1] | | U.S. |
	Number of Employees	Percent of Total	Percent of Total
Construction	7,000	4.3	4.2
Education and Health Services	24,400	15.0	15.5
Financial Activities	9,100	5.6	5.7
Government	17,000	10.4	16.1
Information	2,500	1.5	1.9
Leisure and Hospitality	16,900	10.4	10.2
Manufacturing	12,500	7.7	8.7
Mining and Logging	17,400	10.7	0.6
Other Services	5,100	3.1	3.9
Professional and Business Services	19,500	12.0	13.7
Retail Trade	19,800	12.1	11.4
Transportation and Utilities	4,200	2.6	3.8
Wholesale Trade	7,700	4.7	4.2

Note: Figures cover non-farm employment as of December 2013 and are not seasonally adjusted;
(1) Metropolitan Statistical Area—see Appendix B for areas included
Source: Bureau of Labor Statistics, Current Employment Statistics, Employment, Hours, and Earnings

Occupations with Greatest Projected Employment Growth: 2010 – 2020

Occupation[1]	2010 Employment	2020 Projected Employment	Numeric Employment Change	Percent Employment Change
Registered Nurses	42,440	52,020	9,580	22.6
Personal Care Aides	19,240	27,870	8,630	44.8
Retail Salespersons	61,060	69,500	8,440	13.8
Home Health Aides	13,230	20,480	7,260	54.9
Cashiers	64,410	70,580	6,170	9.6
Food Preparation Workers	27,180	32,890	5,710	21.0
Laborers and Freight, Stock, and Material Movers, Hand	38,610	44,300	5,690	14.8
Waiters and Waitresses	32,700	38,160	5,460	16.7
Combined Food Preparation and Serving Workers, Including Fast Food	24,130	29,570	5,440	22.6
Office Clerks, General	35,500	40,430	4,930	13.9

Note: Projections cover Louisiana; (1) Sorted by numeric employment change
Source: www.projectionscentral.com, State Occupational Projections, 2010–2020 Long-Term Projections

Fastest Growing Occupations: 2010 – 2020

Occupation[1]	2010 Employment	2020 Projected Employment	Numeric Employment Change	Percent Employment Change
Home Health Aides	13,230	20,480	7,260	54.9
Veterinary Technologists and Technicians	1,000	1,540	530	53.2
Interpreters and Translators	560	850	290	51.7
Software Developers, Systems Software	900	1,320	420	46.4
Logisticians	870	1,270	400	45.7
Personal Care Aides	19,240	27,870	8,630	44.8
Market Research Analysts and Marketing Specialists	1,240	1,770	530	43.0
Helpers—Carpenters	1,820	2,570	750	41.3
Computer-Controlled Machine Tool Operators, Metal and Plastic	1,220	1,720	500	41.0
Meeting, Convention, and Event Planners	530	730	210	39.5

Note: Projections cover Louisiana; (1) Sorted by percent employment change and excludes occupations with numeric employment change less than 100
Source: www.projectionscentral.com, State Occupational Projections, 2010–2020 Long-Term Projections

Average Wages

Occupation	$/Hr.	Occupation	$/Hr.
Accountants and Auditors	31.37	Maids and Housekeeping Cleaners	8.58
Automotive Mechanics	19.07	Maintenance and Repair Workers	17.89
Bookkeepers	16.45	Marketing Managers	39.76
Carpenters	17.49	Nuclear Medicine Technologists	n/a
Cashiers	8.98	Nurses, Licensed Practical	18.72
Clerks, General Office	11.42	Nurses, Registered	27.89
Clerks, Receptionists/Information	11.29	Nursing Assistants	9.24
Clerks, Shipping/Receiving	14.48	Packers and Packagers, Hand	9.32
Computer Programmers	23.56	Physical Therapists	38.84
Computer Systems Analysts	29.34	Postal Service Mail Carriers	24.57
Computer User Support Specialists	22.37	Real Estate Brokers	23.35
Cooks, Restaurant	10.05	Retail Salespersons	11.24
Dentists	75.83	Sales Reps., Exc. Tech./Scientific	28.84
Electrical Engineers	n/a	Sales Reps., Tech./Scientific	31.88
Electricians	21.20	Secretaries, Exc. Legal/Med./Exec.	14.31
Financial Managers	44.84	Security Guards	11.22
First-Line Supervisors/Managers, Sales	17.49	Surgeons	71.35
Food Preparation Workers	8.84	Teacher Assistants	10.20
General and Operations Managers	56.92	Teachers, Elementary School	27.40
Hairdressers/Cosmetologists	11.98	Teachers, Secondary School	n/a
Internists	n/a	Telemarketers	11.24
Janitors and Cleaners	9.85	Truck Drivers, Heavy/Tractor-Trailer	19.29
Landscaping/Groundskeeping Workers	10.53	Truck Drivers, Light/Delivery Svcs.	13.58
Lawyers	52.48	Waiters and Waitresses	8.97

Note: Wage data covers the Lafayette, LA Metropolitan Statistical Area—see Appendix B for areas included.
Hourly wages for elementary/secondary school teachers and teacher assistants were calculated by the editors
from annual wage data assuming a 40 hour work week; n/a not available.
Source: Bureau of Labor Statistics, Metro Area Occupational Employment and Wage Estimates, May 2013

RESIDENTIAL REAL ESTATE

Building Permits

Area	Single-Family			Multi-Family			Total		
	2012	2013	Pct. Chg.	2012	2013	Pct. Chg.	2012	2013	Pct. Chg.
City	n/a	n/a	n/a	n/a	n/a	n/a	n/a	n/a	n/a
MSA[1]	1,198	1,399	16.8	145	155	6.9	1,343	1,554	15.7
U.S.	518,695	620,802	19.7	310,963	370,020	19.0	829,658	990,822	19.4

Note: (1) Metropolitan Statistical Area—see Appendix B for areas included; figures represent new, privately-owned housing units authorized (unadjusted data); All permit data are based on estimates with imputation.
Source: U.S. Census Bureau, Manufacturing, Mining, and Construction Statistics, Building Permits, 2012, 2013

Homeownership Rate

Area	2006 (%)	2007 (%)	2008 (%)	2009 (%)	2010 (%)	2011 (%)	2012 (%)	2013 (%)
MSA[1]	n/a	n/a	n/a	n/a	n/a	n/a	n/a	n/a
U.S.	68.8	68.1	67.8	67.4	66.9	66.1	65.4	65.1

Note: (1) Figures cover the Lafayette, LA Metropolitan Statistical Area—see Appendix B for areas included; n/a not available
Source: U.S. Census Bureau, Housing Vacancies and Homeownership Annual Statistics: 2013

Housing Vacancy Rates

Area	Gross Vacancy Rate[2] (%)			Year-Round Vacancy Rate[3] (%)			Rental Vacancy Rate[4] (%)			Homeowner Vacancy Rate[5] (%)		
	2011	2012	2013	2011	2012	2013	2011	2012	2013	2011	2012	2013
MSA[1]	n/a	n/a	n/a	n/a	n/a	n/a	n/a	n/a	n/a	n/a	n/a	n/a
U.S.	14.2	13.8	13.8	11.1	10.8	10.7	9.5	8.7	8.3	2.5	2.0	2.0

Note: (1) Figures cover the Lafayette, LA Metropolitan Statistical Area—see Appendix B for areas included; (2) The percentage of the total housing inventory that is vacant; (3) The percentage of the housing inventory (excluding seasonal units) that is year-round vacant; (4) The percentage of rental inventory that is vacant for rent; (5) The percentage of homeowner inventory that is vacant for sale; n/a not available
Source: U.S. Census Bureau, Housing Vacancies and Homeownership Annual Statistics: 2013

TAXES

State Corporate Income Tax Rates

State	Tax Rate (%)	Income Brackets ($)	Num. of Brackets	Financial Institution Tax Rate (%)[a]	Federal Income Tax Ded.
Louisiana	4.0 - 8.0	25,000 - 200,001	5	4.0 - 8.0	Yes

Note: Tax rates as of January 1, 2014; (a) Rates listed are the corporate income tax rate applied to financial institutions or excise taxes based on income. Some states have other taxes based upon the value of deposits or shares.
Source: Federation of Tax Administrators, "State Corporate Income Tax Rates, 2014"

State Individual Income Tax Rates

State	Tax Rate (%)	Income Brackets ($)	Num. of Brackets	Personal Exempt. ($)[1] Single	Dependents	Fed. Inc. Tax Ded.
Louisiana	2.0 - 6.0	12,500 - 50,001 (b)	3	4,500 (k)	1,000	Yes

Note: Tax rates as of January 1, 2014; Local- and county-level taxes are not included; n/a not applicable; (1) Married joint filers generally receive double the single exemption; (b) For joint returns, taxes are twice the tax on half the couple's income; (k) The amounts reported for Louisiana are a combined personal exemption-standard deduction.
Source: Federation of Tax Administrators, "State Individual Income Tax Rates, 2014"

Various State and Local Tax Rates

State	State and Local Sales and Use (%)	State Sales and Use (%)	Gasoline[1] (¢/gal.)	Cigarette[2] ($/pack)	Spirits[3] ($/gal.)	Wine[4] ($/gal.)	Beer[5] ($/gal.)
Louisiana	8.0	4.00	20.00	0.360	2.50 (f)	0.11	0.32

Note: All tax rates as of January 1, 2014; (1) The American Petroleum Institute has developed a methodology for determining the average tax rate on a gallon of fuel. Rates may include any of the following: excise taxes, environmental fees, storage tank fees, other fees or taxes, general sales tax, and local taxes. In states where gasoline is subject to the general sales tax, or where the fuel tax is based on the average sale price, the average rate determined by API is sensitive to changes in the price of gasoline. States that fully or partially apply general sales taxes to gasoline: CA, CO, GA, IL, IN, MI, NY; (2) The federal excise tax of $1.0066 per pack and local taxes are not included; (3) Rates are those applicable to off-premise sales of 40% alcohol by volume (a.b.v.) distilled spirits in 750ml containers. Local excise taxes are excluded; (4) Rates are those applicable to off-premise sales of 11% a.b.v. non-carbonated wine in 750ml containers; (5) Rates are those applicable to off-premise sales of 4.7% a.b.v. beer in 12 ounce containers; (f) Different rates also applicable according to alcohol content, place of production, size of container, or place purchased (on- or off-premise or onboard airlines).
Source: Tax Foundation, 2014 Facts & Figures: How Does Your State Compare?

State Business Tax Climate Index Rankings

State	Overall Rank	Corporate Tax Index Rank	Individual Income Tax Index Rank	Sales Tax Index Rank	Unemployment Insurance Tax Index Rank	Property Tax Index Rank
Louisiana	33	17	25	50	4	24

Note: The index is a measure of how each state's tax laws affect economic performance. The lower the rank, the more favorable a state's tax system is for business. States without a given tax are given a ranking of 1. The scores/rankings for the District of Columbia do not affect other states. The 2014 index represents the tax climate as of July 1, 2013.
Source: Tax Foundation, State Business Tax Climate Index 2014

COMMERCIAL UTILITIES

Typical Monthly Electric Bills

Area	Commercial Service ($/month) 1,500 kWh	40 kW demand 14,000 kWh	Industrial Service ($/month) 1,000 kW demand 200,000 kWh	50,000 kW demand 15,000,000 kWh
City	197	1,547	18,866	1,268,244
Average[1]	197	1,636	25,662	1,485,307

Note: Based on total rates in effect July 1, 2013; (1) average based on 180 utilities surveyed
Source: Edison Electric Institute, Typical Bills and Average Rates Report, Summer 2013

TRANSPORTATION

Means of Transportation to Work

Area	Car/Truck/Van		Public Transportation			Bicycle	Walked	Other Means	Worked at Home
	Drove Alone	Car-pooled	Bus	Subway	Railroad				
City	80.0	12.2	1.0	0.0	0.0	0.9	1.9	1.2	2.8
MSA[1]	82.6	11.1	0.7	0.0	0.0	0.4	1.7	1.2	2.2
U.S.	76.4	9.7	2.6	1.7	0.5	0.6	2.8	1.3	4.3

Note: Figures are percentages and cover workers 16 years of age and older; (1) Figures cover the Lafayette, LA Metropolitan Statistical Area—see Appendix B for areas included
Source: U.S. Census Bureau, 2010-2012 American Community Survey 3-Year Estimates

Travel Time to Work

Area	Less Than 10 Minutes	10 to 19 Minutes	20 to 29 Minutes	30 to 44 Minutes	45 to 59 Minutes	60 to 89 Minutes	90 Minutes or More
City	18.2	44.5	18.9	11.4	1.9	2.6	2.5
MSA[1]	14.5	37.0	22.9	15.7	4.1	2.6	3.2
U.S.	13.5	29.8	20.9	20.1	7.5	5.6	2.5

Note: Figures are percentages and include workers 16 years old and over; (1) Figures cover the Lafayette, LA Metropolitan Statistical Area—see Appendix B for areas included
Source: U.S. Census Bureau, 2010-2012 American Community Survey 3-Year Estimates

Travel Time Index

Area	1985	1990	1995	2000	2005	2010	2011
Urban Area[1]	n/a	n/a	n/a	n/a	n/a	n/a	n/a
Average[2]	1.09	1.14	1.16	1.19	1.23	1.18	1.18

Note: Travel Time Index—the ratio of travel time in the peak period to the travel time at free-flow conditions. For example, a value of 1.30 indicates a 20-minute free-flow trip takes 26 minutes in the peak. Free-flow speeds (60 mph on freeways and 35 mph on principal arterials) are used as the comparison threshold; (1) Data for the Lafayette, LA urban area was not available; (2) average of 498 urban areas
Source: Texas Transportation Institute, Urban Mobility Report 2012, December 2012

Public Transportation

Agency Name / Mode of Transportation	Vehicles Operated in Maximum Service	Annual Unlinked Passenger Trips (in thous.)	Annual Passenger Miles (in thous.)
Lafayette Transit System			
Bus (directly operated)	13	1,437.2	7,198.7
Bus (purchased transportation)	4	29.3	435.5
Demand Response (purchased transportation)	5	28.3	173.8

Source: Federal Transit Administration, National Transit Database, 2012

Air Transportation

Airport Name and Code / Type of Service	Passenger Airlines[1]	Passenger Enplanements	Freight Carriers[2]	Freight (lbs.)
Lafayette Regional Airport (LFT)				
Domestic service (U.S. carriers - 2013)	9	232,043	3	11,230,465
International service (U.S. carriers - 2012)	0	0	0	0

Note: (1) Includes all U.S.-based major, minor and commuter airlines that carried at least one passenger during the year; (2) Includes all U.S.-based airlines and freight carriers that transported at least one lb. of freight during the year.
Source: Bureau of Transportation Statistics, The Intermodal Transportation Database, Air Carriers: T-100 Domestic Market (U.S. Carriers), 2013; Bureau of Transportation Statistics, The Intermodal Transportation Database, Air Carriers: T-100 International Market (U.S. Carriers), 2012

Other Transportation Statistics

Major Highways:	I-10
Amtrak Service:	Yes
Major Waterways/Ports:	Gulf of Mexico (40 miles)

Source: Amtrak.com; Google Maps

BUSINESSES

Major Business Headquarters

Company Name	Rankings	
	Fortune[1]	Forbes[2]
No companies listed	-	-

Note: (1) Fortune 500—companies that produce a 10-K are ranked 1 to 500 based on 2012 revenue; (2) all private companies with at least $2 billion in annual revenue through the end of their most current fiscal year are ranked 1 to 224; companies listed are headquartered in the city; dashes indicate no ranking
Source: Fortune, "Fortune 500," May 20, 2013; Forbes, "America's Largest Private Companies," December 18, 2013

Minority- and Women-Owned Businesses

Group	All Firms		Firms with Paid Employees			
	Firms	Sales ($000)	Firms	Sales ($000)	Employees	Payroll ($000)
Asian	396	90,192	144	80,346	1,739	23,430
Black	2,131	108,455	151	72,640	1,525	31,327
Hispanic	443	137,108	68	123,280	659	24,084
Women	3,517	833,991	665	756,160	6,398	172,600
All Firms	15,659	16,255,682	4,787	15,627,640	89,598	2,969,477

Note: Figures cover firms located in the city; minority- and women-owned business are defined as firms in which the corresponding group own 51% or more of the stock or equity of the company
Source: U.S. Census Bureau, 2007 Economic Census, Survey of Business Owners (2012 Survey of Business Owners data will be released starting in June 2015)

HOTELS & CONVENTION CENTERS

Hotels/Motels

Area	5 Star		4 Star		3 Star		2 Star		1 Star		Not Rated	
	Num.	Pct.[3]	Num.	Pct.[3]	Num.	Pct.[3]	Num.	Pct.[3]	Num.	Pct.[3]	Num.	Pct.[3]
City[1]	0	0.0	0	0.0	16	18.2	58	65.9	3	3.4	11	12.5
Total[2]	142	0.9	1,005	6.0	5,147	30.9	8,578	51.4	408	2.4	1,397	8.4

Note: (1) Figures cover Lafayette and vicinity; (2) Figures cover all 100 cities in this book; (3) Percentage of hotels which have a given star rating; Star ratings are determined by expedia.com and offer an indication of the general quality of a particular hotel.
Source: expedia.com, April 7, 2014

Major Convention Centers

Name	Overall Space (sq. ft.)	Exhibit Space (sq. ft.)	Meeting Space (sq. ft.)	Meeting Rooms
Cajundome and Convention Center	72,000	37,300	20,000	n/a

Note: Table includes convention centers located in the Lafayette, LA metro area; n/a not available
Source: Original research

Living Environment

COST OF LIVING

Cost of Living Index

Composite Index	Groceries	Housing	Utilities	Trans-portation	Health Care	Misc. Goods/ Services
95.9	90.5	101.5	87.8	104.1	84.8	94.6

Note: The Cost of Living Index measures regional differences in the cost of consumer goods and services, excluding taxes and non-consumer expenditures, for professional and managerial households in the top income quintile. It is based on more than 50,000 prices covering almost 60 different items for which prices are collected three times a year by chambers of commerce, economic development organizations or university applied economic centers in each participating urban area. The numbers shown should be read as a percentage above or below the national average of 100. For example, a value of 115.4 in the groceries column indicates that grocery prices are 15.4% higher than the national average. Small differences in the index numbers should not be interpreted as significant; Figures cover the Lafayette LA urban area.
Source: The Council for Community and Economic Research, ACCRA Cost of Living Index, 2013

Grocery Prices

Area[1]	T-Bone Steak ($/pound)	Frying Chicken ($/pound)	Whole Milk ($/half gal.)	Eggs ($/dozen)	Orange Juice ($/64 oz.)	Coffee ($/11.5 oz.)
City[2]	9.58	1.13	2.81	1.65	3.40	4.00
Avg.	10.19	1.28	2.34	1.81	3.48	4.39
Min.	8.56	0.94	1.44	1.19	2.78	3.40
Max.	14.82	2.28	3.56	3.73	6.23	7.32

Note: (1) Values for the local area are compared with the average, minimum and maximum values for all 327 areas in the Cost of Living Index; (2) Figures cover the Lafayette LA urban area; T-Bone Steak (price per pound); Frying Chicken (price per pound, whole fryer); Whole Milk (half gallon carton); Eggs (price per dozen, Grade A, large); Orange Juice (64 oz. Tropicana or Florida Natural); Coffee (11.5 oz. can, vacuum-packed, Maxwell House, Hills Bros, or Folgers).
Source: The Council for Community and Economic Research, ACCRA Cost of Living Index, 2013

Housing and Utility Costs

Area[1]	New Home Price ($)	Apartment Rent ($/month)	All Electric ($/month)	Part Electric ($/month)	Other Energy ($/month)	Telephone ($/month)
City[2]	298,091	940	-	91.54	44.89	26.12
Avg.	295,864	900	171.38	91.82	70.12	27.73
Min.	185,506	458	117.80	48.81	33.67	17.16
Max.	1,358,917	3,783	441.68	171.40	372.65	39.47

Note: (1) Values for the local area are compared with the average, minimum and maximum values for all 327 areas in the Cost of Living Index; (2) Figures cover the Lafayette LA urban area; New Home Price (2,400 sf living area, 8,000 sf lot, in urban area with full utilities); Apartment Rent (950 sf 2 bedroom/1.5 or 2 bath, unfurnished, excluding all utilities except water); All Electric (average monthly cost for an all-electric home); Part Electric (average monthly cost for a part-electric home); Other Energy (average monthly cost for natural gas, fuel oil, coal, wood, and any other forms of energy except electricity); Telephone (price includes basic monthly rate for a private residential line plus additional local usage charges incurred by a family of four).
Source: The Council for Community and Economic Research, ACCRA Cost of Living Index, 2013

Health Care, Transportation, and Other Costs

Area[1]	Doctor ($/visit)	Dentist ($/visit)	Optometrist ($/visit)	Gasoline ($/gallon)	Beauty Salon ($/visit)	Men's Shirt ($)
City[2]	70.27	72.80	65.20	3.33	32.40	24.46
Avg.	101.40	86.48	96.16	3.44	33.87	26.55
Min.	61.67	50.83	50.12	3.08	18.92	12.48
Max.	182.71	152.50	223.78	4.33	68.22	52.03

Note: (1) Values for the local area are compared with the average, minimum and maximum values for all 327 areas in the Cost of Living Index; (2) Figures cover the Lafayette LA urban area; Doctor (general practitioners routine exam of an established patient); Dentist (adult teeth cleaning and periodic oral examination); Optometrist (full vision eye exam for established adult patient); Gasoline (one gallon regular unleaded, national brand, including all taxes, cash price at self-service pump if available); Beauty Salon (woman's shampoo, trim, and blow-dry); Men's Shirt (cotton/polyester dress shirt, pinpoint weave, long sleeves).
Source: The Council for Community and Economic Research, ACCRA Cost of Living Index, 2013

HOUSING

House Price Index (HPI)

Area	National Ranking[2]	Quarterly Change (%)	One-Year Change (%)	Five-Year Change (%)
MSA[1]	142	-0.08	2.15	3.31
U.S.[3]	–	1.20	7.69	4.18

Note: The HPI is a weighted repeat sales index. It measures average price changes in repeat sales or refinancings on the same properties. This information is obtained by reviewing repeat mortgage transactions on single-family properties whose mortgages have been purchased or securitized by Fannie Mae or Freddie Mac in January 1975; (1) Lafayette, LA Metropolitan Statistical Area—see Appendix B for areas included; (2) Rankings are based on annual percentage change for all metro areas containing at least 15,000 transactions over the last 10 years and ranges from 1 to 283; (3) figures based on a weighted average of Census Division estimates using a seasonally adjusted, purchase-only index; all figures are for the period ending December 31, 2013
Source: Federal Housing Finance Agency, House Price Index, February 25, 2014

Median Single-Family Home Prices

Area	2011	2012	2013p	Percent Change 2012 to 2013
MSA[1]	n/a	n/a	n/a	n/a
U.S. Average	166.2	177.2	197.4	11.4

Note: Figures are median sales prices of existing single-family homes in thousands of dollars; (p) preliminary; n/a not available; (1) Lafayette, LA Metropolitan Statistical Area—see Appendix B for areas included
Source: National Association of Realtors, Median Sales Price of Existing Single-Family Homes for Metropolitan Areas, 4th Quarter 2013

Qualifying Income Based on Median Sales Price of Existing Single-Family Homes

Area	With 5% Down ($)	With 10% Down ($)	With 20% Down ($)
MSA[1]	n/a	n/a	n/a
U.S. Average	45,395	43,006	38,228

Note: Figures are preliminary; Qualifying income is based on a mortgage rate of 4.4%. Monthly principal and interest payment is limited to 25% of income; n/a not available; (1) Lafayette, LA Metropolitan Statistical Area—see Appendix B for areas included
Source: National Association of Realtors, Qualifying Income Based on Median Sales Price of Existing Single-Family Homes for Metropolitan Areas, 4th Quarter 2013

Median Apartment Condo-Coop Home Prices

Area	2011	2012	2013p	Percent Change 2012 to 2013
MSA[1]	n/a	n/a	n/a	n/a
U.S. Average	165.1	173.7	194.9	12.2

Note: Figures are median sales prices of existing apartment condo-coop homes in thousands of dollars; (p) preliminary; n/a not available; (1) Lafayette, LA Metropolitan Statistical Area—see Appendix B for areas included
Source: National Association of Realtors, Median Sales Price of Existing Apartment Condo-Coop Homes for Metropolitan Areas, 4th Quarter 2013

Gross Monthly Rent

Area	Under $200	$200 -299	$300 -499	$500 -749	$750 -999	$1,000 -1,499	$1,500 and up	Median ($)
City	3.0	2.3	8.7	34.9	26.7	18.9	5.5	758
MSA[1]	2.8	3.1	13.6	34.0	24.7	17.6	4.3	732
U.S.	1.7	3.3	8.1	22.7	24.3	25.7	14.3	889

Note: Figures are percentages except for Median; Gross rent is the contract rent plus the estimated average monthly cost of utilities (electricity, gas, and water and sewer) and fuels (oil, coal, kerosene, wood, etc.) if these are paid by the renter (or paid for the renter by someone else); (1) Figures cover the Lafayette, LA Metropolitan Statistical Area—see Appendix B for areas included
Source: U.S. Census Bureau, 2010-2012 American Community Survey 3-Year Estimates

Year Housing Structure Built

Area	2010 or Later	2000 -2009	1990 -1999	1980 -1989	1970 -1979	1960 -1969	1950 -1959	1940 -1949	Before 1940	Median Year
City	0.7	14.2	12.4	16.9	21.6	14.3	11.3	4.1	4.5	1977
MSA[1]	1.6	18.9	15.6	18.4	19.6	10.7	7.8	3.0	4.4	1982
U.S.	0.5	14.9	13.8	13.9	15.9	11.1	10.9	5.5	13.5	1976

Note: Figures are percentages except for Median Year; (1) Figures cover the Lafayette, LA Metropolitan Statistical Area—see Appendix B for areas included
Source: U.S. Census Bureau, 2010-2012 American Community Survey 3-Year Estimates

HEALTH

Health Risk Data

Category	MSA[1] (%)	U.S. (%)
Adults aged 18–64 who have any kind of health care coverage	72.6	79.6
Adults who reported being in good or excellent health	83.9	83.1
Adults who are current smokers	26.0	19.6
Adults who are heavy drinkers[2]	9.0	6.1
Adults who are binge drinkers[3]	18.2	16.9
Adults who are overweight (BMI 25.0 - 29.9)	35.0	35.8
Adults who are obese (BMI 30.0 - 99.8)	29.6	27.6
Adults who participated in any physical activities in the past month	74.0	77.1
Adults 50+ who have ever had a sigmoidoscopy or colonoscopy	52.4	67.3
Women aged 40+ who have had a mammogram within the past two years	73.5	74.0
Men aged 40+ who have had a PSA test within the past two years	53.3	45.2
Adults aged 65+ who have had flu shot within the past year	60.5	60.1
Adults who always wear a seatbelt	n/a	93.8

Note: Data as of 2012 unless otherwise noted; n/a not available; (1) Figures cover the Lafayette, LA Metropolitan Statistical Area—see Appendix B for areas included; (2) Heavy drinkers are classified as males having more than two drinks per day or females having more than one drink per day; (3) Binge drinkers are classified as males having five or more drinks on one occasion or females having four or more drinks on one occasion
Source: Centers for Disease Control and Prevention, Behaviorial Risk Factor Surveillance System, SMART: Selected Metropolitan/Micropolitan Area Risk Trends, 2012

Chronic Health Indicators

Category	MSA[1] (%)	U.S. (%)
Adults who have ever been told they had a heart attack	3.4	4.5
Adults who have ever been told they had a stroke	3.0	2.9
Adults who have been told they currently have asthma	6.8	8.9
Adults who have ever been told they have arthritis	25.1	25.7
Adults who have ever been told they have diabetes[2]	10.3	9.7
Adults who have ever been told they had skin cancer	5.7	5.7
Adults who have ever been told they had any other types of cancer	8.2	6.5
Adults who have ever been told they have COPD	6.4	6.2
Adults who have ever been told they have kidney disease	n/a	2.5
Adults who have ever been told they have a form of depression	13.8	18.0

Note: Data as of 2012 unless otherwise noted; n/a not available; (1) Figures cover the Lafayette, LA Metropolitan Statistical Area—see Appendix B for areas included; (2) Figures do not include pregnancy-related, borderline, or pre-diabetes
Source: Centers for Disease Control and Prevention, Behaviorial Risk Factor Surveillance System, SMART: Selected Metropolitan/Micropolitan Area Risk Trends, 2012

Mortality Rates for the Top 10 Causes of Death in the U.S.

ICD-10[a] Sub-Chapter	ICD-10[a] Code	Age-Adjusted Mortality Rate[1] per 100,000 population	
		County[2]	U.S.
Malignant neoplasms	C00-C97	186.4	174.2
Ischaemic heart diseases	I20-I25	164.3	119.1
Other forms of heart disease	I30-I51	57.0	49.6
Chronic lower respiratory diseases	J40-J47	40.2	43.2
Cerebrovascular diseases	I60-I69	44.0	40.3
Organic, including symptomatic, mental disorders	F01-F09	40.6	30.5
Other degenerative diseases of the nervous system	G30-G31	39.2	26.3
Other external causes of accidental injury	W00-X59	24.8	25.1
Diabetes mellitus	E10-E14	22.4	21.3
Hypertensive diseases	I10-I15	11.5	18.8

Note: (a) ICD-10 = International Classification of Diseases 10th Revision; (1) Mortality rates are a three year average covering 2008-2010; (2) Figures cover Lafayette Parish
Source: Centers for Disease Control and Prevention, National Center for Health Statistics. Compressed Mortality File 1999-2010 on CDC WONDER Online Database, released January 2013. Data are compiled from the Compressed Mortality File 1999-2010, Series 20 No. 2P, 2013.

Mortality Rates for Selected Causes of Death

ICD-10[a] Sub-Chapter	ICD-10[a] Code	Age-Adjusted Mortality Rate[1] per 100,000 population	
		County[2]	U.S.
Assault	X85-Y09	6.5	5.5
Diseases of the liver	K70-K76	8.3	12.4
Human immunodeficiency virus (HIV) disease	B20-B24	5.0	3.0
Influenza and pneumonia	J09-J18	16.7	16.4
Intentional self-harm	X60-X84	10.8	11.8
Malnutrition	E40-E46	Suppressed	0.8
Obesity and other hyperalimentation	E65-E68	*2.6	1.6
Renal failure	N17-N19	22.6	13.6
Transport accidents	V01-V99	15.5	12.6
Viral hepatitis	B15-B19	*1.9	2.2

Note: (a) ICD-10 = International Classification of Diseases 10th Revision; (1) Mortality rates are a three year average covering 2008-2010; (2) Figures cover Lafayette Parish; (*) Unreliable data as per CDC
Source: Centers for Disease Control and Prevention, National Center for Health Statistics. Compressed Mortality File 1999-2010 on CDC WONDER Online Database, released January 2013. Data are compiled from the Compressed Mortality File 1999-2010, Series 20 No. 2P, 2013.

Health Insurance Coverage

Area	With Health Insurance	With Private Health Insurance	With Public Health Insurance	Without Health Insurance	Population Under Age 18 Without Health Insurance
City	82.0	64.1	29.0	18.0	4.3
MSA[1]	83.2	63.8	29.0	16.8	4.1
U.S.	84.9	65.4	30.4	15.1	7.5

Note: Figures are percentages that cover the civilian noninstitutionalized population; (1) Figures cover the Lafayette, LA Metropolitan Statistical Area—see Appendix B for areas included
Source: U.S. Census Bureau, 2010-2012 American Community Survey 3-Year Estimates

Number of Medical Professionals

Area[1]	MDs[2]	DOs[2,3]	Dentists	Podiatrists	Chiropractors	Optometrists
Local (number)	790	9	140	9	68	30
Local (rate[4])	352.3	4.0	61.7	4.0	30.0	13.2
U.S. (rate[4])	267.6	19.6	61.7	5.6	24.7	14.5

Note: Data as of 2012 unless noted; (1) Local data covers Lafayette Parish; (2) Data as of 2011; (3) Doctor of Osteopathic Medicine; (4) rate per 100,000 population
Source: Area Resource File (ARF) 2012-2013. U.S. Department of Health and Human Services, Health Resources and Services Administration, Bureau of Health Professions

EDUCATION

Public School District Statistics

District Name	Schls	Pupils	Pupil/ Teacher Ratio	Minority Pupils[1] (%)	Free Lunch Eligible[2] (%)	IEP[3] (%)
Lafayette Parish	44	30,451	14.9	50.6	53.2	9.5

Note: Table includes school districts with 2,000 or more students; (1) Percentage of students that are not non-Hispanic white; (2) Percentage of students that are eligible for the free lunch program; (3) Percentage of students that have an Individualized Education Program.
Source: U.S. Department of Education, National Center for Education Statistics, Common Core of Data, Local Education Agency (School District) Universe Survey: School Year 2011-2012; U.S. Department of Education, National Center for Education Statistics, Common Core of Data, Public Elementary/Secondary School Universe Survey: School Year 2011-2012

Highest Level of Education

Area	Less than H.S.	H.S. Diploma	Some College, No Deg.	Associate Degree	Bachelor's Degree	Master's Degree	Prof. School Degree	Doctorate Degree
City	13.4	25.8	22.7	5.3	22.2	6.8	2.5	1.3
MSA[1]	15.9	33.5	21.3	4.6	17.5	4.7	1.6	0.9
U.S.	14.1	28.3	21.3	7.8	18.0	7.5	1.9	1.2

Note: Figures cover persons age 25 and over; (1) Figures cover the Lafayette, LA Metropolitan Statistical Area—see Appendix B for areas included
Source: U.S. Census Bureau, 2010-2012 American Community Survey 3-Year Estimates

Educational Attainment by Race

Area	High School Graduate or Higher (%)					Bachelor's Degree or Higher (%)				
	Total	White	Black	Asian	Hisp.[2]	Total	White	Black	Asian	Hisp.[2]
City	86.6	90.8	77.1	87.2	77.2	32.8	39.9	14.7	37.4	28.7
MSA[1]	84.1	88.0	73.4	77.1	70.1	24.7	28.8	12.2	31.3	16.9
U.S.	85.9	88.1	82.5	85.5	63.1	28.6	30.0	18.4	50.2	13.4

Note: Figures shown cover persons 25 years old and over; (1) Figures cover the Lafayette, LA Metropolitan Statistical Area—see Appendix B for areas included; (2) People of Hispanic origin can be of any race
Source: U.S. Census Bureau, 2010-2012 American Community Survey 3-Year Estimates

School Enrollment by Grade and Control

Area	Preschool (%)		Kindergarten (%)		Grades 1 - 4 (%)		Grades 5 - 8 (%)		Grades 9 - 12 (%)	
	Public	Private	Public	Private	Public	Private	Public	Private	Public	Private
City	50.0	50.0	81.3	18.7	78.2	21.8	67.4	32.6	76.3	23.7
MSA[1]	49.1	50.9	82.4	17.6	77.5	22.5	74.3	25.7	79.6	20.4
U.S.	56.9	43.1	87.8	12.2	89.9	10.1	90.0	10.0	90.8	9.2

Note: Figures shown cover persons 3 years old and over; (1) Figures cover the Lafayette, LA Metropolitan Statistical Area—see Appendix B for areas included
Source: U.S. Census Bureau, 2010-2012 American Community Survey 3-Year Estimates

Average Salaries of Public School Classroom Teachers

Area	2012-13		2013-14		Percent Change 2012-13 to 2013-14	Percent Change 2003-04 to 2013-14
	Dollars	Rank[1]	Dollars	Rank[1]		
Louisiana	51,381	25	52,259	24	1.71	37.8
U.S. Average	56,103	–	56,689	–	1.04	21.8

Note: (1) State rank ranges from 1 to 51 where 1 indicates highest salary.
Source: National Education Association, Rankings & Estimates: Rankings of the States 2013 and Estimates of School Statistics 2014, March 2014

412   Lafayette, Louisiana

Higher Education

Four-Year Colleges			Two-Year Colleges			Medical Schools[1]	Law Schools[2]	Voc/ Tech[3]
Public	Private Non-profit	Private For-profit	Public	Private Non-profit	Private For-profit			
1	0	1	2	1	0	0	0	4

Note: Figures cover institutions located within the city limits and include main campuses only; (1) includes schools accredited by the Liaison Committee on Medical Education and the American Osteopathic Association's Commission on Osteopathic College Accreditation; (2) includes ABA-accredited schools, schools with provisional ABA accreditation, and state accredited schools; (3) includes all schools with programs that are less than 2 years.
Source: National Center for Education Statistics, Integrated Postsecondary Education System (IPEDS), 2012-13; Association of American Medical Colleges, Member List, April 24, 2014; American Osteopathic Association, Member List, April 24, 2014; Law School Admission Council, Official Guide to ABA-Approved Law Schools Online, April 24, 2014; Wikipedia, List of Medical Schools in the United States, April 24, 2014; Wikipedia, List of Law Schools in the United States, April 24, 2014

PRESIDENTIAL ELECTION

2012 Presidential Election Results

Area	Obama	Romney	Other
Lafayette Parish	32.2	65.9	1.9
U.S.	51.0	47.2	1.8

Note: Results are percentages and may not add to 100% due to rounding
Source: Dave Leip's Atlas of U.S. Presidential Elections

EMPLOYERS

Major Employers

Company Name	Industry
Acadian Ambulance & Air Med Services	Healthcare/transportation
Cingular Wireless	Telecommunications
ESS Support Services Worldwide	Retail trade
Frank's Casing Crew	Oil and gas
Haliburton Energy SVC	Oil and gas
Island Operating Company	Oil and gas
Lafayette Consolidated Government	Government
Lafayette General Medical Center	Healthcare
Lafayette Parish Government	Government
Mac-Laff	Service
Moncla Well Service	Oil and gas
Omni Energy Services, Corp.	Oil and gas
Our Lady of Lourdes Reg. Med. Ctr.	Healthcare
School Board Lafayette Parish	Education
Stuller	Manufacturing
The Ace Group	Transportation
Univ of LA Lafayette	Education
University Medical Ctr	Healthcare
Walmart Stores	Retail
Women's & Children's Hospital	Healthcare

Note: Companies shown are located within the Lafayette, LA Metropolitan Statistical Area.
Source: Hoovers.com; Wikipedia

PUBLIC SAFETY

Crime Rate

Area	All Crimes	Violent Crimes				Property Crimes		
		Murder	Forcible Rape	Robbery	Aggrav. Assault	Burglary	Larceny -Theft	Motor Vehicle Theft
City	6,181.4	9.0	9.0	164.4	451.8	1,082.6	4,268.6	196.2
Suburbs[1]	n/a	6.6	21.9	66.7	n/a	720.4	1,778.0	n/a
Metro[2]	n/a	7.2	18.6	92.0	n/a	814.4	2,423.8	n/a
U.S.	3,246.1	4.7	26.9	112.9	242.3	670.2	1,959.3	229.7

Note: Figures are crimes per 100,000 population; (1) All areas within the metro area that are located outside the city limits; (2) Figures cover the Lafayette, LA Metropolitan Statistical Area—see Appendix B for areas included
Source: FBI Uniform Crime Reports, 2012

Hate Crimes

Area	Number of Quarters Reported	Bias Motivation				
		Race	Religion	Sexual Orientation	Ethnicity	Disability
City	3	0	0	0	0	0
U.S.	4	2,797	1,099	1,135	667	92

Source: Federal Bureau of Investigation, Hate Crime Statistics 2012

Identity Theft Consumer Complaints

Area	Complaints	Complaints per 100,000 Population	Rank[2]
MSA[1]	268	57.4	227
U.S.	290,056	91.8	-

Note: (1) Figures cover the Lafayette, LA Metropolitan Statistical Area—see Appendix B for areas included; (2) Rank ranges from 1 to 377 where 1 indicates greatest number of identity theft complaints per 100,000 population
Source: Federal Trade Commission, Consumer Sentinel Network Data Book for January–December 2013

Fraud and Other Consumer Complaints

Area	Complaints	Complaints per 100,000 Population	Rank[2]
MSA[1]	1,239	265.5	351
U.S.	1,811,724	595.2	-

Note: (1) Figures cover the Lafayette, LA Metropolitan Statistical Area—see Appendix B for areas included; (2) Rank ranges from 1 to 377 where 1 indicates greatest number of identity theft complaints per 100,000 population
Source: Federal Trade Commission, Consumer Sentinel Network Data Book for January–December 2013

RECREATION

Culture

Dance[1]	Theatre[1]	Instrumental Music[1]	Vocal Music[1]	Series and Festivals	Museums and Art Galleries[2]	Zoos and Aquariums[3]
0	0	1	0	5	8	0

Note: (1) Number of professional perfoming groups; (2) Based on organizations with primary SIC code 8412; (3) AZA-accredited
Source: The Grey House Performing Arts Directory, 2013; Association of Zoos & Aquariums, AZA Member Zoos & Aquariums, April 2014; www.AccuLeads.com, May 1, 2014

Professional Sports Teams

Team Name	League	Year Established
No teams are located in the metro area		

Source: Wikipedia, Major Professional Sports Teams of the United States and Canada, April 25, 2014

CLIMATE

Average and Extreme Temperatures

Temperature	Jan	Feb	Mar	Apr	May	Jun	Jul	Aug	Sep	Oct	Nov	Dec	Yr.
Extreme High (°F)	82	85	91	92	98	103	101	102	99	94	87	85	103
Average High (°F)	61	65	71	79	85	90	91	91	87	80	70	64	78
Average Temp. (°F)	51	54	61	68	75	81	82	82	78	69	59	53	68
Average Low (°F)	41	44	50	57	64	70	73	72	68	57	48	43	57
Extreme Low (°F)	9	13	20	32	44	53	58	59	43	30	21	8	8

Note: Figures cover the years 1948-1995
Source: National Climatic Data Center, International Station Meteorological Climate Summary, 9/96

Average Precipitation/Snowfall/Humidity

Precip./Humidity	Jan	Feb	Mar	Apr	May	Jun	Jul	Aug	Sep	Oct	Nov	Dec	Yr.
Avg. Precip. (in.)	4.9	5.1	4.8	5.5	5.0	4.4	6.6	5.4	4.1	3.1	4.2	5.3	58.5
Avg. Snowfall (in.)	Tr	Tr	Tr	0	0	0	0	0	0	0	Tr	Tr	Tr
Avg. Rel. Hum. 6am (%)	85	85	86	89	91	91	92	93	91	89	88	86	89
Avg. Rel. Hum. 3pm (%)	59	55	52	52	54	57	62	61	59	51	53	57	56

Note: Figures cover the years 1948-1995; Tr = Trace amounts (<0.05 in. of rain; <0.5 in. of snow)
Source: National Climatic Data Center, International Station Meteorological Climate Summary, 9/96

Weather Conditions

Temperature			Daytime Sky			Precipitation		
10°F & below	32°F & below	90°F & above	Clear	Partly cloudy	Cloudy	0.01 inch or more precip.	0.1 inch or more snow/ice	Thunder-storms
< 1	21	86	99	150	116	113	< 1	73

Note: Figures are average number of days per year and cover the years 1948-1995
Source: National Climatic Data Center, International Station Meteorological Climate Summary, 9/96

HAZARDOUS WASTE

Superfund Sites

Lafayette has no sites on the EPA's Superfund Final National Priorities List.
U.S. Environmental Protection Agency, Final National Priorities List, April 26, 2014

AIR & WATER QUALITY

Air Quality Index

Area	Percent of Days when Air Quality was...[2]					AQI Statistics[2]	
	Good	Moderate	Unhealthy for Sensitive Groups	Unhealthy	Very Unhealthy	Maximum	Median
MSA[1]	63.0	36.7	0.3	0.0	0.0	101	44

Note: (1) Data covers the Lafayette, LA Metropolitan Statistical Area—see Appendix B for areas included;
(2) Based on 365 days with AQI data in 2013. Air Quality Index (AQI) is an index for reporting daily air quality.
EPA calculates the AQI for five major air pollutants regulated by the Clean Air Act: ground-level ozone,
particle pollution (aka particulate matter), carbon monoxide, sulfur dioxide, and nitrogen dioxide. The AQI runs
from 0 to 500. The higher the AQI value, the greater the level of air pollution and the greater the health
concern. There are six AQI categories: "Good" AQI is between 0 and 50. Air quality is considered satisfactory;
"Moderate" AQI is between 51 and 100. Air quality is acceptable; "Unhealthy for Sensitive Groups" When
AQI values are between 101 and 150, members of sensitive groups may experience health effects; "Unhealthy"
When AQI values are between 151 and 200 everyone may begin to experience health effects; "Very Unhealthy"
AQI values between 201 and 300 trigger a health alert; "Hazardous" AQI values over 300 trigger warnings of
emergency conditions (not shown).
Source: U.S. Environmental Protection Agency, Air Quality Index Report, 2013

Air Quality Index Pollutants

Area	Percent of Days when AQI Pollutant was...[2]					
	Carbon Monoxide	Nitrogen Dioxide	Ozone	Sulfur Dioxide	Particulate Matter 2.5	Particulate Matter 10
MSA[1]	0.0	0.0	30.4	0.0	69.0	0.5

Note: (1) Data covers the Lafayette, LA Metropolitan Statistical Area—see Appendix B for areas included;
(2) Based on 365 days with AQI data in 2013. The Air Quality Index (AQI) is an index for reporting daily air
quality. EPA calculates the AQI for five major air pollutants regulated by the Clean Air Act: ground-level ozone,
particle pollution (also known as particulate matter), carbon monoxide, sulfur dioxide, and nitrogen dioxide.
The AQI runs from 0 to 500. The higher the AQI value, the greater the level of air pollution and the greater the
health concern.
Source: U.S. Environmental Protection Agency, Air Quality Index Report, 2013

Air Quality Trends: Ozone

	2003	2004	2005	2006	2007	2008	2009	2010	2011	2012
MSA[1]	n/a	n/a	n/a	n/a	n/a	n/a	n/a	n/a	n/a	n/a

Note: (1) Data covers the Lafayette, LA Metropolitan Statistical Area—see Appendix B for areas included; n/a
not available. The values shown are the composite ozone concentration averages among trend sites based on the
highest fourth daily maximum 8-hour concentration in parts per million. These trends are based on sites having
an adequate record of monitoring data during the trend period. Data from exceptional events are included.
Source: U.S. Environmental Protection Agency, Air Quality Monitoring Information, "Air Quality Trends by
City, 2000-2012"

Maximum Air Pollutant Concentrations: Particulate Matter, Ozone, CO and Lead

	Particulate Matter 10 (ug/m³)	Particulate Matter 2.5 Wtd AM (ug/m³)	Particulate Matter 2.5 24-Hr (ug/m³)	Ozone (ppm)	Carbon Monoxide (ppm)	Lead (ug/m³)
MSA[1] Level	73	8.6	18	0.07	n/a	n/a
NAAQS[2]	150	15	35	0.075	9	0.15
Met NAAQS[2]	Yes	Yes	Yes	Yes	n/a	n/a

Note: (1) Data covers the Lafayette, LA Metropolitan Statistical Area—see Appendix B for areas included; Data from exceptional events are included; (2) National Ambient Air Quality Standards; ppm = parts per million; ug/m³ = micrograms per cubic meter; n/a not available.
Concentrations: Particulate Matter 10 (coarse particulate)—highest second maximum 24-hour concentration; Particulate Matter 2.5 Wtd AM (fine particulate)—highest weighted annual mean concentration; Particulate Matter 2.5 24-Hour (fine particulate)—highest 98th percentile 24-hour concentration; Ozone—highest fourth daily maximum 8-hour concentration; Carbon Monoxide—highest second maximum non-overlapping 8-hour concentration; Lead—maximum running 3-month average
Source: U.S. Environmental Protection Agency, Air Quality Monitoring Information, "Air Quality Statistics by City, 2012"

Maximum Air Pollutant Concentrations: Nitrogen Dioxide and Sulfur Dioxide

	Nitrogen Dioxide AM (ppb)	Nitrogen Dioxide 1-Hr (ppb)	Sulfur Dioxide AM (ppb)	Sulfur Dioxide 1-Hr (ppb)	Sulfur Dioxide 24-Hr (ppb)
MSA[1] Level	n/a	n/a	n/a	n/a	n/a
NAAQS[2]	53	100	30	75	140
Met NAAQS[2]	n/a	n/a	n/a	n/a	n/a

Note: (1) Data covers the Lafayette, LA Metropolitan Statistical Area—see Appendix B for areas included; Data from exceptional events are included; (2) National Ambient Air Quality Standards; ppm = parts per million; ug/m³ = micrograms per cubic meter; n/a not available.
Concentrations: Nitrogen Dioxide AM—highest arithmetic mean concentration; Nitrogen Dioxide 1-Hr—highest 98th percentile 1-hour daily maximum concentration; Sulfur Dioxide AM—highest annual mean concentration; Sulfur Dioxide 1-Hr—highest 99th percentile 1-hour daily maximum concentration; Sulfur Dioxide 24-Hr—highest second maximum 24-hour concentration
Source: U.S. Environmental Protection Agency, Air Quality Monitoring Information, "Air Quality Statistics by City, 2012"

Drinking Water

Water System Name	Pop. Served	Primary Water Source Type	Violations[1] Health Based	Violations[1] Monitoring/ Reporting
Lafayette Utilities Water System	151,821	Ground	0	0

Note: (1) Based on violation data from January 1, 2013 to December 31, 2013 (includes unresolved violations from earlier years)
Source: U.S. Environmental Protection Agency, Office of Ground Water and Drinking Water, Safe Drinking Water Information System (based on data extracted February 10, 2014)

Lubbock, Texas

Background

Rarely are the words *West Texas* and *Quaker* used in the same context; however, one of the first settlers in the Lubbock area was a Quaker—Paris Cox, who was looking for farm and ranch land. Originally, the area comprised prime buffalo hunting ground for the Comanche Native Americans, but after the herds were decimated, there was little left for them. Spanish explorers like Francisco Vaquez de Coronado, camped on their way through, looking for the illusive cities of gold.

The Civil War bought a new kind of migration to the country. One way to escape the devastation wrought by the war was to leave the east for new land. And land was ripe for the taking, with the government offering 320 acres to anyone willing to work the land in Texas. It turned out the land was ripe indeed. Draught-resistant soil made for a bounty of cotton.

Lubbock derives its name from a former Texas Ranger and Confederate Officer, Thomas S. Lubbock. It was incorporated in 1909, and soon thereafter, the Santa Fe Railroad helped make Lubbock an important market center, sometimes referred to as the "Hub of the Plains." (To this day, Lubbock's nickname is "Hub City.") A farmer named S. S. Rush is credited with bringing cotton to Texas—an important crop for Lubbock's economy—and a town cotton gin was erected. Cotton production in Lubbock went from four bales in 1902, to over 100,000 by 1932. By 1977, 60% of the state's cotton would come from the Lubbock area, the largest contiguous cotton field in the world.

The Second World War also brought a boon to Lubbock's economy when the U.S. Government developed Lubbock Army Air Field—an advanced training school for would-be pilots, later re-named Reese Air Base. A second base, the South Plains Army Airfield, became a school for training glider pilots, who were charged with silently air dropping supplies to the Allied troops of Europe. Today Lubbock's unique Silent Wings Museum tells their story. The war also increased the demand for cotton, which Lubbock was glad to provide.

Lubbock is a surprising wellspring of music innovation. Rock and Roll legend Buddy Holley was born and raised in Lubbock. Today the Buddy Holly Center highlights his life and his contribution to rock and roll. Though Holly's career was short-lived (Holly died in a plane crash after only a year and a half in the public spotlight), many of today's rock legends, including such greats as Paul McCartney, Keith Richards, Bob Dylan, and Elvis Costello, tribute Holly as one of the greatest influencers in the industry. *Rolling Stone* acknowledged him as one of the top 20 innovators in the history of rock and roll.

With Lubbock's rich music history, comes a rich nightlife. The Depot District, located in the area that surrounds the old railroad depot, is dedicated to music and entertainment. The area is filled with theaters, pubs, nightclubs, upscale restaurants, and cultural attractions, including a winery and radio station. The Buddy Holly Center is also located in the Depot District. Each year, the Lubbock Music Festival, brings a wide variety of top bands and entertainers to the area.

Many institutions of higher learning call Lubbock home. Founded in 1923, Texas Technical University is the only school in Texas to feature an undergraduate university, a medical school, and a Law school at one location. TTU is highly regarded for its research in medicine and technology. The Tech Red Raiders are members of the Division 1, Big 12 Conference for varsity sports.

Lubbock is also the site of one of the first credible UFO sightings. In 1951, numerous residents witnessed the "Lubbock lights," some of whom were highly-regarded Texas Tech scientists. The U.S. Airforce launched an official investigation and concluded that they were not a hoax, though the study failed to explain them. Photographs of these UFO events were published in *Life Magazine*.

Lubbock sits at the southern edge of the western high plains. The climate in Lubbock is semi-arid, and usually warm and dry, but in 1970 a devastating tornado tore through town, destroying over three square miles of the city, and killing 26 people. Damage was estimated to be well over $135 million.

Rankings

Business/Finance Rankings

- Lubbock was the #6-ranked city for savers, according to the finance site GoBankingRates, which considered the prospects for savers in a tough savings economy by looking for higher interest yields, lower taxes, more jobs with higher incomes, and less expensive housing costs. *www.gobankingrates.com, "Best Cities for Saving Money," February 24, 2014*

- The Lubbock metro area appeared on the Milken Institute "2013 Best Performing Cities" list. Rank: #69 out of 200 large metro areas. Criteria: job growth; wage and salary growth; high-tech output growth. *Milken Institute, "Best-Performing Cities 2013," December 2013*

- *Forbes* ranked the 200 most populous metro areas in the U.S. in terms of the "Best Places for Business and Careers." The Lubbock metro area was ranked #73. Criteria: costs (business and living); job growth (past and projected); income growth; educational attainment (college and high school); projected economic growth; cultural and recreational opportunities; net migration patterns; number of highly ranked colleges. *Forbes, "The Best Places for Business and Careers," August 7, 2013*

Children/Family Rankings

- Lubbock was chosen as one of America's 100 best communities for young people. The winners were selected based upon detailed information provided about each community's efforts to fulfill five essential promises critical to the well-being of young people: caring adults who are actively involved in their lives; safe places in which to learn and grow; a healthy start toward adulthood; an effective education that builds marketable skills; and opportunities to help others. *America's Promise Alliance, "100 Best Communities for Young People, 2012"*

Dating/Romance Rankings

- Of the 100 U.S. cities surveyed by *Men's Health* in its quest to identify the nation's best cities for dating and forming relationships, Lubbock was ranked #90 for online dating (#1 = best). *Men's Health, "The Best and Worst Cities for Online Dating," January 30, 2013*

Education Rankings

- *Men's Health* ranked 100 U.S. cities in terms of their education levels. Lubbock was ranked #45 (#1 = most educated city). Criteria: high school graduation rates; school enrollment; educational attainment; number of households who have outstanding student loans; number of households whose members have taken adult-education courses. *Men's Health, "Where School Is In: The Most and Least Educated Cities," September 12, 2011*

Environmental Rankings

- The Lubbock metro area came in at #261 for the relative comfort of its climate on Sperling's list of "chill cities," as measured by the Sperling Heat Index. All 361 metro areas are included. Criteria included daytime high temperatures, nighttime low temperatures, dew point, and relative humidity at the high temperatures. *www.bertsperling.com, "Sperling's Chill Cities," July 18, 2013*

- Sperling's BestPlaces assessed 379 metropolitan areas of the United States for the likelihood of dangerously extreme weather events or earthquakes. In general the Southeast and South-Central regions have the highest risk of weather extremes and earthquakes, while the Pacific Northwest enjoys the lowest risk. Of the least risky metropolitan areas, the Lubbock metro area was ranked #312. *www.bestplaces.net, "Safest Places from Natural Disasters," April 2011*

- The Lubbock metro area was identified as one of nine cities running out of water by *24/7 Wall St.* The area ranked #1. Based on data provided by the U.S. Drought Monitor, a joint program produced by academic and government organizations, *24/7 Wall St.* identified large U.S. urban areas that have been under persistent, serious drought for months. *24/7 Wall St., "Nine Cities Running Out of Water," August 1, 2013*

- Lubbock was selected as one of 22 "Smarter Cities" for energy by the Natural Resources Defense Council. Criteria: investment in green power; energy efficiency measures; conservation. *Natural Resources Defense Council, "2010 Smarter Cities," July 19, 2010*

Food/Drink Rankings

- *Men's Health* ranked 100 major U.S. cities in terms of alcohol intoxication. Lubbock ranked #69 (#1 = most sober).Criteria: binge drinking; alcohol-related traffic accidents, arrests, and fatalities. *Men's Health, "The Drunkest Cities in America," November 19, 2013*

Health/Fitness Rankings

- Lubbock was identified as one of "The 8 Most Artery-Clogging Cities in America." The metro area ranked #3. Criteria: obesity rates; heart disease rates. *Prevention, "The 8 Most Artery-Clogging Cities in America," December 2011*

- *Men's Health* ranked 100 major U.S. cities in terms of the best and worst cities for men. Lubbock ranked #64. Criteria: thirty-three data points were examined covering health, fitness, and quality of life. *Men's Health, "The Best & Worst Cities for Men 2014," December 6, 2013*

- *Men's Health* ranked 100 U.S. cities in terms of their activity levels. Lubbock was ranked #72 (#1 = most active city). Criteria: where and how often residents exercise; percentage of households that watch more than 15 hours of cable television a week and buy more than 11 video games a year; death rate from deep-vein thrombosis, a condition linked to sitting for extended periods of time. *Men's Health, "Where Sit Happens: The Most and Least Active Cities in America," June 20, 2011*

- Lubbock was selected as one of the "20 Most Livable U.S. Cities for Wheelchair Users" by the Christopher & Dana Reeve Foundation. The city ranked #10. Criteria: Medicaid eligibility and spending; access to physicians and rehabilitation facilities; access to fitness facilities and recreation; access to paratransit; percentage of people living with disabilities who are employed; clean air; climate. *Christopher & Dana Reeve Foundation, "20 Most Livable U.S. Cities for Wheelchair Users," July 26, 2010*

Real Estate Rankings

- Lubbock was ranked #109 out of 283 metro areas in terms of house price appreciation in 2013 (#1 = highest rate). *Federal Housing Finance Agency, House Price Index, 4th Quarter 2013*

- Lubbock was selected as one of the best college towns for renters by ApartmentRatings.com." The area ranked #31 out of 87. Overall satisfaction ratings were ranked using thousands of user submitted scores for hundreds of apartment complexes located in cities and towns that are home to the 100 largest four-year institutions in the U.S. *ApartmentRatings.com, "2011 College Town Renter Satisfaction Rankings"*

Safety Rankings

- Allstate ranked the 200 largest cities in America in terms of driver safety. Lubbock ranked #50. Allstate researchers analyzed internal property damage claims over a two-year period from January 2010 to December 2011. A weighted average of the two-year numbers determined the annual percentages. *Allstate, "Allstate America's Best Drivers Report®, August 27, 2013"*

- The National Insurance Crime Bureau ranked 380 metro areas in the U.S. in terms of per capita rates of vehicle theft. The Lubbock metro area ranked #77 (#1 = highest rate). Criteria: number of vehicle theft offenses per 100,000 inhabitants in 2012. *National Insurance Crime Bureau, "Hot Spots 2012," June 26, 2013*

Seniors/Retirement Rankings

- From its Best Cities for Successful Aging indexes, the Milken Institute generated rankings for metropolitan areas, weighing data in eight categories—general indicators, health care, wellness, living arrangements, transportation and general accessibility, financial well-being, education and employment, and community participation. The Lubbock metro area was ranked #17 overall in the small metro area category. *Milken Institute, "Best Cities for Successful Aging," July 2012*

Sports/Recreation Rankings

- Lubbock appeared on the *Sporting News* list of the "Best Sports Cities" for 2011. The area ranked #90 out of 271. Criteria: the magazine takes a 12-month snapshot of each city's sports, putting a heavy premium on regular-season won-lost records (from the most recently completed season). Other criteria include: playoff berths, bowl appearances and tournament bids; championships; applicable power ratings; quality of competition; overall fan fervor (measured in part by attendance); abundance of teams (rewarding quality over quantity); stadium and arena quality; ticket availability and prices; franchise ownership; and marquee appeal of athletes. *Sporting News, "Best Sports Cities 2011," October 4, 2011*

- Lubbock appeared on the *Sporting News* list of the "Best Sports Cities" for 2011. The area ranked #90 out of 271. Criteria: a 12-month snapshot of regular-season won-lost records (from the most recently completed season). Other criteria include: playoff berths, bowl appearances and tournament bids; championships; applicable power ratings; quality of competition; overall fan fervor (measured in part by attendance); abundance of teams (quality over quantity); stadium and arena quality; ticket availability and prices; franchise ownership; and marquee appeal of athletes. *Sporting News, "Best Sports Cities 2011," October 4, 2011*

Women/Minorities Rankings

- Movoto chose five objective criteria to identify the best places for professional women among the largest 100 American cities. Lubbock was among the top ten, at #1, based on commute time, recent job growth, unemployment rank, professional women's groups per capita, and average earnings adjusted for the cost of living. *www.movoto.com, "These Are America's Best Cities for Professional Women," March 5, 2014*

- *Women's Health* examined U.S. cities and identified the 100 best cities for women. Lubbock was ranked #63. Criteria: 30 categories were examined from obesity and breast cancer rates to commuting times and hours spent working out. *Women's Health, "Best Cities for Women 2012"*

Miscellaneous Rankings

- *Men's Health* ranked 100 U.S. cities by their level of sadness. Lubbock was ranked #29 (#1 = saddest city). Criteria: suicide rates; unemployment rates; percentage of households that use antidepressants; percent of population who report feeling blue all or most of the time. *Men's Health, "Frown Towns," November 28, 2011*

Business Environment

CITY FINANCES

City Government Finances

Component	2011 ($000)	2011 ($ per capita)
Total Revenues	471,609	2,170
Total Expenditures	503,077	2,315
Debt Outstanding	1,181,319	5,436
Cash and Securities[1]	933,268	4,294

Note: (1) Cash and security holdings of a government at the close of its fiscal year, including those of its dependent agencies, utilities, and liquor stores.
Source: U.S Census Bureau, State & Local Government Finances 2011

City Government Revenue by Source

Source	2011 ($000)	2011 ($ per capita)
General Revenue		
From Federal Government	14,876	68
From State Government	13,602	63
From Local Governments	0	0
Taxes		
Property	55,065	253
Sales and Gross Receipts	67,249	309
Personal Income	0	0
Corporate Income	0	0
Motor Vehicle License	0	0
Other Taxes	2,494	11
Current Charges	57,677	265
Liquor Store	0	0
Utility	213,763	984
Employee Retirement	22,964	106

Source: U.S Census Bureau, State & Local Government Finances 2011

City Government Expenditures by Function

Function	2011 ($000)	2011 ($ per capita)	2011 (%)
General Direct Expenditures			
Air Transportation	10,084	46	2.0
Corrections	0	0	0.0
Education	0	0	0.0
Employment Security Administration	0	0	0.0
Financial Administration	2,163	10	0.4
Fire Protection	32,042	147	6.4
General Public Buildings	2,848	13	0.6
Governmental Administration, Other	8,409	39	1.7
Health	5,214	24	1.0
Highways	46,069	212	9.2
Hospitals	0	0	0.0
Housing and Community Development	5,648	26	1.1
Interest on General Debt	28,722	132	5.7
Judicial and Legal	5,472	25	1.1
Libraries	3,854	18	0.8
Parking	0	0	0.0
Parks and Recreation	14,665	67	2.9
Police Protection	46,874	216	9.3
Public Welfare	0	0	0.0
Sewerage	32,640	150	6.5
Solid Waste Management	16,238	75	3.2
Veterans' Services	0	0	0.0
Liquor Store	0	0	0.0
Utility	202,173	930	40.2
Employee Retirement	11,077	51	2.2

Source: U.S Census Bureau, State & Local Government Finances 2011

DEMOGRAPHICS

Population Growth

Area	1990 Census	2000 Census	2010 Census	Population Growth (%)	
				1990-2000	2000-2010
City	187,170	199,564	229,573	6.6	15.0
MSA[1]	229,940	249,700	284,890	8.6	14.1
U.S.	248,709,873	281,421,906	308,745,538	13.2	9.7

Note: (1) Figures cover the Lubbock, TX Metropolitan Statistical Area—see Appendix B for areas included
Source: U.S. Census Bureau, Census 1990, 2000, 2010

Household Size

Area	Persons in Household (%)							Average Household Size
	One	Two	Three	Four	Five	Six	Seven or More	
City	30.1	32.8	15.7	12.3	5.4	2.3	1.4	2.51
MSA[1]	28.0	33.0	16.2	12.8	6.1	2.4	1.5	2.57
U.S.	27.6	33.5	15.7	13.2	6.1	2.4	1.5	2.63

Note: (1) Figures cover the Lubbock, TX Metropolitan Statistical Area—see Appendix B for areas included
Source: U.S. Census Bureau, 2010-2012 American Community Survey 3-Year Estimates

Race

Area	White Alone[2] (%)	Black Alone[2] (%)	Asian Alone[2] (%)	AIAN[3] Alone[2] (%)	NHOPI[4] Alone[2] (%)	Other Race Alone[2] (%)	Two or More Races (%)
City	77.3	8.0	2.5	0.5	0.1	8.4	3.2
MSA[1]	79.2	7.2	2.1	0.4	0.1	8.0	3.0
U.S.	74.0	12.6	4.9	0.8	0.2	4.7	2.8

Note: (1) Figures cover the Lubbock, TX Metropolitan Statistical Area—see Appendix B for areas included; (2) Alone is defined as not being in combination with one or more other races; (3) American Indian and Alaska Native; (4) Native Hawaiian and Other Pacific Islander
Source: U.S. Census Bureau, 2010-2012 American Community Survey 3-Year Estimates

Hispanic or Latino Origin

Area	Total (%)	Mexican (%)	Puerto Rican (%)	Cuban (%)	Other (%)
City	33.0	28.5	0.2	0.0	4.3
MSA[1]	33.0	28.8	0.2	0.0	4.0
U.S.	16.6	10.7	1.6	0.6	3.7

Note: Persons of Hispanic or Latino origin can be of any race; (1) Figures cover the Lubbock, TX Metropolitan Statistical Area—see Appendix B for areas included
Source: U.S. Census Bureau, 2010-2012 American Community Survey 3-Year Estimates

Segregation

Type	Segregation Indices[1]				Percent Change		
	1990	2000	2010	2010 Rank[2]	1990-2000	1990-2010	2000-2010
Black/White	n/a	n/a	n/a	n/a	n/a	n/a	n/a
Asian/White	n/a	n/a	n/a	n/a	n/a	n/a	n/a
Hispanic/White	n/a	n/a	n/a	n/a	n/a	n/a	n/a

Note: All figures cover the Metropolitan Statistical Area—see Appendix B for areas included; Figures are based on an analysis of 1990, 2000, and 2010 Census Decennial Census tract data by William H. Frey, Brookings Institution and the University of Michigan Social Science Data Analysis Network. In this analysis all racial groups (whites, blacks, and asians) are non-Hispanic members of those races. Hispanics are shown as a separate category;
(1) Segregation Indices are Dissimilarity Indices that measure the degree to which the minority group is distributed differently than whites across census tracts. They range from 0 (complete integration) to 100 (complete segregation) where the value indicates the percentage of the minority group that needs to move to be distributed exactly like whites; (2) Ranges from 1 (most segregated) to 102 (least segregated); n/a not available.
Source: www.CensusScope.org

Ancestry

Area	German	Irish	English	American	Italian	Polish	French[2]	Scottish	Dutch
City	11.9	9.0	7.4	7.2	1.5	0.9	1.5	1.7	0.9
MSA[1]	12.0	9.4	7.4	7.6	1.4	0.9	1.6	1.7	1.0
U.S.	15.2	11.1	8.2	7.2	5.6	3.1	2.8	1.7	1.4

Note: Figures are the percentage of the total population reporting a particular ancestry. The nine most commonly reported ancestries in the U.S. are shown. Figures include multiple ancestries (e.g. if a person reported being Irish and Italian, they were included in both columns); (1) Figures cover the Lubbock, TX Metropolitan Statistical Area—see Appendix B for areas included; (2) Excludes Basque
Source: U.S. Census Bureau, 2010-2012 American Community Survey 3-Year Estimates

Foreign-Born Population

Area	Any Foreign Country	Mexico	Asia	Europe	Carribean	South America	Central America[2]	Africa	Canada
City	n/a	n/a	n/a	n/a	n/a	n/a	n/a	n/a	n/a
MSA[1]	5.8	2.7	1.8	0.4	0.1	0.2	0.3	0.3	0.1
U.S.	13.0	3.7	3.7	1.6	1.2	0.9	1.0	0.5	0.3

Note: (1) Figures cover the Lubbock, TX Metropolitan Statistical Area—see Appendix B for areas included; (2) Excludes Mexico.
Source: U.S. Census Bureau, 2010-2012 American Community Survey 3-Year Estimates

Marital Status

Area	Never Married	Now Married[2]	Separated	Widowed	Divorced
City	39.9	41.4	2.2	5.7	10.9
MSA[1]	37.0	44.3	2.2	5.9	10.6
U.S.	32.4	48.4	2.2	6.0	11.0

Note: Figures are percentages and cover the population 15 years of age and older; (1) Figures cover the Lubbock, TX Metropolitan Statistical Area—see Appendix B for areas included; (2) Excludes separated
Source: U.S. Census Bureau, 2010-2012 American Community Survey 3-Year Estimates

Age

Area	Under Age 5	Age 5–19	Age 20–34	Age 35–44	Age 45–54	Age 55–64	Age 65–74	Age 75–84	Age 85+	Median Age
City	7.4	21.1	29.0	10.6	11.4	9.6	5.9	3.9	1.4	29.5
MSA[1]	7.1	21.6	26.9	11.0	11.9	10.1	6.1	3.8	1.4	30.6
U.S.	6.4	20.1	20.5	13.1	14.3	12.2	7.3	4.2	1.8	37.3

Note: (1) Figures cover the Lubbock, TX Metropolitan Statistical Area—see Appendix B for areas included
Source: U.S. Census Bureau, 2010-2012 American Community Survey 3-Year Estimates

Gender

Area	Males	Females	Males per 100 Females
City	115,293	118,182	97.6
MSA[1]	143,217	146,468	97.8
U.S.	153,276,055	158,333,314	96.8

Note: (1) Figures cover the Lubbock, TX Metropolitan Statistical Area—see Appendix B for areas included
Source: U.S. Census Bureau, 2010-2012 American Community Survey 3-Year Estimates

Religious Groups by Family

Area	Catholic	Baptist	Non-Den.	Methodist[2]	Lutheran	LDS[3]	Pentecostal	Presbyterian[4]	Muslim[5]	Judaism
MSA[1]	13.4	22.4	7.3	6.6	0.5	1.4	1.9	0.8	1.8	0.1
U.S.	19.1	9.3	4.0	4.0	2.3	2.0	1.9	1.6	0.8	0.7

Note: Figures are the number of adherents as a percentage of the total population; (1) Figures cover the Lubbock, TX Metropolitan Statistical Area—see Appendix B for areas included; (2) Methodist/Pietist; (3) Latter Day Saints; (4) Reformed; (5) Figures are estimates
Source: Association of Statisticians of American Religious Bodies, 2010 U.S. Religion Census: Religious Congregations & Membership Study

Religious Groups by Tradition

Area	Catholic	Evangelical Protestant	Mainline Protestant	Other Tradition	Black Protestant	Orthodox
MSA[1]	13.4	31.5	8.6	4.0	0.7	0.1
U.S.	19.1	16.2	7.3	4.3	1.6	0.3

Note: Figures are the number of adherents as a percentage of the total population; (1) Figures cover the Lubbock, TX Metropolitan Statistical Area—see Appendix B for areas included
Source: Association of Statisticians of American Religious Bodies, 2010 U.S. Religion Census: Religious Congregations & Membership Study

ECONOMY

Gross Metropolitan Product

Area	2011	2012	2013	2014	Rank[2]
MSA[1]	10.3	10.9	11.3	11.7	171

Note: Figures are in billions of dollars; (1) Figures cover the Lubbock, TX Metropolitan Statistical Area—see Appendix B for areas included; (2) Rank is based on 2014 data and ranges from 1 to 363
Source: The United States Conference of Mayors, U.S. Metro Economies: Outlook—Gross Metropolitan Product, with Metro Employment Projections, November 2013

Economic Growth

Area	2011 (%)	2012 (%)	2013 (%)	2014 (%)	Rank[2]
MSA[1]	-2.7	4.3	2.2	1.9	65
U.S.	1.6	2.5	1.7	2.5	–

Note: Figures are real gross metropolitan product (GMP) growth rates and represent annual average percent change; (1) Figures cover the Lubbock, TX Metropolitan Statistical Area—see Appendix B for areas included; (2) Rank is based on 2013 data and ranges from 1 to 363
Source: The United States Conference of Mayors, U.S. Metro Economies: Outlook—Gross Metropolitan Product, with Metro Employment Projections, November 2013

Metropolitan Area Exports

Area	2007	2008	2009	2010	2011	2012	Rank[2]
MSA[1]	859.6	1,016.6	530.4	772.8	966.9	657.9	190

Note: Figures are in millions of dollars; (1) Figures cover the Lubbock, TX Metropolitan Statistical Area—see Appendix B for areas included; (2) Rank is based on 2012 data and ranges from 1 to 369
Source: U.S. Department of Commerce, International Trade Administration, Office of Trade & Industry Information, Manufacturing & Services, data extracted April 1, 2014

INCOME

Income

Area	Per Capita ($)	Median Household ($)	Average Household ($)
City	23,003	42,139	58,725
MSA[1]	23,133	43,414	60,467
U.S.	27,385	51,771	71,579

Note: (1) Figures cover the Lubbock, TX Metropolitan Statistical Area—see Appendix B for areas included
Source: U.S. Census Bureau, 2010-2012 American Community Survey 3-Year Estimates

Household Income Distribution

Area	Under $15,000	$15,000 -24,999	$25,000 -34,999	$35,000 -49,999	$50,000 -74,999	$75,000 -99,000	$100,000 -149,999	$150,000 and up
City	17.5	13.6	12.1	13.6	18.0	10.4	9.1	5.7
MSA[1]	16.7	13.4	12.0	13.8	17.8	10.7	9.7	6.0
U.S.	13.1	11.0	10.5	13.7	18.1	11.9	12.5	9.1

Note: (1) Figures cover the Lubbock, TX Metropolitan Statistical Area—see Appendix B for areas included
Source: U.S. Census Bureau, 2010-2012 American Community Survey 3-Year Estimates

Poverty Rate

Area	All Ages	Under 18 Years Old	18 to 64 Years Old	65 Years and Over
City	22.6	28.5	23.0	7.1
MSA[1]	21.5	27.6	21.5	7.4
U.S.	15.7	22.2	14.6	9.3

Note: Figures are percentage of people whose income during the past 12 months was below the poverty level; (1) Figures cover the Lubbock, TX Metropolitan Statistical Area—see Appendix B for areas included
Source: U.S. Census Bureau, 2010-2012 American Community Survey 3-Year Estimates

Personal Bankruptcy Filing Rate

Area	2008	2009	2010	2011	2012	2013
Lubbock County	1.36	1.50	1.50	1.34	1.33	0.96
U.S.	3.53	4.61	4.97	4.37	3.76	3.29

Note: Numbers are per 1,000 population and include Chapter 7 and Chapter 13 filings
Source: Federal Deposit Insurance Corporation, Regional Economic Conditions, March 20, 2014

EMPLOYMENT

Labor Force and Employment

Area	Civilian Labor Force			Workers Employed		
	Dec. 2012	Dec. 2013	% Chg.	Dec. 2012	Dec. 2013	% Chg.
City	119,336	122,325	2.5	113,737	117,178	3.0
MSA[1]	146,387	150,127	2.6	139,492	143,712	3.0
U.S.	154,904,000	154,408,000	-0.3	143,060,000	144,423,000	1.0

Note: Data is not seasonally adjusted and covers workers 16 years of age and older; (1) Metropolitan Statistical Area—see Appendix B for areas included
Source: Bureau of Labor Statistics, Local Area Unemployment Statistics

Unemployment Rate

Area	2013											
	Jan.	Feb.	Mar.	Apr.	May	Jun.	Jul.	Aug.	Sep.	Oct.	Nov.	Dec.
City	5.4	5.0	5.1	4.7	5.1	6.0	5.7	5.0	4.9	4.6	4.4	4.2
MSA[1]	5.5	5.1	5.3	4.8	5.3	6.1	5.8	5.0	5.0	4.7	4.5	4.3
U.S.	8.5	8.1	7.6	7.1	7.3	7.8	7.7	7.3	7.0	7.0	6.6	6.5

Note: Data is not seasonally adjusted and covers workers 16 years of age and older; All figures are percentages; (1) Metropolitan Statistical Area—see Appendix B for areas included
Source: Bureau of Labor Statistics, Local Area Unemployment Statistics

Employment by Occupation

Occupation Classification	City (%)	MSA[1] (%)	U.S. (%)
Management, Business, Science, and Arts	33.8	33.1	36.0
Natural Resources, Construction, and Maintenance	8.8	10.1	9.1
Production, Transportation, and Material Moving	9.1	9.6	12.0
Sales and Office	27.9	26.8	24.7
Service	20.4	20.3	18.2

Note: Figures cover employed civilians 16 years of age and older; (1) Figures cover the Lubbock, TX Metropolitan Statistical Area—see Appendix B for areas included
Source: U.S. Census Bureau, 2010-2012 American Community Survey 3-Year Estimates

Employment by Industry

| Sector | MSA[1] | | U.S. |
	Number of Employees	Percent of Total	Percent of Total
Construction	n/a	n/a	4.2
Education and Health Services	21,700	16.0	15.5
Financial Activities	7,100	5.2	5.7
Government	28,600	21.1	16.1
Information	3,900	2.9	1.9
Leisure and Hospitality	17,400	12.8	10.2
Manufacturing	4,900	3.6	8.7
Mining and Logging	n/a	n/a	0.6
Other Services	5,500	4.1	3.9
Professional and Business Services	11,000	8.1	13.7
Retail Trade	18,000	13.3	11.4
Transportation and Utilities	4,900	3.6	3.8
Wholesale Trade	6,300	4.6	4.2

Note: Figures cover non-farm employment as of December 2013 and are not seasonally adjusted;
(1) Metropolitan Statistical Area—see Appendix B for areas included; n/a not available
Source: Bureau of Labor Statistics, Current Employment Statistics, Employment, Hours, and Earnings

Occupations with Greatest Projected Employment Growth: 2010 – 2020

Occupation[1]	2010 Employment	2020 Projected Employment	Numeric Employment Change	Percent Employment Change
Combined Food Preparation and Serving Workers, Including Fast Food	243,530	322,520	78,990	32.4
Elementary School Teachers, Except Special Education	166,090	233,860	67,780	40.8
Personal Care Aides	133,820	199,970	66,150	49.4
Retail Salespersons	370,620	433,180	62,560	16.9
Registered Nurses	184,700	245,870	61,160	33.1
Waiters and Waitresses	190,870	244,610	53,730	28.2
Office Clerks, General	262,740	314,810	52,070	19.8
Cashiers	250,510	292,730	42,220	16.9
Home Health Aides	82,420	123,970	41,550	50.4
Customer Service Representatives	200,880	241,030	40,160	20.0

Note: Projections cover Texas; (1) Sorted by numeric employment change
Source: www.projectionscentral.com, State Occupational Projections, 2010–2020 Long-Term Projections

Fastest Growing Occupations: 2010 – 2020

Occupation[1]	2010 Employment	2020 Projected Employment	Numeric Employment Change	Percent Employment Change
Biomedical Engineers	1,440	2,490	1,050	72.9
Diagnostic Medical Sonographers	3,560	5,410	1,850	51.9
Derrick Operators, Oil and Gas	7,190	10,860	3,670	51.1
Home Health Aides	82,420	123,970	41,550	50.4
Personal Care Aides	133,820	199,970	66,150	49.4
Service Unit Operators, Oil, Gas, and Mining	17,870	26,460	8,590	48.0
Special Education Teachers, Middle School	6,170	8,950	2,780	45.1
Special Education Teachers, Preschool, Kindergarten, and Elementary School	12,940	18,750	5,810	44.9
Rotary Drill Operators, Oil and Gas	7,160	10,340	3,180	44.4
Roustabouts, Oil and Gas	17,800	25,580	7,790	43.8

Note: Projections cover Texas; (1) Sorted by percent employment change and excludes occupations with numeric employment change less than 100
Source: www.projectionscentral.com, State Occupational Projections, 2010–2020 Long-Term Projections

Average Wages

Occupation	$/Hr.	Occupation	$/Hr.
Accountants and Auditors	29.12	Maids and Housekeeping Cleaners	8.45
Automotive Mechanics	14.24	Maintenance and Repair Workers	14.17
Bookkeepers	14.57	Marketing Managers	56.59
Carpenters	15.94	Nuclear Medicine Technologists	n/a
Cashiers	8.83	Nurses, Licensed Practical	20.57
Clerks, General Office	13.01	Nurses, Registered	27.47
Clerks, Receptionists/Information	10.76	Nursing Assistants	10.95
Clerks, Shipping/Receiving	13.38	Packers and Packagers, Hand	8.89
Computer Programmers	28.78	Physical Therapists	38.23
Computer Systems Analysts	32.41	Postal Service Mail Carriers	24.89
Computer User Support Specialists	18.01	Real Estate Brokers	n/a
Cooks, Restaurant	9.23	Retail Salespersons	11.69
Dentists	64.36	Sales Reps., Exc. Tech./Scientific	28.05
Electrical Engineers	36.33	Sales Reps., Tech./Scientific	29.00
Electricians	19.77	Secretaries, Exc. Legal/Med./Exec.	13.35
Financial Managers	43.63	Security Guards	11.87
First-Line Supervisors/Managers, Sales	20.57	Surgeons	90.44
Food Preparation Workers	9.10	Teacher Assistants	8.80
General and Operations Managers	47.36	Teachers, Elementary School	21.40
Hairdressers/Cosmetologists	10.62	Teachers, Secondary School	22.50
Internists	n/a	Telemarketers	n/a
Janitors and Cleaners	10.31	Truck Drivers, Heavy/Tractor-Trailer	17.79
Landscaping/Groundskeeping Workers	10.92	Truck Drivers, Light/Delivery Svcs.	14.21
Lawyers	53.47	Waiters and Waitresses	9.03

Note: Wage data covers the Lubbock, TX Metropolitan Statistical Area—see Appendix B for areas included. Hourly wages for elementary/secondary school teachers and teacher assistants were calculated by the editors from annual wage data assuming a 40 hour work week; n/a not available.
Source: Bureau of Labor Statistics, Metro Area Occupational Employment and Wage Estimates, May 2013

RESIDENTIAL REAL ESTATE

Building Permits

Area	Single-Family			Multi-Family			Total		
	2012	2013	Pct. Chg.	2012	2013	Pct. Chg.	2012	2013	Pct. Chg.
City	697	938	34.6	715	1,039	45.3	1,412	1,977	40.0
MSA[1]	752	1,009	34.2	715	1,039	45.3	1,467	2,048	39.6
U.S.	518,695	620,802	19.7	310,963	370,020	19.0	829,658	990,822	19.4

Note: (1) Metropolitan Statistical Area—see Appendix B for areas included; figures represent new, privately-owned housing units authorized (unadjusted data); All permit data are based on estimates with imputation.
Source: U.S. Census Bureau, Manufacturing, Mining, and Construction Statistics, Building Permits, 2012, 2013

Homeownership Rate

Area	2006 (%)	2007 (%)	2008 (%)	2009 (%)	2010 (%)	2011 (%)	2012 (%)	2013 (%)
MSA[1]	n/a	n/a	n/a	n/a	n/a	n/a	n/a	n/a
U.S.	68.8	68.1	67.8	67.4	66.9	66.1	65.4	65.1

Note: (1) Figures cover the Lubbock, TX Metropolitan Statistical Area—see Appendix B for areas included; n/a not available
Source: U.S. Census Bureau, Housing Vacancies and Homeownership Annual Statistics: 2013

Housing Vacancy Rates

Area	Gross Vacancy Rate[2] (%)			Year-Round Vacancy Rate[3] (%)			Rental Vacancy Rate[4] (%)			Homeowner Vacancy Rate[5] (%)		
	2011	2012	2013	2011	2012	2013	2011	2012	2013	2011	2012	2013
MSA[1]	n/a	n/a	n/a	n/a	n/a	n/a	n/a	n/a	n/a	n/a	n/a	n/a
U.S.	14.2	13.8	13.8	11.1	10.8	10.7	9.5	8.7	8.3	2.5	2.0	2.0

Note: (1) Figures cover the Lubbock, TX Metropolitan Statistical Area—see Appendix B for areas included; (2) The percentage of the total housing inventory that is vacant; (3) The percentage of the housing inventory (excluding seasonal units) that is year-round vacant; (4) The percentage of rental inventory that is vacant for rent; (5) The percentage of homeowner inventory that is vacant for sale; n/a not available
Source: U.S. Census Bureau, Housing Vacancies and Homeownership Annual Statistics: 2013

TAXES

State Corporate Income Tax Rates

State	Tax Rate (%)	Income Brackets ($)	Num. of Brackets	Financial Institution Tax Rate (%)[a]	Federal Income Tax Ded.
Texas	(x)	–	–	(x)	No

Note: Tax rates as of January 1, 2014; (a) Rates listed are the corporate income tax rate applied to financial institutions or excise taxes based on income. Some states have other taxes based upon the value of deposits or shares; (x) Texas imposes a Franchise Tax, otherwise known as margin tax, imposed on entities with more than $1,030,000 total revenues at rate of 1%, or 0.5% for entities primarily engaged in retail or wholesale trade, on lesser of 70% of total revenues or 100%of gross receipts after deductions for either compensation or cost of goods sold.
Source: Federation of Tax Administrators, "State Corporate Income Tax Rates, 2014"

State Individual Income Tax Rates

State	Tax Rate (%)	Income Brackets ($)	Num. of Brackets	Personal Exempt. ($)[1] Single	Dependents	Fed. Inc. Tax Ded.
Texas	None	–	–	–	–	–

Note: Tax rates as of January 1, 2014; Local- and county-level taxes are not included; n/a not applicable; (1) Married joint filers generally receive double the single exemption
Source: Federation of Tax Administrators, "State Individual Income Tax Rates, 2014"

Various State and Local Tax Rates

State	State and Local Sales and Use (%)	State Sales and Use (%)	Gasoline[1] (¢/gal.)	Cigarette[2] ($/pack)	Spirits[3] ($/gal.)	Wine[4] ($/gal.)	Beer[5] ($/gal.)
Texas	8.25	6.25	20.00	1.410	2.40 (f)	0.20	0.20

Note: All tax rates as of January 1, 2014; (1) The American Petroleum Institute has developed a methodology for determining the average tax rate on a gallon of fuel. Rates may include any of the following: excise taxes, environmental fees, storage tank fees, other fees or taxes, general sales tax, and local taxes. In states where gasoline is subject to the general sales tax, or where the fuel tax is based on the average sale price, the average rate determined by API is sensitive to changes in the price of gasoline. States that fully or partially apply general sales taxes to gasoline: CA, CO, GA, IL, IN, MI, NY; (2) The federal excise tax of $1.0066 per pack and local taxes are not included; (3) Rates are those applicable to off-premise sales of 40% alcohol by volume (a.b.v.) distilled spirits in 750ml containers. Local excise taxes are excluded; (4) Rates are those applicable to off-premise sales of 11% a.b.v. non-carbonated wine in 750ml containers; (5) Rates are those applicable to off-premise sales of 4.7% a.b.v. beer in 12 ounce containers; (f) Different rates also applicable according to alcohol content, place of production, size of container, or place purchased (on- or off-premise or onboard airlines).
Source: Tax Foundation, 2014 Facts & Figures: How Does Your State Compare?

State Business Tax Climate Index Rankings

State	Overall Rank	Corporate Tax Index Rank	Individual Income Tax Index Rank	Sales Tax Index Rank	Unemployment Insurance Tax Index Rank	Property Tax Index Rank
Texas	11	38	7	36	14	35

Note: The index is a measure of how each state's tax laws affect economic performance. The lower the rank, the more favorable a state's tax system is for business. States without a given tax are given a ranking of 1. The scores/rankings for the District of Columbia do not affect other states. The 2014 index represents the tax climate as of July 1, 2013.
Source: Tax Foundation, State Business Tax Climate Index 2014

COMMERCIAL UTILITIES

Typical Monthly Electric Bills

Area	Commercial Service ($/month)		Industrial Service ($/month)	
	1,500 kWh	40 kW demand 14,000 kWh	1,000 kW demand 200,000 kWh	50,000 kW demand 15,000,000 kWh
City	n/a	n/a	n/a	n/a
Average[1]	197	1,636	25,662	1,485,307

Note: Based on total rates in effect July 1, 2013; (1) average based on 180 utilities surveyed; n/a not available
Source: Edison Electric Institute, Typical Bills and Average Rates Report, Summer 2013

TRANSPORTATION

Means of Transportation to Work

Area	Car/Truck/Van		Public Transportation			Bicycle	Walked	Other Means	Worked at Home
	Drove Alone	Car-pooled	Bus	Subway	Railroad				
City	82.2	10.5	0.9	0.0	0.0	0.5	2.0	0.9	3.0
MSA[1]	82.1	10.5	0.8	0.0	0.0	0.4	1.9	0.9	3.4
U.S.	76.4	9.7	2.6	1.7	0.5	0.6	2.8	1.3	4.3

Note: Figures are percentages and cover workers 16 years of age and older; (1) Figures cover the Lubbock, TX Metropolitan Statistical Area—see Appendix B for areas included
Source: U.S. Census Bureau, 2010-2012 American Community Survey 3-Year Estimates

Travel Time to Work

Area	Less Than 10 Minutes	10 to 19 Minutes	20 to 29 Minutes	30 to 44 Minutes	45 to 59 Minutes	60 to 89 Minutes	90 Minutes or More
City	20.4	58.1	12.9	5.0	1.5	1.0	1.0
MSA[1]	19.5	53.5	15.6	7.5	1.9	1.0	1.1
U.S.	13.5	29.8	20.9	20.1	7.5	5.6	2.5

Note: Figures are percentages and include workers 16 years old and over; (1) Figures cover the Lubbock, TX Metropolitan Statistical Area—see Appendix B for areas included
Source: U.S. Census Bureau, 2010-2012 American Community Survey 3-Year Estimates

Travel Time Index

Area	1985	1990	1995	2000	2005	2010	2011
Urban Area[1]	n/a	n/a	n/a	n/a	n/a	n/a	n/a
Average[2]	1.09	1.14	1.16	1.19	1.23	1.18	1.18

Note: Travel Time Index—the ratio of travel time in the peak period to the travel time at free-flow conditions. For example, a value of 1.30 indicates a 20-minute free-flow trip takes 26 minutes in the peak. Free-flow speeds (60 mph on freeways and 35 mph on principal arterials) are used as the comparison threshold; (1) Data for the Lubbock, TX urban area was not available; (2) average of 498 urban areas
Source: Texas Transportation Institute, Urban Mobility Report 2012, December 2012

Public Transportation

Agency Name / Mode of Transportation	Vehicles Operated in Maximum Service	Annual Unlinked Passenger Trips (in thous.)	Annual Passenger Miles (in thous.)
Citybus	n/a	n/a	n/a

Source: Federal Transit Administration, National Transit Database, 2012

Air Transportation

Airport Name and Code / Type of Service	Passenger Airlines[1]	Passenger Enplanements	Freight Carriers[2]	Freight (lbs.)
Lubbock Preston Smith International Airport (LBB)				
Domestic service (U.S. carriers - 2013)	14	454,123	7	44,067,420
International service (U.S. carriers - 2012)	0	0	0	0

Note: (1) Includes all U.S.-based major, minor and commuter airlines that carried at least one passenger during the year; (2) Includes all U.S.-based airlines and freight carriers that transported at least one lb. of freight during the year.
Source: Bureau of Transportation Statistics, The Intermodal Transportation Database, Air Carriers: T-100 Domestic Market (U.S. Carriers), 2013; Bureau of Transportation Statistics, The Intermodal Transportation Database, Air Carriers: T-100 International Market (U.S. Carriers), 2012

Other Transportation Statistics

Major Highways:	I-27
Amtrak Service:	No
Major Waterways/Ports:	None

Source: Amtrak.com; Google Maps

BUSINESSES

Major Business Headquarters

Company Name	Rankings	
	Fortune[1]	Forbes[2]
No companies listed	-	-

Note: (1) Fortune 500—companies that produce a 10-K are ranked 1 to 500 based on 2012 revenue; (2) all private companies with at least $2 billion in annual revenue through the end of their most current fiscal year are ranked 1 to 224; companies listed are headquartered in the city; dashes indicate no ranking
Source: Fortune, "Fortune 500," May 20, 2013; Forbes, "America's Largest Private Companies," December 18, 2013

Minority- and Women-Owned Businesses

Group	All Firms		Firms with Paid Employees			
	Firms	Sales ($000)	Firms	Sales ($000)	Employees	Payroll ($000)
Asian	449	99,426	(s)	(s)	(s)	(s)
Black	(s)	(s)	(s)	(s)	(s)	(s)
Hispanic	2,464	155,002	223	65,531	729	12,191
Women	4,332	672,719	667	595,008	5,840	145,700
All Firms	19,350	19,394,134	5,426	18,631,615	93,151	2,700,414

Note: Figures cover firms located in the city; minority- and women-owned business are defined as firms in which the corresponding group own 51% or more of the stock or equity of the company; (s) estimates are suppressed when publication standards are not met
Source: U.S. Census Bureau, 2007 Economic Census, Survey of Business Owners (2012 Survey of Business Owners data will be released starting in June 2015)

HOTELS & CONVENTION CENTERS

Hotels/Motels

Area	5 Star		4 Star		3 Star		2 Star		1 Star		Not Rated	
	Num.	Pct.[3]	Num.	Pct.[3]	Num.	Pct.[3]	Num.	Pct.[3]	Num.	Pct.[3]	Num.	Pct.[3]
City[1]	0	0.0	0	0.0	9	16.4	39	70.9	2	3.6	5	9.1
Total[2]	142	0.9	1,005	6.0	5,147	30.9	8,578	51.4	408	2.4	1,397	8.4

Note: (1) Figures cover Lubbock and vicinity; (2) Figures cover all 100 cities in this book; (3) Percentage of hotels which have a given star rating; Star ratings are determined by expedia.com and offer an indication of the general quality of a particular hotel.
Source: expedia.com, April 7, 2014

Major Convention Centers

Name	Overall Space (sq. ft.)	Exhibit Space (sq. ft.)	Meeting Space (sq. ft.)	Meeting Rooms
Lubbock Civic Center	300,000	40,000	n/a	12

Note: Table includes convention centers located in the Lubbock, TX metro area; n/a not available
Source: Original research

Living Environment

COST OF LIVING

Cost of Living Index

Composite Index	Groceries	Housing	Utilities	Trans-portation	Health Care	Misc. Goods/ Services
89.2	90.4	81.4	78.4	95.0	95.6	95.0

Note: The Cost of Living Index measures regional differences in the cost of consumer goods and services, excluding taxes and non-consumer expenditures, for professional and managerial households in the top income quintile. It is based on more than 50,000 prices covering almost 60 different items for which prices are collected three times a year by chambers of commerce, economic development organizations or university applied economic centers in each participating urban area. The numbers shown should be read as a percentage above or below the national average of 100. For example, a value of 115.4 in the groceries column indicates that grocery prices are 15.4% higher than the national average. Small differences in the index numbers should not be interpreted as significant; Figures cover the Lubbock TX urban area.
Source: The Council for Community and Economic Research, ACCRA Cost of Living Index, 2013

Grocery Prices

Area[1]	T-Bone Steak ($/pound)	Frying Chicken ($/pound)	Whole Milk ($/half gal.)	Eggs ($/dozen)	Orange Juice ($/64 oz.)	Coffee ($/11.5 oz.)
City[2]	9.86	1.05	2.63	1.73	3.16	4.04
Avg.	10.19	1.28	2.34	1.81	3.48	4.39
Min.	8.56	0.94	1.44	1.19	2.78	3.40
Max.	14.82	2.28	3.56	3.73	6.23	7.32

Note: (1) Values for the local area are compared with the average, minimum and maximum values for all 327 areas in the Cost of Living Index; (2) Figures cover the Lubbock TX urban area; **T-Bone Steak** *(price per pound);* **Frying Chicken** *(price per pound, whole fryer);* **Whole Milk** *(half gallon carton);* **Eggs** *(price per dozen, Grade A, large);* **Orange Juice** *(64 oz. Tropicana or Florida Natural);* **Coffee** *(11.5 oz. can, vacuum-packed, Maxwell House, Hills Bros, or Folgers).*
Source: The Council for Community and Economic Research, ACCRA Cost of Living Index, 2013

Housing and Utility Costs

Area[1]	New Home Price ($)	Apartment Rent ($/month)	All Electric ($/month)	Part Electric ($/month)	Other Energy ($/month)	Telephone ($/month)
City[2]	242,341	720	-	79.41	39.42	24.00
Avg.	295,864	900	171.38	91.82	70.12	27.73
Min.	185,506	458	117.80	48.81	33.67	17.16
Max.	1,358,917	3,783	441.68	171.40	372.65	39.47

Note: (1) Values for the local area are compared with the average, minimum and maximum values for all 327 areas in the Cost of Living Index; (2) Figures cover the Lubbock TX urban area; **New Home Price** *(2,400 sf living area, 8,000 sf lot, in urban area with full utilities);* **Apartment Rent** *(950 sf 2 bedroom/1.5 or 2 bath, unfurnished, excluding all utilities except water);* **All Electric** *(average monthly cost for an all-electric home);* **Part Electric** *(average monthly cost for a part-electric home);* **Other Energy** *(average monthly cost for natural gas, fuel oil, coal, wood, and any other forms of energy except electricity);* **Telephone** *(price includes basic monthly rate for a private residential line plus additional local usage charges incurred by a family of four).*
Source: The Council for Community and Economic Research, ACCRA Cost of Living Index, 2013

Health Care, Transportation, and Other Costs

Area[1]	Doctor ($/visit)	Dentist ($/visit)	Optometrist ($/visit)	Gasoline ($/gallon)	Beauty Salon ($/visit)	Men's Shirt ($)
City[2]	99.08	77.20	96.47	3.20	35.93	26.92
Avg.	101.40	86.48	96.16	3.44	33.87	26.55
Min.	61.67	50.83	50.12	3.08	18.92	12.48
Max.	182.71	152.50	223.78	4.33	68.22	52.03

Note: (1) Values for the local area are compared with the average, minimum and maximum values for all 327 areas in the Cost of Living Index; (2) Figures cover the Lubbock TX urban area; **Doctor** *(general practitioners routine exam of an established patient);* **Dentist** *(adult teeth cleaning and periodic oral examination);* **Optometrist** *(full vision eye exam for established adult patient);* **Gasoline** *(one gallon regular unleaded, national brand, including all taxes, cash price at self-service pump if available);* **Beauty Salon** *(woman's shampoo, trim, and blow-dry);* **Men's Shirt** *(cotton/polyester dress shirt, pinpoint weave, long sleeves).*
Source: The Council for Community and Economic Research, ACCRA Cost of Living Index, 2013

HOUSING

House Price Index (HPI)

Area	National Ranking[2]	Quarterly Change (%)	One-Year Change (%)	Five-Year Change (%)
MSA[1]	109	2.74	3.67	8.35
U.S.[3]	–	1.20	7.69	4.18

Note: The HPI is a weighted repeat sales index. It measures average price changes in repeat sales or refinancings on the same properties. This information is obtained by reviewing repeat mortgage transactions on single-family properties whose mortgages have been purchased or securitized by Fannie Mae or Freddie Mac in January 1975; (1) Lubbock, TX Metropolitan Statistical Area—see Appendix B for areas included; (2) Rankings are based on annual percentage change for all metro areas containing at least 15,000 transactions over the last 10 years and ranges from 1 to 283; (3) figures based on a weighted average of Census Division estimates using a seasonally adjusted, purchase-only index; all figures are for the period ending December 31, 2013
Source: Federal Housing Finance Agency, House Price Index, February 25, 2014

Median Single-Family Home Prices

Area	2011	2012	2013p	Percent Change 2012 to 2013
MSA[1]	n/a	n/a	n/a	n/a
U.S. Average	166.2	177.2	197.4	11.4

Note: Figures are median sales prices of existing single-family homes in thousands of dollars; (p) preliminary; n/a not available; (1) Lubbock, TX Metropolitan Statistical Area—see Appendix B for areas included
Source: National Association of Realtors, Median Sales Price of Existing Single-Family Homes for Metropolitan Areas, 4th Quarter 2013

Qualifying Income Based on Median Sales Price of Existing Single-Family Homes

Area	With 5% Down ($)	With 10% Down ($)	With 20% Down ($)
MSA[1]	n/a	n/a	n/a
U.S. Average	45,395	43,006	38,228

Note: Figures are preliminary; Qualifying income is based on a mortgage rate of 4.4%. Monthly principal and interest payment is limited to 25% of income; n/a not available; (1) Lubbock, TX Metropolitan Statistical Area—see Appendix B for areas included
Source: National Association of Realtors, Qualifying Income Based on Median Sales Price of Existing Single-Family Homes for Metropolitan Areas, 4th Quarter 2013

Median Apartment Condo-Coop Home Prices

Area	2011	2012	2013p	Percent Change 2012 to 2013
MSA[1]	n/a	n/a	n/a	n/a
U.S. Average	165.1	173.7	194.9	12.2

Note: Figures are median sales prices of existing apartment condo-coop homes in thousands of dollars; (p) preliminary; n/a not available; (1) Lubbock, TX Metropolitan Statistical Area—see Appendix B for areas included
Source: National Association of Realtors, Median Sales Price of Existing Apartment Condo-Coop Homes for Metropolitan Areas, 4th Quarter 2013

Gross Monthly Rent

Area	Under $200	$200 -299	$300 -499	$500 -749	$750 -999	$1,000 -1,499	$1,500 and up	Median ($)
City	1.1	1.5	8.4	34.3	26.5	21.3	6.9	787
MSA[1]	1.1	2.0	9.2	34.1	26.3	20.8	6.6	779
U.S.	1.7	3.3	8.1	22.7	24.3	25.7	14.3	889

Note: Figures are percentages except for Median; Gross rent is the contract rent plus the estimated average monthly cost of utilities (electricity, gas, and water and sewer) and fuels (oil, coal, kerosene, wood, etc.) if these are paid by the renter (or paid for the renter by someone else); (1) Figures cover the Lubbock, TX Metropolitan Statistical Area—see Appendix B for areas included
Source: U.S. Census Bureau, 2010-2012 American Community Survey 3-Year Estimates

Year Housing Structure Built

Area	2010 or Later	2000 -2009	1990 -1999	1980 -1989	1970 -1979	1960 -1969	1950 -1959	1940 -1949	Before 1940	Median Year
City	0.8	17.5	11.6	15.5	18.6	14.1	14.1	4.7	3.0	1978
MSA[1]	0.8	17.3	12.4	15.6	18.0	13.5	13.9	5.0	3.7	1978
U.S.	0.5	14.9	13.8	13.9	15.9	11.1	10.9	5.5	13.5	1976

Note: Figures are percentages except for Median Year; (1) Figures cover the Lubbock, TX Metropolitan Statistical Area—see Appendix B for areas included
Source: U.S. Census Bureau, 2010-2012 American Community Survey 3-Year Estimates

HEALTH

Health Risk Data

Category	MSA[1] (%)	U.S. (%)
Adults aged 18–64 who have any kind of health care coverage	n/a	79.6
Adults who reported being in good or excellent health	n/a	83.1
Adults who are current smokers	n/a	19.6
Adults who are heavy drinkers[2]	n/a	6.1
Adults who are binge drinkers[3]	n/a	16.9
Adults who are overweight (BMI 25.0 - 29.9)	n/a	35.8
Adults who are obese (BMI 30.0 - 99.8)	n/a	27.6
Adults who participated in any physical activities in the past month	n/a	77.1
Adults 50+ who have ever had a sigmoidoscopy or colonoscopy	n/a	67.3
Women aged 40+ who have had a mammogram within the past two years	n/a	74.0
Men aged 40+ who have had a PSA test within the past two years	n/a	45.2
Adults aged 65+ who have had flu shot within the past year	n/a	60.1
Adults who always wear a seatbelt	n/a	93.8

Note: Data as of 2012 unless otherwise noted; n/a not available; (1) Figures cover the Lubbock, TX Metropolitan Statistical Area—see Appendix B for areas included; (2) Heavy drinkers are classified as males having more than two drinks per day or females having more than one drink per day; (3) Binge drinkers are classified as males having five or more drinks on one occasion or females having four or more drinks on one occasion
Source: Centers for Disease Control and Prevention, Behaviorial Risk Factor Surveillance System, SMART: Selected Metropolitan/Micropolitan Area Risk Trends, 2012

Chronic Health Indicators

Category	MSA[1] (%)	U.S. (%)
Adults who have ever been told they had a heart attack	n/a	4.5
Adults who have ever been told they had a stroke	n/a	2.9
Adults who have been told they currently have asthma	n/a	8.9
Adults who have ever been told they have arthritis	n/a	25.7
Adults who have ever been told they have diabetes[2]	n/a	9.7
Adults who have ever been told they had skin cancer	n/a	5.7
Adults who have ever been told they had any other types of cancer	n/a	6.5
Adults who have ever been told they have COPD	n/a	6.2
Adults who have ever been told they have kidney disease	n/a	2.5
Adults who have ever been told they have a form of depression	n/a	18.0

Note: Data as of 2012 unless otherwise noted; n/a not available; (1) Figures cover the Lubbock, TX Metropolitan Statistical Area—see Appendix B for areas included; (2) Figures do not include pregnancy-related, borderline, or pre-diabetes
Source: Centers for Disease Control and Prevention, Behaviorial Risk Factor Surveillance System, SMART: Selected Metropolitan/Micropolitan Area Risk Trends, 2012

Mortality Rates for the Top 10 Causes of Death in the U.S.

ICD-10[a] Sub-Chapter	ICD-10[a] Code	Age-Adjusted Mortality Rate[1] per 100,000 population	
		County[2]	U.S.
Malignant neoplasms	C00-C97	168.0	174.2
Ischaemic heart diseases	I20-I25	121.1	119.1
Other forms of heart disease	I30-I51	67.0	49.6
Chronic lower respiratory diseases	J40-J47	64.8	43.2
Cerebrovascular diseases	I60-I69	45.0	40.3
Organic, including symptomatic, mental disorders	F01-F09	47.7	30.5
Other degenerative diseases of the nervous system	G30-G31	19.5	26.3
Other external causes of accidental injury	W00-X59	29.9	25.1
Diabetes mellitus	E10-E14	37.6	21.3
Hypertensive diseases	I10-I15	16.3	18.8

Note: (a) ICD-10 = International Classification of Diseases 10th Revision; (1) Mortality rates are a three year average covering 2008-2010; (2) Figures cover Lubbock County
Source: Centers for Disease Control and Prevention, National Center for Health Statistics. Compressed Mortality File 1999-2010 on CDC WONDER Online Database, released January 2013. Data are compiled from the Compressed Mortality File 1999-2010, Series 20 No. 2P, 2013.

Mortality Rates for Selected Causes of Death

ICD-10[a] Sub-Chapter	ICD-10[a] Code	Age-Adjusted Mortality Rate[1] per 100,000 population	
		County[2]	U.S.
Assault	X85-Y09	4.8	5.5
Diseases of the liver	K70-K76	19.9	12.4
Human immunodeficiency virus (HIV) disease	B20-B24	3.9	3.0
Influenza and pneumonia	J09-J18	24.0	16.4
Intentional self-harm	X60-X84	14.0	11.8
Malnutrition	E40-E46	*1.9	0.8
Obesity and other hyperalimentation	E65-E68	3.5	1.6
Renal failure	N17-N19	19.1	13.6
Transport accidents	V01-V99	18.8	12.6
Viral hepatitis	B15-B19	4.0	2.2

Note: (a) ICD-10 = International Classification of Diseases 10th Revision; (1) Mortality rates are a three year average covering 2008-2010; (2) Figures cover Lubbock County; (*) Unreliable data as per CDC
Source: Centers for Disease Control and Prevention, National Center for Health Statistics. Compressed Mortality File 1999-2010 on CDC WONDER Online Database, released January 2013. Data are compiled from the Compressed Mortality File 1999-2010, Series 20 No. 2P, 2013.

Health Insurance Coverage

Area	With Health Insurance	With Private Health Insurance	With Public Health Insurance	Without Health Insurance	Population Under Age 18 Without Health Insurance
City	81.7	63.6	28.0	18.3	9.7
MSA[1]	81.2	62.5	28.6	18.8	10.0
U.S.	84.9	65.4	30.4	15.1	7.5

Note: Figures are percentages that cover the civilian noninstitutionalized population; (1) Figures cover the Lubbock, TX Metropolitan Statistical Area—see Appendix B for areas included
Source: U.S. Census Bureau, 2010-2012 American Community Survey 3-Year Estimates

Number of Medical Professionals

Area[1]	MDs[2]	DOs[2,3]	Dentists	Podiatrists	Chiropractors	Optometrists
Local (number)	1,019	36	144	9	45	45
Local (rate[4])	359.6	12.7	50.4	3.1	15.7	15.7
U.S. (rate[4])	267.6	19.6	61.7	5.6	24.7	14.5

Note: Data as of 2012 unless noted; (1) Local data covers Lubbock County; (2) Data as of 2011; (3) Doctor of Osteopathic Medicine; (4) rate per 100,000 population
Source: Area Resource File (ARF) 2012-2013. U.S. Department of Health and Human Services, Health Resources and Services Administration, Bureau of Health Professions

EDUCATION

Public School District Statistics

District Name	Schls	Pupils	Pupil/ Teacher Ratio	Minority Pupils[1] (%)	Free Lunch Eligible[2] (%)	IEP[3] (%)
Lubbock ISD	54	28,790	14.9	72.1	57.0	11.4
Lubbock-Cooper ISD	8	4,269	13.6	39.0	29.6	9.3

Note: Table includes school districts with 2,000 or more students; (1) Percentage of students that are not non-Hispanic white; (2) Percentage of students that are eligible for the free lunch program; (3) Percentage of students that have an Individualized Education Program.
Source: U.S. Department of Education, National Center for Education Statistics, Common Core of Data, Local Education Agency (School District) Universe Survey: School Year 2011-2012; U.S. Department of Education, National Center for Education Statistics, Common Core of Data, Public Elementary/Secondary School Universe Survey: School Year 2011-2012

Best High Schools

High School Name	Rank[1]	Grad. Rate[2] (%)	Coll.[3] (%)	AP/IB/ AICE Tests[4]	AP/IB/ AICE Score[5]	SAT Score[6]	ACT Score[6]
Lubbock H.S.	1452	85	80	0.5	2.6	1610	22.7

Note: (1) Public schools are ranked from 1 to 2,000 based on the following self-reported statistics (with the corresponding weight used in calculating their overall score). Schools that were newly founded and did not have a graduating senior class in 2012 were excluded; (2) Four-year, on-time graduation rate (25%); (3) Percent of 2011 graduates who were accepted to college (25%); (4) AP/IB/AICE tests taken per student (25%); (5) Average AP/IB/AICE exam score (10%); (6) Average SAT and/or ACT score (10%); Percent of students enrolled in at least one AP/IB/AICE course (5%)—data not shown
Source: Newsweek and The Daily Beast, "America's Best High Schools 2013"

Highest Level of Education

Area	Less than H.S.	H.S. Diploma	Some College, No Deg.	Associate Degree	Bachelor's Degree	Master's Degree	Prof. School Degree	Doctorate Degree
City	14.3	24.9	25.2	6.2	19.1	6.6	2.0	1.7
MSA[1]	15.6	25.7	25.1	6.0	18.0	6.2	1.9	1.5
U.S.	14.1	28.3	21.3	7.8	18.0	7.5	1.9	1.2

Note: Figures cover persons age 25 and over; (1) Figures cover the Lubbock, TX Metropolitan Statistical Area—see Appendix B for areas included
Source: U.S. Census Bureau, 2010-2012 American Community Survey 3-Year Estimates

Educational Attainment by Race

Area	High School Graduate or Higher (%)					Bachelor's Degree or Higher (%)				
	Total	White	Black	Asian	Hisp.[2]	Total	White	Black	Asian	Hisp.[2]
City	85.7	88.3	81.9	86.9	68.7	29.5	32.0	12.2	69.7	10.2
MSA[1]	84.4	87.0	79.2	87.5	66.0	27.6	29.8	11.3	68.8	9.4
U.S.	85.9	88.1	82.5	85.5	63.1	28.6	30.0	18.4	50.2	13.4

Note: Figures shown cover persons 25 years old and over; (1) Figures cover the Lubbock, TX Metropolitan Statistical Area—see Appendix B for areas included; (2) People of Hispanic origin can be of any race
Source: U.S. Census Bureau, 2010-2012 American Community Survey 3-Year Estimates

School Enrollment by Grade and Control

Area	Preschool (%)		Kindergarten (%)		Grades 1 - 4 (%)		Grades 5 - 8 (%)		Grades 9 - 12 (%)	
	Public	Private	Public	Private	Public	Private	Public	Private	Public	Private
City	64.5	35.5	88.2	11.8	93.0	7.0	95.8	4.2	97.0	3.0
MSA[1]	64.2	35.8	87.3	12.7	92.5	7.5	95.3	4.7	95.6	4.4
U.S.	56.9	43.1	87.8	12.2	89.9	10.1	90.0	10.0	90.8	9.2

Note: Figures shown cover persons 3 years old and over; (1) Figures cover the Lubbock, TX Metropolitan Statistical Area—see Appendix B for areas included
Source: U.S. Census Bureau, 2010-2012 American Community Survey 3-Year Estimates

Average Salaries of Public School Classroom Teachers

Area	2012-13 Dollars	2012-13 Rank[1]	2013-14 Dollars	2013-14 Rank[1]	Percent Change 2012-13 to 2013-14	Percent Change 2003-04 to 2013-14
Texas	48,819	35	49,270	35	0.92	21.7
U.S. Average	56,103	–	56,689	–	1.04	21.8

Note: (1) State rank ranges from 1 to 51 where 1 indicates highest salary.
Source: National Education Association, Rankings & Estimates: Rankings of the States 2013 and Estimates of School Statistics 2014, March 2014

Higher Education

Four-Year Colleges Public	Four-Year Colleges Private Non-profit	Four-Year Colleges Private For-profit	Two-Year Colleges Public	Two-Year Colleges Private Non-profit	Two-Year Colleges Private For-profit	Medical Schools[1]	Law Schools[2]	Voc/ Tech[3]
2	1	0	0	1	1	1	1	2

Note: Figures cover institutions located within the city limits and include main campuses only; (1) includes schools accredited by the Liaison Committee on Medical Education and the American Osteopathic Association's Commission on Osteopathic College Accreditation; (2) includes ABA-accredited schools, schools with provisional ABA accreditation, and state accredited schools; (3) includes all schools with programs that are less than 2 years.
Source: National Center for Education Statistics, Integrated Postsecondary Education System (IPEDS), 2012-13; Association of American Medical Colleges, Member List, April 24, 2014; American Osteopathic Association, Member List, April 24, 2014; Law School Admission Council, Official Guide to ABA-Approved Law Schools Online, April 24, 2014; Wikipedia, List of Medical Schools in the United States, April 24, 2014; Wikipedia, List of Law Schools in the United States, April 24, 2014

According to *U.S. News & World Report,* the Lubbock, TX metro area is home to one of the best national universities in the U.S.: **Texas Tech University** (#161). The indicators used to capture academic quality fall into a number of categories: assessment by administrators at peer institutions; retention of students; faculty resources; student selectivity; financial resources; alumni giving; high school counselor ratings of colleges; and graduation rate. *U.S. News & World Report, "America's Best Colleges 2014"*

PRESIDENTIAL ELECTION

2012 Presidential Election Results

Area	Obama	Romney	Other
Lubbock County	28.8	69.6	1.6
U.S.	51.0	47.2	1.8

Note: Results are percentages and may not add to 100% due to rounding
Source: Dave Leip's Atlas of U.S. Presidential Elections

EMPLOYERS

Major Employers

Company Name	Industry
American State Bank	Finance
Caprock Home Health Services	Healthcare
City of Lubbock	Government
Convergys Corporation	Call center
Covenant Health System	Healthcare
Frenship ISD	Education
G Boren Services	Recruiting
Interim Healthcare of West Texas	Home health care
Lubbock Christian University	Education
Lubbock Cooper ISD	Education
Lubbock County	Government
Lubbock Independent School District	Education
Lubbock MHMR Center	Government agency
Lubbock State Supported Living Center	Residential care
Messer Auto Group	Vehicle sales and service
Sonic Drive In	Restaurants
SuddenLink Communications	Cable tv services & internet
Texas Dept. of Criminal Justice	Psychiatric/medical facility
Texas Tech University	Education
Texas Tech University Health Sci Ctr	Health sciences
UMC Physician Network Services	Physicians practice management
United Supermarkets	supermarkets
University Medical Center	Healthcare
Walmart	Retail
Wells Fargo Bank	Finance

Note: Companies shown are located within the Lubbock, TX Metropolitan Statistical Area.
Source: Hoovers.com; Wikipedia

PUBLIC SAFETY

Crime Rate

Area	All Crimes	Violent Crimes				Property Crimes		
		Murder	Forcible Rape	Robbery	Aggrav. Assault	Burglary	Larceny -Theft	Motor Vehicle Theft
City	6,000.2	4.6	43.8	137.0	641.5	1,306.3	3,552.9	314.0
Suburbs[1]	2,393.8	1.6	63.4	6.3	247.3	559.6	1,377.6	137.9
Metro[2]	5,242.7	4.0	47.9	109.5	558.7	1,149.4	3,096.0	277.0
U.S.	3,246.1	4.7	26.9	112.9	242.3	670.2	1,959.3	229.7

Note: Figures are crimes per 100,000 population; (1) All areas within the metro area that are located outside the city limits; (2) Figures cover the Lubbock, TX Metropolitan Statistical Area—see Appendix B for areas included
Source: FBI Uniform Crime Reports, 2012

Hate Crimes

Area	Number of Quarters Reported	Bias Motivation				
		Race	Religion	Sexual Orientation	Ethnicity	Disability
City	4	0	0	0	0	0
U.S.	4	2,797	1,099	1,135	667	92

Source: Federal Bureau of Investigation, Hate Crime Statistics 2012

Identity Theft Consumer Complaints

Area	Complaints	Complaints per 100,000 Population	Rank[2]
MSA[1]	164	56.4	237
U.S.	290,056	91.8	-

Note: (1) Figures cover the Lubbock, TX Metropolitan Statistical Area—see Appendix B for areas included; (2) Rank ranges from 1 to 377 where 1 indicates greatest number of identity theft complaints per 100,000 population
Source: Federal Trade Commission, Consumer Sentinel Network Data Book for January–December 2013

Fraud and Other Consumer Complaints

Area	Complaints	Complaints per 100,000 Population	Rank[2]
MSA[1]	836	287.5	325
U.S.	1,811,724	595.2	-

Note: (1) Figures cover the Lubbock, TX Metropolitan Statistical Area—see Appendix B for areas included; (2) Rank ranges from 1 to 377 where 1 indicates greatest number of identity theft complaints per 100,000 population
Source: Federal Trade Commission, Consumer Sentinel Network Data Book for January–December 2013

RECREATION

Culture

Dance[1]	Theatre[1]	Instrumental Music[1]	Vocal Music[1]	Series and Festivals	Museums and Art Galleries[2]	Zoos and Aquariums[3]
0	0	1	0	3	10	0

Note: (1) Number of professional performing groups; (2) Based on organizations with primary SIC code 8412; (3) AZA-accredited
Source: The Grey House Performing Arts Directory, 2013; Association of Zoos & Aquariums, AZA Member Zoos & Aquariums, April 2014; www.AccuLeads.com, May 1, 2014

Professional Sports Teams

Team Name	League	Year Established
No teams are located in the metro area		

Source: Wikipedia, Major Professional Sports Teams of the United States and Canada, April 25, 2014

CLIMATE

Average and Extreme Temperatures

Temperature	Jan	Feb	Mar	Apr	May	Jun	Jul	Aug	Sep	Oct	Nov	Dec	Yr.
Extreme High (°F)	83	87	95	100	104	110	108	106	103	98	86	81	110
Average High (°F)	53	58	66	75	83	91	92	90	84	75	63	55	74
Average Temp. (°F)	39	43	51	61	69	78	80	78	71	61	49	41	60
Average Low (°F)	25	29	36	46	55	64	68	66	59	48	35	27	47
Extreme Low (°F)	-16	-8	2	22	30	45	51	52	33	20	-1	-2	-16

Note: Figures cover the years 1948-1992
Source: National Climatic Data Center, International Station Meteorological Climate Summary, 9/96

Average Precipitation/Snowfall/Humidity

Precip./Humidity	Jan	Feb	Mar	Apr	May	Jun	Jul	Aug	Sep	Oct	Nov	Dec	Yr.
Avg. Precip. (in.)	0.5	0.6	0.8	1.0	2.6	2.9	2.3	2.1	2.3	1.9	0.6	0.5	18.4
Avg. Snowfall (in.)	3	3	2	Tr	0	0	0	0	0	Tr	1	2	10
Avg. Rel. Hum. 6am (%)	73	72	67	68	76	78	75	78	81	78	73	72	74
Avg. Rel. Hum. 3pm (%)	41	40	32	30	35	36	39	41	44	39	38	40	38

Note: Figures cover the years 1948-1992; Tr = Trace amounts (<0.05 in. of rain; <0.5 in. of snow)
Source: National Climatic Data Center, International Station Meteorological Climate Summary, 9/96

Weather Conditions

Temperature			Daytime Sky			Precipitation		
10°F & below	32°F & below	90°F & above	Clear	Partly cloudy	Cloudy	0.01 inch or more precip.	0.1 inch or more snow/ice	Thunder-storms
5	93	79	134	150	81	62	8	48

Note: Figures are average number of days per year and cover the years 1948-1992
Source: National Climatic Data Center, International Station Meteorological Climate Summary, 9/96

HAZARDOUS WASTE

Superfund Sites

Lubbock has no sites on the EPA's Superfund Final National Priorities List.
U.S. Environmental Protection Agency, Final National Priorities List, April 26, 2014

AIR & WATER QUALITY

Air Quality Index

Area	Percent of Days when Air Quality was...[2]					AQI Statistics[2]	
	Good	Moderate	Unhealthy for Sensitive Groups	Unhealthy	Very Unhealthy	Maximum	Median
MSA[1]	92.8	6.9	0.0	0.3	0.0	165	26

Note: (1) Data covers the Lubbock, TX Metropolitan Statistical Area—see Appendix B for areas included; (2) Based on 334 days with AQI data in 2013. Air Quality Index (AQI) is an index for reporting daily air quality. EPA calculates the AQI for five major air pollutants regulated by the Clean Air Act: ground-level ozone, particle pollution (aka particulate matter), carbon monoxide, sulfur dioxide, and nitrogen dioxide. The AQI runs from 0 to 500. The higher the AQI value, the greater the level of air pollution and the greater the health concern. There are six AQI categories: "Good" AQI is between 0 and 50. Air quality is considered satisfactory; "Moderate" AQI is between 51 and 100. Air quality is acceptable; "Unhealthy for Sensitive Groups" When AQI values are between 101 and 150, members of sensitive groups may experience health effects; "Unhealthy" When AQI values are between 151 and 200 everyone may begin to experience health effects; "Very Unhealthy" AQI values between 201 and 300 trigger a health alert; "Hazardous" AQI values over 300 trigger warnings of emergency conditions (not shown).
Source: U.S. Environmental Protection Agency, Air Quality Index Report, 2013

Air Quality Index Pollutants

Area	Percent of Days when AQI Pollutant was...[2]					
	Carbon Monoxide	Nitrogen Dioxide	Ozone	Sulfur Dioxide	Particulate Matter 2.5	Particulate Matter 10
MSA[1]	0.0	0.0	0.0	0.0	100.0	0.0

Note: (1) Data covers the Lubbock, TX Metropolitan Statistical Area—see Appendix B for areas included; (2) Based on 334 days with AQI data in 2013. The Air Quality Index (AQI) is an index for reporting daily air quality. EPA calculates the AQI for five major air pollutants regulated by the Clean Air Act: ground-level ozone, particle pollution (also known as particulate matter), carbon monoxide, sulfur dioxide, and nitrogen dioxide. The AQI runs from 0 to 500. The higher the AQI value, the greater the level of air pollution and the greater the health concern.
Source: U.S. Environmental Protection Agency, Air Quality Index Report, 2013

Air Quality Trends: Ozone

	2003	2004	2005	2006	2007	2008	2009	2010	2011	2012
MSA[1]	n/a	n/a	n/a	n/a	n/a	n/a	n/a	n/a	n/a	n/a

Note: (1) Data covers the Lubbock, TX Metropolitan Statistical Area—see Appendix B for areas included; n/a not available. The values shown are the composite ozone concentration averages among trend sites based on the highest fourth daily maximum 8-hour concentration in parts per million. These trends are based on sites having an adequate record of monitoring data during the trend period. Data from exceptional events are included.
Source: U.S. Environmental Protection Agency, Air Quality Monitoring Information, "Air Quality Trends by City, 2000-2012"

Maximum Air Pollutant Concentrations: Particulate Matter, Ozone, CO and Lead

	Particulate Matter 10 (ug/m³)	Particulate Matter 2.5 Wtd AM (ug/m³)	Particulate Matter 2.5 24-Hr (ug/m³)	Ozone (ppm)	Carbon Monoxide (ppm)	Lead (ug/m³)
MSA[1] Level	n/a	n/a	n/a	n/a	n/a	n/a
NAAQS[2]	150	15	35	0.075	9	0.15
Met NAAQS[2]	n/a	n/a	n/a	n/a	n/a	n/a

Note: (1) Data covers the Lubbock, TX Metropolitan Statistical Area—see Appendix B for areas included; Data from exceptional events are included; (2) National Ambient Air Quality Standards; ppm = parts per million; ug/m³ = micrograms per cubic meter; n/a not available.
Concentrations: Particulate Matter 10 (coarse particulate)—highest second maximum 24-hour concentration; Particulate Matter 2.5 Wtd AM (fine particulate)—highest weighted annual mean concentration; Particulate Matter 2.5 24-Hour (fine particulate)—highest 98th percentile 24-hour concentration; Ozone—highest fourth daily maximum 8-hour concentration; Carbon Monoxide—highest second maximum non-overlapping 8-hour concentration; Lead—maximum running 3-month average
Source: U.S. Environmental Protection Agency, Air Quality Monitoring Information, "Air Quality Statistics by City, 2012"

Maximum Air Pollutant Concentrations: Nitrogen Dioxide and Sulfur Dioxide

	Nitrogen Dioxide AM (ppb)	Nitrogen Dioxide 1-Hr (ppb)	Sulfur Dioxide AM (ppb)	Sulfur Dioxide 1-Hr (ppb)	Sulfur Dioxide 24-Hr (ppb)
MSA[1] Level	n/a	n/a	n/a	n/a	n/a
NAAQS[2]	53	100	30	75	140
Met NAAQS[2]	n/a	n/a	n/a	n/a	n/a

Note: (1) Data covers the Lubbock, TX Metropolitan Statistical Area—see Appendix B for areas included; Data from exceptional events are included; (2) National Ambient Air Quality Standards; ppm = parts per million; ug/m³ = micrograms per cubic meter; n/a not available.
Concentrations: Nitrogen Dioxide AM—highest arithmetic mean concentration; Nitrogen Dioxide 1-Hr—highest 98th percentile 1-hour daily maximum concentration; Sulfur Dioxide AM—highest annual mean concentration; Sulfur Dioxide 1-Hr—highest 99th percentile 1-hour daily maximum concentration; Sulfur Dioxide 24-Hr—highest second maximum 24-hour concentration
Source: U.S. Environmental Protection Agency, Air Quality Monitoring Information, "Air Quality Statistics by City, 2012"

Drinking Water

Water System Name	Pop. Served	Primary Water Source Type	Violations[1] Health Based	Violations[1] Monitoring/ Reporting
Lubbock Public Water System	218,327	Surface	0	0

Note: (1) Based on violation data from January 1, 2013 to December 31, 2013 (includes unresolved violations from earlier years)
Source: U.S. Environmental Protection Agency, Office of Ground Water and Drinking Water, Safe Drinking Water Information System (based on data extracted February 10, 2014)

McAllen, Texas

Background

The largest city in Hidalgo County, Texas, McAllen is located near the tip of southern Texas, across the Rio Grande from Reynosa, Mexico, a location that has been the key to its commercial transformation. The city had begun to grow while agriculture and petroleum were still its economic mainstays, but since the ratification of the North American Free Trade Agreement in 1994, international trade, health care, government administration, and tourism have become its economic engines. Tourism in McAllen has fueled the highest retail spending per capita in Texas.

In 1904 John McAllen, together with his son, James, and other partners, established a town site 8 miles north of the county seat, Hidalgo. In 1907, two miles to the east, William Briggs, O. Jones, and John Closner founded a settlement called East McAllen, while the original town came to be called West McAllen. By 1911 East McAllen had a thousand residents and West McAllen had withered, and the larger town incorporated as the city of McAllen.

John McAllen experimented with growing sugarcane, cotton, alfalfa, broom corn, citrus fruits, grapes, and figs. Eventually farming, mostly by Anglo interests and dependent on the railroad and irrigation systems, displaced ranching as the primary economic activity. By the 1920s the city had some 6,000 residents.

From 1926 McAllen was linked to Reynosa by bridge. The McAllen-Hidalgo-Reynosa International Bridge proved crucial to McAllen after oil was discovered near Reynosa in the late 1940s. The bridge became the second-most-important port of entry into Mexico. Tourism and retail businesses flourished, bolstered by the cheap labor supply.

McAllen's population grew sporadically over the next several decades. In the 1970s and 1980s, however, the population boomed, owing to the *maquiladora* economy (in which U.S. companies take advantage of low labor costs in Mexico, shipping components of manufactured goods across the border to be assembled and shipped back). The McAllen Foreign-Trade Zone (FTZ), created in 1973, was the first inland U.S. foreign trade zone; there is also an FTZ site at McAllen-Miller International Airport. Anzaldúas International Bridge opened in 2009. Today the city is more than three-quarters Hispanic. Thanks to international trade, cross-border commerce, and its concentration of major health-care facilities, McAllen is the U.S. city ranked highest for long-term job growth, according to the U.S. Bureau of Labor Statistics.

South Texas College was founded in 1993. Three of its five campuses are in McAllen, including the Technical Campus. Edinburg-based University of Texas–Pan American has a branch in McAllen.

McAllen's cultural institutions include Quinta Mazatlan, a Spanish Revival Style hacienda built in 1935 and now a sanctuary known for its environmental stewardship programs. Quinta Mazatlan is one of nine Rio Grande Valley preserves administered by the World Birding Center. The oldest stand of native forest in the area is preserved in the McAllen Botanical Garden. Nearby nature preserves include the Edinburg Scenic Wetlands, Santa Ana National Wildlife Refuge, and Bentsen State Park.

McAllen has several notable museums: the International Museum of Art & Science, the Museum of South Texas History, and the McAllen Heritage Center. The Valley Symphony Orchestra and Chorale and two VSO-affiliated youth orchestras perform in McAllen and at the University of Texas–Pan American. An arts scene is coalescing, thanks to the city's Creative Arts Incubator, which sponsors a public art program, studio space for artists and performers, a monthly Artwalk, and a music series. Notable among the region's yearly festivals are the February Borderfest, at Hidalgo, and the mid-March Rio Grande Valley Livestock Show, in Mercedes. The 18.5-acre McAllen Convention Center complex opened in 2007.

The Rio Grande Valley Vipers won the National Basketball Association Development League championship in 2010 and again in 2013. Like the Vipers, the Rio Grande Valley Flash indoor soccer team plays at State Farm Arena in Hidalgo. The Edinburg Roadrunners play at Edinburg Baseball Stadium, which they share with the McAllen Thunder baseball team.

The City of Palms, as McAllen has been known since the 1940s, has sunshine and a warm climate year-round.

Rankings

General Rankings

- McAllen appeared on RelocateAmerica's list of best places to live in America. The annual "Top 100 Places to Live" list recognizes the top communities as nominated by their residents & local businesses. RelocateAmerica's Research Group determined the list based on review of various data gathered for economic, employment, housing, education, industry, opportunity, environment and recreation along with feedback from area leaders and residents. *RelocateAmerica.com, "Top 100 Places to Live for 2011"*

Business/Finance Rankings

- TransUnion ranked the nation's metro areas by average credit score, calculated on the VantageScore system, developed by the three major credit-reporting bureaus—TransUnion, Experian, and Equifax. The McAllen metro area was among the ten cities with the lowest collective credit score, meaning that its residents posed the highest average consumer credit risk. *www.usatoday.com, "Metro Areas' Average Credit Rating Revealed," February 7, 2013*

- Building on the U.S. Department of Labor's Occupational Information Network Data Collection Program, the Brookings Institution defined STEM occupations and job opportunities for STEM workers at various levels of educational attainment. The McAllen metro area was one of the ten metro areas where workers in low-education-level STEM jobs earn the lowest relative wages. *www.brookings.edu, "The Hidden Stem Economy," June 10, 2013*

- Building on the U.S. Department of Labor's Occupational Information Network Data Collection Program, the Brookings Institution defined STEM occupations and job opportunities for STEM workers at various levels of educational attainment. The McAllen metro area was placed among the ten large metro areas with the lowest demand for high-level STEM knowledge. *www.brookings.edu, "The Hidden Stem Economy," June 10, 2013*

- To identify the metro areas with the largest gap in income between rich and poor residents, the 24/7 Wall Street research team used the U.S. Census Bureau's 2012 American Community Survey, an index of income disparity, additional income, poverty, and home-value data. The McAllen metro area placed #10 among metro areas with the widest wealth gap between rich and poor. *247wallst.com, "Cities with the Widest Gap between Rich and Poor," November 4, 2013*

- Council for Community and Economic Research cost-of-living data for the third quarter of 2012 produced a list of the ten most affordable American cities among the 304 cities the council studied. Food items, home purchase or rental, clothing, utilities, services, health care, and other expenses were considered. On the affordability scale, McAllen ranked #6. *CNBC.com, "America's Most Affordable Cities," November 15, 2012*

- McAllen was ranked #43 out of 100 metro areas in terms of economic performance (#1 = best) during the recession and recovery from trough quarter through the second quarter of 2013. Criteria: percent change in employment; percentage point change in unemployment rate; percent change in gross metropolitan product; percent change in House Price Index. *Brookings Institution, MetroMonitor: Tracking Economic Recession and Recovery in America's 100 Largest Metropolitan Areas, September 2013*

- The McAllen metro area was identified as one of 10 best-paying cities for women. The metro area ranked #6. Criteria: *24/7 Wall St.* identified the metropolitan areas that have the smallest pay disparity between men and women by comparing the median earnings for the past 12 months of both men and women working full-time in the country's 100 largest metropolitan statistical areas. *24/7 Wall St., "10 Best-Paying Cities for Women," April 14, 2013*

- For its annual survey of the "10 Cheapest U.S. Cities to Live In," Kiplinger applied Cost of Living Index statistics developed by the Council for Community and Economic Research to U.S. Census Bureau population and median household income data for cities with populations above 50,000. In the resulting ranking, McAllen ranked #2. *Kiplinger.com, "10 Cheapest U.S. Cities to Live In," June 2013*

- McAllen was identified as one of "America's Least Expensive Cities" in 2012. The city ranked #4 out of 5. Criteria: prices of 60 consumer goods and services were compared to the average annual income of professional and managerial households in the top fifth income level. *CNBC, "America's Least Expensive Cities, 2012," January 17, 2012*

- The McAllen metro area appeared on the Milken Institute "2013 Best Performing Cities" list. Rank: #59 out of 200 large metro areas. Criteria: job growth; wage and salary growth; high-tech output growth. *Milken Institute, "Best-Performing Cities 2013," December 2013*

- *Forbes* ranked the 200 most populous metro areas in the U.S. in terms of the "Best Places for Business and Careers." The McAllen metro area was ranked #99. Criteria: costs (business and living); job growth (past and projected); income growth; educational attainment (college and high school); projected economic growth; cultural and recreational opportunities; net migration patterns; number of highly ranked colleges. *Forbes, "The Best Places for Business and Careers," August 7, 2013*

Dating/Romance Rankings

- McAllen was selected as one of the least romantic cities in the U.S. by video-rental kiosk company Redbox. The city ranked #6 out of 10. Criteria: number of romance-related rentals in 2012. *Redbox, "10 Most/Least Romantic Cities," February 12, 2013*

Environmental Rankings

- The McAllen metro area came in at #357 for the relative comfort of its climate on Sperling's list of "chill cities," as measured by the Sperling Heat Index. All 361 metro areas are included. Criteria included daytime high temperatures, nighttime low temperatures, dew point, and relative humidity at the high temperatures. *www.bertsperling.com, "Sperling's Chill Cities," July 18, 2013*

- Sperling's BestPlaces assessed 379 metropolitan areas of the United States for the likelihood of dangerously extreme weather events or earthquakes. In general the Southeast and South-Central regions have the highest risk of weather extremes and earthquakes, while the Pacific Northwest enjoys the lowest risk. Of the least risky metropolitan areas, the McAllen metro area was ranked #314. *www.bestplaces.net, "Safest Places from Natural Disasters," April 2011*

- The McAllen metro area was identified as one of nine cities running out of water by *24/7 Wall St.* The area ranked #3. Based on data provided by the U.S. Drought Monitor, a joint program produced by academic and government organizations, *24/7 Wall St.* identified large U.S. urban areas that have been under persistent, serious drought for months. *24/7 Wall St., "Nine Cities Running Out of Water," August 1, 2013*

- McAllen was selected as one of 22 "Smarter Cities" for energy by the Natural Resources Defense Council. Criteria: investment in green power; energy efficiency measures; conservation. *Natural Resources Defense Council, "2010 Smarter Cities," July 19, 2010*

- The McAllen metro area was selected as one of "America's Cleanest Cities" by *Forbes*. The metro area ranked #1 out of 10. Criteria: toxic releases; air and water quality; per capita spending on Superfund site cleanup. *Forbes.com, "America's Cleanest Cities 2011," March 11, 2011*

- McAllen was highlighted as one of the cleanest metro areas for ozone air pollution in the U.S. during 2008 through 2010. The list represents cities with no monitored ozone air pollution in unhealthful ranges. *American Lung Association, State of the Air 2012*

- McAllen was highlighted as one of the top 25 cleanest metro areas for short-term particle pollution (24-hour PM 2.5) in the U.S. during 2008 through 2010. Monitors in these cities reported no days with unhealthful PM 2.5 levels. *American Lung Association, State of the Air 2012*

Health/Fitness Rankings

- The Gallup-Healthways Well-Being Index tracks Americans' optimism about their communities in addition to their satisfaction with the metro areas in which they live. Gallup researchers asked at least 300 adult residents in each of 189 U.S. metropolitan areas whether their metro was improving. The McAllen metro area placed among the top ten in the percentage of residents who were optimistic about their metro area. *www.gallup.com, "City Satisfaction Highest in Fort Collins-Loveland, Colo.," April 11, 2014*

- Analysts who tracked obesity rates in 189 of the nation's metro areas found that the McAllen metro area was one of the ten communities where residents were most likely to be obese, defined as a BMI score of 30 or above. *www.gallup.com, "Boulder, Colo., Residents Still Least Likely to Be Obese," April 4, 2014*

- McAllen was identified as a "2013 Spring Allergy Capital." The area ranked #4 out of 100. Three groups of factors were used to identify the most severe cities for people with allergies during the spring season: annual pollen levels; medicine utilization; access to board-certified allergists. *Asthma and Allergy Foundation of America, "Spring Allergy Capitals 2013"*

- McAllen was identified as a "2013 Fall Allergy Capital." The area ranked #6 out of 100. Three groups of factors were used to identify the most severe cities for people with allergies during the fall season: annual pollen levels; medicine utilization; access to board-certified allergists. *Asthma and Allergy Foundation of America, "Fall Allergy Capitals 2013"*

- McAllen was identified as a "2013 Asthma Capital." The area ranked #8 out of the nation's 100 largest metropolitan areas. Twelve factors were used to identify the most challenging places to live for people with asthma: estimated prevalence; self-reported prevalence; crude death rate for asthma; annual pollen score; annual air quality; public smoking laws; number of board-certified asthma specialists; school inhaler access laws; rescue medication use; controller medication use; uninsured rate; poverty rate. *Asthma and Allergy Foundation of America, "Asthma Capitals 2013"*

- The McAllen metro area appeared in the 2013 Gallup-Healthways Well-Being Index. The area ranked #147 out of 189. The Gallup-Healthways Well-Being Index score is an average of six sub-indexes, which individually examine life evaluation, emotional health, work environment, physical health, healthy behaviors, and access to basic necessities. Results are based on telephone interviews conducted as part of the Gallup-Healthways Well-Being Index survey January 2–December 29, 2012, and January 2–December 30, 2013, with a random sample of 531,630 adults, aged 18 and older, living in metropolitan areas in the 50 U.S. states and the District of Columbia. *Gallup-Healthways, "State of American Well-Being," March 25, 2014*

Real Estate Rankings

- McAllen was ranked #167 out of 224 metro areas in terms of housing affordability in 2013 by the National Association of Home Builders (#1 = most affordable). The NAHB-Wells Fargo Housing Opportunity Index (HOI) for a given area is defined as the share of homes sold in that area that would have been affordable to a family earning the local median income, based on standard mortgage underwriting criteria. *National Association of Home Builders®, NAHB-Wells Fargo Housing Opportunity Index, 4th Quarter 2013*

- The nation's largest metro areas were analyzed in terms of the worst places to buy foreclosures in 2013. The McAllen metro area ranked #1 out of 20. Criteria: RealtyTrac scored all metro areas with a population of 500,000 or more by summing up four numbers: months' supply of foreclosure inventory; percentage of foreclosure sales; foreclosure discount; percentage increase in foreclosure activity in 2012. *RealtyTrac, "2012 Year-End Metropolitan Foreclosure Market Report," January 28, 2013*

- The McAllen metro area was identified as one of America's most undervalued cities in 2011 by *CNNMoney.com* based on data from Local Market Monitor. Criteria: median home prices; local interest rates; economic and population growth; construction costs; vacancies; household income. *CNNMoney.com, "America's Most Overvalued (and Undervalued) Cities," January 16, 2011*

Safety Rankings

- Allstate ranked the 200 largest cities in America in terms of driver safety. McAllen ranked #36. Allstate researchers analyzed internal property damage claims over a two-year period from January 2010 to December 2011. A weighted average of the two-year numbers determined the annual percentages. *Allstate, "Allstate America's Best Drivers Report®, August 27, 2013"*

- The National Insurance Crime Bureau ranked 380 metro areas in the U.S. in terms of per capita rates of vehicle theft. The McAllen metro area ranked #96 (#1 = highest rate). Criteria: number of vehicle theft offenses per 100,000 inhabitants in 2012. *National Insurance Crime Bureau, "Hot Spots 2012," June 26, 2013*

Seniors/Retirement Rankings

- From its Best Cities for Successful Aging indexes, the Milken Institute generated rankings for metropolitan areas, weighing data in eight categories—general indicators, health care, wellness, living arrangements, transportation and general accessibility, financial well-being, education and employment, and community participation. The McAllen metro area was ranked #44 overall in the large metro area category. *Milken Institute, "Best Cities for Successful Aging," July 2012*

Sports/Recreation Rankings

- McAllen was selected as one of the most playful cities in the U.S. by KaBOOM! The organization's Playful City USA initiative honors cities and towns across the nation for a vision, plan and commitment to creating an agenda for play. Criteria: creating a local play commission or task force; designing an annual action plan for play; conducting a play space audit; outlining a financial investment in play for the current fiscal year; and proclaiming and celebrating an annual "play day." *KaBOOM! National Campaign for Play, "2013 Playful City USA Communities"*

Business Environment

CITY FINANCES

City Government Finances

Component	2011 ($000)	2011 ($ per capita)
Total Revenues	192,488	1,513
Total Expenditures	206,639	1,624
Debt Outstanding	190,212	1,495
Cash and Securities[1]	264,515	2,079

Note: (1) Cash and security holdings of a government at the close of its fiscal year, including those of its dependent agencies, utilities, and liquor stores.
Source: U.S Census Bureau, State & Local Government Finances 2011

City Government Revenue by Source

Source	2011 ($000)	2011 ($ per capita)
General Revenue		
From Federal Government	13,679	108
From State Government	2,154	17
From Local Governments	0	0
Taxes		
Property	32,897	259
Sales and Gross Receipts	63,151	496
Personal Income	0	0
Corporate Income	0	0
Motor Vehicle License	0	0
Other Taxes	1,369	11
Current Charges	48,143	378
Liquor Store	0	0
Utility	13,640	107
Employee Retirement	0	0

Source: U.S Census Bureau, State & Local Government Finances 2011

City Government Expenditures by Function

Function	2011 ($000)	2011 ($ per capita)	2011 (%)
General Direct Expenditures			
Air Transportation	9,967	78	4.8
Corrections	0	0	0.0
Education	0	0	0.0
Employment Security Administration	0	0	0.0
Financial Administration	5,345	42	2.6
Fire Protection	15,042	118	7.3
General Public Buildings	2,192	17	1.1
Governmental Administration, Other	4,961	39	2.4
Health	1,432	11	0.7
Highways	24,074	189	11.7
Hospitals	0	0	0.0
Housing and Community Development	3,474	27	1.7
Interest on General Debt	4,417	35	2.1
Judicial and Legal	4,126	32	2.0
Libraries	5,076	40	2.5
Parking	959	8	0.5
Parks and Recreation	23,822	187	11.5
Police Protection	32,186	253	15.6
Public Welfare	1,505	12	0.7
Sewerage	21,995	173	10.6
Solid Waste Management	15,484	122	7.5
Veterans' Services	0	0	0.0
Liquor Store	0	0	0.0
Utility	19,004	149	9.2
Employee Retirement	0	0	0.0

Source: U.S Census Bureau, State & Local Government Finances 2011

DEMOGRAPHICS

Population Growth

Area	1990 Census	2000 Census	2010 Census	Population Growth (%) 1990-2000	Population Growth (%) 2000-2010
City	86,145	106,414	129,877	23.5	22.0
MSA[1]	383,545	569,463	774,769	48.5	36.1
U.S.	248,709,873	281,421,906	308,745,538	13.2	9.7

Note: (1) Figures cover the McAllen-Edinburg-Mission, TX Metropolitan Statistical Area—see Appendix B for areas included
Source: U.S. Census Bureau, Census 1990, 2000, 2010

Household Size

Area	Persons in Household (%) One	Two	Three	Four	Five	Six	Seven or More	Average Household Size
City	22.0	26.6	18.7	15.1	10.1	5.2	2.3	3.12
MSA[1]	15.4	24.1	17.3	17.1	12.8	7.6	5.7	3.61
U.S.	27.6	33.5	15.7	13.2	6.1	2.4	1.5	2.63

Note: (1) Figures cover the McAllen-Edinburg-Mission, TX Metropolitan Statistical Area—see Appendix B for areas included
Source: U.S. Census Bureau, 2010-2012 American Community Survey 3-Year Estimates

Race

Area	White Alone[2] (%)	Black Alone[2] (%)	Asian Alone[2] (%)	AIAN[3] Alone[2] (%)	NHOPI[4] Alone[2] (%)	Other Race Alone[2] (%)	Two or More Races (%)
City	87.6	1.1	2.8	0.5	0.0	6.6	1.3
MSA[1]	90.8	0.6	1.0	0.4	0.0	6.5	0.7
U.S.	74.0	12.6	4.9	0.8	0.2	4.7	2.8

Note: (1) Figures cover the McAllen-Edinburg-Mission, TX Metropolitan Statistical Area—see Appendix B for areas included; (2) Alone is defined as not being in combination with one or more other races; (3) American Indian and Alaska Native; (4) Native Hawaiian and Other Pacific Islander
Source: U.S. Census Bureau, 2010-2012 American Community Survey 3-Year Estimates

Hispanic or Latino Origin

Area	Total (%)	Mexican (%)	Puerto Rican (%)	Cuban (%)	Other (%)
City	85.1	80.8	0.3	0.2	3.8
MSA[1]	90.8	88.4	0.2	0.1	2.0
U.S.	16.6	10.7	1.6	0.6	3.7

Note: Persons of Hispanic or Latino origin can be of any race; (1) Figures cover the McAllen-Edinburg-Mission, TX Metropolitan Statistical Area—see Appendix B for areas included
Source: U.S. Census Bureau, 2010-2012 American Community Survey 3-Year Estimates

Segregation

Type	Segregation Indices[1] 1990	2000	2010	2010 Rank[2]	Percent Change 1990-2000	Percent Change 1990-2010	Percent Change 2000-2010
Black/White	33.9	48.8	40.7	90	14.8	6.8	-8.1
Asian/White	40.3	41.2	46.7	17	0.9	6.4	5.6
Hispanic/White	37.9	39.5	39.2	69	1.6	1.3	-0.4

Note: All figures cover the Metropolitan Statistical Area—see Appendix B for areas included; Figures are based on an analysis of 1990, 2000, and 2010 Census Decennial Census tract data by William H. Frey, Brookings Institution and the University of Michigan Social Science Data Analysis Network. In this analysis all racial groups (whites, blacks, and asians) are non-Hispanic members of those races. Hispanics are shown as a separate category;
(1) Segregation Indices are Dissimilarity Indices that measure the degree to which the minority group is distributed differently than whites across census tracts. They range from 0 (complete integration) to 100 (complete segregation) where the value indicates the percentage of the minority group that needs to move to be distributed exactly like whites; (2) Ranges from 1 (most segregated) to 102 (least segregated); n/a not available.
Source: www.CensusScope.org

Ancestry

Area	German	Irish	English	American	Italian	Polish	French[2]	Scottish	Dutch
City	4.3	2.5	2.5	1.6	1.2	0.3	2.8	0.2	0.2
MSA[1]	2.7	1.4	1.3	1.1	0.5	0.2	1.0	0.3	0.2
U.S.	15.2	11.1	8.2	7.2	5.6	3.1	2.8	1.7	1.4

Note: Figures are the percentage of the total population reporting a particular ancestry. The nine most commonly reported ancestries in the U.S. are shown. Figures include multiple ancestries (e.g. if a person reported being Irish and Italian, they were included in both columns); (1) Figures cover the McAllen-Edinburg-Mission, TX Metropolitan Statistical Area—see Appendix B for areas included; (2) Excludes Basque
Source: U.S. Census Bureau, 2010-2012 American Community Survey 3-Year Estimates

Foreign-Born Population

Area	Any Foreign Country	Mexico	Asia	Europe	Carribean	South America	Central America[2]	Africa	Canada
City	n/a	n/a	n/a	n/a	n/a	n/a	n/a	n/a	n/a
MSA[1]	29.4	27.4	0.8	0.2	0.1	0.2	0.4	0.0	0.3
U.S.	13.0	3.7	3.7	1.6	1.2	0.9	1.0	0.5	0.3

Note: (1) Figures cover the McAllen-Edinburg-Mission, TX Metropolitan Statistical Area—see Appendix B for areas included; (2) Excludes Mexico.
Source: U.S. Census Bureau, 2010-2012 American Community Survey 3-Year Estimates

Marital Status

Area	Never Married	Now Married[2]	Separated	Widowed	Divorced
City	30.7	50.0	3.9	6.1	9.4
MSA[1]	31.6	52.4	4.2	5.1	6.8
U.S.	32.4	48.4	2.2	6.0	11.0

Note: Figures are percentages and cover the population 15 years of age and older; (1) Figures cover the McAllen-Edinburg-Mission, TX Metropolitan Statistical Area—see Appendix B for areas included; (2) Excludes separated
Source: U.S. Census Bureau, 2010-2012 American Community Survey 3-Year Estimates

Age

Area	Under Age 5	Age 5–19	Age 20–34	Age 35–44	Age 45–54	Age 55–64	Age 65–74	Age 75–84	Age 85+	Median Age
City	7.7	23.8	21.3	13.7	13.0	9.8	6.2	3.1	1.5	32.9
MSA[1]	9.6	28.2	21.2	13.2	10.4	7.9	5.3	3.2	1.1	28.5
U.S.	6.4	20.1	20.5	13.1	14.3	12.2	7.3	4.2	1.8	37.3

Note: (1) Figures cover the McAllen-Edinburg-Mission, TX Metropolitan Statistical Area—see Appendix B for areas included
Source: U.S. Census Bureau, 2010-2012 American Community Survey 3-Year Estimates

Gender

Area	Males	Females	Males per 100 Females
City	64,587	68,133	94.8
MSA[1]	386,944	406,368	95.2
U.S.	153,276,055	158,333,314	96.8

Note: (1) Figures cover the McAllen-Edinburg-Mission, TX Metropolitan Statistical Area—see Appendix B for areas included
Source: U.S. Census Bureau, 2010-2012 American Community Survey 3-Year Estimates

Religious Groups by Family

Area	Catholic	Baptist	Non-Den.	Methodist[2]	Lutheran	LDS[3]	Pentecostal	Presbyterian[4]	Muslim[5]	Judaism
MSA[1]	34.7	4.5	2.8	1.3	0.4	1.3	1.2	0.2	1.0	<0.1
U.S.	19.1	9.3	4.0	4.0	2.3	2.0	1.9	1.6	0.8	0.7

Note: Figures are the number of adherents as a percentage of the total population; (1) Figures cover the McAllen-Edinburg-Mission, TX Metropolitan Statistical Area—see Appendix B for areas included; (2) Methodist/Pietist; (3) Latter Day Saints; (4) Reformed; (5) Figures are estimates
Source: Association of Statisticians of American Religious Bodies, 2010 U.S. Religion Census: Religious Congregations & Membership Study

Religious Groups by Tradition

Area	Catholic	Evangelical Protestant	Mainline Protestant	Other Tradition	Black Protestant	Orthodox
MSA[1]	34.7	9.7	1.9	2.4	<0.1	<0.1
U.S.	19.1	16.2	7.3	4.3	1.6	0.3

Note: Figures are the number of adherents as a percentage of the total population; (1) Figures cover the McAllen-Edinburg-Mission, TX Metropolitan Statistical Area—see Appendix B for areas included
Source: Association of Statisticians of American Religious Bodies, 2010 U.S. Religion Census: Religious Congregations & Membership Study

ECONOMY

Gross Metropolitan Product

Area	2011	2012	2013	2014	Rank[2]
MSA[1]	15.5	16.0	16.5	17.3	130

Note: Figures are in billions of dollars; (1) Figures cover the McAllen-Edinburg-Mission, TX Metropolitan Statistical Area—see Appendix B for areas included; (2) Rank is based on 2014 data and ranges from 1 to 363
Source: The United States Conference of Mayors, U.S. Metro Economies: Outlook—Gross Metropolitan Product, with Metro Employment Projections, November 2013

Economic Growth

Area	2011 (%)	2012 (%)	2013 (%)	2014 (%)	Rank[2]
MSA[1]	1.3	1.8	1.3	3.3	130
U.S.	1.6	2.5	1.7	2.5	–

Note: Figures are real gross metropolitan product (GMP) growth rates and represent annual average percent change; (1) Figures cover the McAllen-Edinburg-Mission, TX Metropolitan Statistical Area—see Appendix B for areas included; (2) Rank is based on 2013 data and ranges from 1 to 363
Source: The United States Conference of Mayors, U.S. Metro Economies: Outlook—Gross Metropolitan Product, with Metro Employment Projections, November 2013

Metropolitan Area Exports

Area	2007	2008	2009	2010	2011	2012	Rank[2]
MSA[1]	4,041.5	4,578.5	3,736.1	4,527.1	4,676.1	5,198.5	52

Note: Figures are in millions of dollars; (1) Figures cover the McAllen-Edinburg-Mission, TX Metropolitan Statistical Area—see Appendix B for areas included; (2) Rank is based on 2012 data and ranges from 1 to 369
Source: U.S. Department of Commerce, International Trade Administration, Office of Trade & Industry Information, Manufacturing & Services, data extracted April 1, 2014

INCOME

Income

Area	Per Capita ($)	Median Household ($)	Average Household ($)
City	21,406	41,375	64,900
MSA[1]	14,073	33,549	48,908
U.S.	27,385	51,771	71,579

Note: (1) Figures cover the McAllen-Edinburg-Mission, TX Metropolitan Statistical Area—see Appendix B for areas included
Source: U.S. Census Bureau, 2010-2012 American Community Survey 3-Year Estimates

Household Income Distribution

Area	Percent of Households Earning							
	Under $15,000	$15,000 -24,999	$25,000 -34,999	$35,000 -49,999	$50,000 -74,999	$75,000 -99,000	$100,000 -149,999	$150,000 and up
City	19.3	13.2	11.0	14.7	15.0	9.5	9.5	7.7
MSA[1]	23.7	15.8	12.2	14.2	15.1	8.1	7.0	3.8
U.S.	13.1	11.0	10.5	13.7	18.1	11.9	12.5	9.1

Note: (1) Figures cover the McAllen-Edinburg-Mission, TX Metropolitan Statistical Area—see Appendix B for areas included
Source: U.S. Census Bureau, 2010-2012 American Community Survey 3-Year Estimates

Poverty Rate

Area	All Ages	Under 18 Years Old	18 to 64 Years Old	65 Years and Over
City	27.2	35.9	24.2	22.1
MSA[1]	35.4	47.2	30.0	24.8
U.S.	15.7	22.2	14.6	9.3

Note: Figures are percentage of people whose income during the past 12 months was below the poverty level; (1) Figures cover the McAllen-Edinburg-Mission, TX Metropolitan Statistical Area—see Appendix B for areas included
Source: U.S. Census Bureau, 2010-2012 American Community Survey 3-Year Estimates

Personal Bankruptcy Filing Rate

Area	2008	2009	2010	2011	2012	2013
Hidalgo County	1.18	1.35	1.30	1.18	0.99	0.82
U.S.	3.53	4.61	4.97	4.37	3.76	3.29

Note: Numbers are per 1,000 population and include Chapter 7 and Chapter 13 filings
Source: Federal Deposit Insurance Corporation, Regional Economic Conditions, March 20, 2014

EMPLOYMENT

Labor Force and Employment

Area	Civilian Labor Force			Workers Employed		
	Dec. 2012	Dec. 2013	% Chg.	Dec. 2012	Dec. 2013	% Chg.
City	61,590	61,903	0.5	57,452	58,083	1.1
MSA[1]	317,468	320,758	1.0	284,246	287,367	1.1
U.S.	154,904,000	154,408,000	-0.3	143,060,000	144,423,000	1.0

Note: Data is not seasonally adjusted and covers workers 16 years of age and older; (1) Metropolitan Statistical Area—see Appendix B for areas included
Source: Bureau of Labor Statistics, Local Area Unemployment Statistics

Unemployment Rate

Area	2013											
	Jan.	Feb.	Mar.	Apr.	May	Jun.	Jul.	Aug.	Sep.	Oct.	Nov.	Dec.
City	7.6	7.3	7.2	7.1	7.3	7.7	7.5	6.9	7.0	6.8	6.4	6.2
MSA[1]	11.6	11.0	10.6	10.5	10.9	11.5	11.3	10.8	10.7	10.1	10.3	10.4
U.S.	8.5	8.1	7.6	7.1	7.3	7.8	7.7	7.3	7.0	7.0	6.6	6.5

Note: Data is not seasonally adjusted and covers workers 16 years of age and older; All figures are percentages; (1) Metropolitan Statistical Area—see Appendix B for areas included
Source: Bureau of Labor Statistics, Local Area Unemployment Statistics

Employment by Occupation

Occupation Classification	City (%)	MSA[1] (%)	U.S. (%)
Management, Business, Science, and Arts	35.7	26.1	36.0
Natural Resources, Construction, and Maintenance	6.2	13.1	9.1
Production, Transportation, and Material Moving	7.7	10.8	12.0
Sales and Office	28.6	26.7	24.7
Service	21.8	23.2	18.2

Note: Figures cover employed civilians 16 years of age and older; (1) Figures cover the McAllen-Edinburg-Mission, TX Metropolitan Statistical Area—see Appendix B for areas included
Source: U.S. Census Bureau, 2010-2012 American Community Survey 3-Year Estimates

Employment by Industry

Sector	MSA[1]		U.S.
	Number of Employees	Percent of Total	Percent of Total
Construction	n/a	n/a	4.2
Education and Health Services	61,200	25.6	15.5
Financial Activities	9,000	3.8	5.7
Government	56,300	23.6	16.1
Information	2,100	0.9	1.9
Leisure and Hospitality	21,300	8.9	10.2
Manufacturing	6,600	2.8	8.7
Mining and Logging	n/a	n/a	0.6
Other Services	6,100	2.6	3.9
Professional and Business Services	15,500	6.5	13.7
Retail Trade	35,700	14.9	11.4
Transportation and Utilities	8,400	3.5	3.8
Wholesale Trade	7,200	3.0	4.2

Note: Figures cover non-farm employment as of December 2013 and are not seasonally adjusted;
(1) Metropolitan Statistical Area—see Appendix B for areas included; n/a not available
Source: Bureau of Labor Statistics, Current Employment Statistics, Employment, Hours, and Earnings

Occupations with Greatest Projected Employment Growth: 2010 – 2020

Occupation[1]	2010 Employment	2020 Projected Employment	Numeric Employment Change	Percent Employment Change
Combined Food Preparation and Serving Workers, Including Fast Food	243,530	322,520	78,990	32.4
Elementary School Teachers, Except Special Education	166,090	233,860	67,780	40.8
Personal Care Aides	133,820	199,970	66,150	49.4
Retail Salespersons	370,620	433,180	62,560	16.9
Registered Nurses	184,700	245,870	61,160	33.1
Waiters and Waitresses	190,870	244,610	53,730	28.2
Office Clerks, General	262,740	314,810	52,070	19.8
Cashiers	250,510	292,730	42,220	16.9
Home Health Aides	82,420	123,970	41,550	50.4
Customer Service Representatives	200,880	241,030	40,160	20.0

Note: Projections cover Texas; (1) Sorted by numeric employment change
Source: www.projectionscentral.com, State Occupational Projections, 2010–2020 Long-Term Projections

Fastest Growing Occupations: 2010 – 2020

Occupation[1]	2010 Employment	2020 Projected Employment	Numeric Employment Change	Percent Employment Change
Biomedical Engineers	1,440	2,490	1,050	72.9
Diagnostic Medical Sonographers	3,560	5,410	1,850	51.9
Derrick Operators, Oil and Gas	7,190	10,860	3,670	51.1
Home Health Aides	82,420	123,970	41,550	50.4
Personal Care Aides	133,820	199,970	66,150	49.4
Service Unit Operators, Oil, Gas, and Mining	17,870	26,460	8,590	48.0
Special Education Teachers, Middle School	6,170	8,950	2,780	45.1
Special Education Teachers, Preschool, Kindergarten, and Elementary School	12,940	18,750	5,810	44.9
Rotary Drill Operators, Oil and Gas	7,160	10,340	3,180	44.4
Roustabouts, Oil and Gas	17,800	25,580	7,790	43.8

Note: Projections cover Texas; (1) Sorted by percent employment change and excludes occupations with numeric employment change less than 100
Source: www.projectionscentral.com, State Occupational Projections, 2010–2020 Long-Term Projections

Average Wages

Occupation	$/Hr.	Occupation	$/Hr.
Accountants and Auditors	26.81	Maids and Housekeeping Cleaners	8.40
Automotive Mechanics	16.00	Maintenance and Repair Workers	11.30
Bookkeepers	13.56	Marketing Managers	n/a
Carpenters	13.93	Nuclear Medicine Technologists	n/a
Cashiers	8.78	Nurses, Licensed Practical	21.91
Clerks, General Office	11.14	Nurses, Registered	31.97
Clerks, Receptionists/Information	9.94	Nursing Assistants	9.83
Clerks, Shipping/Receiving	11.27	Packers and Packagers, Hand	8.67
Computer Programmers	28.68	Physical Therapists	46.12
Computer Systems Analysts	29.92	Postal Service Mail Carriers	24.38
Computer User Support Specialists	18.42	Real Estate Brokers	n/a
Cooks, Restaurant	9.23	Retail Salespersons	9.57
Dentists	96.37	Sales Reps., Exc. Tech./Scientific	25.44
Electrical Engineers	n/a	Sales Reps., Tech./Scientific	n/a
Electricians	15.29	Secretaries, Exc. Legal/Med./Exec.	12.71
Financial Managers	45.55	Security Guards	10.59
First-Line Supervisors/Managers, Sales	18.37	Surgeons	n/a
Food Preparation Workers	8.74	Teacher Assistants	10.30
General and Operations Managers	39.42	Teachers, Elementary School	23.70
Hairdressers/Cosmetologists	12.01	Teachers, Secondary School	25.20
Internists	n/a	Telemarketers	10.62
Janitors and Cleaners	10.13	Truck Drivers, Heavy/Tractor-Trailer	17.51
Landscaping/Groundskeeping Workers	9.71	Truck Drivers, Light/Delivery Svcs.	11.63
Lawyers	61.72	Waiters and Waitresses	8.79

Note: Wage data covers the McAllen-Edinburg-Mission, TX Metropolitan Statistical Area—see Appendix B for areas included. Hourly wages for elementary/secondary school teachers and teacher assistants were calculated by the editors from annual wage data assuming a 40 hour work week; n/a not available.
Source: Bureau of Labor Statistics, Metro Area Occupational Employment and Wage Estimates, May 2013

RESIDENTIAL REAL ESTATE

Building Permits

Area	Single-Family			Multi-Family			Total		
	2012	2013	Pct. Chg.	2012	2013	Pct. Chg.	2012	2013	Pct. Chg.
City	433	374	-13.6	96	145	51.0	529	519	-1.9
MSA[1]	2,833	2,545	-10.2	659	749	13.7	3,492	3,294	-5.7
U.S.	518,695	620,802	19.7	310,963	370,020	19.0	829,658	990,822	19.4

Note: (1) Metropolitan Statistical Area—see Appendix B for areas included; figures represent new, privately-owned housing units authorized (unadjusted data); All permit data are based on estimates with imputation.
Source: U.S. Census Bureau, Manufacturing, Mining, and Construction Statistics, Building Permits, 2012, 2013

Homeownership Rate

Area	2006 (%)	2007 (%)	2008 (%)	2009 (%)	2010 (%)	2011 (%)	2012 (%)	2013 (%)
MSA[1]	n/a	n/a	n/a	n/a	n/a	n/a	n/a	n/a
U.S.	68.8	68.1	67.8	67.4	66.9	66.1	65.4	65.1

Note: (1) Figures cover the McAllen-Edinburg-Mission, TX Metropolitan Statistical Area—see Appendix B for areas included; n/a not available
Source: U.S. Census Bureau, Housing Vacancies and Homeownership Annual Statistics: 2013

Housing Vacancy Rates

Area	Gross Vacancy Rate[2] (%)			Year-Round Vacancy Rate[3] (%)			Rental Vacancy Rate[4] (%)			Homeowner Vacancy Rate[5] (%)		
	2011	2012	2013	2011	2012	2013	2011	2012	2013	2011	2012	2013
MSA[1]	n/a	n/a	n/a	n/a	n/a	n/a	n/a	n/a	n/a	n/a	n/a	n/a
U.S.	14.2	13.8	13.8	11.1	10.8	10.7	9.5	8.7	8.3	2.5	2.0	2.0

Note: (1) Figures cover the McAllen-Edinburg-Mission, TX Metropolitan Statistical Area—see Appendix B for areas included; (2) The percentage of the total housing inventory that is vacant; (3) The percentage of the housing inventory (excluding seasonal units) that is year-round vacant; (4) The percentage of rental inventory that is vacant for rent; (5) The percentage of homeowner inventory that is vacant for sale; n/a not available
Source: U.S. Census Bureau, Housing Vacancies and Homeownership Annual Statistics: 2013

TAXES

State Corporate Income Tax Rates

State	Tax Rate (%)	Income Brackets ($)	Num. of Brackets	Financial Institution Tax Rate (%)[a]	Federal Income Tax Ded.
Texas	(x)	–	–	(x)	No

Note: Tax rates as of January 1, 2014; (a) Rates listed are the corporate income tax rate applied to financial institutions or excise taxes based on income. Some states have other taxes based upon the value of deposits or shares; (x) Texas imposes a Franchise Tax, otherwise known as margin tax, imposed on entities with more than $1,030,000 total revenues at rate of 1%, or 0.5% for entities primarily engaged in retail or wholesale trade, on lesser of 70% of total revenues or 100% of gross receipts after deductions for either compensation or cost of goods sold.
Source: Federation of Tax Administrators, "State Corporate Income Tax Rates, 2014"

State Individual Income Tax Rates

State	Tax Rate (%)	Income Brackets ($)	Num. of Brackets	Personal Exempt. ($)[1] Single	Dependents	Fed. Inc. Tax Ded.
Texas	None	–	–	–	–	–

Note: Tax rates as of January 1, 2014; Local- and county-level taxes are not included; n/a not applicable; (1) Married joint filers generally receive double the single exemption
Source: Federation of Tax Administrators, "State Individual Income Tax Rates, 2014"

Various State and Local Tax Rates

State	State and Local Sales and Use (%)	State Sales and Use (%)	Gasoline[1] (¢/gal.)	Cigarette[2] ($/pack)	Spirits[3] ($/gal.)	Wine[4] ($/gal.)	Beer[5] ($/gal.)
Texas	8.25	6.25	20.00	1.410	2.40 (f)	0.20	0.20

Note: All tax rates as of January 1, 2014; (1) The American Petroleum Institute has developed a methodology for determining the average tax rate on a gallon of fuel. Rates may include any of the following: excise taxes, environmental fees, storage tank fees, other fees or taxes, general sales tax, and local taxes. In states where gasoline is subject to the general sales tax, or where the fuel tax is based on the average sale price, the average rate determined by API is sensitive to changes in the price of gasoline. States that fully or partially apply general sales taxes to gasoline: CA, CO, GA, IL, IN, MI, NY; (2) The federal excise tax of $1.0066 per pack and local taxes are not included; (3) Rates are those applicable to off-premise sales of 40% alcohol by volume (a.b.v.) distilled spirits in 750ml containers. Local excise taxes are excluded; (4) Rates are those applicable to off-premise sales of 11% a.b.v. non-carbonated wine in 750ml containers; (5) Rates are those applicable to off-premise sales of 4.7% a.b.v. beer in 12 ounce containers; (f) Different rates also applicable according to alcohol content, place of production, size of container, or place purchased (on- or off-premise or onboard airlines).
Source: Tax Foundation, 2014 Facts & Figures: How Does Your State Compare?

State Business Tax Climate Index Rankings

State	Overall Rank	Corporate Tax Index Rank	Individual Income Tax Index Rank	Sales Tax Index Rank	Unemployment Insurance Tax Index Rank	Property Tax Index Rank
Texas	11	38	7	36	14	35

Note: The index is a measure of how each state's tax laws affect economic performance. The lower the rank, the more favorable a state's tax system is for business. States without a given tax are given a ranking of 1. The scores/rankings for the District of Columbia do not affect other states. The 2014 index represents the tax climate as of July 1, 2013.
Source: Tax Foundation, State Business Tax Climate Index 2014

COMMERCIAL UTILITIES

Typical Monthly Electric Bills

Area	Commercial Service ($/month) 1,500 kWh	40 kW demand 14,000 kWh	Industrial Service ($/month) 1,000 kW demand 200,000 kWh	50,000 kW demand 15,000,000 kWh
City	n/a	n/a	n/a	n/a
Average[1]	197	1,636	25,662	1,485,307

Note: Based on total rates in effect July 1, 2013; (1) average based on 180 utilities surveyed; n/a not available
Source: Edison Electric Institute, Typical Bills and Average Rates Report, Summer 2013

TRANSPORTATION

Means of Transportation to Work

Area	Car/Truck/Van		Public Transportation			Bicycle	Walked	Other Means	Worked at Home
	Drove Alone	Car-pooled	Bus	Subway	Railroad				
City	75.4	9.5	0.8	0.0	0.0	0.1	1.5	6.7	6.0
MSA[1]	78.4	11.5	0.2	0.0	0.0	0.1	1.2	4.0	4.5
U.S.	76.4	9.7	2.6	1.7	0.5	0.6	2.8	1.3	4.3

Note: Figures are percentages and cover workers 16 years of age and older; (1) Figures cover the McAllen-Edinburg-Mission, TX Metropolitan Statistical Area—see Appendix B for areas included
Source: U.S. Census Bureau, 2010-2012 American Community Survey 3-Year Estimates

Travel Time to Work

Area	Less Than 10 Minutes	10 to 19 Minutes	20 to 29 Minutes	30 to 44 Minutes	45 to 59 Minutes	60 to 89 Minutes	90 Minutes or More
City	17.2	44.4	21.7	10.6	2.1	1.7	2.4
MSA[1]	14.3	38.4	23.0	17.7	2.7	1.8	2.1
U.S.	13.5	29.8	20.9	20.1	7.5	5.6	2.5

Note: Figures are percentages and include workers 16 years old and over; (1) Figures cover the McAllen-Edinburg-Mission, TX Metropolitan Statistical Area—see Appendix B for areas included
Source: U.S. Census Bureau, 2010-2012 American Community Survey 3-Year Estimates

Travel Time Index

Area	1985	1990	1995	2000	2005	2010	2011
Urban Area[1]	1.02	1.02	1.05	1.11	1.13	1.16	1.16
Average[2]	1.09	1.14	1.16	1.19	1.23	1.18	1.18

Note: Travel Time Index—the ratio of travel time in the peak period to the travel time at free-flow conditions. For example, a value of 1.30 indicates a 20-minute free-flow trip takes 26 minutes in the peak. Free-flow speeds (60 mph on freeways and 35 mph on principal arterials) are used as the comparison threshold; (1) Covers the McAllen TX urban area; (2) average of 498 urban areas
Source: Texas Transportation Institute, Urban Mobility Report 2012, December 2012

Public Transportation

Agency Name / Mode of Transportation	Vehicles Operated in Maximum Service	Annual Unlinked Passenger Trips (in thous.)	Annual Passenger Miles (in thous.)
City of McAllen - McAllen Express Transit			
Bus (directly operated)	8	617.7	n/a
Demand Response (directly operated)	2	9.5	n/a

Source: Federal Transit Administration, National Transit Database, 2012

Air Transportation

Airport Name and Code / Type of Service	Passenger Airlines[1]	Passenger Enplanements	Freight Carriers[2]	Freight (lbs.)
McAllen-Miller International Airport (MFE)				
Domestic service (U.S. carriers - 2013)	7	335,325	8	5,938,668
International service (U.S. carriers - 2012)	2	128	3	16,014

Note: (1) Includes all U.S.-based major, minor and commuter airlines that carried at least one passenger during the year; (2) Includes all U.S.-based airlines and freight carriers that transported at least one lb. of freight during the year.
Source: Bureau of Transportation Statistics, The Intermodal Transportation Database, Air Carriers: T-100 Domestic Market (U.S. Carriers), 2013; Bureau of Transportation Statistics, The Intermodal Transportation Database, Air Carriers: T-100 International Market (U.S. Carriers), 2012

Other Transportation Statistics

Major Highways:	Expressway 83E
Amtrak Service:	No
Major Waterways/Ports:	Rio Grande

Source: Amtrak.com; Google Maps

BUSINESSES

Major Business Headquarters

Company Name	Rankings	
	Fortune[1]	Forbes[2]
No companies listed	-	-

Note: (1) Fortune 500—companies that produce a 10-K are ranked 1 to 500 based on 2012 revenue; (2) all private companies with at least $2 billion in annual revenue through the end of their most current fiscal year are ranked 1 to 224; companies listed are headquartered in the city; dashes indicate no ranking Source: Fortune, "Fortune 500," May 20, 2013; Forbes, "America's Largest Private Companies," December 18, 2013

Minority Business Opportunity

McAllen is home to one company which is on the *Hispanic Business* 500 list (500 largest U.S. Hispanic-owned companies based on 2012 revenue): **Galvotec Alloys** (#135). Companies included must show at least 51 percent ownership by Hispanic U.S. citizens, and must maintain headquarters in one of the 50 states or Washington, D.C. *Hispanic Business, "Hispanic Business 500," June 20, 2013*

McAllen is home to one company which is on the *Hispanic Business* Fastest-Growing 100 list (greatest sales growth from 2008 to 2012): **Galvotec Alloys** (#92). Companies included must show at least 51 percent ownership by Hispanic U.S. citizens, and must maintain headquarters in one of the 50 states or Washington, D.C. In addition, companies must have minimum revenues of $200,000 for calendar year 2008. *Hispanic Business, June 20, 2013*

Minority- and Women-Owned Businesses

Group	All Firms		Firms with Paid Employees			
	Firms	Sales ($000)	Firms	Sales ($000)	Employees	Payroll ($000)
Asian	567	245,168	248	229,744	2,094	67,958
Black	(s)	(s)	(s)	(s)	(s)	(s)
Hispanic	8,453	1,632,256	1,344	1,327,110	12,835	272,650
Women	4,346	668,696	686	586,224	6,503	128,807
All Firms	15,161	10,809,367	3,662	10,224,956	60,682	1,514,388

Note: Figures cover firms located in the city; minority- and women-owned business are defined as firms in which the corresponding group own 51% or more of the stock or equity of the company; (s) estimates are suppressed when publication standards are not met Source: U.S. Census Bureau, 2007 Economic Census, Survey of Business Owners (2012 Survey of Business Owners data will be released starting in June 2015)

HOTELS & CONVENTION CENTERS

Hotels/Motels

Area	5 Star		4 Star		3 Star		2 Star		1 Star		Not Rated	
	Num.	Pct.[3]	Num.	Pct.[3]	Num.	Pct.[3]	Num.	Pct.[3]	Num.	Pct.[3]	Num.	Pct.[3]
City[1]	0	0.0	0	0.0	12	15.8	53	69.7	3	3.9	8	10.5
Total[2]	142	0.9	1,005	6.0	5,147	30.9	8,578	51.4	408	2.4	1,397	8.4

Note: (1) Figures cover McAllen and vicinity; (2) Figures cover all 100 cities in this book; (3) Percentage of hotels which have a given star rating; Star ratings are determined by expedia.com and offer an indication of the general quality of a particular hotel. Source: expedia.com, April 7, 2014

Major Convention Centers

Name	Overall Space (sq. ft.)	Exhibit Space (sq. ft.)	Meeting Space (sq. ft.)	Meeting Rooms
McAllen Convention Center	n/a	60,000	25,000	16

Note: Table includes convention centers located in the McAllen-Edinburg-Mission, TX metro area; n/a not available Source: Original research

Living Environment

COST OF LIVING

Cost of Living Index

Composite Index	Groceries	Housing	Utilities	Trans-portation	Health Care	Misc. Goods/Services
87.9	83.3	78.8	99.9	94.6	88.6	90.5

Note: The Cost of Living Index measures regional differences in the cost of consumer goods and services, excluding taxes and non-consumer expenditures, for professional and managerial households in the top income quintile. It is based on more than 50,000 prices covering almost 60 different items for which prices are collected three times a year by chambers of commerce, economic development organizations or university applied economic centers in each participating urban area. The numbers shown should be read as a percentage above or below the national average of 100. For example, a value of 115.4 in the groceries column indicates that grocery prices are 15.4% higher than the national average. Small differences in the index numbers should not be interpreted as significant; Figures cover the McAllen TX urban area.
Source: The Council for Community and Economic Research, ACCRA Cost of Living Index, 2013

Grocery Prices

Area[1]	T-Bone Steak ($/pound)	Frying Chicken ($/pound)	Whole Milk ($/half gal.)	Eggs ($/dozen)	Orange Juice ($/64 oz.)	Coffee ($/11.5 oz.)
City[2]	9.82	1.08	2.70	1.59	3.20	3.85
Avg.	10.19	1.28	2.34	1.81	3.48	4.39
Min.	8.56	0.94	1.44	1.19	2.78	3.40
Max.	14.82	2.28	3.56	3.73	6.23	7.32

Note: (1) Values for the local area are compared with the average, minimum and maximum values for all 327 areas in the Cost of Living Index; (2) Figures cover the McAllen TX urban area; **T-Bone Steak** *(price per pound);* **Frying Chicken** *(price per pound, whole fryer);* **Whole Milk** *(half gallon carton);* **Eggs** *(price per dozen, Grade A, large);* **Orange Juice** *(64 oz. Tropicana or Florida Natural);* **Coffee** *(11.5 oz. can, vacuum-packed, Maxwell House, Hills Bros, or Folgers).*
Source: The Council for Community and Economic Research, ACCRA Cost of Living Index, 2013

Housing and Utility Costs

Area[1]	New Home Price ($)	Apartment Rent ($/month)	All Electric ($/month)	Part Electric ($/month)	Other Energy ($/month)	Telephone ($/month)
City[2]	220,129	795	-	136.74	54.28	21.01
Avg.	295,864	900	171.38	91.82	70.12	27.73
Min.	185,506	458	117.80	48.81	33.67	17.16
Max.	1,358,917	3,783	441.68	171.40	372.65	39.47

Note: (1) Values for the local area are compared with the average, minimum and maximum values for all 327 areas in the Cost of Living Index; (2) Figures cover the McAllen TX urban area; **New Home Price** *(2,400 sf living area, 8,000 sf lot, in urban area with full utilities);* **Apartment Rent** *(950 sf 2 bedroom/1.5 or 2 bath, unfurnished, excluding all utilities except water);* **All Electric** *(average monthly cost for an all-electric home);* **Part Electric** *(average monthly cost for a part-electric home);* **Other Energy** *(average monthly cost for natural gas, fuel oil, coal, wood, and any other forms of energy except electricity);* **Telephone** *(price includes basic monthly rate for a private residential line plus additional local usage charges incurred by a family of four).*
Source: The Council for Community and Economic Research, ACCRA Cost of Living Index, 2013

Health Care, Transportation, and Other Costs

Area[1]	Doctor ($/visit)	Dentist ($/visit)	Optometrist ($/visit)	Gasoline ($/gallon)	Beauty Salon ($/visit)	Men's Shirt ($)
City[2]	70.00	75.33	85.44	3.29	30.83	18.66
Avg.	101.40	86.48	96.16	3.44	33.87	26.55
Min.	61.67	50.83	50.12	3.08	18.92	12.48
Max.	182.71	152.50	223.78	4.33	68.22	52.03

Note: (1) Values for the local area are compared with the average, minimum and maximum values for all 327 areas in the Cost of Living Index; (2) Figures cover the McAllen TX urban area; **Doctor** *(general practitioners routine exam of an established patient);* **Dentist** *(adult teeth cleaning and periodic oral examination);* **Optometrist** *(full vision eye exam for established adult patient);* **Gasoline** *(one gallon regular unleaded, national brand, including all taxes, cash price at self-service pump if available);* **Beauty Salon** *(woman's shampoo, trim, and blow-dry);* **Men's Shirt** *(cotton/polyester dress shirt, pinpoint weave, long sleeves).*
Source: The Council for Community and Economic Research, ACCRA Cost of Living Index, 2013

HOUSING

House Price Index (HPI)

Area	National Ranking[2]	Quarterly Change (%)	One-Year Change (%)	Five-Year Change (%)
MSA[1]	(a)	n/a	0.43	-1.17
U.S.[3]	–	1.20	7.69	4.18

Note: The HPI is a weighted repeat sales index. It measures average price changes in repeat sales or refinancings on the same properties. This information is obtained by reviewing repeat mortgage transactions on single-family properties whose mortgages have been purchased or securitized by Fannie Mae or Freddie Mac in January 1975; (1) McAllen-Edinburg-Mission, TX Metropolitan Statistical Area—see Appendix B for areas included; (2) Rankings are based on annual percentage change for all metro areas containing at least 15,000 transactions over the last 10 years and ranges from 1 to 283; (3) figures based on a weighted average of Census Division estimates using a seasonally adjusted, purchase-only index; all figures are for the period ending December 31, 2013; n/a not available; (a) Not ranked because of increased index variability due to smaller sample size
Source: Federal Housing Finance Agency, House Price Index, February 25, 2014

Median Single-Family Home Prices

Area	2011	2012	2013p	Percent Change 2012 to 2013
MSA[1]	n/a	n/a	n/a	n/a
U.S. Average	166.2	177.2	197.4	11.4

Note: Figures are median sales prices of existing single-family homes in thousands of dollars; (p) preliminary; n/a not available; (1) McAllen-Edinburg-Mission, TX Metropolitan Statistical Area—see Appendix B for areas included
Source: National Association of Realtors, Median Sales Price of Existing Single-Family Homes for Metropolitan Areas, 4th Quarter 2013

Qualifying Income Based on Median Sales Price of Existing Single-Family Homes

Area	With 5% Down ($)	With 10% Down ($)	With 20% Down ($)
MSA[1]	n/a	n/a	n/a
U.S. Average	45,395	43,006	38,228

Note: Figures are preliminary; Qualifying income is based on a mortgage rate of 4.4%. Monthly principal and interest payment is limited to 25% of income; n/a not available; (1) McAllen-Edinburg-Mission, TX Metropolitan Statistical Area—see Appendix B for areas included
Source: National Association of Realtors, Qualifying Income Based on Median Sales Price of Existing Single-Family Homes for Metropolitan Areas, 4th Quarter 2013

Median Apartment Condo-Coop Home Prices

Area	2011	2012	2013p	Percent Change 2012 to 2013
MSA[1]	n/a	n/a	n/a	n/a
U.S. Average	165.1	173.7	194.9	12.2

Note: Figures are median sales prices of existing apartment condo-coop homes in thousands of dollars; (p) preliminary; n/a not available; (1) McAllen-Edinburg-Mission, TX Metropolitan Statistical Area—see Appendix B for areas included
Source: National Association of Realtors, Median Sales Price of Existing Apartment Condo-Coop Homes for Metropolitan Areas, 4th Quarter 2013

Gross Monthly Rent

Area	Under $200	$200 -299	$300 -499	$500 -749	$750 -999	$1,000 -1,499	$1,500 and up	Median ($)
City	2.0	3.5	10.4	41.2	25.3	15.3	2.2	708
MSA[1]	2.8	6.5	18.2	43.1	19.1	8.6	1.7	629
U.S.	1.7	3.3	8.1	22.7	24.3	25.7	14.3	889

Note: Figures are percentages except for Median; Gross rent is the contract rent plus the estimated average monthly cost of utilities (electricity, gas, and water and sewer) and fuels (oil, coal, kerosene, wood, etc.) if these are paid by the renter (or paid for the renter by someone else); (1) Figures cover the McAllen-Edinburg-Mission, TX Metropolitan Statistical Area—see Appendix B for areas included
Source: U.S. Census Bureau, 2010-2012 American Community Survey 3-Year Estimates

Year Housing Structure Built

Area	2010 or Later	2000 -2009	1990 -1999	1980 -1989	1970 -1979	1960 -1969	1950 -1959	1940 -1949	Before 1940	Median Year
City	1.1	27.9	20.7	18.5	18.0	5.6	5.5	1.2	1.4	1990
MSA[1]	1.1	32.1	23.4	19.2	12.2	4.8	3.6	1.8	1.7	1993
U.S.	0.5	14.9	13.8	13.9	15.9	11.1	10.9	5.5	13.5	1976

Note: Figures are percentages except for Median Year; (1) Figures cover the McAllen-Edinburg-Mission, TX Metropolitan Statistical Area—see Appendix B for areas included
Source: U.S. Census Bureau, 2010-2012 American Community Survey 3-Year Estimates

HEALTH

Health Risk Data

Category	MSA[1] (%)	U.S. (%)
Adults aged 18–64 who have any kind of health care coverage	35.4	79.6
Adults who reported being in good or excellent health	71.9	83.1
Adults who are current smokers	14.1	19.6
Adults who are heavy drinkers[2]	n/a	6.1
Adults who are binge drinkers[3]	17.6	16.9
Adults who are overweight (BMI 25.0 - 29.9)	31.2	35.8
Adults who are obese (BMI 30.0 - 99.8)	44.5	27.6
Adults who participated in any physical activities in the past month	63.4	77.1
Adults 50+ who have ever had a sigmoidoscopy or colonoscopy	53.8	67.3
Women aged 40+ who have had a mammogram within the past two years	64.4	74.0
Men aged 40+ who have had a PSA test within the past two years	41.8	45.2
Adults aged 65+ who have had flu shot within the past year	63.8	60.1
Adults who always wear a seatbelt	n/a	93.8

Note: Data as of 2012 unless otherwise noted; n/a not available; (1) Figures cover the McAllen-Edinburg-Mission, TX Metropolitan Statistical Area—see Appendix B for areas included; (2) Heavy drinkers are classified as males having more than two drinks per day or females having more than one drink per day; (3) Binge drinkers are classified as males having five or more drinks on one occasion or females having four or more drinks on one occasion
Source: Centers for Disease Control and Prevention, Behaviorial Risk Factor Surveillance System, SMART: Selected Metropolitan/Micropolitan Area Risk Trends, 2012

Chronic Health Indicators

Category	MSA[1] (%)	U.S. (%)
Adults who have ever been told they had a heart attack	4.3	4.5
Adults who have ever been told they had a stroke	n/a	2.9
Adults who have been told they currently have asthma	3.1	8.9
Adults who have ever been told they have arthritis	21.6	25.7
Adults who have ever been told they have diabetes[2]	13.4	9.7
Adults who have ever been told they had skin cancer	2.6	5.7
Adults who have ever been told they had any other types of cancer	3.8	6.5
Adults who have ever been told they have COPD	3.3	6.2
Adults who have ever been told they have kidney disease	n/a	2.5
Adults who have ever been told they have a form of depression	14.4	18.0

Note: Data as of 2012 unless otherwise noted; n/a not available; (1) Figures cover the McAllen-Edinburg-Mission, TX Metropolitan Statistical Area—see Appendix B for areas included; (2) Figures do not include pregnancy-related, borderline, or pre-diabetes
Source: Centers for Disease Control and Prevention, Behaviorial Risk Factor Surveillance System, SMART: Selected Metropolitan/Micropolitan Area Risk Trends, 2012

Mortality Rates for the Top 10 Causes of Death in the U.S.

ICD-10[a] Sub-Chapter	ICD-10[a] Code	Age-Adjusted Mortality Rate[1] per 100,000 population	
		County[2]	U.S.
Malignant neoplasms	C00-C97	118.4	174.2
Ischaemic heart diseases	I20-I25	134.0	119.1
Other forms of heart disease	I30-I51	31.0	49.6
Chronic lower respiratory diseases	J40-J47	21.3	43.2
Cerebrovascular diseases	I60-I69	32.4	40.3
Organic, including symptomatic, mental disorders	F01-F09	13.6	30.5
Other degenerative diseases of the nervous system	G30-G31	13.6	26.3
Other external causes of accidental injury	W00-X59	11.4	25.1
Diabetes mellitus	E10-E14	24.1	21.3
Hypertensive diseases	I10-I15	6.5	18.8

Note: (a) ICD-10 = International Classification of Diseases 10th Revision; (1) Mortality rates are a three year average covering 2008-2010; (2) Figures cover Hidalgo County
Source: Centers for Disease Control and Prevention, National Center for Health Statistics. Compressed Mortality File 1999-2010 on CDC WONDER Online Database, released January 2013. Data are compiled from the Compressed Mortality File 1999-2010, Series 20 No. 2P, 2013.

Mortality Rates for Selected Causes of Death

ICD-10[a] Sub-Chapter	ICD-10[a] Code	Age-Adjusted Mortality Rate[1] per 100,000 population	
		County[2]	U.S.
Assault	X85-Y09	5.1	5.5
Diseases of the liver	K70-K76	19.6	12.4
Human immunodeficiency virus (HIV) disease	B20-B24	2.1	3.0
Influenza and pneumonia	J09-J18	23.1	16.4
Intentional self-harm	X60-X84	5.2	11.8
Malnutrition	E40-E46	*0.8	0.8
Obesity and other hyperalimentation	E65-E68	*0.8	1.6
Renal failure	N17-N19	16.7	13.6
Transport accidents	V01-V99	11.7	12.6
Viral hepatitis	B15-B19	1.2	2.2

Note: (a) ICD-10 = International Classification of Diseases 10th Revision; (1) Mortality rates are a three year average covering 2008-2010; (2) Figures cover Hidalgo County; (*) Unreliable data as per CDC
Source: Centers for Disease Control and Prevention, National Center for Health Statistics. Compressed Mortality File 1999-2010 on CDC WONDER Online Database, released January 2013. Data are compiled from the Compressed Mortality File 1999-2010, Series 20 No. 2P, 2013.

Health Insurance Coverage

Area	With Health Insurance	With Private Health Insurance	With Public Health Insurance	Without Health Insurance	Population Under Age 18 Without Health Insurance
City	64.4	40.0	29.0	35.6	19.4
MSA[1]	63.5	30.4	37.6	36.5	16.6
U.S.	84.9	65.4	30.4	15.1	7.5

Note: Figures are percentages that cover the civilian noninstitutionalized population; (1) Figures cover the McAllen-Edinburg-Mission, TX Metropolitan Statistical Area—see Appendix B for areas included
Source: U.S. Census Bureau, 2010-2012 American Community Survey 3-Year Estimates

Number of Medical Professionals

Area[1]	MDs[2]	DOs[2,3]	Dentists	Podiatrists	Chiropractors	Optometrists
Local (number)	852	21	190	10	70	50
Local (rate[4])	107.2	2.6	23.6	1.2	8.7	6.2
U.S. (rate[4])	267.6	19.6	61.7	5.6	24.7	14.5

Note: Data as of 2012 unless noted; (1) Local data covers Hidalgo County; (2) Data as of 2011; (3) Doctor of Osteopathic Medicine; (4) rate per 100,000 population
Source: Area Resource File (ARF) 2012-2013. U.S. Department of Health and Human Services, Health Resources and Services Administration, Bureau of Health Professions

EDUCATION

Public School District Statistics

District Name	Schls	Pupils	Pupil/ Teacher Ratio	Minority Pupils[1] (%)	Free Lunch Eligible[2] (%)	IEP[3] (%)
Mcallen ISD	34	25,252	16.0	95.0	n/a	7.6

Note: Table includes school districts with 2,000 or more students; (1) Percentage of students that are not non-Hispanic white; (2) Percentage of students that are eligible for the free lunch program; (3) Percentage of students that have an Individualized Education Program.
Source: U.S. Department of Education, National Center for Education Statistics, Common Core of Data, Local Education Agency (School District) Universe Survey: School Year 2011-2012; U.S. Department of Education, National Center for Education Statistics, Common Core of Data, Public Elementary/Secondary School Universe Survey: School Year 2011-2012

Best High Schools

High School Name	Rank[1]	Grad. Rate[2] (%)	Coll.[3] (%)	AP/IB/ AICE Tests[4]	AP/IB/ AICE Score[5]	SAT Score[6]	ACT Score[6]
James Nikki Rowe H.S.	1856	78	91	0.3	2.0	1393	19.0
McAllen H.S.	1955	80	79	0.3	2.1	1381	18.7
Memorial H.S.	1898	81	79	0.3	1.9	1466	19.5

Note: (1) Public schools are ranked from 1 to 2,000 based on the following self-reported statistics (with the corresponding weight used in calculating their overall score). Schools that were newly founded and did not have a graduating senior class in 2012 were excluded; (2) Four-year, on-time graduation rate (25%); (3) Percent of 2011 graduates who were accepted to college (25%); (4) AP/IB/AICE tests taken per student (25%); (5) Average AP/IB/AICE exam score (10%); (6) Average SAT and/or ACT score (10%); Percent of students enrolled in at least one AP/IB/AICE course (5%)—data not shown
Source: Newsweek and The Daily Beast, "America's Best High Schools 2013"

Highest Level of Education

Area	Less than H.S.	H.S. Diploma	Some College, No Deg.	Associate Degree	Bachelor's Degree	Master's Degree	Prof. School Degree	Doctorate Degree
City	26.1	20.4	21.5	5.3	18.7	4.9	2.4	0.6
MSA[1]	37.7	24.2	17.6	4.4	11.2	3.4	1.0	0.5
U.S.	14.1	28.3	21.3	7.8	18.0	7.5	1.9	1.2

Note: Figures cover persons age 25 and over; (1) Figures cover the McAllen-Edinburg-Mission, TX Metropolitan Statistical Area—see Appendix B for areas included
Source: U.S. Census Bureau, 2010-2012 American Community Survey 3-Year Estimates

Educational Attainment by Race

Area	High School Graduate or Higher (%)					Bachelor's Degree or Higher (%)				
	Total	White	Black	Asian	Hisp.[2]	Total	White	Black	Asian	Hisp.[2]
City	73.9	74.3	91.8	97.5	69.4	26.7	26.3	35.5	69.0	22.4
MSA[1]	62.3	62.9	78.1	93.7	58.3	16.1	16.0	25.2	66.5	13.5
U.S.	85.9	88.1	82.5	85.5	63.1	28.6	30.0	18.4	50.2	13.4

Note: Figures shown cover persons 25 years old and over; (1) Figures cover the McAllen-Edinburg-Mission, TX Metropolitan Statistical Area—see Appendix B for areas included; (2) People of Hispanic origin can be of any race
Source: U.S. Census Bureau, 2010-2012 American Community Survey 3-Year Estimates

School Enrollment by Grade and Control

Area	Preschool (%)		Kindergarten (%)		Grades 1 - 4 (%)		Grades 5 - 8 (%)		Grades 9 - 12 (%)	
	Public	Private	Public	Private	Public	Private	Public	Private	Public	Private
City	74.5	25.5	90.7	9.3	95.6	4.4	93.2	6.8	94.5	5.5
MSA[1]	89.3	10.7	96.7	3.3	97.6	2.4	97.4	2.6	97.1	2.9
U.S.	56.9	43.1	87.8	12.2	89.9	10.1	90.0	10.0	90.8	9.2

Note: Figures shown cover persons 3 years old and over; (1) Figures cover the McAllen-Edinburg-Mission, TX Metropolitan Statistical Area—see Appendix B for areas included
Source: U.S. Census Bureau, 2010-2012 American Community Survey 3-Year Estimates

Average Salaries of Public School Classroom Teachers

Area	2012-13		2013-14		Percent Change 2012-13 to 2013-14	Percent Change 2003-04 to 2013-14
	Dollars	Rank[1]	Dollars	Rank[1]		
Texas	48,819	35	49,270	35	0.92	21.7
U.S. Average	56,103	–	56,689	–	1.04	21.8

Note: (1) State rank ranges from 1 to 51 where 1 indicates highest salary.
Source: National Education Association, Rankings & Estimates: Rankings of the States 2013 and Estimates of School Statistics 2014, March 2014

Higher Education

Four-Year Colleges			Two-Year Colleges			Medical Schools[1]	Law Schools[2]	Voc/ Tech[3]
Public	Private Non-profit	Private For-profit	Public	Private Non-profit	Private For-profit			
1	0	0	0	0	1	0	0	3

Note: Figures cover institutions located within the city limits and include main campuses only; (1) includes schools accredited by the Liaison Committee on Medical Education and the American Osteopathic Association's Commission on Osteopathic College Accreditation; (2) includes ABA-accredited schools, schools with provisional ABA accreditation, and state accredited schools; (3) includes all schools with programs that are less than 2 years.
Source: National Center for Education Statistics, Integrated Postsecondary Education System (IPEDS), 2012-13; Association of American Medical Colleges, Member List, April 24, 2014; American Osteopathic Association, Member List, April 24, 2014; Law School Admission Council, Official Guide to ABA-Approved Law Schools Online, April 24, 2014; Wikipedia, List of Medical Schools in the United States, April 24, 2014; Wikipedia, List of Law Schools in the United States, April 24, 2014

PRESIDENTIAL ELECTION

2012 Presidential Election Results

Area	Obama	Romney	Other
Hidalgo County	70.4	28.6	1.0
U.S.	51.0	47.2	1.8

Note: Results are percentages and may not add to 100% due to rounding
Source: Dave Leip's Atlas of U.S. Presidential Elections

EMPLOYERS

Major Employers

Company Name	Industry
Am-Mex Products	Motor vehicle parts and accessories
City of McAllen	City and town managers' office
County of Hidalgo	Executive offices
Donna Independent School District	Public elementary school
Edcouch-Elsa Independent School District	Public elementary and secondary schools
Edinburg Consol. Ind. School District	Public elementary and secondary schools
Knapp Medical Center	Business services at non-commercial site
La Joya Independent School District	Public elementary and secondary schools
McAllen Independent School District	Public elementary school
McAllen Medical Center	General medical and surgical hospitals
Mercedes Independent School District	Public senior high school
Mid Valley Health System	Investment holding companies, except banks
Mission Consolidated Ind. School District	Public elementary school
Panasonic Industrial Devices Corporation	Audio electronic systems
Pharr-San Juan-Alamo Ind. School District	Public elementary and secondary schools
Sharyland Isb	Public elementary and secondary schools
South Texas College	Junior colleges
Tex-Best Travel Centers	Fast-food restaurant, chain
Texas Regional Delaware Inc.	State commercial banks
TST NA Trim	Personal service agents, brokers, and bureaus
University of Texas - Pan American	College, except junior
Weslaco Independent School District	Public elementary school
Woodcrafters Home Products Holding	Vanities, bathroom: wood

Note: Companies shown are located within the McAllen-Edinburg-Mission, TX Metropolitan Statistical Area.
Source: Hoovers.com; Wikipedia

PUBLIC SAFETY

Crime Rate

Area	All Crimes	Violent Crimes				Property Crimes		
		Murder	Forcible Rape	Robbery	Aggrav. Assault	Burglary	Larceny-Theft	Motor Vehicle Theft
City	4,148.2	0.7	2.2	41.3	78.1	370.5	3,499.9	155.4
Suburbs[1]	4,075.7	4.3	29.5	62.0	263.1	884.6	2,652.8	179.5
Metro[2]	4,087.9	3.7	24.9	58.5	232.0	798.4	2,794.8	175.5
U.S.	3,246.1	4.7	26.9	112.9	242.3	670.2	1,959.3	229.7

Note: Figures are crimes per 100,000 population; (1) All areas within the metro area that are located outside the city limits; (2) Figures cover the McAllen-Edinburg-Mission, TX Metropolitan Statistical Area—see Appendix B for areas included
Source: FBI Uniform Crime Reports, 2012

Hate Crimes

Area	Number of Quarters Reported	Bias Motivation				
		Race	Religion	Sexual Orientation	Ethnicity	Disability
City	4	0	0	0	0	0
U.S.	4	2,797	1,099	1,135	667	92

Source: Federal Bureau of Investigation, Hate Crime Statistics 2012

Identity Theft Consumer Complaints

Area	Complaints	Complaints per 100,000 Population	Rank[2]
MSA[1]	663	85.6	81
U.S.	290,056	91.8	

Note: (1) Figures cover the McAllen-Edinburg-Mission, TX Metropolitan Statistical Area—see Appendix B for areas included; (2) Rank ranges from 1 to 377 where 1 indicates greatest number of identity theft complaints per 100,000 population
Source: Federal Trade Commission, Consumer Sentinel Network Data Book for January–December 2013

Fraud and Other Consumer Complaints

Area	Complaints	Complaints per 100,000 Population	Rank[2]
MSA[1]	1,138	146.9	376
U.S.	1,811,724	595.2	-

Note: (1) Figures cover the McAllen-Edinburg-Mission, TX Metropolitan Statistical Area—see Appendix B for areas included; (2) Rank ranges from 1 to 377 where 1 indicates greatest number of identity theft complaints per 100,000 population
Source: Federal Trade Commission, Consumer Sentinel Network Data Book for January–December 2013

RECREATION

Culture

Dance[1]	Theatre[1]	Instrumental Music[1]	Vocal Music[1]	Series and Festivals	Museums and Art Galleries[2]	Zoos and Aquariums[3]
1	0	0	0	2	1	0

Note: (1) Number of professional perfoming groups; (2) Based on organizations with primary SIC code 8412; (3) AZA-accredited
Source: The Grey House Performing Arts Directory, 2013; Association of Zoos & Aquariums, AZA Member Zoos & Aquariums, April 2014; www.AccuLeads.com, May 1, 2014

Professional Sports Teams

Team Name	League	Year Established
No teams are located in the metro area		

Source: Wikipedia, Major Professional Sports Teams of the United States and Canada, April 25, 2014

CLIMATE

Average and Extreme Temperatures

Temperature	Jan	Feb	Mar	Apr	May	Jun	Jul	Aug	Sep	Oct	Nov	Dec	Yr.
Extreme High (°F)	93	94	106	102	102	102	101	102	99	96	97	94	106
Average High (°F)	70	73	78	83	87	91	93	93	90	85	78	72	83
Average Temp. (°F)	60	63	69	75	80	83	84	85	82	76	68	63	74
Average Low (°F)	51	53	59	66	72	75	76	76	73	66	59	53	65
Extreme Low (°F)	19	22	32	38	52	60	67	63	56	40	33	16	16

Note: Figures cover the years 1948-1990
Source: National Climatic Data Center, International Station Meteorological Climate Summary, 9/96

Average Precipitation/Snowfall/Humidity

Precip./Humidity	Jan	Feb	Mar	Apr	May	Jun	Jul	Aug	Sep	Oct	Nov	Dec	Yr.
Avg. Precip. (in.)	1.4	1.4	0.6	1.5	2.5	2.8	1.8	2.6	5.6	3.2	1.5	1.1	25.8
Avg. Snowfall (in.)	Tr	Tr	0	0	0	0	0	0	0	0	Tr	Tr	Tr
Avg. Rel. Hum. 6am (%)	88	89	88	89	90	91	92	92	91	89	87	87	89
Avg. Rel. Hum. 3pm (%)	62	60	57	58	60	59	54	55	60	58	59	61	59

Note: Figures cover the years 1948-1990; Tr = Trace amounts (<0.05 in. of rain; <0.5 in. of snow)
Source: National Climatic Data Center, International Station Meteorological Climate Summary, 9/96

Weather Conditions

	Temperature			Daytime Sky			Precipitation		
32°F & below	45°F & below	90°F & above	Clear	Partly cloudy	Cloudy	0.01 inch or more precip.	0.1 inch or more snow/ice	Thunder-storms
2	30	116	86	180	99	72	0	27

Note: Figures are average number of days per year and cover the years 1948-1990
Source: National Climatic Data Center, International Station Meteorological Climate Summary, 9/96

HAZARDOUS WASTE

Superfund Sites

McAllen has no sites on the EPA's Superfund Final National Priorities List.
U.S. Environmental Protection Agency, Final National Priorities List, April 26, 2014

AIR & WATER QUALITY

Air Quality Index

Area	Percent of Days when Air Quality was...[2]					AQI Statistics[2]	
	Good	Moderate	Unhealthy for Sensitive Groups	Unhealthy	Very Unhealthy	Maximum	Median
MSA[1]	78.4	21.4	0.3	0.0	0.0	106	36

Note: (1) Data covers the McAllen-Edinburg-Mission, TX Metropolitan Statistical Area—see Appendix B for areas included; (2) Based on 365 days with AQI data in 2013. Air Quality Index (AQI) is an index for reporting daily air quality. EPA calculates the AQI for five major air pollutants regulated by the Clean Air Act: ground-level ozone, particle pollution (aka particulate matter), carbon monoxide, sulfur dioxide, and nitrogen dioxide. The AQI runs from 0 to 500. The higher the AQI value, the greater the level of air pollution and the greater the health concern. There are six AQI categories: "Good" AQI is between 0 and 50. Air quality is considered satisfactory; "Moderate" AQI is between 51 and 100. Air quality is acceptable; "Unhealthy for Sensitive Groups" When AQI values are between 101 and 150, members of sensitive groups may experience health effects; "Unhealthy" When AQI values are between 151 and 200 everyone may begin to experience health effects; "Very Unhealthy" AQI values between 201 and 300 trigger a health alert; "Hazardous" AQI values over 300 trigger warnings of emergency conditions (not shown).
Source: U.S. Environmental Protection Agency, Air Quality Index Report, 2013

Air Quality Index Pollutants

Area	Percent of Days when AQI Pollutant was...[2]					
	Carbon Monoxide	Nitrogen Dioxide	Ozone	Sulfur Dioxide	Particulate Matter 2.5	Particulate Matter 10
MSA[1]	0.0	0.0	33.2	0.0	65.5	1.4

Note: (1) Data covers the McAllen-Edinburg-Mission, TX Metropolitan Statistical Area—see Appendix B for areas included; (2) Based on 365 days with AQI data in 2013. The Air Quality Index (AQI) is an index for reporting daily air quality. EPA calculates the AQI for five major air pollutants regulated by the Clean Air Act: ground-level ozone, particle pollution (also known as particulate matter), carbon monoxide, sulfur dioxide, and nitrogen dioxide. The AQI runs from 0 to 500. The higher the AQI value, the greater the level of air pollution and the greater the health concern.
Source: U.S. Environmental Protection Agency, Air Quality Index Report, 2013

Air Quality Trends: Ozone

	2003	2004	2005	2006	2007	2008	2009	2010	2011	2012
MSA[1]	0.073	0.070	0.069	0.060	0.055	0.058	0.060	0.065	0.062	0.061

Note: (1) Data covers the McAllen-Edinburg-Mission, TX Metropolitan Statistical Area—see Appendix B for areas included. The values shown are the composite ozone concentration averages among trend sites based on the highest fourth daily maximum 8-hour concentration in parts per million. These trends are based on sites having an adequate record of monitoring data during the trend period. Data from exceptional events are included.
Source: U.S. Environmental Protection Agency, Air Quality Monitoring Information, "Air Quality Trends by City, 2000-2012"

Maximum Air Pollutant Concentrations: Particulate Matter, Ozone, CO and Lead

	Particulate Matter 10 (ug/m^3)	Particulate Matter 2.5 Wtd AM (ug/m^3)	Particulate Matter 2.5 24-Hr (ug/m^3)	Ozone (ppm)	Carbon Monoxide (ppm)	Lead (ug/m^3)
MSA[1] Level	69	n/a	n/a	0.061	n/a	n/a
NAAQS[2]	150	15	35	0.075	9	0.15
Met NAAQS[2]	Yes	n/a	n/a	Yes	n/a	n/a

Note: (1) Data covers the McAllen-Edinburg-Mission, TX Metropolitan Statistical Area—see Appendix B for areas included; Data from exceptional events are included; (2) National Ambient Air Quality Standards; ppm = parts per million; ug/m^3 = micrograms per cubic meter; n/a not available.
Concentrations: Particulate Matter 10 (coarse particulate)—highest second maximum 24-hour concentration; Particulate Matter 2.5 Wtd AM (fine particulate)—highest weighted annual mean concentration; Particulate Matter 2.5 24-Hour (fine particulate)—highest 98th percentile 24-hour concentration; Ozone—highest fourth daily maximum 8-hour concentration; Carbon Monoxide—highest second maximum non-overlapping 8-hour concentration; Lead—maximum running 3-month average
Source: U.S. Environmental Protection Agency, Air Quality Monitoring Information, "Air Quality Statistics by City, 2012"

Maximum Air Pollutant Concentrations: Nitrogen Dioxide and Sulfur Dioxide

	Nitrogen Dioxide AM (ppb)	Nitrogen Dioxide 1-Hr (ppb)	Sulfur Dioxide AM (ppb)	Sulfur Dioxide 1-Hr (ppb)	Sulfur Dioxide 24-Hr (ppb)
MSA[1] Level	n/a	n/a	n/a	n/a	n/a
NAAQS[2]	53	100	30	75	140
Met NAAQS[2]	n/a	n/a	n/a	n/a	n/a

Note: (1) Data covers the McAllen-Edinburg-Mission, TX Metropolitan Statistical Area—see Appendix B for areas included; Data from exceptional events are included; (2) National Ambient Air Quality Standards; ppm = parts per million; ug/m^3 = micrograms per cubic meter; n/a not available.
Concentrations: Nitrogen Dioxide AM—highest arithmetic mean concentration; Nitrogen Dioxide 1-Hr—highest 98th percentile 1-hour daily maximum concentration; Sulfur Dioxide AM—highest annual mean concentration; Sulfur Dioxide 1-Hr—highest 99th percentile 1-hour daily maximum concentration; Sulfur Dioxide 24-Hr—highest second maximum 24-hour concentration
Source: U.S. Environmental Protection Agency, Air Quality Monitoring Information, "Air Quality Statistics by City, 2012"

Drinking Water

Water System Name	Pop. Served	Primary Water Source Type	Violations[1]	
			Health Based	Monitoring/ Reporting
McAllen Public Utility	157,125	Surface	0	2

Note: (1) Based on violation data from January 1, 2013 to December 31, 2013 (includes unresolved violations from earlier years)

Source: U.S. Environmental Protection Agency, Office of Ground Water and Drinking Water, Safe Drinking Water Information System (based on data extracted February 10, 2014)

Miami, Florida

Background

While the majority of Miami's residents used to be Caucasian of European descent, the rapidly growing city now consists of a majority of Latinos. The number of Cubans, Puerto Ricans, and Haitians give the city a flavorful mix with a Latin American and Caribbean accent. The City of Miami has three official languages: English, Spanish, and Haitian Creole.

Thanks to early pioneer Julia Tuttle, railroad magnate Henry Flagler extended the East Coast Railroad beyond Palm Beach. Within 15 years of that decision, Miami became known as the "Gold Coast." The land boom of the 1920s brought wealthy socialites, as well as African-Americans in search of work. Pink- and aquamarine-hued art deco hotels were squeezed onto a tiny tract of land called Miami Beach, and the population of the Miami metro area swelled.

Given Miami's origins in a tourist-oriented economy, many of the activities in which residents engage are "leisurely," including swimming, scuba diving, golf, tennis, and boating. For those who enjoy professional sports, the city is host to the following teams: the Miami Dolphins, football; the Florida Marlins, baseball; the Miami Heat, basketball; and the Florida Panthers, hockey. Cultural activities range from the Miami City Ballet and the Coconut Grove Playhouse to numerous art galleries and museums, including the Bass Museum of Art. Visits to the Villa Vizcaya, a gorgeous palazzo built by industrialist James Deering in the Italian Renaissance style, and to the Miami MetroZoo are popular pastimes.

Miami's prime location on Biscayne Bay in the southeastern United States makes it a perfect nexus for travel and trade. The Port of Miami is a bustling center for many cruise and cargo ships. The Port is also a base for the National Oceanic and Atmospheric Administration. The Miami International Airport is a busy destination point to and from many Latin-American and Caribbean countries.

Miami is still at the trading crossroads of the Western Hemisphere as the chief shipment point for exports and imports with Latin America and the Caribbean. One out of every three North American cruise passengers sails from Miami. Miami was also the host city of the 2003 Free Trade Area of the Americas negotiations, and is one of the leading candidates to become the trading bloc's headquarters.

The sultry, subtropical climate against a backdrop of Spanish, art deco, and modern architecture makes Miami a uniquely cosmopolitan city. The Art Deco Historic District, known as South Beach and located on the tip of Miami Beach, has an international reputation in the fashion, film, and music industries. Greater Miami is now a national center for film, television, and print production.

In recent years Miami has witnessed its largest real estate boom since the 1920s, especially in the newly created midtown, north of downtown and south of the Design District. Nearly 25,000 new residential units have been added to the downtown skyline since 2005.

Long, warm summers are typical, as are mild, dry winters. The marine influence is evidenced by the narrow daily range of temperature and the rapid warming of cold air masses. During the summer months, rainfall occurs in early morning near the ocean and in early afternoon further inland. Hurricanes occasionally affect the Miami area, usually in September and October, while destructive tornadoes are quite rare. Funnel clouds are occasionally sighted and a few touch the ground briefly, but significant destruction is unusual. Waterspouts are visible from the beaches during the summer months but seldom cause any damage. During June, July, and August, there are numerous beautiful, but dangerous, lightning events.

Rankings

General Rankings

- Among the 50 largest U.S. cities, Miami placed #22 in Vocativ's "semi-exhaustive, mostly scientific" city Livability Index for people aged 35 and under. Average salary, unemployment rates, rents, and other living costs were considered, along with bike lanes, low-cost broadband, cheap takeout, self-service laundries, the price of a pint of Guinness, music venues, and vintage clothing stores. *vocative.com, "The Livability Index: The Best U.S. Cities for People 35 and Under," November 7, 2013*

- Miami was selected as one of "America's Favorite Cities." The city ranked #30 in the "Quality of Life and Visitor Experience: Cleanliness" category. Respondents to an online survey were asked to rate 35 top urban destinations in the U.S. from a visitor's perspective. Criteria: cleanliness. *Travel + Leisure, "America's Favorite Cities 2013"*

- Miami was selected as one of "America's Favorite Cities." The city ranked #5 in the "Type of Trip: Gay-friendly" category. Respondents to an online survey were asked to rate 35 top urban destinations in the U.S. from a visitor's perspective. Criteria: gay-friendly. *Travel + Leisure, "America's Favorite Cities 2013"*

Business/Finance Rankings

- Recognizing the sizeable percentage of American workers who are self-employed, NerdWallet editors assessed the country's cities according to percentage of freelancers, median rental costs, and affordability of median healthcare costs. By these criteria, Miami placed #3 among the best cities for independent workers. *www.nerdwallet.com, "Best Cities for Freelancers," February 25, 2014*

- In order to help veterans transition from the military to civilian life, USAA and Hiring Our Heroes worked with Sperlings's BestPlaces to develop a list of the major metropolitan areas where military-skills-related employment is strongest. Criteria included job prospects, unemployment, number of government jobs, recent job growth, accessible health resources, and colleges and universities. Metro areas with a violent crime rate or high cost of living were excluded. At #10, the Miami metro area made the top ten. *www.usaa.com, "2013 Best Places for Veterans: Jobs," November 2013*

- Building on the U.S. Department of Labor's Occupational Information Network Data Collection Program, the Brookings Institution defined STEM occupations and job opportunities for STEM workers at various levels of educational attainment. The Miami metro area was placed among the ten large metro areas with the lowest demand for high-level STEM knowledge. *www.brookings.edu, "The Hidden Stem Economy," June 10, 2013*

- To identify the metro areas with the largest gap in income between rich and poor residents, the 24/7 Wall Street research team used the U.S. Census Bureau's 2012 American Community Survey, an index of income disparity, additional income, poverty, and home-value data. The Miami metro area placed #8 among metro areas with the widest wealth gap between rich and poor. *247wallst.com, "Cities with the Widest Gap between Rich and Poor," November 4, 2013*

- Based on a minimum of 500 social media reviews per metro area, the employment opinion group Glassdoor surveyed 50 of the largest U.S. metro areas on measures including compensation and benefits, satisfaction with management, business outlook, and number of employers hiring. The Miami metro area was ranked #38 in overall employee satisfaction. *www.glassdoor.com, "Employment Satisfaction Report Card by City," June 21, 2013*

- The Brookings Institution ranked the 50 largest cities in the U.S. based on income inequality. Miami was ranked #3. (#1 = greatest ineqality). Criteria: the cities were ranked based on the "95/20 ratio." This figure represents the income at which a household earns more than 95 percent of all other households, divided by the income at which a household earns more than only 20 percent of all other households. *Brookings Institution, "Income Inequality in America's 50 Largest Cities, 2007-2012," February 20, 2014*

- Miami was ranked #26 out of 100 metro areas in terms of economic performance (#1 = best) during the recession and recovery from trough quarter through the second quarter of 2013. Criteria: percent change in employment; percentage point change in unemployment rate; percent change in gross metropolitan product; percent change in House Price Index. *Brookings Institution, MetroMonitor: Tracking Economic Recession and Recovery in America's 100 Largest Metropolitan Areas, September 2013*

- The Miami metro area was identified as one of 10 best-paying cities for women. The metro area ranked #9. Criteria: *24/7 Wall St.* identified the metropolitan areas that have the smallest pay disparity between men and women by comparing the median earnings for the past 12 months of both men and women working full-time in the country's 100 largest metropolitan statistical areas. *24/7 Wall St., "10 Best-Paying Cities for Women," April 14, 2013*

- Payscale.com ranked the 20 largest metro areas in terms of wage growth. The Miami metro area ranked #12. Criteria: private-sector wage growth between the 4th quarter of 2012 and the 4th quarter of 2013. *PayScale, "Wage Trends by Metro Area," 4th Quarter, 2013*

- The Miami metro area was identified as one of the most debt-ridden places in America by credit reporting agency Equifax. The metro area was ranked #4. Criteria: proportion of average yearly income owed to credit card companies. *Equifax, "The Most Debt-Ridden Cities in America," February 23, 2012*

- Miami was identified as one of the top 25 U.S. cities with the most credit card debt by credit reporting bureau Experian. The city was ranked #23. *Experian, March 4, 2011*

- Miami was identified as one of the unhappiest cities to work in by CareerBliss.com, an online community for career advancement. The city ranked #9 out of 10. Criteria: independent company reviews from employees all over the country on: relationship with their boss and co-workers; work environment; job resources; compensation; growth opportunities; company culture; company reputation; daily tasks; job control over work performed on a daily basis. *CareerBliss.com, "Top 10 Happiest and Unhappiest Cities to Work in 2014," February 10, 2014*

- The Miami metro area appeared on the Milken Institute "2013 Best Performing Cities" list. Rank: #144 out of 200 large metro areas. Criteria: job growth; wage and salary growth; high-tech output growth. *Milken Institute, "Best-Performing Cities 2013," December 2013*

- *Forbes* ranked the 200 most populous metro areas in the U.S. in terms of the "Best Places for Business and Careers." The Miami metro area was ranked #165. Criteria: costs (business and living); job growth (past and projected); income growth; educational attainment (college and high school); projected economic growth; cultural and recreational opportunities; net migration patterns; number of highly ranked colleges. *Forbes, "The Best Places for Business and Careers," August 7, 2013*

Children/Family Rankings

- Miami was selected as one of the best cities for families to live by *Parenting* magazine. The city ranked #50 out of 100. Criteria: education; health; community; *Parenting's* Culture & Charm Index. *Parenting.com, "The 2012 Best Cities for Families List"*

Culture/Performing Arts Rankings

- Miami was selected as one of "America's Favorite Cities." The city ranked #33 in the "Culture: Museum/Galleries" category. Respondents to an online survey were asked to rate 35 top urban destinations in the U.S. from a visitor's perspective. Criteria: number and quality of museums and galleries. *Travelandleisure.com, "America's Favorite Cities 2013"*

- Miami was selected as one of America's top cities for the arts. The city ranked #7 in the mid-sized city (population 100,000 to 499,999) category. Criteria: readers' top choices for arts travel destinations based on the richness and variety of visual arts sites, activities and events. *American Style, "2012 Top 25 Arts Destinations," June 2012*

Dating/Romance Rankings

- Gizmodo reported on data that Facebook collected on the best American cities for singles. Criteria included highest percentage of single people, the widest single female-to-single male ratio (and vice versa), and the best probability of relationship formation. Among the top 50 American population centers Miami ranked #4. *gizmodo.com, "The Best Places to Find Hot Singles (According to Facebook)," February 13, 2014*

- Miami took the #7 spot on NerdWallet's list of best cities for singles wanting to date, based on the availability of singles; "date-friendliness," as determined by a city's walkability and the number of bars and restaurants per thousand residents; and the affordability of dating in terms of the cost of movie tickets, pizza, and wine for two. *www.nerdwallet.com, "Best Cities for Singles," February 5, 2014*

- Of the 100 U.S. cities surveyed by *Men's Health* in its quest to identify the nation's best cities for dating and forming relationships, Miami was ranked #7 for online dating (#1 = best). *Men's Health, "The Best and Worst Cities for Online Dating," January 30, 2013*

- Miami was selected as one of America's best cities for singles by the readers of *Travel + Leisure* in their annual "America's Favorite Cities" survey. The city was ranked #4 out of 20. *Travel + Leisure, "America's Best Cities for Singles," July 2012*

- Miami was selected as one of the most romantic cities in America by Amazon.com. The city ranked #4 of 20. Criteria: cities with 100,000 or more residents were ranked on their per capita sales of romance novels and relationship books, romantic comedy movies, romantic music, and sexual wellness products. *Amazon.com, "Top 20 Most Romantic Cities in America," February 3, 2014*

- Miami was selected as one of "America's Best Cities for Dating" by *Yahoo! Travel*. Criteria: high proportion of singles; excellent dating venues and/or stunning natural settings. *Yahoo! Travel, "America's Best Cities for Dating," February 7, 2012*

Education Rankings

- *Men's Health* ranked 100 U.S. cities in terms of their education levels. Miami was ranked #100 (#1 = most educated city). Criteria: high school graduation rates; school enrollment; educational attainment; number of households who have outstanding student loans; number of households whose members have taken adult-education courses. *Men's Health, "Where School Is In: The Most and Least Educated Cities," September 12, 2011*

- Miami was selected as one of the most well-read cities in America by Amazon.com. The city ranked #3 of 20. Cities with populations greater than 100,000 were evaluated based on per capita sales of books, magazines and newspapers. *Amazon.com, "The 20 Most Well-Read Cities in America," April 28, 2013*

- Miami was selected as one of America's most literate cities. The city ranked #31 out of the 77 largest U.S. cities. Criteria: number of booksellers; library resources; Internet resources; educational attainment; periodical publishing resources; newspaper circulation. *Central Connecticut State University, "America's Most Literate Cities, 2013"*

Environmental Rankings

- The Miami metro area came in at #342 for the relative comfort of its climate on Sperling's list of "chill cities," as measured by the Sperling Heat Index. All 361 metro areas are included. Criteria included daytime high temperatures, nighttime low temperatures, dew point, and relative humidity at the high temperatures. *www.bertsperling.com, "Sperling's Chill Cities," July 18, 2013*

- Sperling's BestPlaces assessed 379 metropolitan areas of the United States for the likelihood of dangerously extreme weather events or earthquakes. In general the Southeast and South-Central regions have the highest risk of weather extremes and earthquakes, while the Pacific Northwest enjoys the lowest risk. Of the least risky metropolitan areas, the Miami metro area was ranked #313. *www.bestplaces.net, "Safest Places from Natural Disasters," April 2011*

- Miami was identified as one of North America's greenest metropolitan areas. The area ranked #22. The Green City Index is comprised of 31 indicators, and scores cities across nine categories: carbon dioxide; energy; land use; buildings; transport; water; waste; air quality; environmental governance. The 27 largest metropolitan areas in the U.S. and Canada were considered. *Economist Intelligence Unit, sponsored by Siemens, "U.S. and Canada Green City Index, 2011"*

- The U.S. Environmental Protection Agency (EPA) released a list of U.S. metropolitan areas with the most ENERGY STAR certified buildings in 2012. The Miami metro area was ranked #18 out of 25. *U.S. Environmental Protection Agency, "Top Cities With the Most ENERGY STAR Certified Buildings in 2012," March 12, 2013*

- Miami was selected as one of 22 "Smarter Cities" for energy by the Natural Resources Defense Council. Criteria: investment in green power; energy efficiency measures; conservation. *Natural Resources Defense Council, "2010 Smarter Cities," July 19, 2010*

- Miami was selected as one of the five worst summer weather cities in the U.S. by the *Farmers' Almanac.* The city ranked #1. Criteria: average summer and winter temperatures; humidity; precipitation; number of overcast days. The editors only considered cities with populations of 50,000 or more. *Farmers' Almanac, "America's Ten Worst Weather Cities," September 7, 2010*

- Miami was highlighted as one of the top 25 cleanest metro areas for year-round particle pollution (Annual PM 2.5) in the U.S. during 2008 through 2010. The area ranked #25. *American Lung Association, State of the Air 2012*

Food/Drink Rankings

- *Men's Health* ranked 100 major U.S. cities in terms of alcohol intoxication. Miami ranked #6 (#1 = most sober).Criteria: binge drinking; alcohol-related traffic accidents, arrests, and fatalities. *Men's Health, "The Drunkest Cities in America," November 19, 2013*

- Miami was identified as one of "America's Most Caffeinated Cities" by *Bundle.com.* The city was ranked #9 out of 10. The rankings were determined by examining consumer spending at 16 widely known coffee chains during the second quarter of 2011. *Bundle.com, "America's Most Caffeinated Cities," September 19, 2011*

Health/Fitness Rankings

- Analysts who tracked obesity rates in the nation's largest metro areas (those with populations above one million) found that the Miami metro area was one of the ten major metros where residents were least likely to be obese, defined as a BMI score of 30 or above. *www.gallup.com, "Boulder, Colo., Residents Still Least Likely to Be Obese," April 4, 2014*

- For each of the 50 most populous metro areas in the United States, the American College of Sports Medicine's American Fitness Index evaluated infrastructure, community assets, and policies that encourage healthy and fit lifestyles, including preventive health behaviors, levels of chronic disease conditions, health care access, and community resources and policies that support physical activity. The Miami metro area ranked #42 for "community fitness." Personal health indicators were considered as well as community and environmental indicators. *www.americanfitnessindex.org, "ACSM American Fitness Index Health and Community Fitness Status of the 50 Largest Metropolitan Areas," May 2013*

- Miami was identified as one of the 10 most walkable cities in the U.S. by Walk Score, a Seattle-based service that rates the convenience and transit access of 10,000 neighborhoods in 3,000 cities. The area ranked #5 out of the 50 largest U.S. cities. Walk Score measures walkability by analyzing hundreds of walking routes to nearby amenities. Walk Score also measures pedestrian friendliness by analyzing population density and road metrics such as block length and intersection density. *WalkScore.com, March 20, 2014*

- The Miami metro area was identified as one of the worst cities for bed bugs in America by pest control company Orkin. The area ranked #22 out of 50 based on the number of bed bug treatments Orkin performed from January to December 2013. *Orkin, "Chicago Tops Bed Bug Cities List for Second Year in a Row," January 16, 2014*

- Miami was selected as one of the 25 fattest cities in America by *Men's Fitness Online*. It ranked #12 out of America's 50 largest cities. Criteria: fitness centers and sport stores; nutrition; sports participation; TV viewing; overweight/sedentary; junk food; air quality; geography; commute; parks and open space; city recreational facilities; access to healthcare; motivation; mayor and city initiatives; state obesity initiatives. *Men's Fitness, "The Fittest and Fattest Cities in America," March 5, 2012*

- Miami was identified as a "2013 Spring Allergy Capital." The area ranked #71 out of 100. Three groups of factors were used to identify the most severe cities for people with allergies during the spring season: annual pollen levels; medicine utilization; access to board-certified allergists. *Asthma and Allergy Foundation of America, "Spring Allergy Capitals 2013"*

- Miami was identified as a "2013 Fall Allergy Capital." The area ranked #67 out of 100. Three groups of factors were used to identify the most severe cities for people with allergies during the fall season: annual pollen levels; medicine utilization; access to board-certified allergists. *Asthma and Allergy Foundation of America, "Fall Allergy Capitals 2013"*

- Miami was identified as a "2013 Asthma Capital." The area ranked #64 out of the nation's 100 largest metropolitan areas. Twelve factors were used to identify the most challenging places to live for people with asthma: estimated prevalence; self-reported prevalence; crude death rate for asthma; annual pollen score; annual air quality; public smoking laws; number of board-certified asthma specialists; school inhaler access laws; rescue medication use; controller medication use; uninsured rate; poverty rate. *Asthma and Allergy Foundation of America, "Asthma Capitals 2013"*

- *Men's Health* ranked 100 major U.S. cities in terms of the best and worst cities for men. Miami ranked #68. Criteria: thirty-three data points were examined covering health, fitness, and quality of life. *Men's Health, "The Best & Worst Cities for Men 2014," December 6, 2013*

- Miami was selected as one of the best metropolitan areas for hospital care in America by *HealthGrades.com*. The rankings are based on a comprehensive study of patient death and complication rates in the nation's nearly 5,000 hospitals. Hospitals performing in the top 5% nationwide across 26 different medical procedures and diagnoses were identified. *HealthGrades.com* then ranked cities by the highest percentage of these Distinguished Hospitals for Clinical Excellence™. The Miami metro area ranked #16. *HealthGrades.com, "America's Top 50 Cities for Hospital Care," January 21, 2012*

- The American Academy of Dermatology ranked 26 U.S. metropolitan regions in terms of their residents knowledge, attitude and behaviors towards tanning, sun protection and skin cancer detection. The Miami metro area ranked #13. The results of the study are based on an online survey of over 7,000 adults nationwide. *American Academy of Dermatology, "Suntelligence: How Sun Smart is Your City?," May 3, 2010*

- The Miami metro area appeared in the 2013 Gallup-Healthways Well-Being Index. The area ranked #124 out of 189. The Gallup-Healthways Well-Being Index score is an average of six sub-indexes, which individually examine life evaluation, emotional health, work environment, physical health, healthy behaviors, and access to basic necessities. Results are based on telephone interviews conducted as part of the Gallup-Healthways Well-Being Index survey January 2–December 29, 2012, and January 2–December 30, 2013, with a random sample of 531,630 adults, aged 18 and older, living in metropolitan areas in the 50 U.S. states and the District of Columbia. *Gallup-Healthways, "State of American Well-Being," March 25, 2014*

- The Miami metro area was identified as one of "America's Most Stressful Cities" by *Sperling's BestPlaces*. The metro area ranked #3 out of 50. Criteria: unemployment rate; suicide rate; commute time; mental health; poor rest; alcohol use; violent crime rate; property crime rate; cloudy days annually. *Sperling's BestPlaces, www.BestPlaces.net, "Stressful Cities 2012*

- The Miami metro area was identified as one of "America's Most Stressful Cities" by *Forbes*. The metro area ranked #13 out of 40. Criteria: housing affordability; unemployment rate; cost of living; air quality; traffic congestion; sunny days; population density. *Forbes.com, "America's Most Stressful Cities," September 23, 2011*

- *Men's Health* ranked 100 U.S. cities in terms of their activity levels. Miami was ranked #12 (#1 = most active city). Criteria: where and how often residents exercise; percentage of households that watch more than 15 hours of cable television a week and buy more than 11 video games a year; death rate from deep-vein thrombosis, a condition linked to sitting for extended periods of time. *Men's Health, "Where Sit Happens: The Most and Least Active Cities in America," June 20, 2011*

- Miami was selected as one of the "20 Most Livable U.S. Cities for Wheelchair Users" by the Christopher & Dana Reeve Foundation. The city ranked #11. Criteria: Medicaid eligibility and spending; access to physicians and rehabilitation facilities; access to fitness facilities and recreation; access to paratransit; percentage of people living with disabilities who are employed; clean air; climate. *Christopher & Dana Reeve Foundation, "20 Most Livable U.S. Cities for Wheelchair Users," July 26, 2010*

Pet Rankings

- Miami was selected as one of the best cities for dogs by real estate website Estately.com. The city was ranked #14. Criteria: weather; walkability; yard sizes; dog activities; meetup groups; availability of dogsitters. *Estately.com, "17 Best U.S. Cities for Dogs," May 14, 2013*

Real Estate Rankings

- ApartmentList.com calculated the most expensive American cities for renters, comparing median rental prices for studios, one-bedroom units, and two-bedroom units in the nation's 50 most populated cities. Miami placed #8 in the ApartmentList.com ranking. *www.cbsnews.com, "Top 10 Priciest U.S. Cities to Rent an Apartment," July 15, 2013*

- The Miami metro area was identified as #5 among the ten housing markets with the highest percentage of distressed property sales, based on the findings of the housing data website RealtyTrac. Criteria included being sold "short"—for less than the outstanding mortgage balance—or in a foreclosure auction, income and poverty figures, and unemployment data. *247wallst.com, "Cities Selling the Most Distressed Homes," January 23, 2014*

- *U.S. News & World Report* reported TruliaTrends' ranking of the nation's 100 largest metropolitan areas by the strength of their housing markets. Criteria included: sluggish job growth; foreclosure rates; and for-sale housing inventories. The Miami metro area ranked #2 (1 = worst). *U.S. News & World Report, "Struggling Housing Markets Going into 2013," December 20, 2012*

- TheStreet.com ranked the housing market in the nation's five warmest cities. Miami ranked #1. Criteria: mean daily temperature from December to February (1981–2010); the median asking price of homes; and housing supply. *TheStreet.com, "Warm Weather Cities with Blistering-Hot Housing Markets," March 11, 2013*

- Miami was identified as one of the priciest cities to rent in the U.S. The area ranked #4 out of 10. Criteria: rent-to-income ratio. *CNBC, "Priciest Cities to Rent," March 14, 2012*

- Miami was identified as one of the "Top Turnaround Housing Markets for 2012." The area ranked #1 out of 10. Criteria: year-over-year median home price appreciation; year-over-year median inventory age; year-over-year inventory reduction. *AOL Real Estate, "Top Turnaround Housing Markets for 2012," February 4, 2012*

- Miami was ranked #40 out of 283 metro areas in terms of house price appreciation in 2013 (#1 = highest rate). *Federal Housing Finance Agency, House Price Index, 4th Quarter 2013*

- Miami was selected as one of the eight best cities in the U.S. for real estate investment. The city ranked #8. *Association of Foreign Investors in Real Estate, "Ranking of USA Cities for Real Estate Investment, 2013"*

- The Miami metro area was identified as one of the 15 worst housing markets for the next five years." Criteria: projected annualized change in home prices between the fourth quarter 2012 and the fourth quarter 2017. *The Business Insider, "The 15 Worst Housing Markets for the Next Five Years," May 22, 2013*

- The Miami metro area was identified as one of the 20 best housing markets in the U.S. in 2013. The area ranked #13 out of 173 markets with a home price appreciation of 19.7%. Criteria: year-over-year change of median sales price of existing single-family homes between the 4th quarter of 2012 and the 4th quarter of 2013. *National Association of Realtors®, Median Sales Price of Existing Single-Family Homes for Metropolitan Areas, 4th Quarter 2013*

- The Miami metro area was identified as one of the 10 best condo markets in the U.S. in 2013. The area ranked #6 out of 64 markets with a price appreciation of 26.2%. Criteria: year-over-year change of median sales price of existing apartment condo-coop homes between the 4th quarter of 2012 and the 4th quarter of 2013. *National Association of Realtors®, Median Sales Price of Existing Apartment Condo-Coop Homes for Metropolitan Areas, 4th Quarter 2013*

- The Miami metro area was identified as one of the 20 least affordable housing markets in the U.S. in 2013. The area ranked #10 out of 173 markets. Criteria: whether or not a typical family could qualify for a mortgage loan on a typical home. *National Association of Realtors®, Affordability Index of Existing Single-Family Homes for Metropolitan Areas, 2013*

- Miami was ranked #201 out of 224 metro areas in terms of housing affordability in 2013 by the National Association of Home Builders (#1 = most affordable). The NAHB-Wells Fargo Housing Opportunity Index (HOI) for a given area is defined as the share of homes sold in that area that would have been affordable to a family earning the local median income, based on standard mortgage underwriting criteria. *National Association of Home Builders®, NAHB-Wells Fargo Housing Opportunity Index, 4th Quarter 2013*

- Miami was selected as one of the best college towns for renters by ApartmentRatings.com." The area ranked #59 out of 87. Overall satisfaction ratings were ranked using thousands of user submitted scores for hundreds of apartment complexes located in cities and towns that are home to the 100 largest four-year institutions in the U.S. *ApartmentRatings.com, "2011 College Town Renter Satisfaction Rankings"*

- The nation's largest metro areas were analyzed in terms of the percentage of households entering some stage of foreclosure in 2013. The Miami metro area ranked #1 out of 10 (#1 = highest foreclosure rate). *RealtyTrac, "2013 Year-End U.S. Foreclosure Market Report™," January 16, 2014*

- The nation's largest metro areas were analyzed in terms of the best places to buy foreclosures in 2013. The Miami metro area ranked #12 out of 20. Criteria: RealtyTrac scored all metro areas with a population of 500,000 or more by summing up four numbers: months' supply of foreclosure inventory; percentage of foreclosure sales; foreclosure discount; percentage increase in foreclosure activity in 2012. *RealtyTrac, "2012 Year-End Metropolitan Foreclosure Market Report," January 28, 2013*

Safety Rankings

- Symantec, in partnership with Sperling's BestPlaces, ranked the 50 largest cities in the U.S. in terms of their vulnerability to cybercrime. The city ranked #23. Criteria: number of cyberattacks and potential infections; level of Internet access; expenditures on smartphones and computer hardware/software; wireless hotspots; broadband connectivity; Internet usage; online purchases. *Symantec, "Riskiest Online Cities of 2012" February 15, 2012*

- Allstate ranked the 200 largest cities in America in terms of driver safety. Miami ranked #187. Allstate researchers analyzed internal property damage claims over a two-year period from January 2010 to December 2011. A weighted average of the two-year numbers determined the annual percentages. *Allstate, "Allstate America's Best Drivers Report®, August 27, 2013"*

- Miami was identified as one of the most dangerous cities in America by *The Business Insider.* Criteria: cities with 100,000 residents or more were ranked by violent crime rate in 2011. Violent crimes include for murder, rape, robbery, and aggravated assault. The city ranked #17 out of 25. *The Business Insider, "The 25 Most Dangerous Cities in America," November 4, 2012*

- The National Insurance Crime Bureau ranked 380 metro areas in the U.S. in terms of per capita rates of vehicle theft. The Miami metro area ranked #52 (#1 = highest rate). Criteria: number of vehicle theft offenses per 100,000 inhabitants in 2012. *National Insurance Crime Bureau, "Hot Spots 2012," June 26, 2013*

- The Miami metro area was identified as one of the most dangerous metro areas for pedestrians by Transportation for America. The metro area ranked #4 out of 52 metro areas with over 1 million residents. Criteria: area's population divided by the number of pedestrian fatalities in that area. *Transportation for America, "Dangerous by Design 2011"*

Seniors/Retirement Rankings

- The finance website CNNMoney surveyed small U.S. cities that offer exceptional urban amenities at a cost of living somewhat higher than for the top-ten locations but still affordable for retirees. Median home-price figures were supplied by the residential real-estate website Trulia. Miami was among the eight small cities singled out. *money.cnn.com, "Best Places to Retire with a Nice Nest Egg," October 28, 2013*

- From its Best Cities for Successful Aging indexes, the Milken Institute generated rankings for metropolitan areas, weighing data in eight categories—general indicators, health care, wellness, living arrangements, transportation and general accessibility, financial well-being, education and employment, and community participation. The Miami metro area was ranked #38 overall in the large metro area category. *Milken Institute, "Best Cities for Successful Aging," July 2012*

- Bankers Life and Casualty Company, in partnership with Sperling's BestPlaces, ranked the nation's 50 largest metro areas in terms of the "Best U.S. Cities for Seniors." The Miami metro area ranked #35. Criteria: healthcare; transportation; housing; environment; economy; health and longevity; social and spiritual life; crime. *Bankers Life and Casualty Company, Center for a Secure Retirement, "Best U.S. Cities for Seniors 2011," September 2011*

Sports/Recreation Rankings

- According to the personal finance website NerdWallet, the Miami metro area, at #9, is one of the nation's top dozen metro areas for sports fans. Criteria included the presence of all four major sports—MLB, NFL, NHL, and NBA, fan enthusiasm (as measured by game attendance), ticket affordability, and "sports culture," that is, number of sports bars. *www.nerdwallet.com, "Best Cities for Sports Fans," May 5, 2013*

- Miami appeared on the *Sporting News* list of the "Best Sports Cities" for 2011. The area ranked #9 out of 271. Criteria: the magazine takes a 12-month snapshot of each city's sports, putting a heavy premium on regular-season won-lost records (from the most recently completed season). Other criteria include: playoff berths, bowl appearances and tournament bids; championships; applicable power ratings; quality of competition; overall fan fervor (measured in part by attendance); abundance of teams (rewarding quality over quantity); stadium and arena quality; ticket availability and prices; franchise ownership; and marquee appeal of athletes. *Sporting News, "Best Sports Cities 2011," October 4, 2011*

- Miami appeared on the *Sporting News* list of the "Best Sports Cities" for 2011. The area ranked #9 out of 271. Criteria: a 12-month snapshot of regular-season won-lost records (from the most recently completed season). Other criteria include: playoff berths, bowl appearances and tournament bids; championships; applicable power ratings; quality of competition; overall fan fervor (measured in part by attendance); abundance of teams (quality over quantity); stadium and arena quality; ticket availability and prices; franchise ownership; and marquee appeal of athletes. *Sporting News, "Best Sports Cities 2011," October 4, 2011*

- Miami was chosen as one of America's best cities for bicycling. The city ranked #34 out of 50. Criteria: robust cycling infrastructure; vibrant bike culture. The editors only considered cities with populations of 95,000 or more. *Bicycling, "America's Top 50 Bike-Friendly Cities," May 23, 2012*

Transportation Rankings

- NerdWallet surveyed average annual car insurance premiums in 125 U.S. cities to identify the least expensive U.S. cities in which to insure a car. Locations with no-fault insurance laws was a strong determinant. Miami came in at #9 for the most expensive rates. *www.nerdwallet.com, "Best Cities for Cheap Car Insurance," February 3, 2014*

Women/Minorities Rankings

- *Women's Health* examined U.S. cities and identified the 100 best cities for women. Miami was ranked #56. Criteria: 30 categories were examined from obesity and breast cancer rates to commuting times and hours spent working out. *Women's Health, "Best Cities for Women 2012"*

- The Miami metro area appeared on *Forbes'* list of the "Best Cities for Minority Entrepreneurs." The area ranked #56 out of 10. Criteria: 52 metropolitan statistical areas were examined. For each ethnicity (African Americans, Asians and Hispanics), the editors measured housing affordability, population growth, income growth, and entrepreneurship (per capita self-employment). *Forbes, "Best Cities for Minority Entrepreneurs," March 23, 2011*

Miscellaneous Rankings

- The watchdog site Charity Navigator conducts an annual study of charities in the nation's major markets both to analyze statistical differences in their financial, accountability, and transparency practices and to track year-to-year variations in individual communities. The Miami metro area was ranked #26 among the 30 metro markets. *www.charitynavigator.org,* "Metro Market Study 2013," June 1, 2013

- Business Insider reports on the 2013 Trick-or-Treat Index compiled by the real estate site Zillow, which used its own Home Value Index and Walk Score along with population density and local crime stats to determine that Miami ranked #14 for "how much candy it gives out versus how far kids have to walk to get it." Zillow also zeroes in on the best neighborhoods in its top 20 cities. *www.businessinsider.com, "These Are the Best Cities for Trick-or-Treating," October 15, 2013*

- Miami was selected as one of the 10 worst run cities in America by *24/7 Wall St.* The city ranked #4. Criteria: the 100 largest cities in the U.S. were ranked in terms of economy, job market, crime, and the welfare of its residents. *24/7 Wall St., "The Best and Worst Run Cities in America," January 15, 2013*

- Miami appeared on *Travel + Leisure's* list of America's least attractive people. Criteria: cities were selected by readers in their annual America's Favorite Cities survey. The city ranked #6 out of 10. *Travel + Leisure, "America's Most and Least Attractive People," November 2013*

- *Men's Health* ranked 100 U.S. cities by their level of sadness. Miami was ranked #93 (#1 = saddest city). Criteria: suicide rates; unemployment rates; percentage of households that use antidepressants; percent of population who report feeling blue all or most of the time. *Men's Health, "Frown Towns," November 28, 2011*

- Scarborough Research, a leading market research firm, identified the top local markets for lottery ticket purchasers. The Miami DMA (Designated Market Area) ranked in the top 13 with 48% of adults 18+ reporting that they purchased lottery tickets in the past 30 days. *Scarborough Research, January 30, 2012*

- Mars Chocolate North America, the makers of COMBOS®, in partnership with Sperling's BestPlaces, ranked 50 major metro areas in terms of their "manliness." The Miami metro area ranked #36. Criteria: number of professional sports teams; number of nearby NASCAR tracks and racing events; manly lifestyle; concentration of manly retail stores; manly occupations per capita; salty snack sales; "Board of Manliness" rankings. *Mars Chocolate North America, "America's Manliest Cities 2012"*

- Miami was selected as one of the most tattooed cities in America by *Lovelyish.com.* The city was ranked #1. Criteria: number of tattoo shops per capita. *Lovelyish.com, "Top Ten: Most Tattooed Cities in America," October 17, 2012*

- The National Alliance to End Homelessness ranked the 100 most populous metro areas in terms the rate of homelessness. The Miami metro area ranked #38. Criteria: number of homeless people per 10,000 population in 2011. *National Alliance to End Homelessness, The State of Homelessness in America 2012*

- The financial education website CreditDonkey compiled a list of the ten "best" cities of the future, based on percentage of housing built in 1990 or later, population change since 2010, and construction jobs as a percentage of population. Also considered were two more futuristic criteria: number of DeLorean cars available for purchase and number of spaceport companies and proposed spaceports. Miami was scored #6. *www.creditDonkey.com, "In the Future, Almost All of America's 'Best' Cities Will Be on the West Coast, Report Says," February 14, 2014*

Business Environment

CITY FINANCES

City Government Finances

Component	2011 ($000)	2011 ($ per capita)
Total Revenues	884,071	2,158
Total Expenditures	858,727	2,096
Debt Outstanding	854,572	2,086
Cash and Securities[1]	2,619,278	6,393

Note: (1) Cash and security holdings of a government at the close of its fiscal year, including those of its dependent agencies, utilities, and liquor stores.
Source: U.S Census Bureau, State & Local Government Finances 2011

City Government Revenue by Source

Source	2011 ($000)	2011 ($ per capita)
General Revenue		
From Federal Government	99,094	242
From State Government	53,171	130
From Local Governments	42,691	104
Taxes		
Property	292,285	713
Sales and Gross Receipts	85,853	210
Personal Income	0	0
Corporate Income	0	0
Motor Vehicle License	0	0
Other Taxes	44,411	108
Current Charges	106,526	260
Liquor Store	0	0
Utility	0	0
Employee Retirement	126,929	310

Source: U.S Census Bureau, State & Local Government Finances 2011

City Government Expenditures by Function

Function	2011 ($000)	2011 ($ per capita)	2011 (%)
General Direct Expenditures			
Air Transportation	0	0	0.0
Corrections	0	0	0.0
Education	0	0	0.0
Employment Security Administration	0	0	0.0
Financial Administration	15,578	38	1.8
Fire Protection	99,200	242	11.6
General Public Buildings	0	0	0.0
Governmental Administration, Other	13,093	32	1.5
Health	0	0	0.0
Highways	9,881	24	1.2
Hospitals	0	0	0.0
Housing and Community Development	38,032	93	4.4
Interest on General Debt	38,065	93	4.4
Judicial and Legal	5,195	13	0.6
Libraries	0	0	0.0
Parking	35,565	87	4.1
Parks and Recreation	72,182	176	8.4
Police Protection	147,925	361	17.2
Public Welfare	1,097	3	0.1
Sewerage	4,449	11	0.5
Solid Waste Management	22,357	55	2.6
Veterans' Services	0	0	0.0
Liquor Store	0	0	0.0
Utility	237	1	0.0
Employee Retirement	179,185	437	20.9

Source: U.S Census Bureau, State & Local Government Finances 2011

DEMOGRAPHICS

Population Growth

Area	1990 Census	2000 Census	2010 Census	Population Growth (%) 1990-2000	Population Growth (%) 2000-2010
City	358,843	362,470	399,457	1.0	10.2
MSA[1]	4,056,100	5,007,564	5,564,635	23.5	11.1
U.S.	248,709,873	281,421,906	308,745,538	13.2	9.7

Note: (1) Figures cover the Miami-Fort Lauderdale-West Palm Beach, FL Metropolitan Statistical Area—see Appendix B for areas included
Source: U.S. Census Bureau, Census 1990, 2000, 2010

Household Size

Area	Persons in Household (%) One	Two	Three	Four	Five	Six	Seven or More	Average Household Size
City	36.5	29.2	15.7	10.5	4.6	2.1	1.5	2.67
MSA[1]	29.0	31.9	16.5	13.3	5.7	2.3	1.3	2.78
U.S.	27.6	33.5	15.7	13.2	6.1	2.4	1.5	2.63

Note: (1) Figures cover the Miami-Fort Lauderdale-West Palm Beach, FL Metropolitan Statistical Area—see Appendix B for areas included
Source: U.S. Census Bureau, 2010-2012 American Community Survey 3-Year Estimates

Race

Area	White Alone[2] (%)	Black Alone[2] (%)	Asian Alone[2] (%)	AIAN[3] Alone[2] (%)	NHOPI[4] Alone[2] (%)	Other Race Alone[2] (%)	Two or More Races (%)
City	74.8	19.6	0.9	0.1	0.0	3.5	1.0
MSA[1]	71.8	21.1	2.3	0.2	0.0	2.7	1.8
U.S.	74.0	12.6	4.9	0.8	0.2	4.7	2.8

Note: (1) Figures cover the Miami-Fort Lauderdale-West Palm Beach, FL Metropolitan Statistical Area—see Appendix B for areas included; (2) Alone is defined as not being in combination with one or more other races; (3) American Indian and Alaska Native; (4) Native Hawaiian and Other Pacific Islander
Source: U.S. Census Bureau, 2010-2012 American Community Survey 3-Year Estimates

Hispanic or Latino Origin

Area	Total (%)	Mexican (%)	Puerto Rican (%)	Cuban (%)	Other (%)
City	70.4	2.0	2.9	35.0	30.5
MSA[1]	41.9	2.4	3.7	18.1	17.7
U.S.	16.6	10.7	1.6	0.6	3.7

Note: Persons of Hispanic or Latino origin can be of any race; (1) Figures cover the Miami-Fort Lauderdale-West Palm Beach, FL Metropolitan Statistical Area—see Appendix B for areas included
Source: U.S. Census Bureau, 2010-2012 American Community Survey 3-Year Estimates

Segregation

Type	Segregation Indices[1] 1990	2000	2010	2010 Rank[2]	Percent Change 1990-2000	Percent Change 1990-2010	Percent Change 2000-2010
Black/White	71.4	69.2	64.8	23	-2.3	-6.6	-4.3
Asian/White	26.8	33.3	34.2	80	6.4	7.3	0.9
Hispanic/White	32.5	59.0	57.4	8	26.5	24.8	-1.6

Note: All figures cover the Metropolitan Statistical Area—see Appendix B for areas included; Figures are based on an analysis of 1990, 2000, and 2010 Census Decennial Census tract data by William H. Frey, Brookings Institution and the University of Michigan Social Science Data Analysis Network. In this analysis all racial groups (whites, blacks, and asians) are non-Hispanic members of those races. Hispanics are shown as a separate category;
(1) Segregation Indices are Dissimilarity Indices that measure the degree to which the minority group is distributed differently than whites across census tracts. They range from 0 (complete integration) to 100 (complete segregation) where the value indicates the percentage of the minority group that needs to move to be distributed exactly like whites; (2) Ranges from 1 (most segregated) to 102 (least segregated); n/a not available.
Source: www.CensusScope.org

Ancestry

Area	German	Irish	English	American	Italian	Polish	French[2]	Scottish	Dutch
City	2.0	1.7	1.2	4.0	2.2	0.8	0.9	0.2	0.4
MSA[1]	5.5	5.3	3.4	5.4	5.6	2.4	1.4	0.7	0.5
U.S.	15.2	11.1	8.2	7.2	5.6	3.1	2.8	1.7	1.4

Note: Figures are the percentage of the total population reporting a particular ancestry. The nine most commonly reported ancestries in the U.S. are shown. Figures include multiple ancestries (e.g. if a person reported being Irish and Italian, they were included in both columns); (1) Figures cover the Miami-Fort Lauderdale-West Palm Beach, FL Metropolitan Statistical Area—see Appendix B for areas included; (2) Excludes Basque
Source: U.S. Census Bureau, 2010-2012 American Community Survey 3-Year Estimates

Foreign-Born Population

Area	Percent of Population Born in								
	Any Foreign Country	Mexico	Asia	Europe	Carribean	South America	Central America[2]	Africa	Canada
City	58.3	1.1	1.0	1.5	34.0	7.7	12.5	0.2	0.2
MSA[1]	38.5	1.2	1.9	2.2	20.3	7.7	4.2	0.4	0.6
U.S.	13.0	3.7	3.7	1.6	1.2	0.9	1.0	0.5	0.3

Note: (1) Figures cover the Miami-Fort Lauderdale-West Palm Beach, FL Metropolitan Statistical Area—see Appendix B for areas included; (2) Excludes Mexico.
Source: U.S. Census Bureau, 2010-2012 American Community Survey 3-Year Estimates

Marital Status

Area	Never Married	Now Married[2]	Separated	Widowed	Divorced
City	39.9	34.5	4.6	6.9	14.0
MSA[1]	33.9	43.3	3.1	7.0	12.8
U.S.	32.4	48.4	2.2	6.0	11.0

Note: Figures are percentages and cover the population 15 years of age and older; (1) Figures cover the Miami-Fort Lauderdale-West Palm Beach, FL Metropolitan Statistical Area—see Appendix B for areas included; (2) Excludes separated
Source: U.S. Census Bureau, 2010-2012 American Community Survey 3-Year Estimates

Age

Area	Percent of Population									Median Age
	Under Age 5	Age 5–19	Age 20–34	Age 35–44	Age 45–54	Age 55–64	Age 65–74	Age 75–84	Age 85+	
City	6.1	14.8	22.9	15.0	14.2	11.4	7.6	5.7	2.3	39.0
MSA[1]	5.7	18.0	19.4	13.9	14.9	11.8	8.1	5.5	2.5	40.0
U.S.	6.4	20.1	20.5	13.1	14.3	12.2	7.3	4.2	1.8	37.3

Note: (1) Figures cover the Miami-Fort Lauderdale-West Palm Beach, FL Metropolitan Statistical Area—see Appendix B for areas included
Source: U.S. Census Bureau, 2010-2012 American Community Survey 3-Year Estimates

Gender

Area	Males	Females	Males per 100 Females
City	202,143	206,179	98.0
MSA[1]	2,753,497	2,923,911	94.2
U.S.	153,276,055	158,333,314	96.8

Note: (1) Figures cover the Miami-Fort Lauderdale-West Palm Beach, FL Metropolitan Statistical Area—see Appendix B for areas included
Source: U.S. Census Bureau, 2010-2012 American Community Survey 3-Year Estimates

Religious Groups by Family

Area	Catholic	Baptist	Non-Den.	Methodist[2]	Lutheran	LDS[3]	Pente-costal	Presby-terian[4]	Muslim[5]	Judaism
MSA[1]	18.6	5.4	4.2	1.3	0.5	0.5	1.8	0.7	0.9	1.6
U.S.	19.1	9.3	4.0	4.0	2.3	2.0	1.9	1.6	0.8	0.7

Note: Figures are the number of adherents as a percentage of the total population; (1) Figures cover the Miami-Fort Lauderdale-West Palm Beach, FL Metropolitan Statistical Area—see Appendix B for areas included; (2) Methodist/Pietist; (3) Latter Day Saints; (4) Reformed; (5) Figures are estimates
Source: Association of Statisticians of American Religious Bodies, 2010 U.S. Religion Census: Religious Congregations & Membership Study

Religious Groups by Tradition

Area	Catholic	Evangelical Protestant	Mainline Protestant	Other Tradition	Black Protestant	Orthodox
MSA[1]	18.6	11.4	2.5	3.5	1.7	0.3
U.S.	19.1	16.2	7.3	4.3	1.6	0.3

Note: Figures are the number of adherents as a percentage of the total population; (1) Figures cover the Miami-Fort Lauderdale-West Palm Beach, FL Metropolitan Statistical Area—see Appendix B for areas included
Source: Association of Statisticians of American Religious Bodies, 2010 U.S. Religion Census: Religious Congregations & Membership Study

ECONOMY

Gross Metropolitan Product

Area	2011	2012	2013	2014	Rank[2]
MSA[1]	260.7	274.1	283.4	296.1	11

Note: Figures are in billions of dollars; (1) Figures cover the Miami-Fort Lauderdale-West Palm Beach, FL Metropolitan Statistical Area—see Appendix B for areas included; (2) Rank is based on 2014 data and ranges from 1 to 363
Source: The United States Conference of Mayors, U.S. Metro Economies: Outlook—Gross Metropolitan Product, with Metro Employment Projections, November 2013

Economic Growth

Area	2011 (%)	2012 (%)	2013 (%)	2014 (%)	Rank[2]
MSA[1]	1.3	3.5	2.0	2.5	72
U.S.	1.6	2.5	1.7	2.5	–

Note: Figures are real gross metropolitan product (GMP) growth rates and represent annual average percent change; (1) Figures cover the Miami-Fort Lauderdale-West Palm Beach, FL Metropolitan Statistical Area—see Appendix B for areas included; (2) Rank is based on 2013 data and ranges from 1 to 363
Source: The United States Conference of Mayors, U.S. Metro Economies: Outlook—Gross Metropolitan Product, with Metro Employment Projections, November 2013

Metropolitan Area Exports

Area	2007	2008	2009	2010	2011	2012	Rank[2]
MSA[1]	26,197.4	33,411.5	31,175.0	35,866.9	43,129.9	47,858.7	6

Note: Figures are in millions of dollars; (1) Figures cover the Miami-Fort Lauderdale-West Palm Beach, FL Metropolitan Statistical Area—see Appendix B for areas included; (2) Rank is based on 2012 data and ranges from 1 to 369
Source: U.S. Department of Commerce, International Trade Administration, Office of Trade & Industry Information, Manufacturing & Services, data extracted April 1, 2014

INCOME

Income

Area	Per Capita ($)	Median Household ($)	Average Household ($)
City	20,104	28,935	49,640
MSA[1]	26,277	46,867	69,526
U.S.	27,385	51,771	71,579

Note: (1) Figures cover the Miami-Fort Lauderdale-West Palm Beach, FL Metropolitan Statistical Area—see Appendix B for areas included
Source: U.S. Census Bureau, 2010-2012 American Community Survey 3-Year Estimates

Household Income Distribution

Area	Percent of Households Earning							
	Under $15,000	$15,000 -24,999	$25,000 -34,999	$35,000 -49,999	$50,000 -74,999	$75,000 -99,000	$100,000 -149,999	$150,000 and up
City	28.4	16.3	12.4	12.7	12.7	6.0	5.8	5.7
MSA[1]	15.0	12.1	11.3	14.2	17.2	10.5	11.1	8.7
U.S.	13.1	11.0	10.5	13.7	18.1	11.9	12.5	9.1

Note: (1) Figures cover the Miami-Fort Lauderdale-West Palm Beach, FL Metropolitan Statistical Area—see Appendix B for areas included
Source: U.S. Census Bureau, 2010-2012 American Community Survey 3-Year Estimates

Poverty Rate

Area	All Ages	Under 18 Years Old	18 to 64 Years Old	65 Years and Over
City	31.5	45.6	27.0	33.7
MSA[1]	17.3	24.3	15.6	14.7
U.S.	15.7	22.2	14.6	9.3

Note: Figures are percentage of people whose income during the past 12 months was below the poverty level;
(1) Figures cover the Miami-Fort Lauderdale-West Palm Beach, FL Metropolitan Statistical Area—see Appendix B for areas included
Source: U.S. Census Bureau, 2010-2012 American Community Survey 3-Year Estimates

Personal Bankruptcy Filing Rate

Area	2008	2009	2010	2011	2012	2013
Miami-Dade County	n/a	n/a	n/a	n/a	n/a	n/a
U.S.	3.53	4.61	4.97	4.37	3.76	3.29

Note: Numbers are per 1,000 population and include Chapter 7 and Chapter 13 filings; n/a not available
Source: Federal Deposit Insurance Corporation, Regional Economic Conditions, March 20, 2014

EMPLOYMENT

Labor Force and Employment

Area	Civilian Labor Force			Workers Employed		
	Dec. 2012	Dec. 2013	% Chg.	Dec. 2012	Dec. 2013	% Chg.
City	184,999	181,547	-1.9	166,485	167,760	0.8
MD[1]	1,295,038	1,282,132	-1.0	1,174,459	1,194,364	1.7
U.S.	154,904,000	154,408,000	-0.3	143,060,000	144,423,000	1.0

Note: Data is not seasonally adjusted and covers workers 16 years of age and older; (1) Metropolitan Division—see Appendix B for areas included
Source: Bureau of Labor Statistics, Local Area Unemployment Statistics

Unemployment Rate

Area	2013											
	Jan.	Feb.	Mar.	Apr.	May	Jun.	Jul.	Aug.	Sep.	Oct.	Nov.	Dec.
City	10.5	10.6	10.3	9.7	9.7	9.8	9.3	9.4	9.2	9.5	7.9	7.6
MD[1]	9.5	9.0	8.8	8.6	8.7	9.2	8.6	8.6	8.1	8.1	6.9	6.8
U.S.	8.5	8.1	7.6	7.1	7.3	7.8	7.7	7.3	7.0	7.0	6.6	6.5

Note: Data is not seasonally adjusted and covers workers 16 years of age and older; All figures are percentages;
(1) Metropolitan Division—see Appendix B for areas included
Source: Bureau of Labor Statistics, Local Area Unemployment Statistics

Employment by Occupation

Occupation Classification	City (%)	MSA[1] (%)	U.S. (%)
Management, Business, Science, and Arts	27.6	33.2	36.0
Natural Resources, Construction, and Maintenance	12.1	8.8	9.1
Production, Transportation, and Material Moving	10.9	8.7	12.0
Sales and Office	24.3	28.3	24.7
Service	25.1	21.0	18.2

Note: Figures cover employed civilians 16 years of age and older; (1) Figures cover the Miami-Fort Lauderdale-West Palm Beach, FL Metropolitan Statistical Area—see Appendix B for areas included
Source: U.S. Census Bureau, 2010-2012 American Community Survey 3-Year Estimates

Employment by Industry

Sector	MD[1]		U.S.
	Number of Employees	Percent of Total	Percent of Total
Construction	34,900	3.2	4.2
Education and Health Services	166,700	15.3	15.5
Financial Activities	73,800	6.8	5.7
Government	142,400	13.1	16.1
Information	18,200	1.7	1.9
Leisure and Hospitality	128,700	11.8	10.2
Manufacturing	37,300	3.4	8.7
Mining and Logging	400	<0.1	0.6
Other Services	48,200	4.4	3.9
Professional and Business Services	150,400	13.8	13.7
Retail Trade	150,000	13.8	11.4
Transportation and Utilities	66,200	6.1	3.8
Wholesale Trade	73,700	6.8	4.2

Note: Figures cover non-farm employment as of December 2013 and are not seasonally adjusted;
(1) Metropolitan Division—see Appendix B for areas included
Source: Bureau of Labor Statistics, Current Employment Statistics, Employment, Hours, and Earnings

Occupations with Greatest Projected Employment Growth: 2010 – 2020

Occupation[1]	2010 Employment	2020 Projected Employment	Numeric Employment Change	Percent Employment Change
Retail Salespersons	290,200	345,860	55,660	19.2
Combined Food Preparation and Serving Workers, Including Fast Food	154,650	193,760	39,110	25.3
Registered Nurses	165,400	202,190	36,790	22.3
Waiters and Waitresses	174,630	210,650	36,010	20.6
Customer Service Representatives	165,950	194,220	28,260	17.0
Cashiers	200,040	225,430	25,400	12.7
Office Clerks, General	142,480	164,800	22,330	15.7
Landscaping and Groundskeeping Workers	93,350	115,400	22,050	23.6
Postsecondary Teachers	75,610	94,190	18,580	24.6
Cooks, Restaurant	76,000	94,180	18,190	23.9

Note: Projections cover Florida; (1) Sorted by numeric employment change
Source: www.projectionscentral.com, State Occupational Projections, 2010–2020 Long-Term Projections

Fastest Growing Occupations: 2010 – 2020

Occupation[1]	2010 Employment	2020 Projected Employment	Numeric Employment Change	Percent Employment Change
Layout Workers, Metal and Plastic	230	380	150	65.2
Biomedical Engineers	620	990	370	60.2
Helpers—Carpenters	1,120	1,770	650	58.0
Biochemists and Biophysicists	650	1,000	350	53.6
Medical Scientists, Except Epidemiologists	2,850	4,370	1,520	53.5
Helpers—Brickmasons, Blockmasons, Stonemasons, and Tile and Marble Setters	810	1,240	430	52.6
Reinforcing Iron and Rebar Workers	940	1,370	430	46.1
Home Health Aides	28,580	41,010	12,430	43.5
Stonemasons	550	790	240	42.9
Personal Care Aides	16,880	23,920	7,040	41.7

Note: Projections cover Florida; (1) Sorted by percent employment change and excludes occupations with numeric employment change less than 100
Source: www.projectionscentral.com, State Occupational Projections, 2010–2020 Long-Term Projections

Average Wages

Occupation	$/Hr.	Occupation	$/Hr.
Accountants and Auditors	33.25	Maids and Housekeeping Cleaners	9.54
Automotive Mechanics	16.83	Maintenance and Repair Workers	15.19
Bookkeepers	16.90	Marketing Managers	59.68
Carpenters	17.61	Nuclear Medicine Technologists	35.08
Cashiers	9.40	Nurses, Licensed Practical	20.23
Clerks, General Office	13.15	Nurses, Registered	29.53
Clerks, Receptionists/Information	12.06	Nursing Assistants	11.04
Clerks, Shipping/Receiving	13.24	Packers and Packagers, Hand	9.31
Computer Programmers	45.85	Physical Therapists	35.27
Computer Systems Analysts	48.29	Postal Service Mail Carriers	25.08
Computer User Support Specialists	22.69	Real Estate Brokers	n/a
Cooks, Restaurant	11.73	Retail Salespersons	11.23
Dentists	83.10	Sales Reps., Exc. Tech./Scientific	26.45
Electrical Engineers	45.51	Sales Reps., Tech./Scientific	32.81
Electricians	19.99	Secretaries, Exc. Legal/Med./Exec.	14.60
Financial Managers	70.12	Security Guards	10.97
First-Line Supervisors/Managers, Sales	20.88	Surgeons	n/a
Food Preparation Workers	10.36	Teacher Assistants	11.20
General and Operations Managers	61.15	Teachers, Elementary School	23.20
Hairdressers/Cosmetologists	12.33	Teachers, Secondary School	26.50
Internists	98.51	Telemarketers	11.81
Janitors and Cleaners	10.23	Truck Drivers, Heavy/Tractor-Trailer	17.53
Landscaping/Groundskeeping Workers	11.48	Truck Drivers, Light/Delivery Svcs.	14.08
Lawyers	72.84	Waiters and Waitresses	9.76

Note: Wage data covers the Miami-Miami Beach-Kendall, FL Metropolitan Division—see Appendix B for areas included. Hourly wages for elementary/secondary school teachers and teacher assistants were calculated by the editors from annual wage data assuming a 40 hour work week; n/a not available.
Source: Bureau of Labor Statistics, Metro Area Occupational Employment and Wage Estimates, May 2013

RESIDENTIAL REAL ESTATE

Building Permits

Area	Single-Family			Multi-Family			Total		
	2012	2013	Pct. Chg.	2012	2013	Pct. Chg.	2012	2013	Pct. Chg.
City	40	115	187.5	911	4,371	379.8	951	4,486	371.7
MSA[1]	5,089	6,369	25.2	8,172	13,552	65.8	13,261	19,921	50.2
U.S.	518,695	620,802	19.7	310,963	370,020	19.0	829,658	990,822	19.4

Note: (1) Metropolitan Statistical Area—see Appendix B for areas included; figures represent new, privately-owned housing units authorized (unadjusted data); All permit data are based on estimates with imputation.
Source: U.S. Census Bureau, Manufacturing, Mining, and Construction Statistics, Building Permits, 2012, 2013

Homeownership Rate

Area	2006 (%)	2007 (%)	2008 (%)	2009 (%)	2010 (%)	2011 (%)	2012 (%)	2013 (%)
MSA[1]	67.4	66.6	66.0	67.1	63.8	64.2	61.8	60.1
U.S.	68.8	68.1	67.8	67.4	66.9	66.1	65.4	65.1

Note: (1) Figures cover the Miami-Fort Lauderdale-West Palm Beach, FL Metropolitan Statistical Area—see Appendix B for areas included
Source: U.S. Census Bureau, Housing Vacancies and Homeownership Annual Statistics: 2013

Housing Vacancy Rates

Area	Gross Vacancy Rate[2] (%)			Year-Round Vacancy Rate[3] (%)			Rental Vacancy Rate[4] (%)			Homeowner Vacancy Rate[5] (%)		
	2011	2012	2013	2011	2012	2013	2011	2012	2013	2011	2012	2013
MSA[1]	21.0	20.1	20.2	11.7	10.1	10.3	11.8	8.2	6.7	1.8	0.9	1.7
U.S.	14.2	13.8	13.8	11.1	10.8	10.7	9.5	8.7	8.3	2.5	2.0	2.0

Note: (1) Figures cover the Miami-Fort Lauderdale-West Palm Beach, FL Metropolitan Statistical Area—see Appendix B for areas included; (2) The percentage of the total housing inventory that is vacant; (3) The percentage of the housing inventory (excluding seasonal units) that is year-round vacant; (4) The percentage of rental inventory that is vacant for rent; (5) The percentage of homeowner inventory that is vacant for sale
Source: U.S. Census Bureau, Housing Vacancies and Homeownership Annual Statistics: 2013

TAXES

State Corporate Income Tax Rates

State	Tax Rate (%)	Income Brackets ($)	Num. of Brackets	Financial Institution Tax Rate (%)[a]	Federal Income Tax Ded.
Florida	5.5 (f)	Flat rate	1	5.5 (f)	No

Note: Tax rates as of January 1, 2014; (a) Rates listed are the corporate income tax rate applied to financial institutions or excise taxes based on income. Some states have other taxes based upon the value of deposits or shares; (f) An exemption of $50,000 is allowed. Florida's Alternative Minimum Tax rate is 3.3%.
Source: Federation of Tax Administrators, "State Corporate Income Tax Rates, 2014"

State Individual Income Tax Rates

State	Tax Rate (%)	Income Brackets ($)	Num. of Brackets	Personal Exempt. ($)[1] Single	Personal Exempt. ($)[1] Dependents	Fed. Inc. Tax Ded.
Florida	None	–	–	–	–	–

Note: Tax rates as of January 1, 2014; Local- and county-level taxes are not included; n/a not applicable; (1) Married joint filers generally receive double the single exemption
Source: Federation of Tax Administrators, "State Individual Income Tax Rates, 2014"

Various State and Local Tax Rates

State	State and Local Sales and Use (%)	State Sales and Use (%)	Gasoline[1] (¢/gal.)	Cigarette[2] ($/pack)	Spirits[3] ($/gal.)	Wine[4] ($/gal.)	Beer[5] ($/gal.)
Florida	7.0	6.00	36.03	1.339	6.50 (f)	2.25	0.48

Note: All tax rates as of January 1, 2014; (1) The American Petroleum Institute has developed a methodology for determining the average tax rate on a gallon of fuel. Rates may include any of the following: excise taxes, environmental fees, storage tank fees, other fees or taxes, general sales tax, and local taxes. In states where gasoline is subject to the general sales tax, or where the fuel tax is based on the average sale price, the average rate determined by API is sensitive to changes in the price of gasoline. States that fully or partially apply general sales taxes to gasoline: CA, CO, GA, IL, IN, MI, NY; (2) The federal excise tax of $1.0066 per pack and local taxes are not included; (3) Rates are those applicable to off-premise sales of 40% alcohol by volume (a.b.v.) distilled spirits in 750ml containers. Local excise taxes are excluded; (4) Rates are those applicable to off-premise sales of 11% a.b.v. non-carbonated wine in 750ml containers; (5) Rates are those applicable to off-premise sales of 4.7% a.b.v. beer in 12 ounce containers; (f) Different rates also applicable according to alcohol content, place of production, size of container, or place purchased (on- or off-premise or onboard airlines).
Source: Tax Foundation, 2014 Facts & Figures: How Does Your State Compare?

State Business Tax Climate Index Rankings

State	Overall Rank	Corporate Tax Index Rank	Individual Income Tax Index Rank	Sales Tax Index Rank	Unemployment Insurance Tax Index Rank	Property Tax Index Rank
Florida	5	13	1	18	6	16

Note: The index is a measure of how each state's tax laws affect economic performance. The lower the rank, the more favorable a state's tax system is for business. States without a given tax are given a ranking of 1. The scores/rankings for the District of Columbia do not affect other states. The 2014 index represents the tax climate as of July 1, 2013.
Source: Tax Foundation, State Business Tax Climate Index 2014

COMMERCIAL REAL ESTATE

Office Market

Market Area	Inventory (sq. ft.)	Vacancy Rate (%)	Under Construction (sq. ft.)	YTD Net Absorption (sq. ft.)	Total Average Asking Rent ($/sq. ft./year)
Miami	46,798,833	16.7	0	557,599	29.86
National	4,726,900,879	15.0	55,419,286	42,829,434	26.27

Source: Newmark Grubb Knight Frank, National Office Market Report, 4th Quarter 2013

Industrial/Warehouse/R&D Market

Market Area	Inventory (sq. ft.)	Vacancy Rate (%)	Under Construction (sq. ft.)	YTD Net Absorption (sq. ft.)	Total Average Asking Rent ($/sq. ft./year)
Miami	201,865,652	6.1	1,262,062	1,028,477	5.99
National	14,022,031,238	7.9	83,249,164	156,549,903	5.40

Source: Newmark Grubb Knight Frank, National Industrial Market Report, 4th Quarter 2013

**COMMERCIAL
UTILITIES**

Typical Monthly Electric Bills

Area	Commercial Service ($/month)		Industrial Service ($/month)	
	1,500 kWh	40 kW demand 14,000 kWh	1,000 kW demand 200,000 kWh	50,000 kW demand 15,000,000 kWh
City	148	1,190	21,825	839,634
Average[1]	197	1,636	25,662	1,485,307

Note: Based on total rates in effect July 1, 2013; (1) average based on 180 utilities surveyed
Source: Edison Electric Institute, Typical Bills and Average Rates Report, Summer 2013

TRANSPORTATION

Means of Transportation to Work

Area	Car/Truck/Van		Public Transportation			Bicycle	Walked	Other Means	Worked at Home
	Drove Alone	Car-pooled	Bus	Subway	Railroad				
City	69.4	10.4	10.0	0.7	0.2	0.9	4.1	1.4	3.0
MSA[1]	78.3	9.6	3.3	0.3	0.2	0.6	1.8	1.4	4.6
U.S.	76.4	9.7	2.6	1.7	0.5	0.6	2.8	1.3	4.3

Note: Figures are percentages and cover workers 16 years of age and older; (1) Figures cover the Miami-Fort Lauderdale-West Palm Beach, FL Metropolitan Statistical Area—see Appendix B for areas included
Source: U.S. Census Bureau, 2010-2012 American Community Survey 3-Year Estimates

Travel Time to Work

Area	Less Than 10 Minutes	10 to 19 Minutes	20 to 29 Minutes	30 to 44 Minutes	45 to 59 Minutes	60 to 89 Minutes	90 Minutes or More
City	6.3	25.3	28.1	26.3	7.2	5.0	1.8
MSA[1]	7.7	25.1	23.3	27.2	8.8	5.9	2.0
U.S.	13.5	29.8	20.9	20.1	7.5	5.6	2.5

Note: Figures are percentages and include workers 16 years old and over; (1) Figures cover the Miami-Fort Lauderdale-West Palm Beach, FL Metropolitan Statistical Area—see Appendix B for areas included
Source: U.S. Census Bureau, 2010-2012 American Community Survey 3-Year Estimates

Travel Time Index

Area	1985	1990	1995	2000	2005	2010	2011
Urban Area[1]	1.11	1.20	1.21	1.29	1.33	1.25	1.25
Average[2]	1.09	1.14	1.16	1.19	1.23	1.18	1.18

Note: Travel Time Index—the ratio of travel time in the peak period to the travel time at free-flow conditions. For example, a value of 1.30 indicates a 20-minute free-flow trip takes 26 minutes in the peak. Free-flow speeds (60 mph on freeways and 35 mph on principal arterials) are used as the comparison threshold; (1) Covers the Miami FL urban area; (2) average of 498 urban areas
Source: Texas Transportation Institute, Urban Mobility Report 2012, December 2012

Public Transportation

Agency Name / Mode of Transportation	Vehicles Operated in Maximum Service	Annual Unlinked Passenger Trips (in thous.)	Annual Passenger Miles (in thous.)
Miami-Dade Transit (MDT)			
Bus (directly operated)	692	77,828.3	441,667.9
Bus (purchased transportation)	1	30.7	614.9
Demand Response (purchased transportation)	333	1,672.4	21,469.2
Heavy Rail (directly operated)	76	18,706.1	139,721.1
Monorail and Automated Guideway (directly operated)	21	9,102.4	9,738.7
South Florida Regional Transportation Authority (TRI-Rail)			
Bus (purchased transportation)	25	935.9	3,673.9
Commuter Rail (purchased transportation)	40	4,006.0	115,414.2

Source: Federal Transit Administration, National Transit Database, 2012

Air Transportation

Airport Name and Code / Type of Service	Passenger Airlines[1]	Passenger Enplanements	Freight Carriers[2]	Freight (lbs.)
Miami International (MIA)				
Domestic service (U.S. carriers - 2013)	24	9,250,839	18	207,513,494
International service (U.S. carriers - 2012)	15	6,037,354	22	915,543,575

Note: (1) Includes all U.S.-based major, minor and commuter airlines that carried at least one passenger during the year; (2) Includes all U.S.-based airlines and freight carriers that transported at least one lb. of freight during the year.
Source: Bureau of Transportation Statistics, The Intermodal Transportation Database, Air Carriers: T-100 Domestic Market (U.S. Carriers), 2013; Bureau of Transportation Statistics, The Intermodal Transportation Database, Air Carriers: T-100 International Market (U.S. Carriers), 2012

Other Transportation Statistics

Major Highways:	I-95
Amtrak Service:	Yes
Major Waterways/Ports:	Port of Miami; Atlantic Intracoastal Waterway

Source: Amtrak.com; Google Maps

BUSINESSES

Major Business Headquarters

Company Name	Rankings	
	Fortune[1]	Forbes[2]
Brightstar	-	55
Ryder System	404	-
Southern Wine & Spirits	-	32
World Fuel Services	74	-

Note: (1) Fortune 500—companies that produce a 10-K are ranked 1 to 500 based on 2012 revenue; (2) all private companies with at least $2 billion in annual revenue through the end of their most current fiscal year are ranked 1 to 224; companies listed are headquartered in the city; dashes indicate no ranking
Source: Fortune, "Fortune 500," May 20, 2013; Forbes, "America's Largest Private Companies," December 18, 2013

Fast-Growing Businesses

According to *Inc.*, Miami is home to one of America's 500 fastest-growing private companies: **305 Degrees** (#425). Criteria: must be an independent, privately-held, for-profit, U.S. corporation, proprietorship or partnership; revenues must be at least $100,000 in 2009 and $2 million in 2012; must have four-year operating/sales history. Holding companies, regulated banks, and utilities were excluded. *Inc., "America's 500 Fastest-Growing Private Companies," September 2013*

According to *Initiative for a Competitive Inner City (ICIC)*, Miami is home to one of America's 100 fastest-growing "inner city" companies: **Tire Group International** (#59). Companies were ranked by their five-year compound annual growth rate. Criteria for inclusion: company must be headquartered in or have 51 percent or more of its physical operations in an economically distressed urban area; must be an independent, for-profit corporation, partnership or proprietorship; must have 10 or more employees and have a five-year sales history that includes sales of at least $200,000 in the base year and at least $1 million in the current year with no decrease in sales over the two most recent years. *Initiative for a Competitive Inner City (ICIC), "Inner City 100 Companies, 2013"*

Minority Business Opportunity

Miami Beach is home to one company which is on the *Black Enterprise* Industrial/Service 100 list (100 largest companies based on gross sales): **The Peebles Corp.** (#97). Criteria: operational in previous calendar year; at least 51% black-owned and manufactures/owns the product it sells or provides industrial or consumer services. Brokerages, real estate firms and firms that provide professional services are not eligible. *Black Enterprise, B.E. 100s, 2013*

Miami is home to 57 companies which are on the *Hispanic Business* 500 list (500 largest U.S. Hispanic-owned companies based on 2012 revenue): **Brightstar Corp.** (#1); **The Related Group** (#4); **Quirch Foods** (#8); **First Equity Mortgage Bankers** (#27); **BMI Financial Group** (#31); **Precision Trading Corp.** (#40); **MCM** (#44); **El Dorado Furniture Corp.** (#45); **Headquarter Toyota** (#48); **Miami Automotive Retail** (#49); **Refricenter of Miami** (#59); **Machado Garcia Serra** (#72); **Metro Ford** (#89); **Transnational Foods** (#91); **Link Construction Group** (#92); **South Dade Automotive** (#94); **Century Metals & Supplies** (#103); **CSA Holdings** (#111);

John Keeler & Co. (#120); Softech International (#121); Everglades Steel, Medley Steel, Metallic Products (#132); Adonel Concrete Pumping & Finishing of S. Florida (#139); Solo Printing (#142); Ascendant Commercial Insurance Co. (#144); Metric Engineering (#146); Gancedo Lumber Co. (#163); The Intermarket Group (#171); Roach Busters Bug Killers of America (#185); Fru-Veg Marketing (#189); Express Travel (#192); Original Impressions (#201); Protec (#206); Nital Trading Co. (#214); Future Force Personnel (#235); Vina & Sons Food Distributor Corp. (#237); Bermello, Ajamil & Partners (#246); AZF Automotive Group (#286); X-EETO (#287); American Fasteners Corp. (#294); Interamerican Bank (#304); EnviroWaste Services Group (#308); Republica (#311); EYMAQ (#324); Wendium of Florida (#327); Hispanic Group (#329); Farma International (#334); Cherokee Enterprises (#343); Amtec Sales (#351); South Florida Trading Corp. (#362); T&S Roofing Systems (#368); F.R. Aleman & Associates (#396); A-1 Property Services Group (#404); Gomez Ossa International (#433); Honshy Electric Co. (#434); Hernandez & Tacoronte PA (#447); Decorative Sales Assoc. (#484); Dynamic Turbo (#486). Companies included must show at least 51 percent ownership by Hispanic U.S. citizens, and must maintain headquarters in one of the 50 states or Washington, D.C. *Hispanic Business, "Hispanic Business 500," June 20, 2013*

Miami is home to 12 companies which are on the *Hispanic Business* Fastest-Growing 100 list (greatest sales growth from 2008 to 2012): Fru-Veg Marketing (#10); A-1 Property Services Group (#13); Miami Automotive Retail (#39); First Equity Mortgage Bankers (#42); Link Construction Group (#43); Nital Trading Co. (#56); Transnational Foods (#60); MCM (#73); South Florida Trading Corp. (#84); Roach Busters Bug Killers of America (#90); BMI Financial Group (#93); EYMAQ (#100). Companies included must show at least 51 percent ownership by Hispanic U.S. citizens, and must maintain headquarters in one of the 50 states or Washington, D.C. In addition, companies must have minimum revenues of $200,000 for calendar year 2008. *Hispanic Business, June20, 2013*

Minority- and Women-Owned Businesses

Group	All Firms		Firms with Paid Employees			
	Firms	Sales ($000)	Firms	Sales ($000)	Employees	Payroll ($000)
Asian	1,738	629,557	579	586,220	2,895	58,879
Black	9,448	492,059	588	337,832	4,470	75,101
Hispanic	53,234	11,975,646	6,317	10,407,324	35,426	1,127,862
Women	24,414	2,443,049	2,705	1,920,188	14,331	420,472
All Firms	85,143	65,730,894	15,127	62,998,520	321,378	15,801,777

Note: Figures cover firms located in the city; minority- and women-owned business are defined as firms in which the corresponding group own 51% or more of the stock or equity of the company
Source: U.S. Census Bureau, 2007 Economic Census, Survey of Business Owners (2012 Survey of Business Owners data will be released starting in June 2015)

HOTELS & CONVENTION CENTERS

Hotels/Motels

Area	5 Star		4 Star		3 Star		2 Star		1 Star		Not Rated	
	Num.	Pct.[3]	Num.	Pct.[3]	Num.	Pct.[3]	Num.	Pct.[3]	Num.	Pct.[3]	Num.	Pct.[3]
City[1]	9	2.3	77	19.5	161	40.9	106	26.9	13	3.3	28	7.1
Total[2]	142	0.9	1,005	6.0	5,147	30.9	8,578	51.4	408	2.4	1,397	8.4

Note: (1) Figures cover Miami and vicinity; (2) Figures cover all 100 cities in this book; (3) Percentage of hotels which have a given star rating; Star ratings are determined by expedia.com and offer an indication of the general quality of a particular hotel.
Source: expedia.com, April 7, 2014

The Miami-Miami Beach-Kendall, FL metro area is home to seven of the best hotels in the U.S. according to *Travel & Leisure*: Ritz-Carlton, Key Biscayne; Acqualina, Miami; Mandarin Oriental, Miami; Tides South Beach; St. Regis Bal Harbour Resort & Residences; Four Seasons Hotel, Miami; Ritz-Carlton, Miami Beach. Criteria: service; location; rooms; food; and value. The list includes the top 200 hotels in the U.S. *Travel & Leisure, "T+L 500, The World's Best Hotels 2014"*

The Miami-Miami Beach-Kendall, FL metro area is home to three of the best hotels in the world according to *Condé Nast Traveler*: King & Grove Tides South Beach; Mandarin Oriental; The Setai. The selections are based on over 79,000 responses to the magazine's annual Readers' Choice Survey. The list includes the top 200 hotels in the U.S. *Condé Nast Traveler, "Gold List 2014, The World's Best Places to Stay"*

Major Convention Centers

Name	Overall Space (sq. ft.)	Exhibit Space (sq. ft.)	Meeting Space (sq. ft.)	Meeting Rooms
Coconut Grove Convention Center	n/a	150,000	n/a	n/a
Miami Beach Convention Center	1,000,000	500,000	100,000	70

Note: Table includes convention centers located in the Miami-Fort Lauderdale-West Palm Beach, FL metro area; n/a not available

Source: Original research

Living Environment

COST OF LIVING

Cost of Living Index

Composite Index	Groceries	Housing	Utilities	Trans- portation	Health Care	Misc. Goods/ Services
107.2	99.9	118.0	95.7	110.4	104.4	104.3

Note: The Cost of Living Index measures regional differences in the cost of consumer goods and services, excluding taxes and non-consumer expenditures, for professional and managerial households in the top income quintile. It is based on more than 50,000 prices covering almost 60 different items for which prices are collected three times a year by chambers of commerce, economic development organizations or university applied economic centers in each participating urban area. The numbers shown should be read as a percentage above or below the national average of 100. For example, a value of 115.4 in the groceries column indicates that grocery prices are 15.4% higher than the national average. Small differences in the index numbers should not be interpreted as significant; Figures cover the Miami-Dade County FL urban area.
Source: The Council for Community and Economic Research, ACCRA Cost of Living Index, 2013

Grocery Prices

Area[1]	T-Bone Steak ($/pound)	Frying Chicken ($/pound)	Whole Milk ($/half gal.)	Eggs ($/dozen)	Orange Juice ($/64 oz.)	Coffee ($/11.5 oz.)
City[2]	11.10	1.43	2.66	1.91	3.45	3.43
Avg.	10.19	1.28	2.34	1.81	3.48	4.39
Min.	8.56	0.94	1.44	1.19	2.78	3.40
Max.	14.82	2.28	3.56	3.73	6.23	7.32

*Note: (1) Values for the local area are compared with the average, minimum and maximum values for all 327 areas in the Cost of Living Index; (2) Figures cover the Miami-Dade County FL urban area; **T-Bone Steak** (price per pound); **Frying Chicken** (price per pound, whole fryer); **Whole Milk** (half gallon carton); **Eggs** (price per dozen, Grade A, large); **Orange Juice** (64 oz. Tropicana or Florida Natural); **Coffee** (11.5 oz. can, vacuum-packed, Maxwell House, Hills Bros, or Folgers).*
Source: The Council for Community and Economic Research, ACCRA Cost of Living Index, 2013

Housing and Utility Costs

Area[1]	New Home Price ($)	Apartment Rent ($/month)	All Electric ($/month)	Part Electric ($/month)	Other Energy ($/month)	Telephone ($/month)
City[2]	325,413	1,290	150.39	-	-	28.01
Avg.	295,864	900	171.38	91.82	70.12	27.73
Min.	185,506	458	117.80	48.81	33.67	17.16
Max.	1,358,917	3,783	441.68	171.40	372.65	39.47

*Note: (1) Values for the local area are compared with the average, minimum and maximum values for all 327 areas in the Cost of Living Index; (2) Figures cover the Miami-Dade County FL urban area; **New Home Price** (2,400 sf living area, 8,000 sf lot, in urban area with full utilities); **Apartment Rent** (950 sf 2 bedroom/1.5 or 2 bath, unfurnished, excluding all utilities except water); **All Electric** (average monthly cost for an all-electric home); **Part Electric** (average monthly cost for a part-electric home); **Other Energy** (average monthly cost for natural gas, fuel oil, coal, wood, and any other forms of energy except electricity); **Telephone** (price includes basic monthly rate for a private residential line plus additional local usage charges incurred by a family of four).*
Source: The Council for Community and Economic Research, ACCRA Cost of Living Index, 2013

Health Care, Transportation, and Other Costs

Area[1]	Doctor ($/visit)	Dentist ($/visit)	Optometrist ($/visit)	Gasoline ($/gallon)	Beauty Salon ($/visit)	Men's Shirt ($)
City[2]	108.85	98.88	91.33	3.57	58.07	18.10
Avg.	101.40	86.48	96.16	3.44	33.87	26.55
Min.	61.67	50.83	50.12	3.08	18.92	12.48
Max.	182.71	152.50	223.78	4.33	68.22	52.03

*Note: (1) Values for the local area are compared with the average, minimum and maximum values for all 327 areas in the Cost of Living Index; (2) Figures cover the Miami-Dade County FL urban area; **Doctor** (general practitioners routine exam of an established patient); **Dentist** (adult teeth cleaning and periodic oral examination); **Optometrist** (full vision eye exam for established adult patient); **Gasoline** (one gallon regular unleaded, national brand, including all taxes, cash price at self-service pump if available); **Beauty Salon** (woman's shampoo, trim, and blow-dry); **Men's Shirt** (cotton/polyester dress shirt, pinpoint weave, long sleeves).*
Source: The Council for Community and Economic Research, ACCRA Cost of Living Index, 2013

HOUSING

House Price Index (HPI)

Area	National Ranking[2]	Quarterly Change (%)	One-Year Change (%)	Five-Year Change (%)
MD[1]	40	3.08	11.63	-7.55
U.S.[3]	–	1.20	7.69	4.18

Note: The HPI is a weighted repeat sales index. It measures average price changes in repeat sales or refinancings on the same properties. This information is obtained by reviewing repeat mortgage transactions on single-family properties whose mortgages have been purchased or securitized by Fannie Mae or Freddie Mac in January 1975; (1) Miami-Miami Beach-Kendall, FL Metropolitan Division—see Appendix B for areas included; (2) Rankings are based on annual percentage change for all metro areas containing at least 15,000 transactions over the last 10 years and ranges from 1 to 283; (3) figures based on a weighted average of Census Division estimates using a seasonally adjusted, purchase-only index; all figures are for the period ending December 31, 2013
Source: Federal Housing Finance Agency, House Price Index, February 25, 2014

Median Single-Family Home Prices

Area	2011	2012	2013p	Percent Change 2012 to 2013
MSA[1]	181.1	203.1	246.0	21.1
U.S. Average	166.2	177.2	197.4	11.4

Note: Figures are median sales prices of existing single-family homes in thousands of dollars; (p) preliminary; n/a not available; (1) Miami-Fort Lauderdale-West Palm Beach, FL Metropolitan Statistical Area—see Appendix B for areas included
Source: National Association of Realtors, Median Sales Price of Existing Single-Family Homes for Metropolitan Areas, 4th Quarter 2013

Qualifying Income Based on Median Sales Price of Existing Single-Family Homes

Area	With 5% Down ($)	With 10% Down ($)	With 20% Down ($)
MSA[1]	58,767	55,674	49,488
U.S. Average	45,395	43,006	38,228

Note: Figures are preliminary; Qualifying income is based on a mortgage rate of 4.4%. Monthly principal and interest payment is limited to 25% of income; n/a not available; (1) Miami-Fort Lauderdale-West Palm Beach, FL Metropolitan Statistical Area—see Appendix B for areas included
Source: National Association of Realtors, Qualifying Income Based on Median Sales Price of Existing Single-Family Homes for Metropolitan Areas, 4th Quarter 2013

Median Apartment Condo-Coop Home Prices

Area	2011	2012	2013p	Percent Change 2012 to 2013
MSA[1]	84.0	101.3	129.5	27.8
U.S. Average	165.1	173.7	194.9	12.2

Note: Figures are median sales prices of existing apartment condo-coop homes in thousands of dollars; (p) preliminary; n/a not available; (1) Miami-Fort Lauderdale-West Palm Beach, FL Metropolitan Statistical Area—see Appendix B for areas included
Source: National Association of Realtors, Median Sales Price of Existing Apartment Condo-Coop Homes for Metropolitan Areas, 4th Quarter 2013

Gross Monthly Rent

Area	Under $200	$200 -299	$300 -499	$500 -749	$750 -999	$1,000 -1,499	$1,500 and up	Median ($)
City	3.8	5.0	5.0	18.8	25.0	25.8	16.5	922
MSA[1]	1.8	2.2	3.0	10.3	23.3	38.1	21.3	1,103
U.S.	1.7	3.3	8.1	22.7	24.3	25.7	14.3	889

Note: Figures are percentages except for Median; Gross rent is the contract rent plus the estimated average monthly cost of utilities (electricity, gas, and water and sewer) and fuels (oil, coal, kerosene, wood, etc.) if these are paid by the renter (or paid for the renter by someone else); (1) Figures cover the Miami-Fort Lauderdale-West Palm Beach, FL Metropolitan Statistical Area—see Appendix B for areas included
Source: U.S. Census Bureau, 2010-2012 American Community Survey 3-Year Estimates

Year Housing Structure Built

Area	2010 or Later	2000 -2009	1990 -1999	1980 -1989	1970 -1979	1960 -1969	1950 -1959	1940 -1949	Before 1940	Median Year
City	0.6	20.1	5.4	7.6	13.1	10.3	16.1	16.8	10.0	1967
MSA[1]	0.2	14.0	14.9	20.0	22.1	12.8	10.5	3.3	2.2	1980
U.S.	0.5	14.9	13.8	13.9	15.9	11.1	10.9	5.5	13.5	1976

Note: Figures are percentages except for Median Year; (1) Figures cover the Miami-Fort Lauderdale-West Palm Beach, FL Metropolitan Statistical Area—see Appendix B for areas included
Source: U.S. Census Bureau, 2010-2012 American Community Survey 3-Year Estimates

HEALTH

Health Risk Data

Category	MSA[1] (%)	U.S. (%)
Adults aged 18–64 who have any kind of health care coverage	67.9	79.6
Adults who reported being in good or excellent health	81.0	83.1
Adults who are current smokers	13.2	19.6
Adults who are heavy drinkers[2]	4.6	6.1
Adults who are binge drinkers[3]	15.4	16.9
Adults who are overweight (BMI 25.0 - 29.9)	38.8	35.8
Adults who are obese (BMI 30.0 - 99.8)	23.1	27.6
Adults who participated in any physical activities in the past month	74.7	77.1
Adults 50+ who have ever had a sigmoidoscopy or colonoscopy	61.7	67.3
Women aged 40+ who have had a mammogram within the past two years	75.7	74.0
Men aged 40+ who have had a PSA test within the past two years	51.1	45.2
Adults aged 65+ who have had flu shot within the past year	53.0	60.1
Adults who always wear a seatbelt	92.8	93.8

Note: Data as of 2012 unless otherwise noted; (1) Figures cover the Miami-Fort Lauderdale-Miami Beach, FL Metropolitan Statistical Area—see Appendix B for areas included; (2) Heavy drinkers are classified as males having more than two drinks per day or females having more than one drink per day; (3) Binge drinkers are classified as males having five or more drinks on one occasion or females having four or more drinks on one occasion
Source: Centers for Disease Control and Prevention, Behaviorial Risk Factor Surveillance System, SMART: Selected Metropolitan/Micropolitan Area Risk Trends, 2012

Chronic Health Indicators

Category	MSA[1] (%)	U.S. (%)
Adults who have ever been told they had a heart attack	3.8	4.5
Adults who have ever been told they had a stroke	2.4	2.9
Adults who have been told they currently have asthma	5.3	8.9
Adults who have ever been told they have arthritis	21.4	25.7
Adults who have ever been told they have diabetes[2]	10.5	9.7
Adults who have ever been told they had skin cancer	5.9	5.7
Adults who have ever been told they had any other types of cancer	5.7	6.5
Adults who have ever been told they have COPD	6.2	6.2
Adults who have ever been told they have kidney disease	4.0	2.5
Adults who have ever been told they have a form of depression	13.4	18.0

Note: Data as of 2012 unless otherwise noted; (1) Figures cover the Miami-Fort Lauderdale-Miami Beach, FL Metropolitan Statistical Area—see Appendix B for areas included; (2) Figures do not include pregnancy-related, borderline, or pre-diabetes
Source: Centers for Disease Control and Prevention, Behaviorial Risk Factor Surveillance System, SMART: Selected Metropolitan/Micropolitan Area Risk Trends, 2012

Mortality Rates for the Top 10 Causes of Death in the U.S.

ICD-10[a] Sub-Chapter	ICD-10[a] Code	Age-Adjusted Mortality Rate[1] per 100,000 population	
		County[2]	U.S.
Malignant neoplasms	C00-C97	144.4	174.2
Ischaemic heart diseases	I20-I25	128.4	119.1
Other forms of heart disease	I30-I51	36.0	49.6
Chronic lower respiratory diseases	J40-J47	29.0	43.2
Cerebrovascular diseases	I60-I69	31.2	40.3
Organic, including symptomatic, mental disorders	F01-F09	24.9	30.5
Other degenerative diseases of the nervous system	G30-G31	30.3	26.3
Other external causes of accidental injury	W00-X59	14.6	25.1
Diabetes mellitus	E10-E14	23.9	21.3
Hypertensive diseases	I10-I15	21.1	18.8

Note: (a) ICD-10 = International Classification of Diseases 10th Revision; (1) Mortality rates are a three year average covering 2008-2010; (2) Figures cover Miami-Dade County
Source: Centers for Disease Control and Prevention, National Center for Health Statistics. Compressed Mortality File 1999-2010 on CDC WONDER Online Database, released January 2013. Data are compiled from the Compressed Mortality File 1999-2010, Series 20 No. 2P, 2013.

Mortality Rates for Selected Causes of Death

ICD-10[a] Sub-Chapter	ICD-10[a] Code	Age-Adjusted Mortality Rate[1] per 100,000 population	
		County[2]	U.S.
Assault	X85-Y09	9.1	5.5
Diseases of the liver	K70-K76	10.0	12.4
Human immunodeficiency virus (HIV) disease	B20-B24	11.4	3.0
Influenza and pneumonia	J09-J18	9.1	16.4
Intentional self-harm	X60-X84	8.8	11.8
Malnutrition	E40-E46	0.3	0.8
Obesity and other hyperalimentation	E65-E68	1.5	1.6
Renal failure	N17-N19	13.1	13.6
Transport accidents	V01-V99	11.9	12.6
Viral hepatitis	B15-B19	2.1	2.2

Note: (a) ICD-10 = International Classification of Diseases 10th Revision; (1) Mortality rates are a three year average covering 2008-2010; (2) Figures cover Miami-Dade County
Source: Centers for Disease Control and Prevention, National Center for Health Statistics. Compressed Mortality File 1999-2010 on CDC WONDER Online Database, released January 2013. Data are compiled from the Compressed Mortality File 1999-2010, Series 20 No. 2P, 2013.

Health Insurance Coverage

Area	With Health Insurance	With Private Health Insurance	With Public Health Insurance	Without Health Insurance	Population Under Age 18 Without Health Insurance
City	64.7	32.5	35.4	35.3	14.5
MSA[1]	74.3	51.8	30.0	25.7	14.0
U.S.	84.9	65.4	30.4	15.1	7.5

Note: Figures are percentages that cover the civilian noninstitutionalized population; (1) Figures cover the Miami-Fort Lauderdale-West Palm Beach, FL Metropolitan Statistical Area—see Appendix B for areas included
Source: U.S. Census Bureau, 2010-2012 American Community Survey 3-Year Estimates

Number of Medical Professionals

Area[1]	MDs[2]	DOs[2,3]	Dentists	Podiatrists	Chiropractors	Optometrists
Local (number)	8,198	364	1,404	233	441	295
Local (rate[4])	319.4	14.2	54.2	9.0	17.0	11.4
U.S. (rate[4])	267.6	19.6	61.7	5.6	24.7	14.5

Note: Data as of 2012 unless noted; (1) Local data covers Miami-Dade County; (2) Data as of 2011; (3) Doctor of Osteopathic Medicine; (4) rate per 100,000 population
Source: Area Resource File (ARF) 2012-2013. U.S. Department of Health and Human Services, Health Resources and Services Administration, Bureau of Health Professions

Best Hospitals

According to *U.S. News,* the Miami-Miami Beach-Kendall, FL metro area is home to one of the best hospitals in the U.S.: **University of Miami-Jackson Memorial Medical Center** (1 specialty). The hospital listed was nationally ranked in at least one adult specialty. Only 147 hospitals nationwide were nationally ranked in one or more specialties. Eighteen hospitals in the U.S. made the Honor Roll by ranking near the top in at least six specialties.*U.S. News Online, "America's Best Hospitals 2013-14"*

According to *U.S. News,* the Miami-Miami Beach-Kendall, FL metro area is home to two of the best children's hospitals in the U.S.: **Holtz Children's Hospital at UM-Jackson Memorial Hospital; Miami Children's Hospital**. The hospitals listed were highly ranked in at least one pediatric specialty. Eighty-seven hospitals in the U.S. ranked in at least one specialty. Ten children's hospitals in the U.S. made the Honor Roll by ranking near the top in three or more specialties.*U.S. News Online, "America's Best Children's Hospitals 2013-14"*

EDUCATION

Public School District Statistics

District Name	Schls	Pupils	Pupil/ Teacher Ratio	Minority Pupils[1] (%)	Free Lunch Eligible[2] (%)	IEP[3] (%)
Miami-Dade County Public Schools	548	350,239	16.6	91.7	63.2	10.4

Note: Table includes school districts with 2,000 or more students; (1) Percentage of students that are not non-Hispanic white; (2) Percentage of students that are eligible for the free lunch program; (3) Percentage of students that have an Individualized Education Program.
Source: U.S. Department of Education, National Center for Education Statistics, Common Core of Data, Local Education Agency (School District) Universe Survey: School Year 2011-2012; U.S. Department of Education, National Center for Education Statistics, Common Core of Data, Public Elementary/Secondary School Universe Survey: School Year 2011-2012

Best High Schools

High School Name	Rank[1]	Grad. Rate[2] (%)	Coll.[3] (%)	AP/IB/ AICE Tests[4]	AP/IB/ AICE Score[5]	SAT Score[6]	ACT Score[6]
Archimedean Upper Conservatory	54	100	100	1.7	2.7	1654	24.1
Coral Reef Senior H.S.	109	98	97	1.4	2.9	1581	22.4
Design and Architecture Senior High	149	99	98	0.8	3.8	1820	20.0
Dr. Michael M. Krop Senior H.S.	1073	88	97	0.5	3.3	1475	20.8
G Holmes Braddock Senior H.S.	1462	78	93	0.5	2.2	1409	18.8
International Studies Charter H.S.	447	92	100	0.8	3.1	1506	22.5
MAST Academy	76	100	99	1.3	3.0	1690	24.7
Mater Lakes Academy H.S.	1507	85	96	0.3	2.6	1339	18.0
New World School of the Arts	534	99	95	0.6	3.0	1597	23.0
Robert Morgan Educational Center	1441	90	95	0.4	2.3	1413	19.0
School for Advanced Studies	6	100	100	3.3	2.8	1812	26.3
Southwest Miami H.S.	1526	81	91	0.4	3.5	1398	19.0
Young Women's Preparatory Academy	110	95	100	2.0	2.0	n/a	19.2

Note: (1) Public schools are ranked from 1 to 2,000 based on the following self-reported statistics (with the corresponding weight used in calculating their overall score). Schools that were newly founded and did not have a graduating senior class in 2012 were excluded; (2) Four-year, on-time graduation rate (25%); (3) Percent of 2011 graduates who were accepted to college (25%); (4) AP/IB/AICE tests taken per student (25%); (5) Average AP/IB/AICE exam score (10%); (6) Average SAT and/or ACT score (10%); Percent of students enrolled in at least one AP/IB/AICE course (5%)—data not shown; n/a not available
Source: Newsweek and The Daily Beast, "America's Best High Schools 2013"

Highest Level of Education

Area	Less than H.S.	H.S. Diploma	Some College, No Deg.	Associate Degree	Bachelor's Degree	Master's Degree	Prof. School Degree	Doctorate Degree
City	29.6	29.8	11.0	7.2	14.2	4.6	2.7	0.9
MSA[1]	16.4	27.9	18.4	8.5	18.2	6.7	2.7	1.2
U.S.	14.1	28.3	21.3	7.8	18.0	7.5	1.9	1.2

Note: Figures cover persons age 25 and over; (1) Figures cover the Miami-Fort Lauderdale-West Palm Beach, FL Metropolitan Statistical Area—see Appendix B for areas included
Source: U.S. Census Bureau, 2010-2012 American Community Survey 3-Year Estimates

Educational Attainment by Race

Area	High School Graduate or Higher (%)					Bachelor's Degree or Higher (%)				
	Total	White	Black	Asian	Hisp.[2]	Total	White	Black	Asian	Hisp.[2]
City	70.4	71.7	65.4	75.7	66.6	22.4	24.8	9.7	58.8	18.4
MSA[1]	83.6	85.3	77.9	86.7	76.2	28.8	31.4	17.0	48.5	23.4
U.S.	85.9	88.1	82.5	85.5	63.1	28.6	30.0	18.4	50.2	13.4

Note: Figures shown cover persons 25 years old and over; (1) Figures cover the Miami-Fort Lauderdale-West Palm Beach, FL Metropolitan Statistical Area—see Appendix B for areas included; (2) People of Hispanic origin can be of any race
Source: U.S. Census Bureau, 2010-2012 American Community Survey 3-Year Estimates

School Enrollment by Grade and Control

Area	Preschool (%)		Kindergarten (%)		Grades 1 - 4 (%)		Grades 5 - 8 (%)		Grades 9 - 12 (%)	
	Public	Private	Public	Private	Public	Private	Public	Private	Public	Private
City	59.5	40.5	84.8	15.2	87.9	12.1	89.7	10.3	91.2	8.8
MSA[1]	48.7	51.3	82.6	17.4	86.9	13.1	88.2	11.8	88.1	11.9
U.S.	56.9	43.1	87.8	12.2	89.9	10.1	90.0	10.0	90.8	9.2

Note: Figures shown cover persons 3 years old and over; (1) Figures cover the Miami-Fort Lauderdale-West Palm Beach, FL Metropolitan Statistical Area—see Appendix B for areas included
Source: U.S. Census Bureau, 2010-2012 American Community Survey 3-Year Estimates

Average Salaries of Public School Classroom Teachers

Area	2012-13		2013-14		Percent Change 2012-13 to 2013-14	Percent Change 2003-04 to 2013-14
	Dollars	Rank[1]	Dollars	Rank[1]		
Florida	46,598	45	46,691	45	0.20	15.0
U.S. Average	56,103	–	56,689	–	1.04	21.8

Note: (1) State rank ranges from 1 to 51 where 1 indicates highest salary.
Source: National Education Association, Rankings & Estimates: Rankings of the States 2013 and Estimates of School Statistics 2014, March 2014

Higher Education

Four-Year Colleges			Two-Year Colleges			Medical Schools[1]	Law Schools[2]	Voc/ Tech[3]
Public	Private Non-profit	Private For-profit	Public	Private Non-profit	Private For-profit			
2	5	7	4	1	11	2	2	19

Note: Figures cover institutions located within the city limits and include main campuses only; (1) includes schools accredited by the Liaison Committee on Medical Education and the American Osteopathic Association's Commission on Osteopathic College Accreditation; (2) includes ABA-accredited schools, schools with provisional ABA accreditation, and state accredited schools; (3) includes all schools with programs that are less than 2 years.
Source: National Center for Education Statistics, Integrated Postsecondary Education System (IPEDS), 2012-13; Association of American Medical Colleges, Member List, April 24, 2014; American Osteopathic Association, Member List, April 24, 2014; Law School Admission Council, Official Guide to ABA-Approved Law Schools Online, April 24, 2014; Wikipedia, List of Medical Schools in the United States, April 24, 2014; Wikipedia, List of Law Schools in the United States, April 24, 2014

According to U.S. News & World Report, the Miami-Miami Beach-Kendall, FL metro division is home to one of the best national universities in the U.S.: **University of Miami** (#47). The indicators used to capture academic quality fall into a number of categories: assessment by administrators at peer institutions; retention of students; faculty resources; student selectivity; financial resources; alumni giving; high school counselor ratings of colleges; and graduation rate. U.S. News & World Report, "America's Best Colleges 2014"

According to U.S. News & World Report, the Miami-Miami Beach-Kendall, FL metro division is home to one of the top 100 law schools in the U.S.: **University of Miami** (#76). The rankings are based on a weighted average of 12 measures of quality: peer assessment score; assessment score by lawyers/judges; median LSAT scores; median undergrad GPA; acceptance rate; employment rates for graduates; placement success; bar passage rate; faculty resources; expenditures per student; student/faculty ratio; and library resources. U.S. News & World Report, "America's Best Graduate Schools, Law, 2014"

According to *U.S. News & World Report,* the Miami-Miami Beach-Kendall, FL metro division is home to one of the top 100 business schools in the U.S.: **University of Miami** (#91). The rankings are based on a weighted average of the following nine measures: quality assessment; peer assessment; recruiter assessment; placement success; mean starting salary and bonus; student selectivity; mean GMAT and GRE scores; mean undergraduate GPA; and acceptance rate. *U.S. News & World Report, "America's Best Graduate Schools, Business, 2014"*

PRESIDENTIAL ELECTION

2012 Presidential Election Results

Area	Obama	Romney	Other
Miami-Dade County	61.6	37.9	0.4
U.S.	51.0	47.2	1.8

Note: Results are percentages and may not add to 100% due to rounding
Source: Dave Leip's Atlas of U.S. Presidential Elections

EMPLOYERS

Major Employers

Company Name	Industry
Baptist Health South Florida	General medical and surgical hospitals
Baptist Hospital of Miami	General medical and surgical hospitals
County of Miami-Dade	Police protection, county government
County of Miami-Dade	Regulation, administration of transportation
County of, Palm Beach	County supervisors' and executives' office
Florida International University	Colleges and universities
Intercoastal Health Systems	Management services
Miami Dade College	Community college
Mount Sinai Medical Center of Florida	General medical and surgical hospitals
North Broward Hospital District	Hospital, ama approved residency
North Broward Hospital District	General and family practice, physician/surgeon
Royal Caribbean Cruises Ltd.	Computer processing services
Royal Caribbean Cruises Ltd.	Deep sea passenger transportation, except ferry
School Board of Palm Beach County	Public elementary and secondary schools
Style View Products	Storm doors of windows, metal
The Answer Group	Custom computer programming services
University of Miami	Colleges and universities
Veterans Health Administration	General medical and surgical hospitals

Note: Companies shown are located within the Miami-Fort Lauderdale-West Palm Beach, FL Metropolitan Statistical Area.
Source: Hoovers.com; Wikipedia

Best Companies to Work For

Miami Children's Hospital, headquartered in Miami, is among the "100 Best Places to Work in IT." To qualify, companies, both public and private, had to have a minimum of 50 IT employees and were selected based on average salary and bonus increases, the percentage of IT staffers promoted, IT staff turnover rates, training and development programs, and the percentage of women and minorities in IT staff and management positions. In addition, *Computerworld* looked at retention efforts, programs for recognizing and rewarding outstanding performances, and benefits such as flextime, elder care and child care, and reimbursement for college tuition and the cost of pursuing technology certifications. *Computerworld, "100 Best Places to Work in IT 2013"*

PUBLIC SAFETY

Crime Rate

Area	All Crimes	Violent Crimes				Property Crimes		
		Murder	Forcible Rape	Robbery	Aggrav. Assault	Burglary	Larceny -Theft	Motor Vehicle Theft
City	6,547.2	16.7	15.7	505.9	633.8	1,027.0	3,693.9	654.3
Suburbs[1]	4,768.9	6.5	23.2	179.7	356.8	774.8	3,117.7	310.2
Metro[2]	5,053.4	8.1	22.0	231.9	401.1	815.1	3,209.9	365.3
U.S.	3,246.1	4.7	26.9	112.9	242.3	670.2	1,959.3	229.7

Note: Figures are crimes per 100,000 population; (1) All areas within the metro area that are located outside the city limits; (2) Figures cover the Miami-Miami Beach-Kendall, FL Metropolitan Division—see Appendix B for areas included
Source: FBI Uniform Crime Reports, 2012

Hate Crimes

Area	Number of Quarters Reported	Bias Motivation				
		Race	Religion	Sexual Orientation	Ethnicity	Disability
City	4	0	0	0	0	0
U.S.	4	2,797	1,099	1,135	667	92

Source: Federal Bureau of Investigation, Hate Crime Statistics 2012

Identity Theft Consumer Complaints

Area	Complaints	Complaints per 100,000 Population	Rank[2]
MSA[1]	18,941	340.4	1
U.S.	290,056	91.8	-

Note: (1) Figures cover the Miami-Fort Lauderdale-West Palm Beach, FL Metropolitan Statistical Area—see Appendix B for areas included; (2) Rank ranges from 1 to 377 where 1 indicates greatest number of identity theft complaints per 100,000 population
Source: Federal Trade Commission, Consumer Sentinel Network Data Book for January–December 2013

Fraud and Other Consumer Complaints

Area	Complaints	Complaints per 100,000 Population	Rank[2]
MSA[1]	28,103	505.0	17
U.S.	1,811,724	595.2	-

Note: (1) Figures cover the Miami-Fort Lauderdale-West Palm Beach, FL Metropolitan Statistical Area—see Appendix B for areas included; (2) Rank ranges from 1 to 377 where 1 indicates greatest number of identity theft complaints per 100,000 population
Source: Federal Trade Commission, Consumer Sentinel Network Data Book for January–December 2013

RECREATION

Culture

Dance[1]	Theatre[1]	Instrumental Music[1]	Vocal Music[1]	Series and Festivals	Museums and Art Galleries[2]	Zoos and Aquariums[3]
3	2	4	2	4	59	1

Note: (1) Number of professional perfoming groups; (2) Based on organizations with primary SIC code 8412; (3) AZA-accredited
Source: The Grey House Performing Arts Directory, 2013; Association of Zoos & Aquariums, AZA Member Zoos & Aquariums, April 2014; www.AccuLeads.com, May 1, 2014

Professional Sports Teams

Team Name	League	Year Established
Florida Panthers	National Hockey League (NHL)	1993
Miami Dolphins	National Football League (NFL)	1966
Miami Heat	National Basketball Association (NBA)	1988
Miami Marlins	Major League Baseball (MLB)	1993

Note: Includes teams located in the Miami-Fort Lauderdale-West Palm Beach, FL Metropolitan Statistical Area.
Source: Wikipedia, Major Professional Sports Teams of the United States and Canada

CLIMATE

Average and Extreme Temperatures

Temperature	Jan	Feb	Mar	Apr	May	Jun	Jul	Aug	Sep	Oct	Nov	Dec	Yr.
Extreme High (°F)	88	89	92	96	95	98	98	98	97	95	89	87	98
Average High (°F)	75	77	79	82	85	88	89	90	88	85	80	77	83
Average Temp. (°F)	68	69	72	75	79	82	83	83	82	78	73	69	76
Average Low (°F)	59	60	64	68	72	75	76	76	76	72	66	61	69
Extreme Low (°F)	30	35	32	42	55	60	69	68	68	53	39	30	30

Note: Figures cover the years 1948-1990
Source: National Climatic Data Center, International Station Meteorological Climate Summary, 9/96

Average Precipitation/Snowfall/Humidity

Precip./Humidity	Jan	Feb	Mar	Apr	May	Jun	Jul	Aug	Sep	Oct	Nov	Dec	Yr.
Avg. Precip. (in.)	1.9	2.0	2.3	3.0	6.2	8.7	6.1	7.5	8.2	6.6	2.7	1.8	57.1
Avg. Snowfall (in.)	0	0	0	0	0	0	0	0	0	0	0	0	0
Avg. Rel. Hum. 7am (%)	84	84	82	80	81	84	84	86	88	87	85	84	84
Avg. Rel. Hum. 4pm (%)	59	57	57	57	62	68	66	67	69	65	63	60	63

Note: Figures cover the years 1948-1990; Tr = Trace amounts (<0.05 in. of rain; <0.5 in. of snow)
Source: National Climatic Data Center, International Station Meteorological Climate Summary, 9/96

Weather Conditions

Temperature			Daytime Sky			Precipitation		
32°F & below	45°F & below	90°F & above	Clear	Partly cloudy	Cloudy	0.01 inch or more precip.	0.1 inch or more snow/ice	Thunder-storms
< 1	7	55	48	263	54	128	0	74

Note: Figures are average number of days per year and cover the years 1948-1990
Source: National Climatic Data Center, International Station Meteorological Climate Summary, 9/96

HAZARDOUS WASTE

Superfund Sites

Miami has three hazardous waste sites on the EPA's Superfund Final National Priorities List: **Airco Plating Co.; Continental Cleaners; Miami Drum Services**. *U.S. Environmental Protection Agency, Final National Priorities List, April 26, 2014*

AIR & WATER QUALITY

Air Quality Index

Area	Percent of Days when Air Quality was...[2]					AQI Statistics[2]	
	Good	Moderate	Unhealthy for Sensitive Groups	Unhealthy	Very Unhealthy	Maximum	Median
MSA[1]	76.4	22.7	0.8	0.0	0.0	118	41

Note: (1) Data covers the Miami-Fort Lauderdale-West Palm Beach, FL Metropolitan Statistical Area—see Appendix B for areas included; (2) Based on 365 days with AQI data in 2013. Air Quality Index (AQI) is an index for reporting daily air quality. EPA calculates the AQI for five major air pollutants regulated by the Clean Air Act: ground-level ozone, particle pollution (aka particulate matter), carbon monoxide, sulfur dioxide, and nitrogen dioxide. The AQI runs from 0 to 500. The higher the AQI value, the greater the level of air pollution and the greater the health concern. There are six AQI categories: "Good" AQI is between 0 and 50. Air quality is considered satisfactory; "Moderate" AQI is between 51 and 100. Air quality is acceptable; "Unhealthy for Sensitive Groups" When AQI values are between 101 and 150, members of sensitive groups may experience health effects; "Unhealthy" When AQI values are between 151 and 200 everyone may begin to experience health effects; "Very Unhealthy" AQI values between 201 and 300 trigger a health alert; "Hazardous" AQI values over 300 trigger warnings of emergency conditions (not shown).
Source: U.S. Environmental Protection Agency, Air Quality Index Report, 2013

Air Quality Index Pollutants

Area	Percent of Days when AQI Pollutant was...[2]					
	Carbon Monoxide	Nitrogen Dioxide	Ozone	Sulfur Dioxide	Particulate Matter 2.5	Particulate Matter 10
MSA[1]	0.0	1.1	25.5	0.0	73.2	0.3

Note: (1) Data covers the Miami-Fort Lauderdale-West Palm Beach, FL Metropolitan Statistical Area—see Appendix B for areas included; (2) Based on 365 days with AQI data in 2013. The Air Quality Index (AQI) is an index for reporting daily air quality. EPA calculates the AQI for five major air pollutants regulated by the Clean Air Act: ground-level ozone, particle pollution (also known as particulate matter), carbon monoxide, sulfur dioxide, and nitrogen dioxide. The AQI runs from 0 to 500. The higher the AQI value, the greater the level of air pollution and the greater the health concern.
Source: U.S. Environmental Protection Agency, Air Quality Index Report, 2013

Air Quality Trends: Ozone

	2003	2004	2005	2006	2007	2008	2009	2010	2011	2012
MSA[1]	0.066	0.063	0.064	0.074	0.066	0.067	0.062	0.064	0.060	0.062

Note: (1) Data covers the Miami-Fort Lauderdale-West Palm Beach, FL Metropolitan Statistical Area—see Appendix B for areas included. The values shown are the composite ozone concentration averages among trend sites based on the highest fourth daily maximum 8-hour concentration in parts per million. These trends are based on sites having an adequate record of monitoring data during the trend period. Data from exceptional events are included.
Source: U.S. Environmental Protection Agency, Air Quality Monitoring Information, "Air Quality Trends by City, 2000-2012"

Maximum Air Pollutant Concentrations: Particulate Matter, Ozone, CO and Lead

	Particulate Matter 10 (ug/m^3)	Particulate Matter 2.5 Wtd AM (ug/m^3)	Particulate Matter 2.5 24-Hr (ug/m^3)	Ozone (ppm)	Carbon Monoxide (ppm)	Lead (ug/m^3)
MSA[1] Level	73	8.3	20	0.064	2	n/a
NAAQS[2]	150	15	35	0.075	9	0.15
Met NAAQS[2]	Yes	Yes	Yes	Yes	Yes	n/a

Note: (1) Data covers the Miami-Fort Lauderdale-West Palm Beach, FL Metropolitan Statistical Area—see Appendix B for areas included; Data from exceptional events are included; (2) National Ambient Air Quality Standards; ppm = parts per million; ug/m^3 = micrograms per cubic meter; n/a not available.
Concentrations: Particulate Matter 10 (coarse particulate)—highest second maximum 24-hour concentration; Particulate Matter 2.5 Wtd AM (fine particulate)—highest weighted annual mean concentration; Particulate Matter 2.5 24-Hour (fine particulate)—highest 98th percentile 24-hour concentration; Ozone—highest fourth daily maximum 8-hour concentration; Carbon Monoxide—highest second maximum non-overlapping 8-hour concentration; Lead—maximum running 3-month average
Source: U.S. Environmental Protection Agency, Air Quality Monitoring Information, "Air Quality Statistics by City, 2012"

Maximum Air Pollutant Concentrations: Nitrogen Dioxide and Sulfur Dioxide

	Nitrogen Dioxide AM (ppb)	Nitrogen Dioxide 1-Hr (ppb)	Sulfur Dioxide AM (ppb)	Sulfur Dioxide 1-Hr (ppb)	Sulfur Dioxide 24-Hr (ppb)
MSA[1] Level	8	46	n/a	27	n/a
NAAQS[2]	53	100	30	75	140
Met NAAQS[2]	Yes	Yes	n/a	Yes	n/a

Note: (1) Data covers the Miami-Fort Lauderdale-West Palm Beach, FL Metropolitan Statistical Area—see Appendix B for areas included; Data from exceptional events are included; (2) National Ambient Air Quality Standards; ppm = parts per million; ug/m^3 = micrograms per cubic meter; n/a not available.
Concentrations: Nitrogen Dioxide AM—highest arithmetic mean concentration; Nitrogen Dioxide 1-Hr—highest 98th percentile 1-hour daily maximum concentration; Sulfur Dioxide AM—highest annual mean concentration; Sulfur Dioxide 1-Hr—highest 99th percentile 1-hour daily maximum concentration; Sulfur Dioxide 24-Hr—highest second maximum 24-hour concentration
Source: U.S. Environmental Protection Agency, Air Quality Monitoring Information, "Air Quality Statistics by City, 2012"

Drinking Water

Water System Name	Pop. Served	Primary Water Source Type	Violations[1] Health Based	Violations[1] Monitoring/ Reporting
MDWASA - Main System	2,100,000	Ground	0	0

Note: (1) Based on violation data from January 1, 2013 to December 31, 2013 (includes unresolved violations from earlier years)
Source: U.S. Environmental Protection Agency, Office of Ground Water and Drinking Water, Safe Drinking Water Information System (based on data extracted February 10, 2014)

Midland, Texas

Background

In 1881, when Midland Texas might have appeared as a dot on a map, it would have been called the middle of nowhere. In fact, Midland was almost exactly at the midpoint between Fort Worth Texas and El Paso. Today the locals like to tease that Midland is "in the middle of somewhere." Barely a whistle-stop, Midland provided a small shelter where Texas and Pacific Railroad crews could rest and store maintenance equipment. Within ten years, it would become a vital shipping center for the cattle trade.

Little is known about the first inhabitants in the region, though they left plenty of evidence of their existence. The Pecos Trail region is rich with petroglyphs and pictographs. Anthropologists refer to these communities as the Karankawas (hunter-gatherers), and surmise these early scribes are the ancestors of the Comanche, Apache, Kiowa, and Kickapoo nations.

The first westerner to make Midland his permanent home in 1882 was Herman Garrett, a sheep rancher from California. Midland grew quickly. Within three years, 100 families lived there, and by 1900, the population was 1,000. Midland became known as the "Windmill Town," as individual homes built windmills to pump water. After several devastating fires in 1905 and 1909, the town put in a municipal water system and a fire department.

Midland would remain a center of ranching and shipping until May 27, 1923, when a new industry would overrun the town. At 6:00 a.m., in an area just southeast of Midland, the Santa Rita No. 1 "blew." From that time on, Midland's economy and culture would be defined by the price of oil, and its roller coaster ride of market highs and lows. By 1929, there were thirty-six oil companies in Midland. Roads were paved and streetlights were raised as Midland's skyline began to rise from the wide-open landscape. The new Hogal Building was twelve stories high. By 1930, the population blossomed to 5,484. When the Great Depression hit, the demand for petroleum decreased and prices plummeted. By 1932, one third of Midland's workers were unemployed.

World War II brought an increase in oil prices, along with the new Midland Army Air Force Base, a training ground for bomber pilots, giving Midland's economy a much-needed boost. By 1950, 250 oil companies had set up shop in Midland.

In 1972, Midland Community College was founded, and later, a satellite campus in Fort Stockton opened. Twice a year, Midland College hosts free lectures by world-renowned speakers—a Who's Who list of past guest lecturers including such luminaries as Ken Burns, Bill Moyers, Sandra Day O'Connor, Richard Rodriguez, John Updike and Neil deGrasse Tyson.

In recent years, Midland has grabbed headlines due to its association with the Bush family. Laura Bush was born and raised in Midland. Both former presidents George W. Bush, and George H.W. Bush, as well as Barbara and Jeb Bush, lived in Midland. In April of 2006, the George Bush Childhood Home Museum was officially dedicated and has since received over 30,000 visitors.

Midland is a cultural mecca with six museums, as well as a community theater that offers fifteen shows each year. The Midland-Odessa Symphony & Chorale performs eighteen venues each year, with four masterworks, four Pops Concerts, six Chamber Concerts, two Chorale concerts and a youth concert. The Marian Blakemore planetarium offers educational shows and lectures about the history of astronomy.

Midland features a semi-arid climate with long, hot summers and short, moderate winters. The city is occasionally subject to cold waves during the winter, but it rarely sees extended periods of below-freezing cold. Midland receives approximately 14.6 inches of precipitation per year, much of which falls in the summer. Highs exceed 90 °F (32 °C) on 101 days per year, and 100 °F (38 °C) on 16 days.

Rankings

Business/Finance Rankings

- According to data published by the U.S. Conference of Mayors and produced by IHS Global Insight, the Midland metro area was among the metro areas with the fastest-growing GMP (gross metro product) and positive employment trends, at #1. *247wallst.com, "America's Fastest Growing (and Shrinking) Economies," January 31, 2014*

- Based on the Bureau of Labor Statistics (BLS) quarterly reports on employment and wages over fourth-quarter 2011–2012, researchers at 24/7 Wall Street listed the Midland metro area as the #3 metro area for wage growth. *247wallst.com, "American Cities Where Wages Are Soaring," July 15, 2013*

- The Midland metro area appeared on the Milken Institute "2013 Best Performing Cities" list. Rank: #5 out of 179 small metro areas. Criteria: job growth; wage and salary growth; high-tech output growth. *Milken Institute, "Best-Performing Cities 2013," December 2013*

- *Forbes* ranked 184 smaller metro areas in the U.S. in terms of the "Best Small Places for Business and Careers." The Midland metro area was ranked #63. Criteria: costs (business and living); job growth (past and projected); income growth; educational attainment (college and high school); projected economic growth; cultural and recreational opportunities; net migration patterns; number of highly ranked colleges. *Forbes, "The Best Small Places for Business and Careers," August 7, 2013*

Dating/Romance Rankings

- Midland was selected as one of the least romantic cities in the U.S. by video-rental kiosk company Redbox. The city ranked #2 out of 10. Criteria: number of romance-related rentals in 2012. *Redbox, "10 Most/Least Romantic Cities," February 12, 2013*

Environmental Rankings

- The Midland metro area came in at #298 for the relative comfort of its climate on Sperling's list of "chill cities," as measured by the Sperling Heat Index. All 361 metro areas are included. Criteria included daytime high temperatures, nighttime low temperatures, dew point, and relative humidity at the high temperatures. *www.bertsperling.com, "Sperling's Chill Cities," July 18, 2013*

- Sperling's BestPlaces assessed 379 metropolitan areas of the United States for the likelihood of dangerously extreme weather events or earthquakes. In general the Southeast and South-Central regions have the highest risk of weather extremes and earthquakes, while the Pacific Northwest enjoys the lowest risk. Of the least risky metropolitan areas, the Midland metro area was ranked #258. *www.bestplaces.net, "Safest Places from Natural Disasters," April 2011*

- Midland was selected as one of 22 "Smarter Cities" for energy by the Natural Resources Defense Council. Criteria: investment in green power; energy efficiency measures; conservation. *Natural Resources Defense Council, "2010 Smarter Cities," July 19, 2010*

Real Estate Rankings

- The Midland metro area was identified as one of the 15 worst housing markets for the next five years." Criteria: projected annualized change in home prices between the fourth quarter 2012 and the fourth quarter 2017. *The Business Insider, "The 15 Worst Housing Markets for the Next Five Years," May 22, 2013*

- Midland was ranked #195 out of 224 metro areas in terms of housing affordability in 2013 by the National Association of Home Builders (#1 = most affordable). The NAHB-Wells Fargo Housing Opportunity Index (HOI) for a given area is defined as the share of homes sold in that area that would have been affordable to a family earning the local median income, based on standard mortgage underwriting criteria. *National Association of Home Builders®, NAHB-Wells Fargo Housing Opportunity Index, 4th Quarter 2013*

Safety Rankings

- Farmers Insurance, in partnership with Sperling's BestPlaces, ranked metro areas in the U.S. and identified the "Most Secure Places to Live." The Midland metro area ranked #2 out of the top 20 in the small town category (fewer than 150,000 residents). Criteria: economic stability; crime statistics; extreme weather; risk of natural disasters; housing depreciation; foreclosures; air quality; environmental hazards; life expectancy; motor vehicle fatalities; and employment numbers. *Farmers Insurance Group of Companies, "Most Secure U.S. Places to Live in the U.S.," June 25, 2013*

- The National Insurance Crime Bureau ranked 380 metro areas in the U.S. in terms of per capita rates of vehicle theft. The Midland metro area ranked #171 (#1 = highest rate). Criteria: number of vehicle theft offenses per 100,000 inhabitants in 2012. *National Insurance Crime Bureau, "Hot Spots 2012," June 26, 2013*

Seniors/Retirement Rankings

- From its Best Cities for Successful Aging indexes, the Milken Institute generated rankings for metropolitan areas, weighing data in eight categories—general indicators, health care, wellness, living arrangements, transportation and general accessibility, financial well-being, education and employment, and community participation. The Midland metro area was ranked #52 overall in the small metro area category. *Milken Institute, "Best Cities for Successful Aging," July 2012*

- Midland was selected as one of "10 Affordable Cities for Retirement." Criteria: property and sales tax; median home price; cost of living; tax rate on pension and Social Security income; recreation; climate; arts and culture. *AARP The Magazine, "10 Affordable Cities for Retirement," September/October 2011*

Business Environment

CITY FINANCES

City Government Finances

Component	2011 ($000)	2011 ($ per capita)
Total Revenues	162,737	1,567
Total Expenditures	157,576	1,517
Debt Outstanding	130,145	1,253
Cash and Securities[1]	232,092	2,234

Note: (1) Cash and security holdings of a government at the close of its fiscal year, including those of its dependent agencies, utilities, and liquor stores.
Source: U.S Census Bureau, State & Local Government Finances 2011

City Government Revenue by Source

Source	2011 ($000)	2011 ($ per capita)
General Revenue		
From Federal Government	4,186	40
From State Government	3,030	29
From Local Governments	0	0
Taxes		
Property	30,293	292
Sales and Gross Receipts	47,971	462
Personal Income	0	0
Corporate Income	0	0
Motor Vehicle License	0	0
Other Taxes	1,188	11
Current Charges	30,690	295
Liquor Store	0	0
Utility	29,555	285
Employee Retirement	7,251	70

Source: U.S Census Bureau, State & Local Government Finances 2011

City Government Expenditures by Function

Function	2011 ($000)	2011 ($ per capita)	2011 (%)
General Direct Expenditures			
Air Transportation	7,042	68	4.5
Corrections	0	0	0.0
Education	0	0	0.0
Employment Security Administration	0	0	0.0
Financial Administration	7,875	76	5.0
Fire Protection	18,204	175	11.6
General Public Buildings	1,620	16	1.0
Governmental Administration, Other	1,002	10	0.6
Health	4,418	43	2.8
Highways	9,212	89	5.8
Hospitals	0	0	0.0
Housing and Community Development	2,645	25	1.7
Interest on General Debt	3,406	33	2.2
Judicial and Legal	2,856	27	1.8
Libraries	0	0	0.0
Parking	0	0	0.0
Parks and Recreation	13,975	135	8.9
Police Protection	21,151	204	13.4
Public Welfare	0	0	0.0
Sewerage	9,777	94	6.2
Solid Waste Management	7,655	74	4.9
Veterans' Services	0	0	0.0
Liquor Store	0	0	0.0
Utility	31,999	308	20.3
Employee Retirement	4,348	42	2.8

Source: U.S Census Bureau, State & Local Government Finances 2011

DEMOGRAPHICS

Population Growth

Area	1990 Census	2000 Census	2010 Census	Population Growth (%)	
				1990-2000	2000-2010
City	89,358	94,996	111,147	6.3	17.0
MSA[1]	106,611	116,009	136,872	8.8	18.0
U.S.	248,709,873	281,421,906	308,745,538	13.2	9.7

Note: (1) Figures cover the Midland, TX Metropolitan Statistical Area—see Appendix B for areas included
Source: U.S. Census Bureau, Census 1990, 2000, 2010

Household Size

Area	Persons in Household (%)							Average Household Size
	One	Two	Three	Four	Five	Six	Seven or More	
City	24.7	33.0	18.4	12.9	7.1	2.5	1.4	2.77
MSA[1]	24.5	32.8	17.9	13.9	7.1	2.5	1.3	2.78
U.S.	27.6	33.5	15.7	13.2	6.1	2.4	1.5	2.63

Note: (1) Figures cover the Midland, TX Metropolitan Statistical Area—see Appendix B for areas included
Source: U.S. Census Bureau, 2010-2012 American Community Survey 3-Year Estimates

Race

Area	White Alone[2] (%)	Black Alone[2] (%)	Asian Alone[2] (%)	AIAN[3] Alone[2] (%)	NHOPI[4] Alone[2] (%)	Other Race Alone[2] (%)	Two or More Races (%)
City	83.2	8.0	1.9	0.3	0.0	4.9	1.7
MSA[1]	85.1	6.7	1.6	0.4	0.0	4.7	1.5
U.S.	74.0	12.6	4.9	0.8	0.2	4.7	2.8

Note: (1) Figures cover the Midland, TX Metropolitan Statistical Area—see Appendix B for areas included; (2) Alone is defined as not being in combination with one or more other races; (3) American Indian and Alaska Native; (4) Native Hawaiian and Other Pacific Islander
Source: U.S. Census Bureau, 2010-2012 American Community Survey 3-Year Estimates

Hispanic or Latino Origin

Area	Total (%)	Mexican (%)	Puerto Rican (%)	Cuban (%)	Other (%)
City	39.6	37.7	0.0	0.1	1.7
MSA[1]	38.8	36.8	0.1	0.1	1.8
U.S.	16.6	10.7	1.6	0.6	3.7

Note: Persons of Hispanic or Latino origin can be of any race; (1) Figures cover the Midland, TX Metropolitan Statistical Area—see Appendix B for areas included
Source: U.S. Census Bureau, 2010-2012 American Community Survey 3-Year Estimates

Segregation

Type	Segregation Indices[1]				Percent Change		
	1990	2000	2010	2010 Rank[2]	1990-2000	1990-2010	2000-2010
Black/White	n/a	n/a	n/a	n/a	n/a	n/a	n/a
Asian/White	n/a	n/a	n/a	n/a	n/a	n/a	n/a
Hispanic/White	n/a	n/a	n/a	n/a	n/a	n/a	n/a

Note: All figures cover the Metropolitan Statistical Area—see Appendix B for areas included; Figures are based on an analysis of 1990, 2000, and 2010 Census Decennial Census tract data by William H. Frey, Brookings Institution and the University of Michigan Social Science Data Analysis Network. In this analysis all racial groups (whites, blacks, and asians) are non-Hispanic members of those races. Hispanics are shown as a separate category;
(1) Segregation Indices are Dissimilarity Indices that measure the degree to which the minority group is distributed differently than whites across census tracts. They range from 0 (complete integration) to 100 (complete segregation) where the value indicates the percentage of the minority group that needs to move to be distributed exactly like whites; (2) Ranges from 1 (most segregated) to 102 (least segregated); n/a not available.
Source: www.CensusScope.org

Ancestry

Area	German	Irish	English	American	Italian	Polish	French[2]	Scottish	Dutch
City	10.5	7.5	8.1	6.9	1.1	0.5	1.4	1.5	0.9
MSA[1]	10.2	8.0	7.8	6.9	0.9	0.4	1.4	1.7	1.0
U.S.	15.2	11.1	8.2	7.2	5.6	3.1	2.8	1.7	1.4

Note: Figures are the percentage of the total population reporting a particular ancestry. The nine most commonly reported ancestries in the U.S. are shown. Figures include multiple ancestries (e.g. if a person reported being Irish and Italian, they were included in both columns); (1) Figures cover the Midland, TX Metropolitan Statistical Area—see Appendix B for areas included; (2) Excludes Basque
Source: U.S. Census Bureau, 2010-2012 American Community Survey 3-Year Estimates

Foreign-Born Population

Area	Percent of Population Born in								
	Any Foreign Country	Mexico	Asia	Europe	Carribean	South America	Central America[2]	Africa	Canada
City	n/a	n/a	n/a	n/a	n/a	n/a	n/a	n/a	n/a
MSA[1]	n/a	n/a	n/a	n/a	n/a	n/a	n/a	n/a	n/a
U.S.	13.0	3.7	3.7	1.6	1.2	0.9	1.0	0.5	0.3

Note: (1) Figures cover the Midland, TX Metropolitan Statistical Area—see Appendix B for areas included; (2) Excludes Mexico.
Source: U.S. Census Bureau, 2010-2012 American Community Survey 3-Year Estimates

Marital Status

Area	Never Married	Now Married[2]	Separated	Widowed	Divorced
City	30.1	51.8	2.0	5.3	10.8
MSA[1]	28.9	53.3	2.1	5.1	10.6
U.S.	32.4	48.4	2.2	6.0	11.0

Note: Figures are percentages and cover the population 15 years of age and older; (1) Figures cover the Midland, TX Metropolitan Statistical Area—see Appendix B for areas included; (2) Excludes separated
Source: U.S. Census Bureau, 2010-2012 American Community Survey 3-Year Estimates

Age

Area	Percent of Population									Median Age
	Under Age 5	Age 5–19	Age 20–34	Age 35–44	Age 45–54	Age 55–64	Age 65–74	Age 75–84	Age 85+	
City	8.2	21.8	23.6	11.6	12.6	10.9	5.5	4.3	1.5	32.4
MSA[1]	8.2	22.1	22.3	12.0	13.5	11.1	5.5	4.0	1.3	33.1
U.S.	6.4	20.1	20.5	13.1	14.3	12.2	7.3	4.2	1.8	37.3

Note: (1) Figures cover the Midland, TX Metropolitan Statistical Area—see Appendix B for areas included
Source: U.S. Census Bureau, 2010-2012 American Community Survey 3-Year Estimates

Gender

Area	Males	Females	Males per 100 Females
City	55,547	59,258	93.7
MSA[1]	69,616	71,591	97.2
U.S.	153,276,055	158,333,314	96.8

Note: (1) Figures cover the Midland, TX Metropolitan Statistical Area—see Appendix B for areas included
Source: U.S. Census Bureau, 2010-2012 American Community Survey 3-Year Estimates

Religious Groups by Family

Area	Catholic	Baptist	Non-Den.	Methodist[2]	Lutheran	LDS[3]	Pentecostal	Presbyterian[4]	Muslim[5]	Judaism
MSA[1]	22.4	25.3	8.8	4.2	0.7	1.2	1.6	1.9	3.7	<0.1
U.S.	19.1	9.3	4.0	4.0	2.3	2.0	1.9	1.6	0.8	0.7

Note: Figures are the number of adherents as a percentage of the total population; (1) Figures cover the Midland, TX Metropolitan Statistical Area—see Appendix B for areas included; (2) Methodist/Pietist; (3) Latter Day Saints; (4) Reformed; (5) Figures are estimates
Source: Association of Statisticians of American Religious Bodies, 2010 U.S. Religion Census: Religious Congregations & Membership Study

Religious Groups by Tradition

Area	Catholic	Evangelical Protestant	Mainline Protestant	Other Tradition	Black Protestant	Orthodox
MSA[1]	22.4	35.5	7.2	5.4	1.0	<0.1
U.S.	19.1	16.2	7.3	4.3	1.6	0.3

Note: Figures are the number of adherents as a percentage of the total population; (1) Figures cover the Midland, TX Metropolitan Statistical Area—see Appendix B for areas included
Source: Association of Statisticians of American Religious Bodies, 2010 U.S. Religion Census: Religious Congregations & Membership Study

ECONOMY

Gross Metropolitan Product

Area	2011	2012	2013	2014	Rank[2]
MSA[1]	14.7	16.2	17.5	18.7	119

Note: Figures are in billions of dollars; (1) Figures cover the Midland, TX Metropolitan Statistical Area—see Appendix B for areas included; (2) Rank is based on 2014 data and ranges from 1 to 363
Source: The United States Conference of Mayors, U.S. Metro Economies: Outlook—Gross Metropolitan Product, with Metro Employment Projections, November 2013

Economic Growth

Area	2011 (%)	2012 (%)	2013 (%)	2014 (%)	Rank[2]
MSA[1]	6.4	14.4	7.3	4.4	1
U.S.	1.6	2.5	1.7	2.5	–

Note: Figures are real gross metropolitan product (GMP) growth rates and represent annual average percent change; (1) Figures cover the Midland, TX Metropolitan Statistical Area—see Appendix B for areas included; (2) Rank is based on 2013 data and ranges from 1 to 363
Source: The United States Conference of Mayors, U.S. Metro Economies: Outlook—Gross Metropolitan Product, with Metro Employment Projections, November 2013

Metropolitan Area Exports

Area	2007	2008	2009	2010	2011	2012	Rank[2]
MSA[1]	80.2	93.5	75.6	87.2	81.1	104.4	333

Note: Figures are in millions of dollars; (1) Figures cover the Midland, TX Metropolitan Statistical Area—see Appendix B for areas included; (2) Rank is based on 2012 data and ranges from 1 to 369
Source: U.S. Department of Commerce, International Trade Administration, Office of Trade & Industry Information, Manufacturing & Services, data extracted April 1, 2014

INCOME

Income

Area	Per Capita ($)	Median Household ($)	Average Household ($)
City	31,846	59,336	86,405
MSA[1]	31,602	58,875	86,027
U.S.	27,385	51,771	71,579

Note: (1) Figures cover the Midland, TX Metropolitan Statistical Area—see Appendix B for areas included
Source: U.S. Census Bureau, 2010-2012 American Community Survey 3-Year Estimates

Household Income Distribution

Area	Percent of Households Earning							
	Under $15,000	$15,000 -24,999	$25,000 -34,999	$35,000 -49,999	$50,000 -74,999	$75,000 -99,000	$100,000 -149,999	$150,000 and up
City	10.1	9.2	10.0	12.0	20.8	12.3	13.8	12.0
MSA[1]	9.2	9.2	10.4	13.1	20.3	12.0	13.6	12.1
U.S.	13.1	11.0	10.5	13.7	18.1	11.9	12.5	9.1

Note: (1) Figures cover the Midland, TX Metropolitan Statistical Area—see Appendix B for areas included
Source: U.S. Census Bureau, 2010-2012 American Community Survey 3-Year Estimates

Poverty Rate

Area	All Ages	Under 18 Years Old	18 to 64 Years Old	65 Years and Over
City	12.2	18.9	9.6	9.9
MSA[1]	10.8	16.3	8.8	8.5
U.S.	15.7	22.2	14.6	9.3

Note: Figures are percentage of people whose income during the past 12 months was below the poverty level;
(1) Figures cover the Midland, TX Metropolitan Statistical Area—see Appendix B for areas included
Source: U.S. Census Bureau, 2010-2012 American Community Survey 3-Year Estimates

Personal Bankruptcy Filing Rate

Area	2008	2009	2010	2011	2012	2013
Midland County	0.73	0.94	1.17	0.88	0.81	0.38
U.S.	3.53	4.61	4.97	4.37	3.76	3.29

Note: Numbers are per 1,000 population and include Chapter 7 and Chapter 13 filings
Source: Federal Deposit Insurance Corporation, Regional Economic Conditions, March 20, 2014

EMPLOYMENT

Labor Force and Employment

Area	Civilian Labor Force			Workers Employed		
	Dec. 2012	Dec. 2013	% Chg.	Dec. 2012	Dec. 2013	% Chg.
City	75,394	79,562	5.5	73,233	77,357	5.6
MSA[1]	92,254	97,358	5.5	89,593	94,639	5.6
U.S.	154,904,000	154,408,000	-0.3	143,060,000	144,423,000	1.0

Note: Data is not seasonally adjusted and covers workers 16 years of age and older; (1) Metropolitan Statistical Area—see Appendix B for areas included
Source: Bureau of Labor Statistics, Local Area Unemployment Statistics

Unemployment Rate

Area	2013											
	Jan.	Feb.	Mar.	Apr.	May	Jun.	Jul.	Aug.	Sep.	Oct.	Nov.	Dec.
City	3.4	3.2	3.1	3.0	3.4	3.6	3.4	3.2	3.3	3.0	2.9	2.8
MSA[1]	3.4	3.2	3.1	3.0	3.4	3.7	3.5	3.2	3.3	3.1	2.9	2.8
U.S.	8.5	8.1	7.6	7.1	7.3	7.8	7.7	7.3	7.0	7.0	6.6	6.5

Note: Data is not seasonally adjusted and covers workers 16 years of age and older; All figures are percentages;
(1) Metropolitan Statistical Area—see Appendix B for areas included
Source: Bureau of Labor Statistics, Local Area Unemployment Statistics

Employment by Occupation

Occupation Classification	City (%)	MSA[1] (%)	U.S. (%)
Management, Business, Science, and Arts	31.7	30.8	36.0
Natural Resources, Construction, and Maintenance	14.9	14.8	9.1
Production, Transportation, and Material Moving	11.5	12.9	12.0
Sales and Office	27.3	27.1	24.7
Service	14.6	14.4	18.2

Note: Figures cover employed civilians 16 years of age and older; (1) Figures cover the Midland, TX
Metropolitan Statistical Area—see Appendix B for areas included
Source: U.S. Census Bureau, 2010-2012 American Community Survey 3-Year Estimates

Employment by Industry

| Sector | MSA[1] | | U.S. |
	Number of Employees	Percent of Total	Percent of Total
Construction	n/a	n/a	4.2
Education and Health Services	6,900	7.8	15.5
Financial Activities	4,300	4.9	5.7
Government	8,600	9.8	16.1
Information	900	1.0	1.9
Leisure and Hospitality	8,100	9.2	10.2
Manufacturing	3,700	4.2	8.7
Mining and Logging	n/a	n/a	0.6
Other Services	3,100	3.5	3.9
Professional and Business Services	8,800	10.0	13.7
Retail Trade	8,900	10.1	11.4
Transportation and Utilities	4,600	5.2	3.8
Wholesale Trade	5,000	5.7	4.2

Note: Figures cover non-farm employment as of December 2013 and are not seasonally adjusted;
(1) Metropolitan Statistical Area—see Appendix B for areas included; n/a not available
Source: Bureau of Labor Statistics, Current Employment Statistics, Employment, Hours, and Earnings

Occupations with Greatest Projected Employment Growth: 2010 – 2020

Occupation[1]	2010 Employment	2020 Projected Employment	Numeric Employment Change	Percent Employment Change
Combined Food Preparation and Serving Workers, Including Fast Food	243,530	322,520	78,990	32.4
Elementary School Teachers, Except Special Education	166,090	233,860	67,780	40.8
Personal Care Aides	133,820	199,970	66,150	49.4
Retail Salespersons	370,620	433,180	62,560	16.9
Registered Nurses	184,700	245,870	61,160	33.1
Waiters and Waitresses	190,870	244,610	53,730	28.2
Office Clerks, General	262,740	314,810	52,070	19.8
Cashiers	250,510	292,730	42,220	16.9
Home Health Aides	82,420	123,970	41,550	50.4
Customer Service Representatives	200,880	241,030	40,160	20.0

Note: Projections cover Texas; (1) Sorted by numeric employment change
Source: www.projectionscentral.com, State Occupational Projections, 2010–2020 Long-Term Projections

Fastest Growing Occupations: 2010 – 2020

Occupation[1]	2010 Employment	2020 Projected Employment	Numeric Employment Change	Percent Employment Change
Biomedical Engineers	1,440	2,490	1,050	72.9
Diagnostic Medical Sonographers	3,560	5,410	1,850	51.9
Derrick Operators, Oil and Gas	7,190	10,860	3,670	51.1
Home Health Aides	82,420	123,970	41,550	50.4
Personal Care Aides	133,820	199,970	66,150	49.4
Service Unit Operators, Oil, Gas, and Mining	17,870	26,460	8,590	48.0
Special Education Teachers, Middle School	6,170	8,950	2,780	45.1
Special Education Teachers, Preschool, Kindergarten, and Elementary School	12,940	18,750	5,810	44.9
Rotary Drill Operators, Oil and Gas	7,160	10,340	3,180	44.4
Roustabouts, Oil and Gas	17,800	25,580	7,790	43.8

Note: Projections cover Texas; (1) Sorted by percent employment change and excludes occupations with numeric employment change less than 100
Source: www.projectionscentral.com, State Occupational Projections, 2010–2020 Long-Term Projections

Average Wages

Occupation	$/Hr.	Occupation	$/Hr.
Accountants and Auditors	34.93	Maids and Housekeeping Cleaners	9.36
Automotive Mechanics	20.63	Maintenance and Repair Workers	18.71
Bookkeepers	18.08	Marketing Managers	50.77
Carpenters	16.48	Nuclear Medicine Technologists	n/a
Cashiers	9.68	Nurses, Licensed Practical	21.31
Clerks, General Office	16.26	Nurses, Registered	30.14
Clerks, Receptionists/Information	13.36	Nursing Assistants	12.55
Clerks, Shipping/Receiving	n/a	Packers and Packagers, Hand	9.45
Computer Programmers	35.91	Physical Therapists	n/a
Computer Systems Analysts	31.03	Postal Service Mail Carriers	25.01
Computer User Support Specialists	23.54	Real Estate Brokers	22.83
Cooks, Restaurant	11.41	Retail Salespersons	14.55
Dentists	n/a	Sales Reps., Exc. Tech./Scientific	33.58
Electrical Engineers	44.31	Sales Reps., Tech./Scientific	48.05
Electricians	21.13	Secretaries, Exc. Legal/Med./Exec.	15.43
Financial Managers	65.76	Security Guards	12.50
First-Line Supervisors/Managers, Sales	22.28	Surgeons	n/a
Food Preparation Workers	10.27	Teacher Assistants	9.20
General and Operations Managers	58.38	Teachers, Elementary School	23.60
Hairdressers/Cosmetologists	13.68	Teachers, Secondary School	25.80
Internists	n/a	Telemarketers	n/a
Janitors and Cleaners	10.86	Truck Drivers, Heavy/Tractor-Trailer	20.49
Landscaping/Groundskeeping Workers	13.04	Truck Drivers, Light/Delivery Svcs.	15.87
Lawyers	61.47	Waiters and Waitresses	9.80

Note: Wage data covers the Midland, TX Metropolitan Statistical Area—see Appendix B for areas included. Hourly wages for elementary/secondary school teachers and teacher assistants were calculated by the editors from annual wage data assuming a 40 hour work week; n/a not available.
Source: Bureau of Labor Statistics, Metro Area Occupational Employment and Wage Estimates, May 2013

RESIDENTIAL REAL ESTATE

Building Permits

Area	Single-Family			Multi-Family			Total		
	2012	2013	Pct. Chg.	2012	2013	Pct. Chg.	2012	2013	Pct. Chg.
City	599	732	22.2	410	1,092	166.3	1,009	1,824	80.8
MSA[1]	599	732	22.2	410	1,092	166.3	1,009	1,824	80.8
U.S.	518,695	620,802	19.7	310,963	370,020	19.0	829,658	990,822	19.4

Note: (1) Metropolitan Statistical Area—see Appendix B for areas included; figures represent new, privately-owned housing units authorized (unadjusted data); All permit data are based on estimates with imputation.
Source: U.S. Census Bureau, Manufacturing, Mining, and Construction Statistics, Building Permits, 2012, 2013

Homeownership Rate

Area	2006 (%)	2007 (%)	2008 (%)	2009 (%)	2010 (%)	2011 (%)	2012 (%)	2013 (%)
MSA[1]	n/a	n/a	n/a	n/a	n/a	n/a	n/a	n/a
U.S.	68.8	68.1	67.8	67.4	66.9	66.1	65.4	65.1

Note: (1) Figures cover the Midland, TX Metropolitan Statistical Area—see Appendix B for areas included; n/a not available
Source: U.S. Census Bureau, Housing Vacancies and Homeownership Annual Statistics: 2013

Housing Vacancy Rates

Area	Gross Vacancy Rate[2] (%)			Year-Round Vacancy Rate[3] (%)			Rental Vacancy Rate[4] (%)			Homeowner Vacancy Rate[5] (%)		
	2011	2012	2013	2011	2012	2013	2011	2012	2013	2011	2012	2013
MSA[1]	n/a	n/a	n/a	n/a	n/a	n/a	n/a	n/a	n/a	n/a	n/a	n/a
U.S.	14.2	13.8	13.8	11.1	10.8	10.7	9.5	8.7	8.3	2.5	2.0	2.0

Note: (1) Figures cover the Midland, TX Metropolitan Statistical Area—see Appendix B for areas included; (2) The percentage of the total housing inventory that is vacant; (3) The percentage of the housing inventory (excluding seasonal units) that is year-round vacant; (4) The percentage of rental inventory that is vacant for rent; (5) The percentage of homeowner inventory that is vacant for sale; n/a not available
Source: U.S. Census Bureau, Housing Vacancies and Homeownership Annual Statistics: 2013

TAXES

State Corporate Income Tax Rates

State	Tax Rate (%)	Income Brackets ($)	Num. of Brackets	Financial Institution Tax Rate (%)[a]	Federal Income Tax Ded.
Texas	(x)	–	–	(x)	No

Note: Tax rates as of January 1, 2014; (a) Rates listed are the corporate income tax rate applied to financial institutions or excise taxes based on income. Some states have other taxes based upon the value of deposits or shares; (x) Texas imposes a Franchise Tax, otherwise known as margin tax, imposed on entities with more than $1,030,000 total revenues at rate of 1%, or 0.5% for entities primarily engaged in retail or wholesale trade, on lesser of 70% of total revenues or 100% of gross receipts after deductions for either compensation or cost of goods sold.
Source: Federation of Tax Administrators, "State Corporate Income Tax Rates, 2014"

State Individual Income Tax Rates

State	Tax Rate (%)	Income Brackets ($)	Num. of Brackets	Personal Exempt. ($)[1] Single	Personal Exempt. ($)[1] Dependents	Fed. Inc. Tax Ded.
Texas	None	–	–	–	–	–

Note: Tax rates as of January 1, 2014; Local- and county-level taxes are not included; n/a not applicable;
(1) Married joint filers generally receive double the single exemption
Source: Federation of Tax Administrators, "State Individual Income Tax Rates, 2014"

Various State and Local Tax Rates

State	State and Local Sales and Use (%)	State Sales and Use (%)	Gasoline[1] (¢/gal.)	Cigarette[2] ($/pack)	Spirits[3] ($/gal.)	Wine[4] ($/gal.)	Beer[5] ($/gal.)
Texas	8.25	6.25	20.00	1.410	2.40 (f)	0.20	0.20

Note: All tax rates as of January 1, 2014; (1) The American Petroleum Institute has developed a methodology for determining the average tax rate on a gallon of fuel. Rates may include any of the following: excise taxes, environmental fees, storage tank fees, other fees or taxes, general sales tax, and local taxes. In states where gasoline is subject to the general sales tax, or where the fuel tax is based on the average sale price, the average rate determined by API is sensitive to changes in the price of gasoline. States that fully or partially apply general sales taxes to gasoline: CA, CO, GA, IL, IN, MI, NY; (2) The federal excise tax of $1.0066 per pack and local taxes are not included; (3) Rates are those applicable to off-premise sales of 40% alcohol by volume (a.b.v.) distilled spirits in 750ml containers. Local excise taxes are excluded; (4) Rates are those applicable to off-premise sales of 11% a.b.v. non-carbonated wine in 750ml containers; (5) Rates are those applicable to off-premise sales of 4.7% a.b.v. beer in 12 ounce containers; (f) Different rates also applicable according to alcohol content, place of production, size of container, or place purchased (on- or off-premise or onboard airlines).
Source: Tax Foundation, 2014 Facts & Figures: How Does Your State Compare?

State Business Tax Climate Index Rankings

State	Overall Rank	Corporate Tax Index Rank	Individual Income Tax Index Rank	Sales Tax Index Rank	Unemployment Insurance Tax Index Rank	Property Tax Index Rank
Texas	11	38	7	36	14	35

Note: The index is a measure of how each state's tax laws affect economic performance. The lower the rank, the more favorable a state's tax system is for business. States without a given tax are given a ranking of 1. The scores/rankings for the District of Columbia do not affect other states. The 2014 index represents the tax climate as of July 1, 2013.
Source: Tax Foundation, State Business Tax Climate Index 2014

COMMERCIAL UTILITIES

Typical Monthly Electric Bills

Area	Commercial Service ($/month) 1,500 kWh	Commercial Service ($/month) 40 kW demand 14,000 kWh	Industrial Service ($/month) 1,000 kW demand 200,000 kWh	Industrial Service ($/month) 50,000 kW demand 15,000,000 kWh
City	n/a	n/a	n/a	n/a
Average[1]	197	1,636	25,662	1,485,307

Note: Based on total rates in effect July 1, 2013; (1) average based on 180 utilities surveyed; n/a not available
Source: Edison Electric Institute, Typical Bills and Average Rates Report, Summer 2013

TRANSPORTATION

Means of Transportation to Work

Area	Car/Truck/Van		Public Transportation			Bicycle	Walked	Other Means	Worked at Home
	Drove Alone	Car-pooled	Bus	Subway	Railroad				
City	83.9	11.2	0.3	0.0	0.0	0.2	1.1	1.1	2.3
MSA[1]	84.3	10.1	0.2	0.0	0.0	0.2	1.0	1.0	3.3
U.S.	76.4	9.7	2.6	1.7	0.5	0.6	2.8	1.3	4.3

Note: Figures are percentages and cover workers 16 years of age and older; (1) Figures cover the Midland, TX Metropolitan Statistical Area—see Appendix B for areas included
Source: U.S. Census Bureau, 2010-2012 American Community Survey 3-Year Estimates

Travel Time to Work

Area	Less Than 10 Minutes	10 to 19 Minutes	20 to 29 Minutes	30 to 44 Minutes	45 to 59 Minutes	60 to 89 Minutes	90 Minutes or More
City	19.8	48.0	15.8	10.4	1.8	1.8	2.3
MSA[1]	18.2	46.7	17.3	11.1	2.5	1.9	2.3
U.S.	13.5	29.8	20.9	20.1	7.5	5.6	2.5

Note: Figures are percentages and include workers 16 years old and over; (1) Figures cover the Midland, TX Metropolitan Statistical Area—see Appendix B for areas included
Source: U.S. Census Bureau, 2010-2012 American Community Survey 3-Year Estimates

Travel Time Index

Area	1985	1990	1995	2000	2005	2010	2011
Urban Area[1]	n/a	n/a	n/a	n/a	n/a	n/a	n/a
Average[2]	1.09	1.14	1.16	1.19	1.23	1.18	1.18

Note: Travel Time Index—the ratio of travel time in the peak period to the travel time at free-flow conditions. For example, a value of 1.30 indicates a 20-minute free-flow trip takes 26 minutes in the peak. Free-flow speeds (60 mph on freeways and 35 mph on principal arterials) are used as the comparison threshold; (1) Data for the Midland, TX urban area was not available; (2) average of 498 urban areas
Source: Texas Transportation Institute, Urban Mobility Report 2012, December 2012

Public Transportation

Agency Name / Mode of Transportation	Vehicles Operated in Maximum Service	Annual Unlinked Passenger Trips (in thous.)	Annual Passenger Miles (in thous.)
Midland-Odessa Urban Transit District			
Bus (directly operated)	12	479.8	1,439.5
Commuter Bus (purchased transportation)	2	4.2	125.2
Demand Response (directly operated)	6	29.6	149.3

Source: Federal Transit Administration, National Transit Database, 2012

Air Transportation

Airport Name and Code / Type of Service	Passenger Airlines[1]	Passenger Enplanements	Freight Carriers[2]	Freight (lbs.)
Midland International Airport (MAF)				
Domestic service (U.S. carriers - 2013)	10	506,054	5	3,714,965
International service (U.S. carriers - 2012)	0	0	0	0

Note: (1) Includes all U.S.-based major, minor and commuter airlines that carried at least one passenger during the year; (2) Includes all U.S.-based airlines and freight carriers that transported at least one lb. of freight during the year.
Source: Bureau of Transportation Statistics, The Intermodal Transportation Database, Air Carriers: T-100 Domestic Market (U.S. Carriers), 2013; Bureau of Transportation Statistics, The Intermodal Transportation Database, Air Carriers: T-100 International Market (U.S. Carriers), 2012

Other Transportation Statistics

Major Highways:	I-20
Amtrak Service:	No
Major Waterways/Ports:	None

Source: Amtrak.com; Google Maps

BUSINESSES

Major Business Headquarters

Company Name	Rankings	
	Fortune[1]	Forbes[2]
No companies listed	-	-

Note: (1) Fortune 500—companies that produce a 10-K are ranked 1 to 500 based on 2012 revenue; (2) all private companies with at least $2 billion in annual revenue through the end of their most current fiscal year are ranked 1 to 224; companies listed are headquartered in the city; dashes indicate no ranking
Source: Fortune, "Fortune 500," May 20, 2013; Forbes, "America's Largest Private Companies," December 18, 2013

Fast-Growing Businesses

According to *Fortune*, Midland is home to one of the 100 fastest-growing companies in the world: **Concho Resources** (#54). Companies were ranked by their revenue growth rate; their EPS growth rate; and their three-year annualized total return to investors for the period ending June 30, 2013. Criteria for inclusion: a company, foreign or domestic, must trade on a major U.S. stock exchange; must file quarterly reports with the SEC; must have a minimum market capitalization of $250 million; must have a stock price of at least $5 on June 29, 2013; must have been trading continuously since June 30, 2009; must have revenue and net income for the four quarters ended on or before April 30, 2013, of at least $50 million and $10 million, respectively; and must have posted a compound annual growth in revenue and earnings per share of at least 20% annually over the three years ending on or before April 30, 2013. REITs, limited-liability companies, limited parterships, companies about to be acquired, and companies that lost money in the quarter ending April 30, 2013 were excluded. *Fortune, "100 Fastest-Growing Companies," August 29, 2013*

Minority- and Women-Owned Businesses

Group	All Firms		Firms with Paid Employees			
	Firms	Sales ($000)	Firms	Sales ($000)	Employees	Payroll ($000)
Asian	447	119,053	128	79,440	960	22,455
Black	382	27,258	(s)	(s)	(s)	(s)
Hispanic	(s)	(s)	(s)	(s)	(s)	(s)
Women	3,332	554,300	(s)	(s)	(s)	(s)
All Firms	13,791	17,850,108	3,152	16,941,762	54,240	1,932,582

Note: Figures cover firms located in the city; minority- and women-owned business are defined as firms in which the corresponding group own 51% or more of the stock or equity of the company; (s) estimates are suppressed when publication standards are not met
Source: U.S. Census Bureau, 2007 Economic Census, Survey of Business Owners (2012 Survey of Business Owners data will be released starting in June 2015)

HOTELS & CONVENTION CENTERS

Hotels/Motels

Area	5 Star		4 Star		3 Star		2 Star		1 Star		Not Rated	
	Num.	Pct.[3]	Num.	Pct.[3]	Num.	Pct.[3]	Num.	Pct.[3]	Num.	Pct.[3]	Num.	Pct.[3]
City[1]	0	0.0	0	0.0	10	14.5	38	55.1	5	7.2	16	23.2
Total[2]	142	0.9	1,005	6.0	5,147	30.9	8,578	51.4	408	2.4	1,397	8.4

Note: (1) Figures cover Midland and vicinity; (2) Figures cover all 100 cities in this book; (3) Percentage of hotels which have a given star rating; Star ratings are determined by expedia.com and offer an indication of the general quality of a particular hotel.
Source: expedia.com, April 7, 2014

Major Convention Centers

Name	Overall Space (sq. ft.)	Exhibit Space (sq. ft.)	Meeting Space (sq. ft.)	Meeting Rooms
Midland Center	n/a	12,500	n/a	n/a

Note: Table includes convention centers located in the Midland, TX metro area; n/a not available
Source: Original research

Living Environment

COST OF LIVING

Cost of Living Index

Composite Index	Groceries	Housing	Utilities	Trans-portation	Health Care	Misc. Goods/Services
99.4	88.3	100.2	93.2	104.7	95.0	103.7

Note: The Cost of Living Index measures regional differences in the cost of consumer goods and services, excluding taxes and non-consumer expenditures, for professional and managerial households in the top income quintile. It is based on more than 50,000 prices covering almost 60 different items for which prices are collected three times a year by chambers of commerce, economic development organizations or university applied economic centers in each participating urban area. The numbers shown should be read as a percentage above or below the national average of 100. For example, a value of 115.4 in the groceries column indicates that grocery prices are 15.4% higher than the national average. Small differences in the index numbers should not be interpreted as significant; Figures cover the Midland TX urban area.
Source: The Council for Community and Economic Research, ACCRA Cost of Living Index, 2013

Grocery Prices

Area[1]	T-Bone Steak ($/pound)	Frying Chicken ($/pound)	Whole Milk ($/half gal.)	Eggs ($/dozen)	Orange Juice ($/64 oz.)	Coffee ($/11.5 oz.)
City[2]	9.55	1.09	2.05	1.92	3.51	3.94
Avg.	10.19	1.28	2.34	1.81	3.48	4.39
Min.	8.56	0.94	1.44	1.19	2.78	3.40
Max.	14.82	2.28	3.56	3.73	6.23	7.32

*Note: (1) Values for the local area are compared with the average, minimum and maximum values for all 327 areas in the Cost of Living Index; (2) Figures cover the Midland TX urban area; **T-Bone Steak** (price per pound); **Frying Chicken** (price per pound, whole fryer); **Whole Milk** (half gallon carton); **Eggs** (price per dozen, Grade A, large); **Orange Juice** (64 oz. Tropicana or Florida Natural); **Coffee** (11.5 oz. can, vacuum-packed, Maxwell House, Hills Bros, or Folgers).*
Source: The Council for Community and Economic Research, ACCRA Cost of Living Index, 2013

Housing and Utility Costs

Area[1]	New Home Price ($)	Apartment Rent ($/month)	All Electric ($/month)	Part Electric ($/month)	Other Energy ($/month)	Telephone ($/month)
City[2]	260,386	1,215	-	115.78	40.33	24.95
Avg.	295,864	900	171.38	91.82	70.12	27.73
Min.	185,506	458	117.80	48.81	33.67	17.16
Max.	1,358,917	3,783	441.68	171.40	372.65	39.47

*Note: (1) Values for the local area are compared with the average, minimum and maximum values for all 327 areas in the Cost of Living Index; (2) Figures cover the Midland TX urban area; **New Home Price** (2,400 sf living area, 8,000 sf lot, in urban area with full utilities); **Apartment Rent** (950 sf 2 bedroom/1.5 or 2 bath, unfurnished, excluding all utilities except water); **All Electric** (average monthly cost for an all-electric home); **Part Electric** (average monthly cost for a part-electric home); **Other Energy** (average monthly cost for natural gas, fuel oil, coal, wood, and any other forms of energy except electricity); **Telephone** (price includes basic monthly rate for a private residential line plus additional local usage charges incurred by a family of four).*
Source: The Council for Community and Economic Research, ACCRA Cost of Living Index, 2013

Health Care, Transportation, and Other Costs

Area[1]	Doctor ($/visit)	Dentist ($/visit)	Optometrist ($/visit)	Gasoline ($/gallon)	Beauty Salon ($/visit)	Men's Shirt ($)
City[2]	92.67	82.00	94.33	3.32	34.95	22.93
Avg.	101.40	86.48	96.16	3.44	33.87	26.55
Min.	61.67	50.83	50.12	3.08	18.92	12.48
Max.	182.71	152.50	223.78	4.33	68.22	52.03

*Note: (1) Values for the local area are compared with the average, minimum and maximum values for all 327 areas in the Cost of Living Index; (2) Figures cover the Midland TX urban area; **Doctor** (general practitioners routine exam of an established patient); **Dentist** (adult teeth cleaning and periodic oral examination); **Optometrist** (full vision eye exam for established adult patient); **Gasoline** (one gallon regular unleaded, national brand, including all taxes, cash price at self-service pump if available); **Beauty Salon** (woman's shampoo, trim, and blow-dry); **Men's Shirt** (cotton/polyester dress shirt, pinpoint weave, long sleeves).*
Source: The Council for Community and Economic Research, ACCRA Cost of Living Index, 2013

HOUSING

House Price Index (HPI)

Area	National Ranking[2]	Quarterly Change (%)	One-Year Change (%)	Five-Year Change (%)
MSA[1]	(a)	n/a	11.37	26.16
U.S.[3]	–	1.20	7.69	4.18

Note: The HPI is a weighted repeat sales index. It measures average price changes in repeat sales or refinancings on the same properties. This information is obtained by reviewing repeat mortgage transactions on single-family properties whose mortgages have been purchased or securitized by Fannie Mae or Freddie Mac in January 1975; (1) Midland, TX Metropolitan Statistical Area—see Appendix B for areas included; (2) Rankings are based on annual percentage change for all metro areas containing at least 15,000 transactions over the last 10 years and ranges from 1 to 283; (3) figures based on a weighted average of Census Division estimates using a seasonally adjusted, purchase-only index; all figures are for the period ending December 31, 2013; n/a not available; (a) Not ranked because of increased index variability due to smaller sample size
Source: Federal Housing Finance Agency, House Price Index, February 25, 2014

Median Single-Family Home Prices

Area	2011	2012	2013p	Percent Change 2012 to 2013
MSA[1]	n/a	n/a	n/a	n/a
U.S. Average	166.2	177.2	197.4	11.4

Note: Figures are median sales prices of existing single-family homes in thousands of dollars; (p) preliminary; n/a not available; (1) Midland, TX Metropolitan Statistical Area—see Appendix B for areas included
Source: National Association of Realtors, Median Sales Price of Existing Single-Family Homes for Metropolitan Areas, 4th Quarter 2013

Qualifying Income Based on Median Sales Price of Existing Single-Family Homes

Area	With 5% Down ($)	With 10% Down ($)	With 20% Down ($)
MSA[1]	n/a	n/a	n/a
U.S. Average	45,395	43,006	38,228

Note: Figures are preliminary; Qualifying income is based on a mortgage rate of 4.4%. Monthly principal and interest payment is limited to 25% of income; n/a not available; (1) Midland, TX Metropolitan Statistical Area—see Appendix B for areas included
Source: National Association of Realtors, Qualifying Income Based on Median Sales Price of Existing Single-Family Homes for Metropolitan Areas, 4th Quarter 2013

Median Apartment Condo-Coop Home Prices

Area	2011	2012	2013p	Percent Change 2012 to 2013
MSA[1]	n/a	n/a	n/a	n/a
U.S. Average	165.1	173.7	194.9	12.2

Note: Figures are median sales prices of existing apartment condo-coop homes in thousands of dollars; (p) preliminary; n/a not available; (1) Midland, TX Metropolitan Statistical Area—see Appendix B for areas included
Source: National Association of Realtors, Median Sales Price of Existing Apartment Condo-Coop Homes for Metropolitan Areas, 4th Quarter 2013

Gross Monthly Rent

Area	Under $200	$200 -299	$300 -499	$500 -749	$750 -999	$1,000 -1,499	$1,500 and up	Median ($)
City	0.7	0.7	2.8	23.3	29.8	31.4	11.3	939
MSA[1]	0.6	0.9	4.0	24.3	29.1	30.2	10.9	923
U.S.	1.7	3.3	8.1	22.7	24.3	25.7	14.3	889

Note: Figures are percentages except for Median; Gross rent is the contract rent plus the estimated average monthly cost of utilities (electricity, gas, and water and sewer) and fuels (oil, coal, kerosene, wood, etc.) if these are paid by the renter (or paid for the renter by someone else); (1) Figures cover the Midland, TX Metropolitan Statistical Area—see Appendix B for areas included
Source: U.S. Census Bureau, 2010-2012 American Community Survey 3-Year Estimates

Year Housing Structure Built

Area	2010 or Later	2000 -2009	1990 -1999	1980 -1989	1970 -1979	1960 -1969	1950 -1959	1940 -1949	Before 1940	Median Year
City	0.7	12.0	8.4	22.1	18.1	11.9	20.5	4.5	1.7	1976
MSA[1]	0.8	13.6	11.5	22.5	16.5	11.0	17.8	4.3	1.9	1979
U.S.	0.5	14.9	13.8	13.9	15.9	11.1	10.9	5.5	13.5	1976

Note: Figures are percentages except for Median Year; (1) Figures cover the Midland, TX Metropolitan Statistical Area—see Appendix B for areas included
Source: U.S. Census Bureau, 2010-2012 American Community Survey 3-Year Estimates

HEALTH

Health Risk Data

Category	MSA[1] (%)	U.S. (%)
Adults aged 18–64 who have any kind of health care coverage	n/a	79.6
Adults who reported being in good or excellent health	n/a	83.1
Adults who are current smokers	n/a	19.6
Adults who are heavy drinkers[2]	n/a	6.1
Adults who are binge drinkers[3]	n/a	16.9
Adults who are overweight (BMI 25.0 - 29.9)	n/a	35.8
Adults who are obese (BMI 30.0 - 99.8)	n/a	27.6
Adults who participated in any physical activities in the past month	n/a	77.1
Adults 50+ who have ever had a sigmoidoscopy or colonoscopy	n/a	67.3
Women aged 40+ who have had a mammogram within the past two years	n/a	74.0
Men aged 40+ who have had a PSA test within the past two years	n/a	45.2
Adults aged 65+ who have had flu shot within the past year	n/a	60.1
Adults who always wear a seatbelt	n/a	93.8

Note: Data as of 2012 unless otherwise noted; n/a not available; (1) Figures cover the Midland, TX Metropolitan Statistical Area—see Appendix B for areas included; (2) Heavy drinkers are classified as males having more than two drinks per day or females having more than one drink per day; (3) Binge drinkers are classified as males having five or more drinks on one occasion or females having four or more drinks on one occasion
Source: Centers for Disease Control and Prevention, Behaviorial Risk Factor Surveillance System, SMART: Selected Metropolitan/Micropolitan Area Risk Trends, 2012

Chronic Health Indicators

Category	MSA[1] (%)	U.S. (%)
Adults who have ever been told they had a heart attack	n/a	4.5
Adults who have ever been told they had a stroke	n/a	2.9
Adults who have been told they currently have asthma	n/a	8.9
Adults who have ever been told they have arthritis	n/a	25.7
Adults who have ever been told they have diabetes[2]	n/a	9.7
Adults who have ever been told they had skin cancer	n/a	5.7
Adults who have ever been told they had any other types of cancer	n/a	6.5
Adults who have ever been told they have COPD	n/a	6.2
Adults who have ever been told they have kidney disease	n/a	2.5
Adults who have ever been told they have a form of depression	n/a	18.0

Note: Data as of 2012 unless otherwise noted; n/a not available; (1) Figures cover the Midland, TX Metropolitan Statistical Area—see Appendix B for areas included; (2) Figures do not include pregnancy-related, borderline, or pre-diabetes
Source: Centers for Disease Control and Prevention, Behaviorial Risk Factor Surveillance System, SMART: Selected Metropolitan/Micropolitan Area Risk Trends, 2012

Mortality Rates for the Top 10 Causes of Death in the U.S.

ICD-10[a] Sub-Chapter	ICD-10[a] Code	Age-Adjusted Mortality Rate[1] per 100,000 population	
		County[2]	U.S.
Malignant neoplasms	C00-C97	144.3	174.2
Ischaemic heart diseases	I20-I25	129.8	119.1
Other forms of heart disease	I30-I51	46.5	49.6
Chronic lower respiratory diseases	J40-J47	53.3	43.2
Cerebrovascular diseases	I60-I69	47.5	40.3
Organic, including symptomatic, mental disorders	F01-F09	10.4	30.5
Other degenerative diseases of the nervous system	G30-G31	50.6	26.3
Other external causes of accidental injury	W00-X59	20.5	25.1
Diabetes mellitus	E10-E14	21.6	21.3
Hypertensive diseases	I10-I15	14.3	18.8

Note: (a) ICD-10 = International Classification of Diseases 10th Revision; (1) Mortality rates are a three year average covering 2008-2010; (2) Figures cover Midland County
Source: Centers for Disease Control and Prevention, National Center for Health Statistics. Compressed Mortality File 1999-2010 on CDC WONDER Online Database, released January 2013. Data are compiled from the Compressed Mortality File 1999-2010, Series 20 No. 2P, 2013.

Mortality Rates for Selected Causes of Death

ICD-10[a] Sub-Chapter	ICD-10[a] Code	Age-Adjusted Mortality Rate[1] per 100,000 population	
		County[2]	U.S.
Assault	X85-Y09	Suppressed	5.5
Diseases of the liver	K70-K76	19.2	12.4
Human immunodeficiency virus (HIV) disease	B20-B24	Suppressed	3.0
Influenza and pneumonia	J09-J18	44.1	16.4
Intentional self-harm	X60-X84	9.6	11.8
Malnutrition	E40-E46	Suppressed	0.8
Obesity and other hyperalimentation	E65-E68	Suppressed	1.6
Renal failure	N17-N19	12.8	13.6
Transport accidents	V01-V99	24.9	12.6
Viral hepatitis	B15-B19	Suppressed	2.2

Note: (a) ICD-10 = International Classification of Diseases 10th Revision; (1) Mortality rates are a three year average covering 2008-2010; (2) Figures cover Midland County
Source: Centers for Disease Control and Prevention, National Center for Health Statistics. Compressed Mortality File 1999-2010 on CDC WONDER Online Database, released January 2013. Data are compiled from the Compressed Mortality File 1999-2010, Series 20 No. 2P, 2013.

Health Insurance Coverage

Area	With Health Insurance	With Private Health Insurance	With Public Health Insurance	Without Health Insurance	Population Under Age 18 Without Health Insurance
City	79.5	66.3	22.6	20.5	14.6
MSA[1]	78.3	65.8	21.5	21.7	18.2
U.S.	84.9	65.4	30.4	15.1	7.5

Note: Figures are percentages that cover the civilian noninstitutionalized population; (1) Figures cover the Midland, TX Metropolitan Statistical Area—see Appendix B for areas included
Source: U.S. Census Bureau, 2010-2012 American Community Survey 3-Year Estimates

Number of Medical Professionals

Area[1]	MDs[2]	DOs[2,3]	Dentists	Podiatrists	Chiropractors	Optometrists
Local (number)	288	8	68	4	22	18
Local (rate[4])	205.7	5.7	46.3	2.7	15.0	12.3
U.S. (rate[4])	267.6	19.6	61.7	5.6	24.7	14.5

Note: Data as of 2012 unless noted; (1) Local data covers Midland County; (2) Data as of 2011; (3) Doctor of Osteopathic Medicine; (4) rate per 100,000 population
Source: Area Resource File (ARF) 2012-2013. U.S. Department of Health and Human Services, Health Resources and Services Administration, Bureau of Health Professions

EDUCATION

Public School District Statistics

District Name	Schls	Pupils	Pupil/ Teacher Ratio	Minority Pupils[1] (%)	Free Lunch Eligible[2] (%)	IEP[3] (%)
Midland ISD	35	22,628	16.3	68.9	40.8	6.7

Note: Table includes school districts with 2,000 or more students; (1) Percentage of students that are not non-Hispanic white; (2) Percentage of students that are eligible for the free lunch program; (3) Percentage of students that have an Individualized Education Program.
Source: U.S. Department of Education, National Center for Education Statistics, Common Core of Data, Local Education Agency (School District) Universe Survey: School Year 2011-2012; U.S. Department of Education, National Center for Education Statistics, Common Core of Data, Public Elementary/Secondary School Universe Survey: School Year 2011-2012

Highest Level of Education

Area	Less than H.S.	H.S. Diploma	Some College, No Deg.	Associate Degree	Bachelor's Degree	Master's Degree	Prof. School Degree	Doctorate Degree
City	18.0	23.3	28.3	7.2	16.7	4.8	1.1	0.6
MSA[1]	18.5	23.8	27.5	7.3	16.3	4.9	1.0	0.6
U.S.	14.1	28.3	21.3	7.8	18.0	7.5	1.9	1.2

Note: Figures cover persons age 25 and over; (1) Figures cover the Midland, TX Metropolitan Statistical Area—see Appendix B for areas included
Source: U.S. Census Bureau, 2010-2012 American Community Survey 3-Year Estimates

Educational Attainment by Race

Area	High School Graduate or Higher (%)					Bachelor's Degree or Higher (%)				
	Total	White	Black	Asian	Hisp.[2]	Total	White	Black	Asian	Hisp.[2]
City	82.0	83.0	84.0	76.7	59.4	23.2	24.3	15.5	43.1	6.1
MSA[1]	81.5	82.4	83.8	77.6	59.2	22.8	23.8	15.3	45.4	6.8
U.S.	85.9	88.1	82.5	85.5	63.1	28.6	30.0	18.4	50.2	13.4

Note: Figures shown cover persons 25 years old and over; (1) Figures cover the Midland, TX Metropolitan Statistical Area—see Appendix B for areas included; (2) People of Hispanic origin can be of any race
Source: U.S. Census Bureau, 2010-2012 American Community Survey 3-Year Estimates

School Enrollment by Grade and Control

Area	Preschool (%)		Kindergarten (%)		Grades 1 - 4 (%)		Grades 5 - 8 (%)		Grades 9 - 12 (%)	
	Public	Private	Public	Private	Public	Private	Public	Private	Public	Private
City	38.2	61.8	77.7	22.3	89.1	10.9	88.0	12.0	89.3	10.7
MSA[1]	43.2	56.8	81.3	18.7	90.9	9.1	88.7	11.3	87.9	12.1
U.S.	56.9	43.1	87.8	12.2	89.9	10.1	90.0	10.0	90.8	9.2

Note: Figures shown cover persons 3 years old and over; (1) Figures cover the Midland, TX Metropolitan Statistical Area—see Appendix B for areas included
Source: U.S. Census Bureau, 2010-2012 American Community Survey 3-Year Estimates

Average Salaries of Public School Classroom Teachers

Area	2012-13		2013-14		Percent Change 2012-13 to 2013-14	Percent Change 2003-04 to 2013-14
	Dollars	Rank[1]	Dollars	Rank[1]		
Texas	48,819	35	49,270	35	0.92	21.7
U.S. Average	56,103	–	56,689	–	1.04	21.8

Note: (1) State rank ranges from 1 to 51 where 1 indicates highest salary.
Source: National Education Association, Rankings & Estimates: Rankings of the States 2013 and Estimates of School Statistics 2014, March 2014

Higher Education

Four-Year Colleges			Two-Year Colleges			Medical Schools[1]	Law Schools[2]	Voc/ Tech[3]
Public	Private Non-profit	Private For-profit	Public	Private Non-profit	Private For-profit			
1	0	0	0	0	1	0	0	0

Note: Figures cover institutions located within the city limits and include main campuses only; (1) includes schools accredited by the Liaison Committee on Medical Education and the American Osteopathic Association's Commission on Osteopathic College Accreditation; (2) includes ABA-accredited schools, schools with provisional ABA accreditation, and state accredited schools; (3) includes all schools with programs that are less than 2 years.
Source: National Center for Education Statistics, Integrated Postsecondary Education System (IPEDS), 2012-13; Association of American Medical Colleges, Member List, April 24, 2014; American Osteopathic Association, Member List, April 24, 2014; Law School Admission Council, Official Guide to ABA-Approved Law Schools Online, April 24, 2014; Wikipedia, List of Medical Schools in the United States, April 24, 2014; Wikipedia, List of Law Schools in the United States, April 24, 2014

PRESIDENTIAL ELECTION

2012 Presidential Election Results

Area	Obama	Romney	Other
Midland County	18.6	80.1	1.4
U.S.	51.0	47.2	1.8

Note: Results are percentages and may not add to 100% due to rounding
Source: Dave Leip's Atlas of U.S. Presidential Elections

EMPLOYERS

Major Employers

Company Name	Industry
Albertson's	Grocery
Bobby Cox Companies	Retail/ restaurants
City of Odessa	City government
Cudd Energy	Oil & gas
Dixie Electric	Electric
Ector County	Government
Ector County I.S.D.	Public education
Family Dollar	Distribution
Halliburton Services	Oil & gas
HEB	Grocery
Holloman Construction	Oil field construction
Investment Corp. of America	Financial
Lithia Motors	Automotive
Medical Center Hospital	County hospital
Nurses Unlimited	Medical
Odessa College	Education
Odessa Regional Medical Center	Medical
REXtac	Manufacturer
Saulsbury Companies	Electric & construction
Sewell Family of Dealerships	Automotive
Southwest Convenience Stores	Retail/ service
Texas Tech Univ Health Sciences Ctr	Education/ medical
The University of Texas Permian Basin	Education
Walmart	Retail
Weatherford	Oil & gas

Note: Companies shown are located within the Midland, TX Metropolitan Statistical Area.
Source: Hoovers.com; Wikipedia

PUBLIC SAFETY

Crime Rate

Area	All Crimes	Violent Crimes				Property Crimes		
		Murder	Forcible Rape	Robbery	Aggrav. Assault	Burglary	Larceny -Theft	Motor Vehicle Theft
City	2,945.4	3.5	18.2	45.0	277.6	483.4	2,000.2	117.6
Suburbs[1]	2,400.9	3.1	6.3	6.3	191.9	487.7	1,447.5	258.0
Metro[2]	2,828.0	3.4	15.6	36.6	259.1	484.3	1,881.1	147.9
U.S.	3,246.1	4.7	26.9	112.9	242.3	670.2	1,959.3	229.7

Note: Figures are crimes per 100,000 population; (1) All areas within the metro area that are located outside the city limits; (2) Figures cover the Midland, TX Metropolitan Statistical Area—see Appendix B for areas included
Source: FBI Uniform Crime Reports, 2012

Hate Crimes

Area	Number of Quarters Reported	Bias Motivation				
		Race	Religion	Sexual Orientation	Ethnicity	Disability
City	4	0	0	0	0	0
U.S.	4	2,797	1,099	1,135	667	92

Source: Federal Bureau of Investigation, Hate Crime Statistics 2012

Identity Theft Consumer Complaints

Area	Complaints	Complaints per 100,000 Population	Rank[2]
MSA[1]	109	76.9	121
U.S.	290,056	91.8	-

Note: (1) Figures cover the Midland, TX Metropolitan Statistical Area—see Appendix B for areas included; (2) Rank ranges from 1 to 377 where 1 indicates greatest number of identity theft complaints per 100,000 population
Source: Federal Trade Commission, Consumer Sentinel Network Data Book for January–December 2013

Fraud and Other Consumer Complaints

Area	Complaints	Complaints per 100,000 Population	Rank[2]
MSA[1]	529	373.4	166
U.S.	1,811,724	595.2	-

Note: (1) Figures cover the Midland, TX Metropolitan Statistical Area—see Appendix B for areas included; (2) Rank ranges from 1 to 377 where 1 indicates greatest number of identity theft complaints per 100,000 population
Source: Federal Trade Commission, Consumer Sentinel Network Data Book for January–December 2013

RECREATION

Culture

Dance[1]	Theatre[1]	Instrumental Music[1]	Vocal Music[1]	Series and Festivals	Museums and Art Galleries[2]	Zoos and Aquariums[3]
0	0	1	1	0	7	0

Note: (1) Number of professional perfoming groups; (2) Based on organizations with primary SIC code 8412; (3) AZA-accredited
Source: The Grey House Performing Arts Directory, 2013; Association of Zoos & Aquariums, AZA Member Zoos & Aquariums, April 2014; www.AccuLeads.com, May 1, 2014

Professional Sports Teams

Team Name	League	Year Established

No teams are located in the metro area

Source: Wikipedia, Major Professional Sports Teams of the United States and Canada, April 25, 2014

CLIMATE

Average and Extreme Temperatures

Temperature	Jan	Feb	Mar	Apr	May	Jun	Jul	Aug	Sep	Oct	Nov	Dec	Yr.
Extreme High (°F)	84	90	95	101	108	116	112	107	107	100	89	85	116
Average High (°F)	57	62	70	79	86	93	94	93	86	78	66	59	77
Average Temp. (°F)	43	48	55	64	73	80	82	81	74	65	53	46	64
Average Low (°F)	30	34	40	49	59	67	69	68	62	51	39	32	50
Extreme Low (°F)	-8	-11	9	20	34	47	53	54	36	24	13	-1	-11

Note: Figures cover the years 1948-1995
Source: National Climatic Data Center, International Station Meteorological Climate Summary, 9/96

Average Precipitation/Snowfall/Humidity

Precip./Humidity	Jan	Feb	Mar	Apr	May	Jun	Jul	Aug	Sep	Oct	Nov	Dec	Yr.
Avg. Precip. (in.)	0.6	0.6	0.5	0.8	2.1	1.6	1.9	1.7	2.1	1.6	0.6	0.5	14.6
Avg. Snowfall (in.)	2	1	Tr	Tr	0	0	0	0	0	Tr	Tr	1	4
Avg. Rel. Hum. 6am (%)	72	72	65	67	75	76	73	74	79	78	74	71	73
Avg. Rel. Hum. 3pm (%)	38	35	27	27	31	32	34	34	40	37	35	37	34

Note: Figures cover the years 1948-1995; Tr = Trace amounts (<0.05 in. of rain; <0.5 in. of snow)
Source: National Climatic Data Center, International Station Meteorological Climate Summary, 9/96

Weather Conditions

Temperature			Daytime Sky			Precipitation		
10°F & below	32°F & below	90°F & above	Clear	Partly cloudy	Cloudy	0.01 inch or more precip.	0.1 inch or more snow/ice	Thunder-storms
1	62	102	144	138	83	52	3	38

Note: Figures are average number of days per year and cover the years 1948-1995
Source: National Climatic Data Center, International Station Meteorological Climate Summary, 9/96

HAZARDOUS WASTE

Superfund Sites

Midland has one hazardous waste site on the EPA's Superfund Final National Priorities List: **West County Road 112 Ground Water**. *U.S. Environmental Protection Agency, Final National Priorities List, April 26, 2014*

AIR & WATER QUALITY

Air Quality Index

Area	Percent of Days when Air Quality was...[2]					AQI Statistics[2]	
	Good	Moderate	Unhealthy for Sensitive Groups	Unhealthy	Very Unhealthy	Maximum	Median
MSA[1]	n/a	n/a	n/a	n/a	n/a	n/a	n/a

Note: (1) Data covers the Midland, TX Metropolitan Statistical Area—see Appendix B for areas included; (2) Based on days with AQI data in 2013. Air Quality Index (AQI) is an index for reporting daily air quality. EPA calculates the AQI for five major air pollutants regulated by the Clean Air Act: ground-level ozone, particle pollution (aka particulate matter), carbon monoxide, sulfur dioxide, and nitrogen dioxide. The AQI runs from 0 to 500. The higher the AQI value, the greater the level of air pollution and the greater the health concern. There are six AQI categories: "Good" AQI is between 0 and 50. Air quality is considered satisfactory; "Moderate" AQI is between 51 and 100. Air quality is acceptable; "Unhealthy for Sensitive Groups" When AQI values are between 101 and 150, members of sensitive groups may experience health effects; "Unhealthy" When AQI values are between 151 and 200 everyone may begin to experience health effects; "Very Unhealthy" AQI values between 201 and 300 trigger a health alert; "Hazardous" AQI values over 300 trigger warnings of emergency conditions (not shown).
Source: U.S. Environmental Protection Agency, Air Quality Index Report, 2013

Air Quality Index Pollutants

| Area | Percent of Days when AQI Pollutant was...[2] | | | | | |
	Carbon Monoxide	Nitrogen Dioxide	Ozone	Sulfur Dioxide	Particulate Matter 2.5	Particulate Matter 10
MSA[1]	n/a	n/a	n/a	n/a	n/a	n/a

Note: (1) Data covers the Midland, TX Metropolitan Statistical Area—see Appendix B for areas included;
(2) Based on days with AQI data in 2013. The Air Quality Index (AQI) is an index for reporting daily air
quality. EPA calculates the AQI for five major air pollutants regulated by the Clean Air Act: ground-level ozone,
particle pollution (also known as particulate matter), carbon monoxide, sulfur dioxide, and nitrogen dioxide.
The AQI runs from 0 to 500. The higher the AQI value, the greater the level of air pollution and the greater the
health concern.
Source: U.S. Environmental Protection Agency, Air Quality Index Report, 2013

Air Quality Trends: Ozone

	2003	2004	2005	2006	2007	2008	2009	2010	2011	2012
MSA[1]	n/a	n/a	n/a	n/a	n/a	n/a	n/a	n/a	n/a	n/a

Note: (1) Data covers the Midland, TX Metropolitan Statistical Area—see Appendix B for areas included; n/a
not available. The values shown are the composite ozone concentration averages among trend sites based on the
highest fourth daily maximum 8-hour concentration in parts per million. These trends are based on sites having
an adequate record of monitoring data during the trend period. Data from exceptional events are included.
Source: U.S. Environmental Protection Agency, Air Quality Monitoring Information, "Air Quality Trends by
City, 2000-2012"

Maximum Air Pollutant Concentrations: Particulate Matter, Ozone, CO and Lead

	Particulate Matter 10 (ug/m^3)	Particulate Matter 2.5 Wtd AM (ug/m^3)	Particulate Matter 2.5 24-Hr (ug/m^3)	Ozone (ppm)	Carbon Monoxide (ppm)	Lead (ug/m^3)
MSA[1] Level	n/a	n/a	n/a	n/a	n/a	n/a
NAAQS[2]	150	15	35	0.075	9	0.15
Met NAAQS[2]	Yes	Yes	Yes	Yes	Yes	Yes

Note: (1) Data covers the Midland, TX Metropolitan Statistical Area—see Appendix B for areas included; Data
from exceptional events are included; (2) National Ambient Air Quality Standards; ppm = parts per million;
ug/m^3 = micrograms per cubic meter; n/a not available.
Concentrations: Particulate Matter 10 (coarse particulate)—highest second maximum 24-hour concentration;
Particulate Matter 2.5 Wtd AM (fine particulate)—highest weighted annual mean concentration; Particulate
Matter 2.5 24-Hour (fine particulate)—highest 98th percentile 24-hour concentration; Ozone—highest fourth
daily maximum 8-hour concentration; Carbon Monoxide—highest second maximum non-overlapping 8-hour
concentration; Lead—maximum running 3-month average
Source: U.S. Environmental Protection Agency, Air Quality Monitoring Information, "Air Quality Statistics by
City, 2012"

Maximum Air Pollutant Concentrations: Nitrogen Dioxide and Sulfur Dioxide

	Nitrogen Dioxide AM (ppb)	Nitrogen Dioxide 1-Hr (ppb)	Sulfur Dioxide AM (ppb)	Sulfur Dioxide 1-Hr (ppb)	Sulfur Dioxide 24-Hr (ppb)
MSA[1] Level	n/a	n/a	n/a	n/a	n/a
NAAQS[2]	53	100	30	75	140
Met NAAQS[2]	Yes	Yes	Yes	Yes	Yes

Note: (1) Data covers the Midland, TX Metropolitan Statistical Area—see Appendix B for areas included; Data
from exceptional events are included; (2) National Ambient Air Quality Standards; ppm = parts per million;
ug/m^3 = micrograms per cubic meter; n/a not available.
Concentrations: Nitrogen Dioxide AM—highest arithmetic mean concentration; Nitrogen Dioxide
1-Hr—highest 98th percentile 1-hour daily maximum concentration; Sulfur Dioxide AM—highest annual mean
concentration; Sulfur Dioxide 1-Hr—highest 99th percentile 1-hour daily maximum concentration; Sulfur
Dioxide 24-Hr—highest second maximum 24-hour concentration
Source: U.S. Environmental Protection Agency, Air Quality Monitoring Information, "Air Quality Statistics by
City, 2012"

Drinking Water

Water System Name	Pop. Served	Primary Water Source Type	Violations[1]	
			Health Based	Monitoring/ Reporting
City of Midland Water Purification	111,147	Purchased Surface	12	3

Note: (1) Based on violation data from January 1, 2013 to December 31, 2013 (includes unresolved violations from earlier years)
Source: U.S. Environmental Protection Agency, Office of Ground Water and Drinking Water, Safe Drinking Water Information System (based on data extracted February 10, 2014)

Drinking Water

Water System Name	Pop. Served	Primary Water Source Type	Violations, Health Based	Monitoring/ Reporting
City of Midland Water Purification	113,187	Purchased Surface	14	5

Note: (1) Reflects violations from November 1, 2013 to December 31, 2013 (for highest score, lead violations from entire year).

Source: U.S. Environmental Protection Agency, Office of Ground Water and Drinking Water, Safe Drinking Water Information System (based on data extracted February 10, 2014).

Montgomery, Alabama

Background

Montgomery Alabama represents important crossroads in American history, particularly when it comes to race and culture. The French built Fort Toulouse in 1717—a trading post between the French and the Alibamu tribe. But permanent European settlement was slow to take hold, perhaps due to battles and territory disputes that plagued the area. A sophisticated confederacy of tribes known as the Muscogee or Creek, occupied Alabama, Georgia and Florida for centuries. During the war of 1812, civil war broke out in the Creek nation with some tribes resisting western encroachment and others supporting western expansion.

In June 1818, two towns developed along the Alabama River—Alabama Town and New Philadelphia. After a period of rivalry and skirmishes, the two merged in December of 1819. Today, Montgomery streets still reflect the dual nature of the city's founding; streets east of Court Street are aligned on a grid, north-south and east-west, while streets to the west are aligned perpendicular and parallel to the river. Montgomery was named for General George Montgomery who died in the Revolutionary War. Coincidently, Montgomery County was named after an unrelated man, Major Lemuel Montgomery, who died in the Creek civil war.

Once cotton was introduced, Montgomery grew rapidly. In 1821, the steamboat *Harriet* was introduced to the Alabama River, and in 1832, the Montgomery Railroad opened. By 1885 Montgomery introduced the nation's first electric trolley system. Montgomery became the Alabama state capital in 1846. Less than twenty years later, Jefferson Davis would be inaugurated as president of the Confederacy on the steps of the capitol building. For a brief time, Montgomery was the capital of the Confederate States of America, however the provisional Congress realized they needed their capital closer to the Civil War action and moved it to Richmond Virginia. This move saved Montgomery from destruction due to the war—that is, except for self-inflicted destruction. Once Union troops descended upon Montgomery, local citizens burned 40,000 bushels of corn, and more than 100,000 bales of cotton to prevent them from being used by the Union troops. In one of history's great ironies, it was the African-American fire fighter brigade known as the "Grey Eagles" that prevented the town's complete destruction when the flames got out of control.

In the early years of the 20th century, Orville and Wilbur Wright opened a flying school in Montgomery, on a plantation west of town. The same site would become an important aircraft repair facility in World War I, and in World War II, it became an Air Force training ground. Today, Maxwell Air Force Base, Air University is the highest academic branch of the U.S. Air Force, employing over 4,000. The base itself employs 12,000.

Montgomery would make history at another American crossroad—the civil rights movement—that began in December 1955 when Rosa Parks refused to give up her seat on a city bus to a white man. The ensuing bus boycott, organized by Martin Luther King Jr., and E. D. Nixon, would bring the city to its knees, and initiate a process that forever changed America's race relations. In June of 1956, a Montgomery judge, Frank Jonson, ruled that bus segregation was illegal. In an effort to gain equal voting rights, Martin Luther King, Jr. and the Dallas County Voter's League led a large group of marchers from Selma to Montgomery , to deliver a message to Alabama's Governor, George Wallace. King would deliver his famous "How Long? Not Long" speech in support of the disenfranchised black community from the same steps used in the inauguration of Jefferson Davis as President of the Confederacy 104 years earlier. By 1965, President Lyndon B. Johnson would sign the Voting Rights Act, giving equal voting rights to all.

Today, Montgomery celebrates civic renewal and industrial growth, especially in high tech industries. In 2002, Hyundai Motors built their first U.S. factor in the city, and in 2007, they constructed more facilities to manufacture parts and engines for the assembly plant. About 25% of Montgomery's citizens work for the State. Renewed efforts to promote tourism and entertainment have also meant jobs for 8,000. Montgomery has a long list of universities that includes Auburn University, Troy University, Faulkner University, Huntingdon College and Alabama State University—Alabama's oldest university founded for black students.

Rankings

Business/Finance Rankings

- The Montgomery metro area was identified as one of the most debt-ridden places in America by credit reporting agency Equifax. The metro area was ranked #10. Criteria: proportion of average yearly income owed to credit card companies. *Equifax, "The Most Debt-Ridden Cities in America," February 23, 2012*

- Montgomery was identified as one of "America's Hardest-Working Towns." The city ranked #23 out of 25. Criteria: average hours worked per capita; willingness to work during personal time; number of dual income households; local employment rate. *Parade, "What is America's Hardest-Working Town?," April 15, 2012*

- Montgomery was identified as one of the top 25 U.S. cities with the most credit card debt by credit reporting bureau Experian. The city was ranked #24. *Experian, March 4, 2011*

- The Montgomery metro area appeared on the Milken Institute "2013 Best Performing Cities" list. Rank: #182 out of 200 large metro areas. Criteria: job growth; wage and salary growth; high-tech output growth. *Milken Institute, "Best-Performing Cities 2013," December 2013*

- *Forbes* ranked the 200 most populous metro areas in the U.S. in terms of the "Best Places for Business and Careers." The Montgomery metro area was ranked #168. Criteria: costs (business and living); job growth (past and projected); income growth; educational attainment (college and high school); projected economic growth; cultural and recreational opportunities; net migration patterns; number of highly ranked colleges. *Forbes, "The Best Places for Business and Careers," August 7, 2013*

Children/Family Rankings

- Montgomery was selected as one of the best cities for families to live by *Parenting* magazine. The city ranked #84 out of 100. Criteria: education; health; community; *Parenting's* Culture & Charm Index. *Parenting.com, "The 2012 Best Cities for Families List"*

Environmental Rankings

- The Montgomery metro area came in at #283 for the relative comfort of its climate on Sperling's list of "chill cities," as measured by the Sperling Heat Index. All 361 metro areas are included. Criteria included daytime high temperatures, nighttime low temperatures, dew point, and relative humidity at the high temperatures. *www.bertsperling.com, "Sperling's Chill Cities," July 18, 2013*

- Sperling's BestPlaces assessed 379 metropolitan areas of the United States for the likelihood of dangerously extreme weather events or earthquakes. In general the Southeast and South-Central regions have the highest risk of weather extremes and earthquakes, while the Pacific Northwest enjoys the lowest risk. Of the least risky metropolitan areas, the Montgomery metro area was ranked #315. *www.bestplaces.net, "Safest Places from Natural Disasters," April 2011*

- Montgomery was selected as one of 22 "Smarter Cities" for energy by the Natural Resources Defense Council. Criteria: investment in green power; energy efficiency measures; conservation. *Natural Resources Defense Council, "2010 Smarter Cities," July 19, 2010*

- Montgomery was highlighted as one of the top 25 cleanest metro areas for short-term particle pollution (24-hour PM 2.5) in the U.S. during 2008 through 2010. Monitors in these cities reported no days with unhealthful PM 2.5 levels. *American Lung Association, State of the Air 2012*

Health/Fitness Rankings

- The Montgomery metro area appeared in the 2013 Gallup-Healthways Well-Being Index. The area ranked #119 out of 189. The Gallup-Healthways Well-Being Index score is an average of six sub-indexes, which individually examine life evaluation, emotional health, work environment, physical health, healthy behaviors, and access to basic necessities. Results are based on telephone interviews conducted as part of the Gallup-Healthways Well-Being Index survey January 2–December 29, 2012, and January 2–December 30, 2013, with a random sample of 531,630 adults, aged 18 and older, living in metropolitan areas in the 50 U.S. states and the District of Columbia. *Gallup-Healthways, "State of American Well-Being," March 25, 2014*

Real Estate Rankings

- *Kiplinger* looked at metro areas with populations above 250,000 to identify the places in which home prices have declined most, drawing on sales, supply, foreclosure, and market data from Realtors' associations and industry analysts. U.S. Bureau of Labor Statistics unemployment figures were also considered. Montgomery ranked #1. *Kiplinger, "12 Cities Where Home Prices Have Fallen Most," May 2013*

- Montgomery was ranked #230 out of 283 metro areas in terms of house price appreciation in 2013 (#1 = highest rate). *Federal Housing Finance Agency, House Price Index, 4th Quarter 2013*

Safety Rankings

- Allstate ranked the 200 largest cities in America in terms of driver safety. Montgomery ranked #9. Allstate researchers analyzed internal property damage claims over a two-year period from January 2010 to December 2011. A weighted average of the two-year numbers determined the annual percentages. *Allstate, "Allstate America's Best Drivers Report®, August 27, 2013"*

- The National Insurance Crime Bureau ranked 380 metro areas in the U.S. in terms of per capita rates of vehicle theft. The Montgomery metro area ranked #83 (#1 = highest rate). Criteria: number of vehicle theft offenses per 100,000 inhabitants in 2012. *National Insurance Crime Bureau, "Hot Spots 2012," June 26, 2013*

Seniors/Retirement Rankings

- From its Best Cities for Successful Aging indexes, the Milken Institute generated rankings for metropolitan areas, weighing data in eight categories—general indicators, health care, wellness, living arrangements, transportation and general accessibility, financial well-being, education and employment, and community participation. The Montgomery metro area was ranked #205 overall in the small metro area category. *Milken Institute, "Best Cities for Successful Aging," July 2012*

Sports/Recreation Rankings

- Montgomery appeared on the *Sporting News* list of the "Best Sports Cities" for 2011. The area ranked #246 out of 271. Criteria: the magazine takes a 12-month snapshot of each city's sports, putting a heavy premium on regular-season won-lost records (from the most recently completed season). Other criteria include: playoff berths, bowl appearances and tournament bids; championships; applicable power ratings; quality of competition; overall fan fervor (measured in part by attendance); abundance of teams (rewarding quality over quantity); stadium and arena quality; ticket availability and prices; franchise ownership; and marquee appeal of athletes. *Sporting News, "Best Sports Cities 2011," October 4, 2011*

- Montgomery appeared on the *Sporting News* list of the "Best Sports Cities" for 2011. The area ranked #246 out of 271. Criteria: a 12-month snapshot of regular-season won-lost records (from the most recently completed season). Other criteria include: playoff berths, bowl appearances and tournament bids; championships; applicable power ratings; quality of competition; overall fan fervor (measured in part by attendance); abundance of teams (quality over quantity); stadium and arena quality; ticket availability and prices; franchise ownership; and marquee appeal of athletes. *Sporting News, "Best Sports Cities 2011," October 4, 2011*

Transportation Rankings

- NerdWallet surveyed average annual car insurance premiums in 125 U.S. cities to identify the least expensive U.S. cities in which to insure a car. Locations without no-fault insurance laws was a strong determinant. Montgomery came in at #10 for the least expensive rates. *www.nerdwallet.com, "Best Cities for Cheap Car Insurance," February 3, 2014*

Business Environment

CITY FINANCES

City Government Finances

Component	2011 ($000)	2011 ($ per capita)
Total Revenues	294,435	1,443
Total Expenditures	269,657	1,321
Debt Outstanding	371,492	1,820
Cash and Securities[1]	364,036	1,784

Note: (1) Cash and security holdings of a government at the close of its fiscal year, including those of its dependent agencies, utilities, and liquor stores.
Source: U.S Census Bureau, State & Local Government Finances 2011

City Government Revenue by Source

Source	2011 ($000)	2011 ($ per capita)
General Revenue		
From Federal Government	14,402	71
From State Government	12,643	62
From Local Governments	0	0
Taxes		
Property	31,378	154
Sales and Gross Receipts	105,025	515
Personal Income	0	0
Corporate Income	0	0
Motor Vehicle License	0	0
Other Taxes	38,269	188
Current Charges	40,794	200
Liquor Store	0	0
Utility	761	4
Employee Retirement	34,277	168

Source: U.S Census Bureau, State & Local Government Finances 2011

City Government Expenditures by Function

Function	2011 ($000)	2011 ($ per capita)	2011 (%)
General Direct Expenditures			
Air Transportation	0	0	0.0
Corrections	0	0	0.0
Education	0	0	0.0
Employment Security Administration	0	0	0.0
Financial Administration	5,068	25	1.9
Fire Protection	30,098	147	11.2
General Public Buildings	34,001	167	12.6
Governmental Administration, Other	10,334	51	3.8
Health	0	0	0.0
Highways	10,122	50	3.8
Hospitals	0	0	0.0
Housing and Community Development	5,464	27	2.0
Interest on General Debt	10,937	54	4.1
Judicial and Legal	3,685	18	1.4
Libraries	3,237	16	1.2
Parking	3,827	19	1.4
Parks and Recreation	28,014	137	10.4
Police Protection	42,840	210	15.9
Public Welfare	0	0	0.0
Sewerage	0	0	0.0
Solid Waste Management	13,349	65	5.0
Veterans' Services	0	0	0.0
Liquor Store	0	0	0.0
Utility	6,838	34	2.5
Employee Retirement	25,501	125	9.5

Source: U.S Census Bureau, State & Local Government Finances 2011

DEMOGRAPHICS

Population Growth

Area	1990 Census	2000 Census	2010 Census	Population Growth (%)	
				1990-2000	2000-2010
City	190,866	201,568	205,764	5.6	2.1
MSA[1]	305,175	346,528	374,536	13.6	8.1
U.S.	248,709,873	281,421,906	308,745,538	13.2	9.7

Note: (1) Figures cover the Montgomery, AL Metropolitan Statistical Area—see Appendix B for areas included
Source: U.S. Census Bureau, Census 1990, 2000, 2010

Household Size

Area	Persons in Household (%)							Average Household Size
	One	Two	Three	Four	Five	Six	Seven or More	
City	31.5	31.4	17.8	10.7	5.3	1.9	1.3	2.51
MSA[1]	28.3	33.3	17.8	12.3	5.4	1.7	1.3	2.57
U.S.	27.6	33.5	15.7	13.2	6.1	2.4	1.5	2.63

Note: (1) Figures cover the Montgomery, AL Metropolitan Statistical Area—see Appendix B for areas included
Source: U.S. Census Bureau, 2010-2012 American Community Survey 3-Year Estimates

Race

Area	White Alone[2] (%)	Black Alone[2] (%)	Asian Alone[2] (%)	AIAN[3] Alone[2] (%)	NHOPI[4] Alone[2] (%)	Other Race Alone[2] (%)	Two or More Races (%)
City	37.9	56.8	2.3	0.3	0.0	1.2	1.4
MSA[1]	53.0	42.8	1.6	0.3	0.0	0.9	1.4
U.S.	74.0	12.6	4.9	0.8	0.2	4.7	2.8

Note: (1) Figures cover the Montgomery, AL Metropolitan Statistical Area—see Appendix B for areas included;
(2) Alone is defined as not being in combination with one or more other races; (3) American Indian and Alaska
Native; (4) Native Hawaiian and Other Pacific Islander
Source: U.S. Census Bureau, 2010-2012 American Community Survey 3-Year Estimates

Hispanic or Latino Origin

Area	Total (%)	Mexican (%)	Puerto Rican (%)	Cuban (%)	Other (%)
City	3.7	2.3	0.4	0.1	1.0
MSA[1]	3.1	2.0	0.3	0.1	0.7
U.S.	16.6	10.7	1.6	0.6	3.7

Note: Persons of Hispanic or Latino origin can be of any race; (1) Figures cover the Montgomery, AL
Metropolitan Statistical Area—see Appendix B for areas included
Source: U.S. Census Bureau, 2010-2012 American Community Survey 3-Year Estimates

Segregation

Type	Segregation Indices[1]				Percent Change		
	1990	2000	2010	2010 Rank[2]	1990-2000	1990-2010	2000-2010
Black/White	n/a	n/a	n/a	n/a	n/a	n/a	n/a
Asian/White	n/a	n/a	n/a	n/a	n/a	n/a	n/a
Hispanic/White	n/a	n/a	n/a	n/a	n/a	n/a	n/a

Note: All figures cover the Metropolitan Statistical Area—see Appendix B for areas included; Figures are based
on an analysis of 1990, 2000, and 2010 Census Decennial Census tract data by William H. Frey, Brookings
Institution and the University of Michigan Social Science Data Analysis Network. In this analysis all racial
groups (whites, blacks, and asians) are non-Hispanic members of those races. Hispanics are shown as a
separate category;
(1) Segregation Indices are Dissimilarity Indices that measure the degree to which the minority group is
distributed differently than whites across census tracts. They range from 0 (complete integration) to 100
(complete segregation) where the value indicates the percentage of the minority group that needs to move to be
distributed exactly like whites; (2) Ranges from 1 (most segregated) to 102 (least segregated); n/a not available.
Source: www.CensusScope.org

Ancestry

Area	German	Irish	English	American	Italian	Polish	French[2]	Scottish	Dutch
City	3.8	3.5	4.8	13.1	0.8	0.5	1.1	1.3	0.3
MSA[1]	5.5	6.3	6.4	14.9	1.1	0.5	1.3	1.7	0.5
U.S.	15.2	11.1	8.2	7.2	5.6	3.1	2.8	1.7	1.4

Note: Figures are the percentage of the total population reporting a particular ancestry. The nine most commonly reported ancestries in the U.S. are shown. Figures include multiple ancestries (e.g. if a person reported being Irish and Italian, they were included in both columns); (1) Figures cover the Montgomery, AL Metropolitan Statistical Area—see Appendix B for areas included; (2) Excludes Basque
Source: U.S. Census Bureau, 2010-2012 American Community Survey 3-Year Estimates

Foreign-Born Population

Area	\multicolumn{9}{c}{Percent of Population Born in}
	Any Foreign Country	Mexico	Asia	Europe	Carribean	South America	Central America[2]	Africa	Canada
City	n/a	n/a	n/a	n/a	n/a	n/a	n/a	n/a	n/a
MSA[1]	n/a	n/a	n/a	n/a	n/a	n/a	n/a	n/a	n/a
U.S.	13.0	3.7	3.7	1.6	1.2	0.9	1.0	0.5	0.3

Note: (1) Figures cover the Montgomery, AL Metropolitan Statistical Area—see Appendix B for areas included; (2) Excludes Mexico.
Source: U.S. Census Bureau, 2010-2012 American Community Survey 3-Year Estimates

Marital Status

Area	Never Married	Now Married[2]	Separated	Widowed	Divorced
City	39.2	38.3	3.2	6.2	13.1
MSA[1]	33.4	44.4	3.0	6.5	12.7
U.S.	32.4	48.4	2.2	6.0	11.0

Note: Figures are percentages and cover the population 15 years of age and older; (1) Figures cover the Montgomery, AL Metropolitan Statistical Area—see Appendix B for areas included; (2) Excludes separated
Source: U.S. Census Bureau, 2010-2012 American Community Survey 3-Year Estimates

Age

Area	\multicolumn{9}{c}{Percent of Population}	Median Age
	Under Age 5	Age 5–19	Age 20–34	Age 35–44	Age 45–54	Age 55–64	Age 65–74	Age 75–84	Age 85+	
City	7.3	21.3	23.0	12.6	12.9	11.1	6.5	3.9	1.5	34.0
MSA[1]	6.8	20.9	21.3	13.2	14.0	11.6	7.0	3.9	1.4	35.8
U.S.	6.4	20.1	20.5	13.1	14.3	12.2	7.3	4.2	1.8	37.3

Note: (1) Figures cover the Montgomery, AL Metropolitan Statistical Area—see Appendix B for areas included
Source: U.S. Census Bureau, 2010-2012 American Community Survey 3-Year Estimates

Gender

Area	Males	Females	Males per 100 Females
City	97,117	109,229	88.9
MSA[1]	180,522	196,442	91.9
U.S.	153,276,055	158,333,314	96.8

Note: (1) Figures cover the Montgomery, AL Metropolitan Statistical Area—see Appendix B for areas included
Source: U.S. Census Bureau, 2010-2012 American Community Survey 3-Year Estimates

Religious Groups by Family

Area	Catholic	Baptist	Non-Den.	Methodist[2]	Lutheran	LDS[3]	Pentecostal	Presbyterian[4]	Muslim[5]	Judaism
MSA[1]	3.2	35.4	4.0	11.1	0.2	0.9	5.2	1.5	0.3	0.3
U.S.	19.1	9.3	4.0	4.0	2.3	2.0	1.9	1.6	0.8	0.7

Note: Figures are the number of adherents as a percentage of the total population; (1) Figures cover the Montgomery, AL Metropolitan Statistical Area—see Appendix B for areas included; (2) Methodist/Pietist; (3) Latter Day Saints; (4) Reformed; (5) Figures are estimates
Source: Association of Statisticians of American Religious Bodies, 2010 U.S. Religion Census: Religious Congregations & Membership Study

Religious Groups by Tradition

Area	Catholic	Evangelical Protestant	Mainline Protestant	Other Tradition	Black Protestant	Orthodox
MSA[1]	3.2	34.2	11.7	1.6	13.5	<0.1
U.S.	19.1	16.2	7.3	4.3	1.6	0.3

Note: Figures are the number of adherents as a percentage of the total population; (1) Figures cover the Montgomery, AL Metropolitan Statistical Area—see Appendix B for areas included
Source: Association of Statisticians of American Religious Bodies, 2010 U.S. Religion Census: Religious Congregations & Membership Study

ECONOMY

Gross Metropolitan Product

Area	2011	2012	2013	2014	Rank[2]
MSA[1]	15.3	15.4	15.5	16.0	139

Note: Figures are in billions of dollars; (1) Figures cover the Montgomery, AL Metropolitan Statistical Area—see Appendix B for areas included; (2) Rank is based on 2014 data and ranges from 1 to 363
Source: The United States Conference of Mayors, U.S. Metro Economies: Outlook—Gross Metropolitan Product, with Metro Employment Projections, November 2013

Economic Growth

Area	2011 (%)	2012 (%)	2013 (%)	2014 (%)	Rank[2]
MSA[1]	1.1	-0.6	-0.6	1.1	295
U.S.	1.6	2.5	1.7	2.5	–

Note: Figures are real gross metropolitan product (GMP) growth rates and represent annual average percent change; (1) Figures cover the Montgomery, AL Metropolitan Statistical Area—see Appendix B for areas included; (2) Rank is based on 2013 data and ranges from 1 to 363
Source: The United States Conference of Mayors, U.S. Metro Economies: Outlook—Gross Metropolitan Product, with Metro Employment Projections, November 2013

Metropolitan Area Exports

Area	2007	2008	2009	2010	2011	2012	Rank[2]
MSA[1]	1,236.1	1,286.2	1,143.1	1,520.1	1,647.3	1,770.2	109

Note: Figures are in millions of dollars; (1) Figures cover the Montgomery, AL Metropolitan Statistical Area—see Appendix B for areas included; (2) Rank is based on 2012 data and ranges from 1 to 369
Source: U.S. Department of Commerce, International Trade Administration, Office of Trade & Industry Information, Manufacturing & Services, data extracted April 1, 2014

INCOME

Income

Area	Per Capita ($)	Median Household ($)	Average Household ($)
City	23,655	42,403	59,186
MSA[1]	23,860	46,058	61,625
U.S.	27,385	51,771	71,579

Note: (1) Figures cover the Montgomery, AL Metropolitan Statistical Area—see Appendix B for areas included
Source: U.S. Census Bureau, 2010-2012 American Community Survey 3-Year Estimates

Household Income Distribution

Area	Percent of Households Earning							
	Under $15,000	$15,000 -24,999	$25,000 -34,999	$35,000 -49,999	$50,000 -74,999	$75,000 -99,000	$100,000 -149,999	$150,000 and up
City	18.6	12.7	10.3	15.8	17.3	9.7	10.0	5.6
MSA[1]	16.1	11.4	10.8	14.9	18.4	10.8	12.0	5.6
U.S.	13.1	11.0	10.5	13.7	18.1	11.9	12.5	9.1

Note: (1) Figures cover the Montgomery, AL Metropolitan Statistical Area—see Appendix B for areas included
Source: U.S. Census Bureau, 2010-2012 American Community Survey 3-Year Estimates

Poverty Rate

Area	All Ages	Under 18 Years Old	18 to 64 Years Old	65 Years and Over
City	23.3	34.7	21.5	8.7
MSA[1]	18.9	27.7	17.3	9.1
U.S.	15.7	22.2	14.6	9.3

Note: Figures are percentage of people whose income during the past 12 months was below the poverty level;
(1) Figures cover the Montgomery, AL Metropolitan Statistical Area—see Appendix B for areas included
Source: U.S. Census Bureau, 2010-2012 American Community Survey 3-Year Estimates

Personal Bankruptcy Filing Rate

Area	2008	2009	2010	2011	2012	2013
Montgomery County	5.88	7.24	6.89	6.83	7.46	7.61
U.S.	3.53	4.61	4.97	4.37	3.76	3.29

Note: Numbers are per 1,000 population and include Chapter 7 and Chapter 13 filings
Source: Federal Deposit Insurance Corporation, Regional Economic Conditions, March 20, 2014

EMPLOYMENT

Labor Force and Employment

Area	Civilian Labor Force			Workers Employed		
	Dec. 2012	Dec. 2013	% Chg.	Dec. 2012	Dec. 2013	% Chg.
City	93,234	91,988	-1.3	86,867	86,386	-0.6
MSA[1]	168,280	165,988	-1.4	157,029	156,160	-0.6
U.S.	154,904,000	154,408,000	-0.3	143,060,000	144,423,000	1.0

Note: Data is not seasonally adjusted and covers workers 16 years of age and older; (1) Metropolitan Statistical Area—see Appendix B for areas included
Source: Bureau of Labor Statistics, Local Area Unemployment Statistics

Unemployment Rate

Area	2013											
	Jan.	Feb.	Mar.	Apr.	May	Jun.	Jul.	Aug.	Sep.	Oct.	Nov.	Dec.
City	7.9	7.8	7.1	6.2	6.5	7.1	7.0	7.1	7.0	6.8	6.0	6.1
MSA[1]	7.9	7.9	7.0	6.1	6.3	6.9	6.7	7.0	6.8	6.7	5.8	5.9
U.S.	8.5	8.1	7.6	7.1	7.3	7.8	7.7	7.3	7.0	7.0	6.6	6.5

Note: Data is not seasonally adjusted and covers workers 16 years of age and older; All figures are percentages;
(1) Metropolitan Statistical Area—see Appendix B for areas included
Source: Bureau of Labor Statistics, Local Area Unemployment Statistics

Employment by Occupation

Occupation Classification	City (%)	MSA[1] (%)	U.S. (%)
Management, Business, Science, and Arts	35.2	34.2	36.0
Natural Resources, Construction, and Maintenance	6.0	7.3	9.1
Production, Transportation, and Material Moving	12.8	14.6	12.0
Sales and Office	25.8	25.6	24.7
Service	20.3	18.2	18.2

Note: Figures cover employed civilians 16 years of age and older; (1) Figures cover the Montgomery, AL Metropolitan Statistical Area—see Appendix B for areas included
Source: U.S. Census Bureau, 2010-2012 American Community Survey 3-Year Estimates

Employment by Industry

Sector	MSA[1]		U.S.
	Number of Employees	Percent of Total	Percent of Total
Construction	n/a	n/a	4.2
Education and Health Services	18,700	11.0	15.5
Financial Activities	7,400	4.3	5.7
Government	43,000	25.3	16.1
Information	2,200	1.3	1.9
Leisure and Hospitality	15,500	9.1	10.2
Manufacturing	18,400	10.8	8.7
Mining and Logging	n/a	n/a	0.6
Other Services	7,200	4.2	3.9
Professional and Business Services	20,900	12.3	13.7
Retail Trade	19,400	11.4	11.4
Transportation and Utilities	6,100	3.6	3.8
Wholesale Trade	5,300	3.1	4.2

Note: Figures cover non-farm employment as of December 2013 and are not seasonally adjusted;
(1) Metropolitan Statistical Area—see Appendix B for areas included; n/a not available
Source: Bureau of Labor Statistics, Current Employment Statistics, Employment, Hours, and Earnings

Occupations with Greatest Projected Employment Growth: 2010 – 2020

Occupation[1]	2010 Employment	2020 Projected Employment	Numeric Employment Change	Percent Employment Change
Registered Nurses	42,890	55,050	12,160	28.3
Retail Salespersons	56,240	65,530	9,300	16.5
Home Health Aides	11,370	19,230	7,860	69.2
Heavy and Tractor-Trailer Truck Drivers	33,910	40,570	6,660	19.6
Office Clerks, General	36,900	43,290	6,400	17.3
Team Assemblers	27,620	33,900	6,280	22.8
Combined Food Preparation and Serving Workers, Including Fast Food	37,800	43,910	6,110	16.2
Laborers and Freight, Stock, and Material Movers, Hand	34,160	39,010	4,850	14.2
Bookkeeping, Accounting, and Auditing Clerks	29,960	34,360	4,390	14.7
Nursing Aides, Orderlies, and Attendants	22,760	27,110	4,350	19.1

Note: Projections cover Alabama; (1) Sorted by numeric employment change
Source: www.projectionscentral.com, State Occupational Projections, 2010–2020 Long-Term Projections

Fastest Growing Occupations: 2010 – 2020

Occupation[1]	2010 Employment	2020 Projected Employment	Numeric Employment Change	Percent Employment Change
Personal Care Aides	4,200	7,190	2,990	71.3
Home Health Aides	11,370	19,230	7,860	69.2
Occupational Therapy Assistants	400	660	260	64.6
Physical Therapist Assistants	1,330	2,050	720	54.1
Metal-Refining Furnace Operators and Tenders	740	1,120	380	50.4
Physical Therapist Aides	690	1,040	350	50.2
Health Educators	450	670	220	49.1
Helpers—Carpenters	1,190	1,780	590	49.1
Marriage and Family Therapists	350	510	170	48.0
Diagnostic Medical Sonographers	980	1,450	470	47.8

Note: Projections cover Alabama; (1) Sorted by percent employment change and excludes occupations with numeric employment change less than 100
Source: www.projectionscentral.com, State Occupational Projections, 2010–2020 Long-Term Projections

Average Wages

Occupation	$/Hr.	Occupation	$/Hr.
Accountants and Auditors	29.11	Maids and Housekeeping Cleaners	8.80
Automotive Mechanics	19.72	Maintenance and Repair Workers	17.80
Bookkeepers	16.48	Marketing Managers	54.81
Carpenters	15.44	Nuclear Medicine Technologists	n/a
Cashiers	8.81	Nurses, Licensed Practical	18.35
Clerks, General Office	11.66	Nurses, Registered	29.68
Clerks, Receptionists/Information	11.50	Nursing Assistants	11.00
Clerks, Shipping/Receiving	14.13	Packers and Packagers, Hand	9.85
Computer Programmers	37.10	Physical Therapists	38.82
Computer Systems Analysts	32.06	Postal Service Mail Carriers	23.87
Computer User Support Specialists	22.00	Real Estate Brokers	26.74
Cooks, Restaurant	9.21	Retail Salespersons	12.49
Dentists	83.38	Sales Reps., Exc. Tech./Scientific	29.59
Electrical Engineers	50.27	Sales Reps., Tech./Scientific	35.75
Electricians	19.77	Secretaries, Exc. Legal/Med./Exec.	16.22
Financial Managers	52.29	Security Guards	12.16
First-Line Supervisors/Managers, Sales	17.77	Surgeons	n/a
Food Preparation Workers	9.45	Teacher Assistants	9.00
General and Operations Managers	55.87	Teachers, Elementary School	22.80
Hairdressers/Cosmetologists	14.09	Teachers, Secondary School	22.10
Internists	n/a	Telemarketers	8.45
Janitors and Cleaners	9.88	Truck Drivers, Heavy/Tractor-Trailer	18.26
Landscaping/Groundskeeping Workers	10.90	Truck Drivers, Light/Delivery Svcs.	15.61
Lawyers	46.64	Waiters and Waitresses	8.60

Note: Wage data covers the Montgomery, AL Metropolitan Statistical Area—see Appendix B for areas included. Hourly wages for elementary/secondary school teachers and teacher assistants were calculated by the editors from annual wage data assuming a 40 hour work week; n/a not available.
Source: Bureau of Labor Statistics, Metro Area Occupational Employment and Wage Estimates, May 2013

RESIDENTIAL REAL ESTATE

Building Permits

Area	Single-Family			Multi-Family			Total		
	2012	2013	Pct. Chg.	2012	2013	Pct. Chg.	2012	2013	Pct. Chg.
City	218	265	21.6	0	0	-	218	265	21.6
MSA[1]	776	744	-4.1	474	110	-76.8	1,250	854	-31.7
U.S.	518,695	620,802	19.7	310,963	370,020	19.0	829,658	990,822	19.4

Note: (1) Metropolitan Statistical Area—see Appendix B for areas included; figures represent new, privately-owned housing units authorized (unadjusted data); All permit data are based on estimates with imputation.
Source: U.S. Census Bureau, Manufacturing, Mining, and Construction Statistics, Building Permits, 2012, 2013

Homeownership Rate

Area	2006 (%)	2007 (%)	2008 (%)	2009 (%)	2010 (%)	2011 (%)	2012 (%)	2013 (%)
MSA[1]	n/a	n/a	n/a	n/a	n/a	n/a	n/a	n/a
U.S.	68.8	68.1	67.8	67.4	66.9	66.1	65.4	65.1

Note: (1) Figures cover the Montgomery, AL Metropolitan Statistical Area—see Appendix B for areas included; n/a not available
Source: U.S. Census Bureau, Housing Vacancies and Homeownership Annual Statistics: 2013

Housing Vacancy Rates

Area	Gross Vacancy Rate[2] (%)			Year-Round Vacancy Rate[3] (%)			Rental Vacancy Rate[4] (%)			Homeowner Vacancy Rate[5] (%)		
	2011	2012	2013	2011	2012	2013	2011	2012	2013	2011	2012	2013
MSA[1]	n/a	n/a	n/a	n/a	n/a	n/a	n/a	n/a	n/a	n/a	n/a	n/a
U.S.	14.2	13.8	13.8	11.1	10.8	10.7	9.5	8.7	8.3	2.5	2.0	2.0

Note: (1) Figures cover the Montgomery, AL Metropolitan Statistical Area—see Appendix B for areas included; (2) The percentage of the total housing inventory that is vacant; (3) The percentage of the housing inventory (excluding seasonal units) that is year-round vacant; (4) The percentage of rental inventory that is vacant for rent; (5) The percentage of homeowner inventory that is vacant for sale; n/a not available
Source: U.S. Census Bureau, Housing Vacancies and Homeownership Annual Statistics: 2013

TAXES

State Corporate Income Tax Rates

State	Tax Rate (%)	Income Brackets ($)	Num. of Brackets	Financial Institution Tax Rate (%)[a]	Federal Income Tax Ded.
Alabama	6.5	Flat rate	1	6.5	Yes

Note: Tax rates as of January 1, 2014; (a) Rates listed are the corporate income tax rate applied to financial institutions or excise taxes based on income. Some states have other taxes based upon the value of deposits or shares.
Source: Federation of Tax Administrators, "State Corporate Income Tax Rates, 2014"

State Individual Income Tax Rates

State	Tax Rate (%)	Income Brackets ($)	Num. of Brackets	Personal Exempt. ($)[1] Single	Personal Exempt. ($)[1] Dependents	Fed. Inc. Tax Ded.
Alabama	2.0 - 5.0	500 (b) - 3,001 (b)	3	1,500	500 (e)	Yes

Note: Tax rates as of January 1, 2014; Local- and county-level taxes are not included; n/a not applicable; (1) Married joint filers generally receive double the single exemption; (b) For joint returns, taxes are twice the tax on half the couple's income; (e) In Alabama, the per-dependent exemption is $1,000 for taxpayers with state AGI of $20,000 or less, $500 with AGI from $20,001 to $100,000, and $300 with AGI over $100,000.
Source: Federation of Tax Administrators, "State Individual Income Tax Rates, 2014"

Various State and Local Tax Rates

State	State and Local Sales and Use (%)	State Sales and Use (%)	Gasoline[1] (¢/gal.)	Cigarette[2] ($/pack)	Spirits[3] ($/gal.)	Wine[4] ($/gal.)	Beer[5] ($/gal.)
Alabama	10.0	4.00	20.95	0.425	18.23 (g)	1.70	1.05 (q)

Note: All tax rates as of January 1, 2014; (1) The American Petroleum Institute has developed a methodology for determining the average tax rate on a gallon of fuel. Rates may include any of the following: excise taxes, environmental fees, storage tank fees, other fees or taxes, general sales tax, and local taxes. In states where gasoline is subject to the general sales tax, or where the fuel tax is based on the average sale price, the average rate determined by API is sensitive to changes in the price of gasoline. States that fully or partially apply general sales taxes to gasoline: CA, CO, GA, IL, IN, MI, NY; (2) The federal excise tax of $1.0066 per pack and local taxes are not included; (3) Rates are those applicable to off-premise sales of 40% alcohol by volume (a.b.v.) distilled spirits in 750ml containers. Local excise taxes are excluded; (4) Rates are those applicable to off-premise sales of 11% a.b.v. non-carbonated wine in 750ml containers; (5) Rates are those applicable to off-premise sales of 4.7% a.b.v. beer in 12 ounce containers; (g) States where the government controls sales. In these "control states," products are subject to ad valorem mark-up and excise taxes. The excise tax rate is calculated using a methodology developed by the Distilled Spirits Council of the United States; (q) Includes statewide local rate in Alabama ($0.52) and Georgia ($0.53).
Source: Tax Foundation, 2014 Facts & Figures: How Does Your State Compare?

State Business Tax Climate Index Rankings

State	Overall Rank	Corporate Tax Index Rank	Individual Income Tax Index Rank	Sales Tax Index Rank	Unemployment Insurance Tax Index Rank	Property Tax Index Rank
Alabama	21	19	22	37	15	10

Note: The index is a measure of how each state's tax laws affect economic performance. The lower the rank, the more favorable a state's tax system is for business. States without a given tax are given a ranking of 1. The scores/rankings for the District of Columbia do not affect other states. The 2014 index represents the tax climate as of July 1, 2013.
Source: Tax Foundation, State Business Tax Climate Index 2014

COMMERCIAL UTILITIES

Typical Monthly Electric Bills

Area	Commercial Service ($/month) 1,500 kWh	Commercial Service ($/month) 40 kW demand 14,000 kWh	Industrial Service ($/month) 1,000 kW demand 200,000 kWh	Industrial Service ($/month) 50,000 kW demand 15,000,000 kWh
City	239	1,633	18,283	1,181,859
Average[1]	197	1,636	25,662	1,485,307

Note: Based on total rates in effect July 1, 2013; (1) average based on 180 utilities surveyed
Source: Edison Electric Institute, Typical Bills and Average Rates Report, Summer 2013

TRANSPORTATION

Means of Transportation to Work

Area	Car/Truck/Van		Public Transportation			Bicycle	Walked	Other Means	Worked at Home
	Drove Alone	Car-pooled	Bus	Subway	Railroad				
City	85.4	9.8	0.8	0.0	0.0	0.2	1.4	0.3	2.1
MSA[1]	85.8	9.3	0.5	0.0	0.0	0.1	1.1	0.8	2.4
U.S.	76.4	9.7	2.6	1.7	0.5	0.6	2.8	1.3	4.3

Note: Figures are percentages and cover workers 16 years of age and older; (1) Figures cover the Montgomery, AL Metropolitan Statistical Area—see Appendix B for areas included
Source: U.S. Census Bureau, 2010-2012 American Community Survey 3-Year Estimates

Travel Time to Work

Area	Less Than 10 Minutes	10 to 19 Minutes	20 to 29 Minutes	30 to 44 Minutes	45 to 59 Minutes	60 to 89 Minutes	90 Minutes or More
City	13.0	45.7	26.0	10.9	2.1	1.4	0.9
MSA[1]	11.4	34.2	25.9	19.2	5.7	2.4	1.3
U.S.	13.5	29.8	20.9	20.1	7.5	5.6	2.5

Note: Figures are percentages and include workers 16 years old and over; (1) Figures cover the Montgomery, AL Metropolitan Statistical Area—see Appendix B for areas included
Source: U.S. Census Bureau, 2010-2012 American Community Survey 3-Year Estimates

Travel Time Index

Area	1985	1990	1995	2000	2005	2010	2011
Urban Area[1]	n/a	n/a	n/a	n/a	n/a	n/a	n/a
Average[2]	1.09	1.14	1.16	1.19	1.23	1.18	1.18

Note: Travel Time Index—the ratio of travel time in the peak period to the travel time at free-flow conditions. For example, a value of 1.30 indicates a 20-minute free-flow trip takes 26 minutes in the peak. Free-flow speeds (60 mph on freeways and 35 mph on principal arterials) are used as the comparison threshold; (1) Data for the Montgomery, AL urban area was not available; (2) average of 498 urban areas
Source: Texas Transportation Institute, Urban Mobility Report 2012, December 2012

Public Transportation

Agency Name / Mode of Transportation	Vehicles Operated in Maximum Service	Annual Unlinked Passenger Trips (in thous.)	Annual Passenger Miles (in thous.)
Montgomery Area Transit System			
Bus (directly operated)	21	997.4	4,518.2
Demand Response (directly operated)	8	38.7	334.7

Source: Federal Transit Administration, National Transit Database, 2012

Air Transportation

Airport Name and Code / Type of Service	Passenger Airlines[1]	Passenger Enplanements	Freight Carriers[2]	Freight (lbs.)
Montgomery Regional Airport (MGM)				
Domestic service (U.S. carriers - 2013)	10	157,569	3	15,571
International service (U.S. carriers - 2012)	0	0	0	0

Note: (1) Includes all U.S.-based major, minor and commuter airlines that carried at least one passenger during the year; (2) Includes all U.S.-based airlines and freight carriers that transported at least one lb. of freight during the year.
Source: Bureau of Transportation Statistics, The Intermodal Transportation Database, Air Carriers: T-100 Domestic Market (U.S. Carriers), 2013; Bureau of Transportation Statistics, The Intermodal Transportation Database, Air Carriers: T-100 International Market (U.S. Carriers), 2012

Other Transportation Statistics

Major Highways:	I-65; I-85
Amtrak Service:	No
Major Waterways/Ports:	R.E. "Bob" Woodruff Lake

Source: Amtrak.com; Google Maps

BUSINESSES

Major Business Headquarters

Company Name	Rankings	
	Fortune[1]	Forbes[2]
No companies listed	-	-

Note: (1) Fortune 500—companies that produce a 10-K are ranked 1 to 500 based on 2012 revenue; (2) all private companies with at least $2 billion in annual revenue through the end of their most current fiscal year are ranked 1 to 224; companies listed are headquartered in the city; dashes indicate no ranking
Source: Fortune, "Fortune 500," May 20, 2013; Forbes, "America's Largest Private Companies," December 18, 2013

Minority Business Opportunity

Montgomery is home to one company which is on the *Black Enterprise* Industrial/Service 100 list (100 largest companies based on gross sales): **Calhoun Enterprises** (#28). Criteria: operational in previous calendar year; at least 51% black-owned and manufactures/owns the product it sells or provides industrial or consumer services. Brokerages, real estate firms and firms that provide professional services are not eligible. *Black Enterprise, B.E. 100s, 2013*

Montgomery is home to one company which is on the *Black Enterprise* Bank 20 list (20 largest banks based on total assets, capital, deposits and loans, including mortgage-backed securities for the calendar year): **First Tuskegee Bank** (#19). Only commercial banks or savings and loans that are classified by the Federal Reserve as black institutions and have been fully operational for the previous calendar year were considered. *Black Enterprise, B.E. 100s, 2013*

Minority- and Women-Owned Businesses

Group	All Firms		Firms with Paid Employees			
	Firms	Sales ($000)	Firms	Sales ($000)	Employees	Payroll ($000)
Asian	508	168,922	181	155,466	1,241	27,757
Black	7,091	228,293	208	125,690	1,463	34,007
Hispanic	251	136,042	20	121,856	240	13,775
Women	5,946	702,329	517	614,417	4,026	102,601
All Firms	19,203	24,002,003	4,038	23,439,516	99,793	3,490,768

Note: Figures cover firms located in the city; minority- and women-owned business are defined as firms in which the corresponding group own 51% or more of the stock or equity of the company
Source: U.S. Census Bureau, 2007 Economic Census, Survey of Business Owners (2012 Survey of Business Owners data will be released starting in June 2015)

HOTELS & CONVENTION CENTERS

Hotels/Motels

Area	5 Star		4 Star		3 Star		2 Star		1 Star		Not Rated	
	Num.	Pct.[3]	Num.	Pct.[3]	Num.	Pct.[3]	Num.	Pct.[3]	Num.	Pct.[3]	Num.	Pct.[3]
City[1]	0	0.0	0	0.0	13	16.9	49	63.6	2	2.6	13	16.9
Total[2]	142	0.9	1,005	6.0	5,147	30.9	8,578	51.4	408	2.4	1,397	8.4

Note: (1) Figures cover Montgomery and vicinity; (2) Figures cover all 100 cities in this book; (3) Percentage of hotels which have a given star rating; Star ratings are determined by expedia.com and offer an indication of the general quality of a particular hotel.
Source: expedia.com, April 7, 2014

Major Convention Centers

Name	Overall Space (sq. ft.)	Exhibit Space (sq. ft.)	Meeting Space (sq. ft.)	Meeting Rooms
There are no major convention centers located in the metro area				

Source: Original research

Living Environment

COST OF LIVING

Cost of Living Index

Composite Index	Groceries	Housing	Utilities	Trans-portation	Health Care	Misc. Goods/Services
94.4	95.2	85.6	110.2	96.7	84.7	96.7

Note: The Cost of Living Index measures regional differences in the cost of consumer goods and services, excluding taxes and non-consumer expenditures, for professional and managerial households in the top income quintile. It is based on more than 50,000 prices covering almost 60 different items for which prices are collected three times a year by chambers of commerce, economic development organizations or university applied economic centers in each participating urban area. The numbers shown should be read as a percentage above or below the national average of 100. For example, a value of 115.4 in the groceries column indicates that grocery prices are 15.4% higher than the national average. Small differences in the index numbers should not be interpreted as significant; Figures cover the Montgomery AL urban area.
Source: The Council for Community and Economic Research, ACCRA Cost of Living Index, 2013

Grocery Prices

Area[1]	T-Bone Steak ($/pound)	Frying Chicken ($/pound)	Whole Milk ($/half gal.)	Eggs ($/dozen)	Orange Juice ($/64 oz.)	Coffee ($/11.5 oz.)
City[2]	9.42	1.29	2.63	1.95	3.13	3.65
Avg.	10.19	1.28	2.34	1.81	3.48	4.39
Min.	8.56	0.94	1.44	1.19	2.78	3.40
Max.	14.82	2.28	3.56	3.73	6.23	7.32

*Note: (1) Values for the local area are compared with the average, minimum and maximum values for all 327 areas in the Cost of Living Index; (2) Figures cover the Montgomery AL urban area; **T-Bone Steak** (price per pound); **Frying Chicken** (price per pound, whole fryer); **Whole Milk** (half gallon carton); **Eggs** (price per dozen, Grade A, large); **Orange Juice** (64 oz. Tropicana or Florida Natural); **Coffee** (11.5 oz. can, vacuum-packed, Maxwell House, Hills Bros, or Folgers).*
Source: The Council for Community and Economic Research, ACCRA Cost of Living Index, 2013

Housing and Utility Costs

Area[1]	New Home Price ($)	Apartment Rent ($/month)	All Electric ($/month)	Part Electric ($/month)	Other Energy ($/month)	Telephone ($/month)
City[2]	265,245	673	182.72	-	-	29.99
Avg.	295,864	900	171.38	91.82	70.12	27.73
Min.	185,506	458	117.80	48.81	33.67	17.16
Max.	1,358,917	3,783	441.68	171.40	372.65	39.47

*Note: (1) Values for the local area are compared with the average, minimum and maximum values for all 327 areas in the Cost of Living Index; (2) Figures cover the Montgomery AL urban area; **New Home Price** (2,400 sf living area, 8,000 sf lot, in urban area with full utilities); **Apartment Rent** (950 sf 2 bedroom/1.5 or 2 bath, unfurnished, excluding all utilities except water); **All Electric** (average monthly cost for an all-electric home); **Part Electric** (average monthly cost for a part-electric home); **Other Energy** (average monthly cost for natural gas, fuel oil, coal, wood, and any other forms of energy except electricity); **Telephone** (price includes basic monthly rate for a private residential line plus additional local usage charges incurred by a family of four).*
Source: The Council for Community and Economic Research, ACCRA Cost of Living Index, 2013

Health Care, Transportation, and Other Costs

Area[1]	Doctor ($/visit)	Dentist ($/visit)	Optometrist ($/visit)	Gasoline ($/gallon)	Beauty Salon ($/visit)	Men's Shirt ($)
City[2]	77.11	62.45	82.44	3.26	38.33	33.60
Avg.	101.40	86.48	96.16	3.44	33.87	26.55
Min.	61.67	50.83	50.12	3.08	18.92	12.48
Max.	182.71	152.50	223.78	4.33	68.22	52.03

*Note: (1) Values for the local area are compared with the average, minimum and maximum values for all 327 areas in the Cost of Living Index; (2) Figures cover the Montgomery AL urban area; **Doctor** (general practitioners routine exam of an established patient); **Dentist** (adult teeth cleaning and periodic oral examination); **Optometrist** (full vision eye exam for established adult patient); **Gasoline** (one gallon regular unleaded, national brand, including all taxes, cash price at self-service pump if available); **Beauty Salon** (woman's shampoo, trim, and blow-dry); **Men's Shirt** (cotton/polyester dress shirt, pinpoint weave, long sleeves).*
Source: The Council for Community and Economic Research, ACCRA Cost of Living Index, 2013

HOUSING

House Price Index (HPI)

Area	National Ranking[2]	Quarterly Change (%)	One-Year Change (%)	Five-Year Change (%)
MSA[1]	230	-0.17	-0.14	-10.39
U.S.[3]	–	1.20	7.69	4.18

Note: The HPI is a weighted repeat sales index. It measures average price changes in repeat sales or refinancings on the same properties. This information is obtained by reviewing repeat mortgage transactions on single-family properties whose mortgages have been purchased or securitized by Fannie Mae or Freddie Mac in January 1975; (1) Montgomery, AL Metropolitan Statistical Area—see Appendix B for areas included; (2) Rankings are based on annual percentage change for all metro areas containing at least 15,000 transactions over the last 10 years and ranges from 1 to 283; (3) figures based on a weighted average of Census Division estimates using a seasonally adjusted, purchase-only index; all figures are for the period ending December 31, 2013
Source: Federal Housing Finance Agency, House Price Index, February 25, 2014

Median Single-Family Home Prices

Area	2011	2012	2013p	Percent Change 2012 to 2013
MSA[1]	128.2	128.3	133.4	4.0
U.S. Average	166.2	177.2	197.4	11.4

Note: Figures are median sales prices of existing single-family homes in thousands of dollars; (p) preliminary; n/a not available; (1) Montgomery, AL Metropolitan Statistical Area—see Appendix B for areas included
Source: National Association of Realtors, Median Sales Price of Existing Single-Family Homes for Metropolitan Areas, 4th Quarter 2013

Qualifying Income Based on Median Sales Price of Existing Single-Family Homes

Area	With 5% Down ($)	With 10% Down ($)	With 20% Down ($)
MSA[1]	29,856	28,285	25,142
U.S. Average	45,395	43,006	38,228

Note: Figures are preliminary; Qualifying income is based on a mortgage rate of 4.4%. Monthly principal and interest payment is limited to 25% of income; n/a not available; (1) Montgomery, AL Metropolitan Statistical Area—see Appendix B for areas included
Source: National Association of Realtors, Qualifying Income Based on Median Sales Price of Existing Single-Family Homes for Metropolitan Areas, 4th Quarter 2013

Median Apartment Condo-Coop Home Prices

Area	2011	2012	2013p	Percent Change 2012 to 2013
MSA[1]	n/a	n/a	n/a	n/a
U.S. Average	165.1	173.7	194.9	12.2

Note: Figures are median sales prices of existing apartment condo-coop homes in thousands of dollars; (p) preliminary; n/a not available; (1) Montgomery, AL Metropolitan Statistical Area—see Appendix B for areas included
Source: National Association of Realtors, Median Sales Price of Existing Apartment Condo-Coop Homes for Metropolitan Areas, 4th Quarter 2013

Gross Monthly Rent

Area	Under $200	$200 -299	$300 -499	$500 -749	$750 -999	$1,000 -1,499	$1,500 and up	Median ($)
City	1.9	3.6	8.3	30.1	33.4	18.2	4.6	789
MSA[1]	1.8	3.2	9.5	29.8	32.6	18.2	4.9	787
U.S.	1.7	3.3	8.1	22.7	24.3	25.7	14.3	889

Note: Figures are percentages except for Median; Gross rent is the contract rent plus the estimated average monthly cost of utilities (electricity, gas, and water and sewer) and fuels (oil, coal, kerosene, wood, etc.) if these are paid by the renter (or paid for the renter by someone else); (1) Figures cover the Montgomery, AL Metropolitan Statistical Area—see Appendix B for areas included
Source: U.S. Census Bureau, 2010-2012 American Community Survey 3-Year Estimates

Year Housing Structure Built

Area	2010 or Later	2000 -2009	1990 -1999	1980 -1989	1970 -1979	1960 -1969	1950 -1959	1940 -1949	Before 1940	Median Year
City	0.2	11.6	16.1	13.9	20.8	13.1	11.6	5.2	7.6	1976
MSA[1]	0.7	17.2	19.8	13.9	18.5	11.6	8.5	3.7	5.9	1981
U.S.	0.5	14.9	13.8	13.9	15.9	11.1	10.9	5.5	13.5	1976

Note: Figures are percentages except for Median Year; (1) Figures cover the Montgomery, AL Metropolitan Statistical Area—see Appendix B for areas included
Source: U.S. Census Bureau, 2010-2012 American Community Survey 3-Year Estimates

HEALTH

Health Risk Data

Category	MSA[1] (%)	U.S. (%)
Adults aged 18–64 who have any kind of health care coverage	78.8	79.6
Adults who reported being in good or excellent health	78.5	83.1
Adults who are current smokers	23.1	19.6
Adults who are heavy drinkers[2]	7.3	6.1
Adults who are binge drinkers[3]	14.0	16.9
Adults who are overweight (BMI 25.0 - 29.9)	34.4	35.8
Adults who are obese (BMI 30.0 - 99.8)	33.2	27.6
Adults who participated in any physical activities in the past month	72.9	77.1
Adults 50+ who have ever had a sigmoidoscopy or colonoscopy	72.9	67.3
Women aged 40+ who have had a mammogram within the past two years	77.2	74.0
Men aged 40+ who have had a PSA test within the past two years	57.4	45.2
Adults aged 65+ who have had flu shot within the past year	62.4	60.1
Adults who always wear a seatbelt	n/a	93.8

Note: Data as of 2012 unless otherwise noted; n/a not available; (1) Figures cover the Montgomery, AL Metropolitan Statistical Area—see Appendix B for areas included; (2) Heavy drinkers are classified as males having more than two drinks per day or females having more than one drink per day; (3) Binge drinkers are classified as males having five or more drinks on one occasion or females having four or more drinks on one occasion
Source: Centers for Disease Control and Prevention, Behaviorial Risk Factor Surveillance System, SMART: Selected Metropolitan/Micropolitan Area Risk Trends, 2012

Chronic Health Indicators

Category	MSA[1] (%)	U.S. (%)
Adults who have ever been told they had a heart attack	5.9	4.5
Adults who have ever been told they had a stroke	5.3	2.9
Adults who have been told they currently have asthma	7.2	8.9
Adults who have ever been told they have arthritis	30.4	25.7
Adults who have ever been told they have diabetes[2]	14.4	9.7
Adults who have ever been told they had skin cancer	6.6	5.7
Adults who have ever been told they had any other types of cancer	5.0	6.5
Adults who have ever been told they have COPD	9.2	6.2
Adults who have ever been told they have kidney disease	3.2	2.5
Adults who have ever been told they have a form of depression	19.7	18.0

Note: Data as of 2012 unless otherwise noted; (1) Figures cover the Montgomery, AL Metropolitan Statistical Area—see Appendix B for areas included; (2) Figures do not include pregnancy-related, borderline, or pre-diabetes
Source: Centers for Disease Control and Prevention, Behaviorial Risk Factor Surveillance System, SMART: Selected Metropolitan/Micropolitan Area Risk Trends, 2012

Mortality Rates for the Top 10 Causes of Death in the U.S.

ICD-10[a] Sub-Chapter	ICD-10[a] Code	Age-Adjusted Mortality Rate[1] per 100,000 population	
		County[2]	U.S.
Malignant neoplasms	C00-C97	201.1	174.2
Ischaemic heart diseases	I20-I25	88.0	119.1
Other forms of heart disease	I30-I51	89.3	49.6
Chronic lower respiratory diseases	J40-J47	47.2	43.2
Cerebrovascular diseases	I60-I69	51.7	40.3
Organic, including symptomatic, mental disorders	F01-F09	36.6	30.5
Other degenerative diseases of the nervous system	G30-G31	33.4	26.3
Other external causes of accidental injury	W00-X59	19.4	25.1
Diabetes mellitus	E10-E14	49.2	21.3
Hypertensive diseases	I10-I15	35.6	18.8

Note: (a) ICD-10 = International Classification of Diseases 10th Revision; (1) Mortality rates are a three year average covering 2008-2010; (2) Figures cover Montgomery County
Source: Centers for Disease Control and Prevention, National Center for Health Statistics. Compressed Mortality File 1999-2010 on CDC WONDER Online Database, released January 2013. Data are compiled from the Compressed Mortality File 1999-2010, Series 20 No. 2P, 2013.

Mortality Rates for Selected Causes of Death

ICD-10[a] Sub-Chapter	ICD-10[a] Code	Age-Adjusted Mortality Rate[1] per 100,000 population	
		County[2]	U.S.
Assault	X85-Y09	12.4	5.5
Diseases of the liver	K70-K76	11.4	12.4
Human immunodeficiency virus (HIV) disease	B20-B24	7.0	3.0
Influenza and pneumonia	J09-J18	14.1	16.4
Intentional self-harm	X60-X84	9.9	11.8
Malnutrition	E40-E46	*2.1	0.8
Obesity and other hyperalimentation	E65-E68	Suppressed	1.6
Renal failure	N17-N19	22.0	13.6
Transport accidents	V01-V99	12.4	12.6
Viral hepatitis	B15-B19	*2.2	2.2

Note: (a) ICD-10 = International Classification of Diseases 10th Revision; (1) Mortality rates are a three year average covering 2008-2010; (2) Figures cover Montgomery County; (*) Unreliable data as per CDC
Source: Centers for Disease Control and Prevention, National Center for Health Statistics. Compressed Mortality File 1999-2010 on CDC WONDER Online Database, released January 2013. Data are compiled from the Compressed Mortality File 1999-2010, Series 20 No. 2P, 2013.

Health Insurance Coverage

Area	With Health Insurance	With Private Health Insurance	With Public Health Insurance	Without Health Insurance	Population Under Age 18 Without Health Insurance
City	85.3	62.2	35.8	14.7	4.9
MSA[1]	87.0	67.2	32.4	13.0	4.5
U.S.	84.9	65.4	30.4	15.1	7.5

Note: Figures are percentages that cover the civilian noninstitutionalized population; (1) Figures cover the Montgomery, AL Metropolitan Statistical Area—see Appendix B for areas included
Source: U.S. Census Bureau, 2010-2012 American Community Survey 3-Year Estimates

Number of Medical Professionals

Area[1]	MDs[2]	DOs[2,3]	Dentists	Podiatrists	Chiropractors	Optometrists
Local (number)	601	35	142	16	37	35
Local (rate[4])	259.6	15.1	61.9	7.0	16.1	15.3
U.S. (rate[4])	267.6	19.6	61.7	5.6	24.7	14.5

Note: Data as of 2012 unless noted; (1) Local data covers Montgomery County; (2) Data as of 2011; (3) Doctor of Osteopathic Medicine; (4) rate per 100,000 population
Source: Area Resource File (ARF) 2012-2013. U.S. Department of Health and Human Services, Health Resources and Services Administration, Bureau of Health Professions

EDUCATION

Public School District Statistics

District Name	Schls	Pupils	Pupil/ Teacher Ratio	Minority Pupils[1] (%)	Free Lunch Eligible[2] (%)	IEP[3] (%)
Montgomery County	63	31,359	16.9	85.9	67.4	9.8

Note: Table includes school districts with 2,000 or more students; (1) Percentage of students that are not non-Hispanic white; (2) Percentage of students that are eligible for the free lunch program; (3) Percentage of students that have an Individualized Education Program.
Source: U.S. Department of Education, National Center for Education Statistics, Common Core of Data, Local Education Agency (School District) Universe Survey: School Year 2011-2012; U.S. Department of Education, National Center for Education Statistics, Common Core of Data, Public Elementary/Secondary School Universe Survey: School Year 2011-2012

Best High Schools

High School Name	Rank[1]	Grad. Rate[2] (%)	Coll.[3] (%)	AP/IB/ AICE Tests[4]	AP/IB/ AICE Score[5]	SAT Score[6]	ACT Score[6]
Booker T. Washington Magnet H.S.	304	100	98	0.7	2.6	n/a	22.4
Brewbaker Technology Magnet H.S.	1218	72	98	0.9	2.8	n/a	22.5

Note: (1) Public schools are ranked from 1 to 2,000 based on the following self-reported statistics (with the corresponding weight used in calculating their overall score). Schools that were newly founded and did not have a graduating senior class in 2012 were excluded; (2) Four-year, on-time graduation rate (25%); (3) Percent of 2011 graduates who were accepted to college (25%); (4) AP/IB/AICE tests taken per student (25%); (5) Average AP/IB/AICE exam score (10%); (6) Average SAT and/or ACT score (10%); Percent of students enrolled in at least one AP/IB/AICE course (5%)—data not shown; n/a not available
Source: Newsweek and The Daily Beast, "America's Best High Schools 2013"

Highest Level of Education

Area	Less than H.S.	H.S. Diploma	Some College, No Deg.	Associate Degree	Bachelor's Degree	Master's Degree	Prof. School Degree	Doctorate Degree
City	14.5	25.6	22.7	5.7	19.2	9.2	1.8	1.3
MSA[1]	14.8	29.4	22.1	6.7	16.9	7.7	1.5	0.9
U.S.	14.1	28.3	21.3	7.8	18.0	7.5	1.9	1.2

Note: Figures cover persons age 25 and over; (1) Figures cover the Montgomery, AL Metropolitan Statistical Area—see Appendix B for areas included
Source: U.S. Census Bureau, 2010-2012 American Community Survey 3-Year Estimates

Educational Attainment by Race

Area	High School Graduate or Higher (%)					Bachelor's Degree or Higher (%)				
	Total	White	Black	Asian	Hisp.[2]	Total	White	Black	Asian	Hisp.[2]
City	85.5	91.5	81.1	86.4	59.3	31.5	43.0	21.2	50.6	20.2
MSA[1]	85.2	89.7	79.0	86.0	61.4	27.0	32.3	18.4	48.6	19.7
U.S.	85.9	88.1	82.5	85.5	63.1	28.6	30.0	18.4	50.2	13.4

Note: Figures shown cover persons 25 years old and over; (1) Figures cover the Montgomery, AL Metropolitan Statistical Area—see Appendix B for areas included; (2) People of Hispanic origin can be of any race
Source: U.S. Census Bureau, 2010-2012 American Community Survey 3-Year Estimates

School Enrollment by Grade and Control

Area	Preschool (%)		Kindergarten (%)		Grades 1 - 4 (%)		Grades 5 - 8 (%)		Grades 9 - 12 (%)	
	Public	Private	Public	Private	Public	Private	Public	Private	Public	Private
City	52.1	47.9	85.9	14.1	86.4	13.6	83.5	16.5	79.4	20.6
MSA[1]	49.3	50.7	80.1	19.9	83.7	16.3	82.1	17.9	78.0	22.0
U.S.	56.9	43.1	87.8	12.2	89.9	10.1	90.0	10.0	90.8	9.2

Note: Figures shown cover persons 3 years old and over; (1) Figures cover the Montgomery, AL Metropolitan Statistical Area—see Appendix B for areas included
Source: U.S. Census Bureau, 2010-2012 American Community Survey 3-Year Estimates

Average Salaries of Public School Classroom Teachers

Area	2012-13		2013-14		Percent Change 2012-13 to 2013-14	Percent Change 2003-04 to 2013-14
	Dollars	Rank[1]	Dollars	Rank[1]		
Alabama	47,949	39	48,413	40	0.97	26.5
U.S. Average	56,103	–	56,689	–	1.04	21.8

Note: (1) State rank ranges from 1 to 51 where 1 indicates highest salary.
Source: National Education Association, Rankings & Estimates: Rankings of the States 2013 and Estimates of School Statistics 2014, March 2014

Higher Education

Four-Year Colleges			Two-Year Colleges			Medical Schools[1]	Law Schools[2]	Voc/ Tech[3]
Public	Private Non-profit	Private For-profit	Public	Private Non-profit	Private For-profit			
2	3	1	2	0	4	0	1	1

Note: Figures cover institutions located within the city limits and include main campuses only; (1) includes schools accredited by the Liaison Committee on Medical Education and the American Osteopathic Association's Commission on Osteopathic College Accreditation; (2) includes ABA-accredited schools, schools with provisional ABA accreditation, and state accredited schools; (3) includes all schools with programs that are less than 2 years.
Source: National Center for Education Statistics, Integrated Postsecondary Education System (IPEDS), 2012-13; Association of American Medical Colleges, Member List, April 24, 2014; American Osteopathic Association, Member List, April 24, 2014; Law School Admission Council, Official Guide to ABA-Approved Law Schools Online, April 24, 2014; Wikipedia, List of Medical Schools in the United States, April 24, 2014; Wikipedia, List of Law Schools in the United States, April 24, 2014

PRESIDENTIAL ELECTION

2012 Presidential Election Results

Area	Obama	Romney	Other
Montgomery County	61.9	37.6	0.5
U.S.	51.0	47.2	1.8

Note: Results are percentages and may not add to 100% due to rounding
Source: Dave Leip's Atlas of U.S. Presidential Elections

EMPLOYERS

Major Employers

Company Name	Industry
Alabama Power Company	Utilities
Alabama State University	Colleges & universities
Alfa Insurance Companies	Insurance companies/services
Auburn University Montgomery	Colleges & universities
Baptist Health	Hospitals/clinics
Big Lots Stores	Miscellaneous consumer goods
Central Alabama Veteran's Hlth Care Sys	Associations/non-profit
City of Montgomery	Government agency
Creek Casinos	Casinos
GKN Aerospace	Aircraft parts manufacturing
Hyundai Motor Manufacturing Alabama	Automobile manufacturing
International Paper Prattville Mill	Liner board manufacturing
Jackson Hospital & Clinic	Hospitals/clinics
Koch Foods	Poultry processing
Maxwell-Gunter Air Force Base	Federal government
MOBIS Alabama	Cockpit & chassis modules
Montgomery County Commission	Local government
Montgomery Public Schools	Public schools
Neptune Technology Group	Water meters and electronic reading systems mfg
Regions Bank	Banks
Rheem Water Heaters	Water heater manufacturing
State of Alabama	State government
U.S. Postal Service	Shipping services
US Foodservice	Distribution/wholesale food and beverage products
Webster Industries	Plastic freezer and garbage bag manufacturing

Note: Companies shown are located within the Montgomery, AL Metropolitan Statistical Area.
Source: Hoovers.com; Wikipedia

PUBLIC SAFETY

Crime Rate

Area	All Crimes	Violent Crimes				Property Crimes		
		Murder	Forcible Rape	Robbery	Aggrav. Assault	Burglary	Larceny -Theft	Motor Vehicle Theft
City	6,164.5	21.1	19.6	219.6	135.4	1,631.0	3,611.2	526.7
Suburbs[1]	3,134.8	5.3	26.9	55.5	212.7	873.1	1,804.1	157.2
Metro[2]	4,800.7	13.9	22.9	145.7	170.2	1,289.8	2,797.7	360.4
U.S.	3,246.1	4.7	26.9	112.9	242.3	670.2	1,959.3	229.7

Note: Figures are crimes per 100,000 population; (1) All areas within the metro area that are located outside the city limits; (2) Figures cover the Montgomery, AL Metropolitan Statistical Area—see Appendix B for areas included

Source: FBI Uniform Crime Reports, 2012

Hate Crimes

Area	Number of Quarters Reported	Bias Motivation				
		Race	Religion	Sexual Orientation	Ethnicity	Disability
City	n/a	n/a	n/a	n/a	n/a	n/a
U.S.	4	2,797	1,099	1,135	667	92

Note: n/a not available.

Source: Federal Bureau of Investigation, Hate Crime Statistics 2012

Identity Theft Consumer Complaints

Area	Complaints	Complaints per 100,000 Population	Rank[2]
MSA[1]	495	132.2	15
U.S.	290,056	91.8	-

Note: (1) Figures cover the Montgomery, AL Metropolitan Statistical Area—see Appendix B for areas included; (2) Rank ranges from 1 to 377 where 1 indicates greatest number of identity theft complaints per 100,000 population

Source: Federal Trade Commission, Consumer Sentinel Network Data Book for January–December 2013

Fraud and Other Consumer Complaints

Area	Complaints	Complaints per 100,000 Population	Rank[2]
MSA[1]	1,451	387.4	142
U.S.	1,811,724	595.2	-

Note: (1) Figures cover the Montgomery, AL Metropolitan Statistical Area—see Appendix B for areas included; (2) Rank ranges from 1 to 377 where 1 indicates greatest number of identity theft complaints per 100,000 population

Source: Federal Trade Commission, Consumer Sentinel Network Data Book for January–December 2013

RECREATION

Culture

Dance[1]	Theatre[1]	Instrumental Music[1]	Vocal Music[1]	Series and Festivals	Museums and Art Galleries[2]	Zoos and Aquariums[3]
2	1	1	0	1	14	0

Note: (1) Number of professional perfoming groups; (2) Based on organizations with primary SIC code 8412; (3) AZA-accredited

Source: The Grey House Performing Arts Directory, 2013; Association of Zoos & Aquariums, AZA Member Zoos & Aquariums, April 2014; www.AccuLeads.com, May 1, 2014

Professional Sports Teams

Team Name	League	Year Established
No teams are located in the metro area		

Source: Wikipedia, Major Professional Sports Teams of the United States and Canada, April 25, 2014

CLIMATE

Average and Extreme Temperatures

Temperature	Jan	Feb	Mar	Apr	May	Jun	Jul	Aug	Sep	Oct	Nov	Dec	Yr.
Extreme High (°F)	83	85	89	91	98	105	105	104	101	100	87	85	105
Average High (°F)	57	62	69	77	84	90	92	91	87	78	68	60	76
Average Temp. (°F)	47	51	57	65	73	79	82	81	77	66	56	49	65
Average Low (°F)	37	40	46	53	61	68	72	71	66	53	43	38	54
Extreme Low (°F)	0	10	17	28	40	49	60	56	39	26	13	5	0

Note: Figures cover the years 1948-1995
Source: National Climatic Data Center, International Station Meteorological Climate Summary, 9/96

Average Precipitation/Snowfall/Humidity

Precip./Humidity	Jan	Feb	Mar	Apr	May	Jun	Jul	Aug	Sep	Oct	Nov	Dec	Yr.
Avg. Precip. (in.)	4.5	5.1	6.1	4.4	4.0	4.0	5.2	3.4	4.3	2.5	4.1	5.0	52.7
Avg. Snowfall (in.)	Tr	Tr	Tr	Tr	0	0	0	0	0	Tr	Tr	Tr	Tr
Avg. Rel. Hum. 7am (%)	83	82	81	80	80	81	84	86	85	86	86	84	83
Avg. Rel. Hum. 4pm (%)	56	51	48	46	51	54	59	56	55	50	52	56	53

Note: Figures cover the years 1948-1995; Tr = Trace amounts (<0.05 in. of rain; <0.5 in. of snow)
Source: National Climatic Data Center, International Station Meteorological Climate Summary, 9/96

Weather Conditions

Temperature			Daytime Sky			Precipitation		
10°F & below	32°F & below	90°F & above	Clear	Partly cloudy	Cloudy	0.01 inch or more precip.	0.1 inch or more snow/ice	Thunder-storms
< 1	38	82	97	152	116	109	< 1	59

Note: Figures are average number of days per year and cover the years 1948-1995
Source: National Climatic Data Center, International Station Meteorological Climate Summary, 9/96

HAZARDOUS WASTE

Superfund Sites

Montgomery has one hazardous waste site on the EPA's Superfund Final National Priorities List: **T.H. Agriculture & Nutrition Co. (Montgomery Plant).** *U.S. Environmental Protection Agency, Final National Priorities List, April 26, 2014*

AIR & WATER QUALITY

Air Quality Index

Area	Percent of Days when Air Quality was...[2]					AQI Statistics[2]	
	Good	Moderate	Unhealthy for Sensitive Groups	Unhealthy	Very Unhealthy	Maximum	Median
MSA[1]	87.7	12.3	0.0	0.0	0.0	73	37

Note: (1) Data covers the Montgomery, AL Metropolitan Statistical Area—see Appendix B for areas included; (2) Based on 285 days with AQI data in 2013. Air Quality Index (AQI) is an index for reporting daily air quality. EPA calculates the AQI for five major air pollutants regulated by the Clean Air Act: ground-level ozone, particle pollution (aka particulate matter), carbon monoxide, sulfur dioxide, and nitrogen dioxide. The AQI runs from 0 to 500. The higher the AQI value, the greater the level of air pollution and the greater the health concern. There are six AQI categories: "Good" AQI is between 0 and 50. Air quality is considered satisfactory; "Moderate" AQI is between 51 and 100. Air quality is acceptable; "Unhealthy for Sensitive Groups" When AQI values are between 101 and 150, members of sensitive groups may experience health effects; "Unhealthy" When AQI values are between 151 and 200 everyone may begin to experience health effects; "Very Unhealthy" AQI values between 201 and 300 trigger a health alert; "Hazardous" AQI values over 300 trigger warnings of emergency conditions (not shown).
Source: U.S. Environmental Protection Agency, Air Quality Index Report, 2013

Air Quality Index Pollutants

Area	Percent of Days when AQI Pollutant was...[2]					
	Carbon Monoxide	Nitrogen Dioxide	Ozone	Sulfur Dioxide	Particulate Matter 2.5	Particulate Matter 10
MSA[1]	0.0	0.0	66.7	0.0	33.3	0.0

Note: (1) Data covers the Montgomery, AL Metropolitan Statistical Area—see Appendix B for areas included; (2) Based on 285 days with AQI data in 2013. The Air Quality Index (AQI) is an index for reporting daily air quality. EPA calculates the AQI for five major air pollutants regulated by the Clean Air Act: ground-level ozone, particle pollution (also known as particulate matter), carbon monoxide, sulfur dioxide, and nitrogen dioxide. The AQI runs from 0 to 500. The higher the AQI value, the greater the level of air pollution and the greater the health concern.
Source: U.S. Environmental Protection Agency, Air Quality Index Report, 2013

Air Quality Trends: Ozone

	2003	2004	2005	2006	2007	2008	2009	2010	2011	2012
MSA[1]	0.069	0.068	0.069	0.073	0.077	0.069	0.063	0.073	0.069	0.066

Note: (1) Data covers the Montgomery, AL Metropolitan Statistical Area—see Appendix B for areas included. The values shown are the composite ozone concentration averages among trend sites based on the highest fourth daily maximum 8-hour concentration in parts per million. These trends are based on sites having an adequate record of monitoring data during the trend period. Data from exceptional events are included.
Source: U.S. Environmental Protection Agency, Air Quality Monitoring Information, "Air Quality Trends by City, 2000-2012"

Maximum Air Pollutant Concentrations: Particulate Matter, Ozone, CO and Lead

	Particulate Matter 10 (ug/m^3)	Particulate Matter 2.5 Wtd AM (ug/m^3)	Particulate Matter 2.5 24-Hr (ug/m^3)	Ozone (ppm)	Carbon Monoxide (ppm)	Lead (ug/m^3)
MSA[1] Level	28	10.6	20	0.066	n/a	n/a
NAAQS[2]	150	15	35	0.075	9	0.15
Met NAAQS[2]	Yes	Yes	Yes	Yes	n/a	n/a

Note: (1) Data covers the Montgomery, AL Metropolitan Statistical Area—see Appendix B for areas included; Data from exceptional events are included; (2) National Ambient Air Quality Standards; ppm = parts per million; ug/m^3 = micrograms per cubic meter; n/a not available.
Concentrations: Particulate Matter 10 (coarse particulate)—highest second maximum 24-hour concentration; Particulate Matter 2.5 Wtd AM (fine particulate)—highest weighted annual mean concentration; Particulate Matter 2.5 24-Hour (fine particulate)—highest 98th percentile 24-hour concentration; Ozone—highest fourth daily maximum 8-hour concentration; Carbon Monoxide—highest second maximum non-overlapping 8-hour concentration; Lead—maximum running 3-month average
Source: U.S. Environmental Protection Agency, Air Quality Monitoring Information, "Air Quality Statistics by City, 2012"

Maximum Air Pollutant Concentrations: Nitrogen Dioxide and Sulfur Dioxide

	Nitrogen Dioxide AM (ppb)	Nitrogen Dioxide 1-Hr (ppb)	Sulfur Dioxide AM (ppb)	Sulfur Dioxide 1-Hr (ppb)	Sulfur Dioxide 24-Hr (ppb)
MSA[1] Level	n/a	n/a	n/a	n/a	n/a
NAAQS[2]	53	100	30	75	140
Met NAAQS[2]	n/a	n/a	n/a	n/a	n/a

Note: (1) Data covers the Montgomery, AL Metropolitan Statistical Area—see Appendix B for areas included; Data from exceptional events are included; (2) National Ambient Air Quality Standards; ppm = parts per million; ug/m^3 = micrograms per cubic meter; n/a not available.
Concentrations: Nitrogen Dioxide AM—highest arithmetic mean concentration; Nitrogen Dioxide 1-Hr—highest 98th percentile 1-hour daily maximum concentration; Sulfur Dioxide AM—highest annual mean concentration; Sulfur Dioxide 1-Hr—highest 99th percentile 1-hour daily maximum concentration; Sulfur Dioxide 24-Hr—highest second maximum 24-hour concentration
Source: U.S. Environmental Protection Agency, Air Quality Monitoring Information, "Air Quality Statistics by City, 2012"

Drinking Water

Water System Name	Pop. Served	Primary Water Source Type	Violations[1]	
			Health Based	Monitoring/ Reporting
Montgomery Water Works	240,840	Surface	0	0

Note: (1) Based on violation data from January 1, 2013 to December 31, 2013 (includes unresolved violations from earlier years)
Source: U.S. Environmental Protection Agency, Office of Ground Water and Drinking Water, Safe Drinking Water Information System (based on data extracted February 10, 2014)

Nashville, Tennessee

Background

Nashville, the capital of Tennessee, was founded on Christmas Day in 1779 by James Robertson and John Donelson, and sits in the minds of millions as the country music capital of the world. This is the place to record if you want to make it into the country music industry, and where the Grand Ole Opry—the longest-running radio show in the country—still captures the hearts of millions of devoted listeners. It is no wonder, given how profoundly this industry has touched people, names like Dolly, Chet, Loretta, Hank, and Johnny are more familiar than the city's true native sons: Andrew, James, and Sam. Jackson, Polk, and Houston, that is.

Nashville is home to Music Row, an area just to the southwest of downtown with hundreds of businesses related to the country music, gospel music, and contemporary Christian music industries. The USA Network's Nashville Star, a country music singing competition, is also held in the Acuff Theatre. The magnitude of Nashville's recording industry is impressive, but other industries are important to the city, such as health care management, automobile production, and printing and publishing.

Nashville is also a devoted patron of education. The Davidson Academy, forerunner of the George Peabody College for Teachers, was founded in Nashville, as were Vanderbilt and Fisk universities, the latter being the first private black university in the United States. Vanderbilt University and Medical Center is the region's largest non-governmental employer.

Nashville citizens take pride in their numerous museums, including the Adventure Science Center, with its Sudekum Planetarium; the Aaron Douglas Gallery at Fisk University, which features a remarkable collection of African-American art; and the Carl Van Vechten Gallery, also at Fisk University, home to works by Alfred Stieglitz, Picasso, Cezanne, and Georgia O'Keefe. The Cheekwood Botanical Garden and Museum of Art includes 55 acres of gardens and contemporary art galleries.

Gracing the city are majestic mansions and plantations that testify to the mid nineteenth-century splendor for which the South came to be famous. Known as the "Queen of the Tennessee Plantations," the Belle Meade Plantation is an 1853 Greek Revival mansion crowning a 5,400-acre thoroughbred stud farm and nursery. The Belmont Mansion, built in 1850 by Adelicia Acklen, one of the wealthiest women in America, is constructed in the style of an Italian villa and was originally intended to be the summer home of the Acklens. Travelers' Rest Plantation served as a haven for weary travelers, past and present, and is Nashville's oldest plantation home open to the public. It features docents dressed in period costume who explain and demonstrate life in the plantations' heyday. Carnton Plantation was the site of the Civil War's Battle of Franklin, and The Hermitage was the home of Andrew Jackson, the seventh president of the United States. Tennessee's historic State Capitol Building, completed in 1859, has had much of its interior restored to its nineteenth-century appearance.

The Nashville area comprises many urban, suburban, rural, and historic districts, which can differ immensely from each other. Most of the best restaurants, clubs, and shops are on the west side of the Cumberland River, however, the east side encompasses fine neighborhoods, interesting homes, plenty of shopping, and good food, as well. Outdoor activities include camping, fishing, hiking, and biking at the many scenic and accessible lakes in the region.

Located on the Cumberland River in central Tennessee, Nashville's average relative humidity is moderate, as is its weather, with great temperature extremes a rarity. The city is not in the most common path of storms that cross the country, but is in a zone of moderate frequency for thunderstorms.

Rankings

General Rankings

- *Business Insider* projected current trends well into the future to compile its list of the "15 Hottest American Cities of the Future." To such metrics as job and population growth, demographics, affordability, livability, and residents' health and welfare, analysts added innovation in technology and sustainability as well as a culture favoring youth and creativity. Judging by these combined factors, Nashville ranked #9. *Business Insider, "The Fifteen Hottest American Cities of the Future," June 18, 2012*

- Nashville was identified as one of America's fastest-growing major metropolitan areas in terms of population by CNNMoney.com. The area ranked #7 out of 10. Criteria: population growth between July 2012 and July 2013. *CNNMoney, "10 Fastest-Growing Cities," March 28, 2014*

- Among the 50 largest U.S. cities, Nashville placed #25 in Vocativ's "semi-exhaustive, mostly scientific" city Livability Index for people aged 35 and under. Average salary, unemployment rates, rents, and other living costs were considered, along with bike lanes, low-cost broadband, cheap takeout, self-service laundries, the price of a pint of Guinness, music venues, and vintage clothing stores. *vocative.com, "The Livability Index: The Best U.S. Cities for People 35 and Under," November 7, 2013*

- Nashville was selected as one of America's best cities by *Bloomberg Businessweek*. The city ranked #13 out of 50. Criteria: leisure attributes (the number of restaurants, bars, libraries, museums, professional sports teams, and park acres by population); educational attributes (public school performance, the number of colleges, and graduate degree holders); economic factors (2011 income and June and July 2012 unemployment); crime; and air quality. *Bloomberg BusinessWeek, "America's Best Cities," September 26, 2012*

- Nashville was selected as one of America's best river towns by *Outside Magazine*. Criteria: cost of living; cultural vibrancy; job prospects; environmental stewardship; access to the outdoors. *Outside Magazine, "Best Towns 2012," October 2012*

- Nashville was selected as one of "America's Favorite Cities." The city ranked #5 in the "Quality of Life and Visitor Experience: Cleanliness" category. Respondents to an online survey were asked to rate 35 top urban destinations in the U.S. from a visitor's perspective. Criteria: cleanliness. *Travel + Leisure, "America's Favorite Cities 2013"*

- Nashville was selected as one of "America's Favorite Cities." The city ranked #27 in the "Type of Trip: Gay-friendly" category. Respondents to an online survey were asked to rate 35 top urban destinations in the U.S. from a visitor's perspective. Criteria: gay-friendly. *Travel + Leisure, "America's Favorite Cities 2013"*

- The Nashville metro area was selected as one of 10 "Best Value Cities" for 2011 by *Kiplinger.com* The area ranked #3. Criteria: vibrant economy; low cost of living; abundant lifestyle amenities. *Kiplinger.com, "Best Value Cities 2011"*

Business/Finance Rankings

- Recognizing the sizeable percentage of American workers who are self-employed, NerdWallet editors assessed the country's cities according to percentage of freelancers, median rental costs, and affordability of median healthcare costs. By these criteria, Nashville placed #5 among the best cities for independent workers. *www.nerdwallet.com, "Best Cities for Freelancers," February 25, 2014*

- The editors of *Kiplinger's Personal Finance Magazine* named Nashville to their list of ten of the best metro areas for start-ups. Criteria included a well-educated workforce and low living costs for self-employed people, as measured by the Council for Community and Economic Research, as well as areas with lots of start-up investment dollars and low business costs. *www.kiplinger.com, "10 Great Cities for Starting a Business," January 2013*

- Based on a minimum of 500 social media reviews per metro area, the employment opinion group Glassdoor surveyed 50 of the largest U.S. metro areas on measures including compensation and benefits, satisfaction with management, business outlook, and number of employers hiring. The Nashville metro area was ranked #44 in overall employee satisfaction. *www.glassdoor.com, "Employment Satisfaction Report Card by City," June 21, 2013*

- The financial literacy site NerdWallet.com set out to identify the 20 most promising cities for job seekers, analyzing data for the nation's 50 largest cities. Nashville was ranked #12. Criteria: unemployment rate; population growth; median income; selected monthly owner costs. *NerdWallet.com, "Best Cities for Job Seekers," January 7, 2014*

- The Brookings Institution ranked the 50 largest cities in the U.S. based on income inequality. Nashville was ranked #34. (#1 = greatest ineqality). Criteria: the cities were ranked based on the "95/20 ratio." This figure represents the income at which a household earns more than 95 percent of all other households, divided by the income at which a household earns more than only 20 percent of all other households. *Brookings Institution, "Income Inequality in America's 50 Largest Cities, 2007-2012," February 20, 2014*

- CareerBliss, an employment and careers website, analyzed U.S. Bureau of Labor Statistics data, more than 14,000 company reviews from employees and former employees, and job openings over a six-month period to arrive at its list of the 20 worst places in the United States to look for a job. Nashville was ranked #14. *CareerBliss.com, "20 Worst Cities to Find a Job for 2012," October 11, 2012*

- Nashville was ranked #11 out of 100 metro areas in terms of economic performance (#1 = best) during the recession and recovery from trough quarter through the second quarter of 2013. Criteria: percent change in employment; percentage point change in unemployment rate; percent change in gross metropolitan product; percent change in House Price Index. *Brookings Institution, MetroMonitor: Tracking Economic Recession and Recovery in America's 100 Largest Metropolitan Areas, September 2013*

- Nashville was identified as one of America's most frugal metro areas by *Coupons.com*. The city ranked #4 out of 25. Criteria: online coupon usage. *Coupons.com, "Top 25 Most Frugal Cities of 2012," February 19, 2013*

- Nashville was identified as one of America's most frugal metro areas by *Coupons.com*. The city ranked #2 out of 25. Criteria: Grocery IQ and coupons.com mobile app usage. *Coupons.com, "Top 25 Most On-the-Go Frugal Cities of 2012," February 19, 2013*

- The Nashville metro area appeared on the Milken Institute "2013 Best Performing Cities" list. Rank: #14 out of 200 large metro areas. Criteria: job growth; wage and salary growth; high-tech output growth. *Milken Institute, "Best-Performing Cities 2013," December 2013*

- *Forbes* ranked the 200 most populous metro areas in the U.S. in terms of the "Best Places for Business and Careers." The Nashville metro area was ranked #5. Criteria: costs (business and living); job growth (past and projected); income growth; educational attainment (college and high school); projected economic growth; cultural and recreational opportunities; net migration patterns; number of highly ranked colleges. *Forbes, "The Best Places for Business and Careers," August 7, 2013*

Children/Family Rankings

- Nashville was selected as one of the best cities for families to live by *Parenting* magazine. The city ranked #72 out of 100. Criteria: education; health; community; *Parenting's* Culture & Charm Index. *Parenting.com, "The 2012 Best Cities for Families List"*

- Nashville was chosen as one of America's 100 best communities for young people. The winners were selected based upon detailed information provided about each community's efforts to fulfill five essential promises critical to the well-being of young people: caring adults who are actively involved in their lives; safe places in which to learn and grow; a healthy start toward adulthood; an effective education that builds marketable skills; and opportunities to help others. *America's Promise Alliance, "100 Best Communities for Young People, 2012"*

Culture/Performing Arts Rankings

- Nashville was selected as one of "America's Favorite Cities." The city ranked #11 in the "Culture: Museum/Galleries" category. Respondents to an online survey were asked to rate 35 top urban destinations in the U.S. from a visitor's perspective. Criteria: number and quality of museums and galleries. *Travelandleisure.com, "America's Favorite Cities 2013"*

- Nashville was selected as one of America's top cities for the arts. The city ranked #16 in the big city (population 500,000 and over) category. Criteria: readers' top choices for arts travel destinations based on the richness and variety of visual arts sites, activities and events. *American Style, "2012 Top 25 Arts Destinations," June 2012*

Dating/Romance Rankings

- Of the 100 U.S. cities surveyed by *Men's Health* in its quest to identify the nation's best cities for dating and forming relationships, Nashville was ranked #42 for online dating (#1 = best). *Men's Health, "The Best and Worst Cities for Online Dating," January 30, 2013*

- Nashville was selected as one of America's best cities for singles by the readers of *Travel + Leisure* in their annual "America's Favorite Cities" survey. The city was ranked #8 out of 20. *Travel + Leisure, "America's Best Cities for Singles," July 2012*

Education Rankings

- *Men's Health* ranked 100 U.S. cities in terms of their education levels. Nashville was ranked #41 (#1 = most educated city). Criteria: high school graduation rates; school enrollment; educational attainment; number of households who have outstanding student loans; number of households whose members have taken adult-education courses. *Men's Health, "Where School Is In: The Most and Least Educated Cities," September 12, 2011*

- Nashville was selected as one of America's most literate cities. The city ranked #21 out of the 77 largest U.S. cities. Criteria: number of booksellers; library resources; Internet resources; educational attainment; periodical publishing resources; newspaper circulation. *Central Connecticut State University, "America's Most Literate Cities, 2013"*

Environmental Rankings

- The Nashville metro area came in at #230 for the relative comfort of its climate on Sperling's list of "chill cities," as measured by the Sperling Heat Index. All 361 metro areas are included. Criteria included daytime high temperatures, nighttime low temperatures, dew point, and relative humidity at the high temperatures. *www.bertsperling.com, "Sperling's Chill Cities," July 18, 2013*

- Sperling's BestPlaces assessed 379 metropolitan areas of the United States for the likelihood of dangerously extreme weather events or earthquakes. In general the Southeast and South-Central regions have the highest risk of weather extremes and earthquakes, while the Pacific Northwest enjoys the lowest risk. Of the least risky metropolitan areas, the Nashville metro area was ranked #234. *www.bestplaces.net, "Safest Places from Natural Disasters," April 2011*

- Nashville was selected as one of 22 "Smarter Cities" for energy by the Natural Resources Defense Council. Criteria: investment in green power; energy efficiency measures; conservation. *Natural Resources Defense Council, "2010 Smarter Cities," July 19, 2010*

- The Nashville metro area was selected as one of "America's Cleanest Cities" by *Forbes*. The metro area ranked #6 out of 10. Criteria: toxic releases; air and water quality; per capita spending on Superfund site cleanup. *Forbes.com, "America's Cleanest Cities 2011," March 11, 2011*

- Nashville was highlighted as one of the top 25 cleanest metro areas for short-term particle pollution (24-hour PM 2.5) in the U.S. during 2008 through 2010. Monitors in these cities reported no days with unhealthful PM 2.5 levels. *American Lung Association, State of the Air 2012*

Food/Drink Rankings

- *Men's Health* ranked 100 major U.S. cities in terms of alcohol intoxication. Nashville ranked #87 (#1 = most sober).Criteria: binge drinking; alcohol-related traffic accidents, arrests, and fatalities. *Men's Health, "The Drunkest Cities in America," November 19, 2013*

- Nashville was selected as one of the seven best cities for barbeque by *U.S. News & World Report*. The city was ranked #6. *U.S. New & World Report, "America's Best BBQ Cities," February 29, 2012*

Health/Fitness Rankings

- For each of the 50 most populous metro areas in the United States, the American College of Sports Medicine's American Fitness Index evaluated infrastructure, community assets, and policies that encourage healthy and fit lifestyles, including preventive health behaviors, levels of chronic disease conditions, health care access, and community resources and policies that support physical activity. The Nashville metro area ranked #32 for "community fitness." Personal health indicators were considered as well as community and environmental indicators. *www.americanfitnessindex.org, "ACSM American Fitness Index Health and Community Fitness Status of the 50 Largest Metropolitan Areas," May 2013*

- The Nashville metro area was identified as one of the worst cities for bed bugs in America by pest control company Orkin. The area ranked #23 out of 50 based on the number of bed bug treatments Orkin performed from January to December 2013. *Orkin, "Chicago Tops Bed Bug Cities List for Second Year in a Row," January 16, 2014*

- Nashville was identified as one of 15 cities with the highest increase in bed bug activity in the U.S. by pest control provider Terminix. The city ranked #14.Criteria: cities with the largest percentage gains in bed bug customer calls from January–May 2013 compared to the same time period in 2012. *Terminix, "Cities with Highest Increases in Bed Bug Activity," July 9, 2013*

- Nashville was selected as one of the 25 fittest cities in America by *Men's Fitness Online*. It ranked #24 out of America's 50 largest cities. Criteria: fitness centers and sport stores; nutrition; sports participation; TV viewing; overweight/sedentary; junk food; air quality; geography; commute; parks and open space; city recreational facilities; access to healthcare; motivation; mayor and city initiatives; state obesity initiatives. *Men's Fitness, "The Fittest and Fattest Cities in America," March 5, 2012*

- Nashville was identified as a "2013 Spring Allergy Capital." The area ranked #36 out of 100. Three groups of factors were used to identify the most severe cities for people with allergies during the spring season: annual pollen levels; medicine utilization; access to board-certified allergists. *Asthma and Allergy Foundation of America, "Spring Allergy Capitals 2013"*

- Nashville was identified as a "2013 Fall Allergy Capital." The area ranked #24 out of 100. Three groups of factors were used to identify the most severe cities for people with allergies during the fall season: annual pollen levels; medicine utilization; access to board-certified allergists. *Asthma and Allergy Foundation of America, "Fall Allergy Capitals 2013"*

- Nashville was identified as a "2013 Asthma Capital." The area ranked #32 out of the nation's 100 largest metropolitan areas. Twelve factors were used to identify the most challenging places to live for people with asthma: estimated prevalence; self-reported prevalence; crude death rate for asthma; annual pollen score; annual air quality; public smoking laws; number of board-certified asthma specialists; school inhaler access laws; rescue medication use; controller medication use; uninsured rate; poverty rate. *Asthma and Allergy Foundation of America, "Asthma Capitals 2013"*

- *Men's Health* ranked 100 major U.S. cities in terms of the best and worst cities for men. Nashville ranked #41. Criteria: thirty-three data points were examined covering health, fitness, and quality of life. *Men's Health, "The Best & Worst Cities for Men 2014," December 6, 2013*

- Breathe Right Nasal Strips, in partnership with Sperling's BestPlaces, analyzed 50 metro areas and identified those U.S. cities most challenged by chronic nasal congestion. The Nashville metro area ranked #18. Criteria: tree, grass and weed pollens; molds and spores; air pollution; climate; smoking; purchase habits of congestion products; prescriptions of drugs for congestion relief; incidence of influenza. *Breathe Right Nasal Strips, "Most Congested Cities," October 3, 2011*

- The Nashville metro area appeared in the 2013 Gallup-Healthways Well-Being Index. The area ranked #72 out of 189. The Gallup-Healthways Well-Being Index score is an average of six sub-indexes, which individually examine life evaluation, emotional health, work environment, physical health, healthy behaviors, and access to basic necessities. Results are based on telephone interviews conducted as part of the Gallup-Healthways Well-Being Index survey January 2–December 29, 2012, and January 2–December 30, 2013, with a random sample of 531,630 adults, aged 18 and older, living in metropolitan areas in the 50 U.S. states and the District of Columbia. *Gallup-Healthways, "State of American Well-Being," March 25, 2014*

- The Nashville metro area was identified as one of "America's Most Stressful Cities" by *Sperling's BestPlaces*. The metro area ranked #30 out of 50. Criteria: unemployment rate; suicide rate; commute time; mental health; poor rest; alcohol use; violent crime rate; property crime rate; cloudy days annually. *Sperling's BestPlaces, www.BestPlaces.net, "Stressful Cities 2012"*

- *Men's Health* ranked 100 U.S. cities in terms of their activity levels. Nashville was ranked #93 (#1 = most active city). Criteria: where and how often residents exercise; percentage of households that watch more than 15 hours of cable television a week and buy more than 11 video games a year; death rate from deep-vein thrombosis, a condition linked to sitting for extended periods of time. *Men's Health, "Where Sit Happens: The Most and Least Active Cities in America," June 20, 2011*

- *The Daily Beast* identified the 30 U.S. metro areas with the worst smoking habits. The Nashville metro area ranked #15. Sixty urban centers with populations of more than one million were ranked based on the following criteria: number of smokers; number of cigarettes smoked per day; fewest attempts to quit. *The Daily Beast, "30 Cities With Smoking Problems," January 3, 2011*

Pet Rankings

- Nashville was selected as one of the best places to live with pets by *Livability.com*. The city was ranked #9. Criteria: pet-friendly parks and trails; quality veterinary care; active animal welfare groups; abundance of pet boutiques and retail shops; excellent quality of life for pet owners. *Livability.com, "Top 10 Pet Friendly Cities," October 20, 2010*

Real Estate Rankings

- The Nashville metro area was identified as one of the top 20 housing markets to invest in for 2014 by *Forbes*. The area ranked #4. Criteria: high population and job growth; relatively low home prices which are below equilibrium home price (EHP). The EHP is what the average price for a market should be, if speculation, weird distortions in local income, and other factors (like the housing collapse) weren't present in the market. *Forbes.com, "Best Buy Cities: Where to Invest in Housing in 2014," December 25, 2013*

- Nashville was ranked #77 out of 283 metro areas in terms of house price appreciation in 2013 (#1 = highest rate). *Federal Housing Finance Agency, House Price Index, 4th Quarter 2013*

- The Nashville metro area was identified as one of the 15 worst housing markets for the next five years." Criteria: projected annualized change in home prices between the fourth quarter 2012 and the fourth quarter 2017. *The Business Insider, "The 15 Worst Housing Markets for the Next Five Years," May 22, 2013*

- The Nashville metro area was identified as one of the 10 best U.S. markets to invest in single-family homes as rental properties by HomeVestors and Local Market Monitor. The area ranked #4. Criteria: risk-return premium relative to national average. *HomeVestors and Local Market Monitor, "Year-End Top 10 Real Estate Markets," December 20, 2013*

Safety Rankings

- Symantec, in partnership with Sperling's BestPlaces, ranked the 50 largest cities in the U.S. in terms of their vulnerability to cybercrime. The city ranked #36. Criteria: number of cyberattacks and potential infections; level of Internet access; expenditures on smartphones and computer hardware/software; wireless hotspots; broadband connectivity; Internet usage; online purchases. *Symantec, "Riskiest Online Cities of 2012" February 15, 2012*

- Allstate ranked the 200 largest cities in America in terms of driver safety. Nashville ranked #80. Allstate researchers analyzed internal property damage claims over a two-year period from January 2010 to December 2011. A weighted average of the two-year numbers determined the annual percentages. *Allstate, "Allstate America's Best Drivers Report®, August 27, 2013"*

- Nashville was identified as one of the most dangerous cities in America by *The Business Insider*. Criteria: cities with 100,000 residents or more were ranked by violent crime rate in 2011. Violent crimes include for murder, rape, robbery, and aggravated assault. The city ranked #19 out of 25. *The Business Insider, "The 25 Most Dangerous Cities in America," November 4, 2012*

- The National Insurance Crime Bureau ranked 380 metro areas in the U.S. in terms of per capita rates of vehicle theft. The Nashville metro area ranked #188 (#1 = highest rate). Criteria: number of vehicle theft offenses per 100,000 inhabitants in 2012. *National Insurance Crime Bureau, "Hot Spots 2012," June 26, 2013*

- The Nashville metro area was identified as one of the most dangerous metro areas for pedestrians by Transportation for America. The metro area ranked #14 out of 52 metro areas with over 1 million residents. Criteria: area's population divided by the number of pedestrian fatalities in that area. *Transportation for America, "Dangerous by Design 2011"*

Seniors/Retirement Rankings

- From its Best Cities for Successful Aging indexes, the Milken Institute generated rankings for metropolitan areas, weighing data in eight categories—general indicators, health care, wellness, living arrangements, transportation and general accessibility, financial well-being, education and employment, and community participation. The Nashville metro area was ranked #48 overall in the large metro area category. *Milken Institute, "Best Cities for Successful Aging," July 2012*

- *Forbes* selected the Nashville metro area as one of 25 "Best Places for a Working Retirement." Criteria: affordability; improving, above-average economies and job prospects; and a favorable tax climate for retirees. *Forbes.com, "Best Places for a Working Retirement in 2013," February 4, 2013*

- Bankers Life and Casualty Company, in partnership with Sperling's BestPlaces, ranked the nation's 50 largest metro areas in terms of the "Best U.S. Cities for Seniors." The Nashville metro area ranked #28. Criteria: healthcare; transportation; housing; environment; economy; health and longevity; social and spiritual life; crime. *Bankers Life and Casualty Company, Center for a Secure Retirement, "Best U.S. Cities for Seniors 2011," September 2011*

Sports/Recreation Rankings

- *24/7 Wall St.* analysts isolated the ten cities that spent the most public money per capita on sports stadiums, according to 2010 data. Nashville ranked #9. *24/7 Wall St., "Cities Paying the Most for Sports Teams," January 30, 2013*

- Nashville appeared on the *Sporting News* list of the "Best Sports Cities" for 2011. The area ranked #16 out of 271. Criteria: the magazine takes a 12-month snapshot of each city's sports, putting a heavy premium on regular-season won-lost records (from the most recently completed season). Other criteria include: playoff berths, bowl appearances and tournament bids; championships; applicable power ratings; quality of competition; overall fan fervor (measured in part by attendance); abundance of teams (rewarding quality over quantity); stadium and arena quality; ticket availability and prices; franchise ownership; and marquee appeal of athletes. *Sporting News, "Best Sports Cities 2011," October 4, 2011*

- Nashville appeared on the *Sporting News* list of the "Best Sports Cities" for 2011. The area ranked #16 out of 271. Criteria: a 12-month snapshot of regular-season won-lost records (from the most recently completed season). Other criteria include: playoff berths, bowl appearances and tournament bids; championships; applicable power ratings; quality of competition; overall fan fervor (measured in part by attendance); abundance of teams (quality over quantity); stadium and arena quality; ticket availability and prices; franchise ownership; and marquee appeal of athletes. *Sporting News, "Best Sports Cities 2011," October 4, 2011*

- The Nashville was selected as one of the best metro areas for golf in America by *Golf Digest*. The Nashville area was ranked #9 out of 20. Criteria: climate; cost of public golf; quality of public golf; accessibility. *Golf Digest, "The Top 20 Cities for Golf," October 2011*

Women/Minorities Rankings

- *Women's Health* examined U.S. cities and identified the 100 best cities for women. Nashville was ranked #64. Criteria: 30 categories were examined from obesity and breast cancer rates to commuting times and hours spent working out. *Women's Health, "Best Cities for Women 2012"*

- The Nashville metro area appeared on *Forbes'* list of the "Best Cities for Minority Entrepreneurs." The area ranked #64 out of 10. Criteria: 52 metropolitan statistical areas were examined. For each ethnicity (African Americans, Asians and Hispanics), the editors measured housing affordability, population growth, income growth, and entrepreneurship (per capita self-employment). *Forbes, "Best Cities for Minority Entrepreneurs," March 23, 2011*

Miscellaneous Rankings

- *Travel + Leisure* invited readers to rate cities on indicators such as aloofness, "smarty-pants residents," highbrow cultural offerings, high-end shopping, artisanal coffeehouses, conspicuous eco-consciousness, and more in order to identify the nation's snobbiest cities. Cities large and small made the list; among them was Nashville, at #13. *www.travelandleisure.com, "America's Snobbiest Cities, June 2013*

- The watchdog site Charity Navigator conducts an annual study of charities in the nation's major markets both to analyze statistical differences in their financial, accountability, and transparency practices and to track year-to-year variations in individual communities. The Nashville metro area was ranked #28 among the 30 metro markets. *www.charitynavigator.org, "Metro Market Study 2013," June 1, 2013*

- Nashville appeared on *Travel + Leisure's* list of America's most attractive people. Criteria: cities were selected by readers in their annual America's Favorite Cities survey. The city ranked #3 out of 10. *Travel + Leisure, "America's Most and Least Attractive People," November 2013*

- *Men's Health* ranked 100 U.S. cities by their level of sadness. Nashville was ranked #59 (#1 = saddest city). Criteria: suicide rates; unemployment rates; percentage of households that use antidepressants; percent of population who report feeling blue all or most of the time. *Men's Health, "Frown Towns," November 28, 2011*

- The Nashville metro area was selected as one of "The Best U.S. Cities for Bargain Shopping" by *Forbes*. The area ranked #9 out of 10. Criteria: number of outlet stores; gross leasable retail space in major malls; low consumer price index; low sales tax rate. Indicators were examined in the nation's 50 largest metropolitan areas. *Forbes, "The Best U.S. Cities for Bargain Shopping," January 20, 2012*

- Mars Chocolate North America, the makers of COMBOS®, in partnership with Sperling's BestPlaces, ranked 50 major metro areas in terms of their "manliness." The Nashville metro area ranked #4. Criteria: number of professional sports teams; number of nearby NASCAR tracks and racing events; manly lifestyle; concentration of manly retail stores; manly occupations per capita; salty snack sales; "Board of Manliness" rankings. *Mars Chocolate North America, "America's Manliest Cities 2012"*

- Nashville was selected as one of "America's Best Cities for Hipsters" by *Travel + Leisure*. The city was ranked #8 out of 20. Criteria: live music; coffee bars; independent boutiques; best microbrews; offbeat and tech-savvy locals. *Travel + Leisure, "America's Best Cities for Hipsters," November 2013*

- The National Alliance to End Homelessness ranked the 100 most populous metro areas in terms the rate of homelessness. The Nashville metro area ranked #59. Criteria: number of homeless people per 10,000 population in 2011. *National Alliance to End Homelessness, The State of Homelessness in America 2012*

Business Environment

CITY FINANCES

City Government Finances

Component	2011 ($000)	2011 ($ per capita)
Total Revenues	3,998,490	6,768
Total Expenditures	3,945,119	6,678
Debt Outstanding	4,665,176	7,896
Cash and Securities[1]	4,277,011	7,239

Note: (1) Cash and security holdings of a government at the close of its fiscal year, including those of its dependent agencies, utilities, and liquor stores.
Source: U.S Census Bureau, State & Local Government Finances 2011

City Government Revenue by Source

Source	2011 ($000)	2011 ($ per capita)
General Revenue		
From Federal Government	11,292	19
From State Government	555,219	940
From Local Governments	0	0
Taxes		
Property	782,237	1,324
Sales and Gross Receipts	330,590	560
Personal Income	0	0
Corporate Income	0	0
Motor Vehicle License	18,246	31
Other Taxes	34,962	59
Current Charges	327,083	554
Liquor Store	0	0
Utility	1,323,251	2,240
Employee Retirement	442,551	749

Source: U.S Census Bureau, State & Local Government Finances 2011

City Government Expenditures by Function

Function	2011 ($000)	2011 ($ per capita)	2011 (%)
General Direct Expenditures			
Air Transportation	0	0	0.0
Corrections	61,927	105	1.6
Education	829,783	1,404	21.0
Employment Security Administration	0	0	0.0
Financial Administration	29,093	49	0.7
Fire Protection	109,108	185	2.8
General Public Buildings	0	0	0.0
Governmental Administration, Other	24,921	42	0.6
Health	66,029	112	1.7
Highways	46,963	79	1.2
Hospitals	145,217	246	3.7
Housing and Community Development	0	0	0.0
Interest on General Debt	172,310	292	4.4
Judicial and Legal	55,408	94	1.4
Libraries	20,543	35	0.5
Parking	0	0	0.0
Parks and Recreation	80,431	136	2.0
Police Protection	189,956	322	4.8
Public Welfare	32,358	55	0.8
Sewerage	95,796	162	2.4
Solid Waste Management	19,857	34	0.5
Veterans' Services	0	0	0.0
Liquor Store	0	0	0.0
Utility	1,365,169	2,311	34.6
Employee Retirement	179,592	304	4.6

Source: U.S Census Bureau, State & Local Government Finances 2011

DEMOGRAPHICS

Population Growth

Area	1990 Census	2000 Census	2010 Census	Population Growth (%) 1990-2000	Population Growth (%) 2000-2010
City	488,364	545,524	601,222	11.7	10.2
MSA[1]	1,048,218	1,311,789	1,589,934	25.1	21.2
U.S.	248,709,873	281,421,906	308,745,538	13.2	9.7

Note: (1) Figures cover the Nashville-Davidson—Murfreesboro—Franklin, TN Metropolitan Statistical Area—see Appendix B for areas included
Source: U.S. Census Bureau, Census 1990, 2000, 2010

Household Size

Area	Persons in Household (%) One	Two	Three	Four	Five	Six	Seven or More	Average Household Size
City	36.2	32.7	14.1	9.9	4.3	1.6	1.2	2.40
MSA[1]	27.6	34.1	16.1	13.4	5.7	1.8	1.2	2.60
U.S.	27.6	33.5	15.7	13.2	6.1	2.4	1.5	2.63

Note: (1) Figures cover the Nashville-Davidson—Murfreesboro—Franklin, TN Metropolitan Statistical Area—see Appendix B for areas included
Source: U.S. Census Bureau, 2010-2012 American Community Survey 3-Year Estimates

Race

Area	White Alone[2] (%)	Black Alone[2] (%)	Asian Alone[2] (%)	AIAN[3] Alone[2] (%)	NHOPI[4] Alone[2] (%)	Other Race Alone[2] (%)	Two or More Races (%)
City	60.9	28.5	3.1	0.2	0.0	4.9	2.5
MSA[1]	77.5	15.4	2.3	0.3	0.0	2.5	1.9
U.S.	74.0	12.6	4.9	0.8	0.2	4.7	2.8

Note: (1) Figures cover the Nashville-Davidson—Murfreesboro—Franklin, TN Metropolitan Statistical Area—see Appendix B for areas included; (2) Alone is defined as not being in combination with one or more other races; (3) American Indian and Alaska Native; (4) Native Hawaiian and Other Pacific Islander
Source: U.S. Census Bureau, 2010-2012 American Community Survey 3-Year Estimates

Hispanic or Latino Origin

Area	Total (%)	Mexican (%)	Puerto Rican (%)	Cuban (%)	Other (%)
City	10.1	6.3	0.5	0.3	2.9
MSA[1]	6.7	4.2	0.5	0.2	1.8
U.S.	16.6	10.7	1.6	0.6	3.7

Note: Persons of Hispanic or Latino origin can be of any race; (1) Figures cover the Nashville-Davidson—Murfreesboro—Franklin, TN Metropolitan Statistical Area—see Appendix B for areas included
Source: U.S. Census Bureau, 2010-2012 American Community Survey 3-Year Estimates

Segregation

Type	Segregation Indices[1] 1990	2000	2010	2010 Rank[2]	Percent Change 1990-2000	1990-2010	2000-2010
Black/White	60.7	58.1	56.2	49	-2.6	-4.4	-1.9
Asian/White	45.2	44.4	41.0	51	-0.8	-4.2	-3.4
Hispanic/White	24.3	46.0	47.9	34	21.6	23.5	1.9

Note: All figures cover the Metropolitan Statistical Area—see Appendix B for areas included; Figures are based on an analysis of 1990, 2000, and 2010 Census Decennial Census tract data by William H. Frey, Brookings Institution and the University of Michigan Social Science Data Analysis Network. In this analysis all racial groups (whites, blacks, and asians) are non-Hispanic members of those races. Hispanics are shown as a separate category;
(1) Segregation Indices are Dissimilarity Indices that measure the degree to which the minority group is distributed differently than whites across census tracts. They range from 0 (complete integration) to 100 (complete segregation) where the value indicates the percentage of the minority group that needs to move to be distributed exactly like whites; (2) Ranges from 1 (most segregated) to 102 (least segregated); n/a not available.
Source: www.CensusScope.org

Ancestry

Area	German	Irish	English	American	Italian	Polish	French[2]	Scottish	Dutch
City	9.9	9.5	8.4	8.3	2.5	1.1	2.0	2.0	0.9
MSA[1]	11.1	11.5	10.6	14.0	2.7	1.2	2.2	2.4	1.1
U.S.	15.2	11.1	8.2	7.2	5.6	3.1	2.8	1.7	1.4

Note: Figures are the percentage of the total population reporting a particular ancestry. The nine most commonly reported ancestries in the U.S. are shown. Figures include multiple ancestries (e.g. if a person reported being Irish and Italian, they were included in both columns); (1) Figures cover the Nashville-Davidson—Murfreesboro—Franklin, TN Metropolitan Statistical Area—see Appendix B for areas included; (2) Excludes Basque
Source: U.S. Census Bureau, 2010-2012 American Community Survey 3-Year Estimates

Foreign-Born Population

Area	Any Foreign Country	Mexico	Asia	Europe	Carribean	South America	Central America[2]	Africa	Canada
City	12.0	3.4	3.3	0.9	0.3	0.4	1.6	1.9	0.2
MSA[1]	7.4	2.1	2.2	0.7	0.2	0.3	0.9	0.9	0.2
U.S.	13.0	3.7	3.7	1.6	1.2	0.9	1.0	0.5	0.3

Note: (1) Figures cover the Nashville-Davidson—Murfreesboro—Franklin, TN Metropolitan Statistical Area—see Appendix B for areas included; (2) Excludes Mexico.
Source: U.S. Census Bureau, 2010-2012 American Community Survey 3-Year Estimates

Marital Status

Area	Never Married	Now Married[2]	Separated	Widowed	Divorced
City	40.5	39.1	2.5	5.2	12.7
MSA[1]	31.0	49.6	2.0	5.3	12.1
U.S.	32.4	48.4	2.2	6.0	11.0

Note: Figures are percentages and cover the population 15 years of age and older; (1) Figures cover the Nashville-Davidson—Murfreesboro—Franklin, TN Metropolitan Statistical Area—see Appendix B for areas included; (2) Excludes separated
Source: U.S. Census Bureau, 2010-2012 American Community Survey 3-Year Estimates

Age

Area	Under Age 5	Age 5–19	Age 20–34	Age 35–44	Age 45–54	Age 55–64	Age 65–74	Age 75–84	Age 85+	Median Age
City	7.1	17.6	27.2	13.7	13.2	10.9	5.7	3.3	1.4	33.7
MSA[1]	6.8	20.1	21.8	14.2	14.5	11.6	6.4	3.3	1.3	35.9
U.S.	6.4	20.1	20.5	13.1	14.3	12.2	7.3	4.2	1.8	37.3

Note: (1) Figures cover the Nashville-Davidson—Murfreesboro—Franklin, TN Metropolitan Statistical Area—see Appendix B for areas included
Source: U.S. Census Bureau, 2010-2012 American Community Survey 3-Year Estimates

Gender

Area	Males	Females	Males per 100 Females
City	297,280	316,549	93.9
MSA[1]	791,205	827,614	95.6
U.S.	153,276,055	158,333,314	96.8

Note: (1) Figures cover the Nashville-Davidson—Murfreesboro—Franklin, TN Metropolitan Statistical Area—see Appendix B for areas included
Source: U.S. Census Bureau, 2010-2012 American Community Survey 3-Year Estimates

Religious Groups by Family

Area	Catholic	Baptist	Non-Den.	Methodist[2]	Lutheran	LDS[3]	Pentecostal	Presbyterian[4]	Muslim[5]	Judaism
MSA[1]	4.1	25.3	5.8	6.1	0.4	0.8	2.2	2.1	0.4	0.2
U.S.	19.1	9.3	4.0	4.0	2.3	2.0	1.9	1.6	0.8	0.7

Note: Figures are the number of adherents as a percentage of the total population; (1) Figures cover the Nashville-Davidson—Murfreesboro—Franklin, TN Metropolitan Statistical Area—see Appendix B for areas included; (2) Methodist/Pietist; (3) Latter Day Saints; (4) Reformed; (5) Figures are estimates
Source: Association of Statisticians of American Religious Bodies, 2010 U.S. Religion Census: Religious Congregations & Membership Study

Religious Groups by Tradition

Area	Catholic	Evangelical Protestant	Mainline Protestant	Other Tradition	Black Protestant	Orthodox
MSA[1]	4.1	33.0	8.0	1.7	3.4	0.5
U.S.	19.1	16.2	7.3	4.3	1.6	0.3

Note: Figures are the number of adherents as a percentage of the total population; (1) Figures cover the Nashville-Davidson—Murfreesboro—Franklin, TN Metropolitan Statistical Area—see Appendix B for areas included
Source: Association of Statisticians of American Religious Bodies, 2010 U.S. Religion Census: Religious Congregations & Membership Study

ECONOMY

Gross Metropolitan Product

Area	2011	2012	2013	2014	Rank[2]
MSA[1]	84.9	91.1	95.5	100.3	35

Note: Figures are in billions of dollars; (1) Figures cover the Nashville-Davidson—Murfreesboro—Franklin, TN Metropolitan Statistical Area—see Appendix B for areas included; (2) Rank is based on 2014 data and ranges from 1 to 363
Source: The United States Conference of Mayors, U.S. Metro Economies: Outlook—Gross Metropolitan Product, with Metro Employment Projections, November 2013

Economic Growth

Area	2011 (%)	2012 (%)	2013 (%)	2014 (%)	Rank[2]
MSA[1]	3.6	5.4	3.5	3.0	11
U.S.	1.6	2.5	1.7	2.5	–

Note: Figures are real gross metropolitan product (GMP) growth rates and represent annual average percent change; (1) Figures cover the Nashville-Davidson—Murfreesboro—Franklin, TN Metropolitan Statistical Area—see Appendix B for areas included; (2) Rank is based on 2013 data and ranges from 1 to 363
Source: The United States Conference of Mayors, U.S. Metro Economies: Outlook—Gross Metropolitan Product, with Metro Employment Projections, November 2013

Metropolitan Area Exports

Area	2007	2008	2009	2010	2011	2012	Rank[2]
MSA[1]	5,105.9	5,259.5	4,406.6	5,748.5	5,878.7	6,402.1	41

Note: Figures are in millions of dollars; (1) Figures cover the Nashville-Davidson—Murfreesboro—Franklin, TN Metropolitan Statistical Area—see Appendix B for areas included; (2) Rank is based on 2012 data and ranges from 1 to 369
Source: U.S. Department of Commerce, International Trade Administration, Office of Trade & Industry Information, Manufacturing & Services, data extracted April 1, 2014

INCOME

Income

Area	Per Capita ($)	Median Household ($)	Average Household ($)
City	26,412	44,271	62,441
MSA[1]	27,474	51,178	70,435
U.S.	27,385	51,771	71,579

Note: (1) Figures cover the Nashville-Davidson—Murfreesboro—Franklin, TN Metropolitan Statistical Area—see Appendix B for areas included
Source: U.S. Census Bureau, 2010-2012 American Community Survey 3-Year Estimates

Household Income Distribution

Area	Percent of Households Earning							
	Under $15,000	$15,000 -24,999	$25,000 -34,999	$35,000 -49,999	$50,000 -74,999	$75,000 -99,000	$100,000 -149,999	$150,000 and up
City	15.6	12.1	12.0	15.6	18.5	10.3	9.1	6.8
MSA[1]	12.2	10.6	10.8	15.2	18.8	12.3	11.9	8.2
U.S.	13.1	11.0	10.5	13.7	18.1	11.9	12.5	9.1

Note: (1) Figures cover the Nashville-Davidson—Murfreesboro—Franklin, TN Metropolitan Statistical Area—see Appendix B for areas included
Source: U.S. Census Bureau, 2010-2012 American Community Survey 3-Year Estimates

Poverty Rate

Area	All Ages	Under 18 Years Old	18 to 64 Years Old	65 Years and Over
City	19.9	31.8	17.6	9.6
MSA[1]	14.8	21.4	13.4	8.4
U.S.	15.7	22.2	14.6	9.3

Note: Figures are percentage of people whose income during the past 12 months was below the poverty level; (1) Figures cover the Nashville-Davidson—Murfreesboro—Franklin, TN Metropolitan Statistical Area—see Appendix B for areas included
Source: U.S. Census Bureau, 2010-2012 American Community Survey 3-Year Estimates

Personal Bankruptcy Filing Rate

Area	2008	2009	2010	2011	2012	2013
Davidson County	6.61	7.29	6.84	6.49	6.17	5.38
U.S.	3.53	4.61	4.97	4.37	3.76	3.29

Note: Numbers are per 1,000 population and include Chapter 7 and Chapter 13 filings
Source: Federal Deposit Insurance Corporation, Regional Economic Conditions, March 20, 2014

EMPLOYMENT

Labor Force and Employment

Area	Civilian Labor Force			Workers Employed		
	Dec. 2012	Dec. 2013	% Chg.	Dec. 2012	Dec. 2013	% Chg.
City	340,174	331,727	-2.5	319,549	312,959	-2.1
MSA[1]	863,413	841,403	-2.5	811,941	795,197	-2.1
U.S.	154,904,000	154,408,000	-0.3	143,060,000	144,423,000	1.0

Note: Data is not seasonally adjusted and covers workers 16 years of age and older; (1) Metropolitan Statistical Area—see Appendix B for areas included
Source: Bureau of Labor Statistics, Local Area Unemployment Statistics

Unemployment Rate

Area	2013											
	Jan.	Feb.	Mar.	Apr.	May	Jun.	Jul.	Aug.	Sep.	Oct.	Nov.	Dec.
City	6.5	6.3	6.2	6.5	6.7	7.0	6.7	6.9	6.7	6.7	5.8	5.7
MSA[1]	6.6	6.4	6.3	6.4	6.7	7.0	6.8	6.8	6.5	6.6	5.6	5.5
U.S.	8.5	8.1	7.6	7.1	7.3	7.8	7.7	7.3	7.0	7.0	6.6	6.5

Note: Data is not seasonally adjusted and covers workers 16 years of age and older; All figures are percentages; (1) Metropolitan Statistical Area—see Appendix B for areas included
Source: Bureau of Labor Statistics, Local Area Unemployment Statistics

Employment by Occupation

Occupation Classification	City (%)	MSA[1] (%)	U.S. (%)
Management, Business, Science, and Arts	38.4	37.6	36.0
Natural Resources, Construction, and Maintenance	7.1	8.1	9.1
Production, Transportation, and Material Moving	9.8	11.8	12.0
Sales and Office	27.1	26.8	24.7
Service	17.6	15.7	18.2

Note: Figures cover employed civilians 16 years of age and older; (1) Figures cover the Nashville-Davidson—Murfreesboro—Franklin, TN Metropolitan Statistical Area—see Appendix B for areas included
Source: U.S. Census Bureau, 2010-2012 American Community Survey 3-Year Estimates

Employment by Industry

Sector	MSA[1]		U.S.
	Number of Employees	Percent of Total	Percent of Total
Construction	n/a	n/a	4.2
Education and Health Services	127,800	15.4	15.5
Financial Activities	50,800	6.1	5.7
Government	106,200	12.8	16.1
Information	20,400	2.5	1.9
Leisure and Hospitality	88,600	10.7	10.2
Manufacturing	72,600	8.8	8.7
Mining and Logging	n/a	n/a	0.6
Other Services	32,800	4.0	3.9
Professional and Business Services	128,600	15.5	13.7
Retail Trade	89,800	10.8	11.4
Transportation and Utilities	36,000	4.3	3.8
Wholesale Trade	40,500	4.9	4.2

Note: Figures cover non-farm employment as of December 2013 and are not seasonally adjusted;
(1) Metropolitan Statistical Area—see Appendix B for areas included; n/a not available
Source: Bureau of Labor Statistics, Current Employment Statistics, Employment, Hours, and Earnings

Occupations with Greatest Projected Employment Growth: 2010 – 2020

Occupation[1]	2010 Employment	2020 Projected Employment	Numeric Employment Change	Percent Employment Change
Registered Nurses	56,290	69,010	12,720	22.6
Office Clerks, General	64,300	75,450	11,150	17.3
Heavy and Tractor-Trailer Truck Drivers	58,680	69,250	10,570	18.0
Personal Care Aides	15,310	24,380	9,070	59.2
Combined Food Preparation and Serving Workers, Including Fast Food	56,520	64,280	7,750	13.7
Janitors and Cleaners, Except Maids and Housekeeping Cleaners	41,370	48,290	6,920	16.7
Security Guards	21,960	28,260	6,300	28.7
Nursing Aides, Orderlies, and Attendants	29,910	35,570	5,650	18.9
First-Line Supervisors of Office and Administrative Support Workers	31,880	37,210	5,330	16.7
Landscaping and Groundskeeping Workers	16,920	22,210	5,290	31.2

Note: Projections cover Tennessee; (1) Sorted by numeric employment change
Source: www.projectionscentral.com, State Occupational Projections, 2010–2020 Long-Term Projections

Fastest Growing Occupations: 2010 – 2020

Occupation[1]	2010 Employment	2020 Projected Employment	Numeric Employment Change	Percent Employment Change
Personal Care Aides	15,310	24,380	9,070	59.2
Meeting, Convention, and Event Planners	950	1,470	520	55.4
Audiologists	280	410	140	50.2
Glaziers	950	1,400	460	48.2
Software Developers, Systems Software	2,590	3,840	1,250	48.2
Helpers—Pipelayers, Plumbers, Pipefitters, and Steamfitters	1,220	1,770	550	45.1
Physician Assistants	1,550	2,240	690	44.3
Diagnostic Medical Sonographers	1,100	1,560	460	41.8
Security and Fire Alarm Systems Installers	1,340	1,890	550	40.9
Tree Trimmers and Pruners	2,260	3,170	920	40.7

Note: Projections cover Tennessee; (1) Sorted by percent employment change and excludes occupations with numeric employment change less than 100
Source: www.projectionscentral.com, State Occupational Projections, 2010–2020 Long-Term Projections

Average Wages

Occupation	$/Hr.	Occupation	$/Hr.
Accountants and Auditors	32.17	Maids and Housekeeping Cleaners	9.28
Automotive Mechanics	16.82	Maintenance and Repair Workers	17.70
Bookkeepers	17.50	Marketing Managers	48.43
Carpenters	17.16	Nuclear Medicine Technologists	29.04
Cashiers	9.55	Nurses, Licensed Practical	18.85
Clerks, General Office	15.14	Nurses, Registered	28.42
Clerks, Receptionists/Information	13.64	Nursing Assistants	11.87
Clerks, Shipping/Receiving	14.89	Packers and Packagers, Hand	9.83
Computer Programmers	38.24	Physical Therapists	36.18
Computer Systems Analysts	33.90	Postal Service Mail Carriers	24.52
Computer User Support Specialists	21.17	Real Estate Brokers	n/a
Cooks, Restaurant	10.74	Retail Salespersons	12.46
Dentists	96.86	Sales Reps., Exc. Tech./Scientific	27.75
Electrical Engineers	38.25	Sales Reps., Tech./Scientific	34.29
Electricians	20.69	Secretaries, Exc. Legal/Med./Exec.	15.16
Financial Managers	56.15	Security Guards	12.46
First-Line Supervisors/Managers, Sales	19.81	Surgeons	n/a
Food Preparation Workers	9.49	Teacher Assistants	11.10
General and Operations Managers	50.70	Teachers, Elementary School	22.70
Hairdressers/Cosmetologists	13.99	Teachers, Secondary School	23.40
Internists	83.91	Telemarketers	15.24
Janitors and Cleaners	10.51	Truck Drivers, Heavy/Tractor-Trailer	19.93
Landscaping/Groundskeeping Workers	11.95	Truck Drivers, Light/Delivery Svcs.	15.34
Lawyers	52.06	Waiters and Waitresses	8.90

Note: Wage data covers the Nashville-Davidson—Murfreesboro—Franklin, TN Metropolitan Statistical Area—see Appendix B for areas included. Hourly wages for elementary/secondary school teachers and teacher assistants were calculated by the editors from annual wage data assuming a 40 hour work week; n/a not available.
Source: Bureau of Labor Statistics, Metro Area Occupational Employment and Wage Estimates, May 2013

RESIDENTIAL REAL ESTATE

Building Permits

Area	Single-Family			Multi-Family			Total		
	2012	2013	Pct. Chg.	2012	2013	Pct. Chg.	2012	2013	Pct. Chg.
City	1,305	1,824	39.8	1,529	2,142	40.1	2,834	3,966	39.9
MSA[1]	5,340	7,020	31.5	2,907	3,869	33.1	8,247	10,889	32.0
U.S.	518,695	620,802	19.7	310,963	370,020	19.0	829,658	990,822	19.4

Note: (1) Metropolitan Statistical Area—see Appendix B for areas included; figures represent new, privately-owned housing units authorized (unadjusted data); All permit data are based on estimates with imputation.
Source: U.S. Census Bureau, Manufacturing, Mining, and Construction Statistics, Building Permits, 2012, 2013

Homeownership Rate

Area	2006 (%)	2007 (%)	2008 (%)	2009 (%)	2010 (%)	2011 (%)	2012 (%)	2013 (%)
MSA[1]	72.4	70.0	71.3	71.8	70.4	69.6	64.9	63.9
U.S.	68.8	68.1	67.8	67.4	66.9	66.1	65.4	65.1

Note: (1) Figures cover the Nashville-Davidson—Murfreesboro—Franklin, TN Metropolitan Statistical Area—see Appendix B for areas included
Source: U.S. Census Bureau, Housing Vacancies and Homeownership Annual Statistics: 2013

Housing Vacancy Rates

Area	Gross Vacancy Rate[2] (%)			Year-Round Vacancy Rate[3] (%)			Rental Vacancy Rate[4] (%)			Homeowner Vacancy Rate[5] (%)		
	2011	2012	2013	2011	2012	2013	2011	2012	2013	2011	2012	2013
MSA[1]	9.0	8.7	6.6	8.3	8.2	6.4	8.2	8.4	5.3	2.2	1.6	0.9
U.S.	14.2	13.8	13.8	11.1	10.8	10.7	9.5	8.7	8.3	2.5	2.0	2.0

Note: (1) Figures cover the Nashville-Davidson—Murfreesboro—Franklin, TN Metropolitan Statistical Area—see Appendix B for areas included; (2) The percentage of the total housing inventory that is vacant; (3) The percentage of the housing inventory (excluding seasonal units) that is year-round vacant; (4) The percentage of rental inventory that is vacant for rent; (5) The percentage of homeowner inventory that is vacant for sale
Source: U.S. Census Bureau, Housing Vacancies and Homeownership Annual Statistics: 2013

TAXES

State Corporate Income Tax Rates

State	Tax Rate (%)	Income Brackets ($)	Num. of Brackets	Financial Institution Tax Rate (%)[a]	Federal Income Tax Ded.
Tennessee	6.5	Flat rate	1	6.5	No

Note: Tax rates as of January 1, 2014; (a) Rates listed are the corporate income tax rate applied to financial institutions or excise taxes based on income. Some states have other taxes based upon the value of deposits or shares.
Source: Federation of Tax Administrators, "State Corporate Income Tax Rates, 2014"

State Individual Income Tax Rates

State	Tax Rate (%)	Income Brackets ($)	Num. of Brackets	Personal Exempt. ($)[1]		Fed. Inc. Tax Ded.
				Single	Dependents	
Tennessee			State income tax of 6% on dividends and interest income only			

Note: Tax rates as of January 1, 2014; Local- and county-level taxes are not included; n/a not applicable;
(1) Married joint filers generally receive double the single exemption
Source: Federation of Tax Administrators, "State Individual Income Tax Rates, 2014"

Various State and Local Tax Rates

State	State and Local Sales and Use (%)	State Sales and Use (%)	Gasoline[1] (¢/gal.)	Cigarette[2] ($/pack)	Spirits[3] ($/gal.)	Wine[4] ($/gal.)	Beer[5] ($/gal.)
Tennessee	9.25	7.00	21.40	0.620	4.46 (i)	1.27 (m)	1.17 (t)

Note: All tax rates as of January 1, 2014; (1) The American Petroleum Institute has developed a methodology for determining the average tax rate on a gallon of fuel. Rates may include any of the following: excise taxes, environmental fees, storage tank fees, other fees or taxes, general sales tax, and local taxes. In states where gasoline is subject to the general sales tax, or where the fuel tax is based on the average sale price, the average rate determined by API is sensitive to changes in the price of gasoline. States that fully or partially apply general sales taxes to gasoline: CA, CO, GA, IL, IN, MI, NY; (2) The federal excise tax of $1.0066 per pack and local taxes are not included; (3) Rates are those applicable to off-premise sales of 40% alcohol by volume (a.b.v.) distilled spirits in 750ml containers. Local excise taxes are excluded; (4) Rates are those applicable to off-premise sales of 11% a.b.v. non-carbonated wine in 750ml containers; (5) Rates are those applicable to off-premise sales of 4.7% a.b.v. beer in 12 ounce containers; (i) Includes case fees and/or bottle fees which may vary with size of container; (m) Includes case fees and/or bottle fees which may vary with size of container; (t) Includes the wholesale tax rate of 17%, converted into a gallonage excise tax rate.
Source: Tax Foundation, 2014 Facts & Figures: How Does Your State Compare?

State Business Tax Climate Index Rankings

State	Overall Rank	Corporate Tax Index Rank	Individual Income Tax Index Rank	Sales Tax Index Rank	Unemployment Insurance Tax Index Rank	Property Tax Index Rank
Tennessee	15	14	8	43	27	37

Note: The index is a measure of how each state's tax laws affect economic performance. The lower the rank, the more favorable a state's tax system is for business. States without a given tax are given a ranking of 1. The scores/rankings for the District of Columbia do not affect other states. The 2014 index represents the tax climate as of July 1, 2013.
Source: Tax Foundation, State Business Tax Climate Index 2014

COMMERCIAL REAL ESTATE

Office Market

Market Area	Inventory (sq. ft.)	Vacancy Rate (%)	Under Construction (sq. ft.)	YTD Net Absorption (sq. ft.)	Total Average Asking Rent ($/sq. ft./year)
Nashville	48,422,650	9.8	965,486	379,034	19.74
National	4,726,900,879	15.0	55,419,286	42,829,434	26.27

Source: Newmark Grubb Knight Frank, National Office Market Report, 4th Quarter 2013

Industrial/Warehouse/R&D Market

Market Area	Inventory (sq. ft.)	Vacancy Rate (%)	Under Construction (sq. ft.)	YTD Net Absorption (sq. ft.)	Total Average Asking Rent ($/sq. ft./year)
Nashville	213,936,545	9.1	346,488	2,576,102	3.53
National	14,022,031,238	7.9	83,249,164	156,549,903	5.40

Source: Newmark Grubb Knight Frank, National Industrial Market Report, 4th Quarter 2013

COMMERCIAL UTILITIES

Typical Monthly Electric Bills

Area	Commercial Service ($/month)		Industrial Service ($/month)	
	40 kW demand 5,000 kWh	500 kW demand 100,000 kWh	5,000 kW demand 1,500,000 kWh	70,000 kW demand 50,000,000 kWh
City	558	12,480	163,004	3,350,400

Note: Based on rates in effect January 2, 2013
Source: Memphis Light, Gas and Water, 2013 Utility Bill Comparisons for Selected U.S. Cities

TRANSPORTATION

Means of Transportation to Work

Area	Car/Truck/Van		Public Transportation			Bicycle	Walked	Other Means	Worked at Home
	Drove Alone	Car-pooled	Bus	Subway	Railroad				
City	79.2	10.9	2.2	0.0	0.1	0.3	1.9	1.1	4.3
MSA[1]	81.9	10.0	1.1	0.0	0.1	0.2	1.2	1.0	4.6
U.S.	76.4	9.7	2.6	1.7	0.5	0.6	2.8	1.3	4.3

Note: Figures are percentages and cover workers 16 years of age and older; (1) Figures cover the Nashville-Davidson—Murfreesboro—Franklin, TN Metropolitan Statistical Area—see Appendix B for areas included
Source: U.S. Census Bureau, 2010-2012 American Community Survey 3-Year Estimates

Travel Time to Work

Area	Less Than 10 Minutes	10 to 19 Minutes	20 to 29 Minutes	30 to 44 Minutes	45 to 59 Minutes	60 to 89 Minutes	90 Minutes or More
City	8.9	30.8	28.0	23.8	5.2	2.1	1.1
MSA[1]	10.0	27.3	23.0	23.8	9.7	4.5	1.7
U.S.	13.5	29.8	20.9	20.1	7.5	5.6	2.5

Note: Figures are percentages and include workers 16 years old and over; (1) Figures cover the Nashville-Davidson—Murfreesboro—Franklin, TN Metropolitan Statistical Area—see Appendix B for areas included
Source: U.S. Census Bureau, 2010-2012 American Community Survey 3-Year Estimates

Travel Time Index

Area	1985	1990	1995	2000	2005	2010	2011
Urban Area[1]	1.13	1.16	1.19	1.23	1.25	1.23	1.23
Average[2]	1.09	1.14	1.16	1.19	1.23	1.18	1.18

Note: Travel Time Index—the ratio of travel time in the peak period to the travel time at free-flow conditions. For example, a value of 1.30 indicates a 20-minute free-flow trip takes 26 minutes in the peak. Free-flow speeds (60 mph on freeways and 35 mph on principal arterials) are used as the comparison threshold; (1) Covers the Nashville-Davidson TN urban area; (2) average of 498 urban areas
Source: Texas Transportation Institute, Urban Mobility Report 2012, December 2012

Public Transportation

Agency Name / Mode of Transportation	Vehicles Operated in Maximum Service	Annual Unlinked Passenger Trips (in thous.)	Annual Passenger Miles (in thous.)
Metropolitan Transit Authority (MTA)			
Bus (directly operated)	128	9,273.8	47,124.6
Demand Response (directly operated)	50	291.5	3,694.3
Demand Response Taxi (purchased transportation)	52	89.6	672.5

Source: Federal Transit Administration, National Transit Database, 2012

Air Transportation

Airport Name and Code / Type of Service	Passenger Airlines[1]	Passenger Enplanements	Freight Carriers[2]	Freight (lbs.)
Nashville International (BNA)				
Domestic service (U.S. carriers - 2013)	31	5,019,428	12	51,403,666
International service (U.S. carriers - 2012)	9	3,226	0	0

Note: (1) Includes all U.S.-based major, minor and commuter airlines that carried at least one passenger during the year; (2) Includes all U.S.-based airlines and freight carriers that transported at least one lb. of freight during the year.
Source: Bureau of Transportation Statistics, The Intermodal Transportation Database, Air Carriers: T-100 Domestic Market (U.S. Carriers), 2013; Bureau of Transportation Statistics, The Intermodal Transportation Database, Air Carriers: T-100 International Market (U.S. Carriers), 2012

Other Transportation Statistics

Major Highways:	I-24; I-40; I-65
Amtrak Service:	Bus connection
Major Waterways/Ports:	Cumberland River; Port of Nashville

Source: Amtrak.com; Google Maps

BUSINESSES

Major Business Headquarters

Company Name	Rankings	
	Fortune[1]	Forbes[2]
Ardent Health Services	-	216
HCA Holdings	82	-
Ingram Industries	-	215
Vanguard Health Systems	391	-

Note: (1) Fortune 500—companies that produce a 10-K are ranked 1 to 500 based on 2012 revenue; (2) all private companies with at least $2 billion in annual revenue through the end of their most current fiscal year are ranked 1 to 224; companies listed are headquartered in the city; dashes indicate no ranking
Source: Fortune, "Fortune 500," May 20, 2013; Forbes, "America's Largest Private Companies," December 18, 2013

Fast-Growing Businesses

According to *Inc.*, Nashville is home to three of America's 500 fastest-growing private companies: **Value Payment Systems** (#7); **Reboot Marketing** (#304); **Medical Direct Club** (#461). Criteria: must be an independent, privately-held, for-profit, U.S. corporation, proprietorship or partnership; revenues must be at least $100,000 in 2009 and $2 million in 2012; must have four-year operating/sales history. Holding companies, regulated banks, and utilities were excluded. *Inc., "America's 500 Fastest-Growing Private Companies," September 2013*

According to *Initiative for a Competitive Inner City (ICIC)*, Nashville is home to one of America's 100 fastest-growing "inner city" companies: **Zycron** (#64). Companies were ranked by their five-year compound annual growth rate. Criteria for inclusion: company must be headquartered in or have 51 percent or more of its physical operations in an economically distressed urban area; must be an independent, for-profit corporation, partnership or proprietorship; must have 10 or more employees and have a five-year sales history that includes sales of at least $200,000 in the base year and at least $1 million in the current year with no decrease in sales over the two most recent years. *Initiative for a Competitive Inner City (ICIC), "Inner City 100 Companies, 2013"*

Minority Business Opportunity

Nashville is home to one company which is on the *Black Enterprise* Industrial/Service 100 list (100 largest companies based on gross sales): **Zycron** (#68). Criteria: operational in previous calendar year; at least 51% black-owned and manufactures/owns the product it sells or provides industrial or consumer services. Brokerages, real estate firms and firms that provide professional services are not eligible. *Black Enterprise, B.E. 100s, 2013*

Nashville is home to one company which is on the *Black Enterprise* Bank 20 list (20 largest banks based on total assets, capital, deposits and loans, including mortgage-backed securities for the calendar year): **Citizens Savings Bank & Trust Co.** (#14). Only commercial banks or savings and loans that are classified by the Federal Reserve as black institutions and have been fully operational for the previous calendar year were considered. *Black Enterprise, B.E. 100s, 2013*

Minority- and Women-Owned Businesses

Group	All Firms		Firms with Paid Employees			
	Firms	Sales ($000)	Firms	Sales ($000)	Employees	Payroll ($000)
Asian	2,147	605,394	603	527,918	3,935	95,615
Black	7,005	414,476	417	258,896	2,878	74,329
Hispanic	1,868	236,570	199	133,356	1,381	36,780
Women	16,501	5,688,845	1,744	5,198,533	16,705	536,402
All Firms	61,668	80,576,131	13,323	77,992,495	375,494	15,429,858

Note: Figures cover firms located in the city; minority- and women-owned business are defined as firms in which the corresponding group own 51% or more of the stock or equity of the company
Source: U.S. Census Bureau, 2007 Economic Census, Survey of Business Owners (2012 Survey of Business Owners data will be released starting in June 2015)

HOTELS & CONVENTION CENTERS

Hotels/Motels

Area	5 Star		4 Star		3 Star		2 Star		1 Star		Not Rated	
	Num.	Pct.[3]	Num.	Pct.[3]	Num.	Pct.[3]	Num.	Pct.[3]	Num.	Pct.[3]	Num.	Pct.[3]
City[1]	0	0.0	10	4.0	51	20.2	162	64.0	8	3.2	22	8.7
Total[2]	142	0.9	1,005	6.0	5,147	30.9	8,578	51.4	408	2.4	1,397	8.4

Note: (1) Figures cover Nashville and vicinity; (2) Figures cover all 100 cities in this book; (3) Percentage of hotels which have a given star rating; Star ratings are determined by expedia.com and offer an indication of the general quality of a particular hotel.
Source: expedia.com, April 7, 2014

The Nashville-Davidson—Murfreesboro—Franklin, TN metro area is home to two of the best hotels in the U.S. according to *Travel & Leisure*: **Hermitage Hotel**; **Hutton Hotel**. Criteria: service; location; rooms; food; and value. The list includes the top 200 hotels in the U.S. *Travel & Leisure, "T+L 500, The World's Best Hotels 2014"*

Major Convention Centers

Name	Overall Space (sq. ft.)	Exhibit Space (sq. ft.)	Meeting Space (sq. ft.)	Meeting Rooms
Mid-TN Expo Convention Center	40,000	n/a	n/a	n/a
Nashville Convention Center	n/a	118,675	n/a	25

Note: Table includes convention centers located in the Nashville-Davidson—Murfreesboro—Franklin, TN metro area; n/a not available
Source: Original research

Living Environment

COST OF LIVING

Cost of Living Index

Composite Index	Groceries	Housing	Utilities	Transportation	Health Care	Misc. Goods/ Services
87.3	87.8	74.3	87.0	94.1	81.4	95.8

Note: The Cost of Living Index measures regional differences in the cost of consumer goods and services, excluding taxes and non-consumer expenditures, for professional and managerial households in the top income quintile. It is based on more than 50,000 prices covering almost 60 different items for which prices are collected three times a year by chambers of commerce, economic development organizations or university applied economic centers in each participating urban area. The numbers shown should be read as a percentage above or below the national average of 100. For example, a value of 115.4 in the groceries column indicates that grocery prices are 15.4% higher than the national average. Small differences in the index numbers should not be interpreted as significant; Figures cover the Nashville-Franklin TN urban area.
Source: The Council for Community and Economic Research, ACCRA Cost of Living Index, 2013

Grocery Prices

Area[1]	T-Bone Steak ($/pound)	Frying Chicken ($/pound)	Whole Milk ($/half gal.)	Eggs ($/dozen)	Orange Juice ($/64 oz.)	Coffee ($/11.5 oz.)
City[2]	10.63	1.08	2.05	1.73	3.24	4.11
Avg.	10.19	1.28	2.34	1.81	3.48	4.39
Min.	8.56	0.94	1.44	1.19	2.78	3.40
Max.	14.82	2.28	3.56	3.73	6.23	7.32

Note: (1) Values for the local area are compared with the average, minimum and maximum values for all 327 areas in the Cost of Living Index; (2) Figures cover the Nashville-Franklin TN urban area; **T-Bone Steak** *(price per pound);* **Frying Chicken** *(price per pound, whole fryer);* **Whole Milk** *(half gallon carton);* **Eggs** *(price per dozen, Grade A, large);* **Orange Juice** *(64 oz. Tropicana or Florida Natural);* **Coffee** *(11.5 oz. can, vacuum-packed, Maxwell House, Hills Bros, or Folgers).*
Source: The Council for Community and Economic Research, ACCRA Cost of Living Index, 2013

Housing and Utility Costs

Area[1]	New Home Price ($)	Apartment Rent ($/month)	All Electric ($/month)	Part Electric ($/month)	Other Energy ($/month)	Telephone ($/month)
City[2]	200,706	811	-	84.68	57.33	24.16
Avg.	295,864	900	171.38	91.82	70.12	27.73
Min.	185,506	458	117.80	48.81	33.67	17.16
Max.	1,358,917	3,783	441.68	171.40	372.65	39.47

Note: (1) Values for the local area are compared with the average, minimum and maximum values for all 327 areas in the Cost of Living Index; (2) Figures cover the Nashville-Franklin TN urban area; **New Home Price** *(2,400 sf living area, 8,000 sf lot, in urban area with full utilities);* **Apartment Rent** *(950 sf 2 bedroom/1.5 or 2 bath, unfurnished, excluding all utilities except water);* **All Electric** *(average monthly cost for an all-electric home);* **Part Electric** *(average monthly cost for a part-electric home);* **Other Energy** *(average monthly cost for natural gas, fuel oil, coal, wood, and any other forms of energy except electricity);* **Telephone** *(price includes basic monthly rate for a private residential line plus additional local usage charges incurred by a family of four).*
Source: The Council for Community and Economic Research, ACCRA Cost of Living Index, 2013

Health Care, Transportation, and Other Costs

Area[1]	Doctor ($/visit)	Dentist ($/visit)	Optometrist ($/visit)	Gasoline ($/gallon)	Beauty Salon ($/visit)	Men's Shirt ($)
City[2]	78.53	78.20	78.31	3.34	31.00	25.59
Avg.	101.40	86.48	96.16	3.44	33.87	26.55
Min.	61.67	50.83	50.12	3.08	18.92	12.48
Max.	182.71	152.50	223.78	4.33	68.22	52.03

Note: (1) Values for the local area are compared with the average, minimum and maximum values for all 327 areas in the Cost of Living Index; (2) Figures cover the Nashville-Franklin TN urban area; **Doctor** *(general practitioners routine exam of an established patient);* **Dentist** *(adult teeth cleaning and periodic oral examination);* **Optometrist** *(full vision eye exam for established adult patient);* **Gasoline** *(one gallon regular unleaded, national brand, including all taxes, cash price at self-service pump if available);* **Beauty Salon** *(woman's shampoo, trim, and blow-dry);* **Men's Shirt** *(cotton/polyester dress shirt, pinpoint weave, long sleeves).*
Source: The Council for Community and Economic Research, ACCRA Cost of Living Index, 2013

HOUSING

House Price Index (HPI)

Area	National Ranking[2]	Quarterly Change (%)	One-Year Change (%)	Five-Year Change (%)
MSA[1]	77	1.56	5.74	-0.52
U.S.[3]	–	1.20	7.69	4.18

Note: The HPI is a weighted repeat sales index. It measures average price changes in repeat sales or refinancings on the same properties. This information is obtained by reviewing repeat mortgage transactions on single-family properties whose mortgages have been purchased or securitized by Fannie Mae or Freddie Mac in January 1975; (1) Nashville-Davidson—Murfreesboro—Franklin, TN Metropolitan Statistical Area—see Appendix B for areas included; (2) Rankings are based on annual percentage change for all metro areas containing at least 15,000 transactions over the last 10 years and ranges from 1 to 283; (3) figures based on a weighted average of Census Division estimates using a seasonally adjusted, purchase-only index; all figures are for the period ending December 31, 2013
Source: Federal Housing Finance Agency, House Price Index, February 25, 2014

Median Single-Family Home Prices

Area	2011	2012	2013p	Percent Change 2012 to 2013
MSA[1]	151.9	160.6	176.4	9.8
U.S. Average	166.2	177.2	197.4	11.4

Note: Figures are median sales prices of existing single-family homes in thousands of dollars; (p) preliminary; n/a not available; (1) Nashville-Davidson—Murfreesboro—Franklin, TN Metropolitan Statistical Area—see Appendix B for areas included
Source: National Association of Realtors, Median Sales Price of Existing Single-Family Homes for Metropolitan Areas, 4th Quarter 2013

Qualifying Income Based on Median Sales Price of Existing Single-Family Homes

Area	With 5% Down ($)	With 10% Down ($)	With 20% Down ($)
MSA[1]	39,655	37,568	33,393
U.S. Average	45,395	43,006	38,228

Note: Figures are preliminary; Qualifying income is based on a mortgage rate of 4.4%. Monthly principal and interest payment is limited to 25% of income; n/a not available;
(1) Nashville-Davidson—Murfreesboro—Franklin, TN Metropolitan Statistical Area—see Appendix B for areas included
Source: National Association of Realtors, Qualifying Income Based on Median Sales Price of Existing Single-Family Homes for Metropolitan Areas, 4th Quarter 2013

Median Apartment Condo-Coop Home Prices

Area	2011	2012	2013p	Percent Change 2012 to 2013
MSA[1]	n/a	n/a	n/a	n/a
U.S. Average	165.1	173.7	194.9	12.2

Note: Figures are median sales prices of existing apartment condo-coop homes in thousands of dollars; (p) preliminary; n/a not available; (1) Nashville-Davidson—Murfreesboro—Franklin, TN Metropolitan Statistical Area—see Appendix B for areas included
Source: National Association of Realtors, Median Sales Price of Existing Apartment Condo-Coop Homes for Metropolitan Areas, 4th Quarter 2013

Gross Monthly Rent

Area	Under $200	$200 -299	$300 -499	$500 -749	$750 -999	$1,000 -1,499	$1,500 and up	Median ($)
City	2.7	3.1	5.4	28.9	32.1	21.7	6.0	812
MSA[1]	2.3	3.2	6.2	27.6	32.1	22.2	6.4	823
U.S.	1.7	3.3	8.1	22.7	24.3	25.7	14.3	889

Note: Figures are percentages except for Median; Gross rent is the contract rent plus the estimated average monthly cost of utilities (electricity, gas, and water and sewer) and fuels (oil, coal, kerosene, wood, etc.) if these are paid by the renter (or paid for the renter by someone else); (1) Figures cover the Nashville-Davidson—Murfreesboro—Franklin, TN Metropolitan Statistical Area—see Appendix B for areas included
Source: U.S. Census Bureau, 2010-2012 American Community Survey 3-Year Estimates

Year Housing Structure Built

Area	2010 or Later	2000 -2009	1990 -1999	1980 -1989	1970 -1979	1960 -1969	1950 -1959	1940 -1949	Before 1940	Median Year
City	0.6	15.5	11.8	17.2	18.0	13.2	11.8	4.9	6.9	1977
MSA[1]	0.8	21.8	18.8	16.3	15.8	10.4	7.6	3.3	5.3	1985
U.S.	0.5	14.9	13.8	13.9	15.9	11.1	10.9	5.5	13.5	1976

Note: Figures are percentages except for Median Year; (1) Figures cover the Nashville-Davidson—Murfreesboro—Franklin, TN Metropolitan Statistical Area—see Appendix B for areas included
Source: U.S. Census Bureau, 2010-2012 American Community Survey 3-Year Estimates

HEALTH

Health Risk Data

Category	MSA[1] (%)	U.S. (%)
Adults aged 18–64 who have any kind of health care coverage	82.0	79.6
Adults who reported being in good or excellent health	84.7	83.1
Adults who are current smokers	23.7	19.6
Adults who are heavy drinkers[2]	4.5	6.1
Adults who are binge drinkers[3]	16.0	16.9
Adults who are overweight (BMI 25.0 - 29.9)	34.3	35.8
Adults who are obese (BMI 30.0 - 99.8)	29.1	27.6
Adults who participated in any physical activities in the past month	74.3	77.1
Adults 50+ who have ever had a sigmoidoscopy or colonoscopy	71.6	67.3
Women aged 40+ who have had a mammogram within the past two years	75.3	74.0
Men aged 40+ who have had a PSA test within the past two years	53.8	45.2
Adults aged 65+ who have had flu shot within the past year	71.9	60.1
Adults who always wear a seatbelt	94.6	93.8

Note: Data as of 2012 unless otherwise noted; (1) Figures cover the Nashville-Davidson—Murfreesboro, TN Metropolitan Statistical Area—see Appendix B for areas included; (2) Heavy drinkers are classified as males having more than two drinks per day or females having more than one drink per day; (3) Binge drinkers are classified as males having five or more drinks on one occasion or females having four or more drinks on one occasion
Source: Centers for Disease Control and Prevention, Behaviorial Risk Factor Surveillance System, SMART: Selected Metropolitan/Micropolitan Area Risk Trends, 2012

Chronic Health Indicators

Category	MSA[1] (%)	U.S. (%)
Adults who have ever been told they had a heart attack	5.4	4.5
Adults who have ever been told they had a stroke	2.9	2.9
Adults who have been told they currently have asthma	6.7	8.9
Adults who have ever been told they have arthritis	25.2	25.7
Adults who have ever been told they have diabetes[2]	9.4	9.7
Adults who have ever been told they had skin cancer	6.4	5.7
Adults who have ever been told they had any other types of cancer	6.4	6.5
Adults who have ever been told they have COPD	7.3	6.2
Adults who have ever been told they have kidney disease	1.5	2.5
Adults who have ever been told they have a form of depression	16.6	18.0

Note: Data as of 2012 unless otherwise noted; (1) Figures cover the Nashville-Davidson—Murfreesboro, TN Metropolitan Statistical Area—see Appendix B for areas included; (2) Figures do not include pregnancy-related, borderline, or pre-diabetes
Source: Centers for Disease Control and Prevention, Behaviorial Risk Factor Surveillance System, SMART: Selected Metropolitan/Micropolitan Area Risk Trends, 2012

Mortality Rates for the Top 10 Causes of Death in the U.S.

ICD-10[a] Sub-Chapter	ICD-10[a] Code	Age-Adjusted Mortality Rate[1] per 100,000 population	
		County[2]	U.S.
Malignant neoplasms	C00-C97	198.8	174.2
Ischaemic heart diseases	I20-I25	143.1	119.1
Other forms of heart disease	I30-I51	38.5	49.6
Chronic lower respiratory diseases	J40-J47	50.2	43.2
Cerebrovascular diseases	I60-I69	49.0	40.3
Organic, including symptomatic, mental disorders	F01-F09	44.8	30.5
Other degenerative diseases of the nervous system	G30-G31	33.9	26.3
Other external causes of accidental injury	W00-X59	38.0	25.1
Diabetes mellitus	E10-E14	29.2	21.3
Hypertensive diseases	I10-I15	33.0	18.8

Note: (a) ICD-10 = International Classification of Diseases 10th Revision; (1) Mortality rates are a three year average covering 2008-2010; (2) Figures cover Davidson County
Source: Centers for Disease Control and Prevention, National Center for Health Statistics. Compressed Mortality File 1999-2010 on CDC WONDER Online Database, released January 2013. Data are compiled from the Compressed Mortality File 1999-2010, Series 20 No. 2P, 2013.

Mortality Rates for Selected Causes of Death

ICD-10[a] Sub-Chapter	ICD-10[a] Code	Age-Adjusted Mortality Rate[1] per 100,000 population	
		County[2]	U.S.
Assault	X85-Y09	9.9	5.5
Diseases of the liver	K70-K76	12.3	12.4
Human immunodeficiency virus (HIV) disease	B20-B24	6.7	3.0
Influenza and pneumonia	J09-J18	18.3	16.4
Intentional self-harm	X60-X84	12.1	11.8
Malnutrition	E40-E46	*0.8	0.8
Obesity and other hyperalimentation	E65-E68	2.8	1.6
Renal failure	N17-N19	10.4	13.6
Transport accidents	V01-V99	12.5	12.6
Viral hepatitis	B15-B19	4.4	2.2

Note: (a) ICD-10 = International Classification of Diseases 10th Revision; (1) Mortality rates are a three year average covering 2008-2010; (2) Figures cover Davidson County; (*) Unreliable data as per CDC
Source: Centers for Disease Control and Prevention, National Center for Health Statistics. Compressed Mortality File 1999-2010 on CDC WONDER Online Database, released January 2013. Data are compiled from the Compressed Mortality File 1999-2010, Series 20 No. 2P, 2013.

Health Insurance Coverage

Area	With Health Insurance	With Private Health Insurance	With Public Health Insurance	Without Health Insurance	Population Under Age 18 Without Health Insurance
City	82.6	62.5	28.8	17.4	7.6
MSA[1]	86.1	68.8	26.4	13.9	6.0
U.S.	84.9	65.4	30.4	15.1	7.5

Note: Figures are percentages that cover the civilian noninstitutionalized population; (1) Figures cover the Nashville-Davidson—Murfreesboro—Franklin, TN Metropolitan Statistical Area—see Appendix B for areas included
Source: U.S. Census Bureau, 2010-2012 American Community Survey 3-Year Estimates

Number of Medical Professionals

Area[1]	MDs[2]	DOs[2,3]	Dentists	Podiatrists	Chiropractors	Optometrists
Local (number)	3,763	60	468	25	132	92
Local (rate[4])	592.0	9.4	72.1	3.9	20.3	14.2
U.S. (rate[4])	267.6	19.6	61.7	5.6	24.7	14.5

Note: Data as of 2012 unless noted; (1) Local data covers Davidson County; (2) Data as of 2011; (3) Doctor of Osteopathic Medicine; (4) rate per 100,000 population
Source: Area Resource File (ARF) 2012-2013. U.S. Department of Health and Human Services, Health Resources and Services Administration, Bureau of Health Professions

Best Hospitals

According to *U.S. News,* the Nashville-Davidson—Murfreesboro—Franklin, TN metro area is home to one of the best hospitals in the U.S.: **Vanderbilt University Medical Center** (11 specialties). The hospital listed was nationally ranked in at least one adult specialty. Only 147 hospitals nationwide were nationally ranked in one or more specialties. Eighteen hospitals in the U.S. made the Honor Roll by ranking near the top in at least six specialties.*U.S. News Online,* *"America's Best Hospitals 2013-14"*

According to *U.S. News,* the Nashville-Davidson—Murfreesboro—Franklin, TN metro area is home to one of the best children's hospitals in the U.S.: **Monroe Carell Jr. Children's Hospital at Vanderbilt**. The hospital listed was highly ranked in at least one pediatric specialty. Eighty-seven hospitals in the U.S. ranked in at least one specialty. Ten children's hospitals in the U.S. made the Honor Roll by ranking near the top in three or more specialties.*U.S. News Online,* *"America's Best Children's Hospitals 2013-14"*

EDUCATION

Public School District Statistics

District Name	Schls	Pupils	Pupil/ Teacher Ratio	Minority Pupils[1] (%)	Free Lunch Eligible[2] (%)	IEP[3] (%)
Davidson County	144	80,393	15.0	67.8	64.4	11.3

Note: Table includes school districts with 2,000 or more students; (1) Percentage of students that are not non-Hispanic white; (2) Percentage of students that are eligible for the free lunch program; (3) Percentage of students that have an Individualized Education Program.
Source: U.S. Department of Education, National Center for Education Statistics, Common Core of Data, Local Education Agency (School District) Universe Survey: School Year 2011-2012; U.S. Department of Education, National Center for Education Statistics, Common Core of Data, Public Elementary/Secondary School Universe Survey: School Year 2011-2012

Best High Schools

High School Name	Rank[1]	Grad. Rate[2] (%)	Coll.[3] (%)	AP/IB/ AICE Tests[4]	AP/IB/ AICE Score[5]	SAT Score[6]	ACT Score[6]
Hume-Fogg Academic Magnet H.S.*	71	100	98	1.5	3.5	1867	26.8
Martin Luther King, Jr. Academic Magnet School	70	100	100	1.1	3.2	1849	26.5

Note: (1) Public schools are ranked from 1 to 2,000 based on the following self-reported statistics (with the corresponding weight used in calculating their overall score). Schools that were newly founded and did not have a graduating senior class in 2012 were excluded; (2) Four-year, on-time graduation rate (25%); (3) Percent of 2011 graduates who were accepted to college (25%); (4) AP/IB/AICE tests taken per student (25%); (5) Average AP/IB/AICE exam score (10%); (6) Average SAT and/or ACT score (10%); Percent of students enrolled in at least one AP/IB/AICE course (5%)—data not shown; (*) A correction to this school's data was submitted after the list was tabulated and is therefore not reflected in the ranking order
Source: Newsweek and The Daily Beast, "America's Best High Schools 2013"

Highest Level of Education

Area	Less than H.S.	H.S. Diploma	Some College, No Deg.	Associate Degree	Bachelor's Degree	Master's Degree	Prof. School Degree	Doctorate Degree
City	14.2	25.0	20.6	5.6	21.7	8.3	2.5	2.0
MSA[1]	12.8	29.0	21.0	6.3	20.3	7.1	2.0	1.5
U.S.	14.1	28.3	21.3	7.8	18.0	7.5	1.9	1.2

Note: Figures cover persons age 25 and over; (1) Figures cover the Nashville-Davidson—Murfreesboro—Franklin, TN Metropolitan Statistical Area—see Appendix B for areas included
Source: U.S. Census Bureau, 2010-2012 American Community Survey 3-Year Estimates

Educational Attainment by Race

Area	High School Graduate or Higher (%)					Bachelor's Degree or Higher (%)				
	Total	White	Black	Asian	Hisp.[2]	Total	White	Black	Asian	Hisp.[2]
City	85.8	89.0	84.2	80.3	54.9	34.5	40.0	23.3	48.7	11.3
MSA[1]	87.2	88.7	84.1	86.0	59.9	30.9	32.3	23.6	46.3	12.9
U.S.	85.9	88.1	82.5	85.5	63.1	28.6	30.0	18.4	50.2	13.4

*Note: Figures shown cover persons 25 years old and over; (1) Figures cover the
Nashville-Davidson—Murfreesboro—Franklin, TN Metropolitan Statistical Area—see Appendix B for areas
included; (2) People of Hispanic origin can be of any race*
Source: U.S. Census Bureau, 2010-2012 American Community Survey 3-Year Estimates

School Enrollment by Grade and Control

Area	Preschool (%)		Kindergarten (%)		Grades 1 - 4 (%)		Grades 5 - 8 (%)		Grades 9 - 12 (%)	
	Public	Private	Public	Private	Public	Private	Public	Private	Public	Private
City	56.3	43.7	89.2	10.8	87.2	12.8	82.8	17.2	82.4	17.6
MSA[1]	48.4	51.6	89.4	10.6	88.8	11.2	86.4	13.6	85.8	14.2
U.S.	56.9	43.1	87.8	12.2	89.9	10.1	90.0	10.0	90.8	9.2

*Note: Figures shown cover persons 3 years old and over; (1) Figures cover the
Nashville-Davidson—Murfreesboro—Franklin, TN Metropolitan Statistical Area—see Appendix B for areas
included*
Source: U.S. Census Bureau, 2010-2012 American Community Survey 3-Year Estimates

Average Salaries of Public School Classroom Teachers

Area	2012-13		2013-14		Percent Change 2012-13 to 2013-14	Percent Change 2003-04 to 2013-14
	Dollars	Rank[1]	Dollars	Rank[1]		
Tennessee	47,563	40	48,049	43	1.02	19.2
U.S. Average	56,103	–	56,689	–	1.04	21.8

Note: (1) State rank ranges from 1 to 51 where 1 indicates highest salary.
*Source: National Education Association, Rankings & Estimates: Rankings of the States 2013 and Estimates of
School Statistics 2014, March 2014*

Higher Education

Four-Year Colleges			Two-Year Colleges			Medical Schools[1]	Law Schools[2]	Voc/ Tech[3]
Public	Private Non-profit	Private For-profit	Public	Private Non-profit	Private For-profit			
1	10	6	2	2	5	2	3	5

*Note: Figures cover institutions located within the city limits and include main campuses only; (1) includes
schools accredited by the Liaison Committee on Medical Education and the American Osteopathic Association's
Commission on Osteopathic College Accreditation; (2) includes ABA-accredited schools, schools with
provisional ABA accreditation, and state accredited schools; (3) includes all schools with programs that are less
than 2 years.*
*Source: National Center for Education Statistics, Integrated Postsecondary Education System (IPEDS),
2012-13; Association of American Medical Colleges, Member List, April 24, 2014; American Osteopathic
Association, Member List, April 24, 2014; Law School Admission Council, Official Guide to ABA-Approved
Law Schools Online, April 24, 2014; Wikipedia, List of Medical Schools in the United States, April 24, 2014;
Wikipedia, List of Law Schools in the United States, April 24, 2014*

According to *U.S. News & World Report,* the Nashville-Davidson—Murfreesboro—Franklin, TN
metro area is home to one of the best national universities in the U.S.: **Vanderbilt University**
(#17). The indicators used to capture academic quality fall into a number of categories:
assessment by administrators at peer institutions; retention of students; faculty resources; student
selectivity; financial resources; alumni giving; high school counselor ratings of colleges; and
graduation rate. *U.S. News & World Report, "America's Best Colleges 2014"*

According to *U.S. News & World Report,* the Nashville-Davidson—Murfreesboro—Franklin, TN
metro area is home to one of the best liberal arts colleges in the U.S.: **Fisk University** (#146). The
indicators used to capture academic quality fall into a number of categories: assessment by
administrators at peer institutions; retention of students; faculty resources; student selectivity;
financial resources; alumni giving; high school counselor ratings of colleges; and graduation rate.
U.S. News & World Report, "America's Best Colleges 2014"

According to *U.S. News & World Report,* the Nashville-Davidson—Murfreesboro—Franklin, TN metro area is home to one of the top 100 law schools in the U.S.: **Vanderbilt University** (#15). The rankings are based on a weighted average of 12 measures of quality: peer assessment score; assessment score by lawyers/judges; median LSAT scores; median undergrad GPA; acceptance rate; employment rates for graduates; placement success; bar passage rate; faculty resources; expenditures per student; student/faculty ratio; and library resources. *U.S. News & World Report,* *"America's Best Graduate Schools, Law, 2014"*

According to *U.S. News & World Report,* the Nashville-Davidson—Murfreesboro—Franklin, TN metro area is home to one of the top 100 business schools in the U.S.: **Vanderbilt University (Owen)** (#30). The rankings are based on a weighted average of the following nine measures: quality assessment; peer assessment; recruiter assessment; placement success; mean starting salary and bonus; student selectivity; mean GMAT and GRE scores; mean undergraduate GPA; and acceptance rate. *U.S. News & World Report, "America's Best Graduate Schools, Business, 2014"*

PRESIDENTIAL ELECTION

2012 Presidential Election Results

Area	Obama	Romney	Other
Davidson County	58.4	39.9	1.7
U.S.	51.0	47.2	1.8

Note: Results are percentages and may not add to 100% due to rounding
Source: Dave Leip's Atlas of U.S. Presidential Elections

EMPLOYERS

Major Employers

Company Name	Industry
AHOM Holdings	Home health care services
Asurion Corporation	Business services nec
Baptist Hospital	General medical/surgical hospitals
Cannon County Knitting Mills	Apparel and outerwear broadwoven fabrics
County of Rutherford	Public elementary and secondary schools
County of Sumner	Executive offices, local government
Gaylord Entertainment Company	Hotels/motels
Gaylord Opryland USA	Hotels
Ingram Book Company	Books, periodicals, and newspapers
International Automotive	Automotive storage garage
LifeWay Christian Resources of the SBC	Religious organizations
Middle Tennessee State University	Colleges/universities
Newspaper Printing Corporation	Newspapers
Nissan North America	Motor vehicles/car bodies
Primus Automotive Financial Services	Automobile loans including insurance
Psychiatric Solutions	Psychiatric clinic
State Industries	Hot water heaters, household
State of Tennessee	Mentally handicapped home
Tennesee Department of Transportation	Regulation, administration of transportation
Vanderbilt Childrens Hospital	General medical/surgical hospitals
Vanderbilt University	Colleges/universities

Note: Companies shown are located within the Nashville-Davidson—Murfreesboro—Franklin, TN Metropolitan Statistical Area.
Source: Hoovers.com; Wikipedia

Best Companies to Work For

HCA, headquartered in Nashville, is among the "100 Best Places to Work in IT." To qualify, companies, both public and private, had to have a minimum of 50 IT employees and were selected based on average salary and bonus increases, the percentage of IT staffers promoted, IT staff turnover rates, training and development programs, and the percentage of women and minorities in IT staff and management positions. In addition, *Computerworld* looked at retention efforts, programs for recognizing and rewarding outstanding performances, and benefits such as flextime, elder care and child care, and reimbursement for college tuition and the cost of pursuing technology certifications. *Computerworld, "100 Best Places to Work in IT 2013"*

PUBLIC SAFETY

Crime Rate

Area	All Crimes	Violent Crimes				Property Crimes		
		Murder	Forcible Rape	Robbery	Aggrav. Assault	Burglary	Larceny -Theft	Motor Vehicle Theft
City	5,411.9	10.0	50.1	277.7	878.3	923.8	3,041.6	230.5
Suburbs[1]	2,553.5	2.3	23.4	42.1	285.3	479.9	1,613.9	106.7
Metro[2]	3,589.7	5.1	33.0	127.5	500.3	640.8	2,131.5	151.6
U.S.	3,246.1	4.7	26.9	112.9	242.3	670.2	1,959.3	229.7

Note: Figures are crimes per 100,000 population; (1) All areas within the metro area that are located outside the city limits; (2) Figures cover the Nashville-Davidson—Murfreesboro—Franklin, TN Metropolitan Statistical Area—see Appendix B for areas included
Source: FBI Uniform Crime Reports, 2012

Hate Crimes

Area	Number of Quarters Reported	Bias Motivation				
		Race	Religion	Sexual Orientation	Ethnicity	Disability
City	4	7	1	1	1	0
U.S.	4	2,797	1,099	1,135	667	92

Source: Federal Bureau of Investigation, Hate Crime Statistics 2012

Identity Theft Consumer Complaints

Area	Complaints	Complaints per 100,000 Population	Rank[2]
MSA[1]	1,034	61.9	196
U.S.	290,056	91.8	-

Note: (1) Figures cover the Nashville-Davidson—Murfreesboro—Franklin, TN Metropolitan Statistical Area—see Appendix B for areas included; (2) Rank ranges from 1 to 377 where 1 indicates greatest number of identity theft complaints per 100,000 population
Source: Federal Trade Commission, Consumer Sentinel Network Data Book for January–December 2013

Fraud and Other Consumer Complaints

Area	Complaints	Complaints per 100,000 Population	Rank[2]
MSA[1]	7,466	446.8	53
U.S.	1,811,724	595.2	-

Note: (1) Figures cover the Nashville-Davidson—Murfreesboro—Franklin, TN Metropolitan Statistical Area—see Appendix B for areas included; (2) Rank ranges from 1 to 377 where 1 indicates greatest number of identity theft complaints per 100,000 population
Source: Federal Trade Commission, Consumer Sentinel Network Data Book for January–December 2013

RECREATION

Culture

Dance[1]	Theatre[1]	Instrumental Music[1]	Vocal Music[1]	Series and Festivals	Museums and Art Galleries[2]	Zoos and Aquariums[3]
1	7	1	2	5	36	1

Note: (1) Number of professional perfoming groups; (2) Based on organizations with primary SIC code 8412; (3) AZA-accredited
Source: The Grey House Performing Arts Directory, 2013; Association of Zoos & Aquariums, AZA Member Zoos & Aquariums, April 2014; www.AccuLeads.com, May 1, 2014

Professional Sports Teams

Team Name	League	Year Established
Nashville Predators	National Hockey League (NHL)	1998
Tennessee Titans	National Football League (NFL)	1997

Note: Includes teams located in the Nashville-Davidson—Murfreesboro—Franklin, TN Metropolitan Statistical Area.
Source: Wikipedia, Major Professional Sports Teams of the United States and Canada

CLIMATE

Average and Extreme Temperatures

Temperature	Jan	Feb	Mar	Apr	May	Jun	Jul	Aug	Sep	Oct	Nov	Dec	Yr.
Extreme High (°F)	78	84	86	91	95	106	107	104	105	94	84	79	107
Average High (°F)	47	51	60	71	79	87	90	89	83	72	60	50	70
Average Temp. (°F)	38	41	50	60	68	76	80	79	72	61	49	41	60
Average Low (°F)	28	31	39	48	57	65	69	68	61	48	39	31	49
Extreme Low (°F)	-17	-13	2	23	34	42	54	49	36	26	-1	-10	-17

Note: Figures cover the years 1948-1990
Source: National Climatic Data Center, International Station Meteorological Climate Summary, 9/96

Average Precipitation/Snowfall/Humidity

Precip./Humidity	Jan	Feb	Mar	Apr	May	Jun	Jul	Aug	Sep	Oct	Nov	Dec	Yr.
Avg. Precip. (in.)	4.4	4.2	5.0	4.1	4.6	3.7	3.8	3.3	3.2	2.6	3.9	4.6	47.4
Avg. Snowfall (in.)	4	3	1	Tr	0	0	0	0	0	Tr	1	1	11
Avg. Rel. Hum. 6am (%)	81	81	80	81	86	86	88	90	90	87	83	82	85
Avg. Rel. Hum. 3pm (%)	61	57	51	48	52	52	54	53	52	49	55	59	54

Note: Figures cover the years 1948-1990; Tr = Trace amounts (<0.05 in. of rain; <0.5 in. of snow)
Source: National Climatic Data Center, International Station Meteorological Climate Summary, 9/96

Weather Conditions

Temperature			Daytime Sky			Precipitation		
10°F & below	32°F & below	90°F & above	Clear	Partly cloudy	Cloudy	0.01 inch or more precip.	0.1 inch or more snow/ice	Thunder-storms
5	76	51	98	135	132	119	8	54

Note: Figures are average number of days per year and cover the years 1948-1990
Source: National Climatic Data Center, International Station Meteorological Climate Summary, 9/96

HAZARDOUS WASTE

Superfund Sites

Nashville has no sites on the EPA's Superfund Final National Priorities List.
U.S. Environmental Protection Agency, Final National Priorities List, April 26, 2014

AIR & WATER QUALITY

Air Quality Index

Area	Percent of Days when Air Quality was...[2]					AQI Statistics[2]	
	Good	Moderate	Unhealthy for Sensitive Groups	Unhealthy	Very Unhealthy	Maximum	Median
MSA[1]	74.2	25.5	0.3	0.0	0.0	112	43

Note: (1) Data covers the Nashville-Davidson—Murfreesboro—Franklin, TN Metropolitan Statistical Area—see Appendix B for areas included; (2) Based on 365 days with AQI data in 2013. Air Quality Index (AQI) is an index for reporting daily air quality. EPA calculates the AQI for five major air pollutants regulated by the Clean Air Act: ground-level ozone, particle pollution (aka particulate matter), carbon monoxide, sulfur dioxide, and nitrogen dioxide. The AQI runs from 0 to 500. The higher the AQI value, the greater the level of air pollution and the greater the health concern. There are six AQI categories: "Good" AQI is between 0 and 50. Air quality is considered satisfactory; "Moderate" AQI is between 51 and 100. Air quality is acceptable; "Unhealthy for Sensitive Groups" When AQI values are between 101 and 150, members of sensitive groups may experience health effects; "Unhealthy" When AQI values are between 151 and 200 everyone may begin to experience health effects; "Very Unhealthy" AQI values between 201 and 300 trigger a health alert; "Hazardous" AQI values over 300 trigger warnings of emergency conditions (not shown).
Source: U.S. Environmental Protection Agency, Air Quality Index Report, 2013

Air Quality Index Pollutants

Area	Carbon Monoxide	Nitrogen Dioxide	Ozone	Sulfur Dioxide	Particulate Matter 2.5	Particulate Matter 10
MSA[1]	0.0	4.9	37.0	0.0	58.1	0.0

Percent of Days when AQI Pollutant was...[2]

Note: (1) Data covers the Nashville-Davidson—Murfreesboro—Franklin, TN Metropolitan Statistical Area—see Appendix B for areas included; (2) Based on 365 days with AQI data in 2013. The Air Quality Index (AQI) is an index for reporting daily air quality. EPA calculates the AQI for five major air pollutants regulated by the Clean Air Act: ground-level ozone, particle pollution (also known as particulate matter), carbon monoxide, sulfur dioxide, and nitrogen dioxide. The AQI runs from 0 to 500. The higher the AQI value, the greater the level of air pollution and the greater the health concern.
Source: U.S. Environmental Protection Agency, Air Quality Index Report, 2013

Air Quality Trends: Ozone

	2003	2004	2005	2006	2007	2008	2009	2010	2011	2012
MSA[1]	0.076	0.072	0.078	0.078	0.083	0.072	0.064	0.073	0.071	0.077

Note: (1) Data covers the Nashville-Davidson—Murfreesboro—Franklin, TN Metropolitan Statistical Area—see Appendix B for areas included. The values shown are the composite ozone concentration averages among trend sites based on the highest fourth daily maximum 8-hour concentration in parts per million. These trends are based on sites having an adequate record of monitoring data during the trend period. Data from exceptional events are included.
Source: U.S. Environmental Protection Agency, Air Quality Monitoring Information, "Air Quality Trends by City, 2000-2012"

Maximum Air Pollutant Concentrations: Particulate Matter, Ozone, CO and Lead

	Particulate Matter 10 (ug/m³)	Particulate Matter 2.5 Wtd AM (ug/m³)	Particulate Matter 2.5 24-Hr (ug/m³)	Ozone (ppm)	Carbon Monoxide (ppm)	Lead (ug/m³)
MSA[1] Level	34	10.3	19	0.083	2	n/a
NAAQS[2]	150	15	35	0.075	9	0.15
Met NAAQS[2]	Yes	Yes	Yes	No	Yes	n/a

Note: (1) Data covers the Nashville-Davidson—Murfreesboro—Franklin, TN Metropolitan Statistical Area—see Appendix B for areas included; Data from exceptional events are included; (2) National Ambient Air Quality Standards; ppm = parts per million; ug/m³ = micrograms per cubic meter; n/a not available.
Concentrations: Particulate Matter 10 (coarse particulate)—highest second maximum 24-hour concentration; Particulate Matter 2.5 Wtd AM (fine particulate)—highest weighted annual mean concentration; Particulate Matter 2.5 24-Hour (fine particulate)—highest 98th percentile 24-hour concentration; Ozone—highest fourth daily maximum 8-hour concentration; Carbon Monoxide—highest second maximum non-overlapping 8-hour concentration; Lead—maximum running 3-month average
Source: U.S. Environmental Protection Agency, Air Quality Monitoring Information, "Air Quality Statistics by City, 2012"

Maximum Air Pollutant Concentrations: Nitrogen Dioxide and Sulfur Dioxide

	Nitrogen Dioxide AM (ppb)	Nitrogen Dioxide 1-Hr (ppb)	Sulfur Dioxide AM (ppb)	Sulfur Dioxide 1-Hr (ppb)	Sulfur Dioxide 24-Hr (ppb)
MSA[1] Level	12	42	n/a	11	n/a
NAAQS[2]	53	100	30	75	140
Met NAAQS[2]	Yes	Yes	n/a	Yes	n/a

Note: (1) Data covers the Nashville-Davidson—Murfreesboro—Franklin, TN Metropolitan Statistical Area—see Appendix B for areas included; Data from exceptional events are included; (2) National Ambient Air Quality Standards; ppm = parts per million; ug/m³ = micrograms per cubic meter; n/a not available.
Concentrations: Nitrogen Dioxide AM—highest arithmetic mean concentration; Nitrogen Dioxide 1-Hr—highest 98th percentile 1-hour daily maximum concentration; Sulfur Dioxide AM—highest annual mean concentration; Sulfur Dioxide 1-Hr—highest 99th percentile 1-hour daily maximum concentration; Sulfur Dioxide 24-Hr—highest second maximum 24-hour concentration
Source: U.S. Environmental Protection Agency, Air Quality Monitoring Information, "Air Quality Statistics by City, 2012"

Drinking Water

Water System Name	Pop. Served	Primary Water Source Type	Violations[1] Health Based	Monitoring/ Reporting
Nashville Water Dept #1	599,595	Surface	0	0

Note: (1) Based on violation data from January 1, 2013 to December 31, 2013 (includes unresolved violations from earlier years)
Source: U.S. Environmental Protection Agency, Office of Ground Water and Drinking Water, Safe Drinking Water Information System (based on data extracted February 10, 2014)

New Orleans, Louisiana

Background

New Orleans, the old port city upriver from the mouth of the Mississippi River, is on a par with San Francisco and New York City as one of the United States' most interesting cities. The birthplace of jazz is rich in unique local history, distinctive neighborhoods, and an unmistakably individual character.

The failure of the federal levees following Hurricane Katrina in 2005 put 80 percent of the city under floodwaters for weeks. The Crescent City's revival since then is a testament to her unique spirit, an influx of federal dollars, and an outpouring from volunteers ranging from church groups to spring breakers who returned year after year to help rebuild.

New Orleans was founded on behalf of France by the brothers Le Moyne, Sieurs d'Iberville, and de Bienville, in 1718. Despite disease, starvation, and an unwilling working class, New Orleans emerged as a genteel antebellum slave society, fashioning itself after the rigid social hierarchy of Versailles. Even after New Orleans was ceded to Spain after the French & Indian War, this unequal lifestyle, however gracious, persisted.

The port city briefly returned to French control, then became a crown jewel in the 1803 Louisiana Purchase to the U.S. The transfer of control changed New Orleans's Old World isolation. American settlers introduced aggressive business acumen to the area, as well as the idea of respect for the self-made man. As trade opened up with countries around the world, this made for a happy union. New Orleans became "Queen City of the South," growing prosperous from adventurous riverboat traders and speculators, as well as the cotton trade.

Today, much of the city's Old World charm remains, resulting from Southern, Creole, African-American, and European cultures. New Orleans' cuisine, indigenous music, unique festivals, and sultry, pleasing atmosphere, drew more than eight million visitors in 2010.

A major pillar of the city's economy is the enormous tourism trade that includes the Ernest N. Morial Convention Center's numerous convention goers who fill more than 35,000 rooms. A second economic pillar is the Port of New Orleans, one of the nation's leading general cargo ports. In recent years, it has seen $400 million invested in new facilities.

In addition, an influx of mostly young people who arrived after Hurricane Katrina is giving rise to a new start-up spirit. Plus, state tax breaks have helped to turn New Orleans into "Hollywood South," where 35 films were produced in the last few years. New Orleans has given birth to a mother lode of cultural phenomena: Dixieland jazz, musicians Louis Armstrong, Mahalia Jackson, Dr. John, and chefs Emeril Lagasse and John Besh. The city is well aware of its "cultural economy," which employs 12.5 percent of the local workforce. Popular tourist draws include the annual Mardi Gras celebration—which spans two long weekends leading up to Fat Tuesday—and the annual New Orleans Jazz & Heritage Festival. The Louisiana Superdome—renovated and renamed to the Mercedes Benz Superdome, is home to the 2010 Super Bowl champion New Orleans Saints, and hosted the 2013 Super Bowl. A new, nearly $75 million Consolidated Rental Car Facility project is expanding rental capacity and bring scattered facilities under one roof at the Louis Armstrong New Orleans International Airport.

In addition, an effort to boost a medical economy that suffered after Hurricane Katrina is underway with the near completion of a new Louisiana State University teaching hospital.

In his 2011 state of the city address, Mayor Mitch Landrieu said more than $13 billion in investments would unfold in coming years for bridge, airport, road and hospital repairs. School rebuilding was set for a $1.8 billion influx. Since Katrina, the majority of New Orleans public schools have become charter schools—a major experiment that is seeing some success. Higher education campuses include Tulane University (including a medical school and law school), Loyola University, and the University of New Orleans. Louisiana State University has a medical school campus downtown.

Cultural amenities include the New Orleans Museum of Art located in the live-oak filled City Park, the Ogden Museum of Southern Art, and Audubon Park, designed by John Charles Olmsted with its golf course and the Audubon Zoo.

The New Orleans metro area is virtually surrounded by water, which influences its climate. Between mid-June and September, temperatures are kept down by near-daily sporadic thunderstorms. Cold spells sometimes reach the area in winter but seldom last. Frequent and sometimes heavy rains are typical. Hurricane season officially runs from June 1 to November 30 but typically reaches its height in late summer.

Rankings

General Rankings

- New Orleans was selected as one of the best places in the world to visit by *National Geographic Traveler*. The list reflects what's authentic, culturally rich, sustainable and superlative in the world of travel today. *National Geographic Traveler, "2014 Best of the World," December 2013/January 2014*

- New Orleans was selected as one of America's best cities by *Bloomberg Businessweek*. The city ranked #14 out of 50. Criteria: leisure attributes (the number of restaurants, bars, libraries, museums, professional sports teams, and park acres by population); educational attributes (public school performance, the number of colleges, and graduate degree holders); economic factors (2011 income and June and July 2012 unemployment); crime; and air quality. *Bloomberg BusinessWeek, "America's Best Cities," September 26, 2012*

- New Orleans was identified as one of seven American cities that have lost the most people in the past decade. The city ranked #1. Criteria: population change 2000-2009; percent population change 2000-2009; home vacancy rates. *24/7 Wall St., "American Cities that are Running Out of People," January 1, 2011*

- New Orleans was selected as one of "America's Favorite Cities." The city ranked #32 in the "Quality of Life and Visitor Experience: Cleanliness" category. Respondents to an online survey were asked to rate 35 top urban destinations in the U.S. from a visitor's perspective. Criteria: cleanliness. *Travel + Leisure, "America's Favorite Cities 2013"*

- New Orleans was selected as one of "America's Favorite Cities." The city ranked #2 in the "Type of Trip: Gay-friendly" category. Respondents to an online survey were asked to rate 35 top urban destinations in the U.S. from a visitor's perspective. Criteria: gay-friendly. *Travel + Leisure, "America's Favorite Cities 2013"*

- New Orleans was selected as one of the "Best Places to Live" by *Men's Journal*. Criteria: "18 towns were selected that are perfecting the art of living well—places where conservation is more important than development, bike makers and breweries and farmers thrive, and Whole Foods is considered a big-box store." *Men's Journal, "Best Place to Live 2011: Think Small, Live Big," April 2011*

- New Orleans appeared on *Travel + Leisure's* list of the ten best cities in the U.S. and Canada. The city was ranked #6. Criteria: activities/attractions; culture/arts; restaurants/food; people; and value. *Travel + Leisure, "The World's Best Awards 2013"*

- *Condé Nast Traveler* polled 79,268 readers for travel satisfaction. American cities were ranked based on the following criteria: friendliness; atmosphere/ambiance; culture/sites; restaurants; lodging; and shopping. New Orleans appeared in the top 10, ranking #7. *Condé Nast Traveler, Readers' Choice Awards 2013, "Top 10 Cities in the United States"*

Business/Finance Rankings

- Building on the U.S. Department of Labor's Occupational Information Network Data Collection Program, the Brookings Institution defined STEM occupations and job opportunities for STEM workers at various levels of educational attainment. The New Orleans metro area was one of the ten metro areas where workers in low-education-level STEM jobs earn the highest relative wages. *www.brookings.edu, "The Hidden Stem Economy," June 10, 2013*

- CareerBliss, an employment and careers website, analyzed U.S. Bureau of Labor Statistics data, more than 14,000 company reviews from employees and former employees, and job openings over a six-month period to arrive at its list of the 20 worst places in the United States to look for a job. New Orleans was ranked #15. *CareerBliss.com, "20 Worst Cities to Find a Job for 2012," October 11, 2012*

- New Orleans was ranked #6 out of 100 metro areas in terms of economic performance (#1 = best) during the recession and recovery from trough quarter through the second quarter of 2013. Criteria: percent change in employment; percentage point change in unemployment rate; percent change in gross metropolitan product; percent change in House Price Index. *Brookings Institution, MetroMonitor: Tracking Economic Recession and Recovery in America's 100 Largest Metropolitan Areas, September 2013*

- The New Orleans metro area appeared on the Milken Institute "2013 Best Performing Cities" list. Rank: #88 out of 200 large metro areas. Criteria: job growth; wage and salary growth; high-tech output growth. *Milken Institute, "Best-Performing Cities 2013," December 2013*

- *Forbes* ranked the 200 most populous metro areas in the U.S. in terms of the "Best Places for Business and Careers." The New Orleans metro area was ranked #96. Criteria: costs (business and living); job growth (past and projected); income growth; educational attainment (college and high school); projected economic growth; cultural and recreational opportunities; net migration patterns; number of highly ranked colleges. *Forbes, "The Best Places for Business and Careers," August 7, 2013*

Children/Family Rankings

- New Orleans was selected as one of the best cities for families to live by *Parenting* magazine. The city ranked #57 out of 100. Criteria: education; health; community; *Parenting's* Culture & Charm Index. *Parenting.com, "The 2012 Best Cities for Families List"*

Culture/Performing Arts Rankings

- New Orleans was selected as one of 10 best U.S. cities to be a moviemaker. The city was ranked #9. Criteria: film community; access to new films; access to equipment; cost of living; tax incentives. *MovieMaker Magazine, "Top 10 Cities to be a Moviemaker: 2013," March 5, 2013*

- New Orleans was selected as one of "America's Favorite Cities." The city ranked #3 in the "Culture: Museum/Galleries" category. Respondents to an online survey were asked to rate 35 top urban destinations in the U.S. from a visitor's perspective. Criteria: number and quality of museums and galleries. *Travelandleisure.com, "America's Favorite Cities 2013"*

- New Orleans was selected as one of America's top cities for the arts. The city ranked #5 in the mid-sized city (population 100,000 to 499,999) category. Criteria: readers' top choices for arts travel destinations based on the richness and variety of visual arts sites, activities and events. *American Style, "2012 Top 25 Arts Destinations," June 2012*

Dating/Romance Rankings

- New Orleans took the #9 spot on NerdWallet's list of best cities for singles wanting to date, based on the availability of singles; "date-friendliness," as determined by a city's walkability and the number of bars and restaurants per thousand residents; and the affordability of dating in terms of the cost of movie tickets, pizza, and wine for two. *www.nerdwallet.com, "Best Cities for Singles," February 5, 2014*

- Of the 100 U.S. cities surveyed by *Men's Health* in its quest to identify the nation's best cities for dating and forming relationships, New Orleans was ranked #70 for online dating (#1 = best). *Men's Health, "The Best and Worst Cities for Online Dating," January 30, 2013*

- New Orleans was selected as one of America's best cities for singles by the readers of *Travel + Leisure* in their annual "America's Favorite Cities" survey. The city was ranked #1 out of 20. *Travel + Leisure, "America's Best Cities for Singles," July 2012*

- New Orleans was selected as one of "America's Best Cities for Dating" by *Yahoo! Travel*. Criteria: high proportion of singles; excellent dating venues and/or stunning natural settings. *Yahoo! Travel, "America's Best Cities for Dating," February 7, 2012*

Education Rankings

- *Men's Health* ranked 100 U.S. cities in terms of their education levels. New Orleans was ranked #60 (#1 = most educated city). Criteria: high school graduation rates; school enrollment; educational attainment; number of households who have outstanding student loans; number of households whose members have taken adult-education courses. *Men's Health, "Where School Is In: The Most and Least Educated Cities," September 12, 2011*

- New Orleans was selected as one of America's most literate cities. The city ranked #19 out of the 77 largest U.S. cities. Criteria: number of booksellers; library resources; Internet resources; educational attainment; periodical publishing resources; newspaper circulation. *Central Connecticut State University, "America's Most Literate Cities, 2013"*

Environmental Rankings

- The New Orleans metro area came in at #336 for the relative comfort of its climate on Sperling's list of "chill cities," as measured by the Sperling Heat Index. All 361 metro areas are included. Criteria included daytime high temperatures, nighttime low temperatures, dew point, and relative humidity at the high temperatures. *www.bertsperling.com, "Sperling's Chill Cities," July 18, 2013*

- Sperling's BestPlaces assessed 379 metropolitan areas of the United States for the likelihood of dangerously extreme weather events or earthquakes. In general the Southeast and South-Central regions have the highest risk of weather extremes and earthquakes, while the Pacific Northwest enjoys the lowest risk. Of the least risky metropolitan areas, the New Orleans metro area was ranked #326. *www.bestplaces.net, "Safest Places from Natural Disasters," April 2011*

- New Orleans was selected as one of 22 "Smarter Cities" for energy by the Natural Resources Defense Council. Criteria: investment in green power; energy efficiency measures; conservation. *Natural Resources Defense Council, "2010 Smarter Cities," July 19, 2010*

- New Orleans was selected as one of the five worst summer weather cities in the U.S. by the *Farmers' Almanac*. The city ranked #2. Criteria: average summer and winter temperatures; humidity; precipitation; number of overcast days. The editors only considered cities with populations of 50,000 or more. *Farmers' Almanac, "America's Ten Worst Weather Cities," September 7, 2010*

Food/Drink Rankings

- *Men's Health* ranked 100 major U.S. cities in terms of alcohol intoxication. New Orleans ranked #15 (#1 = most sober).Criteria: binge drinking; alcohol-related traffic accidents, arrests, and fatalities. *Men's Health, "The Drunkest Cities in America," November 19, 2013*

Health/Fitness Rankings

- Analysts who tracked obesity rates in the nation's largest metro areas (those with populations above one million) found that the New Orleans metro area was one of the ten major metros where residents were most likely to be obese, defined as a BMI score of 30 or above. *www.gallup.com, "Boulder, Colo., Residents Still Least Likely to Be Obese," April 4, 2014*

- For each of the 50 most populous metro areas in the United States, the American College of Sports Medicine's American Fitness Index evaluated infrastructure, community assets, and policies that encourage healthy and fit lifestyles, including preventive health behaviors, levels of chronic disease conditions, health care access, and community resources and policies that support physical activity. The New Orleans metro area ranked #38 for "community fitness." Personal health indicators were considered as well as community and environmental indicators. *www.americanfitnessindex.org, "ACSM American Fitness Index Health and Community Fitness Status of the 50 Largest Metropolitan Areas," May 2013*

- The New Orleans metro area was identified as one of the worst cities for bed bugs in America by pest control company Orkin. The area ranked #49 out of 50 based on the number of bed bug treatments Orkin performed from January to December 2013. *Orkin, "Chicago Tops Bed Bug Cities List for Second Year in a Row," January 16, 2014*

- New Orleans was selected as one of the 25 fattest cities in America by *Men's Fitness Online*. It ranked #19 out of America's 50 largest cities. Criteria: fitness centers and sport stores; nutrition; sports participation; TV viewing; overweight/sedentary; junk food; air quality; geography; commute; parks and open space; city recreational facilities; access to healthcare; motivation; mayor and city initiatives; state obesity initiatives. *Men's Fitness, "The Fittest and Fattest Cities in America," March 5, 2012*

- New Orleans was identified as one of "The 8 Most Artery-Clogging Cities in America." The metro area ranked #4. Criteria: obesity rates; heart disease rates. *Prevention, "The 8 Most Artery-Clogging Cities in America," December 2011*

- New Orleans was identified as a "2013 Spring Allergy Capital." The area ranked #13 out of 100. Three groups of factors were used to identify the most severe cities for people with allergies during the spring season: annual pollen levels; medicine utilization; access to board-certified allergists. *Asthma and Allergy Foundation of America, "Spring Allergy Capitals 2013"*

- New Orleans was identified as a "2013 Fall Allergy Capital." The area ranked #11 out of 100. Three groups of factors were used to identify the most severe cities for people with allergies during the fall season: annual pollen levels; medicine utilization; access to board-certified allergists. *Asthma and Allergy Foundation of America, "Fall Allergy Capitals 2013"*

- New Orleans was identified as a "2013 Asthma Capital." The area ranked #24 out of the nation's 100 largest metropolitan areas. Twelve factors were used to identify the most challenging places to live for people with asthma: estimated prevalence; self-reported prevalence; crude death rate for asthma; annual pollen score; annual air quality; public smoking laws; number of board-certified asthma specialists; school inhaler access laws; rescue medication use; controller medication use; uninsured rate; poverty rate. *Asthma and Allergy Foundation of America, "Asthma Capitals 2013"*

- *Men's Health* ranked 100 major U.S. cities in terms of the best and worst cities for men. New Orleans ranked #77. Criteria: thirty-three data points were examined covering health, fitness, and quality of life. *Men's Health, "The Best & Worst Cities for Men 2014," December 6, 2013*

- Breathe Right Nasal Strips, in partnership with Sperling's BestPlaces, analyzed 50 metro areas and identified those U.S. cities most challenged by chronic nasal congestion. The New Orleans metro area ranked #3. Criteria: tree, grass and weed pollens; molds and spores; air pollution; climate; smoking; purchase habits of congestion products; prescriptions of drugs for congestion relief; incidence of influenza. *Breathe Right Nasal Strips, "Most Congested Cities," October 3, 2011*

- The New Orleans metro area appeared in the 2013 Gallup-Healthways Well-Being Index. The area ranked #120 out of 189. The Gallup-Healthways Well-Being Index score is an average of six sub-indexes, which individually examine life evaluation, emotional health, work environment, physical health, healthy behaviors, and access to basic necessities. Results are based on telephone interviews conducted as part of the Gallup-Healthways Well-Being Index survey January 2–December 29, 2012, and January 2–December 30, 2013, with a random sample of 531,630 adults, aged 18 and older, living in metropolitan areas in the 50 U.S. states and the District of Columbia. *Gallup-Healthways, "State of American Well-Being," March 25, 2014*

- *Men's Health* ranked 100 U.S. cities in terms of their activity levels. New Orleans was ranked #68 (#1 = most active city). Criteria: where and how often residents exercise; percentage of households that watch more than 15 hours of cable television a week and buy more than 11 video games a year; death rate from deep-vein thrombosis, a condition linked to sitting for extended periods of time. *Men's Health, "Where Sit Happens: The Most and Least Active Cities in America," June 20, 2011*

- New Orleans was selected as one of the "20 Most Livable U.S. Cities for Wheelchair Users" by the Christopher & Dana Reeve Foundation. The city ranked #18. Criteria: Medicaid eligibility and spending; access to physicians and rehabilitation facilities; access to fitness facilities and recreation; access to paratransit; percentage of people living with disabilities who are employed; clean air; climate. *Christopher & Dana Reeve Foundation, "20 Most Livable U.S. Cities for Wheelchair Users," July 26, 2010*

- *The Daily Beast* identified the 30 U.S. metro areas with the worst smoking habits. The New Orleans metro area ranked #24. Sixty urban centers with populations of more than one million were ranked based on the following criteria: number of smokers; number of cigarettes smoked per day; fewest attempts to quit. *The Daily Beast, "30 Cities With Smoking Problems," January 3, 2011*

Real Estate Rankings

- *Forbes* reported that New Orleans ranked #9 on its list of cities where renters could get the best value for their money, based on current rental prices, price per square foot, year-over-year changes in rent cost, and cost of renting compared with the cost of purchasing a home. *www.forbes.com, "Renting? Cities to Get the Most Bang for Your Buck," July 19, 2013*

- Based on the home-price forecasts compiled by the real-estate valuation firm CoreLogic Case-Shiller, the finance website CNNMoney reported that in 2014, the New Orleans metro area is expected to place #3 among American metro areas in terms of increases in residential real estate prices. *money.cnn.com, "10 Hottest Housing Markets for 2014," January 23, 2014*

- New Orleans was ranked #137 out of 283 metro areas in terms of house price appreciation in 2013 (#1 = highest rate). *Federal Housing Finance Agency, House Price Index, 4th Quarter 2013*

Safety Rankings

- Business Insider looked at the FBI's Uniform Crime Report to identify the U.S. cities with the most violent crime per capita, excluding localities with fewer than 100,000 residents. To judge by its relatively high murder, rape, and robbery data, New Orleans was ranked #5 (#1 = worst) among the 25 most dangerous cities. *www.businessinsider.com, "The 25 Most Dangerous Cities in America," June 13, 2013*

- Allstate ranked the 200 largest cities in America in terms of driver safety. New Orleans ranked #156. Allstate researchers analyzed internal property damage claims over a two-year period from January 2010 to December 2011. A weighted average of the two-year numbers determined the annual percentages. *Allstate, "Allstate America's Best Drivers Report®, August 27, 2013"*

- New Orleans was identified as one of the most dangerous mid-size cities in America by CQ Press. All 252 cities with populations of 100,000 to 499,999 that reported crime rates in 2012 for murder, rape, robbery, aggravated assault, burglary, and motor vehicle thefts were ranked. The city ranked #9 out of the top 10. *CQ Press, City Crime Rankings 2014*

- The National Insurance Crime Bureau ranked 380 metro areas in the U.S. in terms of per capita rates of vehicle theft. The New Orleans metro area ranked #56 (#1 = highest rate). Criteria: number of vehicle theft offenses per 100,000 inhabitants in 2012. *National Insurance Crime Bureau, "Hot Spots 2012," June 26, 2013*

- The New Orleans metro area was identified as one of the most dangerous metro areas for pedestrians by Transportation for America. The metro area ranked #15 out of 52 metro areas with over 1 million residents. Criteria: area's population divided by the number of pedestrian fatalities in that area. *Transportation for America, "Dangerous by Design 2011"*

Seniors/Retirement Rankings

- From its Best Cities for Successful Aging indexes, the Milken Institute generated rankings for metropolitan areas, weighing data in eight categories—general indicators, health care, wellness, living arrangements, transportation and general accessibility, financial well-being, education and employment, and community participation. The New Orleans metro area was ranked #34 overall in the large metro area category. *Milken Institute, "Best Cities for Successful Aging," July 2012*

- Bankers Life and Casualty Company, in partnership with Sperling's BestPlaces, ranked the nation's 50 largest metro areas in terms of the "Best U.S. Cities for Seniors." The New Orleans metro area ranked #30. Criteria: healthcare; transportation; housing; environment; economy; health and longevity; social and spiritual life; crime. *Bankers Life and Casualty Company, Center for a Secure Retirement, "Best U.S. Cities for Seniors 2011," September 2011*

Sports/Recreation Rankings

- *24/7 Wall St.* analysts isolated the ten cities that spent the most public money per capita on sports stadiums, according to 2010 data. New Orleans ranked #8. *24/7 Wall St., "Cities Paying the Most for Sports Teams," January 30, 2013*

- New Orleans appeared on the *Sporting News* list of the "Best Sports Cities" for 2011. The area ranked #22 out of 271. Criteria: the magazine takes a 12-month snapshot of each city's sports, putting a heavy premium on regular-season won-lost records (from the most recently completed season). Other criteria include: playoff berths, bowl appearances and tournament bids; championships; applicable power ratings; quality of competition; overall fan fervor (measured in part by attendance); abundance of teams (rewarding quality over quantity); stadium and arena quality; ticket availability and prices; franchise ownership; and marquee appeal of athletes. *Sporting News, "Best Sports Cities 2011," October 4, 2011*

- New Orleans appeared on the *Sporting News* list of the "Best Sports Cities" for 2011. The area ranked #22 out of 271. Criteria: a 12-month snapshot of regular-season won-lost records (from the most recently completed season). Other criteria include: playoff berths, bowl appearances and tournament bids; championships; applicable power ratings; quality of competition; overall fan fervor (measured in part by attendance); abundance of teams (quality over quantity); stadium and arena quality; ticket availability and prices; franchise ownership; and marquee appeal of athletes. *Sporting News, "Best Sports Cities 2011," October 4, 2011*

- New Orleans was selected as one of the most playful cities in the U.S. by KaBOOM! The organization's Playful City USA initiative honors cities and towns across the nation for a vision, plan and commitment to creating an agenda for play. Criteria: creating a local play commission or task force; designing an annual action plan for play; conducting a play space audit; outlining a financial investment in play for the current fiscal year; and proclaiming and celebrating an annual "play day." *KaBOOM! National Campaign for Play, "2013 Playful City USA Communities"*

- New Orleans was chosen as one of America's best cities for bicycling. The city ranked #43 out of 50. Criteria: robust cycling infrastructure; vibrant bike culture. The editors only considered cities with populations of 95,000 or more. *Bicycling, "America's Top 50 Bike-Friendly Cities," May 23, 2012*

Transportation Rankings

- NerdWallet surveyed average annual car insurance premiums in 125 U.S. cities to identify the least expensive U.S. cities in which to insure a car. Locations with no-fault insurance laws was a strong determinant. New Orleans came in at #2 for the most expensive rates. *www.nerdwallet.com, "Best Cities for Cheap Car Insurance," February 3, 2014*

- New Orleans was identified as one of America's worst cities for speed traps by the National Motorists Association. The city ranked #16 out of 25. Criteria: speed trap locations per 100,000 residents. *National Motorists Association, September 2011*

Women/Minorities Rankings

- The Daily Beast surveyed the nation's cities for highest percentage of singles and lowest divorce rate, plus other measures, to determine "emotional intelligence"—happiness, confidence, kindness—which, researchers say, has a strong correlation with people's satisfaction with their romantic relationships. New Orleans placed #19. *www.thedailybeast.com, "Best Cities to Find Love and Stay in Love," February 14, 2014*

- *Women's Health* examined U.S. cities and identified the 100 best cities for women. New Orleans was ranked #70. Criteria: 30 categories were examined from obesity and breast cancer rates to commuting times and hours spent working out. *Women's Health, "Best Cities for Women 2012"*

- The New Orleans metro area appeared on *Forbes'* list of the "Best Cities for Minority Entrepreneurs." The area ranked #70 out of 10. Criteria: 52 metropolitan statistical areas were examined. For each ethnicity (African Americans, Asians and Hispanics), the editors measured housing affordability, population growth, income growth, and entrepreneurship (per capita self-employment). *Forbes, "Best Cities for Minority Entrepreneurs," March 23, 2011*

Miscellaneous Rankings

- *Men's Health* ranked 100 U.S. cities by their level of sadness. New Orleans was ranked #44 (#1 = saddest city). Criteria: suicide rates; unemployment rates; percentage of households that use antidepressants; percent of population who report feeling blue all or most of the time. *Men's Health, "Frown Towns," November 28, 2011*

- The New Orleans metro area was selected as one of "The Best U.S. Cities for Bargain Shopping" by *Forbes*. The area ranked #10 out of 10. Criteria: number of outlet stores; gross leasable retail space in major malls; low consumer price index; low sales tax rate. Indicators were examined in the nation's 50 largest metropolitan areas. *Forbes, "The Best U.S. Cities for Bargain Shopping," January 20, 2012*

- Mars Chocolate North America, the makers of COMBOS®, in partnership with Sperling's BestPlaces, ranked 50 major metro areas in terms of their "manliness." The New Orleans metro area ranked #14. Criteria: number of professional sports teams; number of nearby NASCAR tracks and racing events; manly lifestyle; concentration of manly retail stores; manly occupations per capita; salty snack sales; "Board of Manliness" rankings. *Mars Chocolate North America, "America's Manliest Cities 2012"*

- New Orleans was selected as one of "America's Best Cities for Hipsters" by *Travel + Leisure*. The city was ranked #2 out of 20. Criteria: live music; coffee bars; independent boutiques; best microbrews; offbeat and tech-savvy locals. *Travel + Leisure, "America's Best Cities for Hipsters," November 2013*

- The National Alliance to End Homelessness ranked the 100 most populous metro areas in terms the rate of homelessness. The New Orleans metro area ranked #2. Criteria: number of homeless people per 10,000 population in 2011. *National Alliance to End Homelessness, The State of Homelessness in America 2012*

Business Environment

CITY FINANCES

City Government Finances

Component	2011 ($000)	2011 ($ per capita)
Total Revenues	1,719,191	7,190
Total Expenditures	1,789,163	7,482
Debt Outstanding	1,810,194	7,570
Cash and Securities[1]	1,874,180	7,838

Note: (1) Cash and security holdings of a government at the close of its fiscal year, including those of its dependent agencies, utilities, and liquor stores.
Source: U.S Census Bureau, State & Local Government Finances 2011

City Government Revenue by Source

Source	2011 ($000)	2011 ($ per capita)
General Revenue		
From Federal Government	381,257	1,594
From State Government	285,149	1,192
From Local Governments	0	0
Taxes		
Property	227,490	951
Sales and Gross Receipts	210,764	881
Personal Income	0	0
Corporate Income	0	0
Motor Vehicle License	2,479	10
Other Taxes	25,260	106
Current Charges	294,670	1,232
Liquor Store	0	0
Utility	58,326	244
Employee Retirement	91,032	381

Source: U.S Census Bureau, State & Local Government Finances 2011

City Government Expenditures by Function

Function	2011 ($000)	2011 ($ per capita)	2011 (%)
General Direct Expenditures			
Air Transportation	113,959	477	6.4
Corrections	88,813	371	5.0
Education	0	0	0.0
Employment Security Administration	0	0	0.0
Financial Administration	60,429	253	3.4
Fire Protection	88,400	370	4.9
General Public Buildings	7,379	31	0.4
Governmental Administration, Other	58,870	246	3.3
Health	16,996	71	0.9
Highways	30,994	130	1.7
Hospitals	16,487	69	0.9
Housing and Community Development	309,743	1,295	17.3
Interest on General Debt	107,352	449	6.0
Judicial and Legal	32,896	138	1.8
Libraries	7,624	32	0.4
Parking	3,854	16	0.2
Parks and Recreation	66,785	279	3.7
Police Protection	131,754	551	7.4
Public Welfare	2,124	9	0.1
Sewerage	181,547	759	10.1
Solid Waste Management	40,251	168	2.2
Veterans' Services	0	0	0.0
Liquor Store	0	0	0.0
Utility	93,106	389	5.2
Employee Retirement	55,351	231	3.1

Source: U.S Census Bureau, State & Local Government Finances 2011

DEMOGRAPHICS

Population Growth

Area	1990 Census	2000 Census	2010 Census	Population Growth (%) 1990-2000	Population Growth (%) 2000-2010
City	496,938	484,674	343,829	-2.5	-29.1
MSA[1]	1,264,391	1,316,510	1,167,764	4.1	-11.3
U.S.	248,709,873	281,421,906	308,745,538	13.2	9.7

Note: (1) Figures cover the New Orleans-Metairie, LA Metropolitan Statistical Area—see Appendix B for areas included
Source: U.S. Census Bureau, Census 1990, 2000, 2010

Household Size

Area	Persons in Household (%) One	Two	Three	Four	Five	Six	Seven or More	Average Household Size
City	39.1	30.1	14.9	8.8	4.5	1.4	1.3	2.37
MSA[1]	30.7	32.2	16.6	11.7	5.7	2.0	1.1	2.56
U.S.	27.6	33.5	15.7	13.2	6.1	2.4	1.5	2.63

Note: (1) Figures cover the New Orleans-Metairie, LA Metropolitan Statistical Area—see Appendix B for areas included
Source: U.S. Census Bureau, 2010-2012 American Community Survey 3-Year Estimates

Race

Area	White Alone[2] (%)	Black Alone[2] (%)	Asian Alone[2] (%)	AIAN[3] Alone[2] (%)	NHOPI[4] Alone[2] (%)	Other Race Alone[2] (%)	Two or More Races (%)
City	33.5	60.0	2.9	0.3	0.0	1.7	1.6
MSA[1]	58.4	34.3	2.8	0.4	0.1	2.2	1.7
U.S.	74.0	12.6	4.9	0.8	0.2	4.7	2.8

Note: (1) Figures cover the New Orleans-Metairie, LA Metropolitan Statistical Area—see Appendix B for areas included; (2) Alone is defined as not being in combination with one or more other races; (3) American Indian and Alaska Native; (4) Native Hawaiian and Other Pacific Islander
Source: U.S. Census Bureau, 2010-2012 American Community Survey 3-Year Estimates

Hispanic or Latino Origin

Area	Total (%)	Mexican (%)	Puerto Rican (%)	Cuban (%)	Other (%)
City	5.3	1.6	0.2	0.4	3.1
MSA[1]	8.1	2.0	0.5	0.5	5.0
U.S.	16.6	10.7	1.6	0.6	3.7

Note: Persons of Hispanic or Latino origin can be of any race; (1) Figures cover the New Orleans-Metairie, LA Metropolitan Statistical Area—see Appendix B for areas included
Source: U.S. Census Bureau, 2010-2012 American Community Survey 3-Year Estimates

Segregation

Type	Segregation Indices[1] 1990	2000	2010	2010 Rank[2]	Percent Change 1990-2000	Percent Change 1990-2010	Percent Change 2000-2010
Black/White	68.3	69.2	63.9	28	0.9	-4.4	-5.3
Asian/White	49.6	50.4	48.6	9	0.8	-1.0	-1.8
Hispanic/White	31.1	35.6	38.3	74	4.5	7.2	2.7

Note: All figures cover the Metropolitan Statistical Area—see Appendix B for areas included; Figures are based on an analysis of 1990, 2000, and 2010 Census Decennial Census tract data by William H. Frey, Brookings Institution and the University of Michigan Social Science Data Analysis Network. In this analysis all racial groups (whites, blacks, and asians) are non-Hispanic members of those races. Hispanics are shown as a separate category;
(1) Segregation Indices are Dissimilarity Indices that measure the degree to which the minority group is distributed differently than whites across census tracts. They range from 0 (complete integration) to 100 (complete segregation) where the value indicates the percentage of the minority group that needs to move to be distributed exactly like whites; (2) Ranges from 1 (most segregated) to 102 (least segregated); n/a not available.
Source: www.CensusScope.org

Ancestry

Area	German	Irish	English	American	Italian	Polish	French[2]	Scottish	Dutch
City	6.8	5.9	4.1	3.7	4.2	0.8	6.3	1.0	0.4
MSA[1]	11.3	8.6	5.1	6.0	8.8	0.6	14.9	0.9	0.5
U.S.	15.2	11.1	8.2	7.2	5.6	3.1	2.8	1.7	1.4

Note: Figures are the percentage of the total population reporting a particular ancestry. The nine most commonly reported ancestries in the U.S. are shown. Figures include multiple ancestries (e.g. if a person reported being Irish and Italian, they were included in both columns); (1) Figures cover the New Orleans-Metairie, LA Metropolitan Statistical Area—see Appendix B for areas included; (2) Excludes Basque
Source: U.S. Census Bureau, 2010-2012 American Community Survey 3-Year Estimates

Foreign-Born Population

Area	Percent of Population Born in								
	Any Foreign Country	Mexico	Asia	Europe	Carribean	South America	Central America[2]	Africa	Canada
City	5.8	0.6	2.0	0.8	0.2	0.4	1.4	0.3	0.1
MSA[1]	7.0	0.6	2.0	0.6	0.5	0.4	2.5	0.2	0.1
U.S.	13.0	3.7	3.7	1.6	1.2	0.9	1.0	0.5	0.3

Note: (1) Figures cover the New Orleans-Metairie, LA Metropolitan Statistical Area—see Appendix B for areas included; (2) Excludes Mexico.
Source: U.S. Census Bureau, 2010-2012 American Community Survey 3-Year Estimates

Marital Status

Area	Never Married	Now Married[2]	Separated	Widowed	Divorced
City	48.8	29.7	2.8	6.3	12.3
MSA[1]	36.8	42.0	2.5	6.5	12.2
U.S.	32.4	48.4	2.2	6.0	11.0

Note: Figures are percentages and cover the population 15 years of age and older; (1) Figures cover the New Orleans-Metairie, LA Metropolitan Statistical Area—see Appendix B for areas included; (2) Excludes separated
Source: U.S. Census Bureau, 2010-2012 American Community Survey 3-Year Estimates

Age

Area	Percent of Population									Median Age
	Under Age 5	Age 5–19	Age 20–34	Age 35–44	Age 45–54	Age 55–64	Age 65–74	Age 75–84	Age 85+	
City	6.6	17.8	26.0	12.3	13.7	12.5	6.3	3.3	1.6	34.7
MSA[1]	6.6	19.1	21.6	12.6	14.7	12.8	7.0	3.8	1.6	37.2
U.S.	6.4	20.1	20.5	13.1	14.3	12.2	7.3	4.2	1.8	37.3

Note: (1) Figures cover the New Orleans-Metairie, LA Metropolitan Statistical Area—see Appendix B for areas included
Source: U.S. Census Bureau, 2010-2012 American Community Survey 3-Year Estimates

Gender

Area	Males	Females	Males per 100 Females
City	173,088	186,042	93.0
MSA[1]	578,837	611,325	94.7
U.S.	153,276,055	158,333,314	96.8

Note: (1) Figures cover the New Orleans-Metairie, LA Metropolitan Statistical Area—see Appendix B for areas included
Source: U.S. Census Bureau, 2010-2012 American Community Survey 3-Year Estimates

Religious Groups by Family

Area	Catholic	Baptist	Non-Den.	Methodist[2]	Lutheran	LDS[3]	Pente-costal	Presby-terian[4]	Muslim[5]	Judaism
MSA[1]	31.6	8.4	3.7	2.7	0.8	0.6	2.1	0.5	0.5	0.5
U.S.	19.1	9.3	4.0	4.0	2.3	2.0	1.9	1.6	0.8	0.7

Note: Figures are the number of adherents as a percentage of the total population; (1) Figures cover the New Orleans-Metairie, LA Metropolitan Statistical Area—see Appendix B for areas included; (2) Methodist/Pietist; (3) Latter Day Saints; (4) Reformed; (5) Figures are estimates
Source: Association of Statisticians of American Religious Bodies, 2010 U.S. Religion Census: Religious Congregations & Membership Study

Religious Groups by Tradition

Area	Catholic	Evangelical Protestant	Mainline Protestant	Other Tradition	Black Protestant	Orthodox
MSA[1]	31.6	12.7	4.0	2.1	3.0	0.1
U.S.	19.1	16.2	7.3	4.3	1.6	0.3

Note: Figures are the number of adherents as a percentage of the total population; (1) Figures cover the New Orleans-Metairie, LA Metropolitan Statistical Area—see Appendix B for areas included
Source: Association of Statisticians of American Religious Bodies, 2010 U.S. Religion Census: Religious Congregations & Membership Study

ECONOMY

Gross Metropolitan Product

Area	2011	2012	2013	2014	Rank[2]
MSA[1]	74.3	80.2	83.0	86.2	40

Note: Figures are in billions of dollars; (1) Figures cover the New Orleans-Metairie, LA Metropolitan Statistical Area—see Appendix B for areas included; (2) Rank is based on 2014 data and ranges from 1 to 363
Source: The United States Conference of Mayors, U.S. Metro Economies: Outlook—Gross Metropolitan Product, with Metro Employment Projections, November 2013

Economic Growth

Area	2011 (%)	2012 (%)	2013 (%)	2014 (%)	Rank[2]
MSA[1]	-5.6	7.6	2.5	2.1	50
U.S.	1.6	2.5	1.7	2.5	–

Note: Figures are real gross metropolitan product (GMP) growth rates and represent annual average percent change; (1) Figures cover the New Orleans-Metairie, LA Metropolitan Statistical Area—see Appendix B for areas included; (2) Rank is based on 2013 data and ranges from 1 to 363
Source: The United States Conference of Mayors, U.S. Metro Economies: Outlook—Gross Metropolitan Product, with Metro Employment Projections, November 2013

Metropolitan Area Exports

Area	2007	2008	2009	2010	2011	2012	Rank[2]
MSA[1]	8,449.1	12,664.5	10,145.1	13,964.9	20,336.9	24,359.5	11

Note: Figures are in millions of dollars; (1) Figures cover the New Orleans-Metairie, LA Metropolitan Statistical Area—see Appendix B for areas included; (2) Rank is based on 2012 data and ranges from 1 to 369
Source: U.S. Department of Commerce, International Trade Administration, Office of Trade & Industry Information, Manufacturing & Services, data extracted April 1, 2014

INCOME

Income

Area	Per Capita ($)	Median Household ($)	Average Household ($)
City	25,654	36,004	59,897
MSA[1]	26,159	46,087	65,519
U.S.	27,385	51,771	71,579

Note: (1) Figures cover the New Orleans-Metairie, LA Metropolitan Statistical Area—see Appendix B for areas included
Source: U.S. Census Bureau, 2010-2012 American Community Survey 3-Year Estimates

Household Income Distribution

Area	Percent of Households Earning							
	Under $15,000	$15,000 -24,999	$25,000 -34,999	$35,000 -49,999	$50,000 -74,999	$75,000 -99,000	$100,000 -149,999	$150,000 and up
City	24.5	13.3	11.2	12.7	13.9	8.8	8.3	7.2
MSA[1]	16.8	11.8	11.2	13.6	16.4	11.2	11.4	7.7
U.S.	13.1	11.0	10.5	13.7	18.1	11.9	12.5	9.1

Note: (1) Figures cover the New Orleans-Metairie, LA Metropolitan Statistical Area—see Appendix B for areas included
Source: U.S. Census Bureau, 2010-2012 American Community Survey 3-Year Estimates

Poverty Rate

Area	All Ages	Under 18 Years Old	18 to 64 Years Old	65 Years and Over
City	28.5	42.4	26.0	16.5
MSA[1]	18.8	27.4	17.1	11.5
U.S.	15.7	22.2	14.6	9.3

Note: Figures are percentage of people whose income during the past 12 months was below the poverty level;
(1) Figures cover the New Orleans-Metairie, LA Metropolitan Statistical Area—see Appendix B for areas included
Source: U.S. Census Bureau, 2010-2012 American Community Survey 3-Year Estimates

Personal Bankruptcy Filing Rate

Area	2008	2009	2010	2011	2012	2013
Orleans Parish	1.59	2.12	2.31	2.23	2.04	2.01
U.S.	3.53	4.61	4.97	4.37	3.76	3.29

Note: Numbers are per 1,000 population and include Chapter 7 and Chapter 13 filings
Source: Federal Deposit Insurance Corporation, Regional Economic Conditions, March 20, 2014

EMPLOYMENT

Labor Force and Employment

Area	Civilian Labor Force			Workers Employed		
	Dec. 2012	Dec. 2013	% Chg.	Dec. 2012	Dec. 2013	% Chg.
City	150,567	150,127	-0.3	140,613	141,677	0.8
MSA[1]	544,227	543,640	-0.1	514,276	518,168	0.8
U.S.	154,904,000	154,408,000	-0.3	143,060,000	144,423,000	1.0

Note: Data is not seasonally adjusted and covers workers 16 years of age and older; (1) Metropolitan Statistical Area—see Appendix B for areas included
Source: Bureau of Labor Statistics, Local Area Unemployment Statistics

Unemployment Rate

Area	2013											
	Jan.	Feb.	Mar.	Apr.	May	Jun.	Jul.	Aug.	Sep.	Oct.	Nov.	Dec.
City	8.6	7.0	7.1	7.3	8.2	9.6	9.0	9.0	8.3	7.6	6.8	5.6
MSA[1]	7.2	5.9	6.0	6.2	7.0	7.9	7.2	7.2	6.7	6.3	5.7	4.7
U.S.	8.5	8.1	7.6	7.1	7.3	7.8	7.7	7.3	7.0	7.0	6.6	6.5

Note: Data is not seasonally adjusted and covers workers 16 years of age and older; All figures are percentages;
(1) Metropolitan Statistical Area—see Appendix B for areas included
Source: Bureau of Labor Statistics, Local Area Unemployment Statistics

Employment by Occupation

Occupation Classification	City (%)	MSA[1] (%)	U.S. (%)
Management, Business, Science, and Arts	39.6	34.6	36.0
Natural Resources, Construction, and Maintenance	7.0	11.4	9.1
Production, Transportation, and Material Moving	8.6	10.3	12.0
Sales and Office	20.3	24.2	24.7
Service	24.4	19.5	18.2

Note: Figures cover employed civilians 16 years of age and older; (1) Figures cover the New Orleans-Metairie, LA Metropolitan Statistical Area—see Appendix B for areas included
Source: U.S. Census Bureau, 2010-2012 American Community Survey 3-Year Estimates

Employment by Industry

| Sector | MSA[1] | | U.S. |
	Number of Employees	Percent of Total	Percent of Total
Construction	31,000	5.6	4.2
Education and Health Services	85,300	15.4	15.5
Financial Activities	27,700	5.0	5.7
Government	76,100	13.7	16.1
Information	8,500	1.5	1.9
Leisure and Hospitality	80,500	14.5	10.2
Manufacturing	29,500	5.3	8.7
Mining and Logging	7,700	1.4	0.6
Other Services	20,500	3.7	3.9
Professional and Business Services	72,900	13.2	13.7
Retail Trade	63,400	11.4	11.4
Transportation and Utilities	27,800	5.0	3.8
Wholesale Trade	23,200	4.2	4.2

Note: Figures cover non-farm employment as of December 2013 and are not seasonally adjusted;
(1) Metropolitan Statistical Area—see Appendix B for areas included
Source: Bureau of Labor Statistics, Current Employment Statistics, Employment, Hours, and Earnings

Occupations with Greatest Projected Employment Growth: 2010 – 2020

Occupation[1]	2010 Employment	2020 Projected Employment	Numeric Employment Change	Percent Employment Change
Registered Nurses	42,440	52,020	9,580	22.6
Personal Care Aides	19,240	27,870	8,630	44.8
Retail Salespersons	61,060	69,500	8,440	13.8
Home Health Aides	13,230	20,480	7,260	54.9
Cashiers	64,410	70,580	6,170	9.6
Food Preparation Workers	27,180	32,890	5,710	21.0
Laborers and Freight, Stock, and Material Movers, Hand	38,610	44,300	5,690	14.8
Waiters and Waitresses	32,700	38,160	5,460	16.7
Combined Food Preparation and Serving Workers, Including Fast Food	24,130	29,570	5,440	22.6
Office Clerks, General	35,500	40,430	4,930	13.9

Note: Projections cover Louisiana; (1) Sorted by numeric employment change
Source: www.projectionscentral.com, State Occupational Projections, 2010–2020 Long-Term Projections

Fastest Growing Occupations: 2010 – 2020

Occupation[1]	2010 Employment	2020 Projected Employment	Numeric Employment Change	Percent Employment Change
Home Health Aides	13,230	20,480	7,260	54.9
Veterinary Technologists and Technicians	1,000	1,540	530	53.2
Interpreters and Translators	560	850	290	51.7
Software Developers, Systems Software	900	1,320	420	46.4
Logisticians	870	1,270	400	45.7
Personal Care Aides	19,240	27,870	8,630	44.8
Market Research Analysts and Marketing Specialists	1,240	1,770	530	43.0
Helpers—Carpenters	1,820	2,570	750	41.3
Computer-Controlled Machine Tool Operators, Metal and Plastic	1,220	1,720	500	41.0
Meeting, Convention, and Event Planners	530	730	210	39.5

Note: Projections cover Louisiana; (1) Sorted by percent employment change and excludes occupations with numeric employment change less than 100
Source: www.projectionscentral.com, State Occupational Projections, 2010–2020 Long-Term Projections

Average Wages

Occupation	$/Hr.	Occupation	$/Hr.
Accountants and Auditors	32.37	Maids and Housekeeping Cleaners	9.58
Automotive Mechanics	18.87	Maintenance and Repair Workers	16.78
Bookkeepers	17.21	Marketing Managers	55.25
Carpenters	18.99	Nuclear Medicine Technologists	33.10
Cashiers	9.15	Nurses, Licensed Practical	19.23
Clerks, General Office	12.00	Nurses, Registered	31.68
Clerks, Receptionists/Information	11.82	Nursing Assistants	10.85
Clerks, Shipping/Receiving	15.83	Packers and Packagers, Hand	11.23
Computer Programmers	34.95	Physical Therapists	40.70
Computer Systems Analysts	31.13	Postal Service Mail Carriers	24.16
Computer User Support Specialists	22.56	Real Estate Brokers	n/a
Cooks, Restaurant	11.37	Retail Salespersons	12.89
Dentists	92.33	Sales Reps., Exc. Tech./Scientific	29.58
Electrical Engineers	49.53	Sales Reps., Tech./Scientific	37.42
Electricians	23.96	Secretaries, Exc. Legal/Med./Exec.	15.19
Financial Managers	45.67	Security Guards	13.36
First-Line Supervisors/Managers, Sales	19.27	Surgeons	n/a
Food Preparation Workers	8.63	Teacher Assistants	11.10
General and Operations Managers	52.05	Teachers, Elementary School	22.90
Hairdressers/Cosmetologists	12.66	Teachers, Secondary School	24.70
Internists	106.75	Telemarketers	14.81
Janitors and Cleaners	10.96	Truck Drivers, Heavy/Tractor-Trailer	19.65
Landscaping/Groundskeeping Workers	10.52	Truck Drivers, Light/Delivery Svcs.	16.09
Lawyers	60.17	Waiters and Waitresses	10.29

Note: Wage data covers the New Orleans-Metairie-Kenner, LA Metropolitan Statistical Area—see Appendix B for areas included. Hourly wages for elementary/secondary school teachers and teacher assistants were calculated by the editors from annual wage data assuming a 40 hour work week; n/a not available.
Source: Bureau of Labor Statistics, Metro Area Occupational Employment and Wage Estimates, May 2013

RESIDENTIAL REAL ESTATE

Building Permits

Area	Single-Family			Multi-Family			Total		
	2012	2013	Pct. Chg.	2012	2013	Pct. Chg.	2012	2013	Pct. Chg.
City	690	736	6.7	276	159	-42.4	966	895	-7.3
MSA[1]	2,015	2,441	21.1	278	175	-37.1	2,293	2,616	14.1
U.S.	518,695	620,802	19.7	310,963	370,020	19.0	829,658	990,822	19.4

Note: (1) Metropolitan Statistical Area—see Appendix B for areas included; figures represent new, privately-owned housing units authorized (unadjusted data); All permit data are based on estimates with imputation.
Source: U.S. Census Bureau, Manufacturing, Mining, and Construction Statistics, Building Permits, 2012, 2013

Homeownership Rate

Area	2006 (%)	2007 (%)	2008 (%)	2009 (%)	2010 (%)	2011 (%)	2012 (%)	2013 (%)
MSA[1]	70.3	67.8	68.0	68.2	66.9	63.9	62.4	61.4
U.S.	68.8	68.1	67.8	67.4	66.9	66.1	65.4	65.1

Note: (1) Figures cover the New Orleans-Metairie, LA Metropolitan Statistical Area—see Appendix B for areas included
Source: U.S. Census Bureau, Housing Vacancies and Homeownership Annual Statistics: 2013

Housing Vacancy Rates

Area	Gross Vacancy Rate[2] (%)			Year-Round Vacancy Rate[3] (%)			Rental Vacancy Rate[4] (%)			Homeowner Vacancy Rate[5] (%)		
	2011	2012	2013	2011	2012	2013	2011	2012	2013	2011	2012	2013
MSA[1]	10.7	13.6	13.3	10.3	13.4	12.7	13.1	15.9	11.1	2.1	2.9	1.9
U.S.	14.2	13.8	13.8	11.1	10.8	10.7	9.5	8.7	8.3	2.5	2.0	2.0

Note: (1) Figures cover the New Orleans-Metairie, LA Metropolitan Statistical Area—see Appendix B for areas included; (2) The percentage of the total housing inventory that is vacant; (3) The percentage of the housing inventory (excluding seasonal units) that is year-round vacant; (4) The percentage of rental inventory that is vacant for rent; (5) The percentage of homeowner inventory that is vacant for sale
Source: U.S. Census Bureau, Housing Vacancies and Homeownership Annual Statistics: 2013

TAXES

State Corporate Income Tax Rates

State	Tax Rate (%)	Income Brackets ($)	Num. of Brackets	Financial Institution Tax Rate (%)[a]	Federal Income Tax Ded.
Louisiana	4.0 - 8.0	25,000 - 200,001	5	4.0 - 8.0	Yes

Note: Tax rates as of January 1, 2014; (a) Rates listed are the corporate income tax rate applied to financial institutions or excise taxes based on income. Some states have other taxes based upon the value of deposits or shares.
Source: Federation of Tax Administrators, "State Corporate Income Tax Rates, 2014"

State Individual Income Tax Rates

State	Tax Rate (%)	Income Brackets ($)	Num. of Brackets	Personal Exempt. ($)[1] Single	Personal Exempt. ($)[1] Dependents	Fed. Inc. Tax Ded.
Louisiana	2.0 - 6.0	12,500 - 50,001 (b)	3	4,500 (k)	1,000	Yes

Note: Tax rates as of January 1, 2014; Local- and county-level taxes are not included; n/a not applicable; (1) Married joint filers generally receive double the single exemption; (b) For joint returns, taxes are twice the tax on half the couple's income; (k) The amounts reported for Louisiana are a combined personal exemption-standard deduction.
Source: Federation of Tax Administrators, "State Individual Income Tax Rates, 2014"

Various State and Local Tax Rates

State	State and Local Sales and Use (%)	State Sales and Use (%)	Gasoline[1] (¢/gal.)	Cigarette[2] ($/pack)	Spirits[3] ($/gal.)	Wine[4] ($/gal.)	Beer[5] ($/gal.)
Louisiana	8.75	4.00	20.00	0.360	2.50 (f)	0.11	0.32

Note: All tax rates as of January 1, 2014; (1) The American Petroleum Institute has developed a methodology for determining the average tax rate on a gallon of fuel. Rates may include any of the following: excise taxes, environmental fees, storage tank fees, other fees or taxes, general sales tax, and local taxes. In states where gasoline is subject to the general sales tax, or where the fuel tax is based on the average sale price, the average rate determined by API is sensitive to changes in the price of gasoline. States that fully or partially apply general sales taxes to gasoline: CA, CO, GA, IL, IN, MI, NY; (2) The federal excise tax of $1.0066 per pack and local taxes are not included; (3) Rates are those applicable to off-premise sales of 40% alcohol by volume (a.b.v.) distilled spirits in 750ml containers. Local excise taxes are excluded; (4) Rates are those applicable to off-premise sales of 11% a.b.v. non-carbonated wine in 750ml containers; (5) Rates are those applicable to off-premise sales of 4.7% a.b.v. beer in 12 ounce containers; (f) Different rates also applicable according to alcohol content, place of production, size of container, or place purchased (on- or off-premise or onboard airlines).
Source: Tax Foundation, 2014 Facts & Figures: How Does Your State Compare?

State Business Tax Climate Index Rankings

State	Overall Rank	Corporate Tax Index Rank	Individual Income Tax Index Rank	Sales Tax Index Rank	Unemployment Insurance Tax Index Rank	Property Tax Index Rank
Louisiana	33	17	25	50	4	24

Note: The index is a measure of how each state's tax laws affect economic performance. The lower the rank, the more favorable a state's tax system is for business. States without a given tax are given a ranking of 1. The scores/rankings for the District of Columbia do not affect other states. The 2014 index represents the tax climate as of July 1, 2013.
Source: Tax Foundation, State Business Tax Climate Index 2014

COMMERCIAL UTILITIES

Typical Monthly Electric Bills

Area	Commercial Service ($/month) 1,500 kWh	Commercial Service ($/month) 40 kW demand 14,000 kWh	Industrial Service ($/month) 1,000 kW demand 200,000 kWh	Industrial Service ($/month) 50,000 kW demand 15,000,000 kWh
City	162	1,415	22,201	1,449,742
Average[1]	197	1,636	25,662	1,485,307

Note: Based on total rates in effect July 1, 2013; (1) average based on 180 utilities surveyed
Source: Edison Electric Institute, Typical Bills and Average Rates Report, Summer 2013

TRANSPORTATION

Means of Transportation to Work

| Area | Car/Truck/Van | | Public Transportation | | | Bicycle | Walked | Other Means | Worked at Home |
	Drove Alone	Car-pooled	Bus	Subway	Railroad				
City	70.1	10.4	6.5	0.0	0.0	2.2	5.3	2.3	3.1
MSA[1]	78.9	10.5	2.6	0.0	0.0	0.9	2.6	2.0	2.5
U.S.	76.4	9.7	2.6	1.7	0.5	0.6	2.8	1.3	4.3

Note: Figures are percentages and cover workers 16 years of age and older; (1) Figures cover the New Orleans-Metairie, LA Metropolitan Statistical Area—see Appendix B for areas included
Source: U.S. Census Bureau, 2010-2012 American Community Survey 3-Year Estimates

Travel Time to Work

Area	Less Than 10 Minutes	10 to 19 Minutes	20 to 29 Minutes	30 to 44 Minutes	45 to 59 Minutes	60 to 89 Minutes	90 Minutes or More
City	10.9	35.5	24.9	18.2	4.5	4.2	1.9
MSA[1]	11.1	31.5	21.5	20.1	7.7	5.8	2.2
U.S.	13.5	29.8	20.9	20.1	7.5	5.6	2.5

Note: Figures are percentages and include workers 16 years old and over; (1) Figures cover the New Orleans-Metairie, LA Metropolitan Statistical Area—see Appendix B for areas included
Source: U.S. Census Bureau, 2010-2012 American Community Survey 3-Year Estimates

Travel Time Index

Area	1985	1990	1995	2000	2005	2010	2011
Urban Area[1]	1.21	1.21	1.22	1.22	1.22	1.20	1.20
Average[2]	1.09	1.14	1.16	1.19	1.23	1.18	1.18

Note: Travel Time Index—the ratio of travel time in the peak period to the travel time at free-flow conditions. For example, a value of 1.30 indicates a 20-minute free-flow trip takes 26 minutes in the peak. Free-flow speeds (60 mph on freeways and 35 mph on principal arterials) are used as the comparison threshold; (1) Covers the New Orleans LA urban area; (2) average of 498 urban areas
Source: Texas Transportation Institute, Urban Mobility Report 2012, December 2012

Public Transportation

Agency Name / Mode of Transportation	Vehicles Operated in Maximum Service	Annual Unlinked Passenger Trips (in thous.)	Annual Passenger Miles (in thous.)
New Orleans Regional Transit Authority (NORTA)			
Bus (purchased transportation)	79	16,388.0	56,846.4
Demand Response (purchased transportation)	32	195.7	1,344.8
Streetcar Rail (purchased transportation)	21	7,229.0	13,714.6

Source: Federal Transit Administration, National Transit Database, 2012

Air Transportation

Airport Name and Code / Type of Service	Passenger Airlines[1]	Passenger Enplanements	Freight Carriers[2]	Freight (lbs.)
New Orleans International (MSY)				
Domestic service (U.S. carriers - 2013)	31	4,551,002	16	42,174,851
International service (U.S. carriers - 2012)	11	5,230	3	59,332

Note: (1) Includes all U.S.-based major, minor and commuter airlines that carried at least one passenger during the year; (2) Includes all U.S.-based airlines and freight carriers that transported at least one lb. of freight during the year.
Source: Bureau of Transportation Statistics, The Intermodal Transportation Database, Air Carriers: T-100 Domestic Market (U.S. Carriers), 2013; Bureau of Transportation Statistics, The Intermodal Transportation Database, Air Carriers: T-100 International Market (U.S. Carriers), 2012

Other Transportation Statistics

Major Highways:	I-10; I-59
Amtrak Service:	Yes
Major Waterways/Ports:	Port of New Orleans; Mississippi River

Source: Amtrak.com; Google Maps

BUSINESSES

Major Business Headquarters

Company Name	Rankings	
	Fortune[1]	Forbes[2]
Entergy	261	-

Note: (1) Fortune 500—companies that produce a 10-K are ranked 1 to 500 based on 2012 revenue; (2) all private companies with at least $2 billion in annual revenue through the end of their most current fiscal year are ranked 1 to 224; companies listed are headquartered in the city; dashes indicate no ranking
Source: Fortune, "Fortune 500," May 20, 2013; Forbes, "America's Largest Private Companies," December 18, 2013

Minority Business Opportunity

New Orleans is home to one company which is on the *Black Enterprise* Bank 20 list (20 largest banks based on total assets, capital, deposits and loans, including mortgage-backed securities for the calendar year): **Liberty Bank and Trust Co.** (#4). Only commercial banks or savings and loans that are classified by the Federal Reserve as black institutions and have been fully operational for the previous calendar year were considered. *Black Enterprise, B.E. 100s, 2013*

New Orleans is home to two companies which are on the *Hispanic Business* 500 list (500 largest U.S. Hispanic-owned companies based on 2012 revenue): **Pan-American Life Insurance Group** (#15); **Atlantis International** (#184). Companies included must show at least 51 percent ownership by Hispanic U.S. citizens, and must maintain headquarters in one of the 50 states or Washington, D.C. *Hispanic Business, "Hispanic Business 500," June 20, 2013*

New Orleans is home to one company which is on the *Hispanic Business* Fastest-Growing 100 list (greatest sales growth from 2008 to 2012): **Pan-American Life Insurance Group** (#86). Companies included must show at least 51 percent ownership by Hispanic U.S. citizens, and must maintain headquarters in one of the 50 states or Washington, D.C. In addition, companies must have minimum revenues of $200,000 for calendar year 2008. *Hispanic Business, June20, 2013*

Minority- and Women-Owned Businesses

Group	All Firms		Firms with Paid Employees			
	Firms	Sales ($000)	Firms	Sales ($000)	Employees	Payroll ($000)
Asian	1,403	310,414	388	268,702	1,755	39,419
Black	7,843	497,070	391	345,949	4,728	104,339
Hispanic	1,103	107,771	137	77,257	970	23,102
Women	8,245	1,418,443	1,048	1,236,470	9,907	300,668
All Firms	27,165	28,788,251	6,587	27,896,926	136,637	6,059,640

Note: Figures cover firms located in the city; minority- and women-owned business are defined as firms in which the corresponding group own 51% or more of the stock or equity of the company
Source: U.S. Census Bureau, 2007 Economic Census, Survey of Business Owners (2012 Survey of Business Owners data will be released starting in June 2015)

**HOTELS &
CONVENTION
CENTERS**

Hotels/Motels

Area	5 Star		4 Star		3 Star		2 Star		1 Star		Not Rated	
	Num.	Pct.[3]	Num.	Pct.[3]	Num.	Pct.[3]	Num.	Pct.[3]	Num.	Pct.[3]	Num.	Pct.[3]
City[1]	0	0.0	24	10.4	89	38.5	91	39.4	6	2.6	21	9.1
Total[2]	142	0.9	1,005	6.0	5,147	30.9	8,578	51.4	408	2.4	1,397	8.4

Note: (1) Figures cover New Orleans and vicinity; (2) Figures cover all 100 cities in this book; (3) Percentage of hotels which have a given star rating; Star ratings are determined by expedia.com and offer an indication of the general quality of a particular hotel.
Source: expedia.com, April 7, 2014

The New Orleans-Metairie, LA metro area is home to one of the best hotels in the U.S. according to *Travel & Leisure*: **Windsor Court Hotel**. Criteria: service; location; rooms; food; and value. The list includes the top 200 hotels in the U.S. *Travel & Leisure, "T+L 500, The World's Best Hotels 2014"*

Major Convention Centers

Name	Overall Space (sq. ft.)	Exhibit Space (sq. ft.)	Meeting Space (sq. ft.)	Meeting Rooms
Ernest N. Morial Convention Center	3,000,000	1,100,000	n/a	n/a

Note: Table includes convention centers located in the New Orleans-Metairie, LA metro area; n/a not available
Source: Original research

Living Environment

COST OF LIVING

Cost of Living Index

Composite Index	Groceries	Housing	Utilities	Trans- portation	Health Care	Misc. Goods/ Services
98.4	97.9	95.1	91.3	100.0	103.2	102.1

Note: The Cost of Living Index measures regional differences in the cost of consumer goods and services, excluding taxes and non-consumer expenditures, for professional and managerial households in the top income quintile. It is based on more than 50,000 prices covering almost 60 different items for which prices are collected three times a year by chambers of commerce, economic development organizations or university applied economic centers in each participating urban area. The numbers shown should be read as a percentage above or below the national average of 100. For example, a value of 115.4 in the groceries column indicates that grocery prices are 15.4% higher than the national average. Small differences in the index numbers should not be interpreted as significant; Figures cover the New Orleans LA urban area.
Source: The Council for Community and Economic Research, ACCRA Cost of Living Index, 2013

Grocery Prices

Area[1]	T-Bone Steak ($/pound)	Frying Chicken ($/pound)	Whole Milk ($/half gal.)	Eggs ($/dozen)	Orange Juice ($/64 oz.)	Coffee ($/11.5 oz.)
City[2]	10.81	1.33	2.86	1.87	3.65	3.91
Avg.	10.19	1.28	2.34	1.81	3.48	4.39
Min.	8.56	0.94	1.44	1.19	2.78	3.40
Max.	14.82	2.28	3.56	3.73	6.23	7.32

Note: (1) Values for the local area are compared with the average, minimum and maximum values for all 327 areas in the Cost of Living Index; (2) Figures cover the New Orleans LA urban area; **T-Bone Steak** *(price per pound);* **Frying Chicken** *(price per pound, whole fryer);* **Whole Milk** *(half gallon carton);* **Eggs** *(price per dozen, Grade A, large);* **Orange Juice** *(64 oz. Tropicana or Florida Natural);* **Coffee** *(11.5 oz. can, vacuum-packed, Maxwell House, Hills Bros, or Folgers).*
Source: The Council for Community and Economic Research, ACCRA Cost of Living Index, 2013

Housing and Utility Costs

Area[1]	New Home Price ($)	Apartment Rent ($/month)	All Electric ($/month)	Part Electric ($/month)	Other Energy ($/month)	Telephone ($/month)
City[2]	277,938	861	-	97.49	54.79	24.59
Avg.	295,864	900	171.38	91.82	70.12	27.73
Min.	185,506	458	117.80	48.81	33.67	17.16
Max.	1,358,917	3,783	441.68	171.40	372.65	39.47

Note: (1) Values for the local area are compared with the average, minimum and maximum values for all 327 areas in the Cost of Living Index; (2) Figures cover the New Orleans LA urban area; **New Home Price** *(2,400 sf living area, 8,000 sf lot, in urban area with full utilities);* **Apartment Rent** *(950 sf 2 bedroom/1.5 or 2 bath, unfurnished, excluding all utilities except water);* **All Electric** *(average monthly cost for an all-electric home);* **Part Electric** *(average monthly cost for a part-electric home);* **Other Energy** *(average monthly cost for natural gas, fuel oil, coal, wood, and any other forms of energy except electricity);* **Telephone** *(price includes basic monthly rate for a private residential line plus additional local usage charges incurred by a family of four).*
Source: The Council for Community and Economic Research, ACCRA Cost of Living Index, 2013

Health Care, Transportation, and Other Costs

Area[1]	Doctor ($/visit)	Dentist ($/visit)	Optometrist ($/visit)	Gasoline ($/gallon)	Beauty Salon ($/visit)	Men's Shirt ($)
City[2]	77.67	103.40	77.06	3.30	37.45	32.69
Avg.	101.40	86.48	96.16	3.44	33.87	26.55
Min.	61.67	50.83	50.12	3.08	18.92	12.48
Max.	182.71	152.50	223.78	4.33	68.22	52.03

Note: (1) Values for the local area are compared with the average, minimum and maximum values for all 327 areas in the Cost of Living Index; (2) Figures cover the New Orleans LA urban area; **Doctor** *(general practitioners routine exam of an established patient);* **Dentist** *(adult teeth cleaning and periodic oral examination);* **Optometrist** *(full vision eye exam for established adult patient);* **Gasoline** *(one gallon regular unleaded, national brand, including all taxes, cash price at self-service pump if available);* **Beauty Salon** *(woman's shampoo, trim, and blow-dry);* **Men's Shirt** *(cotton/polyester dress shirt, pinpoint weave, long sleeves).*
Source: The Council for Community and Economic Research, ACCRA Cost of Living Index, 2013

HOUSING

House Price Index (HPI)

Area	National Ranking[2]	Quarterly Change (%)	One-Year Change (%)	Five-Year Change (%)
MSA[1]	137	-0.36	2.30	-0.81
U.S.[3]	–	1.20	7.69	4.18

Note: The HPI is a weighted repeat sales index. It measures average price changes in repeat sales or refinancings on the same properties. This information is obtained by reviewing repeat mortgage transactions on single-family properties whose mortgages have been purchased or securitized by Fannie Mae or Freddie Mac in January 1975; (1) New Orleans-Metairie, LA Metropolitan Statistical Area—see Appendix B for areas included; (2) Rankings are based on annual percentage change for all metro areas containing at least 15,000 transactions over the last 10 years and ranges from 1 to 283; (3) figures based on a weighted average of Census Division estimates using a seasonally adjusted, purchase-only index; all figures are for the period ending December 31, 2013
Source: Federal Housing Finance Agency, House Price Index, February 25, 2014

Median Single-Family Home Prices

Area	2011	2012	2013p	Percent Change 2012 to 2013
MSA[1]	153.0	156.2	164.7	5.4
U.S. Average	166.2	177.2	197.4	11.4

Note: Figures are median sales prices of existing single-family homes in thousands of dollars; (p) preliminary; n/a not available; (1) New Orleans-Metairie, LA Metropolitan Statistical Area—see Appendix B for areas included
Source: National Association of Realtors, Median Sales Price of Existing Single-Family Homes for Metropolitan Areas, 4th Quarter 2013

Qualifying Income Based on Median Sales Price of Existing Single-Family Homes

Area	With 5% Down ($)	With 10% Down ($)	With 20% Down ($)
MSA[1]	36,980	35,034	31,141
U.S. Average	45,395	43,006	38,228

Note: Figures are preliminary; Qualifying income is based on a mortgage rate of 4.4%. Monthly principal and interest payment is limited to 25% of income; n/a not available; (1) New Orleans-Metairie, LA Metropolitan Statistical Area—see Appendix B for areas included
Source: National Association of Realtors, Qualifying Income Based on Median Sales Price of Existing Single-Family Homes for Metropolitan Areas, 4th Quarter 2013

Median Apartment Condo-Coop Home Prices

Area	2011	2012	2013p	Percent Change 2012 to 2013
MSA[1]	167.6	186.7	187.3	0.3
U.S. Average	165.1	173.7	194.9	12.2

Note: Figures are median sales prices of existing apartment condo-coop homes in thousands of dollars; (p) preliminary; n/a not available; (1) New Orleans-Metairie, LA Metropolitan Statistical Area—see Appendix B for areas included
Source: National Association of Realtors, Median Sales Price of Existing Apartment Condo-Coop Homes for Metropolitan Areas, 4th Quarter 2013

Gross Monthly Rent

Area	Under $200	$200 -299	$300 -499	$500 -749	$750 -999	$1,000 -1,499	$1,500 and up	Median ($)
City	2.5	4.6	6.0	18.8	28.7	28.8	10.5	901
MSA[1]	1.7	3.0	5.6	20.7	31.0	28.9	8.9	898
U.S.	1.7	3.3	8.1	22.7	24.3	25.7	14.3	889

Note: Figures are percentages except for Median; Gross rent is the contract rent plus the estimated average monthly cost of utilities (electricity, gas, and water and sewer) and fuels (oil, coal, kerosene, wood, etc.) if these are paid by the renter (or paid for the renter by someone else); (1) Figures cover the New Orleans-Metairie, LA Metropolitan Statistical Area—see Appendix B for areas included
Source: U.S. Census Bureau, 2010-2012 American Community Survey 3-Year Estimates

Year Housing Structure Built

Area	2010 or Later	2000 -2009	1990 -1999	1980 -1989	1970 -1979	1960 -1969	1950 -1959	1940 -1949	Before 1940	Median Year
City	0.8	8.5	3.8	7.2	15.0	11.1	12.3	11.7	29.6	1957
MSA[1]	0.6	13.1	9.6	14.3	19.7	13.8	10.1	6.3	12.4	1974
U.S.	0.5	14.9	13.8	13.9	15.9	11.1	10.9	5.5	13.5	1976

Note: Figures are percentages except for Median Year; (1) Figures cover the New Orleans-Metairie, LA Metropolitan Statistical Area—see Appendix B for areas included
Source: U.S. Census Bureau, 2010-2012 American Community Survey 3-Year Estimates

HEALTH

Health Risk Data

Category	MSA[1] (%)	U.S. (%)
Adults aged 18–64 who have any kind of health care coverage	76.1	79.6
Adults who reported being in good or excellent health	80.7	83.1
Adults who are current smokers	22.8	19.6
Adults who are heavy drinkers[2]	7.9	6.1
Adults who are binge drinkers[3]	19.0	16.9
Adults who are overweight (BMI 25.0 - 29.9)	35.9	35.8
Adults who are obese (BMI 30.0 - 99.8)	28.7	27.6
Adults who participated in any physical activities in the past month	73.8	77.1
Adults 50+ who have ever had a sigmoidoscopy or colonoscopy	66.1	67.3
Women aged 40+ who have had a mammogram within the past two years	79.3	74.0
Men aged 40+ who have had a PSA test within the past two years	49.2	45.2
Adults aged 65+ who have had flu shot within the past year	66.4	60.1
Adults who always wear a seatbelt	95.7	93.8

Note: Data as of 2012 unless otherwise noted; (1) Figures cover the New Orleans-Metairie-Kenner, LA Metropolitan Statistical Area—see Appendix B for areas included; (2) Heavy drinkers are classified as males having more than two drinks per day or females having more than one drink per day; (3) Binge drinkers are classified as males having five or more drinks on one occasion or females having four or more drinks on one occasion
Source: Centers for Disease Control and Prevention, Behaviorial Risk Factor Surveillance System, SMART: Selected Metropolitan/Micropolitan Area Risk Trends, 2012

Chronic Health Indicators

Category	MSA[1] (%)	U.S. (%)
Adults who have ever been told they had a heart attack	4.4	4.5
Adults who have ever been told they had a stroke	3.1	2.9
Adults who have been told they currently have asthma	6.1	8.9
Adults who have ever been told they have arthritis	25.3	25.7
Adults who have ever been told they have diabetes[2]	12.3	9.7
Adults who have ever been told they had skin cancer	5.4	5.7
Adults who have ever been told they had any other types of cancer	5.7	6.5
Adults who have ever been told they have COPD	5.7	6.2
Adults who have ever been told they have kidney disease	1.7	2.5
Adults who have ever been told they have a form of depression	15.3	18.0

Note: Data as of 2012 unless otherwise noted; (1) Figures cover the New Orleans-Metairie-Kenner, LA Metropolitan Statistical Area—see Appendix B for areas included; (2) Figures do not include pregnancy-related, borderline, or pre-diabetes
Source: Centers for Disease Control and Prevention, Behaviorial Risk Factor Surveillance System, SMART: Selected Metropolitan/Micropolitan Area Risk Trends, 2012

Mortality Rates for the Top 10 Causes of Death in the U.S.

ICD-10[a] Sub-Chapter	ICD-10[a] Code	County[2]	U.S.
Malignant neoplasms	C00-C97	202.4	174.2
Ischaemic heart diseases	I20-I25	94.6	119.1
Other forms of heart disease	I30-I51	61.4	49.6
Chronic lower respiratory diseases	J40-J47	25.4	43.2
Cerebrovascular diseases	I60-I69	43.2	40.3
Organic, including symptomatic, mental disorders	F01-F09	26.2	30.5
Other degenerative diseases of the nervous system	G30-G31	21.6	26.3
Other external causes of accidental injury	W00-X59	25.4	25.1
Diabetes mellitus	E10-E14	25.1	21.3
Hypertensive diseases	I10-I15	64.6	18.8

(Age-Adjusted Mortality Rate[1] per 100,000 population)

Note: (a) ICD-10 = International Classification of Diseases 10th Revision; (1) Mortality rates are a three year average covering 2008-2010; (2) Figures cover Orleans Parish
Source: Centers for Disease Control and Prevention, National Center for Health Statistics. Compressed Mortality File 1999-2010 on CDC WONDER Online Database, released January 2013. Data are compiled from the Compressed Mortality File 1999-2010, Series 20 No. 2P, 2013.

Mortality Rates for Selected Causes of Death

ICD-10[a] Sub-Chapter	ICD-10[a] Code	County[2]	U.S.
Assault	X85-Y09	43.8	5.5
Diseases of the liver	K70-K76	15.4	12.4
Human immunodeficiency virus (HIV) disease	B20-B24	16.3	3.0
Influenza and pneumonia	J09-J18	12.8	16.4
Intentional self-harm	X60-X84	10.5	11.8
Malnutrition	E40-E46	*1.4	0.8
Obesity and other hyperalimentation	E65-E68	*1.1	1.6
Renal failure	N17-N19	24.4	13.6
Transport accidents	V01-V99	12.4	12.6
Viral hepatitis	B15-B19	2.3	2.2

(Age-Adjusted Mortality Rate[1] per 100,000 population)

Note: (a) ICD-10 = International Classification of Diseases 10th Revision; (1) Mortality rates are a three year average covering 2008-2010; (2) Figures cover Orleans Parish; (*) Unreliable data as per CDC
Source: Centers for Disease Control and Prevention, National Center for Health Statistics. Compressed Mortality File 1999-2010 on CDC WONDER Online Database, released January 2013. Data are compiled from the Compressed Mortality File 1999-2010, Series 20 No. 2P, 2013.

Health Insurance Coverage

Area	With Health Insurance	With Private Health Insurance	With Public Health Insurance	Without Health Insurance	Population Under Age 18 Without Health Insurance
City	80.8	52.4	36.4	19.2	5.5
MSA[1]	82.9	58.9	33.1	17.1	4.8
U.S.	84.9	65.4	30.4	15.1	7.5

Note: Figures are percentages that cover the civilian noninstitutionalized population; (1) Figures cover the New Orleans-Metairie, LA Metropolitan Statistical Area—see Appendix B for areas included
Source: U.S. Census Bureau, 2010-2012 American Community Survey 3-Year Estimates

Number of Medical Professionals

Area[1]	MDs[2]	DOs[2,3]	Dentists	Podiatrists	Chiropractors	Optometrists
Local (number)	2,546	47	220	14	25	23
Local (rate[4])	705.9	13.0	59.5	3.8	6.8	6.2
U.S. (rate[4])	267.6	19.6	61.7	5.6	24.7	14.5

Note: Data as of 2012 unless noted; (1) Local data covers Orleans Parish; (2) Data as of 2011; (3) Doctor of Osteopathic Medicine; (4) rate per 100,000 population
Source: Area Resource File (ARF) 2012-2013. U.S. Department of Health and Human Services, Health Resources and Services Administration, Bureau of Health Professions

Best Hospitals

According to *U.S. News,* the New Orleans-Metairie, LA metro area is home to one of the best hospitals in the U.S.: **Ochsner Medical Center** (8 specialties). The hospital listed was nationally ranked in at least one adult specialty. Only 147 hospitals nationwide were nationally ranked in one or more specialties. Eighteen hospitals in the U.S. made the Honor Roll by ranking near the top in at least six specialties.*U.S. News Online, "America's Best Hospitals 2013-14"*

EDUCATION

Public School District Statistics

District Name	Schls	Pupils	Pupil/ Teacher Ratio	Minority Pupils[1] (%)	Free Lunch Eligible[2] (%)	IEP[3] (%)
Orleans Parish	19	10,881	15.5	83.5	58.5	9.8
RSD-Algiers Charter Schools Assn	6	3,667	15.3	n/a	83.0	10.0
RSD-Knowledge is Power Program	6	2,462	17.9	98.3	88.7	10.6
RSD-Renew-Reinventing Education	5	2,190	37.7	n/a	91.6	10.7
Recovery School District-Lde	20	7,104	10.0	n/a	84.5	14.5

Note: Table includes school districts with 2,000 or more students; (1) Percentage of students that are not non-Hispanic white; (2) Percentage of students that are eligible for the free lunch program; (3) Percentage of students that have an Individualized Education Program.
Source: U.S. Department of Education, National Center for Education Statistics, Common Core of Data, Local Education Agency (School District) Universe Survey: School Year 2011-2012; U.S. Department of Education, National Center for Education Statistics, Common Core of Data, Public Elementary/Secondary School Universe Survey: School Year 2011-2012

Best High Schools

High School Name	Rank[1]	Grad. Rate[2] (%)	Coll.[3] (%)	AP/IB/ AICE Tests[4]	AP/IB/ AICE Score[5]	SAT Score[6]	ACT Score[6]
Benjamin Franklin H.S.	198	100	100	0.0	3.6	1882	27.0

Note: (1) Public schools are ranked from 1 to 2,000 based on the following self-reported statistics (with the corresponding weight used in calculating their overall score). Schools that were newly founded and did not have a graduating senior class in 2012 were excluded; (2) Four-year, on-time graduation rate (25%); (3) Percent of 2011 graduates who were accepted to college (25%); (4) AP/IB/AICE tests taken per student (25%); (5) Average AP/IB/AICE exam score (10%); (6) Average SAT and/or ACT score (10%); Percent of students enrolled in at least one AP/IB/AICE course (5%)—data not shown
Source: Newsweek and The Daily Beast, "America's Best High Schools 2013"

Highest Level of Education

Area	Less than H.S.	H.S. Diploma	Some College, No Deg.	Associate Degree	Bachelor's Degree	Master's Degree	Prof. School Degree	Doctorate Degree
City	15.9	24.4	22.3	4.4	19.1	7.8	3.9	2.2
MSA[1]	15.5	29.7	22.9	5.5	17.0	5.7	2.5	1.2
U.S.	14.1	28.3	21.3	7.8	18.0	7.5	1.9	1.2

Note: Figures cover persons age 25 and over; (1) Figures cover the New Orleans-Metairie, LA Metropolitan Statistical Area—see Appendix B for areas included
Source: U.S. Census Bureau, 2010-2012 American Community Survey 3-Year Estimates

Educational Attainment by Race

Area	High School Graduate or Higher (%)					Bachelor's Degree or Higher (%)				
	Total	White	Black	Asian	Hisp.[2]	Total	White	Black	Asian	Hisp.[2]
City	84.1	94.7	78.4	71.1	71.4	33.0	59.3	15.1	38.3	29.6
MSA[1]	84.5	88.9	78.5	72.8	71.3	26.3	32.1	14.7	35.6	19.7
U.S.	85.9	88.1	82.5	85.5	63.1	28.6	30.0	18.4	50.2	13.4

Note: Figures shown cover persons 25 years old and over; (1) Figures cover the New Orleans-Metairie, LA Metropolitan Statistical Area—see Appendix B for areas included; (2) People of Hispanic origin can be of any race
Source: U.S. Census Bureau, 2010-2012 American Community Survey 3-Year Estimates

School Enrollment by Grade and Control

Area	Preschool (%)		Kindergarten (%)		Grades 1 - 4 (%)		Grades 5 - 8 (%)		Grades 9 - 12 (%)	
	Public	Private	Public	Private	Public	Private	Public	Private	Public	Private
City	55.7	44.3	70.5	29.5	79.6	20.4	77.4	22.6	79.2	20.8
MSA[1]	54.2	45.8	72.6	27.4	77.5	22.5	75.8	24.2	75.0	25.0
U.S.	56.9	43.1	87.8	12.2	89.9	10.1	90.0	10.0	90.8	9.2

Note: Figures shown cover persons 3 years old and over; (1) Figures cover the New Orleans-Metairie, LA Metropolitan Statistical Area—see Appendix B for areas included
Source: U.S. Census Bureau, 2010-2012 American Community Survey 3-Year Estimates

Average Salaries of Public School Classroom Teachers

Area	2012-13		2013-14		Percent Change 2012-13 to 2013-14	Percent Change 2003-04 to 2013-14
	Dollars	Rank[1]	Dollars	Rank[1]		
Louisiana	51,381	25	52,259	24	1.71	37.8
U.S. Average	56,103	–	56,689	–	1.04	21.8

Note: (1) State rank ranges from 1 to 51 where 1 indicates highest salary.
Source: National Education Association, Rankings & Estimates: Rankings of the States 2013 and Estimates of School Statistics 2014, March 2014

Higher Education

Four-Year Colleges			Two-Year Colleges			Medical Schools[1]	Law Schools[2]	Voc/ Tech[3]
Public	Private Non-profit	Private For-profit	Public	Private Non-profit	Private For-profit			
3	7	0	1	0	1	2	2	5

Note: Figures cover institutions located within the city limits and include main campuses only; (1) includes schools accredited by the Liaison Committee on Medical Education and the American Osteopathic Association's Commission on Osteopathic College Accreditation; (2) includes ABA-accredited schools, schools with provisional ABA accreditation, and state accredited schools; (3) includes all schools with programs that are less than 2 years.
Source: National Center for Education Statistics, Integrated Postsecondary Education System (IPEDS), 2012-13; Association of American Medical Colleges, Member List, April 24, 2014; American Osteopathic Association, Member List, April 24, 2014; Law School Admission Council, Official Guide to ABA-Approved Law Schools Online, April 24, 2014; Wikipedia, List of Medical Schools in the United States, April 24, 2014; Wikipedia, List of Law Schools in the United States, April 24, 2014

According to U.S. News & World Report, the New Orleans-Metairie, LA metro area is home to one of the best national universities in the U.S.: **Tulane University** (#52). The indicators used to capture academic quality fall into a number of categories: assessment by administrators at peer institutions; retention of students; faculty resources; student selectivity; financial resources; alumni giving; high school counselor ratings of colleges; and graduation rate. U.S. News & World Report, "America's Best Colleges 2014"

According to U.S. News & World Report, the New Orleans-Metairie, LA metro area is home to one of the best liberal arts colleges in the U.S.: **Xavier University of Louisiana** (#161). The indicators used to capture academic quality fall into a number of categories: assessment by administrators at peer institutions; retention of students; faculty resources; student selectivity; financial resources; alumni giving; high school counselor ratings of colleges; and graduation rate. U.S. News & World Report, "America's Best Colleges 2014"

According to U.S. News & World Report, the New Orleans-Metairie, LA metro area is home to one of the top 100 law schools in the U.S.: **Tulane University** (#48). The rankings are based on a weighted average of 12 measures of quality: peer assessment score; assessment score by lawyers/judges; median LSAT scores; median undergrad GPA; acceptance rate; employment rates for graduates; placement success; bar passage rate; faculty resources; expenditures per student; student/faculty ratio; and library resources. U.S. News & World Report, "America's Best Graduate Schools, Law, 2014"

According to U.S. News & World Report, the New Orleans-Metairie, LA metro area is home to one of the top 100 business schools in the U.S.: **Tulane University (Freeman)** (#67). The rankings are based on a weighted average of the following nine measures: quality assessment; peer assessment; recruiter assessment; placement success; mean starting salary and bonus; student selectivity; mean GMAT and GRE scores; mean undergraduate GPA; and acceptance rate. U.S. News & World Report, "America's Best Graduate Schools, Business, 2014"

PRESIDENTIAL ELECTION

2012 Presidential Election Results

Area	Obama	Romney	Other
Orleans Parish	80.3	17.7	2.0
U.S.	51.0	47.2	1.8

Note: Results are percentages and may not add to 100% due to rounding
Source: Dave Leip's Atlas of U.S. Presidential Elections

EMPLOYERS

Major Employers

Company Name	Industry
Alton Ochsner Medical Foundation	Home health care services
Avondale Industries of New York	Barges, building and repair
Capital One, National Association	National commercial banks
Chevron USA	Filling stations, gasoline
Childrens Hospital	Childrens hospital
East Jefferson Hospital	General medical/surgical hospitals
Jazz Casino Company LJC	Casino hotel
Lockheed Martin Corporation	Tanks, standard or custom fabricated metal plate 0
Louisiana State University System	University
Medical Ctr of Louisiana at New Orleans	General medical/surgical hospitals
NASA George C Marshall Space Flight Ctr	Space flight operations
Ochsner Clinic Foundation	General medical/surgical hospitals
Ochsner Foundation Hospital	General medical/surgical hospitals
St Tammany Parish Hospital	General medical/surgical hospitals
Tulane University	Colleges/universities
United States Department of the Army	Army
United States Dept of Agriculture	Regulation of agricultural marketing
United States Postal Service	Us postal service
University Healthcare System	General medical/surgical hospitals
US Army Corps of Engineers	Army
West Jefferson Medical Center	General medical/surgical hospitals

Note: Companies shown are located within the New Orleans-Metairie, LA Metropolitan Statistical Area.
Source: Hoovers.com; Wikipedia

Best Companies to Work For

Ochsner Health System, headquartered in New Orleans, is among the "50 Best Employers for Workers Over 50." Criteria: recruiting practices; opportunities for training, education, and career development; workplace accommodations; alternative work options, such as flexible scheduling, job sharing, and phased retirement; employee health and pension benefits; and retiree benefits. Employers with at least 50 employees based in the U.S. are eligible, including for-profit companies, not-for-profit organizations, and government employers. *AARP, "2013 AARP Best Employers for Workers Over 50"*

PUBLIC SAFETY

Crime Rate

Area	All Crimes	Violent Crimes				Property Crimes		
		Murder	Forcible Rape	Robbery	Aggrav. Assault	Burglary	Larceny -Theft	Motor Vehicle Theft
City	4,587.5	53.2	37.5	293.5	431.0	943.3	2,218.7	610.4
Suburbs[1]	3,373.8	6.8	17.4	76.6	241.7	630.4	2,230.2	170.6
Metro[2]	3,734.8	20.6	23.4	141.1	298.0	723.5	2,226.8	301.4
U.S.	3,246.1	4.7	26.9	112.9	242.3	670.2	1,959.3	229.7

Note: Figures are crimes per 100,000 population; (1) All areas within the metro area that are located outside the city limits; (2) Figures cover the New Orleans-Metairie, LA Metropolitan Statistical Area—see Appendix B for areas included
Source: FBI Uniform Crime Reports, 2012

Hate Crimes

Area	Number of Quarters Reported	Race	Religion	Sexual Orientation	Ethnicity	Disability
				Bias Motivation		
City	2	1	0	1	0	0
U.S.	4	2,797	1,099	1,135	667	92

Source: Federal Bureau of Investigation, Hate Crime Statistics 2012

Identity Theft Consumer Complaints

Area	Complaints	Complaints per 100,000 Population	Rank[2]
MSA[1]	976	82.0	101
U.S.	290,056	91.8	-

Note: (1) Figures cover the New Orleans-Metairie, LA Metropolitan Statistical Area—see Appendix B for areas included; (2) Rank ranges from 1 to 377 where 1 indicates greatest number of identity theft complaints per 100,000 population
Source: Federal Trade Commission, Consumer Sentinel Network Data Book for January–December 2013

Fraud and Other Consumer Complaints

Area	Complaints	Complaints per 100,000 Population	Rank[2]
MSA[1]	4,809	404.2	110
U.S.	1,811,724	595.2	-

Note: (1) Figures cover the New Orleans-Metairie, LA Metropolitan Statistical Area—see Appendix B for areas included; (2) Rank ranges from 1 to 377 where 1 indicates greatest number of identity theft complaints per 100,000 population
Source: Federal Trade Commission, Consumer Sentinel Network Data Book for January–December 2013

RECREATION

Culture

Dance[1]	Theatre[1]	Instrumental Music[1]	Vocal Music[1]	Series and Festivals	Museums and Art Galleries[2]	Zoos and Aquariums[3]
1	5	3	2	4	46	2

Note: (1) Number of professional performing groups; (2) Based on organizations with primary SIC code 8412; (3) AZA-accredited
Source: The Grey House Performing Arts Directory, 2013; Association of Zoos & Aquariums, AZA Member Zoos & Aquariums, April 2014; www.AccuLeads.com, May 1, 2014

Professional Sports Teams

Team Name	League	Year Established
New Orleans Pelicans	National Basketball Association (NBA)	2002
New Orleans Saints	National Football League (NFL)	1967

Note: Includes teams located in the New Orleans-Metairie, LA Metropolitan Statistical Area.
Source: Wikipedia, Major Professional Sports Teams of the United States and Canada

CLIMATE

Average and Extreme Temperatures

Temperature	Jan	Feb	Mar	Apr	May	Jun	Jul	Aug	Sep	Oct	Nov	Dec	Yr.
Extreme High (°F)	83	85	89	92	96	100	101	102	101	92	87	84	102
Average High (°F)	62	65	71	78	85	89	91	90	87	80	71	64	78
Average Temp. (°F)	53	56	62	69	75	81	82	82	79	70	61	55	69
Average Low (°F)	43	46	52	59	66	71	73	73	70	59	51	45	59
Extreme Low (°F)	14	19	25	32	41	50	60	60	42	35	24	11	11

Note: Figures cover the years 1948-1990
Source: National Climatic Data Center, International Station Meteorological Climate Summary, 9/96

Average Precipitation/Snowfall/Humidity

Precip./Humidity	Jan	Feb	Mar	Apr	May	Jun	Jul	Aug	Sep	Oct	Nov	Dec	Yr.
Avg. Precip. (in.)	4.7	5.6	5.2	4.7	4.4	5.4	6.4	5.9	5.5	2.8	4.4	5.5	60.6
Avg. Snowfall (in.)	Tr	Tr	Tr	0	0	0	0	0	0	0	0	Tr	Tr
Avg. Rel. Hum. 6am (%)	85	84	84	88	89	89	91	91	89	87	86	85	88
Avg. Rel. Hum. 3pm (%)	62	59	57	57	58	61	66	65	63	56	59	62	60

Note: Figures cover the years 1948-1990; Tr = Trace amounts (<0.05 in. of rain; <0.5 in. of snow)
Source: National Climatic Data Center, International Station Meteorological Climate Summary, 9/96

Weather Conditions

Temperature			Daytime Sky			Precipitation		
10°F & below	32°F & below	90°F & above	Clear	Partly cloudy	Cloudy	0.01 inch or more precip.	0.1 inch or more snow/ice	Thunder-storms
0	13	70	90	169	106	114	1	69

Note: Figures are average number of days per year and cover the years 1948-1990
Source: National Climatic Data Center, International Station Meteorological Climate Summary, 9/96

HAZARDOUS WASTE

Superfund Sites

New Orleans has one hazardous waste site on the EPA's Superfund Final National Priorities List: **Agriculture Street Landfill.** *U.S. Environmental Protection Agency, Final National Priorities List, April 26, 2014*

AIR & WATER QUALITY

Air Quality Index

Area	Percent of Days when Air Quality was...[2]					AQI Statistics[2]	
	Good	Moderate	Unhealthy for Sensitive Groups	Unhealthy	Very Unhealthy	Maximum	Median
MSA[1]	61.4	31.8	6.0	0.8	0.0	200	45

Note: (1) Data covers the New Orleans-Metairie, LA Metropolitan Statistical Area—see Appendix B for areas included; (2) Based on 365 days with AQI data in 2013. Air Quality Index (AQI) is an index for reporting daily air quality. EPA calculates the AQI for five major air pollutants regulated by the Clean Air Act: ground-level ozone, particle pollution (aka particulate matter), carbon monoxide, sulfur dioxide, and nitrogen dioxide. The AQI runs from 0 to 500. The higher the AQI value, the greater the level of air pollution and the greater the health concern. There are six AQI categories: "Good" AQI is between 0 and 50. Air quality is considered satisfactory; "Moderate" AQI is between 51 and 100. Air quality is acceptable; "Unhealthy for Sensitive Groups" When AQI values are between 101 and 150, members of sensitive groups may experience health effects; "Unhealthy" When AQI values are between 151 and 200 everyone may begin to experience health effects; "Very Unhealthy" AQI values between 201 and 300 trigger a health alert; "Hazardous" AQI values over 300 trigger warnings of emergency conditions (not shown).
Source: U.S. Environmental Protection Agency, Air Quality Index Report, 2013

Air Quality Index Pollutants

Area	Percent of Days when AQI Pollutant was...[2]					
	Carbon Monoxide	Nitrogen Dioxide	Ozone	Sulfur Dioxide	Particulate Matter 2.5	Particulate Matter 10
MSA[1]	0.0	1.4	32.1	14.0	52.1	0.5

Note: (1) Data covers the New Orleans-Metairie, LA Metropolitan Statistical Area—see Appendix B for areas included; (2) Based on 365 days with AQI data in 2013. The Air Quality Index (AQI) is an index for reporting daily air quality. EPA calculates the AQI for five major air pollutants regulated by the Clean Air Act: ground-level ozone, particle pollution (also known as particulate matter), carbon monoxide, sulfur dioxide, and nitrogen dioxide. The AQI runs from 0 to 500. The higher the AQI value, the greater the level of air pollution and the greater the health concern.
Source: U.S. Environmental Protection Agency, Air Quality Index Report, 2013

Air Quality Trends: Ozone

	2003	2004	2005	2006	2007	2008	2009	2010	2011	2012
MSA[1]	0.083	0.076	0.076	0.078	0.079	0.070	0.073	0.075	0.073	0.072

Note: (1) Data covers the New Orleans-Metairie, LA Metropolitan Statistical Area—see Appendix B for areas included. The values shown are the composite ozone concentration averages among trend sites based on the highest fourth daily maximum 8-hour concentration in parts per million. These trends are based on sites having an adequate record of monitoring data during the trend period. Data from exceptional events are included.
Source: U.S. Environmental Protection Agency, Air Quality Monitoring Information, "Air Quality Trends by City, 2000-2012"

Maximum Air Pollutant Concentrations: Particulate Matter, Ozone, CO and Lead

	Particulate Matter 10 (ug/m³)	Particulate Matter 2.5 Wtd AM (ug/m³)	Particulate Matter 2.5 24-Hr (ug/m³)	Ozone (ppm)	Carbon Monoxide (ppm)	Lead (ug/m³)
MSA[1] Level	63	12.9	19	0.077	n/a	0.04
NAAQS[2]	150	15	35	0.075	9	0.15
Met NAAQS[2]	Yes	Yes	Yes	No	n/a	Yes

Note: (1) Data covers the New Orleans-Metairie, LA Metropolitan Statistical Area—see Appendix B for areas included; Data from exceptional events are included; (2) National Ambient Air Quality Standards; ppm = parts per million; ug/m³ = micrograms per cubic meter; n/a not available.
Concentrations: Particulate Matter 10 (coarse particulate)—highest second maximum 24-hour concentration; Particulate Matter 2.5 Wtd AM (fine particulate)—highest weighted annual mean concentration; Particulate Matter 2.5 24-Hour (fine particulate)—highest 98th percentile 24-hour concentration; Ozone—highest fourth daily maximum 8-hour concentration; Carbon Monoxide—highest second maximum non-overlapping 8-hour concentration; Lead—maximum running 3-month average
Source: U.S. Environmental Protection Agency, Air Quality Monitoring Information, "Air Quality Statistics by City, 2012"

Maximum Air Pollutant Concentrations: Nitrogen Dioxide and Sulfur Dioxide

	Nitrogen Dioxide AM (ppb)	Nitrogen Dioxide 1-Hr (ppb)	Sulfur Dioxide AM (ppb)	Sulfur Dioxide 1-Hr (ppb)	Sulfur Dioxide 24-Hr (ppb)
MSA[1] Level	8	46	n/a	217	n/a
NAAQS[2]	53	100	30	75	140
Met NAAQS[2]	Yes	Yes	n/a	No	n/a

Note: (1) Data covers the New Orleans-Metairie, LA Metropolitan Statistical Area—see Appendix B for areas included; Data from exceptional events are included; (2) National Ambient Air Quality Standards; ppm = parts per million; ug/m³ = micrograms per cubic meter; n/a not available.
Concentrations: Nitrogen Dioxide AM—highest arithmetic mean concentration; Nitrogen Dioxide 1-Hr—highest 98th percentile 1-hour daily maximum concentration; Sulfur Dioxide AM—highest annual mean concentration; Sulfur Dioxide 1-Hr—highest 99th percentile 1-hour daily maximum concentration; Sulfur Dioxide 24-Hr—highest second maximum 24-hour concentration
Source: U.S. Environmental Protection Agency, Air Quality Monitoring Information, "Air Quality Statistics by City, 2012"

Drinking Water

Water System Name	Pop. Served	Primary Water Source Type	Violations[1] Health Based	Violations[1] Monitoring/ Reporting
New Orleans Algiers Water Works	58,240	Surface	0	0
New Orleans Carrollton WW	291,044	Surface	0	0

Note: (1) Based on violation data from January 1, 2013 to December 31, 2013 (includes unresolved violations from earlier years)
Source: U.S. Environmental Protection Agency, Office of Ground Water and Drinking Water, Safe Drinking Water Information System (based on data extracted February 10, 2014)

Orlando, Florida

Background

The city of Orlando can hold the viewer aghast with its rampant tourism. Not only is it home to the worldwide tourist attractions of Disney World, Epcot Center, and Sea World, but Orlando and its surrounding area also host such institutions as Medieval Times Dinner & Tournament, Wet-N-Wild, Ripley's Believe It or Not Museum, and Sleuths Mystery Dinner Shows, as well as thousands of T-shirt, citrus, and shell vendor shacks.

Orlando has its own high-tech corridor because of the University of Central Florida's College of Optics and Photonics. Manufacturing, government, business service, health care, high-tech research, and tourism supply significant numbers of jobs.

Aside from the glitz that pumps most of the money into its economy, Orlando is also called "The City Beautiful." The warm climate and abundant rains produce a variety of lush flora and fauna, which provide an attractive setting for the many young people who settle in the area, spending their nights in the numerous jazz clubs, restaurants, and pubs along Orange Avenue and Church Street. Stereotypically the land of orange juice and sunshine, Orlando is becoming the city for young job seekers and professionals.

This genteel setting is a far cry from Orlando's rough-and-tumble origins. The city started out as a makeshift campsite in the middle of a cotton plantation. The Civil War and devastating rains brought an end to the cotton trade, and its settlers turned to raising livestock. The transition to a new livelihood did not insure any peace and serenity. Rustling, chaotic brawls, and senseless shootings were everyday occurrences. Martial law had to be imposed by a few large ranch families.

The greatest impetus toward modernity came from the installation of Cape Canaveral, 50 miles away, which brought missile assembly and electronic component production to the area, and Walt Disney World, created out of 27,000 acres of unexplored swampland, which set the tone for Orlando as a tourist-oriented economy.

Orlando is also a major film production site. Nickelodeon, the world's largest teleproduction studio dedicated to children's television programming, is based there, as are the Golf Channel, Sun Sports, House of Moves, and the America Channel. Disney's biggest theme-park competitor, Universal Studios, is also based in Orlando.

The city is also home to a variety of arts and entertainment facilities, including the Amway Arena, part of the Orlando Centroplex, home to the NBA's Orlando Magic and the Orlando Sharks of the Indoor Soccer League. The city vies with Chicago and Las Vegas for hosting the most convention attendees in the United States.

Orlando is surrounded by many lakes. Its relative humidity remains high year-round, though in winter the humidity may drop. June through September is the rainy season, during which time, scattered afternoon thunderstorms are an almost daily occurrence. During the winter months rainfall is light and the afternoons are most pleasant. Hurricanes are not usually considered a threat to the area.

Rankings

General Rankings

- Orlando was identified as one of America's fastest-growing cities in terms of population and economy by *Forbes*. The area ranked #9 out of 20. The 100 most populous metro areas in the U.S. were evaluated on the following criteria: estimated population growth; job growth; gross metropolitan product growth; unemployment; median salaries for college-educated workers. *Forbes, "America's Fastest-Growing Cities 2014," February 14, 2014*

- Orlando was identified as one of America's fastest-growing major metropolitan areas in terms of population by CNNMoney.com. The area ranked #4 out of 10. Criteria: population growth between July 2012 and July 2013. *CNNMoney, "10 Fastest-Growing Cities," March 28, 2014*

- Orlando was selected as one of "America's Favorite Cities." The city ranked #15 in the "Quality of Life and Visitor Experience: Cleanliness" category. Respondents to an online survey were asked to rate 35 top urban destinations in the U.S. from a visitor's perspective. Criteria: cleanliness. *Travel + Leisure, "America's Favorite Cities 2013"*

- Orlando was selected as one of "America's Favorite Cities." The city ranked #29 in the "Type of Trip: Gay-friendly" category. Respondents to an online survey were asked to rate 35 top urban destinations in the U.S. from a visitor's perspective. Criteria: gay-friendly. *Travel + Leisure, "America's Favorite Cities 2013"*

- The U.S. Conference of Mayors and Waste Management sponsor the City Livability Awards Program. The awards recognize and honor mayors for exemplary leadership in developing and implementing programs that improve the quality of life in America's cities. Orlando received an Outstanding Achievement Award in the large cities category. *U.S. Conference of Mayors, "2012 City Livability Awards"*

Business/Finance Rankings

- Orlando was the #10-ranked city for savers, according to the finance site GoBankingRates, which considered the prospects for savers in a tough savings economy by looking for higher interest yields, lower taxes, more jobs with higher incomes, and less expensive housing costs. *www.gobankingrates.com, "Best Cities for Saving Money," February 24, 2014*

- The editors of *Kiplinger's Personal Finance Magazine* named Orlando to their list of ten of the best metro areas for start-ups. Criteria included a well-educated workforce and low living costs for self-employed people, as measured by the Council for Community and Economic Research, as well as areas with lots of start-up investment dollars and low business costs. *www.kiplinger.com, "10 Great Cities for Starting a Business," January 2013*

- In order to help veterans transition from the military to civilian life, USAA and Hiring Our Heroes worked with Sperlings's BestPlaces to develop a list of the major metropolitan areas where military-skills-related employment is strongest. Criteria included job prospects, unemployment, number of government jobs, recent job growth, accessible health resources, and colleges and universities. Metro areas with a violent crime rate or high cost of living were excluded. At #9, the Orlando metro area made the top ten. *www.usaa.com, "2013 Best Places for Veterans: Jobs," November 2013*

- The finance website Wall St. Cheat Sheet reported on the prospects for high-wage job creation in the nation's largest metro areas over the next five years and ranked them accordingly, drawing on in-depth analysis by CareerBuilder and Economic Modeling Specialists International (EMSI). The Orlando metro area placed #7 on the Wall St. Cheat Sheet list. *wallstcheatsheet.com, "Top 10 Cities for High-Wage Job Growth," December 8, 2013*

- Looking at February 2012–2013, 24/7 Wall Street's analysts focused on metro areas where jobs were being added at a faster rate than the labor force was growing to identify the metro areas with the biggest real declines in unemployment. The #7 metro area for gains posted in employment was the Orlando metro area. *247wallst.com, "Cities Where Unemployment Has Fallen the Most," April 16, 2013*

- Based on a minimum of 500 social media reviews per metro area, the employment opinion group Glassdoor surveyed 50 of the largest U.S. metro areas on measures including compensation and benefits, satisfaction with management, business outlook, and number of employers hiring. The Orlando metro area was ranked #6 in overall employee satisfaction. *www.glassdoor.com, "Employment Satisfaction Report Card by City," June 21, 2013*

- In its Competitive Alternatives report, consulting firm KPMG analyzed the 27 largest metropolitan statistical areas according to 26 cost components (such as taxes, labor costs, and utilities) and 30 non-cost-related variables (such as crime rates and number of universities). The business website 24/7 Wall Street examined the KPMG findings, adding to the mix current unemployment rates, GDP, median income, and employment decline during the last recession and "projected" recovery. It identified the Orlando metro area as #3 among the ten best American cities for business. *247wallst.com, "Best American Cities for Business," April 4, 2012*

- Orlando was ranked #22 out of 100 metro areas in terms of economic performance (#1 = best) during the recession and recovery from trough quarter through the second quarter of 2013. Criteria: percent change in employment; percentage point change in unemployment rate; percent change in gross metropolitan product; percent change in House Price Index. *Brookings Institution, MetroMonitor: Tracking Economic Recession and Recovery in America's 100 Largest Metropolitan Areas, September 2013*

- Orlando was identified as one of America's most frugal metro areas by *Coupons.com*. The city ranked #2 out of 25. Criteria: online coupon usage. *Coupons.com, "Top 25 Most Frugal Cities of 2012," February 19, 2013*

- Orlando was identified as one of America's most frugal metro areas by *Coupons.com*. The city ranked #1 out of 25. Criteria: Grocery IQ and coupons.com mobile app usage. *Coupons.com, "Top 25 Most On-the-Go Frugal Cities of 2012," February 19, 2013*

- Orlando was identified as one of the top 25 U.S. cities with the most credit card debt by credit reporting bureau Experian. The city was ranked #25. *Experian, March 4, 2011*

- Orlando was identified as one of the uhappiest cities to work in by CareerBliss.com, an online community for career advancement. The city ranked #2 out of 10. Criteria: independent company reviews from employees all over the country on: relationship with their boss and co-workers; work environment; job resources; compensation; growth opportunities; company culture; company reputation; daily tasks; job control over work performed on a daily basis. *CareerBliss.com, "Top 10 Happiest and Unhappiest Cities to Work in 2014," February 10, 2014*

- The Orlando metro area appeared on the Milken Institute "2013 Best Performing Cities" list. Rank: #98 out of 200 large metro areas. Criteria: job growth; wage and salary growth; high-tech output growth. *Milken Institute, "Best-Performing Cities 2013," December 2013*

- *Forbes* ranked the 200 most populous metro areas in the U.S. in terms of the "Best Places for Business and Careers." The Orlando metro area was ranked #90. Criteria: costs (business and living); job growth (past and projected); income growth; educational attainment (college and high school); projected economic growth; cultural and recreational opportunities; net migration patterns; number of highly ranked colleges. *Forbes, "The Best Places for Business and Careers," August 7, 2013*

Children/Family Rankings

- Orlando was selected as one of the best cities for families to live by *Parenting* magazine. The city ranked #59 out of 100. Criteria: education; health; community; *Parenting's* Culture & Charm Index. *Parenting.com, "The 2012 Best Cities for Families List"*

Culture/Performing Arts Rankings

- Orlando was selected as one of "America's Favorite Cities." The city ranked #34 in the "Culture: Museum/Galleries" category. Respondents to an online survey were asked to rate 35 top urban destinations in the U.S. from a visitor's perspective. Criteria: number and quality of museums and galleries. *Travelandleisure.com, "America's Favorite Cities 2013"*

Dating/Romance Rankings

- Of the 100 U.S. cities surveyed by *Men's Health* in its quest to identify the nation's best cities for dating and forming relationships, Orlando was ranked #4 for online dating (#1 = best). *Men's Health, "The Best and Worst Cities for Online Dating," January 30, 2013*

- Orlando was selected as one of the most romantic cities in America by Amazon.com. The city ranked #6 of 20. Criteria: cities with 100,000 or more residents were ranked on their per capita sales of romance novels and relationship books, romantic comedy movies, romantic music, and sexual wellness products. *Amazon.com, "Top 20 Most Romantic Cities in America," February 3, 2014*

Education Rankings

- *Men's Health* ranked 100 U.S. cities in terms of their education levels. Orlando was ranked #53 (#1 = most educated city). Criteria: high school graduation rates; school enrollment; educational attainment; number of households who have outstanding student loans; number of households whose members have taken adult-education courses. *Men's Health, "Where School Is In: The Most and Least Educated Cities," September 12, 2011*

- Orlando was selected as one of the most well-read cities in America by Amazon.com. The city ranked #5 of 20. Cities with populations greater than 100,000 were evaluated based on per capita sales of books, magazines and newspapers. *Amazon.com, "The 20 Most Well-Read Cities in America," April 28, 2013*

Environmental Rankings

- The Orlando metro area came in at #333 for the relative comfort of its climate on Sperling's list of "chill cities," as measured by the Sperling Heat Index. All 361 metro areas are included. Criteria included daytime high temperatures, nighttime low temperatures, dew point, and relative humidity at the high temperatures. *www.bertsperling.com, "Sperling's Chill Cities," July 18, 2013*

- Sperling's BestPlaces assessed 379 metropolitan areas of the United States for the likelihood of dangerously extreme weather events or earthquakes. In general the Southeast and South-Central regions have the highest risk of weather extremes and earthquakes, while the Pacific Northwest enjoys the lowest risk. Of the least risky metropolitan areas, the Orlando metro area was ranked #341. *www.bestplaces.net, "Safest Places from Natural Disasters," April 2011*

- Orlando was identified as one of North America's greenest metropolitan areas. The area ranked #18. The Green City Index is comprised of 31 indicators, and scores cities across nine categories: carbon dioxide; energy; land use; buildings; transport; water; waste; air quality; environmental governance. The 27 largest metropolitan areas in the U.S. and Canada were considered. *Economist Intelligence Unit, sponsored by Siemens, "U.S. and Canada Green City Index, 2011"*

- Orlando was selected as one of 22 "Smarter Cities" for energy by the Natural Resources Defense Council. Criteria: investment in green power; energy efficiency measures; conservation. *Natural Resources Defense Council, "2010 Smarter Cities," July 19, 2010*

- The Orlando metro area was selected as one of "America's Cleanest Cities" by *Forbes*. The metro area ranked #4 out of 10. Criteria: toxic releases; air and water quality; per capita spending on Superfund site cleanup. *Forbes.com, "America's Cleanest Cities 2011," March 11, 2011*

- Orlando was highlighted as one of the top 25 cleanest metro areas for year-round particle pollution (Annual PM 2.5) in the U.S. during 2008 through 2010. The area ranked #25. *American Lung Association, State of the Air 2012*

Food/Drink Rankings

- *Men's Health* ranked 100 major U.S. cities in terms of alcohol intoxication. Orlando ranked #33 (#1 = most sober).Criteria: binge drinking; alcohol-related traffic accidents, arrests, and fatalities. *Men's Health, "The Drunkest Cities in America," November 19, 2013*

Health/Fitness Rankings

- For each of the 50 most populous metro areas in the United States, the American College of Sports Medicine's American Fitness Index evaluated infrastructure, community assets, and policies that encourage healthy and fit lifestyles, including preventive health behaviors, levels of chronic disease conditions, health care access, and community resources and policies that support physical activity. The Orlando metro area ranked #34 for "community fitness." Personal health indicators were considered as well as community and environmental indicators. *www.americanfitnessindex.org, "ACSM American Fitness Index Health and Community Fitness Status of the 50 Largest Metropolitan Areas," May 2013*

- Orlando was identified as a "2013 Spring Allergy Capital." The area ranked #86 out of 100. Three groups of factors were used to identify the most severe cities for people with allergies during the spring season: annual pollen levels; medicine utilization; access to board-certified allergists. *Asthma and Allergy Foundation of America, "Spring Allergy Capitals 2013"*

- Orlando was identified as a "2013 Fall Allergy Capital." The area ranked #79 out of 100. Three groups of factors were used to identify the most severe cities for people with allergies during the fall season: annual pollen levels; medicine utilization; access to board-certified allergists. *Asthma and Allergy Foundation of America, "Fall Allergy Capitals 2013"*

- Orlando was identified as a "2013 Asthma Capital." The area ranked #62 out of the nation's 100 largest metropolitan areas. Twelve factors were used to identify the most challenging places to live for people with asthma: estimated prevalence; self-reported prevalence; crude death rate for asthma; annual pollen score; annual air quality; public smoking laws; number of board-certified asthma specialists; school inhaler access laws; rescue medication use; controller medication use; uninsured rate; poverty rate. *Asthma and Allergy Foundation of America, "Asthma Capitals 2013"*

- *Men's Health* ranked 100 major U.S. cities in terms of the best and worst cities for men. Orlando ranked #36. Criteria: thirty-three data points were examined covering health, fitness, and quality of life. *Men's Health, "The Best & Worst Cities for Men 2014," December 6, 2013*

- The Orlando metro area appeared in the 2013 Gallup-Healthways Well-Being Index. The area ranked #62 out of 189. The Gallup-Healthways Well-Being Index score is an average of six sub-indexes, which individually examine life evaluation, emotional health, work environment, physical health, healthy behaviors, and access to basic necessities. Results are based on telephone interviews conducted as part of the Gallup-Healthways Well-Being Index survey January 2–December 29, 2012, and January 2–December 30, 2013, with a random sample of 531,630 adults, aged 18 and older, living in metropolitan areas in the 50 U.S. states and the District of Columbia. *Gallup-Healthways, "State of American Well-Being," March 25, 2014*

- The Orlando metro area was identified as one of "America's Most Stressful Cities" by *Sperling's BestPlaces*. The metro area ranked #6 out of 50. Criteria: unemployment rate; suicide rate; commute time; mental health; poor rest; alcohol use; violent crime rate; property crime rate; cloudy days annually. *Sperling's BestPlaces, www.BestPlaces.net, "Stressful Cities 2012"*

- *Men's Health* ranked 100 U.S. cities in terms of their activity levels. Orlando was ranked #48 (#1 = most active city). Criteria: where and how often residents exercise; percentage of households that watch more than 15 hours of cable television a week and buy more than 11 video games a year; death rate from deep-vein thrombosis, a condition linked to sitting for extended periods of time. *Men's Health, "Where Sit Happens: The Most and Least Active Cities in America," June 20, 2011*

- Orlando was selected as one of the "20 Most Livable U.S. Cities for Wheelchair Users" by the Christopher & Dana Reeve Foundation. The city ranked #9. Criteria: Medicaid eligibility and spending; access to physicians and rehabilitation facilities; access to fitness facilities and recreation; access to paratransit; percentage of people living with disabilities who are employed; clean air; climate. *Christopher & Dana Reeve Foundation, "20 Most Livable U.S. Cities for Wheelchair Users," July 26, 2010*

Real Estate Rankings

- On the list compiled by Penske Truck Rental, the Orlando metro area was named the #4 moving destination in 2013, based on one-way consumer truck rental reservations made through Penske's website and reservations call center. *blog.gopenske.com, "Penske Truck Rental's 2013 Top Moving Destinations List," January 22, 2014*

- The Orlando metro area was identified as #2 among the ten housing markets with the highest percentage of distressed property sales, based on the findings of the housing data website RealtyTrac. Criteria included being sold "short"—for less than the outstanding mortgage balance—or in a foreclosure auction, income and poverty figures, and unemployment data. *247wallst.com, "Cities Selling the Most Distressed Homes," January 23, 2014*

- The Orlando metro area was identified as one of the top 20 housing markets to invest in for 2014 by *Forbes*. The area ranked #8. Criteria: high population and job growth; relatively low home prices which are below equilibrium home price (EHP). The EHP is what the average price for a market should be, if speculation, weird distortions in local income, and other factors (like the housing collapse) weren't present in the market. *Forbes.com, "Best Buy Cities: Where to Invest in Housing in 2014," December 25, 2013*

- TheStreet.com ranked the housing market in the nation's five warmest cities. Orlando ranked #3. Criteria: mean daily temperature from December to February (1981–2010); the median asking price of homes; and housing supply. *TheStreet.com, "Warm Weather Cities with Blistering-Hot Housing Markets," March 11, 2013*

- Orlando was identified as one of the "Top Turnaround Housing Markets for 2012." The area ranked #3 out of 10. Criteria: year-over-year median home price appreciation; year-over-year median inventory age; year-over-year inventory reduction. *AOL Real Estate, "Top Turnaround Housing Markets for 2012," February 4, 2012*

- Orlando was ranked #43 out of 283 metro areas in terms of house price appreciation in 2013 (#1 = highest rate). *Federal Housing Finance Agency, House Price Index, 4th Quarter 2013*

- The Orlando metro area was identified as one of the 20 best housing markets in the U.S. in 2013. The area ranked #12 out of 173 markets with a home price appreciation of 19.8%. Criteria: year-over-year change of median sales price of existing single-family homes between the 4th quarter of 2012 and the 4th quarter of 2013. *National Association of Realtors®, Median Sales Price of Existing Single-Family Homes for Metropolitan Areas, 4th Quarter 2013*

- Orlando was ranked #127 out of 224 metro areas in terms of housing affordability in 2013 by the National Association of Home Builders (#1 = most affordable). The NAHB-Wells Fargo Housing Opportunity Index (HOI) for a given area is defined as the share of homes sold in that area that would have been affordable to a family earning the local median income, based on standard mortgage underwriting criteria. *National Association of Home Builders®, NAHB-Wells Fargo Housing Opportunity Index, 4th Quarter 2013*

- Orlando was selected as one of the best college towns for renters by ApartmentRatings.com." The area ranked #62 out of 87. Overall satisfaction ratings were ranked using thousands of user submitted scores for hundreds of apartment complexes located in cities and towns that are home to the 100 largest four-year institutions in the U.S. *ApartmentRatings.com, "2011 College Town Renter Satisfaction Rankings"*

- The nation's largest metro areas were analyzed in terms of the percentage of households entering some stage of foreclosure in 2013. The Orlando metro area ranked #3 out of 10 (#1 = highest foreclosure rate). *RealtyTrac, "2013 Year-End U.S. Foreclosure Market Report™," January 16, 2014*

- The nation's largest metro areas were analyzed in terms of the best places to buy foreclosures in 2013. The Orlando metro area ranked #9 out of 20. Criteria: RealtyTrac scored all metro areas with a population of 500,000 or more by summing up four numbers: months' supply of foreclosure inventory; percentage of foreclosure sales; foreclosure discount; percentage increase in foreclosure activity in 2012. *RealtyTrac, "2012 Year-End Metropolitan Foreclosure Market Report," January 28, 2013*

- The Orlando metro area was identified as one of the 10 best U.S. markets to invest in single-family homes as rental properties by HomeVestors and Local Market Monitor. The area ranked #8. Criteria: risk-return premium relative to national average. *HomeVestors and Local Market Monitor, "Year-End Top 10 Real Estate Markets," December 20, 2013*

Safety Rankings

- Allstate ranked the 200 largest cities in America in terms of driver safety. Orlando ranked #153. Allstate researchers analyzed internal property damage claims over a two-year period from January 2010 to December 2011. A weighted average of the two-year numbers determined the annual percentages. *Allstate, "Allstate America's Best Drivers Report®, August 27, 2013"*

- Orlando was identified as one of the most dangerous cities in America by *The Business Insider.* Criteria: cities with 100,000 residents or more were ranked by violent crime rate in 2011. Violent crimes include for murder, rape, robbery, and aggravated assault. The city ranked #24 out of 25. *The Business Insider, "The 25 Most Dangerous Cities in America," November 4, 2012*

- The National Insurance Crime Bureau ranked 380 metro areas in the U.S. in terms of per capita rates of vehicle theft. The Orlando metro area ranked #108 (#1 = highest rate). Criteria: number of vehicle theft offenses per 100,000 inhabitants in 2012. *National Insurance Crime Bureau, "Hot Spots 2012," June 26, 2013*

- The Orlando metro area was identified as one of the most dangerous metro areas for pedestrians by Transportation for America. The metro area ranked #1 out of 52 metro areas with over 1 million residents. Criteria: area's population divided by the number of pedestrian fatalities in that area. *Transportation for America, "Dangerous by Design 2011"*

Seniors/Retirement Rankings

- From its Best Cities for Successful Aging indexes, the Milken Institute generated rankings for metropolitan areas, weighing data in eight categories—general indicators, health care, wellness, living arrangements, transportation and general accessibility, financial well-being, education and employment, and community participation. The Orlando metro area was ranked #77 overall in the large metro area category. *Milken Institute, "Best Cities for Successful Aging," July 2012*

- Bankers Life and Casualty Company, in partnership with Sperling's BestPlaces, ranked the nation's 50 largest metro areas in terms of the "Best U.S. Cities for Seniors." The Orlando metro area ranked #46. Criteria: healthcare; transportation; housing; environment; economy; health and longevity; social and spiritual life; crime. *Bankers Life and Casualty Company, Center for a Secure Retirement, "Best U.S. Cities for Seniors 2011," September 2011*

- Orlando was identified as one of the most popular places to retire by *Topretirements.com.* The list reflects the 100 cities (out of 900+ total cities reviewed) that visitors to the website are most interested in for retirement. *Topretirements.com, "Most Popular Places to Retire for 2014," February 25, 2014*

Sports/Recreation Rankings

- The sports site Bleacher Report named Orlando as one of the nation's top ten golf cities. Criteria included the concentration of public and private golf courses in a given city and the favored locations of PGA tour events. *BleacherReport.com, "Top 10 U.S. Cities for Golf," September 16, 2013*

- Orlando appeared on the *Sporting News* list of the "Best Sports Cities" for 2011. The area ranked #34 out of 271. Criteria: the magazine takes a 12-month snapshot of each city's sports, putting a heavy premium on regular-season won-lost records (from the most recently completed season). Other criteria include: playoff berths, bowl appearances and tournament bids; championships; applicable power ratings; quality of competition; overall fan fervor (measured in part by attendance); abundance of teams (rewarding quality over quantity); stadium and arena quality; ticket availability and prices; franchise ownership; and marquee appeal of athletes. *Sporting News, "Best Sports Cities 2011," October 4, 2011*

- Orlando appeared on the *Sporting News* list of the "Best Sports Cities" for 2011. The area ranked #34 out of 271. Criteria: a 12-month snapshot of regular-season won-lost records (from the most recently completed season). Other criteria include: playoff berths, bowl appearances and tournament bids; championships; applicable power ratings; quality of competition; overall fan fervor (measured in part by attendance); abundance of teams (quality over quantity); stadium and arena quality; ticket availability and prices; franchise ownership; and marquee appeal of athletes. *Sporting News, "Best Sports Cities 2011," October 4, 2011*

- Orlando was selected as one of the most playful cities in the U.S. by KaBOOM! The organization's Playful City USA initiative honors cities and towns across the nation for a vision, plan and commitment to creating an agenda for play. Criteria: creating a local play commission or task force; designing an annual action plan for play; conducting a play space audit; outlining a financial investment in play for the current fiscal year; and proclaiming and celebrating an annual "play day." *KaBOOM! National Campaign for Play, "2013 Playful City USA Communities"*

- Orlando was chosen as one of America's best cities for bicycling. The city ranked #49 out of 50. Criteria: robust cycling infrastructure; vibrant bike culture. The editors only considered cities with populations of 95,000 or more. *Bicycling, "America's Top 50 Bike-Friendly Cities," May 23, 2012*

- The Orlando was selected as one of the best metro areas for golf in America by *Golf Digest*. The Orlando area was ranked #6 out of 20. Criteria: climate; cost of public golf; quality of public golf; accessibility. *Golf Digest, "The Top 20 Cities for Golf," October 2011*

Transportation Rankings

- Orlando appeared on *Trapster.com's* list of the 10 most-active U.S. cities for speed traps. The city ranked #7 of 10. *Trapster.com* is a community platform accessed online and via smartphone app that alerts drivers to traps, hazards and other traffic issues nearby. *Trapster.com, "Speeders Beware: Cities With the Most Speed Traps," February 10, 2012*

- Orlando was identified as one of America's worst cities for speed traps by the National Motorists Association. The city ranked #3 out of 25. Criteria: speed trap locations per 100,000 residents. *National Motorists Association, September 2011*

Women/Minorities Rankings

- *Women's Health* examined U.S. cities and identified the 100 best cities for women. Orlando was ranked #52. Criteria: 30 categories were examined from obesity and breast cancer rates to commuting times and hours spent working out. *Women's Health, "Best Cities for Women 2012"*

- Orlando was selected as one of the gayest cities in America by *The Advocate*. The city ranked #13 out of 15. This year's criteria include points for a city's LGBT elected officials (and fractional points for the state's elected officials), points for the percentage of the population comprised by lesbian-coupled households, a point for a gay rodeo association, points for bars listed in *Out* magazine's 200 Best Bars list, a point per women's college, and points for concert performances by Mariah Carey, Pink, Lady Gaga, or the Jonas Brothers. The raw score is divided by the population to provide a ranking based on a per capita LGBT quotient. *The Advocate, "2014's Gayest Cities in America" January 6, 2014*

- The Orlando metro area appeared on *Forbes'* list of the "Best Cities for Minority Entrepreneurs." The area ranked #13 out of 10. Criteria: 52 metropolitan statistical areas were examined. For each ethnicity (African Americans, Asians and Hispanics), the editors measured housing affordability, population growth, income growth, and entrepreneurship (per capita self-employment). *Forbes, "Best Cities for Minority Entrepreneurs," March 23, 2011*

Miscellaneous Rankings

- The watchdog site Charity Navigator conducts an annual study of charities in the nation's major markets both to analyze statistical differences in their financial, accountability, and transparency practices and to track year-to-year variations in individual communities. The Orlando metro area was ranked #29 among the 30 metro markets. *www.charitynavigator.org, "Metro Market Study 2013," June 1, 2013*

- Market analyst Scarborough Research surveyed adults who had done volunteer work over the previous 12 months to find out where volunteers are concentrated. The Orlando metro area made the list for highest volunteer participation. *Scarborough Research, "Salt Lake City, UT; Minneapolis, MN; and Des Moines, IA Lend a Helping Hand," November 27, 2012*

- Orlando appeared on *Travel + Leisure's* list of America's least attractive people. Criteria: cities were selected by readers in their annual America's Favorite Cities survey. The city ranked #8 out of 10. *Travel + Leisure, "America's Most and Least Attractive People," November 2013*

- *Men's Health* ranked 100 U.S. cities by their level of sadness. Orlando was ranked #82 (#1 = saddest city). Criteria: suicide rates; unemployment rates; percentage of households that use antidepressants; percent of population who report feeling blue all or most of the time. *Men's Health, "Frown Towns," November 28, 2011*

- Scarborough Research, a leading market research firm, identified the top local markets for lottery ticket purchasers. The Orlando DMA (Designated Market Area) ranked in the top 13 with 48% of adults 18+ reporting that they purchased lottery tickets in the past 30 days. *Scarborough Research, January 30, 2012*

- The Orlando metro area was selected as one of "The Best U.S. Cities for Bargain Shopping" by *Forbes*. The area ranked #1 out of 10. Criteria: number of outlet stores; gross leasable retail space in major malls; low consumer price index; low sales tax rate. Indicators were examined in the nation's 50 largest metropolitan areas. *Forbes, "The Best U.S. Cities for Bargain Shopping," January 20, 2012*

- Mars Chocolate North America, the makers of COMBOS®, in partnership with Sperling's BestPlaces, ranked 50 major metro areas in terms of their "manliness." The Orlando metro area ranked #28. Criteria: number of professional sports teams; number of nearby NASCAR tracks and racing events; manly lifestyle; concentration of manly retail stores; manly occupations per capita; salty snack sales; "Board of Manliness" rankings. *Mars Chocolate North America, "America's Manliest Cities 2012"*

- The National Alliance to End Homelessness ranked the 100 most populous metro areas in terms the rate of homelessness. The Orlando metro area ranked #17. Criteria: number of homeless people per 10,000 population in 2011. *National Alliance to End Homelessness, The State of Homelessness in America 2012*

- The financial education website CreditDonkey compiled a list of the ten "best" cities of the future, based on percentage of housing built in 1990 or later, population change since 2010, and construction jobs as a percentage of population. Also considered were two more futuristic criteria: number of DeLorean cars available for purchase and number of spaceport companies and proposed spaceports. Orlando was scored #4. *www.creditDonkey.com, "In the Future, Almost All of America's 'Best' Cities Will Be on the West Coast, Report Says," February 14, 2014*

Business Environment

CITY FINANCES

City Government Finances

Component	2011 ($000)	2011 ($ per capita)
Total Revenues	754,895	3,312
Total Expenditures	702,130	3,081
Debt Outstanding	1,088,776	4,777
Cash and Securities[1]	1,482,744	6,506

Note: (1) Cash and security holdings of a government at the close of its fiscal year, including those of its dependent agencies, utilities, and liquor stores.
Source: U.S Census Bureau, State & Local Government Finances 2011

City Government Revenue by Source

Source	2011 ($000)	2011 ($ per capita)
General Revenue		
From Federal Government	38,432	169
From State Government	50,691	222
From Local Governments	68,523	301
Taxes		
Property	124,609	547
Sales and Gross Receipts	59,205	260
Personal Income	0	0
Corporate Income	0	0
Motor Vehicle License	0	0
Other Taxes	65,924	289
Current Charges	154,430	678
Liquor Store	0	0
Utility	81	0
Employee Retirement	31,297	137

Source: U.S Census Bureau, State & Local Government Finances 2011

City Government Expenditures by Function

Function	2011 ($000)	2011 ($ per capita)	2011 (%)
General Direct Expenditures			
Air Transportation	0	0	0.0
Corrections	0	0	0.0
Education	0	0	0.0
Employment Security Administration	0	0	0.0
Financial Administration	39,996	175	5.7
Fire Protection	86,359	379	12.3
General Public Buildings	6,549	29	0.9
Governmental Administration, Other	49,912	219	7.1
Health	0	0	0.0
Highways	43,741	192	6.2
Hospitals	0	0	0.0
Housing and Community Development	15,130	66	2.2
Interest on General Debt	36,497	160	5.2
Judicial and Legal	3,736	16	0.5
Libraries	0	0	0.0
Parking	15,302	67	2.2
Parks and Recreation	63,161	277	9.0
Police Protection	123,547	542	17.6
Public Welfare	0	0	0.0
Sewerage	66,404	291	9.5
Solid Waste Management	22,752	100	3.2
Veterans' Services	0	0	0.0
Liquor Store	0	0	0.0
Utility	0	0	0.0
Employee Retirement	40,846	179	5.8

Source: U.S Census Bureau, State & Local Government Finances 2011

DEMOGRAPHICS

Population Growth

Area	1990 Census	2000 Census	2010 Census	Population Growth (%) 1990-2000	Population Growth (%) 2000-2010
City	161,172	185,951	238,300	15.4	28.2
MSA[1]	1,224,852	1,644,561	2,134,411	34.3	29.8
U.S.	248,709,873	281,421,906	308,745,538	13.2	9.7

Note: (1) Figures cover the Orlando-Kissimmee-Sanford, FL Metropolitan Statistical Area—see Appendix B for areas included
Source: U.S. Census Bureau, Census 1990, 2000, 2010

Household Size

Area	Persons in Household (%) One	Two	Three	Four	Five	Six	Seven or More	Average Household Size
City	36.3	33.5	14.4	9.9	3.7	1.3	0.7	2.42
MSA[1]	25.9	35.2	16.6	13.3	5.9	2.0	1.0	2.80
U.S.	27.6	33.5	15.7	13.2	6.1	2.4	1.5	2.63

Note: (1) Figures cover the Orlando-Kissimmee-Sanford, FL Metropolitan Statistical Area—see Appendix B for areas included
Source: U.S. Census Bureau, 2010-2012 American Community Survey 3-Year Estimates

Race

Area	White Alone[2] (%)	Black Alone[2] (%)	Asian Alone[2] (%)	AIAN[3] Alone[2] (%)	NHOPI[4] Alone[2] (%)	Other Race Alone[2] (%)	Two or More Races (%)
City	58.3	29.2	3.4	0.3	0.1	6.1	2.7
MSA[1]	72.4	16.2	4.0	0.3	0.1	4.2	2.9
U.S.	74.0	12.6	4.9	0.8	0.2	4.7	2.8

Note: (1) Figures cover the Orlando-Kissimmee-Sanford, FL Metropolitan Statistical Area—see Appendix B for areas included; (2) Alone is defined as not being in combination with one or more other races; (3) American Indian and Alaska Native; (4) Native Hawaiian and Other Pacific Islander
Source: U.S. Census Bureau, 2010-2012 American Community Survey 3-Year Estimates

Hispanic or Latino Origin

Area	Total (%)	Mexican (%)	Puerto Rican (%)	Cuban (%)	Other (%)
City	26.7	2.9	13.3	1.8	8.7
MSA[1]	26.1	3.2	13.1	2.0	7.7
U.S.	16.6	10.7	1.6	0.6	3.7

Note: Persons of Hispanic or Latino origin can be of any race; (1) Figures cover the Orlando-Kissimmee-Sanford, FL Metropolitan Statistical Area—see Appendix B for areas included
Source: U.S. Census Bureau, 2010-2012 American Community Survey 3-Year Estimates

Segregation

Type	Segregation Indices[1] 1990	2000	2010	2010 Rank[2]	Percent Change 1990-2000	Percent Change 1990-2010	Percent Change 2000-2010
Black/White	59.1	55.9	50.7	69	-3.2	-8.4	-5.2
Asian/White	29.4	35.4	33.9	81	6.0	4.6	-1.4
Hispanic/White	29.2	38.7	40.2	64	9.5	11.0	1.5

Note: All figures cover the Metropolitan Statistical Area—see Appendix B for areas included; Figures are based on an analysis of 1990, 2000, and 2010 Census Decennial Census tract data by William H. Frey, Brookings Institution and the University of Michigan Social Science Data Analysis Network. In this analysis all racial groups (whites, blacks, and asians) are non-Hispanic members of those races. Hispanics are shown as a separate category;
(1) Segregation Indices are Dissimilarity Indices that measure the degree to which the minority group is distributed differently than whites across census tracts. They range from 0 (complete integration) to 100 (complete segregation) where the value indicates the percentage of the minority group that needs to move to be distributed exactly like whites; (2) Ranges from 1 (most segregated) to 102 (least segregated); n/a not available.
Source: www.CensusScope.org

Ancestry

Area	German	Irish	English	American	Italian	Polish	French[2]	Scottish	Dutch
City	8.4	7.0	5.7	6.7	4.1	1.4	1.6	1.2	0.6
MSA[1]	10.9	8.9	7.6	8.3	5.6	2.2	2.3	1.6	1.0
U.S.	15.2	11.1	8.2	7.2	5.6	3.1	2.8	1.7	1.4

Note: Figures are the percentage of the total population reporting a particular ancestry. The nine most commonly reported ancestries in the U.S. are shown. Figures include multiple ancestries (e.g. if a person reported being Irish and Italian, they were included in both columns); (1) Figures cover the Orlando-Kissimmee-Sanford, FL Metropolitan Statistical Area—see Appendix B for areas included; (2) Excludes Basque
Source: U.S. Census Bureau, 2010-2012 American Community Survey 3-Year Estimates

Foreign-Born Population

Area	Percent of Population Born in								
	Any Foreign Country	Mexico	Asia	Europe	Carribean	South America	Central America[2]	Africa	Canada
City	18.9	1.3	2.6	1.3	6.5	5.5	0.8	0.6	0.3
MSA[1]	16.2	1.3	2.8	1.7	4.9	3.7	0.9	0.5	0.4
U.S.	13.0	3.7	3.7	1.6	1.2	0.9	1.0	0.5	0.3

Note: (1) Figures cover the Orlando-Kissimmee-Sanford, FL Metropolitan Statistical Area—see Appendix B for areas included; (2) Excludes Mexico.
Source: U.S. Census Bureau, 2010-2012 American Community Survey 3-Year Estimates

Marital Status

Area	Never Married	Now Married[2]	Separated	Widowed	Divorced
City	43.3	34.9	3.6	5.1	13.0
MSA[1]	34.2	45.9	2.7	5.5	11.7
U.S.	32.4	48.4	2.2	6.0	11.0

Note: Figures are percentages and cover the population 15 years of age and older; (1) Figures cover the Orlando-Kissimmee-Sanford, FL Metropolitan Statistical Area—see Appendix B for areas included; (2) Excludes separated
Source: U.S. Census Bureau, 2010-2012 American Community Survey 3-Year Estimates

Age

Area	Percent of Population									Median Age
	Under Age 5	Age 5–19	Age 20–34	Age 35–44	Age 45–54	Age 55–64	Age 65–74	Age 75–84	Age 85+	
City	7.3	16.9	29.7	14.9	12.9	8.7	5.1	3.1	1.2	32.4
MSA[1]	6.0	20.0	22.0	13.8	14.3	11.2	7.1	4.0	1.6	36.4
U.S.	6.4	20.1	20.5	13.1	14.3	12.2	7.3	4.2	1.8	37.3

Note: (1) Figures cover the Orlando-Kissimmee-Sanford, FL Metropolitan Statistical Area—see Appendix B for areas included
Source: U.S. Census Bureau, 2010-2012 American Community Survey 3-Year Estimates

Gender

Area	Males	Females	Males per 100 Females
City	118,191	125,704	94.0
MSA[1]	1,066,934	1,112,486	95.9
U.S.	153,276,055	158,333,314	96.8

Note: (1) Figures cover the Orlando-Kissimmee-Sanford, FL Metropolitan Statistical Area—see Appendix B for areas included
Source: U.S. Census Bureau, 2010-2012 American Community Survey 3-Year Estimates

Religious Groups by Family

Area	Catholic	Baptist	Non-Den.	Methodist[2]	Lutheran	LDS[3]	Pentecostal	Presbyterian[4]	Muslim[5]	Judaism
MSA[1]	13.2	7.0	5.7	3.0	0.9	1.0	3.2	1.4	1.3	0.3
U.S.	19.1	9.3	4.0	4.0	2.3	2.0	1.9	1.6	0.8	0.7

Note: Figures are the number of adherents as a percentage of the total population; (1) Figures cover the Orlando-Kissimmee-Sanford, FL Metropolitan Statistical Area—see Appendix B for areas included; (2) Methodist/Pietist; (3) Latter Day Saints; (4) Reformed; (5) Figures are estimates
Source: Association of Statisticians of American Religious Bodies, 2010 U.S. Religion Census: Religious Congregations & Membership Study

Religious Groups by Tradition

Area	Catholic	Evangelical Protestant	Mainline Protestant	Other Tradition	Black Protestant	Orthodox
MSA[1]	13.2	17.8	4.8	3.3	1.2	0.3
U.S.	19.1	16.2	7.3	4.3	1.6	0.3

Note: Figures are the number of adherents as a percentage of the total population; (1) Figures cover the Orlando-Kissimmee-Sanford, FL Metropolitan Statistical Area—see Appendix B for areas included
Source: Association of Statisticians of American Religious Bodies, 2010 U.S. Religion Census: Religious Congregations & Membership Study

ECONOMY

Gross Metropolitan Product

Area	2011	2012	2013	2014	Rank[2]
MSA[1]	101.5	106.1	109.8	115.6	30

Note: Figures are in billions of dollars; (1) Figures cover the Orlando-Kissimmee-Sanford, FL Metropolitan Statistical Area—see Appendix B for areas included; (2) Rank is based on 2014 data and ranges from 1 to 363
Source: The United States Conference of Mayors, U.S. Metro Economies: Outlook—Gross Metropolitan Product, with Metro Employment Projections, November 2013

Economic Growth

Area	2011 (%)	2012 (%)	2013 (%)	2014 (%)	Rank[2]
MSA[1]	1.8	3.0	2.2	3.3	64
U.S.	1.6	2.5	1.7	2.5	–

Note: Figures are real gross metropolitan product (GMP) growth rates and represent annual average percent change; (1) Figures cover the Orlando-Kissimmee-Sanford, FL Metropolitan Statistical Area—see Appendix B for areas included; (2) Rank is based on 2013 data and ranges from 1 to 363
Source: The United States Conference of Mayors, U.S. Metro Economies: Outlook—Gross Metropolitan Product, with Metro Employment Projections, November 2013

Metropolitan Area Exports

Area	2007	2008	2009	2010	2011	2012	Rank[2]
MSA[1]	3,045.1	3,388.0	2,947.1	3,453.6	3,230.0	3,850.6	64

Note: Figures are in millions of dollars; (1) Figures cover the Orlando-Kissimmee-Sanford, FL Metropolitan Statistical Area—see Appendix B for areas included; (2) Rank is based on 2012 data and ranges from 1 to 369
Source: U.S. Department of Commerce, International Trade Administration, Office of Trade & Industry Information, Manufacturing & Services, data extracted April 1, 2014

INCOME

Income

Area	Per Capita ($)	Median Household ($)	Average Household ($)
City	24,936	41,266	58,471
MSA[1]	24,156	47,228	64,869
U.S.	27,385	51,771	71,579

Note: (1) Figures cover the Orlando-Kissimmee-Sanford, FL Metropolitan Statistical Area—see Appendix B for areas included
Source: U.S. Census Bureau, 2010-2012 American Community Survey 3-Year Estimates

Household Income Distribution

Area	Percent of Households Earning							
	Under $15,000	$15,000 -24,999	$25,000 -34,999	$35,000 -49,999	$50,000 -74,999	$75,000 -99,000	$100,000 -149,999	$150,000 and up
City	15.4	14.2	12.8	16.0	19.2	8.1	8.3	5.8
MSA[1]	12.4	12.0	12.5	15.4	19.1	11.1	10.7	6.8
U.S.	13.1	11.0	10.5	13.7	18.1	11.9	12.5	9.1

Note: (1) Figures cover the Orlando-Kissimmee-Sanford, FL Metropolitan Statistical Area—see Appendix B for areas included
Source: U.S. Census Bureau, 2010-2012 American Community Survey 3-Year Estimates

Poverty Rate

Area	All Ages	Under 18 Years Old	18 to 64 Years Old	65 Years and Over
City	20.0	31.8	17.1	14.1
MSA[1]	15.9	22.6	14.8	9.0
U.S.	15.7	22.2	14.6	9.3

Note: Figures are percentage of people whose income during the past 12 months was below the poverty level; (1) Figures cover the Orlando-Kissimmee-Sanford, FL Metropolitan Statistical Area—see Appendix B for areas included
Source: U.S. Census Bureau, 2010-2012 American Community Survey 3-Year Estimates

Personal Bankruptcy Filing Rate

Area	2008	2009	2010	2011	2012	2013
Orange County	3.83	6.51	7.70	6.36	5.42	5.04
U.S.	3.53	4.61	4.97	4.37	3.76	3.29

Note: Numbers are per 1,000 population and include Chapter 7 and Chapter 13 filings
Source: Federal Deposit Insurance Corporation, Regional Economic Conditions, March 20, 2014

EMPLOYMENT

Labor Force and Employment

Area	Civilian Labor Force			Workers Employed		
	Dec. 2012	Dec. 2013	% Chg.	Dec. 2012	Dec. 2013	% Chg.
City	137,813	138,700	0.6	127,752	131,373	2.8
MSA[1]	1,149,261	1,156,473	0.6	1,062,530	1,092,651	2.8
U.S.	154,904,000	154,408,000	-0.3	143,060,000	144,423,000	1.0

Note: Data is not seasonally adjusted and covers workers 16 years of age and older; (1) Metropolitan Statistical Area—see Appendix B for areas included
Source: Bureau of Labor Statistics, Local Area Unemployment Statistics

Unemployment Rate

Area	2013											
	Jan.	Feb.	Mar.	Apr.	May	Jun.	Jul.	Aug.	Sep.	Oct.	Nov.	Dec.
City	7.6	7.1	6.7	6.5	6.6	6.6	6.5	6.4	6.1	5.8	5.5	5.3
MSA[1]	7.7	7.2	6.7	6.4	6.6	6.9	6.9	6.6	6.3	6.0	5.9	5.5
U.S.	8.5	8.1	7.6	7.1	7.3	7.8	7.7	7.3	7.0	7.0	6.6	6.5

Note: Data is not seasonally adjusted and covers workers 16 years of age and older; All figures are percentages; (1) Metropolitan Statistical Area—see Appendix B for areas included
Source: Bureau of Labor Statistics, Local Area Unemployment Statistics

Employment by Occupation

Occupation Classification	City (%)	MSA[1] (%)	U.S. (%)
Management, Business, Science, and Arts	35.2	34.2	36.0
Natural Resources, Construction, and Maintenance	6.4	7.6	9.1
Production, Transportation, and Material Moving	7.7	8.7	12.0
Sales and Office	28.0	28.5	24.7
Service	22.6	21.1	18.2

Note: Figures cover employed civilians 16 years of age and older; (1) Figures cover the Orlando-Kissimmee-Sanford, FL Metropolitan Statistical Area—see Appendix B for areas included
Source: U.S. Census Bureau, 2010-2012 American Community Survey 3-Year Estimates

Employment by Industry

| Sector | MSA[1] | | U.S. |
	Number of Employees	Percent of Total	Percent of Total
Construction	53,500	4.9	4.2
Education and Health Services	132,400	12.1	15.5
Financial Activities	71,500	6.5	5.7
Government	119,200	10.9	16.1
Information	23,900	2.2	1.9
Leisure and Hospitality	225,000	20.6	10.2
Manufacturing	39,100	3.6	8.7
Mining and Logging	300	<0.1	0.6
Other Services	35,900	3.3	3.9
Professional and Business Services	179,600	16.4	13.7
Retail Trade	140,100	12.8	11.4
Transportation and Utilities	32,500	3.0	3.8
Wholesale Trade	40,500	3.7	4.2

Note: Figures cover non-farm employment as of December 2013 and are not seasonally adjusted;
(1) Metropolitan Statistical Area—see Appendix B for areas included
Source: Bureau of Labor Statistics, Current Employment Statistics, Employment, Hours, and Earnings

Occupations with Greatest Projected Employment Growth: 2010 – 2020

Occupation[1]	2010 Employment	2020 Projected Employment	Numeric Employment Change	Percent Employment Change
Retail Salespersons	290,200	345,860	55,660	19.2
Combined Food Preparation and Serving Workers, Including Fast Food	154,650	193,760	39,110	25.3
Registered Nurses	165,400	202,190	36,790	22.3
Waiters and Waitresses	174,630	210,650	36,010	20.6
Customer Service Representatives	165,950	194,220	28,260	17.0
Cashiers	200,040	225,430	25,400	12.7
Office Clerks, General	142,480	164,800	22,330	15.7
Landscaping and Groundskeeping Workers	93,350	115,400	22,050	23.6
Postsecondary Teachers	75,610	94,190	18,580	24.6
Cooks, Restaurant	76,000	94,180	18,190	23.9

Note: Projections cover Florida; (1) Sorted by numeric employment change
Source: www.projectionscentral.com, State Occupational Projections, 2010–2020 Long-Term Projections

Fastest Growing Occupations: 2010 – 2020

Occupation[1]	2010 Employment	2020 Projected Employment	Numeric Employment Change	Percent Employment Change
Layout Workers, Metal and Plastic	230	380	150	65.2
Biomedical Engineers	620	990	370	60.2
Helpers—Carpenters	1,120	1,770	650	58.0
Biochemists and Biophysicists	650	1,000	350	53.6
Medical Scientists, Except Epidemiologists	2,850	4,370	1,520	53.5
Helpers—Brickmasons, Blockmasons, Stonemasons, and Tile and Marble Setters	810	1,240	430	52.6
Reinforcing Iron and Rebar Workers	940	1,370	430	46.1
Home Health Aides	28,580	41,010	12,430	43.5
Stonemasons	550	790	240	42.9
Personal Care Aides	16,880	23,920	7,040	41.7

Note: Projections cover Florida; (1) Sorted by percent employment change and excludes occupations with numeric employment change less than 100
Source: www.projectionscentral.com, State Occupational Projections, 2010–2020 Long-Term Projections

Average Wages

Occupation	$/Hr.	Occupation	$/Hr.
Accountants and Auditors	31.58	Maids and Housekeeping Cleaners	9.85
Automotive Mechanics	16.84	Maintenance and Repair Workers	15.16
Bookkeepers	16.23	Marketing Managers	55.71
Carpenters	16.93	Nuclear Medicine Technologists	34.18
Cashiers	9.20	Nurses, Licensed Practical	19.43
Clerks, General Office	13.53	Nurses, Registered	29.70
Clerks, Receptionists/Information	12.58	Nursing Assistants	11.53
Clerks, Shipping/Receiving	12.90	Packers and Packagers, Hand	10.74
Computer Programmers	36.73	Physical Therapists	38.33
Computer Systems Analysts	43.11	Postal Service Mail Carriers	24.73
Computer User Support Specialists	20.29	Real Estate Brokers	47.52
Cooks, Restaurant	11.56	Retail Salespersons	11.24
Dentists	89.42	Sales Reps., Exc. Tech./Scientific	25.68
Electrical Engineers	35.43	Sales Reps., Tech./Scientific	37.45
Electricians	19.06	Secretaries, Exc. Legal/Med./Exec.	14.66
Financial Managers	62.20	Security Guards	11.65
First-Line Supervisors/Managers, Sales	19.56	Surgeons	n/a
Food Preparation Workers	10.38	Teacher Assistants	11.60
General and Operations Managers	54.68	Teachers, Elementary School	22.80
Hairdressers/Cosmetologists	11.54	Teachers, Secondary School	22.10
Internists	75.20	Telemarketers	10.95
Janitors and Cleaners	10.20	Truck Drivers, Heavy/Tractor-Trailer	17.46
Landscaping/Groundskeeping Workers	11.32	Truck Drivers, Light/Delivery Svcs.	15.16
Lawyers	65.35	Waiters and Waitresses	10.98

Note: Wage data covers the Orlando-Kissimmee-Sanford, FL Metropolitan Statistical Area—see Appendix B for areas included. Hourly wages for elementary/secondary school teachers and teacher assistants were calculated by the editors from annual wage data assuming a 40 hour work week; n/a not available.
Source: Bureau of Labor Statistics, Metro Area Occupational Employment and Wage Estimates, May 2013

RESIDENTIAL REAL ESTATE

Building Permits

Area	Single-Family			Multi-Family			Total		
	2012	2013	Pct. Chg.	2012	2013	Pct. Chg.	2012	2013	Pct. Chg.
City	815	1,037	27.2	1,070	1,850	72.9	1,885	2,887	53.2
MSA[1]	7,322	9,222	25.9	4,684	6,341	35.4	12,006	15,563	29.6
U.S.	518,695	620,802	19.7	310,963	370,020	19.0	829,658	990,822	19.4

Note: (1) Metropolitan Statistical Area—see Appendix B for areas included; figures represent new, privately-owned housing units authorized (unadjusted data); All permit data are based on estimates with imputation.
Source: U.S. Census Bureau, Manufacturing, Mining, and Construction Statistics, Building Permits, 2012, 2013

Homeownership Rate

Area	2006 (%)	2007 (%)	2008 (%)	2009 (%)	2010 (%)	2011 (%)	2012 (%)	2013 (%)
MSA[1]	71.1	71.8	70.5	72.4	70.8	68.6	68.0	65.5
U.S.	68.8	68.1	67.8	67.4	66.9	66.1	65.4	65.1

Note: (1) Figures cover the Orlando-Kissimmee-Sanford, FL Metropolitan Statistical Area—see Appendix B for areas included
Source: U.S. Census Bureau, Housing Vacancies and Homeownership Annual Statistics: 2013

Housing Vacancy Rates

Area	Gross Vacancy Rate[2] (%)			Year-Round Vacancy Rate[3] (%)			Rental Vacancy Rate[4] (%)			Homeowner Vacancy Rate[5] (%)		
	2011	2012	2013	2011	2012	2013	2011	2012	2013	2011	2012	2013
MSA[1]	20.1	21.2	20.5	14.0	14.3	15.5	19.0	18.5	14.7	2.5	2.2	2.8
U.S.	14.2	13.8	13.8	11.1	10.8	10.7	9.5	8.7	8.3	2.5	2.0	2.0

Note: (1) Figures cover the Orlando-Kissimmee-Sanford, FL Metropolitan Statistical Area—see Appendix B for areas included; (2) The percentage of the total housing inventory that is vacant; (3) The percentage of the housing inventory (excluding seasonal units) that is year-round vacant; (4) The percentage of rental inventory that is vacant for rent; (5) The percentage of homeowner inventory that is vacant for sale
Source: U.S. Census Bureau, Housing Vacancies and Homeownership Annual Statistics: 2013

TAXES

State Corporate Income Tax Rates

State	Tax Rate (%)	Income Brackets ($)	Num. of Brackets	Financial Institution Tax Rate (%)[a]	Federal Income Tax Ded.
Florida	5.5 (f)	Flat rate	1	5.5 (f)	No

Note: Tax rates as of January 1, 2014; (a) Rates listed are the corporate income tax rate applied to financial institutions or excise taxes based on income. Some states have other taxes based upon the value of deposits or shares; (f) An exemption of $50,000 is allowed. Florida's Alternative Minimum Tax rate is 3.3%.
Source: Federation of Tax Administrators, "State Corporate Income Tax Rates, 2014"

State Individual Income Tax Rates

State	Tax Rate (%)	Income Brackets ($)	Num. of Brackets	Personal Exempt. ($)[1] Single	Dependents	Fed. Inc. Tax Ded.
Florida	None	–	–	–	–	–

Note: Tax rates as of January 1, 2014; Local- and county-level taxes are not included; n/a not applicable; (1) Married joint filers generally receive double the single exemption
Source: Federation of Tax Administrators, "State Individual Income Tax Rates, 2014"

Various State and Local Tax Rates

State	State and Local Sales and Use (%)	State Sales and Use (%)	Gasoline[1] (¢/gal.)	Cigarette[2] ($/pack)	Spirits[3] ($/gal.)	Wine[4] ($/gal.)	Beer[5] ($/gal.)
Florida	6.5	6.00	36.03	1.339	6.50 (f)	2.25	0.48

Note: All tax rates as of January 1, 2014; (1) The American Petroleum Institute has developed a methodology for determining the average tax rate on a gallon of fuel. Rates may include any of the following: excise taxes, environmental fees, storage tank fees, other fees or taxes, general sales tax, and local taxes. In states where gasoline is subject to the general sales tax, or where the fuel tax is based on the average sale price, the average rate determined by API is sensitive to changes in the price of gasoline. States that fully or partially apply general sales taxes to gasoline: CA, CO, GA, IL, IN, MI, NY; (2) The federal excise tax of $1.0066 per pack and local taxes are not included; (3) Rates are those applicable to off-premise sales of 40% alcohol by volume (a.b.v.) distilled spirits in 750ml containers. Local excise taxes are excluded; (4) Rates are those applicable to off-premise sales of 11% a.b.v. non-carbonated wine in 750ml containers; (5) Rates are those applicable to off-premise sales of 4.7% a.b.v. beer in 12 ounce containers; (f) Different rates also applicable according to alcohol content, place of production, size of container, or place purchased (on- or off-premise or onboard airlines).
Source: Tax Foundation, 2014 Facts & Figures: How Does Your State Compare?

State Business Tax Climate Index Rankings

State	Overall Rank	Corporate Tax Index Rank	Individual Income Tax Index Rank	Sales Tax Index Rank	Unemployment Insurance Tax Index Rank	Property Tax Index Rank
Florida	5	13	1	18	6	16

Note: The index is a measure of how each state's tax laws affect economic performance. The lower the rank, the more favorable a state's tax system is for business. States without a given tax are given a ranking of 1. The scores/rankings for the District of Columbia do not affect other states. The 2014 index represents the tax climate as of July 1, 2013.
Source: Tax Foundation, State Business Tax Climate Index 2014

COMMERCIAL REAL ESTATE

Office Market

Market Area	Inventory (sq. ft.)	Vacancy Rate (%)	Under Construction (sq. ft.)	YTD Net Absorption (sq. ft.)	Total Average Asking Rent ($/sq. ft./year)
Orlando	68,394,059	12.2	0	540,836	19.98
National	4,726,900,879	15.0	55,419,286	42,829,434	26.27

Source: Newmark Grubb Knight Frank, National Office Market Report, 4th Quarter 2013

Industrial/Warehouse/R&D Market

Market Area	Inventory (sq. ft.)	Vacancy Rate (%)	Under Construction (sq. ft.)	YTD Net Absorption (sq. ft.)	Total Average Asking Rent ($/sq. ft./year)
Orlando	176,796,958	9.1	58,000	684,089	4.60
National	14,022,031,238	7.9	83,249,164	156,549,903	5.40

Source: Newmark Grubb Knight Frank, National Industrial Market Report, 4th Quarter 2013

COMMERCIAL UTILITIES

Typical Monthly Electric Bills

Area	Commercial Service ($/month)		Industrial Service ($/month)	
	1,500 kWh	40 kW demand 14,000 kWh	1,000 kW demand 200,000 kWh	50,000 kW demand 15,000,000 kWh
City	148	1,190	21,825	839,634
Average[1]	197	1,636	25,662	1,485,307

Note: Based on total rates in effect July 1, 2013; (1) average based on 180 utilities surveyed
Source: Edison Electric Institute, Typical Bills and Average Rates Report, Summer 2013

TRANSPORTATION

Means of Transportation to Work

Area	Car/Truck/Van		Public Transportation			Bicycle	Walked	Other Means	Worked at Home
	Drove Alone	Car-pooled	Bus	Subway	Railroad				
City	78.7	8.9	4.8	0.0	0.0	0.4	2.0	1.6	3.5
MSA[1]	81.2	9.1	2.0	0.0	0.0	0.5	1.2	1.6	4.4
U.S.	76.4	9.7	2.6	1.7	0.5	0.6	2.8	1.3	4.3

Note: Figures are percentages and cover workers 16 years of age and older; (1) Figures cover the Orlando-Kissimmee-Sanford, FL Metropolitan Statistical Area—see Appendix B for areas included
Source: U.S. Census Bureau, 2010-2012 American Community Survey 3-Year Estimates

Travel Time to Work

Area	Less Than 10 Minutes	10 to 19 Minutes	20 to 29 Minutes	30 to 44 Minutes	45 to 59 Minutes	60 to 89 Minutes	90 Minutes or More
City	8.6	33.7	25.7	20.8	5.6	3.0	2.5
MSA[1]	7.6	27.7	23.8	24.8	9.7	4.4	1.9
U.S.	13.5	29.8	20.9	20.1	7.5	5.6	2.5

Note: Figures are percentages and include workers 16 years old and over; (1) Figures cover the Orlando-Kissimmee-Sanford, FL Metropolitan Statistical Area—see Appendix B for areas included
Source: U.S. Census Bureau, 2010-2012 American Community Survey 3-Year Estimates

Travel Time Index

Area	1985	1990	1995	2000	2005	2010	2011
Urban Area[1]	1.12	1.20	1.21	1.25	1.24	1.20	1.20
Average[2]	1.09	1.14	1.16	1.19	1.23	1.18	1.18

Note: Travel Time Index—the ratio of travel time in the peak period to the travel time at free-flow conditions. For example, a value of 1.30 indicates a 20-minute free-flow trip takes 26 minutes in the peak. Free-flow speeds (60 mph on freeways and 35 mph on principal arterials) are used as the comparison threshold; (1) Covers the Orlando FL urban area; (2) average of 498 urban areas
Source: Texas Transportation Institute, Urban Mobility Report 2012, December 2012

Public Transportation

Agency Name / Mode of Transportation	Vehicles Operated in Maximum Service	Annual Unlinked Passenger Trips (in thous.)	Annual Passenger Miles (in thous.)
Central Florida Regional Transportation Authority (Lynx)			
Bus (directly operated)	225	27,271.1	146,785.0
Bus Rapid Transit (directly operated)	7	913.6	666.2
Demand Response (purchased transportation)	220	865.2	9,888.6
Vanpool (purchased transportation)	70	200.1	7,068.5

Source: Federal Transit Administration, National Transit Database, 2012

Air Transportation

Airport Name and Code / Type of Service	Passenger Airlines[1]	Passenger Enplanements	Freight Carriers[2]	Freight (lbs.)
Orlando International (MCO)				
Domestic service (U.S. carriers - 2013)	30	14,959,228	16	127,069,420
International service (U.S. carriers - 2012)	12	312,067	4	381,510

Note: (1) Includes all U.S.-based major, minor and commuter airlines that carried at least one passenger during the year; (2) Includes all U.S.-based airlines and freight carriers that transported at least one lb. of freight during the year.
Source: Bureau of Transportation Statistics, The Intermodal Transportation Database, Air Carriers: T-100 Domestic Market (U.S. Carriers), 2013; Bureau of Transportation Statistics, The Intermodal Transportation Database, Air Carriers: T-100 International Market (U.S. Carriers), 2012

Other Transportation Statistics

Major Highways:	I-4
Amtrak Service:	Yes
Major Waterways/Ports:	None

Source: Amtrak.com; Google Maps

BUSINESSES

Major Business Headquarters

Company Name	Rankings	
	Fortune[1]	Forbes[2]
Darden Restaurants	328	-

Note: (1) Fortune 500—companies that produce a 10-K are ranked 1 to 500 based on 2012 revenue; (2) all private companies with at least $2 billion in annual revenue through the end of their most current fiscal year are ranked 1 to 224; companies listed are headquartered in the city; dashes indicate no ranking Source: Fortune, "Fortune 500," May 20, 2013; Forbes, "America's Largest Private Companies," December 18, 2013

Fast-Growing Businesses

According to *Inc.*, Orlando is home to six of America's 500 fastest-growing private companies: **uBreakiFix** (#13); **Kony** (#28); **Cell Phone Repair** (#201); **Crunchy Logistics** (#254); **Kavaliro** (#438); **GameSim** (#466). Criteria: must be an independent, privately-held, for-profit, U.S. corporation, proprietorship or partnership; revenues must be at least $100,000 in 2009 and $2 million in 2012; must have four-year operating/sales history. Holding companies, regulated banks, and utilities were excluded. *Inc., "America's 500 Fastest-Growing Private Companies," September 2013*

According to Deloitte, Orlando is home to one of North America's 500 fastest-growing high-technology companies: **API Technologies Corp.** (#153). Companies are ranked by percentage growth in revenue over a five-year period. Criteria for inclusion: company must be headquartered within North America; must own proprietary intellectual property or proprietary technology that contributes to a significant portion of the company's operating revenue, or devote a significant proportion of revenues to research and development of technology; must have been in business for a minumum of five years with 2008 operating revenues of at least $50,000 USD/CD and 2012 operating revenues of at least $5 million USD/CD. *Deloitte Touche Tohmatsu, 2013 Technology Fast 500*[TM]

Minority Business Opportunity

Orlando is home to one company which is on the *Black Enterprise* Auto Dealer 60 list (60 largest dealers based on gross sales): **Boyland Auto Group** (#4). Criteria: company must be operational in previous calendar year and be at least 51% black-owned. *Black Enterprise, B.E. 100s, 2013*

Orlando is home to five companies which are on the *Hispanic Business* 500 list (500 largest U.S. Hispanic-owned companies based on 2012 revenue): **Greenway Ford** (#3); **Jardon & Howard Technologies** (#170); **Advanced Xerographics Imaging Systems** (#179); **T&G Constructors** (#202); **US Aluminum Services Corp.** (#361). Companies included must show at least 51 percent ownership by Hispanic U.S. citizens, and must maintain headquarters in one of the 50 states or Washington, D.C. *Hispanic Business, "Hispanic Business 500," June 20, 2013*

Orlando is home to two companies which are on the *Hispanic Business* Fastest-Growing 100 list (greatest sales growth from 2008 to 2012): **US Aluminum Services Corp.** (#16); **Greenway Ford** (#22). Companies included must show at least 51 percent ownership by Hispanic U.S. citizens, and must maintain headquarters in one of the 50 states or Washington, D.C. In addition, companies must have minimum revenues of $200,000 for calendar year 2008. *Hispanic Business, June20, 2013*

Minority- and Women-Owned Businesses

Group	All Firms		Firms with Paid Employees			
	Firms	Sales ($000)	Firms	Sales ($000)	Employees	Payroll ($000)
Asian	1,522	774,833	467	715,806	2,957	77,699
Black	3,685	676,406	267	594,074	4,180	237,447
Hispanic	5,698	763,059	625	612,670	4,149	111,111
Women	8,731	1,491,871	1,376	1,231,467	9,795	283,759
All Firms	30,564	47,965,704	9,019	46,886,322	239,814	9,467,514

Note: Figures cover firms located in the city; minority- and women-owned business are defined as firms in which the corresponding group own 51% or more of the stock or equity of the company
Source: U.S. Census Bureau, 2007 Economic Census, Survey of Business Owners (2012 Survey of Business Owners data will be released starting in June 2015)

HOTELS & CONVENTION CENTERS

Hotels/Motels

Area	5 Star		4 Star		3 Star		2 Star		1 Star		Not Rated	
	Num.	Pct.[3]	Num.	Pct.[3]	Num.	Pct.[3]	Num.	Pct.[3]	Num.	Pct.[3]	Num.	Pct.[3]
City[1]	4	0.8	42	8.0	233	44.6	190	36.4	7	1.3	46	8.8
Total[2]	142	0.9	1,005	6.0	5,147	30.9	8,578	51.4	408	2.4	1,397	8.4

Note: (1) Figures cover Orlando and vicinity; (2) Figures cover all 100 cities in this book; (3) Percentage of hotels which have a given star rating; Star ratings are determined by expedia.com and offer an indication of the general quality of a particular hotel.
Source: expedia.com, April 7, 2014

The Orlando-Kissimmee-Sanford, FL metro area is home to one of the best hotels in the U.S. according to *Travel & Leisure*: **Disney's Grand Floridian Resort & Spa**. Criteria: service; location; rooms; food; and value. The list includes the top 200 hotels in the U.S. *Travel & Leisure, "T+L 500, The World's Best Hotels 2014"*

The Orlando-Kissimmee-Sanford, FL metro area is home to one of the best hotels in the world according to *Condé Nast Traveler*: **Arnold Palmer's Bay Hill Club & Lodge**. The selections are based on over 79,000 responses to the magazine's annual Readers' Choice Survey. The list includes the top 200 hotels in the U.S. *Condé Nast Traveler, "Gold List 2014, The World's Best Places to Stay"*

Major Convention Centers

Name	Overall Space (sq. ft.)	Exhibit Space (sq. ft.)	Meeting Space (sq. ft.)	Meeting Rooms
Orange County Convention Center	n/a	2,100,000	n/a	74

Note: Table includes convention centers located in the Orlando-Kissimmee-Sanford, FL metro area; n/a not available
Source: Original research

Living Environment

COST OF LIVING

Cost of Living Index

Composite Index	Groceries	Housing	Utilities	Trans- portation	Health Care	Misc. Goods/ Services
96.0	96.7	78.6	104.4	98.5	99.3	105.6

Note: The Cost of Living Index measures regional differences in the cost of consumer goods and services, excluding taxes and non-consumer expenditures, for professional and managerial households in the top income quintile. It is based on more than 50,000 prices covering almost 60 different items for which prices are collected three times a year by chambers of commerce, economic development organizations or university applied economic centers in each participating urban area. The numbers shown should be read as a percentage above or below the national average of 100. For example, a value of 115.4 in the groceries column indicates that grocery prices are 15.4% higher than the national average. Small differences in the index numbers should not be interpreted as significant; Figures cover the Orlando FL urban area.
Source: The Council for Community and Economic Research, ACCRA Cost of Living Index, 2013

Grocery Prices

Area[1]	T-Bone Steak ($/pound)	Frying Chicken ($/pound)	Whole Milk ($/half gal.)	Eggs ($/dozen)	Orange Juice ($/64 oz.)	Coffee ($/11.5 oz.)
City[2]	10.72	1.43	2.67	1.94	3.77	3.86
Avg.	10.19	1.28	2.34	1.81	3.48	4.39
Min.	8.56	0.94	1.44	1.19	2.78	3.40
Max.	14.82	2.28	3.56	3.73	6.23	7.32

*Note: (1) Values for the local area are compared with the average, minimum and maximum values for all 327 areas in the Cost of Living Index; (2) Figures cover the Orlando FL urban area; **T-Bone Steak** (price per pound); **Frying Chicken** (price per pound, whole fryer); **Whole Milk** (half gallon carton); **Eggs** (price per dozen, Grade A, large); **Orange Juice** (64 oz. Tropicana or Florida Natural); **Coffee** (11.5 oz. can, vacuum-packed, Maxwell House, Hills Bros, or Folgers).*
Source: The Council for Community and Economic Research, ACCRA Cost of Living Index, 2013

Housing and Utility Costs

Area[1]	New Home Price ($)	Apartment Rent ($/month)	All Electric ($/month)	Part Electric ($/month)	Other Energy ($/month)	Telephone ($/month)
City[2]	214,602	857	171.11	-	-	28.86
Avg.	295,864	900	171.38	91.82	70.12	27.73
Min.	185,506	458	117.80	48.81	33.67	17.16
Max.	1,358,917	3,783	441.68	171.40	372.65	39.47

*Note: (1) Values for the local area are compared with the average, minimum and maximum values for all 327 areas in the Cost of Living Index; (2) Figures cover the Orlando FL urban area; **New Home Price** (2,400 sf living area, 8,000 sf lot, in urban area with full utilities); **Apartment Rent** (950 sf 2 bedroom/1.5 or 2 bath, unfurnished, excluding all utilities except water); **All Electric** (average monthly cost for an all-electric home); **Part Electric** (average monthly cost for a part-electric home); **Other Energy** (average monthly cost for natural gas, fuel oil, coal, wood, and any other forms of energy except electricity); **Telephone** (price includes basic monthly rate for a private residential line plus additional local usage charges incurred by a family of four).*
Source: The Council for Community and Economic Research, ACCRA Cost of Living Index, 2013

Health Care, Transportation, and Other Costs

Area[1]	Doctor ($/visit)	Dentist ($/visit)	Optometrist ($/visit)	Gasoline ($/gallon)	Beauty Salon ($/visit)	Men's Shirt ($)
City[2]	75.96	84.18	62.50	3.34	42.59	36.62
Avg.	101.40	86.48	96.16	3.44	33.87	26.55
Min.	61.67	50.83	50.12	3.08	18.92	12.48
Max.	182.71	152.50	223.78	4.33	68.22	52.03

*Note: (1) Values for the local area are compared with the average, minimum and maximum values for all 327 areas in the Cost of Living Index; (2) Figures cover the Orlando FL urban area; **Doctor** (general practitioners routine exam of an established patient); **Dentist** (adult teeth cleaning and periodic oral examination); **Optometrist** (full vision eye exam for established adult patient); **Gasoline** (one gallon regular unleaded, national brand, including all taxes, cash price at self-service pump if available); **Beauty Salon** (woman's shampoo, trim, and blow-dry); **Men's Shirt** (cotton/polyester dress shirt, pinpoint weave, long sleeves).*
Source: The Council for Community and Economic Research, ACCRA Cost of Living Index, 2013

HOUSING

House Price Index (HPI)

Area	National Ranking[2]	Quarterly Change (%)	One-Year Change (%)	Five-Year Change (%)
MSA[1]	43	1.92	11.31	-20.16
U.S.[3]	–	1.20	7.69	4.18

Note: The HPI is a weighted repeat sales index. It measures average price changes in repeat sales or refinancings on the same properties. This information is obtained by reviewing repeat mortgage transactions on single-family properties whose mortgages have been purchased or securitized by Fannie Mae or Freddie Mac in January 1975; (1) Orlando-Kissimmee-Sanford, FL Metropolitan Statistical Area—see Appendix B for areas included; (2) Rankings are based on annual percentage change for all metro areas containing at least 15,000 transactions over the last 10 years and ranges from 1 to 283; (3) figures based on a weighted average of Census Division estimates using a seasonally adjusted, purchase-only index; all figures are for the period ending December 31, 2013
Source: Federal Housing Finance Agency, House Price Index, February 25, 2014

Median Single-Family Home Prices

Area	2011	2012	2013p	Percent Change 2012 to 2013
MSA[1]	124.9	134.0	160.4	19.7
U.S. Average	166.2	177.2	197.4	11.4

Note: Figures are median sales prices of existing single-family homes in thousands of dollars; (p) preliminary; n/a not available; (1) Orlando-Kissimmee-Sanford, FL Metropolitan Statistical Area—see Appendix B for areas included
Source: National Association of Realtors, Median Sales Price of Existing Single-Family Homes for Metropolitan Areas, 4th Quarter 2013

Qualifying Income Based on Median Sales Price of Existing Single-Family Homes

Area	With 5% Down ($)	With 10% Down ($)	With 20% Down ($)
MSA[1]	38,225	36,213	32,190
U.S. Average	45,395	43,006	38,228

Note: Figures are preliminary; Qualifying income is based on a mortgage rate of 4.4%. Monthly principal and interest payment is limited to 25% of income; n/a not available; (1) Orlando-Kissimmee-Sanford, FL Metropolitan Statistical Area—see Appendix B for areas included
Source: National Association of Realtors, Qualifying Income Based on Median Sales Price of Existing Single-Family Homes for Metropolitan Areas, 4th Quarter 2013

Median Apartment Condo-Coop Home Prices

Area	2011	2012	2013p	Percent Change 2012 to 2013
MSA[1]	n/a	n/a	n/a	n/a
U.S. Average	165.1	173.7	194.9	12.2

Note: Figures are median sales prices of existing apartment condo-coop homes in thousands of dollars; (p) preliminary; n/a not available; (1) Orlando-Kissimmee-Sanford, FL Metropolitan Statistical Area—see Appendix B for areas included
Source: National Association of Realtors, Median Sales Price of Existing Apartment Condo-Coop Homes for Metropolitan Areas, 4th Quarter 2013

Gross Monthly Rent

Area	Under $200	$200 -299	$300 -499	$500 -749	$750 -999	$1,000 -1,499	$1,500 and up	Median ($)
City	0.4	0.9	3.3	15.0	36.4	34.7	9.2	958
MSA[1]	0.5	0.7	2.8	14.4	32.0	38.0	11.6	997
U.S.	1.7	3.3	8.1	22.7	24.3	25.7	14.3	889

Note: Figures are percentages except for Median; Gross rent is the contract rent plus the estimated average monthly cost of utilities (electricity, gas, and water and sewer) and fuels (oil, coal, kerosene, wood, etc.) if these are paid by the renter (or paid for the renter by someone else); (1) Figures cover the Orlando-Kissimmee-Sanford, FL Metropolitan Statistical Area—see Appendix B for areas included
Source: U.S. Census Bureau, 2010-2012 American Community Survey 3-Year Estimates

Year Housing Structure Built

Area	2010 or Later	2000 -2009	1990 -1999	1980 -1989	1970 -1979	1960 -1969	1950 -1959	1940 -1949	Before 1940	Median Year
City	0.2	25.3	15.9	18.1	13.6	8.3	10.8	3.7	4.2	1985
MSA[1]	0.4	27.0	21.0	22.3	13.8	6.5	5.9	1.4	1.7	1989
U.S.	0.5	14.9	13.8	13.9	15.9	11.1	10.9	5.5	13.5	1976

Note: Figures are percentages except for Median Year; (1) Figures cover the Orlando-Kissimmee-Sanford, FL Metropolitan Statistical Area—see Appendix B for areas included
Source: U.S. Census Bureau, 2010-2012 American Community Survey 3-Year Estimates

HEALTH

Health Risk Data

Category	MSA[1] (%)	U.S. (%)
Adults aged 18–64 who have any kind of health care coverage	73.0	79.6
Adults who reported being in good or excellent health	76.8	83.1
Adults who are current smokers	18.7	19.6
Adults who are heavy drinkers[2]	5.7	6.1
Adults who are binge drinkers[3]	17.6	16.9
Adults who are overweight (BMI 25.0 - 29.9)	35.7	35.8
Adults who are obese (BMI 30.0 - 99.8)	28.1	27.6
Adults who participated in any physical activities in the past month	77.7	77.1
Adults 50+ who have ever had a sigmoidoscopy or colonoscopy	72.5	67.3
Women aged 40+ who have had a mammogram within the past two years	76.9	74.0
Men aged 40+ who have had a PSA test within the past two years	53.4	45.2
Adults aged 65+ who have had flu shot within the past year	54.6	60.1
Adults who always wear a seatbelt	94.5	93.8

Note: Data as of 2012 unless otherwise noted; (1) Figures cover the Orlando-Kissimmee, FL Metropolitan Statistical Area—see Appendix B for areas included; (2) Heavy drinkers are classified as males having more than two drinks per day or females having more than one drink per day; (3) Binge drinkers are classified as males having five or more drinks on one occasion or females having four or more drinks on one occasion
Source: Centers for Disease Control and Prevention, Behaviorial Risk Factor Surveillance System, SMART: Selected Metropolitan/Micropolitan Area Risk Trends, 2012

Chronic Health Indicators

Category	MSA[1] (%)	U.S. (%)
Adults who have ever been told they had a heart attack	6.6	4.5
Adults who have ever been told they had a stroke	n/a	2.9
Adults who have been told they currently have asthma	9.5	8.9
Adults who have ever been told they have arthritis	21.9	25.7
Adults who have ever been told they have diabetes[2]	10.2	9.7
Adults who have ever been told they had skin cancer	5.7	5.7
Adults who have ever been told they had any other types of cancer	7.3	6.5
Adults who have ever been told they have COPD	5.9	6.2
Adults who have ever been told they have kidney disease	2.8	2.5
Adults who have ever been told they have a form of depression	18.2	18.0

Note: Data as of 2012 unless otherwise noted; n/a not available; (1) Figures cover the Orlando-Kissimmee, FL Metropolitan Statistical Area—see Appendix B for areas included; (2) Figures do not include pregnancy-related, borderline, or pre-diabetes
Source: Centers for Disease Control and Prevention, Behaviorial Risk Factor Surveillance System, SMART: Selected Metropolitan/Micropolitan Area Risk Trends, 2012

Mortality Rates for the Top 10 Causes of Death in the U.S.

ICD-10[a] Sub-Chapter	ICD-10[a] Code	Age-Adjusted Mortality Rate[1] per 100,000 population	
		County[2]	U.S.
Malignant neoplasms	C00-C97	170.1	174.2
Ischaemic heart diseases	I20-I25	110.8	119.1
Other forms of heart disease	I30-I51	40.6	49.6
Chronic lower respiratory diseases	J40-J47	42.7	43.2
Cerebrovascular diseases	I60-I69	34.6	40.3
Organic, including symptomatic, mental disorders	F01-F09	27.6	30.5
Other degenerative diseases of the nervous system	G30-G31	25.2	26.3
Other external causes of accidental injury	W00-X59	21.4	25.1
Diabetes mellitus	E10-E14	23.5	21.3
Hypertensive diseases	I10-I15	17.9	18.8

Note: (a) ICD-10 = International Classification of Diseases 10th Revision; (1) Mortality rates are a three year average covering 2008-2010; (2) Figures cover Orange County
Source: Centers for Disease Control and Prevention, National Center for Health Statistics. Compressed Mortality File 1999-2010 on CDC WONDER Online Database, released January 2013. Data are compiled from the Compressed Mortality File 1999-2010, Series 20 No. 2P, 2013.

Mortality Rates for Selected Causes of Death

ICD-10[a] Sub-Chapter	ICD-10[a] Code	Age-Adjusted Mortality Rate[1] per 100,000 population	
		County[2]	U.S.
Assault	X85-Y09	7.3	5.5
Diseases of the liver	K70-K76	11.4	12.4
Human immunodeficiency virus (HIV) disease	B20-B24	6.4	3.0
Influenza and pneumonia	J09-J18	11.7	16.4
Intentional self-harm	X60-X84	11.0	11.8
Malnutrition	E40-E46	*0.5	0.8
Obesity and other hyperalimentation	E65-E68	0.9	1.6
Renal failure	N17-N19	13.6	13.6
Transport accidents	V01-V99	12.0	12.6
Viral hepatitis	B15-B19	1.9	2.2

Note: (a) ICD-10 = International Classification of Diseases 10th Revision; (1) Mortality rates are a three year average covering 2008-2010; (2) Figures cover Orange County; (*) Unreliable data as per CDC
Source: Centers for Disease Control and Prevention, National Center for Health Statistics. Compressed Mortality File 1999-2010 on CDC WONDER Online Database, released January 2013. Data are compiled from the Compressed Mortality File 1999-2010, Series 20 No. 2P, 2013.

Health Insurance Coverage

Area	With Health Insurance	With Private Health Insurance	With Public Health Insurance	Without Health Insurance	Population Under Age 18 Without Health Insurance
City	75.2	55.0	26.0	24.8	12.9
MSA[1]	79.3	60.8	27.5	20.7	11.6
U.S.	84.9	65.4	30.4	15.1	7.5

Note: Figures are percentages that cover the civilian noninstitutionalized population; (1) Figures cover the Orlando-Kissimmee-Sanford, FL Metropolitan Statistical Area—see Appendix B for areas included
Source: U.S. Census Bureau, 2010-2012 American Community Survey 3-Year Estimates

Number of Medical Professionals

Area[1]	MDs[2]	DOs[2,3]	Dentists	Podiatrists	Chiropractors	Optometrists
Local (number)	3,125	205	514	48	268	141
Local (rate[4])	267.1	17.5	42.8	4.0	22.3	11.7
U.S. (rate[4])	267.6	19.6	61.7	5.6	24.7	14.5

Note: Data as of 2012 unless noted; (1) Local data covers Orange County; (2) Data as of 2011; (3) Doctor of Osteopathic Medicine; (4) rate per 100,000 population
Source: Area Resource File (ARF) 2012-2013. U.S. Department of Health and Human Services, Health Resources and Services Administration, Bureau of Health Professions

Best Hospitals

According to *U.S. News,* the Orlando-Kissimmee-Sanford, FL metro area is home to one of the best hospitals in the U.S.: **Florida Hospital** (8 specialties). The hospital listed was nationally ranked in at least one adult specialty. Only 147 hospitals nationwide were nationally ranked in one or more specialties. Eighteen hospitals in the U.S. made the Honor Roll by ranking near the top in at least six specialties.*U.S. News Online, "America's Best Hospitals 2013-14"*

According to *U.S. News,* the Orlando-Kissimmee-Sanford, FL metro area is home to one of the best children's hospitals in the U.S.: **Arnold Palmer Medical Center**. The hospital listed was highly ranked in at least one pediatric specialty. Eighty-seven hospitals in the U.S. ranked in at least one specialty. Ten children's hospitals in the U.S. made the Honor Roll by ranking near the top in three or more specialties.*U.S. News Online, "America's Best Children's Hospitals 2013-14"*

EDUCATION

Public School District Statistics

District Name	Schls	Pupils	Pupil/ Teacher Ratio	Minority Pupils[1] (%)	Free Lunch Eligible[2] (%)	IEP[3] (%)
Florida Virtual School	4	2,695	2.2	33.0	n/a	1.7
Orange County Public Schools	249	180,000	15.9	68.7	47.5	12.0

Note: Table includes school districts with 2,000 or more students; (1) Percentage of students that are not non-Hispanic white; (2) Percentage of students that are eligible for the free lunch program; (3) Percentage of students that have an Individualized Education Program.
Source: U.S. Department of Education, National Center for Education Statistics, Common Core of Data, Local Education Agency (School District) Universe Survey: School Year 2011-2012; U.S. Department of Education, National Center for Education Statistics, Common Core of Data, Public Elementary/Secondary School Universe Survey: School Year 2011-2012

Best High Schools

High School Name	Rank[1]	Grad. Rate[2] (%)	Coll.[3] (%)	AP/IB/ AICE Tests[4]	AP/IB/ AICE Score[5]	SAT Score[6]	ACT Score[6]
Timber Creek H.S.	825	93	97	0.7	2.7	1465	20.8

Note: (1) Public schools are ranked from 1 to 2,000 based on the following self-reported statistics (with the corresponding weight used in calculating their overall score). Schools that were newly founded and did not have a graduating senior class in 2012 were excluded; (2) Four-year, on-time graduation rate (25%); (3) Percent of 2011 graduates who were accepted to college (25%); (4) AP/IB/AICE tests taken per student (25%); (5) Average AP/IB/AICE exam score (10%); (6) Average SAT and/or ACT score (10%); Percent of students enrolled in at least one AP/IB/AICE course (5%)—data not shown
Source: Newsweek and The Daily Beast, "America's Best High Schools 2013"

Highest Level of Education

Area	Less than H.S.	H.S. Diploma	Some College, No Deg.	Associate Degree	Bachelor's Degree	Master's Degree	Prof. School Degree	Doctorate Degree
City	11.9	25.2	20.5	10.3	21.1	7.7	2.3	1.0
MSA[1]	12.6	28.5	21.3	9.8	18.4	6.8	1.7	0.9
U.S.	14.1	28.3	21.3	7.8	18.0	7.5	1.9	1.2

Note: Figures cover persons age 25 and over; (1) Figures cover the Orlando-Kissimmee-Sanford, FL Metropolitan Statistical Area—see Appendix B for areas included
Source: U.S. Census Bureau, 2010-2012 American Community Survey 3-Year Estimates

Educational Attainment by Race

Area	High School Graduate or Higher (%)					Bachelor's Degree or Higher (%)				
	Total	White	Black	Asian	Hisp.[2]	Total	White	Black	Asian	Hisp.[2]
City	88.1	91.6	81.8	85.6	79.7	32.1	38.3	16.6	50.4	21.6
MSA[1]	87.4	89.3	82.6	85.4	79.2	27.8	29.4	18.4	45.6	19.1
U.S.	85.9	88.1	82.5	85.5	63.1	28.6	30.0	18.4	50.2	13.4

Note: Figures shown cover persons 25 years old and over; (1) Figures cover the Orlando-Kissimmee-Sanford, FL Metropolitan Statistical Area—see Appendix B for areas included; (2) People of Hispanic origin can be of any race
Source: U.S. Census Bureau, 2010-2012 American Community Survey 3-Year Estimates

School Enrollment by Grade and Control

Area	Preschool (%) Public	Preschool (%) Private	Kindergarten (%) Public	Kindergarten (%) Private	Grades 1 - 4 (%) Public	Grades 1 - 4 (%) Private	Grades 5 - 8 (%) Public	Grades 5 - 8 (%) Private	Grades 9 - 12 (%) Public	Grades 9 - 12 (%) Private
City	49.6	50.4	79.9	20.1	87.1	12.9	88.8	11.2	89.9	10.1
MSA[1]	48.6	51.4	85.4	14.6	88.5	11.5	88.0	12.0	90.7	9.3
U.S.	56.9	43.1	87.8	12.2	89.9	10.1	90.0	10.0	90.8	9.2

Note: Figures shown cover persons 3 years old and over; (1) Figures cover the Orlando-Kissimmee-Sanford, FL Metropolitan Statistical Area—see Appendix B for areas included
Source: U.S. Census Bureau, 2010-2012 American Community Survey 3-Year Estimates

Average Salaries of Public School Classroom Teachers

Area	2012-13 Dollars	2012-13 Rank[1]	2013-14 Dollars	2013-14 Rank[1]	Percent Change 2012-13 to 2013-14	Percent Change 2003-04 to 2013-14
Florida	46,598	45	46,691	45	0.20	15.0
U.S. Average	56,103	–	56,689	–	1.04	21.8

Note: (1) State rank ranges from 1 to 51 where 1 indicates highest salary.
Source: National Education Association, Rankings & Estimates: Rankings of the States 2013 and Estimates of School Statistics 2014, March 2014

Higher Education

Four-Year Colleges Public	Four-Year Colleges Private Non-profit	Four-Year Colleges Private For-profit	Two-Year Colleges Public	Two-Year Colleges Private Non-profit	Two-Year Colleges Private For-profit	Medical Schools[1]	Law Schools[2]	Voc/ Tech[3]
2	2	5	2	0	9	1	2	2

Note: Figures cover institutions located within the city limits and include main campuses only; (1) includes schools accredited by the Liaison Committee on Medical Education and the American Osteopathic Association's Commission on Osteopathic College Accreditation; (2) includes ABA-accredited schools, schools with provisional ABA accreditation, and state accredited schools; (3) includes all schools with programs that are less than 2 years.
Source: National Center for Education Statistics, Integrated Postsecondary Education System (IPEDS), 2012-13; Association of American Medical Colleges, Member List, April 24, 2014; American Osteopathic Association, Member List, April 24, 2014; Law School Admission Council, Official Guide to ABA-Approved Law Schools Online, April 24, 2014; Wikipedia, List of Medical Schools in the United States, April 24, 2014; Wikipedia, List of Law Schools in the United States, April 24, 2014

According to U.S. News & World Report, the Orlando-Kissimmee-Sanford, FL metro area is home to one of the best national universities in the U.S.: **University of Central Florida** (#170). The indicators used to capture academic quality fall into a number of categories: assessment by administrators at peer institutions; retention of students; faculty resources; student selectivity; financial resources; alumni giving; high school counselor ratings of colleges; and graduation rate. U.S. News & World Report, "America's Best Colleges 2014"

PRESIDENTIAL ELECTION

2012 Presidential Election Results

Area	Obama	Romney	Other
Orange County	58.7	40.4	0.9
U.S.	51.0	47.2	1.8

Note: Results are percentages and may not add to 100% due to rounding
Source: Dave Leip's Atlas of U.S. Presidential Elections

EMPLOYERS

Major Employers

Company Name	Industry
Adventist Health System/Sunbelt	General medical and surgical hospitals
Airtran Airways	Air passenger carrier, scheduled
Central Florida Health Alliance	Hospital management
Children & Families, Florida Department	Individual and family services
Cnl Lifestyle Properties	Real estate agents and managers
Connexions	Communication services, nec
Florida Hospital Medical Center	General medical and surgical hospitals
Gaylord Palms Resort & Conv Ctr	Hotel franchised
Leesburg Regional Medical Center	General medical and surgical hospitals
Lockheed Martin Corporation	Aircraft
Marriott International	Hotels and motels
Orlando Health	General medical and surgical hospitals
Rosen 9939	Hotels
Sea World of Florida	Theme park, amusement
Sears Termite & Pest Control	Pest control in structures
Siemens Energy	Power plant construction
Universal City Florida Partners	Amusement parks
University of Central Florida	Colleges and universities
Winter Park Healthcare Group, Ltd	Hospital affiliated with ama residency

Note: Companies shown are located within the Orlando-Kissimmee-Sanford, FL Metropolitan Statistical Area.
Source: Hoovers.com; Wikipedia

Best Companies to Work For

Darden Restaurants, headquartered in Orlando, is among "The 100 Best Companies to Work For." To pick the 100 Best Companies to Work For, *Fortune* partnered with the Great Place to Work Institute. Two hundred fifty seven firms participated in this year's survey. Two-thirds of a company's score is based on the results of the Institute's Trust Index survey, which is sent to a random sample of employees from each company. The questions related to attitudes about management's credibility, job satisfaction, and camaraderie. The other third of the scoring is based on the company's responses to the Institute's Culture Audit, which includes detailed questions about pay and benefit programs, and a series of open-ended questions about hiring practices, internal communication, training, recognition programs, and diversity efforts. Any company that is at least five years old with more than 1,000 U.S. employees is eligible. *Fortune, "The 100 Best Companies to Work For," 2014*

PUBLIC SAFETY

Crime Rate

Area	All Crimes	Violent Crimes				Property Crimes		
		Murder	Forcible Rape	Robbery	Aggrav. Assault	Burglary	Larceny -Theft	Motor Vehicle Theft
City	7,631.2	9.7	41.8	244.6	721.3	1,532.6	4,552.3	529.0
Suburbs[1]	3,577.0	4.3	29.3	105.9	347.0	897.3	1,990.7	202.4
Metro[2]	4,031.1	5.0	30.7	121.4	389.0	968.5	2,277.6	238.9
U.S.	3,246.1	4.7	26.9	112.9	242.3	670.2	1,959.3	229.7

Note: Figures are crimes per 100,000 population; (1) All areas within the metro area that are located outside the city limits; (2) Figures cover the Orlando-Kissimmee-Sanford, FL Metropolitan Statistical Area—see Appendix B for areas included
Source: FBI Uniform Crime Reports, 2012

Hate Crimes

Area	Number of Quarters Reported	Bias Motivation				
		Race	Religion	Sexual Orientation	Ethnicity	Disability
City	4	1	0	1	1	0
U.S.	4	2,797	1,099	1,135	667	92

Source: Federal Bureau of Investigation, Hate Crime Statistics 2012

Identity Theft Consumer Complaints

Area	Complaints	Complaints per 100,000 Population	Rank[2]
MSA[1]	3,193	149.6	11
U.S.	290,056	91.8	-

Note: (1) Figures cover the Orlando-Kissimmee-Sanford, FL Metropolitan Statistical Area—see Appendix B for areas included; (2) Rank ranges from 1 to 377 where 1 indicates greatest number of identity theft complaints per 100,000 population
Source: Federal Trade Commission, Consumer Sentinel Network Data Book for January–December 2013

Fraud and Other Consumer Complaints

Area	Complaints	Complaints per 100,000 Population	Rank[2]
MSA[1]	10,158	475.9	32
U.S.	1,811,724	595.2	-

Note: (1) Figures cover the Orlando-Kissimmee-Sanford, FL Metropolitan Statistical Area—see Appendix B for areas included; (2) Rank ranges from 1 to 377 where 1 indicates greatest number of identity theft complaints per 100,000 population
Source: Federal Trade Commission, Consumer Sentinel Network Data Book for January–December 2013

RECREATION

Culture

Dance[1]	Theatre[1]	Instrumental Music[1]	Vocal Music[1]	Series and Festivals	Museums and Art Galleries[2]	Zoos and Aquariums[3]
2	5	3	1	1	23	3

Note: (1) Number of professional performing groups; (2) Based on organizations with primary SIC code 8412; (3) AZA-accredited
Source: The Grey House Performing Arts Directory, 2013; Association of Zoos & Aquariums, AZA Member Zoos & Aquariums, April 2014; www.AccuLeads.com, May 1, 2014

Professional Sports Teams

Team Name	League	Year Established
Orlando City SC	Major League Soccer (MLS)	2015
Orlando Magic	National Basketball Association (NBA)	1989

Note: Includes teams located in the Orlando-Kissimmee-Sanford, FL Metropolitan Statistical Area.
Source: Wikipedia, Major Professional Sports Teams of the United States and Canada

CLIMATE

Average and Extreme Temperatures

Temperature	Jan	Feb	Mar	Apr	May	Jun	Jul	Aug	Sep	Oct	Nov	Dec	Yr.
Extreme High (°F)	86	89	90	95	100	100	99	100	98	95	89	90	100
Average High (°F)	70	72	77	82	87	90	91	91	89	83	78	72	82
Average Temp. (°F)	59	62	67	72	77	81	82	82	81	75	68	62	72
Average Low (°F)	48	51	56	60	66	71	73	74	72	66	58	51	62
Extreme Low (°F)	19	29	25	38	51	53	64	65	57	44	32	20	19

Note: Figures cover the years 1952-1990
Source: National Climatic Data Center, International Station Meteorological Climate Summary, 9/96

Average Precipitation/Snowfall/Humidity

Precip./Humidity	Jan	Feb	Mar	Apr	May	Jun	Jul	Aug	Sep	Oct	Nov	Dec	Yr.
Avg. Precip. (in.)	2.3	2.8	3.4	2.0	3.2	7.0	7.2	5.8	5.8	2.7	3.5	2.0	47.7
Avg. Snowfall (in.)	Tr	0	0	0	0	0	0	0	0	0	0	0	Tr
Avg. Rel. Hum. 7am (%)	87	87	88	87	88	89	90	92	92	89	89	87	89
Avg. Rel. Hum. 4pm (%)	53	51	49	47	51	61	65	66	66	59	56	55	57

Note: Figures cover the years 1952-1990; Tr = Trace amounts (<0.05 in. of rain; <0.5 in. of snow)
Source: National Climatic Data Center, International Station Meteorological Climate Summary, 9/96

Weather Conditions

Temperature			Daytime Sky			Precipitation		
32°F & below	45°F & below	90°F & above	Clear	Partly cloudy	Cloudy	0.01 inch or more precip.	0.1 inch or more snow/ice	Thunder-storms
3	35	90	76	208	81	115	0	80

Note: Figures are average number of days per year and cover the years 1952-1990
Source: National Climatic Data Center, International Station Meteorological Climate Summary, 9/96

HAZARDOUS WASTE

Superfund Sites

Orlando has two hazardous waste sites on the EPA's Superfund Final National Priorities List: **Chevron Chemical Co. (Ortho Division); City Industries, Inc.** *U.S. Environmental Protection Agency, Final National Priorities List, April 26, 2014*

AIR & WATER QUALITY

Air Quality Index

Area	Percent of Days when Air Quality was...[2]					AQI Statistics[2]	
	Good	Moderate	Unhealthy for Sensitive Groups	Unhealthy	Very Unhealthy	Maximum	Median
MSA[1]	89.3	10.7	0.0	0.0	0.0	97	36

Note: (1) Data covers the Orlando-Kissimmee-Sanford, FL Metropolitan Statistical Area—see Appendix B for areas included; (2) Based on 365 days with AQI data in 2013. Air Quality Index (AQI) is an index for reporting daily air quality. EPA calculates the AQI for five major air pollutants regulated by the Clean Air Act: ground-level ozone, particle pollution (aka particulate matter), carbon monoxide, sulfur dioxide, and nitrogen dioxide. The AQI runs from 0 to 500. The higher the AQI value, the greater the level of air pollution and the greater the health concern. There are six AQI categories: "Good" AQI is between 0 and 50. Air quality is considered satisfactory; "Moderate" AQI is between 51 and 100. Air quality is acceptable; "Unhealthy for Sensitive Groups" When AQI values are between 101 and 150, members of sensitive groups may experience health effects; "Unhealthy" When AQI values are between 151 and 200 everyone may begin to experience health effects; "Very Unhealthy" AQI values between 201 and 300 trigger a health alert; "Hazardous" AQI values over 300 trigger warnings of emergency conditions (not shown).
Source: U.S. Environmental Protection Agency, Air Quality Index Report, 2013

Air Quality Index Pollutants

Area	Percent of Days when AQI Pollutant was...[2]					
	Carbon Monoxide	Nitrogen Dioxide	Ozone	Sulfur Dioxide	Particulate Matter 2.5	Particulate Matter 10
MSA[1]	0.0	0.3	55.6	0.0	44.1	0.0

Note: (1) Data covers the Orlando-Kissimmee-Sanford, FL Metropolitan Statistical Area—see Appendix B for areas included; (2) Based on 365 days with AQI data in 2013. The Air Quality Index (AQI) is an index for reporting daily air quality. EPA calculates the AQI for five major air pollutants regulated by the Clean Air Act: ground-level ozone, particle pollution (also known as particulate matter), carbon monoxide, sulfur dioxide, and nitrogen dioxide. The AQI runs from 0 to 500. The higher the AQI value, the greater the level of air pollution and the greater the health concern.
Source: U.S. Environmental Protection Agency, Air Quality Index Report, 2013

Air Quality Trends: Ozone

	2003	2004	2005	2006	2007	2008	2009	2010	2011	2012
MSA[1]	0.075	0.074	0.080	0.078	0.075	0.069	0.064	0.068	0.072	0.069

Note: (1) Data covers the Orlando-Kissimmee-Sanford, FL Metropolitan Statistical Area—see Appendix B for areas included. The values shown are the composite ozone concentration averages among trend sites based on the highest fourth daily maximum 8-hour concentration in parts per million. These trends are based on sites having an adequate record of monitoring data during the trend period. Data from exceptional events are included.
Source: U.S. Environmental Protection Agency, Air Quality Monitoring Information, "Air Quality Trends by City, 2000-2012"

Maximum Air Pollutant Concentrations: Particulate Matter, Ozone, CO and Lead

	Particulate Matter 10 (ug/m³)	Particulate Matter 2.5 Wtd AM (ug/m³)	Particulate Matter 2.5 24-Hr (ug/m³)	Ozone (ppm)	Carbon Monoxide (ppm)	Lead (ug/m³)
MSA[1] Level	41	7.1	19	0.072	1	n/a
NAAQS[2]	150	15	35	0.075	9	0.15
Met NAAQS[2]	Yes	Yes	Yes	Yes	Yes	n/a

Note: (1) Data covers the Orlando-Kissimmee-Sanford, FL Metropolitan Statistical Area—see Appendix B for areas included; Data from exceptional events are included; (2) National Ambient Air Quality Standards; ppm = parts per million; ug/m³ = micrograms per cubic meter; n/a not available.
Concentrations: Particulate Matter 10 (coarse particulate)—highest second maximum 24-hour concentration; Particulate Matter 2.5 Wtd AM (fine particulate)—highest weighted annual mean concentration; Particulate Matter 2.5 24-Hour (fine particulate)—highest 98th percentile 24-hour concentration; Ozone—highest fourth daily maximum 8-hour concentration; Carbon Monoxide—highest second maximum non-overlapping 8-hour concentration; Lead—maximum running 3-month average
Source: U.S. Environmental Protection Agency, Air Quality Monitoring Information, "Air Quality Statistics by City, 2012"

Maximum Air Pollutant Concentrations: Nitrogen Dioxide and Sulfur Dioxide

	Nitrogen Dioxide AM (ppb)	Nitrogen Dioxide 1-Hr (ppb)	Sulfur Dioxide AM (ppb)	Sulfur Dioxide 1-Hr (ppb)	Sulfur Dioxide 24-Hr (ppb)
MSA[1] Level	5	35	n/a	5	n/a
NAAQS[2]	53	100	30	75	140
Met NAAQS[2]	Yes	Yes	n/a	Yes	n/a

Note: (1) Data covers the Orlando-Kissimmee-Sanford, FL Metropolitan Statistical Area—see Appendix B for areas included; Data from exceptional events are included; (2) National Ambient Air Quality Standards; ppm = parts per million; ug/m³ = micrograms per cubic meter; n/a not available.
Concentrations: Nitrogen Dioxide AM—highest arithmetic mean concentration; Nitrogen Dioxide 1-Hr—highest 98th percentile 1-hour daily maximum concentration; Sulfur Dioxide AM—highest annual mean concentration; Sulfur Dioxide 1-Hr—highest 99th percentile 1-hour daily maximum concentration; Sulfur Dioxide 24-Hr—highest second maximum 24-hour concentration
Source: U.S. Environmental Protection Agency, Air Quality Monitoring Information, "Air Quality Statistics by City, 2012"

Drinking Water

Water System Name	Pop. Served	Primary Water Source Type	Violations[1] Health Based	Violations[1] Monitoring/ Reporting
Orlando Utilities Commission	425,520	Ground	0	0

Note: (1) Based on violation data from January 1, 2013 to December 31, 2013 (includes unresolved violations from earlier years)
Source: U.S. Environmental Protection Agency, Office of Ground Water and Drinking Water, Safe Drinking Water Information System (based on data extracted February 10, 2014)

San Antonio, Texas

Background

San Antonio is a charming preservation of its Mexican-Spanish heritage. Walking along its famous Paseo Del Rio at night, with cream-colored stucco structures, sea shell ornamented facades, and gently illuminating tiny lights is very romantic.

Emotional intensity is nothing new to San Antonio. The city began in the early eighteenth century as a cohesion of different Spanish missions, whose zealous aim was to convert the Coahuiltecan natives to Christianity, and to European ways of farming. A debilitating epidemic, however, killed most of the natives, as well as the missions' goal, causing the city to be abandoned.

In 1836, San Antonio became the site of interest again, when a small band of American soldiers were unable to successfully defend themselves against an army of 4,000 Mexican soldiers, led by General Antonio de Lopez Santa Anna. Fighting desperately from within the walls of the Mission San Antonio de Valero, or The Alamo, all 183 men were killed. This inspired the cry "Remember the Alamo" from the throats of every American soldier led by General Sam Houston, who was determined to wrest Texas territory and independence from Mexico.

Despite the Anglo victory over the Mexicans more than 150 years ago, the Mexican culture and its influence remain strong. We see evidence of this in the architecture, the Franciscan educational system, the variety of Spanish-language media, and the racial composition of the population, in which over half the city's residents are Latino.

This picturesque and practical blend of old and new makes San Antonio unique among American cities.

The city continues to draw tourists who come to visit not just the Alamo, but the nearby theme parks like Six Flags Fiesta Texas and SeaWorld, or to take in the famed River Walk, the charming promenade of shops, restaurants, and pubs. In addition, the city has used ingenuity to diversify its traditional economy. For instance, Kelly Air Force Base, which was decommissioned in 2001, was developed into a successful, nearly 5,000-acre business park, called Kelly USA. The name has since changed to Port San Antonio and a warehouse on the site was used to house refugees from Hurricane Katrina. Businesses at the port receive favorable property tax and pay no state, city or corporate income taxes. Toyota is a major employer in the city.

San Antonio's location on the edge of the Gulf Coastal Plains exposes it to a modified subtropical climate. Summers are hot, although extremely high temperatures are rare. Winters are mild. Since the city is only 140 miles from the Gulf of Mexico, tropical storms occasionally occur, bringing strong winds and heavy rains. Relative humidity is high in the morning, but tends to drop by late afternoon.

Rankings

General Rankings

- San Antonio was identified as one of America's fastest-growing cities in terms of population and economy by *Forbes*. The area ranked #20 out of 20. The 100 most populous metro areas in the U.S. were evaluated on the following criteria: estimated population growth; job growth; gross metropolitan product growth; unemployment; median salaries for college-educated workers. *Forbes, "America's Fastest-Growing Cities 2014," February 14, 2014*

- San Antonio was identified as one of America's fastest-growing major metropolitan areas in terms of population by CNNMoney.com. The area ranked #5 out of 10. Criteria: population growth between July 2012 and July 2013. *CNNMoney, "10 Fastest-Growing Cities," March 28, 2014*

- Among the 50 largest U.S. cities, San Antonio placed #29 in Vocativ's "semi-exhaustive, mostly scientific" city Livability Index for people aged 35 and under. Average salary, unemployment rates, rents, and other living costs were considered, along with bike lanes, low-cost broadband, cheap takeout, self-service laundries, the price of a pint of Guinness, music venues, and vintage clothing stores. *vocative.com, "The Livability Index: The Best U.S. Cities for People 35 and Under," November 7, 2013*

- San Antonio was selected as one of America's best cities by *Bloomberg Businessweek*. The city ranked #30 out of 50. Criteria: leisure attributes (the number of restaurants, bars, libraries, museums, professional sports teams, and park acres by population); educational attributes (public school performance, the number of colleges, and graduate degree holders); economic factors (2011 income and June and July 2012 unemployment); crime; and air quality. *Bloomberg BusinessWeek, "America's Best Cities," September 26, 2012*

- San Antonio appeared on RelocateAmerica's list of best places to live in America. The annual "Top 100 Places to Live" list recognizes the top communities as nominated by their residents & local businesses. RelocateAmerica's Research Group determined the list based on review of various data gathered for economic, employment, housing, education, industry, opportunity, environment and recreation along with feedback from area leaders and residents. *RelocateAmerica.com, "Top 100 Places to Live for 2011"*

- San Antonio was selected as one of "America's Favorite Cities." The city ranked #16 in the "Quality of Life and Visitor Experience: Cleanliness" category. Respondents to an online survey were asked to rate 35 top urban destinations in the U.S. from a visitor's perspective. Criteria: cleanliness. *Travel + Leisure, "America's Favorite Cities 2013"*

- San Antonio was selected as one of "America's Favorite Cities." The city ranked #30 in the "Type of Trip: Gay-friendly" category. Respondents to an online survey were asked to rate 35 top urban destinations in the U.S. from a visitor's perspective. Criteria: gay-friendly. *Travel + Leisure, "America's Favorite Cities 2013"*

Business/Finance Rankings

- The personal finance site NerdWallet scored the nation's 20 largest American cities according to how friendly a business climate they offer to would-be entrepreneurs. Criteria inlcuded local taxes (state, city, payroll, property), growth rate, and the regulatory environment as judged by small business owners. On the resulting list of most welcoming cities, San Antonio ranked #2. *www.nerdwallet.com, "Top 10 Best Cities for Small Business," August 26, 2013*

- The finance website Wall St. Cheat Sheet reported on the prospects for high-wage job creation in the nation's largest metro areas over the next five years and ranked them accordingly, drawing on in-depth analysis by CareerBuilder and Economic Modeling Specialists International (EMSI). The San Antonio metro area placed #1 on the Wall St. Cheat Sheet list. *wallstcheatsheet.com, "Top 10 Cities for High-Wage Job Growth," December 8, 2013*

- Based on a minimum of 500 social media reviews per metro area, the employment opinion group Glassdoor surveyed 50 of the largest U.S. metro areas on measures including compensation and benefits, satisfaction with management, business outlook, and number of employers hiring. The San Antonio metro area was ranked #13 in overall employee satisfaction. *www.glassdoor.com, "Employment Satisfaction Report Card by City," June 21, 2013*

- The financial literacy site NerdWallet.com set out to identify the 20 most promising cities for job seekers, analyzing data for the nation's 50 largest cities. San Antonio was ranked #10. Criteria: unemployment rate; population growth; median income; selected monthly owner costs. *NerdWallet.com, "Best Cities for Job Seekers," January 7, 2014*

- The Brookings Institution ranked the 50 largest cities in the U.S. based on income inequality. San Antonio was ranked #39. (#1 = greatest ineqality). Criteria: the cities were ranked based on the "95/20 ratio." This figure represents the income at which a household earns more than 95 percent of all other households, divided by the income at which a household earns more than only 20 percent of all other households. *Brookings Institution, "Income Inequality in America's 50 Largest Cities, 2007-2012," February 20, 2014*

- San Antonio was ranked #36 out of 100 metro areas in terms of economic performance (#1 = best) during the recession and recovery from trough quarter through the second quarter of 2013. Criteria: percent change in employment; percentage point change in unemployment rate; percent change in gross metropolitan product; percent change in House Price Index. *Brookings Institution, MetroMonitor: Tracking Economic Recession and Recovery in America's 100 Largest Metropolitan Areas, September 2013*

- The San Antonio metro area was identified as one of 10 best-paying cities for women. The metro area ranked #8. Criteria: *24/7 Wall St.* identified the metropolitan areas that have the smallest pay disparity between men and women by comparing the median earnings for the past 12 months of both men and women working full-time in the country's 100 largest metropolitan statistical areas. *24/7 Wall St., "10 Best-Paying Cities for Women," April 14, 2013*

- San Antonio was identified as one of the top 25 U.S. cities with the most credit card debt by credit reporting bureau Experian. The city was ranked #1. *Experian, March 4, 2011*

- The San Antonio metro area appeared on the Milken Institute "2013 Best Performing Cities" list. Rank: #12 out of 200 large metro areas. Criteria: job growth; wage and salary growth; high-tech output growth. *Milken Institute, "Best-Performing Cities 2013," December 2013*

- *Forbes* ranked the 200 most populous metro areas in the U.S. in terms of the "Best Places for Business and Careers." The San Antonio metro area was ranked #11. Criteria: costs (business and living); job growth (past and projected); income growth; educational attainment (college and high school); projected economic growth; cultural and recreational opportunities; net migration patterns; number of highly ranked colleges. *Forbes, "The Best Places for Business and Careers," August 7, 2013*

Children/Family Rankings

- San Antonio was selected as one of the best cities for families to live by *Parenting* magazine. The city ranked #80 out of 100. Criteria: education; health; community; *Parenting's* Culture & Charm Index. *Parenting.com, "The 2012 Best Cities for Families List"*

Culture/Performing Arts Rankings

- San Antonio was selected as one of "America's Favorite Cities." The city ranked #21 in the "Culture: Museum/Galleries" category. Respondents to an online survey were asked to rate 35 top urban destinations in the U.S. from a visitor's perspective. Criteria: number and quality of museums and galleries. *Travelandleisure.com, "America's Favorite Cities 2013"*

- San Antonio was selected as one of America's top cities for the arts. The city ranked #21 in the big city (population 500,000 and over) category. Criteria: readers' top choices for arts travel destinations based on the richness and variety of visual arts sites, activities and events. *American Style, "2012 Top 25 Arts Destinations," June 2012*

Dating/Romance Rankings

- A *Cosmopolitan* magazine article surveyed the gender balance and other factors to arrive at a list of the best and worst cities for women to meet single guys. San Antonio was #9 among the best for single women looking for dates. *www.cosmopolitan.com, "Working the Ratio," October 1, 2013*

- Of the 100 U.S. cities surveyed by *Men's Health* in its quest to identify the nation's best cities for dating and forming relationships, San Antonio was ranked #28 for online dating (#1 = best). *Men's Health, "The Best and Worst Cities for Online Dating," January 30, 2013*

- San Antonio was selected as one of the most romantic cities in America by Amazon.com. The city ranked #1 of 20. Criteria: cities with 100,000 or more residents were ranked on their per capita sales of romance novels and relationship books, romantic comedy movies, romantic music, and sexual wellness products. *Amazon.com, "Top 20 Most Romantic Cities in America," February 3, 2014*

Education Rankings

- *Men's Health* ranked 100 U.S. cities in terms of their education levels. San Antonio was ranked #76 (#1 = most educated city). Criteria: high school graduation rates; school enrollment; educational attainment; number of households who have outstanding student loans; number of households whose members have taken adult-education courses. *Men's Health, "Where School Is In: The Most and Least Educated Cities," September 12, 2011*

- San Antonio was selected as one of America's most literate cities. The city ranked #73 out of the 77 largest U.S. cities. Criteria: number of booksellers; library resources; Internet resources; educational attainment; periodical publishing resources; newspaper circulation. *Central Connecticut State University, "America's Most Literate Cities, 2013"*

Environmental Rankings

- The San Antonio metro area came in at #345 for the relative comfort of its climate on Sperling's list of "chill cities," as measured by the Sperling Heat Index. All 361 metro areas are included. Criteria included daytime high temperatures, nighttime low temperatures, dew point, and relative humidity at the high temperatures. *www.bertsperling.com, "Sperling's Chill Cities," July 18, 2013*

- Sperling's BestPlaces assessed 379 metropolitan areas of the United States for the likelihood of dangerously extreme weather events or earthquakes. In general the Southeast and South-Central regions have the highest risk of weather extremes and earthquakes, while the Pacific Northwest enjoys the lowest risk. Of the least risky metropolitan areas, the San Antonio metro area was ranked #356. *www.bestplaces.net, "Safest Places from Natural Disasters," April 2011*

- San Antonio was selected as one of 22 "Smarter Cities" for energy by the Natural Resources Defense Council. Criteria: investment in green power; energy efficiency measures; conservation. *Natural Resources Defense Council, "2010 Smarter Cities," July 19, 2010*

- San Antonio was highlighted as one of the top 25 cleanest metro areas for short-term particle pollution (24-hour PM 2.5) in the U.S. during 2008 through 2010. Monitors in these cities reported no days with unhealthful PM 2.5 levels. *American Lung Association, State of the Air 2012*

Food/Drink Rankings

- *Men's Health* ranked 100 major U.S. cities in terms of alcohol intoxication. San Antonio ranked #99 (#1 = most sober).Criteria: binge drinking; alcohol-related traffic accidents, arrests, and fatalities. *Men's Health, "The Drunkest Cities in America," November 19, 2013*

- San Antonio was identified as one of "America's Drunkest Cities of 2011" by *The Daily Beast*. The city ranked #5 out of 25. Criteria: binge drinking; drinks consumed per month. *The Daily Beast, "Tipsy Towns: Where are America's Drunkest Cities?," December 31, 2011*

Health/Fitness Rankings

- Analysts who tracked obesity rates in the nation's largest metro areas (those with populations above one million) found that the San Antonio metro area was one of the ten major metros where residents were most likely to be obese, defined as a BMI score of 30 or above. *www.gallup.com, "Boulder, Colo., Residents Still Least Likely to Be Obese," April 4, 2014*

- For each of the 50 most populous metro areas in the United States, the American College of Sports Medicine's American Fitness Index evaluated infrastructure, community assets, and policies that encourage healthy and fit lifestyles, including preventive health behaviors, levels of chronic disease conditions, health care access, and community resources and policies that support physical activity. The San Antonio metro area ranked #48 for "community fitness." Personal health indicators were considered as well as community and environmental indicators. *www.americanfitnessindex.org, "ACSM American Fitness Index Health and Community Fitness Status of the 50 Largest Metropolitan Areas," May 2013*

- San Antonio was selected as one of the 25 fittest cities in America by *Men's Fitness Online*. It ranked #25 out of America's 50 largest cities. Criteria: fitness centers and sport stores; nutrition; sports participation; TV viewing; overweight/sedentary; junk food; air quality; geography; commute; parks and open space; city recreational facilities; access to healthcare; motivation; mayor and city initiatives; state obesity initiatives. *Men's Fitness, "The Fittest and Fattest Cities in America," March 5, 2012*

- San Antonio was identified as a "2013 Spring Allergy Capital." The area ranked #24 out of 100. Three groups of factors were used to identify the most severe cities for people with allergies during the spring season: annual pollen levels; medicine utilization; access to board-certified allergists. *Asthma and Allergy Foundation of America, "Spring Allergy Capitals 2013"*

- San Antonio was identified as a "2013 Fall Allergy Capital." The area ranked #23 out of 100. Three groups of factors were used to identify the most severe cities for people with allergies during the fall season: annual pollen levels; medicine utilization; access to board-certified allergists. *Asthma and Allergy Foundation of America, "Fall Allergy Capitals 2013"*

- San Antonio was identified as a "2013 Asthma Capital." The area ranked #66 out of the nation's 100 largest metropolitan areas. Twelve factors were used to identify the most challenging places to live for people with asthma: estimated prevalence; self-reported prevalence; crude death rate for asthma; annual pollen score; annual air quality; public smoking laws; number of board-certified asthma specialists; school inhaler access laws; rescue medication use; controller medication use; uninsured rate; poverty rate. *Asthma and Allergy Foundation of America, "Asthma Capitals 2013"*

- *Men's Health* ranked 100 major U.S. cities in terms of the best and worst cities for men. San Antonio ranked #62. Criteria: thirty-three data points were examined covering health, fitness, and quality of life. *Men's Health, "The Best & Worst Cities for Men 2014," December 6, 2013*

- Breathe Right Nasal Strips, in partnership with Sperling's BestPlaces, analyzed 50 metro areas and identified those U.S. cities most challenged by chronic nasal congestion. The San Antonio metro area ranked #6. Criteria: tree, grass and weed pollens; molds and spores; air pollution; climate; smoking; purchase habits of congestion products; prescriptions of drugs for congestion relief; incidence of influenza. *Breathe Right Nasal Strips, "Most Congested Cities," October 3, 2011*

- The San Antonio metro area appeared in the 2013 Gallup-Healthways Well-Being Index. The area ranked #75 out of 189. The Gallup-Healthways Well-Being Index score is an average of six sub-indexes, which individually examine life evaluation, emotional health, work environment, physical health, healthy behaviors, and access to basic necessities. Results are based on telephone interviews conducted as part of the Gallup-Healthways Well-Being Index survey January 2–December 29, 2012, and January 2–December 30, 2013, with a random sample of 531,630 adults, aged 18 and older, living in metropolitan areas in the 50 U.S. states and the District of Columbia. *Gallup-Healthways, "State of American Well-Being," March 25, 2014*

- The San Antonio metro area was identified as one of "America's Most Stressful Cities" by *Sperling's BestPlaces*. The metro area ranked #40 out of 50. Criteria: unemployment rate; suicide rate; commute time; mental health; poor rest; alcohol use; violent crime rate; property crime rate; cloudy days annually. *Sperling's BestPlaces, www.BestPlaces.net, "Stressful Cities 2012*

- *Men's Health* ranked 100 U.S. cities in terms of their activity levels. San Antonio was ranked #66 (#1 = most active city). Criteria: where and how often residents exercise; percentage of households that watch more than 15 hours of cable television a week and buy more than 11 video games a year; death rate from deep-vein thrombosis, a condition linked to sitting for extended periods of time. *Men's Health, "Where Sit Happens: The Most and Least Active Cities in America," June 20, 2011*

- *The Daily Beast* identified the 30 U.S. metro areas with the worst smoking habits. The San Antonio metro area ranked #17. Sixty urban centers with populations of more than one million were ranked based on the following criteria: number of smokers; number of cigarettes smoked per day; fewest attempts to quit. *The Daily Beast, "30 Cities With Smoking Problems," January 3, 2011*

Real Estate Rankings

- San Antonio ranked #4 in a *Forbes* study of the rental housing market in the nation's 44 largest metropolitan areas to determine the cities that are best for renters. Criteria: average rent in 2012's first quarter, year-over-year change in that figure, vacancy rate, and average monthly rent payment compared with average monthly mortgage payment. *Forbes.com, "The Best and Worst Cities for Renters," June 14, 2012*

- San Antonio was ranked #117 out of 283 metro areas in terms of house price appreciation in 2013 (#1 = highest rate). *Federal Housing Finance Agency, House Price Index, 4th Quarter 2013*

- San Antonio was ranked #171 out of 224 metro areas in terms of housing affordability in 2013 by the National Association of Home Builders (#1 = most affordable). The NAHB-Wells Fargo Housing Opportunity Index (HOI) for a given area is defined as the share of homes sold in that area that would have been affordable to a family earning the local median income, based on standard mortgage underwriting criteria. *National Association of Home Builders®, NAHB-Wells Fargo Housing Opportunity Index, 4th Quarter 2013*

- San Antonio was selected as one of the best college towns for renters by ApartmentRatings.com." The area ranked #72 out of 87. Overall satisfaction ratings were ranked using thousands of user submitted scores for hundreds of apartment complexes located in cities and towns that are home to the 100 largest four-year institutions in the U.S. *ApartmentRatings.com, "2011 College Town Renter Satisfaction Rankings"*

Safety Rankings

- Symantec, in partnership with Sperling's BestPlaces, ranked the 50 largest cities in the U.S. in terms of their vulnerability to cybercrime. The city ranked #43. Criteria: number of cyberattacks and potential infections; level of Internet access; expenditures on smartphones and computer hardware/software; wireless hotspots; broadband connectivity; Internet usage; online purchases. *Symantec, "Riskiest Online Cities of 2012" February 15, 2012*

- Allstate ranked the 200 largest cities in America in terms of driver safety. San Antonio ranked #141. Allstate researchers analyzed internal property damage claims over a two-year period from January 2010 to December 2011. A weighted average of the two-year numbers determined the annual percentages. *Allstate, "Allstate America's Best Drivers Report®, August 27, 2013"*

- San Antonio was identified as one of the safest large cities in America by CQ Press. All 32 cities with populations of 500,000 or more that reported crime rates in 2012 for murder, rape, robbery, aggravated assault, burglary, and motor vehicle thefts were ranked. The city ranked #10 out of the top 10. *CQ Press, City Crime Rankings 2014*

- The National Insurance Crime Bureau ranked 380 metro areas in the U.S. in terms of per capita rates of vehicle theft. The San Antonio metro area ranked #38 (#1 = highest rate). Criteria: number of vehicle theft offenses per 100,000 inhabitants in 2012. *National Insurance Crime Bureau, "Hot Spots 2012," June 26, 2013*

- The San Antonio metro area was identified as one of the most dangerous metro areas for pedestrians by Transportation for America. The metro area ranked #24 out of 52 metro areas with over 1 million residents. Criteria: area's population divided by the number of pedestrian fatalities in that area. *Transportation for America, "Dangerous by Design 2011"*

Seniors/Retirement Rankings

- For *U.S. News & World Report's* Best Places rankings, the editors sought out affordable cities where retirees spend the least on housing and can live on $75 a day while still having easy access to amenities they want and need, such as recreation, services for seniors, and medical facilities. San Antonio was among the ten cities that best satisfied their criteria. *money.usnews.com, "The Best Places to Retire on $75 a Day," October 15, 2013*

- From its Best Cities for Successful Aging indexes, the Milken Institute generated rankings for metropolitan areas, weighing data in eight categories—general indicators, health care, wellness, living arrangements, transportation and general accessibility, financial well-being, education and employment, and community participation. The San Antonio metro area was ranked #76 overall in the large metro area category. *Milken Institute, "Best Cities for Successful Aging," July 2012*

- The AARP named San Antonio one of the "10 Best Places to Live on $100 a Day." Analysts looked at 200 cities to arrive at their 10-best list. Criteria includes: cost of living; quality-of-life; arts and culture; educational institutions; restaurants; community life; health care; natural setting; sunny days per year; and overall vibe. *AARP The Magazine, "10 Best Places to Live on $100 a Day," July 2012*

- *U.S. News & World Report* listed the best places to retire on an income of $40,000 per year. San Antonio was among the ten cities selected. Criteria: low cost of living; affordable housing; quality of life; accessible major medical facilities; services for seniors; educational institutions; outdoor recreational activities. *U.S. News & World Report, "Best Places to Retire for Under $40,000," October 15, 2012*

- Bankers Life and Casualty Company, in partnership with Sperling's BestPlaces, ranked the nation's 50 largest metro areas in terms of the "Best U.S. Cities for Seniors." The San Antonio metro area ranked #34. Criteria: healthcare; transportation; housing; environment; economy; health and longevity; social and spiritual life; crime. *Bankers Life and Casualty Company, Center for a Secure Retirement, "Best U.S. Cities for Seniors 2011," September 2011*

- San Antonio was identified as one of the most popular places to retire by *Topretirements.com*. The list reflects the 100 cities (out of 900+ total cities reviewed) that visitors to the website are most interested in for retirement. *Topretirements.com, "Most Popular Places to Retire for 2014," February 25, 2014*

Sports/Recreation Rankings

- San Antonio appeared on the *Sporting News* list of the "Best Sports Cities" for 2011. The area ranked #39 out of 271. Criteria: the magazine takes a 12-month snapshot of each city's sports, putting a heavy premium on regular-season won-lost records (from the most recently completed season). Other criteria include: playoff berths, bowl appearances and tournament bids; championships; applicable power ratings; quality of competition; overall fan fervor (measured in part by attendance); abundance of teams (rewarding quality over quantity); stadium and arena quality; ticket availability and prices; franchise ownership; and marquee appeal of athletes. *Sporting News, "Best Sports Cities 2011," October 4, 2011*

- San Antonio appeared on the *Sporting News* list of the "Best Sports Cities" for 2011. The area ranked #39 out of 271. Criteria: a 12-month snapshot of regular-season won-lost records (from the most recently completed season). Other criteria include: playoff berths, bowl appearances and tournament bids; championships; applicable power ratings; quality of competition; overall fan fervor (measured in part by attendance); abundance of teams (quality over quantity); stadium and arena quality; ticket availability and prices; franchise ownership; and marquee appeal of athletes. *Sporting News, "Best Sports Cities 2011," October 4, 2011*

- San Antonio was chosen as a bicycle friendly community by the League of American Bicyclists. A "Bicycle Friendly Community" welcomes cyclists by providing safe accommodation for cycling and encouraging people to bike for transportation and recreation. There are four award levels: Platinum; Gold; Silver; and Bronze. The community achieved an award level of Bronze. *League of American Bicyclists, "Bicycle Friendly Community Master List," Fall 2013*

- San Antonio was selected as one of the most playful cities in the U.S. by KaBOOM! The organization's Playful City USA initiative honors cities and towns across the nation for a vision, plan and commitment to creating an agenda for play. Criteria: creating a local play commission or task force; designing an annual action plan for play; conducting a play space audit; outlining a financial investment in play for the current fiscal year; and proclaiming and celebrating an annual "play day." *KaBOOM! National Campaign for Play, "2013 Playful City USA Communities"*

- San Antonio was chosen as one of America's best cities for bicycling. The city ranked #47 out of 50. Criteria: robust cycling infrastructure; vibrant bike culture. The editors only considered cities with populations of 95,000 or more. *Bicycling, "America's Top 50 Bike-Friendly Cities," May 23, 2012*

Transportation Rankings

- San Antonio was identified as one of America's worst cities for speed traps by the National Motorists Association. The city ranked #13 out of 25. Criteria: speed trap locations per 100,000 residents. *National Motorists Association, September 2011*

Women/Minorities Rankings

- *Women's Health* examined U.S. cities and identified the 100 best cities for women. San Antonio was ranked #44. Criteria: 30 categories were examined from obesity and breast cancer rates to commuting times and hours spent working out. *Women's Health, "Best Cities for Women 2012"*

- San Antonio was selected as one of the 25 healthiest cities for Latinas by *Latina Magazine*. The city ranked #13. Criteria: U.S. cities with populations over 500,000 residents were evaluated on the following criteria: percentage of 18-34 year-olds per city; Latino college graduation rates; number of colleges and universities; affordability; housing costs; income growth over time; average salary; percentage of singles; climate; safety; how the city's diversity compares to the national average; opportunities for minority entrepreneurs. *Latina Magazine, "Top 15 U.S. Cities for Young Latinos to Live In," August 19, 2011*

- San Antonio was selected as one of the best cities for young Latinos in 2013 by mun2, a national cable television broadcast network. The city ranked #1. Criteria: U.S. cities with populations over 500,000 residents were evaluated on the following criteria: number of young latinos; jobs; friendliness; cost of living; fun. *mun2.tv, "Best Cities for Young Latinos 2013*

- The San Antonio metro area appeared on *Forbes'* list of the "Best Cities for Minority Entrepreneurs." The area ranked #1 out of 10. Criteria: 52 metropolitan statistical areas were examined. For each ethnicity (African Americans, Asians and Hispanics), the editors measured housing affordability, population growth, income growth, and entrepreneurship (per capita self-employment). *Forbes, "Best Cities for Minority Entrepreneurs," March 23, 2011*

Miscellaneous Rankings

- *Men's Health* ranked 100 U.S. cities by their level of sadness. San Antonio was ranked #33 (#1 = saddest city). Criteria: suicide rates; unemployment rates; percentage of households that use antidepressants; percent of population who report feeling blue all or most of the time. *Men's Health, "Frown Towns," November 28, 2011*

- San Antonio was selected as one of "America's Best Cities for Hipsters" by *Travel + Leisure*. The city was ranked #16 out of 20. Criteria: live music; coffee bars; independent boutiques; best microbrews; offbeat and tech-savvy locals. *Travel + Leisure, "America's Best Cities for Hipsters," November 2013*

- The National Alliance to End Homelessness ranked the 100 most populous metro areas in terms the rate of homelessness. The San Antonio metro area ranked #51. Criteria: number of homeless people per 10,000 population in 2011. *National Alliance to End Homelessness, The State of Homelessness in America 2012*

Business Environment

CITY FINANCES

City Government Finances

Component	2011 ($000)	2011 ($ per capita)
Total Revenues	4,037,291	3,038
Total Expenditures	4,240,164	3,191
Debt Outstanding	8,949,159	6,734
Cash and Securities[1]	4,231,002	3,184

Note: (1) Cash and security holdings of a government at the close of its fiscal year, including those of its dependent agencies, utilities, and liquor stores.
Source: U.S Census Bureau, State & Local Government Finances 2011

City Government Revenue by Source

Source	2011 ($000)	2011 ($ per capita)
General Revenue		
From Federal Government	100,924	76
From State Government	133,498	100
From Local Governments	35,086	26
Taxes		
Property	379,661	286
Sales and Gross Receipts	307,311	231
Personal Income	0	0
Corporate Income	0	0
Motor Vehicle License	0	0
Other Taxes	35,358	27
Current Charges	509,956	384
Liquor Store	0	0
Utility	2,187,773	1,646
Employee Retirement	197,946	149

Source: U.S Census Bureau, State & Local Government Finances 2011

City Government Expenditures by Function

Function	2011 ($000)	2011 ($ per capita)	2011 (%)
General Direct Expenditures			
Air Transportation	141,399	106	3.3
Corrections	0	0	0.0
Education	0	0	0.0
Employment Security Administration	0	0	0.0
Financial Administration	34,040	26	0.8
Fire Protection	207,233	156	4.9
General Public Buildings	14,099	11	0.3
Governmental Administration, Other	9,137	7	0.2
Health	28,780	22	0.7
Highways	130,975	99	3.1
Hospitals	0	0	0.0
Housing and Community Development	59,608	45	1.4
Interest on General Debt	36,967	28	0.9
Judicial and Legal	20,421	15	0.5
Libraries	31,577	24	0.7
Parking	523	< 1	< 0.1
Parks and Recreation	155,578	117	3.7
Police Protection	294,562	222	6.9
Public Welfare	133,331	100	3.1
Sewerage	263,783	198	6.2
Solid Waste Management	81,268	61	1.9
Veterans' Services	0	0	0.0
Liquor Store	0	0	0.0
Utility	2,316,530	1,743	54.6
Employee Retirement	88,606	67	2.1

Source: U.S Census Bureau, State & Local Government Finances 2011

DEMOGRAPHICS

Population Growth

Area	1990 Census	2000 Census	2010 Census	Population Growth (%)	
				1990-2000	2000-2010
City	997,258	1,144,646	1,327,407	14.8	16.0
MSA[1]	1,407,745	1,711,703	2,142,508	21.6	25.2
U.S.	248,709,873	281,421,906	308,745,538	13.2	9.7

Note: (1) Figures cover the San Antonio-New Braunfels, TX Metropolitan Statistical Area—see Appendix B for areas included
Source: U.S. Census Bureau, Census 1990, 2000, 2010

Household Size

Area	Persons in Household (%)							Average Household Size
	One	Two	Three	Four	Five	Six	Seven or More	
City	28.4	29.5	16.3	13.2	7.2	3.2	2.3	2.80
MSA[1]	25.1	31.2	16.5	14.2	7.4	3.2	2.3	2.83
U.S.	27.6	33.5	15.7	13.2	6.1	2.4	1.5	2.63

Note: (1) Figures cover the San Antonio-New Braunfels, TX Metropolitan Statistical Area—see Appendix B for areas included
Source: U.S. Census Bureau, 2010-2012 American Community Survey 3-Year Estimates

Race

Area	White Alone[2] (%)	Black Alone[2] (%)	Asian Alone[2] (%)	AIAN[3] Alone[2] (%)	NHOPI[4] Alone[2] (%)	Other Race Alone[2] (%)	Two or More Races (%)
City	75.2	6.7	2.2	0.8	0.1	12.3	2.6
MSA[1]	77.7	6.4	2.1	0.7	0.1	10.1	2.9
U.S.	74.0	12.6	4.9	0.8	0.2	4.7	2.8

Note: (1) Figures cover the San Antonio-New Braunfels, TX Metropolitan Statistical Area—see Appendix B for areas included; (2) Alone is defined as not being in combination with one or more other races; (3) American Indian and Alaska Native; (4) Native Hawaiian and Other Pacific Islander
Source: U.S. Census Bureau, 2010-2012 American Community Survey 3-Year Estimates

Hispanic or Latino Origin

Area	Total (%)	Mexican (%)	Puerto Rican (%)	Cuban (%)	Other (%)
City	63.3	57.4	1.1	0.2	4.6
MSA[1]	54.3	48.9	1.0	0.2	4.2
U.S.	16.6	10.7	1.6	0.6	3.7

Note: Persons of Hispanic or Latino origin can be of any race; (1) Figures cover the San Antonio-New Braunfels, TX Metropolitan Statistical Area—see Appendix B for areas included
Source: U.S. Census Bureau, 2010-2012 American Community Survey 3-Year Estimates

Segregation

Type	Segregation Indices[1]				Percent Change		
	1990	2000	2010	2010 Rank[2]	1990-2000	1990-2010	2000-2010
Black/White	56.1	52.8	49.0	73	-3.3	-7.1	-3.8
Asian/White	33.8	35.4	38.3	66	1.6	4.5	2.9
Hispanic/White	52.1	49.7	46.1	43	-2.4	-6.0	-3.6

Note: All figures cover the Metropolitan Statistical Area—see Appendix B for areas included; Figures are based on an analysis of 1990, 2000, and 2010 Census Decennial Census tract data by William H. Frey, Brookings Institution and the University of Michigan Social Science Data Analysis Network. In this analysis all racial groups (whites, blacks, and asians) are non-Hispanic members of those races. Hispanics are shown as a separate category;
(1) Segregation Indices are Dissimilarity Indices that measure the degree to which the minority group is distributed differently than whites across census tracts. They range from 0 (complete integration) to 100 (complete segregation) where the value indicates the percentage of the minority group that needs to move to be distributed exactly like whites; (2) Ranges from 1 (most segregated) to 102 (least segregated); n/a not available.
Source: www.CensusScope.org

Ancestry

Area	German	Irish	English	American	Italian	Polish	French[2]	Scottish	Dutch
City	8.4	4.7	4.0	3.9	1.8	1.1	1.5	1.0	0.5
MSA[1]	12.2	6.1	5.5	4.3	1.9	1.6	2.0	1.2	0.6
U.S.	15.2	11.1	8.2	7.2	5.6	3.1	2.8	1.7	1.4

Note: Figures are the percentage of the total population reporting a particular ancestry. The nine most commonly reported ancestries in the U.S. are shown. Figures include multiple ancestries (e.g. if a person reported being Irish and Italian, they were included in both columns); (1) Figures cover the San Antonio-New Braunfels, TX Metropolitan Statistical Area—see Appendix B for areas included; (2) Excludes Basque
Source: U.S. Census Bureau, 2010-2012 American Community Survey 3-Year Estimates

Foreign-Born Population

Area	Any Foreign Country	\multicolumn{8}{c}{Percent of Population Born in}

Area	Any Foreign Country	Mexico	Asia	Europe	Carribean	South America	Central America[2]	Africa	Canada
City	14.3	10.0	2.1	0.7	0.2	0.3	0.8	0.3	0.1
MSA[1]	12.0	8.1	1.8	0.7	0.2	0.3	0.7	0.2	0.1
U.S.	13.0	3.7	3.7	1.6	1.2	0.9	1.0	0.5	0.3

Note: (1) Figures cover the San Antonio-New Braunfels, TX Metropolitan Statistical Area—see Appendix B for areas included; (2) Excludes Mexico.
Source: U.S. Census Bureau, 2010-2012 American Community Survey 3-Year Estimates

Marital Status

Area	Never Married	Now Married[2]	Separated	Widowed	Divorced
City	35.5	43.4	3.1	5.5	12.5
MSA[1]	31.8	48.7	2.6	5.3	11.6
U.S.	32.4	48.4	2.2	6.0	11.0

Note: Figures are percentages and cover the population 15 years of age and older; (1) Figures cover the San Antonio-New Braunfels, TX Metropolitan Statistical Area—see Appendix B for areas included; (2) Excludes separated
Source: U.S. Census Bureau, 2010-2012 American Community Survey 3-Year Estimates

Age

Area	\multicolumn{9}{c}{Percent of Population}	Median Age

Area	Under Age 5	Age 5–19	Age 20–34	Age 35–44	Age 45–54	Age 55–64	Age 65–74	Age 75–84	Age 85+	Median Age
City	7.4	22.2	23.4	13.0	13.1	10.2	5.9	3.4	1.4	32.8
MSA[1]	7.2	22.3	21.5	13.3	13.5	11.0	6.3	3.5	1.4	34.3
U.S.	6.4	20.1	20.5	13.1	14.3	12.2	7.3	4.2	1.8	37.3

Note: (1) Figures cover the San Antonio-New Braunfels, TX Metropolitan Statistical Area—see Appendix B for areas included
Source: U.S. Census Bureau, 2010-2012 American Community Survey 3-Year Estimates

Gender

Area	Males	Females	Males per 100 Females
City	661,308	696,835	94.9
MSA[1]	1,078,236	1,114,703	96.7
U.S.	153,276,055	158,333,314	96.8

Note: (1) Figures cover the San Antonio-New Braunfels, TX Metropolitan Statistical Area—see Appendix B for areas included
Source: U.S. Census Bureau, 2010-2012 American Community Survey 3-Year Estimates

Religious Groups by Family

Area	Catholic	Baptist	Non-Den.	Methodist[2]	Lutheran	LDS[3]	Pentecostal	Presbyterian[4]	Muslim[5]	Judaism
MSA[1]	28.4	8.5	6.0	3.1	1.7	1.4	1.3	0.8	1.0	0.2
U.S.	19.1	9.3	4.0	4.0	2.3	2.0	1.9	1.6	0.8	0.7

Note: Figures are the number of adherents as a percentage of the total population; (1) Figures cover the San Antonio-New Braunfels, TX Metropolitan Statistical Area—see Appendix B for areas included; (2) Methodist/Pietist; (3) Latter Day Saints; (4) Reformed; (5) Figures are estimates
Source: Association of Statisticians of American Religious Bodies, 2010 U.S. Religion Census: Religious Congregations & Membership Study

Religious Groups by Tradition

Area	Catholic	Evangelical Protestant	Mainline Protestant	Other Tradition	Black Protestant	Orthodox
MSA[1]	28.4	17.0	5.0	3.2	0.4	0.1
U.S.	19.1	16.2	7.3	4.3	1.6	0.3

Note: Figures are the number of adherents as a percentage of the total population; (1) Figures cover the San Antonio-New Braunfels, TX Metropolitan Statistical Area—see Appendix B for areas included
Source: Association of Statisticians of American Religious Bodies, 2010 U.S. Religion Census: Religious Congregations & Membership Study

ECONOMY

Gross Metropolitan Product

Area	2011	2012	2013	2014	Rank[2]
MSA[1]	87.2	92.0	94.1	99.0	36

Note: Figures are in billions of dollars; (1) Figures cover the San Antonio-New Braunfels, TX Metropolitan Statistical Area—see Appendix B for areas included; (2) Rank is based on 2014 data and ranges from 1 to 363
Source: The United States Conference of Mayors, U.S. Metro Economies: Outlook—Gross Metropolitan Product, with Metro Employment Projections, November 2013

Economic Growth

Area	2011 (%)	2012 (%)	2013 (%)	2014 (%)	Rank[2]
MSA[1]	3.9	3.8	1.0	3.2	155
U.S.	1.6	2.5	1.7	2.5	–

Note: Figures are real gross metropolitan product (GMP) growth rates and represent annual average percent change; (1) Figures cover the San Antonio-New Braunfels, TX Metropolitan Statistical Area—see Appendix B for areas included; (2) Rank is based on 2013 data and ranges from 1 to 363
Source: The United States Conference of Mayors, U.S. Metro Economies: Outlook—Gross Metropolitan Product, with Metro Employment Projections, November 2013

Metropolitan Area Exports

Area	2007	2008	2009	2010	2011	2012	Rank[2]
MSA[1]	3,567.8	5,049.5	4,390.0	6,416.2	10,506.5	14,010.2	25

Note: Figures are in millions of dollars; (1) Figures cover the San Antonio-New Braunfels, TX Metropolitan Statistical Area—see Appendix B for areas included; (2) Rank is based on 2012 data and ranges from 1 to 369
Source: U.S. Department of Commerce, International Trade Administration, Office of Trade & Industry Information, Manufacturing & Services, data extracted April 1, 2014

INCOME

Income

Area	Per Capita ($)	Median Household ($)	Average Household ($)
City	22,171	45,074	60,254
MSA[1]	24,522	51,087	68,110
U.S.	27,385	51,771	71,579

Note: (1) Figures cover the San Antonio-New Braunfels, TX Metropolitan Statistical Area—see Appendix B for areas included
Source: U.S. Census Bureau, 2010-2012 American Community Survey 3-Year Estimates

Household Income Distribution

Area	Percent of Households Earning							
	Under $15,000	$15,000 -24,999	$25,000 -34,999	$35,000 -49,999	$50,000 -74,999	$75,000 -99,000	$100,000 -149,999	$150,000 and up
City	15.2	12.5	11.9	15.2	18.5	10.8	10.0	5.9
MSA[1]	12.7	10.9	10.7	14.6	19.0	12.0	12.3	7.7
U.S.	13.1	11.0	10.5	13.7	18.1	11.9	12.5	9.1

Note: (1) Figures cover the San Antonio-New Braunfels, TX Metropolitan Statistical Area—see Appendix B for areas included
Source: U.S. Census Bureau, 2010-2012 American Community Survey 3-Year Estimates

Poverty Rate

Area	All Ages	Under 18 Years Old	18 to 64 Years Old	65 Years and Over
City	20.4	29.7	17.6	13.4
MSA[1]	16.8	24.4	14.6	11.1
U.S.	15.7	22.2	14.6	9.3

Note: Figures are percentage of people whose income during the past 12 months was below the poverty level; (1) Figures cover the San Antonio-New Braunfels, TX Metropolitan Statistical Area—see Appendix B for areas included
Source: U.S. Census Bureau, 2010-2012 American Community Survey 3-Year Estimates

Personal Bankruptcy Filing Rate

Area	2008	2009	2010	2011	2012	2013
Bexar County	1.91	2.39	2.32	2.04	1.80	1.57
U.S.	3.53	4.61	4.97	4.37	3.76	3.29

Note: Numbers are per 1,000 population and include Chapter 7 and Chapter 13 filings
Source: Federal Deposit Insurance Corporation, Regional Economic Conditions, March 20, 2014

EMPLOYMENT

Labor Force and Employment

Area	Civilian Labor Force			Workers Employed		
	Dec. 2012	Dec. 2013	% Chg.	Dec. 2012	Dec. 2013	% Chg.
City	627,542	630,554	0.5	592,131	596,914	0.8
MSA[1]	1,024,714	1,028,922	0.4	966,143	973,947	0.8
U.S.	154,904,000	154,408,000	-0.3	143,060,000	144,423,000	1.0

Note: Data is not seasonally adjusted and covers workers 16 years of age and older; (1) Metropolitan Statistical Area—see Appendix B for areas included
Source: Bureau of Labor Statistics, Local Area Unemployment Statistics

Unemployment Rate

Area	2013											
	Jan.	Feb.	Mar.	Apr.	May	Jun.	Jul.	Aug.	Sep.	Oct.	Nov.	Dec.
City	6.5	6.0	5.8	5.6	6.1	6.5	6.4	5.9	6.1	5.8	5.6	5.3
MSA[1]	6.6	6.1	6.0	5.8	6.2	6.6	6.5	6.0	6.1	5.8	5.6	5.3
U.S.	8.5	8.1	7.6	7.1	7.3	7.8	7.7	7.3	7.0	7.0	6.6	6.5

Note: Data is not seasonally adjusted and covers workers 16 years of age and older; All figures are percentages; (1) Metropolitan Statistical Area—see Appendix B for areas included
Source: Bureau of Labor Statistics, Local Area Unemployment Statistics

Employment by Occupation

Occupation Classification	City (%)	MSA[1] (%)	U.S. (%)
Management, Business, Science, and Arts	33.0	34.7	36.0
Natural Resources, Construction, and Maintenance	10.1	10.3	9.1
Production, Transportation, and Material Moving	9.9	9.9	12.0
Sales and Office	26.4	25.9	24.7
Service	20.5	19.2	18.2

Note: Figures cover employed civilians 16 years of age and older; (1) Figures cover the San Antonio-New Braunfels, TX Metropolitan Statistical Area—see Appendix B for areas included
Source: U.S. Census Bureau, 2010-2012 American Community Survey 3-Year Estimates

Employment by Industry

Sector	MSA[1]		U.S.
	Number of Employees	Percent of Total	Percent of Total
Construction	42,300	4.6	4.2
Education and Health Services	140,300	15.3	15.5
Financial Activities	76,500	8.3	5.7
Government	163,000	17.7	16.1
Information	21,000	2.3	1.9
Leisure and Hospitality	116,300	12.7	10.2
Manufacturing	46,400	5.1	8.7
Mining and Logging	6,100	0.7	0.6
Other Services	34,100	3.7	3.9
Professional and Business Services	111,500	12.1	13.7
Retail Trade	106,700	11.6	11.4
Transportation and Utilities	23,800	2.6	3.8
Wholesale Trade	30,500	3.3	4.2

Note: Figures cover non-farm employment as of December 2013 and are not seasonally adjusted;
(1) Metropolitan Statistical Area—see Appendix B for areas included
Source: Bureau of Labor Statistics, Current Employment Statistics, Employment, Hours, and Earnings

Occupations with Greatest Projected Employment Growth: 2010 – 2020

Occupation[1]	2010 Employment	2020 Projected Employment	Numeric Employment Change	Percent Employment Change
Combined Food Preparation and Serving Workers, Including Fast Food	243,530	322,520	78,990	32.4
Elementary School Teachers, Except Special Education	166,090	233,860	67,780	40.8
Personal Care Aides	133,820	199,970	66,150	49.4
Retail Salespersons	370,620	433,180	62,560	16.9
Registered Nurses	184,700	245,870	61,160	33.1
Waiters and Waitresses	190,870	244,610	53,730	28.2
Office Clerks, General	262,740	314,810	52,070	19.8
Cashiers	250,510	292,730	42,220	16.9
Home Health Aides	82,420	123,970	41,550	50.4
Customer Service Representatives	200,880	241,030	40,160	20.0

Note: Projections cover Texas; (1) Sorted by numeric employment change
Source: www.projectionscentral.com, State Occupational Projections, 2010–2020 Long-Term Projections

Fastest Growing Occupations: 2010 – 2020

Occupation[1]	2010 Employment	2020 Projected Employment	Numeric Employment Change	Percent Employment Change
Biomedical Engineers	1,440	2,490	1,050	72.9
Diagnostic Medical Sonographers	3,560	5,410	1,850	51.9
Derrick Operators, Oil and Gas	7,190	10,860	3,670	51.1
Home Health Aides	82,420	123,970	41,550	50.4
Personal Care Aides	133,820	199,970	66,150	49.4
Service Unit Operators, Oil, Gas, and Mining	17,870	26,460	8,590	48.0
Special Education Teachers, Middle School	6,170	8,950	2,780	45.1
Special Education Teachers, Preschool, Kindergarten, and Elementary School	12,940	18,750	5,810	44.9
Rotary Drill Operators, Oil and Gas	7,160	10,340	3,180	44.4
Roustabouts, Oil and Gas	17,800	25,580	7,790	43.8

Note: Projections cover Texas; (1) Sorted by percent employment change and excludes occupations with numeric employment change less than 100
Source: www.projectionscentral.com, State Occupational Projections, 2010–2020 Long-Term Projections

Average Wages

Occupation	$/Hr.	Occupation	$/Hr.
Accountants and Auditors	33.35	Maids and Housekeeping Cleaners	9.38
Automotive Mechanics	18.10	Maintenance and Repair Workers	14.83
Bookkeepers	17.72	Marketing Managers	53.91
Carpenters	16.84	Nuclear Medicine Technologists	32.77
Cashiers	9.44	Nurses, Licensed Practical	20.50
Clerks, General Office	14.41	Nurses, Registered	31.82
Clerks, Receptionists/Information	11.73	Nursing Assistants	11.69
Clerks, Shipping/Receiving	13.09	Packers and Packagers, Hand	10.18
Computer Programmers	39.12	Physical Therapists	43.27
Computer Systems Analysts	36.21	Postal Service Mail Carriers	24.66
Computer User Support Specialists	20.90	Real Estate Brokers	28.51
Cooks, Restaurant	9.96	Retail Salespersons	12.42
Dentists	89.68	Sales Reps., Exc. Tech./Scientific	27.83
Electrical Engineers	41.41	Sales Reps., Tech./Scientific	41.84
Electricians	20.30	Secretaries, Exc. Legal/Med./Exec.	15.25
Financial Managers	59.79	Security Guards	11.83
First-Line Supervisors/Managers, Sales	22.31	Surgeons	84.64
Food Preparation Workers	9.66	Teacher Assistants	10.80
General and Operations Managers	52.56	Teachers, Elementary School	26.60
Hairdressers/Cosmetologists	13.02	Teachers, Secondary School	27.20
Internists	n/a	Telemarketers	n/a
Janitors and Cleaners	10.50	Truck Drivers, Heavy/Tractor-Trailer	16.40
Landscaping/Groundskeeping Workers	10.98	Truck Drivers, Light/Delivery Svcs.	14.14
Lawyers	54.75	Waiters and Waitresses	9.32

Note: Wage data covers the San Antonio-New Braunfels, TX Metropolitan Statistical Area—see Appendix B for areas included. Hourly wages for elementary/secondary school teachers and teacher assistants were calculated by the editors from annual wage data assuming a 40 hour work week; n/a not available.
Source: Bureau of Labor Statistics, Metro Area Occupational Employment and Wage Estimates, May 2013

RESIDENTIAL REAL ESTATE

Building Permits

Area	Single-Family			Multi-Family			Total		
	2012	2013	Pct. Chg.	2012	2013	Pct. Chg.	2012	2013	Pct. Chg.
City	1,896	2,102	10.9	2,747	16	-99.4	4,643	2,118	-54.4
MSA[1]	5,102	5,827	14.2	2,902	301	-89.6	8,004	6,128	-23.4
U.S.	518,695	620,802	19.7	310,963	370,020	19.0	829,658	990,822	19.4

Note: (1) Metropolitan Statistical Area—see Appendix B for areas included; figures represent new, privately-owned housing units authorized (unadjusted data); All permit data are based on estimates with imputation.
Source: U.S. Census Bureau, Manufacturing, Mining, and Construction Statistics, Building Permits, 2012, 2013

Homeownership Rate

Area	2006 (%)	2007 (%)	2008 (%)	2009 (%)	2010 (%)	2011 (%)	2012 (%)	2013 (%)
MSA[1]	62.6	62.4	66.1	69.8	70.1	66.5	67.5	70.1
U.S.	68.8	68.1	67.8	67.4	66.9	66.1	65.4	65.1

Note: (1) Figures cover the San Antonio-New Braunfels, TX Metropolitan Statistical Area—see Appendix B for areas included
Source: U.S. Census Bureau, Housing Vacancies and Homeownership Annual Statistics: 2013

Housing Vacancy Rates

Area	Gross Vacancy Rate[2] (%)			Year-Round Vacancy Rate[3] (%)			Rental Vacancy Rate[4] (%)			Homeowner Vacancy Rate[5] (%)		
	2011	2012	2013	2011	2012	2013	2011	2012	2013	2011	2012	2013
MSA[1]	11.2	11.3	9.0	10.2	10.4	8.3	9.2	9.0	9.1	1.5	2.7	1.4
U.S.	14.2	13.8	13.8	11.1	10.8	10.7	9.5	8.7	8.3	2.5	2.0	2.0

Note: (1) Figures cover the San Antonio-New Braunfels, TX Metropolitan Statistical Area—see Appendix B for areas included; (2) The percentage of the total housing inventory that is vacant; (3) The percentage of the housing inventory (excluding seasonal units) that is year-round vacant; (4) The percentage of rental inventory that is vacant for rent; (5) The percentage of homeowner inventory that is vacant for sale
Source: U.S. Census Bureau, Housing Vacancies and Homeownership Annual Statistics: 2013

TAXES

State Corporate Income Tax Rates

State	Tax Rate (%)	Income Brackets ($)	Num. of Brackets	Financial Institution Tax Rate (%)[a]	Federal Income Tax Ded.
Texas	(x)	–	–	(x)	No

Note: Tax rates as of January 1, 2014; (a) Rates listed are the corporate income tax rate applied to financial institutions or excise taxes based on income. Some states have other taxes based upon the value of deposits or shares; (x) Texas imposes a Franchise Tax, otherwise known as margin tax, imposed on entities with more than $1,030,000 total revenues at rate of 1%, or 0.5% for entities primarily engaged in retail or wholesale trade, on lesser of 70% of total revenues or 100%of gross receipts after deductions for either compensation or cost of goods sold.
Source: Federation of Tax Administrators, "State Corporate Income Tax Rates, 2014"

State Individual Income Tax Rates

State	Tax Rate (%)	Income Brackets ($)	Num. of Brackets	Personal Exempt. ($)[1] Single	Personal Exempt. ($)[1] Dependents	Fed. Inc. Tax Ded.
Texas	None	–	–	–	–	–

Note: Tax rates as of January 1, 2014; Local- and county-level taxes are not included; n/a not applicable; (1) Married joint filers generally receive double the single exemption
Source: Federation of Tax Administrators, "State Individual Income Tax Rates, 2014"

Various State and Local Tax Rates

State	State and Local Sales and Use (%)	State Sales and Use (%)	Gasoline[1] (¢/gal.)	Cigarette[2] ($/pack)	Spirits[3] ($/gal.)	Wine[4] ($/gal.)	Beer[5] ($/gal.)
Texas	8.25	6.25	20.00	1.410	2.40 (f)	0.20	0.20

Note: All tax rates as of January 1, 2014; (1) The American Petroleum Institute has developed a methodology for determining the average tax rate on a gallon of fuel. Rates may include any of the following: excise taxes, environmental fees, storage tank fees, other fees or taxes, general sales tax, and local taxes. In states where gasoline is subject to the general sales tax, or where the fuel tax is based on the average sale price, the average rate determined by API is sensitive to changes in the price of gasoline. States that fully or partially apply general sales taxes to gasoline: CA, CO, GA, IL, IN, MI, NY; (2) The federal excise tax of $1.0066 per pack and local taxes are not included; (3) Rates are those applicable to off-premise sales of 40% alcohol by volume (a.b.v.) distilled spirits in 750ml containers. Local excise taxes are excluded; (4) Rates are those applicable to off-premise sales of 11% a.b.v. non-carbonated wine in 750ml containers; (5) Rates are those applicable to off-premise sales of 4.7% a.b.v. beer in 12 ounce containers; (f) Different rates also applicable according to alcohol content, place of production, size of container, or place purchased (on- or off-premise or onboard airlines).
Source: Tax Foundation, 2014 Facts & Figures: How Does Your State Compare?

State Business Tax Climate Index Rankings

State	Overall Rank	Corporate Tax Index Rank	Individual Income Tax Index Rank	Sales Tax Index Rank	Unemployment Insurance Tax Index Rank	Property Tax Index Rank
Texas	11	38	7	36	14	35

Note: The index is a measure of how each state's tax laws affect economic performance. The lower the rank, the more favorable a state's tax system is for business. States without a given tax are given a ranking of 1. The scores/rankings for the District of Columbia do not affect other states. The 2014 index represents the tax climate as of July 1, 2013.
Source: Tax Foundation, State Business Tax Climate Index 2014

COMMERCIAL REAL ESTATE

Office Market

Market Area	Inventory (sq. ft.)	Vacancy Rate (%)	Under Construction (sq. ft.)	YTD Net Absorption (sq. ft.)	Total Average Asking Rent ($/sq. ft./year)
San Antonio	27,025,658	14.3	19,065	378,680	20.66
National	4,726,900,879	15.0	55,419,286	42,829,434	26.27

Source: Newmark Grubb Knight Frank, National Office Market Report, 4th Quarter 2013

Industrial/Warehouse/R&D Market

Market Area	Inventory (sq. ft.)	Vacancy Rate (%)	Under Construction (sq. ft.)	YTD Net Absorption (sq. ft.)	Total Average Asking Rent ($/sq. ft./year)
San Antonio	72,157,558	6.2	378,722	2,052,861	5.72
National	14,022,031,238	7.9	83,249,164	156,549,903	5.40

Source: Newmark Grubb Knight Frank, National Industrial Market Report, 4th Quarter 2013

COMMERCIAL UTILITIES

Typical Monthly Electric Bills

Area	Commercial Service ($/month)		Industrial Service ($/month)	
	1,500 kWh	40 kW demand 14,000 kWh	1,000 kW demand 200,000 kWh	50,000 kW demand 15,000,000 kWh
City	n/a	n/a	n/a	n/a
Average[1]	197	1,636	25,662	1,485,307

Note: Based on total rates in effect July 1, 2013; (1) average based on 180 utilities surveyed; n/a not available
Source: Edison Electric Institute, Typical Bills and Average Rates Report, Summer 2013

TRANSPORTATION

Means of Transportation to Work

Area	Car/Truck/Van Drove Alone	Car/Truck/Van Car-pooled	Bus	Subway	Railroad	Bicycle	Walked	Other Means	Worked at Home
City	79.3	11.0	3.2	0.0	0.0	0.2	2.0	1.1	3.1
MSA[1]	79.4	11.1	2.2	0.0	0.0	0.2	1.9	1.2	4.1
U.S.	76.4	9.7	2.6	1.7	0.5	0.6	2.8	1.3	4.3

Note: Figures are percentages and cover workers 16 years of age and older; (1) Figures cover the San Antonio-New Braunfels, TX Metropolitan Statistical Area—see Appendix B for areas included
Source: U.S. Census Bureau, 2010-2012 American Community Survey 3-Year Estimates

Travel Time to Work

Area	Less Than 10 Minutes	10 to 19 Minutes	20 to 29 Minutes	30 to 44 Minutes	45 to 59 Minutes	60 to 89 Minutes	90 Minutes or More
City	10.2	32.0	27.4	21.4	4.6	2.7	1.6
MSA[1]	10.8	29.1	24.7	22.8	6.9	3.8	1.9
U.S.	13.5	29.8	20.9	20.1	7.5	5.6	2.5

Note: Figures are percentages and include workers 16 years old and over; (1) Figures cover the San Antonio-New Braunfels, TX Metropolitan Statistical Area—see Appendix B for areas included
Source: U.S. Census Bureau, 2010-2012 American Community Survey 3-Year Estimates

Travel Time Index

Area	1985	1990	1995	2000	2005	2010	2011
Urban Area[1]	1.06	1.06	1.09	1.19	1.22	1.19	1.19
Average[2]	1.09	1.14	1.16	1.19	1.23	1.18	1.18

Note: Travel Time Index—the ratio of travel time in the peak period to the travel time at free-flow conditions. For example, a value of 1.30 indicates a 20-minute free-flow trip takes 26 minutes in the peak. Free-flow speeds (60 mph on freeways and 35 mph on principal arterials) are used as the comparison threshold; (1) Covers the San Antonio TX urban area; (2) average of 498 urban areas
Source: Texas Transportation Institute, Urban Mobility Report 2012, December 2012

Public Transportation

Agency Name / Mode of Transportation	Vehicles Operated in Maximum Service	Annual Unlinked Passenger Trips (in thous.)	Annual Passenger Miles (in thous.)
VIA Metropolitan Transit (VIA)			
Bus (directly operated)	352	49,322.8	206,931.0
Demand Response (directly operated)	90	505.3	5,600.2
Demand Response (purchased transportation)	102	545.5	6,164.1
Vanpool (purchased transportation)	179	430.8	18,852.0

Source: Federal Transit Administration, National Transit Database, 2012

Air Transportation

Airport Name and Code / Type of Service	Passenger Airlines[1]	Passenger Enplanements	Freight Carriers[2]	Freight (lbs.)
San Antonio International (SAT)				
Domestic service (U.S. carriers - 2013)	29	3,759,648	15	94,591,638
International service (U.S. carriers - 2012)	10	46,537	3	13,046,484

Note: (1) Includes all U.S.-based major, minor and commuter airlines that carried at least one passenger during the year; (2) Includes all U.S.-based airlines and freight carriers that transported at least one lb. of freight during the year.
Source: Bureau of Transportation Statistics, The Intermodal Transportation Database, Air Carriers: T-100 Domestic Market (U.S. Carriers), 2013; Bureau of Transportation Statistics, The Intermodal Transportation Database, Air Carriers: T-100 International Market (U.S. Carriers), 2012

Other Transportation Statistics

Major Highways:	I-10; I-35; I-37
Amtrak Service:	Yes
Major Waterways/Ports:	None

Source: Amtrak.com; Google Maps

BUSINESSES

Major Business Headquarters

Company Name	Rankings	
	Fortune[1]	Forbes[2]
CC Media Holdings	407	-
HE Butt Grocery	-	14
NuStar Energy	389	-
Tesoro	95	-
United Services Automobile Assn	139	-
Valero Energy	9	-

Note: (1) Fortune 500—companies that produce a 10-K are ranked 1 to 500 based on 2012 revenue; (2) all private companies with at least $2 billion in annual revenue through the end of their most current fiscal year are ranked 1 to 224; companies listed are headquartered in the city; dashes indicate no ranking
Source: Fortune, "Fortune 500," May 20, 2013; Forbes, "America's Largest Private Companies," December 18, 2013

Fast-Growing Businesses

According to *Inc.*, San Antonio is home to four of America's 500 fastest-growing private companies: **IT Strategic Performance Firm** (#185); **Vesa Health & Technology** (#229); **Taurean** (#349); **Personalized Prevention** (#485). Criteria: must be an independent, privately-held, for-profit, U.S. corporation, proprietorship or partnership; revenues must be at least $100,000 in 2009 and $2 million in 2012; must have four-year operating/sales history. Holding companies, regulated banks, and utilities were excluded. *Inc., "America's 500 Fastest-Growing Private Companies," September 2013*

According to *Fortune*, San Antonio is home to two of the 100 fastest-growing companies in the world: **Valero Energy** (#29); **Rackspace Hosting** (#96). Companies were ranked by their revenue growth rate; their EPS growth rate; and their three-year annualized total return to investors for the period ending June 30, 2013. Criteria for inclusion: a company, foreign or domestic, must trade on a major U.S. stock exchange; must file quarterly reports with the SEC; must have a minimum market capitalization of $250 million; must have a stock price of at least $5 on June 29, 2013; must have been trading continuously since June 30, 2009; must have revenue and net income for the four quarters ended on or before April 30, 2013, of at least $50 million and $10 million, respectively; and must have posted a compound annual growth in revenue and earnings per share of at least 20% annually over the three years ending on or before April 30, 2013. REITs, limited-liability companies, limited parterships, companies about to be acquired, and companies that lost money in the quarter ending April 30, 2013 were excluded. *Fortune, "100 Fastest-Growing Companies," August 29, 2013*

According to *Initiative for a Competitive Inner City (ICIC)*, San Antonio is home to two of America's 100 fastest-growing "inner city" companies: **InGenesis** (#4); **The Alamo Travel Group** (#97). Companies were ranked by their five-year compound annual growth rate. Criteria for inclusion: company must be headquartered in or have 51 percent or more of its physical operations in an economically distressed urban area; must be an independent, for-profit corporation, partnership or proprietorship; must have 10 or more employees and have a five-year sales history that includes sales of at least $200,000 in the base year and at least $1 million in the current year with no decrease in sales over the two most recent years. *Initiative for a Competitive Inner City (ICIC), "Inner City 100 Companies, 2013"*

According to Deloitte, San Antonio is home to one of North America's 500 fastest-growing high-technology companies: **Rackspace Hosting** (#486). Companies are ranked by percentage growth in revenue over a five-year period. Criteria for inclusion: company must be headquartered within North America; must own proprietary intellectual property or proprietary technology that contributes to a significant portion of the company's operating revenue, or devote a significant proportion of revenues to research and development of technology; must have been in business for a minumum of five years with 2008 operating revenues of at least $50,000 USD/CD and 2012 operating revenues of at least $5 million USD/CD. *Deloitte Touche Tohmatsu, 2013 Technology Fast 500*[TM]

Minority Business Opportunity

San Antonio is home to one company which is on the *Black Enterprise* Industrial/Service 100 list (100 largest companies based on gross sales): **Millennium Steel of Texas L.P.** (#18). Criteria: operational in previous calendar year; at least 51% black-owned and manufactures/owns the product it sells or provides industrial or consumer services. Brokerages, real estate firms and firms that provide professional services are not eligible. *Black Enterprise, B.E. 100s, 2013*

San Antonio is home to 13 companies which are on the *Hispanic Business* 500 list (500 largest U.S. Hispanic-owned companies based on 2012 revenue): **Genesis Networks Telecom Services** (#6); **Ancira Enterprises** (#7); **The Alamo Travel Group LP** (#65); **InGenesis** (#74); **Maldonado Nursery & Landscaping** (#172); **P3S Corp.** (#191); **Davila Pharmacy** (#248); **Garcia Foods** (#256); **Munoz & Co.** (#280); **LuLu's Dessert Corp.** (#387); **IDC** (#407); **J.R. Ramon & Sons** (#412); **Inventiva** (#457). Companies included must show at least 51 percent ownership by Hispanic U.S. citizens, and must maintain headquarters in one of the 50 states or Washington, D.C. *Hispanic Business, "Hispanic Business 500," June 20, 2013*

San Antonio is home to three companies which are on the *Hispanic Business* Fastest-Growing 100 list (greatest sales growth from 2008 to 2012): **InGenesis** (#2); **IDC** (#38); **Visual Net Design** (#55). Companies included must show at least 51 percent ownership by Hispanic U.S. citizens, and must maintain headquarters in one of the 50 states or Washington, D.C. In addition, companies must have minimum revenues of $200,000 for calendar year 2008. *Hispanic Business, June20, 2013*

Minority- and Women-Owned Businesses

Group	All Firms		Firms with Paid Employees			
	Firms	Sales ($000)	Firms	Sales ($000)	Employees	Payroll ($000)
Asian	3,893	1,370,455	1,258	1,273,871	7,827	226,171
Black	3,870	247,723	405	185,861	3,241	73,771
Hispanic	43,099	5,679,041	4,527	4,390,071	49,857	1,143,331
Women	30,581	5,468,661	3,714	4,750,495	40,585	944,051
All Firms	109,186	116,493,946	20,843	112,708,202	560,683	21,250,657

Note: Figures cover firms located in the city; minority- and women-owned business are defined as firms in which the corresponding group own 51% or more of the stock or equity of the company
Source: U.S. Census Bureau, 2007 Economic Census, Survey of Business Owners (2012 Survey of Business Owners data will be released starting in June 2015)

HOTELS & CONVENTION CENTERS

Hotels/Motels

Area	5 Star		4 Star		3 Star		2 Star		1 Star		Not Rated	
	Num.	Pct.[3]	Num.	Pct.[3]	Num.	Pct.[3]	Num.	Pct.[3]	Num.	Pct.[3]	Num.	Pct.[3]
City[1]	0	0.0	16	5.5	84	29.1	167	57.8	8	2.8	14	4.8
Total[2]	142	0.9	1,005	6.0	5,147	30.9	8,578	51.4	408	2.4	1,397	8.4

Note: (1) Figures cover San Antonio and vicinity; (2) Figures cover all 100 cities in this book; (3) Percentage of hotels which have a given star rating; Star ratings are determined by expedia.com and offer an indication of the general quality of a particular hotel.
Source: expedia.com, April 7, 2014

The San Antonio-New Braunfels, TX metro area is home to one of the best hotels in the U.S. according to *Travel & Leisure*: **Hyatt Regency Hill Country Resort & Spa**. Criteria: service; location; rooms; food; and value. The list includes the top 200 hotels in the U.S. *Travel & Leisure, "T+L 500, The World's Best Hotels 2014"*

The San Antonio-New Braunfels, TX metro area is home to two of the best hotels in the world according to *Condé Nast Traveler*: **Hotel Valencia Riverwalk**; **Mokara Hotel & Spa**. The selections are based on over 79,000 responses to the magazine's annual Readers' Choice Survey. The list includes the top 200 hotels in the U.S. *Condé Nast Traveler, "Gold List 2014, The World's Best Places to Stay"*

Major Convention Centers

Name	Overall Space (sq. ft.)	Exhibit Space (sq. ft.)	Meeting Space (sq. ft.)	Meeting Rooms
Henry B. Gonzalez Convention Center	1,300,000	440,000	n/a	59

Note: Table includes convention centers located in the San Antonio-New Braunfels, TX metro area; n/a not available
Source: Original research

Living Environment

COST OF LIVING

Cost of Living Index

Composite Index	Groceries	Housing	Utilities	Transportation	Health Care	Misc. Goods/ Services
88.4	81.4	79.5	82.6	95.5	93.7	96.6

Note: The Cost of Living Index measures regional differences in the cost of consumer goods and services, excluding taxes and non-consumer expenditures, for professional and managerial households in the top income quintile. It is based on more than 50,000 prices covering almost 60 different items for which prices are collected three times a year by chambers of commerce, economic development organizations or university applied economic centers in each participating urban area. The numbers shown should be read as a percentage above or below the national average of 100. For example, a value of 115.4 in the groceries column indicates that grocery prices are 15.4% higher than the national average. Small differences in the index numbers should not be interpreted as significant; Figures cover the San Antonio TX urban area.
Source: The Council for Community and Economic Research, ACCRA Cost of Living Index, 2013

Grocery Prices

Area[1]	T-Bone Steak ($/pound)	Frying Chicken ($/pound)	Whole Milk ($/half gal.)	Eggs ($/dozen)	Orange Juice ($/64 oz.)	Coffee ($/11.5 oz.)
City[2]	9.67	0.99	2.16	1.56	3.38	3.89
Avg.	10.19	1.28	2.34	1.81	3.48	4.39
Min.	8.56	0.94	1.44	1.19	2.78	3.40
Max.	14.82	2.28	3.56	3.73	6.23	7.32

*Note: (1) Values for the local area are compared with the average, minimum and maximum values for all 327 areas in the Cost of Living Index; (2) Figures cover the San Antonio TX urban area; **T-Bone Steak** (price per pound); **Frying Chicken** (price per pound, whole fryer); **Whole Milk** (half gallon carton); **Eggs** (price per dozen, Grade A, large); **Orange Juice** (64 oz. Tropicana or Florida Natural); **Coffee** (11.5 oz. can, vacuum-packed, Maxwell House, Hills Bros, or Folgers).*
Source: The Council for Community and Economic Research, ACCRA Cost of Living Index, 2013

Housing and Utility Costs

Area[1]	New Home Price ($)	Apartment Rent ($/month)	All Electric ($/month)	Part Electric ($/month)	Other Energy ($/month)	Telephone ($/month)
City[2]	222,574	838	-	92.24	36.48	24.49
Avg.	295,864	900	171.38	91.82	70.12	27.73
Min.	185,506	458	117.80	48.81	33.67	17.16
Max.	1,358,917	3,783	441.68	171.40	372.65	39.47

*Note: (1) Values for the local area are compared with the average, minimum and maximum values for all 327 areas in the Cost of Living Index; (2) Figures cover the San Antonio TX urban area; **New Home Price** (2,400 sf living area, 8,000 sf lot, in urban area with full utilities); **Apartment Rent** (950 sf 2 bedroom/1.5 or 2 bath, unfurnished, excluding all utilities except water); **All Electric** (average monthly cost for an all-electric home); **Part Electric** (average monthly cost for a part-electric home); **Other Energy** (average monthly cost for natural gas, fuel oil, coal, wood, and any other forms of energy except electricity); **Telephone** (price includes basic monthly rate for a private residential line plus additional local usage charges incurred by a family of four).*
Source: The Council for Community and Economic Research, ACCRA Cost of Living Index, 2013

Health Care, Transportation, and Other Costs

Area[1]	Doctor ($/visit)	Dentist ($/visit)	Optometrist ($/visit)	Gasoline ($/gallon)	Beauty Salon ($/visit)	Men's Shirt ($)
City[2]	96.00	88.07	85.55	3.33	41.27	27.57
Avg.	101.40	86.48	96.16	3.44	33.87	26.55
Min.	61.67	50.83	50.12	3.08	18.92	12.48
Max.	182.71	152.50	223.78	4.33	68.22	52.03

*Note: (1) Values for the local area are compared with the average, minimum and maximum values for all 327 areas in the Cost of Living Index; (2) Figures cover the San Antonio TX urban area; **Doctor** (general practitioners routine exam of an established patient); **Dentist** (adult teeth cleaning and periodic oral examination); **Optometrist** (full vision eye exam for established adult patient); **Gasoline** (one gallon regular unleaded, national brand, including all taxes, cash price at self-service pump if available); **Beauty Salon** (woman's shampoo, trim, and blow-dry); **Men's Shirt** (cotton/polyester dress shirt, pinpoint weave, long sleeves).*
Source: The Council for Community and Economic Research, ACCRA Cost of Living Index, 2013

HOUSING

House Price Index (HPI)

Area	National Ranking[2]	Quarterly Change (%)	One-Year Change (%)	Five-Year Change (%)
MSA[1]	117	2.81	3.13	6.38
U.S.[3]	–	1.20	7.69	4.18

Note: The HPI is a weighted repeat sales index. It measures average price changes in repeat sales or refinancings on the same properties. This information is obtained by reviewing repeat mortgage transactions on single-family properties whose mortgages have been purchased or securitized by Fannie Mae or Freddie Mac in January 1975; (1) San Antonio-New Braunfels, TX Metropolitan Statistical Area—see Appendix B for areas included; (2) Rankings are based on annual percentage change for all metro areas containing at least 15,000 transactions over the last 10 years and ranges from 1 to 283; (3) figures based on a weighted average of Census Division estimates using a seasonally adjusted, purchase-only index; all figures are for the period ending December 31, 2013
Source: Federal Housing Finance Agency, House Price Index, February 25, 2014

Median Single-Family Home Prices

Area	2011	2012	2013p	Percent Change 2012 to 2013
MSA[1]	152.5	159.5	171.0	7.2
U.S. Average	166.2	177.2	197.4	11.4

Note: Figures are median sales prices of existing single-family homes in thousands of dollars; (p) preliminary; n/a not available; (1) San Antonio-New Braunfels, TX Metropolitan Statistical Area—see Appendix B for areas included
Source: National Association of Realtors, Median Sales Price of Existing Single-Family Homes for Metropolitan Areas, 4th Quarter 2013

Qualifying Income Based on Median Sales Price of Existing Single-Family Homes

Area	With 5% Down ($)	With 10% Down ($)	With 20% Down ($)
MSA[1]	39,586	37,502	33,335
U.S. Average	45,395	43,006	38,228

Note: Figures are preliminary; Qualifying income is based on a mortgage rate of 4.4%. Monthly principal and interest payment is limited to 25% of income; n/a not available; (1) San Antonio-New Braunfels, TX Metropolitan Statistical Area—see Appendix B for areas included
Source: National Association of Realtors, Qualifying Income Based on Median Sales Price of Existing Single-Family Homes for Metropolitan Areas, 4th Quarter 2013

Median Apartment Condo-Coop Home Prices

Area	2011	2012	2013p	Percent Change 2012 to 2013
MSA[1]	n/a	n/a	n/a	n/a
U.S. Average	165.1	173.7	194.9	12.2

Note: Figures are median sales prices of existing apartment condo-coop homes in thousands of dollars; (p) preliminary; n/a not available; (1) San Antonio-New Braunfels, TX Metropolitan Statistical Area—see Appendix B for areas included
Source: National Association of Realtors, Median Sales Price of Existing Apartment Condo-Coop Homes for Metropolitan Areas, 4th Quarter 2013

Gross Monthly Rent

Area	Under $200	$200 -299	$300 -499	$500 -749	$750 -999	$1,000 -1,499	$1,500 and up	Median ($)
City	1.9	3.4	7.0	30.6	30.1	21.6	5.6	801
MSA[1]	1.6	3.1	7.0	28.5	29.3	23.7	6.7	825
U.S.	1.7	3.3	8.1	22.7	24.3	25.7	14.3	889

Note: Figures are percentages except for Median; Gross rent is the contract rent plus the estimated average monthly cost of utilities (electricity, gas, and water and sewer) and fuels (oil, coal, kerosene, wood, etc.) if these are paid by the renter (or paid for the renter by someone else); (1) Figures cover the San Antonio-New Braunfels, TX Metropolitan Statistical Area—see Appendix B for areas included
Source: U.S. Census Bureau, 2010-2012 American Community Survey 3-Year Estimates

Year Housing Structure Built

Area	2010 or Later	2000 -2009	1990 -1999	1980 -1989	1970 -1979	1960 -1969	1950 -1959	1940 -1949	Before 1940	Median Year
City	0.7	18.6	12.5	17.4	17.7	11.2	10.5	5.5	5.8	1980
MSA[1]	1.2	23.9	14.8	16.2	16.4	9.6	8.3	4.5	5.1	1984
U.S.	0.5	14.9	13.8	13.9	15.9	11.1	10.9	5.5	13.5	1976

Note: Figures are percentages except for Median Year; (1) Figures cover the San Antonio-New Braunfels, TX Metropolitan Statistical Area—see Appendix B for areas included
Source: U.S. Census Bureau, 2010-2012 American Community Survey 3-Year Estimates

HEALTH

Health Risk Data

Category	MSA[1] (%)	U.S. (%)
Adults aged 18–64 who have any kind of health care coverage	68.3	79.6
Adults who reported being in good or excellent health	81.0	83.1
Adults who are current smokers	17.7	19.6
Adults who are heavy drinkers[2]	7.3	6.1
Adults who are binge drinkers[3]	20.7	16.9
Adults who are overweight (BMI 25.0 - 29.9)	38.5	35.8
Adults who are obese (BMI 30.0 - 99.8)	28.5	27.6
Adults who participated in any physical activities in the past month	74.7	77.1
Adults 50+ who have ever had a sigmoidoscopy or colonoscopy	66.1	67.3
Women aged 40+ who have had a mammogram within the past two years	69.4	74.0
Men aged 40+ who have had a PSA test within the past two years	40.8	45.2
Adults aged 65+ who have had flu shot within the past year	63.6	60.1
Adults who always wear a seatbelt	96.8	93.8

Note: Data as of 2012 unless otherwise noted; (1) Figures cover the San Antonio, TX Metropolitan Statistical Area—see Appendix B for areas included; (2) Heavy drinkers are classified as males having more than two drinks per day or females having more than one drink per day; (3) Binge drinkers are classified as males having five or more drinks on one occasion or females having four or more drinks on one occasion
Source: Centers for Disease Control and Prevention, Behaviorial Risk Factor Surveillance System, SMART: Selected Metropolitan/Micropolitan Area Risk Trends, 2012

Chronic Health Indicators

Category	MSA[1] (%)	U.S. (%)
Adults who have ever been told they had a heart attack	3.6	4.5
Adults who have ever been told they had a stroke	2.5	2.9
Adults who have been told they currently have asthma	6.2	8.9
Adults who have ever been told they have arthritis	22.1	25.7
Adults who have ever been told they have diabetes[2]	10.3	9.7
Adults who have ever been told they had skin cancer	4.4	5.7
Adults who have ever been told they had any other types of cancer	6.7	6.5
Adults who have ever been told they have COPD	3.3	6.2
Adults who have ever been told they have kidney disease	2.3	2.5
Adults who have ever been told they have a form of depression	16.0	18.0

Note: Data as of 2012 unless otherwise noted; (1) Figures cover the San Antonio, TX Metropolitan Statistical Area—see Appendix B for areas included; (2) Figures do not include pregnancy-related, borderline, or pre-diabetes
Source: Centers for Disease Control and Prevention, Behaviorial Risk Factor Surveillance System, SMART: Selected Metropolitan/Micropolitan Area Risk Trends, 2012

Mortality Rates for the Top 10 Causes of Death in the U.S.

ICD-10[a] Sub-Chapter	ICD-10[a] Code	Age-Adjusted Mortality Rate[1] per 100,000 population	
		County[2]	U.S.
Malignant neoplasms	C00-C97	157.7	174.2
Ischaemic heart diseases	I20-I25	108.6	119.1
Other forms of heart disease	I30-I51	49.8	49.6
Chronic lower respiratory diseases	J40-J47	36.8	43.2
Cerebrovascular diseases	I60-I69	45.4	40.3
Organic, including symptomatic, mental disorders	F01-F09	37.4	30.5
Other degenerative diseases of the nervous system	G30-G31	22.5	26.3
Other external causes of accidental injury	W00-X59	31.3	25.1
Diabetes mellitus	E10-E14	25.4	21.3
Hypertensive diseases	I10-I15	16.1	18.8

Note: (a) ICD-10 = International Classification of Diseases 10th Revision; (1) Mortality rates are a three year average covering 2008-2010; (2) Figures cover Bexar County
Source: Centers for Disease Control and Prevention, National Center for Health Statistics. Compressed Mortality File 1999-2010 on CDC WONDER Online Database, released January 2013. Data are compiled from the Compressed Mortality File 1999-2010, Series 20 No. 2P, 2013.

Mortality Rates for Selected Causes of Death

ICD-10[a] Sub-Chapter	ICD-10[a] Code	Age-Adjusted Mortality Rate[1] per 100,000 population	
		County[2]	U.S.
Assault	X85-Y09	7.2	5.5
Diseases of the liver	K70-K76	21.0	12.4
Human immunodeficiency virus (HIV) disease	B20-B24	3.4	3.0
Influenza and pneumonia	J09-J18	13.3	16.4
Intentional self-harm	X60-X84	10.6	11.8
Malnutrition	E40-E46	1.4	0.8
Obesity and other hyperalimentation	E65-E68	1.9	1.6
Renal failure	N17-N19	19.4	13.6
Transport accidents	V01-V99	12.2	12.6
Viral hepatitis	B15-B19	3.0	2.2

Note: (a) ICD-10 = International Classification of Diseases 10th Revision; (1) Mortality rates are a three year average covering 2008-2010; (2) Figures cover Bexar County
Source: Centers for Disease Control and Prevention, National Center for Health Statistics. Compressed Mortality File 1999-2010 on CDC WONDER Online Database, released January 2013. Data are compiled from the Compressed Mortality File 1999-2010, Series 20 No. 2P, 2013.

Health Insurance Coverage

Area	With Health Insurance	With Private Health Insurance	With Public Health Insurance	Without Health Insurance	Population Under Age 18 Without Health Insurance
City	78.3	57.1	31.4	21.7	11.1
MSA[1]	80.4	61.4	29.7	19.6	10.3
U.S.	84.9	65.4	30.4	15.1	7.5

Note: Figures are percentages that cover the civilian noninstitutionalized population; (1) Figures cover the San Antonio-New Braunfels, TX Metropolitan Statistical Area—see Appendix B for areas included
Source: U.S. Census Bureau, 2010-2012 American Community Survey 3-Year Estimates

Number of Medical Professionals

Area[1]	MDs[2]	DOs[2,3]	Dentists	Podiatrists	Chiropractors	Optometrists
Local (number)	5,495	327	1,362	99	260	241
Local (rate[4])	313.3	18.6	76.3	5.5	14.6	13.5
U.S. (rate[4])	267.6	19.6	61.7	5.6	24.7	14.5

Note: Data as of 2012 unless noted; (1) Local data covers Bexar County; (2) Data as of 2011; (3) Doctor of Osteopathic Medicine; (4) rate per 100,000 population
Source: Area Resource File (ARF) 2012-2013. U.S. Department of Health and Human Services, Health Resources and Services Administration, Bureau of Health Professions

Best Hospitals

According to *U.S. News,* the San Antonio-New Braunfels, TX metro area is home to one of the best hospitals in the U.S.: **University Hospital** (2 specialties). The hospital listed was nationally ranked in at least one adult specialty. Only 147 hospitals nationwide were nationally ranked in one or more specialties. Eighteen hospitals in the U.S. made the Honor Roll by ranking near the top in at least six specialties.*U.S. News Online, "America's Best Hospitals 2013-14"*

EDUCATION

Public School District Statistics

District Name	Schls	Pupils	Pupil/ Teacher Ratio	Minority Pupils[1] (%)	Free Lunch Eligible[2] (%)	IEP[3] (%)
Alamo Heights ISD	5	4,805	14.7	44.2	18.0	6.0
East Central ISD	15	9,462	16.9	78.6	56.6	11.3
Edgewood ISD	19	11,863	16.8	n/a	7.0	9.9
Harlandale ISD	30	14,950	15.5	97.9	n/a	9.3
North East ISD	77	67,439	15.7	69.0	37.5	9.2
Northside ISD	112	98,110	16.7	80.4	43.7	11.7
San Antonio ISD	99	54,394	16.1	97.9	22.7	10.3
South San Antonio ISD	18	9,730	14.7	98.3	4.0	7.5
Southside ISD	9	5,187	15.2	90.8	71.0	9.7
Southwest ISD	17	12,459	16.8	94.7	72.6	10.6

Note: Table includes school districts with 2,000 or more students; (1) Percentage of students that are not non-Hispanic white; (2) Percentage of students that are eligible for the free lunch program; (3) Percentage of students that have an Individualized Education Program.
Source: U.S. Department of Education, National Center for Education Statistics, Common Core of Data, Local Education Agency (School District) Universe Survey: School Year 2011-2012; U.S. Department of Education, National Center for Education Statistics, Common Core of Data, Public Elementary/Secondary School Universe Survey: School Year 2011-2012

Best High Schools

High School Name	Rank[1]	Grad. Rate[2] (%)	Coll.[3] (%)	AP/IB/ AICE Tests[4]	AP/IB/ AICE Score[5]	SAT Score[6]	ACT Score[6]
Alamo Heights H.S.	533	97	92	0.7	3.0	1644	23.9
Claudia Taylor Lady Bird Johnson H.S.	266	100	97	0.6	2.9	1555	24.0
Communications Arts H.S.	118	100	93	1.5	2.6	1663	25.4
Douglas MacArthur H.S.	1740	92	76	0.4	2.4	1517	22.4
Earl Warren High Schoo	1858	96	77	0.3	2.2	967	20.8
International School of the Americas	164	100	98	1.2	2.2	1625	23.8
James Madison H.S.	1399	90	90	0.2	3.0	1433	21.0
Luther Burbank H.S.	1988	90	77	0.4	1.7	873	17.3
Northside Health Careers H.S.	259	100	99	0.7	3.2	1132	25.1
Robert E. Lee H.S.	1623	92	87	0.4	2.2	1412	19.2
Ronald Reagan H.S.	485	94	100	0.6	3.0	1576	23.4
School of Science and Technology San Antonio	261	100	100	0.6	2.7	1642	26.0
Theodore Roosevelt H.S.	1985	88	75	0.1	2.8	1490	19.7
Thomas Edison H.S.	1979	93	85	0.3	1.7	840	16.9
Tom C. Clark H.S.	1882	95	65	0.4	2.8	1030	23.0
Winston Churchill H.S.	699	96	93	0.7	2.9	1567	23.0

Note: (1) Public schools are ranked from 1 to 2,000 based on the following self-reported statistics (with the corresponding weight used in calculating their overall score). Schools that were newly founded and did not have a graduating senior class in 2012 were excluded; (2) Four-year, on-time graduation rate (25%); (3) Percent of 2011 graduates who were accepted to college (25%); (4) AP/IB/AICE tests taken per student (25%); (5) Average AP/IB/AICE exam score (10%); (6) Average SAT and/or ACT score (10%); Percent of students enrolled in at least one AP/IB/AICE course (5%)—data not shown
Source: Newsweek and The Daily Beast, "America's Best High Schools 2013"

Highest Level of Education

Area	Less than H.S.	H.S. Diploma	Some College, No Deg.	Associate Degree	Bachelor's Degree	Master's Degree	Prof. School Degree	Doctorate Degree
City	19.6	25.2	23.9	7.0	15.5	6.1	1.7	1.0
MSA[1]	17.1	25.4	24.0	7.5	16.7	6.7	1.6	1.0
U.S.	14.1	28.3	21.3	7.8	18.0	7.5	1.9	1.2

Note: Figures cover persons age 25 and over; (1) Figures cover the San Antonio-New Braunfels, TX Metropolitan Statistical Area—see Appendix B for areas included
Source: U.S. Census Bureau, 2010-2012 American Community Survey 3-Year Estimates

Educational Attainment by Race

Area	High School Graduate or Higher (%)					Bachelor's Degree or Higher (%)				
	Total	White	Black	Asian	Hisp.[2]	Total	White	Black	Asian	Hisp.[2]
City	80.4	82.1	87.6	85.4	71.5	24.3	26.0	21.5	51.6	13.6
MSA[1]	82.9	84.5	89.3	83.8	72.5	26.0	27.5	23.8	48.5	14.2
U.S.	85.9	88.1	82.5	85.5	63.1	28.6	30.0	18.4	50.2	13.4

Note: Figures shown cover persons 25 years old and over; (1) Figures cover the San Antonio-New Braunfels, TX Metropolitan Statistical Area—see Appendix B for areas included; (2) People of Hispanic origin can be of any race
Source: U.S. Census Bureau, 2010-2012 American Community Survey 3-Year Estimates

School Enrollment by Grade and Control

Area	Preschool (%)		Kindergarten (%)		Grades 1 - 4 (%)		Grades 5 - 8 (%)		Grades 9 - 12 (%)	
	Public	Private	Public	Private	Public	Private	Public	Private	Public	Private
City	64.7	35.3	88.9	11.1	93.6	6.4	92.8	7.2	93.2	6.8
MSA[1]	62.1	37.9	90.1	9.9	92.7	7.3	92.8	7.2	93.1	6.9
U.S.	56.9	43.1	87.8	12.2	89.9	10.1	90.0	10.0	90.8	9.2

Note: Figures shown cover persons 3 years old and over; (1) Figures cover the San Antonio-New Braunfels, TX Metropolitan Statistical Area—see Appendix B for areas included
Source: U.S. Census Bureau, 2010-2012 American Community Survey 3-Year Estimates

Average Salaries of Public School Classroom Teachers

Area	2012-13		2013-14		Percent Change 2012-13 to 2013-14	Percent Change 2003-04 to 2013-14
	Dollars	Rank[1]	Dollars	Rank[1]		
Texas	48,819	35	49,270	35	0.92	21.7
U.S. Average	56,103	–	56,689	–	1.04	21.8

Note: (1) State rank ranges from 1 to 51 where 1 indicates highest salary.
Source: National Education Association, Rankings & Estimates: Rankings of the States 2013 and Estimates of School Statistics 2014, March 2014

Higher Education

Four-Year Colleges			Two-Year Colleges			Medical Schools[1]	Law Schools[2]	Voc/ Tech[3]
Public	Private Non-profit	Private For-profit	Public	Private Non-profit	Private For-profit			
2	6	8	4	0	7	1	1	19

Note: Figures cover institutions located within the city limits and include main campuses only; (1) includes schools accredited by the Liaison Committee on Medical Education and the American Osteopathic Association's Commission on Osteopathic College Accreditation; (2) includes ABA-accredited schools, schools with provisional ABA accreditation, and state accredited schools; (3) includes all schools with programs that are less than 2 years.
Source: National Center for Education Statistics, Integrated Postsecondary Education System (IPEDS), 2012-13; Association of American Medical Colleges, Member List, April 24, 2014; American Osteopathic Association, Member List, April 24, 2014; Law School Admission Council, Official Guide to ABA-Approved Law Schools Online, April 24, 2014; Wikipedia, List of Medical Schools in the United States, April 24, 2014; Wikipedia, List of Law Schools in the United States, April 24, 2014

**PRESIDENTIAL
ELECTION**

2012 Presidential Election Results

Area	Obama	Romney	Other
Bexar County	51.6	47.0	1.4
U.S.	51.0	47.2	1.8

Note: Results are percentages and may not add to 100% due to rounding
Source: Dave Leip's Atlas of U.S. Presidential Elections

EMPLOYERS

Major Employers

Company Name	Industry
Air Force, United States Dept of the	Air force
Baptist Health Systems	Hospital, ama approved residency
Baptist Health Systems	Hospital, med school affiliated with nursing & residency
Boeing Aerospace Operations	Aviation school
Boeing Aerospace Operations	Aircraft and heavy equipment repair services
Christus Santa Rosa Health Care Corp	General medical and surgical hospitals
Continental Automotive Systems	Semiconductors and related devices
Diamond Shamrock Refining & Marketing Co	Gasoline service stations
Northside Independent School District	Personal service agents, brokers and bureaus
Pacific Telesis Group	Telephone communication, except radio
Season Group USA	Electronic circuits
Southwest Research Institute	Commercial physical research
The Scooter Store, Ltd	Medical and hospital equipment
Toyota Motor Manufacturing, Texas	Motor vehicles and car bodies
U of Texas Health Science Center	University
University Health System	General medical and surgical hospitals
University of Texas at San Antonio	University
USAA	Fire, marine, and casualty insurance
Valero Services	Petroleum refining
Veterans Health Administration	Administration of veterans' affairs

Note: Companies shown are located within the San Antonio-New Braunfels, TX Metropolitan Statistical Area.
Source: Hoovers.com; Wikipedia

Best Companies to Work For

NuStar Energy; Rackspace Hosting; USAA, headquartered in San Antonio, are among "The 100 Best Companies to Work For." To pick the 100 Best Companies to Work For, *Fortune* partnered with the Great Place to Work Institute. Two hundred fifty seven firms participated in this year's survey. Two-thirds of a company's score is based on the results of the Institute's Trust Index survey, which is sent to a random sample of employees from each company. The questions related to attitudes about management's credibility, job satisfaction, and camaraderie. The other third of the scoring is based on the company's responses to the Institute's Culture Audit, which includes detailed questions about pay and benefit programs, and a series of open-ended questions about hiring practices, internal communication, training, recognition programs, and diversity efforts. Any company that is at least five years old with more than 1,000 U.S. employees is eligible. *Fortune, "The 100 Best Companies to Work For," 2014*

Rackspace US; USAA, headquartered in San Antonio, are among the "100 Best Places to Work in IT." To qualify, companies, both public and private, had to have a minimum of 50 IT employees and were selected based on average salary and bonus increases, the percentage of IT staffers promoted, IT staff turnover rates, training and development programs, and the percentage of women and minorities in IT staff and management positions. In addition, *Computerworld* looked at retention efforts, programs for recognizing and rewarding outstanding performances, and benefits such as flextime, elder care and child care, and reimbursement for college tuition and the cost of pursuing technology certifications. *Computerworld, "100 Best Places to Work in IT 2013"*

PUBLIC SAFETY

Crime Rate

Area	All Crimes	Violent Crimes				Property Crimes		
		Murder	Forcible Rape	Robbery	Aggrav. Assault	Burglary	Larceny -Theft	Motor Vehicle Theft
City	6,493.0	6.4	39.8	135.1	321.8	1,135.3	4,393.3	461.3
Suburbs[1]	2,776.2	2.9	30.9	30.0	143.8	581.5	1,845.9	141.2
Metro[2]	5,078.7	5.1	36.4	95.1	254.1	924.5	3,424.0	339.5
U.S.	3,246.1	4.7	26.9	112.9	242.3	670.2	1,959.3	229.7

Note: Figures are crimes per 100,000 population; (1) All areas within the metro area that are located outside the city limits; (2) Figures cover the San Antonio-New Braunfels, TX Metropolitan Statistical Area—see Appendix B for areas included
Source: FBI Uniform Crime Reports, 2012

Hate Crimes

Area	Number of Quarters Reported	Bias Motivation				
		Race	Religion	Sexual Orientation	Ethnicity	Disability
City	4	5	5	6	1	0
U.S.	4	2,797	1,099	1,135	667	92

Source: Federal Bureau of Investigation, Hate Crime Statistics 2012

Identity Theft Consumer Complaints

Area	Complaints	Complaints per 100,000 Population	Rank[2]
MSA[1]	1,783	83.2	94
U.S.	290,056	91.8	-

Note: (1) Figures cover the San Antonio-New Braunfels, TX Metropolitan Statistical Area—see Appendix B for areas included; (2) Rank ranges from 1 to 377 where 1 indicates greatest number of identity theft complaints per 100,000 population
Source: Federal Trade Commission, Consumer Sentinel Network Data Book for January–December 2013

Fraud and Other Consumer Complaints

Area	Complaints	Complaints per 100,000 Population	Rank[2]
MSA[1]	8,001	373.4	165
U.S.	1,811,724	595.2	-

Note: (1) Figures cover the San Antonio-New Braunfels, TX Metropolitan Statistical Area—see Appendix B for areas included; (2) Rank ranges from 1 to 377 where 1 indicates greatest number of identity theft complaints per 100,000 population
Source: Federal Trade Commission, Consumer Sentinel Network Data Book for January–December 2013

RECREATION

Culture

Dance[1]	Theatre[1]	Instrumental Music[1]	Vocal Music[1]	Series and Festivals	Museums and Art Galleries[2]	Zoos and Aquariums[3]
1	4	3	1	5	41	2

Note: (1) Number of professional perfoming groups; (2) Based on organizations with primary SIC code 8412; (3) AZA-accredited
Source: The Grey House Performing Arts Directory, 2013; Association of Zoos & Aquariums, AZA Member Zoos & Aquariums, April 2014; www.AccuLeads.com, May 1, 2014

Professional Sports Teams

Team Name	League	Year Established
San Antonio Spurs	National Basketball Association (NBA)	1973

Note: Includes teams located in the San Antonio-New Braunfels, TX Metropolitan Statistical Area.
Source: Wikipedia, Major Professional Sports Teams of the United States and Canada

CLIMATE

Average and Extreme Temperatures

Temperature	Jan	Feb	Mar	Apr	May	Jun	Jul	Aug	Sep	Oct	Nov	Dec	Yr.
Extreme High (°F)	89	97	100	100	103	105	106	108	103	98	94	90	108
Average High (°F)	62	66	74	80	86	92	95	95	90	82	71	64	80
Average Temp. (°F)	51	55	62	70	76	82	85	85	80	71	60	53	69
Average Low (°F)	39	43	50	58	66	72	74	74	69	59	49	41	58
Extreme Low (°F)	0	6	19	31	43	53	62	61	46	33	21	6	0

Note: Figures cover the years 1948-1990
Source: National Climatic Data Center, International Station Meteorological Climate Summary, 9/96

Average Precipitation/Snowfall/Humidity

Precip./Humidity	Jan	Feb	Mar	Apr	May	Jun	Jul	Aug	Sep	Oct	Nov	Dec	Yr.
Avg. Precip. (in.)	1.5	1.8	1.5	2.6	3.8	3.6	2.0	2.5	3.3	3.2	2.3	1.4	29.6
Avg. Snowfall (in.)	1	Tr	Tr	0	0	0	0	0	0	0	Tr	Tr	1
Avg. Rel. Hum. 6am (%)	79	80	79	82	87	87	87	86	85	83	81	79	83
Avg. Rel. Hum. 3pm (%)	51	48	45	48	51	48	43	42	47	46	48	49	47

Note: Figures cover the years 1948-1990; Tr = Trace amounts (<0.05 in. of rain; <0.5 in. of snow)
Source: National Climatic Data Center, International Station Meteorological Climate Summary, 9/96

Weather Conditions

Temperature			Daytime Sky			Precipitation		
32°F & below	45°F & below	90°F & above	Clear	Partly cloudy	Cloudy	0.01 inch or more precip.	0.1 inch or more snow/ice	Thunder-storms
23	91	112	97	153	115	81	1	36

Note: Figures are average number of days per year and cover the years 1948-1990
Source: National Climatic Data Center, International Station Meteorological Climate Summary, 9/96

HAZARDOUS WASTE

Superfund Sites

San Antonio has no sites on the EPA's Superfund Final National Priorities List.
U.S. Environmental Protection Agency, Final National Priorities List, April 26, 2014

AIR & WATER QUALITY

Air Quality Index

Area	Percent of Days when Air Quality was...[2]					AQI Statistics[2]	
	Good	Moderate	Unhealthy for Sensitive Groups	Unhealthy	Very Unhealthy	Maximum	Median
MSA[1]	68.2	29.0	2.7	0.0	0.0	129	45

Note: (1) Data covers the San Antonio-New Braunfels, TX Metropolitan Statistical Area—see Appendix B for areas included; (2) Based on 365 days with AQI data in 2013. Air Quality Index (AQI) is an index for reporting daily air quality. EPA calculates the AQI for five major air pollutants regulated by the Clean Air Act: ground-level ozone, particle pollution (aka particulate matter), carbon monoxide, sulfur dioxide, and nitrogen dioxide. The AQI runs from 0 to 500. The higher the AQI value, the greater the level of air pollution and the greater the health concern. There are six AQI categories: "Good" AQI is between 0 and 50. Air quality is considered satisfactory; "Moderate" AQI is between 51 and 100. Air quality is acceptable; "Unhealthy for Sensitive Groups" When AQI values are between 101 and 150, members of sensitive groups may experience health effects; "Unhealthy" When AQI values are between 151 and 200 everyone may begin to experience health effects; "Very Unhealthy" AQI values between 201 and 300 trigger a health alert; "Hazardous" AQI values over 300 trigger warnings of emergency conditions (not shown).
Source: U.S. Environmental Protection Agency, Air Quality Index Report, 2013

Air Quality Index Pollutants

Area	Percent of Days when AQI Pollutant was...[2]					
	Carbon Monoxide	Nitrogen Dioxide	Ozone	Sulfur Dioxide	Particulate Matter 2.5	Particulate Matter 10
MSA[1]	0.0	0.8	51.0	0.3	47.9	0.0

Note: (1) Data covers the San Antonio-New Braunfels, TX Metropolitan Statistical Area—see Appendix B for areas included; (2) Based on 365 days with AQI data in 2013. The Air Quality Index (AQI) is an index for reporting daily air quality. EPA calculates the AQI for five major air pollutants regulated by the Clean Air Act: ground-level ozone, particle pollution (also known as particulate matter), carbon monoxide, sulfur dioxide, and nitrogen dioxide. The AQI runs from 0 to 500. The higher the AQI value, the greater the level of air pollution and the greater the health concern.
Source: U.S. Environmental Protection Agency, Air Quality Index Report, 2013

Air Quality Trends: Ozone

	2003	2004	2005	2006	2007	2008	2009	2010	2011	2012
MSA[1]	0.082	0.085	0.082	0.083	0.071	0.075	0.070	0.072	0.075	0.079

Note: (1) Data covers the San Antonio-New Braunfels, TX Metropolitan Statistical Area—see Appendix B for areas included. The values shown are the composite ozone concentration averages among trend sites based on the highest fourth daily maximum 8-hour concentration in parts per million. These trends are based on sites having an adequate record of monitoring data during the trend period. Data from exceptional events are included.
Source: U.S. Environmental Protection Agency, Air Quality Monitoring Information, "Air Quality Trends by City, 2000-2012"

Maximum Air Pollutant Concentrations: Particulate Matter, Ozone, CO and Lead

	Particulate Matter 10 (ug/m³)	Particulate Matter 2.5 Wtd AM (ug/m³)	Particulate Matter 2.5 24-Hr (ug/m³)	Ozone (ppm)	Carbon Monoxide (ppm)	Lead (ug/m³)
MSA[1] Level	50	8.7	23	0.087	n/a	n/a
NAAQS[2]	150	15	35	0.075	9	0.15
Met NAAQS[2]	Yes	Yes	Yes	No	n/a	n/a

Note: (1) Data covers the San Antonio-New Braunfels, TX Metropolitan Statistical Area—see Appendix B for areas included; Data from exceptional events are included; (2) National Ambient Air Quality Standards; ppm = parts per million; ug/m³ = micrograms per cubic meter; n/a not available.
Concentrations: Particulate Matter 10 (coarse particulate)—highest second maximum 24-hour concentration; Particulate Matter 2.5 Wtd AM (fine particulate)—highest weighted annual mean concentration; Particulate Matter 2.5 24-Hour (fine particulate)—highest 98th percentile 24-hour concentration; Ozone—highest fourth daily maximum 8-hour concentration; Carbon Monoxide—highest second maximum non-overlapping 8-hour concentration; Lead—maximum running 3-month average
Source: U.S. Environmental Protection Agency, Air Quality Monitoring Information, "Air Quality Statistics by City, 2012"

Maximum Air Pollutant Concentrations: Nitrogen Dioxide and Sulfur Dioxide

	Nitrogen Dioxide AM (ppb)	Nitrogen Dioxide 1-Hr (ppb)	Sulfur Dioxide AM (ppb)	Sulfur Dioxide 1-Hr (ppb)	Sulfur Dioxide 24-Hr (ppb)
MSA[1] Level	4	34	n/a	n/a	n/a
NAAQS[2]	53	100	30	75	140
Met NAAQS[2]	Yes	Yes	n/a	n/a	n/a

Note: (1) Data covers the San Antonio-New Braunfels, TX Metropolitan Statistical Area—see Appendix B for areas included; Data from exceptional events are included; (2) National Ambient Air Quality Standards; ppm = parts per million; ug/m³ = micrograms per cubic meter; n/a not available.
Concentrations: Nitrogen Dioxide AM—highest arithmetic mean concentration; Nitrogen Dioxide 1-Hr—highest 98th percentile 1-hour daily maximum concentration; Sulfur Dioxide AM—highest annual mean concentration; Sulfur Dioxide 1-Hr—highest 99th percentile 1-hour daily maximum concentration; Sulfur Dioxide 24-Hr—highest second maximum 24-hour concentration
Source: U.S. Environmental Protection Agency, Air Quality Monitoring Information, "Air Quality Statistics by City, 2012"

Drinking Water

Water System Name	Pop. Served	Primary Water Source Type	Violations[1]	
			Health Based	Monitoring/ Reporting
San Antonio Water System	1,596,714	Purchased Surface	0	2

Note: (1) Based on violation data from January 1, 2013 to December 31, 2013 (includes unresolved violations from earlier years)

Source: U.S. Environmental Protection Agency, Office of Ground Water and Drinking Water, Safe Drinking Water Information System (based on data extracted February 10, 2014)

Savannah, Georgia

Background

Savannah, at the mouth of the Savannah River on the border between Georgia and South Carolina, is Georgia's second fastest-growing city. It was established in 1733 when General James Oglethorpe landed with a group of settlers in the sailing vessel Anne, after a voyage of more than three months. City Hall now stands at the spot where Oglethorpe and his followers first camped on a small bluff overlooking the river.

Savannah is unique among American cities in that it was extensively planned while Oglethorpe was still in England. Each new settler was given a package of property, including a town lot, a garden space, and an outlying farm area. The town was planned in quadrants, the north and south for residences, and the east and west for public buildings.

The quadrant design was inspired in part by considerations of public defense, given the unsettled character of relations with Native Americans, but in fact an early treaty between the settlers and the Creek Indian Chief Tomochichi allowed Savannah to develop quite peacefully, with little of the hostility between Europeans and Indians that marred much of the development elsewhere in the colonies.

Savannah was taken by the British during the American Revolution, and in the patriotic siege that followed, many lives were lost. Count Pulaski, among other Revolutionary heroes, lost his life during the battle, but Savannah was eventually retaken in 1782 by the American Generals Nathaniel Greene and Anthony Wayne.

In the post-Revolutionary period, Savannah grew dramatically, its economic strength being driven in large part by Eli Whitney's cotton gin. As the world's leader in the cotton trade, Savannah also hosted a great development in export activity, and the first American steamboat built in the United States to cross the Atlantic was launched in its busy port.

Savannah's physical structure had been saved from the worst ravages of war, but the destruction of the area's infrastructure slowed its further development for an extended period, and "sleepy" became a common adjective applied to the once-vibrant economic center. In the long period of slow recovery that followed, one of the great Savannah success stories was the establishment of the Girl Scouts in 1912 by Juliette Gordon Low.

In 1954, an extensive fire destroyed a large portion of the historic City Market, and the area was bulldozed to make room for a parking garage. The Historic Savannah Foundation has worked unceasingly since then to maintain and improve Savannah's considerable architectural charms.

As a result, Savannah's Historic District was designated a Registered National Historic Landmark. Savannah has also been one of the favored sites for movie makers for decades. More than forty major movies have been filmed in Savannah including *Roots* (1976), *East of Eden* (1980), *Forrest Gump* (1994), *Midnight in the Garden of Good and Evil* (1997) and *The Legend of Bagger Vance* (2000), and a segment of the Colbert Report (2005).

Tourism, military services, port operations, and arts & culture industries are major employers in the city. Savannah's port facilities, operated by the Georgia Ports Authority, have seen notable growth in container tonnage in recent years. Garden City Terminal is the fourth largest container port in the United States, and the largest single-terminal operation in North America. Military installations in the area include Hunter Army Airfield and Fort Stewart military bases, employing a combined 42,000 people. Museums include Juliette Gordon Low Museum, Telfair Museum of Art and the Mighty 8th Air Forth Museum.

In addition, the city's beauty draws not just tourists, but conventioneers. The Savannah International Trade & Convention Center is a state-of-the-art facility with more than 100,000 square feet of exhibition space, accommodating nearly 10,000 people.

Colleges and universities in the city include the Savannah College of Art and Design, Savannah State University, and South University.

Savannah's climate is subtropical, with hot summers and mild winters, making the city an ideal locale for all-year outside activities.

Rankings

General Rankings

- Savannah was selected as one of "America's Favorite Cities." The city ranked #6 in the "Quality of Life and Visitor Experience: Cleanliness" category. Respondents to an online survey were asked to rate 35 top urban destinations in the U.S. from a visitor's perspective. Criteria: cleanliness. *Travel + Leisure, "America's Favorite Cities 2013"*

- Savannah was selected as one of "America's Favorite Cities." The city ranked #18 in the "Type of Trip: Gay-friendly" category. Respondents to an online survey were asked to rate 35 top urban destinations in the U.S. from a visitor's perspective. Criteria: gay-friendly. *Travel + Leisure, "America's Favorite Cities 2013"*

- Savannah appeared on *Travel + Leisure's* list of the ten best cities in the U.S. and Canada. The city was ranked #7. Criteria: activities/attractions; culture/arts; restaurants/food; people; and value. *Travel + Leisure, "The World's Best Awards 2013"*

- *Condé Nast Traveler* polled 79,268 readers for travel satisfaction. American cities were ranked based on the following criteria: friendliness; atmosphere/ambiance; culture/sites; restaurants; lodging; and shopping. Savannah appeared in the top 10, ranking #9. *Condé Nast Traveler, Readers' Choice Awards 2013, "Top 10 Cities in the United States"*

Business/Finance Rankings

- Savannah was identified as one of the top 25 U.S. cities with the most credit card debt by credit reporting bureau Experian. The city was ranked #21. *Experian, March 4, 2011*

- The Savannah metro area appeared on the Milken Institute "2013 Best Performing Cities" list. Rank: #94 out of 200 large metro areas. Criteria: job growth; wage and salary growth; high-tech output growth. *Milken Institute, "Best-Performing Cities 2013," December 2013*

- *Forbes* ranked the 200 most populous metro areas in the U.S. in terms of the "Best Places for Business and Careers." The Savannah metro area was ranked #125. Criteria: costs (business and living); job growth (past and projected); income growth; educational attainment (college and high school); projected economic growth; cultural and recreational opportunities; net migration patterns; number of highly ranked colleges. *Forbes, "The Best Places for Business and Careers," August 7, 2013*

Children/Family Rankings

- Savannah was selected as one of the best cities for families to live by *Parenting* magazine. The city ranked #60 out of 100. Criteria: education; health; community; *Parenting's* Culture & Charm Index. *Parenting.com, "The 2012 Best Cities for Families List"*

Culture/Performing Arts Rankings

- Savannah was selected as one of "America's Favorite Cities." The city ranked #10 in the "Culture: Museum/Galleries" category. Respondents to an online survey were asked to rate 35 top urban destinations in the U.S. from a visitor's perspective. Criteria: number and quality of museums and galleries. *Travelandleisure.com, "America's Favorite Cities 2013"*

- Savannah was selected as one of America's top cities for the arts. The city ranked #6 in the mid-sized city (population 100,000 to 499,999) category. Criteria: readers' top choices for arts travel destinations based on the richness and variety of visual arts sites, activities and events. *American Style, "2012 Top 25 Arts Destinations," June 2012*

Dating/Romance Rankings

- Savannah was selected as one of America's best cities for singles by the readers of *Travel + Leisure* in their annual "America's Favorite Cities" survey. The city was ranked #13 out of 20. *Travel + Leisure, "America's Best Cities for Singles," July 2012*

Environmental Rankings

- The Savannah metro area came in at #330 for the relative comfort of its climate on Sperling's list of "chill cities," as measured by the Sperling Heat Index. All 361 metro areas are included. Criteria included daytime high temperatures, nighttime low temperatures, dew point, and relative humidity at the high temperatures. *www.bertsperling.com, "Sperling's Chill Cities," July 18, 2013*

- Sperling's BestPlaces assessed 379 metropolitan areas of the United States for the likelihood of dangerously extreme weather events or earthquakes. In general the Southeast and South-Central regions have the highest risk of weather extremes and earthquakes, while the Pacific Northwest enjoys the lowest risk. Of the least risky metropolitan areas, the Savannah metro area was ranked #266. *www.bestplaces.net, "Safest Places from Natural Disasters," April 2011*

- Savannah was selected as one of 22 "Smarter Cities" for energy by the Natural Resources Defense Council. Criteria: investment in green power; energy efficiency measures; conservation. *Natural Resources Defense Council, "2010 Smarter Cities," July 19, 2010*

- Savannah was highlighted as one of the cleanest metro areas for ozone air pollution in the U.S. during 2008 through 2010. The list represents cities with no monitored ozone air pollution in unhealthful ranges. *American Lung Association, State of the Air 2012*

Health/Fitness Rankings

- The Savannah metro area appeared in the 2013 Gallup-Healthways Well-Being Index. The area ranked #89 out of 189. The Gallup-Healthways Well-Being Index score is an average of six sub-indexes, which individually examine life evaluation, emotional health, work environment, physical health, healthy behaviors, and access to basic necessities. Results are based on telephone interviews conducted as part of the Gallup-Healthways Well-Being Index survey January 2–December 29, 2012, and January 2–December 30, 2013, with a random sample of 531,630 adults, aged 18 and older, living in metropolitan areas in the 50 U.S. states and the District of Columbia. *Gallup-Healthways, "State of American Well-Being," March 25, 2014*

Real Estate Rankings

- Using data from the housing-market research firm RealtyTrac, Yahoo! Finance researchers listed the housing markets in which housing affordability is improving most, factoring in interest rates as well as median home prices. The Savannah metro area was among the most affordable housing markets according to the percentage difference in the income required to buy a home in December 2013 as opposed to in December 2012. *news.yahoo.com, "10 Cities Where Ordinary People Can No Longer Afford Homes," March 5, 2014*

- Savannah was ranked #93 out of 283 metro areas in terms of house price appreciation in 2013 (#1 = highest rate). *Federal Housing Finance Agency, House Price Index, 4th Quarter 2013*

Safety Rankings

- Allstate ranked the 200 largest cities in America in terms of driver safety. Savannah ranked #120. Allstate researchers analyzed internal property damage claims over a two-year period from January 2010 to December 2011. A weighted average of the two-year numbers determined the annual percentages. *Allstate, "Allstate America's Best Drivers Report®, August 27, 2013"*

- The National Insurance Crime Bureau ranked 380 metro areas in the U.S. in terms of per capita rates of vehicle theft. The Savannah metro area ranked #85 (#1 = highest rate). Criteria: number of vehicle theft offenses per 100,000 inhabitants in 2012. *National Insurance Crime Bureau, "Hot Spots 2012," June 26, 2013*

Seniors/Retirement Rankings

- From its Best Cities for Successful Aging indexes, the Milken Institute generated rankings for metropolitan areas, weighing data in eight categories—general indicators, health care, wellness, living arrangements, transportation and general accessibility, financial well-being, education and employment, and community participation. The Savannah metro area was ranked #147 overall in the small metro area category. *Milken Institute, "Best Cities for Successful Aging," July 2012*

- Savannah was identified as one of the most popular places to retire by *Topretirements.com*. The list reflects the 100 cities (out of 900+ total cities reviewed) that visitors to the website are most interested in for retirement. *Topretirements.com, "Most Popular Places to Retire for 2014," February 25, 2014*

Sports/Recreation Rankings

- Savannah appeared on the *Sporting News* list of the "Best Sports Cities" for 2011. The area ranked #225 out of 271. Criteria: the magazine takes a 12-month snapshot of each city's sports, putting a heavy premium on regular-season won-lost records (from the most recently completed season). Other criteria include: playoff berths, bowl appearances and tournament bids; championships; applicable power ratings; quality of competition; overall fan fervor (measured in part by attendance); abundance of teams (rewarding quality over quantity); stadium and arena quality; ticket availability and prices; franchise ownership; and marquee appeal of athletes. *Sporting News, "Best Sports Cities 2011," October 4, 2011*

- Savannah appeared on the *Sporting News* list of the "Best Sports Cities" for 2011. The area ranked #225 out of 271. Criteria: a 12-month snapshot of regular-season won-lost records (from the most recently completed season). Other criteria include: playoff berths, bowl appearances and tournament bids; championships; applicable power ratings; quality of competition; overall fan fervor (measured in part by attendance); abundance of teams (quality over quantity); stadium and arena quality; ticket availability and prices; franchise ownership; and marquee appeal of athletes. *Sporting News, "Best Sports Cities 2011," October 4, 2011*

- Savannah was chosen as a bicycle friendly community by the League of American Bicyclists. A "Bicycle Friendly Community" welcomes cyclists by providing safe accommodation for cycling and encouraging people to bike for transportation and recreation. There are four award levels: Platinum; Gold; Silver; and Bronze. The community achieved an award level of Bronze. *League of American Bicyclists, "Bicycle Friendly Community Master List," Fall 2013*

- Savannah was selected as one of the most playful cities in the U.S. by KaBOOM! The organization's Playful City USA initiative honors cities and towns across the nation for a vision, plan and commitment to creating an agenda for play. Criteria: creating a local play commission or task force; designing an annual action plan for play; conducting a play space audit; outlining a financial investment in play for the current fiscal year; and proclaiming and celebrating an annual "play day." *KaBOOM! National Campaign for Play, "2013 Playful City USA Communities"*

Miscellaneous Rankings

- *Travel + Leisure* invited readers to rate cities on indicators such as aloofness, "smarty-pants residents," highbrow cultural offerings, high-end shopping, artisanal coffeehouses, conspicuous eco-consciousness, and more in order to identify the nation's snobbiest cities. Cities large and small made the list; among them was Savannah, at #12. *www.travelandleisure.com, "America's Snobbiest Cities, June 2013*

- Now an international phenomenon, public St. Patrick's Day celebrations of "everything Irish" typically call forth parades and music and green in unexpected places. In its not-particularly-scientific survey of the St. Patrick's Day scene, the Huffington Post chose the festivities in Savannah as among the world's five best. *www.huffingtonpost.com, "The 5 Best Places to Celebrate St. Patrick's Day," March 10, 2014*

- In *Condé Nast Traveler* magazine's 2013 Readers' Choice Survey, Savannah made the top ten list of friendliest American cities, at #3. *www.cntraveler.com, "The Friendliest and Unfriendliest Cities in the U.S.," July 30, 2013*

- Savannah appeared on *Travel + Leisure's* list of America's most attractive people. Criteria: cities were selected by readers in their annual America's Favorite Cities survey. The city ranked #5 out of 10. *Travel + Leisure, "America's Most and Least Attractive People," November 2013*

- Savannah was selected as one of "America's Best Cities for Hipsters" by *Travel + Leisure*. The city was ranked #13 out of 20. Criteria: live music; coffee bars; independent boutiques; best microbrews; offbeat and tech-savvy locals. *Travel + Leisure, "America's Best Cities for Hipsters," November 2013*

- Savannah was selected as one of the "Top 10 Cities to Defy Death" by *Livability.com*. The city was ranked #9. Criteria includes: extreme sports; surfing; rock-climbing; haunted cities. *Livability.com, "Top 10 Cities to Defy Death," February 22, 2011*

- Savannah was selected as one of America's best-mannered cities. The area ranked #2. The general public determined the winners by casting votes online. *The Charleston School of Protocol and Etiquette, "2012 Most Mannerly City in America Contest," January 31, 2013*

Business Environment

CITY FINANCES

City Government Finances

Component	2011 ($000)	2011 ($ per capita)
Total Revenues	367,949	2,823
Total Expenditures	370,365	2,842
Debt Outstanding	185,102	1,420
Cash and Securities[1]	499,407	3,832

Note: (1) Cash and security holdings of a government at the close of its fiscal year, including those of its dependent agencies, utilities, and liquor stores.
Source: U.S Census Bureau, State & Local Government Finances 2011

City Government Revenue by Source

Source	2011 ($000)	2011 ($ per capita)
General Revenue		
From Federal Government	13,270	102
From State Government	7,862	60
From Local Governments	63,296	486
Taxes		
Property	61,141	469
Sales and Gross Receipts	35,456	272
Personal Income	0	0
Corporate Income	0	0
Motor Vehicle License	0	0
Other Taxes	9,051	69
Current Charges	87,850	674
Liquor Store	0	0
Utility	36,238	278
Employee Retirement	27,711	213

Source: U.S Census Bureau, State & Local Government Finances 2011

City Government Expenditures by Function

Function	2011 ($000)	2011 ($ per capita)	2011 (%)
General Direct Expenditures			
Air Transportation	23,953	184	6.5
Corrections	0	0	0.0
Education	0	0	0.0
Employment Security Administration	0	0	0.0
Financial Administration	5,634	43	1.5
Fire Protection	24,441	188	6.6
General Public Buildings	14,476	111	3.9
Governmental Administration, Other	5,366	41	1.4
Health	0	0	0.0
Highways	12,739	98	3.4
Hospitals	0	0	0.0
Housing and Community Development	31,097	239	8.4
Interest on General Debt	3,697	28	1.0
Judicial and Legal	2,126	16	0.6
Libraries	0	0	0.0
Parking	6,617	51	1.8
Parks and Recreation	20,562	158	5.6
Police Protection	58,546	449	15.8
Public Welfare	925	7	0.2
Sewerage	37,251	286	10.1
Solid Waste Management	24,018	184	6.5
Veterans' Services	0	0	0.0
Liquor Store	0	0	0.0
Utility	43,301	332	11.7
Employee Retirement	17,797	137	4.8

Source: U.S Census Bureau, State & Local Government Finances 2011

DEMOGRAPHICS

Population Growth

Area	1990 Census	2000 Census	2010 Census	Population Growth (%)	
				1990-2000	2000-2010
City	138,038	131,510	136,286	-4.7	3.6
MSA[1]	258,060	293,000	347,611	13.5	18.6
U.S.	248,709,873	281,421,906	308,745,538	13.2	9.7

Note: (1) Figures cover the Savannah, GA Metropolitan Statistical Area—see Appendix B for areas included
Source: U.S. Census Bureau, Census 1990, 2000, 2010

Household Size

Area	Persons in Household (%)							Average Household Size
	One	Two	Three	Four	Five	Six	Seven or More	
City	36.1	31.2	15.5	9.8	4.6	1.7	1.1	2.57
MSA[1]	29.8	33.9	15.4	12.9	5.3	1.7	1.0	2.63
U.S.	27.6	33.5	15.7	13.2	6.1	2.4	1.5	2.63

Note: (1) Figures cover the Savannah, GA Metropolitan Statistical Area—see Appendix B for areas included
Source: U.S. Census Bureau, 2010-2012 American Community Survey 3-Year Estimates

Race

Area	White Alone[2] (%)	Black Alone[2] (%)	Asian Alone[2] (%)	AIAN[3] Alone[2] (%)	NHOPI[4] Alone[2] (%)	Other Race Alone[2] (%)	Two or More Races (%)
City	40.8	54.1	2.4	0.3	0.1	0.7	1.7
MSA[1]	60.8	33.9	2.2	0.3	0.1	1.0	1.7
U.S.	74.0	12.6	4.9	0.8	0.2	4.7	2.8

Note: (1) Figures cover the Savannah, GA Metropolitan Statistical Area—see Appendix B for areas included;
(2) Alone is defined as not being in combination with one or more other races; (3) American Indian and Alaska
Native; (4) Native Hawaiian and Other Pacific Islander
Source: U.S. Census Bureau, 2010-2012 American Community Survey 3-Year Estimates

Hispanic or Latino Origin

Area	Total (%)	Mexican (%)	Puerto Rican (%)	Cuban (%)	Other (%)
City	5.2	3.1	0.8	0.1	1.3
MSA[1]	5.2	3.0	1.0	0.1	1.2
U.S.	16.6	10.7	1.6	0.6	3.7

Note: Persons of Hispanic or Latino origin can be of any race; (1) Figures cover the Savannah, GA
Metropolitan Statistical Area—see Appendix B for areas included
Source: U.S. Census Bureau, 2010-2012 American Community Survey 3-Year Estimates

Segregation

Type	Segregation Indices[1]				Percent Change		
	1990	2000	2010	2010 Rank[2]	1990-2000	1990-2010	2000-2010
Black/White	n/a	n/a	n/a	n/a	n/a	n/a	n/a
Asian/White	n/a	n/a	n/a	n/a	n/a	n/a	n/a
Hispanic/White	n/a	n/a	n/a	n/a	n/a	n/a	n/a

Note: All figures cover the Metropolitan Statistical Area—see Appendix B for areas included; Figures are based
on an analysis of 1990, 2000, and 2010 Census Decennial Census tract data by William H. Frey, Brookings
Institution and the University of Michigan Social Science Data Analysis Network. In this analysis all racial
groups (whites, blacks, and asians) are non-Hispanic members of those races. Hispanics are shown as a
separate category;
(1) Segregation Indices are Dissimilarity Indices that measure the degree to which the minority group is
distributed differently than whites across census tracts. They range from 0 (complete integration) to 100
(complete segregation) where the value indicates the percentage of the minority group that needs to move to be
distributed exactly like whites; (2) Ranges from 1 (most segregated) to 102 (least segregated); n/a not available.
Source: www.CensusScope.org

Ancestry

Area	German	Irish	English	American	Italian	Polish	French[2]	Scottish	Dutch
City	5.0	6.3	5.1	3.8	2.1	0.8	1.5	1.3	0.6
MSA[1]	9.4	9.3	8.3	6.9	2.9	1.1	1.9	2.0	0.9
U.S.	15.2	11.1	8.2	7.2	5.6	3.1	2.8	1.7	1.4

Note: Figures are the percentage of the total population reporting a particular ancestry. The nine most commonly reported ancestries in the U.S. are shown. Figures include multiple ancestries (e.g. if a person reported being Irish and Italian, they were included in both columns); (1) Figures cover the Savannah, GA Metropolitan Statistical Area—see Appendix B for areas included; (2) Excludes Basque
Source: U.S. Census Bureau, 2010-2012 American Community Survey 3-Year Estimates

Foreign-Born Population

Area	Any Foreign Country	Mexico	Asia	Europe	Carribean	South America	Central America[2]	Africa	Canada
City	6.2	2.0	1.9	0.6	0.4	0.4	0.2	0.4	0.2
MSA[1]	5.9	1.5	1.9	0.6	0.5	0.3	0.3	0.6	0.1
U.S.	13.0	3.7	3.7	1.6	1.2	0.9	1.0	0.5	0.3

Note: (1) Figures cover the Savannah, GA Metropolitan Statistical Area—see Appendix B for areas included; (2) Excludes Mexico.
Source: U.S. Census Bureau, 2010-2012 American Community Survey 3-Year Estimates

Marital Status

Area	Never Married	Now Married[2]	Separated	Widowed	Divorced
City	46.9	30.3	2.8	7.0	13.0
MSA[1]	35.3	43.7	2.4	6.0	12.8
U.S.	32.4	48.4	2.2	6.0	11.0

Note: Figures are percentages and cover the population 15 years of age and older; (1) Figures cover the Savannah, GA Metropolitan Statistical Area—see Appendix B for areas included; (2) Excludes separated
Source: U.S. Census Bureau, 2010-2012 American Community Survey 3-Year Estimates

Age

Area	Under Age 5	Age 5–19	Age 20–34	Age 35–44	Age 45–54	Age 55–64	Age 65–74	Age 75–84	Age 85+	Median Age
City	7.1	19.7	28.2	10.8	12.0	10.4	6.1	3.5	2.2	31.2
MSA[1]	6.9	20.2	23.6	12.8	13.2	11.4	6.8	3.6	1.5	34.4
U.S.	6.4	20.1	20.5	13.1	14.3	12.2	7.3	4.2	1.8	37.3

Note: (1) Figures cover the Savannah, GA Metropolitan Statistical Area—see Appendix B for areas included
Source: U.S. Census Bureau, 2010-2012 American Community Survey 3-Year Estimates

Gender

Area	Males	Females	Males per 100 Females
City	66,795	72,872	91.7
MSA[1]	172,578	182,961	94.3
U.S.	153,276,055	158,333,314	96.8

Note: (1) Figures cover the Savannah, GA Metropolitan Statistical Area—see Appendix B for areas included
Source: U.S. Census Bureau, 2010-2012 American Community Survey 3-Year Estimates

Religious Groups by Family

Area	Catholic	Baptist	Non-Den.	Methodist[2]	Lutheran	LDS[3]	Pentecostal	Presbyterian[4]	Muslim[5]	Judaism
MSA[1]	7.1	19.7	6.9	8.9	1.6	1.0	2.4	1.0	0.2	0.8
U.S.	19.1	9.3	4.0	4.0	2.3	2.0	1.9	1.6	0.8	0.7

Note: Figures are the number of adherents as a percentage of the total population; (1) Figures cover the Savannah, GA Metropolitan Statistical Area—see Appendix B for areas included; (2) Methodist/Pietist; (3) Latter Day Saints; (4) Reformed; (5) Figures are estimates
Source: Association of Statisticians of American Religious Bodies, 2010 U.S. Religion Census: Religious Congregations & Membership Study

Religious Groups by Tradition

Area	Catholic	Evangelical Protestant	Mainline Protestant	Other Tradition	Black Protestant	Orthodox
MSA[1]	7.1	25.1	9.5	2.6	8.6	0.1
U.S.	19.1	16.2	7.3	4.3	1.6	0.3

Note: Figures are the number of adherents as a percentage of the total population; (1) Figures cover the Savannah, GA Metropolitan Statistical Area—see Appendix B for areas included
Source: Association of Statisticians of American Religious Bodies, 2010 U.S. Religion Census: Religious Congregations & Membership Study

ECONOMY

Gross Metropolitan Product

Area	2011	2012	2013	2014	Rank[2]
MSA[1]	13.5	14.1	14.3	14.8	147

Note: Figures are in billions of dollars; (1) Figures cover the Savannah, GA Metropolitan Statistical Area—see Appendix B for areas included; (2) Rank is based on 2014 data and ranges from 1 to 363
Source: The United States Conference of Mayors, U.S. Metro Economies: Outlook—Gross Metropolitan Product, with Metro Employment Projections, November 2013

Economic Growth

Area	2011 (%)	2012 (%)	2013 (%)	2014 (%)	Rank[2]
MSA[1]	2.1	2.4	0.0	1.8	245
U.S.	1.6	2.5	1.7	2.5	–

Note: Figures are real gross metropolitan product (GMP) growth rates and represent annual average percent change; (1) Figures cover the Savannah, GA Metropolitan Statistical Area—see Appendix B for areas included; (2) Rank is based on 2013 data and ranges from 1 to 363
Source: The United States Conference of Mayors, U.S. Metro Economies: Outlook—Gross Metropolitan Product, with Metro Employment Projections, November 2013

Metropolitan Area Exports

Area	2007	2008	2009	2010	2011	2012	Rank[2]
MSA[1]	2,520.2	3,598.5	2,724.7	3,459.1	4,140.2	4,116.5	60

Note: Figures are in millions of dollars; (1) Figures cover the Savannah, GA Metropolitan Statistical Area—see Appendix B for areas included; (2) Rank is based on 2012 data and ranges from 1 to 369
Source: U.S. Department of Commerce, International Trade Administration, Office of Trade & Industry Information, Manufacturing & Services, data extracted April 1, 2014

INCOME

Income

Area	Per Capita ($)	Median Household ($)	Average Household ($)
City	18,889	34,832	46,779
MSA[1]	24,759	47,998	63,523
U.S.	27,385	51,771	71,579

Note: (1) Figures cover the Savannah, GA Metropolitan Statistical Area—see Appendix B for areas included
Source: U.S. Census Bureau, 2010-2012 American Community Survey 3-Year Estimates

Household Income Distribution

Area	Under $15,000	$15,000 -24,999	$25,000 -34,999	$35,000 -49,999	$50,000 -74,999	$75,000 -99,000	$100,000 -149,999	$150,000 and up
City	23.0	13.8	13.3	15.1	18.4	7.5	5.7	3.2
MSA[1]	14.6	11.3	11.0	14.8	19.1	11.3	11.3	6.6
U.S.	13.1	11.0	10.5	13.7	18.1	11.9	12.5	9.1

Note: (1) Figures cover the Savannah, GA Metropolitan Statistical Area—see Appendix B for areas included
Source: U.S. Census Bureau, 2010-2012 American Community Survey 3-Year Estimates

Poverty Rate

Area	All Ages	Under 18 Years Old	18 to 64 Years Old	65 Years and Over
City	27.4	42.2	25.1	11.4
MSA[1]	18.0	27.3	16.1	9.0
U.S.	15.7	22.2	14.6	9.3

Note: Figures are percentage of people whose income during the past 12 months was below the poverty level;
(1) Figures cover the Savannah, GA Metropolitan Statistical Area—see Appendix B for areas included
Source: U.S. Census Bureau, 2010-2012 American Community Survey 3-Year Estimates

Personal Bankruptcy Filing Rate

Area	2008	2009	2010	2011	2012	2013
Chatham County	6.33	6.98	6.53	6.21	5.74	5.60
U.S.	3.53	4.61	4.97	4.37	3.76	3.29

Note: Numbers are per 1,000 population and include Chapter 7 and Chapter 13 filings
Source: Federal Deposit Insurance Corporation, Regional Economic Conditions, March 20, 2014

EMPLOYMENT

Labor Force and Employment

Area	Civilian Labor Force			Workers Employed		
	Dec. 2012	Dec. 2013	% Chg.	Dec. 2012	Dec. 2013	% Chg.
City	66,322	64,048	-3.4	59,995	58,835	-1.9
MSA[1]	183,298	177,195	-3.3	168,509	165,250	-1.9
U.S.	154,904,000	154,408,000	-0.3	143,060,000	144,423,000	1.0

Note: Data is not seasonally adjusted and covers workers 16 years of age and older; (1) Metropolitan Statistical Area—see Appendix B for areas included
Source: Bureau of Labor Statistics, Local Area Unemployment Statistics

Unemployment Rate

Area	2013											
	Jan.	Feb.	Mar.	Apr.	May	Jun.	Jul.	Aug.	Sep.	Oct.	Nov.	Dec.
City	9.7	9.0	8.6	8.1	9.0	10.6	10.4	9.3	8.6	8.7	8.1	8.1
MSA[1]	8.3	7.7	7.4	7.1	7.9	8.8	8.6	7.8	7.3	7.5	6.7	6.7
U.S.	8.5	8.1	7.6	7.1	7.3	7.8	7.7	7.3	7.0	7.0	6.6	6.5

Note: Data is not seasonally adjusted and covers workers 16 years of age and older; All figures are percentages;
(1) Metropolitan Statistical Area—see Appendix B for areas included
Source: Bureau of Labor Statistics, Local Area Unemployment Statistics

Employment by Occupation

Occupation Classification	City (%)	MSA[1] (%)	U.S. (%)
Management, Business, Science, and Arts	30.8	33.4	36.0
Natural Resources, Construction, and Maintenance	6.5	9.0	9.1
Production, Transportation, and Material Moving	12.1	12.9	12.0
Sales and Office	25.2	24.6	24.7
Service	25.5	20.2	18.2

Note: Figures cover employed civilians 16 years of age and older; (1) Figures cover the Savannah, GA Metropolitan Statistical Area—see Appendix B for areas included
Source: U.S. Census Bureau, 2010-2012 American Community Survey 3-Year Estimates

Employment by Industry

| Sector | MSA[1] | | U.S. |
	Number of Employees	Percent of Total	Percent of Total
Construction	n/a	n/a	4.2
Education and Health Services	23,700	14.7	15.5
Financial Activities	6,600	4.1	5.7
Government	23,100	14.3	16.1
Information	1,300	0.8	1.9
Leisure and Hospitality	22,600	14.0	10.2
Manufacturing	15,200	9.4	8.7
Mining and Logging	n/a	n/a	0.6
Other Services	7,100	4.4	3.9
Professional and Business Services	20,300	12.6	13.7
Retail Trade	19,700	12.2	11.4
Transportation and Utilities	10,800	6.7	3.8
Wholesale Trade	6,100	3.8	4.2

Note: Figures cover non-farm employment as of December 2013 and are not seasonally adjusted;
(1) Metropolitan Statistical Area—see Appendix B for areas included; n/a not available
Source: Bureau of Labor Statistics, Current Employment Statistics, Employment, Hours, and Earnings

Occupations with Greatest Projected Employment Growth: 2010 – 2020

Occupation[1]	2010 Employment	2020 Projected Employment	Numeric Employment Change	Percent Employment Change
Combined Food Preparation and Serving Workers, Including Fast Food	98,330	120,660	22,330	22.7
Registered Nurses	69,190	90,020	20,830	30.1
Retail Salespersons	143,460	157,600	14,130	9.9
Office Clerks, General	81,710	93,640	11,930	14.6
Postsecondary Teachers	36,620	47,350	10,730	29.3
Waiters and Waitresses	62,600	72,990	10,390	16.6
Customer Service Representatives	91,150	101,390	10,240	11.2
Janitors and Cleaners, Except Maids and Housekeeping Cleaners	73,670	82,570	8,900	12.1
Laborers and Freight, Stock, and Material Movers, Hand	82,360	90,940	8,580	10.4
Elementary School Teachers, Except Special Education	45,250	53,470	8,220	18.2

Note: Projections cover Georgia; (1) Sorted by numeric employment change
Source: www.projectionscentral.com, State Occupational Projections, 2010–2020 Long-Term Projections

Fastest Growing Occupations: 2010 – 2020

Occupation[1]	2010 Employment	2020 Projected Employment	Numeric Employment Change	Percent Employment Change
Biomedical Engineers	170	280	110	64.7
Marriage and Family Therapists	290	460	160	55.3
Home Health Aides	11,790	18,070	6,270	53.2
Diagnostic Medical Sonographers	1,110	1,650	540	48.5
Medical Scientists, Except Epidemiologists	500	730	230	46.6
Personal Care Aides	9,550	13,870	4,320	45.2
Mental Health Counselors	2,030	2,870	840	41.3
Helpers—Carpenters	1,500	2,100	610	40.5
Cardiovascular Technologists and Technicians	1,030	1,400	370	36.0
Medical Secretaries	15,780	21,440	5,660	35.9

Note: Projections cover Georgia; (1) Sorted by percent employment change and excludes occupations with numeric employment change less than 100
Source: www.projectionscentral.com, State Occupational Projections, 2010–2020 Long-Term Projections

Average Wages

Occupation	$/Hr.	Occupation	$/Hr.
Accountants and Auditors	33.25	Maids and Housekeeping Cleaners	8.61
Automotive Mechanics	20.02	Maintenance and Repair Workers	17.38
Bookkeepers	16.14	Marketing Managers	48.96
Carpenters	19.48	Nuclear Medicine Technologists	n/a
Cashiers	9.74	Nurses, Licensed Practical	18.50
Clerks, General Office	12.40	Nurses, Registered	28.25
Clerks, Receptionists/Information	12.80	Nursing Assistants	10.72
Clerks, Shipping/Receiving	17.46	Packers and Packagers, Hand	9.29
Computer Programmers	35.54	Physical Therapists	42.55
Computer Systems Analysts	36.03	Postal Service Mail Carriers	24.73
Computer User Support Specialists	24.38	Real Estate Brokers	28.35
Cooks, Restaurant	9.81	Retail Salespersons	11.52
Dentists	107.80	Sales Reps., Exc. Tech./Scientific	28.61
Electrical Engineers	43.91	Sales Reps., Tech./Scientific	30.20
Electricians	21.99	Secretaries, Exc. Legal/Med./Exec.	15.65
Financial Managers	53.44	Security Guards	14.44
First-Line Supervisors/Managers, Sales	16.91	Surgeons	n/a
Food Preparation Workers	9.75	Teacher Assistants	10.50
General and Operations Managers	45.85	Teachers, Elementary School	26.30
Hairdressers/Cosmetologists	11.05	Teachers, Secondary School	n/a
Internists	n/a	Telemarketers	13.15
Janitors and Cleaners	10.94	Truck Drivers, Heavy/Tractor-Trailer	18.66
Landscaping/Groundskeeping Workers	11.83	Truck Drivers, Light/Delivery Svcs.	16.33
Lawyers	51.02	Waiters and Waitresses	10.07

Note: Wage data covers the Savannah, GA Metropolitan Statistical Area—see Appendix B for areas included. Hourly wages for elementary/secondary school teachers and teacher assistants were calculated by the editors from annual wage data assuming a 40 hour work week; n/a not available.
Source: Bureau of Labor Statistics, Metro Area Occupational Employment and Wage Estimates, May 2013

RESIDENTIAL REAL ESTATE

Building Permits

Area	Single-Family			Multi-Family			Total		
	2012	2013	Pct. Chg.	2012	2013	Pct. Chg.	2012	2013	Pct. Chg.
City	223	265	18.8	160	18	-88.8	383	283	-26.1
MSA[1]	1,263	1,517	20.1	277	233	-15.9	1,540	1,750	13.6
U.S.	518,695	620,802	19.7	310,963	370,020	19.0	829,658	990,822	19.4

Note: (1) Metropolitan Statistical Area—see Appendix B for areas included; figures represent new, privately-owned housing units authorized (unadjusted data); All permit data are based on estimates with imputation.
Source: U.S. Census Bureau, Manufacturing, Mining, and Construction Statistics, Building Permits, 2012, 2013

Homeownership Rate

Area	2006 (%)	2007 (%)	2008 (%)	2009 (%)	2010 (%)	2011 (%)	2012 (%)	2013 (%)
MSA[1]	n/a	n/a	n/a	n/a	n/a	n/a	n/a	n/a
U.S.	68.8	68.1	67.8	67.4	66.9	66.1	65.4	65.1

Note: (1) Figures cover the Savannah, GA Metropolitan Statistical Area—see Appendix B for areas included; n/a not available
Source: U.S. Census Bureau, Housing Vacancies and Homeownership Annual Statistics: 2013

Housing Vacancy Rates

Area	Gross Vacancy Rate[2] (%)			Year-Round Vacancy Rate[3] (%)			Rental Vacancy Rate[4] (%)			Homeowner Vacancy Rate[5] (%)		
	2011	2012	2013	2011	2012	2013	2011	2012	2013	2011	2012	2013
MSA[1]	n/a	n/a	n/a	n/a	n/a	n/a	n/a	n/a	n/a	n/a	n/a	n/a
U.S.	14.2	13.8	13.8	11.1	10.8	10.7	9.5	8.7	8.3	2.5	2.0	2.0

Note: (1) Figures cover the Savannah, GA Metropolitan Statistical Area—see Appendix B for areas included; (2) The percentage of the total housing inventory that is vacant; (3) The percentage of the housing inventory (excluding seasonal units) that is year-round vacant; (4) The percentage of rental inventory that is vacant for rent; (5) The percentage of homeowner inventory that is vacant for sale; n/a not available
Source: U.S. Census Bureau, Housing Vacancies and Homeownership Annual Statistics: 2013

TAXES

State Corporate Income Tax Rates

State	Tax Rate (%)	Income Brackets ($)	Num. of Brackets	Financial Institution Tax Rate (%)[a]	Federal Income Tax Ded.
Georgia	6.0	Flat rate	1	6.0	No

Note: Tax rates as of January 1, 2014; (a) Rates listed are the corporate income tax rate applied to financial institutions or excise taxes based on income. Some states have other taxes based upon the value of deposits or shares.
Source: Federation of Tax Administrators, "State Corporate Income Tax Rates, 2014"

State Individual Income Tax Rates

State	Tax Rate (%)	Income Brackets ($)	Num. of Brackets	Personal Exempt. ($)[1] Single	Dependents	Fed. Inc. Tax Ded.
Georgia	1.0 - 6.0	750 - 7,001 (h)	6	2,700	3,000	No

Note: Tax rates as of January 1, 2014; Local- and county-level taxes are not included; n/a not applicable; (1) Married joint filers generally receive double the single exemption; (h) The Georgia income brackets reported are for single individuals. For married couples filing jointly, the same tax rates apply to income brackets ranging from $1,000, to $10,000.
Source: Federation of Tax Administrators, "State Individual Income Tax Rates, 2014"

Various State and Local Tax Rates

State	State and Local Sales and Use (%)	State Sales and Use (%)	Gasoline[1] (¢/gal.)	Cigarette[2] ($/pack)	Spirits[3] ($/gal.)	Wine[4] ($/gal.)	Beer[5] ($/gal.)
Georgia	7.0	4.00	28.45	0.370	3.79 (f)	1.51	1.01 (q)

Note: All tax rates as of January 1, 2014; (1) The American Petroleum Institute has developed a methodology for determining the average tax rate on a gallon of fuel. Rates may include any of the following: excise taxes, environmental fees, storage tank fees, other fees or taxes, general sales tax, and local taxes. In states where gasoline is subject to the general sales tax, or where the fuel tax is based on the average sale price, the average rate determined by API is sensitive to changes in the price of gasoline. States that fully or partially apply general sales taxes to gasoline: CA, CO, GA, IL, IN, MI, NY; (2) The federal excise tax of $1.0066 per pack and local taxes are not included; (3) Rates are those applicable to off-premise sales of 40% alcohol by volume (a.b.v.) distilled spirits in 750ml containers. Local excise taxes are excluded; (4) Rates are those applicable to off-premise sales of 11% a.b.v. non-carbonated wine in 750ml containers; (5) Rates are those applicable to off-premise sales of 4.7% a.b.v. beer in 12 ounce containers; (f) Different rates also applicable according to alcohol content, place of production, size of container, or place purchased (on- or off-premise or onboard airlines); (q) Includes statewide local rate in Alabama ($0.52) and Georgia ($0.53).
Source: Tax Foundation, 2014 Facts & Figures: How Does Your State Compare?

State Business Tax Climate Index Rankings

State	Overall Rank	Corporate Tax Index Rank	Individual Income Tax Index Rank	Sales Tax Index Rank	Unemployment Insurance Tax Index Rank	Property Tax Index Rank
Georgia	32	8	41	12	24	31

Note: The index is a measure of how each state's tax laws affect economic performance. The lower the rank, the more favorable a state's tax system is for business. States without a given tax are given a ranking of 1. The scores/rankings for the District of Columbia do not affect other states. The 2014 index represents the tax climate as of July 1, 2013.
Source: Tax Foundation, State Business Tax Climate Index 2014

COMMERCIAL UTILITIES

Typical Monthly Electric Bills

Area	Commercial Service ($/month)		Industrial Service ($/month)	
	1,500 kWh	40 kW demand 14,000 kWh	1,000 kW demand 200,000 kWh	50,000 kW demand 15,000,000 kWh
City	250	1,592	30,725	1,512,982
Average[1]	197	1,636	25,662	1,485,307

Note: Based on total rates in effect July 1, 2013; (1) average based on 180 utilities surveyed
Source: Edison Electric Institute, Typical Bills and Average Rates Report, Summer 2013

TRANSPORTATION

Means of Transportation to Work

Area	Car/Truck/Van		Public Transportation			Bicycle	Walked	Other Means	Worked at Home
	Drove Alone	Car-pooled	Bus	Subway	Railroad				
City	75.8	11.1	3.8	0.0	0.0	1.2	4.1	0.8	3.2
MSA[1]	81.5	9.3	1.7	0.0	0.0	0.5	2.0	1.1	3.8
U.S.	76.4	9.7	2.6	1.7	0.5	0.6	2.8	1.3	4.3

Note: Figures are percentages and cover workers 16 years of age and older; (1) Figures cover the Savannah, GA Metropolitan Statistical Area—see Appendix B for areas included
Source: U.S. Census Bureau, 2010-2012 American Community Survey 3-Year Estimates

Travel Time to Work

Area	Less Than 10 Minutes	10 to 19 Minutes	20 to 29 Minutes	30 to 44 Minutes	45 to 59 Minutes	60 to 89 Minutes	90 Minutes or More
City	11.5	42.9	28.3	11.2	3.6	1.6	1.0
MSA[1]	9.3	31.5	29.1	20.1	6.3	2.2	1.4
U.S.	13.5	29.8	20.9	20.1	7.5	5.6	2.5

Note: Figures are percentages and include workers 16 years old and over; (1) Figures cover the Savannah, GA Metropolitan Statistical Area—see Appendix B for areas included
Source: U.S. Census Bureau, 2010-2012 American Community Survey 3-Year Estimates

Travel Time Index

Area	1985	1990	1995	2000	2005	2010	2011
Urban Area[1]	n/a	n/a	n/a	n/a	n/a	n/a	n/a
Average[2]	1.09	1.14	1.16	1.19	1.23	1.18	1.18

Note: Travel Time Index—the ratio of travel time in the peak period to the travel time at free-flow conditions. For example, a value of 1.30 indicates a 20-minute free-flow trip takes 26 minutes in the peak. Free-flow speeds (60 mph on freeways and 35 mph on principal arterials) are used as the comparison threshold; (1) Data for the Savannah, GA urban area was not available; (2) average of 498 urban areas
Source: Texas Transportation Institute, Urban Mobility Report 2012, December 2012

Public Transportation

Agency Name / Mode of Transportation	Vehicles Operated in Maximum Service	Annual Unlinked Passenger Trips (in thous.)	Annual Passenger Miles (in thous.)
Chatham Area Transit Authority (CAT)			
Bus (purchased transportation)	52	3,839.0	13,356.1
Demand Response (purchased transportation)	20	78.9	656.9
Ferryboat (purchased transportation)	1	642.1	244.0

Source: Federal Transit Administration, National Transit Database, 2012

Air Transportation

Airport Name and Code / Type of Service	Passenger Airlines[1]	Passenger Enplanements	Freight Carriers[2]	Freight (lbs.)
Savannah International (SAV)				
Domestic service (U.S. carriers - 2013)	19	797,413	8	5,874,856
International service (U.S. carriers - 2012)	0	0	0	0

Note: (1) Includes all U.S.-based major, minor and commuter airlines that carried at least one passenger during the year; (2) Includes all U.S.-based airlines and freight carriers that transported at least one lb. of freight during the year.
Source: Bureau of Transportation Statistics, The Intermodal Transportation Database, Air Carriers: T-100 Domestic Market (U.S. Carriers), 2013; Bureau of Transportation Statistics, The Intermodal Transportation Database, Air Carriers: T-100 International Market (U.S. Carriers), 2012

Other Transportation Statistics

Major Highways:	I-16; I-95
Amtrak Service:	Yes
Major Waterways/Ports:	Savannah River (Atlantic Ocean)

Source: Amtrak.com; Google Maps

BUSINESSES

Major Business Headquarters

Company Name	Rankings	
	Fortune[1]	Forbes[2]
Colonial Group	-	59

Note: (1) Fortune 500—companies that produce a 10-K are ranked 1 to 500 based on 2012 revenue; (2) all private companies with at least $2 billion in annual revenue through the end of their most current fiscal year are ranked 1 to 224; companies listed are headquartered in the city; dashes indicate no ranking
Source: Fortune, "Fortune 500," May 20, 2013; Forbes, "America's Largest Private Companies," December 18, 2013

Minority- and Women-Owned Businesses

Group	All Firms		Firms with Paid Employees			
	Firms	Sales ($000)	Firms	Sales ($000)	Employees	Payroll ($000)
Asian	639	240,363	290	222,341	3,076	38,001
Black	4,185	316,962	211	193,454	839	21,492
Hispanic	139	47,330	39	39,932	727	6,988
Women	4,332	717,594	628	633,948	7,500	147,281
All Firms	13,717	14,667,749	3,975	14,215,679	89,726	2,944,187

Note: Figures cover firms located in the city; minority- and women-owned business are defined as firms in which the corresponding group own 51% or more of the stock or equity of the company
Source: U.S. Census Bureau, 2007 Economic Census, Survey of Business Owners (2012 Survey of Business Owners data will be released starting in June 2015)

HOTELS & CONVENTION CENTERS

Hotels/Motels

Area	5 Star		4 Star		3 Star		2 Star		1 Star		Not Rated	
	Num.	Pct.[3]	Num.	Pct.[3]	Num.	Pct.[3]	Num.	Pct.[3]	Num.	Pct.[3]	Num.	Pct.[3]
City[1]	0	0.0	10	6.0	48	28.9	91	54.8	4	2.4	13	7.8
Total[2]	142	0.9	1,005	6.0	5,147	30.9	8,578	51.4	408	2.4	1,397	8.4

Note: (1) Figures cover Savannah and vicinity; (2) Figures cover all 100 cities in this book; (3) Percentage of hotels which have a given star rating; Star ratings are determined by expedia.com and offer an indication of the general quality of a particular hotel.
Source: expedia.com, April 7, 2014

The Savannah, GA metro area is home to one of the best hotels in the U.S. according to *Travel & Leisure*: **Bohemian Hotel Savannah Riverfront**. Criteria: service; location; rooms; food; and value. The list includes the top 200 hotels in the U.S. *Travel & Leisure, "T+L 500, The World's Best Hotels 2014"*

Major Convention Centers

Name	Overall Space (sq. ft.)	Exhibit Space (sq. ft.)	Meeting Space (sq. ft.)	Meeting Rooms
Savannah Intl Trade & Convention Center	330,000	100,000	50,000	13

Note: Table includes convention centers located in the Savannah, GA metro area; n/a not available
Source: Original research

Living Environment

COST OF LIVING

Cost of Living Index

Composite Index	Groceries	Housing	Utilities	Trans-portation	Health Care	Misc. Goods/ Services
92.5	91.2	71.5	111.5	102.0	100.1	99.2

Note: The Cost of Living Index measures regional differences in the cost of consumer goods and services, excluding taxes and non-consumer expenditures, for professional and managerial households in the top income quintile. It is based on more than 50,000 prices covering almost 60 different items for which prices are collected three times a year by chambers of commerce, economic development organizations or university applied economic centers in each participating urban area. The numbers shown should be read as a percentage above or below the national average of 100. For example, a value of 115.4 in the groceries column indicates that grocery prices are 15.4% higher than the national average. Small differences in the index numbers should not be interpreted as significant; Figures cover the Savannah GA urban area.
Source: The Council for Community and Economic Research, ACCRA Cost of Living Index, 2013

Grocery Prices

Area[1]	T-Bone Steak ($/pound)	Frying Chicken ($/pound)	Whole Milk ($/half gal.)	Eggs ($/dozen)	Orange Juice ($/64 oz.)	Coffee ($/11.5 oz.)
City[2]	9.54	1.25	2.63	1.65	3.32	4.02
Avg.	10.19	1.28	2.34	1.81	3.48	4.39
Min.	8.56	0.94	1.44	1.19	2.78	3.40
Max.	14.82	2.28	3.56	3.73	6.23	7.32

Note: (1) Values for the local area are compared with the average, minimum and maximum values for all 327 areas in the Cost of Living Index; (2) Figures cover the Savannah GA urban area; **T-Bone Steak** *(price per pound);* **Frying Chicken** *(price per pound, whole fryer);* **Whole Milk** *(half gallon carton);* **Eggs** *(price per dozen, Grade A, large);* **Orange Juice** *(64 oz. Tropicana or Florida Natural);* **Coffee** *(11.5 oz. can, vacuum-packed, Maxwell House, Hills Bros, or Folgers).*
Source: The Council for Community and Economic Research, ACCRA Cost of Living Index, 2013

Housing and Utility Costs

Area[1]	New Home Price ($)	Apartment Rent ($/month)	All Electric ($/month)	Part Electric ($/month)	Other Energy ($/month)	Telephone ($/month)
City[2]	205,496	726	170.47	-	-	33.80
Avg.	295,864	900	171.38	91.82	70.12	27.73
Min.	185,506	458	117.80	48.81	33.67	17.16
Max.	1,358,917	3,783	441.68	171.40	372.65	39.47

Note: (1) Values for the local area are compared with the average, minimum and maximum values for all 327 areas in the Cost of Living Index; (2) Figures cover the Savannah GA urban area; **New Home Price** *(2,400 sf living area, 8,000 sf lot, in urban area with full utilities);* **Apartment Rent** *(950 sf 2 bedroom/1.5 or 2 bath, unfurnished, excluding all utilities except water);* **All Electric** *(average monthly cost for an all-electric home);* **Part Electric** *(average monthly cost for a part-electric home);* **Other Energy** *(average monthly cost for natural gas, fuel oil, coal, wood, and any other forms of energy except electricity);* **Telephone** *(price includes basic monthly rate for a private residential line plus additional local usage charges incurred by a family of four).*
Source: The Council for Community and Economic Research, ACCRA Cost of Living Index, 2013

Health Care, Transportation, and Other Costs

Area[1]	Doctor ($/visit)	Dentist ($/visit)	Optometrist ($/visit)	Gasoline ($/gallon)	Beauty Salon ($/visit)	Men's Shirt ($)
City[2]	113.42	75.53	71.90	3.40	37.25	22.48
Avg.	101.40	86.48	96.16	3.44	33.87	26.55
Min.	61.67	50.83	50.12	3.08	18.92	12.48
Max.	182.71	152.50	223.78	4.33	68.22	52.03

Note: (1) Values for the local area are compared with the average, minimum and maximum values for all 327 areas in the Cost of Living Index; (2) Figures cover the Savannah GA urban area; **Doctor** *(general practitioners routine exam of an established patient);* **Dentist** *(adult teeth cleaning and periodic oral examination);* **Optometrist** *(full vision eye exam for established adult patient);* **Gasoline** *(one gallon regular unleaded, national brand, including all taxes, cash price at self-service pump if available);* **Beauty Salon** *(woman's shampoo, trim, and blow-dry);* **Men's Shirt** *(cotton/polyester dress shirt, pinpoint weave, long sleeves).*
Source: The Council for Community and Economic Research, ACCRA Cost of Living Index, 2013

HOUSING

House Price Index (HPI)

Area	National Ranking[2]	Quarterly Change (%)	One-Year Change (%)	Five-Year Change (%)
MSA[1]	93	1.96	4.73	-12.97
U.S.[3]	–	1.20	7.69	4.18

Note: The HPI is a weighted repeat sales index. It measures average price changes in repeat sales or refinancings on the same properties. This information is obtained by reviewing repeat mortgage transactions on single-family properties whose mortgages have been purchased or securitized by Fannie Mae or Freddie Mac in January 1975; (1) Savannah, GA Metropolitan Statistical Area—see Appendix B for areas included; (2) Rankings are based on annual percentage change for all metro areas containing at least 15,000 transactions over the last 10 years and ranges from 1 to 283; (3) figures based on a weighted average of Census Division estimates using a seasonally adjusted, purchase-only index; all figures are for the period ending December 31, 2013
Source: Federal Housing Finance Agency, House Price Index, February 25, 2014

Median Single-Family Home Prices

Area	2011	2012	2013p	Percent Change 2012 to 2013
MSA[1]	n/a	n/a	n/a	n/a
U.S. Average	166.2	177.2	197.4	11.4

Note: Figures are median sales prices of existing single-family homes in thousands of dollars; (p) preliminary; n/a not available; (1) Savannah, GA Metropolitan Statistical Area—see Appendix B for areas included
Source: National Association of Realtors, Median Sales Price of Existing Single-Family Homes for Metropolitan Areas, 4th Quarter 2013

Qualifying Income Based on Median Sales Price of Existing Single-Family Homes

Area	With 5% Down ($)	With 10% Down ($)	With 20% Down ($)
MSA[1]	n/a	n/a	n/a
U.S. Average	45,395	43,006	38,228

Note: Figures are preliminary; Qualifying income is based on a mortgage rate of 4.4%. Monthly principal and interest payment is limited to 25% of income; n/a not available; (1) Savannah, GA Metropolitan Statistical Area—see Appendix B for areas included
Source: National Association of Realtors, Qualifying Income Based on Median Sales Price of Existing Single-Family Homes for Metropolitan Areas, 4th Quarter 2013

Median Apartment Condo-Coop Home Prices

Area	2011	2012	2013p	Percent Change 2012 to 2013
MSA[1]	n/a	n/a	n/a	n/a
U.S. Average	165.1	173.7	194.9	12.2

Note: Figures are median sales prices of existing apartment condo-coop homes in thousands of dollars; (p) preliminary; n/a not available; (1) Savannah, GA Metropolitan Statistical Area—see Appendix B for areas included
Source: National Association of Realtors, Median Sales Price of Existing Apartment Condo-Coop Homes for Metropolitan Areas, 4th Quarter 2013

Gross Monthly Rent

Area	Under $200	$200 -299	$300 -499	$500 -749	$750 -999	$1,000 -1,499	$1,500 and up	Median ($)
City	2.5	2.8	5.8	21.1	33.6	27.0	7.2	875
MSA[1]	1.8	1.8	5.3	18.7	33.1	32.0	7.4	921
U.S.	1.7	3.3	8.1	22.7	24.3	25.7	14.3	889

Note: Figures are percentages except for Median; Gross rent is the contract rent plus the estimated average monthly cost of utilities (electricity, gas, and water and sewer) and fuels (oil, coal, kerosene, wood, etc.) if these are paid by the renter (or paid for the renter by someone else); (1) Figures cover the Savannah, GA Metropolitan Statistical Area—see Appendix B for areas included
Source: U.S. Census Bureau, 2010-2012 American Community Survey 3-Year Estimates

Year Housing Structure Built

Area	2010 or Later	2000 -2009	1990 -1999	1980 -1989	1970 -1979	1960 -1969	1950 -1959	1940 -1949	Before 1940	Median Year
City	0.8	11.1	7.7	10.6	16.6	13.9	15.3	7.6	16.4	1968
MSA[1]	0.8	24.4	16.6	14.9	13.4	8.6	8.6	4.5	8.2	1985
U.S.	0.5	14.9	13.8	13.9	15.9	11.1	10.9	5.5	13.5	1976

Note: Figures are percentages except for Median Year; (1) Figures cover the Savannah, GA Metropolitan Statistical Area—see Appendix B for areas included
Source: U.S. Census Bureau, 2010-2012 American Community Survey 3-Year Estimates

HEALTH

Health Risk Data

Category	MSA[1] (%)	U.S. (%)
Adults aged 18–64 who have any kind of health care coverage	n/a	79.6
Adults who reported being in good or excellent health	n/a	83.1
Adults who are current smokers	n/a	19.6
Adults who are heavy drinkers[2]	n/a	6.1
Adults who are binge drinkers[3]	n/a	16.9
Adults who are overweight (BMI 25.0 - 29.9)	n/a	35.8
Adults who are obese (BMI 30.0 - 99.8)	n/a	27.6
Adults who participated in any physical activities in the past month	n/a	77.1
Adults 50+ who have ever had a sigmoidoscopy or colonoscopy	n/a	67.3
Women aged 40+ who have had a mammogram within the past two years	n/a	74.0
Men aged 40+ who have had a PSA test within the past two years	n/a	45.2
Adults aged 65+ who have had flu shot within the past year	n/a	60.1
Adults who always wear a seatbelt	n/a	93.8

Note: Data as of 2012 unless otherwise noted; n/a not available; (1) Figures cover the Savannah, GA Metropolitan Statistical Area—see Appendix B for areas included; (2) Heavy drinkers are classified as males having more than two drinks per day or females having more than one drink per day; (3) Binge drinkers are classified as males having five or more drinks on one occasion or females having four or more drinks on one occasion
Source: Centers for Disease Control and Prevention, Behaviorial Risk Factor Surveillance System, SMART: Selected Metropolitan/Micropolitan Area Risk Trends, 2012

Chronic Health Indicators

Category	MSA[1] (%)	U.S. (%)
Adults who have ever been told they had a heart attack	n/a	4.5
Adults who have ever been told they had a stroke	n/a	2.9
Adults who have been told they currently have asthma	n/a	8.9
Adults who have ever been told they have arthritis	n/a	25.7
Adults who have ever been told they have diabetes[2]	n/a	9.7
Adults who have ever been told they had skin cancer	n/a	5.7
Adults who have ever been told they had any other types of cancer	n/a	6.5
Adults who have ever been told they have COPD	n/a	6.2
Adults who have ever been told they have kidney disease	n/a	2.5
Adults who have ever been told they have a form of depression	n/a	18.0

Note: Data as of 2012 unless otherwise noted; n/a not available; (1) Figures cover the Savannah, GA Metropolitan Statistical Area—see Appendix B for areas included; (2) Figures do not include pregnancy-related, borderline, or pre-diabetes
Source: Centers for Disease Control and Prevention, Behaviorial Risk Factor Surveillance System, SMART: Selected Metropolitan/Micropolitan Area Risk Trends, 2012

Mortality Rates for the Top 10 Causes of Death in the U.S.

ICD-10[a] Sub-Chapter	ICD-10[a] Code	Age-Adjusted Mortality Rate[1] per 100,000 population	
		County[2]	U.S.
Malignant neoplasms	C00-C97	174.3	174.2
Ischaemic heart diseases	I20-I25	97.1	119.1
Other forms of heart disease	I30-I51	90.5	49.6
Chronic lower respiratory diseases	J40-J47	44.3	43.2
Cerebrovascular diseases	I60-I69	44.2	40.3
Organic, including symptomatic, mental disorders	F01-F09	32.4	30.5
Other degenerative diseases of the nervous system	G30-G31	20.7	26.3
Other external causes of accidental injury	W00-X59	27.8	25.1
Diabetes mellitus	E10-E14	14.4	21.3
Hypertensive diseases	I10-I15	25.5	18.8

Note: (a) ICD-10 = International Classification of Diseases 10th Revision; (1) Mortality rates are a three year average covering 2008-2010; (2) Figures cover Chatham County
Source: Centers for Disease Control and Prevention, National Center for Health Statistics. Compressed Mortality File 1999-2010 on CDC WONDER Online Database, released January 2013. Data are compiled from the Compressed Mortality File 1999-2010, Series 20 No. 2P, 2013.

Mortality Rates for Selected Causes of Death

ICD-10[a] Sub-Chapter	ICD-10[a] Code	Age-Adjusted Mortality Rate[1] per 100,000 population	
		County[2]	U.S.
Assault	X85-Y09	10.1	5.5
Diseases of the liver	K70-K76	15.4	12.4
Human immunodeficiency virus (HIV) disease	B20-B24	8.5	3.0
Influenza and pneumonia	J09-J18	18.7	16.4
Intentional self-harm	X60-X84	12.8	11.8
Malnutrition	E40-E46	*1.5	0.8
Obesity and other hyperalimentation	E65-E68	*1.5	1.6
Renal failure	N17-N19	17.1	13.6
Transport accidents	V01-V99	15.8	12.6
Viral hepatitis	B15-B19	*1.4	2.2

Note: (a) ICD-10 = International Classification of Diseases 10th Revision; (1) Mortality rates are a three year average covering 2008-2010; (2) Figures cover Chatham County; (*) Unreliable data as per CDC
Source: Centers for Disease Control and Prevention, National Center for Health Statistics. Compressed Mortality File 1999-2010 on CDC WONDER Online Database, released January 2013. Data are compiled from the Compressed Mortality File 1999-2010, Series 20 No. 2P, 2013.

Health Insurance Coverage

Area	With Health Insurance	With Private Health Insurance	With Public Health Insurance	Without Health Insurance	Population Under Age 18 Without Health Insurance
City	78.0	55.8	30.7	22.0	8.9
MSA[1]	80.9	63.8	26.5	19.1	10.1
U.S.	84.9	65.4	30.4	15.1	7.5

Note: Figures are percentages that cover the civilian noninstitutionalized population; (1) Figures cover the Savannah, GA Metropolitan Statistical Area—see Appendix B for areas included
Source: U.S. Census Bureau, 2010-2012 American Community Survey 3-Year Estimates

Number of Medical Professionals

Area[1]	MDs[2]	DOs[2,3]	Dentists	Podiatrists	Chiropractors	Optometrists
Local (number)	931	50	165	18	42	38
Local (rate[4])	342.2	18.4	59.6	6.5	15.2	13.7
U.S. (rate[4])	267.6	19.6	61.7	5.6	24.7	14.5

Note: Data as of 2012 unless noted; (1) Local data covers Chatham County; (2) Data as of 2011; (3) Doctor of Osteopathic Medicine; (4) rate per 100,000 population
Source: Area Resource File (ARF) 2012-2013. U.S. Department of Health and Human Services, Health Resources and Services Administration, Bureau of Health Professions

EDUCATION

Public School District Statistics

District Name	Schls	Pupils	Pupil/ Teacher Ratio	Minority Pupils[1] (%)	Free Lunch Eligible[2] (%)	IEP[3] (%)
Chatham County	55	35,842	13.8	72.0	56.7	10.2

Note: Table includes school districts with 2,000 or more students; (1) Percentage of students that are not non-Hispanic white; (2) Percentage of students that are eligible for the free lunch program; (3) Percentage of students that have an Individualized Education Program.
Source: U.S. Department of Education, National Center for Education Statistics, Common Core of Data, Local Education Agency (School District) Universe Survey: School Year 2011-2012; U.S. Department of Education, National Center for Education Statistics, Common Core of Data, Public Elementary/Secondary School Universe Survey: School Year 2011-2012

Highest Level of Education

Area	Less than H.S.	H.S. Diploma	Some College, No Deg.	Associate Degree	Bachelor's Degree	Master's Degree	Prof. School Degree	Doctorate Degree
City	15.7	31.2	22.4	5.6	16.6	5.7	1.6	1.2
MSA[1]	12.6	28.7	22.8	7.0	18.9	6.9	1.9	1.1
U.S.	14.1	28.3	21.3	7.8	18.0	7.5	1.9	1.2

Note: Figures cover persons age 25 and over; (1) Figures cover the Savannah, GA Metropolitan Statistical Area—see Appendix B for areas included
Source: U.S. Census Bureau, 2010-2012 American Community Survey 3-Year Estimates

Educational Attainment by Race

Area	High School Graduate or Higher (%)					Bachelor's Degree or Higher (%)				
	Total	White	Black	Asian	Hisp.[2]	Total	White	Black	Asian	Hisp.[2]
City	84.3	90.3	79.6	77.5	58.6	25.1	36.7	14.6	32.4	25.5
MSA[1]	87.4	90.1	82.9	78.7	64.5	28.8	33.7	17.8	37.4	25.6
U.S.	85.9	88.1	82.5	85.5	63.1	28.6	30.0	18.4	50.2	13.4

Note: Figures shown cover persons 25 years old and over; (1) Figures cover the Savannah, GA Metropolitan Statistical Area—see Appendix B for areas included; (2) People of Hispanic origin can be of any race
Source: U.S. Census Bureau, 2010-2012 American Community Survey 3-Year Estimates

School Enrollment by Grade and Control

Area	Preschool (%)		Kindergarten (%)		Grades 1 - 4 (%)		Grades 5 - 8 (%)		Grades 9 - 12 (%)	
	Public	Private	Public	Private	Public	Private	Public	Private	Public	Private
City	72.1	27.9	89.2	10.8	92.7	7.3	88.2	11.8	85.9	14.1
MSA[1]	56.0	44.0	91.8	8.2	90.2	9.8	88.3	11.7	85.5	14.5
U.S.	56.9	43.1	87.8	12.2	89.9	10.1	90.0	10.0	90.8	9.2

Note: Figures shown cover persons 3 years old and over; (1) Figures cover the Savannah, GA Metropolitan Statistical Area—see Appendix B for areas included
Source: U.S. Census Bureau, 2010-2012 American Community Survey 3-Year Estimates

Average Salaries of Public School Classroom Teachers

Area	2012-13		2013-14		Percent Change 2012-13 to 2013-14	Percent Change 2003-04 to 2013-14
	Dollars	Rank[1]	Dollars	Rank[1]		
Georgia	52,880	22	52,924	23	0.08	15.1
U.S. Average	56,103	–	56,689	–	1.04	21.8

Note: (1) State rank ranges from 1 to 51 where 1 indicates highest salary.
Source: National Education Association, Rankings & Estimates: Rankings of the States 2013 and Estimates of School Statistics 2014, March 2014

Higher Education

Four-Year Colleges			Two-Year Colleges			Medical Schools[1]	Law Schools[2]	Voc/ Tech[3]
Public	Private Non-profit	Private For-profit	Public	Private Non-profit	Private For-profit			
2	1	4	1	0	1	0	1	2

Note: Figures cover institutions located within the city limits and include main campuses only; (1) includes schools accredited by the Liaison Committee on Medical Education and the American Osteopathic Association's Commission on Osteopathic College Accreditation; (2) includes ABA-accredited schools, schools with provisional ABA accreditation, and state accredited schools; (3) includes all schools with programs that are less than 2 years.
Source: National Center for Education Statistics, Integrated Postsecondary Education System (IPEDS), 2012-13; Association of American Medical Colleges, Member List, April 24, 2014; American Osteopathic Association, Member List, April 24, 2014; Law School Admission Council, Official Guide to ABA-Approved Law Schools Online, April 24, 2014; Wikipedia, List of Medical Schools in the United States, April 24, 2014; Wikipedia, List of Law Schools in the United States, April 24, 2014

PRESIDENTIAL ELECTION

2012 Presidential Election Results

Area	Obama	Romney	Other
Chatham County	55.5	43.5	1.0
U.S.	51.0	47.2	1.8

Note: Results are percentages and may not add to 100% due to rounding
Source: Dave Leip's Atlas of U.S. Presidential Elections

EMPLOYERS

Major Employers

Company Name	Industry
Armstrong Atlantic State University	University
Candler Hospital	General medical and surgical hospitals
City of Savannah	City and town managers' office
City of Savannah	Police protection, local government
Georgia Dept of Public Health	Administration of public health programs
Great Dane Trailers	Trailer parts and accessories
Gulfstream Aerospace Corporation	Aircraft
Honeywell International	Aircraft/aerospace flight instruments & guidance systems
International Paper Company	Paper mills
Kapstone Paper and Packaging Corporation	Stationery stores
Memorial Health University Medical Center	General medical and surgical hospitals
Netjets International	Air transportation, nonscheduled
Saint Joseph's Hospital	General medical and surgical hospitals
Savannah College of Art & Design	Professional schools
Savannah State University	University
St Joseph's/Candler Health System	General medical and surgical hospitals
The Sullivan Group	Employment agencies
United Parcel Service	Mailing and messenger services
Wal-Mart Stores	Department stores, discount
Wells Fargo Insurance Services USA	Insurance brokers, nec

Note: Companies shown are located within the Savannah, GA Metropolitan Statistical Area.
Source: Hoovers.com; Wikipedia

PUBLIC SAFETY

Crime Rate

Area	All Crimes	Violent Crimes				Property Crimes		
		Murder	Forcible Rape	Robbery	Aggrav. Assault	Burglary	Larceny -Theft	Motor Vehicle Theft
City	3,979.1	9.9	10.8	212.3	146.6	900.6	2,413.9	284.9
Suburbs[1]	2,521.7	1.6	27.3	50.0	154.6	538.7	1,626.3	123.4
Metro[2]	3,459.7	7.0	16.7	154.4	149.4	771.6	2,133.2	227.3
U.S.	3,246.1	4.7	26.9	112.9	242.3	670.2	1,959.3	229.7

Note: Figures are crimes per 100,000 population; (1) All areas within the metro area that are located outside the city limits; (2) Figures cover the Savannah, GA Metropolitan Statistical Area—see Appendix B for areas included
Source: FBI Uniform Crime Reports, 2012

Hate Crimes

Area	Number of Quarters Reported	Bias Motivation				
		Race	Religion	Sexual Orientation	Ethnicity	Disability
Area[2]	3	0	0	0	0	0
U.S.	4	2,797	1,099	1,135	667	92

Note: (2) Figures cover Savannah-Chatham Metropolitan.
Source: Federal Bureau of Investigation, Hate Crime Statistics 2012

Identity Theft Consumer Complaints

Area	Complaints	Complaints per 100,000 Population	Rank[2]
MSA[1]	400	115.1	32
U.S.	290,056	91.8	-

Note: (1) Figures cover the Savannah, GA Metropolitan Statistical Area—see Appendix B for areas included; (2) Rank ranges from 1 to 377 where 1 indicates greatest number of identity theft complaints per 100,000 population
Source: Federal Trade Commission, Consumer Sentinel Network Data Book for January–December 2013

Fraud and Other Consumer Complaints

Area	Complaints	Complaints per 100,000 Population	Rank[2]
MSA[1]	1,522	437.8	65
U.S.	1,811,724	595.2	-

Note: (1) Figures cover the Savannah, GA Metropolitan Statistical Area—see Appendix B for areas included; (2) Rank ranges from 1 to 377 where 1 indicates greatest number of identity theft complaints per 100,000 population
Source: Federal Trade Commission, Consumer Sentinel Network Data Book for January–December 2013

RECREATION

Culture

Dance[1]	Theatre[1]	Instrumental Music[1]	Vocal Music[1]	Series and Festivals	Museums and Art Galleries[2]	Zoos and Aquariums[3]
0	0	0	0	3	23	0

Note: (1) Number of professional performing groups; (2) Based on organizations with primary SIC code 8412; (3) AZA-accredited
Source: The Grey House Performing Arts Directory, 2013; Association of Zoos & Aquariums, AZA Member Zoos & Aquariums, April 2014; www.AccuLeads.com, May 1, 2014

Professional Sports Teams

Team Name	League	Year Established
No teams are located in the metro area		

Source: Wikipedia, Major Professional Sports Teams of the United States and Canada, April 25, 2014

CLIMATE

Average and Extreme Temperatures

Temperature	Jan	Feb	Mar	Apr	May	Jun	Jul	Aug	Sep	Oct	Nov	Dec	Yr.
Extreme High (°F)	84	86	91	95	100	104	105	104	98	97	89	83	105
Average High (°F)	60	64	70	78	84	89	92	90	86	78	70	62	77
Average Temp. (°F)	49	53	59	66	74	79	82	81	77	68	59	52	67
Average Low (°F)	38	41	48	54	62	69	72	72	68	57	47	40	56
Extreme Low (°F)	3	14	20	32	39	51	61	57	43	28	15	9	3

Note: Figures cover the years 1950-1995
Source: National Climatic Data Center, International Station Meteorological Climate Summary, 9/96

Average Precipitation/Snowfall/Humidity

Precip./Humidity	Jan	Feb	Mar	Apr	May	Jun	Jul	Aug	Sep	Oct	Nov	Dec	Yr.
Avg. Precip. (in.)	3.5	3.1	3.9	3.2	4.2	5.6	6.8	7.2	5.0	2.9	2.2	2.7	50.3
Avg. Snowfall (in.)	Tr	Tr	Tr	0	0	0	0	0	0	0	Tr	Tr	Tr
Avg. Rel. Hum. 7am (%)	83	82	83	84	85	87	88	91	91	88	86	83	86
Avg. Rel. Hum. 4pm (%)	53	50	49	48	52	58	61	63	62	55	53	54	55

Note: Figures cover the years 1950-1995; Tr = Trace amounts (<0.05 in. of rain; <0.5 in. of snow)
Source: National Climatic Data Center, International Station Meteorological Climate Summary, 9/96

Weather Conditions

Temperature			Daytime Sky			Precipitation		
10°F & below	32°F & below	90°F & above	Clear	Partly cloudy	Cloudy	0.01 inch or more precip.	0.1 inch or more snow/ice	Thunder-storms
< 1	29	70	97	155	113	111	< 1	63

Note: Figures are average number of days per year and cover the years 1950-1995
Source: National Climatic Data Center, International Station Meteorological Climate Summary, 9/96

HAZARDOUS WASTE

Superfund Sites

Savannah has no sites on the EPA's Superfund Final National Priorities List.
U.S. Environmental Protection Agency, Final National Priorities List, April 26, 2014

AIR & WATER QUALITY

Air Quality Index

Area	Percent of Days when Air Quality was...[2]					AQI Statistics[2]	
	Good	Moderate	Unhealthy for Sensitive Groups	Unhealthy	Very Unhealthy	Maximum	Median
MSA[1]	68.2	29.0	2.7	0.0	0.0	131	40

Note: (1) Data covers the Savannah, GA Metropolitan Statistical Area—see Appendix B for areas included;
(2) Based on 365 days with AQI data in 2013. Air Quality Index (AQI) is an index for reporting daily air quality.
EPA calculates the AQI for five major air pollutants regulated by the Clean Air Act: ground-level ozone,
particle pollution (aka particulate matter), carbon monoxide, sulfur dioxide, and nitrogen dioxide. The AQI runs
from 0 to 500. The higher the AQI value, the greater the level of air pollution and the greater the health
concern. There are six AQI categories: "Good" AQI is between 0 and 50. Air quality is considered satisfactory;
"Moderate" AQI is between 51 and 100. Air quality is acceptable; "Unhealthy for Sensitive Groups" When
AQI values are between 101 and 150, members of sensitive groups may experience health effects; "Unhealthy"
When AQI values are between 151 and 200 everyone may begin to experience health effects; "Very Unhealthy"
AQI values between 201 and 300 trigger a health alert; "Hazardous" AQI values over 300 trigger warnings of
emergency conditions (not shown).
Source: U.S. Environmental Protection Agency, Air Quality Index Report, 2013

Air Quality Index Pollutants

Area	Percent of Days when AQI Pollutant was...[2]					
	Carbon Monoxide	Nitrogen Dioxide	Ozone	Sulfur Dioxide	Particulate Matter 2.5	Particulate Matter 10
MSA[1]	0.0	0.0	18.4	25.8	55.9	0.0

Note: (1) Data covers the Savannah, GA Metropolitan Statistical Area—see Appendix B for areas included;
(2) Based on 365 days with AQI data in 2013. The Air Quality Index (AQI) is an index for reporting daily air
quality. EPA calculates the AQI for five major air pollutants regulated by the Clean Air Act: ground-level ozone,
particle pollution (also known as particulate matter), carbon monoxide, sulfur dioxide, and nitrogen dioxide.
The AQI runs from 0 to 500. The higher the AQI value, the greater the level of air pollution and the greater the
health concern.
Source: U.S. Environmental Protection Agency, Air Quality Index Report, 2013

Air Quality Trends: Ozone

	2003	2004	2005	2006	2007	2008	2009	2010	2011	2012
MSA[1]	0.070	0.071	0.068	0.069	0.065	0.067	0.062	0.065	0.065	0.063

Note: (1) Data covers the Savannah, GA Metropolitan Statistical Area—see Appendix B for areas included. The
values shown are the composite ozone concentration averages among trend sites based on the highest fourth
daily maximum 8-hour concentration in parts per million. These trends are based on sites having an adequate
record of monitoring data during the trend period. Data from exceptional events are included.
Source: U.S. Environmental Protection Agency, Air Quality Monitoring Information, "Air Quality Trends by
City, 2000-2012"

Maximum Air Pollutant Concentrations: Particulate Matter, Ozone, CO and Lead

	Particulate Matter 10 (ug/m³)	Particulate Matter 2.5 Wtd AM (ug/m³)	Particulate Matter 2.5 24-Hr (ug/m³)	Ozone (ppm)	Carbon Monoxide (ppm)	Lead (ug/m³)
MSA[1] Level	27	10	24	0.063	n/a	n/a
NAAQS[2]	150	15	35	0.075	9	0.15
Met NAAQS[2]	Yes	Yes	Yes	Yes	n/a	n/a

Note: (1) Data covers the Savannah, GA Metropolitan Statistical Area—see Appendix B for areas included; Data from exceptional events are included; (2) National Ambient Air Quality Standards; ppm = parts per million; ug/m³ = micrograms per cubic meter; n/a not available.
Concentrations: Particulate Matter 10 (coarse particulate)—highest second maximum 24-hour concentration; Particulate Matter 2.5 Wtd AM (fine particulate)—highest weighted annual mean concentration; Particulate Matter 2.5 24-Hour (fine particulate)—highest 98th percentile 24-hour concentration; Ozone—highest fourth daily maximum 8-hour concentration; Carbon Monoxide—highest second maximum non-overlapping 8-hour concentration; Lead—maximum running 3-month average
Source: U.S. Environmental Protection Agency, Air Quality Monitoring Information, "Air Quality Statistics by City, 2012"

Maximum Air Pollutant Concentrations: Nitrogen Dioxide and Sulfur Dioxide

	Nitrogen Dioxide AM (ppb)	Nitrogen Dioxide 1-Hr (ppb)	Sulfur Dioxide AM (ppb)	Sulfur Dioxide 1-Hr (ppb)	Sulfur Dioxide 24-Hr (ppb)
MSA[1] Level	n/a	n/a	n/a	78	n/a
NAAQS[2]	53	100	30	75	140
Met NAAQS[2]	n/a	n/a	n/a	No	n/a

Note: (1) Data covers the Savannah, GA Metropolitan Statistical Area—see Appendix B for areas included; Data from exceptional events are included; (2) National Ambient Air Quality Standards; ppm = parts per million; ug/m³ = micrograms per cubic meter; n/a not available.
Concentrations: Nitrogen Dioxide AM—highest arithmetic mean concentration; Nitrogen Dioxide 1-Hr—highest 98th percentile 1-hour daily maximum concentration; Sulfur Dioxide AM—highest annual mean concentration; Sulfur Dioxide 1-Hr—highest 99th percentile 1-hour daily maximum concentration; Sulfur Dioxide 24-Hr—highest second maximum 24-hour concentration
Source: U.S. Environmental Protection Agency, Air Quality Monitoring Information, "Air Quality Statistics by City, 2012"

Drinking Water

Water System Name	Pop. Served	Primary Water Source Type	Violations[1] Health Based	Violations[1] Monitoring/ Reporting
Savannah-Main	168,958	Ground	0	0

Note: (1) Based on violation data from January 1, 2013 to December 31, 2013 (includes unresolved violations from earlier years)
Source: U.S. Environmental Protection Agency, Office of Ground Water and Drinking Water, Safe Drinking Water Information System (based on data extracted February 10, 2014)

Tallahassee, Florida

Background

Tallahassee is the capital of Florida and located in the northern panhandle of the state in Leon County. In addition to the state government, the city is primarily known as home to Florida State University, with its 40,000 students and 16 colleges. The presence of FSU, as well as other smaller universities, has shaped development of Tallahassee from a small, rural settlement to the modern metropolis that it is today.

After the state of Florida was ceded to United States from Spain in 1821, a governing body was set up to preside over the new territory. The group initially alternated between meetings in St. Augustine and Pensacola-the territory's two largest cities at the time. Eventually Governor William Pope Duval appointed a committee to choose a more central, permanent location for the government. Tallahassee, located between St. Augustine and Pensacola, was incorporated in 1824. The word Tallahassee means "old town" in the language of the Creek Native American tribe that inhabited the area during the 18th century.

Florida State University was founded in 1851, establishing Tallahassee as a city known for education. During the Civil War, Tallahassee was the only Confederate capital city east of the Mississippi not captured by the Union Army. After the war, much of the industry in the southern United States changed. What was once a prosperous region for cotton and tobacco production suffered without slave labor. New industries emerged, including citrus production, cattle ranching and tourism, all of which were well suited to the climate and geography of Tallahassee. The first airport in the city opened in 1929. The 200-acre facility was named Dale Mabry Field after an Army Captain who had grown up in the city.

In 1961, the Tallahassee Regional Airport opened with limited service. In 1989, major passenger service was offered and in 2000, the terminal was renamed Ivan Monroe Terminal. Monroe, the first Tallahassee resident to own his own plane, was also the first manager of Dale Mabry Field-the city's original airport, and adjacent to the site of the present-day Tallahassee Regional. Other transportation services in the city include the StarMetro bus lines and the CSX railroad.

Economic and population growth in recent decades has created the need for more land in the city. During this time, approximately seventy-five square miles have been added to the city by voluntary annexation, in which property owners actively petition for their land to become part of the city. A 25-year-old program to fund new infrastructure and transportation projects via a one cent sales tax has yielded such public gems as the Capital Cascades Park which, at its foundation, is a two-pond storm-water management facility but is also a gathering place with venues such as the Capital City Amphitheater and the 5.2 mile Capital Cascades Trail.

Today, economic activity in Tallahassee is centered primarily on education and research. In addition to Florida State University, the city is home to Florida A&M University, the state's only historically black university that has 11,000 students. In 2014, the 126-year-old institution saw its first woman president, Dr. Elmira Magnum, take the helm. Also here is Tallahassee Community College, home to an Advanced Manufacturing Training Center, a 16,000 square foot facility geared toward high tech and precision manufacturing training, and the Ghazvini Center for Healthcare Education, an 85,000-square foot facility that houses programs in diagnostic medical sonography, nursing, radiologic technology, respiratory care, and emergency medical services. Other higher education offerings in Tallahassee include campuses of Barry University, Embry Riddle Aeronautical University, and Flagler College, among others.

The high-tech industry has grown significantly in recent decades. Recent arrivals include companies such as Bing Energy and SunnyLand Solar that are interested in working with university-based researchers. Also located here are manufacturing facilities for General Dynamics, Land Systems and Danfoss Turbocor.

Major attractions in the Tallahassee area include the Alfred B. Maclay Gardens State Park, the Florida State Capitol, the Lake Jackson Mounds Archaeological State Park, the Mary Brogan Museum of Art and Science and the Tallahassee Museum. Although the city does not host any major professional sports teams, students and residents alike flock to the games of the college teams. The most popular is the division 1 FSU Seminoles football team.

Despite being located in the northern part of the state, Tallahassee is generally hotter in the summer than cities in located on the Florida peninsula. The summer season also brings scattered, severe thunderstorms that develop on the Gulf of Mexico. Winters in the city are usually much cooler than in the rest of Florida. The city does receive occasional snow, but it's usually very light and only occurs once every few years. The city's location near the Gulf of Mexico also means that it sees its share of hurricane activity, but the last direct hit was Hurricane Kate in 1985.

Rankings

Business/Finance Rankings

- Tallahassee was identified as one of the top 25 U.S. cities with the most credit card debt by credit reporting bureau Experian. The city was ranked #14. *Experian, March 4, 2011*

- The Tallahassee metro area appeared on the Milken Institute "2013 Best Performing Cities" list. Rank: #194 out of 200 large metro areas. Criteria: job growth; wage and salary growth; high-tech output growth. *Milken Institute, "Best-Performing Cities 2013," December 2013*

- *Forbes* ranked the 200 most populous metro areas in the U.S. in terms of the "Best Places for Business and Careers." The Tallahassee metro area was ranked #112. Criteria: costs (business and living); job growth (past and projected); income growth; educational attainment (college and high school); projected economic growth; cultural and recreational opportunities; net migration patterns; number of highly ranked colleges. *Forbes, "The Best Places for Business and Careers," August 7, 2013*

Education Rankings

- Tallahassee was selected as one of the most well-read cities in America by Amazon.com. The city ranked #20 of 20. Cities with populations greater than 100,000 were evaluated based on per capita sales of books, magazines and newspapers. *Amazon.com, "The 20 Most Well-Read Cities in America," April 28, 2013*

Environmental Rankings

- The Tallahassee metro area came in at #300 for the relative comfort of its climate on Sperling's list of "chill cities," as measured by the Sperling Heat Index. All 361 metro areas are included. Criteria included daytime high temperatures, nighttime low temperatures, dew point, and relative humidity at the high temperatures. *www.bertsperling.com, "Sperling's Chill Cities," July 18, 2013*

- Sperling's BestPlaces assessed 379 metropolitan areas of the United States for the likelihood of dangerously extreme weather events or earthquakes. In general the Southeast and South-Central regions have the highest risk of weather extremes and earthquakes, while the Pacific Northwest enjoys the lowest risk. Of the least risky metropolitan areas, the Tallahassee metro area was ranked #304. *www.bestplaces.net, "Safest Places from Natural Disasters," April 2011*

- Tallahassee was selected as one of 22 "Smarter Cities" for energy by the Natural Resources Defense Council. Criteria: investment in green power; energy efficiency measures; conservation. *Natural Resources Defense Council, "2010 Smarter Cities," July 19, 2010*

Health/Fitness Rankings

- Tallahassee was identified as one of the top running towns in the southern U.S. by *Running Journal*. The city ranked #2 out of seven. Criteria: training venues; access to running clubs; quality of local running events; specialty running stores; overall social scene. *Running Journal, "Top Running Towns of the South," March 13, 2012*

- The Tallahassee metro area appeared in the 2013 Gallup-Healthways Well-Being Index. The area ranked #125 out of 189. The Gallup-Healthways Well-Being Index score is an average of six sub-indexes, which individually examine life evaluation, emotional health, work environment, physical health, healthy behaviors, and access to basic necessities. Results are based on telephone interviews conducted as part of the Gallup-Healthways Well-Being Index survey January 2–December 29, 2012, and January 2–December 30, 2013, with a random sample of 531,630 adults, aged 18 and older, living in metropolitan areas in the 50 U.S. states and the District of Columbia. *Gallup-Healthways, "State of American Well-Being," March 25, 2014*

Real Estate Rankings

- Using data from the housing-market research firm RealtyTrac, Yahoo! Finance researchers listed the housing markets in which housing affordability is deteriorating most, factoring in interest rates as well as median home prices. The Tallahassee metro area was among the least affordable housing markets according to the percentage difference in the income required to buy a home in December 2013 as opposed to in December 2012. *news.yahoo.com, "10 Cities Where Ordinary People Can No Longer Afford Homes," March 5, 2014*

- Tallahassee was ranked #106 out of 283 metro areas in terms of house price appreciation in 2013 (#1 = highest rate). *Federal Housing Finance Agency, House Price Index, 4th Quarter 2013*

- Tallahassee was ranked #77 out of 224 metro areas in terms of housing affordability in 2013 by the National Association of Home Builders (#1 = most affordable). The NAHB-Wells Fargo Housing Opportunity Index (HOI) for a given area is defined as the share of homes sold in that area that would have been affordable to a family earning the local median income, based on standard mortgage underwriting criteria. *National Association of Home Builders®, NAHB-Wells Fargo Housing Opportunity Index, 4th Quarter 2013*

- Tallahassee was selected as one of the best college towns for renters by ApartmentRatings.com." The area ranked #52 out of 87. Overall satisfaction ratings were ranked using thousands of user submitted scores for hundreds of apartment complexes located in cities and towns that are home to the 100 largest four-year institutions in the U.S. *ApartmentRatings.com, "2011 College Town Renter Satisfaction Rankings"*

Safety Rankings

- Allstate ranked the 200 largest cities in America in terms of driver safety. Tallahassee ranked #67. Allstate researchers analyzed internal property damage claims over a two-year period from January 2010 to December 2011. A weighted average of the two-year numbers determined the annual percentages. *Allstate, "Allstate America's Best Drivers Report®, August 27, 2013"*

- The National Insurance Crime Bureau ranked 380 metro areas in the U.S. in terms of per capita rates of vehicle theft. The Tallahassee metro area ranked #132 (#1 = highest rate). Criteria: number of vehicle theft offenses per 100,000 inhabitants in 2012. *National Insurance Crime Bureau, "Hot Spots 2012," June 26, 2013*

Seniors/Retirement Rankings

- From its Best Cities for Successful Aging indexes, the Milken Institute generated rankings for metropolitan areas, weighing data in eight categories—general indicators, health care, wellness, living arrangements, transportation and general accessibility, financial well-being, education and employment, and community participation. The Tallahassee metro area was ranked #133 overall in the small metro area category. *Milken Institute, "Best Cities for Successful Aging," July 2012*

- Tallahassee was selected as one of "10 Bargain Retirement Spots" by *U.S. News & World Report*. Criteria: cities where home prices are falling fast. *U.S. News & World Report, "10 Bargain Retirement Spots," February 22, 2011*

Sports/Recreation Rankings

- Tallahassee appeared on the *Sporting News* list of the "Best Sports Cities" for 2011. The area ranked #75 out of 271. Criteria: the magazine takes a 12-month snapshot of each city's sports, putting a heavy premium on regular-season won-lost records (from the most recently completed season). Other criteria include: playoff berths, bowl appearances and tournament bids; championships; applicable power ratings; quality of competition; overall fan fervor (measured in part by attendance); abundance of teams (rewarding quality over quantity); stadium and arena quality; ticket availability and prices; franchise ownership; and marquee appeal of athletes. *Sporting News, "Best Sports Cities 2011," October 4, 2011*

- Tallahassee appeared on the *Sporting News* list of the "Best Sports Cities" for 2011. The area ranked #75 out of 271. Criteria: a 12-month snapshot of regular-season won-lost records (from the most recently completed season). Other criteria include: playoff berths, bowl appearances and tournament bids; championships; applicable power ratings; quality of competition; overall fan fervor (measured in part by attendance); abundance of teams (quality over quantity); stadium and arena quality; ticket availability and prices; franchise ownership; and marquee appeal of athletes. *Sporting News, "Best Sports Cities 2011," October 4, 2011*

- Tallahassee was chosen as a bicycle friendly community by the League of American Bicyclists. A "Bicycle Friendly Community" welcomes cyclists by providing safe accommodation for cycling and encouraging people to bike for transportation and recreation. There are four award levels: Platinum; Gold; Silver; and Bronze. The community achieved an award level of Bronze. *League of American Bicyclists, "Bicycle Friendly Community Master List," Fall 2013*

Miscellaneous Rankings

- Bustle.com, a news, entertainment, and lifestyle site for women, studied binge- and heavy drinking rates among nonalcoholics to determine the nation's ten "drunkest" cities. Tallahassee made the list, at #8. *www.bustle.com, "38 Million Americans Have a Problem with Alcohol: The 10 Drunkest American Cities," January 2014*

- Using Musicmetric's Digital Music Index (DMI), CNBC ranked results for music piracy by way of the file-sharing protocol BitTorrent. Tallahassee was ranked #5 among American cities. *CNBC.com, "Florida City Named 'Pirate Capital' of Music World," October 8, 2012*

Business Environment

CITY FINANCES

City Government Finances

Component	2011 ($000)	2011 ($ per capita)
Total Revenues	784,125	4,640
Total Expenditures	809,575	4,791
Debt Outstanding	1,163,881	6,888
Cash and Securities[1]	1,810,140	10,712

Note: (1) Cash and security holdings of a government at the close of its fiscal year, including those of its dependent agencies, utilities, and liquor stores.
Source: U.S Census Bureau, State & Local Government Finances 2011

City Government Revenue by Source

Source	2011 ($000)	2011 ($ per capita)
General Revenue		
From Federal Government	20,332	120
From State Government	34,608	205
From Local Governments	6,961	41
Taxes		
Property	35,287	209
Sales and Gross Receipts	57,650	341
Personal Income	0	0
Corporate Income	0	0
Motor Vehicle License	0	0
Other Taxes	11,150	66
Current Charges	140,396	831
Liquor Store	0	0
Utility	400,087	2,368
Employee Retirement	24,077	142

Source: U.S Census Bureau, State & Local Government Finances 2011

City Government Expenditures by Function

Function	2011 ($000)	2011 ($ per capita)	2011 (%)
General Direct Expenditures			
Air Transportation	12,441	74	1.5
Corrections	0	0	0.0
Education	0	0	0.0
Employment Security Administration	0	0	0.0
Financial Administration	3,954	23	0.5
Fire Protection	28,045	166	3.5
General Public Buildings	0	0	0.0
Governmental Administration, Other	6,192	37	0.8
Health	0	0	0.0
Highways	61,651	365	7.6
Hospitals	0	0	0.0
Housing and Community Development	7,516	44	0.9
Interest on General Debt	2,819	17	0.3
Judicial and Legal	2,042	12	0.3
Libraries	0	0	0.0
Parking	0	0	0.0
Parks and Recreation	20,733	123	2.6
Police Protection	46,740	277	5.8
Public Welfare	0	0	0.0
Sewerage	102,157	605	12.6
Solid Waste Management	19,655	116	2.4
Veterans' Services	0	0	0.0
Liquor Store	0	0	0.0
Utility	407,712	2,413	50.4
Employee Retirement	41,161	244	5.1

Source: U.S Census Bureau, State & Local Government Finances 2011

DEMOGRAPHICS

Population Growth

Area	1990 Census	2000 Census	2010 Census	Population Growth (%)	
				1990-2000	2000-2010
City	128,014	150,624	181,376	17.7	20.4
MSA[1]	259,096	320,304	367,413	23.6	14.7
U.S.	248,709,873	281,421,906	308,745,538	13.2	9.7

Note: (1) Figures cover the Tallahassee, FL Metropolitan Statistical Area—see Appendix B for areas included
Source: U.S. Census Bureau, Census 1990, 2000, 2010

Household Size

Area	Persons in Household (%)							Average Household Size
	One	Two	Three	Four	Five	Six	Seven or More	
City	33.9	33.8	17.3	10.9	2.3	1.2	0.7	2.35
MSA[1]	29.4	35.0	17.0	12.2	3.6	1.7	1.0	2.46
U.S.	27.6	33.5	15.7	13.2	6.1	2.4	1.5	2.63

Note: (1) Figures cover the Tallahassee, FL Metropolitan Statistical Area—see Appendix B for areas included
Source: U.S. Census Bureau, 2010-2012 American Community Survey 3-Year Estimates

Race

Area	White Alone[2] (%)	Black Alone[2] (%)	Asian Alone[2] (%)	AIAN[3] Alone[2] (%)	NHOPI[4] Alone[2] (%)	Other Race Alone[2] (%)	Two or More Races (%)
City	57.2	34.8	3.8	0.4	0.0	1.3	2.5
MSA[1]	61.0	32.5	2.4	0.4	0.0	1.7	2.1
U.S.	74.0	12.6	4.9	0.8	0.2	4.7	2.8

Note: (1) Figures cover the Tallahassee, FL Metropolitan Statistical Area—see Appendix B for areas included;
(2) Alone is defined as not being in combination with one or more other races; (3) American Indian and Alaska Native; (4) Native Hawaiian and Other Pacific Islander
Source: U.S. Census Bureau, 2010-2012 American Community Survey 3-Year Estimates

Hispanic or Latino Origin

Area	Total (%)	Mexican (%)	Puerto Rican (%)	Cuban (%)	Other (%)
City	6.4	1.5	1.5	1.2	2.3
MSA[1]	6.1	2.1	1.2	1.1	1.7
U.S.	16.6	10.7	1.6	0.6	3.7

Note: Persons of Hispanic or Latino origin can be of any race; (1) Figures cover the Tallahassee, FL Metropolitan Statistical Area—see Appendix B for areas included
Source: U.S. Census Bureau, 2010-2012 American Community Survey 3-Year Estimates

Segregation

Type	Segregation Indices[1]				Percent Change		
	1990	2000	2010	2010 Rank[2]	1990-2000	1990-2010	2000-2010
Black/White	n/a	n/a	n/a	n/a	n/a	n/a	n/a
Asian/White	n/a	n/a	n/a	n/a	n/a	n/a	n/a
Hispanic/White	n/a	n/a	n/a	n/a	n/a	n/a	n/a

Note: All figures cover the Metropolitan Statistical Area—see Appendix B for areas included; Figures are based on an analysis of 1990, 2000, and 2010 Census Decennial Census tract data by William H. Frey, Brookings Institution and the University of Michigan Social Science Data Analysis Network. In this analysis all racial groups (whites, blacks, and asians) are non-Hispanic members of those races. Hispanics are shown as a separate category;
(1) Segregation Indices are Dissimilarity Indices that measure the degree to which the minority group is distributed differently than whites across census tracts. They range from 0 (complete integration) to 100 (complete segregation) where the value indicates the percentage of the minority group that needs to move to be distributed exactly like whites; (2) Ranges from 1 (most segregated) to 102 (least segregated); n/a not available.
Source: www.CensusScope.org

Ancestry

Area	German	Irish	English	American	Italian	Polish	French[2]	Scottish	Dutch
City	8.9	9.7	9.6	4.9	4.7	1.9	2.3	2.2	0.9
MSA[1]	9.5	10.0	9.0	6.4	4.2	1.6	2.6	2.7	1.1
U.S.	15.2	11.1	8.2	7.2	5.6	3.1	2.8	1.7	1.4

Note: Figures are the percentage of the total population reporting a particular ancestry. The nine most commonly reported ancestries in the U.S. are shown. Figures include multiple ancestries (e.g. if a person reported being Irish and Italian, they were included in both columns); (1) Figures cover the Tallahassee, FL Metropolitan Statistical Area—see Appendix B for areas included; (2) Excludes Basque
Source: U.S. Census Bureau, 2010-2012 American Community Survey 3-Year Estimates

Foreign-Born Population

Area	Any Foreign Country	Mexico	Asia	Europe	Carribean	South America	Central America[2]	Africa	Canada
City	7.9	0.4	2.9	1.1	1.9	0.7	0.2	0.5	0.2
MSA[1]	6.2	0.7	1.9	0.9	1.3	0.6	0.3	0.4	0.2
U.S.	13.0	3.7	3.7	1.6	1.2	0.9	1.0	0.5	0.3

Note: (1) Figures cover the Tallahassee, FL Metropolitan Statistical Area—see Appendix B for areas included; (2) Excludes Mexico.
Source: U.S. Census Bureau, 2010-2012 American Community Survey 3-Year Estimates

Marital Status

Area	Never Married	Now Married[2]	Separated	Widowed	Divorced
City	56.4	29.0	1.5	3.8	9.4
MSA[1]	43.0	39.3	1.9	4.6	11.1
U.S.	32.4	48.4	2.2	6.0	11.0

Note: Figures are percentages and cover the population 15 years of age and older; (1) Figures cover the Tallahassee, FL Metropolitan Statistical Area—see Appendix B for areas included; (2) Excludes separated
Source: U.S. Census Bureau, 2010-2012 American Community Survey 3-Year Estimates

Age

Area	Under Age 5	Age 5–19	Age 20–34	Age 35–44	Age 45–54	Age 55–64	Age 65–74	Age 75–84	Age 85+	Median Age
City	5.1	20.5	38.4	10.0	9.6	8.3	4.2	2.5	1.4	26.1
MSA[1]	5.5	19.7	27.9	11.7	12.6	11.8	6.2	3.1	1.4	32.2
U.S.	6.4	20.1	20.5	13.1	14.3	12.2	7.3	4.2	1.8	37.3

Note: (1) Figures cover the Tallahassee, FL Metropolitan Statistical Area—see Appendix B for areas included
Source: U.S. Census Bureau, 2010-2012 American Community Survey 3-Year Estimates

Gender

Area	Males	Females	Males per 100 Females
City	87,994	96,085	91.6
MSA[1]	180,521	191,406	94.3
U.S.	153,276,055	158,333,314	96.8

Note: (1) Figures cover the Tallahassee, FL Metropolitan Statistical Area—see Appendix B for areas included
Source: U.S. Census Bureau, 2010-2012 American Community Survey 3-Year Estimates

Religious Groups by Family

Area	Catholic	Baptist	Non-Den.	Methodist[2]	Lutheran	LDS[3]	Pentecostal	Presbyterian[4]	Muslim[5]	Judaism
MSA[1]	4.8	16.1	6.8	9.2	0.5	1.0	2.2	1.6	0.9	0.4
U.S.	19.1	9.3	4.0	4.0	2.3	2.0	1.9	1.6	0.8	0.7

Note: Figures are the number of adherents as a percentage of the total population; (1) Figures cover the Tallahassee, FL Metropolitan Statistical Area—see Appendix B for areas included; (2) Methodist/Pietist; (3) Latter Day Saints; (4) Reformed; (5) Figures are estimates
Source: Association of Statisticians of American Religious Bodies, 2010 U.S. Religion Census: Religious Congregations & Membership Study

Religious Groups by Tradition

Area	Catholic	Evangelical Protestant	Mainline Protestant	Other Tradition	Black Protestant	Orthodox
MSA[1]	4.8	21.9	6.4	3.0	9.2	0.2
U.S.	19.1	16.2	7.3	4.3	1.6	0.3

Note: Figures are the number of adherents as a percentage of the total population; (1) Figures cover the
Tallahassee, FL Metropolitan Statistical Area—see Appendix B for areas included
Source: Association of Statisticians of American Religious Bodies, 2010 U.S. Religion Census: Religious
Congregations & Membership Study

ECONOMY

Gross Metropolitan Product

Area	2011	2012	2013	2014	Rank[2]
MSA[1]	13.3	13.4	13.7	14.2	149

Note: Figures are in billions of dollars; (1) Figures cover the Tallahassee, FL Metropolitan Statistical
Area—see Appendix B for areas included; (2) Rank is based on 2014 data and ranges from 1 to 363
Source: The United States Conference of Mayors, U.S. Metro Economies: Outlook—Gross Metropolitan
Product, with Metro Employment Projections, November 2013

Economic Growth

Area	2011 (%)	2012 (%)	2013 (%)	2014 (%)	Rank[2]
MSA[1]	-0.6	-1.0	0.7	1.7	190
U.S.	1.6	2.5	1.7	2.5	–

Note: Figures are real gross metropolitan product (GMP) growth rates and represent annual average percent
change; (1) Figures cover the Tallahassee, FL Metropolitan Statistical Area—see Appendix B for areas
included; (2) Rank is based on 2013 data and ranges from 1 to 363
Source: The United States Conference of Mayors, U.S. Metro Economies: Outlook—Gross Metropolitan
Product, with Metro Employment Projections, November 2013

Metropolitan Area Exports

Area	2007	2008	2009	2010	2011	2012	Rank[2]
MSA[1]	86.7	119.1	108.1	117.8	118.1	130.8	323

Note: Figures are in millions of dollars; (1) Figures cover the Tallahassee, FL Metropolitan Statistical
Area—see Appendix B for areas included; (2) Rank is based on 2012 data and ranges from 1 to 369
Source: U.S. Department of Commerce, International Trade Administration, Office of Trade & Industry
Information, Manufacturing & Services, data extracted April 1, 2014

INCOME

Income

Area	Per Capita ($)	Median Household ($)	Average Household ($)
City	23,722	38,865	57,787
MSA[1]	24,196	44,647	61,518
U.S.	27,385	51,771	71,579

Note: (1) Figures cover the Tallahassee, FL Metropolitan Statistical Area—see Appendix B for areas included
Source: U.S. Census Bureau, 2010-2012 American Community Survey 3-Year Estimates

Household Income Distribution

Area	Percent of Households Earning							
	Under $15,000	$15,000 -24,999	$25,000 -34,999	$35,000 -49,999	$50,000 -74,999	$75,000 -99,000	$100,000 -149,999	$150,000 and up
City	24.4	11.7	10.6	14.5	14.7	8.5	9.3	6.3
MSA[1]	19.0	10.8	10.7	14.2	17.1	10.9	11.1	6.2
U.S.	13.1	11.0	10.5	13.7	18.1	11.9	12.5	9.1

Note: (1) Figures cover the Tallahassee, FL Metropolitan Statistical Area—see Appendix B for areas included
Source: U.S. Census Bureau, 2010-2012 American Community Survey 3-Year Estimates

Poverty Rate

Area	All Ages	Under 18 Years Old	18 to 64 Years Old	65 Years and Over
City	32.2	30.3	35.2	9.7
MSA[1]	23.8	26.3	25.3	9.5
U.S.	15.7	22.2	14.6	9.3

Note: Figures are percentage of people whose income during the past 12 months was below the poverty level;
(1) Figures cover the Tallahassee, FL Metropolitan Statistical Area—see Appendix B for areas included
Source: U.S. Census Bureau, 2010-2012 American Community Survey 3-Year Estimates

Personal Bankruptcy Filing Rate

Area	2008	2009	2010	2011	2012	2013
Leon County	2.17	2.68	2.70	2.44	1.89	1.72
U.S.	3.53	4.61	4.97	4.37	3.76	3.29

Note: Numbers are per 1,000 population and include Chapter 7 and Chapter 13 filings
Source: Federal Deposit Insurance Corporation, Regional Economic Conditions, March 20, 2014

EMPLOYMENT

Labor Force and Employment

Area	Civilian Labor Force			Workers Employed		
	Dec. 2012	Dec. 2013	% Chg.	Dec. 2012	Dec. 2013	% Chg.
City	94,691	95,773	1.1	88,425	90,725	2.6
MSA[1]	187,562	189,428	1.0	174,929	179,480	2.6
U.S.	154,904,000	154,408,000	-0.3	143,060,000	144,423,000	1.0

Note: Data is not seasonally adjusted and covers workers 16 years of age and older; (1) Metropolitan Statistical Area—see Appendix B for areas included
Source: Bureau of Labor Statistics, Local Area Unemployment Statistics

Unemployment Rate

Area	2013											
	Jan.	Feb.	Mar.	Apr.	May	Jun.	Jul.	Aug.	Sep.	Oct.	Nov.	Dec.
City	6.8	6.4	6.0	5.7	6.3	6.9	6.9	6.2	5.9	5.3	5.4	5.3
MSA[1]	6.8	6.4	5.9	5.6	6.1	6.7	6.7	6.2	5.8	5.3	5.4	5.3
U.S.	8.5	8.1	7.6	7.1	7.3	7.8	7.7	7.3	7.0	7.0	6.6	6.5

Note: Data is not seasonally adjusted and covers workers 16 years of age and older; All figures are percentages;
(1) Metropolitan Statistical Area—see Appendix B for areas included
Source: Bureau of Labor Statistics, Local Area Unemployment Statistics

Employment by Occupation

Occupation Classification	City (%)	MSA[1] (%)	U.S. (%)
Management, Business, Science, and Arts	44.4	42.0	36.0
Natural Resources, Construction, and Maintenance	5.6	7.9	9.1
Production, Transportation, and Material Moving	4.9	6.1	12.0
Sales and Office	25.9	26.4	24.7
Service	19.1	17.7	18.2

Note: Figures cover employed civilians 16 years of age and older; (1) Figures cover the Tallahassee, FL Metropolitan Statistical Area—see Appendix B for areas included
Source: U.S. Census Bureau, 2010-2012 American Community Survey 3-Year Estimates

Employment by Industry

Sector	MSA[1]		U.S.
	Number of Employees	Percent of Total	Percent of Total
Construction	n/a	n/a	4.2
Education and Health Services	19,800	11.6	15.5
Financial Activities	7,400	4.3	5.7
Government	61,100	35.8	16.1
Information	3,400	2.0	1.9
Leisure and Hospitality	18,100	10.6	10.2
Manufacturing	3,000	1.8	8.7
Mining and Logging	n/a	n/a	0.6
Other Services	8,900	5.2	3.9
Professional and Business Services	18,600	10.9	13.7
Retail Trade	18,800	11.0	11.4
Transportation and Utilities	2,000	1.2	3.8
Wholesale Trade	3,400	2.0	4.2

Note: Figures cover non-farm employment as of December 2013 and are not seasonally adjusted;
(1) Metropolitan Statistical Area—see Appendix B for areas included; n/a not available
Source: Bureau of Labor Statistics, Current Employment Statistics, Employment, Hours, and Earnings

Occupations with Greatest Projected Employment Growth: 2010 – 2020

Occupation[1]	2010 Employment	2020 Projected Employment	Numeric Employment Change	Percent Employment Change
Retail Salespersons	290,200	345,860	55,660	19.2
Combined Food Preparation and Serving Workers, Including Fast Food	154,650	193,760	39,110	25.3
Registered Nurses	165,400	202,190	36,790	22.3
Waiters and Waitresses	174,630	210,650	36,010	20.6
Customer Service Representatives	165,950	194,220	28,260	17.0
Cashiers	200,040	225,430	25,400	12.7
Office Clerks, General	142,480	164,800	22,330	15.7
Landscaping and Groundskeeping Workers	93,350	115,400	22,050	23.6
Postsecondary Teachers	75,610	94,190	18,580	24.6
Cooks, Restaurant	76,000	94,180	18,190	23.9

Note: Projections cover Florida; (1) Sorted by numeric employment change
Source: www.projectionscentral.com, State Occupational Projections, 2010–2020 Long-Term Projections

Fastest Growing Occupations: 2010 – 2020

Occupation[1]	2010 Employment	2020 Projected Employment	Numeric Employment Change	Percent Employment Change
Layout Workers, Metal and Plastic	230	380	150	65.2
Biomedical Engineers	620	990	370	60.2
Helpers—Carpenters	1,120	1,770	650	58.0
Biochemists and Biophysicists	650	1,000	350	53.6
Medical Scientists, Except Epidemiologists	2,850	4,370	1,520	53.5
Helpers—Brickmasons, Blockmasons, Stonemasons, and Tile and Marble Setters	810	1,240	430	52.6
Reinforcing Iron and Rebar Workers	940	1,370	430	46.1
Home Health Aides	28,580	41,010	12,430	43.5
Stonemasons	550	790	240	42.9
Personal Care Aides	16,880	23,920	7,040	41.7

Note: Projections cover Florida; (1) Sorted by percent employment change and excludes occupations with numeric employment change less than 100
Source: www.projectionscentral.com, State Occupational Projections, 2010–2020 Long-Term Projections

Average Wages

Occupation	$/Hr.	Occupation	$/Hr.
Accountants and Auditors	26.01	Maids and Housekeeping Cleaners	8.98
Automotive Mechanics	15.45	Maintenance and Repair Workers	14.97
Bookkeepers	15.91	Marketing Managers	50.22
Carpenters	16.16	Nuclear Medicine Technologists	n/a
Cashiers	9.16	Nurses, Licensed Practical	19.16
Clerks, General Office	11.39	Nurses, Registered	27.41
Clerks, Receptionists/Information	12.28	Nursing Assistants	10.92
Clerks, Shipping/Receiving	13.00	Packers and Packagers, Hand	8.94
Computer Programmers	28.72	Physical Therapists	40.08
Computer Systems Analysts	40.01	Postal Service Mail Carriers	24.26
Computer User Support Specialists	18.19	Real Estate Brokers	n/a
Cooks, Restaurant	10.65	Retail Salespersons	11.02
Dentists	101.64	Sales Reps., Exc. Tech./Scientific	21.94
Electrical Engineers	42.41	Sales Reps., Tech./Scientific	33.81
Electricians	17.49	Secretaries, Exc. Legal/Med./Exec.	14.09
Financial Managers	53.63	Security Guards	11.27
First-Line Supervisors/Managers, Sales	19.46	Surgeons	n/a
Food Preparation Workers	9.33	Teacher Assistants	11.90
General and Operations Managers	52.68	Teachers, Elementary School	21.90
Hairdressers/Cosmetologists	12.38	Teachers, Secondary School	22.10
Internists	n/a	Telemarketers	13.78
Janitors and Cleaners	9.91	Truck Drivers, Heavy/Tractor-Trailer	15.22
Landscaping/Groundskeeping Workers	10.83	Truck Drivers, Light/Delivery Svcs.	14.76
Lawyers	52.36	Waiters and Waitresses	9.61

Note: Wage data covers the Tallahassee, FL Metropolitan Statistical Area—see Appendix B for areas included.
Hourly wages for elementary/secondary school teachers and teacher assistants were calculated by the editors
from annual wage data assuming a 40 hour work week; n/a not available.
Source: Bureau of Labor Statistics, Metro Area Occupational Employment and Wage Estimates, May 2013

RESIDENTIAL REAL ESTATE

Building Permits

Area	Single-Family			Multi-Family			Total		
	2012	2013	Pct. Chg.	2012	2013	Pct. Chg.	2012	2013	Pct. Chg.
City	216	293	35.6	692	648	-6.4	908	941	3.6
MSA[1]	468	628	34.2	766	652	-14.9	1,234	1,280	3.7
U.S.	518,695	620,802	19.7	310,963	370,020	19.0	829,658	990,822	19.4

Note: (1) Metropolitan Statistical Area—see Appendix B for areas included; figures represent new, privately-
owned housing units authorized (unadjusted data); All permit data are based on estimates with imputation.
Source: U.S. Census Bureau, Manufacturing, Mining, and Construction Statistics, Building Permits, 2012, 2013

Homeownership Rate

Area	2006 (%)	2007 (%)	2008 (%)	2009 (%)	2010 (%)	2011 (%)	2012 (%)	2013 (%)
MSA[1]	n/a	n/a	n/a	n/a	n/a	n/a	n/a	n/a
U.S.	68.8	68.1	67.8	67.4	66.9	66.1	65.4	65.1

Note: (1) Figures cover the Tallahassee, FL Metropolitan Statistical Area—see Appendix B for areas included;
n/a not available
Source: U.S. Census Bureau, Housing Vacancies and Homeownership Annual Statistics: 2013

Housing Vacancy Rates

Area	Gross Vacancy Rate[2] (%)			Year-Round Vacancy Rate[3] (%)			Rental Vacancy Rate[4] (%)			Homeowner Vacancy Rate[5] (%)		
	2011	2012	2013	2011	2012	2013	2011	2012	2013	2011	2012	2013
MSA[1]	n/a	n/a	n/a	n/a	n/a	n/a	n/a	n/a	n/a	n/a	n/a	n/a
U.S.	14.2	13.8	13.8	11.1	10.8	10.7	9.5	8.7	8.3	2.5	2.0	2.0

Note: (1) Figures cover the Tallahassee, FL Metropolitan Statistical Area—see Appendix B for areas included;
(2) The percentage of the total housing inventory that is vacant; (3) The percentage of the housing inventory
(excluding seasonal units) that is year-round vacant; (4) The percentage of rental inventory that is vacant for
rent; (5) The percentage of homeowner inventory that is vacant for sale; n/a not available
Source: U.S. Census Bureau, Housing Vacancies and Homeownership Annual Statistics: 2013

TAXES

State Corporate Income Tax Rates

State	Tax Rate (%)	Income Brackets ($)	Num. of Brackets	Financial Institution Tax Rate (%)[a]	Federal Income Tax Ded.
Florida	5.5 (f)	Flat rate	1	5.5 (f)	No

Note: Tax rates as of January 1, 2014; (a) Rates listed are the corporate income tax rate applied to financial institutions or excise taxes based on income. Some states have other taxes based upon the value of deposits or shares; (f) An exemption of $50,000 is allowed. Florida's Alternative Minimum Tax rate is 3.3%.
Source: Federation of Tax Administrators, "State Corporate Income Tax Rates, 2014"

State Individual Income Tax Rates

State	Tax Rate (%)	Income Brackets ($)	Num. of Brackets	Personal Exempt. ($)[1] Single	Personal Exempt. ($)[1] Dependents	Fed. Inc. Tax Ded.
Florida	None	–	–	–	–	–

Note: Tax rates as of January 1, 2014; Local- and county-level taxes are not included; n/a not applicable;
(1) Married joint filers generally receive double the single exemption
Source: Federation of Tax Administrators, "State Individual Income Tax Rates, 2014"

Various State and Local Tax Rates

State	State and Local Sales and Use (%)	State Sales and Use (%)	Gasoline[1] (¢/gal.)	Cigarette[2] ($/pack)	Spirits[3] ($/gal.)	Wine[4] ($/gal.)	Beer[5] ($/gal.)
Florida	7.5	6.00	36.03	1.339	6.50 (f)	2.25	0.48

Note: All tax rates as of January 1, 2014; (1) The American Petroleum Institute has developed a methodology for determining the average tax rate on a gallon of fuel. Rates may include any of the following: excise taxes, environmental fees, storage tank fees, other fees or taxes, general sales tax, and local taxes. In states where gasoline is subject to the general sales tax, or where the fuel tax is based on the average sale price, the average rate determined by API is sensitive to changes in the price of gasoline. States that fully or partially apply general sales taxes to gasoline: CA, CO, GA, IL, IN, MI, NY; (2) The federal excise tax of $1.0066 per pack and local taxes are not included; (3) Rates are those applicable to off-premise sales of 40% alcohol by volume (a.b.v.) distilled spirits in 750ml containers. Local excise taxes are excluded; (4) Rates are those applicable to off-premise sales of 11% a.b.v. non-carbonated wine in 750ml containers; (5) Rates are those applicable to off-premise sales of 4.7% a.b.v. beer in 12 ounce containers; (f) Different rates also applicable according to alcohol content, place of production, size of container, or place purchased (on- or off-premise or onboard airlines).
Source: Tax Foundation, 2014 Facts & Figures: How Does Your State Compare?

State Business Tax Climate Index Rankings

State	Overall Rank	Corporate Tax Index Rank	Individual Income Tax Index Rank	Sales Tax Index Rank	Unemployment Insurance Tax Index Rank	Property Tax Index Rank
Florida	5	13	1	18	6	16

Note: The index is a measure of how each state's tax laws affect economic performance. The lower the rank, the more favorable a state's tax system is for business. States without a given tax are given a ranking of 1. The scores/rankings for the District of Columbia do not affect other states. The 2014 index represents the tax climate as of July 1, 2013.
Source: Tax Foundation, State Business Tax Climate Index 2014

COMMERCIAL UTILITIES

Typical Monthly Electric Bills

Area	Commercial Service ($/month) 1,500 kWh	Commercial Service ($/month) 40 kW demand 14,000 kWh	Industrial Service ($/month) 1,000 kW demand 200,000 kWh	Industrial Service ($/month) 50,000 kW demand 15,000,000 kWh
City	n/a	n/a	n/a	n/a
Average[1]	197	1,636	25,662	1,485,307

Note: Based on total rates in effect July 1, 2013; (1) average based on 180 utilities surveyed; n/a not available
Source: Edison Electric Institute, Typical Bills and Average Rates Report, Summer 2013

TRANSPORTATION

Means of Transportation to Work

Area	Car/Truck/Van		Public Transportation			Bicycle	Walked	Other Means	Worked at Home
	Drove Alone	Car-pooled	Bus	Subway	Railroad				
City	81.0	8.2	2.2	0.0	0.0	0.9	3.4	1.2	3.1
MSA[1]	81.8	10.0	1.4	0.0	0.0	0.5	2.2	1.2	3.1
U.S.	76.4	9.7	2.6	1.7	0.5	0.6	2.8	1.3	4.3

Note: Figures are percentages and cover workers 16 years of age and older; (1) Figures cover the Tallahassee, FL Metropolitan Statistical Area—see Appendix B for areas included
Source: U.S. Census Bureau, 2010-2012 American Community Survey 3-Year Estimates

Travel Time to Work

Area	Less Than 10 Minutes	10 to 19 Minutes	20 to 29 Minutes	30 to 44 Minutes	45 to 59 Minutes	60 to 89 Minutes	90 Minutes or More
City	15.6	43.8	23.5	13.0	1.9	1.5	0.7
MSA[1]	11.4	34.4	24.7	20.8	5.7	2.1	0.9
U.S.	13.5	29.8	20.9	20.1	7.5	5.6	2.5

Note: Figures are percentages and include workers 16 years old and over; (1) Figures cover the Tallahassee, FL Metropolitan Statistical Area—see Appendix B for areas included
Source: U.S. Census Bureau, 2010-2012 American Community Survey 3-Year Estimates

Travel Time Index

Area	1985	1990	1995	2000	2005	2010	2011
Urban Area[1]	n/a	n/a	n/a	n/a	n/a	n/a	n/a
Average[2]	1.09	1.14	1.16	1.19	1.23	1.18	1.18

Note: Travel Time Index—the ratio of travel time in the peak period to the travel time at free-flow conditions. For example, a value of 1.30 indicates a 20-minute free-flow trip takes 26 minutes in the peak. Free-flow speeds (60 mph on freeways and 35 mph on principal arterials) are used as the comparison threshold; (1) Data for the Tallahassee, FL urban area was not available; (2) average of 498 urban areas
Source: Texas Transportation Institute, Urban Mobility Report 2012, December 2012

Public Transportation

Agency Name / Mode of Transportation	Vehicles Operated in Maximum Service	Annual Unlinked Passenger Trips (in thous.)	Annual Passenger Miles (in thous.)
City of Tallahassee (StarMetro)			
Bus (directly operated)	58	4,585.6	14,076.4
Demand Response (directly operated)	15	79.2	521.2

Source: Federal Transit Administration, National Transit Database, 2012

Air Transportation

Airport Name and Code / Type of Service	Passenger Airlines[1]	Passenger Enplanements	Freight Carriers[2]	Freight (lbs.)
Tallahassee Regional (TLH)				
Domestic service (U.S. carriers - 2013)	18	335,574	5	8,814,701
International service (U.S. carriers - 2012)	1	2	0	0

Note: (1) Includes all U.S.-based major, minor and commuter airlines that carried at least one passenger during the year; (2) Includes all U.S.-based airlines and freight carriers that transported at least one lb. of freight during the year.
Source: Bureau of Transportation Statistics, The Intermodal Transportation Database, Air Carriers: T-100 Domestic Market (U.S. Carriers), 2013; Bureau of Transportation Statistics, The Intermodal Transportation Database, Air Carriers: T-100 International Market (U.S. Carriers), 2012

Other Transportation Statistics

Major Highways:	I-10
Amtrak Service:	No
Major Waterways/Ports:	None

Source: Amtrak.com; Google Maps

BUSINESSES

Major Business Headquarters

Company Name	Rankings	
	Fortune[1]	Forbes[2]
No companies listed	-	-

Note: (1) Fortune 500—companies that produce a 10-K are ranked 1 to 500 based on 2012 revenue; (2) all private companies with at least $2 billion in annual revenue through the end of their most current fiscal year are ranked 1 to 224; companies listed are headquartered in the city; dashes indicate no ranking
Source: Fortune, "Fortune 500," May 20, 2013; Forbes, "America's Largest Private Companies," December 18, 2013

Minority- and Women-Owned Businesses

Group	All Firms		Firms with Paid Employees			
	Firms	Sales ($000)	Firms	Sales ($000)	Employees	Payroll ($000)
Asian	541	104,534	155	76,732	1,222	15,117
Black	2,581	114,987	(s)	(s)	(s)	(s)
Hispanic	765	88,113	186	73,230	881	21,731
Women	4,816	609,031	921	526,609	5,438	129,271
All Firms	15,791	12,932,947	4,959	12,337,448	86,866	3,001,106

Note: Figures cover firms located in the city; minority- and women-owned business are defined as firms in which the corresponding group own 51% or more of the stock or equity of the company; (s) estimates are suppressed when publication standards are not met
Source: U.S. Census Bureau, 2007 Economic Census, Survey of Business Owners (2012 Survey of Business Owners data will be released starting in June 2015)

**HOTELS &
CONVENTION
CENTERS**

Hotels/Motels

Area	5 Star		4 Star		3 Star		2 Star		1 Star		Not Rated	
	Num.	Pct.[3]	Num.	Pct.[3]	Num.	Pct.[3]	Num.	Pct.[3]	Num.	Pct.[3]	Num.	Pct.[3]
City[1]	0	0.0	1	1.2	16	18.6	59	68.6	3	3.5	7	8.1
Total[2]	142	0.9	1,005	6.0	5,147	30.9	8,578	51.4	408	2.4	1,397	8.4

Note: (1) Figures cover Tallahassee and vicinity; (2) Figures cover all 100 cities in this book; (3) Percentage of hotels which have a given star rating; Star ratings are determined by expedia.com and offer an indication of the general quality of a particular hotel.
Source: expedia.com, April 7, 2014

Major Convention Centers

Name	Overall Space (sq. ft.)	Exhibit Space (sq. ft.)	Meeting Space (sq. ft.)	Meeting Rooms
There are no major convention centers located in the metro area				

Source: Original research

Living Environment

COST OF LIVING

Cost of Living Index

Composite Index	Groceries	Housing	Utilities	Trans-portation	Health Care	Misc. Goods/Services
98.1	99.2	98.2	88.7	101.1	101.4	98.6

Note: The Cost of Living Index measures regional differences in the cost of consumer goods and services, excluding taxes and non-consumer expenditures, for professional and managerial households in the top income quintile. It is based on more than 50,000 prices covering almost 60 different items for which prices are collected three times a year by chambers of commerce, economic development organizations or university applied economic centers in each participating urban area. The numbers shown should be read as a percentage above or below the national average of 100. For example, a value of 115.4 in the groceries column indicates that grocery prices are 15.4% higher than the national average. Small differences in the index numbers should not be interpreted as significant; Figures cover the Tallahassee FL urban area.
Source: The Council for Community and Economic Research, ACCRA Cost of Living Index, 2013

Grocery Prices

Area[1]	T-Bone Steak ($/pound)	Frying Chicken ($/pound)	Whole Milk ($/half gal.)	Eggs ($/dozen)	Orange Juice ($/64 oz.)	Coffee ($/11.5 oz.)
City[2]	10.76	1.37	2.75	1.95	3.58	4.24
Avg.	10.19	1.28	2.34	1.81	3.48	4.39
Min.	8.56	0.94	1.44	1.19	2.78	3.40
Max.	14.82	2.28	3.56	3.73	6.23	7.32

Note: (1) Values for the local area are compared with the average, minimum and maximum values for all 327 areas in the Cost of Living Index; (2) Figures cover the Tallahassee FL urban area; **T-Bone Steak** *(price per pound);* **Frying Chicken** *(price per pound, whole fryer);* **Whole Milk** *(half gallon carton);* **Eggs** *(price per dozen, Grade A, large);* **Orange Juice** *(64 oz. Tropicana or Florida Natural);* **Coffee** *(11.5 oz. can, vacuum-packed, Maxwell House, Hills Bros, or Folgers).*
Source: The Council for Community and Economic Research, ACCRA Cost of Living Index, 2013

Housing and Utility Costs

Area[1]	New Home Price ($)	Apartment Rent ($/month)	All Electric ($/month)	Part Electric ($/month)	Other Energy ($/month)	Telephone ($/month)
City[2]	305,099	820	164.06	-	-	20.00
Avg.	295,864	900	171.38	91.82	70.12	27.73
Min.	185,506	458	117.80	48.81	33.67	17.16
Max.	1,358,917	3,783	441.68	171.40	372.65	39.47

Note: (1) Values for the local area are compared with the average, minimum and maximum values for all 327 areas in the Cost of Living Index; (2) Figures cover the Tallahassee FL urban area; **New Home Price** *(2,400 sf living area, 8,000 sf lot, in urban area with full utilities);* **Apartment Rent** *(950 sf 2 bedroom/1.5 or 2 bath, unfurnished, excluding all utilities except water);* **All Electric** *(average monthly cost for an all-electric home);* **Part Electric** *(average monthly cost for a part-electric home);* **Other Energy** *(average monthly cost for natural gas, fuel oil, coal, wood, and any other forms of energy except electricity);* **Telephone** *(price includes basic monthly rate for a private residential line plus additional local usage charges incurred by a family of four).*
Source: The Council for Community and Economic Research, ACCRA Cost of Living Index, 2013

Health Care, Transportation, and Other Costs

Area[1]	Doctor ($/visit)	Dentist ($/visit)	Optometrist ($/visit)	Gasoline ($/gallon)	Beauty Salon ($/visit)	Men's Shirt ($)
City[2]	102.20	90.72	81.84	3.52	35.06	36.57
Avg.	101.40	86.48	96.16	3.44	33.87	26.55
Min.	61.67	50.83	50.12	3.08	18.92	12.48
Max.	182.71	152.50	223.78	4.33	68.22	52.03

Note: (1) Values for the local area are compared with the average, minimum and maximum values for all 327 areas in the Cost of Living Index; (2) Figures cover the Tallahassee FL urban area; **Doctor** *(general practitioners routine exam of an established patient);* **Dentist** *(adult teeth cleaning and periodic oral examination);* **Optometrist** *(full vision eye exam for established adult patient);* **Gasoline** *(one gallon regular unleaded, national brand, including all taxes, cash price at self-service pump if available);* **Beauty Salon** *(woman's shampoo, trim, and blow-dry);* **Men's Shirt** *(cotton/polyester dress shirt, pinpoint weave, long sleeves).*
Source: The Council for Community and Economic Research, ACCRA Cost of Living Index, 2013

HOUSING

House Price Index (HPI)

Area	National Ranking[2]	Quarterly Change (%)	One-Year Change (%)	Five-Year Change (%)
MSA[1]	106	-0.37	3.76	-20.12
U.S.[3]	–	1.20	7.69	4.18

Note: The HPI is a weighted repeat sales index. It measures average price changes in repeat sales or refinancings on the same properties. This information is obtained by reviewing repeat mortgage transactions on single-family properties whose mortgages have been purchased or securitized by Fannie Mae or Freddie Mac in January 1975; (1) Tallahassee, FL Metropolitan Statistical Area—see Appendix B for areas included; (2) Rankings are based on annual percentage change for all metro areas containing at least 15,000 transactions over the last 10 years and ranges from 1 to 283; (3) figures based on a weighted average of Census Division estimates using a seasonally adjusted, purchase-only index; all figures are for the period ending December 31, 2013
Source: Federal Housing Finance Agency, House Price Index, February 25, 2014

Median Single-Family Home Prices

Area	2011	2012	2013p	Percent Change 2012 to 2013
MSA[1]	143.0	144.9	171.9	18.6
U.S. Average	166.2	177.2	197.4	11.4

Note: Figures are median sales prices of existing single-family homes in thousands of dollars; (p) preliminary; n/a not available; (1) Tallahassee, FL Metropolitan Statistical Area—see Appendix B for areas included
Source: National Association of Realtors, Median Sales Price of Existing Single-Family Homes for Metropolitan Areas, 4th Quarter 2013

Qualifying Income Based on Median Sales Price of Existing Single-Family Homes

Area	With 5% Down ($)	With 10% Down ($)	With 20% Down ($)
MSA[1]	38,802	36,759	32,675
U.S. Average	45,395	43,006	38,228

Note: Figures are preliminary; Qualifying income is based on a mortgage rate of 4.4%. Monthly principal and interest payment is limited to 25% of income; n/a not available; (1) Tallahassee, FL Metropolitan Statistical Area—see Appendix B for areas included
Source: National Association of Realtors, Qualifying Income Based on Median Sales Price of Existing Single-Family Homes for Metropolitan Areas, 4th Quarter 2013

Median Apartment Condo-Coop Home Prices

Area	2011	2012	2013p	Percent Change 2012 to 2013
MSA[1]	71.3	68.7	77.8	13.2
U.S. Average	165.1	173.7	194.9	12.2

Note: Figures are median sales prices of existing apartment condo-coop homes in thousands of dollars; (p) preliminary; n/a not available; (1) Tallahassee, FL Metropolitan Statistical Area—see Appendix B for areas included
Source: National Association of Realtors, Median Sales Price of Existing Apartment Condo-Coop Homes for Metropolitan Areas, 4th Quarter 2013

Gross Monthly Rent

Area	Under $200	$200 -299	$300 -499	$500 -749	$750 -999	$1,000 -1,499	$1,500 and up	Median ($)
City	1.2	1.9	3.8	23.0	29.3	30.7	10.0	923
MSA[1]	1.2	2.1	5.5	23.3	28.6	30.4	8.8	901
U.S.	1.7	3.3	8.1	22.7	24.3	25.7	14.3	889

Note: Figures are percentages except for Median; Gross rent is the contract rent plus the estimated average monthly cost of utilities (electricity, gas, and water and sewer) and fuels (oil, coal, kerosene, wood, etc.) if these are paid by the renter (or paid for the renter by someone else); (1) Figures cover the Tallahassee, FL Metropolitan Statistical Area—see Appendix B for areas included
Source: U.S. Census Bureau, 2010-2012 American Community Survey 3-Year Estimates

Year Housing Structure Built

Area	2010 or Later	2000 -2009	1990 -1999	1980 -1989	1970 -1979	1960 -1969	1950 -1959	1940 -1949	Before 1940	Median Year
City	0.4	20.8	17.5	19.7	17.9	10.1	7.9	3.5	2.1	1984
MSA[1]	0.5	20.7	21.0	20.9	15.8	8.4	6.9	3.1	2.8	1986
U.S.	0.5	14.9	13.8	13.9	15.9	11.1	10.9	5.5	13.5	1976

Note: Figures are percentages except for Median Year; (1) Figures cover the Tallahassee, FL Metropolitan Statistical Area—see Appendix B for areas included
Source: U.S. Census Bureau, 2010-2012 American Community Survey 3-Year Estimates

HEALTH

Health Risk Data

Category	MSA[1] (%)	U.S. (%)
Adults aged 18–64 who have any kind of health care coverage	n/a	79.6
Adults who reported being in good or excellent health	n/a	83.1
Adults who are current smokers	n/a	19.6
Adults who are heavy drinkers[2]	n/a	6.1
Adults who are binge drinkers[3]	n/a	16.9
Adults who are overweight (BMI 25.0 - 29.9)	n/a	35.8
Adults who are obese (BMI 30.0 - 99.8)	n/a	27.6
Adults who participated in any physical activities in the past month	n/a	77.1
Adults 50+ who have ever had a sigmoidoscopy or colonoscopy	n/a	67.3
Women aged 40+ who have had a mammogram within the past two years	n/a	74.0
Men aged 40+ who have had a PSA test within the past two years	n/a	45.2
Adults aged 65+ who have had flu shot within the past year	n/a	60.1
Adults who always wear a seatbelt	n/a	93.8

Note: Data as of 2012 unless otherwise noted; n/a not available; (1) Figures cover the Tallahassee, FL Metropolitan Statistical Area—see Appendix B for areas included; (2) Heavy drinkers are classified as males having more than two drinks per day or females having more than one drink per day; (3) Binge drinkers are classified as males having five or more drinks on one occasion or females having four or more drinks on one occasion
Source: Centers for Disease Control and Prevention, Behaviorial Risk Factor Surveillance System, SMART: Selected Metropolitan/Micropolitan Area Risk Trends, 2012

Chronic Health Indicators

Category	MSA[1] (%)	U.S. (%)
Adults who have ever been told they had a heart attack	n/a	4.5
Adults who have ever been told they had a stroke	n/a	2.9
Adults who have been told they currently have asthma	n/a	8.9
Adults who have ever been told they have arthritis	n/a	25.7
Adults who have ever been told they have diabetes[2]	n/a	9.7
Adults who have ever been told they had skin cancer	n/a	5.7
Adults who have ever been told they had any other types of cancer	n/a	6.5
Adults who have ever been told they have COPD	n/a	6.2
Adults who have ever been told they have kidney disease	n/a	2.5
Adults who have ever been told they have a form of depression	n/a	18.0

Note: Data as of 2012 unless otherwise noted; n/a not available; (1) Figures cover the Tallahassee, FL Metropolitan Statistical Area—see Appendix B for areas included; (2) Figures do not include pregnancy-related, borderline, or pre-diabetes
Source: Centers for Disease Control and Prevention, Behaviorial Risk Factor Surveillance System, SMART: Selected Metropolitan/Micropolitan Area Risk Trends, 2012

Mortality Rates for the Top 10 Causes of Death in the U.S.

ICD-10[a] Sub-Chapter	ICD-10[a] Code	Age-Adjusted Mortality Rate[1] per 100,000 population	
		County[2]	U.S.
Malignant neoplasms	C00-C97	164.3	174.2
Ischaemic heart diseases	I20-I25	90.5	119.1
Other forms of heart disease	I30-I51	44.9	49.6
Chronic lower respiratory diseases	J40-J47	39.4	43.2
Cerebrovascular diseases	I60-I69	42.0	40.3
Organic, including symptomatic, mental disorders	F01-F09	58.3	30.5
Other degenerative diseases of the nervous system	G30-G31	19.8	26.3
Other external causes of accidental injury	W00-X59	20.3	25.1
Diabetes mellitus	E10-E14	17.1	21.3
Hypertensive diseases	I10-I15	21.4	18.8

Note: (a) ICD-10 = International Classification of Diseases 10th Revision; (1) Mortality rates are a three year average covering 2008-2010; (2) Figures cover Leon County
Source: Centers for Disease Control and Prevention, National Center for Health Statistics. Compressed Mortality File 1999-2010 on CDC WONDER Online Database, released January 2013. Data are compiled from the Compressed Mortality File 1999-2010, Series 20 No. 2P, 2013.

Mortality Rates for Selected Causes of Death

ICD-10[a] Sub-Chapter	ICD-10[a] Code	Age-Adjusted Mortality Rate[1] per 100,000 population	
		County[2]	U.S.
Assault	X85-Y09	4.5	5.5
Diseases of the liver	K70-K76	10.2	12.4
Human immunodeficiency virus (HIV) disease	B20-B24	5.3	3.0
Influenza and pneumonia	J09-J18	16.9	16.4
Intentional self-harm	X60-X84	12.1	11.8
Malnutrition	E40-E46	Suppressed	0.8
Obesity and other hyperalimentation	E65-E68	3.6	1.6
Renal failure	N17-N19	9.5	13.6
Transport accidents	V01-V99	12.4	12.6
Viral hepatitis	B15-B19	*2.0	2.2

Note: (a) ICD-10 = International Classification of Diseases 10th Revision; (1) Mortality rates are a three year average covering 2008-2010; (2) Figures cover Leon County; (*) Unreliable data as per CDC
Source: Centers for Disease Control and Prevention, National Center for Health Statistics. Compressed Mortality File 1999-2010 on CDC WONDER Online Database, released January 2013. Data are compiled from the Compressed Mortality File 1999-2010, Series 20 No. 2P, 2013.

Health Insurance Coverage

Area	With Health Insurance	With Private Health Insurance	With Public Health Insurance	Without Health Insurance	Population Under Age 18 Without Health Insurance
City	85.6	72.8	20.1	14.4	5.7
MSA[1]	85.5	69.6	25.2	14.5	6.0
U.S.	84.9	65.4	30.4	15.1	7.5

Note: Figures are percentages that cover the civilian noninstitutionalized population; (1) Figures cover the Tallahassee, FL Metropolitan Statistical Area—see Appendix B for areas included
Source: U.S. Census Bureau, 2010-2012 American Community Survey 3-Year Estimates

Number of Medical Professionals

Area[1]	MDs[2]	DOs[2,3]	Dentists	Podiatrists	Chiropractors	Optometrists
Local (number)	703	20	99	11	50	48
Local (rate[4])	252.6	7.2	34.9	3.9	17.6	16.9
U.S. (rate[4])	267.6	19.6	61.7	5.6	24.7	14.5

Note: Data as of 2012 unless noted; (1) Local data covers Leon County; (2) Data as of 2011; (3) Doctor of Osteopathic Medicine; (4) rate per 100,000 population
Source: Area Resource File (ARF) 2012-2013. U.S. Department of Health and Human Services, Health Resources and Services Administration, Bureau of Health Professions

EDUCATION

Public School District Statistics

District Name	Schls	Pupils	Pupil/ Teacher Ratio	Minority Pupils[1] (%)	Free Lunch Eligible[2] (%)	IEP[3] (%)
FSU Lab Schools	3	2,378	13.3	57.7	n/a	9.9
Leon County Public Schools	61	33,218	16.3	53.4	40.6	15.9

Note: Table includes school districts with 2,000 or more students; (1) Percentage of students that are not non-Hispanic white; (2) Percentage of students that are eligible for the free lunch program; (3) Percentage of students that have an Individualized Education Program.
Source: U.S. Department of Education, National Center for Education Statistics, Common Core of Data, Local Education Agency (School District) Universe Survey: School Year 2011-2012; U.S. Department of Education, National Center for Education Statistics, Common Core of Data, Public Elementary/Secondary School Universe Survey: School Year 2011-2012

Best High Schools

High School Name	Rank[1]	Grad. Rate[2] (%)	Coll.[3] (%)	AP/IB/ AICE Tests[4]	AP/IB/ AICE Score[5]	SAT Score[6]	ACT Score[6]
Florida State University School	472	99	96	0.5	3.7	1540	20.0
Lincoln H.S.	860	84	100	0.9	2.6	1530	21.1

Note: (1) Public schools are ranked from 1 to 2,000 based on the following self-reported statistics (with the corresponding weight used in calculating their overall score). Schools that were newly founded and did not have a graduating senior class in 2012 were excluded; (2) Four-year, on-time graduation rate (25%); (3) Percent of 2011 graduates who were accepted to college (25%); (4) AP/IB/AICE tests taken per student (25%); (5) Average AP/IB/AICE exam score (10%); (6) Average SAT and/or ACT score (10%); Percent of students enrolled in at least one AP/IB/AICE course (5%)—data not shown
Source: Newsweek and The Daily Beast, "America's Best High Schools 2013"

Highest Level of Education

Area	Less than H.S.	H.S. Diploma	Some College, No Deg.	Associate Degree	Bachelor's Degree	Master's Degree	Prof. School Degree	Doctorate Degree
City	7.5	16.4	19.3	8.9	27.1	13.4	3.9	3.4
MSA[1]	11.0	24.7	20.2	7.9	21.0	10.2	2.5	2.5
U.S.	14.1	28.3	21.3	7.8	18.0	7.5	1.9	1.2

Note: Figures cover persons age 25 and over; (1) Figures cover the Tallahassee, FL Metropolitan Statistical Area—see Appendix B for areas included
Source: U.S. Census Bureau, 2010-2012 American Community Survey 3-Year Estimates

Educational Attainment by Race

Area	High School Graduate or Higher (%)					Bachelor's Degree or Higher (%)				
	Total	White	Black	Asian	Hisp.[2]	Total	White	Black	Asian	Hisp.[2]
City	92.5	96.0	85.9	94.1	88.7	47.8	56.0	29.1	77.1	39.2
MSA[1]	89.0	93.1	80.8	92.9	77.9	36.3	41.6	22.6	72.0	28.6
U.S.	85.9	88.1	82.5	85.5	63.1	28.6	30.0	18.4	50.2	13.4

Note: Figures shown cover persons 25 years old and over; (1) Figures cover the Tallahassee, FL Metropolitan Statistical Area—see Appendix B for areas included; (2) People of Hispanic origin can be of any race
Source: U.S. Census Bureau, 2010-2012 American Community Survey 3-Year Estimates

School Enrollment by Grade and Control

Area	Preschool (%)		Kindergarten (%)		Grades 1 - 4 (%)		Grades 5 - 8 (%)		Grades 9 - 12 (%)	
	Public	Private	Public	Private	Public	Private	Public	Private	Public	Private
City	44.3	55.7	80.1	19.9	86.5	13.5	89.7	10.3	90.5	9.5
MSA[1]	55.8	44.2	79.3	20.7	87.2	12.8	86.9	13.1	86.7	13.3
U.S.	56.9	43.1	87.8	12.2	89.9	10.1	90.0	10.0	90.8	9.2

Note: Figures shown cover persons 3 years old and over; (1) Figures cover the Tallahassee, FL Metropolitan Statistical Area—see Appendix B for areas included
Source: U.S. Census Bureau, 2010-2012 American Community Survey 3-Year Estimates

Average Salaries of Public School Classroom Teachers

Area	2012-13		2013-14		Percent Change 2012-13 to 2013-14	Percent Change 2003-04 to 2013-14
	Dollars	Rank[1]	Dollars	Rank[1]		
Florida	46,598	45	46,691	45	0.20	15.0
U.S. Average	56,103	–	56,689	–	1.04	21.8

Note: (1) State rank ranges from 1 to 51 where 1 indicates highest salary.
Source: National Education Association, Rankings & Estimates: Rankings of the States 2013 and Estimates of School Statistics 2014, March 2014

Higher Education

Four-Year Colleges			Two-Year Colleges			Medical Schools[1]	Law Schools[2]	Voc/ Tech[3]
Public	Private Non-profit	Private For-profit	Public	Private Non-profit	Private For-profit			
2	1	1	1	0	0	1	1	3

Note: Figures cover institutions located within the city limits and include main campuses only; (1) includes schools accredited by the Liaison Committee on Medical Education and the American Osteopathic Association's Commission on Osteopathic College Accreditation; (2) includes ABA-accredited schools, schools with provisional ABA accreditation, and state accredited schools; (3) includes all schools with programs that are less than 2 years.
Source: National Center for Education Statistics, Integrated Postsecondary Education System (IPEDS), 2012-13; Association of American Medical Colleges, Member List, April 24, 2014; American Osteopathic Association, Member List, April 24, 2014; Law School Admission Council, Official Guide to ABA-Approved Law Schools Online, April 24, 2014; Wikipedia, List of Medical Schools in the United States, April 24, 2014; Wikipedia, List of Law Schools in the United States, April 24, 2014

According to *U.S. News & World Report*, the Tallahassee, FL metro area is home to one of the best national universities in the U.S.: **Florida State University** (#91). The indicators used to capture academic quality fall into a number of categories: assessment by administrators at peer institutions; retention of students; faculty resources; student selectivity; financial resources; alumni giving; high school counselor ratings of colleges; and graduation rate. *U.S. News & World Report, "America's Best Colleges 2014"*

According to *U.S. News & World Report*, the Tallahassee, FL metro area is home to one of the top 100 law schools in the U.S.: **Florida State University** (#48). The rankings are based on a weighted average of 12 measures of quality: peer assessment score; assessment score by lawyers/judges; median LSAT scores; median undergrad GPA; acceptance rate; employment rates for graduates; placement success; bar passage rate; faculty resources; expenditures per student; student/faculty ratio; and library resources. *U.S. News & World Report, "America's Best Graduate Schools, Law, 2014"*

PRESIDENTIAL ELECTION

2012 Presidential Election Results

Area	Obama	Romney	Other
Leon County	61.3	37.6	1.1
U.S.	51.0	47.2	1.8

Note: Results are percentages and may not add to 100% due to rounding
Source: Dave Leip's Atlas of U.S. Presidential Elections

EMPLOYERS

Major Employers

Company Name	Industry
ACS, A Xerox Company	Print services
Big Bend Hospice	Healthcare
Capital City Bank group	Finance
Capital Health Plan	Healthcare
Capital Regional Medical Center	Healthcare
CenturyLink	Telecommunications
City of Tallahassee	Government
Comcast Cable	Telecommunications & internet
Dale Earnhardt Jr. Chevrolet	Auto dealer
Danfoss Turbocor	Hvac industry
Florida A&M University	Education
Florida Bar	Regulatory agency for lawyers
Florida State University	Education
General Dynamics Land Systems	Manufacturer
Leon County	Government
Leon County Schools	Education
Publix Supermarket	Supermarket
St. Marks Powder	Manufacturer
State of Florida	Government
Tallahassee Community College	Education
Tallahassee Democrat	Newspaper
Tallahassee Memorial HealthCare	Healthcare
Tallahassee Primary Care Associates	Healthcare
Walmart Stores	Retail
Westminister Oaks	Senior care

Note: Companies shown are located within the Tallahassee, FL Metropolitan Statistical Area.
Source: Hoovers.com; Wikipedia

PUBLIC SAFETY

Crime Rate

Area	All Crimes	Violent Crimes				Property Crimes		
		Murder	Forcible Rape	Robbery	Aggrav. Assault	Burglary	Larceny-Theft	Motor Vehicle Theft
City	5,499.3	6.5	62.0	283.1	501.5	1,418.1	2,945.6	282.5
Suburbs[1]	2,719.9	5.3	26.4	45.9	301.0	765.3	1,475.1	100.9
Metro[2]	4,095.2	5.9	44.0	163.3	400.2	1,088.3	2,202.8	190.8
U.S.	3,246.1	4.7	26.9	112.9	242.3	670.2	1,959.3	229.7

Note: Figures are crimes per 100,000 population; (1) All areas within the metro area that are located outside the city limits; (2) Figures cover the Tallahassee, FL Metropolitan Statistical Area—see Appendix B for areas included
Source: FBI Uniform Crime Reports, 2012

Hate Crimes

Area	Number of Quarters Reported	Bias Motivation				
		Race	Religion	Sexual Orientation	Ethnicity	Disability
City	4	1	0	0	0	0
U.S.	4	2,797	1,099	1,135	667	92

Source: Federal Bureau of Investigation, Hate Crime Statistics 2012

Identity Theft Consumer Complaints

Area	Complaints	Complaints per 100,000 Population	Rank[2]
MSA[1]	659	179.4	5
U.S.	290,056	91.8	-

Note: (1) Figures cover the Tallahassee, FL Metropolitan Statistical Area—see Appendix B for areas included; (2) Rank ranges from 1 to 377 where 1 indicates greatest number of identity theft complaints per 100,000 population
Source: Federal Trade Commission, Consumer Sentinel Network Data Book for January–December 2013

Fraud and Other Consumer Complaints

Area	Complaints	Complaints per 100,000 Population	Rank[2]
MSA[1]	1,503	409.1	104
U.S.	1,811,724	595.2	-

Note: (1) Figures cover the Tallahassee, FL Metropolitan Statistical Area—see Appendix B for areas included; (2) Rank ranges from 1 to 377 where 1 indicates greatest number of identity theft complaints per 100,000 population
Source: Federal Trade Commission, Consumer Sentinel Network Data Book for January–December 2013

RECREATION

Culture

Dance[1]	Theatre[1]	Instrumental Music[1]	Vocal Music[1]	Series and Festivals	Museums and Art Galleries[2]	Zoos and Aquariums[3]
1	2	2	1	1	18	0

Note: (1) Number of professional performing groups; (2) Based on organizations with primary SIC code 8412; (3) AZA-accredited
Source: The Grey House Performing Arts Directory, 2013; Association of Zoos & Aquariums, AZA Member Zoos & Aquariums, April 2014; www.AccuLeads.com, May 1, 2014

Professional Sports Teams

Team Name	League	Year Established

No teams are located in the metro area
Source: Wikipedia, Major Professional Sports Teams of the United States and Canada, April 25, 2014

CLIMATE

Average and Extreme Temperatures

Temperature	Jan	Feb	Mar	Apr	May	Jun	Jul	Aug	Sep	Oct	Nov	Dec	Yr.
Extreme High (°F)	83	89	90	95	102	103	103	102	99	94	88	84	103
Average High (°F)	64	67	73	80	86	90	91	91	88	81	72	66	79
Average Temp. (°F)	52	55	61	67	74	80	81	81	78	69	60	54	68
Average Low (°F)	40	42	48	53	62	69	71	72	68	57	47	41	56
Extreme Low (°F)	6	14	20	29	34	46	57	61	40	30	13	10	6

Note: Figures cover the years 1948-1990
Source: National Climatic Data Center, International Station Meteorological Climate Summary, 9/96

Average Precipitation/Snowfall/Humidity

Precip./Humidity	Jan	Feb	Mar	Apr	May	Jun	Jul	Aug	Sep	Oct	Nov	Dec	Yr.
Avg. Precip. (in.)	4.2	5.1	6.0	4.2	4.5	6.8	8.8	7.1	5.7	2.9	3.5	4.5	63.3
Avg. Snowfall (in.)	Tr	Tr	Tr	0	0	0	0	0	0	0	0	Tr	Tr
Avg. Rel. Hum. 7am (%)	86	87	88	89	89	91	93	94	93	90	89	87	90
Avg. Rel. Hum. 4pm (%)	54	51	49	46	50	58	66	64	60	51	52	55	55

Note: Figures cover the years 1948-1990; Tr = Trace amounts (<0.05 in. of rain; <0.5 in. of snow)
Source: National Climatic Data Center, International Station Meteorological Climate Summary, 9/96

Weather Conditions

Temperature			Daytime Sky			Precipitation		
10°F & below	32°F & below	90°F & above	Clear	Partly cloudy	Cloudy	0.01 inch or more precip.	0.1 inch or more snow/ice	Thunderstorms
< 1	31	86	93	175	97	114	1	83

Note: Figures are average number of days per year and cover the years 1948-1990
Source: National Climatic Data Center, International Station Meteorological Climate Summary, 9/96

HAZARDOUS WASTE

Superfund Sites

Tallahassee has no sites on the EPA's Superfund Final National Priorities List.
U.S. Environmental Protection Agency, Final National Priorities List, April 26, 2014

AIR & WATER QUALITY

Air Quality Index

Area	Percent of Days when Air Quality was...[2]					AQI Statistics[2]	
	Good	Moderate	Unhealthy for Sensitive Groups	Unhealthy	Very Unhealthy	Maximum	Median
MSA[1]	83.8	15.3	0.5	0.0	0.3	222	36

Note: (1) Data covers the Tallahassee, FL Metropolitan Statistical Area—see Appendix B for areas included; (2) Based on 365 days with AQI data in 2013. Air Quality Index (AQI) is an index for reporting daily air quality. EPA calculates the AQI for five major air pollutants regulated by the Clean Air Act: ground-level ozone, particle pollution (aka particulate matter), carbon monoxide, sulfur dioxide, and nitrogen dioxide. The AQI runs from 0 to 500. The higher the AQI value, the greater the level of air pollution and the greater the health concern. There are six AQI categories: "Good" AQI is between 0 and 50. Air quality is considered satisfactory; "Moderate" AQI is between 51 and 100. Air quality is acceptable; "Unhealthy for Sensitive Groups" When AQI values are between 101 and 150, members of sensitive groups may experience health effects; "Unhealthy" When AQI values are between 151 and 200 everyone may begin to experience health effects; "Very Unhealthy" AQI values between 201 and 300 trigger a health alert; "Hazardous" AQI values over 300 trigger warnings of emergency conditions (not shown).
Source: U.S. Environmental Protection Agency, Air Quality Index Report, 2013

Air Quality Index Pollutants

Area	Percent of Days when AQI Pollutant was...[2]					
	Carbon Monoxide	Nitrogen Dioxide	Ozone	Sulfur Dioxide	Particulate Matter 2.5	Particulate Matter 10
MSA[1]	0.0	0.0	52.6	0.0	47.4	0.0

Note: (1) Data covers the Tallahassee, FL Metropolitan Statistical Area—see Appendix B for areas included; (2) Based on 365 days with AQI data in 2013. The Air Quality Index (AQI) is an index for reporting daily air quality. EPA calculates the AQI for five major air pollutants regulated by the Clean Air Act: ground-level ozone, particle pollution (also known as particulate matter), carbon monoxide, sulfur dioxide, and nitrogen dioxide. The AQI runs from 0 to 500. The higher the AQI value, the greater the level of air pollution and the greater the health concern.
Source: U.S. Environmental Protection Agency, Air Quality Index Report, 2013

Air Quality Trends: Ozone

	2003	2004	2005	2006	2007	2008	2009	2010	2011	2012
MSA[1]	0.074	0.071	0.070	0.071	0.072	0.071	0.058	0.066	0.065	0.066

Note: (1) Data covers the Tallahassee, FL Metropolitan Statistical Area—see Appendix B for areas included. The values shown are the composite ozone concentration averages among trend sites based on the highest fourth daily maximum 8-hour concentration in parts per million. These trends are based on sites having an adequate record of monitoring data during the trend period. Data from exceptional events are included.
Source: U.S. Environmental Protection Agency, Air Quality Monitoring Information, "Air Quality Trends by City, 2000-2012"

Maximum Air Pollutant Concentrations: Particulate Matter, Ozone, CO and Lead

	Particulate Matter 10 (ug/m^3)	Particulate Matter 2.5 Wtd AM (ug/m^3)	Particulate Matter 2.5 24-Hr (ug/m^3)	Ozone (ppm)	Carbon Monoxide (ppm)	Lead (ug/m^3)
MSA[1] Level	n/a	8.7	18	0.067	n/a	n/a
NAAQS[2]	150	15	35	0.075	9	0.15
Met NAAQS[2]	n/a	Yes	Yes	Yes	n/a	n/a

Note: (1) Data covers the Tallahassee, FL Metropolitan Statistical Area—see Appendix B for areas included; Data from exceptional events are included; (2) National Ambient Air Quality Standards; ppm = parts per million; ug/m^3 = micrograms per cubic meter; n/a not available.
Concentrations: Particulate Matter 10 (coarse particulate)—highest second maximum 24-hour concentration; Particulate Matter 2.5 Wtd AM (fine particulate)—highest weighted annual mean concentration; Particulate Matter 2.5 24-Hour (fine particulate)—highest 98th percentile 24-hour concentration; Ozone—highest fourth daily maximum 8-hour concentration; Carbon Monoxide—highest second maximum non-overlapping 8-hour concentration; Lead—maximum running 3-month average
Source: U.S. Environmental Protection Agency, Air Quality Monitoring Information, "Air Quality Statistics by City, 2012"

Maximum Air Pollutant Concentrations: Nitrogen Dioxide and Sulfur Dioxide

	Nitrogen Dioxide AM (ppb)	Nitrogen Dioxide 1-Hr (ppb)	Sulfur Dioxide AM (ppb)	Sulfur Dioxide 1-Hr (ppb)	Sulfur Dioxide 24-Hr (ppb)
MSA[1] Level	n/a	n/a	n/a	n/a	n/a
NAAQS[2]	53	100	30	75	140
Met NAAQS[2]	n/a	n/a	n/a	n/a	n/a

Note: (1) Data covers the Tallahassee, FL Metropolitan Statistical Area—see Appendix B for areas included; Data from exceptional events are included; (2) National Ambient Air Quality Standards; ppm = parts per million; ug/m³ = micrograms per cubic meter; n/a not available.
Concentrations: Nitrogen Dioxide AM—highest arithmetic mean concentration; Nitrogen Dioxide 1-Hr—highest 98th percentile 1-hour daily maximum concentration; Sulfur Dioxide AM—highest annual mean concentration; Sulfur Dioxide 1-Hr—highest 99th percentile 1-hour daily maximum concentration; Sulfur Dioxide 24-Hr—highest second maximum 24-hour concentration
Source: U.S. Environmental Protection Agency, Air Quality Monitoring Information, "Air Quality Statistics by City, 2012"

Drinking Water

Water System Name	Pop. Served	Primary Water Source Type	Violations[1] Health Based	Violations[1] Monitoring/ Reporting
City of Tallahassee	194,665	Ground	0	1

Note: (1) Based on violation data from January 1, 2013 to December 31, 2013 (includes unresolved violations from earlier years)
Source: U.S. Environmental Protection Agency, Office of Ground Water and Drinking Water, Safe Drinking Water Information System (based on data extracted February 10, 2014)

Tampa, Florida

Background

Although Tampa was visited by Spanish explorers, such as Ponce de Leon and Hernando de Soto as early as 1521, this city, located on the mouth of the Hillsborough River on Tampa Bay, did not see significant growth until the mid-nineteenth century.

Like many cities in northern Florida such as Jacksonville, Tampa was a fort during the Seminole War, and during the Civil War it was captured by the Union Army. Later, Tampa enjoyed prosperity and development when the railroad transported tourists from up north to enjoy the warmth and sunshine of Florida.

Two historical events in the late nineteenth century set Tampa apart from other Florida cities. First, Tampa played a significant role during the Spanish-American War in 1898 as a chief port of embarkation for American troops to Cuba. During that time, Colonel Theodore Roosevelt occupied a Tampa hotel as his military headquarters. Second, a cigar factory in nearby Ybor City, named after owner Vicente Martinez Ybor, was the site where Jose Marti (the George Washington of Cuba) exhorted workers to take up arms against the tyranny of Spanish rule in the late 1800s.

Today, Tampa enjoys its role as a U.S. port and is host to many cruise ships. Major industries in and around Tampa include services, retail trade, government and finance, insurance and real estate. Like most of Florida, its economy is also heavily based on tourism. Significant employers include the Hillsborough County School District, WellCare Health Plan, Raymond James Financial, the University of South Florida, Hillsborough County Government, and MacDill Air Force Base. It is also home to servers at Wikipedia, the online encyclopedia.

The city boasts NFL's Tampa Bay Buccaneers, the Devil Rays baseball team, and the NHL's Lightning. Other attractions include Florida's Latin Quarter known as Ybor City (a National Historic Landmark District), Busch Gardens, and a Museum of Science and Industry. MacDill Air Force Base also hosts a popular air show every year. Tampa hosted the 2012 Republican National Convention.

Tampa has received high marks in various surveys throughout the years, including being top cleanest and outdoor cities, as well as the best place for 20-somethings.

Winters are mild, while summers are long, warm, and humid. Freezing temperatures occur on one or two mornings per year during November through March. A dramatic feature of the Tampa climate is the summer thunderstorm season. Most occur during the late afternoon, sometimes causing temperatures to drop dramatically. The area is vulnerable to tidal surges, as the land has an elevation of less than 15 feet above sea level. The city has not experienced a direct hit from a hurricane since the 1930s.

Rankings

General Rankings

- Tampa was selected as one of America's best cities by *Bloomberg Businessweek*. The city ranked #34 out of 50. Criteria: leisure attributes (the number of restaurants, bars, libraries, museums, professional sports teams, and park acres by population); educational attributes (public school performance, the number of colleges, and graduate degree holders); economic factors (2011 income and June and July 2012 unemployment); crime; and air quality. *Bloomberg BusinessWeek, "America's Best Cities," September 26, 2012*

Business/Finance Rankings

- In order to help veterans transition from the military to civilian life, USAA and Hiring Our Heroes worked with Sperlings's BestPlaces to develop a list of the major metropolitan areas where military-skills-related employment is strongest. Criteria included job prospects, unemployment, number of government jobs, recent job growth, accessible health resources, and colleges and universities. Metro areas with a violent crime rate or high cost of living were excluded. At #7, the Tampa metro area made the top ten. *www.usaa.com, "2013 Best Places for Veterans: Jobs," November 2013*

- Based on a minimum of 500 social media reviews per metro area, the employment opinion group Glassdoor surveyed 50 of the largest U.S. metro areas on measures including compensation and benefits, satisfaction with management, business outlook, and number of employers hiring. The Tampa metro area was ranked #47 in overall employee satisfaction. *www.glassdoor.com, "Employment Satisfaction Report Card by City," June 21, 2013*

- In its Competitive Alternatives report, consulting firm KPMG analyzed the 27 largest metropolitan statistical areas according to 26 cost components (such as taxes, labor costs, and utilities) and 30 non-cost-related variables (such as crime rates and number of universities). The business website 24/7 Wall Street examined the KPMG findings, adding to the mix current unemployment rates, GDP, median income, and employment decline during the last recession and "projected" recovery. It identified the Tampa metro area as #4 among the ten best American cities for business. *247wallst.com, "Best American Cities for Business," April 4, 2012*

- Tampa was ranked #21 out of 100 metro areas in terms of economic performance (#1 = best) during the recession and recovery from trough quarter through the second quarter of 2013. Criteria: percent change in employment; percentage point change in unemployment rate; percent change in gross metropolitan product; percent change in House Price Index. *Brookings Institution, MetroMonitor: Tracking Economic Recession and Recovery in America's 100 Largest Metropolitan Areas, September 2013*

- The Tampa metro area was identified as one of 10 best-paying cities for women. The metro area ranked #10. Criteria: *24/7 Wall St.* identified the metropolitan areas that have the smallest pay disparity between men and women by comparing the median earnings for the past 12 months of both men and women working full-time in the country's 100 largest metropolitan statistical areas. *24/7 Wall St., "10 Best-Paying Cities for Women," April 14, 2013*

- Payscale.com ranked the 20 largest metro areas in terms of wage growth. The Tampa metro area ranked #1. Criteria: private-sector wage growth between the 4th quarter of 2012 and the 4th quarter of 2013. *PayScale, "Wage Trends by Metro Area," 4th Quarter, 2013*

- The Tampa metro area was identified as one of the most affordable metropolitan areas in America by *Forbes*. The area ranked #18 out of 20. Criteria: the 100 largest metro areas in the U.S. were analyzed based on housing affordability and cost-of-living. *Forbes.com, "America's Most Affordable Cities," March 11, 2014*

- Tampa was identified as one of America's most frugal metro areas by *Coupons.com*. The city ranked #3 out of 25. Criteria: online coupon usage. *Coupons.com, "Top 25 Most Frugal Cities of 2012," February 19, 2013*

- Tampa was identified as one of America's most frugal metro areas by *Coupons.com*. The city ranked #4 out of 25. Criteria: Grocery IQ and coupons.com mobile app usage. *Coupons.com, "Top 25 Most On-the-Go Frugal Cities of 2012," February 19, 2013*

- Tampa was identified as one of the uhappiest cities to work in by CareerBliss.com, an online community for career advancement. The city ranked #6 out of 10. Criteria: independent company reviews from employees all over the country on: relationship with their boss and co-workers; work environment; job resources; compensation; growth opportunities; company culture; company reputation; daily tasks; job control over work performed on a daily basis. *CareerBliss.com, "Top 10 Happiest and Unhappiest Cities to Work in 2014," February 10, 2014*

- The Tampa metro area appeared on the Milken Institute "2013 Best Performing Cities" list. Rank: #93 out of 200 large metro areas. Criteria: job growth; wage and salary growth; high-tech output growth. *Milken Institute, "Best-Performing Cities 2013," December 2013*

- *Forbes* ranked the 200 most populous metro areas in the U.S. in terms of the "Best Places for Business and Careers." The Tampa metro area was ranked #63. Criteria: costs (business and living); job growth (past and projected); income growth; educational attainment (college and high school); projected economic growth; cultural and recreational opportunities; net migration patterns; number of highly ranked colleges. *Forbes, "The Best Places for Business and Careers," August 7, 2013*

Children/Family Rankings

- Tampa was selected as one of the best cities for families to live by *Parenting* magazine. The city ranked #45 out of 100. Criteria: education; health; community; *Parenting's* Culture & Charm Index. *Parenting.com, "The 2012 Best Cities for Families List"*

- Tampa was chosen as one of America's 100 best communities for young people. The winners were selected based upon detailed information provided about each community's efforts to fulfill five essential promises critical to the well-being of young people: caring adults who are actively involved in their lives; safe places in which to learn and grow; a healthy start toward adulthood; an effective education that builds marketable skills; and opportunities to help others. *America's Promise Alliance, "100 Best Communities for Young People, 2012"*

Culture/Performing Arts Rankings

- Tampa was selected as one of America's top cities for the arts. The city ranked #3 in the mid-sized city (population 100,000 to 499,999) category. Criteria: readers' top choices for arts travel destinations based on the richness and variety of visual arts sites, activities and events. *American Style, "2012 Top 25 Arts Destinations," June 2012*

Dating/Romance Rankings

- Of the 100 U.S. cities surveyed by *Men's Health* in its quest to identify the nation's best cities for dating and forming relationships, Tampa was ranked #12 for online dating (#1 = best). *Men's Health, "The Best and Worst Cities for Online Dating," January 30, 2013*

Education Rankings

- *Men's Health* ranked 100 U.S. cities in terms of their education levels. Tampa was ranked #51 (#1 = most educated city). Criteria: high school graduation rates; school enrollment; educational attainment; number of households who have outstanding student loans; number of households whose members have taken adult-education courses. *Men's Health, "Where School Is In: The Most and Least Educated Cities," September 12, 2011*

- Tampa was selected as one of America's most literate cities. The city ranked #25 out of the 77 largest U.S. cities. Criteria: number of booksellers; library resources; Internet resources; educational attainment; periodical publishing resources; newspaper circulation. *Central Connecticut State University, "America's Most Literate Cities, 2013"*

Environmental Rankings

- The Tampa metro area came in at #329 for the relative comfort of its climate on Sperling's list of "chill cities," as measured by the Sperling Heat Index. All 361 metro areas are included. Criteria included daytime high temperatures, nighttime low temperatures, dew point, and relative humidity at the high temperatures. *www.bertsperling.com, "Sperling's Chill Cities," July 18, 2013*

- Sperling's BestPlaces assessed 379 metropolitan areas of the United States for the likelihood of dangerously extreme weather events or earthquakes. In general the Southeast and South-Central regions have the highest risk of weather extremes and earthquakes, while the Pacific Northwest enjoys the lowest risk. Of the least risky metropolitan areas, the Tampa metro area was ranked #334. *www.bestplaces.net, "Safest Places from Natural Disasters," April 2011*

- Tampa was selected as one of 22 "Smarter Cities" for energy by the Natural Resources Defense Council. Criteria: investment in green power; energy efficiency measures; conservation. *Natural Resources Defense Council, "2010 Smarter Cities," July 19, 2010*

- Tampa was highlighted as one of the top 25 cleanest metro areas for short-term particle pollution (24-hour PM 2.5) in the U.S. during 2008 through 2010. Monitors in these cities reported no days with unhealthful PM 2.5 levels. *American Lung Association, State of the Air 2012*

Food/Drink Rankings

- *Men's Health* ranked 100 major U.S. cities in terms of alcohol intoxication. Tampa ranked #73 (#1 = most sober).Criteria: binge drinking; alcohol-related traffic accidents, arrests, and fatalities. *Men's Health, "The Drunkest Cities in America," November 19, 2013*

Health/Fitness Rankings

- For each of the 50 most populous metro areas in the United States, the American College of Sports Medicine's American Fitness Index evaluated infrastructure, community assets, and policies that encourage healthy and fit lifestyles, including preventive health behaviors, levels of chronic disease conditions, health care access, and community resources and policies that support physical activity. The Tampa metro area ranked #40 for "community fitness." Personal health indicators were considered as well as community and environmental indicators. *www.americanfitnessindex.org, "ACSM American Fitness Index Health and Community Fitness Status of the 50 Largest Metropolitan Areas," May 2013*

- Tampa was selected as one of the 25 fattest cities in America by *Men's Fitness Online*. It ranked #5 out of America's 50 largest cities. Criteria: fitness centers and sport stores; nutrition; sports participation; TV viewing; overweight/sedentary; junk food; air quality; geography; commute; parks and open space; city recreational facilities; access to healthcare; motivation; mayor and city initiatives; state obesity initiatives. *Men's Fitness, "The Fittest and Fattest Cities in America," March 5, 2012*

- Tampa was identified as a "2013 Spring Allergy Capital." The area ranked #76 out of 100. Three groups of factors were used to identify the most severe cities for people with allergies during the spring season: annual pollen levels; medicine utilization; access to board-certified allergists. *Asthma and Allergy Foundation of America, "Spring Allergy Capitals 2013"*

- Tampa was identified as a "2013 Fall Allergy Capital." The area ranked #71 out of 100. Three groups of factors were used to identify the most severe cities for people with allergies during the fall season: annual pollen levels; medicine utilization; access to board-certified allergists. *Asthma and Allergy Foundation of America, "Fall Allergy Capitals 2013"*

- Tampa was identified as a "2013 Asthma Capital." The area ranked #57 out of the nation's 100 largest metropolitan areas. Twelve factors were used to identify the most challenging places to live for people with asthma: estimated prevalence; self-reported prevalence; crude death rate for asthma; annual pollen score; annual air quality; public smoking laws; number of board-certified asthma specialists; school inhaler access laws; rescue medication use; controller medication use; uninsured rate; poverty rate. *Asthma and Allergy Foundation of America, "Asthma Capitals 2013"*

- *Men's Health* ranked 100 major U.S. cities in terms of the best and worst cities for men. Tampa ranked #54. Criteria: thirty-three data points were examined covering health, fitness, and quality of life. *Men's Health, "The Best & Worst Cities for Men 2014," December 6, 2013*

- Breathe Right Nasal Strips, in partnership with Sperling's BestPlaces, analyzed 50 metro areas and identified those U.S. cities most challenged by chronic nasal congestion. The Tampa metro area ranked #19. Criteria: tree, grass and weed pollens; molds and spores; air pollution; climate; smoking; purchase habits of congestion products; prescriptions of drugs for congestion relief; incidence of influenza. *Breathe Right Nasal Strips, "Most Congested Cities," October 3, 2011*

- The American Academy of Dermatology ranked 26 U.S. metropolitan regions in terms of their residents knowledge, attitude and behaviors towards tanning, sun protection and skin cancer detection. The Tampa metro area ranked #4. The results of the study are based on an online survey of over 7,000 adults nationwide. *American Academy of Dermatology, "Suntelligence: How Sun Smart is Your City?," May 3, 2010*

- The Tampa metro area appeared in the 2013 Gallup-Healthways Well-Being Index. The area ranked #152 out of 189. The Gallup-Healthways Well-Being Index score is an average of six sub-indexes, which individually examine life evaluation, emotional health, work environment, physical health, healthy behaviors, and access to basic necessities. Results are based on telephone interviews conducted as part of the Gallup-Healthways Well-Being Index survey January 2–December 29, 2012, and January 2–December 30, 2013, with a random sample of 531,630 adults, aged 18 and older, living in metropolitan areas in the 50 U.S. states and the District of Columbia. *Gallup-Healthways, "State of American Well-Being," March 25, 2014*

- The Tampa metro area was identified as one of "America's Most Stressful Cities" by *Sperling's BestPlaces*. The metro area ranked #1 out of 50. Criteria: unemployment rate; suicide rate; commute time; mental health; poor rest; alcohol use; violent crime rate; property crime rate; cloudy days annually. *Sperling's BestPlaces, www.BestPlaces.net, "Stressful Cities 2012*

- *Men's Health* ranked 100 U.S. cities in terms of their activity levels. Tampa was ranked #67 (#1 = most active city). Criteria: where and how often residents exercise; percentage of households that watch more than 15 hours of cable television a week and buy more than 11 video games a year; death rate from deep-vein thrombosis, a condition linked to sitting for extended periods of time. *Men's Health, "Where Sit Happens: The Most and Least Active Cities in America," June 20, 2011*

- Tampa was selected as one of the "20 Most Livable U.S. Cities for Wheelchair Users" by the Christopher & Dana Reeve Foundation. The city ranked #12. Criteria: Medicaid eligibility and spending; access to physicians and rehabilitation facilities; access to fitness facilities and recreation; access to paratransit; percentage of people living with disabilities who are employed; clean air; climate. *Christopher & Dana Reeve Foundation, "20 Most Livable U.S. Cities for Wheelchair Users," July 26, 2010*

- *The Daily Beast* identified the 30 U.S. metro areas with the worst smoking habits. The Tampa metro area ranked #19. Sixty urban centers with populations of more than one million were ranked based on the following criteria: number of smokers; number of cigarettes smoked per day; fewest attempts to quit. *The Daily Beast, "30 Cities With Smoking Problems," January 3, 2011*

Real Estate Rankings

- Based on the home-price forecasts compiled by the real-estate valuation firm CoreLogic Case-Shiller, the finance website CNNMoney reported that in 2014, the Tampa metro area is expected to place #6 among American metro areas in terms of increases in residential real estate prices. *money.cnn.com, "10 Hottest Housing Markets for 2014," January 23, 2014*

- On the list compiled by Penske Truck Rental, the Tampa metro area was named the #2 moving destination in 2013, based on one-way consumer truck rental reservations made through Penske's website and reservations call center. *blog.gopenske.com, "Penske Truck Rental's 2013 Top Moving Destinations List," January 22, 2014*

- The Tampa metro area was identified as #4 among the ten housing markets with the highest percentage of distressed property sales, based on the findings of the housing data website RealtyTrac. Criteria included being sold "short"—for less than the outstanding mortgage balance—or in a foreclosure auction, income and poverty figures, and unemployment data. *247wallst.com, "Cities Selling the Most Distressed Homes," January 23, 2014*

- The Tampa metro area was identified as one of the top 20 housing markets to invest in for 2014 by *Forbes*. The area ranked #12. Criteria: high population and job growth; relatively low home prices which are below equilibrium home price (EHP). The EHP is what the average price for a market should be, if speculation, weird distortions in local income, and other factors (like the housing collapse) weren't present in the market. *Forbes.com, "Best Buy Cities: Where to Invest in Housing in 2014," December 25, 2013*

- Tampa ranked #5 in a *Forbes* study of the rental housing market in the nation's 44 largest metropolitan areas to determine the cities that are best for renters. Criteria: average rent in 2012's first quarter, year-over-year change in that figure, vacancy rate, and average monthly rent payment compared with average monthly mortgage payment. *Forbes.com, "The Best and Worst Cities for Renters," June 14, 2012*

- TheStreet.com ranked the housing market in the nation's five warmest cities. Tampa ranked #2. Criteria: mean daily temperature from December to February (1981–2010); the median asking price of homes; and housing supply. *TheStreet.com, "Warm Weather Cities with Blistering-Hot Housing Markets," March 11, 2013*

- Tampa was ranked #47 out of 283 metro areas in terms of house price appreciation in 2013 (#1 = highest rate). *Federal Housing Finance Agency, House Price Index, 4th Quarter 2013*

- Tampa was ranked #108 out of 224 metro areas in terms of housing affordability in 2013 by the National Association of Home Builders (#1 = most affordable). The NAHB-Wells Fargo Housing Opportunity Index (HOI) for a given area is defined as the share of homes sold in that area that would have been affordable to a family earning the local median income, based on standard mortgage underwriting criteria. *National Association of Home Builders®, NAHB-Wells Fargo Housing Opportunity Index, 4th Quarter 2013*

- Tampa was selected as one of the best college towns for renters by ApartmentRatings.com." The area ranked #71 out of 87. Overall satisfaction ratings were ranked using thousands of user submitted scores for hundreds of apartment complexes located in cities and towns that are home to the 100 largest four-year institutions in the U.S. *ApartmentRatings.com, "2011 College Town Renter Satisfaction Rankings"*

- The nation's largest metro areas were analyzed in terms of the percentage of households entering some stage of foreclosure in 2013. The Tampa metro area ranked #6 out of 10 (#1 = highest foreclosure rate). *RealtyTrac, "2013 Year-End U.S. Foreclosure Market Report™," January 16, 2014*

- The nation's largest metro areas were analyzed in terms of the best places to buy foreclosures in 2013. The Tampa metro area ranked #6 out of 20. Criteria: RealtyTrac scored all metro areas with a population of 500,000 or more by summing up four numbers: months' supply of foreclosure inventory; percentage of foreclosure sales; foreclosure discount; percentage increase in foreclosure activity in 2012. *RealtyTrac, "2012 Year-End Metropolitan Foreclosure Market Report," January 28, 2013*

Safety Rankings

- Allstate ranked the 200 largest cities in America in terms of driver safety. Tampa ranked #176. Allstate researchers analyzed internal property damage claims over a two-year period from January 2010 to December 2011. A weighted average of the two-year numbers determined the annual percentages. *Allstate, "Allstate America's Best Drivers Report®, August 27, 2013"*

- The National Insurance Crime Bureau ranked 380 metro areas in the U.S. in terms of per capita rates of vehicle theft. The Tampa metro area ranked #166 (#1 = highest rate). Criteria: number of vehicle theft offenses per 100,000 inhabitants in 2012. *National Insurance Crime Bureau, "Hot Spots 2012," June 26, 2013*

- The Tampa metro area was identified as one of the most dangerous metro areas for pedestrians by Transportation for America. The metro area ranked #2 out of 52 metro areas with over 1 million residents. Criteria: area's population divided by the number of pedestrian fatalities in that area. *Transportation for America, "Dangerous by Design 2011"*

Seniors/Retirement Rankings

- From its Best Cities for Successful Aging indexes, the Milken Institute generated rankings for metropolitan areas, weighing data in eight categories—general indicators, health care, wellness, living arrangements, transportation and general accessibility, financial well-being, education and employment, and community participation. The Tampa metro area was ranked #65 overall in the large metro area category. *Milken Institute, "Best Cities for Successful Aging," July 2012*

- Bankers Life and Casualty Company, in partnership with Sperling's BestPlaces, ranked the nation's 50 largest metro areas in terms of the "Best U.S. Cities for Seniors." The Tampa metro area ranked #44. Criteria: healthcare; transportation; housing; environment; economy; health and longevity; social and spiritual life; crime. *Bankers Life and Casualty Company, Center for a Secure Retirement, "Best U.S. Cities for Seniors 2011," September 2011*

- Tampa was identified as one of the most popular places to retire by *Topretirements.com*. The list reflects the 100 cities (out of 900+ total cities reviewed) that visitors to the website are most interested in for retirement. *Topretirements.com, "Most Popular Places to Retire for 2014," February 25, 2014*

Sports/Recreation Rankings

- Tampa appeared on the *Sporting News* list of the "Best Sports Cities" for 2011. The area ranked #10 out of 271. Criteria: the magazine takes a 12-month snapshot of each city's sports, putting a heavy premium on regular-season won-lost records (from the most recently completed season). Other criteria include: playoff berths, bowl appearances and tournament bids; championships; applicable power ratings; quality of competition; overall fan fervor (measured in part by attendance); abundance of teams (rewarding quality over quantity); stadium and arena quality; ticket availability and prices; franchise ownership; and marquee appeal of athletes. *Sporting News, "Best Sports Cities 2011," October 4, 2011*

- Tampa appeared on the *Sporting News* list of the "Best Sports Cities" for 2011. The area ranked #10 out of 271. Criteria: a 12-month snapshot of regular-season won-lost records (from the most recently completed season). Other criteria include: playoff berths, bowl appearances and tournament bids; championships; applicable power ratings; quality of competition; overall fan fervor (measured in part by attendance); abundance of teams (quality over quantity); stadium and arena quality; ticket availability and prices; franchise ownership; and marquee appeal of athletes. *Sporting News, "Best Sports Cities 2011," October 4, 2011*

- Tampa was selected as one of the most playful cities in the U.S. by KaBOOM! The organization's Playful City USA initiative honors cities and towns across the nation for a vision, plan and commitment to creating an agenda for play. Criteria: creating a local play commission or task force; designing an annual action plan for play; conducting a play space audit; outlining a financial investment in play for the current fiscal year; and proclaiming and celebrating an annual "play day." *KaBOOM! National Campaign for Play, "2013 Playful City USA Communities"*

- The Tampa was selected as one of the best metro areas for golf in America by *Golf Digest*. The Tampa area was ranked #4 out of 20. Criteria: climate; cost of public golf; quality of public golf; accessibility. *Golf Digest, "The Top 20 Cities for Golf," October 2011*

Transportation Rankings

- NerdWallet surveyed average annual car insurance premiums in 125 U.S. cities to identify the least expensive U.S. cities in which to insure a car. Locations with no-fault insurance laws was a strong determinant. Tampa came in at #15 for the most expensive rates. *www.nerdwallet.com, "Best Cities for Cheap Car Insurance," February 3, 2014*

- Tampa was identified as one of America's worst cities for speed traps by the National Motorists Association. The city ranked #7 out of 25. Criteria: speed trap locations per 100,000 residents. *National Motorists Association, September 2011*

Women/Minorities Rankings

- *Women's Health* examined U.S. cities and identified the 100 best cities for women. Tampa was ranked #74. Criteria: 30 categories were examined from obesity and breast cancer rates to commuting times and hours spent working out. *Women's Health, "Best Cities for Women 2012"*

- The Tampa metro area appeared on *Forbes'* list of the "Best Cities for Minority Entrepreneurs." The area ranked #74 out of 10. Criteria: 52 metropolitan statistical areas were examined. For each ethnicity (African Americans, Asians and Hispanics), the editors measured housing affordability, population growth, income growth, and entrepreneurship (per capita self-employment). *Forbes, "Best Cities for Minority Entrepreneurs," March 23, 2011*

Miscellaneous Rankings

- The watchdog site Charity Navigator conducts an annual study of charities in the nation's major markets both to analyze statistical differences in their financial, accountability, and transparency practices and to track year-to-year variations in individual communities. The Tampa metro area was ranked #24 among the 30 metro markets. *www.charitynavigator.org, "Metro Market Study 2013," June 1, 2013*

- *Men's Health* ranked 100 U.S. cities by their level of sadness. Tampa was ranked #97 (#1 = saddest city). Criteria: suicide rates; unemployment rates; percentage of households that use antidepressants; percent of population who report feeling blue all or most of the time. *Men's Health, "Frown Towns," November 28, 2011*

- Mars Chocolate North America, the makers of COMBOS®, in partnership with Sperling's BestPlaces, ranked 50 major metro areas in terms of their "manliness." The Tampa metro area ranked #23. Criteria: number of professional sports teams; number of nearby NASCAR tracks and racing events; manly lifestyle; concentration of manly retail stores; manly occupations per capita; salty snack sales; "Board of Manliness" rankings. *Mars Chocolate North America, "America's Manliest Cities 2012"*

- The National Alliance to End Homelessness ranked the 100 most populous metro areas in terms the rate of homelessness. The Tampa metro area ranked #1. Criteria: number of homeless people per 10,000 population in 2011. *National Alliance to End Homelessness, The State of Homelessness in America 2012*

Business Environment

CITY FINANCES

City Government Finances

Component	2011 ($000)	2011 ($ per capita)
Total Revenues	806,586	2,395
Total Expenditures	750,658	2,229
Debt Outstanding	1,415,674	4,203
Cash and Securities[1]	2,487,995	7,387

Note: (1) Cash and security holdings of a government at the close of its fiscal year, including those of its dependent agencies, utilities, and liquor stores.
Source: U.S Census Bureau, State & Local Government Finances 2011

City Government Revenue by Source

Source	2011 ($000)	2011 ($ per capita)
General Revenue		
From Federal Government	36,092	107
From State Government	53,148	158
From Local Governments	41,192	122
Taxes		
Property	139,391	414
Sales and Gross Receipts	117,069	348
Personal Income	0	0
Corporate Income	0	0
Motor Vehicle License	0	0
Other Taxes	44,816	133
Current Charges	194,402	577
Liquor Store	0	0
Utility	74,304	221
Employee Retirement	49,171	146

Source: U.S Census Bureau, State & Local Government Finances 2011

City Government Expenditures by Function

Function	2011 ($000)	2011 ($ per capita)	2011 (%)
General Direct Expenditures			
Air Transportation	0	0	0.0
Corrections	0	0	0.0
Education	0	0	0.0
Employment Security Administration	0	0	0.0
Financial Administration	19,639	58	2.6
Fire Protection	68,836	204	9.2
General Public Buildings	15,032	45	2.0
Governmental Administration, Other	2,419	7	0.3
Health	0	0	0.0
Highways	56,544	168	7.5
Hospitals	0	0	0.0
Housing and Community Development	36,664	109	4.9
Interest on General Debt	25,325	75	3.4
Judicial and Legal	3,395	10	0.5
Libraries	0	0	0.0
Parking	13,962	41	1.9
Parks and Recreation	53,776	160	7.2
Police Protection	143,059	425	19.1
Public Welfare	0	0	0.0
Sewerage	77,040	229	10.3
Solid Waste Management	61,705	183	8.2
Veterans' Services	0	0	0.0
Liquor Store	0	0	0.0
Utility	67,276	200	9.0
Employee Retirement	61,141	182	8.1

Source: U.S Census Bureau, State & Local Government Finances 2011

DEMOGRAPHICS

Population Growth

Area	1990 Census	2000 Census	2010 Census	Population Growth (%)	
				1990-2000	2000-2010
City	279,960	303,447	335,709	8.4	10.6
MSA[1]	2,067,959	2,395,997	2,783,243	15.9	16.2
U.S.	248,709,873	281,421,906	308,745,538	13.2	9.7

Note: (1) Figures cover the Tampa-St. Petersburg-Clearwater, FL Metropolitan Statistical Area—see Appendix B for areas included
Source: U.S. Census Bureau, Census 1990, 2000, 2010

Household Size

Area	Persons in Household (%)							Average Household Size
	One	Two	Three	Four	Five	Six	Seven or More	
City	36.6	31.2	15.1	10.6	4.2	1.4	0.9	2.44
MSA[1]	32.0	36.0	14.4	10.9	4.2	1.5	0.9	2.48
U.S.	27.6	33.5	15.7	13.2	6.1	2.4	1.5	2.63

Note: (1) Figures cover the Tampa-St. Petersburg-Clearwater, FL Metropolitan Statistical Area—see Appendix B for areas included
Source: U.S. Census Bureau, 2010-2012 American Community Survey 3-Year Estimates

Race

Area	White Alone[2] (%)	Black Alone[2] (%)	Asian Alone[2] (%)	AIAN[3] Alone[2] (%)	NHOPI[4] Alone[2] (%)	Other Race Alone[2] (%)	Two or More Races (%)
City	63.6	26.4	3.5	1.1	0.1	2.6	2.9
MSA[1]	79.9	11.9	2.9	0.5	0.1	2.2	2.5
U.S.	74.0	12.6	4.9	0.8	0.2	4.7	2.8

Note: (1) Figures cover the Tampa-St. Petersburg-Clearwater, FL Metropolitan Statistical Area—see Appendix B for areas included; (2) Alone is defined as not being in combination with one or more other races; (3) American Indian and Alaska Native; (4) Native Hawaiian and Other Pacific Islander
Source: U.S. Census Bureau, 2010-2012 American Community Survey 3-Year Estimates

Hispanic or Latino Origin

Area	Total (%)	Mexican (%)	Puerto Rican (%)	Cuban (%)	Other (%)
City	22.7	2.5	7.2	6.7	6.3
MSA[1]	16.7	3.5	5.3	3.3	4.5
U.S.	16.6	10.7	1.6	0.6	3.7

Note: Persons of Hispanic or Latino origin can be of any race; (1) Figures cover the Tampa-St. Petersburg-Clearwater, FL Metropolitan Statistical Area—see Appendix B for areas included
Source: U.S. Census Bureau, 2010-2012 American Community Survey 3-Year Estimates

Segregation

Type	Segregation Indices[1]				Percent Change		
	1990	2000	2010	2010 Rank[2]	1990-2000	1990-2010	2000-2010
Black/White	69.7	64.6	56.2	50	-5.1	-13.5	-8.3
Asian/White	33.8	35.4	35.3	78	1.6	1.5	-0.1
Hispanic/White	45.3	44.4	40.7	62	-0.9	-4.6	-3.7

Note: All figures cover the Metropolitan Statistical Area—see Appendix B for areas included; Figures are based on an analysis of 1990, 2000, and 2010 Census Decennial Census tract data by William H. Frey, Brookings Institution and the University of Michigan Social Science Data Analysis Network. In this analysis all racial groups (whites, blacks, and asians) are non-Hispanic members of those races. Hispanics are shown as a separate category;
(1) Segregation Indices are Dissimilarity Indices that measure the degree to which the minority group is distributed differently than whites across census tracts. They range from 0 (complete integration) to 100 (complete segregation) where the value indicates the percentage of the minority group that needs to move to be distributed exactly like whites; (2) Ranges from 1 (most segregated) to 102 (least segregated); n/a not available.
Source: www.CensusScope.org

Ancestry

Area	German	Irish	English	American	Italian	Polish	French[2]	Scottish	Dutch
City	8.7	8.0	5.7	5.0	5.9	1.8	1.9	1.4	1.1
MSA[1]	13.4	12.0	9.0	8.8	7.8	3.0	3.1	1.8	1.3
U.S.	15.2	11.1	8.2	7.2	5.6	3.1	2.8	1.7	1.4

Note: Figures are the percentage of the total population reporting a particular ancestry. The nine most commonly reported ancestries in the U.S. are shown. Figures include multiple ancestries (e.g. if a person reported being Irish and Italian, they were included in both columns); (1) Figures cover the Tampa-St. Petersburg-Clearwater, FL Metropolitan Statistical Area—see Appendix B for areas included; (2) Excludes Basque
Source: U.S. Census Bureau, 2010-2012 American Community Survey 3-Year Estimates

Foreign-Born Population

Area	Percent of Population Born in								
	Any Foreign Country	Mexico	Asia	Europe	Carribean	South America	Central America[2]	Africa	Canada
City	15.6	1.1	2.8	1.5	6.3	1.6	1.2	0.7	0.4
MSA[1]	12.7	1.4	2.4	2.4	3.2	1.6	0.6	0.4	0.7
U.S.	13.0	3.7	3.7	1.6	1.2	0.9	1.0	0.5	0.3

Note: (1) Figures cover the Tampa-St. Petersburg-Clearwater, FL Metropolitan Statistical Area—see Appendix B for areas included; (2) Excludes Mexico.
Source: U.S. Census Bureau, 2010-2012 American Community Survey 3-Year Estimates

Marital Status

Area	Never Married	Now Married[2]	Separated	Widowed	Divorced
City	41.2	36.4	3.3	5.6	13.5
MSA[1]	29.8	46.1	2.5	7.5	14.1
U.S.	32.4	48.4	2.2	6.0	11.0

Note: Figures are percentages and cover the population 15 years of age and older; (1) Figures cover the Tampa-St. Petersburg-Clearwater, FL Metropolitan Statistical Area—see Appendix B for areas included; (2) Excludes separated
Source: U.S. Census Bureau, 2010-2012 American Community Survey 3-Year Estimates

Age

Area	Percent of Population									Median Age
	Under Age 5	Age 5–19	Age 20–34	Age 35–44	Age 45–54	Age 55–64	Age 65–74	Age 75–84	Age 85+	
City	6.4	19.7	24.5	13.7	14.3	10.5	5.8	3.7	1.4	34.5
MSA[1]	5.6	17.7	18.5	12.8	14.8	13.1	9.2	5.8	2.6	41.5
U.S.	6.4	20.1	20.5	13.1	14.3	12.2	7.3	4.2	1.8	37.3

Note: (1) Figures cover the Tampa-St. Petersburg-Clearwater, FL Metropolitan Statistical Area—see Appendix B for areas included
Source: U.S. Census Bureau, 2010-2012 American Community Survey 3-Year Estimates

Gender

Area	Males	Females	Males per 100 Females
City	168,972	174,705	96.7
MSA[1]	1,366,313	1,453,069	94.0
U.S.	153,276,055	158,333,314	96.8

Note: (1) Figures cover the Tampa-St. Petersburg-Clearwater, FL Metropolitan Statistical Area—see Appendix B for areas included
Source: U.S. Census Bureau, 2010-2012 American Community Survey 3-Year Estimates

Religious Groups by Family

Area	Catholic	Baptist	Non-Den.	Methodist[2]	Lutheran	LDS[3]	Pente-costal	Presby-terian[4]	Muslim[5]	Judaism
MSA[1]	10.9	7.1	3.8	3.5	1.0	0.6	2.1	1.0	1.3	0.5
U.S.	19.1	9.3	4.0	4.0	2.3	2.0	1.9	1.6	0.8	0.7

Note: Figures are the number of adherents as a percentage of the total population; (1) Figures cover the Tampa-St. Petersburg-Clearwater, FL Metropolitan Statistical Area—see Appendix B for areas included; (2) Methodist/Pietist; (3) Latter Day Saints; (4) Reformed; (5) Figures are estimates
Source: Association of Statisticians of American Religious Bodies, 2010 U.S. Religion Census: Religious Congregations & Membership Study

Religious Groups by Tradition

Area	Catholic	Evangelical Protestant	Mainline Protestant	Other Tradition	Black Protestant	Orthodox
MSA[1]	10.9	13.6	5.2	3.1	1.2	0.8
U.S.	19.1	16.2	7.3	4.3	1.6	0.3

Note: Figures are the number of adherents as a percentage of the total population; (1) Figures cover the Tampa-St. Petersburg-Clearwater, FL Metropolitan Statistical Area—see Appendix B for areas included
Source: Association of Statisticians of American Religious Bodies, 2010 U.S. Religion Census: Religious Congregations & Membership Study

ECONOMY

Gross Metropolitan Product

Area	2011	2012	2013	2014	Rank[2]
MSA[1]	114.4	119.9	125.5	131.5	23

Note: Figures are in billions of dollars; (1) Figures cover the Tampa-St. Petersburg-Clearwater, FL Metropolitan Statistical Area—see Appendix B for areas included; (2) Rank is based on 2014 data and ranges from 1 to 363
Source: The United States Conference of Mayors, U.S. Metro Economies: Outlook—Gross Metropolitan Product, with Metro Employment Projections, November 2013

Economic Growth

Area	2011 (%)	2012 (%)	2013 (%)	2014 (%)	Rank[2]
MSA[1]	1.5	3.1	3.2	2.8	16
U.S.	1.6	2.5	1.7	2.5	–

Note: Figures are real gross metropolitan product (GMP) growth rates and represent annual average percent change; (1) Figures cover the Tampa-St. Petersburg-Clearwater, FL Metropolitan Statistical Area—see Appendix B for areas included; (2) Rank is based on 2013 data and ranges from 1 to 363
Source: The United States Conference of Mayors, U.S. Metro Economies: Outlook—Gross Metropolitan Product, with Metro Employment Projections, November 2013

Metropolitan Area Exports

Area	2007	2008	2009	2010	2011	2012	Rank[2]
MSA[1]	5,711.2	7,153.5	6,463.6	6,633.6	7,736.7	7,190.0	40

Note: Figures are in millions of dollars; (1) Figures cover the Tampa-St. Petersburg-Clearwater, FL Metropolitan Statistical Area—see Appendix B for areas included; (2) Rank is based on 2012 data and ranges from 1 to 369
Source: U.S. Department of Commerce, International Trade Administration, Office of Trade & Industry Information, Manufacturing & Services, data extracted April 1, 2014

INCOME

Income

Area	Per Capita ($)	Median Household ($)	Average Household ($)
City	28,262	41,524	68,107
MSA[1]	26,123	44,959	62,781
U.S.	27,385	51,771	71,579

Note: (1) Figures cover the Tampa-St. Petersburg-Clearwater, FL Metropolitan Statistical Area—see Appendix B for areas included
Source: U.S. Census Bureau, 2010-2012 American Community Survey 3-Year Estimates

Household Income Distribution

Area	Percent of Households Earning							
	Under $15,000	$15,000 -24,999	$25,000 -34,999	$35,000 -49,999	$50,000 -74,999	$75,000 -99,000	$100,000 -149,999	$150,000 and up
City	19.0	12.9	11.8	13.3	15.9	8.5	9.2	9.3
MSA[1]	14.1	12.9	12.2	15.3	18.2	10.7	9.9	6.6
U.S.	13.1	11.0	10.5	13.7	18.1	11.9	12.5	9.1

Note: (1) Figures cover the Tampa-St. Petersburg-Clearwater, FL Metropolitan Statistical Area—see Appendix B for areas included
Source: U.S. Census Bureau, 2010-2012 American Community Survey 3-Year Estimates

Poverty Rate

Area	All Ages	Under 18 Years Old	18 to 64 Years Old	65 Years and Over
City	22.7	31.8	20.2	18.6
MSA[1]	16.1	22.9	15.7	9.3
U.S.	15.7	22.2	14.6	9.3

Note: Figures are percentage of people whose income during the past 12 months was below the poverty level; (1) Figures cover the Tampa-St. Petersburg-Clearwater, FL Metropolitan Statistical Area—see Appendix B for areas included
Source: U.S. Census Bureau, 2010-2012 American Community Survey 3-Year Estimates

Personal Bankruptcy Filing Rate

Area	2008	2009	2010	2011	2012	2013
Hillsborough County	4.09	5.55	6.26	4.84	4.01	3.72
U.S.	3.53	4.61	4.97	4.37	3.76	3.29

Note: Numbers are per 1,000 population and include Chapter 7 and Chapter 13 filings
Source: Federal Deposit Insurance Corporation, Regional Economic Conditions, March 20, 2014

EMPLOYMENT

Labor Force and Employment

Area	Civilian Labor Force			Workers Employed		
	Dec. 2012	Dec. 2013	% Chg.	Dec. 2012	Dec. 2013	% Chg.
City	163,559	164,309	0.5	150,171	154,202	2.7
MSA[1]	1,331,021	1,338,701	0.6	1,226,191	1,259,105	2.7
U.S.	154,904,000	154,408,000	-0.3	143,060,000	144,423,000	1.0

Note: Data is not seasonally adjusted and covers workers 16 years of age and older; (1) Metropolitan Statistical Area—see Appendix B for areas included
Source: Bureau of Labor Statistics, Local Area Unemployment Statistics

Unemployment Rate

Area	2013											
	Jan.	Feb.	Mar.	Apr.	May	Jun.	Jul.	Aug.	Sep.	Oct.	Nov.	Dec.
City	8.4	7.9	7.4	7.1	7.3	7.8	7.9	7.4	7.0	6.6	6.5	6.2
MSA[1]	8.0	7.5	6.9	6.7	6.9	7.3	7.3	7.0	6.7	6.4	6.3	5.9
U.S.	8.5	8.1	7.6	7.1	7.3	7.8	7.7	7.3	7.0	7.0	6.6	6.5

Note: Data is not seasonally adjusted and covers workers 16 years of age and older; All figures are percentages; (1) Metropolitan Statistical Area—see Appendix B for areas included
Source: Bureau of Labor Statistics, Local Area Unemployment Statistics

Employment by Occupation

Occupation Classification	City (%)	MSA[1] (%)	U.S. (%)
Management, Business, Science, and Arts	38.7	35.8	36.0
Natural Resources, Construction, and Maintenance	6.7	8.3	9.1
Production, Transportation, and Material Moving	8.1	8.8	12.0
Sales and Office	26.7	28.8	24.7
Service	19.8	18.3	18.2

Note: Figures cover employed civilians 16 years of age and older; (1) Figures cover the Tampa-St. Petersburg-Clearwater, FL Metropolitan Statistical Area—see Appendix B for areas included
Source: U.S. Census Bureau, 2010-2012 American Community Survey 3-Year Estimates

Employment by Industry

| Sector | MSA[1] | | U.S. |
	Number of Employees	Percent of Total	Percent of Total
Construction	58,100	4.8	4.2
Education and Health Services	189,000	15.8	15.5
Financial Activities	101,100	8.4	5.7
Government	153,600	12.8	16.1
Information	26,100	2.2	1.9
Leisure and Hospitality	130,300	10.9	10.2
Manufacturing	61,700	5.1	8.7
Mining and Logging	500	<0.1	0.6
Other Services	42,000	3.5	3.9
Professional and Business Services	202,900	16.9	13.7
Retail Trade	154,600	12.9	11.4
Transportation and Utilities	28,200	2.4	3.8
Wholesale Trade	50,400	4.2	4.2

Note: Figures cover non-farm employment as of December 2013 and are not seasonally adjusted;
(1) Metropolitan Statistical Area—see Appendix B for areas included
Source: Bureau of Labor Statistics, Current Employment Statistics, Employment, Hours, and Earnings

Occupations with Greatest Projected Employment Growth: 2010 – 2020

Occupation[1]	2010 Employment	2020 Projected Employment	Numeric Employment Change	Percent Employment Change
Retail Salespersons	290,200	345,860	55,660	19.2
Combined Food Preparation and Serving Workers, Including Fast Food	154,650	193,760	39,110	25.3
Registered Nurses	165,400	202,190	36,790	22.3
Waiters and Waitresses	174,630	210,650	36,010	20.6
Customer Service Representatives	165,950	194,220	28,260	17.0
Cashiers	200,040	225,430	25,400	12.7
Office Clerks, General	142,480	164,800	22,330	15.7
Landscaping and Groundskeeping Workers	93,350	115,400	22,050	23.6
Postsecondary Teachers	75,610	94,190	18,580	24.6
Cooks, Restaurant	76,000	94,180	18,190	23.9

Note: Projections cover Florida; (1) Sorted by numeric employment change
Source: www.projectionscentral.com, State Occupational Projections, 2010–2020 Long-Term Projections

Fastest Growing Occupations: 2010 – 2020

Occupation[1]	2010 Employment	2020 Projected Employment	Numeric Employment Change	Percent Employment Change
Layout Workers, Metal and Plastic	230	380	150	65.2
Biomedical Engineers	620	990	370	60.2
Helpers—Carpenters	1,120	1,770	650	58.0
Biochemists and Biophysicists	650	1,000	350	53.6
Medical Scientists, Except Epidemiologists	2,850	4,370	1,520	53.5
Helpers—Brickmasons, Blockmasons, Stonemasons, and Tile and Marble Setters	810	1,240	430	52.6
Reinforcing Iron and Rebar Workers	940	1,370	430	46.1
Home Health Aides	28,580	41,010	12,430	43.5
Stonemasons	550	790	240	42.9
Personal Care Aides	16,880	23,920	7,040	41.7

Note: Projections cover Florida; (1) Sorted by percent employment change and excludes occupations with numeric employment change less than 100
Source: www.projectionscentral.com, State Occupational Projections, 2010–2020 Long-Term Projections

Average Wages

Occupation	$/Hr.	Occupation	$/Hr.
Accountants and Auditors	31.71	Maids and Housekeeping Cleaners	9.39
Automotive Mechanics	17.66	Maintenance and Repair Workers	15.55
Bookkeepers	15.77	Marketing Managers	51.59
Carpenters	16.90	Nuclear Medicine Technologists	36.09
Cashiers	9.29	Nurses, Licensed Practical	19.97
Clerks, General Office	13.20	Nurses, Registered	30.28
Clerks, Receptionists/Information	12.99	Nursing Assistants	11.44
Clerks, Shipping/Receiving	13.32	Packers and Packagers, Hand	9.45
Computer Programmers	35.91	Physical Therapists	37.93
Computer Systems Analysts	40.50	Postal Service Mail Carriers	24.66
Computer User Support Specialists	22.02	Real Estate Brokers	n/a
Cooks, Restaurant	11.10	Retail Salespersons	12.01
Dentists	70.66	Sales Reps., Exc. Tech./Scientific	30.42
Electrical Engineers	42.83	Sales Reps., Tech./Scientific	33.10
Electricians	17.90	Secretaries, Exc. Legal/Med./Exec.	14.48
Financial Managers	57.97	Security Guards	10.79
First-Line Supervisors/Managers, Sales	20.55	Surgeons	103.26
Food Preparation Workers	9.91	Teacher Assistants	10.20
General and Operations Managers	58.67	Teachers, Elementary School	21.00
Hairdressers/Cosmetologists	12.21	Teachers, Secondary School	21.00
Internists	104.44	Telemarketers	12.29
Janitors and Cleaners	10.34	Truck Drivers, Heavy/Tractor-Trailer	17.96
Landscaping/Groundskeeping Workers	10.76	Truck Drivers, Light/Delivery Svcs.	16.34
Lawyers	54.49	Waiters and Waitresses	9.73

Note: Wage data covers the Tampa-St. Petersburg-Clearwater, FL Metropolitan Statistical Area—see Appendix B for areas included. Hourly wages for elementary/secondary school teachers and teacher assistants were calculated by the editors from annual wage data assuming a 40 hour work week; n/a not available.
Source: Bureau of Labor Statistics, Metro Area Occupational Employment and Wage Estimates, May 2013

RESIDENTIAL REAL ESTATE

Building Permits

Area	Single-Family			Multi-Family			Total		
	2012	2013	Pct. Chg.	2012	2013	Pct. Chg.	2012	2013	Pct. Chg.
City	547	686	25.4	1,945	1,168	-39.9	2,492	1,854	-25.6
MSA[1]	5,883	7,314	24.3	4,278	4,838	13.1	10,161	12,152	19.6
U.S.	518,695	620,802	19.7	310,963	370,020	19.0	829,658	990,822	19.4

Note: (1) Metropolitan Statistical Area—see Appendix B for areas included; figures represent new, privately-owned housing units authorized (unadjusted data); All permit data are based on estimates with imputation.
Source: U.S. Census Bureau, Manufacturing, Mining, and Construction Statistics, Building Permits, 2012, 2013

Homeownership Rate

Area	2006 (%)	2007 (%)	2008 (%)	2009 (%)	2010 (%)	2011 (%)	2012 (%)	2013 (%)
MSA[1]	71.6	72.9	70.5	68.3	68.3	68.3	67.0	65.3
U.S.	68.8	68.1	67.8	67.4	66.9	66.1	65.4	65.1

Note: (1) Figures cover the Tampa-St. Petersburg-Clearwater, FL Metropolitan Statistical Area—see Appendix B for areas included
Source: U.S. Census Bureau, Housing Vacancies and Homeownership Annual Statistics: 2013

Housing Vacancy Rates

Area	Gross Vacancy Rate[2] (%)			Year-Round Vacancy Rate[3] (%)			Rental Vacancy Rate[4] (%)			Homeowner Vacancy Rate[5] (%)		
	2011	2012	2013	2011	2012	2013	2011	2012	2013	2011	2012	2013
MSA[1]	20.4	20.8	18.4	14.5	14.2	12.1	11.7	13.0	9.2	3.8	2.0	2.1
U.S.	14.2	13.8	13.8	11.1	10.8	10.7	9.5	8.7	8.3	2.5	2.0	2.0

Note: (1) Figures cover the Tampa-St. Petersburg-Clearwater, FL Metropolitan Statistical Area—see Appendix B for areas included; (2) The percentage of the total housing inventory that is vacant; (3) The percentage of the housing inventory (excluding seasonal units) that is year-round vacant; (4) The percentage of rental inventory that is vacant for rent; (5) The percentage of homeowner inventory that is vacant for sale
Source: U.S. Census Bureau, Housing Vacancies and Homeownership Annual Statistics: 2013

TAXES

State Corporate Income Tax Rates

State	Tax Rate (%)	Income Brackets ($)	Num. of Brackets	Financial Institution Tax Rate (%)[a]	Federal Income Tax Ded.
Florida	5.5 (f)	Flat rate	1	5.5 (f)	No

Note: Tax rates as of January 1, 2014; (a) Rates listed are the corporate income tax rate applied to financial institutions or excise taxes based on income. Some states have other taxes based upon the value of deposits or shares; (f) An exemption of $50,000 is allowed. Florida's Alternative Minimum Tax rate is 3.3%.
Source: Federation of Tax Administrators, "State Corporate Income Tax Rates, 2014"

State Individual Income Tax Rates

State	Tax Rate (%)	Income Brackets ($)	Num. of Brackets	Personal Exempt. ($)[1] Single	Personal Exempt. ($)[1] Dependents	Fed. Inc. Tax Ded.
Florida	None	–	–	–	–	–

Note: Tax rates as of January 1, 2014; Local- and county-level taxes are not included; n/a not applicable;
(1) Married joint filers generally receive double the single exemption
Source: Federation of Tax Administrators, "State Individual Income Tax Rates, 2014"

Various State and Local Tax Rates

State	State and Local Sales and Use (%)	State Sales and Use (%)	Gasoline[1] (¢/gal.)	Cigarette[2] ($/pack)	Spirits[3] ($/gal.)	Wine[4] ($/gal.)	Beer[5] ($/gal.)
Florida	7.0	6.00	36.03	1.339	6.50 (f)	2.25	0.48

Note: All tax rates as of January 1, 2014; (1) The American Petroleum Institute has developed a methodology for determining the average tax rate on a gallon of fuel. Rates may include any of the following: excise taxes, environmental fees, storage tank fees, other fees or taxes, general sales tax, and local taxes. In states where gasoline is subject to the general sales tax, or where the fuel tax is based on the average sale price, the average rate determined by API is sensitive to changes in the price of gasoline. States that fully or partially apply general sales taxes to gasoline: CA, CO, GA, IL, IN, MI, NY; (2) The federal excise tax of $1.0066 per pack and local taxes are not included; (3) Rates are those applicable to off-premise sales of 40% alcohol by volume (a.b.v.) distilled spirits in 750ml containers. Local excise taxes are excluded; (4) Rates are those applicable to off-premise sales of 11% a.b.v. non-carbonated wine in 750ml containers; (5) Rates are those applicable to off-premise sales of 4.7% a.b.v. beer in 12 ounce containers; (f) Different rates also applicable according to alcohol content, place of production, size of container, or place purchased (on- or off-premise or onboard airlines).
Source: Tax Foundation, 2014 Facts & Figures: How Does Your State Compare?

State Business Tax Climate Index Rankings

State	Overall Rank	Corporate Tax Index Rank	Individual Income Tax Index Rank	Sales Tax Index Rank	Unemployment Insurance Tax Index Rank	Property Tax Index Rank
Florida	5	13	1	18	6	16

Note: The index is a measure of how each state's tax laws affect economic performance. The lower the rank, the more favorable a state's tax system is for business. States without a given tax are given a ranking of 1. The scores/rankings for the District of Columbia do not affect other states. The 2014 index represents the tax climate as of July 1, 2013.
Source: Tax Foundation, State Business Tax Climate Index 2014

COMMERCIAL REAL ESTATE

Office Market

Market Area	Inventory (sq. ft.)	Vacancy Rate (%)	Under Construction (sq. ft.)	YTD Net Absorption (sq. ft.)	Total Average Asking Rent ($/sq. ft./year)
Tampa/Saint Petersburg	64,467,038	17.4	0	479,968	20.22
National	4,726,900,879	15.0	55,419,286	42,829,434	26.27

Source: Newmark Grubb Knight Frank, National Office Market Report, 4th Quarter 2013

Industrial/Warehouse/R&D Market

Market Area	Inventory (sq. ft.)	Vacancy Rate (%)	Under Construction (sq. ft.)	YTD Net Absorption (sq. ft.)	Total Average Asking Rent ($/sq. ft./year)
Tampa/Saint Petersburg	245,996,156	9.9	0	702,088	4.26
National	14,022,031,238	7.9	83,249,164	156,549,903	5.40

Source: Newmark Grubb Knight Frank, National Industrial Market Report, 4th Quarter 2013

COMMERCIAL UTILITIES

Typical Monthly Electric Bills

Area	Commercial Service ($/month)		Industrial Service ($/month)	
	1,500 kWh	40 kW demand 14,000 kWh	1,000 kW demand 200,000 kWh	50,000 kW demand 15,000,000 kWh
City	159	1,318	22,534	1,424,212
Average[1]	197	1,636	25,662	1,485,307

Note: Based on total rates in effect July 1, 2013; (1) average based on 180 utilities surveyed
Source: Edison Electric Institute, Typical Bills and Average Rates Report, Summer 2013

TRANSPORTATION

Means of Transportation to Work

Area	Car/Truck/Van		Public Transportation			Bicycle	Walked	Other Means	Worked at Home
	Drove Alone	Car-pooled	Bus	Subway	Railroad				
City	76.5	9.5	3.0	0.1	0.0	1.6	2.4	1.6	5.3
MSA[1]	80.3	9.5	1.3	0.0	0.0	0.8	1.5	1.4	5.2
U.S.	76.4	9.7	2.6	1.7	0.5	0.6	2.8	1.3	4.3

Note: Figures are percentages and cover workers 16 years of age and older; (1) Figures cover the Tampa-St. Petersburg-Clearwater, FL Metropolitan Statistical Area—see Appendix B for areas included
Source: U.S. Census Bureau, 2010-2012 American Community Survey 3-Year Estimates

Travel Time to Work

Area	Less Than 10 Minutes	10 to 19 Minutes	20 to 29 Minutes	30 to 44 Minutes	45 to 59 Minutes	60 to 89 Minutes	90 Minutes or More
City	13.0	34.1	22.6	19.5	5.6	3.4	1.7
MSA[1]	10.5	29.2	22.6	22.6	8.8	4.6	1.8
U.S.	13.5	29.8	20.9	20.1	7.5	5.6	2.5

Note: Figures are percentages and include workers 16 years old and over; (1) Figures cover the Tampa-St. Petersburg-Clearwater, FL Metropolitan Statistical Area—see Appendix B for areas included
Source: U.S. Census Bureau, 2010-2012 American Community Survey 3-Year Estimates

Travel Time Index

Area	1985	1990	1995	2000	2005	2010	2011
Urban Area[1]	1.17	1.21	1.22	1.19	1.22	1.20	1.20
Average[2]	1.09	1.14	1.16	1.19	1.23	1.18	1.18

Note: Travel Time Index—the ratio of travel time in the peak period to the travel time at free-flow conditions. For example, a value of 1.30 indicates a 20-minute free-flow trip takes 26 minutes in the peak. Free-flow speeds (60 mph on freeways and 35 mph on principal arterials) are used as the comparison threshold; (1) Covers the Tampa-St. Petersburg FL urban area; (2) average of 498 urban areas
Source: Texas Transportation Institute, Urban Mobility Report 2012, December 2012

Public Transportation

Agency Name / Mode of Transportation	Vehicles Operated in Maximum Service	Annual Unlinked Passenger Trips (in thous.)	Annual Passenger Miles (in thous.)
Hillsborough Area Regional Transit Authority (HART)			
Bus (directly operated)	153	14,314.6	73,017.4
Demand Response (directly operated)	30	128.8	984.1
Streetcar Rail (directly operated)	3	306.2	523.0

Source: Federal Transit Administration, National Transit Database, 2012

Air Transportation

Airport Name and Code / Type of Service	Passenger Airlines[1]	Passenger Enplanements	Freight Carriers[2]	Freight (lbs.)
Tampa International (TPA)				
Domestic service (U.S. carriers - 2013)	26	8,009,374	12	80,226,224
International service (U.S. carriers - 2012)	8	29,255	3	11,217

Note: (1) Includes all U.S.-based major, minor and commuter airlines that carried at least one passenger during the year; (2) Includes all U.S.-based airlines and freight carriers that transported at least one lb. of freight during the year.
Source: Bureau of Transportation Statistics, The Intermodal Transportation Database, Air Carriers: T-100 Domestic Market (U.S. Carriers), 2013; Bureau of Transportation Statistics, The Intermodal Transportation Database, Air Carriers: T-100 International Market (U.S. Carriers), 2012

Other Transportation Statistics

Major Highways: I-4; I-75
Amtrak Service: Yes
Major Waterways/Ports: Port of Tampa
Source: Amtrak.com; Google Maps

BUSINESSES

Major Business Headquarters

Company Name	Rankings	
	Fortune[1]	Forbes[2]
WellCare Health Plans	345	-

Note: (1) Fortune 500—companies that produce a 10-K are ranked 1 to 500 based on 2012 revenue; (2) all private companies with at least $2 billion in annual revenue through the end of their most current fiscal year are ranked 1 to 224; companies listed are headquartered in the city; dashes indicate no ranking Source: Fortune, "Fortune 500," May 20, 2013; Forbes, "America's Largest Private Companies," December 18, 2013

Fast-Growing Businesses

According to *Inc.*, Tampa is home to three of America's 500 fastest-growing private companies: **LabTech Software** (#53); **Streamline Defense** (#182); **Dynamix Mechanical** (#365). Criteria: must be an independent, privately-held, for-profit, U.S. corporation, proprietorship or partnership; revenues must be at least $100,000 in 2009 and $2 million in 2012; must have four-year operating/sales history. Holding companies, regulated banks, and utilities were excluded. *Inc., "America's 500 Fastest-Growing Private Companies," September 2013*

According to *Fortune*, Tampa is home to one of the 100 fastest-growing companies in the world: **HCI Group** (#13). Companies were ranked by their revenue growth rate; their EPS growth rate; and their three-year annualized total return to investors for the period ending June 30, 2013. Criteria for inclusion: a company, foreign or domestic, must trade on a major U.S. stock exchange; must file quarterly reports with the SEC; must have a minimum market capitalization of $250 million; must have a stock price of at least $5 on June 29, 2013; must have been trading continuously since June 30, 2009; must have revenue and net income for the four quarters ended on or before April 30, 2013, of at least $50 million and $10 million, respectively; and must have posted a compound annual growth in revenue and earnings per share of at least 20% annually over the three years ending on or before April 30, 2013. REITs, limited-liability companies, limited parterships, companies about to be acquired, and companies that lost money in the quarter ending April 30, 2013 were excluded. *Fortune, "100 Fastest-Growing Companies," August 29, 2013*

Minority Business Opportunity

Tampa is home to one company which is on the *Black Enterprise* Industrial/Service 100 list (100 largest companies based on gross sales): **Sun State International Trucks** (#30). Criteria: operational in previous calendar year; at least 51% black-owned and manufactures/owns the product it sells or provides industrial or consumer services. Brokerages, real estate firms and firms that provide professional services are not eligible. *Black Enterprise, B.E. 100s, 2013*

Tampa is home to one company which is on the *Black Enterprise* Auto Dealer 60 list (60 largest dealers based on gross sales): **March Hodge Automotive Group** (#2). Criteria: company must be operational in previous calendar year and be at least 51% black-owned. *Black Enterprise, B.E. 100s, 2013*

Tampa is home to three companies which are on the *Hispanic Business* 500 list (500 largest U.S. Hispanic-owned companies based on 2012 revenue): **Merchandise Partners** (#174); **MarkMaster** (#297); **Diverse ID Products of Florida** (#301). Companies included must show at least 51 percent ownership by Hispanic U.S. citizens, and must maintain headquarters in one of the 50 states or Washington, D.C. *Hispanic Business, "Hispanic Business 500," June 20, 2013*

Minority- and Women-Owned Businesses

Group	All Firms		Firms with Paid Employees			
	Firms	Sales ($000)	Firms	Sales ($000)	Employees	Payroll ($000)
Asian	1,552	605,434	521	483,557	3,663	95,944
Black	4,378	455,594	338	351,483	2,814	63,365
Hispanic	7,947	1,642,003	1,395	1,338,467	7,318	288,902
Women	10,798	3,708,549	1,626	3,373,231	13,263	369,989
All Firms	38,662	67,668,675	11,085	66,207,395	301,427	13,045,436

Note: Figures cover firms located in the city; minority- and women-owned business are defined as firms in which the corresponding group own 51% or more of the stock or equity of the company
Source: U.S. Census Bureau, 2007 Economic Census, Survey of Business Owners (2012 Survey of Business Owners data will be released starting in June 2015)

HOTELS & CONVENTION CENTERS

Hotels/Motels

Area	5 Star		4 Star		3 Star		2 Star		1 Star		Not Rated	
	Num.	Pct.[3]	Num.	Pct.[3]	Num.	Pct.[3]	Num.	Pct.[3]	Num.	Pct.[3]	Num.	Pct.[3]
City[1]	0	0.0	7	4.5	54	34.4	78	49.7	7	4.5	11	7.0
Total[2]	142	0.9	1,005	6.0	5,147	30.9	8,578	51.4	408	2.4	1,397	8.4

Note: (1) Figures cover Tampa and vicinity; (2) Figures cover all 100 cities in this book; (3) Percentage of hotels which have a given star rating; Star ratings are determined by expedia.com and offer an indication of the general quality of a particular hotel.
Source: expedia.com, April 7, 2014

The Tampa-St. Petersburg-Clearwater, FL metro area is home to two of the best hotels in the U.S. according to *Travel & Leisure*: **Sandpearl Resort; Renaissance Vinoy Resort & Golf Club**. Criteria: service; location; rooms; food; and value. The list includes the top 200 hotels in the U.S. *Travel & Leisure, "T+L 500, The World's Best Hotels 2014"*

The Tampa-St. Petersburg-Clearwater, FL metro area is home to one of the best hotels in the world according to *Condé Nast Traveler*: **Sandpearl Resort**. The selections are based on over 79,000 responses to the magazine's annual Readers' Choice Survey. The list includes the top 200 hotels in the U.S. *Condé Nast Traveler, "Gold List 2014, The World's Best Places to Stay"*

Major Convention Centers

Name	Overall Space (sq. ft.)	Exhibit Space (sq. ft.)	Meeting Space (sq. ft.)	Meeting Rooms
Tampa Convention Center	600,000	200,000	42,000	36

Note: Table includes convention centers located in the Tampa-St. Petersburg-Clearwater, FL metro area; n/a not available
Source: Original research

Living Environment

COST OF LIVING

Cost of Living Index

Composite Index	Groceries	Housing	Utilities	Trans-portation	Health Care	Misc. Goods/ Services
92.8	92.7	78.4	93.9	102.3	95.6	99.8

Note: The Cost of Living Index measures regional differences in the cost of consumer goods and services, excluding taxes and non-consumer expenditures, for professional and managerial households in the top income quintile. It is based on more than 50,000 prices covering almost 60 different items for which prices are collected three times a year by chambers of commerce, economic development organizations or university applied economic centers in each participating urban area. The numbers shown should be read as a percentage above or below the national average of 100. For example, a value of 115.4 in the groceries column indicates that grocery prices are 15.4% higher than the national average. Small differences in the index numbers should not be interpreted as significant; Figures cover the Tampa FL urban area.
Source: The Council for Community and Economic Research, ACCRA Cost of Living Index, 2013

Grocery Prices

Area[1]	T-Bone Steak ($/pound)	Frying Chicken ($/pound)	Whole Milk ($/half gal.)	Eggs ($/dozen)	Orange Juice ($/64 oz.)	Coffee ($/11.5 oz.)
City[2]	10.61	1.33	2.58	1.73	3.16	3.60
Avg.	10.19	1.28	2.34	1.81	3.48	4.39
Min.	8.56	0.94	1.44	1.19	2.78	3.40
Max.	14.82	2.28	3.56	3.73	6.23	7.32

*Note: (1) Values for the local area are compared with the average, minimum and maximum values for all 327 areas in the Cost of Living Index; (2) Figures cover the Tampa FL urban area; **T-Bone Steak** (price per pound); **Frying Chicken** (price per pound, whole fryer); **Whole Milk** (half gallon carton); **Eggs** (price per dozen, Grade A, large); **Orange Juice** (64 oz. Tropicana or Florida Natural); **Coffee** (11.5 oz. can, vacuum-packed, Maxwell House, Hills Bros, or Folgers).*
Source: The Council for Community and Economic Research, ACCRA Cost of Living Index, 2013

Housing and Utility Costs

Area[1]	New Home Price ($)	Apartment Rent ($/month)	All Electric ($/month)	Part Electric ($/month)	Other Energy ($/month)	Telephone ($/month)
City[2]	221,461	818	158.03	-	-	24.99
Avg.	295,864	900	171.38	91.82	70.12	27.73
Min.	185,506	458	117.80	48.81	33.67	17.16
Max.	1,358,917	3,783	441.68	171.40	372.65	39.47

*Note: (1) Values for the local area are compared with the average, minimum and maximum values for all 327 areas in the Cost of Living Index; (2) Figures cover the Tampa FL urban area; **New Home Price** (2,400 sf living area, 8,000 sf lot, in urban area with full utilities); **Apartment Rent** (950 sf 2 bedroom/1.5 or 2 bath, unfurnished, excluding all utilities except water); **All Electric** (average monthly cost for an all-electric home); **Part Electric** (average monthly cost for a part-electric home); **Other Energy** (average monthly cost for natural gas, fuel oil, coal, wood, and any other forms of energy except electricity); **Telephone** (price includes basic monthly rate for a private residential line plus additional local usage charges incurred by a family of four).*
Source: The Council for Community and Economic Research, ACCRA Cost of Living Index, 2013

Health Care, Transportation, and Other Costs

Area[1]	Doctor ($/visit)	Dentist ($/visit)	Optometrist ($/visit)	Gasoline ($/gallon)	Beauty Salon ($/visit)	Men's Shirt ($)
City[2]	80.31	89.27	78.38	3.41	39.23	23.60
Avg.	101.40	86.48	96.16	3.44	33.87	26.55
Min.	61.67	50.83	50.12	3.08	18.92	12.48
Max.	182.71	152.50	223.78	4.33	68.22	52.03

*Note: (1) Values for the local area are compared with the average, minimum and maximum values for all 327 areas in the Cost of Living Index; (2) Figures cover the Tampa FL urban area; **Doctor** (general practitioners routine exam of an established patient); **Dentist** (adult teeth cleaning and periodic oral examination); **Optometrist** (full vision eye exam for established adult patient); **Gasoline** (one gallon regular unleaded, national brand, including all taxes, cash price at self-service pump if available); **Beauty Salon** (woman's shampoo, trim, and blow-dry); **Men's Shirt** (cotton/polyester dress shirt, pinpoint weave, long sleeves).*
Source: The Council for Community and Economic Research, ACCRA Cost of Living Index, 2013

HOUSING

House Price Index (HPI)

Area	National Ranking[2]	Quarterly Change (%)	One-Year Change (%)	Five-Year Change (%)
MSA[1]	47	2.63	10.17	-11.07
U.S.[3]	–	1.20	7.69	4.18

Note: The HPI is a weighted repeat sales index. It measures average price changes in repeat sales or refinancings on the same properties. This information is obtained by reviewing repeat mortgage transactions on single-family properties whose mortgages have been purchased or securitized by Fannie Mae or Freddie Mac in January 1975; (1) Tampa-St. Petersburg-Clearwater, FL Metropolitan Statistical Area—see Appendix B for areas included; (2) Rankings are based on annual percentage change for all metro areas containing at least 15,000 transactions over the last 10 years and ranges from 1 to 283; (3) figures based on a weighted average of Census Division estimates using a seasonally adjusted, purchase-only index; all figures are for the period ending December 31, 2013
Source: Federal Housing Finance Agency, House Price Index, February 25, 2014

Median Single-Family Home Prices

Area	2011	2012	2013p	Percent Change 2012 to 2013
MSA[1]	127.8	133.9	142.8	6.6
U.S. Average	166.2	177.2	197.4	11.4

Note: Figures are median sales prices of existing single-family homes in thousands of dollars; (p) preliminary; n/a not available; (1) Tampa-St. Petersburg-Clearwater, FL Metropolitan Statistical Area—see Appendix B for areas included
Source: National Association of Realtors, Median Sales Price of Existing Single-Family Homes for Metropolitan Areas, 4th Quarter 2013

Qualifying Income Based on Median Sales Price of Existing Single-Family Homes

Area	With 5% Down ($)	With 10% Down ($)	With 20% Down ($)
MSA[1]	32,830	31,103	27,647
U.S. Average	45,395	43,006	38,228

Note: Figures are preliminary; Qualifying income is based on a mortgage rate of 4.4%. Monthly principal and interest payment is limited to 25% of income; n/a not available; (1) Tampa-St. Petersburg-Clearwater, FL Metropolitan Statistical Area—see Appendix B for areas included
Source: National Association of Realtors, Qualifying Income Based on Median Sales Price of Existing Single-Family Homes for Metropolitan Areas, 4th Quarter 2013

Median Apartment Condo-Coop Home Prices

Area	2011	2012	2013p	Percent Change 2012 to 2013
MSA[1]	69.1	84.0	91.6	9.0
U.S. Average	165.1	173.7	194.9	12.2

Note: Figures are median sales prices of existing apartment condo-coop homes in thousands of dollars; (p) preliminary; n/a not available; (1) Tampa-St. Petersburg-Clearwater, FL Metropolitan Statistical Area—see Appendix B for areas included
Source: National Association of Realtors, Median Sales Price of Existing Apartment Condo-Coop Homes for Metropolitan Areas, 4th Quarter 2013

Gross Monthly Rent

Area	Under $200	$200 -299	$300 -499	$500 -749	$750 -999	$1,000 -1,499	$1,500 and up	Median ($)
City	1.6	3.6	5.4	19.7	28.9	28.7	12.2	922
MSA[1]	0.9	1.6	4.4	20.8	31.7	29.7	10.9	920
U.S.	1.7	3.3	8.1	22.7	24.3	25.7	14.3	889

Note: Figures are percentages except for Median; Gross rent is the contract rent plus the estimated average monthly cost of utilities (electricity, gas, and water and sewer) and fuels (oil, coal, kerosene, wood, etc.) if these are paid by the renter (or paid for the renter by someone else); (1) Figures cover the Tampa-St. Petersburg-Clearwater, FL Metropolitan Statistical Area—see Appendix B for areas included
Source: U.S. Census Bureau, 2010-2012 American Community Survey 3-Year Estimates

Year Housing Structure Built

Area	2010 or Later	2000 -2009	1990 -1999	1980 -1989	1970 -1979	1960 -1969	1950 -1959	1940 -1949	Before 1940	Median Year
City	0.6	18.4	10.6	13.2	13.7	12.9	16.1	6.1	8.3	1975
MSA[1]	0.4	17.0	14.5	21.7	21.8	11.2	8.6	2.1	2.7	1982
U.S.	0.5	14.9	13.8	13.9	15.9	11.1	10.9	5.5	13.5	1976

Note: Figures are percentages except for Median Year; (1) Figures cover the Tampa-St. Petersburg-Clearwater, FL Metropolitan Statistical Area—see Appendix B for areas included
Source: U.S. Census Bureau, 2010-2012 American Community Survey 3-Year Estimates

HEALTH

Health Risk Data

Category	MSA[1] (%)	U.S. (%)
Adults aged 18–64 who have any kind of health care coverage	76.7	79.6
Adults who reported being in good or excellent health	81.0	83.1
Adults who are current smokers	20.3	19.6
Adults who are heavy drinkers[2]	8.3	6.1
Adults who are binge drinkers[3]	18.9	16.9
Adults who are overweight (BMI 25.0 - 29.9)	32.5	35.8
Adults who are obese (BMI 30.0 - 99.8)	25.1	27.6
Adults who participated in any physical activities in the past month	75.5	77.1
Adults 50+ who have ever had a sigmoidoscopy or colonoscopy	67.2	67.3
Women aged 40+ who have had a mammogram within the past two years	71.4	74.0
Men aged 40+ who have had a PSA test within the past two years	50.7	45.2
Adults aged 65+ who have had flu shot within the past year	56.0	60.1
Adults who always wear a seatbelt	95.0	93.8

Note: Data as of 2012 unless otherwise noted; (1) Figures cover the Tampa-St. Petersburg-Clearwater, FL Metropolitan Statistical Area—see Appendix B for areas included; (2) Heavy drinkers are classified as males having more than two drinks per day or females having more than one drink per day; (3) Binge drinkers are classified as males having five or more drinks on one occasion or females having four or more drinks on one occasion
Source: Centers for Disease Control and Prevention, Behavioral Risk Factor Surveillance System, SMART: Selected Metropolitan/Micropolitan Area Risk Trends, 2012

Chronic Health Indicators

Category	MSA[1] (%)	U.S. (%)
Adults who have ever been told they had a heart attack	5.9	4.5
Adults who have ever been told they had a stroke	2.5	2.9
Adults who have been told they currently have asthma	8.8	8.9
Adults who have ever been told they have arthritis	28.2	25.7
Adults who have ever been told they have diabetes[2]	11.5	9.7
Adults who have ever been told they had skin cancer	7.2	5.7
Adults who have ever been told they had any other types of cancer	7.6	6.5
Adults who have ever been told they have COPD	7.2	6.2
Adults who have ever been told they have kidney disease	1.9	2.5
Adults who have ever been told they have a form of depression	16.6	18.0

Note: Data as of 2012 unless otherwise noted; (1) Figures cover the Tampa-St. Petersburg-Clearwater, FL Metropolitan Statistical Area—see Appendix B for areas included; (2) Figures do not include pregnancy-related, borderline, or pre-diabetes
Source: Centers for Disease Control and Prevention, Behavioral Risk Factor Surveillance System, SMART: Selected Metropolitan/Micropolitan Area Risk Trends, 2012

Mortality Rates for the Top 10 Causes of Death in the U.S.

ICD-10[a] Sub-Chapter	ICD-10[a] Code	Age-Adjusted Mortality Rate[1] per 100,000 population	
		County[2]	U.S.
Malignant neoplasms	C00-C97	178.2	174.2
Ischaemic heart diseases	I20-I25	127.0	119.1
Other forms of heart disease	I30-I51	31.7	49.6
Chronic lower respiratory diseases	J40-J47	48.5	43.2
Cerebrovascular diseases	I60-I69	37.0	40.3
Organic, including symptomatic, mental disorders	F01-F09	35.1	30.5
Other degenerative diseases of the nervous system	G30-G31	30.6	26.3
Other external causes of accidental injury	W00-X59	36.2	25.1
Diabetes mellitus	E10-E14	26.2	21.3
Hypertensive diseases	I10-I15	30.7	18.8

Note: (a) ICD-10 = International Classification of Diseases 10th Revision; (1) Mortality rates are a three year average covering 2008-2010; (2) Figures cover Hillsborough County
Source: Centers for Disease Control and Prevention, National Center for Health Statistics. Compressed Mortality File 1999-2010 on CDC WONDER Online Database, released January 2013. Data are compiled from the Compressed Mortality File 1999-2010, Series 20 No. 2P, 2013.

Mortality Rates for Selected Causes of Death

ICD-10[a] Sub-Chapter	ICD-10[a] Code	Age-Adjusted Mortality Rate[1] per 100,000 population	
		County[2]	U.S.
Assault	X85-Y09	5.3	5.5
Diseases of the liver	K70-K76	12.6	12.4
Human immunodeficiency virus (HIV) disease	B20-B24	5.8	3.0
Influenza and pneumonia	J09-J18	9.5	16.4
Intentional self-harm	X60-X84	13.2	11.8
Malnutrition	E40-E46	0.9	0.8
Obesity and other hyperalimentation	E65-E68	1.8	1.6
Renal failure	N17-N19	10.3	13.6
Transport accidents	V01-V99	13.9	12.6
Viral hepatitis	B15-B19	3.4	2.2

Note: (a) ICD-10 = International Classification of Diseases 10th Revision; (1) Mortality rates are a three year average covering 2008-2010; (2) Figures cover Hillsborough County
Source: Centers for Disease Control and Prevention, National Center for Health Statistics. Compressed Mortality File 1999-2010 on CDC WONDER Online Database, released January 2013. Data are compiled from the Compressed Mortality File 1999-2010, Series 20 No. 2P, 2013.

Health Insurance Coverage

Area	With Health Insurance	With Private Health Insurance	With Public Health Insurance	Without Health Insurance	Population Under Age 18 Without Health Insurance
City	80.2	56.6	31.0	19.8	9.8
MSA[1]	81.8	59.9	34.0	18.2	9.4
U.S.	84.9	65.4	30.4	15.1	7.5

Note: Figures are percentages that cover the civilian noninstitutionalized population; (1) Figures cover the Tampa-St. Petersburg-Clearwater, FL Metropolitan Statistical Area—see Appendix B for areas included
Source: U.S. Census Bureau, 2010-2012 American Community Survey 3-Year Estimates

Number of Medical Professionals

Area[1]	MDs[2]	DOs[2,3]	Dentists	Podiatrists	Chiropractors	Optometrists
Local (number)	3,988	335	620	61	284	143
Local (rate[4])	313.9	26.4	48.4	4.8	22.2	11.2
U.S. (rate[4])	267.6	19.6	61.7	5.6	24.7	14.5

Note: Data as of 2012 unless noted; (1) Local data covers Hillsborough County; (2) Data as of 2011; (3) Doctor of Osteopathic Medicine; (4) rate per 100,000 population
Source: Area Resource File (ARF) 2012-2013. U.S. Department of Health and Human Services, Health Resources and Services Administration, Bureau of Health Professions

Best Hospitals

According to *U.S. News*, the Tampa-St. Petersburg-Clearwater, FL metro area is home to two of the best hospitals in the U.S.: **Moffitt Cancer Center** (1 specialty); **Tampa General Hospital** (6 specialties). The hospitals listed were nationally ranked in at least one adult specialty. Only 147 hospitals nationwide were nationally ranked in one or more specialties. Eighteen hospitals in the U.S. made the Honor Roll by ranking near the top in at least six specialties.*U.S. News Online, "America's Best Hospitals 2013-14"*

According to *U.S. News*, the Tampa-St. Petersburg-Clearwater, FL metro area is home to one of the best children's hospitals in the U.S.: **All Children's Hospital**. The hospital listed was highly ranked in at least one pediatric specialty. Eighty-seven hospitals in the U.S. ranked in at least one specialty. Ten children's hospitals in the U.S. made the Honor Roll by ranking near the top in three or more specialties.*U.S. News Online, "America's Best Children's Hospitals 2013-14"*

EDUCATION

Public School District Statistics

District Name	Schls	Pupils	Pupil/ Teacher Ratio	Minority Pupils[1] (%)	Free Lunch Eligible[2] (%)	IEP[3] (%)
Hillsborough County Public Schools	318	197,041	14.2	61.5	49.2	14.6

Note: Table includes school districts with 2,000 or more students; (1) Percentage of students that are not non-Hispanic white; (2) Percentage of students that are eligible for the free lunch program; (3) Percentage of students that have an Individualized Education Program.
Source: U.S. Department of Education, National Center for Education Statistics, Common Core of Data, Local Education Agency (School District) Universe Survey: School Year 2011-2012; U.S. Department of Education, National Center for Education Statistics, Common Core of Data, Public Elementary/Secondary School Universe Survey: School Year 2011-2012

Best High Schools

High School Name	Rank[1]	Grad. Rate[2] (%)	Coll.[3] (%)	AP/IB/ AICE Tests[4]	AP/IB/ AICE Score[5]	SAT Score[6]	ACT Score[6]
Braulio Alonso High	1836	94	73	0.6	2.0	1349	n/a
C Leon King H.S.	1902	69	68	1.2	2.7	1554	20.4
Chamberlain H.S.	1987	72	76	0.6	3.5	1356	18.5
Freedom H.S.	2000	83	83	0.0	2.5	987	21.0
Gaither H.S.	1644	75	95	0.7	2.2	1398	20.9
H. B. Plant H.S.	371	90	95	1.4	2.6	1569	23.0
TR Robinson H.S.	1635	80	83	0.9	2.2	1483	20.8
Walter L. Sickles H.S.	1784	85	68	0.7	3.2	1439	n/a

Note: (1) Public schools are ranked from 1 to 2,000 based on the following self-reported statistics (with the corresponding weight used in calculating their overall score). Schools that were newly founded and did not have a graduating senior class in 2012 were excluded; (2) Four-year, on-time graduation rate (25%); (3) Percent of 2011 graduates who were accepted to college (25%); (4) AP/IB/AICE tests taken per student (25%); (5) Average AP/IB/AICE exam score (10%); (6) Average SAT and/or ACT score (10%); Percent of students enrolled in at least one AP/IB/AICE course (5%)—data not shown; n/a not available
Source: Newsweek and The Daily Beast, "America's Best High Schools 2013"

Highest Level of Education

Area	Less than H.S.	H.S. Diploma	Some College, No Deg.	Associate Degree	Bachelor's Degree	Master's Degree	Prof. School Degree	Doctorate Degree
City	14.2	27.3	18.2	7.7	20.2	7.8	3.2	1.5
MSA[1]	12.5	30.8	21.6	9.1	17.3	6.1	1.7	0.9
U.S.	14.1	28.3	21.3	7.8	18.0	7.5	1.9	1.2

Note: Figures cover persons age 25 and over; (1) Figures cover the Tampa-St. Petersburg-Clearwater, FL Metropolitan Statistical Area—see Appendix B for areas included
Source: U.S. Census Bureau, 2010-2012 American Community Survey 3-Year Estimates

Educational Attainment by Race

Area	High School Graduate or Higher (%)					Bachelor's Degree or Higher (%)				
	Total	White	Black	Asian	Hisp.[2]	Total	White	Black	Asian	Hisp.[2]
City	85.8	89.4	78.3	84.7	74.5	32.6	39.2	12.2	55.7	17.3
MSA[1]	87.5	88.8	82.6	83.9	75.7	26.0	26.5	18.1	47.4	17.3
U.S.	85.9	88.1	82.5	85.5	63.1	28.6	30.0	18.4	50.2	13.4

*Note: Figures shown cover persons 25 years old and over; (1) Figures cover the Tampa-St.
Petersburg-Clearwater, FL Metropolitan Statistical Area—see Appendix B for areas included; (2) People of
Hispanic origin can be of any race
Source: U.S. Census Bureau, 2010-2012 American Community Survey 3-Year Estimates*

School Enrollment by Grade and Control

Area	Preschool (%)		Kindergarten (%)		Grades 1 - 4 (%)		Grades 5 - 8 (%)		Grades 9 - 12 (%)	
	Public	Private	Public	Private	Public	Private	Public	Private	Public	Private
City	56.7	43.3	92.0	8.0	90.7	9.3	85.7	14.3	92.9	7.1
MSA[1]	58.8	41.2	89.1	10.9	89.4	10.6	88.0	12.0	91.7	8.3
U.S.	56.9	43.1	87.8	12.2	89.9	10.1	90.0	10.0	90.8	9.2

*Note: Figures shown cover persons 3 years old and over; (1) Figures cover the Tampa-St.
Petersburg-Clearwater, FL Metropolitan Statistical Area—see Appendix B for areas included
Source: U.S. Census Bureau, 2010-2012 American Community Survey 3-Year Estimates*

Average Salaries of Public School Classroom Teachers

Area	2012-13		2013-14		Percent Change 2012-13 to 2013-14	Percent Change 2003-04 to 2013-14
	Dollars	Rank[1]	Dollars	Rank[1]		
Florida	46,598	45	46,691	45	0.20	15.0
U.S. Average	56,103	–	56,689	–	1.04	21.8

*Note: (1) State rank ranges from 1 to 51 where 1 indicates highest salary.
Source: National Education Association, Rankings & Estimates: Rankings of the States 2013 and Estimates of
School Statistics 2014, March 2014*

Higher Education

Four-Year Colleges			Two-Year Colleges			Medical Schools[1]	Law Schools[2]	Voc/ Tech[3]
Public	Private Non-profit	Private For-profit	Public	Private Non-profit	Private For-profit			
1	2	8	3	0	4	1	0	6

*Note: Figures cover institutions located within the city limits and include main campuses only; (1) includes
schools accredited by the Liaison Committee on Medical Education and the American Osteopathic Association's
Commission on Osteopathic College Accreditation; (2) includes ABA-accredited schools, schools with
provisional ABA accreditation, and state accredited schools; (3) includes all schools with programs that are less
than 2 years.
Source: National Center for Education Statistics, Integrated Postsecondary Education System (IPEDS),
2012-13; Association of American Medical Colleges, Member List, April 24, 2014; American Osteopathic
Association, Member List, April 24, 2014; Law School Admission Council, Official Guide to ABA-Approved
Law Schools Online, April 24, 2014; Wikipedia, List of Medical Schools in the United States, April 24, 2014;
Wikipedia, List of Law Schools in the United States, April 24, 2014*

According to *U.S. News & World Report,* the Tampa-St. Petersburg-Clearwater, FL metro area is
home to one of the best national universities in the U.S.: **University of South Florida** (#170). The
indicators used to capture academic quality fall into a number of categories: assessment by
administrators at peer institutions; retention of students; faculty resources; student selectivity;
financial resources; alumni giving; high school counselor ratings of colleges; and graduation rate.
U.S. News & World Report, "America's Best Colleges 2014"

According to *U.S. News & World Report,* the Tampa-St. Petersburg-Clearwater, FL metro area is
home to one of the best liberal arts colleges in the U.S.: **Eckerd College** (#141). The indicators
used to capture academic quality fall into a number of categories: assessment by administrators at
peer institutions; retention of students; faculty resources; student selectivity; financial resources;
alumni giving; high school counselor ratings of colleges; and graduation rate. *U.S. News & World
Report, "America's Best Colleges 2014"*

PRESIDENTIAL ELECTION

2012 Presidential Election Results

Area	Obama	Romney	Other
Hillsborough County	52.8	46.2	1.0
U.S.	51.0	47.2	1.8

Note: Results are percentages and may not add to 100% due to rounding
Source: Dave Leip's Atlas of U.S. Presidential Elections

EMPLOYERS

Major Employers

Company Name	Industry
American Staff Management	Employee leasing service
City of Tampa	County supervisor of education, except school board
Diversified Maintenance Systems	Building and maintenance services, nec
Florida Hospital Tampa Bay Division	General medical and surgical hospitals
Granite Services International	Help supply services
H. Lee Moffitt Cancer Center	Physicians' office, including specialists
Honeywell International	Aircraft engines and engine parts
JPMorgan Chase Bank National Association	National commerical banks
Morton Plant Hospital Association	General medical and surgical hospitals
Raymond James & Associates	Security brokers and dealers
Seven-One-Seven Parking Services	Valet parking
SHC Holding	Convalescent home with continuous care
Sykes Enterprisesorporated	Business services, nec
Tech Data Corporation	Computers, peripherals, and software
United States Postal Service	Us postal service
University of South Florida	Colleges and universities
Usani Sub	Television broadcasting stations
Verizon Data Services	Data processing service
Veterans Health Administration	Administration of veterans' affairs
Veterans Health Administration	General medical and surgical hospitals

Note: Companies shown are located within the Tampa-St. Petersburg-Clearwater, FL Metropolitan Statistical Area.
Source: Hoovers.com; Wikipedia

PUBLIC SAFETY

Crime Rate

Area	All Crimes	Violent Crimes				Property Crimes		
		Murder	Forcible Rape	Robbery	Aggrav. Assault	Burglary	Larceny -Theft	Motor Vehicle Theft
City	3,452.2	6.6	12.3	163.4	434.2	705.9	1,956.9	173.1
Suburbs[1]	3,246.9	3.5	26.2	85.1	265.6	672.7	2,043.3	150.5
Metro[2]	3,272.0	3.9	24.5	94.7	286.2	676.7	2,032.7	153.3
U.S.	3,246.1	4.7	26.9	112.9	242.3	670.2	1,959.3	229.7

Note: Figures are crimes per 100,000 population; (1) All areas within the metro area that are located outside the city limits; (2) Figures cover the Tampa-St. Petersburg-Clearwater, FL Metropolitan Statistical Area—see Appendix B for areas included
Source: FBI Uniform Crime Reports, 2012

Hate Crimes

Area	Number of Quarters Reported	Bias Motivation				
		Race	Religion	Sexual Orientation	Ethnicity	Disability
City	4	0	0	0	0	0
U.S.	4	2,797	1,099	1,135	667	92

Source: Federal Bureau of Investigation, Hate Crime Statistics 2012

Identity Theft Consumer Complaints

Area	Complaints	Complaints per 100,000 Population	Rank[2]
MSA[1]	4,328	155.5	10
U.S.	290,056	91.8	-

Note: (1) Figures cover the Tampa-St. Petersburg-Clearwater, FL Metropolitan Statistical Area—see Appendix B for areas included; (2) Rank ranges from 1 to 377 where 1 indicates greatest number of identity theft complaints per 100,000 population
Source: Federal Trade Commission, Consumer Sentinel Network Data Book for January–December 2013

Fraud and Other Consumer Complaints

Area	Complaints	Complaints per 100,000 Population	Rank[2]
MSA[1]	13,820	496.5	19
U.S.	1,811,724	595.2	-

Note: (1) Figures cover the Tampa-St. Petersburg-Clearwater, FL Metropolitan Statistical Area—see Appendix B for areas included; (2) Rank ranges from 1 to 377 where 1 indicates greatest number of identity theft complaints per 100,000 population
Source: Federal Trade Commission, Consumer Sentinel Network Data Book for January–December 2013

RECREATION

Culture

Dance[1]	Theatre[1]	Instrumental Music[1]	Vocal Music[1]	Series and Festivals	Museums and Art Galleries[2]	Zoos and Aquariums[3]
0	5	0	2	0	22	3

Note: (1) Number of professional perfoming groups; (2) Based on organizations with primary SIC code 8412; (3) AZA-accredited
Source: The Grey House Performing Arts Directory, 2013; Association of Zoos & Aquariums, AZA Member Zoos & Aquariums, April 2014; www.AccuLeads.com, May 1, 2014

Professional Sports Teams

Team Name	League	Year Established
Tampa Bay Buccaneers	National Football League (NFL)	1976
Tampa Bay Lightning	National Hockey League (NHL)	1993
Tampa Bay Rays	Major League Baseball (MLB)	1998

Note: Includes teams located in the Tampa-St. Petersburg-Clearwater, FL Metropolitan Statistical Area.
Source: Wikipedia, Major Professional Sports Teams of the United States and Canada

CLIMATE

Average and Extreme Temperatures

Temperature	Jan	Feb	Mar	Apr	May	Jun	Jul	Aug	Sep	Oct	Nov	Dec	Yr.
Extreme High (°F)	85	88	91	93	98	99	97	98	96	94	90	86	99
Average High (°F)	70	72	76	82	87	90	90	90	89	84	77	72	82
Average Temp. (°F)	60	62	67	72	78	81	82	83	81	75	68	62	73
Average Low (°F)	50	52	56	61	67	73	74	74	73	66	57	52	63
Extreme Low (°F)	21	24	29	40	49	53	63	67	57	40	23	18	18

Note: Figures cover the years 1948-1990
Source: National Climatic Data Center, International Station Meteorological Climate Summary, 9/96

Average Precipitation/Snowfall/Humidity

Precip./Humidity	Jan	Feb	Mar	Apr	May	Jun	Jul	Aug	Sep	Oct	Nov	Dec	Yr.
Avg. Precip. (in.)	2.1	2.8	3.5	1.8	3.0	5.6	7.3	7.9	6.5	2.3	1.8	2.1	46.7
Avg. Snowfall (in.)	Tr	Tr	Tr	0	0	0	0	0	0	0	0	Tr	Tr
Avg. Rel. Hum. 7am (%)	87	87	86	86	85	86	88	90	91	89	88	87	88
Avg. Rel. Hum. 4pm (%)	56	55	54	51	52	60	65	66	64	57	56	57	58

Note: Figures cover the years 1948-1990; Tr = Trace amounts (<0.05 in. of rain; <0.5 in. of snow)
Source: National Climatic Data Center, International Station Meteorological Climate Summary, 9/96

Weather Conditions

Temperature			Daytime Sky			Precipitation		
32°F & below	45°F & below	90°F & above	Clear	Partly cloudy	Cloudy	0.01 inch or more precip.	0.1 inch or more snow/ice	Thunder-storms
3	35	85	81	204	80	107	< 1	87

Note: Figures are average number of days per year and cover the years 1948-1990
Source: National Climatic Data Center, International Station Meteorological Climate Summary, 9/96

HAZARDOUS WASTE

Superfund Sites

Tampa has eight hazardous waste sites on the EPA's Superfund Final National Priorities List: **Alaric Area Ground Water Plume; Helena Chemical Co. (Tampa Plant); MRI Corp (Tampa); Peak Oil Co./Bay Drum Co.; Raleigh Street Dump; Reeves Southeastern Galvanizing Corp.; Southern Solvents, Inc.; Stauffer Chemical Co (Tampa).** *U.S. Environmental Protection Agency, Final National Priorities List, April 26, 2014*

AIR & WATER QUALITY

Air Quality Index

Area	Percent of Days when Air Quality was...[2]					AQI Statistics[2]	
	Good	Moderate	Unhealthy for Sensitive Groups	Unhealthy	Very Unhealthy	Maximum	Median
MSA[1]	71.2	27.9	0.8	0.0	0.0	104	43

Note: (1) Data covers the Tampa-St. Petersburg-Clearwater, FL Metropolitan Statistical Area—see Appendix B for areas included; (2) Based on 365 days with AQI data in 2013. Air Quality Index (AQI) is an index for reporting daily air quality. EPA calculates the AQI for five major air pollutants regulated by the Clean Air Act: ground-level ozone, particle pollution (aka particulate matter), carbon monoxide, sulfur dioxide, and nitrogen dioxide. The AQI runs from 0 to 500. The higher the AQI value, the greater the level of air pollution and the greater the health concern. There are six AQI categories: "Good" AQI is between 0 and 50. Air quality is considered satisfactory; "Moderate" AQI is between 51 and 100. Air quality is acceptable; "Unhealthy for Sensitive Groups" When AQI values are between 101 and 150, members of sensitive groups may experience health effects; "Unhealthy" When AQI values are between 151 and 200 everyone may begin to experience health effects; "Very Unhealthy" AQI values between 201 and 300 trigger a health alert; "Hazardous" AQI values over 300 trigger warnings of emergency conditions (not shown).
Source: U.S. Environmental Protection Agency, Air Quality Index Report, 2013

Air Quality Index Pollutants

Area	Percent of Days when AQI Pollutant was...[2]					
	Carbon Monoxide	Nitrogen Dioxide	Ozone	Sulfur Dioxide	Particulate Matter 2.5	Particulate Matter 10
MSA[1]	0.0	0.0	34.0	6.6	59.5	0.0

Note: (1) Data covers the Tampa-St. Petersburg-Clearwater, FL Metropolitan Statistical Area—see Appendix B for areas included; (2) Based on 365 days with AQI data in 2013. The Air Quality Index (AQI) is an index for reporting daily air quality. EPA calculates the AQI for five major air pollutants regulated by the Clean Air Act: ground-level ozone, particle pollution (also known as particulate matter), carbon monoxide, sulfur dioxide, and nitrogen dioxide. The AQI runs from 0 to 500. The higher the AQI value, the greater the level of air pollution and the greater the health concern.
Source: U.S. Environmental Protection Agency, Air Quality Index Report, 2013

Air Quality Trends: Ozone

	2003	2004	2005	2006	2007	2008	2009	2010	2011	2012
MSA[1]	0.077	0.074	0.075	0.074	0.076	0.075	0.064	0.067	0.071	0.066

Note: (1) Data covers the Tampa-St. Petersburg-Clearwater, FL Metropolitan Statistical Area—see Appendix B for areas included. The values shown are the composite ozone concentration averages among trend sites based on the highest fourth daily maximum 8-hour concentration in parts per million. These trends are based on sites having an adequate record of monitoring data during the trend period. Data from exceptional events are included.
Source: U.S. Environmental Protection Agency, Air Quality Monitoring Information, "Air Quality Trends by City, 2000-2012"

Maximum Air Pollutant Concentrations: Particulate Matter, Ozone, CO and Lead

	Particulate Matter 10 (ug/m³)	Particulate Matter 2.5 Wtd AM (ug/m³)	Particulate Matter 2.5 24-Hr (ug/m³)	Ozone (ppm)	Carbon Monoxide (ppm)	Lead (ug/m³)
MSA[1] Level	55	6.9	16	0.074	1	0.98
NAAQS[2]	150	15	35	0.075	9	0.15
Met NAAQS[2]	Yes	Yes	Yes	Yes	Yes	No

Note: (1) Data covers the Tampa-St. Petersburg-Clearwater, FL Metropolitan Statistical Area—see Appendix B for areas included; Data from exceptional events are included; (2) National Ambient Air Quality Standards; ppm = parts per million; ug/m³ = micrograms per cubic meter; n/a not available.
Concentrations: Particulate Matter 10 (coarse particulate)—highest second maximum 24-hour concentration; Particulate Matter 2.5 Wtd AM (fine particulate)—highest weighted annual mean concentration; Particulate Matter 2.5 24-Hour (fine particulate)—highest 98th percentile 24-hour concentration; Ozone—highest fourth daily maximum 8-hour concentration; Carbon Monoxide—highest second maximum non-overlapping 8-hour concentration; Lead—maximum running 3-month average
Source: U.S. Environmental Protection Agency, Air Quality Monitoring Information, "Air Quality Statistics by City, 2012"

Maximum Air Pollutant Concentrations: Nitrogen Dioxide and Sulfur Dioxide

	Nitrogen Dioxide AM (ppb)	Nitrogen Dioxide 1-Hr (ppb)	Sulfur Dioxide AM (ppb)	Sulfur Dioxide 1-Hr (ppb)	Sulfur Dioxide 24-Hr (ppb)
MSA[1] Level	5	34	n/a	110	n/a
NAAQS[2]	53	100	30	75	140
Met NAAQS[2]	Yes	Yes	n/a	No	n/a

Note: (1) Data covers the Tampa-St. Petersburg-Clearwater, FL Metropolitan Statistical Area—see Appendix B for areas included; Data from exceptional events are included; (2) National Ambient Air Quality Standards; ppm = parts per million; ug/m³ = micrograms per cubic meter; n/a not available.
Concentrations: Nitrogen Dioxide AM—highest arithmetic mean concentration; Nitrogen Dioxide 1-Hr—highest 98th percentile 1-hour daily maximum concentration; Sulfur Dioxide AM—highest annual mean concentration; Sulfur Dioxide 1-Hr—highest 99th percentile 1-hour daily maximum concentration; Sulfur Dioxide 24-Hr—highest second maximum 24-hour concentration
Source: U.S. Environmental Protection Agency, Air Quality Monitoring Information, "Air Quality Statistics by City, 2012"

Drinking Water

Water System Name	Pop. Served	Primary Water Source Type	Violations[1] Health Based	Violations[1] Monitoring/ Reporting
City of Tampa Water Department	588,000	Surface	0	0

Note: (1) Based on violation data from January 1, 2013 to December 31, 2013 (includes unresolved violations from earlier years)
Source: U.S. Environmental Protection Agency, Office of Ground Water and Drinking Water, Safe Drinking Water Information System (based on data extracted February 10, 2014)

Appendix A: Comparative Statistics

Population Growth: City

City	1990 Census	2000 Census	2010 Census	Population Growth (%) 1990-2000	2000-2010
Abilene, TX	106,927	115,930	117,063	8.4	1.0
Albuquerque, NM	388,375	448,607	545,852	15.5	21.7
Anchorage, AK	226,338	260,283	291,826	15.0	12.1
Ann Arbor, MI	111,018	114,024	113,934	2.7	-0.1
Athens, GA	86,561	100,266	115,452	15.8	15.1
Atlanta, GA	394,092	416,474	420,003	5.7	0.8
Austin, TX	499,053	656,562	790,390	31.6	20.4
Baltimore, MD	736,014	651,154	620,961	-11.5	-4.6
Billings, MT	81,812	89,847	104,170	9.8	15.9
Boise City, ID	144,317	185,787	205,671	28.7	10.7
Boston, MA	574,283	589,141	617,594	2.6	4.8
Boulder, CO	87,737	94,673	97,385	7.9	2.9
Cape Coral, FL	75,507	102,286	154,305	35.5	50.9
Cedar Rapids, IA	110,829	120,758	126,326	9.0	4.6
Charleston, SC	96,102	96,650	120,083	0.6	24.2
Charlotte, NC	428,283	540,828	731,424	26.3	35.2
Chicago, IL	2,783,726	2,896,016	2,695,598	4.0	-6.9
Cincinnati, OH	363,974	331,285	296,943	-9.0	-10.4
Clarksville, TN	78,569	103,455	132,929	31.7	28.5
Colorado Spgs, CO	283,798	360,890	416,427	27.2	15.4
Columbia, MO	71,069	84,531	108,500	18.9	28.4
Columbus, OH	648,656	711,470	787,033	9.7	10.6
Dallas, TX	1,006,971	1,188,580	1,197,816	18.0	0.8
Davenport, IA	95,705	98,359	99,685	2.8	1.3
Denver, CO	467,153	554,636	600,158	18.7	8.2
Des Moines, IA	193,569	198,682	203,433	2.6	2.4
Durham, NC	151,737	187,035	228,330	23.3	22.1
El Paso, TX	515,541	563,662	649,121	9.3	15.2
Erie, PA	108,718	103,717	101,786	-4.6	-1.9
Eugene, OR	118,073	137,893	156,185	16.8	13.3
Fargo, ND	74,372	90,599	105,549	21.8	16.5
Fayetteville, NC	118,247	121,015	200,564	2.3	65.7
Ft. Collins, CO	89,555	118,652	143,986	32.5	21.4
Ft. Wayne, IN	205,671	205,727	253,691	0.0	23.3
Ft. Worth, TX	448,311	534,694	741,206	19.3	38.6
Gainesville, FL	90,519	95,447	124,354	5.4	30.3
Grand Rapids, MI	189,145	197,800	188,040	4.6	-4.9
Green Bay, WI	96,466	102,313	104,057	6.1	1.7
Greensboro, NC	193,389	223,891	269,666	15.8	20.4
Honolulu, HI	376,465	371,657	337,256	-1.3	-9.3
Houston, TX	1,697,610	1,953,631	2,099,451	15.1	7.5
Huntsville, AL	161,842	158,216	180,105	-2.2	13.8
Indianapolis, IN	730,993	781,870	820,445	7.0	4.9
Jacksonville, FL	635,221	735,617	821,784	15.8	11.7
Kansas City, MO	434,967	441,545	459,787	1.5	4.1
Lafayette, LA	104,735	110,257	120,623	5.3	9.4
Las Vegas, NV	261,374	478,434	583,756	83.0	22.0
Lexington, KY	225,366	260,512	295,803	15.6	13.5
Lincoln, NE	193,629	225,581	258,379	16.5	14.5
Little Rock, AR	177,519	183,133	193,524	3.2	5.7
Los Angeles, CA	3,487,671	3,694,820	3,792,621	5.9	2.6
Louisville, KY	269,160	256,231	597,337	-4.8	133.1
Lubbock, TX	187,170	199,564	229,573	6.6	15.0
Madison, WI	193,451	208,054	233,209	7.5	12.1
Manchester, NH	99,567	107,006	109,565	7.5	2.4

Table continued on next page.

City	1990 Census	2000 Census	2010 Census	Population Growth (%) 1990-2000	Population Growth (%) 2000-2010
McAllen, TX	86,145	106,414	129,877	23.5	22.0
Miami, FL	358,843	362,470	399,457	1.0	10.2
Midland, TX	89,358	94,996	111,147	6.3	17.0
Minneapolis, MN	368,383	382,618	382,578	3.9	-0.0
Montgomery, AL	190,866	201,568	205,764	5.6	2.1
Nashville, TN	488,364	545,524	601,222	11.7	10.2
New Orleans, LA	496,938	484,674	343,829	-2.5	-29.1
New York, NY	7,322,552	8,008,278	8,175,133	9.4	2.1
Oklahoma City, OK	445,065	506,132	579,999	13.7	14.6
Omaha, NE	371,972	390,007	408,958	4.8	4.9
Orlando, FL	161,172	185,951	238,300	15.4	28.2
Oxnard, CA	143,271	170,358	197,899	18.9	16.2
Peoria, IL	114,341	112,936	115,007	-1.2	1.8
Philadelphia, PA	1,585,577	1,517,550	1,526,006	-4.3	0.6
Phoenix, AZ	989,873	1,321,045	1,445,632	33.5	9.4
Pittsburgh, PA	369,785	334,563	305,704	-9.5	-8.6
Portland, OR	485,833	529,121	583,776	8.9	10.3
Providence, RI	160,734	173,618	178,042	8.0	2.5
Provo, UT	87,148	105,166	112,488	20.7	7.0
Raleigh, NC	226,841	276,093	403,892	21.7	46.3
Reno, NV	139,950	180,480	225,221	29.0	24.8
Richmond, VA	202,783	197,790	204,214	-2.5	3.2
Riverside, CA	226,232	255,166	303,871	12.8	19.1
Rochester, MN	74,151	85,806	106,769	15.7	24.4
Salem, OR	112,046	136,924	154,637	22.2	12.9
Salt Lake City, UT	159,796	181,743	186,440	13.7	2.6
San Antonio, TX	997,258	1,144,646	1,327,407	14.8	16.0
San Diego, CA	1,111,048	1,223,400	1,307,402	10.1	6.9
San Francisco, CA	723,959	776,733	805,235	7.3	3.7
San Jose, CA	784,324	894,943	945,942	14.1	5.7
Santa Rosa, CA	123,297	147,595	167,815	19.7	13.7
Savannah, GA	138,038	131,510	136,286	-4.7	3.6
Seattle, WA	516,262	563,374	608,660	9.1	8.0
Sioux Falls, SD	102,262	123,975	153,888	21.2	24.1
Spokane, WA	178,202	195,629	208,916	9.8	6.8
Springfield, MO	142,557	151,580	159,498	6.3	5.2
Tallahassee, FL	128,014	150,624	181,376	17.7	20.4
Tampa, FL	279,960	303,447	335,709	8.4	10.6
Topeka, KS	121,197	122,377	127,473	1.0	4.2
Tulsa, OK	367,241	393,049	391,906	7.0	-0.3
Virginia Beach, VA	393,069	425,257	437,994	8.2	3.0
Washington, DC	606,900	572,059	601,723	-5.7	5.2
Wichita, KS	313,693	344,284	382,368	9.8	11.1
Wilmington, NC	64,609	75,838	106,476	17.4	40.4
Worcester, MA	169,759	172,648	181,045	1.7	4.9
U.S.	248,709,873	281,421,906	308,745,538	13.2	9.7

Source: U.S. Census Bureau, Census 2010, 2000, 1990

Population Growth: Metro Area

Metro Area	1990 Census	2000 Census	2010 Census	Population Growth (%) 1990-2000	Population Growth (%) 2000-2010
Abilene, TX	148,004	160,245	165,252	8.3	3.1
Albuquerque, NM	599,416	729,649	887,077	21.7	21.6
Anchorage, AK	266,021	319,605	380,821	20.1	19.2
Ann Arbor, MI	282,937	322,895	344,791	14.1	6.8
Athens, GA	136,025	166,079	192,541	22.1	15.9
Atlanta, GA	3,069,411	4,247,981	5,268,860	38.4	24.0
Austin, TX	846,217	1,249,763	1,716,289	47.7	37.3
Baltimore, MD	2,382,172	2,552,994	2,710,489	7.2	6.2
Billings, MT	121,499	138,904	158,050	14.3	13.8
Boise City, ID	319,596	464,840	616,561	45.4	32.6
Boston, MA	4,133,895	4,391,344	4,552,402	6.2	3.7
Boulder, CO	208,898	269,758	294,567	29.1	9.2
Cape Coral, FL	335,113	440,888	618,754	31.6	40.3
Cedar Rapids, IA	210,640	237,230	257,940	12.6	8.7
Charleston, SC	506,875	549,033	664,607	8.3	21.1
Charlotte, NC	1,024,331	1,330,448	1,758,038	29.9	32.1
Chicago, IL	8,182,076	9,098,316	9,461,105	11.2	4.0
Cincinnati, OH	1,844,917	2,009,632	2,130,151	8.9	6.0
Clarksville, TN	189,277	232,000	273,949	22.6	18.1
Colorado Spgs, CO	409,482	537,484	645,613	31.3	20.1
Columbia, MO	122,010	145,666	172,786	19.4	18.6
Columbus, OH	1,405,176	1,612,694	1,836,536	14.8	13.9
Dallas, TX	3,989,294	5,161,544	6,371,773	29.4	23.4
Davenport, IA	368,151	376,019	379,690	2.1	1.0
Denver, CO	1,666,935	2,179,296	2,543,482	30.7	16.7
Des Moines, IA	416,346	481,394	569,633	15.6	18.3
Durham, NC	344,646	426,493	504,357	23.7	18.3
El Paso, TX	591,610	679,622	800,647	14.9	17.8
Erie, PA	275,603	280,843	280,566	1.9	-0.1
Eugene, OR	282,912	322,959	351,715	14.2	8.9
Fargo, ND	153,296	174,367	208,777	13.7	19.7
Fayetteville, NC	297,422	336,609	366,383	13.2	8.8
Ft. Collins, CO	186,136	251,494	299,630	35.1	19.1
Ft. Wayne, IN	354,435	390,156	416,257	10.1	6.7
Ft. Worth, TX	3,989,294	5,161,544	6,371,773	29.4	23.4
Gainesville, FL	191,263	232,392	264,275	21.5	13.7
Grand Rapids, MI	645,914	740,482	774,160	14.6	4.5
Green Bay, WI	243,698	282,599	306,241	16.0	8.4
Greensboro, NC	540,257	643,430	723,801	19.1	12.5
Honolulu, HI	836,231	876,156	953,207	4.8	8.8
Houston, TX	3,767,335	4,715,407	5,946,800	25.2	26.1
Huntsville, AL	293,047	342,376	417,593	16.8	22.0
Indianapolis, IN	1,294,217	1,525,104	1,756,241	17.8	15.2
Jacksonville, FL	925,213	1,122,750	1,345,596	21.4	19.8
Kansas City, MO	1,636,528	1,836,038	2,035,334	12.2	10.9
Lafayette, LA	208,740	239,086	273,738	14.5	14.5
Las Vegas, NV	741,459	1,375,765	1,951,269	85.5	41.8
Lexington, KY	348,428	408,326	472,099	17.2	15.6
Lincoln, NE	229,091	266,787	302,157	16.5	13.3
Little Rock, AR	535,034	610,518	699,757	14.1	14.6
Los Angeles, CA	11,273,720	12,365,627	12,828,837	9.7	3.7
Louisville, KY	1,055,973	1,161,975	1,283,566	10.0	10.5
Lubbock, TX	229,940	249,700	284,890	8.6	14.1
Madison, WI	432,323	501,774	568,593	16.1	13.3
Manchester, NH	336,073	380,841	400,721	13.3	5.2

Table continued on next page.

Metro Area	1990 Census	2000 Census	2010 Census	Population Growth (%)	
				1990-2000	2000-2010
McAllen, TX	383,545	569,463	774,769	48.5	36.1
Miami, FL	4,056,100	5,007,564	5,564,635	23.5	11.1
Midland, TX	106,611	116,009	136,872	8.8	18.0
Minneapolis, MN	2,538,834	2,968,806	3,279,833	16.9	10.5
Montgomery, AL	305,175	346,528	374,536	13.6	8.1
Nashville, TN	1,048,218	1,311,789	1,589,934	25.1	21.2
New Orleans, LA	1,264,391	1,316,510	1,167,764	4.1	-11.3
New York, NY	16,845,992	18,323,002	18,897,109	8.8	3.1
Oklahoma City, OK	971,042	1,095,421	1,252,987	12.8	14.4
Omaha, NE	685,797	767,041	865,350	11.8	12.8
Orlando, FL	1,224,852	1,644,561	2,134,411	34.3	29.8
Oxnard, CA	669,016	753,197	823,318	12.6	9.3
Peoria, IL	358,552	366,899	379,186	2.3	3.3
Philadelphia, PA	5,435,470	5,687,147	5,965,343	4.6	4.9
Phoenix, AZ	2,238,480	3,251,876	4,192,887	45.3	28.9
Pittsburgh, PA	2,468,289	2,431,087	2,356,285	-1.5	-3.1
Portland, OR	1,523,741	1,927,881	2,226,009	26.5	15.5
Providence, RI	1,509,789	1,582,997	1,600,852	4.8	1.1
Provo, UT	269,407	376,774	526,810	39.9	39.8
Raleigh, NC	541,081	797,071	1,130,490	47.3	41.8
Reno, NV	257,193	342,885	425,417	33.3	24.1
Richmond, VA	949,244	1,096,957	1,258,251	15.6	14.7
Riverside, CA	2,588,793	3,254,821	4,224,851	25.7	29.8
Rochester, MN	141,945	163,618	186,011	15.3	13.7
Salem, OR	278,024	347,214	390,738	24.9	12.5
Salt Lake City, UT	768,075	968,858	1,124,197	26.1	16.0
San Antonio, TX	1,407,745	1,711,703	2,142,508	21.6	25.2
San Diego, CA	2,498,016	2,813,833	3,095,313	12.6	10.0
San Francisco, CA	3,686,592	4,123,740	4,335,391	11.9	5.1
San Jose, CA	1,534,280	1,735,819	1,836,911	13.1	5.8
Santa Rosa, CA	388,222	458,614	483,878	18.1	5.5
Savannah, GA	258,060	293,000	347,611	13.5	18.6
Seattle, WA	2,559,164	3,043,878	3,439,809	18.9	13.0
Sioux Falls, SD	153,500	187,093	228,261	21.9	22.0
Spokane, WA	361,364	417,939	471,221	15.7	12.7
Springfield, MO	298,818	368,374	436,712	23.3	18.6
Tallahassee, FL	259,096	320,304	367,413	23.6	14.7
Tampa, FL	2,067,959	2,395,997	2,783,243	15.9	16.2
Topeka, KS	210,257	224,551	233,870	6.8	4.2
Tulsa, OK	761,019	859,532	937,478	12.9	9.1
Virginia Beach, VA	1,449,389	1,576,370	1,671,683	8.8	6.0
Washington, DC	4,122,914	4,796,183	5,582,170	16.3	16.4
Wichita, KS	511,111	571,166	623,061	11.7	9.1
Wilmington, NC	200,124	274,532	362,315	37.2	32.0
Worcester, MA	709,728	750,963	798,552	5.8	6.3
U.S.	248,709,873	281,421,906	308,745,538	13.2	9.7

Note: Figures cover the Metropolitan Statistical Area (MSA)—see Appendix B for areas included
Source: U.S. Census Bureau, Census 2010, 2000, 1990

Household Size: City

City	Persons in Household (%)							Average Household Size
	One	Two	Three	Four	Five	Six	Seven or More	
Abilene, TX	29.2	35.3	15.0	11.7	5.3	2.4	1.1	2.55
Albuquerque, NM	33.1	32.6	15.1	11.4	5.0	1.9	0.8	2.43
Anchorage, AK	26.2	32.6	17.6	12.8	5.8	2.7	2.3	2.73
Ann Arbor, MI	38.9	33.4	13.7	9.3	2.3	2.0	0.4	2.24
Athens, GA	32.8	34.3	13.8	12.8	4.1	1.7	0.6	2.66
Atlanta, GA	45.6	29.2	11.8	7.8	3.2	1.6	0.7	2.27
Austin, TX	34.0	32.4	14.9	11.0	4.8	1.6	1.3	2.44
Baltimore, MD	39.4	28.1	15.2	9.1	4.9	1.8	1.6	2.48
Billings, MT	32.5	36.0	13.9	10.5	4.5	1.8	0.8	2.33
Boise City, ID	31.2	34.7	15.3	11.6	4.4	2.0	0.7	2.37
Boston, MA	38.2	31.0	14.5	9.8	3.8	1.7	1.0	2.34
Boulder, CO	32.9	35.5	16.3	11.0	3.6	0.7	0.2	2.24
Cape Coral, FL	22.5	41.3	15.7	11.6	6.1	1.7	1.0	2.84
Cedar Rapids, IA	32.3	34.8	13.9	12.5	4.2	1.7	0.6	2.37
Charleston, SC	35.8	36.2	14.4	9.8	2.9	0.6	0.4	2.25
Charlotte, NC	31.4	31.2	16.0	12.7	5.7	2.2	0.9	2.54
Chicago, IL	36.2	28.0	14.2	10.8	5.8	2.6	2.4	2.59
Cincinnati, OH	43.4	29.1	13.0	8.1	3.2	2.0	1.1	2.22
Clarksville, TN	22.4	31.1	20.8	15.0	6.6	2.4	1.7	2.71
Colorado Spgs, CO	30.0	33.6	15.0	12.6	5.3	2.3	1.1	2.50
Columbia, MO	33.5	32.2	15.5	13.5	3.5	1.3	0.4	2.35
Columbus, OH	36.4	30.7	14.3	10.1	5.4	1.8	1.2	2.40
Dallas, TX	34.7	28.1	13.8	11.5	6.6	3.0	2.3	2.63
Davenport, IA	34.0	34.2	15.6	8.4	5.7	1.2	1.0	2.39
Denver, CO	40.4	31.5	12.3	8.3	4.2	2.0	1.4	2.27
Des Moines, IA	32.2	30.8	15.5	11.6	6.1	2.2	1.6	2.46
Durham, NC	32.2	34.0	15.5	10.6	4.7	2.0	1.0	2.34
El Paso, TX	22.4	26.6	19.0	16.8	9.2	3.7	2.3	3.02
Erie, PA	36.9	31.7	13.9	9.7	4.8	1.5	1.5	2.33
Eugene, OR	32.0	37.7	14.8	9.5	3.7	1.5	0.8	2.28
Fargo, ND	37.9	34.6	14.2	8.5	3.5	1.0	0.3	2.15
Fayetteville, NC	29.7	33.4	17.2	12.5	4.9	1.2	1.0	2.49
Ft. Collins, CO	26.7	36.1	18.1	12.0	4.8	1.5	0.8	2.46
Ft. Wayne, IN	32.2	31.5	16.0	11.4	5.4	2.3	1.2	2.48
Ft. Worth, TX	27.8	27.7	15.7	15.0	8.0	3.5	2.3	2.83
Gainesville, FL	37.0	35.6	14.9	9.1	2.2	0.8	0.3	2.39
Grand Rapids, MI	33.2	30.2	14.3	12.1	5.7	2.6	1.9	2.49
Green Bay, WI	34.9	32.5	12.9	11.1	4.8	2.2	1.6	2.37
Greensboro, NC	34.7	32.7	14.8	10.6	4.5	1.8	0.9	2.35
Honolulu, HI	33.8	31.3	14.5	10.4	4.5	2.4	3.1	2.58
Houston, TX	32.2	28.5	15.3	12.1	7.0	2.8	2.2	2.73
Huntsville, AL	36.7	33.8	13.7	10.2	3.7	1.1	0.6	2.33
Indianapolis, IN	34.3	31.9	14.5	10.5	5.3	2.4	1.2	2.49
Jacksonville, FL	30.6	33.1	16.6	11.7	4.9	2.0	1.2	2.61
Kansas City, MO	35.8	32.2	14.6	10.1	4.5	1.7	1.1	2.38
Lafayette, LA	35.4	32.7	15.4	10.8	3.8	0.7	1.1	2.38
Las Vegas, NV	28.5	31.6	14.8	13.2	6.9	3.0	2.1	2.76
Lexington, KY	33.2	32.7	16.0	11.8	3.9	1.6	0.7	2.36
Lincoln, NE	30.4	36.4	13.5	11.8	4.9	1.8	1.2	2.37
Little Rock, AR	36.0	34.0	14.7	9.1	4.6	0.9	0.7	2.42
Los Angeles, CA	30.4	27.7	15.3	13.2	7.2	3.2	3.1	2.84
Louisville, KY	32.7	32.0	15.7	11.8	5.1	1.7	0.9	2.43
Lubbock, TX	30.1	32.8	15.7	12.3	5.4	2.3	1.4	2.51
Madison, WI	35.6	34.5	14.1	10.6	3.2	1.3	0.6	2.22

Table continued on next page.

City	Persons in Household (%)							Average Household Size
	One	Two	Three	Four	Five	Six	Seven or More	
Manchester, NH	31.3	33.7	16.0	11.5	4.9	1.6	1.0	2.40
McAllen, TX	22.0	26.6	18.7	15.1	10.1	5.2	2.3	3.12
Miami, FL	36.5	29.2	15.7	10.5	4.6	2.1	1.5	2.67
Midland, TX	24.7	33.0	18.4	12.9	7.1	2.5	1.4	2.77
Minneapolis, MN	40.8	31.9	11.1	9.1	3.9	1.3	1.9	2.25
Montgomery, AL	31.5	31.4	17.8	10.7	5.3	1.9	1.3	2.51
Nashville, TN	36.2	32.7	14.1	9.9	4.3	1.6	1.2	2.40
New Orleans, LA	39.1	30.1	14.9	8.8	4.5	1.4	1.3	2.37
New York, NY	32.7	27.9	16.0	12.5	6.0	2.6	2.2	2.65
Oklahoma City, OK	30.5	32.7	15.6	11.5	6.1	2.3	1.2	2.56
Omaha, NE	33.8	32.2	13.2	10.8	6.5	1.8	1.6	2.47
Orlando, FL	36.3	33.5	14.4	9.9	3.7	1.3	0.7	2.42
Oxnard, CA	14.7	21.4	16.0	17.6	13.7	7.4	9.2	3.96
Peoria, IL	35.9	31.7	14.0	10.3	4.9	2.3	1.0	2.34
Philadelphia, PA	39.6	27.7	14.6	9.7	4.9	2.0	1.5	2.58
Phoenix, AZ	28.8	30.1	15.1	13.0	7.0	3.3	2.7	2.81
Pittsburgh, PA	41.7	32.7	13.2	7.9	2.9	1.0	0.6	2.14
Portland, OR	35.4	34.2	14.1	9.8	3.8	1.6	1.2	2.33
Providence, RI	30.5	26.2	18.4	15.2	5.4	2.7	1.6	2.71
Provo, UT	14.9	30.9	16.4	17.9	9.7	6.8	3.4	3.30
Raleigh, NC	33.5	30.9	15.8	12.6	4.6	1.7	0.9	2.45
Reno, NV	33.2	32.8	13.6	11.3	5.5	2.4	1.1	2.50
Richmond, VA	41.8	31.0	13.7	8.3	3.4	1.0	0.8	2.35
Riverside, CA	22.2	25.6	16.2	15.3	10.2	6.1	4.5	3.34
Rochester, MN	31.2	33.5	13.5	13.6	5.5	1.8	1.0	2.44
Salem, OR	29.8	32.2	14.6	12.2	6.1	3.6	1.6	2.57
Salt Lake City, UT	36.6	29.6	14.1	9.9	4.8	2.7	2.4	2.47
San Antonio, TX	28.4	29.5	16.3	13.2	7.2	3.2	2.3	2.80
San Diego, CA	29.2	32.2	15.4	12.7	5.9	2.6	2.0	2.73
San Francisco, CA	39.0	32.8	12.4	9.2	3.4	1.7	1.5	2.33
San Jose, CA	19.6	27.6	18.6	17.9	8.8	3.7	3.7	3.12
Santa Rosa, CA	28.5	32.8	15.5	12.7	6.6	1.8	2.0	2.67
Savannah, GA	36.1	31.2	15.5	9.8	4.6	1.7	1.1	2.57
Seattle, WA	41.9	33.0	12.3	8.4	2.6	1.0	0.7	2.10
Sioux Falls, SD	29.8	35.9	14.0	11.9	4.7	2.2	1.5	2.43
Spokane, WA	34.4	33.4	14.1	10.7	4.6	1.8	1.0	2.30
Springfield, MO	37.7	35.3	13.6	9.6	2.6	0.8	0.4	2.14
Tallahassee, FL	33.9	33.8	17.3	10.9	2.3	1.2	0.7	2.35
Tampa, FL	36.6	31.2	15.1	10.6	4.2	1.4	0.9	2.44
Topeka, KS	36.3	31.9	12.9	10.1	4.5	2.5	1.9	2.32
Tulsa, OK	35.0	32.5	14.1	10.0	5.0	2.1	1.1	2.37
Virginia Beach, VA	23.7	34.7	18.2	13.8	6.3	2.0	1.3	2.64
Washington, DC	46.9	29.1	11.6	7.1	3.0	1.5	0.8	2.21
Wichita, KS	32.2	32.4	14.1	11.3	5.9	2.4	1.7	2.53
Wilmington, NC	34.7	35.6	15.7	10.4	2.2	1.0	0.5	2.23
Worcester, MA	33.4	29.9	15.8	12.4	5.7	1.7	1.1	2.49
U.S.	27.6	33.5	15.7	13.2	6.1	2.4	1.5	2.63

U.S. Census Bureau, 2010-2012 American Community Survey 3-Year Estimates

Household Size: Metro Area

Metro Area	Persons in Household (%)							Average Household Size
	One	Two	Three	Four	Five	Six	Seven or More	
Abilene, TX	28.5	36.8	14.7	11.4	5.4	2.2	1.0	2.55
Albuquerque, NM	29.6	33.5	15.4	12.4	5.7	2.1	1.3	2.56
Anchorage, AK	25.2	33.6	17.4	13.0	5.8	2.7	2.5	2.76
Ann Arbor, MI	32.2	32.7	15.6	12.7	4.4	1.7	0.7	2.45
Athens, GA	27.9	35.3	15.0	14.2	4.8	1.9	0.9	2.75
Atlanta, GA	26.6	31.2	16.8	14.8	6.6	2.5	1.6	2.78
Austin, TX	27.7	32.8	15.7	13.8	6.2	2.3	1.5	2.65
Baltimore, MD	28.6	32.4	16.5	13.2	6.1	2.0	1.2	2.60
Billings, MT	30.0	37.4	13.3	11.6	4.9	1.8	1.0	2.40
Boise City, ID	24.1	34.9	14.7	14.2	7.1	3.2	1.8	2.70
Boston, MA	28.7	32.3	16.0	14.4	5.8	1.9	0.9	2.53
Boulder, CO	28.2	35.5	15.5	13.8	5.0	1.4	0.6	2.42
Cape Coral, FL	28.4	43.5	12.0	9.4	4.1	1.7	0.8	2.62
Cedar Rapids, IA	28.6	36.4	14.4	13.1	5.0	1.8	0.7	2.43
Charleston, SC	28.4	34.4	16.9	12.7	4.9	1.8	0.9	2.57
Charlotte, NC	27.1	32.6	17.0	13.7	6.1	2.3	1.1	2.64
Chicago, IL	28.0	29.8	15.9	14.4	7.1	2.8	1.9	2.73
Cincinnati, OH	28.1	33.8	15.9	13.1	5.7	2.2	1.1	2.57
Clarksville, TN	22.8	32.4	18.9	14.3	7.2	2.6	1.7	2.68
Colorado Spgs, CO	26.4	34.7	15.6	13.6	6.0	2.6	1.2	2.60
Columbia, MO	30.5	33.7	16.5	13.0	4.4	1.3	0.5	2.41
Columbus, OH	29.3	32.8	15.4	13.3	6.0	2.0	1.1	2.54
Dallas, TX	25.3	30.4	16.7	15.1	7.6	3.0	1.9	2.80
Davenport, IA	31.5	35.6	14.4	10.8	5.3	1.4	1.0	2.41
Denver, CO	29.5	33.2	15.1	12.8	5.7	2.3	1.4	2.54
Des Moines, IA	26.9	34.2	16.1	13.7	6.2	1.9	1.0	2.52
Durham, NC	29.7	35.7	15.8	11.6	4.7	1.5	1.0	2.41
El Paso, TX	20.5	25.8	19.3	17.4	10.1	4.1	2.8	3.13
Erie, PA	30.5	34.7	14.8	12.1	5.1	1.7	1.0	2.45
Eugene, OR	28.7	38.7	15.2	10.2	4.5	1.6	1.1	2.38
Fargo, ND	32.9	34.7	14.4	11.4	4.8	1.4	0.4	2.32
Fayetteville, NC	27.3	32.1	18.3	13.7	5.8	1.7	1.2	2.63
Ft. Collins, CO	25.3	39.4	15.9	12.2	4.9	1.5	0.7	2.45
Ft. Wayne, IN	28.2	33.5	15.9	12.8	6.1	2.3	1.2	2.55
Ft. Worth, TX	25.3	30.4	16.7	15.1	7.6	3.0	1.9	2.80
Gainesville, FL	31.6	37.1	15.7	10.1	3.7	1.1	0.7	2.48
Grand Rapids, MI	25.9	33.9	15.5	14.0	6.9	2.6	1.3	2.61
Green Bay, WI	27.9	35.9	14.6	13.2	5.5	1.8	1.0	2.46
Greensboro, NC	29.2	34.4	16.6	12.1	4.8	1.9	1.0	2.47
Honolulu, HI	23.9	30.8	16.8	13.7	6.9	3.4	4.4	3.01
Houston, TX	24.4	29.8	16.9	15.3	8.1	3.2	2.2	2.92
Huntsville, AL	29.4	34.7	15.9	12.7	5.0	1.5	0.8	2.51
Indianapolis, IN	28.4	33.1	16.0	13.1	6.0	2.2	1.1	2.58
Jacksonville, FL	27.6	35.2	16.3	12.7	5.3	1.9	1.0	2.63
Kansas City, MO	28.6	33.9	15.5	13.0	5.8	2.1	1.2	2.54
Lafayette, LA	30.3	32.5	16.7	12.8	5.2	1.4	1.1	2.58
Las Vegas, NV	27.2	32.4	15.5	12.9	6.9	3.1	2.0	2.77
Lexington, KY	30.1	33.7	16.8	12.5	4.5	1.7	0.8	2.43
Lincoln, NE	29.0	36.8	13.6	12.2	5.3	1.9	1.2	2.41
Little Rock, AR	28.9	36.9	15.2	11.9	5.1	1.2	0.8	2.53
Los Angeles, CA	24.7	27.9	16.4	15.4	8.4	3.8	3.4	3.03
Louisville, KY	28.7	34.2	16.2	13.0	5.4	1.7	0.8	2.51
Lubbock, TX	28.0	33.0	16.2	12.8	6.1	2.4	1.5	2.57
Madison, WI	30.1	36.0	14.8	12.2	4.5	1.7	0.7	2.36

Table continued on next page.

Metro Area	Persons in Household (%)							Average Household Size
	One	Two	Three	Four	Five	Six	Seven or More	
Manchester, NH	25.1	35.2	15.9	15.3	5.9	1.7	0.9	2.56
McAllen, TX	15.4	24.1	17.3	17.1	12.8	7.6	5.7	3.61
Miami, FL	29.0	31.9	16.5	13.3	5.7	2.3	1.3	2.78
Midland, TX	24.5	32.8	17.9	13.9	7.1	2.5	1.3	2.78
Minneapolis, MN	28.0	33.6	14.9	14.1	6.0	2.1	1.3	2.54
Montgomery, AL	28.3	33.3	17.8	12.3	5.4	1.7	1.3	2.57
Nashville, TN	27.6	34.1	16.1	13.4	5.7	1.8	1.2	2.60
New Orleans, LA	30.7	32.2	16.6	11.7	5.7	2.0	1.1	2.56
New York, NY	28.0	28.9	16.8	14.8	6.9	2.7	2.0	2.74
Oklahoma City, OK	28.1	34.0	15.9	12.9	5.9	2.2	1.0	2.58
Omaha, NE	28.3	34.1	14.4	13.1	6.6	2.1	1.3	2.55
Orlando, FL	25.9	35.2	16.6	13.3	5.9	2.0	1.0	2.80
Oxnard, CA	20.8	30.6	17.4	15.5	8.5	3.7	3.4	3.07
Peoria, IL	28.8	36.4	14.3	12.2	5.3	1.9	1.1	2.44
Philadelphia, PA	29.5	31.3	16.2	13.6	6.2	2.1	1.2	2.62
Phoenix, AZ	26.6	34.6	14.4	12.8	6.4	3.0	2.2	2.74
Pittsburgh, PA	32.3	35.4	14.8	11.4	4.2	1.3	0.6	2.33
Portland, OR	27.7	34.8	15.3	13.0	5.5	2.1	1.5	2.57
Providence, RI	29.7	32.9	16.3	13.3	5.3	1.6	0.9	2.49
Provo, UT	12.4	26.2	15.9	17.2	12.7	9.0	6.7	3.62
Raleigh, NC	26.2	32.0	17.3	15.1	6.2	2.0	1.1	2.65
Reno, NV	29.0	35.4	14.2	12.4	5.2	2.2	1.6	2.57
Richmond, VA	28.0	34.2	16.4	13.8	5.1	1.6	0.9	2.59
Riverside, CA	20.0	28.0	16.2	16.0	10.3	5.2	4.3	3.30
Rochester, MN	27.6	35.2	13.9	14.7	5.9	1.8	0.8	2.51
Salem, OR	25.3	33.9	15.3	12.6	7.2	3.8	1.9	2.70
Salt Lake City, UT	22.8	29.6	16.0	14.4	8.5	4.7	3.9	3.02
San Antonio, TX	25.1	31.2	16.5	14.2	7.4	3.2	2.3	2.83
San Diego, CA	25.1	32.3	16.3	14.3	6.8	3.0	2.1	2.86
San Francisco, CA	28.7	31.4	15.9	13.9	5.8	2.5	1.8	2.67
San Jose, CA	21.7	29.2	18.5	17.3	7.7	3.0	2.7	2.94
Santa Rosa, CA	28.0	35.1	15.2	12.8	5.8	1.6	1.6	2.60
Savannah, GA	29.8	33.9	15.4	12.9	5.3	1.7	1.0	2.63
Seattle, WA	29.4	33.1	15.9	13.3	5.1	2.0	1.2	2.52
Sioux Falls, SD	27.0	36.0	14.3	13.2	5.8	2.3	1.5	2.52
Spokane, WA	28.9	35.4	14.9	11.9	5.6	2.3	1.0	2.44
Springfield, MO	27.9	37.1	15.7	12.1	4.4	1.6	1.3	2.43
Tallahassee, FL	29.4	35.0	17.0	12.2	3.6	1.7	1.0	2.46
Tampa, FL	32.0	36.0	14.4	10.9	4.2	1.5	0.9	2.48
Topeka, KS	29.4	36.1	13.6	11.9	5.1	2.2	1.7	2.44
Tulsa, OK	28.0	34.6	16.0	12.0	5.9	2.4	1.1	2.54
Virginia Beach, VA	25.9	34.5	17.7	12.9	5.8	1.8	1.3	2.62
Washington, DC	27.6	30.7	16.6	14.4	6.5	2.6	1.6	2.72
Wichita, KS	29.3	33.7	14.1	12.5	6.2	2.8	1.5	2.59
Wilmington, NC	28.2	39.5	15.7	11.0	4.1	1.1	0.4	2.37
Worcester, MA	27.0	32.1	16.7	15.5	6.0	1.9	0.8	2.60
U.S.	27.6	33.5	15.7	13.2	6.1	2.4	1.5	2.63

Note: Figures cover the Metropolitan Statistical Area (MSA)—see Appendix B for areas included
Source: U.S. Census Bureau, 2010-2012 American Community Survey 3-Year Estimates

Race: City

City	White Alone[1] (%)	Black Alone[1] (%)	Asian Alone[1] (%)	AIAN[2] Alone[1] (%)	NHOPI[3] Alone[1] (%)	Other Race Alone[1] (%)	Two or More Races (%)
Abilene, TX	80.3	10.3	1.8	0.5	0.0	4.2	2.9
Albuquerque, NM	69.3	3.3	2.4	4.2	0.1	16.4	4.2
Anchorage, AK	66.1	6.0	8.4	6.7	2.1	1.4	9.3
Ann Arbor, MI	73.9	6.7	14.3	0.2	0.0	0.8	4.1
Athens, GA	65.8	26.2	4.0	0.2	0.0	1.3	2.4
Atlanta, GA	39.3	53.4	3.6	0.2	0.0	1.5	1.9
Austin, TX	72.7	7.9	6.4	0.6	0.1	9.3	2.9
Baltimore, MD	30.1	63.4	2.4	0.3	0.0	1.5	2.3
Billings, MT	89.6	0.8	1.2	4.2	0.1	1.9	2.2
Boise City, ID	89.8	1.5	3.5	0.7	0.2	1.2	3.1
Boston, MA	53.8	25.6	9.2	0.3	0.0	6.7	4.5
Boulder, CO	88.4	1.2	4.4	0.2	0.0	2.5	3.2
Cape Coral, FL	91.2	3.5	1.6	0.5	0.0	1.7	1.4
Cedar Rapids, IA	87.5	6.2	2.0	0.3	0.0	0.9	3.0
Charleston, SC	71.0	25.5	1.3	0.1	0.1	0.4	1.5
Charlotte, NC	53.1	34.8	5.2	0.5	0.1	3.7	2.7
Chicago, IL	47.7	32.5	5.6	0.3	0.0	11.8	2.1
Cincinnati, OH	50.1	44.2	1.9	0.4	0.0	0.9	2.5
Clarksville, TN	66.6	23.0	2.4	1.1	0.4	1.8	4.7
Colorado Spgs, CO	80.6	6.4	2.9	0.6	0.3	4.5	4.8
Columbia, MO	78.8	10.8	5.3	0.2	0.1	1.2	3.7
Columbus, OH	62.1	27.7	4.4	0.2	0.0	2.1	3.5
Dallas, TX	56.5	24.4	2.9	0.3	0.0	13.8	2.0
Davenport, IA	81.4	11.0	2.1	0.4	0.0	1.2	3.8
Denver, CO	72.2	10.0	3.5	1.2	0.1	9.7	3.3
Des Moines, IA	77.9	10.5	4.9	0.5	0.1	3.1	3.1
Durham, NC	46.8	40.2	4.8	0.5	0.1	4.8	2.9
El Paso, TX	81.8	3.4	1.3	0.5	0.1	10.8	2.1
Erie, PA	75.7	16.2	2.1	0.5	0.0	1.8	3.7
Eugene, OR	86.6	1.4	4.1	0.8	0.2	1.9	4.9
Fargo, ND	90.1	2.4	2.7	1.4	0.0	0.7	2.8
Fayetteville, NC	47.1	40.7	2.8	0.8	0.4	2.9	5.2
Ft. Collins, CO	89.6	1.4	2.9	0.4	0.1	1.8	3.7
Ft. Wayne, IN	74.4	16.1	3.2	0.4	0.1	2.3	3.4
Ft. Worth, TX	66.6	18.9	3.8	0.7	0.2	7.5	2.4
Gainesville, FL	65.8	22.8	6.9	0.3	0.1	1.1	3.0
Grand Rapids, MI	69.2	21.0	2.1	0.5	0.0	2.6	4.5
Green Bay, WI	83.7	3.7	4.1	2.8	0.0	1.9	3.9
Greensboro, NC	49.8	40.5	4.2	0.4	0.1	2.6	2.5
Honolulu, HI	17.7	1.7	55.0	0.1	8.1	0.6	16.7
Houston, TX	57.5	23.3	6.1	0.4	0.0	10.9	1.7
Huntsville, AL	62.2	31.0	2.3	0.4	0.1	1.0	3.0
Indianapolis, IN	62.4	27.6	2.1	0.3	0.0	4.7	2.9
Jacksonville, FL	60.5	30.5	4.3	0.3	0.1	1.2	3.2
Kansas City, MO	59.3	29.3	2.6	0.5	0.2	4.4	3.6
Lafayette, LA	64.7	30.7	2.1	0.2	0.0	0.5	1.7
Las Vegas, NV	67.9	10.9	6.2	0.6	0.5	9.4	4.5
Lexington, KY	76.3	14.1	3.4	0.2	0.0	3.0	2.9
Lincoln, NE	87.8	4.0	4.0	0.7	0.1	0.6	2.8
Little Rock, AR	51.4	43.2	3.2	0.3	0.0	0.7	1.1
Los Angeles, CA	52.6	9.4	11.5	0.4	0.2	22.5	3.4
Louisville, KY	71.4	22.7	2.2	0.1	0.0	0.8	2.7
Lubbock, TX	77.3	8.0	2.5	0.5	0.1	8.4	3.2
Madison, WI	79.9	7.6	7.8	0.3	0.0	1.3	3.1

Table continued on next page.

City	White Alone[1] (%)	Black Alone[1] (%)	Asian Alone[1] (%)	AIAN[2] Alone[1] (%)	NHOPI[3] Alone[1] (%)	Other Race Alone[1] (%)	Two or More Races (%)
Manchester, NH	85.9	4.5	4.2	0.2	0.0	2.7	2.5
McAllen, TX	87.6	1.1	2.8	0.5	0.0	6.6	1.3
Miami, FL	74.8	19.6	0.9	0.1	0.0	3.5	1.0
Midland, TX	83.2	8.0	1.9	0.3	0.0	4.9	1.7
Minneapolis, MN	67.6	17.7	5.6	1.5	0.1	3.0	4.4
Montgomery, AL	37.9	56.8	2.3	0.3	0.0	1.2	1.4
Nashville, TN	60.9	28.5	3.1	0.2	0.0	4.9	2.5
New Orleans, LA	33.5	60.0	2.9	0.3	0.0	1.7	1.6
New York, NY	44.0	24.9	12.9	0.4	0.1	14.7	3.1
Oklahoma City, OK	66.9	14.4	3.9	3.1	0.1	4.5	7.0
Omaha, NE	75.8	13.1	2.6	0.8	0.0	4.7	3.0
Orlando, FL	58.3	29.2	3.4	0.3	0.1	6.1	2.7
Oxnard, CA	73.3	2.6	8.0	0.8	0.2	11.4	3.6
Peoria, IL	63.3	27.7	4.8	0.5	0.0	1.0	2.7
Philadelphia, PA	41.3	43.2	6.4	0.3	0.1	6.0	2.6
Phoenix, AZ	77.7	6.8	3.2	1.8	0.2	7.7	2.6
Pittsburgh, PA	66.4	25.1	4.7	0.2	0.0	0.5	3.0
Portland, OR	77.4	6.4	7.3	0.7	0.5	3.6	4.0
Providence, RI	50.4	15.3	6.5	0.9	0.2	22.5	4.3
Provo, UT	87.4	0.8	2.5	0.6	1.3	4.2	3.2
Raleigh, NC	61.0	29.8	4.2	0.3	0.0	2.9	1.9
Reno, NV	78.9	3.2	5.9	1.0	0.7	6.8	3.5
Richmond, VA	43.3	49.5	2.2	0.3	0.0	1.3	3.3
Riverside, CA	66.9	6.2	6.9	1.2	0.2	14.1	4.5
Rochester, MN	82.7	6.3	6.9	0.2	0.0	0.8	3.0
Salem, OR	79.5	1.3	3.0	1.1	1.1	9.7	4.3
Salt Lake City, UT	75.9	3.1	4.7	1.5	2.0	10.3	2.6
San Antonio, TX	75.2	6.7	2.2	0.8	0.1	12.3	2.6
San Diego, CA	63.9	6.8	16.5	0.6	0.4	7.0	4.8
San Francisco, CA	50.3	5.9	33.4	0.4	0.4	5.3	4.1
San Jose, CA	46.6	3.1	32.8	0.7	0.4	11.6	4.7
Santa Rosa, CA	78.7	2.4	5.1	1.4	0.7	8.2	3.6
Savannah, GA	40.8	54.1	2.4	0.3	0.1	0.7	1.7
Seattle, WA	69.9	7.8	14.4	0.8	0.3	1.6	5.2
Sioux Falls, SD	86.4	4.5	2.2	2.9	0.0	2.4	1.6
Spokane, WA	87.1	2.6	2.9	1.8	0.3	1.2	4.1
Springfield, MO	88.9	4.0	2.1	0.7	0.2	0.9	3.2
Tallahassee, FL	57.2	34.8	3.8	0.4	0.0	1.3	2.5
Tampa, FL	63.6	26.4	3.5	1.1	0.1	2.6	2.9
Topeka, KS	75.8	11.1	1.6	1.3	0.0	4.5	5.8
Tulsa, OK	67.0	15.3	2.4	4.3	0.1	4.2	6.6
Virginia Beach, VA	68.4	19.2	6.5	0.3	0.1	1.2	4.4
Washington, DC	39.9	50.3	3.5	0.3	0.0	3.7	2.2
Wichita, KS	74.9	10.9	5.0	1.0	0.0	3.6	4.6
Wilmington, NC	75.3	20.1	1.6	0.3	0.0	1.6	1.2
Worcester, MA	74.3	11.4	6.1	0.3	0.0	3.9	3.9
U.S.	74.0	12.6	4.9	0.8	0.2	4.7	2.8

Note: (1) Alone is defined as not being in combination with one or more other races; (2) American Indian and Alaska Native; (3) Native Hawaiian and Other Pacific Islander
Source: U.S. Census Bureau, 2010-2012 American Community Survey 3-Year Estimates

Race: Metro Area

Metro Area	White Alone[1] (%)	Black Alone[1] (%)	Asian Alone[1] (%)	AIAN[2] Alone[1] (%)	NHOPI[3] Alone[1] (%)	Other Race Alone[1] (%)	Two or More Races (%)
Abilene, TX	83.7	8.1	1.5	0.4	0.0	3.7	2.6
Albuquerque, NM	69.6	2.7	1.8	5.6	0.1	16.4	3.7
Anchorage, AK	70.7	4.8	6.7	6.5	1.7	1.2	8.6
Ann Arbor, MI	74.4	12.2	7.9	0.3	0.0	0.9	4.2
Athens, GA	73.9	19.3	3.2	0.2	0.0	1.2	2.2
Atlanta, GA	56.2	32.7	5.0	0.3	0.0	3.8	2.1
Austin, TX	77.3	7.4	4.9	0.5	0.1	7.2	2.7
Baltimore, MD	62.2	28.7	4.7	0.2	0.0	1.5	2.5
Billings, MT	90.8	0.6	0.9	3.9	0.1	1.6	2.2
Boise City, ID	91.8	0.8	1.9	0.7	0.1	1.8	2.8
Boston, MA	78.7	7.7	6.7	0.2	0.0	3.9	2.8
Boulder, CO	88.0	1.0	4.0	0.3	0.0	3.6	3.0
Cape Coral, FL	84.1	8.2	1.6	0.4	0.0	4.1	1.6
Cedar Rapids, IA	91.6	3.7	1.6	0.3	0.0	0.8	2.1
Charleston, SC	67.0	27.4	1.6	0.4	0.1	1.2	2.3
Charlotte, NC	67.1	23.9	3.3	0.4	0.1	2.8	2.3
Chicago, IL	66.6	17.2	5.8	0.3	0.0	8.1	2.1
Cincinnati, OH	83.1	12.1	2.0	0.2	0.0	0.8	1.8
Clarksville, TN	74.2	18.0	1.7	0.8	0.4	1.3	3.6
Colorado Spgs, CO	82.1	5.9	2.5	0.6	0.3	3.4	5.1
Columbia, MO	83.3	8.9	3.7	0.2	0.0	0.9	3.0
Columbus, OH	77.7	14.9	3.2	0.2	0.0	1.3	2.7
Dallas, TX	69.2	15.0	5.5	0.5	0.1	7.1	2.6
Davenport, IA	86.2	7.1	1.6	0.3	0.0	2.2	2.6
Denver, CO	81.1	5.6	3.7	0.9	0.1	5.3	3.4
Des Moines, IA	87.5	4.7	3.2	0.2	0.1	2.0	2.3
Durham, NC	62.1	26.8	4.4	0.4	0.0	3.8	2.4
El Paso, TX	80.4	3.3	1.1	0.5	0.1	12.4	2.2
Erie, PA	88.3	7.1	1.2	0.3	0.0	0.9	2.2
Eugene, OR	88.9	0.9	2.5	1.1	0.2	2.1	4.2
Fargo, ND	91.5	2.2	1.9	1.2	0.0	0.7	2.4
Fayetteville, NC	51.4	35.8	2.1	2.1	0.3	2.9	5.3
Ft. Collins, CO	90.8	0.9	1.9	0.6	0.1	2.8	2.9
Ft. Wayne, IN	82.6	10.2	2.4	0.3	0.1	1.8	2.6
Ft. Worth, TX	69.2	15.0	5.5	0.5	0.1	7.1	2.6
Gainesville, FL	71.3	19.4	5.1	0.3	0.1	1.0	2.8
Grand Rapids, MI	85.0	8.0	1.9	0.4	0.0	1.8	2.9
Green Bay, WI	90.4	1.9	2.3	2.0	0.0	1.0	2.5
Greensboro, NC	66.0	25.6	3.1	0.4	0.0	2.6	2.2
Honolulu, HI	21.1	2.2	43.7	0.2	9.6	0.9	22.3
Houston, TX	65.7	17.2	6.7	0.4	0.1	7.9	2.0
Huntsville, AL	71.6	22.0	2.1	0.7	0.1	1.2	2.5
Indianapolis, IN	77.5	14.9	2.2	0.2	0.0	2.7	2.4
Jacksonville, FL	70.8	21.6	3.5	0.3	0.1	1.0	2.8
Kansas City, MO	79.4	12.4	2.4	0.5	0.1	2.3	2.8
Lafayette, LA	69.4	26.3	1.4	0.3	0.0	0.5	2.0
Las Vegas, NV	66.6	10.5	8.8	0.6	0.7	8.4	4.4
Lexington, KY	81.8	10.8	2.4	0.2	0.0	2.5	2.3
Lincoln, NE	89.2	3.5	3.6	0.6	0.1	0.5	2.6
Little Rock, AR	73.1	22.6	1.6	0.5	0.0	0.8	1.5
Los Angeles, CA	55.7	6.8	14.9	0.4	0.3	18.2	3.7
Louisville, KY	81.4	13.7	1.6	0.1	0.0	0.9	2.2
Lubbock, TX	79.2	7.2	2.1	0.4	0.1	8.0	3.0
Madison, WI	87.1	4.7	4.3	0.3	0.0	1.2	2.4

Table continued on next page.

Metro Area	White Alone[1] (%)	Black Alone[1] (%)	Asian Alone[1] (%)	AIAN[2] Alone[1] (%)	NHOPI[3] Alone[1] (%)	Other Race Alone[1] (%)	Two or More Races (%)
Manchester, NH	91.1	2.1	3.3	0.2	0.0	1.3	2.0
McAllen, TX	90.8	0.6	1.0	0.4	0.0	6.5	0.7
Miami, FL	71.8	21.1	2.3	0.2	0.0	2.7	1.8
Midland, TX	85.1	6.7	1.6	0.4	0.0	4.7	1.5
Minneapolis, MN	81.5	7.5	5.8	0.6	0.0	1.6	2.9
Montgomery, AL	53.0	42.8	1.6	0.3	0.0	0.9	1.4
Nashville, TN	77.5	15.4	2.3	0.3	0.0	2.5	1.9
New Orleans, LA	58.4	34.3	2.8	0.4	0.1	2.2	1.7
New York, NY	59.3	17.4	10.1	0.3	0.0	10.1	2.8
Oklahoma City, OK	74.2	10.1	2.9	3.6	0.1	2.9	6.3
Omaha, NE	84.3	7.7	2.1	0.6	0.1	2.6	2.5
Orlando, FL	72.4	16.2	4.0	0.3	0.1	4.2	2.9
Oxnard, CA	76.3	1.9	6.9	0.7	0.2	10.0	4.1
Peoria, IL	86.0	9.3	1.9	0.2	0.0	0.7	1.8
Philadelphia, PA	68.5	20.8	5.1	0.2	0.1	3.1	2.3
Phoenix, AZ	80.7	5.1	3.3	2.2	0.2	5.7	2.7
Pittsburgh, PA	87.6	8.2	1.8	0.1	0.0	0.3	1.9
Portland, OR	81.9	2.9	5.9	0.8	0.5	4.2	3.8
Providence, RI	84.1	5.3	2.7	0.3	0.0	4.9	2.6
Provo, UT	91.6	0.6	1.3	0.6	0.9	2.6	2.4
Raleigh, NC	69.9	20.3	4.5	0.3	0.0	2.7	2.2
Reno, NV	81.5	2.4	5.1	1.6	0.6	5.3	3.4
Richmond, VA	63.0	30.0	3.1	0.4	0.0	1.1	2.3
Riverside, CA	64.9	7.4	6.2	1.0	0.3	16.0	4.2
Rochester, MN	88.9	3.9	4.3	0.1	0.0	0.6	2.2
Salem, OR	80.5	0.9	2.0	1.4	0.6	10.5	4.1
Salt Lake City, UT	85.6	1.6	3.2	0.8	1.4	4.8	2.6
San Antonio, TX	77.7	6.4	2.1	0.7	0.1	10.1	2.9
San Diego, CA	71.1	5.1	11.1	0.7	0.4	6.9	4.7
San Francisco, CA	55.0	8.2	23.5	0.5	0.8	7.0	5.1
San Jose, CA	51.4	2.6	31.7	0.6	0.4	9.0	4.4
Santa Rosa, CA	80.2	1.6	4.1	1.3	0.4	8.8	3.6
Savannah, GA	60.8	33.9	2.2	0.3	0.1	1.0	1.7
Seattle, WA	73.0	5.6	11.6	0.9	0.8	2.6	5.5
Sioux Falls, SD	89.9	3.2	1.6	2.1	0.0	1.7	1.5
Spokane, WA	89.1	1.9	2.4	1.4	0.3	1.2	3.7
Springfield, MO	93.2	2.1	1.1	0.5	0.1	0.5	2.4
Tallahassee, FL	61.0	32.5	2.4	0.4	0.0	1.7	2.1
Tampa, FL	79.9	11.9	2.9	0.5	0.1	2.2	2.5
Topeka, KS	84.5	6.3	1.0	1.4	0.0	2.6	4.1
Tulsa, OK	72.9	8.2	1.8	6.9	0.1	2.4	7.7
Virginia Beach, VA	60.2	31.1	3.7	0.3	0.1	1.1	3.5
Washington, DC	55.8	25.6	9.4	0.4	0.0	5.3	3.6
Wichita, KS	81.8	7.5	3.4	0.9	0.0	2.6	3.9
Wilmington, NC	81.3	13.9	0.9	0.4	0.1	1.5	1.9
Worcester, MA	85.8	4.1	4.1	0.2	0.0	3.1	2.6
U.S.	74.0	12.6	4.9	0.8	0.2	4.7	2.8

Note: (1) Figures cover the Metropolitan Statistical Area (MSA)—see Appendix B for areas included; (1) Alone is defined as not being in combination with one or more other races; (2) American Indian and Alaska Native; (3) Native Hawaiian and Other Pacific Islander
Source: U.S. Census Bureau, 2010-2012 American Community Survey 3-Year Estimates

Hispanic Origin: City

City	Hispanic or Latino (%)	Mexican (%)	Puerto Rican (%)	Cuban (%)	Other Hispanic or Latino (%)
Abilene, TX	25.1	22.4	0.5	0.1	2.1
Albuquerque, NM	47.0	24.3	0.4	0.6	21.7
Anchorage, AK	7.9	4.4	1.2	0.2	2.1
Ann Arbor, MI	4.8	2.5	0.2	0.1	2.0
Athens, GA	10.6	7.3	0.3	0.4	2.6
Atlanta, GA	5.7	3.3	0.6	0.2	1.5
Austin, TX	35.0	29.9	0.5	0.5	4.1
Baltimore, MD	4.3	1.3	0.6	0.2	2.3
Billings, MT	5.2	3.8	0.3	0.0	1.1
Boise City, ID	7.5	6.2	0.1	0.1	1.1
Boston, MA	17.7	1.1	5.0	0.4	11.2
Boulder, CO	9.1	6.3	0.2	0.4	2.1
Cape Coral, FL	18.2	1.8	5.3	5.9	5.3
Cedar Rapids, IA	3.6	2.7	0.3	0.0	0.5
Charleston, SC	3.0	1.0	1.0	0.4	0.6
Charlotte, NC	13.2	5.4	1.1	0.4	6.4
Chicago, IL	28.8	21.5	3.8	0.3	3.2
Cincinnati, OH	2.9	1.3	0.3	0.1	1.2
Clarksville, TN	9.7	5.0	2.5	0.1	2.1
Colorado Spgs, CO	16.5	11.1	1.1	0.2	4.2
Columbia, MO	3.6	1.9	0.4	0.4	0.9
Columbus, OH	5.6	3.2	0.7	0.1	1.6
Dallas, TX	42.2	37.5	0.3	0.2	4.3
Davenport, IA	7.9	7.0	0.3	0.1	0.6
Denver, CO	31.7	27.2	0.6	0.1	3.7
Des Moines, IA	11.9	9.7	0.3	0.0	1.9
Durham, NC	13.6	8.0	0.8	0.3	4.6
El Paso, TX	80.0	76.2	1.0	0.3	2.5
Erie, PA	6.7	1.4	4.3	0.1	0.9
Eugene, OR	7.8	6.4	0.3	0.0	1.2
Fargo, ND	2.8	2.0	0.2	0.1	0.5
Fayetteville, NC	10.6	4.2	3.5	0.2	2.7
Ft. Collins, CO	10.5	7.3	0.8	0.2	2.3
Ft. Wayne, IN	7.9	6.2	0.4	0.1	1.2
Ft. Worth, TX	33.9	30.6	0.7	0.2	2.5
Gainesville, FL	10.2	1.2	2.1	2.7	4.1
Grand Rapids, MI	15.6	9.8	1.7	0.3	3.8
Green Bay, WI	12.2	9.6	1.0	0.1	1.6
Greensboro, NC	7.4	4.6	0.6	0.2	2.1
Honolulu, HI	5.6	1.4	1.7	0.1	2.4
Houston, TX	43.9	33.3	0.5	0.3	9.8
Huntsville, AL	6.0	4.0	0.7	0.1	1.2
Indianapolis, IN	9.6	7.3	0.4	0.1	1.9
Jacksonville, FL	8.1	1.8	2.6	1.1	2.6
Kansas City, MO	10.0	7.7	0.4	0.4	1.5
Lafayette, LA	4.4	1.5	0.2	0.2	2.4
Las Vegas, NV	31.8	24.5	1.0	1.1	5.3
Lexington, KY	6.9	5.3	0.3	0.2	1.2
Lincoln, NE	6.4	4.7	0.2	0.1	1.4
Little Rock, AR	5.9	4.1	0.3	0.0	1.5
Los Angeles, CA	48.5	32.7	0.5	0.4	15.0
Louisville, KY	4.6	2.0	0.3	1.4	0.9
Lubbock, TX	33.0	28.5	0.2	0.0	4.3
Madison, WI	6.9	4.6	0.9	0.2	1.1
Manchester, NH	8.5	3.7	2.0	0.1	2.8

Table continued on next page.

City	Hispanic or Latino (%)	Mexican (%)	Puerto Rican (%)	Cuban (%)	Other Hispanic or Latino (%)
McAllen, TX	85.1	80.8	0.3	0.2	3.8
Miami, FL	70.4	2.0	2.9	35.0	30.5
Midland, TX	39.6	37.7	0.0	0.1	1.7
Minneapolis, MN	10.0	6.6	0.5	0.1	2.7
Montgomery, AL	3.7	2.3	0.4	0.1	1.0
Nashville, TN	10.1	6.3	0.5	0.3	2.9
New Orleans, LA	5.3	1.6	0.2	0.4	3.1
New York, NY	28.8	3.9	9.0	0.5	15.4
Oklahoma City, OK	17.7	15.1	0.3	0.1	2.2
Omaha, NE	13.4	10.8	0.4	0.0	2.2
Orlando, FL	26.7	2.9	13.3	1.8	8.7
Oxnard, CA	73.5	69.9	0.4	0.1	3.1
Peoria, IL	5.3	4.5	0.2	0.1	0.6
Philadelphia, PA	12.7	0.9	8.5	0.3	3.0
Phoenix, AZ	39.9	37.0	0.4	0.3	2.2
Pittsburgh, PA	2.6	0.9	0.6	0.2	0.9
Portland, OR	9.9	7.5	0.4	0.3	1.7
Providence, RI	40.2	2.1	8.3	0.4	29.4
Provo, UT	17.2	11.2	0.3	0.2	5.5
Raleigh, NC	11.3	5.2	1.2	0.3	4.6
Reno, NV	25.4	20.3	0.8	0.1	4.2
Richmond, VA	6.3	2.1	0.5	0.1	3.6
Riverside, CA	51.0	45.7	0.5	0.3	4.4
Rochester, MN	5.3	4.2	0.1	0.2	0.8
Salem, OR	20.6	19.0	0.1	0.1	1.5
Salt Lake City, UT	20.9	16.8	0.3	0.0	3.8
San Antonio, TX	63.3	57.4	1.1	0.2	4.6
San Diego, CA	29.5	26.2	0.6	0.2	2.5
San Francisco, CA	15.3	7.4	0.5	0.2	7.1
San Jose, CA	33.3	28.7	0.5	0.2	3.9
Santa Rosa, CA	28.7	24.4	0.5	0.1	3.8
Savannah, GA	5.2	3.1	0.8	0.1	1.3
Seattle, WA	6.5	4.2	0.4	0.2	1.8
Sioux Falls, SD	4.8	2.4	0.1	0.0	2.3
Spokane, WA	5.3	3.8	0.3	0.2	1.1
Springfield, MO	3.9	2.7	0.4	0.0	0.9
Tallahassee, FL	6.4	1.5	1.5	1.2	2.3
Tampa, FL	22.7	2.5	7.2	6.7	6.3
Topeka, KS	13.9	12.3	0.5	0.0	1.0
Tulsa, OK	14.5	12.3	0.4	0.1	1.6
Virginia Beach, VA	6.9	2.1	2.4	0.2	2.3
Washington, DC	9.5	1.5	0.6	0.3	7.2
Wichita, KS	15.5	13.7	0.5	0.1	1.2
Wilmington, NC	5.1	3.2	0.7	0.1	1.1
Worcester, MA	19.9	0.7	12.3	0.1	6.7
U.S.	16.6	10.7	1.6	0.6	3.7

Note: Persons of Hispanic or Latino origin can be of any race
Source: U.S. Census Bureau, 2010-2012 American Community Survey 3-Year Estimates

Hispanic Origin: Metro Area

Metro Area	Hispanic or Latino (%)	Mexican (%)	Puerto Rican (%)	Cuban (%)	Other Hispanic or Latino (%)
Abilene, TX	21.7	19.3	0.4	0.1	1.9
Albuquerque, NM	47.1	23.8	0.4	0.4	22.5
Anchorage, AK	6.9	4.0	1.0	0.2	1.8
Ann Arbor, MI	4.2	2.2	0.4	0.1	1.5
Athens, GA	8.1	5.5	0.4	0.3	2.0
Atlanta, GA	10.5	6.0	0.9	0.4	3.2
Austin, TX	31.7	26.5	0.5	0.4	4.3
Baltimore, MD	4.8	1.3	0.7	0.1	2.6
Billings, MT	4.7	3.6	0.3	0.0	0.8
Boise City, ID	12.7	10.8	0.4	0.1	1.5
Boston, MA	9.3	0.6	2.6	0.2	5.8
Boulder, CO	13.5	10.3	0.3	0.3	2.6
Cape Coral, FL	18.6	5.8	4.3	3.8	4.8
Cedar Rapids, IA	2.5	1.7	0.2	0.0	0.6
Charleston, SC	5.4	3.1	0.8	0.2	1.3
Charlotte, NC	10.0	4.8	0.9	0.3	4.1
Chicago, IL	21.0	16.7	2.1	0.2	2.0
Cincinnati, OH	2.7	1.4	0.3	0.1	0.9
Clarksville, TN	7.2	3.9	1.7	0.0	1.5
Colorado Spgs, CO	15.0	9.6	1.1	0.2	4.1
Columbia, MO	3.0	1.6	0.3	0.3	0.8
Columbus, OH	3.7	2.1	0.5	0.1	1.0
Dallas, TX	27.8	23.8	0.5	0.2	3.3
Davenport, IA	7.9	7.0	0.4	0.1	0.4
Denver, CO	22.7	18.2	0.5	0.1	3.8
Des Moines, IA	6.8	5.3	0.2	0.1	1.3
Durham, NC	11.3	7.0	0.7	0.2	3.4
El Paso, TX	81.7	78.1	0.9	0.2	2.4
Erie, PA	3.5	0.9	1.9	0.1	0.6
Eugene, OR	7.6	6.4	0.3	0.0	1.0
Fargo, ND	2.6	1.9	0.1	0.0	0.4
Fayetteville, NC	10.2	4.1	3.4	0.3	2.4
Ft. Collins, CO	10.7	7.6	0.5	0.1	2.5
Ft. Wayne, IN	6.0	4.7	0.4	0.1	0.8
Ft. Worth, TX	27.8	23.8	0.5	0.2	3.3
Gainesville, FL	8.4	1.3	2.0	2.0	3.2
Grand Rapids, MI	8.6	5.7	0.9	0.2	1.8
Green Bay, WI	6.4	4.7	0.4	0.1	1.1
Greensboro, NC	7.7	5.4	0.7	0.2	1.4
Honolulu, HI	8.5	2.4	2.9	0.1	3.1
Houston, TX	35.7	27.7	0.5	0.3	7.1
Huntsville, AL	4.9	3.4	0.6	0.1	0.8
Indianapolis, IN	6.3	4.6	0.3	0.1	1.3
Jacksonville, FL	7.2	1.6	2.3	0.9	2.3
Kansas City, MO	8.3	6.4	0.3	0.2	1.4
Lafayette, LA	3.7	1.7	0.1	0.1	1.7
Las Vegas, NV	29.5	22.5	1.0	1.1	4.9
Lexington, KY	5.9	4.6	0.3	0.1	0.9
Lincoln, NE	5.8	4.3	0.2	0.1	1.2
Little Rock, AR	4.9	3.7	0.2	0.0	1.0
Los Angeles, CA	44.7	34.9	0.5	0.4	8.9
Louisville, KY	4.1	2.2	0.3	0.7	0.8
Lubbock, TX	33.0	28.8	0.2	0.0	4.0
Madison, WI	5.5	3.9	0.6	0.1	0.9
Manchester, NH	5.5	1.9	1.5	0.1	2.0

Table continued on next page.

Metro Area	Hispanic or Latino (%)	Mexican (%)	Puerto Rican (%)	Cuban (%)	Other Hispanic or Latino (%)
McAllen, TX	90.8	88.4	0.2	0.1	2.0
Miami, FL	41.9	2.4	3.7	18.1	17.7
Midland, TX	38.8	36.8	0.1	0.1	1.8
Minneapolis, MN	5.5	3.8	0.3	0.1	1.3
Montgomery, AL	3.1	2.0	0.3	0.1	0.7
Nashville, TN	6.7	4.2	0.5	0.2	1.8
New Orleans, LA	8.1	2.0	0.5	0.5	5.0
New York, NY	23.3	3.0	6.4	0.7	13.1
Oklahoma City, OK	11.7	9.8	0.3	0.1	1.5
Omaha, NE	9.2	7.3	0.3	0.0	1.5
Orlando, FL	26.1	3.2	13.1	2.0	7.7
Oxnard, CA	40.8	36.2	0.5	0.2	4.0
Peoria, IL	2.9	2.3	0.2	0.0	0.4
Philadelphia, PA	8.1	1.7	4.2	0.2	2.0
Phoenix, AZ	29.7	26.8	0.5	0.2	2.2
Pittsburgh, PA	1.4	0.5	0.4	0.1	0.4
Portland, OR	11.0	8.9	0.3	0.2	1.7
Providence, RI	10.6	0.8	3.4	0.1	6.2
Provo, UT	10.8	7.1	0.2	0.1	3.4
Raleigh, NC	10.3	6.0	1.0	0.3	3.0
Reno, NV	22.5	18.2	0.5	0.2	3.6
Richmond, VA	5.1	1.7	0.8	0.1	2.5
Riverside, CA	47.9	42.3	0.6	0.3	4.6
Rochester, MN	4.2	3.2	0.2	0.1	0.6
Salem, OR	22.3	20.3	0.2	0.0	1.7
Salt Lake City, UT	16.9	12.8	0.3	0.1	3.6
San Antonio, TX	54.3	48.9	1.0	0.2	4.2
San Diego, CA	32.4	29.1	0.7	0.2	2.5
San Francisco, CA	21.8	14.8	0.6	0.2	6.2
San Jose, CA	27.8	23.5	0.4	0.1	3.7
Santa Rosa, CA	25.2	21.2	0.4	0.2	3.4
Savannah, GA	5.2	3.0	1.0	0.1	1.2
Seattle, WA	9.2	6.8	0.5	0.1	1.8
Sioux Falls, SD	3.5	1.8	0.1	0.0	1.7
Spokane, WA	4.7	3.4	0.3	0.1	0.9
Springfield, MO	2.8	1.9	0.2	0.0	0.7
Tallahassee, FL	6.1	2.1	1.2	1.1	1.7
Tampa, FL	16.7	3.5	5.3	3.3	4.5
Topeka, KS	9.1	7.9	0.4	0.0	0.7
Tulsa, OK	8.6	7.1	0.3	0.1	1.1
Virginia Beach, VA	5.6	1.8	1.7	0.2	1.9
Washington, DC	14.2	2.2	0.9	0.3	10.8
Wichita, KS	11.8	10.4	0.4	0.1	0.9
Wilmington, NC	5.4	3.6	0.6	0.1	1.1
Worcester, MA	9.7	0.6	5.3	0.1	3.7
U.S.	16.6	10.7	1.6	0.6	3.7

Note: Persons of Hispanic or Latino origin can be of any race; Figures cover the Metropolitan Statistical Area (MSA)—see Appendix B for areas included
Source: U.S. Census Bureau, 2010-2012 American Community Survey 3-Year Estimates

Age: City

City	Percent of Population							
	Under Age 5	Age 5–19	Age 20–34	Age 35–44	Age 45–54	Age 55–64	Age 65–74	Age 75–84
Abilene, TX	7.4	19.1	27.4	11.2	12.3	10.2	6.4	4.2
Albuquerque, NM	6.9	19.6	23.0	12.8	13.7	11.7	6.7	4.0
Anchorage, AK	7.5	20.8	24.5	13.1	14.7	11.6	4.8	2.3
Ann Arbor, MI	4.1	19.3	38.0	9.8	9.3	9.6	5.3	3.2
Athens, GA	5.9	20.8	37.9	10.2	8.7	7.8	4.9	2.8
Atlanta, GA	6.4	16.4	30.4	15.0	12.2	9.8	5.5	2.8
Austin, TX	7.1	18.3	31.4	15.1	11.9	9.0	4.0	2.2
Baltimore, MD	6.7	18.0	26.2	12.1	13.8	11.4	6.3	3.8
Billings, MT	7.0	18.6	21.5	11.8	13.3	13.0	7.4	4.9
Boise City, ID	6.3	18.2	23.8	13.4	14.1	12.2	6.7	3.4
Boston, MA	5.3	16.8	34.7	12.3	11.3	9.2	5.4	3.3
Boulder, CO	4.2	19.4	35.9	11.4	10.4	9.5	4.9	2.7
Cape Coral, FL	5.9	19.9	14.6	13.1	14.5	14.0	10.4	5.2
Cedar Rapids, IA	7.1	19.5	23.2	12.6	12.9	11.8	6.1	4.6
Charleston, SC	5.7	16.1	30.7	12.3	11.8	11.2	6.9	3.8
Charlotte, NC	7.6	20.1	24.8	15.5	13.3	9.9	4.9	2.7
Chicago, IL	7.0	18.7	27.2	14.1	12.5	10.1	5.7	3.3
Cincinnati, OH	7.2	19.0	27.4	11.3	13.1	11.1	5.8	3.5
Clarksville, TN	9.2	21.8	29.9	13.1	11.0	7.7	4.3	2.2
Colorado Spgs, CO	7.1	20.3	23.0	12.7	14.4	11.4	6.1	3.4
Columbia, MO	6.2	20.6	36.1	9.9	10.1	8.3	4.5	2.9
Columbus, OH	7.7	18.8	29.2	13.6	12.2	9.8	4.9	2.7
Dallas, TX	8.3	20.4	26.4	13.9	12.5	9.4	5.1	2.8
Davenport, IA	6.9	20.1	23.0	12.3	12.8	12.4	6.4	3.9
Denver, CO	7.3	16.6	28.4	15.1	11.8	10.5	5.5	3.2
Des Moines, IA	8.0	20.0	24.3	13.0	13.2	10.5	5.7	3.4
Durham, NC	7.7	18.9	28.1	13.9	12.0	10.1	5.1	2.7
El Paso, TX	7.8	23.9	21.6	12.7	12.8	10.0	6.0	3.9
Erie, PA	7.1	20.5	23.7	11.7	12.8	11.1	6.2	4.4
Eugene, OR	4.8	17.9	28.6	11.7	11.5	12.2	6.9	4.2
Fargo, ND	6.1	17.5	33.1	11.2	11.6	10.4	4.7	3.9
Fayetteville, NC	8.6	19.9	28.3	11.6	11.9	9.5	5.7	3.3
Ft. Collins, CO	6.0	19.8	32.7	11.5	11.5	9.8	4.7	2.5
Ft. Wayne, IN	7.7	21.6	21.0	12.5	13.2	11.5	6.2	4.2
Ft. Worth, TX	8.9	23.1	23.3	14.6	12.7	9.1	4.6	2.6
Gainesville, FL	4.3	18.1	44.0	8.1	7.9	9.2	3.9	3.1
Grand Rapids, MI	7.7	21.1	27.7	11.7	11.2	9.4	4.8	3.9
Green Bay, WI	7.6	20.1	24.1	12.1	13.4	10.9	5.5	3.9
Greensboro, NC	6.5	19.8	24.9	13.0	12.7	11.2	6.0	4.3
Honolulu, HI	5.2	14.8	22.9	12.3	13.7	13.1	8.2	6.2
Houston, TX	7.9	20.5	25.7	14.0	12.8	9.8	5.2	2.8
Huntsville, AL	6.1	18.8	23.0	12.1	14.9	11.1	7.6	4.4
Indianapolis, IN	7.6	20.1	23.9	13.0	13.7	10.9	5.6	3.4
Jacksonville, FL	7.0	19.3	23.0	13.3	14.4	11.7	6.4	3.4
Kansas City, MO	7.3	19.2	23.4	13.4	13.9	11.6	6.0	3.6
Lafayette, LA	5.3	19.9	25.6	12.3	13.9	10.5	6.8	4.0
Las Vegas, NV	7.0	20.4	20.5	14.3	13.7	11.1	7.5	4.1
Lexington, KY	6.4	18.3	27.1	13.3	13.1	11.2	5.9	3.4
Lincoln, NE	7.1	19.7	27.4	11.9	12.1	10.9	5.6	3.6
Little Rock, AR	7.4	19.2	23.3	13.0	13.0	12.3	6.3	3.7
Los Angeles, CA	6.6	19.1	25.3	14.8	13.3	10.2	5.7	3.4
Louisville, KY	6.8	19.3	21.1	12.8	14.6	12.6	6.7	4.2
Lubbock, TX	7.4	21.1	29.0	10.6	11.4	9.6	5.9	3.9
Madison, WI	6.0	17.1	34.6	11.7	11.1	10.0	4.9	3.1

Table continued on next page.

City	Percent of Population							
	Under Age 5	Age 5–19	Age 20–34	Age 35–44	Age 45–54	Age 55–64	Age 65–74	Age 75–84
Manchester, NH	6.3	17.7	23.5	14.5	14.2	11.7	6.7	3.3
McAllen, TX	7.7	23.8	21.3	13.7	13.0	9.8	6.2	3.1
Miami, FL	6.1	14.8	22.9	15.0	14.2	11.4	7.6	5.7
Midland, TX	8.2	21.8	23.6	11.6	12.6	10.9	5.5	4.3
Minneapolis, MN	7.0	17.1	32.0	13.3	12.1	10.1	4.6	2.5
Montgomery, AL	7.3	21.3	23.0	12.6	12.9	11.1	6.5	3.9
Nashville, TN	7.1	17.6	27.2	13.7	13.2	10.9	5.7	3.3
New Orleans, LA	6.6	17.8	26.0	12.3	13.7	12.5	6.3	3.3
New York, NY	6.4	17.6	25.0	14.0	13.4	11.1	6.7	3.9
Oklahoma City, OK	8.0	19.6	24.1	12.6	13.0	11.4	6.1	3.6
Omaha, NE	7.5	20.5	23.9	12.0	13.4	11.3	5.8	3.7
Orlando, FL	7.3	16.9	29.7	14.9	12.9	8.7	5.1	3.1
Oxnard, CA	8.7	23.5	24.6	13.4	12.3	8.9	4.7	2.7
Peoria, IL	7.1	21.3	23.4	11.8	12.1	11.2	6.6	4.4
Philadelphia, PA	6.8	19.1	26.1	12.2	12.7	10.9	6.3	4.0
Phoenix, AZ	7.9	22.7	22.9	14.5	13.3	10.0	5.1	2.6
Pittsburgh, PA	5.0	16.7	30.7	10.1	11.8	11.6	6.8	4.5
Portland, OR	6.0	15.3	26.8	16.2	12.9	12.0	5.8	3.1
Providence, RI	6.1	23.3	30.5	11.8	11.0	8.8	4.3	2.6
Provo, UT	8.6	22.8	44.7	7.0	5.9	5.1	2.9	1.8
Raleigh, NC	7.2	19.9	27.9	15.3	12.3	9.0	4.7	2.6
Reno, NV	6.9	19.5	24.9	12.5	13.0	11.2	6.8	3.6
Richmond, VA	6.5	17.1	30.2	11.5	12.3	11.3	5.8	3.5
Riverside, CA	7.2	23.7	25.2	12.6	13.0	8.9	5.1	2.8
Rochester, MN	7.4	19.3	23.0	12.5	13.8	10.8	6.6	4.3
Salem, OR	7.7	19.9	22.6	12.2	13.2	11.6	7.1	3.8
Salt Lake City, UT	7.7	18.1	31.2	13.4	10.7	9.4	5.0	3.0
San Antonio, TX	7.4	22.2	23.4	13.0	13.1	10.2	5.9	3.4
San Diego, CA	6.3	18.3	27.0	13.9	13.2	10.2	5.8	3.5
San Francisco, CA	4.4	11.0	28.4	16.5	13.7	12.2	6.9	4.7
San Jose, CA	7.1	19.6	22.3	15.5	14.5	10.5	5.9	3.3
Santa Rosa, CA	6.6	19.9	20.8	12.8	14.3	12.4	6.5	4.3
Savannah, GA	7.1	19.7	28.2	10.8	12.0	10.4	6.1	3.5
Seattle, WA	5.3	13.1	29.8	15.9	13.0	11.8	6.0	3.2
Sioux Falls, SD	8.4	18.4	24.8	12.5	13.2	11.4	5.7	3.9
Spokane, WA	7.1	18.1	24.3	12.3	12.8	11.8	6.7	4.8
Springfield, MO	6.2	16.8	29.6	10.8	11.9	10.3	6.8	4.8
Tallahassee, FL	5.1	20.5	38.4	10.0	9.6	8.3	4.2	2.5
Tampa, FL	6.4	19.7	24.5	13.7	14.3	10.5	5.8	3.7
Topeka, KS	7.5	20.0	21.9	11.5	13.0	12.0	6.8	5.1
Tulsa, OK	7.3	20.0	22.9	12.2	13.3	11.7	6.5	4.1
Virginia Beach, VA	6.6	19.6	24.0	13.3	14.5	11.1	6.1	3.5
Washington, DC	5.8	15.0	31.4	13.4	12.3	10.7	6.2	3.5
Wichita, KS	8.1	20.8	22.1	12.4	13.5	11.5	6.2	3.7
Wilmington, NC	5.4	18.0	27.6	11.1	12.7	11.6	7.4	4.3
Worcester, MA	7.0	19.6	25.4	12.3	12.8	10.5	6.1	3.8
U.S.	6.4	20.1	20.5	13.1	14.3	12.2	7.3	4.2

Source: U.S. Census Bureau, 2010-2012 American Community Survey 3-Year Estimates

Age: Metro Area

Metro Area	Under Age 5	Age 5–19	Age 20–34	Age 35–44	Age 45–54	Age 55–64	Age 65–74	Age 75–84
				Percent of Population				
Abilene, TX	6.9	19.9	23.6	11.5	13.0	11.3	7.4	4.7
Albuquerque, NM	6.7	20.3	21.0	12.6	14.1	12.5	7.3	3.9
Anchorage, AK	7.5	21.4	23.2	13.2	14.9	11.8	5.0	2.3
Ann Arbor, MI	5.4	20.3	26.3	12.4	13.4	11.6	6.1	3.0
Athens, GA	6.0	21.1	29.3	11.4	11.6	10.1	6.2	3.0
Atlanta, GA	7.0	21.9	20.9	15.5	14.6	10.8	5.7	2.7
Austin, TX	7.3	20.8	25.3	15.2	13.1	10.0	5.0	2.5
Baltimore, MD	6.2	19.4	20.8	13.0	15.3	12.4	7.0	4.1
Billings, MT	6.5	19.1	19.4	12.0	14.6	13.6	7.8	4.7
Boise City, ID	7.4	22.7	20.6	13.5	13.3	11.2	6.5	3.3
Boston, MA	5.6	18.8	21.1	13.5	15.3	12.3	7.0	4.3
Boulder, CO	5.4	19.9	23.7	13.6	14.5	12.3	6.1	3.0
Cape Coral, FL	5.2	16.3	16.0	11.2	13.0	14.1	13.6	7.5
Cedar Rapids, IA	6.4	20.6	19.7	12.9	14.5	12.1	7.2	4.7
Charleston, SC	6.8	19.1	23.2	13.0	13.8	12.0	7.2	3.4
Charlotte, NC	7.0	21.3	20.8	15.5	14.3	10.9	6.0	3.1
Chicago, IL	6.6	20.9	21.0	13.8	14.4	11.5	6.4	3.6
Cincinnati, OH	6.7	20.8	19.7	13.1	15.0	12.3	6.8	3.9
Clarksville, TN	8.6	21.3	26.3	12.8	12.0	9.4	5.6	3.0
Colorado Spgs, CO	7.0	21.4	22.2	12.8	14.6	11.5	6.1	3.2
Columbia, MO	6.1	20.4	30.1	11.0	12.2	10.3	5.3	3.1
Columbus, OH	6.8	20.4	22.2	14.0	14.2	11.4	6.1	3.4
Dallas, TX	7.6	22.6	21.6	14.8	14.1	10.2	5.4	2.7
Davenport, IA	6.4	19.6	18.7	12.1	14.3	13.3	8.2	4.9
Denver, CO	6.9	20.0	21.7	14.7	14.4	11.7	6.0	3.1
Des Moines, IA	7.5	20.8	21.4	13.8	13.8	11.3	6.2	3.6
Durham, NC	6.4	19.2	23.8	13.5	13.4	11.8	6.7	3.5
El Paso, TX	8.1	25.0	21.7	13.0	12.4	9.5	5.6	3.5
Erie, PA	5.9	20.2	19.9	11.8	14.4	13.2	7.5	4.9
Eugene, OR	5.1	18.0	22.4	11.4	13.2	14.4	8.5	5.0
Fargo, ND	6.8	19.6	28.2	11.9	12.3	10.6	5.3	3.7
Fayetteville, NC	8.6	21.5	25.5	12.5	12.6	9.9	5.5	2.8
Ft. Collins, CO	5.7	19.1	24.4	12.1	13.7	12.8	7.0	3.7
Ft. Wayne, IN	7.2	21.9	19.5	12.7	14.0	12.2	6.7	4.1
Ft. Worth, TX	7.6	22.6	21.6	14.8	14.1	10.2	5.4	2.7
Gainesville, FL	5.3	18.4	31.2	10.3	11.7	11.5	6.3	3.6
Grand Rapids, MI	7.0	21.4	20.9	12.6	14.5	11.8	6.4	3.8
Green Bay, WI	6.6	20.5	19.5	12.9	15.4	12.4	6.8	4.1
Greensboro, NC	6.1	20.2	19.8	13.6	14.4	12.4	7.5	4.5
Honolulu, HI	6.4	18.0	22.4	12.9	13.4	12.1	7.5	4.8
Houston, TX	7.8	22.6	21.9	14.4	13.8	10.6	5.3	2.6
Huntsville, AL	6.2	19.9	20.3	13.3	15.9	11.9	7.2	3.8
Indianapolis, IN	7.2	21.5	20.5	13.8	14.6	11.3	6.2	3.5
Jacksonville, FL	6.4	19.8	20.5	13.3	14.9	12.6	7.3	3.8
Kansas City, MO	7.0	20.7	20.0	13.3	14.7	12.0	6.7	3.8
Lafayette, LA	7.2	20.3	23.7	12.6	14.1	11.3	6.1	3.4
Las Vegas, NV	7.0	20.2	21.6	14.5	13.5	11.3	7.3	3.4
Lexington, KY	6.5	19.3	23.8	13.6	13.8	11.7	6.4	3.6
Lincoln, NE	6.9	20.2	25.5	11.9	12.7	11.4	5.9	3.7
Little Rock, AR	6.8	20.1	21.9	13.1	13.7	11.9	7.1	4.0
Los Angeles, CA	6.5	20.6	22.5	14.3	14.0	10.8	6.1	3.6
Louisville, KY	6.4	19.8	19.6	13.3	15.0	12.8	7.3	4.2
Lubbock, TX	7.1	21.6	26.9	11.0	11.9	10.1	6.1	3.8
Madison, WI	6.1	18.8	24.6	13.0	14.2	12.1	6.1	3.6

Table continued on next page.

Metro Area	Percent of Population							
	Under Age 5	Age 5–19	Age 20–34	Age 35–44	Age 45–54	Age 55–64	Age 65–74	Age 75–84
Manchester, NH	5.8	19.8	18.3	14.0	16.9	12.8	6.8	3.8
McAllen, TX	9.6	28.2	21.2	13.2	10.4	7.9	5.3	3.2
Miami, FL	5.7	18.0	19.4	13.9	14.9	11.8	8.1	5.5
Midland, TX	8.2	22.1	22.3	12.0	13.5	11.1	5.5	4.0
Minneapolis, MN	6.8	20.4	21.1	13.6	15.2	11.7	6.0	3.4
Montgomery, AL	6.8	20.9	21.3	13.2	14.0	11.6	7.0	3.9
Nashville, TN	6.8	20.1	21.8	14.2	14.5	11.6	6.4	3.3
New Orleans, LA	6.6	19.1	21.6	12.6	14.7	12.8	7.0	3.8
New York, NY	6.2	19.0	21.2	13.8	14.7	11.8	7.0	4.3
Oklahoma City, OK	7.2	20.4	22.7	12.5	13.5	11.5	6.7	3.8
Omaha, NE	7.6	21.2	21.6	12.9	14.0	11.5	6.1	3.5
Orlando, FL	6.0	20.0	22.0	13.8	14.3	11.2	7.1	4.0
Oxnard, CA	6.6	21.6	19.9	13.2	14.8	11.7	6.6	3.8
Peoria, IL	6.5	19.9	19.1	12.2	14.1	13.0	7.8	5.1
Philadelphia, PA	6.1	19.9	20.3	12.9	15.1	12.2	7.0	4.4
Phoenix, AZ	7.2	21.6	21.2	13.6	13.0	10.8	7.2	4.0
Pittsburgh, PA	5.1	17.5	18.4	12.0	15.4	14.3	8.5	6.0
Portland, OR	6.4	19.4	21.4	14.5	14.0	12.6	6.6	3.4
Providence, RI	5.4	19.2	19.6	13.0	15.4	12.7	7.4	4.7
Provo, UT	10.9	28.4	27.9	11.3	8.4	6.4	3.8	2.1
Raleigh, NC	7.0	21.6	21.1	15.9	14.5	10.5	5.6	2.7
Reno, NV	6.5	19.4	21.2	13.0	14.2	13.1	7.7	3.6
Richmond, VA	6.1	19.7	20.1	13.6	15.1	12.8	7.1	3.7
Riverside, CA	7.5	24.1	21.2	13.2	13.4	10.1	6.0	3.4
Rochester, MN	7.1	20.3	19.8	12.4	15.1	11.8	7.2	4.3
Salem, OR	7.1	21.7	20.5	12.3	12.6	12.1	7.4	4.2
Salt Lake City, UT	8.6	23.3	24.4	13.4	11.9	9.7	5.0	2.7
San Antonio, TX	7.2	22.3	21.5	13.3	13.5	11.0	6.3	3.5
San Diego, CA	6.6	19.6	24.1	13.4	13.7	11.0	6.1	3.7
San Francisco, CA	5.9	17.4	21.5	14.9	14.8	12.4	7.0	4.0
San Jose, CA	6.9	19.6	21.4	15.4	14.7	10.7	6.2	3.6
Santa Rosa, CA	5.8	18.8	19.4	12.3	14.8	14.5	7.9	4.3
Savannah, GA	6.9	20.2	23.6	12.8	13.2	11.4	6.8	3.6
Seattle, WA	6.4	18.6	22.2	14.6	14.9	12.1	6.2	3.3
Sioux Falls, SD	7.8	20.5	22.0	13.0	14.0	11.3	5.8	3.8
Spokane, WA	6.3	19.6	21.6	12.1	14.0	12.9	7.2	4.3
Springfield, MO	6.4	19.7	22.1	12.1	13.5	11.8	7.7	4.6
Tallahassee, FL	5.5	19.7	27.9	11.7	12.6	11.8	6.2	3.1
Tampa, FL	5.6	17.7	18.5	12.8	14.8	13.1	9.2	5.8
Topeka, KS	6.7	20.4	18.0	11.6	14.6	13.5	8.0	5.0
Tulsa, OK	7.0	21.0	19.9	12.8	14.0	12.1	7.4	4.1
Virginia Beach, VA	6.5	19.9	23.3	12.5	14.6	11.4	6.7	3.8
Washington, DC	6.7	19.5	22.1	14.8	15.1	11.5	6.0	3.0
Wichita, KS	7.6	21.9	20.3	12.1	14.0	11.8	6.4	4.0
Wilmington, NC	5.4	17.3	19.8	12.5	13.6	14.6	10.4	5.0
Worcester, MA	5.8	20.4	18.5	13.7	16.2	12.5	6.7	4.1
U.S.	6.4	20.1	20.5	13.1	14.3	12.2	7.3	4.2

Note: Figures cover the Metropolitan Statistical Area (MSA)—see Appendix B for areas included
Source: U.S. Census Bureau, 2010-2012 American Community Survey 3-Year Estimates

Segregation

Area	Black/White Index[1]	Black/White Rank[2]	Asian/White Index[1]	Asian/White Rank[2]	Hispanic/White Index[1]	Hispanic/White Rank[2]
Abilene, TX	n/a	n/a	n/a	n/a	n/a	n/a
Albuquerque, NM	30.9	99	28.5	93	36.4	79
Anchorage, AK	n/a	n/a	n/a	n/a	n/a	n/a
Ann Arbor, MI	n/a	n/a	n/a	n/a	n/a	n/a
Athens, GA	n/a	n/a	n/a	n/a	n/a	n/a
Atlanta, GA	59.0	41	48.5	10	49.5	27
Austin, TX	50.1	70	41.2	49	43.2	51
Baltimore, MD	65.4	19	43.6	33	39.8	67
Billings, MT	n/a	n/a	n/a	n/a	n/a	n/a
Boise City, ID	30.2	101	27.6	95	36.2	80
Boston, MA	64.0	27	45.4	23	59.6	5
Boulder, CO	n/a	n/a	n/a	n/a	n/a	n/a
Cape Coral, FL	61.6	35	25.3	96	40.2	63
Cedar Rapids, IA	n/a	n/a	n/a	n/a	n/a	n/a
Charleston, SC	41.5	88	33.4	84	39.8	66
Charlotte, NC	53.8	56	43.6	34	47.6	35
Chicago, IL	76.4	3	44.9	26	56.3	10
Cincinnati, OH	69.4	8	46.0	21	36.9	77
Clarksville, TN	n/a	n/a	n/a	n/a	n/a	n/a
Colorado Spgs, CO	39.3	92	24.1	98	30.3	95
Columbia, MO	n/a	n/a	n/a	n/a	n/a	n/a
Columbus, OH	62.2	33	43.3	35	41.5	59
Dallas, TX	56.6	48	46.6	19	50.3	24
Davenport, IA	n/a	n/a	n/a	n/a	n/a	n/a
Denver, CO	62.6	31	33.4	83	48.8	31
Des Moines, IA	51.6	66	35.5	76	46.7	40
Durham, NC	48.1	75	44.0	30	48.0	33
El Paso, TX	30.7	100	22.2	100	43.3	50
Erie, PA	n/a	n/a	n/a	n/a	n/a	n/a
Eugene, OR	n/a	n/a	n/a	n/a	n/a	n/a
Fargo, ND	n/a	n/a	n/a	n/a	n/a	n/a
Fayetteville, NC	n/a	n/a	n/a	n/a	n/a	n/a
Ft. Collins, CO	n/a	n/a	n/a	n/a	n/a	n/a
Ft. Wayne, IN	n/a	n/a	n/a	n/a	n/a	n/a
Ft. Worth, TX	56.6	48	46.6	19	50.3	24
Gainesville, FL	n/a	n/a	n/a	n/a	n/a	n/a
Grand Rapids, MI	64.3	26	43.2	37	50.4	23
Green Bay, WI	n/a	n/a	n/a	n/a	n/a	n/a
Greensboro, NC	54.7	53	47.7	14	41.1	61
Honolulu, HI	36.9	95	42.1	44	31.9	91
Houston, TX	61.4	36	50.4	7	52.5	18
Huntsville, AL	n/a	n/a	n/a	n/a	n/a	n/a
Indianapolis, IN	66.4	15	41.6	47	47.3	37
Jacksonville, FL	53.1	59	37.5	71	27.6	98
Kansas City, MO	61.2	39	38.4	65	44.4	48
Lafayette, LA	n/a	n/a	n/a	n/a	n/a	n/a
Las Vegas, NV	37.6	94	28.8	92	42.0	58
Lexington, KY	n/a	n/a	n/a	n/a	n/a	n/a
Lincoln, NE	n/a	n/a	n/a	n/a	n/a	n/a
Little Rock, AR	58.8	42	39.7	59	39.7	68
Los Angeles, CA	67.8	10	48.4	12	62.2	2
Louisville, KY	58.1	43	42.2	43	38.7	73
Lubbock, TX	n/a	n/a	n/a	n/a	n/a	n/a
Madison, WI	49.6	71	44.2	29	40.1	65
Manchester, NH	n/a	n/a	n/a	n/a	n/a	n/a

Table continued on next page.

Area	Black/White		Asian/White		Hispanic/White	
	Index[1]	Rank[2]	Index[1]	Rank[2]	Index[1]	Rank[2]
McAllen, TX	40.7	90	46.7	17	39.2	69
Miami, FL	64.8	23	34.2	80	57.4	8
Midland, TX	n/a	n/a	n/a	n/a	n/a	n/a
Minneapolis, MN	52.9	60	42.8	39	42.5	54
Montgomery, AL	n/a	n/a	n/a	n/a	n/a	n/a
Nashville, TN	56.2	49	41.0	51	47.9	34
New Orleans, LA	63.9	28	48.6	9	38.3	74
New York, NY	78.0	2	51.9	3	62.0	3
Oklahoma City, OK	51.4	67	39.2	60	47.0	38
Omaha, NE	61.3	38	36.3	74	48.8	30
Orlando, FL	50.7	69	33.9	81	40.2	64
Oxnard, CA	39.9	91	31.2	87	54.6	13
Peoria, IL	n/a	n/a	n/a	n/a	n/a	n/a
Philadelphia, PA	68.4	9	42.3	42	55.1	12
Phoenix, AZ	43.6	86	32.7	85	49.3	28
Pittsburgh, PA	65.8	17	52.4	2	28.6	97
Portland, OR	46.0	81	35.8	75	34.3	83
Providence, RI	53.5	57	40.1	55	60.1	4
Provo, UT	21.9	102	28.2	94	30.9	93
Raleigh, NC	42.1	87	46.7	16	37.1	76
Reno, NV	n/a	n/a	n/a	n/a	n/a	n/a
Richmond, VA	52.4	63	43.9	32	44.9	46
Riverside, CA	45.7	82	40.7	53	42.4	55
Rochester, MN	n/a	n/a	n/a	n/a	n/a	n/a
Salem, OR	n/a	n/a	n/a	n/a	n/a	n/a
Salt Lake City, UT	39.3	93	31.0	88	42.9	53
San Antonio, TX	49.0	73	38.3	66	46.1	43
San Diego, CA	51.2	68	48.2	13	49.6	25
San Francisco, CA	62.0	34	46.6	18	49.6	26
San Jose, CA	40.9	89	45.0	25	47.6	36
Santa Rosa, CA	n/a	n/a	n/a	n/a	n/a	n/a
Savannah, GA	n/a	n/a	n/a	n/a	n/a	n/a
Seattle, WA	49.1	72	37.6	69	32.8	87
Sioux Falls, SD	n/a	n/a	n/a	n/a	n/a	n/a
Spokane, WA	n/a	n/a	n/a	n/a	n/a	n/a
Springfield, MO	n/a	n/a	n/a	n/a	n/a	n/a
Tallahassee, FL	n/a	n/a	n/a	n/a	n/a	n/a
Tampa, FL	56.2	50	35.3	78	40.7	62
Topeka, KS	n/a	n/a	n/a	n/a	n/a	n/a
Tulsa, OK	56.6	47	42.6	40	45.3	45
Virginia Beach, VA	47.8	76	34.3	79	32.2	90
Washington, DC	62.3	32	38.9	64	48.3	32
Wichita, KS	58.0	44	46.5	20	42.3	56
Wilmington, NC	n/a	n/a	n/a	n/a	n/a	n/a
Worcester, MA	52.6	61	45.8	22	52.7	17

Note: Figures are based on an analysis of 1990, 2000, and 2010 Census Decennial Census tract data by William H. Frey, Brookings Institution and the University of Michigan Social Science Data Analysis Network. In this analysis all racial groups (whites, blacks, and asians) are non-Hispanic members of those races. Hispanics are shown as a separate category; All figures cover the Metropolitan Statistical Area (see Appendix B for areas included); (1) Segregation Indices are Dissimilarity Indices that measure the degree to which the minority group is distributed differently than whites across census tracts. They range from 0 (complete integration) to 100 (complete [segregation] where the value indicates the percentage of the minority group that needs to move to be distributed exactly like whites; (2) Ranges from 1 (most segregated) to 102 (least segregated); n/a not available.
Source: www.CensusScope.org

Religious Groups by Family

Area[1]	Catholic	Baptist	Non-Den.	Methodist[2]	Lutheran	LDS[3]	Pentecostal	Presbyterian[4]	Muslim[5]	Judaism
Abilene, TX	5.3	40.3	4.7	6.3	1.1	1.0	1.7	1.0	<0.1	<0.1
Albuquerque, NM	27.2	3.8	4.2	1.5	1.0	2.4	1.5	1.1	0.2	0.3
Anchorage, AK	6.9	5.0	6.4	1.4	1.9	5.1	1.9	0.7	0.2	0.1
Ann Arbor, MI	12.4	2.2	1.6	3.1	2.9	0.9	1.9	3.0	1.3	0.9
Athens, GA	4.4	16.3	2.3	8.4	0.4	0.8	2.8	2.0	0.4	0.2
Atlanta, GA	7.5	17.5	6.9	7.9	0.5	0.8	2.6	1.8	0.8	0.6
Austin, TX	16.0	10.3	4.5	3.6	2.0	1.2	0.8	1.1	1.2	0.3
Baltimore, MD	16.7	4.2	4.8	6.1	2.1	0.5	1.1	1.3	0.5	1.8
Billings, MT	12.1	2.5	3.8	2.1	6.1	4.9	4.1	1.8	<0.1	0.1
Boise City, ID	8.0	2.9	4.2	2.1	1.2	15.9	2.3	0.6	0.1	0.1
Boston, MA	44.4	1.2	1.0	1.0	0.4	0.4	0.6	1.6	0.4	1.4
Boulder, CO	20.1	2.4	4.8	1.8	3.1	3.0	0.5	2.0	0.1	0.8
Cape Coral, FL	16.2	5.0	3.0	2.5	1.2	0.5	4.4	1.4	0.9	0.2
Cedar Rapids, IA	18.8	2.4	3.0	7.3	11.3	0.9	1.8	3.3	0.5	0.1
Charleston, SC	6.2	12.4	7.1	10.0	1.1	1.0	2.0	2.4	0.2	0.3
Charlotte, NC	5.9	17.3	6.8	8.6	1.3	0.8	3.3	4.5	0.2	0.3
Chicago, IL	34.2	3.2	4.5	1.9	3.0	0.4	1.2	1.9	3.3	0.8
Cincinnati, OH	19.1	9.6	3.7	3.9	1.2	0.6	2.2	1.6	0.2	0.5
Clarksville, TN	4.1	30.9	2.3	6.2	0.6	1.5	1.8	1.1	0.1	<0.1
Colorado Spgs, CO	8.4	4.3	7.4	2.4	2.0	3.0	1.1	2.1	0.1	0.1
Columbia, MO	6.6	14.7	5.4	4.3	1.7	1.4	1.1	2.3	0.3	0.3
Columbus, OH	11.8	5.3	3.6	4.7	2.4	0.7	2.0	2.0	0.8	0.5
Dallas, TX	13.3	18.7	7.8	5.3	0.8	1.2	2.2	1.0	2.4	0.4
Davenport, IA	14.9	5.0	2.7	5.3	8.7	0.8	1.4	3.0	0.9	0.1
Denver, CO	16.1	3.0	4.6	1.7	2.1	2.4	1.2	1.6	0.6	0.6
Des Moines, IA	13.6	4.8	3.3	7.0	8.2	1.0	2.4	3.0	0.3	0.3
Durham, NC	5.1	13.9	5.6	8.1	0.5	0.8	1.4	2.5	0.5	0.6
El Paso, TX	43.2	3.8	5.0	0.9	0.3	1.6	1.4	0.2	0.1	0.2
Erie, PA	33.5	2.2	1.7	5.7	3.0	0.6	2.2	2.1	0.7	0.2
Eugene, OR	6.2	3.1	1.9	0.9	1.4	3.7	3.3	0.6	0.1	0.4
Fargo, ND	17.4	0.4	0.5	3.3	32.5	0.6	1.5	1.9	0.1	<0.1
Fayetteville, NC	2.6	14.1	10.5	6.2	0.2	1.4	4.9	2.1	0.2	<0.1
Ft. Collins, CO	11.8	2.2	6.4	4.4	3.5	3.0	4.7	1.9	0.1	<0.1
Ft. Wayne, IN	14.2	6.1	6.8	5.1	8.5	0.4	1.5	1.7	0.3	0.1
Ft. Worth, TX	13.3	18.7	7.8	5.3	0.8	1.2	2.2	1.0	2.4	0.4
Gainesville, FL	7.6	12.3	4.3	6.4	0.5	1.0	3.5	1.1	1.1	0.4
Grand Rapids, MI	17.2	1.7	8.4	3.1	2.1	0.6	1.1	10.0	1.1	0.1
Green Bay, WI	42.0	0.7	3.4	2.2	12.7	0.4	0.6	1.0	0.1	0.1
Greensboro, NC	2.7	12.8	7.4	9.9	0.7	0.8	2.5	3.2	0.6	0.4
Honolulu, HI	18.2	1.9	2.2	0.8	0.3	5.1	4.2	1.5	<0.1	0.1
Houston, TX	17.1	16.0	7.3	4.9	1.1	1.1	1.5	0.9	2.7	0.4
Huntsville, AL	4.0	27.6	3.2	7.5	0.7	1.2	1.2	1.7	0.2	0.2
Indianapolis, IN	10.5	10.3	7.2	5.0	1.7	0.7	1.6	1.7	0.2	0.4
Jacksonville, FL	9.9	18.5	7.8	4.5	0.7	1.1	1.9	1.6	0.6	0.4
Kansas City, MO	12.7	13.2	5.2	5.9	2.3	2.5	2.6	1.6	0.3	0.4
Lafayette, LA	47.0	14.8	4.0	2.6	0.2	0.4	2.9	0.2	0.1	0.1
Las Vegas, NV	18.1	3.0	3.1	0.4	0.7	6.4	1.5	0.2	0.1	0.3
Lexington, KY	6.8	24.9	2.4	5.9	0.4	1.1	2.1	1.4	0.1	0.3
Lincoln, NE	14.8	2.4	1.9	7.2	11.3	1.2	1.4	3.9	0.2	0.2
Little Rock, AR	4.5	25.9	6.1	7.3	0.5	0.9	2.9	0.9	0.1	0.1
Los Angeles, CA	33.8	2.8	3.6	1.1	0.7	1.7	1.8	0.9	0.7	1.0
Louisville, KY	13.7	25.1	1.7	3.7	0.6	0.8	1.0	1.2	0.5	0.4
Lubbock, TX	13.4	22.4	7.3	6.6	0.5	1.4	1.9	0.8	1.8	0.1
Madison, WI	21.8	1.1	1.6	3.7	12.8	0.5	0.4	2.2	0.5	0.5
Manchester, NH	31.2	1.4	2.4	1.2	0.5	0.6	0.5	2.0	0.3	0.5

Table continued on next page.

Area[1]	Catholic	Baptist	Non-Den.	Methodist[2]	Lutheran	LDS[3]	Pente-costal	Presby-terian[4]	Muslim[5]	Judaism
McAllen, TX	34.7	4.5	2.8	1.3	0.4	1.3	1.2	0.2	1.0	<0.1
Miami, FL	18.6	5.4	4.2	1.3	0.5	0.5	1.8	0.7	0.9	1.6
Midland, TX	22.4	25.3	8.8	4.2	0.7	1.2	1.6	1.9	3.7	<0.1
Minneapolis, MN	21.7	2.5	3.0	2.8	14.5	0.6	1.8	1.9	0.4	0.7
Montgomery, AL	3.2	35.4	4.0	11.1	0.2	0.9	5.2	1.5	0.3	0.3
Nashville, TN	4.1	25.3	5.8	6.1	0.4	0.8	2.2	2.1	0.4	0.2
New Orleans, LA	31.6	8.4	3.7	2.7	0.8	0.6	2.1	0.5	0.5	0.5
New York, NY	36.9	1.9	1.8	1.3	0.8	0.4	0.9	1.1	2.3	4.8
Oklahoma City, OK	6.4	25.4	7.1	10.6	0.7	1.3	3.2	1.0	0.2	0.1
Omaha, NE	21.6	4.6	1.8	3.9	7.9	1.8	1.3	2.3	0.5	0.4
Orlando, FL	13.2	7.0	5.7	3.0	0.9	1.0	3.2	1.4	1.3	0.3
Oxnard, CA	28.2	1.9	4.1	1.1	1.5	2.5	1.3	0.7	0.4	0.7
Peoria, IL	11.5	5.5	5.3	5.0	6.1	0.5	1.5	2.8	5.2	0.1
Philadelphia, PA	33.5	3.9	2.9	3.0	1.9	0.3	0.9	2.1	1.3	1.4
Phoenix, AZ	13.4	3.5	5.2	1.0	1.6	6.1	2.9	0.6	0.2	0.3
Pittsburgh, PA	32.8	2.3	2.8	5.7	3.4	0.4	1.1	4.7	0.3	0.7
Portland, OR	10.6	2.3	4.5	1.0	1.6	3.8	2.0	1.0	0.1	0.3
Providence, RI	47.0	1.4	1.2	0.8	0.5	0.3	0.6	1.0	0.1	0.7
Provo, UT	1.3	0.1	0.1	0.2	<0.1	88.6	0.1	0.1	<0.1	<0.1
Raleigh, NC	9.2	12.1	6.0	6.7	0.9	0.9	2.3	2.3	0.9	0.3
Reno, NV	14.3	1.5	3.2	0.9	0.8	4.6	2.0	0.4	0.1	0.2
Richmond, VA	6.0	19.9	5.5	6.1	0.6	1.0	1.8	2.1	2.8	0.4
Riverside, CA	24.8	2.6	5.5	0.6	0.5	2.5	1.6	0.6	0.6	0.1
Rochester, MN	23.4	1.7	4.7	4.9	21.1	1.1	1.3	2.9	0.3	0.2
Salem, OR	16.7	2.2	3.0	1.2	1.7	3.9	3.4	0.7	<0.1	0.1
Salt Lake City, UT	8.9	0.8	0.5	0.5	0.5	58.9	0.7	0.4	0.4	0.1
San Antonio, TX	28.4	8.5	6.0	3.1	1.7	1.4	1.3	0.8	1.0	0.2
San Diego, CA	25.9	2.0	4.8	1.1	1.0	2.3	1.0	0.9	0.7	0.5
San Francisco, CA	20.8	2.5	2.5	2.0	0.6	1.6	1.2	1.1	1.2	0.9
San Jose, CA	26.0	1.4	4.3	1.1	0.6	1.4	1.2	0.7	1.0	0.7
Santa Rosa, CA	22.3	1.4	1.5	0.9	1.0	1.9	0.7	0.9	0.5	0.4
Savannah, GA	7.1	19.7	6.9	8.9	1.6	1.0	2.4	1.0	0.2	0.8
Seattle, WA	12.3	2.2	5.0	1.2	2.1	3.3	2.8	1.4	0.5	0.5
Sioux Falls, SD	14.9	3.0	1.5	3.9	21.4	0.7	1.1	6.2	0.3	0.1
Spokane, WA	13.1	1.9	4.3	1.0	2.9	5.2	2.9	1.5	0.1	0.2
Springfield, MO	4.4	23.2	3.9	4.7	1.4	1.2	9.3	1.1	0.1	0.1
Tallahassee, FL	4.8	16.1	6.8	9.2	0.5	1.0	2.2	1.6	0.9	0.4
Tampa, FL	10.9	7.1	3.8	3.5	1.0	0.6	2.1	1.0	1.3	0.5
Topeka, KS	12.8	9.1	4.1	7.3	3.6	1.5	2.0	1.7	0.1	0.1
Tulsa, OK	5.8	22.9	7.6	9.2	0.8	1.2	3.3	1.3	0.3	0.3
Virginia Beach, VA	6.4	11.6	6.2	5.3	0.7	0.9	1.9	2.0	2.1	0.4
Washington, DC	14.5	7.3	4.9	4.5	1.3	1.2	1.1	1.4	2.4	1.2
Wichita, KS	14.5	13.5	3.2	7.2	1.8	1.4	2.0	1.7	0.2	<0.1
Wilmington, NC	6.2	14.5	4.6	8.5	0.9	1.0	1.1	2.5	0.3	0.1
Worcester, MA	38.4	1.2	1.8	1.0	0.9	0.3	1.1	2.1	0.1	0.5
U.S.	19.1	9.3	4.0	4.0	2.3	2.0	1.9	1.6	0.8	0.7

Note: Figures are the number of adherents as a percentage of the total population; (1) Figures cover the Metropolitan Statistical Area—see Appendix B for areas included; (2) Methodist/Pietist; (3) Latter Day Saints; (4) Reformed; (5) Figures are estimates
Source: Association of Statisticians of American Religious Bodies, 2010 U.S. Religion Census: Religious Congregations & Membership Study

Religious Groups by Tradition

Area	Catholic	Evangelical Protestant	Mainline Protestant	Other Tradition	Black Protestant	Orthodox
Abilene, TX	5.3	47.4	9.0	1.1	0.4	<0.1
Albuquerque, NM	27.2	11.3	3.3	3.9	0.2	0.2
Anchorage, AK	6.9	15.7	3.6	6.8	0.3	0.6
Ann Arbor, MI	12.4	7.3	7.5	3.8	1.6	0.3
Athens, GA	4.4	21.1	9.8	1.7	2.5	0.1
Atlanta, GA	7.5	26.1	9.8	2.9	3.2	0.3
Austin, TX	16.0	16.1	6.3	3.9	1.4	0.1
Baltimore, MD	16.7	9.9	8.3	3.2	3.5	0.5
Billings, MT	12.1	13.7	8.2	5.2	0.1	0.1
Boise City, ID	8.0	13.0	4.4	16.7	<0.1	0.1
Boston, MA	44.4	3.2	4.5	3.4	0.2	1.1
Boulder, CO	20.1	9.8	6.5	4.9	<0.1	0.2
Cape Coral, FL	16.2	14.3	4.6	2.0	0.3	0.2
Cedar Rapids, IA	18.8	13.7	17.5	2.0	0.2	0.2
Charleston, SC	6.2	19.7	11.2	1.9	7.3	0.1
Charlotte, NC	5.9	27.6	13.3	1.7	2.8	0.5
Chicago, IL	34.2	9.8	5.1	5.1	2.1	0.9
Cincinnati, OH	19.1	15.5	7.2	1.6	1.2	0.2
Clarksville, TN	4.1	35.4	7.3	1.7	2.4	<0.1
Colorado Spgs, CO	8.4	15.2	5.4	3.7	0.4	0.1
Columbia, MO	6.6	19.9	10.5	2.3	0.5	0.1
Columbus, OH	11.8	11.9	9.5	3.1	1.1	0.3
Dallas, TX	13.3	28.3	7.0	4.8	1.8	0.2
Davenport, IA	14.9	11.4	15.1	2.4	1.6	0.1
Denver, CO	16.1	11.1	4.5	4.6	0.4	0.3
Des Moines, IA	13.6	12.4	16.8	1.9	0.9	0.1
Durham, NC	5.1	19.4	11.7	2.9	3.1	0.1
El Paso, TX	43.2	10.9	1.3	2.1	0.2	0.1
Erie, PA	33.5	8.4	11.7	1.6	0.9	0.3
Eugene, OR	6.2	9.7	3.4	5.5	0.1	0.1
Fargo, ND	17.4	10.7	30.8	0.9	<0.1	<0.1
Fayetteville, NC	2.6	26.7	7.9	1.8	4.3	0.1
Ft. Collins, CO	11.8	18.8	5.9	4.0	<0.1	0.1
Ft. Wayne, IN	14.2	24.6	9.2	1.0	2.4	0.2
Ft. Worth, TX	13.3	28.3	7.0	4.8	1.8	0.2
Gainesville, FL	7.6	20.4	7.0	4.2	2.2	0.1
Grand Rapids, MI	17.2	20.7	7.6	2.2	1.1	0.2
Green Bay, WI	42.0	14.1	8.1	0.6	<0.1	<0.1
Greensboro, NC	2.7	23.2	14.0	2.2	2.6	0.1
Honolulu, HI	18.2	9.7	2.9	8.4	<0.1	<0.1
Houston, TX	17.1	24.9	6.7	4.9	1.3	0.2
Huntsville, AL	4.0	33.3	9.7	1.9	1.8	0.1
Indianapolis, IN	10.5	18.3	9.6	1.7	1.9	0.3
Jacksonville, FL	9.9	27.1	5.7	2.9	4.2	0.3
Kansas City, MO	12.7	20.6	10.0	3.7	2.6	0.1
Lafayette, LA	47.0	12.8	3.2	0.8	9.3	0.1
Las Vegas, NV	18.1	7.7	1.4	7.6	0.4	0.4
Lexington, KY	6.8	28.3	10.3	1.7	2.1	0.2
Lincoln, NE	14.8	14.8	16.2	2.0	0.1	0.1
Little Rock, AR	4.5	33.9	8.2	1.7	3.5	0.1
Los Angeles, CA	33.8	9.0	2.4	4.6	0.9	0.6
Louisville, KY	13.7	24.5	7.1	2.0	3.0	0.1
Lubbock, TX	13.4	31.5	8.6	4.0	0.7	0.1
Madison, WI	21.8	7.3	15.4	2.3	0.1	0.1
Manchester, NH	31.2	5.1	4.4	1.8	<0.1	0.7

Table continued on next page.

Area	Catholic	Evangelical Protestant	Mainline Protestant	Other Tradition	Black Protestant	Orthodox
McAllen, TX	34.7	9.7	1.9	2.4	<0.1	<0.1
Miami, FL	18.6	11.4	2.5	3.5	1.7	0.3
Midland, TX	22.4	35.5	7.2	5.4	1.0	<0.1
Minneapolis, MN	21.7	12.9	14.5	2.3	0.5	0.2
Montgomery, AL	3.2	34.2	11.7	1.6	13.5	<0.1
Nashville, TN	4.1	33.0	8.0	1.7	3.4	0.5
New Orleans, LA	31.6	12.7	4.0	2.1	3.0	0.1
New York, NY	36.9	4.0	4.1	8.4	1.2	1.0
Oklahoma City, OK	6.4	39.1	9.9	2.8	1.9	0.2
Omaha, NE	21.6	12.1	10.8	3.3	1.5	0.1
Orlando, FL	13.2	17.8	4.8	3.3	1.2	0.3
Oxnard, CA	28.2	8.9	2.7	4.5	0.2	0.2
Peoria, IL	11.5	18.9	11.1	6.2	0.9	0.1
Philadelphia, PA	33.5	6.3	8.9	3.7	1.8	0.4
Phoenix, AZ	13.4	13.2	2.6	7.8	0.2	0.3
Pittsburgh, PA	32.8	7.4	13.8	2.1	0.9	0.7
Portland, OR	10.6	11.7	3.7	5.2	0.2	0.3
Providence, RI	47.0	2.8	4.7	1.6	0.1	0.6
Provo, UT	1.3	0.5	0.1	88.9	<0.1	<0.1
Raleigh, NC	9.2	19.9	10.1	3.3	1.7	0.2
Reno, NV	14.3	7.7	1.9	5.1	0.2	0.1
Richmond, VA	6.0	23.7	13.3	4.6	2.4	0.2
Riverside, CA	24.8	11.5	1.3	3.7	0.8	0.2
Rochester, MN	23.4	19.0	21.1	2.1	<0.1	0.1
Salem, OR	16.7	14.1	3.8	4.2	<0.1	<0.1
Salt Lake City, UT	8.9	2.6	1.3	60.1	0.1	0.5
San Antonio, TX	28.4	17.0	5.0	3.2	0.4	0.1
San Diego, CA	25.9	9.8	2.4	5.2	0.4	0.3
San Francisco, CA	20.8	6.2	3.8	5.2	1.1	0.7
San Jose, CA	26.0	8.2	2.5	6.9	0.1	0.4
Santa Rosa, CA	22.3	5.3	2.4	4.8	<0.1	0.3
Savannah, GA	7.1	25.1	9.5	2.6	8.6	0.1
Seattle, WA	12.3	11.9	4.7	5.9	0.4	0.4
Sioux Falls, SD	14.9	12.9	28.1	1.2	0.1	0.1
Spokane, WA	13.1	12.4	4.9	6.3	0.1	0.2
Springfield, MO	4.4	38.0	7.7	1.4	0.1	<0.1
Tallahassee, FL	4.8	21.9	6.4	3.0	9.2	0.2
Tampa, FL	10.9	13.6	5.2	3.1	1.2	0.8
Topeka, KS	12.8	15.5	12.9	1.8	2.8	<0.1
Tulsa, OK	5.8	34.6	11.3	2.2	1.6	0.1
Virginia Beach, VA	6.4	18.0	9.4	4.0	2.3	0.3
Washington, DC	14.5	12.4	8.8	5.9	2.3	0.6
Wichita, KS	14.5	20.7	11.1	2.4	1.9	0.2
Wilmington, NC	6.2	20.4	10.8	1.7	3.1	0.1
Worcester, MA	38.4	4.7	5.4	2.4	0.1	1.0
U.S.	19.1	16.2	7.3	4.3	1.6	0.3

Note: Figures are the number of adherents as a percentage of the total population; (1) Figures cover the Metropolitan Statistical Area—see Appendix B for areas included; Source: Association of Statisticians of American Religious Bodies, 2010 U.S. Religion Census: Religious Congregations & Membership Study

Ancestry: City

City	German	Irish	English	American	Italian	Polish	French[1]	Scottish	Dutch
Abilene, TX	12.4	9.2	7.3	6.0	1.3	0.6	2.0	1.6	0.8
Albuquerque, NM	10.5	7.8	6.8	3.6	3.2	1.3	2.1	1.8	1.1
Anchorage, AK	17.8	10.9	8.8	5.2	3.4	1.9	3.1	3.0	1.7
Ann Arbor, MI	18.9	9.5	10.3	5.2	5.2	6.5	3.7	3.1	2.4
Athens, GA	9.6	8.1	8.5	10.2	2.0	2.2	1.6	3.5	0.8
Atlanta, GA	6.2	5.0	6.5	7.1	1.9	1.3	1.3	2.1	0.6
Austin, TX	12.6	8.6	8.4	4.0	2.9	1.5	3.1	2.3	0.9
Baltimore, MD	7.5	6.6	3.5	2.3	3.4	2.5	0.7	0.8	0.6
Billings, MT	30.2	12.5	10.3	12.5	3.3	1.7	2.9	2.5	1.8
Boise City, ID	16.6	9.9	13.9	7.2	4.4	1.6	2.3	3.5	2.0
Boston, MA	4.8	15.5	5.3	4.8	8.4	2.6	1.9	1.3	0.5
Boulder, CO	22.6	13.7	13.1	4.7	6.9	4.3	4.3	3.3	2.1
Cape Coral, FL	19.2	16.0	8.9	10.6	12.3	4.5	3.1	1.4	1.4
Cedar Rapids, IA	38.2	17.1	8.8	5.2	2.3	1.7	2.8	1.9	2.4
Charleston, SC	12.2	11.3	11.9	11.4	4.3	1.9	3.0	3.4	1.2
Charlotte, NC	9.9	7.8	7.8	5.0	3.5	1.7	1.5	2.3	0.8
Chicago, IL	7.4	7.5	2.3	1.8	3.9	6.1	0.9	0.6	0.6
Cincinnati, OH	19.1	10.3	5.3	5.2	3.5	1.4	1.5	1.1	0.9
Clarksville, TN	13.7	10.9	6.5	11.9	2.9	1.8	1.8	1.4	1.1
Colorado Spgs, CO	22.1	12.7	10.3	5.7	5.8	2.6	3.3	2.9	2.1
Columbia, MO	27.2	12.0	11.6	4.8	4.2	2.3	3.2	3.4	1.3
Columbus, OH	20.4	12.6	6.8	4.9	5.4	2.2	1.8	1.6	1.2
Dallas, TX	5.9	4.4	5.0	3.2	1.4	0.8	1.4	1.1	0.5
Davenport, IA	33.8	14.9	7.0	6.4	2.4	2.4	2.7	1.0	1.9
Denver, CO	14.5	10.2	8.0	3.2	4.3	2.4	2.4	2.0	1.4
Des Moines, IA	22.9	12.3	8.1	4.7	3.7	1.1	2.0	1.6	3.8
Durham, NC	7.3	5.3	7.6	4.3	2.6	1.6	1.5	1.6	0.8
El Paso, TX	3.7	2.8	1.8	4.3	1.1	0.4	0.7	0.5	0.2
Erie, PA	23.5	14.8	4.5	2.8	12.6	12.6	1.8	0.8	1.3
Eugene, OR	19.6	13.7	11.8	4.7	4.3	2.4	4.0	3.1	2.4
Fargo, ND	41.1	9.4	5.0	2.0	1.3	2.9	3.7	1.1	1.0
Fayetteville, NC	11.0	8.0	5.2	4.7	2.7	1.3	1.5	2.0	0.7
Ft. Collins, CO	27.2	14.1	12.6	4.0	6.3	3.2	3.7	3.2	2.9
Ft. Wayne, IN	26.1	9.3	7.0	14.5	2.3	2.1	3.4	1.3	1.4
Ft. Worth, TX	9.0	7.3	5.7	7.4	1.8	1.0	1.5	1.6	0.8
Gainesville, FL	11.6	10.8	8.5	4.1	5.8	3.2	2.7	2.1	0.7
Grand Rapids, MI	15.9	9.3	6.9	2.8	2.7	7.2	3.0	1.5	14.4
Green Bay, WI	33.5	9.8	3.7	3.5	2.3	10.5	5.5	0.7	3.6
Greensboro, NC	7.7	6.1	8.1	5.2	2.4	1.0	1.2	2.2	0.7
Honolulu, HI	4.0	3.3	2.9	1.2	1.7	0.6	1.2	0.8	0.5
Houston, TX	5.4	3.7	3.9	3.3	1.5	0.9	1.7	0.9	0.5
Huntsville, AL	9.8	8.4	9.5	10.8	2.5	1.1	2.0	2.6	1.1
Indianapolis, IN	16.8	10.5	7.0	7.2	2.3	1.5	1.8	1.5	1.2
Jacksonville, FL	9.4	9.9	8.4	6.0	4.0	1.4	2.2	1.7	0.9
Kansas City, MO	17.0	11.3	7.7	11.1	3.1	1.4	2.3	1.7	1.5
Lafayette, LA	9.8	5.7	6.3	7.0	3.6	0.5	19.8	1.4	0.5
Las Vegas, NV	10.3	8.5	6.1	3.5	6.2	2.7	2.2	1.2	0.9
Lexington, KY	13.8	12.6	11.6	15.7	3.0	1.3	2.0	2.5	1.1
Lincoln, NE	40.7	13.2	9.5	4.4	1.9	2.7	2.7	1.4	2.1
Little Rock, AR	8.2	8.2	8.8	5.5	1.4	0.6	1.6	2.0	0.8
Los Angeles, CA	4.5	3.8	3.2	2.5	2.6	1.6	1.3	0.7	0.5
Louisville, KY	17.1	13.0	8.1	13.5	2.6	0.8	2.0	1.6	1.2
Lubbock, TX	11.9	9.0	7.4	7.2	1.5	0.9	1.5	1.7	0.9
Madison, WI	33.5	12.7	8.7	2.8	4.5	5.2	2.8	1.8	2.1
Manchester, NH	7.6	20.5	9.8	3.1	7.9	4.2	18.1	2.1	0.5
McAllen, TX	4.3	2.5	2.5	1.6	1.2	0.3	2.8	0.2	0.2

Table continued on next page.

City	German	Irish	English	American	Italian	Polish	French[1]	Scottish	Dutch
Miami, FL	2.0	1.7	1.2	4.0	2.2	0.8	0.9	0.2	0.4
Midland, TX	10.5	7.5	8.1	6.9	1.1	0.5	1.4	1.5	0.9
Minneapolis, MN	22.6	10.7	6.0	2.1	2.4	3.8	3.1	1.5	1.6
Montgomery, AL	3.8	3.5	4.8	13.1	0.8	0.5	1.1	1.3	0.3
Nashville, TN	9.9	9.5	8.4	8.3	2.5	1.1	2.0	2.0	0.9
New Orleans, LA	6.8	5.9	4.1	3.7	4.2	0.8	6.3	1.0	0.4
New York, NY	3.1	4.9	1.7	3.7	7.0	2.6	0.8	0.4	0.3
Oklahoma City, OK	12.6	9.8	7.5	7.5	1.5	0.9	2.0	1.9	1.3
Omaha, NE	27.4	15.2	7.9	3.7	4.6	4.3	2.5	1.1	1.6
Orlando, FL	8.4	7.0	5.7	6.7	4.1	1.4	1.6	1.2	0.6
Oxnard, CA	4.3	3.2	2.5	1.4	1.7	0.6	0.8	0.7	0.5
Peoria, IL	21.2	11.5	7.6	4.4	3.2	2.2	2.2	1.1	1.1
Philadelphia, PA	7.6	12.3	2.8	2.2	8.0	3.4	0.7	0.6	0.4
Phoenix, AZ	12.2	8.3	6.5	4.3	4.0	2.3	1.8	1.3	1.1
Pittsburgh, PA	19.6	16.0	4.9	3.7	13.1	7.7	1.6	1.5	0.7
Portland, OR	18.0	12.0	10.9	5.3	4.4	2.1	3.1	3.3	1.8
Providence, RI	3.5	8.8	4.1	1.9	10.1	2.1	3.5	1.2	0.4
Provo, UT	11.1	5.4	23.3	4.4	2.5	0.7	2.6	4.6	1.3
Raleigh, NC	9.7	8.1	9.9	10.0	3.9	1.8	1.8	2.3	0.8
Reno, NV	14.4	12.7	8.3	5.0	7.5	1.8	3.1	1.7	1.4
Richmond, VA	7.0	6.7	8.1	4.0	2.6	1.2	1.6	1.6	0.5
Riverside, CA	8.4	6.6	5.4	3.2	3.5	1.3	2.2	1.2	0.9
Rochester, MN	31.6	10.0	6.2	4.4	1.7	3.4	3.1	1.2	2.1
Salem, OR	20.5	11.6	11.4	4.9	3.2	0.9	3.1	2.7	2.2
Salt Lake City, UT	11.0	6.5	16.2	3.9	3.1	1.1	1.8	3.7	2.2
San Antonio, TX	8.4	4.7	4.0	3.9	1.8	1.1	1.5	1.0	0.5
San Diego, CA	9.7	7.6	6.0	3.2	4.1	1.8	2.1	1.5	0.9
San Francisco, CA	8.0	7.8	5.0	2.1	4.9	1.8	2.2	1.5	0.8
San Jose, CA	6.2	4.6	4.2	1.6	4.2	0.9	1.4	0.9	0.7
Santa Rosa, CA	12.7	10.5	9.1	4.5	8.2	1.3	3.1	2.5	1.9
Savannah, GA	5.0	6.3	5.1	3.8	2.1	0.8	1.5	1.3	0.6
Seattle, WA	15.9	11.4	11.1	3.4	4.4	2.4	3.2	3.2	2.0
Sioux Falls, SD	37.4	10.9	4.8	3.6	1.0	1.6	2.0	1.0	7.3
Spokane, WA	22.7	13.8	10.7	4.9	5.1	1.7	3.4	3.0	1.8
Springfield, MO	18.2	11.9	9.7	24.1	2.7	1.3	2.6	1.7	2.2
Tallahassee, FL	8.9	9.7	9.6	4.9	4.7	1.9	2.3	2.2	0.9
Tampa, FL	8.7	8.0	5.7	5.0	5.9	1.8	1.9	1.4	1.1
Topeka, KS	26.4	14.1	9.7	4.8	2.2	1.0	3.2	1.9	1.9
Tulsa, OK	13.3	11.4	8.8	7.8	1.7	1.0	2.4	2.2	1.7
Virginia Beach, VA	12.9	11.3	9.2	15.0	6.3	2.7	2.7	2.2	1.2
Washington, DC	6.5	6.7	5.3	2.2	3.3	1.8	1.6	1.3	0.5
Wichita, KS	21.3	10.3	8.5	10.0	1.9	0.9	2.6	1.8	1.6
Wilmington, NC	10.6	10.5	10.5	21.0	4.3	1.5	2.3	3.2	1.5
Worcester, MA	3.1	17.3	4.9	2.7	11.1	4.8	8.3	1.2	0.3
U.S.	15.2	11.1	8.2	7.2	5.6	3.1	2.8	1.7	1.4

Note: Figures are the percentage of the total population reporting a particular ancestry. The nine most commonly reported ancestries in the U.S. are shown. Figures include multiple ancestries (e.g. if a person reported being Irish and Italian, they were included in both columns); (1) Excludes Basque
Source: U.S. Census Bureau, 2010-2012 American Community Survey 3-Year Estimates

Ancestry: Metro Area

Metro Area	German	Irish	English	American	Italian	Polish	French[1]	Scottish	Dutch
Abilene, TX	12.1	9.7	7.9	7.3	1.4	0.5	1.9	1.7	0.8
Albuquerque, NM	10.9	7.7	7.0	4.4	3.2	1.5	2.1	1.7	1.0
Anchorage, AK	19.1	11.7	9.0	5.2	3.4	2.2	3.3	3.2	1.9
Ann Arbor, MI	20.8	11.5	10.3	7.0	5.0	6.6	3.4	2.7	2.3
Athens, GA	9.5	9.1	9.7	15.7	2.0	1.6	1.7	3.3	0.7
Atlanta, GA	7.7	7.6	7.6	9.8	2.6	1.3	1.5	1.8	0.8
Austin, TX	15.0	9.1	9.0	4.7	2.9	1.6	2.8	2.2	1.0
Baltimore, MD	18.2	13.6	8.6	5.3	6.5	4.6	1.7	1.7	1.0
Billings, MT	30.7	12.1	10.3	14.2	2.9	1.8	3.0	2.4	2.0
Boise City, ID	16.3	8.8	12.6	12.3	3.2	1.3	2.2	3.0	1.9
Boston, MA	6.4	24.2	10.9	4.5	15.0	3.8	5.7	2.6	0.6
Boulder, CO	22.3	14.0	13.2	5.0	6.1	3.8	3.9	3.6	2.1
Cape Coral, FL	15.8	12.6	9.5	13.6	8.1	3.8	2.9	1.6	1.3
Cedar Rapids, IA	41.7	17.1	9.6	5.7	2.2	1.5	2.9	1.7	2.6
Charleston, SC	11.7	10.3	9.0	13.2	3.6	1.9	2.7	2.6	1.1
Charlotte, NC	11.8	9.5	8.6	8.8	3.8	1.7	1.7	2.5	1.0
Chicago, IL	15.7	12.0	4.5	2.9	7.2	9.5	1.5	1.0	1.3
Cincinnati, OH	29.9	14.4	9.2	11.3	4.1	1.5	2.1	1.8	1.2
Clarksville, TN	13.0	10.5	7.8	16.9	2.8	1.6	1.8	1.9	1.2
Colorado Spgs, CO	22.4	13.2	10.6	6.2	5.2	2.7	3.4	2.9	2.1
Columbia, MO	28.4	12.8	11.4	6.5	3.6	1.7	3.1	3.2	1.3
Columbus, OH	25.5	14.5	9.6	8.0	5.7	2.4	2.2	2.1	1.6
Dallas, TX	10.5	8.2	7.6	6.8	2.2	1.1	2.0	1.7	1.0
Davenport, IA	29.6	14.9	8.7	6.4	2.9	2.4	2.4	1.3	2.1
Denver, CO	19.8	11.8	10.1	5.2	5.3	2.7	2.8	2.4	1.7
Des Moines, IA	30.0	14.0	9.6	5.4	3.2	1.4	2.5	1.6	4.1
Durham, NC	9.6	8.1	11.4	6.9	2.9	1.7	2.0	2.2	1.0
El Paso, TX	3.3	2.6	1.6	3.9	1.0	0.4	0.6	0.4	0.2
Erie, PA	29.5	17.4	7.9	4.9	13.2	12.5	1.8	1.6	1.5
Eugene, OR	19.7	13.3	12.4	5.7	4.1	2.3	3.8	3.0	2.7
Fargo, ND	40.2	8.5	4.6	2.0	1.3	3.1	3.7	1.0	1.0
Fayetteville, NC	9.9	8.1	5.9	7.0	2.9	1.3	1.7	2.1	0.9
Ft. Collins, CO	29.5	13.9	13.5	4.4	5.5	2.9	3.8	3.2	2.8
Ft. Wayne, IN	30.0	9.5	7.5	14.9	2.2	2.3	3.4	1.4	1.5
Ft. Worth, TX	10.5	8.2	7.6	6.8	2.2	1.1	2.0	1.7	1.0
Gainesville, FL	13.3	11.2	10.2	6.1	5.0	2.8	2.7	2.0	1.3
Grand Rapids, MI	21.9	11.5	10.2	5.6	3.0	7.1	3.5	2.0	17.0
Green Bay, WI	39.5	9.8	3.6	4.2	2.5	10.9	5.1	0.8	5.0
Greensboro, NC	8.9	7.0	9.5	10.0	2.4	0.9	1.3	2.2	0.8
Honolulu, HI	5.3	4.1	3.3	1.3	1.9	0.8	1.1	0.8	0.6
Houston, TX	8.9	6.1	5.5	5.0	2.0	1.3	2.3	1.2	0.7
Huntsville, AL	9.5	8.9	9.5	15.8	2.1	1.1	2.1	2.1	1.0
Indianapolis, IN	20.8	12.0	9.8	9.5	2.8	1.9	2.1	2.0	1.7
Jacksonville, FL	11.2	11.8	9.8	8.3	5.1	1.9	2.6	2.1	1.0
Kansas City, MO	23.3	13.7	10.3	9.1	3.4	1.7	2.7	2.1	1.7
Lafayette, LA	8.9	4.9	4.6	8.9	3.1	0.4	22.0	1.1	0.3
Las Vegas, NV	10.8	8.5	6.5	3.8	6.2	2.5	2.2	1.4	1.0
Lexington, KY	13.9	12.8	11.5	20.0	2.6	1.2	1.9	2.6	1.1
Lincoln, NE	42.2	12.8	9.4	4.6	2.0	2.7	2.6	1.5	2.2
Little Rock, AR	10.8	10.8	10.3	11.1	1.8	1.0	2.2	2.0	1.2
Los Angeles, CA	6.2	4.9	4.5	3.1	3.0	1.3	1.5	1.0	0.7
Louisville, KY	19.0	13.5	9.6	17.4	2.3	1.0	2.2	1.7	1.3
Lubbock, TX	12.0	9.4	7.4	7.6	1.4	0.9	1.6	1.7	1.0
Madison, WI	40.5	14.0	9.1	3.4	3.6	4.9	2.9	1.6	2.1
Manchester, NH	8.5	21.9	14.0	4.3	9.9	4.6	15.8	3.4	1.0
McAllen, TX	2.7	1.4	1.3	1.1	0.5	0.2	1.0	0.3	0.2

Table continued on next page.

Metro Area	German	Irish	English	American	Italian	Polish	French[1]	Scottish	Dutch
Miami, FL	5.5	5.3	3.4	5.4	5.6	2.4	1.4	0.7	0.5
Midland, TX	10.2	8.0	7.8	6.9	0.9	0.4	1.4	1.7	1.0
Minneapolis, MN	32.6	12.0	6.1	3.4	2.8	4.7	3.8	1.3	1.6
Montgomery, AL	5.5	6.3	6.4	14.9	1.1	0.5	1.3	1.7	0.5
Nashville, TN	11.1	11.5	10.6	14.0	2.7	1.2	2.2	2.4	1.1
New Orleans, LA	11.3	8.6	5.1	6.0	8.8	0.6	14.9	0.9	0.5
New York, NY	7.1	10.6	3.1	4.0	13.8	4.4	1.0	0.7	0.6
Oklahoma City, OK	14.1	11.4	8.3	9.4	1.8	0.9	2.1	1.9	1.6
Omaha, NE	32.6	15.6	9.0	4.5	4.5	4.1	2.6	1.3	2.0
Orlando, FL	10.9	8.9	7.6	8.3	5.6	2.2	2.3	1.6	1.0
Oxnard, CA	11.7	8.6	8.5	3.4	5.1	1.9	2.3	1.9	1.3
Peoria, IL	32.1	13.7	10.1	9.1	3.9	2.4	2.7	1.7	1.7
Philadelphia, PA	16.8	20.5	7.9	3.5	14.0	5.4	1.5	1.4	1.0
Phoenix, AZ	14.7	9.7	8.4	6.7	4.6	2.6	2.4	1.7	1.4
Pittsburgh, PA	29.0	19.1	8.4	4.6	16.3	9.1	1.9	2.0	1.4
Portland, OR	19.9	11.9	11.3	5.1	4.0	1.9	3.3	3.2	2.2
Providence, RI	5.2	19.0	11.9	3.0	15.5	4.1	11.6	2.0	0.5
Provo, UT	12.0	5.0	28.6	5.4	2.3	0.7	2.1	5.4	2.0
Raleigh, NC	10.7	9.7	11.3	12.2	4.5	2.2	1.9	2.6	1.1
Reno, NV	15.1	12.6	9.6	5.4	7.3	2.0	3.2	2.1	1.5
Richmond, VA	10.3	8.8	12.3	9.1	3.5	1.8	1.9	2.2	0.8
Riverside, CA	8.9	6.4	5.8	3.6	3.4	1.2	1.9	1.2	1.2
Rochester, MN	37.6	10.6	6.5	4.4	1.6	3.2	2.8	1.3	2.3
Salem, OR	20.1	10.5	10.9	5.0	2.7	1.1	3.1	2.5	2.3
Salt Lake City, UT	11.7	6.3	22.0	5.8	3.1	1.0	1.8	4.1	2.5
San Antonio, TX	12.2	6.1	5.5	4.3	1.9	1.6	2.0	1.2	0.6
San Diego, CA	11.0	8.3	8.4	3.1	4.3	1.8	2.3	1.6	1.1
San Francisco, CA	8.6	7.9	6.4	2.6	5.3	1.5	2.0	1.6	0.9
San Jose, CA	7.6	5.7	5.4	2.0	4.6	1.2	1.7	1.2	0.9
Santa Rosa, CA	14.4	12.4	10.1	4.4	9.2	1.7	3.6	2.6	1.8
Savannah, GA	9.4	9.3	8.3	6.9	2.9	1.1	1.9	2.0	0.9
Seattle, WA	17.1	11.1	10.5	4.6	3.8	2.0	3.3	2.8	1.8
Sioux Falls, SD	40.8	10.6	4.7	4.0	1.0	1.6	2.0	0.9	7.5
Spokane, WA	23.8	13.1	11.7	5.4	4.9	1.6	3.6	3.0	1.9
Springfield, MO	20.2	12.1	10.8	19.0	2.6	1.2	2.9	1.8	2.0
Tallahassee, FL	9.5	10.0	9.0	6.4	4.2	1.6	2.6	2.7	1.1
Tampa, FL	13.4	12.0	9.0	8.8	7.8	3.0	3.1	1.8	1.3
Topeka, KS	30.7	14.7	10.4	6.9	2.3	1.2	3.4	1.8	2.1
Tulsa, OK	15.0	12.7	8.9	9.2	1.9	1.0	2.4	2.1	1.8
Virginia Beach, VA	10.9	9.6	9.7	11.6	4.5	2.0	2.1	2.2	1.0
Washington, DC	10.9	9.5	7.8	4.6	4.4	2.3	1.8	1.8	0.8
Wichita, KS	25.2	11.4	9.4	10.8	1.9	1.0	3.0	2.0	1.9
Wilmington, NC	12.0	11.9	11.9	17.8	4.8	1.9	2.5	3.1	1.1
Worcester, MA	6.3	21.6	10.4	3.9	13.8	6.3	14.7	2.4	0.7
U.S.	15.2	11.1	8.2	7.2	5.6	3.1	2.8	1.7	1.4

Note: Figures are the percentage of the total population reporting a particular ancestry. The nine most commonly reported ancestries in the U.S. are shown. Figures include multiple ancestries (e.g. if a person reported being Irish and Italian, they were included in both columns); Figures cover the Metropolitan Statistical Area—see Appendix B for areas included; (1) Excludes Basque
Source: U.S. Census Bureau, 2010-2012 American Community Survey 3-Year Estimates

Foreign-Born Population: City

City	Percent of Population Born in								
	Any Foreign Country	Mexico	Asia	Europe	Carribean	South America	Central America[1]	Africa	Canada
Abilene, TX	n/a	n/a	n/a	n/a	n/a	n/a	n/a	n/a	n/a
Albuquerque, NM	10.5	5.9	2.2	0.9	0.5	0.4	0.3	0.2	0.2
Anchorage, AK	9.4	0.8	5.5	1.2	0.4	0.2	0.3	0.4	0.3
Ann Arbor, MI	17.6	0.3	11.0	3.5	0.2	0.8	0.3	0.6	0.9
Athens, GA	n/a	n/a	n/a	n/a	n/a	n/a	n/a	n/a	n/a
Atlanta, GA	8.2	1.8	2.7	1.3	0.6	0.5	0.3	0.7	0.1
Austin, TX	18.5	9.6	4.7	1.2	0.4	0.4	1.5	0.4	0.2
Baltimore, MD	7.3	0.7	1.9	1.0	1.1	0.5	1.0	1.0	0.1
Billings, MT	n/a	n/a	n/a	n/a	n/a	n/a	n/a	n/a	n/a
Boise City, ID	7.2	1.3	3.0	1.7	0.0	0.1	0.2	0.4	0.4
Boston, MA	26.6	0.4	6.9	3.6	7.9	2.0	2.8	2.6	0.4
Boulder, CO	10.0	2.4	3.5	2.9	0.1	0.4	0.2	0.1	0.3
Cape Coral, FL	13.6	0.5	1.3	3.1	5.1	2.4	0.9	0.1	0.3
Cedar Rapids, IA	n/a	n/a	n/a	n/a	n/a	n/a	n/a	n/a	n/a
Charleston, SC	n/a	n/a	n/a	n/a	n/a	n/a	n/a	n/a	n/a
Charlotte, NC	14.7	3.0	4.1	1.5	0.9	1.3	2.4	1.2	0.2
Chicago, IL	21.1	9.6	4.4	3.8	0.4	1.0	0.9	0.7	0.2
Cincinnati, OH	5.3	0.5	1.6	0.6	0.2	0.2	0.6	1.5	0.2
Clarksville, TN	n/a	n/a	n/a	n/a	n/a	n/a	n/a	n/a	n/a
Colorado Spgs, CO	8.4	2.4	2.2	1.8	0.2	0.3	0.5	0.3	0.4
Columbia, MO	n/a	n/a	n/a	n/a	n/a	n/a	n/a	n/a	n/a
Columbus, OH	10.9	1.6	3.8	0.9	0.5	0.5	0.4	3.1	0.1
Dallas, TX	24.8	17.1	2.6	0.8	0.2	0.5	2.2	1.3	0.2
Davenport, IA	n/a	n/a	n/a	n/a	n/a	n/a	n/a	n/a	n/a
Denver, CO	16.0	9.2	2.7	1.6	0.2	0.3	0.4	1.2	0.3
Des Moines, IA	n/a	n/a	n/a	n/a	n/a	n/a	n/a	n/a	n/a
Durham, NC	14.5	4.5	3.7	1.0	0.3	0.6	2.5	1.4	0.1
El Paso, TX	24.6	22.2	1.0	0.5	0.3	0.2	0.3	0.1	0.1
Erie, PA	n/a	n/a	n/a	n/a	n/a	n/a	n/a	n/a	n/a
Eugene, OR	8.1	2.1	3.6	1.1	0.0	0.2	0.2	0.1	0.5
Fargo, ND	n/a	n/a	n/a	n/a	n/a	n/a	n/a	n/a	n/a
Fayetteville, NC	6.4	0.7	2.2	1.3	0.5	0.6	0.7	0.3	0.1
Ft. Collins, CO	6.0	1.3	2.5	1.0	0.0	0.2	0.3	0.2	0.3
Ft. Wayne, IN	7.3	2.2	2.9	0.9	0.2	0.2	0.5	0.3	0.2
Ft. Worth, TX	17.6	11.5	3.2	0.8	0.2	0.4	0.7	0.6	0.1
Gainesville, FL	12.7	0.4	5.4	1.7	2.0	2.0	0.4	0.4	0.3
Grand Rapids, MI	9.3	3.3	1.9	0.8	0.4	0.2	1.5	0.8	0.4
Green Bay, WI	n/a	n/a	n/a	n/a	n/a	n/a	n/a	n/a	n/a
Greensboro, NC	11.1	2.6	3.6	1.0	0.3	0.6	0.8	1.9	0.2
Honolulu, HI	28.6	0.2	23.8	1.2	0.1	0.2	0.1	0.1	0.3
Houston, TX	28.1	13.4	5.4	1.1	0.5	1.0	5.4	1.1	0.2
Huntsville, AL	6.5	1.6	2.0	0.8	0.5	0.2	0.4	0.9	0.1
Indianapolis, IN	8.4	3.6	2.0	0.5	0.2	0.2	0.8	1.0	0.1
Jacksonville, FL	9.6	0.5	3.7	1.7	1.6	0.9	0.6	0.6	0.2
Kansas City, MO	7.6	2.3	2.0	0.7	0.5	0.3	0.4	1.1	0.1
Lafayette, LA	n/a	n/a	n/a	n/a	n/a	n/a	n/a	n/a	n/a
Las Vegas, NV	21.2	10.3	5.0	1.5	0.8	0.6	2.1	0.4	0.4
Lexington, KY	8.9	3.0	3.2	0.8	0.2	0.3	0.5	0.6	0.2
Lincoln, NE	7.8	1.2	3.9	1.1	0.1	0.2	0.4	0.6	0.1
Little Rock, AR	n/a	n/a	n/a	n/a	n/a	n/a	n/a	n/a	n/a
Los Angeles, CA	38.9	14.2	11.2	2.4	0.3	1.1	8.5	0.7	0.3
Louisville, KY	6.7	0.9	2.1	0.9	1.3	0.2	0.2	0.9	0.1
Lubbock, TX	n/a	n/a	n/a	n/a	n/a	n/a	n/a	n/a	n/a
Madison, WI	11.0	1.8	5.9	1.4	0.1	0.7	0.1	0.7	0.4

Table continued on next page.

City	Any Foreign Country	Mexico	Asia	Europe	Carribean	South America	Central America[1]	Africa	Canada
Manchester, NH	13.0	1.5	3.8	2.5	0.9	1.4	0.3	1.5	1.0
McAllen, TX	n/a	n/a	n/a	n/a	n/a	n/a	n/a	n/a	n/a
Miami, FL	58.3	1.1	1.0	1.5	34.0	7.7	12.5	0.2	0.2
Midland, TX	n/a	n/a	n/a	n/a	n/a	n/a	n/a	n/a	n/a
Minneapolis, MN	14.7	3.0	3.7	1.3	0.2	1.5	0.5	4.3	0.3
Montgomery, AL	n/a	n/a	n/a	n/a	n/a	n/a	n/a	n/a	n/a
Nashville, TN	12.0	3.4	3.3	0.9	0.3	0.4	1.6	1.9	0.2
New Orleans, LA	5.8	0.6	2.0	0.8	0.2	0.4	1.4	0.3	0.1
New York, NY	37.3	2.3	10.3	5.8	10.5	5.1	1.5	1.5	0.3
Oklahoma City, OK	12.2	6.7	3.1	0.4	0.1	0.2	0.9	0.5	0.1
Omaha, NE	9.7	4.5	2.3	0.7	0.1	0.2	0.9	1.0	0.1
Orlando, FL	18.9	1.3	2.6	1.3	6.5	5.5	0.8	0.6	0.3
Oxnard, CA	n/a	n/a	n/a	n/a	n/a	n/a	n/a	n/a	n/a
Peoria, IL	n/a	n/a	n/a	n/a	n/a	n/a	n/a	n/a	n/a
Philadelphia, PA	12.0	0.4	4.7	2.3	2.1	0.8	0.4	1.1	0.1
Phoenix, AZ	20.1	13.3	2.9	1.5	0.3	0.3	0.6	0.6	0.3
Pittsburgh, PA	7.2	0.3	3.9	1.7	0.2	0.3	0.1	0.5	0.2
Portland, OR	13.8	3.0	5.5	2.7	0.2	0.2	0.5	0.8	0.5
Providence, RI	29.8	0.5	4.6	2.2	10.6	1.6	7.5	2.6	0.2
Provo, UT	n/a	n/a	n/a	n/a	n/a	n/a	n/a	n/a	n/a
Raleigh, NC	13.9	3.1	3.7	1.2	0.8	1.0	1.7	2.1	0.3
Reno, NV	16.3	7.7	4.7	1.4	0.1	0.3	1.5	0.2	0.2
Richmond, VA	7.5	1.2	1.6	0.8	0.3	0.3	2.0	1.0	0.2
Riverside, CA	23.4	14.5	4.7	0.8	0.3	0.6	2.0	0.2	0.2
Rochester, MN	12.7	1.6	5.2	1.5	0.2	0.4	0.2	2.8	0.5
Salem, OR	n/a	n/a	n/a	n/a	n/a	n/a	n/a	n/a	n/a
Salt Lake City, UT	17.5	7.0	3.6	2.4	0.3	1.0	0.8	1.2	0.3
San Antonio, TX	14.3	10.0	2.1	0.7	0.2	0.3	0.8	0.3	0.1
San Diego, CA	26.3	9.5	11.8	2.3	0.2	0.6	0.5	0.9	0.4
San Francisco, CA	36.1	2.7	22.8	4.7	0.2	1.2	3.0	0.4	0.6
San Jose, CA	38.5	10.1	23.4	2.0	0.1	0.5	1.1	0.6	0.4
Santa Rosa, CA	18.0	9.9	3.5	1.4	0.1	0.3	1.2	0.8	0.3
Savannah, GA	6.2	2.0	1.9	0.6	0.4	0.4	0.2	0.4	0.2
Seattle, WA	18.1	1.3	10.0	2.5	0.2	0.4	0.4	2.2	0.9
Sioux Falls, SD	n/a	n/a	n/a	n/a	n/a	n/a	n/a	n/a	n/a
Spokane, WA	7.2	0.4	2.4	3.1	0.1	0.2	0.2	0.3	0.5
Springfield, MO	n/a	n/a	n/a	n/a	n/a	n/a	n/a	n/a	n/a
Tallahassee, FL	7.9	0.4	2.9	1.1	1.9	0.7	0.2	0.5	0.2
Tampa, FL	15.6	1.1	2.8	1.5	6.3	1.6	1.2	0.7	0.4
Topeka, KS	n/a	n/a	n/a	n/a	n/a	n/a	n/a	n/a	n/a
Tulsa, OK	10.0	5.7	2.2	0.5	0.1	0.3	0.7	0.3	0.2
Virginia Beach, VA	8.8	0.4	4.6	1.6	0.7	0.5	0.4	0.4	0.2
Washington, DC	13.8	0.5	2.6	2.5	1.3	1.1	3.2	2.2	0.2
Wichita, KS	10.4	4.7	3.8	0.4	0.1	0.2	0.5	0.6	0.1
Wilmington, NC	n/a	n/a	n/a	n/a	n/a	n/a	n/a	n/a	n/a
Worcester, MA	20.3	0.4	5.8	3.7	2.6	2.6	1.0	4.0	0.2
U.S.	13.0	3.7	3.7	1.6	1.2	0.9	1.0	0.5	0.3

Note: (1) Excludes Mexico
Source: U.S. Census Bureau, 2010-2012 American Community Survey 3-Year Estimates

Foreign-Born Population: Metro Area

Metro Area	Any Foreign Country	Mexico	Asia	Europe	Carribean	South America	Central America[1]	Africa	Canada
Abilene, TX	n/a	n/a	n/a	n/a	n/a	n/a	n/a	n/a	n/a
Albuquerque, NM	9.6	6.0	1.6	0.8	0.3	0.3	0.2	0.1	0.2
Anchorage, AK	8.1	0.6	4.5	1.4	0.3	0.2	0.2	0.3	0.3
Ann Arbor, MI	11.2	0.5	6.3	2.0	0.2	0.4	0.4	0.8	0.6
Athens, GA	7.6	2.9	2.3	0.7	0.1	0.5	0.7	0.3	0.2
Atlanta, GA	13.3	3.2	3.9	1.2	1.5	0.9	1.1	1.3	0.2
Austin, TX	14.6	7.5	3.6	1.1	0.3	0.4	1.0	0.4	0.3
Baltimore, MD	9.3	0.5	3.7	1.3	0.7	0.5	1.1	1.2	0.2
Billings, MT	n/a	n/a	n/a	n/a	n/a	n/a	n/a	n/a	n/a
Boise City, ID	6.6	2.9	1.5	1.2	0.1	0.2	0.2	0.2	0.3
Boston, MA	16.8	0.2	5.3	3.3	2.9	1.9	1.4	1.3	0.5
Boulder, CO	10.5	3.7	3.2	2.2	0.1	0.3	0.3	0.2	0.3
Cape Coral, FL	14.9	2.8	1.2	2.3	4.4	1.7	1.4	0.1	0.9
Cedar Rapids, IA	n/a	n/a	n/a	n/a	n/a	n/a	n/a	n/a	n/a
Charleston, SC	5.2	1.5	1.2	1.0	0.3	0.3	0.5	0.1	0.2
Charlotte, NC	10.2	2.6	2.5	1.2	0.6	0.9	1.4	0.7	0.2
Chicago, IL	17.7	7.1	4.6	3.9	0.3	0.6	0.5	0.5	0.2
Cincinnati, OH	4.0	0.5	1.6	0.8	0.1	0.2	0.3	0.5	0.1
Clarksville, TN	n/a	n/a	n/a	n/a	n/a	n/a	n/a	n/a	n/a
Colorado Spgs, CO	7.2	1.8	1.9	1.8	0.2	0.3	0.5	0.3	0.4
Columbia, MO	n/a	n/a	n/a	n/a	n/a	n/a	n/a	n/a	n/a
Columbus, OH	7.0	0.9	2.7	0.8	0.2	0.3	0.3	1.6	0.2
Dallas, TX	17.6	9.2	4.3	0.8	0.2	0.5	1.3	1.0	0.2
Davenport, IA	4.7	1.8	1.3	0.7	0.0	0.2	0.1	0.5	0.1
Denver, CO	12.2	5.6	2.8	1.5	0.1	0.3	0.5	0.9	0.3
Des Moines, IA	7.4	2.0	2.3	1.4	0.0	0.1	0.4	0.8	0.2
Durham, NC	12.3	3.9	3.3	1.2	0.3	0.5	1.8	0.9	0.3
El Paso, TX	25.7	23.5	0.9	0.4	0.2	0.2	0.3	0.0	0.1
Erie, PA	4.1	0.2	1.3	1.7	0.1	0.1	0.1	0.4	0.2
Eugene, OR	5.9	1.9	2.0	1.0	0.0	0.2	0.1	0.1	0.4
Fargo, ND	n/a	n/a	n/a	n/a	n/a	n/a	n/a	n/a	n/a
Fayetteville, NC	5.9	1.1	1.7	1.1	0.5	0.5	0.7	0.3	0.1
Ft. Collins, CO	5.0	1.6	1.5	1.0	0.1	0.2	0.2	0.1	0.2
Ft. Wayne, IN	5.2	1.5	2.0	0.8	0.1	0.1	0.3	0.2	0.1
Ft. Worth, TX	17.6	9.2	4.3	0.8	0.2	0.5	1.3	1.0	0.2
Gainesville, FL	10.3	0.4	3.9	1.6	1.6	1.6	0.4	0.4	0.3
Grand Rapids, MI	6.1	1.6	1.6	1.1	0.4	0.2	0.6	0.4	0.3
Green Bay, WI	4.4	2.0	1.3	0.3	0.1	0.1	0.3	0.2	0.1
Greensboro, NC	8.4	3.0	2.4	0.7	0.2	0.4	0.6	0.9	0.1
Honolulu, HI	19.7	0.2	16.1	0.8	0.2	0.2	0.1	0.1	0.3
Houston, TX	22.1	9.9	5.3	1.0	0.5	0.9	3.4	0.9	0.2
Huntsville, AL	5.1	1.4	1.7	0.7	0.3	0.2	0.2	0.4	0.1
Indianapolis, IN	6.3	2.1	2.0	0.6	0.2	0.2	0.4	0.7	0.1
Jacksonville, FL	7.9	0.4	2.9	1.6	1.2	0.8	0.4	0.4	0.2
Kansas City, MO	6.2	2.1	1.9	0.6	0.2	0.2	0.4	0.6	0.1
Lafayette, LA	n/a	n/a	n/a	n/a	n/a	n/a	n/a	n/a	n/a
Las Vegas, NV	21.7	9.1	6.6	1.7	0.8	0.6	1.8	0.6	0.3
Lexington, KY	6.8	2.5	2.2	0.7	0.2	0.2	0.4	0.4	0.1
Lincoln, NE	6.9	1.1	3.4	1.1	0.1	0.2	0.3	0.5	0.1
Little Rock, AR	4.0	1.6	1.3	0.3	0.1	0.1	0.3	0.1	0.1
Los Angeles, CA	34.1	13.4	12.3	1.7	0.3	0.9	4.3	0.5	0.3
Louisville, KY	4.9	1.0	1.5	0.7	0.7	0.2	0.2	0.5	0.1
Lubbock, TX	5.8	2.7	1.8	0.4	0.1	0.2	0.3	0.3	0.1
Madison, WI	7.1	1.6	3.2	1.0	0.1	0.5	0.1	0.4	0.3

Table continued on next page.

Metro Area	Any Foreign Country	Mexico	Asia	Europe	Carribean	South America	Central America[1]	Africa	Canada
					Percent of Population Born in				
Manchester, NH	8.5	0.7	2.7	1.8	0.5	0.9	0.3	0.6	0.9
McAllen, TX	29.4	27.4	0.8	0.2	0.1	0.2	0.4	0.0	0.3
Miami, FL	38.5	1.2	1.9	2.2	20.3	7.7	4.2	0.4	0.6
Midland, TX	n/a	n/a	n/a	n/a	n/a	n/a	n/a	n/a	n/a
Minneapolis, MN	9.6	1.5	3.8	1.1	0.1	0.5	0.4	2.0	0.3
Montgomery, AL	n/a	n/a	n/a	n/a	n/a	n/a	n/a	n/a	n/a
Nashville, TN	7.4	2.1	2.2	0.7	0.2	0.3	0.9	0.9	0.2
New Orleans, LA	7.0	0.6	2.0	0.6	0.5	0.4	2.5	0.2	0.1
New York, NY	29.0	1.7	8.1	4.8	6.7	4.4	1.9	1.1	0.2
Oklahoma City, OK	7.9	3.8	2.3	0.5	0.1	0.2	0.5	0.4	0.1
Omaha, NE	6.8	2.8	1.9	0.6	0.1	0.1	0.6	0.6	0.1
Orlando, FL	16.2	1.3	2.8	1.7	4.9	3.7	0.9	0.5	0.4
Oxnard, CA	22.8	13.3	5.2	1.6	0.1	0.6	1.3	0.2	0.5
Peoria, IL	3.1	0.6	1.6	0.5	0.1	0.1	0.1	0.1	0.1
Philadelphia, PA	9.7	0.9	3.9	2.0	1.1	0.6	0.4	0.8	0.1
Phoenix, AZ	14.4	8.1	2.8	1.4	0.2	0.3	0.5	0.4	0.6
Pittsburgh, PA	3.2	0.1	1.5	1.0	0.1	0.1	0.1	0.2	0.1
Portland, OR	12.4	3.7	4.4	2.4	0.1	0.2	0.4	0.4	0.5
Providence, RI	12.7	0.2	2.1	4.4	1.8	1.0	1.5	1.4	0.3
Provo, UT	7.2	3.0	1.0	0.6	0.1	1.3	0.5	0.1	0.4
Raleigh, NC	11.8	3.3	3.7	1.1	0.5	0.7	1.1	1.1	0.3
Reno, NV	14.7	7.2	3.9	1.4	0.1	0.2	1.2	0.2	0.3
Richmond, VA	7.2	0.8	2.6	1.1	0.3	0.4	1.1	0.7	0.2
Riverside, CA	21.6	13.1	4.5	0.9	0.2	0.5	1.6	0.3	0.3
Rochester, MN	8.0	1.0	3.2	1.1	0.1	0.2	0.2	1.6	0.3
Salem, OR	12.0	7.9	1.5	1.1	0.1	0.2	0.5	0.2	0.3
Salt Lake City, UT	11.7	4.8	2.4	1.4	0.2	1.0	0.6	0.4	0.3
San Antonio, TX	12.0	8.1	1.8	0.7	0.2	0.3	0.7	0.2	0.1
San Diego, CA	23.4	10.7	8.5	1.9	0.2	0.5	0.5	0.6	0.4
San Francisco, CA	29.9	5.8	16.1	2.9	0.2	1.0	2.5	0.5	0.4
San Jose, CA	36.6	8.2	22.6	2.9	0.1	0.7	1.0	0.5	0.5
Santa Rosa, CA	16.4	9.1	2.9	1.9	0.1	0.3	1.0	0.5	0.3
Savannah, GA	5.9	1.5	1.9	0.6	0.5	0.3	0.3	0.6	0.1
Seattle, WA	17.0	2.6	8.4	2.9	0.1	0.3	0.4	1.2	0.8
Sioux Falls, SD	n/a	n/a	n/a	n/a	n/a	n/a	n/a	n/a	n/a
Spokane, WA	5.7	0.4	1.9	2.3	0.0	0.1	0.1	0.2	0.5
Springfield, MO	2.5	0.4	0.9	0.6	0.1	0.1	0.1	0.2	0.1
Tallahassee, FL	6.2	0.7	1.9	0.9	1.3	0.6	0.3	0.4	0.2
Tampa, FL	12.7	1.4	2.4	2.4	3.2	1.6	0.6	0.4	0.7
Topeka, KS	n/a	n/a	n/a	n/a	n/a	n/a	n/a	n/a	n/a
Tulsa, OK	5.8	2.9	1.5	0.4	0.1	0.2	0.4	0.2	0.2
Virginia Beach, VA	6.2	0.4	2.7	1.1	0.5	0.4	0.5	0.4	0.2
Washington, DC	21.9	0.8	7.8	1.9	1.0	2.3	4.7	3.0	0.2
Wichita, KS	7.3	3.2	2.6	0.5	0.1	0.2	0.3	0.4	0.1
Wilmington, NC	5.0	2.0	0.7	1.0	0.2	0.2	0.5	0.1	0.2
Worcester, MA	11.1	0.2	3.4	2.3	1.0	1.6	0.6	1.4	0.6
U.S.	13.0	3.7	3.7	1.6	1.2	0.9	1.0	0.5	0.3

Note: Figures cover the Metropolitan Statistical Area—see Appendix B for areas included; (1) Excludes Mexico
Source: U.S. Census Bureau, 2010-2012 American Community Survey 3-Year Estimates

Marital Status: City

City	Never Married	Now Married[1]	Separated	Widowed	Divorced
Abilene, TX	35.3	43.2	2.4	6.8	12.2
Albuquerque, NM	35.7	43.0	1.8	5.1	14.4
Anchorage, AK	33.8	47.6	1.7	3.7	13.2
Ann Arbor, MI	56.0	32.7	0.6	3.5	7.2
Athens, GA	56.5	30.1	1.7	4.0	7.7
Atlanta, GA	54.2	26.8	2.6	5.4	11.1
Austin, TX	43.8	39.1	2.3	3.4	11.5
Baltimore, MD	52.1	25.9	4.2	7.1	10.8
Billings, MT	30.3	46.6	1.8	6.6	14.7
Boise City, ID	32.1	47.8	1.1	5.0	14.0
Boston, MA	56.8	28.3	2.9	4.1	7.9
Boulder, CO	54.8	33.7	0.8	2.6	8.0
Cape Coral, FL	25.1	52.3	1.9	7.1	13.7
Cedar Rapids, IA	34.4	46.2	1.8	5.8	11.7
Charleston, SC	44.2	38.1	2.6	5.5	9.5
Charlotte, NC	38.7	43.1	3.2	4.6	10.5
Chicago, IL	48.6	34.3	2.6	5.6	8.8
Cincinnati, OH	51.1	27.7	3.0	5.7	12.6
Clarksville, TN	29.2	52.5	2.8	3.7	11.7
Colorado Spgs, CO	28.8	51.3	2.2	4.7	13.1
Columbia, MO	50.9	35.6	1.4	3.3	8.8
Columbus, OH	43.2	36.8	2.6	4.5	12.8
Dallas, TX	40.5	39.7	3.6	4.9	11.3
Davenport, IA	35.8	43.4	1.2	6.1	13.5
Denver, CO	41.9	38.3	2.3	4.5	13.0
Des Moines, IA	34.9	43.1	2.6	5.9	13.5
Durham, NC	42.0	40.3	2.9	4.7	10.2
El Paso, TX	31.6	47.8	3.5	5.7	11.4
Erie, PA	42.2	36.4	3.5	6.9	11.1
Eugene, OR	42.7	38.0	1.3	5.3	12.7
Fargo, ND	44.2	41.8	0.9	4.3	8.8
Fayetteville, NC	32.8	44.4	3.6	5.7	13.5
Ft. Collins, CO	43.3	43.4	0.7	3.2	9.4
Ft. Wayne, IN	34.3	44.8	1.4	6.2	13.2
Ft. Worth, TX	33.4	46.6	3.1	4.7	12.3
Gainesville, FL	62.5	24.1	1.6	4.0	7.7
Grand Rapids, MI	44.8	36.5	2.5	5.4	10.8
Green Bay, WI	37.3	43.9	1.2	5.4	12.1
Greensboro, NC	41.2	39.4	2.9	5.7	10.7
Honolulu, HI	37.1	43.7	1.5	7.4	10.3
Houston, TX	39.3	41.5	3.6	4.9	10.7
Huntsville, AL	35.3	42.8	2.4	6.2	13.4
Indianapolis, IN	39.0	39.5	2.4	5.4	13.7
Jacksonville, FL	33.5	43.6	2.8	6.0	14.1
Kansas City, MO	38.4	40.4	2.4	5.5	13.2
Lafayette, LA	40.2	38.6	2.2	6.0	13.0
Las Vegas, NV	32.3	44.0	3.0	5.6	15.0
Lexington, KY	37.5	43.3	1.9	4.5	12.8
Lincoln, NE	37.0	46.3	1.4	4.2	11.2
Little Rock, AR	37.0	40.2	2.7	6.0	14.0
Los Angeles, CA	45.5	38.4	2.9	4.7	8.5
Louisville, KY	35.0	42.5	2.4	6.5	13.6
Lubbock, TX	39.9	41.4	2.2	5.7	10.9
Madison, WI	48.2	38.4	1.2	3.3	8.9
Manchester, NH	36.3	43.1	2.2	5.3	13.2
McAllen, TX	30.7	50.0	3.9	6.1	9.4

Table continued on next page.

City	Never Married	Now Married[1]	Separated	Widowed	Divorced
Miami, FL	39.9	34.5	4.6	6.9	14.0
Midland, TX	30.1	51.8	2.0	5.3	10.8
Minneapolis, MN	52.3	32.3	1.6	3.5	10.3
Montgomery, AL	39.2	38.3	3.2	6.2	13.1
Nashville, TN	40.5	39.1	2.5	5.2	12.7
New Orleans, LA	48.8	29.7	2.8	6.3	12.3
New York, NY	44.1	38.6	3.4	5.7	8.1
Oklahoma City, OK	30.7	48.2	2.6	5.4	13.1
Omaha, NE	37.3	42.9	1.9	5.8	12.1
Orlando, FL	43.3	34.9	3.6	5.1	13.0
Oxnard, CA	38.4	46.2	2.7	4.5	8.2
Peoria, IL	40.0	40.5	1.8	6.2	11.4
Philadelphia, PA	51.7	28.9	3.5	7.0	8.9
Phoenix, AZ	38.2	42.8	2.3	4.2	12.5
Pittsburgh, PA	51.5	30.4	2.6	6.7	8.8
Portland, OR	41.0	39.8	1.7	4.6	12.9
Providence, RI	54.3	28.2	3.6	4.8	9.1
Provo, UT	48.8	42.8	0.9	2.3	5.2
Raleigh, NC	41.7	40.8	2.9	4.1	10.5
Reno, NV	35.3	42.4	2.5	4.9	14.9
Richmond, VA	52.3	25.4	4.3	5.9	12.1
Riverside, CA	39.2	43.5	2.6	4.6	10.1
Rochester, MN	32.1	52.3	1.2	4.7	9.7
Salem, OR	30.9	46.5	2.6	5.3	14.7
Salt Lake City, UT	41.7	39.6	2.1	4.4	12.2
San Antonio, TX	35.5	43.4	3.1	5.5	12.5
San Diego, CA	40.8	42.7	2.1	4.6	9.9
San Francisco, CA	47.0	37.8	1.7	5.2	8.2
San Jose, CA	34.3	50.9	1.9	4.5	8.4
Santa Rosa, CA	34.4	45.6	2.1	5.4	12.6
Savannah, GA	46.9	30.3	2.8	7.0	13.0
Seattle, WA	44.0	39.3	1.3	4.2	11.2
Sioux Falls, SD	33.0	49.3	1.2	5.1	11.4
Spokane, WA	33.5	44.1	1.6	6.3	14.4
Springfield, MO	38.3	37.9	2.1	7.1	14.7
Tallahassee, FL	56.4	29.0	1.5	3.8	9.4
Tampa, FL	41.2	36.4	3.3	5.6	13.5
Topeka, KS	31.6	43.4	1.7	7.1	16.2
Tulsa, OK	33.3	42.9	2.6	6.1	15.1
Virginia Beach, VA	30.5	51.0	2.7	4.7	11.0
Washington, DC	58.0	25.1	2.4	5.0	9.5
Wichita, KS	31.7	47.1	2.2	5.6	13.4
Wilmington, NC	41.9	37.9	3.0	5.1	12.2
Worcester, MA	43.5	36.0	2.6	6.5	11.4
U.S.	32.4	48.4	2.2	6.0	11.0

Note: Figures are percentages and cover the population 15 years of age and older; (1) Excludes separated
Source: U.S. Census Bureau, 2010-2012 American Community Survey 3-Year Estimates

Marital Status: Metro Area

Metro Area	Never Married	Now Married[1]	Separated	Widowed	Divorced
Abilene, TX	31.3	46.9	2.3	7.0	12.5
Albuquerque, NM	33.7	45.6	1.8	5.2	13.7
Anchorage, AK	32.4	48.8	1.8	3.7	13.2
Ann Arbor, MI	42.0	43.8	0.9	4.2	9.1
Athens, GA	44.1	40.7	1.7	4.9	8.6
Atlanta, GA	33.9	47.9	2.4	4.7	11.0
Austin, TX	35.8	47.7	2.0	3.6	11.0
Baltimore, MD	35.5	45.7	2.6	6.2	10.1
Billings, MT	27.6	50.7	1.6	6.2	13.9
Boise City, ID	27.0	54.6	1.3	4.7	12.4
Boston, MA	36.2	47.3	1.9	5.6	9.1
Boulder, CO	36.9	48.1	1.1	3.4	10.5
Cape Coral, FL	25.9	50.4	2.1	8.2	13.4
Cedar Rapids, IA	28.8	52.6	1.5	5.8	11.3
Charleston, SC	33.7	46.5	3.2	5.7	10.9
Charlotte, NC	32.1	49.7	3.0	5.1	10.1
Chicago, IL	36.1	47.1	1.9	5.7	9.2
Cincinnati, OH	31.1	49.6	1.9	5.9	11.6
Clarksville, TN	26.5	54.7	2.5	5.1	11.2
Colorado Spgs, CO	27.9	53.7	2.0	4.3	12.0
Columbia, MO	42.0	42.9	1.5	4.2	9.4
Columbus, OH	33.4	47.8	2.0	5.0	11.9
Dallas, TX	31.2	50.7	2.6	4.5	11.1
Davenport, IA	28.9	50.3	1.3	6.9	12.6
Denver, CO	31.5	49.9	1.8	4.3	12.4
Des Moines, IA	28.6	53.4	1.6	5.0	11.4
Durham, NC	37.4	45.4	2.4	5.0	9.8
El Paso, TX	32.1	47.8	3.8	5.5	10.8
Erie, PA	34.3	46.4	2.6	6.9	9.8
Eugene, OR	32.9	45.3	1.6	5.9	14.4
Fargo, ND	38.3	47.9	0.7	4.3	8.8
Fayetteville, NC	31.1	47.2	3.6	5.6	12.6
Ft. Collins, CO	33.1	51.4	1.0	4.0	10.5
Ft. Wayne, IN	29.9	50.9	1.3	5.8	12.1
Ft. Worth, TX	31.2	50.7	2.6	4.5	11.1
Gainesville, FL	45.6	37.9	1.7	4.8	9.9
Grand Rapids, MI	31.5	51.5	1.4	5.0	10.6
Green Bay, WI	30.2	53.6	0.9	5.3	10.0
Greensboro, NC	32.2	47.5	3.3	6.3	10.7
Honolulu, HI	33.8	49.7	1.4	6.2	9.0
Houston, TX	32.4	49.7	2.9	4.6	10.3
Huntsville, AL	29.2	51.1	1.9	5.9	11.9
Indianapolis, IN	31.2	49.2	1.8	5.1	12.7
Jacksonville, FL	30.4	47.6	2.4	5.9	13.7
Kansas City, MO	29.3	50.9	1.9	5.5	12.4
Lafayette, LA	34.6	45.1	2.2	5.8	12.3
Las Vegas, NV	33.2	45.0	2.7	5.1	14.0
Lexington, KY	32.9	47.3	2.1	4.9	12.8
Lincoln, NE	35.2	48.8	1.3	4.1	10.6
Little Rock, AR	29.4	49.1	2.3	5.9	13.2
Los Angeles, CA	39.6	44.2	2.5	5.0	8.7
Louisville, KY	30.2	48.5	2.0	6.2	13.1
Lubbock, TX	37.0	44.3	2.2	5.9	10.6
Madison, WI	35.5	49.3	1.2	4.1	9.8
Manchester, NH	29.5	52.6	1.5	5.1	11.4
McAllen, TX	31.6	52.4	4.2	5.1	6.8

Table continued on next page.

Metro Area	Never Married	Now Married[1]	Separated	Widowed	Divorced
Miami, FL	33.9	43.3	3.1	7.0	12.8
Midland, TX	28.9	53.3	2.1	5.1	10.6
Minneapolis, MN	33.1	51.3	1.3	4.4	10.0
Montgomery, AL	33.4	44.4	3.0	6.5	12.7
Nashville, TN	31.0	49.6	2.0	5.3	12.1
New Orleans, LA	36.8	42.0	2.5	6.5	12.2
New York, NY	37.8	45.5	2.6	6.1	8.0
Oklahoma City, OK	29.4	50.0	2.2	5.7	12.7
Omaha, NE	31.0	51.3	1.5	5.3	11.0
Orlando, FL	34.2	45.9	2.7	5.5	11.7
Oxnard, CA	32.2	50.5	1.9	5.1	10.4
Peoria, IL	28.6	52.0	1.5	6.3	11.5
Philadelphia, PA	36.9	45.4	2.3	6.6	8.9
Phoenix, AZ	33.0	48.0	1.8	5.1	12.2
Pittsburgh, PA	31.6	48.5	2.1	8.1	9.7
Portland, OR	31.4	49.4	1.8	4.8	12.7
Providence, RI	35.0	45.0	2.0	6.7	11.3
Provo, UT	31.8	58.4	1.1	2.6	6.0
Raleigh, NC	31.2	52.2	2.8	4.5	9.4
Reno, NV	30.7	48.0	2.1	4.8	14.4
Richmond, VA	33.7	46.8	2.9	5.8	10.8
Riverside, CA	34.4	47.5	2.7	5.0	10.3
Rochester, MN	28.2	56.5	1.0	4.9	9.4
Salem, OR	29.1	50.9	2.5	5.4	12.2
Salt Lake City, UT	30.8	52.7	1.8	3.9	10.8
San Antonio, TX	31.8	48.7	2.6	5.3	11.6
San Diego, CA	36.0	46.9	1.9	5.0	10.2
San Francisco, CA	36.1	47.2	2.0	5.2	9.5
San Jose, CA	32.6	52.9	1.7	4.6	8.3
Santa Rosa, CA	32.1	47.8	1.9	5.3	13.0
Savannah, GA	35.3	43.7	2.4	6.0	12.8
Seattle, WA	32.2	49.6	1.7	4.5	12.0
Sioux Falls, SD	30.1	53.6	0.9	5.1	10.3
Spokane, WA	30.3	49.5	1.5	5.6	13.2
Springfield, MO	27.6	52.1	1.7	6.4	12.2
Tallahassee, FL	43.0	39.3	1.9	4.6	11.1
Tampa, FL	29.8	46.1	2.5	7.5	14.1
Topeka, KS	26.3	52.3	1.3	6.3	13.8
Tulsa, OK	27.1	51.1	2.1	6.2	13.5
Virginia Beach, VA	32.8	47.6	3.0	5.5	11.0
Washington, DC	36.1	48.2	2.3	4.5	8.9
Wichita, KS	28.5	51.1	1.8	5.8	12.8
Wilmington, NC	28.2	50.9	2.8	6.0	12.1
Worcester, MA	32.8	48.6	1.8	6.1	10.7
U.S.	32.4	48.4	2.2	6.0	11.0

Note: Figures are percentages and cover the population 15 years of age and older; Figures cover the Metropolitan Statistical Area—see Appendix B for areas included; (1) Excludes separated
Source: U.S. Census Bureau, 2010-2012 American Community Survey 3-Year Estimates

Male/Female Ratio: City

City	Males	Females	Males per 100 Females
Abilene, TX	61,444	58,583	104.9
Albuquerque, NM	267,458	284,139	94.1
Anchorage, AK	150,377	145,662	103.2
Ann Arbor, MI	57,616	57,508	100.2
Athens, GA	55,698	61,633	90.4
Atlanta, GA	214,757	217,995	98.5
Austin, TX	413,718	404,518	102.3
Baltimore, MD	292,411	328,432	89.0
Billings, MT	51,343	54,305	94.5
Boise City, ID	104,400	104,892	99.5
Boston, MA	299,769	328,596	91.2
Boulder, CO	50,506	49,897	101.2
Cape Coral, FL	78,211	79,722	98.1
Cedar Rapids, IA	62,523	64,980	96.2
Charleston, SC	58,093	65,133	89.2
Charlotte, NC	363,181	393,544	92.3
Chicago, IL	1,311,742	1,394,239	94.1
Cincinnati, OH	140,714	155,729	90.4
Clarksville, TN	67,056	70,532	95.1
Colorado Spgs, CO	209,996	215,729	97.3
Columbia, MO	52,890	58,314	90.7
Columbus, OH	389,045	410,312	94.8
Dallas, TX	612,684	607,195	100.9
Davenport, IA	49,079	51,564	95.2
Denver, CO	309,777	309,239	100.2
Des Moines, IA	99,913	105,709	94.5
Durham, NC	110,168	123,992	88.9
El Paso, TX	317,940	344,767	92.2
Erie, PA	49,329	52,090	94.7
Eugene, OR	77,558	79,638	97.4
Fargo, ND	53,572	54,180	98.9
Fayetteville, NC	98,609	102,725	96.0
Ft. Collins, CO	72,332	73,903	97.9
Ft. Wayne, IN	122,482	131,313	93.3
Ft. Worth, TX	369,818	392,044	94.3
Gainesville, FL	60,145	65,128	92.3
Grand Rapids, MI	91,725	97,437	94.1
Green Bay, WI	50,917	53,577	95.0
Greensboro, NC	129,218	144,423	89.5
Honolulu, HI	169,148	173,042	97.7
Houston, TX	1,069,485	1,060,631	100.8
Huntsville, AL	88,848	92,886	95.7
Indianapolis, IN	398,657	428,982	92.9
Jacksonville, FL	401,863	427,672	94.0
Kansas City, MO	222,575	239,717	92.8
Lafayette, LA	59,849	61,895	96.7
Las Vegas, NV	298,726	290,815	102.7
Lexington, KY	148,398	152,813	97.1
Lincoln, NE	131,120	131,094	100.0
Little Rock, AR	92,211	103,031	89.5
Los Angeles, CA	1,900,258	1,925,395	98.7
Louisville, KY	291,167	310,503	93.8
Lubbock, TX	115,293	118,182	97.6
Madison, WI	117,449	119,687	98.1
Manchester, NH	54,671	55,208	99.0

Table continued on next page.

City	Males	Females	Males per 100 Females
McAllen, TX	64,587	68,133	94.8
Miami, FL	202,143	206,179	98.0
Midland, TX	55,547	59,258	93.7
Minneapolis, MN	196,165	191,889	102.2
Montgomery, AL	97,117	109,229	88.9
Nashville, TN	297,280	316,549	93.9
New Orleans, LA	173,088	186,042	93.0
New York, NY	3,932,715	4,332,730	90.8
Oklahoma City, OK	291,687	298,605	97.7
Omaha, NE	203,256	213,118	95.4
Orlando, FL	118,191	125,704	94.0
Oxnard, CA	101,827	98,188	103.7
Peoria, IL	54,704	59,694	91.6
Philadelphia, PA	726,023	812,188	89.4
Phoenix, AZ	736,219	731,181	100.7
Pittsburgh, PA	148,144	157,862	93.8
Portland, OR	294,006	300,518	97.8
Providence, RI	86,626	91,673	94.5
Provo, UT	56,618	57,849	97.9
Raleigh, NC	199,292	215,081	92.7
Reno, NV	116,573	112,085	104.0
Richmond, VA	98,377	108,559	90.6
Riverside, CA	154,521	155,272	99.5
Rochester, MN	53,057	54,967	96.5
Salem, OR	76,947	79,208	97.1
Salt Lake City, UT	95,493	92,471	103.3
San Antonio, TX	661,308	696,835	94.9
San Diego, CA	665,894	655,651	101.6
San Francisco, CA	414,137	401,097	103.3
San Jose, CA	487,819	481,505	101.3
Santa Rosa, CA	84,372	85,004	99.3
Savannah, GA	66,795	72,872	91.7
Seattle, WA	308,107	314,166	98.1
Sioux Falls, SD	78,242	78,755	99.3
Spokane, WA	101,738	107,608	94.5
Springfield, MO	77,852	82,896	93.9
Tallahassee, FL	87,994	96,085	91.6
Tampa, FL	168,972	174,705	96.7
Topeka, KS	61,493	66,402	92.6
Tulsa, OK	190,081	203,043	93.6
Virginia Beach, VA	217,519	225,583	96.4
Washington, DC	292,559	326,218	89.7
Wichita, KS	189,420	194,605	97.3
Wilmington, NC	51,786	56,534	91.6
Worcester, MA	85,543	96,801	88.4
U.S.	153,276,055	158,333,314	96.8

Source: U.S. Census Bureau, 2010-2012 American Community Survey 3-Year Estimates

Male/Female Ratio: Metro Area

Metro Area	Males	Females	Males per 100 Females
Abilene, TX	83,952	82,388	101.9
Albuquerque, NM	440,882	455,314	96.8
Anchorage, AK	197,949	189,967	104.2
Ann Arbor, MI	171,853	176,458	97.4
Athens, GA	93,538	101,323	92.3
Atlanta, GA	2,609,093	2,752,059	94.8
Austin, TX	892,059	888,831	100.4
Baltimore, MD	1,316,630	1,417,508	92.9
Billings, MT	78,541	81,633	96.2
Boise City, ID	313,178	314,667	99.5
Boston, MA	2,229,374	2,373,295	93.9
Boulder, CO	150,911	149,770	100.8
Cape Coral, FL	310,415	322,084	96.4
Cedar Rapids, IA	128,955	131,385	98.2
Charleston, SC	333,074	349,170	95.4
Charlotte, NC	872,208	924,551	94.3
Chicago, IL	4,642,475	4,854,112	95.6
Cincinnati, OH	1,046,009	1,092,127	95.8
Clarksville, TN	139,821	140,411	99.6
Colorado Spgs, CO	330,119	329,300	100.2
Columbia, MO	85,543	90,514	94.5
Columbus, OH	912,971	946,726	96.4
Dallas, TX	3,216,334	3,303,515	97.4
Davenport, IA	187,118	194,249	96.3
Denver, CO	1,293,188	1,306,087	99.0
Des Moines, IA	285,448	295,124	96.7
Durham, NC	246,272	267,934	91.9
El Paso, TX	397,109	419,186	94.7
Erie, PA	138,077	142,717	96.7
Eugene, OR	173,728	179,587	96.7
Fargo, ND	106,873	105,898	100.9
Fayetteville, NC	180,157	191,549	94.1
Ft. Collins, CO	151,988	153,347	99.1
Ft. Wayne, IN	204,982	214,270	95.7
Ft. Worth, TX	3,216,334	3,303,515	97.4
Gainesville, FL	129,927	136,437	95.2
Grand Rapids, MI	386,335	393,347	98.2
Green Bay, WI	154,016	154,862	99.5
Greensboro, NC	351,105	379,472	92.5
Honolulu, HI	485,338	481,067	100.9
Houston, TX	3,027,722	3,058,151	99.0
Huntsville, AL	210,052	215,057	97.7
Indianapolis, IN	868,952	910,487	95.4
Jacksonville, FL	663,092	699,558	94.8
Kansas City, MO	1,005,603	1,046,192	96.1
Lafayette, LA	135,466	141,595	95.7
Las Vegas, NV	992,784	981,252	101.2
Lexington, KY	235,376	243,766	96.6
Lincoln, NE	153,781	152,845	100.6
Little Rock, AR	344,604	365,717	94.2
Los Angeles, CA	6,389,104	6,558,230	97.4
Louisville, KY	632,215	661,616	95.6
Lubbock, TX	143,217	146,468	97.8
Madison, WI	286,516	290,329	98.7
Manchester, NH	198,957	202,976	98.0

Table continued on next page.

Metro Area	Males	Females	Males per 100 Females
McAllen, TX	386,944	406,368	95.2
Miami, FL	2,753,497	2,923,911	94.2
Midland, TX	69,616	71,591	97.2
Minneapolis, MN	1,641,004	1,679,186	97.7
Montgomery, AL	180,522	196,442	91.9
Nashville, TN	791,205	827,614	95.6
New Orleans, LA	578,837	611,325	94.7
New York, NY	9,183,572	9,864,595	93.1
Oklahoma City, OK	629,988	646,783	97.4
Omaha, NE	432,704	444,267	97.4
Orlando, FL	1,066,934	1,112,486	95.9
Oxnard, CA	412,614	418,214	98.7
Peoria, IL	185,644	194,274	95.6
Philadelphia, PA	2,894,285	3,101,816	93.3
Phoenix, AZ	2,120,250	2,143,413	98.9
Pittsburgh, PA	1,141,730	1,217,495	93.8
Portland, OR	1,117,800	1,143,348	97.8
Providence, RI	774,756	826,452	93.7
Provo, UT	271,300	269,158	100.8
Raleigh, NC	567,822	595,047	95.4
Reno, NV	216,628	213,213	101.6
Richmond, VA	615,392	655,343	93.9
Riverside, CA	2,139,026	2,159,615	99.0
Rochester, MN	92,501	95,065	97.3
Salem, OR	195,208	198,724	98.2
Salt Lake City, UT	575,758	569,031	101.2
San Antonio, TX	1,078,236	1,114,703	96.7
San Diego, CA	1,576,317	1,563,409	100.8
San Francisco, CA	2,170,877	2,228,334	97.4
San Jose, CA	937,812	930,353	100.8
Santa Rosa, CA	239,948	248,289	96.6
Savannah, GA	172,578	182,961	94.3
Seattle, WA	1,743,562	1,756,070	99.3
Sioux Falls, SD	116,736	116,562	100.1
Spokane, WA	234,592	239,201	98.1
Springfield, MO	215,697	225,114	95.8
Tallahassee, FL	180,521	191,406	94.3
Tampa, FL	1,366,313	1,453,069	94.0
Topeka, KS	114,562	119,954	95.5
Tulsa, OK	464,528	481,216	96.5
Virginia Beach, VA	827,442	856,569	96.6
Washington, DC	2,782,107	2,928,736	95.0
Wichita, KS	309,440	316,500	97.8
Wilmington, NC	180,599	189,112	95.5
Worcester, MA	396,216	407,213	97.3
U.S.	153,276,055	158,333,314	96.8

Note: Figures cover the Metropolitan Statistical Area (MSA)—see Appendix B for areas included
Source: U.S. Census Bureau, 2010-2012 American Community Survey 3-Year Estimates

Gross Metropolitan Product

MSA[1]	2011	2012	2013	2014	Rank[2]
Abilene, TX	5.6	6.0	6.2	6.5	244
Albuquerque, NM	37.9	38.8	39.6	41.5	61
Anchorage, AK	27.9	28.6	29.0	29.6	84
Ann Arbor, MI	18.7	19.3	19.7	20.5	112
Athens, GA	6.6	6.8	7.0	7.3	224
Atlanta, GA	282.0	294.0	304.9	320.9	10
Austin, TX	91.5	98.7	103.2	109.3	31
Baltimore, MD	149.8	157.3	162.1	168.7	19
Billings, MT	8.2	8.5	8.6	8.9	206
Boise City, ID	26.5	27.5	28.2	29.5	85
Boston, MA	323.3	336.2	346.4	361.4	9
Boulder, CO	19.3	20.3	21.0	22.0	105
Cape Coral, FL	20.1	20.9	21.4	22.4	100
Cedar Rapids, IA	14.3	14.8	15.1	15.5	142
Charleston, SC	29.7	31.0	31.8	33.4	74
Charlotte, NC	117.4	125.2	130.5	137.0	22
Chicago, IL	548.5	571.0	585.9	610.4	3
Cincinnati, OH	103.8	108.4	111.2	115.7	29
Clarksville, TN	11.5	11.8	11.9	12.5	163
Colorado Spgs, CO	27.2	28.0	28.6	29.9	83
Columbia, MO	7.0	7.3	7.5	8.0	216
Columbus, OH	95.3	99.7	102.1	106.7	32
Dallas, TX	397.0	418.6	436.4	460.9	6
Davenport, IA	17.9	18.6	18.9	19.4	116
Denver, CO	161.8	167.9	173.3	182.2	18
Des Moines, IA	40.0	42.1	43.9	45.7	57
Durham, NC	38.0	39.7	41.5	43.8	59
El Paso, TX	29.0	29.6	29.8	31.2	78
Erie, PA	9.7	10.0	10.1	10.5	182
Eugene, OR	11.8	12.2	12.4	12.8	160
Fargo, ND	12.3	13.2	14.1	15.0	144
Fayetteville, NC	18.4	18.7	18.8	19.4	116
Ft. Collins, CO	11.9	12.4	12.8	13.4	156
Ft. Wayne, IN	18.2	19.0	19.5	20.1	114
Ft. Worth, TX	397.0	418.6	436.4	460.9	6
Gainesville, FL	10.3	10.5	10.7	11.1	176
Grand Rapids, MI	33.3	35.3	36.8	38.6	65
Green Bay, WI	15.3	15.9	16.3	17.1	131
Greensboro, NC	35.3	36.9	37.9	39.5	64
Honolulu, HI	54.4	56.6	57.6	59.7	51
Houston, TX	425.5	449.7	463.7	488.7	4
Huntsville, AL	21.4	21.7	21.9	22.8	98
Indianapolis, IN	107.2	112.8	116.1	120.9	27
Jacksonville, FL	59.8	62.3	65.1	68.2	47
Kansas City, MO	109.1	113.8	116.6	121.7	25
Lafayette, LA	19.2	17.7	17.2	17.8	126
Las Vegas, NV	92.6	95.6	98.4	103.3	34
Lexington, KY	23.4	23.9	24.7	25.9	90
Lincoln, NE	15.2	15.9	16.2	16.8	133
Little Rock, AR	33.6	34.4	35.1	36.5	68
Los Angeles, CA	732.2	765.7	792.4	827.6	2
Louisville, KY	60.3	63.8	66.5	69.4	46
Lubbock, TX	10.3	10.9	11.3	11.7	171
Madison, WI	36.8	38.0	39.2	40.9	63
Manchester, NH	22.1	22.2	22.3	23.2	97
McAllen, TX	15.5	16.0	16.5	17.3	130

Table continued on next page.

MSA[1]	2011	2012	2013	2014	Rank[2]
Miami, FL	260.7	274.1	283.4	296.1	11
Midland, TX	14.7	16.2	17.5	18.7	119
Minneapolis, MN	207.0	218.5	228.0	237.7	13
Montgomery, AL	15.3	15.4	15.5	16.0	139
Nashville, TN	84.9	91.1	95.5	100.3	35
New Orleans, LA	74.3	80.2	83.0	86.2	40
New York, NY	1,294.2	1,335.1	1,379.7	1,431.3	1
Oklahoma City, OK	61.5	63.3	64.3	66.9	48
Omaha, NE	50.0	51.9	53.1	55.8	52
Orlando, FL	101.5	106.1	109.8	115.6	30
Oxnard, CA	38.3	39.1	39.7	41.5	61
Peoria, IL	19.5	21.3	21.6	22.3	101
Philadelphia, PA	352.3	364.0	373.9	388.4	8
Phoenix, AZ	192.3	201.7	210.1	221.0	14
Pittsburgh, PA	119.3	123.6	126.5	131.5	23
Portland, OR	138.5	147.0	152.6	160.9	20
Providence, RI	67.3	69.5	71.2	73.9	44
Provo, UT	16.1	17.0	17.7	18.7	119
Raleigh, NC	59.0	61.4	63.2	66.8	49
Reno, NV	20.0	20.4	20.7	21.5	108
Richmond, VA	66.6	70.0	71.7	74.4	43
Riverside, CA	110.3	114.0	115.7	121.4	26
Rochester, MN	9.3	9.7	10.0	10.4	185
Salem, OR	12.4	12.7	13.1	13.6	154
Salt Lake City, UT	70.9	74.8	77.5	81.5	42
San Antonio, TX	87.2	92.0	94.1	99.0	36
San Diego, CA	169.9	177.4	182.6	191.7	16
San Francisco, CA	331.0	360.4	377.2	395.4	7
San Jose, CA	167.8	173.9	181.2	191.0	17
Santa Rosa, CA	20.1	20.3	20.6	21.4	110
Savannah, GA	13.5	14.1	14.3	14.8	147
Seattle, WA	243.8	258.8	268.5	281.0	12
Sioux Falls, SD	16.0	16.6	17.6	18.3	123
Spokane, WA	18.6	19.3	19.9	20.7	111
Springfield, MO	15.4	16.2	16.9	17.6	128
Tallahassee, FL	13.3	13.4	13.7	14.2	149
Tampa, FL	114.4	119.9	125.5	131.5	23
Topeka, KS	9.6	9.9	9.9	10.2	192
Tulsa, OK	47.3	47.9	48.2	50.3	54
Virginia Beach, VA	82.1	85.2	87.2	90.2	39
Washington, DC	437.2	446.9	455.8	477.5	5
Wichita, KS	28.6	29.4	29.6	30.8	81
Wilmington, NC	15.1	15.4	15.9	16.6	135
Worcester, MA	29.7	30.5	31.1	32.2	75

*Note: Figures are in billions of dollars; (1) Metropolitan Statistical Area—see Appendix B for areas included;
(2) Rank is based on 2014 data and ranges from 1 to 363.
Source: The United States Conference of Mayors, U.S. Metro Economies: Outlook—Gross Metropolitan Product, with Metro Employment
Projections, November 2013*

Income: City

City	Per Capita ($)	Median Household ($)	Average Household ($)
Abilene, TX	20,195	41,460	54,290
Albuquerque, NM	26,277	46,060	62,606
Anchorage, AK	35,525	74,648	94,517
Ann Arbor, MI	33,992	53,351	76,144
Athens, GA	18,760	32,809	50,939
Atlanta, GA	34,041	44,784	78,505
Austin, TX	30,880	51,668	74,860
Baltimore, MD	23,326	39,788	56,287
Billings, MT	26,568	46,655	62,330
Boise City, ID	27,063	45,985	63,852
Boston, MA	32,886	51,452	78,420
Boulder, CO	36,016	56,205	86,325
Cape Coral, FL	22,522	47,586	59,540
Cedar Rapids, IA	27,884	52,455	65,965
Charleston, SC	31,728	50,602	72,430
Charlotte, NC	30,710	51,209	76,914
Chicago, IL	27,237	45,483	68,868
Cincinnati, OH	24,106	32,591	53,215
Clarksville, TN	20,493	44,760	54,454
Colorado Spgs, CO	28,270	52,896	69,844
Columbia, MO	25,171	41,576	62,641
Columbus, OH	23,609	42,491	55,908
Dallas, TX	26,294	41,745	67,684
Davenport, IA	23,966	42,451	57,089
Denver, CO	32,508	49,049	73,299
Des Moines, IA	23,186	44,292	57,027
Durham, NC	27,001	46,924	65,249
El Paso, TX	19,472	40,920	57,117
Erie, PA	18,207	31,838	42,773
Eugene, OR	25,282	40,435	58,847
Fargo, ND	29,887	45,644	65,527
Fayetteville, NC	22,889	44,472	56,003
Ft. Collins, CO	27,499	51,830	69,242
Ft. Wayne, IN	23,283	43,673	57,396
Ft. Worth, TX	23,597	50,129	65,747
Gainesville, FL	19,445	31,294	48,531
Grand Rapids, MI	19,616	37,791	49,277
Green Bay, WI	23,323	41,404	55,576
Greensboro, NC	24,608	40,323	58,528
Honolulu, HI	29,446	57,452	75,157
Houston, TX	26,335	43,792	69,421
Huntsville, AL	29,484	46,821	68,794
Indianapolis, IN	22,983	40,167	56,113
Jacksonville, FL	24,483	45,577	62,009
Kansas City, MO	26,360	44,277	61,822
Lafayette, LA	27,580	43,928	64,837
Las Vegas, NV	25,045	49,726	66,373
Lexington, KY	28,369	47,785	68,100
Lincoln, NE	25,770	48,295	63,302
Little Rock, AR	28,352	45,267	66,836
Los Angeles, CA	26,913	47,742	74,525
Louisville, KY	25,192	42,609	60,786
Lubbock, TX	23,003	42,139	58,725
Madison, WI	30,386	52,599	69,567
Manchester, NH	27,095	54,122	65,035
McAllen, TX	21,406	41,375	64,900

Table continued on next page.

City	Per Capita ($)	Median Household ($)	Average Household ($)
Miami, FL	20,104	28,935	49,640
Midland, TX	31,846	59,336	86,405
Minneapolis, MN	30,560	48,228	69,624
Montgomery, AL	23,655	42,403	59,186
Nashville, TN	26,412	44,271	62,441
New Orleans, LA	25,654	36,004	59,897
New York, NY	30,826	50,711	79,740
Oklahoma City, OK	24,994	44,519	62,585
Omaha, NE	26,376	46,202	64,411
Orlando, FL	24,936	41,266	58,471
Oxnard, CA	19,835	60,667	74,150
Peoria, IL	26,948	44,061	64,118
Philadelphia, PA	21,292	35,581	52,296
Phoenix, AZ	23,091	44,649	62,918
Pittsburgh, PA	25,927	37,280	57,505
Portland, OR	30,517	49,958	70,209
Providence, RI	21,262	37,654	58,512
Provo, UT	16,506	38,338	55,633
Raleigh, NC	29,277	52,709	72,867
Reno, NV	25,113	44,318	61,643
Richmond, VA	26,231	40,001	60,594
Riverside, CA	21,615	53,893	70,403
Rochester, MN	31,673	61,547	77,129
Salem, OR	22,905	45,215	59,755
Salt Lake City, UT	26,176	42,267	64,133
San Antonio, TX	22,171	45,074	60,254
San Diego, CA	32,086	63,034	85,370
San Francisco, CA	46,580	72,888	106,350
San Jose, CA	32,974	80,155	101,431
Santa Rosa, CA	28,733	58,893	75,670
Savannah, GA	18,889	34,832	46,779
Seattle, WA	41,518	62,617	88,590
Sioux Falls, SD	27,099	50,295	66,148
Spokane, WA	23,567	41,593	54,915
Springfield, MO	20,176	32,359	44,751
Tallahassee, FL	23,722	38,865	57,787
Tampa, FL	28,262	41,524	68,107
Topeka, KS	22,875	39,118	53,735
Tulsa, OK	26,374	40,359	62,060
Virginia Beach, VA	31,431	65,169	82,301
Washington, DC	44,670	64,610	99,781
Wichita, KS	24,123	44,612	60,053
Wilmington, NC	28,552	41,554	64,656
Worcester, MA	23,946	43,999	60,512
U.S.	27,385	51,771	71,579

Source: U.S. Census Bureau, 2010-2012 American Community Survey 3-Year Estimates

Income: Metro Area

Metro Area	Per Capita ($)	Median Household ($)	Average Household ($)
Abilene, TX	21,548	42,724	57,470
Albuquerque, NM	25,545	47,604	64,264
Anchorage, AK	34,076	73,218	91,789
Ann Arbor, MI	32,675	57,548	79,863
Athens, GA	21,698	41,339	59,744
Atlanta, GA	27,642	54,807	75,230
Austin, TX	30,365	58,821	79,799
Baltimore, MD	34,097	67,340	88,089
Billings, MT	26,768	49,610	64,081
Boise City, ID	23,354	48,188	62,610
Boston, MA	37,800	71,375	96,583
Boulder, CO	37,539	66,783	92,309
Cape Coral, FL	26,278	46,022	65,020
Cedar Rapids, IA	28,954	56,667	70,824
Charleston, SC	26,490	50,660	67,011
Charlotte, NC	28,421	52,346	74,162
Chicago, IL	30,112	59,496	81,061
Cincinnati, OH	27,761	53,475	70,905
Clarksville, TN	21,098	44,361	55,912
Colorado Spgs, CO	28,342	55,649	73,248
Columbia, MO	26,057	45,156	65,102
Columbus, OH	28,259	53,717	71,707
Dallas, TX	28,421	57,109	78,238
Davenport, IA	26,698	49,197	64,300
Denver, CO	32,657	61,392	82,057
Des Moines, IA	29,457	59,047	74,101
Durham, NC	29,028	49,965	72,098
El Paso, TX	18,183	39,821	55,130
Erie, PA	23,650	44,475	58,689
Eugene, OR	23,532	41,465	56,155
Fargo, ND	28,997	52,655	68,593
Fayetteville, NC	22,026	44,680	56,594
Ft. Collins, CO	29,717	56,274	73,196
Ft. Wayne, IN	24,905	49,305	63,277
Ft. Worth, TX	28,421	57,109	78,238
Gainesville, FL	24,223	41,405	60,928
Grand Rapids, MI	24,499	50,286	64,332
Green Bay, WI	26,693	51,795	66,183
Greensboro, NC	23,568	42,235	58,207
Honolulu, HI	29,475	70,541	86,889
Houston, TX	28,059	56,080	79,881
Huntsville, AL	29,599	54,407	74,576
Indianapolis, IN	27,291	51,626	70,011
Jacksonville, FL	26,938	50,952	69,112
Kansas City, MO	28,853	55,320	72,650
Lafayette, LA	26,809	47,146	67,314
Las Vegas, NV	25,380	50,943	67,662
Lexington, KY	27,294	48,446	67,120
Lincoln, NE	26,708	51,101	66,578
Little Rock, AR	25,520	47,969	63,248
Los Angeles, CA	28,329	58,377	83,636
Louisville, KY	26,032	47,961	64,793
Lubbock, TX	23,133	43,414	60,467
Madison, WI	32,007	60,308	76,451
Manchester, NH	33,635	69,395	86,470
McAllen, TX	14,073	33,549	48,908

Table continued on next page.

Metro Area	Per Capita ($)	Median Household ($)	Average Household ($)
Miami, FL	26,277	46,867	69,526
Midland, TX	31,602	58,875	86,027
Minneapolis, MN	33,262	65,756	84,643
Montgomery, AL	23,860	46,058	61,625
Nashville, TN	27,474	51,178	70,435
New Orleans, LA	26,159	46,087	65,519
New York, NY	34,738	64,344	93,767
Oklahoma City, OK	25,782	48,618	65,833
Omaha, NE	28,360	55,984	72,066
Orlando, FL	24,156	47,228	64,869
Oxnard, CA	31,960	74,458	96,240
Peoria, IL	27,493	52,705	67,442
Philadelphia, PA	31,569	60,444	82,361
Phoenix, AZ	25,836	51,695	69,492
Pittsburgh, PA	28,881	49,973	67,445
Portland, OR	29,114	56,236	73,797
Providence, RI	29,018	54,674	72,588
Provo, UT	20,109	58,513	72,129
Raleigh, NC	30,039	60,332	79,164
Reno, NV	27,898	51,033	70,341
Richmond, VA	29,527	57,234	76,042
Riverside, CA	21,759	53,855	69,495
Rochester, MN	31,897	63,610	79,757
Salem, OR	21,959	46,214	59,213
Salt Lake City, UT	25,549	59,641	75,575
San Antonio, TX	24,522	51,087	68,110
San Diego, CA	29,483	61,364	81,993
San Francisco, CA	40,165	75,168	105,452
San Jose, CA	39,806	88,446	116,236
Santa Rosa, CA	31,386	61,491	80,775
Savannah, GA	24,759	47,998	63,523
Seattle, WA	34,317	65,710	85,890
Sioux Falls, SD	27,191	54,682	68,473
Spokane, WA	25,279	49,059	62,536
Springfield, MO	22,496	42,305	55,395
Tallahassee, FL	24,196	44,647	61,518
Tampa, FL	26,123	44,959	62,781
Topeka, KS	25,323	48,297	62,038
Tulsa, OK	25,551	47,160	64,227
Virginia Beach, VA	28,418	58,241	73,852
Washington, DC	42,624	88,689	114,231
Wichita, KS	24,782	49,096	63,430
Wilmington, NC	27,541	47,452	65,184
Worcester, MA	30,969	63,687	80,951
U.S.	27,385	51,771	71,579

Note: Figures cover the Metropolitan Statistical Area (MSA)—see Appendix B for areas included
Source: U.S. Census Bureau, 2010-2012 American Community Survey 3-Year Estimates

Household Income Distribution: City

City	Under $15,000	$15,000 -24,999	$25,000 -34,999	$35,000 -49,999	$50,000 -74,999	$75,000 -99,000	$100,000 -149,999	$150,000 and up
				Percent of Households Earning				
Abilene, TX	16.4	13.3	12.7	15.9	19.3	9.8	8.4	4.3
Albuquerque, NM	15.3	12.1	11.8	14.0	17.8	11.1	11.1	6.8
Anchorage, AK	6.3	6.7	7.4	12.1	17.7	14.6	18.6	16.6
Ann Arbor, MI	15.6	9.3	10.7	11.6	17.2	9.8	13.3	12.6
Athens, GA	28.0	13.3	10.7	12.8	15.1	7.1	6.9	6.1
Atlanta, GA	21.5	10.9	9.9	10.9	15.4	8.7	10.2	12.5
Austin, TX	13.4	10.0	10.5	14.8	17.2	11.3	12.3	10.5
Baltimore, MD	22.0	12.6	10.9	13.5	17.2	9.0	8.9	6.0
Billings, MT	13.7	12.3	11.6	15.2	18.9	12.2	10.3	6.0
Boise City, ID	13.4	11.6	12.9	15.9	17.4	10.3	11.3	7.2
Boston, MA	20.6	10.2	7.5	10.8	14.8	10.6	13.1	12.6
Boulder, CO	17.1	9.5	8.5	10.5	15.5	9.5	13.0	16.4
Cape Coral, FL	11.3	11.7	12.9	16.2	20.6	11.9	10.6	4.9
Cedar Rapids, IA	11.5	10.6	10.2	14.4	21.1	14.3	12.3	5.7
Charleston, SC	17.6	9.8	9.6	12.4	16.5	11.8	11.5	10.6
Charlotte, NC	12.8	10.5	10.9	14.6	18.3	11.0	11.7	10.2
Chicago, IL	17.9	12.0	10.5	13.0	16.2	10.4	10.6	9.3
Cincinnati, OH	27.1	14.3	10.7	12.3	14.4	8.2	7.3	5.7
Clarksville, TN	13.9	10.6	12.7	17.8	22.3	11.2	8.4	3.2
Colorado Spgs, CO	11.9	10.8	10.2	14.0	19.6	11.7	13.6	8.2
Columbia, MO	19.7	12.9	10.3	15.0	15.2	9.4	10.5	7.2
Columbus, OH	17.3	12.2	11.8	15.3	18.9	10.8	9.3	4.5
Dallas, TX	16.4	12.9	13.1	14.6	17.1	8.3	8.7	8.9
Davenport, IA	15.3	11.9	14.2	16.1	17.2	11.7	9.9	3.7
Denver, CO	15.2	11.3	10.6	13.7	16.6	11.1	10.9	10.5
Des Moines, IA	14.8	12.3	12.2	15.7	19.6	12.4	9.1	4.0
Durham, NC	14.6	12.2	11.8	14.8	16.7	10.8	11.5	7.7
El Paso, TX	17.4	13.9	12.1	15.5	16.9	9.6	9.2	5.4
Erie, PA	24.4	15.9	13.0	15.6	15.6	8.3	5.3	2.0
Eugene, OR	20.8	11.5	12.2	13.5	16.3	9.7	10.3	5.6
Fargo, ND	12.9	12.1	12.2	16.5	17.8	10.8	10.0	7.7
Fayetteville, NC	14.8	10.3	12.7	17.7	20.9	11.0	8.5	4.1
Ft. Collins, CO	14.0	11.3	8.8	14.2	18.5	12.6	12.5	8.2
Ft. Wayne, IN	14.4	12.2	12.8	16.5	20.7	10.7	8.6	4.1
Ft. Worth, TX	13.6	11.6	10.9	13.7	19.1	12.6	11.7	6.8
Gainesville, FL	27.6	14.0	12.5	12.3	14.5	6.8	7.7	4.5
Grand Rapids, MI	19.0	14.4	12.7	16.1	18.4	9.1	7.7	2.7
Green Bay, WI	15.5	13.2	13.3	18.4	18.2	9.9	7.2	4.4
Greensboro, NC	15.9	14.6	13.8	15.5	16.9	8.9	8.5	6.0
Honolulu, HI	11.9	8.5	9.3	13.9	18.6	13.3	14.3	10.4
Houston, TX	16.1	12.9	12.1	14.0	15.8	9.9	9.7	9.4
Huntsville, AL	16.2	11.7	11.1	13.2	15.8	10.6	12.4	9.1
Indianapolis, IN	16.8	13.5	13.5	15.1	16.9	10.6	8.9	4.7
Jacksonville, FL	15.2	12.1	11.6	14.8	18.6	11.4	10.9	5.5
Kansas City, MO	17.2	11.5	11.6	15.0	17.4	10.7	10.4	6.4
Lafayette, LA	18.5	13.3	9.0	14.0	16.2	9.6	11.0	8.3
Las Vegas, NV	12.7	11.3	11.2	15.1	19.1	12.7	10.6	7.3
Lexington, KY	15.9	11.2	10.8	14.0	16.8	11.1	11.9	8.3
Lincoln, NE	13.6	11.0	12.3	14.9	18.8	12.4	10.7	6.5
Little Rock, AR	16.8	13.4	11.1	12.6	16.4	10.5	10.3	9.0
Los Angeles, CA	15.8	12.1	10.5	13.2	16.2	10.3	11.3	10.7
Louisville, KY	16.9	13.0	11.8	14.7	17.3	10.2	9.9	6.3
Lubbock, TX	17.5	13.6	12.1	13.6	18.0	10.4	9.1	5.7
Madison, WI	14.4	9.7	10.6	12.9	18.4	13.1	12.3	8.5

Table continued on next page.

City	Under $15,000	$15,000 -24,999	$25,000 -34,999	$35,000 -49,999	$50,000 -74,999	$75,000 -99,000	$100,000 -149,999	$150,000 and up
Manchester, NH	11.7	10.5	11.5	12.3	21.6	12.7	13.5	6.2
McAllen, TX	19.3	13.2	11.0	14.7	15.0	9.5	9.5	7.7
Miami, FL	28.4	16.3	12.4	12.7	12.7	6.0	5.8	5.7
Midland, TX	10.1	9.2	10.0	12.0	20.8	12.3	13.8	12.0
Minneapolis, MN	17.1	10.9	9.7	13.6	16.4	11.1	12.2	9.0
Montgomery, AL	18.6	12.7	10.3	15.8	17.3	9.7	10.0	5.6
Nashville, TN	15.6	12.1	12.0	15.6	18.5	10.3	9.1	6.8
New Orleans, LA	24.5	13.3	11.2	12.7	13.9	8.8	8.3	7.2
New York, NY	17.1	11.0	9.4	11.9	15.9	10.5	12.1	12.0
Oklahoma City, OK	14.8	12.3	12.7	15.0	18.1	10.6	10.5	6.1
Omaha, NE	14.3	12.2	12.2	14.5	18.5	11.5	10.4	6.4
Orlando, FL	15.4	14.2	12.8	16.0	19.2	8.1	8.3	5.8
Oxnard, CA	8.7	9.5	8.4	14.5	20.2	14.6	14.9	9.1
Peoria, IL	17.2	12.7	10.7	14.1	17.1	11.2	10.5	6.5
Philadelphia, PA	23.9	13.6	11.8	13.2	15.9	8.9	7.8	4.8
Phoenix, AZ	15.4	11.7	12.1	15.1	17.2	10.7	10.8	7.0
Pittsburgh, PA	21.4	14.5	11.7	13.2	16.5	8.5	7.8	6.5
Portland, OR	15.4	10.6	10.7	13.3	17.2	11.5	12.4	8.9
Providence, RI	25.0	12.6	9.8	13.4	16.2	8.8	8.1	6.1
Provo, UT	18.8	14.3	12.8	14.7	18.8	9.0	7.0	4.5
Raleigh, NC	11.5	9.4	11.8	14.1	19.2	12.2	12.1	9.6
Reno, NV	15.6	12.8	11.7	14.9	17.9	10.1	10.4	6.6
Richmond, VA	20.9	12.8	11.5	15.1	15.8	9.6	7.7	6.5
Riverside, CA	11.5	11.1	10.2	13.5	19.4	12.2	12.9	9.0
Rochester, MN	9.0	9.8	8.9	12.9	19.1	15.4	15.0	9.9
Salem, OR	14.6	11.7	12.3	16.3	19.2	11.1	10.0	4.8
Salt Lake City, UT	17.3	13.2	11.3	14.3	16.9	10.1	9.2	7.7
San Antonio, TX	15.2	12.5	11.9	15.2	18.5	10.8	10.0	5.9
San Diego, CA	11.2	9.0	8.3	12.0	16.8	13.2	15.3	14.2
San Francisco, CA	13.2	8.5	6.9	8.7	13.6	10.7	16.1	22.2
San Jose, CA	8.1	7.5	7.1	10.2	14.4	12.7	18.5	21.4
Santa Rosa, CA	8.9	10.8	9.2	14.5	19.1	13.3	14.2	10.0
Savannah, GA	23.0	13.8	13.3	15.1	18.4	7.5	5.7	3.2
Seattle, WA	12.5	7.8	8.6	11.9	17.0	11.9	15.3	15.2
Sioux Falls, SD	10.7	10.7	12.0	16.3	19.7	13.1	11.1	6.5
Spokane, WA	16.6	13.6	12.8	14.7	19.0	11.0	8.0	4.4
Springfield, MO	20.6	17.8	15.5	15.2	16.6	6.8	4.7	2.9
Tallahassee, FL	24.4	11.7	10.6	14.5	14.7	8.5	9.3	6.3
Tampa, FL	19.0	12.9	11.8	13.3	15.9	8.5	9.2	9.3
Topeka, KS	16.9	13.3	14.2	16.6	18.1	9.5	7.9	3.5
Tulsa, OK	16.8	13.5	13.4	15.7	17.1	8.5	8.0	7.2
Virginia Beach, VA	7.1	6.6	8.6	14.1	21.1	14.7	16.9	11.1
Washington, DC	15.1	7.8	7.1	10.5	14.9	10.8	14.8	19.0
Wichita, KS	14.0	13.0	12.6	15.3	18.6	11.5	9.8	5.2
Wilmington, NC	18.5	13.3	12.4	13.9	15.7	8.5	9.9	7.9
Worcester, MA	18.7	12.6	10.1	13.3	17.5	10.4	10.7	6.7
U.S.	13.1	11.0	10.5	13.7	18.1	11.9	12.5	9.1

Source: U.S. Census Bureau, 2010-2012 American Community Survey 3-Year Estimates

Household Income Distribution: Metro Area

Metro Area	Percent of Households Earning							
	Under $15,000	$15,000 -24,999	$25,000 -34,999	$35,000 -49,999	$50,000 -74,999	$75,000 -99,000	$100,000 -149,999	$150,000 and up
Abilene, TX	15.3	13.3	12.5	15.4	19.6	9.8	9.1	4.9
Albuquerque, NM	14.7	11.9	11.3	14.1	18.1	11.2	11.5	7.2
Anchorage, AK	6.8	7.2	7.3	11.7	18.2	14.6	18.7	15.5
Ann Arbor, MI	12.3	9.5	10.0	12.2	16.7	11.7	14.8	12.9
Athens, GA	20.9	12.3	10.7	13.4	16.4	9.8	9.1	7.4
Atlanta, GA	12.0	9.9	10.1	13.7	18.6	12.0	13.3	10.4
Austin, TX	10.9	8.9	9.4	13.8	18.2	12.8	14.6	11.4
Baltimore, MD	10.3	7.8	8.0	11.1	17.7	13.0	17.1	15.1
Billings, MT	12.5	11.5	11.3	15.0	19.6	12.9	11.4	5.8
Boise City, ID	12.4	11.4	12.2	15.6	20.6	11.3	10.6	6.0
Boston, MA	10.9	7.9	7.3	10.3	15.7	12.8	17.5	17.6
Boulder, CO	10.8	8.4	7.8	12.6	15.2	11.7	16.5	16.9
Cape Coral, FL	11.9	12.5	13.2	16.2	18.9	10.4	10.1	6.8
Cedar Rapids, IA	9.6	9.6	10.1	13.8	21.1	14.5	14.1	7.1
Charleston, SC	13.7	10.9	10.4	14.3	19.4	11.9	11.6	7.9
Charlotte, NC	12.2	10.5	10.4	14.5	18.6	11.8	12.4	9.5
Chicago, IL	11.3	9.6	9.2	12.5	17.8	12.9	14.6	12.1
Cincinnati, OH	12.9	10.6	10.0	13.4	18.7	12.7	12.8	8.8
Clarksville, TN	13.8	12.3	12.6	16.8	21.0	11.4	8.4	3.7
Colorado Spgs, CO	10.6	10.1	9.5	13.9	19.7	12.3	14.9	8.9
Columbia, MO	16.9	12.1	10.4	14.5	17.0	11.4	10.8	6.9
Columbus, OH	12.5	10.2	10.1	13.7	18.9	12.5	13.0	9.0
Dallas, TX	10.4	9.7	10.2	13.6	18.5	12.1	14.4	11.0
Davenport, IA	11.9	11.2	12.1	15.6	19.5	12.5	11.2	6.1
Denver, CO	10.1	8.7	9.2	12.8	18.5	13.1	15.4	12.2
Des Moines, IA	9.4	9.1	10.1	13.6	20.0	14.2	15.0	8.5
Durham, NC	13.8	11.3	11.0	13.9	16.8	11.2	12.2	9.8
El Paso, TX	17.8	14.3	12.7	15.2	17.1	9.3	8.5	5.0
Erie, PA	15.9	12.6	11.5	14.8	19.2	11.3	9.9	4.6
Eugene, OR	17.0	13.1	12.2	15.1	17.9	11.0	9.1	4.5
Fargo, ND	11.5	10.8	11.1	14.5	19.3	13.2	12.4	7.2
Fayetteville, NC	14.9	11.2	12.5	16.3	19.7	11.6	9.7	4.0
Ft. Collins, CO	11.2	10.5	9.1	13.7	18.9	13.7	13.8	9.1
Ft. Wayne, IN	11.6	10.9	11.7	16.5	21.7	12.4	10.2	5.1
Ft. Worth, TX	10.4	9.7	10.2	13.6	18.5	12.1	14.4	11.0
Gainesville, FL	20.6	12.3	10.8	12.8	16.1	10.1	10.5	6.7
Grand Rapids, MI	11.9	11.4	11.6	14.8	20.7	12.8	10.8	5.9
Green Bay, WI	10.7	11.4	10.7	15.3	20.5	13.5	11.7	6.2
Greensboro, NC	15.2	13.1	13.5	15.1	18.2	10.5	9.2	5.4
Honolulu, HI	8.8	6.4	7.4	11.9	18.3	14.5	18.9	13.6
Houston, TX	11.5	10.1	10.2	13.0	17.3	12.0	13.8	12.1
Huntsville, AL	12.5	10.3	9.8	13.6	16.5	12.1	14.7	10.4
Indianapolis, IN	11.9	10.7	11.2	14.5	18.2	12.7	12.8	7.9
Jacksonville, FL	13.2	10.8	10.7	14.5	19.1	12.2	12.1	7.4
Kansas City, MO	11.3	9.7	10.0	14.1	19.1	13.1	14.0	8.6
Lafayette, LA	16.9	12.3	9.7	12.9	17.1	11.0	11.5	8.6
Las Vegas, NV	11.5	10.7	11.7	15.2	19.8	12.6	11.4	7.2
Lexington, KY	15.3	11.0	10.9	14.2	17.4	11.6	12.2	7.4
Lincoln, NE	12.6	10.3	11.7	14.5	19.0	13.0	11.8	7.2
Little Rock, AR	13.7	12.1	11.4	14.4	18.5	12.5	11.3	6.1
Los Angeles, CA	11.7	10.1	9.3	12.6	16.9	11.9	14.4	13.2
Louisville, KY	13.8	11.7	11.2	14.9	18.6	11.9	11.4	6.6
Lubbock, TX	16.7	13.4	12.0	13.8	17.8	10.7	9.7	6.0
Madison, WI	10.3	8.6	9.7	13.1	18.9	14.8	15.3	9.3

Table continued on next page.

Metro Area	Percent of Households Earning							
	Under $15,000	$15,000 -24,999	$25,000 -34,999	$35,000 -49,999	$50,000 -74,999	$75,000 -99,000	$100,000 -149,999	$150,000 and up
Manchester, NH	7.8	8.1	8.3	11.1	18.4	14.5	18.4	13.3
McAllen, TX	23.7	15.8	12.2	14.2	15.1	8.1	7.0	3.8
Miami, FL	15.0	12.1	11.3	14.2	17.2	10.5	11.1	8.7
Midland, TX	9.2	9.2	10.4	13.1	20.3	12.0	13.6	12.1
Minneapolis, MN	9.1	8.0	8.4	12.5	18.5	14.5	16.9	12.2
Montgomery, AL	16.1	11.4	10.8	14.9	18.4	10.8	12.0	5.6
Nashville, TN	12.2	10.6	10.8	15.2	18.8	12.3	11.9	8.2
New Orleans, LA	16.8	11.8	11.2	13.6	16.4	11.2	11.4	7.7
New York, NY	12.3	9.1	8.2	10.8	15.8	11.7	15.4	16.8
Oklahoma City, OK	13.4	11.7	11.6	14.5	18.9	11.6	11.4	6.9
Omaha, NE	10.9	9.8	10.3	13.8	19.5	13.9	13.8	7.9
Orlando, FL	12.4	12.0	12.5	15.4	19.1	11.1	10.7	6.8
Oxnard, CA	7.4	7.8	7.1	11.4	16.8	13.8	18.3	17.5
Peoria, IL	11.4	10.8	10.1	14.6	20.2	13.5	13.4	6.1
Philadelphia, PA	12.1	9.2	9.0	11.9	17.0	12.5	15.2	13.0
Phoenix, AZ	11.9	10.6	11.0	14.9	18.8	12.0	12.8	8.1
Pittsburgh, PA	13.2	12.1	11.1	13.7	18.7	11.9	11.8	7.5
Portland, OR	11.3	9.3	9.9	13.9	19.3	13.2	14.0	9.1
Providence, RI	13.9	10.5	9.1	12.5	17.7	12.4	14.3	9.6
Provo, UT	9.3	9.2	9.1	14.4	23.2	13.9	13.6	7.4
Raleigh, NC	9.6	8.5	10.2	13.1	18.8	13.0	15.2	11.7
Reno, NV	12.6	11.3	10.9	14.3	18.7	11.5	13.2	7.6
Richmond, VA	10.5	8.8	9.9	14.2	18.8	13.2	14.8	9.8
Riverside, CA	11.4	11.0	10.3	13.9	18.6	13.0	13.5	8.4
Rochester, MN	8.4	8.9	8.7	13.3	19.1	15.5	15.9	10.2
Salem, OR	13.5	11.9	12.2	16.0	20.0	11.6	10.5	4.4
Salt Lake City, UT	9.3	9.3	9.3	13.5	21.4	14.1	14.5	8.6
San Antonio, TX	12.7	10.9	10.7	14.6	19.0	12.0	12.3	7.7
San Diego, CA	11.0	8.9	9.2	12.6	17.3	12.8	15.2	13.0
San Francisco, CA	9.6	7.6	7.0	10.1	15.5	11.7	17.2	21.3
San Jose, CA	7.3	6.6	6.3	9.4	13.7	12.0	18.9	25.8
Santa Rosa, CA	8.7	10.0	8.8	13.7	18.2	13.2	15.6	11.8
Savannah, GA	14.6	11.3	11.0	14.8	19.1	11.3	11.3	6.6
Seattle, WA	9.3	7.9	8.3	12.5	18.3	13.6	16.9	13.2
Sioux Falls, SD	9.6	9.5	11.2	15.5	20.3	15.0	12.5	6.4
Spokane, WA	13.8	11.7	11.3	14.1	19.8	12.8	10.7	5.9
Springfield, MO	14.5	13.8	13.1	16.2	19.9	10.4	7.8	4.2
Tallahassee, FL	19.0	10.8	10.7	14.2	17.1	10.9	11.1	6.2
Tampa, FL	14.1	12.9	12.2	15.3	18.2	10.7	9.9	6.6
Topeka, KS	12.8	10.8	12.2	15.9	20.0	12.1	11.3	5.0
Tulsa, OK	13.6	11.8	11.9	15.1	19.0	11.4	10.7	6.5
Virginia Beach, VA	10.1	8.8	9.7	14.2	20.0	13.9	14.7	8.8
Washington, DC	6.5	5.2	5.5	9.3	15.8	13.3	19.9	24.5
Wichita, KS	11.8	12.0	11.6	15.5	19.2	12.9	11.6	5.4
Wilmington, NC	14.4	11.5	11.9	14.4	18.5	11.4	11.7	6.2
Worcester, MA	11.1	9.3	8.3	11.6	17.0	13.5	16.5	12.7
U.S.	13.1	11.0	10.5	13.7	18.1	11.9	12.5	9.1

Note: Figures cover the Metropolitan Statistical Area (MSA)—see Appendix B for areas included
Source: Source: U.S. Census Bureau, 2010-2012 American Community Survey 3-Year Estimates

Poverty Rate: City

City	All Ages	Under 18 Years Old	18 to 64 Years Old	65 Years and Over
Abilene, TX	20.3	23.5	20.9	11.2
Albuquerque, NM	18.3	25.6	17.3	9.0
Anchorage, AK	8.5	12.1	7.4	4.9
Ann Arbor, MI	22.6	14.1	26.8	5.9
Athens, GA	35.8	34.7	39.3	11.2
Atlanta, GA	26.0	39.2	23.1	20.1
Austin, TX	20.1	28.4	18.6	9.3
Baltimore, MD	25.2	36.5	22.8	18.0
Billings, MT	14.5	20.5	13.7	8.5
Boise City, ID	16.1	21.1	16.0	7.1
Boston, MA	22.7	30.4	21.2	20.4
Boulder, CO	23.4	12.2	27.9	6.1
Cape Coral, FL	15.1	21.6	14.5	8.7
Cedar Rapids, IA	12.0	14.0	12.7	5.4
Charleston, SC	21.2	28.8	21.3	10.0
Charlotte, NC	17.8	24.9	16.3	8.2
Chicago, IL	23.3	34.6	20.4	17.2
Cincinnati, OH	31.4	48.1	28.6	13.3
Clarksville, TN	18.9	27.8	16.0	10.2
Colorado Spgs, CO	14.4	20.6	13.1	7.6
Columbia, MO	24.5	17.2	28.9	7.1
Columbus, OH	22.4	31.9	20.7	10.4
Dallas, TX	24.2	37.9	19.9	15.4
Davenport, IA	17.4	25.4	16.4	6.5
Denver, CO	19.7	29.5	17.6	12.8
Des Moines, IA	19.5	29.1	17.8	6.6
Durham, NC	21.1	28.7	19.9	10.1
El Paso, TX	21.9	30.5	18.5	18.4
Erie, PA	28.1	43.1	25.2	14.0
Eugene, OR	25.1	24.1	28.4	10.1
Fargo, ND	15.5	15.1	16.9	6.9
Fayetteville, NC	18.2	26.2	16.2	10.0
Ft. Collins, CO	18.5	13.5	21.5	5.6
Ft. Wayne, IN	18.9	27.5	17.3	8.4
Ft. Worth, TX	19.5	27.0	16.8	12.3
Gainesville, FL	36.1	29.7	40.4	8.9
Grand Rapids, MI	28.3	41.2	26.2	10.2
Green Bay, WI	17.3	24.2	15.8	10.9
Greensboro, NC	19.9	26.3	19.6	9.4
Honolulu, HI	12.1	16.7	11.8	8.6
Houston, TX	23.5	36.3	19.7	14.4
Huntsville, AL	16.6	24.9	15.8	7.3
Indianapolis, IN	21.6	32.5	19.3	9.5
Jacksonville, FL	17.7	25.5	16.2	9.6
Kansas City, MO	20.0	30.4	18.0	9.6
Lafayette, LA	20.6	26.7	20.7	9.4
Las Vegas, NV	17.7	25.7	16.1	10.0
Lexington, KY	18.5	22.1	19.0	7.9
Lincoln, NE	16.3	20.4	16.6	5.6
Little Rock, AR	18.7	27.8	17.1	8.4
Los Angeles, CA	22.5	32.5	20.1	16.1
Louisville, KY	19.3	28.8	17.4	11.1
Lubbock, TX	22.6	28.5	23.0	7.1
Madison, WI	19.4	21.1	21.1	3.7
Manchester, NH	14.2	24.7	12.0	7.7

Table continued on next page.

City	All Ages	Under 18 Years Old	18 to 64 Years Old	65 Years and Over
McAllen, TX	27.2	35.9	24.2	22.1
Miami, FL	31.5	45.6	27.0	33.7
Midland, TX	12.2	18.9	9.6	9.9
Minneapolis, MN	23.1	32.2	21.3	15.9
Montgomery, AL	23.3	34.7	21.5	8.7
Nashville, TN	19.9	31.8	17.6	9.6
New Orleans, LA	28.5	42.4	26.0	16.5
New York, NY	20.8	30.4	18.1	18.5
Oklahoma City, OK	18.7	28.2	16.7	8.0
Omaha, NE	17.5	25.7	15.8	8.7
Orlando, FL	20.0	31.8	17.1	14.1
Oxnard, CA	16.5	23.9	14.0	9.5
Peoria, IL	23.4	34.5	21.9	8.9
Philadelphia, PA	27.3	37.7	25.6	17.2
Phoenix, AZ	23.1	33.1	20.4	11.5
Pittsburgh, PA	22.9	31.7	22.7	13.2
Portland, OR	18.6	24.7	18.0	11.0
Providence, RI	30.0	40.8	27.6	18.2
Provo, UT	32.7	27.4	36.9	4.2
Raleigh, NC	17.3	24.8	15.9	7.4
Reno, NV	19.5	25.0	19.1	10.6
Richmond, VA	26.4	39.0	24.7	15.0
Riverside, CA	19.5	25.7	18.1	11.3
Rochester, MN	10.0	10.9	10.1	7.7
Salem, OR	20.4	29.5	18.9	9.1
Salt Lake City, UT	21.9	28.2	20.9	13.4
San Antonio, TX	20.4	29.7	17.6	13.4
San Diego, CA	16.1	21.8	15.3	9.6
San Francisco, CA	13.8	13.9	13.6	14.8
San Jose, CA	12.5	15.4	11.7	10.4
Santa Rosa, CA	13.5	15.5	14.0	7.3
Savannah, GA	27.4	42.2	25.1	11.4
Seattle, WA	14.4	14.7	14.4	14.0
Sioux Falls, SD	11.7	15.3	11.1	7.5
Spokane, WA	18.7	23.2	18.9	10.4
Springfield, MO	25.2	35.2	25.9	9.5
Tallahassee, FL	32.2	30.3	35.2	9.7
Tampa, FL	22.7	31.8	20.2	18.6
Topeka, KS	21.4	32.1	20.4	6.5
Tulsa, OK	20.3	31.7	18.0	9.6
Virginia Beach, VA	8.3	12.8	7.2	5.0
Washington, DC	18.8	29.3	17.2	12.6
Wichita, KS	17.9	26.0	16.0	9.5
Wilmington, NC	23.1	34.6	22.9	7.8
Worcester, MA	21.3	30.4	19.3	15.1
U.S.	15.7	22.2	14.6	9.3

Note: Figures are percentage of people whose income during the past 12 months was below the poverty level;
Source: U.S. Census Bureau, 2010-2012 American Community Survey 3-Year Estimates

Poverty Rate: Metro Area

Metro Area	All Ages	Under 18 Years Old	18 to 64 Years Old	65 Years and Over
Abilene, TX	18.4	22.2	18.5	11.2
Albuquerque, NM	18.7	26.6	17.4	10.0
Anchorage, AK	8.9	12.6	8.0	4.7
Ann Arbor, MI	15.4	15.9	16.9	5.8
Athens, GA	26.1	24.5	29.3	9.3
Atlanta, GA	16.0	22.5	14.2	9.8
Austin, TX	15.4	20.1	14.7	6.8
Baltimore, MD	11.3	15.2	10.4	8.5
Billings, MT	12.8	17.5	12.1	8.1
Boise City, ID	16.1	21.3	15.4	7.5
Boston, MA	10.5	12.8	10.1	9.1
Boulder, CO	14.4	13.6	16.0	5.4
Cape Coral, FL	16.1	27.3	16.3	6.9
Cedar Rapids, IA	9.7	11.2	9.9	5.7
Charleston, SC	16.1	22.6	15.0	9.2
Charlotte, NC	15.2	20.7	14.1	8.0
Chicago, IL	14.2	20.5	12.7	9.1
Cincinnati, OH	14.3	20.3	13.3	7.4
Clarksville, TN	18.2	26.5	15.9	9.1
Colorado Spgs, CO	12.9	18.2	11.7	7.0
Columbia, MO	19.9	18.1	22.4	7.4
Columbus, OH	15.3	21.0	14.6	7.0
Dallas, TX	15.1	21.8	13.0	9.0
Davenport, IA	12.6	18.8	11.7	6.3
Denver, CO	12.7	17.5	11.6	7.8
Des Moines, IA	11.2	15.5	10.5	5.0
Durham, NC	18.4	24.6	18.1	7.9
El Paso, TX	24.0	33.4	20.2	19.3
Erie, PA	16.6	24.7	15.4	9.1
Eugene, OR	20.8	24.2	22.9	7.9
Fargo, ND	12.4	11.9	13.5	7.1
Fayetteville, NC	18.1	25.0	16.1	11.1
Ft. Collins, CO	14.0	13.7	15.7	5.5
Ft. Wayne, IN	14.7	21.3	13.5	6.6
Ft. Worth, TX	15.1	21.8	13.0	9.0
Gainesville, FL	25.5	25.0	28.5	8.8
Grand Rapids, MI	15.8	22.4	14.8	6.5
Green Bay, WI	11.1	15.1	10.0	8.4
Greensboro, NC	18.0	25.6	17.0	9.7
Honolulu, HI	9.8	13.2	9.3	7.0
Houston, TX	16.8	24.6	14.2	10.5
Huntsville, AL	13.0	18.0	12.2	7.3
Indianapolis, IN	14.4	20.5	13.1	7.1
Jacksonville, FL	15.2	21.1	14.4	8.4
Kansas City, MO	12.8	18.6	11.7	6.5
Lafayette, LA	18.5	25.3	16.9	11.6
Las Vegas, NV	16.1	23.3	14.6	8.8
Lexington, KY	17.2	22.1	17.1	8.4
Lincoln, NE	14.6	17.7	15.1	5.3
Little Rock, AR	14.9	20.4	14.2	7.7
Los Angeles, CA	17.0	23.9	15.3	11.9
Louisville, KY	15.6	22.9	14.1	9.2
Lubbock, TX	21.5	27.6	21.5	7.4
Madison, WI	12.4	14.2	13.1	4.9
Manchester, NH	8.3	12.6	7.3	5.9

Table continued on next page.

Metro Area	All Ages	Under 18 Years Old	18 to 64 Years Old	65 Years and Over
McAllen, TX	35.4	47.2	30.0	24.8
Miami, FL	17.3	24.3	15.6	14.7
Midland, TX	10.8	16.3	8.8	8.5
Minneapolis, MN	10.8	14.4	10.1	7.2
Montgomery, AL	18.9	27.7	17.3	9.1
Nashville, TN	14.8	21.4	13.4	8.4
New Orleans, LA	18.8	27.4	17.1	11.5
New York, NY	14.3	20.1	12.8	11.6
Oklahoma City, OK	16.2	22.7	15.2	7.9
Omaha, NE	12.6	18.1	11.2	7.3
Orlando, FL	15.9	22.6	14.8	9.0
Oxnard, CA	11.1	16.0	9.8	7.4
Peoria, IL	13.6	19.7	12.9	6.6
Philadelphia, PA	13.2	17.8	12.5	8.7
Phoenix, AZ	16.9	24.2	15.8	7.7
Pittsburgh, PA	12.3	17.6	11.9	7.8
Portland, OR	14.1	18.7	13.6	7.9
Providence, RI	13.6	19.1	12.7	9.8
Provo, UT	14.3	12.9	16.3	4.7
Raleigh, NC	12.6	17.5	11.4	7.4
Reno, NV	15.9	22.2	15.1	8.2
Richmond, VA	11.8	15.5	11.4	7.4
Riverside, CA	18.0	25.0	16.3	10.1
Rochester, MN	8.6	9.9	8.3	7.3
Salem, OR	19.3	28.4	18.2	6.7
Salt Lake City, UT	13.3	17.4	12.3	6.3
San Antonio, TX	16.8	24.4	14.6	11.1
San Diego, CA	14.9	19.2	14.4	9.0
San Francisco, CA	11.5	14.2	11.2	9.1
San Jose, CA	10.6	12.8	10.1	8.8
Santa Rosa, CA	12.4	15.2	12.8	6.7
Savannah, GA	18.0	27.3	16.1	9.0
Seattle, WA	11.8	15.6	11.1	8.2
Sioux Falls, SD	9.9	12.3	9.2	8.4
Spokane, WA	15.2	18.1	15.6	8.6
Springfield, MO	17.0	23.4	16.6	8.5
Tallahassee, FL	23.8	26.3	25.3	9.5
Tampa, FL	16.1	22.9	15.7	9.3
Topeka, KS	14.8	22.1	14.2	5.1
Tulsa, OK	15.3	22.4	13.8	8.3
Virginia Beach, VA	11.9	18.0	10.7	6.5
Washington, DC	8.3	10.7	7.8	6.6
Wichita, KS	14.7	20.7	13.3	7.8
Wilmington, NC	16.8	24.4	17.1	7.0
Worcester, MA	11.3	15.1	10.5	8.4
U.S.	15.7	22.2	14.6	9.3

Note: Figures are percentage of people whose income during the past 12 months was below the poverty level;
Figures cover the Metropolitan Statistical Area—see Appendix B for areas included
Source: U.S. Census Bureau, 2010-2012 American Community Survey 3-Year Estimates

Personal Bankruptcy Filing Rate

City	Area Covered	2008	2009	2010	2011	2012	2013
Abilene, TX	Taylor County	2.48	2.42	2.09	2.10	1.87	1.54
Albuquerque, NM	Bernalillo County	2.67	3.44	3.65	3.16	2.73	2.57
Anchorage, AK	Anchorage Borough	1.68	1.79	1.93	1.72	1.19	0.96
Ann Arbor, MI	Washtenaw County	3.98	4.82	4.96	4.03	3.32	2.74
Athens, GA	Clarke County	2.89	3.46	3.52	3.77	3.43	3.31
Atlanta, GA	Fulton County	5.68	7.45	8.21	7.57	6.23	5.48
Austin, TX	Travis County	1.35	1.81	1.86	1.52	1.37	1.08
Baltimore, MD	Baltimore city County	3.08	4.25	5.03	4.87	5.29	5.52
Billings, MT	Yellowstone County	2.34	2.60	3.34	3.32	2.29	2.01
Boise City, ID	Ada County	4.26	6.17	6.11	5.57	4.31	3.75
Boston, MA	Suffolk County	1.95	2.32	2.70	2.32	1.89	1.30
Boulder, CO	Boulder County	2.98	3.92	4.31	3.94	3.10	2.43
Cape Coral, FL	Lee County	4.92	7.38	7.32	5.30	3.73	2.92
Cedar Rapids, IA	Linn County	2.60	3.44	3.17	2.54	2.06	1.93
Charleston, SC	Charleston County	1.45	1.71	1.88	1.51	1.36	1.36
Charlotte, NC	Mecklenburg County	1.98	2.50	2.67	2.23	2.02	1.76
Chicago, IL	Cook County	4.72	6.40	7.44	6.69	6.72	6.90
Cincinnati, OH	Hamilton County	4.67	5.49	5.78	5.14	4.70	4.10
Clarksville, TN	Montgomery County	4.14	4.65	5.02	4.47	4.25	4.24
Colorado Spgs, CO	El Paso County	4.56	5.53	6.05	5.03	4.69	4.11
Columbia, MO	Boone County	5.43	6.39	5.70	4.68	4.19	3.46
Columbus, OH	Franklin County	5.41	6.20	6.22	5.47	4.80	4.46
Dallas, TX	Dallas County	2.39	2.90	2.86	2.64	2.74	2.20
Davenport, IA	Scott County	3.14	3.93	3.91	3.01	2.26	2.23
Denver, CO	Denver County	4.36	5.51	6.28	6.08	5.16	4.60
Des Moines, IA	Polk County	3.92	4.58	4.81	3.51	2.91	2.61
Durham, NC	Durham County	2.35	2.80	2.97	2.70	2.41	2.08
El Paso, TX	El Paso County	2.87	3.71	3.41	3.13	2.99	2.61
Erie, PA	Erie County	3.69	3.33	3.56	3.23	2.70	2.43
Eugene, OR	Lane County	3.25	4.30	4.92	4.14	3.48	3.37
Fargo, ND	Cass County	2.81	3.42	3.29	2.61	2.24	1.88
Fayetteville, NC	Cumberland County	2.87	3.25	3.25	2.99	2.59	2.60
Ft. Collins, CO	Larimer County	4.28	5.37	6.23	5.28	4.39	3.57
Ft. Wayne, IN	Allen County	6.64	8.22	7.67	6.72	5.93	5.90
Ft. Worth, TX	Tarrant County	3.02	3.74	3.76	3.20	3.11	2.57
Gainesville, FL	Alachua County	1.46	1.90	1.99	1.81	1.62	1.29
Grand Rapids, MI	Kent County	3.51	4.78	4.85	3.95	3.51	3.13
Green Bay, WI	Brown County	3.98	4.59	5.02	4.04	3.47	3.17
Greensboro, NC	Guilford County	2.28	2.68	2.54	2.27	2.10	1.87
Honolulu, HI	Honolulu County	1.44	1.98	2.41	2.05	1.65	1.31
Houston, TX	Harris County	1.52	1.78	2.08	1.95	1.64	1.36
Huntsville, AL	Madison County	4.45	4.94	5.11	4.78	4.60	4.26
Indianapolis, IN	Marion County	7.37	8.44	8.65	7.26	6.77	6.22
Jacksonville, FL	Duval County	4.44	5.80	5.97	5.13	4.36	4.39
Kansas City, MO	Jackson County	5.21	5.89	6.43	5.45	5.29	4.67
Lafayette, LA	Lafayette Parish	2.50	2.97	3.00	2.75	2.52	2.25
Las Vegas, NV	Clark County	8.25	12.68	12.54	10.25	7.30	5.54
Lexington, KY	Fayette County	3.59	4.58	4.57	3.93	3.65	3.42
Lincoln, NE	Lancaster County	4.02	4.37	4.43	4.01	3.38	2.79
Little Rock, AR	Pulaski County	6.10	6.81	7.14	6.71	6.38	6.42
Los Angeles, CA	Los Angeles County	3.43	5.57	7.35	6.88	5.49	3.90
Louisville, KY	Jefferson County	5.43	6.05	6.21	5.90	5.35	4.84
Lubbock, TX	Lubbock County	1.36	1.50	1.50	1.34	1.33	0.96
Madison, WI	Dane County	2.66	3.37	3.71	3.00	2.69	2.47
Manchester, NH	Hillsborough County	3.31	3.99	4.62	3.94	3.20	2.50
McAllen, TX	Hidalgo County	1.18	1.35	1.30	1.18	0.99	0.82

Table continued on next page.

City	Area Covered	2008	2009	2010	2011	2012	2013
Miami, FL	Miami-Dade County	n/a	n/a	n/a	n/a	n/a	n/a
Midland, TX	Midland County	0.73	0.94	1.17	0.88	0.81	0.38
Minneapolis, MN	Hennepin County	2.96	3.89	4.22	3.76	3.30	2.82
Montgomery, AL	Montgomery County	5.88	7.24	6.89	6.83	7.46	7.61
Nashville, TN	Davidson County	6.61	7.29	6.84	6.49	6.17	5.38
New Orleans, LA	Orleans Parish	1.59	2.12	2.31	2.23	2.04	2.01
New York, NY	Bronx County	2.01	2.36	2.34	2.21	1.86	1.74
New York, NY	Kings County	1.49	1.82	1.85	1.65	1.29	1.16
New York, NY	New York County	1.42	2.15	1.96	1.77	1.42	1.06
New York, NY	Queens County	1.99	2.56	2.74	2.41	1.94	1.69
New York, NY	Richmond County	1.92	2.85	3.03	2.73	2.23	1.91
Oklahoma City, OK	Oklahoma County	3.76	4.54	4.67	4.15	3.88	3.35
Omaha, NE	Douglas County	4.39	4.43	4.65	4.02	3.69	3.45
Orlando, FL	Orange County	3.83	6.51	7.70	6.36	5.42	5.04
Oxnard, CA	Ventura County	3.17	5.04	6.37	5.96	4.68	3.06
Peoria, IL	Peoria County	5.69	6.14	5.54	4.83	4.07	3.68
Philadelphia, PA	Philadelphia County	2.02	1.88	2.32	2.04	1.97	2.09
Phoenix, AZ	Maricopa County	3.47	6.22	7.82	6.61	5.02	4.11
Pittsburgh, PA	Allegheny County	3.54	3.83	3.70	3.19	2.54	2.39
Portland, OR	Multnomah County	3.18	4.30	4.82	4.40	3.85	3.27
Providence, RI	Providence County	4.49	5.23	5.59	5.09	4.20	3.62
Provo, UT	Utah County	2.64	4.59	5.94	5.78	4.73	3.90
Raleigh, NC	Wake County	2.66	3.45	3.08	2.85	2.68	2.15
Reno, NV	Washoe County	4.27	7.89	8.37	6.59	4.76	3.92
Richmond, VA	Richmond city County	4.41	4.77	5.80	5.13	4.55	4.54
Riverside, CA	Riverside County	5.32	8.64	10.86	9.81	7.19	5.08
Rochester, MN	Olmsted County	2.40	2.87	2.88	2.44	2.09	1.78
Salem, OR	Marion County	4.17	5.37	5.74	4.54	4.49	4.21
Salt Lake City, UT	Salt Lake County	4.10	6.22	7.45	7.58	6.72	6.00
San Antonio, TX	Bexar County	1.91	2.39	2.32	2.04	1.80	1.57
San Diego, CA	San Diego County	4.46	6.50	7.23	6.49	5.22	3.83
San Francisco, CA	San Francisco County	1.52	2.29	2.74	2.29	1.75	1.32
San Jose, CA	Santa Clara County	2.36	3.99	4.91	4.47	3.48	2.40
Santa Rosa, CA	Sonoma County	3.34	4.77	5.38	4.96	3.80	2.62
Savannah, GA	Chatham County	6.33	6.98	6.53	6.21	5.74	5.60
Seattle, WA	King County	2.42	3.76	4.32	4.07	3.48	2.88
Sioux Falls, SD	Minnehaha County	2.84	3.22	3.58	3.23	2.72	2.34
Spokane, WA	Spokane County	4.18	5.42	5.51	4.62	4.11	3.82
Springfield, MO	Christian County	4.51	5.01	5.48	4.36	4.33	3.60
Tallahassee, FL	Leon County	2.17	2.68	2.70	2.44	1.89	1.72
Tampa, FL	Hillsborough County	4.09	5.55	6.26	4.84	4.01	3.72
Topeka, KS	Shawnee County	5.91	6.66	6.65	5.93	5.96	5.24
Tulsa, OK	Tulsa County	3.30	4.23	4.51	3.82	3.54	3.05
Virginia Beach, VA	Virginia Beach city County	4.06	4.99	5.46	5.01	4.57	4.03
Washington, DC	District of Columbia	1.46	1.94	2.13	1.56	1.36	1.27
Wichita, KS	Sedgwick County	3.63	4.42	4.55	4.20	4.00	3.85
Wilmington, NC	New Hanover County	1.90	2.95	3.05	3.12	2.77	2.19
Worcester, MA	Worcester County	3.44	4.37	4.88	3.90	3.24	2.35
U.S.	U.S.	3.53	4.61	4.97	4.37	3.76	3.29

Note: Numbers are per 1,000 population and include Chapter 7 and Chapter 13 filings; n/a not available
Source: Federal Deposit Insurance Corporation, Regional Economic Conditions, March 20, 2014

Building Permits: City

City	Single-Family			Multi-Family			Total		
	2012	2013	Pct. Chg.	2012	2013	Pct. Chg.	2012	2013	Pct. Chg.
Abilene, TX	233	280	20.2	206	2	-99.0	439	282	-35.8
Albuquerque, NM	455	434	-4.6	744	1,040	39.8	1,199	1,474	22.9
Anchorage, AK	497	475	-4.4	35	58	65.7	532	533	0.2
Ann Arbor, MI	12	27	125.0	2	198	9,800.0	14	225	1,507.1
Athens, GA	185	143	-22.7	168	351	108.9	353	494	39.9
Atlanta, GA	359	473	31.8	1,764	5,070	187.4	2,123	5,543	161.1
Austin, TX	2,539	2,573	1.3	7,671	9,261	20.7	10,210	11,834	15.9
Baltimore, MD	164	220	34.1	566	1,037	83.2	730	1,257	72.2
Billings, MT	406	481	18.5	181	558	208.3	587	1,039	77.0
Boise City, ID	580	498	-14.1	157	222	41.4	737	720	-2.3
Boston, MA	40	34	-15.0	1,736	2,527	45.6	1,776	2,561	44.2
Boulder, CO	59	89	50.8	356	789	121.6	415	878	111.6
Cape Coral, FL	330	492	49.1	16	6	-62.5	346	498	43.9
Cedar Rapids, IA	289	242	-16.3	72	245	240.3	361	487	34.9
Charleston, SC	477	576	20.8	338	351	3.8	815	927	13.7
Charlotte, NC	n/a	n/a	n/a	n/a	n/a	n/a	n/a	n/a	n/a
Chicago, IL	317	448	41.3	1,673	2,577	54.0	1,990	3,025	52.0
Cincinnati, OH	83	90	8.4	367	74	-79.8	450	164	-63.6
Clarksville, TN	937	779	-16.9	421	580	37.8	1,358	1,359	0.1
Colorado Spgs, CO	n/a	n/a	n/a	n/a	n/a	n/a	n/a	n/a	n/a
Columbia, MO	733	631	-13.9	304	378	24.3	1,037	1,009	-2.7
Columbus, OH	723	770	6.5	3,286	3,565	8.5	4,009	4,335	8.1
Dallas, TX	936	1,075	14.9	6,149	7,559	22.9	7,085	8,634	21.9
Davenport, IA	128	114	-10.9	60	16	-73.3	188	130	-30.9
Denver, CO	1,056	1,284	21.6	4,522	4,586	1.4	5,578	5,870	5.2
Des Moines, IA	128	184	43.8	236	559	136.9	364	743	104.1
Durham, NC	874	1,112	27.2	1,719	2,636	53.3	2,593	3,748	44.5
El Paso, TX	2,815	2,271	-19.3	1,177	1,408	19.6	3,992	3,679	-7.8
Erie, PA	40	2	-95.0	0	0	-	40	2	-95.0
Eugene, OR	120	182	51.7	383	733	91.4	503	915	81.9
Fargo, ND	403	509	26.3	694	1,146	65.1	1,097	1,655	50.9
Fayetteville, NC	527	437	-17.1	1,356	288	-78.8	1,883	725	-61.5
Ft. Collins, CO	470	612	30.2	674	779	15.6	1,144	1,391	21.6
Ft. Wayne, IN	n/a	n/a	n/a	n/a	n/a	n/a	n/a	n/a	n/a
Ft. Worth, TX	2,716	3,321	22.3	1,485	2,334	57.2	4,201	5,655	34.6
Gainesville, FL	51	63	23.5	225	240	6.7	276	303	9.8
Grand Rapids, MI	45	59	31.1	174	96	-44.8	219	155	-29.2
Green Bay, WI	48	71	47.9	26	105	303.8	74	176	137.8
Greensboro, NC	323	354	9.6	481	614	27.7	804	968	20.4
Honolulu, HI	n/a	n/a	n/a	n/a	n/a	n/a	n/a	n/a	n/a
Houston, TX	3,513	5,198	48.0	9,020	8,845	-1.9	12,533	14,043	12.0
Huntsville, AL	960	1,000	4.2	420	306	-27.1	1,380	1,306	-5.4
Indianapolis, IN	472	562	19.1	79	671	749.4	551	1,233	123.8
Jacksonville, FL	1,310	1,844	40.8	2,499	709	-71.6	3,809	2,553	-33.0
Kansas City, MO	536	703	31.2	525	827	57.5	1,061	1,530	44.2
Lafayette, LA	n/a	n/a	n/a	n/a	n/a	n/a	n/a	n/a	n/a
Las Vegas, NV	1,233	1,517	23.0	75	0	-100.0	1,308	1,517	16.0
Lexington, KY	750	676	-9.9	1,066	223	-79.1	1,816	899	-50.5
Lincoln, NE	704	844	19.9	388	531	36.9	1,092	1,375	25.9
Little Rock, AR	347	356	2.6	323	252	-22.0	670	608	-9.3
Los Angeles, CA	870	1,144	31.5	5,830	7,248	24.3	6,700	8,392	25.3
Louisville, KY	851	938	10.2	1,185	1,289	8.8	2,036	2,227	9.4
Lubbock, TX	697	938	34.6	715	1,039	45.3	1,412	1,977	40.0
Madison, WI	161	217	34.8	1,047	1,018	-2.8	1,208	1,235	2.2

Table continued on next page.

City	Single-Family			Multi-Family			Total		
	2012	2013	Pct. Chg.	2012	2013	Pct. Chg.	2012	2013	Pct. Chg.
Manchester, NH	61	49	-19.7	61	38	-37.7	122	87	-28.7
McAllen, TX	433	374	-13.6	96	145	51.0	529	519	-1.9
Miami, FL	40	115	187.5	911	4,371	379.8	951	4,486	371.7
Midland, TX	599	732	22.2	410	1,092	166.3	1,009	1,824	80.8
Minneapolis, MN	76	146	92.1	3,227	3,176	-1.6	3,303	3,322	0.6
Montgomery, AL	218	265	21.6	0	0	-	218	265	21.6
Nashville, TN	1,305	1,824	39.8	1,529	2,142	40.1	2,834	3,966	39.9
New Orleans, LA	690	736	6.7	276	159	-42.4	966	895	-7.3
New York, NY	280	402	43.6	10,054	17,593	75.0	10,334	17,995	74.1
Oklahoma City, OK	3,260	3,609	10.7	70	804	1,048.6	3,330	4,413	32.5
Omaha, NE	1,305	1,567	20.1	610	1,003	64.4	1,915	2,570	34.2
Orlando, FL	815	1,037	27.2	1,070	1,850	72.9	1,885	2,887	53.2
Oxnard, CA	77	94	22.1	223	276	23.8	300	370	23.3
Peoria, IL	220	147	-33.2	14	6	-57.1	234	153	-34.6
Philadelphia, PA	566	632	11.7	1,609	2,183	35.7	2,175	2,815	29.4
Phoenix, AZ	1,650	1,673	1.4	2,784	1,458	-47.6	4,434	3,131	-29.4
Pittsburgh, PA	137	100	-27.0	0	0	-	137	100	-27.0
Portland, OR	644	763	18.5	1,654	2,992	80.9	2,298	3,755	63.4
Providence, RI	12	16	33.3	3	26	766.7	15	42	180.0
Provo, UT	67	136	103.0	46	51	10.9	113	187	65.5
Raleigh, NC	1,414	1,662	17.5	3,596	2,138	-40.5	5,010	3,800	-24.2
Reno, NV	443	687	55.1	68	426	526.5	511	1,113	117.8
Richmond, VA	119	106	-10.9	721	743	3.1	840	849	1.1
Riverside, CA	190	70	-63.2	168	51	-69.6	358	121	-66.2
Rochester, MN	299	323	8.0	62	44	-29.0	361	367	1.7
Salem, OR	179	283	58.1	200	294	47.0	379	577	52.2
Salt Lake City, UT	41	80	95.1	321	178	-44.5	362	258	-28.7
San Antonio, TX	1,896	2,102	10.9	2,747	16	-99.4	4,643	2,118	-54.4
San Diego, CA	535	821	53.5	2,548	4,487	76.1	3,083	5,308	72.2
San Francisco, CA	22	54	145.5	3,067	4,420	44.1	3,089	4,474	44.8
San Jose, CA	186	274	47.3	3,312	3,429	3.5	3,498	3,703	5.9
Santa Rosa, CA	103	138	34.0	134	347	159.0	237	485	104.6
Savannah, GA	223	265	18.8	160	18	-88.8	383	283	-26.1
Seattle, WA	498	822	65.1	6,799	5,855	-13.9	7,297	6,677	-8.5
Sioux Falls, SD	882	1,025	16.2	459	986	114.8	1,341	2,011	50.0
Spokane, WA	207	321	55.1	176	142	-19.3	383	463	20.9
Springfield, MO	126	152	20.6	646	816	26.3	772	968	25.4
Tallahassee, FL	216	293	35.6	692	648	-6.4	908	941	3.6
Tampa, FL	547	686	25.4	1,945	1,168	-39.9	2,492	1,854	-25.6
Topeka, KS	88	84	-4.5	34	2	-94.1	122	86	-29.5
Tulsa, OK	577	436	-24.4	594	164	-72.4	1,171	600	-48.8
Virginia Beach, VA	594	733	23.4	523	929	77.6	1,117	1,662	48.8
Washington, DC	271	333	22.9	3,552	2,922	-17.7	3,823	3,255	-14.9
Wichita, KS	415	536	29.2	322	200	-37.9	737	736	-0.1
Wilmington, NC	n/a	n/a	n/a	n/a	n/a	n/a	n/a	n/a	n/a
Worcester, MA	44	53	20.5	20	8	-60.0	64	61	-4.7
U.S.	518,695	620,802	19.7	310,963	370,020	19.0	829,658	990,822	19.4

Note: Figures represent new, privately-owned housing units authorized (unadjusted data); All permit data are based on estimates with imputation
Source: U.S. Census Bureau, Manufacturing, Mining, and Construction Statistics, Building Permits, 2012, 2013

Building Permits: Metro Area

Metro Area	Single-Family			Multi-Family			Total		
	2012	2013	Pct. Chg.	2012	2013	Pct. Chg.	2012	2013	Pct. Chg.
Abilene, TX	241	292	21.2	214	14	-93.5	455	306	-32.7
Albuquerque, NM	1,259	1,456	15.6	825	1,150	39.4	2,084	2,606	25.0
Anchorage, AK	530	500	-5.7	45	76	68.9	575	576	0.2
Ann Arbor, MI	262	394	50.4	14	364	2,500.0	276	758	174.6
Athens, GA	447	698	56.2	172	381	121.5	619	1,079	74.3
Atlanta, GA	9,167	14,824	61.7	5,213	9,473	81.7	14,380	24,297	69.0
Austin, TX	8,229	8,941	8.7	11,334	11,911	5.1	19,563	20,852	6.6
Baltimore, MD	3,895	4,617	18.5	2,061	3,452	67.5	5,956	8,069	35.5
Billings, MT	419	974	132.5	202	1,128	458.4	621	2,102	238.5
Boise City, ID	2,887	3,522	22.0	669	843	26.0	3,556	4,365	22.8
Boston, MA	4,126	4,953	20.0	4,725	7,068	49.6	8,851	12,021	35.8
Boulder, CO	471	591	25.5	824	1,034	25.5	1,295	1,625	25.5
Cape Coral, FL	1,806	2,531	40.1	237	645	172.2	2,043	3,176	55.5
Cedar Rapids, IA	617	625	1.3	171	324	89.5	788	949	20.4
Charleston, SC	3,132	3,779	20.7	1,461	1,638	12.1	4,593	5,417	17.9
Charlotte, NC	6,703	8,792	31.2	5,544	5,217	-5.9	12,247	14,009	14.4
Chicago, IL	5,658	7,261	28.3	3,699	4,366	18.0	9,357	11,627	24.3
Cincinnati, OH	2,641	3,308	25.3	963	1,022	6.1	3,604	4,330	20.1
Clarksville, TN	1,387	1,256	-9.4	509	586	15.1	1,896	1,842	-2.8
Colorado Spgs, CO	2,410	2,885	19.7	601	702	16.8	3,011	3,587	19.1
Columbia, MO	916	836	-8.7	312	396	26.9	1,228	1,232	0.3
Columbus, OH	2,913	3,495	20.0	3,898	4,868	24.9	6,811	8,363	22.8
Dallas, TX	18,090	21,224	17.3	16,952	16,686	-1.6	35,042	37,910	8.2
Davenport, IA	545	510	-6.4	141	107	-24.1	686	617	-10.1
Denver, CO	5,606	6,965	24.2	8,154	8,510	4.4	13,760	15,475	12.5
Des Moines, IA	2,809	3,307	17.7	1,358	1,614	18.9	4,167	4,921	18.1
Durham, NC	1,595	1,969	23.4	1,719	2,725	58.5	3,314	4,694	41.6
El Paso, TX	3,176	2,613	-17.7	1,179	1,484	25.9	4,355	4,097	-5.9
Erie, PA	216	258	19.4	272	209	-23.2	488	467	-4.3
Eugene, OR	417	506	21.3	385	743	93.0	802	1,249	55.7
Fargo, ND	1,037	1,395	34.5	1,174	1,698	44.6	2,211	3,093	39.9
Fayetteville, NC	1,376	1,269	-7.8	1,664	621	-62.7	3,040	1,890	-37.8
Ft. Collins, CO	1,139	1,489	30.7	729	888	21.8	1,868	2,377	27.2
Ft. Wayne, IN	694	960	38.3	536	75	-86.0	1,230	1,035	-15.9
Ft. Worth, TX	18,090	21,224	17.3	16,952	16,686	-1.6	35,042	37,910	8.2
Gainesville, FL	397	558	40.6	227	242	6.6	624	800	28.2
Grand Rapids, MI	1,098	1,319	20.1	188	162	-13.8	1,286	1,481	15.2
Green Bay, WI	648	719	11.0	275	551	100.4	923	1,270	37.6
Greensboro, NC	1,183	1,416	19.7	704	616	-12.5	1,887	2,032	7.7
Honolulu, HI	994	1,137	14.4	730	1,504	106.0	1,724	2,641	53.2
Houston, TX	28,628	34,542	20.7	14,662	16,791	14.5	43,290	51,333	18.6
Huntsville, AL	1,927	1,944	0.9	420	306	-27.1	2,347	2,250	-4.1
Indianapolis, IN	4,004	5,014	25.2	990	3,137	216.9	4,994	8,151	63.2
Jacksonville, FL	4,579	6,281	37.2	2,587	1,077	-58.4	7,166	7,358	2.7
Kansas City, MO	3,299	4,229	28.2	1,682	3,303	96.4	4,981	7,532	51.2
Lafayette, LA	1,198	1,399	16.8	145	155	6.9	1,343	1,554	15.7
Las Vegas, NV	6,108	7,067	15.7	1,267	1,506	18.9	7,375	8,573	16.2
Lexington, KY	1,218	1,335	9.6	1,100	319	-71.0	2,318	1,654	-28.6
Lincoln, NE	859	1,052	22.5	390	535	37.2	1,249	1,587	27.1
Little Rock, AR	1,851	1,681	-9.2	1,462	814	-44.3	3,313	2,495	-24.7
Los Angeles, CA	4,946	7,509	51.8	12,501	17,689	41.5	17,447	25,198	44.4
Louisville, KY	2,365	2,551	7.9	1,306	1,466	12.3	3,671	4,017	9.4
Lubbock, TX	752	1,009	34.2	715	1,039	45.3	1,467	2,048	39.6
Madison, WI	865	1,212	40.1	1,577	1,754	11.2	2,442	2,966	21.5

Table continued on next page.

Metro Area	Single-Family			Multi-Family			Total		
	2012	2013	Pct. Chg.	2012	2013	Pct. Chg.	2012	2013	Pct. Chg.
Manchester, NH	365	468	28.2	255	99	-61.2	620	567	-8.5
McAllen, TX	2,833	2,545	-10.2	659	749	13.7	3,492	3,294	-5.7
Miami, FL	5,089	6,369	25.2	8,172	13,552	65.8	13,261	19,921	50.2
Midland, TX	599	732	22.2	410	1,092	166.3	1,009	1,824	80.8
Minneapolis, MN	5,750	7,174	24.8	5,743	4,859	-15.4	11,493	12,033	4.7
Montgomery, AL	776	744	-4.1	474	110	-76.8	1,250	854	-31.7
Nashville, TN	5,340	7,020	31.5	2,907	3,869	33.1	8,247	10,889	32.0
New Orleans, LA	2,015	2,441	21.1	278	175	-37.1	2,293	2,616	14.1
New York, NY	6,815	10,139	48.8	20,097	29,685	47.7	26,912	39,824	48.0
Oklahoma City, OK	5,474	6,359	16.2	1,103	1,146	3.9	6,577	7,505	14.1
Omaha, NE	2,479	3,039	22.6	983	1,425	45.0	3,462	4,464	28.9
Orlando, FL	7,322	9,222	25.9	4,684	6,341	35.4	12,006	15,563	29.6
Oxnard, CA	278	430	54.7	288	571	98.3	566	1,001	76.9
Peoria, IL	638	538	-15.7	89	80	-10.1	727	618	-15.0
Philadelphia, PA	5,175	6,252	20.8	4,095	4,965	21.2	9,270	11,217	21.0
Phoenix, AZ	11,931	12,959	8.6	4,036	5,778	43.2	15,967	18,737	17.3
Pittsburgh, PA	2,918	3,251	11.4	548	1,312	139.4	3,466	4,563	31.7
Portland, OR	4,501	5,717	27.0	3,284	6,013	83.1	7,785	11,730	50.7
Providence, RI	1,144	1,465	28.1	217	509	134.6	1,361	1,974	45.0
Provo, UT	2,226	2,675	20.2	213	748	251.2	2,439	3,423	40.3
Raleigh, NC	6,425	8,034	25.0	6,501	3,397	-47.7	12,926	11,431	-11.6
Reno, NV	777	1,243	60.0	68	477	601.5	845	1,720	103.6
Richmond, VA	2,840	3,555	25.2	1,431	1,450	1.3	4,271	5,005	17.2
Riverside, CA	4,488	6,472	44.2	1,461	2,876	96.9	5,949	9,348	57.1
Rochester, MN	464	594	28.0	62	44	-29.0	526	638	21.3
Salem, OR	395	646	63.5	326	304	-6.7	721	950	31.8
Salt Lake City, UT	2,826	3,447	22.0	1,078	2,081	93.0	3,904	5,528	41.6
San Antonio, TX	5,102	5,827	14.2	2,902	301	-89.6	8,004	6,128	-23.4
San Diego, CA	2,197	2,565	16.8	3,469	5,699	64.3	5,666	8,264	45.9
San Francisco, CA	3,095	3,659	18.2	6,068	7,263	19.7	9,163	10,922	19.2
San Jose, CA	1,501	1,870	24.6	4,031	5,894	46.2	5,532	7,764	40.3
Santa Rosa, CA	312	453	45.2	248	593	139.1	560	1,046	86.8
Savannah, GA	1,263	1,517	20.1	277	233	-15.9	1,540	1,750	13.6
Seattle, WA	8,047	8,773	9.0	9,619	10,744	11.7	17,666	19,517	10.5
Sioux Falls, SD	1,104	1,330	20.5	483	1,079	123.4	1,587	2,409	51.8
Spokane, WA	963	1,299	34.9	390	335	-14.1	1,353	1,634	20.8
Springfield, MO	906	1,098	21.2	660	877	32.9	1,566	1,975	26.1
Tallahassee, FL	468	628	34.2	766	652	-14.9	1,234	1,280	3.7
Tampa, FL	5,883	7,314	24.3	4,278	4,838	13.1	10,161	12,152	19.6
Topeka, KS	270	272	0.7	42	10	-76.2	312	282	-9.6
Tulsa, OK	2,699	3,008	11.4	737	717	-2.7	3,436	3,725	8.4
Virginia Beach, VA	3,534	4,104	16.1	1,849	3,273	77.0	5,383	7,377	37.0
Washington, DC	10,980	13,274	20.9	11,424	10,759	-5.8	22,404	24,033	7.3
Wichita, KS	845	1,163	37.6	465	341	-26.7	1,310	1,504	14.8
Wilmington, NC	2,045	3,141	53.6	1,018	916	-10.0	3,063	4,057	32.5
Worcester, MA	867	1,164	34.3	258	177	-31.4	1,125	1,341	19.2
U.S.	518,695	620,802	19.7	310,963	370,020	19.0	829,658	990,822	19.4

Note: Figures cover the Metropolitan Statistical Area—see Appendix B for areas included; Figures represent new, privately-owned housing units authorized (unadjusted data); All permit data are based on estimates with imputation
Source: U.S. Census Bureau, Manufacturing, Mining, and Construction Statistics, Building Permits, 2012, 2013

Homeownership Rate

Metro Area	2006	2007	2008	2009	2010	2011	2012	2013
Abilene, TX	n/a	n/a	n/a	n/a	n/a	n/a	n/a	n/a
Albuquerque, NM	70.0	70.5	68.2	65.7	65.5	67.1	62.8	65.9
Anchorage, AK	n/a	n/a	n/a	n/a	n/a	n/a	n/a	n/a
Ann Arbor, MI	n/a	n/a	n/a	n/a	n/a	n/a	n/a	n/a
Athens, GA	n/a	n/a	n/a	n/a	n/a	n/a	n/a	n/a
Atlanta, GA	67.9	66.4	67.5	67.7	67.2	65.8	62.1	61.6
Austin, TX	66.7	66.4	65.5	64.0	65.8	58.4	60.1	59.6
Baltimore, MD	72.9	71.2	69.3	67.7	65.7	66.8	66.1	66.0
Billings, MT	n/a	n/a	n/a	n/a	n/a	n/a	n/a	n/a
Boise City, ID	n/a	n/a	n/a	n/a	n/a	n/a	n/a	n/a
Boston, MA	64.7	64.8	66.2	65.5	66.0	65.5	66.0	66.3
Boulder, CO	n/a	n/a	n/a	n/a	n/a	n/a	n/a	n/a
Cape Coral, FL	n/a	n/a	n/a	n/a	n/a	n/a	n/a	n/a
Cedar Rapids, IA	n/a	n/a	n/a	n/a	n/a	n/a	n/a	n/a
Charleston, SC	n/a	n/a	n/a	n/a	n/a	n/a	n/a	n/a
Charlotte, NC	66.1	66.5	65.4	66.1	66.1	63.6	58.3	58.9
Chicago, IL	69.6	69.0	68.4	69.2	68.2	67.7	67.1	68.2
Cincinnati, OH	65.5	67.6	64.7	62.4	62.8	65.2	63.4	63.3
Clarksville, TN	n/a	n/a	n/a	n/a	n/a	n/a	n/a	n/a
Colorado Spgs, CO	n/a	n/a	n/a	n/a	n/a	n/a	n/a	n/a
Columbia, MO	n/a	n/a	n/a	n/a	n/a	n/a	n/a	n/a
Columbus, OH	65.8	66.1	61.2	61.5	62.2	59.7	60.7	60.5
Dallas, TX	60.7	60.9	60.9	61.6	63.8	62.6	61.8	59.9
Davenport, IA	n/a	n/a	n/a	n/a	n/a	n/a	n/a	n/a
Denver, CO	70.0	69.5	66.9	65.3	65.7	63.0	61.8	61.0
Des Moines, IA	n/a	n/a	n/a	n/a	n/a	n/a	n/a	n/a
Durham, NC	n/a	n/a	n/a	n/a	n/a	n/a	n/a	n/a
El Paso, TX	65.0	68.2	64.8	63.8	70.1	72.0	67.4	69.3
Erie, PA	n/a	n/a	n/a	n/a	n/a	n/a	n/a	n/a
Eugene, OR	n/a	n/a	n/a	n/a	n/a	n/a	n/a	n/a
Fargo, ND	n/a	n/a	n/a	n/a	n/a	n/a	n/a	n/a
Fayetteville, NC	n/a	n/a	n/a	n/a	n/a	n/a	n/a	n/a
Ft. Collins, CO	n/a	n/a	n/a	n/a	n/a	n/a	n/a	n/a
Ft. Wayne, IN	n/a	n/a	n/a	n/a	n/a	n/a	n/a	n/a
Ft. Worth, TX	60.7	60.9	60.9	61.6	63.8	62.6	61.8	59.9
Gainesville, FL	n/a	n/a	n/a	n/a	n/a	n/a	n/a	n/a
Grand Rapids, MI	76.5	78.6	77.6	75.6	76.4	76.4	76.9	73.7
Green Bay, WI	n/a	n/a	n/a	n/a	n/a	n/a	n/a	n/a
Greensboro, NC	62.2	62.1	68.0	70.7	68.8	62.7	64.9	67.9
Honolulu, HI	58.4	58.8	57.2	57.6	54.9	54.1	56.1	57.9
Houston, TX	63.5	64.5	64.8	63.6	61.4	61.3	62.1	60.5
Huntsville, AL	n/a	n/a	n/a	n/a	n/a	n/a	n/a	n/a
Indianapolis, IN	79.0	75.9	75.0	71.0	68.8	68.3	67.1	67.5
Jacksonville, FL	70.0	70.9	72.1	72.6	70.0	68.0	66.6	69.9
Kansas City, MO	69.5	71.3	70.2	69.5	68.8	68.5	65.1	65.6
Lafayette, LA	n/a	n/a	n/a	n/a	n/a	n/a	n/a	n/a
Las Vegas, NV	63.3	60.5	60.3	59.0	55.7	52.9	52.6	52.8
Lexington, KY	n/a	n/a	n/a	n/a	n/a	n/a	n/a	n/a
Lincoln, NE	n/a	n/a	n/a	n/a	n/a	n/a	n/a	n/a
Little Rock, AR	n/a	n/a	n/a	n/a	n/a	n/a	n/a	n/a
Los Angeles, CA	54.4	52.3	52.1	50.4	49.7	50.1	49.9	48.7
Louisville, KY	66.4	67.2	67.9	67.7	63.4	61.7	63.3	64.5
Lubbock, TX	n/a	n/a	n/a	n/a	n/a	n/a	n/a	n/a
Madison, WI	n/a	n/a	n/a	n/a	n/a	n/a	n/a	n/a
Manchester, NH	n/a	n/a	n/a	n/a	n/a	n/a	n/a	n/a
McAllen, TX	n/a	n/a	n/a	n/a	n/a	n/a	n/a	n/a

Table continued on next page.

Metro Area	2006	2007	2008	2009	2010	2011	2012	2013
Miami, FL	67.4	66.6	66.0	67.1	63.8	64.2	61.8	60.1
Midland, TX	n/a	n/a	n/a	n/a	n/a	n/a	n/a	n/a
Minneapolis, MN	73.4	70.7	69.9	70.9	71.2	69.1	70.8	71.7
Montgomery, AL	n/a	n/a	n/a	n/a	n/a	n/a	n/a	n/a
Nashville, TN	72.4	70.0	71.3	71.8	70.4	69.6	64.9	63.9
New Orleans, LA	70.3	67.8	68.0	68.2	66.9	63.9	62.4	61.4
New York, NY	53.6	53.8	52.6	51.7	51.6	50.9	51.5	50.6
Oklahoma City, OK	71.8	68.2	69.5	69.0	70.0	69.6	67.3	67.6
Omaha, NE	68.1	67.9	72.5	73.1	73.2	71.6	72.4	70.6
Orlando, FL	71.1	71.8	70.5	72.4	70.8	68.6	68.0	65.5
Oxnard, CA	69.8	71.4	71.7	73.1	67.1	67.0	66.1	66.8
Peoria, IL	n/a	n/a	n/a	n/a	n/a	n/a	n/a	n/a
Philadelphia, PA	73.1	73.1	71.8	69.7	70.7	69.7	69.5	69.1
Phoenix, AZ	72.5	70.8	70.2	69.8	66.5	63.3	63.1	62.2
Pittsburgh, PA	72.2	73.6	73.2	71.7	70.4	70.3	67.9	68.3
Portland, OR	66.0	61.2	62.6	64.0	63.7	63.7	63.9	60.9
Providence, RI	65.5	64.1	63.9	61.7	61.0	61.3	61.7	60.1
Provo, UT	n/a	n/a	n/a	n/a	n/a	n/a	n/a	n/a
Raleigh, NC	71.1	72.8	70.7	65.7	65.9	66.7	67.7	65.5
Reno, NV	n/a	n/a	n/a	n/a	n/a	n/a	n/a	n/a
Richmond, VA	68.9	72.7	72.4	72.2	68.1	65.2	67.0	65.4
Riverside, CA	68.3	66.6	65.8	65.9	63.9	59.2	58.2	56.3
Rochester, MN	n/a	n/a	n/a	n/a	n/a	n/a	n/a	n/a
Salem, OR	n/a	n/a	n/a	n/a	n/a	n/a	n/a	n/a
Salt Lake City, UT	69.6	71.8	72.0	68.8	65.5	66.4	66.9	66.8
San Antonio, TX	62.6	62.4	66.1	69.8	70.1	66.5	67.5	70.1
San Diego, CA	61.2	59.6	57.1	56.4	54.4	55.2	55.4	55.0
San Francisco, CA	59.4	58.0	56.4	57.3	58.0	56.1	53.2	55.2
San Jose, CA	59.4	57.6	54.6	57.2	58.9	60.4	58.6	56.4
Santa Rosa, CA	n/a	n/a	n/a	n/a	n/a	n/a	n/a	n/a
Savannah, GA	n/a	n/a	n/a	n/a	n/a	n/a	n/a	n/a
Seattle, WA	63.7	62.8	61.3	61.2	60.9	60.7	60.4	61.0
Sioux Falls, SD	n/a	n/a	n/a	n/a	n/a	n/a	n/a	n/a
Spokane, WA	n/a	n/a	n/a	n/a	n/a	n/a	n/a	n/a
Springfield, MO	n/a	n/a	n/a	n/a	n/a	n/a	n/a	n/a
Tallahassee, FL	n/a	n/a	n/a	n/a	n/a	n/a	n/a	n/a
Tampa, FL	71.6	72.9	70.5	68.3	68.3	68.3	67.0	65.3
Topeka, KS	n/a	n/a	n/a	n/a	n/a	n/a	n/a	n/a
Tulsa, OK	67.9	66.7	66.8	67.8	64.2	64.4	66.5	64.1
Virginia Beach, VA	68.3	66.0	63.9	63.5	61.4	62.3	62.0	63.3
Washington, DC	68.9	69.2	68.1	67.2	67.3	67.6	66.9	66.0
Wichita, KS	n/a	n/a	n/a	n/a	n/a	n/a	n/a	n/a
Wilmington, NC	n/a	n/a	n/a	n/a	n/a	n/a	n/a	n/a
Worcester, MA	71.0	67.8	68.5	64.4	64.1	65.8	61.9	63.3
U.S.	68.8	68.1	67.8	67.4	66.9	66.1	65.4	65.1

Note: Figures are percentages and cover the Metropolitan Statistical Area—see Appendix B for areas included
Source: U.S. Census Bureau, Housing Vacancies and Homeownership Annual Statistics: 2013

Housing Vacancy Rates

Metro Area[1]	Gross Vacancy Rate[2] (%)			Year-Round Vacancy Rate[3] (%)			Rental Vacancy Rate[4] (%)			Homeowner Vacancy Rate[5] (%)		
	2011	2012	2013	2011	2012	2013	2011	2012	2013	2011	2012	2013
Abilene, TX	n/a	n/a	n/a	n/a	n/a	n/a	n/a	n/a	n/a	n/a	n/a	n/a
Albuquerque, NM	7.1	7.1	8.4	6.3	6.5	7.7	6.9	5.1	7.8	1.4	2.2	2.4
Anchorage, AK	n/a	n/a	n/a	n/a	n/a	n/a	n/a	n/a	n/a	n/a	n/a	n/a
Ann Arbor, MI	n/a	n/a	n/a	n/a	n/a	n/a	n/a	n/a	n/a	n/a	n/a	n/a
Athens, GA	n/a	n/a	n/a	n/a	n/a	n/a	n/a	n/a	n/a	n/a	n/a	n/a
Atlanta, GA	12.8	12.5	12.4	12.4	12.2	11.8	11.6	10.6	10.2	4.3	2.6	2.1
Austin, TX	12.6	12.7	12.5	11.7	11.9	11.9	6.4	9.6	12.1	0.6	1.3	1.1
Baltimore, MD	11.7	11.7	10.5	11.6	11.4	10.2	10.7	9.7	9.5	2.8	2.2	1.8
Billings, MT	n/a	n/a	n/a	n/a	n/a	n/a	n/a	n/a	n/a	n/a	n/a	n/a
Boise City, ID	n/a	n/a	n/a	n/a	n/a	n/a	n/a	n/a	n/a	n/a	n/a	n/a
Boston, MA	8.7	8.6	7.8	6.9	6.9	6.2	5.5	5.9	6.8	1.4	1.3	1.1
Boulder, CO	n/a	n/a	n/a	n/a	n/a	n/a	n/a	n/a	n/a	n/a	n/a	n/a
Cape Coral, FL	n/a	n/a	n/a	n/a	n/a	n/a	n/a	n/a	n/a	n/a	n/a	n/a
Cedar Rapids, IA	n/a	n/a	n/a	n/a	n/a	n/a	n/a	n/a	n/a	n/a	n/a	n/a
Charleston, SC	n/a	n/a	n/a	n/a	n/a	n/a	n/a	n/a	n/a	n/a	n/a	n/a
Charlotte, NC	9.2	8.0	9.3	9.1	7.7	8.7	10.1	6.4	6.4	1.9	1.3	3.5
Chicago, IL	11.8	10.8	10.5	11.6	10.6	10.3	9.9	9.7	10.9	3.6	2.8	2.8
Cincinnati, OH	13.2	11.2	11.2	11.8	9.6	10.0	11.1	9.3	8.9	3.0	1.8	2.6
Clarksville, TN	n/a	n/a	n/a	n/a	n/a	n/a	n/a	n/a	n/a	n/a	n/a	n/a
Colorado Spgs, CO	n/a	n/a	n/a	n/a	n/a	n/a	n/a	n/a	n/a	n/a	n/a	n/a
Columbia, MO	n/a	n/a	n/a	n/a	n/a	n/a	n/a	n/a	n/a	n/a	n/a	n/a
Columbus, OH	11.8	13.7	9.8	11.7	13.7	9.8	8.2	8.3	6.3	3.2	2.3	1.1
Dallas, TX	9.8	8.7	9.0	9.6	8.4	8.8	11.8	9.2	8.2	2.0	2.1	1.9
Davenport, IA	n/a	n/a	n/a	n/a	n/a	n/a	n/a	n/a	n/a	n/a	n/a	n/a
Denver, CO	7.0	6.3	6.3	6.5	5.9	5.5	6.8	4.7	5.3	1.8	1.5	1.2
Des Moines, IA	n/a	n/a	n/a	n/a	n/a	n/a	n/a	n/a	n/a	n/a	n/a	n/a
Durham, NC	n/a	n/a	n/a	n/a	n/a	n/a	n/a	n/a	n/a	n/a	n/a	n/a
El Paso, TX	6.5	4.3	8.8	5.9	4.3	8.6	9.2	8.2	7.9	1.3	0.1	2.9
Erie, PA	n/a	n/a	n/a	n/a	n/a	n/a	n/a	n/a	n/a	n/a	n/a	n/a
Eugene, OR	n/a	n/a	n/a	n/a	n/a	n/a	n/a	n/a	n/a	n/a	n/a	n/a
Fargo, ND	n/a	n/a	n/a	n/a	n/a	n/a	n/a	n/a	n/a	n/a	n/a	n/a
Fayetteville, NC	n/a	n/a	n/a	n/a	n/a	n/a	n/a	n/a	n/a	n/a	n/a	n/a
Ft. Collins, CO	n/a	n/a	n/a	n/a	n/a	n/a	n/a	n/a	n/a	n/a	n/a	n/a
Ft. Wayne, IN	n/a	n/a	n/a	n/a	n/a	n/a	n/a	n/a	n/a	n/a	n/a	n/a
Ft. Worth, TX	9.8	8.7	9.0	9.6	8.4	8.8	11.8	9.2	8.2	2.0	2.1	1.9
Gainesville, FL	n/a	n/a	n/a	n/a	n/a	n/a	n/a	n/a	n/a	n/a	n/a	n/a
Grand Rapids, MI	11.0	8.8	7.2	7.8	6.4	6.2	6.1	5.6	5.1	2.6	2.4	2.5
Green Bay, WI	n/a	n/a	n/a	n/a	n/a	n/a	n/a	n/a	n/a	n/a	n/a	n/a
Greensboro, NC	12.4	12.1	12.5	12.4	12.0	12.4	11.9	7.6	9.6	3.0	3.5	3.0
Honolulu, HI	12.1	10.2	10.9	10.9	8.8	8.6	6.9	6.3	6.0	0.7	1.3	0.9
Houston, TX	11.8	9.8	9.6	11.4	9.4	9.0	16.5	11.4	10.0	2.0	1.9	2.3
Huntsville, AL	n/a	n/a	n/a	n/a	n/a	n/a	n/a	n/a	n/a	n/a	n/a	n/a
Indianapolis, IN	12.4	10.5	9.2	11.9	9.5	8.7	13.1	11.1	10.9	3.4	1.8	1.5
Jacksonville, FL	14.7	15.4	14.2	14.1	14.4	12.7	13.3	11.7	8.4	2.8	1.9	1.5
Kansas City, MO	11.1	10.5	10.8	10.9	10.3	10.4	12.1	11.2	10.1	2.7	1.6	2.0
Lafayette, LA	n/a	n/a	n/a	n/a	n/a	n/a	n/a	n/a	n/a	n/a	n/a	n/a
Las Vegas, NV	16.4	16.2	16.6	16.0	15.0	15.5	12.1	12.8	14.1	4.1	3.4	3.0
Lexington, KY	n/a	n/a	n/a	n/a	n/a	n/a	n/a	n/a	n/a	n/a	n/a	n/a
Lincoln, NE	n/a	n/a	n/a	n/a	n/a	n/a	n/a	n/a	n/a	n/a	n/a	n/a
Little Rock, AR	n/a	n/a	n/a	n/a	n/a	n/a	n/a	n/a	n/a	n/a	n/a	n/a
Los Angeles, CA	6.7	6.2	6.2	6.4	5.9	5.7	5.3	4.9	4.2	1.8	1.3	1.2
Louisville, KY	10.8	10.6	11.0	10.8	10.6	11.0	10.2	7.2	7.8	2.4	2.4	0.8
Lubbock, TX	n/a	n/a	n/a	n/a	n/a	n/a	n/a	n/a	n/a	n/a	n/a	n/a
Madison, WI	n/a	n/a	n/a	n/a	n/a	n/a	n/a	n/a	n/a	n/a	n/a	n/a

Table continued on next page.

Metro Area[1]	Gross Vacancy Rate[2] (%)			Year-Round Vacancy Rate[3] (%)			Rental Vacancy Rate[4] (%)			Homeowner Vacancy Rate[5] (%)		
	2011	2012	2013	2011	2012	2013	2011	2012	2013	2011	2012	2013
Manchester, NH	n/a	n/a	n/a	n/a	n/a	n/a	n/a	n/a	n/a	n/a	n/a	n/a
McAllen, TX	n/a	n/a	n/a	n/a	n/a	n/a	n/a	n/a	n/a	n/a	n/a	n/a
Miami, FL	21.0	20.1	20.2	11.7	10.1	10.3	11.8	8.2	6.7	1.8	0.9	1.7
Midland, TX	n/a	n/a	n/a	n/a	n/a	n/a	n/a	n/a	n/a	n/a	n/a	n/a
Minneapolis, MN	6.6	5.8	5.7	6.1	5.2	5.1	6.7	5.3	5.4	1.8	1.2	0.9
Montgomery, AL	n/a	n/a	n/a	n/a	n/a	n/a	n/a	n/a	n/a	n/a	n/a	n/a
Nashville, TN	9.0	8.7	6.6	8.3	8.2	6.4	8.2	8.4	5.3	2.2	1.6	0.9
New Orleans, LA	10.7	13.6	13.3	10.3	13.4	12.7	13.1	15.9	11.1	2.1	2.9	1.9
New York, NY	10.0	9.8	9.5	8.7	8.4	8.1	6.4	6.4	5.4	2.6	2.2	2.1
Oklahoma City, OK	15.1	12.8	13.0	14.8	12.6	12.6	9.9	10.2	8.7	3.9	2.5	2.0
Omaha, NE	9.3	8.3	7.5	9.0	7.9	6.5	11.1	9.5	6.1	1.9	1.2	1.3
Orlando, FL	20.1	21.2	20.5	14.0	14.3	15.5	19.0	18.5	14.7	2.5	2.2	2.8
Oxnard, CA	7.1	5.5	7.4	4.7	4.6	5.6	3.2	2.3	5.3	0.5	0.5	1.7
Peoria, IL	n/a	n/a	n/a	n/a	n/a	n/a	n/a	n/a	n/a	n/a	n/a	n/a
Philadelphia, PA	10.5	10.2	10.4	10.1	9.8	10.2	12.7	12.6	11.6	1.6	1.9	1.6
Phoenix, AZ	16.7	16.6	18.4	10.8	9.8	11.5	10.9	10.3	9.7	3.1	2.7	2.4
Pittsburgh, PA	12.3	14.4	12.7	11.6	14.1	12.5	6.3	6.4	7.8	2.2	1.3	1.7
Portland, OR	6.5	7.0	6.5	6.3	6.6	6.1	3.4	5.0	3.1	2.0	1.9	1.2
Providence, RI	13.7	13.8	12.3	10.8	10.9	8.9	8.8	8.0	6.6	2.2	2.9	2.3
Provo, UT	n/a	n/a	n/a	n/a	n/a	n/a	n/a	n/a	n/a	n/a	n/a	n/a
Raleigh, NC	9.2	8.5	7.3	9.1	8.2	7.2	8.9	8.8	6.9	2.9	1.9	1.8
Reno, NV	n/a	n/a	n/a	n/a	n/a	n/a	n/a	n/a	n/a	n/a	n/a	n/a
Richmond, VA	12.4	13.8	14.5	12.0	13.0	13.6	13.7	17.5	11.4	2.4	1.4	2.4
Riverside, CA	17.7	17.9	16.2	11.4	12.5	12.9	8.4	9.0	8.6	3.5	3.3	1.8
Rochester, MN	n/a	n/a	n/a	n/a	n/a	n/a	n/a	n/a	n/a	n/a	n/a	n/a
Salem, OR	n/a	n/a	n/a	n/a	n/a	n/a	n/a	n/a	n/a	n/a	n/a	n/a
Salt Lake City, UT	7.5	7.9	7.4	6.4	7.3	6.8	7.4	7.3	6.7	2.2	0.8	1.5
San Antonio, TX	11.2	11.3	9.0	10.2	10.4	8.3	9.2	9.0	9.1	1.5	2.7	1.4
San Diego, CA	9.9	9.1	7.8	9.5	8.6	7.4	6.9	7.1	5.5	1.9	1.4	1.2
San Francisco, CA	8.3	6.9	6.5	8.1	6.8	6.4	6.8	3.2	3.9	1.8	1.0	1.1
San Jose, CA	5.3	3.8	5.0	5.3	3.7	4.9	4.8	3.8	3.0	0.9	0.9	0.6
Santa Rosa, CA	n/a	n/a	n/a	n/a	n/a	n/a	n/a	n/a	n/a	n/a	n/a	n/a
Savannah, GA	n/a	n/a	n/a	n/a	n/a	n/a	n/a	n/a	n/a	n/a	n/a	n/a
Seattle, WA	8.6	8.1	6.9	8.3	8.0	6.6	6.7	5.7	4.3	2.6	2.3	1.7
Sioux Falls, SD	n/a	n/a	n/a	n/a	n/a	n/a	n/a	n/a	n/a	n/a	n/a	n/a
Spokane, WA	n/a	n/a	n/a	n/a	n/a	n/a	n/a	n/a	n/a	n/a	n/a	n/a
Springfield, MO	n/a	n/a	n/a	n/a	n/a	n/a	n/a	n/a	n/a	n/a	n/a	n/a
Tallahassee, FL	n/a	n/a	n/a	n/a	n/a	n/a	n/a	n/a	n/a	n/a	n/a	n/a
Tampa, FL	20.4	20.8	18.4	14.5	14.2	12.1	11.7	13.0	9.2	3.8	2.0	2.1
Topeka, KS	n/a	n/a	n/a	n/a	n/a	n/a	n/a	n/a	n/a	n/a	n/a	n/a
Tulsa, OK	13.2	13.3	12.0	12.7	12.8	11.5	13.0	9.5	10.5	2.5	2.4	2.4
Virginia Beach, VA	10.8	10.8	9.6	10.3	9.5	8.7	9.4	8.7	7.0	3.2	2.9	2.5
Washington, DC	9.6	8.1	8.3	9.4	7.9	8.2	7.9	6.4	7.2	1.8	1.3	1.3
Wichita, KS	n/a	n/a	n/a	n/a	n/a	n/a	n/a	n/a	n/a	n/a	n/a	n/a
Wilmington, NC	n/a	n/a	n/a	n/a	n/a	n/a	n/a	n/a	n/a	n/a	n/a	n/a
Worcester, MA	10.3	10.3	10.8	9.5	9.5	8.6	4.9	3.7	6.4	1.3	2.4	3.1
U.S.	14.2	13.8	13.8	11.1	10.8	10.7	9.5	8.7	8.3	2.5	2.0	2.0

Note: (1) Metropolitan Statistical Area—see Appendix B for areas included; (2) The percentage of the total housing inventory that is vacant; (3) The percentage of the housing inventory (excluding seasonal units) that is year-round vacant; (4) The percentage of rental inventory that is vacant for rent; (5) The percentage of homeowner inventory that is vacant for sale; n/a not available
Source: U.S. Census Bureau, Housing Vacancies and Homeownership Annual Statistics: 2013

Employment by Industry

Metro Area[1]	(A)	(B)	(C)	(D)	(E)	(F)	(G)	(H)	(I)	(J)	(K)	(L)	(M)
Abilene, TX	n/a	19.3	5.6	18.7	1.8	11.2	4.0	n/a	4.1	7.7	12.7	2.8	4.1
Albuquerque, NM	n/a	15.6	4.9	22.6	2.0	10.2	4.5	n/a	3.1	14.6	11.6	2.7	3.0
Anchorage, AK	5.7	16.6	4.6	20.1	2.5	10.0	1.3	2.1	3.8	12.0	12.1	6.5	2.8
Ann Arbor, MI	n/a	12.5	3.9	37.8	1.9	7.3	6.6	n/a	3.4	12.6	8.2	1.8	2.5
Athens, GA	n/a	n/a	n/a	34.6	n/a	10.0	n/a	n/a	n/a	7.9	10.8	n/a	n/a
Atlanta, GA	3.9	12.2	6.5	13.0	3.5	10.2	6.2	<0.1	3.8	18.0	11.1	5.4	6.2
Austin, TX	n/a	11.4	5.6	19.2	2.7	11.8	6.0	n/a	4.3	15.7	11.2	1.7	5.2
Baltimore, MD	n/a	18.9	5.7	17.2	1.2	9.0	4.2	n/a	4.0	16.3	10.8	3.4	3.8
Billings, MT	n/a	17.5	n/a	11.8	n/a	12.6	n/a	n/a	n/a	10.8	n/a	n/a	n/a
Boise City, ID	n/a	15.2	5.3	16.3	1.6	9.2	8.8	n/a	3.5	13.9	12.6	3.1	4.8
Boston, MA[4]	3.1	22.9	8.0	11.3	3.3	9.4	5.2	<0.1	3.9	18.6	8.7	2.3	3.3
Boulder, CO	n/a	12.7	4.2	19.7	4.8	10.6	9.7	n/a	3.2	18.7	9.6	1.0	3.2
Cape Coral, FL	n/a	11.3	5.2	17.5	1.4	15.6	2.2	n/a	4.1	13.0	17.0	1.9	3.0
Cedar Rapids, IA	n/a	14.1	7.4	11.9	3.5	7.9	14.3	n/a	3.6	9.6	12.3	6.6	4.0
Charleston, SC	n/a	11.6	4.1	20.1	1.7	12.1	7.8	n/a	4.2	14.3	12.3	4.5	2.6
Charlotte, NC	n/a	10.1	8.4	14.0	2.5	10.8	8.2	n/a	3.6	16.6	11.4	4.4	5.3
Chicago, IL[2]	3.0	15.5	6.8	12.3	2.0	9.3	8.3	<0.1	4.3	17.9	10.3	4.9	5.4
Cincinnati, OH	n/a	15.4	6.4	12.6	1.4	10.2	10.3	n/a	3.9	16.1	10.4	3.9	5.8
Clarksville, TN	n/a	12.8	3.4	23.6	1.2	12.1	11.1	n/a	3.4	9.7	13.6	2.6	n/a
Colorado Spgs, CO	n/a	12.8	6.4	19.0	2.7	12.4	4.5	n/a	5.9	15.9	11.9	1.7	1.9
Columbia, MO	n/a	n/a	n/a	32.3	n/a	n/a	n/a	n/a	n/a	n/a	12.0	n/a	n/a
Columbus, OH	n/a	14.0	7.6	16.7	1.8	9.8	6.8	n/a	3.8	16.5	10.7	5.0	4.0
Dallas, TX[2]	n/a	12.2	9.0	12.4	3.0	9.7	7.4	n/a	3.5	17.4	10.5	3.9	5.9
Davenport, IA	n/a	n/a	n/a	n/a	n/a	n/a	n/a	n/a	n/a	n/a	n/a	n/a	n/a
Denver, CO	n/a	12.5	7.3	14.3	3.3	10.7	4.9	n/a	3.9	18.0	10.1	3.8	5.0
Des Moines, IA	n/a	14.2	15.3	13.3	2.0	8.6	5.8	n/a	3.9	12.3	11.6	3.0	5.4
Durham, NC	n/a	21.6	4.4	22.5	1.3	8.7	10.3	n/a	3.5	12.4	8.3	1.5	3.2
El Paso, TX	n/a	13.6	4.2	24.0	2.0	10.5	6.0	n/a	3.3	10.3	13.6	4.8	3.4
Erie, PA	n/a	21.3	4.8	12.8	1.0	10.1	17.0	n/a	4.8	7.4	12.2	2.5	3.0
Eugene, OR	3.4	15.8	4.9	21.1	2.2	10.0	8.5	0.6	3.2	10.5	13.5	2.4	3.9
Fargo, ND	n/a	16.2	7.3	13.6	2.4	9.6	7.6	n/a	3.9	11.3	11.9	3.6	6.7
Fayetteville, NC	n/a	11.0	2.8	29.9	1.1	11.2	8.6	n/a	3.8	9.7	13.1	3.6	1.8
Ft. Collins, CO	n/a	9.8	4.1	24.8	1.6	12.0	8.0	n/a	3.7	13.4	12.3	1.8	2.6
Ft. Wayne, IN	n/a	17.9	5.5	10.3	1.5	9.0	16.5	n/a	5.0	9.7	11.1	4.4	5.0
Ft. Worth, TX[2]	n/a	12.6	5.8	13.7	1.4	11.0	10.0	n/a	3.9	11.6	11.4	7.3	4.7
Gainesville, FL	n/a	18.2	4.7	32.4	1.1	10.6	3.5	n/a	3.0	8.7	10.6	2.1	2.1
Grand Rapids, MI	n/a	17.3	5.2	8.1	1.1	9.1	16.9	n/a	4.2	16.6	9.7	2.6	5.6
Green Bay, WI	n/a	13.4	8.1	12.7	1.1	9.3	16.9	n/a	4.7	11.1	9.9	4.6	4.4
Greensboro, NC	n/a	14.0	5.2	13.0	1.4	8.8	15.0	n/a	3.6	14.4	11.0	4.7	5.4
Honolulu, HI	n/a	13.3	4.4	21.8	1.5	14.4	2.5	n/a	4.6	13.8	10.9	4.7	3.1
Houston, TX	6.7	12.0	5.0	13.3	1.2	9.8	9.0	3.8	3.5	15.2	10.5	4.8	5.4
Huntsville, AL	n/a	9.0	2.9	22.9	1.3	8.5	10.7	n/a	3.3	22.7	11.2	1.3	2.7
Indianapolis, IN	4.4	14.5	6.4	12.9	1.7	9.9	8.9	0.1	4.2	15.4	10.7	6.1	4.8
Jacksonville, FL	5.0	14.6	9.8	12.1	1.5	12.0	4.5	0.1	3.3	15.9	12.0	5.2	4.0
Kansas City, MO	n/a	13.8	7.4	14.8	3.0	9.3	7.2	n/a	4.2	16.1	10.7	4.6	5.1
Lafayette, LA	4.3	15.0	5.6	10.4	1.5	10.4	7.7	10.7	3.1	12.0	12.1	2.6	4.7
Las Vegas, NV	4.7	9.4	5.1	11.3	1.1	30.8	2.4	<0.1	2.8	13.1	12.6	4.3	2.4
Lexington, KY	n/a	12.8	3.7	20.7	2.1	9.8	11.2	n/a	3.5	14.1	11.0	3.5	3.7
Lincoln, NE	n/a	15.9	7.8	21.8	1.4	8.8	7.5	n/a	3.8	9.9	11.0	5.9	2.2
Little Rock, AR	n/a	14.8	5.9	20.8	2.1	9.0	5.7	n/a	4.5	13.1	10.9	4.2	4.5
Los Angeles, CA[2]	2.9	17.5	5.0	13.3	4.8	10.5	8.6	0.1	3.5	14.5	10.3	3.8	5.2
Louisville, KY	n/a	13.5	7.0	13.3	1.5	10.1	11.7	n/a	4.0	13.0	10.3	7.3	4.7
Lubbock, TX	n/a	16.0	5.2	21.1	2.9	12.8	3.6	n/a	4.1	8.1	13.3	3.6	4.6
Madison, WI	n/a	11.5	7.8	23.8	3.5	8.4	7.9	n/a	4.9	11.8	10.7	2.4	3.6
Manchester, NH[3]	n/a	19.9	7.1	11.2	3.0	8.4	7.5	n/a	4.5	14.3	13.2	2.6	4.0
McAllen, TX	n/a	25.6	3.8	23.6	0.9	8.9	2.8	n/a	2.6	6.5	14.9	3.5	3.0

Table continued on next page.

Metro Area[1]	(A)	(B)	(C)	(D)	(E)	(F)	(G)	(H)	(I)	(J)	(K)	(L)	(M)
Miami, FL[2]	3.2	15.3	6.8	13.1	1.7	11.8	3.4	<0.1	4.4	13.8	13.8	6.1	6.8
Midland, TX	n/a	7.8	4.9	9.8	1.0	9.2	4.2	n/a	3.5	10.0	10.1	5.2	5.7
Minneapolis, MN	n/a	16.7	7.8	13.3	2.1	9.0	10.2	n/a	4.3	15.2	10.1	3.5	4.5
Montgomery, AL	n/a	11.0	4.3	25.3	1.3	9.1	10.8	n/a	4.2	12.3	11.4	3.6	3.1
Nashville, TN	n/a	15.4	6.1	12.8	2.5	10.7	8.8	n/a	4.0	15.5	10.8	4.3	4.9
New Orleans, LA	5.6	15.4	5.0	13.7	1.5	14.5	5.3	1.4	3.7	13.2	11.4	5.0	4.2
New York, NY[2]	n/a	20.0	9.9	13.6	3.9	9.0	2.9	n/a	4.3	15.9	9.9	3.4	4.1
Oklahoma City, OK	4.5	14.4	5.6	20.9	1.3	10.8	5.8	3.2	3.5	12.1	10.8	2.7	4.4
Omaha, NE	n/a	15.6	8.7	13.5	2.3	9.1	6.7	n/a	3.7	14.8	11.5	5.7	3.5
Orlando, FL	4.9	12.1	6.5	10.9	2.2	20.6	3.6	<0.1	3.3	16.4	12.8	3.0	3.7
Oxnard, CA	4.2	13.8	6.4	15.2	1.7	11.7	10.2	0.4	3.3	12.6	14.1	2.0	4.4
Peoria, IL	n/a	19.1	4.1	11.9	1.2	9.8	15.2	n/a	4.5	11.5	10.3	4.4	4.1
Philadelphia, PA[2]	n/a	22.8	6.8	11.3	1.9	8.6	6.6	n/a	4.4	16.1	10.4	3.3	4.3
Phoenix, AZ	5.0	14.5	8.9	12.8	1.8	10.4	6.3	0.2	3.5	16.4	12.1	3.5	4.5
Pittsburgh, PA	4.5	20.7	6.1	10.5	1.6	9.4	7.6	0.9	4.4	15.0	11.3	3.9	3.9
Portland, OR	4.9	14.7	6.0	13.9	2.2	10.0	11.0	0.1	3.5	14.6	10.8	3.3	5.0
Providence, RI[3]	3.5	22.0	6.2	12.8	1.8	10.8	9.1	<0.1	4.6	11.5	11.7	2.5	3.6
Provo, UT	n/a	22.3	3.3	14.4	4.7	7.3	8.8	n/a	2.2	13.0	12.5	1.3	2.8
Raleigh, NC	n/a	11.9	4.8	16.8	3.3	10.9	5.5	n/a	4.1	19.7	11.5	1.8	4.2
Reno, NV	5.4	11.4	4.7	14.5	0.9	17.2	6.0	0.1	2.9	13.8	11.7	6.9	4.5
Richmond, VA	n/a	14.5	7.5	17.9	1.2	8.9	5.0	n/a	4.9	15.3	11.4	3.3	4.4
Riverside, CA	5.7	14.7	3.3	18.1	0.9	11.4	6.8	0.1	3.2	10.9	14.0	6.5	4.5
Rochester, MN	n/a	40.6	2.4	10.3	1.6	8.5	9.0	n/a	3.5	5.1	11.5	2.3	2.1
Salem, OR	4.4	15.7	4.8	27.9	0.7	8.9	7.4	0.9	3.4	8.5	12.2	2.7	2.4
Salt Lake City, UT	n/a	11.1	7.8	15.3	2.8	9.7	8.2	n/a	3.0	16.3	11.1	4.8	4.7
San Antonio, TX	4.6	15.3	8.3	17.7	2.3	12.7	5.1	0.7	3.7	12.1	11.6	2.6	3.3
San Diego, CA	4.8	13.8	5.4	17.5	1.8	12.5	7.1	<0.1	3.7	16.7	11.2	2.1	3.3
San Francisco, CA[2]	3.6	13.3	7.0	12.4	4.8	13.3	3.5	<0.1	3.9	23.1	8.9	3.8	2.5
San Jose, CA	4.0	15.2	3.4	9.7	6.1	8.8	16.1	<0.1	2.6	19.7	9.2	1.5	3.7
Santa Rosa, CA	5.2	15.9	4.0	17.6	1.4	12.0	10.7	0.1	3.5	10.2	13.1	2.4	4.0
Savannah, GA	n/a	14.7	4.1	14.3	0.8	14.0	9.4	n/a	4.4	12.6	12.2	6.7	3.8
Seattle, WA[2]	4.6	13.1	5.5	13.5	5.7	9.5	11.1	0.1	3.6	15.0	10.7	3.2	4.6
Sioux Falls, SD	n/a	20.6	11.5	9.3	1.9	8.5	9.3	n/a	3.3	9.4	12.6	3.5	5.3
Spokane, WA	n/a	20.9	6.1	16.8	1.3	8.6	7.0	n/a	4.2	10.6	12.3	3.1	4.6
Springfield, MO	n/a	19.2	5.7	14.7	1.9	9.4	6.9	n/a	3.6	12.3	12.7	5.1	5.1
Tallahassee, FL	n/a	11.6	4.3	35.8	2.0	10.6	1.8	n/a	5.2	10.9	11.0	1.2	2.0
Tampa, FL	4.8	15.8	8.4	12.8	2.2	10.9	5.1	<0.1	3.5	16.9	12.9	2.4	4.2
Topeka, KS	n/a	16.0	6.4	23.5	1.3	8.1	6.3	n/a	4.2	11.8	9.9	4.1	3.1
Tulsa, OK	5.0	15.2	5.2	13.5	1.8	8.9	11.7	1.8	3.8	13.3	11.5	4.7	3.6
Virginia Beach, VA	n/a	14.2	4.8	21.0	1.5	10.6	7.2	n/a	4.7	13.6	12.0	3.2	2.6
Washington, DC[2]	n/a	12.7	4.5	23.1	2.4	9.5	1.2	n/a	6.3	22.9	8.7	2.3	2.0
Wichita, KS	n/a	15.2	3.7	14.1	1.5	10.0	17.7	n/a	3.6	11.1	11.3	3.2	3.2
Wilmington, NC	n/a	12.7	4.6	19.3	2.0	14.5	5.1	n/a	3.7	11.7	14.6	3.1	3.2
Worcester, MA[3]	n/a	24.3	5.4	14.9	1.4	8.5	9.5	n/a	3.1	10.2	11.6	3.9	3.9
U.S.	4.2	15.5	5.7	16.1	1.9	10.2	8.7	0.6	3.9	13.7	11.4	3.8	4.2

*Note: All figures are percentages covering non-farm employment as of December 2013 and are not seasonally adjusted;
(1) Figures cover the Metropolitan Statistical Area (MSA) except where noted. See Appendix B for areas included; (2) Metropolitan Division; (3) New England City and Town Area; (4) New England City and Town Area Division; (A) Construction; (B) Education and Health Services; (C) Financial Activities; (D) Government; (E) Information; (F) Leisure and Hospitality; (G) Manufacturing; (H) Mining and Logging; (I) Other Services; (J) Professional and Business Services; (K) Retail Trade; (L) Transportation and Utilities; (M) Wholesale Trade; n/a not available
Source: Bureau of Labor Statistics, Current Employment Statistics, Employment, Hours, and Earnings*

Labor Force, Employment and Job Growth: City

City	Civilian Labor Force			Workers Employed		
	Dec. 2012	Dec. 2013	% Chg.	Dec. 2012	Dec. 2013	% Chg.
Abilene, TX	58,388	59,322	1.6	55,629	56,690	1.9
Albuquerque, NM	257,503	253,224	-1.7	241,594	238,036	-1.5
Anchorage, AK	159,323	158,797	-0.3	151,276	151,438	0.1
Ann Arbor, MI	63,061	63,412	0.6	59,552	59,918	0.6
Athens, GA	69,635	68,686	-1.4	64,973	64,893	-0.1
Atlanta, GA	197,605	193,652	-2.0	176,010	176,555	0.3
Austin, TX	464,387	475,873	2.5	442,621	455,863	3.0
Baltimore, MD	280,654	276,345	-1.5	253,248	252,991	-0.1
Billings, MT	59,074	60,167	1.9	56,680	57,893	2.1
Boise City, ID	111,833	112,063	0.2	105,525	106,950	1.4
Boston, MA	320,515	322,960	0.8	301,058	303,051	0.7
Boulder, CO	61,750	61,918	0.3	58,701	59,321	1.1
Cape Coral, FL	79,099	79,040	-0.1	72,936	74,536	2.2
Cedar Rapids, IA	70,359	72,469	3.0	66,625	69,140	3.8
Charleston, SC	61,564	61,147	-0.7	57,591	58,429	1.5
Charlotte, NC	394,698	391,422	-0.8	363,056	368,591	1.5
Chicago, IL	1,276,070	1,271,227	-0.4	1,151,796	1,150,079	-0.1
Cincinnati, OH	139,839	139,879	0.0	130,211	130,389	0.1
Clarksville, TN	58,343	56,734	-2.8	53,866	52,473	-2.6
Colorado Spgs, CO	208,029	204,653	-1.6	190,227	190,029	-0.1
Columbia, MO	61,533	62,817	2.1	59,235	60,685	2.4
Columbus, OH	426,552	430,423	0.9	403,825	407,115	0.8
Dallas, TX	586,561	596,415	1.7	549,042	561,247	2.2
Davenport, IA	50,302	52,034	3.4	46,893	48,803	4.1
Denver, CO	329,615	328,452	-0.4	303,556	308,202	1.5
Des Moines, IA	104,991	108,232	3.1	98,223	102,321	4.2
Durham, NC	123,995	122,692	-1.1	115,431	116,919	1.3
El Paso, TX	271,850	270,705	-0.4	250,664	251,186	0.2
Erie, PA	48,156	48,060	-0.2	43,940	44,643	1.6
Eugene, OR	80,117	78,516	-2.0	74,788	73,815	-1.3
Fargo, ND	59,587	58,473	-1.9	57,621	56,929	-1.2
Fayetteville, NC	89,479	87,203	-2.5	82,694	82,364	-0.4
Ft. Collins, CO	88,053	86,935	-1.3	82,897	83,067	0.2
Ft. Wayne, IN	121,687	122,979	1.1	111,316	115,180	3.5
Ft. Worth, TX	360,346	368,237	2.2	339,337	348,449	2.7
Gainesville, FL	65,566	65,672	0.2	61,555	62,366	1.3
Grand Rapids, MI	99,786	102,834	3.1	91,273	95,032	4.1
Green Bay, WI	59,228	59,530	0.5	54,082	55,069	1.8
Greensboro, NC	139,545	136,564	-2.1	127,146	127,851	0.6
Honolulu, HI	n/a	n/a	n/a	n/a	n/a	n/a
Houston, TX	1,038,662	1,062,784	2.3	974,997	1,004,714	3.0
Huntsville, AL	90,433	88,011	-2.7	85,419	83,636	-2.1
Indianapolis, IN	422,888	423,668	0.2	385,789	396,511	2.8
Jacksonville, FL	423,087	419,389	-0.9	390,776	395,150	1.1
Kansas City, MO	227,690	227,284	-0.2	210,655	212,790	1.0
Lafayette, LA	63,962	65,811	2.9	61,411	63,563	3.5
Las Vegas, NV	286,848	285,073	-0.6	257,678	259,462	0.7
Lexington, KY	159,498	156,989	-1.6	150,161	148,265	-1.3
Lincoln, NE	152,026	150,990	-0.7	146,998	146,410	-0.4
Little Rock, AR	94,582	93,794	-0.8	88,565	87,934	-0.7
Los Angeles, CA	1,916,100	1,929,831	0.7	1,699,953	1,742,272	2.5
Louisville, KY	368,679	359,327	-2.5	339,507	333,783	-1.7
Lubbock, TX	119,336	122,325	2.5	113,737	117,178	3.0
Madison, WI	144,993	147,223	1.5	138,815	141,727	2.1
Manchester, NH	62,477	61,692	-1.3	58,772	58,550	-0.4

Table continued on next page.

City	Civilian Labor Force			Workers Employed		
	Dec. 2012	Dec. 2013	% Chg.	Dec. 2012	Dec. 2013	% Chg.
McAllen, TX	61,590	61,903	0.5	57,452	58,083	1.1
Miami, FL	184,999	181,547	-1.9	166,485	167,760	0.8
Midland, TX	75,394	79,562	5.5	73,233	77,357	5.6
Minneapolis, MN	215,809	217,300	0.7	204,947	208,040	1.5
Montgomery, AL	93,234	91,988	-1.3	86,867	86,386	-0.6
Nashville, TN	340,174	331,727	-2.5	319,549	312,959	-2.1
New Orleans, LA	150,567	150,127	-0.3	140,613	141,677	0.8
New York, NY	4,028,164	4,037,749	0.2	3,669,066	3,732,938	1.7
Oklahoma City, OK	274,105	280,247	2.2	261,489	266,736	2.0
Omaha, NE	218,683	217,335	-0.6	209,462	208,721	-0.4
Orlando, FL	137,813	138,700	0.6	127,752	131,373	2.8
Oxnard, CA	92,145	91,124	-1.1	81,363	82,560	1.5
Peoria, IL	57,119	55,791	-2.3	51,804	49,990	-3.5
Philadelphia, PA	660,276	642,317	-2.7	590,748	588,476	-0.4
Phoenix, AZ	728,773	725,352	-0.5	677,980	679,012	0.2
Pittsburgh, PA	155,902	153,811	-1.3	144,809	145,348	0.4
Portland, OR	321,366	318,514	-0.9	298,490	299,668	0.4
Providence, RI	81,449	79,843	-2.0	72,508	71,452	-1.5
Provo, UT	55,250	59,507	7.7	52,695	57,575	9.3
Raleigh, NC	222,597	220,426	-1.0	207,564	210,461	1.4
Reno, NV	117,068	115,588	-1.3	105,711	105,752	0.0
Richmond, VA	100,762	101,449	0.7	92,647	94,314	1.8
Riverside, CA	167,284	165,242	-1.2	148,554	150,084	1.0
Rochester, MN	59,183	59,094	-0.2	56,700	56,881	0.3
Salem, OR	74,334	71,837	-3.4	67,821	66,692	-1.7
Salt Lake City, UT	104,296	109,681	5.2	99,376	106,050	6.7
San Antonio, TX	627,542	630,554	0.5	592,131	596,914	0.8
San Diego, CA	715,817	712,880	-0.4	657,354	667,464	1.5
San Francisco, CA	482,376	484,247	0.4	451,368	461,193	2.2
San Jose, CA	480,781	484,451	0.8	440,174	453,654	3.1
Santa Rosa, CA	81,629	81,500	-0.2	75,258	76,868	2.1
Savannah, GA	66,322	64,048	-3.4	59,995	58,835	-1.9
Seattle, WA	372,822	381,488	2.3	352,010	364,929	3.7
Sioux Falls, SD	89,696	91,923	2.5	86,001	88,892	3.4
Spokane, WA	103,149	99,692	-3.4	94,465	92,436	-2.1
Springfield, MO	81,901	82,481	0.7	77,427	78,681	1.6
Tallahassee, FL	94,691	95,773	1.1	88,425	90,725	2.6
Tampa, FL	163,559	164,309	0.5	150,171	154,202	2.7
Topeka, KS	65,108	63,782	-2.0	60,510	60,054	-0.8
Tulsa, OK	191,828	194,571	1.4	182,396	184,737	1.3
Virginia Beach, VA	226,742	228,375	0.7	214,384	217,580	1.5
Washington, DC	371,456	365,540	-1.6	339,415	340,486	0.3
Wichita, KS	184,363	181,136	-1.8	172,236	170,662	-0.9
Wilmington, NC	53,923	52,649	-2.4	49,369	49,596	0.5
Worcester, MA	84,235	84,090	-0.2	77,626	77,344	-0.4
U.S.	154,904,000	154,408,000	-0.3	143,060,000	144,423,000	1.0

Note: Data is not seasonally adjusted and covers workers 16 years of age and older
Source: Bureau of Labor Statistics, Local Area Unemployment Statistics

Labor Force, Employment and Job Growth: Metro Area

Metro Area[1]	Civilian Labor Force			Workers Employed		
	Dec. 2012	Dec. 2013	% Chg.	Dec. 2012	Dec. 2013	% Chg.
Abilene, TX	84,362	85,707	1.6	80,437	81,972	1.9
Albuquerque, NM	400,580	393,881	-1.7	373,825	368,319	-1.5
Anchorage, AK	203,758	203,084	-0.3	192,298	192,504	0.1
Ann Arbor, MI	183,130	184,155	0.6	173,585	174,651	0.6
Athens, GA	114,803	113,199	-1.4	107,437	107,305	-0.1
Atlanta, GA	2,773,421	2,734,954	-1.4	2,540,260	2,548,119	0.3
Austin, TX	972,339	996,173	2.5	923,238	950,857	3.0
Baltimore, MD	1,483,033	1,465,478	-1.2	1,380,763	1,379,362	-0.1
Billings, MT	89,120	90,847	1.9	85,498	87,328	2.1
Boise City, ID	307,922	308,593	0.2	289,070	292,972	1.3
Boston, MA[2]	1,550,680	1,562,753	0.8	1,466,586	1,476,295	0.7
Boulder, CO	181,087	180,906	-0.1	171,073	172,879	1.1
Cape Coral, FL	288,827	288,702	-0.0	266,079	271,916	2.2
Cedar Rapids, IA	142,934	147,236	3.0	135,381	140,490	3.8
Charleston, SC	330,542	328,726	-0.5	307,190	311,663	1.5
Charlotte, NC	928,564	916,145	-1.3	841,635	855,842	1.7
Chicago, IL[2]	4,112,381	4,098,575	-0.3	3,747,045	3,760,120	0.3
Cincinnati, OH	1,081,111	1,073,366	-0.7	1,011,041	1,006,980	-0.4
Clarksville, TN	117,691	114,501	-2.7	108,121	105,574	-2.4
Colorado Spgs, CO	312,941	307,585	-1.7	285,719	285,422	-0.1
Columbia, MO	97,647	99,565	2.0	93,600	95,891	2.4
Columbus, OH	967,106	975,987	0.9	915,289	922,747	0.8
Dallas, TX[2]	2,245,884	2,285,469	1.8	2,113,329	2,160,308	2.2
Davenport, IA	197,858	198,667	0.4	184,080	185,069	0.5
Denver, CO	1,421,045	1,417,353	-0.3	1,315,711	1,335,851	1.5
Des Moines, IA	308,244	318,220	3.2	292,159	304,347	4.2
Durham, NC	276,816	273,704	-1.1	257,103	260,417	1.3
El Paso, TX	323,811	322,443	-0.4	296,188	296,805	0.2
Erie, PA	140,809	140,694	-0.1	129,605	131,678	1.6
Eugene, OR	175,947	171,484	-2.5	162,019	159,911	-1.3
Fargo, ND	118,466	117,176	-1.1	114,045	113,657	-0.3
Fayetteville, NC	165,633	160,669	-3.0	148,798	148,205	-0.4
Ft. Collins, CO	180,270	178,459	-1.0	169,533	169,880	0.2
Ft. Wayne, IN	204,345	206,341	1.0	187,655	194,169	3.5
Ft. Worth, TX[2]	1,123,153	1,148,399	2.2	1,059,051	1,087,543	2.7
Gainesville, FL	142,757	142,789	0.0	134,185	135,953	1.3
Grand Rapids, MI	389,082	402,103	3.3	364,397	379,403	4.1
Green Bay, WI	172,384	174,169	1.0	161,898	164,854	1.8
Greensboro, NC	373,892	364,290	-2.6	337,407	339,279	0.6
Honolulu, HI	459,870	463,811	0.9	440,370	446,131	1.3
Houston, TX	3,055,533	3,131,593	2.5	2,872,966	2,960,533	3.0
Huntsville, AL	211,330	205,600	-2.7	199,598	195,434	-2.1
Indianapolis, IN	903,457	907,894	0.5	832,410	855,545	2.8
Jacksonville, FL	699,589	694,256	-0.8	648,259	655,515	1.1
Kansas City, MO	1,034,701	1,031,930	-0.3	968,609	975,741	0.7
Lafayette, LA	141,028	145,012	2.8	135,418	140,163	3.5
Las Vegas, NV	987,932	983,147	-0.5	889,559	895,716	0.7
Lexington, KY	247,670	243,841	-1.5	232,678	229,740	-1.3
Lincoln, NE	176,663	175,515	-0.6	170,687	170,004	-0.4
Little Rock, AR	340,341	338,060	-0.7	319,225	316,950	-0.7
Los Angeles, CA[2]	4,941,671	4,941,492	-0.0	4,438,759	4,508,710	1.6
Louisville, KY	637,024	626,298	-1.7	588,310	583,770	-0.8
Lubbock, TX	146,387	150,127	2.6	139,492	143,712	3.0
Madison, WI	344,939	349,831	1.4	328,830	335,728	2.1
Manchester, NH	107,832	106,653	-1.1	102,005	101,619	-0.4

Table continued on next page.

Metro Area[1]	Civilian Labor Force			Workers Employed		
	Dec. 2012	Dec. 2013	% Chg.	Dec. 2012	Dec. 2013	% Chg.
McAllen, TX	317,468	320,758	1.0	284,246	287,367	1.1
Miami, FL[2]	1,295,038	1,282,132	-1.0	1,174,459	1,194,364	1.7
Midland, TX	92,254	97,358	5.5	89,593	94,639	5.6
Minneapolis, MN	1,858,152	1,870,263	0.7	1,762,494	1,790,025	1.6
Montgomery, AL	168,280	165,988	-1.4	157,029	156,160	-0.6
Nashville, TN	863,413	841,403	-2.5	811,941	795,197	-2.1
New Orleans, LA	544,227	543,640	-0.1	514,276	518,168	0.8
New York, NY[2]	5,745,485	5,742,363	-0.1	5,247,273	5,334,716	1.7
Oklahoma City, OK	600,367	613,490	2.2	572,314	583,803	2.0
Omaha, NE	461,488	460,949	-0.1	442,331	443,173	0.2
Orlando, FL	1,149,261	1,156,473	0.6	1,062,530	1,092,651	2.8
Oxnard, CA	440,772	438,900	-0.4	402,857	408,786	1.5
Peoria, IL	201,110	196,205	-2.4	184,634	178,165	-3.5
Philadelphia, PA[2]	2,005,235	1,960,037	-2.3	1,843,376	1,836,286	-0.4
Phoenix, AZ	2,042,749	2,033,400	-0.5	1,904,463	1,907,362	0.2
Pittsburgh, PA	1,261,313	1,244,990	-1.3	1,170,044	1,174,397	0.4
Portland, OR	1,178,537	1,164,828	-1.2	1,091,135	1,092,460	0.1
Providence, RI	698,341	687,582	-1.5	632,386	624,667	-1.2
Provo, UT	232,500	250,146	7.6	221,010	241,475	9.3
Raleigh, NC	602,263	595,803	-1.1	557,064	564,840	1.4
Reno, NV	223,265	220,352	-1.3	201,721	201,799	0.0
Richmond, VA	659,432	665,236	0.9	619,573	630,722	1.8
Riverside, CA	1,819,256	1,795,514	-1.3	1,619,017	1,635,688	1.0
Rochester, MN	104,165	103,879	-0.3	99,590	99,909	0.3
Salem, OR	190,388	184,194	-3.3	173,577	170,689	-1.7
Salt Lake City, UT	613,413	645,340	5.2	583,405	622,582	6.7
San Antonio, TX	1,024,714	1,028,922	0.4	966,143	973,947	0.8
San Diego, CA	1,603,528	1,596,937	-0.4	1,472,508	1,495,156	1.5
San Francisco, CA[2]	1,023,133	1,028,522	0.5	960,281	981,184	2.2
San Jose, CA	944,587	953,544	0.9	871,335	898,019	3.1
Santa Rosa, CA	257,011	256,586	-0.2	236,895	241,961	2.1
Savannah, GA	183,298	177,195	-3.3	168,509	165,250	-1.9
Seattle, WA[2]	1,517,566	1,535,481	1.2	1,430,711	1,460,104	2.1
Sioux Falls, SD	131,241	134,415	2.4	125,996	130,230	3.4
Spokane, WA	233,657	226,034	-3.3	214,042	209,444	-2.1
Springfield, MO	223,052	224,783	0.8	210,940	214,358	1.6
Tallahassee, FL	187,562	189,428	1.0	174,929	179,480	2.6
Tampa, FL	1,331,021	1,338,701	0.6	1,226,191	1,259,105	2.7
Topeka, KS	120,621	118,404	-1.8	113,380	112,525	-0.8
Tulsa, OK	450,802	456,837	1.3	426,833	432,310	1.3
Virginia Beach, VA	824,175	828,953	0.6	773,629	785,007	1.5
Washington, DC[2]	2,521,100	2,514,981	-0.2	2,385,023	2,396,147	0.5
Wichita, KS	301,071	295,940	-1.7	283,080	280,493	-0.9
Wilmington, NC	184,167	179,204	-2.7	165,773	166,535	0.5
Worcester, MA	292,613	291,563	-0.4	271,522	270,674	-0.3
U.S.	154,904,000	154,408,000	-0.3	143,060,000	144,423,000	1.0

Note: Data is not seasonally adjusted and covers workers 16 years of age and older; (1) Figures cover the Metropolitan Statistical Area (MSA) except where noted. See Appendix B for areas included; (2) Metropolitan Division; (3) New England City and Town Area; (4) New England City and Town Area Division
Source: Bureau of Labor Statistics, Local Area Unemployment Statistics

Unemployment Rate: City

City	2013											
	Jan.	Feb.	Mar.	Apr.	May	Jun.	Jul.	Aug.	Sep.	Oct.	Nov.	Dec.
Abilene, TX	5.5	5.1	5.0	4.8	5.4	5.9	5.6	5.1	5.1	4.8	4.6	4.4
Albuquerque, NM	6.6	7.0	6.6	5.9	6.2	7.2	7.1	6.3	6.1	6.1	5.7	6.0
Anchorage, AK	5.5	5.1	4.9	4.8	4.7	5.3	4.9	4.7	4.4	4.7	4.6	4.6
Ann Arbor, MI	5.7	5.6	5.4	5.4	6.3	7.2	7.8	6.6	6.0	6.4	5.7	5.5
Athens, GA	6.9	6.4	6.2	5.9	6.6	7.7	7.3	6.6	6.1	6.2	5.4	5.5
Atlanta, GA	11.1	10.3	9.9	9.6	10.4	11.4	10.9	10.4	9.6	9.8	9.1	8.8
Austin, TX	5.5	5.0	4.9	4.7	5.0	5.4	5.2	4.8	5.0	4.8	4.4	4.2
Baltimore, MD	10.5	9.7	9.5	9.3	10.0	11.1	10.7	10.3	9.4	9.9	9.0	8.5
Billings, MT	4.6	4.4	4.4	3.9	3.8	4.4	3.8	3.7	3.6	3.6	3.6	3.8
Boise City, ID	6.3	6.0	5.8	5.5	5.3	5.9	5.7	5.8	5.8	5.7	4.7	4.6
Boston, MA	6.7	5.8	5.8	5.9	6.8	7.8	7.5	7.1	7.0	6.9	6.3	6.2
Boulder, CO	4.9	5.2	5.1	5.0	4.9	6.4	5.5	5.0	4.9	4.7	4.5	4.2
Cape Coral, FL	8.0	7.4	6.9	6.6	6.7	7.1	7.2	6.9	6.5	6.2	6.2	5.7
Cedar Rapids, IA	6.1	5.5	5.1	4.6	4.9	5.1	5.1	5.1	4.6	4.3	4.4	4.6
Charleston, SC	6.6	6.0	5.6	5.2	5.8	6.8	6.1	6.3	5.6	5.2	4.8	4.4
Charlotte, NC	8.5	8.0	7.7	7.4	7.9	8.4	8.4	7.5	6.8	6.9	6.1	5.8
Chicago, IL	10.9	11.3	10.4	10.3	10.7	11.6	11.2	10.9	10.1	9.9	9.6	9.5
Cincinnati, OH	8.6	7.8	7.4	6.9	7.6	8.3	8.0	7.7	8.1	8.1	7.8	6.8
Clarksville, TN	8.2	7.7	7.9	7.5	7.8	9.0	8.3	8.1	8.2	8.9	8.0	7.5
Colorado Spgs, CO	8.7	8.6	8.5	8.0	7.8	9.0	8.3	8.0	7.7	7.4	7.2	7.1
Columbia, MO	4.6	4.5	4.4	4.2	4.6	5.1	5.3	4.9	3.8	3.7	3.5	3.4
Columbus, OH	6.8	6.3	6.1	5.7	6.0	6.4	6.3	6.1	6.5	6.2	6.1	5.4
Dallas, TX	7.3	6.9	6.7	6.5	6.9	7.2	6.9	6.5	6.7	6.4	6.1	5.9
Davenport, IA	7.8	7.3	6.2	5.9	6.0	6.6	6.6	6.1	6.3	6.0	6.2	6.2
Denver, CO	8.1	8.1	7.8	7.3	7.0	7.7	7.2	7.0	6.8	6.3	6.2	6.2
Des Moines, IA	7.3	6.7	6.0	5.4	5.2	5.5	5.4	5.7	5.1	4.8	5.0	5.5
Durham, NC	7.3	6.6	6.4	6.1	6.6	7.0	7.1	6.4	5.6	5.7	4.9	4.7
El Paso, TX	8.7	8.3	8.1	8.0	8.5	9.0	8.6	8.0	8.1	7.8	7.5	7.2
Erie, PA	10.1	9.1	8.7	7.7	7.8	8.7	8.5	8.6	7.6	7.7	8.0	7.1
Eugene, OR	7.8	7.6	7.3	6.8	6.6	7.6	7.8	7.5	6.3	6.2	5.9	6.0
Fargo, ND	4.2	3.8	3.8	3.6	3.0	3.6	3.2	2.9	2.3	2.3	2.3	2.6
Fayetteville, NC	8.2	7.5	7.1	6.8	7.5	8.0	8.1	7.3	6.5	6.5	5.8	5.5
Ft. Collins, CO	6.0	6.1	5.8	5.4	5.2	6.3	5.6	5.2	5.1	4.9	4.7	4.4
Ft. Wayne, IN	9.4	9.2	9.2	8.1	8.1	8.6	9.0	7.5	7.4	7.1	7.2	6.3
Ft. Worth, TX	6.7	6.3	6.3	6.0	6.5	6.9	6.6	6.2	6.1	5.9	5.6	5.4
Gainesville, FL	6.2	5.7	5.4	4.8	5.5	6.3	6.5	5.7	5.5	4.8	5.1	5.0
Grand Rapids, MI	8.8	8.8	8.3	7.9	8.9	9.7	10.0	8.8	8.2	8.7	7.7	7.6
Green Bay, WI	10.1	10.2	9.8	9.2	8.6	9.1	8.6	7.7	7.4	7.3	7.5	7.5
Greensboro, NC	9.8	8.6	8.3	8.0	8.8	9.4	9.2	8.3	7.4	7.6	6.7	6.4
Honolulu, HI	n/a	n/a	n/a	n/a	n/a	n/a	n/a	n/a	n/a	n/a	n/a	n/a
Houston, TX	6.9	6.4	6.2	6.1	6.5	6.9	6.6	6.2	6.3	6.0	5.7	5.5
Huntsville, AL	6.7	6.9	6.0	5.2	5.6	6.2	5.9	5.9	5.6	5.6	4.9	5.0
Indianapolis, IN	9.5	9.3	9.2	8.3	8.4	8.8	8.5	7.9	7.3	7.4	7.4	6.4
Jacksonville, FL	7.9	7.4	6.8	6.7	6.9	7.5	6.9	7.3	6.6	6.3	6.1	5.8
Kansas City, MO	7.5	8.0	7.4	6.8	7.6	7.8	8.4	9.0	7.1	6.5	6.2	6.4
Lafayette, LA	5.5	4.2	4.3	4.6	5.5	6.1	5.4	5.4	4.9	4.7	4.3	3.4
Las Vegas, NV	10.4	10.0	10.0	9.7	9.6	10.4	10.0	10.0	9.7	9.6	8.8	9.0
Lexington, KY	6.5	6.6	6.6	5.9	6.4	7.1	6.4	6.1	6.2	6.4	6.1	5.6
Lincoln, NE	4.0	3.6	3.3	3.2	3.4	3.9	3.9	3.2	3.2	2.9	2.8	3.0
Little Rock, AR	7.2	7.1	6.8	6.4	6.8	7.1	7.1	6.7	6.5	6.4	6.1	6.2
Los Angeles, CA	12.0	11.4	11.0	10.2	10.2	11.3	11.9	11.3	10.3	10.4	10.4	9.7
Louisville, KY	8.3	8.3	8.4	7.5	8.4	9.0	8.7	7.8	7.8	7.8	7.6	7.1
Lubbock, TX	5.4	5.0	5.1	4.7	5.1	6.0	5.7	5.0	4.9	4.6	4.4	4.2
Madison, WI	5.3	5.3	4.7	4.7	4.8	5.1	5.0	4.6	4.2	4.1	4.0	3.7
Manchester, NH	7.0	6.6	6.4	5.5	5.5	5.5	5.4	5.2	5.1	5.2	5.1	5.1

Table continued on next page.

City	2013											
	Jan.	Feb.	Mar.	Apr.	May	Jun.	Jul.	Aug.	Sep.	Oct.	Nov.	Dec.
McAllen, TX	7.6	7.3	7.2	7.1	7.3	7.7	7.5	6.9	7.0	6.8	6.4	6.2
Miami, FL	10.5	10.6	10.3	9.7	9.7	9.8	9.3	9.4	9.2	9.5	7.9	7.6
Midland, TX	3.4	3.2	3.1	3.0	3.4	3.6	3.4	3.2	3.3	3.0	2.9	2.8
Minneapolis, MN	5.7	5.1	5.0	4.7	5.0	5.4	5.3	5.1	4.9	4.5	4.3	4.3
Montgomery, AL	7.9	7.8	7.1	6.2	6.5	7.1	7.0	7.1	7.0	6.8	6.0	6.1
Nashville, TN	6.5	6.3	6.2	6.5	6.7	7.0	6.7	6.9	6.7	6.7	5.8	5.7
New Orleans, LA	8.6	7.0	7.1	7.3	8.2	9.6	9.0	9.0	8.3	7.6	6.8	5.6
New York, NY	9.7	9.2	8.6	8.2	8.6	8.9	9.1	8.8	8.5	8.7	8.0	7.5
Oklahoma City, OK	5.1	4.9	4.6	4.0	4.9	5.4	4.7	4.7	5.0	5.3	4.7	4.8
Omaha, NE	5.0	4.6	4.4	4.1	4.3	4.8	4.8	4.4	4.1	4.0	3.6	4.0
Orlando, FL	7.6	7.1	6.7	6.5	6.6	6.6	6.5	6.4	6.1	5.8	5.5	5.3
Oxnard, CA	12.2	11.1	10.6	9.5	9.1	10.1	10.9	10.7	10.1	10.0	9.9	9.4
Peoria, IL	10.8	11.0	9.6	8.5	8.9	9.9	10.6	9.9	9.7	9.9	10.3	10.4
Philadelphia, PA	11.8	10.6	10.1	9.6	10.1	10.4	10.9	11.1	10.2	10.2	9.6	8.4
Phoenix, AZ	7.3	6.7	6.8	6.8	6.3	7.2	7.1	7.5	7.3	6.9	6.1	6.4
Pittsburgh, PA	8.2	7.3	6.9	6.5	7.0	7.6	7.6	7.9	6.7	6.5	6.4	5.5
Portland, OR	7.9	7.8	7.4	6.7	6.8	7.2	7.2	6.8	6.1	6.2	5.9	5.9
Providence, RI	12.1	11.0	11.0	10.4	11.4	11.0	11.7	11.5	10.8	10.4	9.8	10.5
Provo, UT	5.1	4.9	4.2	4.2	4.6	5.5	4.6	5.0	4.3	4.0	3.1	3.2
Raleigh, NC	7.2	6.6	6.3	6.0	6.6	6.9	6.7	6.2	5.5	5.4	4.8	4.5
Reno, NV	10.6	10.2	10.1	9.9	9.5	10.0	9.4	9.3	9.0	8.9	8.3	8.5
Richmond, VA	8.9	8.0	7.4	7.2	7.7	8.2	8.3	8.1	7.6	7.8	7.3	7.0
Riverside, CA	11.6	11.0	10.6	9.7	9.2	10.3	11.2	10.9	10.2	10.2	9.7	9.2
Rochester, MN	5.2	4.8	4.6	4.4	4.3	4.5	4.4	4.1	4.1	3.6	3.5	3.7
Salem, OR	10.1	9.8	9.4	8.5	8.2	8.8	8.8	8.5	7.3	7.3	7.0	7.2
Salt Lake City, UT	5.1	4.8	4.3	4.1	4.3	4.9	4.2	4.3	4.2	3.9	3.4	3.3
San Antonio, TX	6.5	6.0	5.8	5.6	6.1	6.5	6.4	5.9	6.1	5.8	5.6	5.3
San Diego, CA	8.6	8.0	7.7	7.0	6.8	7.4	7.8	7.5	7.0	7.1	6.9	6.4
San Francisco, CA	6.9	6.3	6.1	5.4	5.3	5.8	6.0	5.7	5.3	5.4	5.2	4.8
San Jose, CA	8.9	8.3	8.0	7.2	6.9	7.6	7.9	7.5	7.1	7.1	6.9	6.4
Santa Rosa, CA	8.3	7.6	7.3	6.5	6.1	6.7	7.1	6.6	6.0	6.1	6.0	5.7
Savannah, GA	9.7	9.0	8.6	8.1	9.0	10.6	10.4	9.3	8.6	8.7	8.1	8.1
Seattle, WA	5.9	5.3	4.7	4.1	4.0	4.8	4.7	5.3	5.0	5.2	4.7	4.3
Sioux Falls, SD	4.6	4.6	4.2	3.7	3.4	3.4	3.2	3.2	3.1	3.0	3.0	3.3
Spokane, WA	9.7	9.7	9.0	7.6	7.8	8.0	8.0	7.2	6.6	6.7	6.7	7.3
Springfield, MO	6.2	6.0	5.7	5.5	5.9	6.2	6.3	6.3	5.1	4.9	4.7	4.6
Tallahassee, FL	6.8	6.4	6.0	5.7	6.3	6.9	6.9	6.2	5.9	5.3	5.4	5.3
Tampa, FL	8.4	7.9	7.4	7.1	7.3	7.8	7.9	7.4	7.0	6.6	6.5	6.2
Topeka, KS	8.1	7.7	7.8	7.0	7.5	7.2	7.7	7.5	7.0	6.4	5.7	5.8
Tulsa, OK	5.5	5.2	5.0	4.4	5.3	5.6	5.0	4.9	5.2	5.5	4.9	5.1
Virginia Beach, VA	5.8	5.4	4.9	4.7	5.3	5.6	5.5	5.2	5.1	5.3	4.9	4.7
Washington, DC	9.4	8.7	8.4	7.9	8.2	8.9	8.9	8.3	8.1	9.0	7.1	6.9
Wichita, KS	7.7	7.2	7.3	6.6	7.3	7.4	7.8	7.5	7.0	6.5	5.6	5.8
Wilmington, NC	9.5	8.8	8.0	7.7	8.2	8.4	8.3	7.4	6.8	7.1	6.1	5.8
Worcester, MA	8.4	7.8	7.9	7.8	8.8	9.8	9.3	8.9	8.7	8.5	8.2	8.0
U.S.	8.5	8.1	7.6	7.1	7.3	7.8	7.7	7.3	7.0	7.0	6.6	6.5

Note: Data is not seasonally adjusted and covers workers 16 years of age and older; All figures are percentages
Source: Bureau of Labor Statistics, Local Area Unemployment Statistics

Unemployment Rate: Metro Area

Metro Area[1]	2013											
	Jan.	Feb.	Mar.	Apr.	May	Jun.	Jul.	Aug.	Sep.	Oct.	Nov.	Dec.
Abilene, TX	5.4	5.1	4.9	4.8	5.3	5.7	5.5	5.0	5.0	4.7	4.5	4.4
Albuquerque, NM	7.2	7.6	7.1	6.4	6.6	7.8	7.8	6.9	6.6	6.6	6.3	6.5
Anchorage, AK	6.3	5.8	5.5	5.3	5.1	5.7	5.3	5.0	4.8	5.0	5.1	5.2
Ann Arbor, MI	5.3	5.3	5.1	5.1	5.9	6.8	7.3	6.2	5.6	6.0	5.3	5.2
Athens, GA	6.5	6.1	5.9	5.5	6.2	7.2	6.9	6.1	5.6	5.8	5.0	5.2
Atlanta, GA	8.7	8.3	7.9	7.6	8.2	8.8	8.6	7.9	7.4	7.7	7.0	6.8
Austin, TX	5.8	5.4	5.3	5.1	5.4	5.8	5.6	5.2	5.3	5.1	4.7	4.5
Baltimore, MD	7.5	7.1	6.9	6.7	7.2	7.9	7.5	7.1	6.6	7.0	6.3	5.9
Billings, MT	4.7	4.6	4.5	3.9	3.7	4.4	3.9	3.8	3.6	3.6	3.6	3.9
Boise City, ID	7.0	6.6	6.1	5.8	5.7	6.2	6.1	6.1	5.9	5.8	5.1	5.1
Boston, MA[2]	6.0	5.4	5.3	5.2	5.7	6.5	6.2	5.8	6.0	6.0	5.5	5.5
Boulder, CO	5.5	5.7	5.4	5.1	5.1	6.1	5.4	5.1	5.0	4.9	4.7	4.4
Cape Coral, FL	7.9	7.4	6.8	6.7	7.0	7.5	7.6	7.3	7.0	6.5	6.3	5.8
Cedar Rapids, IA	6.3	5.7	5.3	4.8	4.6	4.9	4.8	4.9	4.3	4.2	4.2	4.6
Charleston, SC	7.3	6.8	6.4	5.9	6.4	7.3	6.7	6.9	6.3	6.0	5.5	5.2
Charlotte, NC	10.0	9.4	8.8	8.4	8.9	9.3	9.2	8.3	7.6	7.5	6.9	6.6
Chicago, IL[2]	10.0	9.8	9.3	9.1	9.2	10.1	9.6	9.1	8.5	8.5	8.3	8.3
Cincinnati, OH	8.0	7.5	7.2	6.5	6.8	7.3	7.1	6.8	7.1	7.0	6.8	6.2
Clarksville, TN	9.0	8.6	8.4	8.4	8.8	9.5	9.4	8.9	8.7	8.9	8.1	7.8
Colorado Spgs, CO	8.8	8.7	8.6	8.1	7.9	9.1	8.4	8.0	7.8	7.5	7.3	7.2
Columbia, MO	5.1	4.9	4.8	4.4	4.7	5.3	5.5	5.0	4.0	3.9	3.7	3.7
Columbus, OH	7.0	6.4	6.2	5.7	6.0	6.4	6.3	6.0	6.4	6.1	6.1	5.5
Dallas, TX[2]	6.7	6.4	6.2	6.0	6.3	6.7	6.4	6.0	6.1	5.9	5.7	5.5
Davenport, IA	8.3	8.2	7.2	6.2	6.3	6.7	6.9	6.5	6.7	6.7	6.4	6.8
Denver, CO	7.4	7.4	7.2	6.7	6.6	7.3	6.7	6.5	6.4	6.0	5.8	5.8
Des Moines, IA	6.0	5.5	5.0	4.4	4.3	4.7	4.5	4.7	4.2	4.0	4.0	4.4
Durham, NC	7.7	7.0	6.6	6.3	6.8	7.2	7.1	6.4	5.7	5.7	5.1	4.9
El Paso, TX	9.5	9.1	8.9	8.7	9.2	9.8	9.3	8.7	8.8	8.5	8.2	8.0
Erie, PA	9.2	8.2	7.8	7.2	7.1	7.7	7.5	7.6	6.6	6.7	7.1	6.4
Eugene, OR	9.1	8.8	8.4	7.6	7.3	8.1	8.3	8.1	6.9	6.9	6.6	6.7
Fargo, ND	4.7	4.2	4.2	3.9	3.1	3.6	3.2	3.0	2.5	2.3	2.5	3.0
Fayetteville, NC	10.8	10.0	9.6	9.3	9.9	10.4	10.6	9.8	8.9	8.9	8.2	7.8
Ft. Collins, CO	6.2	6.4	6.0	5.5	5.3	6.2	5.6	5.3	5.2	5.1	5.0	4.8
Ft. Wayne, IN	9.1	8.9	8.8	7.6	7.7	8.2	8.5	7.0	7.0	6.6	6.7	5.9
Ft. Worth, TX[2]	6.8	6.2	6.1	5.8	6.2	6.6	6.3	5.9	5.9	5.7	5.5	5.3
Gainesville, FL	6.1	5.6	5.2	4.8	5.3	6.0	6.0	5.5	5.3	4.8	4.9	4.8
Grand Rapids, MI	6.6	6.6	6.2	5.9	6.5	7.1	7.5	6.4	6.0	6.3	5.6	5.6
Green Bay, WI	7.3	7.5	7.0	6.7	6.2	6.5	6.2	5.7	5.4	5.1	5.3	5.3
Greensboro, NC	10.6	9.9	9.4	8.9	9.4	9.7	9.6	8.6	7.9	7.9	7.2	6.9
Honolulu, HI	4.8	4.5	4.4	3.9	4.0	4.7	4.2	3.8	4.1	4.2	4.2	3.8
Houston, TX	6.7	6.3	6.1	6.0	6.3	6.7	6.5	6.1	6.2	5.9	5.6	5.5
Huntsville, AL	6.6	6.8	5.9	5.2	5.5	5.9	5.6	5.8	5.6	5.6	4.8	4.9
Indianapolis, IN	8.7	8.5	8.3	7.4	7.4	7.9	7.5	6.9	6.4	6.5	6.6	5.8
Jacksonville, FL	7.5	7.1	6.5	6.4	6.6	7.0	7.0	6.8	6.4	6.1	5.9	5.6
Kansas City, MO	6.9	7.1	6.6	6.1	6.5	6.6	7.1	7.3	6.0	5.7	5.3	5.4
Lafayette, LA	5.4	4.2	4.3	4.6	5.3	6.0	5.4	5.3	4.8	4.6	4.2	3.3
Las Vegas, NV	10.2	9.8	9.8	9.5	9.3	10.1	9.7	9.6	9.4	9.4	8.6	8.9
Lexington, KY	6.8	6.8	6.8	6.0	6.5	7.3	6.6	6.2	6.4	6.6	6.3	5.8
Lincoln, NE	4.2	3.8	3.4	3.3	3.5	4.0	4.0	3.3	3.2	3.1	2.9	3.1
Little Rock, AR	7.1	7.0	6.7	6.2	6.6	6.7	6.8	6.5	6.4	6.5	6.2	6.2
Los Angeles, CA[2]	10.9	10.2	9.9	9.4	9.7	10.3	10.7	10.2	9.6	9.6	9.1	8.8
Louisville, KY	8.4	8.4	8.3	7.4	8.0	8.5	8.2	7.4	7.4	7.6	7.3	6.8
Lubbock, TX	5.5	5.1	5.3	4.8	5.3	6.1	5.8	5.0	5.0	4.7	4.5	4.3
Madison, WI	5.9	5.9	5.4	5.2	5.0	5.2	4.9	4.5	4.3	4.1	4.1	4.0
Manchester, NH	6.3	6.0	5.8	4.9	4.9	5.0	5.1	4.8	4.7	4.9	4.7	4.7

Table continued on next page.

Metro Area[1]	2013											
	Jan.	Feb.	Mar.	Apr.	May	Jun.	Jul.	Aug.	Sep.	Oct.	Nov.	Dec.
McAllen, TX	11.6	11.0	10.6	10.5	10.9	11.5	11.3	10.8	10.7	10.1	10.3	10.4
Miami, FL[2]	9.5	9.0	8.8	8.6	8.7	9.2	8.6	8.6	8.1	8.1	6.9	6.8
Midland, TX	3.4	3.2	3.1	3.0	3.4	3.7	3.5	3.2	3.3	3.1	2.9	2.8
Minneapolis, MN	6.0	5.5	5.4	5.0	4.7	5.1	5.0	4.7	4.5	4.1	4.0	4.3
Montgomery, AL	7.9	7.9	7.0	6.1	6.3	6.9	6.7	7.0	6.8	6.7	5.8	5.9
Nashville, TN	6.6	6.4	6.3	6.4	6.7	7.0	6.8	6.8	6.5	6.6	5.6	5.5
New Orleans, LA	7.2	5.9	6.0	6.2	7.0	7.9	7.2	7.2	6.7	6.3	5.7	4.7
New York, NY[2]	9.7	9.0	8.4	7.7	8.1	8.5	8.4	8.4	8.2	8.4	7.5	7.1
Oklahoma City, OK	5.2	4.9	4.7	4.1	5.0	5.5	4.8	4.7	5.0	5.4	4.7	4.8
Omaha, NE	5.0	4.6	4.3	4.0	4.1	4.6	4.6	4.2	4.0	3.8	3.6	3.9
Orlando, FL	7.7	7.2	6.7	6.4	6.6	6.9	6.9	6.6	6.3	6.0	5.9	5.5
Oxnard, CA	9.0	8.2	7.8	6.9	6.7	7.4	8.0	7.8	7.4	7.3	7.2	6.9
Peoria, IL	10.1	10.3	8.9	7.9	7.8	8.8	9.4	8.7	8.5	8.7	8.9	9.2
Philadelphia, PA[2]	9.3	8.5	8.0	7.5	7.9	8.2	8.3	8.4	7.5	7.5	7.2	6.3
Phoenix, AZ	7.2	6.7	6.7	6.6	6.2	7.2	7.0	7.4	7.1	6.7	6.0	6.2
Pittsburgh, PA	8.6	7.8	7.1	6.4	6.6	7.2	7.0	7.2	6.2	6.1	6.2	5.7
Portland, OR	8.7	8.5	8.0	7.2	7.1	7.6	7.6	7.3	6.4	6.5	6.3	6.2
Providence, RI	10.6	10.0	9.9	8.9	9.3	8.7	9.4	9.6	8.9	8.6	8.6	9.2
Provo, UT	5.5	5.3	4.5	4.3	4.6	5.3	4.6	4.9	4.3	4.0	3.4	3.5
Raleigh, NC	8.0	7.5	7.1	6.7	7.2	7.5	7.3	6.7	6.1	6.0	5.5	5.2
Reno, NV	10.5	10.1	10.0	9.7	9.3	9.8	9.3	9.1	8.8	8.8	8.2	8.4
Richmond, VA	6.6	6.1	5.6	5.4	6.0	6.3	6.2	6.0	5.7	5.8	5.3	5.2
Riverside, CA	11.5	10.9	10.5	9.6	9.3	10.3	11.0	10.5	9.8	9.8	9.4	8.9
Rochester, MN	5.5	5.1	4.9	4.6	4.3	4.5	4.4	4.1	3.9	3.5	3.4	3.8
Salem, OR	10.1	9.7	9.2	8.4	8.1	8.7	8.6	8.2	7.1	7.3	7.1	7.3
Salt Lake City, UT	5.3	5.0	4.5	4.2	4.4	5.0	4.3	4.5	4.3	4.0	3.5	3.5
San Antonio, TX	6.6	6.1	6.0	5.8	6.2	6.6	6.5	6.0	6.1	5.8	5.6	5.3
San Diego, CA	8.6	8.0	7.7	7.0	6.8	7.4	7.8	7.5	7.0	7.1	6.9	6.4
San Francisco, CA[2]	6.5	6.0	5.8	5.2	5.0	5.6	5.8	5.5	5.1	5.2	5.0	4.6
San Jose, CA	8.2	7.6	7.4	6.6	6.3	6.9	7.2	6.8	6.4	6.4	6.3	5.8
Santa Rosa, CA	8.3	7.6	7.3	6.5	6.1	6.7	7.1	6.6	6.1	6.1	6.0	5.7
Savannah, GA	8.3	7.7	7.4	7.1	7.9	8.8	8.6	7.8	7.3	7.5	6.7	6.7
Seattle, WA[2]	6.1	5.7	5.3	4.8	5.0	5.7	5.6	5.5	5.4	5.5	5.2	4.9
Sioux Falls, SD	4.4	4.4	4.0	3.5	3.3	3.3	3.0	3.0	2.9	2.9	2.9	3.1
Spokane, WA	9.7	9.8	9.0	7.5	7.6	7.9	7.9	7.1	6.6	6.7	6.8	7.3
Springfield, MO	6.2	6.1	5.8	5.4	5.7	6.1	6.2	6.1	5.0	4.7	4.6	4.6
Tallahassee, FL	6.8	6.4	5.9	5.6	6.1	6.7	6.7	6.2	5.8	5.3	5.4	5.3
Tampa, FL	8.0	7.5	6.9	6.7	6.9	7.3	7.3	7.0	6.7	6.4	6.3	5.9
Topeka, KS	7.1	6.7	6.7	6.0	6.5	6.3	6.7	6.4	5.9	5.5	4.8	5.0
Tulsa, OK	5.9	5.7	5.3	4.7	5.6	5.9	5.3	5.2	5.5	5.8	5.3	5.4
Virginia Beach, VA	6.8	6.2	5.7	5.4	6.0	6.3	6.2	5.9	5.7	6.0	5.5	5.3
Washington, DC[2]	5.8	5.5	5.2	5.0	5.5	6.0	5.8	5.5	5.4	5.9	4.9	4.7
Wichita, KS	7.0	6.6	6.7	6.0	6.7	6.6	7.1	6.8	6.3	5.8	5.1	5.2
Wilmington, NC	11.1	10.3	9.2	8.7	9.1	9.4	9.1	8.3	7.7	7.7	7.2	7.1
Worcester, MA	7.9	7.3	7.3	7.0	7.4	8.2	8.0	7.6	7.5	7.5	7.1	7.2
U.S.	8.5	8.1	7.6	7.1	7.3	7.8	7.7	7.3	7.0	7.0	6.6	6.5

Note: Data is not seasonally adjusted and covers workers 16 years of age and older; All figures are percentages; (1) Figures cover the Metropolitan Statistical Area (MSA) except where noted. See Appendix B for areas included; (2) Metropolitan Division; (3) New England City and Town Area; (4) New England City and Town Area Division
Source: Bureau of Labor Statistics, Local Area Unemployment Statistics

Average Hourly Wages: Occupations A – C

Metro Area	Accountants/ Auditors	Automotive Mechanics	Book-keepers	Carpenters	Cashiers	Clerks, Gen. Office	Clerks, Recep./Info.
Abilene, TX	27.43	16.42	14.82	12.98	9.17	13.24	10.53
Albuquerque, NM	30.19	18.65	17.01	18.15	10.12	12.20	12.24
Anchorage, AK	36.17	23.37	20.46	31.31	11.75	19.03	15.50
Ann Arbor, MI	29.53	17.46	17.39	24.50	10.26	14.17	13.07
Athens, GA	26.22	19.62	15.14	13.35	9.24	11.17	12.30
Atlanta, GA	36.56	19.69	18.07	21.86	9.32	13.52	13.47
Austin, TX	32.18	19.17	18.54	17.33	10.12	15.40	12.42
Baltimore, MD	36.00	20.24	20.50	20.24	10.05	15.04	13.46
Billings, MT	33.26	19.76	16.60	19.04	9.90	14.02	12.41
Boise City, ID	31.72	18.99	16.60	16.39	9.96	13.64	12.66
Boston, MA	38.28	21.67	21.66	28.99	10.63	17.12	15.11
Boulder, CO	35.08	18.51	18.63	18.27	10.90	17.84	14.04
Cape Coral, FL	32.91	18.63	16.17	19.17	9.72	13.10	12.80
Cedar Rapids, IA	28.85	17.67	16.95	20.72	8.92	15.50	11.69
Charleston, SC	28.92	20.06	16.48	17.86	9.45	12.58	13.41
Charlotte, NC	35.75	20.32	17.69	17.12	9.50	13.74	13.53
Chicago, IL	35.80	20.80	19.31	28.75	10.46	15.22	14.01
Cincinnati, OH	32.92	16.95	17.65	20.92	9.78	14.81	12.84
Clarksville, TN	28.37	17.07	15.56	18.13	9.05	13.06	11.27
Colorado Spgs, CO	30.13	20.15	16.87	20.22	10.09	14.90	13.08
Columbia, MO	30.34	16.56	18.60	22.31	9.30	13.82	12.84
Columbus, OH	32.32	18.75	20.46	21.36	9.64	14.62	12.91
Dallas, TX	37.07	19.69	18.75	14.51	9.45	15.35	12.97
Davenport, IA	29.86	18.61	15.87	21.53	9.41	13.70	12.43
Denver, CO	35.95	20.23	18.55	19.23	10.44	17.13	14.91
Des Moines, IA	32.54	19.67	17.45	20.38	9.23	15.42	13.64
Durham, NC	35.16	18.90	18.59	18.11	9.33	13.79	13.22
El Paso, TX	28.26	15.93	15.14	13.85	8.90	11.88	10.48
Erie, PA	28.43	15.68	15.06	18.21	8.83	12.89	11.20
Eugene, OR	30.59	17.92	17.64	21.59	10.76	14.63	12.61
Fargo, ND	27.37	19.40	17.12	19.68	9.17	12.50	12.79
Fayetteville, NC	31.00	17.52	15.79	16.06	8.99	12.92	10.88
Ft. Collins, CO	30.42	20.91	16.78	17.36	9.85	15.20	13.23
Ft. Wayne, IN	30.11	17.98	16.19	18.43	8.84	12.35	12.48
Ft. Worth, TX	34.18	19.54	17.62	14.67	10.01	14.85	12.80
Gainesville, FL	27.91	18.50	16.42	17.40	8.96	12.60	11.14
Grand Rapids, MI	34.32	18.09	17.06	19.73	9.35	14.17	13.72
Green Bay, WI	30.58	18.53	16.65	21.53	8.98	14.33	13.62
Greensboro, NC	32.99	20.17	16.88	14.58	8.85	13.23	12.77
Honolulu, HI	29.88	22.71	17.92	33.80	10.80	15.06	13.96
Houston, TX	38.74	19.17	18.62	16.62	9.40	15.80	12.86
Huntsville, AL	32.82	18.14	17.17	16.52	8.84	11.15	11.72
Indianapolis, IN	33.44	22.45	17.96	20.95	9.28	13.29	13.16
Jacksonville, FL	34.05	18.24	16.66	14.81	9.16	13.20	13.25
Kansas City, MO	31.24	19.09	18.28	25.07	9.53	15.10	13.44
Lafayette, LA	31.37	19.07	16.45	17.49	8.98	11.42	11.29
Las Vegas, NV	30.08	20.31	17.75	24.10	10.67	15.05	13.05
Lexington, KY	33.61	17.21	16.87	17.87	9.08	14.05	12.73
Lincoln, NE	29.13	19.63	15.79	16.05	9.12	10.78	12.82
Little Rock, AR	30.95	17.97	16.09	17.27	8.95	12.05	11.66
Los Angeles, CA	37.55	17.81	19.63	25.42	10.79	15.07	13.97
Louisville, KY	30.07	17.02	16.92	18.09	9.39	14.04	12.93
Lubbock, TX	29.12	14.24	14.57	15.94	8.83	13.01	10.76
Madison, WI	33.33	18.35	18.38	24.10	9.61	15.44	13.35
Manchester, NH	34.23	20.10	19.97	22.32	9.31	16.38	13.43

Table continued on next page.

Metro Area	Accountants/ Auditors	Automotive Mechanics	Book-keepers	Carpenters	Cashiers	Clerks, Gen. Office	Clerks, Recep./Info.
McAllen, TX	26.81	16.00	13.56	13.93	8.78	11.14	9.94
Miami, FL	33.25	16.83	16.90	17.61	9.40	13.15	12.06
Midland, TX	34.93	20.63	18.08	16.48	9.68	16.26	13.36
Minneapolis, MN	32.84	19.00	19.10	25.54	10.12	15.43	14.23
Montgomery, AL	29.11	19.72	16.48	15.44	8.81	11.66	11.50
Nashville, TN	32.17	16.82	17.50	17.16	9.55	15.14	13.64
New Orleans, LA	32.37	18.87	17.21	18.99	9.15	12.00	11.82
New York, NY	44.94	20.68	20.95	31.17	10.15	14.82	14.70
Oklahoma City, OK	31.09	18.76	15.97	17.26	9.10	13.43	13.13
Omaha, NE	32.68	19.42	16.45	17.79	9.47	12.68	12.47
Orlando, FL	31.58	16.84	16.23	16.93	9.20	13.53	12.58
Oxnard, CA	35.77	20.57	21.02	23.41	11.68	15.50	14.00
Peoria, IL	35.52	18.17	16.67	24.90	9.92	13.40	12.01
Philadelphia, PA	37.58	19.91	19.61	25.03	10.24	16.19	13.60
Phoenix, AZ	31.32	20.60	17.55	19.17	10.39	16.07	13.44
Pittsburgh, PA	32.64	17.37	16.84	21.51	9.06	14.42	12.31
Portland, OR	31.75	21.10	18.80	20.95	11.73	15.79	13.96
Providence, RI	36.01	18.48	18.82	22.21	10.02	15.77	13.92
Provo, UT	31.69	16.22	16.64	17.39	9.40	12.88	11.93
Raleigh, NC	31.96	21.92	17.94	16.13	9.22	14.19	13.40
Reno, NV	29.02	20.32	18.21	22.23	10.64	16.17	13.46
Richmond, VA	33.61	19.92	17.74	18.44	9.61	14.44	13.22
Riverside, CA	32.45	18.79	18.50	27.31	10.63	14.04	13.07
Rochester, MN	28.78	17.72	18.69	21.97	9.18	13.57	12.60
Salem, OR	30.00	21.24	18.27	19.55	10.96	15.60	13.45
Salt Lake City, UT	34.38	18.42	17.07	17.16	9.72	13.39	12.55
San Antonio, TX	33.35	18.10	17.72	16.84	9.44	14.41	11.73
San Diego, CA	37.37	20.54	19.64	22.65	11.10	14.91	13.74
San Francisco, CA	41.51	26.04	23.77	30.01	12.81	18.99	17.83
San Jose, CA	41.89	24.36	23.39	29.47	12.29	18.73	16.42
Santa Rosa, CA	33.81	21.73	21.06	30.54	12.87	17.20	16.73
Savannah, GA	33.25	20.02	16.14	19.48	9.74	12.40	12.80
Seattle, WA	37.17	22.23	20.39	25.57	13.50	15.80	15.53
Sioux Falls, SD	29.73	19.18	14.71	16.05	9.27	11.41	11.92
Spokane, WA	28.98	20.54	17.42	22.57	11.96	14.21	13.64
Springfield, MO	27.75	15.40	14.45	20.46	9.23	12.72	11.24
Tallahassee, FL	26.01	15.45	15.91	16.16	9.16	11.39	12.28
Tampa, FL	31.71	17.66	15.77	16.90	9.29	13.20	12.99
Topeka, KS	27.11	17.70	15.82	18.91	8.92	13.79	11.64
Tulsa, OK	30.46	17.97	16.51	15.09	8.97	13.00	12.26
Virginia Beach, VA	33.02	20.84	16.69	18.84	9.04	13.39	12.61
Washington, DC	40.82	22.96	21.52	22.03	10.52	17.50	14.93
Wichita, KS	31.45	18.57	16.36	16.62	9.26	13.51	12.50
Wilmington, NC	32.27	20.30	16.48	16.21	9.01	12.75	12.07
Worcester, MA	35.61	20.23	19.02	22.84	10.60	14.94	14.29

Notes: Wage data is for May 2013 and covers the Metropolitan Statistical Area—see Appendix B for areas included; n/a not available
Source: Bureau of Labor Statistics, May 2013 Metro Area Occupational Employment and Wage Estimates

Average Hourly Wages: Occupations C – E

Metro Area	Clerks, Ship./Rec.	Computer Programmers	Computer Systems Analysts	Comp. User Support Specialists	Cooks, Restaurant	Dentists	Electrical Engineers
Abilene, TX	13.69	27.23	32.18	17.64	9.42	103.87	37.88
Albuquerque, NM	13.54	47.92	36.61	21.63	10.71	80.23	49.12
Anchorage, AK	17.87	36.95	36.76	25.36	14.45	104.89	52.25
Ann Arbor, MI	16.95	31.55	35.52	19.32	11.43	77.01	44.17
Athens, GA	13.86	26.99	30.82	17.19	9.71	n/a	33.72
Atlanta, GA	14.19	45.14	36.84	24.72	10.64	91.04	41.62
Austin, TX	13.46	41.66	39.12	23.74	11.05	99.44	47.89
Baltimore, MD	15.88	40.57	42.83	25.20	12.96	88.28	47.30
Billings, MT	13.89	27.07	35.36	20.87	10.53	79.34	35.78
Boise City, ID	13.83	37.50	37.21	19.70	9.63	84.71	44.82
Boston, MA	17.35	40.17	41.42	30.58	13.94	83.35	49.66
Boulder, CO	15.11	54.80	42.01	25.96	11.08	82.37	42.59
Cape Coral, FL	12.50	44.91	45.79	19.67	11.37	47.08	32.63
Cedar Rapids, IA	16.01	31.33	35.96	21.13	9.87	103.77	39.12
Charleston, SC	15.68	32.89	31.81	22.77	10.15	88.16	38.32
Charlotte, NC	14.93	39.57	42.61	24.91	10.66	75.21	42.52
Chicago, IL	15.03	36.41	38.63	25.25	10.92	62.86	43.03
Cincinnati, OH	14.76	34.51	40.85	23.82	10.04	84.46	38.69
Clarksville, TN	15.98	27.53	32.31	18.56	9.56	n/a	35.58
Colorado Spgs, CO	14.64	36.76	45.24	24.10	10.88	94.04	47.09
Columbia, MO	12.88	30.13	37.64	18.56	9.82	73.83	31.64
Columbus, OH	13.64	34.99	38.04	24.30	11.15	91.49	35.80
Dallas, TX	14.76	38.38	41.14	23.30	11.30	103.85	46.81
Davenport, IA	15.24	33.99	39.27	17.76	10.19	n/a	40.13
Denver, CO	15.54	43.75	45.80	26.49	11.49	69.78	42.32
Des Moines, IA	16.41	32.66	37.50	21.53	9.86	87.24	32.11
Durham, NC	14.73	37.11	40.26	27.13	10.37	65.26	40.44
El Paso, TX	12.21	33.64	34.01	21.32	9.33	104.40	45.11
Erie, PA	13.62	36.17	30.92	18.99	10.73	75.00	37.20
Eugene, OR	13.89	28.98	35.12	22.23	10.96	102.79	34.76
Fargo, ND	15.13	24.40	n/a	22.81	10.55	95.87	37.58
Fayetteville, NC	14.96	29.95	34.22	22.55	10.15	96.55	51.65
Ft. Collins, CO	13.21	38.45	43.42	26.39	11.20	70.26	42.77
Ft. Wayne, IN	13.01	29.98	31.36	19.47	9.40	90.74	37.60
Ft. Worth, TX	14.27	39.47	38.95	24.54	10.68	77.20	44.46
Gainesville, FL	14.29	27.73	37.77	19.94	10.26	75.62	36.41
Grand Rapids, MI	15.06	31.17	37.87	22.12	10.84	95.40	39.30
Green Bay, WI	15.06	30.62	32.19	21.37	9.93	92.83	31.83
Greensboro, NC	14.49	36.40	39.01	22.68	10.21	103.71	45.86
Honolulu, HI	15.40	31.10	37.24	24.72	12.49	81.39	40.45
Houston, TX	14.39	39.02	49.83	27.90	10.16	80.85	49.20
Huntsville, AL	15.17	43.90	43.34	21.85	9.95	88.17	48.64
Indianapolis, IN	14.40	31.15	35.31	21.97	11.15	64.38	39.77
Jacksonville, FL	14.27	33.68	37.38	20.85	11.17	75.89	41.44
Kansas City, MO	14.84	34.26	38.11	24.42	10.53	69.78	39.61
Lafayette, LA	14.48	23.56	29.34	22.37	10.05	75.83	n/a
Las Vegas, NV	14.84	35.55	41.40	22.75	13.64	52.27	39.56
Lexington, KY	14.70	30.61	36.66	16.81	10.30	101.69	41.91
Lincoln, NE	14.12	30.60	33.56	20.21	10.52	83.33	38.58
Little Rock, AR	14.06	30.79	32.63	21.07	9.90	93.18	42.51
Los Angeles, CA	14.10	44.05	44.23	26.28	11.18	62.76	53.18
Louisville, KY	14.50	30.71	36.69	21.44	9.81	70.32	39.73
Lubbock, TX	13.38	28.78	32.41	18.01	9.23	64.36	36.33
Madison, WI	14.62	36.41	33.43	22.70	11.37	94.32	37.20
Manchester, NH	15.01	29.13	35.94	23.82	12.00	99.35	41.16

Table continued on next page.

Metro Area	Clerks, Ship./Rec.	Computer Programmers	Computer Systems Analysts	Comp. User Support Specialists	Cooks, Restaurant	Dentists	Electrical Engineers
McAllen, TX	11.27	28.68	29.92	18.42	9.23	96.37	n/a
Miami, FL	13.24	45.85	48.29	22.69	11.73	83.10	45.51
Midland, TX	n/a	35.91	31.03	23.54	11.41	n/a	44.31
Minneapolis, MN	16.20	38.60	39.98	25.36	11.52	91.74	43.80
Montgomery, AL	14.13	37.10	32.06	22.00	9.21	83.38	50.27
Nashville, TN	14.89	38.24	33.90	21.17	10.74	96.86	38.25
New Orleans, LA	15.83	34.95	31.13	22.56	11.37	92.33	49.53
New York, NY	15.85	43.75	47.55	28.67	13.46	69.88	46.38
Oklahoma City, OK	14.49	32.23	34.02	20.60	10.12	57.11	38.18
Omaha, NE	15.05	38.16	36.31	23.39	11.37	90.09	38.09
Orlando, FL	12.90	36.73	43.11	20.29	11.56	89.42	35.43
Oxnard, CA	15.40	43.41	47.37	26.96	11.39	67.98	45.60
Peoria, IL	14.51	31.01	46.10	22.48	10.20	56.10	43.45
Philadelphia, PA	16.57	38.63	44.47	24.11	13.74	85.38	46.41
Phoenix, AZ	14.79	38.36	40.32	23.83	13.64	73.29	47.03
Pittsburgh, PA	15.46	30.77	33.58	22.75	11.71	72.66	41.29
Portland, OR	15.66	35.47	42.35	22.71	11.19	80.83	41.94
Providence, RI	15.08	38.04	38.00	22.97	11.89	n/a	45.34
Provo, UT	12.87	34.15	35.91	21.12	10.55	55.57	38.94
Raleigh, NC	14.05	38.60	40.47	24.88	10.69	92.29	41.46
Reno, NV	15.08	38.61	31.73	20.76	11.56	101.97	41.21
Richmond, VA	15.43	38.28	38.59	24.88	10.79	78.56	40.88
Riverside, CA	14.65	37.70	37.14	24.30	11.10	68.42	46.03
Rochester, MN	14.64	45.51	30.54	23.06	11.93	118.24	41.11
Salem, OR	14.03	36.34	36.82	23.44	11.26	100.20	46.72
Salt Lake City, UT	14.15	38.31	35.07	23.17	12.23	59.22	45.53
San Antonio, TX	13.09	39.12	36.21	20.90	9.96	89.68	41.41
San Diego, CA	16.27	39.34	42.87	24.83	12.10	78.93	49.74
San Francisco, CA	17.20	47.86	49.87	33.43	13.91	79.51	51.79
San Jose, CA	16.72	45.14	50.02	33.75	12.35	70.50	58.37
Santa Rosa, CA	16.13	41.37	39.95	28.35	12.21	89.18	49.08
Savannah, GA	17.46	35.54	36.03	24.38	9.81	107.80	43.91
Seattle, WA	17.86	55.54	48.03	29.07	12.88	94.76	48.66
Sioux Falls, SD	13.65	26.68	31.34	17.35	11.06	87.04	37.79
Spokane, WA	14.45	28.12	36.41	21.15	11.57	118.72	38.21
Springfield, MO	14.37	28.95	28.21	19.79	9.32	79.34	44.48
Tallahassee, FL	13.00	28.72	40.01	18.19	10.65	101.64	42.41
Tampa, FL	13.32	35.91	40.50	22.02	11.10	70.66	42.83
Topeka, KS	18.87	32.30	33.78	20.01	9.14	74.33	38.72
Tulsa, OK	15.09	30.98	34.64	22.38	10.48	78.06	36.72
Virginia Beach, VA	15.44	32.13	39.10	22.42	12.75	73.45	38.98
Washington, DC	16.29	39.90	51.34	29.12	12.80	73.33	52.63
Wichita, KS	14.81	35.15	37.73	17.54	10.18	85.45	43.84
Wilmington, NC	13.42	39.39	37.39	22.14	11.53	87.19	52.57
Worcester, MA	16.08	38.85	41.52	23.76	12.05	88.51	59.16

Notes: Wage data is for May 2013 and covers the Metropolitan Statistical Area—see Appendix B for areas included; n/a not available
Source: Bureau of Labor Statistics, May 2013 Metro Area Occupational Employment and Wage Estimates

Average Hourly Wages: Occupations E – I

Metro Area	Electricians	Financial Managers	First-Line Supervisors/ Mgrs., Sales	Food Preparation Workers	General/ Operations Managers	Hairdressers/ Cosmetolo- gists	Internists
Abilene, TX	18.68	56.69	22.73	9.26	43.14	11.06	n/a
Albuquerque, NM	21.11	50.83	18.13	10.29	47.76	12.28	n/a
Anchorage, AK	35.47	57.95	20.16	12.03	52.42	12.91	94.74
Ann Arbor, MI	33.61	50.43	21.34	11.17	53.18	12.36	n/a
Athens, GA	18.25	48.93	17.60	9.44	43.42	14.05	n/a
Atlanta, GA	22.84	61.89	20.29	10.03	57.36	12.42	112.68
Austin, TX	22.17	65.02	20.04	10.21	57.84	12.37	119.07
Baltimore, MD	26.52	59.94	21.63	11.09	62.50	13.92	101.04
Billings, MT	28.66	55.10	19.36	9.38	45.84	14.66	n/a
Boise City, ID	21.01	46.12	17.49	10.01	40.44	10.09	n/a
Boston, MA	32.11	64.39	22.24	11.68	67.32	15.96	98.46
Boulder, CO	23.32	64.93	20.56	10.22	63.79	15.06	n/a
Cape Coral, FL	16.91	49.70	20.90	10.08	52.27	15.40	102.76
Cedar Rapids, IA	26.44	57.15	19.93	9.74	48.16	11.86	n/a
Charleston, SC	18.98	50.16	19.38	10.20	50.21	11.03	73.51
Charlotte, NC	18.07	67.43	21.23	9.65	63.70	13.62	116.54
Chicago, IL	34.76	63.80	19.83	9.70	52.40	13.91	78.25
Cincinnati, OH	23.81	54.26	18.37	10.45	54.22	12.62	71.31
Clarksville, TN	20.80	29.29	17.04	9.33	36.00	11.81	n/a
Colorado Spgs, CO	22.70	67.65	20.01	10.13	52.86	12.83	n/a
Columbia, MO	25.25	49.57	17.27	9.05	35.78	14.23	n/a
Columbus, OH	22.13	60.47	18.15	10.62	53.60	12.27	87.91
Dallas, TX	20.44	65.14	21.17	9.81	63.07	13.42	94.24
Davenport, IA	28.86	44.57	17.44	9.57	41.80	10.89	n/a
Denver, CO	23.62	69.42	19.79	11.22	63.61	14.12	107.52
Des Moines, IA	24.93	56.76	19.36	9.20	49.48	15.72	100.89
Durham, NC	19.44	61.38	19.43	11.11	64.84	16.36	n/a
El Paso, TX	18.79	48.22	20.29	8.84	47.02	9.84	n/a
Erie, PA	24.09	48.31	18.73	10.73	50.50	11.14	n/a
Eugene, OR	25.78	46.63	18.21	10.19	41.27	13.45	n/a
Fargo, ND	21.93	47.63	18.87	11.81	49.40	12.70	n/a
Fayetteville, NC	20.60	55.58	17.83	10.22	58.29	11.66	n/a
Ft. Collins, CO	22.88	61.98	19.28	11.16	47.99	12.34	n/a
Ft. Wayne, IN	25.72	46.93	19.15	9.80	53.56	11.29	n/a
Ft. Worth, TX	19.21	57.15	21.00	9.59	55.07	12.29	104.23
Gainesville, FL	19.03	61.28	18.58	10.19	50.33	12.75	101.18
Grand Rapids, MI	23.20	46.55	19.01	10.06	52.41	12.20	43.94
Green Bay, WI	24.35	49.56	18.39	10.27	48.10	11.71	n/a
Greensboro, NC	18.65	59.93	20.13	9.69	59.17	12.52	109.09
Honolulu, HI	32.59	45.95	23.31	11.19	48.16	17.49	113.81
Houston, TX	22.65	68.99	21.30	9.38	63.07	14.85	84.76
Huntsville, AL	22.76	57.94	19.98	8.46	65.79	13.19	n/a
Indianapolis, IN	27.18	54.25	19.32	9.40	56.65	13.18	111.80
Jacksonville, FL	19.69	60.52	19.05	9.83	55.77	13.48	100.97
Kansas City, MO	26.99	55.22	18.97	9.93	50.32	10.98	99.62
Lafayette, LA	21.20	44.84	17.49	8.84	56.92	11.98	n/a
Las Vegas, NV	27.14	53.11	20.76	14.18	51.02	10.48	80.44
Lexington, KY	20.66	48.10	17.37	10.18	45.17	13.08	78.65
Lincoln, NE	22.04	58.13	18.37	9.30	50.94	10.89	n/a
Little Rock, AR	21.55	52.25	16.61	8.88	43.41	13.57	82.59
Los Angeles, CA	30.15	70.50	20.81	9.78	61.50	13.44	88.31
Louisville, KY	24.00	48.03	18.48	10.02	46.33	13.37	89.70
Lubbock, TX	19.77	43.63	20.57	9.10	47.36	10.62	n/a
Madison, WI	27.53	55.09	18.93	9.80	52.70	13.76	120.68
Manchester, NH	25.00	55.30	21.01	13.44	56.50	13.23	n/a

Table continued on next page.

Metro Area	Electricians	Financial Managers	First-Line Supervisors/ Mgrs., Sales	Food Preparation Workers	General/ Operations Managers	Hairdressers/ Cosmetologists	Internists
McAllen, TX	15.29	45.55	18.37	8.74	39.42	12.01	n/a
Miami, FL	19.99	70.12	20.88	10.36	61.15	12.33	98.51
Midland, TX	21.13	65.76	22.28	10.27	58.38	13.68	n/a
Minneapolis, MN	28.89	60.96	19.57	11.41	54.40	13.76	95.42
Montgomery, AL	19.77	52.29	17.77	9.45	55.87	14.09	n/a
Nashville, TN	20.69	56.15	19.81	9.49	50.70	13.99	83.91
New Orleans, LA	23.96	45.67	19.27	8.63	52.05	12.66	106.75
New York, NY	37.44	87.96	23.97	11.96	77.74	15.36	80.33
Oklahoma City, OK	20.82	49.30	18.69	9.02	48.80	10.80	77.20
Omaha, NE	22.41	60.10	20.28	8.92	53.69	13.49	98.70
Orlando, FL	19.06	62.20	19.56	10.38	54.68	11.54	75.20
Oxnard, CA	28.21	57.60	23.20	10.59	58.41	13.05	96.37
Peoria, IL	30.48	56.22	17.98	9.69	48.60	9.84	102.78
Philadelphia, PA	30.89	72.36	25.25	11.01	67.69	13.27	101.37
Phoenix, AZ	20.96	54.93	19.12	10.08	52.02	11.97	107.00
Pittsburgh, PA	24.73	60.75	21.60	9.91	57.93	11.63	105.49
Portland, OR	34.72	53.72	19.15	10.58	51.33	14.63	106.69
Providence, RI	26.50	62.42	21.71	11.22	65.06	13.37	79.79
Provo, UT	22.62	55.80	17.68	9.02	40.52	12.61	n/a
Raleigh, NC	18.70	61.21	20.55	10.38	64.35	15.50	120.51
Reno, NV	26.36	47.58	19.88	9.80	51.67	10.72	n/a
Richmond, VA	21.48	61.79	20.33	10.36	58.75	17.09	98.97
Riverside, CA	28.74	53.90	21.11	9.84	52.10	10.26	88.55
Rochester, MN	28.95	51.80	17.51	11.98	41.65	13.47	n/a
Salem, OR	26.97	47.20	18.42	10.34	42.44	13.24	105.60
Salt Lake City, UT	23.13	55.44	20.40	9.67	46.16	14.99	69.36
San Antonio, TX	20.30	59.79	22.31	9.66	52.56	13.02	n/a
San Diego, CA	30.01	62.91	23.00	10.04	58.63	15.76	94.95
San Francisco, CA	40.01	80.75	22.84	11.42	71.88	18.86	73.44
San Jose, CA	30.81	77.44	23.11	10.98	71.60	11.43	88.19
Santa Rosa, CA	33.56	56.45	21.60	10.39	53.03	11.40	118.57
Savannah, GA	21.99	53.44	16.91	9.75	45.85	11.05	n/a
Seattle, WA	33.06	60.02	22.52	12.05	63.97	18.84	97.49
Sioux Falls, SD	20.71	61.26	20.74	9.36	59.52	13.91	n/a
Spokane, WA	23.89	49.78	20.28	10.19	46.58	12.64	78.06
Springfield, MO	21.43	52.66	18.14	8.73	37.73	11.79	n/a
Tallahassee, FL	17.49	53.63	19.46	9.33	52.68	12.38	n/a
Tampa, FL	17.90	57.97	20.55	9.91	58.67	12.21	104.44
Topeka, KS	22.07	48.80	17.77	8.73	42.34	13.85	n/a
Tulsa, OK	22.07	52.38	17.13	9.66	48.38	12.24	84.59
Virginia Beach, VA	21.45	57.11	19.19	9.99	55.74	15.88	89.75
Washington, DC	26.69	69.14	22.09	10.87	68.59	17.40	103.67
Wichita, KS	23.87	45.98	18.79	8.79	50.05	11.93	n/a
Wilmington, NC	18.64	52.06	21.03	10.41	59.01	10.83	n/a
Worcester, MA	32.10	56.15	21.73	10.81	60.60	16.18	n/a

Notes: Wage data is for May 2013 and covers the Metropolitan Statistical Area—see Appendix B for areas included; n/a not available
Source: Bureau of Labor Statistics, May 2013 Metro Area Occupational Employment and Wage Estimates

Average Hourly Wages: Occupations J – N

Metro Area	Janitors/ Cleaners	Landscapers	Lawyers	Maids/ House- keepers	Main- tenance Repairers	Marketing Managers	Nuclear Medicine Technologists
Abilene, TX	9.79	10.35	50.25	8.54	13.87	n/a	n/a
Albuquerque, NM	10.75	11.45	43.99	9.10	17.08	40.40	35.11
Anchorage, AK	13.87	14.07	59.01	10.81	21.64	40.58	n/a
Ann Arbor, MI	12.94	13.36	55.32	10.29	18.10	53.22	32.69
Athens, GA	10.93	10.04	58.06	9.62	16.79	53.90	n/a
Atlanta, GA	11.69	12.60	69.70	9.14	18.34	64.06	34.66
Austin, TX	10.43	12.05	59.97	9.40	17.03	67.44	32.88
Baltimore, MD	11.93	13.56	58.38	10.50	19.11	56.97	38.66
Billings, MT	12.08	12.57	33.40	9.80	15.25	n/a	n/a
Boise City, ID	10.53	12.28	54.04	9.83	15.21	48.83	n/a
Boston, MA	15.25	16.90	67.33	13.66	22.26	67.72	37.12
Boulder, CO	13.23	13.24	63.60	10.02	19.31	69.69	n/a
Cape Coral, FL	11.52	11.41	40.19	10.00	15.96	51.96	36.35
Cedar Rapids, IA	12.63	13.08	46.71	9.96	19.80	53.67	n/a
Charleston, SC	10.54	10.92	48.58	9.35	17.87	53.11	32.35
Charlotte, NC	10.35	10.88	55.60	8.93	18.46	63.83	32.42
Chicago, IL	13.12	12.72	65.83	11.62	20.04	55.55	35.48
Cincinnati, OH	11.35	12.28	54.21	10.52	19.13	57.28	30.29
Clarksville, TN	11.03	11.47	40.52	8.59	16.48	42.15	n/a
Colorado Spgs, CO	13.13	11.67	51.72	9.38	17.31	62.23	n/a
Columbia, MO	12.40	10.68	47.69	9.13	15.74	47.96	n/a
Columbus, OH	11.87	11.91	55.29	9.76	18.14	63.14	31.93
Dallas, TX	10.00	11.31	65.75	9.06	17.50	66.23	33.14
Davenport, IA	11.91	12.11	43.51	9.64	17.03	41.86	n/a
Denver, CO	11.56	13.81	69.19	10.17	18.95	66.34	39.26
Des Moines, IA	11.57	14.89	65.93	10.06	17.28	65.18	32.00
Durham, NC	11.12	13.26	53.74	10.28	20.22	70.91	n/a
El Paso, TX	9.82	9.83	64.13	8.80	12.72	55.22	n/a
Erie, PA	10.54	11.09	56.25	8.84	15.58	56.19	n/a
Eugene, OR	12.52	14.05	45.90	9.99	18.10	36.20	n/a
Fargo, ND	12.26	12.40	52.72	9.71	16.61	47.97	n/a
Fayetteville, NC	10.01	10.33	53.27	8.58	17.19	n/a	28.73
Ft. Collins, CO	11.69	12.64	57.33	9.81	17.22	63.23	n/a
Ft. Wayne, IN	11.19	12.11	60.17	8.75	18.83	45.97	28.70
Ft. Worth, TX	10.62	11.14	54.57	9.18	16.15	53.94	35.60
Gainesville, FL	10.22	11.02	51.94	9.44	16.67	53.76	n/a
Grand Rapids, MI	11.34	12.19	51.01	9.81	18.14	50.88	31.32
Green Bay, WI	11.76	13.86	54.59	9.27	18.63	51.30	n/a
Greensboro, NC	9.70	11.98	56.20	9.06	18.38	62.14	31.19
Honolulu, HI	12.14	13.83	52.23	15.55	20.38	45.86	40.27
Houston, TX	9.66	11.34	76.17	8.98	17.78	70.33	33.26
Huntsville, AL	9.75	10.62	59.69	9.14	19.52	56.43	25.22
Indianapolis, IN	11.70	11.45	49.17	9.14	17.86	52.08	33.00
Jacksonville, FL	11.28	11.69	55.10	9.35	17.27	59.89	34.31
Kansas City, MO	12.04	12.68	60.63	9.63	18.27	53.69	31.60
Lafayette, LA	9.85	10.53	52.48	8.58	17.89	39.76	n/a
Las Vegas, NV	13.88	13.00	59.54	15.10	22.67	55.75	40.01
Lexington, KY	11.35	11.35	47.19	9.22	16.36	49.27	28.83
Lincoln, NE	10.89	11.84	51.53	9.20	18.60	47.20	31.66
Little Rock, AR	10.15	11.41	45.53	8.67	15.30	46.84	32.36
Los Angeles, CA	12.89	13.58	79.15	11.46	20.16	65.55	45.43
Louisville, KY	11.18	12.56	46.86	9.34	18.32	54.14	29.28
Lubbock, TX	10.31	10.92	53.47	8.45	14.17	56.59	n/a
Madison, WI	12.32	14.36	46.97	9.65	18.85	51.85	n/a
Manchester, NH	11.87	17.02	61.67	10.32	20.45	50.26	n/a

Table continued on next page.

Metro Area	Janitors/ Cleaners	Landscapers	Lawyers	Maids/ House- keepers	Main- tenance Repairers	Marketing Managers	Nuclear Medicine Technologists
McAllen, TX	10.13	9.71	61.72	8.40	11.30	n/a	n/a
Miami, FL	10.23	11.48	72.84	9.54	15.19	59.68	35.08
Midland, TX	10.86	13.04	61.47	9.36	18.71	50.77	n/a
Minneapolis, MN	12.43	14.03	63.74	11.09	20.88	61.66	35.28
Montgomery, AL	9.88	10.90	46.64	8.80	17.80	54.81	n/a
Nashville, TN	10.51	11.95	52.06	9.28	17.70	48.43	29.04
New Orleans, LA	10.96	10.52	60.17	9.58	16.78	55.25	33.10
New York, NY	15.78	15.65	79.66	17.16	20.80	85.29	39.70
Oklahoma City, OK	10.13	11.82	47.01	9.21	16.24	45.66	33.57
Omaha, NE	11.13	12.19	49.32	9.46	17.77	52.74	30.46
Orlando, FL	10.20	11.32	65.35	9.85	15.16	55.71	34.18
Oxnard, CA	14.04	14.09	74.49	10.60	19.22	71.85	51.71
Peoria, IL	11.22	12.37	65.50	10.33	19.32	52.74	31.85
Philadelphia, PA	13.88	14.88	68.56	11.45	19.63	80.57	34.14
Phoenix, AZ	11.03	11.21	67.95	9.72	17.62	55.64	38.06
Pittsburgh, PA	12.61	12.40	68.07	10.06	18.75	69.89	27.40
Portland, OR	12.88	13.80	55.70	11.28	19.94	50.31	38.71
Providence, RI	13.33	13.96	47.45	12.21	19.51	58.72	40.30
Provo, UT	10.22	11.48	55.41	9.15	16.24	51.92	n/a
Raleigh, NC	10.37	11.56	58.36	9.57	18.32	64.08	32.80
Reno, NV	10.41	13.39	61.68	10.44	18.21	48.54	n/a
Richmond, VA	11.00	12.01	56.65	9.60	18.31	62.98	30.90
Riverside, CA	13.09	11.85	57.55	10.91	18.73	64.22	46.06
Rochester, MN	13.96	13.84	51.27	12.26	18.91	59.61	n/a
Salem, OR	13.04	12.88	56.65	11.17	17.37	36.97	n/a
Salt Lake City, UT	10.12	12.31	57.91	9.47	17.62	62.76	31.06
San Antonio, TX	10.50	10.98	54.75	9.38	14.83	53.91	32.77
San Diego, CA	12.99	12.94	72.34	10.58	18.90	68.45	36.68
San Francisco, CA	13.55	20.09	81.42	16.90	23.90	83.57	50.86
San Jose, CA	13.14	15.06	94.01	13.74	23.14	88.36	55.61
Santa Rosa, CA	13.39	15.11	77.12	13.34	21.88	61.72	n/a
Savannah, GA	10.94	11.83	51.02	8.61	17.38	48.96	n/a
Seattle, WA	14.60	15.57	62.33	12.07	20.33	67.55	42.21
Sioux Falls, SD	10.88	12.52	48.61	9.38	16.02	51.58	25.69
Spokane, WA	13.46	13.65	48.67	10.56	17.96	54.55	35.02
Springfield, MO	10.85	11.91	42.05	9.03	14.69	39.92	34.09
Tallahassee, FL	9.91	10.83	52.36	8.98	14.97	50.22	n/a
Tampa, FL	10.34	10.76	54.49	9.39	15.55	51.59	36.09
Topeka, KS	11.82	12.38	38.64	9.08	17.69	60.60	n/a
Tulsa, OK	10.41	10.89	57.64	9.03	16.72	46.31	33.07
Virginia Beach, VA	10.22	11.32	61.05	9.68	16.63	55.08	32.47
Washington, DC	12.45	13.26	75.70	11.90	21.37	73.15	38.43
Wichita, KS	10.45	11.56	46.81	9.05	15.68	57.49	32.20
Wilmington, NC	10.91	11.00	45.17	9.04	17.82	50.19	n/a
Worcester, MA	14.17	13.49	60.66	12.18	20.42	62.04	n/a

Notes: Wage data is for May 2013 and covers the Metropolitan Statistical Area—see Appendix B for areas included; n/a not available
Source: Bureau of Labor Statistics, May 2013 Metro Area Occupational Employment and Wage Estimates

Average Hourly Wages: Occupations N – R

Metro Area	Nurses, Licensed Practical	Nurses, Registered	Nursing Assistants	Packers/ Packagers	Physical Therapists	Postal Mail Carriers	R.E. Brokers
Abilene, TX	18.56	28.14	10.88	9.20	40.86	24.24	n/a
Albuquerque, NM	21.69	31.78	13.52	12.32	40.02	24.89	n/a
Anchorage, AK	25.13	40.64	16.92	12.77	48.59	25.49	30.29
Ann Arbor, MI	22.43	32.94	13.87	9.73	37.94	24.63	n/a
Athens, GA	18.64	29.33	9.81	9.29	36.78	23.23	n/a
Atlanta, GA	19.02	30.95	11.11	10.47	37.96	24.72	43.11
Austin, TX	22.05	30.98	11.67	11.34	41.88	25.00	30.32
Baltimore, MD	24.87	34.24	13.96	10.58	39.05	24.68	37.94
Billings, MT	18.43	31.61	12.53	10.98	33.13	24.73	n/a
Boise City, ID	19.45	29.33	11.20	11.43	36.48	24.35	n/a
Boston, MA	25.49	42.35	14.96	10.99	38.80	25.95	63.74
Boulder, CO	21.53	34.08	13.27	10.59	34.04	24.89	29.50
Cape Coral, FL	19.78	28.94	12.72	9.05	40.30	24.25	n/a
Cedar Rapids, IA	17.69	25.65	11.93	8.74	34.36	24.58	n/a
Charleston, SC	20.18	32.16	11.10	9.94	36.90	23.89	26.30
Charlotte, NC	19.86	28.52	11.23	10.76	37.91	24.31	35.01
Chicago, IL	22.53	34.46	12.48	11.00	36.84	25.01	49.15
Cincinnati, OH	20.64	30.08	12.21	10.64	38.29	24.51	23.98
Clarksville, TN	18.75	27.23	11.76	12.86	36.69	24.34	n/a
Colorado Spgs, CO	21.21	31.37	12.78	9.86	37.23	24.74	20.86
Columbia, MO	18.45	27.81	10.90	9.75	31.91	24.25	n/a
Columbus, OH	20.13	30.64	12.13	11.04	36.90	24.08	34.29
Dallas, TX	22.36	33.65	12.32	10.29	45.06	24.91	n/a
Davenport, IA	17.55	26.26	11.72	11.16	37.48	23.98	n/a
Denver, CO	22.89	34.42	14.42	10.29	35.19	24.82	41.76
Des Moines, IA	19.29	26.79	12.14	10.00	36.62	24.62	n/a
Durham, NC	21.76	31.62	12.82	9.49	36.49	24.41	26.03
El Paso, TX	20.50	31.00	10.82	9.06	48.95	23.89	n/a
Erie, PA	18.48	26.75	12.25	11.76	37.13	23.58	n/a
Eugene, OR	22.40	37.50	13.39	10.26	41.40	24.28	31.03
Fargo, ND	18.17	27.67	13.43	8.64	31.95	24.04	n/a
Fayetteville, NC	19.57	29.81	11.33	10.02	38.64	24.08	19.47
Ft. Collins, CO	21.17	30.50	13.44	9.34	32.86	24.95	27.79
Ft. Wayne, IN	18.40	25.17	10.78	10.17	38.22	24.68	n/a
Ft. Worth, TX	22.36	33.60	11.89	11.04	41.45	24.79	n/a
Gainesville, FL	19.90	28.53	10.88	10.59	36.44	23.80	n/a
Grand Rapids, MI	19.05	28.64	12.14	10.98	35.42	23.99	n/a
Green Bay, WI	18.02	27.82	12.31	11.78	39.45	23.63	n/a
Greensboro, NC	19.67	28.80	10.89	9.28	35.43	24.12	22.44
Honolulu, HI	22.43	42.55	13.98	10.44	38.58	26.07	41.96
Houston, TX	22.88	36.56	12.06	11.38	42.08	24.51	48.51
Huntsville, AL	18.73	26.74	10.86	10.78	38.44	23.71	n/a
Indianapolis, IN	20.27	29.90	12.24	11.26	39.04	24.13	60.38
Jacksonville, FL	20.51	30.37	11.57	9.32	46.60	24.69	n/a
Kansas City, MO	19.06	29.88	11.81	11.54	34.37	24.30	24.96
Lafayette, LA	18.72	27.89	9.24	9.32	38.84	24.57	23.35
Las Vegas, NV	26.07	39.12	16.52	11.27	59.64	24.87	54.44
Lexington, KY	18.63	27.91	11.95	9.82	39.27	24.65	n/a
Lincoln, NE	18.23	26.73	12.12	10.11	34.88	24.54	n/a
Little Rock, AR	17.95	28.67	11.01	9.05	35.78	24.18	n/a
Los Angeles, CA	24.62	44.26	13.71	10.33	42.31	25.76	64.57
Louisville, KY	18.93	28.80	11.91	10.54	38.82	24.11	n/a
Lubbock, TX	20.57	27.47	10.95	8.89	38.23	24.89	n/a
Madison, WI	20.97	34.97	13.89	15.06	36.29	24.44	20.83
Manchester, NH	23.10	31.99	13.91	10.50	37.48	25.09	47.44

Table continued on next page.

Metro Area	Nurses, Licensed Practical	Nurses, Registered	Nursing Assistants	Packers/ Packagers	Physical Therapists	Postal Mail Carriers	R.E. Brokers
McAllen, TX	21.91	31.97	9.83	8.67	46.12	24.38	n/a
Miami, FL	20.23	29.53	11.04	9.31	35.27	25.08	n/a
Midland, TX	21.31	30.14	12.55	9.45	n/a	25.01	22.83
Minneapolis, MN	21.08	35.30	14.12	11.24	36.81	24.41	n/a
Montgomery, AL	18.35	29.68	11.00	9.85	38.82	23.87	26.74
Nashville, TN	18.85	28.42	11.87	9.83	36.18	24.52	n/a
New Orleans, LA	19.23	31.68	10.85	11.23	40.70	24.16	n/a
New York, NY	24.60	40.44	16.20	10.81	40.71	25.37	54.98
Oklahoma City, OK	18.99	28.13	10.89	10.81	35.86	24.41	18.85
Omaha, NE	19.69	28.43	13.09	10.20	35.87	24.53	37.40
Orlando, FL	19.43	29.70	11.53	10.74	38.33	24.73	47.52
Oxnard, CA	25.15	36.37	13.40	10.84	41.90	25.49	n/a
Peoria, IL	21.95	26.81	11.43	11.56	33.61	24.34	n/a
Philadelphia, PA	23.18	35.07	13.96	11.90	37.78	24.81	64.60
Phoenix, AZ	25.24	35.12	13.79	11.06	38.46	25.01	44.12
Pittsburgh, PA	19.78	30.04	13.16	12.27	39.28	24.65	71.36
Portland, OR	24.17	40.58	13.87	11.50	37.84	24.51	32.04
Providence, RI	24.60	35.47	13.75	10.48	38.50	24.81	n/a
Provo, UT	19.31	27.31	11.26	10.26	36.46	24.53	21.19
Raleigh, NC	21.13	28.43	11.67	10.48	35.21	24.14	25.34
Reno, NV	26.51	35.25	13.49	11.17	45.80	24.51	n/a
Richmond, VA	19.23	30.32	11.44	12.84	39.35	23.71	27.71
Riverside, CA	22.18	42.37	13.43	11.81	41.17	25.31	n/a
Rochester, MN	22.02	n/a	15.25	10.63	39.57	25.04	n/a
Salem, OR	21.94	37.37	13.40	10.81	40.09	23.63	22.52
Salt Lake City, UT	21.32	29.89	11.31	10.16	40.42	25.05	n/a
San Antonio, TX	20.50	31.82	11.69	10.18	43.27	24.66	28.51
San Diego, CA	23.18	40.60	13.60	10.31	43.73	25.26	36.79
San Francisco, CA	29.97	61.38	20.10	12.74	49.25	26.44	26.40
San Jose, CA	27.94	59.23	16.42	11.17	45.42	26.36	50.01
Santa Rosa, CA	25.85	48.36	15.79	10.34	41.42	25.12	48.60
Savannah, GA	18.50	28.25	10.72	9.29	42.55	24.73	28.35
Seattle, WA	25.93	39.68	14.93	13.41	40.75	25.22	32.78
Sioux Falls, SD	16.79	25.78	11.84	10.60	31.95	24.04	n/a
Spokane, WA	21.55	34.37	12.87	11.06	36.73	24.55	23.22
Springfield, MO	17.12	24.94	10.55	10.77	39.63	24.12	n/a
Tallahassee, FL	19.16	27.41	10.92	8.94	40.08	24.26	n/a
Tampa, FL	19.97	30.28	11.44	9.45	37.93	24.66	n/a
Topeka, KS	19.06	29.36	10.93	15.60	38.36	23.60	n/a
Tulsa, OK	18.83	27.73	10.91	9.53	36.27	24.47	n/a
Virginia Beach, VA	18.26	28.80	11.22	10.43	39.84	24.73	32.08
Washington, DC	22.95	35.74	13.77	10.30	38.69	24.66	34.45
Wichita, KS	19.29	25.51	11.03	9.15	36.26	24.34	26.38
Wilmington, NC	18.86	26.83	11.21	9.61	41.89	23.50	37.64
Worcester, MA	26.36	43.05	15.10	10.06	39.78	24.22	n/a

Notes: Wage data is for May 2013 and covers the Metropolitan Statistical Area—see Appendix B for areas included; n/a not available
Source: Bureau of Labor Statistics, May 2013 Metro Area Occupational Employment and Wage Estimates

Average Hourly Wages: Occupations R – T

Metro Area	Retail Salespersons	Sales Reps., Except Tech./Scien.	Sales Reps., Tech./Scien.	Secretaries, Exc. Leg./ Med./Exec.	Security Guards	Surgeons	Teacher Assistants
Abilene, TX	13.62	23.66	36.44	12.92	10.71	n/a	9.90
Albuquerque, NM	11.74	26.90	39.81	13.97	11.55	n/a	10.10
Anchorage, AK	13.18	25.83	36.45	16.96	13.31	n/a	17.30
Ann Arbor, MI	12.14	32.93	41.15	17.22	16.96	n/a	13.10
Athens, GA	10.51	24.97	n/a	14.32	13.49	n/a	8.70
Atlanta, GA	11.95	30.79	38.95	16.85	11.48	120.81	10.30
Austin, TX	12.53	29.84	37.48	15.77	12.42	n/a	10.60
Baltimore, MD	11.89	33.94	42.30	17.78	14.58	110.84	14.30
Billings, MT	13.88	26.55	n/a	14.44	12.86	n/a	13.50
Boise City, ID	11.90	27.45	29.67	14.49	12.89	n/a	11.10
Boston, MA	12.39	43.10	44.47	21.16	15.06	n/a	14.50
Boulder, CO	13.89	37.59	35.67	17.37	15.01	103.03	15.10
Cape Coral, FL	11.83	24.18	29.78	14.54	11.15	n/a	13.20
Cedar Rapids, IA	11.85	31.08	44.18	14.30	n/a	n/a	12.60
Charleston, SC	11.52	27.76	40.46	15.32	13.52	n/a	11.50
Charlotte, NC	12.10	31.41	40.29	17.10	11.31	n/a	11.20
Chicago, IL	12.33	33.29	37.20	16.95	13.02	115.47	12.30
Cincinnati, OH	11.78	31.64	39.93	15.94	16.47	109.54	12.70
Clarksville, TN	11.36	23.44	52.26	13.22	13.43	n/a	11.10
Colorado Spgs, CO	12.79	30.52	35.26	15.58	13.48	107.95	11.90
Columbia, MO	10.64	23.27	28.42	14.58	13.91	n/a	10.70
Columbus, OH	12.03	29.62	36.19	16.87	12.43	119.77	13.10
Dallas, TX	12.58	33.78	36.24	16.42	13.08	95.05	10.70
Davenport, IA	12.71	28.28	33.17	14.44	12.50	116.62	11.70
Denver, CO	12.80	36.54	48.36	17.96	13.89	111.18	13.30
Des Moines, IA	12.84	35.92	37.24	16.32	16.53	91.11	10.70
Durham, NC	10.89	31.22	45.63	17.51	12.77	113.39	12.20
El Paso, TX	10.96	21.60	38.11	12.87	10.13	n/a	10.60
Erie, PA	11.39	30.08	39.28	13.84	11.23	115.46	10.00
Eugene, OR	13.02	25.11	39.96	16.19	12.41	n/a	13.80
Fargo, ND	13.09	26.62	42.24	15.68	11.95	104.49	12.90
Fayetteville, NC	10.56	24.42	39.94	14.77	15.30	n/a	10.00
Ft. Collins, CO	12.25	26.89	40.29	15.92	10.31	110.38	12.50
Ft. Wayne, IN	11.55	28.96	39.16	15.47	14.83	n/a	11.10
Ft. Worth, TX	11.78	32.63	36.55	15.36	14.30	n/a	8.90
Gainesville, FL	11.11	22.34	33.50	13.86	12.24	n/a	9.40
Grand Rapids, MI	11.77	28.24	37.72	16.53	11.30	n/a	13.00
Green Bay, WI	11.45	32.44	33.42	16.18	13.78	n/a	14.40
Greensboro, NC	12.20	30.40	33.29	15.60	11.06	n/a	10.90
Honolulu, HI	12.25	21.44	33.40	18.43	12.68	n/a	13.40
Houston, TX	12.40	35.33	46.06	16.39	11.75	84.40	9.90
Huntsville, AL	11.46	31.78	37.45	16.94	12.32	n/a	8.70
Indianapolis, IN	12.06	32.67	46.55	16.61	12.49	n/a	11.20
Jacksonville, FL	11.47	28.88	35.44	14.98	10.35	118.25	12.40
Kansas City, MO	12.08	32.16	45.48	15.81	13.84	n/a	11.60
Lafayette, LA	11.24	28.84	31.88	14.31	11.22	71.35	10.20
Las Vegas, NV	13.07	28.96	42.72	18.64	13.22	113.49	15.90
Lexington, KY	11.71	24.93	35.03	15.59	10.51	114.35	14.70
Lincoln, NE	11.07	26.63	n/a	15.31	14.98	n/a	11.80
Little Rock, AR	12.75	27.25	29.86	14.42	12.41	113.90	9.40
Los Angeles, CA	12.39	29.73	38.84	18.27	12.81	111.49	14.10
Louisville, KY	11.51	30.69	44.89	15.00	13.37	118.16	13.80
Lubbock, TX	11.69	28.05	29.00	13.35	11.87	90.44	8.80
Madison, WI	12.09	30.06	41.70	17.17	11.48	n/a	12.80
Manchester, NH	11.99	31.44	38.83	15.96	11.92	105.45	12.90

Table continued on next page.

Metro Area	Retail Salespersons	Sales Reps., Except Tech./Scien.	Sales Reps., Tech./Scien.	Secretaries, Exc. Leg./ Med./Exec.	Security Guards	Surgeons	Teacher Assistants
McAllen, TX	9.57	25.44	n/a	12.71	10.59	n/a	10.30
Miami, FL	11.23	26.45	32.81	14.60	10.97	n/a	11.20
Midland, TX	14.55	33.58	48.05	15.43	12.50	n/a	9.20
Minneapolis, MN	11.44	36.68	44.11	18.95	14.94	119.63	14.40
Montgomery, AL	12.49	29.59	35.75	16.22	12.16	n/a	9.00
Nashville, TN	12.46	27.75	34.29	15.16	12.46	n/a	11.10
New Orleans, LA	12.89	29.58	37.42	15.19	13.36	n/a	11.10
New York, NY	12.84	38.77	46.37	19.00	15.18	98.64	13.90
Oklahoma City, OK	12.73	30.44	32.95	14.90	12.67	114.30	9.70
Omaha, NE	12.29	28.02	34.52	15.61	13.38	n/a	10.20
Orlando, FL	11.24	25.68	37.45	14.66	11.65	n/a	11.60
Oxnard, CA	12.75	32.68	42.86	18.21	12.65	119.04	14.50
Peoria, IL	11.79	28.49	33.56	14.65	16.04	n/a	11.20
Philadelphia, PA	13.07	32.23	49.82	17.47	12.30	120.27	12.90
Phoenix, AZ	11.61	29.76	42.58	16.43	13.52	114.05	11.20
Pittsburgh, PA	12.50	31.81	42.81	15.24	11.90	113.69	11.50
Portland, OR	12.93	32.81	41.56	17.50	13.80	n/a	14.70
Providence, RI	12.48	32.76	41.15	17.93	12.83	116.46	14.50
Provo, UT	12.37	29.40	33.72	14.45	14.08	110.65	11.00
Raleigh, NC	11.79	29.45	41.18	16.28	12.44	n/a	10.80
Reno, NV	12.74	27.70	39.48	17.62	11.51	115.67	12.30
Richmond, VA	12.43	34.63	44.28	16.41	12.89	112.78	10.90
Riverside, CA	12.10	29.92	40.45	17.31	11.51	106.75	14.00
Rochester, MN	11.24	27.21	32.56	17.40	13.32	n/a	12.40
Salem, OR	12.92	25.36	40.96	15.61	14.60	n/a	16.30
Salt Lake City, UT	12.67	34.62	46.90	15.93	14.32	115.18	11.40
San Antonio, TX	12.42	27.83	41.84	15.25	11.83	84.64	10.80
San Diego, CA	13.73	28.45	39.02	18.35	14.03	83.21	14.00
San Francisco, CA	14.53	31.29	47.92	20.71	15.27	93.98	16.60
San Jose, CA	12.94	32.85	58.34	20.56	15.17	114.84	14.40
Santa Rosa, CA	13.67	30.64	46.30	19.16	14.00	118.83	14.30
Savannah, GA	11.52	28.61	30.20	15.65	14.44	n/a	10.50
Seattle, WA	14.69	35.29	45.11	19.62	15.73	115.08	15.80
Sioux Falls, SD	12.34	27.49	43.01	13.16	12.24	n/a	10.90
Spokane, WA	13.16	25.87	46.81	16.12	13.45	n/a	12.90
Springfield, MO	11.82	22.81	30.02	13.13	12.99	n/a	10.40
Tallahassee, FL	11.02	21.94	33.81	14.09	11.27	n/a	11.90
Tampa, FL	12.01	30.42	33.10	14.48	10.79	103.26	10.20
Topeka, KS	11.52	27.70	40.10	14.09	13.94	n/a	10.90
Tulsa, OK	13.25	28.32	41.58	14.04	12.17	79.61	11.00
Virginia Beach, VA	11.29	28.23	42.31	15.60	12.89	111.83	11.80
Washington, DC	12.12	34.08	47.52	20.61	17.82	116.42	14.00
Wichita, KS	12.36	31.22	43.32	14.57	13.43	117.05	10.60
Wilmington, NC	11.87	29.03	35.81	15.03	11.81	n/a	11.60
Worcester, MA	11.90	35.68	38.33	19.68	14.47	116.75	13.60

Notes: Wage data is for May 2013 and covers the Metropolitan Statistical Area—see Appendix B for areas included; hourly wages for teacher assistants were calculated by the editors from annual wage data assuming a 40 hour work week; n/a not available
Source: Bureau of Labor Statistics, May 2013 Metro Area Occupational Employment and Wage Estimates

Average Hourly Wages: Occupations T – Z

Metro Area	Teachers, Elementary School	Teachers, Secondary School	Tele-marketers	Truck Driv., Heavy/ Trac. Trail.	Truck Drivers, Light	Waiters/ Waitresses
Abilene, TX	21.30	22.00	n/a	18.97	11.41	8.74
Albuquerque, NM	21.70	22.40	n/a	19.03	14.14	10.88
Anchorage, AK	32.60	32.60	n/a	25.87	19.18	10.72
Ann Arbor, MI	27.70	29.70	n/a	19.63	17.05	10.14
Athens, GA	25.30	25.30	8.69	20.40	15.44	9.03
Atlanta, GA	26.20	27.10	13.99	20.41	16.93	9.19
Austin, TX	22.70	23.50	13.90	18.67	16.53	9.34
Baltimore, MD	29.50	29.30	12.90	19.80	17.45	9.18
Billings, MT	23.80	26.10	13.73	21.13	16.18	8.99
Boise City, ID	23.60	24.30	12.58	18.08	14.07	8.96
Boston, MA	34.30	35.10	17.08	23.41	18.17	13.50
Boulder, CO	26.60	27.20	12.08	20.68	16.73	12.33
Cape Coral, FL	23.40	24.10	9.65	16.06	14.10	9.67
Cedar Rapids, IA	24.00	23.80	10.54	20.03	16.20	8.74
Charleston, SC	24.70	25.40	9.57	19.36	15.63	9.42
Charlotte, NC	22.10	22.40	13.66	19.37	16.05	9.34
Chicago, IL	28.80	35.80	13.34	23.42	18.67	10.50
Cincinnati, OH	27.20	27.40	13.51	20.10	16.71	9.15
Clarksville, TN	26.60	26.40	n/a	15.41	13.76	9.12
Colorado Spgs, CO	21.60	22.20	12.60	19.36	13.99	9.94
Columbia, MO	21.60	20.90	10.63	19.62	13.15	9.53
Columbus, OH	29.10	29.90	11.74	19.02	16.63	9.37
Dallas, TX	25.00	25.80	n/a	19.20	15.72	10.24
Davenport, IA	26.60	26.10	10.50	19.13	15.78	10.29
Denver, CO	25.50	26.90	13.50	21.35	16.33	10.53
Des Moines, IA	25.20	25.70	15.07	21.18	16.38	9.00
Durham, NC	20.70	21.40	15.76	17.58	17.67	9.40
El Paso, TX	24.60	24.80	9.49	17.61	14.03	8.51
Erie, PA	27.00	24.10	8.65	18.04	15.28	9.07
Eugene, OR	26.90	24.70	12.52	17.32	16.40	10.84
Fargo, ND	24.40	24.00	11.26	18.84	14.90	10.12
Fayetteville, NC	19.20	19.10	8.90	15.43	15.54	9.09
Ft. Collins, CO	22.80	23.30	11.00	17.26	16.25	9.16
Ft. Wayne, IN	24.60	24.80	9.79	19.81	15.74	8.95
Ft. Worth, TX	25.40	26.30	11.19	19.47	15.61	9.29
Gainesville, FL	22.10	24.90	9.47	15.04	15.26	9.90
Grand Rapids, MI	32.70	28.90	11.93	18.72	16.07	9.52
Green Bay, WI	25.70	24.60	12.38	19.49	15.22	8.80
Greensboro, NC	21.60	21.80	11.11	18.90	15.37	8.67
Honolulu, HI	26.30	27.20	11.62	21.37	14.70	12.93
Houston, TX	24.90	25.50	12.17	22.66	16.51	9.73
Huntsville, AL	24.60	24.00	9.29	16.39	14.79	9.19
Indianapolis, IN	25.40	26.00	17.93	20.12	17.28	9.54
Jacksonville, FL	24.10	24.50	10.58	18.75	15.81	9.66
Kansas City, MO	24.30	24.10	13.16	21.38	17.06	9.39
Lafayette, LA	27.40	n/a	11.24	19.29	13.58	8.97
Las Vegas, NV	25.80	26.00	11.88	19.78	16.43	11.11
Lexington, KY	24.00	24.60	n/a	18.81	16.17	8.84
Lincoln, NE	25.10	25.10	10.56	n/a	13.26	8.98
Little Rock, AR	21.80	23.60	8.82	18.66	14.19	8.30
Los Angeles, CA	34.80	33.30	12.66	20.29	16.24	11.07
Louisville, KY	26.60	26.90	12.10	20.93	17.63	9.31
Lubbock, TX	21.40	22.50	n/a	17.79	14.21	9.03
Madison, WI	25.00	27.50	10.87	21.43	17.75	10.35
Manchester, NH	26.30	26.70	15.57	18.63	15.08	11.33

Table continued on next page.

Metro Area	Teachers, Elementary School	Teachers, Secondary School	Tele-marketers	Truck Driv., Heavy/ Trac. Trail.	Truck Drivers, Light	Waiters/ Waitresses
McAllen, TX	23.70	25.20	10.62	17.51	11.63	8.79
Miami, FL	23.20	26.50	11.81	17.53	14.08	9.76
Midland, TX	23.60	25.80	n/a	20.49	15.87	9.80
Minneapolis, MN	31.90	31.20	13.07	21.93	17.93	9.32
Montgomery, AL	22.80	22.10	8.45	18.26	15.61	8.60
Nashville, TN	22.70	23.40	15.24	19.93	15.34	8.90
New Orleans, LA	22.90	24.70	14.81	19.65	16.09	10.29
New York, NY	35.30	37.40	14.62	22.08	17.98	11.50
Oklahoma City, OK	20.80	22.90	10.30	19.01	15.82	9.25
Omaha, NE	22.40	23.40	12.21	19.11	14.67	8.85
Orlando, FL	22.80	22.10	10.95	17.46	15.16	10.98
Oxnard, CA	32.90	31.90	15.69	21.54	18.09	10.01
Peoria, IL	23.80	28.10	12.83	17.46	16.87	10.32
Philadelphia, PA	30.40	31.60	14.56	20.89	17.51	10.38
Phoenix, AZ	20.90	21.00	13.39	20.36	15.72	9.96
Pittsburgh, PA	27.90	29.00	12.88	20.52	15.69	9.69
Portland, OR	27.50	28.00	13.33	19.52	17.07	10.65
Providence, RI	34.70	33.60	15.11	20.27	17.91	10.34
Provo, UT	22.00	23.60	14.09	22.75	13.60	11.15
Raleigh, NC	21.60	22.00	14.65	19.28	16.30	9.47
Reno, NV	25.00	24.10	13.63	21.84	15.47	8.65
Richmond, VA	26.30	26.40	14.06	18.70	16.58	10.48
Riverside, CA	35.10	33.70	11.98	21.73	17.91	9.63
Rochester, MN	25.10	25.20	n/a	18.85	17.53	8.26
Salem, OR	27.20	26.60	10.52	18.24	16.75	10.21
Salt Lake City, UT	26.30	27.50	12.07	19.99	15.18	11.23
San Antonio, TX	26.60	27.20	n/a	16.40	14.14	9.32
San Diego, CA	30.80	33.20	11.55	19.27	16.58	9.95
San Francisco, CA	32.10	33.60	13.93	22.04	19.81	12.13
San Jose, CA	33.30	34.90	14.14	22.03	17.27	10.96
Santa Rosa, CA	22.70	31.00	11.71	22.34	18.16	10.51
Savannah, GA	26.30	n/a	13.15	18.66	16.33	10.07
Seattle, WA	29.10	30.30	13.18	21.75	17.79	14.14
Sioux Falls, SD	20.10	20.00	13.45	19.13	15.04	8.79
Spokane, WA	28.80	29.80	11.23	19.70	17.33	13.14
Springfield, MO	20.70	19.20	10.22	20.44	13.81	9.07
Tallahassee, FL	21.90	22.10	13.78	15.22	14.76	9.61
Tampa, FL	21.00	21.00	12.29	17.96	16.34	9.73
Topeka, KS	24.40	24.70	n/a	17.10	15.21	8.53
Tulsa, OK	22.20	21.60	12.19	19.26	14.05	8.88
Virginia Beach, VA	26.30	27.10	10.10	17.82	15.15	11.28
Washington, DC	32.60	33.60	12.50	19.86	19.19	11.87
Wichita, KS	20.60	23.80	n/a	17.82	13.07	8.96
Wilmington, NC	19.90	19.90	11.55	18.87	15.55	8.84
Worcester, MA	31.10	32.60	18.18	22.87	17.81	12.77

Notes: Wage data is for May 2013 and covers the Metropolitan Statistical Area—see Appendix B for areas included; hourly wages for elementary and secondary school teachers were calculated by the editors from annual wage data assuming a 40 hour work week; n/a not available

Source: Bureau of Labor Statistics, May 2013 Metro Area Occupational Employment and Wage Estimates

Means of Transportation to Work: City

City	Car/Truck/Van		Public Transportation			Bicycle	Walked	Other Means	Worked at Home
	Drove Alone	Car-pooled	Bus	Subway	Railroad				
Abilene, TX	80.3	10.2	1.1	0.0	0.0	0.2	2.9	2.7	2.5
Albuquerque, NM	80.4	9.1	1.9	0.0	0.2	1.2	2.2	1.2	3.8
Anchorage, AK	74.5	12.8	1.9	0.0	0.0	1.3	2.8	2.6	4.0
Ann Arbor, MI	58.4	5.9	9.7	0.1	0.0	4.4	15.4	0.4	5.8
Athens, GA	72.5	10.5	3.0	0.0	0.0	2.1	5.7	1.9	4.2
Atlanta, GA	67.4	7.8	7.0	2.9	0.3	1.0	4.8	1.6	7.3
Austin, TX	72.4	10.6	4.1	0.0	0.1	1.5	2.8	1.9	6.6
Baltimore, MD	59.8	10.2	15.4	1.5	1.0	0.9	6.8	1.7	2.8
Billings, MT	78.8	10.6	1.3	0.0	0.0	1.2	4.0	0.9	3.3
Boise City, ID	78.5	7.4	0.6	0.0	0.0	3.2	3.2	1.3	5.7
Boston, MA	38.1	7.2	13.3	17.7	1.1	1.8	15.3	1.8	3.8
Boulder, CO	52.0	5.8	8.1	0.0	0.0	10.5	9.8	1.4	12.3
Cape Coral, FL	83.7	9.0	0.6	0.0	0.0	0.5	0.8	1.5	4.0
Cedar Rapids, IA	80.3	9.5	1.6	0.0	0.0	0.6	2.9	1.3	3.7
Charleston, SC	76.4	7.2	2.9	0.0	0.0	2.5	5.6	1.1	4.3
Charlotte, NC	76.8	10.1	3.3	0.4	0.1	0.2	2.2	1.1	5.8
Chicago, IL	50.1	9.2	14.1	10.6	1.8	1.4	6.6	1.7	4.4
Cincinnati, OH	72.1	9.7	7.8	0.0	0.0	0.4	5.0	0.8	4.1
Clarksville, TN	84.8	9.8	0.5	0.0	0.0	0.1	2.1	1.1	1.5
Colorado Spgs, CO	79.9	9.9	0.7	0.0	0.0	0.6	2.7	1.1	5.2
Columbia, MO	77.4	9.7	0.9	0.0	0.0	1.5	6.3	0.6	3.6
Columbus, OH	80.3	8.6	3.0	0.0	0.0	0.7	3.0	1.0	3.4
Dallas, TX	77.7	10.7	3.3	0.3	0.3	0.2	1.8	1.6	4.1
Davenport, IA	85.8	7.5	0.7	0.0	0.0	0.4	2.1	0.9	2.6
Denver, CO	69.7	9.4	5.6	0.6	0.3	2.5	4.5	1.3	6.0
Des Moines, IA	79.1	11.7	2.1	0.0	0.0	0.4	2.4	0.8	3.5
Durham, NC	74.8	11.9	3.7	0.0	0.0	1.0	3.3	1.4	4.0
El Paso, TX	79.5	11.2	2.0	0.0	0.0	0.1	1.9	2.6	2.7
Erie, PA	75.7	10.9	4.7	0.0	0.0	0.3	5.4	1.0	2.0
Eugene, OR	66.1	8.2	3.8	0.0	0.0	8.1	6.9	0.8	6.1
Fargo, ND	82.5	7.4	1.1	0.0	0.0	0.9	4.1	1.0	2.9
Fayetteville, NC	80.5	9.8	0.8	0.0	0.0	0.2	4.5	1.3	2.9
Ft. Collins, CO	72.9	8.2	1.5	0.0	0.0	6.4	3.8	1.1	6.1
Ft. Wayne, IN	85.4	7.6	0.7	0.0	0.0	0.3	1.5	0.8	3.7
Ft. Worth, TX	82.0	10.9	0.7	0.0	0.3	0.2	1.2	1.5	3.2
Gainesville, FL	63.4	11.8	7.4	0.0	0.0	6.3	5.2	1.7	4.1
Grand Rapids, MI	74.9	11.4	3.9	0.0	0.0	0.7	3.8	0.7	4.7
Green Bay, WI	81.0	9.4	1.4	0.0	0.0	0.7	2.6	1.9	3.0
Greensboro, NC	81.2	9.6	2.2	0.0	0.0	0.3	2.3	0.9	3.5
Honolulu, HI	57.5	12.6	12.5	0.0	0.0	1.7	9.1	3.4	3.3
Houston, TX	75.8	12.2	4.3	0.0	0.0	0.4	2.1	2.0	3.1
Huntsville, AL	84.7	8.0	0.6	0.0	0.0	0.1	1.3	2.0	3.2
Indianapolis, IN	81.9	9.7	2.0	0.0	0.0	0.5	2.1	0.9	2.9
Jacksonville, FL	80.6	10.3	1.8	0.0	0.0	0.4	1.3	1.1	4.4
Kansas City, MO	80.5	8.5	3.3	0.0	0.0	0.3	2.1	1.2	4.0
Lafayette, LA	80.0	12.2	1.0	0.0	0.0	0.9	1.9	1.2	2.8
Las Vegas, NV	78.1	11.3	3.9	0.0	0.0	0.4	1.8	1.4	3.1
Lexington, KY	79.8	9.8	1.5	0.0	0.0	1.1	3.8	0.7	3.4
Lincoln, NE	80.7	9.9	1.1	0.0	0.0	1.8	2.6	0.6	3.3
Little Rock, AR	84.2	10.6	0.9	0.0	0.0	0.1	1.2	0.6	2.5
Los Angeles, CA	67.0	10.0	10.4	0.6	0.1	1.0	3.7	1.5	5.8
Louisville, KY	81.6	8.3	3.3	0.0	0.0	0.3	2.1	1.3	3.0
Lubbock, TX	82.2	10.5	0.9	0.0	0.0	0.5	2.0	0.9	3.0
Madison, WI	63.6	8.7	8.7	0.0	0.0	5.6	8.9	0.7	3.8

Table continued on next page.

City	Car/Truck/Van		Public Transportation			Bicycle	Walked	Other Means	Worked at Home
	Drove Alone	Car-pooled	Bus	Subway	Railroad				
Manchester, NH	81.0	10.4	1.3	0.1	0.0	0.1	2.9	0.7	3.6
McAllen, TX	75.4	9.5	0.8	0.0	0.0	0.1	1.5	6.7	6.0
Miami, FL	69.4	10.4	10.0	0.7	0.2	0.9	4.1	1.4	3.0
Midland, TX	83.9	11.2	0.3	0.0	0.0	0.2	1.1	1.1	2.3
Minneapolis, MN	61.5	8.0	12.8	0.4	0.5	3.8	6.5	1.2	5.4
Montgomery, AL	85.4	9.8	0.8	0.0	0.0	0.2	1.4	0.3	2.1
Nashville, TN	79.2	10.9	2.2	0.0	0.1	0.3	1.9	1.1	4.3
New Orleans, LA	70.1	10.4	6.5	0.0	0.0	2.2	5.3	2.3	3.1
New York, NY	22.4	4.8	11.7	42.1	1.7	0.9	10.2	2.3	4.0
Oklahoma City, OK	81.9	11.4	0.5	0.0	0.0	0.2	1.7	0.9	3.4
Omaha, NE	81.8	10.2	1.4	0.0	0.0	0.2	2.6	0.8	3.0
Orlando, FL	78.7	8.9	4.8	0.0	0.0	0.4	2.0	1.6	3.5
Oxnard, CA	71.5	21.2	1.5	0.0	0.1	0.6	1.6	0.9	2.6
Peoria, IL	81.3	8.9	3.0	0.0	0.0	0.5	2.6	1.2	2.5
Philadelphia, PA	49.9	9.0	18.7	4.4	2.7	2.0	8.6	1.5	3.0
Phoenix, AZ	75.0	12.1	3.2	0.1	0.0	0.7	1.9	1.8	5.1
Pittsburgh, PA	54.1	10.4	17.3	0.2	0.0	1.5	10.9	1.8	3.8
Portland, OR	58.3	9.0	9.7	0.7	0.2	6.2	5.7	2.5	7.7
Providence, RI	58.8	13.8	7.9	0.1	1.0	1.3	10.2	2.4	4.2
Provo, UT	60.8	14.2	1.7	0.0	0.0	3.4	13.1	1.2	5.7
Raleigh, NC	80.7	9.0	1.8	0.0	0.0	0.6	1.7	1.0	5.1
Reno, NV	76.7	10.4	3.2	0.0	0.0	1.1	3.2	1.9	3.4
Richmond, VA	71.9	10.5	5.3	0.1	0.0	2.1	4.3	1.4	4.4
Riverside, CA	77.1	11.6	2.0	0.0	1.2	0.9	2.7	1.0	3.5
Rochester, MN	75.1	10.2	4.7	0.1	0.0	0.8	3.8	1.1	4.2
Salem, OR	74.7	12.1	1.7	0.0	0.0	1.7	4.8	1.1	3.9
Salt Lake City, UT	67.9	12.5	5.3	0.3	0.2	2.9	5.2	2.6	3.3
San Antonio, TX	79.3	11.0	3.2	0.0	0.0	0.2	2.0	1.1	3.1
San Diego, CA	74.9	9.5	3.7	0.0	0.1	1.0	2.9	1.3	6.6
San Francisco, CA	36.6	7.6	23.4	6.2	1.2	3.6	9.6	4.5	7.1
San Jose, CA	78.4	10.5	2.4	0.1	0.6	0.9	1.6	1.5	4.0
Santa Rosa, CA	78.6	10.3	1.9	0.0	0.0	1.0	2.9	0.8	4.6
Savannah, GA	75.8	11.1	3.8	0.0	0.0	1.2	4.1	0.8	3.2
Seattle, WA	52.0	8.8	17.7	0.4	0.1	3.8	9.1	1.5	6.6
Sioux Falls, SD	84.3	7.8	1.2	0.0	0.0	0.5	2.1	1.3	2.7
Spokane, WA	75.6	10.3	4.0	0.0	0.0	1.1	3.8	0.7	4.5
Springfield, MO	81.9	8.8	0.8	0.0	0.0	0.7	3.4	1.3	3.1
Tallahassee, FL	81.0	8.2	2.2	0.0	0.0	0.9	3.4	1.2	3.1
Tampa, FL	76.5	9.5	3.0	0.1	0.0	1.6	2.4	1.6	5.3
Topeka, KS	80.9	11.9	1.1	0.0	0.0	0.3	2.2	0.8	2.8
Tulsa, OK	81.5	10.8	0.9	0.0	0.0	0.3	1.9	1.1	3.6
Virginia Beach, VA	81.7	8.5	0.8	0.0	0.0	0.6	2.4	1.0	4.9
Washington, DC	34.0	5.9	17.2	20.9	0.4	3.6	11.9	1.3	4.8
Wichita, KS	84.6	9.1	0.6	0.0	0.0	0.3	1.3	1.0	3.0
Wilmington, NC	78.2	9.7	0.7	0.0	0.0	1.4	3.1	1.6	5.3
Worcester, MA	74.7	10.3	2.7	0.2	0.6	0.2	6.3	1.1	3.9
U.S.	76.4	9.7	2.6	1.7	0.5	0.6	2.8	1.3	4.3

Note: Figures are percentages and cover workers 16 years of age and older
Source: U.S. Census Bureau, 2010-2012 American Community Survey 3-Year Estimates

Means of Transportation to Work: Metro Area

Metro Area	Car/Truck/Van		Public Transportation			Bicycle	Walked	Other Means	Worked at Home
	Drove Alone	Car-pooled	Bus	Subway	Railroad				
Abilene, TX	80.1	11.1	0.8	0.0	0.0	0.2	2.5	2.7	2.4
Albuquerque, NM	80.2	9.4	1.4	0.0	0.3	0.9	2.0	1.2	4.5
Anchorage, AK	74.1	12.9	1.8	0.0	0.0	1.1	2.6	3.1	4.4
Ann Arbor, MI	73.0	8.2	4.8	0.0	0.0	1.7	6.6	0.6	5.1
Athens, GA	77.3	9.4	1.8	0.0	0.0	1.3	3.9	1.6	4.7
Atlanta, GA	77.8	10.4	2.3	0.7	0.1	0.2	1.4	1.4	5.7
Austin, TX	75.4	10.9	2.2	0.0	0.1	0.8	2.0	1.6	7.0
Baltimore, MD	76.4	9.4	4.4	0.9	0.8	0.2	2.6	1.1	4.1
Billings, MT	79.4	10.5	1.0	0.0	0.0	0.8	3.6	1.0	3.6
Boise City, ID	78.9	8.5	0.4	0.0	0.0	1.4	2.0	1.8	6.9
Boston, MA	68.8	7.7	4.0	5.5	2.0	0.8	5.4	1.3	4.5
Boulder, CO	65.1	8.2	5.1	0.0	0.0	4.3	4.9	1.3	11.1
Cape Coral, FL	76.6	12.1	1.3	0.0	0.0	1.0	1.0	2.2	5.8
Cedar Rapids, IA	81.2	9.0	1.0	0.0	0.0	0.4	2.7	1.3	4.5
Charleston, SC	80.4	9.0	1.3	0.0	0.0	0.9	3.0	0.9	4.4
Charlotte, NC	79.8	10.0	1.8	0.2	0.1	0.2	1.5	0.9	5.4
Chicago, IL	70.9	8.6	4.6	3.5	3.1	0.6	3.2	1.1	4.3
Cincinnati, OH	83.3	8.2	2.0	0.0	0.0	0.1	2.1	0.6	3.7
Clarksville, TN	82.3	10.4	0.5	0.0	0.0	0.1	2.8	1.2	2.7
Colorado Spgs, CO	77.7	9.7	0.6	0.0	0.0	0.4	4.7	1.0	5.8
Columbia, MO	79.2	10.3	0.6	0.0	0.0	1.0	4.5	0.7	3.7
Columbus, OH	82.4	8.0	1.6	0.0	0.0	0.4	2.2	0.9	4.4
Dallas, TX	81.1	10.2	1.0	0.1	0.3	0.2	1.2	1.3	4.6
Davenport, IA	84.0	8.5	0.9	0.0	0.0	0.4	1.9	1.0	3.3
Denver, CO	76.2	9.3	3.6	0.4	0.2	0.9	2.1	1.2	6.1
Des Moines, IA	83.0	9.2	1.1	0.0	0.0	0.2	1.5	0.7	4.3
Durham, NC	74.0	11.0	4.0	0.0	0.0	1.1	3.0	1.6	5.2
El Paso, TX	79.1	11.2	1.8	0.0	0.0	0.1	2.1	2.8	2.9
Erie, PA	81.2	9.0	1.8	0.0	0.0	0.2	3.9	0.8	3.1
Eugene, OR	71.1	9.8	3.0	0.0	0.0	4.5	4.8	0.9	5.9
Fargo, ND	82.2	7.6	0.8	0.0	0.0	0.6	4.0	0.8	3.9
Fayetteville, NC	82.7	9.6	0.5	0.0	0.0	0.2	3.1	1.5	2.3
Ft. Collins, CO	76.1	8.4	1.0	0.0	0.0	3.8	2.8	1.2	6.8
Ft. Wayne, IN	85.5	7.4	0.4	0.0	0.0	0.3	1.3	0.8	4.2
Ft. Worth, TX	81.1	10.2	1.0	0.1	0.3	0.2	1.2	1.3	4.6
Gainesville, FL	72.9	11.1	4.2	0.0	0.0	3.2	3.1	1.3	4.3
Grand Rapids, MI	82.8	8.9	1.4	0.0	0.0	0.4	1.8	0.6	4.1
Green Bay, WI	82.8	8.2	0.7	0.0	0.0	0.3	2.4	1.1	4.5
Greensboro, NC	83.2	9.7	1.1	0.0	0.0	0.1	1.7	0.7	3.6
Honolulu, HI	64.4	14.7	8.2	0.0	0.0	1.0	5.4	2.8	3.5
Houston, TX	79.9	11.1	2.4	0.0	0.0	0.3	1.4	1.6	3.4
Huntsville, AL	86.3	7.9	0.3	0.1	0.0	0.1	1.1	1.3	2.8
Indianapolis, IN	83.8	8.6	1.1	0.0	0.0	0.3	1.6	0.8	3.7
Jacksonville, FL	81.3	9.8	1.2	0.0	0.0	0.6	1.3	1.2	4.7
Kansas City, MO	83.2	9.0	1.1	0.0	0.0	0.2	1.3	1.0	4.2
Lafayette, LA	82.6	11.1	0.7	0.0	0.0	0.4	1.7	1.2	2.2
Las Vegas, NV	78.8	10.7	3.8	0.0	0.0	0.4	1.8	1.5	3.0
Lexington, KY	80.7	10.0	1.0	0.0	0.0	0.7	3.2	0.6	3.7
Lincoln, NE	80.5	9.9	1.0	0.0	0.0	1.6	2.6	0.6	3.8
Little Rock, AR	84.7	9.9	0.6	0.0	0.0	0.1	1.2	0.9	2.6
Los Angeles, CA	73.8	10.4	5.5	0.3	0.2	0.9	2.7	1.2	5.0
Louisville, KY	83.5	8.8	1.9	0.0	0.0	0.2	1.6	1.0	3.0
Lubbock, TX	82.1	10.5	0.8	0.0	0.0	0.4	1.9	0.9	3.4
Madison, WI	73.9	8.8	4.2	0.0	0.0	2.7	5.1	0.9	4.5

Table continued on next page.

Metro Area	Car/Truck/Van		Public Transportation			Bicycle	Walked	Other Means	Worked at Home
	Drove Alone	Car-pooled	Bus	Subway	Railroad				
Manchester, NH	82.1	8.2	0.8	0.0	0.1	0.0	2.0	0.7	6.1
McAllen, TX	78.4	11.5	0.2	0.0	0.0	0.1	1.2	4.0	4.5
Miami, FL	78.3	9.6	3.3	0.3	0.2	0.6	1.8	1.4	4.6
Midland, TX	84.3	10.1	0.2	0.0	0.0	0.2	1.0	1.0	3.3
Minneapolis, MN	78.2	8.4	4.3	0.1	0.1	0.8	2.2	0.9	4.9
Montgomery, AL	85.8	9.3	0.5	0.0	0.0	0.1	1.1	0.8	2.4
Nashville, TN	81.9	10.0	1.1	0.0	0.1	0.2	1.2	1.0	4.6
New Orleans, LA	78.9	10.5	2.6	0.0	0.0	0.9	2.6	2.0	2.5
New York, NY	50.1	6.7	8.2	18.8	3.6	0.5	6.1	2.0	4.0
Oklahoma City, OK	82.7	10.5	0.4	0.0	0.0	0.3	1.7	1.1	3.4
Omaha, NE	83.4	9.5	0.9	0.0	0.0	0.2	1.8	0.8	3.5
Orlando, FL	81.2	9.1	2.0	0.0	0.0	0.5	1.2	1.6	4.4
Oxnard, CA	75.7	13.3	1.0	0.0	0.3	0.8	2.1	1.1	5.6
Peoria, IL	84.6	8.5	1.1	0.0	0.0	0.3	2.0	0.7	2.9
Philadelphia, PA	73.6	8.0	5.5	1.5	2.2	0.6	3.7	0.9	4.0
Phoenix, AZ	76.6	11.6	1.9	0.1	0.0	0.8	1.5	1.8	5.8
Pittsburgh, PA	77.1	9.1	5.0	0.1	0.0	0.3	3.5	1.3	3.6
Portland, OR	71.2	9.4	4.7	0.5	0.2	2.3	3.5	1.7	6.4
Providence, RI	80.7	8.7	1.7	0.2	0.8	0.3	3.2	1.0	3.3
Provo, UT	73.1	12.8	1.6	0.0	0.0	1.2	4.3	1.0	6.0
Raleigh, NC	81.0	9.1	0.9	0.0	0.0	0.3	1.2	1.2	6.2
Reno, NV	77.8	10.6	2.3	0.0	0.0	0.8	2.2	1.9	4.4
Richmond, VA	81.7	9.4	1.6	0.0	0.0	0.4	1.3	0.8	4.6
Riverside, CA	76.9	14.0	1.1	0.0	0.4	0.4	1.6	1.2	4.3
Rochester, MN	76.9	10.5	3.4	0.1	0.0	0.5	3.0	0.9	4.7
Salem, OR	74.2	13.8	1.3	0.0	0.0	1.1	4.2	1.0	4.3
Salt Lake City, UT	76.2	11.9	2.5	0.2	0.3	0.8	2.1	1.6	4.4
San Antonio, TX	79.4	11.1	2.2	0.0	0.0	0.2	1.9	1.2	4.1
San Diego, CA	76.3	10.0	2.6	0.0	0.3	0.8	2.7	1.3	6.2
San Francisco, CA	61.2	10.1	7.8	5.5	0.9	1.8	4.3	2.1	6.2
San Jose, CA	76.8	10.3	2.1	0.1	0.9	1.8	1.9	1.3	4.8
Santa Rosa, CA	76.3	10.0	1.6	0.0	0.0	1.0	3.0	1.2	6.8
Savannah, GA	81.5	9.3	1.7	0.0	0.0	0.5	2.0	1.1	3.8
Seattle, WA	70.2	10.3	7.7	0.1	0.4	1.1	3.6	1.2	5.4
Sioux Falls, SD	83.4	8.1	0.8	0.0	0.0	0.4	2.2	1.2	3.8
Spokane, WA	76.4	10.3	2.7	0.0	0.0	0.7	3.1	1.0	5.8
Springfield, MO	82.2	9.9	0.4	0.0	0.0	0.3	2.1	1.1	4.0
Tallahassee, FL	81.8	10.0	1.4	0.0	0.0	0.5	2.2	1.2	3.1
Tampa, FL	80.3	9.5	1.3	0.0	0.0	0.8	1.5	1.4	5.2
Topeka, KS	81.6	11.4	0.6	0.0	0.0	0.2	2.0	0.6	3.5
Tulsa, OK	83.0	10.2	0.5	0.0	0.0	0.2	1.3	1.1	3.6
Virginia Beach, VA	80.7	8.7	1.8	0.0	0.0	0.4	2.9	1.1	4.4
Washington, DC	65.8	10.3	5.7	7.8	0.7	0.7	3.3	1.0	4.8
Wichita, KS	85.2	8.6	0.4	0.0	0.0	0.3	1.3	0.9	3.2
Wilmington, NC	79.5	11.8	0.4	0.0	0.0	0.6	1.5	1.3	4.8
Worcester, MA	82.0	8.7	0.8	0.1	0.7	0.2	2.8	0.8	3.9
U.S.	76.4	9.7	2.6	1.7	0.5	0.6	2.8	1.3	4.3

Note: Figures are percentages and cover workers 16 years of age and older; (1) Figures cover the Metropolitan Statistical Area—see Appendix B for areas included
Source: U.S. Census Bureau, 2010-2012 American Community Survey 3-Year Estimates

Travel Time to Work: City

City	Less Than 10 Minutes	10 to 19 Minutes	20 to 29 Minutes	30 to 44 Minutes	45 to 59 Minutes	60 to 89 Minutes	90 Minutes or More
Abilene, TX	24.2	56.3	11.3	3.9	1.7	1.6	1.1
Albuquerque, NM	10.6	37.3	28.6	16.7	3.3	2.0	1.6
Anchorage, AK	16.0	42.9	22.7	12.7	2.7	1.3	1.6
Ann Arbor, MI	17.9	44.4	18.2	10.8	4.7	3.1	0.7
Athens, GA	17.5	49.9	17.2	7.7	2.8	2.9	2.0
Atlanta, GA	8.9	31.5	26.6	20.5	5.6	4.2	2.7
Austin, TX	11.5	34.6	24.1	20.6	4.5	3.2	1.6
Baltimore, MD	7.2	25.6	23.1	23.8	7.5	7.7	5.2
Billings, MT	20.9	50.2	18.8	5.4	1.6	0.8	2.4
Boise City, ID	17.1	45.9	22.4	10.6	1.4	1.2	1.3
Boston, MA	7.9	22.5	20.8	28.3	10.4	8.3	1.8
Boulder, CO	19.8	43.6	16.4	10.6	5.5	2.8	1.2
Cape Coral, FL	8.3	25.9	23.0	26.4	10.1	4.0	2.3
Cedar Rapids, IA	20.5	46.6	17.3	10.5	2.5	1.3	1.3
Charleston, SC	13.0	35.0	28.2	16.0	3.5	2.7	1.6
Charlotte, NC	10.0	30.2	26.5	23.2	5.4	2.5	2.2
Chicago, IL	5.3	18.3	18.6	29.2	13.7	11.2	3.6
Cincinnati, OH	11.7	35.1	26.7	17.7	4.2	2.6	2.0
Clarksville, TN	12.9	35.8	25.5	15.8	5.2	4.0	0.9
Colorado Spgs, CO	14.0	38.6	26.4	14.4	2.9	2.3	1.4
Columbia, MO	18.9	53.2	14.4	8.6	2.8	1.1	1.0
Columbus, OH	10.3	34.7	30.7	18.6	2.8	1.7	1.2
Dallas, TX	9.0	29.6	23.1	25.3	7.0	4.4	1.7
Davenport, IA	18.5	49.3	21.1	7.4	1.6	1.1	1.0
Denver, CO	9.7	31.1	25.2	22.2	6.6	3.8	1.5
Des Moines, IA	15.6	41.3	28.3	10.0	2.6	1.2	0.9
Durham, NC	12.7	40.7	23.6	15.8	3.1	2.2	1.8
El Paso, TX	9.5	32.5	29.2	21.5	3.9	2.1	1.3
Erie, PA	20.0	50.8	15.7	8.8	2.5	1.4	0.7
Eugene, OR	18.8	49.0	20.4	6.9	2.0	2.0	0.9
Fargo, ND	24.7	54.7	13.3	3.2	1.4	1.4	1.3
Fayetteville, NC	17.0	38.5	24.2	12.5	3.8	1.8	2.0
Ft. Collins, CO	18.4	45.3	17.7	10.2	3.2	3.0	2.1
Ft. Wayne, IN	11.2	43.4	29.2	11.1	2.4	1.5	1.2
Ft. Worth, TX	9.2	29.2	23.2	23.3	8.0	5.7	1.5
Gainesville, FL	18.1	50.9	19.3	8.1	1.8	1.2	0.6
Grand Rapids, MI	15.8	44.5	23.2	9.2	3.2	2.9	1.3
Green Bay, WI	18.0	50.0	17.2	8.5	2.8	2.2	1.3
Greensboro, NC	13.0	45.0	22.6	13.4	2.3	1.8	1.9
Honolulu, HI	8.9	36.0	24.7	22.4	4.3	2.9	0.8
Houston, TX	8.6	28.0	24.4	25.2	7.2	5.0	1.7
Huntsville, AL	14.5	45.2	24.9	11.4	1.9	1.0	1.0
Indianapolis, IN	10.9	31.0	29.1	21.1	4.3	2.5	1.0
Jacksonville, FL	8.2	31.3	30.1	22.1	4.7	2.5	1.1
Kansas City, MO	12.1	35.4	26.7	19.3	3.5	1.8	1.2
Lafayette, LA	18.2	44.5	18.9	11.4	1.9	2.6	2.5
Las Vegas, NV	7.7	25.6	28.9	28.6	4.6	2.7	1.9
Lexington, KY	13.0	42.9	25.6	13.1	2.7	1.8	0.9
Lincoln, NE	16.8	46.8	23.0	8.0	2.3	1.9	1.1
Little Rock, AR	15.2	43.8	26.1	10.8	2.1	1.5	0.6
Los Angeles, CA	7.3	24.7	20.3	26.9	9.4	8.5	3.0
Louisville, KY	9.9	33.4	29.7	19.7	3.5	2.0	1.7
Lubbock, TX	20.4	58.1	12.9	5.0	1.5	1.0	1.0
Madison, WI	15.0	42.1	24.6	12.5	2.6	2.0	1.1
Manchester, NH	12.5	41.3	19.3	14.6	5.0	5.0	2.2

Table continued on next page.

City	Less Than 10 Minutes	10 to 19 Minutes	20 to 29 Minutes	30 to 44 Minutes	45 to 59 Minutes	60 to 89 Minutes	90 Minutes or More
McAllen, TX	17.2	44.4	21.7	10.6	2.1	1.7	2.4
Miami, FL	6.3	25.3	28.1	26.3	7.2	5.0	1.8
Midland, TX	19.8	48.0	15.8	10.4	1.8	1.8	2.3
Minneapolis, MN	8.3	35.0	30.4	18.5	3.7	2.8	1.3
Montgomery, AL	13.0	45.7	26.0	10.9	2.1	1.4	0.9
Nashville, TN	8.9	30.8	28.0	23.8	5.2	2.1	1.1
New Orleans, LA	10.9	35.5	24.9	18.2	4.5	4.2	1.9
New York, NY	4.5	13.9	14.7	27.4	15.2	17.9	6.4
Oklahoma City, OK	13.3	37.5	28.3	16.1	2.3	1.3	1.2
Omaha, NE	15.1	43.1	27.0	11.1	1.4	1.3	1.0
Orlando, FL	8.6	33.7	25.7	20.8	5.6	3.0	2.5
Oxnard, CA	9.8	36.8	24.2	19.7	4.6	3.2	1.8
Peoria, IL	16.4	47.4	24.3	6.7	2.4	2.0	0.7
Philadelphia, PA	6.3	20.8	20.1	27.0	12.9	9.2	3.7
Phoenix, AZ	9.1	29.1	25.1	25.8	6.2	3.4	1.3
Pittsburgh, PA	10.9	32.7	25.6	20.5	5.8	3.1	1.4
Portland, OR	9.0	31.3	26.6	21.8	5.9	3.8	1.7
Providence, RI	15.9	41.6	18.4	13.4	4.3	4.3	2.1
Provo, UT	25.3	44.6	16.5	7.0	3.0	2.4	1.2
Raleigh, NC	12.0	36.6	27.3	17.4	3.3	2.2	1.0
Reno, NV	14.8	45.3	22.9	9.2	3.4	3.0	1.4
Richmond, VA	11.6	38.5	26.8	14.9	3.9	2.4	1.9
Riverside, CA	11.1	28.5	19.7	19.2	7.9	8.4	5.2
Rochester, MN	19.9	57.7	12.5	4.7	1.9	2.1	1.2
Salem, OR	17.2	41.3	20.2	12.0	3.9	3.8	1.6
Salt Lake City, UT	14.8	45.9	20.3	11.7	3.6	2.2	1.4
San Antonio, TX	10.2	32.0	27.4	21.4	4.6	2.7	1.6
San Diego, CA	9.1	35.3	28.4	19.5	3.7	2.5	1.5
San Francisco, CA	5.0	22.4	21.6	28.3	10.9	9.4	2.3
San Jose, CA	7.0	28.5	26.0	24.5	6.9	5.4	1.7
Santa Rosa, CA	14.5	41.1	19.6	12.3	4.4	5.3	2.8
Savannah, GA	11.5	42.9	28.3	11.2	3.6	1.6	1.0
Seattle, WA	9.0	28.1	24.4	25.5	7.8	3.8	1.4
Sioux Falls, SD	16.1	55.0	20.4	4.5	1.7	1.5	0.9
Spokane, WA	16.9	39.7	24.2	13.2	2.9	1.6	1.5
Springfield, MO	19.1	46.6	22.7	6.9	2.0	1.7	1.0
Tallahassee, FL	15.6	43.8	23.5	13.0	1.9	1.5	0.7
Tampa, FL	13.0	34.1	22.6	19.5	5.6	3.4	1.7
Topeka, KS	19.3	55.2	15.3	6.3	1.2	1.8	0.9
Tulsa, OK	15.9	43.1	25.1	11.2	2.0	1.5	1.2
Virginia Beach, VA	10.8	31.5	26.1	23.4	5.0	2.2	1.0
Washington, DC	5.3	20.4	23.5	30.8	10.8	6.9	2.2
Wichita, KS	14.0	48.7	24.4	9.7	1.4	1.2	0.7
Wilmington, NC	18.3	50.0	18.1	7.3	3.1	2.1	1.1
Worcester, MA	12.5	39.0	19.2	16.2	6.0	5.2	1.9
U.S.	13.5	29.8	20.9	20.1	7.5	5.6	2.5

Note: Figures are percentages and include workers 16 years old and over
Source: U.S. Census Bureau, 2010-2012 American Community Survey 3-Year Estimates

Travel Time to Work: Metro Area

Metro Area	Less Than 10 Minutes	10 to 19 Minutes	20 to 29 Minutes	30 to 44 Minutes	45 to 59 Minutes	60 to 89 Minutes	90 Minutes or More
Abilene, TX	24.2	47.2	15.5	7.6	2.3	1.8	1.5
Albuquerque, NM	11.1	33.1	25.2	20.0	5.9	2.9	1.8
Anchorage, AK	15.7	40.1	20.9	12.6	4.4	4.2	2.1
Ann Arbor, MI	13.0	34.8	22.9	17.7	6.6	3.9	1.1
Athens, GA	13.7	42.7	21.4	13.1	3.5	3.2	2.4
Atlanta, GA	8.0	23.3	20.2	25.3	11.7	8.6	2.9
Austin, TX	11.3	29.2	22.3	22.9	7.8	4.7	1.8
Baltimore, MD	8.2	23.7	21.5	24.4	10.2	8.1	3.7
Billings, MT	19.2	43.4	21.9	9.0	2.2	1.4	2.9
Boise City, ID	14.6	35.0	25.1	17.6	4.1	2.2	1.3
Boston, MA	10.6	24.1	18.7	24.0	10.9	8.9	2.7
Boulder, CO	15.7	35.3	20.9	16.9	6.0	3.7	1.4
Cape Coral, FL	9.1	28.2	21.6	25.5	8.7	4.4	2.6
Cedar Rapids, IA	19.7	38.1	20.9	13.5	4.3	2.3	1.2
Charleston, SC	10.2	29.8	25.7	21.9	7.5	3.3	1.6
Charlotte, NC	10.3	28.8	23.8	24.1	7.6	3.3	2.0
Chicago, IL	9.1	22.6	18.7	24.8	11.7	9.9	3.2
Cincinnati, OH	11.4	29.1	25.4	22.6	6.9	3.3	1.4
Clarksville, TN	14.8	32.9	23.1	17.7	6.2	3.8	1.5
Colorado Spgs, CO	14.2	35.1	25.2	16.8	4.4	2.7	1.7
Columbia, MO	16.2	45.2	19.4	13.2	3.7	1.2	1.1
Columbus, OH	12.2	30.3	27.0	21.3	5.3	2.5	1.3
Dallas, TX	10.0	26.7	21.3	25.1	9.5	5.6	1.8
Davenport, IA	18.1	39.1	23.8	12.9	2.9	1.8	1.4
Denver, CO	9.1	26.4	23.7	25.6	8.6	4.8	1.9
Des Moines, IA	15.4	36.3	28.5	14.1	3.2	1.5	1.1
Durham, NC	11.4	34.6	25.1	18.9	5.6	3.0	1.5
El Paso, TX	9.8	31.2	28.3	22.5	4.3	2.6	1.4
Erie, PA	19.3	39.2	21.9	14.0	3.1	1.4	1.1
Eugene, OR	17.6	42.2	21.7	11.3	3.0	2.5	1.7
Fargo, ND	22.4	48.6	16.6	7.1	2.2	1.7	1.4
Fayetteville, NC	13.6	33.7	25.7	17.8	4.9	2.1	2.1
Ft. Collins, CO	15.9	38.9	19.2	14.4	5.0	4.2	2.5
Ft. Wayne, IN	12.7	37.0	29.6	14.4	3.4	1.6	1.3
Ft. Worth, TX	10.0	26.7	21.3	25.1	9.5	5.6	1.8
Gainesville, FL	14.0	39.7	23.1	15.8	4.0	2.2	1.2
Grand Rapids, MI	14.5	35.0	25.0	15.9	5.2	2.9	1.5
Green Bay, WI	17.9	40.8	22.0	12.9	3.3	1.9	1.3
Greensboro, NC	12.6	37.6	24.3	17.2	4.3	2.0	1.9
Honolulu, HI	9.7	25.9	20.6	26.6	8.7	6.6	1.8
Houston, TX	8.7	25.2	21.1	25.5	10.3	7.1	2.0
Huntsville, AL	11.6	34.5	27.4	19.1	4.4	1.9	1.1
Indianapolis, IN	11.5	27.3	25.0	24.2	7.4	3.3	1.4
Jacksonville, FL	9.5	28.1	25.9	23.8	7.8	3.7	1.2
Kansas City, MO	13.4	31.4	25.1	20.7	5.8	2.4	1.2
Lafayette, LA	14.5	37.0	22.9	15.7	4.1	2.6	3.2
Las Vegas, NV	8.6	28.8	29.5	24.4	4.4	2.5	1.9
Lexington, KY	15.0	37.3	24.3	16.2	4.1	1.9	1.2
Lincoln, NE	16.7	43.6	23.8	10.2	2.7	2.0	1.2
Little Rock, AR	13.5	33.8	23.4	19.6	5.7	2.7	1.2
Los Angeles, CA	8.3	26.5	20.5	24.8	9.0	8.0	2.9
Louisville, KY	10.5	30.5	27.2	21.6	5.9	2.8	1.7
Lubbock, TX	19.5	53.5	15.6	7.5	1.9	1.0	1.1
Madison, WI	15.5	34.5	24.9	17.0	4.3	2.4	1.4
Manchester, NH	11.0	31.0	20.3	20.0	7.9	7.0	2.8

Table continued on next page.

Metro Area	Less Than 10 Minutes	10 to 19 Minutes	20 to 29 Minutes	30 to 44 Minutes	45 to 59 Minutes	60 to 89 Minutes	90 Minutes or More
McAllen, TX	14.3	38.4	23.0	17.7	2.7	1.8	2.1
Miami, FL	7.7	25.1	23.3	27.2	8.8	5.9	2.0
Midland, TX	18.2	46.7	17.3	11.1	2.5	1.9	2.3
Minneapolis, MN	10.9	28.4	25.1	22.9	7.5	3.9	1.3
Montgomery, AL	11.4	34.2	25.9	19.2	5.7	2.4	1.3
Nashville, TN	10.0	27.3	23.0	23.8	9.7	4.5	1.7
New Orleans, LA	11.1	31.5	21.5	20.1	7.7	5.8	2.2
New York, NY	7.8	19.9	16.8	23.7	11.9	14.0	5.9
Oklahoma City, OK	14.5	33.4	25.0	19.1	4.7	2.0	1.4
Omaha, NE	14.7	37.3	27.1	15.2	3.0	1.6	1.0
Orlando, FL	7.6	27.7	23.8	24.8	9.7	4.4	1.9
Oxnard, CA	14.7	31.7	20.6	18.7	6.4	5.3	2.7
Peoria, IL	16.8	34.9	26.6	14.9	3.4	2.0	1.3
Philadelphia, PA	10.2	25.8	20.3	22.9	10.4	7.4	2.9
Phoenix, AZ	10.0	27.3	23.0	25.3	8.4	4.5	1.5
Pittsburgh, PA	12.8	27.6	21.5	21.6	8.8	5.7	2.0
Portland, OR	11.5	29.1	23.5	22.1	7.7	4.3	1.8
Providence, RI	13.8	32.2	21.2	18.2	6.8	5.3	2.5
Provo, UT	18.9	35.5	20.4	14.3	5.9	3.5	1.5
Raleigh, NC	10.6	29.5	25.6	22.2	7.1	3.5	1.5
Reno, NV	13.0	38.9	25.7	14.0	3.7	2.9	1.8
Richmond, VA	9.4	30.4	27.1	21.9	6.1	2.9	2.2
Riverside, CA	11.0	27.8	17.7	18.7	8.7	10.2	5.9
Rochester, MN	18.6	44.9	20.5	9.7	2.9	2.0	1.5
Salem, OR	17.6	33.9	21.5	15.7	5.2	4.3	1.8
Salt Lake City, UT	11.0	34.1	25.8	19.9	5.2	2.6	1.4
San Antonio, TX	10.8	29.1	24.7	22.8	6.9	3.8	1.9
San Diego, CA	9.6	31.9	26.0	21.0	5.9	3.7	1.9
San Francisco, CA	8.2	25.7	19.2	24.2	10.8	9.3	2.6
San Jose, CA	8.9	30.6	25.1	21.8	6.9	5.0	1.6
Santa Rosa, CA	15.5	33.0	19.3	15.5	6.3	6.5	3.9
Savannah, GA	9.3	31.5	29.1	20.1	6.3	2.2	1.4
Seattle, WA	9.5	25.5	22.1	24.8	9.4	6.3	2.3
Sioux Falls, SD	16.7	45.7	23.9	8.7	2.4	1.5	1.1
Spokane, WA	14.6	36.1	25.0	16.7	4.3	2.0	1.4
Springfield, MO	14.8	35.6	24.0	16.9	4.9	2.1	1.6
Tallahassee, FL	11.4	34.4	24.7	20.8	5.7	2.1	0.9
Tampa, FL	10.5	29.2	22.6	22.6	8.8	4.6	1.8
Topeka, KS	16.9	42.5	21.6	11.6	3.7	2.7	1.2
Tulsa, OK	15.0	33.8	26.0	17.4	4.2	2.3	1.3
Virginia Beach, VA	10.9	32.7	23.6	21.4	6.5	3.3	1.5
Washington, DC	6.4	19.1	18.0	25.7	13.7	12.6	4.3
Wichita, KS	16.1	40.9	24.9	13.8	2.4	1.1	0.8
Wilmington, NC	13.9	38.2	22.7	15.4	4.9	3.1	1.8
Worcester, MA	12.7	27.1	19.4	20.5	9.1	8.4	2.9
U.S.	13.5	29.8	20.9	20.1	7.5	5.6	2.5

Note: Figures are percentages and include workers 16 years old and over; Figures cover the Metropolitan Statistical Area—see Appendix B for areas included
Source: U.S. Census Bureau, 2010-2012 American Community Survey 3-Year Estimates

2012 Presidential Election Results

City	Area Covered	Obama	Romney	Other
Abilene, TX	Taylor County	22.5	76.1	1.4
Albuquerque, NM	Bernalillo County	55.6	39.3	5.1
Anchorage, AK	Districts 18 – 32	41.5	54.5	4.0
Ann Arbor, MI	Washtenaw County	67.0	31.3	1.7
Athens, GA	Clarke County	63.3	34.4	2.4
Atlanta, GA	Fulton County	64.3	34.5	1.2
Austin, TX	Travis County	60.1	36.2	3.6
Baltimore, MD	Baltimore City	87.0	11.3	1.7
Billings, MT	Yellowstone County	38.4	58.9	2.8
Boise City, ID	Ada County	42.7	54.0	3.2
Boston, MA	Suffolk County	77.6	20.8	1.6
Boulder, CO	Boulder County	69.7	27.9	2.4
Cape Coral, FL	Lee County	41.4	57.9	0.7
Cedar Rapids, IA	Linn County	57.9	40.2	1.9
Charleston, SC	Charleston County	50.4	48.0	1.6
Charlotte, NC	Mecklenburg County	60.7	38.2	1.1
Chicago, IL	Cook County	74.0	24.6	1.3
Cincinnati, OH	Hamilton County	51.8	46.9	1.3
Clarksville, TN	Montgomery County	44.0	54.5	1.5
Colorado Spgs, CO	El Paso County	38.1	59.4	2.5
Columbia, MO	Boone County	50.2	47.1	2.7
Columbus, OH	Franklin County	60.1	38.4	1.5
Dallas, TX	Dallas County	57.1	41.7	1.2
Davenport, IA	Scott County	56.1	42.4	1.5
Denver, CO	Denver County	73.5	24.4	2.1
Des Moines, IA	Polk County	56.1	42.0	1.9
Durham, NC	Durham County	75.8	23.0	1.2
El Paso, TX	El Paso County	65.6	33.0	1.3
Erie, PA	Erie County	57.4	41.3	1.3
Eugene, OR	Lane County	59.7	36.4	3.9
Fargo, ND	Cass County	47.0	49.9	3.1
Fayetteville, NC	Cumberland County	59.4	39.7	0.9
Ft. Collins, CO	Larimer County	51.4	45.8	2.7
Ft. Wayne, IN	Allen County	40.9	57.6	1.5
Ft. Worth, TX	Tarrant County	41.4	57.1	1.4
Gainesville, FL	Alachua County	57.9	40.5	1.6
Grand Rapids, MI	Kent County	45.5	53.4	1.0
Green Bay, WI	Brown County	48.6	50.4	1.0
Greensboro, NC	Guilford County	57.7	41.2	1.1
Honolulu, HI	Honolulu County	68.9	29.8	1.3
Houston, TX	Harris County	49.4	49.3	1.3
Huntsville, AL	Madison County	40.0	58.6	1.4
Indianapolis, IN	Marion County	60.2	38.1	1.7
Jacksonville, FL	Duval County	47.8	51.4	0.8
Kansas City, MO	Jackson County	58.7	39.7	1.6
Lafayette, LA	Lafayette Parish	32.2	65.9	1.9
Las Vegas, NV	Clark County	56.4	41.9	1.8
Lexington, KY	Fayette County	49.3	48.3	2.3
Lincoln, NE	Lancaster County	49.0	49.3	1.7
Little Rock, AR	Pulaski County	54.7	43.3	2.0
Los Angeles, CA	Los Angeles County	68.6	29.1	2.3
Louisville, KY	Jefferson County	54.8	43.7	1.4
Lubbock, TX	Lubbock County	28.8	69.6	1.6
Madison, WI	Dane County	71.1	27.6	1.3
Manchester, NH	Hillsborough County	49.7	48.6	1.6
McAllen, TX	Hidalgo County	70.4	28.6	1.0

Table continued on next page.

City	Area Covered	Obama	Romney	Other
Miami, FL	Miami-Dade County	61.6	37.9	0.4
Midland, TX	Midland County	18.6	80.1	1.4
Minneapolis, MN	Hennepin County	62.3	35.3	2.4
Montgomery, AL	Montgomery County	61.9	37.6	0.5
Nashville, TN	Davidson County	58.4	39.9	1.7
New Orleans, LA	Orleans Parish	80.3	17.7	2.0
New York, NY	Bronx County	91.4	8.1	0.5
New York, NY	Kings County	82.0	16.9	1.1
New York, NY	New York County	83.7	14.9	1.3
New York, NY	Queens County	79.1	19.9	1.0
New York, NY	Richmond County	50.7	48.1	1.2
Oklahoma City, OK	Oklahoma County	41.7	58.3	0.0
Omaha, NE	Douglas County	47.2	51.4	1.4
Orlando, FL	Orange County	58.7	40.4	0.9
Oxnard, CA	Ventura County	51.7	46.1	2.2
Peoria, IL	Peoria County	51.3	46.9	1.8
Philadelphia, PA	Philadelphia County	85.3	14.0	0.7
Phoenix, AZ	Maricopa County	43.1	54.9	2.0
Pittsburgh, PA	Allegheny County	56.6	42.2	1.2
Portland, OR	Multnomah County	75.3	20.7	4.0
Providence, RI	Providence County	66.5	31.6	1.9
Provo, UT	Utah County	9.8	88.3	2.0
Raleigh, NC	Wake County	54.9	43.5	1.6
Reno, NV	Washoe County	50.7	47.2	2.1
Richmond, VA	Richmond City	77.0	21.4	1.6
Riverside, CA	Riverside County	48.8	49.2	2.0
Rochester, MN	Olmsted County	50.2	47.0	2.7
Salem, OR	Marion County	46.7	50.2	3.1
Salt Lake City, UT	Salt Lake County	38.8	58.2	3.0
San Antonio, TX	Bexar County	51.6	47.0	1.4
San Diego, CA	San Diego County	51.7	46.2	2.1
San Francisco, CA	San Francisco County	83.4	13.3	3.3
San Jose, CA	Santa Clara County	69.9	27.6	2.5
Santa Rosa, CA	Sonoma County	70.8	26.0	3.2
Savannah, GA	Chatham County	55.5	43.5	1.0
Seattle, WA	King County	68.8	28.8	2.3
Sioux Falls, SD	Minnehaha County	45.3	52.7	2.0
Spokane, WA	Spokane County	45.6	51.6	2.8
Springfield, MO	Christian County	25.8	72.4	1.8
Tallahassee, FL	Leon County	61.3	37.6	1.1
Tampa, FL	Hillsborough County	52.8	46.2	1.0
Topeka, KS	Shawnee County	48.0	49.7	2.2
Tulsa, OK	Tulsa County	36.3	63.7	0.0
Virginia Beach, VA	Virginia Beach City	48.0	50.5	1.6
Washington, DC	District of Columbia	91.1	7.1	1.8
Wichita, KS	Sedgwick County	39.0	58.7	2.3
Wilmington, NC	New Hanover County	47.0	51.5	1.5
Worcester, MA	Worcester County	53.7	44.5	1.8
U.S.	U.S.	51.0	47.2	1.8

Note: Results are percentages and may not add to 100% due to rounding
Source: Dave Leip's Atlas of U.S. Presidential Elections

House Price Index (HPI)

Metro Area[1]	National Ranking[3]	Quarterly Change (%)	One-Year Change (%)	Five-Year Change (%)
Abilene, TX	n/r	n/a	5.43	6.70
Albuquerque, NM	192	-0.50	0.73	-12.18
Anchorage, AK	100	1.15	4.18	4.32
Ann Arbor, MI	53	1.67	9.78	3.91
Athens, GA	85	2.17	5.31	-12.78
Atlanta, GA	66	1.07	7.12	-13.81
Austin, TX	46	2.40	10.34	12.60
Baltimore, MD	144	0.25	2.06	-11.68
Billings, MT	110	-1.21	3.64	4.89
Boise City, ID	31	2.08	13.31	-13.87
Boston, MA[2]	92	1.62	4.78	-0.62
Boulder, CO	57	1.56	9.37	9.08
Cape Coral, FL	39	2.14	11.67	4.86
Cedar Rapids, IA	204	-0.14	0.46	0.69
Charleston, SC	95	-0.30	4.62	-10.06
Charlotte, NC	91	0.84	4.85	-8.42
Chicago, IL[2]	114	1.08	3.37	-17.11
Cincinnati, OH	232	-0.85	-0.23	-6.61
Clarksville, TN	n/r	n/a	-0.03	2.36
Colorado Spgs, CO	116	-0.69	3.14	-2.78
Columbia, MO	175	0.87	1.29	3.61
Columbus, OH	125	0.05	2.90	-2.47
Dallas, TX[2]	70	1.18	6.77	6.22
Davenport, IA	180	-0.64	1.13	2.89
Denver, CO	44	1.58	10.95	11.71
Des Moines, IA	135	0.28	2.38	-0.87
Durham, NC	166	0.37	1.51	-2.44
El Paso, TX	203	-1.67	0.47	-5.06
Erie, PA	n/r	n/a	5.98	9.28
Eugene, OR	71	2.05	6.34	-11.52
Fargo, ND	64	1.47	7.30	11.67
Fayetteville, NC	280	1.32	-3.52	-4.73
Ft. Collins, CO	59	1.58	8.49	9.83
Ft. Wayne, IN	184	0.51	0.97	-0.07
Ft. Worth, TX[2]	82	0.99	5.42	4.04
Gainesville, FL	n/r	n/a	1.04	-23.19
Grand Rapids, MI	76	0.36	5.85	-1.98
Green Bay, WI	260	-0.49	-1.41	-7.47
Greensboro, NC	244	-1.22	-0.57	-6.33
Honolulu, HI	n/a	n/a	n/a	n/a
Houston, TX	69	1.85	6.81	9.89
Huntsville, AL	275	-2.36	-2.87	-6.81
Indianapolis, IN	156	-0.19	1.77	-0.89
Jacksonville, FL	65	1.46	7.30	-18.23
Kansas City, MO	177	-0.52	1.21	-5.53
Lafayette, LA	142	-0.08	2.15	3.31
Las Vegas, NV	5	5.14	24.65	-12.67
Lexington, KY	234	-1.83	-0.28	-2.31
Lincoln, NE	130	0.82	2.64	3.99
Little Rock, AR	221	-0.96	0.08	-0.55
Los Angeles, CA[2]	24	3.91	15.85	6.34
Louisville, KY	155	0.51	1.79	-0.61
Lubbock, TX	109	2.74	3.67	8.35
Madison, WI	164	-0.58	1.61	-3.32
Manchester, NH	158	0.42	1.76	-10.15

Table continued on next page.

Metro Area[1]	National Ranking[3]	Quarterly Change (%)	One-Year Change (%)	Five-Year Change (%)
McAllen, TX	n/r	n/a	0.43	-1.17
Miami, FL[2]	40	3.08	11.63	-7.55
Midland, TX	n/r	n/a	11.37	26.16
Minneapolis, MN	68	0.20	7.00	-7.57
Montgomery, AL	230	-0.17	-0.14	-10.39
Nashville, TN	77	1.56	5.74	-0.52
New Orleans, LA	137	-0.36	2.30	-0.81
New York, NY[2]	146	0.50	2.00	-9.63
Oklahoma City, OK	167	-0.62	1.47	3.64
Omaha, NE	131	0.99	2.60	1.08
Orlando, FL	43	1.92	11.31	-20.16
Oxnard, CA	20	3.60	16.68	6.98
Peoria, IL	217	0.07	0.16	0.07
Philadelphia, PA[2]	138	0.85	2.28	-4.79
Phoenix, AZ	14	3.72	18.13	-6.11
Pittsburgh, PA	132	-0.32	2.57	7.92
Portland, OR	52	1.20	9.84	-6.70
Providence, RI	224	-0.59	0.06	-12.41
Provo, UT	49	1.49	10.02	-7.51
Raleigh, NC	123	-0.09	2.97	-4.52
Reno, NV	11	3.13	20.69	-16.61
Richmond, VA	151	0.26	1.90	-13.49
Riverside, CA	6	5.73	23.29	9.91
Rochester, MN	153	-0.62	1.85	-2.65
Salem, OR	78	1.89	5.73	-16.87
Salt Lake City, UT	56	1.25	9.43	-4.31
San Antonio, TX	117	2.81	3.13	6.38
San Diego, CA	17	3.42	17.14	11.12
San Francisco, CA[2]	21	2.24	16.57	11.98
San Jose, CA	16	2.74	17.32	14.40
Santa Rosa, CA	9	5.16	21.72	6.99
Savannah, GA	93	1.96	4.73	-12.97
Seattle, WA[2]	48	1.67	10.02	-8.70
Sioux Falls, SD	122	-0.09	2.98	3.66
Spokane, WA	195	-1.18	0.66	-15.61
Springfield, MO	190	0.39	0.76	-5.12
Tallahassee, FL	106	-0.37	3.76	-20.12
Tampa, FL	47	2.63	10.17	-11.07
Topeka, KS	174	1.89	1.29	-0.51
Tulsa, OK	241	-1.56	-0.46	0.01
Virginia Beach, VA	237	-0.24	-0.35	-14.40
Washington, DC[2]	90	0.58	5.01	1.34
Wichita, KS	238	-0.82	-0.38	-1.58
Wilmington, NC	179	-0.87	1.20	-19.03
Worcester, MA	168	0.84	1.46	-8.55
U.S.[4]	—	1.20	7.69	4.18

Note: The HPI is a weighted repeat sales index. It measures average price changes in repeat sales or refinancings on the same properties. This information is obtained by reviewing repeat mortgage transactions on single-family properties whose mortgages have been purchased or securitized by Fannie Mae or Freddie Mac in January 1975; (1) figures cover the Metropolitan Statistical Area (MSA) unless noted otherwise—see Appendix B for areas included; (2) Metropolitan Division—see Appendix B for areas included; (3) Rankings are based on annual percentage change, for all MSAs containing at least 15,000 transactions over the last 10 years and ranges from 1 to 283; (4) figures based on a weighted division average; all figures are for the period ended December 31, 2013; n/a not available; n/r not ranked
Source: Federal Housing Finance Agency, House Price Index, February 25, 2014

Year Housing Structure Built: City

City	2010 or Later	2000 -2009	1990 -1999	1980 -1989	1970 -1979	1960 -1969	1950 -1959	Before 1950	Median Year
Abilene, TX	0.7	9.8	8.9	17.2	13.7	12.4	20.4	16.8	1970
Albuquerque, NM	0.2	17.6	15.6	14.8	20.3	10.5	13.1	7.9	1979
Anchorage, AK	0.4	13.2	10.9	24.5	29.9	12.7	6.4	2.0	1980
Ann Arbor, MI	0.0	7.2	10.7	10.2	17.5	19.8	13.5	21.1	1968
Athens, GA	0.2	18.0	19.4	20.9	17.8	10.3	5.8	7.6	1984
Atlanta, GA	0.7	25.2	10.6	8.3	9.5	13.3	12.6	19.8	1975
Austin, TX	0.8	22.5	15.6	20.9	19.7	8.2	6.3	6.1	1985
Baltimore, MD	0.1	3.6	3.3	4.7	5.8	8.6	15.8	58.1	1944
Billings, MT	0.7	14.1	10.4	12.6	20.0	9.3	16.7	16.2	1974
Boise City, ID	0.3	13.5	22.6	14.4	22.3	6.9	7.9	12.1	1981
Boston, MA	0.3	6.7	4.2	5.6	7.0	7.5	7.3	61.4	<1940
Boulder, CO	0.9	10.2	10.3	16.0	24.2	17.6	9.7	11.2	1975
Cape Coral, FL	0.2	45.2	14.5	20.6	12.5	6.1	0.6	0.4	1997
Cedar Rapids, IA	0.4	14.3	13.8	6.9	13.8	14.3	13.8	22.7	1969
Charleston, SC	0.7	25.4	12.5	13.9	9.6	11.0	7.3	19.6	1982
Charlotte, NC	0.7	25.4	20.6	15.7	13.8	10.4	7.3	6.1	1988
Chicago, IL	0.2	8.8	4.1	3.6	6.6	9.7	12.6	54.3	1945
Cincinnati, OH	0.3	4.0	3.3	4.2	8.1	14.2	13.0	52.9	1947
Clarksville, TN	1.7	27.8	22.1	14.5	13.7	9.2	5.8	5.2	1991
Colorado Spgs, CO	0.4	18.2	15.2	19.1	19.3	11.0	8.1	8.6	1982
Columbia, MO	0.7	24.7	18.5	13.8	13.6	13.4	6.5	8.7	1986
Columbus, OH	0.4	12.4	15.7	13.3	14.8	13.5	11.7	18.2	1974
Dallas, TX	0.6	12.8	9.2	17.3	19.7	14.8	13.8	11.8	1975
Davenport, IA	0.3	9.0	6.4	5.3	12.0	12.0	17.2	37.9	1957
Denver, CO	0.8	14.2	6.6	8.3	14.6	12.4	15.6	27.6	1966
Des Moines, IA	0.2	7.9	7.1	6.1	13.3	10.5	15.9	38.9	1957
Durham, NC	1.1	21.7	18.6	17.9	11.4	11.4	6.9	11.0	1985
El Paso, TX	1.5	16.7	13.3	15.2	18.4	12.8	12.9	9.1	1978
Erie, PA	0.1	3.7	2.6	4.3	10.1	7.7	17.9	53.6	1947
Eugene, OR	0.4	13.6	17.5	8.8	23.0	13.4	9.5	13.6	1976
Fargo, ND	0.5	17.8	20.6	14.8	16.6	8.0	8.1	13.6	1983
Fayetteville, NC	0.7	17.7	18.1	16.7	18.9	14.3	8.7	4.9	1982
Ft. Collins, CO	0.4	21.1	20.2	18.4	20.7	7.9	3.5	7.9	1985
Ft. Wayne, IN	0.2	5.9	14.8	12.7	14.2	16.3	12.4	23.5	1969
Ft. Worth, TX	1.1	27.9	11.0	14.8	10.7	9.3	11.9	13.2	1983
Gainesville, FL	0.3	15.4	14.3	19.6	22.8	13.1	7.1	7.3	1980
Grand Rapids, MI	0.2	5.4	6.3	7.0	8.1	10.5	16.9	45.7	1953
Green Bay, WI	0.2	6.8	10.9	10.5	16.0	11.8	17.3	26.6	1965
Greensboro, NC	0.4	15.9	19.2	17.1	16.2	11.7	10.2	9.3	1982
Honolulu, HI	0.5	7.5	8.3	10.0	26.1	22.3	13.2	12.0	1971
Houston, TX	0.7	15.7	8.9	13.9	25.2	14.9	11.2	9.5	1976
Huntsville, AL	0.7	15.3	10.9	16.1	15.4	24.0	10.3	7.3	1975
Indianapolis, IN	0.3	10.5	12.4	11.4	13.5	14.6	14.1	23.3	1969
Jacksonville, FL	0.4	20.9	15.0	16.0	13.8	11.1	12.0	10.8	1981
Kansas City, MO	0.3	11.5	8.8	9.1	11.9	14.4	15.1	29.0	1964
Lafayette, LA	0.7	14.2	12.4	16.9	21.6	14.3	11.3	8.6	1977
Las Vegas, NV	0.4	23.9	33.0	18.4	11.3	7.3	4.5	1.3	1992
Lexington, KY	0.7	16.9	16.2	15.6	15.7	13.4	10.1	11.3	1980
Lincoln, NE	0.3	16.7	14.6	10.2	15.8	11.8	11.9	18.6	1975
Little Rock, AR	0.2	11.4	12.8	17.7	20.9	13.7	10.8	12.6	1976
Los Angeles, CA	0.3	6.4	5.5	10.3	13.5	14.5	18.2	31.3	1960
Louisville, KY	0.2	12.6	11.2	7.2	13.7	14.3	14.8	26.0	1966
Lubbock, TX	0.8	17.5	11.6	15.5	18.6	14.1	14.1	7.7	1978
Madison, WI	0.6	17.2	12.3	10.2	16.2	12.4	11.8	19.4	1974
Manchester, NH	0.1	6.2	6.1	14.2	10.1	6.9	10.1	46.5	1954

Table continued on next page.

City	2010 or Later	2000 -2009	1990 -1999	1980 -1989	1970 -1979	1960 -1969	1950 -1959	Before 1950	Median Year
McAllen, TX	1.1	27.9	20.7	18.5	18.0	5.6	5.5	2.7	1990
Miami, FL	0.6	20.1	5.4	7.6	13.1	10.3	16.1	26.8	1967
Midland, TX	0.7	12.0	8.4	22.1	18.1	11.9	20.5	6.3	1976
Minneapolis, MN	0.2	7.4	3.5	6.7	9.5	7.9	9.7	55.3	1943
Montgomery, AL	0.2	11.6	16.1	13.9	20.8	13.1	11.6	12.8	1976
Nashville, TN	0.6	15.5	11.8	17.2	18.0	13.2	11.8	11.8	1977
New Orleans, LA	0.8	8.5	3.8	7.2	15.0	11.1	12.3	41.3	1957
New York, NY	0.3	6.3	3.5	4.4	7.2	12.5	13.8	52.0	1948
Oklahoma City, OK	1.0	14.3	9.7	15.7	17.4	14.4	11.8	15.7	1975
Omaha, NE	0.2	5.4	9.1	10.2	18.7	15.6	12.9	27.9	1966
Orlando, FL	0.2	25.3	15.9	18.1	13.6	8.3	10.8	7.8	1985
Oxnard, CA	0.2	13.8	9.5	11.6	19.2	22.5	15.8	7.5	1972
Peoria, IL	0.7	9.3	7.8	6.8	15.8	12.6	14.7	32.4	1962
Philadelphia, PA	0.2	3.5	2.7	3.8	7.0	10.7	16.8	55.4	1946
Phoenix, AZ	0.3	18.3	16.2	18.8	20.7	10.0	10.5	5.2	1982
Pittsburgh, PA	0.1	3.9	2.7	4.5	5.8	8.1	13.0	62.0	<1940
Portland, OR	0.3	11.8	8.5	5.6	11.8	9.7	13.1	39.3	1958
Providence, RI	0.1	4.6	2.7	5.3	8.2	6.5	8.4	64.3	<1940
Provo, UT	0.5	14.4	18.5	12.2	19.9	11.6	8.1	14.8	1978
Raleigh, NC	0.8	29.4	21.1	18.4	11.4	8.2	5.3	5.6	1991
Reno, NV	0.7	21.7	18.2	13.8	21.5	9.6	7.0	7.6	1983
Richmond, VA	0.3	6.4	3.7	6.5	12.2	12.3	16.1	42.6	1955
Riverside, CA	0.3	13.1	10.1	14.2	19.8	11.8	18.4	12.2	1974
Rochester, MN	0.7	19.3	15.3	13.7	13.4	13.3	11.3	13.0	1979
Salem, OR	0.3	15.1	16.5	11.8	21.3	9.0	10.4	15.5	1977
Salt Lake City, UT	0.2	6.4	4.9	8.8	12.9	9.3	14.5	42.9	1955
San Antonio, TX	0.7	18.6	12.5	17.4	17.7	11.2	10.5	11.3	1980
San Diego, CA	0.4	10.7	10.9	17.7	22.2	13.2	12.9	12.1	1975
San Francisco, CA	0.2	6.9	4.4	5.1	6.8	8.1	9.5	58.9	1941
San Jose, CA	0.2	10.3	10.4	13.3	24.7	19.9	12.2	8.9	1974
Santa Rosa, CA	0.1	14.0	14.1	17.0	24.0	11.5	8.3	11.0	1978
Savannah, GA	0.8	11.1	7.7	10.6	16.6	13.9	15.3	23.9	1968
Seattle, WA	0.7	14.3	7.8	7.9	9.6	9.6	11.2	39.0	1960
Sioux Falls, SD	1.5	23.1	15.8	11.5	15.8	8.4	8.7	15.1	1982
Spokane, WA	0.3	8.3	9.0	8.4	14.4	6.0	15.8	37.8	1958
Springfield, MO	0.4	12.4	12.8	12.6	18.2	13.6	12.2	17.8	1974
Tallahassee, FL	0.4	20.8	17.5	19.7	17.9	10.1	7.9	5.7	1984
Tampa, FL	0.6	18.4	10.6	13.2	13.7	12.9	16.1	14.4	1975
Topeka, KS	0.3	7.8	8.5	10.8	14.1	16.8	17.0	24.7	1965
Tulsa, OK	0.4	6.4	8.6	14.4	21.6	14.6	17.2	16.7	1971
Virginia Beach, VA	0.4	11.5	13.6	28.7	23.0	13.7	6.6	2.6	1981
Washington, DC	0.3	8.2	3.0	4.4	7.5	12.8	14.0	49.8	1950
Wichita, KS	0.3	11.1	12.1	12.1	13.2	9.1	21.0	21.0	1969
Wilmington, NC	0.4	15.9	23.3	15.5	10.3	9.5	7.6	17.5	1983
Worcester, MA	0.3	4.6	4.4	9.4	8.6	6.3	9.7	56.8	1942
U.S.	0.5	14.9	13.8	13.9	15.9	11.1	10.9	19.0	1976

Note: Figures are percentages except for Median Year
Source: U.S. Census Bureau, 2010-2012 American Community Survey 3-Year Estimates

Year Housing Structure Built: Metro Area

Metro Area	2010 or Later	2000 -2009	1990 -1999	1980 -1989	1970 -1979	1960 -1969	1950 -1959	Before 1950	Median Year
Abilene, TX	0.9	11.2	9.1	17.6	14.9	11.0	17.1	18.1	1973
Albuquerque, NM	0.3	19.1	18.3	16.8	18.4	9.4	10.4	7.4	1983
Anchorage, AK	0.5	18.4	12.5	24.9	26.0	10.4	5.3	1.9	1983
Ann Arbor, MI	0.2	14.8	15.8	10.8	17.5	13.3	11.0	16.5	1975
Athens, GA	0.2	18.8	20.7	20.2	17.6	9.2	5.1	8.2	1985
Atlanta, GA	0.5	27.0	22.3	18.5	13.5	7.9	5.1	5.2	1990
Austin, TX	1.3	31.2	18.9	19.3	14.7	5.5	4.3	4.8	1991
Baltimore, MD	0.4	10.3	13.2	14.2	13.5	10.5	13.9	24.1	1971
Billings, MT	0.8	15.6	11.6	12.7	21.1	7.7	13.1	17.3	1976
Boise City, ID	0.6	28.5	22.8	10.3	17.9	5.0	5.2	9.8	1991
Boston, MA	0.3	8.1	7.1	10.6	11.0	10.4	11.2	41.3	1958
Boulder, CO	0.6	13.5	20.8	16.2	22.6	11.7	5.3	9.2	1981
Cape Coral, FL	0.2	34.4	18.1	21.6	15.8	5.7	2.8	1.4	1992
Cedar Rapids, IA	0.5	15.9	15.2	6.8	14.5	12.1	11.4	23.6	1972
Charleston, SC	0.8	26.3	16.3	17.4	15.9	9.5	6.3	7.5	1986
Charlotte, NC	0.8	27.0	20.8	15.4	12.5	9.2	7.0	7.3	1989
Chicago, IL	0.2	12.1	10.6	8.7	13.8	11.9	13.7	28.9	1966
Cincinnati, OH	0.4	12.8	14.4	10.8	13.3	11.5	12.7	24.2	1971
Clarksville, TN	1.3	23.3	21.8	13.6	14.7	10.2	6.8	8.3	1987
Colorado Spgs, CO	0.7	20.9	16.8	18.3	18.4	9.9	7.2	7.7	1984
Columbia, MO	0.4	21.5	19.6	13.9	17.4	11.7	5.7	9.7	1984
Columbus, OH	0.4	15.5	17.0	11.9	14.6	12.5	11.0	17.1	1976
Dallas, TX	0.9	23.6	16.2	19.7	15.6	9.7	7.9	6.3	1985
Davenport, IA	0.3	8.6	7.5	6.3	13.9	13.4	15.2	34.9	1960
Denver, CO	0.5	18.6	15.5	15.3	19.5	10.5	9.9	10.3	1980
Des Moines, IA	1.2	18.8	14.6	9.3	14.2	9.2	9.9	22.8	1976
Durham, NC	0.9	20.9	19.5	17.7	13.8	10.7	7.3	9.3	1985
El Paso, TX	1.8	19.1	14.6	16.0	17.4	11.5	11.5	8.4	1981
Erie, PA	0.1	7.1	8.8	8.9	14.7	9.7	15.2	35.4	1960
Eugene, OR	0.5	12.9	15.8	9.4	23.4	13.6	9.7	14.7	1975
Fargo, ND	1.0	20.2	17.2	11.4	18.3	8.1	9.0	14.7	1980
Fayetteville, NC	1.4	21.5	21.1	16.3	17.0	11.2	7.2	4.3	1986
Ft. Collins, CO	0.8	21.0	20.3	15.1	21.4	8.0	4.0	9.4	1985
Ft. Wayne, IN	0.4	10.6	15.4	11.5	14.3	14.0	11.2	22.7	1972
Ft. Worth, TX	0.9	23.6	16.2	19.7	15.6	9.7	7.9	6.3	1985
Gainesville, FL	0.5	21.3	20.2	19.8	18.1	9.4	5.5	5.1	1986
Grand Rapids, MI	0.3	12.6	15.5	11.8	13.5	10.4	12.0	23.9	1973
Green Bay, WI	0.5	15.5	16.6	11.2	15.6	9.7	10.2	20.7	1976
Greensboro, NC	0.5	16.4	19.1	15.7	15.4	11.4	10.3	11.2	1981
Honolulu, HI	0.5	11.1	12.5	12.6	25.1	19.3	11.3	7.6	1975
Houston, TX	1.2	25.3	14.4	16.5	20.2	9.6	6.9	5.8	1985
Huntsville, AL	1.2	21.9	18.8	17.5	12.3	15.2	7.3	5.8	1985
Indianapolis, IN	0.7	17.8	17.0	10.9	13.3	11.8	11.0	17.6	1977
Jacksonville, FL	0.5	24.6	17.3	17.8	13.7	8.8	8.9	8.3	1986
Kansas City, MO	0.3	15.0	14.1	12.8	15.8	12.4	12.3	17.3	1975
Lafayette, LA	1.6	18.9	15.6	18.4	19.6	10.7	7.8	7.4	1982
Las Vegas, NV	0.7	34.6	27.9	15.6	12.6	5.3	2.4	0.9	1995
Lexington, KY	0.7	18.5	17.2	15.0	15.6	11.8	8.9	12.3	1981
Lincoln, NE	0.4	16.7	15.0	9.8	16.3	11.2	10.9	19.7	1975
Little Rock, AR	1.2	19.9	17.9	16.7	18.2	10.8	7.8	7.6	1983
Los Angeles, CA	0.3	7.0	7.4	12.7	16.5	16.1	18.9	21.1	1966
Louisville, KY	0.3	15.0	14.6	10.0	15.6	12.7	12.3	19.4	1974
Lubbock, TX	0.8	17.3	12.4	15.6	18.0	13.5	13.9	8.7	1978
Madison, WI	0.5	18.1	15.4	11.0	16.8	10.2	9.1	18.8	1977
Manchester, NH	0.3	10.1	9.7	20.6	15.8	9.5	7.7	26.3	1974

Table continued on next page.

Metro Area	2010 or Later	2000 -2009	1990 -1999	1980 -1989	1970 -1979	1960 -1969	1950 -1959	Before 1950	Median Year
McAllen, TX	1.1	32.1	23.4	19.2	12.2	4.8	3.6	3.5	1993
Miami, FL	0.2	14.0	14.9	20.0	22.1	12.8	10.5	5.5	1980
Midland, TX	0.8	13.6	11.5	22.5	16.5	11.0	17.8	6.2	1979
Minneapolis, MN	0.3	15.3	14.5	14.9	15.5	10.2	10.2	19.1	1977
Montgomery, AL	0.7	17.2	19.8	13.9	18.5	11.6	8.5	9.7	1981
Nashville, TN	0.8	21.8	18.8	16.3	15.8	10.4	7.6	8.6	1985
New Orleans, LA	0.6	13.1	9.6	14.3	19.7	13.8	10.1	18.7	1974
New York, NY	0.3	7.3	5.8	7.4	9.8	13.9	16.8	38.7	1957
Oklahoma City, OK	1.0	16.2	10.7	16.3	18.6	13.6	10.9	12.7	1977
Omaha, NE	0.7	15.8	12.5	10.3	16.1	12.4	9.8	22.4	1973
Orlando, FL	0.4	27.0	21.0	22.3	13.8	6.5	5.9	3.1	1989
Oxnard, CA	0.2	11.4	10.6	16.9	22.7	20.8	10.8	6.6	1975
Peoria, IL	0.3	10.5	8.7	5.8	17.5	12.5	16.1	28.6	1964
Philadelphia, PA	0.3	8.4	8.9	10.0	12.5	12.3	16.1	31.5	1962
Phoenix, AZ	0.5	28.0	20.8	18.6	17.1	7.0	5.5	2.5	1990
Pittsburgh, PA	0.2	6.7	7.5	7.6	11.9	11.1	16.8	38.1	1957
Portland, OR	0.4	16.3	19.0	11.6	18.2	9.3	7.5	17.6	1979
Providence, RI	0.2	6.7	7.5	10.3	12.1	10.3	11.4	41.5	1957
Provo, UT	1.0	31.2	20.8	9.6	15.4	5.8	6.4	9.9	1991
Raleigh, NC	1.0	30.5	25.4	16.8	10.8	6.5	4.1	4.9	1993
Reno, NV	0.5	22.9	19.9	15.9	21.1	8.7	5.5	5.4	1986
Richmond, VA	0.6	16.3	15.3	16.5	16.6	11.0	9.7	13.9	1979
Riverside, CA	0.4	21.8	14.5	22.6	16.4	9.3	8.7	6.2	1984
Rochester, MN	0.6	19.4	15.7	12.3	14.6	11.3	8.9	17.2	1979
Salem, OR	0.5	15.3	18.4	10.5	23.2	9.8	8.4	13.9	1978
Salt Lake City, UT	0.7	17.9	16.9	14.4	19.9	8.6	9.1	12.4	1980
San Antonio, TX	1.2	23.9	14.8	16.2	16.4	9.6	8.3	9.5	1984
San Diego, CA	0.4	12.0	12.1	19.2	24.1	13.0	11.0	8.3	1977
San Francisco, CA	0.3	8.2	7.8	10.6	15.7	13.6	14.5	29.3	1965
San Jose, CA	0.3	9.8	10.5	12.4	22.5	19.1	15.7	9.5	1973
Santa Rosa, CA	0.2	10.8	13.1	18.5	22.1	11.2	9.4	14.7	1977
Savannah, GA	0.8	24.4	16.6	14.9	13.4	8.6	8.6	12.7	1985
Seattle, WA	0.7	16.9	15.7	15.5	15.6	11.8	7.9	15.8	1979
Sioux Falls, SD	1.3	22.8	16.4	10.1	15.0	7.8	8.1	18.5	1981
Spokane, WA	0.6	15.3	13.2	10.2	18.8	6.7	11.8	23.3	1974
Springfield, MO	0.6	21.6	18.6	13.4	16.3	9.0	7.4	13.0	1983
Tallahassee, FL	0.5	20.7	21.0	20.9	15.8	8.4	6.9	5.9	1986
Tampa, FL	0.4	17.0	14.5	21.7	21.8	11.2	8.6	4.7	1982
Topeka, KS	0.3	9.7	11.1	11.0	17.4	14.6	13.0	22.8	1970
Tulsa, OK	0.8	14.9	12.5	15.3	20.5	11.5	11.4	13.3	1977
Virginia Beach, VA	0.5	13.3	14.7	19.5	16.9	13.2	10.6	11.2	1979
Washington, DC	0.6	15.6	14.1	16.7	15.1	13.2	10.2	14.5	1978
Wichita, KS	0.5	12.5	13.6	12.2	13.6	8.5	18.9	20.1	1972
Wilmington, NC	0.6	28.2	24.1	18.0	11.3	6.5	4.5	6.8	1991
Worcester, MA	0.3	8.8	9.4	12.4	10.9	8.2	10.7	39.4	1960
U.S.	0.5	14.9	13.8	13.9	15.9	11.1	10.9	19.0	1976

Note: Figures are percentages except for Median Year; Figures cover the Metropolitan Statistical Area—see Appendix B for areas included
Source: U.S. Census Bureau, 2010-2012 American Community Survey 3-Year Estimates

Highest Level of Education: City

City	Less than H.S.	H.S. Diploma	Some College, No Deg.	Associate Degree	Bachelors Degree	Masters Degree	Profess. School Degree	Doctorate Degree
Abilene, TX	17.7	28.2	25.4	6.6	14.8	5.1	1.3	1.0
Albuquerque, NM	11.3	23.1	25.0	7.7	18.5	9.8	2.4	2.3
Anchorage, AK	7.7	23.2	28.1	8.4	20.5	8.3	2.4	1.3
Ann Arbor, MI	4.0	8.5	13.1	5.0	29.1	24.0	6.4	9.8
Athens, GA	14.2	22.5	17.9	5.0	19.8	12.1	3.1	5.3
Atlanta, GA	12.1	20.4	16.7	4.3	27.7	12.3	4.5	2.0
Austin, TX	13.6	16.8	19.3	5.4	28.5	11.3	2.8	2.3
Baltimore, MD	20.7	29.4	19.5	4.3	14.1	7.7	2.5	1.7
Billings, MT	6.9	30.1	25.4	6.9	22.3	5.3	2.2	1.0
Boise City, ID	6.4	21.2	26.9	8.0	23.8	9.4	2.8	1.5
Boston, MA	15.2	22.7	14.3	4.4	23.8	12.6	4.3	2.7
Boulder, CO	4.3	7.2	13.5	3.6	34.6	22.3	5.7	8.8
Cape Coral, FL	10.2	38.6	23.6	8.0	12.8	4.9	1.1	0.7
Cedar Rapids, IA	7.1	27.0	24.1	10.4	21.8	6.9	1.6	1.0
Charleston, SC	7.7	18.4	18.9	6.9	30.3	11.0	4.4	2.5
Charlotte, NC	11.7	20.4	21.0	7.1	27.3	9.3	2.3	0.8
Chicago, IL	19.2	23.3	18.4	5.4	20.5	9.1	2.9	1.3
Cincinnati, OH	15.5	26.4	20.2	6.7	18.5	8.5	2.6	1.7
Clarksville, TN	8.8	30.6	28.1	8.6	16.0	6.0	1.0	0.8
Colorado Spgs, CO	6.9	21.4	25.2	10.4	22.0	11.0	1.8	1.2
Columbia, MO	6.0	15.1	17.5	5.4	31.1	15.3	3.9	5.6
Columbus, OH	11.7	26.7	22.3	6.9	21.4	7.7	1.8	1.4
Dallas, TX	26.2	22.4	17.8	4.4	18.4	7.0	2.7	1.1
Davenport, IA	9.2	29.6	22.9	12.3	18.2	5.7	1.6	0.5
Denver, CO	14.7	18.6	18.7	5.1	26.2	11.1	3.9	1.7
Des Moines, IA	13.0	32.1	21.8	8.3	17.6	5.2	1.5	0.7
Durham, NC	12.9	17.0	18.2	6.0	25.0	12.8	3.6	4.4
El Paso, TX	23.4	23.9	23.0	7.2	15.1	5.4	1.3	0.7
Erie, PA	13.6	42.4	17.1	6.7	13.2	4.9	1.0	1.2
Eugene, OR	6.7	18.4	28.2	7.4	22.8	10.9	2.8	2.9
Fargo, ND	4.6	19.3	25.6	11.3	25.5	8.4	2.9	2.4
Fayetteville, NC	9.2	25.6	29.5	10.8	16.5	6.1	1.4	1.0
Ft. Collins, CO	4.3	13.5	21.1	9.2	31.9	13.9	2.6	3.5
Ft. Wayne, IN	11.9	29.5	24.1	9.2	17.1	5.9	1.4	0.8
Ft. Worth, TX	20.6	24.3	23.5	5.8	17.7	6.0	1.4	0.8
Gainesville, FL	8.7	20.3	17.8	10.5	20.6	12.0	3.9	6.2
Grand Rapids, MI	16.0	25.2	22.8	7.1	18.9	7.3	1.6	1.0
Green Bay, WI	12.9	33.5	21.5	9.7	16.2	4.6	0.9	0.6
Greensboro, NC	12.6	23.7	21.6	6.5	23.9	8.6	1.7	1.4
Honolulu, HI	11.9	24.7	20.1	8.7	22.6	7.6	2.7	1.7
Houston, TX	24.8	22.4	19.3	4.6	18.0	7.0	2.3	1.5
Huntsville, AL	10.3	20.5	23.4	7.3	23.4	11.0	2.4	1.8
Indianapolis, IN	15.8	29.5	20.7	7.2	17.7	6.4	1.8	0.9
Jacksonville, FL	12.5	29.8	23.8	9.2	17.3	5.1	1.5	0.8
Kansas City, MO	12.5	25.9	23.5	6.8	19.6	8.4	2.3	1.1
Lafayette, LA	13.4	25.8	22.7	5.3	22.2	6.8	2.5	1.3
Las Vegas, NV	17.2	29.7	24.4	7.4	14.0	5.0	1.6	0.7
Lexington, KY	11.3	21.3	20.5	7.1	22.9	10.1	3.6	3.2
Lincoln, NE	6.8	22.8	23.9	10.6	23.3	7.7	2.0	2.8
Little Rock, AR	10.0	22.9	22.3	6.2	23.6	9.0	4.1	1.9
Los Angeles, CA	25.5	19.5	18.1	5.9	20.6	6.5	2.7	1.2
Louisville, KY	13.5	29.9	22.8	6.9	16.0	7.8	2.0	1.2
Lubbock, TX	14.3	24.9	25.2	6.2	19.1	6.6	2.0	1.7
Madison, WI	4.9	16.4	16.8	8.0	29.3	15.5	4.0	5.1
Manchester, NH	13.7	33.0	18.7	8.4	17.9	6.4	1.1	0.7

Table continued on next page.

City	Less than H.S.	H.S. Diploma	Some College, No Deg.	Associate Degree	Bachelors Degree	Masters Degree	Profess. School Degree	Doctorate Degree
McAllen, TX	26.1	20.4	21.5	5.3	18.7	4.9	2.4	0.6
Miami, FL	29.6	29.8	11.0	7.2	14.2	4.6	2.7	0.9
Midland, TX	18.0	23.3	28.3	7.2	16.7	4.8	1.1	0.6
Minneapolis, MN	11.7	17.1	18.4	6.7	29.1	11.0	3.7	2.4
Montgomery, AL	14.5	25.6	22.7	5.7	19.2	9.2	1.8	1.3
Nashville, TN	14.2	25.0	20.6	5.6	21.7	8.3	2.5	2.0
New Orleans, LA	15.9	24.4	22.3	4.4	19.1	7.8	3.9	2.2
New York, NY	20.4	24.8	14.7	6.1	20.2	9.5	3.0	1.3
Oklahoma City, OK	15.0	25.5	25.1	6.4	18.9	6.3	2.0	0.9
Omaha, NE	12.1	23.8	24.8	6.5	21.7	7.4	2.4	1.4
Orlando, FL	11.9	25.2	20.5	10.3	21.1	7.7	2.3	1.0
Oxnard, CA	36.7	20.0	20.3	7.2	11.3	3.3	0.8	0.4
Peoria, IL	11.2	28.1	21.2	7.7	19.3	8.8	2.5	1.2
Philadelphia, PA	19.3	34.7	17.4	5.0	13.6	6.3	2.3	1.3
Phoenix, AZ	19.4	24.3	23.0	7.3	17.1	6.3	1.8	0.8
Pittsburgh, PA	9.7	29.9	17.3	7.7	18.0	10.3	3.4	3.7
Portland, OR	9.6	17.6	22.8	6.8	26.0	11.3	3.9	2.0
Providence, RI	28.2	22.5	16.0	5.4	14.6	7.5	2.9	2.9
Provo, UT	10.2	14.3	28.8	8.3	26.5	7.7	1.7	2.5
Raleigh, NC	10.0	16.4	20.1	7.6	30.8	10.5	2.6	1.9
Reno, NV	15.0	23.7	26.4	6.5	17.8	6.5	2.3	1.8
Richmond, VA	18.8	22.8	18.7	5.4	21.0	9.0	2.9	1.4
Riverside, CA	22.5	23.3	25.0	7.4	12.5	6.4	1.4	1.6
Rochester, MN	6.7	21.1	20.0	11.3	24.4	9.9	4.4	2.2
Salem, OR	13.7	24.4	27.0	8.0	16.4	7.5	2.1	0.9
Salt Lake City, UT	14.7	16.9	21.1	6.5	23.8	9.7	4.0	3.2
San Antonio, TX	19.6	25.2	23.9	7.0	15.5	6.1	1.7	1.0
San Diego, CA	13.0	16.5	21.3	7.9	24.6	10.3	3.3	3.0
San Francisco, CA	13.9	13.6	15.1	5.3	32.1	13.0	4.9	2.2
San Jose, CA	17.5	18.7	18.9	7.6	23.6	10.3	1.7	1.7
Santa Rosa, CA	14.5	20.9	26.0	8.7	19.0	7.3	2.8	0.9
Savannah, GA	15.7	31.2	22.4	5.6	16.6	5.7	1.6	1.2
Seattle, WA	7.0	11.8	17.3	7.2	33.6	14.9	4.7	3.4
Sioux Falls, SD	9.6	28.4	20.1	9.9	21.4	7.2	1.9	1.4
Spokane, WA	8.4	25.1	27.2	10.7	17.8	7.5	2.2	1.3
Springfield, MO	12.5	27.4	26.5	7.2	17.5	5.8	1.7	1.5
Tallahassee, FL	7.5	16.4	19.3	8.9	27.1	13.4	3.9	3.4
Tampa, FL	14.2	27.3	18.2	7.7	20.2	7.8	3.2	1.5
Topeka, KS	11.1	32.3	22.4	7.0	17.1	6.8	2.4	0.9
Tulsa, OK	13.4	25.8	23.8	7.4	19.5	6.6	2.5	1.1
Virginia Beach, VA	6.6	23.2	27.6	10.1	21.1	8.4	2.0	0.9
Washington, DC	12.3	19.0	14.0	3.0	23.1	16.7	8.2	3.7
Wichita, KS	13.0	26.9	25.8	6.4	18.9	6.7	1.4	0.9
Wilmington, NC	11.2	19.5	19.1	10.4	26.2	9.5	2.4	1.7
Worcester, MA	16.1	28.5	17.6	7.9	18.3	8.5	1.8	1.3
U.S.	14.1	28.3	21.3	7.8	18.0	7.5	1.9	1.2

Note: Figures cover persons age 25 and over
Source: U.S. Census Bureau, 2010-2012 American Community Survey 3-Year Estimates

Highest Level of Education: Metro Area

Metro Area	Less than H.S.	H.S. Diploma	Some College, No Deg.	Associate Degree	Bachelors Degree	Masters Degree	Profess. School Degree	Doctorate Degree
Abilene, TX	16.8	30.4	25.5	6.3	14.1	4.8	1.2	0.9
Albuquerque, NM	12.6	25.1	24.8	7.8	16.7	8.9	2.0	2.1
Anchorage, AK	7.7	25.2	28.7	8.6	19.0	7.5	2.2	1.2
Ann Arbor, MI	6.2	16.5	20.0	6.9	24.7	16.0	4.6	5.1
Athens, GA	14.5	26.6	18.9	5.3	17.7	10.5	2.7	3.8
Atlanta, GA	12.5	24.9	20.9	7.0	22.6	8.7	2.2	1.3
Austin, TX	12.1	19.4	21.7	6.5	26.6	9.7	2.3	1.7
Baltimore, MD	11.4	26.5	20.0	6.4	20.4	10.8	2.6	1.9
Billings, MT	7.2	31.3	25.7	7.0	21.1	4.8	2.0	0.9
Boise City, ID	10.0	25.5	27.0	8.2	19.8	6.6	1.8	1.1
Boston, MA	9.4	24.7	15.7	7.2	24.0	13.1	3.2	2.7
Boulder, CO	5.8	13.2	17.5	5.4	32.2	17.0	3.6	5.2
Cape Coral, FL	13.2	33.0	22.0	7.8	15.0	6.0	1.9	1.1
Cedar Rapids, IA	6.6	29.5	23.3	11.4	20.8	6.1	1.5	0.8
Charleston, SC	12.2	26.1	22.3	8.4	20.2	7.8	1.9	1.2
Charlotte, NC	12.8	24.3	21.8	8.1	22.9	7.7	1.7	0.8
Chicago, IL	13.4	25.2	20.3	6.7	21.3	9.4	2.5	1.2
Cincinnati, OH	11.2	31.3	20.2	7.8	18.7	7.9	1.7	1.2
Clarksville, TN	11.6	33.0	27.1	8.2	13.3	5.2	1.1	0.7
Colorado Spgs, CO	6.1	22.3	26.1	10.8	21.3	10.5	1.7	1.3
Columbia, MO	7.1	20.7	18.7	6.2	27.8	12.3	3.2	4.0
Columbus, OH	9.9	28.7	20.8	7.3	21.6	8.2	2.0	1.5
Dallas, TX	16.3	23.0	22.8	6.5	21.2	7.7	1.6	1.0
Davenport, IA	9.9	31.1	23.7	10.5	16.3	6.5	1.4	0.6
Denver, CO	10.5	21.3	21.8	7.5	25.2	10.0	2.5	1.3
Des Moines, IA	7.7	27.2	20.9	10.0	24.3	7.0	1.9	1.0
Durham, NC	12.5	20.1	17.7	6.5	22.7	12.1	3.6	4.7
El Paso, TX	25.8	24.0	22.6	7.0	13.9	4.9	1.1	0.6
Erie, PA	9.5	41.2	16.9	8.0	15.3	6.4	1.6	1.1
Eugene, OR	9.3	25.4	29.8	7.9	16.8	7.2	1.7	1.8
Fargo, ND	5.2	22.4	24.3	12.5	24.6	7.1	2.1	1.8
Fayetteville, NC	11.6	27.1	28.4	10.9	14.8	5.4	1.1	0.7
Ft. Collins, CO	5.3	18.6	23.0	8.9	27.4	11.7	2.3	2.7
Ft. Wayne, IN	10.5	32.4	22.9	9.5	16.3	6.2	1.4	0.7
Ft. Worth, TX	16.3	23.0	22.8	6.5	21.2	7.7	1.6	1.0
Gainesville, FL	9.5	23.0	18.5	10.7	20.0	10.0	3.8	4.6
Grand Rapids, MI	10.7	30.0	23.1	8.6	18.2	6.9	1.6	0.8
Green Bay, WI	9.6	35.0	20.7	10.8	17.0	5.3	1.0	0.6
Greensboro, NC	15.2	29.1	21.6	7.8	18.1	6.2	1.2	0.9
Honolulu, HI	9.7	26.8	22.0	9.9	20.9	7.1	2.3	1.3
Houston, TX	19.0	23.8	22.0	6.2	19.0	6.8	1.9	1.3
Huntsville, AL	11.7	23.7	22.5	7.3	21.7	10.2	1.6	1.4
Indianapolis, IN	11.4	29.6	20.3	7.5	20.4	7.5	2.1	1.2
Jacksonville, FL	11.3	28.9	23.4	9.2	18.8	6.0	1.6	1.0
Kansas City, MO	9.5	26.7	23.6	7.3	21.1	8.7	2.1	1.0
Lafayette, LA	15.9	33.5	21.3	4.6	17.5	4.7	1.6	0.9
Las Vegas, NV	16.1	29.7	25.1	7.1	14.7	4.9	1.6	0.7
Lexington, KY	13.0	25.6	20.7	7.0	19.9	8.7	3.0	2.3
Lincoln, NE	6.6	23.5	23.7	11.0	23.0	7.7	2.0	2.7
Little Rock, AR	11.4	30.7	23.5	6.6	18.1	6.4	2.0	1.2
Los Angeles, CA	21.8	20.0	19.9	7.0	20.5	7.1	2.5	1.3
Louisville, KY	12.7	31.4	22.6	7.4	15.8	7.3	1.9	0.9
Lubbock, TX	15.6	25.7	25.1	6.0	18.0	6.2	1.9	1.5
Madison, WI	5.5	22.6	19.4	9.7	25.3	11.5	3.1	3.0
Manchester, NH	9.2	27.3	18.4	9.6	22.6	10.2	1.5	1.2

Table continued on next page.

Metro Area	Less than H.S.	H.S. Diploma	Some College, No Deg.	Associate Degree	Bachelors Degree	Masters Degree	Profess. School Degree	Doctorate Degree
McAllen, TX	37.7	24.2	17.6	4.4	11.2	3.4	1.0	0.5
Miami, FL	16.4	27.9	18.4	8.5	18.2	6.7	2.7	1.2
Midland, TX	18.5	23.8	27.5	7.3	16.3	4.9	1.0	0.6
Minneapolis, MN	7.0	22.9	21.8	9.6	25.9	9.0	2.5	1.4
Montgomery, AL	14.8	29.4	22.1	6.7	16.9	7.7	1.5	0.9
Nashville, TN	12.8	29.0	21.0	6.3	20.3	7.1	2.0	1.5
New Orleans, LA	15.5	29.7	22.9	5.5	17.0	5.7	2.5	1.2
New York, NY	15.2	26.2	15.7	6.4	21.5	10.5	3.0	1.4
Oklahoma City, OK	12.4	27.4	25.3	6.6	18.5	6.7	1.8	1.2
Omaha, NE	8.9	25.6	24.4	8.1	22.1	7.7	2.0	1.1
Orlando, FL	12.6	28.5	21.3	9.8	18.4	6.8	1.7	0.9
Oxnard, CA	17.5	18.6	24.1	8.5	20.0	7.9	2.3	1.2
Peoria, IL	8.9	32.4	23.5	9.4	17.2	6.4	1.4	0.8
Philadelphia, PA	11.3	31.0	17.9	6.5	20.2	9.0	2.5	1.6
Phoenix, AZ	13.8	24.1	25.5	8.3	18.5	7.1	1.7	1.0
Pittsburgh, PA	8.2	35.9	16.9	9.2	18.5	8.0	1.9	1.4
Portland, OR	9.5	22.4	25.7	8.3	21.6	8.7	2.4	1.4
Providence, RI	16.2	28.1	18.2	8.3	18.0	8.2	1.8	1.2
Provo, UT	6.6	17.9	29.1	10.6	25.1	7.4	1.5	1.8
Raleigh, NC	10.2	20.1	19.6	8.8	27.4	10.0	2.0	1.9
Reno, NV	13.7	25.1	26.8	7.2	17.2	6.3	2.2	1.4
Richmond, VA	13.4	27.1	20.9	6.6	20.4	8.5	2.0	1.2
Riverside, CA	21.4	25.7	25.7	7.7	12.6	4.8	1.3	0.8
Rochester, MN	6.4	25.3	21.1	11.9	22.1	8.3	3.4	1.6
Salem, OR	15.5	26.9	26.9	8.2	14.4	5.9	1.5	0.7
Salt Lake City, UT	11.1	23.3	26.2	8.5	20.2	7.3	2.0	1.4
San Antonio, TX	17.1	25.4	24.0	7.5	16.7	6.7	1.6	1.0
San Diego, CA	14.7	19.2	22.6	9.5	21.1	8.4	2.5	2.0
San Francisco, CA	12.5	17.4	19.1	6.8	26.8	11.4	3.5	2.4
San Jose, CA	13.6	16.0	17.5	7.1	25.6	14.3	2.6	3.2
Santa Rosa, CA	13.1	20.7	25.5	8.7	20.7	7.5	2.7	1.2
Savannah, GA	12.6	28.7	22.8	7.0	18.9	6.9	1.9	1.1
Seattle, WA	8.6	21.6	23.4	9.2	23.8	9.5	2.4	1.6
Sioux Falls, SD	8.4	30.0	20.5	11.0	20.7	6.5	1.7	1.1
Spokane, WA	7.3	25.2	27.4	11.3	18.3	7.4	1.9	1.1
Springfield, MO	11.0	30.6	25.9	7.1	17.2	5.6	1.5	1.1
Tallahassee, FL	11.0	24.7	20.2	7.9	21.0	10.2	2.5	2.5
Tampa, FL	12.5	30.8	21.6	9.1	17.3	6.1	1.7	0.9
Topeka, KS	8.7	34.3	23.5	6.8	17.3	6.6	2.0	0.8
Tulsa, OK	11.9	29.8	24.1	8.4	17.8	5.6	1.6	0.8
Virginia Beach, VA	10.3	26.2	26.0	8.8	18.0	8.0	1.7	1.0
Washington, DC	10.0	19.4	17.4	5.6	24.8	15.5	4.3	2.9
Wichita, KS	11.1	27.8	26.2	7.2	18.9	6.8	1.3	0.8
Wilmington, NC	11.4	25.5	22.6	9.6	20.8	7.3	1.8	1.2
Worcester, MA	10.8	28.4	18.0	9.1	20.8	9.8	1.8	1.4
U.S.	14.1	28.3	21.3	7.8	18.0	7.5	1.9	1.2

Note: Figures cover persons age 25 and over; Figures cover the Metropolitan Statistical Area—see Appendix B for areas included
Source: U.S. Census Bureau, 2010-2012 American Community Survey 3-Year Estimates

School Enrollment by Grade and Control: City

City	Preschool (%)		Kindergarten (%)		Grades 1 - 4 (%)		Grades 5 - 8 (%)		Grades 9 - 12 (%)	
	Public	Private	Public	Private	Public	Private	Public	Private	Public	Private
Abilene, TX	78.7	21.3	99.0	1.0	94.3	5.7	91.9	8.1	94.9	5.1
Albuquerque, NM	58.7	41.3	89.8	10.2	88.7	11.3	89.1	10.9	89.4	10.6
Anchorage, AK	45.2	54.8	89.6	10.4	91.6	8.4	91.8	8.2	91.4	8.6
Ann Arbor, MI	25.6	74.4	88.7	11.3	88.5	11.5	85.1	14.9	89.7	10.3
Athens, GA	60.5	39.5	84.6	15.4	93.9	6.1	86.0	14.0	90.8	9.2
Atlanta, GA	54.6	45.4	82.9	17.1	85.2	14.8	83.6	16.4	81.6	18.4
Austin, TX	48.3	51.7	88.7	11.3	90.4	9.6	90.9	9.1	93.0	7.0
Baltimore, MD	71.0	29.0	83.2	16.8	88.5	11.5	85.3	14.7	87.8	12.2
Billings, MT	40.9	59.1	93.1	6.9	93.8	6.2	93.4	6.6	91.4	8.6
Boise City, ID	58.5	41.5	92.6	7.4	94.7	5.3	95.8	4.2	93.5	6.5
Boston, MA	53.7	46.3	79.9	20.1	84.8	15.2	84.9	15.1	86.5	13.5
Boulder, CO	29.0	71.0	86.2	13.8	87.0	13.0	85.0	15.0	92.8	7.2
Cape Coral, FL	65.6	34.4	92.8	7.2	92.3	7.7	95.2	4.8	93.6	6.4
Cedar Rapids, IA	54.0	46.0	90.3	9.7	83.9	16.1	89.2	10.8	88.7	11.3
Charleston, SC	35.2	64.8	80.4	19.6	81.3	18.7	81.4	18.6	84.2	15.8
Charlotte, NC	39.9	60.1	89.8	10.2	89.0	11.0	87.2	12.8	89.4	10.6
Chicago, IL	65.5	34.5	82.7	17.3	86.8	13.2	87.2	12.8	88.3	11.7
Cincinnati, OH	62.9	37.1	88.1	11.9	78.1	21.9	79.4	20.6	82.1	17.9
Clarksville, TN	60.5	39.5	93.0	7.0	92.8	7.2	94.3	5.7	90.1	9.9
Colorado Spgs, CO	56.9	43.1	93.5	6.5	95.1	4.9	94.7	5.3	92.3	7.7
Columbia, MO	45.8	54.2	85.0	15.0	88.4	11.6	82.6	17.4	93.6	6.4
Columbus, OH	52.3	47.7	88.4	11.6	87.6	12.4	87.4	12.6	88.6	11.4
Dallas, TX	70.8	29.2	89.1	10.9	91.7	8.3	90.3	9.7	90.8	9.2
Davenport, IA	56.5	43.5	87.8	12.2	91.7	8.3	87.4	12.6	94.5	5.5
Denver, CO	57.8	42.2	87.1	12.9	88.8	11.2	87.6	12.4	90.1	9.9
Des Moines, IA	58.2	41.8	87.4	12.6	89.4	10.6	90.2	9.8	92.9	7.1
Durham, NC	48.6	51.4	93.4	6.6	92.0	8.0	88.8	11.2	92.5	7.5
El Paso, TX	80.9	19.1	94.7	5.3	93.9	6.1	94.5	5.5	95.4	4.6
Erie, PA	48.2	51.8	80.9	19.1	85.4	14.6	85.6	14.4	83.3	16.7
Eugene, OR	43.3	56.7	84.2	15.8	86.2	13.8	89.5	10.5	88.7	11.3
Fargo, ND	38.6	61.4	84.2	15.8	80.1	19.9	85.1	14.9	92.1	7.9
Fayetteville, NC	81.6	18.4	92.7	7.3	91.7	8.3	90.0	10.0	90.0	10.0
Ft. Collins, CO	26.0	74.0	96.7	3.3	91.1	8.9	87.6	12.4	98.0	2.0
Ft. Wayne, IN	52.5	47.5	80.8	19.2	83.5	16.5	81.2	18.8	86.7	13.3
Ft. Worth, TX	62.5	37.5	92.7	7.3	91.9	8.1	92.1	7.9	93.2	6.8
Gainesville, FL	51.6	48.4	74.4	25.6	89.6	10.4	90.7	9.3	93.9	6.1
Grand Rapids, MI	71.7	28.3	78.0	22.0	83.7	16.3	84.3	15.7	81.0	19.0
Green Bay, WI	78.5	21.5	88.0	12.0	91.8	8.2	90.6	9.4	90.5	9.5
Greensboro, NC	51.9	48.1	90.9	9.1	92.6	7.4	91.0	9.0	91.0	9.0
Honolulu, HI	34.3	65.7	82.0	18.0	79.3	20.7	78.4	21.6	76.0	24.0
Houston, TX	67.0	33.0	92.2	7.8	93.5	6.5	93.7	6.3	93.1	6.9
Huntsville, AL	37.5	62.5	86.6	13.4	84.7	15.3	81.9	18.1	85.8	14.2
Indianapolis, IN	42.1	57.9	82.3	17.7	89.0	11.0	88.2	11.8	88.3	11.7
Jacksonville, FL	54.8	45.2	84.1	15.9	85.9	14.1	85.3	14.7	84.2	15.8
Kansas City, MO	55.7	44.3	84.4	15.6	84.7	15.3	84.5	15.5	86.4	13.6
Lafayette, LA	50.0	50.0	81.3	18.7	78.2	21.8	67.4	32.6	76.3	23.7
Las Vegas, NV	45.7	54.3	92.5	7.5	93.0	7.0	91.5	8.5	93.9	6.1
Lexington, KY	41.5	58.5	85.4	14.6	86.8	13.2	85.4	14.6	87.7	12.3
Lincoln, NE	45.6	54.4	83.4	16.6	83.5	16.5	84.1	15.9	87.8	12.2
Little Rock, AR	54.1	45.9	88.6	11.4	86.0	14.0	79.6	20.4	82.2	17.8
Los Angeles, CA	63.1	36.9	87.1	12.9	89.3	10.7	88.9	11.1	90.0	10.0
Louisville, KY	45.6	54.4	82.8	17.2	80.4	19.6	80.0	20.0	79.9	20.1
Lubbock, TX	64.5	35.5	88.2	11.8	93.0	7.0	95.8	4.2	97.0	3.0
Madison, WI	37.2	62.8	89.5	10.5	90.8	9.2	88.2	11.8	94.8	5.2
Manchester, NH	50.0	50.0	78.9	21.1	89.9	10.1	91.5	8.5	96.6	3.4

Table continued on next page.

City	Preschool (%)		Kindergarten (%)		Grades 1 - 4 (%)		Grades 5 - 8 (%)		Grades 9 - 12 (%)	
	Public	Private	Public	Private	Public	Private	Public	Private	Public	Private
McAllen, TX	74.5	25.5	90.7	9.3	95.6	4.4	93.2	6.8	94.5	5.5
Miami, FL	59.5	40.5	84.8	15.2	87.9	12.1	89.7	10.3	91.2	8.8
Midland, TX	38.2	61.8	77.7	22.3	89.1	10.9	88.0	12.0	89.3	10.7
Minneapolis, MN	59.1	40.9	86.4	13.6	89.2	10.8	86.9	13.1	90.5	9.5
Montgomery, AL	52.1	47.9	85.9	14.1	86.4	13.6	83.5	16.5	79.4	20.6
Nashville, TN	56.3	43.7	89.2	10.8	87.2	12.8	82.8	17.2	82.4	17.6
New Orleans, LA	55.7	44.3	70.5	29.5	79.6	20.4	77.4	22.6	79.2	20.8
New York, NY	55.0	45.0	79.3	20.7	82.3	17.7	82.3	17.7	83.4	16.6
Oklahoma City, OK	69.8	30.2	91.9	8.1	91.2	8.8	91.2	8.8	91.4	8.6
Omaha, NE	58.1	41.9	80.4	19.6	84.4	15.6	85.2	14.8	88.3	11.7
Orlando, FL	49.6	50.4	79.9	20.1	87.1	12.9	88.8	11.2	89.9	10.1
Oxnard, CA	75.0	25.0	98.0	2.0	94.2	5.8	94.3	5.7	95.9	4.1
Peoria, IL	63.8	36.2	91.6	8.4	84.6	15.4	82.1	17.9	91.8	8.2
Philadelphia, PA	59.2	40.8	82.6	17.4	80.8	19.2	79.1	20.9	82.7	17.3
Phoenix, AZ	59.2	40.8	91.6	8.4	94.1	5.9	94.6	5.4	93.1	6.9
Pittsburgh, PA	61.3	38.7	78.9	21.1	80.8	19.2	78.5	21.5	82.4	17.6
Portland, OR	40.2	59.8	84.7	15.3	89.2	10.8	90.4	9.6	88.3	11.7
Providence, RI	67.8	32.2	84.1	15.9	90.4	9.6	86.3	13.7	86.6	13.4
Provo, UT	44.6	55.4	91.6	8.4	94.3	5.7	92.3	7.7	89.5	10.5
Raleigh, NC	32.1	67.9	88.9	11.1	90.6	9.4	90.7	9.3	93.0	7.0
Reno, NV	57.9	42.1	90.4	9.6	92.6	7.4	93.5	6.5	95.5	4.5
Richmond, VA	52.7	47.3	86.4	13.6	87.2	12.8	87.1	12.9	86.7	13.3
Riverside, CA	72.7	27.3	91.5	8.5	92.9	7.1	93.1	6.9	95.6	4.4
Rochester, MN	50.8	49.2	78.8	21.2	85.8	14.2	88.1	11.9	91.0	9.0
Salem, OR	59.6	40.4	87.5	12.5	94.5	5.5	94.0	6.0	93.7	6.3
Salt Lake City, UT	48.3	51.7	88.3	11.7	92.7	7.3	91.8	8.2	90.5	9.5
San Antonio, TX	64.7	35.3	88.9	11.1	93.6	6.4	92.8	7.2	93.2	6.8
San Diego, CA	54.4	45.6	90.2	9.8	91.4	8.6	93.0	7.0	93.2	6.8
San Francisco, CA	34.6	65.4	70.9	29.1	71.6	28.4	69.9	30.1	81.4	18.6
San Jose, CA	43.6	56.4	83.3	16.7	89.1	10.9	90.7	9.3	90.5	9.5
Santa Rosa, CA	53.8	46.2	90.6	9.4	97.3	2.7	95.6	4.4	91.6	8.4
Savannah, GA	72.1	27.9	89.2	10.8	92.7	7.3	88.2	11.8	85.9	14.1
Seattle, WA	31.8	68.2	75.2	24.8	78.7	21.3	80.3	19.7	80.1	19.9
Sioux Falls, SD	51.9	48.1	84.6	15.4	87.8	12.2	90.8	9.2	92.9	7.1
Spokane, WA	41.1	58.9	85.2	14.8	84.9	15.1	87.9	12.1	91.7	8.3
Springfield, MO	60.8	39.2	90.5	9.5	90.2	9.8	91.5	8.5	91.8	8.2
Tallahassee, FL	44.3	55.7	80.1	19.9	86.5	13.5	89.7	10.3	90.5	9.5
Tampa, FL	56.7	43.3	92.0	8.0	90.7	9.3	85.7	14.3	92.9	7.1
Topeka, KS	71.4	28.6	99.2	0.8	88.4	11.6	90.8	9.2	89.7	10.3
Tulsa, OK	72.5	27.5	88.7	11.3	89.0	11.0	87.8	12.2	87.3	12.7
Virginia Beach, VA	32.8	67.2	81.6	18.4	88.6	11.4	90.6	9.4	92.9	7.1
Washington, DC	71.3	28.7	83.8	16.2	84.0	16.0	79.0	21.0	84.5	15.5
Wichita, KS	66.3	33.7	85.3	14.7	87.2	12.8	86.1	13.9	83.1	16.9
Wilmington, NC	41.8	58.2	82.9	17.1	90.0	10.0	84.2	15.8	86.8	13.2
Worcester, MA	70.2	29.8	93.0	7.0	89.7	10.3	85.6	14.4	87.7	12.3
U.S.	56.9	43.1	87.8	12.2	89.9	10.1	90.0	10.0	90.8	9.2

Note: Figures shown cover persons 3 years old and over
Source: U.S. Census Bureau, 2010-2012 American Community Survey 3-Year Estimates

School Enrollment by Grade and Control: Metro Area

Metro Area	Preschool (%)		Kindergarten (%)		Grades 1 - 4 (%)		Grades 5 - 8 (%)		Grades 9 - 12 (%)	
	Public	Private	Public	Private	Public	Private	Public	Private	Public	Private
Abilene, TX	78.5	21.5	98.4	1.6	94.3	5.7	93.2	6.8	93.9	6.1
Albuquerque, NM	63.1	36.9	88.5	11.5	89.8	10.2	90.3	9.7	90.8	9.2
Anchorage, AK	48.9	51.1	89.2	10.8	90.1	9.9	90.5	9.5	90.3	9.7
Ann Arbor, MI	44.9	55.1	83.7	16.3	88.3	11.7	88.6	11.4	91.2	8.8
Athens, GA	64.4	35.6	87.3	12.7	93.9	6.1	85.7	14.3	89.9	10.1
Atlanta, GA	53.5	46.5	88.5	11.5	90.4	9.6	89.6	10.4	90.9	9.1
Austin, TX	50.8	49.2	88.7	11.3	92.4	7.6	92.4	7.6	93.5	6.5
Baltimore, MD	48.4	51.6	84.3	15.7	87.1	12.9	85.2	14.8	85.5	14.5
Billings, MT	45.7	54.3	92.6	7.4	93.2	6.8	90.8	9.2	89.5	10.5
Boise City, ID	44.8	55.2	92.7	7.3	93.7	6.3	94.4	5.6	93.8	6.2
Boston, MA	41.6	58.4	86.1	13.9	90.4	9.6	88.9	11.1	86.8	13.2
Boulder, CO	44.0	56.0	92.9	7.1	90.8	9.2	88.6	11.4	94.5	5.5
Cape Coral, FL	61.1	38.9	93.7	6.3	93.3	6.7	90.3	9.7	92.5	7.5
Cedar Rapids, IA	57.1	42.9	86.5	13.5	85.3	14.7	89.9	10.1	91.3	8.7
Charleston, SC	46.5	53.5	84.2	15.8	88.2	11.8	89.8	10.2	90.2	9.8
Charlotte, NC	43.5	56.5	90.2	9.8	89.9	10.1	89.3	10.7	89.6	10.4
Chicago, IL	56.7	43.3	85.2	14.8	88.6	11.4	88.8	11.2	91.0	9.0
Cincinnati, OH	48.7	51.3	84.3	15.7	83.4	16.6	82.5	17.5	83.6	16.4
Clarksville, TN	66.8	33.2	88.4	11.6	89.5	10.5	91.4	8.6	89.4	10.6
Colorado Spgs, CO	59.1	40.9	92.1	7.9	92.8	7.2	93.2	6.8	92.6	7.4
Columbia, MO	46.7	53.3	90.6	9.4	89.8	10.2	85.9	14.1	92.3	7.7
Columbus, OH	47.8	52.2	86.4	13.6	88.3	11.7	88.2	11.8	89.8	10.2
Dallas, TX	55.6	44.4	90.2	9.8	92.2	7.8	92.4	7.6	92.7	7.3
Davenport, IA	64.6	35.4	90.4	9.6	92.5	7.5	90.0	10.0	92.6	7.4
Denver, CO	55.9	44.1	89.3	10.7	91.7	8.3	91.4	8.6	91.9	8.1
Des Moines, IA	56.5	43.5	86.2	13.8	90.8	9.2	91.7	8.3	91.5	8.5
Durham, NC	42.9	57.1	92.4	7.6	91.9	8.1	89.8	10.2	91.5	8.5
El Paso, TX	83.8	16.2	95.5	4.5	95.1	4.9	95.4	4.6	96.3	3.7
Erie, PA	50.1	49.9	84.9	15.1	89.2	10.8	89.1	10.9	86.8	13.2
Eugene, OR	49.9	50.1	85.0	15.0	90.9	9.1	91.8	8.2	91.1	8.9
Fargo, ND	50.9	49.1	90.4	9.6	87.5	12.5	91.7	8.3	92.3	7.7
Fayetteville, NC	78.0	22.0	93.6	6.4	91.0	9.0	90.6	9.4	90.4	9.6
Ft. Collins, CO	28.4	71.6	86.2	13.8	92.0	8.0	90.5	9.5	97.1	2.9
Ft. Wayne, IN	47.9	52.1	78.6	21.4	81.8	18.2	80.9	19.1	88.4	11.6
Ft. Worth, TX	55.6	44.4	90.2	9.8	92.2	7.8	92.4	7.6	92.7	7.3
Gainesville, FL	46.5	53.5	82.1	17.9	86.2	13.8	87.8	12.2	86.0	14.0
Grand Rapids, MI	63.4	36.6	85.2	14.8	87.9	12.1	86.3	13.7	86.9	13.1
Green Bay, WI	75.6	24.4	88.7	11.3	89.9	10.1	90.6	9.4	93.0	7.0
Greensboro, NC	57.3	42.7	89.6	10.4	91.8	8.2	91.1	8.9	90.5	9.5
Honolulu, HI	35.2	64.8	82.5	17.5	82.1	17.9	78.4	21.6	76.6	23.4
Houston, TX	57.0	43.0	90.6	9.4	93.8	6.2	94.4	5.6	93.9	6.1
Huntsville, AL	43.8	56.2	84.2	15.8	86.0	14.0	87.4	12.6	87.0	13.0
Indianapolis, IN	43.7	56.3	83.7	16.3	88.8	11.2	90.2	9.8	88.7	11.3
Jacksonville, FL	51.8	48.2	84.9	15.1	86.4	13.6	87.1	12.9	87.3	12.7
Kansas City, MO	52.6	47.4	85.7	14.3	89.0	11.0	88.5	11.5	89.1	10.9
Lafayette, LA	49.1	50.9	82.4	17.6	77.5	22.5	74.3	25.7	79.6	20.4
Las Vegas, NV	53.5	46.5	91.1	8.9	93.7	6.3	94.6	5.4	95.5	4.5
Lexington, KY	45.6	54.4	86.4	13.6	86.6	13.4	85.5	14.5	87.0	13.0
Lincoln, NE	46.2	53.8	82.2	17.8	82.5	17.5	83.5	16.5	87.8	12.2
Little Rock, AR	57.1	42.9	90.0	10.0	88.2	11.8	88.5	11.5	87.7	12.3
Los Angeles, CA	58.9	41.1	88.4	11.6	90.3	9.7	90.7	9.3	92.2	7.8
Louisville, KY	48.3	51.7	84.7	15.3	83.7	16.3	83.2	16.8	83.8	16.2
Lubbock, TX	64.2	35.8	87.3	12.7	92.5	7.5	95.3	4.7	95.6	4.4
Madison, WI	48.9	51.1	89.5	10.5	90.2	9.8	89.3	10.7	94.6	5.4
Manchester, NH	41.4	58.6	74.9	25.1	89.6	10.4	89.7	10.3	91.3	8.7

Table continued on next page.

Metro Area	Preschool (%)		Kindergarten (%)		Grades 1 - 4 (%)		Grades 5 - 8 (%)		Grades 9 - 12 (%)	
	Public	Private	Public	Private	Public	Private	Public	Private	Public	Private
McAllen, TX	89.3	10.7	96.7	3.3	97.6	2.4	97.4	2.6	97.1	2.9
Miami, FL	48.7	51.3	82.6	17.4	86.9	13.1	88.2	11.8	88.1	11.9
Midland, TX	43.2	56.8	81.3	18.7	90.9	9.1	88.7	11.3	87.9	12.1
Minneapolis, MN	52.5	47.5	87.2	12.8	87.5	12.5	88.2	11.8	91.1	8.9
Montgomery, AL	49.3	50.7	80.1	19.9	83.7	16.3	82.1	17.9	78.0	22.0
Nashville, TN	48.4	51.6	89.4	10.6	88.8	11.2	86.4	13.6	85.8	14.2
New Orleans, LA	54.2	45.8	72.6	27.4	77.5	22.5	75.8	24.2	75.0	25.0
New York, NY	49.6	50.4	82.0	18.0	86.1	13.9	86.3	13.7	86.1	13.9
Oklahoma City, OK	71.9	28.1	91.2	8.8	91.8	8.2	91.3	8.7	92.0	8.0
Omaha, NE	53.2	46.8	84.6	15.4	86.6	13.4	86.9	13.1	87.2	12.8
Orlando, FL	48.6	51.4	85.4	14.6	88.5	11.5	88.0	12.0	90.7	9.3
Oxnard, CA	50.8	49.2	90.1	9.9	90.9	9.1	90.3	9.7	90.9	9.1
Peoria, IL	63.8	36.2	90.7	9.3	87.9	12.1	86.7	13.3	92.7	7.3
Philadelphia, PA	43.5	56.5	79.4	20.6	84.3	15.7	83.3	16.7	84.0	16.0
Phoenix, AZ	56.9	43.1	91.3	8.7	93.2	6.8	94.9	5.1	94.1	5.9
Pittsburgh, PA	47.4	52.6	86.1	13.9	87.9	12.1	87.8	12.2	90.4	9.6
Portland, OR	37.7	62.3	84.3	15.7	90.2	9.8	91.6	8.4	91.6	8.4
Providence, RI	49.7	50.3	85.0	15.0	89.3	10.7	90.3	9.7	87.9	12.1
Provo, UT	43.0	57.0	92.7	7.3	95.1	4.9	94.5	5.5	96.0	4.0
Raleigh, NC	33.1	66.9	88.5	11.5	89.9	10.1	89.7	10.3	91.2	8.8
Reno, NV	50.9	49.1	88.6	11.4	92.4	7.6	93.3	6.7	93.6	6.4
Richmond, VA	38.5	61.5	89.4	10.6	90.9	9.1	92.0	8.0	91.4	8.6
Riverside, CA	65.5	34.5	93.1	6.9	94.5	5.5	94.3	5.7	94.6	5.4
Rochester, MN	60.1	39.9	83.3	16.7	88.1	11.9	89.4	10.6	91.9	8.1
Salem, OR	56.4	43.6	88.1	11.9	90.6	9.4	90.4	9.6	93.1	6.9
Salt Lake City, UT	47.3	52.7	90.5	9.5	92.8	7.2	93.2	6.8	93.2	6.8
San Antonio, TX	62.1	37.9	90.1	9.9	92.7	7.3	92.8	7.2	93.1	6.9
San Diego, CA	53.2	46.8	90.8	9.2	92.0	8.0	92.6	7.4	93.4	6.6
San Francisco, CA	40.7	59.3	82.7	17.3	85.2	14.8	85.9	14.1	88.4	11.6
San Jose, CA	34.1	65.9	82.5	17.5	87.1	12.9	88.3	11.7	89.4	10.6
Santa Rosa, CA	43.7	56.3	88.4	11.6	91.9	8.1	92.3	7.7	92.3	7.7
Savannah, GA	56.0	44.0	91.8	8.2	90.2	9.8	88.3	11.7	85.5	14.5
Seattle, WA	40.7	59.3	83.3	16.7	88.9	11.1	89.4	10.6	91.1	8.9
Sioux Falls, SD	53.9	46.1	89.0	11.0	89.2	10.8	90.3	9.7	93.0	7.0
Spokane, WA	39.8	60.2	84.1	15.9	89.0	11.0	89.0	11.0	92.0	8.0
Springfield, MO	63.9	36.1	92.6	7.4	88.8	11.2	88.3	11.7	90.4	9.6
Tallahassee, FL	55.8	44.2	79.3	20.7	87.2	12.8	86.9	13.1	86.7	13.3
Tampa, FL	58.8	41.2	89.1	10.9	89.4	10.6	88.0	12.0	91.7	8.3
Topeka, KS	74.2	25.8	94.8	5.2	88.4	11.6	90.3	9.7	91.1	8.9
Tulsa, OK	71.4	28.6	88.9	11.1	90.9	9.1	89.6	10.4	89.4	10.6
Virginia Beach, VA	53.1	46.9	85.7	14.3	90.2	9.8	91.2	8.8	93.1	6.9
Washington, DC	40.1	59.9	83.6	16.4	87.2	12.8	87.2	12.8	89.0	11.0
Wichita, KS	64.0	36.0	86.1	13.9	88.0	12.0	87.9	12.1	86.7	13.3
Wilmington, NC	46.3	53.7	88.7	11.3	90.2	9.8	91.9	8.1	90.7	9.3
Worcester, MA	54.3	45.7	86.9	13.1	91.4	8.6	91.3	8.7	90.7	9.3
U.S.	56.9	43.1	87.8	12.2	89.9	10.1	90.0	10.0	90.8	9.2

Note: Figures shown cover persons 3 years old and over; Figures cover the Metropolitan Statistical Area—see Appendix B for areas included;
Source: U.S. Census Bureau, 2010-2012 American Community Survey 3-Year Estimates

Educational Attainment by Race: City

City	High School Graduate or Higher (%)					Bachelor's Degree or Higher (%)				
	Total	White	Black	Asian	Hisp.[1]	Total	White	Black	Asian	Hisp.[1]
Abilene, TX	82.3	84.7	71.7	82.6	61.7	22.1	24.2	9.1	30.6	6.8
Albuquerque, NM	88.7	91.4	89.6	83.9	79.1	32.9	37.3	29.6	43.8	17.8
Anchorage, AK	92.3	95.5	87.6	78.1	81.9	32.5	37.3	24.9	23.5	21.2
Ann Arbor, MI	96.0	96.7	91.2	96.3	92.9	69.3	70.0	38.7	84.4	55.8
Athens, GA	85.8	89.8	77.1	92.0	55.6	40.4	52.5	10.9	70.5	10.5
Atlanta, GA	87.9	95.8	81.2	95.6	74.1	46.5	73.0	22.5	82.2	36.2
Austin, TX	86.4	89.2	88.1	92.9	62.5	44.9	49.2	20.9	69.1	17.8
Baltimore, MD	79.3	84.5	76.7	91.5	57.7	26.1	47.1	13.0	70.4	20.1
Billings, MT	93.1	93.9	n/a	76.6	80.9	30.8	31.8	n/a	17.3	13.5
Boise City, ID	93.6	94.5	81.8	83.5	77.9	37.5	38.1	14.0	49.4	17.8
Boston, MA	84.8	91.9	79.7	75.8	66.1	43.4	58.5	17.3	45.8	17.0
Boulder, CO	95.7	97.3	n/a	97.0	61.4	71.3	73.5	n/a	75.0	29.0
Cape Coral, FL	89.8	90.2	88.9	75.9	75.1	19.5	19.9	10.4	29.0	15.3
Cedar Rapids, IA	92.9	93.5	83.3	90.6	65.6	31.4	31.6	14.5	59.1	12.0
Charleston, SC	92.3	96.2	80.1	n/a	89.1	48.2	57.8	15.8	n/a	30.3
Charlotte, NC	88.3	91.5	86.9	84.4	57.5	39.8	50.0	22.8	55.2	15.5
Chicago, IL	80.8	85.1	81.1	85.8	59.3	33.8	45.1	17.6	58.3	12.4
Cincinnati, OH	84.5	89.2	78.3	96.4	57.4	31.3	45.2	11.2	78.1	25.9
Clarksville, TN	91.2	92.4	89.2	86.1	82.3	23.9	25.2	19.4	32.2	17.8
Colorado Spgs, CO	93.1	94.7	91.0	88.5	79.2	36.1	38.7	20.4	36.7	14.7
Columbia, MO	94.0	95.7	84.8	91.0	78.9	56.0	59.0	27.6	71.6	43.1
Columbus, OH	88.3	90.3	85.6	88.6	64.4	32.4	37.2	16.3	63.5	18.5
Dallas, TX	73.8	75.3	82.9	83.1	44.3	29.2	38.0	15.0	56.5	8.2
Davenport, IA	90.8	92.1	85.4	65.1	76.9	26.0	27.7	12.5	23.2	12.4
Denver, CO	85.3	88.7	87.1	77.6	59.0	42.8	49.3	22.1	45.1	10.7
Des Moines, IA	87.0	89.7	82.8	70.9	51.6	24.9	26.7	15.1	25.9	7.0
Durham, NC	87.1	90.2	86.7	94.9	45.1	45.9	58.7	29.6	76.9	13.1
El Paso, TX	76.6	77.4	92.2	87.7	71.6	22.6	22.8	28.6	49.1	17.9
Erie, PA	86.4	88.3	80.9	62.1	71.6	20.3	21.5	13.6	29.9	11.4
Eugene, OR	93.3	93.9	97.5	94.3	68.7	39.4	39.5	21.3	60.3	20.8
Fargo, ND	95.4	96.4	80.7	90.8	83.5	39.2	39.5	33.7	61.7	15.9
Fayetteville, NC	90.8	93.5	88.3	83.4	90.1	25.0	27.9	21.2	37.6	17.0
Ft. Collins, CO	95.7	96.3	86.8	95.3	79.0	51.9	52.9	37.7	59.6	27.0
Ft. Wayne, IN	88.1	90.9	82.3	61.5	61.9	25.3	27.7	11.4	34.2	16.1
Ft. Worth, TX	79.4	81.1	85.2	79.7	51.3	25.9	29.8	16.2	37.5	8.6
Gainesville, FL	91.3	94.3	82.4	95.6	89.3	42.8	50.0	13.6	77.3	43.4
Grand Rapids, MI	84.0	87.5	74.7	64.2	51.7	28.9	34.0	11.2	32.2	8.8
Green Bay, WI	87.1	88.4	85.4	75.7	40.9	22.4	23.9	5.9	19.2	7.4
Greensboro, NC	87.4	91.6	85.6	62.0	53.3	35.6	45.1	23.3	31.7	11.8
Honolulu, HI	88.1	96.4	95.2	85.1	90.2	34.7	48.6	36.9	33.4	26.1
Houston, TX	75.2	75.2	84.4	84.0	51.2	28.9	33.6	19.0	53.4	10.1
Huntsville, AL	89.7	91.7	85.6	89.7	61.3	38.6	44.1	23.7	54.6	19.9
Indianapolis, IN	84.2	86.7	83.3	80.6	49.9	26.9	31.8	14.8	53.9	8.0
Jacksonville, FL	87.5	89.1	84.5	86.0	80.7	24.7	27.2	16.0	44.7	21.0
Kansas City, MO	87.5	91.9	82.4	76.7	64.4	31.3	39.7	14.6	38.5	13.9
Lafayette, LA	86.6	90.8	77.1	87.2	77.2	32.8	39.9	14.7	37.4	28.7
Las Vegas, NV	82.8	84.5	87.3	89.2	57.6	21.4	22.4	16.0	38.2	8.3
Lexington, KY	88.7	91.0	84.1	90.9	51.8	39.8	43.5	17.3	71.1	13.3
Lincoln, NE	93.2	94.6	85.8	72.7	67.5	35.8	36.6	21.5	41.1	19.4
Little Rock, AR	90.0	93.2	85.4	92.1	71.3	38.7	49.6	20.6	64.8	16.2
Los Angeles, CA	74.5	78.7	86.6	89.2	50.5	31.0	36.3	22.6	50.7	9.6
Louisville, KY	86.5	88.2	81.8	74.6	77.0	27.0	29.3	16.5	52.6	22.0
Lubbock, TX	85.7	88.3	81.9	86.9	68.7	29.5	32.0	12.2	69.7	10.2
Madison, WI	95.1	96.4	87.7	88.9	80.4	54.0	55.2	24.7	72.7	30.1
Manchester, NH	86.3	88.2	73.3	68.1	64.7	26.2	26.8	20.2	28.1	13.8

Table continued on next page.

City	High School Graduate or Higher (%)					Bachelor's Degree or Higher (%)				
	Total	White	Black	Asian	Hisp.[1]	Total	White	Black	Asian	Hisp.[1]
McAllen, TX	73.9	74.3	91.8	97.5	69.4	26.7	26.3	35.5	69.0	22.4
Miami, FL	70.4	71.7	65.4	75.7	66.6	22.4	24.8	9.7	58.8	18.4
Midland, TX	82.0	83.0	84.0	76.7	59.4	23.2	24.3	15.5	43.1	6.1
Minneapolis, MN	88.3	93.3	73.7	76.5	53.8	46.2	54.6	14.7	44.9	16.5
Montgomery, AL	85.5	91.5	81.1	86.4	59.3	31.5	43.0	21.2	50.6	20.2
Nashville, TN	85.8	89.0	84.2	80.3	54.9	34.5	40.0	23.3	48.7	11.3
New Orleans, LA	84.1	94.7	78.4	71.1	71.4	33.0	59.3	15.1	38.3	29.6
New York, NY	79.6	86.2	80.5	74.1	63.6	34.0	45.1	20.9	40.5	15.1
Oklahoma City, OK	85.0	87.3	87.6	76.4	49.1	28.1	31.4	18.7	34.9	8.0
Omaha, NE	87.9	91.2	81.7	73.0	48.4	32.8	36.2	15.0	52.2	10.8
Orlando, FL	88.1	91.6	81.8	85.6	79.7	32.1	38.3	16.6	50.4	21.6
Oxnard, CA	63.3	59.9	89.0	89.5	48.4	15.8	14.2	16.4	35.9	7.1
Peoria, IL	88.8	92.1	78.6	93.4	69.2	31.9	35.5	10.2	83.6	12.4
Philadelphia, PA	80.7	86.1	79.9	67.5	60.6	23.5	33.6	12.8	34.3	10.6
Phoenix, AZ	80.6	82.0	85.6	83.9	56.5	26.0	27.4	17.4	50.6	8.3
Pittsburgh, PA	90.3	92.0	84.3	93.0	85.8	35.4	39.8	14.6	79.4	40.6
Portland, OR	90.4	93.4	85.0	77.1	61.7	43.2	46.8	17.7	38.1	20.1
Providence, RI	71.8	79.5	74.2	63.7	54.0	27.9	40.4	15.5	36.1	7.4
Provo, UT	89.8	91.9	n/a	84.4	65.8	38.3	39.3	n/a	48.2	16.7
Raleigh, NC	90.0	93.0	89.0	82.4	50.5	45.9	55.4	28.4	45.0	11.8
Reno, NV	85.0	87.0	83.5	89.1	50.3	28.4	30.3	12.1	39.9	9.1
Richmond, VA	81.2	89.1	74.8	82.9	40.8	34.3	57.1	12.3	59.6	11.2
Riverside, CA	77.5	78.8	92.9	87.6	59.3	21.9	22.0	26.4	43.8	9.2
Rochester, MN	93.3	94.9	72.1	87.4	69.5	41.0	41.6	19.1	51.2	25.6
Salem, OR	86.3	90.4	91.6	90.1	49.5	26.9	29.4	24.7	27.4	10.3
Salt Lake City, UT	85.3	90.8	78.3	83.6	50.9	40.8	44.7	26.8	57.3	12.1
San Antonio, TX	80.4	82.1	87.6	85.4	71.5	24.3	26.0	21.5	51.6	13.6
San Diego, CA	87.0	89.1	89.1	87.4	65.3	41.3	44.7	20.4	47.0	17.3
San Francisco, CA	86.1	94.3	86.8	74.8	74.9	52.2	65.5	23.3	40.4	29.6
San Jose, CA	82.5	84.5	91.9	84.6	63.7	37.3	35.3	28.1	49.7	11.9
Santa Rosa, CA	85.5	88.8	85.0	79.4	59.2	29.9	31.7	26.4	37.5	9.9
Savannah, GA	84.3	90.3	79.6	77.5	58.6	25.1	36.7	14.6	32.4	25.5
Seattle, WA	93.0	96.5	82.4	81.1	78.7	56.6	63.1	21.5	46.1	37.7
Sioux Falls, SD	90.4	92.9	71.4	65.0	52.4	31.9	33.7	13.8	37.5	12.1
Spokane, WA	91.6	92.3	98.7	74.4	78.0	28.7	29.4	25.5	28.4	15.7
Springfield, MO	87.5	88.3	88.1	77.4	63.8	26.4	27.1	17.4	33.9	17.4
Tallahassee, FL	92.5	96.0	85.9	94.1	88.7	47.8	56.0	29.1	77.1	39.2
Tampa, FL	85.8	89.4	78.3	84.7	74.5	32.6	39.2	12.2	55.7	17.3
Topeka, KS	88.9	90.5	85.3	89.1	63.3	27.2	30.0	10.3	61.3	8.3
Tulsa, OK	86.6	88.7	86.7	81.3	55.4	29.6	33.5	16.7	44.0	7.9
Virginia Beach, VA	93.4	94.6	90.1	90.6	91.2	32.5	34.4	23.8	38.3	20.3
Washington, DC	87.7	95.5	82.0	90.5	64.9	51.7	83.6	22.9	76.8	35.7
Wichita, KS	87.0	88.9	86.8	76.9	57.4	27.9	30.4	16.9	28.5	9.6
Wilmington, NC	88.8	92.8	75.0	86.4	56.5	39.8	47.1	10.4	55.7	16.0
Worcester, MA	83.9	86.3	87.8	71.5	63.2	29.9	32.4	20.3	33.8	9.4
U.S.	85.9	88.1	82.5	85.5	63.1	28.6	30.0	18.4	50.2	13.4

Note: Figures shown cover persons 25 years old and over; (1) People of Hispanic origin can be of any race
Source: U.S. Census Bureau, 2010-2012 American Community Survey 3-Year Estimates

Educational Attainment by Race: Metro Area

Metro Area	High School Graduate or Higher (%)					Bachelor's Degree or Higher (%)				
	Total	White	Black	Asian	Hisp.[1]	Total	White	Black	Asian	Hisp.[1]
Abilene, TX	83.2	85.5	69.5	83.4	61.4	20.9	22.4	8.4	31.8	6.2
Albuquerque, NM	87.4	90.3	90.9	85.4	77.2	29.7	33.9	31.5	44.5	15.6
Anchorage, AK	92.3	94.9	87.5	78.2	83.3	29.9	33.3	24.4	23.1	21.5
Ann Arbor, MI	93.8	94.8	88.0	95.5	83.9	50.4	52.1	23.9	79.9	32.2
Athens, GA	85.5	88.7	75.2	89.6	57.2	34.8	40.2	11.2	66.6	10.7
Atlanta, GA	87.5	89.0	88.2	86.9	59.7	34.7	38.5	26.9	52.5	15.6
Austin, TX	87.9	90.0	89.1	92.1	65.8	40.2	42.6	23.1	66.0	17.3
Baltimore, MD	88.6	91.2	83.6	91.1	68.7	35.7	39.9	21.8	61.8	25.4
Billings, MT	92.8	93.3	n/a	79.8	80.1	28.8	29.5	n/a	22.6	10.0
Boise City, ID	90.0	90.8	84.6	84.3	62.8	29.2	29.7	17.4	48.3	9.7
Boston, MA	90.6	93.3	82.1	83.4	68.5	43.0	45.2	22.6	56.7	19.2
Boulder, CO	94.2	95.6	85.4	95.2	62.9	58.1	59.6	37.6	73.2	22.8
Cape Coral, FL	86.8	89.3	71.0	80.9	64.7	24.1	25.6	10.2	37.4	11.3
Cedar Rapids, IA	93.4	93.9	84.3	88.6	72.3	29.1	29.1	17.8	57.9	19.2
Charleston, SC	87.8	91.7	79.0	81.8	70.1	31.1	37.6	14.2	38.4	19.8
Charlotte, NC	87.2	89.1	85.3	84.3	59.0	33.1	36.6	21.7	53.3	15.3
Chicago, IL	86.6	89.7	84.5	90.0	61.6	34.4	37.8	19.8	62.1	12.4
Cincinnati, OH	88.8	89.7	82.8	92.0	69.9	29.5	30.6	15.5	63.8	24.1
Clarksville, TN	88.4	88.9	87.1	85.0	82.0	20.2	20.8	16.0	35.4	14.4
Colorado Spgs, CO	93.9	95.2	92.0	86.6	82.4	34.8	36.8	20.9	36.2	15.5
Columbia, MO	92.9	94.0	84.5	88.8	80.4	47.3	48.4	26.1	68.5	40.7
Columbus, OH	90.1	91.3	85.9	90.2	69.2	33.3	34.7	18.9	67.2	21.8
Dallas, TX	83.7	85.4	88.4	86.9	54.7	31.4	33.4	23.0	54.3	10.9
Davenport, IA	90.1	91.6	80.6	81.2	65.7	24.8	25.5	14.0	53.6	11.0
Denver, CO	89.5	91.5	89.0	84.4	64.6	38.9	41.4	24.4	44.3	12.6
Des Moines, IA	92.3	93.9	85.7	82.2	54.8	34.2	35.3	18.7	43.3	12.4
Durham, NC	87.5	90.3	84.4	91.7	49.4	43.1	49.8	25.6	76.1	12.7
El Paso, TX	74.2	75.4	92.6	88.1	69.1	20.6	21.0	28.2	49.1	16.1
Erie, PA	90.5	91.6	81.7	70.5	74.7	24.4	25.1	13.8	36.3	14.6
Eugene, OR	90.7	91.3	93.9	86.5	66.7	27.5	27.7	22.9	46.8	14.5
Fargo, ND	94.8	95.6	79.2	89.2	81.6	35.6	36.0	27.2	52.6	12.9
Fayetteville, NC	88.4	90.4	87.4	83.3	82.4	22.0	24.3	19.6	32.9	15.0
Ft. Collins, CO	94.7	95.6	89.4	94.8	75.3	44.2	45.1	31.7	54.9	22.1
Ft. Wayne, IN	89.5	91.4	82.7	67.5	64.1	24.6	25.8	12.2	38.5	15.1
Ft. Worth, TX	83.7	85.4	88.4	86.9	54.7	31.4	33.4	23.0	54.3	10.9
Gainesville, FL	90.5	92.9	80.5	93.2	89.3	38.3	42.3	13.0	71.7	44.9
Grand Rapids, MI	89.3	91.0	78.0	70.5	62.3	27.5	28.9	13.1	38.5	11.6
Green Bay, WI	90.4	91.0	81.2	83.6	48.1	23.9	24.2	7.1	36.4	9.6
Greensboro, NC	84.8	86.7	83.8	70.2	54.2	26.4	28.4	20.8	35.9	10.9
Honolulu, HI	90.3	96.4	95.4	87.4	89.4	31.6	43.0	27.8	32.8	20.5
Houston, TX	81.0	81.9	87.6	85.1	57.2	29.0	30.3	23.3	50.6	11.6
Huntsville, AL	88.3	89.0	87.0	85.1	62.5	34.8	36.5	27.2	54.4	19.8
Indianapolis, IN	88.6	90.3	84.3	86.4	56.2	31.2	33.5	17.2	59.0	13.0
Jacksonville, FL	88.7	90.0	84.6	87.5	82.7	27.3	29.4	16.4	45.2	23.7
Kansas City, MO	90.5	92.2	85.4	83.6	66.2	33.0	35.4	17.7	51.0	16.3
Lafayette, LA	84.1	88.0	73.4	77.1	70.1	24.7	28.8	12.2	31.3	16.9
Las Vegas, NV	83.9	85.3	87.8	88.9	60.6	22.0	22.5	16.4	36.8	8.6
Lexington, KY	87.0	88.5	84.3	90.9	51.9	33.8	35.7	16.3	69.2	11.7
Lincoln, NE	93.4	94.6	85.9	72.8	68.5	35.3	35.9	21.4	41.5	21.1
Little Rock, AR	88.6	89.8	85.0	86.1	68.2	27.7	29.6	19.3	52.6	13.8
Los Angeles, CA	78.2	80.9	88.3	86.9	56.6	31.3	33.2	23.8	49.8	10.7
Louisville, KY	87.3	88.2	83.1	80.5	70.1	25.9	26.9	17.0	53.9	17.4
Lubbock, TX	84.4	87.0	79.2	87.5	66.0	27.6	29.8	11.3	68.8	9.4
Madison, WI	94.5	95.3	87.4	89.4	73.3	42.9	43.1	22.8	67.1	23.5
Manchester, NH	90.8	91.5	83.5	84.2	70.1	35.5	35.1	29.5	55.3	19.0

Table continued on next page.

Metro Area	High School Graduate or Higher (%)					Bachelor's Degree or Higher (%)				
	Total	White	Black	Asian	Hisp.[1]	Total	White	Black	Asian	Hisp.[1]
McAllen, TX	62.3	62.9	78.1	93.7	58.3	16.1	16.0	25.2	66.5	13.5
Miami, FL	83.6	85.3	77.9	86.7	76.2	28.8	31.4	17.0	48.5	23.4
Midland, TX	81.5	82.4	83.8	77.6	59.2	22.8	23.8	15.3	45.4	6.8
Minneapolis, MN	93.0	95.2	81.4	79.7	65.1	38.7	40.4	19.8	44.3	17.8
Montgomery, AL	85.2	89.7	79.0	86.0	61.4	27.0	32.3	18.4	48.6	19.7
Nashville, TN	87.2	88.7	84.1	86.0	59.9	30.9	32.3	23.6	46.3	12.9
New Orleans, LA	84.5	88.9	78.5	72.8	71.3	26.3	32.1	14.7	35.6	19.7
New York, NY	84.8	89.3	82.4	82.0	66.8	36.5	41.4	21.9	52.3	16.0
Oklahoma City, OK	87.6	89.1	88.1	79.8	54.8	28.2	29.9	19.9	42.7	10.1
Omaha, NE	91.1	93.0	84.1	78.7	55.6	32.9	34.3	17.9	52.2	12.5
Orlando, FL	87.4	89.3	82.6	85.4	79.2	27.8	29.4	18.4	45.6	19.1
Oxnard, CA	82.5	83.7	93.8	92.1	57.8	31.3	31.4	33.4	56.9	10.8
Peoria, IL	91.1	92.1	79.0	94.2	74.9	25.7	25.9	10.9	76.7	15.8
Philadelphia, PA	88.7	91.6	83.6	82.1	66.3	33.4	37.2	17.3	53.5	14.4
Phoenix, AZ	86.2	87.6	89.1	87.3	62.8	28.4	29.2	22.0	52.7	10.4
Pittsburgh, PA	91.8	92.3	86.7	89.7	84.1	29.8	30.1	15.8	70.5	34.0
Portland, OR	90.5	92.6	86.4	85.4	60.6	34.1	35.0	22.9	45.6	13.8
Providence, RI	83.8	85.5	77.3	78.4	60.4	29.2	30.4	18.9	42.2	11.6
Provo, UT	93.4	94.3	95.5	91.2	71.4	35.7	36.1	50.6	52.5	18.8
Raleigh, NC	89.8	91.9	86.5	91.1	53.2	41.3	44.8	26.2	66.5	12.9
Reno, NV	86.3	87.9	86.1	89.8	52.7	27.2	28.5	14.7	37.1	9.3
Richmond, VA	86.6	89.9	80.5	85.2	55.5	32.0	37.4	17.9	56.6	16.6
Riverside, CA	78.6	80.7	88.3	88.4	60.6	19.4	19.4	20.0	47.1	8.0
Rochester, MN	93.6	94.7	73.4	86.5	71.1	35.4	35.4	18.3	50.2	25.8
Salem, OR	84.5	88.8	93.4	86.7	47.2	22.5	24.5	32.9	32.1	7.7
Salt Lake City, UT	88.9	91.2	81.6	82.2	61.8	31.0	32.1	19.4	44.8	11.4
San Antonio, TX	82.9	84.5	89.3	83.8	72.5	26.0	27.5	23.8	48.5	14.2
San Diego, CA	85.3	86.7	89.7	88.1	62.9	34.1	35.3	21.4	45.0	14.7
San Francisco, CA	87.5	90.9	89.1	84.5	67.5	44.2	48.5	23.6	49.5	18.0
San Jose, CA	86.4	87.7	92.3	89.2	64.8	45.7	43.0	30.0	60.7	13.5
Santa Rosa, CA	86.9	89.8	83.5	82.8	58.4	32.0	34.1	30.2	39.8	10.3
Savannah, GA	87.4	90.1	82.9	78.7	64.5	28.8	33.7	17.8	37.4	25.6
Seattle, WA	91.4	93.5	87.8	85.6	69.7	37.3	38.4	19.9	46.7	17.6
Sioux Falls, SD	91.6	93.5	72.5	66.7	54.4	30.0	31.2	13.3	35.9	13.3
Spokane, WA	92.7	93.4	95.1	80.6	79.1	28.8	29.3	20.1	33.3	15.3
Springfield, MO	89.0	89.4	85.1	85.7	66.2	25.4	25.6	17.4	37.4	19.8
Tallahassee, FL	89.0	93.1	80.8	92.9	77.9	36.3	41.6	22.6	72.0	28.6
Tampa, FL	87.5	88.8	82.6	83.9	75.7	26.0	26.5	18.1	47.4	17.3
Topeka, KS	91.3	92.4	85.8	85.1	66.8	26.7	28.2	10.8	59.1	10.0
Tulsa, OK	88.1	89.4	87.0	82.6	60.7	25.8	27.5	18.5	39.3	10.9
Virginia Beach, VA	89.7	92.2	84.5	88.8	83.3	28.6	32.5	18.8	41.9	21.0
Washington, DC	90.0	93.0	89.5	90.4	64.5	47.6	55.3	30.5	61.6	22.7
Wichita, KS	88.9	90.4	86.3	77.9	61.9	27.8	29.3	17.1	30.1	10.9
Wilmington, NC	88.6	90.5	80.5	92.0	58.5	31.0	34.3	11.1	61.6	12.3
Worcester, MA	89.2	90.7	86.7	83.1	66.4	33.7	34.2	23.7	55.6	13.5
U.S.	85.9	88.1	82.5	85.5	63.1	28.6	30.0	18.4	50.2	13.4

Note: Figures shown cover persons 25 years old and over; Figures cover the Metropolitan Statistical Area—see Appendix B for areas included; (1) People of Hispanic origin can be of any race
Source: U.S. Census Bureau, 2010-2012 American Community Survey 3-Year Estimates

Cost of Living Index

Urban Area	Composite	Groceries	Housing	Utilities	Transp.	Health	Misc.
Abilene, TX	n/a	n/a	n/a	n/a	n/a	n/a	n/a
Albuquerque, NM[1]	92.7	89.8	82.6	89.1	99.9	97.8	99.4
Anchorage, AK	125.7	112.6	154.1	98.9	107.0	139.0	121.8
Ann Arbor, MI	101.7	85.8	112.7	106.6	105.0	99.2	97.0
Athens, GA	n/a	n/a	n/a	n/a	n/a	n/a	n/a
Atlanta, GA	94.9	91.2	87.1	92.0	102.0	102.5	99.6
Austin, TX	92.9	84.0	86.0	91.1	97.2	99.4	99.8
Baltimore, MD	112.6	105.0	154.6	102.5	98.7	95.0	93.4
Billings, MT	n/a	n/a	n/a	n/a	n/a	n/a	n/a
Boise City, ID	93.2	85.6	86.7	87.9	103.7	103.8	97.3
Boston, MA	139.1	125.5	175.3	144.3	104.1	126.1	129.7
Boulder, CO	n/a	n/a	n/a	n/a	n/a	n/a	n/a
Cape Coral, FL	97.4	91.9	93.2	98.1	109.1	98.1	98.3
Cedar Rapids, IA	91.6	86.5	82.1	102.2	94.6	101.5	95.2
Charleston, SC	99.8	104.9	88.8	113.5	95.7	103.0	103.4
Charlotte, NC	95.4	101.6	83.7	106.6	98.4	98.2	97.0
Chicago, IL	114.8	98.1	135.3	98.9	124.1	97.7	109.2
Cincinnati, OH	91.4	92.0	79.0	86.8	105.2	99.8	95.8
Clarksville, TN	n/a	n/a	n/a	n/a	n/a	n/a	n/a
Colorado Springs, CO	95.7	93.5	94.4	101.0	94.4	102.4	95.6
Columbia, MO	95.6	91.3	88.3	98.0	94.3	101.7	102.1
Columbus, OH	86.9	86.5	77.1	96.4	96.2	95.1	87.2
Dallas, TX	95.6	92.3	75.5	106.9	102.2	99.1	106.2
Davenport, IA	95.4	86.6	100.2	85.5	111.2	94.9	92.1
Denver, CO	103.8	93.4	115.5	101.3	94.8	103.7	103.0
Des Moines, IA	90.0	85.2	85.4	89.5	96.1	93.6	92.8
Durham, NC	92.3	100.4	80.2	83.5	98.6	101.7	97.5
El Paso, TX	91.2	90.8	84.0	87.2	97.5	89.9	96.1
Erie, PA	97.8	97.5	94.8	97.1	100.5	94.6	99.9
Eugene, OR	n/a	n/a	n/a	n/a	n/a	n/a	n/a
Fargo, ND	93.5	97.6	83.6	89.4	95.6	111.8	97.4
Fayetteville, NC	n/a	n/a	n/a	n/a	n/a	n/a	n/a
Fort Collins, CO	n/a	n/a	n/a	n/a	n/a	n/a	n/a
Fort Wayne, IN	91.3	82.5	85.0	89.5	104.3	95.8	94.7
Fort Worth, TX	97.1	93.6	85.6	99.6	101.8	104.1	103.9
Gainesville, FL	98.7	97.3	94.1	106.1	104.1	101.2	98.1
Grand Rapids, MI	92.7	84.4	77.6	99.4	106.6	91.8	100.9
Green Bay, WI	93.3	86.4	83.9	101.2	99.5	106.1	96.9
Greensboro, NC[2]	88.1	98.0	69.5	100.3	85.3	102.9	94.0
Honolulu, HI	168.3	154.7	262.4	171.4	126.5	111.3	123.1
Houston, TX	98.8	79.5	107.3	103.2	95.4	96.4	100.2
Huntsville, AL	94.2	89.4	79.1	103.7	98.7	96.2	103.2
Indianapolis, IN	91.6	85.5	80.9	91.3	99.4	115.7	96.1
Jacksonville, FL	94.9	95.2	83.3	105.7	104.7	85.1	98.4
Kansas City, MO	98.9	95.6	91.7	110.6	98.2	96.3	102.9
Lafayette, LA	95.9	90.5	101.5	87.8	104.1	84.8	94.6
Las Vegas, NV	100.4	96.5	99.7	85.3	100.9	103.4	106.4
Lexington, KY	89.4	86.1	75.6	101.0	97.9	94.3	94.1
Lincoln, NE	89.3	87.6	75.6	92.3	96.6	95.0	96.3
Little Rock, AR	97.9	89.2	96.6	110.3	93.3	83.9	102.5
Los Angeles, CA	129.8	102.8	196.8	108.0	111.0	109.5	104.8
Louisville, KY	91.0	85.3	81.6	87.2	101.0	91.2	98.1
Lubbock, TX	89.2	90.4	81.4	78.4	95.0	95.6	95.0
Madison, WI	105.2	90.5	110.4	104.2	106.1	123.9	104.2
Manchester, NH	120.2	98.5	137.9	122.7	101.2	117.7	121.9
McAllen, TX	87.9	83.3	78.8	99.9	94.6	88.6	90.5

Table continued on next page.

Urban Area	Composite	Groceries	Housing	Utilities	Transp.	Health	Misc.
Miami, FL	107.2	99.9	118.0	95.7	110.4	104.4	104.3
Midland, TX	99.4	88.3	100.2	93.2	104.7	95.0	103.7
Minneapolis, MN	109.7	115.4	116.5	97.8	103.6	98.9	109.4
Montgomery, AL	94.4	95.2	85.6	110.2	96.7	84.7	96.7
Nashville, TN	87.3	87.8	74.3	87.0	94.1	81.4	95.8
New Orleans, LA	98.4	97.9	95.1	91.3	100.0	103.2	102.1
New York, NY	170.7	118.7	320.3	124.0	111.9	110.3	119.2
Oklahoma City, OK	89.9	87.8	82.2	91.6	98.9	98.1	91.7
Omaha, NE	86.9	84.3	78.4	91.1	96.6	100.6	87.6
Orlando, FL	96.0	96.7	78.6	104.4	98.5	99.3	105.6
Oxnard, CA	n/a	n/a	n/a	n/a	n/a	n/a	n/a
Peoria, IL	99.2	89.0	100.0	95.9	108.2	95.8	100.8
Philadelphia, PA	120.8	112.8	141.9	128.2	105.1	100.0	114.3
Phoenix, AZ	95.6	93.4	96.2	97.6	95.5	95.8	95.4
Pittsburgh, PA	93.6	94.2	79.3	94.9	104.2	100.9	99.1
Portland, OR	117.1	102.7	142.3	96.6	115.1	117.2	110.1
Providence, RI	125.2	106.9	138.8	133.1	104.2	118.2	128.4
Provo, UT	95.5	88.3	87.1	91.0	111.3	93.1	100.8
Raleigh, NC	93.3	101.7	76.1	105.7	97.8	101.7	96.6
Reno, NV	89.8	90.1	88.1	73.0	103.1	93.3	90.4
Richmond, VA	101.4	98.2	89.4	107.6	99.7	106.5	110.1
Riverside, CA	112.1	104.2	133.9	111.7	111.8	101.3	99.9
Rochester, MN	100.6	95.9	99.3	101.8	101.9	104.8	102.0
Salem, OR	n/a	n/a	n/a	n/a	n/a	n/a	n/a
Salt Lake City, UT	94.1	88.4	90.0	84.2	98.8	96.7	100.5
San Antonio, TX	88.4	81.4	79.5	82.6	95.5	93.7	96.6
San Diego, CA	129.4	101.6	199.0	97.7	113.3	109.7	104.5
San Francisco, CA	160.8	119.2	293.5	95.0	114.9	119.9	116.4
San Jose, CA	148.6	110.4	255.6	123.2	112.1	114.6	106.5
Santa Rosa, CA	n/a	n/a	n/a	n/a	n/a	n/a	n/a
Savannah, GA	92.5	91.2	71.5	111.5	102.0	100.1	99.2
Seattle, WA	118.6	102.6	140.1	97.0	118.3	118.9	114.7
Sioux Falls, SD	97.1	86.3	92.5	107.1	93.7	101.3	102.8
Spokane, WA	95.6	91.8	88.4	91.2	99.5	109.8	100.5
Springfield, MO	88.2	89.8	74.6	92.6	92.5	100.6	93.6
Tallahassee, FL	98.1	99.2	98.2	88.7	101.1	101.4	98.6
Tampa, FL	92.8	92.7	78.4	93.9	102.3	95.6	99.8
Topeka, KS	93.4	87.5	91.4	84.0	94.3	91.8	100.2
Tulsa, OK	88.0	85.5	65.0	96.5	96.3	95.5	100.3
Virginia Beach, VA	n/a	n/a	n/a	n/a	n/a	n/a	n/a
Washington, DC	139.4	107.9	247.5	104.1	105.6	98.6	96.6
Wichita, KS	91.6	88.2	75.6	107.7	96.9	94.8	98.2
Wilmington, NC	98.2	104.8	84.9	107.8	97.8	107.4	102.0
Worcester, MA[3]	104.2	94.3	97.7	117.6	103.8	123.4	106.6
U.S.	100.0	100.0	100.0	100.0	100.0	100.0	100.0

Note: The Cost of Living Index measures regional differences in the cost of consumer goods and services, excluding taxes and non-consumer expenditures, for professional and managerial households in the top income quintile. It is based on more than 50,000 prices covering almost 60 different items for which prices are collected three times a year by chambers of commerce, economic development organizations or university applied economic centers in each participating urban area. The numbers shown should be read as a percentage above or below the national average of 100. For example, a value of 115.4 in the groceries column indicates that grocery prices are 15.4% higher than the national average. Small differences in the index numbers should not be interpreted as significant. In cases where data is not available for the city, data for the metro area or for a neighboring city has been provided and noted below; (1) Rio Rancho NM; (2) Winston-Salem NC; (3) Fitchburg-Leominster MA

Source: The Council for Community and Economic Research (formerly ACCRA), Cost of Living Index, 2013

Grocery Prices

Urban Area	T-Bone Steak ($/pound)	Frying Chicken ($/pound)	Whole Milk ($/half gal.)	Eggs ($/dozen)	Orange Juice ($/64 oz.)	Coffee ($/11.5 oz.)
Abilene, TX	n/a	n/a	n/a	n/a	n/a	n/a
Albuquerque, NM[1]	9.99	0.99	2.38	2.00	3.03	4.59
Anchorage, AK	11.19	1.24	2.43	2.50	4.68	5.50
Ann Arbor, MI	10.09	1.02	2.08	1.70	3.03	4.50
Athens, GA	n/a	n/a	n/a	n/a	n/a	n/a
Atlanta, GA	11.52	1.09	2.22	1.66	3.41	4.93
Austin, TX	8.95	1.25	2.13	1.70	3.17	3.57
Baltimore, MD	10.49	1.39	2.55	2.28	3.57	4.85
Billings, MT	n/a	n/a	n/a	n/a	n/a	n/a
Boise City, ID	9.42	1.02	1.75	1.45	3.38	4.50
Boston, MA	11.49	1.64	2.79	2.99	3.85	5.07
Boulder, CO	n/a	n/a	n/a	n/a	n/a	n/a
Cape Coral, FL	10.66	1.13	2.60	1.79	3.42	4.11
Cedar Rapids, IA	9.76	1.28	1.96	1.63	3.22	4.04
Charleston, SC	10.12	1.46	2.73	1.76	3.54	4.31
Charlotte, NC	9.59	1.42	2.71	1.79	3.44	3.85
Chicago, IL	10.63	1.48	2.11	1.84	3.72	5.86
Cincinnati, OH	10.80	1.40	1.86	1.69	3.62	4.77
Clarksville, TN	n/a	n/a	n/a	n/a	n/a	n/a
Colorado Springs, CO	10.79	1.18	2.05	1.95	3.32	4.90
Columbia, MO	10.53	1.11	2.39	1.69	3.35	4.41
Columbus, OH	10.70	1.11	1.99	1.74	3.27	4.70
Dallas, TX	10.54	1.19	2.18	1.71	3.61	4.46
Davenport, IA	9.57	1.13	2.19	1.52	3.38	4.45
Denver, CO	11.46	1.32	1.98	1.89	3.84	5.11
Des Moines, IA	9.22	1.28	2.03	1.48	3.36	4.20
Durham, NC	10.14	1.46	2.65	1.85	3.46	4.08
El Paso, TX	10.28	1.15	2.13	1.66	3.25	4.96
Erie, PA	10.33	1.33	2.06	1.80	3.29	4.76
Eugene, OR	n/a	n/a	n/a	n/a	n/a	n/a
Fargo, ND	10.24	1.45	2.81	1.58	3.52	4.48
Fayetteville, NC	n/a	n/a	n/a	n/a	n/a	n/a
Fort Collins, CO	n/a	n/a	n/a	n/a	n/a	n/a
Fort Wayne, IN	11.06	0.99	2.05	1.69	3.55	4.60
Fort Worth, TX	9.66	1.29	2.33	1.74	3.35	4.06
Gainesville, FL	10.33	1.31	2.70	1.93	3.67	4.19
Grand Rapids, MI	10.51	1.09	2.10	1.67	3.33	3.89
Green Bay, WI	10.41	1.36	2.27	1.38	3.19	4.02
Greensboro, NC[2]	10.89	1.37	2.68	1.86	3.28	3.75
Honolulu, HI	9.99	2.28	3.56	3.39	5.12	7.32
Houston, TX	9.80	1.00	2.11	1.52	3.16	4.01
Huntsville, AL	10.28	1.19	2.21	1.55	3.35	4.14
Indianapolis, IN	9.71	1.11	2.00	1.71	3.31	4.26
Jacksonville, FL	10.37	1.50	2.66	1.94	3.49	4.07
Kansas City, MO	10.77	1.23	2.55	1.67	3.26	4.39
Lafayette, LA	9.58	1.13	2.81	1.65	3.40	4.00
Las Vegas, NV	9.07	1.26	2.21	1.91	4.03	5.14
Lexington, KY	9.99	1.01	2.11	1.81	3.44	4.09
Lincoln, NE	10.54	1.14	2.04	1.51	3.76	4.79
Little Rock, AR	10.64	1.07	2.08	1.79	3.36	4.00
Los Angeles, CA	10.46	1.48	2.22	2.21	3.50	5.56
Louisville, KY	9.24	0.97	1.99	1.86	3.15	4.42
Lubbock, TX	9.86	1.05	2.63	1.73	3.16	4.04
Madison, WI	10.69	1.47	2.13	1.32	3.53	4.38
Manchester, NH	10.68	1.26	2.22	1.88	2.88	3.81

Table continued on next page.

Urban Area	T-Bone Steak ($/pound)	Frying Chicken ($/pound)	Whole Milk ($/half gal.)	Eggs ($/dozen)	Orange Juice ($/64 oz.)	Coffee ($/11.5 oz.)
McAllen, TX	9.82	1.08	2.70	1.59	3.20	3.85
Miami, FL	11.10	1.43	2.66	1.91	3.45	3.43
Midland, TX	9.55	1.09	2.05	1.92	3.51	3.94
Minneapolis, MN	14.82	2.09	2.34	1.95	3.62	4.68
Montgomery, AL	9.42	1.29	2.63	1.95	3.13	3.65
Nashville, TN	10.63	1.08	2.05	1.73	3.24	4.11
New Orleans, LA	10.81	1.33	2.86	1.87	3.65	3.91
New York, NY	12.32	1.73	2.26	2.61	4.18	5.13
Oklahoma City, OK	9.69	1.26	2.31	1.64	3.40	4.48
Omaha, NE	9.95	1.16	2.09	1.50	3.58	4.35
Orlando, FL	10.72	1.43	2.67	1.94	3.77	3.86
Oxnard, CA	n/a	n/a	n/a	n/a	n/a	n/a
Peoria, IL	10.02	1.02	2.06	1.74	3.60	4.13
Philadelphia, PA	10.56	1.73	2.10	2.30	3.89	4.64
Phoenix, AZ	11.36	1.50	1.87	1.83	3.58	4.83
Pittsburgh, PA	10.53	1.43	2.05	1.69	3.56	4.51
Portland, OR	10.34	1.41	2.00	1.77	3.96	5.20
Providence, RI	11.56	1.36	2.94	2.26	3.29	4.51
Provo, UT	9.31	1.24	2.37	1.73	3.39	6.00
Raleigh, NC	10.51	1.50	2.61	1.98	3.70	4.00
Reno, NV	9.27	1.33	2.10	1.66	3.46	4.72
Richmond, VA	10.12	1.30	2.36	1.74	3.08	4.30
Riverside, CA	9.58	1.47	2.14	2.27	3.81	5.50
Rochester, MN	10.98	1.51	2.08	1.75	3.56	4.62
Salem, OR	n/a	n/a	n/a	n/a	n/a	n/a
Salt Lake City, UT	10.24	1.16	2.09	1.74	3.41	4.97
San Antonio, TX	9.67	0.99	2.16	1.56	3.38	3.89
San Diego, CA	9.77	1.55	2.16	2.09	3.43	5.33
San Francisco, CA	10.46	1.55	2.66	2.86	3.87	6.04
San Jose, CA	10.80	1.29	2.32	2.74	4.03	6.58
Santa Rosa, CA	n/a	n/a	n/a	n/a	n/a	n/a
Savannah, GA	9.54	1.25	2.63	1.65	3.32	4.02
Seattle, WA	11.01	1.52	1.91	1.75	3.97	5.30
Sioux Falls, SD	8.95	1.23	1.97	1.43	3.48	4.10
Spokane, WA	10.08	1.29	2.07	1.63	3.31	4.71
Springfield, MO	10.85	1.17	2.31	1.64	3.45	4.24
Tallahassee, FL	10.76	1.37	2.75	1.95	3.58	4.24
Tampa, FL	10.61	1.33	2.58	1.73	3.16	3.60
Topeka, KS	10.15	1.11	2.17	1.63	3.43	4.23
Tulsa, OK	9.31	1.09	2.34	1.62	3.63	4.01
Virginia Beach, VA	n/a	n/a	n/a	n/a	n/a	n/a
Washington, DC	10.52	1.57	2.58	2.36	3.65	4.93
Wichita, KS	9.47	1.21	2.38	1.68	3.49	4.11
Wilmington, NC	10.88	1.39	2.62	2.10	3.42	4.33
Worcester, MA[3]	9.82	1.41	1.86	1.51	3.28	4.69
Average*	10.19	1.28	2.34	1.81	3.48	4.39
Minimum*	8.56	0.94	1.44	1.19	2.78	3.40
Maximum*	14.82	2.28	3.56	3.73	6.23	7.32

*Note: **T-Bone Steak** (price per pound); **Frying Chicken** (price per pound, whole fryer); **Whole Milk** (half gallon carton); **Eggs** (price per dozen, Grade A, large); **Orange Juice** (64 oz. Tropicana or Florida Natural); **Coffee** (11.5 oz. can, vacuum-packed, Maxwell House, Hills Bros, or Folgers); (*) Values for the local area are compared with the average, minimum, and maximum values for all 327 areas in the Cost of Living Index report; n/a not available; In cases where data is not available for the city, data for the metro area or for a neighboring city has been provided and noted below; (1) Rio Rancho NM; (2) Winston-Salem NC; (3) Fitchburg-Leominster MA*
Source: The Council for Community and Economic Research (formerly ACCRA), Cost of Living Index, 2013

Housing and Utility Costs

Urban Area	New Home Price ($)	Apartment Rent ($/month)	All Electric ($/month)	Part Electric ($/month)	Other Energy ($/month)	Telephone ($/month)
Abilene, TX	n/a	n/a	n/a	n/a	n/a	n/a
Albuquerque, NM[1]	243,339	759	-	102.21	54.04	22.15
Anchorage, AK	476,652	1,277	-	71.12	96.57	26.01
Ann Arbor, MI	338,760	952	-	111.57	68.48	28.21
Athens, GA	n/a	n/a	n/a	n/a	n/a	n/a
Atlanta, GA	239,252	964	-	94.08	58.37	25.06
Austin, TX	234,211	970	-	89.15	36.67	30.94
Baltimore, MD	447,890	1,432	-	90.68	78.22	28.11
Billings, MT	n/a	n/a	n/a	n/a	n/a	n/a
Boise City, ID	260,775	743	-	90.33	59.21	22.95
Boston, MA	482,267	1,863	-	105.74	137.62	38.25
Boulder, CO	n/a	n/a	n/a	n/a	n/a	n/a
Cape Coral, FL	271,536	847	189.95	-	-	20.00
Cedar Rapids, IA	245,521	766	-	96.44	64.02	29.99
Charleston, SC	238,131	1,058	196.23	-	-	28.92
Charlotte, NC	244,676	829	164.64	-	-	31.94
Chicago, IL	398,795	1,175	-	86.36	64.58	30.04
Cincinnati, OH	217,051	847	-	84.01	61.24	23.27
Clarksville, TN	n/a	n/a	n/a	n/a	n/a	n/a
Colorado Springs, CO	270,912	902	-	66.42	59.93	37.45
Columbia, MO	268,483	749	-	88.84	66.30	28.45
Columbus, OH	217,589	784	-	90.95	61.53	27.99
Dallas, TX	214,062	818	-	134.32	46.62	28.15
Davenport, IA	316,168	750	-	66.26	70.13	24.52
Denver, CO	349,490	1,009	-	103.82	63.88	27.61
Des Moines, IA	275,275	636	-	68.04	69.09	27.10
Durham, NC	232,103	802	148.11	-	-	20.37
El Paso, TX	232,054	922	-	97.59	33.67	26.95
Erie, PA	295,090	684	-	98.71	80.68	21.95
Eugene, OR	n/a	n/a	n/a	n/a	n/a	n/a
Fargo, ND	247,098	792	-	63.42	61.61	29.95
Fayetteville, NC	n/a	n/a	n/a	n/a	n/a	n/a
Fort Collins, CO	n/a	n/a	n/a	n/a	n/a	n/a
Fort Wayne, IN	265,671	614	-	66.05	54.95	30.99
Fort Worth, TX	214,551	1,179	-	133.76	46.62	23.34
Gainesville, FL	271,646	900	-	121.68	45.26	31.06
Grand Rapids, MI	220,542	789	-	87.62	73.18	28.01
Green Bay, WI	266,845	624	-	78.44	74.27	31.21
Greensboro, NC[2]	202,750	659	157.77	-	-	29.33
Honolulu, HI	742,651	2,733	364.83	-	-	26.95
Houston, TX	248,558	1,435	-	119.33	45.38	29.59
Huntsville, AL	225,591	815	146.54	-	-	34.39
Indianapolis, IN	224,970	894	-	81.37	66.38	25.68
Jacksonville, FL	216,016	1,037	171.80	-	-	29.58
Kansas City, MO	270,041	845	-	91.98	76.65	33.67
Lafayette, LA	298,091	940	-	91.54	44.89	26.12
Las Vegas, NV	303,436	797	-	117.68	39.76	19.32
Lexington, KY	210,972	792	-	83.74	52.77	34.99
Lincoln, NE	229,001	670	-	69.72	82.55	25.25
Little Rock, AR	291,639	755	-	79.66	64.28	39.47
Los Angeles, CA	552,280	2,051	-	104.77	59.89	32.90
Louisville, KY	233,107	793	-	58.52	65.67	28.66
Lubbock, TX	242,341	720	-	79.41	39.42	24.00
Madison, WI	346,950	866	-	103.82	78.52	25.99
Manchester, NH	389,899	1,378	-	106.64	84.83	36.25

Table continued on next page.

Urban Area	New Home Price ($)	Apartment Rent ($/month)	All Electric ($/month)	Part Electric ($/month)	Other Energy ($/month)	Telephone ($/month)
McAllen, TX	220,129	795	-	136.74	54.28	21.01
Miami, FL	325,413	1,290	150.39	-	-	28.01
Midland, TX	260,386	1,215	-	115.78	40.33	24.95
Minneapolis, MN	342,058	1,100	-	84.79	83.48	25.07
Montgomery, AL	265,245	673	182.72	-	-	29.99
Nashville, TN	200,706	811	-	84.68	57.33	24.16
New Orleans, LA	277,938	861	-	97.49	54.79	24.59
New York, NY	990,514	2,493	-	116.34	103.28	30.33
Oklahoma City, OK	245,212	767	-	78.90	60.11	28.01
Omaha, NE	238,755	688	-	83.48	59.70	26.68
Orlando, FL	214,602	857	171.11	-	-	28.86
Oxnard, CA	n/a	n/a	n/a	n/a	n/a	n/a
Peoria, IL	314,209	723	-	88.85	57.31	29.23
Philadelphia, PA	413,372	1,263	-	123.19	74.37	38.50
Phoenix, AZ	291,667	843	184.23	-	-	21.08
Pittsburgh, PA	220,334	855	-	83.58	77.16	24.95
Portland, OR	345,844	2,029	-	84.72	73.80	26.67
Providence, RI	386,097	1,450	-	117.64	102.89	36.19
Provo, UT	239,391	793	-	63.98	65.56	29.92
Raleigh, NC	228,372	649	-	94.58	65.98	32.33
Reno, NV	249,678	841	-	71.66	51.08	19.43
Richmond, VA	249,778	871	-	85.49	75.66	33.45
Riverside, CA	403,163	1,199	-	110.75	68.55	31.79
Rochester, MN	248,270	1,143	-	79.14	99.35	25.32
Salem, OR	n/a	n/a	n/a	n/a	n/a	n/a
Salt Lake City, UT	257,032	846	-	68.04	62.19	25.17
San Antonio, TX	222,574	838	-	92.24	36.48	24.49
San Diego, CA	584,280	1,790	-	85.70	50.15	32.90
San Francisco, CA	820,479	2,925	-	107.76	57.54	23.96
San Jose, CA	805,160	1,734	-	171.40	57.42	27.52
Santa Rosa, CA	n/a	n/a	n/a	n/a	n/a	n/a
Savannah, GA	205,496	726	170.47	-	-	33.80
Seattle, WA	382,151	1,643	162.36	-	-	25.99
Sioux Falls, SD	287,840	730	-	82.59	67.82	35.71
Spokane, WA	257,960	724	-	55.24	74.78	29.98
Springfield, MO	225,591	652	-	68.72	49.28	33.84
Tallahassee, FL	305,099	820	164.06	-	-	20.00
Tampa, FL	221,461	818	158.03	-	-	24.99
Topeka, KS	270,615	854	-	73.04	65.65	22.99
Tulsa, OK	192,729	604	-	65.78	61.84	34.13
Virginia Beach, VA	n/a	n/a	n/a	n/a	n/a	n/a
Washington, DC	767,485	1,961	-	78.65	97.87	27.32
Wichita, KS	223,589	673	-	85.02	65.61	36.09
Wilmington, NC	259,686	713	181.99	-	-	28.53
Worcester, MA[3]	288,809	881	-	93.43	109.81	29.99
Average*	295,864	900	171.38	91.82	70.12	27.73
Minimum*	185,506	458	117.80	48.81	33.67	17.16
Maximum*	1,358,917	3,783	441.68	171.40	372.65	39.47

Note: **New Home Price** (2,400 sf living area, 8,000 sf lot, in urban area with full utilities); **Apartment Rent** (950 sf 2 bedroom/1.5 or 2 bath, unfurnished, excluding all utilities except water); **All Electric** (average monthly cost for an all-electric home); **Part Electric** (average monthly cost for a part-electric home); **Other Energy** (average monthly cost for natural gas, fuel oil, coal, wood, and any other forms of energy except electricity); **Telephone** (price includes basic monthly rate for a private residential line plus additional local usage charges incurred by a family of four); (*) Values for the local area are compared with the average, minimum, and maximum values for all 327 areas in the Cost of Living Index report; n/a not available; In cases where data is not available for the city, data for the metro area or for a neighboring city has been provided and noted below; (1) Rio Rancho NM; (2) Winston-Salem NC; (3) Fitchburg-Leominster MA
Source: The Council for Community and Economic Research (formerly ACCRA), Cost of Living Index, 2013

Health Care, Transportation, and Other Costs

Urban Area	Doctor ($/visit)	Dentist ($/visit)	Optometrist ($/visit)	Gasoline ($/gallon)	Beauty Salon ($/visit)	Men's Shirt ($)
Abilene, TX	n/a	n/a	n/a	n/a	n/a	n/a
Albuquerque, NM[1]	94.25	95.69	100.00	3.21	22.75	35.86
Anchorage, AK	164.15	125.00	171.58	3.75	44.53	28.42
Ann Arbor, MI	91.51	90.47	98.94	3.62	37.00	23.87
Athens, GA	n/a	n/a	n/a	n/a	n/a	n/a
Atlanta, GA	97.60	99.69	76.89	3.42	42.10	24.19
Austin, TX	100.74	94.53	112.08	3.30	42.60	30.48
Baltimore, MD	82.09	84.36	70.43	3.48	43.32	26.88
Billings, MT	n/a	n/a	n/a	n/a	n/a	n/a
Boise City, ID	116.44	81.53	111.68	3.41	23.14	38.22
Boston, MA	149.00	114.07	120.73	3.61	44.00	36.52
Boulder, CO	n/a	n/a	n/a	n/a	n/a	n/a
Cape Coral, FL	85.97	85.69	86.36	3.54	35.31	20.52
Cedar Rapids, IA	125.28	72.79	105.33	3.32	30.34	25.41
Charleston, SC	95.15	92.47	105.89	3.28	42.50	31.50
Charlotte, NC	98.80	85.07	114.83	3.47	38.80	18.52
Chicago, IL	86.39	99.00	91.00	4.09	40.00	27.30
Cincinnati, OH	98.24	84.06	91.67	3.53	37.20	23.38
Clarksville, TN	n/a	n/a	n/a	n/a	n/a	n/a
Colorado Springs, CO	103.23	91.98	101.47	3.19	36.40	27.29
Columbia, MO	108.83	87.00	86.14	3.28	32.61	23.33
Columbus, OH	99.04	79.19	63.62	3.39	35.40	24.51
Dallas, TX	106.67	86.19	93.70	3.40	39.02	35.25
Davenport, IA	82.50	87.81	73.78	3.38	26.07	23.53
Denver, CO	124.47	80.09	101.09	3.23	39.82	26.93
Des Moines, IA	95.45	76.76	81.53	3.28	27.76	16.82
Durham, NC	95.42	84.50	115.08	3.46	43.75	19.39
El Paso, TX	83.33	77.83	83.33	3.27	32.17	24.94
Erie, PA	94.94	78.51	80.86	3.53	35.71	33.33
Eugene, OR	n/a	n/a	n/a	n/a	n/a	n/a
Fargo, ND	140.61	90.47	78.13	3.30	26.20	27.35
Fayetteville, NC	n/a	n/a	n/a	n/a	n/a	n/a
Fort Collins, CO	n/a	n/a	n/a	n/a	n/a	n/a
Fort Wayne, IN	86.33	85.38	97.33	3.53	20.48	25.77
Fort Worth, TX	96.72	100.50	82.11	3.35	38.39	36.00
Gainesville, FL	93.97	94.69	78.59	3.59	37.00	31.95
Grand Rapids, MI	90.33	77.00	85.60	3.50	37.50	21.91
Green Bay, WI	130.29	82.84	62.79	3.51	27.80	33.15
Greensboro, NC[2]	107.75	83.20	95.40	3.36	36.53	30.24
Honolulu, HI	109.87	86.91	141.39	4.18	51.83	52.03
Houston, TX	90.61	86.57	89.60	3.38	46.10	24.22
Huntsville, AL	79.53	82.56	133.61	3.30	33.00	35.98
Indianapolis, IN	104.10	120.45	85.33	3.45	31.37	30.05
Jacksonville, FL	67.03	88.43	61.02	3.52	43.07	23.47
Kansas City, MO	93.19	86.80	87.96	3.24	24.62	39.97
Lafayette, LA	70.27	72.80	65.20	3.33	32.40	24.46
Las Vegas, NV	112.39	90.21	104.58	3.44	53.46	38.97
Lexington, KY	89.24	89.27	68.33	3.48	37.40	22.79
Lincoln, NE	102.75	72.57	96.67	3.27	28.31	28.81
Little Rock, AR	102.61	50.83	89.44	3.28	40.27	29.29
Los Angeles, CA	100.60	98.13	118.90	3.91	60.61	28.08
Louisville, KY	86.27	86.30	78.43	3.58	33.20	27.66
Lubbock, TX	99.08	77.20	96.47	3.20	35.93	26.92
Madison, WI	182.71	93.56	53.35	3.43	40.07	23.96
Manchester, NH	149.00	98.13	102.96	3.55	38.13	35.78

Table continued on next page.

Urban Area	Doctor ($/visit)	Dentist ($/visit)	Optometrist ($/visit)	Gasoline ($/gallon)	Beauty Salon ($/visit)	Men's Shirt ($)
McAllen, TX	70.00	75.33	85.44	3.29	30.83	18.66
Miami, FL	108.85	98.88	91.33	3.57	58.07	18.10
Midland, TX	92.67	82.00	94.33	3.32	34.95	22.93
Minneapolis, MN	117.48	80.26	79.95	3.40	36.37	24.62
Montgomery, AL	77.11	62.45	82.44	3.26	38.33	33.60
Nashville, TN	78.53	78.20	78.31	3.34	31.00	25.59
New Orleans, LA	77.67	103.40	77.06	3.30	37.45	32.69
New York, NY	108.35	114.81	76.87	3.82	57.93	31.16
Oklahoma City, OK	85.75	102.30	98.78	3.32	35.57	23.89
Omaha, NE	129.33	66.10	98.53	3.24	30.67	18.04
Orlando, FL	75.96	84.18	62.50	3.34	42.59	36.62
Oxnard, CA	n/a	n/a	n/a	n/a	n/a	n/a
Peoria, IL	101.85	71.93	94.85	3.48	23.41	23.01
Philadelphia, PA	118.09	94.76	100.24	3.48	52.14	39.08
Phoenix, AZ	96.94	87.54	89.72	3.37	40.80	19.48
Pittsburgh, PA	94.13	85.40	97.27	3.63	38.37	23.92
Portland, OR	141.65	96.40	123.95	3.77	41.70	31.32
Providence, RI	149.00	96.22	116.67	3.68	45.48	39.46
Provo, UT	98.23	68.48	88.94	3.60	32.11	31.84
Raleigh, NC	97.60	104.92	97.55	3.34	36.53	22.47
Reno, NV	79.00	92.47	108.25	3.61	32.00	19.59
Richmond, VA	90.42	103.67	119.17	3.37	51.78	22.08
Riverside, CA	86.21	92.23	89.25	3.92	36.36	35.82
Rochester, MN	127.22	83.58	86.12	3.43	31.53	27.66
Salem, OR	n/a	n/a	n/a	n/a	n/a	n/a
Salt Lake City, UT	90.00	82.17	90.04	3.27	47.36	21.09
San Antonio, TX	96.00	88.07	85.55	3.33	41.27	27.57
San Diego, CA	103.86	99.93	102.65	3.90	55.35	25.65
San Francisco, CA	130.96	115.18	123.11	3.98	58.61	33.95
San Jose, CA	105.54	113.00	130.31	3.85	46.61	23.88
Santa Rosa, CA	n/a	n/a	n/a	n/a	n/a	n/a
Savannah, GA	113.42	75.53	71.90	3.40	37.25	22.48
Seattle, WA	110.21	116.74	153.83	3.80	47.22	26.09
Sioux Falls, SD	113.50	81.80	97.97	3.32	27.88	25.12
Spokane, WA	127.03	97.07	112.56	3.43	33.95	21.19
Springfield, MO	116.72	78.95	88.78	3.20	30.83	23.74
Tallahassee, FL	102.20	90.72	81.84	3.52	35.06	36.57
Tampa, FL	80.31	89.27	78.38	3.41	39.23	23.60
Topeka, KS	77.57	75.22	110.67	3.21	25.20	34.50
Tulsa, OK	102.58	71.00	79.70	3.08	33.33	23.72
Virginia Beach, VA	n/a	n/a	n/a	n/a	n/a	n/a
Washington, DC	84.40	89.47	72.98	3.73	51.00	26.52
Wichita, KS	89.26	78.01	129.04	3.34	35.62	44.69
Wilmington, NC	120.42	109.38	94.42	3.45	40.62	31.96
Worcester, MA[3]	178.33	105.00	96.94	3.54	31.52	31.35
Average*	101.40	86.48	96.16	3.44	33.87	26.55
Minimum*	61.67	50.83	50.12	3.08	18.92	12.48
Maximum*	182.71	152.50	223.78	4.33	68.22	52.03

*Note: **Doctor** (general practitioners routine exam of an established patient); **Dentist** (adult teeth cleaning and periodic oral examination); **Optometrist** (full vision eye exam for established adult patient); **Gasoline** (one gallon regular unleaded, national brand, including all taxes, cash price at self-service pump if available); **Beauty Salon** (woman's shampoo, trim, and blow-dry); **Men's Shirt** (cotton/polyester dress shirt, pinpoint weave, long sleeves); (*) Values for the local area are compared with the average, minimum, and maximum values for all 327 areas in the Cost of Living Index report; n/a not available; In cases where data is not available for the city, data for the metro area or for a neighboring city has been provided and noted below; (1) Rio Rancho NM; (2) Winston-Salem NC; (3) Fitchburg-Leominster MA*
Source: The Council for Community and Economic Research (formerly ACCRA), Cost of Living Index, 2013

Number of Medical Professionals

City	Area Covered	MDs[1]	DOs[1,2]	Dentists	Podiatrists	Chiropractors	Optometrists
Abilene, TX	Taylor County	205.7	21.8	62.7	6.0	17.2	17.2
Albuquerque, NM	Bernalillo County	404.4	18.8	73.2	7.9	21.7	15.5
Anchorage, AK	Anchorage Borough	305.8	25.7	102.2	4.4	44.9	23.1
Ann Arbor, MI	Washtenaw County	1,125.8	32.4	148.1	5.4	22.5	14.8
Athens, GA	Clarke County	276.6	8.4	52.4	5.0	19.1	16.6
Atlanta, GA	Fulton County	482.7	8.5	64.0	3.9	45.5	13.8
Austin, TX	Travis County	292.5	15.1	62.0	4.5	29.6	15.1
Baltimore, MD	Baltimore City	918.1	15.9	54.5	5.6	9.8	11.1
Billings, MT	Yellowstone County	343.7	18.0	82.3	7.2	32.3	25.0
Boise City, ID	Ada County	274.3	18.0	78.5	3.2	49.4	18.1
Boston, MA	Suffolk County	1,362.0	13.6	166.6	8.8	14.3	28.8
Boulder, CO	Boulder County	360.1	22.0	91.7	4.6	66.5	23.9
Cape Coral, FL	Lee County	176.5	27.3	43.3	7.8	25.9	13.5
Cedar Rapids, IA	Linn County	183.7	15.4	68.8	7.9	49.7	16.3
Charleston, SC	Charleston County	758.6	24.9	100.2	4.9	41.4	19.2
Charlotte, NC	Mecklenburg County	299.1	8.9	65.0	3.3	30.5	12.6
Chicago, IL	Cook County	406.7	22.0	77.9	10.7	23.9	17.0
Cincinnati, OH	Hamilton County	548.1	21.5	66.9	7.7	18.9	16.3
Clarksville, TN	Montgomery County	104.1	18.1	37.3	2.2	14.6	15.1
Colorado Spgs, CO	El Paso County	182.0	25.6	95.6	3.7	36.9	20.5
Columbia, MO	Boone County	763.4	48.8	58.7	5.3	26.7	23.7
Columbus, OH	Franklin County	398.5	59.7	80.5	6.7	22.4	24.2
Dallas, TX	Dallas County	309.1	19.5	71.8	3.7	31.1	11.9
Davenport, IA	Scott County	218.0	47.9	66.4	4.1	155.3	15.4
Denver, CO	Denver County	561.9	25.6	65.4	6.5	28.8	13.7
Des Moines, IA	Polk County	226.4	105.3	65.3	9.5	42.1	22.1
Durham, NC	Durham County	1,118.0	12.0	70.2	5.0	16.0	12.4
El Paso, TX	El Paso County	175.5	13.1	35.4	3.6	8.3	7.7
Erie, PA	Erie County	169.4	97.2	61.6	11.0	35.3	14.6
Eugene, OR	Lane County	244.7	10.5	64.3	2.8	25.4	16.1
Fargo, ND	Cass County	390.2	9.2	70.2	3.2	54.9	26.8
Fayetteville, NC	Cumberland County	193.6	19.5	85.1	6.5	9.6	18.0
Ft. Collins, CO	Larimer County	230.7	24.3	71.8	4.2	50.2	20.0
Ft. Wayne, IN	Allen County	244.6	16.2	56.6	5.0	18.0	21.1
Ft. Worth, TX	Tarrant County	172.6	36.6	51.7	4.1	22.5	12.6
Gainesville, FL	Alachua County	851.6	27.2	153.3	4.4	25.0	13.1
Grand Rapids, MI	Kent County	302.4	54.1	65.8	4.7	27.4	20.7
Green Bay, WI	Brown County	224.0	18.0	63.6	3.6	39.1	18.2
Greensboro, NC	Guilford County	254.1	6.5	52.7	3.8	13.0	10.2
Honolulu, HI	Honolulu County	321.8	13.0	90.4	2.9	15.9	20.9
Houston, TX	Harris County	295.8	9.1	59.9	4.5	20.4	16.9
Huntsville, AL	Madison County	253.8	10.6	54.6	4.1	20.4	16.0
Indianapolis, IN	Marion County	431.2	16.6	76.9	5.3	14.6	17.1
Jacksonville, FL	Duval County	337.6	24.3	65.7	7.6	20.7	14.4
Kansas City, MO	Jackson County	271.3	62.6	73.8	5.3	37.8	16.5
Lafayette, LA	Lafayette Parish	352.3	4.0	61.7	4.0	30.0	13.2
Las Vegas, NV	Clark County	169.5	23.0	55.4	3.6	18.7	11.2
Lexington, KY	Fayette County	679.0	22.9	121.5	7.2	21.3	17.7
Lincoln, NE	Lancaster County	215.7	10.4	87.6	4.4	37.8	19.1
Little Rock, AR	Pulaski County	668.6	11.6	67.9	4.4	17.5	16.2
Los Angeles, CA	Los Angeles County	280.6	10.2	76.0	5.7	25.8	14.9
Louisville, KY	Jefferson County	464.0	12.9	92.2	7.6	28.0	11.6
Lubbock, TX	Lubbock County	359.6	12.7	50.4	3.1	15.7	15.7
Madison, WI	Dane County	554.1	16.5	64.5	4.8	39.7	17.1
Manchester, NH	Hillsborough County	226.7	17.9	73.2	4.7	23.3	17.1
McAllen, TX	Hidalgo County	107.2	2.6	23.6	1.2	8.7	6.2

Table continued on next page.

City	Area Covered	MDs[1]	DOs[1,2]	Dentists	Podiatrists	Chiropractors	Optometrists
Miami, FL	Miami-Dade County	319.4	14.2	54.2	9.0	17.0	11.4
Midland, TX	Midland County	205.7	5.7	46.3	2.7	15.0	12.3
Minneapolis, MN	Hennepin County	471.1	12.8	85.4	3.6	61.1	17.2
Montgomery, AL	Montgomery County	259.6	15.1	61.9	7.0	16.1	15.3
Nashville, TN	Davidson County	592.0	9.4	72.1	3.9	20.3	14.2
New Orleans, LA	Orleans Parish	705.9	13.0	59.5	3.8	6.8	6.2
New York, NY	Kings County	300.2	11.5	59.1	12.3	9.9	9.0
Oklahoma City, OK	Oklahoma County	383.7	41.2	92.8	4.8	24.0	17.9
Omaha, NE	Douglas County	506.9	22.1	81.5	4.3	33.3	17.5
Orlando, FL	Orange County	267.1	17.5	42.8	4.0	22.3	11.7
Oxnard, CA	Ventura County	213.0	8.2	77.5	4.9	33.3	14.7
Peoria, IL	Peoria County	483.1	39.6	64.1	6.9	44.9	18.7
Philadelphia, PA	Philadelphia County	519.0	46.8	62.8	15.8	14.7	14.4
Phoenix, AZ	Maricopa County	234.1	32.0	62.4	5.5	33.1	13.5
Pittsburgh, PA	Allegheny County	598.2	35.3	83.1	10.4	38.9	17.9
Portland, OR	Multnomah County	572.1	29.5	86.3	4.9	60.5	20.6
Providence, RI	Providence County	458.5	15.5	57.1	9.1	18.5	16.1
Provo, UT	Utah County	121.1	14.1	64.3	3.5	23.3	9.1
Raleigh, NC	Wake County	261.0	7.3	63.5	3.2	24.2	15.4
Reno, NV	Washoe County	270.4	17.9	61.3	4.0	25.9	17.5
Richmond, VA	Richmond City	679.8	17.9	123.8	10.0	6.6	12.8
Riverside, CA	Riverside County	113.2	9.6	47.1	2.2	16.2	10.9
Rochester, MN	Olmsted County	2,244.3	48.0	76.1	6.1	35.3	21.1
Salem, OR	Marion County	178.7	10.7	72.5	4.4	26.4	14.3
Salt Lake City, UT	Salt Lake County	354.0	10.4	72.2	5.2	24.3	12.2
San Antonio, TX	Bexar County	313.3	18.6	76.3	5.5	14.6	13.5
San Diego, CA	San Diego County	294.9	14.0	77.4	4.0	30.2	15.6
San Francisco, CA	San Francisco County	790.3	10.3	136.6	9.3	34.8	23.1
San Jose, CA	Santa Clara County	386.0	6.4	104.1	5.4	37.8	22.8
Santa Rosa, CA	Sonoma County	247.8	12.3	84.6	6.1	35.3	15.1
Savannah, GA	Chatham County	342.2	18.4	59.6	6.5	15.2	13.7
Seattle, WA	King County	461.0	12.7	99.1	6.4	41.9	19.2
Sioux Falls, SD	Minnehaha County	330.8	21.5	51.9	4.6	53.0	19.4
Spokane, WA	Spokane County	269.9	20.3	71.2	5.0	27.9	18.5
Springfield, MO	Christian County	96.6	21.6	27.6	0.0	13.8	10.0
Tallahassee, FL	Leon County	252.6	7.2	34.9	3.9	17.6	16.9
Tampa, FL	Hillsborough County	313.9	26.4	48.4	4.8	22.2	11.2
Topeka, KS	Shawnee County	215.7	21.8	58.1	5.6	23.5	26.2
Tulsa, OK	Tulsa County	273.9	104.8	65.6	3.4	36.1	19.9
Virginia Beach, VA	Virginia Beach City	245.2	10.4	69.4	6.7	24.9	13.9
Washington, DC	The District County	797.7	16.8	113.7	8.4	7.6	12.8
Wichita, KS	Sedgwick County	253.2	34.0	55.0	2.2	35.8	24.6
Wilmington, NC	New Hanover County	341.7	20.9	71.2	6.7	32.0	17.2
Worcester, MA	Worcester County	353.1	19.7	65.2	6.1	19.4	17.9
U.S.	U.S.	267.6	19.6	61.7	5.6	24.7	14.5

Note: All figures are rates per 100,000 population; Data as of 2012 unless noted; (1) Data as of 2011; (2) Doctor of Osteopathic Medicine; Source: Area Resource File (ARF) 2012-2013. U.S. Department of Health and Human Services, Health Resources and Services Administration, Bureau of Health Professions

Health Insurance Coverage: City

City	With Health Insurance	With Private Health Insurance	With Public Health Insurance	Without Health Insurance	Population Under Age 18 Without Health Insurance
Abilene, TX	80.8	59.8	33.3	19.2	9.4
Albuquerque, NM	83.9	60.5	34.0	16.1	7.4
Anchorage, AK	83.1	68.2	23.6	16.9	10.1
Ann Arbor, MI	93.9	86.4	17.3	6.1	2.7
Athens, GA	83.5	68.3	22.5	16.5	6.8
Atlanta, GA	80.7	59.8	27.6	19.3	7.2
Austin, TX	78.9	63.0	22.3	21.1	11.2
Baltimore, MD	86.6	54.2	42.1	13.4	5.3
Billings, MT	84.2	67.1	31.3	15.8	9.9
Boise City, ID	84.3	70.9	24.5	15.7	9.6
Boston, MA	94.6	66.0	35.6	5.4	1.5
Boulder, CO	90.9	83.4	14.4	9.1	6.6
Cape Coral, FL	78.8	57.5	34.3	21.2	11.9
Cedar Rapids, IA	91.3	76.1	28.0	8.7	3.0
Charleston, SC	87.2	73.3	24.9	12.8	7.2
Charlotte, NC	82.4	64.7	25.0	17.6	6.9
Chicago, IL	79.9	52.4	33.6	20.1	4.9
Cincinnati, OH	84.2	56.3	36.1	15.8	6.2
Clarksville, TN	87.1	70.7	28.5	12.9	4.0
Colorado Spgs, CO	84.7	69.1	27.0	15.3	8.4
Columbia, MO	89.9	79.7	18.3	10.1	7.0
Columbus, OH	84.5	63.2	29.0	15.5	6.6
Dallas, TX	69.0	45.0	29.9	31.0	16.7
Davenport, IA	87.3	69.2	30.5	12.7	7.3
Denver, CO	82.5	60.7	29.3	17.5	10.2
Des Moines, IA	88.5	64.2	36.3	11.5	4.5
Durham, NC	81.9	63.6	26.5	18.1	9.4
El Paso, TX	73.4	48.1	32.7	26.6	12.8
Erie, PA	88.5	57.2	44.6	11.5	3.5
Eugene, OR	84.4	68.4	27.7	15.6	6.9
Fargo, ND	89.4	79.3	20.4	10.6	6.1
Fayetteville, NC	85.8	66.1	33.0	14.2	5.0
Ft. Collins, CO	88.6	78.0	18.8	11.4	4.8
Ft. Wayne, IN	83.1	61.9	30.8	16.9	10.4
Ft. Worth, TX	75.8	54.8	26.9	24.2	13.0
Gainesville, FL	82.1	69.2	20.1	17.9	7.5
Grand Rapids, MI	87.0	59.5	39.0	13.0	2.6
Green Bay, WI	86.4	61.7	35.2	13.6	6.9
Greensboro, NC	82.6	63.2	28.0	17.4	7.1
Honolulu, HI	92.6	76.0	30.7	7.4	2.9
Houston, TX	70.5	46.4	30.0	29.5	16.7
Huntsville, AL	84.1	69.4	28.6	15.9	4.9
Indianapolis, IN	82.4	58.7	33.1	17.6	9.4
Jacksonville, FL	82.4	62.0	30.1	17.6	8.9
Kansas City, MO	82.8	64.0	28.0	17.2	7.9
Lafayette, LA	82.0	64.1	29.0	18.0	4.3
Las Vegas, NV	76.6	60.1	26.0	23.4	16.5
Lexington, KY	85.6	71.4	23.5	14.4	6.4
Lincoln, NE	88.7	74.6	24.4	11.3	5.6
Little Rock, AR	85.1	63.7	31.7	14.9	6.2
Los Angeles, CA	73.9	48.4	31.2	26.1	10.4
Louisville, KY	85.7	66.1	31.4	14.3	4.9
Lubbock, TX	81.7	63.6	28.0	18.3	9.7
Madison, WI	92.1	80.2	21.9	7.9	3.4
Manchester, NH	86.0	67.0	29.4	14.0	4.0

Table continued on next page.

City	With Health Insurance	With Private Health Insurance	With Public Health Insurance	Without Health Insurance	Population Under Age 18 Without Health Insurance
McAllen, TX	64.4	40.0	29.0	35.6	19.4
Miami, FL	64.7	32.5	35.4	35.3	14.5
Midland, TX	79.5	66.3	22.6	20.5	14.6
Minneapolis, MN	87.4	64.3	30.3	12.6	7.0
Montgomery, AL	85.3	62.2	35.8	14.7	4.9
Nashville, TN	82.6	62.5	28.8	17.4	7.6
New Orleans, LA	80.8	52.4	36.4	19.2	5.5
New York, NY	85.5	54.1	39.1	14.5	4.3
Oklahoma City, OK	79.3	59.7	29.5	20.7	9.6
Omaha, NE	85.1	66.2	28.8	14.9	7.0
Orlando, FL	75.2	55.0	26.0	24.8	12.9
Oxnard, CA	74.4	48.0	32.6	25.6	11.7
Peoria, IL	87.4	62.4	37.0	12.6	2.7
Philadelphia, PA	85.6	55.1	40.8	14.4	4.8
Phoenix, AZ	77.6	52.2	31.9	22.4	15.2
Pittsburgh, PA	89.8	68.7	33.4	10.2	2.9
Portland, OR	83.7	67.1	25.6	16.3	5.1
Providence, RI	79.3	50.9	35.0	20.7	6.0
Provo, UT	82.8	72.0	17.9	17.2	14.9
Raleigh, NC	83.4	68.6	22.5	16.6	9.9
Reno, NV	74.9	60.5	23.5	25.1	22.5
Richmond, VA	83.0	59.0	32.9	17.0	4.7
Riverside, CA	78.1	55.1	29.0	21.9	11.1
Rochester, MN	92.3	78.7	25.3	7.7	3.9
Salem, OR	82.7	62.8	31.9	17.3	7.4
Salt Lake City, UT	78.6	62.3	24.0	21.4	16.0
San Antonio, TX	78.3	57.1	31.4	21.7	11.1
San Diego, CA	82.9	65.9	25.0	17.1	8.5
San Francisco, CA	88.8	70.3	27.0	11.2	4.1
San Jose, CA	85.9	66.7	26.0	14.1	4.7
Santa Rosa, CA	84.2	63.1	31.9	15.8	8.3
Savannah, GA	78.0	55.8	30.7	22.0	8.9
Seattle, WA	88.2	76.4	20.3	11.8	4.9
Sioux Falls, SD	88.7	75.7	24.1	11.3	6.2
Spokane, WA	85.1	61.7	35.5	14.9	5.6
Springfield, MO	82.3	60.9	32.9	17.7	5.4
Tallahassee, FL	85.6	72.8	20.1	14.4	5.7
Tampa, FL	80.2	56.6	31.0	19.8	9.8
Topeka, KS	83.3	63.8	32.6	16.7	9.5
Tulsa, OK	77.6	56.9	30.9	22.4	11.2
Virginia Beach, VA	89.3	80.3	20.4	10.7	4.8
Washington, DC	93.2	69.9	35.0	6.8	2.6
Wichita, KS	83.6	65.3	28.5	16.4	7.0
Wilmington, NC	82.9	65.1	30.3	17.1	6.1
Worcester, MA	95.0	62.8	42.1	5.0	1.9
U.S.	84.9	65.4	30.4	15.1	7.5

Note: Figures are percentages that cover the civilian noninstitutionalized population
Source: U.S. Census Bureau, 2010-2012 American Community Survey 3-Year Estimates

Health Insurance Coverage: Metro Area

Metro Area	With Health Insurance	With Private Health Insurance	With Public Health Insurance	Without Health Insurance	Population Under Age 18 Without Health Insurance
Abilene, TX	80.5	60.3	32.9	19.5	10.8
Albuquerque, NM	83.6	59.7	34.6	16.4	7.4
Anchorage, AK	82.4	67.0	24.1	17.6	10.8
Ann Arbor, MI	92.5	80.9	22.7	7.5	2.3
Athens, GA	84.7	68.9	24.2	15.3	6.1
Atlanta, GA	80.8	65.0	23.5	19.2	9.7
Austin, TX	81.2	67.1	21.9	18.8	10.4
Baltimore, MD	90.8	74.2	28.2	9.2	4.0
Billings, MT	84.5	68.9	29.1	15.5	9.3
Boise City, ID	84.0	68.3	26.4	16.0	8.5
Boston, MA	95.4	77.1	29.4	4.6	1.7
Boulder, CO	89.0	79.0	18.3	11.0	6.8
Cape Coral, FL	78.7	56.6	39.4	21.3	14.2
Cedar Rapids, IA	92.6	78.8	26.9	7.4	2.5
Charleston, SC	82.9	66.7	27.5	17.1	9.8
Charlotte, NC	83.5	66.7	25.5	16.5	7.2
Chicago, IL	85.6	66.4	28.1	14.4	4.2
Cincinnati, OH	88.9	72.6	26.7	11.1	4.9
Clarksville, TN	85.9	69.3	28.8	14.1	6.4
Colorado Spgs, CO	86.1	71.7	25.7	13.9	7.5
Columbia, MO	89.9	78.2	20.7	10.1	5.9
Columbus, OH	88.3	71.4	26.4	11.7	5.0
Dallas, TX	77.7	61.1	23.3	22.3	13.3
Davenport, IA	89.9	72.9	31.9	10.1	4.3
Denver, CO	84.8	69.6	23.6	15.2	9.5
Des Moines, IA	91.9	77.1	26.6	8.1	3.4
Durham, NC	84.5	68.3	26.1	15.5	8.4
El Paso, TX	71.8	45.4	33.0	28.2	13.7
Erie, PA	90.9	69.6	35.9	9.1	2.8
Eugene, OR	83.7	64.3	33.3	16.3	6.9
Fargo, ND	91.4	81.3	20.7	8.6	4.7
Fayetteville, NC	85.2	64.6	32.9	14.8	5.9
Ft. Collins, CO	87.7	75.0	23.3	12.3	6.0
Ft. Wayne, IN	85.6	68.0	27.8	14.4	9.4
Ft. Worth, TX	77.7	61.1	23.3	22.3	13.3
Gainesville, FL	83.8	68.3	25.3	16.2	8.5
Grand Rapids, MI	89.1	70.7	30.7	10.9	3.6
Green Bay, WI	91.1	72.5	29.6	8.9	4.1
Greensboro, NC	83.2	62.5	30.7	16.8	8.0
Honolulu, HI	93.9	79.2	28.8	6.1	2.9
Houston, TX	75.7	57.0	25.0	24.3	14.4
Huntsville, AL	87.4	73.8	26.2	12.6	3.6
Indianapolis, IN	86.2	69.3	26.7	13.8	7.4
Jacksonville, FL	84.1	65.9	29.2	15.9	8.3
Kansas City, MO	86.9	72.9	24.8	13.1	6.8
Lafayette, LA	83.2	63.8	29.0	16.8	4.1
Las Vegas, NV	77.4	62.5	23.9	22.6	16.3
Lexington, KY	85.9	70.4	25.4	14.1	5.9
Lincoln, NE	89.6	76.4	23.6	10.4	5.2
Little Rock, AR	85.3	65.8	31.2	14.7	5.8
Los Angeles, CA	78.6	56.1	28.7	21.4	9.3
Louisville, KY	87.0	70.6	28.7	13.0	5.3
Lubbock, TX	81.2	62.5	28.6	18.8	10.0
Madison, WI	93.1	81.2	23.1	6.9	3.2
Manchester, NH	90.3	76.9	23.6	9.7	2.7

Table continued on next page.

Metro Area	With Health Insurance	With Private Health Insurance	With Public Health Insurance	Without Health Insurance	Population Under Age 18 Without Health Insurance
McAllen, TX	63.5	30.4	37.6	36.5	16.6
Miami, FL	74.3	51.8	30.0	25.7	14.0
Midland, TX	78.3	65.8	21.5	21.7	18.2
Minneapolis, MN	91.5	77.5	24.3	8.5	5.6
Montgomery, AL	87.0	67.2	32.4	13.0	4.5
Nashville, TN	86.1	68.8	26.4	13.9	6.0
New Orleans, LA	82.9	58.9	33.1	17.1	4.8
New York, NY	86.8	64.8	31.3	13.2	4.7
Oklahoma City, OK	82.5	65.0	28.4	17.5	8.5
Omaha, NE	88.8	74.1	25.1	11.2	5.3
Orlando, FL	79.3	60.8	27.5	20.7	11.6
Oxnard, CA	83.7	66.7	26.4	16.3	7.4
Peoria, IL	90.2	72.4	31.6	9.8	2.9
Philadelphia, PA	90.0	72.3	29.4	10.0	4.1
Phoenix, AZ	82.7	61.9	30.7	17.3	12.3
Pittsburgh, PA	91.9	75.5	32.3	8.1	2.8
Portland, OR	85.5	69.9	26.2	14.5	6.4
Providence, RI	91.0	70.6	33.0	9.0	3.5
Provo, UT	86.3	76.3	17.4	13.7	9.7
Raleigh, NC	85.3	71.7	21.9	14.7	8.6
Reno, NV	78.1	63.9	24.0	21.9	18.9
Richmond, VA	87.2	73.1	25.0	12.8	6.3
Riverside, CA	79.2	54.9	31.5	20.8	10.6
Rochester, MN	92.9	80.0	25.0	7.1	4.3
Salem, OR	82.7	62.6	32.9	17.3	7.9
Salt Lake City, UT	83.9	72.0	19.7	16.1	11.6
San Antonio, TX	80.4	61.4	29.7	19.6	10.3
San Diego, CA	82.7	65.6	25.8	17.3	8.8
San Francisco, CA	88.1	71.9	25.7	11.9	5.3
San Jose, CA	88.1	72.2	23.8	11.9	4.2
Santa Rosa, CA	85.6	68.2	29.2	14.4	6.8
Savannah, GA	80.9	63.8	26.5	19.1	10.1
Seattle, WA	87.0	72.8	24.1	13.0	5.5
Sioux Falls, SD	90.5	79.2	22.0	9.5	5.1
Spokane, WA	86.8	66.5	32.9	13.2	4.9
Springfield, MO	84.4	65.8	30.1	15.6	9.9
Tallahassee, FL	85.5	69.6	25.2	14.5	6.0
Tampa, FL	81.8	59.9	34.0	18.2	9.4
Topeka, KS	87.5	72.2	29.8	12.5	7.5
Tulsa, OK	82.0	63.7	29.5	18.0	9.6
Virginia Beach, VA	88.1	74.9	25.2	11.9	5.0
Washington, DC	88.2	76.9	20.7	11.8	5.2
Wichita, KS	85.9	69.7	26.9	14.1	6.5
Wilmington, NC	83.7	66.2	32.5	16.3	7.6
Worcester, MA	96.2	75.9	32.1	3.8	1.3
U.S.	84.9	65.4	30.4	15.1	7.5

Note: Figures are percentages that cover the civilian noninstitutionalized population; Figures cover the Metropolitan Statistical Area (MSA)—see Appendix B for areas included
Source: U.S. Census Bureau, 2010-2012 American Community Survey 3-Year Estimates

Crime Rate: City

City	All Crimes	Violent Crimes				Property Crimes		
		Murder	Forcible Rape	Robbery	Aggrav. Assault	Burglary	Larceny -Theft	Motor Vehicle Theft
Abilene, TX	4,058.0	2.5	31.7	105.9	253.6	865.0	2,656.7	142.6
Albuquerque, NM	6,117.0	7.4	50.2	197.2	494.9	1,205.9	3,666.0	495.4
Anchorage, AK	4,353.1	5.0	101.3	163.1	559.3	387.1	2,859.5	277.8
Ann Arbor, MI	2,567.6	0.9	30.4	43.5	122.6	620.8	1,650.3	99.1
Athens, GA	4,304.6	4.3	40.9	134.5	207.7	978.2	2,732.9	206.0
Atlanta, GA	7,912.5	19.0	25.9	520.8	813.4	1,416.8	3,938.3	1,178.4
Austin, TX	5,628.2	3.7	25.1	117.4	262.6	869.7	4,071.7	277.9
Baltimore, MD	6,065.5	34.9	50.4	576.4	743.6	1,242.3	2,781.4	636.6
Billings, MT	4,871.6	2.8	35.7	63.9	245.4	745.5	3,391.9	386.4
Boise City, ID	2,792.9	0.5	35.4	30.3	201.8	431.5	2,019.2	74.2
Boston, MA	3,744.6	9.0	39.5	302.9	483.6	527.2	2,124.8	257.5
Boulder, CO	3,177.8	0.0	31.9	47.9	168.6	470.8	2,331.0	127.7
Cape Coral, FL	2,349.3	2.5	10.0	25.7	105.2	538.8	1,595.6	71.4
Cedar Rapids, IA	3,955.6	2.3	33.5	75.5	165.9	752.3	2,728.2	197.8
Charleston, SC	2,962.3	9.7	15.3	84.0	130.0	302.0	2,231.6	189.7
Charlotte, NC[1]	4,660.7	7.1	27.6	204.2	367.5	1,081.2	2,707.0	266.1
Chicago, IL	n/a	18.5	n/a	497.6	453.1	839.9	2,684.9	627.7
Cincinnati, OH	7,110.0	15.5	63.5	582.4	313.3	1,851.1	3,912.8	371.4
Clarksville, TN	3,360.6	7.3	33.5	72.1	524.2	710.6	1,891.4	121.6
Colorado Springs, CO	4,595.8	4.2	82.8	121.0	247.3	842.3	2,881.4	416.9
Columbia, MO	4,245.1	2.7	37.1	146.4	244.0	708.6	2,977.1	129.2
Columbus, OH[1]	6,885.1	11.0	71.7	411.9	163.7	1,926.0	3,841.9	459.0
Dallas, TX	5,048.5	12.4	39.1	329.7	293.7	1,296.0	2,508.8	568.8
Davenport, IA	4,636.7	4.0	39.5	149.2	404.2	879.5	2,877.7	282.6
Denver, CO	4,329.7	6.2	59.8	185.3	364.5	816.0	2,313.9	583.9
Des Moines, IA	5,450.3	3.4	48.2	120.5	355.4	1,212.2	3,333.7	377.0
Durham, NC	5,089.5	8.9	26.7	261.1	429.2	1,394.1	2,670.6	298.9
El Paso, TX	2,852.5	3.4	27.2	69.7	322.9	270.3	1,987.3	171.7
Erie, PA	3,891.3	7.8	62.8	168.7	209.9	1,073.8	2,266.3	102.0
Eugene, OR	5,336.5	0.0	45.6	124.0	102.5	958.6	3,830.6	275.2
Fargo, ND	2,940.5	1.8	62.8	41.9	252.2	410.7	2,029.8	141.1
Fayetteville, NC	6,966.7	10.7	34.0	271.9	259.3	1,995.0	4,028.8	367.1
Fort Collins, CO	3,031.1	1.3	29.6	26.9	205.0	401.9	2,271.0	95.4
Fort Wayne, IN	4,070.5	8.6	36.2	174.2	143.8	789.1	2,756.2	162.5
Fort Worth, TX	4,809.5	5.7	50.8	166.2	364.8	1,096.2	2,811.1	314.8
Gainesville, FL	4,764.0	4.7	58.3	134.6	472.3	794.3	3,111.7	188.1
Grand Rapids, MI[1]	4,028.2	5.3	43.1	246.9	447.1	1,038.9	2,074.0	173.0
Green Bay, WI	3,291.9	0.9	41.5	82.0	360.1	621.2	2,083.3	102.8
Greensboro, NC	4,932.0	7.6	25.4	201.4	328.8	1,211.4	2,952.6	205.0
Honolulu, HI	n/a	n/a	n/a	n/a	n/a	n/a	n/a	n/a
Houston, TX	5,938.1	10.0	30.5	431.0	521.0	1,223.1	3,122.2	600.3
Huntsville, AL	5,964.9	7.6	39.2	248.2	628.2	1,178.6	3,476.5	386.5
Indianapolis, IN	6,777.6	11.6	52.0	410.4	711.5	1,761.6	3,282.1	548.4
Jacksonville, FL	4,741.9	11.1	40.6	163.1	402.5	907.9	3,021.8	195.0
Kansas City, MO	6,788.6	22.6	53.0	354.9	832.6	1,500.6	3,251.2	773.6
Lafayette, LA	6,181.4	9.0	9.0	164.4	451.8	1,082.6	4,268.6	196.2
Las Vegas, NV	3,922.2	5.1	40.3	258.5	480.1	961.2	1,725.2	451.9
Lexington, KY	4,784.5	4.0	33.7	200.4	114.4	944.0	3,188.9	299.0
Lincoln, NE	4,247.6	1.1	68.9	74.6	252.9	611.7	3,120.7	117.7
Little Rock, AR	9,376.5	23.0	69.9	411.6	811.0	2,164.7	5,337.8	558.5
Los Angeles, CA	2,750.2	7.8	24.3	233.0	216.1	425.1	1,452.8	391.3
Louisville, KY	4,892.7	9.3	27.5	209.2	352.7	1,051.9	2,913.7	328.3
Lubbock, TX	6,000.2	4.6	43.8	137.0	641.5	1,306.3	3,552.9	314.0
Madison, WI	3,642.0	1.3	48.0	101.5	226.9	674.1	2,483.3	106.9

Table continued on next page.

City	All Crimes	Violent Crimes				Property Crimes		
		Murder	Forcible Rape	Robbery	Aggrav. Assault	Burglary	Larceny -Theft	Motor Vehicle Theft
Manchester, NH	4,064.0	0.9	65.4	186.3	314.4	771.5	2,588.1	137.2
McAllen, TX	4,148.2	0.7	2.2	41.3	78.1	370.5	3,499.9	155.4
Miami, FL	6,547.2	16.7	15.7	505.9	633.8	1,027.0	3,693.9	654.3
Midland, TX	2,945.4	3.5	18.2	45.0	277.6	483.4	2,000.2	117.6
Minneapolis, MN	5,953.0	10.0	103.3	440.5	438.4	1,225.4	3,269.8	465.6
Montgomery, AL	6,164.5	21.1	19.6	219.6	135.4	1,631.0	3,611.2	526.7
Nashville, TN	5,411.9	10.0	50.1	277.7	878.3	923.8	3,041.6	230.5
New Orleans, LA	4,587.5	53.2	37.5	293.5	431.0	943.3	2,218.7	610.4
New York, NY	2,361.5	5.1	14.0	243.7	376.5	224.8	1,398.6	98.8
Oklahoma City, OK	6,860.9	14.3	65.3	203.0	636.5	1,654.4	3,553.0	734.4
Omaha, NE	5,182.9	9.8	44.7	195.0	345.0	792.2	3,139.0	657.2
Orlando, FL	7,631.2	9.7	41.8	244.6	721.3	1,532.6	4,552.3	529.0
Oxnard, CA	2,316.2	4.5	4.0	150.6	139.7	420.2	1,326.6	270.6
Peoria, IL	5,153.2	8.7	21.7	281.0	485.7	1,231.7	2,923.1	201.2
Philadelphia, PA	4,863.7	21.5	57.2	518.8	562.6	780.0	2,507.7	415.9
Phoenix, AZ	4,728.0	8.3	37.4	236.7	354.3	1,205.8	2,401.7	483.8
Pittsburgh, PA	4,177.3	13.1	15.1	363.3	360.4	812.8	2,438.2	174.3
Portland, OR	5,609.5	3.3	38.6	158.9	316.4	747.6	3,745.3	599.5
Providence, RI	5,121.4	9.6	47.2	203.5	376.7	1,084.4	2,745.6	654.4
Provo, UT	2,236.5	0.0	30.8	16.3	80.4	257.5	1,754.8	96.7
Raleigh, NC	3,699.3	4.0	26.9	158.1	234.2	721.8	2,332.9	221.4
Reno, NV	3,737.8	3.0	14.3	141.9	357.9	708.5	2,129.8	382.2
Richmond, VA	5,029.4	20.2	18.3	304.6	305.6	976.9	2,953.8	450.0
Riverside, CA	3,893.4	5.1	24.2	164.9	248.8	716.7	2,262.9	470.8
Rochester, MN	n/a	1.8	n/a	50.7	95.8	455.9	1,968.1	82.0
Salem, OR	4,636.1	4.4	25.4	87.7	240.9	662.8	3,150.9	463.9
Salt Lake City, UT	8,135.0	4.2	63.4	164.2	443.7	947.7	5,625.4	886.4
San Antonio, TX	6,493.0	6.4	39.8	135.1	321.8	1,135.3	4,393.3	461.3
San Diego, CA	2,781.4	3.5	22.7	113.3	273.5	440.9	1,433.6	493.8
San Francisco, CA	5,445.8	8.4	13.2	424.7	257.9	648.1	3,442.6	650.8
San Jose, CA	3,278.2	4.6	28.7	123.7	206.3	533.2	1,484.8	897.0
Santa Rosa, CA	2,606.8	1.2	39.2	73.7	258.1	424.3	1,625.3	184.9
Savannah, GA	3,979.1	9.9	10.8	212.3	146.6	900.6	2,413.9	284.9
Seattle, WA	5,691.3	3.7	19.0	226.7	348.2	1,040.6	3,485.9	567.3
Sioux Falls, SD	3,581.8	1.3	87.8	44.2	265.2	567.7	2,426.8	188.8
Spokane, WA	9,375.3	6.1	38.2	253.1	347.8	1,803.8	5,938.8	987.4
Springfield, MO	10,002.4	9.9	87.6	219.3	674.7	1,376.1	6,981.8	652.9
Tallahassee, FL	5,499.3	6.5	62.0	283.1	501.5	1,418.1	2,945.6	282.5
Tampa, FL	3,452.2	6.6	12.3	163.4	434.2	705.9	1,956.9	173.1
Topeka, KS	5,908.7	11.6	30.3	183.9	373.3	991.1	3,855.1	463.4
Tulsa, OK	6,206.0	10.5	79.2	266.2	634.0	1,563.0	3,048.9	604.2
Virginia Beach, VA	2,787.2	4.7	13.0	72.8	78.9	351.4	2,158.7	107.7
Washington, DC	5,805.9	13.9	37.3	589.1	537.5	556.5	3,510.2	561.3
Wichita, KS	6,195.2	6.0	59.0	128.1	549.4	1,014.2	3,967.6	471.0
Wilmington, NC	5,968.7	7.3	21.0	238.6	298.1	1,548.9	3,513.8	341.0
Worcester, MA	4,469.4	4.4	18.0	228.7	708.3	1,113.3	2,143.0	253.8
U.S.	3,246.1	4.7	26.9	112.9	242.3	670.2	1,959.3	229.7

Note: Figures are crimes per 100,000 population in 2012 except where noted; n/a not available; (1) 2011 data
Source: FBI Uniform Crime Reports, 2012

Crime Rate: Suburbs

Suburbs[1]	All Crimes	Violent Crimes				Property Crimes		
		Murder	Forcible Rape	Robbery	Aggrav. Assault	Burglary	Larceny -Theft	Motor Vehicle Theft
Abilene, TX	1,570.7	0.0	14.3	18.4	136.7	424.3	909.8	67.3
Albuquerque, NM	n/a	3.5	26.8	39.6	407.9	n/a	n/a	203.0
Anchorage, AK	6,012.8	0.0	27.8	55.6	361.5	542.2	4,733.8	292.0
Ann Arbor, MI	2,813.0	1.7	48.5	58.7	233.7	694.7	1,635.9	139.8
Athens, GA	2,849.0	1.3	26.9	26.9	164.3	537.7	1,955.8	136.0
Atlanta, GA	3,431.7	5.0	19.6	122.2	177.0	824.3	1,978.8	304.9
Austin, TX	2,101.1	0.8	25.0	22.2	145.8	402.0	1,434.1	71.2
Baltimore, MD	2,883.2	2.1	16.7	107.8	264.4	456.0	1,886.6	149.5
Billings, MT	1,856.0	0.0	9.0	1.8	152.6	369.8	1,173.9	149.0
Boise City, ID	1,876.3	1.4	28.1	12.6	140.6	408.2	1,221.1	64.2
Boston, MA	2,153.3	1.1	20.2	74.3	235.1	417.0	1,304.8	100.9
Boulder, CO	2,229.6	0.0	20.2	26.6	131.4	342.9	1,609.7	98.9
Cape Coral, FL	2,811.7	8.5	19.4	106.6	282.9	689.3	1,536.5	168.4
Cedar Rapids, IA	n/a	0.8	20.3	3.8	56.3	n/a	757.6	59.3
Charleston, SC	3,850.5	6.4	31.7	91.0	333.2	708.1	2,393.3	286.9
Charlotte, NC[2]	3,228.5	3.0	22.2	60.5	200.4	686.7	2,117.4	138.3
Chicago, IL	n/a	2.1	n/a	59.5	89.8	384.0	1,532.4	94.0
Cincinnati, OH	3,035.0	1.6	27.1	58.7	85.3	623.0	2,145.0	94.3
Clarksville, TN	2,736.0	5.4	30.3	58.2	138.9	676.8	1,699.0	127.3
Colorado Springs, CO	n/a	0.8	37.5	18.6	180.0	n/a	1,051.6	116.4
Columbia, MO	2,658.6	0.0	9.0	32.6	224.3	432.3	1,857.4	103.1
Columbus, OH[2]	2,783.7	1.6	24.5	49.9	64.8	593.9	1,979.6	69.3
Dallas, TX	2,786.9	1.3	20.0	52.8	115.4	573.7	1,846.4	177.1
Davenport, IA	2,352.8	2.1	27.4	33.5	228.2	386.6	1,614.1	60.9
Denver, CO	2,694.1	3.2	38.6	52.8	155.8	400.3	1,836.5	206.9
Des Moines, IA	n/a	0.3	20.8	9.1	127.4	n/a	1,380.7	81.0
Durham, NC	2,848.2	2.1	16.6	38.9	120.7	845.7	1,724.3	99.8
El Paso, TX	2,117.7	3.1	22.4	23.0	237.2	344.1	1,365.0	123.0
Erie, PA	2,267.8	1.7	16.2	28.4	84.7	397.3	1,680.0	59.6
Eugene, OR	3,004.8	3.5	27.3	32.8	144.5	558.9	2,021.9	215.8
Fargo, ND	n/a	0.0	n/a	12.2	116.7	327.6	1,378.9	76.2
Fayetteville, NC	4,535.2	4.7	14.5	112.3	279.8	1,626.5	2,345.6	151.8
Fort Collins, CO	2,363.9	0.6	26.1	21.7	149.7	311.9	1,786.2	67.7
Fort Wayne, IN	1,674.2	1.2	11.6	15.2	61.5	312.5	1,183.7	88.3
Fort Worth, TX	3,143.3	2.6	25.4	63.9	182.3	641.5	2,058.6	168.9
Gainesville, FL	3,054.6	2.8	44.8	58.1	395.2	700.9	1,759.1	93.7
Grand Rapids, MI[2]	2,215.9	1.7	42.7	34.8	138.8	501.1	1,407.6	89.1
Green Bay, WI	1,509.4	2.9	11.8	6.4	78.4	296.8	1,068.7	44.6
Greensboro, NC	3,311.6	5.0	14.5	64.9	169.0	878.4	2,036.5	143.3
Honolulu, HI	n/a	n/a	n/a	n/a	n/a	n/a	n/a	n/a
Houston, TX	n/a	3.3	21.0	104.2	196.8	n/a	1,848.3	256.8
Huntsville, AL	2,284.6	3.3	15.2	37.8	162.2	595.5	1,361.8	108.8
Indianapolis, IN	2,321.3	1.6	15.4	29.1	97.2	388.2	1,675.5	114.4
Jacksonville, FL	2,769.3	3.2	15.8	44.4	287.8	488.2	1,845.6	84.4
Kansas City, MO	3,128.3	3.3	28.1	49.3	178.3	531.9	2,064.1	273.4
Lafayette, LA	n/a	6.6	21.9	66.7	n/a	720.4	1,778.0	n/a
Las Vegas, NV	2,918.4	3.7	27.7	115.8	298.8	642.8	1,532.5	297.1
Lexington, KY	3,732.8	3.4	33.1	53.9	115.1	826.4	2,570.1	130.8
Lincoln, NE	1,819.2	2.2	31.5	9.0	51.7	368.8	1,306.5	49.5
Little Rock, AR	4,463.8	3.9	36.2	76.5	301.6	1,082.0	2,714.2	249.4
Los Angeles, CA	2,788.2	4.9	17.0	162.3	240.4	534.1	1,413.7	415.8
Louisville, KY	2,765.2	2.7	15.8	54.4	153.8	596.5	1,794.6	147.3
Lubbock, TX	2,393.8	1.6	63.4	6.3	247.3	559.6	1,377.6	137.9
Madison, WI	1,998.3	3.2	15.9	14.8	65.7	302.3	1,545.0	51.4

Table continued on next page.

Suburbs[1]	All Crimes	Violent Crimes				Property Crimes		
		Murder	Forcible Rape	Robbery	Aggrav. Assault	Burglary	Larceny -Theft	Motor Vehicle Theft
Manchester, NH	1,982.7	0.0	24.3	24.3	78.7	302.0	1,486.5	67.0
McAllen, TX	4,075.7	4.3	29.5	62.0	263.1	884.6	2,652.8	179.5
Miami, FL	4,768.9	6.5	23.2	179.7	356.8	774.8	3,117.7	310.2
Midland, TX	2,400.9	3.1	6.3	6.3	191.9	487.7	1,447.5	258.0
Minneapolis, MN	n/a	1.2	n/a	45.2	103.0	n/a	1,950.4	158.5
Montgomery, AL	3,134.8	5.3	26.9	55.5	212.7	873.1	1,804.1	157.2
Nashville, TN	2,553.5	2.3	23.4	42.1	285.3	479.9	1,613.9	106.7
New Orleans, LA	3,373.8	6.8	17.4	76.6	241.7	630.4	2,230.2	170.6
New York, NY	n/a	1.9	9.2	94.5	n/a	350.9	1,255.8	102.4
Oklahoma City, OK	3,237.7	2.6	30.0	39.1	157.2	734.5	2,066.9	207.4
Omaha, NE	2,510.9	0.4	31.8	26.7	179.6	470.0	1,579.7	222.6
Orlando, FL	3,577.0	4.3	29.3	105.9	347.0	897.3	1,990.7	202.4
Oxnard, CA	2,024.7	1.9	14.4	49.1	101.0	355.2	1,368.5	134.5
Peoria, IL	2,268.9	3.0	27.2	29.9	183.0	492.0	1,475.9	57.9
Philadelphia, PA	n/a	5.0	15.2	143.1	n/a	418.8	1,822.6	107.3
Phoenix, AZ	n/a	3.7	22.4	69.8	190.0	617.1	2,222.6	n/a
Pittsburgh, PA	n/a	2.9	15.2	48.3	n/a	335.5	1,271.5	61.5
Portland, OR	2,656.0	2.0	29.3	49.4	96.7	451.1	1,785.1	242.5
Providence, RI	2,549.9	1.5	26.8	73.3	201.1	538.3	1,550.7	158.3
Provo, UT	1,846.4	0.9	10.9	11.4	32.2	235.1	1,496.8	59.1
Raleigh, NC	2,170.5	0.5	12.2	30.2	105.8	557.2	1,379.2	85.4
Reno, NV	2,235.1	2.4	25.4	43.5	187.1	513.3	1,286.0	177.3
Richmond, VA	2,356.0	4.1	11.9	51.9	93.3	416.8	1,669.2	108.7
Riverside, CA	3,350.9	4.0	16.6	117.9	224.4	884.2	1,626.9	476.9
Rochester, MN	n/a	1.0	n/a	4.0	60.3	278.5	628.2	57.3
Salem, OR	2,670.7	2.5	20.4	25.8	108.6	475.2	1,812.2	226.0
Salt Lake City, UT	3,936.1	1.8	40.8	54.5	158.5	561.3	2,827.4	291.8
San Antonio, TX	2,776.2	2.9	30.9	30.0	143.8	581.5	1,845.9	141.2
San Diego, CA	2,416.2	3.3	21.2	91.9	228.3	446.5	1,323.2	301.9
San Francisco, CA	2,375.4	1.4	14.7	78.8	158.7	457.4	1,445.3	219.1
San Jose, CA	2,445.6	1.2	15.1	51.2	110.3	451.4	1,557.9	258.4
Santa Rosa, CA	1,818.6	0.6	26.4	32.9	299.3	342.2	996.0	121.2
Savannah, GA	2,521.7	1.6	27.3	50.0	154.6	538.7	1,626.3	123.4
Seattle, WA	3,581.4	2.3	29.2	75.4	115.3	781.6	2,175.9	401.7
Sioux Falls, SD	1,117.5	0.0	24.8	0.0	82.1	301.2	650.7	58.7
Spokane, WA	3,595.3	2.5	21.0	38.7	89.4	868.4	2,292.2	283.1
Springfield, MO	2,288.9	2.1	16.4	8.2	161.4	542.8	1,432.1	125.7
Tallahassee, FL	2,719.9	5.3	26.4	45.9	301.0	765.3	1,475.1	100.9
Tampa, FL	3,246.9	3.5	26.2	85.1	265.6	672.7	2,043.3	150.5
Topeka, KS	2,257.9	2.8	10.3	8.4	174.8	552.3	1,371.0	138.3
Tulsa, OK	2,144.1	2.2	27.8	24.9	165.7	494.1	1,301.5	127.8
Virginia Beach, VA	3,622.0	7.6	23.2	112.7	204.1	598.0	2,516.7	159.6
Washington, DC	2,319.9	2.7	14.9	102.1	118.8	286.0	1,595.7	199.6
Wichita, KS	2,420.4	0.4	24.0	12.4	162.7	528.0	1,582.7	110.3
Wilmington, NC	2,931.5	1.3	22.3	36.0	168.2	641.4	1,949.1	113.2
Worcester, MA	2,007.0	0.9	22.9	35.8	212.6	435.8	1,224.1	74.9
U.S.	3,246.1	4.7	26.9	112.9	242.3	670.2	1,959.3	229.7

Note: Figures are crimes per 100,000 population in 2012 except where noted; n/a not available; (1) All areas within the metro area that are located outside the city limits; (2) 2011 data
Source: FBI Uniform Crime Reports, 2012

Crime Rate: Metro Area

Metro Area[1]	All Crimes	Violent Crimes				Property Crimes		
		Murder	Forcible Rape	Robbery	Aggrav. Assault	Burglary	Larceny -Theft	Motor Vehicle Theft
Abilene, TX	3,336.1	1.8	26.6	80.5	219.6	737.1	2,149.7	120.8
Albuquerque, NM	n/a	5.9	41.2	136.5	461.4	n/a	n/a	382.9
Anchorage, AK	4,429.3	4.8	97.9	158.2	550.2	394.2	2,945.5	278.4
Ann Arbor, MI	2,731.9	1.4	42.5	53.7	197.0	670.3	1,640.7	126.4
Athens, GA	3,724.0	3.1	35.3	91.6	190.4	802.5	2,423.0	178.1
Atlanta, GA	3,792.0	6.1	20.1	154.2	228.2	871.9	2,136.4	375.1
Austin, TX	3,723.9	2.2	25.0	66.0	199.5	617.2	2,647.7	166.3
Baltimore, MD	3,605.5	9.5	24.4	214.2	373.2	634.5	2,089.7	260.1
Billings, MT	3,835.1	1.9	26.5	42.6	213.5	616.4	2,629.5	304.8
Boise City, ID	2,183.2	1.1	30.5	18.5	161.1	416.0	1,488.3	67.6
Boston, MA[2]	2,675.7	3.7	26.5	149.4	316.7	453.2	1,574.0	152.3
Boulder, CO	2,542.8	0.0	24.1	33.6	143.6	385.1	1,848.0	108.4
Cape Coral, FL	2,696.3	7.0	17.0	86.4	238.6	651.8	1,551.2	144.2
Cedar Rapids, IA	n/a	1.5	26.8	39.0	110.1	n/a	1,724.9	127.3
Charleston, SC	3,690.8	7.0	28.8	89.7	296.7	635.1	2,364.2	269.4
Charlotte, NC[3]	3,863.7	4.8	24.6	124.2	274.5	861.7	2,378.9	195.0
Chicago, IL[2]	n/a	8.2	n/a	222.0	224.6	553.1	1,959.9	292.0
Cincinnati, OH	3,603.4	3.5	32.2	131.8	117.1	794.3	2,391.6	133.0
Clarksville, TN	3,058.3	6.4	31.9	65.4	337.7	694.2	1,798.3	124.3
Colorado Springs, CO	n/a	3.0	66.8	84.7	223.5	n/a	2,233.2	310.4
Columbia, MO	3,716.4	1.8	27.7	108.5	237.4	616.5	2,604.0	120.5
Columbus, OH[3]	4,541.3	5.7	44.7	205.0	107.2	1,164.8	2,777.7	236.3
Dallas, TX[2]	3,424.2	4.4	25.4	130.9	165.7	777.2	2,033.1	287.5
Davenport, IA	2,957.7	2.6	30.6	64.1	274.8	517.2	1,948.8	119.6
Denver, CO	3,084.2	3.9	43.6	84.4	205.6	499.5	1,950.4	296.8
Des Moines, IA	n/a	1.4	30.6	48.8	208.6	n/a	2,076.0	186.4
Durham, NC	3,867.3	5.2	21.2	139.9	261.0	1,095.0	2,154.6	190.3
El Paso, TX	2,711.1	3.3	26.3	60.7	306.4	284.5	1,867.5	162.3
Erie, PA	2,856.0	3.9	33.0	79.2	130.0	642.4	1,892.4	75.0
Eugene, OR	4,040.2	2.0	35.4	73.3	125.9	736.4	2,825.0	242.2
Fargo, ND	n/a	0.9	n/a	27.3	185.6	369.8	1,709.7	109.2
Fayetteville, NC	5,860.6	7.9	25.1	199.3	268.6	1,827.4	3,263.1	269.1
Fort Collins, CO	2,684.4	1.0	27.8	24.2	176.3	355.1	2,019.0	81.0
Fort Wayne, IN	3,135.7	5.7	26.6	112.2	111.7	603.2	2,142.8	133.6
Fort Worth, TX[2]	3,707.5	3.6	34.0	98.6	244.1	795.5	2,313.4	218.3
Gainesville, FL	3,858.8	3.7	51.1	94.1	431.5	744.8	2,395.5	138.1
Grand Rapids, MI[3]	2,656.1	2.6	42.8	86.4	213.7	631.7	1,569.5	109.5
Green Bay, WI	2,118.9	2.3	21.9	32.2	174.7	407.7	1,415.6	64.5
Greensboro, NC	3,917.7	6.0	18.6	116.0	228.8	1,003.0	2,379.1	166.3
Honolulu, HI	3,600.7	2.0	22.9	93.8	149.4	606.1	2,315.9	410.5
Houston, TX	n/a	5.7	24.4	219.9	311.6	n/a	2,299.3	378.4
Huntsville, AL	3,867.1	5.1	25.5	128.3	362.6	846.2	2,271.1	228.2
Indianapolis, IN	4,272.0	6.0	31.4	196.0	366.1	989.4	2,378.8	304.4
Jacksonville, FL	3,972.0	8.0	30.9	116.8	357.8	744.0	2,562.7	151.8
Kansas City, MO	3,963.8	7.7	33.8	119.1	327.7	753.0	2,335.0	387.6
Lafayette, LA	n/a	7.2	18.6	92.0	n/a	814.4	2,423.8	n/a
Las Vegas, NV	3,662.5	4.8	37.0	221.6	433.2	878.8	1,675.3	411.8
Lexington, KY	4,394.6	3.7	33.5	146.1	114.7	900.4	2,959.5	236.6
Lincoln, NE	3,897.7	1.3	63.5	65.1	223.9	576.7	2,859.3	107.9
Little Rock, AR	5,815.4	9.1	45.5	168.7	441.8	1,379.9	3,436.0	334.4
Los Angeles, CA[2]	2,773.6	6.0	19.8	189.6	231.0	492.0	1,428.8	406.3
Louisville, KY	3,900.3	6.2	22.0	137.0	260.0	839.5	2,391.7	243.9
Lubbock, TX	5,242.7	4.0	47.9	109.5	558.7	1,149.4	3,096.0	277.0
Madison, WI	2,633.2	2.4	28.3	48.3	128.0	445.9	1,907.4	72.9

Table continued on next page.

Metro Area[1]	All Crimes	Violent Crimes				Property Crimes		
		Murder	Forcible Rape	Robbery	Aggrav. Assault	Burglary	Larceny -Theft	Motor Vehicle Theft
Manchester, NH	2,551.8	0.2	35.5	68.6	143.1	430.3	1,787.7	86.2
McAllen, TX	4,087.9	3.7	24.9	58.5	232.0	798.4	2,794.8	175.5
Miami, FL[2]	5,053.4	8.1	22.0	231.9	401.1	815.1	3,209.9	365.3
Midland, TX	2,828.0	3.4	15.6	36.6	259.1	484.3	1,881.1	147.9
Minneapolis, MN	n/a	2.2	n/a	90.5	141.4	n/a	2,101.5	193.7
Montgomery, AL	4,800.7	13.9	22.9	145.7	170.2	1,289.8	2,797.7	360.4
Nashville, TN	3,589.7	5.1	33.0	127.5	500.3	640.8	2,131.5	151.6
New Orleans, LA	3,734.8	20.6	23.4	141.1	298.0	723.5	2,226.8	301.4
New York, NY[2]	n/a	3.8	12.0	182.6	n/a	276.5	1,340.1	100.3
Oklahoma City, OK	4,915.9	8.0	46.3	115.0	379.2	1,160.6	2,755.3	451.5
Omaha, NE	3,775.9	4.9	37.9	106.4	257.9	622.5	2,317.9	428.4
Orlando, FL	4,031.1	5.0	30.7	121.4	389.0	968.5	2,277.6	238.9
Oxnard, CA	2,094.7	2.5	11.9	73.5	110.3	370.8	1,358.5	167.2
Peoria, IL	3,144.6	4.7	25.5	106.1	274.9	716.6	1,915.3	101.4
Philadelphia, PA[2]	n/a	16.8	45.3	412.6	n/a	678.0	2,314.1	328.7
Phoenix, AZ	n/a	5.3	27.6	127.3	246.6	820.0	2,284.3	n/a
Pittsburgh, PA	n/a	4.2	15.2	89.9	n/a	398.5	1,425.6	76.4
Portland, OR	3,430.8	2.4	31.8	78.1	154.3	528.8	2,299.3	336.1
Providence, RI	2,835.1	2.4	29.1	87.7	220.6	598.8	1,683.2	213.3
Provo, UT	1,929.6	0.7	15.1	12.4	42.5	239.9	1,551.8	67.1
Raleigh, NC	2,717.7	1.8	17.4	76.0	151.7	616.1	1,720.5	134.0
Reno, NV	3,030.9	2.8	19.5	95.6	277.6	616.7	1,732.9	285.8
Richmond, VA	2,806.7	6.8	13.0	94.5	129.1	511.3	1,885.8	166.3
Riverside, CA	3,390.1	4.1	17.1	121.3	226.2	872.1	1,672.8	476.4
Rochester, MN	n/a	1.4	n/a	28.1	78.6	370.3	1,321.6	70.1
Salem, OR	3,448.3	3.3	22.4	50.3	160.9	549.5	2,341.9	320.1
Salt Lake City, UT	4,655.5	2.2	44.7	73.3	207.3	627.5	3,306.8	393.7
San Antonio, TX	5,078.7	5.1	36.4	95.1	254.1	924.5	3,424.0	339.5
San Diego, CA	2,570.5	3.4	21.8	101.0	247.4	444.2	1,369.8	382.9
San Francisco, CA[2]	3,995.9	5.1	13.9	261.3	211.1	558.1	2,499.5	446.9
San Jose, CA	2,877.4	3.0	22.1	88.8	160.1	493.8	1,520.0	589.6
Santa Rosa, CA	2,092.0	0.8	30.9	47.1	285.0	370.7	1,214.3	143.3
Savannah, GA	3,459.7	7.0	16.7	154.4	149.4	771.6	2,133.2	227.3
Seattle, WA[2]	4,067.9	2.6	26.8	110.3	169.0	841.3	2,478.0	439.9
Sioux Falls, SD	2,777.8	0.9	67.2	29.8	205.5	480.8	1,847.3	146.4
Spokane, WA	5,885.8	3.9	27.8	123.6	191.8	1,239.1	3,737.3	562.2
Springfield, MO	5,104.4	5.0	42.4	85.3	348.8	847.0	3,457.8	318.2
Tallahassee, FL	4,095.2	5.9	44.0	163.3	400.2	1,088.3	2,202.8	190.8
Tampa, FL	3,272.0	3.9	24.5	94.7	286.2	676.7	2,032.7	153.3
Topeka, KS	4,252.4	7.6	21.2	104.3	283.2	792.0	2,728.1	315.9
Tulsa, OK	3,844.7	5.7	49.3	125.9	361.8	941.7	2,033.1	327.3
Virginia Beach, VA	3,402.7	6.8	20.5	102.3	171.2	533.2	2,422.7	146.0
Washington, DC[2]	2,800.3	4.3	18.0	169.2	176.5	323.3	1,859.6	249.4
Wichita, KS	4,711.6	3.8	45.2	82.6	397.4	823.1	3,030.2	329.2
Wilmington, NC	4,198.6	3.8	21.7	120.5	222.4	1,020.0	2,601.8	208.3
Worcester, MA	2,537.1	1.6	21.9	77.3	319.3	581.7	1,421.9	113.4
U.S.	3,246.1	4.7	26.9	112.9	242.3	670.2	1,959.3	229.7

Note: Figures are crimes per 100,000 population in 2012 except where noted; n/a not available; (1) Figures cover the Metropolitan Statistical Area except where noted; (2) Metropolitan Division (MD); See Appendix B for counties included in MSAs and MDs; (3) 2011 data Source: FBI Uniform Crime Reports, 2012

Temperature & Precipitation: Yearly Averages and Extremes

City	Extreme Low (°F)	Average Low (°F)	Average Temp. (°F)	Average High (°F)	Extreme High (°F)	Average Precip. (in.)	Average Snow (in.)
Abilene, TX	-7	53	65	76	110	23.6	5
Albuquerque, NM	-17	43	57	70	105	8.5	11
Anchorage, AK	-34	29	36	43	85	15.7	71
Ann Arbor, MI	-21	39	49	58	104	32.4	41
Athens, GA	-8	52	62	72	105	49.8	2
Atlanta, GA	-8	52	62	72	105	49.8	2
Austin, TX	-2	58	69	79	109	31.1	1
Baltimore, MD	-7	45	56	65	105	41.2	21
Billings, MT	-32	36	47	59	105	14.6	59
Boise City, ID	-25	39	51	63	111	11.8	22
Boston, MA	-12	44	52	59	102	42.9	41
Boulder, CO	-25	37	51	64	103	15.5	63
Cape Coral, FL	26	65	75	84	103	53.9	0
Cedar Rapids, IA	-34	36	47	57	105	34.4	33
Charleston, SC	6	55	66	76	104	52.1	1
Charlotte, NC	-5	50	61	71	104	42.8	6
Chicago, IL	-27	40	49	59	104	35.4	39
Cincinnati, OH	-25	44	54	64	103	40.9	23
Clarksville, TN	-17	49	60	70	107	47.4	11
Colorado Springs, CO	-24	36	49	62	99	17.0	48
Columbia, MO	-20	44	54	64	111	40.6	25
Columbus, OH	-19	42	52	62	104	37.9	28
Dallas, TX	-2	56	67	77	112	33.9	3
Davenport, IA	-24	40	50	60	108	31.8	33
Denver, CO	-25	37	51	64	103	15.5	63
Des Moines, IA	-24	40	50	60	108	31.8	33
Durham, NC	-9	48	60	71	105	42.0	8
El Paso, TX	-8	50	64	78	114	8.6	6
Erie, PA	-18	41	49	57	100	40.5	83
Eugene, OR	-12	42	53	63	108	47.3	7
Fargo, ND	-36	31	41	52	106	19.6	40
Fayetteville, NC	-9	48	60	71	105	42.0	8
Fort Collins, CO	-25	37	51	64	103	15.5	63
Fort Wayne, IN	-22	40	50	60	106	35.9	33
Fort Worth, TX	-1	55	66	76	113	32.3	3
Gainesville, FL	10	58	69	79	102	50.9	Trace
Grand Rapids, MI	-22	38	48	57	102	34.7	73
Green Bay, WI	-31	34	44	54	99	28.3	46
Greensboro, NC	-8	47	58	69	103	42.5	10
Honolulu, HI	52	70	77	84	94	22.4	0
Houston, TX	7	58	69	79	107	46.9	Trace
Huntsville, AL	-11	50	61	71	104	56.8	4
Indianapolis, IN	-23	42	53	62	104	40.2	25
Jacksonville, FL	7	58	69	79	103	52.0	0
Kansas City, MO	-23	44	54	64	109	38.1	21
Lafayette, LA	8	57	68	78	103	58.5	Trace
Las Vegas, NV	8	53	67	80	116	4.0	1
Lexington, KY	-21	45	55	65	103	45.1	17
Lincoln, NE	-33	39	51	62	108	29.1	27
Little Rock, AR	-5	51	62	73	112	50.7	5
Los Angeles, CA	27	55	63	70	110	11.3	Trace
Louisville, KY	-20	46	57	67	105	43.9	17
Lubbock, TX	-16	47	60	74	110	18.4	10
Madison, WI	-37	35	46	57	104	31.1	42
Manchester, NH	-33	34	46	57	102	36.9	63

Table continued on next page.

City	Extreme Low (°F)	Average Low (°F)	Average Temp. (°F)	Average High (°F)	Extreme High (°F)	Average Precip. (in.)	Average Snow (in.)
McAllen, TX	16	65	74	83	106	25.8	Trace
Miami, FL	30	69	76	83	98	57.1	0
Midland, TX	-11	50	64	77	116	14.6	4
Minneapolis, MN	-34	35	45	54	105	27.1	52
Montgomery, AL	0	54	65	76	105	52.7	Trace
Nashville, TN	-17	49	60	70	107	47.4	11
New Orleans, LA	11	59	69	78	102	60.6	Trace
New York, NY	-2	47	55	62	104	47.0	23
Oklahoma City, OK	-8	49	60	71	110	32.8	10
Omaha, NE	-23	40	51	62	110	30.1	29
Orlando, FL	19	62	72	82	100	47.7	Trace
Oxnard, CA	27	51	60	68	105	12.0	0
Peoria, IL	-26	41	51	61	113	35.4	23
Philadelphia, PA	-7	45	55	64	104	41.4	22
Phoenix, AZ	17	59	72	86	122	7.3	Trace
Pittsburgh, PA	-18	41	51	60	103	37.1	43
Portland, OR	-3	45	54	62	107	37.5	7
Providence, RI	-13	42	51	60	104	45.3	35
Provo, UT	-22	40	52	64	107	15.6	63
Raleigh, NC	-9	48	60	71	105	42.0	8
Reno, NV	-16	33	50	67	105	7.2	24
Richmond, VA	-8	48	58	69	105	43.0	13
Riverside, CA	24	53	66	78	114	n/a	n/a
Rochester, MN	-40	34	44	54	102	29.4	47
Salem, OR	-12	41	52	63	108	40.2	7
Salt Lake City, UT	-22	40	52	64	107	15.6	63
San Antonio, TX	0	58	69	80	108	29.6	1
San Diego, CA	29	57	64	71	111	9.5	Trace
San Francisco, CA	24	49	57	65	106	19.3	Trace
San Jose, CA	21	50	59	68	105	13.5	Trace
Santa Rosa, CA	23	42	57	71	109	29.0	n/a
Savannah, GA	3	56	67	77	105	50.3	Trace
Seattle, WA	0	44	52	59	99	38.4	13
Sioux Falls, SD	-36	35	46	57	110	24.6	38
Spokane, WA	-25	37	47	57	108	17.0	51
Springfield, MO	-17	45	56	67	113	42.0	18
Tallahassee, FL	6	56	68	79	103	63.3	Trace
Tampa, FL	18	63	73	82	99	46.7	Trace
Topeka, KS	-26	43	55	66	110	34.4	21
Tulsa, OK	-8	50	61	71	112	38.9	10
Virginia Beach, VA	-3	51	60	69	104	44.8	8
Washington, DC	-5	49	58	67	104	39.5	18
Wichita, KS	-21	45	57	68	113	29.3	17
Wilmington, NC	0	53	64	74	104	55.0	2
Worcester, MA	-13	38	47	56	99	47.6	62

Source: National Climatic Data Center, International Station Meteorological Climate Summary, 9/96

Weather Conditions

City	Temperature			Daytime Sky			Precipitation		
	10°F & below	32°F & below	90°F & above	Clear	Partly cloudy	Cloudy	0.01 inch or more precip.	1.0 inch or more snow/ice	Thunder-storms
Abilene, TX	2	52	102	141	125	99	65	4	43
Albuquerque, NM	4	114	65	140	161	64	60	9	38
Anchorage, AK	n/a	194	n/a	50	115	200	113	49	2
Ann Arbor, MI	n/a	136	12	74	134	157	135	38	32
Athens, GA	1	49	38	98	147	120	116	3	48
Atlanta, GA	1	49	38	98	147	120	116	3	48
Austin, TX	< 1	20	111	105	148	112	83	1	41
Baltimore, MD	6	97	31	91	143	131	113	13	27
Billings, MT	n/a	149	29	75	163	127	97	41	27
Boise City, ID	n/a	124	45	106	133	126	91	22	14
Boston, MA	n/a	97	12	88	127	150	253	48	18
Boulder, CO	24	155	33	99	177	89	90	38	39
Cape Coral, FL	n/a	n/a	115	93	220	52	110	0	92
Cedar Rapids, IA	n/a	156	16	89	132	144	109	28	42
Charleston, SC	< 1	33	53	89	162	114	114	1	59
Charlotte, NC	1	65	44	98	142	125	113	3	41
Chicago, IL	n/a	132	17	83	136	146	125	31	38
Cincinnati, OH	14	107	23	80	126	159	127	25	39
Clarksville, TN	5	76	51	98	135	132	119	8	54
Colorado Springs, CO	21	161	18	108	157	100	98	33	49
Columbia, MO	17	108	36	99	127	139	110	17	52
Columbus, OH	n/a	118	19	72	137	156	136	29	40
Dallas, TX	1	34	102	108	160	97	78	2	49
Davenport, IA	n/a	137	26	99	129	137	106	25	46
Denver, CO	24	155	33	99	177	89	90	38	39
Des Moines, IA	n/a	137	26	99	129	137	106	25	46
Durham, NC	n/a	n/a	39	98	143	124	110	3	42
El Paso, TX	1	59	106	147	164	54	49	3	35
Erie, PA	n/a	124	3	57	128	180	165	55	36
Eugene, OR	n/a	n/a	15	75	115	175	136	4	3
Fargo, ND	n/a	180	15	81	145	139	100	38	31
Fayetteville, NC	n/a	n/a	39	98	143	124	110	3	42
Fort Collins, CO	24	155	33	99	177	89	90	38	39
Fort Wayne, IN	n/a	131	16	75	140	150	131	31	39
Fort Worth, TX	1	40	100	123	136	106	79	3	47
Gainesville, FL	n/a	n/a	77	88	196	81	119	0	78
Grand Rapids, MI	n/a	146	11	67	119	179	142	57	34
Green Bay, WI	n/a	163	7	86	125	154	120	40	33
Greensboro, NC	3	85	32	94	143	128	113	5	43
Honolulu, HI	n/a	n/a	23	25	286	54	98	0	7
Houston, TX	n/a	n/a	96	83	168	114	101	1	62
Huntsville, AL	2	66	49	70	118	177	116	2	54
Indianapolis, IN	19	119	19	83	128	154	127	24	43
Jacksonville, FL	< 1	16	83	86	181	98	114	1	65
Kansas City, MO	22	110	39	112	134	119	103	17	51
Lafayette, LA	< 1	21	86	99	150	116	113	< 1	73
Las Vegas, NV	< 1	37	134	185	132	48	27	2	13
Lexington, KY	11	96	22	86	136	143	129	17	44
Lincoln, NE	n/a	145	40	108	135	122	94	19	46
Little Rock, AR	1	57	73	110	142	113	104	4	57
Los Angeles, CA	0	< 1	5	131	125	109	34	0	1
Louisville, KY	8	90	35	82	143	140	125	15	45
Lubbock, TX	5	93	79	134	150	81	62	8	48
Madison, WI	n/a	161	14	88	119	158	118	38	40

Table continued on next page.

City	Temperature			Daytime Sky			Precipitation		
	10°F & below	32°F & below	90°F & above	Clear	Partly cloudy	Cloudy	0.01 inch or more precip.	1.0 inch or more snow/ice	Thunder-storms
Manchester, NH	n/a	171	12	87	131	147	125	32	19
McAllen, TX	n/a	n/a	116	86	180	99	72	0	27
Miami, FL	n/a	n/a	55	48	263	54	128	0	74
Midland, TX	1	62	102	144	138	83	52	3	38
Minneapolis, MN	n/a	156	16	93	125	147	113	41	37
Montgomery, AL	< 1	38	82	97	152	116	109	< 1	59
Nashville, TN	5	76	51	98	135	132	119	8	54
New Orleans, LA	0	13	70	90	169	106	114	1	69
New York, NY	n/a	n/a	18	85	166	114	120	11	20
Oklahoma City, OK	5	79	70	124	131	110	80	8	50
Omaha, NE	n/a	139	35	100	142	123	97	20	46
Orlando, FL	n/a	n/a	90	76	208	81	115	0	80
Oxnard, CA	0	1	2	114	155	96	34	< 1	1
Peoria, IL	n/a	127	27	89	127	149	115	22	49
Philadelphia, PA	5	94	23	81	146	138	117	14	27
Phoenix, AZ	0	10	167	186	125	54	37	< 1	23
Pittsburgh, PA	n/a	121	8	62	137	166	154	42	35
Portland, OR	n/a	37	11	67	116	182	152	4	7
Providence, RI	n/a	117	9	85	134	146	123	21	21
Provo, UT	n/a	128	56	94	152	119	92	38	38
Raleigh, NC	n/a	n/a	39	98	143	124	110	3	42
Reno, NV	14	178	50	143	139	83	50	17	14
Richmond, VA	3	79	41	90	147	128	115	7	43
Riverside, CA	0	4	82	124	178	63	n/a	n/a	5
Rochester, MN	n/a	165	9	87	126	152	114	40	41
Salem, OR	n/a	66	16	78	119	168	146	6	5
Salt Lake City, UT	n/a	128	56	94	152	119	92	38	38
San Antonio, TX	n/a	n/a	112	97	153	115	81	1	36
San Diego, CA	0	< 1	4	115	126	124	40	0	5
San Francisco, CA	0	6	4	136	130	99	63	< 1	5
San Jose, CA	0	5	5	106	180	79	57	< 1	6
Santa Rosa, CA	n/a	43	30	n/a	365	n/a	n/a	n/a	2
Savannah, GA	< 1	29	70	97	155	113	111	< 1	63
Seattle, WA	n/a	38	3	57	121	187	157	8	8
Sioux Falls, SD	n/a	n/a	n/a	95	136	134	n/a	n/a	n/a
Spokane, WA	n/a	140	18	78	135	152	113	37	11
Springfield, MO	12	102	42	113	119	133	109	14	55
Tallahassee, FL	< 1	31	86	93	175	97	114	1	83
Tampa, FL	n/a	n/a	85	81	204	80	107	< 1	87
Topeka, KS	20	123	45	110	128	127	96	15	54
Tulsa, OK	6	78	74	117	141	107	88	8	50
Virginia Beach, VA	< 1	53	33	89	149	127	115	5	38
Washington, DC	2	71	34	84	144	137	112	9	30
Wichita, KS	13	110	63	117	132	116	87	13	54
Wilmington, NC	< 1	42	46	96	150	119	115	1	47
Worcester, MA	n/a	141	4	81	144	140	131	32	23

Note: Figures are average number of days per year
Source: National Climatic Data Center, International Station Meteorological Climate Summary, 9/96

Air Quality Index

MSA[1] (Days[2])	Percent of Days when Air Quality was...					AQI Statistics	
	Good	Moderate	Unhealthy for Sensitive Groups	Unhealthy	Very Unhealthy	Maximum	Median
Abilene, TX (n/a)	n/a	n/a	n/a	n/a	n/a	n/a	n/a
Albuquerque, NM (365)	48.5	50.7	0.8	0.0	0.0	145	51
Anchorage, AK (365)	77.8	20.8	1.1	0.3	0.0	151	29
Ann Arbor, MI (365)	88.2	11.8	0.0	0.0	0.0	87	34
Athens, GA (365)	74.5	25.5	0.0	0.0	0.0	91	39
Atlanta, GA (365)	47.9	51.2	0.5	0.3	0.0	151	52
Austin, TX (365)	73.7	26.0	0.3	0.0	0.0	109	41
Baltimore, MD (365)	58.4	40.3	1.4	0.0	0.0	111	46
Billings, MT (365)	93.2	6.6	0.3	0.0	0.0	101	24
Boise City, ID (365)	80.5	16.2	2.5	0.8	0.0	188	36
Boston, MA (365)	61.1	37.5	1.4	0.0	0.0	116	47
Boulder, CO (363)	81.5	17.4	1.1	0.0	0.0	127	42
Cape Coral, FL (365)	90.1	9.9	0.0	0.0	0.0	77	33
Cedar Rapids, IA (365)	70.1	29.6	0.3	0.0	0.0	122	42
Charleston, SC (365)	83.3	16.7	0.0	0.0	0.0	73	36
Charlotte, NC (365)	76.2	23.8	0.0	0.0	0.0	87	42
Chicago, IL (365)	19.7	77.0	3.0	0.3	0.0	186	60
Cincinnati, OH (365)	42.7	54.2	3.0	0.0	0.0	123	54
Clarksville, TN (365)	76.2	23.8	0.0	0.0	0.0	100	41
Colorado Spgs, CO (365)	69.6	29.0	1.4	0.0	0.0	116	44
Columbia, MO (214)	94.9	5.1	0.0	0.0	0.0	80	37.5
Columbus, OH (365)	66.6	32.9	0.5	0.0	0.0	114	43
Dallas, TX (365)	42.7	48.2	8.8	0.3	0.0	161	54
Davenport, IA (365)	37.5	61.6	0.8	0.0	0.0	126	55
Denver, CO (365)	41.9	51.8	6.3	0.0	0.0	145	54
Des Moines, IA (365)	73.2	26.8	0.0	0.0	0.0	99	41
Durham, NC (365)	84.9	15.1	0.0	0.0	0.0	90	35
El Paso, TX (365)	49.0	48.2	1.9	0.8	0.0	168	51
Erie, PA (365)	54.8	45.2	0.0	0.0	0.0	88	48
Eugene, OR (365)	66.3	27.7	5.8	0.3	0.0	161	36
Fargo, ND (355)	86.8	13.2	0.0	0.0	0.0	88	35
Fayetteville, NC (336)	84.8	15.2	0.0	0.0	0.0	90	37
Ft. Collins, CO (365)	72.3	25.8	1.9	0.0	0.0	140	46
Ft. Wayne, IN (365)	60.0	39.7	0.3	0.0	0.0	104	47
Ft. Worth, TX (365)	42.7	48.2	8.8	0.3	0.0	161	54
Gainesville, FL (365)	91.8	8.2	0.0	0.0	0.0	84	33
Grand Rapids, MI (365)	73.2	26.3	0.5	0.0	0.0	138	39
Green Bay, WI (365)	72.1	26.6	1.4	0.0	0.0	114	40
Greensboro, NC (338)	81.7	18.3	0.0	0.0	0.0	90	38
Honolulu, HI (365)	95.1	4.9	0.0	0.0	0.0	67	30
Houston, TX (365)	46.8	47.9	4.9	0.3	0.0	172	52
Huntsville, AL (336)	90.8	9.2	0.0	0.0	0.0	74	37
Indianapolis, IN (365)	29.0	67.9	3.0	0.0	0.0	124	59
Jacksonville, FL (365)	82.2	17.3	0.5	0.0	0.0	111	38
Kansas City, MO (365)	31.5	57.0	11.2	0.3	0.0	162	58
Lafayette, LA (365)	63.0	36.7	0.3	0.0	0.0	101	44
Las Vegas, NV (365)	43.0	52.6	4.1	0.3	0.0	157	54
Lexington, KY (365)	70.4	29.6	0.0	0.0	0.0	81	42
Lincoln, NE (259)	90.3	9.7	0.0	0.0	0.0	74	34
Little Rock, AR (365)	57.8	41.9	0.3	0.0	0.0	103	47
Los Angeles, CA (365)	7.1	71.5	20.3	1.1	0.0	172	73
Louisville, KY (365)	37.8	57.3	4.9	0.0	0.0	144	55
Lubbock, TX (334)	92.8	6.9	0.0	0.3	0.0	165	26
Madison, WI (365)	68.5	31.5	0.0	0.0	0.0	87	42

Table continued on next page.

MSA[1] (Days[2])	Percent of Days when Air Quality was...					AQI Statistics	
	Good	Moderate	Unhealthy for Sensitive Groups	Unhealthy	Very Unhealthy	Maximum	Median
Manchester, NH (365)	89.6	10.4	0.0	0.0	0.0	84	36
McAllen, TX (365)	78.4	21.4	0.3	0.0	0.0	106	36
Miami, FL (365)	76.4	22.7	0.8	0.0	0.0	118	41
Midland, TX (n/a)	n/a	n/a	n/a	n/a	n/a	n/a	n/a
Minneapolis, MN (365)	63.8	35.6	0.5	0.0	0.0	106	44
Montgomery, AL (285)	87.7	12.3	0.0	0.0	0.0	73	37
Nashville, TN (365)	74.2	25.5	0.3	0.0	0.0	112	43
New Orleans, LA (365)	61.4	31.8	6.0	0.8	0.0	200	45
New York, NY (365)	44.1	51.8	4.1	0.0	0.0	135	53
Oklahoma City, OK (365)	60.8	38.4	0.8	0.0	0.0	122	47
Omaha, NE (365)	54.0	44.9	1.1	0.0	0.0	128	48
Orlando, FL (365)	89.3	10.7	0.0	0.0	0.0	97	36
Oxnard, CA (365)	57.0	41.6	1.4	0.0	0.0	135	48
Peoria, IL (365)	56.7	36.2	5.8	1.4	0.0	183	48
Philadelphia, PA (365)	30.1	66.8	3.0	0.0	0.0	133	57
Phoenix, AZ (365)	9.9	66.3	16.4	5.2	2.2	902	74
Pittsburgh, PA (365)	33.7	61.4	4.7	0.3	0.0	164	56
Portland, OR (365)	66.0	29.6	3.3	1.1	0.0	157	38
Providence, RI (365)	64.1	33.4	2.5	0.0	0.0	145	45
Provo, UT (365)	60.0	29.9	5.8	4.4	0.0	189	47
Raleigh, NC (365)	68.8	31.2	0.0	0.0	0.0	90	43
Reno, NV (365)	50.7	40.5	3.8	1.1	3.8	895	50
Richmond, VA (365)	81.6	18.1	0.3	0.0	0.0	124	39
Riverside, CA (365)	8.2	56.4	27.7	6.8	0.8	455	84
Rochester, MN (365)	80.8	19.2	0.0	0.0	0.0	99	37
Salem, OR (361)	78.7	19.9	1.4	0.0	0.0	123	31
Salt Lake City, UT (365)	61.1	26.6	9.9	2.5	0.0	160	47
San Antonio, TX (365)	68.2	29.0	2.7	0.0	0.0	129	45
San Diego, CA (365)	18.9	75.9	4.7	0.3	0.3	617	61
San Francisco, CA (365)	44.4	53.7	1.9	0.0	0.0	133	53
San Jose, CA (365)	55.9	41.9	1.9	0.3	0.0	152	48
Santa Rosa, CA (365)	81.1	18.9	0.0	0.0	0.0	85	35
Savannah, GA (365)	68.2	29.0	2.7	0.0	0.0	131	40
Seattle, WA (365)	53.4	44.4	2.2	0.0	0.0	149	49
Sioux Falls, SD (365)	77.0	22.7	0.3	0.0	0.0	109	39
Spokane, WA (365)	70.4	29.0	0.3	0.3	0.0	175	39
Springfield, MO (365)	80.8	19.2	0.0	0.0	0.0	80	39
Tallahassee, FL (365)	83.8	15.3	0.5	0.0	0.3	222	36
Tampa, FL (365)	71.2	27.9	0.8	0.0	0.0	104	43
Topeka, KS (365)	90.4	9.6	0.0	0.0	0.0	77	36
Tulsa, OK (365)	54.2	43.8	1.9	0.0	0.0	114	48
Virginia Beach, VA (365)	80.3	19.7	0.0	0.0	0.0	100	39
Washington, DC (365)	53.2	45.5	1.4	0.0	0.0	104	49
Wichita, KS (365)	79.7	20.3	0.0	0.0	0.0	100	39
Wilmington, NC (344)	79.1	20.9	0.0	0.0	0.0	80	38
Worcester, MA (365)	80.8	19.2	0.0	0.0	0.0	97	38

Note: The Air Quality Index (AQI) is an index for reporting daily air quality. EPA calculates the AQI for five major air pollutants regulated by the Clean Air Act: ground-level ozone, particle pollution (also known as particulate matter), carbon monoxide, sulfur dioxide, and nitrogen dioxide. The AQI runs from 0 to 500. The higher the AQI value, the greater the level of air pollution and the greater the health concern. There are six AQI categories: "Good" The AQI is between 0 and 50. Air quality is considered satisfactory; "Moderate" The AQI is between 51 and 100. Air quality is acceptable; "Unhealthy for Sensitive Groups" When AQI values are between 101 and 150, members of sensitive groups may experience health effects; "Unhealthy" When AQI values are between 151 and 200 everyone may begin to experience health effects; "Very Unhealthy" AQI values between 201 and 300 trigger a health alert; "Hazardous" AQI values over 300 trigger health warnings of emergency conditions; Data covers the entire county unless noted otherwise; (1) Data covers the Metropolitan Statistical Area—see Appendix B for areas included; (2) Number of days with AQI data in 2013
Source: U.S. Environmental Protection Agency, Air Quality Index Report, 2013

Air Quality Index Pollutants

MSA[1] (Days[2])	Percent of Days when AQI Pollutant was...					
	Carbon Monoxide	Nitrogen Dioxide	Ozone	Sulfur Dioxide	Particulate Matter 2.5	Particulate Matter 10
Abilene, TX (n/a)	n/a	n/a	n/a	n/a	n/a	n/a
Albuquerque, NM (365)	0.0	0.3	49.0	0.0	33.7	17.0
Anchorage, AK (365)	0.5	0.0	0.0	0.0	69.6	29.9
Ann Arbor, MI (365)	0.0	0.0	83.8	0.0	16.2	0.0
Athens, GA (365)	0.0	0.0	21.6	0.0	78.4	0.0
Atlanta, GA (365)	0.0	1.9	20.8	0.0	77.3	0.0
Austin, TX (365)	0.0	0.3	51.5	0.0	48.2	0.0
Baltimore, MD (365)	0.0	4.4	37.5	0.3	57.8	0.0
Billings, MT (365)	0.0	0.0	0.0	55.1	44.9	0.0
Boise City, ID (365)	0.0	21.6	43.0	0.0	17.0	18.4
Boston, MA (365)	0.0	5.5	21.4	0.8	72.1	0.3
Boulder, CO (363)	0.0	0.0	91.7	0.0	8.0	0.3
Cape Coral, FL (365)	0.0	0.0	57.3	0.0	42.7	0.0
Cedar Rapids, IA (365)	0.0	0.0	28.5	0.0	71.0	0.5
Charleston, SC (365)	0.0	2.5	20.8	0.5	76.2	0.0
Charlotte, NC (365)	0.0	2.7	41.4	0.0	55.3	0.5
Chicago, IL (365)	0.0	7.4	10.7	6.8	69.3	5.8
Cincinnati, OH (365)	0.0	0.8	23.8	15.9	58.1	1.4
Clarksville, TN (365)	0.0	0.0	43.3	1.9	54.8	0.0
Colorado Spgs, CO (365)	0.0	0.0	87.4	9.0	2.7	0.8
Columbia, MO (214)	0.0	0.0	100.0	0.0	0.0	0.0
Columbus, OH (365)	0.0	1.1	34.8	0.0	64.1	0.0
Dallas, TX (365)	0.0	4.7	38.4	0.0	55.6	1.4
Davenport, IA (365)	0.0	0.0	8.5	0.0	65.8	25.8
Denver, CO (365)	0.0	23.0	53.4	1.9	18.1	3.6
Des Moines, IA (365)	0.0	2.2	31.2	0.0	66.6	0.0
Durham, NC (365)	0.0	0.0	31.5	0.3	68.2	0.0
El Paso, TX (365)	0.0	13.4	28.2	0.0	53.7	4.7
Erie, PA (365)	0.0	0.8	23.3	0.0	75.9	0.0
Eugene, OR (365)	0.0	0.0	31.5	0.0	67.9	0.5
Fargo, ND (355)	0.0	2.3	57.2	0.0	37.7	2.8
Fayetteville, NC (336)	0.0	0.0	36.0	0.0	64.0	0.0
Ft. Collins, CO (365)	0.0	0.0	93.7	0.0	4.9	1.4
Ft. Wayne, IN (365)	1.1	0.0	20.8	0.3	77.8	0.0
Ft. Worth, TX (365)	0.0	4.7	38.4	0.0	55.6	1.4
Gainesville, FL (365)	0.0	0.0	53.2	0.0	46.8	0.0
Grand Rapids, MI (365)	0.0	0.0	43.0	0.0	57.0	0.0
Green Bay, WI (365)	0.0	0.0	37.5	13.4	49.0	0.0
Greensboro, NC (338)	0.0	0.0	39.1	0.0	60.7	0.3
Honolulu, HI (365)	0.0	0.0	25.8	0.0	73.2	1.1
Houston, TX (365)	0.0	6.8	26.6	1.6	63.8	1.1
Huntsville, AL (336)	0.0	0.0	61.3	0.0	22.9	15.8
Indianapolis, IN (365)	0.0	0.3	11.2	19.5	69.0	0.0
Jacksonville, FL (365)	0.0	0.3	38.1	6.6	55.1	0.0
Kansas City, MO (365)	0.0	0.5	20.5	27.9	49.0	1.9
Lafayette, LA (365)	0.0	0.0	30.4	0.0	69.0	0.5
Las Vegas, NV (365)	0.0	2.5	59.5	0.0	35.1	3.0
Lexington, KY (365)	0.0	6.0	22.2	1.1	70.1	0.5
Lincoln, NE (259)	0.0	0.0	71.8	0.0	28.2	0.0
Little Rock, AR (365)	0.0	0.8	29.3	0.0	69.9	0.0
Los Angeles, CA (365)	0.0	4.4	33.4	0.0	60.8	1.4
Louisville, KY (365)	0.0	0.5	12.3	17.5	69.6	0.0
Lubbock, TX (334)	0.0	0.0	0.0	0.0	100.0	0.0
Madison, WI (365)	0.0	0.0	37.5	0.0	62.5	0.0

Table continued on next page.

MSA[1] (Days[2])	Percent of Days when AQI Pollutant was...					
	Carbon Monoxide	Nitrogen Dioxide	Ozone	Sulfur Dioxide	Particulate Matter 2.5	Particulate Matter 10
Manchester, NH (365)	0.0	0.0	79.5	0.0	20.5	0.0
McAllen, TX (365)	0.0	0.0	33.2	0.0	65.5	1.4
Miami, FL (365)	0.0	1.1	25.5	0.0	73.2	0.3
Midland, TX (n/a)	n/a	n/a	n/a	n/a	n/a	n/a
Minneapolis, MN (365)	0.0	3.8	36.7	0.5	55.3	3.6
Montgomery, AL (285)	0.0	0.0	66.7	0.0	33.3	0.0
Nashville, TN (365)	0.0	4.9	37.0	0.0	58.1	0.0
New Orleans, LA (365)	0.0	1.4	32.1	14.0	52.1	0.5
New York, NY (365)	0.0	15.1	25.2	0.0	59.7	0.0
Oklahoma City, OK (365)	0.0	5.8	47.9	0.0	46.3	0.0
Omaha, NE (365)	0.0	0.0	19.7	5.8	52.9	21.6
Orlando, FL (365)	0.0	0.3	55.6	0.0	44.1	0.0
Oxnard, CA (365)	0.0	1.6	45.5	0.0	50.4	2.5
Peoria, IL (365)	0.0	0.0	27.1	21.4	51.5	0.0
Philadelphia, PA (365)	0.0	1.6	15.6	0.3	81.9	0.5
Phoenix, AZ (365)	0.0	4.7	19.5	0.0	20.8	55.1
Pittsburgh, PA (365)	0.0	0.3	15.6	7.9	76.2	0.0
Portland, OR (365)	0.0	1.1	41.1	0.0	57.8	0.0
Providence, RI (365)	0.0	0.5	36.7	3.6	58.6	0.5
Provo, UT (365)	0.0	20.3	47.9	0.0	30.7	1.1
Raleigh, NC (365)	0.0	0.0	26.8	0.0	73.2	0.0
Reno, NV (365)	0.0	1.1	48.5	0.0	34.0	16.4
Richmond, VA (365)	0.0	8.2	46.3	1.4	44.1	0.0
Riverside, CA (365)	0.0	4.1	40.5	0.0	38.4	17.0
Rochester, MN (365)	0.0	0.0	40.8	0.0	59.2	0.0
Salem, OR (361)	0.0	0.0	36.0	0.0	64.0	0.0
Salt Lake City, UT (365)	0.0	12.1	54.0	1.4	31.8	0.8
San Antonio, TX (365)	0.0	0.8	51.0	0.3	47.9	0.0
San Diego, CA (365)	0.0	7.1	27.1	0.0	57.5	8.2
San Francisco, CA (365)	0.0	5.2	9.0	0.0	85.8	0.0
San Jose, CA (365)	0.0	0.5	40.5	0.0	58.1	0.8
Santa Rosa, CA (365)	0.0	0.8	51.5	0.0	46.8	0.8
Savannah, GA (365)	0.0	0.0	18.4	25.8	55.9	0.0
Seattle, WA (365)	0.0	0.0	19.5	0.0	80.5	0.0
Sioux Falls, SD (365)	0.0	0.5	58.9	0.0	39.2	1.4
Spokane, WA (365)	0.5	0.0	32.9	0.0	64.1	2.5
Springfield, MO (365)	0.0	0.0	36.7	8.8	54.2	0.3
Tallahassee, FL (365)	0.0	0.0	52.6	0.0	47.4	0.0
Tampa, FL (365)	0.0	0.0	34.0	6.6	59.5	0.0
Topeka, KS (365)	0.0	0.0	83.3	0.0	15.3	1.4
Tulsa, OK (365)	0.0	0.0	37.0	8.2	54.8	0.0
Virginia Beach, VA (365)	0.0	5.8	34.8	9.6	49.9	0.0
Washington, DC (365)	0.0	10.1	32.6	0.0	57.3	0.0
Wichita, KS (365)	0.0	7.9	71.2	0.0	15.3	5.5
Wilmington, NC (344)	0.0	0.0	29.4	6.7	64.0	0.0
Worcester, MA (365)	0.0	3.3	48.8	0.0	47.1	0.8

Note: The Air Quality Index (AQI) is an index for reporting daily air quality. EPA calculates the AQI for five major air pollutants regulated by the Clean Air Act: ground-level ozone, particle pollution (also known as particulate matter), carbon monoxide, sulfur dioxide, and nitrogen dioxide. The AQI runs from 0 to 500. The higher the AQI value, the greater the level of air pollution and the greater the health concern; (1) (1) Data covers the Metropolitan Statistical Area—see Appendix B for areas included; (2) Number of days with AQI data in 2013

Source: U.S. Environmental Protection Agency, Air Quality Index Report, 2013

Air Quality Trends: Ozone

MSA[1]	2003	2004	2005	2006	2007	2008	2009	2010	2011	2012
Abilene, TX	n/a	n/a	n/a	n/a	n/a	n/a	n/a	n/a	n/a	n/a
Albuquerque, NM	0.076	0.071	0.074	0.071	0.070	0.066	0.065	0.066	0.070	0.070
Anchorage, AK	n/a	n/a	n/a	n/a	n/a	n/a	n/a	n/a	n/a	n/a
Ann Arbor, MI	0.091	0.071	0.083	0.076	0.077	0.069	0.065	0.066	0.077	0.085
Athens, GA	0.072	0.078	0.082	0.086	0.083	0.077	0.067	0.073	0.075	0.071
Atlanta, GA	0.083	0.081	0.085	0.092	0.091	0.080	0.072	0.074	0.078	0.077
Austin, TX	0.083	0.081	0.081	0.083	0.073	0.072	0.073	0.072	0.074	0.075
Baltimore, MD	0.083	0.082	0.089	0.089	0.086	0.084	0.072	0.085	0.087	0.083
Billings, MT	n/a	n/a	n/a	n/a	n/a	n/a	n/a	n/a	n/a	n/a
Boise City, ID	n/a	n/a	n/a	n/a	n/a	n/a	n/a	n/a	n/a	n/a
Boston, MA	0.079	0.075	0.082	0.077	0.081	0.072	0.070	0.069	0.066	0.068
Boulder, CO	0.082	0.068	0.076	0.082	0.085	0.076	0.073	0.072	0.076	0.076
Cape Coral, FL	0.074	0.072	0.070	0.070	0.069	0.068	0.062	0.064	0.062	0.063
Cedar Rapids, IA	0.068	0.063	0.073	0.065	0.076	0.063	0.061	0.064	0.064	0.071
Charleston, SC	0.072	0.072	0.073	0.071	0.065	0.069	0.059	0.067	0.066	0.063
Charlotte, NC	0.081	0.078	0.085	0.084	0.088	0.081	0.067	0.076	0.078	0.076
Chicago, IL	0.077	0.067	0.083	0.070	0.079	0.064	0.065	0.070	0.071	0.081
Cincinnati, OH	0.088	0.075	0.085	0.078	0.086	0.075	0.070	0.076	0.080	0.083
Clarksville, TN	n/a	n/a	n/a	n/a	n/a	n/a	n/a	n/a	n/a	n/a
Colorado Spgs, CO	0.077	0.070	0.077	0.072	0.072	0.070	0.060	0.068	0.074	0.075
Columbia, MO	n/a	n/a	n/a	n/a	n/a	n/a	n/a	n/a	n/a	n/a
Columbus, OH	0.088	0.075	0.085	0.077	0.081	0.073	0.070	0.074	0.078	0.079
Dallas, TX	0.089	0.087	0.093	0.089	0.081	0.077	0.080	0.076	0.085	0.083
Davenport, IA	0.072	0.064	0.071	0.065	0.072	0.061	0.061	0.061	0.059	0.069
Denver, CO	0.084	0.068	0.075	0.080	0.079	0.075	0.070	0.072	0.078	0.080
Des Moines, IA	0.061	0.051	0.072	0.064	0.069	0.059	0.061	0.064	0.063	0.070
Durham, NC	0.079	0.072	0.079	0.073	0.077	0.075	0.064	0.072	0.070	0.068
El Paso, TX	0.071	0.074	0.077	0.077	0.074	0.074	0.068	0.068	0.069	0.067
Erie, PA	0.091	0.074	0.086	0.077	0.084	0.074	0.069	0.075	0.072	0.082
Eugene, OR	0.075	0.066	0.068	0.073	0.060	0.059	0.065	0.058	0.059	0.061
Fargo, ND	0.065	0.056	0.061	0.065	0.055	0.055	0.057	0.063	0.057	0.063
Fayetteville, NC	0.084	0.075	0.088	0.073	0.081	0.075	0.066	0.072	0.075	0.069
Ft. Collins, CO	0.081	0.069	0.076	0.077	0.074	0.071	0.066	0.072	0.073	0.077
Ft. Wayne, IN	0.087	0.071	0.081	0.072	0.079	0.068	0.065	0.067	0.071	0.076
Ft. Worth, TX	0.089	0.087	0.093	0.089	0.081	0.077	0.080	0.076	0.085	0.083
Gainesville, FL	0.071	0.075	0.073	0.075	0.078	0.069	0.056	0.069	0.064	0.064
Grand Rapids, MI	0.089	0.070	0.083	0.082	0.085	0.068	0.069	0.068	0.076	0.080
Green Bay, WI	0.087	0.072	0.084	0.072	0.084	0.064	0.068	0.072	0.068	0.083
Greensboro, NC	0.083	0.074	0.078	0.075	0.082	0.084	0.068	0.074	0.071	0.076
Honolulu, HI	0.038	0.046	0.042	0.040	0.033	0.041	0.048	0.047	0.046	0.043
Houston, TX	0.097	0.092	0.087	0.090	0.079	0.074	0.079	0.078	0.082	0.081
Huntsville, AL	0.079	0.077	0.075	0.079	0.082	0.073	0.066	0.071	0.072	0.076
Indianapolis, IN	0.084	0.071	0.080	0.076	0.081	0.070	0.070	0.068	0.071	0.075
Jacksonville, FL	0.071	0.074	0.072	0.074	0.073	0.069	0.061	0.067	0.066	0.060
Kansas City, MO	0.085	0.066	0.082	0.085	0.076	0.067	0.068	0.068	0.074	0.082
Lafayette, LA	n/a	n/a	n/a	n/a	n/a	n/a	n/a	n/a	n/a	n/a
Las Vegas, NV	0.081	0.077	0.082	0.081	0.080	0.073	0.072	0.070	0.074	0.076
Lexington, KY	0.071	0.064	0.078	0.070	0.079	0.070	0.064	0.070	0.074	0.078
Lincoln, NE	0.060	0.056	0.056	0.056	0.054	0.051	0.053	0.050	0.053	0.058
Little Rock, AR	0.075	0.073	0.083	0.083	0.081	0.068	0.072	0.072	0.078	0.078
Los Angeles, CA	0.097	0.088	0.083	0.088	0.084	0.088	0.085	0.073	0.077	0.078
Louisville, KY	0.077	0.071	0.083	0.076	0.083	0.074	0.068	0.075	0.081	0.085
Lubbock, TX	n/a	n/a	n/a	n/a	n/a	n/a	n/a	n/a	n/a	n/a
Madison, WI	0.078	0.065	0.079	0.066	0.079	0.064	0.063	0.062	0.068	0.074
Manchester, NH	0.070	0.071	0.071	0.068	0.074	0.064	0.060	0.063	0.063	0.063
McAllen, TX	0.073	0.070	0.069	0.060	0.055	0.058	0.060	0.065	0.062	0.061

Table continued on next page.

MSA[1]	2003	2004	2005	2006	2007	2008	2009	2010	2011	2012
Miami, FL	0.066	0.063	0.064	0.074	0.066	0.067	0.062	0.064	0.060	0.062
Midland, TX	n/a	n/a	n/a	n/a	n/a	n/a	n/a	n/a	n/a	n/a
Minneapolis, MN	0.073	0.062	0.073	0.068	0.073	0.060	0.062	0.065	0.064	0.068
Montgomery, AL	0.069	0.068	0.069	0.073	0.077	0.069	0.063	0.073	0.069	0.066
Nashville, TN	0.076	0.072	0.078	0.078	0.083	0.072	0.064	0.073	0.071	0.077
New Orleans, LA	0.083	0.076	0.076	0.078	0.079	0.070	0.073	0.075	0.073	0.072
New York, NY	0.089	0.079	0.092	0.087	0.086	0.081	0.072	0.081	0.081	0.079
Oklahoma City, OK	0.079	0.072	0.076	0.081	0.073	0.071	0.072	0.071	0.082	0.078
Omaha, NE	0.067	0.068	0.072	0.070	0.063	0.057	0.057	0.061	0.059	0.068
Orlando, FL	0.075	0.074	0.080	0.078	0.075	0.069	0.064	0.068	0.072	0.069
Oxnard, CA	0.085	0.082	0.077	0.078	0.073	0.077	0.076	0.072	0.072	0.069
Peoria, IL	0.072	0.064	0.075	0.069	0.078	0.064	0.061	0.064	0.068	0.072
Philadelphia, PA	0.085	0.080	0.088	0.083	0.086	0.082	0.069	0.082	0.082	0.081
Phoenix, AZ	0.080	0.073	0.078	0.078	0.073	0.076	0.069	0.072	0.076	0.076
Pittsburgh, PA	0.085	0.074	0.085	0.077	0.078	0.075	0.068	0.075	0.072	0.079
Portland, OR	0.071	0.060	0.059	0.067	0.058	0.062	0.064	0.056	0.056	0.059
Providence, RI	0.089	0.081	0.087	0.082	0.084	0.078	0.068	0.076	0.075	0.077
Provo, UT	0.078	0.069	0.079	0.077	0.077	0.072	0.069	0.070	0.067	0.075
Raleigh, NC	0.086	0.076	0.083	0.074	0.081	0.078	0.067	0.072	0.075	0.073
Reno, NV	0.071	0.069	0.067	0.071	0.069	0.074	0.064	0.067	0.064	0.070
Richmond, VA	0.082	0.076	0.082	0.082	0.081	0.082	0.065	0.078	0.076	0.076
Riverside, CA	0.113	0.102	0.101	0.103	0.100	0.103	0.094	0.092	0.094	0.093
Rochester, MN	n/a	n/a	n/a	n/a	n/a	n/a	n/a	n/a	n/a	n/a
Salem, OR	0.072	0.062	0.063	0.075	0.060	0.066	0.069	0.057	0.057	0.063
Salt Lake City, UT	0.079	0.072	0.084	0.082	0.081	0.075	0.074	0.072	0.074	0.079
San Antonio, TX	0.082	0.085	0.082	0.083	0.071	0.075	0.070	0.072	0.075	0.079
San Diego, CA	0.072	0.076	0.070	0.073	0.073	0.080	0.071	0.069	0.067	0.066
San Francisco, CA	0.067	0.063	0.057	0.067	0.058	0.067	0.066	0.063	0.061	0.059
San Jose, CA	0.080	0.072	0.066	0.080	0.068	0.074	0.072	0.074	0.066	0.065
Santa Rosa, CA	0.057	0.053	0.049	0.053	0.054	0.058	0.052	0.054	0.050	0.050
Savannah, GA	0.070	0.071	0.068	0.069	0.065	0.067	0.062	0.065	0.065	0.063
Seattle, WA	0.072	0.065	0.055	0.068	0.059	0.058	0.061	0.056	0.053	0.058
Sioux Falls, SD	n/a	n/a	n/a	n/a	n/a	n/a	n/a	n/a	n/a	n/a
Spokane, WA	0.074	0.065	0.063	0.066	0.064	0.058	0.057	0.058	0.056	0.063
Springfield, MO	0.072	0.064	0.077	0.074	0.080	0.067	0.062	0.066	0.073	0.075
Tallahassee, FL	0.074	0.071	0.070	0.071	0.072	0.071	0.058	0.066	0.065	0.066
Tampa, FL	0.077	0.074	0.075	0.074	0.076	0.075	0.064	0.067	0.071	0.066
Topeka, KS	n/a	n/a	n/a	n/a	n/a	n/a	n/a	n/a	n/a	n/a
Tulsa, OK	0.083	0.071	0.080	0.082	0.072	0.071	0.071	0.071	0.083	0.084
Virginia Beach, VA	0.081	0.075	0.078	0.074	0.077	0.078	0.065	0.074	0.075	0.069
Washington, DC	0.084	0.080	0.082	0.086	0.084	0.077	0.067	0.080	0.080	0.079
Wichita, KS	0.076	0.061	0.072	0.073	0.063	0.065	0.071	0.073	0.075	0.076
Wilmington, NC	0.076	0.070	0.075	0.072	0.071	0.063	0.060	0.062	0.064	0.064
Worcester, MA	0.080	0.074	0.085	0.077	0.089	0.081	0.077	0.070	0.065	0.070

Note: (1) Data covers the Metropolitan Statistical Area—see Appendix B for areas included; n/a not available. The values shown are the composite ozone concentration averages among trend sites based on the highest fourth daily maximum 8-hour concentration in parts per million. These trends are based on sites having an adequate record of monitoring data during the trend period. Data from exceptional events are included.
Source: U.S. Environmental Protection Agency, Air Quality Monitoring Information, "Air Quality Trends by City, 2000-2012"

Maximum Air Pollutant Concentrations: Particulate Matter, Ozone, CO and Lead

Metro Aea	PM 10 (ug/m³)	PM 2.5 Wtd AM (ug/m³)	PM 2.5 24-Hr (ug/m³)	Ozone (ppm)	Carbon Monoxide (ppm)	Lead (ug/m³)
Abilene, TX	n/a	n/a	n/a	n/a	n/a	n/a
Albuquerque, NM	227	7.4	20	0.077	2	0.01
Anchorage, AK	121	8	33	0.048	6	0.07
Ann Arbor, MI	n/a	9.2	23	0.085	n/a	n/a
Athens, GA	n/a	n/a	n/a	0.071	n/a	n/a
Atlanta, GA	38	11	21	0.088	1	0.03
Austin, TX	32	7.8	17	0.076	0	n/a
Baltimore, MD	31	11.1	25	0.087	2	n/a
Billings, MT	n/a	n/a	n/a	n/a	n/a	n/a
Boise City, ID	182	10.4	41	0.073	2	n/a
Boston, MA	37	9.5	24	0.074	2	n/a
Boulder, CO	43	n/a	n/a	0.076	n/a	n/a
Cape Coral, FL	57	6.7	14	0.065	n/a	n/a
Cedar Rapids, IA	53	9.5	23	0.072	2	n/a
Charleston, SC	41	8.5	21	0.064	n/a	n/a
Charlotte, NC	38	9.6	21	0.085	2	n/a
Chicago, IL	153	11.9	32	0.093	2	0.13
Cincinnati, OH	105	13.9	28	0.091	1	0.01
Clarksville, TN	29	9.9	20	0.078	n/a	n/a
Colorado Spgs, CO	51	n/a	n/a	0.075	1	n/a
Columbia, MO	n/a	n/a	n/a	0.078	n/a	n/a
Columbus, OH	62	10.7	22	0.082	2	0.01
Dallas, TX	66	10.7	22	0.092	1	0.42
Davenport, IA	137	10.4	25	0.072	1	n/a
Denver, CO	103	n/a	37	0.086	2	0.02
Des Moines, IA	49	9.2	21	0.07	1	n/a
Durham, NC	30	8.3	18	0.076	n/a	n/a
El Paso, TX	643	9.9	21	0.074	4	0.03
Erie, PA	32	11.2	25	0.082	1	n/a
Eugene, OR	41	7.6	38	0.062	n/a	n/a
Fargo, ND	92	7.5	23	0.063	0	n/a
Fayetteville, NC	26	8.9	18	0.069	n/a	n/a
Ft. Collins, CO	91	n/a	n/a	0.08	2	n/a
Ft. Wayne, IN	n/a	9.9	26	0.077	2	n/a
Ft. Worth, TX	66	10.7	22	0.092	1	0.42
Gainesville, FL	n/a	7	17	0.064	n/a	n/a
Grand Rapids, MI	35	9.6	29	0.081	1	0.06
Green Bay, WI	n/a	8.7	25	0.086	n/a	n/a
Greensboro, NC	24	8.5	20	0.078	n/a	n/a
Honolulu, HI	36	7.1	15	0.048	1	0
Houston, TX	128	11.8	26	0.087	2	0.01
Huntsville, AL	38	9.3	19	0.076	n/a	0.01
Indianapolis, IN	71	11.7	26	0.084	2	0.04
Jacksonville, FL	55	8	22	0.061	2	0.01
Kansas City, MO	82	9.6	20	0.086	2	0.01
Lafayette, LA	73	8.6	18	0.07	n/a	n/a
Las Vegas, NV	139	8.6	21	0.085	3	n/a
Lexington, KY	30	9.8	19	0.078	n/a	n/a
Lincoln, NE	n/a	8.7	20	0.058	n/a	n/a
Little Rock, AR	36	11.6	27	0.08	1	n/a
Los Angeles, CA	74	12.5	32	0.102	4	0.15
Louisville, KY	46	11.9	24	0.092	2	n/a
Lubbock, TX	n/a	n/a	n/a	n/a	n/a	n/a
Madison, WI	36	9.4	27	0.074	n/a	n/a
Manchester, NH	20	8.2	23	0.073	0	n/a

Table continued on next page.

Metro Aea	PM 10 (ug/m³)	PM 2.5 Wtd AM (ug/m³)	PM 2.5 24-Hr (ug/m³)	Ozone (ppm)	Carbon Monoxide (ppm)	Lead (ug/m³)
McAllen, TX	69	n/a	n/a	0.061	n/a	n/a
Miami, FL	73	8.3	20	0.064	2	n/a
Midland, TX	n/a	n/a	n/a	n/a	n/a	n/a
Minneapolis, MN	70	9.9	25	0.074	2	0.11
Montgomery, AL	28	10.6	20	0.066	n/a	n/a
Nashville, TN	34	10.3	19	0.083	2	n/a
New Orleans, LA	63	12.9	19	0.077	n/a	0.04
New York, NY	73	11.7	26	0.085	3	0.03
Oklahoma City, OK	73	9.8	19	0.081	1	n/a
Omaha, NE	181	11.7	29	0.077	2	0.2
Orlando, FL	41	7.1	19	0.072	1	n/a
Oxnard, CA	76	9.6	19	0.081	n/a	n/a
Peoria, IL	n/a	9.8	21	0.078	2	0.01
Philadelphia, PA	66	16.5	31	0.092	2	0.05
Phoenix, AZ	504	12	29	0.083	3	n/a
Pittsburgh, PA	75	14.3	43	0.085	2	0.19
Portland, OR	33	7.3	23	0.065	2	0.05
Providence, RI	32	7.8	20	0.082	1	n/a
Provo, UT	67	8.1	34	0.077	2	n/a
Raleigh, NC	29	8.5	19	0.075	1	n/a
Reno, NV	194	9.1	26	0.072	2	n/a
Richmond, VA	29	8.9	20	0.078	2	0.01
Riverside, CA	334	15.1	36	0.106	2	0.01
Rochester, MN	n/a	7.8	19	0.069	n/a	n/a
Salem, OR	n/a	n/a	n/a	0.063	n/a	n/a
Salt Lake City, UT	81	8.9	29	0.08	2	0.05
San Antonio, TX	50	8.7	23	0.087	n/a	n/a
San Diego, CA	193	11.1	24	0.08	2	0.17
San Francisco, CA	46	9.5	22	0.072	2	0.33
San Jose, CA	56	9	32	0.072	2	0.12
Santa Rosa, CA	30	8.2	19	0.058	1	n/a
Savannah, GA	27	10	24	0.063	n/a	n/a
Seattle, WA	27	9.7	28	0.071	1	0.06
Sioux Falls, SD	72	8.7	21	0.072	1	n/a
Spokane, WA	84	n/a	n/a	0.063	2	n/a
Springfield, MO	33	10.1	22	0.08	n/a	n/a
Tallahassee, FL	n/a	8.7	18	0.067	n/a	n/a
Tampa, FL	55	6.9	16	0.074	1	0.98
Topeka, KS	47	8.6	18	0.079	n/a	n/a
Tulsa, OK	139	9.7	20	0.085	1	0.01
Virginia Beach, VA	32	8.2	23	0.074	1	n/a
Washington, DC	38	10.3	28	0.09	3	0
Wichita, KS	94	9.3	18	0.081	1	n/a
Wilmington, NC	n/a	6.6	16	0.064	n/a	n/a
Worcester, MA	38	8.8	20	0.07	2	n/a
NAAQS[1]	150	15	35	0.075	9	0.15

Note: Data from exceptional events are included; Data covers the Metropolitan Statistical Area—see Appendix B for areas included; (1) National Ambient Air Quality Standards; ppm = parts per million; ug/m³ = micrograms per cubic meter; n/a not available Concentrations: Particulate Matter 10 (coarse particulate)—highest second maximum 24-hour concentration; Particulate Matter 2.5 Wtd AM (fine particulate)—highest weighted annual mean concentration; Particulate Matter 2.5 24-Hour (fine particulate)—highest 98th percentile 24-hour concentration; Ozone—highest fourth daily maximum 8-hour concentration; Carbon Monoxide—highest second maximum non-overlapping 8-hour concentration; Lead—maximum running 3-month average
Source: U.S. Environmental Protection Agency, Air Quality Monitoring Information, "Air Quality Statistics by City, 2012"

Maximum Air Pollutant Concentrations: Nitrogen Dioxide and Sulfur Dioxide

Metro Area	Nitrogen Dioxide AM (ppb)	Nitrogen Dioxide 1-Hr (ppb)	Sulfur Dioxide AM (ppb)	Sulfur Dioxide 1-Hr (ppb)	Sulfur Dioxide 24-Hr (ppb)
Abilene, TX	n/a	n/a	n/a	n/a	n/a
Albuquerque, NM	14	49	n/a	6	n/a
Anchorage, AK	n/a	n/a	n/a	n/a	n/a
Ann Arbor, MI	n/a	n/a	n/a	n/a	n/a
Athens, GA	n/a	n/a	n/a	n/a	n/a
Atlanta, GA	12	53	n/a	11	n/a
Austin, TX	n/a	n/a	n/a	n/a	n/a
Baltimore, MD	16	56	n/a	19	n/a
Billings, MT	n/a	n/a	n/a	70	n/a
Boise City, ID	n/a	n/a	n/a	6	n/a
Boston, MA	19	49	n/a	21	n/a
Boulder, CO	n/a	n/a	n/a	n/a	n/a
Cape Coral, FL	n/a	n/a	n/a	n/a	n/a
Cedar Rapids, IA	n/a	n/a	n/a	29	n/a
Charleston, SC	7	n/a	n/a	17	n/a
Charlotte, NC	9	n/a	n/a	8	n/a
Chicago, IL	22	63	n/a	108	n/a
Cincinnati, OH	4	29	n/a	85	n/a
Clarksville, TN	n/a	n/a	n/a	55	n/a
Colorado Spgs, CO	n/a	n/a	n/a	n/a	n/a
Columbia, MO	n/a	n/a	n/a	n/a	n/a
Columbus, OH	n/a	n/a	n/a	n/a	n/a
Dallas, TX	12	53	n/a	15	n/a
Davenport, IA	8	34	n/a	12	n/a
Denver, CO	25	72	n/a	39	n/a
Des Moines, IA	8	40	n/a	1	n/a
Durham, NC	n/a	n/a	n/a	n/a	n/a
El Paso, TX	16	59	n/a	5	n/a
Erie, PA	6	31	n/a	19	n/a
Eugene, OR	n/a	n/a	n/a	n/a	n/a
Fargo, ND	5	34	n/a	4	n/a
Fayetteville, NC	n/a	n/a	n/a	4	n/a
Ft. Collins, CO	n/a	n/a	n/a	n/a	n/a
Ft. Wayne, IN	n/a	n/a	n/a	n/a	n/a
Ft. Worth, TX	12	53	n/a	15	n/a
Gainesville, FL	n/a	n/a	n/a	n/a	n/a
Grand Rapids, MI	n/a	n/a	n/a	10	n/a
Green Bay, WI	n/a	n/a	n/a	72	n/a
Greensboro, NC	n/a	n/a	n/a	n/a	n/a
Honolulu, HI	3	19	n/a	16	n/a
Houston, TX	15	60	n/a	29	n/a
Huntsville, AL	n/a	n/a	n/a	n/a	n/a
Indianapolis, IN	10	n/a	n/a	92	n/a
Jacksonville, FL	8	37	n/a	54	n/a
Kansas City, MO	14	53	n/a	167	n/a
Lafayette, LA	n/a	n/a	n/a	n/a	n/a
Las Vegas, NV	14	59	n/a	9	n/a
Lexington, KY	8	45	n/a	15	n/a
Lincoln, NE	n/a	n/a	n/a	n/a	n/a
Little Rock, AR	11	55	n/a	10	n/a
Los Angeles, CA	21	63	n/a	3	n/a
Louisville, KY	11	45	n/a	147	n/a
Lubbock, TX	n/a	n/a	n/a	n/a	n/a
Madison, WI	n/a	n/a	n/a	n/a	n/a
Manchester, NH	n/a	n/a	n/a	4	n/a

Table continued on next page.

Metro Area	Nitrogen Dioxide AM (ppb)	Nitrogen Dioxide 1-Hr (ppb)	Sulfur Dioxide AM (ppb)	Sulfur Dioxide 1-Hr (ppb)	Sulfur Dioxide 24-Hr (ppb)
McAllen, TX	n/a	n/a	n/a	n/a	n/a
Miami, FL	8	46	n/a	27	n/a
Midland, TX	n/a	n/a	n/a	n/a	n/a
Minneapolis, MN	11	57	n/a	16	n/a
Montgomery, AL	n/a	n/a	n/a	n/a	n/a
Nashville, TN	12	42	n/a	11	n/a
New Orleans, LA	8	46	n/a	217	n/a
New York, NY	22	67	n/a	32	n/a
Oklahoma City, OK	9	60	n/a	5	n/a
Omaha, NE	n/a	n/a	n/a	73	n/a
Orlando, FL	5	35	n/a	5	n/a
Oxnard, CA	10	38	n/a	n/a	n/a
Peoria, IL	n/a	n/a	n/a	245	n/a
Philadelphia, PA	18	56	n/a	29	n/a
Phoenix, AZ	26	65	n/a	9	n/a
Pittsburgh, PA	14	50	n/a	117	n/a
Portland, OR	9	36	n/a	5	n/a
Providence, RI	10	40	n/a	65	n/a
Provo, UT	17	66	n/a	n/a	n/a
Raleigh, NC	n/a	n/a	n/a	13	n/a
Reno, NV	14	53	n/a	6	n/a
Richmond, VA	10	51	n/a	21	n/a
Riverside, CA	22	96	n/a	5	n/a
Rochester, MN	n/a	n/a	n/a	n/a	n/a
Salem, OR	n/a	n/a	n/a	n/a	n/a
Salt Lake City, UT	16	54	n/a	20	n/a
San Antonio, TX	4	34	n/a	n/a	n/a
San Diego, CA	20	72	n/a	1	n/a
San Francisco, CA	15	66	n/a	15	n/a
San Jose, CA	13	52	n/a	13	n/a
Santa Rosa, CA	9	36	n/a	n/a	n/a
Savannah, GA	n/a	n/a	n/a	78	n/a
Seattle, WA	n/a	n/a	n/a	19	n/a
Sioux Falls, SD	6	37	n/a	6	n/a
Spokane, WA	n/a	n/a	n/a	n/a	n/a
Springfield, MO	n/a	n/a	n/a	52	n/a
Tallahassee, FL	n/a	n/a	n/a	n/a	n/a
Tampa, FL	5	34	n/a	110	n/a
Topeka, KS	n/a	n/a	n/a	n/a	n/a
Tulsa, OK	9	42	n/a	55	n/a
Virginia Beach, VA	8	41	n/a	56	n/a
Washington, DC	17	51	n/a	12	n/a
Wichita, KS	10	85	n/a	n/a	n/a
Wilmington, NC	n/a	n/a	n/a	47	n/a
Worcester, MA	13	45	n/a	9	n/a
NAAQS[1]	53	100	30	75	140

Note: Data from exceptional events are included; Data covers the Metropolitan Statistical Area—see Appendix B for areas included; (1) National Ambient Air Quality Standards; ppb = parts per billion; n/a not available
Concentrations: Nitrogen Dioxide AM—highest arithmetic mean concentration; Nitrogen Dioxide 1-Hr—highest 98th percentile 1-hour daily maximum concentration; Sulfur Dioxide AM—highest annual mean concentration; Sulfur Dioxide 1-Hr—highest 99th percentile 1-hour daily maximum concentration; Sulfur Dioxide 24-Hr—highest second maximum 24-hour concentration
Source: U.S. Environmental Protection Agency, Air Quality Monitoring Information, "Air Quality Statistics by City, 2012"

Table continued on next page.

Appendix B: Metropolitan Area Definitions

Metropolitan Statistical Areas (MSA), Metropolitan Divisions (MD), New England City and Town Areas (NECTA), and New England City and Town Area Divisions (NECTAD)

Note: In February 2013, the Office of Management and Budget (OMB) announced changes to metropolitan and micropolitan statistical area definitions. Both current and historical definitions are shown below. If the change only affected the name of the metro area, the counties included were not repeated.

Abilene, TX MSA
Callahan, Jones, and Taylor Counties

Albuquerque, NM MSA
Bernalillo, Sandoval, Torrance, and Valencia Counties

Anchorage, AK MSA
Anchorage Municipality and Matanuska-Susitna Borough

Ann Arbor, MI MSA
Washtenaw County

Athens-Clarke County, GA MSA
Clarke, Madison, Oconee, and Oglethorpe Counties

Atlanta-Sandy Springs-Roswell, GA MSA
Barrow, Bartow, Butts, Carroll, Cherokee, Clayton, Cobb, Coweta, Dawson, DeKalb, Douglas, Fayette, Forsyth, Fulton, Gwinnett, Haralson, Heard, Henry, Jasper, Lamar, Meriwether, Morgan, Newton, Paulding, Pickens, Pike, Rockdale, Spalding, and Walton Counties
Previously Atlanta-Sandy Springs-Marietta, GA MSA
Barrow, Bartow, Butts, Carroll, Cherokee, Clayton, Cobb, Coweta, Dawson, DeKalb, Douglas, Fayette, Forsyth, Fulton, Gwinnett, Haralson, Heard, Henry, Jasper, Lamar, Meriwether, Newton, Paulding, Pickens, Pike, Rockdale, Spalding, and Walton Counties

Austin-Round Rock, TX MSA
Previously Austin-Round Rock-San Marcos, TX MSA
Bastrop, Caldwell, Hays, Travis, and Williamson Counties

Baltimore-Columbia-Towson, MD MSA
Previously Baltimore-Towson, MD MSA
Baltimore city; Anne Arundel, Baltimore, Carroll, Harford, Howard, and Queen Anne's Counties

Billings, MT MSA
Carbon and Yellowstone Counties

Boise City, ID MSA
Previously Boise City-Nampa, ID MSA
Ada, Boise, Canyon, Gem, and Owyhee Counties

Boston, MA

Boston-Cambridge-Newton, MA-NH MSA
Peviously Boston-Cambridge-Quincy, MA-NH MSA
Essex, Middlesex, Norfolk, Plymouth, and Suffolk Counties, MA; Rockingham and Strafford Counties, NH

Boston, MA MD
Previously Boston-Quincy, MA MD
Norfolk, Plymouth, and Suffolk Counties

Boston-Cambridge-Nashua, MA-NH NECTA
Includes 157 cities and towns in Massachusetts and 34 cities and towns in New Hampshire
Previously Boston-Cambridge-Quincy, MA-NH NECTA
Includes 155 cities and towns in Massachusetts and 38 cities and towns in New Hampshire

Boston-Cambridge-Newton, MA NECTA Division
Includes 92 cities and towns in Massachusetts
Previously Boston-Cambridge-Quincy, MA NECTA Division
Includes 97 cities and towns in Massachusetts

Boulder, CO MSA
Boulder County

Cape Coral-Fort Myers, FL MSA
Lee County

Cedar Rapids, IA, MSA
Benton, Jones, and Linn Counties

Charleston-North Charleston, SC MSA
Previously Charleston-North Charleston- Summerville, SC MSA
Berkeley, Charleston, and Dorchester Counties

Charlotte-Concord-Gastonia, NC-SC MSA
Cabarrus, Gaston, Iredell, Lincoln, Mecklenburg, Rowan, and Union Counties, NC; Chester, Lancaster, and York Counties, SC
Previously Charlotte-Gastonia-Rock Hill, NC-SC MSA
Anson, Cabarrus, Gaston, Mecklenburg, and Union Counties, NC; York County, SC

Chicago, IL

Chicago-Naperville-Elgin, IL-IN-WI MSA
Previously Chicago-Joliet-Naperville, IL-IN-WI MSA
Cook, DeKalb, DuPage, Grundy, Kane, Kendall, Lake, McHenry, and Will Counties, IL; Jasper, Lake, Newton, and Porter Counties, IN; Kenosha County, WI

Chicago-Naperville-Arlington Heights, IL MD
Cook, DuPage, Grundy, Kendall, Kane, McHenry, and Will Counties
Previously Chicago-Joliet-Naperville, IL MD
Cook, DeKalb, DuPage, Grundy, Kane, Kendall, McHenry, and Will Counties

Lake County-Kenosha County, IL-WI MD
Lake County, IL; Kenosha County, WI

Cincinnati, OH-KY-IN MSA
Previously Cincinnati-Middletown, OH-KY-IN MSA
Dearborn, Ohio, and Union Counties, OH; Boone, Bracken, Campbell, Gallatin, Grant, Kenton, and Pendleton County, KY; Brown, Butler, Clermont, Hamilton, and Warren Counties, IN

Clarksville, TN-KY MSA
Mongomery and Stewart Counties, TN; Christian and Trigg Counties, KY

Colorado Springs, CO MSA
El Paso and Teller Counties

Columbia, MO MSA
Boone and Howard Counties

Columbus, OH MSA
Delaware, Fairfield, Franklin, Licking, Madison, Morrow, Pickaway, and Union Counties

Dallas, TX

Dallas-Fort Worth-Arlington, TX MSA
Collin, Dallas, Denton, Ellis, Hunt, Johnson, Kaufman, Parker, Rockwall, Tarrant, and Wise Counties

Dallas-Plano-Irving, TX MD
Collin, Dallas, Denton, Ellis, Hunt, Kaufman, and Rockwall Counties

Davenport-Moline-Rock Island, IA-IL MSA
Henry, Mercer, and Rock Island Counties, IA; Scott County, IL

Denver-Aurora-Lakewood, CO MSA
Previously Denver-Aurora-Broomfield, CO MSA
Adams, Arapahoe, Broomfield, Clear Creek, Denver, Douglas, Elbert, Gilpin, Jefferson, and Park Counties

Des Moines-West Des Moines, IA MSA
Dallas, Guthrie, Madison, Polk, and Warren Counties

Durham-Chapel Hill, NC MSA
Chatham, Durham, Orange, and and Person Counties

El Paso, TX MSA
El Paso County

Erie, PA MSA
Erie County

Eugene, OR MSA
Previously Eugene-Springfield, OR MSA
Lane County

Fargo, ND-MN MSA
Cass County, ND; Clay County, MN

Fayetteville, NC MSA
Cumberland, and Hoke Counties

Fort Collins, CO MSA
Previously Fort Collins-Loveland, CO MSA
Larimer County

Fort Wayne, IN MSA
Allen, Wells, and Whitley Counties

Fort Worth, TX

Dallas-Fort Worth-Arlington, TX MSA
Collin, Dallas, Denton, Ellis, Hunt, Johnson, Kaufman, Parker, Rockwall, Tarrant, and Wise Counties

Fort Worth-Arlington, TX MD
Hood, Johnson, Parker, Somervell, Tarrant, and Wise Counties

Gainesville, FL MSA
Alachua, and Gilchrist Counties

Grand Rapids-Wyoming, MI MSA
Barry, Kent, Montcalm, and Ottawa Counties

Green Bay, WI MSA
Brown, Kewaunee, and Oconto Counties

Greensboro-High Point, NC MSA
Guilford, Randolph, and Rockingham Counties

Honolulu, HI MSA
Honolulu County

Houston-The Woodlands-Sugar Land-Baytown, TX MSA
Austin, Brazoria, Chambers, Fort Bend, Galveston, Harris, Liberty, Montgomery, and Waller Counties
Previously Houston-Sugar Land-Baytown, TX MSA
Austin, Brazoria, Chambers, Fort Bend, Galveston, Harris, Liberty, Montgomery, San Jacinto, and Waller Counties

Huntsville, AL MSA
Limestone and Madison Counties

Indianapolis-Carmel, IN MSA
Boone, Brown, Hamilton, Hancock, Hendricks, Johnson, Marion, Morgan, Putnam, and Shelby Counties

Jacksonville, FL MSA
Baker, Clay, Duval, Nassau, and St. Johns Counties

Kansas City, MO-KS MSA
Franklin, Johnson, Leavenworth, Linn, Miami, and Wyandotte Counties, KS; Bates, Caldwell, Cass, Clay, Clinton, Jackson, Lafayette, Platte, and Ray Counties, MO

Lafayette, LA MSA
Acadia, Iberia, Lafayette, St. Martin, and Vermilion Parishes

Las Vegas-Henderson-Paradise, NV MSA
Previously Las Vegas-Paradise, NV MSA
Clark County

Lexington-Fayette, KY MSA
Bourbon, Clark, Fayette, Jessamine, Scott, and Woodford Counties

Lincoln, NE MSA
Lancaster and Seward Counties

Little Rock-North Little Rock-Conway, AR MSA
Faulkner, Grant, Lonoke, Perry, Pulaski and Saline Counties, AR

Los Angeles, CA

Los Angeles-Long Beach-Anaheim, CA MSA
Previously Los Angeles-Long Beach-Santa Ana, CA MSA
Los Angeles and Orange Counties

Los Angeles-Long Beach-Glendale, CA MD
Los Angeles County

Anaheim-Santa Ana-Irvine, CA MD
Previously Santa Ana-Anaheim-Irvine, CA MD
Orange County

Louisville/Jefferson, KY-IN MSA
Clark, Floyd, Harrison, Scott, and Washington Counties, IN; Bullitt, Henry, Jefferson, Oldham, Shelby, Spencer, and Trimble Counties, KY

Lubbock, TX MSA
Crosby, Lubbock, and Lynn Counties

Madison, WI MSA
Columbia, Dane, and Iowa Counties

Manchester, NH

Manchester-Nashua, NH MSA
Hillsborough County

Manchester, NH NECTA
Includes 11 cities and towns in New Hampshire
Previously Manchester, NH NECTA
Includes 9 cities and towns in New Hampshire

McAllen-Edinburg-Mission, TX
Hidalgo County

Miami, FL

Miami-Fort Lauderdale-West Palm Beach, FL MSA
Previously Miami-Fort Lauderdale-Pompano Beach, FL MSA
Broward, Miami-Dade, and Palm Beach Counties

Miami-Miami Beach-Kendall, FL MD
Miami-Dade County

Midland, TX MSA
Martin, and Midland Counties

Minneapolis-St. Paul-Bloomington, MN-WI MSA
Anoka, Carver, Chisago, Dakota, Hennepin, Isanti, Le Sueur, Mille
Lacs, Ramsey, Scott, Sherburne, Sibley, Washington, and Wright
Counties, MN; Pierce and St. Croix Counties, WI

Montgomery, AL MSA
Autauga, Elmore, Lowndes, and Montgomery Counties

Nashville-Davidson-Murfreesboro-Franklin, TN MSA
Cannon, Cheatham, Davidson, Dickson, Hickman, Macon, Robertson,
Rutherford, Smith, Sumner, Trousdale, Williamson, and Wilson
Counties

New Orleans-Metarie-Kenner, LA MSA
Jefferson, Orleans, Plaquemines, St. Bernard, St. Charles, St. James,
St. John the Baptist, and St. Tammany Parish
Previously New Orleans-Metarie-Kenner, LA MSA
Jefferson, Orleans, Plaquemines, St. Bernard, St. Charles, St. John the
Baptist, and St. Tammany Parish

New York, NY

New York-Newark-Jersey City, NY-NJ-PA MSA
Bergen, Essex, Hudson, Hunterdon, Middlesex, Monmouth, Morris,
Ocean, Passaic, Somerset, Sussex, and Union Counties, NJ; Bronx,
Dutchess, Kings, Nassau, New York, Orange, Putnam, Queens,
Richmond, Rockland, Suffolk, and Westchester Counties, NY; Pike
County, PA
*Previously New York-Northern New Jersey-Long Island, NY-NJ-PA
MSA*
Bergen, Essex, Hudson, Hunterdon, Middlesex, Monmouth, Morris,
Ocean, Passaic, Somerset, Sussex, and Union Counties, NJ; Bronx,
Kings, Nassau, New York, Putnam, Queens, Richmond, Rockland,
Suffolk, and Westchester Counties, NY; Pike County, PA

New York-Jersey City-White Plains, NY-NJ MD
Bergen, Hudson, Middlesex, Monmouth, Ocean, and Passaic
Counties, NJ; Bronx, Kings, New York, Putnam, Queens, Richmond,
Rockland, and Westchester Counties, NY
Previously New York-Wayne-White Plains, NY-NJ MD
Bergen, Hudson, and Passaic Counties, NJ; Bronx, Kings, New York,
Putnam, Queens, Richmond, Rockland, and Westchester Counties,
NY

Nassau-Suffolk, NY MD
Nassau and Suffolk Counties

Oklahoma City, OK MSA
Canadian, Cleveland, Grady, Lincoln, Logan, McClain, and Oklahoma
Counties

Omaha-Council Bluffs, NE-IA MSA
Harrison, Mills, and Pottawattamie Counties, IA; Cass, Douglas,
Sarpy, Saunders, and Washington Counties, NE

Orlando-Kissimmee-Sanford, FL MSA
Lake, Orange, Osceola, and Seminole Counties

Oxnard-Thousand Oaks-Ventura, CA MSA
Ventura County

Peoria, IL MSA
Marshall, Peoria, Stark, Tazewell, and Woodford Counties

Philadelphia, PA

Philadelphia-Camden-Wilmington, PA-NJ-DE-MD MSA
New Castle County, DE; Cecil County, MD; Burlington, Camden,
Gloucester, and Salem Counties, NJ; Bucks, Chester, Delaware,
Montgomery, and Philadelphia Counties, PA

Philadelphia, PA MD
Delaware and Philadelphia Counties
Previously Philadelphia, PA MD
Bucks, Chester, Delaware, Montgomery, and Philadelphia Counties

Phoenix-Mesa-Scottsdale, AZ MSA
Previously Phoenix-Mesa-Glendale, AZ MSA
Maricopa and Pinal Counties

Pittsburgh, PA MSA
Allegheny, Armstrong, Beaver, Butler, Fayette, Washington, and
Westmoreland Counties

Portland-Vancouver-Hillsboro, OR-WA MSA
Clackamas, Columbia, Multnomah, Washington, and Yamhill
Counties, OR; Clark and Skamania Counties, WA

Providence, RI

Providence-New Bedford-Fall River, RI-MA MSA
Previously Providence-New Bedford-Fall River, RI-MA MSA
Bristol County, MA; Bristol, Kent, Newport, Providence, and
Washington Counties, RI

Providence-Warwick, RI-MA NECTA
Includes 12 cities and towns in Massachusetts and 36 cities and towns
in Rhode Island
Previously Providence-Fall River-Warwick, RI-MA NECTA
Includes 12 cities and towns in Massachusetts and 37 cities and towns
in Rhode Island

Provo-Orem, UT MSA
Juab and Utah Counties

Raleigh, NC MSA
Previously Raleigh-Cary, NC MSA
Franklin, Johnston, and Wake Counties

Reno, NV MSA
Previously Reno-Sparks, NV MSA
Storey and Washoe Counties

Richmond, VA MSA
Amelia, Caroline, Charles City, Chesterfield, Dinwiddie, Goochland,
Hanover, Henrico, King William, New Kent, Powhatan, Prince
George, and Sussex Counties; Colonial Heights, Hopewell,
Petersburg, and Richmond Cities

Riverside-San Bernardino-Ontario, CA MSA
Riverside and San Bernardino Counties

Rochester, MN MSA
Dodge, Fillmore, Olmsted, and Wabasha Counties

Salem, OR MSA
Marion and Polk Counties

Salt Lake City, UT MSA
Salt Lake and Tooele Counties

San Antonio-New Braunfels, TX MSA
Atascosa, Bandera, Bexar, Comal, Guadalupe, Kendall, Medina, and Wilson Counties

San Diego-Carlsbad, CA MSA
Previously San Diego-Carlsbad-San Marcos, CA MSA
San Diego County

San Francisco, CA

San Francisco-Oakland-Hayward, CA MSA
Previously San Francisco-Oakland- Fremont, CA MSA
Alameda, Contra Costa, Marin, San Francisco, and San Mateo Counties

San Francisco-Redwood City-South San Francisco, CA MD
San Francisco and San Mateo Counties

Previously San Francisco-San Mateo-Redwood City, CA MD
Marin, San Francisco, and San Mateo Counties

San Jose-Sunnyvale-Santa Clara, CA MSA
San Benito and Santa Clara Counties

Santa Rosa, CA MSA
Previously Santa Rosa-Petaluma, CA MSA
Sonoma County

Savannah, GA MSA
Bryan, Chatham, and Effingham Counties

Seattle, WA

Seattle-Tacoma-Bellevue, WA MSA
King, Pierce, and Snohomish Counties

Seattle-Bellevue-Everett, WA MD
King and Snohomish Counties

Sioux Falls, SD MSA
Lincoln, McCook, Minnehaha, and Turner Counties

Spokane-Spokane Valley, WA MSA
Pend Oreille, Spokane, and Stevens Counties
Previously Spokane, WA MSA
Spokane County

Springfield, MO MSA
Christian, Dallas, Greene, Polk, and Webster Counties

Tallahassee, FL MSA
Gadsden, Jefferson, Leon, and Wakulla Counties

Tampa-St. Petersburg-Clearwater, FL MSA
Hernando, Hillsborough, Pasco, and Pinellas Counties

Topeka, KS MSA
Jackson, Jefferson, Osage, Shawnee, and Wabaunsee Counties

Tulsa, OK MSA
Creek, Okmulgee, Osage, Pawnee, Rogers, Tulsa, and Wagoner Counties

Virginia Beach-Norfolk-Newport News, VA-NC MSA
Currituck County, NC; Chesapeake, Hampton, Newport News, Norfolk, Poquoson, Portsmouth, Suffolk, Virginia Beach and Williamsburg cities, VA; Gloucester, Isle of Wight, James City, Mathews, Surry, and York Counties, VA

Washington, DC

Washington-Arlington-Alexandria, DC-VA-MD-WV MSA
District of Columbia; Calvert, Charles, Frederick, Montgomery, and Prince George's Counties, MD; Alexandria, Fairfax, Falls Church, Fredericksburg, Manassas Park, and Manassas cities, VA; Arlington, Clarke, Culpepper, Fairfax, Fauquier, Loudoun, Prince William, Rappahannock, Spotsylvania, Stafford, and Warren Counties, VA; Jefferson County, WV
Previously Washington-Arlington-Alexandria, DC-VA-MD-WV MSA
District of Columbia; Calvert, Charles, Frederick, Montgomery, and Prince George's Counties, MD; Alexandria, Fairfax, Falls Church, Fredericksburg, Manassas Park, and Manassas cities, VA; Arlington, Clarke, Fairfax, Fauquier, Loudoun, Prince William, Spotsylvania, Stafford, and Warren Counties, VA; Jefferson County, WV

Washington-Arlington-Alexandria, DC-VA-MD-WV MD
District of Columbia; Calvert, Charles, and Prince George's Counties, MD; Alexandria, Fairfax, Falls Church, Fredericksburg, Manassas Park, and Manassas cities, VA; Arlington, Clarke, Culpepper, Fairfax, Fauquier, Loudoun, Prince William, Rappahannock, Spotsylvania, Stafford, and Warren Counties, VA; Jefferson County, WV
Previously Washington-Arlington-Alexandria, DC-VA-MD-WV MD
District of Columbia; Calvert, Charles, and Prince George's Counties, MD; Alexandria, Fairfax, Falls Church, Fredericksburg, Manassas Park, and Manassas cities, VA; Arlington, Clarke, Fairfax, Fauquier, Loudoun, Prince William, Spotsylvania, Stafford, and Warren Counties, VA; Jefferson County, WV

Wichita, KS MSA
Butler, Harvey, Kingman, Sedgwick, and Sumner Counties

Wilmington, NC MSA
New Hanover and Pender Counties

Worcester, MA

Worcester, MA-CT MSA
Windham County, CT; Worcester County, MA
Previously Worcester, MA MSA
Worcester County

Worcester, MA-CT NECTA
Includes 40 cities and towns in Massachusetts and 8 cities and towns in Connecticut
Previously Worcester, MA-CT NECTA
Includes 37 cities and towns in Massachusetts and 3 cities and towns in Connecticut

Appendix C: Government Type and Primary County

This appendix includes the government structure of each place included in this book. It also includes the county or county equivalent in which each place is located. If a place spans more that one county, the county in which the majority of the population resides is shown.

Abilene, TX
Government Type: City
County: Taylor

Albuquerque, NM
Government Type: City
County: Bernalillo

Anchorage, AK
Government Type: Municipality
Borough: Anchorage

Ann Arbor, MI
Government Type: City
County: Washtenaw

Athens, GA
Government Type: Consolidated
 city-county
County: Clarke

Atlanta, GA
Government Type: City
County: Fulton

Austin, TX
Government Type: City
County: Travis

Baltimore, MD
Government Type: Independent city
County: Baltimore city

Billings, MT
Government Type: City
County: Yellowstone

Boise City, ID
Government Type: City
County: Ada

Boston, MA
Government Type: City
County: Suffolk

Boulder, CO
Government Type: City
County: Boulder

Cape Coral, FL
Government Type: City
County: Lee

Cedar Rapids, IA
Government Type: City
County: Linn

Charleston, SC
Government Type: City
County: Charleston

Charlotte, NC
Government Type: City
County: Mecklenburg

Chicago, IL
Government Type: City
County: Cook

Cincinnati, OH
Government Type: City
County: Hamilton

Clarksville, TN
Government Type: City
County: Montgomery

Colorado Springs, CO
Government Type: City
County: El Paso

Columbia, MO
Government Type: City
County: Boone

Columbus, OH
Government Type: City
County: Franklin

Dallas, TX
Government Type: City
County: Dallas

Davenport, IA
Government Type: City
County: Scott

Denver, CO
Government Type: City
County: Denver

Des Moines, IA
Government Type: City
County: Polk

Durham, NC
Government Type: City
County: Durham

El Paso, TX
Government Type: City
County: El Paso

Erie, PA
Government Type: City
County: Erie

Eugene, OR
Government Type: City
County: Lane

Fargo, ND
Government Type: City
County: Cass

Fayetteville, NC
Government Type: City
County: Cumberland

Fort Collins, CO
Government Type: City
County: Larimer

Fort Wayne, IN
Government Type: City
County: Allen

Fort Worth, TX
Government Type: City
County: Tarrant

Gainesville, FL
Government Type: City
County: Alachua

Grand Rapids, MI
Government Type: City
County: Kent

Green Bay, WI
Government Type: City
County: Brown

Greensboro, NC
Government Type: City
County: Guilford

Honolulu, HI
Government Type: Census Designated Place
 (CDP)
County: Honolulu

Houston, TX
Government Type: City
County: Harris

Huntsville, AL
Government Type: City
County: Madison

Indianapolis, IN
Government Type: City
County: Marion

Jacksonville, FL
Government Type: City
County: Duval

Kansas City, MO
Government Type: City
County: Jackson

Lafayette, LA
Government Type: City
Parish: Lafayette

Las Vegas, NV
Government Type: City
County: Clark

Lexington, KY
Government Type: Consolidated city-county
County: Fayette

Lincoln, NE
Government Type: City
County: Lancaster

Little Rock, AR
Government Type: City
County: Pulaski

Los Angeles, CA
Government Type: City
County: Los Angeles

Louisville, KY
Government Type: Consolidated city-county
County: Jefferson

Lubbock, TX
Government Type: City
County: Lubbock

Madison, WI
Government Type: City
County: Dane

Manchester, NH
Government Type: City
County: Hillsborough

McAllen, TX
Government Type: City
County: Hidalgo

Miami, FL
Government Type: City
County: Miami-Dade

Midland, TX
Government Type: City
County: Midland

Minneapolis, MN
Government Type: City
County: Hennepin

Montgomery, AL
Government Type: City
County: Montgomery

Nashville, TN
Government Type: Consolidated city-county
County: Davidson

New Orleans, LA
Government Type: City
Parish: Orleans

New York, NY
Government Type: City
Counties: Bronx; Kings; New York; Queens;
  Staten Island

Oklahoma City, OK
Government Type: City
County: Oklahoma

Omaha, NE
Government Type: City
County: Douglas

Orlando, FL
Government Type: City
County: Orange

Oxnard, CA
Government Type: City
County: Ventura

Peoria, IL
Government Type: City
County: Peoria

Philadelphia, PA
Government Type: City
County: Philadelphia

Phoenix, AZ
Government Type: City
County: Maricopa

Pittsburgh, PA
Government Type: City
County: Allegheny

Portland, OR
Government Type: City
County: Multnomah

Providence, RI
Government Type: City
County: Providence

Provo, UT
Government Type: City
County: Utah

Raleigh, NC
Government Type: City
County: Wake

Reno, NV
Government Type: City
County: Washoe

Richmond, VA
Government Type: Independent city
County: Richmond city

Riverside, CA
Government Type: City
County: Riverside

Rochester, MN
Government Type: City
County: Olmsted

Salem, OR
Government Type: City
County: Marion

Salt Lake City, UT
Government Type: City
County: Salt Lake

San Antonio, TX
Government Type: City
County: Bexar

San Diego, CA
Government Type: City
County: San Diego

San Francisco, CA
Government Type: City
County: San Francisco

San Jose, CA
Government Type: City
County: Santa Clara

Santa Rosa, CA
Government Type: City
County: Sonoma

Savannah, GA
Government Type: City
County: Chatham

Seattle, WA
Government Type: City
County: King

Sioux Falls, SD
Government Type: City
County: Minnehaha

Spokane, WA
Government Type: City
County: Spokane

Springfield, MO
Government Type: City
County: Christian

Tallahassee, FL
Government Type: City
County: Leon

Tampa, FL
Government Type: City
County: Hillsborough

Topeka, KS
Government Type: City
County: Shawnee

Tulsa, OK
Government Type: City
County: Tulsa

Virginia Beach, VA
Government Type: Independent city
County: Virginia Beach city

Washington, DC
Government Type: City
County: District of Columbia

Wichita, KS
Government Type: City
County: Sedgwick

Wilmington, NC
Government Type: City
County: New Hanover

Worcester, MA
Government Type: City
County: Worcester

Appendix D: Chambers of Commerce & Economic Development Offices

Abilene, TX
Abilene Chamber of Commerce
174 Cypress Street
Suite 200
Abilene, TX 79601
Phone: (325) 677-7241
Fax: (325) 677-0622
www.abilenechamber.com

Albuquerque, NM
Albuquerque Chamber of Commerce
P.O. Box 25100
Albuquerque, NM 87125
Phone: (505) 764-3700
Fax: (505) 764-3714
www.abqchamber.com

Albuquerque Economic Development Dept
851 University Blvd SE
Suite 203
Albuquerque, NM 87106
Phone: (505) 246-6200
Fax: (505) 246-6219
www.cabq.gov/econdev

Anchorage, AK
Anchorage Chamber of Commerce
1016 W Sixth Avenue
Suite 303
Anchorage, AK 99501
Phone: (907) 272-2401
Fax: (907) 272-4117
www.anchoragechamber.org

Anchorage Economic Development
Department
900 W 5th Avenue
Suite 300
Anchorage, AK 99501
Phone: (907) 258-3700
Fax: (907) 258-6646
www.aedcweb.com/aedcdig

Ann Arbor, MI
Ann Arbor Area Chamber of Commerce
115 West Huron
3rd Floor
Ann Arbor, MI 48104
Phone: (734) 665-4433
Fax: (734) 665-4191
www.annarborchamber.org

Ann Arbor Economic Development
Department
201 S Division
Suite 430
Ann Arbor, MI 48104
Phone: (734) 761-9317
www.annarborspark.org

Athens, GA
Athens Area Chamber of Commerce
246 W Hancock Avenue
Athens, GA 30601
Phone: (706) 549-6800
Fax: (706) 549-5636
www.aacoc.org

Athens-Clarke Economic Development
150 E. Hancock Avenue
P.O. Box 1692
Athens, GA 30603
Phone: (706) 613-3810
Fax: (706) 613-3812
www.athensbusiness.org/contact.aspx

Atlanta, GA
Metro Atlanta Chamber of Commerce
235 Andrew Young International Blvd NW
Atlanta, GA 30303
Phone: (404) 880-9000
Fax: (404) 586-8464
www.metroatlantachamber.com/contact_us.html

Austin, TX
Greater Austin Chamber of Commerce
210 Barton Springs Road
Suite 400
Austin, TX 78704
Phone: (512) 478-9383
Fax: (512) 478-6389
www.austin-chamber.org

Baltimore, MD
Baltimore City Chamber of Commerce
312 Martin Luther King Jr Blvd
Baltimore, MD 21201
Phone: (410) 837-7101
Fax: (410) 837-7104
www.baltimorecitychamber.com

City of Baltimore Development Corporation
36 South Charles Street
Suite 1600
Baltimore, MD 21201
Phone: (410) 837-9305
Fax: (410) 837-6363
www.baltimoredevelopment.com

Billings, MT
Billings Area Chamber of Commerce
815 S 27th St
Billings, MT 59101
Phone: (406) 245-4111
Fax: (406) 2457333
www.billingschamber.com

Boise City, ID
Boise Metro Chamber of Commerce
250 S 5th Street
Suite 800
Boise City, ID 83701
Phone: (208) 472-5200
Fax: (208) 472-5201
www.boisechamber.org

Boston, MA
Greater Boston Chamber of Commerce
265 Franklin Street
12th Floor
Boston, MA 02110
Phone: (617) 227-4500
Fax: (617) 227-7505
www.bostonchamber.com

Boulder, CO
Boulder Chamber of Commerce
2440 Pearl Street
Boulder, CO 80302
Phone: (303) 442-1044
Fax: (303) 938-8837
www.boulderchamber.com

City of Boulder Economic Vitality Program
P.O. Box 791
Boulder, CO 80306
Phone: (303) 441-3090
www.bouldercolorado.gov

Cape Coral, FL
Chamber of Commerce of Cape Coral
2051 Cape Coral Parkway East
Cape Coral, FL 33904
Phone: (239) 549-6900
Fax: (239) 549-9609
www.capecoralchamber.com

Cedar Rapids, IA
Cedar Rapids Chamber of Commerce
424 First Avenue NE
Cedar Rapids, IA 52401
Phone: (319) 398-5317
Fax: (319) 398-5228
www.cedarrapids.org

Cedar Rapids Economic Development
50 Second Avenue Bridge, Sixth Floor
Cedar Rapids, IA 52401-1256
Phone: (319) 286-5041
Fax: (319) 286-5141
www.cedar-rapids.org

Charleston, SC
Charleston Metro Chamber of Commerce
P.O. Box 975
Charleston, SC 29402
Phone: (843) 577-2510
www.charlestonchamber.net

Charlotte, NC
Charlotte Chamber of Commerce
330 S Tryon Street
Charlotte, NC 28232
Phone: (704) 378-1300
Fax: (704) 374-1903
www.charlottechamber.com

Charlotte Regional Partnership
1001 Morehead Square Drive
Suite 200
Charlotte, NC 28203
Phone: (704) 347-8942
Fax: (704) 347-8981
www.charlotteusa.com

Chicago, IL
Chicagoland Chamber of Commerce
200 E Randolph Street
Suite 2200
Chicago, IL 60601-6436
Phone: (312) 494-6700
Fax: (312) 861-0660
www.chicagolandchamber.org

City of Chicago Department of Planning
and Development
City Hall, Room 1000
121 North La Salle Street
Chicago, IL 60602
Phone: (312) 744-4190
Fax: (312) 744-2271
www.egov.cityofchicago.org

Cincinnati, OH
Greater Cincinnati Chamber of Commerce
441 Vine Street
Suite 300
Cincinnati, OH 45202
Phone: (513) 579-3100
Fax: (513) 579-3101
www.cincinnatichamber.com

Clarksville, TN
Clarksville Area Chamber of Commerce
25 Jefferson Street
Suite 300
Clarksville, TN 37040
Phone: (931) 647-2331
www.clarksvillechamber.com

Colorado Springs, CO
Greater Colorado Springs Chamber of
Commerce
6 S. Tejon Street
Suite 700
Colorado Springs, CO 80903
Phone: (719) 635-1551
Fax: (719) 635-1571
www.gcsco.wliinc3.com

Greater Colorado Springs Economic
Development Corp
90 South Cascade Avenue
Suite 1050
Colorado Springs, CO 80903
Phone: (719) 471-8183
Fax: (719) 471-9733
www.coloradosprings.org

Columbia, MO
Columbia Chamber of Commerce
300 South Providence Rd.
PO Box 1016
Columbia, MO 65205-1016
Phone: (573) 874-1132
Fax: (573)443-3986
www.columbiamochamber.com

Columbus, OH
Greater Columbus Chamber
37 North High Street
Columbus, OH 43215
Phone: (614) 221-1321
Fax: (614) 221-1408
www.columbus.org

Dallas, TX
City of Dallas Economic Development
Department
1500 Marilla Street
5C South
Dallas, TX 75201
Phone: (214) 670-1685
Fax: (214) 670-0158
www.dallas-edd.org

Greater Dallas Chamber of Commerce
700 North Pearl Street
Suite1200
Dallas, TX 75201
Phone: (214) 746-6600
Fax: (214) 746-6799
www.dallaschamber.org

Davenport, IA
Quad Cities Chamber
331 W. 3rd St.,
Davenport, IA 52801
Phone: (563) 322-1706
www.quadcitieschamber.com

Denver, CO
Denver Metro Chamber of Commerce
1445 Market Street
Denver, CO 80202
Phone: (303) 534-8500
Fax: (303) 534-3200
www.denverchamber.org

Downtown Denver Partnership
511 16th Street
Suite 200
Denver, CO 80202
Phone: (303) 534-6161
Fax: (303) 534-2803
www.downtowndenver.com

Des Moines, IA
Des Moines Downtown Chamber
301 Grand Ave
Des Moines, IA 50309
Phone: (515) 309-3229
www.desmoinesdowtownchamber.com

Greater Des Moines Partnership
700 Locust Street
Suite 100
Des Moines, IA 50309
Phone: (515) 286-4950
Fax: (515) 286-4974
www.desmoinesmetro.com

Durham, NC
Durham Chamber of Commerce
PO Box 3829
Durham, NC 27702
Phone: (919) 682-2133
Fax: (919) 688-8351
www.durhamchamber.org

North Carolina Institute of Minority
Economic Development
114 W Parish Street
Durham, NC 27701
Phone: (919) 956-8889
Fax: (919) 688-7668
www.ncimed.com

El Paso, TX
City of El Paso Department of Economic
Development
2 Civic Center Plaza
El Paso, TX 79901
Phone: (915) 541-4000
Fax: (915) 541-1316
www.elpasotexas.gov

Greater El Paso Chamber of Commerce
10 Civic Center Plaza
El Paso, TX 79901
Phone: (915) 534-0500
Fax: (915) 534-0510
www.elpaso.org

Erie, PA
Erie Regional Chamber and Growth
Partnership
208 E. Bayfront Parkway
Suite 100
Erie, PA 16507
Phone: (814) 454-7191
www.eriepa.com

Eugene, OR
Eugene Area Chamber of Commerce
1401 Williamette Street
Eugene, OR 97401
Phone: (541) 484-1314
Fax: (541) 484-4942
www.eugenechamber.com

Fargo, ND
Chamber of Commerce of Fargo Moorhead
202 First Avenue North
Fargo, ND 56560
Phone: (218) 233-1100
Fax: (218) 233-1200
www.fmchamber.com

Greater Fargo-Moorhead Economic
Development Corporation
51 Broadway, Suite 500
Fargo, ND 58102
Phone: (701) 364-1900
Fax: (701) 293-7819
www.gfmedc.com

Fayetteville, NC
Fayetteville Regional Chamber
1019 Hay Street
Fayetteville, NC 28305
Phone: (910) 483-8133
Fax: (910) 483-0263
www.fayettevillencchamber.org

Fort Collins, CO
Fort Collins Chamber of Commerce
225 South Meldrum
Fort Collins, CO 80521
Phone: (970) 482-3746
Fax: (970) 482-3774
www.fcchamber.org

Fort Wayne, IN
City of Fort Wayne Economic Development
1 Main St
1 Main Street
Fort Wayne, IN 46802
Phone: (260) 427-1111
Fax: (260) 427-1375
www.cityoffortwayne.org

Greater Fort Wayne Chamber of Commerce
826 Ewing Street
Fort Wayne, IN 46802
Phone: (260) 424-1435
Fax: (260) 426-7232
www.fwchamber.org

Fort Worth, TX
City of Fort Worth Economic Development
City Hall
900 Monroe Street, Suite 301
Fort Worth, TX 76102
Phone: (817) 392-6103
Fax: (817) 392-2431
www.fortworthgov.org

Fort Worth Chamber of Commerce
777 Taylor Street
Suite 900
Fort Worth, TX 76102-4997
Phone: (817) 336-2491
Fax: (817) 877-4034
www.fortworthchamber.com

Gainesville, FL
Gainesville Area Chamber of Commerce
300 East University Avenue
Suite 100
Gainesville, FL 32601
Phone: (352) 334-7100
Fax: (352) 334-7141
www.gainesvillechamber.com

Grand Rapids, MI
Grands Rapids Area Chamber of Commerce
111 Pearl Street N.W.
Grand Rapids, MI 49503
Phone: (616) 771-0300
Fax: (616) 771-0318
www.grandrapids.org

Green Bay, WI
Economic Development
100 N Jefferson St
Room 202
Green Bay, WI 54301
Phone: (920) 448-3397
Fax: (920) 448-3063
www.ci.green-bay.wi.us

Green Bay Area Chamber of Commerce
300 N. Broadway
Suite 3A
Green Bay, WI 54305-1660
Phone: (920) 437-8704
Fax: (920) 593-3468
www.titletown.org

Greensboro, NC
Greensboro Area Chamber of Commerce
342 N Elm St.
Greensboro, NC 27401
Phone: (336) 387-8301
Fax: (336) 275-9299
www.greensboro.org

Honolulu, HI
The Chamber of Commerce of Hawaii
1132 Bishop Street
Suite 402
Honolulu, HI 96813
Phone: (808) 545-4300
Fax: (808) 545-4369
www.cochawaii.com

Houston, TX
Greater Houston Partnership
1200 Smith Street
Suite 700
Houston, TX 77002-4400
Phone: (713) 844-3600
Fax: (713) 844-0200
www.houston.org

Huntsville, AL
Chamber of Commerce of
Huntsville/Madison County
225 Church Street
Huntsville, AL 35801
Phone: (256) 535-2000
Fax: (256) 535-2015
www.huntsvillealabamausa.com

Indianapolis, IN
Greater Indianapolis Chamber of Commerce
111 Monument Circle
Suite 1950
Indianapolis, IN 46204
Phone: (317) 464-2222
Fax: (317) 464-2217
www.indychamber.com

The Indy Partnership
111 Monument Circle
Suite 1800
Indianapolis, IN 46204
Phone: (317) 236-6262
Fax: (317) 236-6275
www.indypartnership.com

Jacksonville, FL
Jacksonville Chamber of Commerce
3 Independent Drive
Jacksonville, FL 32202
Phone: (904) 366-6600
Fax: (904) 632-0617
www.myjaxchamber.com

Kansas City, MO
Greater Kansas City Chamber of Commerce
2600 Commerce Tower
911 Main Street
Kansas City, MO 64105
Phone: (816) 221-2424
Fax: (816) 221-7440
www.kcchamber.com

Kansas City Area Development Council
2600 Commerce Tower
911 Main Street
Kansas City, MO 64105
Phone: (816) 221-2121
Fax: (816) 842-2865
www.thinkkc.com

Lafayette, LA
Greater Lafayette Chamber of Commerce
804 East Saint Mary Blvd.
Lafayette, LA 70503
Phone: (337) 233-2705
Fax: (337) 234-8671
www.lafchamber.org

Las Vegas, NV
Las Vegas Chamber of Commerce
6671 Las Vegas Blvd South
Suite 300
Las Vegas, NV 89119
Phone: (702) 735-1616
Fax: (702) 735-0406
www.lvchamber.org

Las Vegas Office of Business Development
400 Stewart Avenue
City Hall
Las Vegas, NV 89101
Phone: (702) 229-6011
Fax: (702) 385-3128
www.lasvegasnevada.gov

Lexington, KY
Greater Lexington Chamber of Commerce
330 East Main Street
Suite 100
Lexington, KY 40507
Phone: (859) 254-4447
Fax: (859) 233-3304
www.commercelexington.com

Lexington Downtown Development
Authority
101 East Vine Street
Suite 500
Lexington, KY 40507
Phone: (859) 425-2296
Fax: (859) 425-2292
www.lexingtondda.com

Lincoln, NE
Lincoln Chamber of Commerce
1135 M Street
Suite 200
Lincoln, NE 68508
Phone: (402) 436-2350
Fax: (402) 436-2360
www.lcoc.com

Little Rock, AR
Little Rock Regional Chamber of
Commerce
One Chamber Plaza
Little Rock, AR 72201-1618
Phone: (501) 374-2001
www.littlerockchamber.com

Los Angeles, CA
Los Angeles Area Chamber of Commerce
350 South Bixel Street
Los Angeles, CA 90017
Phone: (213) 580-7500
Fax: (213) 580-7511
www.lachamber.org

Los Angeles County Economic
Development Corporation
444 South Flower Street
34th Floor
Los Angeles, CA 90071
Phone: (213) 622-4300
Fax: (213) 622-7100
www.laedc.org

Louisville, KY
The Greater Louisville Chamber of
Commerce
614 West Main Street
Suite 6000
Louisville, KY 40202
Phone: (502) 625-0000
Fax: (502) 625-0010
www.greaterlouisville.com

Lubbock, TX
Lubbock Chamber of Commerce
1500 Broadway
Suite 101
Lubbock, TX 79401
Phone: (806) 761-7000
Fax: (806) 761-7013
www.lubbockchamber.com

Madison, WI
Greater Madison Chamber of Commerce
615 East Washington Avenue
P.O. Box 71
Madison, WI 53701-0071
Phone: (608) 256-8348
Fax: (608) 256-0333
www.greatermadisonchamber.com

Manchester, NH
Greater Manchester Chamber of Commerce
889 Elm Street
Manchester, NH 03101
Phone: (603) 666-6600
Fax: (603) 626-0910
www.manchester-chamber.org

Manchester Economic Development Office
One City Hall Plaza
Manchester, NH 03101
Phone: (603) 624-6505
Fax: (603) 624-6308
www.yourmanchesternh.com

Miami, FL
Greater Miami Chamber of Commerce
1601 Biscayne Boulevard
Ballroom Level
Miami, FL 33132-1260
Phone: (305) 350-7700
Fax: (305) 374-6902
www.greatermiami.com

The Beacon Council
80 Southwest 8th Street
Suite 2400
Miami, FL 33130
Phone: (305) 579-1300
Fax: (305) 375-0271
www.beaconcouncil.com

Midland, TX
Midland Chamber of Commerce
109 N. Main
Midland, TX 79701
Phone: (432) 683-3381
Fax: (432) 686-3556
www.midlandtxchamber.com

Minneapolis, MN
Minneapolis Community Development
Agency
Crown Roller Mill
105 5th Avenue South, Suite 200
Minneapolis, MN 55401
Phone: (612) 673-5095
Fax: (612) 673-5100
www.ci.minneapolis.mn.us

Minneapolis Regional Chamber
81 South Ninth Street
Suite 200
Minneapolis, MN 55402
Phone: (612) 370-9100
Fax: (612) 370-9195
www.minneapolischamber.org

Montgomery, AL
Montgomery Area Chamber of Commerce
41 Commerce Street
Montgomery, AL 36104
Phone: (334) 834-5200
www.montgomerychamber.com

Nashville, TN
Nashville Area Chamber of Commerce
211 Commerce Street, Suite 100
Nashville, TN 37201
Phone: (615) 743-3000
Fax: (615) 256-3074
www.nashvillechamber.cm

Tennessee Valley Authority Economic
Development Corp.
P.O. Box 292409
Nashville, TN 37229-2409
Phone: (615) 232-6225
www.tvaed.com

New Orleans, LA
New Orleans Chamber of Commerce
1515 Poydras St, Suite 1010
New Orleans, LA 70112
Phone: (504) 799-4260
Fax: (504) 799-4259
www.neworleanschamber.org

New York, NY
New York City Economic Development
Corporation
110 William Street
New York, NY 10038
Phone: (212) 619-5000
www.nycedc.com

The Partnership for New York City
One Battery Park Plaza
5th Floor
New York, NY 10004
Phone: (212) 493-7400
Fax: (212) 344-3344
www.pfnyc.org

Oklahoma City, OK
Greater Oklahoma City Chamber of
Commerce
123 Park Avenue
Oklahoma City, OK 73102
Phone: (405) 297-8900
Fax: (405) 297-8916
www.okcchamber.com

Omaha, NE
Omaha Chamber of Commerce
1301 Harney Street
Omaha, NE 68102
Phone: (402) 346-5000
Fax: (402) 346-7050
www.omahachamber.org

Orlando, FL
Metro Orlando Economic Development
Commission of Mid-Florida
301 East Pine Street
Suite 900
Orlando, FL 32801
Phone: (407) 422-7159
Fax: (407) 425.6428
www.orlandoedc.com

Orlando Regional Chamber of Commerce
75 South Ivanhoe Boulevard
PO Box 1234
Orlando, FL 32802
Phone: (407) 425-1234
Fax: (407) 839-5020
www.orlando.org

Oxnard, CA
Oxnard Chamber of Commerce
400 E Esplanade Drive
Suite 302
Oxnard, CA 93036
Phone: (805) 983-6118
Fax: (805) 604-7331
www.oxnardchamber.org

Peoria, IL
Peoria Area Chamber
100 SW Water St.
Peoria, IL 61602
Phone: (309) 495-5900
www.peoriachamber.org

Philadelphia, PA
Greater Philadelphia Chamber of
Commerce
200 South Broad Street
Suite 700
Philadelphia, PA 19102
Phone: (215) 545-1234
Fax: (215) 790-3600
www.greaterphilachamber.com

Phoenix, AZ
Greater Phoenix Chamber of Commerce
201 North Central Avenue
27th Floor
Phoenix, AZ 85073
Phone: (602) 495-2195
Fax: (602) 495-8913
www.phoenixchamber.com

Greater Phoenix Economic Council
2 North Central Avenue
Suite 2500
Phoenix, AZ 85004
Phone: (602) 256-7700
Fax: (602) 256-7744
www.gpec.org

Pittsburgh, PA
Allegheny County Industrial Development
Authority
425 6th Avenue
Suite 800
Pittsburgh, PA 15219
Phone: (412) 350-1067
Fax: (412) 642-2217
www.alleghenycounty.us

Greater Pittsburgh Chamber of Commerce
425 6th Avenue
12th Floor
Pittsburgh, PA 15219
Phone: (412) 392-4500
Fax: (412) 392-4520
www.alleghenyconference.org

Portland, OR
Portland Business Alliance
200 SW Market Street
Suite 1770
Portland, OR 97201
Phone: (503) 224-8684
Fax: (503) 323-9186
www.portlandalliance.com

Providence, RI
Greater Providence Chamber of Commerce
30 Exchange Terrace
Fourth Floor
Providence, RI 02903
Phone: (401) 521-5000
Fax: (401) 351-2090
www.provchamber.com

Rhode Island Economic Development
Corporation
Providence City Hall
25 Dorrance Street
Providence, RI 02903
Phone: (401) 421-7740
Fax: (401) 751-0203
www.providenceri.com

Provo, UT
Provo-Orem Chamber of Commerce
51 South University Avenue
Suite 215
Provo, UT 84601
Phone: (801) 851-2555
Fax: (801) 851-2557
www.thechamber.org

Raleigh, NC
Greater Raleigh Chamber of Commerce
800 South Salisbury Street
Raleigh, NC 27601-2978
Phone: (919) 664-7000
Fax: (919) 664-7099
www.raleighchamber.org

Reno, NV
Greater Reno-Sparks Chamber of
Commerce
1 East First Street
16th Floor
Reno, NV 89505
Phone: (775) 337-3030
Fax: (775) 337-3038
www.reno-sparkschamber.org

The Chamber Reno-Sparks-Northern
Nevada
449 S. Virginia St.
2nd Floor
Reno, NV 89501
Phone: (775) 636-9550
www.thechambernv.org

Richmond, VA
Greater Richmond Chamber
600 East Main Street
Suite 700
Richmond, VA 23219
Phone: (804) 648-1234
www.grcc.com

Greater Richmond Partnership
901 East Byrd Street
Suite 801
Richmond, VA 23219-4070
Phone: (804) 643-3227
Fax: (804) 343-7167
www.grpva.com

Riverside, CA
Greater Riverside Chamber of Commerce
3985 University Avenue
Riverside, CA 92501
Phone: (951) 683-7100
Fax: (951) 683-2670
www.riverside-chamber.com

Rochester, MN
Rochester Area Chamber of Commerce
220 South Broadway
Suite 100
Rochester, MN 55904
Phone: (507) 288-1122
Fax: (507) 282-8960
www.rochestermnchamber.com

Salem, OR
Salem Area Chamber of Commerce
1110 Commercial Street NE
Salem, OR 97301
Phone: (503) 581-1466
Fax: (503) 581-0972
www.salemchamber.org

Salt Lake City, UT
Department of Economic Development
451 South State Street, Room 345
Salt Lake City, UT 84111
Phone: (801) 535-6306
Fax: (801) 535-6331
www.slcgov.com/mayor/ED

Salt Lake Chamber
175 E. University Blvd. (400 S)
Suite 600
Salt Lake City, UT 84111
Phone: (801) 364-3631
www.slchamber.com

San Antonio, TX
San Antonio Economic Development
Department
P.O. Box 839966
San Antonio, TX 78283-3966
Phone: (210) 207-8080
Fax: (210) 207-8151
www.sanantonio.gov/edd

The Greater San Antonio Chamber of
Commerce
602 E. Commerce Street
San Antonio, TX 78205
Phone: (210) 229-2100
Fax: (210) 229-1600
www.sachamber.org

San Diego, CA
San Diego Economic Development Corp.
401 B Street
Suite 1100
San Diego, CA 92101
Phone: (619) 234-8484
Fax: (619) 234-1935
www.sandiegobusiness.org

San Diego Regional Chamber of Commerce
402 West Broadway
Suite 1000
San Diego, CA 92101-3585
Phone: (619) 544-1300
Fax: (619) 744-7481
www.sdchamber.org

San Francisco, CA
San Francisco Chamber of Commerce
235 Montgomery Street
12th Floor
San Francisco, CA 94104
Phone: (415) 392-4520
Fax: (415) 392-0485
www.sfchamber.com

San Jose, CA
Office of Economic Development
60 South Market Street
Suite 470
San Jose, CA 95113
Phone: (408) 277-5880
Fax: (408) 277-3615
www.sba.gov

San Jose-Silicon Valley Chamber of
Commerce
310 South First Street
San Jose, CA 95113
Phone: (408) 291-5250
Fax: (408) 286-5019
www.sjchamber.com

Santa Rosa, CA
Santa Rosa Chamber of Commerce
1260 North Dutton Avenue
Suite 272
Santa Rosa, CA 95401
Phone: (707) 545-1414
www.santarosachamber.com

Savannah, GA
Economic Development Authority
131 Hutchinson Island Road
4th Floor
Savannah, GA 31421
Phone: (912) 447-8450
Fax: (912) 447-8455
www.seda.org

Savannah Chamber of Commerce
101 E. Bay Street
Savannah, GA 31402
Phone: (912) 644-6400
Fax: (912) 644-6499
www.savannahchamber.com

Seattle, WA
Greater Seattle Chamber of Commerce
1301 Fifth Avenue
Suite 2500
Seattle, WA 98101
Phone: (206) 389-7200
Fax: (206) 389-7288
www.seattlechamber.com

Sioux Falls, SD
Sioux Falls Area Chamber of Commerce
200 N. Phillips Avenue
Suite 102
Sioux Falls, SD 57104
Phone: (605) 336-1620
Fax: (605) 336-6499
www.siouxfallschamber.com

Spokane, WA
Greater Spokane
801 W Riverside
Suite 100
Spokane, WA 99201
Phone: (509) 624-1393
Fax: (509) 747-0077
www.spokanechamber.org

Springfield, MO
Springfield Area Chamber of Commerce
202 S. John Q. Hammons Parkway
PO Box 1687
Springfield, MO 65806
Phone: (417) 862-5567
www.springfieldchamber.com

Tallahassee, FL
Greater Tallahassee Chamber of Commerce
300 E. Park Avenue
PO Box 1638
Tallahassee, FL 32301
Phone: (850) 224-8116
Fax: (850) 561-3860
www.talchamber.com

Tampa, FL
Greater Tampa Chamber of Commerce
P.O. Box 420
Tampa, FL 33601-0420
Phone: (813) 276-9401
Fax: (813) 229-7855
www.tampachamber.com

Topeka, KS
Greater Topeka Chamber of Commerce/
GO Topeka
120 SE Sixth Avenue
Suite 110
Topeka, KS 66603
Phone: (785) 234-2644
Fax: (785) 234-8656
www.topekachamber.org

Tulsa, OK
Tulsa Regional Chamber
1 West 3rd Street
Suite 100
Tulsa, OK 74103
Phone: (918) 585-1201
Fax: (918) 585-8016
www.tulsachamber.com

Virginia Beach, VA
Hampton Roads Chamber of Commerce
500 East Main St
Suite 700
Virginia Beach, VA 23510
Phone: (757) 664-2531
www.hamptonroadschamber.com

Washington, DC
District of Columbia Chamber of
Commerce
1213 K Street NW
Washington, DC 20005
Phone: (202) 347-7201
Fax: (202) 638-6762
www.dcchamber.org

District of Columbia Office of Planning and
Economic Development
J.A. Wilson Building
1350 Pennsylvania Ave NW, Suite 317
Washington, DC 20004
Phone: (202) 727-6365
Fax: (202) 727-6703
www.dcbiz.dc.gov

Wichita, KS
City of Wichita Economic Development
Department
City Hall, 12th Floor
455 North Main Street
Wichita, KS 67202
Phone: (316) 268-4524
Fax: (316) 268-4656
www.wichitagov.org

Wichita Metro Chamber of Commerce
350 West Douglas Avenue
Wichita, KS 67202
Phone: (316) 265-7771
www.wichitachamber.org

Wilmington, NC
Wilmington Chamber of Commerce
One Estell Lee Place
Wilmington, NC 28401
Phone: (910) 762-2611
www.wilmingtonchamber.org

Worcester, MA
Worcester Regional Chamber of Commerce
446 Main St
Suite 200
Worcester, MA 1608
Phone: (508) 753-2924
Fax: (508) 754-8560
www.worcesterchamber.org

Appendix E: State Departments of Labor

Alabama
Alabama Department of Labor
P.O. Box 303500
Montgomery, AL 36130-3500
Phone: (334) 242-3072
www.Alalabor.state.al.us

Alaska
Dept of Labor and Workforce Devel.
P.O. Box 11149
Juneau, AK 99822-2249
Phone: (907) 465-2700
www.labor.state.AK.us

Arizona
Arizona Industrial Commission
800 West Washington Street
Phoenix, AZ 85007
Phone: (602) 542-4515
www.ica.state.AZ.us

Arkansas
Department of Labor
10421 West Markham
Little Rock, AR 72205
Phone: (501) 682-4500
www.Arkansas.gov/labor

California
Labor and Workforce Development
445 Golden Gate Ave., 10th Floor
San Francisco, CA 94102
Phone: (916) 263-1811
www.labor.CA.gov

Colorado
Dept of Labor and Employment
633 17th St., 2nd Floor
Denver, CO 80202-3660
Phone: (888) 390-7936
www.COworkforce.com

Connecticut
Department of Labor
200 Folly Brook Blvd.
Wethersfield, CT 06109-1114
Phone: (860) 263-6000
www.CT.gov/dol

Delaware
Department of Labor
4425 N. Market St., 4th Floor
Wilmington, DE 19802
Phone: (302) 451-3423
www.Delawareworks.com

District of Columbia
Employment Services Department
614 New York Ave., NE, Suite 300
Washington, DC 20002
Phone: (202) 671-1900
www.DOES.DC.gov

Florida
Agency for Workforce Innovation
The Caldwell Building
107 East Madison St. Suite 100
Tallahassee, FL 32399-4120
Phone: (800) 342-3450
www.Floridajobs.org

Georgia
Department of Labor
Sussex Place, Room 600
148 Andrew Young Intl Blvd., NE
Atlanta, GA 30303
Phone: (404) 656-3011
www.dol.state.GA.us

Hawaii
Dept of Labor & Industrial Relations
830 Punchbowl Street
Honolulu, HI 96813
Phone: (808) 586-8842
wwwHawaii.gov/labor

Idaho
Department of Labor
317 W. Main St.
Boise, ID 83735-0001
Phone: (208) 332-3579
www.labor.Idaho.gov

Illinois
Department of Labor
160 N. LaSalle Street, 13th Floor
Suite C-1300
Chicago, IL 60601
Phone: (312) 793-2800
www.state.IL.us/agency/idol

Indiana
Indiana Government Center South
402 W. Washington Street
Room W195
Indianapolis, IN 46204
Phone: (317) 232-2655
www.IN.gov/labor

Iowa
Iowa Workforce Development
1000 East Grand Avenue
Des Moines, IA 50319-0209
Phone: (515) 242-5870
www.Iowaworkforce.org/labor

Kansas
Department of Labor
401 S.W. Topeka Blvd.
Topeka, KS 66603-3182
Phone: (785) 296-5000
www.dol.KS.gov

Kentucky
Philip Anderson, Commissioner
Department of Labor
1047 U.S. Hwy 127 South, Suite 4
Frankfort, KY 40601-4381
Phone: (502) 564-3070
www.labor.KY.gov

Louisiana
Department of Labor
P.O. Box 94094
Baton Rouge, LA 70804-9094
Phone: (225) 342-3111
www.LAworks.net

Maine
Department of Labor
45 Commerce Street
Augusta, ME 04330
Phone: (207) 623-7900
www.state.ME.us/labor

Maryland
Department of Labor and Industry
500 N. Calvert Street
Suite 401
Baltimore, MD 21202
Phone: (410) 767-2357
www.dllr.state.MD.us

Massachusetts
Dept of Labor & Work Force Devel.
One Ashburton Place
Room 2112
Boston, MA 02108
Phone: (617) 626-7100
www.Mass.gov/eolwd

Michigan
Dept of Labor & Economic Growth
P.O. Box 30004
Lansing, MI 48909
Phone: (517) 335-0400
www.Michigan.gov/cis

Minnesota
Dept of Labor and Industry
443 Lafayette Road North
Saint Paul, MN 55155
Phone: (651) 284-5070
www.doli.state.MN.us

Mississippi
Dept of Employment Security
P.O. Box 1699
Jackson, MS 39215-1699
Phone: (601) 321-6000
www.mdes.MS.gov

Missouri
Labor and Industrial Relations
P.O. Box 599
3315 W. Truman Boulevard
Jefferson City, MO 65102-0599
Phone: (573) 751-7500
www.dolir.MO.gov/lirc

Montana
Dept of Labor and Industry
P.O. Box 1728
Helena, MT 59624-1728
Phone: (406) 444-9091
www.dli.MT.gov

Nebraska
Department of Labor
550 South 16th Street
Box 94600
Lincoln, NE 68509-4600
Phone: (402) 471-9000
www.Nebraskaworkforce.com

Nevada
Dept of Business and Industry
555 E. Washington Ave.
Suite 4100
Las Vegas, NV 89101-1050
Phone: (702) 486-2650
www.laborcommissioner.com

New Hampshire
Department of Labor
State Office Park South
95 Pleasant Street
Concord, NH 03301
Phone: (603) 271-3176
www.labor.state.NH.us

New Jersey
Department of Labor
John Fitch Plaza, 13th Floor
Suite D
Trenton, NJ 08625-0110
Phone: (609) 777-3200
lwd.dol.state.nj.us/labor

New Mexico
Department of Labor
401 Broadway, NE
Albuquerque, NM 87103-1928
Phone: (505) 841-8450
www.dol.state.NM.us

New York
Department of Labor
State Office Bldg. # 12
W.A. Harriman Campus
Albany, NY 12240
Phone: (518) 457-5519
www.labor.state.NY.us

North Carolina
Department of Labor
4 West Edenton Street
Raleigh, NC 27601-1092
Phone: (919) 733-7166
www.nclabor.com

North Dakota
Department of Labor
State Capitol Building
600 East Boulevard, Dept 406
Bismark, ND 58505-0340
Phone: (701) 328-2660
www.nd.gov/labor

Ohio
Department of Commerce
77 South High Street, 22nd Floor
Columbus, OH 43215
Phone: (614) 644-2239
www.com.state.OH.us

Oklahoma
Department of Labor
4001 N. Lincoln Blvd.
Oklahoma City, OK 73105-5212
Phone: (405) 528-1500
www.state.OK.us/~okdol

Oregon
Bureau of Labor and Industries
800 NE Oregon St., #32
Portland, OR 97232
Phone: (971) 673-0761
www.Oregon.gov/boli

Pennsylvania
Dept of Labor and Industry
1700 Labor and Industry Bldg
7th and Forster Streets
Harrisburg, PA 17120
Phone: (717) 787-5279
www.dli.state.PA.us

Rhode Island
Department of Labor and Training
1511 Pontiac Avenue
Cranston, RI 02920
Phone: (401) 462-8000
www.dlt.state.RI.us

South Carolina
Dept of Labor, Licensing & Regulations
P.O. Box 11329
Columbia, SC 29211-1329
Phone: (803) 896-4300
www.llr.state.SC.us

South Dakota
Department of Labor
700 Governors Drive
Pierre, SD 57501-2291
Phone: (605) 773-3682
www.state.SD.us

Tennessee
Dept of Labor & Workforce Development
Andrew Johnson Tower
710 James Robertson Pkwy
Nashville, TN 37243-0655
Phone: (615) 741-6642
www.state.TN.us/labor-wfd

Texas
Texas Workforce Commission
101 East 15th St.
Austin, TX 78778
Phone: (512) 475-2670
www.twc.state.TX.us

Utah
Utah Labor Commission
P.O. Box 146610
Salt Lake City, UT 84114-6610
Phone: (801) 530-6800
Laborcommission.Utah.gov

Vermont
Department of Labor
5 Green Mountain Drive
P.O. Box 488
Montpelier, VT 05601-0488
Phone: (802) 828-4000
www.labor.verMont.gov

Virginia
Dept of Labor and Industry
Powers-Taylor Building
13 S. 13th Street
Richmond, VA 23219
Phone: (804) 371-2327
www.doli.Virginia.gov

Washington
Dept of Labor and Industries
P.O. Box 44001
Olympia, WA 98504-4001
Phone: (360) 902-4200
www.lni.WA.gov

West Virginia
Division of Labor
State Capitol Complex, Building #6
1900 Kanawha Blvd.
Charleston, WV 25305
Phone: (304) 558-7890
www.labor.state.WV.us

Wisconsin
Dept of Workforce Development
201 E. Washington Ave., #A400
P.O. Box 7946
Madison, WI 53707-7946
Phone: (608) 266-6861
www.dwd.state.WI.us

Wyoming
Department of Employment
1510 East Pershing Blvd.
Cheyenne, WY 82002
Phone: (307) 777-7261
www.doe.state.WY.us

Source: U.S. Department of Labor

2014 Title List

Visit **www.GreyHouse.com** for Product Information, Table of Contents and Sample Pages

General Reference

America's College Museums
American Environmental Leaders: From Colonial Times to the Present
An African Biographical Dictionary
An Encyclopedia of Human Rights in the United States
Constitutional Amendments
Encyclopedia of African-American Writing
Encyclopedia of the Continental Congress
Encyclopedia of Gun Control & Gun Rights
Encyclopedia of Invasions & Conquests
Encyclopedia of Prisoners of War & Internment
Encyclopedia of Religion & Law in America
Encyclopedia of Rural America
Encyclopedia of the United States Cabinet, 1789-2010
Encyclopedia of War Journalism
Encyclopedia of Warrior Peoples & Fighting Groups
From Suffrage to the Senate: America's Political Women
Nations of the World
Political Corruption in America
Speakers of the House of Representatives, 1789-2009
The Environmental Debate: A Documentary History
The Evolution Wars: A Guide to the Debates
The Religious Right: A Reference Handbook
The Value of a Dollar: 1860-2009
The Value of a Dollar: Colonial Era
This is Who We Were: A Companion to the 1940 Census
This is Who We Were: The 1920s
This is Who We Were: The 1950s
This is Who We Were: The 1960s
US Land & Natural Resource Policy
Working Americans 1770-1869 Vol. IX: Revolutionary War to the Civil War
Working Americans 1880-1999 Vol. I: The Working Class
Working Americans 1880-1999 Vol. II: The Middle Class
Working Americans 1880-1999 Vol. III: The Upper Class
Working Americans 1880-1999 Vol. IV: Their Children
Working Americans 1880-2003 Vol. V: At War
Working Americans 1880-2005 Vol. VI: Women at Work
Working Americans 1880-2006 Vol. VII: Social Movements
Working Americans 1880-2007 Vol. VIII: Immigrants
Working Americans 1880-2009 Vol. X: Sports & Recreation
Working Americans 1880-2010 Vol. XI: Inventors & Entrepreneurs
Working Americans 1880-2011 Vol. XII: Our History through Music
Working Americans 1880-2012 Vol. XIII: Education & Educators
World Cultural Leaders of the 20ᵗʰ & 21ˢᵗ Centuries

Business Information

Complete Television, Radio & Cable Industry Directory
Directory of Business Information Resources
Directory of Mail Order Catalogs
Directory of Venture Capital & Private Equity Firms
Environmental Resource Handbook
Food & Beverage Market Place
Grey House Homeland Security Directory
Grey House Performing Arts Directory
Hudson's Washington News Media Contacts Directory
New York State Directory
Sports Market Place Directory

Education Information

Charter School Movement
Comparative Guide to American Elementary & Secondary Schools
Complete Learning Disabilities Directory
Educators Resource Directory
Special Education

Health Information

Comparative Guide to American Hospitals
Complete Directory for Pediatric Disorders
Complete Directory for People with Chronic Illness
Complete Directory for People with Disabilities
Complete Mental Health Directory
Diabetes in America: A Geographic & Demographic Analysis
Directory of Health Care Group Purchasing Organizations
Directory of Hospital Personnel
HMO/PPO Directory
Medical Device Register
Older Americans Information Directory

Statistics & Demographics

America's Top-Rated Cities
America's Top-Rated Small Towns & Cities
America's Top-Rated Smaller Cities
American Tally
Ancestry & Ethnicity in America
Comparative Guide to American Hospitals
Comparative Guide to American Suburbs
Profiles of America
Profiles of... Series – State Handbooks
The Hispanic Databook
Weather America

Financial Ratings Series

TheStreet.com Ratings Guide to Bond & Money Market Mutual Funds
TheStreet.com Ratings Guide to Common Stocks
TheStreet.com Ratings Guide to Exchange-Traded Funds
TheStreet.com Ratings Guide to Stock Mutual Funds
TheStreet.com Ratings Ultimate Guided Tour of Stock Investing
Weiss Ratings Consumer Guides
Weiss Ratings Guide to Banks & Thrifts
Weiss Ratings Guide to Credit Unions
Weiss Ratings Guide to Health Insurers
Weiss Ratings Guide to Life & Annuity Insurers
Weiss Ratings Guide to Property & Casualty Insurers

Bowker's Books In Print®Titles

Books In Print®
Books In Print® Supplement
American Book Publishing Record® Annual
American Book Publishing Record® Monthly
Books Out Loud™
Bowker's Complete Video Directory™
Children's Books In Print®
El-Hi Textbooks & Serials In Print®
Forthcoming Books®
Law Books & Serials In Print™
Medical & Health Care Books In Print™
Publishers, Distributors & Wholesalers of the US™
Subject Guide to Books In Print®
Subject Guide to Children's Books In Print®

Canadian General Reference

Associations Canada
Canadian Almanac & Directory
Canadian Environmental Resource Guide
Canadian Parliamentary Guide
Financial Services Canada
Governments Canada
Health Services Canada
Libraries Canada
Major Canadian Cities
The History of Canada

Grey House Publishing | Salem Press | H.W. Wilson
4919 Route, 22 PO Box 56, Amenia NY 12501-0056

2014 Title List

Visit **www.SalemPress.com** for Product Information, Table of Contents and Sample Pages

Literature

American Ethnic Writers
Critical Insights: Authors
Critical Insights: New Literary Collection Bundles
Critical Insights: Themes
Critical Insights: Works
Critical Survey of Drama
Critical Survey of Graphic Novels: Heroes & Super Heroes
Critical Survey of Graphic Novels: History, Theme & Technique
Critical Survey of Graphic Novels: Independents & Underground Classics
Critical Survey of Graphic Novels: Manga
Critical Survey of Long Fiction
Critical Survey of Mystery & Detective Fiction
Critical Survey of Mythology and Folklore: Heroes and Heroines
Critical Survey of Mythology and Folklore: Love, Sexuality & Desire
Critical Survey of Mythology and Folklore: World Mythology
Critical Survey of Poetry
Critical Survey of Poetry: American Poetry
Critical Survey of Poetry: British, Irish & Commonwealth Poets
Critical Survey of Poetry: European Poets
Critical Survey of Poetry: European Poets
Critical Survey of Poetry: Topical Essays
Critical Survey of Poetry: World Poets
Critical Survey of Science Fiction & Fantasy Literature
Critical Survey of Shakespeare's Sonnets
Critical Survey of Short Fiction
Critical Survey of Short Fiction: American Writers
Critical Survey of Short Fiction: British, Irish & Commonwealth Poets
Critical Survey of Short Fiction: European Writers
Critical Survey of Short Fiction: Topical Essays
Critical Survey of Short Fiction: World Writers
Cyclopedia of Literary Characters
Introduction to Literary Context: American Post-Modernist Novels
Introduction to Literary Context: American Short Fiction
Introduction to Literary Context: English Literature
Introduction to Literary Context: World Literature
Magill's Literary Annual 2014
Magill's Survey of American Literature
Magill's Survey of World Literature
Masterplots
Masterplots II: African American Literature
Masterplots II: Christian Literature
Masterplots II: Drama Series
Masterplots II: Short Story Series
Notable African American Writers
Notable American Novelists
Notable Playwrights
Short Story Writers

Science, Careers & Mathematics

Applied Science
Applied Science: Engineering & Mathematics
Applied Science: Science & Medicine
Applied Science: Technology
Biomes and Ecosystems
Careers in Chemistry
Careers in Communications & Media
Careers in Healthcare
Careers in Hospitality & Tourism
Careers in Law & Criminology
Careers in Physics
Computer Technology Inventors
Contemporary Biographies in Chemistry
Contemporary Biographies in Communications & Media
Contemporary Biographies in Healthcare
Contemporary Biographies in Hospitality & Tourism
Contemporary Biographies in Law & Criminology
Contemporary Biographies in Physics
Earth Science
Earth Science: Earth Materials & Resources
Earth Science: Earth's Surface and History
Earth Science: Physics & Chemistry of the Earth
Earth Science: Weather, Water & Atmosphere
Encyclopedia of Energy
Encyclopedia of Environmental Issues
Encyclopedia of Global Resources
Encyclopedia of Global Warming
Encyclopedia of Mathematics and Society
Encyclopedia of the Ancient World
Forensic Science
Internet Innovators
Introduction to Chemistry
Magill's Encyclopedia of Science: Animal Life
Magill's Encyclopedia of Science: Plant life
Magill's Medical Guide
Notable Natural Disasters
Solar System

Health

Addictions & Substance Abuse
Cancer
Complementary & Alternative Medicine
Genetics & Inherited Conditions
Infectious Diseases & Conditions
Magill's Medical Guide
Psychology & Mental Health
Psychology Basics

Grey House Publishing | Salem Press | H.W. Wilson
4919 Route, 22 PO Box 56, Amenia NY 12501-0056

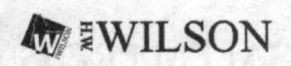
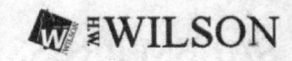

2014 Title List

Visit **www.HwWilsonInPrint.com** for Product Information, Table of Contents and Sample Pages

Current Biography

Current Biography Cumulative Index 1946-2013
Current Biography Magazine
Current Biography Yearbook-2004
Current Biography Yearbook-2005
Current Biography Yearbook-2006
Current Biography Yearbook-2007
Current Biography Yearbook-2008
Current Biography Yearbook-2009
Current Biography Yearbook-2010
Current Biography Yearbook-2011
Current Biography Yearbook-2012
Current Biography Yearbook-2013
Current Biography Yearbook-2014

Core Collections

Senior High Core Collection
Middle & Junior High School Core
Children's Core Collection
Fiction Core Collection
Public Library Core Collection: Nonfiction

Sears List

Sears List of Subject Headings
Sears: Lista de Encabezamientos de Materia

The Reference Shelf

Aging in America
Revisiting Gender
The U.S. National Debate Topic, 2014/2015
Embracing New Paradigms in education
Marijuana Reform
Representative American Speeches 2013-2014
Reality Television
The Business of Food
The Future of U.S. Economic Relations: Mexico, Cuba, and Venezuela
Sports in America
Global Climate Change
Representative American Speeches, 2012-2013
Conspiracy Theories
The Arab Spring
U.S. National Debate Topic: Transportation Infrastructure
Families: Traditional and New Structures
Faith & Science
Representative American Speeches 2011-2012
Social Networking
Dinosaurs
Space Exploration & Development
U.S. Infrastructure
Politics of the Ocean
Representative American Speeches 2010-2011
Robotics
The News and its Future
American Military Presence Overseas
Russia
Graphic Novels and Comic Books
Representative American Speeches 2009-2010

Readers' Guide

Readers Guide to Periodicals Literature
Abridged Readers' Guide to Periodical Literature
Short Story Index

Indexes

Short Story Index
Index to Legal Periodicals & Books

Facts About Series

Facts About the Presidents, Eighth Edition
Facts About China
Facts About the 20th Century
Facts About American Immigration
Facts About World's Languages

Nobel Prize Winners

Nobel Prize Winners, 2002-2013

World Authors

World Authors 2000-2005
World Authors 2006-2013

Famous First Facts

Famous First Facts, Seventh Edition
Famous First Facts About American Politics
Famous First Facts About Sports
Famous First Facts About the Environment
Famous First Facts, International Edition

American Book of Days

The American Book of Days, Fifth Edition
The International Book of Days

Junior Authors & Illustrators

Tenth Book of Junior Authors & Illustrations

Monographs

The Barnhart Dictionary of Etymology
Celebrate the World
Indexing from A to Z
Radical Change: Books for Youth in a Digital Age
The Poetry Break
Guide to the Ancient World

Wilson Chronology

Wilson Chronology of Asia and the Pacific
Wilson Chronology of Human Rights
Wilson Chronology of Ideas
Wilson Chronology of the Arts
Wilson Chronology of the World's Religions
Wilson Chronology of Women's Achievements

Book Review Digest

Book Review Digest, 2014

Grey House Publishing | Salem Press | H.W. Wilson
4919 Route, 22 PO Box 56, Amenia NY 12501-0056

2014 Title List

Visit **www.SalemPress.com** for Product Information, Table of Contents and Sample Pages

History and Social Science

A 2000s in America
50 States
African American History
Agriculture in History (check)
American First Ladies
American Heroes
American Indian Tribes
American Presidents
American Villains
Ancient Greece
Bill of Rights, The
Cold War, The
Defining Documents: American Revolution 1754-1805
Defining Documents: Civil War 1860-1865
Defining Documents: Emergence of Modern America, 1868-1918
Defining Documents: Exploration & Colonial America 1492-1755
Defining Documents: Manifest Destiny 1803-1860
Defining Documents: Reconstruction, 1865-1880
Defining Documents: The 1920s
Defining Documents: The 1930s
Defining Documents: World War I
Eighties in America
Encyclopedia of American Immigration
Fifties in America
Forties in America
Great Athletes
Great Events from History: 17th Century
Great Events from History: 18th Century
Great Events from History: 19th Century
Great Events from History: 20th Century, 1901-1940
Great Events from History: 20th Century, 1941-1970
Great Events from History: 20th Century, 1971-200
Great Events from History: Ancient World
Great Events from History: Middle Ages
Great Events from History: Modern Scandals
Great Events from History: Renaissance & Early Modern Era
Great Lives from History: 17th Century
Great Lives from History: 18th Century
Great Lives from History: 19th Century
Great Lives from History: 20th Century
Great Lives from History: African Americans
Great Lives from History: Ancient World
Great Lives from History: Asian & Pacific Islander Americans
Great Lives from History: Incredibly Wealthy
Great Lives from History: Inventors & Inventions
Great Lives from History: Jewish Americans
Great Lives from History: Latinos
Great Lives from History: Middle Ages
Great Lives from History: Notorious Lives
Great Lives from History: Renaissance & Early Modern Era
Great Lives from History: Scientists & Science
Historical Encyclopedia of American Business
Immigration in U.S. History
Magill's Guide to Military History
Milestone Documents in African American History
Milestone Documents in American History
Milestone Documents in World History
Milestone Documents of American Leaders
Milestone Documents of World Religions
Musicians & Composers 20th Century
Nineties in America
Seventies in America

Sixties in America
Survey of American Industry and Careers
Thirties in America
Twenties in America
U.S. Court Cases
U.S. Laws, Acts, and Treaties
U.S. Legal System
U.S. Supreme Court
United States at War
USA in Space
Weapons and Warfare
World Conflicts: Asia and the Middle East

Grey House Publishing | Salem Press | H.W. Wilson
4919 Route, 22 PO Box 56, Amenia NY 12501-0056